IOWA, KANSAS AND NEBRASKA CIVIL WAR VETERANS

*Compilation of the Death Rolls of the Departments of
Iowa, Kansas and Nebraska, Grand Army of the Republic, 1883-1948*

Dennis Northcott

St. Louis, Mo.
Dennis Northcott
2007

Cover Design: Barbara Northcott

Cover Image: Musicians, members of the Department of Iowa, Grand Army of the Republic, at Iowa State Fair. Des Moines, Iowa, circa 1900. (Grand Army of the Republic Collection [Post 23]: 5000.513; State Historical Society of Iowa, Des Moines)

Northcott, Dennis
    Iowa, Kansas and Nebraska Civil War veterans: compilation of the death rolls of the Departments of Iowa, Kansas and Nebraska, Grand Army of the Republic, 1883-1948 / Dennis Northcott.

1. Grand Army of the Republic, Dept. of Iowa.
2. Grand Army of the Republic, Dept. of Kansas.
3. Grand Army of the Republic, Dept. of Nebraska.
4. Death records—Iowa.
5. Death records—Kansas.
6. Death records—Nebraska.
7. United States—History—Civil War—1861–1865—Registers.
8. Iowa—Genealogy—Sources.
9. Kansas—Genealogy—Sources.
10. Nebraska—Genealogy—Sources.
11. Veterans—Iowa—Registers.
12. Veterans—Kansas—Registers.
13. Veterans—Nebraska—Registers.
    I. Title

ISBN-13: 978-0-9728344-2-1
ISBN-10: 0-9728344-2-7

OTHER TITLES AVAILABLE FROM DENNIS NORTHCOTT

Grand Army of the Republic, Department of Illinois:
Transcription of the Death Rolls, 1879-1947
by Dennis Northcott and Thomas Brooks
(St. Louis, Mo.: Dennis Northcott, 2003), ISBN 0-9728344-0-0

Indiana Civil War Veterans: Transcription of the Death Rolls of the
Department of Indiana, Grand Army of the Republic, 1882-1948
by Dennis Northcott (St. Louis, Mo.: Dennis Northcott, 2005),
ISBN 0-9728344-1-9

COMING NEXT
Compilation of the death rolls of the Department of
Pennsylvania, Grand Army of the Republic

For more information, visit www.ngpublications.com

TABLE OF CONTENTS

INTRODUCTION

The Grand Army of the Republic (G.A.R.) was founded in 1866 in Illinois and became the largest association of Civil War Union veterans. The G.A.R.'s national membership reached its peak in 1890 at 409,489, but as the veterans died, the membership inevitably declined. The national membership dropped to 213,901 in 1910 and 16,597 in 1930. The last surviving G.A.R. member died in 1956.

Those eligible for membership were: "Soldiers and sailors of the United States Army, Navy or Marine Corps, who served between April 12, 1861, and April 9, 1865, in the war for the suppression of the rebellion, and those having been honorably discharged therefrom after such service, and of such state regiments as were called into active service and subject to the orders of U.S. general officers, between the dates mentioned. No person shall be eligible to membership who has, at any time, borne arms against the United States."*

The G.A.R. was organized in departments, most of which comprised one state. These departments published annual reports describing their activities for the preceding year, and these reports usually contain a death roll of the department's members. The *Journal of the 10th Annual Encampment, Department of Iowa, Grand Army of the Republic*, published in 1884, was the first of the Department of Iowa annual reports to contain a death roll of its members. The *Proceedings of the 3rd Annual Encampment of the Grand Army of the Republic, Department of Kansas*, published in 1884, was the first of the Department of Kansas annual reports to contain a death roll of its members. The *Journal of the 8th Annual Encampment, Grand Army of the Republic, Department of Nebraska*, published in 1884, was the first of the Department of Nebraska annual reports to contain a death roll of its members. Thereafter, death rolls were published annually in each department's *Journal of the Annual Encampment*. (The title of these publications varies slightly.) The Department of Kansas did not publish death rolls in its 23rd *Journal* (published in 1904) or its 27th *Journal* (published in 1908). The Department of Nebraska did not publish death rolls in its 14th *Journal* (published in 1890) or its 23rd *Journal* (published in 1899).

To compile these death rolls, the departments requested each of their local chapters, known as "posts," to submit a death roll of its members. Compliance with this request varied from post to post and year to year; some posts submitted incomplete rolls or none at all. The department death rolls published in the *Journal* usually contain the member's name, company, regiment or ship, date of death, and the number of the post to which he belonged. The *Journal* often also includes the member's rank and age. When the *Journal's* death roll contains additional information, such as cause of death, place of death, or place of burial, I recorded this information in the "Company, Regiment or Ship" column.

I compiled the death rolls in this book from *Journals* in the holdings of the Library of Congress, University of Illinois Library, State Historical Society of Iowa Library, Kansas State Historical Society Library, Nebraska State Historical Society Library, and Wisconsin Historical Society Library. This book contains records of more than 36,000 G.A.R. members who served in Civil War units from 37 states and territories. (A statistical summary of the states and territories from which these members served appears in Appendix E.)

In transcribing these death rolls, I made every effort to record the information accurately and completely, with the following two exceptions. Several early Department of Kansas death rolls include notes regarding G.A.R. offices held by members and a note that a member was buried by the post. I did not record this information in this book. Similarly, some of the Department of Nebraska death rolls include the member's dates of Civil War enlistment and discharge, date of muster into the G.A.R., and G.A.R. offices held. I did not record this information in this book. Since the ranks and regiments in the original death rolls were not recorded in a uniform manner, I standardized this information as much as possible. For example, in the original death rolls "Ohio

---

*Membership application of W.A. Hequembourg in Ransom Post No. 131, Department of Missouri, January 9, 1892, Grand Army of the Republic Collection, Missouri Historical Society Archives, St. Louis.

Volunteer Infantry" is variously recorded as "Ohio Vol. Inf.," "Ohio Vol. Inft.," and "O.V.I." In this compilation, I consistently recorded these entries as "Ohio Vol. Inf." When I had any doubt regarding the correct interpretation of an entry, I recorded the information exactly as it appears in the original death roll. Information supplied by me that is not in the original death rolls appears in brackets.

To facilitate sorting, I recorded names such as "La Dee" and "Van Ausdale" as "LaDee" and "VanAusdale," respectively. Occasionally volumes of the *Journal of the Annual Encampment* include obituaries of G.A.R. members that contain additional information about the individual. These names are listed in the death rolls section of this book with a reference to Appendix D, which contains the citation for the number, year and page number of the *Journal* that includes the obituary. I added several cross references in cases in which it appears likely that a member's name was inaccurately recorded in the original death rolls. The final column contains the number and year of the *Journal* from which the entry was extracted. For example, if the last column reads "IA, 24th, 1900," this indicates that the entry was taken from the *Journal of the 24th Annual Encampment, Department of Iowa*, which was published in 1900. Appendices A, B and C contain rosters for the Departments of Iowa, Kansas and Nebraska, which list the number, name, and location of each post.

Users of this compilation should note the following: The death rolls in the *Journal* are usually stated to contain the deaths for the year preceding its publication. The death roll in each *Journal* often contains a title on the first page that reads "Roll of Honor for the Year . . ." or "Memorial Roll for the Year . . ." Within this death roll, entries for each member contain the month and day of death, but in some cases not the year. In this compilation, the year from the title of the death roll has been supplied for each entry in that death roll. For example, the thirty-fourth annual encampment of the Department of Kansas was held May 11–13, 1915. The death roll published in the *Journal of the 34th Annual Encampment* is titled "Memorial Roll, 1914." A death date of January 10 in this death roll has been recorded in this compilation as January 10, 1914. However, it appears likely that occasionally the original death rolls include some submissions of deaths from the early months of the same year of the publication of the *Journal*, in addition to those from the year preceding the publication. Thus, the death date January 10 in the "Memorial Roll, 1914" published in the *Journal of the 34th Annual Encampment* may actually be a record of a death that occurred on January 10, 1915, which would have been recorded in this compilation as occurring on January 10, 1914.

Researchers interested in acquiring selected data in this book arranged in another way (i.e., all the members of a particular post, or all the members of a particular regiment) may contact me at dennis@ngpublications.com.

Dennis Northcott
St. Louis, Missouri
dennis@ngpublications.com

ABBREVIATIONS

Rank

A.A.G. — Assistant adjutant general
Adjt. — Adjutant
AQM — Assistant quartermaster
Asst. — Assistant
Brev. or Bvt. — Brevet
Brig. — Brigadier
Capt. — Captain
Col. — Colonel
Com. Sergt. — Commissary sergeant
Corp. — Corporal
Eng. — Engineer
Gen. — General
Hosp. Stew. — Hospital steward
Lieut. — Lieutenant
Ord. Sergt. — Orderly sergeant
Pvt. — Private
QM — Quartermaster
Sergt. — Sergeant
Surg. — Surgeon

Regiment

Art. — Artillery
Bat./Batt. — Battery
Cav. — Cavalry
Col. — Colored (sometimes may refer to "Colorado")
Eng. — Engineers
Hvy. Art. — Heavy artillery
Inf. — Infantry
Lt. Art. — Light artillery
Mtd. — Mounted
N.G. — National Guard
Prov. — Provisional
Regt. — Regiment
Res. — Reserve
U.S.C. — United States Colored
U.S.C.T. — United States Colored Troops
V.R.C. — Veteran Reserve Corps
Vet. — Veteran
Vol. — Volunteer

HOW TO USE THIS BOOK

1. Locate the name of the G.A.R. member you are researching in the alphabetically arranged death rolls.

2. View the veteran's rank; company, regiment or ship; age; and death date in the appropriate columns. (Please see the Introduction for an important explanation regarding the recording of the death date in this compilation.)

3. Consult the last column to determine from which *Journal of the Annual Encampment* the entry was extracted. For example, if the last column reads "IA, 24th, 1900," this indicates that the entry was taken from the *Journal of the 24th Annual Encampment, Department of Iowa,* published in 1900. In the last column, the abbreviation "KS" stands for Department of Kansas and "NE" stands for Department of Nebraska.

4. To determine the name and location of the G.A.R. post to which the veteran you are researching belonged, consult the "Post" column. If the last column reads "IA," go to Appendix A and look up the post number to determine the name and location of this Department of Iowa post. If the last column reads "KS," go to Appendix B and look up the post number to determine the name and location of this Department of Kansas post. If the last column reads "NE," go to Appendix C and look up the post number to determine the name and location of this Department of Nebraska post.

5. The death rolls compiled in this book were extracted from the many volumes of the *Journal of the Annual Encampment* of the G.A.R. Departments of Iowa, Kansas and Nebraska. In some cases the original records of G.A.R. posts have survived, and these records may contain additional information regarding G.A.R. members. For example, the State Historical Society of Iowa has a sizable collection of post records for the Department of Iowa. To locate these records, researchers may want to try the following:

   • Check the holdings of the state historical society and state archives.
   • Check the holdings of the local library where the G.A.R. post was located.
   • Conduct a keyword search in Internet search engines.
   • Search WorldCat: www.worldcat.org.
   • Search the National Union Catalog of Manuscript Collections: www.loc.gov/coll/nucmc/.
   • Search the Church of Jesus Christ of Latter-Day Saints' Family History Catalog: www.familysearch.org.
   • Contact the local chapter of the Sons of Union Veterans of the Civil War: www.suvcw.org.

Name	Rank	Company, Regiment or Ship	Post*	Age	Death Date†	Journal
Aaker, D.O.	Pvt.	G, 12th Iowa Inf.	168	54	1894 Mar 30	IA, 20th, 1894
Aarl, Geo. W.		G, 7th Kans.	94		1890	KS, 10th, 1891
Aaron, Morris M.		D, 4th Vt. Inf.	25		1913 Jun 5	NE, 38th, 1914
Aarons, Andrew	Pvt.	B, 10th Iowa Inf.	291	58	1895 Jan 5	IA, 21st, 1895
Abarnethy, George			40		1906 Aug 26	NE, 31st, 1907
Abberton, Timothy		K, 53rd Ill. Inf.	63		1886	KS, 6th, 1887
Abbett, W.A.			12		1923 Mar 25	IA, 50th, 1924
Abbey, Aaron	Pvt.	H, 5th Iowa Inf.	212	47	1891 Dec 10	IA, 18th, 1892
Abbey, C.W.		B, 144th Ill.	36		1908[1909?] Jul 17	KS, 29th, 1910
Abbey, Francis		E, 38th Wis.	77		1929 Mar 6	NE, 54th, 1930
Abbey, G.C.	Pvt.	K, 21st Iowa Inf.	74	77	1898 Jan 18	IA, 24th, 1898
Abbey, Gotlieb			159		1925 Oct	IA, 52nd, 1926
Abbey, Orrin		E, 38th Wis.	44		1905 Oct 4	KS, 25th, 1906
Abbey, Thomas	Pvt.	I, 5th Iowa Inf.	212		1916 Sep 18	IA, 43rd, 1917
Abbey, V.		H, 2nd Colo. Cav.	283		1914 Jan 15	KS, 34th, 1915
Abbott, A.A.	Pvt.		57		1930	IA, 57th, 1931
Abbott, A.A.		I, 100th N.Y.	98		1911 Jan 20	KS, 31st, 1912
Abbott, A.J.	Pvt.	C, 2nd Iowa Cav.	190		1908 Jun 7	IA, 35th, 1909
Abbott, A.J.		G, 10th Ind. Cav.	31		1923 May 20	NE, 48th, 1924
Abbott, A.O.	Capt.	H, 1st N.Y. Inf.	31		2nd quarter 1885	IA, 12th, 1886
Abbott, Amos		K, 141st Ohio	240		1913 Dec 27	KS, 33rd, 1914
Abbott, Asbury		G, 44th Ill.	250		1924 Jan 22	KS, 43rd, 1924
Abbott, Dewitt C.		I, 1st Tenn. (died at Knoxville, Tenn.)	32		1892 Oct 28	KS, 12th, 1893
Abbott, E.S.		I, 47th Ill. Inf.	4		1894 Jan 31	NE, 19th, 1895
Abbott, Edwin J.		A, 135th Ohio Inf.	29		1920 Jan 6	IA, 46th, 1920
Abbott, F.M.		K & E, 118th & 153rd Ind.	129		1923 Nov 12	KS, 43rd, 1924
Abbott, G.L.		K, 8th U.S. Vet. Vols.	85		1927 Mar 4	KS, 47th, 1928
Abbott, G.N.		F, 153rd Ind. Inf.	158		1925 Mar 1	KS, 45th, 1926
Abbott, G.W.		C, 6th Mo.	68		1921 Feb 17	KS, 41st, 1922
Abbott, Geo.		13th Kans.	292		1921 May	KS, 41st, 1922
Abbott, Geo. W.		E, 33rd Ill.	85		1917 Nov 23	KS, 37th, 1918
Abbott, H.		M, 4th Mich. Cav.	140		1892 Aug 24	NE, 17th, 1893
Abbott, I.W.	Pvt.	H, 9th Iowa Cav.	11		1929 Mar 1	IA, 56th, 1930
Abbott, J.B.	Band Leader	41st Ohio Inf.	222	59	1894 Mar 13	IA, 21st, 1895
Abbott, J.H.		C, 25th Ind.	59		1892 Sep 9	KS, 12th, 1893
Abbott, J.W.		G, 3rd Tenn.	32		1925 Mar 10	KS, 45th, 1926
Abbott, John		B, 79th Ill.	23		1917 Sep 21	KS, 37th, 1918
Abbott, Joseph		D, 55th Ill.	82		1929 Sep 17	KS, 49th, 1930
Abbott, L.P.	Pvt.	D, 47th Ind. Inf.	211		1927 Jul 9	IA, 54th, 1928
Abbott, Lemuel		G, 7th Ohio	500		1918	KS, 38th, 1919
Abbott, Norris H.		H, 17th Ill.	85		1935 Sep 2	KS, 55th, 1936
Abbott, Othman A.	1st Lieut.	I, 9th Ill. Cav.	11		1935 Jun 24	NE, 60th, 1936
Abbott, S.L.		F, 10th N.Y.	32		1930 Mar 20	KS, 50th, 1931
Abby, Gotleib	Pvt.		159		1926 Sep	IA, 53rd, 1927
Abby, Gottleh	Pvt.	B, 27th Iowa	160		1924 Jan 15	IA, 51st, 1925
Abby, J.S.		4th Ill. Cav.	113		1915 May 8	KS, 35th, 1916
Abel, Jno.		K, 18th Mo. in Ky.	46		1904 Sep 20	KS, 24th, 1905
Abels, Henry		L, 15th Kans.	1		1931 Sep 27	KS, 51st, 1932
Abels, J.F.	Pvt.	92nd Ill. Inf.	71		1926 Nov 22	IA, 53rd, 1927
Abercromly, S.G.		B, 65th Ill. (died of old age)	44	81	1923 Oct 29	NE, 49th, 1925
Abern, John		U.S. Navy	380		1899 Nov 3	KS, 19th, 1900
Abernathy, Alonzo	Pvt.	F, 9th Iowa Inf.	12		1915 Feb 20	IA, 42nd, 1916
Abernathy, George, see Abarnethy, George						
Abernathy, J.L.	Lieut. Col.	8th Kans.	6		1902 Dec 16	KS, 22nd, 1903
Abernathy, W.C.		H, 30th Ill. Inf.	180		1930 Nov 21	KS, 50th, 1931
Abernethy, J.J.	Pvt.	C, 78th Ind. Inf. G, 133rd Ind. Inf.	38		1899	NE, 24th, 1900
Able, A.J.		D, 81st Ind.	19		1918 Jul 3	KS, 38th, 1919
Able, Augustus W.	Pvt.	I, 9th Iowa Inf.	343		1926 Nov 28	IA, 53rd, 1927
Able, Jessie G.		K, 18th Mo. Inf. (died at Clay Center)	88		1895 Nov 11	KS, 15th, 1896
Able, Joseph		D, 13th N.Y.	25		1916 Jul 22	KS, 36th, 1917

*See Appendix A, B or C for roster of post names and locations.
†See Introduction for note regarding recording of death date.

Name	Rank	Company, Regiment or Ship	Post*	Age	Death Date†	Journal
Able, Madison	Pvt.	H, 16th U.S. Inf.	68		1920 Feb 20	IA, 47th, 1921
Abner, William		H, 122nd Ill. Inf.	293		1909 Sep	KS, 29th, 1910
Abney, Joseph		G, 61st Ill.	117		1905 Mar 23	KS, 25th, 1906
Abraham, John B.	Pvt.	7th Ohio	267		1925 Oct 28	IA, 52nd, 1926
Abraham, Lot	Capt.	D, 4th Iowa Cav.	20		1920 Jul 23	IA, 47th, 1921
Abraham, N.W.	Pvt.	H, 47th Iowa Inf.	23		1927 May 27	IA, 54th, 1928
Abram, Dan.	Pvt.		173		1926 Aug 12	IA, 53rd, 1927
Abrams, W.G.	Pvt.	A, 14th Conn.	22		1901 May 28	IA, 28th, 1902
Abrecht, John		E, 2nd N.Y. Inf. 4th N.J. Lt. Art. (died of wounds)	69		1893 Apr 15	NE, 18th, 1894
Aby, A.		A, 13th Ill.	147		1906 Nov 3	KS, 26th, 1907
Achermerhorn, Alonzo		F, 6th Kans.	100		1923 Feb 18	KS, 43rd, 1924
Achler, P.C.	Pvt.	I, 1st Ark. Inf.	398		1904 Feb 14	IA, 31st, 1905
Acker, H.J.		B, 23rd Wis. Inf.	18		1899 Dec 14	KS, 19th, 1900
Acker, James		H, 15th U.S. Inf.	6		1904 Jul 10	KS, 24th, 1905
Acker, John		B, 14th Iowa Inf. (died of heart & lung trouble)	99		1891 May 26	KS, 11th, 1892
Ackerly, D.		K, 19th Mich.	376		1893 Aug 14	KS, 13th, 1894
Ackerly, G.L.			322		1924	KS, 44th, 1925
Ackerman, A.C.		G, 12th Vt.	298		1905 Jul 14	KS, 25th, 1906
Ackerman, Daniel	Pvt.	12th Wis. Battery	42		1912 Dec 22	IA, 39th, 1913
Ackerman, David		I, 28th Penn.	11	67	1915 Feb 4	NE, 40th, 1916
Ackerman, F.			318		1907	NE, 32nd, 1908
Ackerman, Isaac	Pvt.	G, 8th Cav. Co.	176	71	1898 May 10	IA, 25th, 1899
Ackerman, L.J.		E, 32nd Iowa Inf.	68		1917 Oct 9	IA, 44th, 1918
Ackerman, W.H., see Akerman, W.H.						
Ackert, F.H.			94		1917	IA, 44th, 1918
Ackland, James	Pvt.	H, 40th Iowa Inf.	7		1917 Apr 13	IA, 44th, 1918
Ackley, C.T.			36		1929 Dec 24	KS, 49th, 1930
Ackley, Geo.			51		1906	KS, 26th, 1907
Ackley, Henry C.	Pvt.	F, 112th Ill. Inf.	95		1913 Jul 2	IA, 40th, 1914
Ackley, Solomon J.	Pvt.	B, 7th Iowa Inf.	308		1908 Nov 9	IA, 35th, 1909
Acott, John P.	Pvt.	H, 40th Iowa Inf.	7		1920 Feb 2	IA, 47th, 1921
Acres, J.V.		B, 17th Ohio Vol. Inf.	49		1914 Feb 15	KS, 34th, 1915
Acres, Wilson H.		B, 6th Iowa Cav.	190		1918 Sep 15	IA, 45th, 1919
Acton, M.A.	Pvt.	B, 7th Ind. Inf.	347		1907 Jan 13	IA, 34th, 1908
Adair, A.B.		C, 30th Ohio Inf. (died at Independence; buried at Mt. Hope)	4		1894 Mar 15	KS, 14th, 1895
Adair, Arthur		L, 16th N.Y.	88		1928 Apr 4	KS, 48th, 1929
Adair, Austin		B, 46th Ind.	68		1916 Nov 10	KS, 36th, 1917
Adair, James	Pvt.	C, 33rd Iowa Inf.	40		1916 May 27	IA, 43rd, 1917
Adair, John	Pvt.	B, 7th Iowa Inf.	22		1931 Feb 26	IA, 58th, 1932
Adair, Major			28		1927 Jul 5	KS, 47th, 1928
Adair, Thomas	Pvt.	E, 43rd Mo. Inf.	34		1929 Aug 9	IA, 56th, 1930
Adair, Thomas		A, 10th Kans.	68		1913 May 5	KS, 33rd, 1914
Adair, Tom		L, 45th Ind.	36		1906 Aug	KS, 26th, 1907
Adam, Ernest		F, 26th Mo.	256		1897 Dec 9	KS, 17th, 1898
Adams, A.L.	Pvt.	G, 98th N.Y.	235		1921 Aug 27	IA, 48th, 1922
Adams, Abel	Pvt.	F, 31st Iowa Inf.	235		1915 May 24	IA, 42nd, 1916
Adams, Albert M.	Pvt.	F, 2nd Iowa Cav.	193		1915 Jan 4	IA, 42nd, 1916
Adams, Alex	Corp.	A, 100th Penn. Inf.	364		1907 Jun 21	IA, 34th, 1908
Adams, Alex		I, 7th Ill. Inf. (died of dropsy)	69	58	1895 Jul 25	NE, 20th, 1896
Adams, Alfred W.		F, 1st Mass.	18		1899 Jun 30	KS, 19th, 1900
Adams, Amos	Pvt.	I, 88th Penn. Inf.	68		1910 Jul 31	IA, 37th, 1911
Adams, Anderson		H, 46th Ill. (died of heart failure)	354	74	1920 Nov 12	NE, 45th, 1921
Adams, B.F.		H, 2nd Penn. Inf.	66		1914 May 2	KS, 34th, 1915
Adams, B.F.		F, 62nd Ohio Inf. (died of inflammation of bowels)	8	56	1902 Jun	NE, 27th, 1903
Adams, B.H.	Pvt.	E, 79th Ill. Inf.	101		1905 Jan 27	IA, 31st, 1905
Adams, B.P.		A, 1st Ind. Cav.	88		3rd quarter 1884	IA, 11th, 1885
Adams, C.F.	Pvt.	K, 18th Ill. Inf.	29		1910 Jan 16	IA, 37th, 1911
Adams, C.F.		D, 82nd N.Y.			1937 Oct 29	KS, 57th, 1938

*See Appendix A, B or C for roster of post names and locations.
†See Introduction for note regarding recording of death date.

Name	Rank	Company, Regiment or Ship	Post*	Age	Death Date†	Journal
Adams, C.H.		F, 17th Kans.	142		1908 Apr 10	KS, 28th, 1909
Adams, C.M.	Pvt.	B, 32nd Iowa Inf.	42		1926 Jun 5	IA, 53rd, 1927
Adams, Charles		F, 155th Ind.	144		1914 Jan 30	KS, 34th, 1915
Adams, Charles H.		I, D, 1st N.Y. Hvy. Art.	147		1940 Aug 23	NE, 65th, 1941
Adams, Chas. E.		I, 137th Ill. Inf.	180		1929 Dec 23	KS, 49th, 1930
Adams, Chas. H.		1st Ohio	25		1927 Mar 28	NE, 52nd, 1928
Adams, Chas. J.		12th Ohio Battery	62		1904 May 17	KS, 24th, 1905
Adams, Clarendon E.		5th Wis. Battery (died at his home in Los Angeles, California; see Appendix D)	63		1924 Feb 23	NE, 48th, 1924
Adams, D.H.	Pvt.	B, 33rd Iowa Inf.	10		1916 May 30	IA, 43rd, 1917
Adams, Edwin M.	Major	20th Mich.	33		1922 Dec 1	KS, 42nd, 1923
Adams, Eli D.		L, 16th Kans. Cav.	18		1899 Apr 19	KS, 19th, 1900
Adams, Ernest			28		1897 Dec 10	KS, 17th, 1898
Adams, F.M.		E, 6th N.J. Inf. (born in Philadelphia; died in Lincoln, Neb.)	112		1883 Sep 28	NE, 8th, 1884
Adams, Frank J.		E, 3rd V.R.C.	88		1910 Feb 2	KS, 30th, 1911
Adams, G.H.		C, 151st Ind.	132		1910 Dec 5	KS, 30th, 1911
Adams, G.O.		G, 22nd N.Y. Inf. (cause of death: heart)	101	59	1901 Sep	NE, 26th, 1902
Adams, G.W.		F, 146th Ill. Inf. (died of kidney disease)	289	56	1905 May 9	NE, 30th, 1906
Adams, Geo. M.	Pvt.	C, 15th Iowa Inf.	175		1900 Nov	IA, 27th, 1901
Adams, H.I.	Pvt.	C, 8th Ohio Vol. Inf.	125		1924 Mar 27	IA, 51st, 1925
Adams, H.J.		G, 53rd Ind.	4		1931 Apr 13	KS, 51st, 1932
Adams, H.J.		G, 53rd Ind.	4		1931 Apr 13	KS, 52nd, 1933
Adams, H.L.		H, 27th Ill. Inf. (died of paralysis)	9	57	1891[1901?] Jun	NE, 26th, 1902
Adams, H.S.		E, 47th Ind.	130		1926 Mar 8	KS, 46th, 1927
Adams, Henry			168		1908	IA, 35th, 1909
Adams, Henry	Pvt.	A, 9th Wis. Inf.	465		1916 Dec 26	IA, 43rd, 1917
Adams, Israel		C, 17th Penn. Cav. (died of dropsy)	326		1893 Jul 3	NE, 18th, 1894
Adams, J.C.	Capt.	C, 1st Wis.	187		1899	IA, 26th, 1900
Adams, J.L.	Pvt.	C, 14th Iowa Inf.	1		1908 Mar 25	IA, 35th, 1909
Adams, J.M.		A, 123rd Ill. Inf.	94		1919 Feb 19	IA, 46th, 1920
Adams, J.W.		B, 3rd Vt. State Militia	12		1909 Aug 9	KS, 29th, 1910
Adams, J.W.		B, 92nd Ohio K, 42nd Ohio	104		1929 Aug 5	KS, 49th, 1930
Adams, J.W., Dr.	Lieut.	B, 7th Ind. Vols.	12		1901 Sep 13	IA, 28th, 1902
Adams, James	Pvt.	E, 12th Ohio Inf.	231		1904 Dec 17	IA, 31st, 1905
Adams, James		G, 19th Ind.	63		1905 Oct 21	KS, 25th, 1906
Adams, James		C, 24th Iowa Inf., New York (died of old age)	354	93	1919 May 17	NE, 44th, 1920
Adams, James M.		A, 39th Ky.	65		1927 Aug 17	KS, 47th, 1928
Adams, James W.		H, 4th Mo. State Militia Cav.	311		1892 Nov 19	KS, 12th, 1893
Adams, Jas. C.	Capt.	F, 41st Ill. Inf.	216		1902 Nov 10	IA, 29th, 1903
Adams, Jas. F.	Pvt.	F, 40th Iowa Inf.	49		1900 May 9	IA, 27th, 1901
Adams, John		I, 12th Kans. Inf.	18		1908 Nov 23	KS, 28th, 1909
Adams, John D.		H, 151st Ill. (died of paralysis)	23	79	1922 Jun 8	NE, 47th, 1923
Adams, John L.		A, 78th Penn. Inf.	305		1887 Dec 7	KS, 7th, 1888
Adams, John Q.		H, 123rd Ohio Inf.	5		1901 Dec 20	KS, 21st, 1902
Adams, John Q.		H, 123rd Ohio Inf.	31		1901 Dec 21	KS, 21st, 1902
Adams, John Q.		B, 12th Kans. Inf.	12		1911 Nov 30	KS, 31st, 1912
Adams, John W.		47th Ind. Inf.	127		1916 Apr 18	IA, 43rd, 1917
Adams, Joseph	Pvt.	L, 4th Ind. Cav.	321	46	1887 Jan 20	IA, 15th, 1889
Adams, Joseph	Pvt.	A, 32nd Iowa Inf.	66		1914 Oct 2	IA, 41st, 1915
Adams, Joseph		B, 11th Ill. Cav. (died at Goddard)	483		1895 Jul	KS, 15th, 1896
Adams, Joseph W.	Pvt.	M, 2nd Ohio Cav.	88		1913 May 26	IA, 40th, 1914
Adams, L.P.	Corp.	F, 33rd Wis. Inf.	298		1913 Dec 11	IA, 40th, 1914
Adams, L.R.		I, 11th Kans.	35		1908[1909?] Mar 31	KS, 29th, 1910
Adams, M.		10th Ohio	18		1921	IA, 48th, 1922
Adams, Nelson		K, 89th Ohio Vol. Inf.	8		1915 Aug 14	KS, 35th, 1916
Adams, R.B.		I, 26th Mo.	380		1906 Aug 1	KS, 26th, 1907
Adams, Robert		D, 6th Kans. Cav.	49		1898 Nov 27	KS, 18th, 1899
Adams, Robert D.		H, 10th Mich. Cav.	25		1921 Dec 28	KS, 41st, 1922
Adams, Rufus	Pvt.	I, 1st N.Y. Dragoons	420	61	1890 Feb 24	IA, 17th, 1891

*See Appendix A, B or C for roster of post names and locations.
†See Introduction for note regarding recording of death date.

Name	Rank	Company, Regiment or Ship	Post*	Age	Death Date†	Journal
Adams, S.P.	Capt.	Cav.	70	77	1894 Mar 14	IA, 20th, 1894
Adams, S.S.	Pvt.	G, 106th N.Y. Inf.	235		1926 May 23	IA, 53rd, 1927
Adams, Samuel		G, 4th U.S. B, 3rd Wis. Cav. (died at Douglas)	97		1895 Aug 10	KS, 15th, 1896
Adams, Samuel P.	Pvt.	C, 45th Ill. Inf.	22		1898 Jun 23	IA, 25th, 1899
Adams, Shubal P.		provost marshal	70		1894 Apr	IA, 21st, 1895
Adams, T.		I, 14th Ohio	72		1926 Jul 16	KS, 46th, 1927
Adams, Thomas	Pvt.	I, 18th Iowa Inf.	173		1902 Dec 5	IA, 29th, 1903
Adams, Thomas		I, 80th Ill.	1		1918 Jun 8	KS, 38th, 1919
Adams, Thomas		K, 3rd Ky.	59		1927 Dec 29	KS, 47th, 1928
Adams, Thos.	Corp.	K, 112th N.Y. Inf.	88	42	1885 Jul 14	IA, 12th, 1886
Adams, Thos.	Corp.	K, 112th N.Y. Inf.	88	42	1885 Jul 14	IA, 12th, 1886
Adams, Thos. F.			25		1906 Oct 29	KS, 26th, 1907
Adams, W.J.	Pvt.	E, 82nd Ohio Inf.	116		1900 Nov 1	IA, 27th, 1901
Adams, W.T.	Sergt.	E, 96th Ill. Inf.	81		1910 Nov 5	IA, 37th, 1911
Adams, Warren		M, 1st N.Y.	6		1928 Nov 18	KS, 48th, 1929
Adams, William A.		B, 2nd Ohio F, 1st Ohio	104		1920 Dec 5	KS, 40th, 1921
Adams, Willis	Pvt.	F, 9th Ind. Inf.	18		1930 Aug 4	IA, 57th, 1931
Adams, Wm.		F, 155th Penn. Inf.	65		1918 Jun 16	KS, 38th, 1919
Adams, Wm. A.			54		1900 Mar 6	KS, 20th, 1901
Adams, Wm. R.		133rd Ill. (died of senility)	110	80	1911 Nov 17	NE, 36th, 1912
Adamson, Abraham	Pvt.	B, 48th Iowa Inf.	16		1917 Nov 28	IA, 44th, 1918
Adamson, Frank H.		D, 3rd Iowa	18		1906 Apr 10	KS, 26th, 1907
Adamson, V.V.		2nd Kans.	46		1928 Aug 12	KS, 48th, 1929
Adamson, W.	Sergt.	B, 5th Iowa Inf.	16	56	1897 Jan 5	IA, 24th, 1898
Adcock, Adom	Pvt.	I, 8th Iowa Inf.	18		1918 Oct 4	IA, 45th, 1919
Adcock, H.A.	Corp.	E, 36th Iowa Inf.	497		1925 Aug 25	IA, 52nd, 1926
Adderson, J.		G, 9th Ill. Inf.	153		1914 Oct 4	KS, 34th, 1915
Addis, E.S.		B, 6th U.S. Cav.	71		1917 Jun 3	KS, 37th, 1918
Addis, J.B.		K, 12th Kans.	145		1915 Aug 26	KS, 35th, 1916
Adell, Howell G.		A, 19th Iowa Inf. (died of paralysis)	90	66	1910 Sep 7	NE, 35th, 1911
Ades, W.	Pvt.	K, 113th Ill. Inf.	67		1929 Feb 2	IA, 56th, 1930
Adkins, B.B.	Pvt.	B, 10th Iowa	425		1921 Nov 30	IA, 48th, 1922
Adkins, B.B.	Pvt.	B, 10th Iowa	425		1922 Nov 30	IA, 49th, 1923
Adkins, C.J.	Pvt.	I, 83rd Ill. Inf.	127		1906 May 15	IA, 33rd, 1907
Adkins, E.	Pvt.	D, 112th Ill. Inf.	16	72	1897 Jun 2	IA, 24th, 1898
Adkins, F.J.	Sergt.	D, 30th Ky. Inf.	64		1924 Sep 27	IA, 51st, 1925
Adkins, James		I, 9th Mo.	256		1908 Feb	KS, 28th, 1909
Adkinson, A.D.			118		1883	KS, 3rd, 1884
Adkinson, Chauncy		B, 36th Ohio Vol. Inf.	4		1915 Nov 17	KS, 35th, 1916
Adler, H.	Pvt.	M, 2nd Iowa Cav.	22		1921 Mar 4	IA, 48th, 1922
Adrain, A.D.		G, 2nd Ill.	301		1934	KS, 55th, 1936
Adrien, A.	Pvt.	F, 57th Ill. Inf.	111		1921 Feb 10	IA, 48th, 1922
Adsit, H.F.		D, 39th Wis.	49		1915 Nov 14	KS, 35th, 1916
Ady, David	Pvt.	K, 31st Iowa Inf.	18		1918 Jun 24	IA, 45th, 1919
Ady, J.S.	Pvt.		124		1929 May 3	IA, 56th, 1930
Agard, B.E.	Pvt.	C, 6th Iowa Cav.	78	59	1891 Jun 10	IA, 18th, 1892
Agard, Fernando W.	Pvt.	G, 130th N.Y. Vols.	10	55	1900 Mar 14	IA, 26th, 1900
Agard, Norman		A, 32nd Ill.	1		1911 Jan 2	KS, 31st, 1912
Agen, John	Pvt.	A, 14th Iowa Inf.	297		1917 Apr 27	IA, 44th, 1918
Ager, J.H.		H, 15th Wis. Hvy. Art.	25	74	1920 Nov 29	NE, 45th, 1921
Agler, John		B, 4th Iowa Inf.	5	78	1924 May 31	NE, 49th, 1925
Agnew, David B.	Pvt.	I, 22nd Penn. Vol. Cav.	466		1903 Jul 1	IA, 30th, 1904
Agnew, George	Sergt.	C, 4th Iowa Inf.	34		1929 Dec 11	IA, 56th, 1930
Agnew, W.G.		B, 3rd Iowa Inf.	173		1924 Apr 8	IA, 51st, 1925
Agnew, W.G.		B, 3rd Iowa Inf.	173		1923 Apr 8	IA, 50th, 1924
Aiken, Cyrus		G, 16th Vt.	252		1922 Jul 22	KS, 42nd, 1923
Aikins, H.B.	Pvt.	G, 33rd Iowa Inf.	55		1913 Dec 20	IA, 40th, 1914
Aikins, John		K, 28th Iowa Inf.	200		1886	KS, 6th, 1887
Aikman, R.		C, 18th Ind.	32		1927	KS, 47th, 1928
Aimes, C.F.S.		D, 82nd N.Y.			1936 Oct 29	KS, 56th, 1937

Name	Rank	Company, Regiment or Ship	Post*	Age	Death Date†	Journal
Ainsworth, Avery		C, 5th Ill. Cav.	36		1921 May 19	KS, 41st, 1922
Ainsworth, J.S.	Pvt.	H, 6th Vt. Inf.	12		1915 Aug 10	IA, 42nd, 1916
Ainsworth, Oscar	Corp.	A, 32nd Iowa Inf.	58		1909 Dec 7	IA, 36th, 1910
Ainsworth, Wm.		D, 51st Ill.	63		1918 Aug 8	KS, 38th, 1919
Airy, Levi	Pvt.	4th Iowa Bat.	40		1920 Sep 20	IA, 47th, 1921
Aker, —		Kans.	241		1908[1909?] Nov 10	KS, 29th, 1910
Akerman, W.H.		F, 186th N.Y. Vols. (died of Bright's disease)	13	65	1897 Dec 24	NE, 22nd, 1898
Akers, Benjamin F.	Corp.	A, 22nd Iowa Inf. (at large)	448	98	1941 Mar 17	IA, 67th, 1941
Akers, Jonathan		D, 2nd Ill. Cav.	12		1910 May 8	KS, 30th, 1911
Akhurst, John		B & G, 53rd Ill. Inf. (died of heart disease)	187		1891 Dec 28	KS, 11th, 1892
Akin, Alvia D.		H, 46th Ill. (murdered)	193	58	1900 Sep 30	NE, 25th, 1901
Akin, John		7th N.Y. Cav.	65		1916 Nov 1	KS, 36th, 1917
Akins, Joseph		A, 2nd Iowa Inf.	515		1919 Dec 4	IA, 46th, 1920
Akins, W.D.		H, 46th Ill. (died of diseased dig. organs)	209	75	1922 Dec 27	NE, 47th, 1923
Albaugh, Daniel	Pvt.	C, 24th Iowa Inf.	140		1919 Oct 29	IA, 46th, 1920
Albee, A.	Pvt.	H, 18th N.Y. Inf.	337		1920 Aug 5	IA, 47th, 1921
Albee, Anson	Pvt.	D, 50th Wis. Inf.	456		1926 Nov 6	IA, 53rd, 1927
Albee, Edwin W.	Pvt.	A, 44th Iowa Inf.	78		1922 Mar 15	IA, 49th, 1923
Albee, George W.		E, 2nd Wis. Cav. (at large)	149	92	1938 Jan 4	IA, 64th, 1938
Albee, Gilbert		H, 13th N.W.[N.Y.?]	32		1928 Jan 23	KS, 48th, 1929
Albee, Joseph	Pvt.	C, 101st N.Y. Inf.	193		1901 Jun 24	IA, 28th, 1902
Albee, V.W.	Pvt.	E, 1st U.S. Sharpshooters	68		1907 Aug 15	IA, 34th, 1908
Albers, J.L.	Pvt.	C, 66th Ind.	40		1903 Oct	IA, 30th, 1904
Albershardt, L.W.		K, 72nd Ind. (died of heart failure)	13	72	1917 Aug 16	NE, 42nd, 1918
Alberson, R.W.	Pvt.	K, 102nd Iowa Vol. Inf.	108	62	1892 Feb 23	IA, 19th, 1893
Albert, H.W.		died of heart failure	32		1921 Jan 26	NE, 46th, 1922
Albert, J.K.		B, 195th Ohio Vol. Inf.	25		1908 Dec 8	KS, 28th, 1909
Alberts, C.H.			29		1914 Nov 1	IA, 41st, 1915
Albertson, Charley		H, 31st Iowa	25		1911 Mar 15	KS, 31st, 1912
Albertson, David	Pvt.	F, 11th U.S. Inf.	497	59	1896 Oct 24	IA, 23rd, 1897
Albertson, James A.	2nd Lieut.	H, 4th Iowa Cav.	277	52	1894 Jun 21	IA, 21st, 1895
Albertson, Jno.	Drummer	7th Iowa Inf.	434		1925 Nov 4	IA, 52nd, 1926
Albrecht, John, see Abrecht, John						
Albright, A.C.		K, 34th Ohio Inf. (died of paralysis)	13	78	1920 Jun 29	NE, 45th, 1921
Albright, Chas. H.			4		1914 Dec 15	IA, 41st, 1915
Albright, Ezra C.		D, 156th Ind. Inf.	132		1886	KS, 6th, 1887
Albright, Fred		I, 6th Iowa Cav.	13		1931 May 7	NE, 56th, 1932
Albright, Homer		D, 152nd Ill. Inf.	179		1918 Aug 15	KS, 38th, 1919
Albright, J.H.		G, 1st Wis. Hvy. Art.	5		1925	KS, 45th, 1926
Albright, J.S.		D, 70th Ind. Inf.	18		1917 May 26	KS, 37th, 1918
Albright, Jesse		F, 4th Mo. Cav.	17		1912 Jul 18	KS, 32nd, 1913
Albright, Samuel			12		1923 Apr 16	IA, 50th, 1924
Albright, Wm. M.	Pvt.	G, 47th Iowa Inf.		90	1935 Nov 30	IA, 65th, 1939
Albro, James		M, 11th Mich.	12		1912 May 30	KS, 32nd, 1913
Alcorn, James P.		B, 1st Penn. Art.	241		1911 Jan 21	KS, 31st, 1912
Ald, William		F, 77th Ill. Inf.	244		1916 Sep 3	KS, 36th, 1917
Alden, Jonathan		G, 92nd Ohio Inf. (died at Hollenberg)	70		1895 Nov	KS, 15th, 1896
Alden, W.	Pvt.	32nd Mo. Inf.	296	54	1896 Aug 10	IA, 23rd, 1897
Alder, Henry	Pvt.	K, 13th Wis. Inf.	133		1901 Feb 10	IA, 27th, 1901
Alder, J.W.		I, 3rd Wis.	12		1919 Jun 14	KS, 39th, 1920
Alder, John		A, 47th Penn. Inf. (killed in South)	25		1893 Dec 3	KS, 14th, 1895
Alder, L.K.		I, 22nd Ind.	171		1933 May 24	NE, 58th, 1934
Alderman, C.H.		Tenn. Inf.	459		1901 Jul	KS, 21st, 1902
Alderman, Jos. P.	Pvt.	E, 4th Iowa Inf.	30		1918 Jun 25	IA, 45th, 1919
Alderson, Corts	Pvt.	E, 17th Iowa Inf.	69		1923 Apr 13	IA, 50th, 1924
Alderson, M.H.		K, 21st Ky.	127		1924 Jun 4	KS, 44th, 1925
Aldrich, Charles	Adjt.	32nd Iowa Inf.	66		1908 Mar 8	IA, 35th, 1909
Aldrich, Dan'l A.		L, 3rd Ind. Cav.	11	73	1907 Apr 22	NE, 32nd, 1908
Aldrich, Henry	Musician	G, 31st Iowa Inf.	130		1911 May 3	IA, 38th, 1912
Aldrich, Liberty	Pvt.	D, 6th Vt. Inf.	221	68	1887 May 10	IA, 14th, 1888

Name	Rank	Company, Regiment or Ship	Post*	Age	Death Date†	Journal
Aldrich, N.	Pvt.	D, 21st Iowa Inf.	97		1917 Nov 29	IA, 44th, 1918
Aldrich, S.W.		A, 1st R.I. Lt. Art. (died at Hiawatha; buried at Hiawatha)	130		1894 May	KS, 14th, 1895
Aldridge, John	Pvt.	K, 11th Wis. Inf.	3		1904 Feb 18	IA, 31st, 1905
Aldridge, Richard		C, 11th Ill. Cav.	25	82	1917 Feb 10	NE, 42nd, 1918
Aleig, Peter		H, 19th Ohio Inf.	240		1887 May 9	KS, 7th, 1888
Alen, William L.	Pvt.	C, 42nd Ohio Inf.	210		1901 Jul 10	IA, 28th, 1902
Alexander, A.J.		Ky. Mtd. Inf.	1		1902 Sep 24	KS, 22nd, 1903
Alexander, A.P.	Corp.	A, 6th Iowa Inf.	206		1904 Apr	IA, 31st, 1905
Alexander, B.C.			153		1900 Dec 23	KS, 20th, 1901
Alexander, C.F.	Pvt.	G, 14th Iowa Inf.	24		1919 Feb 4	IA, 46th, 1920
Alexander, C.H.		A, 7th Ohio Cav. (died at Clay Centre; buried at Greenwood)	88		1894 Jul 14	KS, 14th, 1895
Alexander, Charles E.		C, 14th Penn.	129		1912 Dec 27	KS, 32nd, 1913
Alexander, Chas.	Pvt.	A, 29th Iowa Inf.	59		1920 Sep 30	IA, 47th, 1921
Alexander, Curtis L.		C, 48th Iowa Inf.	13		1938 Nov 14	NE, 63rd, 1939
Alexander, Edwin		D, 24th Ind.	380		1911 Jul 22	KS, 31st, 1912
Alexander, Geo.	Pvt.	A, 1st Ill. Cav.	78		1906 Sep 2	IA, 33rd, 1907
Alexander, H.S.		D, 160th Ohio Inf.	29	91	1936 Oct 30	IA, 63rd, 1937
Alexander, Isaac		B, 9th Kans. Cav.	15		1913	KS, 33rd, 1914
Alexander, Israel G.		F, 12th Ind. Inf.	32		1908[1909?] May 23	KS, 29th, 1910
Alexander, J.A.		F, 35th Ind.	68		1911 Feb 6	KS, 31st, 1912
Alexander, J.H.	Pvt.	A, 61st Ind. Inf.	124		1916	IA, 43rd, 1917
Alexander, J.M.		F, 12th Ind. Inf.	85		1914 Jun 27	KS, 34th, 1915
Alexander, J.R.		D, 86th Ind.	1		1925 May 2	KS, 45th, 1926
Alexander, J.S.	Capt.	A, 31st Iowa Inf.	206		1915 Jun 29	IA, 42nd, 1916
Alexander, J.T.	Pvt.	F, 54th Ill. Inf.	147		1904-1905	IA, 31st, 1905
Alexander, James	Pvt.	C, 37th Iowa Inf.	170		1st quarter 1886	IA, 12th, 1886
Alexander, James M.		I, 80th Ill.	100		1913 Oct 6	KS, 33rd, 1914
Alexander, James P.	Pvt.	I, 160th Penn. Inf.	414		1912	IA, 39th, 1913
Alexander, John	Pvt.	K, 166th Ohio Inf.	511		1910 Sep 23	IA, 37th, 1911
Alexander, John		E, 18th Wis.	158		1893 Mar 22	KS, 13th, 1894
Alexander, Joseph		F, 164th Ohio	244		1917 Dec 4	KS, 37th, 1918
Alexander, M.L.	Pvt.	G, 9th Iowa Inf.	193		1910 Jun 4	IA, 38th, 1912
Alexander, O.P.	Sergt.	K, 111th Penn. Inf. (died of erysipelas)	43	48	1887 May 8	NE, 12th, 1888
Alexander, Philip	Pvt.	G, 82nd Ohio Inf.	173	61	1898 Oct 31	IA, 25th, 1899
Alexander, Robt. J.		73rd Ill.	33		1906 Sep 2	KS, 26th, 1907
Alexander, S.M.		23rd Ind. Battery Lt. Art.	380		1911 Aug 4	KS, 31st, 1912
Alexander, Silas J.		G, 1st Colo. Cav. (died of heart disease; see also Appendix D)	214		1911 Apr 24	NE, 36th, 1912
Alexander, T.J.	Pvt.	5th Wis. Battery	55		1914 Jun 26	IA, 41st, 1915
Alexander, T.J.		M, 16th Penn. Cav. (died of tuberculosis, bowels)	2	67	1906 Apr 30	NE, 31st, 1907
Alexander, Thomas P.		I, 11th Ind.	202		1913 Feb 27	KS, 32nd, 1913
Alexander, W.D.		A, 110th Ohio Inf.	1		1899 Jun 28	KS, 19th, 1900
Alexander, York		D, 17th U.S.	130		1904 Oct 25	KS, 24th, 1905
Alferd, William J.		D, 11th Ill. Cav.	18		1908 May 10	KS, 28th, 1909
Alford, John W.			337		1917 Nov 17	IA, 44th, 1918
Alford, Lore	Capt.	H, 8th Maine Vols.	68	62	1900 Mar 30	IA, 26th, 1900
Alger, W.S.		B, 115th N.Y.	271	*	1922 Jul 22	IA, 49th, 1923
Algire, W.			68		1916	KS, 36th, 1917
Algood, Robt.	Pvt.	B, 1st Ky. Cav.	40	64	1890 Dec 23	IA, 18th, 1892
Algyer, Hiram	Pvt.	L, 74th N.Y. Lt. Art.	339	51	1887 Feb 3	IA, 14th, 1888
Alher, George K.		P, 4th & 17th U.S.T.	71		1924 Oct 2	KS, 44th, 1925
Aliff, Samuel C.		A, 35th Mo.	263		1908 Nov 14	KS, 28th, 1909
Alkine, C.J.	Pvt.	I, 83rd Ill.	127		1905 May 15	IA, 32nd, 1906
Alkins, Simon		K, 76th Ill. Inf.	113		1909 May 30	KS, 29th, 1910
Allabach, E.W.	Pvt.	A, 52nd Penn. Inf.	12		1912 Apr 23	IA, 39th, 1913
Allard, Daniel	Pvt.	E, 20th Wis. Inf.	235		1900-1901	IA, 27th, 1901
Allbee, J.H.		M, 1st Ill. Art. (Minden)			1943 Nov 12	NE, 70th, 1946
Alldoffer, Newton		I, 82nd Ohio	297		1911 Nov 2	KS, 31st, 1912
Allee, A.		K, 16th Ill. Cav.	110		1906 Jan 10	NE, 31st, 1907

*See Appendix A, B or C for roster of post names and locations.
†See Introduction for note regarding recording of death date.

6

Name	Rank	Company, Regiment or Ship	Post*	Age	Death Date†	Journal
Allee, F.M.		Ind. Battery	408		1906 Feb 17	IA, 32nd, 1906
Allee, F.M.	Pvt.	9th Ind. Battery	408		1906 Feb 17	IA, 33rd, 1907
Allee, Jesse J.	Pvt.	C, 137th Ill.	416		1923 Apr 18	IA, 50th, 1924
Allen, A.		B, 108th Ill.	38		1926 Jul	NE, 51st, 1927
Allen, A.E.			130		1910	IA, 37th, 1911
Allen, A.E.			426		1908	IA, 35th, 1909
Allen, A.F.		Mich. Eng.	12		1917 Nov 24	KS, 37th, 1918
Allen, A.J.	Pvt.		251		1912 Sep 30	IA, 39th, 1913
Allen, A.W.		1st Minn. Lt. Art.	130		1908 Sep 6	KS, 28th, 1909
Allen, Albert	Pvt.	I, 50th Wis. Inf.	200		1916 Jan 16	IA, 42nd, 1916
Allen, Albert S.		F, 82nd Ohio	52		1911 Oct 3	KS, 31st, 1912
Allen, Albion		A, 97th Ill. (died of old age)	38	78	1925 Dec	NE, 50th, 1926
Allen, Alexander	Pvt.	F, 1st Iowa Cav.	63	68	1899 Jun 19	IA, 26th, 1900
Allen, Augustus		F, 26th Ill.	64		1889	KS, 9th, 1890
Allen, B.D.		M, 11th Mo. Cav.	25		1911 Apr 7	KS, 31st, 1912
Allen, B.E.	Pvt.	H, 36th Ill. Inf.	236	89	1931 May 1	IA, 58th, 1932
Allen, Carley B.		B, 9th Kans. Cav.	12		1917 Nov 19	KS, 37th, 1918
Allen, Charles	Pvt.		493		1913	IA, 40th, 1914
Allen, Charles A.		G, 19th Mich. Inf.	88		1930 Jan 4	KS, 50th, 1931
Allen, Charles S.		G, 117th N.Y. (died of paralysis of heart)	22	81	1922 Jul 23	NE, 47th, 1923
Allen, Chas. B.		B, 2nd Kans.	100		1899 Jul 23	KS, 19th, 1900
Allen, D.C.		died of cancer	52	75	1917 Oct 13	NE, 42nd, 1918
Allen, D.E.	Pvt.	F, 8th Iowa Vol. Inf.	167		1903 Dec 7	IA, 30th, 1904
Allen, D.P.		H, 2nd Mich. (died of pneumonia)	32	58	1902 Nov	NE, 27th, 1903
Allen, David S.		E, 7th Ill.	182		1927 Feb 8	NE, 52nd, 1928
Allen, E.T.	Pvt.	F, 46th Iowa Inf.	107		1924 Sep 14	IA, 51st, 1925
Allen, E.W.	Pvt.	B, 45th Iowa Inf.	108		1925 May 4	IA, 52nd, 1926
Allen, Edward P.		E, 13th Ky.	4		1915 Nov 27	KS, 35th, 1916
Allen, Eli P.		C, 7th Mo. State Militia	289		1902 Apr 24	KS, 22nd, 1903
Allen, Eugene	Pvt.	I, 12th Wis. Inf.	235	90	1939 Jan 11	IA, 65th, 1939
Allen, F.D.	Pvt.	H, 8th Iowa Inf.	40		1924 Oct 15	IA, 51st, 1925
Allen, Francis Lossen		H, 146th Ind. (died of paralysis)	60	82	1916 Jun 8	NE, 40th, 1916
Allen, Geo.			235		1911 Jun 26	IA, 38th, 1912
Allen, Geo. W.	Pvt.	M, 8th Ill. Cav.	88		1916 Mar 11	IA, 43rd, 1917
Allen, George	Pvt.	E, 64th Ill. Inf.	81		1919 Nov 14	IA, 46th, 1920
Allen, George W.		A, 110th N.Y.	1		1919 Jan 12	KS, 39th, 1920
Allen, H.B.	Corp.	B, 117th N.Y. Inf.	12	87	1932 Jun 28	IA, 59th, 1933
Allen, H.T.	Pvt.	E, 3rd Ohio Cav.	150		1913 Apr 6	IA, 40th, 1914
Allen, Henry		F, 138th Ill.	at large		1931	NE, 56th, 1932
Allen, Hiram		F, 92nd Ill.	274		1912 Feb 22	KS, 32nd, 1913
Allen, Hugh A.		Mich.	12		1911 Jun 12	KS, 31st, 1912
Allen, Ira J.	Bugler	H, 22nd N.Y. Cav.	31		1917 Jul 30	IA, 44th, 1918
Allen, Isaac E.		G, 76th Penn. Inf. (died of heart trouble)	22	71	1910 Dec 2	NE, 35th, 1911
Allen, J.B.	Pvt.		233		1927 Feb 12	IA, 54th, 1928
Allen, J.C.			55		1930 Aug 14	KS, 50th, 1931
Allen, J.F.		B, 43rd Ind. Inf.	489		1899 Feb 4	KS, 19th, 1900
Allen, Jacob H.		B, 20th Ohio	57		1918 Oct 28	KS, 38th, 1919
Allen, James	Pvt.	K, 5th Penn. Res. Vol. Corps	57		1916 Mar 19	IA, 43rd, 1917
Allen, James		A, 1st Kans.	6		1922 Jun 17	KS, 42nd, 1923
Allen, James H.		H, 79th U.S.C.T.	158		1902	KS, 22nd, 1903
Allen, James M.		A, 23rd Ky.	18		1912 Nov 10	KS, 32nd, 1913
Allen, James M.		K, 16th Ind.	129		1912 Dec 1	KS, 32nd, 1913
Allen, James T.			16		3rd quarter 1883	IA, 10th, 1884
Allen, Jerry		H, 59th U.S.C. Cav. N.C.	46		1904 Oct 29	KS, 24th, 1905
Allen, Jno. M.	2nd Corp.	C & D, 13th Iowa Inf.	68		1925 Feb 9	IA, 52nd, 1926
Allen, John	Pvt.	I, 7th Iowa Inf.	497	74	1896 Dec 12	IA, 23rd, 1897
Allen, John		A, 117th Ill.	125		1912 Jan 19	KS, 32nd, 1913
Allen, John		H, 65th Mo. 75th Wis.	68		1917 Oct 30	KS, 37th, 1918
Allen, John A.		B, 106th Ill.	251		1919 May 19	KS, 39th, 1920
Allen, John D.		D, 7th Ohio	464		1919 Apr 16	KS, 39th, 1920
Allen, John H.	Pvt.	E, 146th Ill. Inf.	162	44	1892 Nov 2	IA, 19th, 1893

*See Appendix A, B or C for roster of post names and locations.
†See Introduction for note regarding recording of death date.

Name	Rank	Company, Regiment or Ship	Post*	Age	Death Date†	Journal
Allen, John U.			144		1913 Jan 2	KS, 33rd, 1914
Allen, Jonah B.		E, 7th Ill. Mt. Inf.	40		1912 Dec 10	KS, 32nd, 1913
Allen, Joseph		B, 40th Ind. Inf.	314		1901 Jan 3	KS, 21st, 1902
Allen, Joseph W.		M, 100th Penn.	14		1913 Aug 5	KS, 33rd, 1914
Allen, L.B.	Pvt.	B, 45th Iowa Inf.	436		1929 Jan 7	IA, 56th, 1930
Allen, L.J.	Capt.	19th Iowa Inf.	40		1902 May 10	IA, 29th, 1903
Allen, M.C.	Pvt.	D, 40th Ohio Inf. (at large)			1931 Jan 23	IA, 58th, 1932
Allen, Mark	Pvt.	B, 1st Iowa Inf.	250		1919 Aug 13	IA, 46th, 1920
Allen, Marshall		F, 7th Ill. Inf.	85		1901 Apr 6	KS, 21st, 1902
Allen, N.M.		M, Ohio	55		1926 Nov 9	KS, 46th, 1927
Allen, Newton		F, 30th Mich. Inf.	88		1909 Jul 3	KS, 29th, 1910
Allen, O.D.		I, 118th Ohio Inf.	158		4th quarter 1884	IA, 11th, 1885
Allen, R.N.		F, 136th Ind.	129		1914 Sep 12	KS, 34th, 1915
Allen, R.S.	Capt.	H, 51st Wis. Inf.	77	62	1887 Dec 2	IA, 14th, 1888
Allen, S.B.		D, 10th Conn.	294		1896 Mar 17	KS, 16th, 1897
Allen, S.E.		C, 146th Ill.	288		1928	NE, 53rd, 1929
Allen, Sanders	Corp.	G, 39th Iowa Inf.	10	67	1898 Dec 14	IA, 25th, 1899
Allen, Silas	Pvt.	H, 87th Inf.	7		1911 Jan 27	IA, 38th, 1912
Allen, Stephen	Pvt.	D, 98th N.Y. Inf.	16		1910 Mar 17	IA, 37th, 1911
Allen, T.C.		D, 147th Ind. (died of hardening of muscles)	76	69	1913 Oct 3	NE, 38th, 1914
Allen, T.J.			32		1911 Sep 13	KS, 31st, 1912
Allen, T.W.		H, 26th Iowa Inf. (died of heart trouble)	22	72	1908 May 30	NE, 33rd, 1909
Allen, Thomas	Pvt.	E, 5th Iowa Cav.	78		1918 Aug 24	IA, 45th, 1919
Allen, Thomas H.		G, 26th Wis. Inf.	52		1929 Jan 9	KS, 49th, 1930
Allen, Thos.	Pvt.	F, 13th Ind. Inf.	40		1904 May 17	IA, 31st, 1905
Allen, Thos. F.	Lieut.	D, 20th Iowa Inf.	339		1907 Apr 29	IA, 34th, 1908
Allen, W.		Kans.	241		1908[1909?] Oct 15	KS, 29th, 1910
Allen, W.E.		B, 145th Ill.	170		1917	KS, 37th, 1918
Allen, W.H.	Pvt.	F, 147th Ill. Inf.	391		1919 Sep 13	IA, 47th, 1921
Allen, W.H.	Pvt.	G, 17th Wis. Inf.	49		1924 Dec 12	IA, 51st, 1925
Allen, W.H.		K, 13th Iowa Vols.	264		1902 Nov	KS, 22nd, 1903
Allen, W.W.		D, 11th Kans.	39		1911 Aug 6	KS, 31st, 1912
Allen, William	Pvt.	C, 34th U.S. Colored Inf.	88		1916 Apr 21	IA, 43rd, 1917
Allen, William		H, 5th Ohio Cav.	5		1912 Jul 22	KS, 32nd, 1913
Allen, William		B, 12th West Va.	100		1915 Aug 22	KS, 35th, 1916
Allen, William G.	Capt.	F, 25th Iowa Inf.	153	68	1895 Jan 17	IA, 21st, 1895
Allen, William H.		A, 45th Ohio	14		1923 Oct 28	KS, 43rd, 1924
Allen, Willis		G, 1st Colored Cav.	27		1885	KS, 5th, 1886
Allen, Wm.		79th —	208		1896	KS, 16th, 1897
Allen, Wm. F.		B, 2nd —	271		1904 Nov 13	KS, 24th, 1905
Allen, Wm. T.	Pvt.	B, 16th Wis. Inf.	230	70	1891 Aug 7	IA, 18th, 1892
Allender, R.B.	Chaplain	22nd Iowa Inf.	100	82	1898 Apr 9	IA, 24th, 1898
Allender, William		K, 134th Ind.	253		1910	KS, 30th, 1911
Allendorf, C.		F, 1st U.S. Art.	36		1898 Dec 25	KS, 18th, 1899
Allensworth, James		D, 108th Ill. Inf.	17		1912 Aug 23	KS, 32nd, 1913
Allerd, Nathaniel	Pvt.	24th Ill.	26		1923 Jan 6	IA, 50th, 1924
Allerts, Henry		H, 7th Ill.	158		1920	KS, 40th, 1921
Alley, Wm. T.	Pvt.	G, 19th Iowa Inf.	2	56	1895 Dec 9	IA, 22nd, 1896
Allgeyer, John	Corp.	E, 21st Iowa Inf.	78		1926 Aug 19	IA, 53rd, 1927
Alline, A.A.	Pvt.	G, 1st Iowa Cav.	91		1923 May 31	IA, 50th, 1924
Allis, Albert		D, 30th Mich. Inf. (nonmember)			1941 Mar	NE, 66th, 1942
Allison, A.	Pvt.	E, 7th Iowa Inf.	56		1916	IA, 43rd, 1917
Allison, Adam C.		E, 115th Ill. (died of old age)	165	84	1918 Mar 21	NE, 43rd, 1919
Allison, David	Sergt.	G, 46th Ill. Inf.	68		1929 Feb 3	IA, 56th, 1930
Allison, Edmund		G, 17th Ill. Cav.	350		1916 Jan 1	KS, 36th, 1917
Allison, George			386		1914	KS, 34th, 1915
Allison, Henry		K, 118th Ill.	101		1902	KS, 22nd, 1903
Allison, Hugh J.	Pvt.	G, 40th Iowa Inf.	205	68	1897 Feb 21	IA, 23rd, 1897
Allison, Jas.	Pvt.	A, 35th Wis. Inf.	101		1902 Feb 22	IA, 29th, 1903
Allison, Jas. H.	Pvt.		247		1902 Jan 26	IA, 29th, 1903
Allison, John E.		I, 21st Penn. Cav.	32		1916 Jun 28	KS, 36th, 1917

Name	Rank	Company, Regiment or Ship	Post*	Age	Death Date†	Journal
Allison, Levy	Pvt.	C, 2nd Ohio Vol. Vet. Cav.	147	69	1900 Feb 28	IA, 26th, 1900
Allison, M.H.		3rd Iowa	92		1926 Mar 16	KS, 46th, 1927
Allison, Samuel V.	Sergt.	I, 42nd Wis.	3		1907 Dec 23	IA, 34th, 1908
Allison, Thos. J.	Pvt.	F, 33rd Iowa Inf.	192		1929 Mar 23	IA, 56th, 1930
Allison, W.G.		F, 1st Ind.	51		1902 May 27	KS, 22nd, 1903
Allison, W.L.		D, 1st Penn.	63		1911 Mar 17	KS, 31st, 1912
Allison, Wm.	Pvt.	F, 33rd Iowa Inf.	138		1912 Dec 6	IA, 40th, 1914
Allmon, Wm.		C, 16th Ohio	55		1896 Nov 27	KS, 16th, 1897
Allpress, H.A.		H, 12th Ill. Cav. (died of heart failure)	130	65	1912 Oct 24	NE, 37th, 1913
Allred, Wm. P.	Pvt.	H, 46th Iowa Inf.	192	92	1939 Mar 4	IA, 65th, 1939
Allslot, John		C, 21st Iowa	51		1920 Feb 20	KS, 40th, 1921
Ally, J.P.		K, 39th Ky.	18		1924 Apr 8	KS, 44th, 1925
Allyn, Chas.	Pvt.	C, 118th Ill. Inf.	190		1913 Mar 23	IA, 40th, 1914
Almond, John K.		H, 54th Ind.	256		1916 May 11	KS, 36th, 1917
Alney, Henry		D, 35th Ind.	70		1885	KS, 5th, 1886
Alor, Wilson H.		A, 7th Ill. Cav. (died of apoplexy)	112	72	1915 Dec 12	NE, 40th, 1916
Alrich, Levi L.		B, 71st Penn.	43		1917 Oct 24	KS, 37th, 1918
Alstrand, Gust.	Pvt.	H, 1st Lt. Art.	236		1925 Apr 16	IA, 52nd, 1926
Alstrum, Jonas		D, 57th Ill. Inf.	88		1917 Feb 15	KS, 37th, 1918
Altamont, Victor	Pvt.	K, 20th Iowa Inf.	382	56	1886 Jul 3	IA, 13th, 1887
Altar, John		I, 101st Penn.	337		1936 Nov	KS, 57th, 1938
Altemus, John	Pvt.	E, 23rd Ill. Inf.	112		1926 Jun 28	IA, 53rd, 1927
Altemus, John	Pvt.	C, 1st Mo. Eng.	112		1930 Jun 28	IA, 57th, 1931
Altenreid, Levi		L, 7th Mo. Cav.	17		1914 Jun 19	KS, 34th, 1915
Alter, I.R.		K, 8th Ohio Inf.	11	66	1910 Nov 8	NE, 35th, 1911
Alter, John		F, 101st Penn.	337		1936 Nov	KS, 56th, 1937
Altermant, Victor, see Altamont, Victor						
Altermut, Victor, see Altamont, Victor						
Althouse, Henry	Pvt.	G, 16th Iowa Inf.	311		1911 Jul 19	IA, 38th, 1912
Altman, D.S.	Chaplain	151st Ill.	18		1893 Nov 11	KS, 13th, 1894
Altman, H.R.		B, 13th Ohio Cav.	250		1901 Nov 21	KS, 21st, 1902
Alusendinger, David	Pvt.	B, 140th N.Y. Inf.	5		1912 Apr 17	IA, 39th, 1913
Alvard, Seth			248		1915	IA, 42nd, 1916
Alverson, H.C.	Pvt.	B, 40th Wis. Inf.	12		1920 Oct 28	IA, 47th, 1921
Alverson, Joseph H.	Pvt.	F, 3rd Iowa Cav. (at large)	107, 393	99 & 9 days	1943 Sep 25	IA, 70th, 1944
Alvis, E.H.	Sergt.	G, 21st Mo.	268		1914 Dec 29	IA, 41st, 1915
Alvis, Ed. H.	Pvt.	G, 21st Mo.	75		1914 Dec 29	IA, 41st, 1915
Alvis, Lewis		D, 58th Ill. Inf. (died of dropsy)	81		1894 Apr 13	NE, 19th, 1895
Alvord, R.A.		E, Col. Inf.	176		1928 May 5	KS, 49th, 1930
Alvord, Theodore		I, 86th Ill.	1		1933 Jan 11	KS, 53rd, 1934
Alwine, Sylvester		C, 134th Penn.	5		1923 Jun 1	KS, 43rd, 1924
Amann, G.		E, 25th Mo.	130		1919 Mar 25	KS, 39th, 1920
Ambler, C.B.		C, 28th Ohio Inf.	32		1918 May 12	KS, 38th, 1919
Amelsburg, B.	Pvt.	K, 54th N.Y. Inf.	165	65	1895 May 11	IA, 22nd, 1896
Ament, Harvey		D, 195th Penn.	71		1897 Mar 25	KS, 17th, 1898
Ament, M.D.	Pvt.	G, 58th Ill. Inf.	153		1929 Feb 10	IA, 56th, 1930
Amer, Elias		C, 178th Penn. Inf.	77		1917 Dec 31	NE, 43rd, 1919
Ames, G.R.		E, 8th Wis.	3		1916 Dec 5	KS, 36th, 1917
Ames, H.S.	Pvt.	I, 11th Mich. Inf.	49		1917 Jun 18	IA, 44th, 1918
Ames, Ira	Pvt.	I, 27th N.Y. Inf. (died of ulceration of stomach)	18	61	1891 Dec 23	NE, 16th, 1892
Ames, John		B, 2nd Colo.	38		1930	KS, 50th, 1931
Ames, Laban L.		E, 8th Wis.	19	67	1910 Apr 29	NE, 34th, 1910
Ames, Nelson	Capt.	G, 4th N.Y. Lt. Art.	94		1907 Mar 7	IA, 34th, 1908
Ames, O.L.		C, 17th Ill.	113		1926 Apr 12	KS, 46th, 1927
Amesby, Lauren	Chaplain	8th Minn.	7		1904 Mar 9	KS, 24th, 1905
Amey, Samuel		D, 151st Penn.	147		1913 Dec 6	KS, 33rd, 1914
Amick, Isaac		K, 79th Ind. Inf. (died of heart disease)	149	70	1906 Sep 7	NE, 31st, 1907
Amick, Jacob		B, 43rd Mo. Inf.	484		1916 Sep 26	KS, 36th, 1917

*See Appendix A, B or C for roster of post names and locations.
†See Introduction for note regarding recording of death date.

9

Name	Rank	Company, Regiment or Ship	Post*	Age	Death Date†	Journal
Amick, John		H, Mo.	42		1930 May 16	KS, 50th, 1931
Amidon, J.R.	Pvt.	I, 3rd Wis. Inf.	235		1912 Jul 1	IA, 39th, 1913
Amlong, R.D.	Pvt.	B, 14th Iowa Inf.	452		1919 Oct 5	IA, 46th, 1920
Amman, W.G.		H, 1st Wis. Hvy. Art. (died of dropsy)	187	60	1897 Nov 21	NE, 22nd, 1898
Ammel, George		L, 2nd Kans. Cav.	318		1908 Jan 27	KS, 28th, 1909
Ammerman, A.B.		D, 21st Mo.	8		1925 Oct 1	KS, 45th, 1926
Ammon, Rufus	Pvt.	C, 1st Cal. Cav.	365		1908 Mar 8	IA, 35th, 1909
Amorine, F.		F, 49th N.Y.	7		1920 Apr 20	KS, 40th, 1921
Amos, Geo.	Pvt.	K, 36th Iowa Inf.	337		1926 Mar 30	IA, 53rd, 1927
Amos, George W.	Chief Bugler	119th Ill.	35		1914 Sep 10	KS, 34th, 1915
Amos, Levi	Pvt.	1st Iowa Battery	254	56	1891 Apr 13	IA, 18th, 1892
Amos, M.S.		F, 126th Ohio	100		1923 Apr 28	KS, 43rd, 1924
Amrstong, H.L.	Pvt.	D, 3rd Iowa Cav.	7		1926 Mar	IA, 53rd, 1927
Amsbaugh, Henry		G, 44th Ind.	113		1919 Aug 10	KS, 39th, 1920
Amsbough, U.H.		C, 102nd Ohio	63		1918 May 8	KS, 38th, 1919
Amy, George		E, 6th Kans. (died suddenly)	32		1890	KS, 10th, 1891
Amy, William		K, 8th Mass. Inf.	71		1900 May 14	KS, 20th, 1901
Anable, John		45th Ill. Inf.	1		1911 1st term	IA, 38th, 1912
Anders, A.A.					1935	KS, 55th, 1936
Anders, C.W.		D, 148th Ill. Inf.	150		1886	KS, 6th, 1887
Anders, J.W.		A, 122nd Ohio (died of Bright's disease)	112		1916 Aug 16	NE, 41st, 1917
Anderson, A.J.		D, 77th Ill.	293		1923 Jun 11	KS, 43rd, 1924
Anderson, A.R.		B, 30th Ind.	57		1914 Aug 14	KS, 34th, 1915
Anderson, Amos J.		E, 9th Iowa Cav.	51		1925 Sep 30	KS, 45th, 1926
Anderson, Andrew J.		A, 17th Ky.	12		1921 Aug 8	KS, 41st, 1922
Anderson, Andrew S.		D, 16th Ill. Inf.	12		1901 Feb 25	KS, 21st, 1902
Anderson, Anton E.	Lieut.	L, 12th Iowa Inf.	168		1910 Sep 8	IA, 37th, 1911
Anderson, Benjamin	Pvt.	G, 32nd Iowa Inf.	105	64	1885 Dec 26	IA, 12th, 1886
Anderson, C.J.	Pvt.	A, 6th Penn. Hvy. Art.	316		1899 Nov 17	IA, 26th, 1900
Anderson, C.L.	Lieut.	G, 3rd Iowa Inf.	49		1915 Apr 22	IA, 42nd, 1916
Anderson, Charles G.		E, 25th Iowa Inf. (died of consumption)	264		1893 Nov 3	NE, 18th, 1894
Anderson, Chas.		F, 11th Ind. Inf. (died of dropsy)	32	67	1902 Mar	NE, 27th, 1903
Anderson, D.B.	Pvt.	I, 46th Iowa	111		1924 Nov 9	IA, 51st, 1925
Anderson, D.C.	Pvt.	C, 19th Iowa Inf.	108		1917 Dec 31	IA, 45th, 1919
Anderson, D.P.	Pvt.	F, 9th Iowa Inf.	216		1915 Feb 19	IA, 42nd, 1916
Anderson, Daniel	Col.	1st Iowa Cav.	337		1901 Feb 4	IA, 27th, 1901
Anderson, Daniel	Col.	1st Iowa Cav.	337		1901 Feb 4	IA, 28th, 1902
Anderson, David G.	Corp.	A, 19th Iowa Inf.	2		1902 Oct 2	IA, 29th, 1903
Anderson, E.W.		K, 14th Ind.	85		1931 Jun 27	KS, 51st, 1932
Anderson, E.W.		K, 14th Ind.	85		1931 Jun 27	KS, 52nd, 1933
Anderson, Eric	Pvt.	K, 7th Ill. Cav.	208		1909 Jan 22	IA, 36th, 1910
Anderson, Ethel			71		1941 Jun 16	KS, 61st, 1942
Anderson, F.		F, 132nd Ill.	25		1934 Feb 11	IA, 61st, 1935
Anderson, F.M.		C, 39th Ill.	354		1905 Sep 28	KS, 25th, 1906
Anderson, G.R.	Musician	K, 136th Ohio Inf.	286	42	1887 Jan 4	IA, 15th, 1889
Anderson, G.S.		E, 14th Ill.	81		1930 Jan 17	KS, 50th, 1931
Anderson, G.W.	Pvt.	K, 65th Ill. Inf.	94	51	1898 Jul 25	IA, 25th, 1899
Anderson, G.W.		A, 188th Ohio	115		1904 Dec 5	KS, 24th, 1905
Anderson, Gabriel		K, 14th U.S.C.T. Tenn.	486		1904 Sep 13	KS, 24th, 1905
Anderson, Geo., Jr.	Pvt.	L, 9th Iowa	425		1922 Oct 10	IA, 49th, 1923
Anderson, Gustavus		D, 37th Ill.	100		1925 Nov 20	KS, 45th, 1926
Anderson, H.C.			232		1914	KS, 34th, 1915
Anderson, H.M.	Sergt.	K, 101st Ill. Inf.	284		1911 Aug 21	IA, 38th, 1912
Anderson, Henry	Pvt.	F, 11th Iowa Inf.	286	44	1889 May 14	IA, 16th, 1890
Anderson, Henry B.		D, 104th Ill. Inf.	25		1917 Aug 1	KS, 37th, 1918
Anderson, Ira W.	Pvt.	E, 45th Iowa	12		1922 May 11	IA, 49th, 1923
Anderson, Israel	Capt.	C, 3rd Iowa Cav.	2		1902 Jun 25	IA, 29th, 1903
Anderson, J.		D, 13th Mo.	41		1888	KS, 8th, 1889
Anderson, J.A.	Pvt.	H, 10th Iowa Inf.	80		1894	IA, 21st, 1895
Anderson, J.A.			3		1884	KS, 4th, 1885
Anderson, J.B.		I, 4th Iowa Cav.	55	91	1934 Aug 4	IA, 61st, 1935
Anderson, J.C.	Pvt.		434		1920 Jan 31	IA, 47th, 1921

*See Appendix A, B or C for roster of post names and locations.
†See Introduction for note regarding recording of death date.

Name	Rank	Company, Regiment or Ship	Post*	Age	Death Date†	Journal
Anderson, J.D.	Pvt.	D, 4th West Va.	356	43	1889 Nov 17	IA, 17th, 1891
Anderson, J.H.	Pvt.	G, 3rd U.S. Art.	2		1920 Apr 11	IA, 47th, 1921
Anderson, J.J.		G, 12th Ind.	99		1893 Sep 17	KS, 13th, 1894
Anderson, J.J.		K, 86th Ill.	4		1918 Feb 6	KS, 38th, 1919
Anderson, J.M.		C, 50th Ind. Inf.	127		1899 Oct 25	KS, 19th, 1900
Anderson, J.M.		C, 9th Iowa Cav.	17		1911 Dec 18	KS, 31st, 1912
Anderson, J. Sid.	Pvt.	A, 1st Ill. Lt. Art.	68		1913	IA, 40th, 1914
Anderson, J.W.		G, 16th Kans.	322		1920 Nov 19	KS, 40th, 1921
Anderson, James	Pvt.	G, 65th Ohio Inf.	452		1905 Mar 31	IA, 32nd, 1906
Anderson, James		I, 5th Iowa	463		1889	KS, 9th, 1890
Anderson, James			334		1894	NE, 19th, 1895
Anderson, James W.		F, 2nd Ill. Cav.	311		1918 Jun 10	KS, 38th, 1919
Anderson, Jas. A.	Pvt.	C, 2nd Iowa Cav.	24		1922 Apr 4	IA, 49th, 1923
Anderson, Jas. S.		Bat., 2nd Kans. State Militia	1		1897 Oct 25	KS, 17th, 1898
Anderson, Jens		B, 15th Wis. Inf.	52	83	1922 Mar 25	NE, 47th, 1923
Anderson, Jno. D.	Pvt.	D, 4th West Va. Cav.	356	41	1889 Nov	IA, 16th, 1890
Anderson, Jno. H.	Pvt.	G, 3rd U.S. Art.	2	49	1890 Feb 2	IA, 16th, 1890
Anderson, Joe		C, 64th Ohio	226		1910 Jul 27	KS, 30th, 1911
Anderson, John			1		1893 Dec 20	KS, 13th, 1894
Anderson, John A.		B, 3rd Cal. (died at Liverpool, England)	100		1892 May 18	KS, 12th, 1893
Anderson, John A.		D, 4th Mo. Cav.	13		1914 Dec 21	KS, 34th, 1915
Anderson, John F.		A, 119th Ill. Inf.	25	75	1920 Apr 22	NE, 45th, 1921
Anderson, Jos.		L, 2nd Iowa Cav.	74		1890 Nov 19	IA, 17th, 1891
Anderson, Jos.	Pvt.	H, 10th Iowa Inf.	23		1918 Jun 13	IA, 45th, 1919
Anderson, Joseph		B, 1st Ky. Cav.	252		1912 Apr 18	KS, 32nd, 1913
Anderson, Lafayette		F, 28th Mass. Inf. (died of apoplexy)	110	51	1900 Oct	NE, 25th, 1901
Anderson, Lewis		E, 108th C. Inf. U.S.	127		1909 Feb 8	KS, 29th, 1910
Anderson, Louis H.		G, 23rd Mo. Inf.	439		1890	KS, 10th, 1891
Anderson, M.			45		1925 Sep 14	IA, 52nd, 1926
Anderson, M.A.	Corp.	B, 45th Ill. Inf.	481	55	1895 Dec 25	IA, 22nd, 1896
Anderson, Martin		B, 11th Kans.	1		1897 Jul 9	KS, 17th, 1898
Anderson, N.	Pvt.	C, 110th Ohio Vol. Inf.	111		3rd quarter 1885	IA, 12th, 1886
Anderson, Nels		F, 89th Ill. Inf. (died of pneumonia)	151	55	1900 Jan 10	NE, 25th, 1901
Anderson, O.B.	Pvt.	B, 12th Iowa Inf.	194		1924	IA, 51st, 1925
Anderson, Ola A.	Lieut.	D, 3rd Inf.	168		1910 Jan 29	IA, 37th, 1911
Anderson, P.B.	Asst. Surg.	8th Minn.	140	71	1899 Jun 17	IA, 26th, 1900
Anderson, P.T.	Pvt.	B, 31st Mo. Inf.	416		1907 Jul 26	IA, 34th, 1908
Anderson, Peter		Henshaw's Battery	193		1900	IA, 27th, 1901
Anderson, R.B.		G, 125th U.S. Cav.	265		1930 Nov 29	NE, 55th, 1931
Anderson, Sam B.		F, 128th Ind. Inf.	92		1934 Jul 6	KS, 54th, 1935
Anderson, T.B.		H, 10th Mo. Inf.	28		1915 Mar 17	KS, 35th, 1916
Anderson, T.T.		A, 3rd Ill.	51		1916 Nov 12	KS, 36th, 1917
Anderson, T.W.		K, 49th Ind.	199		1928 Aug 23	KS, 48th, 1929
Anderson, Thomas	Pvt.	E, 43rd Ind. Inf.	59		1922 Feb 9	IA, 49th, 1923
Anderson, Thomas		H, 10th Wis. Inf.	200	94	1938 Nov 26	IA, 64th, 1938
Anderson, Thomas		A, 61st Ill.	142		1909 Jun 7	KS, 29th, 1910
Anderson, Thomas		G, 15th Kans.	127		1926 Dec 21	KS, 46th, 1927
Anderson, Thomas Jefferson		A, 5th Kans. (died at his home in Topeka)	1		1912 Jan 31	KS, 32nd, 1913
Anderson, Thomas P.	Pvt. Capt.	F, 10th Mo. Inf. 64th U.S.C. Inf. (see Appendix D)	28		1915 Mar 1	KS, 34th, 1915
Anderson, Thos.	Pvt.	H, 10th Wis. Vol. Inf.	216		1904 Mar 19	IA, 30th, 1904
Anderson, Thos.	Pvt.	H, 10th Wis. Inf.	216		1904 Mar 19	IA, 31st, 1905
Anderson, Thos.	Pvt.	G, 18th Iowa Inf.	18		1917 Nov 6	IA, 44th, 1918
Anderson, W.A.	Pvt.	E, 13th Wis. Inf.	236		1929 Feb 15	IA, 56th, 1930
Anderson, W.C.	Pvt.	F, 2nd Kans. Cav.	10		1906 Oct 14	IA, 33rd, 1907
Anderson, W.C.	Pvt.	30th Iowa	170		1922 Oct 14	IA, 49th, 1923
Anderson, W.E.	Pvt.	K, 51st Mo. Inf.	2		1906 Mar 29	IA, 33rd, 1907
Anderson, W.H.			24		1915 Jan 7	IA, 42nd, 1916
Anderson, W.R.		C, 132nd Ohio	447		1916 Nov 19	KS, 36th, 1917
Anderson, W.S.	Seaman	Ozark Gulf Squad	314		1907 Apr 30	IA, 34th, 1908
Anderson, W.S.		G, 113th Ill.	63		1922 Mar 3	KS, 42nd, 1923

Name	Rank	Company, Regiment or Ship	Post*	Age	Death Date†	Journal
Anderson, W.S.		K, 13th M.H. Inf. (cause of death: kidney & heart)	2	63	1909 Oct 27	NE, 34th, 1910
Anderson, William		G, 10th Ill.	258		1923	KS, 43rd, 1924
Anderson, Wm.	Pvt.	L, 7th Iowa Cav.	97		1908 Feb 3	IA, 35th, 1909
Anderson, Wm. G.		H, 60th Ind.	36		1885	KS, 5th, 1886
Anderson, Wm. H.	Pvt.	H, 119th Ill. Inf.	39		1913 Dec 11	IA, 40th, 1914
Andon, C.M.		I, 28th Iowa	150		1915 Nov 26	KS, 35th, 1916
Andre, Jefferson		K, 6th Penn. (died of cancer of the liver)	204	71	1913 Aug 8	NE, 38th, 1914
Andrea, Hugh	Pvt.	H, Iowa Reg.	140		1922 Dec 27	IA, 49th, 1923
Andree, Geo.	Pvt.	D, 6th Iowa Cav.	3		1925 Jul 2	IA, 52nd, 1926
Andres, J.W.		A, 122nd Ohio	13	75	1916	NE, 41st, 1917
Andres, N.K.			262		1904 Aug 28	NE, 29th, 1905
Andrew, Frank		C, 142nd N.Y.	22		1935 Dec 27	NE, 60th, 1936
Andrew, Wm.	Pvt.	I, 79th Ohio	271		1914 Feb 11	IA, 41st, 1915
Andrews, —			182		1916 Jun 16	NE, 41st, 1917
Andrews, A.	Pvt.	D, 71st Ill. Inf.	247		1920 Sep 13	IA, 47th, 1921
Andrews, A.	Pvt.	D, 71st Ill.	247		1920 Sep 13	IA, 48th, 1922
Andrews, A.E.	Pvt.	D, 4th Iowa Cav.	20		1918 Jan	IA, 45th, 1919
Andrews, B.F.	Pvt.	G, 3rd Mo. Cav.	81		1916 Apr 22	IA, 43rd, 1917
Andrews, Chester		location: Steele City			1927 Aug 5	NE, 52nd, 1928
Andrews, E.D.	Pvt.	E, 91st Ill. Inf.	68		1901 Dec 26	IA, 28th, 1902
Andrews, Elias		D, 16th Mo. Cav.	18		1916 Nov 3	KS, 36th, 1917
Andrews, Francis		G, 44th Iowa	246		1928 Mar	KS, 48th, 1929
Andrews, H.C.		D, 8th Iowa Cav.	1		1928 Oct 4	NE, 53rd, 1929
Andrews, Hiram G.		I, 28th Ill. Inf.	11	64	1914 May 4	NE, 39th, 1915
Andrews, J.C.		D, 93rd Ill.	293		1912 Apr 11	KS, 32nd, 1913
Andrews, J.E.	Pvt.	G, 17th Ohio Inf.	18		1920 May	IA, 47th, 1921
Andrews, J.M.	Pvt.	B, 26th Ill. Inf.	267		1929 Dec 11	IA, 56th, 1930
Andrews, J.W.			207		1925 Mar 30	NE, 50th, 1926
Andrews, J.W.		D, 4th Iowa Cav. (died of old age)	207	86	1925 Mar 29	NE, 50th, 1926
Andrews, John	Pvt.	A, 46th Iowa Inf.	124		1910 Feb 16	IA, 37th, 1911
Andrews, John T.		A, 34th Ohio	250		1923 May 11	KS, 43rd, 1924
Andrews, John W.		H, 7th & 44th Wis. (former member; died at Geneva)	22		1935 Aug 11	NE, 60th, 1936
Andrews, Joseph	Pvt.	C, 106th Ill. Inf.	56		1922 Apr 20	IA, 49th, 1923
Andrews, L.D.	Pvt.	B, 27th Wis. Inf.	300		1920 Mar 6	IA, 47th, 1921
Andrews, M.L.	Capt.	B, 29th Iowa Inf.	20	54	1890 Nov 10	IA, 17th, 1891
Andrews, Orson Edgar		K, 141st Ill. Inf.		92	1937 Aug 24	IA, 64th, 1938
Andrews, P.D.		G, 42nd U.S. Col.	158		1922 Aug 13	KS, 42nd, 1923
Andrews, Robt. D.		K, 7th Ohio Cav. (died of old age)	96		1908 Nov 12	NE, 33rd, 1909
Andrews, S.H.		B, 2nd Kans. A, 35th Mass.	12		1900 Jul 28	KS, 20th, 1901
Andrews, Sam'l	Pvt.	D, 32nd Iowa	67		1905 Jan 10	IA, 32nd, 1906
Andrews, Stephen B.		F, 72nd N.Y. Inf.	164		1902 Oct 26	KS, 22nd, 1903
Andrews, T.F.		H, 99th Ill.	4		1910 Sep 9	KS, 30th, 1911
Andrews, W.H.		A, Purnell Legion, Maryland	195	76	1912 Aug 12	NE, 37th, 1913
Andrews, W.W.	Pvt.	H, 12th Mich. Inf.	291	53	1895 Feb 8	IA, 21st, 1895
Andrews, W.W.	Pvt.	E, 46th N.Y. Inf.	181		1925 Jun	IA, 52nd, 1926
Andrus, Walter	Landsman	U.S. Navy	205		1897 Oct 15	NE, 22nd, 1898
Anfenson, Osman	Pvt.	G, 13th Iowa Inf.	365	69	1889 Sep 17	IA, 16th, 1890
Angel, F.C.		C, 6th N.Y. Hvy. Art.	147		1935 Sep 20	KS, 55th, 1936
Angell, A.W.		G, 1st Ill. Cav.	24	59	1900 Apr 4	NE, 25th, 1901
Angelo, S.H.		C, 23rd Iowa Inf.	384		1912 Oct 2	KS, 32nd, 1913
Angelo, W.W.		B, 10th Ill.	491		1911 Aug 30	KS, 31st, 1912
Angford, Silas	Pvt.	H, 19th Iowa Inf.	79		1897 Apr 18	IA, 24th, 1898
Anglund, Eric		D, 57th Ill.	209		1914 Oct 2	KS, 34th, 1915
Angst, Jacob	Pvt.	D, 45th Iowa Inf.	100		1922 May 6	IA, 49th, 1923
Angus, B.F.		H, 12th Penn. Inf. (died of sunstroke)	4	51	1895 Nov 15	NE, 20th, 1896
Ankeny, H.G.	Capt.	H, —	324		1906 Mar 17	IA, 33rd, 1907
Ankeny, Rollin V.	Col. & B.G.	142nd Iowa Vols.	12		1901 Dec 24	IA, 28th, 1902
Ankeny, Seth P.	Pvt.	C, 40th Iowa	40		1907 Mar 1	IA, 34th, 1908
Ankerman, B.F.		F, 5th Penn. Art.	68		1915 Mar 15	IA, 42nd, 1916

*See Appendix A, B or C for roster of post names and locations.
†See Introduction for note regarding recording of death date.

Name	Rank	Company, Regiment or Ship	Post*	Age	Death Date†	Journal
Ankney, Samuel	Pvt.	B, 7th Wis. Inf.	371	72	1894 Oct 9	IA, 21st, 1895
Ankrom, Jesse	Pvt.	D, 53rd R.O.I. Inf.[Ohio Inf.]	107		1925 Jun 14	IA, 52nd, 1926
Anness, John A.	Pvt.	K, 18th Ind. (cause of death: heart)	163	44	1887 Jun	NE, 12th, 1888
Annett, John	Pvt.	E, 60th N.Y. Inf.	277	68	1893 Feb 7	IA, 20th, 1894
Anno, A.S.		A, 39th Mo.	62		1912 Mar 17	KS, 32nd, 1913
Anno, Jno.		G, 43rd Mo.	336		1904 Aug 28	KS, 24th, 1905
Anson, J.W.	Pvt.	D, 37th Iowa Inf.	8		1914 Jul 18	IA, 41st, 1915
Antels, H.H.		B, 22nd Ind. Inf. (died of paralysis)	190	64	1903 Dec 21	NE, 28th, 1904
Anthauer, Andrew		I, 10th Ohio	132		1925 Aug 19	KS, 45th, 1926
Anthony, D.R.		7th Kans.	6		1904 Oct 10	KS, 24th, 1905
Anthony, Edward O.		8th Ind. N.Y. Battery	164		1914 Sep 30	KS, 34th, 1915
Anthony, George T.	Capt.	70th N.Y.	18		1896 Aug 8	KS, 16th, 1897
Anthony, J.M.		A, 7th Kans.	32		1900 Jun 7	KS, 20th, 1901
Anthony, J.R.	Pvt.	A, 20th Iowa Inf.	235		1900-1901	IA, 27th, 1901
Anthony, John	Pvt.	A, 8th Iowa	52		1915 Oct 24	KS, 35th, 1916
Anthony, Richard			275		1919 Dec 7	IA, 46th, 1920
Anthony, Richard			316		1919	IA, 46th, 1920
Anthony, T.F.	Pvt.	E, 69th Ohio Inf.	192	54	1896 Feb 10	IA, 23rd, 1897
Anthony, T.J.		A, 2nd Iowa Cav.	293		1913 Jul 19	KS, 33rd, 1914
Anthony, T.J.		A, 2nd Kans.	25		1913 Jul 19	KS, 33rd, 1914
Anthony, W.H.	Pvt.	H, 54th Ill. (cause of death: lungs)	180	41	1884 Jul 1	NE, 9th, 1885
Antill, John T.		K, 6th West Va. (died of kidney disease)	25	77	1916 Nov 10	NE, 41st, 1917
Antone, George	Pvt.	A, 45th Wis. Inf.	223		1917 Dec 14	IA, 44th, 1918
Antrobus, B.		1st Iowa Art.	147		1911 Jun 3	KS, 31st, 1912
Antwine, Joseph	Pvt.	F, 3rd Iowa Inf.	258		1912 Nov 25	IA, 39th, 1913
Anyan, Wm.		B, 1st Wis. Hvy. Art.	11	84	1911 Sep 16	NE, 36th, 1912
Apel, George	Pvt.	K, 27th Iowa Inf.	90	54	1898 Oct 10	IA, 25th, 1899
Apgar, W.L.	Pvt.	D, 1st N.J. Lt. Art.	12		1906 May 3	IA, 33rd, 1907
Apitz, Chas.		A, 11th N.Y.	12		1906 Jul 12	KS, 26th, 1907
Appelget, Thomas		B, 28th N.J.	47	63	1897 May 19	NE, 22nd, 1898
Appice, S.	Pvt.	Navy	94		1902 Jul 6	IA, 29th, 1903
Appleberry, Frank	Pvt.	C, 38th Iowa Inf.	104		1928 Jul 31	IA, 55th, 1929
Applegarth, R.G.		11th Minn. (died of heart trouble)	180	76	1916 Oct 6	NE, 41st, 1917
Applegate, G.S.	Pvt.	C, 28th Iowa Inf.	127		1920 Oct 10	IA, 47th, 1921
Applegate, J.H.		G, 3rd Ind. Cav.	20		1905 Mar 18	KS, 25th, 1906
Applegate, J.M.		E, 33rd Ind.	113		1926	NE, 51st, 1927
Applegate, James		C, 45th Ky. (died of paralysis)	23	79	1922	NE, 47th, 1923
Applegate, N.S.	Pvt.	E, 9th N.J. Inf.	69		1905 Dec 5	IA, 32nd, 1906
Applegate, Richard		I, 32nd Ohio Inf. (died of stomach trouble)	10	72	1913 Mar 1	NE, 38th, 1914
Applegate, Thomas, see Appelget, Thomas						
Appleton, W.H.			190		1925 Apr	IA, 52nd, 1926
Appleton, W.J.	Lieut.	G, 46th Ill. Inf.	100		1908 Jun 20	IA, 35th, 1909
Appling, W.L.		A, 11th Mo. Inf.	244		1916 Nov 28	KS, 36th, 1917
Arand, Alvin		B, 9th Ohio	9		1919 Aug 6	KS, 39th, 1920
Arbaugh, Jacob	Pvt.	F, 73rd Ind. Inf.	103		1918 Aug 10	IA, 45th, 1919
Arbaugh, Jesse	Pvt.	F, 13th Iowa Inf.	103		1919 Dec 6	IA, 46th, 1920
Arble, W.W.			110		1905	IA, 32nd, 1906
Arbuckle, Daniel		K, 16th Ind. Inf.	32		1920	NE, 45th, 1921
Arch, Geo. M.D.	Pvt.	F, 57th Ill. Inf.	111		1928 Sep 12	IA, 55th, 1929
Archee, James P.		A, 6th Kans.	59		1896 Apr 18	KS, 16th, 1897
Archer, C.		B, 77th Ohio Inf. (died at Concordia)	113		1895 Mar 14	KS, 15th, 1896
Archer, Charles		K, 2nd Neb. Cav.	25	74	1919 Feb 12	NE, 44th, 1920
Archer, John B.		A, 13th Ind. Inf. (died of paralysis)	45		1893 Sep 11	NE, 18th, 1894
Archer, Louis		K, 1st Kans.	132		1910 Oct 29	KS, 30th, 1911
Archer, O.M.	Pvt.	H, 17th Iowa Inf.	158		1926 Apr 18	IA, 53rd, 1927
Archer, Thomas		A, 5th Kans. Cav.	1		1913 Nov 5	KS, 33rd, 1914
Archer, Wm. J.	Corp.	24th Ind. Batt.	201	60	1899 Sep 8	IA, 26th, 1900
Archerd, J.B.		H, 13th Iowa	4		1930 Jun 29	NE, 55th, 1931
Archibald, R.E.	H.S.[Hosp. Stew.?]	K, 8th Iowa Inf.	153		1911 Mar 30	IA, 38th, 1912
Archibald, W.W.	Pvt.	A, 8th Ill. Inf.	5		1913 May 19	IA, 40th, 1914
Ard, W.T.		I, 50th Ind.	11		1904 Sep 16	KS, 24th, 1905

*See Appendix A, B or C for roster of post names and locations.

Name	Rank	Company, Regiment or Ship	Post*	Age	Death Date†	Journal
Ardry, Robert W.		H, 159th Ohio Inf.	65		1925 Jan 19	KS, 45th, 1926
Arel, Wm. A.	Pvt.	M, 8th Iowa	157	49	1887 Mar 19	IA, 15th, 1889
Areman, Adam	Pvt.	1st Minn. Inf.	22		1917 Jun 17	IA, 44th, 1918
Aresmith, J.D.	Pvt.	I, 8th Iowa Cav.	30		1918 Apr 14	IA, 45th, 1919
Arey, M.F.	Pvt.		222	87	1931 Mar 22	IA, 58th, 1932
Arihood, Thos. J.	Pvt.	K, 4th Iowa Cav.		93	1939 May 2	IA, 65th, 1939
Arkey, John	Pvt.	B, 46th Ill. Inf.	57		1902 Aug 11	IA, 29th, 1903
Armann, Henry		D & B, 8th & 5th Ohio (died of old age)	25	72	1916 May 12	NE, 41st, 1917
Armbly, C.J.	Pvt.	E, 47th Wis. Inf.	168		1919	IA, 46th, 1920
Armbus, V.		D, 83rd Penn. Inf. (died of typhoid fever)	28		1894 Jun 11	NE, 19th, 1895
Armes, Edward		B, 6th Tenn.	64		1926 Jun 12	KS, 46th, 1927
Armfulk, Wesley	Pvt.	G, 1st U.S. Sharpshooters	91	56	1898 Oct 6	IA, 25th, 1899
Armitage, P.P.	Pvt.	C, 3rd Iowa Cav.	2	55	1897 Sep 2	IA, 24th, 1898
Armor, T.	Pvt.	G, 4th Iowa Cav.	345	57	1890 Sep 22	IA, 17th, 1891
Armore, W.W.	Pvt.	I, 2nd Neb. Cav.	22		1916 Sep 26	IA, 43rd, 1917
Armour, Geo. W.			235		1915 Dec 18	IA, 42nd, 1916
Armour, Peter		A, 29th Mich. Inf. (died of accident)	23	74	1908 Jan 2	NE, 33rd, 1909
Armstrong, A.D.		D, 27th N.Y. Inf.	22		3rd quarter 1884	IA, 11th, 1885
Armstrong, A.L.	Pvt.	G, 3rd Mich. Inf.	228		1899	NE, 24th, 1900
Armstrong, A.W.	Pvt.	K, Colo. Inf.	452		1922 Oct 19	IA, 49th, 1923
Armstrong, A.W.		D, 2nd Penn.	12		1926 Jun 12	KS, 46th, 1927
Armstrong, Andrew		A, 7th N.Y. Lt. Art.	127		1908 Oct 17	KS, 28th, 1909
Armstrong, Benjamin S.	Pvt.	E, 3rd Iowa Cav. (at large)	100	95	1940 Aug 13	IA, 66th, 1940
Armstrong, Benjamine		E, 13th Ind.	28		1935	KS, 55th, 1936
Armstrong, Christopher		D, 20th N.Y. Cav.	12		1918 May 2	KS, 38th, 1919
Armstrong, D.L.	Pvt.	K, 47th Iowa Inf.	69		1929 Mar 3	IA, 56th, 1930
Armstrong, G.W.		G, 174th Ohio Inf.	40		1899 Jan 30	KS, 19th, 1900
Armstrong, Geo.		C, 4th Ohio Inf.	22		1886	KS, 6th, 1887
Armstrong, Geo. D.		B, 97th Ill. Inf.	57		1900 Oct 5	KS, 20th, 1901
Armstrong, Geo. W.	Pvt.	D, 12th Ohio Cav.	7		1917 Oct 30	IA, 44th, 1918
Armstrong, H.H.		E, 6th West Va.	146		1885	KS, 5th, 1886
Armstrong, H.L.		D, 3rd Iowa Inf.	7		1919 Jan 11	IA, 46th, 1920
Armstrong, H.L., see Amrstong, H.L.						
Armstrong, H.P.	Pvt.	K, 2nd Wis. Cav.	66		1930 Dec 30	IA, 57th, 1931
Armstrong, J.C.	Pvt.	D, 12th Ohio Cav.	7		1898 May 13	IA, 26th, 1900
Armstrong, J.C.		I, 55th Ill. Inf.	46		1900 May 28	KS, 20th, 1901
Armstrong, J.C.		B, 7th Ohio	65		1918 Apr 11	KS, 38th, 1919
Armstrong, J.E.		8th Wis. Battery	284		1912 Jan 3	IA, 39th, 1913
Armstrong, J.E.		I, 50th N.Y. Eng.	18		1924 Jul 4	KS, 44th, 1925
Armstrong, J.E.		D, 8th Iowa Inf.	25		1905 Jan 8	NE, 30th, 1906
Armstrong, J.E.		D, 8th Iowa Cav.	25		1905 Jan 11	NE, 29th, 1905
Armstrong, J.E.		D, 8th Iowa Cav.	25		1905 Jan 8	NE, 31st, 1907
Armstrong, J.H.		H, 75th Ohio	12		1930 Feb 14	KS, 50th, 1931
Armstrong, J.H.	Pvt.	E, 146th Ill. Inf. (died of pneumonia)	179	50	1888 Mar 24	NE, 13th, 1889
Armstrong, J.W.	Pvt.	E, 12th Ohio Cav.	7		1901 Aug 6	IA, 28th, 1902
Armstrong, James	Pvt.	B, 83rd Ill. Inf.	211		1913 Jul 9	IA, 40th, 1914
Armstrong, John C.		I, 135th Ill. Inf.	18		1929 May 17	KS, 49th, 1930
Armstrong, John F.		E, 134th Ill. Inf. (at large)	68	91	1937 Jan 18	IA, 64th, 1938
Armstrong, L.W.	Pvt.	E, 10th Ill. Inf. (at large)			1926 Oct 31	IA, 53rd, 1927
Armstrong, O.F.		D, 6th Kans.	68		1916 Aug 1	KS, 36th, 1917
Armstrong, Richard			52		1926 Nov 19	IA, 53rd, 1927
Armstrong, Robert		1st Iowa Inf.	231		1923 Sep 21	IA, 50th, 1924
Armstrong, Russell B.		B, 2nd Kans. Cav.	303		1901 Jun 7	KS, 21st, 1902
Armstrong, T.		I, 39th Ill. (died of old age)	35	91	1923 May 14	NE, 48th, 1924
Armstrong, Thomas	Pvt.	E, 11th Iowa Inf.	210		1900 Nov 21	IA, 27th, 1901
Armstrong, Thos. J.		G, 117th Ill.	49		1921 Dec 5	KS, 41st, 1922
Armstrong, W.F.	Pvt.	I, 3rd Ohio Inf.	353	55	1897 Feb 14	IA, 24th, 1898
Armstrong, W.H.		I, 154th Ohio Inf.	12		1916 Dec 24	KS, 36th, 1917
Armstrong, Wilson M.		D, 22nd Ill. (died of old age)	77	88	1925 Jun 2	NE, 50th, 1926
Arnell, W.H.		F, 3rd Iowa Cav.	65		3rd quarter 1883	IA, 10th, 1884
Arnell, Wm.	Pvt.	F, 3rd Iowa Cav.	65	57	1883 Sep 20	IA, 14th, 1888

*See Appendix A, B or C for roster of post names and locations.
†See Introduction for note regarding recording of death date.

Name	Rank	Company, Regiment or Ship	Post*	Age	Death Date†	Journal
Arnet, John		A, 77th Ill. Inf.	236	95	1935 Feb 3	IA, 62nd, 1936
Arnett, Jeff		F, 125th U.S. (died of old age)	35	77	1921 Dec 2	NE, 46th, 1922
Arnett, S.C.		I, 15th N.Y. Eng.	25		1922 Jul 15	KS, 42nd, 1923
Arnold, A.J.	Lieut.	2nd Ind. Cav.	250		1899 Mar 29	KS, 19th, 1900
Arnold, Aaron		B, 72nd N.Y.	134		1916	KS, 36th, 1917
Arnold, F.J.		K, 188th N.Y.	244		1918 Feb 25	KS, 38th, 1919
Arnold, Fred L.		B, 2nd Ill. Cav.	185		1913 Oct 22	KS, 33rd, 1914
Arnold, G.F.		I, 10th West Va.	295		1917 Jul	KS, 37th, 1918
Arnold, H.T.		B, 35th Wis. Inf. (died of heart failure)	26	74	1920 Nov 17	NE, 45th, 1921
Arnold, J.E.	Pvt.	F, 1st Iowa Cav.	329	56	1896 Oct 10	IA, 23rd, 1897
Arnold, J.H.		K, 140th Ind. Inf. (killed in storm)	226	53	1902 May	NE, 27th, 1903
Arnold, Jacob		C, 26th Mo. (died of rheumatism)	84	69	1907 Feb	NE, 33rd, 1909
Arnold, James		C, 52nd Ill. Inf.	247		1911	IA, 38th, 1912
Arnold, Jesse W.		H, 4th Iowa	251		1906 Nov 11	KS, 26th, 1907
Arnold, John		C, 1st N.Y.	8		1899 Aug 12	KS, 19th, 1900
Arnold, N.H.		C, 118th N.Y. Inf. (cause of death: heart)	289	68	1903 May 9	NE, 28th, 1904
Arnold, S.A.		F, 59th Ohio Inf.	8		1940 May 2	KS, 60th, 1941
Arnold, S.S.			65		4th quarter 1885	IA, 12th, 1886
Arnold, Wm.		G, 87th Mo. Mil.	130		1936 Sep 17	KS, 56th, 1937
Arnold, Wm.		I, 43rd Mo. (died of influenza)	54	75	1918 Dec 5	NE, 43rd, 1919
Arnold, Wm. M.	Asst. Surg.	51st U.C. Col. Inf.[U.S. Colored Inf.]	8		1915 Dec 2	KS, 35th, 1916
Arrel, Geo. W., see Aarl, Geo. W.						
Arrowood, G.W.	Corp.	A, 6th Ind. Cav.	62		1919 Jul 11	IA, 46th, 1920
Art, W.T.			158		1921 Aug 7	KS, 41st, 1922
Arterburn, Samuel		B, 78th Ill. Inf.	12		1909 Feb 20	KS, 29th, 1910
Arth, Anton		G, 49th Mo.	52		1920 Jul	KS, 40th, 1921
Arth, Jacob		K, 146th Ill.	205		1916 Jun 24	KS, 36th, 1917
Arthur, A.D.	Pvt.	E, 26th Ill. Inf.	135		1917 Jan 11	IA, 44th, 1918
Arthur, A.D.	Pvt.	E, 26th Ill. Inf.	135		1918 Jan 11	IA, 45th, 1919
Arthur, Hugh	Pvt.	F, 26th Ohio Bat.	108		1926 Jun 28	IA, 53rd, 1927
Arthur, J.R.		F, 17th Iowa	132		1902 Nov 25	KS, 22nd, 1903
Arthur, Smith S.	Corp.	M, 8th Ohio Cav.	11	52	1887 Jan 18	IA, 13th, 1887
Arthur, T.J.		A, 206th Penn. Inf.	493		1907 Apr 26	IA, 34th, 1908
Arthur, W.R.	Pvt.	Lt. Art.	11		1930 Sep 21	IA, 57th, 1931
Artlip, David	Pvt.	B, 102nd Ill. Inf.	69		1899	NE, 24th, 1900
Artz, Peter			[89?]		1918	KS, 38th, 1919
Arundson, B.		I, 22nd Wis. Inf.	168		1913 Mar 25	IA, 40th, 1914
Asbell, Chas.		E, 10th Ind. Inf.	158		1930 Jun 15	KS, 50th, 1931
Asbury, Benjamin	Pvt.	E, 37th Iowa Vol. Inf.	286	94	1899	IA, 26th, 1900
Asbury, Page A.		A, 30th Ky.	85		1933 Oct 28	KS, 53rd, 1934
Asbury, W.H.H.	Sergt.	E, 3rd Iowa Cav.	69		1919 Sep 14	IA, 46th, 1920
Asby, William	Lieut.	M, 9th Ill. Cav.	6	60	1897 Jul 20	IA, 24th, 1898
Ascher, H.B.			12		1922 Dec 9	KS, 42nd, 1923
Ascher, Jno.	Pvt.	I, 22nd Iowa Inf.	8		1925 Jun 29	IA, 52nd, 1926
Ash, Ancil O.	Pvt.	E, 47th Wis. Inf.	193	96, 2 mos. & 24 days	1945 Mar 8	IA, 71st, 1945
Ash, G.H.	Pvt.	K, 3rd Minn. Inf.	3		1930 Oct 17	IA, 57th, 1931
Ash, Henry	Pvt.	E, 8th Wis. Inf.	87	55	1892 Jul 28	IA, 19th, 1893
Ash, John			244		1906 Jan	KS, 25th, 1906
Ash, John	Capt.	79th Ohio Inf. (died at his home in Wichita; interred Feb. 6; remains accompanied to grave by Sedgwick County bar)	244		1906 Feb 2	KS, 25th, 1906
Ash, John	Capt.	97th Ohio	244		1906 Feb 2	KS, 25th, 1906
Ash, John Chelton	Pvt.	A, 48th Iowa Inf. (not a G.A.R. member)		97	1940 Dec 14	IA, 67th, 1941
Ash, R.M.	Pvt.	I, 63rd N.H. Inf.	452		1922 Jan 19	IA, 49th, 1923
Ash, Rufus		I, 1st Mo.	174		1900 Oct 30	KS, 20th, 1901
Ashba, Abraham	Pvt.	G, 100th Ind. Inf.	208	64	1894 Feb 19	IA, 21st, 1895
Ashbaugh, John M.		A, 5th Kans.	1		1905 Sep 11	KS, 25th, 1906
Ashbey, J.H.		C, 17th Ill.	113		1927	KS, 47th, 1928

*See Appendix A, B or C for roster of post names and locations.
†See Introduction for note regarding recording of death date.

Name	Rank	Company, Regiment or Ship	Post*	Age	Death Date†	Journal
Ashburn, James	Pvt.	G, 6th Iowa Cav.	124		1929 Oct 22	IA, 56th, 1930
Ashby, M.V.	Pvt.	I, 16th Ill. Inf.	441		1905 Dec 9	IA, 32nd, 1906
Ashby, Milton A.		E, 150th Ill. Inf.	90		1912 Sep 2	KS, 32nd, 1913
Ashby, Thomson		16th Kans.	111		1914 Feb 17	KS, 34th, 1915
Ashcraft, Alonzo P.		D, 7th Ky. Cav.	176		1912 Apr 7	KS, 32nd, 1913
Ashcroft, J.A.		204th Penn. Inf.	130		1900 Aug 6	IA, 27th, 1901
Ashenbeck, Leonard	Pvt.	K, 156th Ill.	377		1901 Oct	IA, 28th, 1902
Asher, James M.			35		1899 Apr 11	KS, 19th, 1900
Asher, Noah		E, 128th Ind. Inf.	17		1899 Aug 13	KS, 19th, 1900
Ashford, T.H.		E, 4th Ky.	51		1928 Mar 21	KS, 48th, 1929
Ashley, A.F.		13th Mo. (died of heart failure)	18	69	1900 Nov 11	NE, 25th, 1901
Ashley, Byron R.		I, 19th Wis.	98		1933	NE, 58th, 1934
Ashley, Charles	Pvt.	I, 9th Iowa Inf.	216		1929 Jan 18	IA, 56th, 1930
Ashline, Geo.			190		1927 Mar 15	IA, 54th, 1928
Ashmore, Samuel	Surg.	15th Kans. Cav.	250		1908[1909?] Jan 19	KS, 29th, 1910
Ashpole, Josiah		B, 110th N.Y.	52		1922 Mar 28	KS, 42nd, 1923
Ashry, J.O.			43		1886	NE, 11th, 1887
Ashtenan, L.N.	Pvt.	I, 3rd N.Y. Inf.	235	63	1896 May 27	IA, 23rd, 1897
Ashton, D.		A, 39th Ill.	83		1918	KS, 38th, 1919
Ashton, G.W.			48		1889	KS, 9th, 1890
Ashton, W.H.		E, 2nd Colo.	100		1927 Oct 14	KS, 47th, 1928
Ashton, Wm.	Pvt. Sergt.	G, 38th Ohio D, U.S. Vet. Eng. (died of rheumatism)	21	50	1886 Jan 5	NE, 10th, 1886
Ashton, Wm. W.			21		1886	NE, 11th, 1887
Ashwell, H.C.	Col.	3rd, 91st, & 145th Ohio	18		1924 Jun 21	KS, 44th, 1925
Asken, Charles		K, 47th Ky. Inf.	493		1930 Mar 30	KS, 50th, 1931
Askew, J.F.	Pvt.	I, 9th Iowa Cav.	42		1927 Jul 12	IA, 54th, 1928
Askey, Samuel	Pvt.	B, 46th Ill. Inf.	57		1916 Aug 22	IA, 43rd, 1917
Askren, Elbert		K, 3rd Col. Cav. (died at Ossawatomie; buried at Des Moines, Iowa)	98		1894 Jun 13	KS, 14th, 1895
Askwith, John D.		M, 21st Penn. Cav.	182		1930 Sep 7	NE, 55th, 1931
Asling, Fredric		C, 9th Kans. Cav. (died of consumption)	132		1890	KS, 10th, 1891
Asmon, Phillip		I, 60th Ind. Inf.	25		1911 Oct 15	KS, 31st, 1912
Asquith, John	Eng.	Miss. Squadron	68		1914	IA, 41st, 1915
Asquith, Theo.	Pvt.	C, 102nd Ill. Inf.	197		1924 Sep 7	IA, 51st, 1925
Assman, Justus		A, 17th Kans. (died at Lawrence)	12		1895 Jul	KS, 15th, 1896
Astel, Wm.		I, 97th Ill.	435		1916 Mar 11	KS, 36th, 1917
Astle, George		I, 97th Ill.	434		1919 Jul 3	KS, 39th, 1920
Atchison, M.		C, 85th Ill.	153		1898 Apr 7	KS, 18th, 1899
Atchley, G.W.			7		1928	IA, 55th, 1929
Aten, B.S.		D, 11th Ill. Cav.	465		1891 Dec 10	KS, 11th, 1892
Aten, H.J.			130		1914 Mar 7	KS, 34th, 1915
Aten, H.J.		G, 85th Ill.	130		1913 Mar 7	KS, 33rd, 1914
Aten, John	Pvt.	F, 82nd Ohio	29		1905 Aug 5	IA, 32nd, 1906
Aten, Samuel	Pvt.	C, 3rd Ill. Cav.	312	66	1900 Apr 29	IA, 26th, 1900
Atenham, Herman		H, 46th Ill. Inf.	177		1899 Nov 24	KS, 19th, 1900
Athearn, Robert C.		D, 103rd Ill. Inf.	85		1914 Aug 26	KS, 34th, 1915
Atherton, C.H.	Musician	C, 65th Ill. Inf.	364		1909 Jul 25	IA, 36th, 1910
Atherton, I.Y.			12		1923 Aug 22	IA, 50th, 1924
Atherton, J.H.	Pvt.	F, 10th Iowa Cav.	412		1911 Jan 21	IA, 37th, 1911
Atherton, John		K, 15th N.Y. Eng. (died of general debility)	118	76	1895 Dec 17	NE, 20th, 1896
Atherton, S.A.	Corp.	A, 2nd N.H. Inf.	78		1900 Apr 4	IA, 27th, 1901
Athey, John W.	Pvt.	E, 39th Iowa Inf.	51	60	1899 Dec 29	IA, 26th, 1900
Athey, Milton J.	Pvt.	H, 3rd Mo. Inf.	314		1926 Nov	IA, 53rd, 1927
Atkins, A.B.			99	72	1911 Nov 1	NE, 36th, 1912
Atkins, L.F.		E, 1st Ohio Lt. Art.	209		1912 Dec 29	KS, 32nd, 1913
Atkinson, A.J.			25	73	1910 Feb 7	NE, 35th, 1911
Atkinson, Chauncy, see Adkinson, Chauncy						
Atkinson, D.E.		H, 100th Penn.	293		1911 May 21	KS, 31st, 1912
Atkinson, E.M., see Aukinson, E.M.						

*See Appendix A, B or C for roster of post names and locations.
†See Introduction for note regarding recording of death date.

16

Name	Rank	Company, Regiment or Ship	Post*	Age	Death Date†	Journal
Atkinson, E.T.	Pvt.	I, 2nd Ill. Art.	5		1899	IA, 26th, 1900
Atkinson, George H.	Pvt.	B, 10th West Va. Inf.	11		1901 Nov	IA, 28th, 1902
Atkinson, Hiram		D, 107th Ill.	50		1921 Sep 29	KS, 41st, 1922
Atkinson, I.N.		A, 7th Mo. Inf. (died of apoplexy)	307	56	1891 Jul 14	NE, 16th, 1892
Atkinson, Jasper		B, 103rd Ill.	142		1910 Jan	KS, 30th, 1911
Atkinson, Jos. F.	Sergt.	H, 11th Ill. Cav.	150		1912 Apr 2	IA, 39th, 1913
Atkinson, Jos. S.	Pvt.	H, 11th Ill. Cav.	130		1912 Apr 2	IA, 39th, 1913
Atkinson, Lewis		I, 13th Ky.	25		1923 Jan 3	KS, 43rd, 1924
Atkinson, M.C.	Pvt.	C, Iowa Inf.	452		1927 Jun 6	IA, 54th, 1928
Atkinson, S.		I, 9th Kans.	40		1899 Jun	KS, 19th, 1900
Atkinson, Samuel		F, 16th Kans.	4		1927 Sep 16	KS, 47th, 1928
Atkinson, Samuel		H, 35th Wis.	129		1936 Jul 20	KS, 56th, 1937
Atkinson, Thos.		C, 76th Penn.	14		1926 Aug 8	KS, 46th, 1927
Atkinson, W.R.			118		1886	KS, 6th, 1887
Atkinson, William		G, 115th Ill. Inf.	50		1925 Dec 25	KS, 45th, 1926
Atkinson, William			17		1933 Jun 20	KS, 53rd, 1934
Atlanta		G, 71st Penn. (died of cerebral softening)	275	83	1922 Dec 31	NE, 47th, 1923
Atmore, E.W.	Pvt.	B, 15th Iowa	7		1903 May 30	IA, 30th, 1904
Aton, William L., see Alen, William L.						
Attebery, Daniel	Corp.	H, 28th Ill. Inf.	306		1905 Sep 5	IA, 32nd, 1906
Attelbury, Thomas	Pvt.	K, 48th Ill. (died of consumption)	75	36	1884 Mar 26	NE, 9th, 1885
Atwater, B.C.	Pvt.	H, 51st Wis. Inf.	141		1929 Apr 4	IA, 56th, 1930
Atwater, Marcus		C, 100th Ind. Inf.	39		1917 Aug 22	KS, 37th, 1918
Atwell, S.M.		C, 131st Ill.	71		1925 Jun 11	KS, 45th, 1926
Atwood, Enoch	Pvt.	92nd Ill. Inf.	286		1913 Jun	IA, 40th, 1914
Atwood, Julius		A, U.S.C.T.	72		1926 Jan 7	KS, 46th, 1927
Atwood, Warren	Pvt.	C, 32nd Mass. (died of dropsy)	42	47	1884 Nov 14	NE, 9th, 1885
Aublen, J.J.	Pvt.	F, 13th Vt.	153		1905 Feb 23	IA, 32nd, 1906
Auchmoody, T.F.		C, 80th N.Y. Inf.	168		1901 May 19	IA, 27th, 1901
Augestine, J.H.		Penn.	94		1921 Dec 24	IA, 48th, 1922
Aughenbaugh, Jacob	Pvt.	G, U.S. Cav.	452		1928 Feb 19	IA, 55th, 1929
Aughey, Daniel S.	Pvt.	H, 2nd Iowa Inf.	108		1922 Jul 22	IA, 49th, 1923
Augustine, J.A.	Pvt.	K, 44th Iowa Inf.	235		1910 Nov 25	IA, 37th, 1911
Augustus, J.C.		A, 8th Ill.	147		1927 May 2	NE, 52nd, 1928
Aukinson, E.M.		B, 4th West Va.	55		1906 Feb 27	KS, 26th, 1907
Aulabaugh, Josiah A.		F, 91st Penn. Inf. (see also Appendix D)	7	91	1935 Sep 4	NE, 60th, 1936
Aulert, Geo.			209		1899	NE, 24th, 1900
Aull, Henry		E, 119th Penn.	87		1921 Aug 24	KS, 41st, 1922
Aulls, Chas. W.	Pvt.	A, 2nd Ill. Cav.	452		1917 May 17	IA, 45th, 1919
Ault, Chas. B.		B, 7th Penn. Cav. (died of smallpox)	45		1894 Jun 21	NE, 19th, 1895
Ault, Fred		C, 85th Ohio Inf.	165		1927 Feb 26	NE, 52nd, 1928
Ault, H.G.		I, 20th N.Y.	25		1930 Jan 4	NE, 55th, 1931
Aumon, John		K, 135th U.S.C. Inf. (died of lung trouble)	47	69	1905 Jan 11	NE, 30th, 1906
Aurand, E.G.	Musician	A, 13th Iowa Inf.	512		1912	IA, 39th, 1913
Aurner, Jacob	Pvt.	12th Kans. Inf.	215		1917 Oct 16	IA, 44th, 1918
Austin, B.F.			287		1889	KS, 9th, 1890
Austin, F.R.		H, 23rd Ill.	68		1917 Apr 1	KS, 37th, 1918
Austin, I.E.		C, 11th Ill.	25		1922 Mar 24	NE, 47th, 1923
Austin, J.E.		C, 11th Ill.	25		1922 Mar 24	NE, 47th, 1923
Austin, J.M.	Lieut.	B, 53rd Ind. Inf.	297		1918 Jan 7	KS, 38th, 1919
Austin, J.W.		A, 89th Ind. Inf.	7		1926 May	NE, 51st, 1927
Austin, John B.	Pvt.	B, 4th West Va. Cav.	116		1912 Mar 3	IA, 39th, 1913
Austin, M.	Pvt.	C, 22nd Mich. Inf.	123		1920 May 12	IA, 47th, 1921
Austin, Robert Augustus		A, 113th —		91	1937 Sep 28	IA, 64th, 1938
Austin, Samuel	Pvt.	I, 7th Mich. Cav. E, 20th Mich. Inf.	60	49	1889 Aug 20	IA, 16th, 1890
Austin, Silas			4		1904 Feb 22	NE, 29th, 1905
Austin, W.A.	Corp.	K, 9th Iowa Inf.	206		1922 Dec 4	IA, 49th, 1923
Austin, W.C.		K, 29th Ind.	386		1913 Nov 25	KS, 33rd, 1914
Auten, Oliver V.		Gunboat *Mound City*	25		1920 Aug 25	KS, 40th, 1921
Autry, George		H, 32nd Iowa Inf.	81	91	1935 May 15	IA, 62nd, 1936

Name	Rank	Company, Regiment or Ship	Post*	Age	Death Date†	Journal
Averill, David	Pvt.	A, 37th Iowa Inf.	118	87	1889 May 21	IA, 16th, 1890
Averill, Jno.	Pvt.	K, 55th Ill. Inf.	68		1925 Aug 26	IA, 52nd, 1926
Avery, A.B.	Bugler	8th Wis. Art.	284		1908 Mar 5	IA, 35th, 1909
Avery, C.D.		12th N.Y. Bat.	113		1910 Oct 24	KS, 30th, 1911
Avery, D.S.		B, 11th Mich.	55		1922 Dec 15	KS, 42nd, 1923
Avery, H.	Pvt.	F, 26th N.Y. Cav.	24		1929 Apr 27	IA, 56th, 1930
Avery, Henry		I, 24th Kans.	429		1908	KS, 28th, 1909
Avery, Henry			429		1911	KS, 31st, 1912
Avery, J.B.			24		1914 Jan 6	KS, 34th, 1915
Avery, J.B.		N.Y.	24		1914 Jan 6	KS, 33rd, 1914
Avery, J.L.	Pvt.	G, 88th Ohio Inf.	18		1899	NE, 24th, 1900
Avery, John	Pvt.	24th N.Y. Inf.	18		1932	IA, 59th, 1933
Avery, John	Pvt.	B, 140th Ill. Inf.		98 & 3 mos.	1944 Jun 29	IA, 70th, 1944
Avery, Minor Mahlon	Pvt.	I, 15th Ill. Inf. (at large)	12	94	1940 Jan 27	IA, 66th, 1940
Avery, Park		H, 12th Vt.	88		1905 Mar 17	KS, 25th, 1906
Avery, Samuel		F, 34th Ill. Inf. (died of old age)	284	82	1910 Apr	NE, 35th, 1911
Avery, Steven, see Avrea, Steven						
Avery, W.H.		E, 115th Ind. Inf.	77		1926 Nov 20	NE, 51st, 1927
Avery, W.R.		C, 66th Ind.	17		1930 Jul 30	KS, 50th, 1931
Avery, Z.		A, 23rd Mich. Inf. (died of heart disease)	11	72	1897 Oct 17	NE, 22nd, 1898
Avey, Samuel		A, 10th Ohio Cav.	35		1933 Mar 31	NE, 58th, 1934
Avey, W.M.	Pvt.	K, 176th Ohio Inf.	40		1920 Jan 22	IA, 47th, 1921
Avrea, Steven		A, 78th Ill.	419		1893 Sep 19	KS, 13th, 1894
Awalt, Jacob		D, 48th Ind.	159		1893 Jan 12	KS, 13th, 1894
Awalt, John		E, 3rd Iowa Cav.	158		1922 Feb 4	KS, 42nd, 1923
Awalt, Mike, see Mike, Awalt						
Axen, Agge		location: Stanton			1926 Nov 4	NE, 52nd, 1928
Axley, Uriah		G, 11th Ill. Inf. (died at Iola)	51		1895 Jun 8	KS, 15th, 1896
Axline, A.		2nd Iowa	242		1897 Mar 4	KS, 17th, 1898
Axtell, John E.		E, 9th Ill. Cav.	163		1927 Dec	NE, 52nd, 1928
Aydelott, Ballenger	Pvt.	D, 40th Iowa Cav.	16		1905 Aug 20	IA, 32nd, 1906
Ayers, Alex. M.		H, 125th Ill.	32		1902 Nov 10	KS, 22nd, 1903
Ayers, D.B.		E, 92nd Ill.	22		1928 Dec 30	NE, 53rd, 1929
Ayers, Edward		G, 1st Mo. Cav.	55		1919 Nov 26	KS, 39th, 1920
Ayers, H.O.	Pvt.	B, 2nd Iowa	31		1926 May 24	IA, 53rd, 1927
Ayers, L.E.	Pvt.	G, 4th Iowa Cav.	7		1925 Mar 6	IA, 52nd, 1926
Ayers, William M.			152		1914 Sep 25	IA, 41st, 1915
Ayes, A.L.		G, 31st Iowa Inf.	80	71	1901 Dec	NE, 26th, 1902
Aylesworth, Thos.	Pvt.	20th Ind. Battery	329		1912 May 23	IA, 39th, 1913
Aylward, M.	Pvt.	E, 47th Ill. Inf.	150		1916 Feb 8	IA, 43rd, 1917
Ayres, Dewitt C.		H, 30th Wis. (died of sverelity)	91	81	1921 Apr 27	NE, 46th, 1922
Ayres, Levi	Pvt.	M, 6th N.Y. Hvy. Art.	377		1903 Mar 1	IA, 30th, 1904
Ayres, Wm. E.	Pvt.	D, 14th Iowa Inf.	56	66	1888 Nov 10	IA, 15th, 1889
Baake, I.H.	Pvt.	G, 7th Wis.	22		1921 Feb 13	IA, 48th, 1922
Babb, D.P.		F, 92nd Ill. Inf. (died of disability)	84	60	1903 Oct 29	NE, 28th, 1904
Babb, Eli		G, 7th Kans.	3		1898 Sep 12	KS, 18th, 1899
Babb, Jos.	Pvt.	I, 4th Minn. Inf.	127		1910 Jan 10	IA, 37th, 1911
Babb, W.I.	QM Sergt.	8th Iowa Cav.	20		1925 Sep 4	IA, 52nd, 1926
Babbitt, Vernon M.		H, 1st N.Y. Inf.	95	64	1906 Dec 15	NE, 31st, 1907
Babcock, A.H.			35		1905	NE, 30th, 1906
Babcock, A.H.			35		1912	NE, 37th, 1913
Babcock, A.S.	Pvt.	D, 57th Penn. Inf.	154		1899 Jul 10	IA, 26th, 1900
Babcock, Amos	Pvt.	F, 35th Iowa Inf.	277		1923 Oct 23	IA, 50th, 1924
Babcock, Clark C.		A, 83rd Ind. Inf.	70		1891 Jun 23	KS, 11th, 1892
Babcock, D.A.	Pvt.	A, 14th Iowa Inf.	93		1906 Mar 7	IA, 33rd, 1907
Babcock, Fred	Pvt.	A, 14th Ill. Inf.	12		1920 Apr 25	IA, 47th, 1921
Babcock, Geo.		C, 15th Ill.		64	1904 Sep 17	NE, 29th, 1905
Babcock, Henry	Corp.	H, 96th N.Y. Inf.	519		1911 Oct 23	IA, 38th, 1912
Babcock, J.R.			235		1913 Jan 17	IA, 40th, 1914
Babcock, L.T.		A, 34th Ill.	380		1898 Mar 26	KS, 18th, 1899

See Appendix A, B or C for roster of post names and locations.
†*See Introduction for note regarding recording of death date.*   18

Name	Rank	Company, Regiment or Ship	Post*	Age	Death Date†	Journal
Babcock, Luke		C, 68th Ohio	463		1914 Jan 28	KS, 34th, 1915
Babcock, M.A.		A, 36th Wis.	209		1919 Dec	KS, 39th, 1920
Babcock, Minard		K, 120th N.Y. Inf.			1929[1928?] Mar	NE, 53rd, 1929
Babcock, P.	Sergt.	A, 10th —	322		1920 Nov 5	IA, 47th, 1921
Babcock, W.G.	Pvt.	F, 3rd Iowa Inf.	190	56	1888 Sep 12	IA, 15th, 1889
Babcock, W.H.	Pvt.	E, 44th Iowa Inf.	222		1914 Jan 5	IA, 42nd, 1916
Babcock, W.H.		K, 1st Vt. Art.	130		1922 Sep 16	KS, 42nd, 1923
Babcock, W.H.		A, 95th Ill. Inf. (died of lung disease)	218	57	1895 Jun 14	NE, 20th, 1896
Baber, W.I.		E, 39th Iowa Inf.	425		1917 Jan 10	IA, 44th, 1918
Baber, William		79th Ill.	4		1915 Mar 4	KS, 35th, 1916
Babson, James E.	Pvt.	B, 31st Wis.	437		1903 Apr 14	IA, 30th, 1904
Bach, Caleb	Pvt.	K, 4th Ill. Cav.	206		1919 Oct 13	IA, 46th, 1920
Bachler, John		A, 1st Va.	26		1911 Sep 6	KS, 31st, 1912
Bachman, Chas.	Pvt.	B, 47th Penn. Inf.	69		1911 Aug 22	IA, 38th, 1912
Bachrode, H.S.	Pvt.	F, 19th Wis. Inf.	12		1920 Oct 10	IA, 47th, 1921
Backenstoce, Edmond		Ind. Bat.	1		1921 Dec 25	KS, 41st, 1922
Backus, C.W.		C, 98th N.Y.	28		1920 Mar 16	KS, 40th, 1921
Backus, Chas. H.		C, 16th Kans. Cav.	85		1919 Jan 23	KS, 39th, 1920
Backus, John		F, 11th Ill. Cav. (died at Topeka; buried at Rochester)	71		1894 Nov 15	KS, 14th, 1895
Backus, L.S.		C, 60th N.Y. Inf. (cause of death: heart)	60	61	1903 Sep 33	NE, 28th, 1904
Bacon, Chas. N.		A, 128th Ohio	1		1920 Feb 27	KS, 40th, 1921
Bacon, Geo. S.	Capt.	C, 29th Iowa Inf.	12		1912 Apr 25	IA, 39th, 1913
Bacon, Henry S.	Pvt.	G, 185th N.Y. Inf.	19		1928 Dec 13	IA, 55th, 1929
Bacon, Isa	Pvt.	K, 48th Mo. Inf.	7		1905 May 15	IA, 32nd, 1906
Bacon, J.M.		F, 12th Ohio Cav.	46		1922 May 15	KS, 42nd, 1923
Bacon, James F.		I, 43rd Ind.	214		1916 May 4	KS, 36th, 1917
Bacon, Joseph	Pvt.	C, 7th Vt.	30		1906 Sep 10	IA, 33rd, 1907
Bacon, Marshall		I, 10th Iowa	25		1922 Mar 21	NE, 47th, 1923
Bacon, Marshall		I, 10th Iowa (not a member; buried by Farragut Post)	25		1922 Mar 21	NE, 47th, 1923
Bacon, Newel A.		K, 93rd Ill. Inf.	25	83	1918 Dec 19	NE, 43rd, 1919
Bacon, W.L.	Pvt.		472		1926 Oct 12	IA, 53rd, 1927
Bacus, A.J.	Blacksmith	D, 3rd Iowa Cav.	67		1920 Nov 20	IA, 47th, 1921
Bacus, J.W.		K, 85th Ind.	23		1919 Jun 7	KS, 39th, 1920
Bader, Geo.		C, 12th Ohio Inf.	24		1892 Mar 16	NE, 17th, 1893
Badger, E.B.		F, 43rd Ind.	25		1926 Sep 24	KS, 46th, 1927
Badger, E.J.		K, 7th Iowa	25		1926 Apr 1	NE, 51st, 1927
Badger, Franklin	Pvt.	11th N.Y. Battery	132		1927 May 6	IA, 54th, 1928
Badger, Samuel	Pvt.	K, 34th Iowa	18		1924 Aug 22	IA, 51st, 1925
Bady, G.W.		D, 54th Ill. Inf. (died of pneumonia)	206		1890	KS, 10th, 1891
Baer, Aaron		A, 14th Wis.	68		1919	KS, 39th, 1920
Baer, Jacob	Pvt.	G, 158th Penn. Inf.	230		1904 Jul 3	IA, 31st, 1905
Baer, Jacob D.		E, 126th Penn. Inf. G, 17th Penn. Cav. (died of paralysis)	10	77	1921 Nov 6	NE, 46th, 1922
Baer, John R.	Pvt.	C, 7th Iowa Inf.	40		1911 May 23	IA, 38th, 1912
Baffrey, John P.		2nd Iowa Bat.	18		1906 Jul 18	KS, 26th, 1907
Baggs, C.H.	Pvt.	E, 50th Iowa Inf.	149		1924 Dec 15	IA, 51st, 1925
Baggs, P.	Pvt.	B, 21st Wis. Inf.	64		1911 Dec 24	IA, 38th, 1912
Baggs, Robert		E, 147th Ohio	17		1919 Apr 24	KS, 39th, 1920
Bagley, E.R.	Pvt.	B, 54th Ill. Inf.	313	56	1893 Jun 27	IA, 20th, 1894
Bagley, Edgar	Pvt.	K, 89th N.Y. Inf.	88		1892 Aug	IA, 19th, 1893
Bagley, George W.	Pvt.	I, 14th Iowa Inf.	1	86	1931 Oct 22	IA, 58th, 1932
Bagley, Jay		I & D, 21st N.Y. Cav.	74		1930	NE, 55th, 1931
Bagley, R.D.	Pvt.	G, 3rd Vt. Inf.	42		1925 Apr 22	IA, 52nd, 1926
Bagley, W.	Pvt.	H, 35th Iowa Inf.	12		1909 Jun 30	IA, 36th, 1910
Bagley, W.E.	Pvt.	C, 21st Iowa Inf.	12		1904 Nov 30	IA, 31st, 1905
Bahn, J.H.	Pvt.		118		1925	IA, 52nd, 1926
Bahne, Wm. H.	Pvt.	F, 13th Ill. Inf.	163		1901 Feb 25	IA, 27th, 1901
Bailey, A.J.	Pvt.	A, — Penn. Reserve	19	64	1896 Dec 31	IA, 23rd, 1897
Bailey, Albert			365		1900 Jun 2	KS, 20th, 1901
Bailey, Alex.		C, 17th Iowa	113		1905 Dec 25	KS, 25th, 1906

Name	Rank	Company, Regiment or Ship	Post*	Age	Death Date†	Journal
Bailey, B.M.		B, 3rd Tenn. Cav., 13th Corps (born in East Tenn.)	103		1883	NE, 8th, 1884
Bailey, Blackwell		C, 10th West Va.	250		1923 Dec 31	KS, 43rd, 1924
Bailey, Bradford		B, 3rd Mich.	288		1925 Feb	KS, 45th, 1926
Bailey, C.P.	Pvt.	H, 15th Iowa Inf.	157		1918 Jun 13	IA, 45th, 1919
Bailey, Chas. W.		A, 3rd Ill.	85		1931 Jan 7	KS, 52nd, 1933
Bailey, Chas. W.		A, 3rd Ill.	85		1931 Jan 7	KS, 51st, 1932
Bailey, Clement J.	Pvt.	L, 6th Iowa Cav.	190		1912 Dec 11	IA, 39th, 1913
Bailey, D.W.		I, 40th Iowa Inf.	128		1900 Dec 24	KS, 21st, 1902
Bailey, David	Pvt.	D, 115th Ohio Inf.	10		1928	IA, 55th, 1929
Bailey, E.A.	Pvt.	D, 4th Iowa Inf.	71		1907 Oct 20	IA, 34th, 1908
Bailey, E.F.		A, 93rd Ill.	72		1928 Feb 28	KS, 48th, 1929
Bailey, E.H.			98		1908 Apr 4	KS, 28th, 1909
Bailey, Ezra	Pvt.	E, 24th Iowa Inf.	343		1908 Apr 21	IA, 35th, 1909
Bailey, Geo. M.	Capt.	5th U.S. Inf.	29		1909 Sep	IA, 36th, 1910
Bailey, Geo. S.		B, 9th Ind. Cav.	11	80	1925 Jan 22	NE, 50th, 1926
Bailey, George W.		A, 18th Ind.	244		1911 Dec 23	KS, 31st, 1912
Bailey, H.A.	1st Sergt.	G, 7th N.Y. Cav.	68	54	1893 Nov 4	IA, 20th, 1894
Bailey, H.U.	Pvt.	C, 27th Iowa Inf.	46		1921 Apr 3	IA, 48th, 1922
Bailey, Ira M.		A, 11th Ill.	81		1918 May 3	KS, 38th, 1919
Bailey, J.R.	Pvt.	K, 2nd Iowa Cav.	157		1909 Aug 5	IA, 36th, 1910
Bailey, J.W.	Pvt.	G, 31st Wis. Inf.	81		1918 Sep 9	IA, 45th, 1919
Bailey, James		K, 30th Iowa Inf.	108		1916 Jan 25	IA, 43rd, 1917
Bailey, Jas. D.	Pvt.	B, 161st Ohio	270		1914 Dec 18	IA, 41st, 1915
Bailey, Jas. G.		Ind.	32		1911 Jun 17	KS, 31st, 1912
Bailey, Jas. M.		E, 149th Ohio	27		1933 Jan 17	KS, 53rd, 1934
Bailey, John A.		E, 14th Ind.	1		1923 Feb 9	KS, 43rd, 1924
Bailey, John G.	Pvt.	H, 95th Ill.	42		1907 May 19	IA, 34th, 1908
Bailey, John I.	Pvt.	B, 46th Inf.	249		1910 Jul 11	IA, 37th, 1911
Bailey, John J.	Pvt.	G, 30th Wis.	58		1922 Nov 27	IA, 49th, 1923
Bailey, John W.	Pvt.	B, 33rd Wis. Inf.	383	57	1893 Aug 6	IA, 20th, 1894
Bailey, L.D.	Pvt.	I, 4th Iowa Cav.	116		1927 Feb 18	IA, 54th, 1928
Bailey, L.T.		1st Mass. Hvy. Art.	456		1924 Feb 10	IA, 51st, 1925
Bailey, Milton W.		I, 160th N.Y. Inf.	88		1908 Jan 3	IA, 35th, 1909
Bailey, Milton W.	Pvt.	D, 9th N.Y. Cav.	88		1908	IA, 35th, 1909
Bailey, Moyor M.		D, 5th Wis.	1		1911 Feb 11	KS, 31st, 1912
Bailey, P.R.	Corp.	A, 118th Ohio	72		1907 Mar 12	IA, 34th, 1908
Bailey, Philip D.	Pvt.	G, 47th Iowa Inf.	255		1917 Jun 14	IA, 44th, 1918
Bailey, S.	Pvt.	B, 18th Wis.	81		1921 Sep 28	IA, 48th, 1922
Bailey, Samuel J.		C, 83rd Ind.	4		1915 Jan 11	KS, 35th, 1916
Bailey, Simes	Pvt.	H, 9th Iowa Inf.	98		1929 Sep 12	IA, 56th, 1930
Bailey, T.L.	Pvt.	E, 1st Mass. Hvy. Art.	456		1926 Jun	IA, 53rd, 1927
Bailey, T.S.			235		1913 Jan 14	IA, 40th, 1914
Bailey, W.F.		25th Iowa	108		1907 May 10	IA, 34th, 1908
Bailey, W.S.	Pvt.	K, 15th Iowa Inf.	254	39	1885 Dec 18	IA, 12th, 1886
Bailey, W.W.	Pvt.	G, 106th N.Y. Inf.	14		1911 May 20	IA, 38th, 1912
Bailey, William T.	Pvt.	F, 2nd Ill. Cav.	94		1932 Jun	IA, 59th, 1933
Bailey, Wm.	Corp.	B, 8th Iowa Inf.	321		1900 Sep 12	IA, 27th, 1901
Bailey, Wm. S.	Pvt.	K, 15th Iowa Inf.	254	40	1885 Dec 13	IA, 17th, 1891
Bailie, Dixon	Pvt.	E, 89th Ill. Inf.	10		1927 Apr	IA, 54th, 1928
Bailor, Jesse	Pvt.	B, 85th Ill. Inf.	153		1908 Sep 12	IA, 35th, 1909
Bailor, William		H, 23rd Ill. Inf. (died of old age)	3	85	1921 Nov 7	NE, 46th, 1922
Baily, S.	Pvt.	G, 4th Ill. Inf.	125		1924 Mar 24	IA, 51st, 1925
Bain, J.D.			52		1884	KS, 4th, 1885
Bain, John		K, 113th N.Y.	67		1934 Jun	IA, 61st, 1935
Bain, John D.		C, 52nd Ill. Inf. (died of cancer of stomach)	60	66	1911 Jan 16	NE, 36th, 1912
Bain, Samuel		A, 36th Iowa Inf.	57		1900 Apr 9	KS, 20th, 1901
Baine, J.G.	Trumpeter	L, 9th Iowa Cav.	7		1906 Oct 11	IA, 33rd, 1907
Bainter, Samuel		C, 11th Ohio Cav.	105		1921	KS, 41st, 1922
Bair, Conrad		C, 12th Kans.	102		1900 May 22	KS, 20th, 1901
Bair, Isaiah F.	Pvt.	K, 22nd Iowa Inf.	452	88	1932 Mar	IA, 59th, 1933
Bair, Jacob, see Bare, Jacob						

Name	Rank	Company, Regiment or Ship	Post*	Age	Death Date†	Journal
Bair, Joseph	Pvt. Pvt.	F, 11th Iowa Inf. 168th Penn. Inf. (at large)	400, 19	97	1940 Apr 15	IA, 66th, 1940
Bair, Wm.	Pvt.	C, 80th Ohio	123	52	1892 Jun 30	IA, 19th, 1893
Baird, Andrew			294		1936	KS, 56th, 1937
Baird, Andrew J.		A, 13th Kans.	127		1923 Jun 23	KS, 43rd, 1924
Baird, B.F.		C, 107th Penn.	71		1926 Nov 25	KS, 46th, 1927
Baird, C.N.	Capt.	E, 129th Ill.	25		1913 Jan 17	NE, 38th, 1914
Baird, Cyrus N.		one of the pioneers of Lancaster County	25		1911	NE, 36th, 1912
Baird, E.D.		K, 145th Penn. Inf.	293		1901 Jul 18	KS, 21st, 1902
Baird, George	Pvt.	A, 14th Iowa Inf.	382		1897 Aug 28	IA, 24th, 1898
Baird, Giles		G, 2nd Ill. Cav.	56		1889	KS, 9th, 1890
Baird, I.W.	Pvt.	D, 37th Iowa Inf.	233		1903 Jun 26	IA, 30th, 1904
Baird, J.C.		112th Ill.	294		1905 Jan	KS, 25th, 1906
Baird, J.M.			1		1922	NE, 47th, 1923
Baird, J.R.		A, 78th Ind.	353		1916 Apr 15	KS, 36th, 1917
Baird, James		C, 30th Ill. (died of insanity)	27	76	1906 Jun 15	NE, 31st, 1907
Baird, Jas. A.		A, 1st Penn. Cav.	191		1890	KS, 10th, 1891
Baird, Jas. S.		83rd Ill. Inf.	55		1922 Sep 16	IA, 49th, 1923
Baird, Jos.	Pvt.	E, 93rd Penn. Inf.	97	58	1891 Dec 18	IA, 18th, 1892
Baird, Joshua M.		D, 24th Ohio	28		1913 Mar 23	KS, 33rd, 1914
Baird, Robert B.	Lieut.	35th Iowa Inf.	231		1910 Aug 18	IA, 37th, 1911
Baird, Robert H.		D, 2nd Kans.	35		1896 Oct 20	KS, 16th, 1897
Baird, S.S.		D, 133rd Ohio Inf.	32		1900 Jul 8	KS, 20th, 1901
Baird, Samuel B.	Pvt.	K, 31st Iowa Inf.	440	77	1898 Jun 2	IA, 25th, 1899
Baird, W.R.	Pvt.	I, 1st Iowa Inf.	78		1909 Oct 9	IA, 36th, 1910
Baker, A.A.		E, 76th N.Y.	65		1921 Oct 22	KS, 41st, 1922
Baker, A.J.	Pvt.	E, 17th Iowa Inf.	122		1911 Apr 23	IA, 38th, 1912
Baker, Abner		A, 40th Ind.	336		1906 Jan 29	KS, 26th, 1907
Baker, Alanson	Pvt.	I, 2nd Neb. Cav.	461		1912 Oct 30	IA, 39th, 1913
Baker, Alanson	Pvt.	I, 2nd Neb. Cav.	461		1911 Oct 30	IA, 38th, 1912
Baker, Albert	Pvt.	M, 8th Ill. Cav.	222		1925 May 9	IA, 52nd, 1926
Baker, Albert E.	Pvt.	H, 29th Wis.	1		1915 Mar 4	KS, 35th, 1916
Baker, Alfred	Pvt.	D, 35th Iowa Inf.	231		1922 Feb 12	IA, 49th, 1923
Baker, Andrew	Pvt.	I, 1st Ind. Hvy. Art.	300		1907 Apr 2	IA, 34th, 1908
Baker, B.B.		I, 4th Iowa Cav. (died of old age)	289		1905	NE, 30th, 1906
Baker, B.B.		I, 4th Iowa Cav. (died of old age)	287		1906	NE, 31st, 1907
Baker, B.T.		K, 26th Iowa Inf.	154		1st quarter 1885	IA, 11th, 1885
Baker, Benj. A.		B, 10th Wis.	25		1923 Aug 5	KS, 43rd, 1924
Baker, Bolin	Pvt.	F, 25th Mo. Inf.	40		1914 Jul 10	IA, 41st, 1915
Baker, Bruce C.		I, 28th Ill.	129		1921 Oct 11	KS, 41st, 1922
Baker, C.D.		B, 2nd Iowa Inf. (died of general debility)	48	78	1922 Oct 4	NE, 47th, 1923
Baker, C.N.		2nd Ohio Battery	38		1919 Jan 26	KS, 39th, 1920
Baker, C.W.	Pvt.	F, 16th Iowa Inf.	94		1925 Jan 31	IA, 52nd, 1926
Baker, Chas.	Pvt.	I, 4th Wis. Cav.	8		1910 Jul 1	IA, 37th, 1911
Baker, Chas. H.	Corp.	B, 5th Minn. Vol. Inf.	74		1903 Sep 19	IA, 30th, 1904
Baker, Conrad		M, 1st Ohio Cav.	66		1919 Aug 2	IA, 46th, 1920
Baker, D.C.		E, 9th Iowa Inf.	44		1899 Aug 7	KS, 19th, 1900
Baker, D.S.	Pvt.	F, 4th Iowa Inf.	14	64	1887 Apr 15	IA, 14th, 1888
Baker, David H.		E, 154th Ohio	17		1897 Dec 2	KS, 17th, 1898
Baker, E.	Pvt.	H, 130th Ohio Vol. Inf.	297		3rd quarter 1885	IA, 12th, 1886
Baker, E.N.		L, 2nd Neb. Cav.	314		1885	KS, 5th, 1886
Baker, E.Y.		A, 68th Ohio	158		1898 Dec 20	KS, 18th, 1899
Baker, F.M.			93		1904	KS, 24th, 1905
Baker, Frank		G, 85th Ohio	85		1912 Jan 19	KS, 32nd, 1913
Baker, G.V.		D, 125th Ill.	51		1898 Jul 17	KS, 18th, 1899
Baker, Geo. D.	Pvt.	B, 44th Iowa Inf.	231		1923 Apr 29	IA, 50th, 1924
Baker, George C.	Corp.	B, 23rd Iowa Inf.	12	49	1894 Mar 23	IA, 21st, 1895
Baker, George E.		F, 5th V.R.C.	348		1892 Sep 10	KS, 12th, 1893
Baker, H.C.		K, 7th Mich.	130		1916 Oct 3	KS, 36th, 1917
Baker, Harrison	Pvt.		122		1925 Feb 1	IA, 52nd, 1926
Baker, Harry		G, 53rd Penn. Inf.	59	71	1897 Aug 15	NE, 22nd, 1898
Baker, Henry		E, 7th Ind. Cav.	158		1913 Jan 11	KS, 33rd, 1914

*See Appendix A, B or C for roster of post names and locations.
†See Introduction for note regarding recording of death date.

Name	Rank	Company, Regiment or Ship	Post*	Age	Death Date†	Journal
Baker, Henry C.		F, 2nd U.S. Cav.	132		1900 Aug 6	KS, 20th, 1901
Baker, Henry L.	Lieut.	F, 15th Kans.	1		1915 Oct 8	KS, 35th, 1916
Baker, Hiram	Pvt.	B, 16th Iowa Inf.	208		1917 Dec 31	IA, 44th, 1918
Baker, I.H.		D, 13th Ill. (died of dropsy)	80	74	1908 Dec 27	NE, 33rd, 1909
Baker, I.L.		H, 21st Kans. State Militia	12		1916 Apr 17	KS, 36th, 1917
Baker, Ira	Pvt.	K, 48th Mo. Inf.	7		1910 Nov 19	IA, 37th, 1911
Baker, Ira G.	Pvt.	D, 2nd Iowa Inf.	255		1913 Jan 31	IA, 40th, 1914
Baker, J.C.	Pvt.	I, 15th Iowa Inf.	497		1908 Aug 1	IA, 35th, 1909
Baker, J.C.		H, 57th Ohio	293		1924	KS, 44th, 1925
Baker, J.F.	Pvt.	C, 29th Mo. Inf.	12		1930 Oct 3	IA, 57th, 1931
Baker, J.J.	Lieut. Col.	19th Mich.	256		1900 Apr 30	KS, 20th, 1901
Baker, J.M.			12		1923 May 8	KS, 43rd, 1924
Baker, J.N.		D, 2nd Ill. Cav.	118		1920 Oct 8	KS, 40th, 1921
Baker, J.S.	Corp.	F, 79th Ill. Inf.	154		1916 Feb 19	IA, 43rd, 1917
Baker, J.T.			168		1909 Dec 4	IA, 36th, 1910
Baker, J.W.		I, 36th Iowa Inf.	122		1st quarter 1885	IA, 11th, 1885
Baker, James D.	Pvt.	H, 4th Iowa Inf.	271	58	1894 Sep 1	IA, 21st, 1895
Baker, James K.P.	Pvt.	D, 20th Iowa Inf.	197		1907 Sep 22	IA, 34th, 1908
Baker, Jerry		L, 72nd Ohio	51		1927	KS, 47th, 1928
Baker, John		F, 39th Iowa Inf.	55		1918 Mar 9	IA, 45th, 1919
Baker, John		D, 16th Kans. Cav.	493		1909 Mar 8	KS, 29th, 1910
Baker, John F.		B, 4th Ohio Cav. (at large)	16	91	1937 Oct 9	IA, 64th, 1938
Baker, John H.	Pvt.	K, 46th Ill. Inf.	68		1918 Mar 13	IA, 45th, 1919
Baker, John S.		F, 4th Ky. Cav.	127		1900 Jul 5	KS, 20th, 1901
Baker, John W.		K, 33rd N.Y.	25		1934 Sep 30	NE, 59th, 1935
Baker, Jos. W.		D, 21st Iowa	113		1907 Feb 15	NE, 32nd, 1908
Baker, Joseph		D, 44th Ohio Inf.	176		1918 Oct 19	KS, 38th, 1919
Baker, Joseph M.		D, 12th Kans.	18		1923 May 8	KS, 43rd, 1924
Baker, Joshua W.		C, 9th Kans. Cav.			1913 Feb 9	KS, 33rd, 1914
Baker, Julius E.	Sergt.	D, 95th Ill. Inf.	141		1916 Jul 2	IA, 43rd, 1917
Baker, Lewis P.		G, 1st U.S. Eng.	85		1918	KS, 38th, 1919
Baker, Lyman M.	Pvt.	H, 93rd Ill. Inf.	16		1918 Feb 7	IA, 45th, 1919
Baker, M.M.		B, 1st Minn. Hvy. Art.	66		1913 Feb 4	KS, 33rd, 1914
Baker, Matthias W.	Pvt.	B, 11th Ill. Cav. (at large)	56	97	1942 Sep 25	IA, 69th, 1943
Baker, Milton		A, 142nd Ind.	25		1923 Feb 18	NE, 47th, 1923
Baker, N.H.	Pvt.	F, 98th Ohio Inf.	19	90	1933 Mar 24	IA, 60th, 1934
Baker, Nathan		A, 121st Ohio	199		1905 Apr 19	KS, 25th, 1906
Baker, Nelson P.		F, 2nd Ohio Cav. D, 4th Ark. Cav. 25th Ohio Bat. (died of Bright's disease)	90	68	1908 Apr 8	NE, 33rd, 1909
Baker, Nelson P.		25th Ohio Bat. 2nd Ohio Cav. D, 4th Ark. Cav. (died of heart trouble)	90	69	1907 Apr 8	NE, 32nd, 1908
Baker, O.E.		D, 141st Ohio Inf.	25		1893 Jul 31	NE, 18th, 1894
Baker, Philemon		A, 146th Ill. Inf.	97		1918 Feb 26	KS, 38th, 1919
Baker, R.R.	Pvt.	23rd Iowa	7		1924 Sep 18	IA, 51st, 1925
Baker, S.F.	Pvt.	G, 3rd Iowa Cav.	79		1899	IA, 26th, 1900
Baker, Samuel		C, 85th Ind. Inf.	51		1901 Jun 13	KS, 21st, 1902
Baker, Seth M.	Pvt.	A, 2nd Neb. Cav.	131		1899	NE, 24th, 1900
Baker, W.F.	Corp.		29		1917 May 5	IA, 44th, 1918
Baker, W.H.	Sergt.	D, 17th Ohio Inf.	12		1918 Dec 19	IA, 45th, 1919
Baker, W.L.		105th Ill. Inf.	505		1908 Jun 27	IA, 35th, 1909
Baker, Washington		D, 46th U.S.C.	321		1904 Nov 29	KS, 24th, 1905
Baker, William E.		H, 12th Ill. Vol. Inf.	4		1885	KS, 5th, 1886
Baker, Wm.	Pvt.	B, 14th Kans. Cav.	117		1884	KS, 4th, 1885
Baker, Wm.		F, 120th Ill.	7		1918	KS, 38th, 1919
Baker, Wm. A.	Pvt.	C, 18th Iowa	208		1903 Jun 7	IA, 30th, 1904
Baker, Wm. A.		A, Ohio Vol. Cav.			1929 Feb 10	NE, 53rd, 1929
Baker, Z.T.	Pvt.	G, 42nd Wis. Inf.	3		1919 Jan 13	IA, 46th, 1920
Balbach, Andrew	Pvt.	H, 3rd Iowa Cav.	2		1909 Jul 28	IA, 36th, 1910
Balch, A.B.		B, 54th Ill.	226		1921 Aug	KS, 41st, 1922
Balch, G.B.		M, 3rd Wis. Cav.	206		1909 Aug 19	KS, 29th, 1910

Name	Rank	Company, Regiment or Ship	Post*	Age	Death Date†	Journal
Balcom, A.H.	Pvt.	F, —	154		1921 Jun 13	IA, 48th, 1922
Balcome, Chas. E.		I, 3rd Iowa	158		1904 Mar 19	KS, 24th, 1905
Balderson, J.M.		A & C, 1st & 14th Ill.	25		1909 Mar 3	KS, 29th, 1910
Baldridge, J.F.		A, 3rd Iowa Cav.	28		1921	KS, 41st, 1922
Baldwin, A.A.		A, 50th Ohio	50		1914 Nov 2	KS, 34th, 1915
Baldwin, A.E.	Sergt.	G, 19th Iowa Inf.	153		1914 Sep 21	IA, 41st, 1915
Baldwin, A.M.		C, 99th Ohio Vol. Inf.	63		1912 Jan 10	KS, 32nd, 1913
Baldwin, A.T.		C, 32nd Iowa	68	96	1934 Nov 4	IA, 61st, 1935
Baldwin, Albert		D, 22nd Ind. (died of apoplexy)	301	70	1911 May 19	NE, 36th, 1912
Baldwin, B.P.	Pvt.	K, 7th N.H.	88		1926 Aug 5	IA, 53rd, 1927
Baldwin, B.S.	Pvt.	K, 91st Ind. Inf.	1		1918 Jun 25	IA, 45th, 1919
Baldwin, C.A.		H, 38th Iowa Inf.	48		1921	IA, 48th, 1922
Baldwin, C.N.		E, —	257		1917 Feb 12	KS, 37th, 1918
Baldwin, Chas. W.	Pvt.	C, 19th Ill.	134		1926 Jan 13	IA, 53rd, 1927
Baldwin, Chester		A, 3rd Iowa Inf. (died of paralysis)	329		1894 Aug 25	NE, 19th, 1895
Baldwin, Cyrus, Jr.		H, 58th Penn. Inf.	351		1891 Aug 19	KS, 11th, 1892
Baldwin, E.E.		P.H.B. Md.[Potomac Home Brigade?]	453		1893 Aug 20	KS, 13th, 1894
Baldwin, Earl	Pvt.	G, 13th Wis. Inf.	68		1926 Sep 27	IA, 53rd, 1927
Baldwin, G.O.		A, 89th Ohio (buried in post grounds)	127		1888	KS, 8th, 1889
Baldwin, G.R.		18th Mich.	32		1888	KS, 8th, 1889
Baldwin, Geo.	Pvt.	9th Iowa Inf.	48		1924 Mar 26	IA, 51st, 1925
Baldwin, H.G.		I, 8th Vt. Inf. (died at Ada; buried at Ada)	266		1894 Apr 6	KS, 14th, 1895
Baldwin, H.H.			236		1917 Feb 8	IA, 44th, 1918
Baldwin, Harry S.		F, 26th Iowa	20		1896 Jan 30	KS, 16th, 1897
Baldwin, Joseph E.		C, 1st Mo.	1		1914 Oct 4	KS, 34th, 1915
Baldwin, L.	Pvt.	K, 6th Iowa Inf.	20		1921 Jan	IA, 48th, 1922
Baldwin, Leander	Pvt.	B, 35th Iowa Inf.	362	64	1897 Dec 2	IA, 24th, 1898
Baldwin, M.T.	Corp.	B, 78th Ill. Inf.	197	66	1897 Apr 21	IA, 24th, 1898
Baldwin, S.	Pvt.	C, 33rd Iowa	425		1924 Jul 4	IA, 51st, 1925
Baldwin, S.	Pvt.	C, 33rd Iowa Inf.	425		1926 Jul 4	IA, 53rd, 1927
Baldwin, S.	Pvt.	C, 33rd Iowa Inf.	425		1925 Jul 4	IA, 52nd, 1926
Baldwin, S.E.		I, 17th Iowa	25		1916 Mar 10	KS, 36th, 1917
Baldwin, S.M.	Sergt.	H, 80th Ohio Inf.	356	67	1895 Feb 1	IA, 22nd, 1896
Baldwin, Simeon M.		H, 73rd Ill. Inf.	64		1899 Apr 13	KS, 19th, 1900
Baldwin, T.F.	2nd Lieut.	D, 14th Iowa Inf.	2		1922 Mar 22	IA, 49th, 1923
Baldwin, T.J., see Balwin, T.J.						
Baldwin, W.	Pvt.		66		1920 Mar 11	IA, 47th, 1921
Bale, John W.		F, 15th Ky. Inf.	72		1929 Apr 20	KS, 49th, 1930
Bales, Asa		H, 59th Ind.	5		1924 Jul 27	KS, 44th, 1925
Bales, Daniel		I, 10th Kans. (died at Chautauqua County; buried at Sedan Cemetery)	74		1894	KS, 14th, 1895
Bales, E.H.		K, 19th Ind.	25		1927 Apr 10	KS, 47th, 1928
Bales, J.H.	Pvt.	H, 33rd Iowa Inf.	154		1911 Dec 19	IA, 38th, 1912
Bales, Jonathan L.	Pvt.	K, 7th Iowa Inf.	143	73	1889 Jul 11	IA, 16th, 1890
Bales, L.R.	Pvt.		11		1919	IA, 46th, 1920
Bales, Samuel		K, 5th Mo. Inf.	66		1899 Sep 30	KS, 19th, 1900
Balfor, William	Pvt.	I, 26th Iowa Inf.	125		1928 Feb 3	IA, 55th, 1929
Balfor, William	Pvt.		125		1929 Feb 3	IA, 56th, 1930
Balfour, Andrew	Pvt.	I, 126th Ill. Inf.	125		1916 Feb 18	IA, 43rd, 1917
Balfour, J.			54		1897 Jun 28	IA, 24th, 1898
Balfour, Walter			116		1912 May 12	IA, 39th, 1913
Balfour, William		I, 45th Ill.	24		1935 Apr 4	NE, 60th, 1936
Balgles, Steven		E, 35th Mo. (died of old age at Soldiers & Sailors Home, Milford)		80	1906 Nov 28	NE, 31st, 1907
Balintine, Henry	Pvt.	B, 7th Ill. Inf.	26		1922 Jan 7	IA, 49th, 1923
Balis, John C.	Pvt.	G, 13th Wis. (died of pneumonia)	114	39	1887 Feb	NE, 12th, 1888
Balkin, A.H.	Capt.	D, 79th Ohio Vol. Inf.	7		1901 Oct 2	IA, 28th, 1902
Ball, A.J.		E, 12th Kans.	32		1935	KS, 55th, 1936
Ball, Benjamin Stamper				91	1937 Feb 27	IA, 64th, 1938
Ball, D.B.		Ves. Gensbock, U.S. Navy, New York (died of old age)	342	84	1919 Dec 12	NE, 44th, 1920
Ball, D.R.		K, 46th Ind. Inf. (died of heart disease)	81	64	1902 Feb	NE, 27th, 1903

Name	Rank	Company, Regiment or Ship	Post*	Age	Death Date†	Journal
Ball, Guy L.		C, 20th Ohio Vol. Inf.	150		1915 Nov 26	KS, 35th, 1916
Ball, Isiah	Pvt.	Ind. Cav.	49		1923 Feb 7	IA, 50th, 1924
Ball, J.M.	Surg.	31st Wis. Inf.	68	85	1897 Aug 25	IA, 24th, 1898
Ball, J.W.		19th Batt. Ind.	16		1928	KS, 48th, 1929
Ball, Jacob G.		A, 148th Ill. Inf. (former member)	1		1939 Feb 1	NE, 64th, 1940
Ball, James W.		K, 10th Iowa Vol. Inf. (died of pneumonia)	265	80	1914 Mar 14	NE, 39th, 1915
Ball, John		I, 1st Penn. Inf. (member at large)	127		1934 Nov 14	KS, 54th, 1935
Ball, John C.		I, 84th Ind. Inf.	108		1925 Feb 7	KS, 45th, 1926
Ball, Joseph	Pvt.	D, 13th Ill. Cav. (died of consumption)	11	63	1887 Aug 13	NE, 12th, 1888
Ball, L.		L, 5th Ind.	130		1921 Mar 12	KS, 41st, 1922
Ball, Nathan W.	Pvt.	E, 18th Iowa Inf.	255	51	1892 Dec 18	IA, 19th, 1893
Ball, O.J.		D, 26th Conn.	24		1919 Jun 5	KS, 39th, 1920
Ball, Rolla B.		A, 3rd Vt. Inf.	14		1912 May 5	KS, 32nd, 1913
Ball, Rufus D.	Pvt.	E, 36th Wis. Inf.	68		1910 Oct 4	IA, 37th, 1911
Ball, Singleton		7th Ky. Cav.	65		1912 Jan 12	KS, 32nd, 1913
Ball, Thomas		I, 47th Iowa	25	74	1916 Jul 19	NE, 41st, 1917
Ball, Thomas S.		K, 10th Ky. Inf.	51		1934 Nov 18	KS, 54th, 1935
Ball, W.C.		45th Iowa	19		1923 Mar 30	IA, 50th, 1924
Ball, Wm. H.		B, 43rd Ind. Inf.	174		1901 Sep 13	KS, 21st, 1902
Ballangh, P.S.	Pvt.	H, 47th N.Y. Inf.	70		1911 Aug 7	IA, 38th, 1912
Ballard, Alonzo		C, 1st U.S. Sharpshooters	363		1917 Jan 1	KS, 36th, 1917
Ballard, E.A.	Pvt.	K, 17th Vt. Inf.	8		1904 Aug 21	IA, 31st, 1905
Ballard, H.C.	Pvt.	B, 69th Ill. Inf.	117		1917 Apr 19	IA, 44th, 1918
Ballard, J.W.	Capt.	B, 47th Ill. Inf.	343	58	1892 Feb 28	IA, 18th, 1892
Ballard, J.W.		I, 191st Ohio Inf.	51		1917	KS, 37th, 1918
Ballard, Y.E.		H, 29th Iowa Inf.	176		1908 Nov 16	KS, 28th, 1909
Ballentyn, H.	Pvt.	B, 15th Ill. Inf.	68		1920 Oct 13	IA, 47th, 1921
Ballewag, F.C.		died of heart failure	177		1909 Feb 17	NE, 33rd, 1909
Balliet, David M.		A, 92nd Ill. Inf. (at large)	68	92	1937 Dec 26	IA, 64th, 1938
Balliet, S.F.	Pvt.	B, 17th Ill. Cav.	12		1910 Apr 24	IA, 37th, 1911
Balliman, W.H.		K, 13th Ill. (died of heart failure)	8	71	1915 Dec 24	NE, 40th, 1916
Ballinger, A.		K, 152nd Ill.	132		1919 Jul 2	KS, 39th, 1920
Ballinger, John		G, 1st Mo. Cav.	257		1914 Aug 23	KS, 34th, 1915
Ballinger, William		I, 55th Penn.	6		1912 Oct 22	KS, 32nd, 1913
Ballinger, Wm.	Lieut.	A, 19th Iowa Inf.	2		1916 Sep 7	IA, 43rd, 1917
Ballinger, Wm.		F, 135th Ind.	8		1928 Aug 20	KS, 48th, 1929
Ballon, A.D.		M, 10th Wis.	116		1899	KS, 19th, 1900
Ballon, R.	Pvt.	K, 4th Iowa	10		1921 Jun 14	IA, 48th, 1922
Ballon, V.A.	Pvt.	F, 2nd Iowa Cav.	31		1906 Jan	IA, 33rd, 1907
Ballou, J.N.	Sergt.	F, 6th Iowa Inf.	440		1918 Dec 23	IA, 45th, 1919
Ballshine, J.	Pvt.	51st Wis. Inf.	68		1925 May 31	IA, 52nd, 1926
Balsley, John W.		G, 32nd Ohio	155		1895 Jan 6	KS, 16th, 1897
Baltimore, John P.	Pvt.	B, 7th Kans. Cav.	137		1912 Mar 3	IA, 39th, 1913
Balwin, T.J.	Capt.	F, 91st Ill. Inf.	424		1905 Oct 15	IA, 32nd, 1906
Bammer, Theodore		H, 124th Ill.	6		1897 Aug 4	KS, 17th, 1898
Bancher, U.		I, 2nd Ohio Inf.	105	68	1903 Sep 19	NE, 28th, 1904
Bancroft, A.R.		C, 17th Kans. Inf. (died of accidental shooting)	55		1890	KS, 10th, 1891
Bancroft, Walter	Pvt.	A, 7th Mo. Cav.	2		1912 May 17	IA, 39th, 1913
Bane, Ephraim		C, 47th Ill. Inf.	17		1912 Nov 29	KS, 32nd, 1913
Bane, Geo.		C, 12th West Va.	19		1928 Jul 15	KS, 48th, 1929
Baner, John H.	Pvt.	I, 25th Iowa Inf.	5		1919 Oct 5	IA, 46th, 1920
Banester, G.W.	Pvt.	B, 6th Iowa	25		1923 May 10	IA, 50th, 1924
Banfill, Geo.			257		1895	KS, 15th, 1896
Bangs, Geo. A.			115		1894	NE, 19th, 1895
Bangs, John C.		L, 1st Maine Cav.	354	76	1911 Nov 9	NE, 36th, 1912
Bangs, L.G.	Pvt.	A, 19th Ill. Inf.	44		1919 Jan 27	IA, 46th, 1920
Bangs, R.R.		L, 1st Maine Cav.	98		1931 Feb 21	NE, 56th, 1932
Bangs, Samuel		G, 12th Wis. (killed by B. & M.)	35	69	1915 Mar 1	NE, 40th, 1916
Banister, A.		K, 36th Iowa Inf.	158		1925 Oct 14	KS, 45th, 1926
Banister, Martin W.	Corp.	B, 147th Ill. Inf.	88		1913 Sep 17	IA, 40th, 1914
Banker, S.O.	Corp.	B, 1st Ohio Cav.	55		1910 Apr 11	IA, 37th, 1911

*See Appendix A, B or C for roster of post names and locations.
†See Introduction for note regarding recording of death date.

Name	Rank	Company, Regiment or Ship	Post*	Age	Death Date†	Journal
Banks, Dan'l		18th U.S.C. Inf.	7		1926 Feb 6	NE, 51st, 1927
Banks, Egbert	Pvt.	E, 11th Iowa Inf.	92	59	1898 Apr 17	IA, 24th, 1898
Banks, Elisha		B, 38th Ind.	84		1909 Mar 22	KS, 29th, 1910
Banks, G.L.		C, 15th Ind.	4		1924 Aug 19	KS, 44th, 1925
Banks, George A.		C, 3rd Kans. State Militia	12		1910 Apr 11	KS, 30th, 1911
Banks, H.A.		A, Missouri Mil.	8		1928 Jul 14	KS, 48th, 1929
Banks, Rivers		C, I.N.C.B.K.S. Ky. (died at Hutchinson)	17		1895 Apr 7	KS, 15th, 1896
Banks, Samuel			147		1912 Jan 12	KS, 32nd, 1913
Banks, W.B.		L, 9th Iowa Cav. (died of lung trouble)	350	69	1911 Oct 18	NE, 36th, 1912
Banks, W.W.			112		1890	NE, 15th, 1891
Banman, John		G, 83rd Ind. (died of throat trouble)	44[24?]	85	1909 Mar 12	NE, 34th, 1910
Banman, Jonas		F, 1st Mo. Inf.	7	53	1895 May	NE, 20th, 1896
Banning, H.	Pvt.	E, 2nd Col. Cav.	384		1910 Nov 22	IA, 37th, 1911
Banning, J.E.	Pvt.	A, 23rd Iowa Inf.	35	65	1890 Dec 9	IA, 17th, 1891
Bannister, Chas.		A, 2nd Neb. Cav. (died of complication of diseases)	131		1894 May 9	NE, 19th, 1895
Bannister, Martin W., see Banister, Martin W.						
Bannister, S.L.		D, 33rd Mo. Inf.	1		1886	KS, 6th, 1887
Bannon, Franklin		C, 11th Ind.	97		1919 Jul 10	KS, 39th, 1920
Banquet, Nick	Sergt.	D, 25th Iowa Inf.	5		1912 Dec 27	IA, 39th, 1913
Banta, B.F.	Pvt.	E, 8th Iowa Inf.	49		1922 Oct 6	IA, 49th, 1923
Banta, J.T.		D, 138th Ill. A, 14th Iowa	13		1933 Apr 12	NE, 58th, 1934
Banta, J.V.		G, 132nd Ind.	173		1923 Jul 21	IA, 50th, 1924
Banton, L.M.	Sergt.	G, 38th Iowa Inf.	48		1915 Jun 24	IA, 42nd, 1916
Bants, J.V.		G, 132nd Ind. Inf.	173		1924 Jul 21	IA, 51st, 1925
Banyard, J.E.	Musician	H, 1st Mo. Inf.	26		1918 Jan 24	IA, 45th, 1919
Barackman, K.H.		D, 7th West Va.	23		1912 Aug 19	KS, 32nd, 1913
Barbee, N.		B, 54th Ohio Inf.	44		1897 Dec 24	NE, 22nd, 1898
Barber, Alonzo S.		E, 22nd Conn. Inf.	25		1911 Sep 8	KS, 31st, 1912
Barber, C.A.		F, 6th Mich.	32	77	1909 Apr 13	NE, 34th, 1910
Barber, C.S.	Pvt.	E, 41st Iowa Inf.	66	52	1894 Oct 30	IA, 21st, 1895
Barber, C.W.		E, 43rd Mo.	100		1926 May 26	KS, 46th, 1927
Barber, Dorr	Corp.	I, 33rd N.Y. Inf.	64		1908 Oct 7	IA, 35th, 1909
Barber, Emory		41st N.Y. Cav. (died of heart failure)	1	83	1919 Dec 29	NE, 45th, 1921
Barber, F.G.		D, 12th Ohio	180		1892 Sep 19	KS, 12th, 1893
Barber, G.D.		I, 29th Wis.	30		1888	KS, 8th, 1889
Barber, G.E.		I, 104th Ohio	25		1931 Apr 25	NE, 56th, 1932
Barber, Geo. E.		B, 15th Ill. Inf.	236	87	1936	IA, 63rd, 1937
Barber, H.E.	Pvt.	M, 8th Ill. Cav.	223	63	1893 Nov 3	IA, 20th, 1894
Barber, Horace		K, 4th Minn. Inf.	292		1919	IA, 46th, 1920
Barber, John		K, 3rd (M) Kans.[Kans. State Militia?]	12		1905 Jan 11	KS, 25th, 1906
Barber, Lander		D, 24th Ky.	289		1893 Jun 26	KS, 13th, 1894
Barber, M.L.		H, — Ind.	63		1912 Sep 26	KS, 32nd, 1913
Barber, N.		died of heart failure	44	54	1896 Dec 24	NE, 21st, 1897
Barber, Nathaniel		C, 2nd Mich.	14		1910 Jul 1	KS, 30th, 1911
Barber, Noyes		29th Ill.	23		1911 Apr 11	KS, 31st, 1912
Barber, Oliver		C, — Kans. (died at Lawrence)	12		1895 Oct	KS, 15th, 1896
Barber, S.J.	Pvt.	A, 9th N.Y. Hvy. Art.	66		1912 Jun 20	IA, 39th, 1913
Barber, Scott	Pvt.	F, 126th N.Y. Inf.	111	96	1933 Dec 10	IA, 60th, 1934
Barber, Thomas J.			25		1910 May 20	NE, 35th, 1911
Barber, W.C.	Pvt.	E, 6th Iowa Cav.	271	85	1933 Nov 4	IA, 60th, 1934
Barber, W.F.		E, 21st Conn. Inf.	88		1886	KS, 6th, 1887
Barber, W.H.	Pvt.	G, 105th Ill. Inf.	132		1910	IA, 37th, 1911
Barber, W.H.		E, 5th U.S. Cav.	46		1916 Mar 6	KS, 36th, 1917
Barbour, James H.	Capt.	K, 1st Del. Inf.	42	94	1938 Nov 22	IA, 64th, 1938
Barchers, E.		D, 4th Mo. Cav.	104		1923 Oct 22	NE, 48th, 1924
Barcies, Sam'l			7		1908	IA, 35th, 1909
Barclay, C.S.	Pvt.	D, 35th Iowa	255		1914 Jun 12	IA, 41st, 1915
Barclay, Geo. E.	Pvt.	E, 90th N.Y. Inf.	503		1904 Aug 13	IA, 31st, 1905
Barclay, Henry	Capt.	25th N.Y. Cav.	23		1912 Feb 29	IA, 39th, 1913

Name	Rank	Company, Regiment or Ship	Post*	Age	Death Date†	Journal
Barclay, Joseph		A, 55th Ill.	464		1914 Mar 25	KS, 34th, 1915
Barclay, Wm. H.	Pvt.	B, 14th Iowa Inf.	267		1916 Apr 25	IA, 43rd, 1917
Barcroft, J.A.	Pvt.	G, 143rd Ohio National Guard	57		1910 Sep 20	IA, 37th, 1911
Barcus, Sam'l A.		D, 21st Ind. Inf.	270		1900 Dec 15	KS, 20th, 1901
Bard, John	Pvt.	K, 61st Ohio Inf. (at large)	321, 24	91	1940 Jan 7	IA, 66th, 1940
Barden, G.W.	Pvt.	H, 31st N.J. Inf.	231		1917 Dec 10	IA, 44th, 1918
Bardoner, Robert		C, 14th Ill.	127		1926 Aug 17	KS, 46th, 1927
Bardwell, A.D.		F, 104th Ill.	4		1926 Aug 19	KS, 46th, 1927
Bardwell, Joseph H.		I, 1st Ohio Lt. Art.	428		1911 Aug 25	KS, 31st, 1912
Bardwell, L.W.	Pvt.	F, 20th Iowa Inf.	206	39	1886 Sep 7	IA, 13th, 1887
Bardwell, P.S.	Surg.	6th Iowa Cav.	206	66	1895 Mar 17	IA, 22nd, 1896
Bardy, Henry M.	Pvt.	B, 12th R.I.	228		1914 Nov 3	IA, 41st, 1915
Bare, J.			197		1921	IA, 48th, 1922
Bare, Jacob	Pvt.	H, 176th Ohio Inf.	443	91	1936 Sep 18	IA, 65th, 1939
Barger, C.D.	Pvt.	L, 13th U.S. Inf.	98		1915 Jan 6	IA, 42nd, 1916
Barger, Clayton		K, 74th Ohio Inf. (died of old age)	31		1919 Jul 28	NE, 44th, 1920
Barger, John	Pvt.	K, 21st Penn. Cav.	163	54	1891 Sep 16	IA, 18th, 1892
Barger, L.G.		C, 47th Iowa Inf.	44		1913 Dec 9	IA, 40th, 1914
Barinsley, Carl	Pvt.	I, 7th U.S. Inf.	452		1906 Oct 20	IA, 33rd, 1907
Bariteau, A.W.		I, 5th N.Y. Hvy. Art. (died of heart failure)	198		1891 Feb 17	KS, 11th, 1892
Barkelow, G.D.		F, 60th Ohio	117		1914 Sep 23	KS, 34th, 1915
Barker, A.F.		H, 15th Kans. Cav.	1		1925 May 22	KS, 45th, 1926
Barker, A.J.		C, 48th Ohio Vol. Inf.	407		1915 Jun 21	KS, 35th, 1916
Barker, Arnold	Sergt.	H, 35th Iowa Cav.	79		1923 Apr 23	IA, 50th, 1924
Barker, Benj.	Pvt.	I, 4th Iowa Inf.	192	74	1894 Jun 19	IA, 21st, 1895
Barker, Chas. P.	Pvt.	E, 132nd —	30		1918 Aug 3	IA, 45th, 1919
Barker, Darwin	Pvt.	F, 67th Ill. Inf.	30		1924 Jan 22	IA, 51st, 1925
Barker, Fred H.		G, 106th Ill.	28		1921 Oct 25	KS, 41st, 1922
Barker, Geo. H.		75th Ill. Inf.	46		1934 Sep 2	KS, 54th, 1935
Barker, George	Pvt.	D, 142nd Ill. Inf. F, 125th Penn. Inf.	88		1929 Oct 30	IA, 56th, 1930
Barker, George W.		A, 8th Ill. Cav. (died of heart failure)	74	49	1895 Jun 5	NE, 20th, 1896
Barker, J.D.		L, 1st Ohio Cav.	49		1912 Jan 19	KS, 32nd, 1913
Barker, J.W.	Pvt.	B, 46th Ill. Inf.	190		1916 Feb 3	IA, 43rd, 1917
Barker, Joseph	Pvt.	G, 22nd Iowa Inf.	298		1911 Jan 9	IA, 38th, 1912
Barker, Oliver J.	Pvt.	I, 4th Iowa Inf.	137		1904 Nov 9	IA, 31st, 1905
Barker, P.B.	Pvt. Sergt.	I, 7th Ind. Inf. B, 4th Ind. Cav.	26	59	1898 Nov 20	IA, 25th, 1899
Barker, R.E.	Corp.	G, 13th Iowa Inf.	296		1908 Jun 16	IA, 35th, 1909
Barker, Samuel T.		D, 11th Kans. Vol. Cav.	3		1914 Aug 31	KS, 34th, 1915
Barker, Vigal	Pvt.	B, 9th Iowa Vol. Inf.	191		1902 Feb 28	IA, 28th, 1902
Barker, W.B.		25th Ohio Bat.	48		1921	IA, 48th, 1922
Barker, W.H.	Pvt.	F, 8th Iowa Inf.	167	67	1896 Jul 8	IA, 23rd, 1897
Barker, W.H.	Pvt.	H, 123rd Penn. Inf.	22		1920 Oct 3	IA, 47th, 1921
Barker, Wm.			130	85	1922 Jun 11	NE, 47th, 1923
Barker, Wm. Henry H.	Corp.	K, 3rd Iowa Cav. (at large)	40, 84	100	1940 Nov 8	IA, 67th, 1941
Barker, Wm. K.	Sergt.	B, 7th Iowa Inf.	216		1902 Nov 11	IA, 29th, 1903
Barkhuff, John	Corp.	F, 33rd Wis. Inf.	59		1903 Aug 3	IA, 30th, 1904
Barkhurst, C.W.		D, 15th Ind.	293		1913 May 12	KS, 33rd, 1914
Barkley, A.J.			67		1922 Dec 19	IA, 49th, 1923
Barkley, J.C.		A, 55th Ill.	464		1914 Mar 25	KS, 33rd, 1914
Barkley, John		Mo.	20		1917 Dec 4	KS, 37th, 1918
Barklow, G.	Pvt.	D, 148th Ind. Inf.	14		1920 Feb 6	IA, 47th, 1921
Barklow, M.B.		G, 35th Iowa Inf.	255		1st quarter 1885	IA, 11th, 1885
Barknell, Alfred		C, 8th Ind.	64		1906 Jan 3	KS, 26th, 1907
Barland, J.A.	Sergt.	A, 77th Penn. Inf.	441		1904 Jul 29	IA, 31st, 1905
Barley, I.N.		F, 134th Ohio	12		1904 Nov 27	KS, 24th, 1905
Barley, John W.		F, 134th Ohio	5		1921 Sep 28	KS, 41st, 1922
Barlow, A.A.		A, Bat. Mo. Res.	257		1925 Jan 14	KS, 45th, 1926
Barlow, A.C.	Surg.	62nd Ohio Inf.	32		1884	KS, 4th, 1885
Barlow, Charles W.	Pvt.	K, 9th Iowa Cav.	452	89	1932 Sep	IA, 59th, 1933
Barlow, Ed			54		1931	IA, 58th, 1932

Name	Rank	Company, Regiment or Ship	Post*	Age	Death Date†	Journal
Barlow, M.J.		M, 9th Kans.	119		1888	KS, 8th, 1889
Barlow, M.J.		M, 9th Kans.	119		1889	KS, 9th, 1890
Barlow, Michael		F, 33rd Mo.	9		1922 Sep 1	KS, 42nd, 1923
Barnard, G.W.		C, 12th Ill. (died of pneumonia)	264	71	1908 Nov 27	NE, 33rd, 1909
Barnard, Geo. A.		1st Mass. Bat. (died at La Crosse)	415		1895 Mar	KS, 15th, 1896
Barnard, Geo. V.	Sergt.	E, 95th Ill. Inf.	489		1911 Dec 25	IA, 38th, 1912
Barnard, George	Pvt.	G, 105th Ill. Inf. (at large)		90	1935 May 14	IA, 65th, 1939
Barnard, J.A.		F, 78th Ohio Inf.	198		1912 Dec 5	KS, 32nd, 1913
Barnard, J.C.		I, 94th Ill.	92		1922 Jan 10	KS, 42nd, 1923
Barnard, J.D.	Pvt.	K, 34th Iowa Inf.	426	54	1896 Jan	IA, 23rd, 1897
Barnard, J.U.		D, 24th Iowa Inf.	4	77	1912 Jun 3	NE, 37th, 1913
Barnard, Levi	Pvt.	A, 11th Iowa Inf.	231		1918 Jan 19	IA, 45th, 1919
Barnard, Samuel			165		1890	NE, 15th, 1891
Barnard, Samuel J.		B, 6th Mich.	72		1889	KS, 9th, 1890
Barnard, William	Pvt.	L, 1st Iowa Cav.	4	64	1886 Dec 20	IA, 13th, 1887
Barnd, James K.		G, 37th Ill.	30		1920 Oct 7	KS, 40th, 1921
Barnes, A.N.	Sergt.	A, 4th Iowa Cav.	69		1914 Dec 23	IA, 41st, 1915
Barnes, A.R.	Pvt.	C, 8th Wis. Inf.	337		1915 Jan 29	IA, 42nd, 1916
Barnes, C.W.		B, 8th N.Y.	255		1909 Dec 27	KS, 29th, 1910
Barnes, Eli		H, 10th Ind.	25		1914 Jan 10	KS, 34th, 1915
Barnes, Eli A.		G, 9th Iowa Cav. (buried August 26, 1923)	11	85	1923 Jul 16	NE, 48th, 1924
Barnes, Ezekiel		H, 36th Ohio Inf. (died of heart failure)	298		1893 Mar 22	NE, 18th, 1894
Barnes, F.M.		H, 100th Ind.	25		1921 Jun 22	KS, 41st, 1922
Barnes, F.M.		M, 5th Ind. Cav. (died of apoplexy)	44	94	1924 Sep 18	NE, 49th, 1925
Barnes, G.L.		F, 2nd Wis.	253		1910	KS, 30th, 1911
Barnes, George		F, 11th Ill. 1st Ill. Bat.	62		1913 Oct 31	KS, 33rd, 1914
Barnes, George W.		C, 28th Iowa	22		1926 Nov 24	NE, 51st, 1927
Barnes, Henry J.			100		1920 Jan 26	KS, 40th, 1921
Barnes, J.A.	Pvt.	E, 115th Ill. Inf.	80		1905 Jan 1	IA, 32nd, 1906
Barnes, J.C.	Capt.	I, 27th Wis. Inf.	259		1916 Jan 27	IA, 43rd, 1917
Barnes, J.D.	Pvt.	K, 20th Iowa Inf.	1	88	1931 Jul 2	IA, 58th, 1932
Barnes, J.H.		A, 97th Ill.	378		1924 Mar 27	KS, 44th, 1925
Barnes, J.P.		B, 4th Kans. Mil.	1		1916 Jun 1	KS, 36th, 1917
Barnes, J.W.	Corp.	C, 34th Iowa Inf.	116		1908 Aug 30	IA, 35th, 1909
Barnes, Job		C, 27th Iowa Inf.	78	96	1935 Jul 4	IA, 62nd, 1936
Barnes, Job		C, 27th Iowa Inf. (at large)		92	1935 Jul 4	IA, 62nd, 1936
Barnes, Josiah		I, 63rd Ind.	1		1918 Apr 14	KS, 38th, 1919
Barnes, L.B.	Pvt.	H, 27th Iowa Cav.	118		1901 Jul	IA, 28th, 1902
Barnes, M.R.		18th U.S. Inf.	7		1926 Mar 5	NE, 51st, 1927
Barnes, Owen		77th Ohio	97		1893 Apr 3	KS, 13th, 1894
Barnes, Samuel		M, 4th Iowa Cav.	19		1907 Dec 29	IA, 34th, 1908
Barnes, Theo. F.		G, 123rd Ill.	[25?]		1923	NE, 48th, 1924
Barnes, Tiram	Pvt.	K, 95th Ill. Inf.	47		1924 May 27	IA, 51st, 1925
Barnes, Uriah		G, 43rd Mo.	12		1925 Oct 24	KS, 45th, 1926
Barnes, W.C.		E, 1st Kans. Inf.	12		1899 Mar 3	KS, 19th, 1900
Barnes, W.C.		E, 92nd Ill. Inf.	28		1916 Feb 19	KS, 36th, 1917
Barnes, W.E.		H, 92nd Ohio	175		1911 Jun 24	KS, 32nd, 1913
Barnes, W.F.			25		1912	IA, 39th, 1913
Barnes, W.R.		K, 29th Iowa	204		1st quarter 1884	IA, 10th, 1884
Barnes, W.R.		I, 18th Ind.	142		1913 Feb 18	KS, 33rd, 1914
Barnes, W.R.		I, 19th Ind.	142		1912 Feb 18	KS, 32nd, 1913
Barnes, William H.		37th N.Y. Art.	4		1915 Jul 27	KS, 35th, 1916
Barnes, Wm.			96		1927 Dec 26	IA, 54th, 1928
Barnes, Wm.		I, 66th Ohio	153		1898 Mar 31	KS, 18th, 1899
Barnes, Wm.		B, 97th Ohio	66		1921 Feb 27	KS, 41st, 1922
Barnes, Z.	Pvt.	C, 40th Iowa	40		1921 Feb 24	IA, 48th, 1922
Barnett, Alexander		D, 7th Ohio Cav.	96		1916 Oct 16	KS, 36th, 1917
Barnett, E.M.		B, 9th Kans. Inf.	4		1914	KS, 34th, 1915
Barnett, J.P.		G, 116th Ill.	25		1908 Oct 1	KS, 28th, 1909
Barnett, James H.	Pvt.	K, 42nd Ind. Inf.	379	52	1894 May 11	IA, 21st, 1895

Name	Rank	Company, Regiment or Ship	Post*	Age	Death Date†	Journal
Barnett, John	Pvt.	A, 25th Wis. Inf.	54	91	1932 Jan 4	IA, 59th, 1933
Barnett, John	Pvt.	A, 25th Wis. Inf.	54	91	1933 Jan 4	IA, 60th, 1934
Barnett, L.A.	Pvt.	C, 16th U.S. Inf. (at large)			1933 May 17	IA, 60th, 1934
Barnett, Michael J.		K, 33rd Ill. Inf. (died of old age)	4	90	1920 Mar 11	NE, 45th, 1921
Barnett, Moses	Pvt.	E, 83rd Ill. Inf.	426	62	1896 Apr 20	IA, 23rd, 1897
Barnett, N.W.		I, 25th Ind.	3		1897 Apr 15	KS, 17th, 1898
Barnett, Oliver P.	Pvt.	L, 8th Iowa Cav.	192		1928 Apr 21	IA, 55th, 1929
Barnett, Thomas J.		H, 38th Ind.	147		1913 Nov 14	KS, 33rd, 1914
Barnett, W.C.	Pvt.	H, 39th Iowa Inf.	12		1919 Jul 30	IA, 46th, 1920
Barnett, W.E.	Pvt.	G, 77th Ill. Inf.	473		1897 Dec 21	IA, 24th, 1898
Barnett, W.T.		D, 26th Ind.	51		1933 Jan 27	KS, 53rd, 1934
Barney, C.E.		K, 108th Ill. (died of heart failure)	1	81	1920 Feb 16	NE, 45th, 1921
Barney, H.F.		C, 132nd Ill.	143		1931 Apr 24	NE, 56th, 1932
Barney, W.W.		C, Mississippi Marine Brigade	293		1922 Aug 17	KS, 42nd, 1923
Barnhart, A.H.	Pvt.	H, 28th N.Y. Lt. Art.	111	91	1933 Dec 29	IA, 60th, 1934
Barnhart, Thompson		G, 69th Ohio (died of typhoid)	32	59	1897 Oct 31	NE, 22nd, 1898
Barnhill, A.J.		E, 117th Ind.	243		1920	KS, 40th, 1921
Barnhill, Allen	Pvt.	D, 39th Iowa Inf.	173	52	1892 Dec 17	IA, 19th, 1893
Barnhill, J.W.		E, 200th Penn. Inf.	129		1934 Sep 8	KS, 54th, 1935
Barnhill, Wm. H.	Pvt.	C, 30th Iowa Inf.	337		1899 Jun 26	IA, 26th, 1900
Barnica, Benjiman			9		1920 Oct	NE, 45th, 1921
Barns, T.J.	Pvt.	E, 120th Ohio Inf.	359		1911 Jan 24	IA, 38th, 1912
Barnsheisel, F.		D, 102nd Ind. Inf.	25		1934 Dec	KS, 54th, 1935
Barnt, Daniel R.	Pvt.	E, 126th Ohio Inf.	343		1914 Jul 10	IA, 41st, 1915
Barnum, H.W.		C, Mass. Militia	7		1924[1923?] Apr 28	NE, 48th, 1924
Barnum, J.	Pvt.	F, 34th Iowa Inf.	452		1921 Nov 1	IA, 48th, 1922
Barothy, Karl		G, 1st Neb. Cav. (Omaha)			1944 Jul 5	NE, 70th, 1946
Barr, Andrew J.	Pvt.	H, 6th Minn. Inf.	66		1913 Sep 18	IA, 40th, 1914
Barr, C.A.					1937 Mar 22	KS, 57th, 1938
Barr, C.A.			497		1936	KS, 56th, 1937
Barr, G.W.	Pvt.	D, 94th N.Y. Inf.	113		1911 Jan	IA, 38th, 1912
Barr, Geo.	Pvt.	B, 93rd Ill. Inf.	98		1927 Dec 10	IA, 54th, 1928
Barr, Geo.			190		1927 Dec 10	IA, 54th, 1928
Barr, Geo. W.	Pvt.	E, 34th Ill.	88		1907 Dec 26	IA, 34th, 1908
Barr, Geo. W.		F, 11th Iowa (died of paralysis)	13	77	1912 Oct 3	NE, 37th, 1913
Barr, H.D.	Sergt.	B, 32nd Iowa Inf.	461		1910 Jan 19	IA, 37th, 1911
Barr, Hanson	Pvt.	C, 68th Ohio Inf.	461		1910 Sep 2	IA, 38th, 1912
Barr, J. Wesley		A, 1st Neb. (died of tuberculosis)	149	72	1912 May 18	NE, 37th, 1913
Barr, L.C.		H, 23rd Ill. Inf. (died of appendicitis)	111	73	1919 Apr 14	NE, 44th, 1920
Barr, Peter	Pvt.	M, 1st Iowa Cav.	88	63	1897 Nov 20	IA, 24th, 1898
Barr, R.	Pvt.	A, 127th Ill. Inf.	64		1920 Mar 4	IA, 47th, 1921
Barr, Thomas	Pvt.	D, 12th Iowa Inf.	500	52	1892 Dec 27	IA, 19th, 1893
Barrackinen, P.			287		1895	NE, 20th, 1896
Barrackman, John A.		D, 7th West Va. Cav.	28		1913 May 17	KS, 33rd, 1914
Barran, James R.		A, 70th Ill. (died of rheumatism)	111	60	1905[1904?] Feb 22	NE, 29th, 1905
Barratt, John		F, 2nd Neb. Cav. (died of complications, old age)	89	81	1919 Aug 27	NE, 44th, 1920
Barrell, Hiram		I, 1st Ind. Cav.	12		1918 Jan 17	KS, 38th, 1919
Barret, J.E.	Pvt.	E, 4th Wis. Cav.	68		1921 Feb 11	IA, 48th, 1922
Barrett, A.R.	Pvt.	C, 6th Iowa Cav.	48		1910	IA, 37th, 1911
Barrett, Abraham	Pvt.	E, 11th Wis. Inf. (died of apoplexy)	87	69	1888 Dec 22	NE, 13th, 1889
Barrett, C.S.		K, 7th Penn.	322		1926	KS, 46th, 1927
Barrett, E.N.	Pvt.	C, 137th Ill. Inf.	8		1901 May 8	IA, 28th, 1902
Barrett, Edward		K, 32nd Ohio Inf. (died at Greensburg)	316		1895 Feb	KS, 15th, 1896
Barrett, Enos		A, 14th Kans.	25		1910 Jul 25	KS, 30th, 1911
Barrett, George		D, 5th Kans.	32		1896 Mar 4	KS, 16th, 1897
Barrett, George W.	Pvt.	E, 3rd Iowa Inf.	329	54	1896 May 4	IA, 23rd, 1897
Barrett, H.G.	Pvt.	I, 37th Iowa Inf.	75		1900 Apr 17	IA, 27th, 1901
Barrett, James		G, 35th Ind. Inf. (died at Osborne; buried at County Cemetery)	69		1894 Dec 5	KS, 14th, 1895
Barrett, James M.		C, 3rd Mo. State Militia	59		1913 Jan 26	KS, 33rd, 1914
Barrett, John		G, 9th Ind. Cav.	79	69	1905 Oct 6	NE, 30th, 1906

*See Appendix A, B or C for roster of post names and locations.
†See Introduction for note regarding recording of death date.

Name	Rank	Company, Regiment or Ship	Post*	Age	Death Date†	Journal
Barrett, John		K, 75th Iowa Inf. (died of old age)	5	84	1924 Sep	NE, 49th, 1925
Barrett, John F.		A, 1st Ohio	188		1917 Feb 2	KS, 36th, 1917
Barrett, John H.			120		1884	KS, 4th, 1885
Barrett, Joseph		F, 25th Ind.	28		1919 Dec 26	KS, 39th, 1920
Barrett, L.C.			193		1908	IA, 35th, 1909
Barrett, S.L.		K, 69th Ohio	25		1914 Apr 29	KS, 34th, 1915
Barrett, S.P.		K, 155th Penn.	38		1927	KS, 47th, 1928
Barrett, Samuel T.		A, 1st Ohio	443		1926 Nov 8	KS, 46th, 1927
Barrett, Thomas		B, 2nd U.S. Cav. Regulars (died of epileptic fits)	2		1893 Jan 29	NE, 18th, 1894
Barrett, Thos.	Chaplain	19th Ind.	32		1904 May 19	KS, 24th, 1905
Barrett, U.D.		I, 10th Iowa	53		1917 Jun 2	KS, 37th, 1918
Barrett, W.H.		E, 11th Iowa	225		1911 Feb 5	KS, 31st, 1912
Barrett, W.H.H.	Pvt.	E, 128th Ohio Inf.	20	60	1898 Apr 7	IA, 24th, 1898
Barrett, Wm.	1st Lieut.	K, 12th Kans. Inf.	242		1899	NE, 24th, 1900
Barrick, A.J.		Penn.	118		1911 Apr 9	KS, 31st, 1912
Barrick, Isaac	Corp.	B, 38th Iowa Inf.	172	58	1892 Oct 4	IA, 19th, 1893
Barrick, J.			7		1900-1901	IA, 27th, 1901
Barrickman, G.W.	Pvt.	C, 17th Iowa	7		1922 Aug 9	IA, 49th, 1923
Barrier, A.W.		C, 115th Ill.	50		1914 Jan 15	KS, 34th, 1915
Barringer, Sam'l E.	Pvt.	C, 5th Iowa Inf.	115		1909 Jun 16	IA, 36th, 1910
Barron, W.R.		F, 11th Kans.	180		1911 Aug 3	KS, 31st, 1912
Barrow, Henry B.	Pvt.	F, 3rd Iowa Cav.	19		1909 Dec 19	IA, 36th, 1910
Barrows, Chas. H.	Pvt.	G, 45th Ill. Inf.	267		1911 Aug 7	IA, 38th, 1912
Barrows, J.A.		D, 101st Ill. Inf. (died of heart failure)	187	69	1906 Nov 9	NE, 31st, 1907
Barrows, James C.		H, 8th Iowa Inf.		93	1937 Nov 7	IA, 64th, 1938
Barrows, P.C.	Pvt.	D, 29th Iowa Inf.	45		1912 Jan 20	IA, 39th, 1913
Barry, N.	Pvt.	K, 31st Iowa Inf.	181	51	1890 Apr 22	IA, 17th, 1891
Barry, Robert C.		E, 13th Conn.	222		1919 Dec 26	KS, 39th, 1920
Barsby, A.	Pvt.	G, 44th Ill. Inf.	83		1909	IA, 36th, 1910
Barslow, Alfred		E, 139th Ill.	25		1927 Jan 8	NE, 52nd, 1928
Bartels, Henry		G, 2nd Ill. Cav.	30		1914 Apr 3	KS, 34th, 1915
Bartemeyer, Fred H.	Pvt.	E, 11th Iowa	1		1928 Feb 15	IA, 55th, 1929
Barter, H.C.		F, 25th Ind.	25		1924 Dec 26	KS, 44th, 1925
Barthalman, Geo. C.		D, 7th Ill. Cav. (died of heart failure)	60	70	1909 Aug 12	NE, 34th, 1910
Bartholoma, O.N.	Col.	U.S.A.	18		1919 Sep 17	IA, 46th, 1920
Bartholomew, A.		Penn.	443		1898 Nov	KS, 18th, 1899
Bartholomew, W.C.		F, 7th Iowa Cav.	10		1934 Mar 9	NE, 59th, 1935
Barthouse, T.J.		C, 185th —	85		1926 Oct 30	KS, 46th, 1927
Bartlebaugh, P.	Pvt.	I, 42nd Penn. Inf.	67		1910 Dec 15	IA, 37th, 1911
Bartleson, E.W.		B, 20th Iowa Inf.	3		1929 Jun 13	KS, 49th, 1930
Bartleson, Harrison C.		H, 13th Iowa Inf.		95	1935 Oct 15	IA, 65th, 1939
Bartlet, E.S.		H, 36th Ill.	132	89	1934 Feb 7	IA, 61st, 1935
Bartlett, A.W.		8th Mass. Inf.	93		1886	KS, 6th, 1887
Bartlett, C.H.	Pvt.	I, 5th Wis. Inf.	193		1911 Feb 1	IA, 38th, 1912
Bartlett, E.J.	Pvt.	A, 12th Wis. Inf.	30		1902 Dec 19	IA, 29th, 1903
Bartlett, George W.		G, 20th Ohio Inf.	294		1912 Jul 10	KS, 32nd, 1913
Bartlett, Henry	Pvt.	B, 11th Ohio Inf.	22		1918 Dec 9	IA, 45th, 1919
Bartlett, J.W.	Pvt.	H, 36th Ohio Inf.	440		1920 Sep 13	IA, 47th, 1921
Bartlett, Lyman	Pvt.	D, 24th Iowa Inf.	8		1899 Aug 29	IA, 26th, 1900
Bartlett, Nimrod		F, 61st Ill.	57		1914 Jan 8	KS, 34th, 1915
Bartlett, Nimrod		F, 61st Ill.	57		1915 Jan 8	KS, 35th, 1916
Bartlett, W.H.		B, 38th Iowa Inf.	68		1915 Jan 20	IA, 42nd, 1916
Bartlett, Wm.	Corp.	F, 4th Iowa Cav.	40		1922 Aug 1	IA, 49th, 1923
Bartley, Jesse B.		A, 49th Penn.	7		1933 Mar 23	NE, 58th, 1934
Bartolet, John	Pvt.	K, 48th Penn. Inf.	22		1911 Jan 9	IA, 38th, 1912
Barton, Alson	Pvt.	D, 7th Minn. Inf.	216		1910 May 22	IA, 37th, 1911
Barton, Benjamin	Pvt.	C, 172nd Ohio Inf.	14	70	1898 Jun 15	IA, 25th, 1899
Barton, George P.	Sergt.	A, 36th Iowa Inf.	143	48	1885 Oct 29	IA, 12th, 1886
Barton, J.L.	Pvt.	K, 7th Ohio Cav. (died of consumption)	35	44	1887 Sep 30	NE, 12th, 1888
Barton, James		C, 15th N.Y. Cav.	25		1935 Apr 8	KS, 55th, 1936
Barton, John W.		E, 15th Iowa Inf.	79		3rd quarter 1883	IA, 10th, 1884

*See Appendix A, B or C for roster of post names and locations.
†See Introduction for note regarding recording of death date.

Name	Rank	Company, Regiment or Ship	Post*	Age	Death Date†	Journal
Barton, T.H.	Pvt.	C, 9th Iowa Cav.	434		1900 Sep 4	IA, 27th, 1901
Barton, Thomas G.		C, 36th Ill. Inf.	337		1891 Jul 19	KS, 11th, 1892
Barton, Thos.	Pvt.	I, 14th Iowa	20		1905	IA, 32nd, 1906
Barton, Thos. S.		I, 130th Penn.	385		1922 Aug 31	KS, 42nd, 1923
Barton, W.R.		I, 172nd Ohio	51		1917 Sep 14	KS, 37th, 1918
Barton, William		E, 122nd Ohio	36		1890	KS, 10th, 1891
Barton, Willion		K, 144th Ill.	64		1923	KS, 43rd, 1924
Barton, Wm. H.		L, 9th Iowa	380		1912 Aug 2	KS, 32nd, 1913
Bartoo, J.K.		H, 86th N.Y. Inf.	8		1901 Aug 28	KS, 21st, 1902
Bartoo, J.L.		not a member of post named, but buried by said post	8		1897	KS, 17th, 1898
Bartow, Thomas C.	Pvt. Pvt. Pvt. Pvt. Pvt.	E, 3rd Penn. Inf. F, 125th Penn. Inf. (at large) M, 20th Penn. Cav. E, 3rd Penn. Hvy. Art. F, 188th Penn. Inf.	88	94	1940 Feb 4	IA, 66th, 1940
Bartow, W.H.		103rd Penn. Inf.	25		1893 Jun 19	NE, 18th, 1894
Bartow, Wm.		I, 16th Kans. M.I.[Kans. State Militia Inf.?]	18		1914 Sep 12	KS, 34th, 1915
Bartram, R.W.		A, 85th Ill. Inf. (died of diabetes)	43		1905 Mar	NE, 30th, 1906
Bartup, Jesse		G, 2nd Ind. Inf. (died of consumption, Soldiers Home, Leavenworth, Kans.)	456		1890	KS, 10th, 1891
Bartz, August		D, 8th Wis.	465		1905 Apr 1	KS, 25th, 1906
Barwick, Joseph S.		F, 3rd Ill. Cav.	25		1915 Jul 4	NE, 40th, 1916
Basch, T.	Pvt.	F, 5th Mo. Cav.	59		1921 Jun 13	IA, 48th, 1922
Bascom, W.H.			52		1923 Mar 9	IA, 50th, 1924
Bascombe, Richard	Pvt. 2nd Lieut.	C, 50th N.Y. Eng. C, 3rd U.S. Colored Inf. (murdered)	69	58	1885 Apr 3	NE, 10th, 1886
Baseman, H.E.		E, 12th Kans. Inf.	32		1935	KS, 55th, 1936
Basemann, H., Sr.	Pvt.	12th Kans. Inf.	32		1884	KS, 4th, 1885
Basey, John		E, 63rd Ind.	26		1921 Jun 30	KS, 41st, 1922
Bash, J.F.		A, 104th Ohio	94		1929 Aug 20	NE, 54th, 1930
Bashaw, Fred		I, 76th Ill.	113		1913 Mar 24	KS, 33rd, 1914
Bashford, George H.		A, 8th Ill. Inf.	484		1914 Feb	KS, 34th, 1915
Bashford, Wm.	Pvt.	A, 8th Iowa Inf.	280	72	1893 Apr 1	IA, 20th, 1894
Basill, Jeremiah	Pvt.	B, 33rd Iowa Inf.	514		1899	IA, 26th, 1900
Basket, J.B.		B, 4th Tenn. Cav.	97		1923 May 2	KS, 43rd, 1924
Baskins, Jacob S.		F, 4th Mo. State Militia	226		1916 Sep	KS, 36th, 1917
Basler, C.D.	Drum Major	27th Penn. (died of pneumonia)	133	58	1887 Dec	NE, 12th, 1888
Basore, William		D, 152nd Ind.			[1938?]	KS, 58th, 1939
Bass, A.J.	Pvt.	D, 33rd Iowa Inf.	40		1926 Nov 16	IA, 53rd, 1927
Bass, D.M.	Pvt.	K, 16th Iowa Inf.	329		1911 Nov 23	IA, 38th, 1912
Bass, Wm.	Pvt.	E, N.Y. Art.	67		1917 Oct 3	IA, 44th, 1918
Bassart, Joseph J.		E, 211th Penn.	265		1893 Sep 16	KS, 13th, 1894
Bassart, Martin	Pvt.	E, 31st Wis. Inf.	230		1913 Apr 22	IA, 40th, 1914
Basseck, W.H.		C, 135th Ohio Inf. (died of Bright's disease)	235		1893 Mar 5	NE, 18th, 1894
Basset, Samuel		A, 26th Mo. (died of broken hip)	52	85	1924 Jan 27	NE, 49th, 1925
Bassett, C.S.	Pvt.	C, 45th Iowa Inf.	254		1925 Nov 7	IA, 52nd, 1926
Bassett, Chas. H.		8th N.Y. Lt. Art.	196		1899 Aug 11	KS, 19th, 1900
Bassett, D.E.		E, 10th Mass.	130		1923 May 13	KS, 43rd, 1924
Bassett, Geo.	Pvt.	C, 19th Ill. Inf.	124		1907 Aug 20	IA, 34th, 1908
Bassett, J.H.		B, 9th Ky. Cav.	266		4th quarter 1884	IA, 11th, 1885
Bassett, S.C.		E, 142nd N.Y.	113		1926 Mar 14	NE, 51st, 1927
Bast, Isaac		D, 2nd U.S.A.	4		1896 Feb 23	KS, 16th, 1897
Bastran, John B.		K, 5th Iowa Cav. (died of membranous croup)	28	67	1913 Nov 1	NE, 38th, 1914
Basye, Joseph		C, 1st Ohio Art. (died of old age)	1	92	1920 Jul 4	NE, 45th, 1921
Batchelder, Adna	Pvt.	A, 16th Iowa Inf.	98		1912 Jul 20	IA, 39th, 1913
Batchelder, F.A.		D, 26th Iowa Inf.	212		1913 Mar 14	IA, 40th, 1914
Batchelder, I.S.		I, 44th Ind.	98		1888	KS, 8th, 1889
Batchelder, Isaac	Pvt.	B, 123rd N.Y. Inf.	461		1916 Jan 15	IA, 43rd, 1917
Batchelor, Geo.	Pvt.	I, 19th Iowa Inf.	177		1907 Feb 28	IA, 34th, 1908

See Appendix A, B or C for roster of post names and locations.
†*See Introduction for note regarding recording of death date.*

Name	Rank	Company, Regiment or Ship	Post*	Age	Death Date†	Journal
Batdorf, J.W.		D, 2nd Iowa Inf.	96		1918 Jan 21	KS, 38th, 1919
Bateman, George C.		C, 20th Kans.	46		1911 Aug 2	KS, 31st, 1912
Bateman, J.W.		D, 33rd Ill. Inf.	4		1925 Nov 30	KS, 45th, 1926
Bateman, James		17th Ill.	25		1905 Jun	NE, 31st, 1907
Baten, Richard			4		1904 Nov	NE, 29th, 1905
Bates, A.J.		K, 1st Mich. Cav.	156		1889	KS, 9th, 1890
Bates, A.J.		L, 11th Mich. Cav.	156		1888	KS, 8th, 1889
Bates, A.M.		B, 1st Ohio Cav.	250		1930 Aug 12	KS, 50th, 1931
Bates, A.M.		B, 1st Ohio Cav.	250		1930[1929?] Aug 12	KS, 49th, 1930
Bates, Byron Dekalb	Pvt.	D, 54th Ill. Inf. (at large)		97	1942 Jul 6	IA, 69th, 1943
Bates, Byron W.		N.Y. Mil. M, N.Y. Riflemen	17		1921 Sep 11	KS, 41st, 1922
Bates, D.D.		C, 18th Wis.	100		1906	KS, 26th, 1907
Bates, F.M.	Pvt.	D, 10th N.Y. Art.	8		1920 Aug 17	IA, 47th, 1921
Bates, F.W.	Musician	38th Iowa Inf.	267		1905 Aug 10	IA, 32nd, 1906
Bates, George G.	Pvt.	I, 14th Penn. Cav.	45	50	1886 Oct 2	IA, 13th, 1887
Bates, H.D.			199		2nd quarter 1884	IA, 11th, 1885
Bates, J.H.			240		1920 Oct	KS, 40th, 1921
Bates, Julius	Pvt.	C, 17th Iowa Inf.	45	60	1888 Feb 6	NE, 13th, 1889
Bates, L.D.	Sergt.	G, 31st Iowa	191		1899	IA, 26th, 1900
Bates, Lyman P.	Pvt.	F, 42nd Ill. Inf.	100		1902 Jun 10	IA, 29th, 1903
Bates, M.A.		B, 95th Ohio	45		1931 Jun 1	NE, 56th, 1932
Bates, N.B.	2nd Asst. Eng.	died of Bright's disease	73	67	1887 Mar	NE, 12th, 1888
Bates, R.C.	Major	2nd D.C. Colored Inf.	42		1884	KS, 4th, 1885
Bates, Reuben		F, 1st Ind. Cav.	27		1893 Jun 22	KS, 13th, 1894
Bates, S.H.		died of debility	95		1903	NE, 28th, 1904
Bates, W.C.	Pvt.		52		1920 Jun	IA, 47th, 1921
Bates, W.E.		D, 10th N.Y. Art.	66		1925 Oct 31	KS, 45th, 1926
Bates, W.P.		H, 35th Iowa Inf. (died of cancer)	63	57	1895 Jul 10	NE, 20th, 1896
Bates, Wm.	Pvt.	H, 38th Wis. Inf.	81		1909 Jun 30	IA, 36th, 1910
Bates, Wm.	Pvt.	I, 16th Wis. Inf.	68		1927 Jan 30	IA, 54th, 1928
Batgos, Steve	Pvt.	D, 10th Iowa	425		1924 May 5	IA, 51st, 1925
Batler, C.P.	Corp.	B, 64th N.Y. Inf.	26		1909 May 31	IA, 36th, 1910
Batman, James E.	Corp.	C, 24th Ind. Inf.	31		1909 Dec	IA, 36th, 1910
Batsen, Charles		H, 21st Ill.	130		1917 Dec 15	KS, 37th, 1918
Batt, Olin			2		1931 Sep 8	KS, 51st, 1932
Batt, Olin			2		1929 Sep 8	KS, 52nd, 1933
Batten, W.A.		C, 50th Ohio	50		1921 Jul 11	KS, 41st, 1922
Batterson, L.C.					1928	NE, 53rd, 1929
Batterson, S.M.	Pvt.	G, 42nd Ind. Inf.	231		1900-1901	IA, 27th, 1901
Batterton, John	Sergt.	B, 30th Iowa Inf.	122		1916 Oct 30	IA, 43rd, 1917
Battin, M.	Pvt.	E, 3rd Iowa Cav.	100		1921 Dec 16	IA, 48th, 1922
Battin, Newt	Lieut.	E, 3rd Iowa Cav.	100	92	1931 Feb 19	IA, 58th, 1932
Battin, Newt.	Lieut.	E, 3rd Iowa Cav.	100		1931 Feb 19	IA, 57th, 1931
Battin, T.W.	Pvt.	G, 18th Ohio Inf.	100	72	1890 Sep 8	IA, 17th, 1891
Battis, William	Pvt.	156th Ill. Inf.	55		1931 Dec	IA, 58th, 1932
Battles, Beniah	Pvt.	B, 14th Iowa Inf.	17		1925	IA, 52nd, 1926
Battles, Otis L.		F, 3rd R.I. Cav. (born in Massachusetts; died of paralysis at Soldiers & Sailors Home Hospital, Burkett; buried at Grand Island, Neb.)		73	1906 Oct 8	NE, 31st, 1907
Battman, Phillip		D, 84th Penn. (died of heart failure)	19	75	1909 Feb	NE, 33rd, 1909
Batton, James A.		B, 10th Kans.	93		1905 Aug 7	KS, 25th, 1906
Batty, Sammel		I, Penn. V.R.C. (died of pneumonia)	110	72	1912 Jan 3	NE, 37th, 1913
Baty, W.A.		B, 24th Ky.	25		1928 May 18	KS, 48th, 1929
Bauer, Adam		2nd Kans. State Militia	71		1900 Oct 30	KS, 20th, 1901
Bauer, Chas.		E, 1st U.S. Reserve Corps	262	71	1915 May 9	NE, 39th, 1915
Bauer, Fred	Pvt.	H, 11th Wis. Inf.	66		1930 Apr 8	IA, 57th, 1931
Bauer, James		A, 4th Ky. Cav. (died of old age)	32		1920	NE, 45th, 1921
Bauer, John H., see Baner, John H.						
Bauer, John N.	Pvt.	Mo. Home Guards	5		1919	IA, 46th, 1920
Baugh, Eli		D, 13th Ky. Cav. (died of heart failure)	81	50	1895 Oct 25	NE, 20th, 1896

Name	Rank	Company, Regiment or Ship	Post*	Age	Death Date†	Journal
Baugh, O.H.		C, 122nd Ill.	301		1922 Mar 15	KS, 42nd, 1923
Baugh, T.W.	Asst. Surg.	52nd Ohio Inf.	40	52	1894 Dec 20	IA, 21st, 1895
Baughart, Isack		G, 52nd Ohio (died of paralysis)	105	78	1914 Jun 19	NE, 39th, 1915
Baughman, A.P.		F, 125th Ill.	8		1929 Sep 22	KS, 50th, 1931
Baughman, Chas.		C, 11th Ind.	417		1927 Sep 28	KS, 47th, 1928
Baughman, D.		I, 41st Ill. Inf.	481		1918 Jun 9	KS, 38th, 1919
Baughman, J.W.		A, 62nd Ohio	25		1923 Feb 3	KS, 43rd, 1924
Baughman, N.M.	Pvt.	G, 4th Iowa Inf.	233		1903 Feb 28	IA, 29th, 1903
Baughman, Paul		I, 44th Ill.	25		1920	KS, 40th, 1921
Baughman, Samuel		C, 66th Ill. Inf. (has of late years made his home in Florida but has maintained his membership in Kansas)			1937 Sep	KS, 57th, 1938
Baughman, Thos.		K, 57th Ind. (died in New Mexico)	231		1892 Oct 12	KS, 12th, 1893
Bauks, Parker M.	Sergt.	G, 105th Ill.	66		1923 Dec 26	IA, 50th, 1924
Baul, H.J.	Pvt.	C, 21st Iowa Inf.	78		1912 Sep 6	IA, 39th, 1913
Baulch, H.			110		1883	KS, 3rd, 1884
Baum, John		I, 1st Mo.	6		1935 Sep 2	KS, 55th, 1936
Bauman, Geo. M.		B, 1st Penn.	66		1893 Jun 22	KS, 13th, 1894
Baumer, J.L.		F, 36th Ind.	2		1904 Jul 7	KS, 24th, 1905
Baumgardner, David		I, 2nd Tenn. Cav.	145		1916 Oct 7	KS, 36th, 1917
Baumgardner, Will.	Pvt.	D, 12th Iowa Inf.	23		1928 Jan 2	IA, 55th, 1929
Baumgartner, A.	Pvt.	Ind. Battery	8	89	1931 Jul 22	IA, 58th, 1932
Baumgartner, M.			222		1918 Nov	IA, 45th, 1919
Baumgartner, M.A.	Pvt.	D, 44th Iowa Inf.	22		1928	IA, 55th, 1929
Bauserman, A.S.	Pvt.	E, 11th Ind. Vol. Inf.	233	56	1898 Jun 26	IA, 25th, 1899
Bauswell, Albert		B, 7th Mo. Cav.	303		1911 Nov 15	KS, 31st, 1912
Baver, Wm.	Pvt.	F, 2nd Iowa Cav.	149		1923 Dec 18	IA, 50th, 1924
Bawker, Simeon	Pvt.	E, 94th N.Y. Inf.	117	76	1899 Nov 8	IA, 26th, 1900
Bax, Adam		D, 7th Mo. A, 40th Mo. (died of chronic diarrhea)	25	87	1915 Dec 17	NE, 40th, 1916
Baxter, A.B.	Pvt.	H, 38th Wis. Inf.	141		1920 Nov 14	IA, 47th, 1921
Baxter, Ben P.		M, 11th Mo. Cav. (died of paralysis)	120	73	1917 Sep 22	NE, 42nd, 1918
Baxter, Daniel		K, 40th U.S. Colored Inf.	180	64	1901 Aug	NE, 26th, 1902
Baxter, Edson		C, 17th Kans.	42		1922 Jul 12	KS, 42nd, 1923
Baxter, Elbert H.	Pvt.	B, 9th Ky. Inf.		93	1935 Dec 2	IA, 65th, 1939
Baxter, Geo.	Pvt.	C, 1st Iowa Inf.	255		1909 Jul 2	IA, 36th, 1910
Baxter, George W.	Pvt.	G, 2nd Mich. Inf.	235	62	1896 Mar 16	IA, 22nd, 1896
Baxter, Henry			154		1894	NE, 19th, 1895
Baxter, James	Pvt.	K, 19th Iowa Inf.	452		1915 Dec 16	IA, 42nd, 1916
Baxter, James	Pvt.	K, 18th Iowa Inf.	452		1916 Mar 11	IA, 43rd, 1917
Baxter, Robert	Lieut.	E, 1st Iowa Cav.	20		1909	IA, 37th, 1911
Baxter, S.S.		E, 30th Mo.	314		1913 Jul 27	KS, 33rd, 1914
Baxter, S.W.		C, 117th Ind.	271		1898 Nov 26	KS, 18th, 1899
Baxter, William	Sergt.	C, 13th Ind. Inf.	180	55	1897 Jul	IA, 24th, 1898
Baxter, William		E, 39th Ill.	100		1915 Oct 10	KS, 35th, 1916
Bayard, O.P.			264		1915 Dec 30	IA, 42nd, 1916
Baylee, R.W.		K, 4th Iowa Cav. (died of heart failure)	60	79	1920 Jul 15	NE, 45th, 1921
Bayless, —	Musician	16th Ill. Inf.	78		1927 Jun 4	IA, 54th, 1928
Bayless, Hiram M.		M, 16th Kans. Cav.	71		1912 Sep 27	KS, 32nd, 1913
Bayless, J.M.		115th Ohio Inf.	132		1929 Jan 2	KS, 49th, 1930
Bayless, Jacob		I, 6th Kans.	274		1885	KS, 5th, 1886
Bayless, Jos.	Vet. Surg.	L, 6th Iowa Cav.	371	53	1888 Aug 6	IA, 15th, 1889
Bayless, W.C.		K, 10th Iowa	4		1918 Jun 26	KS, 38th, 1919
Baylor, Richard	Sergt.	A, 99th N.Y. Vols.	144		1906 Dec 30	IA, 33rd, 1907
Baymuger, J.V.M.		11th Kans. Militia	65		1915 Sep 1	KS, 35th, 1916
Bayne, J.M.			380		1923	KS, 43rd, 1924
Bayne, Samuel H.	Lieut.	I, 96th Ill.	84		1933 Jul 11	NE, 58th, 1934
Bays, Leonard		K, 107th Ill. Inf.	428		1912 Sep 30	KS, 32nd, 1913
Bays, Wm.	Pvt.	6th Ind. Cav.	25		1883	KS, 3rd, 1884
Bazarth, Wesley	Sergt.	G, 4th Iowa Inf.	306		1908 Jan 28	IA, 35th, 1909
Beach, A.W.	Pvt.	F, 20th Wis. Inf.	142		1920 Mar 2	IA, 47th, 1921
Beach, Ben	Col.	11th Iowa Inf.	231		1913 May 16	IA, 40th, 1914

*See Appendix A, B or C for roster of post names and locations.
†See Introduction for note regarding recording of death date.

Name	Rank	Company, Regiment or Ship	Post*	Age	Death Date†	Journal
Beach, Cham B.			25		1910 Jul 7	NE, 35th, 1911
Beach, Clark	Sergt.	I, 29th Ohio Inf.	311		1913 Oct 1	IA, 40th, 1914
Beach, Frank		K, 86th Ill. Inf. (at large)		95	1938 Jan 11	IA, 64th, 1938
Beach, Irwin		H, 19th Ill.	25		1927 Sep 14	KS, 47th, 1928
Beach, Isaac E.		D, 8th Mo. Inf.	77		1918 Jan 7	NE, 43rd, 1919
Beach, J.S.		L, 11th Ohio Cav.	113		1900 Jul 5	KS, 20th, 1901
Beach, James		A, 4th West Va. Inf.	55		1917 Nov 17	KS, 37th, 1918
Beach, N.D.		C, 161st Ohio	53		1912 Oct 15	KS, 32nd, 1913
Beach, R.V.		B, 113th Ill.	218		1928	NE, 53rd, 1929
Beach, Simeon D.			144		1913 Aug 28	KS, 33rd, 1914
Beach, T.B.		F, 14th Iowa (died of senility)	25	82	1921 Dec 28	NE, 46th, 1922
Beach, Thos. H.		B, 9th Ohio Cav.	262	81	1918 Jul 26	NE, 43rd, 1919
Beach, Tom J.		L, 10th Ind. (died of kidney disease)	25	60	1900 Jul 17	NE, 25th, 1901
Beacham, Albert		H, 12th N.Y.	127		1926 Mar 5	KS, 46th, 1927
Beacham, Henry W.		B, 7th Ill. Inf.	236	95	1938 Mar 6	IA, 64th, 1938
Beachell, H.R.		E, 15th Penn. Cav.	38		1932 Mar 9	NE, 57th, 1933
Beachley, N.J.		H, 26th Ind.	25		1908 Jul 10	NE, 33rd, 1909
Beachy, Urias M.		E, 133rd Penn.	18		1912 Mar 18	KS, 32nd, 1913
Beackard, Alfred B.		G, 29th Ill.	257		1893 Dec 27	KS, 13th, 1894
Beacon, James N.		K, 3rd Iowa Cav. (died at Watonga, Oklahoma Terr.; buried at Fairview Cemetery)	45		1894 Aug 11	KS, 14th, 1895
Beadle, Samuel	Pvt.	E, 11th Mo. Cav.	290		1928 Jan 16	IA, 54th, 1928
Beael, James P.		H, 3rd Iowa Cav. (died of natural cause)	26		1910	NE, 35th, 1911
Beagle, J.F.	Pvt.	B, 18th Iowa	497		1924 Mar 12	IA, 51st, 1925
Beakman, Wm.		L, 8th Iowa Cav.	38		1928 Sep 15	NE, 53rd, 1929
Beal, Curtis		F, 50th Ill. Inf., Ohio (died of old age)	354	83	1919 Apr 21	NE, 44th, 1920
Beal, David F.		I & D, 56th & 51st Ill.	79		1904 Dec 9	KS, 24th, 1905
Beal, George	Pvt.	G, 14th Maine Inf.	200		1926 Sep 2	IA, 53rd, 1927
Beal, H.O.			241		1899 Aug 10	KS, 19th, 1900
Beal, J.Q.A.		F, 16th Ill. Cav.	57		1910 Apr 12	KS, 30th, 1911
Beal, John		A, 75th Ill.	4		1915 Dec 10	KS, 35th, 1916
Beal, Lewis H.		H, 1st N.Y. Lt. Art.	199		1927 May 19	KS, 47th, 1928
Beal, Silas		9th Iowa Cav.	98		1927 Jan 7	NE, 51st, 1927
Beal, W.C.		E, 9th Mich.	13		1911	NE, 36th, 1912
Beale, Dennis	Pvt.	D, 13th Ill. Cav.	26		1928	IA, 55th, 1929
Bealer, E.J.C.	Corp.	A, 22nd Iowa Inf.	235		1928 Sep 11	IA, 55th, 1929
Beall, F.M.		L, 7th Iowa Inf.			1928 Jan 19	NE, 53rd, 1929
Beall, T.E.	Corp.	C, U.S. Vol. Marines	167		1899 Feb 21	IA, 26th, 1900
Beals, A.J.		H, 44th Iowa Inf. (died of heart failure)	22	70	1910 Jul 5	NE, 35th, 1911
Bealty, Wm. J.	Pvt.	K, 2nd Ohio Vol. Hvy. Art.	465		1904 Nov 28	IA, 31st, 1905
Beam, John	Pvt.	F, 37th Iowa Inf.	78	79	1893 Jan 13	IA, 19th, 1893
Beam, S.W.		H, 126th Penn. D, 209th Penn. (died of old age)	35	84	1921 Dec 7	NE, 46th, 1922
Beaman, A.R.		F, 62nd Ohio Inf.	54		1886	KS, 6th, 1887
Beaman, Abraham		L, 13th Mo. Cav.	85		1911 Jan 13	KS, 31st, 1912
Beaman, H.S.	Pvt.	I, — Iowa Cav.	155	86	1932 Jan 28	IA, 59th, 1933
Beamer, Wm.		E, 21st Ohio	129		1919 Oct 30	KS, 39th, 1920
Beames, Homer		7th Ohio Cav.	127		1905 Jul 12	KS, 25th, 1906
Beams, J.		Ky.	337		1923 Jan	KS, 43rd, 1924
Beams, James		C, 4th Ky.	337		1924 Jan 11	KS, 44th, 1925
Bean, A.W.	Capt.	D, 7th Wis. Inf.	386		1901 Feb	IA, 28th, 1902
Bean, B.F.	Pvt.	K, 24th Maine	78		1928 Dec 3	IA, 55th, 1929
Bean, Benj. L.		F, 154th Ill. Inf.	118		1923 Jul 1	NE, 48th, 1924
Bean, David C.		F, 42nd Ill.	127		1913 Jan 9	KS, 33rd, 1914
Bean, G.W.		K, 5th Ill. Cav.	28		1920 Feb 16	KS, 40th, 1921
Bean, Horatio			153		1908 Jun 6	IA, 35th, 1909
Bean, J.	Pvt.	F, 28th Iowa Inf.	24		1919 Aug 26	IA, 46th, 1920
Bean, John		H, 145th Ill. Inf.	18		1935 Apr 15	KS, 55th, 1936
Bean, John J.		D, 37th Wis.	25		1915 Dec 18	NE, 40th, 1916
Bean, M.J.	Pvt.	G, 10th Penn. Inf.	158		1906 Apr 20	IA, 33rd, 1907
Bean, M.M.		F, 13th Kans.	93		1893 Dec 9	KS, 13th, 1894

Name	Rank	Company, Regiment or Ship	Post*	Age	Death Date†	Journal
Bean, Nathaniel	Pvt.	I, 185th N.Y. Inf.	353	53	1897 Oct 26	IA, 24th, 1898
Bean, W.O.	Pvt.	H, 22nd Iowa Inf.	193	55	1888 Apr 6	IA, 15th, 1889
Bear, G.N.D.		H, 55th Ill. Inf. (died of heart failure)	114	56	1897 Dec 8	NE, 22nd, 1898
Bear, John	Corp.	H, 120th Ohio Inf.	235		1916 Nov 9	IA, 43rd, 1917
Bear, John		I, 56th Mo.	412		1917 Oct 17	KS, 37th, 1918
Bear, Orange	Pvt.	I, 14th Ill. Cav.	138		1899	NE, 24th, 1900
Bear, W.H.			16		1893 Aug	KS, 13th, 1894
Beard, Acey		A, 157th Ohio Inf.	271		1922 Apr 7	IA, 49th, 1923
Beard, D.H.		A, 175th Ohio Inf.	127		1929	KS, 49th, 1930
Beard, E.H.J.	Pvt.	B, 91st N.Y. Inf.	16		1925 Apr 24	IA, 52nd, 1926
Beard, Edward	Pvt.	K, 2nd Minn. Cav.	452		1928 Dec 15	IA, 55th, 1929
Beard, James		I, 16th Kans.	25		1926 Aug 17	KS, 46th, 1927
Beard, John	Pvt.	G, 39th Iowa Inf.	122		1920	IA, 47th, 1921
Beard, S.W.			78		1904 Jan 3	IA, 30th, 1904
Beard, W.		D, 148th Ill.	377		1906 Apr 22	KS, 26th, 1907
Beard, William		C, 39th Ind.	258		1916 Dec 29	KS, 36th, 1917
Beard, Wm.		1st Ill.	51		1917	KS, 37th, 1918
Beard, Wm. H.		D, 11th Ohio Cav.	131		1909 Jan 31	KS, 29th, 1910
Bearden, E.S.	Sergt.	F, 7th Iowa Inf.	309		1919 Nov	IA, 46th, 1920
Beardley, Chas.		H, 51st N.Y.	25		1930 Jan 5	KS, 50th, 1931
Beardsley, E.			45		1925 Mar 18	IA, 52nd, 1926
Beardsley, J.S.		B, 13th Iowa	25		1927 Oct 11	NE, 52nd, 1928
Beardsley, S.W.		G, 154th N.Y. Inf. (died of Bright's disease)	62	72	1891[1901?] Jan	NE, 26th, 1902
Beardsley, W.W.	Pvt.	F, 8th Iowa Inf.	18		1929 May 4	IA, 56th, 1930
Beardsley, Wm.	Pvt.		231	88	1932 Jul 7	IA, 59th, 1933
Bearman, Henry			277		1926	IA, 53rd, 1927
Beasley, George W.		K, 40th Ind. (former member; died at Lincoln)	21		1935 Apr 20	NE, 60th, 1936
Beasley, W.H.		A, 125th Ind.	94		1921 Dec 16	IA, 48th, 1922
Beasley, W.L.	Pvt.	G, 22nd Iowa Inf.	434	65	1889 Mar 12	IA, 16th, 1890
Beasley, Wm.			67		1922 Feb 18	IA, 49th, 1923
Beasly, John			254		1896 Sep	KS, 16th, 1897
Beasore, Jacob J.		A, Ohio Col.	78		1917 Aug 19	KS, 37th, 1918
Beaston, Joseph		C, 119th Ill.	54		1913 Mar 25	KS, 33rd, 1914
Beatle, David		G, 32nd Iowa Inf.	98		1927 Nov 23	NE, 52nd, 1928
Beatty, A.G.	Pvt.	D, 9th Iowa Inf.	54		1928 Oct 4	IA, 55th, 1929
Beatty, David	Pvt.	I, 21st Iowa Inf.	369		1907 May 18	IA, 34th, 1908
Beatty, George E.		I, 46th Iowa Inf.	110	90	1935 Dec 24	IA, 62nd, 1936
Beatty, H.H.		I, 13th Iowa	23		1917 Jan 25	KS, 37th, 1918
Beatty, Henry	Pvt.	C, 186th Ohio Inf.	322		1916 Oct 21	IA, 43rd, 1917
Beatty, J.			290		1921 Feb 21	IA, 48th, 1922
Beatty, J.F.	Pvt.	I, 13th Iowa Inf.	23		1920 Feb 28	IA, 47th, 1921
Beatty, J.J.		Signal Corps	88		1906 Apr 2	KS, 26th, 1907
Beatty, J.T.		A, 45th Iowa	7		1929 Feb 26	NE, 54th, 1930
Beatty, J.T.		A, 45th Iowa	7		1929 Jan	NE, 53rd, 1929
Beatty, Jas. M.	Pvt.	F, 124th Ill. Inf.	235		1916 Oct 31	IA, 43rd, 1917
Beatty, Jos. H.		H, 125th Penn.	25		1927 Apr 29	NE, 52nd, 1928
Beatty, S.	Pvt.	D, 35th Iowa Inf.	228		1915 Dec 25	IA, 42nd, 1916
Beatty, T.A.	Pvt.	K, 161st Ohio Inf.	466		1913 Oct 14	IA, 40th, 1914
Beatty, T.J.		E, 117th Ohio Inf.	188	61	1902 Sep	NE, 27th, 1903
Beatty, Theodore	Pvt.	E, 2nd Iowa Inf.	12		1917 Sep 15	IA, 44th, 1918
Beatty, William J., see Bealty, Wm. J.						
Beatty, Wm.	Pvt.	7th Iowa Inf.	167		1913 Apr 21	IA, 40th, 1914
Beatty, Wm.	Capt.		8		1915 Mar 16	IA, 42nd, 1916
Beaty, W.T.	Col.	2nd Ohio Inf.	113		1903 Nov 7	NE, 28th, 1904
Beauchamp, F.M.	Sergt.	F, 11th Iowa Inf.	115	48	1889 Apr 16	IA, 16th, 1890
Beauclimp, Wm.	Pvt.	F, 11th Iowa Inf.	213	52	1885 Jul 20	IA, 12th, 1886
Beaven, John H.	Pvt.	A, 50th Ill. Inf.	321		1915 Sep 7	IA, 42nd, 1916
Beaver, Moses W.		5th Kans.	300		1902 Sep 19	KS, 22nd, 1903
Beaver, R.A.	Pvt.	B, 1st Neb. (died of accident)	136	37	1884 Mar 27	NE, 9th, 1885

*See Appendix A, B or C for roster of post names and locations.
†See Introduction for note regarding recording of death date.

34

Name	Rank	Company, Regiment or Ship	Post*	Age	Death Date†	Journal
Beaver, Samuel		C, 71st Ill.	61		1902 Sep 17	KS, 22nd, 1903
Beavers, John		G, 21st Iowa	132		1902 Sep 22	KS, 22nd, 1903
Bebb, E.E.	Sergt.	D, 4th Iowa Cav.	115	60	1892 Mar 5	IA, 18th, 1892
Bebee, S.M.	Pvt.	H, 4th Mich. Cav.	440		1913 May 13	IA, 40th, 1914
Bechtel, George	Musician	16th Ill.	12		1896 Feb 12	KS, 16th, 1897
Bechtel, J.M.	Pvt.	I, 17th Wis. Inf.	5		1926 Sep 14	IA, 53rd, 1927
Bechtel, Samuel	Pvt.	D, 3rd Wis. Inf.	252		1916 Dec 27	IA, 43rd, 1917
Bechthold, Lewis		F, 13th Ind. Inf. (died of dropsy)	124	82	1915 Nov 30	NE, 40th, 1916
Bechtold, Fred	Pvt.	D, 60th Ind. Inf.	34		1930 Feb 20	IA, 57th, 1931
Bechtold, Fred	Pvt.	D, 60th Ind. Inf.	34	86	1931 Feb 20	IA, 58th, 1932
Bechtold, Frederick	Pvt.	D, 60th Ind. Inf.	34, 35		1931 Feb 20	IA, 66th, 1940
Bechtold, Lewis, see Bechthold, Lewis						
Beck, A.N.		C, 1st Ohio	432		1900 Dec 9	KS, 20th, 1901
Beck, A.N.		C, 1st Ohio Inf.	176		1900 Dec	KS, 20th, 1901
Beck, A.P.	Pvt.	A, 89th Ind. Inf.	150	73	1898 Feb 23	IA, 24th, 1898
Beck, C.A.	Pvt.	G, 94th Ill. Inf.	210	66	1896 Nov 12	IA, 23rd, 1897
Beck, C.W.	Pvt.	L, 15th Ill. Cav.	154		1899	NE, 24th, 1900
Beck, Christian	Pvt.	A, Minn. Bat.	22		1926 Nov 14	IA, 53rd, 1927
Beck, Emanuel		A, 88th Ind.	81		1924 May 28	KS, 44th, 1925
Beck, Geo. W.	Pvt.	I, 13th Iowa Inf.	40		1925 Dec 20	IA, 52nd, 1926
Beck, Harmon	Pvt.	G, 104th Ohio Inf.	275	63	1893 Dec 26	IA, 20th, 1894
Beck, Henry A.		G, 1st Ohio Cav.	429		1889	KS, 9th, 1890
Beck, Jas. W.	Pvt.	E, 7th Iowa Inf.	55		1925 Oct	IA, 52nd, 1926
Beck, Jno.		Illinois (Mexican War) (died of cancer)	43		1903	NE, 28th, 1904
Beck, John		D, 57th Ill.	87		1897 Sep 30	KS, 17th, 1898
Beck, John		E, 45th Penn.	32		1900 Dec 29	KS, 20th, 1901
Beck, Joseph			32		1913 Aug 9	KS, 33rd, 1914
Beck, M.	Musician	35th Iowa Inf.	231		1911 Feb 25	IA, 38th, 1912
Beck, M.M.	Capt.	18th Ind. Bat.	46		1931 Feb 3	KS, 51st, 1932
Beck, M.M.	Capt.	18th Ind. Batt.	46		1931 Feb 3	KS, 52nd, 1933
Beck, Martin	Pvt.	H, 11th Iowa Inf.	1		1917 Jun 1	IA, 44th, 1918
Beck, O.I.		H, 136th Ohio	238		1909 May 21	KS, 29th, 1910
Beck, Rob't	Sergt.	G, 27th Iowa Inf.	132	50	1890 Nov 28	IA, 17th, 1891
Beck, S.H.		I, 43rd Ohio Inf.	4		1925 Feb 14	KS, 45th, 1926
Beck, S.J.		F, 2nd Ind. Cav.	25		1923	NE, 48th, 1924
Beck, Sam C.	Pvt.	C, 12th Inf.	267		1904 May 27	IA, 31st, 1905
Beck, Samuel J.	Pvt.	D, 42nd Wis. Inf. (not a G.A.R. member)		93	1941 Nov 18	IA, 67th, 1941
Beck, Samuel James	Pvt.	D, 42nd Wis. Inf. (at large)		93	1941 Nov 18	IA, 68th, 1942
Beck, T.A.		F, 32nd Penn.	1		1928 Jul 4	KS, 48th, 1929
Beck, W.C.		D, 62nd Penn.	65		1911 Aug 27	KS, 31st, 1912
Beck, Wm. H.	Pvt.	F, 23rd N.J. Inf.	29		1911 Jul 17	IA, 38th, 1912
Beckenbaugh, Geo.		F, 1st Ill. Cav.	4	71	1912 Jul 1	NE, 37th, 1913
Becker, A.	Pvt.	B, 129th Ill. Inf.	12		1904 Feb 19	IA, 31st, 1905
Becker, Albert		A, 14th N.Y.	12		1926 Jan 1	KS, 46th, 1927
Becker, C.D.	Pvt.	D, 10th N.Y. Hvy. Art.	68		1919 Sep 18	IA, 46th, 1920
Becker, Jerry	Pvt.	D, 1st Wis. Cav.	25		1924 Jan	IA, 51st, 1925
Becker, P.J.	Pvt.	D, 2nd Iowa Inf.	26		1921 Oct 1	IA, 48th, 1922
Becker, Peter		D, 102nd Ohio Inf.	93		1914 Nov 14	KS, 34th, 1915
Becker, Solomon P.		17th Ohio Battery	85		1905 Mar 24	KS, 25th, 1906
Beckerer, Chas.	Pvt.	2nd Iowa Cav.	316			IA, 47th, 1921
Becket, Edward	Sergt. Sergt. Corp.	I, 1st Iowa Inf. H, 12th Iowa Inf. A, 31st U.S. Inf.	70	54	1894 Oct 18	IA, 21st, 1895
Beckett, George W.		I, 46th Ind. Inf.	127		1912 Dec 20	KS, 32nd, 1913
Beckley, Dan		E, 5th Iowa Inf.	322		1914 Jul 20	KS, 34th, 1915
Beckley, M.P.		I, 7th Minn.	142		1909 Oct 11	KS, 29th, 1910
Beckman, D.	Pvt.	I, 47th Iowa Inf.	40		1911 Feb 13	IA, 38th, 1912
Beckman, Frank	Pvt.	D, 27th Iowa Inf.	120	50	1888 May 22	IA, 15th, 1889
Beckman, Louis		E, 77th Ind.	380		1908 Oct 6	KS, 28th, 1909
Beckman, W.J.		E, 8th Ill.	81		1931 Nov 20	KS, 51st, 1932
Beckman, W.J.		E, 8th Ill.	81		1931 Nov 20	KS, 52nd, 1933

*See Appendix A, B or C for roster of post names and locations.
†See Introduction for note regarding recording of death date.

35

Name	Rank	Company, Regiment or Ship	Post*	Age	Death Date†	Journal
Beckner, F.M.	Pvt.	B, 72nd Ind. Inf.	11		1912 Mar 27	IA, 39th, 1913
Becksted, W.H.		B, 85th Mo. Inf., Ill.	111		1917 Aug 11	KS, 37th, 1918
Becktold, J.G.		8th Kans. Inf. (died at Everest, Kans.)	453		1894 Aug 3	KS, 14th, 1895
Beckwith, John S.		H, 8th Ill. Cav.	25		1921 Mar 15	KS, 41st, 1922
Beckwith, Jos. D.	Pvt.	C, 2nd Vt. Inf. (died of heart failure)	57		1891 Mar 19	NE, 16th, 1892
Beckwith, Sol		G, 150th Penn.	18		1906 Feb 10	KS, 26th, 1907
Beckwith, W.	Capt.	C, 4th Ohio Cav.	20		1905	IA, 32nd, 1906
Bedall, David S.	Corp.	3rd Bat. Wis. Lt. Art.	22		1924 Feb 11	IA, 51st, 1925
Beddingfield, L.L.		E, 16th Mo. Cav.	32		1935	KS, 55th, 1936
Beddy, Robert	Pvt.	I, 7th Ill. Cav.	141		1922 Feb 21	IA, 49th, 1923
Bedell, Albert		F, 78th Ohio	8		1921 Feb 18	KS, 41st, 1922
Bedell, D.E.	Pvt.	C, 22nd Iowa Inf.	410	66	1894 Jul 29	IA, 21st, 1895
Bedell, Edward	Pvt.	K, 55th Penn. Inf.	98		1917 Feb 10	IA, 44th, 1918
Bedell, Gilbert		B, 105th Ill. Inf. (see also Appendix D)	71		1906 Dec 19	KS, 26th, 1907
Bedell, J.J.		G, 44th Iowa Inf.	32		1900 Sep 26	KS, 20th, 1901
Bedford, C.G.	Pvt.	K, 15th Ind.	19		1907 1st term	IA, 34th, 1908
Bedford, D.A.	Pvt.	F, 6th Vt. Inf.	88		3rd quarter 1884	IA, 11th, 1885
Bedford, Wallace S.	Pvt.	K, 39th Ill. Vol. Inf.	505		1903 Jun 1	IA, 30th, 1904
Bedford, Walter	Pvt.	B, 11th Wis. Inf.	124		1894	IA, 20th, 1894
Bedford, Winfield S.		A, Ill. Cav.	11		1917 Nov 7	KS, 37th, 1918
Bedley, David			68		1905 Dec 3	KS, 25th, 1906
Bedor, Peter		K, 3rd Mass.	113		1904 Jun 3	KS, 24th, 1905
Beebe, B.M.	Pvt.	E, 17th Ill. Cav.	5		1907 2nd term	IA, 34th, 1908
Beebe, Chas.	Pvt.	C, 105th Ill. Inf.	212		1910 Apr 7	IA, 37th, 1911
Beebe, David		K, 1st Neb. Inf.	127		1890	KS, 10th, 1891
Beebe, E.N.	Pvt.		38		1910 Oct 10	IA, 37th, 1911
Beebe, G.W.		F, 1st Minn.		86	1934 Jul 2	IA, 61st, 1935
Beebe, Geo.	Pvt.	F, 20th Iowa Inf.	12		1911 Jan 6	IA, 38th, 1912
Beebe, George		33rd N.Y. Inf.	187	76	1920 May 9	NE, 45th, 1921
Beebe, Hiram P.		H, 5th N.H. Inf.	1		1899 Jan 12	KS, 19th, 1900
Beebe, O.R.		E, 151st Ind. (died of general breakdown)	318		1920 Feb 27	NE, 45th, 1921
Beebe, Orasmus	Pvt.	K, 8th Ill. Cav.	23		1930 Nov 30	IA, 57th, 1931
Beebee, L.I.		7th N.Y. Hvy. Art.	17		1919 Dec 22	KS, 39th, 1920
Beeble, John M.	Pvt.	I, 121st Ohio	490	67	1898 Jun	IA, 25th, 1899
Beeby, C.L.			168		1909 Dec 18	IA, 36th, 1910
Beed, J.H.	QM Sergt.	L, 4th Iowa Cav.	81		1921 Dec 15	IA, 48th, 1922
Beeding, Jos. A.	Pvt.	A, 39th Iowa Inf.	55	58	1889 Aug 17	IA, 16th, 1890
Beedle, A.		C, 29th Iowa	86		1921	IA, 48th, 1922
Beedle, A.P.	Sergt.	L, 2nd Conn. Hvy. Art.	100		1921 Jul 13	IA, 48th, 1922
Beedle, B.			290		1923	IA, 50th, 1924
Beedles, Ed		H, 148th N.Y.	50		1906 Sep 14	KS, 26th, 1907
Beedy, J.J.	Musician	A, 27th Iowa Inf.	452		1922 Oct 13	IA, 49th, 1923
Beekey, J.J.	Lieut.	A, 38th Iowa Inf.	48		1916 Mar 30	IA, 43rd, 1917
Beekman, J.V.		C, 47th Ill. Inf.	158		1899 Jun 29	KS, 19th, 1900
Beeks, Sam'l	Pvt.	B, 4th Iowa Cav.	369	49	1890 Jan 26	IA, 17th, 1891
Beeler, Charles		L, 1st Mo. Cav.	8		1886	KS, 6th, 1887
Beeler, John		F, 23rd Ohio	71		1923 Apr 15	KS, 43rd, 1924
Beeler, S.F.		1st Art., Baltimore, Md.	18		1926 Feb 2	KS, 46th, 1927
Beeman, Alonzo		K, N.Y. Hvy. Art.	142		1909 Apr 4	KS, 29th, 1910
Beeman, Carlton I.		C, 50th Mo.	82		1917 Aug 20	KS, 37th, 1918
Beeman, Thomas C.	Pvt.	C, 14th Iowa Inf.	88		1922 May 24	IA, 49th, 1923
Beemer, A.D.		K, 11th Penn. Cav. (died of effect of wound)	214	66	1909 Mar 28	NE, 34th, 1910
Beemer, Everett	Pvt.	C, 156th Ill. Inf.	145		1913 Sep 15	IA, 40th, 1914
Beemer, I.		36th Iowa	290		1921 Nov 21	IA, 48th, 1922
Beemer, Jacob		A, 2nd Iowa Cav. (died of old age)	4	77	1920 Oct 7	NE, 45th, 1921
Beemer, R.M.	Pvt.	D, 6th Iowa Inf.	290		1911 Nov 7	IA, 38th, 1912
Beems, William	Pvt.	H, 13th Mich. Inf.	113	73	1892 Nov 27	IA, 19th, 1893
Been, Jacob		H, 101st Ohio	32		1931 Apr 14	KS, 51st, 1932
Been, Jacob		H, 101st Ohio	32		1931 Apr 14	KS, 52nd, 1933
Beerd, D.W.		H, 7th Penn. Cav. (died of stomach cancer)	15	69	1916 Dec 4	NE, 41st, 1917

Name	Rank	Company, Regiment or Ship	Post*	Age	Death Date†	Journal
Beerman, August		C, 6th Minn. (not a member of the department but living in Nebraska; location: Eustis)			1937 Apr 15	NE, 62nd, 1938
Beers, Anson			90		1911 1st term	IA, 38th, 1912
Beers, George W.		D, 113th Ill.	47		1914 Feb 11	KS, 34th, 1915
Beers, Robert J.		E, 10th Mo. Inf.	80		1921 Mar 7	KS, 41st, 1922
Beese, Carl	Sergt.	C, 24th Iowa Inf.	140	64	1897 Jan 17	IA, 23rd, 1897
Beesley, John		L, 11th Mo. Cav.	113		1902 Sep 13	KS, 22nd, 1903
Beeson, B.A.	Pvt.	B, 2nd Iowa Cav.	94		1929 Jan 5	IA, 56th, 1930
Beeson, S.H.		B, 11th Iowa	25		1928 Feb 2	NE, 53rd, 1929
Beeson, W.B.		I, 8th Iowa Cav.	94		1923 Aug 30	IA, 50th, 1924
Beeth, Z.B.		D, 44th Ohio	17		1919 May 21	KS, 39th, 1920
Beety, S.		G, 99th U.S.	365		1893 May 21	KS, 13th, 1894
Beezley, Paul	Pvt.	F, 20th Ohio Inf.	358		1915 May 3	IA, 42nd, 1916
Beggs, Geo.	Pvt.	B, 105th Ill. Inf.	22		1906 Apr 10	IA, 33rd, 1907
Beggs, Leonard		D, 2nd Iowa Inf. (died of Bright's disease)	22		1893 Aug 9	NE, 18th, 1894
Begley, W.M.		E, 30th Ohio	57		1906 Dec 12	KS, 26th, 1907
Behan, John	QM Sergt.	I, 12th Ill. Cav.	44		1901 Mar 26	IA, 27th, 1901
Behel, Levy H.	Pvt.	D, 323rd Ill. Inf.	452		1924 Apr 28	IA, 51st, 1925
Behm, John G.		A, 58th Ind. Inf.	106		1909 Jan 1	NE, 33rd, 1909
Behrens, John	Sergt.	C, 12th Mo. Inf.	1		1895 Dec 30	IA, 23rd, 1897
Beichtel, F.M., see Biechtel, F.M.						
Beiler, Jas. M.	Pvt.	F, 64th Ohio Inf.	206		1912 Nov 15	IA, 39th, 1913
Beilhardt, John	Pvt.	D, 37th Iowa Inf.	452		1906 Nov 7	IA, 33rd, 1907
Beille, B.F.	Pvt.	2nd Penn. Cav.	108		1932 Feb 11	IA, 59th, 1933
Beitz, Julius	Pvt.	H, 6th Iowa Cav.	212		1912 Apr	IA, 39th, 1913
Beland, Eugene		D, 9th U.S. V. Corps G, 25th Ill. Inf.	25	81	1921 Aug 21	NE, 46th, 1922
Belcher, E.A.	Pvt.	B, 46th Wis. Inf.	193		1910 Mar 21	IA, 37th, 1911
Belcher, W.J.	Pvt.	K, 39th N.J. Inf.	492		1913 Dec 11	IA, 40th, 1914
Belden, S.E.		I, 33rd Ohio	453		1916 Mar 31	KS, 36th, 1917
Belden, William		K, 86th N.Y. (died of Bright's disease)	32	74	1920 Jun 24	NE, 45th, 1921
Belfrage, J.B.	Pvt.	H, 105th Ill. Inf.	22		1917 May 18	IA, 44th, 1918
Belgard, Eliga	Pvt.	A, 151st N.Y. Inf.	497		1925 May 27	IA, 52nd, 1926
Belknap, A.J.	Pvt.	C, 8th Iowa Cav.	254		1902 Sep 9	IA, 29th, 1903
Belknap, F.A.	Pvt.	I, 2nd Wis. Inf.	149		1917 Mar 12	IA, 44th, 1918
Belknap, T.M.	Pvt.	E, 81st Ill. Inf.	200		1910 May 22	IA, 37th, 1911
Belknap, W.H.		A, 13th N.Y.	25		1930 Oct 9	NE, 55th, 1931
Belknap, Wm. W.	Major Gen.		2	61	1890 Oct 13	IA, 17th, 1891
Bell, A.A.		U, 45th Penn. (died of gastric cause)	245	74	1918 Apr 23	NE, 43rd, 1919
Bell, A.J.		H, 35th Ohio Inf. (died of diabetes)	32		1893 Dec 1	NE, 18th, 1894
Bell, A.W.	Pvt.	D, 12th U.S. Inf.	206		1911 Dec 24	IA, 38th, 1912
Bell, Alex. W.		C, 122nd Ohio Inf.	130		1901 Jan 16	KS, 21st, 1902
Bell, Alfred	Pvt.	C, 95th Ill. Inf.	134	53	1890 Aug 31	IA, 17th, 1891
Bell, Alfred H.		B, 46th Ind. (died of Bright's disease)	154	77	1916 Dec 25	NE, 41st, 1917
Bell, Austin		A, 36th Ohio Inf.	68		1891 Oct 15	KS, 11th, 1892
Bell, C.W.	Pvt.	H, 101st Ohio Inf.	145		1918 Mar 28	IA, 45th, 1919
Bell, Columbus		B, 83rd —	208		1896	KS, 16th, 1897
Bell, Darias	Pvt.	D, 3rd Wis. Inf.	68		1918 Dec 26	IA, 45th, 1919
Bell, E.J.		E, 23rd Wis. (died of dropsy)	129	64	1907 Apr 27	NE, 32nd, 1908
Bell, Geo.	Pvt.	F, 1st Ohio Art.	36		1906 May 17	IA, 33rd, 1907
Bell, Geo. H.		K, 25th Iowa	[25?]		1923	NE, 48th, 1924
Bell, George	Pvt.	B, 140th Ohio Inf.	250	70	1896 Aug 21	IA, 23rd, 1897
Bell, George		K, 84th Ill.	307		1896 Dec 9	KS, 16th, 1897
Bell, H.			96		1883	KS, 3rd, 1884
Bell, Isaac		A, 14th Ill.	96		1920 Mar 22	KS, 40th, 1921
Bell, J.A.		I, 22nd Ind.	180		1912 Jul 14	KS, 32nd, 1913
Bell, J.A.			477		1922	KS, 42nd, 1923
Bell, J.B.			11		1927	IA, 54th, 1928
Bell, J.J.		C, 7th Kans. (killed by a bull)	40		1891 Sep 15	KS, 11th, 1892
Bell, J.N.		A, 10th Ill. Cav.	25		1898 Dec 25	KS, 18th, 1899

*See Appendix A, B or C for roster of post names and locations.
†See Introduction for note regarding recording of death date.

37

Name	Rank	Company, Regiment or Ship	Post*	Age	Death Date†	Journal
Bell, J.N.		I, 23rd Ohio	104		1926 Mar 22	KS, 46th, 1927
Bell, James T.	Pvt.	C, 3rd Iowa Inf.	34		1908 May 26	IA, 35th, 1909
Bell, John		B, 28th Wis. Inf.	32		1918 Sep 27	KS, 38th, 1919
Bell, John		C, 11th Ill.	51		1921 May 6	KS, 41st, 1922
Bell, Joseph	Corp.	G, 7th Ill. Inf.	452		1926 Oct 20	IA, 53rd, 1927
Bell, L.B.		I, 12th Iowa	94		1929 Jul 21	NE, 54th, 1930
Bell, L.P.			24		1913 May 27	IA, 40th, 1914
Bell, Lewis		B, 13th Mich.	244		1920 Oct 10	KS, 40th, 1921
Bell, M.R.		K, — Penn.	127		1919 Oct 1	KS, 39th, 1920
Bell, Marion A.		F, 16th Iowa	58		1910 Jan 12	KS, 30th, 1911
Bell, Michael R.		F, 4th Iowa Inf.	52		1889	KS, 9th, 1890
Bell, Ortha C.		B, 10th Ind. Cav. (see also Appendix D)	25	85	1932 May 5	NE, 57th, 1933
Bell, Porter		E, 11th Penn.	40		1916 Nov 26	KS, 36th, 1917
Bell, R.M.		H, 19th Ill. (died at Westport, Mo.)	28		1895 Jul 20	KS, 15th, 1896
Bell, R.P.		H, 2nd Ill.	8		1938[1937?] Dec 11	KS, 57th, 1938
Bell, Robert		G, 59th Ill.	69		1926 Aug 28	KS, 46th, 1927
Bell, Robert F.	Pvt.	H, 38th Iowa Inf.	56	70	1892 Feb 17	IA, 19th, 1893
Bell, Rolando S.		A, 41st Ill. Inf.	244		1916 Sep 7	KS, 36th, 1917
Bell, Russell A.	Pvt.	102nd Ohio Inf.	167		1910 Jun	IA, 37th, 1911
Bell, S.H.			6		1916	IA, 43rd, 1917
Bell, S.S.		A, 70th Ohio Inf.	25		1923	NE, 48th, 1924
Bell, Samuel		E, 4th West Va.	175		1897 Dec	KS, 17th, 1898
Bell, T.J.		B, 101st Penn.	96		1910 Oct 15	KS, 30th, 1911
Bell, Thomas A.	Pvt.	E, 45th Iowa Inf.	245	47	1893 Jan 6	IA, 19th, 1893
Bell, Thos.	Pvt.	K, 2nd Iowa Cav.	19		1903 Aug 18	IA, 30th, 1904
Bell, Thos.	Pvt.	D, 172nd Ohio Inf.	173		1925 Mar 17	IA, 52nd, 1926
Bell, Thos.		E, 10th Ill. Inf.	318		1915 Mar	NE, 40th, 1916
Bell, W.B.	Col.	8th Iowa Inf.	108		1911 Nov 9	IA, 38th, 1912
Bell, W.D.		G, 25th Ind. Inf.	265		1912 Jan 13	KS, 32nd, 1913
Bell, W.H.	Pvt.	B, 17th Ind. Inf.	98		1913 Oct 26	IA, 40th, 1914
Bell, W.R.			134		1900 Jul	IA, 27th, 1901
Bell, W.W.		L, 10th Ill. Cav. (died at Pratt, Kans.; buried at Green Lawn Cemetery)	176		1894 Dec 16	KS, 14th, 1895
Bell, William J.		F, 78th Ind. Inf. (nonmember)			1942 Oct 11	NE, 67th, 1943
Bell, Wm.		C, 1st Tenn.	35	81	1920 Jun 18	NE, 45th, 1921
Bell, Wm. H.	Pvt.	E, 16th Ohio Inf.	491		1905 Apr 11	IA, 31st, 1905
Bell, Wm. Robt.	Pvt.	K, 14th Iowa Inf. A, 14th Resid. Iowa Inf.	440	94	1939 Mar 23	IA, 65th, 1939
Bellamy, Emerson E.		A, 4th Vt. Cav.	265		1926 Sep 26	NE, 51st, 1927
Bellamy, Oliver		C, 104th Penn.	61		1917 May 4	KS, 37th, 1918
Bellany, L.N.	Pvt.	K, 3rd Iowa Cav.	432		1906 May 3	IA, 33rd, 1907
Beller, B.H.		A, 28th Iowa Inf.	116		1906 Aug 12	NE, 31st, 1907
Beller, S.E.		E, 134th N.Y.	68		1917 Jul 2	KS, 37th, 1918
Belles, J.H.	Pvt.	B, 26th Iowa Inf.	497		1929 Jun 22	IA, 56th, 1930
Belles, John		I, 143rd Penn. Inf. (died of cancer)	262	79	1920 Dec 29	NE, 45th, 1921
Bellesfield, D.	Pvt.	E, 8th Wis. Inf.	387	60	1896 May 23	IA, 23rd, 1897
Bellows, B.F.		K, 76th Ohio	4		1921 Feb 10	KS, 41st, 1922
Bellows, Geo. L.	Pvt.	I, 1st Dak. Cav.	11		1899	NE, 24th, 1900
Bellows, Geo. P.	Pvt.	F, 6th Iowa Cav.	194		1925 Mar 6	IA, 52nd, 1926
Bellows, H.C.			144		1884	KS, 4th, 1885
Bellows, W.S.		D, 9th Ohio (died of paralysis)			1924	NE, 49th, 1925
Bells, Ezra	Sergt.	F, 8th Iowa Cav.	208		1917 Mar 4	IA, 44th, 1918
Bellville, Joseph H.		B, 8th Vt.	93		1918 Nov 12	KS, 38th, 1919
Bellville, Samuel		F, 33rd Iowa (died of bilious calculi)	99		1890	KS, 10th, 1891
Belnap, David	Pvt.	E, 23rd Iowa Inf.	12		1926 Nov 17	IA, 53rd, 1927
Belt, Francis I.		I, 5th Mo.	1		1914 Jun 25	KS, 34th, 1915
Belts, G.N.		H, 12th Ill. Cav.	293		1922 Dec 24	KS, 42nd, 1923
Beltz, Abe	Pvt.		116		1914 Sep 15	IA, 41st, 1915
Belvel, H.M.	Pvt.	F, 34th Iowa Inf.	12		1910 Jan 29	IA, 37th, 1911
Belzer, J.E.		33rd Ohio (died of heart trouble)	120	78	1922 Jan 20	NE, 47th, 1923
Bement, A.	Pvt.	D, 143rd N.Y. Inf.	132		1906	IA, 33rd, 1907
Bement, J.H.		D, 51st Mo.	85		1925 Jul 10	KS, 45th, 1926

*See Appendix A, B or C for roster of post names and locations.
†See Introduction for note regarding recording of death date.

Name	Rank	Company, Regiment or Ship	Post*	Age	Death Date†	Journal
Bemis, S.E.	Pvt.	I, 16th N.Y. Inf.	365	57	1896 Dec 22	IA, 23rd, 1897
Bemont, David		G, 19th U.S. Inf.	463		1909 Dec 26	KS, 29th, 1910
Benadom, J.W.	Pvt.	E, 31st Iowa Inf.	130	90	1933 Dec 5	IA, 60th, 1934
Benbo, Berckley	Pvt.	B, 15th Iowa	67		1905 Mar 30	IA, 32nd, 1906
Benbow, R.		D, 9th Kans.	91		1888	KS, 8th, 1889
Bence, Frank	Pvt.	F, 28th Wis.	305		1914 Sep 9	IA, 41st, 1915
Bench, Wm. M.		K, 19th Iowa	65		1918 Jan 21	KS, 38th, 1919
Bendall, William		F, 11th Kans. Cav.	38		1908 Apr 20	KS, 28th, 1909
Bender, Charles H.		A, 10th Conn.	14		1913	KS, 33rd, 1914
Bender, D.A.	Pvt.	A, 129th Ind. Inf.	68		1911 Dec 15	IA, 38th, 1912
Bender, D.M.		I, 12th Ind.	81		1925 Jun 18	KS, 45th, 1926
Bender, James H.		K, 213th Penn. Inf. (born in Pennsylvania; died of pneumonia at Soldiers & Sailors Home Hospital, Burkett; buried at Home Cemetery)		74	1907 Mar 2	NE, 31st, 1907
Bender, Jonathan	Pvt.	C, 31st Ohio Inf.	81		1915 Oct 12	IA, 42nd, 1916
Bender, Martin	Pvt.	A, 46th Ill. Inf.	68		1927 Aug 23	IA, 54th, 1928
Bender, Thomas J.		G, 102nd Penn. Inf. (member at large; died at Fairmount)			1939 Jan 1	NE, 64th, 1940
Benders, I.M.		K, 1st Penn. Res.	71		1916 Feb 23	KS, 36th, 1917
Benedick, R.F.		K, 127th N.Y.	293		1923 Feb 24	KS, 43rd, 1924
Benedick, Thomas	Pvt.	F, 5th Mo. Inf.	56	60	1892 Oct 22	IA, 19th, 1893
Benedict, Abraham		I, 65th Ill.	13	66	1909 Sep 12	NE, 34th, 1910
Benedict, C.B.		B, 9th Ill. Cav.	260		1922 Feb 23	KS, 42nd, 1923
Benedict, D.C.	Pvt.	G, 15th Iowa Inf.	188		1913 Jul 15	IA, 40th, 1914
Benedict, D.E.		C, 14th Wis.	17		1918 Feb 5	KS, 38th, 1919
Benedict, E.F.		C, 112th Ill.	328		1888	KS, 8th, 1889
Benedict, F.M.		E, 38th Iowa	12		1930 Feb 25	KS, 50th, 1931
Benedict, George	Pvt.	A, 11th Iowa Inf.	231		1915 Dec 11	IA, 42nd, 1916
Benedict, George R.		I, 13th Kans.	40		1915 May 26	KS, 35th, 1916
Benedict, Ira J.		H, 147th Ill.	55		1913 May 30	KS, 33rd, 1914
Benedict, J.W.		H, 12th Iowa Inf.	7		1926 May 30	NE, 51st, 1927
Benedict, John		E, 6th Ohio	256		1916 May 1	KS, 36th, 1917
Benedict, John	Pvt. & Corp.	M, 5th Mich. Cav.	70	46	1888 Aug 7	NE, 13th, 1889
Benedict, M.B.			127		1922 Jul 17	KS, 42nd, 1923
Benedict, M.R.		I, 10th Ill. Cav.	12		1916 Jul 1	KS, 36th, 1917
Benedict, S.A.		C, 11th Mich.	12		1915 Apr 4	KS, 35th, 1916
Benedict, W.H.	Pvt.	A, 38th Iowa Inf.	258		1911 Jun 23	IA, 38th, 1912
Benedict, W.T.		I, 9th Iowa	79		1927	KS, 48th, 1929
Benedict, Wm. N.		K, 43rd Wis.	242		1890	KS, 10th, 1891
Benefiel, Isaac		B, 87th Ind.	23		1911 Apr 2	KS, 31st, 1912
Benett, James		19th Iowa	73		1896 May 15	KS, 16th, 1897
Benfer, H.H.		A, 55th Ohio	130		1917 Sep 20	KS, 37th, 1918
Benfer, Henry	2nd Lieut.	G, 172nd Penn. Inf.	36		1918 Feb 23	KS, 38th, 1919
Benfer, John Y.		B, 123rd Ohio	92		1913 Aug 26	KS, 33rd, 1914
Benfield, George		C, 50th Ill. Inf.	260		1902 Jun 1	KS, 22nd, 1903
Benfield, Henry	Pvt.	8th Iowa Inf.	191		1919	IA, 46th, 1920
Benge, Anderson M.		D, 1st Iowa Cav.	55		1918 Jan 6	IA, 45th, 1919
Benge, S.W.			122		1924	IA, 51st, 1925
Benham, P.		G, 30th Ind.	142		1921 Oct 27	KS, 41st, 1922
Beniah, Jno.	Pvt.	G, 47th Iowa Inf.	452		1925 Nov 3	IA, 52nd, 1926
Benidix, William		G, 11th Kans.	225		1923 Nov 7	KS, 43rd, 1924
Benjamin, Fred		A, 157th N.Y. Inf. (died of stomach disease)	13	68	1905 Jan 3	NE, 30th, 1906
Benjamin, G.W.		E, 85th N.Y.	83		1917 Sep 13	KS, 37th, 1918
Benjamin, George		D, 150th Ill. (died of kidney disease)	50	71	1915 Oct	NE, 40th, 1916
Benjamin, George B.		F, 128th Ind.	207		1932	NE, 57th, 1933
Benjamin, Harvey L.	Pvt.	E, 46th Ill. Inf.	74		1922 Jan 17	IA, 49th, 1923
Benjamin, J.B.	Pvt.	L, 6th N.Y.	23		1923 Jan 16	IA, 50th, 1924
Benjamin, James A.		M, 4th Ill. Cav. (died of lightning)	4	50	1895 Jul 28	NE, 20th, 1896
Benjamine, G.E.		I, 46th Ill. Inf.	20		1887 May 10	KS, 7th, 1888
Benne, Henry	Pvt.	D, 4th Iowa Inf.	5		1920 Aug 22	IA, 47th, 1921
Benner, James			5		1933 May 28	KS, 53rd, 1934

*See Appendix A, B or C for roster of post names and locations.
†See Introduction for note regarding recording of death date.

39

Name	Rank	Company, Regiment or Ship	Post*	Age	Death Date†	Journal
Benner, William		E, 5th Ind.	65		1897 Aug 5	KS, 17th, 1898
Bennett, A.		L, 2nd Colo.	239		1897 Jan 31	KS, 17th, 1898
Bennett, A.W.	Pvt.	H, 50th Wis. Inf.	332		1910 Dec 23	IA, 37th, 1911
Bennett, B.S.		K, 104th Penn.	1		1898 Aug 29	KS, 18th, 1899
Bennett, C.W.		K, 52nd Ill.	114		1897 May 9	KS, 17th, 1898
Bennett, C.W.		K, 52nd Ill.	114		1898 May 9	KS, 18th, 1899
Bennett, Charles	Musician	D, 3rd N.J. Inf.	7		1911 Feb 11	IA, 38th, 1912
Bennett, Charles		A, 55th Ill.	297		1913 Sep 23	KS, 33rd, 1914
Bennett, Debit C.		H, 46th Ill.	185		1923 Jan 19	KS, 44th, 1925
Bennett, E.A.	Pvt.	D, 20th Iowa Inf.	392	51	1894 Aug 24	IA, 21st, 1895
Bennett, E.B.	Pvt.	F, 21st Iowa	78		1907 May 7	IA, 34th, 1908
Bennett, F.H.		E, 118th Ill. Inf.	11	68	1910 Jul 18	NE, 35th, 1911
Bennett, G.S.		B, 95th Ill.	108		1917 Sep 2	KS, 37th, 1918
Bennett, Geo.	Pvt.	6th Iowa Cav.	77		1917 Jun 7	IA, 44th, 1918
Bennett, Horace	Pvt.	G, 155th Ill. Inf.	23	87	1932 May	IA, 59th, 1933
Bennett, J.		A, 83rd Ohio	87		1918 Feb 24	KS, 38th, 1919
Bennett, J.H.		K, 177th Ohio Inf. (died of heart failure)	18	76	1896 Dec 29	NE, 21st, 1897
Bennett, J.P.			88		2nd quarter 1883	IA, 10th, 1884
Bennett, J.S.	Pvt.	D, 2nd Iowa Cav.	67		1920 Dec 22	IA, 47th, 1921
Bennett, J.S.		K, 152nd Ohio	17		1918 Feb 4	KS, 38th, 1919
Bennett, Jerry		G, 7th Kans.	321		1905 Sep 9	KS, 25th, 1906
Bennett, John	Pvt.	G, 33rd Mo. Inf.	306		1905 Nov 10	IA, 32nd, 1906
Bennett, John		A, 2nd Wis. Inf.	65	78	1892 Nov 6	KS, 12th, 1893
Bennett, Joseph W.		A, 101st Ind. Inf. (died at Elk Falls, Kans.; buried at Elk Falls Cemetery)	26		1894 Sep 21	KS, 14th, 1895
Bennett, Josiah		G, 15th Ill. Cav.	251		1917 Aug 20	KS, 37th, 1918
Bennett, L.M.	Sergt.	A, 76th Ohio	222		1921 Feb 19	IA, 48th, 1922
Bennett, Martin V.B.		A, 40th Iowa	59		1913 Feb 15	KS, 33rd, 1914
Bennett, Matthew		F, 10th Ind.	26		1913 Jul 5	KS, 33rd, 1914
Bennett, N.E.	Pvt.	G, 46th Iowa Inf.	40		1924 May 26	IA, 51st, 1925
Bennett, N.S.	Seaman	receiving ship	47		1909 Nov 5	KS, 29th, 1910
Bennett, Orin R.		B, 101st Ind.	26		1893 Dec 29	KS, 13th, 1894
Bennett, R.H.	Pvt.	H, 2nd Mo. Cav.	159		1908 Mar 18	IA, 35th, 1909
Bennett, R.M.		G, 17th Ind.	81		1928 Dec 17	KS, 48th, 1929
Bennett, Robert	Pvt.		108		1910 Aug 1	IA, 37th, 1911
Bennett, S.D.		7th Conn. Inf. (died of consumption)	20		1893 Feb 24	NE, 18th, 1894
Bennett, S.J.	Capt.	A, 12th Mo. Cav.	236		1911 May 24	IA, 38th, 1912
Bennett, Samuel B.		E, 2nd Iowa Inf.	32		1916 Sep 20	KS, 36th, 1917
Bennett, Thomas C.		Ohio	116		1909 Mar	KS, 29th, 1910
Bennett, W.H.		K, 14th N.J.	100		1913 Feb 22	KS, 33rd, 1914
Bennett, William	Pvt.	L, 2nd N.Y. Hvy. Art.	35	57	1892 Dec 13	IA, 19th, 1893
Bennett, Wm.		E, 3rd Mich. Inf.	11		1892 Feb	NE, 17th, 1893
Bennett, Wm. A.		H, 8th Wis.	[25?]		1923	NE, 48th, 1924
Bennett, Wm. H.	Pvt.	G, 29th N.Y. Inf.	52		1913 Sep 1	IA, 40th, 1914
Bennett, Wm. R.		E, 143rd N.Y. Inf.	17		1935 Feb 16	KS, 55th, 1936
Benneway, Geo. C.		F, 26th Wis.	60		1924 May 17	NE, 51st, 1927
Benning, A.F.	Pvt.	F, 21st Mo. Inf.	301		1908 Feb 10	IA, 35th, 1909
Benshoof, P.L.	Sergt.	E, 20th Iowa Inf.	16	73	1897 Jun 13	IA, 24th, 1898
Benson, A.P.		D, 71st Mo.	1		1913 Feb 2	KS, 33rd, 1914
Benson, A.W.	Major	154th N.Y. Inf.	18		1916 Jan 1	KS, 36th, 1917
Benson, C.L.	Pvt.	I, 11th Vt. Inf.	2		1902 Jun 9	IA, 29th, 1903
Benson, Daniel	Corp.	G, 96th Ill. Inf.	36		1899	NE, 24th, 1900
Benson, J.V.		A, 164th Ohio (died of paralysis)	29	81	1918 Feb 24	NE, 43rd, 1919
Benson, J.W.		D, 12th Iowa	433		1914 Jul 7	KS, 34th, 1915
Benson, J.Z.	Pvt.	I, 6th Ohio Cav.	452		1925 Sep 5	IA, 52nd, 1926
Benson, Jessey M.		G, 17th Ill.	108		1908 Dec 19	KS, 28th, 1909
Benson, John W.	Pvt.	D, 4th Iowa Cav.	75		1900 Jun 30	IA, 27th, 1901
Benson, Martin	Pvt.	L, 9th Iowa Cav.	127	48	1895 Mar 29	IA, 21st, 1895
Bent, Nathan	Pvt.	F, 3rd Iowa Inf.	276	66	1889 Dec	IA, 16th, 1890
Bentley, Chas. F.		142nd Ill. Inf.	11	64	1908 Jul 15	NE, 33rd, 1909
Bentley, O.F.D.	Pvt.	E, 2nd N.Y. Inf.	209		1905 Jul	IA, 32nd, 1906
Bentley, P.P.		F, 93rd N.Y.	94		1930 Dec 17	NE, 55th, 1931

*See Appendix A, B or C for roster of post names and locations.
†See Introduction for note regarding recording of death date.

Name	Rank	Company, Regiment or Ship	Post*	Age	Death Date†	Journal
Bentley, William		B, 26th Ill. Inf.		96	1937 Jul 21	IA, 64th, 1938
Benton, Almon		I, 2nd Kans. Militia	1		1898 Sep 17	KS, 18th, 1899
Benton, Charles			293		1921	KS, 41st, 1922
Benton, Eli		A, 19th Mich.	25		1919 Jul 24	KS, 39th, 1920
Benton, L.D.	Pvt.	B, 43rd Wis.	235		1923 Feb 12	IA, 50th, 1924
Benton, Levi	Pvt.	D, 46th Ill.	52		1923 Feb 27	IA, 50th, 1924
Benton, R.G.	Pvt.	M, 3rd Iowa Cav.	410		1908 Oct 7	IA, 35th, 1909
Benton, W.R.		E, 62nd Ill. Inf. (died at Oakland, Kans.; buried at Westmoreland, Kans.)	71		1894 Jul 25	KS, 14th, 1895
Benton, Wm. E.	Pvt.	I, 47th Iowa Inf.	1		1925 May 18	IA, 52nd, 1926
Bentz, John	Pvt.	B, 3rd N.Y. Cav.	222		1913 Apr 20	IA, 40th, 1914
Benz, Joseph C.		B, 72nd N.Y. (died of paralysis)	288	79	1920 Oct 12	NE, 45th, 1921
Beraneck, F.A.	Pvt.	A, 22nd Iowa Inf.	8		1917 Nov 17	IA, 44th, 1918
Beranger, Mathias		E, 31st Ohio Inf.	50		1891 Feb 17	KS, 11th, 1892
Berber, John W.		E, 157th Ind.	209		1911 Sep	KS, 31st, 1912
Berberet, M.J.		7th West Va.	132		1921 Oct 5	KS, 41st, 1922
Berdine, G.W.		B, 86th Ill.	25		1911 Feb 5	KS, 31st, 1912
Beregon, Jno.	Pvt.	F, 14th Ill. Inf.	66		1925 Feb 27	IA, 52nd, 1926
Berentz, Jeremiah		C, 12th Ill. Inf.	145		1912 Oct 14	KS, 32nd, 1913
Beresford, C.W.	Drummer	A, 94th N.Y. Inf.	236		1913	IA, 40th, 1914
Berg, C.H.	Pvt.	A, 96th Ill. Inf.	78		1926 Apr 9	IA, 53rd, 1927
Berg, Ed.		3rd Battery, Wis. Lt. Art.	160		1897 Nov 20	KS, 17th, 1898
Bergan, Wm.		H, 14th Ohio (died of old age)	76	84	1918 Sep 18	NE, 43rd, 1919
Berger, B.	Pvt.	K, 31st Ohio Inf.	7		1925 Feb 14	IA, 52nd, 1926
Berger, Benedict	Pvt.	K, 51st Penn. Vols.	12		1926 May 4	IA, 53rd, 1927
Berger, H.C.		C, 130th Penn.	40		1915 Mar 3	NE, 40th, 1916
Berger, John H.		A, 75th Ill.	7		1934 Jul 22	NE, 59th, 1935
Bergesen, L.A.	Pvt.	2nd Ill. Lt. Art.	420	63	1896 Feb 16	IA, 23rd, 1897
Bergh, Wm.	Pvt.	B, 11th Ind. Inf.	220		1884	KS, 4th, 1885
Bergin, J.C.	Pvt.	J, 12th Mich.	223		1907 Sep 28	IA, 34th, 1908
Berington, Thomas			380		1924 Jul 18	KS, 44th, 1925
Berk, J.E.		H, 2nd Ill.	150		1905 Aug	KS, 25th, 1906
Berkey, T.A.H.		G, 63rd Ind. Inf.	25	74	1921 Mar 8	NE, 46th, 1922
Berkhart, Henry	Pvt.	I, 2nd Wis. Inf.	12		1927 Mar 10	IA, 54th, 1928
Berkley, R.J.		A, 7th Mo.	271		1912 May 1	KS, 32nd, 1913
Berkley, W.H.	Musician	F, 8th Vt. Inf.	101		1915 Nov 12	IA, 42nd, 1916
Berkshire, C.H.	Pvt.	A, 62nd Ill. Inf.	358		1913 Jul 14	IA, 40th, 1914
Berkshire, James H.		2nd & 12th Kans.	104		1924 Aug 21	KS, 44th, 1925
Berlew, A.E.		F, 12th Penn. Inf.	76	69	1906 Feb 10	NE, 31st, 1907
Berlin, Edwin		K, 93rd Ill.			1929 Jan 28	NE, 53rd, 1929
Bernard, Henry		D, 58th Ill.	1		1926 Jan 14	KS, 46th, 1927
Bernard, Wm. H.	Pvt.	C, 28th Iowa	127		1923 Mar 18	IA, 50th, 1924
Berner, Chas. H.			14		1923 Apr 6	IA, 50th, 1924
Berner, Chas. H.	Pvt.	B, 1st U.S. (?)	14		1923 Apr 6	IA, 49th, 1923
Bernhard, Jacob		A, 48th Ill. (died of heart failure)	28	76	1909 Oct 12	NE, 34th, 1910
Bernholtz, B.	Pvt.	C, 8th Iowa	44		1905 Nov 13	IA, 32nd, 1906
Bernst, John		G, 4th Mo. Inf. (died at National Home)	380		1895	KS, 15th, 1896
Bero, Ed		B, 8th Kans.	64		1916 Oct 19	KS, 36th, 1917
Berringer, Chas.	Pvt.	C, 5th Wis. Inf.	164		1918 Sep 22	IA, 45th, 1919
Berry, A.P.		13th Iowa Inf.	434		1908 Apr 12	IA, 35th, 1909
Berry, A.W.		B, 11th Penn.	250		1893 Feb 19	KS, 13th, 1894
Berry, Allen J.		K, 5th Ohio	250		1923 Sep 18	KS, 43rd, 1924
Berry, Andrew	Pvt.	A, 14th Iowa Inf.	227	44	1892 Feb 20	IA, 18th, 1892
Berry, C.H.		D, 156th Ill.	96		1910 Nov 7	KS, 30th, 1911
Berry, C.L.		A, 118th Ill.	83		1927 Oct 10	KS, 47th, 1928
Berry, Charles C.		B, 49th Ohio	1		1904 Jul 16	KS, 24th, 1905
Berry, David			25		1928 Jul 31	NE, 53rd, 1929
Berry, David R.		F, 4th Kans. Inf. (died of old age)	84		1909 May 8	NE, 34th, 1910
Berry, F.M.		C, 85th Ill. Inf.	158		1916 Feb 25	KS, 36th, 1917
Berry, Isaac	Pvt.	A, 4th Iowa Inf.	100		1924 Jan 9	IA, 51st, 1925
Berry, J.W.	Pvt.	A, 35th Iowa Inf.	231		1922 Mar 29	IA, 49th, 1923
Berry, James L.	Pvt.	A, 35th Iowa Inf.	231		1902 Oct 23	IA, 29th, 1903

Name	Rank	Company, Regiment or Ship	Post*	Age	Death Date†	Journal
Berry, John	Pvt.	D, 16th Iowa Inf.	370	70	1894 Jun 10	IA, 21st, 1895
Berry, John		D, 151st Ind.	84		1909 Mar 26	KS, 29th, 1910
Berry, John H.		I, 90th Ohio	7		1932 Oct 14	NE, 57th, 1933
Berry, Joseph		H, 3rd Ohio Vol. Inf.	4		1915 Feb 22	KS, 35th, 1916
Berry, Samuel		E, 2nd Kans. Inf.	422		1899 Feb 2	KS, 19th, 1900
Berry, Samuel M.		F, 133rd Ill. Inf.	57		1886	KS, 6th, 1887
Berry, Tho.	Corp.	G, 11th Penn. Inf.	231		1906 Nov 1	IA, 33rd, 1907
Berryhill, John	Pvt.		452	86	1931 Oct 10	IA, 58th, 1932
Berryhill, L.S.	2nd Lieut.	C, 3rd Iowa Cav.	2		1923 Dec 18	IA, 50th, 1924
Berstler, S.J.	Pvt.	I, 38th Iowa Inf.	170		1910 May 15	IA, 37th, 1911
Bert, Soloman	Pvt.	F, 46th —	369		1905 Jun 8	IA, 32nd, 1906
Bertram, Eli S.		Berry's Co., Mo. Cav.	7		1909 Dec 10	KS, 29th, 1910
Bertram, Moses		C, 57th Ill.	132		1902 Oct 28	KS, 22nd, 1903
Bertram, Shelby S.	Corp.	E, 9th Ky. Inf. (at large)	59	97	1941 Mar 15	IA, 67th, 1941
Bertrand, C.P.		C, 18th Ohio Inf.	356		1918 Dec 5	KS, 38th, 1919
Bertsler, Joseph Y.	Sergt.	I, 13th Iowa Vet. Vol. Inf.	170		1902 Jan 17	IA, 28th, 1902
Bertwick, Thomas		D, 8th Kans.	175		1923 Mar 18	KS, 43rd, 1924
Besack, A.J.	Pvt.	C, 88th Ind. Inf.	16		1911 Jan 7	IA, 37th, 1911
Bess, W.H.	Pvt.	D, 17th Iowa Inf.	7		1925 Jul 1	IA, 52nd, 1926
Besser, John	Pvt.	F, 8th Iowa Inf.	167	91	1931 Nov 29	IA, 58th, 1932
Besser, John	Pvt.	F, 8th Iowa Inf.	167		1930 Nov 29	IA, 57th, 1931
Bessey, George A.	Pvt.	F, 17th Iowa	122		1899	IA, 26th, 1900
Best, B.	Pvt.	E, 1st Wis. Inf.	125		1911 Apr 29	IA, 38th, 1912
Best, Campbell H.	Pvt.	B, 11th Iowa Inf.	364		1913 Apr 25	IA, 40th, 1914
Best, John	Pvt.	A, 19th Inf.	519		1906 Feb 6	IA, 33rd, 1907
Best, John	Pvt.	A, 19th Iowa Inf.	268		1906 Feb 6	IA, 33rd, 1907
Best, John H.		A, 13th Kans. Inf.	380		1901 May 21	KS, 21st, 1902
Best, W.K.		C, 106th N.Y.	24		1918 Sep 10	KS, 38th, 1919
Bestivick, James		G, 13th Kans.	175		1897 Oct 4	KS, 17th, 1898
Beswick, A.W.		B, 46th Ill.	85		1915 Apr 15	KS, 35th, 1916
Beswick, J.C.		E, 17th Ill. Inf. B, 102nd Ill. Inf. (died of heart failure)	1	69	1891[1901?] Jun	NE, 26th, 1902
Beswick, William		E, 17th Ill. (died of old age)	109	80	1922 Dec 31	NE, 47th, 1923
Beth, William		A & E, 6th Kans. Cav.	32		1925 Oct 12	KS, 45th, 1926
Bethard, John		A, 10th Ill.	119		1905 Sep 30	KS, 25th, 1906
Bethards, J.W.	Pvt.	K, 88th Ohio Inf.	80		1915	IA, 42nd, 1916
Bethards, John	Pvt.	C, 8th Cav.	251		1918 Dec 30	IA, 45th, 1919
Bethel, James		D, 43rd Ind.	85		1925 Aug 20	KS, 45th, 1926
Bethke, Julius		G, 7th Wis. Inf.		88	1935 Jan 15	IA, 62nd, 1936
Bettersor, John		D, 7th Ill. Cav.	209		1922 Jun 9	KS, 42nd, 1923
Betterton, G.R.		D, 7th Ill. Cav.	209		1912 Apr 19	KS, 32nd, 1913
Bettis, A.		L, 11th Ill.	512	91	1934 Feb 14	IA, 61st, 1935
Betts, John S.		M, 11th Kans. Cav.	250		1925 Feb 9	KS, 45th, 1926
Betts, Martin A.	Pvt.	D, 6th Iowa Cav.	216		1912 Mar 28	IA, 39th, 1913
Bettys, Harry			288		1922	KS, 42nd, 1923
Betz, J.B.	Lieut.	C, 8th Iowa	145		1922 Jul 5	IA, 49th, 1923
Betzer, Aaron R.	Pvt.	H, 34th Iowa Inf.	228		1900 Dec 2	IA, 27th, 1901
Betzhold, John	Pvt.	C, 35th Iowa	231		1903-1904	IA, 30th, 1904
Beurnett, D.M.	Pvt.	G, 151st N.Y. Inf.	149		1925 Feb 5	IA, 52nd, 1926
Beute, Wm.	Pvt.	F, 8th Iowa Cav.	184		1910 Apr 26	IA, 37th, 1911
Bevelle, H.J.		G, 23rd Mo.	1		1910 Jun 15	KS, 30th, 1911
Beveman, S.O.		K, 4th Iowa	93		1904 Mar 25	KS, 24th, 1905
Bevens, S.		Ohio Hvy. Art. (died of demented)	35	82	1922 Dec 21	NE, 47th, 1923
Bever, A.	Pvt.	C, 3rd Mich.	45		1929 Sep 27	IA, 56th, 1930
Bever, Russell B.	Pvt.	123rd Ohio Inf. (not a G.A.R. member)		97	1941 Mar 12	IA, 67th, 1941
Beverage, Samuel	Pvt.	B, 2nd Ohio Art.	271		1931 Mar 16	IA, 58th, 1932
Beveridge, Jacob		A, 60th Ohio	9		1923 Dec 23	KS, 43rd, 1924
Beveridge, James	Pvt.	A, 13th Wis. Inf.	216	55	1897 Feb 23	IA, 23rd, 1897
Beverly, D.C.		G, 52nd Ill.	35		1926 Oct	KS, 46th, 1927
Bevier, H.K.		D, 72nd N.Y. Inf.	11		1938 May 15	NE, 63rd, 1939
Bevington, P.A.	Pvt.	B, 5th Ill. Cav.	39		1917 Jan 14	IA, 44th, 1918
Beyan, C.A.	Capt.	I, 207th Penn. Inf.	107	61	1890 Sep 29	IA, 17th, 1891

Name	Rank	Company, Regiment or Ship	Post*	Age	Death Date†	Journal
Beyer, Anthony	Pvt.	E, 5th Iowa Cav.	78		1918 Feb 10	IA, 45th, 1919
Beyer, Christian C.	Pvt.	I, 8th Calif. Inf.	78	63	1889 Jun 26	IA, 16th, 1890
Beyer, Louis		B, 66th Ill. Inf.	17		prior to 1891	KS, 11th, 1892
Beymer, F.F.		7th Ind. Vol. Bat	51		1914 Nov 4	KS, 34th, 1915
Beymer, G.N.			116		1916 Oct 11	IA, 43rd, 1917
Bianchi, M.		I, 2nd U.S. Art. I, 19th V.R.C. Art. (died of cancer of stomach)	55		1894 Oct 1	NE, 19th, 1895
Bias, Edward		G, 36th Ind.	256		1919 Jul 9	KS, 39th, 1920
Bibbins, W.	Capt.	M, 5th Minn. Cav.	12	53	1896 Jul 7	IA, 23rd, 1897
Bice, Isaac	Pvt.	K, 6th Iowa Inf.	181		1927 Apr	IA, 54th, 1928
Bick, John		B, 1st Iowa Inf. G, 5th Mo. Cav. (died of cancer)	32	67	1908 Feb 17	NE, 33rd, 1909
Bick, Wm.		B, 1st Iowa Inf.	318	79	1916 Feb 18	NE, 41st, 1917
Bickel, D.		A, 3rd V.R.C.	1		1897 Jul 17	KS, 17th, 1898
Bickel, Henry		142nd Penn.	5		1912	KS, 32nd, 1913
Bicken, Jerry	Pvt.	B, —	25		1923 Dec 25	IA, 50th, 1924
Bickert, J.		E, 8th N.Y. Inf. (died of Bright's disease)	95	72	1903 Jan 10	NE, 28th, 1904
Bickett, A.H.	Pvt.	A, 138th Ill. Inf.	96	86	1932 Jul 15	IA, 59th, 1933
Bickford, A.		E, 14th Ill. Inf.	31		1914 Nov 9	KS, 34th, 1915
Bickford, Chas. C.	Pvt.	D, 15th Iowa Inf.	230		1909 Aug 7	IA, 36th, 1910
Bickford, E.	Pvt.	D, 2nd Iowa Inf.	492		1908 Apr 2	IA, 35th, 1909
Bickford, O.	Sergt.	M, 9th N.Y. Hvy. Art.	440		1920 Apr 13	IA, 47th, 1921
Bicklen, L.H.	Pvt.	F, 5th Iowa Cav.	5	49	1887 Oct 8	IA, 14th, 1888
Bickley, T.R.	Pvt.	G, —	69		1927 May 23	IA, 54th, 1928
Bicknell, John		D, 20th N.Y. Cav. (died of asthma)	43		1894 Mar 10	NE, 19th, 1895
Bicknell, M.S.	Pvt.	I, 13th Ind.	263		1921 Apr 3	IA, 48th, 1922
Bicknell, O.P.		B, 22nd Wis. Inf.	127		1891 Aug 14	KS, 11th, 1892
Biddinger, Philip	Pvt.		519		1906 Feb	IA, 33rd, 1907
Bidlake, James	Pvt.	K, 16th Iowa Inf.	18		1928 Jul 19	IA, 55th, 1929
Bidwell, A.J.		F, 153rd Ind.	203		1916 Apr 4	KS, 36th, 1917
Bidwell, B.	Pvt.	K, 1st Minn. Vol. Inf.	219	73	1898 Dec 9	IA, 25th, 1899
Bidwell, F.L.	Pvt.	C, 25th Wis. Inf.	219		1928	IA, 55th, 1929
Bidwell, Lewis N.		I, 144th Ill. Inf.	112		1892 Nov 15	NE, 17th, 1893
Bidwell, William		B, 28th Wis. (Post 336)	167		1905 Jul 22	KS, 25th, 1906
Bidwell, William T.		B, 38th Wis.	336		1905 Jul 22	KS, 25th, 1906
Biechtel, F.M.		D, 112th Ill.	46		1928 Jan 12	KS, 48th, 1929
Bieghler, H.			347		1904 Apr 25	IA, 30th, 1904
Bielly, E.M.	Pvt.	F, 28th Iowa Inf.	343	62	1897 Feb 5	IA, 24th, 1898
Bierce, S.B.		F, 13th Mich. Inf.	13		1928 Oct 4	NE, 53rd, 1929
Bierley, James F.		G, 13th Penn.	6		1923 May 21	KS, 43rd, 1924
Bierring, Jappe	Paymaster	U.S.N., Inf.	1		1910 Aug 26	IA, 37th, 1911
Biers, Fred			44		1924	IA, 51st, 1925
Bies, Joseph		H, 3rd Ill. Cav.	302		1887 Oct 19	KS, 7th, 1888
Bigbee, J.E.		8th Iowa Cav.	145		1906 Jun 5	IA, 33rd, 1907
Bigbee, W.S.		C, 32nd Ohio	116		1916 Feb 5	KS, 36th, 1917
Bigelow, D.A.	Lieut.	A, 124th Ill. Inf.	30	50	1890 Mar 9	IA, 16th, 1890
Bigelow, Elverton	Pvt.	K, 20th Wis. Inf.	97	51	1893 Nov 23	IA, 20th, 1894
Bigelow, R.C.		C, 15th Vt. Inf. (died of dropsy)	73	64	1905 Jul 4	NE, 30th, 1906
Bigger, David		A, 33rd Ill.	318		1915 Feb 6	NE, 40th, 1916
Bigger, L.A.		B, 111th N.Y.	17		1913 Jan 14	KS, 33rd, 1914
Biggs, A.T.		G, 18th Ohio 2nd West Va. Cav.	178		1913 Aug 21	KS, 33rd, 1914
Biggs, J.T.			13		1890 Jun 18	NE, 15th, 1891
Biggs, Washington A.	Pvt.	G, 55th Ill. Inf.	58		1919 Nov 20	IA, 46th, 1920
Bigham, James H.		E, 1st Ill. Inf.	272		1901 Dec 1	KS, 21st, 1902
Bigham, Joseph		A, 3rd Tenn. Cav.	38		1913 Jan 10	KS, 32nd, 1913
Bigham, Robt.		D, 48th Iowa Inf.	69		1922 Apr 14	IA, 49th, 1923
Bigler, John		K, 88th Ill. Inf.	11	68	1908 Jan 29	NE, 33rd, 1909
Bigler, Theodore	Pvt.	E, 1st Iowa Cav.	20		1915 Oct	IA, 42nd, 1916
Bigley, J.L.	Sergt.	C, 8th Iowa Inf.	296		1912 Jun 6	IA, 39th, 1913
Biglow, R.R.	Pvt.	D, 7th Ind. Cav.	74		1917 Mar 6	IA, 44th, 1918

Name	Rank	Company, Regiment or Ship	Post*	Age	Death Date†	Journal
Biglowe, T.A.H.	Musician	45th Ill. Inf.	452		1906 Sep	IA, 33rd, 1907
Bigsby, E.			35		1905 Jul 7	NE, 30th, 1906
Bigsby, E.			35		1905 Jul 2	NE, 37th, 1913
Bilbee, A.P.		I, 78th Ind.	311		1885	KS, 5th, 1886
Biles, Jos.	Pvt.	A, 1st Iowa Inf.	231		1919 Feb 28	IA, 46th, 1920
Bilkey, Joseph	Pvt.	A, 1st Iowa Inf.	231	66	1893 Mar 6	IA, 20th, 1894
Bill, Edwin J.		H & C, 7th Wis. Inf. & 9th Wis. Cav.	354	77	1906 Mar 28	NE, 31st, 1907
Billheimer, H.	Pvt.	E, 32nd Iowa	220		1899 Jun 15	IA, 26th, 1900
Billick, George W.	Pvt.	C, 134th Ill. Inf.	321	93	1939 Jul 28	IA, 65th, 1939
Billick, Josiah		A, 3rd Iowa	36		1906 Jan 17	KS, 26th, 1907
Billig, Daniel		G, 145th Penn.	251		1916 Jan 1	KS, 36th, 1917
Billings, Abraham		K, 12th Iowa Inf. (died of complication)	354	78	1905 Nov 30	NE, 30th, 1906
Billings, Abram		K, 12th Iowa Inf. (died of complication of diseases at Soldiers & Sailors Home, Grand Island; buried in Home Cemetery)	27	78	1905 Nov 30	NE, 30th, 1906
Billings, B.A.	Pvt.	B, 46th Iowa Inf.	132		1914 Sep	IA, 41st, 1915
Billings, C.			342		1899	IA, 26th, 1900
Billings, C.A.	Pvt.	B, 43rd Wis. Inf.	342		1899 Apr 19	IA, 26th, 1900
Billings, C.O.	Pvt.	K, 42nd Wis. Inf.	222		1910	IA, 37th, 1911
Billings, J.		F, 5th Penn. Cav.	262	51	1896 Apr 24	NE, 21st, 1897
Billings, J.M.			236		1925	IA, 52nd, 1926
Billings, John		D, 105th Ill. (died of accident)	154		1905[1904?] Mar	NE, 29th, 1905
Billings, Levi	Pvt.	B, 7th Iowa Cav.	337		1927 Mar 3	IA, 54th, 1928
Billings, Luthur B.			90		1911 1st term	IA, 38th, 1912
Billings, R.	Pvt.	A, 16th Wis. Inf.	154	68	1892 Feb 3	IA, 19th, 1893
Billingsley, L.W.		I, 7th & 4th Ind.	25	75	1916 Feb 19	NE, 41st, 1917
Billiter, William T.		A, 1st Neb. Cav. (born in Indiana; died at Soldiers & Sailors Home Hospital, Burkett; buried at Home Cemetery)		66	1906 Oct 26	NE, 31st, 1907
Bills, C.C.		K, 24th Iowa	25		1913 Jan 27	NE, 38th, 1914
Billsland, Boriah		D, 65th Ind.	53		1910 Dec 13	KS, 30th, 1911
Bilyea, Jesse		E, 130th Ill. Vol. Inf. (died of heart failure)	36	71	1913 Feb 17	NE, 37th, 1913
Binegar, Alfred	Pvt.	H, 27th Ohio Inf.	330		1889 Feb 1	IA, 15th, 1889
Binegar, Geo. W.		C, 28th Iowa Inf.	127		1916 May 21	IA, 43rd, 1917
Binford, Isaac B.	Pvt.	M, 9th Iowa Cav.	137		1904 Nov 9	IA, 31st, 1905
Bing, Charles H.		D & E, 56th Ohio	340		1916 Sep 6	KS, 36th, 1917
Bing, J.R.		H, 29th Mo. (died of dropsy)	25	72	1900 Jan 14	NE, 25th, 1901
Bingaman, Wm.	Pvt.	D, 84th Penn. Inf.	98		1927 Feb 28	IA, 54th, 1928
Bingham, A.J., see Bringham, A.J.						
Bingham, Daniel		C, 46th Iowa	104		1918 Aug 29	KS, 38th, 1919
Bingham, Geo.		C, 106th Ill.	123		1900 Aug 15	KS, 20th, 1901
Bingham, Mathias		G, 161st Ohio Inf. (at large)			1935 Sep	IA, 62nd, 1936
Bingham, S.L.J.		F, 8th Mich. Inf. (died at Nickerson; buried at Wild Meade Cemetery)	83		1894 May 15	KS, 14th, 1895
Binkley, C.P.		B, 11th Penn. Cav.	7		1938 Mar 24	NE, 63rd, 1939
Binney, J.H.		H, 57th Mass. Inf.	147		1901 Mar	NE, 26th, 1902
Birch, T.C.	Pvt.	D, 94th Ill.	322		1924 Apr 22	IA, 51st, 1925
Birch, William	Pvt.	H, 3rd Iowa Cav.	332		1897 Jun 8	IA, 24th, 1898
Birchard, A.T.	Pvt.	32nd Iowa Inf.	94		1913	IA, 40th, 1914
Birchard, C.H.	Pvt.	E, 83rd Penn. Inf.	235	94	1931 Oct 13	IA, 58th, 1932
Bird, C.M.	Sergt.	E, 1st Iowa Cav.	211		1907 Jun 17	IA, 35th, 1909
Bird, Chas. S.	Pvt.	H, 8th Ill. Cav.	231		1915 Jan 15	IA, 42nd, 1916
Bird, E.J.	Pvt.	37th N.Y.	138		1899	NE, 24th, 1900
Bird, Ed.			44		1920	NE, 45th, 1921
Bird, Gullick J.	Pvt.	E, 18th Wis. Inf.	168		1890 Feb 5	IA, 16th, 1890
Bird, H.T.	Hosp. Stew.	8th Iowa Cav.	20		1926 Jul 9	IA, 53rd, 1927
Bird, Jasper N.		E, 9th Kans.	26		1905	KS, 25th, 1906
Bird, P.E.	Pvt.	B, 4th Iowa Inf.	358		1911 Oct 12	IA, 38th, 1912
Bird, R.	Pvt.	B, 19th Iowa Inf.	42		1921 May 10	IA, 48th, 1922
Bird, R.L.	Pvt.	E, 12th Iowa Inf.	452		1915	IA, 42nd, 1916
Bird, Rose			142		1925 Aug 24	KS, 45th, 1926
Bird, T.J.		K, 53rd Ill. (died of consumption)	24	77	1921 Aug 2	NE, 46th, 1922

*See Appendix A, B or C for roster of post names and locations.
†See Introduction for note regarding recording of death date.

Name	Rank	Company, Regiment or Ship	Post*	Age	Death Date†	Journal
Bird, Thomas C.		C, 31st Iowa	158		1911 Aug 6	KS, 31st, 1912
Bird, W.F.		A, 68th Ind.	139		1922 Jul 19	KS, 42nd, 1923
Bird, W.K.	Pvt.	D, 2nd Iowa Inf.	12		1897 Mar 14	IA, 24th, 1898
Birdsall, Geo. B.	Pvt.	H, 15th Ill. Inf.	68		1929 Jan 24	IA, 56th, 1930
Birdsall, Horatio L.		B, 3rd Iowa Cav.	380		1891 Nov 29	KS, 11th, 1892
Birdsell, C.H.	Pvt.	C, 15th Ill. Inf.	206		1912 Aug 8	IA, 39th, 1913
Birdsell, Jas.	Corp.	K, 1st Minn. Inf.	168		1912 Feb 15	IA, 39th, 1913
Birdyl, F.H.	Pvt.	D, 26th Iowa	94		1924 Jun 30	IA, 51st, 1925
Birk, Adam			110		1908	IA, 35th, 1909
Birkinholt, P.	Pvt.	D, 7th Iowa Cav.	84		1933 Jan 2	IA, 60th, 1934
Birney, F.	Pvt.	G, 27th Iowa Inf.	132		1911	IA, 38th, 1912
Birt, C.F.		H, 142nd Penn.	67		1905	KS, 25th, 1906
Birt, J.M.		B, 99th Ill.	81		1930 Jan 26	KS, 50th, 1931
Bisbe, Thaddeus J.		D, 114th N.Y. Inf. (died of paralysis)	136		1894 Jul 3	NE, 19th, 1895
Bisby, Horace J.		D, 1st N.Y. Cav.	289		1902	KS, 22nd, 1903
Bisby, J.E.		K, 92nd Ill.	280		1898 Dec 27	KS, 18th, 1899
Bisell, F.O.	Sergt.	I, 26th Iowa Inf.	36		1908	IA, 35th, 1909
Bish, Lewis		E, 13th Ill. Inf. (at large)		92	1936 Jul 30	IA, 63rd, 1937
Bish, W.G.	Pvt.	E, 15th Penn.	497		1907 Aug 19	IA, 34th, 1908
Bishard, Levi		E, 14th Kans. Cav.	32		1916 Nov 9	KS, 36th, 1917
Bishard, Thomas		A, 6th Kans. Cav.	32		1912 Sep 6	KS, 32nd, 1913
Bishob, J.F.	Lieut.	B, 5th Minn. Inf.	72		1917 May	IA, 44th, 1918
Bishop, A.J.		E, 6th Ohio	47		1909 Feb 16	KS, 29th, 1910
Bishop, Albert			212		1928	IA, 55th, 1929
Bishop, Albert	Pvt.	C, 53rd Wis. Inf.		93	1940 Mar 28	IA, 66th, 1940
Bishop, C.H.		H, 140th Ill. Inf. (died of old age)	1	76	1924 Mar 5	NE, 49th, 1925
Bishop, D.J.	Pvt.	D, Ill. Inf.	31		1923 Nov	IA, 50th, 1924
Bishop, D.W.	Pvt.	M, 4th Ill. Inf.	2		1927 Nov 28	IA, 54th, 1928
Bishop, Frank H.		A, 148th Ill. (died of cancer)	7	53	1897 Jun 21	NE, 22nd, 1898
Bishop, George		D, 113th Ill. Inf. (died of liver disease)	98	71	1895 Jun 26	NE, 20th, 1896
Bishop, H.C.		F, 97th N.Y. Inf. (died of heart failure)	24	62	1896 Oct 20	NE, 21st, 1897
Bishop, Henry	Pvt.	I, 23rd Iowa Inf.	139		1908 Dec 4	IA, 35th, 1909
Bishop, Hiram		I, 14th Vt.	25		1913 Apr 17	NE, 38th, 1914
Bishop, J.		D, 146th Ohio	53		1918 Sep 21	KS, 38th, 1919
Bishop, J.B.	Corp.	E, 79th Ind.	57		1926 Sep	IA, 53rd, 1927
Bishop, J.F.	Capt.	H, 4th Iowa Inf.	12		1912 Mar 20	IA, 39th, 1913
Bishop, J.V.	Pvt.	D, 14th Iowa Inf.	270		1903 Dec 9	IA, 30th, 1904
Bishop, James		E, 138th Ill. Inf. (born in Canada; died in Hebron, Neb.)	17		1883 Dec 14	NE, 8th, 1884
Bishop, James S.	Pvt.	K, 25th Iowa Inf.	384		1901 Nov 24	IA, 28th, 1902
Bishop, John		not a member of post named, but buried by said post	8		1897	KS, 17th, 1898
Bishop, N.J.	Pvt.	C, 184th N.Y. Inf.	81		1928 Mar 25	IA, 55th, 1929
Bishop, P.W.	Chaplain	37th Ill. Inf.	30		1918 Jan 10	IA, 45th, 1919
Bishop, R.H.		G, 15th Kans. Inf.	465		1901 Sep 19	KS, 21st, 1902
Bishop, Stephen A.	Capt.	I, 2nd Iowa Cav.	1	77	1893 Dec 5	IA, 20th, 1894
Bishop, W.H.		G, 67th Ill.	25		1914 Apr 1	KS, 34th, 1915
Bishop, W.O.		K, 97th Ind.	12		1930 Mar 7	KS, 50th, 1931
Bishop, Wm.		B, 48th Wis. Inf.	262	88	1915 Apr	NE, 39th, 1915
Bishopp, Peter	Pvt.	E, 15th Iowa Cav.	69		1903-1904	IA, 30th, 1904
Bisley, M.G.		E, 58th Ind.	42		1923 Feb 6	KS, 43rd, 1924
Bisque, T.J.	Pvt.	G, 57th Ill. Inf.	5		1930 Apr 21	IA, 57th, 1931
Bissel, R.	Pvt.	I, 17th Ill. Cav.	302		1926 Jul 6	IA, 53rd, 1927
Bissell, F.O., see Bisell, F.O.						
Bissell, Hiram	Lieut.	E, 111th Penn. Inf.	24		1930 May	IA, 57th, 1931
Bissell, J.F.	Pvt.	D, 84th Ill. Inf.	69		1908 Feb 28	IA, 35th, 1909
Bissell, W.P.			190		1911 Mar 29	IA, 38th, 1912
Bissell, William		M, 12th Ind.	77		1897 Nov 28	KS, 17th, 1898
Bissinger, Mathias	Pvt.	K, 1st Mo. Inf.	153		1906 Jun 17	IA, 33rd, 1907
Bisson, E.R.		D, 45th Ill. A, 6th Hancock V.C.	9		1931 Jan 3	NE, 56th, 1932
Bissonett, Henry	Pvt.	G, 1st Wis. Hvy. Art.	3	64	1894	IA, 20th, 1894

Name	Rank	Company, Regiment or Ship	Post*	Age	Death Date†	Journal
Biter, Donatus		C, 54th Penn.	363		1913 Sep 12	KS, 33rd, 1914
Bitler, J.J.		F, 39th Mo.	8		1914 Sep 26	KS, 34th, 1915
Bitterly, August		A, 149th N.Y.	12		1896 Nov 11	KS, 16th, 1897
Bittinger, J.M.	Pvt.	I, 94th Ill. Inf.	12		1906 Apr 26	IA, 33rd, 1907
Bittles, William		K, 47th Mass.	1		1897 Nov 17	KS, 17th, 1898
Bittman, Val		F, 2nd Kans. Cav.	38		1911 Jun 12	KS, 31st, 1912
Bitts, James M.		F, 148th Ill.	18		1924 Sep 19	KS, 44th, 1925
Bitzer, Gal	Pvt.	A, 1st Iowa Inf.	231		1914 May 24	IA, 41st, 1915
Bius, R.		D, 43rd Mo.	388		1927 Sep 21	KS, 47th, 1928
Biven, J.B.	Pvt.	E, 36th Iowa Inf.	55		1916 Oct 4	IA, 43rd, 1917
Bivens, James	Pvt. Chief Bugler	H, 138th N.Y. 9th N.Y. Hvy. Art. (died of consumption)	76	47	1884 Apr 26	NE, 9th, 1885
Bivens, John, see Civens, John						
Bivens, William		C, 1st Ohio Lt. Art.	35		1940 Feb 2	NE, 65th, 1941
Bivins, Wm.		K, 7th Ill. Cav. (died of old age)	76	82	1918 Sep 10	NE, 43rd, 1919
Bixby, B.F.	Pvt.	E, 47th Iowa Vols.	408		1914 Nov 21	IA, 41st, 1915
Bixby, D.F.	Pvt.	F, 46th Ill. Inf.	329		1918 Sep 15	IA, 45th, 1919
Bixby, Jos. C.		B, 150th Ohio	7		1928 Dec 18	NE, 53rd, 1929
Bixby, L.L.	Pvt.	D, 10th Vt. Inf.	365		1905 Dec 2	IA, 32nd, 1906
Bixby, Levi	Pvt.	F, 74th Ill. Inf.	91		1923 Dec 29	IA, 50th, 1924
Bixby, Wm.	Pvt.	D, 23rd N.Y. Inf.	98		1917 Nov 3	IA, 44th, 1918
Bixler, A.B.		E, 11th Kans. Cav.	18		1921 Sep 16	KS, 41st, 1922
Bixler, Andrew J.		C, 71st Ohio	25		1923 Dec 1	KS, 43rd, 1924
Bixler, Frederick		K, 22nd Mo. Inf.	153		1909	KS, 29th, 1910
Bixler, Samuel		G, 47th Ill. Inf. (died of hardening of arteries)	82	86	1919	NE, 44th, 1920
Blacheart, George		F, 17th Iowa Inf. (died of gangrene, both feet)	54	81	1924 Aug 15	NE, 49th, 1925
Black, A.	Hosp. Stew.	E, 10th Minn.	332		1899 Oct 18	IA, 26th, 1900
Black, A.H.		F, 3rd Penn. Art.	142		1922 Sep 3	KS, 42nd, 1923
Black, A.M.		G, 36th Ind. (died of age)	18	77	1919 Mar 15	NE, 44th, 1920
Black, Aaron	Musician	35th Ind. Inf.	66		1900 Jun 22	KS, 20th, 1901
Black, Andrew	Pvt.	B, 83rd Ill. Inf.		92	1935 Nov 29	IA, 65th, 1939
Black, C.			265		1923	KS, 43rd, 1924
Black, Calvin			5		1909	KS, 29th, 1910
Black, E.F.	Pvt.		122		1926	IA, 53rd, 1927
Black, G.W., see Bleck, G.W.						
Black, George		I, 118th Ohio	68		1920 Jun 2	KS, 40th, 1921
Black, J.C.	Pvt.	E, 47th Ill. Inf.	11		1899 Nov	IA, 26th, 1900
Black, J.C.	Pvt.	A, 6th Iowa Inf.	500		1919 Jun 30	IA, 46th, 1920
Black, J.C.			72		1883	KS, 3rd, 1884
Black, J.C.			72		1884	KS, 4th, 1885
Black, J.H.		M, 16th Ky. Cav.	123		1913 Nov 11	KS, 33rd, 1914
Black, J.M.	Pvt.	B, 152nd Ill. Inf.	11	58	1892 Oct 26	IA, 19th, 1893
Black, J.P.		F, 135th Ind.	36		1919 Jul 15	KS, 39th, 1920
Black, James D.		D, 14th West Va.	44		1916 Jun 16	KS, 36th, 1917
Black, John		11th Ind.	83		1916 May 16	KS, 36th, 1917
Black, Nirum		A, 105th Ill. Inf.	158		1902 Sep 24	KS, 22nd, 1903
Black, Richard S.		G, 62nd Ill. (died of pneumonia)	111	74	1920 Dec 23	NE, 45th, 1921
Black, S.E.		F, 135th Ill.	66		1916 Sep 27	KS, 36th, 1917
Black, Thomas	Pvt.	F, 11th Iowa Inf.	484	52	1896 May 6	IA, 23rd, 1897
Black, Thomas D.		F, 21st Penn. Cav. (died of old age)	4	76	1910 Jul 1	NE, 35th, 1911
Black, Thomas J.		I, 1st Ohio Cav. (died at Topeka)	116		1895 Oct 3	KS, 15th, 1896
Black, W.C.		C, 8th Kans.	123		1930 May 25	KS, 50th, 1931
Black, W.H.H.		I, 42nd Ind. (died of heart failure)	35	82	1922 Jun 1	NE, 47th, 1923
Black, W.W.		I, 17th Kans.	1		1927 Dec 5	KS, 47th, 1928
Black, William P.	Corp.	I, 40th Iowa Inf.	40		1912 Apr 19	IA, 39th, 1913
Black, Wm. A.		died of general debility	197	72	1917 Mar 14	NE, 42nd, 1918
Blackburn, Abner R.		K, 107th Ohio Inf. (died at Anthony, Kans.; buried at Forest Park Cemetery)	61		1894 Nov 3	KS, 14th, 1895
Blackburn, Andrew		G, 33rd Wis.	90		1921 Mar	KS, 41st, 1922
Blackburn, David	Pvt.	H, 142nd Ohio Vols.	12		1924 Jun 9	IA, 51st, 1925

Name	Rank	Company, Regiment or Ship	Post*	Age	Death Date†	Journal
Blackburn, J.D.			3		1910	NE, 35th, 1911
Blackburn, Jno.		G, 104th Ill. Inf. (died of paralysis)	107	83	1902 Aug	NE, 27th, 1903
Blackledge, Chas.		A, 47th Ind. Inf.	14		1899 May 9	KS, 19th, 1900
Blackley, C.L.		D, 40th Wis.	100		1915 Apr 7	KS, 35th, 1916
Blackman, A.C.	Pvt.	H, 16th Iowa	30		1922 Jan 1	IA, 49th, 1923
Blackman, A.M.		C, 77th Ill.	25		1928 Jun 10	KS, 48th, 1929
Blackman, A.T.	Lieut.	H, 7th Ind. Cav.	93		1916 Apr 5	IA, 43rd, 1917
Blackman, Emerson		D, 39th Ill.	3		1927 Apr 7	KS, 47th, 1928
Blackman, J.	Pvt.	I, 52nd Ill. Inf.	58		1910 Jan 15	IA, 37th, 1911
Blackman, James	Pvt.	I, 52nd Ill. Inf.	58		1910 Jan 15	IA, 36th, 1910
Blackman, William		B, 2nd Ill.	50		1923 May 5	KS, 43rd, 1924
Blackmar, E.C.	Capt.	F, 15th Iowa Inf.	5		1900 Oct 15	IA, 27th, 1901
Blackmar, Wilmon W.		15th Penn. Cav. 1st Va. Vols. (see also Appendix D)			1905 Jul 16	KS, 25th, 1906
Blackmer, Wm. B.	Pvt.	A, 21st Mass. Inf.	359		1909 Jul 22	IA, 36th, 1910
Blackmore, A.C.	Lieut.	I, 64th Inf.	142		1915 Aug 30	IA, 42nd, 1916
Blackmore, A.R.		A, 83rd Ind. Inf.	180		1929	KS, 49th, 1930
Blackmore, J.			70		1890	NE, 15th, 1891
Blackster, H.	Pvt.	B, 28th Iowa Inf.	7		1927 Mar 24	IA, 54th, 1928
Blackston, Chas.	Pvt.	A, 1st Ind. Inf.	164		1906 Jun 16	IA, 33rd, 1907
Blackstone, B.B., see Blockstone, B.B.						
Blackstone, W.C.		N, 3rd Iowa Cav.	5		1892 Jul 23	KS, 12th, 1893
Blackwell, R.D.		H, 11th Ind. Cav.	97		1919 Dec 25	KS, 39th, 1920
Blackwood, B.W.	Pvt.	E, 40th Iowa Inf.	16		1922 Jun 11	IA, 49th, 1923
Blackwood, Geo. R.		F, 39th Mo.	142		1931 Oct 5	KS, 52nd, 1933
Blackwood, Geo. R.		F, 39th Mo.	142		1931 Oct 5	KS, 51st, 1932
Blades, F.S.		K, 3rd Mo. Cav.	14		1917 Dec 7	KS, 37th, 1918
Blades, J.E.			205		1912	IA, 39th, 1913
Blades, Wm.	Pvt.	B, 22nd Wis. Inf.	78	86	1933 Apr 12	IA, 60th, 1934
Blades, Wm.		B, 3rd Mo. Cav.	14		1898 Jul 28	KS, 18th, 1899
Blagett, H.H.	Pvt.	I, 42nd Wis. Inf.	3		1900 Feb	IA, 27th, 1901
Blagg, F.M.	Corp.	180th Battery	22		1906 Dec 13	IA, 33rd, 1907
Blain, James		G, 47th Ohio	25		1935 Jan 16	KS, 55th, 1936
Blain, Wm.	2nd Lieut.	A, 40th Iowa Inf.	49		1905 Oct 31	IA, 32nd, 1906
Blaine, F.M.		E, 5th Ky. Cav.	7		1924[1923?] Apr 28	NE, 48th, 1924
Blaine, L.G.	Pvt.	C, 69th Ill. Inf.	327		1905 Jun 30	IA, 32nd, 1906
Blaine, W.D.	Pvt.	B, 43rd Ohio	203		1923 Nov 23	IA, 50th, 1924
Blair, Alfred		F, 149th Penn.	354	82	1921 Jan 20	NE, 46th, 1922
Blair, Charles		F, 103rd N.Y.	378		1912 Apr 10	KS, 32nd, 1913
Blair, Chas. W.	Major	2nd Kans. Bat.	32		1899 Aug 20	KS, 19th, 1900
Blair, Cyrus		F, 11th Ill. Inf.	32	74	1909 Mar 13	NE, 34th, 1910
Blair, Frank	Pvt.	H, 14th Wis. Inf.	33		1912 Jul 24	IA, 39th, 1913
Blair, G.H.		F, 1st Ill. Lt. Art.	221		1914 Apr 30	KS, 34th, 1915
Blair, Geo. W.	Pvt.	D, 36th Iowa Inf.	40		1909 Apr 2	IA, 36th, 1910
Blair, J.A.	Pvt.	E, 141st Ill. Inf.	15		1926 Feb 22	IA, 53rd, 1927
Blair, J.A.		184th Ohio	20		1914 Mar 28	KS, 34th, 1915
Blair, John			64		1914	KS, 34th, 1915
Blair, John B.	Pvt.	H, 3rd Wis. Inf.	156		1912 Aug 22	IA, 39th, 1913
Blair, John H.		E, 24th Mass. (died of general debility)	25	70	1904 Jan 30	NE, 29th, 1905
Blair, Jonathan		C, 66th Ind. Inf. (died of heart trouble)	64	63	1897 Oct 9	NE, 22nd, 1898
Blair, L.V.	Pvt.	I, 48th Ohio Inf.	11		1918 Apr 29	IA, 45th, 1919
Blair, Levi C.	Pvt.	C, 5th Penn. Cav.	3		1900 Jan 6	IA, 27th, 1901
Blair, Samuel	Pvt.	A, 172nd Ohio Inf.	485	74	1895 Dec 7	IA, 22nd, 1896
Blair, Thomas	Sergt.	B, 10th N.J.	1		1915 Sep 15	KS, 35th, 1916
Blair, W.			55		1929 Dec 4	IA, 56th, 1930
Blair, W.C.		F, 3rd Mo. Cav.	8		1915 Oct 2	KS, 35th, 1916
Blair, William		I, 7th Iowa Cav.		89	1936 Mar 3	IA, 62nd, 1936
Blair, Wm.	Pvt.	C, 19th Iowa Inf.	108		1922 Feb 14	IA, 49th, 1923
Blair, Wm. G.	Pvt.	D, 61st Ill. Inf.	283		1918 Feb 17	IA, 45th, 1919
Blair, Wm. I.		I, 7th Iowa Cav.	197	89	1936 Mar 3	IA, 63rd, 1937
Blake, A.H.	Sergt.	F, 9th Vt.	190		1921 May 2	IA, 48th, 1922

Name	Rank	Company, Regiment or Ship	Post*	Age	Death Date†	Journal
Blake, G.W.	1st Lieut.	K, 2nd Iowa Inf.	18		1900 Dec 20	IA, 27th, 1901
Blake, Henry	Pvt.	A, 11th Wis. Inf.	23		1925 Nov 16	IA, 52nd, 1926
Blake, Hiram	Pvt.	H, 12th Ill. Inf.	30		1908 Jun 19	IA, 35th, 1909
Blake, John B.		C, 55th Ind.	17		1910 Jul 25	KS, 30th, 1911
Blake, T.W.		F, 3rd Iowa Cav. (died of old age)	26	81	1925 Mar 28	NE, 50th, 1926
Blake, W.W.		G, 3rd Wis. Inf.	81		1925 Aug 30	KS, 45th, 1926
Blakeley, E.C.	Pvt.	G, 5th Iowa Inf.	431		1907 Dec 2	IA, 34th, 1908
Blakely, A.J.	Lieut.		64		1922 Jan 30	IA, 49th, 1923
Blakeman, A.	Pvt.	A, 10th Wis. Inf.	86		1900-1901	IA, 27th, 1901
Blaker, B.F.		L, 20th Penn. Cav.	3		1917 Aug 27	KS, 37th, 1918
Blaker, H.W.		L, 20th Penn. Cav.	3		1924 Feb 4	KS, 44th, 1925
Blakeslee, Joseph	Pvt.	G, 31st Iowa Inf.	7		1916 Jul	IA, 43rd, 1917
Blakeslee, Thos., Dr.		F, 95th Ill.	145		1931 Jul 11	KS, 51st, 1932
Blakeslee, Thos., Dr.		F, 95th Ill.	145		1931 Jul 11	KS, 52nd, 1933
Blakesley, Abe.	Sergt.	T, 3rd Iowa Cav.	251		1924 Mar 8	IA, 51st, 1925
Blakesley, Peter		A, 50th Wis.	21		1930	NE, 55th, 1931
Blakesly, Abe	Sergt.	F, 3rd Iowa Cav.	251		1923 Mar 8	IA, 50th, 1924
Blakey, Henry F.		H, 3rd Ill. Cav.	158		1916 Mar 2	KS, 36th, 1917
Blan, Christian		I, 19th Ill.	117		1898 May 27	KS, 18th, 1899
Blanchard, D.A.			45		1916 Jun 23	IA, 43rd, 1917
Blanchard, Daniel M.		D, — Wis.	116		1922 Jan 8	KS, 42nd, 1923
Blanchard, Dave	Pvt.	A, 11th Iowa Inf.	88	54	1889 Oct 17	IA, 16th, 1890
Blanchard, E.L.		E, 3rd Wis. Inf. (died of paralysis)	32		1893 May	NE, 18th, 1894
Blanchard, F.F.		E, 2nd Vt.	113		1922 May 29	NE, 47th, 1923
Blanchard, Horatio		C, 6th Conn. Inf. B, 18th Conn. Inf.	9		1912 Nov 30	KS, 32nd, 1913
Blanchard, John	Pvt.	B, 21st Wis. Inf.	81		1911 Jul 29	IA, 38th, 1912
Blanchard, Joy N.			116		1909	KS, 29th, 1910
Blanchard, Luc. C.	Pvt.	K, 28th Iowa Inf.	40		1908 Mar 1	IA, 35th, 1909
Blanchard, M.V.		K, 7th Kans. Cav. (died of pneumonia)	38	72	1909 Dec 4	NE, 34th, 1910
Blanchard, M.V.		K, 7th Kans. Cav. (died of pneumonia)	38		1908 Dec 4	NE, 33rd, 1909
Blanchard, N.H.	Pvt.	A, 11th Vt. Inf.	440		1917 Jun 15	IA, 44th, 1918
Blanchard, Winfield S.	Pvt.	B, 97th N.Y. Inf.	16	56	1893 Feb 17	IA, 20th, 1894
Bland, J.O.D.			113		1908 Sep 2	KS, 28th, 1909
Blandin, J.F.		D, 9th Iowa Cav.	at large		1930	NE, 55th, 1931
Blaney, James R.		103rd Penn.	126		1902 May 21	KS, 22nd, 1903
Blank, Ernist	Pvt.	C, 6th Iowa Cav.	431		1901 May 15	IA, 28th, 1902
Blank, W.H.	Pvt.		64		1927	IA, 54th, 1928
Blankenship, H.	Pvt.	F, 9th Mich. Cav.	515		1897 May 17	IA, 24th, 1898
Blankenship, John S.		H, 4th Mo.	43		1899 Sep 27	KS, 19th, 1900
Blankenship, N.M.			464		1892 Feb 6	KS, 12th, 1893
Blanvelt, S.L.	Pvt.	D, 3rd Mich. Cav.	346		1899	NE, 24th, 1900
Blasiar, John		C, 154th N.Y.	14		1902 Jun 1	KS, 22nd, 1903
Blasier, Ed.	Lieut.	4th Iowa Cav.	403		1907 Dec 29	IA, 34th, 1908
Blasser, C.H.	Pvt.	E, 20th Iowa Inf.	55		1916 Apr 20	IA, 43rd, 1917
Blatherwick, J.H.	Musician	I, 51st Ill. Inf.	64		1913 Sep 17	IA, 40th, 1914
Blatner, H.	Pvt.	C, 72nd Ill. Inf.	101		1921 Feb 3	IA, 48th, 1922
Blazer, Jefferson		D, 78th Ohio Vol. Inf.	469		1915 Dec 14	KS, 35th, 1916
Bleakley, Joseph		D, 67th Ill.	6		1922 Feb 6	KS, 42nd, 1923
Bleck, G.W.	Sergt.		108		1914	IA, 41st, 1915
Bledsoe, Phillip			111		1913 Jul 20	KS, 33rd, 1914
Bledson, Wm.	Pvt.	C, 47th Ill. Inf.	309		1904 Apr 24	IA, 31st, 1905
Blender, Ed.		A, 55th Ill. (died of dropsy)	59	66	1908 Feb	NE, 33rd, 1909
Blenis, C.	Pvt.	A, 12th Ill. Inf.	68	62	1883[1888?] Mar 17	IA, 15th, 1889
Blesh, David		E, 15th Penn. (died of old age)	82	81	1919 Jun 29	NE, 45th, 1921
Blesh, Rudolph		H, 5th Ind. Cav.	493		1909 Jan 23	KS, 29th, 1910
Blessing, H.W.	Corp.	C, 16th Iowa Inf.	140	41	1886 Dec 8	IA, 14th, 1888
Blessing, H.W.	Corp.	C, 16th Iowa Inf.	140	43	1886 Dec 8	IA, 17th, 1891
Blessing, Henry	Pvt.	F, 13th Iowa Inf.	140		1909 Jul 13	IA, 36th, 1910
Blessing, J.G.	Pvt.	A, 61st Ohio Inf.	231		1910 Mar 25	IA, 37th, 1911
Blessing, Jerry	Pvt.	A, 35th Iowa Inf.	228		1912 Oct 11	IA, 39th, 1913
Blevins, John H.		E, 1st Tenn. Inf.	23		1936 Mar 30	NE, 61st, 1937

*See Appendix A, B or C for roster of post names and locations.
†See Introduction for note regarding recording of death date.

Name	Rank	Company, Regiment or Ship	Post*	Age	Death Date†	Journal
Bline, Charles W.		D, 21st Mo.	55	63	1907 May 12	NE, 32nd, 1908
Blinn, L.B.	Capt.	A, 100th Ohio Inf.	343		1923 Jan 12	IA, 50th, 1924
Blinn, L.B.	Capt.	A, 21st Ohio Inf.	343		1924	IA, 51st, 1925
Bliss, Alvin	Pvt.	C, 3rd Mass. Hvy. Art.	12		1897 Feb 6	IA, 23rd, 1897
Bliss, D.W.		B, 1st West Va.	59		1933 May 12	KS, 53rd, 1934
Bliss, Daniel		H, 10th Wis. Inf.	356		1900 Jun 29	KS, 20th, 1901
Bliss, David G.	1st Lieut.	F, 3rd Wis. I, 42nd Wis.	463		1893 Feb 23	KS, 13th, 1894
Bliss, H.H.		1st Kans. Bat.	18		1923 Jun 7	KS, 43rd, 1924
Bliss, J.L.		G, 4th Wis. (died at Atchison)	336		1895 Apr	KS, 15th, 1896
Bliss, J.V.	Pvt.	D, 78th N.Y.	57		1899 Jul 1	IA, 26th, 1900
Bliss, Jonathon			236		1915	IA, 42nd, 1916
Bliss, Joseph F.		D, 17th Kans.	155		1896 May 7	KS, 16th, 1897
Bliss, M.P.		died of old age	82		1886	NE, 11th, 1887
Bliss, Samuel		10th Kans. (died of paralysis)	118	77	1925 Mar 27	NE, 50th, 1926
Bliss, Uri		3rd Ohio Cav.	155		1935 Jan 27	KS, 54th, 1935
Blitch, H.	Pvt.	B, 13th Maine Inf.	78		1911 Apr 9	IA, 38th, 1912
Bliven, C.B.	Pvt.	I, 2nd Neb. Cav.	22		1916 Sep 22	IA, 43rd, 1917
Blivins, Clark M.		C, 125th Ill. Inf.	49		1891 Apr 9	KS, 11th, 1892
Blizzard, A.C.	Pvt.	D, 11th Iowa Inf.	321		1909 Mar 14	IA, 36th, 1910
Blizzard, J.W.	Sergt.	H, 8th Iowa Inf.	40		1920 Feb 2	IA, 47th, 1921
Blizzard, Rob't D.	Pvt.	A, 9th Iowa Cav.	16		1902 Mar 12	IA, 29th, 1903
Block, Jacob	Pvt.	C, 35th Iowa Inf.	250	77	1896 Jan	IA, 23rd, 1897
Blockart, C.	Pvt.	A, 1st Iowa Inf.	231		1917	IA, 44th, 1918
Blocker, James H.		H, 2nd Kans. Cav.	18	56	1892 Sep 17	KS, 12th, 1893
Blocker, N.C.	Corp.	I, 26th Iowa Inf.	92	66	1897 Jul 2	IA, 24th, 1898
Blockstone, B.B.	Pvt.	G, 12th Maine Inf.	284		1905 Oct 23	IA, 32nd, 1906
Blodgett, Austin	Pvt.	K, 9th Iowa Inf.	212		1915 Jan 5	IA, 42nd, 1916
Blodgett, J.C.	Lieut.	E, 2nd Wis. Cav.	452		1914 Nov	IA, 41st, 1915
Blodgett, J.O.		G, 96th Ill. Inf.	9		1921 Aug 26	NE, 46th, 1922
Blodgett, O.B.	Pvt.	D, 16th Iowa	56		1903 Jan 10	IA, 30th, 1904
Blodgett, Simeon	Pvt.	C, 15th Iowa Inf.	212		1916	IA, 43rd, 1917
Blodgett, W.C.		E, 27th Ind.	265		1917 Feb 12	KS, 37th, 1918
Blodgett, W.H.			515		1910	IA, 37th, 1911
Blodgett, Wm. C.		H, 27th Mich. Inf.	25		1917 Feb 14	KS, 37th, 1918
Blondin, D.C.			177		1904 May 10	NE, 29th, 1905
Blondin, Sam'l F.	Pvt.	3rd Iowa Battery	78	57	1898 Dec 20	IA, 25th, 1899
Blondin, V.R.	Pvt.	K, 14th N.Y. Hvy. Art.	311		1912 Jun 19	IA, 39th, 1913
Blood, H.B.	Capt.	Army of the Potomac	2		1917 Nov 2	IA, 44th, 1918
Blood, J.H.		H, 154th Ill.	51		1915 Jul 11	KS, 35th, 1916
Blood, W.H.		H, 1st Maine	167		1922 Feb 22	KS, 42nd, 1923
Blood, W.O.	Pvt.	M, 8th Iowa Cav.	50	45	1891 Feb 27	IA, 18th, 1892
Bloodgood, A.V.	Pvt.	H, 152nd N.Y. Inf.	98	64	1899 Aug 31	IA, 26th, 1900
Bloodgood, J.W.		B, 52nd Wis.	18		1905 Aug 11	KS, 25th, 1906
Bloom, F.C.	Pvt.	43rd Wis. Inf.	91		1923 Jun 23	IA, 50th, 1924
Bloom, George		C, 32nd Ind.	88		1921 Sep 13	KS, 41st, 1922
Bloom, John	Pvt.	D, 7th Iowa Inf.	231		1911 Apr 18	IA, 38th, 1912
Bloom, Samuel			51		1908 Dec 27	KS, 28th, 1909
Bloomer, Wheeler		B, 48th Ill.	3		1904 Jul 19	KS, 24th, 1905
Bloomfield, Harvey A.	Corp.	G, 21st Mo. Inf. C, 7th Mo. Cav. (at large)	452, 337	98	1940 Jan 10	IA, 66th, 1940
Bloomfield, Wm.	Pvt.	A, Wis. Battery	512		1902 Sep 20	IA, 29th, 1903
Bloss, William R.		E, 74th Ill.	176		1914 Jun 18	KS, 34th, 1915
Blosser, A.		K, 18th Ohio	4		1922 Mar	KS, 42nd, 1923
Blosser, Benoni		C, 71st Ill.	46		1914 Oct 17	KS, 34th, 1915
Blosser, Wm.		H, 15th Ill. Cav.	7		1918	KS, 38th, 1919
Blossom, Abe Bean	Pvt.		108		1920	IA, 46th, 1920
Blossom, William A.		B, 11th Kans.	46		1917 Jan 7	KS, 37th, 1918
Blount, C.Q.		A, 111th N.Y. Inf. (died of apoplexy)	13	76	1923 Sep 18	NE, 48th, 1924
Blout, Allen		C, 17th Ill.	25	77	1913 Dec 21	NE, 38th, 1914
Blout, Allen		C, 17th Ill.	25		1913 Dec 21	NE, 40th, 1916
Blow, Henry	Pvt.	G, 51st Ohio Inf.	18		1902 Oct 25	IA, 29th, 1903

*See Appendix A, B or C for roster of post names and locations.
†See Introduction for note regarding recording of death date.

Name	Rank	Company, Regiment or Ship	Post*	Age	Death Date†	Journal
Blow, J.P.	Pvt.	H, 30th Iowa	155		1903 Feb 9	IA, 30th, 1904
Blower, E.			87		1893 Sep 15	KS, 13th, 1894
Blowers, G.M.		C, 9th Kans. Cav.	147		1908 Mar 23	KS, 28th, 1909
Blowers, Lyman		E, 109th N.Y. (died of heart failure)	35	69	1912 Oct 2	NE, 37th, 1913
Blowers, Lyman J.		G, 44th Ind. Inf. (died of Bright's disease)	10	66	1910 Mar 27	NE, 35th, 1911
Bloxam, Daniel			133		1917	IA, 44th, 1918
Bloyd, J.W.		H, 11th West Va.	57		1920 Aug	KS, 40th, 1921
Bloyer, Jefferson		D, 78th Ohio	469		1913 Dec 14	KS, 33rd, 1914
Blue, D.L.	Pvt.	A, 174th Ohio Inf.	29		1926 Sep 16	IA, 53rd, 1927
Blue, Daniel	Pvt.	D, 2nd Ill. Lt. Art.	319	63	1894 Nov 7	IA, 22nd, 1896
Blue, David	Corp.	G, 118th Ind. Inf.	452		1926 Jun 19	IA, 53rd, 1927
Blue, David		A, 1st Ind. Hvy. Art.	4		1902 Sep 10	KS, 22nd, 1903
Blue, David		D, 94th Ill.	94		1912 Mar 17	KS, 32nd, 1913
Blue, Elias		D, 17th Ind.	63		1913 Jun 27	KS, 33rd, 1914
Blue, Gilbert	Pvt.	M, 2nd Mo. Cav.	306	59	1897 Jun 17	IA, 24th, 1898
Blue, J.L.	Pvt.	K, 3rd Ill. Cav.	57		1926 Dec	IA, 53rd, 1927
Blue, Richard Whiting	Pvt. Sergt. Major, 2nd Lieut. & Capt.	A, 3rd West Va. Inf. 6th West Va. Cav. (see also Appendix D)	3	65	1907 Jan 28	KS, 26th, 1907
Blue, W.J.	Pvt.	E, 29th Ind. Inf.	358		1926	IA, 53rd, 1927
Blumenshine, S.G.		K, 85th Ill.	356		1925 Nov 4	KS, 45th, 1926
Blund, Phillip		G, 14th Penn.	52		1906 Jan 4	KS, 26th, 1907
Blundel, Wm.		A, 17th Mo.	118		1913 Oct 25	KS, 33rd, 1914
Blunk, Joseph	Pvt.	G, 4th Ill.	69		1912 Jul 23	IA, 39th, 1913
Blunk, Mose		D, 10th Inf.	25	84	1918 Mar 16	NE, 43rd, 1919
Blunt, Azariah		G, 4th Ky. Cav.	232		1919 Feb 17	KS, 39th, 1920
Blunt, Isaac	Pvt.	B, 18th Iowa Inf.	59		1920 Jan 26	IA, 47th, 1921
Blush, R.L.	Pvt.	E, 26th Ill. Inf.	74	57	1897 Nov 2	IA, 24th, 1898
Bly, Jas. M.		H, 44th N.Y. Inf. (died of paralysis)	28	80	1921 Oct 19	NE, 46th, 1922
Bly, L.G.		K, 89th Ind.	143		1928	NE, 53rd, 1929
Blyler, F.F.	Pvt.	2nd Iowa Bat.	7		1924 Apr 2	IA, 51st, 1925
Blystone, W.J.		40th Ind. Inf. (see Appendix D)	25		1924 Mar 14	NE, 48th, 1924
Blythe, R.G.	Capt.	D, 1st N.J. Inf.	90	57	1899 Aug 10	IA, 26th, 1900
Boalan, Daniel		C, 21st Ky. Inf.	25	74	1918 Apr 11	NE, 43rd, 1919
Boales, A.C.	Sergt.	A, 108th Ill. Inf.	81		1920 Nov 3	IA, 47th, 1921
Boaltwood, Edwin		D, 27th Mass.	18		1923 Jul 11	KS, 43rd, 1924
Boans, John		A, 47th Ill.	158		1913 May 19	KS, 33rd, 1914
Board, Chas.		G, 5th Colo. Cav.	294		1898 Nov	KS, 18th, 1899
Boarder	Pvt.		253		1926	IA, 53rd, 1927
Boarder, Geo. A.			253		1923 Jul 2	IA, 50th, 1924
Boardman, G.W.		I, 42nd Ill. (died of paralysis)	147	69	1905[1904?] Dec 27	NE, 29th, 1905
Boardman, John	Pvt.		434		1915	IA, 42nd, 1916
Boardway, Peter	Pvt.	A, 64th N.Y. Inf.	190		1913 Jan 27	IA, 40th, 1914
Boatright, J.A.			7		1928 Jan 14	IA, 55th, 1929
Boatright, W.S.			25		1934 Apr	KS, 54th, 1935
Bobbitt, Geo. W.H.		A, 85th Ill. Inf. (died of paralysis)	22	76	1921 Sep 5	NE, 46th, 1922
Boblets, C.H.		Hvy. Art. (died of old age)	1	76	1924 Feb 23	NE, 49th, 1925
Bobrt, D.			265		1923	KS, 43rd, 1924
Bobst, S.B.		G, 2nd Neb. Cav.	66		1933 Feb 5	NE, 58th, 1934
Bock, Chestopher		A, 5th Mo. Cav.	52		1924 Sep 26	KS, 44th, 1925
Bock, F.	Pvt.	F, 2nd Mo. Lt. Art.	58		1920 May 8	IA, 47th, 1921
Bock, J.H.		E, 8th Ind.	51		1910 Jun 27	KS, 30th, 1911
Bockman, George W.		F, 13th Ind.	6		1923 Feb 28	KS, 43rd, 1924
Bockover, S.		A, 2nd Kans.	180		1916 Sep 24	KS, 36th, 1917
Bodcuner, Henry		I, 7th Wis. Inf. D, 42nd Wis. Inf.	14		1890	KS, 10th, 1891
Boddye, Wm.		A, 92nd Ill. Inf.	77		1918	NE, 43rd, 1919
Bode, Lewis P.	Pvt.	C, Mich.	56		1918	IA, 45th, 1919
Bode, Philip		E, 4th Mo. Inf.	380		1909 Apr 12	KS, 29th, 1910
Boden, Henry C.		G, 30th Ill.	63		1928 Oct 28	NE, 53rd, 1929
Boderths, Henry	Pvt.	A, 46th Iowa	29		1923 May 11	IA, 50th, 1924
Bodien, T.			114		1922	NE, 47th, 1923

*See Appendix A, B or C for roster of post names and locations.
†See Introduction for note regarding recording of death date.

Name	Rank	Company, Regiment or Ship	Post*	Age	Death Date†	Journal
Bodkin, Simeon		H, 19th Iowa	57		1922 Jul 21	KS, 42nd, 1923
Bodle, P.S.		C, 8th Ind. Cav.	356		1916 Jun 10	KS, 36th, 1917
Bodles, John R.		H, 83rd Penn.	175		1922 Jan 14	KS, 42nd, 1923
Bodman, H.F.	Pvt.	D, 35th Iowa Inf.	231		1923 Mar 24	IA, 50th, 1924
Bodman, Robt. D.	Fifer	D, 35th Iowa Inf.	231		1927 Feb 19	IA, 54th, 1928
Boegel, H.H.	Pvt.	B, 33rd Iowa	167		1898 Dec 26	IA, 25th, 1899
Boehmler, Charles	Lieut.	K, 3rd Iowa Inf.	222		1917 Nov	IA, 44th, 1918
Boehmler, Jacob	Pvt.	K, 3rd Iowa Inf.	222		1929 Dec 29	IA, 56th, 1930
Boes, Bennett		B, 148th Ind. Inf.	14		1908 Jan 6	KS, 28th, 1909
Boes, Bennett		B, 148th Ind. Inf.	14		1909 Jan 6	KS, 29th, 1910
Bogard, E.	Pvt.	A, 65th Ill.	40		1921 Jan 3	IA, 48th, 1922
Bogardus, J.W.			108		1902 Feb 8	KS, 22nd, 1903
Bogart, E.F.		Ohio	350		1914 Apr 8	KS, 34th, 1915
Bogart, Henry V.		Penn.	101		1897 May	KS, 17th, 1898
Bogart, J.	Pvt.	A, 10th Vt. Inf.	497		1917 Apr 3	IA, 44th, 1918
Bogart, Lou	Pvt.	D, 95th Ill. Inf.	64		1893 Feb 1	IA, 20th, 1894
Bogel, Geo.			79		1917 Jan 20	IA, 44th, 1918
Bogenrief, David		D, 93rd Ill. (died of kidney trouble)	123	79	1922 May 18	NE, 47th, 1923
Boget, E.J.	Capt.	H, 2nd Iowa Cav.	235		1906 Mar 2	IA, 33rd, 1907
Boggs, A.J.	Corp.	G, 32nd Iowa Inf.	200		1921 Jan 3	IA, 48th, 1922
Boggs, A.J.		H, 79th Ill.	4		1922 Jun	KS, 42nd, 1923
Boggs, J.W.		K, 17th Ill.	25		1922 Dec 28	NE, 47th, 1923
Boggs, J.W.		K, 17th Ill.	25		1922 Nov 28	NE, 47th, 1923
Boggs, Theodore		I, 95th Ill.	87		1897 Jan 8	KS, 17th, 1898
Boggs, Theodore		I, 94th Ill.	87		1897 Jan 8	KS, 16th, 1897
Boggs, Wm. R.T.		F, 208th Penn. (former member of department; location: Franklin)			1933 Feb 2	NE, 58th, 1934
Bogley, John P.		G, 40th Wis. E, 46th Wis.	65		1913 Feb 6	KS, 33rd, 1914
Bogue, N.B.	Pvt.	K, 45th Iowa Inf.	2		1919 Oct 10	IA, 46th, 1920
Boham, E.L.		C, 4th Iowa	127		1919 Dec 24	KS, 39th, 1920
Bohannon, A.		A, 139th Ill.	63		1911 May 20	KS, 31st, 1912
Bohannon, G., see Bohannou, G.						
Bohannou, G.		G, 15th Kans. Cav.	12		1908 Dec 19	KS, 28th, 1909
Bohart, Cornelius W.		A, 129th Ind.	9		1929 Jun 17	NE, 54th, 1930
Bohn, Julius		A, 17th Ill.	38		1925 May 12	KS, 45th, 1926
Bohne, A.H.	Pvt.	K, 33rd Ill. Inf. (died of LaGrippe)	11	48	1891 Jul	NE, 16th, 1892
Bohr, Jacob			77		1924 Spring	IA, 51st, 1925
Boice, B.			104		1912 Feb 2	KS, 32nd, 1913
Boice, James Cooper, Dr.		I, 98th Ohio Inf.	108	91	1938 May 17	IA, 64th, 1938
Boice, S.B.		A, 128th Ohio	80		1927	NE, 52nd, 1928
Boice, Thomas R.	Pvt.	B, 14th Iowa Inf.	132		1922 Mar 31	IA, 49th, 1923
Boice, Wesley		K, 137th Ill.	65		1919 Jul	KS, 39th, 1920
Boke, S.F.	Pvt.	D, 35th Iowa Inf.	231		1916 Oct 22	IA, 43rd, 1917
Bolan, M.	Pvt.		24		1907 Feb 1	IA, 34th, 1908
Boland, Peter J.	Pvt.	D, 8th Cal. Inf.	78		1913 Nov 16	IA, 40th, 1914
Boldman, J.Q.			346		1910	IA, 37th, 1911
Bolen, Gilbert		G, 4th Ohio Cav. (died of pneumonia)	2	76	1920 Jan 26	NE, 45th, 1921
Bolen, John		E, 146th Ind.	202		1917 May 28	KS, 37th, 1918
Boles, Clayton E.		I, 6th Kans. Cav.	225		1916 Sep 27	KS, 36th, 1917
Bolin, M.	Pvt.		24		1907 Feb 1	IA, 33rd, 1907
Boling, J.N.	Lieut.	I, 16th Ohio Inf.	235		1926 Mar 18	IA, 53rd, 1927
Boling, S.M.	1st Lieut.	F, 122nd Ohio Inf.	19	59	1893 Oct 12	IA, 20th, 1894
Boller, John		C, 3rd Md. Cav.	132		1912 Jan 19	KS, 32nd, 1913
Boller, Wm.		165th Penn. Inf.	132		1911 Nov 5	KS, 31st, 1912
Bolliers, Wm. W.	Pvt.	F, 2nd Iowa Cav.	97		1902 Sep 14	IA, 29th, 1903
Bolloff, V.	Pvt.	H, 16th Iowa Inf.	259	54	1896 Jan 13	IA, 23rd, 1897
Bolshaw, Joseph		M, 1st N.Y. Eng.	25		1911 Mar 26	NE, 36th, 1912
Bolshaw, Joseph			25		1911	NE, 36th, 1912
Bolsinger, J.K.P.	Pvt.	E, 5th Iowa Cav.	517		1929 Nov 10	IA, 56th, 1930
Bolton, A.H.		D, 84th Ind.	1		1926 Feb 2	NE, 51st, 1927

Name	Rank	Company, Regiment or Ship	Post*	Age	Death Date†	Journal
Bolton, C.S.		F, 21st Ohio	12		1925 Mar 5	KS, 45th, 1926
Bolton, Chas.	Pvt.	B, 43rd Wis. Inf.	67		1909 Nov 14	IA, 36th, 1910
Bolton, Geo. T.	Pvt.	C, 15th Iowa Inf.	11		1915 Apr 1	IA, 42nd, 1916
Bolton, George		A, 98th Ill.	18		1910 Dec 23	KS, 30th, 1911
Bolton, Homer	Pvt.	F, 47th Iowa Inf.	7		1913 Jul 15	IA, 40th, 1914
Bolton, Isaac M.	1st Lieut.	K, 21st Iowa Inf.	142		1900 Nov 10	IA, 27th, 1901
Bolton, James		G, 1st Cav.	4		1917 Mar 26	KS, 37th, 1918
Bolton, John	Pvt.	F, 1st Iowa Cav.	8		1902 Aug 28	IA, 29th, 1903
Bolton, John		F, 5th Penn.	100		1931 May 9	KS, 52nd, 1933
Bolton, John		5th Penn.	100		1931 May 9	KS, 51st, 1932
Bolton, Lewis		I, 71st N.Y. Inf.	14		1899 May 28	KS, 19th, 1900
Boltwood, Fred A.	Pvt.	1st N.Y.	19		1927 Nov 5	IA, 54th, 1928
Boltzell, C.F.		K, 15th Kans. Cav.	289		1900 Aug 19	KS, 20th, 1901
Bomgardner, George W.		H, 8th Iowa Cav. (died at Palco, Kans.; buried at Meade Cemetery)	469		1892 Oct 15	KS, 14th, 1895
Bomgardner, John, see Bumgartner, John						
Bomgardner, John C.		D, 47th Ill.	469		1916 Feb 27	KS, 36th, 1917
Bomine, John			112		1923	IA, 50th, 1924
Bommer, P.J.		A, 9th N.Y.	152		1893 Aug 8	KS, 13th, 1894
Bomount, C.E.	Pvt.		337		1920 Dec 27	IA, 47th, 1921
Bon, William N.		B, 8th Wis. Inf.	78		1912 Feb 3	KS, 32nd, 1913
Bonar, James C.	Sergt.	I, 15th Iowa Inf.	173	45	1886 Oct 29	IA, 13th, 1887
Bond, B.C.		C, 107th Ill. (location: Blair)			1927 Nov 2	NE, 52nd, 1928
Bond, E.W.		F, 140th Ind.	47		1926 Apr 5	KS, 46th, 1927
Bond, Elijah	Pvt.	H, 17th Ill.	47		1905 Apr 4	IA, 32nd, 1906
Bond, H.C.	Pvt.	D, 1st Ohio Lt. Art.	153	86	1932 Dec 7	IA, 59th, 1933
Bond, H.L.		K, 4th Iowa Cav.	26		1936 May 13	NE, 61st, 1937
Bond, Henry J.	Pvt.	G, 2nd N.Y. Cav.	132		1922 Jun 22	IA, 49th, 1923
Bond, John P.	Pvt.	K, 45th Iowa Inf.	2		1911 May 11	IA, 38th, 1912
Bond, Judd L.	Pvt.	H, 15th Ill. (died of blood poison)	123	42	1887 Jun	NE, 12th, 1888
Bond, L.L.	Sergt.	K, 13th Wis.	58		1924 May 27	IA, 51st, 1925
Bond, R.F.		I, 52nd Mass.	14		1906 Nov 27	KS, 26th, 1907
Bond, Richard		B, 11th Wis. Inf.	354	67	1906 Mar 20	NE, 31st, 1907
Bond, Robert			154		1894	NE, 19th, 1895
Bond, Wm.	Pvt.	K, 18th Iowa Inf.	143	69	1892 Feb 22	IA, 18th, 1892
Bondoll, Michael		F, 7th Iowa Inf. (Beatrice)			1948 Dec 24	NE, 73rd, 1949
Bondurat, John M.	Pvt.	D, 51st Mo. Vols.	109[110?]		1899	NE, 24th, 1900
Bone, G.A.W.		A, 36th Wis. Inf. (died at National Home)	244		1895 Nov	KS, 15th, 1896
Bone, Jas.			29		1906 Nov 3	IA, 33rd, 1907
Bone, M.D.			251		1884	KS, 4th, 1885
Bone, Moses	Pvt.	I, 35th Iowa Inf.	127		1908 Jul 16	IA, 35th, 1909
Bone, Samuel		D, 32nd Iowa Inf.	158		1899 May 5	KS, 19th, 1900
Bone, Thos.	Pvt.	I, 36th Iowa	127		1905 May 8	IA, 32nd, 1906
Bonebrake, Ezra		H, 150th Ind.	64		1922 Feb 17	KS, 42nd, 1923
Bonebrake, P.I.		Kans. State Militia	1		1920 Mar 19	KS, 40th, 1921
Bonebrake, P.K.	Sergt.	I, 33rd Iowa Inf.	49	54	1890 Aug 14	IA, 17th, 1891
Boner, Joseph		B, 16th Penn. Inf.	14		1912 Aug 5	KS, 32nd, 1913
Bonewell, John A.	Pvt.	I, 59th Ind. Vol. Inf.	127		1901 Oct 18	IA, 28th, 1902
Bonewell, L.K.		G, 13th Ind. Inf.	85		1912 Jun 25	KS, 32nd, 1913
Bonewell, W.J.		F, 31st Ind.	85		1921 Oct 10	KS, 41st, 1922
Bonham, A.M.		55th Ill. Inf.	29		1919 Sep	IA, 46th, 1920
Bonham, B.A.			29		1908 Jan 25	IA, 35th, 1909
Bonham, B.B.	Pvt.	E, 16th Ill. Inf.	452		1928 Oct 27	IA, 55th, 1929
Bonham, G.D.		F, 12th Iowa Inf.	477		1914 Dec 18	KS, 34th, 1915
Bonham, Geo.	Pvt.	I, 9th Ky. Inf.	377		1916 May 24	IA, 43rd, 1917
Bonham, J.M.	Pvt.	I, 22nd Iowa Inf.	8		1921 Jun 27	IA, 48th, 1922
Bonham, T.C.		B, 43rd Ohio Inf. (died at Meade)	388		1895 Sep	KS, 15th, 1896
Bonine, C.L.		D, U.S. Inf.	7		1924[1923?] Oct 1	NE, 48th, 1924
Bonn, Phillip C.		K, 144th Iowa	28		1922 Jul 22	KS, 42nd, 1923
Bonnell, A.	Pvt.	A, 4th Iowa Inf.	374		1901 Aug 22	IA, 28th, 1902
Bonnell, Chas. W.		A, 7th Mich.	340		1927 Mar 17	KS, 47th, 1928

Name	Rank	Company, Regiment or Ship	Post*	Age	Death Date†	Journal
Bonnell, Jesse	Pvt.	H, 93rd Ill. Inf.	127		1893 Mar 8	IA, 20th, 1894
Bonner, A.	Pvt.	C, 53rd Ind. Inf.	515		1908 May 6	IA, 35th, 1909
Bonney, Byron S.		F, 14th N.Y.	87		1923 May 5	KS, 43rd, 1924
Bonney, T.S.			278		1890	NE, 15th, 1891
Bonnie, John M.	Pvt.	E, 4th Iowa Inf.	26		1914 Sep 1	IA, 41st, 1915
Bonsteel, Henry		E, 151st Ind.	188		1897 Jul 30	KS, 17th, 1898
Bonwell, John C.		D, 175th Ohio	34	92	1934 May 16	IA, 61st, 1935
Bonwell, John C.	Sergt.	A, 175th Ohio Inf. (at large)	34, 35	100, 10 mos. & 27 days	1943 Oct 3	IA, 70th, 1944
Boo, S.L.	Pvt.	C, 63rd Ind. Inf.	466		1917 Apr 15	IA, 44th, 1918
Booen, Jas.	Pvt.	E, 10th Minn. Inf.	142	49	1889 Dec 3	IA, 16th, 1890
Booher, H.	Pvt.	I, 148th Ill. Inf.	39		1921 Oct 15	IA, 48th, 1922
Booie, S.C.	Pvt.	D, 3rd Ohio Cav.	12		1927 Jun 30	IA, 54th, 1928
Booker, Elijah		I, 146th Ill.	71		1926 Feb 22	KS, 46th, 1927
Bookwalter, B.F.	Pvt.	A, 45th Iowa	455		1899 Apr	IA, 26th, 1900
Boomer, A.			342		1899	IA, 26th, 1900
Boomer, Albert, Dr.	Surg.	27th Iowa Vol. Inf.	342	81	1899 Apr 15	IA, 26th, 1900
Boomeville, Gaylor			2		3rd quarter 1883	IA, 10th, 1884
Boon, E.T.		A, 1st Ore. Cav. (died of nervous prostration)	165		1893 Sep 16	NE, 18th, 1894
Boon, Edwin			74		4th quarter 1884	IA, 11th, 1885
Boon, Geo.	Pvt.	D, 143rd Ohio	249		1907 May 4	IA, 34th, 1908
Boone, Hiram		B, 102nd Ill. (former member; died at Mound City, Mo.)	25		1935 Jun	NE, 60th, 1936
Boone, Jesse	Pvt.	D, 32nd Iowa Inf.	67		1929 Sep 4	IA, 56th, 1930
Boone, John C.			38		1915 May	IA, 42nd, 1916
Boone, Lewis A.		K, 98th Ill.	238		1921 Mar 6	KS, 41st, 1922
Boone, Lyler	Pvt.	A, 13th Iowa Inf.	67		1928 Dec 22	IA, 55th, 1929
Boone, T.R.	Seaman		6		1936 Feb 24	KS, 55th, 1936
Boop, George E.		E, 142nd Penn.	20		1916 Jun 25	KS, 36th, 1917
Boorom, John			3		1930 Feb 24	NE, 55th, 1931
Booron, N.M.	1st Lieut.	E, 18th Iowa Inf.	231		1905 Apr 16	IA, 32nd, 1906
Boory, Frederick		D, 162nd Ohio	57		1904 Mar 6	KS, 24th, 1905
Booth, A.	Pvt.	F, 72nd Ill. Inf.	379		1904 Jul 10	IA, 31st, 1905
Booth, B.F.	Pvt.	B, 22nd Iowa Inf.	116		1927 Oct 15	IA, 54th, 1928
Booth, C.M.		A, 8th N.Y. Cav.	83		1925 Mar 15	KS, 45th, 1926
Booth, Everet		G, 139th Ill.	329		1923 Mar 4	IA, 50th, 1924
Booth, Geo. N.		D, 23rd Mass. Inf. (died of insanity)	11	76	1906 Jan 18	NE, 31st, 1907
Booth, George N.		D, 23rd Mass. Inf.	354	75	1906 Jan 18	NE, 31st, 1907
Booth, H.A.		C, 47th Ill. (killed in Colorado)	1		1888	KS, 8th, 1889
Booth, Henry	Pvt.	C, 80th Ill. Inf.	49		1920 May 31	IA, 47th, 1921
Booth, Henry		L, 11th Kans. (see also Appendix D)	8		1898 Feb 14	KS, 18th, 1899
Booth, I.H.		D, 64th Ohio Inf.	25	77	1921 Jul 22	NE, 46th, 1922
Booth, J.H.	Pvt.	H, 27th Iowa Inf.	506		1902 Aug 23	IA, 29th, 1903
Booth, J.J.		H, 32nd Wis.	378		1922 Aug 5	KS, 42nd, 1923
Booth, James		A, 119th Ill.	1		1918 Jun 19	KS, 38th, 1919
Booth, John O.		A, 23rd Iowa Inf.	225		1914 Jan 16	KS, 34th, 1915
Booth, Oscar		B, 1st N.H. Hvy. Art.	23		1939 Feb 17	NE, 64th, 1940
Booth, W.H.H.	Pvt.	6th Wis. Battery	150	49	1890 Sep 24	IA, 17th, 1891
Booth, Wiles S.		24th Ohio	85		1905 Mar 29	KS, 25th, 1906
Boothrog, W.J.	Pvt.	F, 50th N.Y. Eng.	17		1915 Feb 19	IA, 42nd, 1916
Booton, G.W.	Pvt.	A, 4th Ill. Cav.	210		1904 Jun 19	IA, 31st, 1905
Bordeaux, Randall B.		K, 25th Ohio Inf.	25		1917 Nov 22	KS, 37th, 1918
Borden, Samuel		C, 33rd Iowa (died of pneumonia)	10	64	1904 Jun 1	NE, 29th, 1905
Border, John	Pvt.	K, 1st Iowa Cav.	371	53	1892 Dec 13	IA, 19th, 1893
Border, John		I, 140th Penn.	18		1915 Feb 9	KS, 35th, 1916
Border, John M.	Pvt.	F, 99th Ohio Inf.	253		1915 Dec 9	IA, 42nd, 1916
Bordner, H.	Pvt.	D, 11th Mich. Inf.	97		1916 Mar 31	IA, 43rd, 1917
Boregard, Alfred		34th West Va.	28		1928 Mar 6	KS, 48th, 1929
Boremann, C.	Pvt.	H, 59th Ind. Inf.	254		1909 Mar	IA, 36th, 1910

Handwritten note next to "Booth, Geo. N." row: Ho Charles Booth

*See Appendix A, B or C for roster of post names and locations.
†See Introduction for note regarding recording of death date.

53

Name	Rank	Company, Regiment or Ship	Post*	Age	Death Date†	Journal
Borgquest, C.E.	Hosp. Stew.	U.S.A. (died of paralysis)	12	69	1896 Aug 6	NE, 21st, 1897
Boring, David W.		K, 5th Kans.	32		1919 Jun 11	KS, 39th, 1920
Bormann, Jacob	Pvt.	K, 26th Iowa Inf.	327		1903 Jun 6	IA, 30th, 1904
Born, Jacob	Pvt.	A, 23rd Iowa Inf.	30	53	1897 Feb 1	IA, 23rd, 1897
Born, Lawrence L.		E, 11th Ill. Inf.	7		1924[1923?] Jan 1	NE, 48th, 1924
Borschel, Adam	Pvt.	H, 2nd Iowa Cav.	8		1904 Jun 6	IA, 31st, 1905
Borton, Sam			155		1909 Feb 22	IA, 36th, 1910
Borum, T.J.		C, 57th Ind.	142		1892 Jan 8	KS, 12th, 1893
Boseck, Christian				93	1937 Sep 26	IA, 64th, 1938
Boskins, M.B.	Pvt.	K, 7th Iowa Cav.	172		1902 Sep 25	IA, 29th, 1903
Bosleder, Oliver D.	Pvt.	G, 6th Iowa Cav.	452		1912	IA, 39th, 1913
Bosley, H.E.	Pvt.	E, 19th Mich. Inf.	156		1916 Jul 15	IA, 43rd, 1917
Boss, Albert	Pvt.	D, 39th Wis. Inf.	88		1919 May 13	IA, 46th, 1920
Boss, John	Pvt.	D, 27th Iowa Inf.	146	68	1892 Feb 4	IA, 18th, 1892
Boss, S.K.		H, 33rd Ind.	47		1910 Mar 29	KS, 30th, 1911
Bosserman, William		B, 107th Ill. (former member; died at Grafton)	33		1935 Oct	NE, 60th, 1936
Bossert, B.F.	Pvt.	E, 11th Iowa	110		1926 Aug 19	IA, 53rd, 1927
Bossler, John		G, 8th Iowa (died at Stafford)	301		1895 Aug	KS, 15th, 1896
Boston, John A.		B, 75th Ill. Inf. (died of heart disease)	10	82	1913 Jan 27	NE, 38th, 1914
Bostwick, E.M.			107		1884	KS, 4th, 1885
Bosworth, D.S.	1st Lieut.	L, 12th U.S. Colored Art.	30	61	1885 May 13	IA, 12th, 1886
Bosworth, Harvey	Pvt.	E, 7th Ill. Cav.	66		1918 May 1	IA, 45th, 1919
Bosworth, W.A.		C, 87th Ohio Inf.	25		1936 Apr 14	KS, 55th, 1936
Both, John	Pvt.	E, 7th Iowa Inf.	231		1907 Jun 19	IA, 34th, 1908
Botham, Chas.		I, 10th Ind.	1		1926 Mar 3	KS, 46th, 1927
Bothel, Daniel	Sergt.	A, 78th Penn. Inf.	8		1916 Mar 21	IA, 43rd, 1917
Bothwell, Geo. W.	Pvt.	E, 3rd Wis. Inf.	68		1928 Apr 23	IA, 55th, 1929
Botkin, John		G, 7th Iowa Cav. (three years service)	57		1892 Jan 10	KS, 12th, 1893
Botkin, Theo.		F, 8th Ohio Cav.	17		1918 Jan	KS, 38th, 1919
Botkin, Theodosius		F, 44th Ohio Inf. (died at Campbellton, New Brunswick; see Appendix D)		72	1918 May	KS, 38th, 1919
Botsford, Gideon B.		E, 12th Conn. Vols.	209		1917 May 1	KS, 37th, 1918
Botsford, John		G, 17th Ill.	142		1930 Apr 17	KS, 50th, 1931
Bott, V.T.	Pvt.	F, 34th Iowa Inf.	192		1917 Mar 25	IA, 44th, 1918
Bottom, Benjamin		K, 49th Penn.	1		1921 Dec 4	KS, 41st, 1922
Bottomly, Wm.		1st Minn. Hvy. Art.	158		1918 Jan	KS, 38th, 1919
Bottomstone, G.W.	Sergt.	E, 9th Penn. Cav.	130	91	1931 Mar 13	IA, 58th, 1932
Botts, Sheppard	Pvt.	C, 23rd Iowa Inf.	7		1919 Jun 14	IA, 46th, 1920
Boucher, W.F.			94		1919	IA, 46th, 1920
Bouck, Geo.	Pvt.	D, 44th Iowa Inf.	68		1911 Jan 16	IA, 38th, 1912
Bouden, Asher H.		D, 91st Ill. Inf.	88		1914 May 28	KS, 34th, 1915
Boudinett, C.T.		C, 11th Ind. Inf.	110	77	1918 Mar 9	NE, 43rd, 1919
Boughton, Corydon	Lieut.	D, 8th Wis. Inf.	247		1918 Apr 20	IA, 45th, 1919
Boughton, Mervin	Pvt.	K, 22nd Wis. Inf.	66		1923 Feb 10	IA, 50th, 1924
Boughton, Philo K.	Corp.	E, 105th Ohio	71		1901 Sep	IA, 28th, 1902
Boulding, W.F.	Pvt.	F, 111th Ill. Inf.	452		1928 Aug 19	IA, 55th, 1929
Boulton, C.S.		F, 21st Ohio Inf.	12		1925 Mar 5	KS, 44th, 1925
Boulware, G.R.		G, 146th Ill.	28		1918 Mar 14	KS, 38th, 1919
Bound, W.J.		B, 64th Ill. (died at Fontana)	102		1895 Nov 9	KS, 15th, 1896
Bounslot, Sam'l	Pvt.	H, 26th Iowa Inf.	25		1912	IA, 39th, 1913
Bouplon, John	Sergt.	G, 125th N.Y. Inf.	36		1914 Feb 8	IA, 40th, 1914
Bourison, Andrew		H, 72nd Ind. (died of old age)	111	76	1913 Jul 17	NE, 38th, 1914
Bourless, Peter		K, 43rd Ill. Inf. (died of dropsy)	24	65	1896 Mar 6	NE, 21st, 1897
Bourne, B.F.		F, 20th Ind. Inf.	66		1917 Oct 9	KS, 37th, 1918
Bourne, J.C.	Sergt.	B, 27th N.Y. Inf.	71		1916 May 28	IA, 43rd, 1917
Bourne, N.R.	Pvt.	G, 5th Mo. Cav.	81		1920 Sep 13	IA, 47th, 1921
Bourow, D.W.		F, 4th Ohio	18		1906 Feb 20	KS, 26th, 1907
Bousquet, J.J.	1st Lieut.	3rd Iowa Inf. U.S.C.T.	404		1921 Jul 31	IA, 49th, 1923
Boutell, John A.		B, 4th Mich. Cav.	23		1923 Jul 12	KS, 43rd, 1924
Boutman, Aaron	Corp.	H, 33rd Ill.	283		1924 Feb 26	IA, 51st, 1925
Bouton, Albert Q.		B, 12th Mich. Inf.	10		1921 Feb 9	NE, 46th, 1922

*See Appendix A, B or C for roster of post names and locations.
†See Introduction for note regarding recording of death date.

Name	Rank	Company, Regiment or Ship	Post*	Age	Death Date†	Journal
Bovee, A.M.		E, 7th Ill. Inf.	52	62	1900 Dec 25	NE, 25th, 1901
Bovee, W.R.	Lieut.	2nd Neb.	46		1899	NE, 24th, 1900
Bovee, William H.	Pvt.	B, 65th Ill. Inf.	452		1912 Oct 22	IA, 39th, 1913
Boveid, Frank			267		1922 Apr 5	IA, 49th, 1923
Bowar, Thomas B.	Pvt.	D, 10th N.Y. Hvy. Art.	112	54	1891 Sep 6	NE, 16th, 1892
Bowden, A.S.			289		1912	KS, 32nd, 1913
Bowden, C.A.		B, 3rd Minn.	438		1888	KS, 8th, 1889
Bowdish, Asa		B, 105th Penn. Inf. (died of old age)	89		1894 Dec 14	NE, 19th, 1895
Bowdish, Francis M.		F, 10th Ind.	90		1935 Aug 9	KS, 55th, 1936
Bowe, Romanzo	Pvt.	D, 28th Iowa Inf.	98		1927 Apr 27	IA, 54th, 1928
Bowels, John A.		E, 68th Ill.	251		1920 Dec 29	KS, 40th, 1921
Bowen, A.B.	Pvt.	U.S. Navy	74		1925 Apr 16	IA, 52nd, 1926
Bowen, Aretius	Surg.	2nd Neb. Inf. (died of old age)	24	80	1895 Aug 5	NE, 20th, 1896
Bowen, Brice B.	Pvt.	L, 4th Wis. Cav.	197		1925 Mar 5	IA, 52nd, 1926
Bowen, D.R.	Pvt.	K, 3rd Wis. Cav.	147		1919 Mar 21	IA, 46th, 1920
Bowen, David		K, 139th Ill.	11		1933 Oct 17	NE, 58th, 1934
Bowen, David W.		B, 38th Penn. Inf.	1		1886	KS, 6th, 1887
Bowen, J.W.			48		1906 Aug	IA, 33rd, 1907
Bowen, James H.		D, 41st Ill.	65		1911 Aug 20	KS, 31st, 1912
Bowen, Jesse	Pvt.	E, 3rd Iowa Inf.	305		1920 Sep	IA, 47th, 1921
Bowen, John	Corp.	I, 40th Iowa Inf.	40		1914 Aug 19	IA, 41st, 1915
Bowen, Noah	Pvt.	D, 2nd Ohio Cav.	154		1916 Aug 2	IA, 43rd, 1917
Bowen, Wm. M.	Musician	C, 28th Iowa Inf.	127		1904 Jan 8	IA, 31st, 1905
Bower, Frank		L, 9th Mich.	42		1913 Jun 14	KS, 33rd, 1914
Bower, George A.		H, 149th Ohio	50		1914 Oct 1	KS, 34th, 1915
Bower, H.T.		K, 24th Iowa Inf. (died of old age)	77	87	1924 Mar 26	NE, 49th, 1925
Bower, J.A.	Pvt.	I, 36th Iowa Inf.	186		1906 Dec 24	IA, 33rd, 1907
Bower, Myer	Pvt.	B, 37th Ind. Inf.	2		1916 May 1	IA, 43rd, 1917
Bower, W.H.		B, 2nd Kans.	100		1912 May 19	KS, 32nd, 1913
Bowerman, B.F.			380		1917	KS, 37th, 1918
Bowerman, F.		K, 105th Ill. Inf.	7	83	1925 Jan 18	NE, 50th, 1926
Bowers, E.A.		E, 95th Ill. Inf.	71		1917 Feb 20	KS, 37th, 1918
Bowers, E.A.		G, 56th Ill.	380		1920 Jul 19	KS, 40th, 1921
Bowers, H.W.		A, 10th Ill. (died of general breaking down)	81	76	1914 Oct 12	NE, 39th, 1915
Bowers, J.N.	Pvt.	K, 163rd Ohio	22		1921 Jun 10	IA, 48th, 1922
Bowers, Jacob		H, 1st Mr. Inf.	38		1929 Jan 23	NE, 53rd, 1929
Bowers, John		B, 47th Ill.	113		1905 Jul 24	KS, 25th, 1906
Bowers, Joseph	Pvt.	C, 92nd Ill. Inf.	101		1911 Apr 9	IA, 38th, 1912
Bowers, Joseph D.		F, 12th West Va. Inf. (died of diabetes)	34	57	1897 Oct 13	NE, 22nd, 1898
Bowers, Joseph M.		K, 11th Ind.	1		1924 Feb 1	KS, 44th, 1925
Bowers, Marion		D, 16th Ill.	412		1922 Mar 20	KS, 42nd, 1923
Bowers, R.S.	Pvt.	C, 32nd Iowa Inf.	134		1909 Nov 1	IA, 36th, 1910
Bowers, W.J.	Corp.	F, 32nd Iowa Inf.	154		1926 Sep 9	IA, 53rd, 1927
Bowersock, D.C.		B, 152nd Ohio	44		1931 Aug 21	KS, 52nd, 1933
Bowersock, D.C.		B, 152nd Ohio	44		1931 Aug 21	KS, 51st, 1932
Bowersock, John B.			44		1939 Oct 5	KS, 59th, 1940
Bowersox, James	Pvt.	E, 149th Ind.	1		1907 Nov 15	IA, 34th, 1908
Bowie, Thomas C., Dr.		B, 76th Ohio	82		1919 Dec 28	KS, 39th, 1920
Bowie, Thomas O.		B, 76th Ohio	82		1919 Dec 28	KS, 40th, 1921
Bowie, Titus	Pvt.	G, 182nd Ohio Inf.	103	49	1894 Jul 26	IA, 21st, 1895
Bowker, H.H.		E, 15th Ill. Inf. (died of heart failure)	32	56	1900 Sep 27	NE, 25th, 1901
Bowker, Joseph	Pvt.	F, 42nd Ohio Inf.	16	64	1899 Mar 26	IA, 25th, 1899
Bowland, A.E.		H, 44th Ill.	301		1926 Jun 6	KS, 46th, 1927
Bowles, J.A.	Sergt.	K, 21st Penn. Cav.	23		1935 Jan 28	NE, 60th, 1936
Bowles, Stephen H.		B, 89th N.Y. (died of apoplexy)	39	74	1919 Dec	NE, 45th, 1921
Bowles, Thomas A.		A, 10th Ohio Cav.	25		1912 Oct 11	KS, 32nd, 1913
Bowley, A.		D, 154th Ind. Inf. (died at Maple City)	158		1895 Feb 14	KS, 15th, 1896
Bowling, Isaac W.		K, 45th Ky. Cav.	25	78	1917 Dec 20	NE, 42nd, 1918
Bowlsby, B.F.			55		1920	IA, 47th, 1921
Bowlus, J.W.	Lieut. Col.	25th Ohio Vol. Inf.	32		1901 Sep	KS, 21st, 1902
Bowman, A.J.	Pvt.	C, 6th Iowa Inf.	141		1930 Jul 23	IA, 57th, 1931

Name	Rank	Company, Regiment or Ship	Post*	Age	Death Date†	Journal
Bowman, A.J.		C, 67th Ohio	177		1897 Dec 3	KS, 17th, 1898
Bowman, Benj. F.		B, 31st Mo.	380		1916 Aug 15	KS, 36th, 1917
Bowman, Chas. F.		H, 13th Mich.	25	75	1917 Mar 10	NE, 42nd, 1918
Bowman, E.	Pvt.	B, 24th Iowa Inf.	440		1918 Mar 27	IA, 45th, 1919
Bowman, Elias Wesley		A, 14th Ill. Cav. (see also Appendix D)	25	85	1929 Apr 29	KS, 49th, 1930
Bowman, Gabril	Pvt.	A, 7th Iowa Inf.	231		1919 Apr 17	IA, 46th, 1920
Bowman, Geo.			515		1914 Sep 29	IA, 41st, 1915
Bowman, Geo.			515		1913 Sep 29	IA, 40th, 1914
Bowman, Godfrey	Pvt.	H, 13th Iowa Inf.	222		1913 Sep 1	IA, 40th, 1914
Bowman, H.C.			5		1923 Jun 9	IA, 50th, 1924
Bowman, I.	Pvt.	D, 4th Iowa Inf.	15		1904 Apr 25	IA, 31st, 1905
Bowman, I.D.		A, 67th Ind.	4		1917 Dec 16	KS, 37th, 1918
Bowman, J.H.		K, 3rd Penn.	85		1930 Aug 6	KS, 50th, 1931
Bowman, Jacob	Musician	A, 11th Iowa Inf.	196		1912	IA, 39th, 1913
Bowman, John	Chaplain	49th N.Y. Inf.	222		1903 Jan 20	IA, 29th, 1903
Bowman, John	Pvt.		231		1933 Oct 20	IA, 60th, 1934
Bowman, Joseph		E, 184th Ohio	25		1928 Jan 13	KS, 48th, 1929
Bowman, M.T.V.	Col.	1st Maine Cav.	12		1901 Aug 26	IA, 28th, 1902
Bowman, R.D.		K, 124th Ind. Inf. (died at Lamar, Kans.; buried at Halls Cemetery)	350		1894 Mar 13	KS, 14th, 1895
Bowman, Sam'l M.			235		1923 Dec 29	IA, 50th, 1924
Bowman, Samuel			180		1923 Apr 7	KS, 43rd, 1924
Bowman, T.B.	Pvt.	K, 1st Iowa Cav.	200		1913 Sep 27	IA, 40th, 1914
Bowman, Thos.	1st Lieut.	B, 4th Iowa Cav.	67		1904 Jul 2	IA, 31st, 1905
Bowman, U.J.	Pvt.	F, 15th Ill. Inf.	154		1924 May 2	IA, 51st, 1925
Bowman, W.P.	Pvt.	K, 1st Wis. Hvy. Art.	124		1917 Apr 26	IA, 44th, 1918
Bowman, William H.	Sergt.	B, 92nd Ohio Inf.	35		1917 Jun 28	IA, 44th, 1918
Bown, T.W.	Major	146th Ohio	42		1924 Nov 13	KS, 44th, 1925
Bowne, W.B.	Pvt.	D, 23rd N.J.	72		1914 Dec 3	IA, 41st, 1915
Bowne, Z.	Pvt.	A, 11th Mo. Inf.	66		1914 Nov 7	IA, 41st, 1915
Bowns, George			29		4th quarter 1884	IA, 11th, 1885
Bowser, Geo. W.		C, 9th Mich.	25		1916 Sep 3	KS, 36th, 1917
Box, Martin V.	Pvt.	K, 4th Iowa Cav.	104		1924 Jul 8	IA, 51st, 1925
Boyce, Benj.		A, 2nd Ill.	244		1926 Nov	KS, 46th, 1927
Boyce, Mortimer D.	Corp.	F, 134th Ill. Inf.	416		1925 Oct 19	IA, 52nd, 1926
Boyce, W.H.	Pvt.	A, 20th Iowa Inf.	235		1916 Nov 11	IA, 43rd, 1917
Boyd, Alex. B.		I, 6th Iowa	1		1922 Sep 28	KS, 42nd, 1923
Boyd, B.B.		B, 1st N.Y. Eng.	12		1910 Aug 4	KS, 30th, 1911
Boyd, Enoch	Pvt.	B, 192nd Ill. Inf.	222	85	1931 Jan 9	IA, 58th, 1932
Boyd, Geo. L.		D, 11th Ill.	19		1918 May 10	KS, 38th, 1919
Boyd, George	Pvt.	K, 32nd Iowa Inf.	439		1893 Dec 30	IA, 20th, 1894
Boyd, George S.		C, 138th Ill.	257		1916 Jan	KS, 36th, 1917
Boyd, Haley C.	Pvt.	K, 27th Iowa Inf.	512	65	1897 Sep 10	IA, 24th, 1898
Boyd, Henry		B, 45th Iowa Inf. (at large)			1932 Jan 10	IA, 59th, 1933
Boyd, Israel, Col.	Pvt.	K, 1st Kans. Inf.	10		1917 Oct 16	IA, 44th, 1918
Boyd, J.M.		E, 63rd Penn.	13	63	1909 Feb 13	NE, 34th, 1910
Boyd, J.N.	Corp.	K, 7th Penn. Cav.	88		1921 May 15	IA, 48th, 1922
Boyd, John			269		4th quarter 1885	IA, 12th, 1886
Boyd, John		I, 55th Mass.	72		1910 Jan 26	KS, 30th, 1911
Boyd, John C.		E, 48th Ill. Inf. (died at Cimarron, Kans.; buried at Cimarron Cemetery)	365		1894 Apr 19	KS, 14th, 1895
Boyd, Newton		K, 6th Ohio	17		1909 Sep 27	KS, 29th, 1910
Boyd, R.G.	Pvt.	H, 15th Iowa Inf.	397		1907 Nov 16	IA, 34th, 1908
Boyd, R.M.		H, 2nd Ohio	279		1910 Mar 25	KS, 32nd, 1913
Boyd, Robert M.	Pvt.	K, 6th Iowa Cav.	219		1922 Feb 9	IA, 49th, 1923
Boyd, Robt. M.	Pvt.	D, 69th Ill. Inf.	81		1899	NE, 24th, 1900
Boyd, S.L.		G, 21st Penn. Cav. (died of accident)	262	49	1897 Nov 29	NE, 22nd, 1898
Boyd, S.T.		I, 120th Ohio Inf.	117		1886	KS, 6th, 1887
Boyd, Samuel		B, 169th Ohio	68		1927 Feb 27	KS, 47th, 1928
Boyd, T.W.			68		1912 Feb 21	KS, 32nd, 1913
Boyd, Thomas		I, 5th Kans. Cav.	447		1920 Mar 14	KS, 40th, 1921
Boyd, Thomas E.		M, 6th Kans.	1		1923 Sep 26	KS, 43rd, 1924

Name	Rank	Company, Regiment or Ship	Post*	Age	Death Date†	Journal
Boyd, W.M.		B, 48th Iowa Inf.	253		1911 Jul 3	IA, 38th, 1912
Boyd, W.O.	Sergt.	H, 11th Minn. Inf.	30		1920 Aug 15	IA, 47th, 1921
Boyd, W.T.			123		1895	KS, 15th, 1896
Boyd, William A.		H, 7th Iowa	302		1897 Jan 16	KS, 17th, 1898
Boyd, Wm.	Pvt.	K, 33rd Iowa Inf.	40		1920 Mar 26	IA, 47th, 1921
Boyd, Wm. S.		B, 99th Ohio	40		1926 Feb 14	KS, 46th, 1927
Boyden, Daniel		B, 73rd Ill.	66		1898 Dec 24	KS, 18th, 1899
Boyden, John H.	Pvt.	A, 28th Iowa Inf.	98		1917 Dec 24	IA, 44th, 1918
Boydeton, Ben F.	Pvt.	C, 28th Iowa Inf.	69	45	1891 Feb 15	IA, 18th, 1892
Boydston, Geo.	Lieut.	A, 47th Iowa	49		1926 Aug 31	IA, 53rd, 1927
Boyer, Adam		A, 148th Penn.	63		1919 Oct 2	KS, 39th, 1920
Boyer, Benj.	Pvt.	D, 15th Iowa Inf.	369		1902 Sep 6	IA, 29th, 1903
Boyer, D.A.	Pvt.	A, 25th Iowa Inf.	108	88	1931 Jul 12	IA, 58th, 1932
Boyer, D.W.	Pvt.	B, 7th Ill. Cav.	154		1917 Jan 25	IA, 44th, 1918
Boyer, Emanuel	Pvt.	E, 53rd Ind. Inf.	124		1922 Jul 19	IA, 49th, 1923
Boyer, G.W.	Pvt.	C, 14th Ill. Inf.	316		1926 Mar 15	IA, 53rd, 1927
Boyer, G.W.		D, 3rd Ill. Cav.	116		1921 May 6	KS, 41st, 1922
Boyer, G.W.		I, 26th Wis. Inf. (died of old age)	197	72	1901 Apr	NE, 26th, 1902
Boyer, J.A.	Capt.	A, 8th Iowa Inf.	108		1917 Nov 2	IA, 44th, 1918
Boyer, J.F.		C, 8th Iowa Inf. (died of brain fever)	298	56	1895 Dec 28	NE, 20th, 1896
Boyer, Jacob B.		F, 84th — (died of Bright's disease)	13	70	1910 Jun 8	NE, 35th, 1911
Boyer, John F.	Corp.	E, 146th Ill. Inf.	267		1911 May 3	IA, 38th, 1912
Boyer, John J.		C, 142nd Ill. Inf. (member at large; location: Pawnee City)			1938 Sep 30	NE, 63rd, 1939
Boyer, L.M.	Pvt.	A, 19th Iowa Inf.	440		1927 Jun 8	IA, 54th, 1928
Boyer, Leonard		7th Kans.	130		1906 Jul 26	KS, 26th, 1907
Boyer, M.	Pvt.	C, 1st Iowa Cav.	153		1900 Sep	IA, 27th, 1901
Boyer, O.	Pvt.	G, 46th Ill. Inf.	57		1921 Nov 21	IA, 48th, 1922
Boyer, Sam'l	Pvt.	E, 52nd Penn. Inf.	68		1911 Mar 5	IA, 38th, 1912
Boyer, Wm. H.		H, 82nd Ohio	25		1931 Feb 23	NE, 56th, 1932
Boyer, Wm. W.		G, 89th Ohio	500		1917 Oct 18	KS, 37th, 1918
Boyers, Benson		B, 7th West Va. Vols. (died of heart disease)	10		1912 May 25	NE, 37th, 1913
Boyes, Harrison H.	Lieut.	B, 2nd Iowa Cav.	31		1917 Mar 14	IA, 44th, 1918
Boylan, Alvoy	Sergt.	K, 34th Iowa Inf.	18		1909	IA, 36th, 1910
Boyland, T.J.	Pvt.	D, 46th Iowa	190		1922 Feb 17	IA, 49th, 1923
Boyle, A.		C, 147th Ohio	231		1888	KS, 8th, 1889
Boyle, B.F.		F, 103rd Penn. Inf.	93		1912 Jul 23	KS, 32nd, 1913
Boyle, Charles		C, 20th Wis.	47		1897 Mar 1	KS, 17th, 1898
Boyle, James	Pvt.	A, 25th N.Y. Inf.	297		1922 Feb 20	IA, 49th, 1923
Boyle, James A.		L, 2nd U.S. Cav. E, 100th Penn. Inf. (died of dropsy)	215		1890	KS, 10th, 1891
Boyle, Thos.	Pvt.	3rd Iowa Battery	337		1913 Sep 30	IA, 40th, 1914
Boyles, C.W.	Pvt.	A, 17th Iowa Inf.	515		1905	IA, 32nd, 1906
Boyles, R.S.		I, 5th Iowa	12		1898 Sep 5	KS, 18th, 1899
Boynton, Henry W.	H.S.[Hosp. Stew.?]	H, 28th Iowa Inf.	343		1918 Jan 21	IA, 45th, 1919
Boynton, J.S.		F, 27th Ohio Inf.	85		1899 Feb 24	KS, 19th, 1900
Boynton, J.W.	Pvt.	C, 3rd Wis. Cav.	68		1916 Nov 5	IA, 43rd, 1917
Boynton, Nels G.	Pvt.	H, 15th Iowa Inf.	59		1909 Jan 24	IA, 36th, 1910
Bozarts, S.S.		H, 11th Iowa	71		1923 Aug 10	KS, 43rd, 1924
Bozle, J.M.		C, 142nd Ohio	114		1912 Nov 27	KS, 32nd, 1913
Braasch, C.W.		B, 26th Wis. Inf.	109	65	1907 Aug 11	NE, 32nd, 1908
Brabdt, A.V.			40		1906 Jun 20	NE, 31st, 1907
Brace, G.C.	Pvt.	H, 92nd Ill. Inf.	469		1910 Sep 18	IA, 37th, 1911
Brace, J.H.	Pvt.	C, 29th Iowa Inf.	83		1909 Sep 20	IA, 36th, 1910
Brace, M.P.	Pvt.	F, 15th Ohio	83		1924 May 25	IA, 51st, 1925
Brace, S.U.	Pvt.	A, 11th Ill. Inf.	165		1918	IA, 45th, 1919
Bracken, Jas. L.		C, Ill. Inf.	24		1923 Mar 26	IA, 50th, 1924
Bracken, R.P.		G, 92nd Ohio	13		1936 Dec 14	NE, 61st, 1937
Brackett, A.R.	Pvt.	E, U.S. Art.	12		1924 Jun 21	IA, 51st, 1925
Brackett, Sam'l	Pvt.	I, 32nd Wis.	23		1905	IA, 32nd, 1906
Bracy, Geo.		K, 83rd U.S.C.T.	52		1917 May 25	KS, 37th, 1918

Name	Rank	Company, Regiment or Ship	Post*	Age	Death Date†	Journal
Bradberry, D.	Pvt.	B, 30th Iowa Inf.	100	68	1895 Jul 7	IA, 22nd, 1896
Bradburg, Joseph		B, 10th Kans.	88		1906 May 11	KS, 26th, 1907
Bradbury, J.W.		20th Ind.	40		1905 Mar 21	IA, 32nd, 1906
Bradbury, W.H.		B, 129th Ill. Inf.	1		1900 Nov 3	KS, 20th, 1901
Braden, Robt.			167		1927	IA, 54th, 1928
Brader, George W.	Corp.	E, 8th Wis. Inf.	111		1897 Apr 20	IA, 24th, 1898
Brader, Richard			111		1917 Feb 5	IA, 44th, 1918
Bradfield, A.	Lieut.	F, 39th Iowa Inf.	82	64	1888 Dec 4	IA, 15th, 1889
Bradfield, H.	Pvt.	G, 1st Iowa Cav.	154		1919 Jun 30	IA, 46th, 1920
Bradfield, W.	Pvt.	F, 3rd Iowa Cav.	192		1918 Nov 21	IA, 45th, 1919
Bradford, A.J.		K, 2nd Col. Cav.	159		1893 Dec 24	KS, 13th, 1894
Bradford, Albert	Corp.	F, 29th Wis. Inf.	132	43	1887 Dec 24	IA, 14th, 1888
Bradford, Aloin		F, 39th Iowa	18		1911 Jul 26	KS, 31st, 1912
Bradford, B.		E, 3rd Mich. Cav.	288		1924 Dec 27	KS, 44th, 1925
Bradford, E.			112		1923	IA, 50th, 1924
Bradford, Heath	Pvt.	D, 100th Ill. Inf.	101		1923 Jun 14	IA, 50th, 1924
Bradford, Hiram		B, 103rd Ohio	72		1910 Oct 25	KS, 30th, 1911
Bradford, J.		F, Ohio (died at Centropolis)	18		1895 Nov	KS, 15th, 1896
Bradford, M.		F, 49th Ill.	132		1924 Mar 28	KS, 44th, 1925
Bradford, Sidney	Corp.	A, 8th Ill.	465		1914 Oct 31	IA, 41st, 1915
Bradford, Thos.	Pvt.	A, 45th Ill. Inf.	155		1901 Feb 9	IA, 27th, 1901
Bradford, Trunnell	Pvt.	B, 18th Mo. Inf.	17		1902 Feb 26	IA, 29th, 1903
Bradford, V.	Pvt.	B, 114th Ill. Inf.	112		1910 Feb 8	IA, 37th, 1911
Bradford, W.		D, 25th Ill.	132		1888	KS, 8th, 1889
Bradford, Ward		C, 6th Mo. Inf.	11		1900 Aug 16	KS, 20th, 1901
Bradgeman, J.	Pvt.	G, 35th Iowa	452		1921 Aug 2	IA, 48th, 1922
Bradley, C.C.	Pvt.	A, 4th Iowa Cav.	190		1906 Dec	IA, 33rd, 1907
Bradley, Frank	Pvt.	B, 1st N.Y. Cav.	12		1909 Oct 7	IA, 36th, 1910
Bradley, J.R.		F, 1st U.S. Vol. En., Virginia	38		1885	KS, 5th, 1886
Bradley, J.T.		A, 70th Ohio Inf.	81		1916 May 23	KS, 36th, 1917
Bradley, Jacob S.			[77?]		1904[1905?] Jan 11	KS, 24th, 1905
Bradley, John		A, — Mich. Cav. (born in Buffalo, N.Y.; died in Omaha)	7		1883 Sep 2	NE, 8th, 1884
Bradley, John L.	Pvt. & Corp.	H, 122nd Ill. (died of typhoid fever)	16	43	1884 Feb 10	NE, 9th, 1885
Bradley, Joseph	Pvt.	B, 177th N.Y. Inf.	19		1918 Jul 9	IA, 45th, 1919
Bradley, Lucien		B, 12th Ind.	1		1931 Jan 30	KS, 51st, 1932
Bradley, P.H.	Pvt.	G, 6th Iowa Cav.	23		1919 Jun	IA, 46th, 1920
Bradley, R.J.		A, 1st Mich. Art. (died of heart disease)	24		1902 Feb	NE, 27th, 1903
Bradley, S.D.		G, 7th Iowa Cav. (died at Salina)	127		1895 Oct 6	KS, 15th, 1896
Bradley, W.E.	Pvt.	F, 15th Ill. Inf.	414		1903 Feb 15	IA, 30th, 1904
Bradshaw, C.B.	Capt.	F, 24th Iowa Inf.	343		1916	IA, 43rd, 1917
Bradshaw, Chas.			116		1928 May 22	IA, 55th, 1929
Bradshaw, Henry		E, 8th Mo. Cav. (died at Galena, Kans.; buried at Galena Cemetery)	54		1894 Jul 28	KS, 14th, 1895
Bradshaw, L.H.	Pvt.	A, 2nd Ill. Cav.	12		1924 Dec 26	IA, 51st, 1925
Bradshaw, Smith		K, 79th U.S. Cav.	18		1923 Apr 8	KS, 43rd, 1924
Bradshaw, W.S.			22		1898 Nov 15	KS, 18th, 1899
Brady, Daniel		died of consumption	3		1886 Apr 8	NE, 11th, 1887
Brady, Hugh		G, 64th Ill.	185		1920 Sep 12	KS, 40th, 1921
Brady, James L.		I, 94th Ohio Inf.	12		1914 May 24	KS, 34th, 1915
Brady, John	Pvt.	A, 32nd N.Y. Art.	83		1905 Nov 1	IA, 32nd, 1906
Brady, John L.		C, 1st Del.	174		1914 Oct 19	KS, 34th, 1915
Brady, John T.	Pvt.	K, 15th Iowa Inf.	49		1915 Jan 22	IA, 42nd, 1916
Brady, Joseph	Pvt.	C, 14th Iowa Inf.	74		1925 Apr 2	IA, 52nd, 1926
Brady, M.	Pvt.	D, 2nd Iowa Inf.	12		1920 Aug 6	IA, 47th, 1921
Brady, M.		M, 1st Ill. Art. (died from wounds)	263		1888	KS, 8th, 1889
Brady, P.P.		F, 38th Ill.	322		1904 Mar	KS, 24th, 1905
Brady, Patrick		G, 10th Ill.	117		1926 Jun 6	KS, 46th, 1927
Brady, W.R.		H, 30th Iowa Inf.	52		1908 Nov 17	KS, 28th, 1909
Brady, Wm.	Pvt.	C, 21st Iowa Inf.	190		1926 Dec 1	IA, 53rd, 1927
Bragdon, B.F.			147		1919 Sep 11	KS, 39th, 1920
Bragg, Minton F.		I, 25th Ill.	447		1926 Aug 18	KS, 46th, 1927

*See Appendix A, B or C for roster of post names and locations.
†See Introduction for note regarding recording of death date.

Name	Rank	Company, Regiment or Ship	Post*	Age	Death Date†	Journal
Bragg, T.N.		C, 91st Ill. Inf.	111		1918 Feb 8	IA, 45th, 1919
Bragger, F.O.	Pvt.	B, Wis.	101		1923 Sep 3	IA, 50th, 1924
Brainard, Jas. F.	Pvt.	G, 5th Iowa Inf.	235		1915 May 4	IA, 42nd, 1916
Brainard, Jesse		B, 4th Ill. Cav.	17		1917 Feb 6	KS, 37th, 1918
Brainard, M.C.	Pvt.	F, 141st Ill. Inf.	12		1917 Jun 8	IA, 44th, 1918
Brainerd, William		B, 1st Mo. Eng.	311		1913 Mar 5	KS, 33rd, 1914
Braininger, Peter	Pvt.	E, 15th Ill. Inf.	147		1910 May 31	IA, 37th, 1911
Brakeman, L.D.		H, 169th Penn. Inf. (died of old age)	32	80	1905 Aug 28	NE, 30th, 1906
Braley, J.S.	Pvt.	C, 79th Ill. Inf.	3		1919 Dec 8	IA, 46th, 1920
Braman, W.B.		F, 71st Ill. Inf.	293		1909 Feb 25	KS, 29th, 1910
Bramble, I.F.	Pvt.	104th Ill.	248		1922 Feb 4	IA, 49th, 1923
Bramer, Daniel D.		C, 21st Ohio Inf. (died of heart failure)	10	65	1900 Jan 22	NE, 25th, 1901
Bramer, L.	Pvt.	E, 30th Iowa Inf.	376	46	1888 Jul 11	IA, 17th, 1891
Bramer, Laf.	Pvt.	E, 30th Iowa Inf.	376	46	1888 Jul 11	IA, 15th, 1889
Bramhall, F.M.	Pvt.	C, 92nd Ill. Inf.	98		1930 Dec 19	IA, 57th, 1931
Bramhall, I.N.		F, 17th Iowa Inf. (killed on railroad)	118	76	1920 Jun 1	NE, 45th, 1921
Brammer, Henry		H, 2nd Kans. Cav.	260		1898 Nov 6	KS, 18th, 1899
Brammer, W.A.	Pvt.	D, 22nd Ky.	27		1899 Mar 1	IA, 26th, 1900
Brams, F.I.		A, 11th U.S. Col. Art.	132		1909 Feb 1	KS, 29th, 1910
Branch, Arthur A.	Pvt.	K, 6th Mich. Cav.	67	43	1892 Apr 27	IA, 19th, 1893
Branch, M.L.	Lieut.	A, 184th N.Y. Inf.	58		1915 Mar 28	IA, 42nd, 1916
Branch, Phineas C.		G, 13th Iowa Inf.	14		1912 Jan 2	KS, 32nd, 1913
Brand, Thos.	Sergt.	D, 19th Wis.	314		1924 May 17	IA, 51st, 1925
Brandis, August	Pvt.	L, 6th Iowa Cav.	247		1909 May 17	IA, 36th, 1910
Brandon, C.D.		A, 13th Ill.	225		1906 Aug 26	KS, 26th, 1907
Brandon, Chas.	Pvt.	E, 28th Wis.	22		1922 Dec 23	IA, 49th, 1923
Brandon, Jos.	Pvt.	K, 9th Iowa Cav.	78		1929 Jul 15	IA, 56th, 1930
Brandon, Nathanial		B, 4th Tenn. Cav.	97		1890	KS, 10th, 1891
Brandt, F.G.	1st Lieut.	U.S.A.	78		1905 Mar 31	IA, 32nd, 1906
Brandt, J.H.		C, 43rd Penn. (died of rheumatism)	245	73	1918 Mar 13	NE, 43rd, 1919
Brandt, John H.	Pvt.	C, 1st Iowa Cav.	5		1911 Apr 29	IA, 38th, 1912
Brandt, Michael		E, 3rd Penn. Art.	25		1929 May 24	NE, 54th, 1930
Brandt, Wm.			175		1916	KS, 36th, 1917
Brandts, Wm.			152		1890 May 11	NE, 15th, 1891
Branhagen, Anders T.		E, 38th Iowa Inf.		92 & 10 mos.	1937 Aug 11	IA, 64th, 1938
Brann, Richard W.		I, 21st Ind.	33		1923 Nov 17	KS, 43rd, 1924
Brannan, John		I & C, 2nd & 75th Ohio Vol. Inf.	64		1908 Apr 21	KS, 28th, 1909
Brannan, Joseph M.		I, 72nd Ind.	388		1918 Feb 22	KS, 38th, 1919
Brannan, L.H.	Pvt.	G, 14th Iowa Inf.	24	86	1933 Oct 20	IA, 60th, 1934
Brannen, Wm.		I, 18th Iowa Inf. (died of heart disease)	55		1894 Sep 3	NE, 19th, 1895
Brannigan, John		C, 4th Ill. Cav.	500		1914 Apr 14	KS, 34th, 1915
Branning, N.B.	Pvt.	G, 51st Wis.	30		1926 Sep 18	IA, 53rd, 1927
Brannon, John					1903 Dec 20	IA, 30th, 1904
Brannon, T.S.	Corp.	C, 10th Iowa Inf.	93		1915 Jan 12	IA, 42nd, 1916
Branny, John		I, 107th Ohio Inf.	32		1908[1909?] Jun 10	KS, 29th, 1910
Branson, N.T.		F, 12th Ill. Inf. (died of softening of brain)	106	71	1901 Apr	NE, 26th, 1902
Brant, Zinri		G, 152nd Ill. Inf.	91		1891 Aug 4	KS, 11th, 1892
Brantam, Wm.		B, 13th Kans.	87		1906 Nov 12	KS, 26th, 1907
Brashear, W.F.		F, 154th Ill.	139		1911 Nov 15	KS, 31st, 1912
Brashelier, Henry	.	L, 3rd Mass. Hvy. Art.	64		1920 Dec 31	KS, 40th, 1921
Brasher, Ed.	Pvt.	M, 3rd Iowa Inf.	122		1909	IA, 36th, 1910
Brasier, —			4		1923 Sep 8	KS, 43rd, 1924
Brasier, Andrew			25		1937 Mar 22	KS, 57th, 1938
Brass, S.L.		D, 1st Mich. Cav. (died of heart disease)	81	71	1902 Aug	NE, 27th, 1903
Brassfield, G.M.		M, 3rd Mo. Cav.	53		1923 Jul 10	KS, 43rd, 1924
Brasted, I.H.	Pvt.	L, 1st N.Y. Art.	12		1921 May 15	IA, 48th, 1922
Bratcher, J.E.		A, 17th Ky.	378		1913 May 25	KS, 33rd, 1914
Brates, G.E.		E, 2nd Kans.	132		1888	KS, 8th, 1889
Bratley, Joseph		5th Wis. Cav.	25		1929 Jan 10	KS, 49th, 1930
Bratnober, R.	Pvt.	K, 44th Wis. Inf.	68		1925 Feb 16	IA, 52nd, 1926

Name	Rank	Company, Regiment or Ship	Post*	Age	Death Date†	Journal
Braton, Wm.			38		1911 1st term	IA, 38th, 1912
Bratt, Jos. M.		A, 5th Iowa Cav. (died of old age)	47	83	1913 Aug 27	NE, 38th, 1914
Bratt, W.A.	2nd Lieut.	H, 14th Wis. Inf.	276		1900 Jan 20	IA, 27th, 1901
Bratt, W.H.	Pvt.	I, 16th Iowa	68		1906 Dec 14	IA, 33rd, 1907
Bratton, John M.		E, 12th Kans.	35		1915 Oct 24	KS, 35th, 1916
Braught, S.M.		G, 17th Iowa	118		1908 Nov 9	KS, 28th, 1909
Brawley, Geo. S.		H, 23rd Mo.	25		1904 Dec 13	KS, 24th, 1905
Brawley, Mark A.		G, 137th Ohio	53		1923 Jul 15	KS, 43rd, 1924
Brawrie, Howard		K, 30th Penn.	43		1906 Jul 2	KS, 26th, 1907
Bray, Andrew J.	Pvt.	H, 4th Iowa Cav.	294	51	1893 May 17	IA, 20th, 1894
Bray, Enos		B, 85th Mo.	81		1928 Jul 18	KS, 48th, 1929
Bray, Henry	Pvt.	F, 76th Ill. Inf. (at large)	68	99	1943 May 8	IA, 69th, 1943
Bray, J.G.		F, 165th Ill.	113		1914 Oct 22	KS, 34th, 1915
Bray, John		F, 152nd Ind. Inf.	79		1893 Jul 31	NE, 18th, 1894
Bray, Levi H.	Pvt.	B, 22nd Iowa Inf.	333		1913 Jun 1	IA, 40th, 1914
Bray, W.H.	Pvt.	D, 46th Iowa Inf.	46		1916 Mar 26	IA, 43rd, 1917
Brayman, W.B.		19th Ohio	65		1904 Feb 29	KS, 24th, 1905
Brayward, J.P.		A, 3rd Wis. Inf. (died at Indiana, Kans.; buried at Indiana Cemetery)	182		1894 Jun 11	KS, 14th, 1895
Brazelton, John	Surg.	134th Ind.	318		1912	NE, 37th, 1913
Bready, John E.	Lieut.	H, 14th Penn. Cav.	78		1912 Jun 5	IA, 39th, 1913
Breaithwaite, John W.	Lieut.	M, 6th West Va.	127		1913 Nov 18	KS, 33rd, 1914
Breat, H.I.	Pvt.		116		1920	IA, 47th, 1921
Brecher, R.		B, 36th Ill. Inf.	80	91	1935 Jun 30	IA, 62nd, 1936
Brechter, Geo. F.	Pvt.	A, 8th Mich. Cav.	329		1913 Oct 13	IA, 40th, 1914
Breckenbride, D.L.	Pvt.	A, 142nd Ohio Inf.	418		1912 May 13	IA, 39th, 1913
Breckenridge, A.	Pvt.	F, 148th Ohio Inf.	286	65	1897 Feb 5	IA, 23rd, 1897
Breckenridge, Hugh	Pvt.	F, 148th Ohio Inf.	286		1900 Nov 2	IA, 27th, 1901
Breckenridge, John		8th Wis. Bat.	168		1899 Apr 21	IA, 26th, 1900
Breckon, J.W.		died of paralysis	23	78	1913 Oct 15	NE, 38th, 1914
Breckon, W.J.	Pvt.	G, 1st Mo. Cav.	231		1899 Jun 12	IA, 26th, 1900
Breed, A.		A, 20th Iowa	9		1909 Jan	NE, 33rd, 1909
Breeding, Alexander	Sergt.	A, 3rd Iowa Inf.	100		1914 Aug 8	IA, 41st, 1915
Breeley, James E.			158		1913	IA, 40th, 1914
Breemen, Solomon		F, 4th Iowa Cav.	8		1891 Jan 24	KS, 11th, 1892
Brees, S.W.		F, 18th Iowa (died of pneumonia)	35	76	1918 Mar 26	NE, 43rd, 1919
Breese, A.M.		C, 15th Ohio	201		1927 Aug 11	KS, 47th, 1928
Breese, Edward	Pvt.	I, 22nd Iowa Inf.	8		1908 May 25	IA, 35th, 1909
Breese, Israel	Pvt.	B, 25th Wis. Inf.	57		1931 Dec 12	IA, 58th, 1932
Breese, J.M.	Pvt.	I, 1st Neb. Inf.	30		1919 Sep 25	IA, 46th, 1920
Breese, Thomas		B, 12th Kans. Inf.	12		1911 Apr 5	KS, 31st, 1912
Brehm, S.H.		E, 130th Penn. Inf. (died at Hutchinson, Kans.; buried at East Side Cemetery)	17		1894 Aug 20	KS, 14th, 1895
Breisch, J.F.		B, 1st Md.	1		1897 Jan 7	KS, 17th, 1898
Breitenstein, William	Pvt.	B, 3rd Iowa Cav.	254	98	1939 Oct 1	IA, 66th, 1940
Breithaupt, Chas.		F, 13th Iowa Inf.	25		1940 Jul	NE, 65th, 1941
Breman, B.F.	Pvt.	I, 15th Iowa Inf.	82		1917 Feb 26	IA, 44th, 1918
Bremer, Conrad	Corp.	C, 35th Iowa Inf.	231		1915 Nov 26	IA, 42nd, 1916
Brenbarger, Isaac		C, 191st Ohio Inf. (died of pneumonia)	52		1902 Feb	NE, 27th, 1903
Brendle, Emil	Sergt.	82nd Ill. Inf.	235		1906 Jan 6	IA, 33rd, 1907
Breneman, Benj.	Pvt.	F, 24th Iowa Inf.	30		1908 Jun 1	IA, 35th, 1909
Brennan, Michael			227		1921 Dec 10	NE, 47th, 1923
Brennan, Thomas		E, 7th Kans. Inf.	117		1886	KS, 6th, 1887
Brenneman, Fred	Pvt.	H, 28th Iowa Inf.	321		1909 Mar 14	IA, 36th, 1910
Brenner, Jacob		D, 201st Penn. Inf.	233	90	1935 Mar 2	IA, 62nd, 1936
Brenner, Jacob		D, 93rd Ill.	100		1919 Aug 26	KS, 39th, 1920
Brentnall, James O.		I, 1st Wis.	1		1911 Apr 12	KS, 31st, 1912
Brenton, A.P.		G, 58th Ind.	50		1920 Feb 24	KS, 40th, 1921
Brenton, O.L.		A, 3rd Ind.	18		1927 Sep 26	KS, 47th, 1928
Brenton, W.H.	Pvt.	D, 2nd Iowa Inf.	230	53	1893 Dec 10	IA, 20th, 1894
Bressner, John		C, 14th Ill.	50		1923 May 5	KS, 43rd, 1924
Breston, Nicholas		Post No. 29, Dept. of Missouri			1890	KS, 10th, 1891

Name	Rank	Company, Regiment or Ship	Post*	Age	Death Date†	Journal
Bretsford, A.N.		126th Ill. Inf.	24		1923 Apr 25	IA, 50th, 1924
Brett, John			187		1894 May 4	NE, 19th, 1895
Bretweiser, Leonard					1935	KS, 55th, 1936
Brewer, A.P.		F, 167th Ohio Inf.	12		1908 Apr 10	KS, 28th, 1909
Brewer, G.W.		C, 75th Ind. Inf. (died at Pittsburg, Kans.)	65		1894 Jan	KS, 14th, 1895
Brewer, H.W.		L, 2nd Cal. Cav.	117		1916 Sep 16	KS, 36th, 1917
Brewer, Ira		D, 28th Iowa Inf. (died of paralysis)	89	77	1922 Jan 17	NE, 47th, 1923
Brewer, J.A.	Capt.	C, 23rd Mo. Inf.	12		1918 Jan 31	IA, 45th, 1919
Brewer, J.H.C.		6th Md.	89		1927 Dec 15	KS, 48th, 1929
Brewer, J.W.	Pvt.	F, 150th Ohio Inf.	192		1919 Dec 8	IA, 46th, 1920
Brewer, John		B, 80th Ind.	42		1912 Apr 1	KS, 32nd, 1913
Brewer, John S.	Pvt.	F, 7th Iowa Cav.	48	72	1891 Aug	IA, 18th, 1892
Brewer, L.		D, 1st Mich. E. and M.[Engineers & Mechanics]	43		1892 Jul 2	NE, 17th, 1893
Brewer, L.H.		I, 149th Ill.	127		1920 Dec 15	KS, 40th, 1921
Brewer, Stephen	Pvt.	A, 11th Iowa Inf.	231		1902 Aug 12	IA, 29th, 1903
Brewer, Stephen		A, 12th Ill. Inf.	387		1887 Dec 27	KS, 7th, 1888
Brewer, Stephen		D, 12th Ill.	387		1888	KS, 8th, 1889
Brewer, Thomas J.		L, 1st Ind. Lt. Art.	65		1913 Jul 3	KS, 33rd, 1914
Brewer, Thos. H.		C, 69th Ind.	450		1897 Aug 24	KS, 17th, 1898
Brewer, W.W.		F, 9th Iowa	7		1930 Jan 5	NE, 55th, 1931
Brewerton, S.S.		F, 117th Ill.	42		1911 Oct 7	KS, 31st, 1912
Brewster, A.		I, 15th N.Y. Cav.	35		1932 Feb 5	NE, 57th, 1933
Brewster, Caleb		K, 69th N.Y.	64		1927 Mar 29	KS, 47th, 1928
Brewster, Henry	Pvt.	D, 24th Wis. Inf.	165		1900 Jan 15	IA, 27th, 1901
Brewster, J.H.		E, 80th Ohio	4		1916 Mar 8	KS, 36th, 1917
Brewster, J.M.			6		1925	IA, 52nd, 1926
Brewster, Robert E.		E, 8th N.Y. 74th N.Y.	3		1892 Jul 28	KS, 12th, 1893
Brewster, S.G.		A, 34th Ind. Inf. (died at Topeka)	71		1895 Nov 7	KS, 15th, 1896
Brewster, Thos. K.	Pvt.	A, 131st Ohio National Guard	40		1904 Oct 23	IA, 31st, 1905
Briant, Joseth		G, 77th Penn.	115		1908 Oct 23	KS, 28th, 1909
Briar, James	Pvt.	A, 27th Iowa Inf.	194		1928 Jan 23	IA, 55th, 1929
Brice, Frederick H.		F, 16th Ill. Inf.	290		1913 Aug 7	IA, 40th, 1914
Brice, Thos.	Pvt.	H, 92nd Ill. Inf.	24		1919 Apr 2	IA, 46th, 1920
Brickle, P.		F, 85th — (died of dropsy)	43	57	1903 Oct 14	NE, 28th, 1904
Brickley, James J.	Pvt.	B, 9th Iowa Inf.	191		1902 Apr 4	IA, 28th, 1902
Bricksey, Wm.	Pvt.	C, 8th Mo. Cav.	67		1912 Jun 7	IA, 39th, 1913
Bridal, John G.			434		1907	IA, 34th, 1908
Bridell, Isaac	Pvt.	I, 3rd Minn. Inf.	299	59	1889 Jan 25	IA, 17th, 1891
Bridenstein, Levi		F, 69th Ohio	147		1917 Apr 27	KS, 37th, 1918
Bridenstine, Abraham		F, 74th Ind.	244		1912 Mar 13	KS, 32nd, 1913
Bridgeman, John	Pvt.	B, 51st Ind. Inf.	59		1926 Nov 7	IA, 53rd, 1927
Bridges, Geo. O.		G, 11th Kans. Cav.	147		1918 Aug 15	KS, 38th, 1919
Bridges, James A.	Pvt.	K, 14th Iowa Inf.	157		1907	IA, 34th, 1908
Bridges, James A.	Corp.	G, 45th Iowa Inf.	157		1907 Jan 15	IA, 34th, 1908
Bridges, Robert		A, 6th Tenn. Inf.	90		1917 Mar 14	KS, 37th, 1918
Bridges, Thomas H.		L, 5th Kans. Cav.	97		1917 Jun 12	KS, 37th, 1918
Bridget, John		I, 4th Ind. Cav. (died of Bright's disease)	59	68	1897 Jun 12	NE, 22nd, 1898
Bridgford, Wm.	Pvt.	C, 18th N.Y. Inf.	152		1909 Nov 7	IA, 36th, 1910
Brien, J.O.		F, 10th Ill. Cav.	95		1892 Aug 26	NE, 17th, 1893
Brier, J.A.	Pvt.	K, 142nd Ind. Inf.	19	85	1932 Jan 4	IA, 59th, 1933
Brieton, J.N.		A, 1st Kans.	17		1920 Jan 14	KS, 40th, 1921
Briggs, Alvin		D, 10th Kans.	10		1892 Oct 28	KS, 12th, 1893
Briggs, Chester J.	Wagoner	D, 16th Vt. M.	59		1905 Jan 19	IA, 31st, 1905
Briggs, E.C.	Pvt.	A, 12th N.Y. Inf.	92	55	1897 Jul 29	IA, 24th, 1898
Briggs, Edward R.		F, 1st Ore. Cav. (died of old age)	354	82	1919 Apr 2	NE, 44th, 1920
Briggs, Elijah	Pvt.		206		1920 Nov 10	IA, 47th, 1921
Briggs, Geo. O.	Pvt.	M, 1st Mex. Cav.	78		1907 Feb 15	IA, 34th, 1908
Briggs, George			115		1899 Aug 25	IA, 26th, 1900
Briggs, J.M.	Sergt.	K, 14th Penn. Cav.	50		1911 2nd term	IA, 38th, 1912
Briggs, James S.	Pvt.	A, U.S.P.G.[U.S. Provost Guard?]	235		1913 Oct 31	IA, 40th, 1914

Name	Rank	Company, Regiment or Ship	Post*	Age	Death Date†	Journal
Briggs, John		K, 35th Iowa	107		1914 Jan 28	KS, 34th, 1915
Briggs, Jos. W.		B, 13th Ohio	68		1922 Jan 11	KS, 42nd, 1923
Briggs, Lauren	Pvt.	C, 1st Iowa Cav.	11		1897 May	IA, 24th, 1898
Briggs, Levi	Pvt.	E, 12th Ind. Cav.	452	86	1931 Oct 22	IA, 58th, 1932
Briggs, M.C.		B, 116th N.Y.	25		1915	NE, 40th, 1916
Briggs, O.F.	QM	19th Iowa Inf.	497		1925 Oct 6	IA, 52nd, 1926
Briggs, Oren		C, 1st Wis.	174		1917 Dec 18	KS, 37th, 1918
Briggs, Y.S.			17		1911 Dec 29	KS, 31st, 1912
Brigham, C.B.		H, 4th N.H. Inf. (died of La Grippe)	44	68	1896 May 26	NE, 21st, 1897
Brigham, J.H.		G, 10th N.Y.	147		1922 Dec 28	KS, 42nd, 1923
Bright, J.G.		H, 50th Ind. Inf.	25		1901 Nov	KS, 21st, 1902
Bright, J.H.	Pvt.	K, 4th Iowa Cav.	56		1917 Dec 28	IA, 44th, 1918
Bright, J.M.		43rd Mo.	28		1928 Oct 29	KS, 48th, 1929
Bright, John			193		1912 May 14	KS, 32nd, 1913
Bright, Leb		K, 4th Iowa Cav.	56	90	1934 Jul 24	IA, 61st, 1935
Bright, Lewis		C, 7th Ind. Cav.	28		1921 Oct 25	KS, 41st, 1922
Bright, S.		H, 8th Wis. Inf. (died of old age)	80	85	1895 May 28	NE, 20th, 1896
Brighthill, D.J.	Pvt.	G, 127th Penn. Inf.	78		1924 Oct 8	IA, 51st, 1925
Brightwell, Geo. W.	Pvt.	G, 118th Ill. Inf.	208		1903 Feb 14	IA, 29th, 1903
Briles, B.W.	Pvt.	A, 102nd Ill. Inf.	5		1904 Sep 11	IA, 31st, 1905
Briley, Ira	Pvt.	A, 23rd Iowa Inf.	329		1910 Dec 10	IA, 37th, 1911
Briley, S.H.	Pvt.	A, 34th Iowa Inf.	312		1909 May 22	IA, 36th, 1910
Brill, J.R.	Pvt.	B, 148th Ohio Inf.	40		1920 Jul 14	IA, 47th, 1921
Brill, W.E.	Sergt.	F, 23rd Wis. Inf.	348		1909 Aug 27	IA, 36th, 1910
Brill, W.H.	Pvt.	A, 33rd Wis. Inf.	22		1909 Feb 19	IA, 36th, 1910
Brimkin, A.			377		1907	IA, 34th, 1908
Brimmerman, H.J.		E, 156th Ohio	47		1921 Oct 7	KS, 41st, 1922
Brindle, Sam'l		109th Penn.	8		1927 Jul 31	KS, 47th, 1928
Brinenstall, R.R.	Pvt.	K, 2nd Ill. Lt. Art.	441		1900 Nov 1	IA, 27th, 1901
Bringham, A.J.	Pvt.	H, 1st Minn. Inf.	179		1907 Jan 3	IA, 34th, 1908
Bringle, I.J.		B, 7th Ind.	17		1921 Dec 15	KS, 41st, 1922
Brink, J.R.			440		1910 Dec 6	IA, 37th, 1911
Brinkerhoff, J.W.		E, Penn. Inf.	18		1929 Mar 7	KS, 49th, 1930
Brinkerhoff, S.S.			32		1883	KS, 3rd, 1884
Brinnerman, John		E, 28th Iowa	25		1924 Jan 7	KS, 44th, 1925
Brinson, Wm.	Pvt.	F, 4th Iowa Inf.	55		1929 Dec	IA, 57th, 1931
Brisben, John		39th Iowa Inf.	297		1917 Dec 28	IA, 44th, 1918
Brisben, John J.		K, 39th Iowa Inf.	297		1918 Dec 28	IA, 45th, 1919
Brisco, Abijah		A, 1st N.Y. (died of old age)	8	90	1916 Nov 30	NE, 41st, 1917
Briscoe, Wm. H.		D, 84th Ill. Inf.	303		1900 Jul 18	KS, 20th, 1901
Brister, John		B, 30th Ill. (died in Oklahoma)	99		1892 Nov 17	KS, 12th, 1893
Bristol, Cicero		46th Iowa Inf.	25	80	1917 Jul 30	NE, 42nd, 1918
Bristol, L.F.	Pvt.	I, 9th Ill. Cav.	222		1920 Apr 17	IA, 47th, 1921
Bristow, George W.		1st Ind. Iowa	25		1925 Dec 23	KS, 45th, 1926
Bristow, J.J.	Pvt.	K, 81st Ind. Inf.	97		1906 May 8	IA, 33rd, 1907
Bristow, Wm.		K, 24th Ky. Inf.	40		1921 Mar 15	KS, 41st, 1922
Britell, O.		D, 75th Ill. (died of paralysis)	327	60	1911 Oct 14	NE, 36th, 1912
Britt, John		K, 34th Iowa	17		1915 Jan 15	KS, 35th, 1916
Britt, Leroy F.		B, 29th Iowa (died of paralysis)	262	54	1900 Nov 13	NE, 25th, 1901
Brittan, H.P.		C, 35th N.Y. Inf.	235		1915 Jun 26	IA, 42nd, 1916
Brittian, Alfred	Pvt.	A, 39th Iowa Inf.	55		1913 Oct 23	IA, 40th, 1914
Brittian, Parks	Pvt.	29th Iowa Inf.	440		1910 Mar 24	IA, 37th, 1911
Brittingham, Jerry		D, 135th Ill. Inf. (died of paralysis)	332		1893 Mar 14	NE, 18th, 1894
Britton, C.H.	Pvt.	H, 127th Ill. Inf.	22		1918 Jul 16	IA, 45th, 1919
Britton, D.T.		I, 169th Ohio Inf. (died at Eldorado)	154		1895 Oct 3	KS, 15th, 1896
Broadbent, Andrew			311		1898 Jun 20	KS, 18th, 1899
Broadbent, Geo. W.	Pvt.	F, 9th Iowa Inf.	192		1909 Nov 12	IA, 36th, 1910
Broadstone, Allen H.		E, 195th Penn.	251		1914 Mar 10	KS, 34th, 1915
Broadstone, John		D, 73rd Ind. Inf.	127[?]		1893 Jan 31	IA, 20th, 1894
Broady, Frederick		K, 129th Ill. Inf. (died of lingering illness)	47	72	1914 Jun 29	NE, 39th, 1915
Brobst, A.B.	Pvt.	L, 9th Iowa Cav.	49		1929 Jan 12	IA, 56th, 1930
Brobst, Sol	Pvt.	H, 7th Ohio Inf.	12		1919 Apr 17	IA, 47th, 1921

*See Appendix A, B or C for roster of post names and locations.
†See Introduction for note regarding recording of death date.

Name	Rank	Company, Regiment or Ship	Post*	Age	Death Date†	Journal
Brobst, Solomon	Pvt.	H, 7th Ohio Inf.	452		1919 Apr 7	IA, 46th, 1920
Brock, C.H.	Capt.	B, 2nd Iowa Cav.	94		1925 Nov 14	IA, 52nd, 1926
		I, 8th Iowa Cav.				
Brock, C.L.	Pvt.	I, 104th Ill. Inf.	141		1915 Jan 2	IA, 42nd, 1916
Brock, George	Pvt.	F, 17th Ill. Cav.	78		1901 Aug 8	IA, 28th, 1902
Brock, J.F.	Sergt.	A, 39th Iowa	55		1899	IA, 26th, 1900
Brock, J.K.	Pvt.	B, 2nd Iowa Cav.	155		1916 Jan 4	IA, 42nd, 1916
Brock, J.K.	Pvt.	B, 2nd Iowa Cav.	155		1916 Jan 4	IA, 43rd, 1917
Brock, John R.		E, 10th Penn. Inf.	9		1927 May 21	NE, 52nd, 1928
Brock, Philip H.		D, 23rd Iowa	256		1931 Jul 24	NE, 56th, 1932
Brockaway, Wm.	Pvt.	B, 35th Iowa	12		1907 Feb 2	IA, 34th, 1908
Brocke, Robert			77		1924	NE, 49th, 1925
Brockelsberg, Fred'ck	Pvt.	H, 4th Minn. Inf.	2		1901 Nov 4	IA, 28th, 1902
Brocklesby, William		D, 1st Kans.	12		1905 Aug 18	KS, 25th, 1906
Brockman, John M.		1st Neb.		65	1907	NE, 31st, 1907
		5th Iowa Cav. (see Appendix D)				
Brockway, A.C.	Pvt.	A, 49th Mass. Inf.	71		1916 Dec 21	IA, 43rd, 1917
Brockway, Geo. A.	Pvt.	B, 35th Iowa Vols.	12		1907 Feb 21	IA, 34th, 1908
Brockway, H.N.	Capt.	B, 32nd Iowa Inf.	485		1906 Jun 7	IA, 33rd, 1907
Brockway, J.N.		I, 9th Iowa Cav.	34	92	1934 Apr 11	IA, 61st, 1935
Brockway, Jed	Pvt.	D, 47th Iowa Inf.	23	88	1933 Sep 27	IA, 60th, 1934
Brockway, N.	Pvt.	E, 19th Iowa Inf.	7		1910 Aug 29	IA, 37th, 1911
Brockway, William S.		A, 10th Conn. Inf.	68		1925 Jun 18	KS, 45th, 1926
Broderick, Case		2nd Kans. Art.	46		1920 Apr 1	KS, 40th, 1921
Broderick, Edw.		F, 37th Wis.	113		1920 Oct	NE, 45th, 1921
Brodock, H.H.		F, 4th Mich.	158		1911 Apr 20	KS, 31st, 1912
Brodway, Charles	Pvt.	E, 10th —	455	52	1894 Apr	IA, 21st, 1895
Brody, J.K.	Pvt.	C, 47th Ill. Inf.	98		1918 Oct 26	IA, 45th, 1919
Brody, Thos. T.	Pvt.	C, Ohio E.	40		1923 Sep 11	IA, 50th, 1924
Broerman, Wm.	Pvt.	B, 61st Penn. Inf.	7		1915 Nov 6	IA, 42nd, 1916
Brokall, E.E.		I, 58th Ohio	256		1920 Jan 12	KS, 40th, 1921
Broker, Charles		C, 33rd Ohio	89		1905 Jul 3	KS, 25th, 1906
Bromley, Owen	Pvt.	E, 2nd Iowa	12		1907 Aug 9	IA, 34th, 1908
Bromley, T.C.	Pvt.		132		1914 Mar 19	IA, 41st, 1915
Bromwell, J.F.		C, 33rd Ind.	55		1915 Apr 1	KS, 35th, 1916
Bronaugh, R.M.		E, 13th Kans.	92		1922 Feb 10	KS, 42nd, 1923
Bronaugh, Robert M.		E, 13th Kans.	92		1921 Feb 10	KS, 41st, 1922
Bronson, Frank	2nd Lieut.	33rd Ind.	72		1913 Jan 13	KS, 33rd, 1914
Bronson, Jas. W.	Pvt.	K, 24th Iowa Vols.	130	52	1898 Oct	IA, 25th, 1899
Bronson, Joseph		E, 5th Mass.	22		1913	KS, 33rd, 1914
Bronson, L.H.	Pvt.	G, 1st Iowa Cav.	68		1916 Dec 20	IA, 43rd, 1917
Bronson, M.J.	Pvt.	12th Wis. Inf.	222	49	1892 Mar 14	IA, 18th, 1892
Bronson, M.L.		I, 42nd Ind. Inf.	236		1899 Apr 30	KS, 19th, 1900
Bronson, T.S.		I, 7th Kans. Cav.	130		1908 Jan 15	KS, 28th, 1909
Brook, G.W.		D, 15th Ky. Inf.	154		1886	KS, 6th, 1887
Brook, John P.		I, 35th Ohio	25	74	1916 Jun 10	NE, 41st, 1917
Brook, P.R.	QM	3rd Kans. State Militia	12		1916 Dec 13	KS, 36th, 1917
Brookhauser, J.J.	Capt.	C, U.S. Col. Inf.	59	94	1932 Dec 9	IA, 59th, 1933
Brooking, James	Pvt.	H, 55th Ky. Inf.	92	56	1897 Jul 10	IA, 24th, 1898
Brookings, Walter S.	Pvt.	E, 113th Ill. Inf.	396	46	1892 Jun 28	IA, 19th, 1893
Brookins, Richard (colored)	Pvt.	K, 123rd U.S.C.T. (not a G.A.R. member)		94	1941 Jan 12	IA, 67th, 1941
Brookiry, Robt. L.		D, 1st Mo. Cav.	128		1893 Oct 15	KS, 13th, 1894
Brookman, J.H.	Pvt.	G, 47th Ill. Inf.	212		1912 Mar	IA, 39th, 1913
Brookman, J.H.	Sergt.	H, 6th Mo. Inf.	440		1919 Apr 16	IA, 46th, 1920
Brookman, J.W.		C, 144th Ill.	265		1927 Dec 27	KS, 47th, 1928
Brooks, Chas. E.	Pvt.	E, 28th Wis. Inf.	42		1919 Apr 26	IA, 46th, 1920
Brooks, Chas. G.		G, 24th Ind.	153		1898 Dec 25	KS, 18th, 1899
Brooks, Daniel	Pvt.	K, 6th Iowa Inf.	384	57	1887 Jul 16	IA, 14th, 1888
Brooks, Daniel T.		C, 30th Ohio	3		1913 Feb 18	KS, 33rd, 1914
Brooks, E.M.			6		1925	IA, 52nd, 1926
Brooks, Frank D.		A, 167th Ohio	12		1925 Oct 22	KS, 45th, 1926
Brooks, Geo. B.		I, 94th N.Y. Inf.	83		1929 Dec 23	KS, 49th, 1930

Name	Rank	Company, Regiment or Ship	Post*	Age	Death Date†	Journal
Brooks, Geo. M.		D, 69th Ind.	127		1917 Jun 5	KS, 37th, 1918
Brooks, H.B.			32		1921 Feb 20	NE, 46th, 1922
Brooks, H.P.			371		1909	IA, 36th, 1910
Brooks, Harry D.		B, 97th N.Y. Inf.	25	76	1918 Dec 11	NE, 43rd, 1919
Brooks, Harvey	Pvt.	H, 146th Ill. Inf.	300		1902 Jul 27	IA, 29th, 1903
Brooks, Henry L.		A, 32nd Wis.	380		1905 Jan 25	KS, 25th, 1906
Brooks, J.A.			44		1921 Jan 8	KS, 41st, 1922
Brooks, J.H.		F, 22nd N.J. (died of pneumonia)	110	67	1910 Apr 25	NE, 35th, 1911
Brooks, J.P.			72		1884	KS, 4th, 1885
Brooks, J.S.		A, 13th Iowa Inf. (died of old age)	327	75	1903 Feb 28	NE, 28th, 1904
Brooks, Jas.			12		1922 Feb 3	KS, 42nd, 1923
Brooks, Jas. W.	Lieut.	I, 3rd Ill. Inf.	247		1907 Mar 9	IA, 34th, 1908
Brooks, John	Pvt.	E, 9th Iowa Inf.	168	54	1895 Oct 26	IA, 22nd, 1896
Brooks, John		E, 22nd Iowa Inf. (died of general debility)	25	71	1896 Oct 2	NE, 21st, 1897
Brooks, Joseph		C, 30th Ohio Inf.	318		1909 Dec 3	NE, 34th, 1910
Brooks, Luman A.	Pvt.	I, 12th Iowa Inf.	177		1909 Dec 13	IA, 36th, 1910
Brooks, M.	Capt.	I, 8th Kans. Inf. (at large)		94 & 4 mos.	1936 May 28	IA, 63rd, 1937
Brooks, M.	Capt.	I, 8th Kans. Inf. (at large)		94 & 4 mos.	1936 May 25	IA, 62nd, 1936
Brooks, R.C.		G, 96th Inf. (died of cancer)	115		1910 Sep 18	NE, 35th, 1911
Brooks, Richard H.	Pvt.	M, Iowa Cav.	452		1916 Jan 26	IA, 43rd, 1917
Brooks, Seth	Pvt.	D, 52nd Wis. Inf.	88		1924 Dec 24	IA, 51st, 1925
Brooks, Socrates		B, ?5th Ohio (died of kidney trouble)	118	72	1919 Feb 1	NE, 44th, 1920
Brooks, Theo.	Pvt.	K, 57th Ill. Inf.	231		1912 Jun 19	IA, 39th, 1913
Brooks, Thomas	Pvt.	E, 143rd Penn. Inf.	7		1930 Mar 4	IA, 57th, 1931
Brooks, Thomas		E, 23rd Ill. (died of stomach trouble)	34	82	1913 Nov 30	NE, 38th, 1914
Brooks, Thomas E.		I, 140th N.Y. Inf., 5th Corps (born in Monroe Co., N.Y.; died in Blair, Neb.)	52		1883 Oct 3	NE, 8th, 1884
Brooks, William		F, 42nd Mo.	91		1897 Jun 26	KS, 17th, 1898
Broomhall, Thomas S.		L, 9th Iowa Cav.	147		1934 Sep 7	NE, 59th, 1935
Broomhower, Isaac			187		1907 2nd term	IA, 34th, 1908
Brooms, Geo.	Pvt.	E, Inf.	40		1923 May 11	IA, 50th, 1924
Brophy, J.T.	Pvt.	A, 22nd Iowa Inf.	8	73	1897 Dec 17	IA, 24th, 1898
Broshar, Levi	Sergt.	F, 36th Iowa Inf.	398		1903 Nov 10	IA, 30th, 1904
Brosius, C.C.		H, 14th Penn.	2		1905 Dec 10	KS, 25th, 1906
Brosius, Joseph L.		A, 32nd Ohio Inf.	1		1902 May 20	KS, 22nd, 1903
Bross, Harmon		B or G, 18th Mich. (see also Appendix D)	25	92	1928 Jan 8	NE, 53rd, 1929
Brosseau, George	Sergt.	K, 23rd Mich. Inf.	206		1918 Jul 26	IA, 45th, 1919
Brost, John	Pvt.	K, 35th Wis.	78		1923 Oct 22	IA, 50th, 1924
Brother, Chas.		U.S. Marines	12		1917 Nov 21	IA, 45th, 1919
Brother, Ferd	Surg.	8th Mo.	35	87	1920 Dec 7	NE, 45th, 1921
Brothers, E.H.			488		1892 Jan	KS, 12th, 1893
Brothers, E.W.W.			50		1892	KS, 12th, 1893
Brotherton, D.		D, 17th Mich.	5		1897 Jan 2	KS, 17th, 1898
Brotherton, Miles		H, 106th Ill. Inf. (died of paralysis)	22	86	1925 Jan 5	NE, 50th, 1926
Brott, James A.	Pvt.	D, 83rd Ill. Inf.	67		1901 May 27	IA, 28th, 1902
Brott, Thomas		1st Col. Cav.	132		1911 Apr 18	KS, 31st, 1912
Brotts, H.A.		H, 8th Ohio	179		1919	KS, 39th, 1920
Brotzer, Lewis	Pvt.	20th Iowa Inf.	20		1914	IA, 41st, 1915
Brougher, Ira		F, 130th Penn.	52		1920 May 17	KS, 40th, 1921
Broughton, Jas. S.		B, 6th Mich.	12		1906 Oct 24	KS, 26th, 1907
Broughton, John A.		B, 49th Ill.	9		1921 Dec 19	KS, 41st, 1922
Broughton, Will. H.		F, 145th Penn. Inf.	63		1899 Dec 3	KS, 19th, 1900
Brower, B.E.	Adjt.	14th Wis.	295		1897 Dec 18	KS, 17th, 1898
Browley, Mark A.		G, 137th Ohio	53		1922 Jun 15	KS, 42nd, 1923
Brown, A.B.	Pvt.	C, 13th Iowa Inf.	11		1915 May 7	IA, 42nd, 1916
Brown, A.D.		G, 33rd Ill. Inf. (died of rheumatism)	80		1906 Jan 14	NE, 31st, 1907
Brown, A.F.	Pvt.	I, 60th Ohio Inf.	67		1912 May 31	IA, 39th, 1913
Brown, A.H.	Pvt.	A, 5th Iowa Inf.	147		1903 Jun 18	IA, 30th, 1904
Brown, A.H.	Wagoner	G, 151st Ill. Inf.	403		1917 Mar 11	IA, 44th, 1918
Brown, A.J.	Pvt.	B, 12th Ohio Inf.	94		1920 May 16	IA, 47th, 1921

*See Appendix A, B or C for roster of post names and locations.
†See Introduction for note regarding recording of death date.

64

Name	Rank	Company, Regiment or Ship	Post*	Age	Death Date†	Journal
Brown, A.J.		K, 48th Ind.	92		1893 Nov 22	KS, 13th, 1894
Brown, A.S.	Pvt.	G, 2nd Iowa Cav.	212		1899 Aug 13	IA, 26th, 1900
Brown, Agustus C.		G, 122nd Ill. Inf.	9		1901 Nov 1	KS, 21st, 1902
Brown, Alba		C, 5th Iowa Cav.	25	82	1917 Feb 5	NE, 42nd, 1918
Brown, Alex	Pvt.	E, 15th Iowa Inf.	79		1910 Aug 10	IA, 37th, 1911
Brown, Alex H.	Pvt.	H, 45th Ill. Inf.	34		1914 Nov 23	IA, 41st, 1915
Brown, Alexander		B, 64th Ill. Inf.	47		1909 Jan 21	KS, 29th, 1910
Brown, Alfred		L, 9th Kans.	180		1913 Jun 18	KS, 33rd, 1914
Brown, Alfred		I, 53rd Ohio	23		1933 Feb 28	NE, 58th, 1934
Brown, Allen		E, 29th Ind.	250		1919 Mar 12	KS, 39th, 1920
Brown, Alonzo		L, 10th N.Y. Hvy. Art.	142		1923 Dec 3	KS, 43rd, 1924
Brown, Alva	Pvt.	C, 14th Ill. Inf.	40		1910 Dec 23	IA, 37th, 1911
Brown, Anderon	Pvt.	D, 50th Ind. Inf.	283		1916 Feb 29	IA, 43rd, 1917
Brown, Andrew J.	Pvt.	F, 27th Iowa Inf.	190		1912 Nov 22	IA, 39th, 1913
Brown, Andrew J.		A, 8th Ill. Cav.	28		1923 Mar 1	KS, 43rd, 1924
Brown, B.B.	Pvt.	B, 4th Iowa Inf.	166		1915 Apr 27	IA, 42nd, 1916
Brown, B.F.	Pvt.	A, Ill. Lt. Art.	40		1917 Sep 14	IA, 44th, 1918
Brown, B.F.		D, 87th Ind.	1		1913 Dec 2	KS, 33rd, 1914
Brown, B.G.			96		1925 Mar 6	IA, 52nd, 1926
Brown, B.L.	Pvt.	H, 84th Ill. Inf.	324		1912 Aug 22	IA, 39th, 1913
Brown, C.B.		K, 33rd N.Y.	129		1933 Jul 1	KS, 53rd, 1934
Brown, C.C.		C, 50th Wis. Inf.	477		1914 Mar 20	KS, 34th, 1915
Brown, C.E.		G, 80th Ill. Inf.	11	84	1923 Jul 5	NE, 48th, 1924
Brown, C.F.	Pvt.	A, 93rd N.Y. Inf.	68	94	1931 Jun 9	IA, 58th, 1932
Brown, C.M.	Pvt.	Ohio Inf.	167		1913 May 8	IA, 40th, 1914
Brown, C.O.C.	Corp.	M, 3rd Ill. Cav.	192		1914 Nov 3	IA, 41st, 1915
Brown, C.P.		19th Ind.	85		1926 Nov 23	KS, 46th, 1927
Brown, C.R.	Pvt.	32nd Iowa	22		1922 Dec 23	IA, 49th, 1923
Brown, C.R.		1st Neb. Cav.	63		1924 Nov 18	KS, 44th, 1925
Brown, Calvin	Sergt.	D, 3rd Iowa Vol. Inf.	168		1901 Sep 4	IA, 28th, 1902
Brown, Charles	Pvt.	Cogswell's Ind. Battery	97	67	1897 Dec 11	IA, 24th, 1898
Brown, Charles		I, 99th U.S.	10		1905 Dec 29	KS, 25th, 1906
Brown, Chas.			111		1922	KS, 42nd, 1923
Brown, Chas. H.		M, 9th Kans.	370		1906 Apr	KS, 26th, 1907
Brown, Chas. M.			23		1883	KS, 3rd, 1884
Brown, Chris.	Sergt.	G, 33rd Wis. Inf.	267		1908 Sep 26	IA, 35th, 1909
Brown, Conrad	Fifer	C, 35th Iowa	223		1922 May 19	IA, 49th, 1923
Brown, Courtland		F, 59th Ohio	257		1923 Mar 5	KS, 43rd, 1924
Brown, Cylon L.	Pvt.	H, 8th Iowa Inf.	346		1918 Sep 25	IA, 45th, 1919
Brown, D.O.	Pvt.	H, 8th Mich. Inf.	29		1923 Mar 23	IA, 50th, 1924
Brown, David A.		D, 206th Penn.	25		1920 Jul 19	KS, 40th, 1921
Brown, David S.	Pvt.	D, 52nd Ill. Inf.	408		1904 May 27	IA, 31st, 1905
Brown, Delos M.		F, 8th Mich. (cause of death: heart)	35	74	1915 Nov 20	NE, 40th, 1916
Brown, Dennis		8th Iowa Inf.	108		1916 Feb 25	IA, 43rd, 1917
Brown, Dudley	Pvt.	B, 29th Ohio	147		1923 Jun 23	IA, 50th, 1924
Brown, E.	Pvt.	C, 25th Ind. Inf.	79		1909 Jan 14	IA, 36th, 1910
Brown, E.E.	Pvt.	H, 2nd Iowa Inf.	130		1910	IA, 37th, 1911
Brown, E.S.			3		1921 Jun 3	IA, 48th, 1922
Brown, Ed S.		F, 47th U.S. Col. Inf.	17		prior to 1891	KS, 11th, 1892
Brown, Ed. J.		G, 1st Neb. Cav. (died of stomach trouble)	110		1916 Mar 13	NE, 41st, 1917
Brown, Ed. S.	Pvt.	A, 137th Ill. Inf.	88	87	1933 Jun 10	IA, 60th, 1934
Brown, Edmund		K, 12th Ky.	36		1923 Apr 15	KS, 43rd, 1924
Brown, Edwin	Pvt.	D, 1st Iowa Cav.	149	61	1895 Apr 3	IA, 22nd, 1896
Brown, Edwin	Pvt.	B, 7th Iowa	181		1905 Jan 29	IA, 32nd, 1906
Brown, Edwin F.		H, 151st Ill. Inf. (Lincoln)			1943 May 5	NE, 70th, 1946
Brown, Edwin F.		H, 151st Ill. Inf. (see also Appendix D)	25		1943 May 5	NE, 67th, 1943
Brown, Edwin G.		G, 137th Ohio	147		1917 Jul 27	KS, 37th, 1918
Brown, Elijah		4th Iowa Inf.	356		1900 Nov 30	KS, 20th, 1901
Brown, Elizah			309		1922	IA, 49th, 1923
Brown, Erastus	Pvt.	M, 3rd Iowa Cav.	398		1911 Aug 13	IA, 38th, 1912
Brown, Ezekial		I, 86th Ill. Inf. (died of heart failure)	47	73	1911 Dec 1	NE, 36th, 1912
Brown, Ezra		K, 4th Mich. (died of army wound)	60	81	1919 Apr 8	NE, 44th, 1920

*See Appendix A, B or C for roster of post names and locations.

†See Introduction for note regarding recording of death date.   65

Name	Rank	Company, Regiment or Ship	Post*	Age	Death Date†	Journal
Brown, F.A.	Pvt.	H, 105th Ohio Inf.	233		1913 Oct 17	IA, 40th, 1914
Brown, F.B.	2nd Lieut.	C, 28th Wis. Inf.	82	44	1887 Dec 6	IA, 15th, 1889
Brown, F.J.		G, 33rd Ill. Inf. (died of accident)	34	62	1891[1901?] Nov	NE, 26th, 1902
Brown, F.M.		B, 57th Ohio	256		1919 Aug 1	KS, 39th, 1920
Brown, Finley		D, 9th Ind. Cav.	4		1916 Mar 17	KS, 36th, 1917
Brown, Foster D.	Pvt.	B, 47th Mo. Inf.	16		1915 Jul 2	IA, 42nd, 1916
Brown, Francis H.		G, 76th —	332		1896 Mar 21	KS, 16th, 1897
Brown, Francis H.	Pvt.	C, 34th Ill. (died of rheumatism)	25	47	1884 Mar 30	NE, 9th, 1885
Brown, Francis M.	Pvt.	I, 46th —	470		1919 May 28	IA, 46th, 1920
Brown, Frank	Pvt.	A, 19th Iowa Inf.	248		1924 Nov 3	IA, 51st, 1925
Brown, Frank		H, 35th Wis.	37		1926 Jan 9	KS, 46th, 1927
Brown, Frank E.	Pvt.	E, 194th N.Y. Inf.	66		1927 Sep 8	IA, 54th, 1928
Brown, Fritz W.		G, 21st Ill.	214		1898 Oct 3	KS, 18th, 1899
Brown, G.J.		A, 160th N.Y. Inf. (died of heart disease)	42		1894 Jan 26	NE, 19th, 1895
Brown, G.O.	Pvt.	B, 32nd Iowa Inf.	42		1916 Sep 29	IA, 43rd, 1917
Brown, G.R.	Pvt.	B, 132nd Ill. Inf.	152		1915 Mar 10	IA, 42nd, 1916
Brown, G.R.		K, 74th Ohio Inf. (died of abscess)	204		1893 Nov 19	NE, 18th, 1894
Brown, G.W.	Pvt.	D, 154th Ind. Inf.	7		1905 Nov	IA, 32nd, 1906
Brown, Geo.			290		1908	IA, 35th, 1909
Brown, Geo. H.	Musician	127th Penn.	2		1898 Oct 10	KS, 18th, 1899
Brown, Geo. W.	Sergt.	B, 22nd Iowa Inf.	8		1923 Sep 18	IA, 50th, 1924
Brown, George	Pvt.	H, 25th Wis. Inf.	46	87	1931 Aug 27	IA, 58th, 1932
Brown, George		B, 6th Mich. Inf. (died at Leavenworth; buried at Mt. Muncie Cemetery)	6		1894 Nov 20	KS, 14th, 1895
Brown, George		G, 111th N.Y.	47		1913 Jan 24	KS, 33rd, 1914
Brown, George S.		B, 21st Wis.	17		1913 Feb 7	KS, 33rd, 1914
Brown, H.A.	Eng.	on sloop of war	233		1919 Apr 10	IA, 46th, 1920
Brown, H.C.	Pvt.	1st N.H. Inf.	81		1929 Mar 3	IA, 56th, 1930
Brown, H.D.	Corp.	D, 12th Ill. Cav.	81		1915 Mar 7	IA, 42nd, 1916
Brown, H.H.		L, 7th Penn.	81		1906 Jan 1	KS, 26th, 1907
Brown, H.H.		B, 141st Ohio	81		1933 Mar 3	KS, 53rd, 1934
Brown, H.L.		D, 17th Md. Inf.	61		1929 Dec 10	KS, 49th, 1930
Brown, H.P.		C, 16th Iowa Inf.	1	92	1936 Jul 14	IA, 63rd, 1937
Brown, H.W.		E, 65th N.Y.	25		1908	NE, 33rd, 1909
Brown, H.W.		B, 32nd Ill.	40	70	1915 Nov 16	NE, 40th, 1916
Brown, Harvey	Pvt.	D, 2nd Iowa Inf.	55		1919 Oct 3	IA, 46th, 1920
Brown, Henry	Pvt.	B, 36th Iowa Inf.	398		1900 Feb 19	IA, 27th, 1901
Brown, Henry	Pvt.	B, 60th U.S.C. Inf.	254		1920 Jun 23	IA, 47th, 1921
Brown, Henry	Pvt.	L, 26th N.Y. Cav.	1		1923 Jun 22	IA, 50th, 1924
Brown, Henry		H, 10th Ohio Cav. (died of heart disease)	287		1889	KS, 9th, 1890
Brown, Henry F.		F, 18th Wis. Inf.	112	72	1916 Apr 26	NE, 41st, 1917
Brown, Henty M.	Musician	A, 176th Ohio Inf.	6	88	1931 Apr 9	IA, 58th, 1932
Brown, Hiram		I, 8th Ohio	412		1918	KS, 38th, 1919
Brown, Hiram D.		F, 15th Iowa	130		1909 Nov 15	KS, 29th, 1910
Brown, Hugh, Major	2nd Lieut.	E, 15th Iowa Inf.	79		1901 Nov 30	IA, 28th, 1902
Brown, J.		B, 23rd Mo. Inf.	36		1900 Sep 14	KS, 21st, 1902
Brown, J.A.		G, 23rd Ohio Inf.	117		1916 Jan 1	KS, 36th, 1917
Brown, J.B.	Pvt.		206		1920 Apr 14	IA, 47th, 1921
Brown, J.B.	Pvt.	E, 1st Mo. Cav.	12	95	1933 Mar 18	IA, 60th, 1934
Brown, J.C.			167		1923 Aug 28	IA, 50th, 1924
Brown, J.C.		D, 6th Ky.	17		1921 Jan 1	KS, 41st, 1922
Brown, J.C.		C, 92nd Ill. Inf. (died of paralysis)	24	69	1902 Feb	NE, 27th, 1903
Brown, J.D.		A, 21st Iowa Inf.	59	94 & 4 mos.	1936 Feb 27	IA, 63rd, 1937
Brown, J.D.		A, 21st Iowa Inf.		94 & 4 mos.	1936 Feb 27	IA, 62nd, 1936
Brown, J.E.		D, 46th Ill.	35	95	1919 Nov 11	NE, 44th, 1920
Brown, J.G.		55th Ill. Cav.	94		1921 Oct 31	IA, 48th, 1922
Brown, J.H.			235		1917 Sep 17	IA, 44th, 1918
Brown, J.H.		K, 14th Vt.	293		1912 Jan 9	KS, 32nd, 1913
Brown, J.J.		H, 1st Colo. Cav.	63		1892 Apr 24	KS, 12th, 1893
Brown, J.M.	1st Lieut.	A, 3rd Iowa Cav.	100		1900 May 30	IA, 27th, 1901

Name	Rank	Company, Regiment or Ship	Post*	Age	Death Date†	Journal
Brown, J.M.			96		1918 Jan 12	IA, 45th, 1919
Brown, J.M.		H, 77th Ill.	253		1888	KS, 8th, 1889
Brown, J.P.	Pvt.		66		1920 Jan 12	IA, 47th, 1921
Brown, J.R.	Pvt.	G, 32nd Iowa Inf.	449		1902 Mar 13	IA, 29th, 1903
Brown, J.R.		D, 4th Ohio	243		1920	KS, 40th, 1921
Brown, J.W.	Pvt.	C, 14th Iowa Inf.	48		1918 Oct 27	IA, 45th, 1919
Brown, J.W.	Corp.	F, 26th Iowa	12		1922 Dec 18	IA, 49th, 1923
Brown, J.W.		H, 114th Ohio	52		1898 Feb 23	KS, 18th, 1899
Brown, J.W.		I, 15th Iowa	18		1919 Jul 22	KS, 39th, 1920
Brown, Jacob		I, 125th Ill.	156		1905 Nov 15	KS, 25th, 1906
Brown, Jacob, Sr.			236		1915	IA, 42nd, 1916
Brown, Jacob M.		D, 33rd Ind.	250		1924 Jul 12	KS, 44th, 1925
Brown, James		B, 8th Ohio Inf. (died at National Home)	380		1895 May	KS, 15th, 1896
Brown, James			25		1913 Jun 2	KS, 33rd, 1914
Brown, James		1st Mo. Bat. (died of general debility)	25	84	1896 Nov 9	NE, 21st, 1897
Brown, James B.		L, 10th N.Y. Cav.	4		1914 Aug 3	KS, 34th, 1915
Brown, James M.	Capt.	F, 29th Iowa Inf.	116		1913 Oct 5	IA, 40th, 1914
Brown, James M.		E, 11th Ill.	82		1913 Jul 19	KS, 33rd, 1914
Brown, James W.		H, 46th Ind. Inf. (died at Oketa)	9		1895 Jun	KS, 15th, 1896
Brown, Jas. Lewis		D, 144th Ind. Vol. Inf.	143		1924 Sep 22	NE, 51st, 1927
Brown, Jas. M.	Pvt.	G, 20th Iowa Inf.	16		1927 Jul 2	IA, 54th, 1928
Brown, Jas. R.		D, 11th Penn. Inf.	25		1934 Aug	KS, 54th, 1935
Brown, Jas. U.		C, 1st West Va. Inf.	35		1917 May 24	KS, 37th, 1918
Brown, Jas. W.		E, 23rd Wis. Inf. (died of heart disease)	392		1891 Dec 24	KS, 11th, 1892
Brown, Jesse	Pvt.	96th Ohio	108		1907 Jul 24	IA, 34th, 1908
Brown, Jno. C.	Pvt.	G, 10th Iowa Inf.	169	50	1888 Oct 14	IA, 17th, 1891
Brown, Jno. D.	Capt.	B, U.S. Colored Inf. (at large)		96 & 4 mos.	1936 Feb 27	IA, 62nd, 1936
Brown, Jno. D.	Capt.	B, U.S. Colored Inf. (at large)		94 & 4 mos.	1936 Feb 22	IA, 63rd, 1937
Brown, Jno. F.	Corp.	D, 4th Ind. Cav.	257	52	1888 Dec 13	IA, 15th, 1889
Brown, John		H, 94th Ill. Inf.	156		1922 Jan 8	IA, 49th, 1923
Brown, John		U.S. Navy	380		1896 Jun 21	KS, 16th, 1897
Brown, John			488		1920 Jul	KS, 40th, 1921
Brown, John		A, 13th Ind. Inf.	250		1930[1929?] Oct 18	KS, 49th, 1930
Brown, John		I, 13th Ind. Inf.	250		1930 Oct 18	KS, 50th, 1931
Brown, John		E, 120th Ill.	46		1928 Dec 27	KS, 48th, 1929
Brown, John		14th Ohio Battery (died of old age)	77	78	1924 Dec 31	NE, 49th, 1925
Brown, John		141st Ohio Inf.	20		1916	IA, 43rd, 1917
Brown, John B.		K, 20th Iowa Inf.	1		1923 May 5	IA, 50th, 1924
Brown, John C.	Pvt.	E, 7th Ohio	354		1914 Sep 14	KS, 34th, 1915
Brown, John C.		B, 206th Penn.	66		1897 May 18	KS, 17th, 1898
Brown, John D.		E, 37th Iowa Inf.	40		1909 Oct 26	IA, 36th, 1910
Brown, John F.	Pvt.	E, 42nd Wis. Inf. (died of cancer of face)	60	78	1922 Jul 16	NE, 47th, 1923
Brown, John F.		H, 150th Ill. Inf.	12		1909 Dec 28	KS, 29th, 1910
Brown, John H.		I, 110th Penn. Inf.	7		1924[1923?] Nov 11	NE, 48th, 1924
Brown, John J.		G, 3rd Iowa Cav.	19	58	1896 Apr 3	IA, 22nd, 1896
Brown, John L.	Sergt. 1st Lieut.	K, 138th U.S. Colored Inf.				
Brown, John L.		G, 6th Kans. Inf.	51		1886	KS, 6th, 1887
Brown, John M.	Pvt.	A, 34th Iowa Inf.	312		1909 Aug 19	IA, 36th, 1910
Brown, John P.	Corp.	I, 89th Ohio Inf.	11	92	1936 Jun 16	IA, 65th, 1939
Brown, John S.		D, 6th Vt.	35		1908[1909?] May 13	KS, 29th, 1910
Brown, John W.	Pvt.	B, 36th Iowa Inf.	337		1912 Mar 22	IA, 39th, 1913
Brown, John W.		C, 6th Ohio Cav.	47		1909 Mar 27	KS, 29th, 1910
Brown, Jos.	Pvt.	E, 47th Ill. Cav.	465		1909 May 7	IA, 36th, 1910
Brown, Jos.		K, 84th Ill. Inf. (died of complications)	95	78	1902 Aug	NE, 27th, 1903
Brown, Joseph	Pvt.	C, 4th Iowa Cav.	137		1907 Dec 22	IA, 34th, 1908
Brown, Joseph		D, 72nd Ind. (died from lung disease)	289		1889	KS, 9th, 1890
Brown, Joseph L.		L, 1st Minn.	51		1916 Jul 25	KS, 36th, 1917
Brown, Josephus		H, 63rd Ohio Inf.	36		1925 Nov 15	KS, 45th, 1926
Brown, Joshuah H.		H, 84th Ill.	218		1928 Dec 22	NE, 53rd, 1929

*See Appendix A, B or C for roster of post names and locations.
†See Introduction for note regarding recording of death date.

67

Name	Rank	Company, Regiment or Ship	Post*	Age	Death Date†	Journal
Brown, K.W.	Pvt.	I, 35th N.Y. Vols.	30		1926 Apr 30	IA, 53rd, 1927
Brown, L.T.	Capt.	H, 68th Ill. Inf.	16	65	1887 Jan 31	IA, 14th, 1888
Brown, Leonard	Pvt.	F, 47th Iowa Inf.	12		1914 Aug 24	IA, 41st, 1915
Brown, Leroy T.	Capt.	H, 68th Ill. Inf.	16	65	1887 Jan 31	IA, 13th, 1887
Brown, Levi T.		M, 9th Iowa	50		1916 Mar 28	KS, 36th, 1917
Brown, Lucius R.		C, 8th Ill. Cav.	91	76	1916 Apr 21	NE, 41st, 1917
Brown, M.G.	Pvt.	H, 4th Mich.	493		1907 Nov 27	IA, 34th, 1908
Brown, Manford			437		1921 Feb 7	KS, 41st, 1922
Brown, Merrett S.	Corp.	K, 7th Iowa Inf.	292		1916 Jul 3	IA, 43rd, 1917
Brown, Monroe		A, 18th U.S.	[17?]		1909 Feb 9	KS, 29th, 1910
Brown, Myron J.		K, 96th Ill. Inf.	26		1928 Dec 19	NE, 53rd, 1929
Brown, N.B.		B, 101st Ill.	113		1910 Jan 1	KS, 30th, 1911
Brown, N.D.			12		1922 May 9	KS, 42nd, 1923
Brown, N.G.		B, 33rd Ohio	51		1927	KS, 47th, 1928
Brown, N.K.		A, 8th Minn. (died of softening of brain)	43	82[?]	1897 May 5	NE, 22nd, 1898
Brown, Nathan	Pvt.	A, 1st Neb. Cav.	210		1901 Sep 16	IA, 28th, 1902
Brown, Nathan	Pvt.	A, 8th Iowa	57		1922 Jan 12	IA, 49th, 1923
Brown, Nelson	Pvt.	F, 13th Iowa Inf.	1		1920 Jul 15	IA, 47th, 1921
Brown, O.H.		G, 8th Iowa Cav.	118	61	1908 Nov	NE, 33rd, 1909
Brown, O.L.F.	Capt.	G, 149th N.Y. Inf.	12		1908 Jun 15	IA, 35th, 1909
Brown, O.P.	Pvt.	C, 39th Ill. Inf.	26		1918 Apr 6	IA, 45th, 1919
Brown, O.R.		B, 125th Ohio Inf.	292		1902 May 13	KS, 22nd, 1903
Brown, Oscar F.		E, 1st Miss. Cav. (born in New York; died at Central City, Neb.; buried at Schuyler, Neb.)		74	1906 Oct 12	NE, 31st, 1907
Brown, P.L.	1st Sergt.	B, 36th Wis. Inf.	56	74	1895 Mar 12	IA, 22nd, 1896
Brown, Peter		E, 13th Iowa Inf. (at large)		90	1935 Dec 15	IA, 62nd, 1936
Brown, Peter		H, 28th Ill. Inf. (died of heart failure)	104	65	1897 Dec 27	NE, 22nd, 1898
Brown, Porter		8th Iowa Inf.	167		1922 Jun 25	IA, 49th, 1923
Brown, R.C.	Pvt.	D, 142nd Ill. Inf.	364	48	1895 Jun 12	IA, 22nd, 1896
Brown, R.M.		H, 26th Ind.	40		1916 May 12	KS, 36th, 1917
Brown, Resin	Pvt.	G, 20th Ohio Inf.	167		1925 May 29	IA, 52nd, 1926
Brown, Robert			47		1907 Mar 13	IA, 34th, 1908
Brown, Robert		F, 21st Iowa Inf.	68		1917 Sep 10	IA, 44th, 1918
Brown, Robert		Kans.	241		1908[1909?] Jun 4	KS, 29th, 1910
Brown, Robert			13		1905	NE, 30th, 1906
Brown, Robert S.		K, 152nd Ill. Inf.	345		1899 Oct	KS, 19th, 1900
Brown, S.F.	Pvt.	17th Ohio Inf.	27		1926 Jan	IA, 53rd, 1927
Brown, S.J.			167		1924 Jan 22	IA, 51st, 1925
Brown, S.M.	Corp.	F, 30th Iowa Inf.	497		1926 Apr 10	IA, 53rd, 1927
Brown, S.S.		B, 119th Ill. (died of heart failure)	40	84	1924 Jun 20	NE, 49th, 1925
Brown, S.W.	Pvt.	H, 96th Ill. Inf.	141	64	1894 Apr 17	IA, 21st, 1895
Brown, S.W.	Sergt.	G, 31st Wis. Inf.	58		1929 Mar 3	IA, 56th, 1930
Brown, Samuel	Pvt.	F, 13th Mo. Inf.	384	78	1888 Jul 10	IA, 15th, 1889
Brown, Sidney B.		K, 50th Ill.	65		1910 Feb 20	KS, 30th, 1911
Brown, Stephen		B, 12th Mich.	52		1911 Dec 11	KS, 31st, 1912
Brown, Stephen H.	Musician	I, 34th Ind. Inf.	349	51	1894 Jul 16	IA, 21st, 1895
Brown, Sylvester		N.Y. Cav.	55		1934 Aug 9	KS, 54th, 1935
Brown, T.A.	Pvt.	G, 13th Iowa Inf.	7		1887 Oct 18	IA, 14th, 1888
Brown, T.C.	Pvt.	H, 24th Iowa Inf.	235		1926 Jan 15	IA, 53rd, 1927
Brown, Theo.		9th Wis. Lt. Art.	40		1924 May 3	KS, 44th, 1925
Brown, Theodore		74th Ind.	28		1928 Mar 18	KS, 48th, 1929
Brown, Thomas	Pvt.	E, 75th Ill. Inf.	364		1923 Apr 5	IA, 50th, 1924
Brown, Thomas		I, 13th Iowa	303		1917 Jan 18	KS, 36th, 1917
Brown, Thomas		D, 8th Iowa Cav.	84		1918 Apr 10	KS, 38th, 1919
Brown, Thomas J.	Pvt.	A, 137th Ill. Inf.	88		1928 Sep 3	IA, 55th, 1929
Brown, Virgil A.		C, 6th Ind.	113		1920 Apr 27	KS, 40th, 1921
Brown, Volney N.	Pvt.	G, 9th Iowa Inf.	48		1915 Feb 4	IA, 42nd, 1916
Brown, W.	Pvt.	13th Colo. Art.	88		1921 Apr 24	IA, 48th, 1922
Brown, W.B.		B, 3rd Mo. Cav.	23		1913 Dec 15	IA, 40th, 1914
Brown, W.B.	Bugler	M, 1st Ill. Art.	26		1911 Sep 23	IA, 38th, 1912
Brown, W.E.	Lieut.	8th U.S.C. Hvy. Art.	10		1917 Feb 21	IA, 44th, 1918

Name	Rank	Company, Regiment or Ship	Post*	Age	Death Date†	Journal
Brown, W.E.		30th Wis.	28		1918 Jan 1	KS, 38th, 1919
Brown, W.H.	Pvt.	L, 9th Iowa Cav.	440		1908 May 31	IA, 35th, 1909
Brown, W.H.	Pvt.	D, 28th Iowa Inf.	98		1911 Apr 2	IA, 38th, 1912
Brown, W.H.		H, 38th Wis.	195		1885	KS, 5th, 1886
Brown, W.H.		B, 3rd Conn. Inf.	1		1896 Nov 26	KS, 16th, 1897
Brown, W.H.		1st Kans. Battery	407		1908	KS, 28th, 1909
Brown, W.H.		H, 78th Ind.	464		1913 Aug 4	KS, 33rd, 1914
Brown, W.H.H.			12		1923 Mar 28	IA, 50th, 1924
Brown, W.L.		102nd Ohio	49		1923 Jul 17	IA, 50th, 1924
Brown, W.P.	Corp.	H, 118th Ill. Inf.	28		1909 Sep	IA, 36th, 1910
Brown, W.P.		F, 10th Iowa	100		1908 Mar 25	KS, 28th, 1909
Brown, W.S.		A, 70th N.J.	28		1919 Jul 10	KS, 39th, 1920
Brown, W.S.		A, 18th Ohio	130		1923 Feb 15	KS, 43rd, 1924
Brown, W.V.			122		1912	IA, 39th, 1913
Brown, W.W.	Pvt.	G, 9th Ind. Inf.	22		1909 Jan 18	IA, 36th, 1910
Brown, W.W.	Corp.	E, 44th Ohio Inf.	40		1915 May 2	IA, 42nd, 1916
Brown, Walter	Pvt.		316		1923 Jul 26	IA, 50th, 1924
Brown, William			83		1893 Oct 19	KS, 13th, 1894
Brown, William		U.S. Navy	72		1912 Sep 17	KS, 32nd, 1913
Brown, William		K, 13th Iowa Inf.	158		1916 Feb 17	KS, 36th, 1917
Brown, William		I, 7th Ill. Cav. (died of complication of diseases)	43	58	1904 Sep 8	NE, 29th, 1905
Brown, William A.		F, 1st Mo. Cav.	209		1909 Apr 21	KS, 29th, 1910
Brown, William H.	Pvt.	K, 15th Ill. Inf.	364		1916 Oct 14	IA, 43rd, 1917
Brown, Willis		B, 83rd U.S.C.T.	52		1919 Dec 16	KS, 39th, 1920
Brown, Wm.	Lieut.	B, 22nd Penn. Inf.	7		1910 Jan 16	IA, 37th, 1911
Brown, Wm.		G, 104th Penn. (died of old age)	338	73	1920 Sep 18	NE, 45th, 1921
Brown, Wm. D.		A, 3rd Iowa	59		1931 Dec 12	KS, 51st, 1932
Brown, Wm. D.		A, 3rd Iowa	59		1931 Dec 12	KS, 52nd, 1933
Brown, Wm. F.	Pvt.	H, 45th Ill.	127		1907 Dec 15	IA, 34th, 1908
Brown, Wm. J.	Pvt.	F, 2nd Iowa Cav.	8		1913	IA, 40th, 1914
Brown, Wm. S.	Pvt.	A, 30th Iowa	2	55	1891 May 29	IA, 18th, 1892
Brown, Wright H.		K, 14th Vt.	12		1912 Jan 8	KS, 32nd, 1913
Browne, Charles		D, 14th Ill.	111		1921	KS, 41st, 1922
Browne, Elliott L.		A, 12th Ill. Cav. (died of accident)	16	76	1921 Jun 24	NE, 46th, 1922
Browne, H.W.		1st Ill.	430		1892 Nov 5	KS, 12th, 1893
Brownell, E.	Pvt.	A, 99th N.Y.	55		1921 Jan 26	IA, 48th, 1922
Brownell, G.W.			265		1906 Nov 27	KS, 26th, 1907
Brownell, Stephen P.			147		1884	KS, 4th, 1885
Brownell, Wm. H.	Pvt.	L, 9th Mich. Cav.	88		1923 Sep 17	IA, 50th, 1924
Brownfield, B.B.	Sergt.	D, 1st Wis. Hvy. Art.	84		1902 Jan 13	IA, 28th, 1902
Brownfield, J.A.	Pvt.	D, 1st Wis. Hvy. Art.	12		1904 Apr 16	IA, 31st, 1905
Brownhall, Robert H.	Pvt.	3rd Ill. Cav.	122		1923 Aug 2	IA, 50th, 1924
Brownhouse, Geo. S.	Pvt.	A, 51st Ohio	122		1923 Mar 29	IA, 50th, 1924
Browning, A.H.	Pvt.	G, 86th Ohio Inf.	400	89	1931 May 8	IA, 58th, 1932
Browning, Henry		I, 79th U.S.C.T.	34	52	1897 Jan 30	NE, 22nd, 1898
Browning, J.H.		E, 151st Ill. (cause of death: kidney)	32	75	1915 Jan 16	NE, 40th, 1916
Browning, John W.		I, 124th Ill.	18		1922 Aug 15	KS, 42nd, 1923
Browning, John W.		C, 124th Ill.	18		1923 Aug 15	KS, 43rd, 1924
Browning, Joshua	Sergt.	D, 168th Ill. Inf.	250		1918 Jan 19	KS, 38th, 1919
Browning, S.R.		B, 43rd Ind.	129		1918 Feb 22	KS, 38th, 1919
Browning, W.H.		E, 41st Wis.	322	94	1934 Sep 27	IA, 61st, 1935
Brownlee, E.S.	Pvt.	F, 140th Ill. Inf.	135		1920 Apr 10	IA, 47th, 1921
Brownlee, E.S.		F, 140th Ill. Inf.	135		1919 Apr 10	IA, 46th, 1920
Brownlee, T.W.		F, 73rd Ill.	4		1920 Sep 15	KS, 40th, 1921
Brownlee, Walter		H, 14th Kans.	292		1898 Oct 21	KS, 18th, 1899
Brownlee, Wm. H.		A, 54th Ill.	60		1916 Nov 2	KS, 36th, 1917
Brownswell, Wm.	Corp.	B, 35th Iowa Inf.	231		1918 Mar 19	IA, 45th, 1919
Browser, Benj.	Pvt.	F, 42nd Ohio Inf.	7		1917 Oct 7	IA, 44th, 1918
Brubaker, Abram	Pvt.	C, 75th Ohio Inf.	12		1918 Dec 24	IA, 45th, 1919
Bruce, C.		K, 95th Ill.	3		1898 Feb 3	KS, 18th, 1899
Bruce, David K.	Pvt.	H, 75th Ill. Inf.	89		1916 Dec 13	IA, 43rd, 1917

*See Appendix A, B or C for roster of post names and locations.
†See Introduction for note regarding recording of death date.

Name	Rank	Company, Regiment or Ship	Post*	Age	Death Date†	Journal
Bruce, F.J.		C, 2nd Ohio Cav.	127		1911 May 11	KS, 31st, 1912
Bruce, F.M.	Pvt.	I, 4th Iowa Cav.	55		1918 Jul 21	IA, 45th, 1919
Bruce, J.R.	Pvt.	4th Iowa Inf.	55		1910 Sep 15	IA, 37th, 1911
Bruce, James	Pvt.	G, 64th Ill. Inf.	156		1916 Feb 28	IA, 43rd, 1917
Bruce, John W.		G, 39th or 82nd Ind.	98		1927 Nov 27	NE, 52nd, 1928
Bruce, John W.		39th Ind.	98		1928 Jan 4	NE, 53rd, 1929
Bruce, M.H.		C, 83rd Ill.	25		1930 Feb 10	KS, 50th, 1931
Bruce, M.R.	1st Lieut.	A, 2nd Ind. D, 42nd Mo.	1		1888	KS, 8th, 1889
Bruce, R. (C)	Pvt.	B, 11th U.S. Inf.	12		1920 Apr 20	IA, 47th, 1921
Bruch, David	Pvt.	I, 153rd Penn. Inf.	235		1915 May 29	IA, 42nd, 1916
Bruck, Lawrence		A, 20th Ill. Inf. (died in railroad accident)	1	54	1891[1901?] Nov	NE, 26th, 1902
Bruck, Oliver		C, 11th N.Y. Inf.	25	73	1918 Apr 28	NE, 43rd, 1919
Brucker, Louis		E, 25th Iowa Inf. (died of complication of diseases at Soldiers & Sailors Home, Grand Island; buried at Riverdale, Neb.)	21	62	1905 Sep 11	NE, 30th, 1906
Bruen, Chas.	Pvt.	D, Bord Brig.	22		1921 Oct 9	IA, 48th, 1922
Bruenger, Peter		F, 50th Ill. (died of paralysis)	201	79	1920 Jan	NE, 45th, 1921
Bruett, Chas.	Pvt.	H, 117th Ill.	55		1926 Nov 15	IA, 53rd, 1927
Bruihl, Herman			462		1911 Sep 29	KS, 31st, 1912
Bruitt, John	Pvt.	I, 33rd Iowa Inf.	49		1917 Jan 30	IA, 44th, 1918
Brula, Anthony	Pvt.	F, 45th Ill. Inf.	78	95	1931 Oct 27	IA, 58th, 1932
Brula, Edward	Pvt.	C, 16th Ill. Inf.	267		1916 Jun 9	IA, 43rd, 1917
Brumfield, J.W.		H, 11th Ky. Cav.	462		1914 May 13	KS, 34th, 1915
Brumfield, S.J.	Pvt.	C, 73rd Ind. Inf.	26		1919 Nov 14	IA, 46th, 1920
Brumley, H.	Pvt.	I, 92nd N.Y.	68		1921 Aug 29	IA, 48th, 1922
Brummage, R.F.		G, 88th Ohio Inf.	293		1916 Nov 18	KS, 36th, 1917
Brummett, Marion		C, 35th Mo.	113		1920 Dec 26	KS, 40th, 1921
Brump, M.V.	Pvt.	G, 47th Iowa	11		1921 Apr 11	IA, 48th, 1922
Brunais, Jos.	Pvt.	B, 15th U.S. Inf.	132		1908 Apr 21	IA, 35th, 1909
Brundage, Joseph W.		K, 92nd Ill. Mtd. Inf. I, 65th Ill. Inf.	236 375	92	1938 Jun 23	IA, 64th, 1938
Brundage, S.S.		C, 105th Ill.	25		1919 May 26	KS, 39th, 1920
Brundidge, H.A.		H, 25th Wis.	242		1915 Aug 15	KS, 35th, 1916
Bruner, A.		D, 175th Ohio	32		1925 May 1	KS, 45th, 1926
Bruner, A.B.		H, 34th Ky.	40		1922 Mar 15	KS, 42nd, 1923
Bruner, Charles W.	Pvt.	B, 86th Ohio Inf.	44		1928 Jul 29	IA, 55th, 1929
Bruner, E.P.		K, 23rd Ind.	55		1920 Feb 4	KS, 40th, 1921
Bruner, Isaac		K, 9th Ill. Cav.	7	87	1937 Jan 8	IA, 64th, 1938
Bruner, J.M.		M, 10th Ind.	57		1928 Apr 23	KS, 48th, 1929
Bruner, Perry	Pvt.	C, 71st Ill. Inf.	35		1917 Feb 22	IA, 44th, 1918
Bruner, S.	Pvt.	F, 28th Iowa Inf.	94		1920 Dec 11	IA, 47th, 1921
Bruner, Samuel		H, 12th Ky. Cav.	74		1917 Nov 4	KS, 37th, 1918
Brunk, Wm.		B, 53rd Ill. (died of heart trouble)	27	78	1914 Mar 23	NE, 39th, 1915
Brunn, C.F.		Indiana	377		1916	KS, 36th, 1917
Brunn, Charles	Pvt.	C, 31st Iowa Inf.	68		1912 Nov 19	IA, 39th, 1913
Brunnemer, J.O.		G, 136th Ind.	58		1916 Jan 1	KS, 36th, 1917
Brunner, Henry		D, 103rd N.Y. Inf.	147		1916 Sep 20	KS, 36th, 1917
Brunner, J.	Pvt.	E, 14th Iowa Inf.	16		1920 Apr 15	IA, 47th, 1921
Brunskill, James	Pvt.	C, 21st Iowa	78		1923 Oct 19	IA, 50th, 1924
Brunson, John	Pvt.	F, 12th Ill. Inf.	432	71	1895 Apr 10	IA, 22nd, 1896
Brunt, J.M.		F, 33rd Iowa	100		1924 Apr 10	KS, 44th, 1925
Brunt, S.W.	Pvt.	D, 13th Iowa Inf.	167	92	1933 Dec 16	IA, 60th, 1934
Brusean, Wm.		F, 6th Kans. Cav.	347		1892 Jan 13	KS, 12th, 1893
Brush, B.L.			23		1888	KS, 8th, 1889
Brussman, Chas. D.		H, 26th Ohio Inf. (died at Topeka)	1		1895 May 3	KS, 15th, 1896
Bruyn, S.T.	Pvt.	K, 143rd Penn. Inf.	235		1912 Aug 13	IA, 39th, 1913
Bryan, A.A.	Pvt.	F, 10th Iowa Inf.	127		1917 Feb 23	IA, 44th, 1918
Bryan, Albert, see Bryon, Albert						
Bryan, Asbury		E, 137th Ohio (died of asthma)	24	73	1918 Nov 4	NE, 43rd, 1919
Bryan, Daniel	Pvt.	G, 133rd Ohio Inf.	139		1907 Feb 16	IA, 33rd, 1907
Bryan, Ellis, see Bryon, Ellis						

*See Appendix A, B or C for roster of post names and locations.
†See Introduction for note regarding recording of death date.

Name	Rank	Company, Regiment or Ship	Post*	Age	Death Date†	Journal
Bryan, H.E.	Pvt.	I, 21st Iowa	190		1924 Dec 27	IA, 51st, 1925
Bryan, Henry		H, 68th U.S. Col.	321		1925 Mar 18	KS, 45th, 1926
Bryan, J.H.		B, 85th Penn.	17		1919 Nov 24	KS, 39th, 1920
Bryan, J.M.			52		1910	IA, 37th, 1911
Bryan, J.M.		H, 154th Ind.	74		1915 Dec 4	KS, 35th, 1916
Bryan, J.W.		D, 2nd Ohio	117		1929 Jun 20	KS, 49th, 1930
Bryan, Jos.		K, 48th Ill. Inf.	263		1892 Nov 29	NE, 17th, 1893
Bryan, L.M.		A, 155th Ind. Inf.	11	61	1861 Jun 24	NE, 34th, 1910
Bryan, P.L.	Pvt.	B, 34th Iowa Inf.	7		1917 May 11	IA, 44th, 1918
Bryan, Patrick		died of old age	105	84	1914	NE, 39th, 1915
Bryan, S.H.		G, 1st West Va. Cav.	206		1898 Nov 13	KS, 18th, 1899
Bryan, T.E.	Pvt.	K, 21st Iowa Cav.	90	53	1897 Dec 26	IA, 24th, 1898
Bryan, W.B.	Corp.	K, 96th Ill. Inf.	81		1919 Feb 10	IA, 46th, 1920
Bryan, W.H.	Lieut.	D, 5th Ky. Cav.	27		1930 Nov 3	IA, 57th, 1931
Bryant, A.B.		F, 30th N.J.	117		1923 May 26	KS, 43rd, 1924
Bryant, Allen		G, 79th Ill.	51		1898 Oct 8	KS, 18th, 1899
Bryant, B.A.	Pvt.	B, 32nd Iowa Inf.	42	60	1895 Sep 23	IA, 22nd, 1896
Bryant, Benjamin	Pvt.	B, 30th Iowa Inf.	100		1902 Feb 15	IA, 29th, 1903
Bryant, C.A.		C, 20th Wis. (died of paralysis)	5	81	1924 Nov 23	NE, 49th, 1925
Bryant, D.G.		12th Ohio	202		1916 Nov 29	KS, 36th, 1917
Bryant, Eli	Pvt.	G, 36th Iowa Inf.	122		1911 Apr 30	IA, 38th, 1912
Bryant, F.B.		C, 12th Wis. Inf.	7		1928 Nov 19	NE, 53rd, 1929
Bryant, Hiram D.	Pvt.	F, 53rd Penn. Inf.	410		1900 Mar 31	IA, 27th, 1901
Bryant, Joseph, see Briant, Joseth						
Bryant, Joseph J.			219		1926	IA, 53rd, 1927
Bryant, Peter		K, 93rd Ill.	46		1912 Aug 3	KS, 32nd, 1913
Bryant, Samuel			12		1913 Apr 30	KS, 33rd, 1914
Bryant, W.B.	Sergt.	I, 124th Ind. Inf.	203		1925 Aug 5	IA, 52nd, 1926
Bryant, W.C.	Pvt.	E, 2nd Wis. Inf.	222		1905 Nov 6	IA, 32nd, 1906
Bryant, W.C.		H, 7th Kans. Cav.	176		1911 Nov 12	KS, 31st, 1912
Bryant, Wm.	Pvt.	G, 36th Iowa Inf.	122		1910 Feb 2	IA, 37th, 1911
Bryden, James		I, 7th Mo. Inf.	32		1916 Jun 5	KS, 36th, 1917
Bryon, Alanson	Pvt.	B, 40th Iowa Inf.	127		1913 Jun 6	IA, 40th, 1914
Bryon, Albert		F, 168th Ohio Inf.	295		1899 Jul 27	KS, 19th, 1900
Bryon, Ellis		F, 106th —	43		1908 Sep 5	KS, 28th, 1909
Bryon, J.P.		5th Ohio Inf.	25		1903 Sep 13	NE, 28th, 1904
Bryson, David	Corp.	I, 75th Ill. Inf. (see also Appendix D)	13		1939 Jan 29	NE, 64th, 1940
Bryson, John			500		1910	IA, 37th, 1911
Bryson, John, see Byrson, John						
Bster, Samuel M.		A, 70th Ohio	18		1924	KS, 44th, 1925
Buchan, E.A.	Pvt.	E, 52nd Ill. Inf.	267		1906 Jun 19	IA, 33rd, 1907
Buchan, W.J.		H, 42nd Ohio	28		1922 Mar 22	KS, 42nd, 1923
Buchanan, A., see Buchannan, A.						
Buchanan, G.W.	Pvt.	D, 15th Iowa Inf.	231		1911 Jan 30	IA, 38th, 1912
Buchanan, J.J.		A, 3rd Mo.	13	72	1918 Apr 22	NE, 43rd, 1919
Buchanan, U.		B, 18th Penn. Cav. (died of Bright's disease)	192	70	1903 Aug 8	NE, 28th, 1904
Buchanan, Wm.		I, 16th Ohio	1		1896 Sep 2	KS, 16th, 1897
Buchanan, Wm. M.	Pvt.	B, 153rd Ill. Inf.	503		1915 Jul 6	IA, 42nd, 1916
Buchannan, A.		C, 16th Kans.	117		1896 Oct 10	KS, 16th, 1897
Buchannan, Robert L.		F, 9th Ky. Inf. (died at smallpox hospital, St. Louis, Mo.)	294		1890	KS, 10th, 1891
Buchanon, J.Y.	Pvt.	G, 8th Iowa Cav.	74		1920 Dec 30	IA, 47th, 1921
Bucharrad, James	Pvt.	C, 6th Iowa Inf.	154		1911 May 7	IA, 38th, 1912
Bucher, Fred		A, 57th Ill. (died of old age)	18	74	1904 Jun 6	NE, 29th, 1905
Bucher, T.W.	Pvt.	E, 4th Ohio Inf.	493		1912 Mar	IA, 39th, 1913
Buchler, Sabastion	Pvt.	A, 24th Ind. Battery	117	55	1899 Mar 12	IA, 25th, 1899
Buchman, A.	Pvt.	G, 9th Iowa Vol. Inf.	118		1899 Apr 21	IA, 26th, 1900
Buchoff, Paul	Lieut.	E, 13th Iowa	141		1905 Jun 20	IA, 32nd, 1906
Buchtel, Wm. D.		D, 128th Ind. (former member of department; location: North Platte)			1933	NE, 58th, 1934

*See Appendix A, B or C for roster of post names and locations.

†See Introduction for note regarding recording of death date.

Name	Rank	Company, Regiment or Ship	Post*	Age	Death Date†	Journal
Buchtell, Al.		C, 72nd Ohio	180		1904 May 2	KS, 24th, 1905
Buck, A.H.	Pvt.	E, 45th Ill.	30		1926 Jan 19	IA, 53rd, 1927
Buck, Arthur G.	Pvt.	C, 45th Iowa Inf.	2	48	1890 Oct 21	IA, 17th, 1891
Buck, C.H.		C, 2nd Ill. Lt. Art.	89		1928 Aug 28	NE, 53rd, 1929
Buck, E.		A, 107th Ill.	196		1916 May 16	KS, 36th, 1917
Buck, F.A., Dr.		D, — Maine	89		1906 Dec 13	KS, 26th, 1907
Buck, Geo. W.		B, 120th Ind.	50		1917 Oct 29	KS, 37th, 1918
Buck, George, Jr.		H, 2nd Vt.	25		1927 Apr 2	NE, 52nd, 1928
Buck, H.A.		F, 3rd Kans.	1		1921 Sep 2	KS, 41st, 1922
Buck, J.A.	Pvt.	G, 113th Ill. Inf.	236		1930 Sep 19	IA, 57th, 1931
Buck, J.H.	Pvt.	K, 78th N.Y. Inf.	452		1922 Feb 8	IA, 49th, 1923
Buck, J. Jay		I, 101st U.S.C.T.	55		1917 Sep 4	KS, 37th, 1918
Buck, J.M.		A, 3rd Ill. Inf.	98		1930 Jan	KS, 50th, 1931
Buck, J.S.		L, 14th Ill. Cav. (died of consumption)	7		1893 Nov 18	NE, 18th, 1894
Buck, John		11th Ill.	12		1917 Dec 6	KS, 37th, 1918
Buck, Joseph		F, 107th Ill. Inf.	25		1917 Jan 1	KS, 37th, 1918
Buck, L.D.		A, 20th Ohio	51		1917 Mar 11	KS, 37th, 1918
Buck, Lorenzo		E, 7th West Va. Cav.	335		1904 Dec 27	KS, 24th, 1905
Buck, M.			211		1921	IA, 48th, 1922
Buck, Max		E, 26th Mich. Inf. (died at Burlingame; buried at Burlingame Cemetery)	35		1894 Feb 6	KS, 14th, 1895
Buck, Reuben		B, 23rd Wis. Inf.	85		1914 Mar 10	KS, 34th, 1915
Buck, W.H.		E, 74th Ill. Inf. (died at Larned, Kans.; buried at Garfield, Kans.)	8		1894 Jul 5	KS, 14th, 1895
Buckels, Henry C.		K, 6th Mich. Inf.	8		1914 Dec 16	KS, 34th, 1915
Buckeridge, R.W.		A, 29th Ill. Inf.	239		1891 Feb	KS, 11th, 1892
Buckert, Frank		39th Ill.	7		1925 Mar 8	NE, 50th, 1926
Buckingham, Chancy		C, 46th Ohio Inf.	25		1917 Dec 8	KS, 37th, 1918
Buckler, G.W.	Pvt.	128th Ohio	40		1923 Jun 13	IA, 50th, 1924
Buckler, Geo.	Pvt.	H, 1st Iowa Inf.	78		1913 May 4	IA, 40th, 1914
Bucklew, John	Pvt.	K, 78th Ill. Inf.	5	66	1887 Dec 27	IA, 14th, 1888
Buckley, Alva D.		B, 53rd Ohio	[18?]		1909 Dec 4	KS, 29th, 1910
Buckley, Andrew	Pvt.	A, 18th Iowa Inf.	88		1911 Feb 13	IA, 38th, 1912
Buckley, Daniel	Pvt.	I, 75th Ill. Inf.	88		1915 Dec 2	IA, 42nd, 1916
Buckley, Elisha	Pvt.	I, 75th Ill. Inf.	327	80	1893 Mar 8	IA, 19th, 1893
Buckley, Ike		died of paralysis	84	69	1910 Dec 31	NE, 35th, 1911
Buckley, Isaac		died of paralysis	84		1911 Jan 2	NE, 36th, 1912
Buckley, J.L.	Corp.	K, 22nd Inf.	364		1925 Nov 11	IA, 52nd, 1926
Buckley, Merrill	Pvt.	E, 46th Ill. Inf.	452		1912 Nov 21	IA, 39th, 1913
Buckley, R.K.	Pvt.	139th Ill. Inf.	17		1919 May 26	IA, 46th, 1920
Buckley, Wm.		died of sickness	190		1920	NE, 45th, 1921
Bucklin, Hiram		E, 2nd R.I.	18		1922 Mar 20	KS, 42nd, 1923
Bucklin, Mason C.	Pvt.	A, 8th Vt. Inf.	196		1901 Mar 10	IA, 27th, 1901
Buckman, A.H.		A, 32nd Ohio	1		1919 Jul 3	KS, 39th, 1920
Buckmaster, A.	Pvt.	4th Iowa Battery (died of consumption)	118	39	1884 Feb 1	NE, 9th, 1885
Buckner, Allen		79th Ill. (see also Appendix D)	40	70	1900 Nov 9	KS, 20th, 1901
Buckner, Chas.			22		1926	KS, 46th, 1927
Buckner, Enos		I, 79th Ill.	16		1898 Aug	KS, 18th, 1899
Buckner, Robt. W.		K, 5th Ky. Inf.	98		1928 Aug 21	NE, 53rd, 1929
Buckner, Russell	Pvt.	K, 30th Wis. Inf.	165	56	1893 Feb 10	IA, 20th, 1894
Buckner, W.T.		F, 175th Ohio	25		1930 Jan 10	KS, 50th, 1931
Buckworth, L.M.	Corp.	E, 34th Iowa	18		1907 Sep 25	IA, 34th, 1908
Budd, Aso M.	Pvt.	K, 97th Ind. Inf.	154		1903 Dec 23	IA, 30th, 1904
Budd, D.B.		I, 7th Kans. Cav.	93		1902	KS, 22nd, 1903
Budd, Will H.	Pvt.	K, 31st Iowa Inf.	212		1917 Nov 9	IA, 44th, 1918
Buddin, S.P.	Pvt.	E, 21st Ind. Inf.	324		1902 Jul 19	IA, 29th, 1903
Budwell, Elijah	Pvt.	C, 30th Iowa Inf.	363		1906 Dec 20	IA, 33rd, 1907
Budworth, I.N.		I, 20th Wis. Inf. (died at Clifton)	24		1895 Oct	KS, 15th, 1896
Buehler, Lenard	Pvt.	H, 1st Iowa Inf.	78		1916 Mar 13	IA, 43rd, 1917
Buehner, John		B, 2nd Ohio (died of paralysis)	25		1916 Aug 27	NE, 41st, 1917
Buel, C.	Pvt.	E, 146th Ill. Inf.	45		1909 Aug	IA, 36th, 1910
Buel, Marcus		D, 38th Mich.	443		1910 May 11	KS, 30th, 1911

Name	Rank	Company, Regiment or Ship	Post*	Age	Death Date†	Journal
Buel, Samuel T.	Lieut.	1st & 2nd Vt. Inf.	228		1913 Apr 26	IA, 40th, 1914
Buell, A.G.		G, 80th Ill. Inf.	11	84	1925 Aug 23	NE, 50th, 1926
Buell, FitzRoy		K, 10th Ill.	340		1916 Jun	KS, 36th, 1917
Buell, J.F.		F, 114th N.Y. Inf.	1		1916 Jul 16	KS, 36th, 1917
Buelter, Samuel		died of heart failure	66	74	1910 Sep 23	NE, 35th, 1911
Buffington, Geo.		E, 161st Ohio	118	95	1917 Oct 7	NE, 42nd, 1918
Buffington, H.V.			69		1906	IA, 33rd, 1907
Buffington, J.A.		D, 32nd Iowa	85		1931 Mar 4	KS, 51st, 1932
Buffington, J.A.		D, 32nd Iowa	85		1931 Mar 4	KS, 52nd, 1933
Buffington, S.A.			101		1915 Apr 26	IA, 42nd, 1916
Buffum, Joseph W.		G, 83rd Ill. Inf. (died of general breakdown, old age)	47	80	1914 Feb 3	NE, 39th, 1915
Bugbee, Geo. C.	Pvt.	H, 49th N.Y. Inf.	88		1918 Aug 14	IA, 46th, 1920
Bugbee, George E.		D, 1st Maine	256		1913 Oct 2	KS, 33rd, 1914
Bugbee, Orange		A, 25th Mich.	244		1917 Oct 15	KS, 37th, 1918
Bugbee, Ossian	Sergt.	I, 3rd Wis. Inf. (cause of death: kidneys)	25	45	1887 Dec 23	NE, 12th, 1888
Bugh, Alfred		D, 62nd Ohio Inf.	262	79	1914 Sep 5	NE, 39th, 1915
Buhre, Charles E.		C, 22nd Wis. Inf.	1		1916 Feb 16	KS, 36th, 1917
Buhrle, Leonard			55		1926 Apr 25	KS, 46th, 1927
Buker, Decatur		A, 88th Ohio	85		1936 Apr 30	KS, 56th, 1937
Bulcher, Preston		A, 2nd Ill. Cav.	74		1930	KS, 50th, 1931
Bulger, Samuel			32		1914 Apr 24	KS, 34th, 1915
Bull, C.H.		A, 10th N.Y. Hvy. Art.	25		1927 Nov 4	NE, 52nd, 1928
Bull, J.G.	Pvt.	94th Ohio Inf.	343		1906 Dec 5	IA, 33rd, 1907
Bull, Stephen		G, 186th N.Y.	35		1926 Nov 17	NE, 51st, 1927
Bull, Wm. E.		E, 2nd N.Y. (died of general disability)	84	80	1907 Jan	NE, 33rd, 1909
Bullard, J.C.			251		1912 Aug 7	IA, 39th, 1913
Bullen, O.L.	Pvt.	D, Wis. Inf.	132		1923 Aug 10	IA, 50th, 1924
Bullene, L.		E, 3rd Kans. State Militia	12		1915 Apr 2	KS, 35th, 1916
Bulley, Samuel		I, 4th Mass.	17		1916 Mar 18	KS, 36th, 1917
Bullington, Levi		A, 30th Ky.	85		1923 Jun 5	KS, 43rd, 1924
Bullington, Robt.		A, 30th Ky.	174		1904 May 28	KS, 24th, 1905
Bullis, Allen	Pvt.	E, 19th Wis. Inf.	9		1918 Feb 16	IA, 45th, 1919
Bullis, Chas. N.		G, 18th Wis.	5		1918 Dec 7	KS, 38th, 1919
Bullis, J.W.	Corp.	C, 104th Ill. Inf.	141		1923 Dec 7	IA, 50th, 1924
Bullis, O.B.		B, 35th Wis.	380		1920 May 5	KS, 40th, 1921
Bullitt, H.G.		K, 9th U.S. Cav.	25	74	1921 Mar 21	NE, 46th, 1922
Bullitt, H.G.		K, 7th U.S. Cav.	25	74	1921 Mar 21	NE, 46th, 1922
Bullman, Aaron	Corp.	D, 10th Iowa Inf.	100	78	1890 Jul 17	IA, 17th, 1891
Bullock, Adnah David	Pvt.	A, 1st N.Y. Lt. Art. (at large)	6, 50	95	1941 Oct 11	IA, 67th, 1941
Bullock, C.R.	Pvt.	F, 37th Ill. Inf.	137	62	1885 Dec 31	IA, 12th, 1886
Bullock, George K.		2nd Inf.	354	68	1906 Jan 7	NE, 31st, 1907
Bullock, H.D.	Pvt.		466		1927	IA, 54th, 1928
Bullock, H.D.	Pvt.	D, 30th Ohio Inf.	466		1926 Mar 30	IA, 53rd, 1927
Bullock, Norman	Pvt.	I, 7th R.I. Inf.	98		1915 Dec 4	IA, 42nd, 1916
Bullock, S.A.			170		1899	IA, 26th, 1900
Bullock, William		B, 2nd Iowa Cav.	32		1938 Aug 3	NE, 63rd, 1939
Bulluff, Victor	Pvt.	H, 16th Iowa Inf.	259	54	1896 Jan 13	IA, 22nd, 1896
Bumerat, M.L.		G, 134th Ohio	32		1919 Oct 14	KS, 39th, 1920
Bumgardner, Geo., see Bumgartner, Geo.						
Bumgartner, Geo.	Pvt.	B, 3rd West Va. Inf.	173		1900 Apr	IA, 27th, 1901
Bumgartner, J.	Pvt.	F, 45th Iowa Inf.	5		1910 Jan 5	IA, 37th, 1911
Bumgartner, John	Pvt.	E, 46th Iowa Inf.	235		1899 May 30	IA, 26th, 1900
Bump, Horace		A, 15th Iowa	132		1902 Jun 1	KS, 22nd, 1903
Bump, John A.		D, 111th N.Y. Inf.	20		1913	IA, 40th, 1914
Bunam, R.B.		H, 14th Kans. Inf. (died at Oskaloosa; buried at Pleasant View Cemetery)	155		1894 Dec 31	KS, 14th, 1895
Bunc, W.D.	Pvt.	F, 28th Iowa Inf.	452		1925	IA, 52nd, 1926
Bunce, D.R.			89		1917 Jan 24	IA, 44th, 1918
Bunce, Edgar H.		11th Wis. (died of paralysis)	50	67	1910 Dec 3	NE, 35th, 1911
Bunce, Edwin	Pvt.	F, 28th Iowa Inf.	452		1924 Nov 9	IA, 51st, 1925

Name	Rank	Company, Regiment or Ship	Post*	Age	Death Date†	Journal
Bunce, F.E.	Pvt.	M, 1st Iowa Cav.	141		1918 Mar 11	IA, 45th, 1919
Bunce, Milo			14		1915 Nov 28	IA, 42nd, 1916
Bunce, William	Sergt.	E, 5th Iowa Inf.	63	66	1893 May 22	IA, 20th, 1894
Bunch, E.T.	Pvt.	G, 6th Mo. Cav.	26		1922 Nov 26	IA, 49th, 1923
Bundy, A.D.	Pvt.	G, 1st Wis. Inf.	77		1913 Feb 21	IA, 40th, 1914
Bundy, Wm. Henry		H, 23rd Ill. Inf. (died of old age, debility)	77	83	1911 Dec 27	NE, 36th, 1912
Bunes, J.W.	Sergt.	G, 3rd Iowa Cav.	79		1909 Apr 11	IA, 36th, 1910
Bunger, J.D.	Corp.	G, 118th Ill. Inf.	235		1906 May 31	IA, 33rd, 1907
Bunker, A.		E, 15th Iowa Inf.	1		1925 Jun 13	KS, 45th, 1926
Bunker, David		C, 104th Ill.	12		1905 Oct 10	KS, 25th, 1906
Bunker, Dell		D, 9th Mich.	147		1927 Mar 3	KS, 47th, 1928
Bunker, H.M.	Pvt.	G, 92nd Ill. Inf.	200		1918 May 30	IA, 45th, 1919
Bunker, John		B, 25th Ind.	25		1924 Oct 2	KS, 44th, 1925
Bunker, John C.		H, 30th Iowa Inf.	240		1913 Jan 24	KS, 32nd, 1913
Bunker, John C.		K, 30th Iowa	240		1913 Jan 24	KS, 33rd, 1914
Bunker, L.S.	Pvt.	F, 3rd Wis. Cav.	66		1911 Dec 2	IA, 38th, 1912
Bunnell, Byron L.		H, 26th Iowa Inf.		96	1936 May 7	IA, 62nd, 1936
Bunnell, J.A.	Pvt.	L, 9th Iowa Cav.	123		1906 Nov 29	IA, 33rd, 1907
Bunnell, Moses L.	Musician	B, 74th Ohio Vols.	12		1914 Nov 27	IA, 41st, 1915
Bunner, Joseph	Pvt.	B, 8th Ill. Cav.	68		1905 Oct 28	IA, 32nd, 1906
Bunniner, Isaac		E, 148th Ind.	4		1913 Jan 6	KS, 33rd, 1914
Bunninghoff, T.C.		B, 11th Md.	25	78	1919 Oct 1	NE, 44th, 1920
Buntin, A.E.		G, 23rd Mo.	45		1914 Dec 24	KS, 34th, 1915
Bunting, Henry		108th Ill. Inf.	11	66	1908 Nov 27	NE, 33rd, 1909
Bunting, W.M.		G, 102nd Ill. Inf.	10	81	1920 Nov 20	NE, 45th, 1921
Bunton, A.W.		C, 46th Iowa	90		1933 Jun 10	KS, 53rd, 1934
Bunton, G.	Pvt.		155		1899	NE, 24th, 1900
Burbank, D.S.	Sergt.	G, 20th Wis.	68		1923 Jan 5	IA, 50th, 1924
Burbank, Jerome	Sergt.	33rd Wis. Inf.	267	70	1897 May 26	IA, 24th, 1898
Burch, C.S.			10		1920 Aug 24	NE, 45th, 1921
Burch, F.A.	Pvt.	C, 23rd Iowa Inf.	7	53	1888 Jun 23	IA, 15th, 1889
Burch, Frank		A, 10th Ind.	203		1925 May 15	KS, 45th, 1926
Burch, Frank		A, 10th Ind.	203		1924 May 15	KS, 44th, 1925
Burch, Geo. B.		G, 42nd Ind. (died of heart failure)	226	67	1909 Jan 12	NE, 34th, 1910
Burch, H.S.		E, 1st Wis. Cav.	32		1926 Aug 15	NE, 51st, 1927
Burch, James P.	Pvt.	B, 5th Mich. Cav.	154		1907 Mar 20	IA, 34th, 1908
Burch, W.A.		2nd Lt. Art.	63		1912 Mar 31	KS, 32nd, 1913
Burch, Wm.		8th Ohio	17		1904 Feb	KS, 24th, 1905
Burchard, E.H.		B, 29th Iowa Inf.	262	54	1896 Aug 4	NE, 21st, 1897
Burcher, Thos. B.		B, 50th Penn. Inf. (died of softening of brain)	11	62	1897 Dec 31	NE, 22nd, 1898
Burd, Alex. N.		F, 2nd Iowa Cav.	25		1894 Aug 13	NE, 19th, 1895
Burdell, Isaac	Pvt.	I, 3rd Maine Inf.	299	56	1889 Jan 25	IA, 16th, 1890
Burden, Edward		E, 27th Ohio C, 43rd Ind.	293		1917 Oct 8	KS, 37th, 1918
Burden, H.F.L.	Capt.	E, 44th Iowa Inf.	220	64	1897 May 4	IA, 23rd, 1897
Burden, Henry		B, 17th Va. U.S. Inf. (died of pneumonia)	107	71	1913 Oct 11	NE, 38th, 1914
Burden, John			99		1916 Aug 26	KS, 36th, 1917
Burdett, John P.		B, 3rd Ky.	57		1923 Jun 25	KS, 43rd, 1924
Burdick, C.W.	Lieut.	D, 3rd Iowa Inf.	168		1913 Mar 7	IA, 40th, 1914
Burdick, D.L.		G, 8th Minn. Inf. (died of inflammation of kidneys)	95		1893 Mar 17	NE, 18th, 1894
Burdick, Eli H.	Corp.	B, 8th Ill. Cav.	88		1916 Nov 21	IA, 43rd, 1917
Burdick, Frank J.				90	1938 Mar 30	IA, 64th, 1938
Burdick, G.D.	Pvt.	L, 6th Mich. Cav.	228		1899	NE, 24th, 1900
Burdick, G.L.	Pvt.	A, 33rd Iowa Inf.	49		1920 Mar 2	IA, 47th, 1921
Burdick, Jared		I, 49th Wis. Inf. (died of paralysis of bladder)	60	68	1897 Dec 27	NE, 22nd, 1898
Burdick, John			151		1908 May 23	KS, 28th, 1909
Burdick, O.N.		I, 26th N.Y. Inf., 1st Corps (born in Bridgewater, N.Y., Sept. 10, 1842; died in Fairmount, Neb.)	18		1883 Sep 17	NE, 8th, 1884
Burdick, Z.C.			389		1924 Feb 27	IA, 51st, 1925

Name	Rank	Company, Regiment or Ship	Post*	Age	Death Date†	Journal
Burdict, T.W.	Capt.	D, 6th Iowa Cav.	168	61	1898 Jul 16	IA, 25th, 1899
Burel, C.E.	Pvt.		14		1925 Dec 12	IA, 52nd, 1926
Burent, E.T.		D, 115th Ill.	375		1909 Jun 28	KS, 29th, 1910
Burg, C.H.		C, 7th Ohio	71		1923 Jan 13	KS, 43rd, 1924
Burge, Alfred	Pvt.	C, 40th Ill. Inf. (died of consumption)	13	47	1887 Sep	NE, 12th, 1888
Burge, Clancy		K, 103rd Ill.	85		1905 Feb 13	KS, 25th, 1906
Burge, F.M.		B, 151st Ill.	85		1913 Feb 23	KS, 33rd, 1914
Burge, Geo. W.		E, 27th Ind. Inf.	1		1899 May 2	KS, 19th, 1900
Burge, Henry		I, 155th Ind.	358		1916 Jan 8	KS, 36th, 1917
Burge, Henry J.		B, 6th Ind. Inf. (died of gunshot wound)	77	72	1908 Dec 3	NE, 33rd, 1909
Burge, James J.		G, 2nd Iowa Inf.	79		1916 Nov 15	NE, 41st, 1917
Burge, Wm.	Pvt.	K, 11th Iowa Inf.	140		1907 Jan 11	IA, 33rd, 1907
Burgen, C.Y.	Capt.	H, 4th Iowa Inf.	324		1916 Oct 23	IA, 43rd, 1917
Burgener, Henry		K, 20th Ind.	36		1929 Apr 6	KS, 49th, 1930
Burger, A.M.	Pvt.	G, 158th Penn.	230		1899 Dec 11	IA, 26th, 1900
Burger, August	Corp.	B, 15th Iowa	55		1926 Aug 5	IA, 53rd, 1927
Burger, Wm.	Pvt.	G, 8th Mich. Inf.	22		1910 Dec 3	IA, 37th, 1911
Burgers, Jesse	Sergt.	I, 27th Iowa	187		1914 Jan 15	IA, 41st, 1915
Burges, Truman	Pvt.	K, Wis. Hvy. Art.	389		1914 Feb 17	IA, 41st, 1915
Burgess, C.M.	Corp.	D, 45th Iowa Inf.	100		1907 Feb 11	IA, 34th, 1908
Burgess, Fred W.	Pvt.	G, 61st Ill. Inf.	2		1919 Jan 20	IA, 46th, 1920
Burgess, George W., Rev.		A, 10th Kans.	18		1913 Feb 21	KS, 33rd, 1914
Burgess, J.R.			12		1923 Nov	IA, 50th, 1924
Burgess, James		A, 7th & 124th Ind.	1		1912 Feb 20	KS, 32nd, 1913
Burgess, John	Chaplain	30th Iowa Inf.	2	76	1897 May 6	IA, 23rd, 1897
Burgess, John T.		G, 7th Mo. Cav.	170		1910 Jul 10	KS, 30th, 1911
Burgess, T.W.	Capt.	30th Iowa Inf.	244		1914 Sep	KS, 34th, 1915
Burgess, Truman	Pvt.	K, 1st Wis. Hvy. Art.	389		1914 Feb 17	IA, 40th, 1914
Burgess, Walter	Pvt.	I, 7th Iowa Cav.	22		1922 Aug 21	IA, 49th, 1923
Burgess, William		G, 2nd Wis. Cav. (former member)	89		1940 Sep 17	NE, 65th, 1941
Burget, L.		K, 39th Ill.	100		1915 Jan 4	KS, 35th, 1916
Burgett, A.G.		E, 78th Ill.	75		1909 Apr 10	KS, 29th, 1910
Burgett, William	Pvt.	I, 2nd Iowa Inf.	228	66	1893 Feb 23	IA, 20th, 1894
Burgette, Samuel		C, 107th Ill. Inf. (died at Cheney)	325		1895 Mar	KS, 15th, 1896
Burghart, Geo.		K, 24th Wis.	90		1927 Feb 7	KS, 47th, 1928
Burgin, Jesse W.	Pvt.	H, 105th Ill. Inf.	66	53	1898 Jun 13	IA, 25th, 1899
Burgoon, William		H, 10th Kans.	18		1923 May 21	KS, 43rd, 1924
Buriss, O.Z.		B, 15th Ohio Inf. (died at Council Grove)	7		1895 Jan 8	KS, 15th, 1896
Burk, James H.			96		1922 May 21	IA, 49th, 1923
Burk, John		I, 2nd Kans. Cav.	28		1915 Jun 25	KS, 35th, 1916
Burk, M.M.		C, 73rd Ind. Inf.	289		1894	NE, 19th, 1895
Burk, O.P.		H, 47th Ill. Inf.	25	89	1917 Aug 3	NE, 42nd, 1918
Burk, S.	Pvt.	G, 1st Iowa Cav.	154		1921 Mar 13	IA, 48th, 1922
Burk, T.F.		A, 116th Ill.	4		1917 Jun 13	KS, 37th, 1918
Burk, Thomas		G, 11th Ill.	164		1914 Apr 13	KS, 34th, 1915
Burk, Wm. M.		H, 51st Mo.	45		1928	NE, 53rd, 1929
Burke, A.A.			44		1921 Jun 13	KS, 41st, 1922
Burke, E.H.	Pvt.		489		1923 Apr 22	IA, 52nd, 1926
Burke, E.W.	Pvt.	C, 11th Ill. Inf.	267		1925 Apr 22	IA, 52nd, 1926
Burke, G.P.		C, 118th Ohio (died of ptomaine poisoning)	23	73	1915 Sep 5	NE, 40th, 1916
Burke, J.H.		K, 19th Mo.	130		1926 Jul 2	KS, 46th, 1927
Burke, James		F, 10th Kans.	336		1898 Jul 25	KS, 18th, 1899
Burke, James A.		F, 106th Ill.	18		1919 Sep 28	KS, 39th, 1920
Burke, James H.		E, 44th N.Y. Inf. (see also Appendix D)	35		1906 Aug 14	KS, 26th, 1907
Burke, Patrick		F, 189th Ohio	380		1898 Nov 15	KS, 18th, 1899
Burke, Wm. J.		E, 106th N.Y. Inf. (died of indigestion)	23		1924 Feb 15	NE, 48th, 1924
Burkepile, Jacob B.		H, 133rd Penn.	147		1904 Jul 6	KS, 24th, 1905
Burkerd, N.C.		F, 41st Ill. Inf. (died of gallstones)	134	63	1903 Jun 13	NE, 28th, 1904
Burkert, Theo. E.		E, 205th Penn.	42		1931 Jan 13	KS, 51st, 1932
Burkert, Theo. E.		E, 205th Penn.	42		1931 Jan 13	KS, 52nd, 1933
Burket, John S.		K, 29th Iowa	214		1919	KS, 39th, 1920

*See Appendix A, B or C for roster of post names and locations.
†See Introduction for note regarding recording of death date.

Name	Rank	Company, Regiment or Ship	Post*	Age	Death Date†	Journal
Burket, M.D.	Pvt.	E, 33rd Iowa Inf.	40		1906	IA, 33rd, 1907
Burkett, Daniel		B, 84th Ind.	437		1922 Nov 15	KS, 42nd, 1923
Burkett, Geo. M.	Pvt.	D, 12th Penn.	230		1924 Jan 6	IA, 51st, 1925
Burkett, H.L.		B, 13th Ill. Inf. (cause of death: heart)	262	59	1901 May	NE, 26th, 1902
Burkett, Henry	Pvt.	D, 14th U.S. Inf.	230		1926 Jan 13	IA, 53rd, 1927
Burkett, John S.		K, 29th Iowa	214		1918	KS, 38th, 1919
Burkett, Pleas. J.M.		E, 138th Ind. Vol. Inf.	1		1909 Jul 3	KS, 29th, 1910
Burkey, Leve		B, 90th Ohio	119		1889	KS, 9th, 1890
Burkhard, Andrew		I, 5th Iowa	1		1917 Apr 18	KS, 37th, 1918
Burkhart, Andrew	Pvt.	L, 1st Wis. Inf.	12		1911 Jan 9	IA, 38th, 1912
Burkhart, Chas.		K, 3rd Mich. Cav. (died of apoplexy)	26	87	1917 Dec 1	NE, 42nd, 1918
Burkhart, J.C.	Pvt.	A, 20th Iowa Inf.	239		1910 Jun	IA, 38th, 1912
Burkhart, John	Pvt.	E, 16th Iowa Inf.	231		1922 Sep 3	IA, 49th, 1923
Burkholder, A.M.		E, 7th Ill.	66		1897 Dec 8	KS, 17th, 1898
Burkholder, Wm.		A, 99th Penn. Inf.	47		1917 Jan 25	KS, 36th, 1917
Burkit, F.M.	Pvt.	B, 19th Iowa Inf.	57		1916 Jan 28	IA, 43rd, 1917
Burleson, David G.	Sergt.	D, 11th Mich. Inf.	11	56	1899 Dec 6	IA, 26th, 1900
Burlet, Joseph	Pvt.	E, 21st Iowa Inf.	78		1916 Sep 9	IA, 43rd, 1917
Burley, A.D.	Pvt.	A, 153rd Ill. Inf.	155		1927 Nov 12	IA, 54th, 1928
Burley, A.H.	Pvt.		118		1927	IA, 54th, 1928
Burley, Hiram		Ind. Battery	208		1886	KS, 6th, 1887
Burlingame, E.H.		I, 2nd Iowa	52		1906 Apr 22	KS, 26th, 1907
Burlingame, G.M.			23		1922	NE, 47th, 1923
Burlingame, John H.	Pvt.	I, 156th Ill. Inf.	25	97 & 2 days	1945 Mar 10	IA, 71st, 1945
Burlingham, R.E.	Corp.	C, 6th Iowa Cav.	48		1900 Aug 4	IA, 27th, 1901
Burlinghame, C.E.	Corp.	G, 26th Ill. Inf.	88	58	1895 Mar 10	IA, 21st, 1895
Burmaster, Chas. E.		B, 11th Vt. Inf. (died of paralysis)	110		1916 Feb 17	NE, 41st, 1917
Burmeister, H.	Pvt.		116		1921 Aug 31	IA, 48th, 1922
Burmont, Peter		D, 137th Ind. (died of pneumonia)	134	81	1925 Dec 1	NE, 50th, 1926
Burnan, Robert			83		1916 May 21	KS, 36th, 1917
Burnap, W.A.	Pvt.	I, 2nd Iowa Cav.	101		1923 Mar 11	IA, 50th, 1924
Burnell, C.P.		D, 40th Ky. A, 18th Ky.	78		1913 Jul 24	KS, 33rd, 1914
Burnell, Gilbert		E, 12th Inf. (died of diabetes at Soldiers & Sailors Home, Grand Island; buried in Grand Island Cemetery)	2	62	1905 Jan 26	NE, 30th, 1906
Burner, Isaac		I, 92nd Ill.	25		1904 May 23	NE, 29th, 1905
Burnes, C.P.	Pvt.	C, 17th Ill. Cav.	81		1920 Sep 24	IA, 47th, 1921
Burnes, D.M.	Pvt.	G, 87th Penn. Inf.	1		1930 Apr 1	IA, 57th, 1931
Burnes, J.M.		C, 62nd Ill. Inf.	314		1899 Sep 3	KS, 19th, 1900
Burnes, W.E.		A, 7th Mo.	17		1930 May 15	KS, 50th, 1931
Burnett, Chas. H.		G, 64th Ill.	22		1930 Mar 31	NE, 55th, 1931
Burnett, D.M., see Beurnett, D.M.						
Burnett, Daniel D.		L, 7th Ill. Cav. (not a member of the G.A.R.)	18		1912 Mar 16	KS, 32nd, 1913
Burnett, E.C.		12th Ind. Cav.	81		1917 May 2	KS, 37th, 1918
Burnett, Elliott R.		A, 29th Mich. Inf. (died of old age, paralysis at Soldiers & Sailors Home, Grand Island; buried in Home Cemetery)	18	79	1905 Aug 13	NE, 30th, 1906
Burnett, J.E.		44th Ohio Inf.	25		1904 Dec 3	NE, 29th, 1905
Burnett, Jesse F.		H, 118th Ill.	34		1911 Nov 18	KS, 31st, 1912
Burnett, Joseph		E, 1st Mich.	294		1924 May 24	KS, 44th, 1925
Burnett, L.C.		Gunboat *Wisconsin*	239		1922 Mar 24	KS, 42nd, 1923
Burnett, Lewis C.		Boat *Avenger*	239		1922 Mar 24	KS, 41st, 1922
Burnett, Richard		36th Ohio	452	88	1934 Nov 19	IA, 61st, 1935
Burnett, Robt.	Pvt.	35th Ohio Inf.	452		1930 Apr 7	IA, 57th, 1931
Burnett, S.H.	Pvt.	K, 5th Ky.	363	59	1898 Sep 24	IA, 25th, 1899
Burnett, Theo.	Pvt.	K, 43rd Ind.	108		1923 May 20	IA, 50th, 1924
Burnett, Virgil		G, 137th & 149th Ind.	114		1897 Jun 14	KS, 17th, 1898
Burnett, William		E, 41st Ill.	72		1912 Feb 26	KS, 32nd, 1913
Burnette, Elisha	Pvt.	I, 64th Ohio Inf.	49		1897 Jun 11	IA, 24th, 1898

*See Appendix A, B or C for roster of post names and locations.
†See Introduction for note regarding recording of death date.

Name	Rank	Company, Regiment or Ship	Post*	Age	Death Date†	Journal
Burney, A.J.		I, 9th Iowa Inf.	147		1921 Apr 3	KS, 41st, 1922
Burney, C.F.		C, 12th Kans. Inf.	18		1917 Jan 25	KS, 37th, 1918
Burnham, Adam	Pvt.	D, 40th Iowa Inf.	16		1899 Jan 4	IA, 26th, 1900
Burnham, Geo. A.		F, 4th Iowa Cav.	44		1899 Jun 1	KS, 19th, 1900
Burnham, Geo. E.		C, 154th Ohio Inf.	47		1909 Jul 27	KS, 29th, 1910
Burnham, R.R.			155		1896	KS, 16th, 1897
Burnham, Sumner W.		C, 17th Maine	25		1913 Jan 29	NE, 38th, 1914
Burns, E.C.		B, 4th Mich. (died of dropsy)	311	69	1907 May 28	NE, 32nd, 1908
Burns, G.W.	1st Lieut. Capt.	F, 1st Neb. Inf. A, 8th Iowa Cav.	11	60	1892 Sep 28	IA, 19th, 1893
Burns, G.W.		B, 70th Ohio	4		1928 Jun 19	KS, 48th, 1929
Burns, Geo. W.		A, 7th Ill.	74		1917 Mar 8	KS, 37th, 1918
Burns, H.T.	Pvt.	B, 39th Iowa Inf.	230		1911 Jan 19	IA, 38th, 1912
Burns, J.D.	Sergt.	B, 198th Ohio Inf.	71		1915 Dec 22	IA, 42nd, 1916
Burns, J.J.	Pvt.	G, 128th N.Y. Inf.	78		1906 Oct 22	IA, 33rd, 1907
Burns, James	Pvt.	F, 14th Iowa Inf.	177		1911 Apr 10	IA, 38th, 1912
Burns, Jno.	Sergt.	F, Navy	7		1921	IA, 48th, 1922
Burns, John	Pvt.	K, 8th Ind. Bat.	125		1920 Aug 1	IA, 47th, 1921
Burns, John		I, 12th Kans. Cav.	96		1918 Sep 12	KS, 38th, 1919
Burns, John	Pvt.	H, 57th Ill. Inf.	193		1899	NE, 24th, 1900
Burns, John D.		I, 11th Wis. Inf.	278		1918 Aug 15	KS, 38th, 1919
Burns, John M.		E, 3rd West Va.	52		1917 Jul 19	KS, 37th, 1918
Burns, Martin		B, 44th N.Y. (died of old age)	318		1922 Jul	NE, 47th, 1923
Burns, Patrick		D, 5th N.Y. Art. B, 2nd U.S. Scout	304	60	1895 Jun 15	NE, 20th, 1896
Burns, R.G.		A, 7th Ill.	4		1928 Oct 3	KS, 48th, 1929
Burns, R.H.	Pvt.	N.Y. Inf.	7	90 & 4 mos.	1931 Mar 31	IA, 58th, 1932
Burns, Robert	Pvt.	G, 2nd Iowa Inf.	16		1910 Feb 20	IA, 37th, 1911
Burns, Squire		H, 7th Wis. Inf.	250		1930[1929?] May 9	KS, 49th, 1930
Burns, Squire		H, 7th Wis. Inf.	250		1930 May 9	KS, 50th, 1931
Burns, W.J.			28		1883	KS, 3rd, 1884
Burns, W.M.		G, 1st Mass. Cav. (died of old age)	206	73	1909 Nov 14	NE, 34th, 1910
Burnside, John A.	Pvt.	D, 18th Mo. Inf.	497		1908 Mar 1	IA, 35th, 1909
Burnside, Sylvester		D, 83rd Ill. Inf. (died of general decline)	226	66	1906 Nov 1	NE, 31st, 1907
Burnsill, A.E.		K, 88th Penn. Inf. (died of paralysis)	79	71	1901 Nov	NE, 26th, 1902
Burr, Charles E.		2nd Penn. Hvy. Art.	25		1927 Dec 8	NE, 52nd, 1928
Burr, Fred P.			12		1923 Oct 19	KS, 43rd, 1924
Burr, G.W.	Pvt.	A, 1st N.Y. Dragoons	54		1906 Nov 17	IA, 33rd, 1907
Burr, J.N.		B, 120th Ind.	14		1919 Apr 29	KS, 39th, 1920
Burr, J.W.	Capt.	F, 45th Ill. Inf.	98		1918 Oct 16	IA, 45th, 1919
Burr, John B.	Pvt.	A, 36th Ill. Inf.	1		1916 Jul 30	IA, 43rd, 1917
Burr, Levi P.	Pvt.	H, 45th Ill. Inf.	8		1928 May 27	IA, 55th, 1929
Burr, Lewis H.		F, 12th Kans. Cav.	25		1911 Oct 21	KS, 31st, 1912
Burr, Norvill L.		B, 21st N.Y.	1		1911 Jun 2	KS, 31st, 1912
Burr, O.		K, 144th N.Y.	105		1892 May	KS, 12th, 1893
Burr, R.E.	Pvt.	I, 28th Wis. Inf.	197	46	1887 Jul 28	IA, 14th, 1888
Burr, Rufus H.		A, 50th Ohio D, 177th Ohio	1		1919 Nov 30	KS, 39th, 1920
Burr, W.H.		K, 26th N.Y. Inf.	13	72	1913 Mar 21	NE, 38th, 1914
Burrell, John		C, 29th Wis.	9		1932	NE, 58th, 1934
Burrell, Robert		D, 72nd Ill. Inf.	26		1922 Apr 15	IA, 49th, 1923
Burres, W.L.	2nd Lieut.	A, 147th Ind.	81		1922 Jan 31	IA, 49th, 1923
Burrill, Ed.		H, 2nd Iowa Inf. H, 15th Ill. Inf. (died of stomach troubles)	102	67	1901 Feb	NE, 26th, 1902
Burris, B.H.		H, 77th Ohio	22		1892 Jan 6	KS, 12th, 1893
Burris, Daniel		H, 2nd Kans. Cav. (died of paralysis)	354	75[?]	1913 Oct 10	NE, 38th, 1914
Burris, Josiah F.		A, 39th Ind.	1		1911 Jan 2	KS, 31st, 1912
Burris, Nelson	Pvt.	A, 57th Ind. Inf.	40		1913 Dec 14	IA, 40th, 1914
Burriss, O.Z., see Buriss, O.Z.						
Burroughs, William		K, 41st Mo.	354	76	1921 Jan 10	NE, 46th, 1922
Burrows, C.E.		I, 2nd Ill. Cav.	25		1909 Dec 27	KS, 29th, 1910
Burrows, Chas. H.		C, 124th Ill.	93		1922 Jun 14	KS, 42nd, 1923

*See Appendix A, B or C for roster of post names and locations.
†See Introduction for note regarding recording of death date.

Name	Rank	Company, Regiment or Ship	Post*	Age	Death Date†	Journal
Burrows, Geo. W.	Pvt.	G, 2nd Iowa Inf.	100	42	1887 Nov 8	IA, 14th, 1888
Burrows, J.E.	Pvt.	I, 140th Ill. Inf.	250		1913 May 20	IA, 40th, 1914
Burrows, W.C.	Musician	H, 136th Ohio Inf.	210	83	1897 Mar 24	IA, 23rd, 1897
Burrows, Wm. T.	Pvt.	C, 4th Ill.	78		1923 Feb 20	IA, 50th, 1924
Burrus, Robt. R.	Musician	10th Ill. Inf.	5		1911 May 9	IA, 38th, 1912
Bursly, John	Pvt.	H, 75th Ill. Inf.	212	60	1889 Feb 24	IA, 16th, 1890
Burson, Charles		E, 87th Ohio Inf.	255		1931 May 2	KS, 51st, 1932
Burson, David	1st Lieut.	C, 143rd Ohio Inf.	6	72	1894 Feb 12	IA, 20th, 1894
Burst, Nelson		G, 51st Wis.	77		1885	KS, 5th, 1886
Burt, A., Jr.			429		1901 Apr 5	KS, 21st, 1902
Burt, A.L.	Pvt.	G, 8th Iowa Cav.	74	50	1896 Jul 28	IA, 23rd, 1897
Burt, Adrain	Pvt.	I, 3rd Ohio Inf.	68		1917 May 5	IA, 44th, 1918
Burt, B. Franklin	Pvt.	B, 23rd Penn. Inf.	515		1918 Mar 8	IA, 45th, 1919
Burt, Cyrus		K, 6th Cal. Inf.	4		1899 Apr 28	KS, 19th, 1900
Burt, G.G.	Pvt.	H, 14th Iowa	7		1905 Feb 9	IA, 32nd, 1906
Burt, J.A.		I, 33rd Ind.	153		1905 Nov 16	KS, 25th, 1906
Burt, J.M.		B, 4th Wis. Cav.	465		1917 Oct 27	KS, 37th, 1918
Burt, James W.		H, 95th Penn. Inf. (died of fever)	22	72	1919 Jul 28	NE, 44th, 1920
Burt, John	Pvt.	F, 30th N.J. Inf.	40		1913 Jan 3	IA, 40th, 1914
Burt, M.L.		2nd Ill. Art.	25		1908 Jul 21	NE, 33rd, 1909
Burt, W.W.		K, 123rd Ind.	4		1921 Dec 17	KS, 41st, 1922
Burtch, John		76th Ky.	443		1910 Apr 24	KS, 30th, 1911
Burtch, Z.			4		1914 Mar 30	IA, 41st, 1915
Burton, David		B, 91st N.Y. Inf. (died of heart failure)	130	75	1913 Jul 25	NE, 38th, 1914
Burton, Eli M.		H, 67th Ind.	113		1908 Feb 14	NE, 33rd, 1909
Burton, Francis M.		C, 139th Ill.	7		1931 Aug 27	NE, 56th, 1932
Burton, George		2nd Ohio Battery	113		1912 Sep 17	KS, 32nd, 1913
Burton, H.V.		F, 9th Ill. Cav.	293		1925 Feb 25	KS, 45th, 1926
Burton, Irvin		G, 1st Ky. Cav.	42		1917 Apr 16	KS, 37th, 1918
Burton, J.N.		I, 112th Ill.	63		1921 Sep 25	KS, 41st, 1922
Burton, James H.		F, 11th Mo. Cav. Indiana	46		1904 Nov 15	KS, 24th, 1905
Burton, L.G.	Pvt.	I, 38th Iowa Inf.	216		1911 Mar 27	IA, 38th, 1912
Burton, P.D.	Pvt.	14th Ohio Batt.	64		1929	IA, 56th, 1930
Burton, R.D.		I, 24th Ind. Inf. H, 67th Ind. Inf.	136		1920 Apr 4	NE, 45th, 1921
Burton, Samuel	Pvt.	C, 98th Ohio Inf.	67		1901 Feb	IA, 28th, 1902
Burton, Seth		I, 26th Mo.	380		1889	KS, 9th, 1890
Burton, W.J.		A, 8th Ill.	98		1904 Sep 9	KS, 24th, 1905
Burton, William R.		E, 23rd Ind.	13		1935 May 24	NE, 60th, 1936
Burtz, Ambrose, see Butrz, Ambrose						
Burwell, Daniel M.		D, 111th Ohio Inf.	206		1900 Mar 11	KS, 20th, 1901
Burwell, J.		I, 14th Ohio	81		1928 May 9	NE, 53rd, 1929
Busby, Geo.	Pvt.	I, 114th Ohio	329		1923 Oct 26	IA, 50th, 1924
Busby, Thomas		B, 48th Ind. Inf.	1		1921 May 28	KS, 41st, 1922
Busch, Jacob	Pvt.	A, 40th Mo. Inf.	2		1917 Jan 4	IA, 44th, 1918
Busch, John		F, 3rd & 28th N.Y.	62		1893 Jun 12	KS, 13th, 1894
Busesam, Ruborn		E, 43rd Ind.	293		1922 Mar 26	KS, 42nd, 1923
Busey, John A.		died of blood poison	35		1886 Dec 6	NE, 11th, 1887
Bush, A.M.	Pvt.	E, 11th Mich. Inf.	77		1905 Oct 25	IA, 32nd, 1906
Bush, Charles		I, 1st Md. Inf.	127		1909 Dec 29	KS, 29th, 1910
Bush, Colby		B, 9th Mo. State Militia	132		1914 May 11	KS, 34th, 1915
Bush, Curtis	Seaman	gunboat	88	59	1897 Aug 6	IA, 24th, 1898
Bush, D.E.		K, 30th Iowa	51		1927	KS, 47th, 1928
Bush, E.S.			383		1918	IA, 45th, 1919
Bush, H.H.	Capt.	D, 17th Ill. Inf.	485		1905 Sep 14	IA, 32nd, 1906
Bush, J.R.		C, 12th Mo.	69		1926 May 30	KS, 46th, 1927
Bush, Jacob		K, 112th Ill. (cause of death: heart)	25	63	1900 Jan 26	NE, 25th, 1901
Bush, Jas. Wm.		K, 54th Mass. Inf.	25	74	1918 Apr 22	NE, 43rd, 1919
Bush, John		C, 2nd Ohio Art. H, 97th Ohio Inf.	7	92	1937 May 6	IA, 64th, 1938
Bush, John		H, 19th Ind. (died of dropsy)		67	1909 Dec 13	NE, 34th, 1910

Name	Rank	Company, Regiment or Ship	Post*	Age	Death Date†	Journal
Bush, John		E, 36th Ill. (died of paralysis)	165	75	1915 Oct 5	NE, 40th, 1916
Bush, Moses	Pvt.	I, 60th U.S.C.T. Inf.	1		1914 Jul 22	IA, 41st, 1915
Bush, Rickard	Pvt.	A, 6th U.S.C. Hvy. Art.	1		1904 Aug 13	IA, 31st, 1905
Bushey, Calvin			194		1936 Sep 7	KS, 56th, 1937
Bushly, W.J.	Pvt.	Signal Service	215		1914 Apr 23	IA, 41st, 1915
Bushman, Daniel	Pvt.	L, 17th Ill. Cav.	154		1905 Nov 18	IA, 32nd, 1906
Bushman, Henry		15th Ohio Inf.	80		1911	IA, 38th, 1912
Bushnell, A.L.	Pvt.	G, 24th N.Y. Cav.	140		1924 Dec 16	IA, 51st, 1925
Bushnell, Edwin		I, 10th Mich. Cav.	90		1922 Dec 1	KS, 42nd, 1923
Bushnell, George Shipman	Pvt.	E, 46th Iowa Inf. (at large)	235	94, 10 mos. & 18 days	1943 Dec 29	IA, 70th, 1944
Bushnell, J.P.	Pvt.	D, 44th Wis. Inf.	12		1927 Apr 30	IA, 54th, 1928
Bushong, G.W.		F, 10th Iowa	17		1909 Apr 23	KS, 29th, 1910
Bushong, William A.		E, 3rd Ohio Cav.	18		1915 Sep 25	KS, 35th, 1916
Bussard, A.	Pvt.	G, 28th Ill. Inf.	7		1910 May 18	IA, 37th, 1911
Bussart, F.A.		6th Ohio Lt. Art.	3		1918 Aug 13	KS, 40th, 1921
Bussert, Carlisle		I, 39th M.O. Inf. (died of kidney trouble)	190		1891 Mar 13	KS, 11th, 1892
Bussinger, M.C.		K, 85th Ind. Inf.	17		1925 Dec 18	KS, 45th, 1926
Busten, W.S.	Pvt.	C, 13th Wis. Inf.	30		1920 Feb 7	IA, 47th, 1921
Butchen, —			2		1924	IA, 51st, 1925
Butcher, A.		Ind. Inf.	25		1919 May 10	KS, 39th, 1920
Butcher, John	Pvt.	I, 2nd Mich. Cav.	147		1905 Dec 20	IA, 32nd, 1906
Butcher, W.T.			98		1913 Dec 25	KS, 33rd, 1914
Buterbaugh, J.L.		D, 78th Penn.	206		1930 Nov 14	NE, 55th, 1931
Buthbough, Sam		E, 34th Ill. (died of age)	18	75	1919 Nov 21	NE, 44th, 1920
Butin, C.J.		D, 3rd Iowa Cav.	98		1921	KS, 41st, 1922
Butlar, O.D.		D, 51st Ill. Inf.	9		1911 Apr 27	NE, 36th, 1912
Butler, A.		E, 11th Mo.	209		1922 Aug 26	KS, 42nd, 1923
Butler, Alonzo	Pvt.	B, 11th Iowa Inf.	292		1909 Oct 6	IA, 36th, 1910
Butler, Anson R.	3rd Sergt.	H, 26th Iowa Inf.	92		1901 Apr 26	IA, 27th, 1901
Butler, Ben		H, 60th Ill.	147		1913 Mar 22	KS, 33rd, 1914
Butler, Ben B.		B, 2nd Iowa	17		1919 Apr 1	KS, 39th, 1920
Butler, Charles		E, 5th U.S. Art.	66		1902 Feb	KS, 22nd, 1903
Butler, Chas.		C, 9th Ohio Cav.	462		1911 Mar 26	KS, 31st, 1912
Butler, David L., see Buttler, David L.						
Butler, F.A.		A, 100th Ill.	304		1924 Aug 18	KS, 44th, 1925
Butler, Fred	Sergt.	C, 33rd Iowa Inf.	40		1929 Nov 7	IA, 56th, 1930
Butler, George		C, 96th Ohio	474		1914 Oct 31	KS, 34th, 1915
Butler, Gilford		C, 138th U.S. Colored	127		1905 May 26	KS, 25th, 1906
Butler, I.	Pvt.	F, 44th Wis. Inf.	142		2nd quarter 1885	IA, 12th, 1886
Butler, J.M.		D, 50th Ind. Inf. 1st Cav.	25		1919 Apr 14	NE, 44th, 1920
Butler, Jacob	Capt.	I, 1st Neb. Inf.	11		1912 Oct 24	IA, 39th, 1913
Butler, Jas. G.		C, 22nd N.J. Vols.	22		1906 Mar 7	KS, 26th, 1907
Butler, John H.		C, 5th Iowa Inf.	7		1925 May 23	NE, 50th, 1926
Butler, John L.		E, 11th Kans. Cav.	249		1916 Jun 10	KS, 36th, 1917
Butler, Joseph		G, 120th Ind. Inf. (died of heart disease)	324		1894 Jan 3	NE, 19th, 1895
Butler, Louis		C, U.S. Cav.	17		1923 Jan 28	KS, 43rd, 1924
Butler, M.V.	Pvt.	F, 5th Iowa Inf.	249		1926 Jun 13	IA, 53rd, 1927
Butler, Maron		cause of death: unknown, old age	256		1917	NE, 42nd, 1918
Butler, Moses	Pvt.	A, 14th Iowa	92		1922 Mar 20	IA, 49th, 1923
Butler, O.D., see Butlar, O.D.						
Butler, R.P.	Pvt.	G, 28th Iowa Inf.	403		1912 Sep 5	IA, 39th, 1913
Butler, S.C.		I, 97th Ind. Inf. (died of pneumonia)	95	65	1895 Feb 1	NE, 20th, 1896
Butler, T.A.		C, 138th Ill. Inf.	20		1899 Mar 4	KS, 19th, 1900
Butler, W.H.			29		1914 Oct 3	IA, 41st, 1915
Butler, W.H.		F, 180th Ill.	85		1926 Mar 15	KS, 46th, 1927
Butler, W.J.		8th Mo.	388		1925	KS, 45th, 1926
Butler, Washington		B, 7th Iowa Cav. 14th Iowa Inf.	314		1901 Nov 24	KS, 21st, 1902

*See Appendix A, B or C for roster of post names and locations.
†See Introduction for note regarding recording of death date.

Name	Rank	Company, Regiment or Ship	Post*	Age	Death Date†	Journal
Butler, William M.		K, 19th Ill.	92		1917 May 19	KS, 37th, 1918
Butler, Wm. A.	Pvt.	G, 120th Ind. (died of wounds)	95	39	1884 Feb 2	NE, 9th, 1885
Butler, Wm. H.		D, 135th Ohio Inf. (at large)	139		1938 May 28	IA, 64th, 1938
Butler, Wm. H.		D, 135th Ohio Inf.	30, 139	89	1938 May 28	IA, 65th, 1939
Butrz, Ambrose		I, 10th Ill. Inf.	354	81	1914 Dec 26	NE, 40th, 1916
Butt, Jacob H.		I, 126th Penn.	63		1913 Sep 3	KS, 33rd, 1914
Butter, Samuel		C, 44th Iowa Inf. G, 24th Iowa Cav.	9		1920 Feb 9	KS, 40th, 1921
Butterfield, D.G.		H, 26th Iowa Inf. (at large)			1936	IA, 63rd, 1937
Butterfield, J.A.			98		1927 Jan	IA, 54th, 1928
Butterfield, J. Ware	Capt.	D, 12th N.H.	1		1915 Jun 12	KS, 35th, 1916
Butterfield, James	Pvt.	I, 10th Ill. Cav.	233	54	1894 Aug 6	IA, 21st, 1895
Butterfield, W.E.	Pvt.	H, 13th U.S. Eng.	181		1922 Jun 7	IA, 49th, 1923
Buttermore, Henry		C, 14th Ill.	258		1927	KS, 47th, 1928
Butters, Willard	Pvt.	A, 7th Mass. Cav.	212		1926 Feb 16	IA, 53rd, 1927
Buttingham, J.		D, 135th Ill. Inf. (died of paralysis)	287		1893 Mar 3	NE, 18th, 1894
Buttler, David L.		A, 14th Kans.	65		1924 Feb	KS, 44th, 1925
Buttles, Charles		E, 38th Ohio	293		1921 Sep 14	KS, 41st, 1922
Buttles, Frank		H, 113th Ohio	380		1905 Aug 8	KS, 25th, 1906
Buttolph, A.M.	Pvt.	D, 28th Iowa Inf.	349		1910 Sep 13	IA, 37th, 1911
Button, A.M.		G, 146th Ill.	59		1896 Apr 20	KS, 16th, 1897
Button, Henry		I, 3rd Ohio	18		1937 Oct 7	KS, 57th, 1938
Buttorff, W.K.			19		1921 Oct 26	IA, 48th, 1922
Buttre, C.W.			200		1924 Jul 24	IA, 51st, 1925
Butts, C.M.	Pvt.	B, 4th Iowa Inf.	371		1913 Sep	IA, 40th, 1914
Butts, D.E.		42nd Ill.	117		1925 Oct 21	KS, 45th, 1926
Butts, J.A.		B, 50th Ohio	139		1928 May 26	KS, 48th, 1929
Butts, J.P.		F, 151st Ill. Inf.	7		1926	NE, 51st, 1927
Butts, L.A.	Lieut.	K, 85th N.Y. Inf.	208		1910 Dec 30	IA, 37th, 1911
Butts, L.A.	Pvt.	6th Iowa Cav.	495		1916 Nov	IA, 43rd, 1917
Buttus, J.F.	Pvt.	I, Iowa Cav.	22		1916 Sep 28	IA, 43rd, 1917
Buuth, F.H.	Pvt.	F, 4th Wis. Inf.	267		1918 Aug 9	IA, 45th, 1919
Buxton, Singleton		E, 18th Mo.	17		1913 Apr 9	KS, 33rd, 1914
Buzbee, B.F.		G, 10th Kans.	39		1914 Oct 2	KS, 34th, 1915
Buzley, H.F.	Pvt.	H, 78th Ill. Inf.	11		1915 Dec 24	IA, 42nd, 1916
Buzley, J.F.		F, 38th Ill.	49		1896 Nov 25	KS, 16th, 1897
Bybee, J.C.		A, 100th Ohio	380		1919 Aug	KS, 39th, 1920
Byer, Jabez D.	Corp.	D, 27th Iowa Inf.	299	56	1897 Sep 18	IA, 24th, 1898
Byer, Wm.	Pvt.	E, 41st Mo. Inf.	78	86	1933 Oct 6	IA, 60th, 1934
Byerly, Cyrus P.		A, 37th Ill. (former member; died at Norfolk)	109		1936 May 4	NE, 61st, 1937
Byerly, W.P.	V.S.	1st Iowa Cav.	78		1910 Jan 18	IA, 37th, 1911
Byers, Byron	Pvt.	I, 16th Ind. Inf.	497		1908 Aug 14	IA, 35th, 1909
Byers, David	Pvt.	A, 37th Ill. Inf.	321	52	1892 Jan 13	IA, 18th, 1892
Byers, J.C.		D, 21st Cav.	95	74	1920	NE, 45th, 1921
Byers, J.D.	Corp.	I, 20th Penn. Cav.	112		1909 Aug 15	IA, 36th, 1910
Byers, Jacob	Pvt.	F, 65th Ohio Inf.	59		1923 Jul 30	IA, 50th, 1924
Byers, John	Pvt.	G, 9th Ind. Inf.	5		1915 Jan 10	IA, 42nd, 1916
Byers, John T.		I, 13th Iowa (died of heart failure)	26	85	1915 Nov 23	NE, 40th, 1916
Byers, Samuel W.	Pvt.	C & K, 38th Iowa	132		1902 May 4	IA, 28th, 1902
Byford, John R.	Pvt.	A, 37th Iowa Inf.	68		1900 Dec 27	IA, 27th, 1901
Byington, J.G.		I, U.S. Inf. (died at the Military Home in Leavenworth)	6		1936 Mar or Feb 30	KS, 55th, 1936
Bykerk, Cornelius		I, 187th N.Y. Inf. (died of cancer of stomach)	312		1906 Jun 10	NE, 31st, 1907
Byng, E.F.		C, 26th Iowa Inf.	235	97	1936 Sep 23	IA, 63rd, 1937
Bynn, Samuel		E, 34th Iowa	36		1927 Dec 31	KS, 47th, 1928
Byrd, Herman	Artificer	C, 1st Mo. Eng.	34		1914 Aug 24	IA, 41st, 1915
Byrd, S.L.		L, 4th Iowa Bat. (died of old age)	120		1915 Dec	NE, 40th, 1916
Byrne, Sylvester	Pvt.	E, 35th Iowa Inf.	231		1906 Sep 17	IA, 33rd, 1907
Byrnes, Albert J.		G, 147th Ill.	388		1918 Sep 20	KS, 38th, 1919
Byrnes, Geo. W.	Pvt.	D, 26th Iowa Inf.	92		1909 Jul 25	IA, 36th, 1910

*See Appendix A, B or C for roster of post names and locations.
†See Introduction for note regarding recording of death date.

Name	Rank	Company, Regiment or Ship	Post*	Age	Death Date†	Journal
Byrnes, J.S.	Pvt.	M, 6th Iowa Cav.	78	63	1888 Feb 7	IA, 15th, 1889
Byrns, John		I, 124th Ohio Inf.	283		1st quarter 1885	IA, 11th, 1885
Byrns, Wm.	Pvt.	D, 119th Ill. Inf.	23		1916 Jan 17	IA, 43rd, 1917
Byrns, Wm.	Pvt.	A, 15th —	23		1923 Oct 24	IA, 50th, 1924
Byron, James W.		E, 63rd Ill. Inf.	49		1887	KS, 7th, 1888
Byrson, John	Pvt.	D, 92nd Ill. Inf.	271		1905 Dec 17	IA, 32nd, 1906
Bywater, A.	Pvt.	H, 6th Iowa Inf.	94		1930 Feb 3	IA, 57th, 1931
Cabb, J.P.		B, 34th Ohio	17		1910 Jan	KS, 30th, 1911
Caber, Lafayette		I, 3rd Ill. Art.	302		1899	KS, 19th, 1900
Cable, Geo.		A, 99th Ohio Inf.	164		1900 Dec 9	KS, 20th, 1901
Cachelin, Urban		K, 1st Mo. Art.	52		1928 Jan 6	NE, 52nd, 1928
Cachlin, Urban		K, 1st Mo. Art.	52		1929 Jan 23	NE, 53rd, 1929
Cacy, James S.		L, 16th Ill. Cav. (died of disease of liver)	42	51	1897 Sep 25	NE, 22nd, 1898
Cade, B.F.		D, 19th Kans.	221		1913 Sep 27	KS, 33rd, 1914
Cade, Chas.			45		1923 May 9	IA, 50th, 1924
Cade, Chas. W.		49th Penn.	87		1919 Dec 25	KS, 39th, 1920
Cade, William		H, 36th Iowa Inf. (died of pneumonia)	84		1909 Jan 2	NE, 34th, 1910
Cadle, C.F.	Pvt.	A, 2nd Iowa Cav.	231		1922 Nov 5	IA, 49th, 1923
Cadwallader, C.S.		K, 32nd Iowa	25		1936 Jan 24	NE, 61st, 1937
Cadwallader, John W.		A, 55th Ill. Inf.	25	76	1911 Nov 17	NE, 36th, 1912
Cadwell, C.N.	Pvt.	A, 1st Wis. Cav.	38		1921 Mar 19	IA, 48th, 1922
Cadwell, E.J.	Pvt.		56		1926 Oct 20	IA, 53rd, 1927
Cady, Chas.	Pvt.	K, 19th Iowa Inf.	7		1915 May 29	IA, 42nd, 1916
Cady, E.J.		D, 30th Wis. Inf.	1		1886	KS, 6th, 1887
Cady, Geo. W.			14		1923 Dec 8	IA, 50th, 1924
Cady, George W.		B, 1st Mo. State Militia	12		1913 Sep 9	KS, 33rd, 1914
Cady, L.L.	Pvt.	C, 104th Ill. Inf.	431		1891 Apr 15	IA, 17th, 1891
Cady, O.L.		K, 146th N.Y. Inf.	25	75	1921 Jan 25	NE, 46th, 1922
Caffee, W.H.			173		1927 Sep 10	IA, 54th, 1928
Cafferty, D.N.	Pvt.	B, 57th Ill. Inf.	233		1911 Jan 29	IA, 38th, 1912
Cafferty, James		C, 1st N.Y. Cav.	63		1917 Jul 13	KS, 37th, 1918
Caffey, H.M.		K, 52nd Ind.	344	75	1892 Nov 17	KS, 12th, 1893
Caffman, A.		A, 23rd Iowa Inf.	110		1886	KS, 6th, 1887
Cahail, W.H.	Pvt.	H, 2nd Iowa	52		1923 Jan 22	IA, 50th, 1924
Cahill, C.	Pvt.	G, 26th Iowa Inf.	327		1920 Feb 8	IA, 47th, 1921
Cahill, John	Pvt.	I, 7th Iowa Inf.	168	56	1891 Dec 10	IA, 18th, 1892
Cahill, John	Pvt.	31st Iowa Inf.	236		1906	IA, 33rd, 1907
Cahill, John W.		B, 33rd Iowa	25		1912 Aug 18	KS, 32nd, 1913
Cahill, Richard		B, 151st N.Y.	1		1922 Mar 3	KS, 42nd, 1923
Cahill, Wm.		E, 30th Ill. Inf.	22		1886	KS, 6th, 1887
Cahon, Fred.	Pvt.	I, 134th Ill. Inf.	39		1927 Oct 9	IA, 54th, 1928
Cahoon, C.R.	Corp.	I, 76th Ill. Inf.	193		1918 Feb 15	IA, 45th, 1919
Cain, A.J.	Pvt.	I, 34th Ill. Inf.	334	58	1893 Dec 21	IA, 20th, 1894
Cain, Dennis	Corp.	A, 12th Ill. Cav.	93		1912	IA, 39th, 1913
Cain, Geo. H.		B, 11th Kans.	144		1928	KS, 48th, 1929
Cain, James		A, 62nd Penn.	27		1924 Mar 3	KS, 44th, 1925
Cain, John		N, 2nd Colo.	[4?]		1920 Aug 26	KS, 40th, 1921
Cain, M.J.	Lieut.	K, 39th Iowa Inf.	321		1913 Apr 4	IA, 40th, 1914
Cain, R.M.		M, 2nd Neb. Cav. (cause of death: heart)	55	66	1903 Jun 27	NE, 28th, 1904
Cain, S.R.	Pvt.	B, 34th Iowa Inf.	169	76	1899 Apr 9	IA, 26th, 1900
Cain, T.C.		A, 34th Ind.	185		1923 Apr 7	KS, 43rd, 1924
Cain, Wesley A.		K, 36th Iowa	25		1916 Aug 11	KS, 36th, 1917
Cain, William S.		C, 8th & 12th Kans.	93		1920 Apr 6	KS, 40th, 1921
Cain, Wm. H.		K, 74th Ill.	66		1918 Nov 20	KS, 38th, 1919
Cair, W.H.		K, 74th Ill.	377		1918 Nov 20	KS, 38th, 1919
Cairns, Alexander		E, 14th Ill.	85		1913 Jan 11	KS, 33rd, 1914
Cakens, K.J.		K, 24th Iowa (died of Bright's disease)	32	74	1920 Feb 14	NE, 45th, 1921
Calahan, Cornelius	Pvt.	D, 2nd Kans. Cav.	78		1915 Mar 31	IA, 42nd, 1916
Calder, Daniel R.		E, 20th Ohio	354		1922 Nov 30	NE, 47th, 1923
Calderhead, W.A.		H, 126th Ohio	9		1928 Dec 18	KS, 48th, 1929
Caldwell, A.B.		A, 2nd U.S.	17		1920 Sep 14	KS, 40th, 1921
Caldwell, Alix	Corp.	K, 4th V.R.C.	13		1914 Nov 21	IA, 41st, 1915

*See Appendix A, B or C for roster of post names and locations.
†See Introduction for note regarding recording of death date.

Name	Rank	Company, Regiment or Ship	Post*	Age	Death Date†	Journal
Caldwell, David		H, 1st Penn.	25		1915 Mar 27	NE, 40th, 1916
Caldwell, E.	Pvt.	H, 32nd Iowa Inf.	81		1902 Oct 27	IA, 29th, 1903
Caldwell, Jackson N.		C, 83rd Ill.	100		1929 Feb 11	KS, 49th, 1930
Caldwell, John C.		11th Maine Inf.	1		1912 Aug 31	KS, 32nd, 1913
Caldwell, John N.		E, 86th Ind.	81		1914 Nov 4	KS, 34th, 1915
Caldwell, John S.		D, 145th Ind. Inf.	12		1901 May 5	KS, 21st, 1902
Caldwell, Lafe	Pvt.	M, 9th Penn. Cav.	7		1917 May 20	IA, 44th, 1918
Caldwell, Smith T.		died at Edgar, Neb.	16	58	1903 Mar 15	NE, 27th, 1903
Caldwell, T.J.	Surg.	23rd Iowa Inf.	45		1906 Jun 16	IA, 33rd, 1907
Caldwell, T.T.		H, 9th Penn.	47		1910 Mar 23	KS, 30th, 1911
Caldwell, Wm. H.		36th Iowa	250		1913 Jul 25	KS, 33rd, 1914
Cale, J.B.		H, 101st Penn.	28		1922 Apr 30	KS, 42nd, 1923
Cale, J.P.		H, 79th Ill.	25		1920 Dec 14	KS, 40th, 1921
Caley, J.C.	Pvt.	I, 29th Ohio Inf.	59		1921 May 21	IA, 48th, 1922
Caley, Lewis		B, 43rd Wis.	35		1928 Jan 2	NE, 53rd, 1929
Calhoon, J.	Sergt.	G, 5th I.C.[Iowa Cav.?]	141		1915 Mar 30	IA, 42nd, 1916
Calhoun, David B.		B, 155th Ohio	27		1913 Feb 3	KS, 33rd, 1914
Calhoun, J., see Calhoon, J.						
Calhoun, J.W.		C, 17th Ohio	85		1926 Dec 15	KS, 46th, 1927
Calhoun, N.C.		G, 2nd Ill. Art.	9		1921 Jul 31	KS, 41st, 1922
Calhoun, O.R.B.		C, 61st Penn. Inf. (died of heart failure)	1		1894 Jul 29	NE, 19th, 1895
Calhoun, Robt. Y.		A, 13th Ind. Cav.	32		1901 Nov 18	KS, 21st, 1902
Calhoun, S.S.	Corp.	H, 7th Iowa Inf.	333		1897 Dec 12	IA, 24th, 1898
Calin, E.	Pvt.	D, 57th Ill. Inf.	375		1906 Nov 8	IA, 33rd, 1907
Calintzky, Henry R.T.		D, 13th Ill. Inf. (died at Chanute, Kans.; buried at Elmwood Cemetery)	129		1894 Sep 2	KS, 14th, 1895
Calis, William		L, 20th Mich. Eng.	123		1914 Sep 10	KS, 34th, 1915
Calking, R.			50		1920	IA, 47th, 1921
Calkins, A.A.		7th Minn. (died of complication)	154		1905[1904?] Mar 14	NE, 29th, 1905
Calkins, C.P.			236		1922	IA, 49th, 1923
Calkins, E.R.	Sergt.	D, 8th Wis. Lt. Art.	141		1919 Aug 19	IA, 46th, 1920
Calkins, H.F.		F, 2nd Conn. Inf.	244		1916 Dec 24	KS, 36th, 1917
Calkins, M.B.			5		1923 Jul 6	IA, 50th, 1924
Calkins, Riley	Drummer	K, 24th Iowa Inf.	130	79	1899 Mar 17	IA, 25th, 1899
Calkins, Royal D.			127		1920 Feb 18	KS, 40th, 1921
Calkins, Russell W.	Lieut.	K, 139th Ill. Inf.	50		1923 Mar 3	IA, 50th, 1924
Calkins, W.S.		I, 30th Wis.	25		1914 Mar 21	KS, 34th, 1915
Calkins, William			64		1914 Jan 2	KS, 34th, 1915
Call, John	Pvt.	C, 6th Mich. Inf.	222		1924 Nov 29	IA, 51st, 1925
Calla, Isaac		B, 46th Ill. Inf.	124		1928 Apr	IA, 55th, 1929
Callaghan, John	Pvt.	I, 69th N.Y.	383	55	1891 Jun 20	IA, 18th, 1892
Callaham, Andrew M.		H, 73rd Ind.	1		1902 Jul 13	KS, 22nd, 1903
Callahan, A.C.		B, 6th Iowa Cav.	18	92	1935 Dec 23	IA, 62nd, 1936
Callahan, B.A.	Sergt.	B, U.S. Cav.	2		1923 Jan 22	IA, 50th, 1924
Callahan, Charles C.			28		1925 Dec 12	KS, 45th, 1926
Callahan, Geo.	Pvt.	F, 4th Minn.	18		1907 Aug 11	IA, 34th, 1908
Callahan, J.D.	Pvt.	F, 7th Mass. Inf.	78		1910 Mar 3	IA, 37th, 1911
Callan, J.L.D.		D, 101st Ill. Inf.	64		1886	KS, 6th, 1887
Calland, H.S.		D, 92nd Ohio	35	77	1923 Mar 4	NE, 48th, 1924
Callender, J.M.		E, 97th Penn.	9		1923 Feb 4	KS, 43rd, 1924
Callender, Wm.	Pvt.	D, 2nd Iowa Inf.	12		1930 May 5	IA, 57th, 1931
Calleson, V.L.	Pvt.	I, 77th Ill.	55		1921 Oct 30	IA, 48th, 1922
Callicott, Thos.			156		1924 Dec 26	IA, 51st, 1925
Callison, Claiborn	Pvt.	B, 28th Iowa Inf.	16		1903 Mar 6	IA, 30th, 1904
Calloup, John		F, 69th Mo.	15[14?]		1896 May 21	KS, 16th, 1897
Callow, Wm.		F, 4th Mo.	428		1906 Nov 29	KS, 26th, 1907
Calloway, Daniel		K, 15th Kans. Cav.	32		1912 Oct 28	KS, 32nd, 1913
Callowway, Jesse C.	Pvt.	C, 40th Iowa Inf.	40		1919 Dec 21	IA, 46th, 1920
Calonkey, Henry Peter	Pvt.	C, 140th Ill. Inf.	252	92	1940 Apr 10	IA, 66th, 1940
Calvert, A.W.		B, 140th Penn.	180		1916 Dec 4	KS, 36th, 1917
Calvert, J.D.		C, 43rd Ind.	126		1902 Feb 3	KS, 22nd, 1903
Calvert, J.E.			180		1923 Jan 4	KS, 43rd, 1924

Name	Rank	Company, Regiment or Ship	Post*	Age	Death Date†	Journal
Calvert, J.G.		I, 3rd Iowa Cav.	196		1912 Feb 29	IA, 39th, 1913
Calvert, Jasper		13th Kans.	292		1921 May	KS, 41st, 1922
Calvert, John	Pvt.	B, 43rd Wis. Inf.	78		1918 Feb 15	IA, 45th, 1919
Calvin, J.W.		D, 91st Ind.	85		1923 Apr 16	KS, 43rd, 1924
Calvin, John		H, 34th Iowa	100		1912 Jan 22	KS, 32nd, 1913
Calvin, John		A, 18th U.S. Col. Inf.	321		1915 Dec 20	KS, 35th, 1916
Calvin, L.J.		K, 33rd Ohio	18		1922 Nov 18	KS, 42nd, 1923
Calvin, P.Y.	Pvt.	K, 10th Penn.	22		1922 May 12	IA, 49th, 1923
Calvin, Sam'l	Pvt.	C, 44th Iowa Inf.	8		1911 Apr 19	IA, 38th, 1912
Cam, G.N.		F, 21st Ohio (died of old age)	30	78	1921	NE, 46th, 1922
Caman, A.W.		E, 60th N.Y.	35		1931	NE, 56th, 1932
Camble, Patrick		G, 4th Ohio	43		1925 Apr 4	KS, 45th, 1926
Cameron, James	Pvt.	B, 79th N.Y. Inf.	1		1899 Dec 18	IA, 26th, 1900
Cameron, Jas. N.	Pvt.	E, 38th Iowa Inf.	168		1900 Jul 16	IA, 27th, 1901
Cameron, John H.		C, 2nd Wis. Cav. (location: Blair)			1927 Jul 2	NE, 52nd, 1928
Cameron, Peter		F, 7th Wis.	118	63	1905[1904?] Jan 15	NE, 29th, 1905
Cameron, S.		H, 21st Mo. Inf.	14		1888	KS, 8th, 1889
Cameron, T.W.		F, 44th Ill. Inf. (died of pneumonia)	4	63	1902 Feb	NE, 27th, 1903
Cameron, W.T.	Lieut.	143rd Ohio Inf.	130		1920	IA, 47th, 1921
Camery, Denton, see Carney, Denton						
Camin, Wm.		E, 20th Wis. Inf. (died of dropsy)	197	73	1905 Dec 7	NE, 30th, 1906
Cammack, F.M.		F, 69th Ind.	4		1893 Oct	KS, 13th, 1894
Cammeron, J.T.		A, 3rd Kans. Inf.	12		1899 Jan 12	KS, 19th, 1900
Camon, A.W.		E, 60th N.Y.	35		1932 Dec	NE, 57th, 1933
Camp, E.T.		C, 2nd Penn. Art. (died of heart trouble)	63	75	1920 Mar 14	NE, 45th, 1921
Camp, H.E.	Pvt.	C, 24th Ohio Vols.	68		1914	IA, 41st, 1915
Camp, Harry E.		C, 24th Ohio Inf.	68		1915 Jan 8	IA, 42nd, 1916
Camp, Isaac	Pvt.	B, 12th Ill. Inf.	242		1911 Feb 15	IA, 37th, 1911
Camp, John			55		1918 Oct 27	KS, 38th, 1919
Camp, Milton H.	Pvt.	D, 38th Iowa	168	61	1891 Jun 12	IA, 18th, 1892
Camp, Myron		H, 32nd Ill.	352		1895 Feb 3	KS, 16th, 1897
Camp, Thos. P.	Muster	11th Wis. Inf.	40		1924 Mar 24	IA, 51st, 1925
Campbel, John P.		H, 1st R.I. Lt. Art.	63		1924 Feb 6	KS, 44th, 1925
Campbell, A.		M, 6th Mich. Cav. (died at Cherryvale)	142		1895 Sep 9	KS, 15th, 1896
Campbell, A.B.	Pvt.	C, 66th Ill. Inf.	26		1913 May 27	IA, 40th, 1914
Campbell, A.B.		died recently in Chicago, the victim of a combination of misfortunes that became too heavy for him to carry				KS, 17th, 1898
Campbell, A.H.	Pvt.	B, 72nd Ohio	25		1923 Oct 18	IA, 50th, 1924
Campbell, A.S.		G, 11th Iowa Inf.	191		1886	KS, 6th, 1887
Campbell, A.V.	Pvt.	A, 40th Iowa Inf.	313	53	1895 Sep 15	IA, 22nd, 1896
Campbell, Alex	Pvt.	C, 2nd Iowa Inf.	110	63	1891 Nov 29	IA, 18th, 1892
Campbell, Alfred B.		A, 11th Wis.	88		1911 May 20	KS, 31st, 1912
Campbell, Anderson			184		1918	KS, 38th, 1919
Campbell, Brayton	Pvt.	H, 76th N.Y. Inf.	42		1904 Jul 6	IA, 31st, 1905
Campbell, C.C.		A, 2nd Ill.	25		1910 Jul 25	KS, 30th, 1911
Campbell, C.E.		B, 9th N.Y. Inf.	17		1929 Oct 7	KS, 49th, 1930
Campbell, Calvin B.	Pvt.	D, 19th Iowa Inf.	19		1925 Mar 5	IA, 52nd, 1926
Campbell, Charles		D, 81st Ohio Inf.	47		1929 Nov 3	KS, 49th, 1930
Campbell, Charles H.	Pvt.	K, 29th Wis.	68		1923 Apr 14	IA, 50th, 1924
Campbell, Charles L.		G, 77th Ill. (died of fall concussion)	19	66	1907 May 21	NE, 32nd, 1908
Campbell, D.		196th Ohio	36		1910 May 26	KS, 30th, 1911
Campbell, D.S.	Pvt. Pvt.	H, 7th Penn. Inf. C, 49th Penn. Inf.	56	58	1898 Mar 15	IA, 24th, 1898
Campbell, Daniel	Pvt.	D, 30th Mich. Inf.	394	51	1897 Nov 20	IA, 24th, 1898
Campbell, Daniel	Pvt.	H, 8th Iowa Cav.	337	50	1894 Feb 11	IA, 21st, 1895
Campbell, E.B.	Sergt.	I, 12th Iowa Inf.	365	64	1897 Sep 19	IA, 24th, 1898
Campbell, E.P.		Penn.	116	83	1914 May 13	NE, 39th, 1915
Campbell, Eldridge			153		1902	NE, 27th, 1903
Campbell, Ellis	Pvt.	H, 13th Iowa Inf.	246		1901-1902	IA, 28th, 1902
Campbell, F.M.		E, 12th Ill. Inf.	123		1929 May 4	KS, 49th, 1930

Name	Rank	Company, Regiment or Ship	Post*	Age	Death Date†	Journal
Campbell, F.T.	Pvt.	C, 23rd Iowa Inf.	284		1906 Dec 15	IA, 33rd, 1907
Campbell, Francis		H, 11th Kans. Cav.	1		1887 Feb 13	KS, 7th, 1888
Campbell, Frank	Pvt.	K, 67th Ohio Inf.	25		1912 Jun 1	IA, 39th, 1913
Campbell, Franklin	Col.	Ill.	122		1889	KS, 9th, 1890
Campbell, Geo.		C, 33rd Mo.	129		1928 May 31	KS, 48th, 1929
Campbell, Geo.		C, 33rd Mo.	129		1928 May 31	KS, 50th, 1931
Campbell, Geo. W.		C, 141st Ohio	20		1897 Feb 4	KS, 17th, 1898
Campbell, George		G, 129th Ill. Inf.	12		1908 Nov 13	KS, 28th, 1909
Campbell, George P.		D, 34th Ohio Inf.	88		1912 Aug 29	KS, 32nd, 1913
Campbell, H.S.		E, 83rd Penn. Inf.	117		1890	KS, 10th, 1891
Campbell, Hugh C.		C, 6th Vt. Inf.	145		1912 Oct 18	KS, 32nd, 1913
Campbell, J.B.			264		1905 Jun 27	IA, 32nd, 1906
Campbell, J.B.		F, 11th Kans.	180		1916 Oct 7	KS, 36th, 1917
Campbell, J. Clark	Corp.	C, 9th Iowa Cav.	19		1925 Aug 26	IA, 52nd, 1926
Campbell, J.H.		F, 33rd Ohio	329	88	1934 Jun 22	IA, 61st, 1935
Campbell, J.M.		I, 23rd Ky.	4		1913 Feb 7	KS, 33rd, 1914
Campbell, J.M.			180		1923 May 12	KS, 43rd, 1924
Campbell, J.W.	Sergt.	7th Iowa Cav.	434		1915 Jan	IA, 42nd, 1916
Campbell, Jacob		B, 54th Ohio	47		1914 Nov 28	KS, 34th, 1915
Campbell, James		D, 35th Mo.	65		1897 Dec 25	KS, 17th, 1898
Campbell, James M.		C, 39th Iowa Inf. (died of cancer bladder)	15	66	1911 Oct 17	NE, 36th, 1912
Campbell, Jas.	Pvt.	H, 27th Iowa	81		1905 Jan 26	IA, 32nd, 1906
Campbell, Jno.	Pvt.	G, 35th Iowa Inf.	261		1930 Dec 14	IA, 57th, 1931
Campbell, Jno. M.	Pvt.	D, 1st West Va. Art.	64	87	1933 Apr 4	IA, 60th, 1934
Campbell, Joel	Pvt.	G, 30th Iowa Inf.	20		1932	IA, 59th, 1933
Campbell, John			417		1917	IA, 44th, 1918
Campbell, John	Pvt.	I, 33rd Wis. Vol. Inf.	125		1924 Feb 4	IA, 51st, 1925
Campbell, John		C, 6th U.S. Inf.	196		1893 Jul 16	KS, 13th, 1894
Campbell, John		B, 68th Ill.	27		1918 Dec 22	KS, 38th, 1919
Campbell, John B.		K, 12th Ohio Inf.	303		1901 Dec 19	KS, 21st, 1902
Campbell, John C.		108th U.S. Col. Inf.	18		1929 Feb 20	KS, 49th, 1930
Campbell, John H.		B, 11th Kans. Cav. (died at Ontario, Kans.; buried at Ontario Cemetery)	167		1894 Jun 21	KS, 14th, 1895
Campbell, John P., see Campbel, John P.						
Campbell, John R.		C, 119th Ill.	47		1937 Nov 17	NE, 62nd, 1938
Campbell, John W.	Sergt.	I, 7th Cav.	434		1916	IA, 43rd, 1917
Campbell, John W.	Pvt.	I, 130th Ind. Inf.	66		1899	NE, 24th, 1900
Campbell, Joseph R.		1st or 2nd Neb. (killed by street car)	115		1911 Mar 24	NE, 36th, 1912
Campbell, L., M.D.	Pvt.	B, 36th Iowa Inf.	69	54	1897 Dec 1	IA, 24th, 1898
Campbell, L.A.	Pvt.	A, 169th N.Y. Inf.	68	49	1893 May	IA, 20th, 1894
Campbell, L.C.		B, 101st Ind. Inf. (died at Sedgwick; buried at Pleasant Valley Cemetery)	285		1894 Apr 4	KS, 14th, 1895
Campbell, Luther D., see Campell, Luther D.						
Campbell, Luther D.		F, 28th Iowa Inf. (died of paralysis)	130	67	1910 Jul 10	NE, 35th, 1911
Campbell, N.A.		K, 47th Ind. (died of paralysis)	60	74	1919 Apr 20	NE, 44th, 1920
Campbell, Oliver C.		I, 9th Vt. Inf.	110	88	1920 Feb 5	NE, 45th, 1921
Campbell, Patrick, see Camble, Patrick						
Campbell, Peter D.	Pvt.	A, 1st Vol. Eng.	113	49	1892 Sep 14	IA, 19th, 1893
Campbell, Robert A.		K, 24th Ohio (see also Appendix D)	17		1923 Jan 12 or 20	KS, 43rd, 1924
Campbell, Robert C.		D, 13th Ohio	18		1909 Jun 2	KS, 29th, 1910
Campbell, S.M.	Pvt.	B, 3rd Iowa Cav.	497		1921 Feb 6	IA, 48th, 1922
Campbell, S.R.			130		1911 Oct 11	IA, 38th, 1912
Campbell, S.S.		G, 129th Ill.	12		1912 Nov 29	KS, 32nd, 1913
Campbell, Sam'l	Pvt.	K, 42nd Wis. Inf.	291	63	1889 Sep 3	IA, 16th, 1890
Campbell, Samuel P.		A, 11th Kans. Cav.	336		1900 Jan 7	KS, 20th, 1901
Campbell, T.			44	80	1924 Nov 2	NE, 49th, 1925
Campbell, T.F.	Pvt.	K, 4th Iowa Cav.	20		1925 Mar 27	IA, 52nd, 1926
Campbell, Thomas	Pvt.	B, 16th Ohio	110		1907 Oct 7	IA, 34th, 1908
Campbell, Thomas		E, 8th Ind. Cav. 39th Ind. Inf. (died at Argentine)	463		1895 Oct	KS, 15th, 1896

*See Appendix A, B or C for roster of post names and locations.
†See Introduction for note regarding recording of death date.

Name	Rank	Company, Regiment or Ship	Post*	Age	Death Date†	Journal
Campbell, Thomas		A, 26th Iowa	32		1905 Mar 4	KS, 25th, 1906
Campbell, W.A.		M, 4th N.Y. Cav.	28		1894 Jul 3	KS, 14th, 1895
Campbell, W.B.		M, 6th Kans. Cav.	25		1936 Mar	KS, 55th, 1936
Campbell, W.C.		B, 52nd Ind.	100		1913 Aug 18	KS, 33rd, 1914
Campbell, W.E.		A, 53rd Wis.	66		1913 May 11	KS, 33rd, 1914
Campbell, W.P.		M, 6th Ky. Cav.			1936 Apr	KS, 57th, 1938
Campbell, W.T.		H, 140th Ill.	25		1928 Mar 6	NE, 53rd, 1929
Campbell, W.W.	Pvt.	G, 15th Iowa Inf.	116		1921 Jan 28	IA, 48th, 1922
Campbell, William	Pvt.	2nd Iowa Cav.	12		1919 Apr 18	IA, 46th, 1920
Campbell, William		F & I, 26th Mo.	110		1916 Dec 16	KS, 36th, 1917
Campbell, Wm.			113		1906	KS, 26th, 1907
Campbell, Wm.		D, 118th Ind. A, 142nd Ind.	9		1931 Jan 5	NE, 56th, 1932
Campbell, Wm. H.		B, 4th Iowa Inf.	29		1925 May 17	IA, 52nd, 1926
Campbell, Wm. J.		H, 13th Kans. Inf. (died of general breakdown)	275	67	1910 Mar 26	NE, 35th, 1911
Campbell, Zachariah		E, 25th Ill.	201		1921 Jul 20	KS, 41st, 1922
Campell, Luther D.		F, 28th Iowa Inf. (died of paralysis)	130	67	1910 Jul 10	NE, 37th, 1913
Campion, M.M.		B, 1st Iowa	3		1930 Jul 9	NE, 55th, 1931
Campton, A.		B, 1st Mich.	132		1888	KS, 8th, 1889
Campton, Thos.		G, 4th Penn. Cav. K, 134th Penn. Inf. (died of old age)	262	77	1901 Oct	NE, 26th, 1902
Camron, Peter		G, 102nd Ill. Inf. (died of fever)	3	73	1905 Jan	NE, 30th, 1906
Canada, W.A.		G, 28th Ill.	407		1915 Mar 5	KS, 35th, 1916
Canada, W.H.			7		1909 Jan 10	IA, 36th, 1910
Canaday, M.D.		H, 5th Kans. Cav.	203		1915 Oct 5	KS, 35th, 1916
Canan, John W.			45		1923 Mar 24	IA, 50th, 1924
Cane, E.T.	Pvt.	G, 46th Iowa Inf.	297		1925 Nov 19	IA, 52nd, 1926
Cane, John			107		1894	NE, 19th, 1895
Canedy, J.M.		C, 115th Ill.			1928 Mar 24	NE, 53rd, 1929
Canfer, D.		A, 34th Ind.	35	84	1923 Mar 4	NE, 48th, 1924
Canfield, Alvin	Pvt.	D, 7th Minn.	22		1926 Oct 2	IA, 53rd, 1927
Canfield, D.W.	Pvt.	C, 146th Ill. Inf.	271		1903 Dec 31	IA, 31st, 1905
Canfield, G.C.	Pvt.	K, 46th Ill. Inf.	222		1910	IA, 37th, 1911
Canfield, J.	Pvt.	B, 2nd Iowa Cav.	94		1913	IA, 40th, 1914
Canfield, J.		B, 2nd Iowa Cav.	94		1921 Aug 17	IA, 48th, 1922
Canfield, Jno. S.		G, 114th Ill. Inf. (died of heart failure)	110	59	1902 Jan	NE, 27th, 1903
Canfield, Leman		K, 1st N.J. Cav. (died of cancer)	62	74	1918 Jun 3	NE, 43rd, 1919
Canfield, R.A.		E, 12th Conn.	25		1930 Jul 8	KS, 50th, 1931
Canfield, Robert		D, 12th Ill. Cav.	46		1916 Jan 8	KS, 36th, 1917
Canfield, W.H.	Pvt.	A, 19th U.S. Inf.	156		1909 Oct 31	IA, 36th, 1910
Canine, C.	Pvt.	G, 33rd Iowa Inf.	12		1910 Jul 20	IA, 37th, 1911
Cann, R.F.		G, 72nd Ind.	25		1928 Feb 18	KS, 48th, 1929
Cannady, James H.		D, 14th Ill. Inf.	6		1930 Feb 4	KS, 51st, 1932
Cannell, John		I, 6th Wis.	318		1913 Sep	NE, 38th, 1914
Cannett, Wm.		16th Ind. Battery	435		1908 Feb 12	KS, 28th, 1909
Canning, Ed A.	Lieut.	E, 6th Iowa Inf.	337		1916 Apr 25	IA, 43rd, 1917
Cannon, J.W.		I, 3rd Mo.	300		1897 Feb	KS, 17th, 1898
Cannon, John H., see Canon, John H.						
Cannon, John H.		E, 16th Ill. (former member of department)			1932 Oct 25	NE, 57th, 1933
Cannon, L.B.	Pvt.	G, 22nd Iowa	1		1907 Feb 13	IA, 34th, 1908
Cannon, Lewis S.		K, 8th Ind. Inf. (died at Independence; buried at Mt. Hope Cemetery)	4		1894 Mar 23	KS, 14th, 1895
Cannon, R.			10		1927 Jan 1	KS, 47th, 1928
Canny, Thomas	Pvt.	H, 102nd Ill. Inf.	5		1915 Apr 29	IA, 42nd, 1916
Canon, John H.		D, 7th Ill. Cav. C, 138th Ill. Inf.	250		1925 Jan 21	KS, 45th, 1926
Canon, William H.		E, 4th Mo. State Militia Cav.	474		1914 Mar 9	KS, 34th, 1915
Canot, Henry		C, 26th Ill.	142		1889	KS, 9th, 1890
Canover, Samuel B.			206		1884	KS, 4th, 1885
Cansdel, A.		B, 3rd Kans.	153		1898 Nov 17	KS, 18th, 1899

*See Appendix A, B or C for roster of post names and locations.
†See Introduction for note regarding recording of death date.

Name	Rank	Company, Regiment or Ship	Post*	Age	Death Date†	Journal
Canteen, J.J.	Pvt. Capt.	K, 137th N.Y. D, 137th N.Y. (died of asthma)	104	42	1884 Mar 5	NE, 9th, 1885
Canter, Nathan	Pvt.	E, 6th Ind. Inf.	10		1899 Mar	IA, 26th, 1900
Canterbery, J.M.	Pvt.	I, 189th Ohio Inf.	19		1927 Apr 18	IA, 54th, 1928
Cantlin, J.R.		A, 104th Ill. Inf. (died of apoplexy)	52		1902 Oct	NE, 27th, 1903
Cantonwine, David	Pvt.	G, 5th Iowa Inf.	98		1917 Dec 8	IA, 44th, 1918
Cantrall, Jesse		114th Ill.	104		1910 Aug 15	KS, 30th, 1911
Cantz, Andrew	Pvt.	F, 3rd Iowa Cav.	19		1918 Apr 13	IA, 45th, 1919
Capin, Geo. W.	Pvt.	H, 2nd Iowa Inf.	108		1923 May 11	IA, 50th, 1924
Capley, Isaac	Lieut.	G, 89th Ill. Inf.	408		1905 Nov 23	IA, 32nd, 1906
Cappel, W.H.		95th Ill.	47		1910 Jun 6	KS, 30th, 1911
Capper, F.A.		U.S. Navy	19		1916	KS, 36th, 1917
Cappey, G.W.		E, U.S. Cav.	53		1913 Mar 17	KS, 32nd, 1913
Capps, Prior		B, 14th Kans. (died at Arcadia)	472		1895 Nov	KS, 15th, 1896
Capron, A.J.		I, 50th N.Y. Eng.	250		1920 Jun 23	KS, 40th, 1921
Capwell, John	Pvt.	D, 13th Wis. Inf.	22		1924 Feb 30	IA, 51st, 1925
Caraher, Mathew	Pvt.	T, 26th Iowa	92		1922 Mar 2	IA, 49th, 1923
Caraway, W.A.	Pvt.	6th Iowa Cav.	66		1915 Apr 26	IA, 42nd, 1916
Carbaugh, Geo.		K, 4th Penn. Inf.	394		1899 Feb 5	KS, 19th, 1900
Carberry, A.M.	Pvt.	B, 14th Iowa	142		1923 Feb 27	IA, 50th, 1924
Carberry, F.W.	Pvt.	I, 1st Iowa Inf.	75		1903 Nov 26	IA, 30th, 1904
Carbott, Bej.		H, 13th Kans.	113		1905 May 17	KS, 25th, 1906
Card, Frank	Pvt.	13th Iowa Inf.	94		1913	IA, 40th, 1914
Card, J.S.		I, 1st Ohio Lt. Art.	22		1888	KS, 8th, 1889
Card, J.S.		I, 1st Ohio Art.	22		1888 Jun 19	KS, 12th, 1893
Card, Job	Pvt.	B, 5th N.Y.	6		1901 Aug 15	IA, 28th, 1902
Card, William	Pvt.	I, 27th Ohio Inf.	209		1900-1901	IA, 27th, 1901
Card, Wm.	Pvt.	G, 18th Mich. Inf.	465		1911 Dec 30	IA, 38th, 1912
Cardell, H.H.	Lieut.	E, 4th Iowa Cav.	26	49	1890 Feb 9	IA, 16th, 1890
Carden, Robert	Pvt.	I, 42nd Wis. Inf.	66		1913 Sep 26	IA, 40th, 1914
Carder, Peter	Pvt.	I, 28th Iowa Inf.	292		1913 Oct 9	IA, 40th, 1914
Cardiff, John W.		B, 11th Ind. Inf. (died of age, etc.)	77	83	1916 Mar 31	NE, 41st, 1917
Care, H.C.	Pvt.	E, 148th Penn. Inf.	222		1917 Mar	IA, 44th, 1918
Carey, Anson		K, 6th Mich. Cav. (died of dyspepsia at Soldiers & Sailors Home, Grand Island; buried in Home Cemetery)	7	81	1905 Mar 10	NE, 30th, 1906
Carey, Archibald		A, 3rd Ky. Cav.	295		4th quarter 1884	IA, 11th, 1885
Carey, B.F.		B, 36th Ill. Inf. (died of La Grippe)	32	61	1891[1901?] Sep	NE, 26th, 1902
Carey, Daniel		F, 88th Ohio Inf. B, 60th Ohio Inf. (former member of department; location: Hebron)	17		1937 Dec 15	NE, 63rd, 1939
Carey, David		B, 153rd Ind.	251		1917 Mar 14	KS, 37th, 1918
Carey, Elial	Pvt.	K, 31st Iowa Inf.	30		1900 Dec 17	IA, 27th, 1901
Carey, Joel	Pvt.	C, 18th Conn. Inf.	57		1919 Sep 4	IA, 46th, 1920
Carey, L.D.		B, 58th Penn. Inf. (died of paralysis)	77	75	1921 Apr 1	NE, 46th, 1922
Carey, Patrick	Pvt.	H, 17th Ill. Inf.	186	49	1886 Feb 16	IA, 13th, 1887
Carey, Phillip	Pvt.	58th Ohio Inf.	108		1915 Aug 27	IA, 42nd, 1916
Cargill, Alex	Sergt.	B, 20th Iowa Inf.	235		1916 Jan 16	IA, 43rd, 1917
Cargill, R.		G, 48th Ill. Inf. (died of heart trouble)	289	67	1908 Apr 4	NE, 33rd, 1909
Carhart, John E.	Corp.	E, 6th Iowa Cav.	337		1929 Aug 7	IA, 56th, 1930
Carl, J.H.	Pvt.	C, 8th Iowa Inf.	231		1922 Nov 25	IA, 49th, 1923
Carl, James	Pvt.	H, 105th Penn. Inf.	231		1927 Oct 10	IA, 54th, 1928
Carle, John	Pvt.	K, 12th Ohio Inf.	161	49	1887 Mar 5	IA, 13th, 1887
Carle, Uriah		I, 120th N.Y.	1		1919 May 18	KS, 39th, 1920
Carley, Stephen	Pvt.	D, 29th Iowa Inf.	50		1893 Mar 6	IA, 20th, 1894
Carlile, Daniel		I, 40th Iowa Inf.	127		1929	KS, 49th, 1930
Carlile, Wm.		I, 40th Iowa	93		1892 Nov 15	KS, 12th, 1893
Carlin, Chester C.		B, 121st N.Y.	238		1923 Aug 5	KS, 43rd, 1924
Carlisle, David	Pvt.	B, 4th Mich. Inf.	26		1889 Dec 13	IA, 17th, 1891
Carll, Benj. P.		B, 7th Mo. Cav.	7		1927 Dec 30	NE, 52nd, 1928
Carlot, M.C.		3rd Iowa Cav.	497		1910 Nov 20	IA, 37th, 1911
Carlton, Abner G.		C, 116th Ohio	147		1885	KS, 5th, 1886
Carlton, C.		D, 6th N.Y.	51		1927	KS, 47th, 1928

*See Appendix A, B or C for roster of post names and locations.

†See Introduction for note regarding recording of death date.   86

Name	Rank	Company, Regiment or Ship	Post*	Age	Death Date†	Journal
Carlton, E.O.	Pvt.	C, 16th U.S. Inf.	152	53	1892 May 28	IA, 19th, 1893
Carlton, George W.	Pvt.	K, 5th Iowa Inf.	299	60	1897 Jun 9	IA, 24th, 1898
Carlton, H.H.			11		1913	IA, 40th, 1914
Carlton, James M.			54		1905 Mar 26	KS, 25th, 1906
Carlton, John			349		1912	IA, 39th, 1913
Carlton, L.L.		E, 36th Ohio Inf. (died at Manhattan)	271		1895 Sep	KS, 15th, 1896
Carlton, Perry E.		D, 104th N.Y.	11	84	1915 Jul 23	NE, 40th, 1916
Carlton, R.A.	Hosp. Stew.	B, 2nd Iowa Cav.	141		1908 Mar 13	IA, 35th, 1909
Carlton, Robert E.		B, 7th Ky.	65		1928 Aug 9	KS, 48th, 1929
Carlton, Samuel O.		H, 9th Iowa Inf.	173	95	1936 Dec 28	IA, 63rd, 1937
Carman, Henry C.		D, 5th Mo. Cav.	47		1938 Oct 28	NE, 63rd, 1939
Carman, J.B.	Pvt.	I, 7th Iowa Inf.	107		1930 Jun 30	IA, 57th, 1931
Carman, J.W.			158		1919 Feb 18	IA, 46th, 1920
Carman, Robert		D, 88th Penn.	432		1889	KS, 9th, 1890
Carmean, S.H.		D, 21st Kans. State Militia	12		1912 Jun 15	KS, 32nd, 1913
Carmer, L.L.		E, 8th Ill. (died at Gypsum)	465		1895 Apr	KS, 15th, 1896
Carmichael, A.W.		I, 2nd Iowa Cav. (died of pneumonia)	89		1923 Nov 27	NE, 48th, 1924
Carmichael, J.W.		C, 97th Ind. (died of apoplexy)	13	77	1921 Aug 27	NE, 46th, 1922
Carmichael, M.A.		7th Ind. Battery (see also Appendix D)	179		1902 Aug 27 or 28	KS, 22nd, 1903
Carmichael, S.E.	Pvt.	K, 34th Iowa Inf.	417	71	1898 Mar 11	IA, 24th, 1898
Carmichael, W.E.	Lieut.	H, 18th N.Y. Inf.	88		1897 Oct 6	IA, 24th, 1898
Carmichal, J.J.		H, 46th Ill. (died of cancer)	35	79	1922 Sep 25	NE, 47th, 1923
Carmine, James			85		1884	KS, 4th, 1885
Carmony, J.W.		D, 104th Ill. Inf.	77		1923 May 14	NE, 48th, 1924
Carnahan, A.S.			269		4th quarter 1885	IA, 12th, 1886
Carnahan, Andrew	Pvt.	E, 40th Iowa Inf.	16		1916 Jul 26	IA, 43rd, 1917
Carnahan, E.L., see Garnahan, E.L.						
Carnahan, J.G.		E, 9th Ill.	35	78	1915 Aug 8	NE, 40th, 1916
Carnahan, Martin E.		F, 106th Ill.	335		1911 Jul 27	KS, 31st, 1912
Carnahan, Pollard		K, 9th Ky.	100		1926 Apr 26	KS, 46th, 1927
Carnahan, S.P.		L, 1st Iowa Cav.	97		1922 Jun 25	KS, 42nd, 1923
Carnahan, W.A.		E, 38th Ohio	380		1920 Jul 14	KS, 40th, 1921
Carne, C.F.	Pvt.	F, 20th Iowa Inf.	150		1899	NE, 24th, 1900
Carner, L.		I, 8th Ill.	23		1904 Oct 2	KS, 24th, 1905
Carnes, Isiah B.	Sergt.	E, 40th Iowa Inf.	16		1913	IA, 40th, 1914
Carnes, Josephus V.		B, 29th Iowa	25		1934 Dec 20	NE, 59th, 1935
Carnes, Leonard		C, 97th Ohio Vol. Inf.	32		1915 Jun 7	KS, 35th, 1916
Carney, Ab. T.	Pvt.	11th Ohio Battery	327		1904 Mar 3	IA, 31st, 1905
Carney, Denton	Corp.	K, 47th Iowa Inf.	343		1911 Dec 11	IA, 38th, 1912
Carney, Henry		E, 167th Ohio	47		1913 Aug 18	KS, 33rd, 1914
Carney, J.H.		B, 108th N.Y.	74		1913 Oct 14	KS, 33rd, 1914
Carney, John W.	Pvt.	E, 4th Iowa Cav.	95		1913 Apr 30	IA, 40th, 1914
Carnfield, R.B.		1st Ark. (killed by accident)	187		1889	KS, 9th, 1890
Carnine, John C.		K, 11th Kans. Cav.	35		1919 Dec 2	KS, 39th, 1920
Carnine, Peter M.		H, 9th Kans. Cav.	55		1918 Nov 5	KS, 38th, 1919
Carns, John B.		C, 119th Ill. Inf.	90		1929 Jan 16	KS, 49th, 1930
Carny, A.M.		C, 75th Ill.	424		1924 Dec 2	KS, 44th, 1925
Carpenter, A.B.	Pvt.	D, 19th U.S. Inf.	231	49	1891 Apr 11	IA, 18th, 1892
Carpenter, A.B.	Pvt.	D, 19th U.S. Inf.	231	49	1891 Apr 11	IA, 17th, 1891
Carpenter, Abraham		E, 138th Penn.	25		1933 Aug	KS, 53rd, 1934
Carpenter, Alden	Pvt.	I, 49th Mass. Inf.	118		1910 Dec 2	IA, 37th, 1911
Carpenter, C.		K, 108th Kans.	236		1893 Nov 8	KS, 13th, 1894
Carpenter, Chapin H.		F, 8th Kans. Inf.	28		1914 Feb 7	KS, 34th, 1915
Carpenter, Chas. L.	Pvt.	I, 17th Iowa Inf.	2		1912 Aug 28	IA, 39th, 1913
Carpenter, D.D.		A, 33rd Ill. Inf.	87		1914 Dec 17	KS, 34th, 1915
Carpenter, E.J.	Pvt.	F, 36th Ohio Inf.	231		1914 Feb 10	IA, 41st, 1915
Carpenter, Edwin H.	Pvt.	H, 106th N.Y. Inf.	7	53	1895 Apr 26	IA, 22nd, 1896
Carpenter, Fred. D.		D, 102nd Penn. Vol. Inf. (died of old age)	77	72	1908 Apr	NE, 33rd, 1909
Carpenter, Geo. D.		C, 60th Ill. U.S. Colored	185		1885	KS, 5th, 1886
Carpenter, Geo. W.	Pvt.	D, 46th Ill. Inf.	12		1915 Nov 24	IA, 42nd, 1916
Carpenter, George		F, 56th Iowa	57		1919 Apr 9	KS, 39th, 1920

Name	Rank	Company, Regiment or Ship	Post*	Age	Death Date†	Journal
Carpenter, George		B, 1st Md. Cav.	92		1923 Jun 12	KS, 43rd, 1924
Carpenter, George D.		D, 72nd Ill. Inf.	185		1886	KS, 6th, 1887
Carpenter, H.		E, 2nd Wis.	77	92	1934 Jul	IA, 61st, 1935
Carpenter, H.B.	Pvt.	B, 2nd Wis. Cav.	104		1911	IA, 38th, 1912
Carpenter, H.M.		B, 15th Mass.	13		1933 Oct 7	NE, 58th, 1934
Carpenter, Henry		F, 2nd Wis.	100		1913 Oct 24	KS, 33rd, 1914
Carpenter, Hezekiah P.				94	1937 Aug 21	IA, 64th, 1938
Carpenter, Hiram S.	Pvt.	I, 147th Ill. Inf. (at large)		89	1936 Mar 10	IA, 65th, 1939
Carpenter, James C.		C, 39th Iowa Inf.	7		1912 Oct 15	KS, 32nd, 1913
Carpenter, Jas. T.	Pvt.	D, 7th Vt. Inf.	30		1919 Dec 4	IA, 46th, 1920
Carpenter, Jesse		K, 118th Ind.	49		1914 Jan 14	KS, 34th, 1915
Carpenter, John		C, 42nd Ind.	46		1921 Jul 31	KS, 41st, 1922
Carpenter, John		Neb.	118	64	1908	NE, 33rd, 1909
Carpenter, John C.	Col.	67th Penn.	129		1921 May 21	KS, 41st, 1922
Carpenter, John H.	Pvt.	F, 40th Iowa Inf.	49		1914 Oct 6	IA, 41st, 1915
Carpenter, John J.	Pvt.	B, 21st Iowa Vol. Inf.	259		1903 Nov 9	IA, 30th, 1904
Carpenter, Joseph		I, 33rd Wis.	138		1897 Oct	KS, 17th, 1898
Carpenter, Jud		D, 188th N.Y. (died of heart trouble)	83	77	1922 Dec 12	NE, 47th, 1923
Carpenter, Judson		D, 188th Inf.	10	77	1922 Dec 12	NE, 47th, 1923
Carpenter, Luther R.		I, 90th Ohio	40		1910 Jun 16	KS, 30th, 1911
Carpenter, Lyman S.	Pvt.	H, 13th U.S. Inf.	181		1915 Oct 28	IA, 42nd, 1916
Carpenter, M.V.	Pvt.	G, 48th Ind. Inf.	12		1919 Dec 27	IA, 46th, 1920
Carpenter, Nelson		B, 135th Ill.	25	80	1915 Feb 16	NE, 40th, 1916
Carpenter, O.S.	Major	142nd N.Y. Inf.	17		1911 Jan 13	KS, 31st, 1912
Carpenter, P.V.	Pvt.	K, 10th Iowa Inf.	158		1905 Oct 2	IA, 32nd, 1906
Carpenter, Q.A.	Pvt.	E, 1st Wis. Inf.	125		1912 Feb 25	IA, 39th, 1913
Carpenter, Robert	Capt.	A, 10th —	12		1919 Nov 3	KS, 39th, 1920
Carpenter, T.A.	Pvt.	A, 12th Ill. Cav.	236	98	1931 Apr 20	IA, 58th, 1932
Carpenter, T.J.	Pvt.	C, 7th Ill. Inf.	91		1928 Oct 12	IA, 55th, 1929
Carpenter, W.L.	Pvt.	G, 32nd Iowa Inf.	12		1916[1915?] Aug 26	IA, 42nd, 1916
Carpenter, Walter	Sergt.	L, 1st Wis. Cav.	141		1922 Dec 3	IA, 49th, 1923
Carpenter, Willet		1st Iowa Cav.	116		1916	IA, 43rd, 1917
Carper, A.S.	Musician	I, 16th Ill. Inf.	7		1910 May 11	IA, 37th, 1911
Carr, A.M.		E, 117th Ill.	142		1913 Mar 3	KS, 33rd, 1914
Carr, Andrew		E, 117th Ill.	142		1913 Mar 2	KS, 32nd, 1913
Carr, Benjamin F.	Pvt.	M, 11th Mo. Cav.	40		1916 Jan 29	IA, 43rd, 1917
Carr, C.C.C.		F, 1st U.S. Cav.	6		1914 Jul 24	KS, 34th, 1915
Carr, C.M.	Pvt.	L, 8th Ill. Cav.	68		1926 Oct 23	IA, 53rd, 1927
Carr, G.L.		F, 30th Wis.	68		1929 Dec 4	KS, 49th, 1930
Carr, Garrin H.	Pvt.	C, 37th Iowa Inf.	170	67	1894	IA, 20th, 1894
Carr, Geo. T.B.		22nd Ind. Inf.	354	68	1906 Aug 18	NE, 31st, 1907
Carr, Geo. W.		D, 7th Ind. Cav.	11		1929 Jul	NE, 54th, 1930
Carr, George T.B.		22nd Ind. Inf. (born in Kentucky; died of dropsy at Soldiers & Sailors Home Hospital, Burkett; buried at Kearney, Neb.)		68	1906 Aug 18	NE, 31st, 1907
Carr, H.H.		B, 15th N.Y. Inf.	25		1934 Jul	KS, 54th, 1935
Carr, Horace M.	Chaplain	3rd Ill. Cav.	64		1922 Nov 7	KS, 42nd, 1923
Carr, Hugh	Pvt.	C, 13th Ill. Inf.	133		1913 Nov 22	IA, 40th, 1914
Carr, I.N.			112		1923	IA, 50th, 1924
Carr, J.A.			285		1924 May	IA, 51st, 1925
Carr, James	Sergt.	F, 2nd Iowa Inf.	254		1905 Mar 6	IA, 32nd, 1906
Carr, Jno. W.	Pvt.	I, 48th Ind.	40		1923 Jun 2	IA, 50th, 1924
Carr, John W.	Capt.	C, 28th Iowa Inf.	127		1929 Mar 13	IA, 56th, 1930
Carr, Thomas	Pvt.	I, 22nd Iowa Inf.	40		1909 Apr 4	IA, 36th, 1910
Carr, William H.		A, 34th Iowa Inf. (died of heart failure)	55	73	1912 Jun 23	NE, 37th, 1913
Carrico, Andrew		A, 9th Ky. Cav.	93		1915 Dec 13	KS, 35th, 1916
Carrier, A.S.	Pvt.	D, 8th Mich. Cav.	86		1923 Jun 20	IA, 50th, 1924
Carrier, Frank		K, 31st Ill. (died of paralysis)	13	81	1921 Jan 16	NE, 46th, 1922
Carrier, Octave		E, 1st Mo. Art.	6		1914 Nov 9	KS, 34th, 1915
Carries, Joe		A, 79th Ky. Inf. (died at Leavenworth; buried at Mt. Muncie Cemetery)	208		1894 Jul 13	KS, 14th, 1895
Carrigan, J.R.		F, 205th Penn. Inf. (killed by cars)	289	60	1905 May 13	NE, 30th, 1906

Name	Rank	Company, Regiment or Ship	Post*	Age	Death Date†	Journal
Carrigg, Thomas C.		G, 7th Kans. Cav.	293		1920 Jun 2	KS, 40th, 1921
Carringer, William H.		F, 25th Iowa	57		1924 May 11	KS, 44th, 1925
Carrington, Charles	Pvt.	C, 74th Ill.	332		1901 Jun 22	IA, 28th, 1902
Carris, L.		N.Y. Art.	83		1916 Mar 1	KS, 36th, 1917
Carris, S.D.	Corp.	C, 8th Iowa Inf.	333		1927 Feb 7	IA, 54th, 1928
Carris, William	Sergt.	C, 8th Iowa Inf.	333		1918 Feb 2	IA, 45th, 1919
Carrol, W.M.	Pvt.	H, 17th Kans. Cav.	147		1921 Sep 5	IA, 48th, 1922
Carrol, Wesley			186		1899 Apr 12	KS, 19th, 1900
Carroll, Dennis		G, 2nd Penn.	380		1905 Dec 23	KS, 25th, 1906
Carroll, G.W.		A, 1st Ohio Inf.	66		1918 Oct 17	KS, 38th, 1919
Carroll, G.W.		A, 1st Ohio	142		1918 Oct 17	KS, 38th, 1919
Carroll, Geo. R.	Chaplain	24th Iowa Inf.	130	64	1895 Dec 11	IA, 22nd, 1896
Carroll, H.E.	Pvt.	K, 15th N.Y.	339		1904 Apr 11	IA, 31st, 1905
Carroll, Matthey			64		1903-1904	IA, 30th, 1904
Carroll, Patrick	Corp.	E, 35th Iowa Inf.	88		1915 Dec 2	IA, 42nd, 1916
Carroll, S.S.	Pvt.	D, Monongahela Guards	40	54	1890 Mar	IA, 18th, 1892
Carroll, Thos.			13	70	1913 Aug 13	NE, 38th, 1914
Carroll, W.J.	Pvt.	K, 2nd Iowa	57		1905 Aug	IA, 32nd, 1906
Carron, A.W.			69		1883	KS, 3rd, 1884
Carrothers, Z.			265		1923	KS, 43rd, 1924
Carruthers, L.	Capt.	I, 33rd Iowa Inf.	49	61	1895 Apr 17	IA, 22nd, 1896
Carsner, David	Pvt.	149th Penn. Inf.	53		1909 Jun 3	IA, 36th, 1910
Carsob, John		M, 4th Iowa Cav.	440		1915 Mar 13	IA, 42nd, 1916
Carson, A.C.		I, 13th Kans.	79		1925 Jul	KS, 45th, 1926
Carson, Abel	Corp.	K, 170th Ohio Inf.	17		1916 Sep 10	IA, 43rd, 1917
Carson, Allen C.		K, 9th Ill. Inf.	127		1918 Dec 2	KS, 38th, 1919
Carson, Geo.	Capt.	K, 12th Ind. Inf.	29		1920 Feb 18	IA, 46th, 1920
Carson, H.P.	Pvt.	H, — U.S. Colored Inf.	153	58	1895 Jun 11	IA, 22nd, 1896
Carson, J.A.	Lieut.	I, 97th Ohio Inf.	74		1918 Dec 2	IA, 45th, 1919
Carson, J.R.		E, 32nd Ohio	158		1934 Dec 2	KS, 55th, 1936
Carson, J.W.	Pvt.	D, 139th Ill. Inf.	5	89	1933 Dec 16	IA, 60th, 1934
Carson, J.W.	Pvt.	F, 11th Ind. Inf.	5		1929 Jan 20	IA, 57th, 1931
Carson, James			264		1913	IA, 40th, 1914
Carson, John		A, 10th Ind.	19		1913 Aug 16	KS, 33rd, 1914
Carson, John		C, 61st Ill. Inf.	11	76	1907 Dec 29	NE, 33rd, 1909
Carson, John M.		A, 101st Ind.	19		1914 Aug 16	KS, 34th, 1915
Carson, Joseph		B, 2nd Iowa	1		1917 Feb 9	KS, 37th, 1918
Carson, R.B.	Corp.	G, 2nd Iowa Inf.	434		1929 Sep 15	IA, 56th, 1930
Carson, R. Beecher	Pvt.	G, 2nd Iowa Inf. (at large)	434	93	1935 Sep 11	IA, 65th, 1939
Carson, Robert M.		C, 128th Ohio	22		1933 Nov 10	NE, 58th, 1934
Carson, S.F.		C, 10th Kans. Inf.	111		1935 Jul 5	KS, 55th, 1936
Carson, Samuel S.		H, 5th Iowa	35		1918 Oct 28	KS, 38th, 1919
Carson, T.D.	Pvt.	F, 124th Ill. Inf.	230	56	1892 Oct	IA, 19th, 1893
Carson, W.I.		I, 42nd Ill. (died of paralysis)	22	85	1925 Feb 14	NE, 50th, 1926
Carson, W.L.	Pvt.	K, 13th Iowa Inf.	79		1902 Oct 10	IA, 29th, 1903
Carson, William F.		C, 77th Ill.	17		1924 Aug 13	KS, 44th, 1925
Carson, Wm. G.	Pvt.	H, 135th Ohio Inf.	22		1925 Feb 19	IA, 52nd, 1926
Carter, A.	Pvt.	D, 100th Ill.	12		1921 Apr 3	IA, 48th, 1922
Carter, A.H.		K, 40th Wis.	5		1927 Dec 8	NE, 52nd, 1928
Carter, Alfred	Pvt.	G, 9th Iowa Cav.	231		1923 Feb 17	IA, 50th, 1924
Carter, Amos C.	Pvt.	E, 146th Ill. Inf.	190		1917 Feb 27	IA, 44th, 1918
Carter, Anderson S.		I, 13th Ind.	32		1920 Feb 11	KS, 40th, 1921
Carter, Aris B.		K, 3rd Iowa Cav.	293		1922 Nov 16	KS, 42nd, 1923
Carter, B.P.	Pvt.	A, 39th Iowa Inf.	158		1916 Dec 17	IA, 43rd, 1917
Carter, Chalen		D, 8th Kans.	256		1917 Feb 2	KS, 37th, 1918
Carter, Chas. J.	Pvt.	C, 2nd Iowa Inf.	440		1925 Jul 21	IA, 52nd, 1926
Carter, Darius					1937 Jan 12	IA, 64th, 1938
Carter, David J.	Pvt.	H, 19th Iowa Inf.	301		1900 Oct 12	IA, 27th, 1901
Carter, E.M.			168		1909 Oct 30	IA, 36th, 1910
Carter, Ed S.	Pvt.	C, 45th Iowa Inf.	2		1912 Jun 7	IA, 39th, 1913
Carter, Francis		D, 3rd Wis.	374		1893 Dec 3	KS, 13th, 1894
Carter, G.A.		G, 34th Ill.	65		1910 Jul 14	KS, 30th, 1911

*See Appendix A, B or C for roster of post names and locations.

†See Introduction for note regarding recording of death date.

89

Name	Rank	Company, Regiment or Ship	Post*	Age	Death Date†	Journal
Carter, G.W.	Pvt.	18th Penn. Cav.	29		1924 Sep 24	IA, 51st, 1925
Carter, Geo.	Pvt.	D, 75th Ohio Inf.	15		1906 Apr 4	IA, 33rd, 1907
Carter, Geo. H.			173		1914	IA, 41st, 1915
Carter, Geo. W.	Pvt.	F, 30th Iowa Inf.	434		1913 Sep	IA, 40th, 1914
Carter, George W.		A, 21st Mich.	207		1931 Oct 11	NE, 56th, 1932
Carter, Harrison	Pvt.	G, 23rd Iowa Inf.	84		1910 Apr 28	IA, 37th, 1911
Carter, J.B.		C, 86th Ohio	59		1931 Feb 8	KS, 51st, 1932
Carter, J.B.		C, 86th Ohio	59		1931 Feb 8	KS, 52nd, 1933
Carter, J.M.	Pvt.	F, 14th Iowa Inf.	284		1911 Jul 21	IA, 38th, 1912
Carter, J.N.		E, 1st Ind. Hvy. Art.	129		1916 Sep 2	KS, 36th, 1917
Carter, J.R.		K, 96th Ohio Inf.	59		1930 Dec	KS, 50th, 1931
Carter, J.W.			173		1913	IA, 40th, 1914
Carter, J.W.		D, 18th Maine	51		1921 Jan 29	KS, 41st, 1922
Carter, James	Musician	I, 22nd Ohio Inf.	74		1918 Oct 12	IA, 45th, 1919
Carter, James		B, 36th Wis. Inf.	113		1934 Jan 27	KS, 54th, 1935
Carter, Jas. H.	Corp.	F, 93rd Ohio	2		1910 Jul 10	IA, 37th, 1911
Carter, Jas. P.		G, 11th Ill. Cav.	9		1911 Jun 17	NE, 36th, 1912
Carter, Jasper		K, 1st Ind. Hvy. Art.	66		1916 Aug	KS, 36th, 1917
Carter, John	Pvt.	A, 29th U.S.C. Inf.	1		1915 May 28	IA, 42nd, 1916
Carter, John		F, 79th Kans. Inf.	321		1902 Jan 29	KS, 22nd, 1903
Carter, John F.		I, 11th Kans. Cav.	1		1914 Mar 31	KS, 34th, 1915
Carter, Joseph		K, 23rd Mo. Inf.	93		1912 Mar 26	KS, 32nd, 1913
Carter, O.N.		C, 13th Ohio	497		1911 Sep 23	KS, 31st, 1912
Carter, Orrin B.		C, 4th Iowa Cav.	52		1923 Nov 26	KS, 43rd, 1924
Carter, Peter	Pvt.	I, 21st Iowa	22		1924 Jun 26	IA, 51st, 1925
Carter, R.		A, 5th Tenn.	32		1896 Oct 10	KS, 16th, 1897
Carter, Richard	Pvt.		512		1920 Mar 31	IA, 47th, 1921
Carter, S.N.		D, 29th Iowa	76		1933	KS, 53rd, 1934
Carter, T.M.		I, 37th Ill.	23		1931 May 26	KS, 52nd, 1933
Carter, T.M.		I, 37th Ill.	23		1931 May 26	KS, 51st, 1932
Carter, T.W.			24		1908 Feb 19	IA, 35th, 1909
Carter, Thomas M.		B, 2nd Neb. Cav.	52	86	1922 Mar 16	NE, 47th, 1923
Carter, W.H.	Pvt.	B, 93rd Ill. Inf.	7		1910 Jul 21	IA, 37th, 1911
Carter, W.L.		E, 13th Ky.	337		1926 Nov 26	KS, 46th, 1927
Carter, William		A, 2nd Iowa Cav.	85		1923 Nov 2	KS, 43rd, 1924
Carter, William A.	Corp.	D, 20th Iowa Inf.	123	65	1900 Feb 28	IA, 26th, 1900
Carter, William J.		M, 4th Iowa Cav.	1		1899 Jan 29	KS, 19th, 1900
Carter, Wm. F.		29th Ind. Inf.	15		1908	NE, 33rd, 1909
Cartiff, W.H.		E, 17th Kans.	493		1926 Apr 29	KS, 46th, 1927
Cartlidge, Edward J.		B, 1st Mo. Inf.	1		1899 Mar 29	KS, 19th, 1900
Carton, L.H.		I, 116th Ohio	129		1904 Jun 26	KS, 24th, 1905
Cartright, Orville		J, 61st U.S.C.	180		1908	KS, 28th, 1909
Caruthers, Jas.	Pvt.		186		1925 Jun 18	IA, 52nd, 1926
Carver, G.R.		I, 22nd Kans.	53		1925 Sep 18	KS, 45th, 1926
Carver, J.		C, 7th Iowa	40	87	1934 Sep 9	IA, 61st, 1935
Carver, Jas. M.		M, 9th Kans. Vol. Cav.	3		1917 Nov 19	KS, 37th, 1918
Carver, K.K.	Pvt.	G, 76th Ind. Inf.	78	46	1887 Nov 13	IA, 14th, 1888
Carver, Michael		B, 124th Ind.	243		1916 Oct 8	KS, 36th, 1917
Carver, T.C.	Pvt.	B, 28th Wis. Inf.	236		1910 Aug 30	IA, 37th, 1911
Cary, Alfred		K, 11th Kans.	39		1913 Jul 20	KS, 33rd, 1914
Cary, Carr		G, 13th Ind.	136		1898 Apr 27	KS, 18th, 1899
Cary, George W.		K, 16th Kans.	18		1911 Jun 21	KS, 31st, 1912
Cary, Reuben		F, 1st Kans. Inf.	486		1899 Sep 11	KS, 19th, 1900
Cary, T.C.		I, 15th Ohio (died from wounds)	350		1888	KS, 8th, 1889
Casad, A.S.		C, 147th Ind.	76		1919 Nov 26	KS, 39th, 1920
Casad, Don S.	Pvt.	A, 149th Ohio Inf.	110		1928 Oct 22	IA, 55th, 1929
Casad, O.S.		B, 62nd Ill.	65		1928 May 25	KS, 48th, 1929
Case, A.E.		K, 187th Penn.	42		1929 Jan 4	KS, 49th, 1930
Case, Allen		B, 115th N.Y.	25		1919 Jan 8	KS, 39th, 1920
Case, Benson	Pvt.	D, Ill.	243		1923	IA, 50th, 1924

Name	Rank	Company, Regiment or Ship	Post*	Age	Death Date†	Journal
Case, C.M.		Vt., U.S. Ship *Anacosta* (died at Enterprise, Kans.; buried at Enterprise Cemetery)	396		1894 Jun 29	KS, 14th, 1895
Case, Chas.		H, 125th Ill. Inf.	66		1899 May 27	KS, 19th, 1900
Case, Emery	Pvt.	E, 177th Ohio Inf.	64		1919 Sep 28	IA, 46th, 1920
Case, H.L.	Pvt.	G, 5th N.Y. Cav.	12		1929 Nov 23	IA, 56th, 1930
Case, I.W.	Pvt.	F, 147th Penn. Inf.	329	53	1895 Feb 10	IA, 21st, 1895
Case, J.E.		B, 75th Ill. Inf. (died of bronchitis)	21	68	1905 Sep 12	NE, 30th, 1906
Case, S.G.		C, 27th N.Y. Inf.	7		1928 Aug 3	NE, 53rd, 1929
Case, S.P.	Pvt.	C, 46th Ind. Inf.	55		1921 Sep 6	IA, 48th, 1922
Case, Scott	Pvt.	C, 11th Wis. Inf.	124		1926 Jun 27	IA, 53rd, 1927
Case, T.D.		D, 112th Ill. (died of apoplexy)	44	79	1924 Oct 18	NE, 49th, 1925
Case, W.W.	Pvt.	B, 16th Iowa Inf.	34		1929 Oct 5	IA, 56th, 1930
Case, William	Pvt.	B, 1st Bat. 13th U.S. Reg.	104	95	1935 May 22	IA, 65th, 1939
Casebeer, George		D, 47th Iowa Inf.	252		1912 Apr 4	KS, 32nd, 1913
Casebeer, Jacob B.	Capt.	D, 24th Iowa Inf.	235	55	1889 Dec 18	IA, 16th, 1890
Cased, John W.	Lieut.	A, 5th Iowa Inf.	110		1907 Jul 27	IA, 34th, 1908
Casey, Comrade			265		1913 Nov 22	KS, 33rd, 1914
Casey, D.B.	Pvt.	G, 3rd Ill. Cav.	300		1921 Jul 23	IA, 48th, 1922
Casey, David	Pvt.	I, 63rd Ohio	156		1922 Jan 19	IA, 49th, 1923
Casey, H.	Pvt.	G, 31st Ohio	86		1905 Oct 10	IA, 32nd, 1906
Casey, Henry		I, 15th Ill.	147		1917 Jun 9	KS, 37th, 1918
Casey, Israel		not a member of post named, but buried by said post	266		1897	KS, 17th, 1898
Casey, James S., see Cacy, James S.						
Casey, John		A, 8th Mo. Cav.	18		1937 Dec 16	KS, 56th, 1937
Casey, M.	Pvt.	K, 1st Iowa Cav.	49		1908 Mar 28	IA, 35th, 1909
Casey, Thos.		B, 18th U.S. Inf.	380		1898 Jun 8	KS, 18th, 1899
Casford, Henry T.		H, 151st Ill. Inf. (died of heart trouble)	47	63	1906 Apr 6	NE, 31st, 1907
Cash, H.R.		L, 1st Ohio Art.	463		1929 Feb 6	KS, 49th, 1930
Caskey, Hugh		F, 70th N.Y. Inf.	250		1914 Jul 13	KS, 34th, 1915
Caskey, Jas. O.		9th Kans.	87		1900 Jan 23	KS, 20th, 1901
Caskey, John		F, 126th Ohio	28		1924 Sep 20	KS, 44th, 1925
Caslin, John M.		D & H, 1st & 16th Ill., & Penn. Cav.	14		1912 Nov 13	KS, 32nd, 1913
Casman, Israel		K, 33rd Ill. (died of paralysis)	47	75	1919 Jan 3	NE, 44th, 1920
Cason, Thomas J.		H, 118th Ill.	58		1916 Apr 17	KS, 36th, 1917
Caspen, Frank		K, 8th Iowa Cav. (at large)			1932 Feb 28	IA, 59th, 1933
Cass, Henry	Pvt.	F, 16th Wis. Inf.	88		1919 Nov 27	IA, 46th, 1920
Cass, J.M.	Pvt.	H, 4th Wis. Inf.	68		1922 Jul 12	IA, 49th, 1923
Cass, Lewis	Pvt.	A, 52nd Wis. Inf.	220	48	1889 Dec 5	IA, 16th, 1890
Cassaday, Louis		C, 26th Ohio Vol. Inf.	28		1915 Dec 20	KS, 35th, 1916
Cassatt, Samuel		H, 87th Penn.	63		1918 Feb 6	KS, 38th, 1919
Cassel, A.B.	Pvt.	C, 8th Iowa Cav.	485	76	1895 Apr 20	IA, 21st, 1895
Cassel, Thos. K.	Pvt.	G, 13th Iowa Inf.	296		2nd quarter 1885	IA, 12th, 1886
Cassell, John N.		G, 20th Ohio Inf. (died of paralysis & general debility)	44	79	1914 Oct 21	NE, 39th, 1915
Cassell, Wm. H.	Pvt.	77th Ill. Inf.	23		1918 Jun 11	IA, 45th, 1919
Casselman, Ezra		5th Iowa Cav.	24		1920	NE, 45th, 1921
Cassen, Jas. M.		F, 88th Ill.	18		1930 Jan 25	KS, 50th, 1931
Cassett, D.C.	Corp.	K, 184th Penn.	324		1921 Jul 7	IA, 48th, 1922
Cassidy, R.T.		B, 163rd West Va. M.	17		1915 Jan 11	KS, 35th, 1916
Cassidy, T.B.	Pvt.	K, 4th Iowa Inf.	34	61	1890 Oct 10	IA, 17th, 1891
Cast, James W.	Pvt.	H, 48th Ohio Inf.	20		1912 Dec 26	IA, 39th, 1913
Casteel, Ely		A, 87th Ill.	125		1910 Jun	KS, 30th, 1911
Casteel, J.A.		E, 25th Iowa Inf. (died of cancer of stomach)	352	65	1908 May 4	NE, 33rd, 1909
Casterline, T.C.		G, 1st N.J.	253		1910	KS, 30th, 1911
Casterline, Wm.			113		1883	KS, 3rd, 1884
Castle, D.R.			457		1913	IA, 40th, 1914
Castle, David		I, 6th Vt.	147		1917 Nov 3	KS, 37th, 1918
Castle, E.S.		B, 5th Mo. Cav.	292		1898 Mar 9	KS, 18th, 1899
Castle, Geo. H.	Pvt.	A, 59th Ill. Inf.	56		1927 Jul 6	IA, 54th, 1928

Name	Rank	Company, Regiment or Ship	Post*	Age	Death Date†	Journal
Castle, Henry A.		A, 164th N.Y.	339		1920 Dec 21	KS, 40th, 1921
Castle, L.G.			3		1910	NE, 35th, 1911
Castle, Samuel		G, 128th Ind.	25		1932 Dec 14	NE, 57th, 1933
Castle, T.O.		I, 128th Ohio Inf.	66		1902 Apr	KS, 22nd, 1903
Castor, Robert		F, 69th Ind. Inf.	25		1917 Jan 1	KS, 37th, 1918
Caswell, Charles	Pvt.	F, 12th N.Y. Cav.	132		1925 May 8	IA, 52nd, 1926
Caswell, David J.		G, 27th Iowa (died of cancer of stomach)	274	76	1907 Oct 12	NE, 32nd, 1908
Caswell, E.A.		61st Penn.	77		1927	KS, 47th, 1928
Caswell, George H.		H, 59th Ind.	147		1933 Apr 11	NE, 58th, 1934
Caswell, O.	Lieut.	D, 5th Iowa Inf.	94		1906	IA, 33rd, 1907
Caswell, Russell W.		A, 84th Ill. Inf.	25		1917 Jul 15	KS, 37th, 1918
Caswell, Wm.		I, 3rd N.Y.	25		1922 Dec 17	KS, 42nd, 1923
Cates, Cornelius	Pvt.	E, 10th Iowa Inf.	34		1924 Oct 15	IA, 51st, 1925
Cates, V.	Corp.	C, 9th Iowa Inf.	54		1907 Jun 15	IA, 34th, 1908
Cating, C.M.	Pvt.		16		1912 Nov 27	IA, 39th, 1913
Cation, William			72		1911 Nov 23	KS, 31st, 1912
Catlett, W.O.	Pvt.	C, 94th Ill. Inf.	12	57	1886 Sep 27	IA, 13th, 1887
Catlin, J.E., see Cattlin, J.E.						
Catois, C.	Pvt.	B, 1st Mo. Eng.	187	67	1889 Feb 24	IA, 17th, 1891
Catois, Clement	Pvt.	B, 1st Mo. Eng.	187	67	1889 Feb 24	IA, 16th, 1890
Caton, Daniel		H, 45th Mo. Inf.	293		1929	KS, 49th, 1930
Caton, John		F, 38th Ill. Inf.	89		1908 Jun 14	KS, 28th, 1909
Caton, John			380		1924 Nov 2	KS, 44th, 1925
Catron, A.S.		D, 2nd Iowa	25		1926 Dec 12	KS, 46th, 1927
Catt, John		D, 63rd Ind.	32		1898 Jun 11	KS, 18th, 1899
Catt, Thos. H.		F, 10th Ind. Cav.	[25?]		1923	NE, 48th, 1924
Cattlin, J.E.	1st Lieut.	I, 45th Penn. Inf.	98		1905 Dec 3	IA, 32nd, 1906
Catton, John W.			90		1911 1st term	IA, 38th, 1912
Caufield, D.F.		L, Mich. Cav. (died of paralysis)	20	85	1907 Aug 22	NE, 32nd, 1908
Cauger, James A.		14th Ind. Batt.	25		1933 Aug 20	NE, 58th, 1934
Caughell, Jacob	Sergt.	D, 35th Ohio Inf.	57		1914 Oct 2	IA, 41st, 1915
Caughey, William		I, 30th Wis.	25		1914 Mar 21	KS, 34th, 1915
Caughron, Samuel		G, 27th Ind.	51		1923 Feb 7	KS, 43rd, 1924
Caught, David		G, 17th Ky.	119[129?]		1906 Jan 5	KS, 26th, 1907
Caul, Henry	Pvt.	D, 52nd Ill. Inf.	12		1926 Mar 29	IA, 53rd, 1927
Causey, Enoch		F, 38th Ind.	3		1898 Apr 16	KS, 18th, 1899
Cavalier, L.	Pvt.	K, 92nd Ill. Inf.	327		1913 Jun 12	IA, 40th, 1914
Cavana, Lewis			18		1911 2nd term	IA, 38th, 1912
Cavaness, A.A.B.		1st Kans. Battery	40		1916 Apr 18	KS, 36th, 1917
Cave, Albert	Pvt.	H, 39th Iowa Inf.	43		1909 Sep	IA, 36th, 1910
Cave, D.H.		A, 32nd Ill. (killed by accident)	129		1889	KS, 9th, 1890
Cave, Dennis W.		145th Ill.	[25?]		1923	NE, 48th, 1924
Cave, George	Pvt.	K, 4th Wis. Cav.	25		1924 Aug	IA, 51st, 1925
Cave, J.J.		D, 153rd Ill.	352		1932 Sep 28	NE, 57th, 1933
Cave, P.H.	Pvt.	G, 9th Iowa Inf.	68		1923 Mar 18	IA, 50th, 1924
Cave, W.R.	Pvt.	G, 32nd Iowa	220		1905 Jul 2	IA, 32nd, 1906
Cave, William A.	Q.M.S.	C, 116th Ind. Inf.	12		1928 Sep 13	IA, 55th, 1929
Cavender, A.L.		I, 140th Ohio	36		1906 Jul	KS, 26th, 1907
Cavender, Green		E, 3rd Iowa Cav.	250		1912 Dec 31	KS, 32nd, 1913
Cavender, John		G, 8th Iowa Inf.	238		1899 Jul 3	KS, 19th, 1900
Cavenis, M.V.			40		1899 Jan 11	KS, 19th, 1900
Caveny, John L.		I, 126th Penn.	36		1920 Oct 4	KS, 40th, 1921
Caver, John C.	Pvt.	I, 6th Penn. Cav.	5	64	1895 May 28	IA, 22nd, 1896
Caves, R.T.		G, 74th Ohio (not a member of Farragut Post)	25		1913 Nov 20	NE, 38th, 1914
Caves, Robert P.		G, 74th Ohio	318		1912	NE, 37th, 1913
Cavett, A.J.		K, 7th Iowa Cav.	29		1919 Oct 14	IA, 46th, 1920
Cavett, Thos. W.		I, 38th Ill.	25		1927 Aug 29	NE, 52nd, 1928
Cavinee, Sol.	Pvt.	K, 4th Iowa Cav.	20		1920 Dec	IA, 47th, 1921
Caviness, D.W.	Pvt.	A, 2nd Iowa Cav.	19		1914 Mar 25	IA, 41st, 1915
Cavire, J.E.	Bugler	I, 9th Iowa Cav.	49		1919 Aug 21	IA, 46th, 1920
Cavney, Jacob		E, 164th Ohio Inf.	127		1909 Aug 21	KS, 29th, 1910

*See Appendix A, B or C for roster of post names and locations.
†See Introduction for note regarding recording of death date.

Name	Rank	Company, Regiment or Ship	Post*	Age	Death Date†	Journal
Cavrier, W.H.	Pvt.	I, 3rd Wis. Inf.	54		1906 Jul 28	IA, 33rd, 1907
Caw, Geo. F.		A, 147th Ohio	134		1921 Dec	KS, 41st, 1922
Caylor, W.H.		G, 131st Ohio	68		1909 May	KS, 29th, 1910
Cayott, L.P.		K, 3rd Penn.	96		1919 May 29	KS, 39th, 1920
Cayton, William			12		1923 Feb 9	KS, 43rd, 1924
Caywood, H.V.		K, 11th Ind. Inf. (died at Altoona)	243		1895 Jul	KS, 15th, 1896
Ceathubee, J.M.		D, 83rd Ill.	48		1921	IA, 48th, 1922
Ceis, Daniel	Pvt.	B, 28th Iowa Vol. Inf.	233		1902 Feb 11	IA, 28th, 1902
Cell, Geo. W.	Pvt.	I, 22nd Iowa Cav.	255		1924 Sep 20	IA, 51st, 1925
Cell, John		E, 191st Penn.	1		1911 Jan 5	KS, 31st, 1912
Center, H.H.		105th —	94		1919 Feb	IA, 46th, 1920
Center, W.H.		F, 11th Ill.	17		1926 Dec 6	KS, 46th, 1927
Ceperly, D.I.	Drummer	K, 113th Ill. Inf.	419		1902 Feb 13	IA, 29th, 1903
Cessna, Jonathan		E, 54th Ill. Inf. (died at Winfield)	85		1895 Mar 12	KS, 15th, 1896
Chace, W.H.		N.Y.	105		1917 Dec 10	KS, 37th, 1918
Chadburn, A.S.	Lieut. Col.	88th Ill. Inf.	98		1900 Dec 28	IA, 27th, 1901
Chadburn, Wm.		B, 11th Kans. Cav.	25		1912 Nov 9	KS, 32nd, 1913
Chadsey, A.N.		C, 119th Ill.	56		1898 Dec 5	KS, 18th, 1899
Chadwell, Thomas H.		C, 61st Ill.	18		1910 Jun 4	KS, 30th, 1911
Chadwick, Allen		on gunboat *Lexington*	[303?]		1905	KS, 25th, 1906
Chadwick, Chas.			12		1922 Mar 4	KS, 42nd, 1923
Chadwick, E.B.	Pvt.	10th Iowa Inf.	167		1913 Jun 27	IA, 40th, 1914
Chadwick, H.L.		E, 13th Ill. Inf.	110	74	1915 Sep	NE, 41st, 1917
Chadwick, John J.	Pvt.	B, 14th Iowa Inf.	240	90	1935 Apr 1	IA, 65th, 1939
Chadwick, Levi		G, 1st Mo. Cav. (died of old age)	36	84	1913 Jul	NE, 38th, 1914
Chadwick, W.H.		C, Mich. Eng. Corps (died of pneumonia)	13	69	1916 Jan 7	NE, 41st, 1917
Chafa, Geo. W.	Pvt.	B, 10th N.Y. Hvy. Art.	36	47	1890 Dec 26	IA, 18th, 1892
Chaffee, Edward			338		1909 Aug 10	IA, 36th, 1910
Chaffin, F.M.		D, 2nd Ark. Inf.	293		1914 Nov 27	KS, 34th, 1915
Chafin, Phillip	Pvt.	C, 78th Ill. Inf.	305	54	1894 May 15	IA, 21st, 1895
Chalis, Ed.		E, 62nd Ohio Inf. (died of paralysis)	96[95?]	80	1920 Feb 20	NE, 45th, 1921
Chalk, Wm.		I, 24th Iowa Inf. (died of disease of bowels)	304		1894 Aug 25	NE, 19th, 1895
Chalmers, Thomas J.		K, 122nd Ohio (not a member of the G.A.R.)	18		1912 Oct 2	KS, 32nd, 1913
Chamber, J.A.		C, 12th Kans.	50		1909 Apr 5	KS, 29th, 1910
Chamberlain, A.	Pvt.	G, 1st Wis. Cav.	493		1905 Jul 3	IA, 32nd, 1906
Chamberlain, A.C.		A, 23rd Iowa	190		1930	NE, 55th, 1931
Chamberlain, Abijah		17th Ohio Lt. Art.	117		1911 May 28	KS, 31st, 1912
Chamberlain, Albert B.		D, 133rd Ill.	25	74	1916	NE, 41st, 1917
Chamberlain, Calos	Pvt.	M, 3rd N.Y. Art.	267		1904 Jun 30	IA, 31st, 1905
Chamberlain, D.W., see Chomberlain, D.W.						
Chamberlain, E.			124		1923 Feb 17	IA, 50th, 1924
Chamberlain, Ira D.		K, 8th Ind.	380		1896 Mar 13	KS, 16th, 1897
Chamberlain, Isaac		M, 1st Maine Cav. (died of old age)	193	83	1916 Jun 18	NE, 41st, 1917
Chamberlain, J.C.		G, 46th Ind.	265		1890	KS, 10th, 1891
Chamberlain, Lewis		E, 146th Ohio	104		1910 Sep 17	KS, 30th, 1911
Chamberlain, P.R.	Pvt.	B, 44th Wis. Inf.	383		1904 May 8	IA, 31st, 1905
Chamberlin, Andre C.		A, 23rd Iowa (former member of Nebraska Dept.; location: Alma)	190		1937 Oct 22	NE, 62nd, 1938
Chamberlin, J.R.			29		1915 Jan 23	IA, 42nd, 1916
Chamberlin, Stillman		36th Mass. Inf.	36		1901 Jan 2	KS, 21st, 1902
Chamberlin, W.H.		B, 146th Ohio	104		1925 Mar 12	KS, 45th, 1926
Chambers, A.J.	Corp.	E, 72nd Ind. Inf.	271		1900 Dec 3	IA, 27th, 1901
Chambers, Alexander		A, 36th Ill. Inf.	197	70	1912 Oct 22	NE, 37th, 1913
Chambers, Columbus		F, 40th Iowa	18		1922 Oct 11	IA, 49th, 1923
Chambers, Edward		F, 6th Ohio	96		1924 Jun 14	KS, 44th, 1925
Chambers, G.N.		C, 48th Ind.	10		1926 Apr 15	NE, 51st, 1927
Chambers, Henry	Pvt.	K, 27th Iowa Inf.	479	59	1891 Nov 3	IA, 18th, 1892
Chambers, J.		A, 66th Ill.	72		1888	KS, 8th, 1889
Chambers, J.D.	Pvt.	I, 25th Ill. Inf.	67	62	1896 Jul 12	IA, 23rd, 1897
Chambers, J.H.	Pvt.	K, 17th Ill. Inf.	347		1905 Sep 16	IA, 32nd, 1906

Name	Rank	Company, Regiment or Ship	Post*	Age	Death Date†	Journal
Chambers, Jas. C.	Pvt.	I, 3rd Iowa Inf.	90	69	1898 Dec 20	IA, 25th, 1899
Chambers, John H.		H, 74th Ill.	214		1915 Sep 22	KS, 36th, 1917
Chambers, John K.		K, 94th Ill.	25		1921 Aug 12	KS, 41st, 1922
Chambers, N.N.		K, 3rd Kans. Militia	12		1920 Dec 3	KS, 40th, 1921
Chambers, R.B.	Pvt.	H, 15th N.Y. Inf.	357	64	1895 Apr 10	IA, 22nd, 1896
Chambers, Robert H.	Pvt.	K, 3rd Iowa Cav.	317	79	1893 Jun 12	IA, 20th, 1894
Chambers, Sam'l	Pvt.	E, —	515		1911 Jul 22	IA, 38th, 1912
Chambers, W.B.		G, 11th Ind.	85		1927 Oct 5	KS, 47th, 1928
Chambers, William		A, 66th Ill.	196		1902 Jul 2	KS, 22nd, 1903
Champ			134	75	1916 Aug 12	NE, 41st, 1917
Champaigne, Peter		A, 12th Ill.	9		1924 Apr 20	KS, 44th, 1925
Champion, T.J.		C, 148th N.Y. Inf. (died at Eldorado; buried at Bellvista Cemetery)	66		1894 Apr 22	KS, 14th, 1895
Champlain, W.	Pvt.	G, 9th Iowa Cav.	452		1910 Apr	IA, 37th, 1911
Champlin, C.A.		H, 15th Ill. Cav.	87		1890	KS, 10th, 1891
Champlin, Henry A.		K, 10th Wis.	85		1890	KS, 10th, 1891
Champlin, Lester		A, 42nd Ill.	164		1917 Feb 18	KS, 36th, 1917
Chamring, J.W.	Pvt.		115		1921 Sep 23	IA, 48th, 1922
Chance, Abisolon			451		1893	KS, 13th, 1894
Chance, Nathan			25		1940 Jan	KS, 60th, 1941
Chance, T.C.	Pvt.	H, 11th Ohio Cav.	43		1916 Dec 9	IA, 43rd, 1917
Chancellor, Cornelius S.		10th Ohio Bat.	117		1905 Jan 3	KS, 25th, 1906
Chancy, Thomas	Pvt.	K, 23rd Wis. Inf.	101		1927 Feb 16	IA, 54th, 1928
Chandler, Amariah		H, 10th Mass. Inf. (at large)		100	1938 Jan 2	IA, 64th, 1938
Chandler, Andrew		K, 47th Wis.	25		1913 Jan 21	NE, 38th, 1914
Chandler, B.	Corp.	I, 14th Iowa Inf.	20		1910 Jun	IA, 37th, 1911
Chandler, B.	Corp.	H, 28th Ill. Inf.	10		1925	IA, 52nd, 1926
Chandler, Burt	Pvt.	I, 14th Iowa Inf.	20		1910 Sep	IA, 37th, 1911
Chandler, D.J.		C, 51st Ohio Vol. Inf.	135		1899 Sep 6	KS, 19th, 1900
Chandler, D.L.		1st Ind.	341		1892 May 5	KS, 12th, 1893
Chandler, E.B.	Musician	F, 52nd Ill. Inf.	88		1918 Oct 15	IA, 46th, 1920
Chandler, E.G.		E, 1st Maine Cav.	330		1901 Oct 15	IA, 28th, 1902
Chandler, G.G.			110		1913	IA, 40th, 1914
Chandler, John	Pvt.	C, 3rd Mo. Cav.	49		1920 Mar 27	IA, 47th, 1921
Chandler, John		E, 70th Ill. (died of heart trouble)	180	75	1923	NE, 48th, 1924
Chandler, M.		E, 5th Ill. Cav.	12		1904 Apr	KS, 24th, 1905
Chandler, Thos.	Pvt.	D, 24th Iowa Vol. Inf.	112		1926	IA, 53rd, 1927
Chandler, Thos.	Pvt.	C, 28th Wis. Inf.	19		1899	NE, 24th, 1900
Chandler, W.H.	Pvt.	C, 4th Iowa Cav.	26		1933 Oct 6	IA, 60th, 1934
Chaney, A.J.		L, 4th Mo.	68		1923 Sep 24	KS, 43rd, 1924
Chaney, Frederick E.		C, 16th Iowa Inf. (died at Wichita; buried at Wichita, Kans.)	57		1894 Dec 26	KS, 14th, 1895
Chaney, G.C.		167th Ohio	4		1918 Feb 4	KS, 38th, 1919
Chaney, J.H.	Sergt.	C, 24th Ohio Bat.	12		1918 Apr 12	IA, 45th, 1919
Chaney, James S.		B, 57th Ill. Inf.	191		1917 Feb 25	KS, 37th, 1918
Chaney, John	2nd Lieut.	H, 34th Iowa Inf.	173	66	1898 Apr 9	IA, 24th, 1898
Chaney, R.T.		D, 116th Ohio	1		1897 Jul 21	KS, 17th, 1898
Chaney, T.M.	Pvt.	M, 11th Mo. Cav.	11	73	1894 Apr 16	IA, 20th, 1894
Chantland, P.H.	2nd Lieut.	E, 15th Wis. Inf.	236		1905 Jul 10	IA, 32nd, 1906
Chapel, Edwin	Pvt.	I, 9th Iowa Inf.	216		1910 Jun 27	IA, 37th, 1911
Chapel, J.L.			190		1906 Oct	IA, 33rd, 1907
Chapel, R.H.		G, 13th Wis. Inf.	147		1918 Sep 27	KS, 38th, 1919
Chapin, A.T.		H, 4th Maine Bat.	5	82	1925 Apr 13	NE, 50th, 1926
Chapin, Alvah L.		20th Conn. Inf.	12		1917 Dec 17	IA, 44th, 1918
Chapin, C.O.		K, 10th Ill.	17		1921 Jul 13	KS, 41st, 1922
Chapin, Edward R.		B, 4th Wis. Inf.	85		1918 Jun 30	KS, 38th, 1919
Chapin, Henry T.	Corp.	D, 42nd Ohio Inf.	64		1919 Oct 10	IA, 46th, 1920
Chapin, J.R.	Pvt.	I, 2nd Ill. Inf.	156		1921 May 22	IA, 48th, 1922
Chapin, James A.	Pvt.	H, 1st Va. Inf.	59		1913 Apr 17	IA, 40th, 1914
Chapin, Jas. P.	Pvt.	C, 3rd Minn. Inf.	24		1909 Jul 11	IA, 36th, 1910
Chapin, John	Pvt.	C, 31st Iowa	165		1903 May 16	IA, 30th, 1904
Chapin, W.E.	Pvt.	B, 29th Wis. Inf.	12		1905 Sep 14	IA, 32nd, 1906

Name	Rank	Company, Regiment or Ship	Post*	Age	Death Date†	Journal
Chapin, W.F.		K, 148th N.Y. Inf.	7		1925 Oct 20	KS, 45th, 1926
Chapin, W.H.		I, 3rd N.Y. (died of la grippe)	47		1916 Apr 25	NE, 41st, 1917
Chaplain, B.F.	Pvt.	C, 13th Iowa Inf.	18		1900 Apr 19	IA, 27th, 1901
Chaplan, A.W.			226		1901 Jul	KS, 21st, 1902
Chaplin, J.M.	Pvt.	C, 33rd Iowa Inf.	175	56	1892 May 24	IA, 19th, 1893
Chapman, Abijah W.		K, 8th Ind.	18		1923 Jan 21	KS, 43rd, 1924
Chapman, C.C.		E, 3rd Iowa 3rd U.S.	55		1920 Mar 30	KS, 40th, 1921
Chapman, C.W.	Pvt.	A, 9th Iowa Cav.	231		1916 Dec 24	IA, 43rd, 1917
Chapman, Calvin	Lieut.	Indian Scouts	24		1928 Aug 29	NE, 53rd, 1929
Chapman, Chas. H.	Pvt.	G, 150th Ill. Inf.	292		1911 May 2	IA, 38th, 1912
Chapman, D.		D, 10th Ill. (died from wound)	117		1888	KS, 8th, 1889
Chapman, E.A.	Pvt.	K, 150th Ohio Inf.	222		1922 May 29	IA, 49th, 1923
Chapman, Ed E.		G, 30th Iowa	1		1925	KS, 45th, 1926
Chapman, F.D.		B, — N.Y.	286		1905	KS, 25th, 1906
Chapman, F.M.	Pvt.	I, Sharpshooters	231		1920 Jun 25	IA, 47th, 1921
Chapman, J.B.		D, 53rd Ind.	322		1912 Oct 2	KS, 32nd, 1913
Chapman, J.L.		F, 14th N.Y. Art.	38		1911 Jun 25	KS, 31st, 1912
Chapman, J.N.		A, 121st Ohio	142		1931 Apr 22	KS, 52nd, 1933
Chapman, J.N.		A, 121st Ohio	142		1931 Apr 22	KS, 51st, 1932
Chapman, J.W.		E, 72nd Ill. Inf.	380		1909 Mar 11	KS, 29th, 1910
Chapman, James S.		D, 5th Ohio	184		1921 Feb 13	KS, 41st, 1922
Chapman, John		C, 85th Ohio Inf. (died at Hutchinson)	17		1895 Sep 20	KS, 15th, 1896
Chapman, Justice	Pvt.	I, 95th Ill. Inf.	243		1926 Feb 4	IA, 53rd, 1927
Chapman, Lyman	Pvt.	D, 16th Iowa Inf.	267		1910 Dec 18	IA, 37th, 1911
Chapman, M.J.		E, 16th Ohio	223		1896 Feb 20	KS, 16th, 1897
Chapman, O.C.		B, 7th Mich.	42		1911 Mar 13	KS, 31st, 1912
Chapman, O.J.	Pvt.	A, 9th Iowa Cav.	235		1916 Aug 3	IA, 43rd, 1917
Chapman, R.N.	Corp.	K, 24th Ohio Inf.	12		1925 Jan 30	IA, 52nd, 1926
Chapman, S.B.		C, 13th Iowa Inf. (died of gastritis)	44	65	1905 Feb 6	NE, 30th, 1906
Chapman, S.L.		C, 6th Mich.	123		1899 Nov 24	KS, 19th, 1900
Chapman, Samuel	Pvt.	G, 50th Ill. Inf.	86		1897 Jan	IA, 24th, 1898
Chapman, Samuel		H, 140th Penn.	328		1902 Dec 12	KS, 22nd, 1903
Chapman, W.D.		K, 62nd Penn.	32		1919 Jan 15	NE, 44th, 1920
Chapman, W.H.		I, 4th Ohio Inf.	13	73	1918 Aug 7	NE, 43rd, 1919
Chapman, W.S.		D, 16th Iowa Inf.	1		1940 May 30	KS, 60th, 1941
Chapman, Wm. A.	Pvt.	I, 145th Ill. Inf.	5	50	1897 Nov 9	IA, 24th, 1898
Chapman, Wm. A.		B, 17th Kans.	155		1914 Nov 19	KS, 34th, 1915
Chapman, Wm. C.		K, 10th Ill. (died of age)	4	80	1914 Mar 16	NE, 39th, 1915
Chapman, Wm. S.	Pvt.	I, 23rd Iowa Inf.	12		1908 Feb 9	IA, 35th, 1909
Chapmen, Wells H.	Pvt.	159th Ohio	138		1914 Apr 9	IA, 41st, 1915
Chappel, Jesse		D, 82nd Ind. Inf.	25	75	1911 Oct 20	NE, 36th, 1912
Chappell, H.H.		H, 122nd N.Y. Inf. (died of rheum dropsy)	191	64	1903 May 18	NE, 28th, 1904
Chappell, Jesse			25		1911	NE, 36th, 1912
Chappell, S.	Pvt.	I, 202nd Penn. Inf.	18		1917 Nov 19	IA, 44th, 1918
Chard, B.F.			311		1913	KS, 33rd, 1914
Charles, James		A, 1st Penn. Cav.	2		1893 Oct 22	NE, 18th, 1894
Charles, T.J.		I, 27th N.Y.	25		1930 Nov 5	NE, 55th, 1931
Charleston, J.W.			4		1928	NE, 53rd, 1929
Charlesworth, F.		A, 6th Ill. Cav.	147		1901 May 4	KS, 21st, 1902
Charlton, Chas.		D, 7th West Va. Cav.	185		1919 Oct 22	KS, 39th, 1920
Charlton, J.B.	Lieut.	I, 18th Iowa Inf.	101		1907 Apr 23	IA, 34th, 1908
Charpie, A.B.	Musician	51st Ind.	265		1916 Dec 5	KS, 36th, 1917
Charro, R.	Seaman	Mound City	42		1920 Jul 19	IA, 47th, 1921
Charter, Charles W.		Kans.	241		1908[1909?] Feb 1	KS, 29th, 1910
Chartier, Dositee		G, 22nd Mich.	395		1900 Nov 18	KS, 20th, 1901
Chase, A.E.		D, 39th Iowa Inf.	251	55	1890 Oct 30	IA, 17th, 1891
Chase, A.W.	Pvt.	F, 65th Ill.	235		1922 Jul 6	IA, 49th, 1923
Chase, Aaron		I, 1st Mich.	17		1913 Apr 3	KS, 33rd, 1914
Chase, Alvin H.	Pvt.	H, 39th Iowa Vols.	43		1901 May 29	IA, 28th, 1902
Chase, C.L.		H, 40th Mass.	36		1917 Sep 18	KS, 37th, 1918
Chase, C.W.	Corp.	G, 12th N.H. Inf.	88		1907 Aug 10	IA, 34th, 1908

*See Appendix A, B or C for roster of post names and locations.
†See Introduction for note regarding recording of death date.

95

Name	Rank	Company, Regiment or Ship	Post*	Age	Death Date†	Journal
Chase, D.P.		B, 1st Va. Cav.	374		1914 Dec 19	KS, 34th, 1915
Chase, D.W.	Pvt.	D, 36th Mass. Inf.	101		1915 Dec 8	IA, 42nd, 1916
Chase, Daniel	Pvt.	F, 2nd Mass. Inf.	101	77	1891 Dec 2	IA, 18th, 1892
Chase, E.H.	Pvt.	A, 2nd Ill. Art.	516		1903 Dec 19	IA, 30th, 1904
Chase, E.R.	Capt.	F, 11th Wis. Inf.	78		1899 Sep 8	IA, 26th, 1900
Chase, F.M.		B, 29th Maine	7		1920 Jun 28	KS, 40th, 1921
Chase, G.B.		C, 4th Mich. Cav. (member at large)			1934 Oct 8	NE, 59th, 1935
Chase, G.W.		4th Mich.	132		1922 May 20	KS, 42nd, 1923
Chase, Geo.	Pvt.	B, 129th Ohio Inf.	130		1910	IA, 37th, 1911
Chase, George H.		E, 2nd Iowa	34		1924 Jul 20	KS, 44th, 1925
Chase, Harlow			64		1917 May 11	IA, 44th, 1918
Chase, Harvey	Pvt.	C, 9th Iowa Inf.	367		1912	IA, 39th, 1913
Chase, Harvey		C, 9th Iowa Inf.	367		1913 Jan	IA, 40th, 1914
Chase, Isaac M.		D, 33rd Wis.	25		1916 Aug 9	KS, 36th, 1917
Chase, J.	Pvt.	A, 39th Iowa Inf.	55		1905 Aug 4	IA, 32nd, 1906
Chase, J.A.	Pvt.	D, 153rd Ill. Inf.	26		1911 Feb 12	IA, 38th, 1912
Chase, J.C.		H, 1st Wis. Cav.	46		1916 Jul 4	KS, 36th, 1917
Chase, John B.		I, —	134		1911 Nov 11	KS, 31st, 1912
Chase, John J.	Pvt.	E, 36th Iowa Inf.	497		1918 Jun 17	IA, 45th, 1919
Chase, John W.	Pvt.	G, 125th Ill. Inf.	12		1919 Dec 23	IA, 46th, 1920
Chase, John W.	Pvt.	D, 145th Ill. Inf.	12		1915 Dec 23	IA, 42nd, 1916
Chase, Lemuel		I, 8th Penn. Cav.	52		1911 Jun 15	KS, 31st, 1912
Chase, Oscar	Pvt.	7th N.Y. Sharpshooters	25	52	1889 May 24	IA, 16th, 1890
Chase, R.C.		D, 3rd N.Y. Cav.	130		1915 Jan 10	KS, 35th, 1916
Chase, R.L.	Pvt.	D, 3rd N.Y. Cav.	7		1928 Jan 2	IA, 55th, 1929
Chase, Thurston		H, 13th Kans. Inf. (died at Hiawatha; buried at Hiawatha Cemetery)	130		1894 Oct 19	KS, 14th, 1895
Chastine, Reuben		C, 53rd Ky. Inf. (died at Ft. Scott; buried at National Cemetery)	486		1894 Nov 19	KS, 14th, 1895
Chatfield, Beecher	Sergt.	D, 11th Iowa Inf.	78	59	1893 Jan 24	IA, 19th, 1893
Chatfield, M.M.	Pvt.	B, 1st Iowa Cav.	147		1911 Jan 10	IA, 38th, 1912
Chatman, L.		H, 1st Mo.	49		1925 Oct	KS, 45th, 1926
Chatt, Thomas P.		I, 13th Ill.	32		1919 Feb 3	KS, 39th, 1920
Chatterton, Frank		C, 8th N.Y. Art.	179		1913 Mar 2	KS, 33rd, 1914
Chatterton, Wm.	Pvt.	B, 8th Iowa Inf.	231		1912 Dec 27	IA, 39th, 1913
Chears, A.S.		K, 1st Ohio Cav.	8		1915 Mar 18	KS, 35th, 1916
Cheasbrau, Ezra		M, 10th N.Y. Hvy. Art. (died of dropsy)	65	80	1897 Sep 28	NE, 22nd, 1898
Chedester, Ben. F.	Pvt.	I, 7th Iowa Inf.	313		1907 Mar 28	IA, 34th, 1908
Cheedle, Dean	1st Sergt.	K, 6th Iowa Cav.	206		1897 Jan 29	IA, 24th, 1898
Cheek, J.W.	Pvt.	G, 15th Iowa	12		1922 Sep 11	IA, 49th, 1923
Cheeney, H.A.		H, 77th Ind. G, 10th Ind.	52		1913 Mar 24	KS, 33rd, 1914
Cheeney, J.H.	Pvt.	E, 15th Iowa Inf.	79		1916	IA, 43rd, 1917
Cheeny, A.E.	Pvt. & 1st Lieut.	H, 20th Wis. Inf. (died of erysipelas)	44	45	1887 May 18	NE, 12th, 1888
Cheeseman, W.		G, 133rd Ohio	240		1909 Nov 21	KS, 29th, 1910
Cheever, A.B.		H, 4th Ill. Cav.	57		1918 Aug 18	KS, 38th, 1919
Cheil, Harry		K, 13th Kans.	130		1916 Mar 27	KS, 36th, 1917
Chelsey, F.G.	6-Corp.	D, 9th Iowa Cav.	108		1925 Jul 30	IA, 52nd, 1926
Chenawith, Samuel		B, 4th Mo. Cav.	85		1923 Sep 1	KS, 43rd, 1924
Cheney, A.H.	Major	41st U.S.C.T.	124		1926 Apr 30	IA, 53rd, 1927
Cheney, B.F.	1st Lieut.	G, 9th Iowa Cav.	3		1899 Mar	IA, 26th, 1900
Cheney, Ithmer	Pvt.	B, 11th Iowa Inf.	292		1910 Apr 20	IA, 37th, 1911
Cheney, J.H., see Cheeney, J.H.						
Cheney, John T.	Pvt.	1st Ill. Art.	22		1901 Oct 16	IA, 28th, 1902
Cheney, M.B.		G, 154th N.Y.	25		1915 Jul 14	NE, 40th, 1916
Cheney, Thomas			298		1897	NE, 22nd, 1898
Cheney, William T.		H, 9th Ill. Inf.	87		1914 Sep 28	KS, 34th, 1915
Chenoweth, Noah		K, 1st Ind. Cav.	30		1912 Jan 9	KS, 32nd, 1913
Chenoweth, Wm.		F, 19th Iowa Inf.	32		1916 Mar 28	KS, 36th, 1917
Chenowith, J.D.	Pvt.	E, 7th Iowa Inf.	2		1923 Jan 17	IA, 50th, 1924
Cheput, Joseph		B, 37th Ill. Inf. (died at Aurora)	326		1895 Mar	KS, 15th, 1896
Cherrie, M.	Capt.	K, 3rd Iowa Cav.	49		1899 Dec 16	IA, 26th, 1900

*See Appendix A, B or C for roster of post names and locations.
†See Introduction for note regarding recording of death date.

Name	Rank	Company, Regiment or Ship	Post*	Age	Death Date†	Journal
Cherry, A.B.			1		1890	NE, 15th, 1891
Cherry, B.F.	Pvt.		108		1910 Jul 5	IA, 37th, 1911
Cherry, David		F, 17th Ohio	25		1936	KS, 56th, 1937
Cherry, James M.		L, 11th Mo. Cav.	32		1915 Oct 18	KS, 35th, 1916
Cherry, John		died by falling off porch	89	80	1915 Dec 15	NE, 40th, 1916
Cherry, M.C.		C, 14th Ill.	114		1898	KS, 18th, 1899
Cherry, Wm.		I, 1st Wis.	59	74	1909 May 31	NE, 34th, 1910
Chesebro, Ezra, see Cheasbrau, Ezra						
Chesley, F.G., see Chelsey, F.G.						
Chesley, F.W.	Pvt.	E, 142nd Penn. Inf.	244		1926 Jun 14	IA, 53rd, 1927
Chesney, William	Sergt.	D, 13th Iowa Inf.	333		1919 May 4	IA, 46th, 1920
Chester, Henry	Seaman	Navy	22		3rd quarter 1885	IA, 12th, 1886
Chester, T.			71		1888	KS, 8th, 1889
Chestnut, J.W.	Pvt.	K, 22nd Penn. Cav.	135		1901 Dec	IA, 28th, 1902
Cheuvrant, M.E.		A, 7th West Va.	25	71	1919 May 19	NE, 44th, 1920
Chevuront, Thomas J.		F, 9th Mo. Cav. (died of general debility)	149	71	1914 Feb 10	NE, 38th, 1914
Chewning, Geo. W.	Musician	F, 42nd Wis. Inf.	78		1908 Jul 5	IA, 35th, 1909
Chickering, E.	Pvt.	B, 2nd N.H. Inf.	235		1921 Nov 30	IA, 48th, 1922
Chidester, Ben. F., see Chedester, Ben. F.						
Chidester, H.M.	Pvt.	A, 36th Iowa Inf.	337		1925 Sep 19	IA, 52nd, 1926
Chilcott, N.G.		E, 1st Iowa Cav.	34		1922 Feb 7	KS, 42nd, 1923
Chilcotte, E.		B, 129th Ill.	38		1911 Jul 6	KS, 31st, 1912
Child, S.M.	Pvt.	K, 32nd Iowa Inf.	83		1915 Mar 21	IA, 42nd, 1916
Childers, A.		D, 132nd Ill.	464		1911 Dec 22	KS, 31st, 1912
Childers, B.F.		G, 8th Mo.	153		1897 Oct 17	KS, 17th, 1898
Childers, David J.	Pvt.	C, 140th Ill. Inf.	259		1909 Oct 19	IA, 36th, 1910
Childers, M.A.		C, 9th Tenn.	38		1913 Apr 24	KS, 33rd, 1914
Childers, Richard		B, 154th Ill.	66		1918 Feb 12	KS, 38th, 1919
Childers, Silas		C, 42nd Mo.	185		1913 Dec 14	KS, 33rd, 1914
Childers, T.D.		C, 11th Kans.	464		1893 Dec 9	KS, 13th, 1894
Childress, C.H.		C, 30th Wis.	63		1933 Feb 28	NE, 58th, 1934
Childress, G.T.			233		1923 Sep 6	IA, 50th, 1924
Childress, H.J.	Pvt.	H, 28th Iowa Inf.	22		1902 Sep 30	IA, 29th, 1903
Childreth, E.D.		E, 11th Kans.	55		1928 Apr 22	KS, 48th, 1929
Childs, A.M.	Pvt.	C, 6th Iowa Cav.	12	56	1897 Feb 7	IA, 23rd, 1897
Childs, A.P.		cause of death: heart	109	66	1902 Aug	NE, 27th, 1903
Childs, C.O.		Battery J, 12th Ohio (died of paralysis)	28	73	1914 Jun 25	NE, 39th, 1915
Childs, E.V.		A, 21st Wis. Inf. (died of paralysis)	182	68	1868[1906?] Aug 13	NE, 31st, 1907
Childs, G.H.	Capt.	F, 21st Iowa Inf.	452		1922 Feb 22	IA, 49th, 1923
Childs, H.P.		H, 137th Ind.	19		1892 Aug 17	KS, 12th, 1893
Childs, Myron		D, 4th Vt.	71		1918 Mar 5	KS, 38th, 1919
Childs, O.M.			116	79	1915 Apr 7	NE, 39th, 1915
Childs, W.H.		H, 29th Mich.	265		1922 Aug 7	KS, 42nd, 1923
Chill, Alfred		I, 7th Kans.	283		1906 Jan 20	KS, 26th, 1907
Chill, Z.		A, 10th Kans.	74		1913 Aug 8	KS, 33rd, 1914
Chilson, Albert	Pvt.	4th Ind. Bat. Iowa Lt. Art. (at large)		93	1939 Jan 4	IA, 65th, 1939
Chilson, James M.		C, 129th Ind.	198		1914 Feb 22	KS, 34th, 1915
Chinkchank, A.W.		D, 23rd Ohio Inf.	262	67	1905 May 17	NE, 30th, 1906
Chinn, John		H, 12th Ky. Cav.	240		1917 Nov 19	KS, 37th, 1918
Chipman, N.J.		K, 76th Ill. Inf.	5		1925	KS, 45th, 1926
Chisholm, A.W.	Pvt.	E, 43rd Mass. Inf.	105		1899	NE, 24th, 1900
Chisman, Palmer	Capt.	B, 7th Ind.	497		1925 Apr 16[?]	IA, 52nd, 1926
Chisman, William H.		I, 83rd Ind.	105		1925 Apr 25	KS, 45th, 1926
Chittenden, E.F.		B, 14th Ill. Inf. (died of old age)	32	79	1912 May 30	NE, 37th, 1913
Chittenden, J.W.		H, 38th Ill.	145		1909 May 15	KS, 29th, 1910
Chitwood, J.M.		K, 111th Ill.	17		1927 Oct 9	KS, 47th, 1928
Choate, John R.		I, 2nd Tenn. Inf.	90		1917 Mar 18	KS, 37th, 1918
Choate, M.M.		6th Iowa Inf.	94		1923 Dec 12	IA, 50th, 1924
Chomberlain, D.W.			91		2nd quarter 1883	IA, 10th, 1884

*See Appendix A, B or C for roster of post names and locations.
†See Introduction for note regarding recording of death date.

Name	Rank	Company, Regiment or Ship	Post*	Age	Death Date†	Journal
Choote, B.F.		I, 19th Maine Inf.	328		1901 Dec 26	KS, 21st, 1902
Choplin, William R.		G, 2nd Ill. Art.	252		1886	KS, 6th, 1887
Chown, J.J.	Pvt.	B, 100th Ill. Inf.	314	53	1887 Aug 22	IA, 14th, 1888
Chriner, Isaac			74		1925 Jan 19	KS, 45th, 1926
Chrisler, Helmus	Pvt.	C, 107th N.Y. Inf.	6		1926	IA, 53rd, 1927
Chrisler, John A.		K, 24th Ind. Vols.	170		1902 Apr 30	KS, 22nd, 1903
Christ, Jacob B.		F, 49th Penn. Inf. (died at Beattie, Kans.; buried at Dunkard Cemetery)	101		1894 Dec 1	KS, 14th, 1895
Christ, William		D, 104th Penn. Inf. (died at Saw Log)	353		1895 Nov	KS, 15th, 1896
Christian, Christian		G, 20th Ill. (died of old age)	75	75	1904 Oct 30	NE, 29th, 1905
Christian, James		C, S. U.S. Vols. (died at Arkansas City)	158		1895 Apr 14	KS, 15th, 1896
Christiance, Peter B.		H, 45th Ill. Inf. (died of paralysis)	10		1893 Oct 21	NE, 18th, 1894
Christianson, E.	Sergt.	I, 2nd Iowa Inf.	92		1913 Feb 20	IA, 40th, 1914
Christianson, John		A, 148th Ill. Inf. (died at Osage City; buried at Swedish Cemetery)	11		1894 Mar 4	KS, 14th, 1895
Christie, Benj.	Pvt.	K, 1st Cav.	153		1924	IA, 51st, 1925
Christie, Chas.		C, 20th Mass. Inf. (died of rheumatism)	34		1894 Oct 1	NE, 19th, 1895
Christie, F.	Pvt.	A, 1st Conn. Cav.	247		1921 Jun 2	IA, 48th, 1922
Christie, Wm.	Pvt.	C, 23rd Iowa Inf.	7		1919 Sep 27	IA, 46th, 1920
Christie, Wm. H.		H, 75th Ill. Inf.	110		1908 May 28	NE, 33rd, 1909
Christman, Augustus	Pvt.	A, 44th Iowa Inf.	78	58	1894 Sep 7	IA, 21st, 1895
Christman, H.	Pvt.	C, 71st N.Y. Inf.	30		1901 Oct 25	IA, 28th, 1902
Christneau, J.H.	Pvt.	A, 33rd Iowa	49		1921 Dec 25	IA, 48th, 1922
Christofel, Frederick	Lieut.	K, 15th Iowa Inf.	49		1915 Oct 16	IA, 42nd, 1916
Christopher, Henry	Chief bugler	13th Colored Hvy. Art.	70	60	1889 May 8	IA, 16th, 1890
Christy, Frank		B, 1st Mich.	256		1910 Apr 27	KS, 30th, 1911
Christy, G.W.		B, 47th Iowa	35		1905 Mar 27	KS, 25th, 1906
Christy, Henry E.		K, 40th Iowa (died of Bright's disease)	51	62	1900 Feb 27	NE, 25th, 1901
Christy, M.C.	Corp.	D, 8th Iowa Cav.	12		1909 May 31	IA, 36th, 1910
Christy, T.A.	Pvt.	F, 32nd Iowa Inf.	22		1930 Jan 25	IA, 57th, 1931
Christy, T.W.		C, 31st Ill.	113		1925 Mar 30	KS, 45th, 1926
Christy, W.D.	Corp.	G, 116th Ohio Inf.	440		1916 Aug 2	IA, 43rd, 1917
Christy, W.D.	Pvt.	D, 2nd Iowa Inf.	12		1919 Jun 30	IA, 46th, 1920
Chritchfield, John			25		1936	KS, 56th, 1937
Chubb, C.C.			165		1911	IA, 38th, 1912
Church, A.N.	Pvt.	E, 33rd Iowa Inf.	40		1910 Nov 8	IA, 37th, 1911
Church, Alonzo H.		G, 114th Ill. Inf. (died of stomach trouble; see also Appendix D)	69	50	1894[1895] Jan 8	NE, 19th, 1895
Church, Andrew H.		H, 86th Ill. Inf.	25		1938 Apr 4	NE, 63rd, 1939
Church, C.	Pvt.	C, 147th Ill. Inf.	497		1916 Sep 10	IA, 43rd, 1917
Church, C.A.	Pvt.		247		1927	IA, 54th, 1928
Church, Charles M.		D, 19th Wis. Inf.	147		1901 Jul 8	KS, 21st, 1902
Church, Edw. A.		K, 57th Ill.	25		1927 Aug 10	NE, 52nd, 1928
Church, Geo. W.		A, 5th Ohio Cav. (died of pneumonia)	273	64	1902 Oct	NE, 27th, 1903
Church, George	Pvt.		377		1927 Feb 8	IA, 54th, 1928
Church, H.G.		K, 24th N.Y. Cav.	12		1899 Jul 21	KS, 19th, 1900
Church, Henry	Pvt.	M, 2nd Wis. Cav.	23		1897 May 10	IA, 24th, 1898
Church, Jacob			42		1908	IA, 35th, 1909
Church, Jas.		H, 1st Ill.	259		1906 Oct 6	KS, 26th, 1907
Church, Lewis		Illinois	377		1916	KS, 36th, 1917
Church, Nathan	Pvt.	E, 12th Iowa Inf.	307		1905 Nov 24	IA, 32nd, 1906
Church, Othell		F, 39th Iowa	88		1887 Apr 6	KS, 7th, 1888
Church, Philander		K, 12th Iowa	32		1928 Dec 7	NE, 53rd, 1929
Church, Philander P.		I, 50th Ohio Inf. (died of heart trouble)	90	67	1910 Oct 20	NE, 35th, 1911
Church, Samuel			34		1924 Jul 7	KS, 44th, 1925
Church, W.S.		B, 2nd Neb. (died of general debility)	129	76	1907 Sep 17	NE, 32nd, 1908
Church, Wm.	Pvt.	F, 50th Ill.	515		1899 Oct 7	IA, 26th, 1900
Church, Wm. W.	Pvt.	K, 6th Iowa Cav.	509		1899 Feb 15	IA, 26th, 1900
Churcher, J.H.	Pvt.	I, 2nd Iowa Inf.	88		1909 Apr	IA, 36th, 1910
Churchers, Robert		D, 100th U.S.C.T.	486		1900 Apr 8	KS, 20th, 1901
Churches, James	Pvt.	M, 1st Wis. Cav.	240		1906	IA, 33rd, 1907
Churchill, A.S.		K, 22nd Wis. Inf. (died of pneumonia)	262	74	1920 May 12	NE, 45th, 1921

*See Appendix A, B or C for roster of post names and locations.
†See Introduction for note regarding recording of death date.

98

Name	Rank	Company, Regiment or Ship	Post*	Age	Death Date†	Journal
Churchill, Henry		B, 25th Md.	77		1926 Sep 30	KS, 46th, 1927
Churchill, John N.		K, 74th Ill.	25	77	1913 Feb 20	NE, 38th, 1914
Churchill, Justin	Pvt.	L, 7th Iowa Cav.	188		1913 Jul 6	IA, 40th, 1914
Churchtown, John		G, 156th Ind. Inf. (died at Fawn Creek; buried at Robbins Cemetery)	153		1894 Nov	KS, 14th, 1895
Chute, Andrew	Pvt.	E, 17th Wis. Inf.	42		1902 Dec 19	IA, 29th, 1903
Cilliny, A.J.	Pvt.	A, 39th Ill. Inf.	190		1925 Dec 23	IA, 52nd, 1926
Cines, W.	Pvt.	K, 45th Iowa Inf.	79		1926 Sep 26	IA, 53rd, 1927
Civens, John		B, 11th Kans. Cav.	328		1889	KS, 9th, 1890
Cjaplinski, Andrew		B, 27th Ohio	27		1920 Sep 21	KS, 40th, 1921
Claflin, A.A.	Pvt.	G, 33rd Ill. Inf.	66		1915 Aug 29	IA, 42nd, 1916
Clagg, Wm. H.			91		1912	IA, 39th, 1913
Clain, John		G, 72nd Ind.	64		1916 Nov 21	KS, 36th, 1917
Clampit, R.M.	Pvt.	F, 39th Iowa Inf.	7		1908 Jun 19	IA, 35th, 1909
Clampitt, D.W.		B, 118th Ill.	68		1917 Dec 1	KS, 37th, 1918
Clancy, A.H.		E, 193rd Ohio Inf.	52		1930 Apr 4	KS, 50th, 1931
Clancy, Z.R.	Pvt.	B, 62nd Ohio Inf.	56		1913 Sep 7	IA, 40th, 1914
Clanin, John L.	Pvt.	1st Iowa Art.	292		1913 Jan 6	IA, 40th, 1914
Clanton, T.H.		G, 23rd Iowa Inf. (died of disease of lung)	3		1891 July	KS, 11th, 1892
Clapp, W.H.	Pvt.	C, 51st Mass.	22		1924 Nov 5	IA, 51st, 1925
Clapper, Frank		F, 40th Wis.	171		1933 Feb 28	NE, 58th, 1934
Clapper, J.M.	Pvt.	E, 159th Ohio Inf.	233		1908 Nov 6	IA, 35th, 1909
Clapperbon, Alexander		E, — N.Y. Inf.	6		1900 Mar 10	KS, 20th, 1901
Clapsottle, J.E.			23		1907 May 12	IA, 34th, 1908
Clarey, E.B.	Sergt.	H, West Va. Inf.	230		1900 Feb 19	IA, 27th, 1901
Clark, A.D.	Pvt.	H, 1st Wis. Inf.	68		1918 Jan 6	IA, 45th, 1919
Clark, A.D.	Pvt.	H, 42nd Wis. Inf.	165		1922	IA, 49th, 1923
Clark, A.L.		B, 43rd Wis. Inf.	78	91	1936 Oct 9	IA, 63rd, 1937
Clark, A.M.		G, 127th Penn.	110		1918 Apr 21	NE, 43rd, 1919
Clark, A.O.	Pvt.	H, 75th Ill. Inf.	64	45	1887 Nov 28	IA, 14th, 1888
Clark, A.R.		G, 2nd Iowa Cav.	14		1920 Sep 4	KS, 40th, 1921
Clark, A.S.	Bugler	E, 1st Wis. Cav.	42		1911 Dec 3	IA, 38th, 1912
Clark, Albert M.		H, 15th Iowa Inf.	94	93	1937 Apr 22	IA, 64th, 1938
Clark, Alfred W.	Pvt.	B, 43rd Wis. Inf.	78	91	1936 Oct 9	IA, 65th, 1939
Clark, Almeron F.		E, 194th Ohio (died of dropsy at Soldiers & Sailors Home, Milford)		65	1906 Jul 15	NE, 31st, 1907
Clark, Alva		I, 92nd Ohio	311		1912 Aug 31	KS, 32nd, 1913
Clark, Amos		I, 129th Ill. Inf. (died of heart failure)	173		1893 Feb 27	NE, 18th, 1894
Clark, Andrew R.		G, 129th Ohio Inf. (former member of department; location: Lincoln)	318, 274		1938 Jan 14	NE, 63rd, 1939
Clark, Arthur	Pvt.	93rd N.Y. Inf.	300		1905 Mar 10	IA, 32nd, 1906
Clark, Asbury		F, 86th Ill. Inf. (died at Nickerson; buried at Wild Meade Cemetery)	83		1894 Apr 15	KS, 14th, 1895
Clark, Augustus N.		K, 2nd R.I. Inf.	380		1901 Jul 12	KS, 21st, 1902
Clark, Bernard		L, 6th Kans.	380		1897 May 27	KS, 17th, 1898
Clark, Boryman		86th —	89		1908	KS, 28th, 1909
Clark, C.C.	Pvt.	E, 8th N.Y. Cav.	247		1907 Jul 14	IA, 34th, 1908
Clark, C.D.		A, 12th Ill. Cav.	47		1922 Mar 26	KS, 42nd, 1923
Clark, C.H.			212		1928	IA, 55th, 1929
Clark, C.M.		H, 88th Ill. Inf.	25	79	1919 Apr 30	NE, 44th, 1920
Clark, Calvin P.	Pvt.	F, 12th Mich. Inf.	193		1917 Feb 5	IA, 44th, 1918
Clark, Carlton		G, 1st Ill. Cav.	55		1917 Jul 3	KS, 37th, 1918
Clark, Charles Armory	Pvt., Major & Lieut. Col.	6th Maine (see Appendix D)			1913 Dec 22	IA, 40th, 1914
Clark, Chas. A.		C, 32nd Iowa Inf. (died of age, heart & stomach)	77	84	1916 Dec 5	NE, 41st, 1917
Clark, Chas. V.	Musician	1st Brigade, 3rd Division, 15th Army Corps	81		1902 Jun 28	IA, 29th, 1903
Clark, Cornelius	Musician	H, 31st Iowa Inf. C, 17th Iowa Inf.	1	92	1937 Oct 8	IA, 65th, 1939
Clark, Cornelius M.		H, 63rd Ohio	123		1937 Feb 7	KS, 57th, 1938
Clark, Cornelius M.		H, 63rd Ohio	123		1937 Feb 7	KS, 56th, 1937

*See Appendix A, B or C for roster of post names and locations.
†See Introduction for note regarding recording of death date.

99

Name	Rank	Company, Regiment or Ship	Post*	Age	Death Date†	Journal
Clark, Curtis	Capt.	H, 7th Iowa Cav. F, 3rd Iowa Cav.	18	71	1896 Apr 15	IA, 23rd, 1897
Clark, D.B.	Capt.	H, 15th Iowa Inf.	29		1897 Oct 1	IA, 24th, 1898
Clark, Daniel		A, 194th Penn.	63		1920 Dec 4	KS, 40th, 1921
Clark, David	Sergt.	H, 153rd N.Y. Inf.	125		1926 Jun 23	IA, 53rd, 1927
Clark, David H.	Pvt.	K, 2nd Iowa Inf.	173		1899 Dec 10	IA, 26th, 1900
Clark, Denzel J.	Pvt.	H, 37th N.Y. Vols.	284	58	1898 Sep 21	IA, 25th, 1899
Clark, Duane L.		G, 114th N.Y.	55		1919 Nov 26	KS, 39th, 1920
Clark, E.F.		H, 6th Mass.	6		1918	KS, 38th, 1919
Clark, E.F.A.		I, 129th Penn.	1		1918 Sep 12	KS, 38th, 1919
Clark, E.H.		G, 27th Ill.	130		1922 Jan 13	KS, 42nd, 1923
Clark, E.J.		died of wound	35		1890	KS, 10th, 1891
Clark, E.S.		G, 46th Ill.	40		1922 Mar 13	KS, 42nd, 1923
Clark, Edward		C, 8th P.R.[Penn. Res.?]	9		1920 Dec	NE, 45th, 1921
Clark, Elander		F, 36th Ohio	17		1924 Jun 24	KS, 44th, 1925
Clark, Eli		H, 67th Ind.	71		1893 Dec 7	KS, 13th, 1894
Clark, Emanuel		F, 31st Ohio	68		1919 Sep 28	KS, 39th, 1920
Clark, F.G.	Lieut.	G, 16th Vt. Inf.	235		1921 Feb 3	IA, 48th, 1922
Clark, F.L.		C, 7th Ohio (died at Girard, Kans.)	32		1892 Jan 28	KS, 12th, 1893
Clark, Frank		F, 4th Mich.	74		1896 Aug 29	KS, 16th, 1897
Clark, Frederick H.		E, 9th Vt. Inf. (died of chronic diarrhea)	89	62	1906 Dec 17	NE, 31st, 1907
Clark, G.A.		E, 39th Ill. Inf.	23		1923 Jun 11	NE, 48th, 1924
Clark, G.W.		H, 38th Ohio Inf.	18		1917 Dec 6	KS, 37th, 1918
Clark, Geo. C.	Pvt.	B, 33rd Wis.	14		1907 Sep	IA, 34th, 1908
Clark, Geo. H.		K, 1st Wis.	1		1917 Jun 30	KS, 37th, 1918
Clark, Geo. R.	Corp.	I, 25th Wis. Inf.	78		1923 Jan 22	IA, 50th, 1924
Clark, Geo. W.		C, 27th Ill.	147		1918 Aug 12	KS, 38th, 1919
Clark, George	Sergt.	H, 150th Ill. Inf.	247		1911 Jan 19	IA, 38th, 1912
Clark, George	Pvt.	A, 31st Iowa Inf.	235		1918 Sep 22	IA, 45th, 1919
Clark, H.A.		C, 68th Ill.	55		1923 Sep 29	KS, 43rd, 1924
Clark, H.M.		I, 11th Ohio Inf.	353		1899 Nov 22	KS, 19th, 1900
Clark, H.P.	Pvt.	K, 13th Wis. Inf.	68		1928 Sep 5	IA, 55th, 1929
Clark, H.S.		E, 3rd M. Kans.[Kansas State Militia?]	12		1908 Jan 4	KS, 28th, 1909
Clark, Harvey			236		1925	IA, 52nd, 1926
Clark, Henry		I, 36th Ohio Vol. Inf.	49		1914 Mar 16	KS, 34th, 1915
Clark, Henry		C, 8th Kans. Hvy. Art. (died of stomach trouble)	69		1894 Oct 8	NE, 19th, 1895
Clark, Hiram N.		F, 34th Ill.	18		1910 Jul 20	KS, 30th, 1911
Clark, Horace		G, 5th U.S.C. Cav.	321		1904 Apr 26	KS, 24th, 1905
Clark, Ira B.		F, 11th Penn. Cav.	241		1912 Apr 6	KS, 32nd, 1913
Clark, Isaac	Pvt.	C, 4th Iowa Inf.	264		1904 Nov 17	IA, 31st, 1905
Clark, J.	Pvt.	A, 6th Ind. Cav.	37		1906	IA, 33rd, 1907
Clark, J.C.	Pvt.	M, 17th Ill. Cav.	46		1911 Jan 16	IA, 38th, 1912
Clark, J.D.	Pvt.	B, 7th Iowa Cav.	111		1929 Aug 30	IA, 56th, 1930
Clark, J.F.		K, 101st Penn. Inf. (died of paralysis)	96	56	1901 Jul	NE, 26th, 1902
Clark, J.H.	Pvt.	G, 3rd Iowa Inf.	116		1910 Nov 26	IA, 37th, 1911
Clark, J.H.	QM Sergt.	D, 7th Iowa Cav.	1	86	1931 Jun 7	IA, 58th, 1932
Clark, J.J.		F, 6th N.Y.	19		1898 Jan 9	KS, 18th, 1899
Clark, J.M.		C, 73rd Ind.	81		1923 Feb 9	KS, 43rd, 1924
Clark, J.R.		F, 125th Ohio Inf.	3		1900 Nov 27	KS, 20th, 1901
Clark, J.S.	Pvt.	D, 11th Iowa Inf.	211	62	1895 May 22	IA, 22nd, 1896
Clark, J.S.			255		1923 May 10	KS, 43rd, 1924
Clark, J.T.		B, 8th Cal. Inf.	36		1911 May 8	KS, 31st, 1912
Clark, J.T.		G, 6th Va. (died of cancer)	101	72	1912 Apr 26	NE, 37th, 1913
Clark, J.W.	Pvt.	2nd Ind. Legion	276		1897-1898	IA, 24th, 1898
Clark, J.W.	Pvt.	2nd Ind. Legions	276	63	1896 Dec 9	IA, 23rd, 1897
Clark, J.W.	Pvt.	E, 44th Iowa Inf.	3		1913 Apr 4	IA, 40th, 1914
Clark, Jacob	Pvt.	L, 7th Ill. Cav.	348	69	1895 Jun 24	IA, 22nd, 1896
Clark, James			1		1910 May 12	KS, 30th, 1911
Clark, James		K, 102nd Ill.	40		1915 Sep 18	KS, 35th, 1916
Clark, James A.	Musician	K, 47th Iowa Inf.	111		1916 Jul 24	IA, 43rd, 1917
Clark, James R.			61		4th quarter 1883	IA, 10th, 1884

*See Appendix A, B or C for roster of post names and locations.
†See Introduction for note regarding recording of death date.

Name	Rank	Company, Regiment or Ship	Post*	Age	Death Date†	Journal
Clark, James W.		E, 66th Penn.	1		1922 Feb 28	KS, 42nd, 1923
Clark, Jeptha	Pvt.	H, 7th Iowa Inf.	84		1914 Jul 19	IA, 41st, 1915
Clark, Jno. F.	Pvt.	B, 36th Iowa Inf.	477	76	1890 Dec 19	IA, 17th, 1891
Clark, John	Pvt.	H, 12th Ill. Cav.	348		1905 Aug 19	IA, 32nd, 1906
Clark, John		I, 30th Ill.	51		1912 Jul 9	KS, 32nd, 1913
Clark, John A.			235		1913 Mar 13	IA, 40th, 1914
Clark, John C.		F, 73rd Ohio	129		1896 May 17	KS, 16th, 1897
Clark, John K.	Corp.	H, 79th Ill. Inf.	66		1900 Nov 17	IA, 27th, 1901
Clark, John L.		C, Ill. Art. (died of cancer)	8		1906 Aug 8	NE, 31st, 1907
Clark, John P.	Pvt.	G, 8th Penn. Cav.	216	60	1899 Jan 12	IA, 25th, 1899
Clark, John R.	Pvt. & 2nd Lieut. 1st Lieut.	B, 15th Ohio Inf. A, 15th Ohio Inf. (see also Appendix D)	25	47	1890 Aug 2	NE, 15th, 1891
Clark, Judson		F, 27th Iowa Inf. (died of paralysis)	77	79	1921 Jul 26	NE, 46th, 1922
Clark, L.M.	Pvt.	H, 5th Ill. Cav.	88		1905 Dec 8	IA, 32nd, 1906
Clark, Lake		G, 107th Ill. Inf. (died at Dunavant; buried at Spring Grove Cemetery)	168		1894 Jan 17	KS, 14th, 1895
Clark, Leander	Capt.	C, 24th Iowa Inf.	343		1910 Dec 23	IA, 37th, 1911
Clark, M.		D, 10th Kans.	12		1912 Apr 12	KS, 32nd, 1913
Clark, M.J.		G, 42nd Penn.	71		1905 Dec 13	KS, 25th, 1906
Clark, M.O.		G, 32nd Iowa Inf.	231		1899 May 20	KS, 19th, 1900
Clark, M.R.		I, 83rd Penn.	25		1916 Jan 3	KS, 36th, 1917
Clark, Mack		C, 1st U.S.C.T.	47		1916 May	KS, 36th, 1917
Clark, Malcolm	Pvt.	39th & 51st Wis. Inf.	290		1926 Feb 15	IA, 54th, 1928
Clark, Matt			187		1917	IA, 45th, 1919
Clark, Moses	Capt.	34th Iowa	116		1914 Aug 27	IA, 41st, 1915
Clark, Nelson	Pvt.	F, 171st Ohio Inf.	22		1920 Dec 19	IA, 47th, 1921
Clark, O.J.	Pvt.	K, 38th Iowa Inf.	118		1926 Aug 1	IA, 53rd, 1927
Clark, O.P.	Pvt.	E, 124th Ind. Inf.	97	45	1888 Sep 8	IA, 15th, 1889
Clark, Oliver E.		F, 3rd Kans. (died at Wakarusa; buried at Wakarusa)	12		1894 Sep 1	KS, 14th, 1895
Clark, Oren	Pvt.	F, 81st Ohio	511		1903 Sep 23	IA, 30th, 1904
Clark, Osborn	Musician		54		1914 Sep 5	IA, 41st, 1915
Clark, Peter T.		H, 2nd Ill. Art. (died at Cameron, Mo.)	93		1895 May 22	KS, 15th, 1896
Clark, Plinney F.	Pvt.	L, 2nd Minn. Cav.	193		1907 May 26	IA, 34th, 1908
Clark, R.A.		I, 119th Ill. Inf.	97	79	1924 Mar 8	NE, 49th, 1925
Clark, R.B.	Pvt.	E, 28th Iowa Inf.	8		1918 May 26	IA, 45th, 1919
Clark, Reason		B, 83rd U.S. Col. Inf.	236		1891 May 12	KS, 11th, 1892
Clark, Robert	Pvt.	C, 46th Ill. Inf.	156		1917 Apr 22	IA, 44th, 1918
Clark, Robert		H, 103rd Ill.	190		1916 Nov 21	KS, 36th, 1917
Clark, S.		F, 3rd Kans.	12		1893 Apr	KS, 13th, 1894
Clark, S.L.			80		1918	IA, 45th, 1919
Clark, S.W.		K, Ind. Bat.	115		1922 Mar 14	KS, 42nd, 1923
Clark, Samuel G.		F, 28th Iowa Inf.	85		1916 Oct 9	KS, 36th, 1917
Clark, Samuel K.		B, 128th Penn.	93		1921 Sep 17	KS, 41st, 1922
Clark, Silas		H, 170th Ohio (died of paralysis)	13	77	1912 Aug 23	NE, 37th, 1913
Clark, Simeon		F, 28th U.S.A.	352		1896 Jul 2	KS, 16th, 1897
Clark, Smith	Pvt.	H, 13th Iowa Inf.	253		1905 Sep	IA, 32nd, 1906
Clark, T.C.		8th Iowa Cav.	25		1904 Feb 23	NE, 29th, 1905
Clark, Thad's S.	Pvt.	C, 25th Iowa Inf.	246	66	1898 Dec 10	IA, 25th, 1899
Clark, Thomas R.		H, 77th Ill. Inf.	239		1912 Nov 19	KS, 32nd, 1913
Clark, Thos.		G, 3rd Mo.	180		1922 Aug 9	KS, 42nd, 1923
Clark, Thos. A.	Corp.	G, 6th Iowa Inf.	235	54	1892 Apr 24	IA, 18th, 1892
Clark, Thos. C.		8th Iowa (died of pneumonia)	318	74	1904 Feb 22	NE, 29th, 1905
Clark, U.	Sergt.	G, 124th Ill. Inf.	358		1914 Dec 8	IA, 41st, 1915
Clark, W.B.		B, 26th Mass. Inf.	16		1925 Jun 20	KS, 45th, 1926
Clark, W.C.		H, 16th Ohio	18		1923 Feb 7	KS, 43rd, 1924
Clark, W.H.		Mo.	251		1919 Jun 20	KS, 39th, 1920
Clark, W.H.		E, 103rd Dragoons	83		1924 Aug 15	KS, 44th, 1925
Clark, W.H.H.		B, 33rd Mo.	51		1924 Dec 27	KS, 44th, 1925
Clark, W.S.	Capt.	E, 18th Maine	12	53	1891 Apr 26	IA, 18th, 1892
Clark, W.W.	Pvt.	D, 22nd Iowa Inf.	235		1921 Aug 10	IA, 48th, 1922
Clark, W.W.		I, 135th Ill.	25		1896 Apr	KS, 16th, 1897

*See Appendix A, B or C for roster of post names and locations.
†See Introduction for note regarding recording of death date.

101

Name	Rank	Company, Regiment or Ship	Post*	Age	Death Date†	Journal
Clark, W.W.		F, 29th Ind.	493		1910 Aug 10	KS, 30th, 1911
Clark, Walden		G, 16th Mo. (died of Bright's disease)	95	76	1920 Sep 9	NE, 45th, 1921
Clark, Walter M.		D, 12th Kans. Inf.	18		1916 Nov 1	KS, 36th, 1917
Clark, William	Pvt.	M, 11th Mo. Cav.	97	62	1894 Sep 24	IA, 21st, 1895
Clark, Wilson		G, 1st Iowa Cav. (died of general disability)	77	79	1916 Jun 4	NE, 41st, 1917
Clark, Wm.	Pvt.	M, 2nd Col. Cav.	502		1905 Sep 22	IA, 32nd, 1906
Clark, Wm.	Pvt.	C, 126th N.Y. Inf.	48		1916 Mar 23	IA, 43rd, 1917
Clark, Wm.	Pvt.	G, 27th Iowa Inf.	132		1926 Feb 1	IA, 53rd, 1927
Clark, Wm.		Mich. Art.	93		1926 Jul 18	KS, 46th, 1927
Clark, Wm. H.	Pvt.	G, 28th Wis. Inf.	26		1918 Mar 1	IA, 45th, 1919
Clark, Wm. H.		F, 83rd Ill.	18		1912 Jun 7	KS, 32nd, 1913
Clark, Wm. H.		G, 5th Iowa Inf. (died of asthma)	89	73	1916 Jan 7	NE, 41st, 1917
Clark, Wm. L.		I, 86th Ill. Inf. (died of nepthietis)	169	67	1905 Jun 12	NE, 30th, 1906
Clarke, Ben. S.		D, 7th Ill.	25		1908	NE, 33rd, 1909
Clarke, Edwin M.		K, 101st Ill.	68		1922 Feb 25	KS, 42nd, 1923
Clarke, G.W.		G, 6th Kans. Cav.	54		1899 Jun 29	KS, 19th, 1900
Clarke, H.D.		I, 24th Iowa Inf. (died of general debility)	77	79	1921 Jul 22	NE, 46th, 1922
Clarke, H.W.		E, 50th N.Y. Eng.	13	73	1920 Nov 19	NE, 45th, 1921
Clarke, W.J.			14		1883	KS, 3rd, 1884
Clarke, W.T.	2nd Lieut.	H, 1st Neb.	12	58	1890 Aug 16	IA, 17th, 1891
Clarke, Wm. M.		E, 10th Ill. Inf.	12		1902 Jul 23	KS, 22nd, 1903
Clarkson, R.P.	Sergt.	A, 12th Iowa Vols.	12		1905 Oct 3	IA, 32nd, 1906
Clarkson, Thaddeus S.	Adjt. Major	Battery A, 1st Ill. Art. 13th Ill. Cav. 3rd Ark. Cav. (see Appendix D)	110		1915 Jan 16	NE, 39th, 1915
Clarkson, Thomas	Pvt.	F, 198th Penn. Inf.	301	48	1895 Jan 6	IA, 21st, 1895
Clarno, Valentine		C, 3rd Wis. Inf.	11	67	1911 Mar 25	NE, 36th, 1912
Clarridge, N.P.	Pvt.	B, 19th Iowa Inf.	279	54	1898 Jan 18	IA, 24th, 1898
Classen, J.B.	Pvt.	D, 34th Ill. Inf.	94		1927 Mar 21	IA, 54th, 1928
Classer, Warren	1st Lieut.	C, 142nd Ind. Inf.	12		1904 Aug 16	IA, 31st, 1905
Claudell, J.T.		G, 81st Ind.	184		1914 Oct 21	KS, 34th, 1915
Claugh, A.W.	Pvt.	A, 12th Iowa Inf.	5		1913 Sep 27	IA, 40th, 1914
Claunch, Eli	Bugler	A, 7th Mo. Inf.	164		1913 Sep 20	IA, 40th, 1914
Claver, Charles	Pvt.	E, 6th Iowa Inf.	337		1915 Mar 15	IA, 42nd, 1916
Claver, Chas. H.	Pvt.	E, 6th Iowa Inf.	337		1916	IA, 43rd, 1917
Claver, Jas. W.	Pvt.	C, 8th Iowa Cav.	337		1912 Jun 22	IA, 39th, 1913
Clawson, A.N.	Musician	A, 129th Ind. Inf.	452		1916 Nov 13	IA, 43rd, 1917
Clawson, Henry			3		1908	NE, 33rd, 1909
Clay, C.H.		13th N.H. Inf. (died of pneumonia)	[187?]	64	1902 Mar	NE, 27th, 1903
Clay, D.A.	Pvt.	B, 24th Iowa Inf.	130		1915 Sep 21	IA, 42nd, 1916
Clay, F.M.		E, 3rd Ohio Cav.	111		1926 Oct 15	NE, 51st, 1927
Clay, G.W.		E, Ark. Art.	293		1924 May 10	KS, 44th, 1925
Clay, H.W.	Pvt.	K, 44th Ohio Inf.	7		1916 Aug 4	IA, 43rd, 1917
Clay, Henry		H, U.S.A.	453		1927 Dec 19	KS, 47th, 1928
Clay, Hiram	Pvt.	B, 7th Iowa Inf.	308		1905 Mar 19	IA, 32nd, 1906
Clay, J.W.		H, 197th Ohio	38		1917 May 19	KS, 37th, 1918
Clay, J.W.		H, 4th Minn.	293		1925 May 21	KS, 45th, 1926
Clay, Nicholas		F, 36th Ohio	142		1898 Aug 10	KS, 18th, 1899
Clay, Thomas		C, 111th U.S.A.	123		1896 Nov	KS, 16th, 1897
Clay, W.H.	Sergt.	K, 1st West Va.	180		1899	NE, 24th, 1900
Claybagh, Henry	Pvt.	A, 8th Iowa Cav.	248		1911 Jul 27	IA, 38th, 1912
Claybough, C.T.		I, 15th Mo. Cav.	85		1922 Feb 4	KS, 42nd, 1923
Claycomb, W.O.		A, 83rd Ill.	50		1912 Aug 2	KS, 32nd, 1913
Clayd, Benj.	Pvt.	A, 7th Iowa Cav.	497		1916 Mar 16	IA, 43rd, 1917
Claypool, J.W.		K, 70th Ind.	83		1897 May 22	KS, 17th, 1898
Claypool, J.W.		K, 143rd Ill. (died of broken hip)	35	77	1922 Jun 21	NE, 47th, 1923
Claypool, N.B.	Pvt.	K, 21st Ill. Inf.	81		1917 Jun 15	IA, 44th, 1918
Claypool, Phillip		C, 76th Ohio	46		1920 Dec 26	KS, 40th, 1921
Clayton, Alexander		G, 29th Ohio	89		1893 Jun 22	KS, 13th, 1894
Clayton, B.E.			185		1884	KS, 4th, 1885
Clayton, C.C.			309		1922	IA, 49th, 1923

*See Appendix A, B or C for roster of post names and locations.
†See Introduction for note regarding recording of death date.

Name	Rank	Company, Regiment or Ship	Post*	Age	Death Date†	Journal
Clayton, David	Pvt.	B, 5th Ohio Cav.	30		1928 Jun 14	IA, 55th, 1929
Clayton, I.R.		A, 151st Ill.	35		1932 Jun	NE, 57th, 1933
Clayton, John	QM	1st Kans.	52		1905 Aug 23	KS, 25th, 1906
Clayton, R.M.	Pvt.	B, 43rd Ohio	121		1901 Mar 13	IA, 28th, 1902
Clayton, T.C.	Pvt.	B, 4th Iowa Inf.	452		1911 Sep 21	IA, 38th, 1912
Cleal, Alfred		D, 5th Kans. Vol. Cav.	32		1908 Aug 14	KS, 28th, 1909
Clearman, L.A.		H, 2nd Iowa	8	87	1934 Nov 7	IA, 61st, 1935
Clearwater, Henry	Pvt.	G, 107th Ill. Inf.	392		1900-1901	IA, 27th, 1901
Clearwater, Henry	Pvt.	C, 10th Ill. Inf.	392		1900 Jun	IA, 27th, 1901
Clearwater, R.H.			17		1933 Oct 15	KS, 53rd, 1934
Cleary, Wm.	Pvt.	C, 18th Wis. Inf.	165		1918	IA, 45th, 1919
Cleaveland, A.B.		I, 15th Ill. Inf. (died of wound)	119		1893 Jul 19	NE, 18th, 1894
Cleaveland, Henry		H, 1st Ohio	8		1914 Mar 10	KS, 34th, 1915
Cleaveland, J.M.		C, 37th Ill.	180		1914 Mar 7	KS, 34th, 1915
Cleaver, J.J.	Pvt.	I, 8th Iowa Cav.	242		1911 Sep 2	IA, 38th, 1912
Cleer, C.H.		H, 8th Maine Inf. (died of Bright's disease)	147	78	1919 Oct 25	NE, 44th, 1920
Clegg, Sam'l		B, 185th Ohio Vol. Inf.	159		1899 Mar 27	KS, 19th, 1900
Cleighton, J.W.		K, 73rd Ind.	293		1925 Jan 5	KS, 45th, 1926
Cleinstaber, George F.		C, 3rd Ill. Cav.	85		1923 Feb 25	KS, 43rd, 1924
Cleland, C.G.	Pvt.	G, 7th Wis. Res.	39	49	1893 May 13	IA, 20th, 1894
Cleland, Robert		G, 194th N.Y. Inf. (former member of department; died at Bellwood)	83		1939 Jul 11	NE, 64th, 1940
Clellan, Andrew S.		C, 185th Ohio	58		1922 Jul 21	KS, 42nd, 1923
Clem, H.C.		1st Miss. (Colored)	129		1918 Nov 29	KS, 38th, 1919
Clem, Wm. R.C.		Regular Army	4		1887 Feb 20	KS, 7th, 1888
Clemens, Daniel		H, 2nd Neb. Cav.	44		1895 Jan	KS, 15th, 1896
Clemens, J.					1885	KS, 5th, 1886
Clemenson, Clem.		F, 10th Kans. Inf.	130		1901 Aug 8	KS, 21st, 1902
Clement, Allen		B, 12th U.S.C.	62		1896 Dec 15	KS, 16th, 1897
Clement, George H.		I, 9th Ind. Cav.	452	93	1938 Apr 4	IA, 64th, 1938
Clement, J.W.	Pvt.	D, 9th Penn. Inf.	356		1897 Dec	IA, 24th, 1898
Clements, C.		A, 2nd Mass. Art. (died at National Military Home)	380		1888	KS, 8th, 1889
Clements, D.D.			311		1917 Sep 10	KS, 37th, 1918
Clements, Geo. W.		D, 33rd Wis. Inf.	130		1934 Sep 23	KS, 54th, 1935
Clements, Isaac			417		1917	IA, 44th, 1918
Clements, John	Corp.	C, 21st Iowa Inf.	259		1900 Oct 21	IA, 27th, 1901
Clements, Joshua D.		A, 7th Ind. Inf. (died at Smith County, Kans.; buried at Fairview Cemetery)	45		1894 Jul 29	KS, 14th, 1895
Clements, Richard	Pvt.	K, 103rd Ind. Inf.	107		1906 Oct 1	IA, 33rd, 1907
Clements, W.H.		D, 39th Ill.	25		1922 Jun 10	NE, 52nd, 1928
Clemer, T.A.		C, 91st Ohio	356		1912 Oct 15	KS, 32nd, 1913
Clemmor, C.L.		I, 49th N.Y.	294		1905	KS, 25th, 1906
Cleveland, Aaron E.	Pvt.	E, 1st Wis. Cav.	55	92	1939 Jan 7	IA, 65th, 1939
Cleveland, B.F.		A, 3rd N.Y. Lt. Art.	192		1894 May 31	NE, 19th, 1895
Cleveland, Chas.	Fireman	U.S.S. Dak.	86		1924 May 6	IA, 51st, 1925
Cleveland, D.W.	Pvt.	A, 21st Iowa Inf.	78		1910 Aug 29	IA, 37th, 1911
Cleveland, David H.		H, — Mich.	293		1917 Jan 26	KS, 37th, 1918
Cleveland, E.		I & F, 14th Mich. Cav.	110	86	1905 Aug 29	NE, 30th, 1906
Cleveland, James		2nd Maine	18		1905 Jun 11	KS, 25th, 1906
Cleveland, K.E.		H, 157th Ill. Inf.	25	69	1917 Aug 20	NE, 42nd, 1918
Cleveland, S.J.		I, 153rd Ill. Inf. (died of pneumonia)	9	78	1921 Dec 24	NE, 46th, 1922
Cleveland, Wm. H.	Pvt.	E, 27th Ill. Inf.	52		1910 Sep 12	IA, 37th, 1911
Cleveland, Wm. P.		A, 1st Ohio Cav.	25		1917 Jan 1	KS, 37th, 1918
Clevenger, William A.		C, 2nd Kans. Cav.	200		1905 Nov 27	KS, 25th, 1906
Clever, J.L.		K, 26th Wis. (died of heart trouble)	78	78	1918 Mar 17	NE, 43rd, 1919
Clewell, J.D.	Pvt.		96		1920 Sep 10	IA, 47th, 1921
Clews, John		I, 7th Penn. Cav.	82		1911 Feb 9	KS, 31st, 1912
Click, B.F.		F, 8th Ohio Inf.	3		1902 Dec 31	KS, 22nd, 1903
Click, R.C.		C, 2nd Colo. Cav.	81		1913 May 8	KS, 33rd, 1914
Clifford, E.K.	Sergt.	K, 29th Wis. Inf.	489		1911 Oct 18	IA, 38th, 1912
Clifford, Pearson N.		I, 27th Ky. Inf.	191		1916 May 27	KS, 36th, 1917

*See Appendix A, B or C for roster of post names and locations.
†See Introduction for note regarding recording of death date.
103

Name	Rank	Company, Regiment or Ship	Post*	Age	Death Date†	Journal
Clifford, Wm. M.		B, 11th Iowa Inf.	292		1907 Nov 29	IA, 34th, 1908
Clift, J.W.			85		1920 Apr 28	KS, 40th, 1921
Clifton, Silas		A, 31st Ind.	1		1923 Apr 23	KS, 43rd, 1924
Clikinmallie, Peter		F, 53rd Ill.	8		1893 Oct 29	KS, 13th, 1894
Clime, H.M.		H, 186th Penn. Inf.	250		1930 Dec 31	KS, 50th, 1931
Cline, A.J.			122		1925 Sep 9	IA, 52nd, 1926
Cline, C.R.		D, 24th Ky. Inf.	97		1916 Mar 26	KS, 36th, 1917
Cline, D.O.	Pvt.	42nd Ill. Inf.	167		1915 Jul 14	IA, 42nd, 1916
Cline, D.W.			32		1911 Aug 9	KS, 31st, 1912
Cline, Daniel		A, 72nd Ind.	4		1909 Sep	KS, 29th, 1910
Cline, Daniel I.		H, 75th Ohio Inf.	32		1899 Apr 18	KS, 19th, 1900
Cline, E.M.	Pvt.	D, 32nd Iowa Inf.	67		1921 Sep 6	IA, 48th, 1922
Cline, George W.		A, 4th Mo.	225		1925 Dec 19	KS, 45th, 1926
Cline, H.M.		H, 186th Penn. Inf.	250		1940[1929?], Dec 41	KS, 49th, 1930
Cline, Harlow		E, 2nd Kans.	1		1918 Jun 19	KS, 38th, 1919
Cline, Henry		A, 19th Iowa	378		1923	KS, 43rd, 1924
Cline, J.H.		E, 38th Ind. Inf. (died of disability)	84	73	1912 May 13	NE, 37th, 1913
Cline, J.J.		C, — Mo. Cav.	297		1912 Feb 23	KS, 32nd, 1913
Cline, J.L.		A, 5th Penn. Art. (died of Bright's disease)	13	68	1895 Jul 15	NE, 20th, 1896
Cline, Jacob		H, 33rd Iowa Inf.	51		1892 Jun 19	NE, 17th, 1893
Cline, James L.		C, 29th Ind. Inf.	6		1891 Oct 12	KS, 11th, 1892
Cline, John			127		1922 Jul 1	KS, 42nd, 1923
Cline, Joseph				91	1937 Jul 5	IA, 64th, 1938
Cline, Thomas O.		G, 7th West Va.	38		1916 May 28	KS, 36th, 1917
Cline, William H.		A, 107th Ill.	69	90	1934 Dec 25	IA, 61st, 1935
Cline, Wm.	Pvt.	D, 32nd Iowa Inf.	67		1909 Oct 2	IA, 36th, 1910
Cline, Wm. H.		A, 107th Ill. Inf.	69	90	1934 Dec 25	IA, 62nd, 1936
Cline, Wm. R.	Pvt.	F, 4th Iowa Inf.	55	62	1893 Jul 1	IA, 20th, 1894
Clinebell, Wm. L.		9th Mo. Cav.	500		1923	KS, 43rd, 1924
Cling, C.J.	Sergt.	C, 43rd Ill. Inf.	375		1911 Jun 5	IA, 38th, 1912
Clingan, R.L.		G, 13th Iowa Inf.	174		3rd quarter 1883	IA, 10th, 1884
Clinger, Alfred B.		I, 128th Ind.	91	76	1922 Oct 5	NE, 47th, 1923
Clingman, Stephen		E, 146th Ill.	10		1932 Aug 1	NE, 57th, 1933
Clinkenbeard, Thos. L.		D, 1st Ky.	1		1909 Mar 23	KS, 29th, 1910
Clinkinbeard, J.W.	Pvt.	D, 9th Iowa Cav.	7	86	1931 Jun 3	IA, 58th, 1932
Clinton, Madison M.		B, 1st Mo. Eng.	17		1914 Dec 1	KS, 34th, 1915
Clinton, Patrick	Fireman	Navy, South Atlantic Squadron	302	54	1899 May 25	IA, 26th, 1900
Clippenger, John	Pvt.	C, 22nd Iowa	16		1907 Sep 19	IA, 34th, 1908
Clippinger, Geo.			105		1921	KS, 41st, 1922
Clithert, James		C, 57th Ill.	113		1911 Jan 6	KS, 31st, 1912
Clock, H.C.	Capt.	C, 6th Iowa Inf.	81		1919 Sep 3	IA, 46th, 1920
Clockentagel, Fred	Pvt.	E, 10th Iowa Inf.	112 .		1931 Feb 11	IA, 58th, 1932
Cloe, E.B.		I, 151st Ohio	46		1905 Jan 3	KS, 25th, 1906
Clogston, J.B.		H, 11th Kans.	50		1902 Feb 18	KS, 22nd, 1903
Clogston, Lewis		C, 2nd Kans.	112		1896 Jul 28	KS, 16th, 1897
Clogston, Thos. P.	Sergt.	F, 45th Ill. Inf.	206		1909 Oct 17	IA, 36th, 1910
Clore, George		B, 1st Mo.	255		1925 Oct 10	KS, 45th, 1926
Clore, Henry		F, 2nd Mo.	255		1926 May 7	KS, 46th, 1927
Close, F.L.		G, 18th Ill.	53		1935 Apr 20	KS, 55th, 1936
Close, John A.			4		1904 Apr	NE, 29th, 1905
Close, John W.	Pvt.	I, 36th Iowa Inf.	122		1915 Nov 2	IA, 42nd, 1916
Close, Levi		A, 55th Ohio	130		1905 Nov 20	KS, 25th, 1906
Close, W.B.		M, 2nd Ill. Cav.	302		1900 Nov 14	KS, 20th, 1901
Clossen, S.C.	Pvt.	B, 2nd Iowa Inf.	2		1927 Dec 27	IA, 54th, 1928
Clothier, A.		I, 115th N.Y.	354	73	1911 Mar 3	NE, 36th, 1912
Clothier, S.		G, 2nd Ill. (died of heart trouble)	301	75	1915 Feb 26	NE, 41st, 1917
Clothier, Solomon		G, 2nd Ill. Lt. Art. (died of heart failure)	301	74	1916 Feb 26	NE, 40th, 1916
Clothier, Theodore	Pvt.	G, 31st Iowa Inf.	191		1916 Sep 23	IA, 43rd, 1917
Cloton, Holmes W.		D, Signal Corps, Ohio (not a member of the G.A.R.)	18		1912 Aug 21	KS, 32nd, 1913
Clouch, C.C.		C, 13th Kans.	191		1897 Oct 17	KS, 17th, 1898

*See Appendix A, B or C for roster of post names and locations.
†See Introduction for note regarding recording of death date.

Name	Rank	Company, Regiment or Ship	Post*	Age	Death Date†	Journal
Cloud, A.			118		1st quarter 1884	IA, 10th, 1884
Cloud, A.P.	Corp.	E, 11th Ind. Inf.	434		1920 Mar 8	IA, 47th, 1921
Cloud, Thomas		C, 119th Ind. Cav. (died at Leavenworth, Kans.)	293		1892 Nov 21	KS, 12th, 1893
Cloud, Thos.	Pvt.		156		1920	IA, 47th, 1921
Clough, J.E.	Pvt.	D, 74th Ind. Inf.	261		1925 Apr 22	IA, 52nd, 1926
Clough, W.A.	Pvt.	B, 4th Ohio Cav.	22		1920 Mar 26	IA, 47th, 1921
Cloughwell, Thos.		G, 1st Conn. Inf. (died of paralysis of bowels)	96		1893 Apr	NE, 18th, 1894
Clouse, George N.		D, 4th Iowa Cav.	250		1914 Jul 15	KS, 34th, 1915
Clouse, George W.		K, 129th Ind.	105		1897 Dec	KS, 17th, 1898
Clover, M.A.		H, 28th Ill.	129		1933 Aug 3	KS, 53rd, 1934
Clow, Nelson B.	Pvt.	F, 34th Iowa Inf.	63		1918 Jun 12	IA, 45th, 1919
Clune, Thomas	Pvt.	A, 8th Iowa Cav.	15		1930 Jul 6	IA, 57th, 1931
Clutter, Geo. W.		4th Iowa Cav.	110		1908 Dec 9	NE, 33rd, 1909
Clutter, George W.		C, 21st Iowa Inf. (died of pneumonia)	129	89	1915 Jun 14	NE, 41st, 1917
Clymer, J.V.			17		1902 Jul 9	KS, 22nd, 1903
Clymer, Peter	Pvt.	D, 13th U.S. Inf.	296		1907 May 19	IA, 34th, 1908
Coap, Nathan P.		K, 161st Ohio	148		1897 Dec 20	KS, 17th, 1898
Coater, George W.		E, 25th Mo.	17		1924 Dec 16	KS, 44th, 1925
Coates, H.J.		Bat. L, 5th Wis. (died of heart failure)	107	70	1910 Dec 22	NE, 35th, 1911
Coates, J.S.	Pvt.	C, 27th Iowa	72		1905 Nov 8	IA, 32nd, 1906
Coates, J.W.			7		1926 Mar 3	IA, 53rd, 1927
Coates, S.K.		I, 11th Ill.	108	87	1934 Jul 8	IA, 61st, 1935
Coats, J.J.	Pvt.	B, 28th Iowa Inf.	145		1917 Mar 2	IA, 44th, 1918
Cobb, A.L.	Pvt.	K, 4th Iowa Inf.	10		1915 Jul 11	IA, 42nd, 1916
Cobb, Abner		C, 38th Ohio Inf.	477		1914 Dec 6	KS, 34th, 1915
Cobb, Amasa	Gen.	5th & 52nd Wis.	25		1905 Jul 6	NE, 31st, 1907
Cobb, Amasa	Col.	5th & 52nd Wis.	25		1905 Jul 6	NE, 30th, 1906
Cobb, Daniel			94		1917 Jul 28	IA, 44th, 1918
Cobb, E.C.	Pvt.	I, 12th Iowa Inf.	2		1919 Mar 12	IA, 46th, 1920
Cobb, E.K.		B, 57th Ill. (died of gallstones)	22	65	1908 Oct 22	NE, 33rd, 1909
Cobb, Eliott A.	Pvt.	A, 55th Ohio Inf.	197		1925 Jan 12	IA, 52nd, 1926
Cobb, Geo.	Pvt.	A, 12th Iowa Inf.	154		1920 Jan 15	IA, 47th, 1921
Cobb, Jared A.	Pvt.	I, 24th Iowa Inf.	101		1929	IA, 56th, 1930
Cobb, Loran	Sergt.	D, 33rd Wis. Inf.	298		1904 Apr 25	IA, 31st, 1905
Cobb, S.M.	Sergt. M.	35th Iowa Inf.	231	74	1892 Dec 12	IA, 19th, 1893
Cobb, W.	Pvt.	F, 29th Iowa Inf.	10		1922 Feb 12	IA, 49th, 1923
Cobb, Wm. H.	Pvt.	C, 126th Ill. Inf.	110	57	1895 Apr 18	IA, 22nd, 1896
Cobbs, S.C.		H, 6th Mo. State Militia	50		1908 Aug	KS, 28th, 1909
Cobe, F.A.		F, 38th Ohio	132		1912 Sep 20	KS, 32nd, 1913
Cobilena, Louis	Pvt.	K, 2nd R.I. Inf.	2		1912 Jan 26	IA, 39th, 1913
Cobin, James			100		1886	KS, 6th, 1887
Cobun, Marcellus H.		B, 14th West Va.	175		1916 May 16	KS, 36th, 1917
Coburn, F.D.		F, 135th Ill.	1		1924 May 10	KS, 44th, 1925
Coburn, F.J.			235		1915 Aug 26	IA, 42nd, 1916
Coburn, J.S.	Pvt.	K, 13th Ky. Inf.	29		1928 Apr 28	IA, 55th, 1929
Coburn, John	Pvt.	D, 22nd Wis. Inf.	94	89	1931 Jun 14	IA, 58th, 1932
Coburn, Wm.		A, 14th Iowa Inf.	110		1908 Jul 28	NE, 33rd, 1909
Cochran, Alexander		A, 12th Ill. Inf.	17		1912 Oct 21	KS, 32nd, 1913
Cochran, Chas.	Sergt.	F, 12th Kans.	314		1916	KS, 36th, 1917
Cochran, Chas. M.			294		1923 Oct 12	KS, 43rd, 1924
Cochran, F.P.		E, 15th Ohio	1		1917 Sep 26	KS, 37th, 1918
Cochran, Henry		C, 184th N.Y.	23	57	1907 Sep 12	NE, 32nd, 1908
Cochran, J.B.		A, 142nd Ohio Inf.	41		1902 Nov 23	KS, 22nd, 1903
Cochran, J.R.S.		D, 13th Iowa (died of heart failure)	25		1916 Jul 21	NE, 41st, 1917
Cochran, James		G, 59th Ohio Inf. (died of paralysis)	309	71	1897 Nov 4	NE, 22nd, 1898
Cochran, Lewis	Corp.	E, 33rd Iowa Inf.	40	43	1890 Nov	IA, 18th, 1892
Cochran, M.B.		L, 16th Ill. Cav.	17		1934 Sep 20	KS, 54th, 1935
Cochran, W.B.		H, 25th Ill. Cav.	56		1914 Nov	KS, 34th, 1915
Cochran, William		H, 14th Ill. Cav.	42		1917 Apr 5	KS, 37th, 1918
Cochran, William C.		D, 13th Iowa	147		1924 Nov 10	KS, 44th, 1925

*See Appendix A, B or C for roster of post names and locations.
†See Introduction for note regarding recording of death date.
105

Name	Rank	Company, Regiment or Ship	Post*	Age	Death Date†	Journal
Cochran, Wm. F.		G, 102nd Ill. Inf.	69		1913 Feb 10	KS, 32nd, 1913
Cochrane, M.B.	Pvt.	I, 1st Iowa Cav.	8	70	1898 May 29	IA, 25th, 1899
Cochron, J.T.	Capt.	E, 33rd Iowa Inf.	40		1910 Dec 8	IA, 37th, 1911
Cochrun, Thomas	Corp.	G, 4th Iowa Inf.	316		1905 Sep 11	IA, 32nd, 1906
Cockerhaven, J.P.	Pvt.		512		1921 Feb 2	IA, 48th, 1922
Cocklin, Abraham		I, 13th Iowa (died of Bright's disease)	111	75	1917	NE, 42nd, 1918
Cocklin, Wm. L.	Pvt.	I, 23rd Iowa Inf.	9		1920[1919?] Sep 17	IA, 46th, 1920
Cockrell, Geo. C.		97th Ill. Inf. (died of old age)	110	75	1912 Apr 4	NE, 37th, 1913
Cockrell, Jesse		C, 122nd Ill.	171		1920 Dec 1	KS, 41st, 1922
Cockriel, Morgan		E, 16th Kans.	238		1924 Feb 21	KS, 44th, 1925
Cockwell, H.		D, 29th Iowa	271		1903-1904	IA, 30th, 1904
Cocrayn, W.J.	Pvt.	E, 15th Iowa Inf.	5		1901 Mar 23	IA, 27th, 1901
Coddington, Daniel S.		B, 18th Mo. Inf. H, 46th Iowa Inf.	1		1886	KS, 6th, 1887
Coddington, J.D.		F, 18th Mo.	71		1925 May 2	KS, 45th, 1926
Coddington, John	Pvt.	H, 34th Ill. Inf.	503		1904 May 11	IA, 31st, 1905
Coddington, John		F, 37th Wis.	118		1930 Jul 24	NE, 55th, 1931
Coddington, Thos. S.		C, 54th Ohio Vol. Inf.	1		1909 May 2	KS, 29th, 1910
Coder, Ellis		F, 106th Penn. Inf.	7		1926 May 5	NE, 51st, 1927
Coder, Jacob F.		D, 36th Iowa	31		1916 Jul 16	KS, 36th, 1917
Coder, Simon		I, 125th Penn.	13		1896 May 8	KS, 16th, 1897
Codling, William	Corp.	E, 5th Iowa Inf.	367	72	1894 Oct 29	IA, 21st, 1895
Codlins, Robert	Pvt.	I, 24th Iowa Inf.	74		1900 Dec 25	IA, 27th, 1901
Cody, A.O.		F, 39th Ind. Inf.	96		1918 Jul 26	KS, 38th, 1919
Coe, Edward	Musician	A, 105th Ill. Inf.	501		1912 Sep 2	IA, 39th, 1913
Coe, G.T.			173		1884	KS, 4th, 1885
Coe, H.P.		K, 16th Iowa Inf.	15		1900 Aug 30	KS, 21st, 1902
Coe, H.P.		K, 16th Iowa Inf.	148		1900 Aug 30	KS, 20th, 1901
Coe, Henry L.		L, 16th Kans.	18		1910 Jul 5	KS, 30th, 1911
Coe, I.S.		C, 33rd Mo. Inf.	51		1908 Apr 18	KS, 28th, 1909
Coe, Jas. H.	Capt.	I, 23rd Iowa Inf.	201		1889 Apr 22	IA, 17th, 1891
Coe, Justine E.		H, 11th Iowa Inf.	231	92	1937 Jul 19	IA, 64th, 1938
Coe, Samuel	Pvt.	D, 10th Iowa Inf.	67		1910 Dec 20	IA, 37th, 1911
Coe, W.O.		J, 4th Ill. Cav. (died of pneumonia)	94	92	1922 Sep 10	NE, 47th, 1923
Coen, P.H.		C, 16th Ill.	447		1914 Dec 27	KS, 34th, 1915
Coen, W.S.		5th Iowa Cav.	69		1900 Jan 25	IA, 27th, 1901
Coffee, Robert	Corp.	A, 93rd Ill. Inf.	154		1920 Apr 22	IA, 47th, 1921
Coffee, W.H.H.		G, 13th Ind. Inf.	64		1908 Sep 7	KS, 28th, 1909
Coffeen, H.L.	Pvt.	D, 43rd Wis. Inf.	168		1911 Sep 17	IA, 38th, 1912
Coffeen, Seth		D, 10th Ind.	12		1934 Nov	IA, 61st, 1935
Coffeen, W.G.		C, 88th Ill.	46		1921 Jan 15	KS, 41st, 1922
Coffern, David		B, 5th Wis.	3		1922 Feb 15	KS, 42nd, 1923
Coffey, William B.		F, 5th Conn. Inf.	25		1911 Sep 21	NE, 36th, 1912
Coffield, A.H.		B, 101st Ill.	129		1919 May 23	KS, 39th, 1920
Coffield, B.H.	Pvt.	C, 116th Ohio Inf.	454		1913 Dec 24	IA, 40th, 1914
Coffield, J.C.		H, 9th Kans. Cav.	51		1923 Aug	KS, 43rd, 1924
Coffin, A.		A, 23rd Iowa Inf.	110		1887	KS, 7th, 1888
Coffin, E.	Pvt.	H, 8th Iowa Inf.	40		1920 May 3	IA, 47th, 1921
Coffin, Geo.		I, 101st Ill. Inf.	55		1900 Jun 12	KS, 20th, 1901
Coffin, J.L., M.D.	Pvt. Capt.	G, 2nd Wis. Inf. D, 10th Wis. Inf.	40	77	1893 Dec 28	IA, 20th, 1894
Coffin, Jno. L.	Pvt.	E, 23rd Ind. Inf.	40	53	1885 Jul 16	IA, 14th, 1888
Coffin, John	Capt.	B, U.S. Inf.	40		2nd quarter 1885	IA, 12th, 1886
Coffin, John	Pvt.	H, 15th Ill. Inf.	193		1896 Mar 17	IA, 23rd, 1897
Coffin, Jos. Raymond	Pvt.	D, 38th Ind. Inf. (at large)	20	97	1943 Apr 10	IA, 69th, 1943
Coffin, L.S.	Chaplain	32nd Iowa Inf.	236		1915 Jan 15	IA, 42nd, 1916
Coffin, Michael	Pvt.	D, 8th Iowa Inf.	1		1903 Aug 14	IA, 30th, 1904
Coffin, Warren D.	Pvt.	B, 7th Ill. Inf. L, 7th Ill. Cav.	165	58	1887 Dec 16	IA, 15th, 1889
Coffin, Wm.		C, 37th Iowa Inf.	45		1927 Feb 14	IA, 54th, 1928
Coffland, B.W.		G, 90th Ohio	453		1905	KS, 25th, 1906
Coffman, A.J.		B, 97th Ind.	255		1914 May 7	KS, 34th, 1915

*See Appendix A, B or C for roster of post names and locations.
†See Introduction for note regarding recording of death date.

Name	Rank	Company, Regiment or Ship	Post*	Age	Death Date†	Journal
Coffman, Andrew J.	Pvt.	G, 10th Iowa Inf.	275		1907 Aug 7	IA, 34th, 1908
Coffman, E.C.		G, 11th Ind.	178		1913 Jun 5	KS, 33rd, 1914
Coffman, Isaac		A, 22nd Ind. Inf.	35		1886	KS, 6th, 1887
Coffman, J.H.	Pvt.	A, 16th Penn. Cav.	56		1916	IA, 43rd, 1917
Coffman, J.S.	Pvt.		316		1910 Apr	IA, 37th, 1911
Coffman, Jacob	Corp.	L, 2nd Neb. Cav. (died of cancer)	45	50	1885 Oct 20	NE, 10th, 1886
Coffman, Jesse H.		B, 73rd Ill.	55		1911 Sep 18	KS, 31st, 1912
Coffman, Peter		A, 5th Ohio	35		1930 Jan 16	KS, 50th, 1931
Coffman, Samuel		B, 28th Penn.	46		1929 Sep 15	KS, 49th, 1930
Coffman, Victor H.		34th Iowa	262		1908	NE, 33rd, 1909
Coffman, W.A.		9th Ind. Cav.	108	90	1936 Mar 16	IA, 63rd, 1937
Coffman, W.A.		9th Ind. Cav.		90	1936 Mar 15	IA, 62nd, 1936
Coffman, W.H.		I, 11th Kans. Cav.	147		1921 Aug 10	KS, 41st, 1922
Coffman, Wm.	Pvt.	E, 34th Iowa Inf.	190		1924 Jan 13	IA, 51st, 1925
Coghlan, John		K, 63rd N.Y. Inf. (died at National Home)	380		1895 Sep	KS, 15th, 1896
Cogil, Moses Y.		F, 28th Ill.	32		1927	NE, 52nd, 1928
Coglyn, C.H.		B, 88th Ill. Inf.	31		1900 Apr	IA, 27th, 1901
Cogswell, Louis S.		E, 18th Ill.	85		1908 Mar 26	KS, 28th, 1909
Cohnan, Howard M.		A, 55th Ohio (died of Bright's disease)	139	63	1900 Nov 5	NE, 25th, 1901
Colbert, J.L.		C, 9th Ill.	100		1913 Nov	KS, 33rd, 1914
Colbert, Jesse			188		1909	IA, 36th, 1910
Colburn, Amos	Pvt.	D, 10th N.Y. Art.	68		1919 Apr 6	IA, 46th, 1920
Colburn, C.G.		E, 112th Ill.	257		1914 Jul 4	KS, 34th, 1915
Colburn, Everett		G, 11th Kans. (died at Paine County, O.T.; buried on his claim)	100		1894 Sep 10	KS, 14th, 1895
Colburn, H.	Pvt.	K, 83rd Penn. Inf.	22		1909 Sep 21	IA, 36th, 1910
Colburn, H.C.		G, 89th Ind.	464		1908 Aug	KS, 28th, 1909
Colburn, W.F.	Lieut.	K, 153rd Ill. Inf.	68		1914 Mar	IA, 41st, 1915
Colby, A.	Pvt.	18th Ind. Battery	267		1908 Dec 15	IA, 35th, 1909
Colby, H.M.	Pvt.	G, 8th Mich.	111		1921 Dec 28	IA, 48th, 1922
Colby, J.P.	Pvt.	H, 13th Wis. Inf.	357		1901 Feb 5	IA, 27th, 1901
Colcord, E.H.	Pvt.	K, 112th Ill. Inf.	98		1916 Dec 4	IA, 43rd, 1917
Colcord, Geo. F.	Pvt.	G, 63rd Ohio Inf.	219		1902 Feb 9	IA, 29th, 1903
Cold, J.F.G.	Pvt.	G, 177th Ohio Inf.	71		1910 Nov 2	IA, 37th, 1911
Coldren, E.V.	Musician	10th Iowa	1		1913 Jul 17	KS, 33rd, 1914
Coldren, J.N.	Lieut.	A, 20th Iowa	8		1905 Jun 28	IA, 32nd, 1906
Cole, A.G.		D, 145th Penn.	69		1918 Apr 23	KS, 38th, 1919
Cole, A.J.	Pvt.	C, 48th Wis.	142		1907 Mar 13	IA, 34th, 1908
Cole, Andrew C.		G, 2nd Penn. Cav.	132		1917 Jul 12	KS, 37th, 1918
Cole, Charles		D, 4th N.Y. Hvy. Art.	274		1916 Jun	KS, 36th, 1917
Cole, Chester C.	Pvt.	E, 5th Iowa Cav.	452		1916 May 13	IA, 43rd, 1917
Cole, D.R.		3rd Ind. Cav.	28		1918 Mar 1	KS, 38th, 1919
Cole, David P.		F, 123rd Ill. Inf.	25		1917 Oct 4	KS, 37th, 1918
Cole, E.B.	Pvt.	I, 9th Iowa Vol. Inf.	216		1923 Apr 12	IA, 50th, 1924
Cole, Edgar			431		1913 Sep 15	IA, 40th, 1914
Cole, Elijah H.	Pvt.	B, 28th Iowa Inf.	34		1911 Nov 22	IA, 38th, 1912
Cole, Elisha	Lieut.	4th U.S. Art.	117		1897 Jul 22	KS, 17th, 1898
Cole, Erwin R.		A, 55th Ohio	12		1911 May 1	KS, 31st, 1912
Cole, F.M.		F, 6th Penn.	235		1890	KS, 10th, 1891
Cole, G.L.		E, 29th Iowa Inf. (died of old age)	35	82	1910 Aug 28	NE, 35th, 1911
Cole, George Spencer			99		1916 May 14	KS, 36th, 1917
Cole, H.C.	Pvt.	G, 48th Wis.	22		1922 Feb 7	IA, 49th, 1923
Cole, Harris	Pvt.	C & E, 34th Ill. Inf. (at large)	12	92	1941 Jun 17	IA, 67th, 1941
Cole, Henry E.	Pvt.	B, 28th Iowa Inf.	34	58	1895 Apr 20	IA, 22nd, 1896
Cole, Henry M.	Pvt.	D, 40th Iowa Inf.	305		1919	IA, 46th, 1920
Cole, Ira L.	Pvt.	D, 21st Iowa Inf.	259		1902 May 7	IA, 29th, 1903
Cole, Irving		B, 123rd Ohio	85		1920 Dec 23	KS, 41st, 1922
Cole, J.	Pvt.	B, 9th Iowa Cav.	10		1920 Jan 15	IA, 47th, 1921
Cole, J.N.		F, 6th & 3rd West Va.	32		1918 Aug 24	KS, 38th, 1919
Cole, J.S.	Pvt.	H, 15th Iowa Inf.	54		1906 Sep 6	IA, 33rd, 1907
Cole, J.W.		A, 12th Kans.	54		1919 Aug 2	KS, 39th, 1920
Cole, James F.		K, 24th Mo.	134		1897 Aug 12	KS, 17th, 1898

*See Appendix A, B or C for roster of post names and locations.
†See Introduction for note regarding recording of death date.

Name	Rank	Company, Regiment or Ship	Post*	Age	Death Date†	Journal
Cole, Jesse	Pvt.	8th Wis. Inf.	94		1913	IA, 40th, 1914
Cole, John			236		1921 May 28	KS, 41st, 1922
Cole, John F.		H, 18th Minn. Indiana (died of old age, general debility)	27	77	1900 Jul 15	NE, 25th, 1901
Cole, John W.		B, 140th Ind.	129		1913 Feb 18	KS, 32nd, 1913
Cole, Joseph		K, 1st Kans.	85		1890	KS, 10th, 1891
Cole, L.W.F.		19th N.Y. Bat. (cause of death: heart)	195	65	1901 Jul	NE, 26th, 1902
Cole, M.G.	Pvt.	G, 1st Wis. Cav.	77		1902 Dec 4	IA, 29th, 1903
Cole, N.A.	Pvt.		31		1920 Feb 20	IA, 47th, 1921
Cole, P.B.	Pvt.	G, 96th Ill. Inf.	3		1923 Nov 1	IA, 50th, 1924
Cole, Richard		107th Ill. Inf.	16		1902 Jun 19	KS, 22nd, 1903
Cole, S.C.		A, 123rd Ohio	37		1927 Jun	NE, 52nd, 1928
Cole, S.G.	Capt.	136th N.Y. Inf.	267		1906 Nov 17	IA, 33rd, 1907
Cole, Samuel		H, 55th Penn. Inf.	54	93	1938 Mar 11	IA, 64th, 1938
Cole, T.O.		K, 96th Ohio	52		1921 Jan 17	KS, 41st, 1922
Cole, T.R.	Pvt.	B, 36th Iowa Inf.	49		1920 Apr 14	IA, 47th, 1921
Cole, Thos.			89		1918 Oct 18	KS, 38th, 1919
Cole, W.	Pvt.	F, 85th Ind. Inf.	10		1925 May 3	IA, 52nd, 1926
Cole, Wm. M.	Pvt.	D, 20th Iowa Inf.	327	68	1889 Dec 3	IA, 16th, 1890
Cole, Wm. W.		E, 12th Kans.	12		1906 Dec 10	KS, 26th, 1907
Colegrove, H.P.		S.M., 44th Ind.	52		1920	KS, 40th, 1921
Coleman, A.D.	Drummer	A, 18th Iowa Inf.	40		1906	IA, 33rd, 1907
Coleman, Amos		D, 1st Neb. Cav.	3		1932 Mar 4	NE, 57th, 1933
Coleman, Asa		2nd Neb.	120		1927 Apr 15	NE, 51st, 1927
Coleman, D.F.	Pvt.	K, 8th Iowa Inf.	153		1911 Sep 21	IA, 38th, 1912
Coleman, Daniel	Pvt.	C, 26th Iowa Inf.	401	53	1886 Jul 7	IA, 13th, 1887
Coleman, Ellis C.		F, 31st N.J. Inf. (died of pneumonia)	149	86	1924 Nov 24	NE, 49th, 1925
Coleman, Geo.		I, 70th Ind.	17		1928 Sep 9	KS, 48th, 1929
Coleman, Henry			32		1887	KS, 7th, 1888
Coleman, James	Pvt.	I, 180th Ohio Inf.	206		1918 Nov 30	IA, 45th, 1919
Coleman, James		K, 13th Kans.	93		1909 Jan 27	KS, 29th, 1910
Coleman, John N.	Pvt.	G, 44th Ill. Inf. K, 95th Ill. Inf. (at large)	104	94	1939 Mar 7	IA, 65th, 1939
Coleman, R.M.J.	Pvt.	K, 113th Ohio Inf.	7		1929 Feb 7	IA, 56th, 1930
Coleman, Richard E.		D, 136th Ill. Inf. (Lincoln)			1947 Mar 16	NE, 73rd, 1949
Coleman, S.A.		L, 9th Penn. Cav.	25	64	1903 Mar 15	NE, 28th, 1904
Coleman, Stephen	Pvt.	I, 7th Iowa Cav.	22		1911 Mar 25	IA, 38th, 1912
Coleman, T.M.		A.S. Stevenson's staff, Ohio (died at National Home)	36		1895 Sep	KS, 15th, 1896
Coleman, W.F.	Asst. Surg.	17th Iowa Inf.	168	61	1886 Apr 21	IA, 13th, 1887
Coleman, Wesley		F, 33rd Ind. Inf. (died at Ottawa)	18		1895 Sep	KS, 15th, 1896
Coleman, Wesley		A, 68th Ill. Inf.	428		1912 Oct 30	KS, 32nd, 1913
Coleman, William		G, 79th Kans.	321		1909 Oct 18	KS, 29th, 1910
Coleman, William H.		E, 209th Penn. Inf.	32		1941 Jul 22	NE, 66th, 1942
Coleman, William L.		D, 103rd Ill. Inf.	127		1908 Jan 2	KS, 28th, 1909
Coleman, Wm.	Pvt.	H, 6th Iowa	358		1907 Nov 2	IA, 34th, 1908
Colenso, John	Pvt.	G, 1st Ohio Lt. Art.	59		1926 Jun 29	IA, 53rd, 1927
Colenstine, E.		U.S. Marines	72		1916 Apr 27	KS, 36th, 1917
Coles, John O.	Lieut.	K, 46th Iowa Inf.	18		1913 Sep 10	IA, 40th, 1914
Coles, John W.		H, 46th Iowa	1		1910 Jul 17	KS, 30th, 1911
Coleson, E.W.		E, 78th Ohio	158		1923 Apr 23	KS, 43rd, 1924
Colford, John		B, 10th N.Y. Inf. (died of tuberculosis)	166		1895 Sep 28	NE, 20th, 1896
Colgan, John		B, 1st Ind. Hvy. Art.	332		1892 Aug 1	KS, 12th, 1893
Colgrove, A.E.	Corp.	I, 27th Iowa Inf.	194		1902 Jul 2	IA, 29th, 1903
Colgrove, H.P., see Colegrove, H.P.						
Colin, Dow	Pvt.	K, Ill. Cav.	22		1923 Jun	IA, 50th, 1924
Colip, W.A.	Pvt.	G, 19th Iowa Inf.	153		1913 Feb 6	IA, 40th, 1914
Coll, W.J.	Pvt.	H, 116th Ohio Inf.	440		1928 Dec 18	IA, 55th, 1929
Collar, J.A.		Battery B, 3rd Ill.	147		1911 Apr 2	KS, 31st, 1912
College, John			45		1908	IA, 36th, 1910
Coller, Samuel P.		G, 9th Ill. Cav. (died at Jetmore, Kans.; buried at City Cemetery)	82		1894 Sep 22	KS, 14th, 1895

*See Appendix A, B or C for roster of post names and locations.
†See Introduction for note regarding recording of death date.

Name	Rank	Company, Regiment or Ship	Post*	Age	Death Date†	Journal
Collett, J.B.		E, 22nd Ill.	66		1911 Jun 24	KS, 31st, 1912
Collett, W.J.		E, 6th Iowa Inf. (died of paralysis)	13	82	1923 Sep 23	NE, 48th, 1924
Collie, James		D, 10th Kans.	78		1915 Sep 16	KS, 35th, 1916
Collie, William		B, 11th Kans.	58		1914 Oct 16	KS, 34th, 1915
Collier, A.D.	Pvt.	K, 1st Iowa Inf.	22		1918 Jan 17	IA, 45th, 1919
Collier, C.W.	Pvt.	I, 43rd Ill. Inf.	1	42	1887 Nov 16	IA, 14th, 1888
Collier, John H.		D, 52nd Ohio Inf.	1		1899 Feb 25	KS, 19th, 1900
Collier, Robt.		D, 57th Ind. Inf.	25		1934 Dec	KS, 54th, 1935
Collins, Albert	Pvt.	F, 38th Wis. Inf.	267	52	1898 May 5	IA, 24th, 1898
Collins, Allen B.	Corp.	F, 7th Iowa Inf.	452		1903 Jul 1	IA, 30th, 1904
Collins, Benj.	Pvt.	I, 110th Ill.	93		1899 Aug 30	IA, 26th, 1900
Collins, C.	Pvt.	F, 19th Ind.	337	48	1891 Jan 17	IA, 17th, 1891
Collins, C.C.	Corp.	F, 28th Iowa Inf.	125		1911 Apr 22	IA, 38th, 1912
Collins, C.C.		A, 101st Penn. Inf. (see also Appendix D)	12		1927 Jan 4 or 24	KS, 47th, 1928
Collins, C.P.	Sergt.	E, 12th Iowa Inf.	3		1908 Apr 8	IA, 35th, 1909
Collins, Chas. G.		B, 4th Ill. Cav. (died of apoplexy)	110	54	1897 Nov 8	NE, 22nd, 1898
Collins, D.O.	Corp.	F, 64th Ill. Inf.	133	52	1887 Apr 29	IA, 14th, 1888
Collins, Geo.		A, 52nd Ill. (died of apoplexy)	13	74	1922 Feb 18	NE, 47th, 1923
Collins, Geo. F.		D, 14th Ill.	175		1927 Jul 8	KS, 47th, 1928
Collins, Geo. T.		F, 45th Iowa	18		1930 Mar 18	KS, 50th, 1931
Collins, Hiram	Pvt.	A, 30th Iowa Inf.	2	47	1891 Aug 16	IA, 18th, 1892
Collins, I.W.	Pvt.	L, 13th Wis. Cav.	154		1908 Sep 2	IA, 35th, 1909
Collins, Ira F.		D, 114th Ill.	175		1927 Nov 8	KS, 47th, 1928
Collins, J.A.M.	Pvt.	A, 2nd Iowa Inf.	2		1916 May 23	IA, 43rd, 1917
Collins, J.P.	Clerk	unassigned	4		1926 Jun 11	KS, 46th, 1927
Collins, Jacob	Pvt.	I, 21st Iowa Inf.	78		1906 Apr 17	IA, 33rd, 1907
Collins, James C.		H, 15th Penn. Cav.	96		1917 Feb 7	KS, 37th, 1918
Collins, Jesse		100th Ind.	111		1921 Sep 23	KS, 41st, 1922
Collins, John H.		G, 42nd Mo. Inf.		89	1938 Jan 15	IA, 64th, 1938
Collins, John M.	Sergt.	K, 12th Ohio Cav.	40		1922 Sep 19	IA, 49th, 1923
Collins, Levi		B, 8th Ind.	412		1919 Sep	KS, 39th, 1920
Collins, Norman	Sergt.	K, 116th Ill. Inf.	177		1907 May 24	IA, 34th, 1908
Collins, Richard		C, 132nd N.Y.	293		1917 May 5	KS, 37th, 1918
Collins, Samuel M.	Pvt.	F, 21st Iowa Inf.	78		1918 Feb 10	IA, 45th, 1919
Collins, Sylvester W.		K, 29th Ohio	374		1900 Nov 16	KS, 20th, 1901
Collins, Truvee			235		1930 Feb 22	IA, 57th, 1931
Collins, W.B.	Pvt.	F, 7th Mo. Inf.	2		1931	IA, 59th, 1933
Collins, W.H.		K, 7th Penn. Cav.	96		1913 Oct 4	KS, 33rd, 1914
Collins, W.T.		H, 14th Kans. Cav.	174		1918	KS, 38th, 1919
Collins, Willis J.	Pvt.	C, 7th Iowa Cav.	88		1908 Jan 1	IA, 35th, 1909
Collison, John N.		A, 2nd Maine	17		1915 Mar 18	KS, 35th, 1916
Collister, J.C.	Sergt.	G, 23rd Ill.	124		1931	IA, 58th, 1932
Collumber, Wm.		B & F, 13th Ohio Vol. Inf.	99		1899 Jan 24	KS, 19th, 1900
Colman, Sam'l	Pvt.	H, 29th U.S. Colored	1		1911 Sep 30	IA, 38th, 1912
Colnon, T.B.		G, 1st Neb. Cav.	58		1925	NE, 51st, 1927
Colony, O.L.P.		K, 1st Kans.	100		1919 Jun 26	KS, 39th, 1920
Colson, Angelo		A, 3rd West Va.	78		1925 Jan 2	KS, 44th, 1925
Colt, A.P.		32nd Ill.	412		1917 Oct 25	KS, 37th, 1918
Colt, J.H.		E, 1st Wis.	85		1906 Mar 10	KS, 26th, 1907
Colton, Andrew		I, 15th Kans. (died at Bigelow, Kans.; buried at Antioch Cemetery)	330		1894 Jun 30	KS, 14th, 1895
Colton, E.J.		F, 15th Ill. Iowa (cause of death: broken down)	1	84	1920 Feb 11	NE, 45th, 1921
Columbus, Holman		A, 16th Mo. Cav.	142		1923 Sep 29	KS, 43rd, 1924
Colvig, Geo. W.		B, 3rd Mo. Cav.	23		1914	IA, 41st, 1915
Colville, B.P.		G, 1st Iowa Cav.	71		1916 Jan	KS, 36th, 1917
Colville, George W.	Capt.	H, 3rd Iowa Inf.	40		4th quarter 1885	IA, 12th, 1886
Colvin, Wm. S.	Sergt.	B, 16th Penn. Cav.	300	66	1898 Dec 29	IA, 25th, 1899
Colwell, J.M.	Musician	2nd Iowa Cav.	314	45	1887 Mar 21	IA, 14th, 1888
Colyar, I.	Pvt.	B, 5th Iowa Inf.	7		1925 Dec 16	IA, 52nd, 1926
Colyer, J.P.		4th Kans.	129		1923 Jan 29	KS, 43rd, 1924
Colyer, J.W.		F, 102nd Ohio	7		1920 Nov 6	KS, 40th, 1921

*See Appendix A, B or C for roster of post names and locations.
†See Introduction for note regarding recording of death date.
109

Name	Rank	Company, Regiment or Ship	Post*	Age	Death Date†	Journal
Coman, Wm. L.		D, 3rd Colo.	160		1918 Dec 10	KS, 38th, 1919
Combs, Frank		C, 12th U.S. Colored Inf.	321		1902 Feb 17	KS, 22nd, 1903
Combs, James		F, 10th N.Y. Art.	91	75	1919 Apr 7	NE, 44th, 1920
Combs, M.J.		C, 2nd Neb. Cav.	284		1926 Jan 5	NE, 51st, 1927
Combs, W.J.		M, 15th Kans. Cav.	55		1918 Feb 14	KS, 38th, 1919
Comby, J.J.			463		1924 Feb 22	KS, 44th, 1925
Comegys, D.R.	Pvt.	B, 19th Iowa Inf.	22		1918 Jul 10	IA, 45th, 1919
Comer, Robert			240		1918 Feb 20	KS, 41st, 1922
Comes, Robert		Ind.	240		1919	KS, 39th, 1920
Comferd, David		B, 8th Ky.	57		1922 Mar 21	KS, 42nd, 1923
Comley, Jesse R.	Pvt.	H, 3rd Penn. Prov. Cav.	359	54	1898 Nov 15	IA, 25th, 1899
Commean, J.D.		I, 4th Tenn.	187	78	1920 Jan 11	NE, 44th, 1920
Commons, William		D, 5th Kans. Cav.	32		1919 Mar 8	KS, 39th, 1920
Commoran, E.F.	Pvt.	A, 39th Iowa Inf.	55	89	1931 Feb 8	IA, 58th, 1932
Commuck, Thos. M.	Pvt.	H, 29th Wis. Inf.	141	53	1889 Jun 22	IA, 16th, 1890
Comp, Jas. M.	Pvt.	B, 120th Ill.	55		1919 Sep 6	IA, 46th, 1920
Comper, A.		D, 101st Penn. Inf.	18	63	1902 Feb	NE, 27th, 1903
Compton, David		H, 25th Iowa	87		1917 Jun 28	KS, 37th, 1918
Compton, G.H.	Pvt.	A, 152nd Ind. Inf.	440		1923 Oct 29	IA, 50th, 1924
Compton, John		I, 16th Kans.	18		1909 May 6	KS, 29th, 1910
Compton, Orville		B, 16th N.Y.	25		1936 Mar 3	NE, 61st, 1937
Comro, Adolph		H, 16th Ill. Vol. Inf.	9		1917 Dec 2	KS, 37th, 1918
Comstock, Geo. B.		F, 88th Ill. Inf.	110		1906 Mar 19	NE, 31st, 1907
Comstock, Geo. E.	Pvt.	C, 12th Iowa Inf.	46		1911 Jan 16	IA, 38th, 1912
Comstock, J.C.	Pvt.	G, 45th Iowa Inf.	5		1910 Sep 14	IA, 37th, 1911
Comstock, John C.		F, 21st Mo. Inf.	405		1899 Jan 23	KS, 19th, 1900
Comstock, R.C.	Saddler	F, 5th Mich. Cav.	173	64	1893 Mar 24	IA, 19th, 1893
Comstock, R.E.			25		1910 Jul 26	NE, 35th, 1911
Comstock, W.R.	Pvt.	D, 24th N.Y.	1		1915 Apr 4	KS, 35th, 1916
Comstock, Win. S.	Pvt.	H, 3rd Penn. Art.	465	52	1898 Sep 25	IA, 25th, 1899
Conard, John		F, 4th Iowa	18		1892 Nov 26	KS, 12th, 1893
Conarty, John		K, 20th Ind. Inf.	209		1929	KS, 49th, 1930
Conawa, S.A.		Ohio	292		1921	KS, 43rd, 1924
Condra, Isaac N.	Pvt.	B, 47th Iowa Inf.	186		1915 Aug 13	IA, 42nd, 1916
Condray, William		F, 6th Cal.	271		1917 Nov 5	KS, 37th, 1918
Condron, W.T.	Pvt.	K, 20th Iowa Inf.	322		1929	IA, 56th, 1930
Cone, A.B.			5		1925 May 8	IA, 52nd, 1926
Cone, E.W.		A, 7th Kans.	111		1908 Aug 14	NE, 33rd, 1909
Cone, John P.		E, 12th Kans. Inf.	12		1925 Jan 2	KS, 44th, 1925
Cone, John P.		E, 12th Kans.	12		1925 Jan 2	KS, 45th, 1926
Cone, O.B.	Corp.	K, 9th Iowa Inf.	206		1899 May 20	IA, 26th, 1900
Cone, Ryron	Pvt.	F, 20th Iowa Inf.	206		1909 Oct 9	IA, 36th, 1910
Cone, W.D., Dr.			115		1899 Dec 1	IA, 26th, 1900
Cone, W.P.		A, 36th Iowa	52		1922 Dec 27	KS, 43rd, 1924
Conell, Charles		B, 44th Iowa Inf. (died of paralysis)	95	76	1920 Sep 9	NE, 45th, 1921
Conery, John	Pvt.	I, 24th Iowa Inf.	74		1906 Apr 15	IA, 33rd, 1907
Coney, E.J.		F, 11th Mich.	18		1918 Mar 8	KS, 38th, 1919
Coney, Patrick H.		H, 111th N.Y.	1		1932 Jul 24	KS, 52nd, 1933
Confare, N.H.	Pvt.	K, 124th Ind. Inf.	31		1919 Dec 30	IA, 46th, 1920
Congdon, David		H, 142nd Ohio	17		1911 Feb 22	KS, 31st, 1912
Congelan, Thos.		F, 179th Ohio	46		1898 Jan 10	KS, 18th, 1899
Conger, G.M.	Pvt.	E, 17th Iowa Inf.	107		1909 Oct	IA, 36th, 1910
Conger, John	Pvt.	E, 3rd Wis. Cav.	206		1908 May 30	IA, 35th, 1909
Conine, B.J.	Pvt.	1st Iowa Art.	297		1931 Dec 2	IA, 58th, 1932
Conine, I.V.			6		1921	IA, 48th, 1922
Conine, Jacob		C, 27th Ohio	32		1924 May 14	KS, 44th, 1925
Conkle, Joseph		H, 21st Ohio G, 17th Ohio (died at Hallowell)	200		1895 Sep	KS, 15th, 1896
Conkle, William		B, 126th Ill. Inf.	52		1899 Aug 31	KS, 19th, 1900
Conklin, B.F.		A, 9th Kans.	50		1919 Mar 30	KS, 39th, 1920
Conklin, D.E.	Capt.	I, 13th Iowa Inf.	108		1913	IA, 40th, 1914
Conklin, Dyar A.		H, 2nd Colo. Cav.	354	87	1918 Jan 12	NE, 43rd, 1919

Name	Rank	Company, Regiment or Ship	Post*	Age	Death Date†	Journal
Conklin, Elias	Pvt.	C, 15th Iowa Inf.	323	40	1887 Dec 18	IA, 14th, 1888
Conklin, Elijah		C, 33rd Ohio	25		1932 Dec 29	NE, 57th, 1933
Conklin, George W.		D, 47th Ohio	98	89	1934 Mar 19	IA, 61st, 1935
Conklin, H.C.	Pvt.	C, 44th Iowa Inf.	147		1910 Oct 31	IA, 37th, 1911
Conklin, J.L.		I, 128th Ohio	1		1904 Dec 23	KS, 24th, 1905
Conklin, J.S.	Pvt.	K, 136th Ohio Inf.	333	74	1900 Jan 8	IA, 26th, 1900
Conklin, Joseph E.		K, 67th Ill. B, 135th Ill.	25		1913 Oct 14	KS, 33rd, 1914
Conklin, Samuel		K, 141st Penn. Inf. (died at Norton County, Kans.; buried at Edmond Cemetery)	312		1894 Aug 27	KS, 14th, 1895
Conklin, W.W.	Pvt.	F, 1st Iowa Inf.	7		1908 Oct 29	IA, 35th, 1909
Conlan, Patrick		I, 57th Ohio	65		1912 Sep 12	KS, 32nd, 1913
Conley, A.G.	Pvt.	D, 47th Ill. Inf.	29		1932 Nov 22	IA, 59th, 1933
Conley, Andrew	Pvt.	A, 15th Iowa Inf.	420	96	1935 Jun 24	IA, 65th, 1939
Conley, D.R.			131		1893	NE, 18th, 1894
Conley, David		H, 24th Ind.	3	70	1908	NE, 33rd, 1909
Conley, David W.	Pvt.	I, 22nd Iowa Inf.	192		1911 May 26	IA, 38th, 1912
Conley, Dennis	Sergt.	D, 12th Iowa Inf.	1		1899	IA, 26th, 1900
Conley, Ezra		G, 29th Iowa	25		1928 May 10	NE, 53rd, 1929
Conley, Mike		F, 19th Ohio Inf.	18		1917 Mar 8	KS, 37th, 1918
Conley, S.R.	Pvt.	D, 22nd Iowa Inf.	49		1918 Jul 9	IA, 45th, 1919
Conlin, J.M.	Pvt.	K, 160th N.Y. Inf.	69		1911 Jan 2	IA, 38th, 1912
Conn, James J.		E, 7th Iowa Cav.	78		1914 Sep	KS, 34th, 1915
Conn, Robt.	Sergt.	E, 24th Iowa Inf.	235		1917 Jun 5	IA, 44th, 1918
Conn, Thos.	Corp.	A, 30th Iowa Inf.	2	53	1887 May 29	IA, 14th, 1888
Conn, W.C.		D, 144th Ohio	123		1900 Sep	KS, 20th, 1901
Connell, Geo.		Keene (at large)			1935	KS, 55th, 1936
Connell, Geo.		member at large			1934	KS, 54th, 1935
Connell, John	Col.	28th Iowa	343	68	1891 Jun 10	IA, 18th, 1892
Connell, Richard	Pvt.	D, 1st U.S. Art.	337		1908 Dec 26	IA, 35th, 1909
Connelly, Jeptha J.		1st Ind. Cav.	58		1911 Jun 29	KS, 31st, 1912
Connelly, John		U.S. Navy	354	78	1906 Mar 26	NE, 31st, 1907
Connelly, William		I, 31st Ind. Inf.	500		1915 Oct 2	KS, 36th, 1917
Conner, A.	Corp.	D, 21st Iowa Inf.	82		1906 Jan 27	IA, 33rd, 1907
Conner, Aaron	Corp.	D, 21st Iowa	82		1907 Jan 27	IA, 34th, 1908
Conner, Amos		H, 12th Mich. Cav.	235		1906 Oct 24	IA, 33rd, 1907
Conner, B.	Pvt.	E, 35th Iowa	231		1921 Jul 29	IA, 48th, 1922
Conner, J.L.	Pvt.	D, 139th Ind. Inf.	49		1918 Feb 23	IA, 45th, 1919
Conner, Jabez W.	Musician	A, 140th Ill. Inf.	327		1908 May 19	IA, 35th, 1909
Conner, James		E, 9th Ky.	85		1928 Nov 28	KS, 48th, 1929
Conner, John		D, 36th Ohio Vol. Inf.	14		1914 Apr 21	KS, 34th, 1915
Conner, John D.		C, 13th Iowa Inf.	431		1902 Nov 4	KS, 22nd, 1903
Conner, Levi L.	Musician	C, 172nd Ohio Inf.	81	90	1937 Sep 27	IA, 64th, 1938
Conner, O.			[36?]		1908[1909?] Aug 10	KS, 29th, 1910
Conner, W.A.	Pvt.	F, 2nd Minn. Cav.	7		1925 Apr 16	IA, 52nd, 1926
Conner, William Frank		E, 111th Penn. Inf.	67 & 329	90	1937 Nov 14	IA, 64th, 1938
Conner, Wm.	Pvt.	D, 13th N.Y. Cav.	12		1904 Feb 9	IA, 31st, 1905
Conners, Isaac S.	Pvt.	29th U.S. Cav.	70		1908 Jun 25	IA, 35th, 1909
Connet, Andrew J.		A, 3rd Iowa Cav.			1928 Dec 17	NE, 53rd, 1929
Connett, John	Pvt.	A, 36th Iowa Inf.	337	74	1897 Feb 27	IA, 23rd, 1897
Conningham, B.G.	Sergt.	G, 9th Iowa Cav.	81		1920 Jun 22	IA, 47th, 1921
Connor, Alexander		M, 6th Kans.	153		1897 May 10	KS, 17th, 1898
Connor, C.W.	Pvt.	I, 2nd Iowa Cav.	284		1905 Sep 12	IA, 32nd, 1906
Connor, E.W.	Musician	B, 35th Iowa Inf.	446	64	1896 Oct 30	IA, 23rd, 1897
Connor, Ed.		A, 27th Iowa Inf.	193		1895	IA, 23rd, 1897
Connor, J.	Pvt.	D, 15th Iowa (died of rheumatism)	230	56	1887 May	NE, 12th, 1888
Connor, M.E.		E, 11th Kans. Cav.	18		1924 Aug 7	KS, 44th, 1925
Connor, Thomas	Pvt.	I, 2nd Iowa Cav.	190		1914 Sep 26	IA, 41st, 1915
Connors, F.J.		F, 46th Iowa Vol. Inf.	303		1908 Mar 17	KS, 28th, 1909
Connrardy, John B.	Pvt.	A, 16th U.S. Inf.	35		1914 Nov 2	IA, 41st, 1915
Conon, Nathan	Corp.	G, 141st Ill.	465		1922 Oct	IA, 49th, 1923
Conover, Henry		B, 99th Ill.	147		1904 Oct 2	KS, 24th, 1905

*See Appendix A, B or C for roster of post names and locations.
†See Introduction for note regarding recording of death date.

Name	Rank	Company, Regiment or Ship	Post*	Age	Death Date†	Journal
Conover, Henry		B, 35th Iowa	106		1913 Aug 21	KS, 33rd, 1914
Conover, Oliver		G, 139th Ill.	127		1934 May 28	KS, 55th, 1936
Conover, Oliver		C, 139th Ill.	107		1934 May 22 or 28	KS, 54th, 1935
Conover, Oliver		G, 139th Ill. Inf. (member at large)	127		1934 May 28	KS, 54th, 1935
Conoway, A.M.		D, 7th West Va.	148		1905 Jul 7	KS, 25th, 1906
Conquest, R.			13		1886	NE, 11th, 1887
Conrad, Edwin		F, 10th Mich. Art.	12		1925 Apr 6	IA, 52nd, 1926
Conrad, Ezra		D, 86th Ill.	79		1916 May 23	NE, 41st, 1917
Conrad, H.G.		E, 134th Ind.	4		1928 Oct 8	KS, 48th, 1929
Conrad, J.		C, 42nd Ind. Inf. (died of pneumonia)	306		1893 Mar 7	NE, 18th, 1894
Conrad, James	Pvt.	D, 46th Iowa Inf.	47		1925 Mar 12	IA, 52nd, 1926
Conrad, John C.	Pvt.	I, 10th Maine. Inf.	88		1907 Apr 24	IA, 34th, 1908
Conrad, Sam'l	Pvt.	H, 23rd Iowa Inf.	440		1918 Jul 7	IA, 45th, 1919
Conrad, Samuel W.	Pvt.	D, 1st Iowa Cav.	116	50	1892 Jun 10	IA, 19th, 1893
Conrad, W.J.	Musician	35th Ill. Inf.	235		1916 Apr 30	IA, 43rd, 1917
Conrad, Wesley		K, U.S. Vet. Vols.	85		1927 Apr 12	KS, 47th, 1928
Conrad, William F.	Pvt.	G, 25th Iowa Vol. Inf. (see also Appendix D)	7		1901 Dec 20	IA, 28th, 1902
Conrey, W.P.		1st Kans. Battery	264		1898 May 31	KS, 18th, 1899
Conrod, W.S.		C, 2nd Ohio	42		1911 Sep 13	KS, 31st, 1912
Conroe, I.		E, 41st N.Y. Inf.	36		1900 Apr 17	KS, 20th, 1901
Conroy, P.S.		C, 10th Ohio	203		1898 Oct 21	KS, 18th, 1899
Consadine, P.		C, 14th Iowa	380		1898 Sep 27	KS, 18th, 1899
Consigny, Eugene A.	Pvt.	M, 1st Vt. Cav. (see also Appendix D)	123		1900 Aug 8	IA, 27th, 1901
Consigny, Geo. J.	Pvt.	K, 2nd Vt. Inf.	235		1917 May 10	IA, 44th, 1918
Constant, A.J.			235		1894	NE, 19th, 1895
Constant, Wm. R.		A, 73rd Ill.	175		1919 Mar 3	KS, 39th, 1920
Constantine, U.		H, 11th Kans.	38		1931 Jul	KS, 51st, 1932
Constantine, U.		H, 11th Kans.	38		1931 Jul	KS, 52nd, 1933
Contel, B.		9th Iowa Cav. (died of paralysis)	52	83	1903 Jul 30	NE, 28th, 1904
Converse, Louis N.	Pvt.	A, 46th Iowa Inf.	78		1919 Feb 18	IA, 46th, 1920
Converse, Peter		K, 28th Mich. Inf.	47		1894 Apr 28	NE, 19th, 1895
Convey, M.		I, 6th Iowa Cav.	235		1914 Oct 16	IA, 41st, 1915
Conwall, J.W.	Pvt.	B, 8th Iowa Cav.	337		1924	IA, 51st, 1925
Conway, A.M., see Conoway, A.M.						
Conway, C.M.	Sergt.	E, 35th Ind. Inf.	56		1919 Jun 20	IA, 46th, 1920
Conway, H.B.	Pvt.	I, 142nd Ohio	67		1907 Dec 25	IA, 34th, 1908
Conway, H.V.	Sergt.	H, 142nd Penn. Inf.	67		1908 Jan 16	IA, 35th, 1909
Conway, James		A, 10th N.Y. Cav.	380		1909 Aug 7	KS, 29th, 1910
Conway, Patrick		U.S.N.	12		1913 Aug 28	KS, 33rd, 1914
Conway, Peter	Pvt.	E, 24th Ind. Inf.	67	61	1893 May 14	IA, 21st, 1895
Conway, Peter	Pvt.	C, 24th Ind. Inf.	67	61	1893 May 19	IA, 20th, 1894
Conway, Samuel		F, 28th Ill.	52		1902	KS, 22nd, 1903
Conway, Samuel		F, 28th Ill. Inf.	52		1901 Oct 10	KS, 21st, 1902
Conway, Wm.	Pvt.	G, 149th Penn. Inf.	359		1917 Aug 27	IA, 44th, 1918
Conwell, James S.		G, 2nd Kans. Inf.	1		1901 Jun 21	KS, 21st, 1902
Conwell, Jas. M.		E, 11th Kans. Inf.	55		1891 Dec 7	KS, 11th, 1892
Conwell, R.T.	Pvt.	E, 11th Kans.	1		1915 Feb 7	KS, 35th, 1916
Conwell, W.F.		B, 17th Ind. (died of heart trouble)	88	75	1921 Nov 9	NE, 46th, 1922
Conwell, W.H.	Pvt.	B, 3rd Iowa Inf.	49		1906 Jan 29	IA, 33rd, 1907
Conwell, Wm. E.		D, 11th Kans. Cav.	155		1914 Nov 30	KS, 34th, 1915
Cony, Willard	Pvt.	6th Ohio Battery	62		1914 Nov 22	IA, 41st, 1915
Conyell, John		C, 155th Ill. Inf. (died at Oak Valley)	217		1895 Apr	KS, 15th, 1896
Cook, A.			98		1911 Jun 9	KS, 31st, 1912
Cook, A.D.	Pvt. Col.	E, 23rd Maine — (died of apoplexy)	31	48	1885 Jan 23	NE, 10th, 1886
Cook, A.S.	Pvt.	D, 52nd Ill. Inf.	55		1908 Sep 9	IA, 35th, 1909
Cook, Adrian		H, 88th Ill. Inf. (died of old age)	204	93	1913 Mar 26	NE, 38th, 1914
Cook, Archibald	Pvt.	2nd Penn. Cav.	29		1924 Mar 4	IA, 51st, 1925
Cook, B.O.			110		1908	IA, 35th, 1909
Cook, Benj.		I, 106th N.Y.	355		1902 Aug	KS, 22nd, 1903

*See Appendix A, B or C for roster of post names and locations.
†See Introduction for note regarding recording of death date.

112

Name	Rank	Company, Regiment or Ship	Post*	Age	Death Date†	Journal
Cook, Bradford Pierce		F, 56th Mass. Inf. (died of heart disease; see also Appendix D)	214		1911 Jun 2	NE, 36th, 1912
Cook, C.C., Dr.		died of erysipelas	36	59	1904 Sep 30	NE, 29th, 1905
Cook, C.H.	Pvt.	Battery L, 1st N.Y. Lt. Art.	466		1917 May 4	IA, 44th, 1918
Cook, Cassius M.		C, 1st Penn.	32		1930 Jun 18	KS, 50th, 1931
Cook, Charles A.		D, 7th Vt.	36		1924 Jul 4	KS, 44th, 1925
Cook, Charles W.	Pvt.	B, 124th Ill. Inf.	238	55	1895 May 25	IA, 22nd, 1896
Cook, Chas. E.	Musician	I, 19th Ill. Inf.	67		1900 Dec 5	IA, 27th, 1901
Cook, Curtis	Pvt.	I, 6th Ohio Cav.	231		1915 Jun 26	IA, 42nd, 1916
Cook, D.S.			31		1886	NE, 11th, 1887
Cook, Daniel C.		K, 72nd & 44th Ind.	25	77	1919 Sep 9	NE, 44th, 1920
Cook, Daniel D.		C, Cass Co., Mo., Vols. (died of old age, comp. diseases at Soldiers & Sailors Home, Grand Island; buried in Home Cemetery)	4	85	1905 Feb 21	NE, 30th, 1906
Cook, David		K, 2nd Iowa	155		1928 May 6	KS, 48th, 1929
Cook, E.C.	Corp.	H, 28th Iowa Inf.	321		1915 Jun 1	IA, 42nd, 1916
Cook, Enos	Pvt.	K, 6th Iowa Inf.	178		1917	IA, 44th, 1918
Cook, F.A.			11		1913	IA, 40th, 1914
Cook, Frank		D, 125th Ill. Vol. Inf.	322		1916 Dec 18	KS, 36th, 1917
Cook, G.W.		A, 38th Iowa	322		1920 Apr 14	KS, 40th, 1921
Cook, Geo.			417		1917	IA, 44th, 1918
Cook, Geo. W.	Pvt.	A, 113th Ill. Inf.	29		1913 Feb 13	IA, 40th, 1914
Cook, Geo. W.A.	Pvt.	B & M, 2nd Colo. Cav.	4	97	1939 Jul	IA, 65th, 1939
Cook, H.H.	Pvt.	E, 35th N.J. Inf.	10		1911 Jan 9	IA, 37th, 1911
Cook, Henry	Pvt.	C, 42nd Ind.	264	68	1899 Jan 1	IA, 25th, 1899
Cook, Henry		G, 2nd N.Y.	5		1923 Nov 27	KS, 43rd, 1924
Cook, Henry H.		C, 58th Ill.	18		1911 Oct 28	KS, 31st, 1912
Cook, J.B.	Col.	4th Ill. Cav.	118		1921 Aug 18	KS, 41st, 1922
Cook, J.B.		A, 11th Kans.	257		1923 Feb 11	KS, 43rd, 1924
Cook, J.D.		E, 11th Ind.	433		1897 Jul 29	KS, 17th, 1898
Cook, J.H.	Pvt.	A, 39th Iowa Inf.	359		1897-1898	IA, 24th, 1898
Cook, J.H.	Pvt.	K, 4th Iowa Cav.	208		1907 Feb 21	IA, 33rd, 1907
Cook, J.L.		G, 169th Ohio	115		1913 Jun 4	KS, 33rd, 1914
Cook, J.S.	Pvt.	K, 30th Iowa	57		1926 Jan	IA, 53rd, 1927
Cook, J.S.B.	Pvt.	E, 43rd Wis. Inf.	3		1914 Oct 14	IA, 41st, 1915
Cook, Jacob	Pvt.	A, 144th Ind. Inf.	231		1914 Oct 20	IA, 41st, 1915
Cook, James	Pvt.	I, 7th Colo. Vols.	97		1914 Jul 30	IA, 41st, 1915
Cook, James	Pvt.		98		1929 Jun 24	IA, 56th, 1930
Cook, James F.	Pvt.	K, 4th Iowa Cav.	208		1907 Feb 21	IA, 34th, 1908
Cook, James H.		E, 2nd Wis. Cav. (died at Topeka; buried at Topeka Cemetery)	1		1894 Sep 19	KS, 14th, 1895
Cook, James P.		12th Iowa Inf.	116	79	1913 Jan 20	NE, 39th, 1915
Cook, James W.	Pvt.	A, 12th Iowa Inf.	31		1909 Feb	IA, 36th, 1910
Cook, John	Pvt.	13th Mich. Lt. Art.	92		1912 Jan 21	IA, 39th, 1913
Cook, John		B, 1st West Va. Art.	67		1899 Jun 23	KS, 19th, 1900
Cook, John		I, 80th Ohio	180		1911 Sep 23	KS, 31st, 1912
Cook, John		I, 138th Penn.	158		1920 Apr	KS, 40th, 1921
Cook, John B.	Pvt. Col.	K, 1st Maine Inf. 5th U.S. Colored Inf. (see also Appendix D)	44	52	1892 Oct 14	IA, 19th, 1893
Cook, John C.		H, 42nd Mo. Inf.	14		1885	KS, 5th, 1886
Cook, John E.		E, 13th Mass.	25		1911 Jan 10	NE, 36th, 1912
Cook, John R.	Pvt.	F, 38th Iowa Inf.	48		1918 Nov 18	IA, 45th, 1919
Cook, John R.		E, 12th Kans. Cav.	293		1917 Mar 25	KS, 37th, 1918
Cook, Joseph	Pvt.	H, 45th Ill. Inf.	321	75	1899 Apr 26	IA, 25th, 1899
Cook, Joseph		I, 2nd Penn. Hvy. Art.	251		1892 Aug 4	KS, 12th, 1893
Cook, Joseph S.		F, 8th Penn. Res. Corps	52	84	1922 Jul 3	NE, 47th, 1923
Cook, L.H.	Pvt.	H, 46th Ill. Inf.	193		1905 Oct 3	IA, 32nd, 1906
Cook, Luther W.		K, 30th Iowa	25		1911 Jun 28	KS, 31st, 1912
Cook, O.H.P.		C, 29th Iowa	78		1918 Oct 6	KS, 38th, 1919
Cook, Peter D.			256		1890	KS, 17th, 1898
Cook, Philip R.		E, 61st Ill. Inf. (died of heart disease)	311		1891 Oct 18	KS, 11th, 1892
Cook, Phillip		F, 151st N.Y.	74		1927	KS, 47th, 1928

*See Appendix A, B or C for roster of post names and locations.
†See Introduction for note regarding recording of death date.

Name	Rank	Company, Regiment or Ship	Post*	Age	Death Date†	Journal
Cook, S.E.		died of short sickness	32		1911 Feb 7	NE, 36th, 1912
Cook, Samuel B.		Ind. (killed by horse)	32		1890	KS, 10th, 1891
Cook, Samuel R.		E, 75th Ill.	21		1904 Mar 10	KS, 24th, 1905
Cook, Thomas		U.S.C.T.	321		1897	KS, 17th, 1898
Cook, Thomas		H, 3rd Wis. Cav.	57		1925 Oct 20	KS, 45th, 1926
Cook, Thos. J.	Corp.	K, 4th Iowa Inf.	10		1908 Jul 20	IA, 35th, 1909
Cook, W.C.		D, 137th Ill.	75		1917 Dec 26	KS, 37th, 1918
Cook, W.D.		K, 6th Ill.	218		1896 Jul 1	KS, 16th, 1897
Cook, W.E.		F, 10th Ind.	293		1927	KS, 47th, 1928
Cook, W.J.			279		1911 Jun 27	KS, 32nd, 1913
Cook, W.W.		G, 2nd Vt.	132		1916 Nov 6	KS, 36th, 1917
Cook, William		C, 192nd Ohio Inf.	113		1899 Feb	KS, 19th, 1900
Cook, William		K, 35th Iowa (died of old age)	112	86	1910 Dec 27	NE, 35th, 1911
Cook, Wm.	Pvt.	D, 74th Ill. Inf.	159		1915 Jan 13	IA, 42nd, 1916
Cook, Wm. H.	Pvt.	I, 58th Penn. Inf.	132		1908 Oct 12	IA, 35th, 1909
Cooke, George		E, 59th N.Y. Inf.	6		1909 Dec 11	KS, 29th, 1910
Cooksey, John	Pvt.		79		1912 Feb	IA, 39th, 1913
Cool, D.	Mechanic	48th N.Y. Bat.	270		1920 Jan 7	IA, 47th, 1921
Cool, Delos	Pvt.	D, 1st N.Y. Art.	270		1920 Jan 7	IA, 46th, 1920
Cool, John	Lieut.	I, 8th Ill. Cav.	123	74	1898 Nov 29	IA, 25th, 1899
Coolbaugh, H.C.	Pvt.	G, 2nd Ill. Art.	210		1911 Apr 27	IA, 38th, 1912
Cooley, B.		G, 50th Ill.	54		1923	KS, 43rd, 1924
Cooley, Chas. H.	Pvt.	B, 50th Wis. Inf.	101		1922 Jun 23	IA, 49th, 1923
Cooley, E.E.	Major	Commissary of S[ubsistence?]	168	68	1895 Feb 1	IA, 21st, 1895
Cooley, George			42		1890 Feb 19	NE, 15th, 1891
Cooley, Gilbert	Lieut.	D, 21st Iowa Cav.	259		1910 Dec 14	IA, 37th, 1911
Cooley, Isaac	Pvt.	F, 40th Iowa Inf.	49		1918 Jun 11	IA, 45th, 1919
Cooley, J.C.		C, 11th Kans. Inf.	196		1891 Oct 19	KS, 11th, 1892
Cooley, James	Pvt.	C, 32nd Iowa Inf.	68		1915 Aug 6	IA, 42nd, 1916
Cooley, James			145		1914 Jul 9	KS, 34th, 1915
Cooley, John		C, 61st Ill. Inf.	240		1899 May 1	KS, 19th, 1900
Cooley, Lewis		F, 86th N.Y.	25		1933 Jan 17	NE, 58th, 1934
Cooley, N.	Pvt.	A, 150th Ind. Inf.	154		1920 Oct 5	IA, 47th, 1921
Cooley, R.S.		H, 6th Ohio Cav.	38		1928 Aug 4	NE, 53rd, 1929
Cooley, Rufus	Chaplain	47th Wis. Inf.	25		1894 Mar 18	NE, 19th, 1895
Cooley, S.H.		I, 42nd Ill. Inf. (died of old age)	111	86	1903 Dec 21	NE, 28th, 1904
Cooley, Sam'l C.	Pvt.	B, 6th Kans. Cav.	325		1910 Nov 26	IA, 37th, 1911
Cooley, Thomas		E, 21st Ky. Inf.	97		1902 Oct 27	KS, 22nd, 1903
Cooley, Wm. F.		A, 10th Ind. Inf.	244		1901 Sep 10	KS, 21st, 1902
Cooling, A.A.	Pvt.	B, 92nd Ill. Inf.	250	57	1900 Jan 19	IA, 26th, 1900
Cooling, A.A.	Pvt.	B, 92nd Ill. Inf.	250		1900 Jun 11	IA, 27th, 1901
Coombs, Wm. H.	Pvt.	H, 10th Iowa Inf.	25		1912 Jul 4	IA, 39th, 1913
Coomes, C.H.	Pvt.	I, 76th Mass.	22		1926 Oct 10	IA, 53rd, 1927
Cooms, Thos. W.		A, 152nd Ind. Inf.	209		1929	KS, 49th, 1930
Coon, A.F.	Capt.	E, 4th Penn. Cav. (died of cancer on face)	10	82	1897 Nov 27	NE, 22nd, 1898
Coon, Benjamin		B, 138th Ill. Inf.	43		1885	KS, 5th, 1886
Coon, C.B.		K, 8th Penn.	7		1928 Dec 1	NE, 53rd, 1929
Coon, David L.		G, 1st Ohio Cav.	32		1919 Oct 5	KS, 39th, 1920
Coon, E.G.		I, 94th N.Y. Inf.	12		1909 Dec 26	KS, 29th, 1910
Coon, E.M.		H, 13th Mich.	61		1928 Dec 12	KS, 48th, 1929
Coon, H.F.		I, 7th West Va. Cav. 12th Iowa Inf.	68		4th quarter 1884	IA, 11th, 1885
Coon, M.L.		A, 105th Penn. Inf.	388		1891 Sep 6	KS, 11th, 1892
Coon, W.A.		F, 17th Ill. Cav.	13	68	1911 Jul 4	NE, 36th, 1912
Coon, William		E, 153rd Ill.	25		1933 Jul 13	NE, 58th, 1934
Coones, Reuben	Corp.	C, 33rd Iowa Inf.	40		1912 Nov 21	IA, 39th, 1913
Coons, I.A.	Surg.	38th Ohio Inf.	104		1886	KS, 6th, 1887
Coons, J.B.		14th & 38th Ohio	104		1924 Jan 9	KS, 44th, 1925
Coons, J.W.		2nd Iowa Battery	55		1886	KS, 6th, 1887
Coons, John		D, 20th Iowa	8		1918 Feb 22	KS, 38th, 1919
Coonts, Jacob		B, 160th Ohio	463		1910 Jul 3	KS, 30th, 1911
Cooper, Albert	Pvt.	I, 20th Iowa Inf.	206	53	1887 Sep 14	IA, 15th, 1889

Name	Rank	Company, Regiment or Ship	Post*	Age	Death Date†	Journal
Cooper, Albert	Sergt.	H, 33rd Iowa Inf.	40		1930 Apr 11	IA, 57th, 1931
Cooper, Albert		M, 9th Kans. Cav.	248		1891	KS, 11th, 1892
Cooper, C.D.	Pvt.	G, 11th Mo. Cav.	107		1920 Oct 11	IA, 47th, 1921
Cooper, C.H.	Pvt.	H, 146th Ind. Inf.	363		1912 Feb 6	IA, 39th, 1913
Cooper, C.M.		H, 6th Iowa	32		1926 Feb 20	NE, 51st, 1927
Cooper, C.P.			142		1925 Jul 7	KS, 45th, 1926
Cooper, Chancy		D, 1st Ill.	493		1926 Nov 22	KS, 46th, 1927
Cooper, Chas.	Pvt.	F, 103rd Ohio Inf.	259		1911 Jan 3	IA, 38th, 1912
Cooper, Chas. H.			32		1911 Apr 12	KS, 31st, 1912
Cooper, D.C.	Capt.	1st U.S. Cav.	364		1907 Jun 20	IA, 34th, 1908
Cooper, David		E, 6th Ind. Inf. (died of old age)	96	79	1918 Apr 23	NE, 43rd, 1919
Cooper, Don C.		I, 62nd Ill.	303		1920 Aug 10	KS, 40th, 1921
Cooper, Edwin R. (alias Harry Rivers)		4th Wis. Art. (died of paralysis)	118		1920 Feb 13	NE, 45th, 1921
Cooper, G.M.		G, 23rd Wis. Inf. (died of pneumonia)	22	64	1907 Oct 12	NE, 32nd, 1908
Cooper, George	Pvt.	A, 15th Iowa Inf.	74		1926 Aug 5	IA, 53rd, 1927
Cooper, Henry	Pvt.	E, 60th U.S.C. Inf.	40		1907 Nov 30	IA, 34th, 1908
Cooper, Henry C.		H, 11th Ill. Cav.	118		1935 Jun 29	NE, 60th, 1936
Cooper, Isaac C.		6th Ind.	35		1908 Feb 6	NE, 33rd, 1909
Cooper, Isaih		K, 99th Ill. Inf.	123		1895	KS, 15th, 1896
Cooper, J.B.		H, 35th Mo. Inf.	464		1899 May 14	KS, 19th, 1900
Cooper, J.C.			75		1920	NE, 45th, 1921
Cooper, J.F.		A, 56th Ill.	147		1913 May 29	KS, 33rd, 1914
Cooper, J.K.	Pvt.	D, 1st Md. Inf.	29	86	1931 Jul 26	IA, 58th, 1932
Cooper, J.M.		K, 16th Ill.	123		1914 Nov 18	KS, 34th, 1915
Cooper, James M.	Lieut.	A, 33rd Iowa Inf.	49		1915 Aug 29	IA, 42nd, 1916
Cooper, Jerry	Pvt.	A, 41st Wis. Inf.	78		1928 Jan	IA, 55th, 1929
Cooper, John	Pvt.	C, 6th Iowa Cav.	192	74	1897 Feb 22	IA, 23rd, 1897
Cooper, John	Corp.	K, 6th Iowa Cav.	206		1903 Feb 6	IA, 30th, 1904
Cooper, John I.		K, 4th Mo.	283		1914 Nov 24	KS, 34th, 1915
Cooper, John K.	Pvt.	H, 40th Ind. Inf.	208		1897 Mar 4	IA, 24th, 1898
Cooper, John R.	Pvt.	H, 2nd Iowa Inf.	108	96	1939 Dec 18	IA, 66th, 1940
Cooper, Joseph		I, 97th Ohio	288		1921 Jul 1	KS, 41st, 1922
Cooper, Joseph H.		K, 9th Kans. Cav.	151		1910 Mar 25	KS, 30th, 1911
Cooper, LeRoy D.	Pvt.	5th Ohio Battery	324	89	1933 Mar 24	IA, 60th, 1934
Cooper, Levi		E, 131st Ohio Inf.	147		1908 Apr 22	KS, 28th, 1909
Cooper, M.			288		1922	KS, 42nd, 1923
Cooper, Martin	Corp.	F, 10th N.Y. Art.	151	55	1894	IA, 20th, 1894
Cooper, R.H.	Sergt.	Penn. Art.	55		1927 Oct 18	IA, 54th, 1928
Cooper, R.M.	Pvt.	G, 7th Iowa Inf.	472	53	1891 Oct 14	IA, 18th, 1892
Cooper, Sam F.	Sergt.	G, Mo.	50		1924 Jul 19	IA, 51st, 1925
Cooper, Sampson	Pvt.	E, 6th Iowa Inf.	337		1906 Sep 3	IA, 33rd, 1907
Cooper, Thomas		C, 4th Ind.	52		1904 Apr 16	KS, 24th, 1905
Cooper, W.C.		6th Mo. Cav.	17		1922 Nov 8	KS, 42nd, 1923
Cooper, W.F.	Pvt.	D, 166th Ohio	101		1901 Sep 19	IA, 28th, 1902
Cooper, W.J.		K, 89th Ill.	25		1913 Dec 19	NE, 38th, 1914
Cooper, William B.		I, 32nd Ind.	18		1923 Jul 1	KS, 43rd, 1924
Cooper, Wm.		B, 2nd Ky.	322		1926	KS, 46th, 1927
Cooper, Wm. A.	Pvt.	G, 35th Iowa Vols.	12		1907 Jul 31	IA, 34th, 1908
Cooper, Wm. H.		C, 102nd Ill.	211		1885	KS, 5th, 1886
Cooprider, Presley		A, 133rd Ind.	52		1927 Dec 2	KS, 47th, 1928
Coover, Edward	Pvt.	G, 47th Iowa Inf.	233		1926 Jun 26	IA, 53rd, 1927
Coover, F.M.		8th Ohio Bat.	85		1914 Jun 2	KS, 34th, 1915
Coover, Samuel		F, 17th Penn. Cav.	115		1899	KS, 19th, 1900
Cope, Ben			17		1919 Aug 22	IA, 46th, 1920
Cope, Charles	Sergt.	G, 2nd Iowa Cav.	255		1917 Apr 8	IA, 44th, 1918
Cope, Chas. E.		M, 1st Ill. Lt. Art.	7		1924[1923] Dec 17	NE, 48th, 1924
Cope, James A.		E, 12th Wis. Inf. (died of cancer)	95		1894 Feb 12	NE, 19th, 1895
Copeland, G.M.		H, 11th Kans. Cav.	71		1916 Jan 12	KS, 36th, 1917
Copeland, Henry E.		died at Lawrence	365		1895 Aug	KS, 15th, 1896
Copeland, Hugh W.	Pvt.	E, 29th Iowa Inf.	35		1915 Aug 26	IA, 42nd, 1916
Copeland, J.A.		G, 21st Ill.	32		1925 Jan 1	KS, 45th, 1926

Name	Rank	Company, Regiment or Ship	Post*	Age	Death Date†	Journal
Copeland, J.M.		Ill.	239		1922 Jan 3	KS, 42nd, 1923
Copeland, John M.		H, 1st Ill. Cav.	239		1922 Jan 3	KS, 41st, 1922
Copeland, John W.	Sergt.	A, 55th Ind. Inf.	19	65	1895 Dec 3	IA, 22nd, 1896
Copeland, Levi M.		I, 69th Ind.	91		1931 Feb	NE, 56th, 1932
Copeland, M.N.		A, 107th Ill.	435		1897 Nov 20	KS, 17th, 1898
Copeland, Robert	Pvt.	D, 15th Iowa Inf.	54		1922 Nov 29	IA, 49th, 1923
Copeland, Thos.		D, — Ind.	245	79	1913 Oct 31	NE, 38th, 1914
Copeland, W.B.			38		1910 May	IA, 37th, 1911
Copeland, W.E.		K, 150th Ohio Inf.	50		1930	KS, 50th, 1931
Copeland, W.M.		D, 17th Kans.	221		1913 May 30	KS, 33rd, 1914
Copeland, William K.		C, 14th Kans. (died at National Home)	428		1895 Sep	KS, 15th, 1896
Copes, Wm. J.			32		1914 Jul 27	KS, 34th, 1915
Copestake, J.C.	Asst. Surg.	114th Ill. Inf.	30		1917 Sep 18	IA, 44th, 1918
Copley, W.W.	Pvt.	E, 112th Ill. Inf.	408		1911 Apr 26	IA, 38th, 1912
Copp, Charles S.	Pvt.	I, 1st Mo. Inf. (died of manapata)	90	38	1884 Dec 12	NE, 9th, 1885
Copp, Henry H.		I, 1st Mo. Eng. (former member of department; died at Brewster)	257		1939	NE, 64th, 1940
Coppage, J.F.		B, 1st Ky. Cav.	3		1914 Mar	KS, 34th, 1915
Coppel, Alfred		E, 54th Ill. Inf.	18		1899 May 18	KS, 19th, 1900
Copper, Jos.	Corp.	C, 43rd Wis. Inf.	7		1913 Jan 13	IA, 40th, 1914
Coppers, Harry	Pvt.	S, 155th Penn. Vol. Inf.	109		1924 Dec 12	IA, 51st, 1925
Copple, J.H.		I, 141st Ohio	322		1913 May 3	KS, 33rd, 1914
Coppock, J.J.	Pvt.	L, 19th Ohio Cav.	22		1909 Jan 11	IA, 36th, 1910
Coppock, T.S.	Pvt.	H, 2nd Iowa Inf.	19		1926 Oct 24	IA, 53rd, 1927
Coppock, Wm.	Pvt.		108		1910 Sep	IA, 37th, 1911
Copson, David	Musician	A, 22nd Ind. Inf.	204		1916 Feb 22	IA, 43rd, 1917
Corabie, Simon			158		1913	IA, 40th, 1914
Corben, Edwin	Pvt.	F, 3rd Mich. Cav.	1		1915 Jul 24	KS, 35th, 1916
Corbett, James		L, 11th Penn. Cav.	36		1920 Jan 25	KS, 40th, 1921
Corbin, A.M.		G, 31st Wis.	13	75	1921 Jan 24	NE, 46th, 1922
Corbin, D.A.	Pvt.	G, 2nd Iowa Cav.	231		1917	IA, 44th, 1918
Corbin, Elbert		B, 1st N.Y. Lt. Art.	11	78	1915 Jan 14	NE, 40th, 1916
Corbin, Eli		L, 17th Ill. Cav.	84		1912 Jun 30	KS, 32nd, 1913
Corbin, J.W.	Pvt.	B, 4th Iowa Cav.	190		1930 Apr 23	IA, 57th, 1931
Corbin, James C.	Pvt.	G, 2nd Iowa Cav. (at large)	231	94	1940 Feb 16	IA, 66th, 1940
Corbin, John P.	Pvt.	G, 1st Cav.	238	51	1899 Dec 20	IA, 26th, 1900
Corbin, L.S.	Pvt.	2nd Iowa Inf.	167		1911 Jul	IA, 38th, 1912
Corbin, Levi		B, 5th N.Y. Cav.	22		1942 Dec 20	NE, 67th, 1943
Corbin, M.M.		G, 12th Kans.	12		1900 Nov 25	KS, 20th, 1901
Corbin, Nathon		M, Ill. Mo. Cav. (died of heart trouble)	152	68	1909 Oct 9	NE, 34th, 1910
Corbin, Parker		E, 76th Ill.	1		1911 Nov 18	KS, 31st, 1912
Corby, Peter		F, 1st Mich. Inf. (died at Harper, Kans.; buried at Harper Cemetery)	251		1894 Sep 3	KS, 14th, 1895
Corcoran, Daniel	Pvt.	Ship Richmond	40	66	1894 Aug	IA, 21st, 1895
Corcoran, M.			42		1st quarter 1885	IA, 11th, 1885
Cordell, Alfred	Pvt.	H, 27th Iowa Inf.	68		1918 Apr 14	IA, 45th, 1919
Cordeman, D.	Farrier	L, 6th Iowa Cav.	284		1929 Mar 29	IA, 56th, 1930
Cordes, B.H.		T, 6th Mo.	388		1927 Nov 2	KS, 47th, 1928
Cordiff, C.F.	Pvt.	E, 58th Ohio	57		1924 Jan 30	IA, 51st, 1925
Cordley, Rich, Dr.		D, 21st Kans.	12		1904 Jun 10	KS, 24th, 1905
Cordon, Isaac N.		M, 16th Kans.	46		1926 Aug 20	KS, 46th, 1927
Core, I.N.		H, 40th Iowa Inf.	5		1899 Oct 22	KS, 19th, 1900
Core, J.W.		K, 3rd West Va.	75		1911 Feb 11	KS, 31st, 1912
Core, S.P.			108		1899 Oct	IA, 26th, 1900
Corey, —		Kans.	241		1908[1909?] Nov 12	KS, 29th, 1910
Corey, Elias		G, 109th Ill. Inf. (died of consumption)	262	69	1896 Jul 6	NE, 21st, 1897
Corey, H.		K, 7th Iowa Cav.	284		1921 Jan 17	IA, 48th, 1922
Corey, Henry	Drummer	G, 36th Ohio Inf.	434		1926 May 16	IA, 53rd, 1927
Corey, Herman F.		M, 1st Mich. Eng.	64		1937 Dec 27	KS, 56th, 1937
Corey, John L.		A, 32nd Mass.	25		1927 Nov 20	NE, 52nd, 1928
Corey, John U.		H, 6th Minn.	293		1925 May 21	KS, 45th, 1926
Corey, John W.	Corp.	C, 4th Iowa Cav.	363		1912 Jul 2	IA, 39th, 1913

*See Appendix A, B or C for roster of post names and locations.
†See Introduction for note regarding recording of death date.

116

Name	Rank	Company, Regiment or Ship	Post*	Age	Death Date†	Journal
Corey, S.L.		44th Wis. Inf.	25		1905 Jan 24	NE, 30th, 1906
Corey, S.L.		44th Wis.	25		1905 Jan 24	NE, 31st, 1907
Corey, Stephen T.		I, 44th Wis. Inf.	75	61	1905 Jan 23	NE, 30th, 1906
Corforan, Gaines		B, 8th Iowa	69		1927 Feb 27	KS, 51st, 1932
Corforan, Gaines		B, 8th Iowa	69		1927 Feb 27	KS, 52nd, 1933
Coriell, Charles, see Conell, Charles						
Corkdale, George C.		C, 124th Penn. Inf.	225		1925 Dec 21	KS, 45th, 1926
Corkery, Dennis		G, 5th N.Y.	185		1931	KS, 52nd, 1933
Corkery, Dennis		G, 5th N.Y.	185		1931	KS, 51st, 1932
Corkhill, T.E.	Chaplain	25th Iowa Inf.	20	76	1897-1898	IA, 24th, 1898
Corkill, T.C.		K, 134th Ill.	255		1915 Jun 20	KS, 35th, 1916
Corkins, L.A.			[89]		1923	KS, 43rd, 1924
Corless, John		E, 179th Penn. (died of heart & old age)	133	89	1920 Oct 11	NE, 45th, 1921
Corley, Joel		C, 25th Ind.	14		1923 Aug 23	KS, 43rd, 1924
Corlis, Francis	Pvt.	C, 6th Mich. Inf.	465		1926 Jun	IA, 53rd, 1927
Corlis, S.H.		I, 44th Inf. (died of rheumatism)	177	73	1913 Jan 27	NE, 38th, 1914
Corman, J.S.		C, 97th Penn.	66		1920 Jan 13	KS, 40th, 1921
Cormish, Amos G.		E, 47th Ill.	218	76	1907 Jan 9	NE, 32nd, 1908
Cormony, W.A.		D, 60th Ohio	32		1920 Jun 19	KS, 40th, 1921
Corn, C.F.		D, 147th Ind. Inf.	142		1925 Nov 24	KS, 45th, 1926
Corn, James		B, 51st Ind.	42		1917 Nov 26	KS, 37th, 1918
Cornelius, George W.		I, 150th Ill.	375		1913 Aug 9	KS, 33rd, 1914
Cornelius, P.W.		E, 83rd Ohio Inf. (died at Americus)	249		1895 Mar	KS, 15th, 1896
Cornelius, Peter		G, 2nd Ind. Cav.	241		1916 Jul 23	KS, 36th, 1917
Cornell, D.E.		7th N.Y.	28		1911 Feb 27	KS, 31st, 1912
Cornell, Daniel		3rd Battery Wis. Lt. Art. (died of cancer)	40		1894 Jan 5	NE, 19th, 1895
Cornell, H.P.	1st Sergt.	C, 112th N.Y.	318		1914 Dec 2	NE, 39th, 1915
Cornell, Ira P.			488		1892 Jan	KS, 12th, 1893
Cornell, James	Sergt.	C, 133rd Penn. Inf.	291	77	1897 Oct 7	IA, 24th, 1898
Cornell, James		K, 128th Ohio (died of cancer)	84	65	1908 Mar	NE, 33rd, 1909
Corner, Samuel		H, 175th Penn.	40	75	1920 Feb 13	NE, 45th, 1921
Corney, C.B.	Pvt.	A, 5th N.H. Inf.	84		1913 Aug 21	IA, 40th, 1914
Corning, Cyrus		I, — Wis. Art.	1		1911 Jan 23	KS, 31st, 1912
Corning, Dwight		B, 102nd Ill.	49		1916 Jan 26	KS, 36th, 1917
Cornish, A.L.	Pvt.	D, 6th Iowa Inf.	233	54	1899 Jun 13	IA, 26th, 1900
Cornish, Ebenezer W.		E, 155th Penn. (died of indigestion)	118	83	1905[1904?] Dec 30	NE, 29th, 1905
Corns, Martin Henry	Pvt.	E, 15th Iowa Inf. (at large)		91	1936 Apr 25	IA, 65th, 1939
Cornvill, Wm. T.	Cook	U.S. Navy, gunboat Brilliant	49		1915 Jul 30	KS, 35th, 1916
Cornwell, John		I, 5th Ill.	66		1896 Jan 12	KS, 16th, 1897
Corp, Frederick	Surg.	2nd Wis. Inf.	338		1904 Jan 28	IA, 31st, 1905
Corp, I.A.		U.S. Navy, Ship 14	68		1924 Apr 15	KS, 44th, 1925
Corpman, J.L.	Pvt.	Ohio	108		1920 Apr 13	IA, 47th, 1921
Corpstein, John	Pvt.	E, 5th Iowa Cav.	78		1918 Sep 21	IA, 45th, 1919
Correll, Chas.	Pvt.	A, 1st Mo. Inf.	251		1913 May 30	IA, 40th, 1914
Correll, D.H.	Pvt.	F, 26th Iowa Inf.	206		1915 Feb 15	IA, 42nd, 1916
Correll, Frederick	Pvt.	F, 185th Ohio Inf.	102	61	1897 Dec 23	IA, 24th, 1898
Correll, Samuel		I, 24th Iowa	81		1923 Jul 30	KS, 43rd, 1924
Correy, John G.	1st Asst. Eng.	Boat Diana	73	70	1894 Mar 1	IA, 21st, 1895
Corrigan, Thos.			7		1909 Nov 4	IA, 36th, 1910
Corrin, Edward	Pvt.	D, 15th Iowa Inf.	222		1924 Oct 27	IA, 51st, 1925
Corrington, Benton	Pvt.	E, 86th Ill. Inf.	31		1910 Feb	IA, 37th, 1911
Corry, Joshua M.		G, 130th Ill.	94		1916 Sep 23	KS, 36th, 1917
Cort, Abe	Pvt.	B, 57th Ill.	23		1923 Sep 8	IA, 50th, 1924
Cortright, J.R.	Pvt.	A, 75th Ill. Inf.	56		1920 Apr 11	IA, 47th, 1921
Cortright, James L.	Pvt.	H, 44th Iowa Inf.	236	89	1935 Dec 31	IA, 65th, 1939
Corwin, H.E.	Pvt.	C, 100th Ill. Inf.	68		1930 Jan 17	IA, 57th, 1931
Corwin, J.E.		A, 97th Ind. Inf.	92		1902 Nov 11	KS, 22nd, 1903
Corwin, Jacob M.		Hvy. Art.	170		1928 Oct 2	IA, 55th, 1929
Corwin, James W.		D, 15th Ohio Vols.	247		1902	KS, 22nd, 1903
Corwin, S.C.		B, 17th Ohio Inf.	25		1902 Sep 12	KS, 22nd, 1903
Corwin, W.E.	Pvt.	D, 30th Iowa Inf.	516		1905 Nov 6	IA, 32nd, 1906

Name	Rank	Company, Regiment or Ship	Post*	Age	Death Date†	Journal
Cory, D.W.		G, 11th Ind. Inf. (died of old age)	256	80	1921 Dec 12	NE, 46th, 1922
Cory, John L.			7		1927 Sep 19	NE, 52nd, 1928
Cory, L.C.		I, 27th N.Y. Cav.	17		1922 Jan 11	KS, 42nd, 1923
Cory, P.G.		L, 6th Mich. Cav.	1		1890	KS, 10th, 1891
Cory, W.W.	Ensign	Navy	69		1914 Jan 16	IA, 41st, 1915
Coryell, Henry		A, 34th Ill.	27		1919 Sep 23	KS, 39th, 1920
Coryell, John S.		C, 10th Mich.	132		1902 Mar 21	KS, 22nd, 1903
Cosgrove, William		G, 11th Kans. (died at Soldiers' Home, Leavenworth)	132		1893	KS, 13th, 1894
Cosley, Frank D.			12		1922 Jun 28	KS, 42nd, 1923
Cosmer, Adam			27		1914	NE, 39th, 1915
Cossitt, John M.			25		1913 Apr 14	KS, 33rd, 1914
Cossman, Nich		A, 8th Ill.	52		1927 Nov 30	KS, 47th, 1928
Costello, John		O, 151st Ill.	142		1930 Jun 15	KS, 50th, 1931
Coswell, D.E.		E, 4th Ohio	293		1924	KS, 44th, 1925
Cotten, Byron	Pvt.	A, 24th Iowa Inf.	163		1907 Dec 3	IA, 34th, 1908
Cotten, C.E.	Pvt.	A, 11th Ill. Inf.	497		1910 Dec 4	IA, 37th, 1911
Cotten, W.H.		F, 36th Ill.	17		1913 Jun 3	KS, 33rd, 1914
Cotter, James	Pvt.	B, 8th Iowa Cav.	337	56	1897 Jun 12	IA, 24th, 1898
Cotterman, Benton		B, 2nd Ohio (died of general breakdown)	42	79	1919 Jul 13	NE, 44th, 1920
Cotterman, W. Andrew		E, 133rd Ill.	19		1917 Nov 14	KS, 37th, 1918
Cottingham, D.	Pvt.	E, 43rd Wis. Inf.	78		1921 Jan 19	IA, 48th, 1922
Cottington, Levi	Pvt.	F, 3rd Wis. Cav.	66		1927 Jun 14	IA, 54th, 1928
Cottington, O.S.	Pvt.	K, 10th Wis. Inf.	105	63	1890 May 23	IA, 17th, 1891
Cottman, James D.		C, 11th Ind. Inf.	25		1917 Jan 1	KS, 37th, 1918
Cottman, James D.		C, 11th Ind.	25		1916 Dec 30	KS, 36th, 1917
Cotton, A.	Pvt.	4th West Va. Inf.	497		1918 Dec 5	IA, 45th, 1919
Cotton, A.B.		K, 27th Iowa	147		1917 Aug 11	KS, 37th, 1918
Cotton, George		B, 1st Maine	57		1915 Feb 12	KS, 35th, 1916
Cotton, Owen W.		B, 5th Mich.	25		1930 Oct 14	NE, 55th, 1931
Cotton, W.S.	Corp.	B, 24th Iowa Inf.	14	61	1892 Apr 9	IA, 18th, 1892
Cotton, Winfield S.	Corp.	B, 24th Iowa Inf.	14	62	1892 Apr 9	IA, 19th, 1893
Cottrell, Z.E.	Sergt.	B, 23rd Iowa	68		1922 Dec 31	IA, 49th, 1923
Coublin, Wm.	Pvt.	B, 6th Iowa	173		1905 Jan 28	IA, 32nd, 1906
Couch, C.B.			32		1922	NE, 47th, 1923
Couch, Isaac M.		E, 44th Mo.	61		1911	KS, 31st, 1912
Couch, John	Pvt.	F, 98th Ohio Inf.	55		1913 Mar 9	IA, 40th, 1914
Couch, Josephus			147		1912 Nov 25	KS, 32nd, 1913
Couch, Rufus B.	Pvt.	K, 101st Ohio Vol. Inf.	511	68	1900 Mar 3	IA, 26th, 1900
Couch, Stanford G.	Sergt.	K, 20th Wis. Inf.	97		1909 Jun 28	IA, 36th, 1910
Couch, W.S.		C, 23rd Iowa	147		1921 May 15	KS, 41st, 1922
Couchnet, August		I, 27th Wis.	464		1910 Dec 11	KS, 30th, 1911
Coudron, Andrew	Pvt.	K, 10th Minn. Inf.	22		1908 Sep 16	IA, 35th, 1909
Coudry, John		E, 5th Kans. Cav.	[100?]		1914 Feb 13	KS, 34th, 1915
Couger, David H.		H, 36th Iowa	147		1925 Dec 26	KS, 45th, 1926
Couley, David C.		A, 24th Ind. (died of old age)	25	74	1908 Dec 14	NE, 33rd, 1909
Couley, John	Pvt.	K, 9th Iowa Battery (died of consumption)	182	44	1887 Mar	NE, 12th, 1888
Coulson, George S.		E, 78th Ohio	46		1925 Mar 29	KS, 45th, 1926
Coulson, Jackson		H, 166th Penn.	63		1920 Mar 28	KS, 40th, 1921
Coulter, Edwin	Capt.	20th Iowa Inf.	235		1910 Feb 7	IA, 37th, 1911
Coulter, J.N.	Pvt.	G, 10th Iowa Inf.	116		1906 Nov 9	IA, 33rd, 1907
Coulter, M.W.	Pvt.	E, 30th Ill. Inf.	25		1890 Jul 6	KS, 11th, 1892
Coulter, O.H.		50th Ill. Inf. (died at Santa Ana, California)		65	1912 Jan 12	KS, 31st, 1912
Coulter, Robert		I, 104th Ohio (died of old age)	35	90	1920 Jan 20	NE, 45th, 1921
Coulter, W.A.		E, 1st Iowa Cav. (died of old age)	50	85	1914 Oct 17	NE, 39th, 1915
Coulter, William		K, 34th Iowa	36		1890	KS, 10th, 1891
Coulthurst, Henry	Pvt.	C, 50th Wis.	324		1914 Aug 16	IA, 41st, 1915
Council, Milton		D, 24th Wis.	1		1926 May 26	KS, 46th, 1927
Council, Thos.	Pvt.	E, 39th Iowa Inf.	26		1909 May 27	IA, 36th, 1910
Counhoven, John	Marine		141		1903 Nov 29	IA, 31st, 1905
Counhover, John E.	Landsman		462		1903 Nov 22	IA, 30th, 1904

*See Appendix A, B or C for roster of post names and locations.
†See Introduction for note regarding recording of death date.

Name	Rank	Company, Regiment or Ship	Post*	Age	Death Date†	Journal
Counslee, James M.	Pvt.	F, 39th Iowa	55		1901 Dec 16	IA, 28th, 1902
Counter, David	1st Sergt.	E, 66th Ill. Inf.	66		1897 May 19	IA, 24th, 1898
Counts, S.T.		I, 42nd Ohio	40		1921 Mar 21	KS, 41st, 1922
Counts, W.H.		A, 20th Ind.	85		1922 Feb 21	KS, 42nd, 1923
Coup, J.D.	Pvt.	K, 5th Penn. Cav.	10		1929 Apr 21	IA, 56th, 1930
Coupland, Wm.		F, 16th Ill.	64		1926 Sep 29	KS, 46th, 1927
Courson, Samuel		H, 83rd Ill.	18		1919 Nov 27	KS, 39th, 1920
Courter, E.		G, 96th Ohio	232		1908 Aug 23	KS, 28th, 1909
Courtney, Cyrus		Y, 14th West Va.	116		1927 Jan 9	KS, 47th, 1928
Courtney, J.H.	Sergt.	K, 31st Iowa Inf.	130		1918 Aug 6	IA, 45th, 1919
Courtney, John H.		F, 6th West Va. (served five years)	19		1889	KS, 9th, 1890
Courtney, Nathan W.		B & L, 2nd & 4th West Va.	142		1913 Nov 9	KS, 33rd, 1914
Courtright, J.	Pvt.	D, 113th Ill.	452		1921 Oct 19	IA, 48th, 1922
Courtright, Jas. S.	Pvt.	B, 15th Iowa Inf.	457		1912 Feb 4	IA, 39th, 1913
Courtright, W.C.		C, 45th Mo. Inf.	4		1915 Apr 8	KS, 35th, 1916
Courtwright, A.L.		C, 6th Mo. Cav.	4		1923 Mar 2	KS, 43rd, 1924
Courtwright, G.A.	Pvt.	B, 15th Ill.	210	71	1900 Apr 9	IA, 26th, 1900
Courtwright, Peter		L, 2nd Mo. Cav.	217		1899	NE, 24th, 1900
Cousins, E.B.	Sergt.	B, 24th Iowa Inf.	34		1921 Oct 3	IA, 48th, 1922
Cousins, John		C, 21st Iowa	75		1919 May 20	KS, 39th, 1920
Cousins, L.B.		B, 41st & 89th Ohio Inf.	29		1925 May 17	IA, 52nd, 1926
Covel, Orin M.	Pvt.	K, 22nd Wis. Inf.	25		1927 Oct	IA, 54th, 1928
Covell, Hiram B.		A, 1st N.Y. Dragoons	82		1908 Aug 9	KS, 28th, 1909
Covell, Thomas		F, 46th Ill. Inf.	25		1925 Feb 26	KS, 45th, 1926
Cover, D.M.V.B.		K, 55th Ohio Inf. (died of paralysis)	412		1891 Aug 30	KS, 11th, 1892
Cover, Wm.			25		1924 Jul	IA, 51st, 1925
Covert, John S.		H, 1st Ohio Lt. Art.	190		1921 May 28	KS, 41st, 1922
Covert, Peter		H, 5th Mo.	123		1926 Nov 10	KS, 46th, 1927
Covert, Truman	Pvt.	C, —	133		1907 Jan 29	IA, 34th, 1908
Covey, John R.	Pvt.	F, 18th N.Y. Cav.	216	63	1896 Mar 25	IA, 22nd, 1896
Covill, J.A.	Corp.	A, 35th Iowa Inf.	231		1905 Mar 7	IA, 32nd, 1906
Covolt, B.D.		D, 3rd Md.	89		1926	KS, 46th, 1927
Cowan, Geo.		D, 9th Ill. Cav.	35		1904 Dec 18	KS, 24th, 1905
Cowan, Geo. G.	Pvt.	H, 7th Iowa	497		1922 Oct 29	IA, 49th, 1923
Cowan, H.H.		F, 34th Ill. Inf. (died of pneumonia)	169	60	1901 Jun	NE, 26th, 1902
Cowan, John C.		A, 23rd Ohio	262	75	1918 Dec 14	NE, 43rd, 1919
Cowan, Jos.	Sergt.	B, 3rd Wis. Cav.	219		1913 May 24	IA, 40th, 1914
Cowan, Richard	Pvt.	G, 1st Ill. Cav.	12	58	1898 Jul 27	IA, 25th, 1899
Cowan, T.S.		L, 74th Ill.		70	1909 Dec 12	NE, 34th, 1910
Cowan, W.B.	Pvt.	F, 6th Iowa Cav.	194		1928 Sep 10	IA, 55th, 1929
Cowan, W.R.	Pvt.	K, 33rd Iowa Inf.	40		1926 Sep 6	IA, 53rd, 1927
Cowdan, J.T.		150th Ill.	295		1917 Feb	KS, 37th, 1918
Cowden, W.P.	Sergt.	F, 140th Ill. Inf.	135		1919 Oct 2	IA, 47th, 1921
Cowden, W.P.		F, 140th Ill. Inf.	135		1919 Oct 2	IA, 46th, 1920
Cowder, Nathan		E, 5th Ill. Cav. (died at asylum)	354	69	1913[1912?] Sep 11	NE, 37th, 1913
Cowdery, J.A.		B, 2nd West Va. Cav.	20		1921 Oct 26	KS, 41st, 1922
Cowels, C.H.		A, 1st N.Y. Art.	251		1913 Apr 13	KS, 33rd, 1914
Cowen, H.		H, 37th Ind. Inf.	252		1908 Dec 7	KS, 28th, 1909
Cowgill, J.E.	Pvt.	H, 46th Iowa Inf. A, 14th Iowa Inf.	1		1927 Jan	IA, 54th, 1928
Cowgill, J.W.		D, 53rd Ind.	96		1927 Aug 18	KS, 47th, 1928
Cowgill, M.	Capt.	F, 60th Ohio	271		1921 Apr 7	IA, 48th, 1922
Cowgill, Thos. G.	Pvt.	E, 1st Del. Cav.	22		1903 Feb 3	IA, 30th, 1904
Cowin, E.F.	Pvt.	A, 177th Ohio	68		1907 Apr 29	IA, 34th, 1908
Cowles, D.B.	Pvt.	D, Brack. Div. Minn. Cav.	69		1925 May 14	IA, 52nd, 1926
Cowles, H.R.	Capt.	H, 2nd Iowa Inf.	108	59	1892 Apr 13	IA, 19th, 1893
Cowles, W.D.			346		1910	IA, 37th, 1911
Cowley, A.J.			187		1917	IA, 45th, 1919
Cowley, W.J.		H, 20th Iowa Inf.	51		1917	KS, 37th, 1918
Cowley, W.R.		C, 84th Ohio	59		1914 Jul 14	KS, 34th, 1915
Cowman, Thomas J.	Pvt.	B, 3rd Iowa Inf.	27		1917 Apr 22	IA, 44th, 1918
Cowman, W.P.	Sergt.	G, 18th Inf.	359		1905 Dec 24	IA, 32nd, 1906

*See Appendix A, B or C for roster of post names and locations.
†See Introduction for note regarding recording of death date.

Name	Rank	Company, Regiment or Ship	Post*	Age	Death Date†	Journal
Cowman, William M.	Pvt.	A, 47th Iowa Inf.	27	94	1940 Feb 4	IA, 66th, 1940
Cown, F.P.		F, 36th Ohio Inf.	11	75	1910 Apr 5	NE, 35th, 1911
Cox, A.		I, 55th Mass.	158		1921 Aug 19	KS, 41st, 1922
Cox, A.I.		D, 20th Ind. Inf.	91		1887 Feb 25	KS, 7th, 1888
Cox, Aaron		D, 79th Ohio	418		1924 Oct 25	KS, 44th, 1925
Cox, Aaron		D, 79th Ohio Inf.	418		1925 Oct 25	KS, 45th, 1926
Cox, Andrew		B, 20th Ohio	255		1909 Jul 3	KS, 29th, 1910
Cox, Anthony			32		1913 Oct 28	KS, 33rd, 1914
Cox, C.		A, 10th Iowa Inf.	284		1921 Oct 21	IA, 48th, 1922
Cox, D.A.			86		1907 2nd term	IA, 34th, 1908
Cox, Daniel M.	Pvt.	D, 14th Ill. Inf.	440		1913 Nov	IA, 40th, 1914
Cox, Elie		E, 6th Kans.	370		1896 Apr 4	KS, 16th, 1897
Cox, Geo. H.	Pvt.	G, 126th Ill. Inf.	88	50	1892 Jul 12	IA, 19th, 1893
Cox, Geo. W.			182		1904	IA, 31st, 1905
Cox, Geo. W.		I, 48th Ill.	25		1922 Feb 21	NE, 47th, 1923
Cox, George		H, 16th U.S. Cav.	15		1911 Nov 14	KS, 31st, 1912
Cox, George W.		I, 48th Ill. (not a member; buried by Farragut Post)	25		1922 Feb 21	NE, 47th, 1923
Cox, Grandville		C, 11th West Va.	55		1928 Nov 9	KS, 48th, 1929
Cox, H.D.		H, 123rd Ill.	32		1906 Oct 16	KS, 26th, 1907
Cox, Henry		F, 134th Ohio	5		1923 Dec 19	KS, 43rd, 1924
Cox, Hosea J.		Indiana	57	76	1922 Aug	NE, 47th, 1923
Cox, Isaiah		H, 11th Kans. Inf.	1		1899 Jan 3	KS, 19th, 1900
Cox, J.L.		E, 7th Mo. Cav.	435		1916 Feb 10	KS, 36th, 1917
Cox, J.R.		I, 4th West Va.	66		1916 Jan 8	KS, 36th, 1917
Cox, J.R.		I, 153rd Ind. Inf. (died of cancer of throat)	110	69	1902 Mar	NE, 27th, 1903
Cox, J.T.		A, 1st Indian	98		1888	KS, 8th, 1889
Cox, Jacob D.	Pvt.	D, 6th Iowa Inf.	398		1902 Jul 21	IA, 29th, 1903
Cox, James			143		1911	IA, 38th, 1912
Cox, James W.	Musician	G, 17th Iowa Inf.	404		1925 Nov 15	IA, 52nd, 1926
Cox, Jas. W.	Corp.	C, 3rd Iowa Cav.	2	75	1891 Sep 17	IA, 18th, 1892
Cox, Jesse		M, 2nd Mo. Lt. Art.	38		1922 Aug 2	KS, 42nd, 1923
Cox, Jesse		A, 4th Kans. M.[Kans. State Militia?]	38		1921 Aug 12	KS, 41st, 1922
Cox, John			338		1909 Apr	IA, 36th, 1910
Cox, John S.		B, 119th Ill.	28		1896 Aug 7	KS, 16th, 1897
Cox, John W.	Pvt.	C, 112th Ill. Inf.	12		1930 Aug 16	IA, 57th, 1931
Cox, L.A.	Pvt.	C, 3rd Iowa Cav.	2		1905 Jan 27	IA, 32nd, 1906
Cox, Mark		H, 7th Mo. Cav.	49		1917 Jun 27	KS, 37th, 1918
Cox, Merryman	Pvt.	I, 10th Iowa Inf.	253		1916 Feb 2	IA, 43rd, 1917
Cox, Milton		G, 5th Iowa Inf. (died of old age)	89	82	1921 May 26	NE, 46th, 1922
Cox, R.L.		F, 84th Ill. Inf. (died of dropsy)	32	73	1902 Jun	NE, 27th, 1903
Cox, Recompense		K, 55th Ind.	209		1916 Apr 18	KS, 36th, 1917
Cox, Thomas		H, 139th Ill. Inf.	25		1911 Mar 23	NE, 36th, 1912
Cox, Thomas J.		C, 125th Ill. Inf.	88		1908 Feb 17	KS, 28th, 1909
Cox, Thos. W.	Drummer	G, 33rd Iowa Inf.	404		1908 Jan 29	IA, 35th, 1909
Cox, W.A.H.	Pvt.	D, 44th Mo. Eng.	56		1920 Jul 12	IA, 47th, 1921
Cox, W.A.J.		D, 52nd Ind.	73		1913 Jan 25	KS, 32nd, 1913
Cox, W.B.			84		1927 Jul 21	NE, 52nd, 1928
Cox, W.E.		B, 34th Ill. Inf.	13	65	1911 Oct 15	NE, 36th, 1912
Cox, W.F.		H, 63rd Ill.	65		1911 Jan 20	KS, 31st, 1912
Cox, W.J.		D, 140th Ind. Inf. (died at Reno County, Kans.; buried at Avery Cemetery)	14		1894 Aug 28	KS, 14th, 1895
Cox, W.M.W.		86th —	89		1908	KS, 28th, 1909
Cox, Will		B, 91st Ill.	257		1925 Aug 21	KS, 45th, 1926
Cox, William	Pvt.	A, 78th Ill. Inf. (died of rheumatism)	28	59	1887 Jan 2	NE, 12th, 1888
Cox, William H.		H, 12th Iowa Inf.		92	1937 Feb 25	IA, 64th, 1938
Cox, Wm.	Pvt.	F, 3rd Iowa Inf.	48	64	1891 Feb	IA, 18th, 1892
Cox, Wm.	Pvt.	G, 22nd Wis. Inf.	101		1910 Sep 17	IA, 37th, 1911
Coy, Geo.		E, 11th Ind.	90		1933 Apr 21	KS, 53rd, 1934
Coy, Wm.	Pvt.	I, 97th Ohio Inf.	271		1888 Aug	IA, 15th, 1889
Coykendall, C.W.		D, 53rd Ill.	44		1896 Nov 8	KS, 16th, 1897
Coykendall, M.J.	Pvt.	55th Ill. Inf.	379		1911 1st term	IA, 38th, 1912

*See Appendix A, B or C for roster of post names and locations.
†See Introduction for note regarding recording of death date.

120

Name	Rank	Company, Regiment or Ship	Post*	Age	Death Date†	Journal
Coyle, James		H, 1st Ky. Cav.	38		1911 Nov 29	KS, 31st, 1912
Coyle, John		A, 2nd N.J.	142		1913 Nov 25	KS, 33rd, 1914
Coyle, Peter		40th Inf. (died by automobile)	5	80	1922 Jul 4	NE, 47th, 1923
Coyne, Bartley		K, 2nd Iowa	1		1924 Nov 11	KS, 44th, 1925
Coyne, John		B, 23rd Ind.	1		1922 Aug 27	KS, 42nd, 1923
Coyne, John Wesley, see Koin, John W.						
Coyner, James		B, 30th Iowa	142		1928 Dec 9	KS, 48th, 1929
Cozad, B.F.	Pvt.	A, 47th Inf.	472		1907 Dec 11	IA, 34th, 1908
Cozad, F.W.	Capt.	B, 40th Iowa Inf.	16		1918	IA, 45th, 1919
Cozad, W.N.	Pvt.	K, 4th Iowa Inf.	57		1913 Mar 28	IA, 40th, 1914
Cozier, B.F.W.	Chaplain	3rd Ohio	12		1903 May 31	IA, 30th, 1904
Cozine, Geo. A.		20th Ind. Bat.	233		1900 Nov 14	KS, 20th, 1901
Cozine, John S.		E, 10th Ky. Inf.	25		1891 Jan 7	KS, 11th, 1892
Crabb, John H.		D, 6th Mich. Hvy. Art.	9		1921 Sep 3	KS, 41st, 1922
Crabbs, J.M.		K, 89th Ind. Inf.	242		1894 Mar 17	KS, 14th, 1895
Crabill, George	Pvt.	G, 4th Ore. Inf.	11		1899 Feb 9	IA, 26th, 1900
Crable, John J.		E, 47th Iowa (former member; died at Grand Island)	24		1936	NE, 61st, 1937
Crabtree, C.C.	Pvt.	H, 44th Wis.	68		1924 May 15	IA, 51st, 1925
Crabtree, Jno. G.	Pvt.	D, 42nd Wis.	436		1903 Aug 1	IA, 30th, 1904
Crabtree, John S.		M & C, 10th Ill.	380		1913 Dec 7	KS, 33rd, 1914
Crabtree, Joseph	Pvt.	E, 18th Iowa	283		1903 Jul 20	IA, 30th, 1904
Cracklin, J.	Capt.	D, 2nd Kans.	12		1888	KS, 8th, 1889
Cracraft, A.W.		187th Ohio	175		1918 Jan	KS, 38th, 1919
Craddock, John W.	Pvt.	E, 18th Iowa Inf.	231		1912 Aug 14	IA, 39th, 1913
Cradit, N.C.		K, 16th Kans.	40		1905 Mar 21	KS, 25th, 1906
Cradwick, Clark	Musician	K, 35th Iowa Inf.	39		1917 Dec 2	IA, 44th, 1918
Craft, Fred J.	Pvt.	C, 52nd Ill. Inf.	5	60	1896 Mar 13	IA, 22nd, 1896
Craft, Samuel H.		A, 5th Kans. Cav.	328		1918 Feb 8	KS, 38th, 1919
Cragg, Harry P.	Pvt.	L, 4th Iowa Cav.	465		1910 Dec 9	IA, 37th, 1911
Cragg, John	Pvt.	C, 2nd Iowa Cav.	452		1922 Apr 11	IA, 49th, 1923
Craig, A.W.			98		1908 Apr 18	KS, 28th, 1909
Craig, Absolom W.		G, 67th Ohio	339		1921 Apr 21	KS, 41st, 1922
Craig, H.R.		E, 7th Ohio Cav.			1928 May 23	NE, 53rd, 1929
Craig, I.H.	Pvt.	A, 23rd Iowa Inf.	30		1912 Jul 9	IA, 39th, 1913
Craig, J.J.		E, 193rd Ohio Inf.	18		1929 Mar 28	KS, 49th, 1930
Craig, James B.		E, 16th Iowa	65		1916 Jan 12	KS, 36th, 1917
Craig, James G.		G, 58th Ill.	185		1925 Jan 24	KS, 45th, 1926
Craig, James M.		H, 23rd Ohio	2		1923 Jul 2	KS, 43rd, 1924
Craig, Jno. R.		B, 10th Ill.	35		1926 Jan 1	NE, 51st, 1927
Craig, John T.		I, 6th Ind.	356		1909 Dec 3	KS, 29th, 1910
Craig, Josiah	Pvt.	H, 2nd Iowa Cav.	12	37	1887 Jul 25	IA, 15th, 1889
Craig, Louis		D, 7th Iowa (died of influenza)	77	75	1919 Dec 3	NE, 44th, 1920
Craig, Riley			338		1909 Jul 20	IA, 36th, 1910
Craig, Robert A.		G, 114th Ill.	85		1913 May 15	KS, 33rd, 1914
Craig, Robt.		L, 11th Penn. Cav.	38		1904 May 26	KS, 24th, 1905
Craig, S.H.	Capt.	B, 4th Iowa	29		1905 Aug 5	IA, 32nd, 1906
Craig, Thomas		I, 19th Ill.	76		1914 Jan 22	KS, 34th, 1915
Craig, W.F.	Capt.		306		1906 Oct 12	IA, 33rd, 1907
Craig, W.L.		C, 3rd Ill. Cav. (died in Colorado)	23		1889	KS, 9th, 1890
Craig, W.W.			272		1908	NE, 33rd, 1909
Craig, William		G, 28th N.Y.	328		1905 Aug 2	KS, 25th, 1906
Craig, Wm.		I, 24th Iowa	59		1918 Jan 31	KS, 38th, 1919
Crain, T.W.		H, 5th Ill.	64		1923 Jun 24	KS, 43rd, 1924
Crain, William		F, 2nd Ill. Cav.	118		1912 Jan 30	KS, 32nd, 1913
Craithorm, Frank			98		1909 Jul 6	KS, 29th, 1910
Crales, D.W.			145		1914 Jun 18	KS, 34th, 1915
Crall, Matthias		F, 33rd Wis.	81		1924 Jul 25	KS, 44th, 1925
Cram, Geo. W.	Pvt.	F, 5th Wis. Inf.	247		1926 May	IA, 53rd, 1927
Cramblet, E.B.	Pvt.	A, 78th Ohio Inf.	30	92	1933 Apr 2	IA, 60th, 1934
Cramer, A.B.	Pvt.	H, 4th Cav.	500		1924	IA, 51st, 1925

*See Appendix A, B or C for roster of post names and locations.
†See Introduction for note regarding recording of death date.

Name	Rank	Company, Regiment or Ship	Post*	Age	Death Date†	Journal
Cramer, A.J.		C, 12th Kans. Inf.	97		1917 Oct 11	KS, 37th, 1918
Cramer, Christian		E, 19th U.S.	32		1905 Feb 4	KS, 25th, 1906
Cramer, F.E.		D, 128th N.Y. Inf.	143		1892 Dec 10	NE, 17th, 1893
Cramer, F.M.		A, 15th Kans.	96		1920 Jul 20	KS, 40th, 1921
Cramer, J.E.		B, 135th Ill. Inf.	7	79	1925 Jul 7	NE, 50th, 1926
Cramer, John W.	Pvt.	F, 43rd Wis. Inf.	230		1908 Nov 24	IA, 35th, 1909
Cramer, Maley		E, 138th Ill.	90		1928 Jan 5	KS, 48th, 1929
Cramer, Peter		B, 52nd Ill. Inf.	71		1891 Dec 18	KS, 11th, 1892
Cramer, S.M.		D, 18th Ohio	12		1913 Aug 15	KS, 33rd, 1914
Cramlet, J.B.	Pvt.		96		1921 Jan 14	IA, 48th, 1922
Crammer, Hiram		A, 60th N.Y. Inf.	378		1900 Oct 16	KS, 20th, 1901
Crammer, L.	Pvt.	D, 25th Iowa Inf.	1		1929 Aug 11	IA, 56th, 1930
Cramphin, Jas. H.		H, 64th Ill. Inf.	25	79	1919 Jan 1	NE, 44th, 1920
Crance, H.C.	Pvt.	A, 109th N.Y.	172		1907 Sep 13	IA, 34th, 1908
Crandal, H.C.	Pvt.	B, 1st Iowa Cav.	267		1908 Jan 18	IA, 35th, 1909
Crandall, Benj. F.		F, 1st Penn.	1		1911 Sep 21	KS, 31st, 1912
Crandall, C.		C, 81st Ind.	265		1917 Feb 2	KS, 37th, 1918
Crandall, Cyrus		C, 81st Ind. Inf.	25		1917 Feb 17	KS, 37th, 1918
Crandall, E.		died of old age	57	83	1919 About Oct	NE, 44th, 1920
Crandall, George B.		D, 19th Mich. Inf.	58		1925 Jan 16	KS, 45th, 1926
Crandall, J.F.		38th Ind.	130		1913 Jun 24	KS, 33rd, 1914
Crandall, Jas. R.		D, 2nd Neb. Cav. (died of heart failure)	7	74	1902 Apr	NE, 27th, 1903
Crandall, P.W.		52nd Wis. Inf. (died of heart failure)	57	74	1917 Apr 24	NE, 42nd, 1918
Crandall, Robert W., see Crandell, Robert W.						
Crandell, —	Pvt.	A, 102nd Ill. Inf.	233		1926 Feb 5	IA, 53rd, 1927
Crandell, James F.		2nd Ky. Art.	130		1914 Jun 24	KS, 34th, 1915
Crandell, Robert W.		F, 73rd Ind.	36		1923 May 27	KS, 43rd, 1924
Crandle, E.H.	Pvt.	D, 10th Ill. Inf.	40	55	1894 Jan 3	IA, 20th, 1894
Crane, Augustus A.		H, 120th N.Y.	453		1921 Dec 14	KS, 41st, 1922
Crane, B.H.	Lieut.	B, 25th Iowa Inf.	20	49	1887 Dec 21	IA, 14th, 1888
Crane, D.O.		A, 2nd, 5th Kans.	1		1918 May 3	KS, 38th, 1919
Crane, Edward P.		E, 6th Mo. Inf.	84	93	1935 Jun 18	IA, 62nd, 1936
Crane, Edward P.		E, 6th Mo. Inf.		93	1936[1935?] Jun 14	IA, 62nd, 1936
Crane, F.L.			1		1884	KS, 4th, 1885
Crane, Harvey D.		C, 18th Iowa	25		1910 Dec 30	KS, 30th, 1911
Crane, Henry		L, 15th Ill. Cav.	339		1899 Sep	KS, 19th, 1900
Crane, I.K.	Pvt.	I, 12th Iowa Inf.	74	74	1894 Aug 21	IA, 21st, 1895
Crane, J.F.G.	Pvt.	B, 44th Iowa Inf.	211	39	1887 Aug 18	IA, 14th, 1888
Crane, J.G.	Capt.	K, 37th Iowa Inf.	1		1905 Nov 8	IA, 32nd, 1906
Crane, John		K, 5th Mich.	76		1933	KS, 53rd, 1934
Crane, Stephen		D, 7th Wis.	57		1920 Oct 10	KS, 40th, 1921
Craner, John	Capt.	A or B, 9th Ind. Inf. (was severely wounded at Chickamauga)	110		1902 Jun or Jul 28	KS, 22nd, 1903
Crangle, Wm. F.		E, 60th N.Y.	35		1929	NE, 54th, 1930
Crans, A.W.	Corp.	I, 82nd N.Y. Inf.	1		1917 Oct 24	IA, 44th, 1918
Cranshaw, Titus		B, 3rd N.Y. Inf.	185		1917 Mar 30	KS, 37th, 1918
Cranston, David J.	Pvt.	H, 26th Iowa	92		1922 Dec 1	IA, 49th, 1923
Cranston, Thos.		A, 3rd Ind. Cav.	156		1899 May 8	KS, 19th, 1900
Crapo, Philip M.		E, 3rd Mich. Inf. (see Appendix D)			1903 Sep 20	IA, 30th, 1904
Crappa, P.M.	Pvt.	E, 3rd Mass. Vol. Inf.	5		1903 Sep 20	IA, 30th, 1904
Crary, A.B.		E, 138th Ohio Inf.	63		1901 Feb 9	KS, 21st, 1902
Crasthwade, A.C.		D, 103rd Penn. Inf.	318	75	1917 Mar 3	NE, 42nd, 1918
Cratsenberg, A.J.	Sergt.	F, 186th N.Y. Inf.	168		1910 Aug 12	IA, 37th, 1911
Cratty, Wm.		E, 33rd Iowa Inf. (cause of death: heart)	327	77	1903 Jan 19	NE, 28th, 1904
Craul, Geo. W.	Pvt.	H, 128th Penn. Inf.	74		1912 Feb 12	IA, 39th, 1913
Craushaw, J.R.	Pvt.	C, 23rd Iowa Inf.	7		1905 Dec	IA, 32nd, 1906
Crauther, Daniel	Pvt.	C, 5th Ill. Cav.	42		1912 Sep 28	IA, 39th, 1913
Craven, C.C.	Pvt.	C, 28th Iowa Inf.	127		1919 Nov 1	IA, 46th, 1920
Cravens, Thomas		C, 23rd Ill.	18		1913 Aug 31	KS, 33rd, 1914
Craw, M.J.		Wis. (died of cancer of stomach)	82		1894 May 8	NE, 19th, 1895
Craw, R.B.			[89]		1923	KS, 43rd, 1924

*See Appendix A, B or C for roster of post names and locations.
†See Introduction for note regarding recording of death date.

122

Name	Rank	Company, Regiment or Ship	Post*	Age	Death Date†	Journal
Crawfor, John	Pvt.	G, 2nd Iowa Cav.	452		1903-1904	IA, 30th, 1904
Crawford, A.	Pvt.	A, 32nd Ohio	48		1901 Oct	IA, 28th, 1902
Crawford, A.J.		H, 1st Vt.	115		1918 Jun 11	KS, 38th, 1919
Crawford, Augustien		I, 9th Mo. Cav. (died of general debility)	84	74	1912 Feb 10	NE, 37th, 1913
Crawford, C.F.		E, 141st Ill. Inf.	57		1887 Mar 5	KS, 7th, 1888
Crawford, C.H.		H, 4th Ohio Inf.	47		1929 Apr 7	KS, 49th, 1930
Crawford, Chas.		B, 18th Iowa Inf. (died of heart failure)	171	80	1922 Feb 25	NE, 50th, 1926
Crawford, Chas. T.		died of old age	171		1922 Feb 25	NE, 47th, 1923
Crawford, D.C.		E, 105th Penn.	25		1922 Dec 29	NE, 47th, 1923
Crawford, D.C.		E, 105th Penn.	25		1922 Dec 29	NE, 47th, 1923
Crawford, E.B.		H, 51st Ohio Vols.	301		1886	KS, 6th, 1887
Crawford, E.H.		C, 69th Ill.	81		1906 Jan 9	KS, 26th, 1907
Crawford, E.M.	Pvt.	I, 25th Iowa	108		1923 Feb 25	IA, 50th, 1924
Crawford, G.W.	Pvt.	H, 73rd —	83		1923	IA, 50th, 1924
Crawford, Geo. F.		E, 146th N.Y. (died at Atchison)	336		1895 Nov	KS, 15th, 1896
Crawford, H.R.		B, 141st N.J.	132		1888	KS, 8th, 1889
Crawford, Henry	Pvt.	D, 78th Ohio Inf.	98		1911 Apr 14	IA, 38th, 1912
Crawford, J.B.	Pvt.	A, 75th Ill. Inf.	88		1919 Apr 26	IA, 46th, 1920
Crawford, J.H.		E, 122nd Ill. Inf.	147		1914 Nov 7	KS, 34th, 1915
Crawford, J.L.	Pvt.	H, 3rd Iowa Cav.	12		1929 Dec 3	IA, 56th, 1930
Crawford, J.W.		K, 2nd Ill. D, 13th Ill.	193		1912 Oct 25	KS, 32nd, 1913
Crawford, Jas.		A, 2nd Neb. Cav. (died of general debility)	197	69	1905 Feb 9	NE, 30th, 1906
Crawford, Morris J.		A, 166th Ohio	18		1926 Dec 19	KS, 46th, 1927
Crawford, N.S.		H, 23rd Ohio	85		1917 May 4	KS, 37th, 1918
Crawford, N.T.		A, 55th Ind. (died of heart trouble)	274	69	1910 Feb 26	NE, 34th, 1910
Crawford, P.W.	Pvt.	A, 3rd Iowa Inf.	78		1910 Dec 9	IA, 37th, 1911
Crawford, Philip S.		E, 11th Kans. Cav.	1		1886	KS, 6th, 1887
Crawford, S.J.	Col.	19th Kans.	1		1913 Oct 21	KS, 33rd, 1914
Crawford, Saml.	Pvt.	E, 20th Iowa Inf.	285	55	1891 Jul 29	IA, 18th, 1892
Crawford, T.M.	Sergt.	B, 1st Iowa	97		1903 Apr 3	IA, 30th, 1904
Crawford, Thomas	Pvt.	B, 2nd Ohio Inf.	66		1916 Mar 6	IA, 43rd, 1917
Crawford, W.A.		A, 3rd Colo. Cav.	147		1930 Oct 11	NE, 55th, 1931
Crawford, W.B.			321		1904-1905	IA, 31st, 1905
Crawford, W.B.		F, 28th Ill.	49		1919 Aug 29	KS, 39th, 1920
Crawford, W.C.		G, 49th Ohio Inf.	71		1918 Nov 22	KS, 38th, 1919
Crawford, W.H.	Pvt.	D, 8th Iowa	1		1922 May 16	IA, 49th, 1923
Crawford, W.N.	Pvt.	H, 28th Iowa Inf.	321	42	1887 Aug 10	IA, 14th, 1888
Crawford, W.N.	Pvt.	H, 28th Iowa Inf.	321	49	1st quarter 1887	IA, 14th, 1888
Crawford, William H.		E & C, 12th Ill. Cav.	64		1901 Dec	KS, 21st, 1902
Crawford, Wm.	Pvt.	I, 22nd Iowa Inf.	140	60	1899 Sep 13	IA, 26th, 1900
Cray, Zeohaniah	Pvt.	G, 2nd Iowa Cav.	8		1923 Oct 24	IA, 50th, 1924
Crea, A.B.	Capt.	F, 22nd Iowa Inf.	8		1901 Apr 2	IA, 28th, 1902
Creager, Geo. W.		G, 7th Kans. Cav.	170		1904 Jul 27	KS, 24th, 1905
Creager, Peter			207		1913 Jul 19	NE, 38th, 1914
Creagor, John		8th Wis. Bat.	127		1915	KS, 36th, 1917
Creal, Wm.	Pvt.	D, 14th Iowa Inf.	241	72	1896 Feb 6	IA, 23rd, 1897
Cree, J.M.	Pvt.	H, 4th U.S. Cav.	141		1927 Sep 1	IA, 54th, 1928
Creek, S.L.	Pvt.	F, 3rd Iowa Cav.	19		1930 Mar 4	IA, 57th, 1931
Creg, Green		B, 79th Ark. (Colored) (died at Lawrence, Kans.; buried at Lawrence, Oak Hill)	365		1894 Oct 31	KS, 14th, 1895
Creger, Levi A.	Pvt.	I, 152nd Ind. Vol. Inf.	5		1903 Jun 1	IA, 30th, 1904
Creger, S.M.			449		Winter 1902	IA, 30th, 1904
Creghton, Joseph	Fifer	C, 30th Iowa Inf.	153		1923 May 22	IA, 50th, 1924
Cregs, S.B.	Pvt.	B, 142nd Ohio Inf.	127		1913 Mar 2	IA, 40th, 1914
Creigh, Thomas A.		died at his home in Omaha (see Appendix D)			1909 May 16	NE, 34th, 1910
Creighton, Boyd		E, 33rd Wis. Inf.	117		1899 Mar 18	KS, 19th, 1900
Creighton, David	Pvt.	E, 12th Iowa Inf.	81		1919 May 22	IA, 46th, 1920
Creighton, George F.		I, 16th Ill.	1		1916 Mar 24	KS, 36th, 1917
Creighton, Henry		E, 134th N.Y.	3		1936 Mar 23	NE, 61st, 1937

*See Appendix A, B or C for roster of post names and locations.
†See Introduction for note regarding recording of death date.
123

Name	Rank	Company, Regiment or Ship	Post*	Age	Death Date†	Journal
Creighton, J.W., see Cleighton, J.W.						
Creighton, W.A.		B, 70th Ind.	251		1921 Nov 29	KS, 41st, 1922
Creighton, W.S.			445		1924 Sep 11	IA, 51st, 1925
Creit, Frank		F, 7th U.S.C.I.	321		1930 Jun 23	KS, 50th, 1931
Creits, S.F.	3rd Class Musician	Penn. Vols.	412		1903 Aug 20	IA, 30th, 1904
Creitz, L.F.	1st Lieut. Pvt.	35th Iowa Inf. A, 1st Iowa Inf.	250	61	1895 Feb 20	IA, 21st, 1895
Crelley, James		5th U.S.B.[U.S. Battery]	65		1921 Oct 22	KS, 41st, 1922
Crenshan, D.L.		L, 2nd Wis.	49		1885	KS, 5th, 1886
Crepps, Fred		E, 103rd Ohio Inf.	25	89	1935 Jan 21	IA, 62nd, 1936
Cress, A.G.		G, 209th Penn.	100		1915 Jul 3	KS, 35th, 1916
Cress, David F.	Pvt. Sergt.	F, 10th Ill. Inf. D, 2nd Mo. Cav.	2	52	1891 Dec 3	IA, 22nd, 1896
Cressler, C.W.	Pvt.	G, 77th Penn.	111		1926 Mar 22	IA, 53rd, 1927
Cresswell, J.S.	Pvt.	H, 76th Penn. Inf.	204		1909 Oct 7	IA, 36th, 1910
Creswell, Wm.	Pvt.	K, 20th Iowa Inf.	513	58	1895 Feb 19	IA, 22nd, 1896
Cretcher, J.C.		G, 95th Ohio	255		1914 Mar 8	KS, 34th, 1915
Cretors, J.H.		B, 79th Ohio Inf.	440	94	1938 Jan 31	IA, 64th, 1938
Cretzmyer, S.	Pvt.	C, 16th Iowa Inf.	267		1920	IA, 47th, 1921
Creuss, David		K, 33rd Ill.	130		1924 Aug 12	KS, 44th, 1925
Creviston, Harvey			226		1901 Dec 31	KS, 21st, 1902
Creviston, M.D.		K, 132nd Ind.	100		1908 Sep 7	KS, 28th, 1909
Criddebo, M.	Pvt.	D, 36th Iowa Inf.	122		1920	IA, 47th, 1921
Crigles, James W.		C, 112th Ill. Inf. (died of heart failure)	15	74	1911 May 5	NE, 36th, 1912
Criley, E.B.	Pvt.	H, 32nd Iowa Inf.	69		1912 Dec 15	IA, 39th, 1913
Criley, J.W.		Penn. & Ohio (died of consumption)	43		1909	NE, 34th, 1910
Crill, C.W.	Pvt.	K, 8th Iowa	12	66	1890 May 3	IA, 17th, 1891
Crippen, D.H.	Sergt.	A, 3rd Ohio Cav.	264	56	1896 Jan 10	IA, 22nd, 1896
Crippen, Edgar D.	Pvt.	M, 6th Iowa Cav.	31		1918 Jul 21	IA, 45th, 1919
Crippen, John T.	Chaplain	117th N.Y. Inf.	400		1912 May 13	IA, 39th, 1913
Crippen, L.		A, 5th Ohio Inf.	36		1911 Jan 12	KS, 31st, 1912
Cripps, Benj.		E, 11th Kans.	418		1927 Mar 1	KS, 47th, 1928
Cripps, Walter J.	Capt.	10th Mo. 2nd Mo. Cav.	4		1916 Nov 30	KS, 36th, 1917
Crisler, James A.		B, 34th Ind. Inf.	408		1899 Mar 22	KS, 19th, 1900
Crisler, O.F.		F, 154th Ill. (died of heart failure)	165	79	1909 Jan 3	NE, 34th, 1910
Crisman, Wm.	Pvt.	B, 24th Iowa Inf.	6		1926 Aug	IA, 53rd, 1927
Crisp, Wm.		D, 18th Mich. Inf. (died of pneumonia)	26	91	1925 Mar 31	NE, 50th, 1926
Crispin, Cal. H.	Pvt.	E, 23rd Iowa Inf.	59		1925	IA, 52nd, 1926
Criss, George		A, 50th Ind.	42	80	1922 Jan 2	NE, 47th, 1923
Criss, Isaac	Pvt.	A, 14th West Va. Inf.	284		1902 Nov 14	IA, 29th, 1903
Criss, J.A.			73		1884	KS, 4th, 1885
Criss, St.		E, 2nd West Va.	12		1936	KS, 55th, 1936
Crissinger, E.W.	Pvt.	B, 45th Iowa Inf.	108		1932 Jun 22	IA, 59th, 1933
Crist, Geo. W.		I, 14th Kans.	251		1920 Dec 29	KS, 40th, 1921
Crist, Hiram N.		I, 1st Penn.	69		1922 Jan 20	KS, 42nd, 1923
Crist, J.H.	Pvt.	A, 12th Iowa Inf.	154		1926 Apr 1	IA, 53rd, 1927
Cristal, Harmon		G, 8th Kans.	283		1910	KS, 30th, 1911
Criswell, J.M.		K, 30th Iowa	41		1888	KS, 8th, 1889
Criswell, John		K, 91st Ill.	85		1928 May 13	KS, 48th, 1929
Criswell, R.H.	Sergt.	A, 99th Ill. Inf.	154	55	1888 Sep	NE, 13th, 1889
Criswell, William	Pvt.	K, 20th Iowa Inf.	513	52	1895 Feb 19	IA, 21st, 1895
Critchett, E.	Pvt.	C, 7th Iowa Inf.	40		1920 Mar 14	IA, 47th, 1921
Critchfield, Jacob			292		1890	NE, 15th, 1891
Crittenden, J.	Pvt.	G, 121st N.Y. Inf.	88	63	1897 Apr 3	IA, 23rd, 1897
Crittenden, Lewit C.		C, 2nd Kans. Cav.	18		1908 Nov 13	KS, 28th, 1909
Critton, J.R.		A, 2nd Ky.	201		1906 Oct 15	KS, 26th, 1907
Critzer, D.W.		I, 2nd Colo. Cav.	132		1886	KS, 6th, 1887
Critzer, L.W.		B, 150th Ind. Inf.	25		1917 May 14	KS, 37th, 1918
Critzer, Otho D.		A, 10th Ill. Inf. (died at San Antonio, Tex.; buried at Mt. Hope Cemetery)	72		1894 Jan 11	KS, 14th, 1895
Croasdale, B.F.	Corp.	C, 3rd Penn. Rec.	139		1916 Oct 13	IA, 43rd, 1917

See Appendix A, B or C for roster of post names and locations.
†*See Introduction for note regarding recording of death date.*

Name	Rank	Company, Regiment or Ship	Post*	Age	Death Date†	Journal
Crocker, A.J.		G, 2nd Ill. Art.	55		1917 Nov 9	KS, 37th, 1918
Crocker, R.B.		K, 30th Ill.	10		1930 Mar 3	NE, 55th, 1931
Crocker, S.E.		H, 25th Wis.	7		1931 Mar 24	NE, 56th, 1932
Crocket, David		H, 133rd Ind.	129		1928 Feb 23	KS, 50th, 1931
Crocket, John		A, 185th Ohio	64		1924 Dec 22	KS, 44th, 1925
Crockett, David		H, 133rd Ind.	129		1928 Feb 23	KS, 48th, 1929
Crockett, John H.		I, 18th Ky. Inf.	65		1899 Feb 26	KS, 19th, 1900
Crofford, Stephen	Pvt.	H, 4th Iowa Inf.	314		1913 Jun 10	IA, 40th, 1914
Crofoot, Wm.	Pvt.	D, 15th Iowa Inf.	63		1927 May 18	IA, 54th, 1928
Croft, H.B.	Sergt.	C, 13th Wis. Inf.	358		1926 Mar 11	IA, 53rd, 1927
Croft, Wm.		L, 6th Mich.	13		1930 Feb 15	NE, 55th, 1931
Croiser, Cassius M.	Pvt.	K, 21st Iowa Inf.	342	52	1897 Dec 20	IA, 24th, 1898
Croley, J.B.			35		1910 May	NE, 35th, 1911
Croll, Henry C.		I, 167th Penn. Inf.	333		1886	KS, 6th, 1887
Cromfane, N.H.	Pvt.		31		1920 Dec 30	IA, 47th, 1921
Crommett, Robt.		E, 7th Maine Inf.	14		1890 Mar 12	KS, 12th, 1893
Cromwell, F.C.	Pvt.	A, 12th Iowa Inf.	193		1905 Mar 25	IA, 32nd, 1906
Cromwell, G.F.	Pvt.	I, 46th Iowa Inf.	250	51	1897 Feb 8	IA, 23rd, 1897
Cromwell, Henry C.		E, 124th Ind. (died of general disability)	22	75	1917 Jan 9	NE, 42nd, 1918
Cromwell, Henry C.		E, 124th Ind. (died of old age)	22	75	1917 Jan 9	NE, 41st, 1917
Cromwell, Newton		D, 16th Iowa Inf.	52		1930 Feb 11	KS, 50th, 1931
Cromwell, Samuel T.		A, 43rd Ind. Inf.	250		1915 Oct 10	KS, 36th, 1917
Cronch, James B.	Pvt.	F, 11th Iowa Inf.	108	57	1897 Dec 4	IA, 24th, 1898
Crone, Cristian	Pvt.	C, 13th Wis. Inf.	503		1922 Jan 27	IA, 49th, 1923
Crone, T.H.	Pvt.	B, 7th Ill. Inf.	108		1899 Jul 26	IA, 26th, 1900
Croner, Franklin		B, 40th Ill.	17		1909 Oct 16	KS, 29th, 1910
Cronk, Gilbert G.	Pvt.	B, 96th Ohio Inf.	234		1899 Mar 2	IA, 26th, 1900
Cronk, John		F, 37th Ill.	69		1918 Jan 12	KS, 38th, 1919
Cronn, Wm. P.	Pvt.	K, 10th N.Y. Cav.	42		1911 Aug 27	IA, 38th, 1912
Crook, C.N.		B, 112th Ill.	300		1889	KS, 9th, 1890
Crook, J.H.	Pvt.	H, 158th Ill. Inf.	236	89	1931 Feb 20	IA, 58th, 1932
Crookes, John W.		F, 126th Ohio	68		1917 Oct 29	KS, 37th, 1918
Crookham, J.C.	Sergt. Capt.	C, 7th Iowa Inf. 7th U.S.C. Art.	40		1912 Nov 1	IA, 39th, 1913
Crooks, Andrew D.		E, 88th Ill.	246		1910 Dec 26	KS, 30th, 1911
Crooks, Daniel J.		A, 25th Ohio	101		1897 Oct 16	KS, 17th, 1898
Crooks, Frank	Pvt.	G, 46th Ohio	98		1905 Aug 11	IA, 32nd, 1906
Crooks, J.B.	Pvt.	Penn.	108		1917 Feb 8	IA, 44th, 1918
Crooks, William		I, 46th Wis. Inf. (died of abscess of liver)	87		1893 Oct 7	NE, 18th, 1894
Crookshank, A.W.		D, 23rd Ohio	262	67	1911 May 17	NE, 36th, 1912
Crookshank, Benj. M.	Pvt.	I, 85th Ohio Inf. (at large)	155	95	1941 Jul 9	IA, 67th, 1941
Crooms, John		D, 4th Ky. Cav.	17		1922 Jul 3	KS, 42nd, 1923
Crop, David	Pvt.	E, 106th Ill.	451		1903-1904	IA, 30th, 1904
Croply, James	Pvt.	K, 7th Iowa Cav.	8		1909 Jan 3	IA, 36th, 1910
Cropp, George	Pvt.	B, 21st Iowa Inf.	130		1929 Nov 3	IA, 56th, 1930
Cropt, Michael	Pvt.	M, 4th Iowa Cav.	363		1904 Dec 28	IA, 31st, 1905
Crosby, D.H.		C, 42nd Wis.	184		1922 Dec 31	KS, 42nd, 1923
Crosby, G.P.		A, 38th Iowa	47		1924 Feb 11	KS, 44th, 1925
Crosby, James			132		1920 Mar 13	KS, 40th, 1921
Crosby, John L.		C, 10th N.H. Vols.	311		1902 Feb 25	KS, 22nd, 1903
Crosby, L.E.	Pvt.	H, 42nd Wis. Inf.	222		1917 Oct	IA, 44th, 1918
Crosby, Philus S.	Pvt.	H, 21st Iowa Inf.	190		1917 Jun 25	IA, 44th, 1918
Crosby, William		B, 17th Kans.	225		1900 Jul 5	KS, 20th, 1901
Crose, B.R.	Pvt.	D, 72nd Ind. Inf.	23		1929 Sep 21	IA, 56th, 1930
Crosen, T.H.	Pvt.	A, 30th Ill. Inf.	55		1917 Aug 11	IA, 44th, 1918
Crosier, F.E.		D, 3rd N.Y. Cav.	81		1930 Nov 15	NE, 55th, 1931
Crosier, George R.		E, 61st Ill.	7		1934	NE, 59th, 1935
Crosier, George R.		E, 61st Ill.	7		1935 Jan 10	NE, 60th, 1936
Crosley, Geo. W.	Col.	5th Iowa Inf.	66		1913 Dec 27	IA, 40th, 1914
Crosley, Lawrence	Pvt.	G, 4th Iowa Cav.	170	59	1895 Mar 4	IA, 21st, 1895
Crosoley, D.S.	Pvt.	K, 34th Iowa	18		1907 Aug 19	IA, 34th, 1908
Cross, C.B.			205		1916 Nov 1	KS, 36th, 1917

*See Appendix A, B or C for roster of post names and locations.
†See Introduction for note regarding recording of death date.

Name	Rank	Company, Regiment or Ship	Post*	Age	Death Date†	Journal
Cross, C.F.		C, 63rd Penn.	65		1913 Apr 2	KS, 33rd, 1914
Cross, C.H.	Pvt.	G, 7th Iowa Inf.	34	53	1894 Nov 21	IA, 21st, 1895
Cross, C.M.	Pvt.	K, 104th Ohio Inf.	26		1919 Mar 27	IA, 46th, 1920
Cross, Charles W.		L, 3rd Mo.	238		1919 Apr 16	KS, 39th, 1920
Cross, Charles W.		L, 3rd Mo. Militia	238		1920 Apr 16	KS, 40th, 1921
Cross, Chas. E.	Pvt.	B, 7th Ill. Cav.	206		1927 Jan 23	IA, 54th, 1928
Cross, David J.			86		1893	NE, 18th, 1894
Cross, Edwin T.		L, 6th Iowa Cav.	82		1909 Sep 25	KS, 29th, 1910
Cross, G.F.		G, 44th Iowa	32		1932 Feb 17	NE, 57th, 1933
Cross, George		I, 24th Iowa Inf.	77	79	1920 Sep 2	NE, 45th, 1921
Cross, H.C.		F, 153rd Ohio Inf. (died at Machinac, Mich.; buried at Maplewood Cemetery)	55		1894 Sep 5	KS, 14th, 1895
Cross, John		H, 34th Ill.	32		1926	NE, 51st, 1927
Cross, Levi	Pvt.	A, 11th Iowa Inf.	231		1909 May 6	IA, 36th, 1910
Cross, Milton		H, 15th U.S.C.T.	321		1899 Jun 27	KS, 19th, 1900
Cross, Perry		F, 35th Iowa Inf. (died of old age)	79	84	1917 Apr 9	NE, 42nd, 1918
Cross, Robt. S.	Pvt.	E, 19th Ohio Inf.	26		1927 Dec 13	IA, 54th, 1928
Cross, Samuel K.		E, 2nd Kans. Inf. A, 2nd Kans. Cav. (died at Galveston, Tex.)	1		1895 Jul	KS, 15th, 1896
Cross, Thomas		I, 9th Kans. Cav. (died at Topeka, Kans.; buried at Topeka Cemetery)	71		1894 Mar 3	KS, 14th, 1895
Cross, Thos.	Pvt.	C, 34th Iowa Inf.	116		1904 Oct 29	IA, 31st, 1905
Cross, W.J.		I, 185th Ill.	265		1926 Feb 17	KS, 46th, 1927
Cross, Walter P.		H, 16th Wis.	47		1922 Feb 12	KS, 42nd, 1923
Cross, William N.		I, 9th N.Y. Cav. (died of pneumonia)	32	66	1910 Nov 28	NE, 35th, 1911
Cross, Wm.	Pvt.	B, 34th Ill.	46		1921 Apr 12	IA, 48th, 1922
Crosser, S.B.	Pvt.	F, 15th Iowa Inf.	379		1910 Aug 18	IA, 37th, 1911
Crosser, W.A.	Pvt.	B, 77th Ohio Inf.	159		1917 Jul 14	IA, 44th, 1918
Crossfield, Malon B.		B, 2nd Mo. Cav.	176		1918 Feb 14	KS, 38th, 1919
Crossley, J.W.	Pvt.	D, 99th Ill.	55		1926 Oct 26	IA, 53rd, 1927
Crossly, Chas. F.		A, 24th N.Y. Inf.	25		1904 Feb 6	NE, 29th, 1905
Crossman, John T.		G, 10th Penn. V.R.C.	11		1914 Dec 2	KS, 34th, 1915
Crossnaith, G.B.	Pvt.	D, 75th Iowa Inf.	248		1906 Jun 15	IA, 33rd, 1907
Crosswaith, G.B.	Pvt.	H, 12th Ill. Inf.	348		1905 Aug 19	IA, 33rd, 1907
Crosthwait, H.W.	Corp.	D, 138th Ill. Inf.	453	63	1891 May 11	IA, 18th, 1892
Crosthwait, H.W.	Major	H, 102nd Ill. Inf.	57		1915 Nov 8	IA, 42nd, 1916
Crouch, Andrew W.	Pvt.	G, 1st Wis. Cav.	91	95, 10 mos. & 26 days	1945 Jan 11	IA, 71st, 1945
Crouch, Chas. P.		A, 48th Ind.	18		1918 Mar 17	KS, 38th, 1919
Crouch, Elias S.		G, 142nd Ill.	46		1912 Nov 21	KS, 32nd, 1913
Crouch, F.L.	Pvt.	K, 92nd Ill. Inf.	15		1927 Jun 18	IA, 54th, 1928
Crouch, H.B.	Corp.	L, 2nd Ky. Cav.	67		1915	IA, 42nd, 1916
Crouch, Joseph		E, 83rd Ind.	17		1916 May 30	KS, 36th, 1917
Crouch, L.P.	Chaplain	55th Ill.	60		1914	NE, 39th, 1915
Crouch, Thos. A.		A, 3rd Ill. Cav.	25		1930 Aug 3	NE, 55th, 1931
Crouch, W.A.	Pvt.	A, 27th Iowa Inf.	284		1899 Dec 17	IA, 26th, 1900
Crouch, William	Pvt.	A, 26th Ind. Inf.	358		1915 Apr 14	IA, 42nd, 1916
Crouse, E.H.		A, 38th Ohio Foot Bat.	31	83	1924 Oct 14	NE, 49th, 1925
Crouse, Eli	Pvt.	E, 206th Penn. Inf.	222		1929 Jan 12	IA, 56th, 1930
Crouse, Obediah	Pvt.	D, 31st Ind. Inf.	155		1900 Jul 3	IA, 27th, 1901
Crouse, Walter K.		H, 46th Wis. Inf. (died of heart failure)	229	48	1895 May 28	NE, 20th, 1896
Crouse, William	Pvt.	K, 37th Iowa Inf.	513	85	1897 Aug 10	IA, 24th, 1898
Crovost, F.C.		A, 83rd Ill. Inf. (died at Mound City, Kans.; buried at National Cemetery)	33		1894 May 8	KS, 14th, 1895
Crow, B.F.		C, 133rd Ill.	2	88	1934 Apr 29	IA, 61st, 1935
Crow, Henry		C, 91st Ohio	257		1917 Nov 4	KS, 37th, 1918
Crow, James			22		1883	KS, 3rd, 1884
Crow, Jesse N.		F, 18th Iowa Inf.	496		1916 Mar 28	KS, 36th, 1917
Crow, John W.		C, 1st Kans. Militia	170		1915 Jun 25	KS, 35th, 1916
Crow, M.		K, 92nd Ohio	17		1904 Oct 14	KS, 24th, 1905

*See Appendix A, B or C for roster of post names and locations.
†See Introduction for note regarding recording of death date.

Name	Rank	Company, Regiment or Ship	Post*	Age	Death Date†	Journal
Crow, R.B., see Craw, R.B.						
Crow, Robert		I, 3rd Mo. Cav.	175		1910 Mar 10	KS, 32nd, 1913
Crow, Samuel	Pvt.	B, 6th Iowa Inf.	73		1910 Jun	IA, 37th, 1911
Crow, Stephen	Pvt.	A, 61st Ill. Inf.	86		1904 Dec 16	IA, 31st, 1905
Crow, W.G.	Corp.	D, 6th Iowa Inf.	73		1911	IA, 38th, 1912
Crow, W.H.	Pvt.	K, 8th Iowa Inf.	1		1929 Jan 11	IA, 56th, 1930
Crow, W.H.			50		1892	KS, 12th, 1893
Crow, W.Y.		E, 91st Kans.	256		1919 Jul 8	KS, 39th, 1920
Crowder, J.H.	Musician	18th Ind.	59		1907 Mar 22	IA, 34th, 1908
Crowder, T.N.		I, 11th Iowa G, 45th Iowa	12		1930 Nov 14	KS, 50th, 1931
Crowe, Abijah			85		1920 Feb 28	KS, 40th, 1921
Crowe, J.E.	Pvt.	K, 15th Iowa Inf.	193		1912 May	IA, 39th, 1913
Crowell, E.	Pvt.	G, 27th Iowa	377		1921 Apr 23	IA, 48th, 1922
Crowell, Ed	Pvt.	G, 27th Iowa	377		1922 Apr 23	IA, 49th, 1923
Crowell, J.B.		C, 3rd West Va. Cav.	203		1914 Jul 5	KS, 34th, 1915
Crowell, L.N.		G, 51st Ohio Inf.	329		1913 Jun 15	IA, 40th, 1914
Crowell, O.P.		G, 33rd Ill.	147		1922 Oct 11	KS, 42nd, 1923
Crowell, S.W.	Pvt.	G, 27th Iowa Inf.	377		1915 May 15	IA, 42nd, 1916
Crowell, S.W.	Pvt.	E, 44th Iowa Inf.	235		1929 May 3	IA, 56th, 1930
Crowell, V.B.	Pvt.	C, 8th Iowa Cav.	337		1911 Sep 28	IA, 38th, 1912
Crowell, W.W.	Pvt.		54		1915 Sep 30	IA, 42nd, 1916
Crowell, W.W.	Pvt.	K, 9th Iowa Cav.	54		1916 Sep 30	IA, 43rd, 1917
Crowelts, Dan		E, 137th Penn. (died of operation)	1	85	1920 Mar 15	NE, 45th, 1921
Crowl, L.W.		L, 11th Kans. Cav.	151		1913 Sep	KS, 33rd, 1914
Crowley, J.J.		E, 47th N.Y.	7		1897 Dec 21	KS, 17th, 1898
Crown, L.F.	Pvt.	F, 148th Ill. Inf.	515		1905 May 20	IA, 32nd, 1906
Crowther, Daniel, see Crauther, Daniel						
Croxell, Leander	Pvt.	E, 34th Iowa Inf.	298		1917 Jan 16	IA, 44th, 1918
Crozer, James G.	Pvt.	C, 26th Iowa Inf.	235		1919 May 1	IA, 46th, 1920
Crozet, Charles	Pvt.	I, 24th Penn. Inf.	452	87	1931 Mar 19	IA, 58th, 1932
Crozier, G.W.	Pvt.	A, 7th Iowa Cav.	49		1929 May 30	IA, 56th, 1930
Crozier, John A.	Sergt.	H, 17th Iowa Inf.	337		1928 Nov 20	IA, 55th, 1929
Crozier, M.W.	Sergt.	H, 33rd Iowa Inf.	40		1927 Mar 28	IA, 54th, 1928
Crozier, Thomas	Corp.	G, 47th Iowa Inf.	8		1917 Mar 31	IA, 44th, 1918
Cruden, Wm.	Pvt.	G, 17th Conn. Inf.	200		1927 Feb 22	IA, 54th, 1928
Crull, Jerry B.	Pvt.	K, 1st Mo. Eng.	153	82	1894 May 31	IA, 21st, 1895
Crum, Huston		205th Penn. (not a member of the department but living in Nebraska; location: Lincoln)			1937 Jan 23	NE, 62nd, 1938
Crumb, Albert J.		G, 31st Iowa Inf.	20		1891 Nov 30	KS, 11th, 1892
Crume, John S.		C, 2nd Neb. Cav.	554[354?]	79	1906 Feb 26	NE, 31st, 1907
Crump, Henry C.		F, 39th Ind.	271		1897 Jan 4	KS, 17th, 1898
Crundon, R.C.		A, 110th N.Y.	64		1920 Oct 17	KS, 40th, 1921
Crutchfield, J.H.		N, 54th Ind.	158		1905 Sep	KS, 25th, 1906
Crutchfield, John W.	Pvt.	F, 16th Ill. Inf.	153		1909 Dec 11	IA, 36th, 1910
Crutchfield, Nathan	Sergt.	C, 16th Ill. Inf.	153		1919 Dec 1	IA, 46th, 1920
Crutchfield, William		F, 3rd Kans. State Militia	12		1917 Mar 21	KS, 37th, 1918
Cruze, Thomas		U.S. Navy	100		1933 Mar 17	KS, 53rd, 1934
Cruzen, Benj. F.	Pvt.	K, 33rd Iowa Inf.	40	88	1933 Apr 19	IA, 60th, 1934
Crystal, John		C, 23rd Iowa (died of Bright's disease)	354	76	1904 Jan 15	NE, 29th, 1905
Cryth, G.W.	M. Sergt.	F, 4th Iowa Cav.	107		1920 Jul 10	IA, 47th, 1921
Cubberly, Jesse	Pvt.	G, 3rd Iowa Cav.	79		1911 Feb 13	IA, 38th, 1912
Cuddington, Miner		A, 1st N.Y. Art.	23	65	1904 Oct 16	NE, 29th, 1905
Cudgell, R.J.		F, 3rd Iowa Cav.	19		1921 Apr 4	IA, 48th, 1922
Cudworth, J.	1st Lieut.	C, 35th N.Y. Inf.	4	54	1897 Jul 5	IA, 24th, 1898
Cue, Joseph			25		1913 May 13	KS, 33rd, 1914
Culberson, M.R.		F, 6th Ohio	20		1896 Sep 12	KS, 16th, 1897
Culbertson, A.	Pvt.	H, 47th Ohio	497		1923 Nov 21	IA, 50th, 1924
Culbertson, C.J.	Sailor	Gulf Squadron	68	68	1899 Jun 23	IA, 26th, 1900
Culbertson, W.L.	Pvt.	G, 20th Iowa Inf.	44		1908 Oct 19	IA, 35th, 1909

*See Appendix A, B or C for roster of post names and locations.
†See Introduction for note regarding recording of death date.

127

Name	Rank	Company, Regiment or Ship	Post*	Age	Death Date†	Journal
Culin, Franklin		H, 2nd Neb. Cav.	251		1901 Nov 29	KS, 21st, 1902
Cullen, Frank	Pvt.	A, 2nd Iowa Cav.	231		1913 Jul 29	IA, 40th, 1914
Culler, Geo. W.		B, 149th Ind. Inf. (died of pneumonia)	5	72	1905 Feb 10	NE, 30th, 1906
Cullimore, J.W.		F, 1st Mo. Cav.	5			
Cullins, Wm.			316		1921	KS, 41st, 1922
Cullmary, David	Pvt.	H, 6th Iowa Cav.	88	83	1917 Oct 9	KS, 37th, 1918
Cully, Albert	2nd Lieut.	K, 147th Ind. Inf.	7	44	1887 Dec 24	IA, 14th, 1888
Culp, C.W.		D, 50th Ill.	147		1888 Apr 13	IA, 15th, 1889
Culp, Charles C.		A, 25th Ohio Inf.	127		1925 Dec 12	KS, 45th, 1926
Culp, S.L.	Pvt.	G, 19th Ind.	231		1916 Aug 1	KS, 36th, 1917
Culton, J.C.	Capt.	E, 86th Ill. Inf.	29		1923 May 29	IA, 50th, 1924
Culver, A.M.	Pvt.	H, 141st Ohio	118		1925 Apr 25	IA, 52nd, 1926
Culver, A.S.	Pvt., Landsman	Navy	34		1907 Apr 10	IA, 34th, 1908
Culver, D.F.	Pvt.	G, 38th Iowa Inf.	12	51	1921 Jun 19	IA, 48th, 1922
Culver, E.C.		13th Ill. (died of pneumonia)	42		1897 Aug 3	IA, 24th, 1898
Culver, E.R.	Pvt.	H, 9th Iowa Inf.	40		1907 Oct 15	NE, 32nd, 1908
Culver, Elijah C.		C, 138th Ind. Inf.	329		1928 Mar 9	IA, 55th, 1929
Culver, George	Pvt.	D, 3rd Iowa Inf.	168	93	1937 Aug 13	IA, 64th, 1938
Culver, Jacob H.	Musician	K, 1st Wis. Inf. (died at East San Diego; see Appendix D)	56	61	1895 Oct 26	IA, 22nd, 1896
Culver, Joseph F.		A, 129th Ill. Inf.	464	76	1921 Aug 19	NE, 46th, 1922
Culver, Joseph F.		A, 129th Ill. Inf.	55		1899 Jan 29	KS, 19th, 1900
Culver, Orren		E, 11th Iowa Inf.	137		1899 Jan 20	KS, 19th, 1900
Culver, W.F.	Pvt.	A, 6th Wis. Inf.	247		1892 Jul 26	NE, 17th, 1893
Culver, W.H.	Pvt.	F, 50th N.Y. Eng.	512		1912 Jul 12	IA, 39th, 1913
Culver, Wm. W.	Pvt.	A, 23rd Wis. Inf.	101		1918 Aug 20	IA, 45th, 1919
Culver, Zed		G, 5th Tenn. Cav.	293		1923 Jun 17	IA, 50th, 1924
Culverson, Wm.			11		1918 Jan 5	KS, 38th, 1919
Cumback, A.		A, 13th N.J.	293		1913 Nov 10	IA, 40th, 1914
Cumberland, J.S.		G, 192nd Ohio	127		1913 Jun 20	KS, 33rd, 1914
Cumberland, J.S.		G, 192nd Ohio	127		1931 Feb 28	KS, 52nd, 1933
Cumings, Caleb		K, 25th Wis.	20		1931 Feb 28	KS, 51st, 1932
Cumins, J.B.	Pvt.	D, 32nd Iowa Inf.	67		1892 Feb 19	KS, 12th, 1893
Cumming, W.G.	Lieut. Col.	1st Vt. Cav.	88		1916	IA, 43rd, 1917
Cummings, B.I.	Pvt.	B, 46th Iowa	263		1911 May 10	IA, 38th, 1912
Cummings, Chas. P.	Sergt.	A, 1st Ohio Art.	94	48	1923 Feb 24	IA, 50th, 1924
Cummings, Cornelius		I, 2nd Penn.	88		1890 Jan 3	IA, 16th, 1890
Cummings, D.		C, 11th Iowa Inf. (died of peritonitis)	228		1905 Nov 27	KS, 25th, 1906
Cummings, H.J.B.	Capt.	F, 4th Iowa Inf.	55		1894 May 7	NE, 19th, 1895
Cummings, Jas.	Pvt.	C, 49th Wis. Inf.	42		1909 Apr 16	IA, 36th, 1910
Cummings, Jas. A.	Pvt.	B, 60th N.Y. Inf.	1		1911 Mar 9	IA, 38th, 1912
Cummings, L.	Pvt.	E, 94th N.Y.	10		1920 Dec 19	IA, 47th, 1921
Cummings, L.J.	Pvt.	D, 1st Vt. Cav.	88		1921 Aug	IA, 48th, 1922
Cummings, Seth		D, 20th Iowa Inf.	324		1919 Jul 5	IA, 46th, 1920
Cummings, T.K.		H, 44th Ohio Inf.	25	82	1917 Jan 12	IA, 44th, 1918
Cummings, Thomas	Pvt.	E, 38th Iowa Inf.	216		1921 Sep 20	NE, 46th, 1922
Cummings, W.A.		G, 11th Penn.	142		1917 Mar 31	IA, 44th, 1918
Cummings, W.G.	Pvt.	D, 25th Ohio Inf.	98		1929 Sep 12	KS, 49th, 1930
Cummings, W.J.		M, 5th Kans.	12		1925 May 27	IA, 52nd, 1926
Cummings, William		E, 82nd Ind. Inf.	356		1919 Aug 26	KS, 39th, 1920
Cummins, Ephriam	Capt.	F, 8th Iowa Cav.	398	59	1918 Sep 18	KS, 38th, 1919
Cummons, I.B.	Pvt.	D, 32nd Iowa Inf.	67		1891 Aug 6	IA, 18th, 1892
Cuningham, A.M.		F, 16th Penn.	143		1915	IA, 42nd, 1916
Cunming, Thos.	Corp.	B, 28th Wis. Inf.	289	47	1928	NE, 53rd, 1929
Cunnine, E.J.		A, 53rd Ill. Inf. (died of hemorrhage)	282		1888 Jul 20	IA, 15th, 1889
Cunningham, A.		G, 4th Iowa Cav.	207		1893 Sep 12	NE, 18th, 1894
Cunningham, A.F.		I, 134th Penn. Inf.	18		1932	NE, 57th, 1933
Cunningham, A.G.	Pvt.	B, 45th Zouaves	108		1917 Apr 17	KS, 37th, 1918
Cunningham, A.M.			3		1920 Jun 26	IA, 47th, 1921
Cunningham, A.M., see Cuningham, A.M.					1921 Apr 22	IA, 48th, 1922

*See Appendix A, B or C for roster of post names and locations.
†See Introduction for note regarding recording of death date.
128

Name	Rank	Company, Regiment or Ship	Post*	Age	Death Date†	Journal
Cunningham, A.W.		F, 88th Ill. G, 15th V.R.C. (died of blood poison in old wound)	40		1890	KS, 10th, 1891
Cunningham, Alex		A, 47th Ill. Inf. (died of apoplexy)	112	75	1915 Dec 26	NE, 40th, 1916
Cunningham, Alonzo		G, 4th Iowa Cav. (former member of department; died at Imperial)	301		1939 May 21	NE, 64th, 1940
Cunningham, B.G., see Conningham, B.G.						
Cunningham, E.W.		D, 101st Ohio	55		1905 Aug 16	KS, 25th, 1906
Cunningham, Geo.	Pvt.		211		1920	IA, 47th, 1921
Cunningham, J.A.	Lieut.		108		1911 Jul 3	IA, 38th, 1912
Cunningham, J.A.		F, 134th Ind.	142		1928 Nov 2	KS, 48th, 1929
Cunningham, J.R.	Pvt.	I, 126th Ill. Inf.	1		1897 Feb 10	IA, 24th, 1898
Cunningham, James	Pvt.	F, 26th Iowa Inf.	78		1923 Jun 2	IA, 50th, 1924
Cunningham, James S.		D, 8th Mo.	16		1921 Apr 1	KS, 41st, 1922
Cunningham, John		G, 5th Ky.	362		1919 Dec 22	KS, 39th, 1920
Cunningham, M.	Pvt.	B, 1st Iowa Cav.	184		1911 Aug 16	IA, 38th, 1912
Cunningham, P.W.	Pvt.	E, 11th Minn.	34		1923 Apr 11	IA, 50th, 1924
Cunningham, P.W.		E, 11th Minn. (died of heart failure)	13	80	1923 Apr 10	NE, 48th, 1924
Cunningham, S.C.		E, 7th Ill.	85		1922 May 15	KS, 42nd, 1923
Cunningham, Sam		I, 98th Ohio	59		1933 Apr 13	KS, 53rd, 1934
Cunningham, T.C.	QM Sergt.	B, 134th Ind. Inf.	98	57	1899 Nov 27	IA, 26th, 1900
Cunningham, W.O.		D, 22nd Ind. 6th U.S. Cav.	158		1918 Dec 11	KS, 38th, 1919
Cunningham, W.S.		D, 138th Ill. Inf. (died of general debility)	182	74	1919 Aug 7	NE, 44th, 1920
Cunningham, Wm.	Pvt.		321		1910 Aug 8	IA, 37th, 1911
Cunningham, Wm.	Pvt.	K, 59th Ill. Inf.	337		1926 Jan	IA, 53rd, 1927
Cunningham, Wm.	Pvt.	G, 106th Ill. Inf.	127		1926 Mar 13	IA, 53rd, 1927
Cupp, A.W.			54		1917	KS, 37th, 1918
Cupp, Jonah	Pvt.	K, 171st Penn. Inf.	324		1928 Aug 13	IA, 55th, 1929
Cuppett, D.L.	Sergt.	G, 9th Iowa Inf.	247		1921 Apr 10	IA, 48th, 1922
Cupps, Caleb		E, 136th Ind. Inf.	354		1886	KS, 6th, 1887
Cure, Sellick		M, N.Y. Eng.	65[85]		1926 Feb 2	KS, 46th, 1927
Curler, Chas. Sylvanus	Pvt.	I, 192nd N.Y. Inf. (at large)	26	95, 1 mo. & 9 days	1944 Jan 5	IA, 70th, 1944
Curley, Thomas		I, 126th Ind. Inf.	1		1887 Sep 17	KS, 7th, 1888
Curlice, John N.		D, 138th Ill.	129		1918 Aug 1	KS, 38th, 1919
Curnutt, Henry G.		E, 72nd Ind.	17		1925 Feb 15	KS, 45th, 1926
Curran, J.D.	Pvt.	F, 1st Neb. Cav.	209		1901 Aug 19	IA, 28th, 1902
Curran, John	Corp.	C, 17th Wis.	94		1924 May 13	IA, 51st, 1925
Curran, John		H, 37th Ill. Inf. (died of heart failure)	111	73	1919 Jan 3	NE, 43rd, 1919
Curran, John		H, 37th Ill. Inf. (died of accident)	111	73	1919 Jan 3	NE, 44th, 1920
Current, Isaac	Pvt.	K, 48th Mo. Inf.	49	93	1939 Apr 20	IA, 65th, 1939
Current, W.	Pvt.	I, 24th Iowa Inf.	74		1926 Apr 5	IA, 53rd, 1927
Currie, A.J.		B, 30th Iowa Inf.	25		1893 Feb 9	NE, 18th, 1894
Currier, A.C.		G, 11th Mich.	14		1898 Jan 8	KS, 18th, 1899
Currier, A.E.			32		1914 Sep 19	KS, 34th, 1915
Currier, A.N.	Pvt.	C, 8th Iowa Inf.	8		1909 May 16	IA, 36th, 1910
Currier, E.F.		G, 16th Ill.	180		1920	KS, 40th, 1921
Currier, Geo.	Pvt.	H, 13th Inf.	80		1923 Jul 3	IA, 50th, 1924
Curry, A.E.			56		1913	KS, 33rd, 1914
Curry, A.F.		A, 10th West Va.	45		1931 Aug	KS, 52nd, 1933
Curry, A.F.		A, 10th West Va.	45		1931 Aug	KS, 51st, 1932
Curry, Allen	Pvt.	K, 134th Ind.	52		1915 Aug 22	KS, 35th, 1916
Curry, Chas.	Pvt.	A, 2nd Ill. Cav.	102		1904 Dec 31	IA, 31st, 1905
Curry, D.J.	Pvt.	K, 33rd Ill. Inf.	472		1919 Aug 14	IA, 46th, 1920
Curry, E.W.	Pvt.	L, 3rd Iowa Cav.	251	49	1896 Nov 18	IA, 23rd, 1897
Curry, Frank S.		F, 36th Ind.	12		1913 Mar 3	KS, 33rd, 1914
Curry, G.W.		F, 55th Ohio Inf.	36		1901 Jul 15	KS, 21st, 1902
Curry, Geo. W.		C, 9th Ill. Cav.	4		1923 Jan 14	NE, 48th, 1924
Curry, J.A.		M & C, 10th Ill. Cav.	56		1913 Mar 10	KS, 32nd, 1913
Curry, M.G.		G, 36th Ill.	19		1918 Feb 25	KS, 38th, 1919

Name	Rank	Company, Regiment or Ship	Post*	Age	Death Date†	Journal
Curry, N.G.	Pvt.	B, 4th Iowa Inf.	12		1927 Nov 9	IA, 54th, 1928
Curry, N.G.		C, West Va. Cav.	19		1919 Feb 1	KS, 39th, 1920
Curry, Owen		J, 27th N.Y.	134	70	1915 Jan 11	NE, 39th, 1915
Curry, R.		C, 8th Ind. Inf.	156		1888	KS, 8th, 1889
Curry, R.A.		C, 2nd Ill. Cal.[Cav.] (died of paralysis)	144	55	1900 Oct 7	NE, 25th, 1901
Curry, Robt.		L, 8th Ind. Inf.	156		1889	KS, 9th, 1890
Curs, Charles		E, 13th Kans. Inf. (died at Waterville, Kans.; buried at Riverside Cemetery)	260		1894 Sep 1	KS, 14th, 1895
Curtis, A.B.		F, 20th Ohio	117		1906 May 12	KS, 26th, 1907
Curtis, Andrew		H, 12th Ind. Cav.	18		1922 Mar 12	KS, 42nd, 1923
Curtis, D.F.	Pvt.	E, 8th Ohio Inf.	250		1900 Jun 24	IA, 27th, 1901
Curtis, D.F.	Pvt.	F, 21st Wis. (cause of death: shot accidentally)	36	43	1884 Nov 3	NE, 9th, 1885
Curtis, George P.		D, 45th Ill.	88		1919 Oct 19	KS, 39th, 1920
Curtis, H.A.	Corp.	C, 24th Iowa	222		1921 Sep 17	IA, 48th, 1922
Curtis, H.G.	Pvt.	K, 46th Iowa Inf.	18		1904 Feb 29	IA, 31st, 1905
Curtis, I.S.		L, 149th Ill.	1		1927 Oct 28	KS, 47th, 1928
Curtis, J.T.		E, 51st Penn.	293		1902 Aug 18	KS, 22nd, 1903
Curtis, M.J.	Pvt.	B, 8th Ill. Cav.	12	55	1892 Jan 28	IA, 19th, 1893
Curtis, M.M.	Pvt.	D, 26th Iowa Inf.	22		1917 Mar 30	IA, 44th, 1918
Curtis, Nathan	Pvt.	B, 26th Iowa Inf.	247		1916 Oct 20	IA, 45th, 1919
Curtis, Orlanda		D, 70th Ill. (died of tumor)	207	71	1913 Mar 2	NE, 38th, 1914
Curtis, R.B.	Corp.	K, 45th Iowa Inf.	254		1917 Dec 31	IA, 44th, 1918
Curtis, Samuel R.	Pvt.	B, 102nd Ill. Inf.	34		1910 Mar 13	IA, 37th, 1911
Curtis, Samuel S.		3rd Colo. Inf.	110	83	1920 Mar 5	NE, 45th, 1921
Curtis, Theo.		I, 184th N.Y.	432		1898 Nov 6	KS, 18th, 1899
Curtis, W.D.		E, 13th N.Y. Cav.	25		1923 Nov 27	KS, 43rd, 1924
Curtis, W.O.		C, 9th Iowa Inf.	54		1912 Mar 15	IA, 39th, 1913
Curtis, Wilber			54		1929 Nov 27	IA, 56th, 1930
Curtis, Z.T.	Hosp. Stew.		63		1917 Jan 4	KS, 37th, 1918
Curtiss, Robert B.		A, 10th Kans. Vol. Inf. (former member of department; died at Nebraska City)	24		1939 Jan 14	NE, 64th, 1940
Curtright, David		G, 17th Ky.	129		1905 Jan 5	KS, 25th, 1906
Curwell, Ezra	Pvt.	I, 45th Iowa Inf.	440		1916 Mar 31	IA, 43rd, 1917
Curyes, C.T.	Pvt.	F, 151st Ill. Inf.	236		1933 May	IA, 60th, 1934
Cushing, Frank L.		E, 13th Mass.	380		1912 Mar 5	KS, 32nd, 1913
Cushman, Egbert	Pvt.	D, 26th Iowa Inf.	92		1910 Oct 7	IA, 37th, 1911
Cushman, Myron		H, 8th Ill. Cav.	122		1916 Oct 27	KS, 36th, 1917
Cussins, James		G, 2nd Iowa (died of erysipelas)	35	77	1917 Feb 23	NE, 42nd, 1918
Custer, Aaron	Pvt.	59th Ohio	84		1907 Aug 17	IA, 34th, 1908
Custer, C.C.			32		1922 Oct 21	NE, 47th, 1923
Custer, Henry	Pvt.	A, 29th Iowa Inf.	197		1926 Oct 9	IA, 53rd, 1927
Custer, John L.		G, 79th Penn.	12		1924 Aug 28	KS, 44th, 1925
Custer, Matt	Capt.	H, 10th Iowa Inf.	23		1927 Jan 20	IA, 54th, 1928
Custer, Noble V.			498		1927	KS, 47th, 1928
Custiss, Asher		G, 153rd Ohio Inf.	128		1891 Dec 19	KS, 11th, 1892
Cutler, Alfred		B, 9th Kans.	12		1915 Jul 24	KS, 35th, 1916
Cutler, B.F.	Pvt.	L, 4th Iowa Cav.	510	64	1896 Jan 7	IA, 22nd, 1896
Cutler, Chas. C.	Pvt.	F, 2nd Iowa Cav.	78		1920 Jan 18	IA, 47th, 1921
Cutler, Ezekiel	Major	31st Iowa Inf.	168	66	1893 Nov 1	IA, 20th, 1894
Cutler, G.L.	Pvt.	F, 2nd Iowa Cav.	247		1920 Dec 26	IA, 48th, 1922
Cutler, G.L.	Pvt.	F, 2nd Iowa Cav.	247		1920 Dec 26	IA, 47th, 1921
Cutler, James G.		G, 4th Wis. Cav.	26		1912 Jan 20	KS, 31st, 1912
Cutler, Robt. E.		H, 163rd Ohio	32		1935 Dec 23	NE, 60th, 1936
Cutler, W.H.		H, 8th Wis. Inf. (died of dropsy)	13	64	1905 Apr 16	NE, 30th, 1906
Cutshall, S.L.	Pvt.	B, 4th Iowa Cav.	124	87	1933 Sep 29	IA, 60th, 1934
Cutsinger, George W.		I, 2nd Mo. Cav.	171		1931	NE, 56th, 1932
Cuttell, D.F.O.	Pvt.	A, 24th Iowa Inf.	124		1917 Nov 7	IA, 44th, 1918
Cutter, T.D.	Pvt.	D, 22nd Wis. Vols.	97		1914 Jun 26	IA, 41st, 1915
Cutting, Dean	Corp.	K, 52nd Ill. Inf.	70	57	1892 Aug 20	IA, 19th, 1893
Cutting, H.P.		Iowa (died of liver disease)	59		1905 Oct 8	NE, 30th, 1906
Cutting, Otis S.		K, 25th Mass.	182		1897 Mar 9	KS, 17th, 1898

*See Appendix A, B or C for roster of post names and locations.
†See Introduction for note regarding recording of death date.

Name	Rank	Company, Regiment or Ship	Post*	Age	Death Date†	Journal
Cutts, D.N.		5th Vt. Inf. (died of general debility)	25	65	1896 Jul 27	NE, 21st, 1897
Cyphers, Jos. L.	Pvt.	D, 103rd Ill. Inf.	20	58	1891 Mar 26	NE, 16th, 1892
Dabbs, John T.		H, 33rd Mo.	35	70	1915 Feb 1	NE, 40th, 1916
Dabid, John Miles		C, 49th Penn.	36		1916 Jul 4	KS, 36th, 1917
Dabney, J.W.	Pvt.	I, 4th Iowa Inf.	55		1902 Mar 30	IA, 29th, 1903
Dacheson, A.	Pvt.	E, 11th Penn. Inf.	108		1918 May 29	IA, 45th, 1919
Daft, Wm. H.	Pvt.	I, 47th Ill. Inf.	253		1910 Dec 23	IA, 37th, 1911
Dagget, John			63		1907 Jun	NE, 32nd, 1908
Daggett, L.H.		E, 4th Iowa	51		1921 Feb 4	KS, 41st, 1922
Daggett, W.L.	Corp.	C, 47th Iowa Inf.	19	69	1895 Jun 15	IA, 22nd, 1896
Daggy, James H.		B, 137th Ind.	265		1936 Aug 8	NE, 61st, 1937
Dagle, Frank	Corp.	E, 2nd Wis. Inf.	12		1928 Oct 31	IA, 55th, 1929
Dagnan, Wm.			222		1917 Jan 16	IA, 44th, 1918
Daharsh, E.N.		I, 1st Wis. Inf.	7		1926 Jul 27	NE, 51st, 1927
Daharsh, Edward		E, 186th Ohio	154		1930 Jan 11	NE, 55th, 1931
Dahl, O.H.			168		3rd quarter 1883	IA, 10th, 1884
Dahlberg, R.N.	Pvt.	C, 2nd Iowa Inf.	12		1929 Jan 29	IA, 56th, 1930
Dahm, Frederick		2nd Col. Battery	52		1929 Nov 22	KS, 49th, 1930
Daigh, David		E, 114th Ill. Inf.	81		1934 Mar 27	KS, 54th, 1935
Daikam, John	Sergt.	H, 34th Iowa Inf.	216	67	1897 Mar 22	IA, 23rd, 1897
Dailey, E.J.		C, 17th Ill. Cav.	75		1902 Nov 4	KS, 22nd, 1903
Dailey, Geo. W.		D, 17th Kans.	1		1926 Mar 7	KS, 46th, 1927
Dailey, John F.			14		1917 May 8	IA, 44th, 1918
Dailey, M.		D, 1st Mo.	147		1931 Dec 16	KS, 52nd, 1933
Dailey, M.		D, 1st Mo.	147		1931 Dec 16	KS, 51st, 1932
Dailey, Samuel		E, 123rd Ill.	57		1916 Dec 19	KS, 36th, 1917
Dailey, Thomas A.		C, 1st Mo. Eng.	14		1913 Nov 14	KS, 33rd, 1914
Dailey, Thos. H.		H, Wis. Inf. (died of paralysis)	110	68	1913 Dec 27	NE, 38th, 1914
Dailey, Wm.			137		1908 Apr 5	IA, 35th, 1909
Daily, Geo.	Pvt.	M, 2nd Neb. Cav.	33		1906 Nov	IA, 33rd, 1907
Daily, H.B.		E, 15th Iowa (died of heart failure)	155		1897 May 7	NE, 22nd, 1898
Dake, A.J.		Q, 27th N.Y. Dragoons (died of paralysis)	13	75	1914 Oct 17	NE, 39th, 1915
Dake, Isiah		E, 30th Wis. Inf.	250		1901 Dec 3	KS, 21st, 1902
Dakin, C.C.		M, 2nd Cal. Inf.	66		1911 Jan 18	IA, 38th, 1912
Dakin, J.B.	Corp.	C, 72nd Ill. Inf.	42	60	1896 Mar 1	IA, 22nd, 1896
Dalaney, S.S.			244		1904 Sep	KS, 24th, 1905
Dalby, S.J.	Pvt.	B, 40th Iowa Inf.	29		1919 Dec 31	IA, 47th, 1921
Dalby, S.S.			173		1922 Jul 5	IA, 49th, 1923
Dale, Charles		H, 132nd Ohio (died of pneumonia)	182	75	1904 Mar 17	NE, 29th, 1905
Dale, David	Pvt.	B, 11th Iowa	12		1922 Jan 14	IA, 49th, 1923
Dale, David		E, 72nd Ind.	1		1892 Aug 15	KS, 12th, 1893
Dalgreen, —		C, 55th[?] Ill. Cav. (died of old age)	55	80	1919	NE, 44th, 1920
Dallas, A.M.	Pvt.	C, 1st Ill. Inf.	71		1910 Sep 3	IA, 37th, 1911
Dallison, S.J.	Sergt.	F, 29th Iowa Cav.	10		1919 Sep 28	IA, 46th, 1920
Dally, John	Pvt.	H, 11th Iowa Inf.	7		1929 May 2	IA, 56th, 1930
Dalrymple, D.W.	Sergt.	H, 16th Wis. Inf.	12		1916 Aug 2	IA, 43rd, 1917
Dalrymple, G.D.	Pvt.	6th Wis. Inf.	88	91	1933 Apr 25	IA, 60th, 1934
Dalrymple, I.N.			239		1914 Jun 3	KS, 34th, 1915
Dalton, H.S.	Pvt.	A, 32nd Ill. Inf.	32		1884	KS, 4th, 1885
Dalton, P.F.	Pvt.	G, 117th Ohio	91		1922 Jul 16	IA, 49th, 1923
Daly, C.C.	Pvt.	F, 3rd Iowa Cav.	2	48	1891 Feb 24	IA, 18th, 1892
Daly, J.C.		A, 1st Bat. Cav. (died of cancer)	41		1923 Oct 20	NE, 48th, 1924
Dalziel, James S.		F, 1st Minn. Art.	52		1921 Jul 18	KS, 41st, 1922
Damewood, Francis A.		F, 4th Iowa Cav. (see also Appendix D)	25		1931 Jun 4	NE, 56th, 1932
Damewood, R.S.		F, 29th Iowa Inf.	243		1914 Oct 19	KS, 34th, 1915
Damold, Benton L.	Pvt.	K, 2nd Iowa Cav.	34		1918 Mar 12	IA, 45th, 1919
Damond, Ben.			100		1897 Jan 29	KS, 17th, 1898
Damoude, Edwin		D, 3rd Wis.	131		1929 Oct 17	KS, 49th, 1930
Dan, F.D.		101st Penn.	245	77	1916 Jan 13	NE, 40th, 1916
Dana, D.E.			5		1926 Apr 20	IA, 53rd, 1927
Dance, John	Capt.	K, 8th Iowa Cav.	140		1905	IA, 32nd, 1906
Dancer, John R.		C, 29th N.J.	15		1914 Mar 19	KS, 34th, 1915

*See Appendix A, B or C for roster of post names and locations.
†See Introduction for note regarding recording of death date.
131

Name	Rank	Company, Regiment or Ship	Post*	Age	Death Date†	Journal
Dane, S.	Pvt.		222		1907 2nd term	IA, 34th, 1908
Dane, W.H.		A, 72nd Ill.	244		1923 Nov 27	KS, 43rd, 1924
Danenbaugh, T.J.	Pvt.	K, 22nd Wis. Inf.	166		1904 Oct 26	IA, 31st, 1905
Danforth, L.F.		I, 24th Vt.	156		1924 Dec 8	IA, 51st, 1925
Danger, Henry	Pvt.	B, 11th Iowa Inf.	154		1915 Nov 10	IA, 42nd, 1916
Danham, John S.		I, 31st Iowa Inf. (died of old age)	354	78	1912 Sep 11	NE, 37th, 1913
Danhauer, John E.		D, 115th Ind.	23		1931 Dec 7	NE, 56th, 1932
Danhaur, D.H.	Adjt.	122nd Ohio	19		1896 Mar 14	KS, 16th, 1897
Daniel, Robert	Sergt.	3rd Mo. Cav.	27		1922 Aug	IA, 49th, 1923
Daniel, S.A.		E, 3rd Iowa Inf.	12		1908 Jan 10	KS, 28th, 1909
Daniel, T.J.	Pvt.	E, 23rd Mo. Inf.	410		1909 Oct 15	IA, 36th, 1910
Daniel, W.A.	Sergt.	28th Iowa Inf.	125		1912 Feb	IA, 39th, 1913
Daniels, C.H.		A, 9th Md.	38		1913	KS, 33rd, 1914
Daniels, Chas. B.		A, 1st Wis. Inf.	96		1887 Oct 9	KS, 7th, 1888
Daniels, J., see Danils, J.						
Daniels, James	Pvt.	H, 102nd Ill. Inf.	435	48	1893 Apr 15	IA, 20th, 1894
Daniels, James	Pvt.		270		1910	IA, 37th, 1911
Daniels, John D.		C, 2nd Kans. Inf.	185		1886	KS, 6th, 1887
Daniels, Levi		F, 11th Kans. Cav.	180		1913 Feb 2	KS, 33rd, 1914
Daniels, Percy	Col.	7th R.I.	49		1916 Feb 14	KS, 36th, 1917
Daniels, S.	Pvt.	G, 56th Ill. Inf. G, 23rd Ill. Inf.	98	83	1895 Apr 2	IA, 22nd, 1896
Daniels, S.L.	Pvt.	I, 46th Iowa Inf.	5		1929 Jan 20	IA, 56th, 1930
Daniels, Samuels	Pvt.	K, 1st Iowa Inf.	206		1918	IA, 45th, 1919
Daniels, T.T.		C, 2nd Ill. Inf. (died of paralytic stroke)	180	76	1916 Jul 4	NE, 41st, 1917
Daniels, W.A.		I, 43rd Mo.	225		1928	KS, 48th, 1929
Daniels, W.B.		13th U.S. Inf.	42	58	1891[1901?] Nov	NE, 26th, 1902
Daniels, Wm. H.		B, 31st Ind.	92		1922 Dec 3	KS, 42nd, 1923
Danielson, Daniel		D, 57th Ill.	87		1920 Jun 25	KS, 40th, 1921
Danils, J.		M, 4th Mo. M. Inf. (cause of death: heart)	52	65	1903 Oct 29	NE, 28th, 1904
Danis, Daniel		C, 132nd N.Y.	164		1889	KS, 9th, 1890
Danner, Chas. C., see Dauner, Chas. C.						
Danner, S.T.		A, 12th U.S. Colored	36		1919 Mar 20	KS, 39th, 1920
Dannivick, O.M.		C, 13th Kans. Inf. (died at Norton County, Kans.; buried at Edmond Cemetery)	312		1894 Aug 3	KS, 14th, 1895
Dano, J.P.	Pvt.	F, 15th N.Y. Art.	505		1905 Dec 17	IA, 32nd, 1906
Dansdiehl, John		2nd Iowa Cav.	144		1917 Oct 22	IA, 44th, 1918
Danskin, Alex	Pvt.	D, 37th Iowa Inf.	233		1911 Jul 6	IA, 38th, 1912
Dansworth, A.J.		F, 50th Ill.	17		1922 Apr 22	KS, 42nd, 1923
Danville, Henry	Pvt.	C, 127th Ill. Inf.	91		1900 Aug 8	IA, 27th, 1901
Darbell, William		C, 9th Kans. Cav.	500		1929 Feb 10	KS, 49th, 1930
Darby, W.A.			337		1911 Mar 25	KS, 31st, 1912
Darby, William		H, 195th Ohio Vols.	358		1902 Jun 22	KS, 22nd, 1903
Darland, Henry	Pvt.	I, 28th Iowa Inf.	144		1916 Apr 4	IA, 43rd, 1917
Darling, P.S.		K, 46th Ill. Inf.	428		1912 Nov 18	KS, 32nd, 1913
Darnell, A.M.	Pvt. Lieut.	D, 36th Iowa Inf. K, 54th U.S.C. Inf.	40		1912 Dec 21	IA, 39th, 1913
Darnell, J.A.	Pvt.	C, 28th Iowa Inf.	55		1911 Jun 29	IA, 38th, 1912
Darnell, James		G, 61st Ill. Inf. (died of paralysis)	73	63	1897 Aug 8	NE, 22nd, 1898
Darnell, Sumner		F, 86th Ill. Inf.	10		1921 Feb 12	NE, 46th, 1922
Darnell, Wm.	Pvt.	C, 7th Iowa Inf.	82		1912	IA, 39th, 1913
Darner, Austin		B, 88th Ill. Inf.	491		1909 Jan 15	KS, 29th, 1910
Darr, John C.		96th Ill.	55		1921 Jun 15	KS, 41st, 1922
Darr, Thos. M.		K, 83rd Ill.	114		1889	KS, 9th, 1890
Darrah, Alexander				82, 6 mos. & 8 days	1937 Jan 20	IA, 64th, 1938
Darrow, J.L.		C, 117th Ill. (died of pneumonia)	289	73	1909 Dec 6	NE, 34th, 1910
Darrow, William H.	Asst. Surg.	C, 5th Iowa Inf.	115	56	1894 Jul 15	IA, 21st, 1895
Darrt, A.F.		B, 20th Ind.	185		1923 Apr 18	KS, 43rd, 1924
Dart, Wilson	Pvt.	D, 34th Iowa Inf.	32		1899	NE, 24th, 1900
Darwell, Samuel		not a member of Farragut Post	25		1913	NE, 38th, 1914

*See Appendix A, B or C for roster of post names and locations.
†See Introduction for note regarding recording of death date.

Name	Rank	Company, Regiment or Ship	Post*	Age	Death Date†	Journal
Dashler, Chas. H.		B, 75th Ohio	57		1905 Nov 10	KS, 25th, 1906
Daskan, Jas. Sylvester	Pvt.	D, 3rd Iowa Inf.	168	51	1892 Oct 7	IA, 19th, 1893
Dauber, Fred		H, 7th Ohio Cav.	250		1915 Oct 25	KS, 36th, 1917
Daubersmith, F.F.	Pvt.	I, 3rd Iowa	216		1914 Jul 31	IA, 41st, 1915
Daugherty, David H.		E, 11th Mo. Cav.	59		1902 Oct 4	KS, 22nd, 1903
Daugherty, J.F.	Capt.	H, 10th Mo. Inf.	2		1920 May 8	IA, 47th, 1921
Daugherty, John, Dr.	Pvt.	K, 8th Iowa Cav.	238	58	1889 Sep 30	IA, 16th, 1890
Daugherty, M.	Pvt.	B, 13th Iowa Inf.	31	60	1886 Feb 23	IA, 12th, 1886
Daugherty, M.T.	Pvt.	B, 10th Kans.	497		1906 Mar 27	IA, 34th, 1908
Daugherty, Patrick		H, 5th Mo.	19		1893 Feb 26	KS, 13th, 1894
Daugherty, Thos.		E, 2nd Mo.	117		1897 Jul 20	KS, 17th, 1898
Daulby, Wiley L.		L, 8th Ind. Cav.	150		1902 Feb 25	KS, 22nd, 1903
Daulphin, C.D.		I, 1st Kans. Inf. (died of old age)	182	82	1918 Nov 4	NE, 43rd, 1919
Daun, J.B.		died of general debility	35		1910	NE, 35th, 1911
Dauner, Chas. C.	Pvt.	E, 152nd Ill. Inf.	231	61	1892 Aug 17	IA, 19th, 1893
Daupee, D.M.		C, 9th Iowa Cav.	488		1935 Jul 23	KS, 55th, 1936
Dauphin, C.D., see Daulphin, C.D.						
Daury, Eli	Capt.	A, 2nd Iowa Inf.	122		1905 Apr 27	IA, 32nd, 1906
Dauson, B.S.	Pvt.	2nd Ill. Cav.	29		1905	IA, 32nd, 1906
Dautel, Geo.		A, 39th Penn. Inf.	63		1886	KS, 6th, 1887
Davalaar, John	Sergt.	1st Mo. Lt. Art.	396	53	1892 May 29	IA, 19th, 1893
Davalt, Samuel	Pvt.	G, 21st Mo. Inf.	40		1926 Jul 2	IA, 53rd, 1927
Davdison, S.P.		D, 147th Ill.	25		1927 Dec 11	KS, 47th, 1928
Davenport, A.B.		A, 35th Mo.	174		1902 Oct 16	KS, 22nd, 1903
Davenport, D.L.		A, 162nd N.Y.	38		1917 Oct 6	KS, 37th, 1918
Davenport, F.	Pvt.	B, 31st Iowa Inf.	222		1903 Jan 9	IA, 29th, 1903
Davenport, G.A.	Pvt.	G, 11th Ill. Inf.	102		1911 Dec 30	IA, 38th, 1912
Davenport, Geo. W.			25	67	1910 May 8	NE, 35th, 1911
Davenport, J.M.		L, 9th Mo. Cav. (died at Linwood)	333		1895 Sep	KS, 15th, 1896
Davenport, W.S.		F, 148th Ill. Inf. (died of accident)	301	63	1903 Jan 22	NE, 28th, 1904
Davenport, W.W.		D, 24th Ohio	57		1918 Jun 19	KS, 38th, 1919
Davey, Jas.	Pvt.	K, 132nd Ill. Inf.	352	47	1892 Mar 31	IA, 18th, 1892
David, D.H.		B, 5th Mo. Cav.	190		1913 Aug 16	KS, 33rd, 1914
David, Daniel		C, 56th N.Y.	44		1921 Apr 31	KS, 41st, 1922
David, David W.		D, 51st Ill. Inf. (died of paralysis at Soldiers & Sailors Home, Grand Island; buried in York, Neb.)	10	65	1905 May 21	NE, 30th, 1906
David, I.B.		A, 30th Ill. Inf.	25	82	1918 Jan 3	NE, 43rd, 1919
David, J.F.		Bader, Iowa	284	80	1924 Sep 16	NE, 49th, 1925
David, J.W.	Pvt.	B, 30th Wis.	436		1922 Apr 22	IA, 49th, 1923
David, John F.		H, 62nd Ill. Inf. H, 12th Ill. Cav. (died of old age)	284	84	1925 May 6	NE, 50th, 1926
David, John Miles, Dabid, John Miles						
David, R.G.		B, 5th Mo. State Militia Cav.	196		1892 Oct 24	KS, 12th, 1893
David, T.W.	Pvt.	I, 27th Iowa Inf.	194		1908 Jul 16	IA, 35th, 1909
Davidson, B.O.	Pvt.	F, 6th Iowa Inf.	173	62	1887 Aug 13	IA, 14th, 1888
Davidson, Charles L.	Pvt.	A, 25th Iowa Inf. (died at his home in Hull, Iowa; buried in Hope Cemetery at Hull)	76	53	1898 Mar 15	IA, 24th, 1898
Davidson, Geo. N.	Pvt.	H, 7th Penn. Cav.	320	48	1892 Oct 18	IA, 19th, 1893
Davidson, J.B.	Pvt.	F, 151st Ill. Inf.	434		1920 May 1	IA, 47th, 1921
Davidson, J.G.	Lieut.	E, 25th Iowa Inf.	5	54	1891 Jan 11	IA, 17th, 1891
Davidson, J.G.	Pvt.	G, 36th Iowa	57		1921 Nov 23	IA, 48th, 1922
Davidson, J.W.		A, 153rd Ill.	50		1924 Jun 5	KS, 44th, 1925
Davidson, Jas.	1st Lieut.	G, 52nd Ill. Inf.	176	54	1890 Jun 15	IA, 17th, 1891
Davidson, John		G, 99th Ohio Inf.	448		1901 Sep 25	KS, 21st, 1902
Davidson, John		B, 123rd Ind.	418		1926	KS, 46th, 1927
Davidson, John		C, 6th Wis.	132		1926 Dec 15	KS, 46th, 1927
Davidson, John A.		F, 106th Ill. Inf.	335		1925 Apr 25	KS, 45th, 1926
Davidson, John E.	Corp.	D, 39th Iowa Inf.	320	59	1890 Oct 7	IA, 18th, 1892
Davidson, M.A.		A, 108th Ill. Inf.	11	60	1896 Aug 14	NE, 21st, 1897
Davidson, M.G.		C, 19th Iowa Inf.	83		1929 Feb 1	KS, 49th, 1930

*See Appendix A, B or C for roster of post names and locations.
†See Introduction for note regarding recording of death date.

Name	Rank	Company, Regiment or Ship	Post*	Age	Death Date†	Journal
Davidson, Nicholas		C, 12th Ind.	103		1926 Aug 24	KS, 47th, 1928
Davidson, R.W.		A, 108th Ill.	25		1926 Dec 10	NE, 51st, 1927
Davidson, Robert	Sergt.	C, 25th Iowa Inf.	246		1907 Aug	IA, 34th, 1908
Davidson, S.H.	Pvt.	23rd Iowa	7		1899 May 20	IA, 26th, 1900
Davidson, Samuel	Sergt.	H, 151st Ohio Inf.	246	56	1897 Nov 16	IA, 24th, 1898
Davidson, Searles			[22]		1929	KS, 49th, 1930
Davidson, W.A.		D, 1st Ohio	12		1904 Sep 22	KS, 24th, 1905
Davidson, W.T.		B, 5th Penn.	63		1920 Dec 3	KS, 40th, 1921
Davidson, W.W.		G, 12th Ill. Cav.	395		1936 Jan 5	KS, 55th, 1936
Davidson, Webster	Pvt.	H, 15th Iowa Inf.	236		1903 Aug 1	IA, 30th, 1904
Davies, A.O.			17		1902 Jul 16	KS, 22nd, 1903
Davies, David W.		D, 4th U.S.	100		1912 Aug 26	KS, 32nd, 1913
Davies, Jos. S.	Pvt.	E, 7th Ill.	29		1923 Dec 16	IA, 50th, 1924
Davin, Richard		C, 40th N.Y. Inf.	8		1899 Feb 13	KS, 19th, 1900
Davis, A.C.		G, 113th Ill.	85		1905 Oct	KS, 25th, 1906
Davis, A.C., Dr.	Surg.	48th U.S.C.T.	250		1915 Apr 24	KS, 36th, 1917
Davis, A.M.	Corp.	D, 7th Ill. Cav.	14		1922 Mar 25	IA, 49th, 1923
Davis, A.R.		A, 116th Ill. Inf.	118		1886	KS, 6th, 1887
Davis, A.R.		A, 116th Ill. Inf.	118		1885	KS, 5th, 1886
Davis, Amasa A.		K, 6th Wis. Inf. (died at Hot Springs, Ark.; buried at Prairie View Cemetery)	158		1894 Apr 16	KS, 14th, 1895
Davis, Andrew S.	Corp.	E, 4th Iowa Vols.	12		1898 Nov 24	IA, 25th, 1899
Davis, B.B.		K, 122nd Ill.	265		1911 Jun 9	KS, 31st, 1912
Davis, B.C.			170		1915	IA, 42nd, 1916
Davis, B.R.	Pvt.	D, 28th Ill. Inf.	231		1922 Jan 25	IA, 49th, 1923
Davis, C.		H, 12th Maine Inf.	36		1911 Dec 13	KS, 31st, 1912
Davis, C.A.	Pvt.	K, 1st Wis. Hvy. Art.	5		3rd quarter 1885	IA, 12th, 1886
Davis, C.C.		F, 86th Ill. Inf. (died of heart failure)	10	74	1913 Jul 3	NE, 38th, 1914
Davis, C.H.	Pvt.	K, 27th Iowa Inf.	77		1912 Nov 17	IA, 39th, 1913
Davis, C.M.	Pvt.	D, 32nd Iowa Inf.	67		1920 Dec 18	IA, 47th, 1921
Davis, C.W.	Pvt.	F, 2nd Iowa Cav.	140		1920 Jul 30	IA, 47th, 1921
Davis, Charles		65th U.S. Col. Inf.	413	97	1935 May 16	IA, 65th, 1939
Davis, Charles		M, 3rd Ill. Cav.	225		1920 Aug 23	KS, 40th, 1921
Davis, Charles		B, 51st Ind.	243		1920	KS, 40th, 1921
Davis, Charles			7		1925 Oct 26	NE, 50th, 1926
Davis, Charles F.	Pvt.	B, 16th Iowa Inf.	240	64	1897 Jan 13	IA, 23rd, 1897
Davis, Chas. H.		C, 1st Md.	25		1913 Mar 19	NE, 38th, 1914
Davis, Clarkson		H, 7th Wis.	5		1936 Jan 8	KS, 57th, 1938
Davis, Clinton		G, 121st Ohio (died of Bright's disease)	60	76	1914 Jul 20	NE, 39th, 1915
Davis, D.D.		E, 7th Iowa	71		1898 Oct 17	KS, 18th, 1899
Davis, D.F.		G, 29th Iowa	74		1912 Jul 11	KS, 32nd, 1913
Davis, Daniel	Pvt.	F, 47th Iowa Inf.	12		1927 Apr 13	IA, 54th, 1928
Davis, David	Pvt.	F, 1st Ind. Hvy Art.	100		1919 Jul 7	IA, 46th, 1920
Davis, David N.		51st Ill. Inf.	32		1905 May 22	NE, 30th, 1906
Davis, Dennis	Corp.	F, 191st Ohio Inf.	418		1905 Jun 20	IA, 32nd, 1906
Davis, Dennis	2nd Lieut.	B, 3rd Ind.	40		1922 Nov 25	IA, 49th, 1923
Davis, E.	Pvt.	H, 37th Ind. Inf.	119	42	1887 Jul 23	IA, 14th, 1888
Davis, E.H.			3		1883	KS, 3rd, 1884
Davis, E.W.		19th Ohio Bat.	46		1917 Jan 30	KS, 37th, 1918
Davis, Edmund B.	Pvt.	E, 25th Iowa Inf. (at large)		97	1941 May 30	IA, 67th, 1941
Davis, Edward		Ill.	461		1914 Dec 5	KS, 34th, 1915
Davis, Edward C.	Pvt.	L, 11th Mo. Cav.	12		1911 Jun 22	IA, 38th, 1912
Davis, Elihu		F, 23rd Iowa	77		1890	KS, 10th, 1891
Davis, Enoch	Pvt.	G, 6th Iowa Inf.	8		1899 May 14	IA, 26th, 1900
Davis, F.M.	Capt.	D, 29th Iowa Inf.	324		1917 Sep 16	IA, 44th, 1918
Davis, Francis		G, 9th Mo. Cav.	46		1912 Apr 6	KS, 32nd, 1913
Davis, Francis L.	Pvt.	E, 5th N.Y. Cav.	59		1917 Jun 3	IA, 44th, 1918
Davis, Friend	Pvt.	E, 37th Iowa	288	81	1898 Sep 15	IA, 25th, 1899
Davis, G.D.	Pvt.	D, 37th Ind. Inf.	156		1908 Nov 1	IA, 35th, 1909
Davis, G.W.			56		1905 Mar 1	IA, 32nd, 1906
Davis, G.W.	Pvt.	I, 5th U.S. Cav.	44		1920 May 25	IA, 47th, 1921
Davis, G.W.			69		1918 Dec 27	KS, 38th, 1919

*See Appendix A, B or C for roster of post names and locations.
†See Introduction for note regarding recording of death date.

Name	Rank	Company, Regiment or Ship	Post*	Age	Death Date†	Journal
Davis, Geo.	Pvt.	D, 113th Ill.	298		1903 Mar 7	IA, 30th, 1904
Davis, Geo. V.	Blacksmith	E, 9th Iowa Cav.	496		1900 May 16	IA, 27th, 1901
Davis, Geo. W.	Corp.	F, 11th Mich. Cav.	88		1923 Sep 23	IA, 50th, 1924
Davis, Geo. W.		E, 2nd E.S.[Eastern Shore] Md. Vols.	241		1902 Dec 13	KS, 22nd, 1903
Davis, Geo. W.		A, 16th Kans. (died of old age)	35	86	1922 Nov 29	NE, 47th, 1923
Davis, George W.		M, 6th Kans.	155		1910 Sep 4	KS, 30th, 1911
Davis, H.H.	Pvt.	A, 22nd Wis. Inf.	247	68	1899 Jun 18	IA, 26th, 1900
Davis, H.I.	1st Lieut.	K, 93rd Ill. Inf.	64		1924 Feb 1	IA, 51st, 1925
Davis, H.J.		E, 78th Ohio	115		1921 Aug 1	KS, 41st, 1922
Davis, Harry D.		A, 15th Ohio Vol. Inf.	1		1908 Aug 18	KS, 28th, 1909
Davis, Henry H.		B, 120th Ohio (died of congestion of bowels)	151	55	1900 Oct 6	NE, 25th, 1901
Davis, Henry J.		A, 48th Penn. (former member of Nebraska Dept.; location: Mason City)	237, 339		1937 Jan 29	NE, 62nd, 1938
Davis, Hermin R.		H, 145th Ind.	119		1923 Mar 29	KS, 43rd, 1924
Davis, Hiram E.		F, 8th Mich. Cav.	250		1915 May 22	KS, 36th, 1917
Davis, I.A.		M, 15th Kans. Vol. Cav.	3		1914 Feb	KS, 34th, 1915
Davis, I.R.		K, 156th Ill.	113		1914 Oct 17	KS, 34th, 1915
Davis, Ira A.		H, 21st Iowa	17		1915 Oct 29	KS, 35th, 1916
Davis, J.A.		E, 36th Wis.	25		1931 Jul 9	NE, 56th, 1932
Davis, J.B.	Pvt.	B, 34th Iowa	7		1899 Feb 11	IA, 26th, 1900
Davis, J.B.			87		1884	KS, 4th, 1885
Davis, J.D.		N.J.	264		1905 May 12	KS, 25th, 1906
Davis, J.H.	Lieut.	B, 2nd Iowa Inf.	1		1909 Dec 13	IA, 36th, 1910
Davis, J.J.		C, 39th Iowa	114		1909 Aug 18	KS, 29th, 1910
Davis, J.J.			68		1926 Dec 15	KS, 46th, 1927
Davis, J.L.		B, 15th Penn. Inf.	120	67	1911 Oct 6	NE, 36th, 1912
Davis, J.M.	Pvt.	K, 94th N.Y. Inf.	22		1913 Feb	IA, 40th, 1914
Davis, J.M.		F, 54th Iowa	18		1921 Mar 22	KS, 41st, 1922
Davis, J.M.		D, 9th Iowa	8		1927 Jan 8	KS, 47th, 1928
Davis, J.M.		E, 13th Ohio	25		1915 Jul 14	NE, 40th, 1916
Davis, J.R.	Pvt.	F, 39th Ind. Inf.	55		1921 Aug 26	IA, 48th, 1922
Davis, J.S.	Pvt.	F, 1st Iowa Cav.	16		1905 Aug 2	IA, 32nd, 1906
Davis, J.T.		L, Maine Bat.	36		1899 Jan 8	KS, 19th, 1900
Davis, J.W.	Pvt.	C, 16th Ky. Inf.	29	87	1933 Apr 19	IA, 60th, 1934
Davis, J.W.		G, 89th Ill. Inf.	11		1926 Feb 6	NE, 51st, 1927
Davis, Jacob	Pvt.		66		1920 Mar 22	IA, 47th, 1921
Davis, James	Pvt.	H, 35th Iowa Inf.	228	77	1899 Mar 13	IA, 25th, 1899
Davis, James H.		B, 57th Mass.	113		1907 Dec 9	NE, 32nd, 1908
Davis, James P.		A, 17th Ohio	8		1897 Aug 9	KS, 17th, 1898
Davis, James W.		L, 4th Mo. Inf.	153		1914 Dec 29	KS, 34th, 1915
Davis, Jas. T.M.		E, 47th Ind.	105		1897 Jun	KS, 17th, 1898
Davis, Joel H.		E, 82nd Ind. Inf.	25	74	1917 Mar 24	NE, 42nd, 1918
Davis, John			36		1911 Jan 12	KS, 31st, 1912
Davis, John			12		1923 Mar 15	KS, 43rd, 1924
Davis, John A.	Pvt.	H, 129th Ill. Inf.	11		1910 Jan	IA, 37th, 1911
Davis, John L.		D, 22nd Ill.	1		1919 May 3	KS, 39th, 1920
Davis, John W.	Pvt.	H, 47th Ohio	332	79	1899 Aug 12	IA, 26th, 1900
Davis, John W.	Pvt.	C, 120th Ohio Inf.	108		1927 Jan 7	IA, 54th, 1928
Davis, John W.	Pvt.	F, 17th Iowa Inf.	109		1887 Dec 7	IA, 14th, 1888
Davis, Joseph		E, 188th Ohio Inf.	328		1887 Sep 11	KS, 7th, 1888
Davis, Joseph A.	Pvt.	A, 9th Iowa Inf.	12		1915 Feb 19	IA, 42nd, 1916
Davis, Joseph B.	Lieut.	F, 96th N.Y. Cav.	5		1901 Feb 10	IA, 27th, 1901
Davis, Joseph J.		C, 17th Ill.	311		1885	KS, 5th, 1886
Davis, Joshua	Pvt.	D, 107th Ill. Inf.	7		1913 Jun 25	IA, 40th, 1914
Davis, Joshua B.	Chaplain Major & Lieut. Col.	8th N.Y. Cav. (Morrison's Black Horse) A & E, 122nd N.Y. Vols. (see Appendix D)	90	56	1889 Aug 22	NE, 14th, 1890
Davis, Josiah			192		1900-1901	IA, 27th, 1901
Davis, Josiah			47		1911 1st term	IA, 38th, 1912
Davis, Justus V.		C, 59th Ind.	303		1911 Aug 21	KS, 31st, 1912
Davis, L.B.	1st Lieut.	A, 50th Ind. Inf.	55	57	1889 Apr 30	IA, 16th, 1890

Name	Rank	Company, Regiment or Ship	Post*	Age	Death Date†	Journal
Davis, L.F.		G, 187th Penn. Inf.	78		1908 Dec 29	KS, 28th, 1909
Davis, L.M.		F, 125th Ohio Inf.	92		1925 Mar 6	KS, 45th, 1926
Davis, L.N.	Pvt.	F, 42nd Ind. Inf.	67	44	1889 Feb 7	IA, 15th, 1889
Davis, Leander S.		E, D.C. & 50th Ohio (died of cancer)	57	58	1904 Aug 7	NE, 29th, 1905
Davis, Lyman		H, 14th R.I. Art.	17		1912 Jul 17	KS, 32nd, 1913
Davis, M.H.	Pvt.	G, 17th Iowa Inf.	17		1911 Sep 17	IA, 38th, 1912
Davis, M.L.	Pvt.	E, 1st Del. Inf.	107		1909 Apr	IA, 36th, 1910
Davis, Madison Bartlett	1st Sergt.	I, 1st N.H. Cav. (see also Appendix D)	22		1914 Jul 8 or 28	IA, 41st, 1915
Davis, Marion Taylor		Iowa Southern Border Brigade (at large)		93	1940 Dec 7	IA, 67th, 1941
Davis, N.E.	Pvt.	I, 103rd Penn. Inf.	321	48	1893 Dec 26	IA, 20th, 1894
Davis, Napoleon B.		C, Ill. Bat.	85		1917 Jun 7	KS, 37th, 1918
Davis, Nathan M.		I, 57th Ill. Inf.	20		1931	KS, 51st, 1932
Davis, O.F.	Pvt.	F, 4th Iowa Inf.	184		1908 Nov 22	IA, 35th, 1909
Davis, O.F.	Pvt.	F, 117th Ind. Inf.	40		1930	IA, 57th, 1931
Davis, Oliver P.		H, 42nd Mo. Inf.	388		1886	KS, 6th, 1887
Davis, Owen L.		C, 11th Kans.	55		1922 Mar 25	KS, 42nd, 1923
Davis, P.T.J.		D, 525th Ind.	4		1926 Aug 2	KS, 46th, 1927
Davis, Phillip		A, 78th Ill. Inf. (died of chronic diarrhea)	309	67	1895 Jun 23	NE, 20th, 1896
Davis, R.H.	Pvt.	B, 71st Ill. Inf.	93		1913 Sep 30	IA, 40th, 1914
Davis, R.M.		F, 5th Minn. Inf.	57	84	1917 Mar 5	NE, 42nd, 1918
Davis, Robt. H.		A, 13th West Va. Inf.	78		1917 Aug 8	KS, 37th, 1918
Davis, Roger		D, 10th Ohio	25		1933 Feb	KS, 53rd, 1934
Davis, Rosser	Pvt.	D, 171st Ohio Inf.	40		1915 Dec 26	IA, 42nd, 1916
Davis, Royal M.		F, 184th N.Y. Inf. (nonmember)			1940	NE, 65th, 1941
Davis, Russell P.		1st Ind. Hvy. Art.	303		1897 Feb 22	KS, 17th, 1898
Davis, S.A.	Pvt.	K, 22nd Wis.	81		1921 Mar 4	IA, 48th, 1922
Davis, S.B.		U.S. Navy	74		1914 Feb 23	KS, 34th, 1915
Davis, S.J.		2nd Iowa Cav.	284		1918 Feb 1	IA, 45th, 1919
Davis, S.L.		G, 16th Kans. Inf.	313		1886	KS, 6th, 1887
Davis, Sam'l	Pvt.	E, 68th U.S.C.	7		1907 Jan	IA, 34th, 1908
Davis, Sam'l		B, 8th Ill. Cav.	35		1926 May 25	NE, 51st, 1927
Davis, Sam'l R.	Pvt.	B, 22nd Ohio Inf.	389		1913 Oct 4	IA, 40th, 1914
Davis, Samuel		I, 36th Iowa Inf.	186		3rd quarter 1883	IA, 10th, 1884
Davis, Samuel	Pvt.	I, 36th Iowa Inf.	186		1883 Jul	IA, 13th, 1887
Davis, Samuel D.		D, 76th Ohio Inf. (see Appendix D)		61	1907 Jan 13	NE, 31st, 1907
Davis, Samuel S.		D, 10th R.I. Inf.	32		1899 Apr 19	KS, 19th, 1900
Davis, Samuel T.		E, 21st Ill. Inf.	32		1891 Dec 20	KS, 11th, 1892
Davis, Silas C.		F, 8th Mo. Inf.	200		1902 Mar 4	KS, 22nd, 1903
Davis, Stephen	Saddler	H, 2nd Neb. Cav.	59		1911 Aug 4	IA, 38th, 1912
Davis, Stephen		I, 7th Ky.	408		1890	KS, 10th, 1891
Davis, Sylvester		D, 97th Ind.	7		1911 Mar 10	KS, 31st, 1912
Davis, T.B.		A, 10th Kans.	55		1924 Jun 1	KS, 44th, 1925
Davis, T.C.		I, 68th Ind.	47		1921 Oct 4	KS, 41st, 1922
Davis, T.D.		I, 22nd Iowa Inf.	8	93	1936 Feb 19	IA, 63rd, 1937
Davis, T.D.		I, 22nd Iowa Inf.		93	1936 Feb 19	IA, 62nd, 1936
Davis, T.E.	Pvt.	E, 1st Cal. Inf.	452		1907 Jun 31	IA, 34th, 1908
Davis, T.G.	Pvt.	B, 29th Iowa	22		1923 Jul	IA, 50th, 1924
Davis, T.J.		I, 1st Cav.	232		1904	KS, 24th, 1905
Davis, T.M.			266		1897	KS, 17th, 1898
Davis, Tamerlane	Pvt.	E, 42nd Mo. Inf.	67		1917 Jul 17	IA, 44th, 1918
Davis, Thomas	Pvt.	Ill.	23		1901-1902	IA, 28th, 1902
Davis, Thomas	Pvt.	C, 30th Iowa Inf.	157		1909 Aug 22	IA, 36th, 1910
Davis, Thomas	Pvt.	E, 60th Ohio	12		1912 Aug 9	IA, 39th, 1913
Davis, Thomas E.		E, 27th Ohio Vol. Inf.	14		1915 Aug 29	KS, 35th, 1916
Davis, Thos.		H, 141st Penn.	453		1922	KS, 42nd, 1923
Davis, U.S.		C, 3rd U.S. Cav.	242		1886	KS, 6th, 1887
Davis, W.A.R.	Pvt.	A, 14th Penn. Cav. G, 7th Penn. Cav.	22		1928	IA, 55th, 1929
Davis, W.B.	1st Lieut.	A, 24th Iowa Inf.	34		1928	IA, 55th, 1929
Davis, W.C.		K, 7th Iowa Inf.	173		1907 Dec 12	IA, 34th, 1908
Davis, W.D.		F, 13th Iowa Inf. (died of cancer)	11	65	1900 May 2	NE, 25th, 1901
Davis, W.E.	Lieut.	D, — Iowa Inf.	12	87	1932 Apr 14	IA, 59th, 1933

*See Appendix A, B or C for roster of post names and locations.
†See Introduction for note regarding recording of death date.

136

Name	Rank	Company, Regiment or Ship	Post*	Age	Death Date†	Journal
Davis, W.G.	Sergt.	I, 8th Kans. Cav.	2		1906 Oct 6	IA, 33rd, 1907
Davis, W.H.	Pvt.	B, 126th Ill. Inf.	231		1904 Jun 6	IA, 31st, 1905
Davis, W.H.	Pvt.	K, 12th Iowa Inf.	7		1914 Nov 18	IA, 41st, 1915
Davis, W.H.	Pvt.	I, 32nd Ohio Inf.	130		1929 Jun 17	IA, 56th, 1930
Davis, W.H.		I, 12th Ill. Cav.	65	56	1892 Dec 8	KS, 12th, 1893
Davis, W.H.		119 No record	64		1925	KS, 45th, 1926
Davis, W.J.		E, 6th Mo.	129		1904 Feb 6	KS, 24th, 1905
Davis, W.J.			7		1918	KS, 38th, 1919
Davis, W.L.	Pvt.	D, 2nd Iowa Inf.	12		1915 Jan 15	IA, 42nd, 1916
Davis, W.L.	Sergt.	B, 35th Iowa Inf.	235		1925 Mar 5	IA, 52nd, 1926
Davis, W.P.		F, 118th Ohio Inf.	262	69	1904 Aug 16	NE, 29th, 1905
Davis, Werter E.		16th Kans. Cav.	40		1893 Jun 22	KS, 13th, 1894
Davis, William		B, 16th N.Y. Art. (died of pneumonia)	12	75	1900 Feb 22	NE, 25th, 1901
Davis, William E.	Pvt.	D, 171st Ohio Inf.	35		1917 Feb 7	IA, 44th, 1918
Davis, William H.		H, 31st Wis. Inf. (died of heart trouble)	48	82	1925 Oct 10	NE, 50th, 1926
Davis, Willis	Sergt.	B, 35th Iowa Inf.	64		1908 Feb 10	IA, 35th, 1909
Davis, Willis		C, 57th Ill. Inf. (died of paralysis)	22	72	1916 Apr 27	NE, 41st, 1917
Davis, Wm.	1st Lieut.	1st U.S. Inf.	235		1906 Jan 26	IA, 33rd, 1907
Davis, Wm.	Pvt.	K, 11th Penn. Cav.	259		1910 Aug 23	IA, 37th, 1911
Davis, Wm.	Pvt.	B, 4th Ohio Inf.	512		1922 Dec 27	IA, 49th, 1923
Davis, Wm.		Kans.	241		1908[1909?] Aug 15	KS, 29th, 1910
Davis, Wm.		H, 7th Ind.	51		1922 Nov 21	KS, 42nd, 1923
Davis, Wm. B.	Pvt.	A, 24th Iowa Inf.	34		1927 Jul 27	IA, 54th, 1928
Davison, A.W.		D, 102nd Ill. Inf. (died at Mitchell County; buried at Highland Cemetery)	173		1894	KS, 14th, 1895
Davison, Chas. P.	Pvt.	A, 8th Iowa	92		1922 Mar 12	IA, 49th, 1923
Davison, J.H.	Sailor	U.S. Navy	88		1925 May 29	IA, 52nd, 1926
Davison, J.M.	Pvt.	D, 13th Iowa	64		1905	IA, 32nd, 1906
Davison, J.N.	Pvt.	F, 112th Ill. Inf.	192		1922 Mar 22	IA, 49th, 1923
Davison, Joseph		D, 2nd Kans.	318		1906 Oct 14	KS, 26th, 1907
Davison, Morris		A, 7th Kans.	191		1897 Mar 26	KS, 17th, 1898
Davison, W.R.	Pvt.	C, 118th Ill. Inf.	122		1919	IA, 46th, 1920
Davison, W.S.		D, 21st Penn. Cav.	474		1919 Sep 26	KS, 39th, 1920
Davison, W.W.	Pvt.	B, 7th Wis. Inf. A & B, 177th Penn. Inf.	22		1930	IA, 57th, 1931
Davisson, John S.	Corp.	I, 9th Iowa Cav. (see also Appendix D)	7		1941 May 20	NE, 66th, 1942
Davy, Geo. P.		H, 2nd Mich.	13		1916	NE, 41st, 1917
Dawdy, G.L.		D, 129th Ill.	5		1922 Sep 20	KS, 42nd, 1923
Dawley, H.		H, 8th N.Y.	293		1911 Apr 28	KS, 31st, 1912
Dawley, John Murray		D, 8th Iowa Inf.	235 452	94	1938 Mar 20	IA, 64th, 1938
Daws, Alfred			52		1916 Dec 18	IA, 43rd, 1917
Daws, James M.	Musician		45		1913 Nov 17	IA, 40th, 1914
Daws, Thos.	Pvt.	G, 46th Ill. Inf.	216		1908 Feb 29	IA, 35th, 1909
Dawson, B.S., Dauson, B.S.			23		1890	NE, 15th, 1891
Dawson, Daniel			231	55	1893 Mar	IA, 20th, 1894
Dawson, Eli	Sergt.	G, 26th Ind. Inf.	287		1913 Sep	NE, 38th, 1914
Dawson, F.M.		A, 39th Ohio	6		1923	IA, 50th, 1924
Dawson, I.S.			108	87	1933 Nov 15	IA, 60th, 1934
Dawson, J.A.	Pvt.	G, 19th Iowa Inf.	25		1905 Oct 25	NE, 30th, 1906
Dawson, J.O.		U.S. Navy	25		1905 Oct 25	NE, 31st, 1907
Dawson, J.O.		U.S. Navy	36		1898 Mar 18	KS, 18th, 1899
Dawson, James		I, 6th Iowa Cav.	250	66	1898 Dec 8	IA, 25th, 1899
Dawson, Jasper	Pvt.	H, 2nd Iowa Cav.			1929 Jan 4	NE, 53rd, 1929
Dawson, John L.			110		1918 Sep 2	KS, 38th, 1919
Dawson, John W.		G, Mo. State Militia	52		1920 Jun 24	KS, 40th, 1921
Dawson, John W.		M, 2nd Iowa Cav.	45		1925 Sep 11	IA, 52nd, 1926
Dawson, M.			17		1915 May 27	KS, 35th, 1916
Dawson, R.H.	Hosp. Stew.	U.S.A.	18		1905 Oct 27	KS, 25th, 1906
Dawson, Robert D.		A, 4th Ky.	25	80	1917 Oct 23	NE, 42nd, 1918
Dawson, T.B.		101st Penn. Inf.	104		1883	KS, 3rd, 1884
Dawson, T.J.						

*See Appendix A, B or C for roster of post names and locations.
†See Introduction for note regarding recording of death date.

137

Name	Rank	Company, Regiment or Ship	Post*	Age	Death Date†	Journal
Dawson, T.W.		H, 29th Ill. Inf.	297		1916 Apr 12	KS, 36th, 1917
Dawson, W.		E, 15th Ohio	133		1921 Feb	IA, 48th, 1922
Dawson, Washington	Pvt.	C, 94th Ill. Inf.	31		1902 Nov 13	IA, 29th, 1903
Dawson, William Jackson		E, 8th Iowa Inf.	363	89	1937 Jan 31	IA, 64th, 1938
Day, A.J.		H, 11th Penn. Inf. (died of long sickness)	32	72	1911 Mar	NE, 36th, 1912
Day, Aaron W.	Pvt.	A, 24th Iowa Inf.	163	61	1887 Feb 10	IA, 15th, 1889
Day, Aaron W.	Pvt.	A, 24th Iowa Inf.	163	61	1887 Feb 10	IA, 13th, 1887
Day, Amos D.		L, 3rd Ohio	339		1928 Aug 20	KS, 48th, 1929
Day, Benj. F.	Pvt.	G, 29th Iowa Inf.	96	61	1893 Mar 25	IA, 19th, 1893
Day, Capt.			25		1906	KS, 26th, 1907
Day, David		K, 31st Ind.	72		1937 Jan 8	KS, 57th, 1938
Day, David R.	Corp.	D, 7th Iowa Inf.	56		1903 Jul 1	IA, 30th, 1904
Day, E.	Pvt.	F, 77th Ohio	271		1921 Dec 26	IA, 48th, 1922
Day, E.P.	Pvt.	E, 18th Iowa Inf.	231		1910 May 22	IA, 37th, 1911
Day, Edward H.		B, 40th Iowa Inf. (died of sickness)	209	78	1911 Feb 1	NE, 36th, 1912
Day, Frank G.	Sergt.	L, 10th Ky. Cav.	2		1900 Jun 10	IA, 27th, 1901
Day, G.D.	Pvt.	I, 21st Ind.	3		1930 Sep 14	KS, 51st, 1932
Day, G.D.		I, 21st Ind.	3		1930 Sep 14	KS, 52nd, 1933
Day, Geo. A.	Lieut. Col.	91st Ill. Cav.	190	62	1891 Jan 27	IA, 18th, 1892
Day, George	Pvt.	I, 12th Wis. Inf.	23		1930 Apr 3	IA, 57th, 1931
Day, Handy S.		C, 12th Ohio	71		1913 Dec 1	KS, 33rd, 1914
Day, J.H.		B, 2nd Calif. Cav. (died of heart trouble)	7	59	1897 Aug 27	NE, 22nd, 1898
Day, J.H.		A, 51st Ill. Inf. (died of complication)	262	78	1920 May 6	NE, 45th, 1921
Day, James J.		K, 6th Ohio Cav.	113		1914 Apr 5	KS, 34th, 1915
Day, Jemes G.	Capt.	F, 15th Iowa Inf.	12		1898 May 1	IA, 24th, 1898
Day, John		K, 21st Ind.	72		1926 Jun 11	KS, 46th, 1927
Day, John			32		1922 Oct 15	NE, 47th, 1923
Day, Joseph		F, 173rd Ohio	252		1909 May 5	KS, 29th, 1910
Day, Lemuel	Pvt.	H, 53rd Ind.	11		1921 Apr 11	IA, 48th, 1922
Day, N.A.		F, 36th Mo.	1		1925 Jun 14	NE, 50th, 1926
Day, R.H.		K, 102nd Ill.	20		1915 Jan 31	KS, 35th, 1916
Day, S.H.		H, 62nd Ill.	293		1922 May 3	KS, 42nd, 1923
Day, Stephen A.		B, 40th Iowa	106		1889	KS, 9th, 1890
Day, T.W.	Pvt.	B, 18th Iowa Inf.	297		1913 Mar 8	IA, 40th, 1914
Day, W.H.	Major	K, 10th Ohio Cav.	78		1921 Feb 12	IA, 48th, 1922
Day, W.W.		F, 70th Ind.	63		1912 Jun 17	KS, 32nd, 1913
Day, Wilburn		D, 34th Ind. Inf. (at large)		92	1937 Jan 24	IA, 64th, 1938
Day, William	Pvt.	C, 14th Wis. Inf.	7		1894 Mar 28	IA, 21st, 1895
Daylor, Thos.			179		1909	IA, 36th, 1910
Dayton, Geo. B.	Pvt.	C, 2nd Iowa Inf.	88		1918 Feb 2	IA, 46th, 1920
Dayton, Lyman I.	Pvt.	F, 10th N.Y. Hvy. Art.	321		1913 May 1	IA, 40th, 1914
Deach, S.R.		D, 1st Ill. Cav.	58		1934 Sep 11	KS, 54th, 1935
Deacon, J.R.	Pvt.	C, 1st Wis. Cav.	72		1887 Aug	IA, 15th, 1889
Deal, Jacob		I, 41st Ohio	52		1911 Apr 20	KS, 31st, 1912
Deal, Jno. K.	Pvt.	C, 88th Ind. Inf.	44	48	1892 May 23	IA, 19th, 1893
Deal, M.D.	Pvt.	E, 3rd Iowa Inf.	30		1904 May 24	IA, 31st, 1905
Deamer, John			12		1922 Apr 16	KS, 42nd, 1923
Dean, Albert A.			14		1905 Nov 28	KS, 25th, 1906
Dean, D.R.	Pvt.	H, 93rd Ill. Inf.	127		1913 May 23	IA, 40th, 1914
Dean, Daniel	Pvt.	M, 1st Iowa Cav.	88	78	1895 May 21	IA, 22nd, 1896
Dean, E.R.		N, G, Mich. Cav. (died of heart trouble)	10		1906 Jun 8	NE, 31st, 1907
Dean, Geo.			290		1923	IA, 50th, 1924
Dean, Geo. H.		D, 1st West Va.	100		1919 Mar 15	KS, 39th, 1920
Dean, Geo. P.		H, 8th Mich. Cav.	11		1926 Sep 30	NE, 51st, 1927
Dean, H.F.	Sergt.	H, 26th Iowa Inf.	83		1908 Dec 22	IA, 35th, 1909
Dean, Henry H.	Col.	146th Ill. Inf.	214		1899	NE, 24th, 1900
Dean, Israel A.	Pvt.	H, 7th Iowa Inf.	40		1904 Sep 15	IA, 31st, 1905
Dean, J.A.	Lieut.	B, 124th Ill. Inf.	22		1920 Mar 13	IA, 47th, 1921
Dean, J.S.W.		M, 3rd West Va. Cav.	40		1917 Jun 24	KS, 37th, 1918
Dean, J.W.	Sergt.	G, 18th Iowa Inf.	330		1887 Jun 20	IA, 15th, 1889
Dean, Jas. H.	Pvt.	C, 23rd Iowa Inf.	7		1917 May 27	IA, 44th, 1918
Dean, L.	Pvt.	M, 1st Iowa Cav.	332		1930 Jun 22	IA, 57th, 1931

*See Appendix A, B or C for roster of post names and locations.
†See Introduction for note regarding recording of death date.

Name	Rank	Company, Regiment or Ship	Post*	Age	Death Date†	Journal
Dean, L.E.	Pvt.	M, 1st Iowa Cav.	88		1892-1893	IA, 19th, 1893
Dean, M.			122		1927	IA, 54th, 1928
Dean, Martin	Pvt.	M, 6th Va. Inf.	9		1915 Jul	IA, 42nd, 1916
Dean, Martin G.	Chaplain	145th N.Y.	1		1915 Dec 28	KS, 35th, 1916
Dean, Nelson		I, 16th Mich.	82		1923 Sep 14	KS, 43rd, 1924
Dean, W.L.	Pvt.	I, 23rd Penn. Inf.	9		1911	IA, 38th, 1912
Dean, W.O.	Pvt.	A, 32nd Iowa Inf.	149		1912 Dec 12	IA, 40th, 1914
Dean, William		C, 23rd Iowa Inf.	209		1912 Aug 8	KS, 32nd, 1913
Dean, William G.		M, 5th Mo. Cav.	380		1901 Mar 20	KS, 21st, 1902
Dearborn, T.H.	Capt.	K, 6th N.H. Inf.	57		1916 Apr 21	IA, 43rd, 1917
Deardorf, James	Pvt.	I, 63rd Ohio Inf.	200		1927 Dec 28	IA, 54th, 1928
Deardorff, Elmer E.		C, 4th Ind. Cav.	358		1902 Mar 20	KS, 22nd, 1903
Deardurff, Eli	Pvt.	M, 4th Iowa Cav.	5		1903 Sep 21	IA, 30th, 1904
Dearinger, C.M.		E, 40th Iowa Inf.	25	90	1936 Nov 14	IA, 63rd, 1937
Deater, John	Pvt.	D, 4th Iowa Cav.	188		1913 Jun 10	IA, 40th, 1914
Deaton, F.K.	Lieut.	34th Iowa	425		1904 May 4	IA, 31st, 1905
Deaton, James		D, 101st Ill. Inf.	8		1899 Jan 6	KS, 19th, 1900
Deaver, G.W.			239		1905	IA, 32nd, 1906
Deaver, L.T.	Pvt.	I, 1st Ohio Hvy. Art.	440		1920 Feb 29	IA, 47th, 1921
DeBarrows, F.A.		I, 130th Ill.	1		1897 Apr 19	KS, 17th, 1898
Debette, Wm.		D, 16th Ill.	7		1898 Sep 2	KS, 18th, 1899
DeBois, John P.		C, 15th Ohio	465		1912 Dec 5	KS, 32nd, 1913
DeBore, John	Corp.	D, 8th Mich. Inf.	171		1916 Feb 28	KS, 36th, 1917
DeBow, A.M., see DoBow, A.M.						
Debow, Nason		A, 13th Mo. Cav.	7		1925 May 26	NE, 50th, 1926
Debruler, Alfred		F, 10th Ind. Cav.	265		1934 Dec 4	NE, 59th, 1935
DeBruler, J.N.		F, 17th Ind. V.R.C.	4		1902 Feb 12	KS, 22nd, 1903
Debyell, William		C, 39th Ohio	6		1897 Sep 10	KS, 17th, 1898
Dech, W.H.		I, 1st Penn. Rifles	31		1926 Aug 31	NE, 51st, 1927
Deck, Isaac		K, 7th Mo.	242		1898 Oct 6	KS, 18th, 1899
Deck, J.J.		D, 34th Ill.	31	78	1917 Dec 3	NE, 42nd, 1918
Deck, John	Pvt.	C, 2nd Iowa Inf.	372	62	1896 Dec 28	IA, 23rd, 1897
Decker, E.C.		G, 187th Penn. Inf.	22	90	1936 Aug 4	IA, 63rd, 1937
Decker, Eli		A, 183rd Ohio Inf.	11	80	1921 Apr 29	NE, 46th, 1922
Decker, Elias C.		G, 187th Penn. Inf.	22	96	1936 Jul 27	IA, 63rd, 1937
Decker, Geo.		E, 2nd Conn. (cause of death: demented)	35	75	1922 May 14	NE, 47th, 1923
Decker, J.C.			45		1917 Feb 11	IA, 44th, 1918
Decker, John		G, 83rd Ind. Inf. (died of old age)	24	78	1902 Jun	NE, 27th, 1903
Decker, L.F.		L, 2nd Wis. Cav.	78		1908 Oct 4	KS, 28th, 1909
Decker, Norman		G, 21st Mich.	113		1902 Oct 30	KS, 22nd, 1903
Decker, S.B.		K, 134th Ill. Inf.	68		1917 Nov 1	IA, 44th, 1918
Decker, S.W.	Pvt.	H, 7th Iowa Cav.	40		1890 Aug 22	IA, 17th, 1891
Decker, Theo. J.		C, 97th Ohio Inf. (died in Ohio)	17		1895 Sep	KS, 15th, 1896
Decker, William		B, 87th Ohio Inf. (died at Alta Vista; buried at Pleasant Mound Cemetery)	60		1894 Apr 10	KS, 14th, 1895
Decker, Wm.	Pvt.	C, 9th Iowa Inf.	54		1911 Mar 20	IA, 38th, 1912
Decker, Zachariah		B, 16th Kans.	293		1925 Apr 10	KS, 45th, 1926
Deckered, J.R.	Steward	E, 29th Ind. Inf.	452		1922 Mar 12	IA, 49th, 1923
DeCoursey, J.L.	Pvt.	I, 56th Penn. Inf.	12	87	1933 Feb	IA, 60th, 1934
Dee, C.F.	Corp.	Kans. State Militia	321		1916 Mar 29	IA, 43rd, 1917
Dee, Henry			24		1926	IA, 53rd, 1927
Dee, James			24		1926	IA, 53rd, 1927
Deeble, C.W.		F, 73rd Ohio	462		1911 Feb 16	KS, 31st, 1912
Deeds, Hiram		E, 23rd Ohio	258		1917 Nov 23	KS, 37th, 1918
Deel, James A.		L, 115th Ill.	40		1920 Feb 22	KS, 40th, 1921
Deemer, I.W.	Sergt.	H, 10th Iowa Inf.	156		1918 Aug 16	IA, 45th, 1919
Deemer, Joe	Pvt.	H, 10th Iowa Inf.	7		1921	IA, 48th, 1922
Deeter, C.H.		B, 11th Ohio Inf.	413		1901 Jun 18	KS, 21st, 1902
Deets, Aaron	Pvt.	A, 2nd Conn. Cav.	452		1924 May 27	IA, 51st, 1925
Deets, Frank	Pvt.	B, 10th Iowa Inf.	425		1914 Sep 23	IA, 41st, 1915
Deffer, Augustus		A, 1st Dist. of Columbia	77		1938 Feb 22	NE, 63rd, 1939

*See Appendix A, B or C for roster of post names and locations.
†See Introduction for note regarding recording of death date.
139

Name	Rank	Company, Regiment or Ship	Post*	Age	Death Date†	Journal
DeFord, Franklin			12		1923 Nov 18	IA, 50th, 1924
DeFord, H.S., Dr.	Asst. Surg.	U.S. Navy	18		1900 May 23	KS, 20th, 1901
Deford, Henry		6th Ill. Art. Henshaw's Battery	10		1936 May 1	NE, 61st, 1937
Deford, John H.			79		1927	IA, 54th, 1928
Deford, John W.		F, Penn. Res.	18		1913 Dec 3	KS, 33rd, 1914
Deford, T.J.	Pvt.	A, 53rd Ill. Inf.	7		1920 Jul 30	IA, 47th, 1921
Defore, W.L.	Pvt.	D, 32nd Iowa Inf.	67	60	1887 Nov 7	IA, 14th, 1888
DeForrest, J.W.	Pvt.	C, 2nd N.Y. Inf.	452		1910 Aug	IA, 37th, 1911
Defriez, J.G.	Pvt.	G, 136th Ohio Inf.	436		1917 Dec 8	IA, 44th, 1918
DeGree, Eli		A, 6th Vt.	36		1923 Apr 28	KS, 43rd, 1924
Degroff, J.N.	Pvt.	B, Dragout	154		1923 Jun 12	IA, 50th, 1924
DeGroote, Daniel	Pvt.	H, 1st Wis. Inf.	193		1911 Aug 28	IA, 38th, 1912
Degrow, Geo. W.	Pvt.	D, 153rd Ill. Inf.	267		1904 Apr 9	IA, 31st, 1905
DeHanen, Geo.	Pvt.	A, 138th Penn.	16		1922 Oct 20	IA, 49th, 1923
Dehart, Geo.	Pvt.	E, 15th —	79		1920 Feb	IA, 47th, 1921
DeHart, J.M.	Pvt.	H, 7th Mo. Cav.	433		1910 Sep 14	IA, 37th, 1911
DeHarty, T.B.			22		1905	IA, 32nd, 1906
DeHaven, A. Leroy	Sergt.	I, 2nd Ohio Art.	300		1909 May 6	IA, 36th, 1910
DeHaven, J.C.	1st Lieut.	E, 6th Iowa Cav.	29		1925 Feb 25	IA, 52nd, 1926
Dehnio, Peter	Pvt.	D, 98th N.Y. Inf.	4	51	1893 Dec 2	IA, 20th, 1894
Dehorda, Edward	Pvt.	A, 15th Mo. Inf.	317	78	1894 Feb 27	IA, 20th, 1894
Deibler, Geo. W.		D, 167th Penn. Inf.	100		1891 Nov 19	KS, 11th, 1892
Deighton, James	Pvt.	E, 19th Iowa Inf.	56	88	1931 Jul 4	IA, 58th, 1932
Deighton, Samuel		E, 78th Ill.	52		1921 Jan 2	KS, 41st, 1922
Deihl, E.P.		D, 50th Mo.	68		1908 Mar 21	KS, 28th, 1909
Deihl, Henry		A, 151st Ill. Inf. (died of stomach trouble)	63		1907 Oct 12	NE, 32nd, 1908
Deihl, Henry E.A.	Pvt.	H, 27th Iowa Inf.	63		1915 May 17	IA, 42nd, 1916
Deiter, J.N.		L, 1st U.S. Cav.	88		1928 Jun 26	KS, 48th, 1929
Deitrich, J.E.		H, 15th Kans.	148		1899 May 7	KS, 19th, 1900
Deitz, Alonzo	Pvt.	D, 27th Iowa Inf.	452		1904 Aug 27	IA, 31st, 1905
Deitz, H.		died of old age	101	84	1914 Oct 10	NE, 39th, 1915
Deitz, L.A.		G, 4th Kans.	114		1896 Feb 3	KS, 16th, 1897
Deitz, L.J.	Pvt.	F, 21st U.S. Inf.	134		1927 Nov 14	IA, 54th, 1928
Deitz, L.J.	Pvt.	F, 21st U.S. Inf.	134		1925 Nov 14	IA, 52nd, 1926
DeJean, Geo. W.			83		1922	IA, 49th, 1923
DeKuck, S.	Pvt.	G, 33rd Iowa	404		1924 Oct 7	IA, 51st, 1925
Delaney, F.P.	Pvt.	F, 17th Wis.	54		1905 Apr 2	IA, 32nd, 1906
Delaney, Patrick		I, 7th Kans. Cav.	380		1886	KS, 6th, 1887
Delano, R.D.		B, 49th Ind.	17		1913 Feb 17	KS, 33rd, 1914
Delano, S.B.		K, 108th N.Y.	497		1917 Jan 11	KS, 37th, 1918
Delano, W.L.		M, 11th Kans. Cav.	18		1917 Feb 2	KS, 37th, 1918
Delany, Thomas E.	Pvt.	B, 12th Ill. Inf.	503		1919 Nov 7	IA, 46th, 1920
DeLapp, James	Pvt.	D, 6th Iowa Inf.	170		1885 Oct 8	IA, 12th, 1886
Delay, George		I, 36th Iowa	434		1919 Feb 4	KS, 39th, 1920
Delay, Reuben		I, 3rd Iowa Cav.	71		1900 Aug 24	KS, 20th, 1901
Deleplain, I.V.	Pvt.	I, 91st Ohio Inf.	110		1904 Mar 15	IA, 31st, 1905
Deley, Geo.	Pvt.		211		1920	IA, 47th, 1921
Delk, S.B.	Corp.	D, 39th Iowa Inf.	173		1910 Oct 19	IA, 37th, 1911
Dell, Frank		F, 70th N.Y.	52		1905 Mar 13	KS, 25th, 1906
Dell, George	Pvt.	A, 36th Ill. Inf.	216		1925 Jan 17	IA, 52nd, 1926
Dellenger, W.S.		G, 113th Ohio	301		1924 Oct 8	KS, 44th, 1925
Dellenger, Wm.		M, 2nd U.S. Battery	301		1902 Nov 22	KS, 22nd, 1903
Dellinger, J.H.		I, 58th Ind.	466		1918 Jan 17	KS, 38th, 1919
DeLong, Amos		D, 124th N.Y.	62		1898 Apr 17	KS, 18th, 1899
DeLong, Dan J.	Pvt.		11		1916 Aug 6	IA, 43rd, 1917
DeLong, Fenton S.	Pvt.	I, 15th Iowa Inf.	12	56	1892 Jun 27	IA, 19th, 1893
DeLong, G.E.		K, 6th Iowa	415		1895 Apr 22	KS, 17th, 1898
DeLong, Geo.		77th Ill. Inf. (died of cancer)	25		1903 Mar	NE, 28th, 1904
DeLong, Gilbert E.		K, 6th Iowa Inf. (died at Dighton)	415		1895 Apr	KS, 15th, 1896
Delong, Gipson		K, 34th Ill. Cav. (died of general disability)	21	87	1920 Apr 6	NE, 45th, 1921
DeLong, Henry		3rd Iowa Battery	29		1927 May 12	IA, 54th, 1928
Delong, John A.	Pvt.	F, 90th Ohio Inf.	337	57	1894 May 4	IA, 21st, 1895

*See Appendix A, B or C for roster of post names and locations.
†See Introduction for note regarding recording of death date.

Name	Rank	Company, Regiment or Ship	Post*	Age	Death Date†	Journal
DeLong, Joseph	Pvt.	I, 23rd Ohio Inf.	427	46	1887 Jul 27	IA, 14th, 1888
DeLong, N.R.	Pvt.	E, 38th Iowa Inf.	98		1915 May 27	IA, 42nd, 1916
Delong, T.E.		C, 33rd Iowa Inf.			1929 Jan 8	NE, 53rd, 1929
DeLong, Wm.		I, 35th Iowa Inf.	292		1899 Jul 10	KS, 19th, 1900
Delp, M.	Pvt.	13th Wis. Inf.	80		1919 Nov 25	IA, 46th, 1920
Delp, Michael		E, 126th Penn.	241		1920 Dec 23	KS, 40th, 1921
DeMarsh, John	Pvt.	B, 57th N.Y. Inf.	19		1917 Dec 16	IA, 44th, 1918
Demary, Christ		K, 6th N.H.	8	75	1913 Aug	NE, 38th, 1914
Dement, D.R.			96		1910 Jan 1	IA, 37th, 1911
Deming, Wm. P.		I, 11th Kans.	35		1916 May 24	KS, 36th, 1917
Demmony, Henry M.		F, 36th Ohio	203		1913 Jul 25	KS, 33rd, 1914
Demo, M.	Pvt.	A, 14th N.Y. Art.	42		1920 Oct 19	IA, 47th, 1921
Demoney, J.H.		B, 21st Mo.	63		1918 Apr 5	KS, 38th, 1919
DeMoss, D.P.		A, 35th Ill.	49		1921 Nov 18	KS, 41st, 1922
DeMoss, Nelson		A, 35th Ill.	49		1905 May 15	KS, 25th, 1906
Demoss, William		C, 11th Kans. Cav.	105		1893 Oct 28	KS, 13th, 1894
DeMoss, Wm. A.		B, 117th Ind.	1		1897 Jan 1	KS, 17th, 1898
Dempsey, Geo. P.	Pvt.	K, 12th Wis. Inf.	452		1917 Nov 24	IA, 44th, 1918
Dempsey, John		G, 5th Iowa (died of old age)	82	84	1920 Jun 5	NE, 45th, 1921
Dempster, John A.		I, 52nd Ill. Inf. (died of Bright's disease; see also Appendix D)	110	74	1914 Dec 21	NE, 39th, 1915
DeMuth, Jacob	Pvt.	G, 2nd Iowa Inf.	100		1920 Aug 12	IA, 47th, 1921
Demuth, John A.	Lieut.	G, 2nd Iowa Inf.	337		1928 Dec 1	IA, 55th, 1929
DeNarce, Joe	Pvt.		167		1920 Apr 4	IA, 47th, 1921
Denbo, John M.		D, 144th Ind.	52		1916 Oct 21	KS, 36th, 1917
Dence, Frank M.	Artificer	B, 1st Mo. Eng.	2	46	1889 Oct 30	IA, 16th, 1890
Deney, Mathias		E, 17th Kans. Inf.	25		1911 Jan 4	KS, 31st, 1912
Denham, George W.		I, 132nd Ill.	25		1933 Jan 10	NE, 58th, 1934
Deniaus, Oliver		B, 104th Ohio	311		1918 Apr 1	KS, 38th, 1919
Denick, V.	Pvt.	A, 24th Iowa Inf.	164		1917 Aug 25	IA, 44th, 1918
Denil, Wm. H.		E, 12th Mich.	11	73	1916 May 8	NE, 41st, 1917
Denison, J.L.		9th Kans.	311		1908 Aug 14	KS, 28th, 1909
Denison, James S.	Pvt.	K, 1st Ill.	237		1901 Jun 1	IA, 28th, 1902
Denison, W.W.		I, 11th Ind. Cav.	1		1935 Jul 3	KS, 56th, 1937
Deniston, J.		H, 4th Wis.	301		1934	KS, 55th, 1936
Denmey, Henry			373		4th quarter 1884	IA, 11th, 1885
Denning, C.H.		B, 10th Tenn.	25		1930 Oct 30	KS, 50th, 1931
Denning, Geo. P.	Pvt.	3rd Iowa Battery	50		1923 Feb 11	IA, 50th, 1924
Denning, George		C, 51st Mo. Inf.	129		1925 Feb 9	KS, 45th, 1926
Denning, J.A.		B, 170th Ohio	399		1898 Dec 2	KS, 18th, 1899
Denning, Newt		G, 74th Ohio	17		1922 Aug 5	KS, 42nd, 1923
Dennis, A.E.	Musician	A, 30th N.J. Inf.	404		1916 May 7	IA, 43rd, 1917
Dennis, A.Z.	Pvt.	I, 33rd Iowa Inf.	16		1920 Nov 8	IA, 47th, 1921
Dennis, Adam		B, Merrill's White Horse Mo. Vols.	22		1886	KS, 6th, 1887
Dennis, Cronin		A, 13th Kans.	191		1905 Apr 7	KS, 25th, 1906
Dennis, G. St., see St. Dennis, G.						
Dennis, Geo. W.	Sergt.	C, 7th Iowa Cav.	466		1909 Jul 6	IA, 36th, 1910
Dennis, I.V.	Capt.	G, 22nd Iowa Inf.	8	73	1894 Dec	IA, 21st, 1895
Dennis, J.B.	Sergt.	B, 184th Ill. Inf.	125		1911 May 9	IA, 38th, 1912
Dennis, J.W.		K, 123rd Ind. (died of lung trouble)	47		1916 Jun 29	NE, 41st, 1917
Dennis, Jno. B.		G, 6th Mass. Inf. (died of heart disease)	262		1894 Dec 26	NE, 19th, 1895
Dennis, Julius	Pvt.	M, 11th Mo. Cav.	68	84	1931 Feb 16	IA, 58th, 1932
Dennis, Oliver P.		location: Basset			1926 May 4	NE, 52nd, 1928
Dennis, Sam. W.		A, 8th Iowa Inf.	282		1892 Jul 6	NE, 17th, 1893
Dennis, T.		B, 13th Iowa	122		1898	KS, 18th, 1899
Dennis, Travis		B, 13th Iowa	122		1897 Sep 20	KS, 17th, 1898
Dennis, W.H.		B, 38th Ohio	74		1921 Jun 1	KS, 41st, 1922
Dennison, F.W.		I, 112th N.Y.	250		1931 Jan 10	KS, 52nd, 1933
Dennison, F.W.		I, 112th N.Y.	250		1931 Jan 10	KS, 51st, 1932
Dennison, G.A.		I, 6th Iowa Cav.	265		1900 Jul 3	KS, 20th, 1901
Dennison, Geo. E.		B, 6th Kans. Cav.	54		1885	KS, 5th, 1886

*See Appendix A, B or C for roster of post names and locations.
†See Introduction for note regarding recording of death date.
141

Name	Rank	Company, Regiment or Ship	Post*	Age	Death Date†	Journal
Dennison, Jas.		H, 10th N.Y.	25		1933 Sep 25	KS, 53rd, 1934
Dennison, Martin	Pvt.	A, 25th Iowa Inf.	108		1905 Aug 19	IA, 32nd, 1906
Dennison, W.W.		I, 11th Kans.	1		1936[1935?] Jul 4	KS, 55th, 1936
Denny, A.J.					1935	KS, 55th, 1936
Denny, George		C, 51st Mo.	129		1925 Feb 9	KS, 44th, 1925
Denny, Henry			182		1903	NE, 28th, 1904
Denny, J.M.		K, 35th Ohio Inf. (died at Gardner, Kans.; buried at Gardner Cemetery)	447		1894 Sep 30	KS, 14th, 1895
Denny, J.S.		C, 14th Wis.	22		1888	KS, 8th, 1889
DeNorth, M.	Pvt.	C, 21st Iowa Inf.	78		1921 May 19	IA, 48th, 1922
Denpter, W.		I, 62nd Ohio	4		1923 Nov 26	KS, 43rd, 1924
Densmore, Wm. H.		K, 134th Ohio	16		1936 Sep 16	KS, 56th, 1937
Dent, Thomas W.	Pvt.	I, 35th Wis. Inf.	42		1932 Jan 26	IA, 59th, 1933
Dentler, Wallace W.		H, 53rd Penn. Inf.	64		1887	KS, 7th, 1888
Denton, J.C.		F, 142nd Penn.	8		1888	KS, 8th, 1889
Denton, J.H.		C, 19th Ind.	147		1927 Sep 19	KS, 47th, 1928
Denton, J.R.		E, 3rd Mo.	4		1927 Jan 1	KS, 47th, 1928
Denton, James		D, 21st Mo.	153		1898 Oct 27	KS, 18th, 1899
DeObert, Frederick		M, 9th N.J. Inf. K, 100th Ind.	1		1916 Dec 30	KS, 36th, 1917
Deppen, Isaac N.		F, 48th Ind.	122		1914 Feb 16	KS, 34th, 1915
DePue, D.J.		143rd Penn. Inf. (died of heart failure)	25	77	1921 Feb 28	NE, 46th, 1922
Depue, Lewis		I, 15th Ill.	158		1913 Dec	KS, 33rd, 1914
DePue, Stephen	Pvt.	A, 24th Iowa Inf.	22		1913 May 14	IA, 40th, 1914
DePui, Thomas E.		29th Penn.	1		1913 Apr 21	KS, 33rd, 1914
Deputy, Solomon	Sergt.		86		1913 Aug 15	IA, 40th, 1914
Depuy, I.		K, 67th Ill. Inf. (died of dropsy)	106	68	1906 Jun 17	NE, 31st, 1907
DeQuazie, J.O.		C, 139th Ind. (died of paralysis)	39	68	1914 Jul 7	NE, 39th, 1915
Derby, Chas. W.	Pvt.	D, 11th Iowa	250		1914 Feb 6	IA, 41st, 1915
Derby, John		E, 12th Ill. Cav.	36		1914 Jun 5	KS, 34th, 1915
Derby, M.R., see Durby, M.R.						
Derby, W.H.		G, 10th Mich.	12		1904 Feb 15	KS, 24th, 1905
Derdrick, Herbert		C, 100th Ill.	134		1911 Jan 7	KS, 31st, 1912
Derickson, K.E.	Pvt.	G, 52nd Ind. Inf.	10		1912 May 22	IA, 39th, 1913
Deringer, James L.		I, 10th Ind. Inf. (died of pneumonia)	12		1893 Dec 7	NE, 18th, 1894
Derkin, Fritz		B, 7th Mo. Cav.	301		1914 Jun 11	KS, 34th, 1915
Dermad, C.J.		G, — (died of paralysis)	59	76	1910 Jul	NE, 35th, 1911
Dermar, Henry		M, 6th N.Y. Cav.	354	67	1906 Mar 12	NE, 31st, 1907
Dermer, Joseph			32		1922 Jun 10	NE, 47th, 1923
Dernux, Geo. F.		K, 35th Iowa	380		1906 Nov 12	KS, 26th, 1907
DeRoss, David E.		L, 2nd Mo. Lt. Art. E, 5th Mo. Cav.	244		1916 Mar 26	KS, 36th, 1917
Derr, Horace		C, 143rd Ill. Inf.	158		1925 Nov 24	KS, 45th, 1926
Derrickson, Dwight	Drummer	B, 23rd Iowa Inf.	51		1915 Mar 7	IA, 42nd, 1916
Derrington, T.H.		D, 8th Cal.	127		1917 May 28	KS, 37th, 1918
Derry, Samuel			241		1909 Feb 15	KS, 29th, 1910
Dersch, C.L.		B, 4th Mo. Inf.	96		1886	KS, 6th, 1887
Desbrow, T.A.		194th Ohio Inf.	14		1924 Sep	KS, 45th, 1926
Deseler, Tom B.		I, 7th Ohio	301		1924 Jun 22	KS, 44th, 1925
DeSilva, J.W.	Corp.	F, 102nd N.Y.	197		1899 Mar 21	IA, 26th, 1900
Desmond, Dan			109		1890	NE, 15th, 1891
Desmond, Jas.	Farrier	E, 3rd Iowa Cav.	70	74	1892 May 8	IA, 19th, 1893
Dessinger, H.D.		203rd Penn.	236		1934 Apr 8	IA, 61st, 1935
Destoval, Charles	Pvt.	9th Iowa Cav.	63		1917 Dec 13	IA, 44th, 1918
Detar, Josiah		E, 6th Iowa	90		1937 Aug 22	KS, 57th, 1938
DeTar, Josiah		E, 6th Iowa Inf.	90		1935	KS, 55th, 1936
DeTar, Josiah N.		E, 6th Iowa	90		1936 Jul 27	KS, 56th, 1937
Detrick, J.J.			80		1912	IA, 39th, 1913
Detro, James			154		1884	KS, 4th, 1885
Detwiler, A.N.	Pvt.	H, 2nd Iowa Cav.	34		1921 May 29	IA, 48th, 1922
Detwiler, H.R.	Pvt.	H, 14th Iowa Cav.	234	47	1889 Oct 27	IA, 16th, 1890
Detwiler, H.R.	Pvt.	F, 14th Iowa Inf.	234		1889 Oct 27	IA, 17th, 1891

Name	Rank	Company, Regiment or Ship	Post*	Age	Death Date†	Journal
Detwiler, Z.R.		G, 13th Iowa	38		1928 Dec 12	KS, 48th, 1929
Deune, Geo.		G, 1st N.M. Cav.	421		1887 Dec 30	KS, 7th, 1888
Deupree, Moses T.	Pvt.	B, 29th Iowa Inf.	15		1926 Oct 7	IA, 53rd, 1927
DeVault, Hiram		D, 194th Ohio Inf.	100	90	1938 Jan 15	IA, 64th, 1938
Deve, Ewin		A, 20th Ohio	322		1906 Apr 26	KS, 26th, 1907
DeVean, Andrew		K, 2nd Kans.	6		1915 Sep 29	KS, 35th, 1916
Develbis, Isaac T.		H, 1st Md. Inf. (died at Ellinwood, Kans.; buried at Ellinwood Cemetery)	48		1894 Aug 14	KS, 14th, 1895
Devendorf, Henry X.		K, 142nd N.Y. Inf.	1		1912 Jul 2	KS, 32nd, 1913
Dever, Jesse		13th Ind. Bat.	88		1918 Jul 1	KS, 38th, 1919
Dever, Richard W.		G, 15th Ohio Inf.		94 & 10 mos.	1938 Sep 18	IA, 64th, 1938
Dever, Samuel		K, 20th Ohio Inf. (died at Argentine, Kans.; buried at Junction Cemetery)	463		1894 Jul 3	KS, 14th, 1895
Devereaux, Pat		A, 6th Kans.	497		1914 Apr 22	KS, 34th, 1915
Devine, James	Pvt.	A, 115th Ill. Inf.	57		1920 May 25	IA, 47th, 1921
Devine, Jno.	1st Lieut.	F, 32nd Iowa Inf.	94	61	1887 Oct 31	IA, 14th, 1888
Devinney, Jno.	Pvt.	C, 195th Penn. Inf.	91		1925 Oct 9	IA, 52nd, 1926
Devitt, Clark		H, 75th Ind.	211		1889	KS, 9th, 1890
Devlin, Peter	Pvt.	F, 73rd Penn. Cav.	176	66	1889 Dec 22	IA, 16th, 1890
Devore, Adam		I, 3rd Ohio (not a member of the G.A.R.)	18		1912 Feb 17	KS, 32nd, 1913
Devore, D.	Pvt.	C, 15th Iowa Inf.	7		1921	IA, 48th, 1922
Devore, J.L.		G, 179th Ohio Inf. (died at Butler, Kans.; buried at Florence)	202		1894 Aug 3	KS, 14th, 1895
Devore, Philip		D, 115th Ind.	293		1925 Mar 6	KS, 45th, 1926
DeVore, Phillip			64		1930 Sep	KS, 50th, 1931
DeVoss, Peter	Pvt.	G, 43rd Wis. Inf.	217		1891 Dec 14	IA, 18th, 1892
Dew, C.E.		B, 145th Ill.	28		1888	KS, 8th, 1889
Dew, J.S.		D, 85th Ill. Inf. (died of old age)	47		1916 Mar 14	NE, 41st, 1917
Dewees, Geo. W.			14		1905 Sep 14	KS, 25th, 1906
Deweese, J.B.	Pvt.	D, 33rd Iowa Inf.	40		1928 Nov 22	IA, 55th, 1929
Deweese, Josiah F.		I, 12th Kans.	104		1893 Nov 2	KS, 13th, 1894
Deweese, S.P.		D, 17th Kans.	491		1912 May 4	KS, 32nd, 1913
Deweese, Thos. R.	Pvt.	D, 1st Ill. Lt. Art.	59		1925 Feb 22	IA, 52nd, 1926
Dewein, Geo. I.			5		1925 May 6	IA, 52nd, 1926
Dewess, Samuel		K, 59th Ind.	38		1925 Oct 26	KS, 45th, 1926
Dewey, A.R.	Pvt.	D, 103rd Ohio	108		1905	IA, 32nd, 1906
Dewey, Edward A.		G, 31st Iowa Inf.	68		1938 Aug 18	NE, 63rd, 1939
Dewey, G.A.		D, 11th Kans.	293		1927	KS, 47th, 1928
Dewey, George M.		E, 67th N.Y.	129		1912 Oct 26	KS, 32nd, 1913
Dewey, I.B.			35		1910	NE, 35th, 1911
Dewey, J.C.		F, 55th Ill. Inf.	25	88	1920 Mar 9	NE, 45th, 1921
Dewey, Jacob D.	Pvt.	D, 151st N.Y.	440		1903 Jun 26	IA, 30th, 1904
Dewey, L.E.		F, 2nd Ohio U.S.	25	75	1918 Feb 11	NE, 43rd, 1919
Dewey, R.M.		B, 12th Ill. Inf.	68		1917 Nov 12	IA, 44th, 1918
Dewey, W.B.	Pvt.	B, 41st Ohio Inf.	337		1905 Dec 20	IA, 32nd, 1906
Dewey, W.H.		H, 66th Ill.	96		1920	KS, 40th, 1921
Dewitt, F.		B, 153rd — Inf.	250		1912 May 23	KS, 32nd, 1913
DeWitt, James P.		K, 2nd Iowa Inf.	13		1932 May 31	NE, 57th, 1933
DeWitt, R.M.	Pvt.	C, 9th N.Y. Art.	7	45	1895 Jan 7	IA, 21st, 1895
DeWitt, W.	Pvt.	B, 91st Ohio Inf.	339		1908 Jan 13	IA, 35th, 1909
DeWitt, Wm.		D, 47th Ohio	68		1918 Apr 11	KS, 38th, 1919
DeWolf, H.C.	2nd Lieut.	F, 6th Ohio Cav.	27	52	1897 Aug 25	IA, 24th, 1898
DeWolf, John	Pvt.	G, 22nd Iowa Inf.	8	54	1891 Dec 15	IA, 18th, 1892
DeWolf, Ransom		B, 17th Ill. Cav. (died of paralysis)	11	54	1900 Nov 23	NE, 25th, 1901
DeWoody, Geo. W.		H, 4th Penn.	18		1926 Sep	KS, 46th, 1927
Dewr, Thos.		8th Ill.	132		1922 Jun 11	KS, 42nd, 1923
Dews, Chas. T.		G, 35th Ohio	12		1930 Feb 1	KS, 50th, 1931
Dexter, Knight	Sergt.	C, 10th Iowa Inf.	343		1918 Jun	IA, 45th, 1919
Dexter, Rodney	Pvt.	B, 100th N.Y. Inf.	222		1918 Dec	IA, 45th, 1919
Dexter, Simon	Lieut.	D, 34th Ill.	42		1907 Aug 27	IA, 34th, 1908
Dey, J.B.	Pvt.	C, 2nd Iowa Inf.	108		1931 Jul 30	IA, 58th, 1932

*See Appendix A, B or C for roster of post names and locations.
†See Introduction for note regarding recording of death date.

143

Name	Rank	Company, Regiment or Ship	Post*	Age	Death Date†	Journal
DeYoung, A.		L, 2nd Ill., F.A.[Lt. Art.]	132		1923 Apr 24	KS, 43rd, 1924
Dial, Martin L.	Pvt.	E, 31st Iowa Inf.	298	55	1897 Oct 20	IA, 24th, 1898
Diamond, A.J., see Dimond, A.J.						
Dibble, Richard		H, 1st Wis.	35		1908 Oct 23	NE, 33rd, 1909
Dibert, M.H.		H, 12th Penn. Cav.	132		1916 Nov 22	KS, 36th, 1917
Dice, H.W.		C, 132nd Ill. Inf.	17		1914 Mar 17	KS, 34th, 1915
Dice, Isaac	Pvt.	101st Penn. Inf.	204		1916 Mar 28	IA, 43rd, 1917
Dich, F.M.		B, 124th Ind.	255		1910 Oct 6	KS, 30th, 1911
Dick, A.C.		I, 21st Wis.	36		1910 Mar 30	KS, 30th, 1911
Dick, Henry	Pvt.	B, 16th Penn. Inf.	324	90	1935 Aug 27	IA, 65th, 1939
Dick, L.F.		H, 57th Ind.	81		1939 Apr 4	KS, 59th, 1940
Dick, S.M.		D, 12th Ky.	57		1925 Dec 16	KS, 45th, 1926
Dickenson, A.		3rd Wis. Cav.	129		1929 Mar 29	KS, 49th, 1930
Dickenson, B.	Pvt.	E, 23rd Wis. Inf.	24	85	1931 Sep 29	IA, 58th, 1932
Dickenson, C.R.	Pvt.	D, 5th Iowa Cav.	88		1912 Mar 13	IA, 39th, 1913
Dickenson, E.H.	Pvt.	E, 5th Iowa Cav.	78		1926 Jan 22	IA, 53rd, 1927
Dickerson, A.N.	Pvt.	E, 23rd Wis. Inf.	452	86	1931 Sep 14	IA, 58th, 1932
Dickerson, D.H.		C, 103rd Penn.	71		1898 Oct 17	KS, 18th, 1899
Dickerson, D.R.		B, 1st Mo. Eng.	256		1922 Dec 23	KS, 42nd, 1923
Dickerson, Wm.	Pvt.	E, 31st Iowa Inf.	4		1897-1898	IA, 24th, 1898
Dickey, C.H.	Pvt.	D, 9th Iowa Inf.	31		1925 Jan 1	IA, 52nd, 1926
Dickey, E.S.	Capt.		29		1911 Oct 18	IA, 38th, 1912
Dickey, J.H.		A, 1st Mo. Inf.	51		1901 Aug 2	KS, 21st, 1902
Dickey, J.S.		6th Iowa Cav.	129		1929 Jun 16	KS, 49th, 1930
Dickey, M.B.		I, 147th Ind. Inf.	244		1900	KS, 20th, 1901
Dickey, R.C.	Pvt.	K, 26th Iowa Inf.	164		1926 Jan 2	IA, 53rd, 1927
Dickey, W.A.	Pvt.	B, — Iowa Inf.	7	87	1932 Feb 7	IA, 59th, 1933
Dickey, W.C.		12th Kans.	4		1917 Apr 10	KS, 37th, 1918
Dickey, W.G.		A, 121st Penn. Inf.	215		1886	KS, 6th, 1887
Dickey, W.W.		C, 20th Ohio	104		1910 Jul 30	KS, 30th, 1911
Dickins, R.	Pvt.	E, 60th U.S.C. Inf.	7		1920 Aug 4	IA, 47th, 1921
Dickinson, Chester L.	Pvt.	I, 6th Mich. Hvy. Art.	440	92	1940 Jan 1	IA, 66th, 1940
Dickinson, G.H.	Pvt.	F, 31st Iowa Inf.	110		1904 Mar 1	IA, 31st, 1905
Dickinson, G.W.		C, 72nd Ill.	72		1919 Dec 14	KS, 39th, 1920
Dickinson, J.			267		1921 Jul 26	IA, 48th, 1922
Dickinson, John W.		B, 43rd Wis. Inf. (died of epilepsy)	38	67	1911 Sep 11	NE, 36th, 1912
Dickinson, L.D.	Pvt.	A, 2nd Iowa Cav.	165		1924 Nov 25	IA, 51st, 1925
Dickinson, N.P.		F, 1st Cav.	134		1925	NE, 50th, 1926
Dickinson, S.S.		K, 2nd Mich.	8		1928 Dec 6	KS, 48th, 1929
Dickinson, Thomas		G, 78th Ill.	57		1913 Sep 21	KS, 33rd, 1914
Dickman, Chas. W.		D, 18th Ind.	74		1889	KS, 9th, 1890
Dickman, Wm. H.			200		1926 Feb 1	IA, 53rd, 1927
Dickson, A.B.		L, 8th Ill. Cav.	123		1914 Jan 27	NE, 39th, 1915
Dickson, A.J.	Pvt.	D, 134th Penn. Inf.	16		1902 Feb 5	IA, 29th, 1903
Dickson, Dennis		A, 141st Ill. Inf.	330		1887 Oct 4	KS, 7th, 1888
Dickson, E.			7		1919	IA, 46th, 1920
Dickson, John		C, 1st Conn.	46		1898 Apr 29	KS, 18th, 1899
Dickson, Wm.	Sergt.	G, 31st Wis. Inf.	91	71	1895 Jun 12	IA, 22nd, 1896
Dicus, W.C.		F, 2nd Iowa	142		1929 Jun 8	KS, 49th, 1930
Diddy, Jno. W.	Pvt.	C, 39th Iowa Inf.	26		1929 Jan 29	IA, 56th, 1930
Diefenderfer, Isaac	Pvt.	I, 135th Ohio	78		1901 Sep 13	IA, 28th, 1902
Diehl, Alfred J.	Sergt.	B, 86th Ill. Inf.	18		1916 Jan 26	KS, 36th, 1917
Diehl, Amos	Pvt.	D, 165th Penn. Inf.	235		1912 Oct 18	IA, 39th, 1913
Diehl, Andrew	Corp.	D, 92nd Ill. Inf.	155		1928 Jul 13	IA, 55th, 1929
Diehl, Christian		H, 10th Ill.	25		1929 Oct 25	NE, 54th, 1930
Diehl, E.P., see Deihl, E.P.						
Diehl, Hamilton	Pvt.	C, 165th Penn. Inf.	235		1917 Feb 8	IA, 44th, 1918
Diehl, Henry		D, 4th Mo. Cav.	127		1917 Aug 21	KS, 37th, 1918
Diehl, John	Pvt.	F, 6th Iowa Inf.	173		1909	IA, 36th, 1910
Diehl, S.D.		A, 30th Ill.	186		1885	KS, 5th, 1886

Name	Rank	Company, Regiment or Ship	Post*	Age	Death Date†	Journal
Diehl, Simon		F, 83rd Ill. Inf. (died at Girard, Kans.; buried at Girard Cemetery)	49		1894 Dec 15	KS, 14th, 1895
Diel, Emanuell	Seaman	Navy, Penn.	43		1904 Jan 27	KS, 24th, 1905
Diener, John F.		F, 7th Penn. Cav. (see also Appendix D)	25	72	1918 Jan 23	NE, 43rd, 1919
Dierdorff, E.H.		F, 50th Ill. Inf.	18		1929 Mar 1	KS, 49th, 1930
Dietrick, D.		G, 158th Penn.	132		1923 Jun 17	KS, 43rd, 1924
Diffenbaugh, David		Ohio	437		1917 Oct 2	KS, 37th, 1918
Diffendaffer, Wm.		G, 20th Iowa (died of old age)	25	83	1916 Dec 1	NE, 41st, 1917
Digby, John		E, 26th Iowa Inf., England (died of old age)	354	80	1919 Apr 22	NE, 44th, 1920
Diggins, Fred		A, 95th Ill.	385		1914 Mar 10	KS, 33rd, 1914
Diggins, G.H.	Pvt.	2nd Ill. Art.	124		1916	IA, 43rd, 1917
Diggs, Hiram C.		B, 3rd Iowa (died of old age)	35	80	1915 May 13	NE, 40th, 1916
Dighton, Richard		D, 50th Ill.	52		1916 Feb 6	KS, 36th, 1917
Dignon, Michael		K, 6th Minn.	1		1902 Feb 6	KS, 22nd, 1903
Dikeman, Wm.		G, 12th Kans. Inf.	146		1892 Feb 11	NE, 17th, 1893
Dilgert, Adam		B, 25th Mo. Inf. (died at Atchison, Kans.; buried at Mt. Vernon Cemetery)	93		1894 Apr 1	KS, 14th, 1895
Dill, Benj. F.		F, 8th Ind.	25		1929 Jan 9	NE, 54th, 1930
Dill, J.W.		E, 8th Iowa	129		1933 Feb 24	KS, 53rd, 1934
Dill, Mark		I, 25th Iowa	75		1905 Nov 28	KS, 25th, 1906
Dill, Wm. A.		F, 44th Ind. (not a member; buried by Farragut Post)	25		1922 Aug 24	NE, 47th, 1923
Dill, Wm. A.		F, 44th Ind.	25		1922 Aug 24	NE, 47th, 1923
Dillenbeck, C.B.			66		1925 Jul 8	KS, 45th, 1926
Diller, H.	Pvt.	C, 158th Penn.	452		1921 Sep 18	IA, 48th, 1922
Diller, J.K.		C, 101st Penn.	77		1929 Dec 12	NE, 54th, 1930
Diller, S.W.			245		1890	NE, 15th, 1891
Diller, W.H.		Penn. (died of consumption)	245	61	1906 Sep 6	NE, 31st, 1907
Dilley, D.M.	Pvt.	D, 33rd Iowa Inf.	40		1920 Jul 30	IA, 47th, 1921
Dilley, Gustus		B, 19th Ohio	55		1906 Jan 18	KS, 26th, 1907
Dilley, J.W.	Pvt.	L, 8th Iowa Cav.	240		1930 Jan 26	IA, 57th, 1931
Dilley, James M.		83rd Penn.	354		1914 Sep 22	KS, 34th, 1915
Dillhorn, N.B.		H, 11th Ill. Inf.	157		1902 Dec 12	KS, 22nd, 1903
Dillinbeck, Jerome		I, 14th N.Y.	66		1921 Jun 18	KS, 41st, 1922
Dilling, Henry A.		K, 186th Ohio	374		1916 Jul 21	KS, 36th, 1917
Dillinger, G.W.	Pvt.	A, 70th Ohio Inf.	322		1910 Dec 2	IA, 37th, 1911
Dillinger, Geo.	Pvt.	F, 158th Penn. Inf.	29	60	1895 Jun 11	IA, 22nd, 1896
Dillinger, T.L.		D, 13th Ind.	293		1924	KS, 44th, 1925
Dillingham, J.	Pvt.	B, 100th Ill. Inf.	7		1910 Sep 24	IA, 37th, 1911
Dillion, Thomas		A, 2nd Ky.	71		1906 Nov 10	KS, 26th, 1907
Dillman, Samuel A.		K, 10th Iowa	34		1919 Apr 21	KS, 39th, 1920
Dillon, A.C.		E, 196th Ohio	69		1925 Jan 2	KS, 44th, 1925
Dillon, A.C.		E, 196th Ohio	69		1923 Jun 2	KS, 46th, 1927
Dillond, J.	Pvt.	E, 12th Mo. Cav.	7		1914 Dec 13	IA, 41st, 1915
Dillow, Bradford D.		A, 149th Ind.	90		1923 Mar 18	KS, 43rd, 1924
Dills, W.P.	Pvt.	A, 78th Ind.	203		1921 Apr 15	IA, 48th, 1922
Dills, Watson P.	Pvt.	A, 78th Ind. Inf.	203		1920 Apr 15	IA, 46th, 1920
Dillsworth, Benj. F.		I, 29th Ind.	59		1890	KS, 10th, 1891
Dillts, James		D, 103rd Ill.	85		1923 Jan 1	KS, 43rd, 1924
Dilly, Isaac		H, 130th Ind.	130		1911 May	KS, 31st, 1912
Dilts, D.L.	Pvt.	F, 5th Penn. Res. Vol. Corps	50		1908 Apr 16	IA, 35th, 1909
Dilts, James S.		I, 135th Penn.	125		1913 Feb 6	KS, 33rd, 1914
Diltz, D.L., see Dilts, D.L.						
Diltz, H.A.		A, 71st Ill.	142		1910 Sep	KS, 30th, 1911
Dilworth, C.H.	Pvt.	E, 124th Penn. Inf.	7		1904 Mar 8	IA, 31st, 1905
Dilworth, C.J.		Cal., 85th Ill. (died of old age at his residence in Omaha; buried in Wyuka Cemetery in Lincoln)	25	72	1900 Feb 3	NE, 25th, 1901
Dilworth, Emmon		B, 84th Ill. Inf. (died at Beloit, Kans.; buried at Vermont, Ill.)	147		1894 Apr 5	KS, 14th, 1895
Dilworth, W.S.		G, 8th Ill. Inf. (died of heart failure)	169	73	1915 Jan 6	NE, 39th, 1915
Dimick, Wm. H.		D, 19th Ind. Inf. (died of pneumonia)	38	68	1910 Jan 16	NE, 35th, 1911

Name	Rank	Company, Regiment or Ship	Post*	Age	Death Date†	Journal
Dimmett, S.T.		F, 72nd Ind.	265		1917 Sep 4	KS, 37th, 1918
Dimmick, Hiram H.	Sergt.	22nd Wis. Inf.	35		1909 Dec 8	IA, 36th, 1910
Dimmitt, Geo. M.	Pvt.	D, 44th Iowa Inf.	12		1911 Apr 23	IA, 38th, 1912
Dimond, A.J.	Pvt.	C, 45th Iowa Inf.	2		1923 Jun 16	IA, 50th, 1924
Dimond, W.W.		G, 83rd Penn.	232		1911 Mar 8	KS, 31st, 1912
Dine, J.C.	Pvt.	A, 123rd Ind.	98		1924 Dec	IA, 51st, 1925
Dinelbiss, G.R.	Pvt.	C, 47th Ill. Inf.	333		1920 Aug 29	IA, 47th, 1921
Dinges, A.K.		G, 93rd Ill. Inf. (died of paralysis)	129	64	1903 May 1	NE, 28th, 1904
Dingman, J.L.		B, 9th Minn. Inf. (died of exhaustion)	18	68	1903 May 2	NE, 28th, 1904
Dingman, M.V.		C, 20th Mass. Inf.	127		1900 Jan 5	KS, 20th, 1901
Dingmon, C.R.	Pvt.	H, 76th N.Y. Inf.	117	43	1888 Mar 28	IA, 15th, 1889
Dinsmore, H.H.		G, 123rd Penn.	132		1913 Oct 5	KS, 33rd, 1914
Dinsmore, J.S.		E, 12th N.H. Inf. (died of Bright's disease)	47	73	1902 Dec	NE, 27th, 1903
Dinsmore, Theodore		K, 1st N.H. Hvy. Art.	64		1900 May 19	KS, 20th, 1901
Dinsmore, Wm. L.	Pvt.	I, 9th Ill. Inf. I, 7th Iowa Inf.	135	55	1893 Oct 16	IA, 20th, 1894
Dinwiddie, W.A.	Sergt.	28th Iowa Inf.	222		1901 Nov 2	IA, 28th, 1902
Dipman, E.L.		E, 57th Ohio	8		1935	KS, 55th, 1936
Dipman, Ernest		E, 57th Ohio	8		1935 Aug	KS, 56th, 1937
Dipman, Ernest		E, 57th Ohio	8		1937 Aug	KS, 57th, 1938
Disart, Lee		38th Iowa	48		1923 Jan 1	IA, 50th, 1924
Disbrow, W.D.		B, 2nd M.	1		1900 Jun 21	KS, 20th, 1901
Discus, John	Pvt.	Ill. Inf.	9		1917 Feb 25	IA, 43rd, 1917
Disney, A.A.		I, 2nd Kans. State Militia	71		1902 Apr 29	KS, 22nd, 1903
Distil, Peter	Pvt.	K, 16th Iowa Inf.	2		1908 Feb 8	IA, 35th, 1909
Ditch, John			25		1913 Mar 29	KS, 33rd, 1914
Ditman, John F.		F, 35th Ind.	74		1890	KS, 10th, 1891
Ditmons, Samuel F.		D, 9th Kans. Cav.	461		1901 Jul 24	KS, 21st, 1902
Ditson, W.A.		H, 133rd Ill.	7		1920 Aug 26	KS, 40th, 1921
Ditson, W.S.		H, 133rd Ill.	117		1920 Aug 30	KS, 43rd, 1924
Dittemore, T.E.		D, 49th Ind.	50		1911	KS, 31st, 1912
Dittman, Frank	Sergt.	G, 1st Iowa Inf.	1		1904 Mar 5	IA, 31st, 1905
Ditus, Fred		F, 156th Ill. Inf.	227		1887 Nov 15	KS, 7th, 1888
Diver, Merrick R.		A, 69th Ill.	25		1929 Feb 19	KS, 49th, 1930
Divine, John		I, 23rd Mo. Inf.	275		1892 Dec 10	KS, 12th, 1893
Dix, Alpheus W.	Pvt.	H, 20th Iowa Inf.	509	68	1897 Jan 12	IA, 23rd, 1897
Dix, James H.	Pvt.	C, 51st Mo. Inf.	231		1912 Aug 18	IA, 39th, 1913
Dixen, John V.		104th Ill.	295		1917 Jan	KS, 37th, 1918
Dixen, Luther	Pvt.	A, 33rd Ill. Inf.	12		1900 Apr 7	IA, 27th, 1901
Dixon, Austin E.		18th Mo. Inf. (not a member of the department but living in Nebraska; location: Alma)			1937 Oct 26	NE, 62nd, 1938
Dixon, E.M.		I, 3rd Ill.	40		1924 Mar 3	KS, 44th, 1925
Dixon, George		F, 77th Ill. Inf.	28		1914 Aug 31	KS, 34th, 1915
Dixon, J.A.		D, 1st Minn.	240		1909 Mar 29	KS, 29th, 1910
Dixon, J.B.	Pvt.	A, 32nd Iowa Inf.	465	79	1897 Dec 9	IA, 24th, 1898
Dixon, J.H.		C, 15th Iowa	27		1915 Nov 24	KS, 35th, 1916
Dixon, James				96	1937 Aug 26	IA, 64th, 1938
Dixon, John	Pvt.	A, 32nd Iowa Inf.	67		1928 Sep 22	IA, 55th, 1929
Dixon, John		B, 104th Ill.	295		1917 Jan 8	KS, 36th, 1917
Dixon, Joseph		G, 73rd Ohio	38		1916	KS, 36th, 1917
Dixon, Joseph H.		D, 18th Iowa Inf.	100	69	1910	NE, 35th, 1911
Dixon, M.A.			45		1908 Aug 13	NE, 33rd, 1909
Dixon, S.H.		H, 4th Ky. Cav.	71		1925 Oct 20	KS, 45th, 1926
Dixon, S.M.		A, 49th Ohio	4		1916 Jun 23	KS, 36th, 1917
Dixon, S.Y.E.		H, 72nd Ind.	88		1888	KS, 8th, 1889
Dixon, Seth	Pvt.	F, 20th Ohio Vol. Inf.	84		1924 Aug	IA, 51st, 1925
Dixon, Thomas			386		1912 Dec 3	KS, 32nd, 1913
Dixon, Wm. E.		G, 17th Iowa Inf.	318	69	1916 Aug 16	NE, 41st, 1917
Dixson, Frank W.		B, 173rd Penn.	260		1905 Feb 23	KS, 25th, 1906
Doak, Nathan		C, 6th West Va.	113		1920 Feb 25	KS, 40th, 1921
Doak, Robert	Corp.	I, 66th Ohio Inf.	40		1927 Aug 10	IA, 54th, 1928

Name	Rank	Company, Regiment or Ship	Post*	Age	Death Date†	Journal
Doak, Wm.	Pvt.	I, 10th Iowa Inf.	16		1912 Feb 15	IA, 39th, 1913
Doan, M.S.	Sergt.	K, 39th Iowa	39		1905 Jun 7	IA, 32nd, 1906
Doan, Thomas J.	Pvt.	D, 70th Ind. Inf.	7	56	1895 Mar 2	IA, 21st, 1895
Doan, W.H.	Pvt.	C, 17th Ind. Inf.	55		1921 Apr 28	IA, 48th, 1922
Doan, William			[22]		1929	KS, 49th, 1930
Doane, C.N.	Pvt.	E, 36th Ill. Inf.	432		1916 Mar 28	IA, 43rd, 1917
Doane, C.W.	Pvt.	34th Iowa Inf.	116		1917 Nov 21	IA, 44th, 1918
Doane, Eleazor B.		K, 19th Iowa Inf.	320		1886	KS, 6th, 1887
Doane, Philip L.		E, 13th M.O. Inf.	71		1891 Apr 27	KS, 11th, 1892
Dobbin, Alexander		A, 123rd N.Y. Inf.	266	94	1938 Feb 28	IA, 64th, 1938
Dobbins, James O.	Pvt.	B, 19th Ohio Inf.	11		1917 Jun 4	IA, 44th, 1918
Dobbs, L.D.		K, 11th Penn. Res. Corps	12		1918 May 20	KS, 38th, 1919
Dobie, G.W.	Pvt.	D, 13th Iowa Inf.	167	64	1889 Aug 27	IA, 16th, 1890
DoBow, A.M.		C, 29th N.J.	71		1927 Feb 6	KS, 47th, 1928
Dobson, Adam		H, 10th Ill.	18		1911 Jun 30	KS, 31st, 1912
Dobson, John S.		3 years' service; no record	4		1922 Mar	KS, 42nd, 1923
Dobson, Robert		G, 91st Ill.	4		1915 Jun 7	KS, 35th, 1916
Dobson, S.J.		C, 46th Wis. Inf. (died of heart disease)	25	62	1902 Sep	NE, 27th, 1903
Dobson, T.C.		H, 12th Mo.	380		1897 Aug 15	KS, 17th, 1898
Dobson, Thomas		A, 61st Ill.	377		1893 Jan 18	KS, 13th, 1894
Dobson, Warrington			94		4th quarter 1884	IA, 11th, 1885
Dobyns, J.B.		E, 6th Kans.	23		1919 Nov 2	KS, 39th, 1920
Docker, S.E.	Pvt.	K, 134th Ill. Inf.	53	40	1890 Feb 1	IA, 16th, 1890
Dockery, Austin	Pvt.	C, 145th Ind. Inf.	235		1924 Feb 7	IA, 51st, 1925
Dodd, Brint		G, 51st Ark.	10		1912 Jan 5	KS, 32nd, 1913
Dodd, H.H.		C, 90th Ohio Cav.	4		1908 Jul 20	KS, 28th, 1909
Dodd, I.N.		K, 8th Mo.	158		1890	KS, 10th, 1891
Dodd, Jeremiah M.		F, 52nd Ill.	147		1929 Feb 15	NE, 54th, 1930
Dodd, John	Pvt.	G, —	74		1925 Jul 3	IA, 52nd, 1926
Dodd, John		I, 9th Kans.	322		1906 Sep 1	KS, 26th, 1907
Dodd, John W.		C, 7th Ind. Inf. (died of influenza)	77	77	1919 Sep 28	NE, 44th, 1920
Dodd, R.P.		C, 31st Ill.	25		1914 Jan 1	KS, 34th, 1915
Dodd, Samuel		1st Kans. Bat.	18		1921 Aug 12	KS, 41st, 1922
Dodd, Theo. F.C.		B, 73rd Ind.	243		1905 Mar 9	KS, 25th, 1906
Dodd, W.	Corp.	A, 3rd Iowa Cav.	100		1921 Apr 19	IA, 48th, 1922
Dodder, Silas		E, 21st Kans.	12		1925 Feb 3	KS, 46th, 1927
Dodds, John C.		H, 26th Mo. Inf.	229		1891 Aug	KS, 11th, 1892
Dodds, Joseph C.		G, 172nd Ohio Inf.	12		1917 Dec 14	KS, 37th, 1918
Dodds, W.D.		D, Penn. R.V. Cav.	9	82	1921 Nov 4	NE, 46th, 1922
Dodds, W.R.	Pvt.	B, 2nd Iowa Inf.	382		1904 Apr 6	IA, 31st, 1905
Doden, Geo. A.	Pvt.	F, 15th Ill. Inf.	74		1925 Feb 2	IA, 52nd, 1926
Dodge, Charles			25		1928	IA, 55th, 1929
Dodge, Daniel C.		G, 64th Ill. Inf.	67	90	1938 Mar 27	IA, 64th, 1938
Dodge, Erie	Pvt.	48th Iowa Inf.	66		1915 Jun 27	IA, 42nd, 1916
Dodge, Gardener		L, 9th Iowa Cav.	16	91	1935 Jun 21	IA, 62nd, 1936
Dodge, Grenville M.	Gen.		29		1916 Jan 13	IA, 43rd, 1917
Dodge, H.D.		A, 16th Kans.	40		1914 Mar 11	KS, 34th, 1915
Dodge, Henry	Pvt.	H, 4th Iowa Cav.	132	57	1895 Jul 5	IA, 22nd, 1896
Dodge, J.G.		H, 11th Kans. Cav.	147		1900 Mar 3	KS, 20th, 1901
Dodge, John	Pvt.	H, 4th Iowa Cav.	348		1902 Jun 8	IA, 29th, 1903
Dodge, Levi	Pvt.	B, 38th Iowa Inf.	172	75	1893 Feb 7	IA, 19th, 1893
Dodge, W.W.	Pvt.		244		1916	IA, 43rd, 1917
Dodge, Wm. H.	Lieut.	F, 37th Wis. Inf.	12		1912 Oct 24	IA, 39th, 1913
Dodson, C.C.		F, 74th Ohio Inf.	11	79	1918 May 7	NE, 43rd, 1919
Dodson, J.M.	Pvt.	C, 5th Iowa Inf.	115		1923 Nov 8	IA, 50th, 1924
Dodson, T.M.		H, 7th Ind. Inf.	244		1918 May 12	KS, 38th, 1919
Dodson, Wm.		L, 10th Mo. Cav.	293		1922 Sep 10	KS, 42nd, 1923
Dodt, C.	Pvt.	B, 22nd Iowa Inf.	8	62	1896 Jan 8	IA, 23rd, 1897
Doege, Joseph		B, 13th Mo.	12		1910 Dec 26	KS, 30th, 1911
Doessu, W.W.		C, 8th Kans.	65		1908 Nov 21	KS, 28th, 1909
Dofflemeyer, F.M.			25		1913 Feb 14	KS, 33rd, 1914
Doggett, W.A.		A, 19th Ill.	25	82	1921 Dec 5	NE, 46th, 1922

*See Appendix A, B or C for roster of post names and locations.
†See Introduction for note regarding recording of death date.

Name	Rank	Company, Regiment or Ship	Post*	Age	Death Date†	Journal
Doghtmeyer, Edwin		B, 12th Ill. Cav.	28		1924 Sep 30	KS, 44th, 1925
Doherty, James	Pvt.	K, 31st Iowa Inf.	387		1901 Mar 21	IA, 28th, 1902
Dohrer, John	Pvt.	A, 22nd Iowa Inf.	8		1910 Jun 12	IA, 37th, 1911
Dohrmann, Fred	Pvt.	E, 26th Iowa Inf.	327		1903 Sep 10	IA, 30th, 1904
Doing, Hiram		4th Ind. Lt. Art.	25		1929 Jun 10	NE, 54th, 1930
Dolan, L.B.		F, 8th Ill. Cav.	378		1912 May 15	KS, 32nd, 1913
Dolan, Patrick	Pvt.	26th Iowa Inf.	164		1922 May 8	IA, 49th, 1923
Doland, John		E, 2?d Ill. Inf.	11		1892 Dec 22	NE, 17th, 1893
Doles, J.A.		G, 22nd Ohio	435		1922 Dec 23	KS, 42nd, 1923
Doling, Julius C.	Corp.	D, 32nd Wis. Inf.	219		1910 Aug	IA, 37th, 1911
Doll, D.	Pvt.	B, 26th Ill. Inf.	154		1916 Nov 7	IA, 43rd, 1917
Dollbee, P.A.		K, 14th Iowa	12		1897 Nov 13	KS, 17th, 1898
Dolliffe, Franklin	Pvt.	I, 44th Wis.	67		1907 Feb 9	IA, 34th, 1908
Dollins, John S.		A, 62nd Penn.	453		1914 Jun 1	KS, 34th, 1915
Dolman, E.F.		G, 84th Ill. (killed by cars)	24		1905 Aug 27	KS, 25th, 1906
Dolphin, John, see John, Dolphin						
Dolphin, Wm.	Corp.	F, 2nd N.Y. Cav.	12		1907 May 4	IA, 34th, 1908
Dolsby, Martin		G, 33rd Ind.	209		1923 Mar 23	KS, 43rd, 1924
Dolson, E.B.		1st Ohio Hvy. Art.	57		1897 Mar 26	KS, 17th, 1898
Dolson, H.I.		E, 2nd Mo.	90		1933 Jul 9	KS, 53rd, 1934
Dolson, N.I.		F, 2nd Mo. Cav.	90		1935	KS, 55th, 1936
Dombaugh, Uriah		K, 77th Ill.	61		1911	KS, 31st, 1912
Donaghue, M.	Pvt.	B, 2nd Iowa Inf.	270	43	1886 Mar 25	IA, 13th, 1887
Donahoo, Robt.		I, 14th Ill. Cav. (died of stroke of paralysis)	107	84	1909 Mar 19	NE, 33rd, 1909
Donahue, James		E, 18th Ill. Inf. (died of chronic diarrhea)	112	67	1901 Jan	NE, 26th, 1902
Donahue, Jas. R.	Pvt.	B, 30th Iowa Inf.	2	62	1899 Aug 14	IA, 26th, 1900
Donahue, Thomas		K, 5th U.S. Cav. (died of general delilty[debility?])	4	83	1912 Aug 17	NE, 37th, 1913
Donahue, W.A.	1st Lieut.	B, 60th Ohio Inf.	237	63	1891 Aug	IA, 18th, 1892
Donahugh, Josiah	Pvt.	F, 16th Iowa Inf.	31		1911 Mar	IA, 38th, 1912
Donald, Thomas J.		C, 28th Penn.	308		1912 Nov 5	KS, 32nd, 1913
Donaldson, C.D.		G, 30th Iowa	19		1907	IA, 34th, 1908
Donaldson, Chas. N.	Pvt.	10th N.Y. Art.	410		1917 Jul 30	IA, 44th, 1918
Donaldson, E.B.	Pvt.	E, 50th Mass.	123		1905 Jun 30	IA, 32nd, 1906
Donaldson, G.	Pvt.	A, 7th Wis. Inf.	101		1920 Apr 1	IA, 47th, 1921
Donaldson, Jno. A.	Pvt.	B, 45th Iowa Inf.	108		1927 Nov 13	IA, 54th, 1928
Donaldson, John			55		1924 Oct 25	IA, 51st, 1925
Donaldson, Louis		D, 63rd Ohio	113		1910 Feb 10	KS, 30th, 1911
Donaldson, Samuel	Pvt.	84th Ind. Inf.	16		1912 Apr 13	IA, 39th, 1913
Donaldson, T.W.			22		1884	KS, 4th, 1885
Donavan, W.J.		I, 110th Ohio	28		1898 Jun 16	KS, 18th, 1899
Donelson, Lester		K, 136th Ohio	257		1925 Aug 12	KS, 45th, 1926
Doner, Adam	Pvt.	H, 1st Iowa Inf.	78		1911 Apr 17	IA, 38th, 1912
Doner, E.D.		C, 115th Penn.	115		1915 Oct 8	KS, 35th, 1916
Doner, Joseph	Pvt.	F, 16th Iowa Inf.	147		1914 Aug	IA, 41st, 1915
Donivan, D.	Pvt.	F, 26th Ill. Inf.	26		1918 Mar 8	IA, 45th, 1919
Donkleman, Henry	Pvt.	A, 6th Iowa Cav.	118		1926 Aug 28	IA, 53rd, 1927
Donley, J.H.		5th Ind. Art.	130		1917 Sep 26	KS, 37th, 1918
Donly, Samuel		K, 75th Ind.	258		1925 Sep 16	KS, 45th, 1926
Donnell, John			437		1914	KS, 34th, 1915
Donnell, O.	Pvt.	I, 1st Iowa Cav.	165		1920 May 31	IA, 47th, 1921
Donnell, Robt. L.	Pvt.	1st Iowa Cav.	108		1922 Mar 17	IA, 49th, 1923
Donnelly, Douglas V.		C, 5th N.Y.	25		1924 May 22	KS, 44th, 1925
Donner, A.R.	Pvt.	C, 5th Iowa Cav.	263	47	1890 Apr	IA, 17th, 1891
Donner, Henry	Pvt.	B, 29th Iowa Inf.	204		1909 Jul	IA, 36th, 1910
Donnon, Aquilla	Pvt.	K, 2nd Iowa Cav.	1		1897 Feb 10	IA, 24th, 1898
Donnon, W.G.	Lieut.	H, 27th Iowa Inf.	54		1908 Dec 4	IA, 35th, 1909
Donnovan, L.			35		1911 Jul 18	NE, 36th, 1912
Donovan, A.J.	Pvt.	A, 32nd Mass. Inf.	72	53	1889 Aug 11	IA, 16th, 1890
Donovan, Chas. B.	Pvt.	M, 20th N.Y. Cav.	140	53	1892 May	IA, 19th, 1893
Donovan, L., see Donnovan, L.						

Name	Rank	Company, Regiment or Ship	Post*	Age	Death Date†	Journal
Dood, C.B.	Pvt.	B, 50th Ill. Inf.	1		3rd quarter 1885	IA, 12th, 1886
Doogs, Charles	Pvt.	K, 13th Ohio Vol. Inf.	123		1901 May 1	IA, 28th, 1902
Dooley, J.K.		G, 30th Ind. (died of old age)	13	86	1919 Mar 9	NE, 44th, 1920
Dooley, James	Pvt.		12		1930 Feb 12	IA, 57th, 1931
Dooley, M.H.		H, 11th Minn. Inf.	147		1902 Apr 15	KS, 22nd, 1903
Dooley, Patrick	Pvt.	K, 153rd Ill. Inf.	150		1901 May 31	IA, 28th, 1902
Dooley, T.E.	Pvt.	D, 22nd Iowa Inf.	67		1904 Nov 16	IA, 31st, 1905
Doolittle, Columbus	Pvt.	E, 15th Iowa Inf.	384		1910 May 20	IA, 37th, 1911
Doolittle, E.W.	Pvt.	B, 64th Ill. Inf.	12		1919 Nov 25	IA, 46th, 1920
Doolittle, H.A.	Pvt.	1st Wis. Hvy. Art.	118		1927 Dec 30	IA, 54th, 1928
Doolittle, H.G.			118		1915	IA, 42nd, 1916
Doolittle, Henry		G, 9th Ill. Cav.	225		1911 Oct 13	KS, 31st, 1912
Doolittle, Russell C.		D, 11th Ill. Cav.	175		1912 Nov 9	KS, 32nd, 1913
Doolittle, Wm. A.	Pvt.	K, 5th Iowa Inf. (at large)			1933 Jan 10	IA, 60th, 1934
Doolittle, Wm. A.		K, 5th Iowa Inf. (at large)			1932 Jan 10	IA, 59th, 1933
Doope, Simon M.	Pvt.	E, 150th Ill. Inf.	55	91	1938 Jul 14	IA, 65th, 1939
Door, Edward		G, 141st Ohio (died of stroke of apoplexy)	123	76	1922 May 19	NE, 47th, 1923
Dora, B.F.	Lieut.	34th Iowa	18		1907 Jun 11	IA, 34th, 1908
Doran, A.J.		C, 157th N.Y. Inf.	18		1929 Dec 22	KS, 49th, 1930
Doran, F.W.	Capt.	E, 35th Iowa Inf.	250		1910 Sep 22	IA, 37th, 1911
Doran, Henry		A, 40th Ohio	191		1922 Dec 23	KS, 42nd, 1923
Doran, John		C, 53rd Ill. Inf. (cause of death: kidney & bladder)	205	63	1895 Jan 5	NE, 20th, 1896
Doran, John A.		G, 9th Penn.	25		1897 May 25	KS, 17th, 1898
Doran, M.	Sergt.	D, 2nd Md. Inf.	73		1911 Apr 20	IA, 38th, 1912
Dore, H.C.	Pvt.	— Ohio Inf.	250	50	1896 Mar 4	IA, 23rd, 1897
Doreland, John			132		1917 May 1	KS, 37th, 1918
Dorlan, P.S.	Pvt.	I, 3rd Iowa	68		1905 Jun 3	IA, 32nd, 1906
Dorley, John	Pvt.	K, 16th Iowa Inf.	425		1919 Jan 19	IA, 46th, 1920
Dorman, G.		I, 8th Ill.	243		1920	KS, 40th, 1921
Dorman, Jerry M.	Pvt.	E, 3rd N.Y. Cav.	46		1924 Oct 17	IA, 51st, 1925
Dorman, L.C.	Pvt.	G, 8th N.Y. Hvy. Art.	26	88	1932 May 4	IA, 59th, 1933
Dorman, W.J.	Pvt.	G, 28th Iowa Inf.	26	54	1892 Jan 21	IA, 18th, 1892
Dorn, David H.		B, 34th Ill. Inf. (died of heart trouble)	35	72	1913 May 4	NE, 38th, 1914
Dorrance, Delos	Pvt.	E, 126th Ill. Inf.	382	47	1885 Jul 15	IA, 12th, 1886
Dorrance, E.F.		B, 1st Conn. Cav.	158		1922 Jan 18	KS, 42nd, 1923
Dorrents, James H.		F, 4th Iowa Inf. (died of dropsy)	354	79	1918 Nov 3	NE, 43rd, 1919
Dorsay, J.A.		F, 1st Va.	32		1933 May 6	KS, 53rd, 1934
Dorsey, A.			378		1924	KS, 44th, 1925
Dorsey, F.J.		D, 116th Ind.	51		1920 Apr 17	KS, 40th, 1921
Dorsey, Geo. W.E.		C, 6th West Va. (died of atheroma)	4	68	1911 Jun 12	NE, 36th, 1912
Dorsey, George W.E.		congressman from the third district; died at Salt Lake City	4		1911 Jun 12	NE, 36th, 1912
Dorsey, J.A.		F, 1st Va.	32		1934 Oct 9	KS, 54th, 1935
Dorsey, J.L.		F, 147th Ohio	97		1935 Jun 19	NE, 60th, 1936
Dorsey, N.		G, 5th Ill.	32		1927	NE, 52nd, 1928
Dorsey, N.		G, 50th Ill.	32		1926 Dec 10	NE, 51st, 1927
Dorsey, Samuel		G, 11th West Va. Inf. (died of Bright's disease)	315	66	1895 Nov 30	NE, 20th, 1896
Dorst, Henry	1st Lieut.	7th Ohio Bat.	78		1916 Feb 8	KS, 36th, 1917
Dorty, Wm. H.H.		A, 1st Minn.	328		1906 Apr 14	KS, 26th, 1907
Dorwoard, S.S.	Pvt.	E, 29th Wis. Inf.	97		1910 Sep 6	IA, 37th, 1911
Dory, Wm.			22		1906	KS, 26th, 1907
Dose, Fred	Pvt.	G, 1st Iowa Inf.	1		1904 Nov 4	IA, 31st, 1905
Doss, Thomas E.S.			487		1910	IA, 37th, 1911
Doster, A.F.		M, 13th Ind.	1		1933 Feb 25	KS, 53rd, 1934
Doster, B.F.		G, 66th Ohio	18		1923 Jan 7	KS, 43rd, 1924
Dotey, Louis		E, 35th Ill.	119		1892 Jul 7	KS, 12th, 1893
Dother, Jacob	Pvt.	B, 6th Iowa Cav.	182		1904	IA, 31st, 1905
Dotson, Chas.		E, 6th West Va.	113		1899 Feb	KS, 19th, 1900
Dotson, George Sydney		E, 7th Ill. Cav.		90	1937 Jun 16	IA, 64th, 1938
Dotson, J.M.	Pvt.	2nd Iowa Cav.	115		1921 Nov 8	IA, 48th, 1922

Name	Rank	Company, Regiment or Ship	Post*	Age	Death Date†	Journal
Dotson, John	Pvt.	H, 4th Iowa Cav.	398		1910 Mar 3	IA, 37th, 1911
Dotson, Samuel Scott		L, 1st Ohio Cav. (died of pneumonia)	25		1916 Feb 4	NE, 41st, 1917
Dotts, Wm.	Pvt.	G, 51st Ohio Inf.	288	45	1892 Feb 20	IA, 18th, 1892
Dotty, J.F.		B, 26th Ohio Inf.	1		1891 Feb 27	KS, 11th, 1892
Doty, Andrew	Pvt.	G, 38th Iowa Inf.	48	62	1893 Sep 18	IA, 20th, 1894
Doty, F.M.		B, 187th & 83rd Ohio	52		1924 Dec 15	KS, 44th, 1925
Doty, G.W.		H, N.Y. Art.	35		1911 Jun 30	KS, 31st, 1912
Doty, Isaac			29		1917	IA, 44th, 1918
Doty, James N.		Mich.	10	81	1922 Jul 22	NE, 47th, 1923
Doty, John			305		1903-1904	IA, 30th, 1904
Doty, L.M.	Pvt.	A, 84th Ind.	43		1926 Dec 14	IA, 53rd, 1927
Doty, Morris		G, 93rd Ohio	123		1916 Dec 24	KS, 36th, 1917
Doty, William		F, 5th N.Y. Cav.	500		1930 Dec 11	KS, 50th, 1931
Doubleday, J.M.		D, 20th Ind.	27		1937 Jun 8	KS, 56th, 1937
Doud, E. Jackson			132		2nd quarter 1883	IA, 10th, 1884
Douer, John	Pvt.	H, 69th Ill. Inf.	337		1905 Dec 25	IA, 32nd, 1906
Dougherty, E.J.	Pvt.	L, 3rd Iowa Cav.	97		1908 Oct 19	IA, 35th, 1909
Dougherty, James L.		F, 47th Ind.	55		1919 Oct 2	KS, 39th, 1920
Dougherty, William		G, 19th Penn. Inf. (at large)	78	92	1937 Aug 10	IA, 64th, 1938
Doughman, S.H.	Pvt.	D, 33rd Iowa Inf.	49		1911 Oct 11	IA, 38th, 1912
Douglas, A.L.		L, 1st Maine Cav.	25		1913 May 2	NE, 38th, 1914
Douglas, B.F.		H, 29th —	320		1896 Mar 5	KS, 16th, 1897
Douglas, Chas. H.		H, 66th Ill. Inf.	131		1908 Aug 27	NE, 33rd, 1909
Douglas, D.		C, 34th Iowa Inf.	7		1919 Feb 2	IA, 46th, 1920
Douglas, D.W.	Corp.	B, 16th U.S. Inf.	194		1913 Nov 6	IA, 40th, 1914
Douglas, G.E.		E, 15th N.Y. Inf.	13	64	1907 Sep 8	NE, 32nd, 1908
Douglas, H.			45		1925 Feb 10	IA, 52nd, 1926
Douglas, I.M.		F, 51st Wis.	13	74	1918 Jun 22	NE, 43rd, 1919
Douglas, J.E.	Pvt.	H, 20th Iowa Inf.	16	63	1896 Jun 15	IA, 23rd, 1897
Douglas, J.W.		L, 2nd Ill. Cav.	32		1927	NE, 52nd, 1928
Douglas, Thos. N.		F, 23rd Ill. Inf.	94		1927 Jan 10	NE, 52nd, 1928
Douglas, William A.		A, 1st Mo. Cav.	46		1919 Feb 21	KS, 39th, 1920
Douglass, Edward F.	Pvt.	C, 39th Ill. Inf. (at large)	293, 261	92	1940 Mar 16	IA, 66th, 1940
Douglass, J.W.			85		1902 Nov 7	KS, 22nd, 1903
Douglass, L.H.		G, 12th Ind. Inf. (died of insanity)	98		1893 May 3	NE, 18th, 1894
Douglass, Stephen		A, 5th U.S. Art.	321		1904 Oct 30	KS, 24th, 1905
Douglass, W.H.	Pvt.	E, 157th N.Y.	10		1907 Aug 27	IA, 34th, 1908
Douglass, Wm.		G, 40th Ohio	180		1896 Feb 3	KS, 16th, 1897
Dougle, John W.	Pvt.	I, 164th Ohio Inf.	81		1913 Nov 25	IA, 40th, 1914
Dourity, Harden		D, 10th Kans.	236		1923 Apr 15	KS, 43rd, 1924
Douthart, I.W.		D, 13th Iowa	130		1924 Mar 22	KS, 44th, 1925
Douthitt, A.P.		E, 21st Ohio	85		1933 Apr 6	KS, 53rd, 1934
Douthitt, Wm. P.		E, 2nd Kans. State Militia	1		1897 Nov 28	KS, 17th, 1898
Dovlin, John		I, 53rd Ill.	251		1920 Oct 15	KS, 40th, 1921
Dow, A.B.		C, 30th Ohio	176		1913 Jan 31	KS, 33rd, 1914
Dow, Chas. H.		D, 59th Ind.	113		1907 Mar 2	NE, 32nd, 1908
Dow, D.W.	Lieut.	G, 44th Iowa Inf.	81		1918 Aug 18	IA, 45th, 1919
Dow, Ichabod	Pvt.	D, 46th Iowa Inf.	271		1910 Jul 1	IA, 37th, 1911
Dow, Isaac W.		F, 9th Kans. Cav.	73		1913 Sep 27	KS, 33rd, 1914
Dow, J.E.		G, 15th Maine	112		1911 Jun 13	KS, 31st, 1912
Dow, John	Pvt.	M, 3rd Kans. Cav.	150		1923 Dec	IA, 50th, 1924
Dowd, Philander		B, 12th Ill.	68		1931 Dec 31	NE, 57th, 1933
Dowdell, Joseph S.		I, 14th Ind. Inf. E, 115th Ind. Inf. E, 149th Ind. Inf.	250		1900 Aug 17	KS, 20th, 1901
Dowding, Jacob E.	Pvt.	C, 3rd Iowa Inf.	25	48	1889 Mar 16	IA, 16th, 1890
Dowding, Joseph		A, 2nd U.S. Bat.	55		1918 Jul 31	IA, 45th, 1919
Dowdy, Warren		G, 125th Ohio	1		1904 Dec 10	KS, 24th, 1905
Dowel, S.F.	Pvt.	B, 18th Iowa Inf.	7		1920 Apr 21	IA, 47th, 1921
Dowers, James		E, 35th Ill. Inf.	10		1924 Apr 19	NE, 48th, 1924
Dowler, J.J.		A, 45th Ohio	50		1911	KS, 31st, 1912
Dowler, Wm.		E, 7th West Va.	85		1922 Jun 5	KS, 42nd, 1923

*See Appendix A, B or C for roster of post names and locations.
†See Introduction for note regarding recording of death date.

150

Name	Rank	Company, Regiment or Ship	Post*	Age	Death Date†	Journal
Dowling, John	Pvt.	B, 12th Iowa Inf.	194		1915 Jan 23	IA, 42nd, 1916
Dowling, M.M.	Pvt.	B, 105th Penn. Inf.	194	62	1892 Aug 10	IA, 19th, 1893
Dowling, N.H.		I, 55th Ill.	352		1933 Oct 25	NE, 58th, 1934
Downard, A.L.	Pvt.	B, 3rd Iowa Cav.	233		1908 Sep 1	IA, 35th, 1909
Downard, E.R.		B, 45th Ohio	17		1923 Feb 22	KS, 43rd, 1924
Downell, B.J.		C, U.S. Hvy. Art.	100		1930 Apr 29	KS, 50th, 1931
Downer, B.F.		C, 30th Iowa (died of army wound)	120	65	1910	NE, 35th, 1911
Downer, Geo.	Pvt.	F, 44th Iowa Inf.	74		1917 May 12	IA, 44th, 1918
Downer, J.B.	Capt.	K, 136th U.S. Inf.	231		1911 Feb 8	IA, 38th, 1912
Downer, James W.		D, 79th Penn. Inf.	2		1902 Jan 12	KS, 22nd, 1903
Downes, Wm.			132		1922 May 23	KS, 42nd, 1923
Downey, R.T.	Pvt.	C, 48th Iowa Inf.	116		1926 Sep 20	IA, 53rd, 1927
Downey, Wm.	Corp.	17th Ind. Battery	302		1908 Mar 31	IA, 35th, 1909
Downhe, Cyrus	Pvt.	D, 9th Iowa Inf.	144		1916 Jan 9	IA, 43rd, 1917
Downie, Robert		C, 1st Colo.	35		1898 Dec 17	KS, 18th, 1899
Downing, B.H.		D, 40th Penn. Vol. Inf.	25		1908 Nov 14	KS, 28th, 1909
Downing, D.J.		B, 17th Ind.	57		1920 Oct 7	KS, 40th, 1921
Downing, D.M.		C, 15th Ind.	54		1920 May 31	KS, 40th, 1921
Downing, Geo. W.	Pvt.	C, 43rd Mo. Inf.	144	46	1891 Dec 9	IA, 18th, 1892
Downing, George C.		O, Ohio Battery Lt. Art.	1		1908 Feb 14	KS, 28th, 1909
Downing, P.J.	Pvt.	H, 13th Iowa	52		1921 Sep 21	IA, 48th, 1922
Downing, Thomas		M, 48th Iowa	4		1926 Mar 3	KS, 46th, 1927
Downing, W.H.	Pvt.	E, 33rd Iowa Inf.	40		1924 Mar 9	IA, 51st, 1925
Downing, Walter			333		1913	IA, 40th, 1914
Downs, B.P.	Corp.	E, 93rd Ind. Inf.	337		1904 Oct 18	IA, 31st, 1905
Downs, D.D.	Lieut.	C, 75th Ind. Inf.	40		1916 Aug 4	IA, 43rd, 1917
Downs, Eli A.		E, 32nd Ill.	19		1916	KS, 36th, 1917
Downs, Franklin S.		F, 3rd Iowa Inf.	48	95	1938 Mar 28	IA, 64th, 1938
Downs, J.P.		M, 12th Mo. Cav.	337		1889	KS, 9th, 1890
Downs, Jas.		A, 8th Mo.	380		1906 Nov 1	KS, 26th, 1907
Downs, L.L.	Pvt.	G, 95th Ill. Inf.	220		1927 May 31	IA, 54th, 1928
Downs, Levi M.		E, 71st Ill.	35		1916 Jul 24	KS, 36th, 1917
Downs, Theo.	Pvt.	B, 14th U.S. Battery	170	85	1931 Apr 2	IA, 58th, 1932
Dowrin, W.J.		A, 37th Ind.	17		1923 Apr 25	KS, 43rd, 1924
Dows, S.L.			235		1908 Apr	IA, 35th, 1909
Dowse, Lewis R.		F, 60th Mass.	98		1931 Jan 7	NE, 56th, 1932
Doxsee, Harvey L.		F, 97th Ill. (former member; died at Callaway)	264		1936 Jun	NE, 61st, 1937
Doyd, Farmer J.	Pvt.	C, 40th Ind. Inf.	12	50	1892 Mar 4	IA, 19th, 1893
Doyle, James Emery		E, 59th Ind.	35	86	1915 Nov 23	NE, 40th, 1916
Doyle, Jas. H.		C, 11th Kans. Cav.	55		1898 Jun 12	KS, 18th, 1899
Doyle, Lawrence	Pvt.	C, 14th Iowa Inf.	1	96	1932 Oct 22	IA, 59th, 1933
Doyle, Michael			38		1911 1st term	IA, 38th, 1912
Doyle, Michael		H, 53rd Ill.	1		1928 Apr 4	KS, 48th, 1929
Drabek, J.F.		I, 6th Iowa Cav.	7		1926	NE, 51st, 1927
Draine, John (colored)	Pvt.	E, 65th U.S.C.T. (at large)	413	96	1940 Feb 28	IA, 66th, 1940
Drake, A.B.		F, 105th Ohio Inf.	88		1909 Sep 30	KS, 29th, 1910
Drake, A.K.	Pvt.	D, 3rd Iowa Inf.	168		1917 Jan 3	IA, 44th, 1918
Drake, Benjamin F.		16th Ind. (died of old age)	47	85	1921 Dec 30	NE, 46th, 1922
Drake, C.L.	Pvt.	I, 12th Ill. Inf.	197		1910 Sep 23	IA, 37th, 1911
Drake, David N.		G, 55th Ill. Vol. Inf.	25		1908 Jul	KS, 28th, 1909
Drake, E.E.		B, 142nd N.Y.	25		1927 Apr 28	KS, 47th, 1928
Drake, F.M.	Brig. Gen.	36th Iowa Inf.	122		1903 Nov 20	IA, 30th, 1904
Drake, F.W.	Pvt.	G, 7th Mich. Inf.	496	73	1894 Oct 15	IA, 21st, 1895
Drake, G.G.			311		1884	KS, 4th, 1885
Drake, H.F.	Pvt.	E, 79th Ohio Inf.	88		1921 Nov 15	IA, 48th, 1922
Drake, H.F.		D, 2nd Kans. Cav.	293		1904 May 10	KS, 24th, 1905
Drake, Henry	Pvt.	B, 65th Ill. Inf.	231		1913 May 21	IA, 40th, 1914
Drake, J.C.			134		1890	NE, 15th, 1891
Drake, J.M.		F, 88th Ill.	18		1916 May 17	KS, 36th, 1917
Drake, John			77		1896 Sep 6	KS, 16th, 1897
Drake, John T.	Lieut. Col.	10th Iowa Inf.	321		1907 Feb 12	IA, 34th, 1908

Name	Rank	Company, Regiment or Ship	Post*	Age	Death Date†	Journal
Drake, Jos. W.		E, 9th Kans. Cav.	51		1901 Oct 7	KS, 21st, 1902
Drake, M.L.		H, 45th Ohio	32		1928 Jul 8	KS, 48th, 1929
Drake, Phillip	Pvt.	I, 2nd Iowa Inf.	88	64	1886 Jan 31	IA, 12th, 1886
Drake, Phineas Henry	Pvt.	M, 11th Ill. Cav. (at large)	263	100, 7 mos. & 3 days	1944 Apr 3	IA, 70th, 1944
Drake, Robert		11th Kans.	7		1905 Mar 15	KS, 25th, 1906
Drake, Robert G.		died at his home, 410 South 19th Street, Lincoln			1923 Sep 26	NE, 48th, 1924
Drake, Robt. R.		E, 100th Ohio	147		1893 Nov	KS, 13th, 1894
Drake, S.		A, 77th Ill. (died of cancer)	1	82	1924 Jul 27	NE, 49th, 1925
Drake, T.S.			104		1912 Sep 19	KS, 32nd, 1913
Drake, Theo.	Pvt.	B, 3rd Wis. Inf.	58		1925 Mar 27	IA, 52nd, 1926
Drake, Thomas		G, 4th Mo.	250		1919 Oct 1	KS, 39th, 1920
Drake, W.C.		Ill.	54		1904 Nov 9	KS, 24th, 1905
Drake, W.H.	Pvt.	H, 140th Ind. Inf.	174	47	1888 Mar 31	IA, 15th, 1889
Drake, W.S.		A, 160th N.Y.	42		1893 Oct 27	KS, 13th, 1894
Draper, A.P.		F, 10th Ind.	382		1893 Aug 23	KS, 13th, 1894
Draper, Anderson		D, 10th Iowa	174		1918	KS, 38th, 1919
Draper, C.R.		A, 45th Ill. Inf. (died of heart trouble)	120	67	1916 Oct 19	NE, 41st, 1917
Draper, E.W.		H, 12th Mo.	51		1915 Dec 14	KS, 35th, 1916
Draper, H.C.	Sergt.	E, 3rd Mo.	150		1918	KS, 38th, 1919
Draper, O.D.			25		1919 Nov 21	KS, 39th, 1920
Draper, Robert A.		C, 8th Mo. Cav.	123		1912 Aug 5	KS, 32nd, 1913
Draper, W.	Pvt.	Ohio	108		1920 Jul 22	IA, 47th, 1921
Draper, W.T.		C, 3rd — (died of Bright's disease)	40	66	1910 Oct 22	NE, 35th, 1911
Draper, William		L, 1st Kans.	12		1919 Nov 12	KS, 39th, 1920
Drapers, John			233		1924	IA, 51st, 1925
Drayer, John		F, 39th Ohio Inf.	71		1912 Jan 25	KS, 32nd, 1913
Drazey, Stephen		I, 42nd Ill. (killed by runaway team)	411		1890	KS, 10th, 1891
Drees, Jacob W.			424		1921	KS, 41st, 1922
Dreibelbis, Orlando		E, 151st Penn.	46		1913 Nov 21	KS, 33rd, 1914
Dreman, J.P.	Pvt.	H, 136th Penn. (died of consumption)	172	47	1887	NE, 12th, 1888
Dresser, Virgil		C, 19th Kans.	6		1913 Feb 8	KS, 33rd, 1914
Dressie, W.W., see Doessu, W.W.						
Drew, Charles J.	Seaman	U.S.N.	1		1916 Jan 7	KS, 36th, 1917
Drew, Charles P.		I, 11th Kans. Cav.	1		1916 Jan 31	KS, 36th, 1917
Drew, Frank	Pvt.	F, 1st Minn. Inf.	512		1910 Feb 1	IA, 37th, 1911
Drew, S.B.	Pvt.	B, 63rd Ohio Inf.	16		1902 Feb 24	IA, 29th, 1903
Drew, Samuel		G, 84th Penn. Inf. (see rec. National Military Home Post hos.)	380		1890	KS, 10th, 1891
Drew, W.G.		I, 11th Kans.	35		1904 Aug 16	KS, 24th, 1905
Drexler, Jno. C.	Pvt.	H, 14th Iowa Inf.	212		1929 Jan 2	IA, 56th, 1930
Driesbach, Charles S.		F, 132nd Penn. Inf.	71		1916 Nov 30	KS, 36th, 1917
Drinkwalter, L.S.	Pvt.	G, 1st Iowa Cav. (died of pneumonia)	122	48	1884 Jan 1	NE, 9th, 1885
Dripps, Joseph H.	Pvt.	L, 6th Iowa Cav.	92		1907 Mar	IA, 34th, 1908
Driscal, Murthy	Pvt.	K, 2nd Iowa Inf.	87		1900 Sep 18	IA, 27th, 1901
Driscall, Charles		B, 211th Penn. Inf. (died of old age; resident of Soldiers & Sailors Home, Grand Island; died in Johnstown, Penn.)	3	81	1905 Feb 3	NE, 30th, 1906
Driscoll, James K.		G, 2nd Ind. Inf.	284	93	1938 Mar 10	IA, 64th, 1938
Driver, Isaiah		A, 142nd Ind. Inf.	14		1914 May 14	KS, 34th, 1915
Droneberger, H.P.			38		1924 Feb 25	KS, 44th, 1925
Droneberger, H.P.			38		1925 Feb 25	KS, 45th, 1926
Drown, Daniel B.	Pvt.	E, 106th Ill. Inf.	12		1912 Jun 4	IA, 39th, 1913
Droz, E.H.		I, 13th Iowa Inf.	85		1899 Feb 21	KS, 19th, 1900
Druckheimmer, G.		A, 165th N.Y.	380		1897 May 7	KS, 17th, 1898
Drum, Chas.		D, 145th Penn.	77		1922 Jun 14	KS, 42nd, 1923
Drum, D.D.		H, 15th Kans. Cav.	111		1917 Feb 12	KS, 37th, 1918
Drum, Edward		B, 16th Kans.	247		1916 Oct 7	KS, 36th, 1917
Drumhiller, Wm.		D, 5th Mo. Inf.	177		1901 Feb 13	KS, 21st, 1902
Drummond, J.A.	Pvt.	H, 19th Iowa Inf.	79		1915 Oct	IA, 42nd, 1916

Name	Rank	Company, Regiment or Ship	Post*	Age	Death Date†	Journal
Drummond, J.T.	Pvt.	K, 4th Iowa Cav.	20	66	1890 May 29	IA, 17th, 1891
Drummond, Wm.	Pvt.	E, 13th U.S. Inf.	369		1925 Jan 22	IA, 52nd, 1926
Drummons, James		I, 72nd Ind.	64		1916 Jul 4	KS, 36th, 1917
Drurey, E.G.	Pvt.	F, 1st Mass. Inf.	130		1928 Dec 17	IA, 55th, 1929
Drury, J.M.		D, 1st Mo.	147		1919 Oct 6	KS, 39th, 1920
Druse, E.H.	Pvt.	A, 5th Minn. Cav.	42		1931 Jan 2	IA, 57th, 1931
Druse, Geo.		E, 1st Mich.	71		1931 Jan 5	KS, 51st, 1932
Druse, Geo.		E, 1st Mich.	71		1931 Jan 5	KS, 52nd, 1933
Drustic, Mathias		L, 2nd Ky. Cav.	353		1918 Mar 23	KS, 38th, 1919
Dryden, Carleton	Capt.	F, 10th Iowa Inf.	5	89	1931 Jun 30	IA, 58th, 1932
Dryden, D.F.	Corp.	19th Ohio Battery	29		1908	IA, 35th, 1909
Dryden, H.B.	Pvt.	G, 11th Ohio Cav.	127		1927 Mar 9	IA, 54th, 1928
Dryden, H.C.		16th Kans.	129		1923 Mar 10	KS, 43rd, 1924
Dryden, J.F.	Pvt.	H, 2nd Ohio Art.	127		1921 Jul 26	IA, 48th, 1922
Dryden, J.H.	Pvt.	A, 48th Ohio Inf.	40		1925 Mar 1	IA, 52nd, 1926
Drydon, Robt.		A, 54th Ill. Inf. (died of heart failure)	250	69	1902 Oct	NE, 27th, 1903
Duball, Geo.		K, 79th U.S.C.T.	10		1927 Dec 10	KS, 47th, 1928
Dubbs, C.F.			50		1st quarter 1883	IA, 10th, 1884
Dubois, Ferdinand	Pvt.	D, 12th Iowa	58		1926 Jul 24	IA, 53rd, 1927
Dubois, Geo. H.	Sergt.	G, 1st Iowa Cav.	190		1918 Oct 29	IA, 45th, 1919
Dubois, L.K.		K, 24th Iowa Inf. (died at Lenora, Kans.; buried at Lenora)	182		1894 Aug 16	KS, 14th, 1895
Dubrow, C.D.		H, 15th Ohio Inf.	129		1925 Feb 12	KS, 45th, 1926
Duchesne, Henry C.	Pvt.	C, 77th Ill.	52		1915 Sep 5	KS, 35th, 1916
Duck, W.		A, 88th Ind. (died of Bright's disease)	231	64	1908 Feb 4	NE, 33rd, 1909
Duckeshire, Merit			106		1884	KS, 4th, 1885
Duckworth, D.A.	Corp.	G, 2nd Iowa Inf.	79	49	1891 Nov 21	IA, 18th, 1892
Duckworth, H.H.			122		1924	IA, 51st, 1925
Duckworth, J.		K, 3rd Ill.	311		1927	KS, 47th, 1928
Duckworth, P.		G, 120th Ind. Inf.	53		1925 Jul 15	KS, 45th, 1926
Duda, Frank		55th N.Y. Ind. Battery	294		1909 Nov 15	KS, 29th, 1910
Duden, W.M.			232		1914	KS, 34th, 1915
Dudley, A.J.	Pvt.	K, 138th Ill. Inf.	23		1920 Jun 21	IA, 47th, 1921
Dudley, Edgar S.		I, 1st N.Y. Art.	214	62	1911 Jan 9	NE, 36th, 1912
Dudrew, Charles D.		H, 55th Ohio	129		1925 Feb 13	KS, 44th, 1925
Dudway, Geo.		F, 73rd Ill.	1		1922 Jul 29	KS, 42nd, 1923
Dueese, W.H.	Pvt.	G, 101st Ill. Inf.	291		1910 Oct 10	IA, 37th, 1911
Duelam, C.		106th N.Y. Lt. Art.	286		1905	KS, 25th, 1906
Duell, Thomas		C, 50th Ohio	100		1923 Mar 22	KS, 43rd, 1924
Duenbortle, Fred	Pvt.	H, 144th Ill. Inf.	348	56	1892 Oct 30	IA, 19th, 1893
Duessler, John J.		A, 55th Ohio	1		1922 Jan 30	KS, 42nd, 1923
Duff, James A.		D, 10th Kans.	40		1911 Jan 27	KS, 31st, 1912
Duff, Jas.		18th Ohio Battery	147		1926 Dec 7	KS, 46th, 1927
Duff, S.L.		E, Penn.	18		1922 Jan 22	KS, 42nd, 1923
Duffey, Andrew		D, 77th Ill.	120		1898 Dec 22	KS, 18th, 1899
Duffey, M.			457		1907	IA, 34th, 1908
Duffield, Geo.	Capt., Major, & Lieut. Col.	E, 3rd Iowa Cav.	100	71	1898 Jul 20	IA, 25th, 1899
Duffield, H.P.	Corp.	137th Ill. Inf.	56		1919 Aug 6	IA, 46th, 1920
Duffield, John	Sergt.	G, 2nd Iowa Inf.	100		1919 Apr 1	IA, 46th, 1920
Duffield, Samuel		F, 1st U.S. Cav.	476		1899 Aug 10	KS, 19th, 1900
Dufford, George		H, 15th N.J.	8		1924 May 23	KS, 44th, 1925
Duffy, John		C, 7th Penn.	474		1896 Jul 4	KS, 16th, 1897
Duffy, John S.		A, 118th Ill. Vols.	247		1902	KS, 22nd, 1903
Dufoe, N.H.	Lieut.	E, 42nd Ill. Inf.	222	66	1898 Mar 4	IA, 24th, 1898
Dugan, D.W.		H, 11th Mo. Cav.	59		1934 May 25	KS, 54th, 1935
Dugan, Geo.	Sergt.	I, 151st Ill. Inf.	10		1918 Oct 21	IA, 45th, 1919
Dugan, John	Pvt.	D, 124th Ill. Inf.	414	49	1890 Dec 12	IA, 17th, 1891
Dugdale, Peter		H, 13th Ill.	9		1923 Oct 5	KS, 43rd, 1924
Duigle, Frank	Pvt.		118		1929	IA, 56th, 1930
Duish, James W.		E, 21st Ohio Vols.	28		1911 Oct 18	KS, 31st, 1912
Duiston, E.W.	Pvt.	G, 42nd Wis. Inf.	132	64	1892 Jan 24	IA, 18th, 1892

Name	Rank	Company, Regiment or Ship	Post*	Age	Death Date†	Journal
Duke, J.C.	Pvt.	G, 22nd Iowa Inf.	56		1917	IA, 44th, 1918
Duke, John H.		H, 13th West Va.	303		1913 Feb 11	KS, 33rd, 1914
Duke, Taylor	Pvt.	A, 57th U.S. Colored	7		1922 Apr 12	IA, 49th, 1923
Duke, Zennis	Pvt.	C, 32nd Iowa Inf.	68		1925 Jun 19	IA, 52nd, 1926
Dulin, Wm.		E, 120th Ohio	129		1917 Jun 6	KS, 37th, 1918
Dull, Fisher	Pvt.	E, 45th Wis. Inf.	22		1913 May 22	IA, 40th, 1914
Dull, George		D, 124th Penn.	171		1919 Aug 15	KS, 39th, 1920
Dull, John			204		1914 Sep	IA, 42nd, 1916
Dull, Joseph		B, 129th Ohio	337		1926 May 30	KS, 46th, 1927
Dull, S.H.		G, 51st Ohio	17		1911 Oct 29	KS, 31st, 1912
Dumans, T.			122		1883	KS, 3rd, 1884
Dumas, Simeon		G, 14th N.Y. Hvy. Art. (died of grip, stomach trouble)	112		1894 Dec 23	NE, 19th, 1895
Dumenil, J.M.		M, 5th Ohio Cav.	71		1914 Feb 18	KS, 34th, 1915
Dumigan, Hugh F.		H, 38th N.Y. Inf.	49		1892 Feb 29	KS, 12th, 1893
Dumm, J.W.		C, 116th Ohio	7		1905 Dec 30	KS, 25th, 1906
Dummitt, William	Pvt.	H, 6th Iowa Inf.	339		1915	IA, 42nd, 1916
Dumont, T.R.	Pvt.	A, 18th Iowa Inf.	400		1915	IA, 42nd, 1916
Dun, John H.	Pvt.	K, 45th Iowa Inf.	516	82	1896 Dec 30	IA, 23rd, 1897
Dunable, W.J.		E, 39th Ill.	88		1896 Dec 3	KS, 16th, 1897
Dunahugh, Alex	Pvt.	H, 22nd Iowa Inf.	31		1905 Nov 25	IA, 32nd, 1906
Dunbar, A.F.		D, 9th Kans. Cav.	96		1914 Jan 4	KS, 34th, 1915
Dunbar, B.S.		E, 1st Colo. Cav.	271		1913 Oct 5	KS, 33rd, 1914
Dunbar, F.D.	Pvt.	I, 4th Ill. Cav.	97		1911 May 11	IA, 38th, 1912
Dunbar, F.M.	Pvt.	C, 7th Iowa Inf.	26		1920 Apr 5	IA, 47th, 1921
Dunbar, H.P.	Pvt.	I, 40th Inf.	22		1916 Jul 8	IA, 43rd, 1917
Dunbar, Henry		A, 11th Ill. Cav. (died of heart trouble)	96	71	1918 Jan 24	NE, 43rd, 1919
Dunbar, Richard		B, 18th Wis.	64		1926 Jun 9	KS, 46th, 1927
Dunbar, Richard		B, 18th —	64		1925	KS, 45th, 1926
Dunbar, William	Pvt.	L, 1st Ill. Art.	42		1901 Feb 17	IA, 28th, 1902
Dunbas, F.M.			43		1921 May 2	IA, 48th, 1922
Duncan, A.J.		F, 17th Penn.	71		1926 Jun 26	KS, 46th, 1927
Duncan, A.L.	Pvt.	C, 11th Iowa Inf.	4	50	1895 May 1	IA, 22nd, 1896
Duncan, Alex.	Pvt.	F, 29th Iowa Inf.	248		1924 Oct 5	IA, 51st, 1925
Duncan, B.F.		B, 25th Ill.	34		1918	KS, 38th, 1919
Duncan, B.F., see Dunsan, B.F.						
Duncan, C.S.		A, 3rd Kans. State Militia	12		1904 Apr 14	KS, 24th, 1905
Duncan, David D.		M, 5th Ind. Cav.	25		1912 Oct 30	KS, 32nd, 1913
Duncan, E.O.	Pvt.	A, 44th Iowa Inf.	78		1900 Mar 16	IA, 27th, 1901
Duncan, Elias		I, 11th Ill. Cav.	209		1929	KS, 49th, 1930
Duncan, Fred S.	Pvt.	G, 35th Iowa	231		1903-1904	IA, 30th, 1904
Duncan, H.S.		C, 11th Iowa Inf.	290		1913 Nov 2	IA, 40th, 1914
Duncan, J.C.		E, 98th Kans.	158		1885	KS, 5th, 1886
Duncan, J.J.	Pvt.	D, 100th Penn. Inf.	96		1925 Jun 13	IA, 52nd, 1926
Duncan, J.L.	Lieut.	G, 46th Iowa	337		1907 Feb 5	IA, 34th, 1908
Duncan, J.P.	Pvt.	H, 135th Ill. Inf.	58		1911 Aug 19	IA, 38th, 1912
Duncan, J.P.		K, 11th Ind.	51		1921 Jul 24	KS, 41st, 1922
Duncan, J.R.		H, 143rd Ohio	378		1928	KS, 48th, 1929
Duncan, J.R.		H, 143rd Ohio	378		1927	KS, 47th, 1928
Duncan, James	Pvt.	B, 45th Iowa Inf.	263		1923 Jun 1	IA, 50th, 1924
Duncan, Jas. A.		3rd Iowa Cav. (location: Grand Island)			1927 Jan 10	NE, 52nd, 1928
Duncan, John	Pvt.	G, 11th Iowa Inf.	231		1929 Feb 17	IA, 56th, 1930
Duncan, John		B, 10th Ind.	87		1885	KS, 5th, 1886
Duncan, John E.	1st Lieut.	D, 23rd Wis. Inf.	30		1900 Oct 6	IA, 27th, 1901
Duncan, John W.		F, 29th M.O. Inf.	307		1891 Oct	KS, 11th, 1892
Duncan, N.H.		D, 46th Ill.	4		1918 Jun 5	KS, 38th, 1919
Duncan, Noah		I, 46th Ohio	252		1916 Nov 25	KS, 36th, 1917
Duncan, Perry		D, 11th Iowa Inf.	231	91	1935 May 14	IA, 62nd, 1936
Duncan, Perry		G, 11th Iowa	231	91	1934 May 14	IA, 61st, 1935
Duncan, R.J.		A, 11th Kans. Cav.	160		1914 Dec 10	KS, 34th, 1915
Duncan, W.F.	Corp.	C, 82nd Ill. Inf.	191		1903 Jun 26	IA, 30th, 1904
Duncan, W.M.		F, 206th Penn.	88		1911 Oct 22	KS, 31st, 1912

*See Appendix A, B or C for roster of post names and locations.
†See Introduction for note regarding recording of death date.

Name	Rank	Company, Regiment or Ship	Post*	Age	Death Date†	Journal
Duncanson, J.A.	Pvt.	I, 11th Minn. Inf.	30		1917	IA, 44th, 1918
Duncomb, Elizabeth, Mrs.		Civil War nurse (nonmember; died at Upland)			1936 Mar 6	NE, 61st, 1937
Dundore, W.E.	Pvt.	K, 167th Penn. Inf.	26		1925 Feb 18	IA, 52nd, 1926
Dune, Fred	Pvt.	D, 27th Iowa Inf.	146		1904 Aug 27	IA, 31st, 1905
Duner, Payson		F, 37th Wis. (died of cancer)	35	76	1920 Jan 22	NE, 45th, 1921
Dunfee, J.		G, 63rd Ind.	51		1902 Oct 15	KS, 22nd, 1903
Dungan, B.F.		I, 17th Ill. Inf.	25		1929 Sep 19	KS, 49th, 1930
Dungan, Francis	Pvt.	E, 6th Iowa Cav.	97		1904 Jan 11	IA, 31st, 1905
Dungan, J.R.			5		1918 Nov 19	IA, 45th, 1919
Dungan, W.O.		A, 30th Ill.	91	83	1922 Mar 8	NE, 47th, 1923
Dungan, W.S.	Col.	34th Iowa Inf.	18		1913 May 5	IA, 40th, 1914
Dungan, Wm.		B, 5th Iowa	13		1926 Feb 7	NE, 51st, 1927
Dunham, A.	Lieut.	F, 12th Iowa Inf.	190		1910 Dec 31	IA, 37th, 1911
Dunham, David H.		D, 25th Mich. Inf.	64		1911 Sep 9	KS, 31st, 1912
Dunham, Fred H.		H, 150th Ohio	258		1913 Jun 15	KS, 33rd, 1914
Dunham, G.C.	Pvt.	F, 26th Mich. Inf.	12		1905 May 14	IA, 32nd, 1906
Dunham, J.L.	Pvt.	F, 42nd Wis. Inf.	391		1920 Oct 16	IA, 47th, 1921
Dunham, W.W.		F, 30th Wis.	57		1916 Jan 20	KS, 36th, 1917
Dunker, Thos. H.	Pvt.		159		1904-1905	IA, 31st, 1905
Dunkerly, John		Penn.	65		1909 Oct	KS, 29th, 1910
Dunkle, A.T.	Pvt.	C, 13th Mich.	40		1923 Mar 29	IA, 50th, 1924
Dunkle, David		H, 13th Iowa Inf. (died of old age, chronic diarrhea at Soldiers & Sailors Home, Grand Island; buried in Omaha, Neb.)	11	72	1905 Jun 10	NE, 30th, 1906
Dunlap, A.T.	Pvt.	I, 16th Iowa Inf.	270		1929 Jul 3	IA, 56th, 1930
Dunlap, Alvin H.		K, 2nd Iowa Inf.	88		1917 Jun 28	KS, 37th, 1918
Dunlap, Benj. J.		G, 44th Mo. Inf.	250		1915 Mar 23	KS, 36th, 1917
Dunlap, Chas.		C, 48th Ind. (died of heart trouble)	120	75	1922 Oct 28	NE, 47th, 1923
Dunlap, D.O.		C, 136th Ohio	63		1923 Nov 28	KS, 43rd, 1924
Dunlap, H.L.		G, — U.S.	1		1904 Apr 6	KS, 24th, 1905
Dunlap, James H.	Sergt.	D, 29th Ind. Inf.	11		1910 Sep 24	IA, 37th, 1911
Dunlap, James R.		F, 7th Ind. Inf.	51		1934 Feb 1	KS, 54th, 1935
Dunlap, John		B, 5th Ill.	127		1906 Oct 10	KS, 26th, 1907
Dunlap, John		E, 1st Nev. Cav.	14		1918 Jan 15	KS, 38th, 1919
Dunlap, L.S.		K, 34th Iowa	25		1923 Mar 17	KS, 43rd, 1924
Dunlap, S.M.	Pvt.	H, 8th Iowa Inf.	12	86	1932 Mar 7	IA, 59th, 1933
Dunlap, T.		I, 78th Penn.	88		1888	KS, 8th, 1889
Dunlap, T.J.		U.S. Navy	78		1907 Oct 17	IA, 34th, 1908
Dunlap, W.D.		B, 147th Ill.	40	72	1919 Feb 7	NE, 44th, 1920
Dunlap, W.L.		I, 56th Ill. Inf. (died of old age)	47	79	1904 Jan 22	NE, 29th, 1905
Dunlavy, H.F.	Musician	G, 2nd Iowa Inf.	10		1915 Dec 3	IA, 42nd, 1916
Dunlavy, John		D, 115th Ind.	36		1922 Jun 26	KS, 43rd, 1924
Dunlavy, John		D, 115th Ind.	100		1922 Jun 26	KS, 42nd, 1923
Dunlavy, Levi	Pvt.	B, 30th Iowa Inf.	10	45	1889 Feb 12	IA, 15th, 1889
Dunmore, J.H.	Pvt.	A, 140th Ill. Inf.	88	85 & 9 mos.	1932 Dec 20	IA, 59th, 1933
Dunn, A.W.	Capt.	B, 11th Ill. Cav.	192		1913 Apr 26	IA, 40th, 1914
Dunn, Charles F.	Pvt.	B, 9th Iowa Cav. (not a member in Iowa at time of death)	235	92	1940 May 31	IA, 67th, 1941
Dunn, Charles F.		B, 9th Iowa Cav.	7		1939 May 31	NE, 64th, 1940
Dunn, David D.		C, 13th Wis. (died of Bright's disease at Soldiers & Sailors Home, Milford)		72	1906 Sep 9	NE, 31st, 1907
Dunn, Elijah		I, 141st Ill.	262	68	1914 Nov 3	NE, 39th, 1915
Dunn, Finley		B, 145th Penn.	25		1930 Aug 25	NE, 55th, 1931
Dunn, Geo. H.		F, 27th Mich.	493		1921 Oct 8	KS, 41st, 1922
Dunn, George E.		D, 95th Ill. Inf. H, 8th Ill. Cav.	71		1901 Apr 10	KS, 21st, 1902
Dunn, Henry		A, 24th Iowa Inf.	164		1912 Aug 16	IA, 39th, 1913
Dunn, Henry		G, 186th Ohio Inf. (cause of death: heart)	77	59	1901 Jun	NE, 26th, 1902
Dunn, Hiram	Sergt.	F, 25th Iowa Inf.	275	55	1889 Aug 9	IA, 16th, 1890
Dunn, J.A.		Ill.	356		1912	KS, 32nd, 1913
Dunn, J.M.		A, 97th Ill.	257		1917 Nov 27	KS, 37th, 1918

*See Appendix A, B or C for roster of post names and locations.
†See Introduction for note regarding recording of death date.

155

Name	Rank	Company, Regiment or Ship	Post*	Age	Death Date†	Journal
Dunn, J.P.			17		1933 Oct 14	KS, 53rd, 1934
Dunn, James	Pvt.	E, 1st Wis. Inf.	68		1925 Oct 6	IA, 52nd, 1926
Dunn, John		C, 6th Kans. Cav.	18		1918 Jun 8	KS, 38th, 1919
Dunn, John H.		C, 19th Ohio	262		1919 Sep 2	NE, 44th, 1920
Dunn, John M.	Musician	I, 1st Iowa Inf.	231	68	1895 Jan 26	IA, 22nd, 1896
Dunn, Peter N.		U.S. Marine Corps	193		1917	IA, 44th, 1918
Dunn, Robert		I, R.I. Art.	12		1924 Feb 5	KS, 44th, 1925
Dunn, S.C.	1st Sergt.	H, 11th Iowa Inf.	231		1899 Jan 4	IA, 26th, 1900
Dunn, Samuel H.		I, 37th Ind. Inf.	12		1909 Jul 18	KS, 29th, 1910
Dunn, W.H.		I, 58th Vt. Inf.	262	74	1919 Jan 31	NE, 43rd, 1919
Dunn, W.H.		G, 125th Penn.	262		1919 Jan 31	NE, 44th, 1920
Dunn, W.W.		C, 49th Iowa Inf. (died of chronic diarrhea)	191	32	1903 Dec 18	NE, 28th, 1904
Dunn, William	Pvt.	H, 45th Wis. Inf.	216		1925 Feb 8	IA, 52nd, 1926
Dunn, William		K, 3rd Iowa Cav.	14		1914 Aug 20	KS, 34th, 1915
Dunn, Wm. C.	Pvt.	D, 5th Wis. Battery	45		1912 Feb 3	IA, 39th, 1913
Dunnell, L.W.		G, 3rd Colo.	203		1922 Dec 22	KS, 42nd, 1923
Dunnett, D.W.			17		1903[1902?] Apr 21	KS, 22nd, 1903
Dunning, Chas.		D, 6th Mich.	38		1930 Feb	NE, 55th, 1931
Dunning, D.D.	Lieut.	B, 8th Ill. Cav.	111		1911 Jan 10	IA, 38th, 1912
Dunning, E.N.	Pvt.	B, 41st Wis. Inf.	236		1927 Sep 16	IA, 54th, 1928
Dunning, W.J.		A, 35th N.J.	100		1926 Jan 18	KS, 46th, 1927
Dunning, Wm. H.		I, 73rd Ill. Inf.	133	63	1901 Apr	NE, 26th, 1902
Dunnivan, Dan			12		1922 Mar 18	KS, 42nd, 1923
Dunsan, B.F.		F, 4th Mo. Cav.	127		1908 Mar 16	KS, 28th, 1909
Dunstan, Samuel		C, 31st Wis.	226		1904 Apr 26	KS, 24th, 1905
Dunster, Isaiah H.	Pvt.	A, 8th Iowa Inf.	88		1916 Nov 29	IA, 43rd, 1917
Dunster, T.E.		U.S. Navy	19		1891 May 15	KS, 11th, 1892
Dunston, John		I, 7th Ill. Cav.	309		1912 Sep 21	KS, 32nd, 1913
Dunsworth, J.T.		D, 32nd Ill. Inf.	435		1918 Apr 17	KS, 38th, 1919
Dunton, C.P.	Pvt.	K, 21st Iowa	190		1921 Aug 21	IA, 48th, 1922
Dunton, Milton		G, 2nd Ill. Lt. Art.	7		1926 Sep 25	NE, 51st, 1927
Dunton, Robt.		E, 18th Iowa	73		1898 Sep 1	KS, 18th, 1899
DuPont, Cassius		16th Ill.	116		1927 Apr 2	KS, 47th, 1928
Duran, Alfred		D, 10th Ill. Inf. (died of heart disease)	147		1893 Nov 9	NE, 18th, 1894
Durand, Amos M.	Surg.	50th Ind. Inf.	25		1891 Jul 8	KS, 11th, 1892
Durand, F.M.		58th Ind. Inf.	17		1914 Jan 15	KS, 34th, 1915
Durand, O.H.	Sergt.	see Appendix D	77		1917 Mar 14	NE, 41st, 1917
Durand, Oliver H.		G, 115th Ill. (died of acute indigestion)	79	75	1917 Mar 11	NE, 42nd, 1918
Durand, W.W.	Pvt.	F, 93rd Ill. Inf.	88		1918 Jul 22	IA, 46th, 1920
Durant, A.H.	Pvt.	A, 32nd Iowa Inf.	165		1906 Jul 21	IA, 33rd, 1907
Durant, W.E.		B, 33rd Ill.	88		1928 Dec 6	KS, 48th, 1929
Durberrow, John		F, 49th Ohio Inf.	293		1925 Oct 3	KS, 45th, 1926
Durbin, Henry		C, 10th Ind.	257		1926 Jan 24	KS, 46th, 1927
Durby, M.R.	Sergt.	C, 32nd Wis. Inf.	193		1909 Aug 11	IA, 36th, 1910
Duree, James		H, 146th Ohio	71		1919 Dec 8	KS, 39th, 1920
Durell, W.R.		C, 111th Ill. Inf.	422		1914 Nov 10	KS, 34th, 1915
Durem, N.P.			153		1884	KS, 4th, 1885
Durest, Mathias	Sergt.	K, 9th Wis. Inf.	149		1917 Jun 24	IA, 44th, 1918
Durgan, W.O.		F, 2nd Mo.	265		1919	KS, 39th, 1920
Durghart, A.		B, 173rd Ohio	290		1895 Aug 29	KS, 16th, 1897
Durgin, John C.	Pvt.	K, 21st Wis. Inf.	339		1915	IA, 42nd, 1916
Durgin, N.S.	Pvt.	D, 5th N.H. Inf.	216		1920 Dec 12	IA, 47th, 1921
Durgwall, John	Pvt.	H, 29th Wis. Inf.	97	75	1898 Jan 2	IA, 24th, 1898
Durham, C.J.			97		1911 May 24	KS, 31st, 1912
Durham, L.L.	Corp.	C, 6th Iowa Inf.	395	67	1897 Mar 11	IA, 24th, 1898
Durham, Samuel		M, 6th Kans.	51		1917 May 11	KS, 37th, 1918
Durien, Andrew		F, 158th Penn.	18		1922 Apr 10	KS, 42nd, 1923
Durisch, T.S.		B, 8th Iowa Inf.	25	74	1921 Jun 27	NE, 46th, 1922
Durkee, Geo. F.		9th Vt.	58		1892 Feb 29	KS, 12th, 1893
Durkee, H.	Pvt.	B, 5th & 2nd Wis.	377		1899 Jun 23	IA, 26th, 1900

*See Appendix A, B or C for roster of post names and locations.
†See Introduction for note regarding recording of death date.

156

Name	Rank	Company, Regiment or Ship	Post*	Age	Death Date†	Journal
Durkee, Miles F.		B, 12th Inf. (died at Soldiers & Sailors Home, Grand Island; buried at Ulysses, Neb.)	24	71	1905 Oct 18	NE, 30th, 1906
Durkee, Miles F.		B, 12th Minn. Inf. (died of paralysis)	73	71	1905 Oct 18	NE, 30th, 1906
Durkin, Michael		5th Penn. Cav.	67		1899 Feb 12	KS, 19th, 1900
Durkin, Pat		A, 143rd Penn. Vol. Inf.	63		1916 Feb 21	KS, 36th, 1917
Durrand, James W.			25		1925[1935?] Oct 17	KS, 55th, 1936
Durstin, Martin V.	Pvt.	B, 147th Ill. Inf.	80	46	1888 Feb 11	IA, 16th, 1890
Durston, E.W., see Duiston, E.W.						
Duryea, A.P.		A, 5th N.Y.	69		1920 Oct 28	KS, 40th, 1921
Dust, David	Pvt.	M, 9th Iowa Cav.	68		1909 Oct 22	IA, 36th, 1910
Dutch, Peter		H, 48th Ind. Inf. (died of hemorrhage bladder)	270		1892 Jul 1	KS, 12th, 1893
Dutcher, D.H.	Pvt.	G, 126th Ill. Inf.	8		1902 Aug 29	IA, 29th, 1903
Dutcher, John	Pvt.	B, 43rd Mo. Mtd. Inf.	66	60	1898 Jun 23	IA, 25th, 1899
Dutcher, John A.		A, 1st N.Y.	420		1898 Aug 13	KS, 18th, 1899
Dutro, Franklin		C, 66th Ill. Inf. (at large)			1932	IA, 59th, 1933
Dutton, H.A.		I, 11th Kans. Cav.	35		1919 Feb 7	KS, 39th, 1920
Dutton, J.C.		D, 7th Mich. Inf. (at large)		96	1935 Dec 21	IA, 62nd, 1936
Dutton, James C.		A, 99th Ind. Inf. (died of disease of lungs)	289		1891 Apr 23	KS, 11th, 1892
Dutton, L.K.	Corp.	39th Ohio	40	51	1890 Jan 23	IA, 18th, 1892
Dutton, S.J.	Lieut.	A, 48th Iowa Inf.	40		1930 May 19	IA, 57th, 1931
Dutton, S.W.		K, 7th Iowa Inf. (died of consumption)	45		1894 Dec 5	NE, 19th, 1895
Duval, Jesse W.		H, 7th Iowa Cav.	167		1911 Dec 25	KS, 31st, 1912
Duval, V.A.	Pvt.	E, 25th Ohio Inf.	298	54	1895 Jan 18	IA, 22nd, 1896
Duvall, J.F., Dr.	Surg.	105th Ill.	28		1913 Feb 20	KS, 33rd, 1914
Dvan, G.	Pvt.		156		1920	IA, 47th, 1921
Dwiggins, Cyrus		G, 75th Ind.	1		1921 Sep	KS, 41st, 1922
Dwiggins, Joseph	Pvt.	A, 1st Iowa Cav.	14		1918 Jun 11	IA, 45th, 1919
Dwire, Benjamin F.	Pvt.	K, 9th Ind. Inf.	156		1893 Jul 4	IA, 20th, 1894
Dwire, John	Farrier	F, 4th Iowa Cav.	107		1915 Jun 21	IA, 42nd, 1916
Dwyer, Edwin	Pvt.	C, 1st Wis. Cav. (died of fever)	140	53	1887 Nov	NE, 12th, 1888
Dwyer, M.		D, 115th Ind.	4		1896 Oct 21	KS, 16th, 1897
Dwyer, Wm.	Pvt.	E, 47th Ill. Vol. Inf.	465	56	1898 Dec 29	IA, 25th, 1899
Dwyer, Wm.		C, 78th N.Y.	380		1896 Nov 18	KS, 16th, 1897
Dyart, Alex		died in asylum	185		1893 Sep 25	KS, 13th, 1894
Dye, B.F.		H, 3rd West Va. Cav.	364		1916 Mar	KS, 36th, 1917
Dye, F.		130th Ill.	247		1908[1909?]	KS, 29th, 1910
Dye, James			23		1899	NE, 24th, 1900
Dye, L.C.		H, 100th Ill. Inf. (died at Crawford County; buried at Union Cemetery)	49		1894 Jul 1	KS, 14th, 1895
Dye, Nathan		K, 187th Ohio Inf. (died of heart disease)	321	73	1895 May 5	NE, 20th, 1896
Dye, Pearson	Pvt.	D, 16th Iowa Inf.	244	56	1898 May 10	IA, 24th, 1898
Dye, William H.		I, 7th Ohio Bat.	72		1913 Jan 27	KS, 33rd, 1914
Dyer, Dennis			322		1919 Sep 5	IA, 46th, 1920
Dyer, Henry A.	Pvt.	C, 21st Iowa Inf. (see also Appendix D)	42		1912 Jul 24	IA, 39th, 1913
Dyer, J.H.	Corp.	E, 1st Ill. Lt. Art.	271		1903 Mar 10	IA, 30th, 1904
Dyer, James A.	Pvt.	B, 6th Iowa Cav.	42		1907 Jan 24	IA, 34th, 1908
Dyer, John		K, 18th Ohio Inf. 2nd West Va. Cav.	85		1918 Jul 26	KS, 38th, 1919
Dyer, John			40		1919 Mar 23	KS, 39th, 1920
Dyer, N.C.		H, 141st Penn.	63		1921 Oct 24	KS, 41st, 1922
Dyer, W.R.			67		1922 May 3	IA, 49th, 1923
Dyers, J.F.		G, 25th Ill. Inf. (died of paralysis)	13	63	1905 Oct 19	NE, 30th, 1906
Dyke, E.B.	Pvt.	C, 47th Iowa Inf.	3	54	1897 Oct 29	IA, 24th, 1898
Dykeman, Geo. W.	Sergt.	D, 13th Wis. Inf.	77	65	1893 Aug 15	IA, 20th, 1894
Dyman, Jas.		K, 100th Ohio	14		1906 Sep 6	KS, 26th, 1907
Dysart, Gideon	Trumpeter	G, 7th Iowa Cav.	12		1928 May 27	IA, 55th, 1929
Dysart, Wm.		F, 310th Ohio Inf. (died of old age)	63	87	1924 Dec 13	NE, 49th, 1925
Dyson, J.H.	Pvt.	D, 6th Iowa Cav.	408	59	1888 Oct 5	IA, 15th, 1889
Dytch, John	Pvt.	G, 32nd Wis.	42		1903 Sep 20	IA, 30th, 1904
Dziewanowfki, K.	Pvt.	6th Wis. Batt.	42		1929 Jun 14	IA, 56th, 1930

*See Appendix A, B or C for roster of post names and locations.
†See Introduction for note regarding recording of death date.

Name	Rank	Company, Regiment or Ship	Post*	Age	Death Date†	Journal
Eade, John	Pvt.	G, 57th Ill.	231		1923 Sep 3	IA, 50th, 1924
Eads, George			231		1929 Apr 28	IA, 56th, 1930
Eads, William	Pvt.	F, 36th Iowa Inf.	398	66	1893 Jan 18	IA, 19th, 1893
Eagal, Jos. P.	Pvt.	I, 44th Iowa Inf.	1		1923 Nov 4	IA, 50th, 1924
Eager, Amos	Pvt.	I, 124th N.Y. Inf.	177		1906 Apr 17	IA, 33rd, 1907
Eager, Amos		D, 7th Wis.	25		1932 Aug 5	NE, 57th, 1933
Eager, Peter, Dr.		H, 7th N.Y. Inf.	28			KS, 7th, 1888
Eagle, John A.		A, 10th Penn. Vol. Inf.	63		1887	KS, 7th, 1888
Eagle, T.A.		I, 16th Ohio	244		1912 May 16	KS, 32nd, 1913
Eagle, T.A.		I, 16th Ohio	244		1931 Aug 2	KS, 52nd, 1933
Eakins, Geo. P.	Sergt.	D, 5th Iowa Inf.	88	55	1931 Aug 2	KS, 51st, 1932
Eakins, S.R.		B, 70th Ohio	74		1892 Apr 2	IA, 19th, 1893
Ealey, G.B.		H, 86th Ohio	28		1921 Jun 30	KS, 41st, 1922
Eames, J.B.		L, 3rd Ill. Cav.	1		1904 May 4	KS, 24th, 1905
Earhart, C.	Pvt.	C, 35th Ind. Inf.	38		1918 Mar 6	KS, 38th, 1919
Earhart, E.H.		A, 37th Ill. Inf.	12		1908 May 1	IA, 35th, 1909
Earhart, Geo. A.	Pvt.	D, 1st Iowa Cav.	235		1925 Sep 24	IA, 52nd, 1926
Earhart, Wm.	Pvt.	C, 198th Ohio Inf.	77		1924 Sep 15	IA, 51st, 1925
Earl, Erain	Pvt.	E, 28th Mich. Inf.	231		1933 Jan 25	IA, 60th, 1934
Earl, George		D, 7th Ill. Cav. (died of old age)	143	89	1925 Feb 17	IA, 52nd, 1926
Earl, Henry	Pvt.	M, 3rd Mich. Cav.	231		1922 Aug 20	NE, 47th, 1923
Earl, Irving		K, 11th —	350		1915 Oct 18	IA, 42nd, 1916
Earl, John			142		1899 Apr 10	KS, 19th, 1900
Earl, W.H.		4th Ind. Battery	75		1925 Jul 4	KS, 45th, 1926
Earl, W.H.		D, 12th Kans.	36		1885	KS, 5th, 1886
Earle, J.J.	Pvt.	F, 3rd Iowa Inf.	48	92	1929 Feb 19	KS, 49th, 1930
Earlenbugh, Andrew		C, 125th Penn.	2		1932 Jan 28	IA, 59th, 1933
Earls, Wm. D.		H, 104th Ill. Inf. (died of asthma)	41	63	1918 Dec 23	KS, 38th, 1919
Earlwine, Thos.	Pvt.	G, 8th Kans. Inf.	103		1905 Aug 24	NE, 30th, 1906
Early, Geo. G.	Sergt.	I, 3rd Ohio Inf.	16		1915 Jul 31	IA, 42nd, 1916
Earnest, Wm. H., Dr.	Pvt. Pvt.	D, 150th Ohio D, 189th Ohio Inf.	186, 192	96, 3 mos. & 6 days	1913 Jan 4 1945 Mar 4	IA, 40th, 1914 IA, 71st, 1945
Earnst, Albert		B, 12th Ill. Cav.	25	92	1918 Feb 2	NE, 43rd, 1919
Earp, F.			45		1921 Jan 27	IA, 48th, 1922
Ears, Fred	Pvt.	I, 32nd Iowa Inf.	1		1905 Mar 14	IA, 32nd, 1906
Earwood, E.	Corp.	I, 36th Ohio Inf.	349		1910 Feb 13	IA, 37th, 1911
Easha, Jos.	Pvt.	A, 105th Ill. Inf.	68		1908 Aug 29	IA, 35th, 1909
Eason, Jas. H.		C, 1st Ky. Cav.	18		1917 Jun 5	KS, 37th, 1918
East, Henry		K, 149th Ind. Inf.	57	77	1902 Jun	NE, 27th, 1903
Easter, Franklin		G, 108th Ill. Inf. (died of heart failure)	152	60	1905[1904?] Jun 27	NE, 29th, 1905
Easter, S.R.	Corp.	A, 175th Ohio	127		1924 May 4	IA, 51st, 1925
Easterly, A.N.	Pvt.	B, 24th Iowa Inf.	228		1918 Jan 22	IA, 45th, 1919
Easterly, J.N.	Pvt.	A, 13th Iowa Inf.	400		1921 Jun 2	IA, 48th, 1922
Easterly, W.H.	Corp.	F, 13th Iowa Inf.	88		1930 Feb 15	IA, 57th, 1931
Eastin, W.M.		K, 62nd Ill.	252		1920 Feb 11	KS, 40th, 1921
Eastland, Geo. J.	Pvt.	D, 13th Iowa	104		1926 Jan 31	IA, 53rd, 1927
Eastlick, A.S.		E, 148th Ill.	87		1911 Apr 6	KS, 31st, 1912
Eastling, William		G, 30th Ill. Inf.	477		1925	KS, 45th, 1926
Eastman, A.J.		B, 49th Wis. Inf.	477		1914 Mar 8	KS, 34th, 1915
Eastman, C.		B, 34th Ill. Inf. (died of old age)	152		1908 Mar 1	NE, 33rd, 1909
Eastman, Chas.			44		1901	NE, 26th, 1902
Eastman, D.W.	1st Lieut. & Adjt.	H, Merrill's Horse (died at his home in Enid, Okla.) (see Appendix D)			1912 Jun 23	KS, 32nd, 1913
Eastman, G.W.		H, 150th Penn. Inf. (died of pneumonia)	110		1893 Dec 26	NE, 18th, 1894
Eastman, Ira		B, 6th Mich.	28		1900 Mar 23	KS, 20th, 1901
Eastman, J.O.		I, 93rd Ill. (died of heart trouble)	2	72	1915 Jul 16	NE, 40th, 1916
Eastman, John		D, 114th Ill.	51		1933 Jul 10	KS, 53rd, 1934
Eastman, N.B.		C, 39th Maine	127		1896 Sep 16	KS, 16th, 1897
Eastman, Reuben		K, 34th Ill.	12		1915 Aug 4	NE, 35th, 1916
Eastman, S.B.		Mich. Art.	24	68	1912 Aug 8	NE, 37th, 1913
Eastman, Samuel D.		C & B, 23rd & 48th Wis.	25		1913 May 22	NE, 38th, 1914

*See Appendix A, B or C for roster of post names and locations.
†See Introduction for note regarding recording of death date.
158

Name	Rank	Company, Regiment or Ship	Post*	Age	Death Date†	Journal
Eastmond, J.S.		C, 48th Ill.	50		1908 Jan 13	KS, 28th, 1909
Easton, Alex		E, 34th Ohio	42		1929 Mar 6	KS, 49th, 1930
Easton, C.H.		D, 8th Ill.	237		1898 Apr 6	KS, 18th, 1899
Easton, James	1st Lieut.	G, 135th Ill. Vols.	59		1901 Dec 10	IA, 28th, 1902
Easton, John A.		Y, 4th Iowa Inf. (died of heart failure)	47	78	1919 Mar 12	NE, 44th, 1920
Eastwood, D.			6		1921	IA, 48th, 1922
Eastwood, Daniel	Pvt.		6		1923	IA, 50th, 1924
Easty, Martin J.	Pvt.	I, 24th Iowa Inf.	74	50	1894 Aug 23	IA, 21st, 1895
Eaton, A.A.	Pvt.	F, 8th Iowa Inf.	514		1899	IA, 26th, 1900
Eaton, C.B.	Pvt.	B, Ill. Art.	190		1905 Jul 27	IA, 32nd, 1906
Eaton, David			74		1905	IA, 32nd, 1906
Eaton, Edwin	Pvt.	F, 9th Iowa Cav.	77		1900 Dec 17	IA, 27th, 1901
Eaton, Frank		I, 4th Mich. Cav. (died of consumption)	262	59	1911 Nov 1	NE, 36th, 1912
Eaton, Frank		I, 4th Mich. Cav. (died of consumption)	262	59	1905 Nov 1	NE, 30th, 1906
Eaton, Geo. L.	Pvt.	C, 36th N.H. Inf.	497		1913 Oct 30	IA, 40th, 1914
Eaton, Henry	Pvt.	D, 10th Ind.	12		1926 Jun 18	IA, 53rd, 1927
Eaton, Henry		G, 9th Ind. (died of hemorrhage of bowels)	245	70	1908 Jul 12	NE, 33rd, 1909
Eaton, Henry W.		B, 45th Inf. (died of heart failure)	149	70	1916 Jan 29	NE, 41st, 1917
Eaton, Ira K.	Sergt.	B, 36th Ohio Inf.	152		1908	IA, 35th, 1909
Eaton, J.C.	Pvt.	H, 33rd Iowa Inf.	145		1913 Feb	IA, 40th, 1914
Eaton, J.S.		E, 50th Mass. (died of old age)	327	86	1913 Dec 19	NE, 38th, 1914
Eaton, J.W.		9th Ohio	129		1923 Dec 29	KS, 43rd, 1924
Eaton, Jasper	Bugler	I, 2nd Iowa Cav.	333		1903 Nov 30	IA, 30th, 1904
Eaton, Levi J.		H, 8th Iowa	115		1918 Oct 25	KS, 38th, 1919
Eaton, M.D.		H, 34th Iowa	115		1930 Jan	KS, 50th, 1931
Eaton, M.D.		E, 34th Iowa	112		1931 Jan 6	KS, 51st, 1932
Eaton, M.D.		E, 34th Iowa	112		1931 Jan 6	KS, 52nd, 1933
Eaton, O.M.		H, 2nd U.S. Sharpshooters	7		1927 May 21	NE, 52nd, 1928
Eaton, P.B.		H, 11th Ill. Cav.	87		1909 Feb 23	KS, 29th, 1910
Eaton, Thomas			29		1927 May 7	IA, 54th, 1928
Eaton, U.H.	Capt.	I, 18th Ill. Inf.	71	69	1898 Oct 1	IA, 25th, 1899
Eaton, W.H.			417		1917	IA, 44th, 1918
Eayres, Nelson P.	Corp.	F, 10th Wis. Inf.	97		1909 Aug 7	IA, 36th, 1910
Ebarhart, Albert G.	Musician	C, 2nd Iowa Inf.	343	62	1897 Jan 19	IA, 24th, 1898
Ebeling, John		A, 44th Ill.	107		1918	KS, 38th, 1919
Ebenizer, H.		K, 139th Ill. Inf. (died of disease of bowels)	23	58	1902 Aug	NE, 27th, 1903
Ebenstine, C.F.		B, 69th Ind.	123		1898 Dec 26	KS, 18th, 1899
Eberhardt, Chris			127		1922 Dec 26	KS, 42nd, 1923
Eberhart, A.C.		D, 10th Ill. Inf. (died of long sickness)	32	79	1911	NE, 36th, 1912
Eberhart, Albert G., see Ebarhart, Albert G.						
Eberhart, Charles		A, 37th Ohio Inf.	380		1902 Oct 10	KS, 22nd, 1903
Eberhart, Fred			236		1914 May 6	IA, 41st, 1915
Eberhart, Gustavus A.	Lieut. Col.	33rd Iowa Inf.	12		1916 Jun 30	IA, 43rd, 1917
Eberhart, John		H, 8th Iowa Cav.	239		1914 Nov 9	KS, 34th, 1915
Eberhart, John		D, 35th Iowa Inf. (died of old age)	34		1903	NE, 28th, 1904
Eberhart, Jos. E.		H, 37th Ill. Inf. (died of complications)	159	63	1901 Jul	NE, 26th, 1902
Eberhart, W.A.P.	Chaplain	1st Penn. Art.	235	80	1899 Feb 15	IA, 25th, 1899
Eberline, Ferdinand		A, 58th Ohio	385		1913 Jun 20	KS, 33rd, 1914
Eberly, Henry S.			519		1916	IA, 43rd, 1917
Eberly, John	Corp., Comm. Sergt., QM Sergt.	F, 19th Ohio Inf. (see Appendix D)	190		1914 Apr 3	NE, 38th, 1914
Eberly, P.C.	Pvt.	A, 22nd Iowa	22		1923 Nov 26	IA, 50th, 1924
Eberly, Samuel		A, 169th Ohio	25		1926 Oct 24	KS, 46th, 1927
Ebersole, C.A.	Pvt.	D, 32nd Iowa Inf.	4		1897-1898	IA, 24th, 1898
Ebersole, John W.	Pvt.	B, 142nd Penn. Inf.	343		1910 Sep 26	IA, 37th, 1911
Ebersole, W.O.		B, 1st Colo. Cav. (died of paralysis)	63	80	1920 Apr 1	NE, 45th, 1921
Eberstein, Henry		C, 1st Mich.	68		1922 Apr 1	KS, 42nd, 1923
Ebert, Henry	Pvt.		57		1929	IA, 56th, 1930
Ebert, Henry A.		I, 116th Ill.	129		1927 Jan 19	KS, 50th, 1931
Ebert, Henry I.		I, 116th Ill.	129		1927 Jan 19	KS, 48th, 1929

*See Appendix A, B or C for roster of post names and locations.
†See Introduction for note regarding recording of death date.

159

Name	Rank	Company, Regiment or Ship	Post*	Age	Death Date†	Journal
Ebling, John		9th Ill. Cav.	435		1914 Mar 27	KS, 34th, 1915
Ebright, Phillip		C, 140th Ohio	69		1911 Jul 16	KS, 31st, 1912
Eby, A.F.		G, 54th Ind.	23		1920 Jan 15	KS, 40th, 1921
Eby, E.N.		A, 107th Ill.	42		1909 Mar 28	KS, 29th, 1910
Eby, Henry M.		D, 2nd Neb. Cav. (died of heart failure)	55	73	1911 Jan 4	NE, 36th, 1912
Eby, John		K, 47th Ill.	3		1913 Apr 29	KS, 33rd, 1914
Eby, Nathan J.		B, 7th Ill.	17		1918 Mar 21	KS, 38th, 1919
Eby, W.H.		C, 64th Ohio	12	92	1934 Sep 30	IA, 61st, 1935
Eccarius, John	Pvt.	G, 135th Ohio Inf.	22		1911	IA, 38th, 1912
Echler, Henry	Pvt.	I, 4th Iowa	190		1904 Oct 10	IA, 31st, 1905
Eck, Alfred		A, 6th Penn.	12		1921 Aug 9	KS, 41st, 1922
Eckart, Seb.		K, 17th Mo. Inf.	146		2nd quarter 1884	IA, 11th, 1885
Eckart, Wm. F.		E, 11th Kans.	457		1905	KS, 25th, 1906
Eckdall, Jonas		2nd Ill. Lt. Art.	55		1914 Nov 21	KS, 34th, 1915
Eckel, Chas.		1st Wis. Hvy. Art.	66		1918 Nov	KS, 38th, 1919
Eckels, Amos		E, 103rd Penn.	176		1919 Feb 4	KS, 39th, 1920
Ecker, Alonzo	Pvt.	M, 3rd N.Y. Lt. Art.	147	67	1900 Feb 19	IA, 26th, 1900
Ecker, Geo. W.		F, 3rd Iowa	87		1922 Apr 4	KS, 42nd, 1923
Ecker, John			371		1909	IA, 36th, 1910
Eckerman, Jerry B.			108		1922 Oct 3	IA, 49th, 1923
Eckersly, Henry H.	Corp.	U.S. Marines	247		1917 Oct 26	IA, 44th, 1918
Eckerson, J.C.	Pvt.	E, 13th Iowa Inf.	452		1920 Dec 30	IA, 47th, 1921
Eckerson, Sherod A.	Sergt.	A, 10th Wis.	12		1909 Apr 7	IA, 36th, 1910
Eckert, J.F.		G, 70th Ohio	57		1912 Jun 6	KS, 32nd, 1913
Eckhardt, A.		H, 4th Ill. Cav. (died of cancer)	95	63	1905 Sep	NE, 30th, 1906
Eckhart, Elius					1929 Feb 6	NE, 53rd, 1929
Eckles, Charles	Capt.	B, 34th Iowa Inf.	94		1932 Jul 9	IA, 59th, 1933
Eckles, Elkanah		L, 8th Mo.	75		1912 Aug 29	KS, 32nd, 1913
Eckles, W.T.		L, 8th Mo. Cav.	53		1910 Oct 26	KS, 30th, 1911
Eckley, Jas.		E, 4th Ky.	4		1918 Feb 20	KS, 38th, 1919
Eckley, P.L.		F, 8th Iowa Inf.	167		4th quarter 1883	IA, 10th, 1884
Eckman, B.	Pvt.	H, 45th Ill. Inf.	451	72	1896 Mar 16	IA, 23rd, 1897
Eckroat, Chris.			69		1899	IA, 26th, 1900
Eckroat, John	Pvt.	C, 33rd Iowa Inf.	40		1904 Sep 16	IA, 31st, 1905
Ecord, James			380		1925 May 5	KS, 45th, 1926
Edaburn, Benjamin	Pvt.	I, 81st Ohio Inf.	440	54	1897 Apr 2	IA, 23rd, 1897
Eddinger, Wm.	Pvt.	I, 152nd Ohio Inf.	332	55	1887 Sep 3	IA, 14th, 1888
Eddy, A.		E, 95th Ill.	113	83	1908 Nov 19	NE, 33rd, 1909
Eddy, A.J.	Pvt.	F, 14th Iowa Inf.	34		1910 Oct 20	IA, 37th, 1911
Eddy, Geo. B.		I, 8th Vt. C, 41st Ill. Inf. (death not reported till 1889)	14		1889	KS, 9th, 1890
Eddy, H.C.		K, 11th Minn.	236	90	1934 Nov 8	IA, 61st, 1935
Eddy, Henry H.	1st Lieut.	F, 93rd Ill. Inf.	98		1900 Dec 26	IA, 27th, 1901
Eddy, James	Pvt.	15th Ohio Battery	94		1906	IA, 33rd, 1907
Eddy, John		L, 1st U.S. Eng.	17		1910 Aug 22	KS, 30th, 1911
Eddy, L.	Pvt.	G, 8th Iowa Inf.	40		1920 Jan 29	IA, 47th, 1921
Eddy, Lander A.		D, 116th Ohio	11[12?]		1911 Apr 24	KS, 31st, 1912
Eddy, N.E.		K, 70th Ind.	85		1926 Feb 19	KS, 46th, 1927
Eddy, Samuel	Pvt.	I, 3rd Iowa Cav.	519		1906 Jun 20	IA, 33rd, 1907
Eddy, W.A.	Pvt.	G, 105th Ill. Inf.	12		1928 Aug 15	IA, 55th, 1929
Eddy, Wm.	Pvt.	B, 42nd Ohio	81		1905 Mar 1	IA, 32nd, 1906
Eddy, Wm. L.		K, 25th Mass. Inf.	49		1935 Apr 9	KS, 55th, 1936
Edelblute, W.H.		G, 11th Kans.	100		1908 May 28	KS, 28th, 1909
Edelman, G.			164		1921 Aug 7	IA, 48th, 1922
Edenburn, Jas. W.		I, 23rd Ill. (died of stomach trouble)	63		1915 Oct 8	NE, 40th, 1916
Ederer, Andrew	Pvt.	I, 15th Mo. Inf.	2	47	1887 May 14	IA, 14th, 1888
Edgar, George B.		D, 1st Kans. State Militia	12		1912 Jan 16	KS, 32nd, 1913
Edgar, Samuel		died of paralysis	84		1911 Mar 19	NE, 36th, 1912
Edgarton, John	Pvt.	F, 89th Ill. Inf.	40	79	1879 Feb 24	IA, 18th, 1892
Edger, Chas. W.	Pvt.	E, 13th Wis. Inf.	452		1927 Jul 3	IA, 54th, 1928
Edgerley, F.W.		I, 132nd Ill.	142		1905 Feb 24	KS, 25th, 1906

*See Appendix A, B or C for roster of post names and locations.
†See Introduction for note regarding recording of death date.

Name	Rank	Company, Regiment or Ship	Post*	Age	Death Date†	Journal
Edgerton, A.S.		I, 29th Iowa	84		1911 Jul 26	KS, 31st, 1912
Edgerton, G.H.		E, 112th Ill. (died of paralysis)	13	81	1923 Dec 10	NE, 48th, 1924
Edgerton, John, see Edgarton, John						
Edgerton, Joseph V.	Pvt.	D, 34th Iowa Inf.	309		1915 Aug 29	IA, 42nd, 1916
Edgeton, Charles	Pvt.	D, 92nd Ill. Inf.	252		1900 Nov 7	IA, 27th, 1901
Edgington, Abraham		C, 129th Ill.	68		1918 Aug 2	KS, 38th, 1919
Edgington, F.M.	Pvt.	F, 35th Iowa Inf.	231		1912 Mar 15	IA, 39th, 1913
Edgington, S.R.	Capt.	A, 12th Iowa Inf.	154	56	1888 May 20	IA, 15th, 1889
Edgington, W.W.	Lieut.	B, 24th Iowa Inf.	68		1912 Jul 24	IA, 39th, 1913
Edgren, A.H.	1st Lieut.	B, 99th N.Y. Inf. (cause of death: heart)	214		1903 Dec 10	NE, 28th, 1904
Edie, J.S.		1st & 2nd Kans.	314		1892	KS, 12th, 1893
Edinborough, C.D.	Pvt.	C, 65th N.Y. Inf.	152	54	1892 Nov 17	IA, 19th, 1893
Edington, John F.	Pvt.	B, 24th Iowa	68		1907 Nov 7	IA, 34th, 1908
Edington, P.A.	Sergt.	H, 90th Ohio Inf.	72		1912 Jun 9	IA, 39th, 1913
Edminister, J.D.			63		1907 Nov	NE, 32nd, 1908
Edmiston, J.M.		I, 173rd Ohio Inf. (died at Burden, Kans.; buried at Burden Cemetery)	172		1894 Nov 24	KS, 14th, 1895
Edmiston, Miles B.		H, 39th Ill. Inf. (died at Paola)	117		1895 May 3	KS, 15th, 1896
Edmonds, Geo.			122		1912	IA, 39th, 1913
Edmonds, Robt. L.	Pvt.	F, 23rd Iowa Inf.	11		1915 Dec 22	IA, 42nd, 1916
Edmondson, Eli		I, 53rd Ohio	458		1891 Jun 9	KS, 16th, 1897
Edmondson, James M.		I, 63rd Ohio	458		1916	KS, 36th, 1917
Edmonson, E.	Pvt.	C, 40th Ind.	203		1921 Aug 25	IA, 48th, 1922
Edmonson, G.A.	Pvt.	D, 22nd Iowa Inf.	231		1920 Sep 2	IA, 47th, 1921
Edmonson, Henry B.	Pvt.	I, 12th Iowa Inf.	177		1910 Sep 18	IA, 37th, 1911
Edmonson, James		I, 129th Ill. Inf.	[18?]		1901 Apr 24	KS, 21st, 1902
Edmunds, D.R.	R. Major	E, 35th Ky. Inf.	91		1927 Sep 3	IA, 54th, 1928
Edmunds, E.E.		H, 40th Ind. Inf.	10	70	1913 May 5	NE, 38th, 1914
Edsall, Peter		E, 30th Ind.	90		1928 Apr 26	KS, 48th, 1929
Edson, John	Pvt.	E, 10th Minn. Inf.	101		1928 May 31	IA, 55th, 1929
Edson, John	Pvt.	E, 10th Minn. Inf.	101		1927 May 31	IA, 54th, 1928
Edson, Samuel	Pvt.	F, 16th V.R.C.	284		1919 Aug 20	IA, 46th, 1920
Edson, Willis		A, 84th Ill.	1		1911 May 1	KS, 31st, 1912
Edson, Wm.	Pvt.	I, 32nd Iowa Inf.	370	65	1895 Feb 22	IA, 22nd, 1896
Edwards, A.F.		L, 1st Ky. Cav.	81		1919 Dec 2	KS, 39th, 1920
Edwards, A.H., see Ewards, A.H.						
Edwards, Abraham	Pvt.	K, 60th U.S.C.T.	459		1900 Jul 11	IA, 27th, 1901
Edwards, Abram	Pvt.	K, 60th U.S.C. Inf.	459		1900 Jul 11	IA, 27th, 1901
Edwards, B.		B, 116th Ohio	38		1913 Jul 23	KS, 33rd, 1914
Edwards, B.W.		A, 18th Ill.	251		1923 Sep 25	KS, 43rd, 1924
Edwards, C.		K, 39th Mo.	50		1911	KS, 31st, 1912
Edwards, C.L.		D, 37th Mass. Inf.	12		1916 Nov 22	KS, 36th, 1917
Edwards, D.F.		G, 49th Wis. (died of heart failure)	82		1904 Oct 9	NE, 29th, 1905
Edwards, D.L.	Pvt.	K, 55th Penn. Inf.	197		1926 Jun 27	IA, 53rd, 1927
Edwards, E.		F, 112th N.Y.	17		1923 Dec 4	KS, 43rd, 1924
Edwards, E.L.	Pvt.	G, 28th Iowa Inf.	403		1899 Nov	IA, 26th, 1900
Edwards, Edward	Pvt.	K, 21st Wis. Inf.	150	67	1896 Jan 9	IA, 22nd, 1896
Edwards, F.J.			65		1924 Aug 21	KS, 44th, 1925
Edwards, Frank		L, 11th Kans.	126		1908 Jul 5	KS, 28th, 1909
Edwards, G.M.		L, 2nd Mo. Art.	293		1925 Jul 26	KS, 45th, 1926
Edwards, Geo. L.	Pvt.	D, 2nd Iowa Cav.	6		1927 Jun 10	IA, 54th, 1928
Edwards, Hardin		86th Ill.	14		1910	KS, 30th, 1911
Edwards, Harry	Musician	H, 20th Penn. Cav.	88		1907 Sep 18	IA, 34th, 1908
Edwards, Henry		E, 18th Ind.	129		1904 Jun 25	KS, 24th, 1905
Edwards, Henry		I, 40th N.J.	171		1904 Apr 30	KS, 24th, 1905
Edwards, J.B.	Pvt.	C, 31st Iowa Inf.	68		1910 Feb 17	IA, 37th, 1911
Edwards, J.B.	Pvt.	B, 18th Iowa Inf.	51		1916 Nov 11	IA, 43rd, 1917
Edwards, J.E.	Pvt.	C, 44th Iowa Inf.	78		1912 Oct 3	IA, 39th, 1913
Edwards, J.J.		F, 1st Wis.	55		1906 Feb 21	KS, 26th, 1907

*See Appendix A, B or C for roster of post names and locations.
†See Introduction for note regarding recording of death date.

161

Name	Rank	Company, Regiment or Ship	Post*	Age	Death Date†	Journal
Edwards, J.M.		D, 8th Tenn. A, 3rd N.C.	448		1924 Aug 16	KS, 44th, 1925
Edwards, J.W.		B, 36th Ill.	84		1909 Apr 30	KS, 29th, 1910
Edwards, J.W.		G, 124th Ill.	35		1933 Jan 6	NE, 58th, 1934
Edwards, Joe A.	Pvt.	B, 139th Ill. Inf.	8	53	1898 Aug 5	IA, 25th, 1899
Edwards, John		D, 18th Ill.	72		1913 Aug 11	KS, 33rd, 1914
Edwards, John		G, 95th Ohio	448		1918 May 22	KS, 38th, 1919
Edwards, John		F, 22nd Wis.	55		1933 Jan 9	KS, 53rd, 1934
Edwards, John		B, 186th Iowa Inf. N.Y.	89	72	1919 Nov 1	NE, 44th, 1920
Edwards, John R.	Pvt.	B, 18th U.S. Colored Inf.	57	47	1886 Sep 13	IA, 13th, 1887
Edwards, Jonathan	Pvt.	C, 135th Ohio Inf.	497		1915 Aug 9	IA, 42nd, 1916
Edwards, Jonathan		I, 1st Neb. Cav.	7		1937 Oct 25	NE, 62nd, 1938
Edwards, Jos. W.		I, 55th Ill.	303		1898 Nov 11	KS, 18th, 1899
Edwards, L.L.	Pvt.	F, 34th Ill. Inf.	440		1929[1928?] Jul 9	IA, 55th, 1929
Edwards, L.L.	Pvt.	F, 34th Ill. Inf.	452		1928 Aug 29	IA, 55th, 1929
Edwards, Moses	Pvt.	K, 36th Iowa	337		1907 Apr 7	IA, 34th, 1908
Edwards, O.		L, 15th Penn. Cav.	191		1888	KS, 8th, 1889
Edwards, Oran		J, 29th Ind. (died of old age)	55	73	1920	NE, 45th, 1921
Edwards, P.L.		A, 66th Ill.	51		1916 Oct 29	KS, 36th, 1917
Edwards, P.L.		66th Ill.	4		1916 Nov 2	KS, 36th, 1917
Edwards, R.B.			55		1930 Sep 36	KS, 50th, 1931
Edwards, R.J.		F, 22nd Wis.	55		1917 Mar 4	KS, 37th, 1918
Edwards, W.P.			14		1883	KS, 3rd, 1884
Edwards, W.R.	Pvt.	D, 10th Vt.	42		1921 Jul 18	IA, 48th, 1922
Edwards, William	Pvt.	C, 18th Iowa Inf.	18		1925 Dec 12	IA, 52nd, 1926
Edwards, William S.	Pvt.		183		1886 Oct 8	IA, 13th, 1887
Edwards, Wm.		2nd Miss. Cav.	434		1924 May 17	IA, 51st, 1925
Edwards, Wm.		F, 51st Ill.	58		1921 Mar 7	KS, 41st, 1922
Edwin, Foster	Sergt.	G, 145th Ill.	68		1924 Jan 26	IA, 51st, 1925
Eells, Dan'l		I, 24th Iowa Inf.	25	73	1913 Mar 3	NE, 38th, 1914
Efner, H.S.	Pvt.	K, 28th Iowa Inf.	16		1919	IA, 46th, 1920
Efner, William E.		C, 8th Ill. Cav. (former member)	249		1941 Jul 16	NE, 66th, 1942
Efnor, Chas. V.	Pvt.	D, 93rd Ind. Inf.	515		1917 Jun 20	IA, 44th, 1918
Egan, E.B.		E, 41st Mo.	262		1919 Jun 29	NE, 44th, 1920
Egbert, C.J.		C, 23rd Mo.	13	71	1914 Oct 16	NE, 39th, 1915
Egbert, Henry	Pvt.	I, 34th Iowa Inf.	7	91	1933 Feb 6	IA, 60th, 1934
Egbert, Thos. W.		A, 72nd Ohio Inf. (died of old age)	63	82	1904 Mar 7	NE, 29th, 1905
Egenes, A.G.	Corp.	E, 91st Ill. Inf.	439		1908 Aug 30	IA, 35th, 1909
Egestone, Amos D.	Pvt.	B, 31st Iowa Inf.	68	55	1898 Sep 25	IA, 25th, 1899
Eggar, Jurgen	Pvt.	H, 76th Ill. Inf.	327		1912 Oct 31	IA, 39th, 1913
Eggen, D.C.		H, 13th Iowa	100		1923 Feb 22	KS, 43rd, 1924
Eggert, Henry W.		B, 12th Kans.	12		1928 Feb 28	KS, 48th, 1929
Eggleston, —			265		1921	KS, 41st, 1922
Eggleston, B.B.	Col.	1st Ohio Cav.	25		1891 May 27	KS, 11th, 1892
Eggleston, B.F.		D, 12th U.S. Inf.	127		1891 Feb 12	KS, 11th, 1892
Eggleston, Ben.		A, 38th Ill.	111		1897 Feb 20	KS, 17th, 1898
Eggleston, J.S.	Pvt.	I, 54th Ill. Inf.	22		1913 Mar 19	IA, 40th, 1914
Eggleston, Leroy	Pvt.	E, 7th Wis. Inf.	489		1909	IA, 36th, 1910
Eggleston, O.F.	Pvt.	I, 9th Iowa Inf.	98		1925 Aug 10	IA, 52nd, 1926
Egloff, Wm.	Pvt.	E, 29th Iowa Inf.	209		1905 May	IA, 32nd, 1906
Ehler, William		F, 54th Penn. Vols.	1		1909 Dec 2	KS, 29th, 1910
Ehrett, John		A, 43rd Mo. Inf.	93		1914 Feb 11	KS, 34th, 1915
Ehrhardt, John A.	Pvt.	F, 52nd Ill. Inf. (see Appendix D)	190		1925 Nov 6	NE, 50th, 1926
Ehrman, Henry	Pvt.	E, 8th Iowa Cav.	177	43	1890 Dec 23	IA, 17th, 1891
Eichhoff, W.F.	Musician	7th Iowa Inf.	231		1908 May 9	IA, 35th, 1909
Eichhorn, George		L, 5th Penn. Cav.	257		1914 May 30	KS, 34th, 1915
Eichoff, August	Pvt.	D, 12th Iowa Inf. (at large)	231	93	1940 Dec 27	IA, 67th, 1941
Eicholtz, W.H.		B, 87th Penn. Inf.	63		1909 Sep 21	KS, 29th, 1910
Eifer, Henry		I, 155th Ill.	25		1922 May 14	KS, 42nd, 1923
Eighmey, H.B.	Pvt.	H, 16th Iowa Inf.	68		1926 Jan 7	IA, 53rd, 1927
Eighmey, J.J.		H, 52nd Ill.	209		1914 Oct 1	KS, 34th, 1915
Eighmey, P.P.	Pvt.	A, 32nd Iowa Inf.	68	58	1900 Feb 8	IA, 26th, 1900

See Appendix A, B or C for roster of post names and locations.
†*See Introduction for note regarding recording of death date.*

Name	Rank	Company, Regiment or Ship	Post*	Age	Death Date†	Journal
Eile, Jos.		E, 1st Ohio Hvy. Art.	20		1904 Sep 20	KS, 24th, 1905
Eilerts, Gerd B.		A, 101st Ill.	36		1924 May 13	KS, 44th, 1925
Einhrllig, Chas.		gunboat	2[32?]		1917 Jan 6	KS, 37th, 1918
Einsphar, H. Fred		Navy	155		1920	NE, 45th, 1921
Eisele, Charles		C, 131st Penn. Inf.	88		1917 Jul 18	KS, 37th, 1918
Eisenbuen, John	Pvt.		2		1931 Dec 31	IA, 58th, 1932
Eisentrout, Geo.	Musician	K, 20th Ill.	22		1926 Oct 18	IA, 53rd, 1927
Eisler, John		died of pneumonia	308	77	1921 Dec 11	NE, 46th, 1922
Eisley, Paulis		H, 58th Ohio	142		1922 Sep 19	KS, 42nd, 1923
Ekard, M.A.		I, 83rd Ind.	69		1909 Nov 28	KS, 29th, 1910
Ela, C.N.		I, 1st N.H. Inf.	1		1902 Jan 10	KS, 22nd, 1903
Elam, Alex.		H, 35th Ill.	17		1922 Jan 17	KS, 42nd, 1923
Elam, G.W.		A, — Mo.	271		1893 Dec 26	KS, 13th, 1894
Elbut, Henry		B, 11th Ind. Cav. (died of consumption)	2		1894 Feb 28	NE, 19th, 1895
Elder, D.C.			108		1900	IA, 27th, 1901
Elder, Dan		1st Iowa Cav.	66		1922 Jan 31	KS, 42nd, 1923
Elder, David P.		H, 133rd Penn.	250		1923 Mar 4	KS, 43rd, 1924
Elder, Hugh A.		A, — Art.	54		1899 Jul 24	KS, 19th, 1900
Elder, John			127		1923 Feb 28	KS, 43rd, 1924
Elder, John W.		H, 7th Wis. Inf.	174		1900 Feb 14	KS, 20th, 1901
Elder, Thos.	Pvt.	H, 13th Iowa Inf.	337		1905 May 6	IA, 32nd, 1906
Elderd, N.E.	Pvt.	K, 105th Ohio Inf.	68		1920 Mar 28	IA, 47th, 1921
Elderkin, D.C.	Pvt.	F, 100th Ill. Inf.	222		1912 Nov 13	IA, 39th, 1913
Elderkin, O.C.	Pvt.	B, Penn. Inf.	216	52	1895 May 25	IA, 22nd, 1896
Eldred, E.M.		F, 3rd Mich. Inf.	269		1901 Feb 10	KS, 21st, 1902
Eldridge, A.	Pvt.	G, 8th Ohio Inf.	418		1909 Oct 3	IA, 36th, 1910
Eldridge, Geo. I.		E, 9th Kans.	51		1917 Jan 28	KS, 37th, 1918
Eldridge, J.L.		A, 6th Mass.	71		1913 Jun 19	KS, 33rd, 1914
Eldridge, James	Pvt.	B, 8th U.S. Inf.	519		1920 Feb 20	IA, 46th, 1920
Eldridge, M.P.	Pvt.	A, 92nd Ill. Inf.	167	82	1897 Mar 16	IA, 24th, 1898
Eldridge, S.W.	QM	2nd Kans. Inf.	12		1899 Jan 16	KS, 19th, 1900
Elgen, C.		F, —	16		1888	KS, 8th, 1889
Elicker, Jacob	Pvt.	G, 133rd Penn.	231		1914 Nov 1	IA, 41st, 1915
Elipal, S.	Corp.	E, 4th Mo. Cav.	283		1921 Sep 25	IA, 48th, 1922
Elison, C.S.		K, — (died of old age)	180	94	1922 Sep	NE, 48th, 1924
Elison, C.S.		K, 5th U.S. Art., Penn.	180	90	1922 Jul 28	NE, 47th, 1923
Elkins, Calvin P.		F, 3rd Tenn.	7		1930 Aug 8	NE, 55th, 1931
Elkins, D.B.		2nd Ky. Art.	130		1916 Nov 4	KS, 36th, 1917
Elkins, J.			88		1884	KS, 4th, 1885
Elkins, R.A.		I, 8th Vt. Inf.	429		1908	KS, 28th, 1909
Ell, John C.		B, 92nd Ill. Inf. (died of gallstones)	62	73	1916 Jan 13	NE, 41st, 1917
Elledge, Wm. H.		F, 137th Ill. (died of Bright's disease)	15	73	1920 Jul 4	NE, 45th, 1921
Eller, Cleveland		K, 9th Iowa Cav.	10		1929 Mar 30	NE, 54th, 1930
Eller, J.W.		H, 10th Ind. Inf.	7	81	1925 Sep 1	NE, 50th, 1926
Ellerman, H.	Pvt.	D, 114th Ill. Inf.	62		1920 Oct 4	IA, 47th, 1921
Ellerman, H.	Pvt.	D, 114th Ill.	62		1921 Oct 4	IA, 48th, 1922
Ellerman, H.	Pvt.	D, —	62		1923 Oct 4	IA, 50th, 1924
Ellerman, Henry		A, 11th Kans.	278		1925 Nov 9	KS, 45th, 1926
Ellerton, F.M.	Pvt.	K, 6th Iowa Inf.	434		1925 Dec 24	IA, 52nd, 1926
Ellett, D.C.	Pvt.		26		1925 Feb 25	IA, 52nd, 1926
Elling, Richard O.		A, 2nd Cal.	30		1905 Nov 15	KS, 25th, 1906
Ellinger, Martin L.		D, —	18		1910 Feb 26	KS, 30th, 1911
Ellingson, Thomas	Pvt.	C, 12th Wis. Inf.	365		1899 Aug	IA, 26th, 1900
Ellingsson, Kittle	Pvt.	H, 1st Minn. Inf.	168		1919	IA, 46th, 1920
Ellington, J.M.	Capt.	A, 41st Ind. Cav.	96		1913 Nov 26	IA, 40th, 1914
Elliot, Henry	Pvt.	21st Ill. Inf.	12		1888 Dec 28	IA, 15th, 1889
Elliot, J.B.		Iowa	69	83	1925	NE, 50th, 1926
Elliot, J.S.	2nd Lieut.	H, 29th Iowa Inf.	56	66	1891 Dec 6	IA, 18th, 1892
Elliott, David H.		G, 15th Iowa Inf.	242		1899 Jun 12	KS, 19th, 1900
Elliott, David Stewart		E, 76th Penn. Inf. (born December 23, 1843; killed in battle at Manila, Philippine Islands; see also Appendix D)	153		1899 Feb 28	KS, 19th, 1900

*See Appendix A, B or C for roster of post names and locations.
†See Introduction for note regarding recording of death date.

163

Name	Rank	Company, Regiment or Ship	Post*	Age	Death Date†	Journal
Elliott, Franklin		A, 36th Ind.	59		1919 Apr 2	KS, 39th, 1920
Elliott, Freeman	Sergt.	G, 15th Ill. Cav.	31		1902 Dec 24	IA, 29th, 1903
Elliott, G.W.	Pvt.	C, 55th Ill.	66		1921 Aug 5	IA, 48th, 1922
Elliott, Geo. N.		A, 39th Iowa Inf.	1		1899 Dec 29	KS, 19th, 1900
Elliott, H.C.		M, 1st Ind. Cav.	96		1925 Jan 20	KS, 45th, 1926
Elliott, J.B.	Pvt.	K, 28th Iowa Inf.	106	60	1896 Jan	IA, 23rd, 1897
Elliott, J.D.		C, 3rd Ill. Cav.	356		1904 Nov 17	KS, 24th, 1905
Elliott, Jack	Pvt.	E, 144th N.Y. Inf.	98		1931 Feb 10	IA, 58th, 1932
Elliott, James		I, 74th Ill. Inf.	464		1899 Nov 10	KS, 19th, 1900
Elliott, Jas.	Corp.	B, 52nd Wis.	16		1903 Jul 21	IA, 30th, 1904
Elliott, Joel		9th Ind. Bat.	96		1924 Jun 6	KS, 44th, 1925
Elliott, John	Pvt.	A, 10th Ill. Inf.	100		1918	IA, 45th, 1919
Elliott, John	Pvt.	B, 2nd Kans. M.	1		1915 Feb 23	KS, 35th, 1916
Elliott, John		G, 10th Ind. Inf.	96		1917 Nov 1	KS, 37th, 1918
Elliott, John B.		C, 4th West Va.	61		1921 Aug 30	KS, 41st, 1922
Elliott, John C.	Pvt.	C, 3rd Iowa Cav.	100		1916 Aug	IA, 43rd, 1917
Elliott, John C.		died of nervous prostration	37	66	1891 Dec 3	NE, 16th, 1892
Elliott, John U.		K, 19th Ohio	318		1898 Sep 15	KS, 18th, 1899
Elliott, Kier	Pvt.	K, 11th Ill. Cav.	39		1917 May 2	IA, 44th, 1918
Elliott, M.S.		T, 54th Ill.	339		1927 Mar 20	KS, 47th, 1928
Elliott, Mathew	Pvt.	A, 19th Ind. Inf.	425		1911 Aug 4	IA, 38th, 1912
Elliott, Milton S.		I, 54th Ill.	339		1927 Mar 22	KS, 48th, 1929
Elliott, Peter		H, 11th Kans.	1		1904 May 11	KS, 24th, 1905
Elliott, Robt. J.		E, 12th Ill.	150		1898 May 15	KS, 18th, 1899
Elliott, S.M.	Pvt.	I, 3rd Iowa Inf.	7	65	1895 Dec 20	IA, 22nd, 1896
Elliott, Samuel	Pvt.	G, 75th Ill. Inf.	356	53	1896 Jun 7	IA, 23rd, 1897
Elliott, Scott		B, 1st Col. Cav.	19		1925 Feb 10	KS, 44th, 1925
Elliott, T.L.		D, 9th Iowa Cav.	409		1894 Nov 29	KS, 14th, 1895
Elliott, Thos. F.	Pvt.		164		1927 Nov 20	IA, 54th, 1928
Elliott, W.H.		D, 17th Penn. Cav.	9		1906 Feb 19	KS, 26th, 1907
Elliott, W.H.		G, 7th Mo. Cav.	17		1928 Aug 16	KS, 48th, 1929
Elliott, W.M.		E, 58th Mo.	10		1925 Jul 15	KS, 45th, 1926
Elliott, W.W.	Pvt.		186		1927	IA, 54th, 1928
Elliott, W.W.	Pvt.		186		1930	IA, 57th, 1931
Elliott, Wm.	Sergt.	A, 5th Iowa Inf.	8		1905 Sep 8	IA, 32nd, 1906
Elliott, Wm.	Pvt.		144		1920 Dec 17	IA, 47th, 1921
Ellis, A.A.		M, 12th Ind.	12		1913 Jan 27	KS, 33rd, 1914
Ellis, A.G.	Pvt.	H, 22nd N.Y. Cav.	95	43	1888 Apr 21	IA, 15th, 1889
Ellis, A.H.		K, 36th Iowa Inf.	147		1902 Sep 26	KS, 22nd, 1903
Ellis, A.M.		M, 3rd Kans. State Militia	12		1902 Sep 26	KS, 22nd, 1903
Ellis, Abraham B.		D, 2nd Kans.	167		1906 Dec 6	KS, 26th, 1907
Ellis, C.M.		E, 9th Kans.	74		1919 Nov 5	KS, 39th, 1920
Ellis, Clark	Pvt.	C, 29th Iowa Inf.	139		1912 Jul 12	IA, 39th, 1913
Ellis, D.G.	Pvt.	C, 9th Iowa Cav.	68		1916 Apr 9	IA, 43rd, 1917
Ellis, D.W.		A, 93rd Ohio Inf.	62		1928 Sep 3	NE, 53rd, 1929
Ellis, E.T.		B, 17th Kans. Cav.	46		1913 Jul 29	KS, 33rd, 1914
Ellis, F.B.		Kans.	74		1893 Apr 5	KS, 13th, 1894
Ellis, Geo. W.	Musician	D, 79th Ohio Inf.	497		1912 Feb 20	IA, 39th, 1913
Ellis, George W.		G, 70th Ohio	57		1923 Nov 5	KS, 43rd, 1924
Ellis, H.B.			387		1910	IA, 37th, 1911
Ellis, H.B.	Pvt.		387		1911	IA, 38th, 1912
Ellis, H.M.			180		1919 Feb 12	KS, 39th, 1920
Ellis, Henry		G, 57th Ind.	185		1922 Nov 4	KS, 42nd, 1923
Ellis, Henry H.		F, 181st Ohio	185		1914 Aug 18	KS, 34th, 1915
Ellis, Horton	Pvt.	H, 4th Penn. Res.	190	60	1893 Dec 6	IA, 20th, 1894
Ellis, J.H.		K, 56th Penn.	388		1917 Feb 28	KS, 37th, 1918
Ellis, James			40		1902	KS, 22nd, 1903
Ellis, James L.		I, 3rd Mo. Mil.	15		1915 May 31	KS, 35th, 1916
Ellis, John		77th Ill.	176		1931 Oct	KS, 52nd, 1933
Ellis, John G.		G, 130th Ill. Inf. G, 77th Ill. Inf.	176		1931 Oct 10	KS, 51st, 1932
Ellis, John H.	Pvt.		137		1911 Jan 3	IA, 38th, 1912

*See Appendix A, B or C for roster of post names and locations.
†See Introduction for note regarding recording of death date.

164

Name	Rank	Company, Regiment or Ship	Post*	Age	Death Date†	Journal
Ellis, Joseph		M, 21st Penn.	35	71	1915 Mar 25	NE, 40th, 1916
Ellis, Joseph		B, 47th Ill. (died of apoplexy)	89	70	1915 Mar 25	NE, 40th, 1916
Ellis, Linza	Pvt.	I, 47th Iowa Inf.	40		1926 Jun 28	IA, 53rd, 1927
Ellis, M.J.	Sergt.	K, 29th Wis. Inf.	12		1925 Apr 23	IA, 52nd, 1926
Ellis, P.V.	Pvt.	C, 2nd West Va. Cav.	167		1903 Dec 24	IA, 30th, 1904
Ellis, R.			156		1924 Apr 6	IA, 51st, 1925
Ellis, Rolla	Corp.	G, 11th Ind. Zouaves	287	67	1893 Mar	IA, 20th, 1894
Ellis, S.	Pvt.		24		1916	IA, 43rd, 1917
Ellis, S.L.		H, 33rd Ill. Inf.	185		1917 Jun 18	KS, 37th, 1918
Ellis, Samuel		B, 13th Penn. Cav. (former member; died at McCook)	207		1935 Jan 6	NE, 60th, 1936
Ellis, Thomas		M, 126th Ind.	129		1904 Apr 10	KS, 24th, 1905
Ellison, H.D.		D, 8th Kans. Cav. (died of heart disease)	38		1891 Nov 4	KS, 11th, 1892
Ellison, Jas.	Pvt.	C, 23rd Wis. Inf.	267		1908 Apr 25	IA, 35th, 1909
Ellliott, Hiram	Pvt.	H, 6th Ind. Cav.	234	56	1894 Apr 4	IA, 21st, 1895
Ellsbury, J.T., see Elsbury, J.T.						
Ellsmaker, T.G.	Mate & Boatswain	N.Y.	28		1906	KS, 26th, 1907
Ellsworth, H.M.	Pvt.	F, 14th Iowa Inf.	329		1904 May 9	IA, 31st, 1905
Ellsworth, J.W.	Pvt.	B, 3rd Vt. Inf.	64		1910 May 4	IA, 37th, 1911
Ellsworth, M.L.		D, 141st Penn. (died of apoplexy)	90	62	1904 Oct 1	NE, 29th, 1905
Ellwanger, H.H.	Pvt.	E, 5th Iowa Cav.	78		1920 Aug 2	IA, 47th, 1921
Elmer, W.P.		B, 36th Wis.	154		1932	NE, 57th, 1933
Elmour, J.M.		G, 65th Ind.	27		1911 Jan	KS, 31st, 1912
Elphic, James			46		1906 Jun 3	IA, 33rd, 1907
Elrod, J.	Pvt.	F, 20th Iowa Inf.	206		1910 Dec 12	IA, 37th, 1911
Elrod, M.F.			400		1909	IA, 36th, 1910
Elrod, T.H.		F, 2nd Iowa	127		1920 Feb 2	KS, 40th, 1921
Elrod, Wm.	Musician	E, 6th Penn. Art.	84		1905 Nov 15	IA, 32nd, 1906
Elrode, John			3		1883	KS, 3rd, 1884
Elsberry, Z.V.	Pvt.	H, 24th Iowa Inf.	206		1908 Jan 24	IA, 35th, 1909
Elsbury, J.T.		E, 17th Ill. Cav. (died of blood poison)	39		1923	NE, 48th, 1924
Elsbury, John F.	Pvt.	F, 93rd Ill.	156		1899 Feb 26	IA, 26th, 1900
Elsen, David		H, 11th Iowa (died of heart trouble)	5	66	1910 Nov 3	NE, 35th, 1911
Elsher, M.D.	Pvt.	I, 20th Iowa Inf.	14		1921 Aug 16	IA, 48th, 1922
Elsner, C.A.	Pvt.	L, 2nd Iowa Cav.	74	71	1896 Dec 17	IA, 23rd, 1897
Elston, C.M.			129		1898 Aug 6	KS, 18th, 1899
Elston, John		I, 5th Kans. Cav.	447		1920 Nov 28	KS, 40th, 1921
Elsworth, E.R.	Pvt.	F, 14th Iowa Inf.	235		1911 Jul 18	IA, 38th, 1912
Elsworth, H.L.		G, 26th Mo. Inf.	464		1899 Aug 13	KS, 19th, 1900
Elward, J.H.	Major	43rd Ill.	17		1909 Dec 27	KS, 29th, 1910
Elwell, E.B.		D, 7th Ill.	18		1915 Nov 23	KS, 35th, 1916
Elwell, James H.		D, 7th Ill.	18		1910 Sep 14	KS, 30th, 1911
Elwell, Jos. O.	Sergt.	I, 123rd Ill. Inf.	211		1909	IA, 36th, 1910
Elwell, L.E.			512		1923	IA, 50th, 1924
Elwell, W.P.	Pvt.	K, 14th Ohio Inf.	452		1929 Feb 20	IA, 56th, 1930
Elwood, Ashford B.		175th Ohio (died at Sulphur Springs, Mo.)	169		1894 Nov 11	KS, 14th, 1895
Elwood, Fred M.	Sergt.	H, 1st Neb.	201		1899	NE, 24th, 1900
Ely, Daniel		5th Mo. Battery	19	67	1904 Nov 18	NE, 29th, 1905
Ely, E.S.		H, 154th N.Y.	473		1893 Dec 7	KS, 13th, 1894
Ely, Ellison	Corp.	H, 51st Ill. Inf.	465	53	1896 Mar 14	IA, 23rd, 1897
Ely, Eugene H.	Sergt.	C, 3rd Wis. Cav.	8		1910 Nov 11	IA, 37th, 1911
Ely, George	Pvt.	F, 112th Ill. Inf.	66		1912 Jul 1	IA, 39th, 1913
Ely, Jno. W.		D, 1st Wis. Art.	85		1886	KS, 6th, 1887
Ely, R.	Pvt.	I, 11th Iowa Inf.	176	71	1895 Oct 5	IA, 22nd, 1896
Ely, W.C.		F, 146th Ohio	35		1908 Nov	KS, 28th, 1909
Embree, A.S.		A, 40th Ind. Inf.	1		1921 Oct 18	KS, 41st, 1922
Embree, D.T.	Pvt.	C, 5th N.Y. Hvy. Art.	483		1901 Nov 24	IA, 28th, 1902
Embree, H.A.	Pvt.	C, 5th N.Y. Art.	472		1913 Dec 16	IA, 40th, 1914
Embree, J.C.		H, 78th Ill.	293		1927	KS, 47th, 1928
Embree, James Asbury		H, 2nd Iowa Inf.	108	89	1937 Jun 30	IA, 64th, 1938
Embree, Oliver		G, 170th Ohio Inf.	293		1929	KS, 49th, 1930

*See Appendix A, B or C for roster of post names and locations.
†See Introduction for note regarding recording of death date.

Name	Rank	Company, Regiment or Ship	Post*	Age	Death Date†	Journal
Emerson, J.W.			293		1926 Dec 31	KS, 46th, 1927
Emerson, M.H.	Pvt.	I, 1st Wis. Inf.	42		1910 Dec 21	IA, 37th, 1911
Emerson, W.A.	Pvt.	G, 3rd U.S. Col.	88		1926 Mar 29	IA, 53rd, 1927
Emerson, Wesley C., Rev.		K, 33rd Ohio	18		1913 Feb 6	KS, 33rd, 1914
Emerson, Wm.		L, 1st Ind. Hvy. Art. (died of physical & mental disease)	69	50	1895 Apr 10	NE, 20th, 1896
Emert, William M.	Pvt.	C, 34th Ill. Inf.	7	43	1885 Nov 18	IA, 12th, 1886
Emery, Benj.	Pvt.	12th Wis. Battery	521		1904 Oct 21	IA, 31st, 1905
Emery, D.W.		D, 2nd Colo. Cav.	85		1905 Oct 13	KS, 25th, 1906
Emery, Dan T.		E, 118th Ill.	17		1919 Jan 14	KS, 39th, 1920
Emery, E.F.		C, 92nd Ill. Mtd. Inf.	88		1901 Mar 30	IA, 27th, 1901
Emery, I.M.		A, 128th Ill.	158		1922 Nov 23	KS, 42nd, 1923
Emery, J.A.		K, 16th Iowa Inf.	67		4th quarter 1884	IA, 11th, 1885
Emery, John T.		H, 107th Ohio	18		1923 May 9	KS, 43rd, 1924
Emery, M.L.		D, 3rd Colo. Vols.	90		1902 Oct 26	KS, 22nd, 1903
Emery, Perry		F, 1st Ill. Cav. (died of heart trouble)	35	78	1913 Apr 27	NE, 38th, 1914
Emery, S.A.	Corp.	A, 22nd Wis. Inf.	476		1900 Nov 26	IA, 27th, 1901
Emery, Samuel A.	Seaman	Mississippi Squadron	47		1920 Jul 28	KS, 40th, 1921
Emery, T.L.	Pvt.	A, 2nd Iowa Cav.	363		1908 Feb 13	IA, 35th, 1909
Emery, W.C.		D, 157th Penn. Inf. (died of phys. collapse)	10	74	1905 Mar 23	NE, 30th, 1906
Emery, W.T.	Pvt.	K, 33rd Iowa Inf.	452		1914 Dec	IA, 41st, 1915
Emery, William		E, 30th Ill.	113		1911 Apr 28	KS, 31st, 1912
Emes, Elias B.	Pvt.	A, 34th Ohio Inf. E, 34th Ohio Inf.	155	90	1936 Feb 18	IA, 65th, 1939
Emigh, Joshua		D, 2nd West Va.	14		1897 Apr 24	KS, 17th, 1898
Emilton, C.N.	Pvt.	I, 21st Wis. Inf.	86		1916 Mar 9	IA, 43rd, 1917
Emm, Otto			120		1883	KS, 3rd, 1884
Emmens, Albert		A, 96th Ohio Vol. Inf.	250		1916 Jan 12	KS, 36th, 1917
Emmerson, C.D.		N.Y. (died of old age)	318		1921 Dec 23	NE, 46th, 1922
Emmerson, L.M.		A, 11th Mich.	65		1919 Aug 3	KS, 39th, 1920
Emmert, Jonathan		H, 1st Penn.	175		1909 Feb 12	KS, 32nd, 1913
Emmet, John			125		1908 Jun 16	IA, 35th, 1909
Emmons, Charles		L, 10th Ky. Cav.	25		1914 Nov 3	KS, 34th, 1915
Emmons, Edward		H, 110th N.Y.	1		1920 Jan 20	KS, 40th, 1921
Emmons, W.W.		K, 11th Kans.	271		1912 Jul 22	KS, 32nd, 1913
Emms, S.R.	Pvt.	B, 29th Ohio Inf.	26	87	1933 Feb 2	IA, 60th, 1934
Emon, J.		C, 101st Ill.	325		1888	KS, 8th, 1889
Emory, E.F., see Emery, E.F.						
Emory, W.H.	Pvt.	K, 1st N.H. Inf.	59		1907 Apr 5	IA, 34th, 1908
Enderly, Fred		H, 2nd Ky.	294		1892 Aug 25	KS, 12th, 1893
Enders, Jesse		3rd Iowa Inf.	116	65	1905[1904?] Nov 17	NE, 29th, 1905
Enderton, J.	Sergt.	F, 27th Mass. Inf.	124		1931 May 13	IA, 58th, 1932
Endres, Michael		E, 84th Penn.	25		1927 Mar 21	NE, 52nd, 1928
Endsley, Gilson		I, 1st Mo. Cav.	106		1890	KS, 10th, 1891
Endsley, H.		E, 35th Ill. Inf.	75		1899 Aug 31	KS, 19th, 1900
Endsley, Wm.		K, 75th Ind.	12		1920 Apr 3	KS, 40th, 1921
Enfield, Charles		C, 52nd Ohio Inf.	23		1914	IA, 41st, 1915
Engel, R.B., Rev.		G, 155th Ohio	61		1912 Feb 9	KS, 32nd, 1913
England, Emor		B, 12th Ohio Cav.	62		1911 May 11	KS, 31st, 1912
England, Geo. W.	Pvt.	D, 3rd Iowa Cav.	100		1928 Oct 31	IA, 55th, 1929
England, James		B, 130th Ind.	85		1931 May 16	KS, 51st, 1932
England, James		B, 130th Ind.	85		1931 May 16	KS, 52nd, 1933
England, James K.P.	Pvt.	I, 1st Iowa Cav.		91	1936 Sep 10	IA, 65th, 1939
Engle, F.J.		F, 8th Ind.	25	64	1904 May 20	NE, 29th, 1905
Engle, John	Sergt.	A, 14th Mich. Inf.	18		1905 Mar 15	IA, 32nd, 1906
Engle, John A.		E, 8th Ill. Cav.	68		1921 Apr 12	KS, 41st, 1922
Engle, Soloman		E, 51st Penn.	12		1927 Mar 4	KS, 47th, 1928
Engle, W.R.		B, 4th West Va. Cav.	334		1893 Dec 22	KS, 13th, 1894
Englebert, J. Lee	Lieut. Col.	G, 3rd Penn. Cav.	12	47	1888 Dec 22	IA, 15th, 1889
Englebright, Henry		E, 3rd Ohio Cav.	185		1913 Dec 28	KS, 33rd, 1914
Engledinger, Pete			167		1928 Feb 28	IA, 55th, 1929
Englehardt, Paul		A, 57th Ill.	61		1924 Oct 26	KS, 44th, 1925

*See Appendix A, B or C for roster of post names and locations.
†See Introduction for note regarding recording of death date.

Name	Rank	Company, Regiment or Ship	Post*	Age	Death Date†	Journal
Englehart, George		I, 60th Ohio	25		1934 Feb 20	NE, 59th, 1935
Engleman, L.D.		E, 58th Ind. Inf. (former member)	231		1940 Jan 23	NE, 65th, 1941
Engler, G.W.		H, 143rd Penn.	260		1918 Nov 12	KS, 38th, 1919
English, A.	Pvt.	4th Wis. Bat.	31		1923 Feb	IA, 50th, 1924
English, David			140		1919	IA, 46th, 1920
English, James		I, 45th Penn.	50		1920 Jul 10	KS, 40th, 1921
English, James		K, 11th Kans. Cav.	71		1925 May 31	KS, 45th, 1926
English, W.D.			7		1916 Jan 13	IA, 43rd, 1917
English, W.R.	Capt.	A, 4th Iowa Inf.	19		1897 May 29	IA, 24th, 1898
English, W.W.		H, 71st Ind. (cause of death: heart)	25	67	1900 Aug 9	NE, 25th, 1901
Enise, Mathew		F, 27th Wis.	25	88	1920 Jan 11	NE, 45th, 1921
Enloe, Benj. F.		E, 3rd Ill. Cav.	61		1921 Aug 8	KS, 41st, 1922
Enlow, F.U.		E, 11th Wis.	243		1912	IA, 39th, 1913
Ennis, J.K.	Pvt.	C, 24th Mich. Cav.	452	85	1931 Jun 9	IA, 58th, 1932
Eno, Louis			371		1915	IA, 42nd, 1916
Enochs, J.M.		L, 1st Iowa Cav.	303		1904 Nov 16	KS, 24th, 1905
Enocks, A.O.		E, 1st Va.	256		1891 Jul 25	KS, 11th, 1892
Ensign, A.W.		F, 1st Ind. Cav.	25		1892	NE, 17th, 1893
Ensign, E.W.	Pvt.	E, 44th Iowa	243		1921 Jul 22	IA, 48th, 1922
Ensign, E.W.		F, 1st Mich. Bat.	100		1922 May 15	KS, 42nd, 1923
Ensign, G.D.		K, 11th Ky.	71		1920 Mar 2	KS, 40th, 1921
Ensign, H.D.	Pvt.	14th Independent Ohio Lt. Art.	67	58	1898 Oct 3	IA, 25th, 1899
Ensign, N.R.		K, 83rd Ill. Inf.	336		1899 Oct 12	KS, 19th, 1900
Ensign, Orin S.		29th Iowa Inf.	466		1911 Feb	IA, 38th, 1912
Enslow, C.C.		C, 77th Ill. (cause of death: heart)	25	52	1900 Sep 4	NE, 25th, 1901
Enslow, H.S.		D, 152nd Ill.	18		1920 Dec	KS, 41st, 1922
Enslow, T.F.		I, 17th Iowa	at large		1931 Dec 21	NE, 56th, 1932
Ensminger, H.		F, 78th Ill.	17		1927 Feb 2	KS, 47th, 1928
Ensminger, H.C.	Pvt.	B, 71st Ind. Inf.	7	42	1886 Dec	IA, 13th, 1887
Entrikin, Joseph		F, 10th Ohio Cav.	118	71	1917 Sep	NE, 42nd, 1918
Envill, Moses	Pvt.	G, 25th Wis. Inf.	88		1918 Dec 13	IA, 46th, 1920
Enyart, Alonzo			115		1914	IA, 41st, 1915
Enyart, Harvey		D, 13th Iowa Inf.	73		1917 Sep 19	IA, 44th, 1918
Enyart, John			318		1906 Apr	NE, 31st, 1907
Enyert, Milton		F, 131st Ind.	100		1931 Feb 19	KS, 52nd, 1933
Enyert, Milton		F, 131st Ind.	100		1931 Jan 19	KS, 51st, 1932
Eoers, E.			17		1901 Sep 13	KS, 21st, 1902
Eoyes, N.		D, 7th Mich.	52		1928 Sep 12	NE, 53rd, 1929
Epla, W.H.			440		1911 Jun 16	IA, 38th, 1912
Epley, Geo. W.		E, 3rd Iowa Cav. (died of paralysis)	22	78	1920 Oct 8	NE, 45th, 1921
Epp, Adam	Pvt.	D, 2nd Wis. Cav.	503	59	1893 Dec 12	IA, 20th, 1894
Epperson, John	Pvt.	K, 33rd Iowa Inf.	29		1928 Dec 19	IA, 55th, 1929
Epperson, W.N.		A, 16th Kans.	251		1923 Aug 5	KS, 43rd, 1924
Epple, David		H, Kimball's Missouri State Militia	36		1904 Nov 14	KS, 24th, 1905
Epply, J.H.	Pvt.	E, 12th Ill. Inf.	267	86	1931 Feb 7	IA, 58th, 1932
Epply, J.H.	Pvt.	E, 12th Ill. Inf.	267		1931 Feb 7	IA, 57th, 1931
Erendine, F.M.		A, 1st Ark.	54		1905 Feb 15	KS, 25th, 1906
Erickson, J.A.	Pvt.	F, 16th Ill. Inf.	57		1911 Feb 23	IA, 38th, 1912
Erickson, John M.	Pvt.	H, 112th Ill. Inf.	375		1912 Nov 8	IA, 39th, 1913
Erickson, N.	Sergt.	D, 36th Ill. Inf.	439	52	1895 Mar 19	IA, 22nd, 1896
Erickson, William, see Erricson, Wm.						
Ernest, A.		G, 7th Cal. Inf.	17		1888	KS, 8th, 1889
Ernest, Daniel		D, 6th Kans. Cav.	3		1912 Oct 30	KS, 32nd, 1913
Ernest, Jacob		H, 146th Ill.	32		1920 Sep 29	KS, 40th, 1921
Ernshaw, Jas.	Pvt.	E, 127th Ill. Inf.	134		1920 Nov	IA, 47th, 1921
Ernst, Albert, see Earnst, Albert						
Ernst, J.H.	Corp.	D, 7th Ohio	48		1926 Mar 17	IA, 53rd, 1927
Ernst, Jos.	Pvt.	E, 16th Iowa Inf.	87	57	1893 Aug 20	IA, 20th, 1894
Errett, Russell H.	Pvt.	F, 66th Ill. Inf.	16		1909 Jan 30	IA, 36th, 1910
Errett, W.H.	Pvt.	I, 126th Ill.	197		1923 Aug 16	IA, 50th, 1924
Erricson, Wm.	Pvt.	D, 26th Ill. Inf.	16		1906 Mar 15	IA, 33rd, 1907

*See Appendix A, B or C for roster of post names and locations.
†See Introduction for note regarding recording of death date.

Name	Rank	Company, Regiment or Ship	Post*	Age	Death Date†	Journal
Erskine, W., see Erskune, W.						
Erskune, W.	Pvt.	D, 114th N.Y. Inf.	5		1908 Jul 17	IA, 35th, 1909
Erthum, Peter C.		died of paralysis	22	80	1908 Oct 12	NE, 33rd, 1909
Erving, F.W.	Pvt.	F, 6th West Va.	7		1921	IA, 48th, 1922
Erwin, Hugh		A, 24th Ind.	32		1905 Feb 13	KS, 25th, 1906
Erwin, L.M.		C, 65th Ohio	57		1923 Dec 25	KS, 43rd, 1924
Escke, Bernard	Sergt.	G, 20th Iowa Inf.	1	64	1893 Nov 27	IA, 20th, 1894
Escue, Sandy	Pvt.	A, 60th U.S. Col.	452		1893	IA, 20th, 1894
Eshbaugh, Frank	Pvt.	6th Iowa Cav.	24		1908	IA, 35th, 1909
Eshbaugh, Joseph		K, 2nd Penn.	51		1906	IA, 33rd, 1907
Eshbaugh, Wm.	Pvt.	2nd Iowa Cav.	452		1921 Nov 19	KS, 41st, 1922
Eshe, Joseph		C, 179th Penn.	115		1915	IA, 42nd, 1916
Esheick, Henry	Pvt.	K, 15th Ill. Inf.	101	63	1917 Nov 29	KS, 37th, 1918
Esher, John U.		E, 11th Iowa (died of typhoid fever)	180	60	1892 Jul 3	IA, 19th, 1893
Eskridge, C.V.		A, 11th Kans.	55		1897 Sep 2	NE, 22nd, 1898
Esnay, James	Pvt.	H, 24th Iowa	163		1900 Jul 15	KS, 20th, 1901
Espy, Chas.	Pvt.	G, —	122		1903 Mar 26	IA, 30th, 1904
Espy, George W.		D, 59th Ohio	25		1911 Apr 15	IA, 38th, 1912
Essex, Alex	Pvt.	G, 15th Iowa	7		1925 Jan 8	KS, 45th, 1926
Essex, J.	Pvt.	D, 32nd Ill. Inf.	111		1922 Aug 8	IA, 49th, 1923
Essex, J.P.		Fremont Rangers	61		1908 Sep 29	IA, 35th, 1909
Essley, John F.		G, 27th Ill. 9th Ill. Inf.	36		4th quarter 1883	IA, 10th, 1884
Esslinger, Ed.	Pvt.	33rd Wis.	102		1921 Jan 27	KS, 41st, 1922
Esslinger, Eman	Pvt.	33rd Wis. Inf.	102		1907 Dec 8	IA, 34th, 1908
Esslinger, S.	Pvt.		81		1909 Nov 10	IA, 36th, 1910
Estabrook, Geo.		B, 64th Ill. (died of apoplexy)	112	76	1930	IA, 57th, 1931
Estabrook, George		B, 64th Ill. (died of apoplexy)	112	76	1918 Dec 5	NE, 44th, 1920
Estel, A.		K, 139th Ill.	94		1918 Dec 5	NE, 43rd, 1919
Estelle, Lee S.		Mississippi Squadron (died of general breakdown; see also Appendix D)	262	74	1921 Aug 13	IA, 48th, 1922
Estep, Enoch		D, 6th Kans.	3		1920 Oct 10	NE, 45th, 1921
Estep, J.N.		M, 39th Ind.	76		1906 Dec 20	KS, 26th, 1907
Ester, Wm. J.		I, 10th Mich.	85		1918 Jul 28	KS, 38th, 1919
Esters, Elijah	Pvt.	G, 18th Iowa	29		1905 Nov 1	KS, 25th, 1906
Estes, E.A.J.	Sergt.	B, 7th Wis. Inf.	159		1923 Dec 18	IA, 50th, 1924
Estes, Geo. M.	Pvt.	H, 39th Iowa Inf.	14		1908 Jan 8	IA, 35th, 1909
Estes, Madison		E, 6th Mo.	172		1919 Sep	IA, 46th, 1920
Estes, W.T.		B, 150th Ill. Inf.	25	71	1928 Dec 3	KS, 48th, 1929
Estes, Wm. M.		G, 23rd Mo.	170		1918 May 14	NE, 43rd, 1919
Estle, William	Pvt.	B, 7th Iowa Vol. Cav.	84		1909 Mar	KS, 29th, 1910
Esty, H.B.		I, 17th Ill.	50		1928 Mar 15	IA, 55th, 1929
Esty, H.S.			188		1908 Jan 1	KS, 28th, 1909
Etchen, John P.		B, 57th Ohio	153		1915	IA, 42nd, 1916
Etchison, Samuel		F, 65th Ind. Inf. (died of old age)	105	76	1912 Jan 9	KS, 32nd, 1913
Etchison, Samuel		F, 65th Ind. (died of old age)	105	82	1913 Aug 28	NE, 38th, 1914
Etgetmills, John		B, 64th Ill. Inf.	91		1914	NE, 39th, 1915
Ethorton, Jas. A.		K, 8th Tenn.	269		1896 Sep 26	NE, 21st, 1897
Ethridge, N.C.		H, N.Y. (Douglas Bat.)	127		1906 Oct 29	KS, 26th, 1907
Ethridge, S.S.	Pvt.	F, 47th Iowa Inf.	12		1905 Feb 19	KS, 25th, 1906
Etter, Francis M.		A, 122nd Ill.	27		1909 Jun 7	IA, 36th, 1910
Etter, Fred J.		G, 15th N.Y. Cav. (died of Bright's disease)	2	70	1910 Dec 13	KS, 30th, 1911
Ettinger, A.L.	Capt.	A, 166th Penn. Inf.	68		1906 Nov 17	NE, 31st, 1907
Eubanks, Jesse D.		I, 47th Iowa Inf.	25		1929 Jan 11	IA, 56th, 1930
Eull, Simon	Pvt.	A, 1st Wis. Inf.	371		1921 Jun 13	KS, 41st, 1922
Eustis, George D.	Corp.	C, 106th N.Y. Inf.	14		1897 Apr 5	IA, 24th, 1898
Eustler, Charles	Pvt.	A, 11th Iowa Inf.	231		1917 Dec 16	IA, 44th, 1918
Eustler, D.F.	Pvt.	A, 11th Iowa Inf.	231		1926 Dec 29	IA, 53rd, 1927
Eva, Henry		H, 2nd Ill. Art.	63		1917 Sep 10	IA, 44th, 1918
Eva, John	Pvt.	F, 3rd Wis. Inf.	97		1916 Dec 10	KS, 36th, 1917
Evan, C.			96		1902 Sep 25	IA, 29th, 1903
					1914 Jul 5	IA, 41st, 1915

See Appendix A, B or C for roster of post names and locations.
†*See Introduction for note regarding recording of death date.*

Name	Rank	Company, Regiment or Ship	Post*	Age	Death Date†	Journal
Evanes, Evan S.	Pvt.	H, 46th Iowa Inf.	137		1916 Apr 14	IA, 43rd, 1917
Evans, A.	Pvt.	B, 47th Ill. Inf.	165		1924	IA, 51st, 1925
Evans, A.N.	Pvt.	I, 25th Iowa Vol. Inf.	108		1924 Oct 2	IA, 51st, 1925
Evans, Amos H.	Pvt.	D, 3rd N.J. Inf.	2		1919 Jul 25	IA, 46th, 1920
Evans, B.B.		R, 103rd Penn. E, 193rd Penn.	12		1927 Nov 1	KS, 47th, 1928
Evans, B.F.		D, 69th Ohio (died of stomach trouble)	13	84	1922 Mar 10	NE, 47th, 1923
Evans, Chas. W.		C, 20th Mass. Inf. C, 10th Mass. Inf. G, 37th Mass. Inf.	64		1900 Sep 30	KS, 20th, 1901
Evans, Daniel		F, 10th Ohio	277		1897 Feb 17	KS, 17th, 1898
Evans, David			316		1906	IA, 33rd, 1907
Evans, David		F, 36th Iowa	100		1912 Oct 19	KS, 32nd, 1913
Evans, Edward		B, 132nd Ill. Inf.	378		1886	KS, 6th, 1887
Evans, Eldon C.	Pvt.	A, 15th Iowa	40		1923 Apr 3	IA, 50th, 1924
Evans, F.H.	Pvt.	G, 39th Iowa Inf.	55		1908 Sep 29	IA, 35th, 1909
Evans, F.J.	Pvt.	A, 1st N.Y. Art.	141		1917 May 22	IA, 44th, 1918
Evans, F.W.	Chaplain	35th Ind. Inf.	7		1908 Sep 3	IA, 35th, 1909
Evans, Frank		B, 144th Ill.	130		1926 Dec 24	KS, 46th, 1927
Evans, G.W.	Pvt.	H, 96th Ill. Inf.	130		1919 Dec 20	IA, 46th, 1920
Evans, Geo. E.		E, 142 —	111		1927 Sep 8	KS, 47th, 1928
Evans, Geo. W.		H, 123rd N.Y.	251		1921 Nov 28	KS, 41st, 1922
Evans, George		G, 12th Ind. Cav.	60		1932 Dec 5	NE, 57th, 1933
Evans, George H.		B, 87th Ind.	1		1905 Aug 8	KS, 25th, 1906
Evans, George H., Mrs.		one of the originators of Decoration Day	12		1st quarter 1884	IA, 10th, 1884
Evans, H.A.	Pvt.	I, 35th Iowa Inf.	19	42	1887 Dec 22	NE, 12th, 1888
Evans, Henry		G, 46th Ind.	1		1898 Mar 28	KS, 18th, 1899
Evans, I.W.		H, 194th N.Y. Inf.	354	70	1906 Oct 18	NE, 31st, 1907
Evans, Inman	2nd Lieut.	B, 13th Iowa Inf.	16		1910 Aug 21	IA, 37th, 1911
Evans, Isaac W.		F, 194th N.Y. Inf. (born in New York; died at Soldiers & Sailors Home Hospital, Burkett; buried at Home Cemetery)		72	1906 Oct 18	NE, 31st, 1907
Evans, Isaiah D.		E, 49th Wis. (member at large; died at Lincoln)			1935 Jan 10	NE, 60th, 1936
Evans, J.A.	Pvt.	D, 83rd Ill. Inf.	39		1931 Sep 5	IA, 58th, 1932
Evans, J.A.	Pvt. & Corp.	D, 9th Ind. Inf. (died of heart disease)	35	46	1887 Jan 17	NE, 12th, 1888
Evans, J.H.	Capt.	G, 31st Iowa Inf.	40		1908 Jul 9	IA, 35th, 1909
Evans, J.K.			265		1923	KS, 43rd, 1924
Evans, J.P.	Sergt.	I, 117th Ill. Inf.	124	56	1898 Oct 30	IA, 25th, 1899
Evans, J.W.			380		1924 Jul 24	KS, 44th, 1925
Evans, James			44		1883	KS, 3rd, 1884
Evans, James B.		H, 2nd Kans. C, 2nd Kans.	250		1913 Dec 12	KS, 33rd, 1914
Evans, Jeremiah	Pvt.	I, 35th Iowa Inf.	255		1918 Jan	IA, 45th, 1919
Evans, Jeremiah		E, 5th N.Y. Art.	343		1886	KS, 6th, 1887
Evans, Jesse		M, 12th Mo.	241		1921 May 29	KS, 41st, 1922
Evans, Jno. W.	Pvt.	I, 37th Iowa Inf.	403	75	1888 Dec 28	IA, 17th, 1891
Evans, John			69		1899 Dec 12	IA, 26th, 1900
Evans, John		1st Colo. Battery	117		1912 Feb 26	KS, 32nd, 1913
Evans, John B.	Pvt.	B, 10th Ind. Inf.	343		1924	IA, 51st, 1925
Evans, John P.	Pvt.	Ind.	343		1923 Jan 31	IA, 50th, 1924
Evans, John W.	Pvt.	D, 14th Wis. Inf.	186		1915 Jan 3	IA, 42nd, 1916
Evans, Jonas H.		H, 103rd Ill. (former member; died at Fairbury)	77		1936 Feb 3	NE, 61st, 1937
Evans, Joseph S.	Pvt.	E, 39th Ill. Inf.	66	92	1933 Dec 15	IA, 60th, 1934
Evans, Joshua		K, 6th Ind. Inf.	19		1910 Sep 9	KS, 30th, 1911
Evans, Josiah L.	Pvt.	D, 6th Iowa Cav.	216	59	1899 Apr 15	IA, 25th, 1899
Evans, M.V.B.	Pvt.	I, 8th Iowa Cav.	155		1920 Feb 26	IA, 47th, 1921
Evans, Melvin		Iowa			1913 Jun 21	KS, 33rd, 1914
Evans, Philander		A, 109th N.Y.	293		1921 Jan 17	KS, 41st, 1922
Evans, R.P.		A, 15th Kans.	256		1911 Jul 26	KS, 31st, 1912
Evans, R.W.		E, 2nd Colo. Cav.	294		1912 Mar	KS, 32nd, 1913
Evans, R.W.		F, 18th Ohio	18		1922 May 12	KS, 42nd, 1923

*See Appendix A, B or C for roster of post names and locations.

†See Introduction for note regarding recording of death date.

Name	Rank	Company, Regiment or Ship	Post*	Age	Death Date†	Journal
Evans, S.C.	QMS	1st N.Y. Battery	23	68	1907 Feb 2	NE, 32nd, 1908
Evans, S.J.		C, 1st Cor. Ill.	15		1904 Nov 12	KS, 24th, 1905
Evans, S.M.	Pvt.	H, 15th Ind. Inf.	98		1908 Jan 9	IA, 35th, 1909
Evans, S.P.		37th Iowa	69		1903-1904	IA, 30th, 1904
Evans, Samuel		A, 1st Mo.	209		1908 Jun 4	KS, 28th, 1909
Evans, Thomas	Pvt.	A, 17th Ky. Inf.	14		1910	IA, 37th, 1911
Evans, Thomas		F, 46th Penn. Inf.	12		1908 Mar 28	KS, 28th, 1909
Evans, Torrence		I, 32nd Ill.	25		1897 Sep 29	KS, 17th, 1898
Evans, W.F.	Pvt.	F, 29th Iowa Inf.	10		1926	IA, 53rd, 1927
Evans, W.G.		C, 135th Ind.	265		1926 Aug 13	KS, 46th, 1927
Evans, W.O.	Major	140th Ill. Inf.	131	57	1895 May 22	IA, 22nd, 1896
Evans, W.S.		F, 4th Ind. Cav.	4		1899 Nov 22	KS, 19th, 1900
Evans, W.T.	Surg.	Art. & 15th V.R.C. 19th Ohio Hvy. Art.	64		1892 Jan 7 or 8	KS, 12th, 1893
Evans, Willard M.					1928 Dec 24	NE, 53rd, 1929
Eveland, John L.		A, 40th N.Y.	25		1926 Nov 13	NE, 51st, 1927
Eveland, Peter		E, 18th Iowa	123		1933 Jan 2	NE, 58th, 1934
Evens, A.L.		H, 44th Ill.	63		1926 Apr 27	KS, 46th, 1927
Evens, J.M.	Pvt.		31		1920 Nov 22	IA, 47th, 1921
Everest, A.S.		C, 56th Ohio Inf. (died at Atchison; buried at Mt. Vernon)	336		1894 Dec 21	KS, 14th, 1895
Everet, John		H, 104th Ill.	52		1923 Aug 29	KS, 43rd, 1924
Everett, Elmer		H, 83rd Ill.	17		1921 May 22	KS, 41st, 1922
Everett, Henry		B, 104th Ill.	52		1922 Nov 25	KS, 42nd, 1923
Everett, J.F.	Pvt.	F, 4th Iowa Cav.	40		1909 Nov 23	IA, 36th, 1910
Everett, J.S.	Corp.	G, 40th Iowa Inf.	96	54	1897 Apr 17	IA, 24th, 1898
Everett, John	Pvt.	C, 210th Penn. Inf.	18		1908	IA, 35th, 1909
Everett, Thomas	Pvt.	F, 6th Iowa Cav.	24		1929	IA, 56th, 1930
Everett, Wm.	Pvt.	D, 9th Ind. Inf.	26		1918 Mar 1	IA, 45th, 1919
Everett, Wm. S.	Sergt.	23rd Iowa	6		1903-1904	IA, 30th, 1904
Everette, Martin S.		G, 53rd Ohio	256		1938 Jan 17	KS, 57th, 1938
Everetts, Harlow	Pvt.	G, 12th Ind. Cav.	46		1926 Nov 8	IA, 53rd, 1927
Everhard, W.H.	Sergt.	E, 87th Ohio Inf.	1		1910 Dec 23	IA, 37th, 1911
Everhart, Charles S.		C, 145th Ind.	465		1914 Aug 21	KS, 34th, 1915
Everhart, Jacob		C, 165th Penn.	3		1913 Jun 1	KS, 33rd, 1914
Everhart, James	Pvt.	E, 57th Ohio Inf.	215	73	1895 Oct 26	IA, 22nd, 1896
Everhart, John	Pvt.	F, 26th Iowa	159		1914 Dec 27	IA, 41st, 1915
Everingham, W.H.	Pvt.	I, 9th Iowa Inf.	277	75	1897 Dec 10	IA, 24th, 1898
Everitt, William H.		H, 4th Mo. (died at Hallowell, Kans.; buried at McKee Cemetery)	200		1894 Nov 26	KS, 14th, 1895
Everman, W.F.	Pvt.	H, 8th Iowa Cav.	122		1910 Mar 27	IA, 37th, 1911
Evers, E., see Eoers, E.						
Eversoll, Joshua	Pvt.	I, 118th Ill. Inf.	347		1899 Dec 17	IA, 26th, 1900
Everst, David		D, 13th Wis.	25		1931 Mar 22	NE, 56th, 1932
Everts, Herbert Newell		H, 6th Minn. Inf.	168	93	1937 Jan 25	IA, 64th, 1938
Ewald, Nicholas		G, 50th Ill. Inf.	208	96	1937 Aug 14	IA, 64th, 1938
Ewalt, Jake			44	79	1924 Oct 28	NE, 49th, 1925
Ewards, A.H.	Pvt.	G, 139th Ill.	34		1923 Mar 1	IA, 50th, 1924
Ewart, A.J.		B, 123rd Ill.	1		1910 Dec 24	KS, 30th, 1911
Ewen, James		G, 18th Mo.	1		1926 Mar 5	KS, 46th, 1927
Ewing, A.O.		A, 10th Wis. Inf.	1		1936 Jul 12	KS, 57th, 1938
Ewing, F.P.		10th Ohio	245		1897 Jan 29	KS, 16th, 1897
Ewing, F.P.		10th Ohio	245		1897 Jan 30	KS, 17th, 1898
Ewing, Geo. W.			204		1891 Oct 26	IA, 18th, 1892
Ewing, Henry A.		E, 14th Ill. Inf.	51		1934 Dec 6	KS, 54th, 1935
Ewing, J.K.	Pvt.	A, 104th Ill. Inf.	271		1930 Apr 3	IA, 57th, 1931
Ewing, John		C, 115th U.S. Colored Inf. (died at Dighton; buried at Dighton Cemetery)	415		1894 Nov 12	KS, 14th, 1895
Ewing, John J.		F, 38th Ill.	145		1911 Jul 28	KS, 31st, 1912
Ewing, John T.		H, 5th Penn. Art.	12		1910 Dec 12	KS, 30th, 1911
Ewing, Nelson			123		1895	KS, 15th, 1896
Ewing, Nelson		A, 11th U.S.A.	123		1896	KS, 16th, 1897

*See Appendix A, B or C for roster of post names and locations.
†See Introduction for note regarding recording of death date.

Name	Rank	Company, Regiment or Ship	Post*	Age	Death Date†	Journal
Ewing, Robert		H, 43rd Ind.	32		1921 Mar 15	KS, 41st, 1922
Ewing, Robt. E.	Sergt.	I, 4th Iowa Cav.	12		1918 May 6	IA, 45th, 1919
Ewing, S.M.		K, 126th Ill. Inf.	147		1909 Feb 7	KS, 29th, 1910
Ewing, T.H.		206th Penn. (died of old age)	265	80	1913	NE, 39th, 1915
Eye, Wm.		K, 10th Kans.	283		1898 Jun 4	KS, 18th, 1899
Eyerly, George	Pvt.	E, 40th Iowa Inf.	55		1927 May 5	IA, 54th, 1928
Eyestone, Amos D., see Egestone, Amos D.						
Eyestone, J.		E, 10th Ill. Cav.	65		1898 Apr 9	KS, 18th, 1899
Eyestone, Jno. W.	Lieut.	K, 13th Iowa Inf.	400		1930 Feb 19	IA, 57th, 1931
Eyler, O.H.		F, 7th Ohio Cav.	68		1893 Nov 4	KS, 13th, 1894
Eynon, John		D, 172nd N.Y.	3		1892 Feb 19	KS, 12th, 1893
Fabrick, G.A.	Pvt.	E, 100th Ill. Inf.	222		1928 Dec 27	IA, 55th, 1929
Fackler, Enoch		D, 208th Penn.	209		1914 Jun 7	KS, 34th, 1915
Fackler, James W.	Pvt.	B, 22nd Iowa Inf.	8		1912 Jun 20	IA, 39th, 1913
Fadden, J.S.	Pvt.	B, 10th Wis. Inf.	124		1922 Dec 15	IA, 49th, 1923
Fagan, Ben		24th Mass. (was a prisoner at Tyler, Tex., for 10 months; died at Enid, Okla.; leaves a wife & son)	22	59	1902 Dec 1	KS, 22nd, 1903
Fagan, Hugh	Pvt.	I, 21st Iowa Inf.	369		1913 Sep 25	IA, 40th, 1914
Fagan, J.J.	Pvt.	I, 21st Iowa Inf.	369		1921 Oct 29	IA, 48th, 1922
Fagan, Thos.	Lieut.	A, 7th Iowa Inf.	231		1907 May 4	IA, 34th, 1908
Fagan, W.F.		H, 11th Kans.	71		1920 May 18	KS, 40th, 1921
Fagen, Ezra B.	Pvt.	F, 47th Iowa Inf.	12		1913 Jul 26	IA, 40th, 1914
Fague, Michael		E, 44th Iowa (died of old age)	308	89	1909 Oct 21	NE, 34th, 1910
Fahnstock, S.J.		A, 15th Penn. Inf.	7		1919 Feb 22	IA, 46th, 1920
Failor, B.M.	Surg.	19th Ohio Inf.	16		1901 Sep 30	IA, 28th, 1902
Failor, Emanuel		K, 64th Ohio	238		1916 Oct 27	KS, 36th, 1917
Failor, S.	Pvt.	Dodge Brig. Band	16		1921 Sep 24	IA, 48th, 1922
Fain, Geo.		B, 19th Ky. Inf.	26		1889	KS, 9th, 1890
Fair, E.W.		G, 66th Ohio	142		1914 Nov 19	KS, 34th, 1915
Fair, Lyman		G, 92nd Ill.	175		1923 Jan 1	KS, 43rd, 1924
Fair, W.H.		G, 71st Ohio	158		1935 Jan 1	KS, 55th, 1936
Fairbank, C.W.	Pvt.	H, N.Y. Inf.	124		1922 Jan 19	IA, 49th, 1923
Fairbanks, A.	Pvt.	A, 47th Ill. Inf. (died of hemorrhage of bowels)	306	53	1891 Apr 6	NE, 16th, 1892
Fairbanks, D.		A, 154th N.Y. Inf. (died at Blue Rapids)	328		1895 Mar	KS, 15th, 1896
Fairbanks, J.C.	Pvt.	H, 86th N.Y. Inf.	319	59	1890 Sep 7	IA, 17th, 1891
Fairbanks, N.D.		K, 4th N.Y. Cav.	19		1892 Jun 24	KS, 12th, 1893
Fairbanks, W.H.		B, 67th Penn. Inf.	206		1892 Dec	NE, 17th, 1893
Fairbrother, Geo. W.		D, Mo. State Militia Cal.[Cav.] (died of old age)	309	72	1900 Jun 3	NE, 25th, 1901
Fairbrother, Hiram	Pvt.	H, 15th Iowa Inf.	68		1909 Feb 10	IA, 36th, 1910
Fairchild, E.R.		G, 13th Kans.	53		1921 Oct 22	KS, 41st, 1922
Fairchild, H.C.		I, 7th Iowa	25		1922 Apr 11	KS, 42nd, 1923
Fairchild, John		A, 4th Iowa Cav. (died of surgical operation)	52		1894 Aug	NE, 19th, 1895
Fairchilds, J.B.		I, 7th Ind.	4		1906 Sep 14	KS, 26th, 1907
Fairchilds, Lee	Sergt.	E, 133rd N.Y. Inf.	34	56	1886 Nov 6	IA, 13th, 1887
Fairleigh, D.J.		F, 71st Ind.	4		1927 Dec 20	KS, 47th, 1928
Fairleigh, Leander		H, 14th Ind.	4		1915 Jan 9	KS, 35th, 1916
Fairman, J.W.	Pvt.	L, 4th Iowa Cav.	193		1911 May 5	IA, 38th, 1912
Fairweather, John	Lieut.	I, 1st Minn. Hvy. Art.	25		1912	IA, 39th, 1913
Fairweather, John	Corp.	E, 124th Ill. Inf.	25		1912	IA, 39th, 1913
Fakiner, Justus		A, 29th N.Y. Inf.	28		1917 Oct 27	KS, 37th, 1918
Falconer, Chas.		I, 4th Iowa Inf.	190		1918 Apr 21	IA, 45th, 1919
Falconer, Reuben		I, 36th Iowa (died of cancer of stomach)	4	66	1908 Nov 7	NE, 33rd, 1909
Falconer, William P.		L, 4th Ind. Cav.	275		1886	KS, 6th, 1887
Fales, Emerson F.	Pvt.	E, 4th Maine Inf.	34	61	1894 Jul 11	IA, 21st, 1895
Falkender, John		D, 3rd Penn.	138		1885	KS, 5th, 1886
Falkner, Chas.			457		1918	IA, 45th, 1919
Falls, J.W.		E, 57th Ind.	243		1920	KS, 40th, 1921
Falsted, J.		G, 2nd Neb. Cav. (died of disability)	84	79	1908 Jan	NE, 33rd, 1909

Name	Rank	Company, Regiment or Ship	Post*	Age	Death Date†	Journal
Fancett, Thomas B.	Pvt.	C, 24th Iowa Inf.	110	58	1895 Apr 3	IA, 21st, 1895
Fancher, Abram A.	Corp.	K, 1st Wis. Cav.	29		1925 Mar 9	IA, 52nd, 1926
Fancher, Elias B.	Corp., Sergt., 2nd Lieut., & 1st Lieut.	K, 22nd Wis. D, 36th Wis. (see also Appendix D)	25		1926 Jan 31	NE, 51st, 1927
Fancher, Henry		F, 87th Ind.	19		1918 Jun 10	KS, 38th, 1919
Fanger, Henry	Pvt.	F, 10th Iowa Inf.	327		1923 Feb 27	IA, 50th, 1924
Fangler, Geo.	Corp.	A, 21st Iowa Inf.	78		1900 Apr 28	IA, 27th, 1901
Fangmire, Wm.	Pvt.	F, 35th Iowa Inf.	231		1919 Mar 24	IA, 46th, 1920
Fannace, E.E.		F, 75th Ill. Inf.	113		1918 Oct 1	KS, 38th, 1919
Fannin, M.C.	Pvt.	E, 7th Iowa Inf.	2		1920 Nov 20	IA, 47th, 1921
Fanning, Joseph			254		1897 Jul 25	KS, 17th, 1898
Fansey, John	Pvt.	C, 4th Penn. Cav.	440	54	1895 Jun 1	IA, 22nd, 1896
Fantroy, Henry		B, 116th U.S. Col.	257		1925 Jun 15	KS, 45th, 1926
Fantroy, Joseph		B, 116th U.S. Col.	257		1924 Jun 11	KS, 44th, 1925
Farass, J.A.		A, — Ohio	14		1931	KS, 51st, 1932
Farass, J.A.		A, — Ohio	14		1932	KS, 52nd, 1933
Fard, T.P.			167		1919 Mar 31	IA, 46th, 1920
Farier, R.P.		1st Iowa	244		1926 Aug 2	KS, 46th, 1927
Farioin, Jos. C.	Pvt.	L, 1st Wis. Lt. Art.	153		1912 Dec 10	IA, 39th, 1913
Faris, J.C.			96		1916 Feb 6	IA, 43rd, 1917
Farison, W.H.		K, 5th Mo. Inf.	356		1901 Dec 17	KS, 21st, 1902
Farland, Thos.	Pvt.	D, 42nd Wis. Inf.	140		1924 Dec 24	IA, 51st, 1925
Farlemire, N.	Major	4th Ind. Cav.	122		4th quarter 1883	IA, 10th, 1884
Farley, B.F.		I, 69th Ill.	32	76	1916 Jan 17	NE, 41st, 1917
Farley, F.H.	Pvt.	I, 13th Iowa	22		1922 Jun 14	IA, 49th, 1923
Farley, J.W.		I, 13th Iowa	63		1908 Apr 7	KS, 28th, 1909
Farley, James	Pvt.	B, 11th Iowa Inf.	233		1903 Mar 7	IA, 29th, 1903
Farley, James M.	Corp.	D, 2nd Minn. Inf.	43		1899	NE, 24th, 1900
Farley, Joe		F, 11th Iowa	238		1912 Jul	KS, 32nd, 1913
Farley, Mat.	Pvt.	G, 15th Iowa Inf.	425	46	1891 Oct 4	IA, 18th, 1892
Farley, Owen	Pvt.	G, 20th Iowa Inf.	415	43	1889 May 26	IA, 16th, 1890
Farley, Patrick		C, 2nd U.S. Inf. (died of old age)	9		1921 Jul 21	NE, 46th, 1922
Farley, W.	Pvt.	B, 142nd Ill.	300		1921 Sep 2	IA, 48th, 1922
Farlin, Horace	Pvt.	C, 119th Ill. Inf.	271		1905 Jun 13	IA, 32nd, 1906
Farlowe, N.M.		F, 13th Ind. Cav.	4		1920 Mar 27	KS, 40th, 1921
Farmer, A.			226		1926 Dec 12	KS, 46th, 1927
Farmer, C.H.		K, 42nd Ill.	139		1888	KS, 8th, 1889
Farmer, J.J.		C, 2nd Kans.	129		1906 Sep 19	KS, 26th, 1907
Farmer, J.Q.G.		C, 2nd Kans.	129		1905 Sep 19	KS, 25th, 1906
Farmer, Jas. D.	Pvt.	I, 1st Minn. Inf.	217		1892-1893	IA, 19th, 1893
Farmer, John A.		H, 68th Ind.	42		1912 Feb 15	KS, 32nd, 1913
Farmer, John W.	Corp.	B, 40th Iowa Inf.	127		1900 Jul 14	IA, 27th, 1901
Farmer, L.W.	Pvt.	B, 40th Iowa Inf.	127		1897 Jan 9	IA, 23rd, 1897
Farmer, Mat	Pvt.	H, 42nd Wis. Inf.	142		1918 Nov 11	IA, 45th, 1919
Farmer, P.S.	Pvt.	G, 49th Wis. Inf.	42		1927 Mar 30	IA, 54th, 1928
Farmer, Samuel	Pvt.	B, 48th Iowa Inf.	149		1928 Aug	IA, 55th, 1929
Farmer, Thos.	Pvt.	C, 1st Wis. Inf.	235		1900-1901	IA, 27th, 1901
Farmwith, W.C.	Pvt.	D, 8th N.Y. Inf.	68		1920 Oct 9	IA, 47th, 1921
Farner, John		B, 13th Ohio	13		1933 Oct 8	NE, 58th, 1934
Farnesworth, E.M.	Corp.	D, 3rd Iowa Inf.	168		1890 Jan 23	IA, 16th, 1890
Farney, Isaiah		B, 185th Ohio	337		1927	KS, 47th, 1928
Farnham, O.	Corp.	B, 42nd Wis. Inf.	16		1911 Jun 25	IA, 38th, 1912
Farnsworth, G.W.	Pvt.	H, 34th Mass. Inf.	135		1921 Apr 24	IA, 48th, 1922
Farnsworth, H.A.	Corp.	A, 16th Iowa Inf.	88		1909 Sep 19	IA, 36th, 1910
Farnsworth, Henry C.		G, 18th Iowa Inf.	250		1917 Oct 3	KS, 37th, 1918
Farnsworth, John	Pvt.	D, 174th Ohio Inf.	94	83	1931 Sep 9	IA, 58th, 1932
Farnsworth, R.N.		G, 3rd Vt.	370		1897 Jan 31	KS, 17th, 1898
Farnsworth, Russell		F, 123rd N.Y.	379		1896 Oct 23	KS, 16th, 1897
Farnsworth, T.H.	Pvt.	B, 4th Maine Inf.	22		1911 Jun 4	IA, 38th, 1912
Faroute, John A.	Pvt.	F, 4th Iowa Inf.	55		1915 Aug 10	IA, 42nd, 1916
Farr, Charles H.		B, 2nd Mo. Cav.	46		1916 Jul 28	KS, 36th, 1917
Farr, J.L.	Pvt.	M, 2nd Cal. Cav.	154	60	1888 Feb 14	IA, 15th, 1889

*See Appendix A, B or C for roster of post names and locations.
†See Introduction for note regarding recording of death date.

Name	Rank	Company, Regiment or Ship	Post*	Age	Death Date†	Journal
Farr, Nathan L.		H, 33rd Ind.	55		1913 Sep 23	KS, 33rd, 1914
Farram, Simon		B, 8th Ill. Cav.	88		1912 Sep 26	KS, 32nd, 1913
Farran, Thomas		E, 140th N.Y. (died of softening of brain)	5	68	1910 Dec 18	NE, 35th, 1911
Farrand, J.W.		D, 18th Iowa	147		1911 Apr 17	KS, 31st, 1912
Farrand, Jas. F.	Pvt.	B, 21st Iowa (died of hernia)	170	42	1884 Jan 19	NE, 9th, 1885
Farrar, L.P.		H, Iowa R. Regt.	7	62	1904 Mar 12	NE, 29th, 1905
Farrell, Geo. W.		F, 1st Ill. Lt. Art.	80		1903-1904	IA, 30th, 1904
Farrell, Gregory		D, 28th N.Y. Inf. (died of kidney trouble)	2	49	1896 Oct 10	NE, 21st, 1897
Farrell, Isaac L.	Pvt.	A, 1st Iowa Cav.	170	54	1891 Dec 30	IA, 19th, 1893
Farrell, J.B.		G, 98th Ohio	98		1927 Dec 9	NE, 52nd, 1928
Farrell, J.W.		E, 26th Ill.	100		1926 May 13	KS, 46th, 1927
Farrell, James	Pvt.	A, 46th Ill. Inf.	206		1919 Mar 5	IA, 46th, 1920
Farrell, John	Sergt.	K, 4th —	18		1905 Dec 18	IA, 32nd, 1906
Farrell, W.P.			71		1928 Mar 26	KS, 48th, 1929
Farrell, William		B, 23rd Ind. Inf.	380		1909 Feb 15	KS, 29th, 1910
Farrier, T.D.	Pvt.	D, 11th Iowa Inf.	110		1917 Dec 15	IA, 44th, 1918
Farrington, J.L.	Pvt.	B, 126th Ill. Inf.	141		1928 Jul 17	IA, 55th, 1929
Farris, J.H.	Corp.	C, 9th Iowa Cav.	251		1915 Apr 9	IA, 42nd, 1916
Farris, Matthew J.	Pvt.	F, 49th Mich.	54		1926 Mar 16	IA, 53rd, 1927
Farris, Oratis N.		C, 1st Ky.	253		1910	KS, 30th, 1911
Farris, Samuel		F, 36th Ohio	142		1909 Jan 3	KS, 29th, 1910
Farris, William J.		D, 6th Mo.	42		1928 Mar 11	NE, 52nd, 1928
Fass, Joseph		G, 1st Wis. Art. (died of paralysis)	182	76	1918 Jan 16	NE, 43rd, 1919
Fast, Luther	Pvt.	B, 16th Ohio Inf.	49		1930 Jan 16	IA, 57th, 1931
Fast, Wm. A.	Pvt.	E, 16th Iowa	334	51	1890 Jun 24	IA, 17th, 1891
Fath, Jacob	Pvt.	G, 19th Iowa Inf.	231		1922 Nov 23	IA, 49th, 1923
Fatty, Charles		D, 16th Ind.	12		1925 Dec 19	KS, 45th, 1926
Fatzer, Jacob		E, 29th Ill. Vol. Inf.	241		1916 Apr	KS, 36th, 1917
Faulhanber, C.	Pvt.	K, 2nd Iowa Inf.	70	62	1896 Nov 1	IA, 23rd, 1897
Faulk, J.H.		F, 100th Ind. Inf.	225		1914 Dec 15	KS, 34th, 1915
Faulkender, G.T.		K, 99th Ill.	46		1908 Aug 28	KS, 28th, 1909
Faulkes, Ed. O.	Pvt.	A, 11th Mich. Cav.	17		1924 Mar 22	IA, 51st, 1925
Faulkner, Frank J.		D, 156th Ind. Inf.	9		1911 Jul 2	KS, 31st, 1912
Faulkner, Jesse		H, 59th Ill.	59		1923 Jul 30	KS, 43rd, 1924
Faulkner, Lemuel	Chaplain		464		1905	KS, 25th, 1906
Faulkner, T.F.	Pvt.	H, 115th Ind. Inf.	192		1923 Apr 16	IA, 50th, 1924
Faulteroy, William		H, 101st U.S.C.I.	153		1914 Mar 7	KS, 34th, 1915
Fauquer, O.H.	Pvt.	B, 40th Iowa Inf.	127	52	1890 Jun 8	IA, 18th, 1892
Faurot, J.P.		F, 6th N.Y. Art.	407		1908	KS, 28th, 1909
Faus, Jacob		D, West Va. Inf. (died of Bright's disease)	133	67	1911 Aug 14	NE, 37th, 1913
Faust, Samuel		E, 129th Penn.	129		1923 Jun 12	KS, 43rd, 1924
Faust, W.M.		G, 6th Iowa Cav.	78		3rd quarter 1884	IA, 11th, 1885
Fawcett, Asa		K, 42nd Ohio	17		1921 Dec 19	KS, 41st, 1922
Fawcett, Jacob		I, 16th Wis. Inf.	7		1928 Apr 18	NE, 53rd, 1929
Faxon, Joseph		A, 1st N.Y. Art.	354	74	1911 Mar 19	NE, 36th, 1912
Fay, D.H.		S, 31st N.Y.	71		1928 Dec 8	KS, 48th, 1929
Fay, Henry W.		K, 47th Iowa	97		1935 Jan 10	NE, 60th, 1936
Fay, Lewis		A, 13th Kans.	76		1887 Sep 10	KS, 7th, 1888
Fay, Patrick		G, 3rd Ill.	93		1909 May 23	KS, 29th, 1910
Fay, Walter F.		C, 14th & 32nd Wis. (not a member of the G.A.R.)	4		1912 May 25	KS, 32nd, 1913
Fayran, J.H.	Pvt.	H, 56th Ill. Inf.	492		1906 Nov 13	IA, 33rd, 1907
Feaks, Wm.	Pvt.	M, 13th N.Y. Cav.	[152/153?]		1912 Nov 27	IA, 39th, 1913
Fear, F., Dr.			247		1902	KS, 22nd, 1903
Fear, J.H.	Pvt.	B, 33rd Iowa Inf.	167	90	1933 Sep 2	IA, 60th, 1934
Fearing, W.G.		D, 16th Iowa Inf.	12		1908 May 9	KS, 28th, 1909
Fearn, A.C.			168		1908	IA, 35th, 1909
Fearn, E.I.	Pvt. & Sergt.	I, 6th Wis. (died of chronic diarrhea)	80	55	1885 Dec 11	NE, 10th, 1886
Fears, James		A, 14th U.S. Inf.	354	79	1906 Jul 7	NE, 31st, 1907

Name	Rank	Company, Regiment or Ship	Post*	Age	Death Date†	Journal
Fears, James		A, 14th U.S. Colored Inf. (born in Virginia; died of heart failure at Soldiers & Sailors Home Hospital, Burkett; buried at Grand Island, Neb.)		79	1906 Jul 7	NE, 31st, 1907
Feaster, J.H.		G, 75th Ill. Inf.	107		1892 Mar 19	NE, 17th, 1893
Feather, P.W.		K, 22nd Wis.	100	71	1905 Jan 1	NE, 29th, 1905
Feathers, J.M.		F, 17th West Va. (died of debility)	1	75	1918 Apr 3	NE, 43rd, 1919
Fedbaugh, G.		B, 8th Iowa Inf.	92		1905 Nov 3	IA, 32nd, 1906
Fee, John F.	Pvt.	G, 40th Iowa Inf.	49		1914 Dec 17	IA, 41st, 1915
Fee, Syl.		B, 68th Ill. Inf.	38		1899 Feb 7	KS, 19th, 1900
Fee, T.M.	Capt.	G, 36th Iowa Inf.	122		1910 Apr 12	IA, 37th, 1911
Fee, W.			132		1923	IA, 50th, 1924
Fee, W.F.	Pvt.	D, 4th Wis. Inf.	90		1908 Dec 7	IA, 35th, 1909
Feegans, H.G.	Pvt.	G, 95th Ill. Inf.	125		1921 Feb 1	IA, 48th, 1922
Feehan, John	Pvt.	E, 50th Ill.	69		1923 Aug 2	IA, 50th, 1924
Feenan, M.J.		M, 6th Iowa Cav.	7		1928 May 17	NE, 53rd, 1929
Fegan, Jos. D.	Capt.	B, 26th Iowa Inf.	88		1913 Sep 2	IA, 40th, 1914
Fehr, A.	Pvt.		29		1916 Apr 1	IA, 43rd, 1917
Fehr, Benj.			73		1914	IA, 41st, 1915
Fehr, Owen			14		1884	KS, 4th, 1885
Feifer, W.F.			2		1926 Aug 21	IA, 53rd, 1927
Feighan, John W.	Col.	born April 5, 1845; died in Spokane, Washington (see also Appendix D)			1898 May 28	KS, 18th, 1899
Feigley, J.C.			7		1893 May 21	KS, 13th, 1894
Feihler, Henry			40		1897 Mar 16	KS, 17th, 1898
Feist, Phillip	Pvt.	B, 123rd Penn.	1		1915 Apr 7	KS, 35th, 1916
Felcher, John	Pvt.	G, 27th Iowa Inf.	132	69	1895 Feb 18	IA, 21st, 1895
Feldpausch, G.	Pvt.	B, 8th Iowa Vol. Inf.	92		1906 Nov 4	IA, 33rd, 1907
Felker, J.S.	Pvt.	K, 12th Maine Inf.	40	55	1892 Oct 14	IA, 19th, 1893
Fell, A.B.		C, 19th Penn.	265		1927 Sep 19	KS, 47th, 1928
Fell, S.T.	Pvt.	G, 139th Ill. Inf.	19		1929 Oct 28	IA, 56th, 1930
Feller, Fredrick G.		F, 19th Ohio	34		1913 Sep 23	KS, 33rd, 1914
Felling, N.			233		1906 Jun 3	IA, 33rd, 1907
Fellows, J.B.		B, 53rd Ill. Inf.	4		1914 Feb 5	KS, 34th, 1915
Fellows, W.E.	Pvt.	I, 71st N.Y. Inf.	327	88	1895 Mar 2	IA, 22nd, 1896
Felson, S.T.			97		1883	KS, 3rd, 1884
Felt, G.W.		E, 24th N.Y. Inf. (died of abdominal tumor)	63		1893 May 21	NE, 18th, 1894
Felt, Peter F.		F, 78th Ill.	127		1919 Jun 16	KS, 39th, 1920
Felter, Joshua		A, 1st N.Y. Eng. (died of consumption)	118	67	1897 Mar	NE, 22nd, 1898
Felton, C.K.		F, 56th Penn. Inf.	250		1886	KS, 6th, 1887
Felton, D.B.	Pvt.	H, 9th Iowa Cav.	43	49	1897 Feb 2	IA, 23rd, 1897
Felton, J.B.		B, 14th West Va. Inf.	87		1917 Jul 27	KS, 37th, 1918
Feltz, Anton			461		1917	IA, 44th, 1918
Feltz, Anton			333		1917	IA, 44th, 1918
Feltz, Anton	Pvt.	Chicago Bat.	333		1916	IA, 43rd, 1917
Felwack, L.	Pvt.	K, 42nd Wis. Inf.	377		1918 Aug 9	IA, 45th, 1919
Fender, E.		F, 9th Kans.	73		1888	KS, 8th, 1889
Fenenden, E.	Pvt.	G, 8th V.R.C.	42		1911 Apr 3	IA, 38th, 1912
Fenk, Wm. D.		A, 185th N.Y.	[25?]		1923	NE, 48th, 1924
Fenn, Amos A.		C, 19th Kans.	6		1913	KS, 33rd, 1914
Fenn, E.B., Dr.		C, 4th Iowa	19		1892 May 30	KS, 12th, 1893
Fenn, Isaac		K, 11th Kans.	68		1928 Jun 15	KS, 48th, 1929
Fenn, Leno E.		C, 33rd Iowa	332		1896 Oct 16	KS, 16th, 1897
Fenner, James W.	Pvt.	B, 16th Ohio Inf.	16		1909 Oct 18	IA, 36th, 1910
Fenstemaker, Lewis		D, 34th Ill.	12		1913 Feb 7	KS, 33rd, 1914
Fenton, Aug.	Pvt.	F, 12th Ill. Inf.	68		1925 Mar 31	IA, 52nd, 1926
Fenton, J.H.	Pvt.	I, 9th Iowa Inf.	118	54	1890 Aug 29	IA, 17th, 1891
Fenton, J.H.			6		1917 Feb 26	KS, 37th, 1918
Fenton, Lewis H.	Pvt.	I, 6th Ind. Battery	20		1925 Oct 29	IA, 52nd, 1926
Fenton, Otis J.	Lieut.		169		1903 Nov 10	IA, 30th, 1904
Fenton, Samuel H.		K, 3rd Penn. Cav. (died at Wichita)	25		1895 Jul	KS, 15th, 1896
Fenton, W.H.		H, 81st Ohio	1		1931 Apr 26	KS, 51st, 1932

See Appendix A, B or C for roster of post names and locations.
†See Introduction for note regarding recording of death date.*

Name	Rank	Company, Regiment or Ship	Post*	Age	Death Date†	Journal
Fenton, William		C, 77th Ohio Inf.	49		1900 Sep 30	KS, 20th, 1901
Fenull, John		1st & 4th Mass. Cav. (died of old age)	318	77	1919 Feb 8	NE, 44th, 1920
Fenwick, Wm.		I, 39th Iowa	83		1922 Mar 8	KS, 42nd, 1923
Fepler, Henry		55th Ill. Inf.	19	70	1911 Feb 25	NE, 36th, 1912
Ferdinand	Pvt.	B, 3rd Mo. Cav.	22		1911 Sep 25	IA, 38th, 1912
Ferdryce, J.G.	Pvt.		108		1914 Sep	IA, 41st, 1915
Fergus, A.R.		F, 151st Ind. (died of general decline)	13	83	1909 Jan 23	NE, 34th, 1910
Ferguson, A.		25th Iowa Inf.	108		1913	IA, 40th, 1914
Ferguson, A.J.	Pvt.	F, 121st Ohio Inf.	84		1912 Jul 26	IA, 39th, 1913
Ferguson, A.J.		8th Iowa Cav.	5	79	1922 Jul 8	NE, 47th, 1923
Ferguson, Amos B.		B, 20th N.Y. Inf.	380		1909 May 28	KS, 29th, 1910
Ferguson, B.F.		C, 2nd Neb. (died of dropsy, Bright's disease)	66	80	1897 Nov 31	NE, 22nd, 1898
Ferguson, Bradner	Pvt.	B, 12th Iowa Inf.	461	51	1893 Nov	IA, 20th, 1894
Ferguson, C.A.	Pvt.	2nd Iowa Battery	45		1931 May 13	IA, 58th, 1932
Ferguson, Charles		M, 7th Iowa Cav.	23	90	1938 Mar 28	IA, 64th, 1938
Ferguson, D.G.	Pvt.	C, 44th Wis.	30		1905 Feb 24	IA, 32nd, 1906
Ferguson, D.H.		A, 92nd Ill. Inf.	298		1908 Sep 23	IA, 35th, 1909
Ferguson, David	Pvt.	H, 35th Iowa Inf.	34		1885 Aug 7	IA, 12th, 1886
Ferguson, David, see Furguson, David						
Ferguson, H.B.		A, 48th Ohio	203		1922 Feb 16	KS, 42nd, 1923
Ferguson, Harvey T.		F, 1st Ill. Lt. Art. (died of heart failure)	114	66	1910 Sep 16	NE, 35th, 1911
Ferguson, Hill	Sergt.	H, 35th Reg.	228		1923 Apr 14	IA, 50th, 1924
Ferguson, J.	Pvt.	G, 7th Mich. Battery	410	74	1895 Aug 20	IA, 22nd, 1896
Ferguson, J.B.	Lieut. & Major	148th & 206th Penn. Inf.	25		1911 Feb 6	NE, 36th, 1912
Ferguson, J.E.		I, 20th Ind.	47		1930	KS, 51st, 1932
Ferguson, J.E.		I, 20th Ind.	47		1930	KS, 52nd, 1933
Ferguson, J.F.		H, 4th Ill. Cav.	13		1933 May 1	NE, 58th, 1934
Ferguson, J.M.		U.S. Signal Corps	13		1931 Feb 13	NE, 56th, 1932
Ferguson, J.P.	Sergt.	G, 31st Iowa Inf.	13		1904 Jun 17	IA, 31st, 1905
Ferguson, J.S.	Capt.		515		1916 Dec 5	IA, 43rd, 1917
Ferguson, James		K, 38th Ohio	113		1911 Apr 6	KS, 31st, 1912
Ferguson, Jas. E.		I, 20th Ind.	47		1927 Dec 8	KS, 47th, 1928
Ferguson, Jesse J.		B, 10th Ind. Inf. (died of stomach trouble)	112	74	1915 Apr 20	NE, 40th, 1916
Ferguson, John			[65?]		1918 Dec 8	KS, 38th, 1919
Ferguson, John M.	Pvt.	A, 141st Penn. (died of consumption)	67	49	1884 Mar 25	NE, 9th, 1885
Ferguson, John S.	Pvt.	F, 28th Iowa Inf.	515		1915 Dec 5	IA, 42nd, 1916
Ferguson, L.	Pvt.	M, 7th Iowa Cav.	152		1920 Feb 22	IA, 47th, 1921
Ferguson, Levi		F, 117th Ind.	57		1911 Aug 15	KS, 31st, 1912
Ferguson, N.		K, 66th Ind.	498		1910 Aug 29	KS, 33rd, 1914
Ferguson, N.M.		G, 15th Ill. (died of cancer)	32	75	1915 Aug 23	NE, 40th, 1916
Ferguson, N.W.	Pvt.	K, Ohio Inf.	25		1924 Dec 29	IA, 51st, 1925
Ferguson, Nathaniel		K, 66th Ind.	498		1910 Aug 29	KS, 30th, 1911
Ferguson, R., see Furguson, R.						
Ferguson, S.C.			94		1919	IA, 46th, 1920
Ferguson, T.T.			340		1890	KS, 10th, 1891
Ferguson, T.T.		D & C, 191st Ohio	340		1918 Mar 22	KS, 38th, 1919
Ferguson, Thomas H.			283	63	1907 Mar 13	KS, 26th, 1907
Ferguson, W.M.		H, 4th Cav.	77		1922 Jul 20	KS, 42nd, 1923
Ferguson, W.P.	Pvt.	G, 1st U.S. Eng.	56		1910 Oct 15	IA, 37th, 1911
Ferman, Jacob	Pvt.		54		1925 Nov 23	IA, 52nd, 1926
Fern, Benjamin	Pvt.	C, 21st Iowa Inf.	78		1900 Oct 29	IA, 27th, 1901
Fernald, Chas.	Pvt.	K, 8th Wis. Inf.	493		1916 Feb	IA, 43rd, 1917
Fernis, Geo. H.	Pvt.	112th Ill. Inf.	11		1916 Dec 10	IA, 43rd, 1917
Fernold, Charles	Pvt.	6th Wis. Bat.	493		1915	IA, 42nd, 1916
Ferrel, Jos.		I, 13th Ohio Inf.	262	78	1914 Dec 23	NE, 39th, 1915
Ferrell, John	Pvt.		66		1920 Aug 25	IA, 47th, 1921
Ferren, W.H.	Capt.	Ill. Inf.	92		1914 Apr 16	IA, 41st, 1915
Ferrier, J., see Frerris, J.						
Ferrier, John		H, 86th Ohio Inf.	25	86	1919 Feb 4	NE, 44th, 1920
Ferris, Andrew	Pvt.	K, 1st M.S.S.[U.S. Sharpshooters?]	88		1922 May 25	IA, 49th, 1923

*See Appendix A, B or C for roster of post names and locations.
†See Introduction for note regarding recording of death date.

Name	Rank	Company, Regiment or Ship	Post*	Age	Death Date†	Journal
Ferris, D.C.			192		1903-1904	IA, 30th, 1904
Ferris, Edwin	Pvt.	A, 29th Iowa	502		1907 Jul 5	IA, 34th, 1908
Ferris, Geo.		H, 9th Ohio	271		1922 Dec 30	IA, 49th, 1923
Ferris, John	Pvt. & Seaman		2		1920 Nov 20	IA, 47th, 1921
Ferris, John H.		I, 9th Ill. Cav.	45		1925 Oct 26	KS, 45th, 1926
Ferris, O.B.	Pvt.	18th Ind. Battery	222		1905 Nov 21	IA, 32nd, 1906
Ferris, S.W.	Pvt.	H, 2nd Ill. Lt. Art.	81		1920 May 24	IA, 47th, 1921
Ferriss, B.F.	Pvt.	F, 1st Colo. Cav.	81		1929 Jun 28	IA, 56th, 1930
Ferry, Joseph		C, 1st Ill. Art.	159		1886	KS, 6th, 1887
Fessenden, C.B.		D, 43rd Mass.	81		1926 Jan 12	KS, 46th, 1927
Fessenden, Wm. P.		K, 4th U.S.	18		1922 Aug 8	KS, 42nd, 1923
Fessender, J.		E, 128th Ind.	150		1888	KS, 8th, 1889
Fessendey, Chas. B.	Pvt.	E, 78th Ill. Inf. (died of asthma)	256	57	1888 Sep	NE, 13th, 1889
Fessler, Leopold		A, 5th Mo.	36		1920 Dec 22	KS, 40th, 1921
Fethers, Stephen		Ohio (died of old age)	318	70	1907 Aug 15	NE, 32nd, 1908
Fetrow, J.R.		K, 130th Penn.	125		1910	KS, 30th, 1911
Fetrow, John R.		K, 130th Penn. Vol. Inf.	25		1908 Aug 30	KS, 28th, 1909
Fetrow, Wm.		K, 2nd Iowa Cav. (died of pneumonia)	89		1923 Mar 23	NE, 48th, 1924
Fetter, Clifford		F, 17th Ohio	18		1933 Nov 24	KS, 53rd, 1934
Fetter, Jacob		E, 19th Iowa	303		1912 Nov 18	KS, 32nd, 1913
Fetter, Thos. S.		C, 197th Penn.	5		1893 Mar	KS, 13th, 1894
Fetterly, N.D.		C, 29th Ill. (died of hardening of arteries)	62	81	1921 Feb 9	NE, 46th, 1922
Fetterman, Cyrus		B, 33rd Ill.	25	80	1915 Feb 25	NE, 40th, 1916
Fetters, W.	Pvt.	A, 2nd Ind. Cav.	231		1930 Dec 23	IA, 57th, 1931
Fetters, W.H.		B, 30th Ind. Inf. (Stromsburg)			1947 May 19	NE, 73rd, 1949
Fetz, David		G, 16th Penn. Cav.	318	77	1911 Jun 27	NE, 36th, 1912
Fetzer, Henry		B, 9th Wis.	62		1933 Mar	NE, 58th, 1934
Feuston, James		M, 13th Ky. Ind. Cav. (cause of death: heart)	308	67	1914 Oct	NE, 39th, 1915
Fevner, J.D.	Pvt.	D, 12th Iowa Inf.	31		1905 Jan 29	IA, 32nd, 1906
Fey, A.H.	Pvt.	B, 105th Ill.	111		1926 Jan 24	IA, 53rd, 1927
Fichter, Jacob H.		K, 49th N.J. Inf. (died of old age)	143	88	1922 Jul 7	NE, 47th, 1923
Fickel, Joel	Sergt.	C, 62nd Ohio Inf.	12		1930 Apr 17	IA, 57th, 1931
Fickel, M.		A, 60th Ohio	117		1918 Apr	KS, 38th, 1919
Fickes, D.D.	Pvt.	D, 126th Penn. Inf.	8		1906 Oct 20	IA, 33rd, 1907
Fickey, James A.	Pvt.	K, 45th —	79		1917 Nov 11	IA, 44th, 1918
Fickle, Wm.		66th Ohio	1		1904 Sep 11	KS, 24th, 1905
Fiddock, J.A.		D, 64th Ill.	63		1918 Apr 17	KS, 38th, 1919
Fidler, Chas.		F, 22nd Ind.	63		1921 Mar 5	KS, 41st, 1922
Fidler, John	1st Lieut.	D, 25th Iowa Inf.	1		1897 Mar 22	IA, 24th, 1898
Fie, John		D, 6th Penn.	293		1898 Jun	KS, 18th, 1899
Fiege, Christian		D, 12th Mo.	52		1916 Aug 1	KS, 36th, 1917
Field, C.E.	Pvt.		434		1920 Aug 22	IA, 47th, 1921
Field, Chas. D.	Sergt.	C, 13th Ill. Cav.	149		1912 Feb 9	IA, 39th, 1913
Field, George		L, 1st Mo. Cav.	129		1909 Oct 28	KS, 29th, 1910
Field, George W.		A, 121st U.S. Inf. (died of paralysis)	262	55	1897 Feb 27	NE, 22nd, 1898
Field, Henry A.	Pvt.	E, 1st Iowa Inf.	64		1924 Mar 13	IA, 51st, 1925
Field, W.E.		D, 52nd Mass.	25		1930 Mar 26	NE, 55th, 1931
Fields, A.A.		K, 1st Ohio Art.	293		1914 Apr 9	KS, 34th, 1915
Fields, Edgar D.	Pvt.	I, 10th N.Y. Art.	168	47	1893 Oct 23	IA, 20th, 1894
Fields, Henry	Pvt.		110		1919 Jan 6	IA, 46th, 1920
Fields, Hiram	Pvt.	K, 21st Iowa Inf.	212		1910 Jun 29	IA, 37th, 1911
Fields, Jesse		A, 2nd Wis. Cav. (died of old age)	182	89	1918 Jan 31	NE, 43rd, 1919
Fields, Michael		I, 15th Kans.	220		1896 Jan 20	KS, 16th, 1897
Fields, Stephen A.		D, 2nd Ill. Art.	154		1886	KS, 6th, 1887
Fields, W.H.		G, 5th Conn. Inf.	380		1917 Nov 15	KS, 37th, 1918
Fife, Samuel	Pvt.	F, 39th Ind. Inf.	158		1917	IA, 44th, 1918
Fife, Wm.			42		1883	KS, 3rd, 1884
Fifer, William		H, 100th Ind.	56	76	1915 Nov 10	NE, 40th, 1916
Fifield, Clinton		F, 46th Iowa Inf.	216	92	1935 Oct 11	IA, 62nd, 1936
Fifield, Jas. R.	Pvt.	F, 60th N.Y.	243		1924 Apr 29	IA, 51st, 1925
Fifield, Wm.			29		1905	IA, 32nd, 1906

Name	Rank	Company, Regiment or Ship	Post*	Age	Death Date†	Journal
Figgers, Jas.		E, 65th N.Y.	301		1926 Feb 9	KS, 46th, 1927
Figgins, Daniel			211		1915	IA, 42nd, 1916
Fight, John		A, 29th Wis.	45		1931 Sep 5	NE, 56th, 1932
Filbey, I.F.		I, 4th Iowa Inf. (died at Platsmouth, Neb.; buried at Platsmouth Cemetery)	283		1894 Apr 15	KS, 14th, 1895
File, Egbert H.		K, 15th N.Y.	117		1906 May 23	KS, 26th, 1907
Filkins, Andrew		B, 33rd N.Y.	84		1904 Dec 26	KS, 24th, 1905
Fill, Jno. K.	Pvt.	F, 2nd Iowa Inf.	452		1927 May 21	IA, 54th, 1928
Filley, Geo. W.		F, 1st Mass. Cav.	260		1902 Mar 5	KS, 22nd, 1903
Filley, H.W.		A, 2nd Mo. (died at Burlingame; buried at Burlingame Cemetery)	35		1894 Oct 14	KS, 14th, 1895
Fillmore, Luther S.	Sergt.	N.Y. Art.	63		1916 Jan 19	IA, 43rd, 1917
Filloon, R.T.	Pvt.	E, 24th Iowa Inf.	418		1908	IA, 35th, 1909
Filmore, John		G, 132nd N.Y.	7	67	1904 May 8	NE, 29th, 1905
Filson, Caspar	Pvt.	C, 2nd Iowa Inf.	110	70	1895 Apr 14	IA, 22nd, 1896
Filson, Thos. B.		D, 138th Ill.	129		1922 Jan 25	KS, 42nd, 1923
Finasty, J.W.	Pvt.	D, 63rd Ill. Inf.	49		1920 Feb 16	IA, 47th, 1921
Finch, A.D.		C, 7th Penn.	25		1922 Oct 25	NE, 47th, 1923
Finch, A.D.		C, 7th Penn. Cav.	25		1922 Oct 25	NE, 47th, 1923
Finch, A.J.		B, 43rd N.Y.	293		1923 Jul 16	KS, 43rd, 1924
Finch, C.L.		D, 9th Kans. Inf.	170		1901 Oct 24	KS, 21st, 1902
Finch, C.M.		E, 5th Mich.	493		1919 Apr 3	KS, 39th, 1920
Finch, Eddie S.		H, 87th Ind.	5		1923 Mar 9	KS, 43rd, 1924
Finch, G.B.	Lieut.	A, 4th Wis. Cav.	46		1912 Jun 18	IA, 39th, 1913
Finch, Henry	Corp.	K, 25th Wis. Inf.	63	48	1888 Dec 14	IA, 15th, 1889
Finch, Henry	Pvt.	K, 25th Wis. Inf.	63	45	1888 Dec 14	IA, 17th, 1891
Finch, Irvan	Pvt.	B, 9th Iowa	160		1924	IA, 51st, 1925
Finch, James F.		G, 11th Kans. Cav. (died at National Home)	380		1895 Aug	KS, 15th, 1896
Finch, James H.		D, 13th Kans.	85		1885	KS, 5th, 1886
Finch, John D.	Pvt.	K, 18th Iowa Inf.	125		1923 Apr 1	IA, 50th, 1924
Finch, L.E.			35		1899 Mar 21	KS, 19th, 1900
Finch, R.J.		E, 6th Iowa Cav. (former member; died at Arapahoe)	120		1936 Feb 21	NE, 61st, 1937
Fincher, A.T.		F, 12th Penn.	12		1921 Feb 8	KS, 41st, 1922
Fincher, John D.		H, 132nd Penn.	12		1917 Nov 19	KS, 37th, 1918
Findley, David		I, 211th Penn.	41		1919 Feb 26	KS, 39th, 1920
Findley, R.S.	Pvt.	C, 126th Penn. Inf.	173		1900 Aug 3	IA, 27th, 1901
Findley, S.S.		A, 138th Ill.	25		1919 Apr 19	KS, 39th, 1920
Fine, Joseph		F, 113th U.S.C.T.	3		1921 Nov 22	KS, 41st, 1922
Finefield, E.W.	Pvt.	G, 6th Iowa Inf.	8		1918 Nov 29	IA, 45th, 1919
Finefrock, M.L.		F, 47th Ohio	158		1930 Oct 3	KS, 50th, 1931
Finerty, P.H.	Pvt.	C, 45th Iowa Inf.	2		1906 Jan 16	IA, 33rd, 1907
Finigan, John	Corp.	D, 5th Penn. Cav.	4	66	1896 Feb 14	IA, 22nd, 1896
Finigan, P.H.	Pvt.	I, 2nd Penn. Cav.	127		1896 Jul 23	IA, 23rd, 1897
Fink, A.W.	Pvt.	E, 10th Ill. Inf.	71		1919 Jun 20	IA, 46th, 1920
Fink, S.	Pvt.		173		1921 Mar 10	IA, 48th, 1922
Fink, S.E.		122nd Ill.	85		1912 Aug 18	KS, 32nd, 1913
Fink, W.W.			12		1923 Aug 26	IA, 50th, 1924
Fink, William		died at Nora	15		1914	NE, 39th, 1915
Finkinkiller, Andrew		B, 1st Iowa Cav.	7		1935 Oct 7	NE, 60th, 1936
Finkle, W.H.		G, 26th Ind.	458		1916	KS, 36th, 1917
Finlaw, J.P.			17		1933 Apr 25	KS, 53rd, 1934
Finlay, James		A, 123rd Ill.	51		1923 Aug 10	KS, 43rd, 1924
Finlay, John	Pvt.	E, 7th Iowa Inf.	2	62	1893 Aug 5	IA, 20th, 1894
Finley, A.P.		A, 3rd Ill. Cav.	43		1918	KS, 38th, 1919
Finley, Andrew M.		H, 10th Mich. (died of apoplexy)	40	74	1908 Aug 24	NE, 33rd, 1909
Finley, D.M.	Sergt.	F, 13th Mo. Cav.	369		1908 Mar 16	IA, 35th, 1909
Finley, David Alexander		D, 47th Iowa Inf. (at large)	222	90	1937 Mar 25	IA, 64th, 1938
Finley, Hiram	Corp.	A, 14th Iowa Inf. (at large)	114	101	1943 Mar 25	IA, 69th, 1943
Finley, Jas. H.	Pvt.	B, 36th Iowa Inf.	497		1913 Dec 14	IA, 40th, 1914
Finley, John	Pvt.	C, 2nd Iowa Cav.	93		1917	IA, 44th, 1918

Name	Rank	Company, Regiment or Ship	Post*	Age	Death Date†	Journal
Finley, John H.	Pvt.	D, 14th Iowa Inf.	114	56	1896 Oct 4	IA, 23rd, 1897
Finley, John L.		L, 2nd Mass. Cav.	294		1916 Jun 4	KS, 36th, 1917
Finley, Samuel S.	Pvt.	K, 3rd Iowa Cav.	153		1908 Oct 14	IA, 35th, 1909
Finley, T.J.	Pvt.	K, 21st Ohio Inf.	118		1909 Nov 23	IA, 36th, 1910
Finley, Wm.	Capt.	12th Iowa Inf.	369		1909 Dec 13	IA, 36th, 1910
Finn, Carl		drowned	94		1883	KS, 3rd, 1884
Finn, Jasper A.		A, 16th Kans. Inf.	201		1901 Nov	KS, 21st, 1902
Finn, Thomas	Pvt.	D, 5th U.S. Art.	247		1906 Aug 19	IA, 33rd, 1907
Finn, Timothy	2nd Lieut.	D, 6th Iowa Cav.	168		1902 Dec 22	IA, 29th, 1903
Finn, William		E, 1st Ill. Art.	255		1929 Jul 19	KS, 49th, 1930
Finnemore, A.J.		2nd Ky. Bat. 15th R.I. Inf. (died of rheumatism, heart)	207	59	1901 Sep	NE, 26th, 1902
Finney, A.		C, 137th Ind.	132		1926 Jan 21	KS, 46th, 1927
Finney, D.W.		A, 85th Ind. Inf.	73		1916 Nov 1	KS, 36th, 1917
Finney, James		K, 78th N.Y. Inf. (died of dropsy at Soldiers & Sailors Home, Grand Island; buried in Home Cemetery)	26	75	1905 Oct 27	NE, 30th, 1906
Finney, James		K, 28th N.Y. Inf. (died of dropsy)	11	75	1905 Oct 27	NE, 30th, 1906
Finnup, Fred		E, 9th Ohio Inf.	357[257?]		1914 Apr 6	KS, 34th, 1915
Finton, M.E.	Pvt.	F, 31st Iowa	74		1923 May 2	IA, 50th, 1924
Firestine, Joseph	Pvt.	B, 4th Iowa Cav.	190		1923 Feb 19	IA, 50th, 1924
Firevoid, John		K, 88th Ohio Vol. Inf.	100		1915 May 4	KS, 35th, 1916
Firman, James	Pvt.	D, 21st Iowa Inf.	452		1931 Mar 6	IA, 58th, 1932
Firman, James H.	Pvt.	D, 21st Iowa Inf. 34th/38th Consolidated Iowa (at large)	299	94	1943 May 21	IA, 69th, 1943
First, Octalona		A, 75th Ohio	247		1910 Feb 6	KS, 30th, 1911
Fischer, Dan		C, 27th Penn.	118		1926 Aug 20	NE, 51st, 1927
Fischer, Julius		M, 3rd Kans. State Militia	12		1902 Sep 9	KS, 22nd, 1903
Fischer, W.M.			12		1922 May 7	KS, 42nd, 1923
Fiscus, Francis M.		A, 134th Ind.	265		1931	NE, 56th, 1932
Fiscus, Jake		D, 140th Ind. Inf.	79		1925 May	KS, 45th, 1926
Fish, A.P.			36		1890	NE, 15th, 1891
Fish, E.F.	Pvt.	E, 3rd Iowa	197	98	1933 Feb 18	IA, 60th, 1934
Fish, E.H.	Pvt.	A, 6th Mich. Inf.	181		1916 Dec 4	IA, 43rd, 1917
Fish, James F.		H, 6th Ind.	113		1910 Nov 20	KS, 30th, 1911
Fish, Lewis	Pvt.	C, 20th Iowa Inf.	92		1909 May 16	IA, 36th, 1910
Fish, M.E.	Lieut.	C, 5th Vt. Inf.	88		1910 May 13	IA, 37th, 1911
Fish, Marion		E, 1st N.Y. Dragoons (died of old age)	55	78	1920	NE, 45th, 1921
Fish, Mortmer A.		K, 42nd Ill.	52		1923 Nov 6	KS, 43rd, 1924
Fish, T.			500		1900-1901	IA, 27th, 1901
Fish, Thomas J.		A, 1st Mo.	1		1924 Mar 8	KS, 44th, 1925
Fish, Warren		C, 64th Ill. Inf. (died of paralysis)	147	68	1903 Oct 22	NE, 28th, 1904
Fish, Wm. L.		G, 88th Ill. Inf.	71		1891 Jun 28	KS, 11th, 1892
Fishback, J.B.		L, 1st Ky. Cav.	25		1920 Jan 25	KS, 40th, 1921
Fishburn, Wm.	Pvt.	A, 35th Iowa Inf.	231		1929 Jul 13	IA, 56th, 1930
Fishel, Robert	Lieut.	H, 12th Iowa Inf.	190		1917 May 23	IA, 44th, 1918
Fishell, Peter H.	Corp.	G, 87th Ohio Inf.	206		1916 Dec 30	IA, 43rd, 1917
Fisher, A.	Pvt.	K, 12th Wis. Inf.	93		1906 Oct 17	IA, 33rd, 1907
Fisher, A.B.		C, 166th Ohio Vol. Inf.	265		1915 Mar 27	KS, 35th, 1916
Fisher, A.H.	Pvt.	B, 22nd Iowa Inf.	8		1926 Sep 10	IA, 53rd, 1927
Fisher, Abram C.		K, 9th Iowa Cav. (died of pneumonia)	60	78	1915 Nov 19	NE, 40th, 1916
Fisher, Alpheus		I, 12th Kans. Inf.	117		1916 Dec 21	KS, 36th, 1917
Fisher, B.G.	Pvt.		122		1915 Jan 25	IA, 42nd, 1916
Fisher, C.G.		C, 28th Ohio Inf. (died of heart disease)	24		1903 Oct 5	NE, 28th, 1904
Fisher, Charles		E, 17th Wis.	87		1911 Oct 29	KS, 31st, 1912
Fisher, Conrad		18th Mo.	166		1906 Sep 9	KS, 26th, 1907
Fisher, Conrad G.		A, 16th Iowa Inf. (died of paralysis)	110	72	1916 Jul 23	NE, 41st, 1917
Fisher, E.B.		D, 23rd Mo.	55		1921 Jun 29	KS, 41st, 1922
Fisher, E.H.	Sergt.	B, 13th Iowa Inf.	511		1903 Aug 11	IA, 30th, 1904
Fisher, E.H.			305		1903-1904	IA, 30th, 1904
Fisher, Elijah R.		G, 70th Ind. Inf. (died at Beloit, Kans.; buried at Elmwood Cemetery)	147		1894 Apr 8	KS, 14th, 1895
Fisher, Emmanuel	Chaplain	D, 138th Penn.	209		1905 Oct 3	KS, 25th, 1906

*See Appendix A, B or C for roster of post names and locations.
†See Introduction for note regarding recording of death date.

Name	Rank	Company, Regiment or Ship	Post*	Age	Death Date†	Journal
Fisher, Francis		A, 1st Iowa Inf.	231		1923 Nov 6	IA, 50th, 1924
Fisher, Frank	Pvt.	H, 13th Iowa Inf.	4		1905	IA, 32nd, 1906
Fisher, Geo. M.		G, 86th Ind.	34		1917	KS, 37th, 1918
Fisher, Geo. W.		K, 138th Ind.	1		1922 Mar 9	KS, 42nd, 1923
Fisher, George		E, 85th Penn. Inf.	32		1938 Jan 27	NE, 63rd, 1939
Fisher, George W.		G, 33rd Mo. Inf.	380		1914 Oct 27	KS, 34th, 1915
Fisher, H.	Pvt.		66		1901 Jul 22	IA, 28th, 1902
Fisher, H.C.			71		1883	KS, 3rd, 1884
Fisher, H.H.	Lieut.	G, 2nd Ill. Lt. Art.	132		1920 Jan 21	IA, 47th, 1921
Fisher, H.J.		not a member of post named, but buried by said post	63		1897	KS, 17th, 1898
Fisher, Henry	Pvt.	L, 3rd Iowa Cav.	312		1912 Apr 8	IA, 39th, 1913
Fisher, Hugh D.		5th Kans. Cav. (see also Appendix D)	1		1905 Oct 29	KS, 25th, 1906
Fisher, I.J.		D, 186th Ohio Inf.	57		1930 Feb 3	KS, 50th, 1931
Fisher, J.		K, 17th Ind.	66		1888	KS, 8th, 1889
Fisher, J.A.		H, 116th Ind. Inf. (died at Tyrone, Kans.; buried at Liberal Cemetery)	205		1894 Sep 15	KS, 14th, 1895
Fisher, J.C.	Pvt.	H, 178th Ohio Inf.	34	88	1933 Oct 4	IA, 60th, 1934
Fisher, J.W.	Pvt.	G, 3rd Iowa Vols.	12		1903 Jan 13	IA, 30th, 1904
Fisher, J.W.	Pvt.	G, 3rd Iowa Vols.	12		1903 Jul 13	IA, 30th, 1904
Fisher, J.W.	Pvt.	H, 86th Ind. Inf.	173		1919 Sep 26	IA, 46th, 1920
Fisher, Jacob					1929 Feb 20	NE, 53rd, 1929
Fisher, Jno. B.	Pvt.	H, 28th Ohio Inf.	8		1925 Nov 28	IA, 52nd, 1926
Fisher, John	Sergt.	H, 7th Mich. Cav.	88		1914 Aug 3	IA, 41st, 1915
Fisher, John			87		1883	KS, 3rd, 1884
Fisher, John		M, 4th Mo.	18		1912 May 27	KS, 32nd, 1913
Fisher, John		E, 38th Ohio	25		1922 Mar 12	KS, 42nd, 1923
Fisher, John		K, 136th Penn. (died of accident)	25	71	1915 Nov 23	NE, 40th, 1916
Fisher, Joseph	Lieut.	B, 16th Iowa Inf.	1		1904 Mar 7	IA, 31st, 1905
Fisher, Julius	Pvt.	G, 1st Iowa Inf.	1		1917 Sep 13	IA, 44th, 1918
Fisher, Lee T.	Sergt.	I, 148th Ind. Inf.	176		1918 Dec 31	KS, 38th, 1919
Fisher, Linford	Pvt.	D, 25th Ohio Inf.	7		1913 Aug 13	IA, 40th, 1914
Fisher, Moleston		E, 108th Ill.	122		1914 Nov 26	KS, 34th, 1915
Fisher, N.B.			7		1917 Jun 2	IA, 44th, 1918
Fisher, Oliver B.	Band Master	12th Ind.	14		1896 Apr 6	KS, 16th, 1897
Fisher, Peter	Pvt.	G, 37th Iowa	20	95	1890 Oct 8	IA, 17th, 1891
Fisher, Philip		F, 31st Wis. Inf.	77		2nd quarter 1884	IA, 11th, 1885
Fisher, R.H.		A, 5th Ind. Cav.	453		1889	KS, 9th, 1890
Fisher, R.P.		I, 29th Ohio (was West Va. Lt. Art. Bat. H)	278		1905 Jul 31	KS, 25th, 1906
Fisher, Samuel		D, 2nd Kans. A, 9th Kans.	12		1913 Sep 7	KS, 33rd, 1914
Fisher, Solomon		G, 114th Md.	89		1898 Nov 22	KS, 18th, 1899
Fisher, T.J.		B, 77th N.Y.	113		1907 Jan 24	NE, 32nd, 1908
Fisher, T.P.	Pvt.	E, 17th Iowa Inf.	440		1901 Jul 17	IA, 28th, 1902
Fisher, Thomas	Pvt.	F, 2nd Iowa Cav.	66		1927 Feb 11	IA, 54th, 1928
Fisher, W.	Pvt.	G, 128th Ohio Inf.	59		1921 May 20	IA, 48th, 1922
Fisher, W.R.		D, 80th Ohio	209		1911	KS, 31st, 1912
Fisher, W.T.		B, —	485		1900 Dec	KS, 21st, 1902
Fisher, William T.		B, 24th Mo.	485		1900 Dec 12	KS, 20th, 1901
Fisher, Wm.	Pvt.	B, 104th Ohio	191		1904 Mar 9	IA, 30th, 1904
Fisher, Wm.	Pvt.	M, 100th Ohio Inf.	191		1904 Mar 9	IA, 31st, 1905
Fisher, Wm.	Pvt.	A, 1st Iowa Inf.	94		1906	IA, 33rd, 1907
Fisher, Wm.	Pvt.	H, 35th Iowa Inf.	236		1912 Oct 9	IA, 39th, 1913
Fisher, Wm.		D, 3rd Penn.	63		1939 Sep 1	KS, 59th, 1940
Fisher, Wm. N.	Pvt.	G, 27th Iowa Inf.	3	68	1897 Feb 10	IA, 24th, 1898
Fisk, D.G.		E, 12th Mass. (cause of death: heart)	35	78	1915 Jan 7	NE, 40th, 1916
Fisk, D.M.	Capt.	E, 30th Ill.	29		1921 Jul 24	IA, 48th, 1922
Fisk, George		B, 3rd Kans. State Militia	12		1910 Apr 24	KS, 30th, 1911
Fisk, James		E, 30th Maine (died of softening of brain)	21	76	1920 Jul 13	NE, 45th, 1921
Fisk, James			89		1919 Jul 14	NE, 44th, 1920
Fisk, Jas. W.		A, ?0th Maine (died of general debility)	21	75	1919 Jul 13	NE, 44th, 1920

Name	Rank	Company, Regiment or Ship	Post*	Age	Death Date†	Journal
Fisk, John		E, 36th Ohio (died of paralysis)	40		1924 Oct 3	NE, 49th, 1925
Fisk, K.M.		G, 92nd N.Y.	293		1913 Feb 1	KS, 33rd, 1914
Fisk, M.			243		1922	KS, 42nd, 1923
Fisk, O.		B, 9th Ind. Cav.	17		1925 Dec 27	KS, 45th, 1926
Fisk, P.G.		M, 1st Wis. Cav. (died of Bright's disease)	142	64	1901 Mar	NE, 26th, 1902
Fisk, R.S.		K, 14th Ind.	243		1920	KS, 40th, 1921
Fisk, Simon J.		H, 106th N.Y. Vols.	134		1909 May 5	KS, 29th, 1910
Fiske, Edward		Maine	18		1905 Oct 13	KS, 25th, 1906
Fiss, Thomas J.		G, 46th Iowa	25	76	1910 Dec 11	NE, 35th, 1911
Fissel, Wm. B.		G, 91st Penn.	176		1918 Nov 17	KS, 38th, 1919
Fitch, A.L.		F, 14th Ohio Batt. Lt. Art.	1		1928 Jan 7	NE, 53rd, 1929
Fitch, Ed			50		1912	IA, 39th, 1913
Fitch, G.W.		G, 62nd Ill. Inf.	48		1921	IA, 48th, 1922
Fitch, Gilbert		dropped dead	354		1925	NE, 50th, 1926
Fitch, J.H.	Pvt.	A, 4th Iowa Cav.	48	84	1932 Jun 15	IA, 59th, 1933
Fitch, J.M.		149th Ind.	12		1912 Mar 26	KS, 32nd, 1913
Fitch, J.T.	Pvt.	D, 17th Iowa Inf.	10		1900 Dec 24	IA, 27th, 1901
Fitch, James		D, 191st Ohio Cav.	47		1912 Jun 25	KS, 32nd, 1913
Fitch, James E.		C, 14th Ky. (died of paralysis)	23	79	1922 Aug	NE, 47th, 1923
Fitch, James F.		F, 17th Ind. Inf. (died of paralysis)	315	69	1895 Jan 27	NE, 20th, 1896
Fitch, John			205		1884	KS, 4th, 1885
Fitch, John		H, 31st Iowa	25		1924 Dec 29	KS, 44th, 1925
Fitch, Luthur	Pvt.	B, 37th Ill. Inf.	452		1910 May	IA, 37th, 1911
Fitch, M.B.	Pvt.	H, 18th Iowa Inf.	168		1914 Dec 12	IA, 41st, 1915
Fitch, Robert	Pvt.	C, 182nd Ohio Inf.	233		1913 Jun 15	IA, 40th, 1914
Fitch, U.C.		B, 6th Iowa Inf.	323		4th quarter 1884	IA, 11th, 1885
Fitch, W.H.	Sergt.	E, 11th Md. Inf.	10		1918 Sep 22	IA, 45th, 1919
Fitch, Wm. H.	Capt.	A, 60th N.Y.	156		1907 Jul 27	IA, 34th, 1908
Fitchpatrick, J.M.		I, 8th Iowa Cav. (died of accident)	17	7?	1920 Sep 19	NE, 45th, 1921
Fite, Andrew		66th Ind.	4		1916 Sep 20	KS, 36th, 1917
Fithian, Wm. C.		B, 138th Ohio National Guard	55		1914 Dec 15	KS, 34th, 1915
Fitkins, F.F.	Pvt.	B, 31st Iowa Inf.	452		1924 Nov 25	IA, 51st, 1925
Fitsimmons, Thos.		F, 35th Iowa Inf.	231		1923 Oct 1	IA, 50th, 1924
Fitten, T.H.			35		1908	NE, 33rd, 1909
Fitterington, H.H.		D, 135th Penn.	130		1926 May 17	KS, 46th, 1927
Fitts, J.C.		D, 3rd N.J. Vols.	132		1902 Jul 11	KS, 22nd, 1903
Fitts, Jno. A.	Pvt.	A, 13th Iowa Inf.	141		1925 Mar 20	IA, 52nd, 1926
Fitts, Mort B.		G, 135th Ill.	52		1924 Jan 7	KS, 44th, 1925
Fitz, J.W.		A, 13th Iowa Inf.	23		1915 Aug 6	IA, 42nd, 1916
Fitzgerald, A.		B, 18th Ohio	429		1908	KS, 28th, 1909
Fitzgerald, A.			429		1911	KS, 31st, 1912
Fitzgerald, A.		B, 18th Ohio Inf.	429		1917 Jun 12	KS, 37th, 1918
Fitzgerald, H.C.H.			25	82	1918 Feb 26	NE, 43rd, 1919
Fitzgerald, J.H.	Sergt.	A, 11th Penn. Cav.	12		1908 Nov 11	IA, 35th, 1909
Fitzgerald, John C.	Lieut.	A, 140th Ill. Inf.	418		1904 Oct 23	IA, 31st, 1905
Fitzgerald, Patrick		B, 57th Ill. (died of general debility)	140		1920 Oct 18	NE, 45th, 1921
Fitzgerald, Peter		I, 28th Iowa Inf.	292		3rd quarter 1884	IA, 11th, 1885
Fitzgerald, Phillip		U.S. Navy	454		1893 Dec 17	KS, 13th, 1894
Fitzgerald, R.P.	Pvt.	A, 140th Ill. Inf.	418		1915 Oct 24	IA, 42nd, 1916
Fitzgerald, W.E.		7th Mo. Cav. D, 118th Ill.	1		1919 May 18	KS, 39th, 1920
Fitzgerald, Wm.	Pvt.	E, 10th Ohio Inf.	367		1912	IA, 39th, 1913
Fitzgerald, Wm.	Pvt.	E, 10th Ohio Inf.	367		1913 May	IA, 40th, 1914
Fitzgerald, Wm.			383		1918	IA, 45th, 1919
Fitzgerald, Wm.		F, 89th Iowa	17		1910 Jul 22	KS, 30th, 1911
Fitzpatrick, J.A.	Corp.	E, 3rd Iowa Inf.	31		1922 Feb 5	IA, 49th, 1923
Fitzpatrick, John		I, 1st Md.	100		1912 Apr 2	KS, 32nd, 1913
Fitzpatrick, Michael	Pvt.	E, 35th Iowa Inf.	231		1916 May 17	IA, 43rd, 1917
Fitzsimmons, Thomas		G, 3rd U.S. Inf. (died at Oskaloosa, Kans.)	71		1894 Oct 20	KS, 14th, 1895
Fitzsimmons, Thos., see Fitsimmons, Thos.						
Fitzwaters, G.W.		B, 4th Mo. State Militia	113		1887 Mar 4	KS, 7th, 1888

*See Appendix A, B or C for roster of post names and locations.
†See Introduction for note regarding recording of death date.

Name	Rank	Company, Regiment or Ship	Post*	Age	Death Date†	Journal
Fivecoat, Michael		L, 10th Ind. Cav.	25		1930 Oct 1	NE, 55th, 1931
Fizell, W.T.	Pvt.	K, 29th Wis. Inf.	124		1911 Jun 5	IA, 38th, 1912
Flack, J.W.		I, 40th Ohio Inf.	51		1925 May	KS, 45th, 1926
Flack, John N.		F, 52nd Ill. Inf. (death by accident)	88		1891 Dec 11	KS, 11th, 1892
Flad, John M.		B, 10th Kans.	260		1898 Feb 15	KS, 18th, 1899
Flagle, C.H.		C, 93rd Ill. Inf. (died of epilepsy)	157	65	1905 Aug 20	NE, 30th, 1906
Flaherty, Edward	Pvt.	I, 32nd Iowa Inf.	236		1900 May	IA, 27th, 1901
Flaize, R.		18th Ohio	79		1905 Nov 26	KS, 25th, 1906
Flam, J.B.	Pvt.	C, 25th Iowa Inf.	20		1908	IA, 35th, 1909
Flanagan, Jas. N.	Pvt.	G, 40th Iowa Inf.	330	66	1891 Sep 11	IA, 18th, 1892
Flanagan, Thos., see Flannagan, Thos.						
Flanders, Alden		C, 4th Ind.	22		1916 Mar 7	KS, 36th, 1917
Flanders, Charles		I, 16th Kans. Cav.	117		1914 Oct 28	KS, 34th, 1915
Flanders, John		B, 77th Ohio	22		1905 Aug 30	KS, 25th, 1906
Flanders, Orin		K, 78th Ill.	123		1910 Feb 20	KS, 30th, 1911
Flanders, Wm. B.		B, 2nd Kans.	127		1906 Jul 30	KS, 26th, 1907
Flanigan, Wm.	Pvt.	G, 47th Wis. Inf.	78		1916 Mar 27	IA, 43rd, 1917
Flanigan, Wm. B.		G, 24th Mich. Inf.	1	91	1936 Dec 16	IA, 63rd, 1937
Flannagan, Thos.		H, 9th Ill. Cav.	32		1920 Aug 19	NE, 45th, 1921
Flasner, Harrison		B, 57th Ill.	123		1910 Mar 27	KS, 30th, 1911
Flathers, Ira C.	Corp.	K, 47th Iowa Inf.	94		1912 Jan 14	IA, 39th, 1913
Flaugh, Wm.	Pvt.	B, 13th Iowa Inf.	36		1911 May 18	IA, 38th, 1912
Flaugher, D.S.		D, 10th Kans. Inf.	7		1936 Nov 2	NE, 61st, 1937
Flausburg, John		D, 11th Ill.	5		1927 Dec 17	KS, 47th, 1928
Fleanor, James		H, 17th Ky.	477		1938 Jan 29	KS, 59th, 1940
Flechsig, August	Pvt.	G, 16th Iowa Inf.	78		1922 Nov 17	IA, 49th, 1923
Fleck, M.		F, 113th Ill.	38		1902 Oct 7	KS, 22nd, 1903
Fleck, M.F.		B, 78th Penn.	303		1920 Feb 7	KS, 40th, 1921
Fleece, J.C.		K, 6th Cal.	158		1906 Apr 2	KS, 26th, 1907
Fleener, J.H.		C, 12th Ind.	36		1929 Sep 9	KS, 49th, 1930
Fleener, W.P.		G, 76th Ill. Inf.	66		1918 Jan 23	KS, 38th, 1919
Fleenor, William		F, 66th Ind.	433		1916 Sep 4	KS, 36th, 1917
Fleerckin, J.B.		H, 12th Iowa Inf.	272	64	1896 Feb 16	NE, 21st, 1897
Fleishhour, Ed		A, 2nd Cav. (died of cancer)	133	80	1915 Aug 31	NE, 40th, 1916
Fleming, A.N.			325		1902 Jul 13	KS, 22nd, 1903
Fleming, Charles	Corp.	F, 32nd Iowa Inf.	193		1910 Sep 11	IA, 37th, 1911
Fleming, Franklin F.		D, 13th Iowa	23		1921 Aug 13	KS, 41st, 1922
Fleming, Geo. W.	Pvt.	F, 25th Iowa Inf.	8		1910 Jan 17	IA, 37th, 1911
Fleming, J.M.		F, 7th Kans. Cav.	6		1918	KS, 38th, 1919
Fleming, Jacob		1st Kans. Art.	129		1923 May 16	KS, 43rd, 1924
Fleming, James		C, 15th Kans. Cav.	117		1898 Apr 23	KS, 18th, 1899
Fleming, John			70		1908 Dec 7	IA, 35th, 1909
Fleming, Joseph		I, 195th Penn.	209		1902 May 17	KS, 22nd, 1903
Fleming, Justin	Pvt.	I, 47th Iowa Inf.	39		1927 Nov 14	IA, 54th, 1928
Fleming, L.C.		D, 133rd Ohio	47		1911 Jan 7	KS, 31st, 1912
Fleming, Milton K.		L, 7th Ind. (died of heart failure)	77		1912 Nov 12	NE, 37th, 1913
Fleming, Nicholas, see Flemming, Nicholas						
Fleming, W.B.		A, 187th Ohio	158		1927 Jun 9	KS, 47th, 1928
Fleming, W.H.		A, 1st Mo. Cav.	3		1925 Jan 17	KS, 45th, 1926
Fleming, W.H.		D, 152nd Ill. Inf. (died of old age)	129	79	1906	NE, 31st, 1907
Fleming, W.W.		K, 6th Ind. Cav.	117		1911 Aug 16	KS, 31st, 1912
Fleming, Wm. W.		K, 188th Ohio	85		1920 Dec 21	KS, 41st, 1922
Flemming, J.N.	Pvt.	G, 23rd Iowa Inf.	27		1927 Jan 9	IA, 54th, 1928
Flemming, Jno.	Pvt.	H, 119th Ill. Inf.	112		1927 May 2	IA, 54th, 1928
Flemming, Nicholas	Musician	Navy	380		1925 Jun 19	KS, 45th, 1926
Fleneker, A.W.		B, 3rd Ill. Cav.	69		1887	KS, 7th, 1888
Flennikan, Henry C.		K, 26th Ill.	69		1902 Nov 30	KS, 22nd, 1903
Flesher, W.M.		K, 47th Iowa	23		1922 Apr 13	KS, 42nd, 1923
Fletcher, C.P.		D, 6th Minn.	388		1912 Oct 2	KS, 32nd, 1913
Fletcher, C.W.	Sergt.	F, 2nd N.H. Inf.	22		1906 Oct 17	IA, 33rd, 1907

*See Appendix A, B or C for roster of post names and locations.
†See Introduction for note regarding recording of death date.

Name	Rank	Company, Regiment or Ship	Post*	Age	Death Date†	Journal
Fletcher, Charles		L, 14th Conn.	142		1913 Nov 21	KS, 33rd, 1914
Fletcher, Hatton		E, 10th Kans.	12		1936	KS, 55th, 1936
Fletcher, Isadore	Pvt.	H, 13th Ohio Cav.	269		1905 Feb 24	IA, 31st, 1905
Fletcher, J.C.		I, 3rd Iowa Cav.	35		1930 Jun	NE, 55th, 1931
Fletcher, Jesse		E, 11th Mo.	87		1897 Apr 12	KS, 17th, 1898
Fletcher, John J.		F, 132nd Ind. Inf.	28		1914 Dec 11	KS, 34th, 1915
Fletcher, Jonathan N.		I, 103rd N.Y. F, 1st N.Y. Vet. Cav.	25		1934 Sep 27	NE, 59th, 1935
Fletcher, R.R., see Flettcher, R.R.						
Fletcher, S.W.		H, 1st Vt.	7		1920 Jun 27	KS, 40th, 1921
Fletcher, Warren H.		G, 5th N.H. Bat.	88		1913 Mar 4	KS, 33rd, 1914
Fletcher, Wm. B.		H, 11th Mo. Cav.	25		1911 Feb 9	KS, 31st, 1912
Flettcher, R.R.			52		1890 Jan	NE, 15th, 1891
Flicher, Isadore	Pvt.	L, 6th Iowa Cav.	259		1905 Feb 5	IA, 32nd, 1906
Flick, Wm.		E, 20th Penn. Cav.	25		1894 Jul 8	NE, 19th, 1895
Fligar, Joseph		C, 78th Ohio	294		1925 Dec	KS, 45th, 1926
Fligar, Joseph		C, 78th Ohio	294		1927 Dec	KS, 47th, 1928
Flinn, A.	Pvt.		45		1920 Oct 10	IA, 47th, 1921
Flinn, John W.	Sergt.	D, 22nd Iowa Inf.	297		1930 Jan 25	IA, 57th, 1931
Flinn, Patrick		C, 5th Ky. Cav.	25		1899	NE, 24th, 1900
Flint, Ali F.		25th Independent Battery Ohio Lt. Art.	23		1940 Sep 1	NE, 65th, 1941
Flint, C.E.		H, 22nd Iowa Inf. (died of typhoid fever)	242	65	1902 Sep	NE, 27th, 1903
Flint, Charles A.	Pvt.	B, 53rd Ill. Inf.	343		1919 Mar 29	IA, 46th, 1920
Flint, George W.		H, 22nd Iowa (died of cancer of bowels)	43	62	1897 Apr 17	NE, 22nd, 1898
Flint, J.H.	R.Q.M.	26th Iowa Inf.	88	65	1891 Sep 21	IA, 18th, 1892
Flint, John B.		I, 142nd Ill.	1		1931 Oct	NE, 56th, 1932
Flint, Larkin S.		F, 43rd Mo.	4		1932 May 6	NE, 57th, 1933
Flinton, Nelson		A, 10th Vt.	1		1930 Jan 8	KS, 50th, 1931
Flippin, C.A.		A, 14th U.S. Inf.	11		1930 Dec 5	NE, 55th, 1931
Flitch, Sylvester		A, 2nd Ohio Cav.	99		1900 Dec 12	KS, 20th, 1901
Flock, Geo.		I, 6th Iowa A. & I. (died of pneumonia)	32	66	1902 Nov	NE, 27th, 1903
Flood, Jas. H.	Pvt.	K, 4th Iowa Inf.	57		1912 May 18	IA, 39th, 1913
Flora, A.M.	Lieut. Col.	B, 46th Ind.	55		1893 Aug 18	KS, 13th, 1894
Florence, F.B.	Pvt.	B, 32nd Iowa Inf.	42		1919 Jan 17	IA, 46th, 1920
Florence, H.F.	Pvt.	H, 4th Iowa Cav.	42		1920 May 27	IA, 47th, 1921
Flory, John J.		H, 6th Md.	46		1919 Sep 4	KS, 39th, 1920
Flory, M.K.		A, 30th Ill.	415		1897 Apr 3	KS, 17th, 1898
Flott, John		B, 12th Mo. Cav.	250		1927 May 12	KS, 47th, 1928
Flower, W.S.	Pvt.	B, 17th Mich. Inf.	465		1930 Jan 5	IA, 56th, 1930
Flowers, D.M.	Corp.	I, 77th Ohio Inf.	324		1912 Dec 20	IA, 39th, 1913
Flowers, Geo. W.	Pvt.	G, 67th N.Y. Inf.	66		1916 Jan 31	IA, 43rd, 1917
Floyd, C.H.	1st Lieut. & Adjt.	D, 50th Ill.	113		1888	KS, 8th, 1889
Floyd, Isiah	Pvt.	B, —	244		1908 Nov 21	IA, 35th, 1909
Floyd, J.F.		E, 120th Ill.	147		1888	KS, 8th, 1889
Floyd, J.P.		F, 12th West Va.	18		1928 Mar 18	KS, 48th, 1929
Floyd, M.	Pvt. Pvt.	E, 5th Ohio Cav. K, 12th Ohio Cav. (cause of death: stomach)	63	70	1887 Sep	NE, 12th, 1888
Floyd, Thos. J.		K, 12th Ohio Cav.	85		1908 May 31	KS, 28th, 1909
Floyd, William D.		I, 7th Kans. Cav.	448		1920 Dec 1	KS, 40th, 1921
Floyd, Wm. C.	Pvt.	F, 23rd Iowa Inf.	452		1908	IA, 35th, 1909
Flucard, John	Sergt.	I, 29th Ind. Inf.	110[109?]		1899	NE, 24th, 1900
Fluent, J.F.		G, 9th Iowa Cav.	28	62	1906 Dec 28	NE, 31st, 1907
Fluent, Joseph F.		G, 9th Iowa Cav. (born in New York; died of too free use of pat[ent] medicine at Soldiers & Sailors Home Hospital, Burkett; buried at Home Cemetery)		61	1906 Dec 29	NE, 31st, 1907
Fluke, John		E, — Ill.	36		1913 Mar 16	KS, 33rd, 1914
Fluke, William W.		E, 1st Iowa	1		1909 Apr 22	KS, 29th, 1910
Flummer, Sylvester	Pvt. Recruit	K, 118th Ind. Inf. 13th Ind. Inf. (at large)		98	1943 Mar 10	IA, 69th, 1943
Fluskey, B.H.		B, 1st Ill. Bat. (died of blood poison)	250	68	1902 Jan	NE, 27th, 1903

*See Appendix A, B or C for roster of post names and locations.
†See Introduction for note regarding recording of death date.

Name	Rank	Company, Regiment or Ship	Post*	Age	Death Date†	Journal
Flusky, B.H.		B, 1st Ill. Art. (died of blood poison)	250	64	1901 Dec	NE, 26th, 1902
Flynn, John		E, 1st Mo. Cav. (died at Atchison)	336		1895 Feb	KS, 15th, 1896
Flynn, Michael		B, 53rd Ind.	380		1905 Apr 19	KS, 25th, 1906
Flynn, Patrick, see Flinn, Patrick						
Flynn, Peter	Pvt.	H, 2nd Iowa Cav.	455		1904 Jun 30	IA, 31st, 1905
Focht, Jacob	Pvt.	F, 106th Penn. Inf.	57		1900 Nov 2	IA, 27th, 1901
Fodge, J.M.		2nd Iowa Cav.	98		1928 Sep 9	NE, 53rd, 1929
Foeling, Jno.		C, 2nd Mo.	93		1905 Dec 29	KS, 25th, 1906
Fogarty, Edward	Pvt.	I, 32nd Iowa Inf.	193		1909 Jul 8	IA, 36th, 1910
Fogg, D.W.	Pvt.	E, 17th Ill. Inf.	17		1916 Aug 21	IA, 43rd, 1917
Fogo, David		D, 11th Wis. Inf.	186		1914 Dec 31	KS, 34th, 1915
Fogwell, Samuel		G, 152nd Ind.	1		1916 Jan 6	KS, 36th, 1917
Folden, O.B.		A, 91st Reg. (died of fever)	22	70	1910 Oct 16	NE, 35th, 1911
Foldin, R.R.	Pvt.	B, 193rd Ohio Inf.	122		1899	NE, 24th, 1900
Foley, J.W.		I, 10th Mo. Inf.	262	71	1915 Apr	NE, 39th, 1915
Foley, John	Pvt.	E, 35th Iowa Inf.	231		1911 Jan 5	IA, 38th, 1912
Foley, John F., see Foly, John F.						
Foley, Thomas	Artificer	2nd Iowa Bat.	12		1915 Apr 21	IA, 42nd, 1916
Folger, A.S.	Pvt.	K, 162nd Ind. Inf.	108		1910 Apr 6	IA, 37th, 1911
Follet, L.M.	Pvt.	C, 44th Wis. Inf.	154		1916 Dec 12	IA, 43rd, 1917
Follet, W.R.	Musician	B, 29th Iowa Inf.	204	59	1897 May 24	IA, 24th, 1898
Follett, Joseph M.		H, 33rd Ill. (died of heart failure)	25		1908 Oct 5	NE, 33rd, 1909
Folliam, Jas. M.		K, 79th Ill.	40		1906 Jul 29	KS, 26th, 1907
Folmer, John M.		G, 3rd Ind. Cav.	81		1915 Nov 22	KS, 35th, 1916
Folsom, DeWitte C.	Capt.	C, 1st Mo. Eng. D, 4th U.S. Inf. (1848)	250		1914 Mar 19	KS, 34th, 1915
Folsom, William H.		G, 13th Tenn.	55		1915 Aug 5	KS, 35th, 1916
Folts, Geo.		B, 40th Wis.	32		1926 Mar 19	NE, 51st, 1927
Foltz, David M.		D, 37th Penn. B, 201st Penn.	250		1925 May 13	KS, 45th, 1926
Foltz, Louis			61		1891[1901?] Sep	NE, 26th, 1902
Foly, John F.		A, 1st Ohio Lt. Art.	1		1896 Apr 22	KS, 16th, 1897
Fonda, E.R.		D, 147th N.Y. Inf.	29		1919 Aug	IA, 46th, 1920
Fonda, James	Pvt.	E, 27th Iowa	74		1923 Feb 21	IA, 50th, 1924
Fonda, Wm.	Pvt.	G, 7th N.Y. Hvy. Art.	262	59	1886 Feb 15	IA, 14th, 1888
Fondray, W.E.		H, 16th Ky.	203		1916 May 23	KS, 36th, 1917
Fonger, Wm.		E, 12th N.Y. Cav.	180		1922 Dec 20	KS, 42nd, 1923
Fonts, J.H.		E, 29th Ind.	69		1918 Nov 28	KS, 38th, 1919
Fontz, W.L.		K, 25th Ohio	87		1920 Sep 3	KS, 40th, 1921
Fookes, James H.		E, 18th U.S. Inf.	25		1912 Nov 6	KS, 32nd, 1913
Foot, George		C, 62nd Ill.	256		1916 Nov 20	KS, 36th, 1917
Foot, M.B.		E, 115th N.Y.	13	78	1918 Feb 7	NE, 43rd, 1919
Foot, M.V.	Pvt.	D, 111th Ohio Inf.	314		1910 Nov 28	IA, 37th, 1911
Foot, O.F.		G, 7th Penn. Cav. (died of cancer in stomach)	134		1894 Oct 31	NE, 19th, 1895
Foote, Charles A.	Pvt.	H, 2nd Mich. Inf.	324	94	1936 Mar 19	IA, 65th, 1939
Foote, D.		7th Kans. Inf. (died of paralysis)	43		1903	NE, 28th, 1904
Foote, L.R.	Pvt.	M, 8th Iowa Cav.	153		1904 Apr 10	IA, 31st, 1905
Foote, O.F.		G, 7th Penn. Cav. (died of cancer of stomach)	134		1893 Oct 31	NE, 18th, 1894
Foote, W.D.	Sergt.	B, 9th N.Y. Cav.	7	52	1888 Apr 29	IA, 15th, 1889
Foote, W.P.		F, 16th N.Y. Inf.	4		1926 Feb 16	NE, 51st, 1927
Foote, Wilbert	Pvt.	H, 142nd Ohio National Guard	408		1912 Feb 8	IA, 39th, 1913
Footwiles, J.N.	Pvt.	F, 2nd Iowa Inf.	57		1908 Nov 2	IA, 35th, 1909
Forame, W.H.	Pvt.	D, 36th Ind.	49		1907 Jan 10	IA, 34th, 1908
Forbes, A.			290		1886	KS, 6th, 1887
Forbes, Andrew		F, 8th Ill.	482		1897 Oct 9	KS, 17th, 1898
Forbes, Daniel		E, 58th Ill.	121		1897 Dec 18	KS, 17th, 1898
Forbes, H.P.	Pvt.	I, 46th Ill. Inf.	23		1928 Jan 20	IA, 55th, 1929
Forbes, Ira			113		1908 Oct 17	KS, 28th, 1909
Forbes, J.A.		L, 1st Vt.	147		1926 Jul 8	KS, 46th, 1927

*See Appendix A, B or C for roster of post names and locations.
†See Introduction for note regarding recording of death date.

Name	Rank	Company, Regiment or Ship	Post*	Age	Death Date†	Journal
Forbes, J.A.		F, 42nd Ill. (died of Bright's disease)	35	77	1920 Dec 9	NE, 45th, 1921
Forbes, J.B.		G, 157th N.Y. Inf.	216[218?]		1928 Jan 5	NE, 52nd, 1928
Forbes, James	Pvt.	H, 8th Ind. Inf.	167		1927 Jul 19	IA, 54th, 1928
Forbes, James		K, 5th N.Y. Inf.	380		1908 Nov 21	KS, 28th, 1909
Forbes, Lewis		G, 15th N.J. Inf. (died of diabetes)	68	75	1906 Dec 25	NE, 31st, 1907
Forbes, N.S.		B, 26th Ill.	193		1929 Oct 14	NE, 54th, 1930
Forbes, Reuben		D, 11th Iowa Inf.	110	76	1914 Mar 29	NE, 39th, 1915
Forbes, Robt.		L, 2nd Neb. Cav.	1		1899 Dec 9	KS, 19th, 1900
Forbes, Sherman		D, 49th N.Y.	25		1933 Mar 11	NE, 58th, 1934
Forbes, T.H.	Corp.	H, 25th Iowa Inf.	440		1919 May 25	IA, 46th, 1920
Force, H.C.		L, 5th Ill. Cav.	23		1918 Nov 14	KS, 38th, 1919
Force, I.N.	Pvt.	K, 14th Mich.	329		1924 Jul 18	IA, 51st, 1925
Force, J.A.		H, 22nd N.Y. Cav. (died of paralysis)	8		1893 May 29	NE, 18th, 1894
Force, Jefferson	Pvt.	A, 45th Iowa Inf.	26	84	1931 Jun 17	IA, 58th, 1932
Forcht, Frederick		F, 64th Ill.	131		1919 May 22	KS, 39th, 1920
Forcum, W.M.		B, 7th Del.	248		1898 Dec 25	KS, 18th, 1899
Ford, A.	Pvt.	H, 45th Iowa Inf.	22		1920 Feb 4	IA, 47th, 1921
Ford, A.H.		C, 16th Kans. Inf.	111		1886	KS, 6th, 1887
Ford, Abejah		A, 66th Ill. Inf.	94		1923 Feb 23	IA, 50th, 1924
Ford, Abraham		K, 45th Iowa Inf.	40		1927 Oct 5	IA, 54th, 1928
Ford, Amos	Corp.	D, 11th Iowa Inf.	64		1915 Oct 12	IA, 42nd, 1916
Ford, C.		A, 1st Ky. Art. (died of pneumonia)	245		1902 Sep	NE, 27th, 1903
Ford, Caswell P.	Lieut. Col.	25th Ill. Inf.	65		1911 Dec 29	KS, 31st, 1912
Ford, Chas.	Pvt.	A, 28th Iowa Inf.	98		1906 May 2	IA, 33rd, 1907
Ford, Daniel	Pvt.	B, 2nd Iowa Inf.	110		1923 Dec 19	IA, 50th, 1924
Ford, Daniel		H, 12th Ohio Cav.	9		1918 Aug 20	KS, 38th, 1919
Ford, Franklin		F, 13th Ohio	130		1917 Jun 6	KS, 37th, 1918
Ford, Geo.	Pvt.	D, 9th Iowa Inf.	104		1906 Jan	IA, 33rd, 1907
Ford, H.		L, 14th Ill.	132		1926 Feb 2	KS, 46th, 1927
Ford, H.C.	Sergt.	I, 72nd N.Y. Inf.	86		1915 Jun 16	IA, 42nd, 1916
Ford, I.H.	Sergt.	I, 2nd Iowa Cav.	152		1906 Dec 29	IA, 33rd, 1907
Ford, I.S.	Pvt.	F, 4th Iowa Inf.	452		1929 Jul 10	IA, 56th, 1930
Ford, J.C.	Capt.	H, 21st Va. Cav.	12		1899 Jul 1	IA, 26th, 1900
Ford, J.G.			515		1909 Jul 12	IA, 36th, 1910
Ford, James		C, 12th Kans.	145		1917 Jan 6	KS, 37th, 1918
Ford, James E.		K, 4th Iowa	462		1898 Oct	KS, 18th, 1899
Ford, Jerome C.		H, 36th Ill. Inf. (died of heart trouble)	22	68	1908 Mar 27	NE, 33rd, 1909
Ford, Jno. T.	Pvt.	F, 29th Iowa Inf.	248	50	1890 Jan 22	IA, 16th, 1890
Ford, John C.	Pvt.	D, 13th Mass. Inf.	2		1913 Jan 14	IA, 40th, 1914
Ford, John C.		C, 85th Ill.	399		1914 Mar 15	KS, 33rd, 1914
Ford, Joseph H.H.		G, 13th Kans.	92		1921 Feb 23	KS, 41st, 1922
Ford, Oscar F.	Sergt.	A, 8th Iowa Inf. H, 26th Iowa Inf.	196		1899 Apr 11	IA, 26th, 1900
Ford, P.O.		C, 13th Ky. Inf.	14		1902 Oct 31	KS, 22nd, 1903
Ford, R.E.	Pvt.	F, 44th Ind. Inf.	7	59	1894 Feb 17	IA, 21st, 1895
Ford, T.F.			167		1919 Mar 31	IA, 46th, 1920
Ford, T.O.			267		1921 Jul 19	IA, 48th, 1922
Ford, Thomas			3		1884	KS, 4th, 1885
Ford, Wm. M.		I, 1st Kans. Mtd. Inf.	7		1924[1923?] Dec 10	NE, 48th, 1924
Forder, J.E.	Bugler	E, 1st Iowa Inf.	515		1911 May 24	IA, 38th, 1912
Fordham, G.M.	Pvt.	G, 47th Ill. Inf.	231		1905 Dec 7	IA, 32nd, 1906
Fordice, Geo. W.			337		1917 Nov 14	IA, 44th, 1918
Fordyce, J.G., see Ferdryce, J.G.						
Forehand, L.D.	Pvt.	C, 1st N.H. Cav.	64		1920 Dec 7	IA, 47th, 1921
Forehand, L.D.		E, 5th N.H. (died of smallpox)	1	76	1918 May 27	NE, 43rd, 1919
Foreman, Alfred		E, 15th Ill. Inf. (died of heart failure)	130	71	1911 Aug 16	NE, 36th, 1912
Foreman, Alfred		E, 15th Ill.	130	74	1911 Aug 16	NE, 37th, 1913
Foreman, B.F.	Pvt.	I, 93rd Ill. Inf.	12		1926 May 17	IA, 53rd, 1927
Foreman, George		A, 201st Penn.	2		1924 Dec 25	KS, 44th, 1925
Foreman, George L.		A, 77th Ohio	7		1913 Apr 4	KS, 33rd, 1914
Foreman, J.J.		D, 4th Ohio	25		1919 Dec 9	KS, 39th, 1920

*See Appendix A, B or C for roster of post names and locations.
†See Introduction for note regarding recording of death date.
184

Name	Rank	Company, Regiment or Ship	Post*	Age	Death Date†	Journal
Foreman, Thos. C.	Pvt.	I, 7th Ill. Cav.	12		1913 Jul 3	IA, 40th, 1914
Foresman, James		E, 47th Iowa Inf.	55		1912 Jan 17	IA, 39th, 1913
Forest, C.M.	Pvt.	D, 22nd Iowa Inf.	337		1908 Dec 21	IA, 35th, 1909
Foresyth, Geo. W.	Pvt.	G, 31st Wis. Inf.	91		1913 Nov 28	IA, 40th, 1914
Forg, Sunbert		H, 121st Penn. Inf.	7		1925 May 21	NE, 50th, 1926
Forgey, A.J.		B, 46th Ind. Inf.	240		1916 Feb 22	KS, 36th, 1917
Forgey, A.J.		B, 46th Ind.	240		1915 Jan 22	KS, 35th, 1916
Forgey, A.W.		G, 76th Ind.	98		1896 May	KS, 16th, 1897
Forgy, John D.	Pvt.	B, 46th Ind. Inf.	12	44	1887 May 19	IA, 15th, 1889
Forman, Aaron M.		1st S.M. Cav.	4		1918 Mar 20	KS, 38th, 1919
Forman, Chas.	Pvt.	C, 3rd Iowa Cav.	2		1925 Dec 2	IA, 52nd, 1926
Forman, E.A.		C, 23rd Mich.	18		1909 Mar 21	KS, 29th, 1910
Forman, John		E, 1st Mo.	4		1933 Feb 6	KS, 53rd, 1934
Forman, William H.	Pvt.	C, 3rd Iowa Cav.	2	75	1897 Mar 10	IA, 23rd, 1897
Forney, A.C.	Pvt.	I, 80th Ohio Inf.	173		1918	IA, 45th, 1919
Forney, Aaron H.		I, 156th Ill. Inf.	69		1899 Sep 29	KS, 19th, 1900
Forney, Geo. H.		I, 12th Ill. Inf. (died of paralysis)	4		1894	NE, 19th, 1895
Forney, John M.	Pvt.	I, 90th Ohio Cav.	321		1909 Jun 29	IA, 36th, 1910
Forrest, F.R.		P, 192nd Penn.	463		1922 Apr 28	KS, 42nd, 1923
Forrest, Frank			463		1923	KS, 43rd, 1924
Forrester, A.B.	Pvt.	E, 8th Ill. Inf.	98		1927 Dec 11	IA, 54th, 1928
Forrester, J.W.	Pvt.	A, 23rd Iowa Inf.	45		1928 Nov 5	IA, 55th, 1929
Forrester, T.G.		B, 4th Iowa	71		1904 Feb 16	KS, 24th, 1905
Forscutt, M.H.		E, 3rd Calif. Inf. (died of general debility)	24		1903 Oct 18	NE, 28th, 1904
Forscythe, J.D.		D, 8th Iowa	17		1909 Apr 23	KS, 29th, 1910
Forsee, Olof		D, 57th Ill.	127		1928 Sep 15	KS, 48th, 1929
Forsyth, —			95		1914	NE, 39th, 1915
Forsyth, A.P.		I, 97th Ind.	4		1906 Sep 3	KS, 26th, 1907
Forsyth, A.W.			253		1923 Nov 17	IA, 50th, 1924
Forsyth, E.L.		H, 7th Ill.	71		1919 Jul 12	KS, 39th, 1920
Forsyth, Geo. W., see Foresyth, Geo. W.						
Forsyth, J.M.	Pvt.	M, 4th N.Y. Cav.	24		1921 Nov 4	IA, 48th, 1922
Forsyth, Jacob		G, 20th Iowa Inf.	25	82	1918 Dec 8	NE, 43rd, 1919
Forsyth, R.M.		D, 8th Iowa Inf.	57		1902 Oct 10	KS, 22nd, 1903
Forsythe, J.D., see Forscythe, J.D.						
Forsythe, John		E, 13th Iowa Inf. (died of abscess of liver)	123		1893 Jun 9	NE, 18th, 1894
Forsythe, John		E, 13th Iowa Inf. (died of general debility)	123		1894 Jun 9	NE, 19th, 1895
Forsythe, T.J.	Sergt.	E, 7th Iowa Cav.	434		1927 Oct 19	IA, 54th, 1928
Fortier, Eloy		K, 147th Ill. Inf.	17		1917 Mar 17	KS, 37th, 1918
Fortner, Church	Corp.	1st Iowa Bat.	267		1915 Aug 11	IA, 42nd, 1916
Fortney, A.		B, 4th West Va. Cav.	115		1922 Dec	KS, 42nd, 1923
Fortney, Jasper			32		1914 Feb 6	KS, 34th, 1915
Forward, M.		2nd Mich. Cav.	28		1918 Dec 29	KS, 38th, 1919
Fosbury, E.		23rd Iowa (died of old age)	318		1921 Dec 2	NE, 46th, 1922
Fosdick, M.	Pvt.	F, 95th Ill. Inf.	284		1920	IA, 47th, 1921
Fosket, B.		87th Iowa	114	75	1916 Mar	NE, 41st, 1917
Foskett, H.B.	Chaplain	124th Ill. Inf.	56	67	1892 Sep 3	IA, 19th, 1893
Foskett, Wm.		B, 2nd Ill. Cav.	265		1929 Jul 10	NE, 54th, 1930
Fosler, C.		I, 185th Ohio	13		1931 Jul 2	NE, 56th, 1932
Fosler, Geo.			3		1928 Nov	NE, 53rd, 1929
Fosler, George		B, 46th Ill.	3		1931 Apr 18	NE, 56th, 1932
Foss, Alven B.		H, 96th Ill.	459		1921 Apr 5	KS, 41st, 1922
Foss, Francis M.		E, 13th Ind.	8		1913 Apr 4	KS, 33rd, 1914
Foss, Ransom		B, 34th Ill. Vet. Inf. (born in Ohio; died of diabetes at Soldiers & Sailors Home Hospital, Burkett; buried in Home Cemetery)		72	1906 Jun 30	NE, 31st, 1907
Foss, Wm. H.		E, 3rd Ind.	36		1885	KS, 5th, 1886
Foster, A.C.		C, 7th Kans.	130		1921 Jul 4	KS, 41st, 1922
Foster, A.M.	Pvt.	H, 33rd Iowa Inf.	12		1913 Jan 11	IA, 40th, 1914
Foster, A.N.			72		1884	KS, 4th, 1885

Name	Rank	Company, Regiment or Ship	Post*	Age	Death Date†	Journal
Foster, A.W.		G, 14th Ind.	14		1893 Jul 27	KS, 13th, 1894
Foster, Asa		B, 151st N.Y.	132		1902 Dec 16	KS, 22nd, 1903
Foster, B.S.		C, 7th Kans.	130		1920 Nov 30	KS, 40th, 1921
Foster, C.P.	Pvt.	H, 43rd Wis. Inf.	123		1917 Apr 5	IA, 44th, 1918
Foster, C.W.	Capt.	D, 76th U.S.C.T.	391		1917 Jan 20	IA, 44th, 1918
Foster, Charles H.	Pvt.	C, 89th Ill. Inf.	59	67	1894 Dec 6	IA, 21st, 1895
Foster, D.W.		A, 27th Ohio			1928 Nov 20	NE, 53rd, 1929
Foster, Daniel		A, 27th Ohio	45		1928 Nov 12	NE, 53rd, 1929
Foster, E.M.			40		1906 Mar 3	NE, 31st, 1907
Foster, Ed. P.		E, 93rd Ind. Inf.	441		1902	KS, 22nd, 1903
Foster, Edwin		H, 34th Ill.	4		1913 Nov 4	KS, 33rd, 1914
Foster, Edwin, see Edwin, Foster						
Foster, F.W.	Pvt.	D, 8th Wis. Inf.	75	55	1891 Jul 8	IA, 18th, 1892
Foster, F.W.	1st Lieut.	A, 9th Iowa Inf.	267	52	1892 Sep 5	IA, 19th, 1893
Foster, George		E, 8th Ill. Cav. (died of accident)	27		1893 Oct 15	NE, 18th, 1894
Foster, H.C.		B, 83rd Ill.	271	90	1934 Apr 21	IA, 61st, 1935
Foster, Homer			371		1909	IA, 36th, 1910
Foster, I.G.		G, 112th Ill. Inf. (died of hardening of arteries)	15	71	1914 Oct 2	NE, 39th, 1915
Foster, Isaac	Pvt.	G, 28th Ill. Inf.	231		1929 Nov 6	IA, 56th, 1930
Foster, J.A.	Sergt.	E, 4th Penn. Cav.	258		1913 Jan 14	IA, 39th, 1913
Foster, J.A.	Sergt.	E, 4th Penn. Cav.	258		1913 Jan 14	IA, 40th, 1914
Foster, J.B.	Pvt.	A, 33rd Iowa Inf.	209		1904 May 19	IA, 31st, 1905
Foster, J.E.		B, 184th Ohio	166		1918 Jan 5	KS, 38th, 1919
Foster, J.H.	Sergt.	E, 20th Iowa Inf.	135		1921 Jul 23	IA, 48th, 1922
Foster, J.S.	Pvt.	A, 44th Wis. Inf.	223	45	1891 Feb 24	IA, 18th, 1892
Foster, J.S.		D, 12th Kans.	18		1906 Dec 2	KS, 26th, 1907
Foster, J.W.	Pvt.	A, 110th N.Y. Inf.	236		1912 Aug 7	IA, 39th, 1913
Foster, James W.		K, 11th Penn.	175		1908 Sep 2	KS, 32nd, 1913
Foster, Jeremiah	Pvt.	B, 44th Iowa Inf.	231		1902 Jul 14	IA, 29th, 1903
Foster, John	Pvt.	L, N.Y. Mt. Rifle	8		1914 Nov 25	IA, 41st, 1915
Foster, Johnathan	Pvt.	G, 21st Iowa Inf.	78		1916 Mar 7	IA, 43rd, 1917
Foster, Joseph		E, 163rd Ohio	293		1927	KS, 47th, 1928
Foster, L.Y.	Pvt.	M, 2nd Iowa Cav.	78		1912 Aug 5	IA, 39th, 1913
Foster, Louis		F, 12th Kans. (died in California)	247		1892 Jul 13	KS, 12th, 1893
Foster, M.L., Dr.		A, 138th Ohio Inf.	18		1934 Jan 23	KS, 54th, 1935
Foster, Maynard Wright		E, 61st Ill. Inf.	25	72	1921 Mar 10	NE, 46th, 1922
Foster, O.	Pvt.	B, 48th Wis. Inf.	118		1906 Jul 8	IA, 33rd, 1907
Foster, Ozro B.		C, 48th Ind.	98		1932	NE, 57th, 1933
Foster, R.S.		G, 113th Ohio	72		1919 Nov 23	KS, 39th, 1920
Foster, Richard			17		1934 Jul 21	KS, 54th, 1935
Foster, Robert B.	Pvt.	E, 146th Ill.	66		1926 Feb 21	IA, 53rd, 1927
Foster, Robt.		E, 92nd Ohio	104		1904 Jul	KS, 24th, 1905
Foster, Rubon			158		1919 Jan 22	IA, 46th, 1920
Foster, Samuel		B, 79th U.S. Col.	453		1925 Feb 20	KS, 45th, 1926
Foster, Samuel		B, 79th U.S.C.	453		1926 Feb 20	KS, 46th, 1927
Foster, Simon S.		H, 98th Ill.	1		1904 Jul 14	KS, 24th, 1905
Foster, Sol H.	Pvt.	E, 28th Wis. Inf.	29		1924 Jul 6	IA, 51st, 1925
Foster, T.C.		B, 41st Ill. Inf. (died of paralysis)	107	67	1903 Nov 20	NE, 28th, 1904
Foster, T.M.	Pvt.	E, 149th Ill. Inf.	284		1928	IA, 55th, 1929
Foster, Thomas	Sergt.	D, 6th Iowa Inf.	434		1901 Aug 14	IA, 28th, 1902
Foster, Traverse T.	Pvt.	I, 4th Iowa Inf.	192	65	1894 Mar 16	IA, 21st, 1895
Foster, W.J.		L, 2nd Mich. Cav.	447		1923 Aug 11	KS, 43rd, 1924
Foster, W.L.		H, 49th Colored Inf.	152		1897 Feb 18	KS, 17th, 1898
Foster, William		A, 126th Ohio (died of heart failure)	41	67	1907 Apr 6	NE, 32nd, 1908
Foster, William H.		B, 44th Iowa Inf.	29	96	1938 Jun 13	IA, 64th, 1938
Foster, Wm.		K, 20th Maine	100		1926 Nov 15	KS, 46th, 1927
Fotherston, Gabriel		B, 83rd Ark.	10		1912 Apr 12	KS, 32nd, 1913
Foughty, John	Pvt.	B, 47th Ohio	81		1924 Feb 6	IA, 51st, 1925
Foulks, C.M.		C, 102nd Ohio	1		1897 May 13	KS, 17th, 1898
Fountain, C.			41		1920	KS, 40th, 1921

*See Appendix A, B or C for roster of post names and locations.
†See Introduction for note regarding recording of death date.

Name	Rank	Company, Regiment or Ship	Post*	Age	Death Date†	Journal
Fountain, Cyril		A, 57th N.Y.	41		1919 Oct 21	KS, 39th, 1920
Fountain, Isaac		K, 85th Ill. Inf. (died of old age)	13	82	1920 Jul 4	NE, 45th, 1921
Fountain, Pierson	Sergt.	D, 55th Mass. Inf.	197		1910 Aug 10	IA, 37th, 1911
Fountain, Wm. H.		H, 18th Ohio Cav. I & B, 2nd West Va. Cav.	66		1914 Dec 22	KS, 34th, 1915
Fouse, D.S.	Capt.	54th Penn. Inf.	140		1912 Mar 3	IA, 39th, 1913
Foust, Ben.	Pvt.	C, 44th Iowa Inf.	270		1924 Jul 1	IA, 51st, 1925
Foust, Henry		M, 8th Iowa Cav. (member at large)			1936 Oct 13	NE, 61st, 1937
Fouts, David		G, 35th Mo. Inf. (died at Colyer, Kans.; buried at WaKeeney Cemetery)	107		1894 Nov 23	KS, 14th, 1895
Fouts, Joseph			515		1916 Jan 29	IA, 43rd, 1917
Fouts, Reuben		F, 36th Iowa Inf. (died of pneumonia)	74	58	1895 Mar 20	NE, 20th, 1896
Fouts, William P.		I, 5th Iowa Cav.	354	84	1914 Oct 28	NE, 40th, 1916
Fowble, John W.	Pvt.	M & K, 2nd Penn. Hvy. Art. B, 22nd Penn. Cav.	206	90	1935 Nov 16	IA, 65th, 1939
Fowle, J.	Corp.	I, 22nd Iowa Inf.	8		1905 Jul 6	IA, 32nd, 1906
Fowler, Ban			116		1920	IA, 47th, 1921
Fowler, D.P.	Pvt.	F, 27th Iowa Inf.	346		1903 Feb 16	IA, 29th, 1903
Fowler, E.M.	Pvt.	B, 98th Ohio Inf.	24	44	1889 Jul 31	IA, 16th, 1890
Fowler, Eli		C, 11th Kans.	55		1924 May 13	KS, 44th, 1925
Fowler, Ezra		K, 105th Ohio	25		1927 Jun 10	KS, 47th, 1928
Fowler, J.M.		H, 27th Ind. Inf.	7		1926 Apr 27	NE, 51st, 1927
Fowler, J.W.		C, 98th Ill. Inf.	50		1925 Jul 29	KS, 45th, 1926
Fowler, James			190		1927 Nov 29	IA, 54th, 1928
Fowler, James A.			79		1927	IA, 54th, 1928
Fowler, Joe		F, 47th Ill.	308		1906 Sep 10	KS, 26th, 1907
Fowler, John R.	Pvt.	B, 23rd Ohio	81		1924 Mar 18	IA, 51st, 1925
Fowler, O.S.	Corp.	K, 13th Ill. Inf.	346		1903 Feb 2	IA, 29th, 1903
Fowler, Wm. P.	Pvt.	D, 9th Ill. Cav.	404		1923 Dec 3	IA, 50th, 1924
Fowler, Wm. S.			117		1883	KS, 3rd, 1884
Fowlks, J.W.	Pvt.	D, 43rd Ind. Inf.	54		1929 Mar 27	IA, 56th, 1930
Fox, A.H.		K, 4th Mich. Cav. (died of heart failure)	35	66	1911 Apr 19	NE, 36th, 1912
Fox, Amos W.		B, 101st Ohio	77		1896 Nov	KS, 16th, 1897
Fox, Austin	Pvt.	F, 3rd Ill.	133		1926 Apr 16	IA, 53rd, 1927
Fox, Basil	Pvt.	H, 17th Iowa Inf.	59		1910 Jan 16	IA, 37th, 1911
Fox, Charles B.		10th Iowa	25		1910 Sep 7	NE, 35th, 1911
Fox, Chas. B.		K, Ind. Hvy. Art.	7		1906 Apr 13	NE, 31st, 1907
Fox, Chas. E.	Pvt.	I, 8th Iowa (died of rheumatism)	207	64	1887 Jul	NE, 12th, 1888
Fox, Cyrus	Pvt.	C, 7th Iowa Inf. (member of Dept. of Nebraska)	187	96	1942 Jun 12	IA, 69th, 1943
Fox, Cyrus		C, 7th Iowa Inf. (member at large)			1942 Jun 12	NE, 67th, 1943
Fox, Dennis	Pvt.	G, 42nd Mo. Inf.	452	47	1892 Oct 16	IA, 19th, 1893
Fox, Dorns M.	Col.	27th Mich. Vols.	12		1901 Nov 14	IA, 28th, 1902
Fox, Edgar		F, 95th Ill. (died of heart trouble)	20	70	1909 Oct 4	NE, 34th, 1910
Fox, Elias	Pvt.	F, 18th Iowa Inf.	122		1920	IA, 47th, 1921
Fox, Elmore		3rd Penn. Hvy. Art.	66		1921 Sep 8	KS, 41st, 1922
Fox, Geo. H.		F, 66th N.Y.	72		1920 Dec 5	KS, 40th, 1921
Fox, George			72		1922 Dec 5	KS, 43rd, 1924
Fox, George R.			97		1911 May 24	KS, 31st, 1912
Fox, George W.	Pvt.	D, 30th Iowa Inf.	40		1914 Apr 30	IA, 41st, 1915
Fox, H.C.			190		1st quarter 1885	IA, 11th, 1885
Fox, J.T.		G, 25th Ill.	5		1928 Nov 17	KS, 48th, 1929
Fox, James	Pvt.	B, 2nd U.S. Cav.	26		1916 Jan 12	IA, 43rd, 1917
Fox, James H.		1st Wis. Cav.	58		1911 Oct 29	KS, 31st, 1912
Fox, John			230		1916 May 27	IA, 43rd, 1917
Fox, John W.		D, 11th Wis. (cause of death: heart)	25	57	1900 Aug 3	NE, 25th, 1901
Fox, Jonas G.	Pvt.	C, 34th Penn. Inf.	98	84	1931 Apr 20	IA, 58th, 1932
Fox, Joseph W.		H, 13th Ind.	132		1914 Apr 19	KS, 34th, 1915
Fox, Joseph W.		D, 40th Ind.	132		1914 Aug 18	KS, 34th, 1915
Fox, Marshall D.		A, 11th Iowa Inf. (at large)	117	95	1937 Oct 12	IA, 64th, 1938
Fox, O.W.		K, 14th Wis. Inf.	1		1901 Dec 2	KS, 21st, 1902
Fox, Paul	Pvt.	A, 116th Ind. Inf. (at large)	22	92	1939 Dec 10	IA, 66th, 1940

*See Appendix A, B or C for roster of post names and locations.
†See Introduction for note regarding recording of death date.

187

Name	Rank	Company, Regiment or Ship	Post*	Age	Death Date†	Journal
Fox, S.		G, 114th Ill.	5		1930 Nov 6	NE, 55th, 1931
Fox, Samuel		13th Mo. Inf.	51		1914 Oct	KS, 34th, 1915
Fox, Samuel		D, 155th Penn. Inf.	12		1925 Oct 25	KS, 45th, 1926
Foxworthy, P.E.		H, 33rd Ind. Inf.	113		1914 Mar 29	NE, 39th, 1915
Foy, David		I, 46th Iowa (died of old age)	26	83	1918 Mar	NE, 43rd, 1919
Foy, Lewis		H, 123rd Ohio	18		1936 Apr 12	KS, 56th, 1937
Foy, N.C.		H, 13th Iowa Inf.	11	84	1923 Jan 23	NE, 48th, 1924
Fozier, Chas. W.		D, 2nd Kans.	132		1899 Jan	KS, 19th, 1900
Frabrick, L.N.	Pvt.	1st Minn. Battery	222		1911 Aug 13	IA, 38th, 1912
Frack, L.S.	Pvt.	F, 32nd Ohio Inf.	231		1913 Nov 10	IA, 40th, 1914
Fracker, E.G.	Lieut.	G, 6th Iowa Inf.	8		1900 Feb 25	IA, 27th, 1901
Frager, Elias S.		H, 3rd Ohio Cav.	167		1913 Jul 14	KS, 33rd, 1914
Frager, Jacob	Teamster	K, 6th Iowa Cav.	206		1899 Dec 11	IA, 26th, 1900
Frahm, Gust.		D, 13th Kans.	260		1906 Aug 17	KS, 26th, 1907
Frahm, Jacob		D, 43rd Ill. (died of old age)	318	83	1925 Feb 2	NE, 49th, 1925
Frain, C.D.		E, 49th Penn.	297		1904 Aug 28	KS, 24th, 1905
Frakes, A.J.	Pvt.	H, 32nd Iowa Inf.	66		1916 Nov 23	IA, 43rd, 1917
Fraley, J.D.	Pvt.	H, 13th Iowa Inf.	94	83	1933 Jun 1	IA, 60th, 1934
Fralick, David			380		1918	KS, 38th, 1919
Frallick, David			380		1917	KS, 37th, 1918
Frame, J.L.		G, 30th Iowa Inf.	79		1893 Jun 24	NE, 18th, 1894
Frame, James	Pvt.		173		1926 Apr 10	IA, 53rd, 1927
Frame, James T.		H, 12th Ohio	303		1913 Nov 30	KS, 33rd, 1914
Frame, Oliver	Pvt.	K, 38th Iowa	57		1899 Feb 17	IA, 26th, 1900
France, Aquila	Pvt.	E, 37th Wis. Inf.	66		1911 Sep 10	IA, 38th, 1912
France, J.R.		B, Minn. Cav. Bat.	113		1903	NE, 28th, 1904
France, R.	Pvt.	C, 18th Wis. Inf.	465		1920 Jul 1	IA, 47th, 1921
France, Wm.	Pvt.	B, 13th N.Y.S.N.G.[N.Y. State National Guard] (died of heart disease)	110	44	1888 Sep	NE, 13th, 1889
Frances, Geo. H.		E, 78th N.Y. K, 102nd N.Y.	453		1929 Sep 10	KS, 49th, 1930
Francis, A.I.	Pvt.	E, 5th Ill. Inf.	181	64	1891 Dec 17	IA, 18th, 1892
Francis, Chas.		I, 2nd Mich. Cav. (died of kidney disease)	13	67	1906 Oct 28	NE, 31st, 1907
Francis, Edward			129		1901 Sep 22	KS, 21st, 1902
Francis, J.P.		I, 85th Ohio	83		1928 Feb 20	KS, 48th, 1929
Francis, J.S.	Pvt.	A, 28th Iowa Inf.	204		1912 Jul 10	IA, 39th, 1913
Francis, R.H.		E, 12th Ind. Cav.	255		1913 Sep 8	KS, 33rd, 1914
Francis, S.A.	Pvt.	A, 2nd Neb.	44		1899	NE, 24th, 1900
Francis, W.H.	Pvt.	A, 28th Iowa Inf.	204		1911 Jun 10	IA, 38th, 1912
Franey, Patrick H.		A, 16th Minn.	158		1915 Jun 11	KS, 35th, 1916
Frank, C.A.			72		1911 Feb 19	KS, 31st, 1912
Frank, Ernest	Pvt.	K, 17th Ind. Inf.	170	63	1891 Apr 13	IA, 18th, 1892
Frank, H.H.	Pvt.	G, 34th Ill. Inf.	275	42	1887 Dec 13	IA, 14th, 1888
Frank, J.E.	Pvt.	E, 1st Iowa Cav.	57		1907 Sep 1	IA, 34th, 1908
Frank, Jos. W.		D, 4th Iowa Cav. (died of stroke)	1	76	1919 Jan 18	NE, 44th, 1920
Frank, O.F.	Pvt.	A, 11th Ill. Inf.	178		1917 Sep 9	IA, 44th, 1918
Frank, S.S.		C, 11th Wis.	57		1917 Mar 8	KS, 37th, 1918
Frank, Simon R.B.	Corp.	C, 57th Ill. Inf.	56		1916	IA, 43rd, 1917
Frank, W.H.		F, 1st Neb. (died of heart trouble)	111	79	1925 Apr 16	NE, 50th, 1926
Frank, William			315		1884	KS, 4th, 1885
Frank, William		G, 144th Ohio	134		1898 Nov 22	KS, 18th, 1899
Franke, Charles		I, 1st Kans. Inf.	6		1910 May 16	KS, 30th, 1911
Frankeberger, John W.		B, 129th Ind. (former member; died at Sterling)	99		1935 Nov 30	NE, 60th, 1936
Frankee, Conrad		I, — Ill.	52		1892 Aug 15	KS, 12th, 1893
Franken, B.	Steward	H, 33rd Iowa Inf.	167		1906 Sep 11	IA, 33rd, 1907
Frankenberger, F.P.		D, 38th Wis. Inf.	81		1925 Dec 7	KS, 45th, 1926
Frankfire, Jacob		F, 86th Ohio Inf.	25	69	1913 Jan 21	NE, 38th, 1914
Frankfurter, David		H, 45th Ohio	at large		1929 Sep 3	NE, 55th, 1931
Franklin, Chas. R.	Pvt.	3rd Iowa Battery	377	45	1888 Feb 25	IA, 15th, 1889
Franklin, J.T.		G, 8th Tenn. Inf.	91		1923	NE, 48th, 1924
Franklin, Sanford E.		G, 47th Ill.	91		1905 Aug 15	KS, 25th, 1906

*See Appendix A, B or C for roster of post names and locations.
†See Introduction for note regarding recording of death date.

Name	Rank	Company, Regiment or Ship	Post*	Age	Death Date†	Journal
Franklin, Simeon		C, 116th Ky.	127		1913 Sep 21	KS, 33rd, 1914
Franklin, Squire	Pvt.	E, 3rd Mo. Cav.	306	58	1892 Jul 6	IA, 19th, 1893
Franklin, V.		H, 198th Penn.	207	73	1913 Oct 12	NE, 38th, 1914
Franklin, W.A.	1st Sergt.	J, 9th Iowa Cav.	81		1901 Mar 18	IA, 28th, 1902
Franklin, W.B.		A, 2nd Neb.	262	58	1904 Aug 19	NE, 29th, 1905
Franklin, W.L.	Corp.	E, 39th Iowa Inf.	23		1912 May	IA, 39th, 1913
Franks, Joseph	Pvt.	H, 12th Iowa Inf.	346		1915	IA, 42nd, 1916
Fransue, Henry W.		I, 52nd Ill. Inf. (died of gunshot wound)	39	64	1907 Dec 12	NE, 32nd, 1908
Frantz, A.J.		I, 3rd Md.	13		1929 Oct 26	NE, 54th, 1930
Frantz, David		D, 130th Penn.	12		1918 Aug 6	KS, 38th, 1919
Frantz, L.F.	Pvt.	E, 6th Ky. Cav.	10		1920 Dec 20	IA, 47th, 1921
Frantz, W.F.	Pvt.	G, 44th Iowa Inf.	311		1906 Aug 4	IA, 33rd, 1907
Frantz, Wm.	Pvt.	B, 13th Iowa	123		1903 Mar 27	IA, 30th, 1904
Frantz, Wm. M.		D, 145th Ill.	81		1931 May 1	NE, 56th, 1932
Franz, Michael P.	Pvt. Pvt.	A, 20th Iowa Inf. H, 29th Iowa Inf.	19, 235	100, 8 mos. & 3 days	1945 Jun 17	IA, 71st, 1945
Frase, B.B.	Pvt.	H, 16th Iowa Inf.	12		1902 Oct 6	IA, 29th, 1903
Frasenger, Gus	Pvt.	H, 6th Iowa Cav.	206		1900 Nov	IA, 27th, 1901
Fraser, D.H.		I, 11th Kans. Cav.	160		1916 Mar 8	KS, 36th, 1917
Fraser, John A.		I, 127th Ill. Inf.	130		1901 May 21	KS, 21st, 1902
Fraser, William W.		I, 97th Ill.	18		1915 Feb 9	KS, 35th, 1916
Fraser, Wm.		I, 3rd Iowa Cav.	447		1921 Apr 26	KS, 41st, 1922
Frasier, Jas.		C, 79th Ind.	25		1908 Apr 11	NE, 33rd, 1909
Frasker, C.W.	Lieut.	C, 16th Iowa Vols.	12		1926 Dec 20	IA, 53rd, 1927
Fraton, John	Pvt.	D, 7th Kans. Cav.	142		1920 May 2	IA, 47th, 1921
Fratz, John	Pvt.	E, 8th Iowa Inf.	206		1908 Apr 27	IA, 35th, 1909
Fravord, H.A.	Pvt.	B, 2nd Ohio Cav.	48		1920 Feb 2	IA, 46th, 1920
Frayne, R.T.		F, 22nd Ky. Inf.	17		prior to 1891	KS, 11th, 1892
Frazee, G.M.		G, 10th Mo. Inf.	136		4th quarter 1884	IA, 11th, 1885
Frazee, J.W.	Pvt.	K, 8th Iowa Inf.	446		1910 Oct 8	IA, 37th, 1911
Frazee, Jerome Wiltse		K, 48th Mo. (died of old age)	84	93	1924 Dec 1	NE, 49th, 1925
Frazell, Frank		F, 2nd Kans.	258		1892 Jan 19	KS, 12th, 1893
Frazell, J.A.D.		F, 2nd Kans. Inf.	88		1889	KS, 9th, 1890
Frazer, Donald	Pvt.	E, 4th Iowa Cav.	321		1909 Sep 8	IA, 36th, 1910
Frazer, J.B.		H, 3rd Ohio Cav.	5		1918 Apr 28	KS, 38th, 1919
Frazer, Joseph	Pvt.	G, 15th Ohio Inf. (died of wounds)	18	64	1891 Aug 13	NE, 16th, 1892
Frazer, Pearl E.		L, 6th Ohio Vol. Cav.	30		1915 Nov 19	KS, 35th, 1916
Frazey, H.P.	Pvt.	Penn.	79		1915	IA, 42nd, 1916
Frazier, Albert		K, 122nd Ohio	50		1927	KS, 47th, 1928
Frazier, C.B.		C, 5th Mich.	114		1896 Oct 16	KS, 16th, 1897
Frazier, Chas.		M.S. Col.	17		1917 Sep 6	KS, 37th, 1918
Frazier, Geo. R.			197		1925 Jan 30	IA, 52nd, 1926
Frazier, Geo. W.		E, 76th Ill. Inf. (died of Bright's disease)	266		1894 Aug 13	NE, 19th, 1895
Frazier, J. Warren		E, 3rd Ohio	4		1898 May 3	KS, 18th, 1899
Frazier, James		4th & 194th Iowa Vol. Inf.	9		1908	NE, 33rd, 1909
Frazier, N.G.		E, 21st Kans.	450		1898 Dec 10	KS, 18th, 1899
Frazier, T.J.	Pvt.	C, 13th Iowa	59		1905 May 31	IA, 32nd, 1906
Frazier, T.J.		H, 23rd Mo.	491		1919 Aug 16	KS, 39th, 1920
Frazier, Thomas	Corp.	D, 14th Iowa Inf.	338		3rd quarter 1885	IA, 12th, 1886
Frazier, Wm. W.	Pvt.	C, 29th Iowa Inf.	59		1926 Sep 13	IA, 53rd, 1927
Frazur, S.E.		H, 7th Ill.	185		1908	KS, 28th, 1909
Freak, John		C, 75th Ill.	293		1906 May 23	KS, 26th, 1907
Freake, Abram	Pvt.	D, 17th Iowa Inf.	19	94	1932 Mar 28	IA, 59th, 1933
Frear, David	Pvt.	C, 5th Penn. Cav.	147		1899 Sep 19	IA, 26th, 1900
Frease, J.A.		G, 105th Penn.	4		1906 Jan 4	KS, 26th, 1907
Frease, Joseph	Pvt.	I, 12th Ill. Inf.	111		1919 Nov 28	IA, 46th, 1920
Frease, William	Pvt.	I, 12th Ill. Inf.	321		1906 Dec 18	IA, 33rd, 1907
Freder, J.		Mo.	333		1899 Apr 16	KS, 19th, 1900
Frederick, A.E.			127		1925 Mar 10	KS, 45th, 1926
Frederick, C.H.		F, 14th U.S. Inf. (died of paresis)	110	71	1902 Jul	NE, 27th, 1903
Frederick, Charles		L, 4th U.S. Inf.	77		1924 Feb 3	KS, 44th, 1925

*See Appendix A, B or C for roster of post names and locations.
†See Introduction for note regarding recording of death date.

Name	Rank	Company, Regiment or Ship	Post*	Age	Death Date†	Journal
Frederick, John		McLaughlin's Ohio Cav. (died of heart failure)	38	73	1909 Nov 13	NE, 34th, 1910
Frederick, John B.		I, 30th Kans.	309		1909 Oct 21	KS, 29th, 1910
Frederickson, C.		G, 9th Kans.	98		1898 Sep 18	KS, 18th, 1899
Frederickson, H.C.	Pvt.	I, 126th Ill. Inf.	34		1909 Jul 13	IA, 36th, 1910
Fredrick, John		F, 82nd Ill. (died of cancer)	35	75	1921 Aug 27	NE, 46th, 1922
Free, F.A.	Pvt.	92nd Ill. Inf.	26		1929 Jan 18	IA, 56th, 1930
Free, Francis A.		G, 65th Ill. Inf.	26		1928 Jan 19	IA, 55th, 1929
Free, John			193		1908	IA, 35th, 1909
Free, Wm. Z.		I, 8th Iowa Inf.	344		1909 Aug 18	KS, 29th, 1910
Freed, O.D.	Pvt.	20th Ind. Battery	30		1925 Jul 3	IA, 52nd, 1926
Freel, B.		H, 34th Iowa Inf. (died of paralysis)	32	72	1912 Feb 13	NE, 37th, 1913
Freel, James M.		B, 34th Iowa Inf. C, 34th & 38th Iowa Inf.		90	1937 Dec 24	IA, 64th, 1938
Freeland, D.S.		G, 4th Wis. Cav. (died of sciatic rheumatism)	303	61	1895 Feb 11	NE, 20th, 1896
Freeland, J.D.		D, 155th Penn. Inf.	245		1st quarter 1885	IA, 11th, 1885
Freeland, W.S.	Pvt.	C, 8th Iowa	153		1926 Sep 16	IA, 53rd, 1927
Freeler, Thos. J.		H, 58th Ind.	25		1911 May 9	KS, 31st, 1912
Freely, James		B, 9th Ill. Cav.	134		1921 Oct 3	KS, 41st, 1922
Freeman, C.E.	Seaman	U.S. Navy	88		1918 Dec 19	IA, 46th, 1920
Freeman, D.N.		F, 130th Ill.	132		1916 Feb 12	KS, 36th, 1917
Freeman, D.R.	Pvt.	D, 7th Wis. Inf.	200		1926 Mar	IA, 53rd, 1927
Freeman, Dan			35		1908 Dec 31	NE, 33rd, 1909
Freeman, E.J.	Pvt.	A, 61st Ill. Inf.	34		1923 Aug 18	IA, 50th, 1924
Freeman, Edgar	Pvt.	K, 38th Iowa	223	46	1891 May 20	IA, 18th, 1892
Freeman, Frank	Pvt.	B, 44th Iowa Inf.	231		1930 Feb 7	IA, 57th, 1931
Freeman, G.W.	Pvt.	Art.	270		1913 Jul	IA, 40th, 1914
Freeman, G.W.			157		1887 Nov 30	KS, 7th, 1888
Freeman, George D.	Sharpshooter	27th Mich.	27		1913 Oct 27	KS, 33rd, 1914
Freeman, H.E.	Pvt.	M, 14th N.Y. Hvy. Art.	2		1910 Sep 4	IA, 37th, 1911
Freeman, Ira R.	Pvt.	Kans.	116		1914 Jul 3	IA, 41st, 1915
Freeman, J.	Pvt.	D, 47th Iowa Inf.	54		1915 Jul 5	IA, 42nd, 1916
Freeman, J.D.	Sergt.	D, 8th Minn. Inf.	101		1906 Oct 3	IA, 33rd, 1907
Freeman, J.G.		A, 180th Ohio	4		1898 Jul 13	KS, 18th, 1899
Freeman, J.R.	Pvt.	F, 4th Iowa Cav.	324		1918 Sep 13	IA, 45th, 1919
Freeman, James E.		G, 11th Kans.	100		1922 Dec 17	KS, 42nd, 1923
Freeman, John F.	Pvt.	I, 25th Wis. Inf.	88		1919 Apr 21	IA, 46th, 1920
Freeman, John H.		G, 30th Iowa	251		1913 Dec 28	KS, 33rd, 1914
Freeman, John M.		D, 3rd N.Y. Cav.	32		1901 Apr 30	KS, 21st, 1902
Freeman, L.C.		A, 36th Ind. Inf.	118		1917 May 10	KS, 37th, 1918
Freeman, R.A.		B, 70th Ill.	50		1911	KS, 31st, 1912
Freeman, W.S.	Bugler	B, 8th Ill. Cav.	91		1930 Feb 16	IA, 57th, 1931
Frees, Peter		E, 11th Mich. Inf.	24		1920	NE, 45th, 1921
Freese, Asjen	Pvt.	F, 15th Ill. Inf.	71		1910 May 31	IA, 37th, 1911
Freestone, John	Pvt.	G, 2nd Col. Cav.	12		1920 Jul 4	IA, 47th, 1921
Freeze, W.H.			45		1922 Aug 25	NE, 47th, 1923
Freiberger, John		D, 32nd Mass. Inf.	380		1900 Apr 19	KS, 20th, 1901
Freidlie, Casper		K, 33rd Ohio Inf. (died at Elmo)	219		1895 Oct	KS, 15th, 1896
Freman, T.C.		K, 5th Ariz.	4		1924 Nov 5	KS, 44th, 1925
Fremuth, Geo.		G, 12th Mo.	293		1906	KS, 26th, 1907
Fren, C.E.		B, 93rd Ill. Inf.	489		1917	IA, 44th, 1918
French, Alfred D.	Pvt.	A, 89th Ill. Inf.	15	96	1939 Jun 1	IA, 65th, 1939
French, Alfred Newton		B, 19th Ohio Inf.	94	100 & 9 mos.	1938 Oct 17	IA, 64th, 1938
French, C.H.	Pvt.	F, 89th N.Y.	235		1923 Sep 18	IA, 50th, 1924
French, Ed		B, 11th Ill. Cav.	19		1908 Nov 22	KS, 28th, 1909
French, Ephrem	Pvt.	G, 146th N.Y. Inf.	22		1908 Dec 28	IA, 35th, 1909
French, Franklin F.	Pvt.	I, 29th Wis. Inf.	193		1917 Apr 21	IA, 44th, 1918
French, George B.		F, 26th Penn. Cav. (died of pneumonia)	4	72	1910 Dec 29	NE, 35th, 1911
French, I.M.	Corp.	F, 31st Iowa	130		1912 Sep 16	IA, 39th, 1913
French, J.N.	Pvt.	D, 117th N.Y. Inf.	206		1904 Jan 1	IA, 31st, 1905

*See Appendix A, B or C for roster of post names and locations.
†See Introduction for note regarding recording of death date.
190

Name	Rank	Company, Regiment or Ship	Post*	Age	Death Date†	Journal
French, J.R.		A, 26th Ky. Inf. (died of chronic diarrhea)	52		1902 Sep	NE, 27th, 1903
French, James W.		A, 109th U.S.C.T.	64		1919 Sep 23	KS, 39th, 1920
French, Jno.		H, 11th N.Y.	142		1904 Nov 26	KS, 24th, 1905
French, John	Sergt.	A, 37th Ind. Inf.	168		1910 Nov 10	IA, 37th, 1911
French, John	Pvt.	D, 9th Vt. Inf.	311		1916 Aug 28	IA, 43rd, 1917
French, John W.		A, 2nd Ill. (died of tuberculosis)	60	72	1910 Apr 8	NE, 35th, 1911
French, Judson	Musician	I, 36th Wis. Inf.	512		1916 May 1	IA, 43rd, 1917
French, L.	Asst. Surg.	31st Iowa Inf.	1		1910 Sep 19	IA, 37th, 1911
French, Lewis S.	Pvt.	D, 38th Wis. Inf.	386		1900 Sep 13	IA, 27th, 1901
French, O.L.	1st Lieut.	75th Ill. Inf.	59		1905 May 15	IA, 32nd, 1906
French, S.D.	Pvt.	F, N.Y. Inf.	132		1925 Dec 6	IA, 52nd, 1926
French, S.T.		E, 13th Iowa	187		1897 Nov 9	KS, 17th, 1898
French, Thos. G.	Pvt.	A, 102nd Ill. Inf.	2		1918 Nov 7	IA, 45th, 1919
French, W.K.		37th Ill.	36		1912 Nov 29	KS, 32nd, 1913
French, W.W.	Pvt.	A, 34th Ill. Inf.	81		1920 Jan 9	IA, 47th, 1921
French, William		G, 63rd Ind.	63		1921 Nov 12	KS, 41st, 1922
Frerris, J.		A, 29th Ind.	353		1889	KS, 9th, 1890
Freshwater, A.		H, 3rd Iowa Cav.	19		1907 Mar 13	IA, 34th, 1908
Freshwater, Wm.	Pvt.	4th Iowa Inf.	96		1912 May 7	IA, 39th, 1913
Fressler, D.P.		E, 208th Penn.	249		1900 Aug 16	KS, 20th, 1901
Fretz, J.		D, 26th Ky. Inf.	12		1918 May 14	KS, 38th, 1919
Fretz, J.K.		H, 147th Ohio Inf. (died of heart failure)	66	70	1895 Aug 30	NE, 20th, 1896
Frew, Patrick		K, 40th Ky. Inf.	1		1901 Mar 11	KS, 21st, 1902
Frey, Emanuel		I, 2nd Iowa Cav.	14		1914 Jul 26	KS, 34th, 1915
Frey, Frank		I, 31st Wis.	201		1919 Nov 9	KS, 39th, 1920
Frey, J.A.	Pvt.	G, 156th Ill.	22		1926 Apr 11	IA, 53rd, 1927
Frey, James		F, 126th Ohio	354	87	1921 Jan 12	NE, 46th, 1922
Frey, Samuel			333		1912	IA, 39th, 1913
Fribley, James J.		H, 16th Ohio	123		1923 Sep 7	KS, 43rd, 1924
Frick, A.J.			298		1904 Dec 29	IA, 31st, 1905
Friddle, William		D, 21st Ill. Inf.	74		1909 May 29	KS, 29th, 1910
Frie, F.A.			4		1910 May 12	KS, 30th, 1911
Fried, Richard T.		A, 46th Ind. (died of dropsy)	25	71	1915 Jul 15	NE, 40th, 1916
Fried, Wm.		A, Ill. Franklin (Taylor Engineer Corps) (died of cancer)	4	73	1914 Jul 21	NE, 39th, 1915
Friedell, G.	Pvt.	I, 4th U.S. Cav.	78		1920 Jun 13	IA, 47th, 1921
Friedlin, Nick	Pvt.	D, 37th Iowa	146		1905 Jun 5	IA, 32nd, 1906
Friedline, Samuel		C, 141st Ohio	295		1897 Dec 14	KS, 17th, 1898
Friedlings, M.H.		B, 118th Ind.	477		1931 Jul 26	KS, 51st, 1932
Friedlings, M.H.		B, 118th Ind.	477		1931 Jul 26	KS, 52nd, 1933
Friend, Chas. C.		F, 37th Ky.	35		1937 Oct 21	KS, 57th, 1938
Friend, G.W.		E, 114th Ill.	57		1912 Jul 8	KS, 32nd, 1913
Friend, Levi F.	Pvt.	E, 148th Ind. Inf.	59		1910 Dec 5	IA, 37th, 1911
Friesel, W.H.		K, 62nd Penn. Inf. (Weeping Water)			1943 Jan 28	NE, 70th, 1946
Frink, A.			109		1906 Oct 19	IA, 33rd, 1907
Frink, George D.			94		1899	IA, 26th, 1900
Frisbee, M.B.	Capt.	G, 75th N.Y. Art.	408		1906 May 8	IA, 33rd, 1907
Frisbie, B.R.	Pvt.	K, 46th Ill. Inf.	48		1908 Sep 26	IA, 35th, 1909
Frissel, Alonzo J.		B, 140th Ohio	380		1911 Aug 5	KS, 31st, 1912
Fritag, August		H, 6th Ohio	18		1905 Apr 17	KS, 25th, 1906
Frits, James		F, 16th Ill.	138		1897 Nov	KS, 17th, 1898
Fritscher, Walter M.			5		1909 Apr 4	IA, 36th, 1910
Fritton, John		F, 91st N.Y.	42	79	1920 Oct 17	NE, 45th, 1921
Fritts, George		C, 12th Kans.	102		1893 Sep 30	KS, 13th, 1894
Fritz, Ammon		F, 132nd Penn. Inf.	25		1929 May 23	KS, 49th, 1930
Fritz, E.		B, 150th Ind.	185		1908 Nov 15	KS, 28th, 1909
Fritz, Frederick		F, 182nd Ohio Inf.	303		1900 Jul 27	KS, 20th, 1901
Fritz, George H.		B, 32nd Ohio Inf.	88		1930	KS, 50th, 1931
Fritz, H.C.		G, 192nd Penn. Vol. Inf.	63		1916 Apr 12	KS, 36th, 1917
Fritz, Louis		M, 5th U.S. Cav. (died of old age)	12		1893 Apr	NE, 18th, 1894
Fritz, Michael	Pvt.	C, 26th Wis. Inf.	215	49	1890 Dec 14	IA, 18th, 1892
Fritzer, Peter		E, 104th Ohio	25		1935 May 5	NE, 60th, 1936

*See Appendix A, B or C for roster of post names and locations.
†See Introduction for note regarding recording of death date.
191

Name	Rank	Company, Regiment or Ship	Post*	Age	Death Date†	Journal
Frizell, John		A, 60th Ill.	71		1914 May 1	KS, 34th, 1915
Frizzel, Allen	Pvt.	A, 5th Ohio Inf.	16		1918	IA, 45th, 1919
Frodsham, Samuel	Hosp. Stew.	12th Mo. Inf.	71		1901 Jun 4	KS, 21st, 1902
Frohardt, R.			429		1911	KS, 31st, 1912
Frohart, Augustus		K, 24th Ill.	429		1908	KS, 28th, 1909
From, James		B, 46th Ill. (died of nephritis)	10	72	1912 Mar 19	NE, 37th, 1913
Froment, Wm.			337		1911 Dec 25	KS, 31st, 1912
Frost, —			139	69	1905	NE, 30th, 1906
Frost, Benj. A.		Ohio (not a member of the G.A.R.)	18		1912 Nov 1	KS, 32nd, 1913
Frost, C.E.	Pvt.	C, Va. Inf.	153		1914 Nov 14	IA, 41st, 1915
Frost, David		11th Kans.	464		1917 Dec	KS, 37th, 1918
Frost, Frederick W.	Pvt.	1st Independent Battery	40		1914 May 25	IA, 41st, 1915
Frost, H.L.	Pvt.	B, 1st N.H. Hvy. Art.	6	84	1931 Jun 21	IA, 58th, 1932
Frost, James R.	Sergt.	F, 35th Ohio Inf.	78		1912 Dec 24	IA, 39th, 1913
Frost, Lewis H.		F, 1st Neb.	380		1904 Jun 11	KS, 24th, 1905
Frost, Luther		A, 119th Ill. Inf. (died at Great Bend)	52		1895 Aug	KS, 15th, 1896
Frost, M.N.		E, 11th Kans. Cav.	55		1929	KS, 49th, 1930
Frost, Marcus O.		D, 10th Mo.	1		1909 May 14	KS, 29th, 1910
Frost, O.		I, 7th N.Y.		73	1909 Dec 13	NE, 34th, 1910
Frost, S.B.	Pvt.	C, 3rd Mass. Lt. Art.	139		1912 Dec 11	IA, 39th, 1913
Frost, Sam'l B.	Pvt.	C, 3rd Mass. Lt. Art.	452		1912 Dec 11	IA, 39th, 1913
Frost, Spencer	Corp.	53rd Mass. Inf.	149		1912 Apr 19	IA, 40th, 1914
Frost, W.H.		A, 92nd Ill.	4		1913 Apr 18	KS, 33rd, 1914
Fruitts, N.H.		L, 2nd Ohio	4		1918 Jun 30	KS, 38th, 1919
Frum, S.B.	Pvt.	C, 14th Wis. Inf.	364		1909 Aug 27	IA, 36th, 1910
Frush, Geo.	Pvt.		64		1927	IA, 54th, 1928
Fry, A.B.		F, 1st Ohio Cav.	113		1919 Mar 18	KS, 39th, 1920
Fry, B.D.		A, 56th Ohio	85		1928 Apr 15	KS, 48th, 1929
Fry, Bartlett, see Tyler (or Fry), Bartlett						
Fry, Fountain Miller		Ind.		91	1938 Oct 11	IA, 64th, 1938
Fry, Geo. T.	Pvt.	B, 43rd Ind. Inf.	64		1926 Jun 26	IA, 53rd, 1927
Fry, Geo. W.		K, 53rd Penn.	249		1927 Nov 20	KS, 47th, 1928
Fry, Geo. W.	Corp.	F, 1st Ill. Cav.	11		1899	NE, 24th, 1900
Fry, Henry	Pvt.	I, 6th Wis. Inf.	187		1910	IA, 37th, 1911
Fry, J.D.		K, 116th Ill.	293		1916 Aug 17	KS, 36th, 1917
Fry, Jas. M.	Pvt.	E, 7th Iowa Cav.	19		1926 Jul 4	IA, 53rd, 1927
Fry, John	Pvt.	D, 33rd Iowa	144		1922	IA, 49th, 1923
Fry, John C.	Pvt.	C, 45th Iowa Inf.	2		1912 Nov 3	IA, 39th, 1913
Fry, Lewis W.	Pvt.	K, 1st Mo. Eng.	137		1904 Aug 22	IA, 31st, 1905
Fry, Marion		L, 84th Ill.	25		1920	KS, 40th, 1921
Fry, Theodore		G, 47th Iowa	120		1915 Dec	NE, 40th, 1916
Fry, Ulrich	Pvt.	H, 22nd Ill. Inf.	168		1910 Jun 20	IA, 37th, 1911
Fry, Wm. L.	Sergt.	I, 12th Iowa	111	61	1898 Aug 14	IA, 25th, 1899
Fryar, Jackson		D, 128th Ind.	37		1913	KS, 33rd, 1914
Fryar, L.F.		A, 37th Ill. (died of cancer)	13	77	1922 Sep 12	NE, 47th, 1923
Frye, O.B.	Pvt.	I, 44th Ohio	12		1920 Jul 20	IA, 48th, 1922
Frye, Thos.	Pvt.	B, 44th Iowa Inf.	231		1917 Dec 7	IA, 44th, 1918
Fryer, Andrew J.		K, 78th Ill. Inf.	51		1891 Dec 19	KS, 11th, 1892
Fuegol, Herman	Pvt.	1st Iowa Inf.	452		1906 Jan	IA, 33rd, 1907
Fugard, Samuel C.	2nd Lieut.	C, 22nd Iowa Inf.	432	71	1894 May 10	IA, 21st, 1895
Fugate, John		E, 11th Ohio	47		1927 Jun 6	KS, 47th, 1928
Fugate, Josiah	Pvt.	G, 4th Iowa Cav.	481	71	1891 May 14	IA, 18th, 1892
Fulder, William		H, 156th Ill. (died of heart & kidney)	77	82	1924 Nov 2	NE, 49th, 1925
Fulk, James		13th U.S. Inf.	17		1910 Sep 18	KS, 30th, 1911
Fulkerson, W.F.		B, 157th Penn.	18		1902 Dec 27	KS, 22nd, 1903
Fullen, W.T.		F, 93rd Ind.	344		1920 May 5	KS, 40th, 1921
Fullen, Wash. J.	Pvt.	F, 12th Ill.	22	60	1898 Aug 20	IA, 25th, 1899
Fuller, A.		G, 14th Maine	62		1897 Feb	KS, 17th, 1898
Fuller, A.		G, 14th Maine	55		1897	KS, 17th, 1898
Fuller, A.M.		E, 10th Ill.	1		1920 Jun 12	KS, 40th, 1921
Fuller, Arthur		I, 53rd Ill.	265		1932 Apr 11	NE, 57th, 1933

*See Appendix A, B or C for roster of post names and locations.
†See Introduction for note regarding recording of death date.

192

Name	Rank	Company, Regiment or Ship	Post*	Age	Death Date†	Journal
Fuller, B.H.		K, 3rd Vt. Inf. (cause of death: lungs)	95	71	1901 Jan	NE, 26th, 1902
Fuller, Boston R.		B, 123rd Ill.	18		1909 May 8	KS, 29th, 1910
Fuller, C.M.	Pvt.	E, 78th Ohio	324		1907 Mar 16	IA, 34th, 1908
Fuller, Cash. D.		F, 11th Mich.	25		1929 Sep 8	NE, 54th, 1930
Fuller, Charles M.		F, 1st N.Y. Cav.	58		1924 Aug 14	KS, 44th, 1925
Fuller, Clark	Pvt.	I, 32nd Iowa Inf.	236		1895 Oct 20	IA, 22nd, 1896
Fuller, D.E.		D, 169th Ill.	242		1892	KS, 12th, 1893
Fuller, D.M.			67		1913 Apr 7	IA, 40th, 1914
Fuller, E.E.	Hosp. Stew.	3rd Iowa Cav.	2	75	1897 Nov 18	IA, 24th, 1898
Fuller, E.M.	Pvt.	A, 20th Ill. Inf.	12		1915 Dec 19	IA, 42nd, 1916
Fuller, G.H.	Pvt.	C, 27th Iowa Inf.	342		1908 Jan 31	IA, 35th, 1909
Fuller, G.W.	Pvt.	C, 12th Wis. Inf.	58		1920 Aug 30	IA, 47th, 1921
Fuller, Geo. E.	Pvt.	F, 1st R.I.L. & S.L.	165	50	1889 Dec 31	IA, 16th, 1890
Fuller, Geo. W.		C, 135th Ill.	[25?]		1923	NE, 48th, 1924
Fuller, H.	Pvt.	B, 44th N.Y.	112		1903 May 3	IA, 30th, 1904
Fuller, J.C.	Pvt.	F, 45th Iowa Inf.	5		1915 Jul 20	IA, 42nd, 1916
Fuller, J.N.			35		1905	NE, 30th, 1906
Fuller, J.N.			35		1912	NE, 37th, 1913
Fuller, John W.	Pvt.	H, 36th Iowa Inf.	497	92	1938 Dec 14	IA, 65th, 1939
Fuller, Jos.	Pvt.	I, 11th Ill. Cav.	2	46	1888 Apr 19	IA, 15th, 1889
Fuller, Leroy			96		1916	IA, 43rd, 1917
Fuller, M.M.		C, 176th N.Y.	171		1911 Jan 6	KS, 31st, 1912
Fuller, Nathan	Pvt.	I, 32nd Ill. Inf.	40		1930 May 30	IA, 57th, 1931
Fuller, Nelson A.	Pvt.	E, 38th Ohio Inf.	62		1919 Jun 29	IA, 46th, 1920
Fuller, S.H.		G, 130th Ind.	18		1926 Nov 15	KS, 46th, 1927
Fuller, S.L.	Pvt.	D, 30th Wis. Inf.	7	41	1893 Jan 24	IA, 19th, 1893
Fuller, Sidney	Pvt.	L, 2nd Iowa Cav.	221	43	1885 Nov 17	IA, 12th, 1886
Fuller, W.J.		I, 1st Mo. Bat.	28		1906 May 31	KS, 26th, 1907
Fuller, Wm.		I, 32nd Ill. (died of old age)	47	80	1921 Jan 1	NE, 46th, 1922
Fuller, Wm. F.	Pvt.	N.Y. Cav.	248		1922 Mar 4	IA, 49th, 1923
Fullerton, Arch		B, 18th Iowa	52		1920	KS, 40th, 1921
Fullerton, John	Sergt.	17th Iowa Inf.	286		1911	IA, 38th, 1912
Fullerton, John S.		9th Ind. B.	220		1896 Jul 18	KS, 16th, 1897
Fullerton, W.B.		F, 82nd Ind.			1913 Oct 16	KS, 33rd, 1914
Fullmer, Diebold		H, 54th Ill.	25		1909 Sep 9	KS, 29th, 1910
Fulman, F.	Pvt.	I, 20th Ind. Inf.	153		1910 Apr 23	IA, 37th, 1911
Fulmer, Geo. W.		D, Penn. Battery	98	85	1935 Mar 16	IA, 62nd, 1936
Fulmer, J.F.	Pvt.	35th Penn. Reserve C.	231		1917	IA, 44th, 1918
Fulmer, Jno. G.	Sergt.	H, 17th Mich. Inf.	284	57	1888 Apr 16	IA, 15th, 1889
Fulton, A.		D, 106th N.Y.	456	91	1934 Jul	IA, 61st, 1935
Fulton, A.C.		A, 34th Ind.	68		1917 Oct 1	KS, 37th, 1918
Fulton, Alexander	Pvt.	I, 141st Ohio Vol. Inf.	5		1903 Dec 13	IA, 30th, 1904
Fulton, Geo. W.		E, 21st Miss. Inf.	241		1890	KS, 10th, 1891
Fulton, Henry	Pvt.	B, 13th Iowa Inf.	177		1912 Jan 11	IA, 39th, 1913
Fulton, Henry	Pvt.	B, 13th Iowa Inf.	177		1913 Jun 11	IA, 40th, 1914
Fulton, J.R.	Pvt.	C, 126th Penn. Inf.	430	51	1891 Oct 17	IA, 18th, 1892
Fulton, J.T.	Pvt.	B, 19th Iowa	19		1924	IA, 51st, 1925
Fulton, J.W.			100		1915 Aug 15	KS, 35th, 1916
Fulton, Jas.	Pvt.	I, 10th Ill. Cav.	97	61	1891 Jul 25	IA, 18th, 1892
Fulton, John A.		A, 4th Penn.	175		1912 May 14	KS, 32nd, 1913
Fulton, Joseph T.		H, 105th Ill.	1		1897 Jan 16	KS, 17th, 1898
Fulton, Joseph W.		B, 53rd Ohio	25		1916 Jul 15	KS, 36th, 1917
Fulton, Oliver C.	Pvt.	K, 45th Iowa Inf.	452		1916 Feb 16	IA, 43rd, 1917
Fulton, R.H.	Pvt.	D, 206th Penn. Inf.	11		1907 Jun 8	IA, 34th, 1908
Fulton, Reed		H, 191st Penn. (died of heart failure)	195	77	1921 May 19	NE, 47th, 1923
Fulton, S.A.		G, 125th Penn.	9		1893 Apr 26	KS, 13th, 1894
Fulton, W.H.	Pvt.		251		1914 Oct 13	IA, 41st, 1915
Fulton, W.S.	Pvt.	I, 156th Ill. Inf.	177	56	1896 Jan 14	IA, 23rd, 1897
Fulton, Wm.	Corp.	C, 11th Iowa Vol. Inf.	108		1924 Apr 5	IA, 51st, 1925
Fultz, Manfard M.	Pvt.	16th Kans. (not member of the post, but buried by it)	[64?]		1885	KS, 5th, 1886
Fultz, Wm. S.	Pvt.	D, 11th Iowa Inf.	231		1915 Sep 19	IA, 42nd, 1916

*See Appendix A, B or C for roster of post names and locations.
†See Introduction for note regarding recording of death date.

Name	Rank	Company, Regiment or Ship	Post*	Age	Death Date†	Journal
Fuman, W.A.		E, 4th N.J.	294		1927 Dec	KS, 47th, 1928
Funk, A.W.			56		1886	NE, 11th, 1887
Funk, Adam		B, Mo. Militia	147		1908 Apr 9	KS, 28th, 1909
Funk, Adam		I, 48th Ind.	81		1923 Jul 11	KS, 43rd, 1924
Funk, George W.		E, 7th Iowa Cav.	25	93	1936 Mar 1	IA, 63rd, 1937
Funk, George W.		B, 14th Iowa Inf.		93	1936 Mar 1	IA, 62nd, 1936
Funk, H.C.		U.S. Navy	12		1912 Feb 28	KS, 32nd, 1913
Funk, Henry		D, 201st Penn. Inf.	110		1917 Jan 8	IA, 44th, 1918
Funk, J.A.	Pvt.		403		1918 Jul 27	IA, 45th, 1919
Funk, J.H.	Drummer	D, 49th Ohio Inf.	12		1920 Feb 3	IA, 47th, 1921
Funk, J.T.			143		1915 May	NE, 40th, 1916
Funk, John	Pvt.	E, 73rd Iowa Inf.	56		1928 Nov 24	IA, 55th, 1929
Funk, John M.		K, 65th Ohio	112		1913 Sep 14	NE, 38th, 1914
Funk, John N.		F, 151st Ohio	92		1922 Oct 20	KS, 42nd, 1923
Funk, Martin		A, 28th N.Y.	170		1916 Mar 13	KS, 36th, 1917
Funk, Martin		K, 35th Iowa	25		1926 Oct 6	KS, 46th, 1927
Funk, Otto	Pvt.	E, 8th Ill. Cav. (died of throat cancer)	74	50	1885 Nov 27	NE, 10th, 1886
Funk, P.C.		A, 3rd Ohio Cav.	111		1933 Apr	NE, 58th, 1934
Funk, S.G.	Sergt.	31st —	37		1921 Jan 16	IA, 48th, 1922
Funk, S.K.		E, 206th Penn.	12		1935	KS, 55th, 1936
Funk, Samuel	Pvt.	F, 40th Iowa Inf.	22		1927 Oct 29	IA, 54th, 1928
Funk, W.N.	Pvt.	D, 142nd Ill.	242	58	1890 Jul 17	IA, 17th, 1891
Funkhouser, J.T.		F, 36th Iowa	8		1915 May 19	KS, 35th, 1916
Funnell, H.	Pvt.	K, 32nd Wis. Inf.	343	50	1890 Sep 15	IA, 17th, 1891
Funston, R.B.	Pvt.	H, 2nd Iowa Inf.	363	53	1888 Dec 26	IA, 15th, 1889
Funston, T.H.		E, 18th Ohio	51		1931 May 27	KS, 51st, 1932
Funston, T.H.		E, 18th Ohio	51		1931 May 27	KS, 52nd, 1933
Funston, T.L.		A, 94th Ill. Inf.	185		1901 Feb 12	KS, 21st, 1902
Fuqua, Wm. M.		A, Mo. State Militia	293		1918 Aug 8	KS, 38th, 1919
Fuquay, J.F.	Pvt.	F, 57th Ill.	452		1914 Dec	IA, 41st, 1915
Furbush, J.F.	Pvt.	B, 28th Maine Inf.	3		1908 Feb 27	IA, 35th, 1909
Furguson, David		M, 4th Ill.	18		1909 Feb 25	KS, 29th, 1910
Furguson, R.		D, 2nd Kans.	276		1896 Feb 29	KS, 16th, 1897
Furguson, Robert		C, 116th Ind.	141		1906 Dec 31	KS, 26th, 1907
Furley, C.C.	Asst. Surg.	2nd Cal. Cav.	25		1902 Jul 6	KS, 22nd, 1903
Furman, Jas.		C, 42nd Ill. Inf.	440		1913 Sep 2	IA, 40th, 1914
Furman, Morris	Pvt.	D, 34th Ill. Inf.	414		1916 Apr 29	IA, 43rd, 1917
Furman, W.A.		E, 4th N.J.	294		1925 Dec	KS, 45th, 1926
Furnas, A.J.	Pvt.		115		1917 Dec 30	IA, 44th, 1918
Furnas, David		I, 85th Ind.	25		1913 Jul 4	KS, 33rd, 1914
Furness, H.N.		C, 105th Ill. Inf.	59		1925 Nov 5	KS, 45th, 1926
Furr, John A.		D, 94th Ill. (died of heart trouble)	301	74	1911 Apr 1	NE, 36th, 1912
Furrow, G.W.	Corp.	H, 8th Ind. Inf.	414		1907 Apr 10	IA, 34th, 1908
Furrow, Joseph	Pvt.	A, 2nd Ohio Inf.	235		1920 Jun 18	IA, 47th, 1921
Furry, William		C, 54th Ill.	68		1920 Aug 30	KS, 40th, 1921
Furstenberg, Joseph		F, 2nd Wis. Inf.	135	96	1937 Nov 13	IA, 64th, 1938
Fuson, Milton		B, 4th Ohio	20		1919 Jun 4	KS, 39th, 1920
Fuson, W.H.			197		1884	KS, 4th, 1885
Fussell, Joshua L.		D, 34th Ind. (died of old age)	22	88	1915 Mar 1	NE, 40th, 1916
Fusselman, Warren		K, 14th Ohio (died of paralysis)	273		1912 Mar 4	NE, 37th, 1913
Fustel, John	Pvt.	A, 35th Va.	231		1922 May 10	IA, 49th, 1923
Fye, Daniel		H, 26th Ill. (location: Marquette)			1928 Jan 8	NE, 52nd, 1928
Fyfe, Morris M.	Pvt.	4th Wis. Inf.	416		1913 Aug 31	IA, 40th, 1914
Gabel, Frederick	Corp.	E, 43rd Ill. Inf.	231		1913 Mar 20	IA, 40th, 1914
Gable, D.S.			188		1909	IA, 36th, 1910
Gable, Wm. H.	Corp.	C, 5th Kans. Vol. Cav.	108		1924 Dec 2	IA, 51st, 1925
Gableman, Alex	Pvt.	C, 7th Iowa Cav.	100		1925 Nov 15	IA, 52nd, 1926
Gabrial, Elias		D, 24th Iowa	311		1924 Jul 26	KS, 44th, 1925
Gabriel, Geo. W.		D, 1st Kans. Inf.	64		1930 Apr	KS, 50th, 1931
Gabriel, George	Pvt.	C, 2nd Iowa Cav.	112		1915 Apr 17	IA, 42nd, 1916
Gabriel, Hiram	Pvt.	A, 1st Iowa Cav.	2		1901 Aug 25	IA, 28th, 1902
Gabrielson, John	Pvt.	C, 2nd Iowa Inf.	375		1908 May 8	IA, 35th, 1909

*See Appendix A, B or C for roster of post names and locations.
†See Introduction for note regarding recording of death date.

Name	Rank	Company, Regiment or Ship	Post*	Age	Death Date†	Journal
Gadbury, John	Pvt.		24		1912 Feb 20	IA, 39th, 1913
Gaddis, J.J.		C, 1st Ohio Cav.	65		1917 Sep 10	KS, 37th, 1918
Gades, J.R.	Pvt.	I, 19th Iowa Inf.	452		1915	IA, 42nd, 1916
Gafferty, Smith	Pvt.	I, 16th Ohio	55		1899	IA, 26th, 1900
Gaffy, Thos.	Pvt.	K, 20th Wis. Cav.	408	61	1890 Dec 30	IA, 17th, 1891
Gage, Alonzo		A, 14th Vt. (died of old age)	289	91	1911 May 3	NE, 36th, 1912
Gage, Guilford G.		Topeka Battery, Kansas Bat.	1		1899 May 19	KS, 19th, 1900
Gage, I.P.		B, 3rd Vt. Inf. (died of old age)	4	73	1922 Sep 25	NE, 47th, 1923
Gage, James D.		1st N.H. Cav. (see Appendix D)	98		1924 Feb 26	NE, 48th, 1924
Gage, L.T.		K, 121st Ohio	1		1922 Jul 12	KS, 42nd, 1923
Gage, Norris L.		G, 105th Ohio	1		1918 Nov 12	KS, 38th, 1919
Gage, Roy	Pvt.	8th Ill. Cav.	123	44	1890 Sep 1	IA, 17th, 1891
Gage, W.C.		A, 2nd Vt. (died of pneumonia)	289	77	1920 Dec 4	NE, 45th, 1921
Gage, William		G, 8th Mich.	52		1924 Sep 17	KS, 44th, 1925
Gageby, J.W.			24		1911 Mar 23	IA, 38th, 1912
Gager, John	Pvt.	G, 2nd Kans. Cav.	216		1929 May 30	IA, 56th, 1930
Gager, John P.		G, 2nd Kans. Cav.	216	90	1937 May 20	IA, 64th, 1938
Gager, John T.	Corp.	B, 105th Ill. Inf.	216, 171	99	1939 Nov 24	IA, 66th, 1940
Gahan, James		A, 14th Kans.	271		1906 Jul 3	KS, 26th, 1907
Gahan, M.J.		13th N.Y. Art.	11	63	1908 Jul 18	NE, 33rd, 1909
Gaines, Chas. J., see Ganes, Chas. J.						
Gaines, E.T.	Pvt.	K, 16th Ill. Inf.	154		1897-1898	IA, 24th, 1898
Gaines, F.M.		B, 20th Ky.	65		1928 Jan 12	KS, 48th, 1929
Gaines, Geo. W.		E, 2nd Mo. Cav.	46		1928 Dec 31	KS, 48th, 1929
Gaines, J.W.	Pvt.	A, 19th Iowa Vol. Inf.	12		1899 Apr 8	IA, 26th, 1900
Gaines, John		H, 12th U.S. Colored Inf.	241		1900 Jun 21	KS, 20th, 1901
Gaines, John W.			12		1923 Jan 21	KS, 43rd, 1924
Gaines, Richard	Pvt.		19		1916 Sep 29	IA, 43rd, 1917
Gainforth, Thomas		G, 44th Wis. (died of old age)	111	87	1920 Mar 19	NE, 45th, 1921
Gaither, B.E.		G, 23rd Ind.	13	80	1923 Dec 3	NE, 48th, 1924
Gaither, Rodolph		K, 30th Ill.	59		1911 Oct 5	KS, 31st, 1912
Gaius, W.F.		B, 130th Ill.	52	72	1913 Apr 27	NE, 38th, 1914
Galager, G.L.		D, 25th Ill.	105		1924 Nov	KS, 43rd, 1924
Gale, Henry		A, 55th Ohio (died of cancer)	207		1920 Dec 16	NE, 45th, 1921
Gale, Joseph W.			434		1914	IA, 41st, 1915
Galer, Joseph C.		B, 64th Ill. Inf. (died of accidental gunshot)	60	75	1917[1916?] May 24	NE, 41st, 1917
Gall, M.S.	Pvt.	E, 7th Mo. Inf.	75		1906 Oct 23	IA, 33rd, 1907
Gallager, P.C.			35		1905	NE, 30th, 1906
Gallager, P.C.			35		1912	NE, 37th, 1913
Gallagher, H.H.			157		1887 Apr 13	KS, 7th, 1888
Gallagher, Jas.		Ohio (died of pneumonia)	318		1921 May 27	NE, 46th, 1922
Gallagher, T.F.	Capt.	K, 30th Iowa	108		1903-1904	IA, 30th, 1904
Gallagher, Wm.	Pvt.	F, 37th Ill. Inf.	327		1897 Oct 13	IA, 24th, 1898
Gallaher, George	Pvt.	K, 11th Iowa Inf.	157		1919 Sep	IA, 46th, 1920
Gallantine, Willia B.		A, 7th West Va.	60	75	1919 Jul 1	NE, 44th, 1920
Gallaway, Geo.		B, 8th Ill.	86		1922	KS, 42nd, 1923
Galletine, Joseph		A, 7th West Va.	13		1936 Feb 10	NE, 61st, 1937
Galley, Jacob		A, 72nd Ill. (died of heart trouble)	15	78	1919 Sep 21	NE, 44th, 1920
Galley, James H.		K, 2nd Neb. Cav.	9		1930 Mar 24	NE, 55th, 1931
Galligher, John		2nd Mass. Hvy. Art.	256		1900 Jan	KS, 20th, 1901
Gallino, Wm. W.		G, 47th Ill.	370		1896 Oct 13	KS, 16th, 1897
Gallion, Elijah	Pvt.	G, 14th Iowa Inf.	343	47	1888 Jun 28	IA, 15th, 1889
Gallion, Thomas		C, 67th Ohio	433		1912 Oct 16	KS, 32nd, 1913
Galloup, John		F, 69th Mo.	200		1896 May 21	KS, 16th, 1897
Gallup, H.C.		B, 88th Ill.	17		1921 Jul 16	KS, 41st, 1922
Gamble, James	Lieut.	D, 4th Iowa	49		1926 Nov 25	IA, 53rd, 1927
Gamble, John M.	Pvt.	D, 171st Penn. Vol. Inf. (died of paralysis)	163	72	1891 Jan 31	NE, 16th, 1892
Gamble, Le Roy	Pvt.	B, 25th Iowa Inf.	116	90	1933 Apr 26	IA, 60th, 1934
Gamble, M.	Pvt.	E, 47th Iowa Inf.	55	87	1931 Oct 30	IA, 58th, 1932
Gamble, O.P.		E, 159th Penn.	4		1916 May 13	KS, 36th, 1917

*See Appendix A, B or C for roster of post names and locations.
†See Introduction for note regarding recording of death date.

195

Name	Rank	Company, Regiment or Ship	Post*	Age	Death Date†	Journal
Gamble, W.O.		C, 112th Ill. (died of cancer)	5	68	1910 May 22	NE, 35th, 1911
Gamble, Wm.	Pvt.	G, 149th N.Y. Inf.	193		1911 Jun 2	IA, 38th, 1912
Gamble, Xenophen		E, 140th Penn. Inf.	55		1925 Mar 4	KS, 45th, 1926
Gambrel, Henry		I, 46th Mo. Inf.	293		1914 Nov 6	KS, 34th, 1915
Games, R.C.		F, 34th Iowa	399		1915 Sep 29	KS, 35th, 1916
Gammil, James M.		M, 3rd Iowa Cav.	207		1931 Jun 2	NE, 56th, 1932
Gammon, Michael		H, 10th Ind. Inf. (killed by lightning)	132		1890 Jul 4	KS, 10th, 1891
Gammon, Warren			12		1923 Oct 24	IA, 50th, 1924
Gander, James H.		B, 78th Ohio	40		1927 Oct 16	KS, 47th, 1928
Gander, S.H.	Pvt.	I, 29th Iowa Inf.	37		1906	IA, 33rd, 1907
Ganes, Chas. J.	Pvt.	I, 142nd Ill. Inf.	78		1912 Mar 30	IA, 39th, 1913
Gange, William	Pvt.	I, 5th Wis. Inf. (at large)	3	102	1940 Jan 1	IA, 66th, 1940
Gann, L.O.	Pvt.	B, 33rd Iowa Inf.	12		1919 Dec 4	IA, 46th, 1920
Gannaway, Robert			64		1928	IA, 55th, 1929
Gano, Charles		G, 58th Ill.	17		1918 Apr 10	KS, 38th, 1919
Gano, James		K, 32nd Wis. Inf. (died of general debility)	77	77	1921 May 23	NE, 46th, 1922
Ganoe, James	Pvt.	D, 94th Ill.	300		1907 Jul 9	IA, 34th, 1908
Ganoe, Jas.	Pvt.	E, 39th Iowa Inf.	23		1925 Apr 29	IA, 52nd, 1926
Ganoe, L.	Pvt.	C, 41st Ill.	298		1907 Oct	IA, 34th, 1908
Ganson, W.L.		D & G, 10th Ill.	87		1926 Feb 25	KS, 46th, 1927
Gantz, Lewis	Pvt.	H, 28th Iowa Inf.	97	47	1887 May 28	IA, 14th, 1888
Gapin, John		K, 25th Ill. Inf.	51		1930 Mar 31	KS, 50th, 1931
Garber, Abram		I, 3rd Mo. Inf. (died of rheumatism)	138		1893 May 27	NE, 18th, 1894
Garber, Jos.		D, 27th Iowa Inf.	80		1906 Jul 18	NE, 31st, 1907
Garber, S.A.	Pvt.	B, 19th Iowa Inf.	110	49	1892 Sep 1	IA, 19th, 1893
Garber, William	Pvt.	F, 74th Ill. Inf.	102	71	1897 Nov 25	IA, 24th, 1898
Garbey, S.P.		H, 18th Ohio Inf. I, 53rd Ohio Inf. (died of general debility)	289	58	1895 Feb 16	NE, 20th, 1896
Garbison, Jacob B.	Pvt.	D, 34th Iowa Inf.	275	57	1892 Jan 23	IA, 18th, 1892
Gard, B.G.	Pvt.	H, 15th Iowa Inf.	235	88	1933 Mar 5	IA, 60th, 1934
Gard, D.M.			293		1931	KS, 51st, 1932
Gard, S.J.	Corp.	A, 72nd Ind. Inf.	285		1906 Dec 10	IA, 33rd, 1907
Garden, Robt. I.	Pvt.	B, 3rd Iowa Inf.	40		1918 Oct 26	IA, 45th, 1919
Gardener, I.N.	Pvt.	A, 88th Ohio Inf.	358		1926 Sep 5	IA, 53rd, 1927
Gardner, Andrew		6th Wis. Bat.	68		1917 Oct 23	IA, 44th, 1918
Gardner, B.F.		I, 15th Ill.	11		1928	NE, 53rd, 1929
Gardner, Baylis D.	Pvt.	K, 7th Mo. Cav.	205	52	1893 Jan 13	IA, 20th, 1894
Gardner, C.H.	Pvt.	I, 65th Ill. Inf.	34		1920 Jan 23	IA, 47th, 1921
Gardner, C.L.	Pvt.	I, 37th Iowa Inf.	64		1921 Feb 17	IA, 48th, 1922
Gardner, C.M.	Pvt.	F, 38th Ill. Inf.	26		1909 Apr 20	IA, 36th, 1910
Gardner, Chas. L.	Pvt.	I, 37th Iowa Inf.	64		1914	IA, 41st, 1915
Gardner, E.A.	Pvt.	I, Wis. Inf.	277		1906 Dec 20	IA, 33rd, 1907
Gardner, Eliga		K, 102nd Ind.	113		1918 May 28	KS, 38th, 1919
Gardner, Geo. Q.	Capt.	5th Wis. Lt. Art.	168	54	1894 May 20	IA, 20th, 1894
Gardner, George	Pvt.	C, 52nd Ohio Inf.	55		1932 Nov 1	IA, 59th, 1933
Gardner, George H.		I, 7th Ill. Cav.	311		1885	KS, 5th, 1886
Gardner, Henry		D, 58th Ill. Inf.	85		1908 Aug 2	KS, 28th, 1909
Gardner, J.E.		E, 125th Penn. Inf. (died of insanity)	25	69	1903 Mar	NE, 28th, 1904
Gardner, J.M.	Pvt.	B, 9th Ill. Cav.	452		1912 Jun 21	IA, 39th, 1913
Gardner, J.M.		E, 12th Ill. Cav.	288	79	1920 Nov	NE, 45th, 1921
Gardner, James		U.S. Navy	336		1909 Jan 20	IA, 36th, 1910
Gardner, Jno. O.		A, 9th Maine	130		1904 Mar 2	KS, 24th, 1905
Gardner, John	Capt.	5th Ind.	12		1926 Mar 5	KS, 46th, 1927
Gardner, L.		E, 5th Wis. Inf.	141		1899	IA, 26th, 1900
Gardner, L.R.		D, 145th Ohio	96		1916 Jun 15	KS, 36th, 1917
Gardner, Layfette	Pvt.	G, 3rd Ohio River Defense	79	68	1891 Aug	NE, 16th, 1892
Gardner, M.W.	Pvt.	B, 212th N.Y.	22		1923 May	IA, 50th, 1924
Gardner, Malilow	Pvt.	H, 39th Ill. Inf.	271		1913 Sep 13	IA, 40th, 1914
Gardner, Milton	Pvt.	C, 30th Wis. Inf.	54		1909 Nov 23	IA, 36th, 1910
Gardner, O.L.		I, 8th Ill. Cav. (died at Louisburg)	252		1895 Dec	KS, 15th, 1896
Gardner, Robert		A, 45th Ohio Inf.	4		1887 May 20	KS, 7th, 1888
Gardner, Rollin E.	Pvt.	K, 3rd Iowa Cav.	12, 49	92	1939 Aug 5	IA, 65th, 1939

*See Appendix A, B or C for roster of post names and locations.
†See Introduction for note regarding recording of death date.

196

Name	Rank	Company, Regiment or Ship	Post*	Age	Death Date†	Journal
Gardner, S.C.	Sergt.	A, 25th Iowa Inf.	108		1918 Dec 13	IA, 45th, 1919
Gardner, Sam'l C.	Pvt.	B, 1st Lieut. Art.	12		1922 Feb 25	IA, 49th, 1923
Gardner, T.J.	Pvt.	B, 33rd Iowa Inf.	40		1914 Aug 15	IA, 41st, 1915
Gardner, Theodore		1st Bat. Kans. Art.	12		1929 Sep 28	KS, 49th, 1930
Gardner, Thos. S.	Pvt.	B, 32nd Iowa Vol. Inf.	101	78	1898 Dec 8	IA, 25th, 1899
Gardner, W.A.	Sergt.	H, 124th Ill. Inf.	7		1908 Oct 16	IA, 35th, 1909
Gardner, W.B.		8th Mich. Cav.	311		1901	NE, 26th, 1902
Gardner, W.H.		E, 30th Mass. Inf. (died of paralysis)	110	60	1902 Jun	NE, 27th, 1903
Gardner, W.M.		C, 195th Ohio	4		1917 Apr 6	KS, 37th, 1918
Gardner, W.V.	Pvt.	B, 47th Wis.	134		1923 Mar 22	IA, 50th, 1924
Gardner, W.W.	Capt.	D, 100th U.S. Colored	147		1913 Mar 24	IA, 40th, 1914
Gardner, Whitman	Pvt.	I, 129th Ind. Inf.	7		1916 Jan 5	IA, 43rd, 1917
Gardon, J.W.			29		1919 Jun	IA, 46th, 1920
Garey, Simon G.		H, 3rd Iowa	85		1904 Nov 20	KS, 24th, 1905
Garhan, John S.		F, 51st Mo. Inf. (died of old age)	52	88	1925 May 31	NE, 50th, 1926
Garison, Sam		175th —	134	79	1916 Dec 4	NE, 41st, 1917
Gariss, Jacob		F, 2nd Neb. Cav. (died of dropsy)	47	71	1904 Apr 7	NE, 29th, 1905
Garland, W.H.	Sergt.	B, 4th Iowa Cav.	111		1917 Jun 3	IA, 44th, 1918
Garlick, J.M.	Pvt.	I, 153rd N.Y. Inf.	235	88	1932 Nov 26	IA, 59th, 1933
Garlinhouse, D.	Sergt.	I, 2nd Iowa Cav.	176	62	1896 Nov 9	IA, 23rd, 1897
Garlock, Perry		M.M.M. Mo.[Enrolled Mo. Militia?]	17		1929 Feb 28	KS, 49th, 1930
Garlock, W.E.	Sergt.	K, 42nd Ohio Inf.	12		1930 Dec 29	IA, 57th, 1931
Garlove, L.S.		D, 32nd N.Y.	130		1904 Oct 24	KS, 24th, 1905
Garlow, Charles H.		B, 13th Maine Hvy. Art.	468		1902 Dec 13	KS, 22nd, 1903
Garlow, John W.	Corp.	A, 144th N.Y. Inf.	193		1897 Aug 17	IA, 24th, 1898
Garman, William	Pvt.	A, 104th Ohio Inf.	42		1925 Nov 30	IA, 52nd, 1926
Garme, J.W.	Corp.	25th Inf.	115		1921 May 9	IA, 48th, 1922
Garn, Henry		I, 8th N.Y. Inf. (died of rheumatism)	11	64	1906 Jun 13	NE, 31st, 1907
Garnahan, E.L.		F, 106th Ill.	244		1924 Mar 20	KS, 44th, 1925
Garner, B.		E, 20th Wis. (died of old age)	312	78	1904 Nov 1	NE, 29th, 1905
Garner, E.C.		I, 10th Ind. Cav.	98		1909 Jan 23	KS, 29th, 1910
Garner, Frank E.			60		1884	KS, 4th, 1885
Garner, J.C.	Pvt.	C, 55th Ill. Inf.	267	87	1931 Jul 12	IA, 58th, 1932
Garner, J.W.	Pvt.	F, 18th Ohio Inf.	22		1929 Jan	IA, 56th, 1930
Garner, John A.	Pvt.	D, 161st Ohio Inf.	297		1929 Apr 14	IA, 56th, 1930
Garner, S.H.	Pvt.	I, 16th Iowa Inf.	10		1928	IA, 55th, 1929
Garner, W.F.	Pvt.	D, 19th Iowa	57		1926 Oct	IA, 53rd, 1927
Garner, W.H.	Pvt.	H, 38th Iowa Inf.	170		1901 Mar 22	IA, 28th, 1902
Garnett, Wm. G.	Pvt.	H, 16th Iowa	127	53	1891 Jun 8	IA, 18th, 1892
Garretson, Edwin	Pvt.	21st Penn. Cav.	206		1916 Nov 28	IA, 43rd, 1917
Garrett, J.C.	Pvt.	G, 18th Iowa Inf.	17		1919 Sep 22	IA, 46th, 1920
Garrett, J.W.		D, 11th Kans.	39		1922 Jun 13	KS, 42nd, 1923
Garrett, Jas.	Pvt.	D & I, 78th Ohio & 149th Ind.	239	64	1899 Mar 18	IA, 25th, 1899
Garrett, Jos.	Middy	U.S.S. Ver.	75	53	1891 Jun 8	IA, 18th, 1892
Garrett, Reuben	Pvt.	K, 1st Mo. Lt. Art.	12	62	1892 Mar 20	IA, 19th, 1893
Garrett, W.A.	Pvt.	H, 5th N.Y. Cav.	12		1921 Feb 13	IA, 48th, 1922
Garrett, W.A.A.	Sergt. Pvt.	55th Conn. Inf. E, 1st Conn. Cav.	12		1928 Jun 26	IA, 55th, 1929
Garrett, William		A, 78th Penn.	1		1920 Jun 2	KS, 40th, 1921
Garrett, Wm. S.		C, 12th Mo. Cav.	303		1917 Mar 4	KS, 36th, 1917
Garrettson, John	Pvt.	G, 33rd Iowa Inf.	49		1913 Nov 7	IA, 40th, 1914
Garring, John	Pvt.	F, 10th Iowa Inf.	127	54	1893 Nov 14	IA, 20th, 1894
Garris, John A.		E, 9th Ind. Cav.	180		1905 Dec 20	KS, 25th, 1906
Garris, Peter L.	Pvt.	K, 48th Ill. Inf.	266	51	1893 Dec 3	IA, 20th, 1894
Garrison, A.W.	Pvt.		86		1918 Apr 20	IA, 45th, 1919
Garrison, B.F.	Sergt.	B, 68th Ill. Inf.	440		1912 May 22	IA, 39th, 1913
Garrison, E.	Pvt.	I, 47th Ind. Inf.	136	49	1891 Aug 28	IA, 18th, 1892
Garrison, Homer			49		1926 Feb 12	IA, 53rd, 1927
Garrison, I.P.		H, E.M.M. Ind.	4		1899 Jun 30	KS, 19th, 1900
Garrison, J.W.		E, 8th Mo. Cav.	180		1930 Sep 10	KS, 50th, 1931
Garrison, John M.		B, 23rd Wis. Inf.	235		1915 Jun 28	IA, 42nd, 1916
Garrison, L.W.	Pvt.	B, 11th Iowa Inf.	7		1915 Jun 14	IA, 42nd, 1916

Name	Rank	Company, Regiment or Ship	Post*	Age	Death Date†	Journal
Garrison, R.M.	Pvt.	I, 70th Ind. Inf.	235		1928 Jan 12	IA, 55th, 1929
Garrison, S.		B, 33rd Iowa Inf. (died of stomach trouble)	134	77	1919 Jul 21	NE, 44th, 1920
Garrison, W.E.		L, 8th Mo. Cav. (died at Edgerton)	313		1895 Sep	KS, 15th, 1896
Garrison, W.E.			17		1911 Sep 1	KS, 31st, 1912
Garrison, W.H.	Pvt.	F, 1st Ill. Lt. Art.	122		1899	NE, 24th, 1900
Garrison, W.S.		G, 31st Iowa Inf.	130	88	1935 Feb 15	IA, 62nd, 1936
Garritson, L.G.		I, 40th Ind.	[25?]		1923	NE, 48th, 1924
Garrow, Stephen	Pvt.	A, 13th N.D.	1		1922 Jul 26	IA, 49th, 1923
Garside, Samuel	Pvt.	C, 12th Ill. Inf.	302	62	1895 Jan 1	IA, 21st, 1895
Garsuch, John		8th Mich. (died of paralysis stroke)	155	73	1909 Feb 6	NE, 34th, 1910
Garten, D.N.		C, 4th Mo. Cav.	36		1912 Dec 11	KS, 32nd, 1913
Garten, James L.		C, 1st Ind. Cav.	374		1916 Feb 9	KS, 36th, 1917
Gartin, George	Pvt.	C, 13th Iowa Inf.	96		1928 Oct 25	IA, 55th, 1929
Gartner, Henry		C, 3rd Ill. Cav.	11		1894 Jan 10	NE, 19th, 1895
Garton, James A.		died of Bright's disease	89		1908	NE, 33rd, 1909
Garton, W.J.	Pvt.	F, 33rd Iowa Inf.	12		1916 Apr 28	IA, 43rd, 1917
Garvench, Aaron		I, 136th Ohio	90		1926 May	KS, 46th, 1927
Garver, David		C, 77th Penn.	259		1918 Mar 4	KS, 38th, 1919
Garver, Jacob	Pvt.	E, 45th Iowa	246		1899 Jun 30	IA, 26th, 1900
Garver, Joseph		K, 156th Ill. Inf.	337		1918 Aug 12	IA, 45th, 1919
Garver, Peter	Pvt.	B, 24th Iowa Inf. (at large)	7, 12	98	1942 Feb 15	IA, 68th, 1942
Garver, W.F.		18th Ind. Batt. Art.	66		1936 Jul 27	NE, 61st, 1937
Garver, Wm.		E, 10th Iowa	17		1928 Apr 27	KS, 48th, 1929
Garvey, Martin		B, 10th Ill. Cav.	52		1914 May 20	KS, 34th, 1915
Garvey, Martin		B, 10th Ill. Cav.	293		1914 May 20	KS, 34th, 1915
Garvies, William J.		H, 14th N.Y. Cav.	88		1910 Nov 10	KS, 30th, 1911
Garvin, Al.		H, 146th Ill.	292		1939 Jun 17	KS, 59th, 1940
Garvin, P.C.		51st Mass. Inf.	53		1885	KS, 5th, 1886
Garwood, Cyrus		I, 8th Iowa (died of old age)	4	78	1924 Nov 10	NE, 49th, 1925
Garwood, Gilbert		E, 131st Ind.	198		1921 Dec 9	KS, 41st, 1922
Gary, John B.	Pvt.	E, 46th Iowa Vol. Inf. E, 147th Ill. Vol. Inf.	250	49	1898 Oct 17	IA, 25th, 1899
Gary, Riley	Pvt.	D, 24th Iowa Inf.	391		1916 Mar 11	IA, 43rd, 1917
Gaskell, Fred. A.		D, 7th Kans. Cav.	65		1911 Dec 18	KS, 31st, 1912
Gaskell, Israel	Pvt.	D, 2nd Iowa Inf.	255		1908 Feb 20	IA, 35th, 1909
Gaskill, Asberry		K, 4th Iowa	293		1925 May 21	KS, 45th, 1926
Gaskill, James	Pvt.	A, 1st U.S. Art. (served 29 years; died of heart disease)	2	52	1887 Mar 17	NE, 12th, 1888
Gaskill, S.N.	Pvt.	B, 1st Mo. Cav.	408		1905 Nov 3	IA, 32nd, 1906
Gass, George S.	Pvt.	A, 22nd Penn. Cav.	20		1932	IA, 59th, 1933
Gassford, Wm.		C, 2nd Ind. Cav.	354		1905 Jul 17	NE, 30th, 1906
Gast, Henry	Pvt.	I, 27th Iowa Inf.	90		1912 Sep 28	IA, 39th, 1913
Gast, Herman	Pvt.	G, 19th Iowa Inf.	153		1929 Feb 24	IA, 56th, 1930
Gast, John M.	Pvt.	G, 20th Iowa Inf.	88		1918 Oct 12	IA, 46th, 1920
Gaston, Chas. W.	Pvt.	E, 88th Iowa	170		1924 Mar 30	IA, 51st, 1925
Gaston, D.		C, 7th Kans. Cav.	429		1908	KS, 28th, 1909
Gaston, David			429		1911	KS, 31st, 1912
Gaston, E.C.		H, 33rd Iowa Inf.	7	87	1925 Sep 23	NE, 50th, 1926
Gaston, J.H.		L, 97th Ind.	253		1910	KS, 30th, 1911
Gaston, J.N.	Pvt.	C, 7th Iowa Inf.	67		1920 Feb 9	IA, 47th, 1921
Gaston, Joseph		H, 3rd Iowa	286		1905	KS, 25th, 1906
Gaston, Robert		A, 7th Kans.	130		1906 Sep 8	KS, 26th, 1907
Gaston, S.M.	Musician	E, 88th Ohio Inf.	2		1927 Jul 28	IA, 54th, 1928
Gaston, W.H.	Pvt.	F, 47th Iowa Inf.	12		1906 Nov 19	IA, 33rd, 1907
Gaston, William		A, 30th Ohio	301		1885	KS, 5th, 1886
Gaston, William		D, 12th Ill. Inf.	58		1929 Jun 20	KS, 49th, 1930
Gatch, C.H.	1st Lieut.	K, 133rd Ohio Inf.	12		1897 Jul 1	IA, 24th, 1898
Gatch, L.B.			39		1922 Jan 6	IA, 48th, 1922
Gatch, S.S.	Pvt.	B, 52nd Ill.	39		1922 Jan 6	IA, 49th, 1923
Gatchell, Enos B.		F, 90th Ohio	9		1926 Feb 11	KS, 46th, 1927
Gatchell, Theodore	Pvt.	I, 5th Md. Vols.	12		1901 Nov 7	IA, 28th, 1902

*See Appendix A, B or C for roster of post names and locations.
†See Introduction for note regarding recording of death date.
198

Name	Rank	Company, Regiment or Ship	Post*	Age	Death Date†	Journal
Gatchill, J.B.		I, 15th Ohio F, 55th Ohio	1		1896 Jul 17	KS, 16th, 1897
Gates, A.H.		H, 9th Iowa Inf.	168		1918	IA, 45th, 1919
Gates, A.M.	Pvt.	H, 138th Ill. Inf.	230		1910 Jan 28	IA, 37th, 1911
Gates, Albert E.	Musician	A, 116th Ohio Inf.	255	99	1943 Nov 9	IA, 70th, 1944
Gates, Charles L.		C, 58th Ill. Inf.	101		1937 Jul 4	IA, 64th, 1938
Gates, E.F.		E, 39th Ill.	25		1926 Mar 7	NE, 51st, 1927
Gates, Elmer		24th Mich. Inf.	129		1934 Aug 1	KS, 54th, 1935
Gates, H.M.	Pvt.	K, 14th Wis. Inf.	22		1920 Oct 8	IA, 47th, 1921
Gates, Henry H.		G, 92nd Ill.	118		1933 Nov 6	NE, 58th, 1934
Gates, Horace S.	Pvt.	K, 39th Wis. Inf.	235		1913 Oct 31	IA, 40th, 1914
Gates, Jacob		8th Ill.	59		1896 May 4	KS, 16th, 1897
Gates, John H.		I, 11th Ill.	100		1901 Jun 3	KS, 22nd, 1903
Gates, John M.	Capt.	A, 6th Iowa Cav.	92	75	1893 Jun 17	IA, 20th, 1894
Gates, Joseph		E, 76th Penn. Inf.	294		1894 Aug	KS, 14th, 1895
Gates, Levi	Pvt.	B, 36th Iowa Inf.	497		1919 Mar 29	IA, 46th, 1920
Gates, Mathias		F, 38th Ill. Inf.	25		1929 Nov 7	KS, 49th, 1930
Gates, Peter		G, 16th Ohio	179		1893 Mar 28	KS, 13th, 1894
Gates, Robert T.		E, 65th Ind.	500		1920	KS, 40th, 1921
Gates, Stephen		D, 18th Ohio	85		1896 Sep 12	KS, 16th, 1897
Gates, W.B.		G, 3rd Ohio	18		1927 Jan 13	KS, 47th, 1928
Gates, W.H.	Pvt.	B, 4th Iowa Cav.	118		1899 Mar 13	IA, 26th, 1900
Gates, W.P.		D, 133rd Penn. Vols.	429		1908	KS, 28th, 1909
Gates, W.P.			429		1911	KS, 31st, 1912
Gates, Wm.	Pvt.	C, 20th N.Y. Inf.	206		1911 Dec 26	IA, 38th, 1912
Gather, Simon		F, 82nd Ohio	55		1927 Mar 16	KS, 47th, 1928
Gatter, R.A.		H, Ohio (died of cancer)	37		1902 Jul	NE, 27th, 1903
Gauger, John	Pvt.	F, 9th Ill. Cav.	193		1907 Jun 18	IA, 34th, 1908
Gaughan, Dennis		B, 4th Mo. Cav.	7	82	1895 Oct 18	NE, 20th, 1896
Gault, Ezekeil		21st Penn.	85		1922 Jan 18	KS, 42nd, 1923
Gault, J.G.	Pvt.	K, 40th Iowa Inf.	98		1910 Oct 21	IA, 37th, 1911
Gaunt, J.T.	Sergt.	C, 33rd Iowa Inf.	55		1909 Oct 4	IA, 36th, 1910
Gaunt, O.E.	Pvt.	E, 83rd Ind. Inf.	94		1918 Jun 10	IA, 45th, 1919
Gaunt, William			69	89	1925 Sep 27	NE, 50th, 1926
Gaunt, Wm.	Pvt.	I, 22nd Iowa Inf.	8	64	1890 Jan 25	IA, 16th, 1890
Gausnell, W.T.		I, 16th Kans. Cav.	250		1922 Mar 6	KS, 42nd, 1923
Gay, A.E.	Pvt.	H, 3rd Ohio Cav.	94		1915 Mar 27	IA, 42nd, 1916
Gay, E.L.		G, 1st Mass. Cav.	30		1908	KS, 28th, 1909
Gay, John	Musician	25th Iowa Inf.	115		1919 Oct 27	IA, 46th, 1920
Gay, Robt.	Pvt.		147	63	1891 Aug 17	IA, 18th, 1892
Gay, Thomas	Pvt.	B, 68th Ill. Inf.	18		1908	IA, 35th, 1909
Gay, Wm. M.	Bugler	136th N.Y. Inf.	193		1900 Dec 16	IA, 27th, 1901
Gayhart, Peter		D, 25th Mo. Inf. A, B & D, 1st Mo. Eng.	71		1900 Oct 24	KS, 20th, 1901
Gaylor, T.M.	Corp.	B, 122nd Ohio Inf.	252	54	1894 Apr 14	IA, 21st, 1895
Gaylord, A.E.	Pvt.	U.S. Signal Corps	192	86	1932 May 23	IA, 59th, 1933
Gaylord, C.M.	Pvt.	K, 76th N.Y. Inf.	42	68	1895 Mar 12	IA, 21st, 1895
Gaylord, Henry		B, 138th Ind.	55		1915 Sep 8	KS, 35th, 1916
Gaylord, Theo.		A, 64th Ill.	126		1906 Jan 7	KS, 25th, 1906
Gayt, T.S.		F, 118th Ill.	265		1904 Dec 17	KS, 24th, 1905
Gear, J.M.		G, 151st Ind. Inf. (died of cholera morbus)	245		1893 Oct 17	NE, 18th, 1894
Gearhart, Adam		G, 10th Ill.	59		1913 Aug 29	KS, 33rd, 1914
Gearhart, John W.		D, 32nd Ill.	156		1906 Dec 6	KS, 26th, 1907
Gearhart, Wm.		D, 11th Mo.	293		1906 Feb 14	KS, 26th, 1907
Gearkee, J.H.	Sergt. Major	B, 1st Iowa Inf. 22nd Iowa Inf.	8		1904 Dec 4	IA, 31st, 1905
Geary, J.B.	Pvt.	B, 3rd Iowa Battery	16		1905 Jun 10	IA, 32nd, 1906
Geary, William G.		H, 145th Ohio	92		1920 Dec 24	KS, 40th, 1921
Geaugue, Louis		E, 38th Ohio	63		1923 Feb 23	KS, 42nd, 1923
Gebhardt, W.A.		K, 15th Iowa Inf.	22		1891 Dec 23	KS, 12th, 1893
Gebhart, W.A.		K, 15th Iowa Inf.	22		1891 Dec 23	KS, 11th, 1892
Geddes, Charles		I, 16th Iowa	35		1932 Feb 29	NE, 57th, 1933

Name	Rank	Company, Regiment or Ship	Post*	Age	Death Date†	Journal
Geddes, James Loraine	Brev. Brig. Gen.	D, 8th Iowa Inf. (see also Appendix D)	30	60	1887 Feb 21	IA, 14th, 1888
Geddings, J.R.		95th Ill. Inf.	86		1906 Mar 2	IA, 33rd, 1907
Gedney, Joseph B.	Capt.	I, 36th Iowa Inf.	122	68	1893 Jul 27	IA, 20th, 1894
Gee, A.C.	Pvt.	M, 2nd Ill. Cav.	49		1906 Dec 11	IA, 33rd, 1907
Gee, H.S.	Bugler	K, 6th Penn. Cav.	98		1902 Dec 18	IA, 29th, 1903
Gee, Isaac		K, 24th Iowa Inf.	58		1912 Jan 4	KS, 32nd, 1913
Gee, Nicholas		A, 4th U.S. Art. (died at Russell)	164		1895 Feb 20	KS, 15th, 1896
Geer, A.W.		D, 42nd Wis.	92		1928 Apr 29	KS, 48th, 1929
Geer, Lewis C.		F, 105th Ill.	241		1913 Feb 17	KS, 33rd, 1914
Geer, Philander C.		D, 134th Ohio	191		1914 Oct 17	KS, 34th, 1915
Geer, William E.		E, 166th Ohio	259		1924 Jun 28	KS, 44th, 1925
Gehmet, Kenry		C, 8th Kans.	278		1892 Jan 29	KS, 12th, 1893
Gehring, John D.		C, 27th Wis.	12		1912 Oct 13	KS, 32nd, 1913
Geiger, F.	Pvt.	A, 1st Iowa Inf. E, 18th Iowa Inf.	231	59	1896 Jul 17	IA, 23rd, 1897
Geiger, Joseph	2nd Lieut.	H, 1st Iowa Inf.	70	71	1897 Jan 1	IA, 23rd, 1897
Geiger, S.P.	Pvt.	F, 24th Iowa Inf.	400	85	1931 Oct 15	IA, 58th, 1932
Geil, Joseph		D, 8th Ohio Inf.	12	96	1938 Aug 5	IA, 64th, 1938
Geisen, Jacob		E, 19th Kans.	47		1925 May 16	KS, 45th, 1926
Geiser, Fred	Pvt.	C, 45th Iowa Inf.	2		1912 Jan 2	IA, 39th, 1913
Geisinher, Caleb		4th Wis. Bat.	417		1929 Jun 11	KS, 49th, 1930
Geist, W.J.			132		1917 May 9	KS, 37th, 1918
Geist, William		B, 82nd Penn. Inf.	14		1890 Jan 8	KS, 11th, 1892
Geist, Wm.		B, 82nd Penn. Inf.	14		1890 Jan 8	KS, 12th, 1893
Geister, Peter		G, 2nd U.S. Art.	6		1912	KS, 32nd, 1913
Geitz, Wm.		I, 5th Mo. Cav.	1		1921 Mar 19	KS, 41st, 1922
Gellatly, John		cause of death: heart	77		1901 Dec	NE, 26th, 1902
Gellison, F.W.		I, 13th Kans.	175		1923 Feb 13	KS, 43rd, 1924
Gender, Fred		B, 101st Ill. Inf.	38		1925 Nov 8	KS, 45th, 1926
Gensel, J.W.		A, 30th Ohio	92		1893 May 6	KS, 13th, 1894
Gensirt, Fred	Pvt.	D, 2nd Cal. Inf.	68		1911 Feb 8	IA, 38th, 1912
Gentle, Stephen		C, 1st Ky. Cav.	32		1924 Apr 17	KS, 44th, 1925
Gentry, J.R.	Pvt.	L, 9th Iowa Cav.	12		1921 Nov 16	IA, 48th, 1922
Gentry, Jacob M.		G, 6th Tenn. (former member; died at Norman)	91		1936 Feb 12	NE, 61st, 1937
Gentry, Sylvester P.		I, 87th Ill.	85		1925 Oct 18	KS, 45th, 1926
George, A.B.	Lieut.	A, 48th Mass.	12		1924 Jun 22	IA, 51st, 1925
George, Christy		D, 64th Ill.	10	75	1922 Jul 18	NE, 47th, 1923
George, Daniel		C, 8th Ill. Inf.	117		1886	KS, 6th, 1887
George, H.W.		6th Mass. Lt. Art.	98		1926 Feb 7	NE, 51st, 1927
George, Henry M.		F, 12th Ill.	47		1914 Mar 3	KS, 34th, 1915
George, Isaac N.			25		1913 May 14	KS, 33rd, 1914
George, J.W.	Pvt.	G, 17th Iowa Inf.	40		1928 Apr 11	IA, 55th, 1929
George, Jas. W.		F, 15th West Va. Inf.	251		1908[1909?] Dec 1	KS, 29th, 1910
George, John F.		A, 2nd Mass. Inf.	3		1886	KS, 6th, 1887
George, John F.		A, 2nd Mass. (died at Soldiers' Home, Leavenworth)	3		1886	KS, 12th, 1893
George, John S.	Pvt.	A, 4th Mass. Art.	55		1916 Oct 21	IA, 43rd, 1917
George, Justice	Pvt.	Penn.	251		1916 Aug 24	IA, 43rd, 1917
George, Paul			236		1924	IA, 51st, 1925
George, S.S., Dr.	Major	5th N.Y.	244		1931 Feb 8	KS, 51st, 1932
George, S.S., Dr.	Major	5th N.Y.	244		1931 Feb 8	KS, 52nd, 1933
George, Thos. B.		A, 4th Mass. Hvy Art.	113		1907 Apr 4	NE, 32nd, 1908
George, W.W.H.		H, 12th Kans.	32		1923 Dec 1	KS, 43rd, 1924
George, Wm.		H, 144th Ind. Inf.	311		1918 Dec 22	KS, 38th, 1919
George, Wm.	Pvt. & Corp.	B, 5th Wis. (died of diabetes)	76	44	1884 Nov 25	NE, 9th, 1885
George, Wm. B.	Pvt.	L, 14th Iowa Inf.	7		1927 Apr 2	IA, 54th, 1928
George, Wm. S.		H, 36th Iowa Inf.	250		1918 Apr 30	KS, 38th, 1919
George, Wm. T.	Capt.	A, 143rd N.Y. Inf.	337		1900 Aug 19	IA, 27th, 1901
Gephart, H.H.	Pvt.	A, 53rd Ill.	57		1921 Oct 12	IA, 48th, 1922
Gephart, Philip		I, 21st Ohio	4		1916 Nov 23	KS, 36th, 1917
Gephart, Phillip		I, 21st Ohio	4		1917 Nov 23	KS, 37th, 1918

*See Appendix A, B or C for roster of post names and locations.
†See Introduction for note regarding recording of death date.
200

Name	Rank	Company, Regiment or Ship	Post*	Age	Death Date†	Journal
Geraty, Fernard		53rd Ohio	118		1896	KS, 16th, 1897
Gerbuick, George		I, 75th Ind. Inf.	1		1929 Mar 21	KS, 49th, 1930
Gere, Asa O.		A, 54th Ill. Inf. (died at his home in Stafford, Kans.)			1941 Mar 2	KS, 60th, 1941
Gere, Charles H.		buried at Wyuka Cemetery at Lincoln	214		1904 Oct 4	NE, 29th, 1905
Gere, F.A.			417		1916	IA, 43rd, 1917
Gerecke, Robert		I, 2nd Ky. 187th N.Y.	82		1912 Jun 30	KS, 32nd, 1913
Gereeke, Herman		B, 16th Iowa (former member; died at Norfolk)	109		1936 May	NE, 61st, 1937
Gerkin, Henry		F, 13th Mo. Calif.	49		1930 Nov 20	KS, 50th, 1931
Gerkin, Wm.		F, 17th Ind. (died of Bright's disease)	174	68	1912 Jul 6	NE, 37th, 1913
Gerlach, Joseph		C, 12th Mo. Inf.	8		1887 May 4	KS, 7th, 1888
German, A.			13		1916	NE, 41st, 1917
German, Abel	Sergt.	D, 92nd Ill.	147		1904 Sep 19	KS, 24th, 1905
German, John		H, 6th Ill. Cav. (died at Andover)	121		1895	KS, 15th, 1896
Gern, Stephen	Pvt.	I, 14th Wis. Inf.	5		1903-1904	IA, 30th, 1904
Gero, Joseph G.		F, 76th Ill.	253		1910	KS, 30th, 1911
Gerrard, G.W.	Pvt.	E, 105th Ill. Inf.	30	59	1898 Mar 14	IA, 24th, 1898
Gertenbach, W.	Pvt.	B, 35th Iowa Inf.	231		1920 Jun 16	IA, 47th, 1921
Gertevitt, Samuel	Pvt.	F, 100th Ohio Inf. (killed by stallion)	307	55	1891 May 23	NE, 16th, 1892
Gertin, A.		D, 34th Iowa	298		1908	NE, 33rd, 1909
Gerver, J.D.		I, 98th Ill. Inf. (died of general debility)	207		1893 Jul 22	NE, 18th, 1894
Gessman, O.M.		G, 169th Ohio Inf. E, 186th Ohio Inf. (died of appendicitis)	180	58	1895 Nov 4	NE, 20th, 1896
Gest, Hiram	Pvt.	F, 116th Ill. Inf.	156		1904 Feb 10	IA, 31st, 1905
Getchel, C.S.		H, 28th Maine Inf.	68	78	1902 Jun	NE, 27th, 1903
Getchel, Chas. O.		Wis.	136	69	1904	NE, 29th, 1905
Getchell, Charles	Pvt.	F, 3rd Maine Inf.	206	63	1894 Sep 30	IA, 21st, 1895
Gettert, Peter		C, 16th Iowa Inf.	231	93	1935 May 30	IA, 62nd, 1936
Getty, J.H.		A, 16th Iowa Inf.	18		1939 Jul 13	KS, 60th, 1941
Getty, John		E, 188th Penn. Inf.	22		1889	KS, 9th, 1890
Getty, L.N.	Pvt.	D, 8th Iowa Cav.	40		1929 Mar 3	IA, 56th, 1930
Getz, Joseph		E, 53rd Penn.	36		1913 Mar 4	KS, 33rd, 1914
Gewinner, Geo.	Musician	99th N.Y. Inf. 4th Mass. Cav.	7		1894 Jan	NE, 19th, 1895
Geyler, J.G.		C, 2nd Kans. Cav.	132		1900 Dec 19	KS, 20th, 1901
Gher, Samuel		I, 100th Ind. Inf. (died of cancer of stomach)	190	59	1900 Nov 2	NE, 25th, 1901
Ghorn, J.B.		B, 107th Penn.	51		1920 Dec 15	KS, 40th, 1921
Ghrist, F. David	Sergt.	B, 28th Penn. Inf.	49		1924 Feb 12	IA, 51st, 1925
Gibb, A.P.		1st Bat. Wis. Art.	160		1913	KS, 33rd, 1914
Gibben, J.K.		A, 11th Penn.	74		1923 Jul 31	KS, 43rd, 1924
Gibbert, Geo. E.		13th Wis. Bat. (died of short sickness)	32	67	1911 Jan 10	NE, 36th, 1912
Gibbon, W.H.	Surg.	15th Iowa Inf.	18	63	1895 Oct 2	IA, 22nd, 1896
Gibboney, F.E.			96		1917 Jan 16	IA, 44th, 1918
Gibbons, F.A.		H, 63rd Ohio Inf.	123		1895	KS, 15th, 1896
Gibbons, Michael		H, 65th N.Y. (died of heart failure)	274	65	1907 Jun 16	NE, 32nd, 1908
Gibbons, S.G.	Pvt.	A, 16th Ohio Inf.	67		1924 Oct 31	IA, 51st, 1925
Gibbons, Thos. J.	Pvt.	B, 7th Iowa Inf.	216	66	1891 Oct 15	IA, 18th, 1892
Gibbons, W.B.		I, 25th Iowa Inf. (died of accident)	94	70	1903 Nov 5	NE, 28th, 1904
Gibbony, James	Pvt.	F, 13th Iowa Inf.	140		1913 Oct 2	IA, 40th, 1914
Gibbs, Alfred		C, 21st Mich.	293		1927	KS, 47th, 1928
Gibbs, Cyrus P.		D, 6th Iowa Cav.	168		3rd quarter 1884	IA, 11th, 1885
Gibbs, E.C.	Pvt.	A, 192nd Penn. Inf.	271		1926 Jul 2	IA, 53rd, 1927
Gibbs, F.M.	Pvt.	I, 4th Iowa Inf.	192		1919 Aug 4	IA, 46th, 1920
Gibbs, Gannell		K, 125th Ill.	184		1922 Oct 3	KS, 42nd, 1923
Gibbs, P.T.	Pvt.	G, 24th Ill. Inf.	67		1920 Feb 8	IA, 47th, 1921
Gibbs, Richard	Pvt.	D, 5th Mo. Cav.	56	56	1890 Oct 25	IA, 17th, 1891
Gibbs, T.W.		C, 68th Ind.	142		1917 May 17	KS, 37th, 1918
Gibbs, V.C.		F, 19th Iowa	5		1934 Feb 3	IA, 61st, 1935
Gibbs, W.F.	Capt.	D, 16th Wis. Inf.	133		1905 Nov 15	IA, 32nd, 1906
Gibbs, W.T.		H, 134th Ill.	47		1931 Nov 15	NE, 56th, 1932

*See Appendix A, B or C for roster of post names and locations.
†See Introduction for note regarding recording of death date.

Name	Rank	Company, Regiment or Ship	Post*	Age	Death Date†	Journal
Gibbs, William		D, 7th N.Y. Hvy. Art.	1		1899 Jan 10	KS, 19th, 1900
Gibbson, Wm.		A, 3rd Ill. Cav.	12		1906 May 2	KS, 26th, 1907
Gibeaut, Chas. L.	Lieut.	A, 21st Iowa Inf.	77		1916 Jul 29	IA, 43rd, 1917
Gibelstein, Anton	Pvt.	M, 2nd Mo. Art.	88		1917 Aug 12	IA, 44th, 1918
Gibford, D.L.	Pvt.	K, 28th Iowa Inf.	16		1917 Dec 5	IA, 44th, 1918
Gibler, William H.		B, 23rd Ind. Inf.	6		1925 Jul 29	KS, 45th, 1926
Gibson, A.D.	Pvt.	C, Penn. Art.	81		1931 May 22	IA, 58th, 1932
Gibson, A.P.	Capt.	I, 45th Ind.	129		1906 Jun 17	KS, 26th, 1907
Gibson, A.W.		I, 33rd Iowa	226		1893 Mar 10	KS, 13th, 1894
Gibson, B.W.	Pvt.	H, 24th Iowa Inf.	270		1913 Nov	IA, 40th, 1914
Gibson, C.W.		H, 14th Wis. Inf.	71		1st quarter 1885	IA, 11th, 1885
Gibson, Charles	Pvt.	C, 19th Iowa Inf.	452	87	1931 Jul 10	IA, 58th, 1932
Gibson, Charles	Pvt.	C, 19th Iowa Inf.	452		1930 Jul 10	IA, 57th, 1931
Gibson, D. Charles	Pvt.	E, 18th Iowa Inf. C, 10th Iowa Inf.	452		1929 Nov 19	IA, 56th, 1930
Gibson, Edward G.		D, 1st N.Y. Inf.	23		1914	IA, 41st, 1915
Gibson, Francis	Wagoner	G, 1st Maine Inf.	58		1918	IA, 45th, 1919
Gibson, Francis N.		9th N.H.	25		1905 Jul 14	NE, 31st, 1907
Gibson, Francis N.		M, D, 9th N.H. Inf.	25		1905 Jul 10	NE, 30th, 1906
Gibson, G.W.	Pvt.	B, 3rd Iowa Cav.	100		1924 Oct 10	IA, 51st, 1925
Gibson, G.W.		B, 103rd Penn.	97		1923 May 9	KS, 43rd, 1924
Gibson, Geo. N.		D, 33rd Ill.	50		1920 May 20	KS, 40th, 1921
Gibson, J.D.		B, 9th Kans.	249		1889	KS, 9th, 1890
Gibson, J.G.	Pvt.	K, 31st Iowa Inf.	9		1920[1919?] Oct 12	IA, 46th, 1920
Gibson, J.S.		B, 2nd Neb. Cav.	110		1906 Mar 31	NE, 31st, 1907
Gibson, J.W.		B, 1st Mo. 2nd Ohio	63		1897 Nov 7	KS, 17th, 1898
Gibson, James	Corp.	F, 13th Iowa Inf.	270		1928 Jul 6	IA, 55th, 1929
Gibson, James		F, 2nd Mo. Inf.	246		1887 Nov 29	KS, 7th, 1888
Gibson, John			305		1916	IA, 43rd, 1917
Gibson, Joseph P.		C, 4th Tenn. Cav.	174		1901 Jan 9	KS, 21st, 1902
Gibson, S.B.		B, 1st Ohio Cav.	244		1917 Jun 3	KS, 37th, 1918
Gibson, S.G.		I, 40th Ill. Inf.	25		1916	NE, 43rd, 1919
Gibson, Sam'l M.	Pvt.	M, 2nd Iowa Cav.	269		1909 Sep 30	IA, 36th, 1910
Gibson, Seymour		K, 9th N.Y. Art.	87		1891 Apr 4	KS, 11th, 1892
Gibson, Stephen W.		B, 59th Ill.	25		1926 Jul 4	KS, 46th, 1927
Gibson, T.	Pvt.	G, 75th Ill. Inf.	262	38	1887 Aug 19	IA, 14th, 1888
Gibson, T.J.		C, 9th Iowa	27		1928 Apr 9	KS, 48th, 1929
Gibson, Valentine			127		1916 May 8	KS, 36th, 1917
Gibson, Wm.	Pvt.	A, 33rd Iowa Inf.	40		1899 Aug 16	IA, 26th, 1900
Gibson, Wm., see Gibbson, Wm.						
Giddings, Calvin	Pvt.	D, 93rd Ill. Inf.	30		1902 Feb 25	IA, 29th, 1903
Giddings, J.R., see Geddings, J.R.						
Giddings, Jerome W.		C, 142nd Ind.	25		1922 Apr 20	KS, 42nd, 1923
Giddings, Joseph		K, 11th Wis.	98		1931 Aug 13	NE, 56th, 1932
Giddins, F.G.		E, 156th Ill.	202		1885	KS, 5th, 1886
Gideon, Thomas W.			256		1884	KS, 4th, 1885
Gidley, R.L.	Corp.	I, 2nd Wis. Inf.	204	49	1887 May 4	IA, 14th, 1888
Giesler, Fred	Pvt.	C, 35th Iowa Inf. (at large)	231	95	1939 Jul 6	IA, 65th, 1939
Giey, Robert A.		E, 1st Ind. Art.	32		1924 Oct 14	KS, 44th, 1925
Giffen, A.H.L.		D, 7th Ill. Cav.	412		1913 May	KS, 33rd, 1914
Giffen, W.M.	Sergt.	H, 24th Iowa Inf.	212		1906 Apr 3	IA, 33rd, 1907
Giffin, M.B.		M, —	318	80	1919 Apr 14	NE, 44th, 1920
Gifford, Collins F.		D, 9th Vt. Inf.	171		1899 Dec 2	KS, 19th, 1900
Gifford, Fred		93rd Ill.	113		1923	KS, 43rd, 1924
Gifford, G.W.		D, 93rd Ohio	3		1933 Oct 11	KS, 53rd, 1934
Gifford, Henry	Pvt.	M, 8th Ill. Cav.	261		1904 Aug 20	IA, 31st, 1905
Gifford, I.B.	Pvt.	A, 30th Iowa Inf.	66	77	1896 Nov 9	IA, 23rd, 1897
Gifford, J.D.	Pvt.	H, 92nd Ill. Inf.	125		1928 Jan 10	IA, 55th, 1929
Gifford, John	Pvt.	A, 38th Iowa Inf.	216		1907 Jul 21	IA, 34th, 1908

*See Appendix A, B or C for roster of post names and locations.
†See Introduction for note regarding recording of death date.

202

Name	Rank	Company, Regiment or Ship	Post*	Age	Death Date†	Journal
Gifford, W.M.		G, 89th Ind. Inf.	25	74	1920 Feb 2	NE, 45th, 1921
Gift, Chas.	Pvt.	H, 15th Iowa Inf.	19	57	1898 Aug 30	IA, 25th, 1899
Gift, Joseph		B, 19th Iowa	34		1910 Dec 27	KS, 30th, 1911
Giger, W.H.	Pvt.	I, 115th Ill. Inf.	343	56	1891[?]	IA, 22nd, 1896
Gilam, Sylvester	Pvt.	I, 10th Wis. Inf.	59		1923	IA, 50th, 1924
Gilbert, A.G.		C, 3rd Ill. Cav.	58		1926	NE, 51st, 1927
Gilbert, Amasa	Pvt.	C, 18th Iowa Inf.	208		1910 Apr 12	IA, 37th, 1911
Gilbert, Austin B.	Pvt.	A, 11th Iowa Inf.	100		1919 Nov 30	IA, 46th, 1920
Gilbert, Charles		K, 65th N.Y. Inf.	135		1900 Dec 14	KS, 20th, 1901
Gilbert, Chas. H.	Pvt.	F, 46th Iowa Inf.	71		1904 Nov 6	IA, 31st, 1905
Gilbert, D.W.		D, 24th Ohio	57		1918 Feb 11	KS, 38th, 1919
Gilbert, E.B.			7		1918 Sep 4	IA, 45th, 1919
Gilbert, Frank	Pvt.	H, 10th Ill. Inf.	68		1910 Dec 30	IA, 37th, 1911
Gilbert, G.M.	Pvt.	B, 16th Vt. Inf.	22		1918 May 11	IA, 45th, 1919
Gilbert, H.A.		E, 61st N.Y. Inf.	39		1918 Jul 28	IA, 45th, 1919
Gilbert, Henry W.		A, 1st N.Y. Eng. (died of old age, general dis.)	110	85	1917 Dec 23	NE, 42nd, 1918
Gilbert, Hollis		K, 135th Ohio	16		1902 Apr 3	KS, 22nd, 1903
Gilbert, J.C.		C, 10th Iowa Inf. (died of cancer of liver)	111	60	1900 Jun 8	NE, 25th, 1901
Gilbert, J.M.	Pvt.	D, 22nd Ky. Inf.	30		1913 Nov 3	IA, 40th, 1914
Gilbert, J.W.	Pvt.	K, 45th Iowa Inf.	73		1899	IA, 26th, 1900
Gilbert, James M.	Corp.	K, 1st Iowa Inf.	261		1919 Dec 17	IA, 46th, 1920
Gilbert, L.		G, — Minn. Art.	56		1906	KS, 26th, 1907
Gilbert, Leroy A.		H, 21st Iowa Inf.	68		1939 Jun 7	NE, 64th, 1940
Gilbert, M.B.		H, 8th Iowa Cav. (died at Soldier Home)	174		1893 Jan 22	KS, 13th, 1894
Gilbert, Mark	Lieut.	E, 9th Iowa Cav.	48		1918 Apr 3	IA, 45th, 1919
Gilbert, Moses		H, 99th Ind.	339		1885	KS, 5th, 1886
Gilbert, Nathan	Pvt.	H, 1st Iowa Inf.	208		1906 Mar 19	IA, 33rd, 1907
Gilbert, Nathan	Corp.	H, 1st Iowa Cav.	208		1906 Mar 19	IA, 32nd, 1906
Gilbert, O.T.	Pvt.	A, 132nd Ind. Inf.	8	50	1894 Oct	IA, 21st, 1895
Gilbert, Piere	Pvt.	G, 95th Ill. Inf.	42		1923 Apr 3	IA, 50th, 1924
Gilbert, S.	Sergt.	C, 19th Mich. Inf.	52		1899	NE, 24th, 1900
Gilbert, Sam		F, 9th Minn.	54		1904 May 28	KS, 24th, 1905
Gilbert, T.J.		G, 77th N.Y. (prisoner of war)	182		1891 Aug 21	KS, 11th, 1892
Gilbert, W.F.			5		1923 May 19	IA, 50th, 1924
Gilbert, W.H.	Musician	A, 19th Ill. Inf.	54		1905 Nov 14	IA, 32nd, 1906
Gilbert, Wm.		C, 51st Ind.	64		1922 Oct 16	KS, 42nd, 1923
Gilchrest, J.G.	Pvt.	A, 7th Penn. Inf.	8		1906 Mar 22	IA, 33rd, 1907
Gilchrist, Geo.	Lieut.	K, 33rd Iowa Inf.	40		1913 Feb 19	IA, 40th, 1914
Gilchrist, Jas.		E, 12th Kans.	67		1899 Apr 13	KS, 19th, 1900
Gilchrist, John R.		F, 106th Ill.	335		1911 Sep 22	KS, 31st, 1912
Gilchrist, Wm. H.		K, 53rd Penn.	55		1914 Jan 31	KS, 34th, 1915
Gileran, M.M.	Pvt.	E, 47th Iowa Inf.	55		1930 Mar 30	IA, 57th, 1931
Giles, J.G.	Sergt.	1st Ohio Art.	186		1910 Aug 1	IA, 37th, 1911
Giles, John R.		H, 47th Ill. Inf.	7		1924[1923?] Mar 10	NE, 48th, 1924
Giles, R.M.		15th Kans. Cav.	74		1909 Jun 16	KS, 29th, 1910
Gilespie, Henry		F, 71st Ill. Inf. (died of heart disease)	392		1891 Jan 29	KS, 11th, 1892
Gilfett, I.	Pvt.	A, 3rd Iowa Cav.	79		1921 Nov 20	IA, 48th, 1922
Gilfillan, J.E.		C, 53rd Ohio	68		1898 Dec 10	KS, 18th, 1899
Gilgas, J.W.		G, 113th U.S.C.T. Inf.	6		1930 Nov 25	KS, 51st, 1932
Gilger, John W.	Pvt.	L, 11th Penn. Cav.	238		1900 Feb 17	IA, 27th, 1901
Gilham, W.	Pvt.	D, 18th Ill. Inf.	39		1921 Dec 7	IA, 48th, 1922
Gilimvater, I.A.		I, 119th Ill.	254		1892 Oct 10	KS, 12th, 1893
Gilkerson, T.S.		A, 31st Ind.	35		1914 Nov 25	KS, 34th, 1915
Gilkerson, Thos.		I, 43rd Mo.	25		1930 May 26	NE, 55th, 1931
Gill, J.B.	Pvt.	M, 17th Ill. Cav.	236		1921 Aug 8	IA, 48th, 1922
Gill, J.H.		D, 150th Ind.	4		1928 May 1	KS, 48th, 1929
Gill, James H.		B, 8th Mo. Cav.	90		1925 Jul 17	KS, 45th, 1926
Gill, Jesse T.		T, 12th Tenn.	256		1892 Mar 14	KS, 12th, 1893
Gill, Samuel			350		1922	KS, 42nd, 1923
Gill, T.H.		D, 205th Penn.	118		1934 Jan 20	NE, 59th, 1935
Gill, W.H.		E, 19th Iowa	8		1888	KS, 8th, 1889

*See Appendix A, B or C for roster of post names and locations.
†See Introduction for note regarding recording of death date.

Name	Rank	Company, Regiment or Ship	Post*	Age	Death Date†	Journal
Gill, W.H.		B, 30th Wis.	12		1915 Jan 16	KS, 35th, 1916
Gill, William M.		H, 136th Ohio	123		1910 Sep 6	KS, 30th, 1911
Gillam, Isaac	Pvt.	K, 22nd Iowa Inf.	450	68	1892 Feb 10	IA, 19th, 1893
Gillam, Sylvester, see Gilam, Sylvester						
Gilland, Seth M.		14th Mich. Battery Lt. Art.	380		1909 Dec 31	KS, 29th, 1910
Gillany, M.		H, 3rd N.Y.	32		1888	KS, 8th, 1889
Gillaspie, J.	Pvt.	I, 19th Iowa Inf.	177	44	1891 Jan 25	IA, 17th, 1891
Gillaspie, James	Pvt.	A, 16th Iowa	55		1916 Feb 16	IA, 43rd, 1917
Gillem, Isaac	Pvt.	K, 22nd Iowa Inf.	450	68	1892 Feb 10	IA, 18th, 1892
Gillenwater, E.W.		A, 15th Kans.	293		1927	KS, 47th, 1928
Giller, W.H.	Pvt.	D, 11th Iowa	231		1923 Sep 9	IA, 50th, 1924
Gillespie, D.C.	Pvt.	E, 12th Wis.	124		1926 Apr 16	IA, 53rd, 1927
Gillespie, H.J.		K, 14th Kans. Cav.	130		1912 Mar 7	KS, 32nd, 1913
Gillespie, Hamilton G.		B, 50th Ohio Inf.	110	85	1921 Oct 11	NE, 46th, 1922
Gillespie, Henry, see Gilespie, Henry						
Gillespie, John		1st Neb. Inf. 2nd Neb. Cav. (died of disease of lungs)	214	64	1897 Dec 19	NE, 22nd, 1898
Gillespie, Leander	Pvt.	B, 25th Iowa	18		1924 Mar 22	IA, 51st, 1925
Gillespie, Robert G.		F, 52nd Ohio	247		1913 Nov 21	KS, 33rd, 1914
Gillespie, Thos.		C, 13th U.S. Colored Inf.	321		1902 Oct 6	KS, 22nd, 1903
Gillespie, Wm.		C, 1st Neb.	25		1913 Jan 10	NE, 38th, 1914
Gillett, Andrian		I, 19th Ohio Inf.	354	71	1911 May 19	NE, 36th, 1912
Gillett, Anson Wolcott		G, 59th N.Y. Inf. (at large)	68	91	1937 Apr 15	IA, 64th, 1938
Gillett, Geo. M.	Pvt.	F, 29th Iowa Inf.	10	53	1888 Jul 27	IA, 15th, 1889
Gillett, Henry A.	Pvt.	I, 3rd Wis. Inf.	42		1923 Mar 18	IA, 50th, 1924
Gillett, J.C.	Pvt.	3rd Iowa Cav.	167		1905 Nov 7	IA, 32nd, 1906
Gillett, Jasper W.		E, 17th Ill. Inf.	64		1901 Oct 25	KS, 21st, 1902
Gillett, Joseph		F, 14th Iowa Inf.	39		1918 Apr 24	IA, 45th, 1919
Gillett, Jules		C, 108th Ill.	89		1930 Mar 16	KS, 50th, 1931
Gillette, Geo. R.	Musician	94th Ohio Inf. (died of paralysis)	91		1894 Sep 17	NE, 19th, 1895
Gillette, Omar		E, 1st Ohio Inf. (died at Kingman)	265		1895 Dec	KS, 15th, 1896
Gillette, P.H.	Pvt.		493		1921 Apr 18	IA, 48th, 1922
Gillette, William		I, 83rd Ill. Inf.	7		1899 Jun 18	KS, 19th, 1900
Gilley, M.	Pvt.	F, 1st Mo. Eng.	68		1919 Jun 24	IA, 46th, 1920
Gilley, Stephen	Pvt.	3rd Iowa Lt. Art. (at large)	68, 187	97, 3 mos. & 14 days	1943 Dec 28	IA, 70th, 1944
Gillhaur, John H.		F, 117th Ill. Inf.	12		1908 Dec 12	KS, 28th, 1909
Gillian, C.A.	Pvt.	E, 5th Iowa Cav.	78		1925 Oct 23	IA, 52nd, 1926
Gillickson, John			87		1920 Aug 20	KS, 40th, 1921
Gilliespie, J.F.		E, 13th Iowa Inf.	31	93	1935 Jul 9	IA, 62nd, 1936
Gilligan, P.H.	Pvt.	A, 102nd Ill. Inf.	440	52	1889 Sep 6	IA, 16th, 1890
Gillihan, C.		F, 6th Kans. Cav.	51		1899 Sep 13	KS, 19th, 1900
Gillihan, J.G.	Pvt.	E, 15th Iowa Inf.	21	65	1885 Apr 21	IA, 12th, 1886
Gillilan, G.D.	Pvt.	F, 20th Iowa Inf.	212		1907 Apr 29	IA, 34th, 1908
Gilliland, Hugh		A, 1st Ohio Hvy. Art.	18		1915 Dec 23	KS, 35th, 1916
Gilliland, J.P.		A, 7th Ind. Inf.	227		1892 Jun 8	NE, 17th, 1893
Gilliland, John	Capt.	D, 194th Ohio Inf.	114		1899	NE, 24th, 1900
Gillis, C.B.		D, 18th Mich.	52		1927 Aug	KS, 47th, 1928
Gillis, H.T.			32		1913 Feb 15	KS, 33rd, 1914
Gillis, W.H.		C, 95th Ill.	89		1928 Dec 10	KS, 48th, 1929
Gillispie, James E.	Sergt.	I, 1st Ky. Vols.	1	36	1891 Mar 4	NE, 16th, 1892
Gillispie, M.	Pvt.	F, 51st Ill. Inf.	192		1930 Jun 10	IA, 57th, 1931
Gillispie, R.J.			187		1917	IA, 45th, 1919
Gillispie, William	Pvt.	H, 17th Vt. Inf.	400		1915	IA, 42nd, 1916
Gillman, E.M.	Corp.	G, 129th Ill.	512		1907 Apr 17	IA, 34th, 1908
Gillman, J.D.		E, 2nd U.S. Sharpshooters, Berdens, Vt.	84		1926 Nov 3	NE, 51st, 1927
Gillmore, Daniel Webster		L, 2nd Wis. Cav.	440 57	92	1938 Feb 10	IA, 64th, 1938
Gillmore, John		A, 3rd Kans. State Militia	12		1909 Jul 20	KS, 29th, 1910

Name	Rank	Company, Regiment or Ship	Post*	Age	Death Date†	Journal
Gilluly, James		G, 11th Mich.	12		1898 Jun 11	KS, 18th, 1899
Gilluly, W.F.		U.S.	155		1919 Nov 2	KS, 39th, 1920
Gillum, A.N.		H, 12th Ill. Cav.	196		1916 Mar 10	KS, 36th, 1917
Gilman, Francis		2nd Iowa Bat.	110		1913 Mar 21	KS, 33rd, 1914
Gilman, H.H.		C, 118th Ill. Inf.	4		1916 May 25	IA, 43rd, 1917
Gilman, J.D., see Gillman, J.D.						
Gilman, W.H.	Pvt.	C, 145th Penn.	22		1926 May 20	IA, 53rd, 1927
Gilmartin, Jas.	Pvt.	B, 9th Ill. Cav.	236		1900 Apr	IA, 27th, 1901
Gilmer, R.A.		G, 127th Penn. Inf.	158		1912 Dec 13	KS, 32nd, 1913
Gilmon, Isaac	Lieut.	C, 2nd Iowa Cav.	58		1909 Apr 8	IA, 36th, 1910
Gilmore, A.C.		H, 12th Iowa Inf.	51		1891 Dec 18	KS, 11th, 1892
Gilmore, A.P.		A, 6th Iowa	49		1896 Aug 12	KS, 16th, 1897
Gilmore, Alfred B.		K, 6th Iowa	58		1896 Oct 5	KS, 16th, 1897
Gilmore, C.H.		H, 9th Ill. Inf. (died of paralysis)	147	72	1911 Nov 1	NE, 36th, 1912
Gilmore, Elias		I, 100th Penn.	7		1928 Dec 26	NE, 53rd, 1929
Gilmore, J.A.		E, 9th Ill.	180		1911 May 8	KS, 31st, 1912
Gilmore, J.E.	Pvt.	K, 24th Iowa Inf.	492		1904 Apr 15	IA, 31st, 1905
Gilmore, J.P.			197		1921 Oct 14	IA, 48th, 1922
Gilmore, J.R.		G, 53rd Ill. Inf. (died of erysipelas)	174	62	1901 Feb	NE, 26th, 1902
Gilmore, Jack P.	Pvt.	died of consumption	95	46	1885 Apr 16	NE, 10th, 1886
Gilmore, Luther		F, 149th Ill.	64		1909 Apr 15	KS, 29th, 1910
Gilmore, Myron		B, 96th Ill.	1		1918 Dec 14	KS, 38th, 1919
Gilmore, R.G.		D, 83rd Penn. (died of old wounds)	35	81	1922 May 1	NE, 47th, 1923
Gilmore, R.N.		K, 102nd Ill.	180		1916 Dec 11	KS, 36th, 1917
Gilmore, Samuel		I, 39th Ill.	100		1922 Jun 23	KS, 42nd, 1923
Gilmore, W.M.		F, 41st Ill. Inf.	25		1904 Jun 7	NE, 29th, 1905
Gilmore, Wm.		H, 2nd Neb.	45		1928	NE, 53rd, 1929
Gilmore, Wm. H.	Pvt.	A, 9th Ill. Cav.	127		1926 Mar 2	IA, 53rd, 1927
Gilpatrick, J.H.	Lieut. Col.	2nd Kans.	6		1913 Jun 10	KS, 33rd, 1914
Gilpin, Emanuel		I, 123rd Ill.	293		1922 Jun 7	KS, 42nd, 1923
Gilpin, T.C.	Major	E, 3rd Iowa Cav.	55		1916 Dec 21	IA, 43rd, 1917
Gilroy, G.W.			177		1904 Mar 18	NE, 29th, 1905
Gilson, Leonard		C, 30th Iowa	34		1913 Jul 18	KS, 33rd, 1914
Gilson, Pinbroke E.		D, 12th Wis. Inf.	25	72	1913 Mar 27	NE, 38th, 1914
Giltner, Alex	Pvt.	E, 22nd Iowa Inf.	107		1912 Nov 20	IA, 39th, 1913
Giltner, Conrad		E, 17th Ill. (died of cancer)	118	78	1919 Dec	NE, 44th, 1920
Giltner, John	Pvt.	E, 22nd Iowa Inf.	107		1919 Dec 24	IA, 46th, 1920
Gimmer, James	Pvt.	D, 6th Iowa Inf.	122		1926 Apr 13	IA, 53rd, 1927
Gingery, C.C.		H, 104th Ohio Inf.	25	83	1920 Jun 1	NE, 45th, 1921
Gingery, Samuel		C, 13th Ohio Inf.	25		1911 Feb 6	KS, 31st, 1912
Gingrey, J.M.	Pvt.	G, 134th Ohio Inf.	72		1913 Apr 6	IA, 40th, 1914
Gingrich, Simson		C, 208th Penn. Inf.	257		1925 May 7	KS, 45th, 1926
Ginter, Geo.		D, 78th Penn.	20		1928 Jul 9	KS, 48th, 1929
Ginter, Peter	Pvt.	L, 1st Iowa Cav.	78		1915 Nov 19	IA, 42nd, 1916
Gion, Frank		F, 35th Wis. Inf. (died of heart disease)	142	54	1901 Dec	NE, 26th, 1902
Gipe, S.S.		L, 21st Penn. Cav.	63		1921 Sep 22	KS, 41st, 1922
Gippe, F.		C, 2nd Colo. Cav. (died of heart disease)	104		1893 Feb 14	NE, 18th, 1894
Gipple, I.	Pvt.	K, 8th Iowa Inf.	153		1929 Jan 24	IA, 56th, 1930
Girsehman, A.			5		1928 Jul 1	IA, 55th, 1929
Girton, J.S.	Pvt.	F, 12th Iowa Inf.	63	52	1891 Feb 18	IA, 18th, 1892
Gist, Geo. V.	Pvt.	D, 38th Wis. Inf.	101		1922 Oct 3	IA, 49th, 1923
Gist, W.W.	Pvt.	D, 26th Ohio	222		1923 Jun 8	IA, 50th, 1924
Gittins, M.H.	Pvt.	I, 61st Penn. Inf.	1		1929 Dec 28	IA, 56th, 1930
Given, Josiah	Col.	7th Ohio Inf. (see also Appendix D)	12		1908 Feb 3	IA, 35th, 1909
Givens, Edward		B, 93rd Ill.	25		1928 Dec 19	NE, 53rd, 1929
Givens, Geo.		F, 54th Ind.	1		1928 Dec 13	KS, 48th, 1929
Givens, Samuel		L, 1st Ill. Lt. Art. (died of heart disease)	334	70	1895 Dec 8	NE, 20th, 1896
Givins, Robert			365		1900 Aug 20	KS, 20th, 1901
Givler, Jas.	Pvt.	149th Penn. Inf.	195	47	1892 Feb 4	IA, 18th, 1892
Glace, J.A.		M, 21st Penn. Cav.	88		1923 Nov 10	KS, 43rd, 1924
Gladden, L.W.		G, 12th Ind.	185		1915 Jul 31	KS, 35th, 1916
Gladfetter, G.	Pvt.	G, 36th Iowa Inf.	122		1920	IA, 47th, 1921

*See Appendix A, B or C for roster of post names and locations.
†See Introduction for note regarding recording of death date.

205

Name	Rank	Company, Regiment or Ship	Post*	Age	Death Date†	Journal
Gladwin, Wm. E.	Pvt.	F, 24th Conn. Inf.	40		1904 Aug 9	IA, 31st, 1905
Glancey, C.A.		G, 105th Ohio	25		1929 Mar 23	KS, 49th, 1930
Glanvill, Amos Edward		F, 10th Minn.	399		1916 Sep 30	KS, 36th, 1917
Glanz, Christian	Pvt.	I, 65th Ill. Inf.	12		1926 Nov 12	IA, 53rd, 1927
Glasby, C.		A, 8th Wis.	113		1899 Oct 31	KS, 19th, 1900
Glaser, August		I, 2nd Mo. Inf.	127		1917 May 4	KS, 37th, 1918
Glasgow, Charles Andrew		A, 4th Iowa Cav.		94	1937 Dec 5	IA, 64th, 1938
Glasgow, J.T.		4th Iowa Bat.	344		1919 Apr 30	KS, 39th, 1920
Glasgow, Wm.		F, 4th Iowa Cav.	344		1909 Sep 17	KS, 29th, 1910
Glason, A.S.		Wis. (died of debility)	139	69	1903 May 24	NE, 28th, 1904
Glass, James	Pvt.	C, 9th Ohio Cav.	127	49	1887 Aug 25	IA, 14th, 1888
Glass, John		F, 6th U.S. Cav. (died of paralysis)	8		1893 Nov 29	NE, 18th, 1894
Glass, Thos. E.		E, 23rd Ind. Inf.	25		1923	NE, 48th, 1924
Glass, W.B.		A, 126th Ohio Vol. Inf.	150		1915 Mar 14	KS, 35th, 1916
Glass, William		K, 36th Iowa (died of heart failure)	43	80	1897 Nov 26	NE, 22nd, 1898
Glasscock, A.C.		F, 1st West Va.	103		1926 Mar 29	KS, 47th, 1928
Glasser, H.H.		115th Ohio Inf. (cause of death: heart)	291	70	1901 Apr	NE, 26th, 1902
Glassner, Theodore F.		C, 33rd Ind.	203		1924 May 15	KS, 44th, 1925
Glauder, Charles		B, 35th Mo. Inf.	23		1911 Apr 8	KS, 31st, 1912
Glaze, Geo. P.		A, 9th Mo. State Mil.	25		1892 Dec 19	KS, 12th, 1893
Glaze, M.L.		H, 194th Ohio Vol. Inf.	20		1900 Jan 4	KS, 20th, 1901
Glazier, L.C.		G, 35th Ind.	461		1898 Jul 20	KS, 18th, 1899
Gleason, A.S., see Glason, A.S.						
Gleason, Chas. H.		G, 19th Mich. Inf.	25	84	1919 Jan 12	NE, 44th, 1920
Gleason, Horace W.	Pvt.	G, 12th N.H. Inf.	40		1911 Apr 20	IA, 38th, 1912
Gleason, J.A.	Sergt.	K, 105th Ill. Inf.	259	58	1894 May 30	IA, 21st, 1895
Gleason, Josiah		I, 28th Wis.	147		1911 Mar 6	KS, 31st, 1912
Gleason, M.		G, 106th Ill. Inf. (died of dropsy)	25		1903 Apr 24	NE, 28th, 1904
Gleason, Wm. H.			147		1926 Mar 15	KS, 46th, 1927
Glen, R.R.	Pvt.	C, 4th Iowa Inf.	130		1923 Mar 14	IA, 50th, 1924
Glendening, H.C.		A, 32nd Wis.	36		1912 Aug 9	KS, 32nd, 1913
Glendenning, J.E.		E, 33rd Iowa	1		1913 Mar 16	KS, 33rd, 1914
Glenn, Chas. C.	Pvt.	T, 18th Iowa Vols.	17		1924 Nov 22	IA, 51st, 1925
Glenn, D.		F, 32nd Ill.	130		1920 Jul 17	KS, 40th, 1921
Glenn, Edward A.	Sergt.	E, 39th Iowa Inf.	22		1916 Apr 13	IA, 43rd, 1917
Glenn, H.S.	Sergt.	B, 76th Penn. Inf.	18		1905 Jul 5	IA, 32nd, 1906
Glenn, J.V.		K, 3rd Iowa Cav. (died of chronic diarrhea)	115	77	1902 Sep	NE, 27th, 1903
Glenn, James		C, 134th Ind.	74		1910 Dec 14	KS, 30th, 1911
Glenn, James		Lt. Art.	77		1918 Aug 25	NE, 43rd, 1919
Glenn, Jas. R.		I, 135th Ill.	18		1928 Sep 14	KS, 48th, 1929
Glenn, L.B.	Pvt.	E, 43rd Ind. Inf.	12	88	1932 Mar 14	IA, 59th, 1933
Glenn, Lawrence		C, 30th Mo. Inf.	69		1922 Mar 22	IA, 49th, 1923
Glenn, William		A, 2nd Wis.	36		1927 Jun 23	KS, 47th, 1928
Glick, Daniel	Pvt.	F, 36th Iowa Inf.	122		1928 Dec	IA, 55th, 1929
Glick, Frederick		L, 1st Mo. Eng.	132		1934 Dec 25	KS, 54th, 1935
Glick, Geo. W.		G, 18th Kans. (ex-gov.)	93		1911 Apr 14	KS, 31st, 1912
Glick, John W.		G, 47th Penn. Inf. (died of old age)	110	71	1913 Apr 26	NE, 38th, 1914
Glidden, John	Pvt.	F, 7th Iowa Cav.	25		1912	IA, 39th, 1913
Glines, E.B.		C, 11th N.H. Inf. (died of debility)	125	72	1903 Dec 13	NE, 28th, 1904
Glines, E.P.		E, 3rd Wis.	84		1926 Nov 1	NE, 51st, 1927
Glines, S.W.		G, 7th Mo.	36		1914 May 31	KS, 34th, 1915
Gloss, Benj. F.	Pvt.	H, 13th Iowa Inf.	155		1926 Jan 25	IA, 53rd, 1927
Glotfelty, Nelson	Pvt.	U.S.S. Benton	232	51	1893 Nov 2	IA, 20th, 1894
Glover, A.S.		2nd N.Y.	32		1905 Nov 13	KS, 25th, 1906
Glover, Eli		B, 2nd Neb. Cav. (died of lung disease)	62	51	1895 Sep 8	NE, 20th, 1896
Glover, James R.		K, 84th Ill.	316		1893 Sep 9	KS, 13th, 1894
Glover, James R.		K, 84th Ill. Inf. (died at Greensburg, Mo.; buried at Greensburg Cemetery)	316		1893 Sep	KS, 14th, 1895
Glover, S.C.		E, 10th Ill.	64		1922 Mar 18	KS, 42nd, 1923
Glover, William C.	Sergt.	F, 24th Iowa Inf.	206		1915 Oct 30	IA, 42nd, 1916
Glover, Wm.		B, 83rd Ill.	17		1904 May	KS, 24th, 1905
Gluck, A.		1st Ark.	294		1917 Sep 20	KS, 37th, 1918

*See Appendix A, B or C for roster of post names and locations.
†See Introduction for note regarding recording of death date.

Name	Rank	Company, Regiment or Ship	Post*	Age	Death Date†	Journal
Gobin, John K.		B, 93rd Tenn.	176		1930 Dec 3	KS, 50th, 1931
Goble, Ayers		D, 34th Ill. (died of paralysis)	13	65	1909 Mar 7	NE, 34th, 1910
Goble, Enos	Pvt.	F & I, 21st Mich. (died of dysentery)	70	59	1887 Feb	NE, 12th, 1888
Goble, H.W.	Pvt.	B, 34th Iowa Inf.	7		1930 Dec 27	IA, 57th, 1931
Goble, Hiram	Pvt.		7		1931	IA, 58th, 1932
Goble, J.M.	Pvt.	A, 21st Iowa Inf.	90	52	1891 Jun 2	IA, 18th, 1892
Goble, James		K, 23rd Ind. (died of congestion of bowels)	32	65	1897 Jun 14	NE, 22nd, 1898
Goble, John D.		C, 8th Iowa Inf. (at large)	290	90	1937 Apr 23	IA, 64th, 1938
Goddard, A.		96th Ill.	235		1914 Dec 21	IA, 41st, 1915
Goddard, Geo. V.R.	Pvt.	H, 33rd Ill. Inf.	440		1917 Dec 23	IA, 44th, 1918
Godding, A.R.			132		4th quarter 1884	IA, 11th, 1885
Godding, Wm.			10		1907 May 13	IA, 34th, 1908
Godell, J.C.		C, 3rd Vt.	407		1908	KS, 28th, 1909
Godell, J.C.		I, 51st Ill. (died of gunshot wounds)	1	80	1925 Oct 30	NE, 50th, 1926
Godfrey, A.S.		21st Wis.	25		1905 Sep 17	NE, 31st, 1907
Godfrey, A.S.		21st Wis. Inf.	25		1905 Sep 17	NE, 30th, 1906
Godfrey, Dolly	Pvt.	K, 12th Iowa Inf.	212		1919 Sep 1	IA, 46th, 1920
Godfrey, Emmond J.			25		1913 Apr 10	NE, 38th, 1914
Godfrey, Geo. L.	Pvt.	D, 2nd Iowa Inf.	12		1915 Apr 24	IA, 42nd, 1916
Godfrey, John D.		B, 11th Ind. Inf. (killed by cyclone)	305		1892 Mar 31	KS, 12th, 1893
Godfrey, John W.	Capt.		487		1894 Dec 3	IA, 21st, 1895
Godfrey, Lewis	Pvt.	D, 18th Iowa	440		1922 Jul 13	IA, 49th, 1923
Godfrey, M.	Pvt.	D, 17th Iowa	5		1921 Nov 23	IA, 48th, 1922
Godfrey, T., see Godrey, T.						
Godley, James	Pvt.	K, 52nd Ind. Inf.	19	56	1893 Apr 22	IA, 20th, 1894
Godley, M.L.	1st Lieut.	E, 17th Iowa Inf.	73	66	1896 Sep 14	IA, 23rd, 1897
Godlove, Henry		K, 11th Kans.	39		1914 Oct 6	KS, 34th, 1915
Godrey, T.		I, 33rd Iowa	115		1922 May 3	KS, 42nd, 1923
Godskisen, S.		M, 1st Mo. Battery	88		3rd quarter 1883	IA, 10th, 1884
Goernhardt, J.C.			25		1905 Jan	NE, 30th, 1906
Goernhardt, J.C.		42nd Wis.	25		1905 Jan	NE, 31st, 1907
Goff, A.H.		E, 1st Penn. Bat.	407		1899 Apr 21	KS, 19th, 1900
Goff, Edmond		C, 3rd Mich.	71		1923 Nov 10	KS, 43rd, 1924
Goff, H.A.		D, 133rd Ind.	25		1922 Nov 16	NE, 47th, 1923
Goff, H.A.		D, 133rd Ind. (not a member; buried by Farragut Post)	25		1922 Nov 16	NE, 47th, 1923
Goff, James O.	Pvt.	H, 39th Ill. Inf.	63	62	1895 Dec 9	IA, 22nd, 1896
Goff, John W.		G, 146th N.Y.	4		1934 Jul 16	NE, 59th, 1935
Goff, William C.		K, 108th Ohio	6		1924 Aug 3	KS, 44th, 1925
Gogall, A.		D, 15th Conn.	1		1892 Jul 29	KS, 12th, 1893
Goit, E.D.	2nd Lieut.	H, 24th N.Y. Inf.	66	66	1891 Dec 25	IA, 18th, 1892
Gold, Peter		A, 153rd Penn.	165		1927 Aug 6	NE, 52nd, 1928
Golden, Chas. M.	Pvt.	D, 20th Iowa Inf.	12		1911 Sep 16	IA, 38th, 1912
Golden, Daniel		L, 6th Penn. Hvy. Art.	85		1928 May 25	KS, 48th, 1929
Golden, Jno. A.	Pvt.	F, 142nd Ill. Inf.	66		1925 Nov 16	IA, 52nd, 1926
Golden, Peter	Pvt.	K, 88th Ill.	88		1914 Dec 23	IA, 41st, 1915
Goldeng, M.		E, 8th Mo.	17		1918 Apr 12	KS, 38th, 1919
Goldier, Peter			24		1907 Mar 16	IA, 34th, 1908
Goldin, Geo. W.		F, 56th Penn.	13	79	1918 Aug 28	NE, 43rd, 1919
Golding, Eli		I, 118th Ind. I, 154th Ind.	60		1926 Sep 15	NE, 51st, 1927
Goldrick, P.G.		H, 32nd Mo.	7		1893 Nov 15	KS, 13th, 1894
Goldsberg, Cyrus P.		G, 9th Iowa Cav.	315		1899 May 4	KS, 19th, 1900
Goldsberry, A.E.		127th Ill. Inf.	47		1910 Oct 27	IA, 37th, 1911
Goldsberry, George W.		G, 72nd Ind.	59		1913 Mar 5	KS, 33rd, 1914
Goldsberry, John	Pvt.	B, 6th Kans. Cav.	122		1916 Jun 6	IA, 44th, 1918
Goldsberry, Theo.		I, 51st Mo. Inf. (at large)		89	1936 Nov 13	IA, 63rd, 1937
Goldsberry, Theodore	Pvt.	I, 51st Mo. Inf. Unassigned, 55th Mo. Inf.		89	1936 Nov 13	IA, 65th, 1939
Goldsberry, Theodore			59		1930 Nov 28	KS, 50th, 1931
Goldsmith, E.P.	Pvt.	A, 1st Del. Cav.	324		1903 Jul	IA, 30th, 1904
Goldsmith, James		D, 80th Ind. Inf.	74		1891 Aug 21	KS, 11th, 1892

Name	Rank	Company, Regiment or Ship	Post*	Age	Death Date†	Journal
Goltry, Jacob F.	Corp.	C, 37th Ind. Inf.	208		1914 Oct 15	IA, 42nd, 1916
Goneley, J.	Pvt.	F, 23rd Iowa Inf.	271		1921 Mar 3	IA, 48th, 1922
Gonsalus, A.C.	Pvt.	F, 9th Iowa Inf.	48		1908 Dec 15	IA, 35th, 1909
Gonsky, John		B, 8th Kans.	39		1904 Dec 30	KS, 24th, 1905
Gonzales, Samuel		K, 190th Penn.	75		1885	KS, 5th, 1886
Good, Arnold	Pvt.	A, 33rd Wis. Inf.	182	63	1894 Jun 19	IA, 21st, 1895
Good, E.F.		B, 135th Ill.	75		1921 Jul 22	KS, 41st, 1922
Good, George W.		E, 75th Ind.	110		1890	KS, 10th, 1891
Good, Jacob R.		F, 3rd Cal. Cav. (died at Lawrence, Kans.; buried at Oak Hill Cemetery)	12		1894 Jun 15	KS, 14th, 1895
Good, John C.	Pvt.	D, 47th Iowa Inf.	68	93	1939 Jan 29	IA, 65th, 1939
Good, John L.	Corp.	I, 177th Penn. Inf.	67		1928 Jun 8	IA, 55th, 1929
Good, Joseph	Pvt.	F, 7th Iowa Cav.	155	41	1886 Sep 10	IA, 13th, 1887
Good, Robt.	Pvt.	U.S.C. Inf.	251		1911 Jun 13	IA, 38th, 1912
Good, Wm.	Pvt.	E, 4th Iowa Cav.	253		1920 Aug 31	IA, 47th, 1921
Goodale, J.		C, 11th Ind. Cav.	8		1916 Jul 21	KS, 36th, 1917
Goodale, N.	Corp.	I, 5th N.Y. Art.	242	65	1889 Nov 15	IA, 17th, 1891
Goodale, Nathan	Corp.	I, 5th N.Y. Hvy. Art.	242	65	1889 Nov 15	IA, 16th, 1890
Goodale, Simon	Pvt.	H, 115th Ill. (died of fever sore)	95	67	1885 Sep 25	NE, 10th, 1886
Goodale, Wm. H.	Pvt.	K, 2nd Iowa Inf.	17	49	1890 Sep 18	IA, 17th, 1891
Goodall, W.B.		K, 9th Ind. Cav. (died of acute hepatitis)	110		1893 Aug 29	NE, 18th, 1894
Goodapple, Henry	Sergt.	D, 148th Ill. Inf.	235		1913 Jul 20	IA, 40th, 1914
Goodbrake, S.F.	1st Lieut.	7th Ill. Cav.	132		1911 Nov 3	KS, 31st, 1912
Goode, John T.	Pvt.	B, 41st Ohio	209		1904-1905	IA, 31st, 1905
Goodell, Andrew J.	Pvt.	E, 113th Ill. Inf.	124		1926 Nov 3	IA, 53rd, 1927
Goodell, Elson		K, 17th Wis. (not a member of the G.A.R.)	4		1912 May 17	KS, 32nd, 1913
Goodell, L.H.	Pvt.	C, 32nd Ill. Inf.	192		1922 May 27	IA, 49th, 1923
Gooden, Wm.	Pvt.	H, 65th Ohio Vol. Inf.	32		1884	KS, 4th, 1885
Goodenough, A.C.	Pvt.	A, 186th N.Y. Inf.	2		1908 Apr 13	IA, 35th, 1909
Goodenough, E.H.	Pvt.	I, 38th Iowa Inf.	49	69	1897 Dec 8	IA, 24th, 1898
Goodenough, M.	Pvt.	D, 20th N.Y. Cav.	235		1916 Sep 1	IA, 43rd, 1917
Gooder, J.W.	Corp.	D, 39th Wis. Inf.	512		1926 Jan 15	IA, 53rd, 1927
Gooder, J.W.	Corp.	D, 39th Wis. Inf.	512		1925 Jan 15	IA, 52nd, 1926
Goodger, Lester		C, 15th Ind. Inf. (died of wounds)	78	82	1922 Nov 18	NE, 47th, 1923
Goodhue, Jas. Henry	Sergt.	K, 8th Iowa Cav.	235	92	1938 Dec 1	IA, 65th, 1939
Goodie, Jno. E.		A, 80th Ill.	25		1922 May 26	NE, 47th, 1923
Goodie, John E.		A, 80th Ill. (not a member; buried by Farragut Post)	25		1922 May 26	NE, 47th, 1923
Goodim, Jas. W.		I, 36th Iowa Inf.	7		1926 Dec 30	NE, 51st, 1927
Goodin, Alf.	Lieut.	B, 82nd Ohio Inf.	31		1908 Nov 12	IA, 35th, 1909
Goodin, Samuel		F, 160th Ohio	88		1911 Dec 17	KS, 31st, 1912
Goodin, Wm.	Pvt.	A, 1st Iowa Cav.	254		1917 Apr 23	IA, 44th, 1918
Gooding, Fred	Pvt.	E, 77th Ill. Inf.	197		1914 Nov 2	IA, 41st, 1915
Goodlander, John W.		F, 8th Ind. Inf.	88		1909 Sep 27	KS, 29th, 1910
Goodlove, W.H.	Pvt.	H, 24th Iowa Inf.	212		1916	IA, 43rd, 1917
Goodman, Chas. F.	Hosp. Stew.	67th N.Y. Inf. (cause of death: kidneys)	110	60	1895 Jan 11	NE, 20th, 1896
Goodman, D.B.	Pvt.	F, 1st Neb. Inf.	11		1908 Sep	IA, 35th, 1909
Goodman, Daniel		D, 18th Ill.	24	70	1912 Apr 5	NE, 37th, 1913
Goodman, H.B.	Pvt.	D, 144th N.Y. Inf.	39		1909 Dec 5	IA, 36th, 1910
Goodman, Herbert		E, 133rd Ill. A, 149th Ill.	19		1919 Dec 21	KS, 39th, 1920
Goodman, James G.	Pvt.	B, 95th Ill. Inf.	39	58	1894 Oct 12	IA, 21st, 1895
Goodman, Jno.		E, 83rd Ill.	380		1904 Jun 2	KS, 24th, 1905
Goodman, John			4		1884	KS, 4th, 1885
Goodman, John F.	Pvt.	C, 105th & 156th Penn. Inf.	66	90	1932 Oct 31	IA, 59th, 1933
Goodman, Thomas	Sergt.	H, 67th Ohio Inf.	233		1910 Jan 15	IA, 37th, 1911
Goodman, Thomas		6th Wis. Bat. (died of heart failure)	47	77	1919 Dec 1	NE, 44th, 1920
Goodnight, Porter		F, 54th Ill.	57		1889	KS, 9th, 1890
Goodnow, Frank	Corp.	A, 124th Ill. Inf.	59		1914 Sep 14	IA, 41st, 1915
Goodnow, P.	Pvt.	D, 98th N.Y. Inf.	305		1919 Jul 26	IA, 46th, 1920
Goodrean, Jos.		C, 12th Ill. Inf. (died of complications)	159	72	1901 Jul	NE, 26th, 1902
Goodrell, W.H.	Pvt.	G, 140th Penn. Inf.	8	57	1897-1898	IA, 24th, 1898

*See Appendix A, B or C for roster of post names and locations.
†See Introduction for note regarding recording of death date.
208

Name	Rank	Company, Regiment or Ship	Post*	Age	Death Date†	Journal
Goodrell, W.H.	Capt.	B, 15th Iowa Inf.	8	56	1897 Jul 5	IA, 24th, 1898
Goodrich, C.B.		A, 156th Ill.	12		1910 Aug 21	KS, 30th, 1911
Goodrich, D.B.	Pvt.	88th Ill.	204		1907 Jan	IA, 34th, 1908
Goodrich, Daniel K.	Pvt.	C, 1st Mo. Lt. Art.	48	56	1893 Sep 22	IA, 20th, 1894
Goodrich, E.F.			12		1923 Jan 18	KS, 43rd, 1924
Goodrich, Ezra	Pvt.	B, 24th Iowa Inf.	231		1920 Nov 18	IA, 47th, 1921
Goodrich, Frederick	Pvt.	3rd Minn. Lt. Art.	92		1901 Mar 6	IA, 27th, 1901
Goodrich, J.	Pvt.	4th Md. Cav.	57		1921 Nov 3	IA, 48th, 1922
Goodrich, J.P.		I, 121st Ohio Inf. (died of paralysis)	57		1902 Nov	NE, 27th, 1903
Goodrich, John		I, 3rd Cal.	18		1911 Jan 19	KS, 31st, 1912
Goodrich, L.B.		F, 45th Wis.	55		1933 Sep 15	KS, 53rd, 1934
Goodrich, L.B.		F, 45th Wis. Inf.	55		1933 Sep 15	KS, 55th, 1936
Goodrich, M.J.	Pvt.	E, 144th Penn. Inf.	493		1915 Dec 31	IA, 42nd, 1916
Goodrich, W.	Pvt.	H, 13th Ill. Cav.	111		1921 Feb 21	IA, 48th, 1922
Goodrich, W.B.	Sergt.	B, 26th Iowa Inf.	456		1913 May 22	IA, 40th, 1914
Goodrich, W.D.		C, 1st Wis.	335		1924 Jan 29	KS, 44th, 1925
Goodrich, W.H.	Pvt.	C, 5th N.Y. Art.	46		1913 Feb 4	IA, 40th, 1914
Goodrich, W.W.	Pvt.	D, 32nd Iowa Inf.	347		1910 Jun	IA, 37th, 1911
Goodrich, Ward		F, 147th Ill. (died of old age)	182	72	1918 Apr 5	NE, 43rd, 1919
Goodrich, William			[85]		1923	KS, 43rd, 1924
Goodrick, E.L.	Pvt.	K, 13th Wis. Inf.	22	46	1887 Apr 1	IA, 13th, 1887
Goodrick, H.B.	Pvt. Lieut.	B, 11th Iowa Inf. D, 70th U.S. Colored (died of consumption)	44	51	1887 Sep 29	NE, 12th, 1888
Goodson, John D.	Surg.	72nd Ohio	14[15?]		1896 Nov 20	KS, 16th, 1897
Goodwater, Thurman	Pvt.	F, 46th Iowa Inf.	364		1917 Feb 11	IA, 44th, 1918
Goodwin, B.F.		C, 8th N.Y. Hvy. Art.	130		1916 Jul 10	KS, 36th, 1917
Goodwin, Dave		H, 11th Mo. Cav.	4		1925 Oct 30	KS, 45th, 1926
Goodwin, E.A.	Pvt.	F, 99th N.Y. Inf.	452		1910 Aug	IA, 37th, 1911
Goodwin, E.A.		F, 1st Ill. Cav.	253		1886	KS, 6th, 1887
Goodwin, Edwin	Pvt.	D, 22nd Wis. Inf.	47	61	1890 Jan 7	IA, 16th, 1890
Goodwin, Elliott	Pvt.	D, 28th Iowa Inf.	98		1917 Nov 13	IA, 44th, 1918
Goodwin, G.W.	Pvt.	F, 1st La. Ill.	22		1921 Jun 2	IA, 48th, 1922
Goodwin, Ira			199		1924 Feb 22	KS, 46th, 1927
Goodwin, Isaac	Lieut.	I, 34th Ind. Inf.	75		1899	NE, 24th, 1900
Goodwin, J.P.	Pvt.	36th Iowa Inf.	434		1905 Nov 22	IA, 32nd, 1906
Goodwin, Jesse O.		I, 15th Ind. C, 25th Ky.	25		1927 Apr 5	NE, 52nd, 1928
Goodwin, John	Pvt.	F, 34th Iowa Inf.	197	68	1890 May 9	IA, 17th, 1891
Goodwin, John	Pvt.	I, 18th Iowa Inf.	112	65	1892 Jun 2	IA, 19th, 1893
Goodwin, John		K, 69th Ohio (died of heart failure)	342	77	1913 Oct 27	NE, 38th, 1914
Goodwin, King H.		I, 8th Iowa Cav.	190		1918 Jul 31	IA, 45th, 1919
Goodwin, M.J.	Pvt.	A, 77th N.Y. Inf.	452		1920 Oct 12	IA, 47th, 1921
Goodwin, T.J.		A, 18th Ill.	28		1922 May 9	KS, 42nd, 1923
Goodwin, William		I, 2nd Kans. Cav.	74		1909 May 2	KS, 29th, 1910
Goodwin, Wm. C.		K, 92nd N.Y.	110		1913 May 10	KS, 33rd, 1914
Goody, Robert	Pvt.	B, 22nd Iowa Inf.	8		1923 Mar 4	IA, 50th, 1924
Goodyear, Jas.		B, 17th Mich. Cav.	244		1918 Mar 3	KS, 38th, 1919
Goodykoontz, D.F.	Pvt.	B, 12th Iowa Inf.	329		1919 Oct 27	IA, 46th, 1920
Gookin, T.		D, 8th Iowa	18		1921 Jan 20	IA, 48th, 1922
Goold, C.A.		G, 129th Ill. Inf. (died at Vernal, Utah)	473		1895 Sep	KS, 15th, 1896
Goorich, Silas	Pvt.	F, 91st N.Y. Inf.	226	78	1892 Sep 19	IA, 19th, 1893
Gorden, B.F.	Pvt.	D, 36th Iowa	138		1914 Apr 6	IA, 41st, 1915
Gorden, D.R.		D, 126th Penn.	63		1935 Apr 7	KS, 55th, 1936
Gorden, J.W.	Pvt.	K, 75th Ill.	98		1907 Dec 24	IA, 34th, 1908
Gorden, Thomas		A, 13th Kans.	10		1897 Nov 6	KS, 17th, 1898
Gorden, Thos.		C, 11th Kans. Cav.	295		1898 Feb	KS, 17th, 1898
Gordon, A.W.		K, 139th Ind.	63		1905 Apr 19	KS, 25th, 1906
Gordon, Abram	Sergt.	B, 150th Ill. Inf.	39		1927 May 8	IA, 54th, 1928
Gordon, Alex	Pvt.	C, 28th Iowa Inf.	127	62	1888 Mar 16	IA, 15th, 1889
Gordon, Alex	Pvt.	C, 28th Iowa Inf.	127	62	1888 Mar 16	IA, 18th, 1892
Gordon, Azra Blake		E, 171st Ohio	32		1919 Feb 24	KS, 39th, 1920

Name	Rank	Company, Regiment or Ship	Post*	Age	Death Date†	Journal
Gordon, C.W.		C, 93rd Penn. (died of heart trouble)	352	72	1918 May 17	NE, 43rd, 1919
Gordon, D.		C, 129th Ill.	59		1888	KS, 8th, 1889
Gordon, Howard	Pvt.	H, 8th Iowa Cav.	122		1911 Apr 30	IA, 38th, 1912
Gordon, Howard	Pvt.	H, 8th Iowa Inf.	122		1916 Aug 6	IA, 43rd, 1917
Gordon, J.A.		F, 39th Iowa Inf.	55		1918 Mar 10	IA, 45th, 1919
Gordon, J.S.			80		1915	IA, 42nd, 1916
Gordon, James	Pvt.	A, 5th Minn. Inf.	12	84	1931 Sep 6	IA, 58th, 1932
Gordon, Jasper H.	Pvt.	K, 33rd Iowa Inf.	40	68	1893 Nov 11	IA, 20th, 1894
Gordon, Jno. W.		L, Cav.	29		1927 Mar 15	IA, 54th, 1928
Gordon, John		E, 39th Ill. Inf. (died at Oak Hill)	304		1895 Mar	KS, 15th, 1896
Gordon, John F.		I, 23rd Mo. Inf. (collapsed)	61		1908 Oct 3	NE, 33rd, 1909
Gordon, John M.		I, 11th Kans. Cav.	71		1901 Jan 2	KS, 21st, 1902
Gordon, R.G.		H, 2nd Neb. Cav. (died of rheumatism)	61		1893 Aug	NE, 18th, 1894
Gordon, S.I.		C, 15th U.S. Inf.	7		1926 May 11	NE, 51st, 1927
Gordon, Samuel	2nd Lieut.	F, 11th Iowa Inf.	108		1922 Dec 3	IA, 49th, 1923
Gordon, Wm.	Sergt.	H, 47th Ill. Inf.	316		1896 Sep 12	IA, 23rd, 1897
Gordon, Wm.	Pvt.	I, 7th Ind. Inf.	98		1909 Sep 28	IA, 36th, 1910
Gore, Frank		G, 11th Ind. (died of old age)	25	80	1916 Apr 29	NE, 41st, 1917
Gore, J.W.	Col.	2nd Conn.	63		1892 Aug 6	KS, 12th, 1893
Gore, John	Pvt.	D, 13th Ohio Cav.	12		1929 Sep 28	IA, 56th, 1930
Gore, John W.		D, 4th Ind. Cav.	147		1930 Jan 28	KS, 50th, 1931
Gore, M.H.		K, 37th Ky. Inf.	413		1901 Mar 6	KS, 21st, 1902
Gore, Robert S.		D, 48th Ill. Inf. (former member)	297		1941 Jul 3	NE, 66th, 1942
Gorham, James H.		F, 5th Ind. Cav.	1		1899 Jun 12	KS, 19th, 1900
Gork, John	Pvt.	F, 44th Ill. Inf.	440		1904 Sep 5	IA, 31st, 1905
Gorlock, David	Pvt.	I, 30th Wis. Inf.	101		1910 Oct 2	IA, 37th, 1911
Gorman, Edward	Pvt.	B, 92nd Ill. Inf.	236		1911 Nov 2	IA, 38th, 1912
Gorman, James		D, 97th Penn.	66		1920 Jan 30	KS, 40th, 1921
Gorman, James		B, 102nd Ill.	293		1921 Sep 21	KS, 41st, 1922
Gorman, Jas. A.	Pvt.	E, 15th Ohio Vol. Inf.	11		1903 Jan 3	IA, 30th, 1904
Gormely, J.M.		C, 182nd —	17		1909 Mar 17	KS, 29th, 1910
Gormley, J.M.		C, 9th Iowa Cav.	293		1908 May 12	KS, 28th, 1909
Gormley, J.W.		M, 21st Penn. Cav.	18		1917 Feb 9	KS, 37th, 1918
Gorrell, J.R.	Surg.	129th Ind. Inf.	16		1916	IA, 43rd, 1917
Gorrell, Oliver			12		1923 Aug 30	IA, 50th, 1924
Gorrell, W.W.	Pvt.	E, 42nd Ill. Inf.	11	59	1893 Sep 9	IA, 20th, 1894
Gorsuch, Andrew		I, 26th Iowa	50		1908 Jan 27	KS, 28th, 1909
Gorsuch, E.W.	Pvt.	B, 40th Iowa Inf.	127	57	1886 Jul 25	IA, 18th, 1892
Gorsuch, John, see Garsuch, John						
Gorsuch, S.D.		E, 2nd Iowa	113		1917 Nov 25	KS, 37th, 1918
Gorsuch, Thos. B.	Pvt.	B, 40th Iowa	127	54	1884 Dec 29	IA, 18th, 1892
Goshorn, John S.	Capt.	E, 47th Iowa Inf.	55		1917 Jul 29	IA, 44th, 1918
Gosnell, Wm. M.	Pvt.	A, 35th Ill. Inf.	88		1918 Sep 30	IA, 46th, 1920
Goss, A.R.	Pvt.	E, 5th Iowa Inf.	63		1909 Sep 17	IA, 36th, 1910
Goss, David		D, 6th Kans. Vol. Cav.	3		1917 May 24	KS, 37th, 1918
Goss, H.W.	Pvt.	B, 4th Iowa Inf.	29		1904	IA, 31st, 1905
Goss, James		D, 6th Kans. Cav.	3		1926 Aug 10	KS, 46th, 1927
Goss, Thomas		D, 6th Kans. Vol. Cav.	3		1914 Nov 13	KS, 34th, 1915
Gossage, Jackson		I, 5th Ky. Cav.	40		1917 Oct 24	KS, 37th, 1918
Gossage, Jackson		I, 5th Ky. Cav.	500		1917 Aug 9	KS, 37th, 1918
Gossage, John	Pvt.	C, 43rd Iowa Inf.	497		1916 Dec 22	IA, 44th, 1918
Gossard, Jas. C.	Pvt.	D, 10th Iowa Cav.	323		1924 Aug 5	IA, 51st, 1925
Gossard, T.M.	Corp.	D, 10th Iowa Inf.	30	47	1890 Apr 11	IA, 17th, 1891
Gosser, Peter		F, 115th Ohio	2		1909 Feb 19	KS, 29th, 1910
Gossett, Wm. N.	Pvt.	C, 5th Tenn. (died of chronic diarrhea)	163	42	1884 Sep 25	NE, 9th, 1885
Gossom, Jackson		D, 115th U.S. Colored Inf.	127		1897 Dec 4	KS, 17th, 1898
Gosting, Edward	Pvt.	K, 21st Iowa Inf.	190		1913 Jan 30	IA, 40th, 1914
Gottbracht, Adolph	Sergt.	B, 16th Iowa Inf.	231		1915 Jul 19	IA, 42nd, 1916
Gottlirt, —	Pvt.	G, 153rd Ill.	3		1907 Sep 29	IA, 34th, 1908
Goudie, Jno. S.	Pvt.	A, 8th Iowa Cav.	248	56	1887 Apr 22	IA, 14th, 1888
Goughnour, B.P.	Pvt.	C, 8th Iowa Art.	28		1903 Apr	IA, 30th, 1904

*See Appendix A, B or C for roster of post names and locations.
†See Introduction for note regarding recording of death date.
210

Name	Rank	Company, Regiment or Ship	Post*	Age	Death Date†	Journal
Goughour, J.	Bugler	G, 3rd Iowa Cav.	28		1906 May 12	IA, 33rd, 1907
Goul, James W.		B, 89th Ind. Cav.	65		1915 Jun 14	KS, 35th, 1916
Gould, Benjamin L.		F, 13th & 25th Ill.	18		1924 Mar 8	KS, 44th, 1925
Gould, C.A., see Goold, C.A.						
Gould, C.H.		C, 16th Wis. Inf. (died of paralysis)	25	65	1903 Jun 4	NE, 28th, 1904
Gould, E.E.	Pvt.	K, 74th Ill. Inf.	149		1914 Aug 25	IA, 41st, 1915
Gould, F.T.		I, 39th Wis. Inf.	116		1906 Aug 27	NE, 31st, 1907
Gould, Geo. R.		A, 13th Wis.	12		1904 Nov 11	KS, 24th, 1905
Gould, George W.		A, 11th Mo. Inf. (died at Parsons)	64		1895 Sep	KS, 15th, 1896
Gould, H.G.	Pvt.		2		1927 Sep 20	IA, 54th, 1928
Gould, J.F.		K, 3rd Ill. Inf.	49		1930 Sep	KS, 50th, 1931
Gould, James	Pvt.	D, 15th Iowa Inf.	322		1914 Feb 9	IA, 41st, 1915
Gould, John H.	Pvt.	E, 93rd Ill. Inf.	9	83	1892 Aug 19	IA, 19th, 1893
Gould, John H.		C, 72nd Ill.	65		1918 Jan 15	KS, 38th, 1919
Gould, L.E.	Pvt.		42		1918 Jun 14	IA, 45th, 1919
Gould, L.J.		A, 1st La. Cav.	34		1929	KS, 49th, 1930
Gould, L.J.		A, 1st La. Cav.	34		1934	KS, 55th, 1936
Gould, S.F.		C, 2nd Minn. Cav.	203		1923 Jan 19	KS, 43rd, 1924
Gould, T.B.	Pvt.	E, 2nd —	147		1924 Dec 5	IA, 51st, 1925
Gould, Theodore O.		H, 3rd N.J. Inf.	32		1916 Jul 3	KS, 36th, 1917
Gouldin, Silas W.	Pvt.	E, 10th Ill. Inf.	440		1927 Feb 2	IA, 54th, 1928
Goulsby, James M.		A, 7th Mo. Cav. (died of disability)	84	70	1913 Dec 20	NE, 38th, 1914
Gove, Charles H.	1st Lieut.	101st Ill.	132		1911 Apr 18	KS, 31st, 1912
Gove, G.S.	Capt.	K, 5th N.H. Inf.	329		1918 Feb 7	IA, 45th, 1919
Gow, Allen		A, 31st Maine Inf.	25		1893 Jul 17	NE, 18th, 1894
Gow, W.G.	Pvt.	K, 8th N.H. Inf.	94		1925 Sep 25	IA, 52nd, 1926
Gowdey, John B.	Pvt.	H, 20th Ill. Inf. (at large)	36	93	1935 Jan 23	IA, 65th, 1939
Gowkov, William		A, 1st Neb. Inf. (died of hemorrhage)	2	74	1921 Nov 10	NE, 46th, 1922
Gowland, Frank	Pvt.	K, 100th Ill. Inf.	94	46	1889 Jan 9	IA, 15th, 1889
Gozine, Samuel	Pvt.	D, 24th Iowa Inf.	8		1910 Feb 4	IA, 37th, 1911
Grabendyke, William G.		C, 124th Ill.	18		1915 Feb 19	KS, 35th, 1916
Graber, H.	Pvt.	I, 27th Iowa Inf.	200		1917 Jan 5	IA, 44th, 1918
Grabham, John		E, 96th Ill. Inf.	50		1900 Sep 25	KS, 20th, 1901
Grabill, Paul	Pvt.	G, 74th Ohio Inf.	12		1910 May 20	IA, 37th, 1911
Grace, A.J.		C, 20th Iowa Inf.	23		1913 Nov 19	IA, 40th, 1914
Grace, George		H, 55th Ind.	244		1917 Jun 11	KS, 37th, 1918
Grace, J.B.		G, 5th Ind.	32		1902 Nov 25	KS, 22nd, 1903
Grace, J.L.	Pvt.	L, 14th Ill. Cav.	7		1907 Sep 14	IA, 34th, 1908
Grace, Phillip			399		1922 Dec 5	IA, 49th, 1923
Grace, William	Pvt.	E, 28th Iowa Inf.	403		1897 Sep 28	IA, 24th, 1898
Graden, John		C, 103rd Penn.	448		1908 Mar 1	KS, 28th, 1909
Graff, Andrew A.		M, 4th Mich.	57		1935 Nov 20	KS, 55th, 1936
Graff, Cyrus		C, 119th Ill. Inf. (died of heart failure)	47	74	1911 Aug 5	NE, 36th, 1912
Graff, D.W.	Pvt.	L, 2nd Ill. Cav.	284		1918 Dec 1	IA, 45th, 1919
Graff, H.C.	Sergt.	K, 3rd Mo. Cav.	284	40	1889 Mar 8	IA, 15th, 1889
Graff, Henry C.		C, 15th Ohio	6		1927 Sep 15	KS, 47th, 1928
Graff, Joseph		M, 1st Mo. Cav. (died of heart failure)	108	76	1910 Aug 28	NE, 35th, 1911
Graff, Val	Sergt.	G, 12th Mo. Cav.	11		1921 Oct 9	IA, 48th, 1922
Graffin, G.B.		H, 50th Ohio	17		1923 Jul 11	KS, 43rd, 1924
Grafton, Daniel S.		A, 3rd Iowa Cav. (died of heart disease)	112		1894 Jan 4	NE, 19th, 1895
Gragg, Mortimer		K, 1st N.Y.	1		1922 Jul 8	KS, 42nd, 1923
Graham, A.J.	Pvt.		81		1931 Jul 5	IA, 58th, 1932
Graham, A.J.	Pvt. Pvt.	F, 135th Penn. F, 13th Penn. (died of poisoning)	163	55	1887 Nov	NE, 12th, 1888
Graham, A.W.		D, 68th Ohio	40		1923 May 25	KS, 43rd, 1924
Graham, Alex	Pvt.	H, 2nd Iowa Inf.	12		1910 Nov 4	IA, 37th, 1911
Graham, B.D.		H, 86th N.Y. F, 19th N.Y. U.S.C.	92		1928 Oct 30	KS, 48th, 1929
Graham, B.J.	Pvt.	D, 8th Iowa Cav.	153		1927 Mar 15	IA, 54th, 1928
Graham, C.H.		16th Kans.	40		1916 Feb 16	KS, 36th, 1917
Graham, C.W.	Pvt.	I, 26th Ohio	50		1906 Mar 7	IA, 33rd, 1907
Graham, D.R.	Pvt.	G, 83rd Penn. Inf.	20		1911 Feb	IA, 38th, 1912

Name	Rank	Company, Regiment or Ship	Post*	Age	Death Date†	Journal
Graham, Daniel	Pvt.	M, 8th Iowa Cav.	153		1927 Sep 19	IA, 54th, 1928
Graham, E.	Pvt.	E, 2nd Iowa Inf.	515		1909 Jul 8	IA, 36th, 1910
Graham, E.		D, 144th N.Y. (died of old age)	299	82	1911 Sep 3	NE, 36th, 1912
Graham, Edward C.		G, 10th Iowa Inf.	240		1902 Dec 25	KS, 22nd, 1903
Graham, Elijah		K, 145th Ind. Inf. (died at Norton County, Kans.; buried at Edmond Cemetery)	312		1894 Dec 20	KS, 14th, 1895
Graham, Enoch C.	Pvt.	G, 10th Iowa Inf.	116		1912 Jul 21	IA, 39th, 1913
Graham, Frances		E, 114th Ohio Vol. Inf.	252		1915 Jan 15	KS, 35th, 1916
Graham, G.E.	Pvt.	I, 45th Ill. Inf.	306		1906 Dec 8	IA, 33rd, 1907
Graham, G.W.	Lieut.	C, 19th Ky. Inf. (died of old age)	1	87	1919 May 26	NE, 44th, 1920
Graham, George		K, 87th Ill. Inf.	87		1890	KS, 10th, 1891
Graham, George		G, 122nd Ohio	87		1895 Dec 12	KS, 16th, 1897
Graham, H.	Pvt.	A, 2nd Minn. Cav.	194		1930 Apr 2	IA, 57th, 1931
Graham, H.D.		C, 11th Ill.	54		1913 Feb 3	KS, 33rd, 1914
Graham, H.H.		D, 126th Ohio	81		1921 Jul 15	KS, 41st, 1922
Graham, H.R.		not a member of the G.A.R.	76		1912	KS, 32nd, 1913
Graham, H.S.		K, 40th Iowa Inf.	116		1924 Mar 6	IA, 51st, 1925
Graham, Henry		A, 4th Ohio	66		1911 Apr 29	IA, 38th, 1912
Graham, Henry C.		C, 46th Ind. Inf.			1936 Apr	IA, 62nd, 1936
Graham, I.H.		G, 5th Conn. Inf.	380		1917 Mar 16	KS, 37th, 1918
Graham, J.	Pvt.	A, 16th Ill.	452		1921 Jul 13	IA, 48th, 1922
Graham, J.A.	Pvt.	E, 12th Iowa Inf.	122		1911 Apr 11	IA, 38th, 1912
Graham, J.C.			76		1911	KS, 31st, 1912
Graham, J.F.		F, 166th Ohio National Guard	85		1902 Mar 28	KS, 22nd, 1903
Graham, J.S.		E, 25th Ohio	244		1913 Oct 27	KS, 33rd, 1914
Graham, James	Sergt.	7th Wis. Battery	48		1905 May 1	IA, 32nd, 1906
Graham, James E.		H, 199th Penn.	190		1896 May 1	KS, 16th, 1897
Graham, Jerome	Pvt.	D, 12th Ind. Cav.	440		1908 Jul 19	IA, 35th, 1909
Graham, John F.	Pvt.	Ohio	333		1918 Aug 10	IA, 45th, 1919
Graham, John W.		C, 40th Iowa	89		1905 Jun 6	KS, 25th, 1906
Graham, Leander		G, 25th Ind.	294		1909 Dec 20	KS, 29th, 1910
Graham, Manoah		F, 36th Iowa Inf. (died at Washington; buried at Washington Cemetery)	44		1894 Aug 20	KS, 14th, 1895
Graham, Mathew Joseph		G, 10th Ill. Inf.	55	98	1937 Jan 10	IA, 64th, 1938
Graham, Millon	Pvt.	B, 86th Ill.	19		1905 Mar 27	IA, 32nd, 1906
Graham, N.B.		B, 6th Ind.	500		1917 Aug 11	KS, 37th, 1918
Graham, Napoleon		C, 83rd Ohio (died of consumption)	81	74	1922 Jun 2	NE, 47th, 1923
Graham, Oscar	Pvt.	G, 3rd Iowa Cav.	79	48	1st quarter 1889	IA, 16th, 1890
Graham, Oscar		G, 3rd Iowa Cav.	79		3rd quarter 1884	IA, 11th, 1885
Graham, Robert B.		E, 67th Ill.	25		1913 Feb 8	NE, 38th, 1914
Graham, Rubin		A, 98th Ill.	32		1930 Jun 20	KS, 50th, 1931
Graham, S.J.	Sergt.	G, 50th Ill. Inf.	29		1920 Apr 20	IA, 47th, 1921
Graham, T.J.	Pvt.	K, 7th Iowa Inf.	285	56	1890 Nov 10	IA, 17th, 1891
Graham, Thos.	Sergt.	K, 2nd Wis. Inf.	168		1911 Dec 8	IA, 38th, 1912
Graham, Thos. N., see Grayham, Thos. N.						
Graham, W.W.		A, 107th Ill.	185		1927 Mar 5	KS, 47th, 1928
Graham, William		10th N.Y. Hvy. Art.	130		1932 Jan 4	NE, 57th, 1933
Graham, Wm. A.	Pvt.	G, 85th Penn. Inf.	245	49	1892 Feb 26	IA, 19th, 1893
Graham, Wm. I.	Pvt.	G, 45th Iowa Inf.	157		1917 Sep 2	IA, 45th, 1919
Granahan, A.	Pvt.	A, 38th Iowa Inf.	452		1915	IA, 42nd, 1916
Granaman, Henry	Pvt.	D, 25th Iowa Inf.	157		1919 Oct 8	IA, 46th, 1920
Granaman, William	Pvt.	F, 45th Iowa Inf.	157		1917 Dec 5	IA, 45th, 1919
Grand, Christian		E, 107th Penn.	51		1905 May 6	KS, 25th, 1906
Grandon, Ezekiel	Pvt.	D, 5th Iowa Cav.	452		1915 Aug 20	IA, 42nd, 1916
Grandstaff, James	Pvt.	I, 29th Iowa Inf.	251		1919 Dec	IA, 46th, 1920
Grandt, Henry	Pvt.	E, 26th Iowa Inf.	505	65	1897 Oct 26	IA, 24th, 1898
Grandy, John	Pvt.	M, 1st Iowa Cav.	90	58	1895 Apr 28	IA, 22nd, 1896
Grane, H.H.		E, 49th Mo.	150		1905 Nov 8	KS, 25th, 1906
Granger, A.E.	Pvt.	G, 153rd Ill.	48		1924 Jun 5	IA, 51st, 1925
Granger, C.T.	Capt.	K, 27th Iowa Inf.	194		1915 Oct 26	IA, 42nd, 1916
Granger, T.P.	Musician	21st Ohio Inf.	159		1908 Apr 12	IA, 35th, 1909

Name	Rank	Company, Regiment or Ship	Post*	Age	Death Date†	Journal
Grannaman, John	Pvt.	F, 45th Iowa Inf.	5		1913 Aug 18	IA, 40th, 1914
Grannis, H.J.	Pvt.	C, 12th Iowa Inf.	46		1908 Oct 13	IA, 35th, 1909
Gransby, Albert	Pvt.	C, 30th Iowa Inf.	452		1912 Aug 25	IA, 39th, 1913
Grant, Benjamin F.		G, 5th Ind. Cav.	64		1923 Feb 19	KS, 43rd, 1924
Grant, Chas.		D, 18th Ohio Inf.	8		1918 Feb 24	KS, 38th, 1919
Grant, E.R.	Capt.	I, 49th U.S. Colored	39		1890 Dec 21	IA, 17th, 1891
Grant, Edward	Pvt.	G, 2nd Iowa Cav.	382		1897 Aug 10	IA, 24th, 1898
Grant, George W.	Pvt.	H, 44th Iowa 100 Day Vols.	473		1902 Feb 5	IA, 28th, 1902
Grant, H.D.		D, 4th Mich. Cav.	4		1922 Nov	KS, 42nd, 1923
Grant, Isaac M.		K, 38th Ohio	36		1922 Dec 20	KS, 42nd, 1923
Grant, James L.		D, 39th Ill.	143		1929 Apr 1	NE, 54th, 1930
Grant, Joseph H.		H, 7th Ind.	23		1916 Apr ?4	KS, 36th, 1917
Grant, M.S.	Brig. Gen.	1st Kans.	6		1914	KS, 34th, 1915
Grant, S.	Pvt.	F, 29th Iowa Inf.	10		1910 Feb	IA, 37th, 1911
Grant, Sam			25	71	1910 Jan 17	NE, 35th, 1911
Grant, Waldo K.		D, 1st Iowa Cav.	171		1940 Jan 31	NE, 65th, 1941
Grant, Wm.	Capt.	F, 4th U.S.C. Art.	90		1904 Sep 14	IA, 31st, 1905
Grantham, C.F.		F, 48th Mo.	19		1927 Oct 13	KS, 47th, 1928
Grantham, R.R.C.			12		1923 Oct 3	IA, 50th, 1924
Grapins, T.L.		K, 143rd Penn. (died of heart failure)	28	67	1909 Nov 16	NE, 34th, 1910
Grash, H.I.F.		F, 13th Md.	25		1914 Oct 2	KS, 34th, 1915
Grasle, Gustave	Pvt.	1st Mich. Lt. Art.	88		1910 Jul 8	IA, 37th, 1911
Grass, Daniel		H, 61st Ill. Inf. (died at Coffeyville; buried at Independence, Kans.)	153		1894 Dec 21	KS, 14th, 1895
Grass, Daniel		65th Ill. (died at Independence)	4		1895	KS, 15th, 1896
Grass, Francis	Pvt.	2nd Iowa Battery	29		1904 Apr 29	IA, 31st, 1905
Grasser, Ferdinand			58		1893	NE, 18th, 1894
Grassfield, David	Pvt.	F, 20th Iowa Inf.	4	62	1893 Mar 4	IA, 19th, 1893
Grate, Levi		G, 130th Ill. (killed by accident)	262	65	1900 Sep 30	NE, 25th, 1901
Gratigny, A.F.		C, 56th Ohio Inf. (died at Atchison; buried at Mt. Vernon Cemetery)	336		1894 Dec 21	KS, 14th, 1895
Grattan, Marvin Trask	Landsman	U.S. Navy (served on *U.S.S. Ouichita, Great Western* and *Clara Dolsen*) (at large)	122, 452	91	1940 Feb 23	IA, 66th, 1940
Gravel, Joseph		B, 134th Ill.	36		1921 Nov 24	KS, 41st, 1922
Graven, Clark		A, 166th Ohio Inf. (at large)	23	92	1937 Jun 11	IA, 64th, 1938
Graves, C.B.		9th Kans. Cav.	55		1912 Mar 25	KS, 32nd, 1913
Graves, C.E.	Lieut.	B, 15th Md. Inf.	14		1929	IA, 56th, 1930
Graves, C.P.	Pvt.	A, 13th U.S. Inf.	30		1917 Jan 13	IA, 44th, 1918
Graves, C.R.	Pvt.	A, 94th Ill. Inf.	179		1903 Jul 8	IA, 30th, 1904
Graves, Charles		L, 14th Ill. Cav. (at large)			1932 Apr 26	IA, 59th, 1933
Graves, E.A.			80		1918	IA, 45th, 1919
Graves, George W.		G, 3rd Ill. Cav.	93		1914 Mar 21	KS, 34th, 1915
Graves, Harley		C, 6th Iowa Cav.	352		1931 Jul 9	NE, 56th, 1932
Graves, I.K.	Landsman	U.S. Navy	262	60	1911 Apr 9	NE, 36th, 1912
Graves, Ira		I, 2nd Mich.	26[25?]		1915 Feb 3	NE, 40th, 1916
Graves, J.H.		F, 12th Mo.	477		1926 Nov 19	KS, 46th, 1927
Graves, J.K.		U.S. Navy	262	60	1905 Apr 9	NE, 30th, 1906
Graves, J.W.		D, 51st Ohio	209		1914 Mar 8	KS, 34th, 1915
Graves, J.W.		B, 2nd Ind. Cav.	97		1923 Aug 29	KS, 43rd, 1924
Graves, John B.		B, 15th Ky. Cav.	380		1909 Mar	KS, 29th, 1910
Graves, Johnson		F, 23rd Iowa Inf.		99	1938 Jul 31	IA, 64th, 1938
Graves, L.B.		L, 24th Maine	81		1900 Aug 18	KS, 20th, 1901
Graves, N.	Pvt.	G, 143rd —	466		1905 Jul 26	IA, 32nd, 1906
Graves, S.V.R.	Pvt.	B, 47th Wis. Inf.	134		1922 Jun 2	IA, 49th, 1923
Graves, Steven			240		1921 Feb 3	KS, 41st, 1922
Graves, W.J.	Pvt.	B, 48th Iowa Inf.	18	86	1931 Feb	IA, 58th, 1932
Graves, Z.H.	Artificer	3rd Iowa Bat.	475	75	1893 Apr 11	IA, 20th, 1894
Gravet, Samson		B, 13th Kans. Inf.	18		1908 Jul 17	KS, 28th, 1909
Grawe, J.F.	Pvt.	G, 91st Ill. Inf.	267	89	1933 Feb 24	IA, 60th, 1934
Gray, Amos	Pvt.	F, 33rd Iowa Inf.	40	85	1931 May 27	IA, 58th, 1932
Gray, C.M.		I, 58th Ind.	129		1905 Dec 30	KS, 25th, 1906

*See Appendix A, B or C for roster of post names and locations.
†See Introduction for note regarding recording of death date.

Name	Rank	Company, Regiment or Ship	Post*	Age	Death Date†	Journal
Gray, C.M.G.		I, 58th Ind.	129		1906 Dec 30	KS, 26th, 1907
Gray, David O.		F, 13th Mich.	52		1918 Dec 4	KS, 38th, 1919
Gray, George			294		1913 Mar	KS, 33rd, 1914
Gray, George C.		K, 11th Mass.	52		1923 Jun 1	KS, 43rd, 1924
Gray, H.H.	QM	9th Iowa Cav.	267	42	1885 Sep 29	IA, 12th, 1886
Gray, H.W.	Pvt. Bvt. Col.	A, 6th Iowa 6th Iowa (died of pneumonia)	19	69	1885 Apr 28	NE, 10th, 1886
Gray, J.L.	Pvt.	I, 73rd Ohio Vols.	12		1906 Jun 1	IA, 33rd, 1907
Gray, J.M.		I, 123rd Ill.	239		1897 Dec 5	KS, 17th, 1898
Gray, J.W.		F, 11th Ohio Cav.	50		1917 Dec 11	KS, 37th, 1918
Gray, Jas. A.		B, 4th Iowa Cav. (died of accident)	169	73	1914 Mar 7	NE, 39th, 1915
Gray, Jesse		I, —	7		1925 Feb 16	KS, 45th, 1926
Gray, John			23		1907 May 12	IA, 34th, 1908
Gray, John	Pvt.	H, 16th U.S. Inf.	118		1909 Nov 8	IA, 36th, 1910
Gray, John		Mass. Bat.	59		1927 Jul 11	KS, 47th, 1928
Gray, John		A, 17th Ind. Inf. (died of pneumonia)	180	72	1915 Dec 26	NE, 40th, 1916
Gray, John S.	Capt.	C, 19th Iowa Inf.	108		1917 Dec 15	IA, 44th, 1918
Gray, Joseph	Sergt.	F, 17th Iowa Inf.	122	66	1896 Jan 29	IA, 23rd, 1897
Gray, Joseph		F, 5th Wis.	15		1914 Oct 13	KS, 34th, 1915
Gray, L.D.		I, 13th Iowa	35		1931 Apr	NE, 56th, 1932
Gray, L.M.	Corp.	A, 95th Ill.	117		1903 Mar 23	IA, 30th, 1904
Gray, Mahlon F.	Pvt.	K, 83rd Ill. Inf.	321	52	1896 Sep 16	IA, 23rd, 1897
Gray, N.E.	Pvt.	C, 25th Iowa Inf.	132		1929 May 19	IA, 56th, 1930
Gray, Nelson A.	Pvt.	7th Wis. Inf.	441		1909 Jan 1	IA, 35th, 1909
Gray, O.	Pvt.	G, 32nd Regt.	236		1905 Jul 2	IA, 32nd, 1906
Gray, R.	Surg.	21st Ohio Inf. (died of dropsy)	31	65	1895 Jun 28	NE, 20th, 1896
Gray, R.		D, 124th Ill. Inf. (died of strang. hernia)	60	73	1903 Sep 26	NE, 28th, 1904
Gray, S.S.		E, 8th Tenn.	153		1897 Dec 6	KS, 17th, 1898
Gray, S.W.	Lieut.		337		1926 Apr 26	IA, 53rd, 1927
Gray, W.		G, 95th Ill.	113		1918 Jan 19	KS, 38th, 1919
Gray, W.A.			337		1917 Jun 9	IA, 44th, 1918
Gray, W.H.		E, 87th Penn. Inf. (died at National Military Home; buried at Military Home Cemetery)	380		1894 Sep 14	KS, 14th, 1895
Gray, W.H.H.		A, 45th Ill.	122		1923 Apr 26	KS, 43rd, 1924
Gray, W.P.		C, 15th Kans.	294		1906 Jun 2	KS, 26th, 1907
Gray, Walter S.			515		1918 Dec 29	IA, 45th, 1919
Gray, William		K, 43rd Ind.	64		1890	KS, 10th, 1891
Gray, William		I, —	7		1922 Jan 1	KS, 45th, 1926
Gray, Wm.	Pvt.	C, 12th Wis. Inf.	11		1910 Feb	IA, 37th, 1911
Gray, Wm. A.		K, 202nd Penn. Inf.	100	90	1910	NE, 35th, 1911
Gray, Wm. H.		D, 1st Cal.	25		1926 Nov 28	KS, 46th, 1927
Grayham, G.W.		G, 11th Ind. Inf. K, 43rd Ind. Inf. (died of Bright's disease)	335	56	1895 Dec 17	NE, 20th, 1896
Grayham, Thos. N.		G, 15th Ind.	12		1911 Feb 4	KS, 31st, 1912
Grayson, James	Pvt.	B, 11th Ill. Cav.	208		1907 Feb	IA, 33rd, 1907
Grayson, James	Pvt.	B, 11th Ill. Cav.	208		1907 Feb 16	IA, 34th, 1908
Grealey, W.M.	Capt.	A, 121st N.Y. Inf.	30		1917 Feb 15	IA, 44th, 1918
Greaser, Michael G.		C, Ohio Ind. Battery (died at Denver, Colo.; buried at Riverside Cemetery)	1		1894 Aug 20	KS, 14th, 1895
Greater, James M.		B, 2nd Neb. Cav.	25		1913 Apr 10	NE, 38th, 1914
Greathouse, Leonard		C, 8th Kans.	93		1912 Dec 22	KS, 32nd, 1913
Grebe, Geo. W.		A, 82nd Ind.	129		1918 Sep 8	KS, 38th, 1919
Greek, D.		C, 9th Iowa	25		1919 Jan	KS, 39th, 1920
Greeley, Benj.	Pvt.	C, 21st Iowa Inf.	78		1911 Feb 25	IA, 38th, 1912
Greeley, Otis	Corp.	B, 32nd Iowa Inf.	180	54	1885 May 14	IA, 12th, 1886
Green, A.G.		K, 41st Ill.	57		1917 Feb 14	KS, 37th, 1918
Green, Abram		F, 113th U.S.C.	321		1904 Dec 4	KS, 24th, 1905
Green, Albert	Pvt.	B, 9th Iowa Inf.	191		1918 Mar 5	IA, 45th, 1919
Green, Albert R.		9th Kans. Cav. (died at Hood River, Ore.; see Appendix D)		76	1918 Jun 15	KS, 38th, 1919
Green, Alfred	Corp.	H, 19th Iowa	66		1907 May 18	IA, 34th, 1908
Green, Alonzo J.	Pvt.	M, 4th Iowa Cav.	19		1929 Jun 11	IA, 56th, 1930

*See Appendix A, B or C for roster of post names and locations.
†See Introduction for note regarding recording of death date.

Name	Rank	Company, Regiment or Ship	Post*	Age	Death Date†	Journal
Green, B.D.		H, 94th Ill.	83		1918	KS, 38th, 1919
Green, B.F.		D, 79th Ill. Inf.	18		1914 Dec 23	KS, 34th, 1915
Green, Benton			6		1908	IA, 35th, 1909
Green, Caleb	Pvt.	F, 102nd Ill. Inf.	14		1910 Nov 20	IA, 37th, 1911
Green, Charles E.		H, Mo. Cav.	158		1915 Apr 8	KS, 35th, 1916
Green, Chas.	Pvt.	B, 7th Iowa Inf.	122		1920	IA, 47th, 1921
Green, D.A.		H, 12th Ind.	127		1926 Jan 5	KS, 46th, 1927
Green, D.J.		B, 81st Ind.	51		1920 Jan 4	KS, 40th, 1921
Green, D.M.	Pvt.	E, 34th N.Y. Inf.	124		1916	IA, 43rd, 1917
Green, Daniel	Pvt.	G, 6th Iowa Inf.	8		1919 Jun 1	IA, 46th, 1920
Green, David	Pvt.	G, 47th Iowa Inf.	364		1920 Jan 28	IA, 47th, 1921
Green, David		G, 21st Ohio	130		1904 Mar 3	KS, 24th, 1905
Green, David C.		F, 88th Ohio	49		1921 Mar 22	KS, 41st, 1922
Green, Doctor		D, 84th Ind.	54		1921	KS, 41st, 1922
Green, E.D.		I, 25th Mich.	57		1916 Nov 16	KS, 36th, 1917
Green, Francis		I, 1st Ind.	88		1897 Oct 26	KS, 17th, 1898
Green, Francis M.		H, 68th Ill. (not a member of the G.A.R.)	129		1912 Jul 5	KS, 32nd, 1913
Green, Geo. W.	Pvt.	E, 197th Ohio Inf.	95		1913 Feb 10	IA, 40th, 1914
Green, George B.		G, 20th Mich.	18		1910 Mar 29	KS, 30th, 1911
Green, H.	Lieut.	F, 49th Wis.	124		1921 Nov 16	IA, 48th, 1922
Green, H.			284		1890	NE, 15th, 1891
Green, H.C.		K, 1st R.I. Inf. (died of catarrh of bowels)	228	62	1903 Dec 15	NE, 28th, 1904
Green, H.M.			57		1921 Nov 13	KS, 41st, 1922
Green, Henry		E, 4th Ky. Inf.	46		1921 May 12	KS, 41st, 1922
Green, Henry J.		H, 11th Ill.	199		1909 Aug 14	KS, 29th, 1910
Green, Isaac		G, 5th Tenn.	256		1900 Jan 27	KS, 20th, 1901
Green, J.A.		B, 11th Iowa	220		1888	KS, 8th, 1889
Green, J.E.		I, 147th Ill. (at large)			1933 Sep 24	NE, 58th, 1934
Green, J.L.	Pvt.	H, 23rd Iowa Inf.	441		1907 Dec 3	IA, 34th, 1908
Green, J.P.		K, 33rd Ohio	244		1911 Aug 6	KS, 31st, 1912
Green, Jacob	Pvt.	A, 57th Ind.	40		1903 Oct	IA, 30th, 1904
Green, James		B, 23rd Ohio Inf. (died of blood poison)	70		1893 Nov 5	NE, 18th, 1894
Green, James E.	Pvt.	A, 3rd Wis. Inf.	42		1931 Jan 23	IA, 57th, 1931
Green, James E.	Pvt.	A, 3rd Wis. Inf.	42	86	1931 Jan 23	IA, 58th, 1932
Green, John	Pvt.	G, 33rd Iowa Inf.	387	71	1897 Jan 15	IA, 24th, 1898
Green, John		I, 21st N.J.	354		1928 Oct 21	KS, 48th, 1929
Green, John, see Greene, John						
Green, John A.		K, 16th Iowa Inf.	25		1916 May 9	NE, 41st, 1917
Green, John D.			104		1924 Jan 4	KS, 43rd, 1924
Green, John M.		116th Ill. Inf.	264		1900 Nov 2	KS, 20th, 1901
Green, Joseph D.		12th Mass.	103		1916 Jul	KS, 36th, 1917
Green, L.N.	Pvt.	H, 9th Iowa Inf.	342		1905 Jul 7	IA, 32nd, 1906
Green, Lewis N.		A, 73rd Ind.	18		1924	KS, 44th, 1925
Green, Merritt		Engineer Corps	94		1923 Oct 24	IA, 50th, 1924
Green, Michael		A, 116th Ill.	498		1912 Aug 13	KS, 32nd, 1913
Green, Moses			25		1927 Sep 9	KS, 47th, 1928
Green, Newton	Pvt.	K, 21st Iowa Inf.	342		1905 Aug 24	IA, 32nd, 1906
Green, O.M.		F, 110th N.Y.	258		1922	KS, 43rd, 1924
Green, Percy B.		D, 83rd Ohio	25		1910 Dec 30	KS, 30th, 1911
Green, Perry O.		L, 45th Iowa Inf. (Lincoln)			1944 Sep 21	NE, 70th, 1946
Green, Peter		6th Wis. Lt. Art. (died of pneumonia)	60		1923 Feb 14	NE, 48th, 1924
Green, Philip		F, 83rd —	208		1896	KS, 16th, 1897
Green, R. Botts	Pvt.	K, 83rd U.S.C.	497		1919 Apr 12	IA, 46th, 1920
Green, S.J.		K, 47th Iowa	17		1930 Jul 8	KS, 50th, 1931
Green, Sam'l S.	Pvt.	F, 57th Ill. Inf.	12		1911 Feb 1	IA, 38th, 1912
Green, Samuel	Pvt.	E, 28th Iowa Inf.	8		1902 Jan 8	IA, 28th, 1902
Green, Thomas	Pvt.	4th Mo. State Militia	10		1926 Mar 9	IA, 53rd, 1927
Green, W.H.	Pvt.	C, 31st Wis. Inf.	134		1908 Sep 23	IA, 35th, 1909
Green, Wayland		B, 6th U.S. Inf. (at large)			1932 Jun 27	IA, 59th, 1933
Green, Webster		C, 86th Ill.	51		1920 Jan 3	KS, 40th, 1921
Green, Wilbur Maxson		E, 1st Wis. Cav. (former member; died at North Loup)	57		1936 Sep 12	NE, 61st, 1937

Name	Rank	Company, Regiment or Ship	Post*	Age	Death Date†	Journal
Green, William		C, 13th U.S. Inf. (died at Baxter Springs; buried at Baxter Springs Cemetery)	123		1894	KS, 14th, 1895
Green, William		C, 37th Wis. Inf.	250		1925 Jun 8	KS, 45th, 1926
Green, William H.	Sergt.	E, 92nd Ohio Vol. Inf.	191		1901 Jun 16	IA, 28th, 1902
Green, Wm.		C, 27th Iowa	12		1935	KS, 55th, 1936
Greene, Albert R.		A, 9th Kans. Cav.	481		1918 Jan 5	KS, 38th, 1919
Greene, H.M.	Lieut. Col.	2nd Kans. State Militia	12		1900 Nov 29	KS, 20th, 1901
Greene, John	Pvt.	K, 48th U.S. Colored Inf.	343	44	1885 Oct 2	IA, 12th, 1886
Greene, O.N.		F, 110th N.Y.	258		1922 Dec 8	KS, 42nd, 1923
Greene, Wm. H.		K, 202nd Penn.	19		1914 Apr 3	KS, 34th, 1915
Greenely, Wm.	Pvt.	K, 9th Iowa	64		1927 Feb	IA, 54th, 1928
Greenfield, John	Pvt.	C, 122nd Ill. Inf.	71		1901 Nov 13	IA, 28th, 1902
Greenfield, Peter	Pvt.	F, 14th Iowa	206		1907 Sep 17	IA, 34th, 1908
Greenfield, Wm.	Pvt.	B, 22nd Penn. Cav.	384	56	1889 Feb 11	IA, 15th, 1889
Greenhalgh, J.J.		G, 8th Kans.	199		1917 Dec 1	KS, 37th, 1918
Greenholgt, John		K, 77th Ill. (died of heart, rheumatism)	131	68	1917 Jan 25	NE, 42nd, 1918
Greenings, John		H, 129th Ind.	293		1920 Feb 3	KS, 40th, 1921
Greenla, H.U.	Pvt.	A, 16th Penn. Cav.	10		1906 Sep 11	IA, 33rd, 1907
Greenland, Geo. F.		A, 81st Penn. (died of heart failure)	226	66	1909 Jun 13	NE, 34th, 1910
Greenleaf, L.A.	Pvt.	C, 28th Iowa Inf.	16		1919	IA, 46th, 1920
Greenlee, James	Pvt.	B, 152nd Ill. Inf.	172	66	1892 Sep 6	IA, 19th, 1893
Greenlee, John		I, 50th Ill. Inf.	14		1918 May 20	KS, 38th, 1919
Greenly, I.W.	Sergt.	F, 2nd Kans. Inf.	97		1901 Sep 14	IA, 28th, 1902
Greeno, H.A.			25	70	1910 Mar 28	NE, 35th, 1911
Greenough, Christ		C, 8th Kans.	142		1885	KS, 5th, 1886
Greenwald, Charles	Pvt.	H, 48th Ind. Inf.	78		1928 Feb 12	IA, 55th, 1929
Greenwalt, H.A., see Greenwdt, H.A.						
Greenwalt, John	Pvt.	A, 96th Ill. Inf.	78		1908 Mar 2	IA, 35th, 1909
Greenwalt, Wm. K.		C, 8th Kans.	93		1893 Dec 29	KS, 13th, 1894
Greenway, R.H.	Pvt.	L, 9th Iowa Cav.	330		1904 Aug 23	IA, 31st, 1905
Greenwdt, H.A.		E, 112th Ill. (died of old age)	76	60	1913 Aug 28	NE, 38th, 1914
Greenwood, Chas.	Major	38th Ohio Inf.	139		1899	NE, 24th, 1900
Greenwood, Geo. W.		C, 11th Ill.	1		1927 Jan 30	KS, 47th, 1928
Greenwood, H.A.		K, 8th Cav.	115		1908 Oct 19	NE, 33rd, 1909
Greenwood, L.	Pvt.	F, 148th Ill. Inf.	22		1909 Apr 25	IA, 36th, 1910
Greer, A.C.		F, 5th Ind. Cav.	4		1917 Jan 29	KS, 37th, 1918
Greer, Daniel		C, 27th Ind. Inf.	63		1909 Feb 14	KS, 29th, 1910
Greer, Dillon B.	Pvt.	B, 84th Ill. Inf.		88	1936 Jul 10	IA, 65th, 1939
Greer, John I.		F, 90th Ind.	4		1896 Jan 17	KS, 16th, 1897
Greer, Robert F.	Sergt.	D, 6th Iowa Cav.	168	59	1898 May 12	IA, 24th, 1898
Gregg, A.		D, Mo. Home Guards	322		1922 Jan 23	KS, 42nd, 1923
Gregg, Anthony D.		G, 65th N.Y.	25		1932 Mar 10	NE, 57th, 1933
Gregg, E.A.	Sergt.	F, 36th Iowa Inf.	452		1905 Jan 24	IA, 32nd, 1906
Gregg, Geo. A.	Pvt.	I, Navy	94		1903 Sep 13	IA, 30th, 1904
Gregg, Geo. W.		C, 102nd Ill. (died of erysipelas)	26	81	1920 Jan 7	NE, 44th, 1920
Gregg, Geo. W.		C, 102nd Ill. (died of erysipelas)	26	81	1920 Jan 7	NE, 45th, 1921
Gregg, J.H.	Pvt.	D, 6th Mich. Inf.	322		1913 Apr 2	IA, 40th, 1914
Gregg, James M.	Pvt.	G, 30th Iowa Inf.	19		1929 Feb 7	IA, 56th, 1930
Gregg, Ruben, Rev.		C, 124th Ill.	221		1909 Nov	KS, 29th, 1910
Gregg, Rufus C.		E, 48th Wis.	60		1934 Jun 6	NE, 59th, 1935
Gregg, Samuel		B, 63rd Ohio	311		1919 Jan 4	KS, 39th, 1920
Gregg, Samuel		B, 63rd Ohio Inf.	311		1918 Jan 4	KS, 38th, 1919
Gregg, T.P.	Pvt.	B, 3rd Iowa Inf.	156		1901 Mar 3	IA, 28th, 1902
Gregg, Thos. C.	Pvt.	H, 51st Ill. Inf.	322		1903 Jun 6	IA, 30th, 1904
Gregg, Tom			322		1904-1905	IA, 31st, 1905
Gregory, B.F.	Pvt.	D, 34th Iowa Inf.	30	53	1886 Jul 27	IA, 13th, 1887
Gregory, Edward	Pvt.	H, 45th Wis. Inf.	156		1919 Nov 27	IA, 46th, 1920
Gregory, F.M.	Capt.	I, 8th Ill. Cav.	42		1911 May 23	IA, 38th, 1912
Gregory, G.L.	Pvt.	B, 6th Iowa Cav.	3		1910 Dec 17	IA, 37th, 1911
Gregory, George		C, 16th Ind.	25		1937 Jul 23	KS, 57th, 1938
Gregory, H.W.		L, 11th Kans. Cav.	256		1918 Oct 31	KS, 38th, 1919

Name	Rank	Company, Regiment or Ship	Post*	Age	Death Date†	Journal
Gregory, Jeremiah		G, 42nd Ind.	85		1927 Oct 1	KS, 47th, 1928
Gregory, John C.		E, 81st Ill.	1		1911 Feb 7	KS, 31st, 1912
Gregory, Jos.	Pvt.	I, 70th Ind. Inf.	2		1908 May 8	IA, 35th, 1909
Gregory, Joseph		H, 128th Ind. Inf.	37		1934 Dec 28	KS, 54th, 1935
Gregory, Julius	Pvt.	M, 2nd Mich. Cav.	92		1904 Feb 27	IA, 30th, 1904
Gregory, Milton		C, 18th Mo.	4		1926 Jan 8	KS, 46th, 1927
Gregory, O.P.		D, 24th Ohio	180		1920 Mar 15	KS, 40th, 1921
Gregory, Omer		H, 166th Ohio	17		1922 Jan 7	KS, 42nd, 1923
Gregory, S.T.	Pvt.	D, 39th Ill. Inf.	22		1909 Oct 8	IA, 36th, 1910
Gregory, U.		F, 43rd Wis. Inf. (died of heart failure)	109	64	1896 Jul 25	NE, 21st, 1897
Gregory, W.S.		I, 107th N.Y.	8		1910 Sep 22	KS, 30th, 1911
Grensolis, S.J.	Pvt.	D, 12th Ill. Inf.	235	64	1897 Feb 20	IA, 23rd, 1897
Grent, Nicholas	Pvt.	A, 31st Wis. Inf.	42		1916 Mar 3	IA, 43rd, 1917
Gresham, T.H.		C, 45th Mo. Inf.	1		1918 Jul 26	KS, 38th, 1919
Gresham, Wm.			3		1908	NE, 33rd, 1909
Gress, Fred		I, 11th Penn.	12		1928 Jul 1	KS, 48th, 1929
Gressel, Alfred		K, 63rd Ill. Inf. I, 66th Ill. Vet. Inf.	57		1890	KS, 10th, 1891
Grest, John		I, 28th Wis.	335		1896 Nov 12	KS, 16th, 1897
Grest, Oliver E.		B, 104th Ill.	47		1919 Oct 21	KS, 39th, 1920
Gretsinger, N.B.	Pvt.	A, 1st Miss. Marine	31		1919 Aug 21	IA, 46th, 1920
Gretten, M.	Pvt.	F, 37th Ill. Inf.	89		1908 May 4	IA, 35th, 1909
Greubner, Fred	Pvt.	D, 8th Ill. Cav.	236		1926 Oct 17	IA, 53rd, 1927
Grewell, Brinton T.	Pvt.	G, 35th Mo. Inf.	249		1928 Sep 25	IA, 55th, 1929
Grewell, Ezekiel		B, 51st Ohio	453		1908 Aug 3	KS, 28th, 1909
Grey, G.A.	Capt.	H, 20th Iowa Inf.	206		1904 Feb 6	IA, 31st, 1905
Grey, S.P.		H, 40th Iowa	51		1908 Oct 17	KS, 28th, 1909
Gribble, E.M.		E, 6th West Va.	166		1905 May 4	KS, 25th, 1906
Grice, A.J.		F, 27th Ohio	293		1913 Jan 31	KS, 33rd, 1914
Grice, D.G.		E, 39th Ill. Inf.	80		1892 Nov 9	NE, 17th, 1893
Grice, George		G, 128th Ill. Inf.	71		1925 Oct 25	KS, 45th, 1926
Grice, H.R.		G, 2nd Kans. Cav.	240		1917 Aug 23	KS, 37th, 1918
Grice, Thomas		E, 21st Ill.	17		1916 Jun 18	KS, 36th, 1917
Gridley, C.B.	Sergt.	D, 9th Iowa Inf.	130		1928 Jan 1	IA, 55th, 1929
Grieg, George		E, 2nd N.Y. Art.	13		1931 Aug 7	NE, 56th, 1932
Grier, David M.	Pvt.	H, 30th Iowa Inf.	40		1914 Oct 13	IA, 41st, 1915
Grier, J.S.		G, 16th Ohio Inf. (died of enlargement of liver & stricture)	20		1894 Jan 4	NE, 19th, 1895
Grier, P.E.	1st Lieut.	F, 23rd Iowa	56		1903 Feb 7	IA, 30th, 1904
Griest, Wm. P.		I, 200th Penn.	152		1885	KS, 5th, 1886
Griffeth, Wm. F.		G, 35th Iowa Inf. (died of pneumonia)	36	62	1895 Dec 24	NE, 20th, 1896
Griffin, A.A.		B, 7th Kans. Cav.	225		1921 Apr 12	KS, 41st, 1922
Griffin, A.B.		I, 100th U.S.	88		1905 Feb 26	KS, 25th, 1906
Griffin, C.A.		G, 85th Penn.	129		1937	KS, 57th, 1938
Griffin, C.L.		I, 7th Iowa Inf.	147		1914 Apr 21	KS, 34th, 1915
Griffin, Calvin W.		K, 17th Ill.	129		1921 Jun 17	KS, 41st, 1922
Griffin, E.J.		C, 74th Ill.	7		1906 May 14	KS, 26th, 1907
Griffin, E.P.		G, 8th Wis. Inf.	7		1926 Feb 19	NE, 51st, 1927
Griffin, Elias J.		E, 123rd Ill.	[18?]		1909 Oct 6	KS, 29th, 1910
Griffin, John	Pvt.	D, 65th N.Y. Inf.	1		1913 Nov 9	IA, 40th, 1914
Griffin, John B.	Pvt.	E, 20th Conn. Inf.	206		1915 Oct 21	IA, 42nd, 1916
Griffin, M.			98		1913	KS, 33rd, 1914
Griffin, M.E.	2nd Sergt.	F, 21st Iowa Inf.	124		1925 Oct 14	IA, 52nd, 1926
Griffin, O.C.	Pvt.	E, 171st Ohio Inf.	98		1929 Mar 15	IA, 56th, 1930
Griffin, Robert		H, 36th N.Y.	8		1930 Feb 16	KS, 50th, 1931
Griffin, S.F.	Pvt.	D, 31st Iowa Inf.	238		1907 Jan 3	IA, 33rd, 1907
Griffin, W.C.		I, 11th Ill.	264		1914 Jan 19	KS, 33rd, 1914
Griffin, W.H.		A, 11th West Va.	85		1927 Oct 5	KS, 47th, 1928
Griffin, W.J.		Navy	298		1888	KS, 8th, 1889
Griffin, W.T.		L, 15th Kans.	12		1919 Jun 13	KS, 39th, 1920
Griffin, William		K, 129th Ill.	47		1911 May 29	KS, 31st, 1912
Griffin, Wm.			7		1885 Apr 19	NE, 10th, 1886

Name	Rank	Company, Regiment or Ship	Post*	Age	Death Date†	Journal
Griffin, Wm.		B, 23rd Wis. Inf. (died of old age)	313	78	1901 Jun	NE, 26th, 1902
Griffis, W.B.	Pvt.	D, 36th Iowa	40		1921 Dec 15	IA, 48th, 1922
Griffith, A.H.		D, 21st Mo.	57		1919 Oct 15	KS, 39th, 1920
Griffith, A.K.		A, 209th Penn. Inf. (cause of death: heart)	25	59	1903 Dec 25	NE, 28th, 1904
Griffith, A.P.	Pvt.	I, 13th Iowa Inf.	30		1915 Nov 14	IA, 42nd, 1916
Griffith, Amos	Pvt.	A, 122nd Penn. Inf.	139	80	1898 Jan 15	IA, 24th, 1898
Griffith, B.B.	Pvt.	B, 98th Ohio	197		1901 Jan 4	IA, 28th, 1902
Griffith, B.B., see Guffith, B.B.						
Griffith, B.F.		D, 1st Iowa Cav.	7		1926 May 19	NE, 51st, 1927
Griffith, Chas. W.	Corp.	G, 4th Ind. Inf.	12		1914 Oct 26	IA, 41st, 1915
Griffith, D.G.	Sergt.	B, 2nd N.Y. Art.	184		1910 Aug 27	IA, 37th, 1911
Griffith, E.	Pvt.	I, 139th Ohio Inf.	7		1895 Apr 3	IA, 22nd, 1896
Griffith, E.F.	Pvt.	B, 113th Penn. Inf.	465		1916 Aug 18	IA, 43rd, 1917
Griffith, Edward		B, 46th Wis. Inf.	171		1929 Dec 25	KS, 50th, 1931
Griffith, Eli W.		F, 10th Iowa Inf. (died at National Military Home; buried at Leavenworth Home Cemetery)	7		1894 Nov 19	KS, 14th, 1895
Griffith, F.M.	Capt.	D, 2nd Iowa Cav.	7	55	1892 Jan 22	IA, 18th, 1892
Griffith, Franklin		D, 132nd Ill. (died of stroke)	36	76	1924 May 14	NE, 49th, 1925
Griffith, H.V.			7		1918 Sep 4	IA, 45th, 1919
Griffith, J.A.	Corp.	B, 44th Ind. Inf.	452		1922 Nov 21	IA, 49th, 1923
Griffith, J.M.		71st Ind. Inf.	55		1912 May 12	KS, 32nd, 1913
Griffith, J.W.		G, 32nd Ohio Vol. Inf.	1		1890	KS, 10th, 1891
Griffith, James		I, 8th N.Y. Cav.	224		2nd quarter 1884	IA, 11th, 1885
Griffith, Jas. F.	Pvt.	I, 8th N.Y. Cav.	224	41	1884 Jun 15	IA, 17th, 1891
Griffith, John	Pvt.	C, 45th —	2		1921 Feb 11	IA, 48th, 1922
Griffith, Joseph W., Dr.		D, 185th Ohio Inf.		89	1937 Sep 19	IA, 64th, 1938
Griffith, M.A.			113		1908 Oct 3	KS, 28th, 1909
Griffith, Melville	Pvt.	G, 9th Iowa Cav.	54		1922 May 8	IA, 49th, 1923
Griffith, Milo H.		C, 186th Ohio	147		1916 Apr 2	KS, 36th, 1917
Griffith, Myron C.	Pvt.	F, 13th Wis. Inf.	34		1922 Apr 7	IA, 49th, 1923
Griffith, Noah		C, 15th Ill.	51		1919 Oct 13	KS, 39th, 1920
Griffith, Simon		F, 12th N.Y. Inf. (died at Bradford)	75		1895 Sep 8	KS, 15th, 1896
Griffith, W.C.		A, 209th Penn. Inf. (cause of death: heart)	25	61	1903 Dec 3	NE, 28th, 1904
Griffith, W.P.		D, 7th Iowa	8		1918 Jan 27	KS, 38th, 1919
Griffith, William		I, 11th Kans. Inf.	68		1914 Aug 15	KS, 34th, 1915
Griffiths, H.F.	Capt.	E, 4th Iowa Inf.	12	60	1885 Jul 20	IA, 12th, 1886
Griffiths, John D.		C, 31st Wis. (former member of department)			1932 Jun	NE, 57th, 1933
Griffiths, W.L.		B, 4th Mass.	1		1898 Feb 23	KS, 18th, 1899
Griffitt, John W.		G, 174th Ohio (died of pneumonia)	188	55	1900 Apr 13	NE, 25th, 1901
Griggs, A.O.		F, 2nd Mich. (Colored)	66		1905 Feb 21	KS, 25th, 1906
Griggs, Andrew	Pvt.	F, 48th Wis.	155		1922 Jul 29	IA, 49th, 1923
Griggs, Geo. H.	Pvt.	K, 12th Vt. Inf.	147	56	1898 Aug 3	IA, 25th, 1899
Griggs, J.M.		F, 119th Ill. Inf.	250		1901 Jun 30	KS, 21st, 1902
Griggs, L.T.			35		1908	NE, 33rd, 1909
Griggs, T.V.	Pvt.	C, 21st Mo. Inf.	2	70	1899 Dec 14	IA, 26th, 1900
Griggs, William M.		B, 140th Penn. Inf.	62		1899 Sep 30	KS, 19th, 1900
Griggsby, J.W.		G, 10th Ind. Cav.	251		1929	KS, 49th, 1930
Griggsby, Robt.			54		1902 Feb 9	KS, 22nd, 1903
Grigsby, D.W.		C, 42nd Ind. (killed in Chicago)	360		1893 Oct 27	KS, 13th, 1894
Grigsby, John W.		K, 46th Ill.	44		1932 Feb 17	NE, 57th, 1933
Grigsby, L.M.	Pvt.	I, 11th Kans. Cav.	12		1929 Jul 16	IA, 56th, 1930
Grim, John		K, 6th Iowa	68		1913 May 11	KS, 33rd, 1914
Grim, P.P.		K, 11th Kans. Inf.	39		1912 Jun 30	KS, 32nd, 1913
Grimer, J.A.			23		1906 Dec 16	IA, 33rd, 1907
Grimes, D.C.	Pvt.	22nd Penn. Cav.	26		1923 Nov 3	IA, 50th, 1924
Grimes, Henry H.		K, 45th Ill.	25		1908	NE, 33rd, 1909
Grimes, J.T.		A, 12th Ill. Cav.	130		1919 Dec 18	KS, 39th, 1920
Grimes, John L.		58th[?] Ohio Inf.	25	87	1919 Feb 25	NE, 44th, 1920
Grimes, John Wesley	Pvt.	B, 148th Ind. Inf. (member of Dept. of California)	6, 302	98	1943 Mar 25	IA, 69th, 1943

*See Appendix A, B or C for roster of post names and locations.
†See Introduction for note regarding recording of death date.
218

Name	Rank	Company, Regiment or Ship	Post*	Age	Death Date†	Journal
Grimes, M.D.		K, 18th Iowa	34		1890	KS, 10th, 1891
Grimes, M.L.	Pvt.	K, 30th Ohio Inf.	292	46	1893 Oct	IA, 20th, 1894
Grimes, Reuben	Pvt.	F, 20th Iowa Inf.	110		1901 Mar 14	IA, 27th, 1901
Grimes, Washington	Pvt.	D, 45th Iowa Inf.		94	1939 Sep 19	IA, 66th, 1940
Grimes, William		D, 11th Ohio Cav.	45		1914	KS, 34th, 1915
Grimins, Henry		E, 8th Kans.	35		1905 Dec 4	KS, 25th, 1906
Grimm, Joseph	Pvt.	B, 16th Penn. Cav.	68	86	1933 Feb 25	IA, 60th, 1934
Grimshaw, Samuel		B, 52nd Ohio	46		1918 Nov 9	KS, 38th, 1919
Grimsley, Wm. R.	Pvt.	D, 24th Ky. Inf.	97	62	1892 Nov 5	IA, 19th, 1893
Grimsly, John		B, 10th Ky.	5		1927 May 10	NE, 52nd, 1928
Grimstead, B.R.		E, 3rd Iowa Cav. (at large)			1936 Dec 9	IA, 63rd, 1937
Grimstead, Charles R.			1		1925	KS, 45th, 1926
Grimstead, Thos. F.	Pvt.	K, 21st Ind. Art.	100		1900 Feb 15	IA, 27th, 1901
Grindle, E.W.		A, 77th Ohio	5		1918 Nov 2	KS, 38th, 1919
Grindle, J.H.		20th Ind. Bat.	435		1890	KS, 10th, 1891
Grinn, Jonathan		C, 83rd Ill. Inf. (died of paralysis)	47	75	1906 Jan 11	NE, 31st, 1907
Grinnell, A.		A, — N.Y. (died of old age)	55	77	1924 Mar	NE, 49th, 1925
Grinnell, Burritt J.	Corp.	B, 5th Vt. Inf.	193		1917 Apr 7	IA, 44th, 1918
Grinnell, C.H.	Pvt.	M, 14th N.Y. Hvy. Art.	440		1911 Dec 19	IA, 38th, 1912
Grinnell, Esra H.			64		1901 Aug 16	IA, 28th, 1902
Grinnell, J.L.	Surg.	34th Ind.	89		1891 Dec 16	KS, 11th, 1892
Grinstaff, M.L.		G, 2nd Mo. Cav.	42		1921 Jun 29	KS, 41st, 1922
Grinstead, E.W.	Pvt.	B, 2nd Mo.	73	74	1891 May 6	IA, 18th, 1892
Grinstead, T.F.	Pvt.	K, 21st Art.	100	69	1900 Feb 15	IA, 26th, 1900
Gripp, Jacob F.	Pvt.	H, 29th Iowa Inf.	297		1908 Jun 13	IA, 35th, 1909
Grismore, C.W.	Pvt.	G, 54th Ind. Inf.	192		1919	IA, 46th, 1920
Grissen, J.J.			71		1884	KS, 4th, 1885
Grissom, James	Pvt.	G, 152nd Ill. Inf.	491	70	1896 Jan 2	IA, 22nd, 1896
Grissom, Morris		B, 130th Ill.	90		1893 Jan 9	KS, 13th, 1894
Grisson, E.W.		M, 13th Ill.	32		1930 Jan 25	KS, 50th, 1931
Griswall, John		K, V.R.C. (died of vericose veins)	284		1910	NE, 35th, 1911
Griswold, Asahel E.	Pvt.	C, 13th U.S. Inf.	77	50	1889 Aug 10	IA, 16th, 1890
Griswold, C.D.	Pvt.	E, 4th Iowa Cav.	321		1911 Jun 20	IA, 38th, 1912
Griswold, Hurlbut (Hurley) Edward	Pvt.	C, 118th Ill. Inf. (see also Appendix D)	6		1908 Sep 18 or 19	IA, 35th, 1909
Griswold, Roswell		M, 14th N.Y. (died of paralysis)	38	86	1911 Jan 31	NE, 36th, 1912
Griswold, W.W.	Col.	152nd Ind.	51		1893 Jun 23	KS, 13th, 1894
Groat, J.H.		F, 31st Iowa	5		1930 Oct 24	NE, 55th, 1931
Groat, James M.	Pvt.	E, 21st N.Y. Cav.	68		1912 Apr 18	IA, 39th, 1913
Groat, Thos. C.	Pvt.	B, 23rd Ky. Inf.	258		1909 Jan 10	IA, 36th, 1910
Groff, David S.		G, 197th Ohio (former member of department)			1932 Feb 1	NE, 57th, 1933
Grogan, Isom C.		B, 1st Nev. Cav. (died of Bright's disease)	129	50	1895 Jan 9	NE, 20th, 1896
Grogger, Paul		F, 2nd E. Tenn.	46		1921 Mar 20	KS, 41st, 1922
Groin, D.L.		B, 144th Ind.	378		1922 Aug 27	KS, 42nd, 1923
Gronan, W. Otto	Lieut.	C, 45th N.Y. Inf.	1		1916 Jul 26	IA, 43rd, 1917
Groner, George	Pvt.	4th Wis. Bat.	436		1915 Mar 10	IA, 42nd, 1916
Groom, Charles C.		4th Ill.	165	75	1910 Oct 1	NE, 35th, 1911
Groom, J.W.		M, 11th Ill.	85		1928 May 18	KS, 48th, 1929
Groom, Wm.		E, 50th Ill.	5		1937 Jan 26	KS, 57th, 1938
Groomes, Elias		G, 194th Ohio	308		1911 Dec 17	KS, 31st, 1912
Groomes, W.N.		H, 80th Ill.	38		1924 Feb 22	KS, 44th, 1925
Grooms, T.C.		B, 6th Ohio (died in Osage, I.T.)	99		1892 Jul 9	KS, 12th, 1893
Groover, Isaac		D, 146th Ill.	117		1913 Oct 14	KS, 33rd, 1914
Grooves, D.	Musician	K, 9th Iowa Cav.	7		1907 Apr 19	IA, 34th, 1908
Gropes, Samuel	Pvt.	K, 21st Iowa Inf.	451	53	1891 Dec 26	IA, 19th, 1893
Grosch, Sam'l F.		G, 35th Ohio Inf.	1		1902 Oct 6	KS, 22nd, 1903
Groscup, David	Sergt.	C, 42nd Ohio	55		1907 Dec 28	IA, 34th, 1908
Groscup, Samuel	Pvt.	D, 176th Ohio Inf.	1		1899	NE, 24th, 1900
Grosenbaugh, A.	Pvt.	F, 126th Ohio Inf.	236		1926 Nov 21	IA, 53rd, 1927
Gross, C.H.	Pvt.	D, 9th Iowa Cav.	7		1929 Jul 23	IA, 56th, 1930
Gross, Edward B.			65		1918 Nov 24	KS, 38th, 1919

Name	Rank	Company, Regiment or Ship	Post*	Age	Death Date†	Journal
Gross, M.D.			45		1924 Dec 29	IA, 51st, 1925
Gross, Wendall		A, 127th Penn.	265		1926 Apr 28	NE, 51st, 1927
Grossman, Max.		5th N.Y. Inf.	18		1901 Dec 25	KS, 21st, 1902
Grossman, W.M.		A, 3rd Ill. Cav.	290		1889	KS, 9th, 1890
Grosvenor, Gordon		E, 5th Kans. State Militia	12		1914 Mar 13	KS, 34th, 1915
Grosvenor, R.L.			94		1899	IA, 26th, 1900
Grotowold, Oto	Pvt.		5		1929 May 3	IA, 56th, 1930
Groucek, Robert		F, 152nd Ind. (died of paralysis)	174	73	1913 Jan 1	NE, 37th, 1913
Grove, Benovil	Saddler	K, 9th Iowa Cav.	333	76	1900 Feb 19	IA, 26th, 1900
Grove, Hans A.	Pvt. Pvt.	A, 16th U.S. Inf. D, 3rd Iowa Inf.	78		1919 Nov 7	IA, 46th, 1920
Grove, Henry C.		G, 191st Ohio	129		1931 Nov 29	KS, 51st, 1932
Grove, Henry C.		G, 191st Ohio	129		1931 Nov 29	KS, 52nd, 1933
Grove, Isaac	Pvt.	I, 140th Ill.	242		1914 Jul 11	IA, 41st, 1915
Grove, James E.		G, 147th Ill.	85		1916 Sep 12	KS, 36th, 1917
Grovenberg, A.		B, 22nd Ill.	76		1914 Feb 15	KS, 34th, 1915
Grover, A.F.		E, 1st Bat.	5		1910 Dec 4	KS, 30th, 1911
Grover, A.H.	Pvt.	I, 31st Iowa Inf.	181		1906 May 12	IA, 33rd, 1907
Grover, Benjamin Harry		H, 116th N.Y. Inf.	143	93	1937 Jul 19	IA, 64th, 1938
Grover, Edward L.	Pvt.	E, 27th Wis. Inf.	97	51	1897 Jul 27	IA, 24th, 1898
Grover, H.H.		I, 25th Maine	85		1921 Oct 12	KS, 41st, 1922
Groves, Andrew H.	Pvt.	G, 12th Iowa Inf.	168		1908 Jun 17	IA, 35th, 1909
Groves, C.W.		L, 118th Ind.	1		1908 Oct 16	KS, 28th, 1909
Groves, Daniel C.			265		1918 May 13	KS, 38th, 1919
Groves, Geo. W.		K, 193rd Ind.	142		1893 Nov 5	KS, 13th, 1894
Groves, H.J.	Pvt.		22		1927 Feb 11	IA, 54th, 1928
Groves, John Harris		C, 7th Iowa Inf.		89	1937 Feb 27	IA, 64th, 1938
Groves, R.J.		D, 13th Kans.	93		1915 Jul 17	KS, 35th, 1916
Grow, Allen D.		D, 10th Wis. Inf. (at large)		94 & 7 mos.	1935 Dec 16	IA, 62nd, 1936
Grubb, Allen		E, 100th Ind.	244		1916 Mar 13	KS, 36th, 1917
Grubb, J.L.	Corp.	C, 5th Iowa Inf.	153		1907 Apr 10	IA, 34th, 1908
Grubb, Preston		E, 50th Wis.	250		1890	KS, 10th, 1891
Grubb, W.H.		E, 30th Ohio	50		1908 Dec 31	KS, 28th, 1909
Grubb, W.M.		B, 9th West Va.	134		1916 Jan	KS, 36th, 1917
Grubbs, John		G, 4th Ky. Inf. A, 30th Ky. Inf.	22		1928 Dec	IA, 55th, 1929
Grubbs, John W.		F, 21st Ind. Hvy. Art.	37		1919 Nov 1	KS, 39th, 1920
Gruber, Geo. W.			55		1926 Feb 27	KS, 46th, 1927
Gruber, William D.		E, 88th Ill.	57		1925 Apr 7	KS, 45th, 1926
Gruener, M.			12		1923 Mar 2	IA, 50th, 1924
Gruger, Francis R.	Hosp. Stew.	United States	69		1899 Feb 23	KS, 19th, 1900
Grumerman, John	Pvt.	G, 15th Mo. Inf.	78		1915 May 28	IA, 42nd, 1916
Grun, M.		A, 116th Ill.	498		1912 Aug 1	KS, 33rd, 1914
Grunan, P.		Penn. Marines (died of heart failure)	134	75	1920 Apr 19	NE, 45th, 1921
Grund, H.P.		K, 33rd Ill.	49		1922 May 22	KS, 42nd, 1923
Grupe, Durbin	Pvt.	G, 25th Iowa Inf.	1		1933 Feb 15	IA, 60th, 1934
Gruver, Isaac, see Groover, Isaac						
Gruwell, Daniel			216		1922	NE, 47th, 1923
Guaion, Joseph			108		1899	IA, 26th, 1900
Guard, Thos. B.		A, 9th N.Y. Cav.	1		1902 Jun 25	KS, 22nd, 1903
Gubbins, J.	Sergt.	D, 26th Iowa	92		1921 Mar 3	IA, 48th, 1922
Guches, Geo.	Pvt.	F, 6th Iowa Inf.	173		1906	IA, 33rd, 1907
Gudgel, Jacob		A, 58th Ind.	88		1905 Nov 7	KS, 25th, 1906
Gudgill, J.D.	Pvt.	F, 3rd Iowa Cav.	19	55	1888 Mar 26	IA, 15th, 1889
Gue, F.A.		died of old age	47	75	1920 Jun 3	NE, 45th, 1921
Gue, Peter L.		G, 86th Ind. (location: Tecumseh)			1927	NE, 52nd, 1928
Gueller, John		I, 81st Ill.	14		1893 Nov 26	KS, 13th, 1894
Guenther, Chas. W.	Pvt.	A, 86th Ohio	156		1907 Dec 3	IA, 34th, 1908
Guenther, Theadore		D, 41st N.Y. Inf.	456		1890	KS, 10th, 1891
Guerney, G.A.	Pvt.	I, 26th Iowa Inf.	427	50	1893 Apr 5	IA, 20th, 1894

Name	Rank	Company, Regiment or Ship	Post*	Age	Death Date†	Journal
Guernsey, A.W.	Lieut.	B, 16th Penn. Cav.	24		1911 Mar 29	IA, 38th, 1912
Guernsey, Moses H.	Pvt.	A, 23rd Wis. Inf.	419	46	1891 Nov 21	IA, 18th, 1892
Guesnier, Francis		G, 41st Wis. Inf.	90		1934 Jul 10	KS, 54th, 1935
Guess, John		E, 14th Ind.	69		1925[1924?] Sep 28	KS, 44th, 1925
Guest, J.A.		N.Y. Inf.	5		1906 Nov 11	IA, 33rd, 1907
Guest, T.H.		G, 116th Ind. H, 150th Ind.	74		1914 Feb 26	KS, 34th, 1915
Guesz, John		E, 14th Ind.	69		1923 Sep 28	KS, 46th, 1927
Guffey, John W.		K, 53rd Ill. Inf.	250		1914 Mar 21	KS, 34th, 1915
Guffin, A.Y.		F, 2nd N.Y. Cav.	12		1906 Dec 25	KS, 26th, 1907
Guffith, B.B.	Pvt.	B, 40th Iowa	127		1921 Nov 8	IA, 48th, 1922
Guffy, J.T.		D, 69th Ill.	34		1917	KS, 37th, 1918
Guffy, Joseph		A, 57th Ohio	92		1920 Feb 23	KS, 40th, 1921
Guge, W.H.		D, 53rd Ind. Inf.	31		1925 Aug 24	IA, 52nd, 1926
Guilbert, E.A.	Capt.	A, 46th Iowa Inf.	78		1900 Mar 4	IA, 27th, 1901
Guild, Edward	Corp.	I, 22nd Wis. Inf.	236		1900 May	IA, 27th, 1901
Guile, T.M.	Pvt.	G, 54th Ill. Inf.	39		1897 May 17	IA, 24th, 1898
Guilford, George	Sergt.	C, 10th Iowa Inf.	83		1916 Mar 23	IA, 43rd, 1917
Guilford, John	Pvt.	C, 2nd Wis.	392		1904 Aug 30	IA, 31st, 1905
Guilliams, B.C.	Pvt.	F, 4th Iowa Inf.	158		1917 Jun 12	IA, 44th, 1918
Guinn, Alfred H.	Pvt.	E, 2nd Neb. Cav.	210		1902 Nov 22	IA, 29th, 1903
Guinn, Peter	Pvt.	D, 12th Ill. Cav.	168		1915 May 12	IA, 42nd, 1916
Guinn, R.F.		G, 61st Ind.	65		1927 Dec 18	KS, 47th, 1928
Guinn, R.J.F.	Pvt.	K, 180th Ohio Inf.	86	66	1893 Dec 8	IA, 20th, 1894
Guinnan, B.		K, 93rd Ohio Inf. (killed by railroad accident)	380		1888	KS, 8th, 1889
Guinor, C.A.	Pvt. & Corp.	B, 129th Ill. Inf. (cause of death: poisoned)	40	53	1887 Dec 4	NE, 12th, 1888
Guist, W.H.			164		1921 Aug 17	IA, 48th, 1922
Guittar, Theo.		2nd Iowa Bat.	29		1920 Apr 22	IA, 46th, 1920
Gulfard, A.H.	Pvt.	3rd Iowa Battery	78		1927 Jan 12	IA, 54th, 1928
Gulick, H.S.	Sergt.	C, 26th Iowa Inf.	296		1896 May 12	IA, 23rd, 1897
Gulick, John	Pvt.	K, 16th Iowa Inf.	347		1900 May 22	IA, 27th, 1901
Gullranson, H.	Pvt.	D, 3rd Iowa Inf.	168	51	1888 Aug 6	IA, 15th, 1889
Gumerman, J.J.		B, 111th Ill.	59		1896 Feb 23	KS, 16th, 1897
Gump, Fred	Pvt.	D, 17th West Va.	186		1905 Jul 20	IA, 32nd, 1906
Gump, I.	Pvt.	D, 17th Inf.	186		1921 Mar 19	IA, 48th, 1922
Gunder, Jacob	Pvt.	E, 34th Ill. Vols.	89		1914 Aug 22	IA, 41st, 1915
Gunder, Jos.	Pvt.	G, 1st Penn. Cav.	7	58	1891 Jul 27	IA, 18th, 1892
Gunn, —			464		1917	KS, 37th, 1918
Gunney, A.L.		2nd N.Y. Cav.	25		1925 Apr 25	KS, 45th, 1926
Gunning, J.T.	Corp.	A, 15th Iowa Inf.	235	68	1896 Sep 27	IA, 23rd, 1897
Gunselman, V.	Pvt.		122		1913 Jun 13	IA, 40th, 1914
Gunter, M.G.	Pvt.		186		1927	IA, 54th, 1928
Gunther, J.W.	Sergt.	I, Mo. Inf.	153		1905 Sep 20	IA, 32nd, 1906
Guptil, W.B.		I, 11th Wis. Inf. (died at Leavenworth)	117		1895 Aug 31	KS, 15th, 1896
Gupton, Solomon	Pvt.	I, 12th U.S. Colored Inf.	1		1906 May 21	KS, 26th, 1907
Gurberson, S.S.	Pvt.	A, 39th Iowa Inf.	55		1908 Aug 24	IA, 35th, 1909
Gurdy, Henry H.	Pvt.	B, 49th Wis. Inf.	375		1900 Mar 10	IA, 27th, 1901
Gurney, A.H.	Sergt.	F, 5th Wis. Inf.	66		1910 Nov 19	IA, 37th, 1911
Gurnsey, Phineas B.		C, 17th Ill. Cav.	265		1935 Jan 15	NE, 60th, 1936
Gurtler, Fred H.		B, 2nd Md. Mt. Inf.	250		1916 Jul 21	KS, 36th, 1917
Gurtner, Henry R.	Pvt.	A, 35th Iowa Inf.	231	101	1935 Feb 14	IA, 65th, 1939
Gushard, Isaac	Pvt.	E, 55th Ill. Inf.	68		1930 Nov 23	IA, 57th, 1931
Gushard, Samuel	Pvt.	H, 17th Ill. Cav.	68		1928 Feb 28	IA, 55th, 1929
Gustue, John		I, 112th Ill. (died of old age)	151	84	1910 Dec 29	NE, 35th, 1911
Gutchers, I.J.		H, 9th Ill. (died of cancer)	22	74	1917 Aug 25	NE, 42nd, 1918
Gutherie, P.J.	Corp.	B, 92nd Ill. Inf.	234		1911 Mar 14	IA, 38th, 1912
Guthrie, A.W.			7		1909 Mar 24	IA, 36th, 1910
Guthrie, F.H.			227		1921 Jul 15	NE, 47th, 1923
Guthrie, Fred	Pvt.	B, 13th Iowa Inf.	52		1913 Jan 22	IA, 40th, 1914
Guthrie, J.H.	Pvt.	H, 44th Iowa Inf.	252	44	1889 Feb 27	IA, 16th, 1890
Guthrie, J.M.	Pvt.	D, 5th Iowa Cav.	206		1911 Aug 26	IA, 38th, 1912

*See Appendix A, B or C for roster of post names and locations.
†See Introduction for note regarding recording of death date.
221

Name	Rank	Company, Regiment or Ship	Post*	Age	Death Date†	Journal
Guthrie, J.W.	Surg.	20th Ohio Inf.	10		1911 Sep 27	IA, 38th, 1912
Guthrie, John	Capt.	103rd Ill. Inf.	108		1918 Feb 20	IA, 45th, 1919
Guthrie, John		D, 46th Ind. Inf. (see also Appendix D)	71		1906 Jul 1	KS, 26th, 1907
Guthrie, Lewis		K, 44th Ind.	301		1926 May 14	KS, 46th, 1927
Guthrie, St. Clair		A, 17th Conn.	7		1920 Sep 3	KS, 40th, 1921
Guthrie, Thos. E.			452		1916 May 9	IA, 43rd, 1917
Guthrie, W.S.	Pvt.	L, 1st Iowa Cav.	235		1929 Jun	IA, 56th, 1930
Guthrie, Wm.	Pvt.	F, 40th Iowa Inf.	452		1900 Apr 8	IA, 27th, 1901
Guthrie, Wm. D.	Pvt.	C, 15th Ind. Inf.	170	49	1892-1893	IA, 19th, 1893
Guttery, Charles		D, 140th Penn.	106		1911 Aug 14	KS, 31st, 1912
Gutzmer, D.		K, — N.Y. Cav.	66		1892 Aug 30	NE, 17th, 1893
Gutzy, Sam'l		E, 28th Iowa Inf. (died of ulcer)	296	63	1901 Jan	NE, 26th, 1902
Guy, Harrison		F, 99th Ohio	85		1897 Jul 5	KS, 17th, 1898
Guy, J.B.	Pvt.	C, 34th —	275		1914 Aug	IA, 41st, 1915
Guy, James		K, 136th Ill.	18		1902 Aug 16	KS, 22nd, 1903
Guy, James W.	Pvt.	E, 12th Kans. Inf.	400		1925 May 29	IA, 52nd, 1926
Guy, John L.		E, 18th Ohio Inf.	1		1899 Oct 21	KS, 19th, 1900
Guy, Moss		I, 4th Ind. Cav.	11		1887 Apr 12	KS, 7th, 1888
Guy, W.H.		E, 32nd Ind. Inf.	289		1902 Oct	KS, 22nd, 1903
Guyer, J.W.		H, 17th Wis.	69		1916 Oct 8	KS, 36th, 1917
Gwin, James M.		D, 50th Ind.	23		1917 Jun 20	KS, 37th, 1918
Gwynn, W.T.		I, 93rd N.Y.	129		1906 Jul 16	KS, 26th, 1907
Gylois, James		C, 105th Penn. Inf. (died of general breakdown)	52	70	1917 May	NE, 42nd, 1918
Haag, Thos. G.	Pvt.	B, 26th Ill. Inf.	57		1908 Apr	IA, 35th, 1909
Haak, F.		B, 8th Iowa Inf.	1		1915 Jan 11	IA, 42nd, 1916
Haakenson, A.	Pvt.	K, 11th Wis. Inf.	22		1917 May 31	IA, 44th, 1918
Haakinson, Ed.	Pvt.	C, 1st Wis. Inf.	22		1920 Oct 4	IA, 47th, 1921
Haaman, Franklin		E, 4th Va.	408		1893 Jul 15	KS, 13th, 1894
Haas, Adam		H, 2nd Ohio Inf.	17		1914 Sep 2	KS, 34th, 1915
Haas, George		G, 2nd Kans.	40		1905 Mar 13	KS, 25th, 1906
Haas, Jacob	Corp.	D, 6th Iowa Cav.	168		1901 Apr 17	IA, 27th, 1901
Haas, Louis		B, 12th Kans. Inf.	12		1908 Sep 18	KS, 28th, 1909
Haas, Wm.		B, 120th Ill.	19		1909 Feb 27	KS, 29th, 1910
Habee, Abert		I, 1st N.J.	28		1904 May 14	KS, 24th, 1905
Haber, Chas.	Pvt.	E, 11th Penn. Inf.	88		1905 Dec 4	IA, 32nd, 1906
Habler, J.E.		U.S. Rose Chaplain	244		1905 Apr 20	KS, 25th, 1906
Hackenbush, H.C.F.			6		1912 Nov 12	KS, 32nd, 1913
Hacker, A.B.		E, 93rd Ind.	81		1921 Jan 8	KS, 41st, 1922
Hacker, I.G.		C, 38th Mass.	100		1925 Aug 14	KS, 45th, 1926
Hacker, W.G.		B, 15th West Va. Inf.	25		1911 Apr 14	KS, 31st, 1912
Hackett, Henry		K, 110th Ohio	68		1920 Jan 27	KS, 40th, 1921
Hackett, Henry L.	Pvt.	B, 2nd Minn. Inf.	295		1889 Jul 25	IA, 16th, 1890
Hackett, Roland		C, 118th Ind. Inf.	1		1929 Mar 18	KS, 49th, 1930
Hackett, Timothy		A, Battalion, Bourbon County, Kans.	32		1908[1909?] Jul 28	KS, 29th, 1910
Hackett, Wm. G.		K, 1st Neb.	117		1890	KS, 10th, 1891
Hackler, James F.		A, 2nd Mo. State Militia	142		1904 Sep	KS, 24th, 1905
Hackley, Thomas	Pvt.	F, 79th U.S. Colored Inf.	40		1918 Mar 1	IA, 45th, 1919
Hackney, A.J.		E, 7th Ill.	57		1935 Jan 18	KS, 55th, 1936
Hackney, W.P.		H, 7th Ill.	85		1926 Jul 26	KS, 46th, 1927
Hackstedt, Wm.		B, 50th Ill.	55		1917 Mar 1	KS, 37th, 1918
Hackthorn, G.H.	Pvt.	K, —	14		1925	IA, 52nd, 1926
Hackthorn, H.J.	Pvt.	E, 3rd Iowa Inf.	14	79	1898 Apr 5	IA, 24th, 1898
Hacles, Geo.			79		1922 Dec 10	KS, 42nd, 1923
Hadden, John C.		I, 27th Ind. Vol. Inf. (died of heart failure)	115	70	1911 Jan 20	NE, 36th, 1912
Hadden, Levi M.		H, 10th Kans.	129		1905 Jul 11	KS, 25th, 1906
Hadden, M.			321		1922 Aug	KS, 42nd, 1923
Hadens, Isaac	Pvt.		156		1920	IA, 47th, 1921
Hadley, Addison		D, 101st Ind.	142		1897 Jul 9	KS, 17th, 1898
Hadley, Allen		K, 149th Ind.	44		1923 Jan 7	KS, 43rd, 1924
Hadley, E.D.			12		1923 May 27	IA, 50th, 1924
Hadley, Geo. W.	Pvt.	C, 41st Wis.	98		1919	IA, 46th, 1920

*See Appendix A, B or C for roster of post names and locations.
†See Introduction for note regarding recording of death date.

Name	Rank	Company, Regiment or Ship	Post*	Age	Death Date†	Journal
Hadley, H.B.		I, 30th Maine Inf. (died of old age)	4	74	1920 Sep 26	NE, 45th, 1921
Hadley, L.P.		36th Ind.	17		1921 Jun 11	KS, 41st, 1922
Hadley, Robert		A, 13th Ill.	22		1926	KS, 46th, 1927
Hadley, S.J.		7th Iowa	435		1913 Apr 24	KS, 33rd, 1914
Hadley, W.T.			79		1905 Jun 22	KS, 25th, 1906
Hadley, Wm. H.		F, 175th Ohio	7		1904 Nov 13	KS, 24th, 1905
Hadlock, Ewins S.		E, 25th Mich.	238		1906 Feb 22	KS, 26th, 1907
Haenss, B.D.	Pvt.	D, 20th N.Y. Inf.	206		1926 Oct 27	IA, 53rd, 1927
Hafer, Geo. W.	Pvt.	E, 36th Wis. Inf.	68		1910 Apr 21	IA, 37th, 1911
Hafferd, Geo.		B, 17th Ind. Inf.	19		1886	KS, 6th, 1887
Haffey, P.A.	Pvt.	E, 142nd Ill.	147		1923 Dec 4	IA, 50th, 1924
Hagadorn, M.K.		G, 97th Penn.	98		1932	NE, 57th, 1933
Hagan, C.J., M.D.	Asst. Surg.	46th Ohio	2		1903 Nov 30	IA, 30th, 1904
Hagan, Jasper	Sergt.	G, 4th Iowa Inf.	96	57	1892 Feb 16	IA, 18th, 1892
Hagan, John		I, 4th N.Y. Cav.	252		1908 Apr 14	KS, 28th, 1909
Hagan, Joseph	Pvt.	G, 47th Iowa	7		1922 Sep 8	IA, 49th, 1923
Hagat, Jesse			338		1899	IA, 26th, 1900
Hageman, T.C.		A, 40th N.Y.	207		1930 Aug 6	NE, 55th, 1931
Hageman, Van			3		1910	NE, 35th, 1911
Hagen, Jas.	Pvt.	K, 40th Iowa Inf.	235		1908 Jul 10	IA, 35th, 1909
Hagenbaugh, Eli T.	Pvt.	B, 25th Iowa Inf.	8		1917 Mar 10	IA, 44th, 1918
Hager, Horace E.		B, 9th Iowa	7		1913 Oct 15	KS, 33rd, 1914
Hager, Jas. W.	Pvt.	I, 29th Iowa Inf.	359		1907 Nov 27	IA, 34th, 1908
Hager, O.P.		K, 6th Penn. (died of old age)	32	84	1915 Jul 20	NE, 40th, 1916
Hager, Otto C.		D, 45th Ill.	93		1911 May 30	KS, 31st, 1912
Hagerman, James		G, 13th Ill. Cav.	39		1917 May 15	KS, 37th, 1918
Hagermaster, Henry	Pvt.	H, 38th Ill. Inf.	271		1927 Nov 8	IA, 54th, 1928
Hagerty, John			25		1910 Jan 19	NE, 35th, 1911
Haggard, C.G.		I, 3rd Cav.	32		1920	NE, 45th, 1921
Haggard, J.R.		C, 129th Ill. (died of heart failure)	25	74	1915 Jul 14	NE, 40th, 1916
Haggard, Wm. H.		B, 1st Minn. Mt. Reg.	110	64	1905 Oct 25	NE, 30th, 1906
Haggerty, D.W.	Pvt.	F, 10th Ill. Inf.	2		1917 Jul 10	IA, 44th, 1918
Haggerty, James	Pvt.	E, 90th Ill. Inf.	147		1915 May 14	IA, 42nd, 1916
Hagie, Adam	Pvt.	D, 4th Penn. Cav.	111	87	1894 Apr 16	IA, 21st, 1895
Hagity, James	Pvt.		104		1920	IA, 47th, 1921
Hagler, Isaac			127		1922 Dec 31	KS, 42nd, 1923
Hagler, V.W.		I, 30th Ill. Inf. (died of consumption)	107		1893 Jan 27	NE, 18th, 1894
Hagler, W.J.		K, 9th Ill. Inf.	127		1901 Dec 26	KS, 21st, 1902
Hagne, Geo. M.		G, 2nd N.H. Inf.	262	62	1905 Dec 31	NE, 30th, 1906
Hagner, D.H.		A, 132nd Ill.	23		1893	KS, 13th, 1894
Hagsdale, G.H.	Pvt.	C, 13th Iowa Inf.	12		1924 Mar 13	IA, 51st, 1925
Hague, D.T.	Pvt.		96		1920 Feb 8	IA, 47th, 1921
Hague, J.		B, 88th Ohio Inf.	20		1887 Dec 28	KS, 7th, 1888
Hague, Lewis C.	Pvt.	C, 43rd Mo. Inf.	56		1924 Dec	IA, 51st, 1925
Hahen, John		G, 1st Neb. Cav. (died of kick by horse)	55	76	1905 Jul 5	NE, 30th, 1906
Hahmon, Martain		C, 21st Iowa	53		1909 Feb 9	KS, 29th, 1910
Hahn, Ashford		H, 43rd Ind. (died at Lawrence)	12		1895 Dec	KS, 15th, 1896
Hahn, Chas.		E, 61st Ohio	39		1919 Dec 8	KS, 39th, 1920
Hahn, Geo.		K, 8th Iowa	10		1926 Oct 15	NE, 51st, 1927
Hahn, Jeremiah	Pvt.	A, 35th Penn. Inf.	1		1927 Jul 9	IA, 54th, 1928
Hahn, Saml. C.	Pvt.	A, 45th Iowa Inf.	18		1925 Sep 25	IA, 52nd, 1926
Hahnen, Jacob F.	Corp.	D, 2nd Iowa Cav.	12	53	1892 Dec 15	IA, 19th, 1893
Haid, Stephen		E, 76th Germany	38		1908[1909?] Dec 22	KS, 29th, 1910
Haigh, J.D.		H, 89th Ill. Inf.	18		1917 Apr 4	KS, 37th, 1918
Haigh, Uriah		I, 13th Kans.	167		1913 May 8	KS, 33rd, 1914
Haigh, William		H, 21st Iowa Inf.	190		1918 Jul 12	IA, 45th, 1919
Haight, George	Pvt.		25	92 & 9 mos.	1931 Feb 1	IA, 58th, 1932
Haight, N.A.			85		1893 Jul 3	KS, 13th, 1894
Haigler, John Wesley	Pvt.	K, 30th Iowa Inf.	167	96	1939 Dec 25	IA, 66th, 1940
Haile, Charles	Corp.	B, 9th Iowa Cav.	40		1930 May 20	IA, 57th, 1931
Haily, John H.	Pvt.	E, 58th Ill. Inf.	297		1908 Feb 5	IA, 35th, 1909

*See Appendix A, B or C for roster of post names and locations.
†See Introduction for note regarding recording of death date.

Name	Rank	Company, Regiment or Ship	Post*	Age	Death Date†	Journal
Hain, F.M.	1st Sergt.	C, 46th Iowa Inf.	26	56	1892 Dec 19	IA, 19th, 1893
Hainer, D.W.		B, 9th Ind.	55		1924 Nov 4	KS, 44th, 1925
Haines, A.W.		A, 23rd Iowa (died of heart trouble)	180	66	1904 Aug 30	NE, 29th, 1905
Haines, B.B.		G, 47th Iowa	4		1923 Aug 4	KS, 43rd, 1924
Haines, C.T.		I, 33rd Iowa	17		1926 Sep 23	KS, 46th, 1927
Haines, Geo. W.	Pvt.	H, 8th Ind. Inf.	7		1912 May 26	IA, 39th, 1913
Haines, Isaac W.	Pvt.	M, 9th Ohio Cav.	249		1918 Aug 10	IA, 45th, 1919
Haines, J.F.	Pvt.	G, 7th Iowa Cav.	10	53	1898 Apr 9	IA, 24th, 1898
Haines, J.R.		88th Ohio	366		1893 May 17	KS, 13th, 1894
Haines, Jas. M.	Pvt.	A, 97th Penn. Inf.	235		1916 Feb 20	IA, 43rd, 1917
Haines, Robert		H, 128th Ohio	1		1926 Mar 24	NE, 51st, 1927
Haines, Samuel J.			49		1883	KS, 3rd, 1884
Haines, W.S.	Pvt.	G, 51st Ind. Inf.	69	66	1891 Nov 23	IA, 18th, 1892
Haines, W.S.		K, 29th Ind. (died of pneumonia)	180	80	1922 Dec	NE, 48th, 1924
Hainlin, Frederick		C, 5th Mo. Cav.	91		1902 Mar 26	KS, 22nd, 1903
Hainline, A.J.	Pvt.	D, 124th Ill. Inf.	234		1908 Jan 8	IA, 35th, 1909
Hainline, N.G.		I, 11th Ill. Cav.	244		1919 May 9	KS, 39th, 1920
Hains, William		E, 19th Mich. Inf.	55		1891 Aug 6	KS, 11th, 1892
Hair, John		H, 126th Penn. (died of dropsy)	124	77	1897 Feb 27	NE, 22nd, 1898
Hair, L.W.		F, 49th N.Y.	49		1922 Aug 25	KS, 42nd, 1923
Hair, W.O.		E, 121st Ohio Inf.	16		1925 Apr 5	KS, 45th, 1926
Haise, G.A.	Asst. Surg.	1st U.S.	164		1911 Dec 11	KS, 31st, 1912
Hake, Levi G.		G, 200th Penn.	251		1931 Sep 27	KS, 52nd, 1933
Hakeman, Geo.	Pvt.	C, 24th Iowa Inf.	339		1913 Feb 15	IA, 39th, 1913
Halbert, Esor		H, 33rd Ind.	147		1911 Oct 7	KS, 31st, 1912
Halbert, T.H.			113		1925 Mar 29	KS, 45th, 1926
Hale, C.D.		C, 192nd Ohio	127		1906 Oct 19	KS, 26th, 1907
Hale, David D.		H, 1st Ohio Lt. Art.	85		1919 Nov 28	KS, 39th, 1920
Hale, Elias M.	Pvt.	G, 11th Ill. Vol. Cav.	254		1901 Dec 30	IA, 28th, 1902
Hale, H.W.		T, 74th Mo.	145		1918	KS, 38th, 1919
Hale, J.S.		B, 106th Ill.	209		1888	KS, 8th, 1889
Hale, L.L.		C, 13th Wis.	47		1930	KS, 52nd, 1933
Hale, L.L.		C, 13th Wis.	47		1930	KS, 51st, 1932
Hale, M.M.		K, 35th Ohio	1		1914 Oct 17	KS, 34th, 1915
Hale, Ripley A.	Corp.	D, 21st Iowa Inf.	259	67	1893 Sep 13	IA, 20th, 1894
Hale, Wm.		F, 190th Kans.	190		1926 Jul 25	KS, 46th, 1927
Hales, Townsend P.		H, 25th Iowa Inf.	85		1916 Nov 19	KS, 36th, 1917
Haley, Dan	Pvt.	I, 17th Vt. Inf.	7	84	1932 Oct 15	IA, 59th, 1933
Halfhill, Wm.		F, 13th Ohio	66		1911 Aug 25	KS, 31st, 1912
Haliday, N.M.		F, 31st Neb Ind. Inf. (died of heart & stomach trouble)	118	64	1908 Dec 16	NE, 33rd, 1909
Hall, A.C.	Pvt.	A, 1st Ill. Art.	7		1905 Jul	IA, 32nd, 1906
Hall, A.O.	Musician	K, 32nd Iowa Inf.	30	71	1897 Oct 10	IA, 24th, 1898
Hall, Adam		B, 28th Iowa Inf. (died of heart trouble)	10	76	1906 Dec 14	NE, 31st, 1907
Hall, Alonzo		A, 8th Ill. Cav.	25		1892	NE, 17th, 1893
Hall, Beley		E, 153rd Ind.	89		1918	KS, 38th, 1919
Hall, Bird P.		B, 44th Mo. Inf. (died of heart disease)	318	66	1909 Dec 26	NE, 34th, 1910
Hall, Cyrus W.	Pvt.	A, 17th Ill. Cav.	39		1912 Oct 29	IA, 39th, 1913
Hall, D.F.	Musician	G, 27th Iowa Inf.	132		1910	IA, 37th, 1911
Hall, D.H.	Pvt.	I, 8th Wis. Inf.	48	87	1931 Jan 24	IA, 58th, 1932
Hall, D.H.	Pvt.	I, 8th Wis. Inf.	48		1931 Jan 24	IA, 57th, 1931
Hall, Daniel	Pvt.	5th or 7th Minn. Inf.	512		1910 Feb	IA, 37th, 1911
Hall, Daniel F.		C, B.B. Co., Kans.	32		1908[1909?] Sep 8	KS, 29th, 1910
Hall, E.	Pvt.	F, 36th Ill. Inf.	111		1921 May 20	IA, 48th, 1922
Hall, E.L.	Pvt.	A, 153rd Ill. Inf.	78		1917 Nov 18	IA, 44th, 1918
Hall, E.M.		D, 1st Mo. Eng.	12		1904 Aug 19	KS, 24th, 1905
Hall, E.P.		L, 4th N.M.	25		1927 May 3	KS, 47th, 1928
Hall, E.W.		A, 2nd Ill. Cav.	51		1915 Jan 12	KS, 35th, 1916
Hall, F.D.	Pvt.	D, 7th Iowa Inf.	132		1910	IA, 37th, 1911
Hall, G.H.	Pvt.	F, 3rd Wis. Inf.	416	58	1899 Jun 1	IA, 26th, 1900
Hall, G.W.	Pvt.	D, 1st Colo.	197	67	1890 Mar 11	IA, 17th, 1891
Hall, Geo. C.		I, 16th Wis. Inf. (died of pneumonia)	24	54	1896 Mar 25	NE, 21st, 1897

*See Appendix A, B or C for roster of post names and locations.
†See Introduction for note regarding recording of death date.

Name	Rank	Company, Regiment or Ship	Post*	Age	Death Date†	Journal
Hall, Geo. M.	Pvt.	K, 47th Iowa Inf.	386		1917 Mar 20	IA, 44th, 1918
Hall, Geo. R.	Capt.	E, 123rd N.Y. Inf.	8		1915 Dec 19	IA, 42nd, 1916
Hall, Geo. V.		F, 2nd Neb. Cav.	25	79	1921 Jun 18	NE, 46th, 1922
Hall, Geo. W.	Pvt.	9th Iowa Cav.	141		1923 May 30	IA, 50th, 1924
Hall, Geo. W.			7		1909 Nov 12	IA, 36th, 1910
Hall, H.O.		E, 105th Ill. Inf. (died of old age)	21	83	1919 Aug 23	NE, 44th, 1920
Hall, H.S.		43rd U.S. Colorado	12		1908 Jul 1	KS, 28th, 1909
Hall, H.W.		B, 71st Ohio Inf.	17		1914 Nov 12	KS, 34th, 1915
Hall, Harry	Corp.	F, 27th Wis.	68	70	1900 May 16	IA, 26th, 1900
Hall, Henry		C, 9th Ind.	175		1897 Oct 14	KS, 17th, 1898
Hall, I.		H, 84th Ind.	8		1897 Feb 9	KS, 17th, 1898
Hall, I.B.		I, 88th Ill.	83		1924 Sep 28	KS, 44th, 1925
Hall, Isaac W.		F, 77th Penn. (at large)	164		1924 Dec 14	KS, 46th, 1927
Hall, Isaac W.		F, 77th Penn. Inf. (at large)			1925 Dec 14	KS, 45th, 1926
Hall, J.		8th Mich. (died of Bright's disease)	92	71	1907 May 25	NE, 32nd, 1908
Hall, J.C.		K & A, 34th Iowa Inf. (died of heart disease)	228	65	1905 Nov 1	NE, 30th, 1906
Hall, J.D.	Pvt.	K, 65th Ill. Inf.	26		1916 May 1	IA, 43rd, 1917
Hall, J.D.		I, 78th Penn.	71		1905 Oct 9	KS, 25th, 1906
Hall, J.F.	Pvt.	I, 13th Iowa Inf.	305		1919 Jun 19	IA, 46th, 1920
Hall, J.G.		22nd Ind.	25		1916 Aug 16	NE, 41st, 1917
Hall, J.S.	Corp.	B, 1st Dak.	86		1921 Mar 26	IA, 48th, 1922
Hall, J.W.	Sergt.	F, 8th Iowa Cav.	398		1913 Mar 31	IA, 40th, 1914
Hall, James	Pvt.	C, 31st Ohio Inf.	100		1920 Oct 4	IA, 47th, 1921
Hall, James A.	Pvt.	I, 20th Iowa Inf.	296		1905 Jun	IA, 32nd, 1906
Hall, James L.	Pvt.	A, 78th Penn. Inf.	30		1915 Jul 12	IA, 42nd, 1916
Hall, Jas.	Pvt.	C, 2nd Iowa Cav.	94		1920 Oct 23	IA, 47th, 1921
Hall, Joel		G, 51st Ohio	447		1905 Oct 12	KS, 25th, 1906
Hall, John		2nd Iowa Cav.	144		1917 Feb 9	IA, 44th, 1918
Hall, John	Pvt.	F, 15th Iowa Inf.	56		1928 Jul 24	IA, 55th, 1929
Hall, John		H, 185th Ohio Inf.	289		1900 Jun 15	KS, 20th, 1901
Hall, John		B, 3rd Iowa Inf.	25		1899 Aug 25	KS, 19th, 1900
Hall, John, Sr.	Corp.	B, 40th Iowa Inf.	127	75	1898 Dec 12	IA, 25th, 1899
Hall, John H.	Pvt.	F, 2nd Iowa Inf.	461		1901 Jan 3	IA, 28th, 1902
Hall, John H.		C, 144th Ill. Inf.	85		1901 May 22	KS, 21st, 1902
Hall, John J.		K, 6th Ky. Cav. (died at Great Falls)	25		1895 Jul	KS, 15th, 1896
Hall, John R.	Musician	B, 13th Iowa Inf.	84		1917 Oct 23	IA, 44th, 1918
Hall, Jos. L.		H, 1st Iowa Cav.	97		1918 Nov 23	KS, 38th, 1919
Hall, Joseph		9th Ill.	174		1905 Sep 22	KS, 25th, 1906
Hall, L.M.		A, 1st Mass. Cav.	17		1928 Feb 27	KS, 48th, 1929
Hall, L.S.	Pvt.	C, 142nd Ohio Vol. Inf.	343		1901 Mar 3	IA, 28th, 1902
Hall, Lester		F, 56th N.Y.	132		1912 Jul 15	KS, 32nd, 1913
Hall, Mosley E.	Pvt.	G, 5th U.S. Art.	23		1924 Mar 24	IA, 51st, 1925
Hall, Oliver L.		H, 83rd Penn. Inf. (died at Parsons, Kans.; buried at Oakwood Cemetery)	64		1894 Jul 21	KS, 14th, 1895
Hall, R.C.	Corp.	B, 20th Iowa	235		1923 Sep 30	IA, 50th, 1924
Hall, R.S.	Pvt.	A, 26th Mich. Inf.	440	62	1899 Mar 22	IA, 25th, 1899
Hall, R.W.		Kans. State Militia	255		1904 Jul 10	KS, 24th, 1905
Hall, Richard	Pvt.	K, 9th Ohio Cav.	108		1930 Sep 30	IA, 57th, 1931
Hall, Richard M.	Pvt.	B, 66th Ohio	143		1907 Aug 6	IA, 34th, 1908
Hall, S.B.	Pvt.	E, 1st Wis. Cav.	461		1917 Feb 20	IA, 44th, 1918
Hall, S.E.		8th Iowa Cav.	448		1914 Sep	KS, 34th, 1915
Hall, S.O.		B, 17th Ill. Cav. (died of consumption)	112	51	1895 Nov 16	NE, 20th, 1896
Hall, S.R.		C, 15th Kans. Cav.	55		1920 Jun 19	KS, 40th, 1921
Hall, S.S.		F, 103rd Ohio	35		1911 Oct 16	KS, 31st, 1912
Hall, Samuel		C, 91st Ill.	100		1915 Sep 13	KS, 35th, 1916
Hall, Samuel G.		K, 65th N.Y. Vols.	3		1924 Apr 9	KS, 44th, 1925
Hall, T.J.	Pvt.	H, 101st Ohio Inf.	69		1917 Aug 6	IA, 44th, 1918
Hall, Thos. P.		10th Kans.	55		1904 Dec 22	KS, 24th, 1905
Hall, W.C.	Musician	C, 1st Iowa Cav.	360	49	1885 Oct 12	IA, 12th, 1886
Hall, W.F.	Pvt.	C, 5th Iowa Inf.	115		1923	IA, 50th, 1924
Hall, W.F.		G, 115th Ill. Inf.	8		1925 Mar 28	KS, 45th, 1926

*See Appendix A, B or C for roster of post names and locations.
†See Introduction for note regarding recording of death date.

225

Name	Rank	Company, Regiment or Ship	Post*	Age	Death Date†	Journal
Hall, William	Pvt.	E, 10th Iowa Inf.	68		1919 Jun 14	IA, 46th, 1920
Hall, William V.		D, 10th Kans. Inf.	191		1899 Oct 5	KS, 19th, 1900
Hall, Wm.	Sergt.	C, 192nd Penn. Inf.	457		1906 Nov	IA, 33rd, 1907
Hall, Wm.		1st Neb. (died of stomach trouble)	24		1908 Nov 26	NE, 33rd, 1909
Hall, Wm. C.	Musician	1st Iowa Cav.	360		[1889?]	IA, 17th, 1891
Hallaway, S.H.		E, 33rd Iowa (died of old age)	120	79	1913 Oct	NE, 38th, 1914
Halle, Wm.		K, 12th Kans. Inf.	32		1912 Nov 6	KS, 32nd, 1913
Hallenbeck, Aaron	Pvt.	A, 16th Wis.	88		1914 Aug 24	IA, 41st, 1915
Hallenbeck, Andrew	Pvt.	M, 10th N.Y. Hvy. Art.	22		1907 2nd term	IA, 34th, 1908
Haller, Samuel G.		9th Wis. Batt.	52		1931 May 6	NE, 56th, 1932
Hallett, David E.	Pvt.	H, 7th Iowa Cav.	284	89	1936 Oct 24	IA, 65th, 1939
Hallett, M.C.		H, 2nd Iowa Cav.	474		1916 Dec 9	KS, 36th, 1917
Hallett, S.M.	Pvt.	M, 1st Minn. Ref.	235		1921 Mar 31	IA, 48th, 1922
Hallett, Sam'l		F, 6th Iowa Cav. (location: Lynch)			1926	NE, 52nd, 1928
Hallett, Warren	Mate	U.S. Navy (died of paralysis)	38		1895 Jul 20	NE, 20th, 1896
Halley, B.F.	Lieut.	U.S. Inf.	92		1914 Apr 11	IA, 41st, 1915
Halley, John S.	Pvt.	H, 4th Vt. Inf.	68		1913	IA, 40th, 1914
Halley, Lewis R.		B, 122nd Ill. Inf.	100		1914 Jul 2	KS, 34th, 1915
Hallick, A.M.	Pvt.	K, 65th Ill. Inf.	80		1917 Dec 26	IA, 44th, 1918
Halliday, A.R.		I, 53rd Ohio	81		1926 Oct 12	KS, 46th, 1927
Halliday, M.H.	Sergt.	C, 51st Ohio Inf.	1		1916 Aug 7	IA, 43rd, 1917
Hallock, H.K.		F, 10th Mich. Cav.	13	75	1920 Nov 24	NE, 45th, 1921
Hallock, Henry S.		K, 30th Iowa Inf.	1		1929 Jan 15	KS, 49th, 1930
Hallowell, J.R.		31st Ind.	25		1898	KS, 18th, 1899
Hallyon, H.		D, 9th Kans.	380		1916 Aug 15	KS, 36th, 1917
Halman, John	Pvt.	D, 38th Iowa Inf.	216		1930 Oct 6	IA, 57th, 1931
Halsey, M.W.	Pvt.	C, 91st Ill.	50		1921 Oct 28	IA, 48th, 1922
Halsey, Wm. M.		C, 63rd Ohio	52		1917 Aug 29	KS, 37th, 1918
Halstead, James M.		G, 144th N.Y.	250		1921 Dec 20	KS, 41st, 1922
Halstead, Jonathan		H, 99th Ill. Inf. (died of dropsy)	11	76	1913 Nov 7	NE, 38th, 1914
Halstead, Otis	Sergt.	I, 4th Ill. Cav.	228		1899	NE, 24th, 1900
Halstead, Samuel	Pvt.	C, 3rd Md. Inf.	7		1898 Feb 12	IA, 26th, 1900
Halsted, Charles H.		A, 52nd Ill. Inf. (former member)	47		1941 Mar 26	NE, 66th, 1942
Haltom, John	Pvt.	G, 11th Iowa Inf.	37		1919 Jan 1	IA, 45th, 1919
Halverson, Henry	Pvt.	E, 43rd Ill. Inf.	233	59	1895 Apr 7	IA, 21st, 1895
Halverson, Jno.	Pvt.	I, 38th Iowa Inf.	216		1925 Mar 28	IA, 52nd, 1926
Halverson, Paul	Pvt.	I, 27th Iowa Inf.	194		1900-1901	IA, 27th, 1901
Halverstadt, S.S.			85		1920 May 26	KS, 40th, 1921
Ham, Alonzo		17th N.Y. Battery	328		1905 Nov 27	KS, 25th, 1906
Ham, D.M.		M, 4th Ill. Cav.	97		1902 Mar 24	KS, 22nd, 1903
Ham, John		K, 43rd Ind. Inf. (died of heart failure)	35	68	1912 Jan 13	NE, 37th, 1913
Ham, Joseph A.	Boy	U.S. Navy	250		1923 Sep 27	KS, 43rd, 1924
Haman, August	Pvt.	16th Regulars	168		1920 Jun 15	IA, 47th, 1921
Hambleton, J.G.		C, 88th Ohio Vol. Inf.	4		1915 Dec 31	KS, 35th, 1916
Hamblin, A.A.		A, 97th Ind.	4		1917 Jun 14	KS, 37th, 1918
Hamblin, Geo. W.		F, 4th Kans.	18		1902 Jan 13	KS, 22nd, 1903
Hambsch, Phillip	Pvt.	A, 83rd Ill. Inf.	204		1913 Apr	IA, 40th, 1914
Hamersly, M.G.			448		1921	KS, 41st, 1922
Hamill, David B.	Lieut.	C, 45th Iowa Inf.	2		1916 Sep 17	IA, 43rd, 1917
Hamill, James		C, 11th Kans. Cav.	464		1902 Dec 2	KS, 22nd, 1903
Hamilton, A.	Pvt.	C, 1st Ill. Inf.	57		1913 Sep 28	IA, 40th, 1914
Hamilton, A.H.	Major	36th Iowa Inf.	69		1918 Nov 17	IA, 45th, 1919
Hamilton, A.H.	Major	36th Iowa Inf.	69		1919 Nov 17	IA, 46th, 1920
Hamilton, Albert		G, 40th Ind.	155		1912 Jul 31	KS, 32nd, 1913
Hamilton, Andrew	Pvt.	G, 18th Ind. Inf.	15		1930 Jul 23	IA, 57th, 1931
Hamilton, Chas. C.	Capt.	I, 152nd N.Y. Inf. (at large)	30	101	1941 Apr 8	IA, 67th, 1941
Hamilton, D.H.	Capt.	G, 55th Ind. Inf.	440	64	1894 Dec 15	IA, 22nd, 1896
Hamilton, D.P.	Wagoner	F, 10th Vt. Inf.	386		1909 Oct 4	IA, 36th, 1910
Hamilton, Edgar C.	Pvt.	E, 47th Wis. Inf.	42	53	1893 Jan 7	IA, 19th, 1893
Hamilton, Henry		K, 4th Ind. Cav.	380		1924 Dec 24	KS, 44th, 1925
Hamilton, Henry C.		H, 39th Mo. Inf. (died of rheumatism)	11	79	1924 Apr 14	NE, 49th, 1925
Hamilton, I.T.	Lieut. Col.	110th Penn.	85		1919 Mar 2	KS, 39th, 1920

*See Appendix A, B or C for roster of post names and locations.
†See Introduction for note regarding recording of death date.
226

Name	Rank	Company, Regiment or Ship	Post*	Age	Death Date†	Journal
Hamilton, J.H.		A, 10th Ind. Inf.	232		1886	KS, 6th, 1887
Hamilton, J.H.		D, 30th Ill.	293		1926	KS, 46th, 1927
Hamilton, J.W.		M, 11th Ind. Cav.	42		1912 Feb 14	KS, 32nd, 1913
Hamilton, J.W.		E, 57th Ill.	24		1924	KS, 44th, 1925
Hamilton, Jacob			188		1909 Feb 14	IA, 36th, 1910
Hamilton, James			493		1905 Dec	IA, 32nd, 1906
Hamilton, John	Pvt.	E, 113th Ill. Inf.	55		1914 Aug 31	IA, 41st, 1915
Hamilton, John		E, 89th Ill. Inf.	55		1891 Feb 26	KS, 11th, 1892
Hamilton, John R.		B, 17th Ind. Inf.	209		1912 Aug 19	KS, 32nd, 1913
Hamilton, Joseph D.		A, 18th Mo. (died of heart trouble)	22	81	1925 Jun 19	NE, 50th, 1926
Hamilton, N.B.		H, 33rd Ill. Inf.	7	58	1896 Jul 28	NE, 21st, 1897
Hamilton, Norman A.		134th N.Y. (died of palsy)	95	77	1912 Nov 29	NE, 37th, 1913
Hamilton, Robert	Pvt.	G, 8th Iowa Inf. G, 28th Iowa Inf.	233	61	1895 Feb 14	IA, 21st, 1895
Hamilton, S.A.		C, 2nd Iowa Inf.	11	65	1909 Jan 1	NE, 34th, 1910
Hamilton, S.H.		12th Wis. Bat.	5		1930 Dec 25	KS, 50th, 1931
Hamilton, T.	Pvt.	F, 2nd U.S. Col.	485		1910 Nov 9	IA, 37th, 1911
Hamilton, T.D.		G, 8th Iowa Inf. G, 19th U.S. Inf.	1		1886	KS, 6th, 1887
Hamilton, T.M.		M, 2nd Iowa	180		1912 Jul 2	KS, 32nd, 1913
Hamilton, Thomas		H, 2nd Ill. Cav. (died at St. John, Kans.; buried at St. John Cemetery)	103		1894 Feb 25	KS, 14th, 1895
Hamilton, Thomas		died of paralysis	217	67	1909 Oct 4	NE, 34th, 1910
Hamilton, W.D.		F, 11th Kans.	180		1925 Aug	KS, 45th, 1926
Hamilton, W.E.	Pvt.	45th Iowa Inf.	116		1929 Oct 16	IA, 56th, 1930
Hamilton, W.H.	Pvt.	E, 137th Ill.	40		1903 Oct 25	IA, 30th, 1904
Hamilton, W.H.	Pvt.	C, 9th N.Y. Cav.	30		1920 Jul 14	IA, 47th, 1921
Hamilton, W.J.			173		1914 Oct 17	IA, 41st, 1915
Hamilton, W.J.			108		1916 Apr 2	IA, 43rd, 1917
Hamilton, W.S.			207		1913 Jan 23	NE, 38th, 1914
Hamilton, William	Pvt. 1st Lieut.	G, 1st Mo. Cav. A, 1st Mo. Cav.	154	47	1888 Dec	NE, 13th, 1889
Hamilton, Wm.	Pvt.	E, 7th Iowa Cav.	68		1912 Dec 17	IA, 39th, 1913
Hamlin, H.A.	Pvt.	G, 3rd Iowa Cav.	516		1907 May 6	IA, 35th, 1909
Hamlin, H.H.	Pvt.	H, 10th Wis. Inf.	132		1930 Mar 4	IA, 57th, 1931
Hamlin, Horace W.		67th N.Y.	52		1913 Dec 15	KS, 33rd, 1914
Hamlin, Isaac		B, 91st Penn.	117		1916 Jan 1	KS, 36th, 1917
Hamlin, J.M.	Lieut.	B, 36th Ohio Inf.	18		1918 Jun 6	IA, 45th, 1919
Hamlin, James A.		U.S. Navy	12		1929 Sep 20	KS, 49th, 1930
Hamlin, William		H, 17th Iowa Inf.	108		1902 May 4	KS, 22nd, 1903
Hamman, W.F.		D, 115th Ill.	268		1920 Sep 9	KS, 40th, 1921
Hammed, Ben.		F, 76th Ill.	169		1897 Mar 22	KS, 17th, 1898
Hammell, D.	Pvt.	I, 14th Iowa Inf.	20		1920 May 22	IA, 47th, 1921
Hammell, Wm.		F, 121st Ohio Inf.	25		1894 Apr 20	NE, 19th, 1895
Hammell, Zack		F, 121st Ohio (died of pneumonia)	25	54	1900 Jan 26	NE, 25th, 1901
Hammer, Alfred		K, 50th Wis. Inf.		89	1937 Oct 4	IA, 64th, 1938
Hammer, G.B.	Capt.	B, 12th Penn. Cav.	7		1898 Jun 27	IA, 26th, 1900
Hammer, Henry	Pvt.	L, 3rd Mich. Cav.	282	50	1887 Jul 31	IA, 14th, 1888
Hammer, Jacob		G, 47th Ind.	484		1913 Jan 7	KS, 33rd, 1914
Hammer, John M.		7th Iowa Cav.	7		1928 Mar	IA, 55th, 1929
Hammitt, B.F.	Pvt.	I, 2nd Iowa Cav.	418		1909 Feb	IA, 36th, 1910
Hammitt, B.F.	Corp.	I, 2nd Iowa Inf.	418		1908 Dec 7	IA, 35th, 1909
Hammitt, O.H.P.		F, 75th Ind. Inf. (died at St. John, Kans.; buried at St. John Cemetery)	103		1894 Aug 7	KS, 14th, 1895
Hammitt, S.R.		D, 145th Ill. Inf. (at large)		89	1936 Jul 29	IA, 63rd, 1937
Hammon, Andrew	Pvt.	C, 15th I.[Iowa ?] Inf.	70	55	1884 Aug 10	NE, 9th, 1885
Hammond, Aug. J.	Sergt.	E, 5th Iowa Cav.	78		1922 Feb 5	IA, 49th, 1923
Hammond, Geo.	Pvt.	B, 9th Iowa Inf.	191		1906 Nov 17	IA, 33rd, 1907
Hammond, Geo.	Pvt.	K, 6th Iowa Cav.	211		1919 Jan	IA, 46th, 1920
Hammond, Geo. M.	Pvt.	B, 5th Iowa Inf.	7		1911 Aug 2	IA, 38th, 1912
Hammond, Henry		A, 38th Ind.	76		1931 Jun 14	NE, 56th, 1932
Hammond, J.T.	Pvt.	B, 1st Dakota	97	44	1891 Jun 10	IA, 18th, 1892
Hammond, J.W.	Col.	65th Ind. Inf.	40		1904 Apr 11	IA, 31st, 1905

Name	Rank	Company, Regiment or Ship	Post*	Age	Death Date†	Journal
Hammond, John A.		D, 26th Ill.	64		1885	KS, 5th, 1886
Hammond, John M.			17		1902 Mar	KS, 22nd, 1903
Hammond, M.	Pvt.	D, 21st Wis. Inf.	222		1909 Dec 20	IA, 36th, 1910
Hammond, S.	Pvt.	D, 31st Iowa Inf.	206		1911 Jan 9	IA, 38th, 1912
Hammond, W.F.		F, 16th Ky. Inf.	51		1908 May 9	KS, 28th, 1909
Hammond, William H.		A, 5th Penn. Inf.	13		1893 Aug 19	NE, 18th, 1894
Hammond, Wm.		C, 9th Ind. Cav.	55		1936 Feb 22	KS, 55th, 1936
Hammons, Charles B.		B, 3rd Ill. Cav.	500		1913 Mar 15	KS, 33rd, 1914
Hamnell, John W.	Corp.	I, 102nd Ill. Inf.	125		1919 Jun 27	IA, 46th, 1920
Hamon, Archer		E, 4th Mo. Cav.	74		1913 Aug 28	KS, 33rd, 1914
Hampson, Frank		M, 9th Iowa Inf.	422		1892 Dec 2	KS, 12th, 1893
Hampton, E.P.		B, 9th Mich. Cav. (born in Lawrence, Mich.; died in Exeter, Neb.)	76		1883 Nov 20	NE, 8th, 1884
Hampton, Geo. W.	Pvt.	E, 19th U.S.	435	62	1892 Jul 2	IA, 19th, 1893
Hampton, H.L.		K, 37th Ind.	18		1922 Feb 16	KS, 42nd, 1923
Hampton, John		H, 1st Iowa Cav. (died of heart failure)	32	60	1897 Aug 3	NE, 22nd, 1898
Hampton, L. Ed.	Pvt.	A, 97th Penn. Inf.	5	59	1900 Jan 23	IA, 26th, 1900
Hampton, Michael		E, 1st Ill. Cav.	482		1921 Oct 17	KS, 41st, 1922
Hampton, W.H.			5		1926 Aug 9	IA, 53rd, 1927
Hampton, William			55		1925 Feb 5	KS, 45th, 1926
Hamren, John R.	Seaman	U.S.S. Stars and Stripes	298		1901 Feb 7	IA, 28th, 1902
Hamrick, W.G.		H, 39th Ohio Inf. (died at Soldiers' Home, Dayton, Ohio)	14		1892 Oct 27	KS, 12th, 1893
Hamstreet, D.W.	Pvt.	I, 16th Wis. Inf.	101		1925 Mar 20	IA, 52nd, 1926
Hanawalt, G.P.	Surg.	U.S.A.	12		1912 Jun 19	IA, 39th, 1913
Hanaway, Ezekiel		C, 10th Kans.	497		1917 Dec 31	KS, 37th, 1918
Hanback, Lewis		K, 27th Ill. (see also Appendix D)	463		1897 Aug 30	KS, 17th, 1898
Hanback, Wm. H.	Pvt.	K, 6th Cal. Vols.	516		1900 Jan 13	IA, 27th, 1901
Hanblen, J.P.	Pvt.	F, 16th Maine Inf.	22		1911 Feb 17	IA, 38th, 1912
Hanbrack, Chas.		H, 43rd Ill. (died of heart failure)	13	72	1910 Mar	NE, 35th, 1911
Hance, Jno.	Sergt.	K, 1st Ill. Cav.	294	55	1888 Feb 5	IA, 15th, 1889
Hance, John	Sergt.	K, 1st Ill. Cav.	294	55	1888	IA, 17th, 1891
Hanchett, J.H.	Pvt.	F, 72nd N.Y. Inf.	267	48	1888 Nov 25	IA, 15th, 1889
Hanchett, L.S.	Pvt.	G, 49th N.Y. Inf.	267	51	1894 May 12	IA, 20th, 1894
Hanchett, L.S.	Pvt.	G, 49th N.Y. Inf.	267	51	1894 May 12	IA, 21st, 1895
Hanchett, P.		C, 7th Vt. (died of stomach trouble)	201	73	1918 Mar 28	NE, 42nd, 1918
Hancock, A.A.		36th Iowa Inf. (died of old age)	43	83	1902 Oct	NE, 27th, 1903
Hancock, Benj. G.		B, 11th Ky. Cav.	127		1918 Aug 6	KS, 38th, 1919
Hancock, Frederick	Capt.		177		1903 Oct 4	IA, 30th, 1904
Hancock, G.	Pvt. & Sergt.	D, 4th Wis. Cav. (died of wounds)	163	48	1887 Apr	NE, 12th, 1888
Hancock, J.J.		Mo.	85		1911 May 8	KS, 31st, 1912
Hancock, John H.	Corp.	E, 127th Ill. Inf.	98		1901 Jan 12	IA, 27th, 1901
Hancock, M.N.	Pvt.	E, 27th Iowa Inf.	495		1907 Jun 18	IA, 34th, 1908
Hancock, Samuel		H, 97th Ind. Inf. (died of old age)	124	75	1901 Sep	NE, 26th, 1902
Hancock, Thos.		B, 17th Ill.	68		1904 Jan 5	KS, 24th, 1905
Hancock, Thos. J.	Pvt.	A, 16th U.S. Inf.	194		1925 Feb 10	IA, 52nd, 1926
Hand, Erastus	Pvt.	H, 112th Ill. Inf.	1		1917 Dec 8	IA, 44th, 1918
Hand, Geo. H.	Pvt.	H, 15th Ill. Cav.	56		1904 Aug 7	IA, 31st, 1905
Hand, Giles F.	Major	55th Ill. Inf.	56		1926 Jun 2	IA, 53rd, 1927
Hand, T.B.		G, 78th Ill. Inf.	17		1912 Jan 29	KS, 32nd, 1913
Handig, Leander W.		H, 5th Wis. Inf. (died of heart failure)	60	67	1910 Feb 3	NE, 35th, 1911
Handley, Wm.	Pvt.	B, 112th Ill. Inf.	196		1904 Dec 11	IA, 31st, 1905
Handlon, Thomas	Pvt.	G, 44th Ill. Inf.	42		1915 Aug 7	IA, 42nd, 1916
Handy, E.S.		F, 79th Ill. Inf.	17		1914 May 19	KS, 34th, 1915
Handy, Emanual		A, 82nd Ohio	236		1922 Dec 8	KS, 43rd, 1924
Handy, Emanuel		K, 108th U.S.A.	236		1922 Dec 8	KS, 42nd, 1923
Hanen, Lewis	Pvt.	F, 76th Ill.	66		1923 Jun 6	IA, 50th, 1924
Haner, Eugene E.	Capt.	D, 6th Iowa	122		1922 May 29	IA, 49th, 1923
Haner, G.W.		I, 15th Iowa Inf. (died of cancer)	32		1905 Jul 22	NE, 30th, 1906
Haner, Geo. R.	Sergt.	1st N.Y. Art.	267		1911 Apr 11	IA, 38th, 1912
Haner, John		C, 40th Iowa	468		1896 May 25	KS, 16th, 1897
Hanes, Alex B.		H, 54th Ill.	92		1923 Aug 8	KS, 43rd, 1924

Name	Rank	Company, Regiment or Ship	Post*	Age	Death Date†	Journal
Hanes, Charles		B, 81st Ohio	211		1892 Aug 23	KS, 12th, 1893
Hanes, Jonathan C.	Pvt.	A, 23rd Iowa Inf.	12	94	1939 Feb 20	IA, 65th, 1939
Haney, Charles		C, 129th Ill.	25	77	1916 Mar 31	NE, 41st, 1917
Haney, Damiel		A, 1st Kans. Battery	35		1916 Aug 13	KS, 36th, 1917
Haney, Francis	Pvt.	K, 1st Wis. Hvy. Art.	22		1913 Sep 26	IA, 40th, 1914
Haney, Hebos F.			25		1913 May 1	NE, 38th, 1914
Haney, Henry C.	Pvt.	B, 103rd Ill. Inf.	231		1915 Apr 5	IA, 42nd, 1916
Haney, Wm.		G, 18th U.S. Inf. (died of Bright's disease)	85		1905 Dec 8	NE, 30th, 1906
Haney, Wm.		G, 18th Wis. (died of Bright's disease)	35		1905 Dec 8	NE, 37th, 1913
Hanford, R.R.	Pvt.	G, 13th Iowa Inf.	98		1917 Jan 26	IA, 44th, 1918
Hanger, B.O.	Pvt.	D, 10th Iowa Inf.	12		1918 Dec 18	IA, 45th, 1919
Hanger, E.P.		I, 143rd Ill. Inf.	68		1926 Jan 3	NE, 51st, 1927
Hanger, E.P.		I, 148th Ill. Inf.	68	79	1926 Jan 31	NE, 50th, 1926
Hanger, Wm.			7		1900-1901	IA, 27th, 1901
Haniden, John			89		1912	IA, 39th, 1913
Haning, Eliphaz	Pvt.	H, 40th Iowa	253		1899 Nov 27	IA, 26th, 1900
Haning, John A.		G, 16th Ky.	62		1926 Mar 27	NE, 51st, 1927
Hanke, Robert	Pvt.	I, 24th Ill. Inf.	434	67	1895 Dec 25	IA, 23rd, 1897
Hankins, Casius E.	Pvt.	E, 151st Ill. Inf.	284	40	1886 Aug 24	IA, 13th, 1887
Hankins, W.N.		C, 69th Ind. Inf.	265		1891 Feb 18	KS, 11th, 1892
Hanks, George	Pvt.	B, 13th Iowa Inf.	39		1927	IA, 54th, 1928
Hanlan, James B.		B, 25th Iowa	65		1911 Apr 3	KS, 31st, 1912
Hanley, Geo.		G, 20th Ill.	1		1933 Jun 2	KS, 53rd, 1934
Hanley, Harry	Sergt.	M. Corps	263		1923	IA, 50th, 1924
Hanlin, Ephraim		E, 1st Ohio Cav.	315		1898 Mar 3	KS, 18th, 1899
Hanlon, Michael	Pvt.	A, 24th Iowa Inf.	164		1900 Mar 24	IA, 27th, 1901
Hanly, David	Pvt.	D, 15th U.S. Inf.	44		1911 Jul 9	IA, 38th, 1912
Hann, H.T.	Pvt.	C, 7th Iowa Vol. Inf.	209		1902 Jan 22	IA, 28th, 1902
Hanna, A.	Pvt.	E, —	122		1913 Oct 21	IA, 40th, 1914
Hanna, David		G, 37th Ind.	23		1906 Feb 22	KS, 26th, 1907
Hanna, G.A.	Pvt.	A, 65th Ill. Inf.	24		1921 Mar 21	IA, 48th, 1922
Hanna, Geo. B.		F, 129th Ill.	117		1918 Mar 18	KS, 38th, 1919
Hanna, H.C.		F, 129th Ohio	117		1921 May 23	KS, 43rd, 1924
Hanna, James G.		C, 128th Ohio	130		1936 Dec 8	KS, 56th, 1937
Hanna, John	Pvt.	E, 100th Penn. Inf.	192		1925 Aug 20	IA, 52nd, 1926
Hanna, Jos.	Pvt.	K, 24th Iowa Inf.	130		1919 Apr 28	IA, 46th, 1920
Hanna, K.J.			255		1916	IA, 43rd, 1917
Hanna, P.B.		C, 179th Ohio	25		1910 Sep 7	KS, 30th, 1911
Hanna, R.H.		G, 8th Penn. Inf.	440		1913 Sep 9	IA, 40th, 1914
Hanna, Samuel B.		A, 39th Ky.	104		1890	KS, 10th, 1891
Hanna, Thomas	Pvt.	E, 100th Penn. Inf.	165		1912 May 5	IA, 39th, 1913
Hanna, William	Pvt.		81		1930	IA, 57th, 1931
Hanna, Wm. S.	Pvt.	G, 13th Iowa Inf.	98	56	1895 May 1	IA, 22nd, 1896
Hannah, Francis H.		B, 73rd Ill.	7		1904 Jan 4	KS, 24th, 1905
Hannah, J.S.		H, 65th Ill. Inf. (died at Blue Rapids; buried at Prospect Hill Cemetery)	328		1894 Mar 5	KS, 14th, 1895
Hannah, John G.		A, 10th Iowa Inf.	294		1887 Feb 18	KS, 7th, 1888
Hannamon, Jno.	Pvt.	D, 27th Iowa Inf.	120	56	1885 Sep 20	IA, 12th, 1886
Hannan, Chas. H.		E, 2nd Col.	12		1927 Mar 24	KS, 47th, 1928
Hanner, Enoch	Pvt.	I, 36th Iowa Inf.	186		1892 Feb 14	IA, 19th, 1893
Hannigan, W.E.		D, 25th Ill. Inf.	150		1918	KS, 38th, 1919
Hannon, Edward	Pvt.	K, 1st Iowa Cav.	12		1890 Jun 30	IA, 17th, 1891
Hannon, Michael	Pvt.	G, 11th Ill. Cav.	78	60	1893 Jul 17	IA, 20th, 1894
Hannon, Tobias		died of old age	143		1916 Jun	NE, 41st, 1917
Hannum, J.F.		C, 30th Iowa	113		1913 Sep 10	KS, 33rd, 1914
Hanover, J.A.		H, 52nd Ill.	477		1912 Aug 30	KS, 32nd, 1913
Hanover, Joseph			380		1923	KS, 43rd, 1924
Hansel, David	Pvt.	B, 5th Iowa Inf.	497		1925 Mar 2	IA, 52nd, 1926
Hansell, Sam'l	Pvt.	K, 1st Ill. Cav.	261		1903 Oct 18	IA, 30th, 1904
Hanselman, David		A, 115th Ohio	37		1919 Mar 30	KS, 39th, 1920
Hansen, Andred		K, 95th Ohio	129		1896 Feb 29	KS, 16th, 1897

*See Appendix A, B or C for roster of post names and locations.
†See Introduction for note regarding recording of death date.

229

Name	Rank	Company, Regiment or Ship	Post*	Age	Death Date†	Journal
Hansen, F.	Pvt.	Ind. Battery 3rd N.Y. Inf.	327	75	1897 Apr 21	IA, 24th, 1898
Hansen, Peter	Pvt.	E, 5th Iowa Cav.	70	49	1891 Dec 31	IA, 18th, 1892
Hansen, Wm. K.	Pvt.	4th Wis. Lt. Art.	131		1899	NE, 24th, 1900
Hanshaw, J.H.		H, 133rd Ill. Inf. (died of paralysis)	13	72	1913 May 14	NE, 38th, 1914
Hansknecht, Ed'd	Pvt.	A, 1st N.J. Art.	5	64	1899 Feb 23	IA, 25th, 1899
Hanson, A.		K, 28th Wis.	50		1924 Dec 7	KS, 44th, 1925
Hanson, B.	Pvt.	A, 72nd Ill. Inf.	259		1911 Apr 2	IA, 38th, 1912
Hanson, Edward	Pvt.	H, 16th U.S. Regulars	168	44	1890 Jun 10	IA, 17th, 1891
Hanson, Geo.		E, 55th Ill. Inf.	18		1899 Nov 6	KS, 19th, 1900
Hanson, Geo. W.		G, 115th Ill. Inf. D, 98th Ill. Inf.	12		1900 Jul 9	KS, 20th, 1901
Hanson, John	Sergt.	58th Ohio Inf.	98		1906 Sep 26	IA, 33rd, 1907
Hanson, L.P.	Seaman	U.S. Navy	452		1919 Jan 22	IA, 46th, 1920
Hanson, Mark		1st Neb. Inf.	110		1908 Feb 25	NE, 33rd, 1909
Hanson, Stener	Pvt.	G, 22nd Wis. Inf.	365	60	1893 Aug	IA, 20th, 1894
Hant, Jacob B.		G, 10th Ohio Cav.	11		1918 Feb 26	KS, 38th, 1919
Hanthorn, J.		H, 12th Iowa Inf.	15	67	1903 Nov 8	NE, 28th, 1904
Hantz, Alex		F, 87th Penn.	83		1926 Jun 15	KS, 46th, 1927
Hantz, John	Pvt.	G, 44th Iowa Inf.	231		1927 Oct 6	IA, 54th, 1928
Hanup, J.		F, 184th N.Y.	36		1888	KS, 8th, 1889
Hanway, John S.		A, 3rd Kans. Inf.	18		1908 Jan 1	KS, 28th, 1909
Happertin, John		C, 7th Penn. Cav. (died of cancer of stomach)	201		1893 Aug 28	NE, 18th, 1894
Happle, Geo.		A, 102nd Ill.	76		1893 Sep 6	KS, 13th, 1894
Harbaugh, H.H.		B, 14th Ill.	85		1929 Jan 29	KS, 49th, 1930
Harbaugh, J.M.		H, 6th West Va. (died of hardening of arteries)	111	71	1917 Dec 23	NE, 42nd, 1918
Harber, E.		D, 2nd Ill. Inf. (died of cancer)	63	52	1895 Jun 8	NE, 20th, 1896
Harbert, Richard J.	Sergt.	A, 37th Iowa Inf.	400	82	1889 Apr 10	IA, 16th, 1890
Harbert, Seth T.		A, 4th Mo. Cav.	32		1889	KS, 9th, 1890
Harbeson, W.A.		H, 9th Penn. Cav.	12		1909 Apr 16	KS, 29th, 1910
Harbet, J.D.	Pvt.	22nd Iowa Inf.	314		1915	IA, 42nd, 1916
Harbin, Berry A.J.		E, 35th Ill. Inf.	225		1916 Dec 25	KS, 36th, 1917
Harbin, Calvin		D, 4th Kans. Inf.	65		1917 Nov 21	KS, 37th, 1918
Harbison, Robt. F.	Sergt.	G, 3rd Iowa Inf.	12	53	1898 Mar 13	IA, 24th, 1898
Harbison, Wesley		F, 20th Iowa	59		1930 Sep 4	KS, 50th, 1931
Harbison, Wm.	Sergt.	A, 6th Iowa Inf.	206		1902 Jul 6	IA, 29th, 1903
Harbour, Noah	Pvt.	9th Iowa	497		1923 Aug 13	IA, 50th, 1924
Hard, J.S.	Pvt.	H, 32nd Iowa Inf.	81		1901 Jul 23	IA, 28th, 1902
Hard, John		G, 94th N.Y. (hurt from fall)	42		1907 Oct 15	NE, 32nd, 1908
Harden, Erastus	Pvt.	H, 145th Ohio	68	73	1898 Oct 1	IA, 25th, 1899
Harden, T.J.	Pvt.	C, 28th Iowa	127		1924 Sep 12	IA, 51st, 1925
Harden, Timothy	Pvt.	K, 31st Wis. Inf.	371		1885 May 30	IA, 12th, 1886
Hardenbrook, Geo.			305		1916	IA, 43rd, 1917
Hardenbrook, John		H, 137th Ind. Inf. (at large)		91	1938 May 5	IA, 64th, 1938
Hardenbrook, R.L.	Pvt.	F, 83rd Ill. Inf.	10		1913 Nov 6	IA, 40th, 1914
Harder, A.C.	Pvt.	G, 130th Penn. Inf.	59	58	1897 Oct 7	IA, 24th, 1898
Harder, Charles		F, 139th Ill. Inf. (died of stoppage of bowels)	37	60	1904 Nov 4	NE, 29th, 1905
Harder, Peter		E, 12th Mo.	15		1898 Jan 14	KS, 17th, 1898
Hardesty, William		34th Iowa	116		1914 Oct	KS, 34th, 1915
Hardey, Geo. H.	Sergt.	D, 5th Wis. Inf.	133		1925 Nov 29	IA, 52nd, 1926
Hardin, A.J.	Pvt.	3rd Iowa Cav.	2		1923 Oct 27	IA, 50th, 1924
Hardin, Abe	Pvt.	I, 46th Iowa Inf.	359		1912 Sep 16	IA, 39th, 1913
Hardin, David C.		B, 1st Mo.	18		1906 Mar 27	KS, 26th, 1907
Hardin, Isaac	Pvt.	G, 8th Iowa Inf.	233	44	1887 Jan 12	IA, 13th, 1887
Hardin, John B.		H, 13th Ind. Inf.	85		1914 Feb 18	KS, 34th, 1915
Hardin, John E.		E, 14th Ill. Inf.	51		1891 Nov 2	KS, 11th, 1892
Hardin, R.C.		A, 30th Ill. Inf. (died of chronic dis.)	226	57	1902 Jun	NE, 27th, 1903
Harding, B.J.	Sergt.	C, 6th Ind. Cav.	235		1927 Jul 19	IA, 54th, 1928
Harding, Benj.	Pvt.		322		1915 Jun 29	IA, 42nd, 1916
Harding, H.N.		49th Wis.	320		1892 Jul 8	KS, 12th, 1893

*See Appendix A, B or C for roster of post names and locations.
†See Introduction for note regarding recording of death date.

Name	Rank	Company, Regiment or Ship	Post*	Age	Death Date†	Journal
Harding, John	Pvt.	F, 13th Ky. Cav.	164		1913 Mar 29	IA, 40th, 1914
Harding, John H.		74th Ohio	12		1910 Dec 21	KS, 30th, 1911
Harding, Louis		D, 1st Wis.	47		1896 Mar 21	KS, 16th, 1897
Harding, O.		A, 146th Ill.	134		1885	KS, 5th, 1886
Harding, T.D.		C, 11th Mich. Inf. (died of old age)	24	85	1900 Sep 25	NE, 25th, 1901
Harding, Thomas			8		1918	KS, 38th, 1919
Harding, Tyler	Pvt.	E, 1st Mass. Cav.	12		1918 Dec 26	IA, 45th, 1919
Harding, W.A.	Corp.	D, 114th Ill.	57		1922 Aug 20	IA, 49th, 1923
Harding, W.A.	Pvt.	D, 114th Ill. Inf.	57	90	1933 Sep	IA, 60th, 1934
Harding, W.F.	Pvt.	A, 3rd Colo. Cav.	12		1904 Oct 12	IA, 31st, 1905
Harding, W.H.	Pvt.	C, 8th Iowa Inf.	108		1917 Nov 7	IA, 44th, 1918
Harding, W.H.	Pvt.	A, 33rd Iowa Inf.	12		1929 Jul 23	IA, 56th, 1930
Harding, Z.N.		H, 3rd Wis.	355		1897 Sep 11	KS, 17th, 1898
Hardman, David			38		1912	IA, 39th, 1913
Hardsock, E.E.		F, 150th Ill.	49		1913 Sep 26	KS, 33rd, 1914
Hardwick, John			75		1912 Sep 20	IA, 39th, 1913
Hardy, H.E.	Pvt.	B, 42nd Wis.	314	66	1891 Jun 24	IA, 18th, 1892
Hardy, H.H.		H, 41st Ill. Inf.	174		1901 Dec 5	KS, 21st, 1902
Hardy, James			100		1919 Jul 9	KS, 39th, 1920
Hardy, John			116		1884	KS, 4th, 1885
Hardy, Joseph D.		F, 118th N.Y.	130		1904 Jul 3	KS, 24th, 1905
Hardy, Noah		C, 11th Ill.	17		1920 Feb 16	KS, 40th, 1921
Hardy, Otis B.		L, 3rd Mass. Cav.	203		1900 Nov 8	KS, 20th, 1901
Hardy, Robt.		B, 4th West Va.	55		1902 Oct 6	KS, 22nd, 1903
Hardy, W.P.	2nd Lieut.	H, 46th Ill. Inf.	193		1905 Sep 3	IA, 32nd, 1906
Hare, A.M.	Col.	11th Iowa	231		1903-1904	IA, 30th, 1904
Hare, D.L.	Pvt.	I, 4th Iowa Inf.	288	52	1891 Jul 8	IA, 18th, 1892
Hare, George W.		I, 45th Ill.	65		1915 Mar 4	KS, 35th, 1916
Harger, B.M.	Pvt.	A, 44th Iowa Inf.	78		1918 Jan 19	IA, 45th, 1919
Harger, W.P.	Pvt.	D, 149th Ind. Inf.	111		1899	NE, 24th, 1900
Harges, S.M.	Pvt.	B, 10th Iowa Inf.	425		1918	IA, 45th, 1919
Hargis, Andrew T.		A, 9th Mo. Inf.	292		1901 Sep 26	KS, 21st, 1902
Hargis, Daniel H.		A, 9th Mo. Cav.	292		1904 Dec 1	KS, 24th, 1905
Hargis, S.	Sergt.	10th Iowa Inf.	425		1925	IA, 52nd, 1926
Hargis, Thos. J.		K, 115th Ill.	46		1918 Nov 10	KS, 38th, 1919
Hargrave, E.B.		C, 3rd Ill. Cav.	28		1912 Jun 21	KS, 32nd, 1913
Hargraves, Richard		K, 38th Mass. Inf.	394		1889	KS, 11th, 1892
Hargrove, John		C, 148th Ind.	289		1893 Aug 30	KS, 13th, 1894
Harich, Jacob	Pvt.	A, 19th Iowa Inf.	2	49	1892 Jun 21	IA, 19th, 1893
Haring, Wm. G.	Pvt.	I, 83rd Penn. Inf.	88		1919 Mar 27	IA, 46th, 1920
Harkart, F.G.		C, 5th Iowa	6		1904 Aug 18	KS, 24th, 1905
Harker, Daniel P.	Pvt.	I, 28th Iowa Inf.	234		1907 2nd term	IA, 34th, 1908
Harkins, Dennis		C, 14th N.Y. Cav.	127		1901 Sep 29	KS, 21st, 1902
Harkley, Samuel		K, 11th N.Y.	12		1910 Jan 7	KS, 30th, 1911
Harkness, David	Pvt.	G, 9th Iowa Inf.	219		1919 Nov	IA, 46th, 1920
Harkness, Edwin R.		A, 5th Minn.	120		1893	KS, 13th, 1894
Harkness, J.L.		K, 22nd Iowa	44		1905 Oct 27	KS, 25th, 1906
Harlan, A.W.	Pvt.	F, 21st Mo. Inf.	268		1911 Apr 30	IA, 38th, 1912
Harlan, H.M.	Pvt.	E, 33rd Iowa Inf.	144		1918 Feb 4	IA, 45th, 1919
Harlan, Isaiah		9th Iowa	246		1928	IA, 55th, 1929
Harlan, J.A.	Corp.	A, 39th Iowa	80		1924 Oct 19	IA, 51st, 1925
Harlan, James	Pvt.	D, 44th Iowa Inf.	400	88	1933 Dec 13	IA, 60th, 1934
Harlan, Jamison		K, 4th Iowa Cav.	56		1887	KS, 7th, 1888
Harlan, Jos.	Pvt.	H, 47th Ill. Inf.	14		1911 May 18	IA, 38th, 1912
Harlan, Joshua		I, 9th Ind. Cav.	44		1904 Jul 31	KS, 24th, 1905
Harlan, Noah		G, 7th Iowa	25		1928 Jul 23	NE, 53rd, 1929
Harlan, Valentine			173		1922 Aug 10	IA, 49th, 1923
Harley, J.A.	Pvt.	105th Penn. Inf.	108		1931 May 28	IA, 58th, 1932
Harley, J.M.		I, 53rd Ill.	104		1927	KS, 46th, 1927
Harley, M.	Pvt.	I, 16th Wis. Inf.	485		1910 Jul 8	IA, 37th, 1911
Harlow, Larkin W.	Pvt.	K, 36th Iowa Inf.	40		1924 May 29	IA, 51st, 1925
Harman, H.D.		D, 14th Kans.	12		1927 Jul 11	KS, 47th, 1928

*See Appendix A, B or C for roster of post names and locations.
†See Introduction for note regarding recording of death date.

231

Name	Rank	Company, Regiment or Ship	Post*	Age	Death Date†	Journal
Harman, Isiah	Pvt.	E, 2nd Iowa Cav.	92		1923 Mar 26	IA, 50th, 1924
Harmen, Jacob	Pvt.	C, 5th Iowa Cav.	349	43	1893 Jun 22	IA, 20th, 1894
Harmer, Fred	Pvt.	B, 24th N.Y. Cav.	220		1913 Feb 13	IA, 40th, 1914
Harmer, N.M.		118th Penn. Inf.	381		1886	KS, 6th, 1887
Harmes, Charles		Ord. Corps Reg's	6		1901 Oct 20	KS, 21st, 1902
Harmes, H.	Pvt.	E, 16th Iowa	184		1903 Feb 25	IA, 30th, 1904
Harming, Geo.		I, 14th Ill.	49		1918 Nov 23	KS, 38th, 1919
Harmon, A.W.	Pvt.	C, 14th Iowa Inf.	42	87	1931 Dec 8	IA, 58th, 1932
Harmon, Chas. R.	Pvt.	E, 44th Iowa	243		1924 Apr 29	IA, 51st, 1925
Harmon, D.B.	Pvt.		219		1925	IA, 52nd, 1926
Harmon, David W.		I, 130th Ind.	257		1928	KS, 48th, 1929
Harmon, E.	Pvt.	A, 35th Iowa Inf.	452		1928 Mar 5	IA, 55th, 1929
Harmon, E.C.	Pvt.	C, 11th U.S. Inf.	77		1926 Jan 22	IA, 53rd, 1927
Harmon, Eli		I, 192nd Penn.	30		1917 Aug 10	KS, 37th, 1918
Harmon, Elijah		I, 18th Mo.	123		1925 Oct 29	KS, 45th, 1926
Harmon, Geo. M.	Pvt.	G, 14th Ky. Cav.	34		1911 Nov 18	IA, 38th, 1912
Harmon, George		E, 83rd Ill.	25		1909 Jul 25	KS, 29th, 1910
Harmon, Henry	Pvt.	E, 4th Iowa Cav.	321		1927 Apr 28	IA, 54th, 1928
Harmon, Henry	Pvt.	E, 4th Iowa Cav.	321		1928 Apr 28	IA, 55th, 1929
Harmon, I.M.		B, 1st Tenn.	3		1916 Jan 1	KS, 36th, 1917
Harmon, J.C.	Pvt.	F, 75th Ill. Inf.	222		1912 Oct 3	IA, 39th, 1913
Harmon, J.C.	Pvt.	D, 1st Col. Cav.	22		1930 Mar	IA, 57th, 1931
Harmon, J.H.		27th Ind.	317		1893 Jun 6	KS, 13th, 1894
Harmon, Jas. W.			45		1926 Mar 16	IA, 53rd, 1927
Harmon, John			171		1908 Apr	NE, 33rd, 1909
Harmon, John		C, 78th Ill. Inf. (died of old age)	89	83	1919 Dec 24	NE, 44th, 1920
Harmon, Lyman A.		B, 2nd Neb. Cav. (died of old age)	4	78	1910 Nov 20	NE, 35th, 1911
Harmon, M.		died of natural causes	5	79	1922 Apr 20	NE, 47th, 1923
Harmon, Nathan E.		K, 142nd Ill. Inf. (of Wichita, Kans.)	25		1911 Aug 3 (or 13)	KS, 31st, 1912
Harmon, Pat	Pvt.	H, 12th Iowa Inf.	131		1908	IA, 35th, 1909
Harmon, S.L.	Pvt.	C, 1st Mass. Cav.	43		1907 Dec	IA, 34th, 1908
Harmon, S.T.	Pvt.	A, 13th Iowa	140		1923	IA, 50th, 1924
Harmon, Wm.	Pvt.	E, 7th Iowa Inf.	515		1904 Nov 10	IA, 31st, 1905
Harmony, W.J.		B, 6th Mo.	17		1921 Nov 27	KS, 41st, 1922
Harms, A.C.	Sergt.	F, 3rd Vt. Inf.	154		1912 Nov 27	IA, 39th, 1913
Harms, O.		B, 43rd Ill.	75		1907 Sep 23	NE, 32nd, 1908
Harn, Jason		F, 38th Ill.	36		1922 Jul 27	KS, 42nd, 1923
Harned, M.R.	Pvt.	A, 33rd Iowa Inf.	12		1924 Oct 8	IA, 51st, 1925
Harned, W.F.	Chaplain	24th Ind. Inf.	7		1913 Jan 7	IA, 40th, 1914
Harned, Z.T.			167		1919 Jan 13	IA, 46th, 1920
Harner, Henry		C, 35th Ind.	88		1906 Jan 27	KS, 26th, 1907
Harner, John		I, Ind. Bat.	100		1923	KS, 43rd, 1924
Harner, John D.	Pvt.	I, 4th Iowa Cav.	288	55	1896 Apr 1	IA, 23rd, 1897
Harners, James		D, 11th Kans. Inf.	225		1914 Jan 15	KS, 34th, 1915
Harness, James		D, 11th Kans.	225		1897 Dec 6	KS, 17th, 1898
Harney, H.	Pvt.	I, 25th Wis. Inf.	78		1924 Jul 8	IA, 51st, 1925
Harney, J.M.		H, 106th Ill. Vols. (died of old age)	188	7?	1910 Sep 21	NE, 35th, 1911
Harns, E.A.		A, 89th N.Y.	8		1897	KS, 17th, 1898
Harns, T.C.		A, 154th N.Y. Inf. (died of paralysis)	89	81	1919 Dec 1	NE, 44th, 1920
Harold, Jonathan		I, 28th Iowa (died of old age)		81	1924 Sep 14	NE, 49th, 1925
Harp, J.M.			380		1917	KS, 37th, 1918
Harp, Jas.		K, 70th Ohio Inf.	74		1903 Sep 18	IA, 30th, 1904
Harper, —			433		1923	KS, 43rd, 1924
Harper, A.M.	Pvt.	D, 16th Ohio Inf.	314	46	1887 Oct 23	IA, 14th, 1888
Harper, A.Y.	Sergt.	B, 63rd Ill.	302		1922 Jun	IA, 49th, 1923
Harper, Alexander	Pvt.	D, 8th Iowa Vol. Inf.	98		1903 Jan 27	IA, 30th, 1904
Harper, Burris		G, 5th Mo. Cav.	164		1899 Oct 22	KS, 19th, 1900
Harper, D.C.		C, 39th Iowa Inf.	45		1927 Jan 27	IA, 54th, 1928
Harper, David C.		K, 6th Kans.	71		1924 Mar 31	KS, 44th, 1925
Harper, G.W.	Pvt.		52		1907 Mar	IA, 34th, 1908
Harper, Geo.	Sergt.	K, 16th Inf.	337		1924 Jul	IA, 51st, 1925
Harper, I.	Pvt.	1st Ill. Hvy. Art.	305	65	1895 Apr 22	IA, 22nd, 1896

*See Appendix A, B or C for roster of post names and locations.
†See Introduction for note regarding recording of death date.
232

Name	Rank	Company, Regiment or Ship	Post*	Age	Death Date†	Journal
Harper, Jas.	Corp.	4th Iowa Inf.	192		1903 Sep 5	IA, 30th, 1904
Harper, Jas.	1st Sergt.	A, 7th Iowa Cav.	56		1900 Jan 9	IA, 27th, 1901
Harper, John		G, 104th Ohio Inf. (buried at Shawnee)	318		1894 May 15	KS, 14th, 1895
Harper, John C.		H, 4th West Va. Cav.	62	77	1922 Apr 25	NE, 47th, 1923
Harper, John L.		I, 12th West Va.	54		1885	KS, 5th, 1886
Harper, L.P.		G, 13th Wis. Inf.	185	72	1909 Sep 19	NE, 34th, 1910
Harper, Milan A.		B, 70th Ill.	251		1914 Nov 14	KS, 34th, 1915
Harper, Philip	Musician	42nd Ohio L, 8th Ohio Cav.	10		1933 Feb 27	NE, 58th, 1934
Harper, R.F.		G, 11th Kans.	100		1915 Jun 28	KS, 35th, 1916
Harper, S.E.		D, 15th Mo.	293		1910 Dec 8	KS, 30th, 1911
Harper, Samuel Houston	Capt.	46th U.S.C. Inf. (see also Appendix D)	69		1911 Dec 17	IA, 38th, 1912
Harper, Thos. V.		E, 1st Ohio	14		1897 Nov 25	KS, 17th, 1898
Harper, W.E.	Pvt.	D, 8th Iowa Cav.	173		1917	IA, 44th, 1918
Harpster, Fred		U.S. Signal Service	40		1913 Aug 4	KS, 33rd, 1914
Harpster, Geo. W.		L, 27th Penn. Cav. (died of consumption)	62	58	1891[1901?] Jan	NE, 26th, 1902
Harr, J.G.		A, 14th Mo.	8		1923 Jul 24	KS, 43rd, 1924
Harr, John	Pvt.	C, 2nd Mo. Inf.	254		1904 Mar 23	IA, 31st, 1905
Harrah, Albert	Pvt.	B, 46th Iowa Inf.	16		1906 Dec 1	IA, 33rd, 1907
Harrell, Edmund M.		I, 18th Iowa	5		1911 Aug 29	KS, 31st, 1912
Harrell, John P.			12		1936 Sep 5	KS, 56th, 1937
Harrier, Adam	Pvt.	K, 82nd Penn. Inf.	235		1911 Sep 7	IA, 38th, 1912
Harriman, Charles Allison		G, 18th N.H. Inf. G, 3rd Brigade, 9th Corps		91	1937 Jun 10	IA, 64th, 1938
Harrington, C.J.	Pvt.	K, 6th Penn. Res. Vol. Corps	222	47	1888 Aug 29	IA, 15th, 1889
Harrington, Eldred		Wis. Battery	130		1909 Nov 7	KS, 29th, 1910
Harrington, J.R.	Pvt.	2nd Iowa Lt. Art.	67		1928 Sep 6	IA, 55th, 1929
Harrington, Jas. D.	Pvt.	B, 27th Iowa	22		1926 Sep 9	IA, 53rd, 1927
Harrington, M.J.	Pvt.	G, 31st N.Y.	74		1923 May 27	IA, 50th, 1924
Harrington, W.L.		I, 51st Ohio Inf.		90	1936 Apr 16	IA, 62nd, 1936
Harrington, W.L.		I, 51st Ohio Inf.	1	90	1935 Apr 16	IA, 62nd, 1936
Harris, A.D.	Pvt.	I, 22nd Wis. Inf.	12		1928 Apr 14	IA, 55th, 1929
Harris, A.L.		A, 33rd Ind.	12		1924 Aug 7	KS, 44th, 1925
Harris, Aaron		F, 7th Iowa (died of heart failure)	179	66	1913 Aug 4	NE, 38th, 1914
Harris, C.H.	Lieut.	K, 11th Ky. Cav.	66		1913 Jan 20	IA, 40th, 1914
Harris, C.O.	Pvt.	I, 16th Wis. Inf.	124		1910 Nov 13	IA, 37th, 1911
Harris, C.S.	Sergt.	H, 8th Ind. Cav.	403	63	1893 Apr 4	IA, 20th, 1894
Harris, C.W.	Pvt.	A, 2nd Iowa Cav.	132		1905 Oct 31	IA, 32nd, 1906
Harris, Charles		A, 46th Iowa (see also Appendix D)	55	73	1920 Jan 27 or 28	KS, 40th, 1921
Harris, Charles		A, 9th Ill. Inf.	25	77	1911 Sep 17	NE, 36th, 1912
Harris, Charles H.	Pvt.	H, 112th Ill.	1		1928 Dec 15	IA, 55th, 1929
Harris, Danl.	Pvt.	K, 154th Ohio Inf.	12		1927 Jan 2	IA, 54th, 1928
Harris, David	Pvt.	K, 28th Iowa Inf.	16		1913	IA, 40th, 1914
Harris, Ed. V.		K, 1st Calif. Inf.	11		1929 Sep	NE, 54th, 1930
Harris, Elam H.		C, 130th Ind. Inf.	55		1899 Jan 23	KS, 19th, 1900
Harris, Elon		C, 130th Ind. Inf.	464		1899 Jan 23	KS, 19th, 1900
Harris, Fred	Sergt.	H, 1st Neb. Cav.	116		1925 Oct 23	IA, 52nd, 1926
Harris, Fred A.		2nd Iowa Cav.	133		1892	IA, 19th, 1893
Harris, G.		D, 12th Kans.	40		1888	KS, 8th, 1889
Harris, I.H.	Pvt.	G, 98th Ohio Inf.	192		1911 Jul 21	IA, 38th, 1912
Harris, I.H.		K, 25th Mich.	314		1898 Jan 30	KS, 18th, 1899
Harris, Isaac		K, 8th Mo. (death from fall)	440		1889	KS, 9th, 1890
Harris, J.E.		E, 36th Ohio	12		1936	KS, 55th, 1936
Harris, J.H.W.		85th Ind. Inf.	77		1918	NE, 43rd, 1919
Harris, J.K.	Pvt.	B, 29th Ind. Inf.	127		1920 Jun 28	IA, 47th, 1921
Harris, J.L.	Pvt.	I, 14th Ill. Inf.	10	60	1891 Jul 13	IA, 18th, 1892
Harris, J.M.	Pvt.	K, 16th Iowa Inf.	67		1930 Oct	IA, 57th, 1931
Harris, J.R.		G, 13th Kans.	148		1892 Aug 22	KS, 12th, 1893
Harris, J.S.		E, 77th N.Y.	113		1901 May 15	KS, 22nd, 1903
Harris, J.T.	Pvt.		2		1924 Feb 12	IA, 51st, 1925
Harris, J.U.	Pvt.	M, 7th Mo. Cav.	122		1913 Sep 2	IA, 40th, 1914
Harris, Jack		B, 14th U.S. Colored	321		1886	KS, 6th, 1887

Name	Rank	Company, Regiment or Ship	Post*	Age	Death Date†	Journal
Harris, James A.		G, 13th Kans. Inf.	148		1900 Jul 22	KS, 20th, 1901
Harris, James G.	Pvt.	B, 5th Kans. Cav.	251		1911 Oct 21	IA, 38th, 1912
Harris, James R.		L, 2nd Ill.	61		1902 Nov 6	KS, 22nd, 1903
Harris, Jeremiah		F, 5th U.S.	486		1911 Oct 27	KS, 31st, 1912
Harris, Jno.		G, Mo. Hvy. Art.	15	63	1903 Jul 2	NE, 28th, 1904
Harris, John		F, 20th Wis. Inf. (died at Coyville, Kans.; buried at Coyville, Kans.)	248		1894 Sep 16	KS, 14th, 1895
Harris, John		H, 79th Ohio Inf.	180	75	1902 Dec	NE, 27th, 1903
Harris, John J.		B, 1st Cal. Cav.	3		1893 Sep 28	KS, 13th, 1894
Harris, John P.		1st Bat. Kans. Lt. Art. (see also Appendix D)	18		1917 Feb 21 or 29	KS, 37th, 1918
Harris, John P.		F, 85th Ind. Inf. (died of old age)	77	78	1911 Jul 20	NE, 36th, 1912
Harris, John W.		C, 6th Md.	4		1931 Feb 5	NE, 56th, 1932
Harris, Joseph		G, 62nd Ill. Inf. (died of general debility)	174	72	1897 Dec 3	NE, 22nd, 1898
Harris, Joseph F.		A, 4th Mo.	265		1926 Dec 20	KS, 46th, 1927
Harris, L.D.		I, 58th Ill.	262		1919 Feb 19	NE, 44th, 1920
Harris, L.M.	Corp.	F, 2nd Iowa Cav.	66		1913 Mar 14	IA, 40th, 1914
Harris, Milo R.		L, 1st Kans.	18		1924 Jul 30	KS, 44th, 1925
Harris, N.		F, 50th Ill.	186		1926 Jan 30	KS, 46th, 1927
Harris, Newton P.	Pvt.	H, 118th N.Y. Inf.	42		1928 Apr 16	IA, 55th, 1929
Harris, P.M.	Pvt.	D, 4th Iowa Inf.	248		1921 Dec 8	IA, 48th, 1922
Harris, P.M.	Pvt.	4th Iowa Inf.	248		1922 Dec 8	IA, 49th, 1923
Harris, P.P.	Pvt.	F, 14th Iowa Inf.	8	43	1888 Jan 18	IA, 15th, 1889
Harris, Phillip		B, 86th Ohio Inf.	89		1908 Aug 5	KS, 28th, 1909
Harris, R.S.		L, 3rd Ind. Cav.	56		1886	KS, 6th, 1887
Harris, Richard	Pvt.	A, 6th Iowa Inf.	206	80	1893 Dec 6	IA, 20th, 1894
Harris, Robert		C, 19th Ind.	25		1922 Apr 22	KS, 42nd, 1923
Harris, Robert O.		B, 48th Mo.	156		1897 Mar 10	KS, 17th, 1898
Harris, S.H.		K, 1st Iowa Cav. (died of paralysis)	180	70	1915 Sep 27	NE, 40th, 1916
Harris, S.W.	Pvt.	M, 1st Iowa Cav.	216		1922 Jul 12	IA, 49th, 1923
Harris, T.G.		E, 137th Ind. Inf.	90		1936 Feb 18	KS, 55th, 1936
Harris, Thomas Glenn		F, 137th Ind.	90		1936 Feb 2	KS, 56th, 1937
Harris, Thos. J.		F, 137th Ind.	90		1937 Feb 18	KS, 57th, 1938
Harris, W.C.		A, 4th Kans. Inf.	12		1909 Jan 16	KS, 29th, 1910
Harris, W.F.		K, 115th Ill.	43		1906 Aug 5	KS, 26th, 1907
Harris, W.H.		K, 83rd Ill. Inf. (died at Topeka)	71		1895 May 1	KS, 15th, 1896
Harris, Walter J.			25		1890	NE, 15th, 1891
Harris, William H.	Sergt.	K, 69th Ohio Inf.	6	55	1894 Nov	IA, 21st, 1895
Harris, Wm. E.		A, 157th Ind. Inf.	55		1917 Jul 23	KS, 37th, 1918
Harrison, A.L.			39		3rd quarter 1883	IA, 10th, 1884
Harrison, Andrew	Pvt.	H, 7th Iowa Cav.	24	87	1932 Jan	IA, 59th, 1933
Harrison, B.D.K.		1st Ohio Battery	4		1910 Nov 2	KS, 30th, 1911
Harrison, C.S.		M, 11th Kans. Cav.	50		1905 Feb 23	KS, 25th, 1906
Harrison, Dan	Pvt.	C, 98th Ohio Inf.	50		1924 Mar 18	IA, 51st, 1925
Harrison, David		G, 29th Penn.	412		1923 Oct	KS, 43rd, 1924
Harrison, E.O.		E, 137th Ohio	25		1928 Jan 28	KS, 48th, 1929
Harrison, E.W.	Pvt.	G, 18th U.S. Inf.	329		1913 Sep 8	IA, 40th, 1914
Harrison, Franklin		M, 11th Kans.	25		1922 Mar 20	KS, 42nd, 1923
Harrison, Geo. W.		K, 7th Iowa	337		1926 Dec 29	KS, 46th, 1927
Harrison, H.J.	Pvt.	E, 12th Iowa	68		1907 Feb 22	IA, 34th, 1908
Harrison, J.		K, 11th Ind. Cav.	28		1914 Dec 23	KS, 34th, 1915
Harrison, J.M.	Pvt.	K, 46th Iowa Inf.	18		1932 Jun 25	IA, 59th, 1933
Harrison, J.P.		L, 5th Ind. Cav.	18		1917 Oct 2	KS, 37th, 1918
Harrison, J.S.	Pvt.	C, 8th Ill. Cav.	88	52	1888 Aug 10	IA, 15th, 1889
Harrison, J.S.		E, 56th N.Y.	1		1922 Jun 6	KS, 42nd, 1923
Harrison, J.W.		B, 116th Ohio	25		1929 Feb 6	KS, 49th, 1930
Harrison, Jackson		E, 40th Col. U.S.	59		1924 Feb 7	KS, 44th, 1925
Harrison, James A.			17		1901	KS, 21st, 1902
Harrison, John		L, 11th Kans.	100		1912 Mar 15	KS, 32nd, 1913
Harrison, John N.	Sergt.	K, 39th (8th Cav.) Ind. Inf. (died in Long Beach, Cal.; funeral in Ottawa; buried at Princeton)	18		1926 Feb 14	KS, 46th, 1927

*See Appendix A, B or C for roster of post names and locations.
†See Introduction for note regarding recording of death date.
234

Name	Rank	Company, Regiment or Ship	Post*	Age	Death Date†	Journal
Harrison, R.L.		H, 2nd Ohio Art. (died of pneumonia)	11	54	1891[1901?] Feb	NE, 26th, 1902
Harrison, Robert		G, 24th Mo. Inf.	251		1899 Jul 8	KS, 19th, 1900
Harrison, Robert G.		120th Ind.	72		1910 Jul 28	KS, 30th, 1911
Harrison, T.M.			105		1912 May 27	KS, 32nd, 1913
Harrison, T.W.		E, 10th Wis.	1		1910 May 21	KS, 30th, 1911
Harrison, Thos.		K, 8th Ind.	18		1937 Aug 14	KS, 56th, 1937
Harrison, Thos. C.		D, 5th Kans.	202		1900 Dec	KS, 20th, 1901
Harrison, Virgil			123		1920 Aug 7	KS, 40th, 1921
Harrison, W.H.	Pvt.	H, 9th Ill. Cav.	440		1929 Jan 8	IA, 55th, 1929
Harrison, W.H.	Pvt.	F, 74th Penn. Inf.	20	56	1891 Apr 3	NE, 16th, 1892
Harrison, W.M.	Pvt.	E, 10th Wis. Inf.	150		1906 May 13	IA, 33rd, 1907
Harrison, Walter		I, 18th U.S.	17		1924 Feb 28	KS, 44th, 1925
Harrison, Wm. H.		H, 3rd Mo. (died of paralysis)	118	81	1922 Jan 6	NE, 47th, 1923
Harrison, Wm. M.	Pvt.	E, 10th Wis.	105		1906 May 13	IA, 32nd, 1906
Harrison, Wm. S.		K, 94th Ill. Inf.	2		1916 Dec 3	KS, 36th, 1917
Harriston, W.H.			111		1916	KS, 36th, 1917
Harrod, Allen	Pvt.	K, 15th Iowa Inf.	332		1912 Nov 15	IA, 39th, 1913
Harrold, A.B.		F, 41st Ill. Inf.	334		1900 Jul 9	KS, 20th, 1901
Harroms, Chas. H.	Pvt.	I, 31st Iowa Inf.	88	72	1898 Feb 3	IA, 24th, 1898
Harrop, Thos.		D, 36th Ill.	25		1913 Sep 6	NE, 38th, 1914
Harryman, Jos.		F, 123rd Ind.	75		1907 Mar 15	NE, 32nd, 1908
Harsey, Samuel	Pvt.	K, 19th Inf.	519		1906 Sep 3	IA, 33rd, 1907
Harsh, Jas. B.	Sergt.	K, 148th Ill. Inf.	440		1923 Jun 19	IA, 50th, 1924
Harshbarger, W.H.		G, 11th Kans.	28		1906 May 20	KS, 26th, 1907
Harshbarger, Wm.		B, 7th Ind.	102		1906 Nov 24	KS, 26th, 1907
Harshberger, Henry	Sergt.	B, 36th Iowa Inf.	156		1916 Jan 1	IA, 43rd, 1917
Harsley, Jo.	Pvt.	C, 16th Iowa Inf.	26		1920 Apr 15	IA, 47th, 1921
Harst, Jacob		K, 54th Ind.	180		1922 Jul 25	KS, 42nd, 1923
Harstook, Daniel		F, 55th Ill. Inf.	1		1915 Dec 7	IA, 42nd, 1916
Hart, A.R.	Sergt.	A, 44th Ill. Inf.	88		1925 Dec 17	IA, 52nd, 1926
Hart, Andrew A.	Pvt.	K, 104th Ill. Inf.	130		1894 Jan 20	IA, 20th, 1894
Hart, C.B.		G, 3rd N.Y.	354	75	1908 Oct 12	NE, 33rd, 1909
Hart, Charles		A, 2nd Ill. Inf.	56	92	1936 Feb 3	IA, 63rd, 1937
Hart, Charles L.		G, 16th Conn.	91		1905 Oct 13	KS, 25th, 1906
Hart, Charles P.		A, 23rd N.Y. Inf.	474		1908 Jan 15	KS, 28th, 1909
Hart, D.S.		D, 123rd Ill. Inf. (died in Oklahoma Terr.)	85		1893 Dec	KS, 14th, 1895
Hart, Daniel		F, 5th Iowa Inf.	144		3rd quarter 1884	IA, 11th, 1885
Hart, E.	Pvt.	F, 6th Iowa Inf.	173		1920 Jul 20	IA, 47th, 1921
Hart, E.C.	Pvt.	A, 22nd Iowa Inf.	198	50	1890	IA, 17th, 1891
Hart, Geo. W.	Pvt.	M, 2nd N.Y. Hvy. Art.	329		1913 Apr 21	IA, 40th, 1914
Hart, George	Pvt.	I, 32nd Iowa Inf.	236		1928 May 13	IA, 55th, 1929
Hart, George W.	Corp.	I, 4th Iowa Cav. (at large)	211	93	1936 Jan 31	IA, 65th, 1939
Hart, H.L.		55th Ill.	36		1912 Feb 11	KS, 32nd, 1913
Hart, J.B.	Pvt.	37th Iowa	20		1905	IA, 32nd, 1906
Hart, J.C.		E, 107th Ill.	81		1917 Apr 24	KS, 37th, 1918
Hart, J.H.	Pvt.	G, —	64		1921 Aug 23	IA, 48th, 1922
Hart, James		B, 18th Ohio (died of accident)	43	68	1910 Dec 2	NE, 35th, 1911
Hart, James D.		C, 16th Wis.	58		1930 May 1	NE, 55th, 1931
Hart, John		F, 44th Ind. Inf.	123		1914 Apr 6	NE, 39th, 1915
Hart, John E.		E, 117th Ohio	28		1910 Oct 3	KS, 30th, 1911
Hart, John S.	Pvt.	F, 33rd Iowa Inf.	137	72	1886 Feb 21	IA, 12th, 1886
Hart, Jonas D.	Lieut.	I, 54th U.S. Inf.	466		1913 Jun 12	IA, 40th, 1914
Hart, Joseph	Sergt.	B, 9th Ill. Cav.	250	64	1892 May 4	IA, 19th, 1893
Hart, M.M.		E, 9th Kans. Cav.	51		1910 Jun 19	KS, 30th, 1911
Hart, P.F.		K, 137th N.Y. Inf.	1		1912 Feb 7	IA, 39th, 1913
Hart, Peter	Pvt.	D, 12th Ind. Cav.	124		1926 Aug 8	IA, 53rd, 1927
Hart, Riley S.		B, 10th Wis.	58		1935 Apr 15	NE, 60th, 1936
Hart, Sarah Elizabeth		nurse			1937 Mar 20	IA, 64th, 1938
Hart, Thomas B.		A, 4th Ky. Cav.	459		1914 Jan 19	KS, 34th, 1915
Harter, C.A.	Pvt.	K, 10th N.Y.	100		1923 Jun 11	IA, 50th, 1924
Harter, C.L.		T, 167th Ohio	85		1930 Jan 8	KS, 50th, 1931
Harter, P.			12		1923 Dec 5	IA, 50th, 1924

*See Appendix A, B or C for roster of post names and locations.
†See Introduction for note regarding recording of death date.

Name	Rank	Company, Regiment or Ship	Post*	Age	Death Date†	Journal
Harter, Wm. F.					1929 Jan 15	NE, 53rd, 1929
Hartford, Henry	Lieut. Col.	8th N.J.	17		1919 Oct 4	KS, 39th, 1920
Harth, Chas. H.		H, 72nd N.Y. (died of pneumonia)	28	74	1913 Jan 18	NE, 38th, 1914
Hartkop, Fred	Pvt.	C, 14th Iowa Inf.	1		1918 Jul 9	IA, 45th, 1919
Hartley, C.T.	Pvt.	A, 64th Ill. Inf.	196		1904 May 26	IA, 31st, 1905
Hartley, John P.		G, 69th Ind. Inf.	123		1899 Aug 23	KS, 19th, 1900
Hartly, Jos.		H, 15th Kans. (died of heart disease)	201		1889	KS, 9th, 1890
Hartly, George			35		1897 Mar 11	NE, 22nd, 1898
Hartman, A.A.		K, 46th Ill.	8		1918 Oct 3	KS, 38th, 1919
Hartman, Adam	Drummer	C, 35th Iowa Inf.	231		1922 Apr 6	IA, 49th, 1923
Hartman, Chas.		B, 4th Mo. Cav.	173		1885	KS, 5th, 1886
Hartman, Chris	Pvt.	D, 1st Neb.	262		1899	NE, 24th, 1900
Hartman, Christian		9th Wis.	63		1924 Mar 10	KS, 44th, 1925
Hartman, Frank		G, 1st Ill. Art.	13		1893 Apr 28	NE, 18th, 1894
Hartman, Fred		F, 13th Kans.	93		1909 Nov 20	KS, 29th, 1910
Hartman, J.W.	Pvt.	D, 46th Iowa Inf.	124		1920 Oct 10	IA, 47th, 1921
Hartman, Jno. G.	Pvt.	B, 18th Ohio Inf.	141		1925 Dec 11	IA, 52nd, 1926
Hartman, L.C.		C, 78th N.Y. Inf. (died at Pueblo, Colo.; buried at Pueblo, Colo.)	294		1894 Aug	KS, 14th, 1895
Hartman, O.S.	Pvt.	H, 24th Iowa Inf.	452		1927 May 29	IA, 54th, 1928
Hartman, Reuben	Pvt.	D, 11th Iowa Inf.	441		1902 Jun 14	IA, 29th, 1903
Hartman, W.H.	Pvt.	B, 34th Iowa	425		1922 Jan 20	IA, 49th, 1923
Hartmann, Geo.	Pvt.	F, 2nd Mo. Inf.	78		1906 Feb 28	IA, 33rd, 1907
Hartnett, Charles H.		B, 11th Kans.	301		1893 Mar	KS, 13th, 1894
Hartnug, F.W.	Lieut.	C, 9th Ill. Cav.	322		1914 Aug 18	IA, 41st, 1915
Hartsell, Phil			24		1915 Oct 11	IA, 42nd, 1916
Hartshorn, Abury	Pvt.	B, 4th Minn. Inf.	496		1892 Jul	IA, 19th, 1893
Hartshorn, Wm. W.		C, 50th Ill.	52		1918 May 6	KS, 38th, 1919
Hartshough, W.D.	Pvt.	F, 2nd Iowa Inf.	101		1920 Oct 6	IA, 47th, 1921
Hartsock, Frank	Corp.	A, 33rd Wis. Inf.	149		1912 May 4	IA, 40th, 1914
Hartsock, Joseph	1st Lieut.	K, 55th Ill. Inf.	1		1897 May 23	IA, 24th, 1898
Hartson, P.M.	Corp.	H, 19th Iowa Inf.	79		1915 Dec	IA, 42nd, 1916
Hartsough, Walter	Sergt.	K, 16th Ill. Cav.	186	55	1892 Jul 2	IA, 19th, 1893
Hartung, Jacob	Pvt.	E, 107th Penn. Inf.	7	86	1932 Dec 1	IA, 59th, 1933
Hartwell, B.F.		F, 81st Ohio (died of consumption)	160		1889	KS, 9th, 1890
Hartwell, G.W.		E, 98th Ill.	83		1898 Aug 13	KS, 18th, 1899
Hartwell, P.A.	Pvt.	E, 74th Ill. Inf.	42		1906 Jul 1	IA, 33rd, 1907
Hartwell, R.B.		B, 28th Iowa	35	76	1922 Sep 27	NE, 47th, 1923
Hartwell, S.W.	Pvt.	H, 32nd Iowa Inf.	277		1902 Nov 4	IA, 29th, 1903
Hartwig, William			72		1923 Mar 19	KS, 43rd, 1924
Hartz, J.C.		49th Ohio (died of dropsy)	312	70	1908	NE, 33rd, 1909
Hartz, Wm.		H, 49th Ohio	25	77	1919 Jun 25	NE, 44th, 1920
Hartzel, R.M.		G, 39th Ohio	498		1918 Nov 14	KS, 38th, 1919
Hartzel, Seth	Sergt.	C, 2nd Iowa Cav.	34		1916 Nov 28	IA, 43rd, 1917
Hartzel, W.L.	Pvt.	I, 145th Ill. Inf.	316		1931	IA, 58th, 1932
Hartzell, Samuel		E, 44th Ind.	57		1919 Dec 6	KS, 39th, 1920
Hartzell, Solomon			227		1921 Feb 3	NE, 47th, 1923
Harvey, A.J.	Pvt.	A, 31st Iowa Inf.	181		1925 Sep 1	IA, 52nd, 1926
Harvey, Albert B.	Pvt.	M, 17th Ill. Cav.	12		1912 May 25	IA, 39th, 1913
Harvey, C.D.			112		1911 Mar 2	IA, 38th, 1912
Harvey, Calvin		H, 26th Ohio Inf.	32		1916 May 2	KS, 36th, 1917
Harvey, George E.	Asst. Surg.	100th Ill. Inf. (died at Assoria, Kans.; buried at Highland Cemetery)	132		1894 Sep	KS, 14th, 1895
Harvey, H.C.		A, 62nd Ohio	383		1926 Nov 10	KS, 46th, 1927
Harvey, H.L.		F, 8th Iowa Regt. (died of dropsy)	94	68	1911 Apr 22	NE, 36th, 1912
Harvey, Henry		Wis. (died of old age)	201	80	1907 Feb 13	NE, 32nd, 1908
Harvey, J.R.		E, 44th Iowa	355		1917 Apr 3	KS, 37th, 1918
Harvey, J.T.	Lieut.	E, 15th Ind.	39		1907 2nd term	IA, 34th, 1908
Harvey, Jas. H.		K, 9th Iowa (died of old age)	96		1922	NE, 47th, 1923
Harvey, Jesse E.		E, 30th Iowa Inf.	108	97	1938 Jan 7	IA, 64th, 1938
Harvey, John		D, 99th Ind. Inf.	289		1899 Sep 23	KS, 19th, 1900
Harvey, John W.	Lieut.	18th Iowa Inf.	251		1913 Feb 28	IA, 40th, 1914

*See Appendix A, B or C for roster of post names and locations.
†See Introduction for note regarding recording of death date.

Name	Rank	Company, Regiment or Ship	Post*	Age	Death Date†	Journal
Harvey, N.C.	Pvt.	H, 2nd Wis. Inf.	124		1909 Mar 24	IA, 36th, 1910
Harvey, S.T.		B, 4th Ohio Cav.	47		1921 Aug 7	KS, 41st, 1922
Harvey, T.H.		C, 69th Ohio	32		1921 May 28	KS, 41st, 1922
Harvey, W.A.	Pvt.	I, 130th Penn. Inf.	454	73	1896 Aug 3	IA, 23rd, 1897
Harvey, W.C.		U.S. Navy	18		1921 Mar 7	KS, 41st, 1922
Harvey, W.H.		B, 17th Ill. (died of old age)	4	76	1924 Apr 4	NE, 49th, 1925
Harvey, W.M.	Pvt.	I, 36th Iowa Inf.	325	46	1887 Jul 8	IA, 14th, 1888
Harvey, W.M.	Pvt.	K, 46th Iowa Inf.	18		1897 Dec 9	IA, 24th, 1898
Harvey, W.W.		A, 3rd Wis. Inf., 20th Corps (born in Maine; died in New Mexico)	80		1883 Jun	NE, 8th, 1884
Harvey, Wm.	Pvt.	A, 14th Iowa	16		1923 Sep 29	IA, 50th, 1924
Harvey, Wm. H.	Pvt.	I, 18th Iowa Inf.	112		1930 May	IA, 57th, 1931
Harvison, John	Pvt.	C, 8th Ill. Cav.	298	60	1897 Jan 3	IA, 23rd, 1897
Harwood, F.W.	Pvt.	I, 2nd Wis. Cav.	235		1918 Feb 19	IA, 45th, 1919
Harwood, N.S.		G, 9th Iowa (cause of death: heart)	25	52	1900 Jan 5	NE, 25th, 1901
Harwood, R.		6, 110th Penn.	32	70	1919 May 24	NE, 44th, 1920
Hasbrook, J.D.	Capt.	D, 156th N.Y. Inf.	137		1905 Jan 29	IA, 32nd, 1906
Haseloh, Fred A.		F, 15th Mo.	60		1925 Apr 16	NE, 51st, 1927
Haselton, P.	Corp.	F, 39th Iowa Inf.	175	66	1887 Feb 9	IA, 13th, 1887
Hashberger, H.D.		D, 21st Ohio	34	68	1910 Apr 6	NE, 35th, 1911
Hashman, Lew		I, 39th Ill. Inf.	18		1917 Apr 5	KS, 37th, 1918
Haskell, B.A.		D, 142nd N.Y. (died of paralysis)	40	78	1924 Jan 13	NE, 49th, 1925
Haskell, E.A.		B, 7th Iowa Cav.	33		2nd quarter 1884	IA, 11th, 1885
Haskell, Jno. L.	Pvt.	C, 26th Iowa Inf.	88	60	1889 Nov 8	IA, 16th, 1890
Haskell, John D.	Band	11th U.S.	63		1924 Sep 20	KS, 44th, 1925
Haskell, M.M.	Chaplain		340		1890	KS, 10th, 1891
Haskell, Orrin D.		H, 12th Kans.	88		1911 Dec 6	KS, 31st, 1912
Haskell, T.H.		A, 2nd Kans.	1		1898 Feb 14	KS, 18th, 1899
Haskell, William		F, 67th Ill.	93		1902	KS, 22nd, 1903
Haskill, Caleb T.		G, 9th Ind. Inf.	64		1886	KS, 6th, 1887
Haskin, Edward		B, 44th Wis. Inf. (at large)		100 & 4 mos.	1936 Jan 16	IA, 62nd, 1936
Haskin, Edward		B, 44th Wis. Inf. (at large)		100 & 5 mos.	1936 Apr 9	IA, 63rd, 1937
Haskin, Frederick		C, 141st Ill.	28		1915 Nov 27	KS, 35th, 1916
Haskin, W.H.	Pvt.	B, 43rd Wis. Inf.	149		1918 Mar 6	IA, 45th, 1919
Haskins, A.	Pvt.	D, 21st Iowa Inf.	346		1921 Nov 13	IA, 48th, 1922
Haskins, A.D.	Pvt.	K, 3rd Wis. Inf.	26		1921 Jan 17	IA, 48th, 1922
Haskins, C.V.	Pvt.	F, 103rd Ill. Inf.	56		1913 Jul 8	IA, 40th, 1914
Haskins, Edward		B, 44th Wis. Inf.		100 & 5 mos.	1936 Apr 9	IA, 62nd, 1936
Haskins, F.M.			14		1899	IA, 26th, 1900
Haskins, John		C, 60th U.S.C.T.	236		1899	KS, 19th, 1900
Haskins, M.S.		2nd Ind.	64		1914 Nov	KS, 34th, 1915
Haskins, Owen	Pvt.	D, 26th Iowa Inf.	49		1922 Jan 17	IA, 49th, 1923
Haskins, P.A.		A, 21st Wis.	145		1885	KS, 5th, 1886
Haskins, W.C.	Corp.	F, Ind. Colored Ark.	1		1907 Dec 6	IA, 34th, 1908
Haskins, W.F.	Pvt.	D, 57th Ill. Inf.	441		1908 Nov 30	IA, 35th, 1909
Haskinson, John		I, 7th Iowa	28		1915 Dec 11	KS, 35th, 1916
Haslet, C.B.		D, 8th Kans. Vols.	53		1902 Jan 15	KS, 22nd, 1903
Hasley, J.L.	Pvt.	I, 61st Ill. Inf.	10		1927 Jul	IA, 54th, 1928
Haslin, P.I.			19		1909 Jul 7	IA, 36th, 1910
Hasned, Z.T.			167		1919 Jan 13	IA, 46th, 1920
Hass, B.S.		F, 83rd Penn. Inf.	262	70	1911 Jun 30	NE, 36th, 1912
Hass, B.S.		F, 83rd Penn. Inf.	262	70	1905 Jun 30	NE, 30th, 1906
Hass, G.R.	Pvt.	A, 155th Ind.	94		1924 May 30	IA, 51st, 1925
Hass, Geo. W.		K, 104th Ill. (died of paralysis)	13	75	1917 Aug 24	NE, 42nd, 1918
Hass, George	Pvt.	A, 102nd Ohio Inf.	96	90	1933 Oct 26	IA, 60th, 1934
Hass, J.M.		E, 9th Ky. Cav.	4		1900 Apr 9	KS, 20th, 1901
Hass, T.O.			335		1886	KS, 6th, 1887
Hasselbaum, Wm.		G, 82nd Ill. Reg.	77		1918 May	NE, 43rd, 1919
Hassell, D.			5		1923 Mar 24	IA, 50th, 1924

Name	Rank	Company, Regiment or Ship	Post*	Age	Death Date†	Journal
Hasselman, Ben	Artificer	B, 1st N.Y. Eng.	5		1902 Dec 9	IA, 29th, 1903
Hastie, David	Pvt.	D, 2nd Iowa Inf.	26	70	1898 May 22	IA, 25th, 1899
Hastie, Phil	Pvt.	K, 20th Iowa Inf.	425		1915 Dec 17	IA, 42nd, 1916
Hastings, A.G.		C, 31st Iowa Inf.	25		1894 Jul 10	NE, 19th, 1895
Hastings, Ben A.	Sergt.	G, 184th N.Y. Inf.	88		1916 Oct 20	IA, 43rd, 1917
Hastings, D.C.	Surg.	27th Iowa Inf.	381	58	1888 Sep 9	IA, 15th, 1889
Hastings, Henry		died of heart trouble	10		1906 Apr 14	NE, 31st, 1907
Hastings, Joseph	Pvt.	D, 1st U.S. Hvy. Art.	6		1929 Oct 13	IA, 56th, 1930
Hastings, L.D.		6th Iowa (died of stomach trouble)	44	65	1900	NE, 25th, 1901
Hastings, L.M.	Pvt.	C, 9th Iowa Cav.	173		1901 Sep 26	IA, 28th, 1902
Hastings, L.R.		G, 10th Kans.	341		1889	KS, 9th, 1890
Hastings, L.R.		H, 4th Kans.	341		1888	KS, 8th, 1889
Hastings, L.R.		H, 4th Kans. Inf.	341		1886	KS, 6th, 1887
Hastings, L.R.		G, 10th Kans.	341		1886 Mar 12	KS, 11th, 1892
Hastings, L.R.		H, 10th Kans.	341		1886 Mar 26	KS, 12th, 1893
Haswell, Arthur	Pvt.	H, 28th Iowa Inf.	66	63	1895 Feb 13	IA, 21st, 1895
Haswell, John		K, 133rd Ill. Inf.	18		1899 Sep 15	KS, 19th, 1900
Hatch, F.C.		H, 2nd N.Y. Cav.	74		1915 Jul 10	KS, 35th, 1916
Hatch, F.W.		F, 64th Ill. Inf.	66		1918 Jul 6	KS, 38th, 1919
Hatch, Henry	Pvt.	C, 9th Iowa Inf.	165		1918	IA, 45th, 1919
Hatch, J.S.		A, 10th Kans.	12		1936	KS, 55th, 1936
Hatch, M.C.	Pvt.	K, 148th Ill. Inf.	440		1919 Aug 22	IA, 46th, 1920
Hatch, S.		I, 16th Ill.	283		1888	KS, 8th, 1889
Hatch, S.		I, 16th Ill. Inf.	283		1887 Nov 15	KS, 7th, 1888
Hatch, S.		I, 16th Ill. Inf. (died of disease of stomach)	283		1887 Oct 25	KS, 11th, 1892
Hatch, Thos. C.		B, 73rd Ill. Inf.	25	75	1921 Mar 6	NE, 46th, 1922
Hatch, Thos. H.		E, 47th Ill.	25		1927 Oct 7	NE, 52nd, 1928
Hatcher, E.R.	Pvt.	H, 47th Iowa Inf.	40		1929 Jan 14	IA, 56th, 1930
Hatcher, R.H.	Pvt.	G, 23rd Iowa	17		1921 Aug 2	IA, 48th, 1922
Hatchett, E.R.		H, 4th Mo.	244		1912 Oct	KS, 32nd, 1913
Hatfield, George		D, 47th Ill.	469		1922 Feb 23	KS, 41st, 1922
Hatfield, George		H, 89th Ohio Inf.	28		1925 Apr 1	KS, 45th, 1926
Hatfield, Henry		F, 49th Ohio	69		1912 Jun 11	KS, 32nd, 1913
Hatfield, L.S.		G, 5th Iowa	97		1888	KS, 8th, 1889
Hatfield, Marshall			371		1904 Oct	IA, 31st, 1905
Hatfield, Samuel M.		D, 47th Ind.	35		1919 Dec 14	KS, 39th, 1920
Hathaway, A.W.	Pvt.	B, 9th Vt. Inf.	235		1924 Jan 14	IA, 51st, 1925
Hathaway, C.E.		D, 2nd Ind. Cav.	38		1924 Jul 7	KS, 44th, 1925
Hathaway, D.A.		F, 25th Ind. Inf. (died at Cheney)	325		1895 Mar	KS, 15th, 1896
Hathaway, G.Z.		F, 9th Kans. Cav.	73		1916 May 16	KS, 36th, 1917
Hathaway, Geo.	Pvt.	39th Iowa Inf.	45		1912 May 29	IA, 39th, 1913
Hathaway, J.S.	Sergt.	A, 26th Ind.	195		1907 Jun 15	IA, 34th, 1908
Hathaway, Leonard	Lieut.	K, 7th Mass. Inf.	465		1912 May 24	IA, 39th, 1913
Hathaway, N.R.	Corp.	G, 2nd Ill. Lt. Art.	22	89	1932 Dec 25	IA, 59th, 1933
Hattchet, J.T.		E, 116th Ill.	203		1922 Sep 8	KS, 42nd, 1923
Hattery, Andrew		D, 87th Ind. Inf.	324		1887 Dec 19	KS, 7th, 1888
Hattery, W.M.	Pvt.	A, 42nd Ohio Inf.	68		1913	IA, 40th, 1914
Hattman, Chas.	Pvt.	F, 2nd Mo. Art.	184		1903 Nov 29	IA, 30th, 1904
Hatton, G.W.	Pvt.	D, 35th Iowa Inf.	231		1922 Dec 29	IA, 49th, 1923
Hatton, J.W.	Steward	31st Ohio	44		1905 Dec 16	IA, 32nd, 1906
Hatton, Joseph S.	Pvt.	I, 6th Iowa Cav.	357	51	1887 Mar 12	IA, 13th, 1887
Hauber, Wm.		E, 35th Mo.	130		1921 Mar 5	KS, 41st, 1922
Haug, Gottlieb		G, 127th Ind. Inf.	6		1925 Aug 22	KS, 45th, 1926
Haugh, J.H.			171		1904 Jan 3	IA, 31st, 1905
Haughey, J.T.		C, 12th Kans. Inf. (died at Paola)	117		1895 Apr 14	KS, 15th, 1896
Haughey, Jacob		B, 183rd Ohio	25		1927 Jul 25	KS, 47th, 1928
Haughn, S.I.			233		1922 Dec 17	IA, 49th, 1923
Haulmann, Henry	Pvt.	H, 21st Penn. Inf.	7		1912 Nov 11	IA, 39th, 1913
Haun, Simeon S.		B, 57th Penn. Inf.	130 235 400	96	1938 Feb 10	IA, 64th, 1938
Hause, John A.		E, 154th Ohio Inf.	151		1912 Jul 17	KS, 32nd, 1913

*See Appendix A, B or C for roster of post names and locations.
†See Introduction for note regarding recording of death date.
238

Name	Rank	Company, Regiment or Ship	Post*	Age	Death Date†	Journal
Hause, Milton		C, 126th Penn.	63		1917 Feb 18	KS, 37th, 1918
Hauser, Robert B.		died of consumption	147		1891 Sep 4	KS, 11th, 1892
Haven, N.C.	Pvt.	B, 13th Iowa Inf.	253	72	1892 Apr 4	IA, 18th, 1892
Haven, S.W.	Pvt.	G, 27th Iowa Inf.	377	67	1894	IA, 20th, 1894
Havener, George J.	Pvt.	I, 4th Iowa Inf.	192		1901 Feb 1	IA, 28th, 1902
Havens, A.D.		F, 96th Ohio	39		1928 Feb 21	NE, 53rd, 1929
Havens, Ben	Pvt.	G, 9th Iowa Cav.	141		1931 Feb 12	IA, 58th, 1932
Havens, Benj. F.		C, 122nd Ill.	244		1912 Mar 9	KS, 32nd, 1913
Havens, C.			209		1901-1902	IA, 28th, 1902
Havens, Geo. C.	Pvt.	25th Iowa Inf.	39		1909 Sep 16	IA, 36th, 1910
Havens, J.O.	1st Lieut.	G, 96th Ill.	291		1903 Nov 11	IA, 30th, 1904
Havens, Jasper	Pvt.	M, 4th Ill. Cav.	7	53	1895 Sep 12	IA, 22nd, 1896
Haver, Geo. R.	Pvt.	F, 36th Iowa	398		1914 Aug 23	IA, 41st, 1915
Haverhill, A.H.	Pvt.	G, 19th Iowa Inf.	153		1912 Oct 19	IA, 40th, 1914
Haverly, D.M.		G, 8th Iowa Inf.	7		1927 Mar 23	NE, 52nd, 1928
Haverly, O.E.	Pvt.	B, 28th Iowa	30		1922 Feb 2	IA, 49th, 1923
Haviland, W.H.	Corp.	K, 23rd Ill. Inf.	182	43	1888 Jun 6	IA, 15th, 1889
Haw, Alonzo		17th N.Y. Battery	328		1904 Nov 27	KS, 24th, 1905
Haw, Charles		F, —	53		1917 Nov 19	KS, 37th, 1918
Haw, Geo.	Lieut.	B, 33rd Wis. Inf.	69		1911 Sep 10	IA, 38th, 1912
Haward, Chas. W.	Sergt.	D, 4th N.J. Lt. Art.	515		1914 Dec 13	IA, 41st, 1915
Hawes, Le Roy		M, 5th N.Y. Cav.	25		1923	NE, 48th, 1924
Hawes, LeRoy	Pvt.	M, 5th N.Y. Cav.	29		1923 Dec 15	IA, 50th, 1924
Hawk, D.L.			258		1916	KS, 36th, 1917
Hawk, David A.		G, 11th Penn. Cav.	25		1911 Feb 1	KS, 31st, 1912
Hawk, E.H.		D, 26th U.S. Inf.	375		1915 Feb 2	KS, 35th, 1916
Hawk, F.M.		I, 75th Ohio	27		1924 Sep 3	KS, 44th, 1925
Hawk, George W.		I, 25th Ill. Inf.	64		1912 Apr 5	KS, 32nd, 1913
Hawk, Hugh		B, 21st Ind. Inf.	14		1890 Jul 13	KS, 12th, 1893
Hawk, J.B.		H, 47th Ohio Inf.	11	62	1908 Apr 14	NE, 33rd, 1909
Hawk, Michael	Pvt. Pvt.	I, 78th Ohio Inf. K, 1st U.S. Inf.	22	93	1940 Nov 16	IA, 67th, 1941
Hawk, V.D.		H, 59th Ill.	298		1910 Jul 16	KS, 30th, 1911
Hawk, William		D, 9th Kans. Cav.	51		1892 Mar 11	KS, 12th, 1893
Hawkes, E.H.		D, 25th U.S. Inf.	375		1914 Feb 20	KS, 34th, 1915
Hawkes, S.W.	Pvt.	E, 118th Ill. Inf.	2		1906 Sep 27	IA, 33rd, 1907
Hawkins, A.J.	Pvt.	A, 10th Iowa Inf.	347		1897 Jun 16	IA, 24th, 1898
Hawkins, Albert	Pvt.	C, 7th Wis. Inf.	244	49	1894 Nov 24	IA, 21st, 1895
Hawkins, Alfred		H, 8th Kans. (died of heart failure)	302		1904	NE, 29th, 1905
Hawkins, B.J.		I, 9th Mo. Cav.	117		1916 Mar 14	KS, 36th, 1917
Hawkins, C.Z.	Sergt.		30		1923 Apr 17	IA, 50th, 1924
Hawkins, Chas. F.		H, 24th N.Y.	107		1897 Mar 27	KS, 17th, 1898
Hawkins, D.		D, 4th Mo. (died at Burden)	172		1895 Nov 22	KS, 15th, 1896
Hawkins, Daniel		D, 20th Ind.	81		1916 Oct 4	KS, 36th, 1917
Hawkins, F.E.		C, 166th Ohio	249		1917 Dec 25	KS, 37th, 1918
Hawkins, Frank		Mich. Eng.	17		1919 Apr 6	KS, 39th, 1920
Hawkins, Geo.	Pvt.	I, 16th Ill.	12		1924 Aug 31	IA, 51st, 1925
Hawkins, Geo. C.	Pvt.	C, 1st Iowa Cav.	440	63	1898 Mar 16	IA, 24th, 1898
Hawkins, J.			215		1883	KS, 3rd, 1884
Hawkins, J.W.		I, 12th Kans.	68		1929 Feb 19	KS, 49th, 1930
Hawkins, Jas.	Pvt.	C, 1st Maine Art.	364	74	1888 Jun 24	IA, 15th, 1889
Hawkins, John		C, 84th Ill.	71		1920 Sep 4	KS, 40th, 1921
Hawkins, L.H.		F, 16th Ind.	129		1914 Jul 15	KS, 34th, 1915
Hawkins, Levi D.		E, 42nd Ill. Inf.	90		1912 Mar 1	KS, 32nd, 1913
Hawkins, M.J.		A, 33rd Ohio Inf.	1		1886	KS, 6th, 1887
Hawkins, Marflitt	Sergt.	G, 94th Ohio Vol. Inf.	1		1915 Jun 21	KS, 35th, 1916
Hawkins, O.H.		H, 2nd Wis.	45		1906 Feb 15	KS, 26th, 1907
Hawkins, S.E.	Pvt.	C, 15th Iowa Inf.	12		1904 Sep 3	IA, 31st, 1905
Hawkins, T.G.		E, 19th Ohio Inf. (died of cancer stomach)	62	79	1920 Dec 14	NE, 45th, 1921
Hawkins, Wm.	Pvt.	K, 31st Iowa Inf.	111	61	1891 Jan 26	IA, 18th, 1892
Hawks, C.B.	Pvt.	B, 45th Ill. Inf.	42		1922 Mar 22	IA, 49th, 1923
Hawks, F.S.		B, 124th Ill.	7		1921	IA, 48th, 1922

Name	Rank	Company, Regiment or Ship	Post*	Age	Death Date†	Journal
Hawks, Geo. W.		F, 22nd Ind. (died from wounds)	418		1889	KS, 9th, 1890
Hawkshurst, J.P.			118		1909	IA, 36th, 1910
Hawley, E.J.	Pvt.	I, 52nd Ill. Inf.	67	50	1888 Mar 10	IA, 15th, 1889
Hawley, Frank D.	Pvt.	L, 8th Iowa Cav.	130		1901 Aug 15	IA, 28th, 1902
Hawley, Geo. R.	Pvt.	B, 44th Iowa Inf.	231		1918 Oct 24	IA, 45th, 1919
Hawley, Price	Corp.	B, 73rd Ind. Inf.	452		1926 Jul 18	IA, 53rd, 1927
Hawley, Wm.	Pvt.	A, 100th Ill.	500		1907 Jan 29	IA, 34th, 1908
Hawley, Wm. C.	Pvt.	F, 9th Ill. Inf.	5		1909 May 2	IA, 36th, 1910
Hawlk, L.A.	Pvt.	I, 35th Iowa Inf.	7		1921	IA, 48th, 1922
Hawn, Aug.	Pvt.	K, 12th Ind. Inf.	16		1920 Dec 20	IA, 47th, 1921
Haworth, W.H.		H, 18th Ohio	32		1925 Mar 15	KS, 45th, 1926
Hawthorn, W.E.	Corp.	K, 13th Iowa Inf.	455	72	1894 Jul 23	IA, 21st, 1895
Hawthorne, Wm.		Navy	50		1922 Jul 31	KS, 42nd, 1923
Hay, Beriah	Pvt.	F, 50th Ill. Inf.	88	51	1889 Apr 7	IA, 16th, 1890
Hay, J.M.			265		1913 Feb 2	KS, 33rd, 1914
Hay, P.H.		A, 23rd Mo.	293		1919 Jun 17	KS, 39th, 1920
Hay, S.D.	Pvt.	E, 28th Wis. Inf.	391		1918 Feb 10	IA, 45th, 1919
Hay, Sam'l			45		1916 Jun 10	IA, 43rd, 1917
Hay, W.T.	Pvt.	A, 10th Wis. Inf.	391		1915 Aug 3	IA, 42nd, 1916
Haycock, George A.	Pvt.	I, 9th Iowa Cav.	12		1928 Apr 6	IA, 55th, 1929
Haycraft, Joel M.		F, 2nd Minn. Inf.	324		1886	KS, 6th, 1887
Hayden, Alfred R.	Pvt.	A, 55th Ill.	193		1907 Jan 4	IA, 34th, 1908
Hayden, B.T.	Capt.	A, 7th Ky.	301		1898 Jul 6	KS, 18th, 1899
Hayden, E.E.		D, 59th Ill. Inf. (died at Topeka; buried at Topeka Cemetery)	1		1894 Jan 10	KS, 14th, 1895
Hayden, Elijah	Pvt.	F, 32nd Iowa Inf.	154		1917 Apr 17	IA, 44th, 1918
Hayden, G.M.		F, 51st Penn. Inf. (died at Topeka)	71		1895 May 9	KS, 15th, 1896
Hayden, George W.		A, 17th Ind. Inf.	17		1917 Mar 9	KS, 37th, 1918
Hayden, H.		C, 33rd Wis. Inf.	36		1911 Apr 3	KS, 31st, 1912
Hayden, Henry		I, 2nd Mo.	64		1934 Mar 25	NE, 59th, 1935
Hayden, James	Seaman	Steamer *Pensacola*	396	51	1886 Nov 29	IA, 17th, 1891
Hayden, James	Seaman	U.S. frigate *Colorado*	396	50	1886 Nov 29	IA, 13th, 1887
Hayden, James		G, 7th Iowa Cav. (at large)	154	91	1937 May 16	IA, 64th, 1938
Hayden, L.M.		H, 10th Kans.	129		1906 Jul 11	KS, 26th, 1907
Hayden, S.E.	Pvt.	G, 132nd Ill. Inf.	440		1930 Sep 12	IA, 57th, 1931
Hayden, Warren		G, 187th Ohio Inf. (died of heart disease)	201		1889	KS, 9th, 1890
Hayden, Wm.	Pvt.	I, 8th Iowa Cav.	184		1911 Dec 22	IA, 38th, 1912
Hayes, A.O.		A, 3rd Ind.	218		1896 Jun 24	KS, 16th, 1897
Hayes, Ben F.		C, 54th Ill.	25		1921 Nov 23	KS, 41st, 1922
Hayes, Bennel		E, 9th Ind. Cav.	25		1923	NE, 48th, 1924
Hayes, E.R.	Pvt.	1st Ohio Bat.	49	47	1896 Feb 26	IA, 23rd, 1897
Hayes, F.S.	Sergt.	F, 157th N.Y. Inf.	124		1910 Feb 16	IA, 37th, 1911
Hayes, George A.		1st U.S. Eng. Corps	164		1911 Dec 11	KS, 32nd, 1913
Hayes, H.R.		B, 6th Ohio Cav.	1		1887 Aug 14	KS, 7th, 1888
Hayes, Jas. K.P.		G, 23rd Iowa	[25?]		1923	NE, 48th, 1924
Hayes, John E.		K, 8th Iowa	214		1916 May 9	KS, 36th, 1917
Hayes, John F.	Pvt.	2nd Battery V.R.C.	88		1910 Sep 20	IA, 37th, 1911
Hayes, Noah S.		E, 36th Ind.	25		1929 Aug 6	NE, 54th, 1930
Hayes, Orrin	Pvt.	D, 40th Wis. Inf.	67		1917 Dec 4	IA, 44th, 1918
Hayes, S.A.	Corp.	C, 36th Iowa Inf.	398		1916 Aug 10	IA, 43rd, 1917
Hayes, S.W.		I, 34th Ohio	63		1918 Dec 21	KS, 38th, 1919
Hayes, Sam'l A.		F, 64th Ohio Inf.	174		1900 Nov 1	KS, 20th, 1901
Hayes, T.H.	Pvt.	K, 46th Ill.	74		1921 Mar 10	IA, 48th, 1922
Hayes, W.H.	Pvt.	L, 3rd Colo. Cav.	458	61	1890 Mar 6	IA, 16th, 1890
Hayes, W.H.		K, 1st N.H. Hvy. Art.	81		1920 Jan 24	KS, 40th, 1921
Hayes, W.Q.		B, 48th Ill.	256		1917 Jan 19	KS, 37th, 1918
Hayes, Zaccheus		I, 8th Ill. Cav.	117		1900 Jan 13	KS, 20th, 1901
Hayhey, Jas.			80		1922 Apr	IA, 49th, 1923
Hayle, James	Pvt.	G, 72nd Ill. Inf.	4		1899	NE, 24th, 1900
Hayner, H.C.	Pvt.	G, 135th Penn. Inf.	440	87	1931 Jan 5	IA, 58th, 1932
Hayner, H.C.	Pvt.	G, 135th Penn. Inf.	440		1931 Jan 5	IA, 57th, 1931
Haynes, F.V.		A, 51st Ind.	184		1920 Jun 21	KS, 40th, 1921

Name	Rank	Company, Regiment or Ship	Post*	Age	Death Date†	Journal
Haynes, Jesse	Pvt.	G, 98th Ohio	7		1903 Apr 14	IA, 30th, 1904
Haynes, Philip		E, 5th U.S.C.I.	127		1929	KS, 49th, 1930
Haynes, Phillips		E, 5th U.S. Col. Inf.	127		1928 Dec 30	KS, 48th, 1929
Haynes, W.H.		I, 2nd Ill.	177		1899 May 4	KS, 19th, 1900
Haynes, W.L.		K, 135th Ind. Cav.	1		1918 Mar 8	KS, 38th, 1919
Haynes, Wm.		K, 3rd Tenn.	74		1898	KS, 18th, 1899
Haynie, T			123		1895	KS, 15th, 1896
Hays, A.H.		Kans.	74		1893 Jul 16	KS, 13th, 1894
Hays, C.R.		M, 2nd Mich. Cav.	27		1912 Jul 28	KS, 32nd, 1913
Hays, D.F.	Pvt.	E, 4th Iowa Cav.	64		1930 Nov 6	IA, 57th, 1931
Hays, George W.		F, 10th Iowa	357		1900 Jun 5	KS, 20th, 1901
Hays, Homer		F, 1st Kans. Inf.	12		1892 Aug 2	KS, 12th, 1893
Hays, Hysom		C, 2nd — Cav.	240		1901 Feb 3	KS, 21st, 1902
Hays, J.B.		E, 9th Kans. Cav.	51		1885	KS, 5th, 1886
Hays, J.B.		G, 60th Ohio	4		1913 Jul 21	KS, 33rd, 1914
Hays, John		B, 5th Kans. (died in Oklahoma Terr.)	74		1894 Dec 9	KS, 14th, 1895
Hays, John L.			23		1924 Aug 31	KS, 44th, 1925
Hays, Loren			49		1926 Oct 15	IA, 53rd, 1927
Hays, M.	Pvt.	F, 1st Iowa Cav.	63		1920 Apr 28	IA, 47th, 1921
Hays, Merritt		E, 4th Mass.	64		1885	KS, 5th, 1886
Hays, Rhody P.		H, 3rd Penn. Art.	276		1886	KS, 6th, 1887
Hays, Robert		H, — Conn. Art. & Inf.	32		1905 Dec 5	KS, 25th, 1906
Hays, Robert		C, 30th Ind.	145		1909 Apr 13	KS, 29th, 1910
Hays, Sam			429		1911	KS, 31st, 1912
Hays, Samuel		I, 149th N.Y.	429		1908	KS, 28th, 1909
Hays, Samuel		I, 199th N.Y.	429		1918 May 2	KS, 38th, 1919
Hays, Thomas			231		1929 Jan 2	IA, 55th, 1929
Hays, Wm. M.	Sergt.	E, 4th Iowa Cav.	64		1911 Jun 20	IA, 38th, 1912
Hays, Wm. M.	Seaman	Steamer *Fairy*, U.S. Navy	12		1892 Feb 29	KS, 12th, 1893
Hayse, Alex		C, 26th Mich.	234		1893 Jan 11	KS, 13th, 1894
Hayse, Austin Q.		A, 196th Ohio	17		1925 Apr 29	KS, 45th, 1926
Hayson, Wm.		F, 33rd Ill.	35		1926 Sep	KS, 46th, 1927
Haythorn, Oscar			244		1905 Jan 1	KS, 25th, 1906
Hayward, E.B.	Major	5th N.Y. Cav.	1		1927 Feb 3	IA, 54th, 1928
Hayward, Geo.	Pvt.	E, 2nd Iowa Cav.	123		1910 Nov 24	IA, 37th, 1911
Hayward, M.L.	Capt.	H, 5th N.Y. Cav.	24		1899	NE, 24th, 1900
Hayward, W.B.	Pvt.	B, 29th Iowa Inf.	97		1908 Mar 10	IA, 35th, 1909
Haywood, John	Pvt.	B, 10th Ind. Inf.	55		1916 Jun 16	IA, 43rd, 1917
Haywood, W.T.	Pvt.	F, 44th Mass. Inf.	12		1911 Apr 18	IA, 38th, 1912
Hayworth, George		E, 39th Ill. (not a member of the department but living in Nebraska; location: McCool)			1937 Jan 20	NE, 62nd, 1938
Hazard, Carlos	Pvt.	M, 1st Wis. Art.	22		1911 Jan 18	IA, 38th, 1912
Haze, George	Pvt.	M, Ill. Inf.	219		1917 Jan 12	IA, 44th, 1918
Hazel, Robert		E, 45th Ill.	130		1921 Jan 12	KS, 41st, 1922
Hazelbaker, S.J.		K, 18th Ill.	3		1922 Sep 23	KS, 42nd, 1923
Hazell, Jno.	Pvt.	I, 46th Wis. Inf.	441	58	1888 Jan 18	IA, 15th, 1889
Hazelton, F.S.		I, 39th Wis.	117		1913 Jan 14	KS, 33rd, 1914
Hazelton, Geo.		F, 48th Ohio Inf.	498		1930	KS, 50th, 1931
Hazelton, James		C, 48th Ind.	32		1896 Apr 25	KS, 16th, 1897
Hazelton, O.S.		died of old age	62	82	1908 Nov 22	NE, 33rd, 1909
Hazelton, T.W.	Sergt.	D, 21st Iowa Inf.	168		1910 May 31	IA, 37th, 1911
Hazen, E.H.			12		1923 Aug 3	IA, 50th, 1924
Hazen, H.W.		D, 44th Ill. Inf.	4		1899 Apr 30	KS, 19th, 1900
Hazen, James		144th Ill.	163		1904 Mar 17	KS, 24th, 1905
Hazen, R.S.	Pvt.	G, 7th Iowa Cav.	88		1906 Apr 25	IA, 33rd, 1907
Hazle, James H.		M, 1st Ohio Cav.	130		1912 Aug	KS, 32nd, 1913
Hazlet, Gilbert	Sergt.	C, 12th —	356		1911 Jul 2	IA, 38th, 1912
Hazleton, J.H.	Pvt.	D, 106th Penn. Inf.	235		1928 May 3	IA, 55th, 1929
Hazlett, R.M.		G, 206th Penn. (died of paralysis)	22		1918 Aug 6	NE, 43rd, 1919
Hazlett, Wm.	Pvt.	C, 15th Iowa Inf.	167		1911 Aug	IA, 38th, 1912
Heacock, D.B.			29		1904 Jan 4	IA, 31st, 1905

*See Appendix A, B or C for roster of post names and locations.
†See Introduction for note regarding recording of death date.

Name	Rank	Company, Regiment or Ship	Post*	Age	Death Date†	Journal
Heacock, James H.		I, 29th Ill.	55		1917 Jul 2	KS, 37th, 1918
Heacock, Jas.		7th Ohio Bat.	81		1917 Sep 24	KS, 37th, 1918
Head, Albert	Capt.	H, 10th Iowa	12		1922 Oct 18	IA, 49th, 1923
Head, C.B.		died of pneumonia	37	75	1904 Apr 28	NE, 29th, 1905
Head, James					1935	KS, 55th, 1936
Head, Malon	Lieut.	F, 10th Iowa Inf.	23		1920 Jan 17	IA, 47th, 1921
Head, Moses		F, 60th N.Y. Inf. (cause of death: heart)	143	61	1903 Oct 5	NE, 28th, 1904
Headfirst, R.	Pvt.	D, Bat. B, Minn.	236	56	1886 Nov 18	IA, 13th, 1887
Headington, E.		B, 30th Ohio	53		1888	KS, 8th, 1889
Headle, J.C.			173		1910	IA, 37th, 1911
Headley, Thos. J.			287		1925	NE, 50th, 1926
Headley, W.E.		5th Iowa Battery	147		1908 Jun 3	KS, 28th, 1909
Heald, A.E.		7th Iowa Cav.	48		1902 Oct 24	IA, 29th, 1903
Heald, Clark		A, 7th Iowa Cav.	47		1900 Sep 27	KS, 20th, 1901
Heald, Seth	Pvt.	G, 34th Iowa Inf.	1		1915 May 31	IA, 42nd, 1916
Heald, Wm. A.		B, 1st Ohio	39		1911 Jan 20	KS, 31st, 1912
Healey, Edward		G, 1st Wis. E, 1st Vol. Inf. (died of accidental strangulation)	56	70	1908 Jun 18	NE, 33rd, 1909
Healy, Francis M.		I, 31st Wis. Inf.	4	65	1913 Mar 5	NE, 38th, 1914
Heard, Wm. A.	Corp.	G, 8th Iowa Cav.	74	52	1895 Aug 28	IA, 22nd, 1896
Hearling, Gus.			91		1915	IA, 42nd, 1916
Hearn, John					1929 Jan 23	NE, 53rd, 1929
Hearn, M.O.	Pvt.	F, 153rd Ill. Inf.	78		1911 Apr 7	IA, 38th, 1912
Hearn, Patrick	Pvt.	A, 35th Iowa Inf.	231		1904 Oct 9	IA, 31st, 1905
Heasley, J.T.		D, 83rd Penn. (died of pneumonia)	2	78	1921 Oct 12	NE, 46th, 1922
Heastan, B.F.		A, 7th Kans. Cav.	191		1909 Aug 9	KS, 29th, 1910
Heaster, John B.		D, 2nd Iowa Inf.	9		1913 Nov 17	KS, 33rd, 1914
Heaston, David F.		B, 170th Ohio National Guard	12		1929 Jun 10	KS, 49th, 1930
Heath, A.T.		E, 143rd Ill.	311		1919 Jul 14	KS, 39th, 1920
Heath, Bradford	Pvt.	D, 100th Ill. Inf.	101		1926 Jun 22	IA, 53rd, 1927
Heath, C.H.	Sergt.	E, 28th Wis. Inf.	277		1899 Jun 14	IA, 26th, 1900
Heath, C.P.	Pvt.	G, 2nd Wis.	22		1901 Mar 21	IA, 28th, 1902
Heath, Elias M.		D, 2nd Mich. Vol. Cav.	196		1892 Jan 19	KS, 12th, 1893
Heath, G.W.	Musician	H, 60th Vet. Inf.	493		1908 Jun 13	IA, 35th, 1909
Heath, H.B.	Pvt.	H, 6th Iowa Cav.	23		1920 Jan 4	IA, 47th, 1921
Heath, J.K.P.		K, 24th Mich.	129		1913 Sep 15	KS, 33rd, 1914
Heath, Jas. D.		A, 72nd Ill.	25		1930 Jan 15	NE, 55th, 1931
Heath, Joseph T.	Pvt.	D, 8th Iowa Inf.	500		1928 Dec 24	IA, 55th, 1929
Heath, L.F.	Pvt.	D, 177th Ohio Inf.	40		1910 Apr 7	IA, 37th, 1911
Heath, Miles		H, 112th N.Y. Inf., 2nd Corps (born in New York, April 25, 1843; died in Belvidere, Neb.)	17		1883 Aug 18	NE, 8th, 1884
Heath, N.G.	Pvt.	52nd Ill. Inf.	137		1919 Jul 18	IA, 46th, 1920
Heath, R.D.		G, 89th N.Y.	147		1913 Dec 23	KS, 33rd, 1914
Heath, R.J.	Lieut.	A, 34th Ill. Inf.	154		1915 Mar 4	IA, 42nd, 1916
Heath, T.R.		L, 5th Ind. Cav.	96		1925 Nov 28	KS, 45th, 1926
Heath, V.	Surg.	K, 33rd Wis. Inf.	332	57	1891 Oct 26	IA, 18th, 1892
Heath, W.W.			243		1922 Apr 21	KS, 42nd, 1923
Heather, W.Y.		C, 8th Ill. Cav. (died of peritonitis)	21	80	1908 Dec 17	NE, 33rd, 1909
Heatherly, E.F.		A, 4th Tenn. Cav.	256		1918 Apr 23	KS, 38th, 1919
Heathman, S.E.	Pvt.	I, 2nd Wis. Cav.	452		1929 Feb 24	IA, 56th, 1930
Heaton, A.W.		G, 91st Ill. Inf. (died at Manchester, Ill.)	117		1895 Feb	KS, 15th, 1896
Heaton, C.M.		B, 18th Ohio	258		1922 Jun	KS, 42nd, 1923
Heaton, Chas. M.		D, 18th Ohio	258		1921 Dec 11	KS, 41st, 1922
Heaton, F.M.	Pvt.	A, 1st Iowa Inf.	231		1900-1901	IA, 27th, 1901
Heaton, J.		A, 116th Ind.	22		1888	KS, 8th, 1889
Heaton, James		D, 135th Ind.	25		1926 Jan 3	NE, 51st, 1927
Heaton, Jno.		D, 40th Ind.	68		1904 Aug 24	KS, 24th, 1905
Heaton, Peter A.	Pvt.	K, 6th —	212		1919 May 13	IA, 46th, 1920
Heaton, Peter A.	Pvt.	K, 6th Iowa Cav.	212		1919 Apr 10	IA, 46th, 1920
Heaton, W.H.	Pvt.	E, 30th Iowa Inf.	26		1920 Apr 23	IA, 47th, 1921

Name	Rank	Company, Regiment or Ship	Post*	Age	Death Date†	Journal
Heaygry, David E.			35		1897 Jan 11	NE, 22nd, 1898
Hebard, E.A., see Hebbard, E.A.						
Hebard, Wm.	Pvt.	E, 4th Wis. Inf.	132		1910	IA, 37th, 1911
Hebb, Edward T.		I, 1st Ind. Cav.	27		1917 Jun 17	KS, 37th, 1918
Hebb, Joseph		A, 55th Ill.	110		1917 Nov 11	KS, 37th, 1918
Hebbard, E.A.		B, 25th Iowa (not a member of Farragut Post)	25		1913 Apr 6	NE, 38th, 1914
Hebeschen, Nicholas		G, 14th Wis.	127		1924 Jan 17	KS, 44th, 1925
Heck, C.		F, —	18		1892 Apr 4	KS, 12th, 1893
Heck, Frank N.		C, 18th Kans.	18		1910 Oct 29	KS, 30th, 1911
Heck, Samuel K.		I, 101st Penn. (fell dead while feeding his cattle)	31		1890	KS, 10th, 1891
Heckard, L.F.		K, 83rd Penn.	17		1916 Jul 19	KS, 36th, 1917
Hecker, Wm. C.		C, 2nd Iowa Inf. (died of cancer of stomach)	133	70	1908 Nov 28	NE, 33rd, 1909
Heckert, P.H.		B, 2nd Iowa	153		1897 Oct 3	KS, 17th, 1898
Heckerthorn, O.W.		F, 34th Iowa	87		1908 Jul 29	KS, 28th, 1909
Heckler, Geo. W.	Pvt.	C, 1st Iowa Inf.	231		1915 Aug 21	IA, 42nd, 1916
Heckman, L.S.		E, 46th Penn.	4		1911 Nov 24	KS, 31st, 1912
Heckmot, Francis W.	Cook	Gunboat *Noga*	18		1906 Jan 20	KS, 26th, 1907
Hedden, A.D.		A, 52nd Penn. (died of pneumonia)	94	80	1922 Dec 11	NE, 47th, 1923
Hedden, R.B.	Corp.	B, 1st Iowa Cav.	40		1904 Jun 10	IA, 31st, 1905
Hederhorst, Fred		K, 43rd Ill.	76		1911	KS, 31st, 1912
Hedge, A.		B, 80th Ohio Inf.	80	51	1895 Oct 13	NE, 20th, 1896
Hedge, George E.	Pvt.	G, 44th Iowa Inf.	7	72	1892 Nov 9	IA, 19th, 1893
Hedge, H.B.	Sergt.	Ringgold Cav.	12		1918 Jan 23	IA, 45th, 1919
Hedge, J.C.		H, 2nd Penn. Cav. (died of old age)	13	80	1925 Jan 16	NE, 50th, 1926
Hedge, Porter		E & C, 142nd & 51st Ohio Inf. (died of paralysis)	214	54	1903 Sep 5	NE, 28th, 1904
Hedges, Geo.		K, 9th Ohio Cav.	23		1918 Oct 23	KS, 38th, 1919
Hedges, Jesse	Pvt.	C, 26th Iowa Inf.	88	53	1895 Feb 10	IA, 21st, 1895
Hedges, Jester	Pvt.	8th Iowa	127		1923 Jan 16	IA, 50th, 1924
Hedges, M.T.		K, 26th Ill.	36		1913 Feb 15	KS, 33rd, 1914
Hedges, Salem		C, 123rd Ill.	458		1916	KS, 36th, 1917
Hedges, Thomas		E, 18th Ohio Inf. (died of blood poison)	47	69	1906 Mar 22	NE, 31st, 1907
Hedinger, Chas.	Surg.	2nd Colo. Cav.	84		1918 Dec 13	KS, 38th, 1919
Hedrick, Henry	Corp.	H, 46th Iowa Inf.	189	78	1889 Mar	IA, 16th, 1890
Hedrick, J.H.		E, 137th Ill.	142		1937 Jan 22	KS, 57th, 1938
Hedrick, J.H.		E, 137th Ill.	142		1936 Jan 22	KS, 56th, 1937
Hedrick, J.H.		D, 11th Ill. Inf.	17		1938 Jan 28	KS, 59th, 1940
Hedrick, J.M.	1st Lieut.	D, 15th Iowa Inf.	69	55	1886 Oct 3	IA, 13th, 1887
Hedrick, J.M.	Capt.	I, 4th Ohio	17		1938 Jan 25	KS, 57th, 1938
Hedrick, John E.		D, 11th Ill. Cav. (died of heart disease)	17		1891 Dec 13	KS, 11th, 1892
Hedrick, Joseph		C, 137th Ill. Inf.	145		1936 Jan 22	KS, 55th, 1936
Hedrick, Samuel	Pvt.	A, 23rd Mo. Inf.	17		1914 Dec 14	IA, 41st, 1915
Hedrick, T.N.	Capt.	D, 15th Iowa Inf.	10		2nd quarter 1885	IA, 12th, 1886
Hedrix, S.H.	Pvt.	C, 23rd Mo. Inf.	192	88	1933 Aug 15	IA, 60th, 1934
Heels, R.T.		H, 133rd Ill. Inf.	142		1901 Mar 14	KS, 21st, 1902
Heffelbower, E.W.		F, 207th Penn. (died of kidney trouble)	26	74	1914 Mar 11	NE, 39th, 1915
Heffelfinger, E.M.	Pvt.	A, 146th Ill.	71		1901 Jul 4	IA, 28th, 1902
Heffelfinger, John		G, 142nd Ill.	71	91	1934 Jun 12	IA, 61st, 1935
Hefflefinger, L.	Corp.	L, 3rd Penn. Cav.	57		1910 Jun 15	IA, 37th, 1911
Hefflin, S.G.	Pvt.	B, 102nd Ill. Inf.	197		1910 Apr 28	IA, 37th, 1911
Heflen, J.M.			441		1907 1st term	IA, 34th, 1908
Hefley, John M.	Pvt.	I, 32nd Iowa Inf.	150	67	1894 Aug 10	IA, 21st, 1895
Hefman, John	Pvt.	B, 7th Mo. Cav.	212		1913 Mar 8	IA, 40th, 1914
Hefner, N.H.	Pvt.	K, 3rd Ill. Cav.	56		1915 Nov 17	IA, 42nd, 1916
Heft, E.	Pvt.	E, 34th Iowa Inf.	414		1900 Jul 12	IA, 27th, 1901
Heft, J.B.			29		1902 Apr 6	IA, 29th, 1903
Heft, Peter		29th Iowa Inf.	29		1913	IA, 40th, 1914
Hefton, A.W.		B, 18th Ill.	32		1929 Jan 7	KS, 49th, 1930

Name	Rank	Company, Regiment or Ship	Post*	Age	Death Date†	Journal
Hefty, Jacob		1st U.S. Cav.	271		1903 Jun 21	IA, 30th, 1904
Heggstrand, Geo. W.		A, 148th Ill. Inf.	127		1909 Jun 25	KS, 29th, 1910
Heickox, Geo. M.	Pvt.	I, 1st Ill. Art.	190		1911 Mar	IA, 38th, 1912
Heidebrek, Frederick		E, 4th Ohio Cav.	22		1894 Jul 5	KS, 14th, 1895
Heidelbaugh, Alex	Pvt.	F, 35th Iowa Inf.	231		1920 Sep 22	IA, 47th, 1921
Heideman, Fred	Pvt.	D, 8th Ill. Cav.	267	66	1897 Apr 28	IA, 23rd, 1897
Heidt, Ludwig	Pvt.	E, 26th Iowa Inf. (at large)			1933 Feb 7	IA, 60th, 1934
Heidt, Ludwig		E, 26th Iowa Inf. (at large)			1932 Feb 7	IA, 59th, 1933
Heightshoe, I.F.	Pvt.	D, 31st Ohio Inf.	108		1911 Oct 4	IA, 38th, 1912
Heihnhamer, Jacob	Pvt.	K, 6th Iowa Cav.	206		1918 Jan	IA, 45th, 1919
Heil, John	Pvt.	I, 25th Wis. Inf.	78		1915 Feb 14	IA, 42nd, 1916
Heil, Peter		A, 5th Kans.	1		1919 May 3	KS, 39th, 1920
Heilman, C.E.		G, 49th Wis. (not a member of Farragut Post)	25		1913 Mar 14	NE, 38th, 1914
Heim, Geo.	Pvt.	L, 5th Iowa Cav.	78		1900 Feb 7	IA, 27th, 1901
Heimbaugh, J.M.	Pvt.	G, 86th Ill. Inf.	231		1920 Oct 27	IA, 47th, 1921
Hein, John		A, 85th Ill. (died of heart failure)	60		1923 May 8	NE, 48th, 1924
Heinan, John		A, 114th Ill.	92		1923 Nov 17	KS, 43rd, 1924
Heinbach, John	Pvt.	C, 8th N.Y. Cav.	327		1901 Jun 1	IA, 28th, 1902
Heinbaugh, Sol	Pvt.	I, 52nd Penn. Inf.	452		1917 Sep 25	IA, 44th, 1918
Heinberg, Louis	Pvt.	I, 23rd Wis. Inf.	168		1906 Jul 11	IA, 33rd, 1907
Heine, F.		A, 119th Ill. Inf.	4		1892 Apr 20	NE, 17th, 1893
Heinecke, E.D.		F, 76th Ill.	58		1917 Aug 14	KS, 37th, 1918
Heinemyer, Chas.		D, 133rd Penn. (died of Bright's disease)	27	69	1906 May 1	NE, 31st, 1907
Heines, George B.		L, 11th Kans.	271		1897 Feb 11	KS, 17th, 1898
Heinrich, Frederick		E, 59th Ill.	45		1925	NE, 50th, 1926
Heinrick, Godlieb			25		1908 Feb	KS, 28th, 1909
Heins, John Frederick		K, 1st U.S. Eng.	153	96	1937 Nov 14	IA, 64th, 1938
Heintz, Michael		H, 26th Ill. Inf.	39		1914 Dec 15	KS, 34th, 1915
Heise, David		A, 14th Kans.	92		1925 Jan 22	KS, 45th, 1926
Heisler, David Augustus		I, 2nd Penn. Hvy. Art.	29	91	1937 May 27	IA, 64th, 1938
Heisler, E.F.		A, 6th Kans.	28		1922 May 21	KS, 42nd, 1923
Heisler, G.F.	Pvt.	E, 13th Iowa Inf.	15		1904 Jan	IA, 31st, 1905
Heisser, A.		F, 7th Mo.	352		1898 May 24	KS, 18th, 1899
Heit, John G.		I, 3rd Mo.	64		1910 Mar 7	KS, 30th, 1911
Heitz, Charles			32		1913 Mar 30	KS, 33rd, 1914
Heitz, F.		A, 166th Ill. Inf.	32		1925 Aug 31	KS, 45th, 1926
Heki, George F.		I, 150th Ill. Inf.		91	1937 Jul 7	IA, 64th, 1938
Helder, Phil. C.		K, 42nd Ind.	100		1924 Oct 16	KS, 44th, 1925
Heldridge, Jas.	Corp.	I, 38th Iowa Inf.	223		1907 Feb 26	IA, 35th, 1909
Helfenbine, John		B, 4th Mo. Cav. (died of rheumatism & disability)	84	75	1912 Jun 11	NE, 37th, 1913
Helfer, Jesse		32nd Iowa Inf.	17		1902	NE, 27th, 1903
Heller, David		K, 4th Kans. Cav. (died of Bright's disease)	274	71	1905 Nov 26	NE, 30th, 1906
Heller, Flavius J.		D, 25th Ohio	43		1910 Sep 12	KS, 30th, 1911
Heller, Godleib		C, 6th Mo. Inf.	132		1909 Jul 27	KS, 29th, 1910
Heller, Jacob B.	Pvt.	C, 49th —	466		1906 Aug 16	IA, 33rd, 1907
Heller, Joel	Pvt.	G, 13th Iowa Inf.	98	71	1893 Dec 28	IA, 20th, 1894
Heller, John	Pvt.	C, 178th Penn. Inf.	125		1918 Sep 22	IA, 45th, 1919
Heller, Lewis		A, 100th N.Y. Inf.	23		1914	IA, 41st, 1915
Heller, Marcus	Pvt.	F, 35th Iowa Inf.	231	43	1891 Nov 4	IA, 18th, 1892
Heller, Robert	Pvt.	A, 9th Iowa Cav.	123	43	1887 Jun 20	IA, 14th, 1888
Heller, T.C.		G, 2nd Iowa Cav. (died of accident)	25	60	1902 Dec	NE, 27th, 1903
Helligas, David	Pvt.	C, 8th Iowa Inf.	321		1913 May 17	IA, 40th, 1914
Hellyer, David		B, 73rd Ill.	130		1905 May 25	KS, 25th, 1906
Helm, Anthony	Pvt.	C, 10th U.S. Inf.	5		1890 Jul 30	IA, 17th, 1891
Helm, David		B, 83rd Ind.	1		1920 Jul 7	KS, 40th, 1921
Helme, Alonzo		F, 34th Mass. Inf.	57		1890	KS, 10th, 1891
Helme, James		G, 7th Kans.	40		1917 Mar 19	KS, 37th, 1918
Helmer, J.W.	Musician	Band, 25th Ind. Inf.	228	43	1886 Mar 27	IA, 13th, 1887
Helmer, Theodore		E, 29th Iowa	380		1889	KS, 9th, 1890

Name	Rank	Company, Regiment or Ship	Post*	Age	Death Date†	Journal
Helmerick, R.G.		D, 26th Ill.	407		1917 Nov 1	KS, 37th, 1918
Helmerick, R.L.		D, 126th Ill.	407		1908	KS, 28th, 1909
Helmick, Jacob		B, 6th Mich. Cav.	190		1921 Oct 13	KS, 41st, 1922
Helmo, John	Pvt.	A, 21st Ohio Vol. Inf.	98	63	1898 Nov 4	IA, 25th, 1899
Helms, F.M.	Pvt.	A, 10th Iowa Inf.	347		1912	IA, 39th, 1913
Helms, George		I, 89th Ind. Inf.	112		1887 Jan 5	KS, 7th, 1888
Helms, R.W.	Pvt.	H, 1st U.S. Sharpshooters	48		1912 Dec 31	IA, 39th, 1913
Helphenstine, P.H.			111		1914	KS, 34th, 1915
Helphrey, Dan	Pvt.	E, 1st Iowa Cav.	20		1916	IA, 43rd, 1917
Helphrey, F.P.	Pvt.	E, 1st Iowa Cav.	20		1921 Feb	IA, 48th, 1922
Helphrey, Israel	Pvt.	A, 23rd Iowa Inf.	300		1925 Dec 16	IA, 52nd, 1926
Helphrey, Peter	Pvt.	E, 23rd Iowa Inf.	16		1920 Aug 2	IA, 47th, 1921
Helrick, Elias J.		B, 133rd Penn.	301		1893 Nov 18	KS, 13th, 1894
Helt, T.H.		A, 7th Ill.	64		1923 Jun 27	KS, 43rd, 1924
Heltinger, Geo.		C, 24th Iowa	72		1920 Oct 15	KS, 40th, 1921
Heltzel, John A.		F, 11th Mo. Cav.	147		1924 Apr 21	KS, 44th, 1925
Heltzel, John A.		F, 11th Mo. Cav.	147		1922 Dec 25	KS, 42nd, 1923
Helvery, Charles W.		H, 7th Mo. State Militia	380		1918	KS, 38th, 1919
Helwick, E.B.		C, 19th Iowa	44		1914 Oct 24	KS, 34th, 1915
Heman, H.L.	Pvt.	K, 1st Iowa Cav.	495		1916 Dec	IA, 43rd, 1917
Hembree, Wm. B.	Pvt.		248		1922 Jul 29	IA, 49th, 1923
Hemenover, David			7		1926	IA, 53rd, 1927
Hemenway, H.C.	Lieut.	C, 27th Iowa Vols.	222		1922 Jan 27	IA, 49th, 1923
Hemerling, F.M.	Sergt.	D, 39th —	222		1910 Sep 14	IA, 37th, 1911
Heminger, A.T.	1st Sergt.	A, 121st Ohio Vol. Inf.	423		1899 Oct 22	KS, 19th, 1900
Hemingway, C.E.		C, 153rd Ill. Inf.	68		1926 Jul 24	NE, 51st, 1927
Hemmelder, A.H.	Pvt.	E, 5th Iowa Cav.	78		1908 Apr 1	IA, 35th, 1909
Hemminger, Calvin		B, 129th Ohio	129		1921 Oct 21	KS, 41st, 1922
Hemminger, John S.		D, 1st Penn. Cav.	58		1912 Jan 16	KS, 32nd, 1913
Hemphill, Isaac			12		1922 Sep 17	KS, 42nd, 1923
Hemphill, John		L, 11th Kans.	25		1916 Jan 20	KS, 36th, 1917
Hemphill, R.C.		D, 13th Penn. Cav. (died of leakage of heart)	35	76	1918 Jan 24	NE, 43rd, 1919
Hemphill, William			37		1926	IA, 53rd, 1927
Hemphry, J.	Pvt.	A, 24th Iowa Inf.	163		1910 Mar 1	IA, 37th, 1911
Hemry, Charles W., Rev.		D, 99th Ohio Vol. Inf. (see Appendix D)		82	1924 Jul 10	NE, 49th, 1925
Hemstock, G.W.	Corp.	A, Ill. Cav.	31		1923 Sep	IA, 50th, 1924
Hemstreet, M.	Lieut.	G, 157th N.Y.	30		1906 Feb 8	IA, 33rd, 1907
Hen, Fred		G, 83rd Ind.	24	74	1910 Sep 30	NE, 35th, 1911
Hench, Thomas	Pvt.	C, 21st Penn. Cav.	74		1927 Dec 11	IA, 54th, 1928
Hencley, S.C.	Pvt.	F, 11th Iowa Inf.	249		1912 May 21	IA, 39th, 1913
Hendershott, Geo. W.		Ind. (died of sun stroke)	30	66	1906 Aug 17	NE, 31st, 1907
Henderson, A.J.	Pvt.	I, 9th Mo. Cav.	11		1899	NE, 24th, 1900
Henderson, D.B.	Pvt.	G, 16th Ohio Inf.	81	88	1933 Jul 8	IA, 60th, 1934
Henderson, David B.	Lieut.	C, 12th Iowa Inf.	78		1906 Feb 25	IA, 33rd, 1907
Henderson, E.T.	Pvt.	K, 33rd Iowa Inf.	40		1925 Mar 3	IA, 52nd, 1926
Henderson, Edgar	Major	11th Ind. Cav.	265		1891 Jun 5	KS, 11th, 1892
Henderson, H.C.	1st Lieut.	C, 34th Iowa Inf.	29	59	1888 Jul 18	IA, 15th, 1889
Henderson, Ira		B, 37th Ky. Inf.	99		1900 Dec 1	KS, 20th, 1901
Henderson, J.			3		1908	NE, 33rd, 1909
Henderson, J.E.		B, 60th Ohio	51		1926 Mar 9	KS, 46th, 1927
Henderson, J.H.		G, 2nd Penn. Art.	59		1921 Feb 24	KS, 41st, 1922
Henderson, J.H.		B, 60th Ohio Inf. (of Iola; he contracted a fatal cold attending the Harrison funeral Feb. 19, 1926; his wife died three days later; both are buried in Iola cemetery)			1926 Mar 9	KS, 45th, 1926
Henderson, J.H.		F, 206th Penn. (died of pneumonia)	218		1916 Aug 19	NE, 41st, 1917
Henderson, J.R.	Pvt.	C, 36th Ill. Inf.	96		1900 Feb 9	IA, 27th, 1901
Henderson, James		K, 128th Ohio	145		1898 Jan 23	KS, 18th, 1899
Henderson, James		F, 36th Iowa	45		1916 Jun 9	KS, 36th, 1917
Henderson, Jas.	Pvt.	E, 27th Iowa Inf.	25		1924 Jun	IA, 51st, 1925
Henderson, Jesse		H, 91st Ind.	1		1927 May 3	KS, 47th, 1928

Name	Rank	Company, Regiment or Ship	Post*	Age	Death Date†	Journal
Henderson, John	Pvt.	62nd Penn. Inf.	283		1913 Jun 14	IA, 40th, 1914
Henderson, John	Pvt.	D, 12th N.Y. Inf.	512		1917 Aug 3	IA, 44th, 1918
Henderson, John M.		C, 112th Ill. Inf.	157		1891 Sep 28	KS, 11th, 1892
Henderson, John M.		H, 75th Ohio	7		1911 Aug 10	KS, 31st, 1912
Henderson, Johnson	Pvt.	D, 5th Mo. State Militia	6		1899	NE, 24th, 1900
Henderson, Joseph		G, 6th Ind. Inf.	113		1918 Jul 25	KS, 38th, 1919
Henderson, Justus		D, 24th Iowa Inf.	79		1899 Apr 13	KS, 19th, 1900
Henderson, Lars	Pvt.	I, 16th Iowa Inf.	439		1908 Jan 30	IA, 35th, 1909
Henderson, N.W.		G, 20th Iowa Inf. (died of fever)	318	60	1903 Oct 4	NE, 28th, 1904
Henderson, P.P.	Col.	10th Iowa Inf.	116		1908 Jan 4	IA, 35th, 1909
Henderson, R.A.	Pvt.	C, 36th Ill. Inf.	290		1926 Jan 26	IA, 53rd, 1927
Henderson, Robert			316		1912 Jan 3	IA, 39th, 1913
Henderson, S.	Pvt.	A, 11th Iowa Inf.	197		1910 Apr 22	IA, 37th, 1911
Henderson, S.C.	Sergt.	50th Ohio Cav.	364	72	1897 Sep 27	IA, 24th, 1898
Henderson, Samuel	Pvt.	B, 35th Iowa Inf.	197		1904 May 10	IA, 31st, 1905
Henderson, Samuel J.		C, 81st Ill. Inf. (died of heart failure)	22	71	1913 Dec 2	NE, 38th, 1914
Henderson, Thomas E.		C, 2nd U.S. Vets.	167		1912 Feb 17	KS, 32nd, 1913
Henderson, Thomas M.		D, 30th Iowa	18		1923 Oct 27	KS, 43rd, 1924
Henderson, W.F.		C, 63rd Ind. Inf.	311		1918 Aug 22	KS, 38th, 1919
Henderson, William		B, 33rd Iowa	170		1923 May 17	KS, 43rd, 1924
Henderson, Wm. P.	Capt.	G, 2nd Ark. Inf.	235	48	1893 May 22	IA, 20th, 1894
Henderson, Zma	Sergt.	A, 12th Ill. Inf.	223		1905 Aug 22	IA, 32nd, 1906
Hendickson, H.H.		G, 2nd Iowa Inf.	32		1899 Jun 12	KS, 19th, 1900
Hendrick, E.M.		H, 46th Iowa Inf.	173		1923 Apr 18	IA, 50th, 1924
Hendrick, E.M.			173		1924 Feb 6	IA, 51st, 1925
Hendrick, G.		E, 76th Ohio Inf.	329	64	1896 Feb 16	NE, 21st, 1897
Hendrick, N.	Pvt. Pvt.	G, 70th Ill. E, 66th Ill. (cause of death: lungs)	66	42	1887 Jan	NE, 12th, 1888
Hendrick, S.P.		G, 134th Ind.	31	79	1924 Dec 19	NE, 49th, 1925
Hendrick, Wm.	Pvt.	F, 35th Iowa	231		1923 Jan 11	IA, 50th, 1924
Hendricks, H.W.		B, 42nd Ill.	25		1926 Aug 1	KS, 46th, 1927
Hendricks, J.W.			235		1913 Jan 16	IA, 40th, 1914
Hendricks, Jno.		D, 19th Ill.	1		1904 Dec 5	KS, 24th, 1905
Hendricks, John A.	Pvt.	E, 84th Penn. Inf.	90		1899	NE, 24th, 1900
Hendricks, John J.		K, 21st Ind.	142		1897 Dec 20	KS, 17th, 1898
Hendrickson, F.A.	Pvt.	5th Wis. Bat.	168		1920 Aug 20	IA, 47th, 1921
Hendrickson, J.C.		G, 15th Wis.	30	91	1934 Nov 20	IA, 61st, 1935
Hendrickson, Jno. A.		C, 3rd Iowa Cav.	380		1904 Aug 12	KS, 24th, 1905
Hendrickson, P.		B, 6th Mo. Inf.	271		1888	KS, 8th, 1889
Hendrickson, W.H.		F, 7th Ill. Cav.	252		1925 Jul 1	KS, 45th, 1926
Hendrix, F.C.	Sergt.	B, 13th Ind.	364		1914 Aug 9	IA, 41st, 1915
Hendrix, H.H.	Pvt.	E, 46th Iowa Inf.	154		1911 Jan 22	IA, 38th, 1912
Hendrix, J.W.		E, 2nd Kans. Inf.	111		1887 Jan 15	KS, 7th, 1888
Hendrix, James C.		D, 54th Ky.	63		1894 Jun 6	KS, 14th,.1895
Hendrix, Silas		C, 12th Mo.	25		1922 Jul 26	KS, 42nd, 1923
Hendrix, William M.		C, 7th Tenn.	459		1892 Jun 29	KS, 12th, 1893
Hendrix, Wm.		M, 15th Kans.	3		1920 May 21	KS, 40th, 1921
Hendry, James M.		E, 3rd Kans. (died at Lawrence)	12		1895 Feb	KS, 15th, 1896
Hendryx, J.G.		H, 9th Mich.	11		1929 Nov	NE, 54th, 1930
Henesy, Jno.			190		1925 Oct 1	IA, 52nd, 1926
Henete, Jno. B.		I, 1st Kans.	93		1905 Apr 3	KS, 25th, 1906
Hengue, Nathaniel	Pvt.	K, 42nd Ill. Inf.	132	67	1891 Aug 3	IA, 18th, 1892
Henion, J.B.	Pvt.	G, 17th Ill. Cav.	321		1912 Mar 19	IA, 39th, 1913
Henkel, Peter		E, 12th Mich. (died of old age)	2	80	1921 Jun 12	NE, 46th, 1922
Henkle, Conrad	Musician	D, 10th Ill. Cav.	516		1912 Mar 12	IA, 39th, 1913
Henkle, Henry C.		D, 28th Iowa Inf.	98	94	1938 Mar 26	IA, 64th, 1938
Henkle, Seth V.		A, 183rd Ohio	46		1921 May 29	KS, 41st, 1922
Henley, Elias	Pvt.	22nd Ind. Bat. Lt. Art.	40		1912 Dec 16	IA, 39th, 1913
Henley, Geo. W.	Sergt.	E, 5th Iowa Cav.	78		1913 May 9	IA, 40th, 1914
Henley, Henry	Pvt.	G, 52nd Ind. Inf.	40		1913 Apr 4	IA, 40th, 1914
Henley, John		B, 9th Kans. Cav.	50		1914 Feb 1	KS, 34th, 1915
Henn, Chas.		I, 188th Penn. Inf.	7		1923 Sep	NE, 48th, 1924

Name	Rank	Company, Regiment or Ship	Post*	Age	Death Date†	Journal
Henn, John	Pvt.	D, 87th Penn. Vol. Inf.	247		1903 Feb 24	IA, 30th, 1904
Hennecker, Ed.	Sergt.	A, 2nd Iowa Cav.	231		1914 Jun 16	IA, 41st, 1915
Hennen, M.B.		G, 8th Ill. Cav.	334		1892 Oct 5	KS, 12th, 1893
Hennesey, Michael		G, 4th Iowa Cav.	71		1898 Aug 7	KS, 18th, 1899
Henney, Cyrus L.	Pvt.	I, 3rd Ohio Cav.	17		1928 Jul 8	IA, 55th, 1929
Henney, Thomas	Pvt.	A, 44th Iowa	78		1900 Jul 14	IA, 27th, 1901
Hennig, C.	Pvt.	B, 6th Iowa Cav.	78		1913 Jan 11	IA, 40th, 1914
Hennigh, David		E, 1st Penn.	175		1921 Apr 18	KS, 41st, 1922
Hennimon, Christ		A, 2nd Neb. Cav. (died of old age)	133	80	1913 Jul 8	NE, 38th, 1914
Henning, C.E.		G, 120th Ind.	74		1904 Aug 22	KS, 24th, 1905
Henning, J.H.		B, 18th Ohio Inf.	66		1909 Mar 5	KS, 29th, 1910
Henning, John			1		1924 Feb 25	NE, 49th, 1925
Henninger, Geo.	Pvt.	C, 9th Ill. Cav.	17		1918 Jan 17	IA, 45th, 1919
Hennis, Albert	Pvt.	D, 69th Ohio Inf.	420	72	1894 Apr 15	IA, 21st, 1895
Hennissey, G.		K, 2nd Ind. Cav.	98		1919 Sep 19	KS, 39th, 1920
Hennway, Thomas		F, 35th Iowa	172		1913 Mar 5	KS, 32nd, 1913
Henrich, Charles		D, 27th Iowa Inf.	8	92	1937 Feb 9	IA, 64th, 1938
Henrich, Fred	Pvt.	D, 54th Ohio Inf.	29	65	1895 Dec 24	IA, 22nd, 1896
Henrie, J.C.		B, 124th Ill. Inf.	25		1929 Aug 25	KS, 49th, 1930
Henry, Aaron		A, 203rd Penn.	10		1927 Jan 1	NE, 51st, 1927
Henry, Aaron		A, 203rd Penn.	10		1927 Jan 1	NE, 52nd, 1928
Henry, Alpheus	Pvt.	A, 7th Iowa Cav.	222		1911 Nov 30	IA, 38th, 1912
Henry, C.W.	Sergt.	C, 88th N.D. Cav.	7		1905 Oct	IA, 32nd, 1906
Henry, David		24th U.S. Col. Inf.	115		1922 Dec 1	KS, 42nd, 1923
Henry, David P.		H, 11th Mo. Inf. (died of exposure, army)	47	72	1905 Jan 20	NE, 30th, 1906
Henry, E.D.		B, 51st Ind.	344		1928 Feb 21	KS, 48th, 1929
Henry, Edson		I, 66th Ind. Inf.	68	83	1925 Aug	NE, 50th, 1926
Henry, Elisha		F, 15th Kans. Cav.	28		1911 Dec 3	KS, 31st, 1912
Henry, G.E.	Pvt.	K, 146th Ill.	150		1921 May 28	IA, 48th, 1922
Henry, George	Pvt.	B, 3rd Iowa Inf.	49		1901 Jan 5	IA, 28th, 1902
Henry, Hamilton H.		F, 2nd Ohio	61		1917 Sep 12	KS, 37th, 1918
Henry, Isaac		E, 12th Wis. (died of old age at Soldiers & Sailors Home, Milford)		86	1907 Apr 4	NE, 31st, 1907
Henry, J.P.	Pvt.	C, 10th Iowa Inf.	314		1912 May 20	IA, 39th, 1913
Henry, J.W.	Pvt.	G, 13th Iowa Inf.	69		1911 Jun 1	IA, 38th, 1912
Henry, J.W.	Pvt.	I, 94th Ill. Inf.	37		1925 Jan 7	IA, 52nd, 1926
Henry, James		A, 28th Ill.	47		1931 Sep 27	NE, 56th, 1932
Henry, Job	Pvt.	Perry Volunteer Militia	321	48	1887 May	IA, 14th, 1888
Henry, John	Pvt.	B, 16th Iowa Inf.	188		1903 Dec 7	IA, 30th, 1904
Henry, John A.		B, 5th Iowa Cav. (died of paralysis)	7	63	1897 Sep 12	NE, 22nd, 1898
Henry, John M.		K, 3rd Kans.	12		1925 Nov 4	KS, 45th, 1926
Henry, John W.	Pvt.	K, 33rd Iowa Inf.	40		1929 Dec 11	IA, 56th, 1930
Henry, Jules		H, 114th Ill.	57		1917 Jul 8	KS, 37th, 1918
Henry, N.D.	Pvt.	E, 11th Iowa Inf.	88		1910 Jun 7	IA, 37th, 1911
Henry, Oscar	Pvt.	A, 18th Ind. Inf.	74	50	1894 Sep 22	IA, 21st, 1895
Henry, P.	Pvt.	H, 3rd N.Y. Inf.	12		1920 Jan 19	IA, 47th, 1921
Henry, R.J.		C, 62nd Penn.	68		1916 Jul 18	KS, 36th, 1917
Henry, Theo. P.	Sergt.	K, 2nd Iowa Inf.	516		1900 Jan 23	IA, 27th, 1901
Henry, W.B.		F, 120th U.S.A.	19		1910 Feb 1	KS, 30th, 1911
Henry, W.C.	Capt.	7th Kans. Cav.	25		1903	NE, 28th, 1904
Henry, W.C.		K, 19th N.Y. (died of kidney trouble)	18	61	1904 May 14	NE, 29th, 1905
Henry, W.R.		E, 23rd Iowa Inf.	32		1887	KS, 7th, 1888
Henry, Wm. A.		G, 47th Iowa	25		1913 Dec 3	NE, 38th, 1914
Henry, Wm. G.	Pvt.	E, 115th Ill.	150		1923 Jun 10	IA, 50th, 1924
Henry, Wm. J.		G, 7th V.R.C.	87		1891 Nov 21	KS, 11th, 1892
Henry, Wm. L.	Pvt.	18th Ind. Art.	192		1924 Feb 22	IA, 51st, 1925
Henshaw, B.C.		G, 34th Ohio	257		1928	KS, 48th, 1929
Henshaw, Newton	QM Sergt.	12th Kans. Inf. (died at Eudora, Kans.; buried at Eudora Cemetery)	333		1894 Jul 9	KS, 14th, 1895
Henshaw, W.N.			6		1921	IA, 48th, 1922
Henshaw, W.N.	Pvt.	B, 2nd Iowa Cav.	6		1923	IA, 50th, 1924
Hensley, Geo.		E, 49th Ind.	69		1923 Jul 11	KS, 46th, 1927

*See Appendix A, B or C for roster of post names and locations.
†See Introduction for note regarding recording of death date.
247

Name	Rank	Company, Regiment or Ship	Post*	Age	Death Date†	Journal
Hensley, George		E, 49th Ind.	69		1923 Jul 11	KS, 44th, 1925
Hensley, J.M.		A, 21st Iowa Inf. (died at Lyons, Kans.; buried at Lyons Cemetery)	20		1894 Oct 9	KS, 14th, 1895
Hensley, S.C.	Pvt.	K, 11th Iowa Inf.	249		1912 May 21	IA, 40th, 1914
Hensley, W.H.			25		1900 Mar	KS, 20th, 1901
Hensley, W.N.		B, 9th Ky. Cav.	9		1929 Jun 30	NE, 54th, 1930
Hensley, W.W.		25th Ill.	23		1914 Jun 22	KS, 34th, 1915
Hensley, William		E, 38th Ill.	185		1924 May 16	KS, 44th, 1925
Henson, Enoch		D, 5th Kans.	158		1900 Sep 15	KS, 20th, 1901
Henson, Henry	Corp.	C, 14th Iowa Inf.	111		1915 May 15	IA, 42nd, 1916
Henthorn, Wm. H.		H, 27th Iowa Inf. G, 44th Iowa	250		1918 May 28	KS, 38th, 1919
Henton, Robert, see Hinton, Robert						
Hentz, Phillip		1st Colo. Cav.	65		1916 Feb	KS, 36th, 1917
Henzel, Ernest	Pvt.	E, 32nd Wis. Inf.	22		1925 Aug 18	IA, 52nd, 1926
Henzie, Gus		C, 1st Wis. Inf.	56		1914 Jan 1	KS, 34th, 1915
Hepburn, H.S.	Capt.	K, 160th N.Y. Inf.	1		1910 Jul 30	IA, 37th, 1911
Hepburn, W.P.	Lieut. Col.	2nd Iowa Cav.	11		1916 Feb 7	IA, 43rd, 1917
Hepner, D.W.		D, 29th Ind. Inf.	110	93	1936 Feb 12	IA, 63rd, 1937
Hepner, D.W.		D, 29th Ind. Inf.		93	1936 Feb 12	IA, 62nd, 1936
Hepner, E.		A, 208th Penn.	94		1921 Mar 28	IA, 48th, 1922
Heppenstahl, Geo.	Pvt.	G, 2nd Iowa Cav.	255		1899 Dec	IA, 26th, 1900
Heppy, C.	Pvt.	F, 16th Iowa Inf.	231		1921 Jan 12	IA, 48th, 1922
Hepworth, Jeremiah		K, 1st Kans. Inf. (died at Osage City)	11		1895 Oct	KS, 15th, 1896
Herbert, G.W.		E, 102nd Ill.	158		1922 May 26	KS, 42nd, 1923
Herbert, Wm.		B, 23rd Iowa	7		1922 Nov 18	IA, 49th, 1923
Herbert, Wm. M.		A, 1st Minn.	36		1927 Mar 1	KS, 47th, 1928
Herbst, John			147		1925	IA, 52nd, 1926
Herchenbach, G.		A, 1st Mo. Lt. Art.	380		1897 Aug 19	KS, 17th, 1898
Herd, G.W.		G, 132nd Ill.	63		1923 Jan 16	KS, 43rd, 1924
Herd, Sidney		1st Kans. Bat.	12		1917 Nov 13	KS, 37th, 1918
Herdman, Henry			11		1890	NE, 15th, 1891
Hergenrother, J.		I, 6th Iowa Cav. (died of diabetes)	60		1893 Oct 3	NE, 18th, 1894
Herick, H.G.		D, 124th N.Y.	463		1917 Jun 29	KS, 37th, 1918
Heriman, J.C.D.		D, 30th Iowa Inf.	49		1918 Nov 28	KS, 38th, 1919
Heritage, Lemuel T.		C, 11th Kans. H, 8th Kans.	55		1913 Jan 25	KS, 33rd, 1914
Herkelman, Carl	Pvt.	G, 2nd Cal. Inf.	74		1917 Oct 1	IA, 44th, 1918
Herkes, J.P.	Pvt.	E, 21st Iowa Inf.	70		1904 Oct 22	IA, 31st, 1905
Herman, Adam		A, 40th Wis.	147		1911 Apr 15	KS, 31st, 1912
Herman, E.A.	Pvt.	E, 1st N.J. Inf.	22		1913 Dec 4	IA, 40th, 1914
Herman, Frederick	Pvt.	E, —	234		1907 Feb 20	IA, 34th, 1908
Herman, J.V.	Pvt.	F, 7th Ill. Cav.	328	52	1890 Jan 24	IA, 17th, 1891
Herman, John	Pvt.	G, 25th Iowa	157		1907 Sep 12	IA, 34th, 1908
Herman, W.W.		M, 1st Ohio Cav.	35		1914 Dec 9	KS, 34th, 1915
Hermance, H.B.	Sergt.	H, 19th Ohio Inf.	297		1904 Nov 7	IA, 31st, 1905
Hermance, N.E.	Pvt.	K, 128th N.Y. Inf.	377		1901 Nov	IA, 28th, 1902
Hermer, Robt.			32		1921 Aug 23	NE, 46th, 1922
Herod, R.W.		7th Iowa Cav.	311		1921	KS, 41st, 1922
Herold, Henry	Sergt.	F, 9th Ind. Inf.	12		1925 May 3	IA, 52nd, 1926
Herold, William		H, 43rd Iowa Inf.	51		1925 Sep 11	KS, 45th, 1926
Herr, Ben.	Pvt.	D, 11th Iowa Inf.	255		1924 Aug 19	IA, 51st, 1925
Herr, Daniel W.			1		1884	KS, 4th, 1885
Herrell, John		L, 3rd Ark.	12		1935	KS, 55th, 1936
Herreman, D.B.	Pvt.	I, 49th Wis. Inf.	101		1917 Sep 17	IA, 44th, 1918
Herren, I.H.		I, 6th Iowa Inf. (born in Cayuga Co., N.Y.; died in Polk Co., Neb.)	26		1883	NE, 8th, 1884
Herren, Wm.	Pvt.	C, 105th Ill. Inf.	132	57	1889 Feb 1	IA, 15th, 1889
Herrick, A.J.		G, 11th Mich. Cav. (died of cancer)	28		1894 Jun 12	NE, 19th, 1895
Herrick, C.F.	Capt.	D, 47th Iowa Inf.	54		1905 Apr 2	IA, 32nd, 1906
Herrick, Ervin		died of indigestion	92	66	1912 Jan	NE, 37th, 1913
Herrick, H.G.		D, 124th N.Y.	463		1922	KS, 42nd, 1923

Name	Rank	Company, Regiment or Ship	Post*	Age	Death Date†	Journal
Herrick, H.G., see Herick, H.G.						
Herrick, James A.			298		1904-1905	IA, 31st, 1905
Herrick, Leonard		H, 4th Minn. Inf.	36		1914 Oct 8	KS, 34th, 1915
Herrick, Oscar D.		K, 9th Ill. Cav.	25		1934 May 2	NE, 59th, 1935
Herrick, Pierce		A, 1st Penn. Inf.	8		1887 Apr 25	KS, 7th, 1888
Herring, Benj.	Pvt.	B, 22nd Wis. Inf.	97	70	1896 May 23	IA, 23rd, 1897
Herring, Eugene	Pvt.		512		1930 Jun 9	IA, 57th, 1931
Herring, Isaac	Pvt.	D, 17th Iowa Vols.	12		1903 May 12	IA, 30th, 1904
Herring, Jacob		K, 40th Ohio Cav.	51		1908 Jan 10	KS, 28th, 1909
Herring, John		G, 40th Penn. Inf.	51		1915 Jan 6	KS, 35th, 1916
Herring, Milton	Pvt.	H, 34th Iowa	7		1903 Dec 10	IA, 30th, 1904
Herring, Robert	Pvt.	H, 34th Iowa Inf.	18		1900 Oct 18	IA, 27th, 1901
Herrington, Ezeriah	Pvt.	A, 1st Dak.	132		1905 Apr 24	IA, 32nd, 1906
Herrington, F.		C, 3rd Wis.	12		1925 Apr 1	KS, 45th, 1926
Herrington, Freman		C, 3rd Wis. Cav.	12		1925 Apr 1	KS, 44th, 1925
Herrington, Wm. F.		I, 142nd Ohio (died of old age)	25	82	1916 Mar 31	NE, 41st, 1917
Herriott, J.F.		G, 45th Ind. Cav.	1		1925	KS, 45th, 1926
Herriott, John	Pvt.	K, 1st Penn. Res. Cav.	14		1918 Sep 24	IA, 45th, 1919
Herrm, A.M.		H, 5th Cal.	352		1888	KS, 8th, 1889
Herrold, J.	Pvt.	B, 9th Ind. Inf.	12		1920 Nov 15	IA, 47th, 1921
Herrold, Wm.	Pvt.	D, 138th Ind. Inf.	284		1915 Sep 25	IA, 42nd, 1916
Herron, J.B.		E, 137th Ill.	17		1913 Jan 23	KS, 33rd, 1914
Herron, J.R.		A, 9th Iowa	25		1926 Feb 6	NE, 51st, 1927
Herron, James	Pvt.	A, 3rd Iowa	78		1928 Aug 15	IA, 55th, 1929
Herron, John	Pvt.	D, 32nd Iowa	329		1899 Sep 29	IA, 26th, 1900
Herron, John W.		I, 152nd Ill.	293		1920 Nov 21	KS, 40th, 1921
Herron, Leander		C, 83rd Penn.	8		1937 Apr 5	NE, 62nd, 1938
Herron, R.B.		14th Ky. Inf.	4		1899 Mar 25	KS, 19th, 1900
Herron, Sanuel	Pvt.	K, 11th Ohio	188		1914 Jan 21	IA, 41st, 1915
Hershberger, H.	Pvt.	G, 8th Iowa Inf.	265	66	1896 Jun 14	IA, 23rd, 1897
Hershey, J.G.		member at large			1934	KS, 54th, 1935
Hershey, J.G.		Whitewater (at large)			1934	KS, 55th, 1936
Hershman, E.B.		G, 147th Ind. Inf.	1	89	1935 Jul 3	IA, 62nd, 1936
Hersley, C.H.		A, 6th Kans. (died of LaGrippe)	32		1890	KS, 10th, 1891
Herstrom, Carl		I, 29th Mich. Inf.	139		1899 Nov 19	KS, 19th, 1900
Hertzler, Ephraim		C, 101st Penn.	12		1930 Apr 16	KS, 50th, 1931
Hertzog, Henry	Pvt.	E, 26th Wis. Inf. E, 45th Wis. Inf.	90	54	1893 Jul 7	IA, 20th, 1894
Hervey, J.		A, 68th Ind.	18		1921	IA, 48th, 1922
Hervey, James	Hosp. Stew.	1st Iowa Cav.	78		1901 Dec 18	IA, 28th, 1902
Heryford, Henry		L, 6th Kans. Cav.	72		1892 Jun 7	KS, 12th, 1893
Heskett, Thos. E.		D, 82nd Ind. Inf.	25	76	1920 Jul 7	NE, 45th, 1921
Heskett, Wm.			192		1914 Mar 14	IA, 41st, 1915
Hess, A.	Pvt.	G, 20th Iowa Inf.	206		1908 Jun 15	IA, 35th, 1909
Hess, Aaron		B, 46th Ill.	28		1925 Sep 9	KS, 45th, 1926
Hess, Anson P.	Sergt.	A, 101st Ind. Inf.	60		1899	NE, 24th, 1900
Hess, Conrad			51		1905	KS, 25th, 1906
Hess, Daniel		E, 91st Ill.	28		1915 Apr 19	KS, 35th, 1916
Hess, Finley	Pvt.	M, 3rd Ind. Cav.	32		1884	KS, 4th, 1885
Hess, Fred C.	Pvt.	C, 104th Ill. Inf.	71		1916 Nov 27	IA, 43rd, 1917
Hess, J.			452		1915	IA, 42nd, 1916
Hess, Jacob	Pvt.	C, 35th Iowa Inf.	231		1915 Aug 15	IA, 42nd, 1916
Hess, James		I, 4th N.Y. Cav.	100		1920 Jan 24	KS, 40th, 1921
Hess, Lewis	Pvt.	176th N.C. Battery	2		1905 Jun 6	IA, 32nd, 1906
Hess, Phillip		F, 1st Ill. Cav. (died of suicide)	35	68	1912 Jan 1	NE, 37th, 1913
Hess, W.H.	Sergt.	C, 1st Mo.	117		1926 Oct 20	IA, 53rd, 1927
Hess, W.H.		B, 88th Ohio	13	67	1911 Oct 22	NE, 36th, 1912
Hess, William J.		F, 4th Iowa Inf. (died at Alden)	14		1895 Jul	KS, 15th, 1896
Hess, Wm. W.	Pvt.	C, 14th West Va. Inf.	116	92	1933 Apr 16	IA, 60th, 1934
Hesse, F.C.	Pvt.	G, 7th Iowa Inf.	12	55	1890 Nov 28	IA, 17th, 1891
Hesse, Fred	Pvt.	D, 3rd Iowa Cav.	100		1919 Jan 27	IA, 46th, 1920
Hesser, J.C.	Pvt.	D, 15th Ohio Inf.	231		1922 May 17	IA, 49th, 1923

*See Appendix A, B or C for roster of post names and locations.
†See Introduction for note regarding recording of death date.

Name	Rank	Company, Regiment or Ship	Post*	Age	Death Date†	Journal
Hesser, J.C.	Pvt.	A, 7th Iowa	231		1923 Feb 6	IA, 50th, 1924
Hesson, Edward	Pvt.	A, 6th Md. Inf.	16		1919	IA, 46th, 1920
Hester, Charles	Pvt.	I, 148th Ill. Inf. (at large)	116, 173, 189	98 & 20 days	1944 Jun 28	IA, 70th, 1944
Heston, Geo. W.	Pvt.	C, 71st Penn. Inf.	58		1902 Apr 17	IA, 29th, 1903
Hetrick, Samuel		H, 125th Ohio Inf.	172		1900 Nov 27	KS, 20th, 1901
Hettich, Charles W.		E, 4th Mo. Cav.	12		1901 Oct 20	KS, 21st, 1902
Hetzell, John	Sergt.	B, 3rd Penn. Res.	18		1916 Jan 15	KS, 36th, 1917
Heubner, L.A.	Pvt.	B, 45th Iowa Inf.	12		1929 Nov 7	IA, 56th, 1930
Heustes, George F.	Pvt.	E, 20th Ind.	1		1915 Jan 24	KS, 35th, 1916
Heustes, William E.		F, 5th Kans. Cav.	55		1924 May 24	KS, 44th, 1925
Heuston, J.C.	Pvt.	C, 8th Iowa Cav.	69		1931 Apr 13	IA, 58th, 1932
Heverdine, Robert	Pvt.	G, 25th Ill. Inf.	322		1902 Jun 1	IA, 29th, 1903
Hewett, A.		B, 2nd Maine Bat. (cause of death: heart)	46		1903 Oct 18	NE, 28th, 1904
Hewett, C.O.	Pvt.	D, 21st Iowa Inf.	346		1900 Dec 13	IA, 27th, 1901
Hewett, Jos.			116		1917 Feb 7	IA, 44th, 1918
Hewins, E.M.		D, 19th Kans. Cav.	99		1898 Dec 12	KS, 18th, 1899
Hewit, E.C.		K, 118th Ill.	293		1917 Oct 7	KS, 37th, 1918
Hewitt, Ben F.		H, 110th Penn.	68		1896 Aug 12	KS, 16th, 1897
Hewitt, H.H.	Pvt.	M, 4th Ill. Cav. (died of pneumonia)	162	44	1884 Feb 10	NE, 9th, 1885
Hewitt, Harvey W.		D, 75th Ill.	354		1926 May 28	NE, 51st, 1927
Hewitt, J.A.		I, 12th West Va.	130		1928 Jan 5	KS, 48th, 1929
Hewitt, James S.	Pvt.	H, 3rd Iowa Vol. Cav.	309	77	1898 Oct 21	IA, 25th, 1899
Hewitt, R.H.		A, 1st Wis. Inf.	43		1902 Sep 28	KS, 22nd, 1903
Hey, Geo.	Pvt.	E, 24th Ohio Inf.	92		1906 Oct 25	IA, 33rd, 1907
Heyer, Charles	Pvt.	E, 3rd N.J. Cav.	5	58	1899 May 11	IA, 25th, 1899
Heywood, C.L.		G, 18th Maine A, 1st Lieut & Sergt. Sergt. Major 1st M.H.A.[Hvy. Art.]	250		1928 Jan 10	KS, 48th, 1929
Heywood, Geo. W.		G, 65th Ill. Inf. (died of hemorrhage)	302	73	1913 Sep 7	NE, 38th, 1914
Hezikiah	Pvt.	C, 116th Ind. Inf.	122		1916 Apr 17	IA, 43rd, 1917
Hiads, Erastus F.		B, 46th Ill. Inf.	88		1909 Nov 21	KS, 29th, 1910
Hiatt, Benjamin A.		C, 19th Ky. (died of Bright's disease)	44	72	1913 Dec 22	NE, 38th, 1914
Hiatt, D.D.	Corp.	H, 11th Kans.	256		1899	KS, 19th, 1900
Hiatt, Elijah			449		Winter 1902	IA, 30th, 1904
Hiatt, Enoch			12		1923	IA, 50th, 1924
Hiatt, J.W.		B, 40th Iowa Inf. (died of heart disease)	52		1894 Apr 16	NE, 19th, 1895
Hiatt, Jas. W.	Pvt.	B, 40th Iowa	40		1923 Apr 17	IA, 50th, 1924
Hiatt, Stephen A.		C, 118th Ind.	39		1927 Nov 24	NE, 52nd, 1928
Hibbard, A.N.	Pvt.	F, 132nd Ill. Inf.	279		1915 Feb 16	IA, 42nd, 1916
Hibbard, H.W.			349		1905	IA, 32nd, 1906
Hibbard, J.E.		8th Kans. Inf.	139	70	1905 Feb 23	NE, 30th, 1906
Hibbard, Lawrence		G, 18th Wis. Inf. (born in Canada; died & buried at Harvard, Neb.)		75	1907 Feb 8	NE, 31st, 1907
Hibbard, Reuben		F, 12th Ky. Art. (died at Girard, Kans.; buried at Girard Cemetery)	49		1894 Oct 15	KS, 14th, 1895
Hibbard, Richard		B, 147th Ill.	1		1932 Jun 7	NE, 57th, 1933
Hibbels, Chas.	Pvt.	M, 9th Ohio Cav.	100		1900 Apr 18	IA, 27th, 1901
Hibberd, E.S.		C, 2nd Ill. Cav.	49		1925 Mar 25	KS, 45th, 1926
Hibbert, T.E.		A, 137th Penn. Inf. C, 2nd Penn. Vet. Art. (see Appendix D)	100		1905 Mar 3	NE, 29th, 1905
Hibbetts, Charles	Pvt.	M, 9th Ohio Cav.	100	70	1900 Apr 18	IA, 26th, 1900
Hibbs, C.W.			295		1884	KS, 4th, 1885
Hibbs, John		I, 40th Ind.	72		1913 Apr 19	KS, 33rd, 1914
Hickcox, A.B.		2nd Kans. Lt. Art.	1		1898 Apr 28	KS, 18th, 1899
Hickerson, G.P.		I, 10th Ill. (died at Beverly, Kans.; buried at Monroe Cemetery)	422		1894 Apr 19	KS, 14th, 1895
Hickey, Daniel	Pvt.	H, 55th Ill.	231		1922 Jun 3	IA, 49th, 1923
Hickey, J.F.	Surg.	60th Ohio	129		1906 Mar 13	KS, 26th, 1907
Hickey, James	Pvt.	E, 169th N.Y.	1		1922 May 12	IA, 49th, 1923
Hickey, John F.		8th & 60th Ohio	129		1905 Mar 13	KS, 25th, 1906
Hickle, J.H.	Pvt.	E, 32nd Iowa Inf.	220		1927 Oct 26	IA, 54th, 1928

Name	Rank	Company, Regiment or Ship	Post*	Age	Death Date†	Journal
Hicklin, J.H.	Pvt.	G, 19th Iowa Inf.	153		1907 May 11	IA, 34th, 1908
Hickman, A.J.			173		1922 Feb 10	IA, 49th, 1923
Hickman, G.W.	Pvt.	C, 53rd Ky.	16		1905 Mar 31	IA, 32nd, 1906
Hickman, J.F.		I, 133rd Ill. Inf. (died of cerebral apoplexy)	60		1894 Nov 29	NE, 19th, 1895
Hickman, Jas.			340		1890	KS, 10th, 1891
Hickman, John W.	Pvt.	D, 138th Ill. Vol. Inf.	5	52	1899 Feb 22	IA, 25th, 1899
Hickman, Joseph	Pvt.	G, 3rd Mo. Cav.	423		1889 Dec 23	IA, 16th, 1890
Hickman, L.T.		H, 68th Ill.	3		1913 Jan 20	KS, 33rd, 1914
Hickman, W.B.		C, 9th Ill.	17		1927 Dec 12	KS, 47th, 1928
Hickman, Wm.		H, 6th Mo. Cav.	63		1918 Dec 26	KS, 38th, 1919
Hickmaster, Henry	Pvt.	K, 2nd Wis. Inf.	184	66	1888 Mar 10	IA, 15th, 1889
Hickok, C.B.	Pvt.	C, 67th Ill. Inf.	377	56	1890 May 25	IA, 17th, 1891
Hickok, C.G.		C, 176th Ohio Inf.	9		1927 Apr 14	NE, 52nd, 1928
Hickok, J.J.	Pvt.	C, 92nd Ill. Inf.	25	60	1890 Nov 29	IA, 17th, 1891
Hickok, William	Pvt.	K, 14th Mich. Cav.	132		1919 Nov 28	IA, 46th, 1920
Hickox, A.A.		C, 11th Kans.	55		1896 Jan 13	KS, 16th, 1897
Hickox, Geo. M., see Heickox, Geo. M.						
Hicks, Alfred	Corp.	M, 8th Iowa Cav.	452		1926 May 31	IA, 53rd, 1927
Hicks, C.	Pvt.	D, 25th Mich.	452		1921 Jun 19	IA, 48th, 1922
Hicks, D.N.		A, 6th Kans.	132		1919 Jul 20	KS, 39th, 1920
Hicks, Geo.	Capt.	C, 9th West Va. Inf.	440		1919 Aug 29	IA, 46th, 1920
Hicks, George		K, 116th U.S.C. (died at Kansas City)	10		1895 Jun	KS, 15th, 1896
Hicks, George W.	Pvt.	K, 114th Ill. Inf.	358	62	1894 Jun 3	IA, 21st, 1895
Hicks, H.G.		10th N.Y.	302		1922	NE, 47th, 1923
Hicks, J.B.		B, 4th Mo.	77		1928 Jun 10	KS, 48th, 1929
Hicks, J.M.	Pvt.	B, 21st Iowa Inf.	258		1915 Mar 8	IA, 42nd, 1916
Hicks, J.M.	Pvt.	B, 21st Iowa Inf.	258		1916 Mar 8	IA, 43rd, 1917
Hicks, J.W.		D, 2nd Colo.	147		1926 Feb 9	KS, 46th, 1927
Hicks, James		1st Wis. Inf.	219		1910 Aug	IA, 37th, 1911
Hicks, Lorenzo D.		D, 79th Ill.	340		1916 Dec	KS, 36th, 1917
Hicks, W.		M, 15th Kans. Cav.	51		1920 Dec 9	KS, 40th, 1921
Hicks, W.W.		C, 2nd Kans. Cav.	132		1912 Nov 12	KS, 32nd, 1913
Hicks, William			275		1911 1st term	IA, 38th, 1912
Hickson, Hiram	Pvt.		137		1919 Jan 17	IA, 46th, 1920
Hicock, Joel R.	Corp.	C, 12th Ill. Cav.	172	56	1892 Jul 27	IA, 19th, 1893
Hicok, Charles B.	Pvt.	G, 27th Iowa Inf.	132		1908 Apr 14	IA, 35th, 1909
Hiddleson, J.B.		D, 92nd Ohio	7		1930 Jul 11	NE, 55th, 1931
Hidlebaugh, David	Sergt.	F, 35th Iowa Inf.	264	58	1894 Jul 21	IA, 21st, 1895
Hiegier, Francis		G, 5th Mo.	380		1896 Aug 31	KS, 16th, 1897
Hiekox, G.R.	Corp.	A, 46th Iowa Inf.	101		1908 Oct 20	IA, 35th, 1909
Higbee, Joseph	Pvt.	F, 19th Iowa	19		1907 1st term	IA, 34th, 1908
Higbie, Lewis D.		85th Ind.	497		1916 Feb 29	KS, 36th, 1917
Higby, A.S.		C, 18th Ind.	32		1925 Apr 30	KS, 45th, 1926
Higday, J.W.		F, 33rd Wis.	3		1926 Jun 19	KS, 46th, 1927
Higgason, F.M.		C, 33rd Ill.	25	81	1915 Mar 10	NE, 40th, 1916
Higgenfolter, Alex	Pvt.	E, 15th Mo. Inf.	244		1897-1898	IA, 24th, 1898
Higginbotham, R.M.	Pvt.	G, 1st Iowa Cav.	154		1919 May 7	IA, 46th, 1920
Higgins, A.C.		H, 11th Mo. Inf. (died at Neodesha; buried at Neodesha Cemetery)	145		1894 May 9	KS, 14th, 1895
Higgins, A.D.		I, 1st Mo. Inf.	184		1888	KS, 8th, 1889
Higgins, Chas. F.	Pvt.	K, 195th Ohio	68		1924 Jun 13	IA, 51st, 1925
Higgins, F.M.		A, 2nd Wis. Vols.	92		1902 Dec 24	KS, 22nd, 1903
Higgins, G.H.	Pvt.	F, 8th Iowa Inf.	40	69	1890 Apr 25	IA, 18th, 1892
Higgins, J.A.	Bugler	13th Kans. Cav.	4		1914	KS, 34th, 1915
Higgins, J.C.	Pvt.	D, 20th Iowa Inf.	93		1905 Jul 4	IA, 32nd, 1906
Higgins, John			174		1898 Jun 28	KS, 18th, 1899
Higgins, L.H.		67th Col. Inf.	35		1917 Oct 9	KS, 37th, 1918
Higgins, Lewis C.		A, 135th Ill. Inf. E, 14th Ill. Inf. (died of disease contracted in service)	301		1890	KS, 10th, 1891
Higgins, M.		H, 120th Ind. Inf. (died of consumption)	24	51	1895 Aug 9	NE, 20th, 1896

Name	Rank	Company, Regiment or Ship	Post*	Age	Death Date†	Journal
Higgins, M.J.	Sergt.	F, 5th Del. Inf.	204	55	1897 Aug 1	IA, 24th, 1898
Higgins, Patrick		F, 5th Ohio	65		1922 Nov 28	KS, 42nd, 1923
Higgins, T.L.		H, 15th Va.	28		1900 Mar 10	KS, 20th, 1901
Higgins, T.P.		F, 43rd Mo. Inf. (died at Alton, Kans.; buried at Cedarville Cemetery)	184		1894 Feb 25	KS, 14th, 1895
Higgins, Thomas	Sergt.	E, 7th U.S. Inf.	383	69	1896 Dec 11	IA, 23rd, 1897
Higgins, Thomas	Pvt.	K, 33rd Iowa Inf.	40		1909 May 21	IA, 36th, 1910
Higgins, Thomas		L, 2nd Mass. Art.	32		1920 Nov 29	KS, 40th, 1921
Higgins, W.H.		A, 29th Wis. Inf.	282		1st quarter 1885	IA, 11th, 1885
Higgins, W.W.		F, 5th Ill. Inf.	7		1927 Jan	NE, 52nd, 1928
High, Henry		3rd Penn.	115		1927	KS, 47th, 1928
High, Hiram B.		F, 20th Mich.	28		1914 Nov 16	KS, 34th, 1915
High, S.Y.		A, 76th Penn.	250		1920 Jan 7	KS, 40th, 1921
High, T.C.		A, 25th Ohio	4		1920 Nov 18	KS, 40th, 1921
Highberger, R.K.	Pvt.	H, 7th Iowa Cav.	68		1916 Jul 31	IA, 43rd, 1917
Highland, Cyrus	Pvt.	H, 156th Ill. Inf.	30	89	1932 May 21	IA, 59th, 1933
Highley, G.W.		H, 58th Ohio	180	65	1897	NE, 22nd, 1898
Highley, Jacob C.	Pvt.	C, 16th Iowa	1		1924 Dec 5	IA, 51st, 1925
Hight, B.W.		K, 2nd Vt. Inf.	29		1918 Feb 10	IA, 45th, 1919
Hight, Geo. H.	Pvt.	H, 4th Iowa Inf.	324		1926 Mar 19	IA, 53rd, 1927
Hight, Harvey	Pvt.	D, 52nd Ill.	34		1926 Mar 11	IA, 53rd, 1927
Hight, Isaac	Pvt.	B, 5th Ohio Cav.	235		1925 Jul 2	IA, 52nd, 1926
Hight, Jacob		D, 151st Ind.	158		1905 Dec 15	KS, 25th, 1906
Hight, Jacob		D, 151st Ind.	158		1926 Sep 18	KS, 46th, 1927
Higland, Ole	Pvt.		66		1920 Jan 6	IA, 47th, 1921
Higlefield, Geo.			9		1883	KS, 3rd, 1884
Higley, Darwin		C, 11th Ohio	214		1918	KS, 38th, 1919
Higley, Darwin		C, 11th Ohio	214		1918 Jul	KS, 39th, 1920
Higley, M.A.	Pvt.	A, 15th Iowa Inf.	235		1900-1901	IA, 27th, 1901
Higley, Sheldon	Pvt.	E, 68th Ohio Inf.	496		1902 Sep 27	IA, 29th, 1903
Higley, W.H.			28		1900 Jan 12	KS, 20th, 1901
Hilbert, C.		A, 45th Ill.	375		1898 Dec 27	KS, 18th, 1899
Hilbert, Henry		H, 138th Penn.	259		1920 Feb 25	KS, 40th, 1921
Hilbert, M.	Hosp. Stew.	1st Ark. Cav.	91		1922 Jun 19	IA, 49th, 1923
Hilbert, Sol		C, 11th Ind.	85		1930 May 8	KS, 50th, 1931
Hild, John	Pvt.	A, 146th Ill. Inf.	125		1930	IA, 57th, 1931
Hildebrand, David	Sergt.	F, 2nd Penn. Res. Inf.	18		1916 Sep 25	KS, 36th, 1917
Hildebrand, S.M., see Mildebrand, S.M.						
Hilderbrand, J.A.		C, 15th Mich. Inf.	235	92	1936 Aug 24	IA, 63rd, 1937
Hileman, Elijah		B, 18th Wis. Inf.	87		1892 Sep 12	NE, 17th, 1893
Hileman, M.	Pvt.	H, 96th Ill. Inf.	235		1915 Apr 11	IA, 42nd, 1916
Hileman, N.			277		1917	IA, 44th, 1918
Hiles, George		H, 6th Mo.	472		1893 Aug 22	KS, 13th, 1894
Hilgardner, Henry		D, 6th West Va.	303		1896 Jun 13	KS, 16th, 1897
Hilker, Wm.	Pvt.	K, 112th Ill. Inf.	17		1923 Mar	IA, 50th, 1924
Hill, A.	Pvt.	A, 12th Ill. Cav.	343	49	1891[?]	IA, 22nd, 1896
Hill, A.W.	Pvt.	H, 72nd Penn. Inf.	452		1915 Aug 27	IA, 42nd, 1916
Hill, Adison			199		1915	IA, 42nd, 1916
Hill, B.F.	Pvt.	H, 12th Iowa Inf.	2		1905 Feb 27	IA, 32nd, 1906
Hill, Benjamin	Pvt.	H, 35th Iowa Inf.	228		1918 Mar 8	IA, 45th, 1919
Hill, C.C.	Pvt.	C, 39th Iowa	175	54	1890 Oct 22	IA, 17th, 1891
Hill, C.W.	Sergt.	C, 4th Iowa Inf.	12		1925 Apr 5	IA, 52nd, 1926
Hill, Calvin H.		A, 52nd Ohio Inf.	336		1900 Oct 4	KS, 20th, 1901
Hill, Charles		A, 8th Iowa Inf.	32		1931 Dec 6	NE, 56th, 1932
Hill, Charles H.	Pvt.	G, 15th Ill. Inf.	71	54	1893 Dec 6	IA, 20th, 1894
Hill, D.J.		I, 22nd Ohio	32		1912 Dec 16	KS, 32nd, 1913
Hill, E.		K, L, West Va.	17		1928 Dec 24	KS, 48th, 1929
Hill, Edgar S.		G, 4th Calif.	154		1929 Aug 5	NE, 54th, 1930
Hill, Edward		B, 3rd U.S. Colored (died at Kansas City, Kans.; buried at Oak Grove Cemetery)	10		1894 Mar 30	KS, 14th, 1895
Hill, Edwin			105		1912 May 31	KS, 32nd, 1913

*See Appendix A, B or C for roster of post names and locations.
†See Introduction for note regarding recording of death date.
252

Name	Rank	Company, Regiment or Ship	Post*	Age	Death Date†	Journal
Hill, F.C.	Pvt.	E, 117th N.Y.	22		1899	IA, 26th, 1900
Hill, Francis M.		I, 147th Ind.	49		1911 Sep 5	KS, 31st, 1912
Hill, G.H.		B, 46th Iowa Inf.	12		1925 Nov 25	IA, 52nd, 1926
Hill, Geo. A.	Pvt.	A, 34th Ill. Inf.	88		1922 Jun 9	IA, 49th, 1923
Hill, George		U.S. Navy Bacon Squadron	2		1907 Mar 9	IA, 34th, 1908
Hill, George		G, 2nd Wis.	185		1923 Apr 6	KS, 43rd, 1924
Hill, George C.	Pvt.	M, 1st Wis. Cav.	88		1919 Dec 30	IA, 46th, 1920
Hill, H.A.		B, 47th Mo.	25		1910 Jul 25	KS, 30th, 1911
Hill, H.B.		dropped dead	318		1923 Dec 1	NE, 48th, 1924
Hill, H.D.		B, 32nd Ohio	40		1913 Feb 8	KS, 33rd, 1914
Hill, H.H.		B, 14th Ky.	36		1908 Jun 3	KS, 28th, 1909
Hill, Hallock		G, 51st N.Y.	1		1925 Oct 20	KS, 45th, 1926
Hill, Harry		M, 14th N.Y. Hvy. Art.	17		1925 Feb 9	KS, 45th, 1926
Hill, Henry			55		1927 May 9	IA, 54th, 1928
Hill, I.A.		A, 43rd Wis. (former member; died at Minden)	91		1936	NE, 61st, 1937
Hill, I.H.	Pvt.	C, 1st Colo. Cav. (died of consumption)	62	56	1884 Feb 3	NE, 9th, 1885
Hill, J.	Pvt.	C, 92nd Ind. Inf.	134		1904 Dec	IA, 31st, 1905
Hill, J.A.	Corp.	G, 2nd Mo. Cav.	237		1897 Dec 21	IA, 24th, 1898
Hill, J.B.	Pvt.	I, 1st Wis. Cav.	88		1921 Feb 15	IA, 48th, 1922
Hill, J.E.	Pvt.	Neb. Inf.	11		1916 Dec 26	IA, 43rd, 1917
Hill, J.L.		C, 44th Mo.	[40?]		1914 Feb 5	KS, 34th, 1915
Hill, J.M.	Pvt.	B, 46th Iowa Inf.	263	49	1897 Jan 24	IA, 23rd, 1897
Hill, J.N.	Pvt.	A, 60th Ohio	440		1903-1904	IA, 30th, 1904
Hill, J.R.	Pvt.	E, 7th Iowa Cav.	68		2nd quarter 1885	IA, 12th, 1886
Hill, J.W.		F, 18th Iowa Inf. (died of heart trouble)	120		1913 Sep	NE, 38th, 1914
Hill, Jacob		D, 1st Wis. Hvy. Art.	140	77	1923 Dec 29	NE, 49th, 1925
Hill, James			369			IA, 26th, 1900
Hill, James		I, 3rd Wis. Inf. (Albion)			1944 Apr 13	NE, 70th, 1946
Hill, James A.		F, 102nd Ill. Inf. (died of cancer)	84	80	1925 Feb 15	NE, 50th, 1926
Hill, James C.		G, 1st Mo. Cav.	127		1913 Oct	IA, 40th, 1914
Hill, Jesse R.		F, 116th Ill. (died of paralysis)	20	63	1907 Apr 27	NE, 32nd, 1908
Hill, John	Pvt.	C, 35th Iowa Inf.	1		1924 Feb 12	IA, 51st, 1925
Hill, John			77		1924 Jan 15	IA, 51st, 1925
Hill, John F.	Sergt.	F, 14th Iowa Inf.	35		1915 Jun 12	IA, 42nd, 1916
Hill, John H.	Pvt.	C, 4th Ill. Cav.	236		1909	IA, 36th, 1910
Hill, John H.		G, 10th Ind.	20		1922 Jan 21	KS, 42nd, 1923
Hill, John O.		A, 77th Ind.	391		1889	KS, 9th, 1890
Hill, John W.	Pvt.	C, 12th Iowa Inf.	365		1910 Mar 22	IA, 37th, 1911
Hill, Joseph		A, 13th Kans.	46		1912 Nov 16	KS, 32nd, 1913
Hill, Levi D.		G, 132nd Ill.	127		1921 Jun 19	KS, 41st, 1922
Hill, Lewis	Capt.	E, 2nd Neb. Cav. (died of pneumonia)	84	83	1921 Oct 9	NE, 46th, 1922
Hill, M.S.	Pvt.	C, 117th Ill.	343		1907 Oct 21	IA, 34th, 1908
Hill, Mortimer V.		E, 28th N.Y. Inf. E, 15th N.Y. Cav.	10	83	1921 Aug 10	NE, 46th, 1922
Hill, N.O.		E, 9th Ind. Cav.	120		1927 Jul 24	NE, 52nd, 1928
Hill, Norman		K, 100th Ohio Inf.	146		1899 Apr 6	KS, 19th, 1900
Hill, O.C.		A, 42nd Ohio Inf.	130		1899 Jun 30	KS, 19th, 1900
Hill, Preston K.	Pvt.	H, — Ill. Inf.	26	88	1932 Nov 7	IA, 59th, 1933
Hill, Robert		B, 65th Ill. Inf.	12		1924 Apr 8	KS, 44th, 1925
Hill, Sylvender	Pvt.	A, 51st Wis. Inf.	101		1913 Apr 22	IA, 40th, 1914
Hill, Sylvester P.		L, 2nd Ind. Cav.	1		1925 Jun 2	KS, 45th, 1926
Hill, T.F.	Teamster	C, 29th Iowa Inf.	38		1921 Sep 17	IA, 48th, 1922
Hill, T.T.		C, 142nd N.Y.	22		1936 Mar 23	NE, 61st, 1937
Hill, T.W.		I, 48th Ill.	177		1897 May 3	KS, 17th, 1898
Hill, Thomas		D, 2nd Vt.	18		1911 Jan 29	KS, 31st, 1912
Hill, Thomas B.		E, 39th Ohio Inf. (died at Crawford County, Kans.; buried at Girard Cemetery)	49		1894 Nov 1	KS, 14th, 1895
Hill, W.C.		K, 177th Penn.	244		1904 Oct 18	KS, 24th, 1905
Hill, W.E.	Pvt.	B, 138th Ill. Inf.	16		1917 Jan 9	IA, 44th, 1918
Hill, W.N.		E, 59th Ind. Inf.	79		1900	KS, 20th, 1901
Hill, Walter F.		D, 178th Ohio (died of paralysis)	8	73	1916 Aug 20	NE, 41st, 1917

*See Appendix A, B or C for roster of post names and locations.
†See Introduction for note regarding recording of death date.

Name	Rank	Company, Regiment or Ship	Post*	Age	Death Date†	Journal
Hill, William H.		B, 22nd Iowa Inf.	158		1916 Feb 25	KS, 36th, 1917
Hill, Wm.		C, 149th Ill.	134		1904 Jun 5	KS, 24th, 1905
Hill, Wm.		C, 149th Ill.	88		1904 Jun 1	KS, 24th, 1905
Hill, Wm.	Capt.	B, 8th Mo. Inf.	145		1918 Aug 6	KS, 38th, 1919
Hill, Wm. H.	Sergt.	D, 19th Wis. Inf.	267	73	1888 May 17	IA, 15th, 1889
Hillard, William		F, 3rd Ill. Cav.	25		1923 Apr 17	KS, 43rd, 1924
Hiller, Alfred		E, 3rd Mass.	3		1936 Mar 22	NE, 61st, 1937
Hillery, David	Pvt.	C, 50th Wis. Inf.	179		1926 Dec 21	IA, 53rd, 1927
Hillhouse, John		K, 18th Mo. Inf.	239		1892 Aug 1	KS, 12th, 1893
Hilliard, Aaron	Pvt.	E, 15th Iowa Inf.	177		1913 Sep 11	IA, 40th, 1914
Hilliard, James		U.S. Marines (died at Westmoreland; buried at Westmoreland Cemetery)	151		1894 Jan 24	KS, 14th, 1895
Hilliker, John A.		I, 27th Mich.	113		1900 Sep 24	KS, 20th, 1901
Hilling, Geo. W.	Pvt.	Iowa	29		1908 Nov 9	IA, 35th, 1909
Hillinger, John		B, 11th Penn.	1		1923 Jul 16	KS, 43rd, 1924
Hillis, D.B.	Lieut. Col.	17th Iowa Inf.	2		1900 Sep 9	IA, 27th, 1901
Hillis, J.G.	Pvt.	G, 17th Iowa	497		1921 Jul	IA, 48th, 1922
Hillman, Charles		D, 8th Ill. Inf.	98		1916 Jan 3	KS, 36th, 1917
Hillman, J.M.		C, 10th Iowa Cav.	221		1909 Apr 29	KS, 29th, 1910
Hillman, R.L.		L, 3rd Mass. (at time discharged 1st Lieut., Company F, 2nd Mass.)	47		1890	KS, 10th, 1891
Hills, Geo.	Pvt.	F, 26th N.Y.	22		1921 Apr 12	IA, 48th, 1922
Hills, Henry A.		F, 33rd N.Y.	191		1919 Feb 12	KS, 39th, 1920
Hills, Levi		F, 11th Ill. Inf.	69		1899 Jul 15	IA, 26th, 1900
Hills, M.S.		C, 95th Ill. (died of old age)	90	76	1920 Dec 11	NE, 45th, 1921
Hills, William	Pvt.	D, 102nd Ill. Inf.	248		1916 Nov 24	IA, 43rd, 1917
Hillver, E.D.		E, 5th Kans.	1		1892 Dec 11	KS, 12th, 1893
Hilly, F.M.		F, 14th Ill.	251		1916 Dec 31	KS, 36th, 1917
Hillyard, P.	Pvt.	D, 25th Iowa	384		1903 Jun 5	IA, 30th, 1904
Hilman, D.C.		H, 7th Iowa	79		1889	KS, 9th, 1890
Hiltabidel, Geo. A.		D, 104th Ohio	142		1897 Feb	KS, 17th, 1898
Hilter, Nathan		I, 152nd Ohio	17		1926 Sep 2	KS, 46th, 1927
Hilton, Geo.	Pvt.	G, 15th Iowa Inf.	169	54	1886 Nov 26	IA, 17th, 1891
Hilton, J.K.	Pvt.	F, 4th Iowa Cav.	107		1909 Mar	IA, 36th, 1910
Hilton, M.J.	Pvt.		231		1933	IA, 60th, 1934
Hilton, William		9th Maine Inf.	97		1934 Apr 22	KS, 55th, 1936
Hilts, John		C, 2nd Mo. Cav.	61		1924 Oct 26	KS, 44th, 1925
Hiltz, William		H, 15th Mo.	380		1890	KS, 10th, 1891
Hilyard, W.L.		A, 25th Ill.	63		1933 Sep 12	NE, 58th, 1934
Himebaugh, H.H.	Pvt.	C, 44th Iowa Inf.	66		1913 Mar 14	IA, 40th, 1914
Himes, Chas. F.		B, 37th Ill.	35		1919 Mar 14	KS, 39th, 1920
Himes, F.			164		1913	KS, 33rd, 1914
Himes, J.M.	Pvt.	E, 33rd Iowa Inf.	12		1929 Jul 23	IA, 56th, 1930
Hinate, A.		C, 3rd Iowa Cav. (died of paralysis)	228	60	1901 Oct	NE, 26th, 1902
Hinchcliffe, R.L.			144		1908 Jan	IA, 35th, 1909
Hinchliffe		B, 4th Iowa Inf.	8	90	1936 Dec 30	IA, 63rd, 1937
Hinckley, E.C.		E, 13th Ill.	12		1905 Feb 15	KS, 25th, 1906
Hinckley, W.H.		A, 7th Iowa	1		1889	KS, 9th, 1890
Hinderer, N.O.		G, 185th Ohio	25		1928 Jul 20	KS, 48th, 1929
Hindley, Edwin		K, 39th Ohio (location: Blair)			1927 Jun 15	NE, 52nd, 1928
Hindman, D.R.	Lieut.	H, 19th Wis. Inf.	67		1908 Apr 17	IA, 35th, 1909
Hindman, D.R.	Pvt.	B, 2nd Penn. Inf.	206		1918 Feb 25	IA, 45th, 1919
Hindman, H.	Pvt.	D, 46th Iowa Inf.	10		1910 Mar	IA, 37th, 1911
Hindman, Lorenzo W.		C, 9th Kans.	[40?]		1914 Oct 3	KS, 34th, 1915
Hindman, Samuel		19th Ind.	71		1904 Oct 4	KS, 24th, 1905
Hinds, Erastus F., see Hiads, Erastus F.						
Hine, Colin E.	Pvt.	G, 8th Wis. (died of epilepsy)	25	47	1884 Oct 4	NE, 9th, 1885
Hine, Daniel		L, 3rd Iowa Cav.	251		3rd quarter 1884	IA, 11th, 1885
Hine, L.	Pvt.	H, 43rd Wis. Inf.	112		1899	NE, 24th, 1900
Hinebaugh, Jacob		124th Ohio	443		1910 Sep 4	KS, 30th, 1911

*See Appendix A, B or C for roster of post names and locations.
†See Introduction for note regarding recording of death date.

Name	Rank	Company, Regiment or Ship	Post*	Age	Death Date†	Journal
Hineman, William		E, 49th Ohio Inf. (died at Elm Creek; buried at Gypsum Hill)	127		1894 Feb 2	KS, 14th, 1895
Hiner, Sylvester		D, 15th West Va. Inf.	25		1925 Sep 3	KS, 45th, 1926
Hines, Barney	Pvt.	H, 13th Ill. Inf.	87	53	1893 Dec 25	IA, 20th, 1894
Hines, Edward		E, 27th Mo. (cause of death: hurt in runaway)	226	67	1911 Oct 25	NE, 36th, 1912
Hines, Francis M.		C, 119th Ind.	493		1921 Nov 6	KS, 41st, 1922
Hines, Isaac				92	1937 Jul 3	IA, 64th, 1938
Hines, Isaac		G, 38th Ill.	28		1925 Feb 12	KS, 45th, 1926
Hines, Jno.		8th Ohio	17		1904 Feb 27	KS, 24th, 1905
Hines, Shelton		D, 13th Ky. Cav. (died of wounds)	155	63	1908 Nov 10	NE, 33rd, 1909
Hines, Thos.	Pvt.	A, 31st Iowa Inf.	1		1919 Oct 1	IA, 46th, 1920
Hines, Wm.		B, 69th Ind.	490		1906 Nov 13	KS, 26th, 1907
Hinkel, Comrade			477		1919 Aug	KS, 39th, 1920
Hinkle, Con	Pvt.	C, 35th Iowa Inf.	231	63	1890 Jun 12	IA, 18th, 1892
Hinkle, Emanuel		F, 107th Ill.	264		1898 Jun 26	KS, 18th, 1899
Hinkle, Geo. W.	Pvt.	I, 45th Iowa Inf.	192		1933 May 13	IA, 60th, 1934
Hinkle, J.C.	Pvt.	A, 1st Iowa Cav. (at large)			1933 Jul 30	IA, 60th, 1934
Hinkle, William		D, 61st Penn.	303		1919 May 18	KS, 39th, 1920
Hinks, John B.		B, 5th Mich. Inf.	236	93	1937 May 14	IA, 64th, 1938
Hinkson, Jno. W.	Pvt.	D, 4th Iowa Cav.	20		1924 Dec 29	IA, 51st, 1925
Hinman, David		D, 1st Kans. Inf.	12		1917 Feb 6	KS, 37th, 1918
Hinman, David S.	Pvt.	K, 6th Iowa Cav.	235	62	1899 Sep 24	IA, 26th, 1900
Hinman, Lewis	Pvt.	D, 32nd Iowa Inf.	372	49	1892 Jan 22	IA, 18th, 1892
Hinman, S.N.	Lieut.	C, 1st Conn. Cav.	247		1919 Jul 9	IA, 46th, 1920
Hinman, S.N.	Lieut.	C, 1st Conn. Cav.	247		1919 Jul 9	IA, 46th, 1920
Hinsdale, J.W.		A, 4th Mich.	388		1911	KS, 31st, 1912
Hinson, John	Pvt.	C, 25th Iowa Inf.	2		1917 Feb 11	IA, 44th, 1918
Hinton, Eli		F, 13th Kans. Cav. (died at Logan, Kans.; buried at Logan Cemetery)	177		1894 Oct 3	KS, 14th, 1895
Hinton, Robert		H, 12th H.D. Ky.[12th Ky. Hvy. Art.]	486		1904 Dec 27	KS, 24th, 1905
Hirsh, H.H.		K, 1st Ohio Cav.	18		1913 Jul 10	KS, 33rd, 1914
Hirst, P.			8		1886 May 5	NE, 11th, 1887
Hirth, John		A, 46th N.Y.	17		1921 Mar 13	KS, 41st, 1922
Hiscox, Daniel P.			25		1928	IA, 55th, 1929
Hise, J.G.		E, 1st Iowa Cav.	108		1916 Jun 15	IA, 43rd, 1917
Hiseg, W.H.		7th Mo. Cav.	27		1908[1909?] Sep	KS, 29th, 1910
Hisel, William	Pvt.	F, 174th Ohio Inf.	231		1925 Aug 31	IA, 52nd, 1926
Hisey, Solomon		A, 121st Ohio	68		1914 Oct 4	KS, 34th, 1915
Hisler, E.S.		14th Lt. Art.	147		1929 Jul 8	KS, 49th, 1930
Hislop, M.L.		1st Iowa Inf.	231	65	1902 Feb	NE, 27th, 1903
Hitch, O.G.		A, 5th Ohio Vol. Cav.	49		1914 Feb 5	KS, 34th, 1915
Hitchcock, A.A.	Pvt.	I, 29th Wis. Inf.	339		1915	IA, 42nd, 1916
Hitchcock, A.C.	Sergt.	B, 19th Wis. Inf.	168	63	1897 Aug 16	IA, 24th, 1898
Hitchcock, C.H.	Pvt.	I, 14th Vt. Inf.	12		1921 Jul 8	IA, 48th, 1922
Hitchcock, C.P.		I, 61st Ill. Inf.	201	56	1901 Nov	NE, 26th, 1902
Hitchcock, Chancey	Pvt.	H, 7th Wis.	22		1922 Jun 20	IA, 49th, 1923
Hitchcock, H.F.	Lieut.	C, 76th Ill. Inf.	11		1919 Aug 14	IA, 46th, 1920
Hitchcock, J.F.	Pvt.	L, 3rd Iowa Cav.	12		1918 Jan 23	IA, 45th, 1919
Hitchcock, L.J.		F, 5th Mo. (died of heart failure)	84	86	1924 Nov 16	NE, 49th, 1925
Hitchcock, Levi J.		F, 5th Mo. Cav. (died of paralytic stroke)	84	86	1925 Nov 16	NE, 50th, 1926
Hitchcock, O.H.	S. & C.	H & K, 95th & 15th Ill. Inf.	168	65	1898 Jun 6	IA, 25th, 1899
Hitchcock, Richard			52		1892 Nov 19	KS, 12th, 1893
Hitchcock, S.L.		D, 151st N.Y.	142		1923 Jul 17	KS, 43rd, 1924
Hitchings, John	Pvt.	H, 1st Iowa Cav.	54	86	1933 Aug 28	IA, 60th, 1934
Hitchings, John		H, 1st Iowa	81		1933 Aug 28	KS, 53rd, 1934
Hitchings, Martin V.	Pvt.	K, 34th Iowa Inf.	63		1917 Dec 27	IA, 45th, 1919
Hite, Abram			153		1884	KS, 4th, 1885
Hite, J.I.		A, 34th —	461		1899 Apr 29	KS, 19th, 1900
Hite, J.N.	Pvt.	L, 4th Iowa Cav.	97	56	1886 Jun 16	IA, 13th, 1887
Hite, John S.	Pvt.	G, 112th Ill. Inf.	95	49	1893 Oct 28	IA, 20th, 1894
Hite, Nate	Pvt.	D, 24th Inf.	116		1925 Sep 26	IA, 52nd, 1926

*See Appendix A, B or C for roster of post names and locations.

255

†See Introduction for note regarding recording of death date.

Name	Rank	Company, Regiment or Ship	Post*	Age	Death Date†	Journal
Hite, Nathan	Pvt.	B, 25th Iowa Inf.	309		1925 Sep 26	IA, 52nd, 1926
Hite, Swan P.		H, 108th Ill. (died of old age)	359	78	1910 Dec 17	NE, 35th, 1911
Hitland, B.G.		I, 67th Ill. Inf.	101		1914 Oct 6	IA, 41st, 1915
Hits, Joseph		K, 27th Ill.	40	78	1917 Feb 19	NE, 42nd, 1918
Hitz, C.		I, 12th Wis. Bat.	49		1918 Nov 17	KS, 38th, 1919
Hitz, John		F, 17th Mo. Inf.	375		1886	KS, 6th, 1887
Hively, H.C.		C, 17th Ind.	118		1922 Nov 12	KS, 42nd, 1923
Hixon, D.S.		A, 48th Ohio	255		1905 Nov 16	KS, 25th, 1906
Hixson, James		F, 14th Iowa	90		1928 Jan 22	KS, 48th, 1929
Hoag, Benj. S.		F, 128th N.Y. (died of dis[ease?] contracted in serv[ice?])	54	75	1912 Jul 28	NE, 37th, 1913
Hoag, J.M.		9th N.Y. Art.	74		1917 Dec 12	IA, 44th, 1918
Hoag, Orie		D, 12th Kans.	322		1921 Nov 2	KS, 41st, 1922
Hoag, S.C.		H, 47th Ind.	132		1918	KS, 38th, 1919
Hoag, Wm.		B, 6th N.Y.	32		1902 Aug 13	KS, 22nd, 1903
Hoagland, Henry	Pvt.	E, 137th Ill. Inf.	365		1909 Sep 14	IA, 36th, 1910
Hoagland, Henry V.		F, 7th Ill. Inf. (see also Appendix D)	25		1930 Feb 14	NE, 55th, 1931
Hoagland, I.P.		H, 132nd Penn. Inf.	13	74	1916 Apr 6	NE, 41st, 1917
Hoagland, Joseph S.		see Appendix D	69	73	1920 Jul 31	NE, 45th, 1921
Hoagland, M.		I, 57th Ill.	17		1926 Jun 23	KS, 46th, 1927
Hobart, F.E.	Pvt.	F, 17th Iowa Inf.	20	59	1889 Apr 5	IA, 16th, 1890
Hobart, Frank		D, 64th Ill. Inf.	147		1935 Nov 25	KS, 55th, 1936
Hobart, Seth S.	Pvt.	I, 8th Iowa Inf.	88		1917 Jan 4	IA, 44th, 1918
Hobble, P.R.		D, 13th Ohio (see also Appendix D)	294	80	1918 Mar 6 or 7	KS, 38th, 1919
Hobbs, Albert		D, 64th Ill. (died at Girard)	49		1895 Jul	KS, 15th, 1896
Hobbs, Harley S.		A, 151st N.Y. Inf.	354	70	1914 Nov 12	NE, 40th, 1916
Hobbs, I.F.	Capt.	G, 111th Maine	156		1899 Jun 8	IA, 26th, 1900
Hobbs, J.W.	Artificer	17th Ind. Battery	12		1910 Aug 29	IA, 37th, 1911
Hobbs, James			384		1909	IA, 36th, 1910
Hobbs, John W.		I, 2nd Iowa Cav.	44		1914	NE, 39th, 1915
Hobbs, W.S.		B, 20th Ill. Inf.	66		1916 Dec 1	KS, 36th, 1917
Hobbs, William F.		E, 10th Ohio Cav.	55		1911 Jan 15	KS, 31st, 1912
Hobbs, Wm. H.		C, 5th West Va.	40		1917 Feb 8	KS, 37th, 1918
Hobert, James		I, 185th N.Y. Inf. (died of consumption)	262		1894 Jun 13	NE, 19th, 1895
Hobert, W.K.	Pvt.	F, 1st Iowa Inf.	20		1922 Feb 10	IA, 49th, 1923
Hoblet, D.	Pvt.	H, 12th Ill. Cav.	22		1920 Oct 5	IA, 47th, 1921
Hoblit, W.H.		H, 12th Ill.	13		1914	NE, 39th, 1915
Hobson, Aaron	Pvt.	G, 3rd Mo. Cav.	287	57	1889 Jun 19	IA, 16th, 1890
Hobson, Aaron	Pvt.	G, 3rd Minn. Cav.	287	56	1889 Jun 19	IA, 17th, 1891
Hobson, C.	Pvt.	I, 4th Iowa Cav.	11		1904 Oct 28	IA, 31st, 1905
Hobson, J.T.	Pvt.	E, 6th Iowa Cav.	57		1909 Aug 24	IA, 36th, 1910
Hobson, James M.		50th Ind. Inf.	55		1912 Jan 18	IA, 39th, 1913
Hoch, Isaac	Sergt. Lieut.	D, 29th Iowa Inf. G, 3rd U.S. Inf. (at large)	175, 45	99	1939 Dec 19	IA, 66th, 1940
Hock, Josegh	Pvt.	G, 57th Ill. Inf.	5	57	1889 May 6	IA, 16th, 1890
Hockaday, William			190		1927 Nov 9	IA, 54th, 1928
Hockart, J.L.		I, 2nd Ind. Battery	7		1928 Oct 2	IA, 55th, 1929
Hocke, Henry	Pvt.	A, 35th Iowa Inf.	231		1925 Jul 3	IA, 52nd, 1926
Hockenburg, James			44		1899	NE, 24th, 1900
Hocker, Philip		E, 8th Ind. (died of old age)	318		1924 Sep 9	NE, 49th, 1925
Hocket, Henry		B, 4th Iowa	51		1916 Nov 25	KS, 36th, 1917
Hockett, Ansel B.		I, 2nd Kans.	94		1917 Jul 25	KS, 37th, 1918
Hockett, Eleazor		E, 39th Iowa Inf.	23		1914	IA, 41st, 1915
Hockett, Henry		G, 4th Iowa Cav.	179		1916 Nov 25	KS, 36th, 1917
Hockett, Wyatt		F, 124th Ind. Inf.	350		1900 Dec 23	KS, 20th, 1901
Hocum, A.H.	Pvt.	E, 1st Wis. Inf.	512		1916 Oct 22	IA, 43rd, 1917
Hodge, Chas. W.		D, 55th Ind. G, 115th Ind. I, 17th Ind.	14		1908 Mar 12	KS, 28th, 1909
Hodge, Com.	Pvt.		116		1914 Mar 28	IA, 41st, 1915
Hodge, David	Pvt.	1st Iowa Cav.	69		1904 Oct 14	IA, 31st, 1905
Hodge, E.A.		F, 6th Minn.	42		1911 May 5	KS, 31st, 1912

*See Appendix A, B or C for roster of post names and locations.
†See Introduction for note regarding recording of death date.
256

Name	Rank	Company, Regiment or Ship	Post*	Age	Death Date†	Journal
Hodge, J.B.		37th Ind.	160		1888	KS, 8th, 1889
Hodge, William H.		I, 5th Kans. Cav.	18		1915 Jun 30	KS, 35th, 1916
Hodge, Wm. S.		K, 51st Ohio	63		1904 Sep 9	KS, 24th, 1905
Hodges, Charles	Pvt.	D, 39th —	426		1901 Jun 20	IA, 28th, 1902
Hodges, David H.		K, 16th Kans. Inf.	[18?]		1918 Jul 14	KS, 38th, 1919
Hodges, F.L.	Pvt.	C, 48th Wis. Inf.	314		1910	IA, 37th, 1911
Hodges, Geo. W.	Pvt.	K, 40th Iowa	49		1923 Feb 7	IA, 50th, 1924
Hodges, George N.		I, 2nd Ill. Lt. Art.	17		1912 Oct 8	KS, 32nd, 1913
Hodges, Henry F.	Pvt.	A, 139th Ill. Inf.	7		1930 May 16	IA, 57th, 1931
Hodges, Lewis C.			316		1908	IA, 35th, 1909
Hodges, Milton	Pvt.	A, 33rd Iowa	49		1926 Dec 19	IA, 53rd, 1927
Hodges, W.C.		A, 31st Ill.	139		1921 Feb 8	KS, 41st, 1922
Hodges, W.E.	Sergt.	C, 7th Iowa Inf.	40		1909	IA, 36th, 1910
Hodgin, John	Pvt.	H, 24th Iowa Inf.	4	50	1895 Feb 16	IA, 22nd, 1896
Hodgson, G.H.	Sergt.	F, 37th Wis. Inf. C, 13th Wis. Inf.	30	53	1894 Jun 10	IA, 21st, 1895
Hodgson, William		E, 4th Minn. Inf.	17		1925 Nov 24	KS, 45th, 1926
Hodkins, George		A, 5th Mo. Inf. (died of rheumatism)	53	75	1895 Mar 11	NE, 20th, 1896
Hodsell, Chas.		M, 2nd Penn. (died of paralysis)	318		1915 Nov 19	NE, 40th, 1916
Hodsell, I.D.		M, Hvy. Art.	17		1911 May 17	KS, 31st, 1912
Hodson, David	Pvt.	K, 3rd Iowa Cav.	18		1900 Nov 18	IA, 27th, 1901
Hodson, F.F.		D, 28th Iowa Inf.	241		1918 Jun	KS, 38th, 1919
Hoeb, A.		A, 76th Ill.	170		1914 Feb 2	KS, 34th, 1915
Hoeflinger, Geo.	Pvt.	A, 31st Iowa Inf.	509		1900 Oct	IA, 27th, 1901
Hoelinger, Joseph		B, 74th Penn. (died of disability)	84	72	1907 Feb	NE, 33rd, 1909
Hoeppner, Theo.		F, 31st Ind. Inf.	64		1937 May 5	KS, 56th, 1937
Hoerner, D.G.		E, 12th Ill. Cav.	104		1929	NE, 54th, 1930
Hoerner, George W.	Corp.	H, 12th Iowa Inf.	78	63	1894 Aug 26	IA, 21st, 1895
Hofer, John J.		D, 1st Mo. Eng.	250		1919 Mar 13	KS, 39th, 1920
Hoff, Henry		I, 107th Ohio	125		1912	KS, 32nd, 1913
Hoff, Samuel M.	Pvt.	G, 1st Iowa Cav.	68		1916 Aug 19	IA, 43rd, 1917
Hoffa, D.	Pvt.	E, 5th Penn. Inf.	68		1921 Aug 3	IA, 48th, 1922
Hoffa, Henry	Pvt.	D, 142nd Ill.	71		1907 Jul 29	IA, 34th, 1908
Hoffaker, W.		B, 6th Mo. Cav. (died at Tribune)	475		1895 Aug	KS, 15th, 1896
Hoffan, W.H.		B, 147th Inf.		89	1936[1935?] Dec 9	IA, 62nd, 1936
Hoffbauer, Hugo	Lieut.	A, 14th Iowa Inf.	1		1921 Mar 14	IA, 48th, 1922
Hoffer, Jacob		C, 38th Ohio Inf. (died at Fort Scott)	32		1895 Oct	KS, 15th, 1896
Hoffer, Michael		B, 3rd Md. Potomac Home Brigade Inf.	26		1934 Jun 13	NE, 59th, 1935
Hoffhines, Jonas	Pvt.	C, 88th Ohio Inf. (at large)	251	100	1940 Oct 22	IA, 67th, 1941
Hoffman, A.S.	Surg.	1st Ky. Cav.	89		1891 Oct	KS, 11th, 1892
Hoffman, Adam	Pvt.	B, 78th Penn. Inf.	236		1931	IA, 58th, 1932
Hoffman, Aug.	Sailor	Gunboat Chippewa	22		1919 Apr 5	KS, 39th, 1920
Hoffman, C.		K, 202nd Penn. Inf. (died of hernia)	23	72	1896 May 1	NE, 21st, 1897
Hoffman, C.A.	Pvt.	H, 1st Wis. Cav.	68		1904 Jun 17	IA, 31st, 1905
Hoffman, C.P.	Pvt.	K, 15th Iowa Inf.	193		1912 Mar 21	IA, 39th, 1913
Hoffman, Corn		D, 143rd Germ.	429		1908	KS, 28th, 1909
Hoffman, E.H.		11th Mo. Inf. (cause of death: heart)	7	60	1891[1901?] Oct	NE, 26th, 1902
Hoffman, Edw. J.		A, 34th N.Y. Inf.	25		1917 Feb 12	NE, 42nd, 1918
Hoffman, F.	Pvt.	A, 2nd Iowa Inf.	2	53	1895 Jun 13	IA, 22nd, 1896
Hoffman, Fred		A, 22nd Ohio	90		1935 Oct 5	KS, 55th, 1936
Hoffman, Gilbert O.		B, 6th Wis.	293		1925 Mar 14	KS, 45th, 1926
Hoffman, J.F.		H, 87th Penn.	81		1930 Feb 14	KS, 50th, 1931
Hoffman, Jno.		D, 5th Mo.	380		1904 Aug 24	KS, 24th, 1905
Hoffman, John	Pvt.	E, 16th Iowa Inf.	6		1927 Apr 11	IA, 54th, 1928
Hoffman, John	Pvt.	A, 44th Iowa Inf.	1		1930 Aug 5	IA, 57th, 1931
Hoffman, John		B, 43rd Ill.	36		1929 Jul 5	KS, 49th, 1930
Hoffman, John S.	Corp.	G, 26th Ind. Inf.	51		1917 Oct 21	IA, 44th, 1918
Hoffman, Joseph H.	Pvt.	G, 5th Wis. Bat.	267		1901 Oct 12	IA, 28th, 1902
Hoffman, Louis	Pvt.	B, 66th Ill. Sharpshooters	345	46	1888 Sep 17	IA, 15th, 1889
Hoffman, M.A.		Bat., 12th N.Y.	318		1888	KS, 8th, 1889
Hoffman, Nicolas	Pvt.	E, 21st Iowa Inf.	297		1925 Apr 5	IA, 52nd, 1926
Hoffman, Oliver			429		1911	KS, 31st, 1912

*See Appendix A, B or C for roster of post names and locations.
†See Introduction for note regarding recording of death date.

257

Name	Rank	Company, Regiment or Ship	Post*	Age	Death Date†	Journal
Hoffman, P.B.	Pvt.	44th Ill. Inf.	78		1908 Jan 2	IA, 35th, 1909
Hoffman, Peter		E, 29th Iowa	69		1898 Aug 21	KS, 18th, 1899
Hoffman, Peter		Neb.	118	72	1908	NE, 33rd, 1909
Hoffman, Phillip	Pvt.	C, 3rd Iowa Inf.	230	57	1898 Jul 9	IA, 25th, 1899
Hoffman, Valentine		A, 8th Ill.	12		1915 Apr 24	KS, 35th, 1916
Hoffman, W.H.		B, 147th N.Y. Inf.	7	89	1935 Dec 9	IA, 62nd, 1936
Hoffman, Wm.	Pvt.	G, 19th Iowa Inf.	231	91	1932 Mar 2	IA, 59th, 1933
Hoffman, Wm. F.		K, 180th Ohio Inf.	28		1912 Aug 28	KS, 32nd, 1913
Hoffmaster, A.W.	Asst. Surg.	8th Mo. Inf.	170	70	1896 May 16	IA, 23rd, 1897
Hoffmaster, R.T.	Pvt.	K, 18th Iowa Inf.	231		1919 Apr 19	IA, 46th, 1920
Hoffnal, S.B.		A, 55th Ohio Vol. Inf.	63		1914 Jun 28	KS, 34th, 1915
Hofins, J.T.		F, 43rd Wis. Inf. (died at Concordia)	113		1894 Dec 25	KS, 14th, 1895
Hofman, Sanford	Pvt.	K, 26th Iowa Inf.	398		1903 Jun 12	IA, 30th, 1904
Hofmaster, Augustus	Pvt.	B, 46th Ill. Inf.	90		1918 Aug 12	IA, 45th, 1919
Hogaboom, E.B.	Sergt.	G, 10th N.Y. Cav.	113	76	1896 Oct 20	IA, 23rd, 1897
Hogan, A.A.		C, 122nd Ill.	32		1923 Oct 13	KS, 43rd, 1924
Hogan, A.J.		H, 12th Kans.	74		1922 Sep 25	KS, 42nd, 1923
Hogan, A.M.	Pvt.	H, 2nd Ill. Cav.	127	59	1897 Jan 8	IA, 23rd, 1897
Hogan, B.R.		K, 9th Iowa Cav.	44		1916 Jun 17	KS, 36th, 1917
Hogan, C.H.		A, 89th Ohio	4		1906 Jan 24	KS, 26th, 1907
Hogan, I.J.	Pvt.	1st N.E. Mtd. H.G.[Northeast Mounted Home Guard]	516		1908 Mar 23	IA, 35th, 1909
Hogan, Martin		C, 2nd Iowa Cav.	12		1925 Feb 5	IA, 52nd, 1926
Hogan, Michael		B, 23rd Wis. Inf. (died of dropsy)	380		1891 Sep 11	KS, 11th, 1892
Hogan, S.R.		K, 31st Wis.	38		1904 Feb 22	KS, 24th, 1905
Hogan, Thomas		C, 58th Ill.	11		1921 Feb 15	KS, 41st, 1922
Hogancamp, David	Pvt.	F, 56th N.Y. Inf.	97		1904 Mar 10	IA, 31st, 1905
Hoganson, Ole	Sergt.	G, 13th Wis. Inf.	370	55	1897 Feb 3	IA, 23rd, 1897
Hogeboom, H.H.	Pvt.	K, 57th Ill. Inf.	22		1933 Feb 7	IA, 60th, 1934
Hogeboom, William F.		D, 2nd Neb. Cav. (died of heart failure)	55	71	1911 Aug 6	NE, 36th, 1912
Hogelin, Amos		K, 98th Ill.	139		1916 Oct 2	KS, 36th, 1917
Hoggard, C.D.	Musician	B, 118th Ill. Inf.	316		1899 May 17	IA, 26th, 1900
Hogin, George B.	Pvt., Comm. Sergt., 2nd Lieut., 1st Lieut. & Capt.	D, 13th Iowa Inf. (see Appendix D)	16	57	1895 Feb 6	IA, 21st, 1895
Hogland, B.L.		B, 38th Wis.	85		1911 Jun 7	KS, 31st, 1912
Hogle, Sanford	Pvt.	A, 16th Iowa Inf.	81		1915 Apr 6	IA, 42nd, 1916
Hogoboom, J.		C, 6th Mich. Inf. (died of old age)	76	76	1911 Aug 12	NE, 36th, 1912
Hogsett, John W.		G, 10th Ind.	258		1914 Dec 4	KS, 34th, 1915
Hogue, Elijah	Major	1st Bt., 9th Ohio	255		1899 Nov 23	IA, 26th, 1900
Hogue, George M.		G, 2nd N.H. Art.	262	62	1911 Dec 31	NE, 36th, 1912
Hogue, Harvey S.		G, 115th Ohio Inf.	191		1914 Feb 23	KS, 34th, 1915
Hogue, I.R.	Pvt.	50th Ohio Inf.	96		1929 Feb 4	IA, 56th, 1930
Hogue, J.C.		K, 14th Ind. Inf.	209		1929	KS, 49th, 1930
Hogue, J.M.		E, 12th Ill.	129		1919 Dec 23	KS, 39th, 1920
Hogue, John N.		B, 83rd Ill.	17		1926 Feb 24	KS, 46th, 1927
Hogue, Samuel R.			104		1923 Feb 26	KS, 43rd, 1924
Hogue, T.P.		D, 52nd Ill.	23		1928 Oct 20	NE, 53rd, 1929
Hohnbaum, Wm.		Bat. L, 3rd Penn. Art. (died of dropsy)	41	72	1919 Dec 29	NE, 44th, 1920
Hoit, Awasa	Pvt.	C, 7th Iowa Inf.	94		1927 Apr 10	IA, 54th, 1928
Hojack, James		I, 25th Ind. Inf.	22	78	1924 Dec 22	NE, 49th, 1925
Hoke, Henry		A, 1st Ind.	382		1896 Jul 13	KS, 16th, 1897
Hokinson, J.V.	Pvt.	C, 4th Iowa Cav.	440		1928 Nov 29	IA, 55th, 1929
Hol, M.G.		G, 33rd Iowa Inf. (at large)		89	1935 Dec 15	IA, 62nd, 1936
Holbert, M.		F, 11th West Va. Inf.	100		1915 Aug 16	KS, 35th, 1916
Holbrock, A.N.	Pvt.	M, 7th Iowa Cav.	512		1914 Apr 10	IA, 41st, 1915
Holbroke, C.D.	Pvt.	B, 39th Iowa Inf.	324		1897 Mar 24	IA, 24th, 1898
Holbrook, Alex	Sergt.	H, 101st Ill.	284		1907 Sep 23	IA, 34th, 1908
Holbrook, August		G & H, 5th[?] N.Y. Inf. & 14th N.Y. Hvy. Art.	25		1911 Mar 26	NE, 36th, 1912
Holbrook, J.M.		F, 27th Iowa	190		1st quarter 1884	IA, 10th, 1884
Holbrook, Jas. E., see Holdbrook, Jas. E.						

*See Appendix A, B or C for roster of post names and locations.
†See Introduction for note regarding recording of death date.

258

Name	Rank	Company, Regiment or Ship	Post*	Age	Death Date†	Journal
Holcomb, Chas. R.	Pvt.	H, 2nd Ohio Cav.	67		1926 Dec 27	IA, 53rd, 1927
Holcomb, Isaac N.		I, 27th Ill.	214		1916 Jan 3	KS, 36th, 1917
Holcomb, J.L.		D, 30th Ohio	51		1917 Apr 27	KS, 37th, 1918
Holcomb, J.W.		K, 169th Penn.	130		1918 Feb 21	KS, 38th, 1919
Holcomb, Lester	Pvt.	C, 13th Ill. Inf.	68		1929 Sep 5	IA, 56th, 1930
Holcomb, Lewis		D, 16th Iowa Inf.	168		1918	IA, 45th, 1919
Holcomb, Perry W.	Pvt.	G, 10th Mich. Cav. (at large)	192	93	1940 Jan 12	IA, 66th, 1940
Holcomb, Solomon		K, 15th Iowa Inf. (died of general disability)	209	68	1904 Dec 10	NE, 29th, 1905
Holcomb, William		F, 118th Ill.	87		1908 Mar 10	KS, 28th, 1909
Holdbrook, Geo.			105		1904 Nov 12	KS, 24th, 1905
Holdbrook, Jas. E.		K, 34th Iowa	336		1906 May 30	KS, 26th, 1907
Holden, C.C.	Pvt.	B, 90th N.Y. Inf.	173		1906	IA, 33rd, 1907
Holden, H.W.		H, 21st Mass. Inf.	29		1919 Sep 27	IA, 46th, 1920
Holden, J.G.		K, 13th Wis.	23		1926	NE, 51st, 1927
Holden, John	Pvt.	B, 5th Kans. Cav.	251		1911 Nov 12	IA, 38th, 1912
Holden, John	Pvt.	H, 84th Ill. Inf.	96		1929 Jun 4	IA, 56th, 1930
Holden, John		F, 114th U.S.C.I.	321		1930 Oct 22	KS, 50th, 1931
Holden, Levi P.	Major	F, 20th Ill. & 88th Ill.	81		1901 Nov 13	IA, 28th, 1902
Holden, Lucius		H, 33rd Mass.	100		1931 Jan 5	KS, 52nd, 1933
Holden, Lucius		H, 33rd Mass.	100		1931 Jan 5	KS, 51st, 1932
Holderman, Dan	Capt.	F, 131st Ohio	68		1898 May 30	KS, 18th, 1899
Holderness, Elisha		B, 8th Ill. Cav. (died of paralysis)	73	60	1897 Dec 4	NE, 22nd, 1898
Holdridge, D. Cyrus		I, Wis. (died of pneumonia)	150	71	1905[1904?] Feb 7	NE, 29th, 1905
Hole, Henry F.		K, 17th Ill.	77		1929 May 27	NE, 54th, 1930
Hole, R.D.		K, 94th Ohio Inf.	4		1902 Jun 1	KS, 22nd, 1903
Holenbeck, Geo. H.	Pvt.	H, 8th Mo. Inf.	157		1907 Apr	IA, 34th, 1908
Holinghead, Geo. W.	Pvt.	K, Iowa Cav.	49		1923 Dec 27	IA, 50th, 1924
Hollahan, John		E, 140th & 15th Ill.	25		1915 May 9	NE, 40th, 1916
Hollan, Samuel	Sergt.	H, 20th Iowa Inf.	235	65	1897 Feb 11	IA, 23rd, 1897
Holland, E.C.		G, 7th Iowa Cav.	305		1921 Sep 29	IA, 48th, 1922
Holland, E.V.			170		1926 Mar 29	IA, 53rd, 1927
Holland, J.H.	Pvt.	A, 61st Mass. Vols.	12		1903 Dec 30	IA, 30th, 1904
Holland, J.H.			337		1911	KS, 31st, 1912
Holland, J.H.		C, 18th Ill.	25		1929 Dec 4	NE, 54th, 1930
Holland, P.H.	Landsman	Steamer *Peosta*	70		1908 Nov 11	IA, 35th, 1909
Hollaway, A.	Pvt.	C, 39th Iowa Inf.	320	57	1890 Aug 7	IA, 17th, 1891
Hollaway, Samuel	Pvt.	F, 143rd Ohio Inf.	255	57	1896 Apr 10	IA, 23rd, 1897
Hollenbach, J.F.		36th Ohio (died of pneumonia)	114		1916 Jan	NE, 41st, 1917
Hollenback, Clark W.		A, 12th Kans.	26		1913 Jun 18	KS, 33rd, 1914
Hollenbeck, B.F.		H, 12th Kans. Inf.	318		1918 Jun 21	KS, 38th, 1919
Hollenbeck, Bradford L.		E, 124th Ind. Inf.	36		1914 Oct 29	KS, 34th, 1915
Hollenbeck, C.W.		H, 12th Kans.	26		1917	KS, 37th, 1918
Hollenbeck, J.C.	Pvt.	8th Wis. Hvy. Art.	22		1933 Jan 10	IA, 60th, 1934
Hollenbeck, James A.		H, 1st Minn. Cav.	90		1919 Jan 9	KS, 40th, 1921
Holley, Albert		I, 77th Ind. Inf. (died of insanity)	180	69	1902 Apr	NE, 27th, 1903
Hollicke, Thomas		D, 2nd Ill.	25		1897 Sep 27	KS, 17th, 1898
Holliday, A.S.	Pvt.	B, 84th Ill. Inf.	440		1931 Oct 5	IA, 58th, 1932
Holliday, D.E.		C, 91st Ohio	337		1926 Jul 20	KS, 46th, 1927
Holliday, D.M.		I, 77th Ind.	251		1916 Mar 10	KS, 36th, 1917
Holliday, F.C.				90	1937 Jan 6	IA, 64th, 1938
Holliday, H.B.		A, 173rd Ohio Inf. (died of heart failure)	35	67	1911 Nov 10	NE, 36th, 1912
Holliday, J.C.	Pvt.	A, 28th Ill. Inf.	12		1917 Jun 13	IA, 44th, 1918
Holliday, John O.	Capt.	B, 2nd Minn. Inf.	147		1912 Sep 22	IA, 39th, 1913
Holliday, Thomas		E, 95th Ill.	142		1910 Jan 30	KS, 30th, 1911
Holling, John	Pvt.	F, 2nd Mo. Inf.	1		1905 Mar 2	IA, 32nd, 1906
Hollingshead, John C.		F, 9th Kans. Cav.	244		1914 Jan	KS, 34th, 1915
Hollingshead, Wm.		I, 3rd Wis. Inf. (died of pneumonia)	275	81	1910 Dec 15	NE, 35th, 1911
Hollingsworth, A.J.		C, 22nd Ill.	113		1914 Jan 5	KS, 34th, 1915
Hollingsworth, Chas.	Pvt.	G, 142nd Ill.	81		1923 Dec 18	IA, 50th, 1924
Hollingsworth, E.	Pvt.	A, 39th Iowa Inf.	39		1920	IA, 47th, 1921
Hollingsworth, Geo.	Pvt.	F, 43rd Ohio Cav.	412		1910 Mar 7	IA, 37th, 1911

*See Appendix A, B or C for roster of post names and locations.
†See Introduction for note regarding recording of death date.
259

Name	Rank	Company, Regiment or Ship	Post*	Age	Death Date†	Journal
Hollingsworth, Levi	Pvt.	F, 98th Ohio Inf.	334		1900 Oct 19	IA, 27th, 1901
Hollingsworth, Nelson		E, 10th Ill.	19		1932[1931?] Aug 25	KS, 51st, 1932
Hollingsworth, Nelson		E, 10th Ill.	19		1931 Aug 25	KS, 52nd, 1933
Hollingsworth, Rob't			25		1890 Apr 11	NE, 15th, 1891
Hollis, E.B.	Musician	20th Ill. Inf.	7		1918 Mar 10	IA, 45th, 1919
Hollis, J.M.		B, — Ill.	51		1931 Feb 1	KS, 52nd, 1933
Hollis, J.M.		B, — Ill.	51		1931 Feb 1	KS, 51st, 1932
Hollis, Jas. C.		H, 123rd Ind.	116		1926 Jul 14	KS, 46th, 1927
Hollis, Thos.		I, 149th Ohio	303		1902 Mar 16	KS, 22nd, 1903
Hollisler, A.D.		K, 39th Ohio Inf.	71		1909 Feb 26	KS, 29th, 1910
Hollister, Brad		C, 13th Wis. Inf.	25		1923	NE, 48th, 1924
Hollister, John L.		F, 36th Ohio	1		1919 Dec 28	KS, 39th, 1920
Holloway, Chester		E, 93rd Ohio	113		1932 Apr 8	NE, 57th, 1933
Holloway, Collins		F, 3rd (M) Kans.[Kans. State Militia?]	12		1905 Oct 5	KS, 25th, 1906
Holloway, Elisha		G, 7th Mo.	[87?]		1919 Dec 16	KS, 39th, 1920
Holloway, Henry D.		I, 63rd Ill.	6		1912 Jan 23	KS, 32nd, 1913
Holloway, J.O.		C, 138th Ind.	12		1928 Oct 27	KS, 48th, 1929
Holloway, James C.		E, 11th Kans. Cav.	145		1911 Jan 9	KS, 31st, 1912
Holloway, L.L.		H, 2nd Kans.	9		1930 May 6	KS, 50th, 1931
Holloway, R.E.			64		1917	KS, 37th, 1918
Holloway, Samuel	Pvt.	K, 44th Mo. Inf.	43		1928 Apr 25	IA, 55th, 1929
Hollowbaugh, Edward		G, 1st Mich. Lt. Art.	354	67	1911 Jul 17	NE, 36th, 1912
Hollowell, Austin E.	Pvt.	B, 3rd Iowa Cav.	2		1916 Mar 2	IA, 43rd, 1917
Holman, Edwin T.		H, 23rd N.J.	6		1925 Mar 21	KS, 45th, 1926
Holman, F.H.	Pvt.	B, 27th Iowa	68		1907 Feb 28	IA, 34th, 1908
Holman, Harrison West	1st Lieut.	U.S. Signal Corps (see also Appendix D)	54	63	1905 Mar 5	IA, 31st, 1905
Holman, Henry		D, 47th Iowa Inf.	94	91	1935 Aug 13	IA, 62nd, 1936
Holman, J.A.		C, 23rd Penn. Cav.	66		1922 Apr 3	IA, 49th, 1923
Holman, J.W.	Pvt.	F, 17th Iowa Inf.	122		1910 May 13	IA, 37th, 1911
Holman, Philip		D, 15th Ill.	90		1926	KS, 46th, 1927
Holman, W.J.	Landsman	U.S. Navy	235	38	1888 Jul 6	IA, 15th, 1889
Holmburg, L.N.		The comrades of Post 87 chartered a train, and about 100 of them went to Lindsburg and buried their comrade in accordance with the rules and regulations.	87		1883	KS, 3rd, 1884
Holmes, Alfred			386		1912 Oct 30	KS, 32nd, 1913
Holmes, Alfred A.		B, 73rd Ill.	130		1896 Apr 6	KS, 16th, 1897
Holmes, B.A.		C, 6th Kans. State Militia	3		1892 May 29	KS, 12th, 1893
Holmes, Byron		A, 2nd West Va.	52		1917 Oct 12	KS, 37th, 1918
Holmes, Charles A.	Capt.	F, 29th Wis. Inf. (died of pneumonia)	47	68	1908 Dec 13	NE, 33rd, 1909
Holmes, Charles J.		C, 135th Ind.	355		1914 Jul 10	KS, 34th, 1915
Holmes, D.	Hosp. Stew.	11th Ill. Inf. (died at Topeka, Kans.; buried at Topeka Cemetery)	1		1894 Nov 9	KS, 14th, 1895
Holmes, G.B.	Pvt.	D, 1st Wis. Cav.	7	50	1888 Aug 4	IA, 15th, 1889
Holmes, G.L.		E, 1st West Va.	257		1919 Dec 1	KS, 39th, 1920
Holmes, Henry (Col.)					1938 Mar 17	IA, 64th, 1938
Holmes, J.B.W.		C, 150th Ind.	205		1919 Dec 1	KS, 39th, 1920
Holmes, J.E.		B, 154th Ill.	17		1930 Nov 1	KS, 50th, 1931
Holmes, James T.		E, 14th Kans. Cav.	497		1912 Dec 10	KS, 32nd, 1913
Holmes, Jas.	Sergt.	C, 6th Iowa Cav.	48		1901 Aug	IA, 28th, 1902
Holmes, John	Pvt.	C, 64th Ill. Inf.	56		1914 Oct 9	IA, 41st, 1915
Holmes, John		H, 35th Mo. Inf.	93		1912 Jun 14	KS, 32nd, 1913
Holmes, John		G, 44th N.Y. Inf. (died of pneumonia)	94	73	1911 Dec 28	NE, 36th, 1912
Holmes, John B.		D, 36th Ohio	20		1892 Sep 8	KS, 12th, 1893
Holmes, P.	1st Lieut.	A, 186th N.Y. Inf.	88		1905 Oct 13	IA, 32nd, 1906
Holmes, Paschal	Pvt.	C, 21st Mo. Inf.	254		1923 Feb 23	IA, 50th, 1924
Holmes, Phillip H.		K, 27th Ill. Inf.	28		1912 Sep 15	KS, 32nd, 1913
Holmes, R.M.		B, 2nd Ohio Cav. (died of old age)	96	81	1919 May 31	NE, 44th, 1920
Holmes, Thomas		H, 40th N.Y. Inf. (died of old age)	45	57	1900 Feb	NE, 25th, 1901
Holmes, W.M.		K, U.S. Art.		93	1936 Feb 25	IA, 62nd, 1936
Holmes, W.M.		K, U.S. Art.	80	93	1936 Feb 25	IA, 63rd, 1937
Holmes, W.W.	Musician	15th Ohio. Vol. M.	58		1913 Feb 8	IA, 40th, 1914

*See Appendix A, B or C for roster of post names and locations.
†See Introduction for note regarding recording of death date.

260

Name	Rank	Company, Regiment or Ship	Post*	Age	Death Date†	Journal
Holmes, Wm.		C, 144th Ill.	17		1927 Nov 6	KS, 47th, 1928
Holmon, S.	Pvt. Sergt.	A, 20th Ind. Inf. A, 2nd Ind. Inf. (died of fever)	23	49	1885 Nov 11	NE, 10th, 1886
Holms, A.A.	Corp.	D, 19th Iowa Inf.	497		1917 Jun 6	IA, 44th, 1918
Holsapple, John A.	Corp.	H, 26th Iowa Vol. Inf.	92		1901 Jul 9	IA, 28th, 1902
Holster, John F.		K, 30th Ohio (died of heart failure)	339	63	1907 Dec 15	NE, 32nd, 1908
Holston, J.T.			265		1917 Feb 21	KS, 37th, 1918
Holt, G.W.	Pvt.	D, 146th Ill.	377		1907 Mar 27	IA, 34th, 1908
Holt, G.W.	Sergt.	K, 4th Iowa Cav.	57		1913 Feb 22	IA, 40th, 1914
Holt, H.E.		H, 86th N.Y.	338		1912 Dec 29	NE, 37th, 1913
Holt, H.H.	Pvt.	L, 2nd Maine Cav. (died of wounds in leg received during war)	35	43	1891 Nov 5	NE, 16th, 1892
Holt, Henry T.		C, 9th Minn.	46		1908 Feb 24	KS, 28th, 1909
Holt, Homer H.	Pvt.	D, 140th Ill.	1		1928 Jul 24	IA, 55th, 1929
Holt, J.B.		L, 6th N.Y. (died of complication of diseases)	195	73	1914 Aug 18	NE, 39th, 1915
Holt, Joel		G, 1st N.H. Cav.	147		1892 May 27	KS, 12th, 1893
Holt, Joseph S.		H, 1st Ind.	200		1906 Feb 8	KS, 26th, 1907
Holt, Joshua J.		C, G, 2nd U.S. Art.	32		1924 Sep 15	KS, 44th, 1925
Holt, Newton			241		1885	KS, 5th, 1886
Holt, S.E.G.		C, 11th Kans. Cav.	196		1902 Jun 22	KS, 22nd, 1903
Holthansen, Nicholas		Wis.	28		1920 Jan 20	KS, 40th, 1921
Holton, E.J.		K, 76th Ill.	85		1917 Aug 8	KS, 37th, 1918
Holton, J.S.	Pvt.	H, 13th Iowa Inf.	86		1910 Dec 27	IA, 38th, 1912
Holton, John	Pvt.	G, 11th Iowa Inf.	37		1919 Jan 1	IA, 46th, 1920
Holtorf, John C.		C, 29th Md. Inf.	110	69	1905 Jun 27	NE, 30th, 1906
Holtz, David		K, 6th Ind. Cav.	25		1898 Dec 1	KS, 18th, 1899
Holtz, Ernest	Pvt.	A, 36th Ill. Inf.	455		1908	IA, 35th, 1909
Holtzafel, Thomas		I, 8th Conn. Inf.	8		1902 Feb 7	KS, 22nd, 1903
Holtzshor, E.		F, 10th Conn.	175		1912 Apr 27	KS, 32nd, 1913
Holubar, Jos.	Pvt.	K, 22nd Iowa Inf.	8		1919 Mar 9	IA, 46th, 1920
Holzhaner, J.C.	Pvt.	I, 11th Ill. Inf.	56		1906 Jun 8	IA, 33rd, 1907
Homan, Carl		A, 58th Penn. Inf.	43		1887 Mar 11	KS, 7th, 1888
Homan, I.T.	Pvt.	B, 78th Ind. Inf.	324		1905 Oct 4	IA, 32nd, 1906
Homan, Jesse		8th Ind. Lt. Art.	324		1916 May 29	IA, 43rd, 1917
Homersham, James		Chicago Merchant Battery (Art.), Illinois (died of old age)	148	82	1913 Dec 28	NE, 39th, 1915
Homes, Benj.		F, 36th Ill. Inf.	153		1900 Jun 15	KS, 20th, 1901
Homewood, L.M.		B, 18th Iowa Inf.	211		1923 May 12	IA, 50th, 1924
Homey, James O.		D, 17th Ill.	64		1885	KS, 5th, 1886
Homeyer, H.	Pvt.	B, 4th M.R.C.[V.R.C.?] (cause of death: lungs)	24	50	1887 Jul 20	NE, 12th, 1888
Hon, J.V.		E, 53rd Ind. Inf.	244		1900	KS, 20th, 1901
Honess, Robt.	Pvt.	G, 74th N.Y. Inf.	222		1926 Feb 24	IA, 53rd, 1927
Honnold, Arthur J.	Pvt.	B, 48th Iowa Inf.	84		1919 Mar 11	IA, 46th, 1920
Honnold, Jesse	Pvt.	C, 51st Ohio Vols.	84		1923 Oct 31	IA, 50th, 1924
Honnold, John W.	1st Lieut.	F, 65th Ind. Inf.	84		1905 Mar 4	IA, 31st, 1905
Honnold, Samuel H.		E, 160th Ohio Inf.	68		1925 Sep 8	KS, 45th, 1926
Honstead, F.C.		E, 118th Ohio Vol. Inf.	39		1915 Jan 30	KS, 35th, 1916
Honza, John W.		A, 22nd Iowa Inf. (died of pneumonia)	7	51	1895 Mar 25	NE, 20th, 1896
Hoobens, W.W.	Sergt.	B, 8th N.Y.	137		1923 Dec 31	IA, 50th, 1924
Hood, Calvin		F, 10th Kans.	55		1910 Nov 12	KS, 30th, 1911
Hood, David		K, 10th Ky.	100		1921 Aug 20	KS, 41st, 1922
Hood, F.Q.		I, 151st Ohio	46		1902 Nov 15	KS, 22nd, 1903
Hood, George F.		E, 11th Mo.	17		1921 Feb 19	KS, 41st, 1922
Hood, George W.		C, 89th Ill. Inf.	14		1921 Nov 7	KS, 41st, 1922
Hood, Jas. H.	Pvt.	B, 23rd Penn. Inf.	12		1908 Oct 14	IA, 35th, 1909
Hood, John	Pvt.	H, 5th Iowa Cav.	74		1922 Mar 22	IA, 49th, 1923
Hood, John A.		H, 101st Ill.	481		1913 Sep 21	KS, 33rd, 1914
Hood, S.H.		G, 155th Ind.	127		1918 Apr 6	KS, 38th, 1919
Hood, Samuel			294		1913 Apr 22	KS, 33rd, 1914
Hood, Samuel		C, 14th Penn. Cal.[Cav.] (died of heart trouble)	216	59	1900 Sep 28	NE, 25th, 1901

*See Appendix A, B or C for roster of post names and locations.
†See Introduction for note regarding recording of death date.

Name	Rank	Company, Regiment or Ship	Post*	Age	Death Date†	Journal
Hood, Solomon		F, 9th West Va.	315		1898 Feb 10	KS, 18th, 1899
Hood, Wm.		G, 34th Iowa	52		1906 Mar 21	KS, 26th, 1907
Hooge, B.F.		C, 104th N.Y.	59		1896 Nov 11	KS, 16th, 1897
Hooghkirk, C.H.	Pvt.	I, 149th N.Y.	519		1924 Feb 20	IA, 51st, 1925
Hook, Calvin	Pvt.	F, 16th Wis.	22		1922 Mar 31	IA, 49th, 1923
Hook, D.C.	Pvt.		316		1910 Jun	IA, 37th, 1911
Hook, G.W.	Pvt.	D, 11th Ohio Cav.	71		1921 Jun 20	IA, 48th, 1922
Hook, James	Pvt.	Ohio	424		1905 Jul	IA, 32nd, 1906
Hook, Mathew		C, 27th Iowa	59		1928 Sep 10	KS, 48th, 1929
Hook, Norman R.	Lieut.	C, 33rd Iowa Inf.	40		1911 Jun 3	IA, 38th, 1912
Hooke, John		K, 16th Iowa Inf.	231		1924 Feb 23	IA, 51st, 1925
Hooker, E.H.		I, 14th Ind.	32		1925 May 3	KS, 45th, 1926
Hooker, William			83		1907 Mar 9	IA, 34th, 1908
Hooly, S.V.			43		1916 Nov 30	IA, 43rd, 1917
Hoon, James	Sergt.		29		1917 Jun 2	IA, 44th, 1918
Hoon, Silas	Pvt.	A, 5th Iowa Vol. Inf.	110		1902 Feb 15	IA, 28th, 1902
Hoop, Joseph		A, 76th Ill.	65		1910 Jun 19	KS, 30th, 1911
Hooper, Thos. B.		B, 14th Kans. Cav.	90		1918 Jul 20	KS, 38th, 1919
Hooper, Wm.	Pvt.	C, 43rd Penn. Inf.	230		1904 May	IA, 31st, 1905
Hooper, Z.		I, 110th Ohio	85		1929 Feb 18	KS, 49th, 1930
Hoopes, Thos. J.M.	Pvt.	U.S. Marine Corps	231		1909 Jun 14	IA, 36th, 1910
Hoops, T.J.			7		1902 Sep 17	IA, 29th, 1903
Hoops, W.Y.			211		1915	IA, 42nd, 1916
Hoor, Joseph	Capt.	C, U.S. Inf.	78		1914 Dec 19	IA, 41st, 1915
Hoosier, Jas.	Pvt.		436		1926 Mar 28	IA, 53rd, 1927
Hooton, H.L.		D, 7th Ind. 1st V.R.C.	43		1919	KS, 39th, 1920
Hoover, A.A.		D, 18th Iowa	18		1926 Apr 3	KS, 46th, 1927
Hoover, Abraham		C, 18th Ohio Inf.	117		1892 Mar 24	KS, 12th, 1893
Hoover, C.H.		F, 13th Iowa Inf. (died of Bright's disease)	107	58	1901 Sep	NE, 26th, 1902
Hoover, Charles W.		I, 140th Ill. (member at large; died at Narka, Kans.)			1935 May 10	NE, 60th, 1936
Hoover, Christain		C, 11th Ill.	35		1897 Dec 15	KS, 17th, 1898
Hoover, Daniel	Pvt.	G, 12th Ind. Inf.	12		1916 Mar 13	IA, 43rd, 1917
Hoover, Henry		K, 11th Kans. Cav.	39		1915 Jan 7	KS, 35th, 1916
Hoover, Jasper			32		1913 Apr 9	KS, 33rd, 1914
Hoover, Jerome		D, 17th Kans.	93		1911 Oct 11	KS, 31st, 1912
Hoover, John D.	Pvt.	C, 76th Penn. Inf.	64		1924 Oct 1	IA, 51st, 1925
Hoover, John S.		31st Ill. (died of kidney trouble)	22	73	1906 Aug 2	NE, 31st, 1907
Hoover, John W.		H, 11th Ind.	63		1917 Jul 26	KS, 37th, 1918
Hoover, Jos.	Pvt.	B, 10th Ill. Inf.	154		1905 Dec 11	IA, 32nd, 1906
Hoover, Joseph		42nd Ohio	216		1928 Apr 20	NE, 53rd, 1929
Hoover, Phil.		B, 104th Ohio Inf. (died of appendicitis)	81	59	1901 Apr	NE, 26th, 1902
Hoover, Samuel G.		F, 94th Ill.	25		1913 Dec 4	KS, 33rd, 1914
Hoover, W.C.		M, 15th Kans.	199		1928 Jan 19	KS, 48th, 1929
Hoover, W.D.	Surg.		117		1899	KS, 19th, 1900
Hoover, William		F, 31st Ohio Inf.	127		1908 Dec 28	KS, 28th, 1909
Hoover, William		D, 1st Kans.	493		1910 Dec 16	KS, 30th, 1911
Hoover, Wm. H.	Pvt.	F, 148th Ind. Inf.	347		1901 Dec 23	IA, 28th, 1902
Hoozer, J.T.		Penn. (died of old age)	106	80	1906 Jan 1	NE, 31st, 1907
Hopbell, H.S.	Pvt.	D, 4th Iowa Cav.	20		1920 May	IA, 47th, 1921
Hope, Charles C.	Pvt.	H, 77th Ill. Inf.	205	50	1895 Jun 13	IA, 22nd, 1896
Hopfee, Christopher	Pvt.	C, 8th Iowa Vol. Inf.	451	83	1899 Dec 12	IA, 26th, 1900
Hopkins, Albert C.		I, 11th Wis. Inf.	132		1904 Oct 11	IA, 31st, 1905
Hopkins, C.B.	Corp.	H, 58th Penn. Inf.	130		1912 Feb 7	IA, 39th, 1913
Hopkins, C.M.	Pvt.	B, 51st Ohio Inf.	81		1919 Nov 19	IA, 46th, 1920
Hopkins, Chris.	Corp.	A, 22nd Wis. Inf.	452		1926 Mar 14	IA, 53rd, 1927
Hopkins, Elijah J.		B, 6th Mo. Inf.	55		1917 Jul 10	KS, 37th, 1918
Hopkins, G.H.		died of apoplexy	318		1906 Apr 2	NE, 31st, 1907
Hopkins, H.H.	Pvt.	I, 11th Wis. Inf.	132		1906 Mar 8	IA, 33rd, 1907
Hopkins, Isaac		H, 3rd Ill.	22		1906 Mar 12	KS, 26th, 1907
Hopkins, Isaac		I, 11th Minn.	65		1916 Oct 25	KS, 36th, 1917

See Appendix A, B or C for roster of post names and locations.
†*See Introduction for note regarding recording of death date.*

Name	Rank	Company, Regiment or Ship	Post*	Age	Death Date†	Journal
Hopkins, J.F.	Pvt.	A, 5th Minn. Inf.	22		1913 Apr 6	IA, 40th, 1914
Hopkins, James	Pvt.	A, Ky. Inf.	8		1920 Apr 9	IA, 47th, 1921
Hopkins, James M.		C, 3rd Ill. Cav.	145		1917 Dec 19	KS, 37th, 1918
Hopkins, John B.		I, 41st Ill.	20		1925	KS, 45th, 1926
Hopkins, L.B.			12		1910 Dec 22	KS, 30th, 1911
Hopkins, Luke	Pvt.	D, 30th Ohio Inf.	271		1927 Nov 14	IA, 54th, 1928
Hopkins, M.G.		C, 72nd Ill. Inf. (died of pneumonia)	208	57	1901 Mar	NE, 26th, 1902
Hopkins, Nye B.	Pvt.	F, 196th Ohio Inf.	330, 49	91	1939 May 17	IA, 65th, 1939
Hopkins, O.B.		location: Orleans			1927	NE, 52nd, 1928
Hopkins, P.W.	Pvt.	H, 44th Iowa Inf.	238		1904 Aug 19	IA, 31st, 1905
Hopkins, Sam		G, 15th Tenn.	123		1914 Jun 10	KS, 34th, 1915
Hopkins, T.M.	1st Sergt.	G, 21st Iowa Inf.	78		1899 May 18	IA, 26th, 1900
Hopkins, Thos. J.	Pvt.	E, 6th Mo. Cav.	231		1922 Mar 15	IA, 49th, 1923
Hopkins, W.G.	Pvt.	K, 10th Iowa Inf.	30		1889 Apr 14	IA, 16th, 1890
Hopkins, W.H.	Pvt.	A, 9th Iowa Inf.	117		1911 Sep 10	IA, 38th, 1912
Hopkins, W.H.		K, 33rd Ind.	20		1928 Oct 3	KS, 48th, 1929
Hopkins, W.R.		I, 12th Mo. Cav.	257		1913 Dec 10	KS, 33rd, 1914
Hopkinson, Alva	Pvt.	H, 11th Iowa Vol. Inf.	110	58	1899 Aug 7	IA, 26th, 1900
Hopkinson, Perry		E, 18th Iowa	5		1934 Feb 5	IA, 61st, 1935
Hoppa, Ernest	Pvt.	A, 92nd Ill. Vol. Inf.	216	60	1899 Apr 20	IA, 25th, 1899
Hoppe, Fred'k W.		D, 5th Iowa Cav. (died of age & other causes)	77	78	1916 Oct 27	NE, 41st, 1917
Hoppe, H.A.		5th Iowa Cav. (died of complication)	77	65	1908 May 5	NE, 33rd, 1909
Hoppe, Herman		died of diverse causes	77		1910	NE, 35th, 1911
Hoppe, J.B.		B, 22nd N.J.	453		1925 Sep 17	KS, 45th, 1926
Hopper, A.M.		H, 2nd Ill. Cav.	257		1924 Feb 15	KS, 44th, 1925
Hopper, J.F.		A, 4th N.Y. Cav.	262	84	1919 Feb 21	NE, 43rd, 1919
Hopper, J. Francis		A, 4th Iowa Cav.	262		1919 Feb 21	NE, 44th, 1920
Hopper, James		D, 18th Mo.	477		1912 Feb 17	KS, 32nd, 1913
Hopper, James F.		I, 123rd Ill.	64		1919 Dec 18	KS, 39th, 1920
Hopper, Jas. F.		E, 6th Tenn.	164		1890	KS, 10th, 1891
Hopper, Martin		K, 37th Wis.	199		1909 Jul 4	KS, 29th, 1910
Hopper, Robert		G, 41st Ill. Inf. (died of old age)	318		1923 Sep	NE, 48th, 1924
Hopper, Robt.		G, 41st Ill.	[25?]		1923	NE, 48th, 1924
Hopper, Samuel		D, 145th Ind. Inf. (died of pneumonia)	118	72	1920 Oct 10	NE, 46th, 1922
Hopper, Samuel		D, 145th Ind. Inf. (died of pneumonia)	118	71	1920 Oct 10	NE, 45th, 1921
Hopper, William		E, 6th Tenn.	2		1931 Aug 7	KS, 52nd, 1933
Hopper, William		E, 6th Tenn.	2		1931 Aug 7	KS, 51st, 1932
Hopper, Wm.	Pvt.	B, 24th Iowa Inf.	23		1917 Sep 6	IA, 44th, 1918
Hopping, George M.		K, 85th Ill. Inf. (died of pneumonia)	95	62	1906 Jan 10	NE, 31st, 1907
Hopping, T.J.		I, 28th Ill.	17		1913 Aug 27	KS, 33rd, 1914
Hopple, John		C, 192nd Ohio	57		1916 Jul 19	KS, 36th, 1917
Hopson, Addison	Pvt.	B, 35th Iowa Inf.	231		1918 Dec 15	IA, 45th, 1919
Hopt, Charles		F, N.Y. Hvy. Art. (died of apoplexy)	187	84	1922 Dec 4	NE, 47th, 1923
Hopt, Chas.		15th N.Y. Hvy. Art. (died of disability)	187		1923	NE, 48th, 1924
Hopt, Chas.		15th N.Y. Hvy. Art. (died of old age)	318	92	1922 Dec 4	NE, 47th, 1923
Horack, F.J.	Pvt.	E, 46th Iowa Inf.	8		1915 Jun 18	IA, 42nd, 1916
Horak, Wesley	Pvt.	H, 22nd Iowa	235		1923 Apr 6	IA, 50th, 1924
Horan, Mathew		Vol. Inf.	92		1924 Jul 16[?]	IA, 51st, 1925
Horbin, Geo. W.	Hosp. Stew.	D, 24th Iowa Inf.	68		1923 Nov 10	IA, 50th, 1924
Hord, S.H.		C, 112th Ill.	127		1918 Apr 6	KS, 38th, 1919
Horford, I.N.		D, 34th Iowa	74		1914 Jul 2	KS, 34th, 1915
Horine, Harrison		B, 46th Ind.	52		1904 Oct 2	KS, 24th, 1905
Hormell, H.L.		D, 20th Ill.	16		1921 Oct 3	KS, 41st, 1922
Horn, F.W.	Pvt.	G, 197th Penn. Inf.	3		1913 Sep 20	IA, 40th, 1914
Horn, Fritz	Pvt.	E, 26th Iowa Inf.	88		1920 Jun 26	IA, 47th, 1921
Horn, Henry		H, 9th Ohio	57		1917 Jan 31	KS, 37th, 1918
Horn, Henry		K, 48th Wis. Inf. (member at large)			1940 Nov 5	NE, 65th, 1941
Horn, Perry E.		A, 61st Penn.	52		1914 May 20	KS, 34th, 1915
Horn, Perry E.		A, 24th Iowa	17		1919 Aug 14	KS, 39th, 1920
Horn, Samuel A.		C, 7th Iowa	31		1915 Dec 15	KS, 35th, 1916
Horn, William	Pvt.	C, 24th Iowa Inf.	235	88	1932 Aug	IA, 59th, 1933

Name	Rank	Company, Regiment or Ship	Post*	Age	Death Date†	Journal
Hornady, W.A.		G, 75th Ohio (died of paralysis)	12	70	1916 Nov 18	NE, 41st, 1917
Hornbaker, David R.	Pvt.	F, 2nd Iowa Inf.	177	50	1892 Feb 17	IA, 18th, 1892
Hornbaker, F.D.		I, 145th Ind.	17		1920 Mar 3	KS, 40th, 1921
Hornbeck, John		E, 56th N.Y.	25		1922 May 5	KS, 42nd, 1923
Hornby, O.T.		G, 17th Ind. Inf.	19		1912 Jul 8	KS, 32nd, 1913
Hornby, Wm. L.	Pvt.	1st Iowa Cav.	20		1915 Dec	IA, 42nd, 1916
Horne, O.		G, 100th Ill. Inf. (died of cardiac dropsy)	21	64	1905 Dec 15	NE, 30th, 1906
Horner, C.M.		B, 142nd Penn. Inf.	5		1929 Nov 1	KS, 49th, 1930
Horner, Charles	Pvt.		2		1932	IA, 59th, 1933
Horner, David	Pvt.	I, 3rd Iowa Inf.	479		1915	IA, 42nd, 1916
Horner, Edward		C, 3rd Va. Cav.	25		1924 Mar 24	KS, 44th, 1925
Horner, George	Pvt.	C, 15th Ill. Inf.	111	74	1891 Nov 18	IA, 18th, 1892
Horner, George D.		H, 83rd Ill. Inf.	17		1917 Jul 23	KS, 37th, 1918
Horner, J.F.	Pvt.	I, 21st Iowa Inf.	78		1913 Sep 5	IA, 40th, 1914
Horner, Jacob	Pvt.	K, 10th Iowa Inf.	31		1902 Oct 8	IA, 29th, 1903
Horner, James		C, 61st Ohio	38		1921 Jul	KS, 41st, 1922
Horner, James S.			199		1919	IA, 46th, 1920
Horner, John	Pvt.	E, 55th Ohio Inf.	235	54	1888 Mar 30	IA, 15th, 1889
Horner, Landon			122		1925 Dec 10	IA, 52nd, 1926
Horner, S.W.		I, 2nd Wis. Inf.	257		1921 Jan 13	KS, 41st, 1922
Horner, William		H, 5th Wis. Reorg.	112		1937 Aug 2	NE, 62nd, 1938
Horney, Iredell A.		B, 4th Ill.	176		1917 Jul 6	KS, 37th, 1918
Hornick, John	Pvt.	E, 26th Ill. Inf.	22		1911 Sep 19	IA, 38th, 1912
Hornish, J.M.		F, 8th Iowa	409		1891 Jul	KS, 13th, 1894
Hornish, William		I, 40th Iowa (died at Lowell)	406		1895	KS, 15th, 1896
Horr, Jesse		D, 14th Kans. Cav.	28		1913 May 14	KS, 33rd, 1914
Horr, Warren		4th Ind. Cav. (died at Sterling)	14		1895 Aug	KS, 15th, 1896
Horsch, John C.		Batt. C, 2nd Penn. Hvy. Art. (nonmember of department; died at Lincoln)			1935	NE, 60th, 1936
Horsefull, W.M.	Pvt.	I, 20th Wis. Inf.	147		1920 Sep 20	IA, 47th, 1921
Horsley, W.H.			94		1916 Jun	IA, 43rd, 1917
Horton, C.C.	Lieut. Col.	2nd Iowa Cav.	452		1916 Apr 21	IA, 43rd, 1917
Horton, Charles		54th N.Y.	104		1905 Nov 17	KS, 25th, 1906
Horton, Chas. H.	Pvt.	K, 8th N.Y. Inf.	68	36	1888 Jan 17	IA, 15th, 1889
Horton, Delos J.	Pvt.	C, 109th N.Y. Inf.	489		1917 Apr 30	IA, 44th, 1918
Horton, E.V.		A, 116th N.Y.	187		1904 Nov 8	KS, 24th, 1905
Horton, E.W.	Pvt.	B, 45th Iowa Inf.	231		1917	IA, 44th, 1918
Horton, Ezra		D, 8th Kans.	12		1906 Feb 4	KS, 26th, 1907
Horton, Geo. W.		D, 3rd Wis. Inf. (died of paralysis)	61	75	1908 Aug 2	NE, 33rd, 1909
Horton, J.A.		C, 133rd Penn.	76		1931 Dec 3	NE, 56th, 1932
Horton, James Polk		H, 29th Ind. Inf.	61		1901 Dec 18	KS, 21st, 1902
Horton, Jeremiah		H, 26th Ind. Inf.	82		1914 Oct 24	KS, 34th, 1915
Horton, Laurens Jackson		H, 4th Iowa Cav. (died of heart failure; see also Appendix D)	190		1906 Sep 6 or 16	NE, 31st, 1907
Horton, N.P.		H, 11th Kans. Cav.	250		1913 Feb 4	KS, 33rd, 1914
Horton, Oliver			291		1919	IA, 46th, 1920
Horton, Timothy		F, 30th Iowa Inf.	46		1934 Sep 3	KS, 54th, 1935
Hosea, T.M.		D, 49th Ind.	42		1909 Oct 29	KS, 29th, 1910
Hoserfield, J.H.		K, 170th Ohio Inf.	35		1901 Jul 25	KS, 21st, 1902
Hosfelt, Geo.	Pvt.	H, 12th Ill.	302	58	1891 Sep 3	IA, 18th, 1892
Hosic, Allen T.		K, 1st West Va. Cav. (died of paralysis; died in Lincoln)	47	78	1913 Sep 19	NE, 38th, 1914
Hosie, J.W.		F, 1st Ohio Art.	63		1923 Feb 17	KS, 43rd, 1924
Hosier, A.E.	Pvt.	C, 30th Ill. Inf.	440		1927 Mar 29	IA, 54th, 1928
Hoskins, James H.	Pvt.	J, 12th Ill. Inf.	322		1915 Dec 15	IA, 42nd, 1916
Hoskins, Oscar		G, 5th U.S.C.T.	132		1912 Aug 5	KS, 32nd, 1913
Hoskins, Shadrock	Surg.	14th Iowa Inf.	462	65	1892 Sep 14	IA, 19th, 1893
Hoskins, W.D.			39		1923	IA, 50th, 1924
Hoskinson, C.W.		A, 1st Iowa	37		1927 May 11	KS, 47th, 1928
Hoskinson, J.M.		H, 44th Mo. Cav.	180		1913 Aug 10	KS, 33rd, 1914
Hosler, Henry		F, 25th Iowa Inf.	231		1924 Nov 20	IA, 51st, 1925
Hosley, Andrew I.		E, 82nd Ill.	171		1922 May 26	KS, 42nd, 1923

*See Appendix A, B or C for roster of post names and locations.
†See Introduction for note regarding recording of death date.
264

Name	Rank	Company, Regiment or Ship	Post*	Age	Death Date†	Journal
Hosley, Martin S.		D, 42nd Penn. (died at Edson, Kans.; buried at Edson Cemetery)	428		1894 May	KS, 14th, 1895
Hoss, T.O.		D, 49th Ill. Inf.	293		1914 Oct 8	KS, 34th, 1915
Hossley, Z.		D, 51st Ill. Inf.	66		1919 Aug 10	IA, 46th, 1920
Hostetter, Albert K.	Pvt.	D, 15th Iowa Inf.	64		1915 Oct 20	IA, 42nd, 1916
Hostetter, Christopher		G, 48th Ind. Inf. (died of heart failure)	11	65	1911 Feb 2	NE, 36th, 1912
Hostetter, W.C.	Pvt.	H, 46th Ill.	94		1907 Feb 16	IA, 34th, 1908
Hotaling, Oscar		E, 39th Ohio Inf.	68	74	1909 Oct 6	NE, 34th, 1910
Hotchkiss, Chas.	Pvt.	B, 140th Ill. Inf.	23		1923 Mar 26	IA, 50th, 1924
Hotchkiss, J.C.	Pvt.	B, 4th Mich. Inf.	12		1920 May 12	IA, 47th, 1921
Hotchkiss, L.L.	Corp.	F, 10th Iowa Inf.	94		1912 Jan 18	IA, 39th, 1913
Hotchkiss, S.B.		A, 23rd N.J.	85		1922 Mar 24	KS, 42nd, 1923
Hotchkiss, W.Y.	Pvt.	D, 15th Iowa Inf.	42		1926 Dec 26	IA, 53rd, 1927
Hotopp, H.J.	Capt.	D, 8th Ill. Cav.	155		1906 Jun 7	IA, 33rd, 1907
Hottel, W.H.		G, 197th Penn. Inf.	7	94	1935 Aug 3	IA, 62nd, 1936
Hottes, John		K, 47th Wis. (died of old age)	4	80	1908	NE, 33rd, 1909
Hotze, C.A.		H, 54th Ky. Mtd. (former member of Nebraska Dept.; location: Indianola)	154		1937 Sep 25	NE, 62nd, 1938
Houck, Alexander	Pvt.	C, 144th N.Y.	54		1923 Nov 28	IA, 50th, 1924
Houck, D.B.	Sergt.	E, 84th Penn.	7		1899	NE, 24th, 1900
Houck, Henry C.	Pvt.	K, 28th Iowa Inf.	16		1912 Oct 25	IA, 39th, 1913
Houck, L.F.	Pvt.	F, 132nd Ohio Inf.	66		1910 Apr 15	IA, 37th, 1911
Hough, C.H.	Pvt.	1st Ill. Bat.	22		1915 Mar 15	IA, 42nd, 1916
Hough, E.G.		F, 9th Iowa	51		1920 Jun 11	KS, 40th, 1921
Hough, James H.	Pvt.	B, 7th Ill. Cav.	452		1906 Apr 27	IA, 33rd, 1907
Hough, Jerry	Pvt.	D, 2nd Mo. Cav.	10		1919 Apr 7	IA, 46th, 1920
Hougham, Wilson T.		I, 18th Iowa Inf.	403	92	1938 Aug 29	IA, 64th, 1938
Houghland, D.R.		2nd Mo. State Militia	68		1922 Sep 1	KS, 42nd, 1923
Houghtelin, John E.		B, 156th N.Y.	64		1921 Jun 6	KS, 41st, 1922
Houghton, D.W.		I, 144th N.Y.	1		1913 Feb 13	KS, 33rd, 1914
Houghton, Joab			344		1916	KS, 36th, 1917
Houghton, V.W.			180		1923 Jun 29	KS, 43rd, 1924
Houghton, Wm. H.		K, 27th Iowa	147		1928 Jan 7	KS, 48th, 1929
Houlton, W.M.		K, 22nd Ohio	63		1918 Feb 13	KS, 38th, 1919
Houps, Michael	Sergt.	E, 21st Iowa Inf.	78		1903 Jan 16	IA, 29th, 1903
House, Alphonso M.	Drummer	E, 31st Iowa Inf.	228		1915 Feb 25	IA, 42nd, 1916
House, B.F.		H, 28th Ill.	311		1898 Dec 17	KS, 18th, 1899
House, G.W.	Pvt.	F, 31st Iowa Inf.	74	65	1896 Jan 17	IA, 22nd, 1896
House, J.H.		K, 20th Wis.	123		1912 May 11	KS, 33rd, 1914
House, Jacob		A, 3rd Kans. State Militia	12		1913 Aug 25	KS, 33rd, 1914
House, Jeremiah	Pvt.	F, 38th Iowa Inf.	48		1916 Mar 29	IA, 43rd, 1917
House, John		not a member of the G.A.R.	76		1912	KS, 32nd, 1913
House, W.A.	Pvt.	M, 2nd Iowa Cav.	16	87	1931 Nov 29	IA, 58th, 1932
Householder, J.M.		K, 2nd Ohio	85		1923 Mar 6	KS, 43rd, 1924
Householder, J.M., see Housholder, J.M.						
Householder, Jas. M.	Pvt.	H, 44th Iowa Inf.	67		1901 Jun 25	IA, 28th, 1902
Householder, Jos. W.		I, 52nd Ohio Inf.	88		1909 Oct 27	KS, 29th, 1910
Housel, J.V.		I, 13th Iowa Vol. Inf.	64		1929 Mar 4	NE, 53rd, 1929
Houseman, Geo. W.		G, 34th Ind.	17		1925 Feb 9	KS, 45th, 1926
Houseman, N.Y.		Iowa (died of heart trouble)	97	72	1917 Dec 16	NE, 43rd, 1919
Houser, Daniel	Corp.	L, 7th Iowa Cav.	22		1929 Feb	IA, 56th, 1930
Houser, Daniel	Pvt.	K, Iowa Cav.	22		1930 Feb	IA, 57th, 1931
Houser, David L.	Drummer	D, 14th Iowa Inf.	8		1913 Jul 17	IA, 40th, 1914
Houser, E.			190		1925 Feb 25	IA, 52nd, 1926
Houser, George		I, 67th Ind. Inf.	264		1892 Mar 5	KS, 12th, 1893
Houser, George W.		H, 77th Penn.	61		1916 May 1	KS, 36th, 1917
Houser, J.F.	Pvt.	1st Wis. Battery	8	56	1893 Jan 8	IA, 19th, 1893
Houser, J.M.		H, 29th Iowa	13		1926 Jun 15	NE, 51st, 1927
Houser, James	Corp.	B, 7th Iowa Cav.	40		1910 Mar 31	IA, 37th, 1911
Houser, M.		G, 98th Ill. Inf.	38	77	1909 Jul 8	NE, 34th, 1910
Houser, Thompson	Pvt.	I, 3rd Mo. Inf.	267		1916 Dec 30	IA, 43rd, 1917

Name	Rank	Company, Regiment or Ship	Post*	Age	Death Date†	Journal
Houser, W.H.		H, 97th Penn. Inf.	11		1919 Jan 22	NE, 44th, 1920
Houseworth, James W.		B, 81st Ind.	25		1916 Oct 5	KS, 36th, 1917
Housholder, J.M.		F, 5th Del.	91	82	1917 Jun 22	NE, 42nd, 1918
Housholder, L.B.	Capt.	A, 36th Ill.	516		1922 Mar 2	IA, 49th, 1923
Housman, William		C, 96th Ohio Reg. (died of general debility & kidney)	8	79	1913 Aug 15	NE, 38th, 1914
Houss, E.W.	Pvt.	19th Ohio Inf.	2		1919 Jul 11	IA, 46th, 1920
Houston, Aquella P.		I, 94th Ill.	25		1913 Apr 27	NE, 38th, 1914
Houston, D.W.		G, 7th Kans.	180		1915 Dec 2	KS, 35th, 1916
Houston, John		C, 8th Tenn.	484		1916 May 10	KS, 36th, 1917
Houston, John A.					1928	NE, 53rd, 1929
Houston, Robert			142		1884	KS, 4th, 1885
Houston, S.A.			12		1922 Aug 25	KS, 42nd, 1923
Houston, Samuel	Major	I, 25th Ill. Inf.	8		1891 Aug 3	KS, 11th, 1892
Houston, Thos. J.	Pvt.	A, 26th Iowa Inf.	74		1918 Nov 16	IA, 45th, 1919
Houze, Edward	Pvt.	D, 7th Ind. Inf.	49		1924 Jun 17	IA, 51st, 1925
Hover, A.W.		Osage Battalion	35		1893 Feb 16	KS, 13th, 1894
Hover, Henry		D, 85th Ind.	119		1921 Mar 31	KS, 41st, 1922
Hover, O.H.		C, 12th Wis. Inf.	50		1918 Jan 10	KS, 38th, 1919
Hovey, B.L.	Pvt.	G, 27th Iowa Inf.	284		1916 Oct 9	IA, 43rd, 1917
Hovey, Hardin		I, 78th Ill.	93		1892 Mar 15	KS, 12th, 1893
Hovey, L.B.		F, 16th Ill. Inf.	207		1931 Sep 7	NE, 56th, 1932
Hovey, N.K.		C, 9th Iowa Inf.	54		1912 May 27	IA, 39th, 1913
Hovey, W.W.	Eng.	1st Asst., U.S. Navy	2	68	1896 Nov 5	IA, 23rd, 1897
How, James		H, 25th Mo. (died of chronic diarrhea)	199		1890	KS, 10th, 1891
Howalo, Chris.		K, 10th Mich.	25		1918 Sep 5	KS, 38th, 1919
Howard, A.H.	Pvt.	K, 112th Ind. Inf.	16		1915 Dec 6	IA, 42nd, 1916
Howard, Abner		D, 83rd Ind.	50		1913 Dec 7	KS, 33rd, 1914
Howard, Alford		H, 22nd N.Y.	100		1915 Nov 13	KS, 35th, 1916
Howard, Andrew C.		H, 2nd Del.	463		1904 Aug 13	KS, 24th, 1905
Howard, C.C.	Pvt.	H, 12th Ill. Cav.	26		1922 May 20	IA, 49th, 1923
Howard, C.E.			515		1915 Dec 12	IA, 42nd, 1916
Howard, Charles L.		F, 16th Iowa Inf.	452	92	1938 Sep 6	IA, 64th, 1938
Howard, Chas. T.	Pvt.	G, 7th Ill. Cav.	56		1904 Jul 6	IA, 31st, 1905
Howard, Chas. W.		1st Iowa	1		1927 Sep 4	KS, 47th, 1928
Howard, D.J.		G, 121st Ohio E, 88th Ohio	39		1918 Jan 10	KS, 38th, 1919
Howard, David B.		M, 9th Ill. Cav.	25	71	1916 Oct 4	NE, 41st, 1917
Howard, Ezra E.		A, Ky. Green R. Batt.	16		1929 Jul	NE, 54th, 1930
Howard, F.A.	Pvt.	C, 23rd Iowa Inf.	7		1926 May	IA, 53rd, 1927
Howard, Frank M.	Pvt.	A, 156th Ill. Inf.	206		1927 May 16	IA, 54th, 1928
Howard, G.W.		D, 49th Ill.	13	74	1907 Apr 9	NE, 32nd, 1908
Howard, Harden	Pvt.	A, 135th Ind. Inf.	7		1917 Jan 7	IA, 44th, 1918
Howard, J.B.	Sergt.	I, 1st Iowa Inf.	78		1912 Apr 10	IA, 39th, 1913
Howard, J.H.		C, 13th Ky. Inf.	142		1901 Sep 8	KS, 21st, 1902
Howard, J.L.		F, 2nd Ind.	1		1908 Nov 26	KS, 28th, 1909
Howard, J.W.			7		1918 Aug 6	IA, 45th, 1919
Howard, John	Pvt.	A, 95th Ill. Inf.	216	52	1893 Sep 18	IA, 20th, 1894
Howard, John		B, 31st Minn.	232		1911 Dec 1	KS, 31st, 1912
Howard, John		L, 11th Kans.	271		1916 Mar 19	KS, 36th, 1917
Howard, John W.	Sergt.	I, 125th Ill. Inf.	18		1916 Oct 31	KS, 36th, 1917
Howard, Jordan T.		I, 47th Ill.	142		1908 Apr 8	KS, 28th, 1909
Howard, P.P.	Pvt.	D, 7th Iowa Cav.	337		1924 Dec	IA, 51st, 1925
Howard, Robert		C, 23rd Iowa Inf.	347		1912	IA, 39th, 1913
Howard, S.A.	Pvt.	F, 111th Penn. Inf.	29		1931	IA, 58th, 1932
Howard, S.N.	Sergt.	I, 2nd Iowa Inf.	164		1912 Jan 27	IA, 38th, 1912
Howard, Samuel T.		I, 47th Ill.	40		1918 Jan 18	KS, 38th, 1919
Howard, T.C.	Pvt.	A, 23rd Mich. Inf.	235		1928 Sep 3	IA, 55th, 1929
Howard, W.H.		K, 4th Iowa Cav.	155		1904 Sep 25	KS, 24th, 1905
Howard, W.H.		B, 20th Mich.	56		1912 Jan 6	KS, 31st, 1912
Howard, William	Corp.	D, 6th Vt. Inf.	233	63	1897 Jun 21	IA, 24th, 1898
Howarth, Henry			270		1890 Oct 13	NE, 15th, 1891

*See Appendix A, B or C for roster of post names and locations.
†See Introduction for note regarding recording of death date.

266

Name	Rank	Company, Regiment or Ship	Post*	Age	Death Date†	Journal
Howarth, I.J.					1929 Jan 7	NE, 53rd, 1929
Howarth, James			264		1917	IA, 44th, 1918
Howdesheldt, Wm.		I, 36th Iowa Inf. (at large)		100	1936 Jan 30	IA, 63rd, 1937
Howdesheldt, Wm.		I, 36th Iowa Inf. (at large)		100	1936 Jan 30	IA, 62nd, 1936
Howe, A.H.	Pvt.	D, 166th Ohio Inf.	298		1910 Jul 1	IA, 37th, 1911
Howe, A.W.		A, 85th N.Y.	98		1898 Jan 15	KS, 18th, 1899
Howe, C.M.	Capt.	C, 25th Mich. Inf. (of Salina; buried at Manhattan)			1927 Feb 2	KS, 46th, 1927
Howe, C.M.		C, 25th Mich.	100		1927 Mar 28	KS, 47th, 1928
Howe, Chas.	Pvt.	F, 7th Iowa Cav.	216		1903 Apr 18	IA, 30th, 1904
Howe, Francis	Sergt.	L, 13th N.Y. Hvy. Art.	123		1908 May 28	IA, 35th, 1909
Howe, Geo.		K, 101st Ill. (died of paralysis)	44	76	1913 Nov 7	NE, 38th, 1914
Howe, Geo. Marion	Pvt.	D, 155th Ill. Inf.	353	91	1939 Jun 6	IA, 65th, 1939
Howe, George		G, 5th Mo. Mil.	4	75	1913 Nov 7	NE, 38th, 1914
Howe, H.S.	Pvt.	E, 73rd Penn. Inf.	231		1919 Jan 29	IA, 46th, 1920
Howe, J.E.		A, 132nd Ind.	293		1922 Dec 14	KS, 42nd, 1923
Howe, James	Sergt.	B, 8th Ill. Cav.	222		1925 Nov 4	IA, 52nd, 1926
Howe, Jessie		G, 45th Iowa Inf.	147		1934 Jan 9	KS, 54th, 1935
Howe, Joel C.		K, 13th Iowa	184		1913 Oct 18	KS, 33rd, 1914
Howe, Joel W.	Pvt.	C, 105th Ill.	48		1924 Nov 15	IA, 51st, 1925
Howe, John A.		F, 13th Mass. Inf. (died at Marlboro, Mass.; buried at Marlboro, Mass.)	19		1894 Jun 24	KS, 14th, 1895
Howe, John W.		C, 30th Iowa Inf.	445	94	1937 Aug 30	IA, 64th, 1938
Howe, Jonathan D.		D, 79th Ohio	260		1910 Aug 14	KS, 30th, 1911
Howe, Martin		D, 34th Ohio Inf.	25	75	1920 Dec 17	NE, 45th, 1921
Howe, Orlando C.		L, 9th Iowa Cav.	174		1899 Aug 24	KS, 19th, 1900
Howe, P.D.C. Church	Pvt. Lieut., QM, Capt. & Major	G, 6th Mass. Inf. 15th Mass. Inf. (see Appendix D)		75	1915 Oct 7	NE, 40th, 1916
Howe, S.H.		E, 15th Iowa	71		1906 Dec 27	KS, 26th, 1907
Howe, Samuel T.		B, 189th Ohio	1		1922 May 13	KS, 42nd, 1923
Howe, W.P.	Pvt.	F, 1st Iowa Inf.	20		1908 Jun	IA, 35th, 1909
Howe, Wm. H.	Pvt.	A, 38th Iowa Inf.	171	52	1890 Aug 20	IA, 17th, 1891
Howell, D.T.		I, 32nd Iowa Inf.	193		3rd quarter 1884	IA, 11th, 1885
Howell, David		F, 36th Iowa	52		1914 Jul 23	KS, 34th, 1915
Howell, P.S.		H, 39th Iowa Inf.	209		1912 Sep 17	KS, 32nd, 1913
Howell, R.A.		A, 1st Kans.	25		1913 Oct 21	KS, 33rd, 1914
Howell, Thos. G.		E, 4th Kans. Inf. (died of old age)	110	75	1912 Jun 3	NE, 37th, 1913
Howenden, Adam	Pvt.	H, 34th N.Y. Inf.	505		1900 May 27	IA, 27th, 1901
Howerton, Willis		B, 26th Ky.	52		1913 Feb 21	KS, 33rd, 1914
Howerton, Willis	Pvt.	D, 36th Ky. Inf.	52		1915 Feb 21	KS, 35th, 1916
Howes, James		A, 120th Ind.	4		1924 Jun 1	KS, 44th, 1925
Howes, Lewis E.	Corp.	H, 118th N.Y.	151	63	1899 Feb 9	IA, 26th, 1900
Howeshell, J.R.	Pvt.	G, 27th Iowa Inf.	132		1918	IA, 45th, 1919
Howey, D.R.		I, 102nd Ill. Inf.	13		1928 Jan 29	NE, 53rd, 1929
Howie, John	Pvt.	A, 3rd Iowa Cav.	100	76	1898 Aug 3	IA, 25th, 1899
Howke, C.A.		I, 16th Ind.	129		1904 Mar 8	KS, 24th, 1905
Howland, A.		I, 24th Ill. (died of Bright's disease)	100	71	1904 Mar 5	NE, 29th, 1905
Howland, Geo.	Pvt.	A, N.Y.	222		1917 Oct	IA, 44th, 1918
Howland, J.C.		G, 26th Ind.	56		1889	KS, 9th, 1890
Howland, J.H.		E, 9th Kans.	51		1917 Dec 19	KS, 37th, 1918
Howland, Levi	Pvt.	I, 39th Ohio Inf.	286	48	1888 Dec 26	IA, 15th, 1889
Howland, S.P.		B, 4th Mich. Inf.	81		1928 Nov 3	NE, 53rd, 1929
Howlett, Charles H.		G, 5th N.Y.	64		1910 Jan 20	KS, 30th, 1911
Howlett, J.W.	Pvt.	F, 20th Iowa Inf.	206		1915 May 1	IA, 42nd, 1916
Howlett, James	Pvt.	D, 2nd Iowa Inf.	35		1894 Apr	IA, 21st, 1895
Hows, John H.		H, 12th Ind.	250		1923 Nov 23	KS, 43rd, 1924
Hoxie, C.W.		I, 13th Mich.	124		1934 Dec 18	IA, 61st, 1935
Hoxie, H.B.	Pvt.	D, 75th N.Y. Inf.	68		1926 Apr 29	IA, 53rd, 1927
Hoxie, R.L.	Bugler	E, 1st Iowa Cav.	8		1930 Apr 29	IA, 57th, 1931
Hoyle, Edmund			30		1895	NE, 20th, 1896
Hoysington, David B.		11th N.Y.	87		1887 Nov 17	KS, 7th, 1888

*See Appendix A, B or C for roster of post names and locations.
†See Introduction for note regarding recording of death date.
267

Name	Rank	Company, Regiment or Ship	Post*	Age	Death Date†	Journal
Hoyt, C.H.		A, 19th Kans. Inf.	12		1934 Aug 25	KS, 54th, 1935
Hoyt, D.C.		B, 29th Iowa	177		1897	KS, 17th, 1898
Hoyt, D.H.			22		1926	KS, 46th, 1927
Hoyt, E.T.	Pvt.	K, 3rd Iowa Inf.	22		1930 Sep 8	IA, 57th, 1931
Hoyt, Hollis K.		E, 9th Vt.	344		1925 Feb 19	KS, 45th, 1926
Hoyt, J.M.	Pvt.	H, 18th Iowa Inf.	6		1929 Oct 14	IA, 56th, 1930
Hoyt, Jacob	Sergt.	E, 4th Iowa Inf.	233		1931 Mar 17	IA, 58th, 1932
Hoyt, John	Pvt.	F, 33rd Wis. Inf.	298		1908 Jan 15	IA, 35th, 1909
Hoyt, T.			168		1908	IA, 35th, 1909
Hoyt, Thos.	Pvt.	B, 1st Iowa Inf.	8		1921 Sep 4	IA, 48th, 1922
Hoyt, W.F.	Adjt.	K, 6th Iowa Cav.	269		1912 Feb 1	IA, 38th, 1912
Hoyt, William	Pvt.	A, 2nd Iowa Inf.	2		1922 Apr 26	IA, 49th, 1923
Hubbard, Allison	Pvt.	L, 7th Ill. Cav.	377	52	1888 May 21	IA, 15th, 1889
Hubbard, Alonzo H.		E, 12th Ind.	380		1904 Apr 13	KS, 24th, 1905
Hubbard, Chas. O.		D, 7th Wis. Cav.	47		1921 Sep 5	KS, 41st, 1922
Hubbard, E.B.		H, 9th Ohio Cav. (died of chronic diarrhea)	104		1893 Jan 8	NE, 18th, 1894
Hubbard, Frank S.			38		1919	IA, 46th, 1920
Hubbard, Gideon M.		F, 56th Ohio	41		1896 Sep	KS, 16th, 1897
Hubbard, J.B.	Sergt.	K, 13th & M.S.M. Mo. Cav.	434		1927 Jun 10	IA, 54th, 1928
Hubbard, J.H.	Pvt.	I, 3rd Iowa Inf.	68		1911 Jul 11	IA, 38th, 1912
Hubbard, Jacob P.		F, 2nd Ill. Cav.	32		1916 Jan 5	KS, 36th, 1917
Hubbard, N.D.	Pvt.	D, 11th Ind. Cav. (died of typhoid fever)	35	52	1891 Jun 20	NE, 16th, 1892
Hubbard, R.C.	Capt.	C, 72nd U.S.C.	7		1907 Mar 16	IA, 34th, 1908
Hubbard, Robert T.		A, 15th U.S.B. (died of general debility)	48	81	1922 Jun 28	NE, 47th, 1923
Hubbard, S.M.					1896	KS, 16th, 1897
Hubbard, T.A.		B, 13th Mich.	57		1919 Nov 8	KS, 39th, 1920
Hubbard, W.L.		34th Ill. Inf.	113		1909 Apr 20	KS, 29th, 1910
Hubbard, Wm.	Pvt.	E, 6th Minn. Inf.	365		1915 Mar 16	IA, 42nd, 1916
Hubbell, G.		D, 192nd Ohio	197	87	1934 Jul 5	IA, 61st, 1935
Hubbell, H.E.		F, 97th Ind.	23		1919 Mar 9	KS, 39th, 1920
Hubbell, Julias C.		H, 56th N.Y.	82		1924 Aug 13	KS, 44th, 1925
Hubbell, Willard O.	Lieut.	C, 12th Kans.	1		1916 Feb 5	KS, 36th, 1917
Hubbert, Joseph P.		F, 2nd Ill.	32		1915 Jan 5	KS, 35th, 1916
Hubbord, J.W.		H, 27th Ky.	293		1922 Feb 26	KS, 42nd, 1923
Hubel, Peter		F, 33rd Ind.	41		1904	KS, 24th, 1905
Hubert, John H.			11		1930	IA, 57th, 1931
Hubler, Wm.	Pvt.	G, 173rd Iowa	110		1905 Oct 15	IA, 32nd, 1906
Hublitz, Phil.	Pvt.	C, 7th Ill. Cav. (died of consumption)	188	47	1887 Aug	NE, 12th, 1888
Hubner, C.F.	Pvt.	E, 28th Iowa Inf.	8		1910 Mar 7	IA, 37th, 1911
Hucke, Conrad	Sadler	A, 9th Iowa Cav.	250		1919 Jul	IA, 46th, 1920
Huckelberry, A.J.		D, 4th Ind.	17		1924 Jan 4	KS, 44th, 1925
Huckins, Lorenzo Dow	Pvt.	I, 38th Iowa Inf. F, 34th Iowa Inf.	3	97	1938 Dec 30	IA, 65th, 1939
Huckstadt, Emil		E, 2nd Ohio Cav.	38		1918 Aug 21	KS, 38th, 1919
Hud, S.R.		F, 3rd Ky. Inf.	457		1891 May 7	KS, 11th, 1892
Huddeston, E.			12		1922 Jan 12	KS, 42nd, 1923
Huddleson, D.C.			301		1899	NE, 24th, 1900
Huddleson, J.D.		B, 24th Ind.	4		1924 Jul 1	KS, 44th, 1925
Huddleston, P.A.		I, 119th Ill.	474		1892 Dec 21	KS, 12th, 1893
Huddleston, W.	Pvt.	H, 13th —	145		1921 May	IA, 48th, 1922
Hudgel, William Jeptha		D, 39th Iowa Inf.	22	97	1938 Jul 12	IA, 64th, 1938
Hudgell, Joseph	Pvt.	B, 19th Iowa Inf.	19		1914 Mar 10	IA, 41st, 1915
Hudley, H.C.		D, 16th Wis. Inf.	25		1891 Feb 15	KS, 11th, 1892
Hudnall, W.C.		H, 85th Ill.	7		1933 Jun 9	NE, 58th, 1934
Hudson, B.		6th Kans.	32		1935 Aug 31	KS, 55th, 1936
Hudson, B.F.		46th U.S.C. Inf.	93		1912 May 24	KS, 32nd, 1913
Hudson, D.H.		A, 18th Ohio Inf.	40		1927 Sep 6	IA, 54th, 1928
Hudson, D.W.	Pvt.	E, 13th Iowa Inf.	51		1925 Sep 23	IA, 52nd, 1926
Hudson, Edward G.		1st Ill. Art.	36		1917 Aug 29	KS, 37th, 1918
Hudson, George M.		K, 17th Iowa Inf. (died of heart disease)	311		1891 Aug 20	KS, 11th, 1892
Hudson, H.		G, 68th U.S. Colored Inf.	104		1888	KS, 8th, 1889
Hudson, J.M.		F, 1st Mich. Cav.	49		1913 Oct 2	KS, 33rd, 1914

Name	Rank	Company, Regiment or Ship	Post*	Age	Death Date†	Journal
Hudson, Jno.		D, 145th Ill.	25		1922 Jan 13	NE, 47th, 1923
Hudson, John			100		1884	KS, 4th, 1885
Hudson, John		D, 145th Ill. (not a member; buried by Farragut Post)	25		1922 Jan 13	NE, 47th, 1923
Hudson, Joseph Kennedy	Gen.	see Appendix D	1	67	1907 May 5	KS, 26th, 1907
Hudson, M., Dr.		K, 202nd Penn. Inf.	12		1909 Aug 12	KS, 29th, 1910
Hudson, M.F.		K, 202nd Penn.	69		1909 Aug 12	KS, 29th, 1910
Hudson, R.D.		D, 4th Ind. Cav.	158		1922 May 7	KS, 42nd, 1923
Hudson, T.E.B.	Pvt.	C, 74th Ill. Inf.	81		1921 Oct 25	IA, 48th, 1922
Hudson, W.H.		D, 9th Ky. Cav.	180		1920 Jan 6	KS, 40th, 1921
Hudson, Willis		B, 9th Ind.	77		1927 Dec 11	KS, 48th, 1929
Hue, H.	Pvt.	D, 8th Ill. Cav.	68		1921 Dec 20	IA, 48th, 1922
Huehn, P.C.	Pvt.	A, 8th Iowa Inf.	92		1906 Feb 14	IA, 33rd, 1907
Huellar, John		6th Ind. Bat.	89		1899 Mar 1	KS, 19th, 1900
Huene, O.E.	Pvt.	K, 23rd Ohio Inf.	190		1926 Dec 26	IA, 53rd, 1927
Hueston, M.D.	Pvt.	B, 11th Mo. Cav.	190		1926 Jan 2	IA, 53rd, 1927
Huett, Lewis	Pvt.	A, 30th Iowa Inf.	170		1919 Jan 18	IA, 46th, 1920
Huey, Benj.		C, 62nd Penn.	38		1900 Nov 22	KS, 20th, 1901
Huey, J.W.		F, 80th Ill. Inf.	59		1916 Oct 10	KS, 36th, 1917
Huey, T.B.	Pvt.	8th Wis. Lt. Art.	1		1915 Aug 10	IA, 42nd, 1916
Huey, Thos.		G, 11th Kans. Inf.	420		1899 Sep	KS, 19th, 1900
Huff, Elder J.		D, 2nd Neb. Cav.	7		1929 Feb 2	NE, 53rd, 1929
Huff, Geo. A.	Pvt.	E, 66th Ind. Inf.	68		1916 Aug 9	IA, 43rd, 1917
Huff, George		D, 7th Ill.	68		1927 Jun 20	KS, 47th, 1928
Huff, Henry	Pvt.	K, 16th Iowa Inf.	43		1929	IA, 56th, 1930
Huff, J.A.		H, 25th Ohio Inf.	28		1936 Jun 7	KS, 55th, 1936
Huff, James		D, 2nd Neb. Cav.	7		1929 Feb 2	NE, 54th, 1930
Huff, John		C, 11th Wis. Inf.	74	92	1936 Nov 12	IA, 63rd, 1937
Huff, John A.		F, 14th Kans.	117		1896 Oct 14	KS, 16th, 1897
Huff, Levi C.	Pvt.	E, 63rd Ind. Inf.	29	51	1895 Nov 12	IA, 22nd, 1896
Huff, Nathan		D, 28th Iowa	209		1905 Jan 15	KS, 25th, 1906
Huff, Samuel G.		B, 182nd Ohio	40		1927 Jun 4	KS, 47th, 1928
Huffaker, James		B, Mo. Mil.	100		1920 Apr 2	KS, 40th, 1921
Huffaker, Thomas W.	Pvt.	I, 18th Mo. Inf.	325		1902 Nov 5	IA, 29th, 1903
Huffman, Alex	Pvt.	M, 1st Ill. Battery	8		1911 Feb 1	IA, 38th, 1912
Huffman, D.B.	Corp.	B, 27th Ill.	231		1921 Jun 19	IA, 48th, 1922
Huffman, D.J.		G, 126th N.Y.	260		1923 Jun 10	KS, 43rd, 1924
Huffman, G.D.	Pvt.	H, 51st Ohio Inf.	114		1897-1898	IA, 24th, 1898
Huffman, G.M.		H, 22nd Iowa	1		1932 Jan 13	KS, 52nd, 1933
Huffman, George T.		I, 86th Ind.	85		1924 Apr 6	KS, 44th, 1925
Huffman, H.B.		D, 172nd Ohio National Guard	55		1896 Jul 19	KS, 16th, 1897
Huffman, Hiram		E, 138th Ind. Inf.	8		1902 Aug 4	KS, 22nd, 1903
Huffman, J.		D, 6th Ind. Inf. A, 5th Ind. Cav. (wounded at Chickamauga)	311		1888	KS, 8th, 1889
Huffman, J.E.	Pvt.	F, 44th Ind. Inf.	22		1908	IA, 35th, 1909
Huffman, J.E.	Pvt.	A, 13th Ind. Inf.	22		1908 Dec 21	IA, 35th, 1909
Huffman, J.S.	Pvt.	I, 160th Ohio Inf.	497		1928 Jan 7	IA, 55th, 1929
Huffman, Jacob	Pvt.	F, 1st Ill. Art.	68		1920 Oct 12	IA, 47th, 1921
Huffman, Jas.	Pvt.	F, 97th Ind. Inf.	317	59	1885 Nov 14	IA, 14th, 1888
Huffman, Jno.	Pvt.	F, 31st Ind. Inf.	197		1930 Mar 9	IA, 57th, 1931
Huffman, John		H, 17th Ohio	83		1926 Feb 20	KS, 46th, 1927
Huffman, O.		D, 28th Iowa	23		1892 Sep 5	KS, 12th, 1893
Huffman, Peter		I, 53rd Ohio	83		1905 Mar 22	KS, 25th, 1906
Huffman, V.J.		G, 169th Ohio	46		1913 Jan 27	KS, 33rd, 1914
Hufstedler, Wm. M.	Pvt.	G, 25th Iowa Inf.	19		1918 Sep 25	IA, 45th, 1919
Hugar, Jacob			130		1922 Oct 24	NE, 47th, 1923
Hugenin, J.L.		C, 153rd N.Y.	64		1905 Jul 26	KS, 25th, 1906
Hugg, Fred		C, 62nd Ill. Inf.	8		1887 Feb	KS, 7th, 1888
Huggins, John		D, 15th U.S.	25		1916 Mar 11	KS, 36th, 1917
Huggins, Josiah		E, 8th Ind. Inf.	190		1918 Jul 6	IA, 45th, 1919
Hughe, Stephen F.		K, 5th Tenn.	6		1928 Jul 1	KS, 48th, 1929

*See Appendix A, B or C for roster of post names and locations.
†See Introduction for note regarding recording of death date.
269

Name	Rank	Company, Regiment or Ship	Post*	Age	Death Date†	Journal
Hughes, A.D.		E, 22nd Ill.	24		1888	KS, 8th, 1889
Hughes, Andrew		D, 155th Ill.	85		1923 Feb 17	KS, 43rd, 1924
Hughes, C.			211		1921	IA, 48th, 1922
Hughes, Clinton D.		L, 1st Ohio Hvy. Art. (died of insanity)	90	62	1906 Aug 30	NE, 31st, 1907
Hughes, Cyrus		I, 12th Ill.	18		1927 May 20	KS, 47th, 1928
Hughes, E.S.		Kans.	477		1920	KS, 40th, 1921
Hughes, Emery		E, 126th Ill.	238		1915 Jan 26	KS, 35th, 1916
Hughes, F.T.			2		1926 Oct 21	IA, 53rd, 1927
Hughes, G.W.		E, 4th Mich.	75		1905 Apr 20	KS, 25th, 1906
Hughes, H.R.	Pvt.	C, 2nd Iowa Cav.	91		1920 Oct 23	IA, 47th, 1921
Hughes, Henry		F, 23rd Ohio	477		1927 Jan 25	KS, 47th, 1928
Hughes, Henry W.			144		1913 Jul 14	KS, 33rd, 1914
Hughes, J.C.		A, 97th Ohio	18		1923 Jan 24	KS, 43rd, 1924
Hughes, James	Pvt.	G, 139th N.Y. Inf.	29	87	1896 May 29	IA, 23rd, 1897
Hughes, James M.		E, 2nd Iowa Inf.	19		1st quarter 1884	IA, 10th, 1884
Hughes, Jas. R.		A, — Mo.	28		1906 Feb 5	KS, 26th, 1907
Hughes, Jesse M.	Pvt.	G, 43rd Wis. Inf.	11		1917 Sep 2	IA, 44th, 1918
Hughes, John F.		A, 121st Penn. Inf.	87		1914 Jul 2	KS, 34th, 1915
Hughes, John R.	Pvt.	I, 22nd Iowa Inf.	8		1913 Oct 28	IA, 40th, 1914
Hughes, John W.		I, 17th Ill. Cav.	17		1935 Mar 10	NE, 60th, 1936
Hughes, Joseph B.	Pvt.	E, 15th N.J. Inf.	452		1916 Jan 16	IA, 43rd, 1917
Hughes, Joseph R.		F, 13th Ind. Inf. (died at Soldiers & Sailors Home, Grand Island; buried in Willard, Mo.)	16	82	1905 Jul 24	NE, 30th, 1906
Hughes, Sam M.		D, —			1937 Apr 8	KS, 57th, 1938
Hughes, Sam. M.			497		1936	KS, 56th, 1937
Hughes, William		B, 3rd (M) Kans.[Kans. State Militia?]	12		1905 Oct 2	KS, 25th, 1906
Hughes, Wm.			44		1883	KS, 3rd, 1884
Hughlin, Chas.	Pvt.	11th Ohio Inf.	375		1904 Oct 24	IA, 31st, 1905
Hughs, Felix	Pvt.	E, 28th Iowa Inf.	364		1911 Jun 3	IA, 38th, 1912
Hughs, John		I, 31st Ind.	113		1911 Jul 11	KS, 31st, 1912
Hughs, Joseph		F, 6th Ind. Cav. (died of paralysis)	354	82	1905 Jul 19	NE, 30th, 1906
Hughs, Thomas		A, Mo. Vol. Cav. (died of heart failure; died at Soldiers & Sailors Home, Milford)		78	1906 Jun 8	NE, 31st, 1907
Hugs, Simon	Pvt.	H, 9th Iowa Inf.	132		1913 Jan 23	IA, 40th, 1914
Hugus, J.W.	Seaman	Gunboat *Louisiana*	32		1918 Feb 11	KS, 38th, 1919
Huhenes, John	Pvt.	M, 6th West Va. Inf.	48		1908 Oct 31	IA, 35th, 1909
Huhn, John	Pvt.	G, 4th Md. Inf.	31		1906 Nov	IA, 33rd, 1907
Huie, John		B, 4th Iowa Cav. (at large)			1932 Apr 29	IA, 59th, 1933
Huink, Herman	Pvt.	A, 9th Iowa Inf.	231		1918 Jul 15	IA, 45th, 1919
Huitson, Robert		F, 77th Ill.	6		1913 Apr 19	KS, 33rd, 1914
Hulbert, E.J.		A, 11th Ill. Inf. (died at Andale, Kans.; buried at Mt. Hope Cemetery)	354		1894 Oct 31	KS, 14th, 1895
Hulbert, Henry		B, 18th Mo. Vol. Inf. (died of old age, general debility)	77	86	1922 Aug 11	NE, 47th, 1923
Hulburt, J.B.	Pvt.	D, 32nd Iowa	347		1914 Aug 23	IA, 41st, 1915
Hulburt, J.H.		F, 95th Ill. Inf. (died of cancer)	262	75	1920 Jul 7	NE, 45th, 1921
Hulburt, Milton		F, 1st Ohio Cav. (died at Sylvan Grove; buried at Wilson Cemetery)	115		1894 Aug 28	KS, 14th, 1895
Hule, W.J.	Sergt.	I, 1st West Va. Cav.	67		1910 Mar 11	IA, 37th, 1911
Huler, Wm. B.		82nd Ill.	94		1905 Mar 2	KS, 25th, 1906
Hulett, L.D.		B, 13th Ill. (died of long con't sickness)	110	74	1917 Jan 15	NE, 42nd, 1918
Hulett, William		B, 140th Ill. Inf.		91	1936 May 29	IA, 62nd, 1936
Hulett, Wm.		B, 140th Ill. Inf.	30	91	1935 May 29	IA, 62nd, 1936
Hulick, Jos.		C, 1st Mo. Eng. (born in Indiana, 1835; died in Dorchester)	107		1883 Feb 2	NE, 8th, 1884
Huling, Alden S.		30th N.Y.	1		1912 Dec 11	KS, 32nd, 1913
Huling, Moses		B, 23rd Wis.	25		1927 Mar 13	NE, 52nd, 1928
Hulit, William A.		A, 64th Ohio	303		1919 Jun 21	KS, 39th, 1920
Hulitt, Richard	Corp.	K, 20th Iowa Inf.	362	76	1895 Aug 30	IA, 22nd, 1896
Hulka, Frank C.		C, 10th Iowa Inf.	24	97	1938 Feb 2	IA, 64th, 1938
Hull, Aholiab	Pvt.	D, 33rd Iowa Inf.	40		1916 Jan 21	IA, 43rd, 1917
Hull, Dwight G.	Boy & Yeoman	U.S. Navy (died of accidental poisoning)	7	43	1887 Mar 4	NE, 12th, 1888

*See Appendix A, B or C for roster of post names and locations.
†See Introduction for note regarding recording of death date.

Name	Rank	Company, Regiment or Ship	Post*	Age	Death Date†	Journal
Hull, F.M.			114		1884	NE, 9th, 1885
Hull, F.W.		D, 32nd Iowa Inf., 16th Corps (born Feb. 14, 1835; died in Orleans)	114		1883 Dec 24	NE, 8th, 1884
Hull, H.C.		K, 11th Kans.	133		1902 May	KS, 22nd, 1903
Hull, H.W.	Pvt.	F, 13th Iowa Inf.	347		1912	IA, 39th, 1913
Hull, J.A.T.	Capt.	C, 23rd Iowa Inf.	7		1928 Sep 26	IA, 55th, 1929
Hull, J.D.		A, 151st Ind. Inf.	66		1909 Jan 18	KS, 29th, 1910
Hull, Joel		A, 41st Ill.	129		1912 Sep 17	KS, 32nd, 1913
Hull, John		K, 3rd West Va. Cav.	110		1921 Mar 5	KS, 41st, 1922
Hull, L.B.		K, 11th Ohio Cav.	97		1902 Jun 14	KS, 22nd, 1903
Hull, L.R.		A, 11th Kans. Cav.	155		1925 Apr 17	KS, 45th, 1926
Hull, Lyman		A, 38th Wis.	100		1920 Nov 29	KS, 40th, 1921
Hull, Lyman		A, 38th Wis.	429		1920 Nov 27	KS, 40th, 1921
Hull, M.B.		E, 6th Wis.	100		1920 Apr 15	KS, 40th, 1921
Hull, N.H.		D, 76th N.Y.	57		1918 Mar 19	KS, 38th, 1919
Hull, Quincy A.	Pvt.	D, 61st Ill.	1		1906 Aug 31	KS, 26th, 1907
Hull, Simon		B, 17th Kans.	160		1885	KS, 5th, 1886
Hull, VanRensler J.		D, 90th Iowa Art. (died of paralysis)	112		1924 Dec 18	NE, 49th, 1925
Hull, Warren W.		I, 73rd Ohio Inf.	196		1912 Mar 14	IA, 39th, 1913
Hullett, William		45th Minn.	8		1902 Jul 4	KS, 22nd, 1903
Hulley, C.A.	Pvt.	C, 39th Iowa Inf.	6		1914 Oct 20	IA, 41st, 1915
Hullinger, S.P.	Pvt.	D, 151st Ohio Inf.	15		1928 Mar 4	IA, 55th, 1929
Hulse, H.H.	Pvt.	25th Ohio Battery	31		1905 May 7	IA, 32nd, 1906
Hulse, Joseph	Pvt.	B, 74th Ill. Inf.	321		1900 May 20	IA, 27th, 1901
Hulse, L.		D, 80th Ill.	76		1919 Jul 2	KS, 39th, 1920
Hultz, J.		D, 92nd Ill. (killed at Beloit)	383		1888	KS, 8th, 1889
Hultz, S.		H, 62nd Penn.	295		1888	KS, 8th, 1889
Humbert, H.C.	Capt.	E, 22nd Iowa Inf.	107		1908 Jan 7	IA, 35th, 1909
Humbert, J.N.		D, 133rd Penn. Inf. R, 5th Penn. Hvy. Art.	429		1908	KS, 28th, 1909
Humbert, J.N.		D, 133rd Penn.	429		1920 Feb 3	KS, 40th, 1921
Humbert, S.B.	Pvt.	B, 30th Wis. Inf.	22		1933 May 23	IA, 60th, 1934
Humbert, Solomon B.		B, 31st Iowa Inf.	222	96	1938 Sep 20	IA, 64th, 1938
Humberton, Sam.			429		1911	KS, 31st, 1912
Humes, George		C, 47th Ind. (died at Bunker Hill)	152		1895 Mar 17	KS, 15th, 1896
Humes, Josiah		K, 121st Ohio	4		1926 Jan 3	KS, 46th, 1927
Humeston, K.J.	Pvt.	K, 36th Iowa Inf.	204		1915 Nov 27	IA, 42nd, 1916
Humfreville, D.W.		E, 94th Ohio	260		1917 Jun 15	KS, 37th, 1918
Humfrey, John		H, 11th Ill. Inf. (at large)	11	91, 11 mos. & 19 days	1938 Sep 11	IA, 64th, 1938
Humfries, E.L.		E, 99th Ind.	325		1911 Aug 25	KS, 31st, 1912
Hummel, Christien	Landsman	Navy	100		1917 Jul 15	IA, 44th, 1918
Hummel, G.F.	Pvt.	D, 40th Ill. Cav.	66		1910 Sep 10	IA, 37th, 1911
Hummel, Peter			22		1920 Jan 8	KS, 40th, 1921
Hummel, Wesley G.		M, 12th Ill. Cav.	25		1937 Mar 3	NE, 62nd, 1938
Hummell, Daniel			170		1899	KS, 19th, 1900
Hummell, Wm.			5		1929 Feb 14	IA, 56th, 1930
Humphrees, Thos.		H, 19th Iowa	30		1927 Feb 2	KS, 47th, 1928
Humphrey, Benj.	Pvt.	G, 63rd Ohio Inf.	16		1906 Jul 2	IA, 33rd, 1907
Humphrey, C.C.			465		1912 Oct 11	IA, 39th, 1913
Humphrey, Chas.		G, 93rd Ill.	58		1904 Jan 5	KS, 24th, 1905
Humphrey, E.G.		D, 22nd Conn.	7		1930 Mar 31	NE, 55th, 1931
Humphrey, E.J.	Pvt.	E, 40th Iowa Inf.	425		1918 Dec 23	IA, 45th, 1919
Humphrey, G.G.		B, 94th Ill.	337		1902 Aug 23	KS, 22nd, 1903
Humphrey, Geo. C.		B, 75th Ohio Inf. (died of heart trouble)	11	79	1925 Jan 22	NE, 50th, 1926
Humphrey, Geo. M.		H, 2nd Wis. Inf. (died of Bright's disease)	95		1894 Nov 17	NE, 19th, 1895
Humphrey, H.		H, 176th Ohio	81		1930 Aug 9	KS, 50th, 1931
Humphrey, H.A.		K, 82nd Ohio	461		1912 Apr 6	KS, 32nd, 1913
Humphrey, Hugh			316		1928	IA, 55th, 1929
Humphrey, J.J.	Corp.	G, 112th Ill.	305	73	1898 Oct 31	IA, 25th, 1899
Humphrey, J.M.	Pvt.	K, 8th Iowa Inf.	39		1920	IA, 47th, 1921

Name	Rank	Company, Regiment or Ship	Post*	Age	Death Date†	Journal
Humphrey, Jno. W.	Pvt.	I, 9th Iowa Inf.	216	85	1898 Oct 3	IA, 25th, 1899
Humphrey, Linnill		A, 10th Kans.	218		1885	KS, 5th, 1886
Humphrey, Lyman W.		I, 76th Ohio Vol. Inf.	4		1915 Sep 13	KS, 35th, 1916
Humphrey, Miles	Pvt.	B, 5th Iowa Inf.	16		1909 Nov 16	IA, 36th, 1910
Humphrey, Milton			11		1925	IA, 52nd, 1926
Humphrey, Milton			11		1927	IA, 54th, 1928
Humphrey, Theophilus	Lieut. Col.	171st Penn.	1		1906 Aug 31	KS, 26th, 1907
Humphrey, Thomas		H, 19th Iowa	30		1927 Feb 5	KS, 46th, 1927
Humphrey, W.T.		G, 8th Ill.	44		1896 Jan 20	KS, 16th, 1897
Humphrey, W.T.R.	Pvt.	I, 44th Iowa Inf.	133		1925 Apr 5	IA, 52nd, 1926
Humphrey, W.W.		K, 1st Penn. Rifles	47		1899 Oct 31	KS, 19th, 1900
Humphrey, Watson		A, 13th Iowa (died of old age)	55	76	1911 Sep 22	NE, 36th, 1912
Humphrey, Wm.		G, 6th Kans.	55		1921 Jul 9	KS, 41st, 1922
Humphreys, C.N.		3rd N.Y. Bat.	6		1917	KS, 37th, 1918
Humphreys, E.	Pvt.	B, 2nd Neb. (died of general debility)	52	64	1884 Mar 15	NE, 9th, 1885
Humphreys, E.L., see Humfries, E.L.						
Humphreys, William	Pvt. Pvt.	D, 1st Ohio Hvy. Art. (at large) D, 117th Ohio Inf.	309, 18	96	1941 Jan 25	IA, 67th, 1941
Humphries, C.N.		L, 3rd Reg. Bat.	6		1918	KS, 38th, 1919
Humphry, J.W.			32		1911 Feb 19	KS, 31st, 1912
Humphry, John	Pvt.	E, 40th Iowa Inf.	45		1912 Mar 5	IA, 39th, 1913
Humpton, L.E.	Pvt.	A, 97th Penn. Inf.	5		1900-1901	IA, 27th, 1901
Hundertmark, Henry		11th Ind.	258		1912 Jul 6	KS, 32nd, 1913
Hundley, Wm. H.	Pvt.	I, 3rd Mo. Cav.	71		1913 Oct 12	IA, 40th, 1914
Hungate, Andrew J.		E, 37th Ind.	1		1904 Oct 30	KS, 24th, 1905
Hungerford, D.A.		K, 8th Vt. Inf.	11	91	1917 Aug 9	NE, 42nd, 1918
Hungerford, G.B.	Pvt.	D, 8th Minn. Inf.	217		3rd quarter 1885	IA, 12th, 1886
Hunley, C.W.		D, 118th Ill. Inf., 16th Corps (born and died in Quincy, Ill.)	70		1883	NE, 8th, 1884
Hunn, Michael	Pvt.	F, 3rd Mo. Inf.	231		1922 Apr 9	IA, 49th, 1923
Hunnicutt, Daniel B.		D, 79th Ohio Inf.	12		1929 Aug 10	KS, 49th, 1930
Hunnius, A.		E, 64th N.Y.	6		1923 Feb 21	KS, 43rd, 1924
Hunsberger, J.B.		Miss. Squadron, Kans.	354		1935 Nov 27	KS, 55th, 1936
Hunsburger, J.B.		Miss. Squadron	354		1936 Nov 27	KS, 57th, 1938
Hunt, A.L.		C, 2nd Mo. Cav.			1913 Nov 15	KS, 33rd, 1914
Hunt, Alex			98		1913	KS, 33rd, 1914
Hunt, Alonzo		I, 2nd Kans.	57		1928 Feb 16	KS, 48th, 1929
Hunt, Andrew M.	Pvt.	F, 7th Minn. Vols.	132		1902 May 6	IA, 28th, 1902
Hunt, Aretas		A, 155th Ill.	68		1917 Dec 18	KS, 37th, 1918
Hunt, C.P.	Pvt.	C, 32nd Iowa Inf.	68		1908 Apr 28	IA, 35th, 1909
Hunt, Cyrus L.		I, 79th Ohio	14		1898 Jan 27	KS, 18th, 1899
Hunt, Eugene	Pvt.	E, 112th Ill. Inf.	430	50	1887 Oct 29	IA, 14th, 1888
Hunt, H.H.	Asst. Surg.	21st Iowa Inf.	54	68	1896 Aug 24	IA, 23rd, 1897
Hunt, Harrison H.		13th Ky.	337		1927 Jan 25	KS, 47th, 1928
Hunt, Henry A.		C, 104th N.Y. Inf.	250		1908 May	KS, 28th, 1909
Hunt, J.	Pvt.	C, 18th Inf.	173		1921 Nov 18	IA, 48th, 1922
Hunt, J.A.		A, 94th Ill. Inf.	155		1929 Dec 31	KS, 49th, 1930
Hunt, J.F.		C, 3rd N.Y. Cav.	75		1926	NE, 51st, 1927
Hunt, Jacob S.			51		1886	NE, 11th, 1887
Hunt, Jas.	Pvt.	M, 2nd Calif. Cav.	267	54	1889 Jul 17	IA, 16th, 1890
Hunt, Jefferson	Pvt.	F, 40th Iowa Inf.	49		1912 Nov 14	IA, 39th, 1913
Hunt, John W.	Pvt.	F, 10th Ind. Inf.	338	50	1892 Dec 18	IA, 19th, 1893
Hunt, Jonathan		G, 10th Ohio	40		1908[1909?] Feb 28	KS, 29th, 1910
Hunt, Joshua		K, 152nd Ind.	250		1916 Mar 24	KS, 36th, 1917
Hunt, L.M.			44		1901	NE, 26th, 1902
Hunt, S.	Pvt.		472		1910 Mar 15	IA, 37th, 1911
Hunt, S.H.		A, 54th Ind.	96		1923 Feb 24	KS, 43rd, 1924
Hunt, Samuel		F, 127th Ill.	314		1916 Mar 11	KS, 36th, 1917
Hunt, Thomas	Pvt.	I, 9th Iowa Cav.	100		1899 Oct 4	IA, 26th, 1900
Hunt, W.E.			43		1886	NE, 11th, 1887
Hunt, W.J.	Sergt.	84th Ill.	170		1905 Jun	IA, 32nd, 1906

Name	Rank	Company, Regiment or Ship	Post*	Age	Death Date†	Journal
Hunter, A.	4th Sergt.	E, 15th Iowa Inf.	108		1925 Nov 27	IA, 52nd, 1926
Hunter, A.C.	Pvt.	H, 26th Iowa Inf.	92	55	1895 Apr 1	IA, 22nd, 1896
Hunter, C.E.	Pvt.	C, 8th Iowa Cav.	383		1924 Nov 15	IA, 51st, 1925
Hunter, Charles W.			50		1884	KS, 4th, 1885
Hunter, Chas. H.	Pvt.	B, 35th Iowa Inf.	231		1908 Feb 22	IA, 35th, 1909
Hunter, Daniel		G, 72nd Ind. (died at Holton)	46		1895 Dec	KS, 15th, 1896
Hunter, Daniel		B, 2nd Minn. Inf. (died at Minneapolis)	47		1895 Jul	KS, 15th, 1896
Hunter, David	Pvt.	F, 47th Iowa Inf.	7		1918 Apr 16	IA, 45th, 1919
Hunter, Geo. B.	Lieut.	B, 13th Iowa Inf.	16		1908 Jun 22	IA, 35th, 1909
Hunter, Geo. M.	Pvt.	F, 22nd Iowa Vol. Inf.	8		1924 Apr 24	IA, 51st, 1925
Hunter, George A.		B, 10th Kans.	130		1936 Mar 20	KS, 56th, 1937
Hunter, H.		G, Kans.	365		1889	KS, 9th, 1890
Hunter, H.S.	Pvt.	S, 130th Ohio Vols.	416		1915 Jan 11	IA, 41st, 1915
Hunter, J.R.C.	Capt.	A, 12th Iowa Inf.	66		1917 Jan 9	IA, 44th, 1918
Hunter, James C.		A, 33rd Ind.	209		1893 Dec 9	KS, 13th, 1894
Hunter, James L.			16		3rd quarter 1883	IA, 10th, 1884
Hunter, John		E, 11th Wis.	209		1911	KS, 31st, 1912
Hunter, John		B, 18th N.Y.	27		1933 Jul 1	KS, 53rd, 1934
Hunter, Joseph	Pvt.	H, 211th Penn. Inf.	7	55	1887 Jul 17	IA, 14th, 1888
Hunter, Joseph F.	Corp.	A, 33rd Iowa Inf.	330		1902 Dec 30	IA, 29th, 1903
Hunter, Miller C.	Pvt.	E, 76th Ind. Inf.	49		1910 Oct 7	IA, 37th, 1911
Hunter, Olander		D, 77th Ohio	51		1916 Feb 23	KS, 36th, 1917
Hunter, Olarnder		D, 77th Ohio Vol. Inf.	51		1915 Feb 23	KS, 35th, 1916
Hunter, Robert	Landsman	U.S. Navy	111		1912 Dec 19	IA, 39th, 1913
Hunter, Robert		C, 49th U.S.C.T.	132		1902 Apr 16	KS, 22nd, 1903
Hunter, S.		L, 2nd Neb.	130		1927 Jan 16	KS, 48th, 1929
Hunter, Stephen		L, 2nd Neb.	130		1928 Jan 16	KS, 47th, 1928
Hunter, Thomas		D, 74th Ohio Inf.	100		1914 Dec 5	KS, 34th, 1915
Hunter, W.H.		D, 13th Mo.	71		1897 Feb 9	KS, 17th, 1898
Hunter, W.H.		B, 66th Ind.	64		1904 Jan 14	KS, 24th, 1905
Hunter, W.T.			197		1884	KS, 4th, 1885
Hunter, Wells L.	Pvt.	10th N.Y. Inf.	16		1916	IA, 43rd, 1917
Hunter, William		B, 3rd Mass. Cav. (died of cancer of stomach)	50	79	1897 Jan 15	NE, 22nd, 1898
Hunting, S.S.	Chaplain	27th Mich. Inf.	12	62	1894 Jun 2	IA, 21st, 1895
Hunting, W.H.	Corp.	M, 1st Iowa Cav.	88		1928 May 2	IA, 55th, 1929
Huntington, Geo. W.	Pvt.	D, 15th Ill. Inf.	58		1915 Apr 20	IA, 42nd, 1916
Huntington, J.W.	Pvt.	D, 23rd Wis. Inf.	23	88	1933 Feb 21	IA, 60th, 1934
Huntington, W.W.A.	Musician	F, 26th Iowa Inf.	92		1914 Mar 7	IA, 41st, 1915
Huntington, Ward		G, 2nd Col. Cav.	32		1912 Dec 2	KS, 32nd, 1913
Huntley, A.J.	Pvt.	F, 121st N.Y.	22		1921 May 13	IA, 48th, 1922
Huntley, C.M.	Pvt.	I, 147th Ill. Inf.	141		1922 Oct 22	IA, 49th, 1923
Huntley, J.W.		C, 10th Kans.	8		1890	KS, 10th, 1891
Huntley, John	Corp.	E, 29th Ind. Inf.	38		1920 Jul 18	IA, 47th, 1921
Huntley, Jonathan	Pvt.	C, 2nd Mich. Cav.	264	55	1899 Nov 4	IA, 26th, 1900
Huntley, L.S.			18		1926	IA, 53rd, 1927
Huntley, O.D.	Pvt.	E, 10th Iowa Inf.	455		1908	IA, 35th, 1909
Huntley, O.V.	Pvt.	10th Iowa Inf.	455		1907 2nd term	IA, 34th, 1908
Huntling, Benj.	Corp.	C, 3rd Iowa Inf.	216	63	1896 Jul 7	IA, 23rd, 1897
Hunton, George E.		G, 1st Maine Cav.	63		1916 Feb 18	KS, 36th, 1917
Huntoon, Andrew J.		B, 2nd Kans.	1		1902 May 27	KS, 22nd, 1903
Huntoon, Joel	Pvt.	H, 11th Kans.	1		1906 Oct 3	KS, 26th, 1907
Huntoon, Sylvester A.		C, 14th Ill. Cav.	110	77	1920 Apr 7	NE, 45th, 1921
Huntsinger, Henry J.		A, 48th Ind.	91		1927 Oct 24	NE, 52nd, 1928
Huntsinger, Isaac		A, 72nd Ind.	47		1923 Oct 16	KS, 43rd, 1924
Huntsinger, L.P., Rev.		I, 79th Ind.	25		1922 Nov 30	KS, 42nd, 1923
Huntsinger, S.K.		A, 72nd Ill.	25		1913 Dec 11	NE, 38th, 1914
Huntsman, H.C.	1st Asst. Surg.	5th Iowa Inf.	40	57	1887 Jan 14	IA, 14th, 1888
Hunwick, Edwin	Pvt.	A, 46th Iowa	78		1907 Mar 14	IA, 34th, 1908
Hunzicker, Casper		H, 33rd Mo.	434		1889	KS, 9th, 1890
Hupp, E.	Pvt.	K, 16th Penn. Cav.	153		1917 Feb 23	IA, 44th, 1918
Hupp, George		F, 121st Ohio	36		1917 Jul 5	KS, 37th, 1918

*See Appendix A, B or C for roster of post names and locations.
†See Introduction for note regarding recording of death date.

Name	Rank	Company, Regiment or Ship	Post*	Age	Death Date†	Journal
Hupp, W.H.			188		1909 Feb 24	IA, 36th, 1910
Hupp, W.W.		B, 15th Kans.	370		1912 Aug 11	KS, 32nd, 1913
Hurbert, Delos	Corp.	F, 109th N.Y.	362	46	1890 Jun 7	IA, 17th, 1891
Hurd, A.C.		L, 5th Kans.	250		1928 Dec 21	KS, 48th, 1929
Hurd, George		I, 3rd Kans. State Militia Cal.	12		1925 Mar 2	KS, 44th, 1925
Hurd, George		I, 3rd Kans. State Militia	12		1925 Mar 2	KS, 45th, 1926
Hurd, George		B, 37th Ill. Inf.	25		1894 Oct 27	NE, 19th, 1895
Hurd, J.D.		H, 5th Iowa	56		1906 Sep 30	KS, 26th, 1907
Hurd, Thomas		H, 139th Ill.	57		1920 Jul 2	KS, 40th, 1921
Hurd, W.H.	Sergt.	A, 3rd N.Y. Inf.	222		1920 Nov 7	IA, 47th, 1921
Hurd, W.J.C.		B, 140th Ill.	46		1902 Oct 23	KS, 22nd, 1903
Hurd, William C.			50		1884	KS, 4th, 1885
Hurgins, David		C, 23rd Iowa	63		1904 Jun 25	KS, 24th, 1905
Hurlbert, A.E.		M, 1st Mich. Cav.	25	54	1902 May	NE, 27th, 1903
Hurlbert, Delos, see Hurbert, Delos						
Hurlbert, Eli A.		C, 2nd Wis. Inf.	127		1929 Dec 4	KS, 49th, 1930
Hurlburt, E.C.	Pvt.	H, 3rd Iowa Cav.	515		1900 Dec 16	IA, 27th, 1901
Hurlbut, Delos, see Hurbert, Delos						
Hurlbut, E.C.	Pvt.	H, 3rd Iowa Cav.	515		1900 Dec 10	IA, 28th, 1902
Hurlbut, Fredrick		C, 22nd Calif.	40	60	1916 Sep 2	NE, 41st, 1917
Hurlbut, Jacob C.		E, 1st Iowa Cav. (died of stomach trouble)	149	68	1908 Apr 23	NE, 33rd, 1909
Hurley, Horace		K, 140th Ohio	132		1918	KS, 38th, 1919
Hurley, R.F.		A, 54th Ill.	158		1920 Jan 10	KS, 40th, 1921
Hurley, Timothy		H, 19th Mich. Inf.	303		1901 Jan 16	KS, 21st, 1902
Hurling, Fred			72		1923 Dec 29	KS, 43rd, 1924
Huron, Geo. A.		I, 7th Ind.	1		1927 Jun 21	KS, 47th, 1928
Hurry, Wm. H.H.		F, 57th Penn. Inf.	28		1912 Oct 25	KS, 32nd, 1913
Hursh, Jacob		E, 158th Penn. (nonmember of department; died at Lincoln)			1935 Jul 1	NE, 60th, 1936
Hurst, A.G.	Pvt.	K, 17th Iowa Inf.	97	63	1894 Dec 27	IA, 22nd, 1896
Hurst, Bennett		E, 115th Ill.	4		1918 Mar 2	KS, 38th, 1919
Hurst, Harry	Pvt.	I, 16th Wis.	68		1924 Aug 20	IA, 51st, 1925
Hurst, James		A, 85th Ohio	250		1890	KS, 10th, 1891
Hurst, Keenan		K, 27th Ohio	23		1927 Nov 1	KS, 47th, 1928
Hurt, H.S.		E, 7th Iowa Cav.	7		1928 Nov 23	IA, 55th, 1929
Hurt, Wm. S.		B, 2nd Ill. Cav. (former member of department; location: Clay Center)			1934 Jan 8	NE, 58th, 1934
Huskamp, Luke			2		1908 Dec 13	IA, 35th, 1909
Husmand, G.F.	Pvt.	44th Iowa Inf.	220		1897 Dec 1	IA, 24th, 1898
Huss, G.W.	Pvt.		7		1921	IA, 48th, 1922
Husselton, Henry B.		F, 12th Ind.	117		1912 Oct 21	KS, 32nd, 1913
Husseman, Joseph	Pvt.	D, 31st Iowa Inf.	68		1930 Jun 25	IA, 57th, 1931
Hussey, Frank D.	Pvt.	U.S. Signal Corps	7	49	1896 Apr 17	IA, 22nd, 1896
Hussong, Calvin	Pvt.	A, 23rd Iowa Inf.	30		1904 May 3	IA, 31st, 1905
Hustead, Geo. W.	Pvt.	G, 8th Iowa Inf.	233		1915 Mar 3	IA, 42nd, 1916
Husted, Hoyt L.	Pvt.	H, 2nd Ohio Cav.	84		1912 Mar 1	IA, 39th, 1913
Husted, J.M.		K, 192nd N.Y.	38		1900 Apr 19	KS, 20th, 1901
Husted, Marcus		Ill.	468		1893 Dec 13	KS, 13th, 1894
Husted, Thomas M.		C, 30th Iowa	62		1885	KS, 5th, 1886
Husted, Thos.	Pvt.	B, 18th Iowa Inf.	55		1913 Oct 5	IA, 40th, 1914
Huston, Abe	Pvt.	G, 70th Ill. Inf.	23		1920 Mar 29	IA, 47th, 1921
Huston, Armstrong		D, 38th Ind. (died of heart trouble)	22	85	1925 Aug 2	NE, 50th, 1926
Huston, David A.		A, 22nd Penn. Cav.	85		1900 Aug 22	KS, 20th, 1901
Huston, E.S.	Pvt.	I, 39th Iowa Inf.	5		1915 Dec 5	IA, 42nd, 1916
Huston, Frank M.	Pvt.		410		1911 Feb	IA, 38th, 1912
Huston, Geo. W.		G, 149th Ohio Inf.	56		1925 Nov 15	IA, 52nd, 1926
Huston, J.H.	Pvt.	13th Cav. H.M.	108		1924 Jul 20	IA, 51st, 1925
Huston, J.M.		C, 41st Ohio	25		1922 Dec 29	KS, 42nd, 1923
Huston, James M.		C, 41st Ohio	244		1923 Dec 29	KS, 43rd, 1924
Huston, James O.		B, 66th Ind. Inf. (died of paralysis heart)	22	72	1909 Aug 27	NE, 34th, 1910

Name	Rank	Company, Regiment or Ship	Post*	Age	Death Date†	Journal
Huston, Jefferson		B, 2nd Ill. Art.	17		1913 Jan 22	KS, 33rd, 1914
Huston, Matt		B, 6th Ind. Cav.	87		1927 Jul 6	KS, 47th, 1928
Huston, Robert		A, 9th Kans.	397		1892	KS, 12th, 1893
Huston, Thos.	Pvt.	D, 15th Ill. Inf.	141		1920 Jan 5	IA, 47th, 1921
Hutchenson, Perry		E, 13th Kans.	9		1914 Dec 29	KS, 34th, 1915
Hutchin, W.W.		E, 6th Kans.	170		1914 May 12	KS, 34th, 1915
Hutchins, E.R.	Pvt.	I, 1st Mass. Inf.	12		1921 Apr 5	IA, 48th, 1922
Hutchins, H.H.	Pvt.	K, 1st Iowa	74		1927 Feb 1	IA, 54th, 1928
Hutchins, J.E.		I, 7th Kans.	453		1919 Oct 3	KS, 39th, 1920
Hutchins, M.S.		K, 153rd Ill.	249		1905 Nov 30	KS, 25th, 1906
Hutchins, Sparhawk	Musician	8th Wis. Inf.	22		1915 May 10	IA, 42nd, 1916
Hutchinson, Alex.			236		1924	IA, 51st, 1925
Hutchinson, C.C.		F, 17th Penn. Cav.	63		1919 Nov 12	KS, 39th, 1920
Hutchinson, D.M.		K, 8th Iowa Inf.	97		1916 Mar 16	KS, 36th, 1917
Hutchinson, David		17th Ind. Battery	238		1901 Feb 3	KS, 21st, 1902
Hutchinson, David F.	Pvt.	I, 27th Ill. Inf.	28	51	1886 Mar 6	IA, 13th, 1887
Hutchinson, Dillman		I, 36th Iowa Inf.	25		1911 Aug 17	NE, 36th, 1912
Hutchinson, Eli Merritt	Pvt.	K, 27th Iowa Inf.	90	101	1939 Dec 26	IA, 66th, 1940
Hutchinson, H.		2nd Neb.	302		1927 Feb 9	NE, 52nd, 1928
Hutchinson, I.	Pvt.	C, 20th Iowa Inf.	94		1920 Mar 2	IA, 47th, 1921
Hutchinson, J.B.		I, 15th Penn. Inf.	87		1909 May 17	KS, 29th, 1910
Hutchinson, J.M.	Pvt.	D, 6th Iowa Inf.	325		1912 Aug 27	IA, 39th, 1913
Hutchinson, Jas. J.		K, 199th Penn.	134		1897 Nov 10	KS, 17th, 1898
Hutchinson, Joseph		B, 12th Wis. Inf. (died of old age)	265	80	1926 Feb 22	NE, 50th, 1926
Hutchinson, Joseph S.		I, 126th Ill.	428		1913 Aug 13	KS, 33rd, 1914
Hutchinson, M.S.		G, 130th Ill.	25		1936	KS, 56th, 1937
Hutchinson, N.R.	Corp.	H, 10th Iowa Inf.	156		1912 Dec 31	IA, 39th, 1913
Hutchinson, T.W.		D, Penn.	18		1926 Apr 29	KS, 46th, 1927
Hutchinson, W.B.		A, 17th Kans. Inf. (died at Wichita, Kans.; buried at Maple Grove)	25		1894 Jun 19	KS, 14th, 1895
Hutchinson, Wm.			236		1914 Oct 31	IA, 41st, 1915
Hutchison, E.W.		K, 2nd Neb. Cav. (died of pneumonia at Soldiers & Sailors Home, Milford)		77	1907 Apr 17	NE, 31st, 1907
Hutchison, J. Alonzo		D, 134th Ind.	98		1936 Jun 11	NE, 61st, 1937
Hutchison, J.G.	Capt.	I, 28th Penn. Inf.	69		1910 Apr 9	IA, 37th, 1911
Hutchison, J.G.		B, 1st Mo. State Militia	57		1919 Jan 10	KS, 39th, 1920
Hutigan, Emory	Pvt.	Mo. Company	49		1924 Jun 21	IA, 51st, 1925
Hutinger, Peter	Corp.	I, 126th Ohio Inf.	338		1904 Oct 18	IA, 31st, 1905
Hutsell, H.S.		A, 75th Ind. Inf.	85		1914 Mar 11	KS, 34th, 1915
Hutson, John		K, 13th Iowa (former member of Nebraska Dept.; location: Long Pine)	124		1937 Feb 27	NE, 62nd, 1938
Hutton, C.J.		15th Mo. Cav.	74		1930	KS, 50th, 1931
Hutton, David L.		E, 9th Kans. Cav.	51		1910 Dec 2	KS, 30th, 1911
Hutton, Emmett R.		I, 94th Ill.	17		1924 Apr 11	KS, 44th, 1925
Hutton, George	Pvt.	A, 14th Mich. Inf.	78	91	1931 Oct 16	IA, 58th, 1932
Hutton, H.W.		G, 3rd Iowa Cav. (died of pneumonia)	95	65	1901 Jan	NE, 26th, 1902
Hutton, J.C.	Pvt.	C, 12th Penn. Inf.	7		1920 Feb 28	IA, 47th, 1921
Hutton, J.P.	Pvt.	E, 3rd Col. Cav.	59		1928 Apr 25	IA, 55th, 1929
Hutton, Wm. L.		E, 25th Ohio Inf.	172		1929 Jan 15	KS, 49th, 1930
Huxford, George	Pvt.	K, 16th Iowa Inf.	235		1926 Dec 7	IA, 53rd, 1927
Huyck, Isaac		A, — U.S. Inf.	95	79	1920	NE, 45th, 1921
Huyck, John H.	Pvt. Pvt.	E, 134th Ill. Inf. (at large) G, 49th Wis. Inf.	159	95	1942 Feb 10	IA, 68th, 1942
Huycle, S.M.	Capt.	I, 27th U.S.C. Inf. I, 14th Ohio Inf.	149	79	1897 Apr 5	IA, 24th, 1898
Hyatt, A.H.			47		2nd quarter 1883	IA, 10th, 1884
Hyatt, A.H.	Pvt.	B, 40th Iowa Inf.	16		1915 Apr 5	IA, 42nd, 1916
Hyatt, A. Jackson		A, 11th Iowa Inf.	5		1940 Jan 13	NE, 65th, 1941
Hyatt, D.K.		F, 1st M.R.N.Y.[N.Y. Mtd. Rifles]	250		1922 Mar 5	KS, 42nd, 1923
Hyatt, J.H.		I, 6th Iowa Inf.	93		1st quarter 1884	IA, 10th, 1884
Hyatt, J.W.		H, 31st Wis. (died of perilants)	318	68	1913 Aug 3	NE, 38th, 1914
Hyde, Aaron	Pvt.	A, 16th U.S. Inf.	146	56	1896 May 25	IA, 23rd, 1897
Hyde, Addison	Pvt.	D, 16th Iowa Inf.	146	70	1894 Jan 18	IA, 21st, 1895

*See Appendix A, B or C for roster of post names and locations.
†See Introduction for note regarding recording of death date.

Name	Rank	Company, Regiment or Ship	Post*	Age	Death Date†	Journal
Hyde, Addison	Pvt.	D, 16th Iowa Inf.	146	71	1894 Jan 8	IA, 20th, 1894
Hyde, C.E.		D, 1st N.Y. Dragoons	7		1929 Jan 23	NE, 54th, 1930
Hyde, Edwin	Pvt.	K, 1st Iowa Cav.	168		1907 Dec 13	IA, 34th, 1908
Hyde, Geo. N.		K, 1st Wis. Inf. (died of paralysis)	354	69	1912 Jul 9	NE, 37th, 1913
Hyde, George	Commissary Sergt.	F, 8th Ill. Cav.	12		1890	KS, 10th, 1891
Hyde, H.A.		died of kidney disease	112	68	1902 Oct	NE, 27th, 1903
Hyde, James W.		C, 128th Ind.	25		1935 Jul	NE, 60th, 1936
Hyde, John H.		H, 103rd Ill.	167		1896 Feb 24	KS, 16th, 1897
Hyde, N.M.		H, 3rd Mo.	226		1925 Jul 16	KS, 45th, 1926
Hyde, Reuben C.	Pvt.	E, 21st Ohio Inf.	54		1904 Sep 18	IA, 31st, 1905
Hyde, S.P.	Pvt.	F, 4th N.Y. Hvy. Art.	101		1899 Dec 24	IA, 26th, 1900
Hyde, T.B.	Pvt.	A, 129th Ohio Inf.	466		1919 Aug 29	IA, 46th, 1920
Hyde, Thos. W.	Chaplain	E, 30th Iowa Inf.	12		1920 Mar 3	IA, 47th, 1921
Hyde, W.W.	Pvt.	F, 4th N.Y. Art.	101		1920 Aug 7	IA, 47th, 1921
Hyden, Edward	Pvt.	G, 132nd Ind. Inf.	55		1925 Oct	IA, 52nd, 1926
Hyden, J. Albert, Rev.		appointed hospital chaplain, 1863-65, Knoxville, Tenn., by A. Lincoln	[18?]		1909	KS, 29th, 1910
Hydinger, William		5th West Va. Cav.		96	1938 Jun 24	IA, 64th, 1938
Hydom, J.H.		F, 11th Kans.	180		1896 Jan 31	KS, 16th, 1897
Hyett, John		B, 9th Iowa Cav.	262	72	1904 Jan 1	NE, 29th, 1905
Hysham, S.H.	Sergt.	D, 21st Iowa Inf.	101		1910 Dec 10	IA, 37th, 1911
Hysie, David	Pvt.	K, 142nd Penn.	4		1922 Jan 25	IA, 49th, 1923
Hyter, G.W.	Pvt.	D, 184th Ohio Inf.	394		1909 Aug	IA, 36th, 1910
Hyzer, W.W.	Capt.	3rd Mich. Art.	52		1917 Jun	IA, 44th, 1918
Ichl, John	Pvt.	A, 31st Iowa Inf.	206		1919 Apr 18	IA, 46th, 1920
Iden, John T.		H, 7th Ill. Inf.	134		1912 Dec 2	KS, 32nd, 1913
Ihde, Henry	Pvt.	K, 29th Wis. Inf.	81		1911 Jan 25	IA, 38th, 1912
Ihringer, August		K, 20th N.Y. Inf.	25	89	1917 Jul 30	NE, 42nd, 1918
Ijams, Isaac			17		1911 Sep 6	KS, 31st, 1912
Ijams, W.H.			173		1914 Oct	IA, 41st, 1915
Ilgin, David M.		G, 93rd Ill. (died of catarrh of stomach)	54	81	1918 Apr 27	NE, 43rd, 1919
Iliff, J.N.	Pvt.	E, 9th Iowa Cav.	452		1918 Oct 10	IA, 45th, 1919
Iliff, T.C.		A, 62nd Ohio Vol. Inf.	63		1909 Dec 28	KS, 29th, 1910
Iliff, W.I.		K, 28th Iowa Inf.	130		1908 May 7	KS, 28th, 1909
Imel, John	Pvt.	E, 27th Wis. Inf.	3		1912 Dec 27	IA, 39th, 1913
Imhof, A.	Pvt.	F, 5th Iowa Cav.	70	52	1891 Jan 5	IA, 17th, 1891
Immel, Peter		G, 127th Ind.	353		1918 Jul 29	KS, 38th, 1919
Immerman, John	Pvt.	C, 3rd Ill. Cav.	116	84	1932 Jun 10	IA, 59th, 1933
Inbody, Louis		B, 9th Iowa Cav. (died of hardening of arteries)	41	75	1921 Feb 12	NE, 46th, 1922
Inby, S.W.		C, 54th Ind.	4		1920 Dec 23	KS, 40th, 1921
Inches, David		C, 44th Iowa Inf.	14		1914 Nov 10	KS, 34th, 1915
Incho, A.J.		B, 100th Ohio Inf.	4		1934	KS, 54th, 1935
Infield, Henry			152		1914 Nov 30	IA, 41st, 1915
Ingald, L.B.	Lieut.	F, 146th Ind. Inf.	159		1908 May 15	IA, 35th, 1909
Ingalls, E.B.	Pvt.	E, 65th Ill. Inf.	56		1912	IA, 39th, 1913
Ingalls, J.B., Dr.		D, 54th Ill.	8		1913 Jul 27	KS, 33rd, 1914
Ingalls, John J.	Judge Advocate General	staff of General Deitzler	93		1900 Aug 16	KS, 20th, 1901
Ingalls, R.W.	Pvt.	A, 40th Ohio (died of disability)	102	51	1887 Jul	NE, 12th, 1888
Ingel, Henry S.		C, 123rd Ill.	23		1922 Feb 16	KS, 42nd, 1923
Ingels, James W.		F, 2nd Ohio Art.	238		1919 Jun 3	KS, 39th, 1920
Inger, J.D.	Pvt.	B, 1st Iowa Cav.	267		1912 Mar 12	IA, 39th, 1913
Ingersoll, A.M.			4		1914 Oct 18	IA, 41st, 1915
Ingersoll, David		B, 102nd Ill. Inf. (died at Blue Rapids; buried at Cottage Hill Cemetery)	328		1894 Jul 15	KS, 14th, 1895
Ingersoll, E.M.	Pvt.	C, 45th Iowa Inf.	2		1922 Oct 24	IA, 49th, 1923
Ingersoll, G.W.	Pvt.	E, 17th Ohio Inf.	343		1915 May 24	IA, 42nd, 1916
Ingersoll, Melvin		E, 3rd Mo. Inf.	52		1912 Feb 18	KS, 32nd, 1913
Ingersoll, O.		A, 11th Ill.	158		1923 Feb 23	KS, 43rd, 1924
Ingerson, Harvey	Pvt.	I, 14th N.Y. Hvy. Art.	22		1904 Feb 7	IA, 31st, 1905
Ingham, John E.		F, 93rd Ill.	318	71	1911 Nov 30	NE, 36th, 1912

*See Appendix A, B or C for roster of post names and locations.
†See Introduction for note regarding recording of death date.
276

Name	Rank	Company, Regiment or Ship	Post*	Age	Death Date†	Journal
Ingham, John E.		93rd Ill. Inf.	25		1911 Nov 30	NE, 36th, 1912
Ingham, S.A.		G, Wis. Battery	44		1919 Dec 3	KS, 39th, 1920
Ingleman, A.P.		E, 39th Ill.	248		1893 Jan 27	KS, 13th, 1894
Ingman, J.T.	Pvt.	H, 42nd Ohio Inf.	271		1913 Sep 25	IA, 40th, 1914
Ingmire, Elias M.		H, 63rd Ohio Inf.	90		1918 May 16	KS, 38th, 1919
Ingraham, James	Pvt.	F, 1st Minn. Inf.	180	63	1897 Jun 2	IA, 24th, 1898
Ingraham, W.H.		H, 32nd Iowa (died of consumption)	318		1908 Jun 24	NE, 33rd, 1909
Ingram, A.		H, 11th Ill. Cav.	284		1918 Jun 22	IA, 45th, 1919
Ingram, Elias M.		H, 63rd Ohio	90		1918 May 16	KS, 40th, 1921
Ingram, Geo.	Pvt.	G, 79th Ill. Inf.	186		1913 Jul 9	IA, 40th, 1914
Ingram, James		F, 159th Ohio	5		1924 Nov 17	KS, 44th, 1925
Ingram, Jonathan B.		H, 37th Ill. Inf. (former member)	13		1940 Aug 4	NE, 65th, 1941
Ingram, Y.S.		D, 6th Ind. Cav.	244		1929 Jan 17	KS, 49th, 1930
Ingrim, Joseph Thos.	Pvt.	2nd Battery, Iowa Art. (at large)	245, 20	95	1940 May 8	IA, 66th, 1940
Inlay, Edgar	Corp.	C, 175th N.Y. Inf.	519		1910 Apr 20	IA, 37th, 1911
Inman, Charles			235		1908 Sep 18	IA, 35th, 1909
Inman, David M., see Tuman, David M.						
Inman, John C., see Innman, John C.						
Inman, John R.		B, 5th Mich. Inf. (died at Phillips County; buried at Long Island Cemetery)	181		1894 Dec 2	KS, 14th, 1895
Inman, Ovid	Pvt.	A, 28th Iowa Inf.	98		1912 Jan 15	IA, 39th, 1913
Innes, Alexander		F, 40th U.S.C.T.	25		1885	KS, 5th, 1886
Inness, William		15th U.S. Cav.	25		1911 Feb 4	KS, 31st, 1912
Innis, Thomas	Pvt.	F, 11th Ind. Cav.	108		1931 Mar 24	IA, 58th, 1932
Innman, John C.			371		1915	IA, 42nd, 1916
Inskeep, Oliver W.		K, 132nd Ohio	497		1911 Nov 17	KS, 31st, 1912
Ioerson, Albert	Pvt.	K, 12th Wis. Inf.	101		1906 Jun 14	IA, 33rd, 1907
Ira, J.B.		H, 73rd Ohio	20		1922 May 1	KS, 42nd, 1923
Irby, Thomas K.	Pvt.	F, 15th Iowa Inf.	15	47	1886 Nov 17	IA, 13th, 1887
Irelan, James	Pvt.	H, 6th Ky. Cav. (cause of death: heart)	75	47	1887 Jan	NE, 12th, 1888
Ireland, H.C.	Pvt.	G, 117th N.Y. Inf.	3		1919 Jul 25	IA, 46th, 1920
Ireland, J.W.		I, 28th Iowa	25		1926 Feb 28	NE, 51st, 1927
Ireland, James		K, 11th Ill. Inf. (died of hardening of arteries)	77	77	1913 Aug 7	NE, 38th, 1914
Ireland, John	Pvt.	E, 67th Ind.	52		1922 Jul 9	IA, 49th, 1923
Ireland, John		A, 118th Ind. Inf.	57		1900 Feb 3	KS, 20th, 1901
Ireland, Joseph	Pvt.	D, 2nd Mo. State Militia Cav.	515		1901 Apr 30	IA, 28th, 1902
Ireland, Peter		F, 154th Ill. Inf.	65		1899 Feb 12	KS, 19th, 1900
Ireland, W.T.		H, 5th Iowa Cav. (died of pneumonia)	55	80	1911 Jan 20	NE, 36th, 1912
Iretoon, William		11th Mich.	14		1926 Feb 11	KS, 46th, 1927
Irish, Calvin		dropped dead	354		1925	NE, 50th, 1926
Irish, Chauncey		Bat. E, 7th Penn.	1		1914 Jun 24	KS, 34th, 1915
Irish, John		A, 2nd U.S. Art. (born in New York; died of alcoholism at Soldiers & Sailors Home Hospital, Burkett; buried at Home Cemetery)		72	1907 Jan 8	NE, 31st, 1907
Irons, Leander		C, 76th Ill. Inf.	110		1906 Oct	NE, 31st, 1907
Irvin, James	Pvt.	F, 23rd Iowa Inf.	56		1929 Dec	IA, 56th, 1930
Irvin, Jas. A.	Pvt.	C, 9th Iowa Inf.	40		1916 Jan 2	IA, 43rd, 1917
Irvin, Wm.	Pvt.	D, 18th Iowa Inf.	18		1918 Mar	IA, 45th, 1919
Irvin, Wm.			25		1926 Apr 14	NE, 51st, 1927
Irvine, I.	Pvt.	A, 130th Penn. Inf.	22		1901 Feb	IA, 28th, 1902
Irwin, B.			63		1907 May	NE, 32nd, 1908
Irwin, David	Pvt.	G, 15th Ohio Inf.	253		1904 Sep	IA, 31st, 1905
Irwin, H.			209		1901-1902	IA, 28th, 1902
Irwin, J.C.	Capt.	A, 18th Ohio	1		1888	KS, 8th, 1889
Irwin, J.M.		A, 22nd Ill.	65		1926 Nov 13	KS, 46th, 1927
Irwin, J.N.	Sergt.	C, 45th Iowa Inf.	2		1905 Dec 22	IA, 32nd, 1906
Irwin, Jas.	Pvt.	K, 7th Iowa Cav.	22		1910 Apr 2	IA, 37th, 1911
Irwin, John	Pvt.	M, 15th Penn. Cav.	1		1933	IA, 60th, 1934
Irwin, Lott. W.	Pvt.	K, 15th Ill. Inf.	194		1925 Apr 19	IA, 52nd, 1926

*See Appendix A, B or C for roster of post names and locations.
†See Introduction for note regarding recording of death date.

Name	Rank	Company, Regiment or Ship	Post*	Age	Death Date†	Journal
Irwin, M.E.	Pvt.	M, 11th N.Y. Cav.	78		1908 Jan 5	IA, 35th, 1909
Irwin, Orville C.		E, 12th Kans.	12		1898 Nov 12	KS, 18th, 1899
Irwin, S.T.	Pvt.	H, 45th Iowa Inf.	153	86	1933 Feb 7	IA, 60th, 1934
Irwin, Steward		K, 1st Iowa	92		1909 Jan	KS, 29th, 1910
Irwin, W.H.	Musician	48th Ill.	12		1915 May 15	KS, 35th, 1916
Irwin, Wm.	Pvt.	H, 2nd Bat. Penn. Vols.	207		1899	NE, 24th, 1900
Isbel, N.H.			45		1923	NE, 48th, 1924
Isbell, J.R.	Pvt.	B, 12th Ind. Cav.	386	66	1892 Nov 2	IA, 19th, 1893
Isely, C.H.		F, 2nd Kans. Cav.	25		1919 Aug 8	KS, 39th, 1920
Iseminger, W.G.	Pvt.	I, 73rd Ind. Inf.	17		1927 May 16	IA, 54th, 1928
Isenberg, Samuel D.		B, 7th Ill. Inf. (died of stricture of oesophagus)	270		1892 Apr 23	KS, 12th, 1893
Isenhart, Francis M.	Pvt.	K, 75th Ill. Inf.	394	97	1938 Dec 17	IA, 65th, 1939
Isenhour, D.		A, 123rd Ill.	311		1919 Dec 14	KS, 39th, 1920
Isham, I.O.	Pvt.	D, 46th Wis. Inf.	365		1906 Aug 6	IA, 33rd, 1907
Isham, W.M.	Pvt.	G, U.S. Sharpshooters	12		1917 Jan 13	IA, 44th, 1918
Isiomon, B.F.		15th Iowa (cause of death: stomach & heart)	44	59	1900 Sep	NE, 25th, 1901
Isley, H.H.		F, 89th Iowa	256		1938 Apr 20	KS, 57th, 1938
Ismear, Edward	Pvt.	D, —	68		1899	IA, 26th, 1900
Israel, Charles J.		C, 1st Mo. Lt. Art.	1		1933 Dec 19	NE, 58th, 1934
Israel, Isaac		E, 12th West Va.	244		1929 Feb 8	KS, 49th, 1930
Israel, Martin		134th Ind. Inf.	69		1912 May 4	IA, 39th, 1913
Israel, W.T.	Pvt.	E, 2nd Iowa Inf.	18		1917 Jan 9	IA, 44th, 1918
Ittner, John		B, Fremont's Body Guard	32		1936 Mar 6	NE, 61st, 1937
Iuscho, Edwin		G, 128th Ohio	14		1904 Jun 19	KS, 24th, 1905
Ivers, Joseph	Pvt.	K, 10th Iowa Inf.	26, 12	92	1937 Sep 7	IA, 66th, 1940
Iverson, Albert, see Ioerson, Albert						
Ives, Charles			103		1922 Dec 10	KS, 42nd, 1923
Ives, Charles P.	Capt.	115th U.S. Col. Inf. H, 1st N.Y.	40		1913 Oct 29	KS, 33rd, 1914
Ives, Chas. W.		G, 95th Ill.	36		1927 Mar 25	KS, 47th, 1928
Ives, I.C.		K, 19th Iowa	1		1925	KS, 45th, 1926
Ives, Joseph	Pvt.	K, 10th Iowa Inf.	12		1927 Sep 7	IA, 54th, 1928
Ives, Oliver P.	Pvt.	E, 122nd N.Y. Inf.	168	71	1890 Oct 3	IA, 17th, 1891
Ives, William H.			108		1899	IA, 26th, 1900
Ives, Wm. H.	Pvt.	K, 8th Iowa Vol. Cav.	110	55	1899 Aug 10	IA, 26th, 1900
Ivey, J.A.		B, 43rd Wis.	37		1921 Jul	KS, 41st, 1922
Iwig, Samuel		B, 108th Ill.	71		1931 Mar 17	KS, 51st, 1932
Iwig, Samuel		B, 108th Ill.	71		1931 Mar 17	KS, 52nd, 1933
Izzard, Isaac		D, 12th Mo. Cav.	9		1886	KS, 6th, 1887
Jaberg, N.H.	Pvt.	Independent Inf. (at large)	52	90	1935 Mar 15	IA, 65th, 1939
Jack, D.L.		E, 92nd Ohio	68		1929 Feb 25	KS, 49th, 1930
Jack, David		L, 1st Iowa Cav.	302		1934 Jan 20	NE, 59th, 1935
Jack, Thomas		C, 142nd N.Y. Inf.	196		1912 Nov 20	IA, 39th, 1913
Jack, Wm.			440		1910 Jul 6	IA, 37th, 1911
Jackman, Moses A.	Pvt.	A, 12th Ill.	12		1907 Jan 1	IA, 34th, 1908
Jackman, R.C.		G, 82nd Ind.	25		1910 Oct 7	KS, 30th, 1911
Jackman, Wm.		K, 12th Kans.	32		1922 Jul 13	KS, 42nd, 1923
Jacks, George S.	Pvt.	H, 33rd Ill. Inf.	66		1929 Nov 29	IA, 56th, 1930
Jackson, A.B.		I, 50th Penn. Inf.	142		1901 Nov 15	KS, 21st, 1902
Jackson, A.C.		C, 54th Ind.	176		1919 Aug 15	KS, 39th, 1920
Jackson, A.C.		D, 8th Ohio	47		1930	KS, 52nd, 1933
Jackson, A.C.		D, 8th Ohio	47		1930	KS, 51st, 1932
Jackson, A.M.		K, 78th Ohio Inf.	158		1912 Apr 26	KS, 32nd, 1913
Jackson, A.P.	Sergt.	C, 30th Iowa Inf.	157	40	1885 Jul 11	IA, 12th, 1886
Jackson, Andrew	Pvt.	D, 64th Ind. Inf.	204		1917 Dec 5	IA, 44th, 1918
Jackson, Andrew		A, 48th U.S.C. (died at Kansas City)	10		1895 Dec	KS, 15th, 1896
Jackson, Andrew		C, 8th Ind.	232		1918 Dec 31	KS, 38th, 1919
Jackson, Andrew		C, 7th Iowa Cav. (died of softening of tissues)	147	60	1906 Aug 17	NE, 31st, 1907
Jackson, B.	Pvt.		18		1920 May 2	IA, 47th, 1921

*See Appendix A, B or C for roster of post names and locations.
†See Introduction for note regarding recording of death date.

Name	Rank	Company, Regiment or Ship	Post*	Age	Death Date†	Journal
Jackson, Dan'l	Pvt.	I, 38th Wis. Inf.	416		1916 Oct 8	IA, 43rd, 1917
Jackson, E.C.		K, 12th Vt. Inf.	52		1928 Feb 1	NE, 53rd, 1929
Jackson, E.G.		3rd Battery, Wis. Lt. Art.	380		1900 Dec 12	KS, 20th, 1901
Jackson, E.G.		K, 14th U.S. Res.	25		1929 Apr 7	KS, 49th, 1930
Jackson, Edwin		H, 2nd Ill. Cav.	110		1906 Feb 13	NE, 31st, 1907
Jackson, Fred		A, 116th N.Y.	87		1930 Aug 28	KS, 50th, 1931
Jackson, G.R.	Sergt.	C, 175th Ohio Inf.	166	43	1894 Jan 16	IA, 20th, 1894
Jackson, G.W.	Lieut.	4th Iowa Battery	23		1910 May 31	IA, 37th, 1911
Jackson, G.W.		9th Ind. Cav.	85		1912 Feb 8	KS, 32nd, 1913
Jackson, Geo. W.			64		1883	KS, 3rd, 1884
Jackson, George M.		D, 2nd Mass.	64		1885	KS, 5th, 1886
Jackson, George W.	Pvt.	B, 3rd Ill. Cav.	254		1901 Jun 28	IA, 28th, 1902
Jackson, H.E.		A, 12th Iowa	1		1928 Nov 23	KS, 48th, 1929
Jackson, H.L.	Pvt.	5th Ind. Cav.	23		1918 Feb 28	IA, 45th, 1919
Jackson, J.A.	Wagoner	D, 12th Wis. Inf.	124		1911 Feb 11	IA, 38th, 1912
Jackson, J.E.B.			59		1930 Jan 24	KS, 50th, 1931
Jackson, J.F.		C, 27th Iowa Inf.	113		3rd quarter 1883	IA, 10th, 1884
Jackson, J.J.	Pvt.	G, 113th Ill. Inf.	465		1915 May 10	IA, 42nd, 1916
Jackson, J.M.	Pvt.	G, 14th Ill. Inf.	5		1910 May 18	IA, 37th, 1911
Jackson, J.W.	Pvt.	96th Ohio	109		1907 Jul 24	IA, 34th, 1908
Jackson, J.W.		F, 43rd Ind.	11		1889	KS, 9th, 1890
Jackson, J.W.		G, 124th Ill.	35		1926 Oct 25	NE, 51st, 1927
Jackson, James	Pvt.	K, 21st Iowa Inf.	124		1925 Jul 15	IA, 52nd, 1926
Jackson, James		H, 28th Iowa	77	79	1919 Dec 17	NE, 44th, 1920
Jackson, James H.	Pvt.	H, 25th Wis. Inf. (at large)	78	96	1940 Oct 27	IA, 67th, 1941
Jackson, Jefferson		died of asthma	147		1891 Jan 11	KS, 11th, 1892
Jackson, Jesse	Pvt.	F, 11th Iowa	7		1922 Apr 24	IA, 49th, 1923
Jackson, John C.		A, 121st Ohio	176		1906 Mar 3	KS, 26th, 1907
Jackson, John William	Sergt. Sergt. Major	E, 89th Ind. Inf. 26th Ind. Inf. (former member)	20	99	1942 Jan 3	IA, 68th, 1942
Jackson, Joseph		D, 124th Ill. Inf.	4		1900 Aug 14	KS, 20th, 1901
Jackson, Joseph		E, 89th Ind.	43		1913 Jul 30	KS, 33rd, 1914
Jackson, Lewis		G, 79th Kans.	321		1904 Oct 3	KS, 24th, 1905
Jackson, M.E.	Corp.	E, 36th Iowa Inf.	497		1915 Mar 19	IA, 42nd, 1916
Jackson, M.V.			50		1908 Aug	KS, 28th, 1909
Jackson, Milton	Pvt.	C, 26th Iowa Vol. Inf.	88	56	1900 Mar 13	IA, 26th, 1900
Jackson, Nelson	Pvt.	E, 128th Ind. Inf.	55		1933 Jun 2	IA, 60th, 1934
Jackson, Peter	Pvt.	A, 60th U.S. Colored	413	42	1890 Dec	IA, 17th, 1891
Jackson, Preston	Corp.	D, 50th U.S.C. Inf.	7		1913 Feb 4	IA, 40th, 1914
Jackson, R.S.	Pvt.	G, 140th Penn. Inf.	343		1913 Dec 5	IA, 40th, 1914
Jackson, Ralph	Pvt.	F, 40th Mo. Inf.	78		1905 Jun 12	IA, 32nd, 1906
Jackson, Rich		I, 5th U.S. Col. Hvy. Art.	18		1915 Jul 24	KS, 35th, 1916
Jackson, Richard		E, 36th Iowa	25		1910 Jul 25	KS, 30th, 1911
Jackson, Romanza A.	Pvt.	I, 11th N.Y. Cav.		96	1939 Jan 30	IA, 65th, 1939
Jackson, Rufus		L, 14th U.S. Art.	25		1915 Sep 2	NE, 40th, 1916
Jackson, S.C.		G, 1st Tenn. Inf.	328		1901 Dec 3	KS, 21st, 1902
Jackson, Thomas Jefferson	Col.	11th U.S. Colored (colored troops, Ft. Pillow massacre, all killed but 2; see also Appendix D)	36		1905 Nov 1	KS, 25th, 1906
Jackson, Thos. A.	Pvt.	B, 18th Wis. Inf.	68		1908 Feb 14	IA, 35th, 1909
Jackson, Thos. B.		C, 184th Penn. Inf.	89		1918 Dec 12	KS, 38th, 1919
Jackson, Tom					1905 Oct 31	KS, 25th, 1906
Jackson, W.N.		35th N.Y. Inf.	113		1903	NE, 28th, 1904
Jackson, W.W.	Pvt.	E, 134th N.Y. Inf.	58		1908 Feb 12	IA, 35th, 1909
Jackson, Wm.		E, 8th Ind. Cav.	4		1922 Sep	KS, 42nd, 1923
Jackson, Z.E.		K, 3rd Iowa Inf.	25		1911 Jun 28	NE, 36th, 1912
Jacob, Frederick	Pvt.	B, 31st Iowa Inf.	68		1910 Nov 25	IA, 37th, 1911
Jacobs, A.G.		B, 6th Ohio Cav.	453		1922 Sep 9	KS, 42nd, 1923
Jacobs, Adelbert	Pvt.	F, 75th Ill. Vol. Inf.	222		1899 Feb 15	IA, 25th, 1899
Jacobs, B.F.		F, 14th Iowa	260		1914 May 10	KS, 34th, 1915
Jacobs, Dan		H, 25th Ill.	10	82	1920 Dec 27	NE, 45th, 1921
Jacobs, Henry T.		G, 91st N.Y. Inf.	380		1902[1908?] Jan 22	KS, 28th, 1909

See Appendix A, B or C for roster of post names and locations.
†See Introduction for note regarding recording of death date.*

Name	Rank	Company, Regiment or Ship	Post*	Age	Death Date†	Journal
Jacobs, J.L.		A, 12th Ill.	289		1898 Jun 22	KS, 18th, 1899
Jacobs, J.W.		A, 16th Kans.	54		1920 Mar 10	KS, 40th, 1921
Jacobs, Jeremiah	Pvt.		2		1924 Dec	IA, 51st, 1925
Jacobs, John H.K.	Pvt.	K, 1st Penn. Reserves (died of bronchial disease)	7	51	1891 Feb 11	NE, 16th, 1892
Jacobs, L.D.		A, 26th Penn.	55		1904 Apr 28	KS, 24th, 1905
Jacobs, Noah	Pvt.	F, 8th Iowa Inf.	167		1925 Jun 20	IA, 52nd, 1926
Jacobs, Peter	Pvt.	E, 1st Wis. Inf.	8		1901 Nov 29	IA, 28th, 1902
Jacobs, W.C.	Drummer	E, 8th Iowa Inf.	49		1923 Dec 28	IA, 50th, 1924
Jacobs, Wm.		C, 2nd Neb. Cav.	5		1920 Jul 16	KS, 40th, 1921
Jacobson, Christian	Pvt.	D, Wis. Inf.	101		1926 Dec 25	IA, 53rd, 1927
Jacobson, Hans	Pvt.	C, 15th Wis. Inf.	216		1903 Jul 18	IA, 30th, 1904
Jacoby, J.	Pvt.	I, 25th Iowa Inf.	5		1904 Apr 7	IA, 31st, 1905
Jacoby, Jas. A.			29		1912 Nov 16	IA, 39th, 1913
Jacoby, John		G, 153rd Penn.	63		1911 Aug 3	KS, 31st, 1912
Jacoby, S.R.		G, 4th Iowa Inf. (died of Bright's disease)	38	80	1903 Jul 19	NE, 28th, 1904
Jacoby, Wm.		Navy	52		1922 Jun 21	IA, 49th, 1923
Jacquemin, Geo.		K, 11th Kans.	155		1923 May 12	KS, 43rd, 1924
Jaeger, Nick	1st Sergt.	B, 16th Iowa Inf.	73	52	1897 Mar 23	IA, 24th, 1898
Jager, John		19th Iowa Inf.	138		1916 May 17	IA, 43rd, 1917
Jaggard, Henry C.		A, 2nd Ill. Lt. Art.	7		1912 Oct 30	KS, 32nd, 1913
Jaggard, Thomas		A, 2nd Ill. Lt. Art.	55		1914 Mar 24	KS, 34th, 1915
Jahnel, Frank			77		1927 May	IA, 54th, 1928
Jaiser, Jacob	Pvt.	B, 10th Kans. (not member of the post, but buried by it)	[64?]		1885	KS, 5th, 1886
Jakway, G.H.		C, 27th Iowa Inf. (at large)			1936 Apr 26	IA, 63rd, 1937
Jakway, G.H.		C, 27th Iowa Inf. (at large)			1936 Apr 26	IA, 62nd, 1936
James, Albert		C, 12th Penn.	321		1905 Dec 1	KS, 25th, 1906
James, C.H.	Pvt.		371		1902 Nov 11	IA, 29th, 1903
James, Chas. S.	Pvt.	I, 27th Mich. Inf. (died of consumption)	81	73	1888 Oct 20	NE, 13th, 1889
James, Clem	Pvt.	33rd Ohio Inf.	231		1912 Feb 3	IA, 39th, 1913
James, Dicus	Pvt.	E, 28th Iowa Vol. Inf.	8		1924 Oct 14	IA, 51st, 1925
James, E.W.	Pvt.	H, 63rd Ohio	86		1921 Aug 8	IA, 48th, 1922
James, Enoch		D, 3rd Wis. Cav. (died at Osage City)	11		1895 Aug	KS, 15th, 1896
James, Geo. W.		B, 14th Iowa Inf.	225		1916 Dec 18	KS, 36th, 1917
James, Geo. W.		K, 60th Mo. State Militia	73		1898 Aug 6	KS, 18th, 1899
James, George W.		K, 24th Iowa Inf.	130	94	1937 Oct 5	IA, 64th, 1938
James, George W.		B, 93rd Ill.	293		1923 Feb 1	KS, 43rd, 1924
James, Horace		I, 32nd N.Y.	260		1928 Mar 2	KS, 49th, 1930
James, J.C.		A, 74th Iowa Inf.	231		1924 Mar 18	IA, 51st, 1925
James, J.N.	Pvt.	E, 193rd Ohio Inf.	440		1918 Jun 9	IA, 45th, 1919
James, J.P.	1st Lieut.	E, 4th Hvy. Art.	154		1903 Aug 20	IA, 30th, 1904
James, J.T.		C, 4th Va. U.S. Art.	370		1906 Nov 27	KS, 26th, 1907
James, James		K, 23rd Ohio Inf.	66		1902 Dec 20	KS, 22nd, 1903
James, Jesse	Pvt.	I, 2nd Iowa Cav.	110	43	1886 May 12	IA, 13th, 1887
James, Jno. A.	Pvt.	I, 140th Ill. Inf.	452		1927 May 13	IA, 54th, 1928
James, John	Pvt.	G, 21st Mo.	58		1924 Jan 2	IA, 51st, 1925
James, John			493		1924	KS, 44th, 1925
James, John M.	Pvt.	K, 2nd Ohio Vol. Hvy. Art.	515		1904 Nov 28	IA, 31st, 1905
James, Joseph		I, 3rd Iowa Cav.	440		1913 Nov 27	IA, 40th, 1914
James, Lott	Pvt.	E, 45th Penn. Inf.	52	50	1887 Sep 29	IA, 14th, 1888
James, Lyman H.		G, 15th Iowa Inf. (died of stomach trouble)	149	75	1915 Nov 11	NE, 40th, 1916
James, M.W.		D, 7th Ill. Cav.	44		1926	NE, 51st, 1927
James, Orville	Pvt.	A, 12th Ohio Cav.	80		1929 Sep 18	IA, 56th, 1930
James, P.H.		I, 26th Ohio Inf. (died of heart trouble)	35	71	1913 Dec 17	NE, 38th, 1914
James, R.C.	Pvt.	I, 47th Ill. Inf.	472		1919	IA, 46th, 1920
James, S.A.		A, 78th Ill.	97		1897 Jul 15	KS, 17th, 1898
James, S.C.	Corp.	B, 1st Berdan Sharpshooters	122		1907 May 11	IA, 34th, 1908
James, S.P.	Pvt.	D, 6th Iowa Inf.	14		1911 Sep 5	IA, 38th, 1912
James, Samuel		I, 4th Penn. Cav. (died of cancer throat)	77		1910 Oct 24	NE, 35th, 1911
James, Stephen	Pvt.	I, 15th Iowa Inf.	55		1910 Mar 9	IA, 37th, 1911

*See Appendix A, B or C for roster of post names and locations.
†See Introduction for note regarding recording of death date.

Name	Rank	Company, Regiment or Ship	Post*	Age	Death Date†	Journal
James, Thomas M.	1st Lieut. 2nd Lieut.	D, 1st Ohio Hvy. Art. B, 119th Ohio	250		1918 Dec 7	KS, 38th, 1919
James, W.H.	Pvt.	H, 9th Iowa Inf.	234	64	1894 Jul 17	IA, 21st, 1895
James, Walter		B, 38th Iowa Inf.	130	95	1935 Apr 19	IA, 62nd, 1936
James, William	Pvt.	I, 13th Wis. Inf.	132		1897 Mar 9	IA, 24th, 1898
James, Wm. H.	Pvt.	A, 11th U.S. Inf.	5		1901 Jun 30	IA, 28th, 1902
Jameson, B.W.		E, 83rd Ind.	206		1927 Feb	NE, 51st, 1927
Jameson, Jacob		K, 47th Ill. Inf. (died at Cherokee; buried at Cherokee Cemetery)	56		1894 Mar	KS, 14th, 1895
Jameson, John			177		1st quarter 1886	IA, 12th, 1886
Jameson, John H.		I, 19th Iowa	65		1913 Dec 19	KS, 33rd, 1914
Jameson, R.M.	Pvt.	I, 31st Iowa Inf.	74		1923 Sep 10	IA, 50th, 1924
Jameson, S.A.	Pvt.	G, 7th Iowa Cav.	66		1910 Feb 4	IA, 37th, 1911
Jamieson, N.	Corp.	G, 15th Ind. Inf.	17		1905 Nov 27	IA, 32nd, 1906
Jamis, Charles		I, 93rd Ohio Vol. Inf.	63		1912 Dec 13	KS, 32nd, 1913
Jamison, I.E.	Pvt.	E, 44th Iowa Inf.	243		1901-1902	IA, 28th, 1902
Jamison, J.M.	Capt.	G, 174th Penn. Inf.	231		1899 Jul 10	IA, 26th, 1900
Jamison, James M.		27th Ind.	25		1916 Jan 31	KS, 36th, 1917
Jamison, Josiah C.	Pvt.	E, 15th Iowa Inf.	12		1911 Jan 15	IA, 38th, 1912
Jane, Warren	C. Sergt.	K, 22nd Wis. Inf.	132		1919 Jun 9	IA, 46th, 1920
Janes, Alfred		K, 11th Ill. Cav. (died of dropsy)	107	66	1905[1904?] Nov 29	NE, 29th, 1905
Janes, Daniel	Pvt.	F, 8th-11th Md. Inf.	12		1917 Sep 6	IA, 44th, 1918
Jansen, John	Pvt.	E, 10th Iowa Inf.	78		1900 Jun 13	IA, 27th, 1901
Jany, Peter W.		F, 77th Ill.	51		1922 Mar 10	KS, 42nd, 1923
Japhet, Wm.		B, 64th N.Y. Inf. (died of wounds)	32	79	1895 Jul 12	NE, 20th, 1896
Japp, Christian	Pvt.	1st Mo. Lt. Art. Battery	1		1907 May 2	IA, 34th, 1908
Jaques, A.W.	Pvt.	I, 45th Iowa Inf.	19		1917	IA, 44th, 1918
Jaques, F.A.		A, 38th Ohio	130		1928 Dec 30	KS, 48th, 1929
Jaques, W.H.C.	Capt.	B, 56th U.S.C.	69		1917 Nov 2	IA, 44th, 1918
Jaquett, Asbury		E, 7th West Va.	45		1929	NE, 54th, 1930
Jarboe, A.M.		not a member of post named, but buried by said post	35		1897	KS, 17th, 1898
Jarboe, H.L.		H, 11th Wis.	16		1920 Oct 20	KS, 41st, 1922
Jarnell, S.		E, 25th Kans.	336		1888	KS, 8th, 1889
Jarnigan, H.A.		H, 40th —	84		1918 Mar 22	IA, 45th, 1919
Jarrett, C.		U.S.C.T.	321		1897	KS, 17th, 1898
Jarrett, Crab		F, 113th Ill. Inf.	270		1902 Aug 28	KS, 22nd, 1903
Jarrett, H.H.		died of general debility	197	74	1916 Sep 13	NE, 41st, 1917
Jarvis, Alva H.			267		1926 Nov 11	IA, 53rd, 1927
Jarvis, Charles	Pvt.	B, 4th Iowa Inf.	193		1899 Nov 5	IA, 26th, 1900
Jarvis, J.B.	Pvt.	E, 18th Iowa Inf.	231		1909 Apr 1	IA, 36th, 1910
Jarvis, John M.		G, 72nd Ill.	265		1916 Dec 19	KS, 36th, 1917
Jarvis, John O.		A, 1st Ohio	386[286?]		1897 Jan 30	KS, 16th, 1897
Jarvis, William	Sergt.	E, 4th Wis. Inf.	472		1901 Aug 11	IA, 28th, 1902
Jay, A.L.		E, 1st Iowa Cav. (died of old age)	190		1920 Mar 4	NE, 45th, 1921
Jay, E.T.		K, 46th Iowa	32		1927	KS, 47th, 1928
Jay, J.H.		E, 17th Ill. Cav.	32		1925 May 22	KS, 45th, 1926
Jay, Levi			20		1884	KS, 4th, 1885
Jay, Thomas	Pvt.	K, 34th Ohio Inf.	7		1916 Mar 4	IA, 43rd, 1917
Jay, Wesley H.	Pvt.	A, 45th Iowa Inf. (at large)	34	97	1943 Jan 15	IA, 69th, 1943
Jaycox, John W.			22		1925 Oct 25	KS, 45th, 1926
Jayne, D.T.	Pvt.	A, 36th Ill.	124		1898 Aug	IA, 25th, 1899
Jayne, Henry D.		E, 13th N.Y. Inf. (died of old age)	111	96	1919 May 12	NE, 44th, 1920
Jayne, John E.	Pvt.	D, 24th Iowa Inf.	8		1911 Jan 26	IA, 38th, 1912
Jayne, S.	Pvt.	C, 9th N.Y. Hvy. Art.	217	70	1895 Jan 20	IA, 22nd, 1896
Jayne, W.H.		C, 6th Penn. Inf. (died of dropsy)	318	83	1906 Dec 8	NE, 31st, 1907
Jeanguent, Eugene		L, 1st Ohio Art.	82		1929 Feb 4	KS, 48th, 1929
Jeannin, C.P.	Pvt.	H, 1st Minn. Inf.	68		1911 Dec 19	IA, 38th, 1912
Jeff, W.E.		G, —	17		1909 Dec 27	KS, 29th, 1910
Jeffcoat, Amanza		I, 76th Ill. Inf.	63		1934 Dec 29	KS, 54th, 1935
Jeffcoat, D.H.		I, 76th Ill. Inf.	63		1916 Dec 4	KS, 36th, 1917
Jeffcoat, John		B, 113th Ill. Inf. (died of grip)	110	65	1900 Apr 24	NE, 25th, 1901

See Appendix A, B or C for roster of post names and locations.
†*See Introduction for note regarding recording of death date.*

Name	Rank	Company, Regiment or Ship	Post*	Age	Death Date†	Journal
Jefferies, W.T.		B, 50th Ohio	293		1924	KS, 44th, 1925
Jeffers, A.M.		E & F, 77th Ohio	13	78	1921 Jan 12	NE, 46th, 1922
Jeffers, Aaron		F, 15th Mich.	83		1926 Feb 8	KS, 46th, 1927
Jeffers, Allen	Pvt.	I, 30th Ind. Inf.	511		1913 Nov 17	IA, 40th, 1914
Jeffers, Jas. H.	Corp.	B, 6th Ind. Cav.	297		1924 May 9	IA, 51st, 1925
Jeffers, Wm.		H, 147th Ind. Inf.	83		1934 Aug 3	KS, 54th, 1935
Jefferson, Charles		H, 158th Ill.	57		1934 Jun 13	IA, 61st, 1935
Jefferson, John A.	Corp.	B, 3rd Iowa Cav.	359		1918 Nov 17	IA, 45th, 1919
Jefferson, Reuben		D, 51st Ill.	4		1913 Feb 1	KS, 33rd, 1914
Jefferson, Thomas		123rd U.S. Inf., Kentucky (died of old age)	354	82	1919 May 11	NE, 44th, 1920
Jeffery, George		A, 9th Mich.	76		1914 Apr 18	KS, 34th, 1915
Jeffery, Jeremiah		C, 8th Iowa Cav.	284		1929 Sep 9	NE, 54th, 1930
Jeffery, John	Pvt.	I, 25th Wis. Inf.	377		1917	IA, 44th, 1918
Jeffery, Martin		E, 43rd Wis.	38	73	1916	NE, 41st, 1917
Jeffords, Edward	Pvt.	25th Wis. Inf.	277		1904-1905	IA, 31st, 1905
Jeffrey, W.O.		I, 145th Ill.	81		1931 Dec 7	KS, 51st, 1932
Jeffrey, W.O.		I, 145th Ill.	81		1931 Dec 7	KS, 52nd, 1933
Jeffrey, W.R.	Sergt.	C, 19th Iowa Inf.	108		1922 Dec 8	IA, 49th, 1923
Jeffries, A.C.			1		1930 Oct 12	KS, 50th, 1931
Jeffries, Benj. A.	Pvt.	I, 40th Wis. Inf.	461	48	1895 Mar 13	IA, 21st, 1895
Jeffries, Geo. B.		E, 9th Mo. Inf.	118		1886	KS, 6th, 1887
Jeffries, J.		186th N.Y. Inf. (died of loco motoratoxin)	192	74	1903 Apr 25	NE, 28th, 1904
Jeffries, John			40	52	1894 Oct 20	IA, 21st, 1895
Jehl, Ansel		B, 48th Ill.	86		1922 Sep 13	KS, 42nd, 1923
Jehring, Jno.	Musician	45th Ill. Inf.	1		1925 Jun 22	IA, 52nd, 1926
Jelf, W.H.		C, 51st Ind.	74		1914 Jan 23	KS, 34th, 1915
Jellison, Jno. W.	Corp.	E, 27th Maine Inf. K, 9th Maine Inf.	206		1927 Oct 31	IA, 54th, 1928
Jellison, John			7		1918 Nov 5	IA, 45th, 1919
Jellison, R.T.		I, 13th Kans.	44		1921 Oct 10	KS, 41st, 1922
Jenison, J.M.			12		1923 Jun 11	KS, 43rd, 1924
Jenkin, Elijah		A, 37th Ind. Inf.	29		1925 Dec 24	IA, 52nd, 1926
Jenkins, A.H.		K, 8th Ohio	85		1912 Feb 17	KS, 33rd, 1914
Jenkins, Al.	Pvt.		493		1904 Nov 8	IA, 31st, 1905
Jenkins, Andrew		194th Ohio Inf.	14		1924 Sep	KS, 45th, 1926
Jenkins, C.J.	Pvt.	I, 186th N.Y. Inf.	284		1900 Jan 30	IA, 27th, 1901
Jenkins, Daniel B.		M, 3rd Iowa Cav. (nonmember; died at Grand Island)			1936 May 11	NE, 61st, 1937
Jenkins, E.W.		G, 5th Kans. Cav.	388		1916 Dec 4	KS, 36th, 1917
Jenkins, Hiram		B, 124th Ind.	47		1923 May 5	KS, 43rd, 1924
Jenkins, Isadore N.		B, 28th Iowa Inf. (died of old age)	28	81	1910 Nov 13	NE, 35th, 1911
Jenkins, J.M.	Surg.	134th Ill. Inf.	461	55	1894 Jan 30	IA, 20th, 1894
Jenkins, James		B, 4th U.S. Art.	22		1932 Mar 24	NE, 57th, 1933
Jenkins, Jas. W.	Sergt.	B, 5th Ohio Cav.	12	52	1892 Jun 11	IA, 19th, 1893
Jenkins, Joseph		E, 36th Ind.	17		1921 Jun 7	KS, 41st, 1922
Jenkins, Lloyd		C, 29th Iowa Inf.	293		1901 May 28	KS, 21st, 1902
Jenkins, Philip R.	Pvt.		45		1922 Feb 12	IA, 49th, 1923
Jenkins, T.B.		A, 18th Ohio Inf.	91		1891 Oct 5	KS, 11th, 1892
Jenkins, W.G.	Pvt.	D, 2nd Iowa Inf.	83		1901-1902	IA, 28th, 1902
Jenkins, W.W.		A, 8th N.Y. Cav.	42		1918 Nov 12	KS, 38th, 1919
Jenkins, Wm.	Corp.	E, 6th Iowa Inf.	275	66	1890 May 22	IA, 17th, 1891
Jenkins, Wm.		M, 1st Iowa Cav.	339		1899 Oct	KS, 19th, 1900
Jenkinson, Jas.	Pvt.	B, 32nd Iowa Inf.	42	60	1893 Mar 15	IA, 19th, 1893
Jenkinson, L.C.		C & H, 3rd Wis. Cav.	355		1921 Jan 14	KS, 41st, 1922
Jenks, George		D, 28th Iowa Inf. (at large)	156	95 & 10 mos.	1937 Jan 1	IA, 64th, 1938
Jenks, George		D, 28th Iowa Inf.	28	96	1936 Dec 31	IA, 63rd, 1937
Jenks, Joppa	Musician	D, 28th Iowa Inf.	98		1915 Nov 7	IA, 42nd, 1916
Jenne, N.F.		B, 2nd Mich. Cav.	289		1898 Jun 25	KS, 18th, 1899
Jenne, Oscar		C, 36th Ill. Inf. (died of consumption)	95	62	1905 Jun 24	NE, 30th, 1906
Jenner, A.	Pvt.	G, 129th Ohio Inf.	116		1921 Jan 26	IA, 48th, 1922

*See Appendix A, B or C for roster of post names and locations.
†See Introduction for note regarding recording of death date.
282

Name	Rank	Company, Regiment or Ship	Post*	Age	Death Date†	Journal
Jenner, Chas.		D, 5th Mich. Inf.	354	68	1911 May 4	NE, 36th, 1912
Jenness, F.J.	Pvt.	K, 16th Penn. Inf.	68		1920 Jan 29	IA, 47th, 1921
Jennewin, J.J.	1st Lieut.	A, 1st West Va. Cav.	194	69	1896 Jul 16	IA, 23rd, 1897
Jenning, Ben	Pvt.	C, 23rd Iowa Inf.	7		1921	IA, 48th, 1922
Jennings, A.J.		E, 12th Kans. Inf.	12		1917 Dec 12	KS, 37th, 1918
Jennings, Chas.	Pvt.	L, 9th Iowa Vol. Cav.	16		1918	IA, 45th, 1919
Jennings, Chas.	Pvt.	L, 9th Iowa Cav.	16		1920 Nov 8	IA, 47th, 1921
Jennings, Geo.	Pvt.	F, 3rd Iowa Cav.	251		1924 Jan 23	IA, 51st, 1925
Jennings, Geo.	Pvt.	F, 3rd Iowa Cav.	251		1923 Jan 23	IA, 50th, 1924
Jennings, George		B, 112th Ill. Inf.	56		1912	KS, 32nd, 1913
Jennings, George			56		1913	KS, 33rd, 1914
Jennings, H.C.		A, 7th Kans. Cav. (died of paralysis)	48	56	1895 Oct 30	NE, 20th, 1896
Jennings, Henry	Lieut.	I, 53rd Ill.	83		1907 Sep 18	IA, 34th, 1908
Jennings, J.B.	Corp.	G, 44th Ill. Inf.	222		1918 Sep 28	IA, 45th, 1919
Jennings, J.W.	Musician	B, 22nd Iowa Inf.	497		1912 Nov 26	IA, 39th, 1913
Jennings, John A.		A, 38th Ind.	1		1926 Feb 20	NE, 51st, 1927
Jennings, John B.	Pvt.	I, 29th Wis. Inf.	94	40	1882 Dec 20	IA, 14th, 1888
Jennings, John J.		E, 10th Mich.	64		1937 Oct 10	KS, 57th, 1938
Jennings, John M.		K, 74th Ind.	38		1930 Dec	KS, 52nd, 1933
Jennings, John M.		K, 74th Ind.	38		1930 Dec	KS, 51st, 1932
Jennings, R.F.	Pvt.	K, 16th Maine Inf.	42	60	1896 Apr 18	IA, 23rd, 1897
Jennings, S.T.	1st Lieut.	D, 99th N.Y. Inf.	94	55	1891 Jul 20	IA, 18th, 1892
Jennings, W.F.	Pvt.	A, 162nd N.Y. Inf.	254		1912 Dec 14	IA, 39th, 1913
Jennings, W.H.		C, 11th Iowa	25		1930 Dec 29	NE, 55th, 1931
Jennings, Wiley	Pvt.	D, Ill.	243		1923	IA, 50th, 1924
Jennings, William		G, 74th Ohio	17		1920 Jan 23	KS, 40th, 1921
Jennisen, G.F.	Pvt.	K, 13th Vt. Inf.	42		1920	IA, 47th, 1921
Jennison, William		C, 17th N.Y.	380		1897 May 1	KS, 17th, 1898
Jenson, F.W.	Pvt.	A, 13th Ill. Cav.	68		1911 Jul 31	IA, 38th, 1912
Jericho, G.	Pvt.	Sturgis Rifles	20		1910 Jun	IA, 37th, 1911
Jernigan, L.	Capt.	1st Ark. Cav.	65		1913 Jun 5	KS, 33rd, 1914
Jerolaman, —	Pvt.	A, 30th N.J.	222		1923 Sep 17	IA, 50th, 1924
Jeroleman, D.E.	Pvt.	A, 30th N.J. Inf.	222		1917 Mar 17	IA, 44th, 1918
Jesmark, H.		B, 28th Wis.	147		1911 Jul 23	KS, 31st, 1912
Jessup, A.L.	Pvt.	4th Iowa Art.	40		1910 May 8	IA, 37th, 1911
Jessup, S.P.		E, 8th Iowa Inf.	56		1889	KS, 9th, 1890
Jester, J.B.	Capt.	K, 12th Va. Inf.	231		1905 Jan 25	IA, 32nd, 1906
Jester, James M.		I, 60th Ohio Inf.	7		1938 Jun 5	NE, 63rd, 1939
Jewel, James Esom	Pvt. Pvt.	C, 27th Iowa Inf. C, 12th Iowa Inf.	54	92	1939 Nov 8	IA, 66th, 1940
Jewell, A.F.	Corp.	2nd Iowa Bat. Lt. Art.	23		1933 Apr 18	NE, 58th, 1934
Jewell, A.R.		F, 3rd Mo.	26	91	1934 Jan 7	IA, 61st, 1935
Jewell, A.S.			38		1919	IA, 45th, 1919
Jewell, B.W.	Pvt.	F, 1st Mass. Inf.	190		1929 May 10	IA, 56th, 1930
Jewell, Chas. P.		B, 11th Kans.	328		1885	KS, 5th, 1886
Jewell, Crews		C, 31st Ill. Inf.	129		1934 Feb 8	KS, 54th, 1935
Jewell, Geo. W.		E, 2nd Ill. Cav. (died of consumption)	89	64	1909 Nov 21	NE, 34th, 1910
Jewell, Hiram B.		G, 35th Iowa Inf.	302		1940 Apr	NE, 65th, 1941
Jewell, Jardus	Pvt.	K, 92nd Ill. Inf.	112		1899	NE, 24th, 1900
Jewell, Lewis R.		L, 6th Kans. Cav.	472		1899 Feb 12	KS, 19th, 1900
Jewell, W.D.		I, 84th Ind.	17		1930 Dec 17	KS, 50th, 1931
Jewet, Moses	Pvt.	K, Mo. Eng.	231		1923 Feb 26	IA, 50th, 1924
Jewett, A.V.		H, 2nd Ill. Cav.	63		1919 Jun 24	KS, 39th, 1920
Jewett, G.H.		E, 142nd N.Y. Inf. (died of Bright's disease)	46	63	1908 Sep	NE, 34th, 1910
Jewett, G.H.		85th N.Y. (died of diabetes)	46		1908 Oct	NE, 33rd, 1909
Jewett, H.C.		10th Ohio	4		1930 Dec 6	KS, 50th, 1931
Jewett, Henry C.		U.S. Navy	36		1921 Apr 30	KS, 41st, 1922
Jewett, John E.		E, 3rd Ohio Inf. (died at Lawrence)	12		1895 Oct	KS, 15th, 1896
Jewett, N.	Pvt.	B, 3rd Ohio Inf.	18		1908	IA, 35th, 1909
Jewett, Victor	Pvt.	K, 24th Iowa Inf.	43		1919 Jun 1	IA, 46th, 1920
Jeys, Thomas	Pvt.	A, 48th Iowa Inf.	116		1906 Dec 28	IA, 33rd, 1907

Name	Rank	Company, Regiment or Ship	Post*	Age	Death Date†	Journal
Jimmison, W.E.		G, 58th Ill.	85		1913 Jun 14	KS, 33rd, 1914
Jirk, J.W.	Pvt.	A, 153rd Penn. Inf.	466		1920 Feb 10	IA, 47th, 1921
Jobbins, Albert	Pvt.	E, 1st Wis. Hvy. Art.	10		1924 Sep 20	IA, 51st, 1925
Jobe, Henry	Pvt.	E, 95th Ill. Inf.	58		1912 Dec 13	IA, 39th, 1913
Jobe, J.M.	Pvt.		48		1929	IA, 56th, 1930
Jobes, A.H.		D, 6th West Va.	17		1913 Mar 31	KS, 33rd, 1914
Jobes, William H.H.	Pvt.	A, 2nd Iowa Cav.	359		1901 Mar 19	IA, 28th, 1902
Joel, Whitney	Pvt.	F, 6th Minn.	56		1903 May 7	IA, 30th, 1904
Johannes, Fred			32		1913 May 19	KS, 33rd, 1914
John, C.C.	Pvt.	K, 26th Ind. Inf.	10		1915 Aug 11	IA, 42nd, 1916
John, Dolphin	Pvt.	A, 21st Iowa Inf.	176		1899	IA, 26th, 1900
John, G.A.	Pvt.	K, 1st Iowa Inf.	400		1921 Aug 25	IA, 48th, 1922
John, Jas.	Pvt.	I, 36th Iowa Inf.	20		1908 Apr	IA, 35th, 1909
John, William		E, 37th Ohio	17		1927 Aug 27	KS, 47th, 1928
Johns, D.	Pvt.	E, 3rd Iowa Inf.	23		1924 Apr 28	IA, 51st, 1925
Johns, D.T.			32		1912 Mar 11	NE, 37th, 1913
Johns, David			477		1922	KS, 42nd, 1923
Johns, J.M.		G, 43rd Ind. Inf.	127		1891 Sep 24	KS, 11th, 1892
Johns, James F.		F, 2nd Wis. Cav.	399		1918	KS, 38th, 1919
Johns, James W.		E, 47th Ohio	125		1910 Dec 15	KS, 30th, 1911
Johns, John			380		1923	KS, 43rd, 1924
Johns, Lewis A.		B, 20th Ohio Inf.	129		1934 Jan 19	KS, 54th, 1935
Johns, S.L.		Navy	24		1920	NE, 45th, 1921
Johns, T.W.	Pvt.	C, 141st Ohio Inf.	97		1911 Mar 3	IA, 38th, 1912
Johnson, A.	Pvt.	F, 13th Iowa Inf.	103	54	1890 Jul 27	IA, 17th, 1891
Johnson, A.	Pvt.	I, 15th Mich. Inf.	123		1920 Dec 7	IA, 47th, 1921
Johnson, A.	Sergt.	A, 17th Iowa Inf.	2		1921 Jan	IA, 48th, 1922
Johnson, A.		F, 23rd Iowa (died of old age infirmities)	188	83	1917 Jun 8	NE, 42nd, 1918
Johnson, A.D.	Pvt.	C, 11th Iowa Inf.	290		1913 Apr 6	IA, 40th, 1914
Johnson, A.D.		D, 63rd Ohio	4		1923 May 12	KS, 43rd, 1924
Johnson, A.F.	Pvt.	A, 7th Iowa Inf.	231		1919 May 28	IA, 46th, 1920
Johnson, A.H.		C, 15th Wis.	158		1905 Nov	KS, 25th, 1906
Johnson, A.H.		K, 13th Mich.	271		1912 Jan 15	KS, 32nd, 1913
Johnson, A.J.	Pvt.	C, 153rd Ill. Inf.	82		1914 Dec 25	IA, 41st, 1915
Johnson, A.M.			165		1913	IA, 40th, 1914
Johnson, A.S.	Musician	6th Iowa Inf.	173		1899 Nov 20	IA, 26th, 1900
Johnson, A.S.	Pvt.	G, 22nd Penn. Cav.	7		1924 Sep 13	IA, 51st, 1925
Johnson, A.S.		I, 129th Ohio	49		1933 Feb 21	KS, 53rd, 1934
Johnson, Aaron C.	Capt. Lieut. Col.	D, 25th Ohio Inf. 25th Ohio Vol. Inf. (died of heart disease)	96	65	1888 Oct	NE, 13th, 1889
Johnson, Albert		A, 7th N.H. Inf. (died of consumption)	40		1893 Jul 21	NE, 18th, 1894
Johnson, Alex.		D, 36th Iowa Inf. (died of heart failure)	304	73	1895 May 10	NE, 20th, 1896
Johnson, Alex. W.		D, 1st N.Y. Cav.	380		1899 Jul 22	KS, 19th, 1900
Johnson, Alexander I.		F, 14th N.J.	112		1932 Oct 23	NE, 57th, 1933
Johnson, Alpine A.		3rd Ky. Cav.	97		1893 Dec 31	KS, 13th, 1894
Johnson, Amos	Pvt.	I, 4th Ohio Inf.	23		1903 Dec 28	IA, 30th, 1904
Johnson, Amos		F, 41st Ill.	52		1927 Nov 13	KS, 47th, 1928
Johnson, Andrew		H, 79th U.S.C.T.	3		1898 May 23	KS, 18th, 1899
Johnson, Andrew		D, 57th Ill.	171		1911 Jan 21	KS, 31st, 1912
Johnson, Andrew		I, 79th Ill.	[18?]		1909 Jul 21	KS, 29th, 1910
Johnson, Andrew		C, 60th Mass. Inf. (died of catarrh)	4	67	1902 Jun	NE, 27th, 1903
Johnson, Andrew		G, 38th Ill.	130		1928	NE, 52nd, 1928
Johnson, Andrew M.	Pvt.	G, 124th Ill. Inf.	347	60	1893 May 10	IA, 20th, 1894
Johnson, Asahel Alanson	Pvt.	D, 5th Wis. Inf. (at large)	179	97	1940 Jan 9	IA, 66th, 1940
Johnson, B.F.					[1938?]	KS, 58th, 1939
Johnson, B.L.		A, 15th Kans.	96		1897 Oct 7	KS, 17th, 1898
Johnson, B.M.	Pvt.	C, 38th Iowa Inf.	377		1913 Apr 19	IA, 40th, 1914
Johnson, B.T.		B, 9th Kans.	1		1928 Mar 10	KS, 48th, 1929
Johnson, Beckwith		E & D, 14th Kans.	332		1895 Dec 31	KS, 16th, 1897
Johnson, Benj. W.	Pvt.	E, 1st N.Y. Lt. Art.	77		1901 Jul 14	IA, 28th, 1902
Johnson, C.A.			67		1914 Dec 2	IA, 41st, 1915
Johnson, C.A.	Pvt.	D, 4th Wis. Cav.	190		1922 Sep 3	IA, 49th, 1923

*See Appendix A, B or C for roster of post names and locations.
†See Introduction for note regarding recording of death date.

Name	Rank	Company, Regiment or Ship	Post*	Age	Death Date†	Journal
Johnson, C.B.			6		1918	IA, 45th, 1919
Johnson, C.J.	Seaman	U.S. Navy	56		1917	IA, 44th, 1918
Johnson, C.P.	Pvt.	C, 43rd Ill. Inf.	375		1911 May 19	IA, 38th, 1912
Johnson, C.W.		E, 130th Ill. Inf.	130		1900 Nov 30	KS, 21st, 1902
Johnson, Caswell		D, 1st U.S. Hvy. Art.	321		1909 Dec 18	KS, 29th, 1910
Johnson, Chancy	Pvt.	A, 165th Ill. Inf.	512	88	1932 May 2	IA, 59th, 1933
Johnson, Charles	Pvt.	F, 146th Ind. Inf.	173		1897 Aug 28	IA, 24th, 1898
Johnson, Charles O.		H, 28th Ill. (former member; died at Wahoo)	90		1935 Jun 30	NE, 60th, 1936
Johnson, Chas.	Pvt.	113th Ill. Inf.	34		1910 Dec 20	IA, 37th, 1911
Johnson, Chas.		C, 105th Ill. (died of heart failure)	107	72	1916 Dec 1	NE, 41st, 1917
Johnson, Chas. T.		H, 40th Iowa	15		1918 Jul 4	KS, 38th, 1919
Johnson, Chas. W.			130		1900 Nov 20	KS, 20th, 1901
Johnson, D.	Pvt.	D, 11th Ill.	68		1921 Jun 21	IA, 48th, 1922
Johnson, D.	Pvt.	C, 7th N.Y. Cav.	68		1925 Jul 14	IA, 52nd, 1926
Johnson, D.A.	Pvt.	A, 54th Ohio Inf.	127	53	1884 Nov 27	IA, 18th, 1892
Johnson, Daniel	Pvt.	A, 20th Iowa Inf.	400		1907 Oct	IA, 34th, 1908
Johnson, David A.	Pvt.	A, 74th Ohio Inf.	127	58	1889 Aug 1	IA, 16th, 1890
Johnson, David H.	Sergt.	D, 39th Iowa Inf.	173	46	1886 Dec 28	IA, 13th, 1887
Johnson, E.E.		G, 1st Colo.	422		1899 Jun 8	KS, 19th, 1900
Johnson, E.G.		A, 11th Ky.	32		1912 Nov 25	KS, 32nd, 1913
Johnson, Eli		H, 5th West Va.	25		1926 Jan 6	KS, 46th, 1927
Johnson, Elias		E, 161st Ohio Inf.	123		1895	KS, 15th, 1896
Johnson, F.A.	Pvt.	B, 72nd Ill. Inf.	440		1900 Oct 31	IA, 27th, 1901
Johnson, F.M.	Lieut.	63rd U.S.C.T.	75		1911 Jul	IA, 38th, 1912
Johnson, F.T.		B, 12th Ind.	201		1926 Feb 5	KS, 46th, 1927
Johnson, Finley P.			147		1932 Oct 22	NE, 57th, 1933
Johnson, G.D.			64		1906 Feb 12	IA, 33rd, 1907
Johnson, G.H.T., Dr.		D, 110th Ill.	93		1917 Feb 24	KS, 37th, 1918
Johnson, G.W.		G, 40th Ill.	100		1896 Jul 24	KS, 16th, 1897
Johnson, G.W.			5		1896 Aug 23	KS, 16th, 1897
Johnson, G.W.		D, 8th Kans.	92		1928 Feb 27	KS, 48th, 1929
Johnson, G.Y.		H, 73rd Ill.	130		1909 Nov 27	KS, 29th, 1910
Johnson, Geo. C.	Sergt. Major	C, 47th Ill. Inf.	40		1925 Jan 12	IA, 52nd, 1926
Johnson, Geo. D.		Mo. Cav.	380		1921 Nov 28	KS, 41st, 1922
Johnson, Geo. S.		B, 1st Del. Cav.	18		1922 Jun 11	KS, 42nd, 1923
Johnson, Geo. W.		L, Mo. State Militia Cav.	92		1926 Jan 23	KS, 46th, 1927
Johnson, George	Pvt.	A, 169th Ohio Inf.	55		1915 May 15	IA, 42nd, 1916
Johnson, George		U.S.C.T.	25		1916 Dec 1	KS, 36th, 1917
Johnson, George			111		1924	KS, 44th, 1925
Johnson, George	Corp.	D, 48th Ill. (see also Appendix D)	118		1935 May 29	NE, 60th, 1936
Johnson, H.	Pvt.	D, 21st Ill. Inf.	222		1920 Dec 16	IA, 47th, 1921
Johnson, H.H.	Pvt.	A, 25th Ill. Inf.	66	44	1887 Dec 9	IA, 14th, 1888
Johnson, H.M.	Pvt.	L, —	236		1908 Mar	IA, 35th, 1909
Johnson, H.S.	Pvt.	A, 14th Ill. Cav.	135		1890 Jan 21	IA, 17th, 1891
Johnson, H.S.		E, 3rd Ill. Cav.	97		1916 Nov 15	KS, 36th, 1917
Johnson, Harry		H, 1st Neb. (died of pneumonia)	25	54	1900 May 22	NE, 25th, 1901
Johnson, Henry	Pvt.	E, 91st Ill. Inf.	365		1913 Sep 17	IA, 40th, 1914
Johnson, Henry		I, 1st Cal. Inf.	132		1930 Apr 15	KS, 50th, 1931
Johnson, Henry A.			127		1922 Apr 22	KS, 42nd, 1923
Johnson, High		C, 68th Ohio	17		1909 Jan 4	KS, 29th, 1910
Johnson, Hiram		A, 113th Ark. (died at Lawrence)	365		1895 May	KS, 15th, 1896
Johnson, Howard	Pvt.	F, 21st Iowa	222		1899 Jan	IA, 26th, 1900
Johnson, Howard	Pvt.	F, 21st Iowa Vols.	222		1899 Jan 23	IA, 25th, 1899
Johnson, Howard		E, 39th Ill.	38		1924 May 17	KS, 44th, 1925
Johnson, I.N.		F, 51st Mo.	49		1916 Feb 6	KS, 36th, 1917
Johnson, Isaac		H, 3rd Ill.	14		1918 Sep 3	KS, 38th, 1919
Johnson, Isaac C.		H, 14th Ind. Inf.	25	74	1918 Jun 29	NE, 43rd, 1919
Johnson, Isaac H.	Corp.	I, 26th Iowa Inf.	111		1922 Mar 10	IA, 49th, 1923
Johnson, Iver	Pvt.	I, 23rd Wis. Inf.	35	53	1893 Nov 29	IA, 21st, 1895
Johnson, J.A.		H, 9th Minn. Inf.	440		1913 Jul 22	IA, 40th, 1914

*See Appendix A, B or C for roster of post names and locations.
†See Introduction for note regarding recording of death date.

285

Name	Rank	Company, Regiment or Ship	Post*	Age	Death Date†	Journal
Johnson, J. Arrell		E, 4th Kans. (died at Topeka, Kans.; buried at Topeka Cemetery)	250		1894 Jun 30	KS, 14th, 1895
Johnson, J.C.	Pvt.	E, 11th Iowa Inf.	110		1886 Oct 4	IA, 14th, 1888
Johnson, J.C.	Pvt.	E, 11th Iowa Inf.	110		1886 Oct 4	IA, 13th, 1887
Johnson, J.D.	Pvt.	C, 196th Ohio Inf.	102	65	1896 Feb 17	IA, 23rd, 1897
Johnson, J.F.		F, 1st Minn. Hvy. Art.	147		1923 May 25	NE, 48th, 1924
Johnson, J.M.	Pvt.	B, 18th Iowa Inf.	376	50	1888	IA, 17th, 1891
Johnson, J.N.		G, 2nd Ill. Cav.	324		1917 May 22	IA, 44th, 1918
Johnson, J.O.	Pvt.	L, 12th Iowa Inf.	168		1910 Jan 2	IA, 37th, 1911
Johnson, J.P.	Pvt.	H, 177th Ohio Inf.	181	73	1894 Dec 8	IA, 21st, 1895
Johnson, J.P.		B, 2nd Kans. Cav. 2nd Kans. Bat.	342		1916 Aug 1	KS, 36th, 1917
Johnson, J.S.		116th Ohio	89		1918	KS, 38th, 1919
Johnson, J.W.			96		1906	IA, 33rd, 1907
Johnson, J.W.	Pvt.	E, 20th Iowa Inf.	127		1914 Oct	IA, 41st, 1915
Johnson, J.W.		D, 180th Ohio	3		1928 Nov 23	KS, 48th, 1929
Johnson, J.W.			40		1906 Nov 14	NE, 31st, 1907
Johnson, J. Weber		D, 72nd Ind.	51		1926 Nov 13	KS, 46th, 1927
Johnson, Jacob		H, K, 51st Ill. 4th U.S. Cav.	14		1914 Jun 9	KS, 34th, 1915
Johnson, James	Corp.	E, 129th Ill. Inf.	512		1917 Feb 18	IA, 44th, 1918
Johnson, James		B, 111th Ill.	59		1909 Oct 21	KS, 29th, 1910
Johnson, James		I, 21st Ky.	145		1911 May 6	KS, 31st, 1912
Johnson, James H.	Pvt.		4		1900-1901	IA, 27th, 1901
Johnson, James H.	Pvt.	I, 46th Iowa	23		1922 Jul 11	IA, 49th, 1923
Johnson, James H.			150		1884	KS, 4th, 1885
Johnson, James P.			8		1899	NE, 24th, 1900
Johnson, James R.		K, 11th Ill.	25	73	1915 Apr 14	NE, 40th, 1916
Johnson, James S.		C, 6th Kans.	111		1893 Dec 27	KS, 13th, 1894
Johnson, James T.		G, 10th Mo. (not a member of Farragut Post)	25		1913 May 15	NE, 38th, 1914
Johnson, James W.		D, 67th Ind. (died of apoplexy at Soldiers & Sailors Home, Milford)		62	1906 Nov 14	NE, 31st, 1907
Johnson, Jas. M.	Pvt.	B, 18th Iowa Inf.	11	55	1888 Sep 25	IA, 15th, 1889
Johnson, Jno.		F, 7th Wis.	147		1904 Apr 11	KS, 24th, 1905
Johnson, Jno. M.	Pvt.	I, 82nd Ill. Inf.	66		1928 Dec 3	IA, 55th, 1929
Johnson, Jno. S.		C, 6th Kans. Cav.	111		1889	KS, 9th, 1890
Johnson, John	Pvt.	H, 18th Iowa Inf.	48	47	1887 Jun 25	IA, 14th, 1888
Johnson, John	Pvt.	B, 95th Ill.	142		1905 Apr 4	IA, 32nd, 1906
Johnson, John	Pvt.	A, 43rd Ill. Inf.	347		1905 Jan 31	IA, 32nd, 1906
Johnson, John		30th Iowa Inf.	20		1916	IA, 43rd, 1917
Johnson, John		F, 69th Mo.	17		1918 Aug 2	KS, 38th, 1919
Johnson, John		A, 97th Ind.	175		1924 May 12	KS, 44th, 1925
Johnson, John			106		1899	NE, 24th, 1900
Johnson, John		F, 44th Inf. (died of old age)	32	78	1913 Jul 21	NE, 38th, 1914
Johnson, John B.		A, 55th Ill. Inf. D, 137th Ill. Inf.	1		1899 May 18	KS, 19th, 1900
Johnson, John B.	Pvt.	B, 2nd Iowa Inf.	147		1917 Jan 24	IA, 44th, 1918
Johnson, John C.		L, 8th Ind. Cav.	303		1911 Jan 20	KS, 31st, 1912
Johnson, John C.		K, 132nd Ill. Inf.	1		1929 Apr 16	KS, 49th, 1930
Johnson, John E.	Corp.	E, 3rd Vt. Inf.	12		1917 Feb 5	IA, 44th, 1918
Johnson, John G.		F, 3rd Ill. Cav.	147		1938 Jul 17	NE, 63rd, 1939
Johnson, John H.		K, 12th Iowa	46		1918 Jun 5	KS, 38th, 1919
Johnson, John O.	Pvt.	K, 10th Iowa Inf.	234		1911 Dec 8	IA, 38th, 1912
Johnson, John W.	Pvt.	K, 10th Ill.	234		1922 Sep 14	IA, 49th, 1923
Johnson, Joseph C.		G, 13th Mo. Cav. (died of accident)	218	84	1921 Oct	NE, 46th, 1922
Johnson, L.C.	Pvt.		173		1926 Aug 9	IA, 53rd, 1927
Johnson, L.H.	Pvt.	K, 92nd Ohio Inf.	7		1913 Sep 23	IA, 40th, 1914
Johnson, L.H.		148th Ill.	129		1914 Jul 14	KS, 34th, 1915
Johnson, L.H.		C, 1st Conn. Cav.	257		1913 Jul 26	KS, 33rd, 1914
Johnson, L.W.	Sergt.	E, 125th Ill. Inf.	322		1913 Jan 15	IA, 40th, 1914
Johnson, Levi F.		H, 78th Ohio Inf.	85		1918 Apr 14	KS, 38th, 1919
Johnson, Luter R.		G, 58th Ill.	25		1916 Jan 15	KS, 36th, 1917

*See Appendix A, B or C for roster of post names and locations.
†See Introduction for note regarding recording of death date.

Name	Rank	Company, Regiment or Ship	Post*	Age	Death Date†	Journal
Johnson, M.B.	Pvt.	C, 38th Iowa Inf.	337		1913 Apr 19	IA, 40th, 1914
Johnson, M.C.	Pvt.	F, 1st Neb. Inf.	11	54	1899 Oct 3	IA, 26th, 1900
Johnson, M.W.		C, 1st Iowa	147		1925 Mar 22	KS, 45th, 1926
Johnson, Martin W.		C, 15th Ohio Inf.	109	95	1938 Mar 11	IA, 64th, 1938
Johnson, N.		D, 49th N.Y. (died of apoplexy)	32	69	1910 Jan	NE, 35th, 1911
Johnson, Nelson M.		A, 5th Kans. Inf.	1		1901 Apr 5	KS, 21st, 1902
Johnson, Newton S.	Sergt.	E, 1st Wis. Cav.	100		1911 Mar 11	IA, 38th, 1912
Johnson, O.			72		1883	KS, 3rd, 1884
Johnson, O.			72		1884	KS, 4th, 1885
Johnson, O.D.	Pvt.	15th Ind. Battery	86		1910 Jan 1	IA, 37th, 1911
Johnson, Owen O.		G, 2nd Col.	114		1906 Jun 27	KS, 26th, 1907
Johnson, Oxley		D, 23rd Mo.	145		1919 Sep 27	KS, 39th, 1920
Johnson, P.B.		H, 13th Iowa	25		1897 Feb 21	KS, 17th, 1898
Johnson, Peter		E, 15th Wis. Inf.	174		4th quarter 1883	IA, 10th, 1884
Johnson, Porter C.		B, 3rd Penn. Reserves (died of pneumonia while chaplain of the state penitentiary)	47	77	1914 Jan 20	NE, 39th, 1915
Johnson, R.C.		D, 2nd N.Y. Cav.	36		1912 Oct 5	KS, 32nd, 1913
Johnson, R.L.	Pvt.	C, —	445		1923 Nov 14	IA, 50th, 1924
Johnson, Robert H.	Pvt.	H, 179th Ohio Vol. Inf.	257		1901 Jun 28	IA, 28th, 1902
Johnson, Robert H.		G, 30th Ind. Inf.	25		1917 Oct 2	KS, 37th, 1918
Johnson, Robt.		L, 3rd Iowa Cav. (died of Bright's disease)	187	71	1917 Oct	NE, 42nd, 1918
Johnson, S.H.	Pvt.	G, 58th Ill. Inf.	2		1920 Apr 9	IA, 47th, 1921
Johnson, S.M.	Lieut.	D, 54th U.S.C.	414		1911 1st term	IA, 38th, 1912
Johnson, Sam'l	Pvt.	K, 6th Iowa	29		1923 Apr 11	IA, 50th, 1924
Johnson, Samuel		H, 8th U.S.C.T.	88		1905 Dec 20	KS, 25th, 1906
Johnson, Samuel		H, 17th Ill. Cav.	9		1920 Jan 6	KS, 40th, 1921
Johnson, Scott	Pvt.		290		1929 Mar 9	IA, 56th, 1930
Johnson, Simeon			59		1917 Sep 18	KS, 37th, 1918
Johnson, Sml.	Pvt.	F, 24th Iowa Inf.	140		1925 Jun 16	IA, 52nd, 1926
Johnson, T.B.	Pvt.	D, 96th Ohio Inf.	23	50	1891 Sep 11	IA, 18th, 1892
Johnson, T.B.		G, 39th Ill. Inf.	15		1893 Aug 21	NE, 18th, 1894
Johnson, T.J.	Pvt.	I, 24th N.Y. Inf.	365		1909 Oct 7	IA, 36th, 1910
Johnson, T.J.		D, 45th Mo.	18		1925 Jun	KS, 45th, 1926
Johnson, T.L.		B, 54th Ill. Inf. (at large)			1925 Nov 26	KS, 45th, 1926
Johnson, Theadore F.		E, 138th Ill.	60		1926 Jan 2	NE, 51st, 1927
Johnson, Theo.		E, 139th Ind.	145		1918 Jul 12	KS, 38th, 1919
Johnson, Thomas		4th Iowa Cav.	76		1886	KS, 6th, 1887
Johnson, Thos.	Corp.	A, 67th Penn. Inf.	40		1916 May 25	IA, 43rd, 1917
Johnson, Thos. B.		E, 11th Mo.	44		1927 Dec 31	NE, 52nd, 1928
Johnson, Thos. L.		B, 156th Ill.	6		1922 Mar 19	KS, 42nd, 1923
Johnson, U.	Pvt.	C, 19th Iowa Inf.	8	66	1887 Jun 17	IA, 14th, 1888
Johnson, U.S.	Pvt.	B, 28th Penn. Inf.	343	79	1887 Jul 17	IA, 14th, 1888
Johnson, W.A.		15th Ind. Battery	256		1905 Dec 8	KS, 25th, 1906
Johnson, W.A.	Pvt.	H, 80th Ohio Inf.	151		1899	NE, 24th, 1900
Johnson, W.B.	Pvt.	G, 9th Iowa Cav.	81		1900 Jul 15	IA, 27th, 1901
Johnson, W.C.	Pvt.	82nd Ill. Inf.	132		1914 Aug	IA, 41st, 1915
Johnson, W.D.		B, 33rd Ill.	89		1922 Aug	KS, 42nd, 1923
Johnson, W.E.		A, 2nd Ohio	85		1919 Nov 15	KS, 39th, 1920
Johnson, W.H.	Capt.	F, 144th N.Y. Inf.	236		1911 Jun 6	IA, 38th, 1912
Johnson, W.H.	Pvt.	K, 148th Ill. Inf.	284		1932 Dec 18	IA, 59th, 1933
Johnson, W.H.	1st Lieut. & QM	97th Ind.	1		1888	KS, 8th, 1889
Johnson, W.H.		K, 66th Ind.	129		1906 Sep 19	KS, 26th, 1907
Johnson, W.H.		C, 116th Ill.	301		1923 Jan 25	KS, 43rd, 1924
Johnson, W.H.		E, 2nd Kans. Cav.	127		1927 May 14	KS, 47th, 1928
Johnson, W.H.		G, 13th Mich. Inf. (died of pneumonia)	32	67	1891[1901?] Sep	NE, 26th, 1902
Johnson, W.I.		H, 3rd Iowa Cav. (died of heart failure)	1	52	1895 Sep 1	NE, 20th, 1896
Johnson, W.L.		K, 72nd Ind.	17		1917 Dec 23	KS, 37th, 1918
Johnson, W.M.	Pvt.	K, 13th Ill. Inf.	14		1925	IA, 52nd, 1926
Johnson, W.W.	Pvt.	E, 46th Ill. Inf.	64	43	1889 May 5	IA, 16th, 1890
Johnson, Walter	Pvt.	1st Penn. Reserves	231		1920 Feb 9	IA, 47th, 1921
Johnson, Weslay		C, 15th Kans. Cav.	74		1935	KS, 55th, 1936
Johnson, Wesley			94		1935	KS, 55th, 1936

*See Appendix A, B or C for roster of post names and locations.
†See Introduction for note regarding recording of death date.

Name	Rank	Company, Regiment or Ship	Post*	Age	Death Date†	Journal
Johnson, Wesley		C, 96th N.Y. Inf.	4		1923 Oct 29	NE, 48th, 1924
Johnson, Willard P.			17		1941 Apr 14	KS, 61st, 1942
Johnson, William	Pvt.	H, 194th Ohio Inf.	186	54	1896 May 18	IA, 23rd, 1897
Johnson, William		G, 136th Ind.	49		1919 Jun 25	KS, 39th, 1920
Johnson, Wm.	Pvt.	H, 6th Mich. Inf.	14		1913 Oct 30	IA, 40th, 1914
Johnson, Wm.			45		1926 Sep 20	IA, 53rd, 1927
Johnson, Wm.	Pvt.	I, 106th Ill. Inf. (cause of death: accident)	41	42	1887 Jul 23	NE, 12th, 1888
Johnson, Wm.		H, 79th Ill. Inf. (died of dropsy)	207	68	1901 May	NE, 26th, 1902
Johnson, Wm. A.	Pvt.	D, 145th Ohio Inf.	40		1922 Jan 26	IA, 49th, 1923
Johnson, Wm. F.		C, 37th Ind. Inf.	35		1916 Apr 8	KS, 36th, 1917
Johnson, Wm. H.		A, 137th Ill. Inf.	5		1887 Jul 31	KS, 7th, 1888
Johnson, Wm. H.		G, 13th Mich. (died of heart failure at Soldiers & Sailors Home, Milford)		71	1906 Dec 6	NE, 31st, 1907
Johnson, Wm. H.		M, 3rd Iowa Cav.	127		1920 Feb 21	KS, 40th, 1921
Johnson, Wm. L.	Pvt.	A, 36th N.Y. Inf.	321	92	1938 Sep 19	IA, 65th, 1939
Johnson, Wm. M.		A, 18th Mo. Inf.	75		1918 Apr 9	KS, 38th, 1919
Johnson, Worthy A.	Pvt.	A, 148th Ohio Inf.	40		1904 Mar 2	IA, 31st, 1905
Johnston, A.M.		I, 141st Ohio	119		1897 Jan 18	KS, 17th, 1898
Johnston, B.A.	Commissary Sergt.	24th Kans. State Militia	32		1915 Jun 6	KS, 35th, 1916
Johnston, C.K.	Pvt.	F, 36th Ill. Inf.	236		1927 Feb 13	IA, 54th, 1928
Johnston, D.B.		F, 135th Ill.	127		1924 Oct 9	KS, 44th, 1925
Johnston, David H.		K, 8th Mo. Inf.	23		1931 Sep 13	NE, 56th, 1932
Johnston, David Hurst			177		1906	KS, 26th, 1907
Johnston, Francis E.		D, 9th Iowa (died of cancer)	15	76	1920 Sep 19	NE, 45th, 1921
Johnston, Frederick	Pvt.		158		1927 Mar 31	IA, 54th, 1928
Johnston, George		G, 145th Ill.	57		1915 Oct 27	KS, 35th, 1916
Johnston, H.		H, 11th Kans.	291		1888	KS, 8th, 1889
Johnston, J.H.		G, 126th Ill. Inf.	94	96	1935 Oct 26	IA, 62nd, 1936
Johnston, J.K.		I, 2nd Art. Battery	7		1885	KS, 5th, 1886
Johnston, J.M.	Pvt.	E, 8th Iowa Inf.	14		1916 Apr 20	IA, 43rd, 1917
Johnston, J.M.			96		1917 Mar 22	IA, 44th, 1918
Johnston, J.M.	Pvt.	K, 14th Iowa Inf.	12		1919 Apr 6	IA, 46th, 1920
Johnston, J.T.	Sergt.	G, 4th Mo. State Militia	10		1918 Apr 12	IA, 45th, 1919
Johnston, J.W.	Capt.	E, 12th Ohio	44		1914 Mar 29	KS, 34th, 1915
Johnston, James D.	Pvt.	K, 36th Iowa	40		1907 Dec 13	IA, 34th, 1908
Johnston, John F.			287		1899	KS, 19th, 1900
Johnston, John W.	Capt.	E, 12th Ohio Cav.	44		1913 Mar 29	KS, 33rd, 1914
Johnston, Joseph H.		G, 126th Ill. Inf.	94	96	1935 Oct 26	IA, 65th, 1939
Johnston, Owen Z.		D, 11th Ill. Inf.		91 & 7 mos.	1937 Feb 26	IA, 64th, 1938
Johnston, R.H.	Pvt.	L, 3rd Iowa Cav.	195	61	1897 Nov 30	IA, 24th, 1898
Johnston, Simeon		B, 14th Penn. Cav.	81		1933 Mar 10	NE, 58th, 1934
Johnston, T.K.		D, 26th Minn.	380		1913 Jul 17	KS, 33rd, 1914
Johnston, W.H.		A, 120th Ill.	8		1906 Nov 21	KS, 26th, 1907
Johnston, Wm.	Pvt.	B, 2nd Wis. Inf.	505		1906 Jun 13	IA, 33rd, 1907
Johnston, Wm.			277		1911 2nd term	IA, 38th, 1912
Joiner, B.A.	Pvt.	M, 11th Mo. Inf.	122		1905 Oct 16	IA, 32nd, 1906
Jolley, J.M.			45		1926 Aug 9	IA, 53rd, 1927
Jolley, M.P.		A, 126th Ohio	63		1922 Dec 8	KS, 42nd, 1923
Jollman, John	Pvt.	A, 1st Minn. Inf.	267		1902 Jun 18	IA, 29th, 1903
Jolls, Levi	Pvt.	C, 32nd Ill. Inf.	68	90	1933 Jun 12	IA, 60th, 1934
Jolly, N.J.		117th Ind. Inf.	173		1917	IA, 44th, 1918
Jolly, Z.T.			173		1915	IA, 42nd, 1916
Jones, A.			143		1890	NE, 15th, 1891
Jones, A.A.		A, 4th Mich. Cav.	322		1910 Jul 30	KS, 30th, 1911
Jones, A.A.		F, 63rd Ohio Inf.	12		1934 Feb 4	KS, 54th, 1935
Jones, A.C.			27		1884	KS, 4th, 1885
Jones, A.H.	Pvt.	A, 25th Wis. Inf.	392		1908 Nov 3	IA, 35th, 1909
Jones, A.H.		I, 61st N.Y. (died of congestion of brain)	32	74	1913 Jan 10	NE, 38th, 1914
Jones, A.H.		I, 61st N.Y. Inf. (died of congestion of brain)	10	74	1913 Jan 10	NE, 38th, 1914
Jones, A.J.		C, 3rd Ill. Cav.	498		1910 May 19	KS, 30th, 1911

*See Appendix A, B or C for roster of post names and locations.
†See Introduction for note regarding recording of death date.
288

Name	Rank	Company, Regiment or Ship	Post*	Age	Death Date†	Journal
Jones, A.J.		3rd Ill. Cav.	498		1910 May 19	KS, 33rd, 1914
Jones, A.L.		3rd, 36th, & 34th Ohio (died of old age)	32	79	1915 Jun 8	NE, 40th, 1916
Jones, Aaron		G, 87th Ind.	142		1909 Jul 8	KS, 29th, 1910
Jones, Aaron		G, 29th Ill.	49		1913	KS, 33rd, 1914
Jones, Aaron Matt	Pvt.	G, 211th Penn. Inf.	124	93	1936 Jun 22	IA, 65th, 1939
Jones, Abner		F, 91st Ill.	303		1916 Mar 4	KS, 36th, 1917
Jones, Albert	Pvt.	A, 23rd Iowa Inf.	12		1919 Aug 10	IA, 46th, 1920
Jones, Alexander	Pvt.	G, 27th Iowa Inf.	132		1903 Jan 11	IA, 29th, 1903
Jones, Alonzo	Pvt.	C, 33rd Iowa Inf.	40		1916 Jan 14	IA, 43rd, 1917
Jones, Alvin	Lieut.	B, 3rd Vt. Inf.	127		1917 Sep 27	IA, 44th, 1918
Jones, Andrew W.		G, 23rd Iowa	176		1915 May 28	KS, 35th, 1916
Jones, Asa	Pvt.	G, 2nd Ill. Cav.	245	57	1890 Feb 12	IA, 17th, 1891
Jones, Asa	Pvt.	B, 18th Iowa Inf.	173	64	1898 May 6	IA, 24th, 1898
Jones, B.B.		K, 13th Ky. Inf.	42		1918 May 9	KS, 38th, 1919
Jones, B.F.	Corp.	B, 1st Va. Cav.	145		1916 Apr 9	IA, 43rd, 1917
Jones, B.W.	Pvt.	A, 44th Iowa Inf.	78		1911 Oct 10	IA, 38th, 1912
Jones, C.B.		B, 25th Ohio Inf.	18		1917 Apr 26	KS, 37th, 1918
Jones, C.M.		D, 20th Mich. Inf.	25		1899 Aug 21	KS, 19th, 1900
Jones, C.R.		A, 14th Ill.	1		1919 May 27	KS, 39th, 1920
Jones, C.T.	Pvt.	H, 2nd Iowa Inf.	7		1915 Sep 15	IA, 42nd, 1916
Jones, C.T.		A, 101st Ill.	63		1922 Oct 27	KS, 42nd, 1923
Jones, Cass		F, 2nd Kans. Cav.	84		1927 Sep 9	NE, 52nd, 1928
Jones, Chas. L.	Pvt.	I, 2nd Iowa Cav.	105		1912 Apr 6	IA, 39th, 1913
Jones, D.A.	Pvt.	D, 28th Iowa Inf.	98		1913 May 8	IA, 40th, 1914
Jones, D.D.		C, 27th Ohio Inf.	440		1915 Jul 30	IA, 42nd, 1916
Jones, D.K.	Pvt.	A, 2nd Iowa Inf.	116		1908 Nov 11	IA, 35th, 1909
Jones, D.L.		B, 65th Ill. Inf.	94	93	1935 Jan 14	IA, 62nd, 1936
Jones, D.L.		C, 9th Tenn.	38		1885	KS, 5th, 1886
Jones, Danford M.		C, 142nd Ill.	134		1919 Aug 12	KS, 39th, 1920
Jones, Danl. W.	Pvt.	E, 6th U.S. Cav.	40	54	1888	IA, 18th, 1892
Jones, David		2nd U.S. Inf. (died of old age)	69	73	1908 Oct 31	NE, 33rd, 1909
Jones, David F.		A, 145th Ohio Inf. A, 185th Ohio Inf. (died by fall from scaffold at work)	55		1890	KS, 10th, 1891
Jones, Delivan		E, 105th Ohio	318		1892 Sep 4	KS, 12th, 1893
Jones, E.B.		H, 93rd Ill.	46		1927 Jul 21	KS, 47th, 1928
Jones, E.C.		I, 18th Ill.	61		1932 Jun 22	KS, 53rd, 1934
Jones, E.D.		A, 23rd Ind. (died of old age)	13	82	1919 Jan 10	NE, 44th, 1920
Jones, E.J.B.		F, 10th Kans.	55		1910 Nov 12	KS, 30th, 1911
Jones, E.L.		A, 3rd Kans. State Militia	12		1911 Nov 4	KS, 31st, 1912
Jones, E.S.		B, 151st Ind. (died of old age)	169	86	1914 May 2	NE, 39th, 1915
Jones, Ed. F.		I, 7th Iowa	46		1898 Jul 9	KS, 18th, 1899
Jones, Elias W.		E, 5th Mo. Inf. (died of paralysis)	354	76	1905 Mar 10	NE, 30th, 1906
Jones, Ellis		A, 9th Kans. Vol. Cav.	196		1892 Jan 1	KS, 12th, 1893
Jones, Ellis W.		E, 5th Mo. Inf. (died of paralysis at Soldiers & Sailors Home, Grand Island; buried in Home Cemetery)	6	76	1905 Mar 10	NE, 30th, 1906
Jones, Ezekiel	Pvt.	D, 27th Iowa Inf.	292	88	1888 Jul 7	IA, 15th, 1889
Jones, Ezekiel D.		D, 15th Iowa Inf.	127		1919[1916?] Jun 7	KS, 36th, 1917
Jones, F.J.		dropped dead	354		1925	NE, 50th, 1926
Jones, Francis	Pvt.	B, 21st Wis. Inf.	36		1912 Mar 13	IA, 38th, 1912
Jones, Frank H.	Pvt.	A, 1st Iowa Cav.	2		1903 Feb 19	IA, 30th, 1904
Jones, Frank H.	Pvt.	A, 1st Iowa Cav.	2		1903 Feb 19	IA, 29th, 1903
Jones, G.B.	Pvt.	D, 2nd Mo. Cav.	192	44	1887 Nov 16	IA, 14th, 1888
Jones, Geo. F.		A, 122nd Ill.	63		1917 May 19	KS, 37th, 1918
Jones, George A.		I, 10th Mich. Inf.	477		1934 May 31	KS, 54th, 1935
Jones, George W.		C, 16th Ind.	17		1915 Sep 7	KS, 35th, 1916
Jones, H., Dr.		I, 112th Ill.	20		1893 Mar 8	KS, 13th, 1894
Jones, H.A.	Pvt.	G, 17th V.R.C.	81		1906 Nov 30	IA, 33rd, 1907
Jones, H.L.	Pvt.	K, 2nd Iowa Inf.	127		1925 Mar 3	IA, 52nd, 1926
Jones, H.S.		Indian wars	50		1917 Nov 3	KS, 37th, 1918
Jones, Harvey F.		I, 122nd Ill. Inf.	231		1886	KS, 6th, 1887

Name	Rank	Company, Regiment or Ship	Post*	Age	Death Date†	Journal
Jones, Henry	Pvt.		52		1920 Jul	IA, 47th, 1921
Jones, Henry		C, 44th Mo.	147		1924 Apr 24	KS, 44th, 1925
Jones, Henry		M, 2nd Neb. Cav. (died of disease of liver)	95	57	1902 Sep	NE, 27th, 1903
Jones, Henry		M, 2nd Mo. Cav. (born in Ohio, Jan. 8, 1836; died in Bainbridge)	94		1883 Oct 21	NE, 8th, 1884
Jones, I.		G, 56th Penn. Inf. (died of heart failure)	118	80	1906 Jan 1	NE, 31st, 1907
Jones, Isaiah		C, 7th Kans.	55		1911 Aug 28	KS, 31st, 1912
Jones, J.B.	Pvt.	C, 39th Wis. Inf.	12		1905 Sep 24	IA, 32nd, 1906
Jones, J.B.		A, 30th Ind. Inf.	180		1930 Dec 9	KS, 50th, 1931
Jones, J.D.		C, 8th Ill.	81		1928 Jul 16	KS, 48th, 1929
Jones, J.E.		A, 110th Ill.	63		1905 Jun 2	KS, 25th, 1906
Jones, J.F.	Pvt.	G, 114th Ohio Inf.	55		1910 Apr 2	IA, 37th, 1911
Jones, J.H.	Pvt.	M, 8th Iowa Cav.	17		1911 Nov 13	IA, 38th, 1912
Jones, J.J.		B, 65th Ill. C, 2nd Iowa	97		1919 Oct 1	KS, 39th, 1920
Jones, J.L.		B, 152nd Ill.	1		1892 Oct 13	KS, 12th, 1893
Jones, J.L.			118		1910 Nov 10	KS, 30th, 1911
Jones, J.M.	Pvt.	F, 129th Ill.	30		1906 Feb 22	IA, 33rd, 1907
Jones, J.M.	Paymaster	U.S.	66		1917 Feb 10	IA, 44th, 1918
Jones, J.M.		K, 47th Ill. Inf.	40	73	1920 Dec 21	NE, 45th, 1921
Jones, J.P.	Pvt.	B, 2nd Iowa Cav.	50		1915 Apr 28	IA, 42nd, 1916
Jones, J.R.	Capt.	E, 32nd Iowa Inf.	220	51	1889 Sep 5	IA, 16th, 1890
Jones, J.R.		B, 16th Ky.	18		1915 Jun 30	KS, 35th, 1916
Jones, J. Truman	Pvt.	G, 15th Iowa Inf.	7		1926 Sep	IA, 53rd, 1927
Jones, J.W.	Pvt.	F, 47th Iowa Inf.	17		1919 Jan 9	IA, 46th, 1920
Jones, Jacob H.		H, 17th Ohio Inf.	26		1892 Oct 15	NE, 17th, 1893
Jones, James		K, 112th Ill. Inf.	7		1922 Aug 19	KS, 45th, 1926
Jones, James		C, 40th Ind. (died of fall from wagon)	121	59	1897 May 3	NE, 22nd, 1898
Jones, James C.		C, 2nd Mo. Cav.	18		1913 Jul 21	KS, 33rd, 1914
Jones, James E.		F, 6th Kans. Cav.	88		1914 Aug 22	KS, 34th, 1915
Jones, James E.			107		1905	NE, 30th, 1906
Jones, James J.	Pvt.	C, 31st Wis. Inf.	40		1911 Feb 6	IA, 38th, 1912
Jones, Jas. L.		A, 8th Ill.	293		1906 Nov 7	KS, 26th, 1907
Jones, Jesse	Pvt.	40th Ind. Inf.	69		1925 Mar 21	IA, 52nd, 1926
Jones, John	Pvt.	83rd Ill. Inf.	56		1922 Nov 3	IA, 49th, 1923
Jones, John		G, 91st Inf. (died at Morehead)	480		1895 Nov	KS, 15th, 1896
Jones, John		D, 40th U.S. Cav.	236		1905 Aug 22	KS, 25th, 1906
Jones, John D.	Pvt.	I, 24th Ind. Inf.	11		1917 Nov 28	IA, 44th, 1918
Jones, John H.		E, 4th Tenn. Cav.	7		1911 Jan 31	KS, 31st, 1912
Jones, John M.		K, 146th Ill. Inf. (died of general debility)	133	75	1920 Nov 21	NE, 45th, 1921
Jones, John M.		G, 16th Wis. Inf.	87		1899 Jan 24	KS, 19th, 1900
Jones, John T.	Pvt.	K, 8th Iowa Cav.	8		1914 Aug 27	IA, 41st, 1915
Jones, John W.	Pvt.	B, 134th Ind. Inf.	81	41	1890 Oct 20	IA, 17th, 1891
Jones, John W.		E, 167th Ohio Inf.	25		1917 Jan 1	KS, 37th, 1918
Jones, Joseph		Ohio	139	61	1905	NE, 30th, 1906
Jones, Joseph A.		D, 74th Ind.	153		1898 Oct 5	KS, 18th, 1899
Jones, L.	Pvt.	K, 28th Iowa	16		1921 Feb 3	IA, 48th, 1922
Jones, L.D.		B, 107th Ill. Inf.	59		1916 Oct 31	KS, 36th, 1917
Jones, L.W.		58th Ill.	137		1888	KS, 8th, 1889
Jones, Leander		A, 123rd Ind. Inf.	11	73	1917 Mar 10	NE, 42nd, 1918
Jones, Lemon		K, 130th Ind.	74		1898 Apr 28	KS, 18th, 1899
Jones, Levi	Pvt.	D, 32nd Iowa Inf.	300	61	1888 Mar	IA, 15th, 1889
Jones, M.C.	Pvt.	K, 7th Vt. Inf.	30	44	1887 May 28	IA, 14th, 1888
Jones, Marshall		E, 42nd Ind. Inf. (died of epilepsy)	35	71	1912 Feb 3	NE, 37th, 1913
Jones, Milton	Sergt.		124		1923 May 11	IA, 50th, 1924
Jones, Morton H.	1st Lieut.	D, 45th Iowa Inf.	100	71	1899 May 25	IA, 26th, 1900
Jones, O.H.		C, 118th Ind.	11		1889	KS, 9th, 1890
Jones, Ora		A, 3rd Cal.	45		1906 Nov 13	KS, 26th, 1907
Jones, Philip I.		K, 9th Iowa Cav.	265		1927 Mar 30	NE, 51st, 1927
Jones, Richard	Pvt.	G, 75th Ill. Inf.	74		1900 Sep 13	IA, 27th, 1901
Jones, Robert S.	Pvt.	E, 4th Iowa Cav.	12		1914 Nov 27	IA, 41st, 1915
Jones, S.A.		A, 18th U.S. Inf.	262	74	1914 May 17	NE, 39th, 1915

*See Appendix A, B or C for roster of post names and locations.
†See Introduction for note regarding recording of death date.

Name	Rank	Company, Regiment or Ship	Post*	Age	Death Date†	Journal
Jones, S.B.		D, 8th Iowa	57		1914 Sep 19	KS, 34th, 1915
Jones, S.C.	Lieut.	A, 22nd Iowa Inf.	8	94	1932 Dec 27	IA, 59th, 1933
Jones, Sam'l		117th Ill. Inf. (cause of death: heart)	25		1903 Sep 1	NE, 28th, 1904
Jones, Samuel	Pvt.	E, 13th Ill.	1		1922 Jul 11	IA, 49th, 1923
Jones, Samuel H.		A, 7th Ind. Cav.	1		1922 May 30	KS, 42nd, 1923
Jones, Sanduskey		G, 94th Ohio	250		1906 Jun 8	KS, 26th, 1907
Jones, Seth		H, 40th Iowa	17		1910 Jul 25	KS, 30th, 1911
Jones, Stephen		D, 2nd Maine Cav.	143		1925 Jul 7	NE, 51st, 1927
Jones, Stephen B.		D, 1st N.Y. Lt. Art. (died of heart disease, asthma, dropsy)	60	76	1916 Jun 25	NE, 40th, 1916
Jones, Sylvester		F, 30th Iowa	25		1928 Jan 4	NE, 53rd, 1929
Jones, T.C.		A, 146th N.Y.	129		1902 Sep 2	KS, 22nd, 1903
Jones, T.H.	Pvt.	H, 22nd Wis. Inf.	124		1915	IA, 42nd, 1916
Jones, T.J.	Pvt.	B, 77th Ohio Inf.	26		1902 Jul 13	IA, 29th, 1903
Jones, Theo.	Pvt.	A, 9th Iowa Cav.	255		1924 Dec 11	IA, 51st, 1925
Jones, Theo.	Corp.	A, 9th Iowa Cav.	255		1923	IA, 50th, 1924
Jones, Thomas		F, 14th Kans.	221		1913 Sep 23	KS, 33rd, 1914
Jones, Thomas H.		B, 15th Mo. Cav.	500		1914 Jun 19	KS, 34th, 1915
Jones, Thomas J.	Pvt.	B, 10th Iowa Inf.	74	56	1893 Aug 13	IA, 21st, 1895
Jones, Thomas M.	Pvt.	C, 14th Ill. (not member of the post, but buried by it)	[64?]		1885	KS, 5th, 1886
Jones, Thos.		D, 2nd Ind.	239		1898 Dec 4	KS, 18th, 1899
Jones, Thos.		G, 2nd Minn.	25		1927 Aug 28	NE, 52nd, 1928
Jones, Thos. A.	Corp.	F, 26th N.Y. Inf.	82		1911 Sep 16	IA, 38th, 1912
Jones, Thos. S.		G, 63rd Ind. Inf.	25	78	1916	NE, 44th, 1920
Jones, U.G.		U.S. Navy	28		1918 Jan 2	KS, 38th, 1919
Jones, Virgil A.		52nd Ky. Inf. (died of pneumonia)	38	73	1911 Mar 26	NE, 36th, 1912
Jones, W.B.	Pvt.	K, 27th Iowa	223		1914 Feb 14	IA, 41st, 1915
Jones, W.C.		143rd Ohio National Guard	124		1926 Jan 26	IA, 53rd, 1927
Jones, W.E.		A, 12th Wis.	235		1914 Aug 15	IA, 41st, 1915
Jones, W.G.	Asst. Surg.	14th Ky. Cav.	25		1889	KS, 9th, 1890
Jones, W.H.		B, 2nd Mich. Inf.	216		1st quarter 1884	IA, 10th, 1884
Jones, W.H.	Pvt.	G, 74th Ohio Inf.	153		1913 Jun 25	IA, 40th, 1914
Jones, W.H.	Pvt.	E, 45th Iowa Inf.	170	84	1931 Jun 25	IA, 58th, 1932
Jones, W.H.			185		1896 Jun 22	KS, 16th, 1897
Jones, W.H.		H, 57th Ohio	19		1913 May 31	KS, 33rd, 1914
Jones, W.H.	Paymaster	Ohio	19		1914 May 31	KS, 34th, 1915
Jones, W.L.			371		1906	IA, 33rd, 1907
Jones, W.N.		B, 9th Mich. Cav.	12		1914 Apr 25	KS, 34th, 1915
Jones, W.O.		83rd Ill. (died of old age)	82	79	1909 Dec 29	NE, 34th, 1910
Jones, W.T.		L, 15th Kans. Cav.	40		1919 Jan 12	KS, 39th, 1920
Jones, Walter N.	Pvt.	D, 113th Ill.	40		1899 Jun 23	IA, 26th, 1900
Jones, William		C, 84th Ind.	303		1912 Jun 5	KS, 32nd, 1913
Jones, William A.		K, 99th Ind.	117		1897 Mar 24	KS, 17th, 1898
Jones, William D.		G, 14th Ill.	127		1924 May 9	KS, 44th, 1925
Jones, William H.		E, 3rd Vt. Inf. (nonmember)			1941 Nov 17	NE, 66th, 1942
Jones, Wm.	Pvt.	G, 46th Iowa Inf.	398		1908 Apr 3	IA, 35th, 1909
Jones, Wm.	Lieut. Col.	40th Ohio Inf.	440		1914 Nov 12	IA, 41st, 1915
Jones, Wm.	Pvt.	H, Iowa	98		1924 Dec	IA, 51st, 1925
Jones, Wm.		H, 52nd Iowa	55		1921 Dec 18	KS, 41st, 1922
Joor, C.	Pvt.	K, 32nd Iowa Inf.	31		2nd quarter 1885	IA, 12th, 1886
Jordan, —			11		1913	IA, 40th, 1914
Jordan, Cornelius	Pvt.	B, 17th Wis. Inf.	67	42	1887 Sep 4	IA, 15th, 1889
Jordan, Cornelius	Pvt.	B, 17th Wis. Inf.	67	46	1887 Sep 4	IA, 14th, 1888
Jordan, D.C.	Capt.	G, 40th Iowa Inf. (died of rheumatism & comp.)	10	78	1910 Aug 10	NE, 35th, 1911
Jordan, Foster	Pvt.	I, 14th Penn.	52		1915 Dec 19	KS, 35th, 1916
Jordan, Frank			5		1929 Aug 3	IA, 56th, 1930
Jordan, H.B.	Sergt.	E, 30th Iowa Inf.	363		1909 Sep 9	IA, 36th, 1910
Jordan, Hugh	Corp.	H, 18th Iowa Inf.	118	44	1887 Jul 14	IA, 14th, 1888
Jordan, Isaac B.	Corp.	G, 2nd Mass. Cav.	441		1899 Jun 8	IA, 26th, 1900
Jordan, J.H.	Pvt.	E, 13th Ill. Inf.	1		1926 Mar 22	IA, 53rd, 1927

Name	Rank	Company, Regiment or Ship	Post*	Age	Death Date†	Journal
Jordan, J.L.	Pvt.	I, 88th Penn. Inf.	84	72	1895 Mar 29	IA, 22nd, 1896
Jordan, J.M.			92		1913	IA, 40th, 1914
Jordan, John	Pvt.	17th Ind.	69		1924 Jun 8	IA, 51st, 1925
Jordan, M.A.			89		1912 May 6	KS, 32nd, 1913
Jordan, M.L.	3rd Corp.	G, 9th Iowa Inf.	68		1925 Feb 14	IA, 52nd, 1926
Jordan, Nathan		I, 19th Mass.	147		1926 Jan	KS, 46th, 1927
Jordan, Patrick		C, 3rd Mich. Inf.	147		1902 Jan 7	KS, 22nd, 1903
Jordan, Stephen	Sergt.	D, 130th Ohio Vol. Inf.	339	44	1885 Dec 2	IA, 12th, 1886
Jordan, T.W., see Rordan, T.W.						
Jordan, W.S.	Lieut.	22nd Ind. Inf.	11		1912 Jan 29	IA, 39th, 1913
Jordan, Wade H.		H, 21st Penn.	25	79	1915 Apr 28	NE, 40th, 1916
Jorden, Zachariah W.		F, 2nd Ohio Art.	289		1886	KS, 6th, 1887
Jordon, E.T.	Pvt.	C, 102nd Ill.	127		1924 Nov 6	IA, 51st, 1925
Jordon, Henry C.	Pvt.	A, 23rd Iowa Inf.	12		1918 Nov 24	IA, 45th, 1919
Jorgensen, Christian		G, 39th Inf. (died of dropsy, heart trouble at Soldiers & Sailors Home, Grand Island; buried at Hastings, Neb.)	20	67	1905 Aug 29	NE, 30th, 1906
Jorgenson, C.J.			13		1905	NE, 30th, 1906
Jorstead, Jno. S.		E, 89th Ill.	25	74	1917 Mar 17	NE, 42nd, 1918
Jory, John	Pvt.	F, 45th Ill. Inf.	234		1915 Nov 25	IA, 42nd, 1916
Joseph, Abraham C.		K, 11th Ind. Inf. 11th U.S. Inf. K, 20th U.S. Inf. (died at Topeka, Kans.; buried at Topeka Cemetery)	1		1894 Jun 15	KS, 14th, 1895
Joseph, Elmer		G, 53rd Penn.	87		1925 Jun 24	KS, 45th, 1926
Joseph, H.C.			519		1916	IA, 43rd, 1917
Joseph, Leonidas W.		K, 129th Ohio A, 42nd Ohio A, 30th Ill. (died at Soldiers Home, Leavenworth, Kans.)	336		1890	KS, 10th, 1891
Josephus			27		1909	IA, 36th, 1910
Joslin, J.F.		C, 31st Ind. Inf.	65		1912 Sep 12	KS, 32nd, 1913
Joslin, O.N.		C, 15th Mich.	83		1924 Nov 28	KS, 44th, 1925
Joslin, Thos. H.	Corp.	E, 33rd Wis. Inf.	452		1926 Sep 14	IA, 53rd, 1927
Joslyn, Fred		C, 116th N.Y. (died of general debility)	95	78	1920 Jan 8	NE, 45th, 1921
Joslyn, H.M.		111th N.Y.	129		1917 Jan 23	KS, 37th, 1918
Joslyn, J.	Pvt.	E, 13th Wis. Inf.	73		1910 Nov	IA, 37th, 1911
Josselyn, S.T.		C, 13th Ill. Inf.	110	63	1905 Apr 4	NE, 30th, 1906
Jossinger, Henry	Pvt.	G, 8th Iowa Inf.	1		1906 Aug 28	IA, 33rd, 1907
Jost, August		C, 5th Mo.	28		1924 Jun 3	KS, 44th, 1925
Jost, Jacob	Pvt.	A, 29th N.Y. Inf.	200		1915 Oct 7	IA, 42nd, 1916
Joute, P.F.	Pvt.	A, 60th Ohio Inf.	127	50	1889 Jun 25	IA, 16th, 1890
Joute, P.F.	Drum Major	60th Ohio Inf.	127	44	1888 Sep 8	IA, 18th, 1892
Jowler, George W.		H, 44th Ill.	196		1911 Jun 25	KS, 31st, 1912
Joy, Henry			152		1914 Aug 11	IA, 41st, 1915
Joy, J.P.		H, 4th Ohio	69		1923 Sep 26	KS, 44th, 1925
Joy, James		L, 15th Kans.	1		1926 Aug 2	KS, 46th, 1927
Joy, Joseph		H, 4th Ohio	69		1923 Sep 26	KS, 46th, 1927
Joy, Lenard	Band	34th Iowa	116		1924 Oct 24	IA, 51st, 1925
Joyce, Edward	Pvt.	L, 10th Ky. Cav.	150	51	1893 Feb 4	IA, 19th, 1893
Joyce, Edward	Corp.	L, 10th Ky. Cav.	150	51	1894 Feb 4	IA, 20th, 1894
Joyce, Geo.		E, 46th Iowa	94		1929 Jul 23	NE, 54th, 1930
Joyse, David		D, 6th Ohio Inf.	1		1893 Dec 5	NE, 18th, 1894
Juckett, F.H.	Pvt.	E, 77th N.Y. Inf.	235		1924 Oct 10	IA, 51st, 1925
Judd, A.H.		F, 1st Penn. Cav.	76		1912	KS, 32nd, 1913
Judd, D.B.	Pvt.	E, 128th Ohio Inf.	72		1911 Oct 27	IA, 38th, 1912
Judd, Edwin		8th Ill.	238		1928 May 1	KS, 48th, 1929
Judd, Nez		G, 3rd Ill. Cav.	156		1905 Aug 3	KS, 25th, 1906
Judd, Oliver H.		A, 36th Ill. Vol. Inf.	132		1909 Mar 13	KS, 29th, 1910
Judd, R.M.	Pvt.	M, 1st Wis. Cav.	512		1902 Nov 2	IA, 29th, 1903
Judd, Reuben		H, 71st Ind.	114		1909 Jun 23	KS, 29th, 1910
Judd, S.J.		1st Mass. Hvy. Art.	127		1911 Feb 1	KS, 31st, 1912

*See Appendix A, B or C for roster of post names and locations.
†See Introduction for note regarding recording of death date.

Name	Rank	Company, Regiment or Ship	Post*	Age	Death Date†	Journal
Judd, Wm.	Pvt.	I, 49th Wis. Inf.	216	56	1887 May 21	IA, 14th, 1888
Judiesch, August F.	Pvt.	A, 9th Iowa Cav.	1, 55	91	1939 Sep 29	IA, 66th, 1940
Judkins, M.W.	Pvt.	G, 15th Iowa Inf.	116	59	1897 Jan 15	IA, 23rd, 1897
Judson, D.J.		I, 26th N.Y. Inf. (died of jaundice)	80	69	1901 Jan	NE, 26th, 1902
Judson, Harlow E.		I, 8th Iowa	43		1924 Feb 5	KS, 43rd, 1924
Judson, Hosa. F.		H, 1st Minn. (died of heart failure)	147	65	1900 Nov 8	NE, 25th, 1901
Judson, I.B.	Pvt.	4th Lt. Art.	337		1924 Nov	IA, 51st, 1925
Judson, W.A.			456		1924	IA, 51st, 1925
Juelfs, Jacob	Pvt.	L, 10th Ill. Inf.	93		1918 Nov 6	IA, 45th, 1919
Juett, Chas. M.		K, 4th Iowa Cav.	44	75	1914 Dec 10	NE, 39th, 1915
Juhnke, A.F.		25th Mich.	354		1927 Aug 13	NE, 52nd, 1928
Julian, Amos	Pvt.	H, 112th Ill. Inf.	66		1910 Jan 26	IA, 37th, 1911
Julian, J.P.		B, 5th Ohio	38		1892 Apr 15	KS, 12th, 1893
Julian, Stephen		C, 13th Iowa Inf.	18		3rd quarter 1884	IA, 11th, 1885
Julian, Steven H.		E, — Tenn.	145		1913 Oct	KS, 33rd, 1914
Julian, William		K, 132nd Ind.	464		1914 Oct 19	KS, 34th, 1915
Julison, Wm.	Pvt.	B, 29th Ohio	68		1923 Jan 21	IA, 50th, 1924
Jump, O.P.		C, 42nd Mo. Inf. (at large)		87	1935 Nov 27	IA, 62nd, 1936
Juneau, H.		B, 10th Wis.	294		1921 Feb 4	KS, 41st, 1922
Jungk, August	Pvt.	H, 1st Iowa Inf.	146	60	1896 Jul 19	IA, 23rd, 1897
Junkins, John S.	Pvt.	B, 98th Ill. Inf.	337		1928 Feb 2	IA, 55th, 1929
Junkins, W.W.		Kans. State Militia	40		1919 Jun 3	KS, 39th, 1920
Jury, Theodore		A, 208th Penn.	22		1922 Jun 22	KS, 42nd, 1923
Justice, Benj.			211		1928	IA, 55th, 1929
Justice, John S.		C, 5th Ky. Cav.	11		1905 Jul 19	KS, 25th, 1906
Justice, L.J.	Pvt.	E, 46th Ill.	247	52	1891 Jan 14	IA, 17th, 1891
Justis, S.M.		B, 35th Ind. Inf. (died at Hollenberg)	70		1894 Dec 9	KS, 14th, 1895
Justus, Isaac	Pvt.	H, 32nd Iowa	81		1905 Jul 16	IA, 32nd, 1906
Justus, James			41		1920	KS, 40th, 1921
Kaemps, L.W.		C, 46th Ind.	32		1936	KS, 57th, 1938
Kafer, Christian			291		1919	IA, 46th, 1920
Kahler, Charles F.	Pvt.	C, 14th Iowa	1		1928 May 31	IA, 55th, 1929
Kahler, Henry	Pvt.	C, 14th Iowa Inf.	1		1915 Jul 28	IA, 42nd, 1916
Kahler, Martin J.	Pvt.	E, 115th Ohio Inf.	228	53	1895 Nov 12	IA, 22nd, 1896
Kahley, Henry	Pvt.	G, 93rd Ill. Inf.	12		1904 Sep 17	IA, 31st, 1905
Kaiser, H.B.		E, 144th Ill.	40	83	1916 Jan 9	NE, 41st, 1917
Kaiser, Peter		A, 3rd Mo.	18		1940 May 9	KS, 60th, 1941
Kaiser, Peter		45th & 58th N.Y. (died of heart failure)	55	70	1910 Aug 8	NE, 35th, 1911
Kaizer, Jacob		C, 75th Ohio	55		1893 Dec 2	KS, 13th, 1894
Kakoa, Michael	Corp.	I, 8th Iowa Inf.	208		1909 Apr 4	IA, 35th, 1909
Kalb, A.		K, 116th Ohio Vol. Inf.	40		1915 Mar 1	KS, 35th, 1916
Kale, James	Pvt.	A, 39th Iowa Inf.	55		1917 Jun 26	IA, 44th, 1918
Kaler, Samuel		L, 12th Ohio	1		1930 Feb 8	KS, 50th, 1931
Kaler, William		F, 9th Ind.	79		1927	KS, 48th, 1929
Kaley, Abram		I, 53rd Penn. Inf.	25	78	1918	NE, 43rd, 1919
Kalsom, S.V.	Pvt.	C, 7th Iowa	30		1926 Apr 8	IA, 53rd, 1927
Kamberling, H.	Pvt.	A, 13th Iowa Inf.	400	72	1896 Oct 16	IA, 23rd, 1897
Kamery, James	Corp.	F, 15th Ill. Inf.	154		1920 Mar 25	IA, 47th, 1921
Kan, Henry	Sergt.	H, 1st Neb. Cav.	210	54	1896 Nov 9	IA, 23rd, 1897
Kanaga, P.B.			17		1901	KS, 21st, 1902
Kanaval, G.W.		F, 80th Ohio Inf.	255		1931 Jan	KS, 51st, 1932
Kane, Ansel J.		H, 30th Mich.	250		1898 Sep 21	KS, 18th, 1899
Kane, Henry		A, 24th Iowa Inf.	147		1916 Oct 24	KS, 36th, 1917
Kane, John	Pvt.	C, 1st Iowa Inf.	231	54	1891 Nov 9	IA, 18th, 1892
Kaness, Henry			94		1890	NE, 15th, 1891
Kannoe, Theodore		E, 7th Iowa Cav. (died of heart disease)	354	70	1918 Feb 22	NE, 43rd, 1919
Kantz, Peter		2nd Mo. Cav.	65		1918 Sep 14	KS, 38th, 1919
Kargus, August	Pvt.	E, 9th Wis. Inf.	391	46	1886 Sep 2	IA, 13th, 1887
Karner, Wilson S.		D, 3rd Ohio Inf. (died of disability)	84	70	1913 Jul 2	NE, 38th, 1914
Karnes, Jasper	Pvt.	C, 118th Ill. Inf.	57		1925 Mar 23	IA, 52nd, 1926
Karns, John S.		I, 175th Ohio Inf.	324		1917 Feb 16	IA, 44th, 1918
Karr, Joseph	Pvt.	C, 38th Wis. Inf.	101		1917 Aug 3	IA, 44th, 1918

See Appendix A, B or C for roster of post names and locations.
†See Introduction for note regarding recording of death date.

Name	Rank	Company, Regiment or Ship	Post*	Age	Death Date†	Journal
Karr, R.E.		H, 57th Ohio	252		1888	KS, 8th, 1889
Karsh, Michael	Pvt.	K, 21st & 34th Iowa	336	83	1899 Mar 9	IA, 25th, 1899
Karst, Geo.	Pvt.	D, 9th Iowa Inf.	141		1923 Apr 14	IA, 50th, 1924
Karstadt, Wm.		H, 15th Kans. Cav.	215		1889	KS, 9th, 1890
Karsteen, C.H.		B, 1st Neb. (died of hernia)	24	75	1910 Aug 16	NE, 35th, 1911
Karton, Anson		B, 51st Wis. Inf. (died of chronic diarrhea)	75		1894 Aug 12	NE, 19th, 1895
Karwarth, Henry	Sergt.	E, 20th Iowa Inf.	1		1927 May 26	IA, 54th, 1928
Kasper, F.W.	Pvt.	C, 2nd Iowa Inf.	231		1916 Jan 3	IA, 43rd, 1917
Kassey, Henry		G, 12th Kans. Inf.	456		1889	KS, 9th, 1890
Kassing, Henry		K, 12th Iowa Inf. (died of old age)	89	87	1921 Jan 18	NE, 46th, 1922
Kasson, C.D.	Pvt.	C, 22nd N.Y. Inf.	324		2nd quarter 1885	IA, 12th, 1886
Kasson, W.O.		E, 6th U.S. Cav.	235		1914 Oct 11	IA, 41st, 1915
Kasterholtz, Levi			45		1908 Dec 7	NE, 33rd, 1909
Kaston, C.	Pvt.	A, Wis. Inf.	170		1922 Feb 19	IA, 49th, 1923
Katch, W.E.		G, 86th Ohio	100		1933 Jul 12	KS, 53rd, 1934
Kates, R.		C, 89th Ind. Inf.	236		1899 Jun 30	KS, 19th, 1900
Kates, W.H.		A, 180th Ohio Inf. (died of chronic diarrhea)	274		1893 Jul 25	NE, 18th, 1894
Kating, C.M.	Pvt.	E, 40th Iowa Inf.	16		1913 Nov 27	IA, 40th, 1914
Katterman, C.E.		A, 208th Penn. Inf.	25		1935 Mar 28	KS, 55th, 1936
Kauffman, Sol.		L, 3rd —	180		1909 Dec 22	KS, 29th, 1910
Kaufman, J.		D, 151st Penn. (died of lung trouble)	100	69	1904 Mar 14	NE, 29th, 1905
Kaufman, T.F.	Col.	29th Penn. Inf.	247		1912 Oct 21	IA, 39th, 1913
Kautch, Joseph		G, 193rd Ohio	75		1910 Feb 11	NE, 35th, 1911
Kavanagh, Bryan		45th Ill. (died of general debility)	169	84	1922	NE, 47th, 1923
Kavanaugh, John		L, 9th Ill. Cav.	47		1933 Nov 20	NE, 58th, 1934
Kavhr, August		A, 11th Mich. P.G. (died of cancer of stomach)	274	63	1908 Jan 6	NE, 33rd, 1909
Kay, Ezra P.		G, 13th Penn. Inf.	6		1914 Apr 13	KS, 34th, 1915
Kay, John		C, 18th Penn.	88		1897 Sep 1	KS, 17th, 1898
Kayes, F.S.	Pvt.	B, 4th Iowa Inf.	197		1930 Oct 25	IA, 57th, 1931
Kaylor, George A.		K, 18th Ind. Inf. (died of old age)	60	83	1924 Oct 26	NE, 49th, 1925
Kaylor, Henry	Pvt.	H, 45th Ill.	68		1924 Mar 21	IA, 51st, 1925
Kaylor, James C.			147		1884	KS, 4th, 1885
Kays, George W.	Pvt. Pvt.	A, 41st Wis. Inf. K, 47th Wis. Inf. (at large)	54	93	1941 Apr 24	IA, 67th, 1941
Keables, B.F.	Surg.	3rd Iowa Inf.	404		1911 May 14	IA, 38th, 1912
Keables, C.F.		C, 18th Conn.	147		1924 Feb 1	KS, 44th, 1925
Keagan, H.L.W.		D, 9th Kans. Cav. (died at Iola)	51		1895 Apr	KS, 15th, 1896
Keaggll, George			65		1924 Aug 21	KS, 44th, 1925
Keagle, Levi S.	Chaplain	I, 45th Ohio Vol. Inf.	98		1901 Dec 12	IA, 28th, 1902
Kealey, Michael		E, 13th Wis. Inf. (died of old age)	111	86	1914 May 20	NE, 39th, 1915
Keane, John	Pvt.	A, 11th Mass. Inf.	150		1907 Dec 19	IA, 34th, 1908
Kear, R.C.		A, 15th Penn. Cav.	127		1890	KS, 10th, 1891
Kearby, J.W.	Pvt.	D, 32nd Iowa Inf.	67		1921 Jun 11	IA, 48th, 1922
Kearney, Francis	Pvt.	G, 6th Iowa Cav.	342	84	1892 Dec 21	IA, 19th, 1893
Kearney, M.	Pvt.	B, 83rd N.Y. Inf.	78		1913 Jan 5	IA, 40th, 1914
Kearns, Delos		I, 141st Ill. (died of paralysis)	44	63	1908 Mar 20	NE, 33rd, 1909
Kearns, John V.	Pvt.	H, 13th U.S. Inf.	66	88	1931 Dec 25	IA, 58th, 1932
Kearns, S.A.	Pvt.	E, 17th Ohio Inf.	452		1929 Jan 27	IA, 56th, 1930
Keath, Gabriel F.		D, 12th Kans.	26		1893 Aug 16	KS, 13th, 1894
Keating, John	Corp.	F, 11th Iowa Inf.	108	58	1893 Nov 13	IA, 20th, 1894
Keck, John Sloan	1st Lieut.	G, 4th Iowa Cav. Vet. Vols.	177	58	1892 Nov 29	IA, 19th, 1893
Keck, Phill	Pvt.	K, 34th Ohio Vol. Inf.	1		1915 Oct 31	KS, 35th, 1916
Keckvort, Albert	Pvt.	B, 86th Ind. Inf.	78		1911 Jul 6	IA, 38th, 1912
Keeble, Frank	Sergt.	B, 98th N.Y. Inf.	7		1919 Feb 18	IA, 46th, 1920
Keefer, W.C.		12th Kans.	25		1905 Sep	NE, 31st, 1907
Keefer, W.C.		12th Kans. Inf. (died of accident)	25		1905 Sep	NE, 30th, 1906
Keegan, R.E.	Pvt.	C, 3rd Ill. Inf.	363		1905 Oct 23	IA, 32nd, 1906
Keeks, John		H, 35th Wis.	6		1926 Apr 5	KS, 46th, 1927
Keeler, A.R.		K, 33rd Ind. Inf.	88		1902 Sep 22	KS, 22nd, 1903
Keeler, Clinton		19th Ind. Bat.	52		1896 Dec 6	KS, 16th, 1897

*See Appendix A, B or C for roster of post names and locations.
†See Introduction for note regarding recording of death date.

Name	Rank	Company, Regiment or Ship	Post*	Age	Death Date†	Journal
Keeler, E.		B, 58th Ind.	112		1889	KS, 9th, 1890
Keeler, James	Pvt.	F, 193rd N.Y. Inf.	327	69	1897 Apr 5	IA, 24th, 1898
Keeley, C.H.	Lieut.	F, 1st Mo. Cav.	17		1909 Nov 15	IA, 36th, 1910
Keeley, Francis	Pvt.	B, 26th Iowa Inf.	74		1927 Dec 9	IA, 54th, 1928
Keeling, W.H.		13th Inf. (died of old age)	84	84	1920 Mar 6	NE, 45th, 1921
Keelor, Urias		G, 2nd Ind. Cav. (born in Indiana; died of paralysis at Soldiers & Sailors Home Hospital, Burkett; buried at Home Cemetery)		68	1907 Feb 6	NE, 31st, 1907
Keen, Almond E.	Pvt.	G, 40th Wis. Inf. (at large)	78	95	1943 May 24	IA, 69th, 1943
Keen, James		G, 5th W. Na.[West Va.?]	145		1906 Oct 13	KS, 26th, 1907
Keen, Louis			371		1906	IA, 33rd, 1907
Keen, Thos.		K, 17th Kans.	23		1917 Feb 8	KS, 37th, 1918
Keenam, Pat	Pvt.	E, 35th Iowa	231		1914 Feb 5	IA, 41st, 1915
Keenan, M.T.	Pvt.	D, 36th Iowa Inf.	138		1909 Dec 16	IA, 37th, 1911
Keener, Geo. I.		E, 14th Penn. Cav.	88		1902	KS, 22nd, 1903
Keener, I.G.		E, 116th Ohio (died of pneumonia)	5		1890	KS, 10th, 1891
Keener, W.H.		A, 16th Ind. Inf.	47		1921 Dec 4	KS, 41st, 1922
Keeney, M.T.	Pvt.	H, 52nd Penn. Inf.	364		1917 Mar 31	IA, 44th, 1918
Keeney, William P.		B, 10th Iowa Inf.		94	1938 May 6	IA, 64th, 1938
Keeny, E.J.		B, 7th Ill.	180		1909 Jul 20	KS, 29th, 1910
Keeny, F.M.	Pvt.	9th Penn.	264[364]		1921	IA, 48th, 1922
Keeper, Alex		C, 100th Penn.	72		1926 Aug 17	KS, 46th, 1927
Keeper, William F.		D, 20th Ill.	167		1905 Dec 2	KS, 25th, 1906
Keerer, Barney			12		1886	NE, 11th, 1887
Keerl, Henry	Pvt.	B, 32nd Iowa Inf.	42		1906 Dec 22	IA, 33rd, 1907
Keeslar, Daniel			139		1924 Nov 1	KS, 44th, 1925
Keeth, James		F, 5th Kans. Cav.	334		1900 Apr	KS, 20th, 1901
Keeve, H.A.		E, 7th Ill.	63		1913 Aug 9	KS, 33rd, 1914
Keever, W.H.		A, 17th U.S. Inf.	57		1898 May 30	KS, 18th, 1899
Keffer, J.W.		E, 52nd Ind.	257		1922 Jun 9	KS, 42nd, 1923
Kehler, Herman B.			374		1906	KS, 26th, 1907
Keiber, Friedrich		E, 148th Ill. (former member of Nebraska Dept.; location: Crab Orchard)	19		1937 May 18	NE, 62nd, 1938
Keiderling, Chas.	Corp.	D, 35th N.J. Inf.	68		1925 Sep 16	IA, 52nd, 1926
Keim, Geo. W.		E, 30th Ind. (died of paralysis)	22	75	1917 May 14	NE, 42nd, 1918
Keim, George W.		E, 30th Ind. (died of heart failure)	22	75	1917 May 14	NE, 41st, 1917
Keirns, Wm.		I, 137th Ill.	19		1907 Aug 1	IA, 34th, 1908
Keiser, Henry	Pvt.	55th Ill. Inf.	267		1906 Sep 9	IA, 33rd, 1907
Keister, O.B.	Pvt.	C, 50th Wis. Inf.	149		1917 Mar 27	IA, 44th, 1918
Keister, Phillip	Musician	36th Iowa Inf.	69		1900 Apr	IA, 27th, 1901
Keister, Wm. A.	1st Sergt.	G, 22nd Iowa Inf.	200		1902 Feb 12	IA, 28th, 1902
Keiter, C.I.	Sergt.	G, 142nd Ill. Inf.	71		1914 Jan 3	IA, 41st, 1915
Keith, F.L.	Sergt.	A, 13th Iowa Inf.	206		1893 Feb 10	IA, 20th, 1894
Keith, H.	Pvt.	I, 18th U.S.C. Inf.	20		1921 Jan	IA, 48th, 1922
Keith, J.W.		G, 145th Ind.	100		1888	KS, 8th, 1889
Keith, John W.		A, 13th Mich.	25		1889	KS, 9th, 1890
Keith, John W.			294		1921 Jun 11	KS, 41st, 1922
Keith, Melvin	Pvt.	H, 44th Iowa Inf.	347		1901 Apr 3	IA, 27th, 1901
Keith, W.B.	Pvt.	B, 35th Ind. Inf.	29	88	1933 Nov 20	IA, 60th, 1934
Keith, William S.		G, 18th Ohio	93		1918 Mar 4	KS, 38th, 1919
Keith, Wm.		K, 42nd Ind.	24		1908 Dec 25	NE, 33rd, 1909
Keithler, John		A, 29th Iowa	2		1934 Jun 11	IA, 61st, 1935
Keithly, Perry C.		C, 78th Ill. Inf.	85		1934 Feb 7	KS, 54th, 1935
Keizer, Jacob			232		1893 Nov 29	KS, 13th, 1894
Keley, P.	Pvt.	K, 92nd Ill. Inf.	111		1902 Dec 30	IA, 29th, 1903
Kelian, C.		Marine (buried by post)	339		1888	KS, 8th, 1889
Kell, Peter O.	Lieut.	Miss. Squadron	170		1910 Dec 6	IA, 37th, 1911
Kellam, George M.		B, 2nd Kans.	1		1912 Nov 12	KS, 32nd, 1913
Kellams, John R.		H, 49th Ind.	85		1913 Jan 19	KS, 33rd, 1914
Kellar, J.C.		D, 10th N.Y.	18		1911 Jan 25	KS, 31st, 1912
Kellar, James G.		A, 4th Ill.	64		1928 Dec 20	KS, 48th, 1929

Name	Rank	Company, Regiment or Ship	Post*	Age	Death Date†	Journal
Kellar, W.F.		F, 131st Penn.	8		1917 Mar 30	KS, 37th, 1918
Kelleher, M.		H, 37th Ill.	35		1914 Nov 25	KS, 34th, 1915
Kelleher, Michael		C, 45th Iowa Inf.	2		1913	IA, 40th, 1914
Kellen, Patrick	Pvt.	K, 6th Iowa Cav.	270		1914 Nov 27	IA, 41st, 1915
Kellenberger, J.H.	Pvt.	B, 3rd Iowa Inf.	64		1923	IA, 50th, 1924
Keller, A.J.	Pvt.	B, 6th Iowa Cav.	206		1912 Sep 15	IA, 39th, 1913
Keller, Abraham		D, 91st Ohio	83		1933 Dec 13	KS, 53rd, 1934
Keller, Adam	Pvt.	I, 74th Ill. Inf.	68		1908 Oct 31	IA, 35th, 1909
Keller, Alex.		I, 1st N.Y. Cav.	52		1921 Mar 28	KS, 41st, 1922
Keller, Amos	Pvt.	Penn. Cav.	108		1922 Apr 15	IA, 49th, 1923
Keller, B.F.			5		1928 Mar 8	IA, 55th, 1929
Keller, C.P.		D, 63rd Ill. Inf.	50		1914 Apr 24	KS, 34th, 1915
Keller, Daniel		K, 158th Penn.	115		1939 Jun 10	KS, 59th, 1940
Keller, David J.		H, 16th Kans.	6		1915 Sep 4	KS, 35th, 1916
Keller, Edmond		K, 86th Ill.	63		1896 Jul 9	KS, 16th, 1897
Keller, H.B.F.		1st Kans.	18		1930 Jan 5	KS, 50th, 1931
Keller, H.D.	Musician	1st Iowa Cav.	153		1908 Jun 11	IA, 35th, 1909
Keller, Henry	Pvt.	B, 38th Iowa Inf.	267		1902 Aug 27	IA, 29th, 1903
Keller, Henry		I, 9th Ill.	115		1939 Dec 31	KS, 59th, 1940
Keller, James		151st Penn.	1		1920 Dec 20	KS, 40th, 1921
Keller, John	Pvt.	A, 31st Iowa Inf.	206		1913 Dec 1	IA, 40th, 1914
Keller, John		A, 39th Mo.	203		1926 Feb 10	KS, 46th, 1927
Keller, Miton		M, 8th Ill. Cav.	116		1899 Aug 17	KS, 19th, 1900
Keller, S.S.	Pvt.	I, 165th Penn. Inf.	29		1930 Aug 11	IA, 57th, 1931
Keller, Thos.	Pvt.	B, 7th Ill. (died of freezing)	247	64	1888 Jan	NE, 12th, 1888
Keller, William H.		K, 86th Ill.	265		1926 Apr 11	NE, 51st, 1927
Kelley, A.J.		G, 149th Ind.	17		1915 Mar 20	KS, 35th, 1916
Kelley, A.R.		G, 19th Ohio Inf. (member at large)	65		1934 Jan 26	KS, 54th, 1935
Kelley, Bernard		F, 103rd Ill.	1		1926 May 16	KS, 46th, 1927
Kelley, Charles		D, 1st Ohio	14		1896 Oct 2	KS, 16th, 1897
Kelley, Chas.	Pvt.	A, 52nd Ill. Inf.	152		1905 Apr 5	IA, 32nd, 1906
Kelley, D.A.		died of heart trouble	77		1919 Dec 10	NE, 44th, 1920
Kelley, E.A.		E, 105th Ohio Inf.	378		1902 Dec 14	KS, 22nd, 1903
Kelley, E.R.		I, 2nd Mo.	265		1928 Jun 18	KS, 48th, 1929
Kelley, Eli		G, 128th Ohio	247		1911 Mar 18	KS, 31st, 1912
Kelley, Ely M.		A, 2nd Ark.	125		1910	KS, 30th, 1911
Kelley, Geo.		H, 13th Mo. Cav.	500		1917 Oct 28	KS, 37th, 1918
Kelley, Geo. W.	Pvt.		30		1916 Nov 15	IA, 43rd, 1917
Kelley, George		F, 21st Ohio	265		1908 Jun 24	KS, 28th, 1909
Kelley, H.B.		C, 1st Iowa Cav.	293		1921 Oct 3	KS, 41st, 1922
Kelley, Harrison		5th Kans.	108		1897 Jul 24	KS, 17th, 1898
Kelley, J.B.	Pvt.	M, 8th Iowa Cav.	452		1920 Feb 19	IA, 47th, 1921
Kelley, J.B.		C, 2nd Iowa	76		1906 Nov 7	KS, 26th, 1907
Kelley, J.J.	Col.	107th Ill. Inf. (cause of death: heart)	214	75	1903 Jan 20	NE, 28th, 1904
Kelley, James	Pvt.	C, 11th Ind. Inf.	29		1920 Jan 1	IA, 47th, 1921
Kelley, James			293[493?]		1905 Dec 23	KS, 25th, 1906
Kelley, James L.		B, 97th Ill.	42		1922 Jan 26	KS, 41st, 1922
Kelley, James T.		I, 1st Ind. Cav.	380		1891 Jul 18	KS, 11th, 1892
Kelley, Joel	Pvt.	K, 16th Wis. Inf.	81		1906 Nov 19	IA, 33rd, 1907
Kelley, Joseph	Pvt.	A, 12th Mich. Inf.	7		1901 Jul 1	IA, 28th, 1902
Kelley, P., see Keley, P.						
Kelley, Patrick		E, 70th Ill. Inf.	354	70	1906 Jan 9	NE, 31st, 1907
Kelley, Peter			161		1899	KS, 19th, 1900
Kelley, S.P.	Pvt.	A, 9th Iowa	269		1902 Jan 1	IA, 28th, 1902
Kelley, S.P.	Lieut.	A, 4th Iowa Cav.	271		1921 Feb 7	IA, 48th, 1922
Kelley, Samuel Washington		G, 141st Ill. Inf.	54	91	1937 Oct 15	IA, 64th, 1938
Kelley, Thomas J.	Pvt.	E, 13th Iowa Inf.	250		1913 Sep 29	IA, 40th, 1914
Kelley, Thos. G.	Sergt.	H, 40th Ill. Inf.	69		1917 Aug	IA, 44th, 1918
Kelley, W.H.	Sergt.	A, 9th Ohio Cav.	26		1921 Jan 20	IA, 48th, 1922
Kelley, W.L.		F, 1st Ohio Lt. Art.	18		1921 Aug 18	KS, 41st, 1922
Kelley, W.R.	Pvt.		167		1916 Dec 15	IA, 43rd, 1917
Kelley, W.T.		E, 39th Ill. Inf. (died of dropsy)	136	67	1905 Dec 12	NE, 30th, 1906

*See Appendix A, B or C for roster of post names and locations.
†See Introduction for note regarding recording of death date.

Name	Rank	Company, Regiment or Ship	Post*	Age	Death Date†	Journal
Kelley, William	Pvt.	A, 14th Iowa Inf.	68		1901 Jan 23	IA, 27th, 1901
Kelley, William		C, 5th Mo.	294		1905 Sep 17	KS, 25th, 1906
Kelley, Wm.	Pvt.	F, 34th Iowa Inf.	192		1916 Jan 11	IA, 43rd, 1917
Kelley, Wm. A.	Pvt.	K, 3rd Iowa Cav.	49		1913 May 28	IA, 40th, 1914
Kelley, Wm. B.	Capt.	19th Ky. Inf. (killed by cars)	301		1891 Nov 9	KS, 11th, 1892
Kelling, Albert	Pvt.	A, 4th Mich. Cav.	22		1908 Jun 19	IA, 35th, 1909
Kellogg, A.F.		G, 10th Mass.	66		1922	IA, 49th, 1923
Kellogg, C.F.	Sergt.	C, 21st Iowa	88		1926 Feb 12	IA, 53rd, 1927
Kellogg, C.R.	Capt.	I, 11th Ind. Inf.	68	60	1897 May 29	IA, 24th, 1898
Kellogg, E.		H, 11th Mo.	239		1897 Jul 25	KS, 17th, 1898
Kellogg, Geo. M.	Surg.	U.S. Vols.	2		1904 Aug 18	IA, 31st, 1905
Kellogg, H., see Kelogg, H.						
Kellogg, H.C.	Corp.	A, 11th Iowa Inf.	452		1926 Feb 23	IA, 53rd, 1927
Kellogg, H.W.		A, 105th Ill. Inf.	23		1908 Nov 20	IA, 35th, 1909
Kellogg, Hiram	Pvt.	C, 5th Iowa Cav.	515	60	1898 Dec 15	IA, 25th, 1899
Kellogg, J.J.		B, 118th Ill. Inf.	108		1916 May 18	IA, 43rd, 1917
Kellogg, Lewis F.	Pvt.	H, 86th Ill. Inf.	197		1929 Nov	IA, 56th, 1930
Kellogg, T.P.	Pvt.	C, 29th Penn. Inf.	86		1908 Jul 27	IA, 35th, 1909
Kellogg, W.P.	Pvt.	H, 26th Ill.	197		1914 Aug 7	IA, 41st, 1915
Kellough, A.		C, 14th Iowa	49		1914	KS, 34th, 1915
Kellsal, Geo. W.	1st D.S.	L, 2nd Iowa Cav.	481	61	1898 Nov 19	IA, 25th, 1899
Kelly, A.C.	Pvt.	G, 44th Iowa Inf.	231		1927 Jun 14	IA, 54th, 1928
Kelly, A.R.		G, 19th Ohio	65		1934 Jan 26	KS, 55th, 1936
Kelly, Ambrose W.		D, 120th Ill.	51		1922 Mar 18	KS, 42nd, 1923
Kelly, Bernard	Pvt. & Capt.	F, 103rd Ill. Inf. (see Appendix D)			1926 Mar 18	KS, 45th, 1926
Kelly, D.J.		B, 11th Ind. Cav.	113		1900 Jan 16	KS, 20th, 1901
Kelly, Frank	Musician	25th Wis. Inf.	451		1910 Jul 22	IA, 37th, 1911
Kelly, Geo. W.		H, 145th Ind.	25		1926 Sep 15	KS, 46th, 1927
Kelly, Horace B.		K, 3rd Wis. Inf. (at large)		93 & 6 mos.	1935 Aug 2	IA, 62nd, 1936
Kelly, J.L.	Sergt.	M, 4th Iowa Cav.	5		1926 Oct 22	IA, 53rd, 1927
Kelly, J.S.	Pvt.	F, 35th Iowa Inf.	153	86	1931 Mar 14	IA, 58th, 1932
Kelly, James			500		1918	KS, 38th, 1919
Kelly, James M.		I, 18th Ohio	66		1913 Oct 11	KS, 33rd, 1914
Kelly, Jno.		K, 105th Penn.	209		1904 Sep 2	KS, 24th, 1905
Kelly, John		F, 19th Ohio Inf.	71		1912 Aug 15	KS, 32nd, 1913
Kelly, John M.		G & F, 68th Ill.	57		1896 Oct 15	KS, 16th, 1897
Kelly, P., see Keley, P.						
Kelly, Reynolds L.		F, 45th Ind.	25		1920 Mar 4	KS, 40th, 1921
Kelly, Thomas		D, 76th Penn. Inf. (died at National Home)	380		1895 Feb	KS, 15th, 1896
Kelly, W.A.	Pvt.	F, 12th Penn. Cav.	329		1905 Sep 25	IA, 32nd, 1906
Kelly, W.V.		I, 70th Ind.	17		1930 Sep 22	KS, 50th, 1931
Kelly, William H.		I, 36th Iowa (died of general disability)	301	67	1911 Mar 28	NE, 36th, 1912
Kelly, Wm.		D, 36th Ohio	14		1898 Jul 27	KS, 18th, 1899
Kelmar, Reinhard	Pvt.	K, 21st Iowa Inf.	342	80	1897 Jun 12	IA, 24th, 1898
Kelogg, H.		A, 105th Ill.	68		1926 Apr 9	KS, 46th, 1927
Kelper, Kris	Pvt.		24		1916	IA, 43rd, 1917
Kelsall, George W., see Kellsal, Geo. W.						
Kelsey, Austin H.		K, 2nd Kans. Cav.	38		1920 Feb 22	KS, 40th, 1921
Kelsey, D.E.		B, 83rd Ind.	1		1904 Oct 1	KS, 24th, 1905
Kelsey, E.A.	Pvt.	C, 27th N.Y. Inf.	240		1913 Jul 17	IA, 40th, 1914
Kelsey, F.	Pvt.	I, 14th N.Y. Inf.	22		1931 Mar 24	IA, 58th, 1932
Kelsey, F.M.	Pvt.	B, 27th Mo.	69		1907 Dec 30	IA, 34th, 1908
Kelsey, Geo. D.		E, 15th Ohio	123		1928 Jan 23	KS, 48th, 1929
Kelsey, Henry		K, 15th Ill.	293		1912 Mar 11	KS, 32nd, 1913
Kelsey, J.C.		A, 17th Kans.	130		1928 May 27	KS, 48th, 1929
Kelsey, J.F.		D, 12th Kans.	1		1923 May 13	KS, 43rd, 1924
Kelsey, James	Pvt.	G, 23rd Ill.	67		1926 Dec 5	IA, 53rd, 1927
Kelsey, Reason D.		F, 73rd Ill.	14		1922 Jun 18	KS, 42nd, 1923
Kelsey, S.H.		I, 84th Ind.	68		1908 Jun 5	KS, 28th, 1909
Kelsey, Scott R.	Seaman	Indiana	1		1936 Apr 8	KS, 55th, 1936

*See Appendix A, B or C for roster of post names and locations.

†See Introduction for note regarding recording of death date.

Name	Rank	Company, Regiment or Ship	Post*	Age	Death Date†	Journal
Kelsey, Thomas		D, 12th Kans. Inf.	18		1935 May 13	KS, 55th, 1936
Kelsey, William		9th Iowa	185		1913 Jan 16	KS, 33rd, 1914
Kelsey, Wm.	Sergt.	C, 78th Ind. Inf.	135		1916	IA, 43rd, 1917
Kelso, J. Seaton	Asst. Surg.	2nd Wis. Inf.	311	70	1892 Feb 12	IA, 18th, 1892
Kelty, S.D.			500		1910	IA, 37th, 1911
Kem, Calvin P.		I, 12th Ind. Cav.	163		1892 Jul 28	NE, 17th, 1893
Kemball, J.M.		G, 11th Kans.	100		1922 Mar 19	KS, 42nd, 1923
Kemble, J.F.		I, 8th Kans.	25		1923	NE, 48th, 1924
Kemble, W.A.	Pvt.	Penn. Inf.	67	94	1931 May 18	IA, 58th, 1932
Kemp, A.P.			158		1899 Dec 23	KS, 19th, 1900
Kemp, George C.			32		1913 Aug 8	KS, 33rd, 1914
Kemp, J.A.	Pvt.	E, 98th Ohio	110		1923 May 24	IA, 50th, 1924
Kemp, John		D, 2nd Kans. State Militia	250		1915 Feb 18	KS, 36th, 1917
Kemp, Sumner	Pvt.	A, 12th Iowa Inf.	436		1920 May 7	IA, 47th, 1921
Kemp, Thos. J.		I, 11th Kans.	278		1921	KS, 41st, 1922
Kemp, William		K, 12th Iowa	355		1918 Dec 3	KS, 38th, 1919
Kemper, D.F.		B, 1st Mo. Cav.	129	62	1903 Oct 1	NE, 28th, 1904
Kemper, J.M.		C, 18th Iowa Inf. (died of cancer)	18	68	1911 Jul 13	NE, 36th, 1912
Kempin, L.A.		F, 129th Ill.	259		1929 May 15	KS, 50th, 1931
Kemple, C.B.		D, 86th Ill. Inf. (died of paralysis)	13	84	1913 Mar 18	NE, 38th, 1914
Kempt, Murphey		B, 9th Ky. (died at Ft. Scott, Kans.)	32		1892 Nov	KS, 12th, 1893
Kemptner, Edw. G.	Pvt.	A, 35th Iowa Inf.	231		1911 May 15	IA, 38th, 1912
Kempton, John W.		L, 6th Mass.	1		1923 Apr 7	KS, 43rd, 1924
Kempton, Seth T.	Pvt.	1st Iowa Cav.	324		1927 Jan 4	IA, 54th, 1928
Kenayer, Eli	Pvt.		2		1932	IA, 59th, 1933
Kenburg, Adam L.		G, 83rd Penn.	182	78	1918	NE, 43rd, 1919
Kendal, F.C.		F, 10th Kans.	74		1914 Aug 30	KS, 34th, 1915
Kendal, W.R.	Pvt.	I, 21st Iowa Inf.	78		1909 Oct 15	IA, 36th, 1910
Kendall, A.R.	Pvt.	A, 37th Ill. Inf.	59	45	1886 Jul 11	IA, 13th, 1887
Kendall, E.L.	Musician	6th Iowa Inf.	18		1900 May 6	IA, 27th, 1901
Kendall, Edw.	Pvt.	A, 11th Penn. Cav.	236		1923 May 3	IA, 50th, 1924
Kendall, H.L.	Sergt.	E, 13th Ill. Inf.	108		1916 Nov 13	IA, 43rd, 1917
Kendall, J.H.		E, 138th Ill. Inf.	29		1921 Jul 27	IA, 48th, 1922
Kendall, James P.		G, 99th Ind.	12		1911 Aug 29	KS, 31st, 1912
Kendall, N.B.		G, 39th Ill.	25		1913 Dec 17	NE, 38th, 1914
Kendall, N.R.		C, 17th Mich.	380		1922 Jul 20	KS, 42nd, 1923
Kendall, P.S.	Pvt.	B, 78th Ind. Inf.	57		1913 Mar 29	IA, 40th, 1914
Kendall, Robert		G, 118th Ill. Inf.	24		1892 Apr 2	NE, 17th, 1893
Kendall, Stephen		D, 38th Wis. (died of pneumonia)	19	63	1907 May 9	NE, 32nd, 1908
Kendell, W.K.			153		1906	KS, 26th, 1907
Kendelspire, Geo.	Pvt.	H, 8th Mo. Inf.	124		1909 Apr 26	IA, 36th, 1910
Kendig, G.W.		B, 1st Penn.	69		1909 Sep 18	KS, 29th, 1910
Kendig, J.B.	Pvt.	G, 122nd Penn. Inf.	511		1911 Aug 2	IA, 38th, 1912
Kendig, O.L.		C, 33rd Iowa	49		1923 Oct 4	IA, 50th, 1924
Kendrew, John		G, 187th Penn.	77		1913 Oct 27	KS, 33rd, 1914
Kendrick, Augustus E.		B, 14th Ky.	255		1908 Jan 30	KS, 28th, 1909
Kendrick, N.H.		A, 16th Ill.	74		1929	KS, 49th, 1930
Kenedy, D.A.	Pvt.	B, 28th Iowa Inf.	314		1905 Oct 24	IA, 32nd, 1906
Kenedy, Ezra		A, 4th Ky.	174		1905 Dec 20	KS, 25th, 1906
Kenedy, M.H.		I, 100th Ind.	25		1893 Jul 13	KS, 13th, 1894
Keneston, S.B.	Pvt.	H, 92nd Ill. Inf.	261		1930 Apr 11	IA, 57th, 1931
Kenfield, W.M.		B, 57th Ill. Inf. (cause of death: heart)	140	59	1901 Jan	NE, 26th, 1902
Keniston, Uriah B.	Pvt.	F, 105th Ill. Inf.	461	95	1935 Apr 18	IA, 65th, 1939
Kenley, James		I, 22nd Ill.	169		1885	KS, 5th, 1886
Kenlim, John	Pvt.	B, 12th Ill. Inf.	193		1911 Jan 24	IA, 38th, 1912
Kennard, R.B.		C, 63rd Ohio	409		1888	KS, 8th, 1889
Kennealy, Thos.	Pvt.	H, 16th U.S. Inf.	259		1913 Jun 12	IA, 40th, 1914
Kennedy, D.A., see Kenedy, D.A.						
Kennedy, D.G.		L, 21st Kans.	40		1906 Jan 18	KS, 26th, 1907
Kennedy, E.R.		F, 6th Iowa Inf.	25	77	1921 Jun 26	NE, 46th, 1922
Kennedy, Edward	Pvt.	B, 32nd Wis. Inf.	466		1923 May	IA, 50th, 1924

*See Appendix A, B or C for roster of post names and locations.
†See Introduction for note regarding recording of death date.
298

Name	Rank	Company, Regiment or Ship	Post*	Age	Death Date†	Journal
Kennedy, Frank		H, 147th Ill. Inf.	231		1924 Feb 24	IA, 51st, 1925
Kennedy, Gayen G.	Pvt.	K, 27th Iowa Inf. (at large)	77	98	1940 Dec 19	IA, 67th, 1941
Kennedy, Geo. S.		H, 109th U.S. Inf.	262	52	1897 Oct 21	NE, 22nd, 1898
Kennedy, George W.	Pvt.	D, 81st Ohio Inf.	98		1928 Sep 14	IA, 55th, 1929
Kennedy, George W.		H, 38th Ohio	88		1911 Aug 9	KS, 31st, 1912
Kennedy, J.F.	Pvt.	H, 34th Ill. Inf.	461		1923 May 31	IA, 50th, 1924
Kennedy, J.H.		B, 126th Ind.	180		1916 Dec 17	KS, 36th, 1917
Kennedy, J.M.		A, 5th U.S. Cav.	18		1917 Apr 24	KS, 37th, 1918
Kennedy, J.T.	Pvt.	I, 10th Iowa Inf.	16		1913 Nov 8	IA, 40th, 1914
Kennedy, James	Pvt.	I, 77th N.Y. Inf.	52		1915 Jul 10	IA, 42nd, 1916
Kennedy, James		G, 68th Ohio	22		1930 Oct 9	NE, 55th, 1931
Kennedy, James M.	Sergt.	D, 187th Penn.	242	59	1900 Mar 24	IA, 26th, 1900
Kennedy, James R.		D, 28th Iowa Inf. (died of broken limb)	4	63	1897 Dec 14	NE, 22nd, 1898
Kennedy, Jefferson		B, 6th Kans. Cav.	68		1925 Dec 31	KS, 45th, 1926
Kennedy, Jesse		C, 40th N.Y. Inf. (died of wounds)	321		1893	NE, 18th, 1894
Kennedy, Jno.		L, 14th Kans. Cav.	151		1904 Feb 15	KS, 24th, 1905
Kennedy, John		D, 69th Ill.	240		1915 Jan 23	KS, 35th, 1916
Kennedy, John M.		F, 16th Kans.	256		1924 Oct 2	KS, 44th, 1925
Kennedy, L.L.		D, 61st Ill.	228		1923 Nov 29	IA, 50th, 1924
Kennedy, M.L.			173		1913	IA, 40th, 1914
Kennedy, Michael		M, 2nd Neb. Cav.	1		1893 Aug	NE, 18th, 1894
Kennedy, Miles H.		I, 129th Ill.	18		1911 Sep 19	KS, 31st, 1912
Kennedy, N.R.	Pvt.	K, 13th Ind. Inf.	68		1920 Jul 13	IA, 47th, 1921
Kennedy, O.P.		F, 3rd Kans. State Militia	12		1917 Apr 25	KS, 37th, 1918
Kennedy, Patrick		L, 1st N.Y. Art.	335		1919 Jun 10	KS, 39th, 1920
Kennedy, R.F.		D, 21st Ind. Inf.	114		1886	KS, 6th, 1887
Kennedy, R.H.		A, 18th Ohio	20		1925 Dec 26	KS, 45th, 1926
Kennedy, Robt.		F, 83rd —	321		1896 Aug 11	KS, 16th, 1897
Kennedy, S.L.	Pvt.	I, 12th Iowa Inf.	235		1917 Nov 15	IA, 44th, 1918
Kennedy, T.H.	Major	12th Kans. Inf.	12		1890	KS, 10th, 1891
Kennedy, Thomas	Pvt.	B, 1st Ky. Inf.	159		1897 Oct 15	IA, 24th, 1898
Kennedy, W.D.		G, 23rd Mo.	435		1918 Feb 7	KS, 38th, 1919
Kennedy, W.M.	Pvt.	A, 7th Iowa Inf.	231		1915 May 21	IA, 42nd, 1916
Kennedy, Wm. D.		E, 63rd Ohio Inf.	154		1901 Sep	NE, 26th, 1902
Kennedy, Wm. H.H.	Pvt.	H, 34th Ill. Inf.		98	1939 May 24	IA, 65th, 1939
Kennely, R.C.	Pvt.	K, 205th Penn. Inf.	12		1929 Dec 31	IA, 56th, 1930
Kennen, J.C.	Capt.	F, 8th Iowa Inf.	98		1906 Jan 2	IA, 33rd, 1907
Kennerly, John		C, 13th Mo. Cav.	160		1908 Dec 19	KS, 28th, 1909
Kennett, —			71		1928	IA, 55th, 1929
Kenney, Samuel	Pvt.	H, 75th Ill.			1902 Apr 3	IA, 28th, 1902
Kenney, Wesley	Pvt.	I, 100th Ill. Inf.	11		1915 Apr 23	IA, 42nd, 1916
Kennison, Edwin			485		1901	KS, 21st, 1902
Kenny, John L.	Lieut.	A, 50th U.S. Col. Inf.	375		1910 Apr 11	IA, 37th, 1911
Kenoyer, Elyah		15th Ind.	17		1904 Jan	KS, 24th, 1905
Kent, Charles		D, 5th Mich. (died of gastratagia at Soldiers & Sailors Home, Milford)		75	1906 Apr 14	NE, 31st, 1907
Kent, Chas. W.		D, 137th Ill.	90		1927 Aug 6	KS, 47th, 1928
Kent, E.D.		died of pneumonia	32	71	1908 Nov 22	NE, 33rd, 1909
Kent, Elmer T.		H, 17th Ill.	90		1923 Dec 8	KS, 43rd, 1924
Kent, H.E.		H, 3rd Penn. Art.	11	77	1910 Aug 4	NE, 35th, 1911
Kent, J.E.	Pvt.	F, 7th Iowa Inf.	26		1929 Sep 15	IA, 56th, 1930
Kent, J.L.			81		1923	NE, 48th, 1924
Kent, John W.		G, 10th Kans.	78		1905 Jul 30	KS, 25th, 1906
Kent, Wm.		H, 27th Ind. (died of heart failure)	84	71	1908 Feb	NE, 33rd, 1909
Kentnir, Alex.	Corp.	F, 142nd Ill. Inf.	211	52	1898 Jul 3	IA, 25th, 1899
Kenton, Wm. H.		H, 86th Ohio	256		1911 Nov 8	KS, 31st, 1912
Kenworthy, D.E.		15th Ind. Bat.	[4?]		1918 Feb 13	KS, 38th, 1919
Kenworthy, David Clark	Pvt.	H, 1st Iowa Cav.	337	99	1938 Oct 10	IA, 65th, 1939
Kenworthy, J.W.		A, 85th Ohio	76		1927	KS, 47th, 1928
Kenworthy, Joseph Edwin	Pvt.	B, 185th Ohio Inf. (at large)		94	1942 Jun 17	IA, 69th, 1943
Kenworthy, S.B.	Pvt.	B, 10th Iowa Inf.	12		1930 Feb 20	IA, 57th, 1931
Kenyon, E.H.	Corp.	F, 3rd Iowa Inf.	46		1912 Nov 4	IA, 39th, 1913

*See Appendix A, B or C for roster of post names and locations.
†See Introduction for note regarding recording of death date.

Name	Rank	Company, Regiment or Ship	Post*	Age	Death Date†	Journal
Kenyon, J.R.		E, 28th Wis. Inf.	277		1st quarter 1885	IA, 11th, 1885
Kenyon, N.H.	Pvt.	B, 105th Ill. Inf.	6		1930 Aug 30	IA, 57th, 1931
Kenyon, P.W.			232		1914	KS, 34th, 1915
Kenyon, Wm.	Pvt.	E, 41st Ind. Vol. Inf.	419	66	1898 Sep	IA, 25th, 1899
Kenyon, Wm. A.		A, 38th Ind. Inf.	279		1886	KS, 6th, 1887
Keohler, J.	Pvt.	C, West Va.	190		1930 Jan 2	IA, 57th, 1931
Keough, John	Pvt.	B, 8th Iowa Inf.	452		1910 May	IA, 37th, 1911
Keown, Wm. W.		D, 5th Mo.	187		1889	KS, 9th, 1890
Kephart, James	Pvt.	C, 13th U.S. Inf.	66	90	1932 Apr 27	IA, 59th, 1933
Kepler, Charles W.	Capt.	A, 13th Iowa Inf.	400		1923 Mar 30	IA, 50th, 1924
Kepler, L. Monroe		F, 24th Ill. (died of erysipelas)	107	78	1916 Dec 6	NE, 41st, 1917
Keplinger, L.W.		A, 32nd Ill.	28		1928 Dec 14	KS, 48th, 1929
Kepner, Robert	Pvt.	G, 7th Iowa Inf.	233		1929 Oct 8	IA, 56th, 1930
Keppart, H.C.		L, 1st Ohio	180		1896 Sep 11	KS, 16th, 1897
Kepperling, R.L.		C, 36th Penn.	132		1923 Oct 10	KS, 43rd, 1924
Kercheval, J.A.	Lieut.	I, 143rd Ill.	22		1921 Jun 15	IA, 48th, 1922
Kerfer, Matthies	Pvt.	A, 1st Iowa Inf.	231	63	1895 Feb 11	IA, 22nd, 1896
Kerlin, W.W.	Surg.		80		1913 Dec 8	IA, 40th, 1914
Kern, Andrew	Pvt.	B, 183rd N.Y. Inf.	68		1917 Jun 5	IA, 44th, 1918
Kern, Fred	Pvt.	E, 16th Iowa Inf.	235	48	1899 Feb 6	IA, 25th, 1899
Kern, J.F.	Pvt.	G, 19th —	115		1907 Jun 19	IA, 34th, 1908
Kern, Martin		G, 9th Kans. Cav.	72		1910 May 16	KS, 30th, 1911
Kern, Solomon			40		1902	KS, 22nd, 1903
Kern, William		B, 1st Minn. Inf. (born in Canada; died of senility at Soldiers & Sailors Home Hospital, Burkett; buried at Home Cemetery)		77	1906 Dec 25	NE, 31st, 1907
Kerns, Darius P.	Pvt.	F, 83rd Ill. Inf.	324	95	1939 Jul	IA, 65th, 1939
Kerns, Darius P.	Pvt.	F, 83rd Ill. Inf.	324	95	1939 Jul 29	IA, 66th, 1940
Kerns, John		C, 10th Ohio Cav.	257		1898 Mar 27	KS, 18th, 1899
Kerns, Joseph H.	Corp.	B, 31st Wis. Vol. Inf.	242	68	1899 May 10	IA, 26th, 1900
Kerns, Lemuel		I, 13th Iowa Inf.	18		1918 Feb 10	KS, 38th, 1919
Kerns, W.J.			141		1894	NE, 19th, 1895
Kerr, Alexander		K, 8th Iowa	14		1928 Feb 23	KS, 48th, 1929
Kerr, Daniel	Lieut.	G, 117th Ill. Inf.	71		1916 Oct 8	IA, 43rd, 1917
Kerr, David A.	Sergt.	A, 1st Iowa Cav.	2		1911 Aug 30	IA, 38th, 1912
Kerr, E.B.	Capt.	30th Iowa	167		1914 Jan 22	IA, 41st, 1915
Kerr, Ed.		H, 6th Kans.	300		1893 Dec 27	KS, 13th, 1894
Kerr, Geo. H.	Pvt.	H, 44th Iowa Inf.	234		1911 Sep 1	IA, 38th, 1912
Kerr, H.C.		B, 168th Ohio Inf.	13	69	1916 Nov 12	NE, 41st, 1917
Kerr, Henry		B, 97th Penn.	258		1927	KS, 47th, 1928
Kerr, J.S.		F, 55th Ind. Inf.	132		1929 Jan 18	KS, 49th, 1930
Kerr, J.T.		F, 2nd Tenn.	244		1928 Jun 5	KS, 48th, 1929
Kerr, James	Pvt.	A, 2nd Iowa Inf.	2		1916	IA, 43rd, 1917
Kerr, James		L, 2nd Penn. Hvy. Art.	1		1918 Jan 30	KS, 38th, 1919
Kerr, James P.	Sergt.	G, 140th Penn. Inf.	8	63	1897 Sep 2	IA, 24th, 1898
Kerr, Jas. D.		K, 89th N.Y. (pensioner)	167		1889	KS, 9th, 1890
Kerr, John B.	Pvt.	B, 14th Iowa Inf.	240		1922 Mar 16	IA, 49th, 1923
Kerr, L.J.	Pvt.	I, 6th Mo. Inf.	68		1906 Aug 7	IA, 33rd, 1907
Kerr, Levi H.	Pvt.	G, 15th Iowa Inf.	169		1905 May 15	IA, 32nd, 1906
Kerr, R.N.		A, 70th Ohio	180		1911 Apr 23	KS, 31st, 1912
Kerr, Richard W.	Corp.	A, 188th N.Y. Inf.	139		1912 Mar 12	IA, 40th, 1914
Kerr, S.J.	Pvt.	D, Lt. Art.	261		1926 Aug 14	IA, 53rd, 1927
Kerr, Thomas	Pvt.	B, Iowa Inf.	84		1910 Apr 19	IA, 37th, 1911
Kerr, W.H.		C, 36th Ind. Inf. (died of heart failure)	84	72	1914 May 1	NE, 39th, 1915
Kerritt, Mathew S.		H, 3rd Colo.	493		1922 Nov 29	KS, 42nd, 1923
Kerschner, Levi		I, 156th Ill. (died of kidney & gallstones)	342	76	1913 Jul 15	NE, 38th, 1914
Kersey, Isaac	Pvt.	B, 70th Ind. Inf.	10		1911 Mar 16	IA, 37th, 1911
Kersey, J.H.	Pvt.		14		1899	IA, 26th, 1900
Kersey, R.B.		I, 73rd Ind.	38		1908[1909?] Aug 29	KS, 29th, 1910
Kershner, D.C.		B, 38th Ill.	209		1922 May 15	KS, 42nd, 1923
Kersler, Steve	Sergt.		29		1917 Jun 30	IA, 44th, 1918

*See Appendix A, B or C for roster of post names and locations.
†See Introduction for note regarding recording of death date.

Name	Rank	Company, Regiment or Ship	Post*	Age	Death Date†	Journal
Kerwin, Martin	Pvt.	F, 27th Iowa Inf.	78		1906 Aug 7	IA, 33rd, 1907
Kerwood, Theo.		B, 106th Ill.	32	75	1919 Oct 28	NE, 44th, 1920
Kesecker, Geo.	Pvt.	C, 12th Ohio Cav.	20		1910 May 22	IA, 37th, 1911
Kesler, Elias	Pvt.	I, 23rd Mo. Inf.	223		1918 Jul 13	IA, 45th, 1919
Kesler, J.M.		I, 153rd Penn. (died from wound)	152		1888	KS, 8th, 1889
Kesler, Willis		H, 117th Ind.	127		1923 Mar 12	KS, 43rd, 1924
Kesselring, Jno.	Pvt.	B, 37th Ind. Inf.	24		1925	IA, 52nd, 1926
Kesselring, Joseph			52		1928	IA, 55th, 1929
Kessler, Adam		G, 58th Ill.	130		1917 Jun 4	KS, 37th, 1918
Kessler, Frank	Pvt.	I, 2nd Iowa Inf.	1		1905 Sep 10	IA, 32nd, 1906
Kessler, J.M., see Kesler, J.M.						
Kessler, M.		B, 104th Ill. Inf. (died of dropsy)	207	64	1896 Nov 26	NE, 21st, 1897
Kessler, Martin		D, 30th Ind.	51		1922 Feb 14	KS, 42nd, 1923
Kessler, W.R.		H, 79th Ohio	25		1923 Jan 5	KS, 43rd, 1924
Kester, Benj. H.	Pvt.	I, 4th Iowa Inf.	473		1923 Dec 20	IA, 50th, 1924
Kester, S.M.	Pvt.	H, 1st Iowa Cav.	337		1907 Nov 17	IA, 34th, 1908
Kester, Wm.	Pvt.	E, 46th Iowa Inf.	244		1905 Nov 14	IA, 32nd, 1906
Kesterson, Geo.		E, 76th Ind.	142		1928 Jan 12	KS, 48th, 1929
Kesterton, Jas.	Pvt.	E, 2nd Minn. Inf.	168		1900 Mar 25	IA, 27th, 1901
Kestner, Henry			139		1890	NE, 15th, 1891
Ketcham, Ira P.	Pvt.	H, 8th N.Y. Inf.	18	52	1892 Aug 14	IA, 19th, 1893
Ketchem, L.M.	Pvt.	F, 35th Mo. Inf.	156		1905 Aug 3	IA, 32nd, 1906
Ketcheson, J.C.		G, 8th Ill. Cav.	6		1918 Apr 10	KS, 38th, 1919
Ketchum, H.E.	Pvt.	K, 3rd Minn. Inf.	22		1912 Jan 1	IA, 38th, 1912
Kettell, Henry	Pvt.	B, 24th Iowa Inf.	152		1909 Oct 26	IA, 36th, 1910
Kettell, Wm.	Pvt.	C, 2nd Iowa Inf.	110		1906 Aug 9	IA, 33rd, 1907
Kettenring, Fred P.	Capt.	B, 8th Iowa Vet. Inf.	92		1901 Feb 21	IA, 27th, 1901
Ketterman, Geo.		F, 64th Ill.	51		1922 May 14	KS, 42nd, 1923
Ketzler, Alonzo		B, 50th Ill. Inf.	25		1901 Nov 2	KS, 21st, 1902
Ketzler, Geo.		B, 50th Ill. Inf.	25		1929 May 19	KS, 49th, 1930
Ketzmaller, Frank		H, 13th Kans. Inf.	191		1901 May 4	KS, 21st, 1902
Kewbanks, John W.		E, 14th Kans.	65		1924 Jul 23	KS, 44th, 1925
Keyes, C.C.	Pvt.	F, 29th Iowa Inf.	235	78	1898 May 5	IA, 24th, 1898
Keyes, J.B.		E, 5th Kans.	145		1906 Dec 12	KS, 26th, 1907
Keyes, L.J.	Lieut.	C, 55th Ill. Inf.	90		1908 Oct 28	IA, 35th, 1909
Keyes, Norman D.		G, 40th Wis. Inf. (died of pneumonia)	23	51	1900 Jan 11	NE, 25th, 1901
Keyes, S.P.		H, 211th Penn.	17		1920 Nov 5	KS, 40th, 1921
Keyes, Samuel L.		I, 151st Ill.	129		1908 Jan 13	KS, 28th, 1909
Keyhue, James		F, 6th Kans.	38		1920 Nov 10	KS, 40th, 1921
Keymme, Anthony		Telegraph Corps, Mo.	468		1904 Nov 26	KS, 24th, 1905
Keys, A.G.		C, 34th Iowa	71		1927 Jul 25	KS, 47th, 1928
Keys, A.N.	Pvt.	F, 60th Ohio Inf.	440		1917 Jan 15	IA, 44th, 1918
Keys, E.F.		A, 136th Penn.	38		1917 Dec 7	KS, 37th, 1918
Keys, Ira	Pvt.	24th Ohio Art.	271		1904 Apr 1	IA, 31st, 1905
Keys, N.A.	Pvt.	Burlington	5		1933 Feb 18	IA, 60th, 1934
Keyser, John		E, 44th Mo.	378		1923	KS, 43rd, 1924
Keyser, Wilton W.		A, 13th Kans.	241		1908 Oct 22	KS, 29th, 1910
Keysor, P.C.		U.S. Navy	7	54	1895 Aug	NE, 20th, 1896
Keyte, W.J.		F, 135th Ill.	87		1928 Oct 20	KS, 48th, 1929
Keyte, Wm. R.	Sergt.	E, 50th Ill. Inf.	12		1915 Jan 6	IA, 42nd, 1916
Kibbe, Wm. E.		D, 16th Kans.	18		1922 Feb 26	KS, 42nd, 1923
Kibbey, Meigs	Pvt.	K, 44th Iowa Inf.		90	1937 Dec 3	IA, 65th, 1939
Kibbie, A.E.	Pvt.	1st Minn. Lt. Art.	92		1884	KS, 4th, 1885
Kibbie, A.E.			92		1884	KS, 4th, 1885
Kibbie, W.E.		D, 12th Kans.	111		1922	KS, 42nd, 1923
Kibler, George	Pvt.	E, 22nd Iowa Inf.	233		1931 Mar 8	IA, 58th, 1932
Kidd, Thos.	Pvt.	F, 9th Ill. Inf.	7		1913 Aug 5	IA, 40th, 1914
Kidder, Albert E.		A, 1st Neb. Cav.	209		1910 Apr 5	KS, 30th, 1911
Kidder, Orange		C, 16th Ky. (died of disability)	84	78	1907 Feb	NE, 33rd, 1909
Kidder, Sherbon		K, 13th Mich. (died of old age)	89	84	1919 Jul 4	NE, 44th, 1920
Kidder, Sherburne		K, 13th Mich. (died of old age)	82	84	1919 Jul 4	NE, 45th, 1921
Kiebel, H.I.	Pvt.	D, 16th U.S. Cav.	70		1919 Apr 6	IA, 46th, 1920

Name	Rank	Company, Regiment or Ship	Post*	Age	Death Date†	Journal
Kiebler, Thomas T.		B, 101st Penn. Inf.	34		1916 Dec 18	KS, 36th, 1917
Kiefer, Geo. W.		C, 57th Penn. Inf.	12		1909 Jan 16	KS, 29th, 1910
Kiefner, Henry	Pvt.	C, 35th Iowa Inf.	231		1923 May 17	IA, 50th, 1924
Kieger, W.	Pvt.	K, 8th Inf.	333		1907 Apr	IA, 34th, 1908
Kiehle, J.D.	Pvt.	B, 16th Wis. Inf.	7		1910 Apr 14	IA, 37th, 1911
Kiene, F.A.		I, 49th Ohio	1		1924 May 13	KS, 44th, 1925
Kiene, Peter	Pvt.	E, 16th Iowa Inf.	78		1912 Dec 6	IA, 39th, 1913
Kiersch, Nicholas		I, 13th Iowa Inf.		93	1938 Feb 21	IA, 64th, 1938
Kiersey, E.D.	1st Lieut.	H, 80th Ill. Inf.	150		1899 Mar 13	KS, 19th, 1900
Kiersey, Geo. W.		H, 46th Ill.	250		1919 Feb 28	KS, 39th, 1920
Kiester, Henry C.		I, 88th Penn. Inf. (former member of department; location: Albion)	140		1938 Feb 25	NE, 63rd, 1939
Kiger, Moses	Pvt.	Ohio Inf.	19		1923	IA, 50th, 1924
Kiger, W.R.		D, 47th Ill.	71		1904 Mar 9	KS, 24th, 1905
Kighley, Geo. F.	Pvt.	C, 55th Inf.	153		1918 Nov	IA, 45th, 1919
Kiisel, Henry	Pvt.	B, 13th Iowa Inf.	16		1902	IA, 29th, 1903
Kikendall, J.S.	Pvt.	D, 114th Ill.	57		1922 Apr 26	IA, 49th, 1923
Kilborn, Daniel	Pvt.	D, 12th Ill. Cav.	97		1900 Sep 15	IA, 27th, 1901
Kilborne, Daniel	Pvt.	D, 12th Ill. Cav.	97		1900 Aug 15	IA, 27th, 1901
Kilbourne, J.E.	Pvt.	K, 18th Iowa Inf.	110	50	1892 Apr 2	IA, 18th, 1892
Kilcore, J.M.	Pvt.	A, 25th Iowa Inf.	108	53	1895 Apr 4	IA, 21st, 1895
Kilcoyne, J.		Navy	4		1893 Oct	KS, 13th, 1894
Kildon, Jos. C.		E, 3rd West Va. Cav. (died of Bright's disease)	57		1902 Nov	NE, 27th, 1903
Kile, A.C.	Pvt.	H, 84th Ill. Inf.	231		1913 Oct 12	IA, 40th, 1914
Kile, E.N.	Pvt.	H, 84th Ill. Inf.	26	89	1931 Mar 12	IA, 58th, 1932
Kilgone, Wm.		D, 103rd Penn. Inf. (died of heart disease)	10	65	1912 May 14	NE, 37th, 1913
Kilgore, A.C.		I, 18th Iowa Inf. (died of typhoid fever)	262	59	1905 May 24	NE, 30th, 1906
Kilgore, Coe		A, 95th Ill. (died of rheumatism & old age)	1	89	1925 May 16	NE, 50th, 1926
Kilgore, E.	Pvt.	F, 32nd Iowa Inf.	156		1904 Apr 28	IA, 31st, 1905
Kilgore, Geo. S.		B, 168th Ohio (died of pneumonia)	13	74	1917 Oct 24	NE, 42nd, 1918
Kilgore, H.H.	Corp.	H, 31st Iowa Inf.	440		1919 Jan 20	IA, 46th, 1920
Kilgore, M.M.		I, 18th Iowa (died of typhoid fever)	262	59	1911 May 24	NE, 36th, 1912
Kilgore, W.E.		B, 86th Ohio	66		1899 Nov 30	KS, 19th, 1900
Kilian, C.		K, 7th N.J. Inf.	231		1924 May 9	IA, 51st, 1925
Killduff, J.T.	Pvt.	H, 11th Ill. Cav.	16		1920 Nov 22	IA, 47th, 1921
Killen, Robert	Pvt. Pvt.	F, 37th Ky. Inf. E, 55th Ky. Inf. (at large)	309	96	1941 Jan 25	IA, 67th, 1941
Killerlain, T.	Pvt.	K, 40th Wis. Inf.	46		1924 Nov 29	IA, 51st, 1925
Killfoil, Christ		B, 67th Ill.	17		1916 Oct 23	KS, 36th, 1917
Killfoil, Christopher		B, 62nd Ill. Inf.	82		1916 Oct 22	KS, 36th, 1917
Killian, C., see Kilian, C.						
Killian, Jno. N.		D, 8th Ind. Art.	25		1886	KS, 6th, 1887
Killian, Wm. E.		Neb. (died of cancer)	118	62	1908 Apr 12	NE, 33rd, 1909
Killion, B.		F, 28th Ind.	129		1908 Aug 22	KS, 28th, 1909
Killion, William B.		F, 28th Ill. Inf. (died at Caney, Kans.; buried at Caney Cemetery)	477		1894 Apr 5	KS, 14th, 1895
Killman, Clinton DeWitt				89	1938 Feb 3	IA, 64th, 1938
Kilmer, Aug.	Pvt.		2		1924 Nov 24	IA, 51st, 1925
Kilmer, Jesse	Pvt.	B, 57th Ill. Inf.	230		1911 Jan 4	IA, 38th, 1912
Kilpatrick, A.		E, 48th Ind. (died in Indiana)	110		1892	KS, 12th, 1893
Kilpatrick, James		F, 3rd Mo.	110		1905 Dec 31	KS, 25th, 1906
Kilpatrick, John M.	Pvt.	A, 28th Iowa Inf.	166		1914 Nov 19	IA, 41st, 1915
Kimball, A.B.	Pvt.	1st Wis. Cav.	434		1921 Mar 25	IA, 48th, 1922
Kimball, D.H.		G, 10th Mich. Cav. (died at Delphos)	116		1895 Aug 16	KS, 15th, 1896
Kimball, David P.	Corp.	M, 2nd Iowa Cav.	269		1907 Nov 1	IA, 34th, 1908
Kimball, E.A.	Pvt.	F, 64th Ill. Inf.	193	78	1895 Dec 25	IA, 23rd, 1897
Kimball, F.W.	Pvt.	F, 188th N.Y. Inf.	102		1900 Sep 2	IA, 27th, 1901
Kimball, G.M.	Pvt.	B, 19th Mass. Inf.	78		1921 Jun 6	IA, 48th, 1922
Kimball, H.			434		1904-1905	IA, 31st, 1905
Kimball, Jerome		K, 35th Iowa Inf. (died of old age)	171		1923 May 26	NE, 48th, 1924
Kimball, Jerome		K, 35th Iowa Inf. (died of paralysis)	171		1923 May 26	NE, 50th, 1926

*See Appendix A, B or C for roster of post names and locations.
†See Introduction for note regarding recording of death date.
302

Name	Rank	Company, Regiment or Ship	Post*	Age	Death Date†	Journal
Kimball, Jos.	Pvt.	M, 2nd Iowa Cav.	461		1910 Apr 25	IA, 37th, 1911
Kimball, Jos. H.		A, 49th Ohio	81		1906 Jun 2	KS, 26th, 1907
Kimball, S.A.	Pvt.	A, 57th Penn. Inf.	163	58	1887 May 17	IA, 15th, 1889
Kimball, Samuel		C, 3rd Kans. State Militia	12		1897 Mar 31	KS, 17th, 1898
Kimberly, W.S.	Pvt.	F, 1st Iowa Cav.	94	90	1933 Aug 16	IA, 60th, 1934
Kimblade, John		G, 4th Iowa	87		1908 Nov 30	KS, 28th, 1909
Kimble, E.M.		B, 2nd Ill.	45		1913 Mar 4	KS, 33rd, 1914
Kimbley, Wm. H.	Pvt.	A, 24th Ind.	127		1922 Apr 1	IA, 49th, 1923
Kimbrough, And.	Pvt.	G, 9th Ohio Cav.	235		1923 Dec 31	IA, 50th, 1924
Kimbrough, Noah	Corp.	C, 62nd U.S.C. Inf.	40		1918 May 27	IA, 45th, 1919
Kime, E.H.	Pvt.	B, 2nd Penn. Cav.	78		1912 Dec 17	IA, 39th, 1913
Kime, N.F.			233		1907 1st term	IA, 34th, 1908
Kimes, Lebanon		7th Iowa Cav.	73		1917	IA, 44th, 1918
Kimes, W.D.			25	65	1910 Feb 8	NE, 35th, 1911
Kimler, Ben F.	Pvt.	E, 6th Iowa Inf.	313		1912 Jan 22	IA, 39th, 1913
Kimler, Joseph		H, 102nd Ill.	185		1919 Jan 19	KS, 39th, 1920
Kimmel, David		K, 10th Mo. Inf.	262	66	1897 Jul 14	NE, 22nd, 1898
Kimmel, Oliver P.	Pvt.	B, 64th Ill. Inf.	57		1902	IA, 29th, 1903
Kimmell, F.		G, 30th Ill. Inf. (died of dropsy)	105		1894 Dec 12	NE, 19th, 1895
Kimmell, Jonathan		K, 10th Mo.	230		1885	KS, 5th, 1886
Kimmer, Wesley	Pvt.	E, 35th Wis. Inf.	59		1923 Oct 11	IA, 50th, 1924
Kimmerly, D.J.		A, 13th N.Y. (died of old age)	35	79	1918 Jan 19	NE, 43rd, 1919
Kimmey, J.H.		F, 4th Del.	129		1917 Apr 9	KS, 37th, 1918
Kimport, Martin	Pvt.	A, 13th Iowa Inf.	251		1915 Aug 10	IA, 42nd, 1916
Kimsey, Jas.	Pvt.	F, 3rd Iowa Cav.	309		1900-1901	IA, 27th, 1901
Kimsey, M.A.		F, 15th Ky.	85		1926 Mar 24	KS, 46th, 1927
Kinard, Geo. H.	Pvt.	H, 23rd Iowa Inf.	55		1922 Jul 14	IA, 49th, 1923
Kincaid, Joseph		H, 7th Ohio	3		1922 May 4	KS, 42nd, 1923
Kindal, Richard H.		G, 11th Kans.	100		1923 Jan 23	KS, 43rd, 1924
Kindblade, G.A.		G, 4th Iowa	87		1921 Feb 21	KS, 41st, 1922
Kinder, J.A.		D, 18th Mo.	325		1916 Aug 2	KS, 36th, 1917
Kindred, D.R.		G, 50th Ind. Inf.	45		1917 Sep 26	KS, 37th, 1918
Kindred, Edward	Pvt.	G, 50th Ill. Inf.	84	65	1892 Jan 31	IA, 18th, 1892
Kindred, Scott	Pvt.	F, 93rd Ind. Inf.	84		1912 Aug 11	IA, 39th, 1913
Kinell, R.	Pvt.	L, 2nd Minn. Inf.	377		1915 Jul 17	IA, 42nd, 1916
Kinert, S.T.		C, 152nd Penn.	265		1917 May 25	KS, 37th, 1918
Kinert, Samuel		C, 158th Penn.	251		1917 Apr 28	KS, 37th, 1918
Kines, Lebenor		H, 7th Iowa Cav.	73		1916	IA, 43rd, 1917
Kiney, J.G.	Pvt.	3rd Iowa Cav.	122		1920	IA, 47th, 1921
King, A.B.		C, 62nd Ohio	25		1916 Feb 7	KS, 36th, 1917
King, A.G.		C, 9th Ill. Cav.	23	64	1909 Nov 29	NE, 34th, 1910
King, A.P.	Pvt.	B, 22nd Iowa Inf.	234		1913 Aug 20	IA, 40th, 1914
King, Abram		U.S. Navy	142		1916 Sep 18	KS, 36th, 1917
King, Adam		C, 19th Kans.	1		1898 Dec 19	KS, 18th, 1899
King, Alanson T.		E, 24th Iowa Inf.	452	92	1937 Aug 8	IA, 64th, 1938
King, Benjamin		I, 9th Kans. Cav.	66		1912 Apr 26	KS, 32nd, 1913
King, Benjamin		I, 6th Iowa Cav.	11		1893 Oct 17	NE, 18th, 1894
King, C.D.	Pvt.	E, 22nd Iowa Vol. Inf.	107	63	1898 Jul 27	IA, 25th, 1899
King, C.O.	Pvt.	C, 3rd Mich. Cav.	123	50	1887 Feb 24	IA, 14th, 1888
King, C.P.		C, 14th Iowa Inf. (died of paralysis)	22	75	1919 Apr 15	NE, 44th, 1920
King, Charles	Pvt.	C, 9th Iowa Cav.		94	1939 Oct 5	IA, 66th, 1940
King, Charles H.		B, 15th Iowa Inf.	388		1916 Feb 12	KS, 36th, 1917
King, Chas. P.	Capt.	G, 8th Wis. Inf.	15		1900 Apr 11	IA, 27th, 1901
King, D.A.		A, 19th Iowa	8		1889	KS, 9th, 1890
King, D.E.			45		1923 Mar 1	IA, 50th, 1924
King, D.H.	Pvt.	H, 33rd Wis.	124		1914 Sep 20	IA, 41st, 1915
King, David	Pvt.	C, 24th Iowa Inf.	235		1924 Jan 21	IA, 51st, 1925
King, David A.		A, 19th Iowa	8		1890	KS, 10th, 1891
King, David A.		A, 19th Iowa Inf.	8		1889 Jan 26	KS, 11th, 1892
King, E.			322		1924	KS, 44th, 1925
King, E.H.	Pvt.	D, 35th Iowa Inf.	231		1918 Feb 14	IA, 45th, 1919
King, E.H.	Pvt.	G, 38th Iowa Inf.	497		1920 Nov 30	IA, 47th, 1921

Name	Rank	Company, Regiment or Ship	Post*	Age	Death Date†	Journal
King, Edgar O.		B, 146th N.Y.	210		1893 Oct 1	KS, 13th, 1894
King, F.M.	Pvt.	H, 21st Iowa Inf.	2		1920 Feb 11	IA, 47th, 1921
King, Francis M.	Pvt.	E, 151st Ill. Inf.	279		1903 Oct 7	IA, 30th, 1904
King, G.W.		G, 148th Ill. Inf.	28		1900 May 21	KS, 20th, 1901
King, Geo.	Pvt.	G, 5th Iowa Inf.	296		1905 Sep 15	IA, 32nd, 1906
King, Geo.	Pvt.	F, 45th Ill. Inf.	88		1925 Apr 13	IA, 52nd, 1926
King, Geo. T.	Pvt.	D, 47th Iowa Inf.	54		1911 Dec 2	IA, 38th, 1912
King, Geo. W.	Pvt.	A, 2nd Iowa Cav.	1		1919 Sep 18	IA, 46th, 1920
King, Geo. Wm.		I, 115th Ind. Inf.	40		1908[1909?] Aug 9	KS, 29th, 1910
King, George A.	Pvt.	K, 148th Ill. Vol. Inf.	56		1901 Oct 18	IA, 28th, 1902
King, George H.	Pvt.		337		1929 Jan 4	IA, 56th, 1930
King, Henry B.			44		1910	IA, 37th, 1911
King, J.H.		E, 36th Ohio	250		1922 Jun 8	KS, 42nd, 1923
King, J.M.		A, 3rd Iowa Cav.	4		1898 Sep 8	KS, 18th, 1899
King, J.M.		K, 53rd Ill. (died of hardening of arteries)	52	82	1919 Aug 1	NE, 44th, 1920
King, J.W.	Pvt.	C, 9th Iowa Inf.	193		1908 Sep 1	IA, 35th, 1909
King, James	Pvt.	L, Cav.	69		1927 Dec 22	IA, 54th, 1928
King, James		E, 18th U.S.	129		1904 Aug 28	KS, 24th, 1905
King, James		A, 35th Ind. (died of cancer)	118		1894 Apr 7	NE, 19th, 1895
King, James K.		36th Iowa	69		1922 Dec 25	IA, 49th, 1923
King, James L.			127		1936	KS, 56th, 1937
King, Jeremiah		H, 17th Iowa Inf.		95	1938 Jun 20	IA, 64th, 1938
King, Jerome	Pvt.	F, 6th Iowa Cav.	1		1916 Mar 28	IA, 43rd, 1917
King, Jno. S.	Pvt.		54		1925 Mar 24	IA, 52nd, 1926
King, John	1st Lieut.	B, 53rd Ill.	329	74	1890 Nov 24	IA, 17th, 1891
King, John	Pvt.	F, 48th Ind.	54		1907 Mar 13	IA, 34th, 1908
King, John		E, 10th Ohio	123		1914 Dec 20	KS, 34th, 1915
King, John S.		B, 94th N.Y. Inf.	11		1926 Mar 30	NE, 51st, 1927
King, L.A.		died of heart disease	32		1905 Oct 13	NE, 30th, 1906
King, Lewis		F, Iowa	99		1896 Nov 29	KS, 16th, 1897
King, Lyman	Pvt.	C, 25th Ohio Inf.	466		1903 Jan 8	IA, 29th, 1903
King, Martin V.		F, 29th Iowa (died of paralysis; see also Appendix D)	22	74	1918 Jul 10	NE, 43rd, 1919
King, P.B.		D, 48th Ill.	64		1928	KS, 48th, 1929
King, Perry	Pvt.	B, 168th Ohio	19		1923 Dec 30	IA, 50th, 1924
King, Peter		A, 83rd U.S.C.I.	180		1912 Dec 3	KS, 32nd, 1913
King, Shepherd H.		D, 6th Minn. (died of paresis)	25	81	1916 Nov 27	NE, 41st, 1917
King, Simpson		B, 82nd Ind. (location: Loup City)			1927 Jul 17	NE, 52nd, 1928
King, Sylvester M.	Pvt.	E, 20th Ill. Inf.	337		1909 Dec 1	IA, 36th, 1910
King, T.N.		D, 2nd Ky.	74		1916 Oct 17	KS, 36th, 1917
King, Thos.		K, 19th Ohio (died of old age)	129	86	1922 Aug 7	NE, 47th, 1923
King, W.B.	Pvt.	B, —	67		1910 May 18	IA, 37th, 1911
King, W.C.		B, 125th Ill. Inf.	81		1925 Nov	KS, 45th, 1926
King, W.S.	Pvt.	E, 27th Iowa Inf.	452		1914 Aug	IA, 41st, 1915
King, W.S.C.	Pvt.	I, 45th Ohio Inf.	22	87	1932 May 22	IA, 59th, 1933
King, W.T.		A, 93rd Ohio	258		1888	KS, 8th, 1889
King, William B.		B, 61st Ill.	52		1919 Dec 13	KS, 39th, 1920
King, Wm.		E, 114th Ill. Inf.	17		1914 Dec 24	KS, 34th, 1915
Kingery, John	Pvt.	E, 106th Ill. Inf.	84		1927 Nov 11	IA, 54th, 1928
Kingery, Peter		F, 81st Ind.	318	78	1917 Oct 1	NE, 42nd, 1918
Kingsberry, John	Pvt.	D, 31st Iowa	23		1926 Mar 28	IA, 53rd, 1927
Kingsberry, N.E.		B, 3rd Penn.	32		1889	KS, 9th, 1890
Kingsberry, Robt.			122		1927	IA, 54th, 1928
Kingsburg, Elisha		E, 34th Ill.	23		1896 Oct 16	KS, 16th, 1897
Kingsburry, Ben		E, 74th Ill. Inf.	30		1913 Oct 23	IA, 40th, 1914
Kingsbury, Robt.	Pvt.	36th Iowa Inf.	122		1928	IA, 55th, 1929
Kingsland, William W.		1st N.Y. Cav.	200		1905 Jan 18	KS, 25th, 1906
Kingsley, R.			134	75	1916 Jun 10	NE, 41st, 1917
Kingsolver, J.M.	Corp.	K, 10th Iowa Inf.	56	90	1932	IA, 58th, 1932
Kingsworth, G.W.	Pvt.	I, 7th Iowa Cav.	22	99	1933 Sep 10	IA, 60th, 1934
Kinkead, James W.		K, 8th Iowa Cav.	7	64	1906 Jul 31	NE, 31st, 1907
Kinkead, John		C, 189th N.Y. Inf.	25		1935 Dec 31	KS, 55th, 1936

Name	Rank	Company, Regiment or Ship	Post*	Age	Death Date†	Journal
Kinkead, John			204		1894	NE, 19th, 1895
Kinkead, L.	Corp.	E, 8th Iowa Inf.	12		1908 Dec 11	IA, 35th, 1909
Kinley, D.R.	Pvt.	A, 6th Iowa Cav.	206		1923 Mar 4	IA, 50th, 1924
Kinley, O.C.		I, 10th Iowa Inf.	24		1923 Aug 27	IA, 50th, 1924
Kinlode, Isaac			44		1901	NE, 26th, 1902
Kinman, John	Pvt.	E, 11th Iowa Inf.	23		1929 Oct 2	IA, 56th, 1930
Kinmouth, O.F.	Pvt.	C, 14th Ill. Inf.	208		1905 Oct 25	IA, 32nd, 1906
Kinnaman, Zach.	Pvt.	G, 12th Ind. Vol. Inf.	210	79	1899 Mar 24	IA, 26th, 1900
Kinnard, Geo. H., see Kinard, Geo. H.						
Kinne, Isaac	Pvt.	H, 7th Wis. Vet. Inf.	150		1902 Jan 18	IA, 28th, 1902
Kinney, Asa		B, 4th Wis. Inf.	164		1889	KS, 9th, 1890
Kinney, Asa		B, 4th Wis. Inf.	164		1886	KS, 6th, 1887
Kinney, Asa		B, 4th Wis. Inf.	164		1886 Oct 3	KS, 11th, 1892
Kinney, Asa		B, 4th Wis. Inf.	164		1886 Oct 2	KS, 12th, 1893
Kinney, Asa		B, 4th Wis.	164		1897 Oct 3	KS, 17th, 1898
Kinney, B.C.		H, 1st Mich. Lt. Art. (died at Parsons)	64		1895 Oct	KS, 15th, 1896
Kinney, Charles H.		C & K, 96th Ohio Vol. Inf. (member at large; died at Raymond; see also Appendix D)		93	1939 Feb 20	NE, 64th, 1940
Kinney, George W.	Pvt.	G, 2nd Vt. Inf.	31	51	1894 Aug 21	IA, 21st, 1895
Kinney, H.W.		G, 15th N.J. (died of old age)	1	88	1920 May 27	NE, 45th, 1921
Kinney, Ira G.	Pvt.	D, 9th Mich. Cav.	29	88	1933 Sep 1	IA, 60th, 1934
Kinney, Isaac		184th Penn.	36		1927 Sep 1	KS, 47th, 1928
Kinney, J.G., see Kiney, J.G.						
Kinney, John		E, 8th Penn. Res. Inf.	6		1929 Aug 15	KS, 49th, 1930
Kinney, Milon		H, 19th Ohio Inf. (died of heart disease)	102	70	1911 Aug 24	NE, 36th, 1912
Kinney, Park		H, 80th Ohio	29	62	1908 Sep 1	NE, 33rd, 1909
Kinney, T.J.			206		1927	IA, 56th, 1930
Kinney, Thos. J.	Pvt.	L, 8th Iowa Cav.	206		1927 Jul 17	IA, 54th, 1928
Kinney, William		K, 4th Iowa	153		1905 May 15	KS, 25th, 1906
Kinney, William		23rd N.Y. Lt. Art. (cause of death: kidney)	15	75	1914 May 13	NE, 39th, 1915
Kinnie, Howard	Pvt.	D, 6th Iowa Cav.	216		1919 Mar 19	IA, 46th, 1920
Kinnion, J.J.		G, 8th Kans. Inf.	201		1900 Dec 13	KS, 21st, 1902
Kinny, Asa		B, 4th Wis.	164		1896 Oct 3	KS, 16th, 1897
Kinpfer, Gottleip		I, 1st Kans. Inf. (died of injuries received being thrown from buggy)	456		1890	KS, 10th, 1891
Kinsey, E.L.		H, 45th Iowa	49		1915 Oct 26	KS, 35th, 1916
Kinsey, G.W.	Pvt.	C, 189th Ohio	56		1905 Mar 7	IA, 32nd, 1906
Kinsey, Henry		A, 74th Ind.	47		1927 Feb 25	KS, 47th, 1928
Kinsey, L.B.	Pvt.	P, 51st Ohio Inf.	26		1922 Mar 22	IA, 49th, 1923
Kinsey, W.A.	Pvt.	D, 2nd Iowa Inf.	12		1915 May 20	IA, 42nd, 1916
Kinsley, Jason	Pvt.	K, 1st Iowa Cav.	371		1903 Sep 3	IA, 30th, 1904
Kinsman, N.	Sergt.	H, 61st Ill. (died of consumption)	163	63	1887 Jan	NE, 12th, 1888
Kinter, C.	Pvt.	D, 83rd Penn. Inf.	512		1916 Nov 28	IA, 43rd, 1917
Kintsel, Israel	1st Sergt.	A, 35th Iowa	231		1923 Aug 31	IA, 50th, 1924
Kinzie, Godfrey		K, 63rd Ind. Inf.	130		1934 Jun 28	KS, 54th, 1935
Kious, John W.		I, 154th Ind. (not a member of the G.A.R.)	18		1912 Apr 3	KS, 32nd, 1913
Kipling, R.B.		M, 12th Ind. Cav.	40	75	1920 Apr 17	NE, 45th, 1921
Kiplinger, Samuel	Pvt.	A, 48th Ind. Inf.	441	55	1895 Jun 8	IA, 22nd, 1896
Kipp, John J.		D, 102nd Ill. Inf.	25	84	1920 Nov 19	NE, 45th, 1921
Kipp, Theodore		G, 128th N.Y.	118		1936 Jan	NE, 61st, 1937
Kipper, Preston		3rd U.S. Hvy. Art.	127		1924 Sep 20	KS, 44th, 1925
Kirby, A.R.		H, 33rd Iowa Inf.	147		1909 Jan 13	KS, 29th, 1910
Kirby, Barton		K, 29th Mich.	83		1927 Feb 6	KS, 47th, 1928
Kirby, David		K, 11th Ind.	51		1916 Nov 12	KS, 36th, 1917
Kirby, F.M.		A, 35th Ill. Inf.	25		1929 Jul 4	KS, 49th, 1930
Kirby, John A.		I, 5th Kans.	150		1896	KS, 16th, 1897
Kirby, John N.		B, 118th Ill. Inf.	354	65	1906 Mar 16	NE, 31st, 1907
Kirby, John R.		H, 1st Neb.	71		1893 Oct 23	KS, 13th, 1894
Kirby, William	Pvt.	A, 33rd Ky. Inf.	88		1930 Jul 30	IA, 57th, 1931
Kirchmond, Wm. S.	Pvt.	H, 2nd Iowa Cav.	53	48	1890 Jan 4	IA, 16th, 1890

*See Appendix A, B or C for roster of post names and locations.
†See Introduction for note regarding recording of death date.

305

Name	Rank	Company, Regiment or Ship	Post*	Age	Death Date†	Journal
Kirchoff, Henry		M, 2nd Col.	4		1910 Jun 8	KS, 30th, 1911
Kirk, Buchan C.		B, 1st Ohio Lt. Art.	64		1922 Oct 22	KS, 42nd, 1923
Kirk, Charles		H, 95th Ill.	21		1931 Jun 29	NE, 56th, 1932
Kirk, Chas. W.	Pvt.	H, 23rd Iowa Inf.	12		1915 Jun 6	IA, 42nd, 1916
Kirk, Cyrus	Corp.	E, Purnell Legion Mo.	12		1912 Nov 29	IA, 39th, 1913
Kirk, Enos H.		E, 80th Ind. (died of prostate gland)	15	77	1911 Oct 26	NE, 36th, 1912
Kirk, J.H.	Pvt.	D, 111th —	234		1920 Feb 13	IA, 47th, 1921
Kirk, J.T.		I, 139th Ill.	44		1919 Apr 28	KS, 39th, 1920
Kirk, J.W.	Pvt.	A, 153rd Penn. Inf.	466		1920 Feb 10	IA, 46th, 1920
Kirk, J.W.	Pvt.	D, 1st Iowa Cav.	452		1928 Oct 24	IA, 55th, 1929
Kirk, J.W.		D, 1st Iowa	452	91	1934 Jan 10	IA, 61st, 1935
Kirk, James V.			55		1917 Jun 26	IA, 44th, 1918
Kirk, M.L.	Mate	Volunteer	69		1914 Aug 30	IA, 41st, 1915
Kirk, Mason H.		B, 21st Ind.	57		1923 Nov 8	KS, 43rd, 1924
Kirk, O.D.		E, 135th Ind.	25		1919 Jun 30	KS, 39th, 1920
Kirk, Robert		C, 15th Kans. Cav. (died at Rest)	270		1895 Aug	KS, 15th, 1896
Kirk, Sherman		C, 8th Iowa Inf.	45		1887 Sep 26	KS, 7th, 1888
Kirk, Thomas		A, 37th Ind. (died of cancer)	113	67	1905[1904?] Dec 9	NE, 29th, 1905
Kirk, Vincent		B, 53rd Ind.	265		1912 Oct 8	KS, 32nd, 1913
Kirk, W.H.		G, 9th Iowa Inf.	20		1912 Feb 15	KS, 32nd, 1913
Kirk, W.R.			251		1884	KS, 4th, 1885
Kirk, Wm.	Pvt.	H, 110th N.Y. Inf.	66		1912 Oct 29	IA, 39th, 1913
Kirk, Wm.		I, 53rd Ill. Inf. (died of old age)	32		1908 Apr 5	NE, 33rd, 1909
Kirk, Z.		A, 1st Neb. Inf. (died of old age)	21	71	1905 Nov 6	NE, 30th, 1906
Kirkendall, J.D.	Capt.	I, 41st Ohio Inf.	211	56	1887 Apr 17	IA, 14th, 1888
Kirkham, C.C.		D, 12th Kans. Inf.	18		1916 Mar 31	KS, 36th, 1917
Kirkham, Oscar		I, 5th Mo. Cav.	28		1902 Jan 14	KS, 22nd, 1903
Kirkland, G.W.	Pvt.	G, 12th Iowa Inf.	168		1914 Dec 12	IA, 41st, 1915
Kirkland, Geo.	Pvt.	B, 13th Wis. Inf.	168		1916 Jul	IA, 43rd, 1917
Kirkland, John		C, 10th Kans.	111		1919 Mar 5	KS, 39th, 1920
Kirkpatric, G.	Pvt.	C, 127th Ill. Inf.	493		1920 Dec	IA, 47th, 1921
Kirkpatrick, A.M., Dr.		K, 98th Ill.	51		1916 Jan 11	KS, 36th, 1917
Kirkpatrick, E.A.		B, 2nd Neb.	45		1928	NE, 53rd, 1929
Kirkpatrick, E.S.		E, 7th Ohio	96		1935 Dec 21	KS, 55th, 1936
Kirkpatrick, E.T.	Pvt.	A, 2nd Iowa	443	48	1893 Apr 13	IA, 20th, 1894
Kirkpatrick, Geo.		F, 37th Ill. Inf. (died of old age)	171		1923 Sep 24	NE, 48th, 1924
Kirkpatrick, Geo. E.		K, 162nd Ohio	25		1916 Sep 18	KS, 36th, 1917
Kirkpatrick, Geo. W.		F, 37th Ill. Inf. (died of paralysis)	171	80	1923 Sep 24	NE, 50th, 1926
Kirkpatrick, J.A.		K, 4th Iowa Inf.	17		1929 Jun 30	KS, 49th, 1930
Kirkpatrick, J.C.	Pvt.		71		1913 Apr 14	IA, 40th, 1914
Kirkpatrick, J.E.		A, 36th Ill. Inf.	11	65	1905 Jun 13	NE, 30th, 1906
Kirkpatrick, J.H.			64		1928	IA, 55th, 1929
Kirkpatrick, J.H.		C, 189th N.Y. Inf.	25		1934 Nov	KS, 54th, 1935
Kirkpatrick, J.W.		B, 93rd Ill.	50		1914 Jun 4	KS, 34th, 1915
Kirkpatrick, James		E, 156th Ohio Inf. (died of pneumonia)	94	85	1911 Dec 26	NE, 36th, 1912
Kirkpatrick, James E.		M, 10th Ill. Cav. (died of heart failure at Soldiers & Sailors Home, Grand Island; buried in Home Cemetery)	12	67	1905 Jun 13	NE, 30th, 1906
Kirkpatrick, L.N.	Pvt.	A, 28th Iowa Inf.	98		1918 Sep 7	IA, 45th, 1919
Kirkpatrick, Milton		I, 30th Ill. Inf.	112		1886	KS, 6th, 1887
Kirkpatrick, S.S.			98		1909 Apr 5	KS, 29th, 1910
Kirkpatrick, Theo. E.		D, 1st Ohio Hvy. Art.	25		1923 Feb 2	KS, 43rd, 1924
Kirkpatrick, W.H.		M, 5th Ohio Cav. (died at Haven, Kans.; buried at Mt. Hope Cemetery)	435		1894 Apr 22	KS, 14th, 1895
Kirkpatrick, Welington		B, 13th Kans.	46		1928 Dec 15	KS, 48th, 1929
Kirkpatrick, William		A, 154th Ohio	221		1905 Dec	KS, 25th, 1906
Kirkpatrick, Wm.	Pvt.	H, 12th Iowa Inf.	40		1906 Sep 19	IA, 33rd, 1907
Kirkpatrick, Wm. R.		A, 32nd Mo. Militia	1		1912 Feb 3	KS, 32nd, 1913
Kirkrice, Anderson		B, 12th Ind.	115		1906 Mar 6	KS, 26th, 1907
Kirkwood, A.	Pvt.	F, 37th Iowa Inf.	409	77	1887 Aug 12	IA, 15th, 1889
Kirkwood, A.W.		B, 84th Ind.	9		1916 Apr 19	KS, 36th, 1917
Kirkwood, J.C.		D, 9th Iowa	375		1904 Dec 15	KS, 24th, 1905

*See Appendix A, B or C for roster of post names and locations.
†See Introduction for note regarding recording of death date.

Name	Rank	Company, Regiment or Ship	Post*	Age	Death Date†	Journal
Kirls, Sherman		C, 5th Iowa	63		1921 Mar 8	KS, 41st, 1922
Kirsch, Andrew	Pvt.	6th Mo. Inf.	231		1909 Apr 14	IA, 36th, 1910
Kirschner, Jacob		B, 1st Mo. Inf.	85		1914 Jul 25	KS, 34th, 1915
Kirthar, W.H.		G, 8th Mich. Inf. (died of old age)	284		1923 May 21	NE, 48th, 1924
Kirtland, —		H, 105th Ill.	32	73	1916 Jan 1	NE, 41st, 1917
Kirtley, Benj.		C, 109th U.S. Colored Inf.	127		1900 Jul 6	KS, 20th, 1901
Kirtley, Thomas		B, 24th N.Y. Cav. (died of paralysis)	216		1924	NE, 49th, 1925
Kirtly, William			37		1926	IA, 53rd, 1927
Kiser, C.E.		H, 17th Iowa	43		1917 Dec 30	KS, 37th, 1918
Kisner, Amos	Pvt.	B, 7th Penn. Cav.	42		1921 May 21	IA, 48th, 1922
Kisor, Nicholas	Pvt.	F, 10th Iowa Inf.	144		1906 Jul 30	IA, 33rd, 1907
Kissel, J.B.	Pvt.	K, 8th Iowa Cav.	29	92	1933 Dec 22	IA, 60th, 1934
Kissick, Robert	Lieut.	113th U.S.C. Inf.	40		1917 Aug 24	IA, 44th, 1918
Kissick, W.L.	Pvt.	C, 16th Iowa	40		1921 Jan 12	IA, 48th, 1922
Kistler, L.K.		F, 208th Penn.	260		1923 Apr 5	KS, 43rd, 1924
Kistner, Frank	Pvt.	C, 133rd Penn. Inf.	68		1916 Dec 1	IA, 43rd, 1917
Kistner, Thomas		A, 1st Ohio Cav.	25		1919 Jan 8	KS, 39th, 1920
Kitch, Josephus		E, 91st Ohio Inf. (died at Douglas)	97		1895 Aug 1	KS, 15th, 1896
Kitchell, C.W.		G, 15th Iowa Inf.	55		1918 Mar 3	IA, 45th, 1919
Kitchen, Joseph C.		D, 45th Ohio	257		1916 Jun 1	KS, 36th, 1917
Kiteninger, Sylvester	Pvt.	D, 11th Wis. Inf.	22		1913 Apr 24	IA, 40th, 1914
Kitselman, J.C.	Pvt.	A, 69th Ind. Inf.	18		1897 Jun 8	IA, 24th, 1898
Kitson, John	Pvt.	A, 188th Penn. Inf. (died of pneumonia)	263	61	1891 Mar 31	NE, 16th, 1892
Kitterman, Geo.		H, 36th Iowa Inf.	69		1922 Oct 27	IA, 49th, 1923
Kitterman, Sam			69		1925	IA, 52nd, 1926
Kitterman, W.H.	Capt.		497		1928	IA, 55th, 1929
Kittridge, John		D, 2nd Maine	158		1915 Apr 13	KS, 35th, 1916
Kitzleman, R.M.		A, 21st Penn.	66		1914 Aug 8	KS, 34th, 1915
Kivits, A.P.		C, 23rd Mo.	12	90	1934 Mar 26	IA, 61st, 1935
Kizer, S.B.		B, 16th U.S. Inf.	80		1940 Aug 26	NE, 65th, 1941
Klassey, Thos.		G, 31st Wis.	26	73	1917 Jul 19	NE, 42nd, 1918
Klasson, M.		C, 12th Kans.	117		1916 Apr 8	KS, 36th, 1917
Klauser, Emanuel		H, 54th Ill. Inf.	85		1916 Dec 27	KS, 36th, 1917
Kleckner, I.F.	Corp.	B, 46th Ill. Inf.	396	48	1891 Mar 4	IA, 17th, 1891
Kleckner, N.J.		150th Penn. Inf.	173		1917	IA, 44th, 1918
Kleckner, W.S.		8th Mo. Inf.	379		1908 Sep 25	IA, 35th, 1909
Kleese, Isaac	Pvt.	106th Penn. Inf.	108		1920 Dec 9	IA, 47th, 1921
Kleffman, Samuel		G, 47th Ill.	140	81	1922 Mar 20	NE, 49th, 1925
Klein, Henry H.	Pvt.	D, 1st Iowa Inf.	297		1912 Oct 29	IA, 39th, 1913
Klein, Louis		B, 32nd Ind.	8		1890	KS, 10th, 1891
Kleippine, Theo.	Pvt.	E, 26th Iowa Inf.	88	86	1933 Oct 30	IA, 60th, 1934
Klenk, John	Pvt.	F, 22nd Iowa Inf.	183	60	1894 Mar 20	IA, 21st, 1895
Kleny, Daniel		A, 1st Ind. Mo.	8		1896 Sep 5	KS, 16th, 1897
Klie, Joseph		K, 8th N.Y.	412		1913 Jul	KS, 33rd, 1914
Kline, Carl	Pvt.	K, 7th Wis. Inf.	247		1891	IA, 18th, 1892
Kline, Ed D.		E, 7th Md.	63		1913 Oct 29	KS, 33rd, 1914
Kline, Geo. W.			291		1919	IA, 46th, 1920
Kline, John	Pvt.	G, 16th Iowa Inf.	78		1906 Jul 12	IA, 33rd, 1907
Kline, Levi		F, 73rd Ill.	42		1916 May 17	KS, 36th, 1917
Kline, Peter	Pvt.	E, 40th Iowa	511		1907 Jul 9	IA, 34th, 1908
Kline, Valentine		C, 18th Ill.	96		1928 Dec 22	KS, 48th, 1929
Kline, Wm. I.		B, 40th Wis.	35		1926 Oct	KS, 46th, 1927
Klinefelter, J.K.		I, 13th Kans. Inf.	130		1902 Mar 4	KS, 22nd, 1903
Klinefelter, Michael		I, 136th Ohio Inf.	130		1935 Feb 10	KS, 55th, 1936
Kling, J.W.	Pvt.	F, 6th Iowa Inf.	11		1919 Oct 14	IA, 46th, 1920
Kling, J.W.			96		1919 Oct 14	IA, 46th, 1920
Klingarman, J.F.	Pvt.	C, 34th Penn. Inf.	68		1928 Dec 22	IA, 55th, 1929
Klingensmith, J.			38		1910 Jul 16	KS, 30th, 1911
Klingerman, S.L.	Pvt.	K, 5th Penn. Hvy. Art.	68		1920 Jul 13	IA, 47th, 1921
Klingerman, W.L.		E, 1st Iowa Cav.	13	68	1907 Aug 9	NE, 32nd, 1908
Klingle, George A.		H, 47th Ind. Inf.	85		1901 Feb 8	KS, 21st, 1902
Klingman, H.C.	Pvt.	A, 176th Ohio Inf.	12		1917 Oct 9	IA, 44th, 1918

See Appendix A, B or C for roster of post names and locations.
†*See Introduction for note regarding recording of death date.*   307

Name	Rank	Company, Regiment or Ship	Post*	Age	Death Date†	Journal
Kliper, E.	Pvt.	B, 35th Iowa Inf.	231		1926 Aug 5	IA, 53rd, 1927
Klise, C.J.	Pvt.	I, 46th Iowa Inf.	11		1928 Feb	IA, 55th, 1929
Klise, D.E.		G, 31st Iowa Inf.	180		1915 Sep 14	KS, 35th, 1916
Klise, George	Pvt.		516		1925	IA, 52nd, 1926
Klontz, George		G, 46th Ill.	122		1914 Jan 3	KS, 34th, 1915
Klopp, B.J.	Pvt.	C, 9th Iowa Inf.	10		1913 Nov 3	IA, 40th, 1914
Klopp, Henry			150		1884	KS, 4th, 1885
Kluetsch, J.D.			25		1894 Jan 28	NE, 19th, 1895
Klumke, J.H.	Pvt.	F, 7th Iowa Inf.	306		1905 Oct 27	IA, 32nd, 1906
Klump, W.B.	Pvt.	28th Penn. Militia	31		1917 Jun 10	IA, 44th, 1918
Klutes, Chas.		11th Mich. Cav.	134		1887 Jan 25	KS, 7th, 1888
Klutzbaugh, Simon		45th Ill. Inf.	72		1918 Dec 13	KS, 38th, 1919
Knap, Leonard	Pvt.	D, 36th Inf.	519		1906 Jun 24	IA, 33rd, 1907
Knapp, A.C.		D, 29th U.S.C.T.	151		1897 Nov 19	KS, 17th, 1898
Knapp, A.W.		died of apoplexy	98	82	1922 Dec 23	NE, 47th, 1923
Knapp, Alonzo		K, 44th Iowa Inf.	293		1931 Nov 13	KS, 51st, 1932
Knapp, C.M.		2nd Colo.	74		1898	KS, 18th, 1899
Knapp, C.W.			100		1884	KS, 4th, 1885
Knapp, Caleb	Pvt.	F, 37th Iowa Inf.	78		1897 Aug 30	IA, 24th, 1898
Knapp, E.A.	Pvt.	A, 5th Minn.	372		1901 Mar 2	IA, 28th, 1902
Knapp, Francis		A, 10th Kans. Inf.	18		1914 Dec 3	KS, 34th, 1915
Knapp, Franklin			187		1883	KS, 3rd, 1884
Knapp, G.W.		C, 7th Ind.	57		1936 Jan	KS, 55th, 1936
Knapp, Geo. W.	Pvt.	K, 11th Iowa Inf.	231		1907 Feb 5	IA, 34th, 1908
Knapp, Geo. W.		C & F, 7th Ind. Inf.	57		1934 Mar 15	KS, 54th, 1935
Knapp, Henry E.		I, 16th —	209		1904 Jan 11	KS, 24th, 1905
Knapp, J.M.		L, 1st N.Y. Cav.	25		1913 Sep 1	KS, 33rd, 1914
Knapp, Jacob R.		3rd Iowa Bat.	81		1897 Oct 9	IA, 24th, 1898
Knapp, John	Pvt.	G, 8th Ill. Cav.	242	60	1897 Jul 13	IA, 24th, 1898
Knapp, John W.		A, 20th Mich.	1		1937 Feb 24	KS, 57th, 1938
Knapp, John Wesley		A, 20th Mich.	1		1937 Feb 4	KS, 56th, 1937
Knapp, Noah	Pvt.	C, 13th Wis. Inf.	3		1911 Nov 29	IA, 38th, 1912
Knapp, S.H.	Pvt.	I, 61st Ill. Inf.	71		1921 Jun 30	IA, 48th, 1922
Knapp, Thos. J.	Pvt.	D, 8th Iowa Inf.	156		1927	IA, 54th, 1928
Knapp, W.A.	Pvt.	G, 21st Mo. Inf.	398		1905 Dec 8	IA, 32nd, 1906
Knapp, W.M.		M, 9th Ohio Cav.	51		1908 Mar 19	KS, 28th, 1909
Knarr, Solomon		11th Penn.	58		1896 May 18	KS, 16th, 1897
Knatt, J.E.	Pvt.	I, 46th Iowa Inf.	147		1902 Aug 9	IA, 29th, 1903
Knauer, Ernest	Pvt.	E, 120th N.Y. Inf.	12		1912 Jan 4	IA, 39th, 1913
Knaup, Theo.	Pvt.	D, 1st Iowa Inf.	5		1913 Dec 28	IA, 40th, 1914
Knauss, A.J.	Pvt.		108		1927 Jan 17	IA, 54th, 1928
Knauss, Chas. H.		B, 47th Penn.	17		1921 Jul 13	KS, 41st, 1922
Knedler, G.W.		K, 81st Ohio Inf.	283		1912 Nov 10	KS, 32nd, 1913
Kneeland, E.S.		F, 1st Mass.	44		1914 Jan 12	KS, 34th, 1915
Kneese, Henry	Pvt.	I, 11th Iowa Inf.	231		1909 May 31	IA, 36th, 1910
Kneese, M.M.	Pvt.	H, 11th Iowa Inf.	231	41	1886 Dec 17	IA, 14th, 1888
Kneese, M.S.	Pvt.	H, 11th Iowa Inf.	231	44	1886 Dec 17	IA, 13th, 1887
Knickerbacker, James	Pvt.	G, 53rd Ill. Inf.	431		1901 Jan 31	IA, 28th, 1902
Knifkin, Henry	Pvt.	6th Iowa Cav.	54		1890 Aug 20	IA, 17th, 1891
Knight, A.B.	Pvt.	E, 24th Iowa Inf.	418	61	1893 Feb 23	IA, 19th, 1893
Knight, C.A.	Pvt.	H, 129th Ind. Inf.	96	86	1932 Feb 5	IA, 59th, 1933
Knight, C.A.	Pvt.	H, 129th Ind. Inf.	96	86	1933 Feb 5	IA, 60th, 1934
Knight, D.R.	Pvt.	I, 36th Iowa Inf.	16		1922 Oct 13	IA, 49th, 1923
Knight, E.T.	Pvt.	A, 36th Iowa Cav.	337		1927 Aug 26	IA, 54th, 1928
Knight, G.W.	Pvt.	D, 8th Iowa Inf.	18		1917 Dec 16	IA, 44th, 1918
Knight, H.G.		E, 32nd Iowa Inf.	25		1905 Apr 20	NE, 30th, 1906
Knight, J.H.		F, 28th Penn. Inf. (died of general debility)	25	67	1896 Oct 17	NE, 21st, 1897
Knight, J. Lee	Sergt.	A, 72nd Ind.	1		1915 Jun 27	KS, 35th, 1916
Knight, J.W.	Pvt.	F, 30th Ill. Inf.	30		1926 May 15	IA, 53rd, 1927
Knight, James M.		Mo. Reg.	292		1934 Jan	KS, 54th, 1935
Knight, Job		B, 17th Ill.	496		1912 Aug 20	KS, 32nd, 1913
Knight, John	1st Lieut.	E, 7th Iowa Inf.	2	49	1887 Feb 11	IA, 13th, 1887

Name	Rank	Company, Regiment or Ship	Post*	Age	Death Date†	Journal
Knight, John F.		M, 15th Kans. Cav.	32		1924 Aug 26	KS, 44th, 1925
Knight, John W.		C, 30th Iowa Inf.	25		1941 Aug 29	NE, 66th, 1942
Knight, M.		L, 11th Kans. Cav.	462		1892 Oct 10	KS, 12th, 1893
Knight, Milton	Corp.	L, 8th Iowa Cav.	55		1922 Jan 11	IA, 49th, 1923
Knight, N.G.		E, 32nd Iowa	25		1905 Apr 24	NE, 31st, 1907
Knight, N.G.		E, 32nd Iowa Inf.	25		1905 Apr 20	NE, 31st, 1907
Knight, Norman D.		D, 4th West Va.	37		1923 Oct 31	KS, 43rd, 1924
Knight, S.Y.	Pvt.	L, 3rd Iowa Vet. Cav.	379		1904 Mar 17	IA, 30th, 1904
Knight, Thomas H.		D, 36th Iowa	180		1931	KS, 51st, 1932
Knight, Thomas H.		D, 36th Iowa	180		1931	KS, 52nd, 1933
Knight, W.C.			92		1900 Jan 27	IA, 27th, 1901
Knight, Wes	Pvt.	C, 4th Wis. Inf.	200		1917 Oct 3	IA, 44th, 1918
Knight, William J.		D, 96th N.Y.	85		1915 Dec 25	KS, 35th, 1916
Knight, Wm.			441		1907 1st term	IA, 34th, 1908
Knight, Z.C.	Pvt.	I, 31st Ill. Inf.	132		1917 Sep	IA, 44th, 1918
Knightly, John		B, 23rd Mo.	290		1889	KS, 9th, 1890
Knipe, Wm.		M, 20th Kans.	100		1921 May 20	KS, 41st, 1922
Kniskers, L.		U.S. Navy	88		1910 Apr 17	IA, 37th, 1911
Knittle, August		I, 2nd U.S. Cav.	11	70	1897 Feb 16	NE, 22nd, 1898
Knoff, Jacob	Pvt.	B, 126th Ill.	43		1922 Mar 12	IA, 49th, 1923
Knoll, Geo. W.		K, 3rd N.Y. Cav.	380		1901 Mar 8	KS, 21st, 1902
Knoll, Jeremiah		F, 167th Penn.	47		1921 Dec 25	KS, 41st, 1922
Knopf, John		E, 13th Mo.	31		1920 Oct 10	KS, 40th, 1921
Knott, J.M.	Capt.	G, 186th Ohio	22		1921 May 13	IA, 48th, 1922
Knott, John	Pvt.	C, 38th Iowa	267		1903-1904	IA, 30th, 1904
Knott, John		D, 142nd Ohio	355		1898 Oct 3	KS, 18th, 1899
Knouf, George	Pvt.	G, 24th Iowa Vol. Inf.	420		1901 Jun 26	IA, 28th, 1902
Knouse, David		D, 20th Iowa Inf. (died of dropsy)	115	62	1905[1904?] Nov 18	NE, 29th, 1905
Knouse, David S.	Capt.	F, 40th Ohio	14		1896 Mar 25	KS, 16th, 1897
Knouse, J.S.	Pvt.	C, 14th Iowa Inf.	250		1919 May 27	IA, 46th, 1920
Knouse, M.		A, 21st Iowa Inf.	440		1915 Mar 7	IA, 42nd, 1916
Knowles, Albert W.	QMS	U.S. Navy	1		1916 Oct 6	KS, 36th, 1917
Knowles, J.R.	Pvt.	E, 50th Wis. Inf.	23		1916 Jan 20	IA, 43rd, 1917
Knowles, Jacob		K, 114th Ill.	25		1930 Apr 9	KS, 50th, 1931
Knowles, John	Pvt.	I, 3rd Iowa Cav.	398		1909 Jul 30	IA, 36th, 1910
Knowles, John A.		A, 112th N.Y. Inf.	337		1899 Sep 2	KS, 19th, 1900
Knowles, Leonard	Pvt.	B, 31st Iowa Inf.	458	67	1895 Apr 3	IA, 21st, 1895
Knowles, S.	Pvt.	C, 22nd Wis. Inf.	493		1899	IA, 26th, 1900
Knowles, W.F.	Pvt.	B, 52nd Penn. Inf.	22		1925 Feb 4	IA, 52nd, 1926
Knowles, W.H.		A, 9th Mich.	35		1929	NE, 54th, 1930
Knowlin, James L.	Pvt.	G, 7th N.Y. Cav.	58		1899	NE, 24th, 1900
Knowlton, Henry A.		G, 8th Iowa Cav. (at large)	78	89	1937 Jan 27	IA, 64th, 1938
Knowlton, W.I.	Pvt.	D, 2nd Colo. Inf.	215		1911 Sep 16	IA, 38th, 1912
Knowlton, Wm. H.		H, 3rd N.H. Inf.	88		1914 Apr 30	KS, 34th, 1915
Knox, A.J.		C, 1st Cal.	55		1922 Jan 5	KS, 42nd, 1923
Knox, Donald			63		1884	KS, 4th, 1885
Knox, J.M.		A, 124th Ill. Inf.	55		1936 Jan 30	KS, 55th, 1936
Knox, James R.		D, 9th Penn. Inf.	271		1901 Apr 5	KS, 21st, 1902
Knox, John	Pvt.	K, 40th Ill. Inf.	290		1915 Sep 1	IA, 42nd, 1916
Knox, John M.		G, 18th Mo. (died of senility)	187	77	1920 Jul 31	NE, 45th, 1921
Knox, N.N.		I, 42nd Iowa Inf. (died of general disability)	180	70	1919 Nov 1	NE, 44th, 1920
Knox, Ohio	Sergt.	E, 16th Ohio Inf.	29		1920 Feb 10	IA, 46th, 1920
Knox, Rob.	Pvt.		66		1920 Sep 9	IA, 47th, 1921
Knox, Wm. E.	Corp.	D, 14th Ky. Cav.	299		1899	NE, 24th, 1900
Knudson, O.G.	Pvt.	C, 7th Iowa Inf.	66		1910 Feb 15	IA, 37th, 1911
Knuth, Wm.	Pvt.	D, 57th Ill.	98		1919	IA, 46th, 1920
Knypers, James		B, 7th Iowa Cav.	11		1893 Feb 20	NE, 18th, 1894
Koaf, Henry	Pvt.	D, 25th Iowa Inf.	157		1917 Sep 11	IA, 45th, 1919
Kobi, Nicholas		K, 51st Ohio Inf.	63		1899 May 14	KS, 19th, 1900
Koch, Adolph	Pvt.	A, 16th Iowa Inf.	240		1916 Jun 1	IA, 43rd, 1917
Koch, Allen		D, 48th Penn. (died of suicide)	110	66	1911 Mar 31	NE, 36th, 1912

*See Appendix A, B or C for roster of post names and locations.
†See Introduction for note regarding recording of death date.
309

Name	Rank	Company, Regiment or Ship	Post*	Age	Death Date†	Journal
Koch, Geo.	Pvt.	A, 46th Iowa Inf.	70		1908	IA, 35th, 1909
Koch, Geo.		M, 7th Ill. Cav.	64		1921 Apr 23	KS, 41st, 1922
Koch, Peter	Pvt.	I, 2nd Mo. Inf.	75		1912 Apr 11	IA, 39th, 1913
Koch, Wm. G.	Pvt.	B, 49th Ind. Inf.	1		1921 Jun 17	IA, 48th, 1922
Kochel, Samuel		F, 48th Ohio	354		1920 Aug 18	KS, 40th, 1921
Kocher, Wm. H.		E, 46th Wis. Inf.	111		1914 Jun 20	NE, 39th, 1915
Kock, Victor		G, 1st Neb.	262	52	1900 Jan 27	NE, 25th, 1901
Kockwood, John N.		E, 16th Ill.	89		1885	KS, 5th, 1886
Koehler, J., see Keohler, J.						
Koehler, John	Pvt.	B, 44th Iowa Inf. (promoted to U.S.C.T. as captain)	231		1925 Dec 1	IA, 52nd, 1926
Koehler, Wm.	Pvt.	I, 12th Iowa Inf.	78		1916 Jun 2	IA, 43rd, 1917
Koehn, William		E, 27th Iowa Inf. (at large)			1932	IA, 59th, 1933
Koentz, J.P.		K, 11th Kans.	39		1911 Apr 26	KS, 31st, 1912
Koeplin, Phillip H.		A, 170th Ohio Inf. (died of lung trouble)	11	82	1924 Dec 24	NE, 49th, 1925
Koerber, John			39		1894	NE, 19th, 1895
Koerney, James		F, 1st Del.	7		1927 Jan 26	NE, 52nd, 1928
Koester, Martin			321		1904-1905	IA, 31st, 1905
Kohe, Daniel F.	Pvt.	F, 13th Iowa Inf.	140		1913 Aug 20	IA, 40th, 1914
Kohlstead, Fred	Pvt.	5th Minn. Battery	365		1913 Jul 8	IA, 40th, 1914
Kohnle, John		H, 2nd Ill. Cav.	37		1918 Oct 24	KS, 38th, 1919
Koin, John W.		E, 46th Ill. Inf.	94	89	1937 Mar 10	IA, 64th, 1938
Kolb, E.M.	Pvt.	E, 38th Wis. Inf.	314		1911 Jul 31	IA, 38th, 1912
Koller, Earnest			42		1909 Oct 11	IA, 36th, 1910
Kolling, Henry		I, 5th Ohio Reg.	362		1918 Feb 23	KS, 38th, 1919
Kolp, H.A.	Corp.	C, 2nd Iowa Cav.	125	90	1932 Dec 29	IA, 59th, 1933
Kondewry, Wm.	Pvt.	I, 7th Iowa Cav.	22		1917 Sep 9	IA, 44th, 1918
Kooch, Frederick	Pvt.	C, 2nd Iowa Vol. Inf.	98	62	1899 Jul	IA, 26th, 1900
Koolbeck, John	Pvt.	J, 4th Iowa	197		1923 Jul 21	IA, 50th, 1924
Koons, J.H.	Pvt.	H, 1st Ind. Art.	7		1912 Mar 19	IA, 39th, 1913
Koons, Loyal		F, 131st Ohio	114		1897 Oct 21	KS, 17th, 1898
Koontz, A.J.		I, 152nd Ind.	25		1913 Dec 24	NE, 38th, 1914
Koontz, Alpheus, see Kooutz, Alpheus						
Koontz, Jaspar N.		5th Ind. Lt. Art.	25	68	1911 Oct 19	NE, 36th, 1912
Kooutz, Alpheus	Pvt.	I, 19th Ohio Inf.	337	44	1888 Mar 9	IA, 15th, 1889
Koozer, Daniel	Pvt.		425		1901 Apr 3	IA, 28th, 1902
Koozer, F.M.		A & D, 47th Ill. Inf. (died of paralysis)	22	77	1909 Jul 29	NE, 34th, 1910
Koppenhofer, J.		H, 131st Penn. Inf. (died of paralysis)	24	56	1896 Sep 15	NE, 21st, 1897
Kopping, Geo.	Pvt.	E, 8th Iowa Inf.	231		1917	IA, 44th, 1918
Kopsa, John	Pvt.	A, 13th U.S.A.	8		1919 Nov 29	IA, 46th, 1920
Korbel, Mike		B, 17th Ill.	25		1926 Mar 28	NE, 51st, 1927
Korn, Leander	Pvt.	I, 18th Mo.	100		1923 Dec 8	IA, 50th, 1924
Korns, Jacob C.	Pvt.	B, 46th Iowa Inf.	64		1930 Mar 25	IA, 57th, 1931
Korns, Robert		G, 51st Ohio	63		1906 Apr 15	KS, 26th, 1907
Korsmeyer, F.A.		A, 136th Ind. Inf.	25		1923	NE, 48th, 1924
Kortz, James G.		G, 39th & 7th Iowa Inf.	1		1902 Dec 8	KS, 22nd, 1903
Koss, Peter	Pvt.	B, 13th N.D.	124		1905 Dec	IA, 32nd, 1906
Kosta, A.	Pvt.	28th Iowa Inf.	24		1918 Mar 28	IA, 45th, 1919
Kothe, Gustave C.			127		1922 Dec 20	KS, 42nd, 1923
Kotsch, Frank			292		1913	KS, 33rd, 1914
Kounts, Thompson F.	Pvt.	I, 13th Iowa Inf.	177	45	1887 Mar 27	IA, 13th, 1887
Krabiel, C.C.	Corp.	F, 50th Ill. Inf.	55	46	1893 Apr 22	IA, 20th, 1894
Kracraft, Lewis		H, 119th Ill.	25		1911 Jan 10	KS, 31st, 1912
Kraft, R.A.		I, 1st Kans.	35		1908[1909?] Mar 14	KS, 29th, 1910
Krager, Lewis		I, 49th Mo.	47		1928 Mar 8	KS, 48th, 1929
Kraig, John C.		A, 29th Mich.	85		1898 Oct 6	KS, 18th, 1899
Krallman, Wm.		B, Ind. Penn. Art.	67		1899 Mar 18	KS, 19th, 1900
Kramer, Adam	2nd Lieut.	M, 2nd U.S. Colored Cav.	8		1901 Nov 10	IA, 28th, 1902
Kramer, Benj. F.	Pvt.	B, 26th Ill. Inf.	485		1901 Dec 31	IA, 28th, 1902
Kramer, Cornelius		C, 47th Penn.	308		1911 Oct 21	KS, 31st, 1912
Kramer, David E.		G, 57th Ohio Inf.	36		1914 Nov 6	KS, 34th, 1915

*See Appendix A, B or C for roster of post names and locations.
†See Introduction for note regarding recording of death date.

Name	Rank	Company, Regiment or Ship	Post*	Age	Death Date†	Journal
Kramer, H.T.		G, 12th Ohio Inf.	25		1908 Dec 22	KS, 28th, 1909
Kramer, H.T.		G, 12th Ohio Inf.	25		1908 Dec 22	KS, 29th, 1910
Kramer, J.H.		6th Ind. Bat.	8		1918 May 13	IA, 45th, 1919
Kramer, J.H.		6th Ohio Battery	25	75	1918 May 13	NE, 43rd, 1919
Kramer, Zachariah		H, 17th Penn.	293		1920 Apr 5	KS, 40th, 1921
Kranert, Wm.	Pvt.	I, 41st N.Y. Inf.	371		1913 Jul 5	IA, 40th, 1914
Krape, A.C.		E, 7th Penn. Inf.	180		1929	KS, 49th, 1930
Krapfel, John W.		G, 1st Iowa Cav.	68		1918 Jun 6	IA, 45th, 1919
Kraul, Chas.			5		1917	IA, 44th, 1918
Kraut, L.	Pvt.	A, 148th Ill. Inf.	235		1921 Oct 6	IA, 48th, 1922
Kraysher, Wesley	Pvt.	C, 39th Iowa	45		1905 Feb 3	IA, 32nd, 1906
Kreachbaum, David		E, 58th Ohio	22		1935 Jun 15	NE, 60th, 1936
Kreamer, Aug.	Pvt.	I, 32nd Iowa Inf.	236		1925 Apr 18	IA, 52nd, 1926
Kreamer, G.W.	Pvt.		35		1905 Feb 4	IA, 33rd, 1907
Kreamer, Wm.	Pvt.	B, 26th Ill. Inf.	6		1927 Dec 6	IA, 54th, 1928
Krebbs, James		G, 8th Wis.	15		1914 Oct 19	KS, 34th, 1915
Krebs, F.D.		H, 6th Penn. Inf.	453		1889	KS, 9th, 1890
Krebs, Gotleib	Pvt.	D, 29th Iowa Inf.	324	54	1888 May 4	IA, 15th, 1889
Krebs, Josiah		D, 208th Penn. Inf.	308		1900 Jun 24	KS, 20th, 1901
Kreech, John H.	Pvt.	I, 7th Iowa Inf.	235		1926 Jan 5	IA, 53rd, 1927
Krege, Chas.	Sergt.	K, 17th Mo. Inf.	78	67	1891 May 17	IA, 18th, 1892
Kreiger, Henry		H, 89th Ohio Inf.	6		1891 Sep 11	KS, 11th, 1892
Kreigh, Elias		30th Ind.	350		1921 Jul 28	KS, 41st, 1922
Kreker, C.F.		H, 7th U.S. Inf. (died of cancer)	84	75	1911 Nov 13	NE, 36th, 1912
Krell, Frederick	Pvt.	I, 16th Iowa Cav.	8	57	1892 Nov 24	IA, 19th, 1893
Krell, George		F, 16th U.S. Inf.	13		1930 Aug 9	NE, 55th, 1931
Krell, John Henry	Sergt.	A, 73rd Ohio Inf.	55		1914 Jun 4	IA, 41st, 1915
Kremmer, Aug.	Sergt.	M, 8th Iowa Cav.	249		1926 Oct 22	IA, 53rd, 1927
Kreninger, Henry		G, 22nd Wis. Inf.	104	91	1935 Apr 27	IA, 62nd, 1936
Kress, M.N.		E, 1st Penn. Cav. (died of paralysis)	13	77	1919 Jul 4	NE, 44th, 1920
Kretschman, F.	Pvt.	D, 26th Wis. Inf.	267	44	1886 Jun 13	IA, 13th, 1887
Kretzer, G.R.		G, 54th Penn.	4		1912 Aug 2	KS, 32nd, 1913
Krick, Edward		H, 91st Ind. Inf.	91	74	1917 Jan 4	NE, 42nd, 1918
Krider, Joseph		K, 201st Penn.	81		1906 Oct 3	KS, 26th, 1907
Krieble, Karl		E, 10th Wis. Inf. (died of old age)	133	82	1918 Apr 24	NE, 43rd, 1919
Kries, R.B.	Pvt.	C, 13th U.S. Inf.	78		1912 Jun 30	IA, 39th, 1913
Krise, Abe	Pvt.	208th —	201		1917 Dec 10	IA, 44th, 1918
Krishbaum, John		E, 58th Ohio	25		1919 Jun 2	NE, 44th, 1920
Kristie, A.N.	Pvt.	B, 45th Inf.	108		1923 Mar 21	IA, 50th, 1924
Kroger, M.	Pvt.	F, 2nd Mo. Bat.	125		1921 Dec 27	IA, 48th, 1922
Kroghn, Peter	Pvt.	G, 1st Ill. Battery	270	70	1897 Apr 7	IA, 24th, 1898
Kroh, Henry	P. Corp.	I, 10th Iowa Inf.	16		1905 Dec 2	IA, 32nd, 1906
Krohn, George			371		1910	IA, 38th, 1912
Kron, L.J.	Pvt.	G, 153rd Ill. Inf.	81		1927 Dec 5	IA, 54th, 1928
Kron, Peter F.			12		1923 Jun 15	KS, 43rd, 1924
Krone, D.C.		E, 41st Ill.	4		1922 Jun	KS, 42nd, 1923
Krone, D.C.		E, 41st Ill.	4		1921 Apr 26	KS, 41st, 1922
Krone, D.H.		41st Ill.	4		1918 Jan 22	KS, 38th, 1919
Kroniger, Henry J.	Pvt.	G, 22nd Wis. Inf.	104	90	1935 Apr 27	IA, 65th, 1939
Krouse, Martin	Pvt.	D, 86th Ill. Inf.	192		1907 Nov 26	IA, 33rd, 1907
Krouskup, G.W.	Pvt.	A, 39th Ill. Inf.	372	53	1893 Apr 1	IA, 20th, 1894
Krouskup, John			321		1922 Jan 15	IA, 49th, 1923
Kruckman, F.W.	Pvt.	B, 46th Wis. Inf.	236		1915 Jan 9	IA, 42nd, 1916
Krudewig, Wm.	Pvt.	I, 7th Iowa Cav.	22		1917 Sep 9	IA, 44th, 1918
Krudwig, Mathius		E, 34th Wis.	145		1915 Apr 19	KS, 35th, 1916
Krug, John V.		C, 8th Ohio Battery	1		1885	KS, 5th, 1886
Kruger, Charles	Pvt.	E, 21st Iowa Inf.	78		1915 Jul 12	IA, 42nd, 1916
Kruger, K.C.	Pvt.	C, 46th Ill. Inf.	71		1912 Jul 14	IA, 39th, 1913
Krugg, J.A.	Seaman	Gulf Squadron	329	50	1886 Feb 4	IA, 14th, 1888
Krum, Urias		16th N.Y. Bat.	353		1918 Feb 7	KS, 38th, 1919
Kubick, John	Pvt.	E, 4th Mo. Inf.	8		1908 Mar 26	IA, 35th, 1909
Kuchel, August	Pvt.	G, 20th Iowa Inf.	423		1908 Dec 21	IA, 35th, 1909

*See Appendix A, B or C for roster of post names and locations.
†See Introduction for note regarding recording of death date.

Name	Rank	Company, Regiment or Ship	Post*	Age	Death Date†	Journal
Kueger, Otto		E, 37th Ill.	[51?]		1937 Sep 7	KS, 56th, 1937
Kuehner, Frank	Pvt.	I, 35th Ind. Inf.	7		1917 Sep 28	IA, 44th, 1918
Kuer, Nicholas	Pvt.	F, 10th Iowa Inf.	127		1906 Jul 30	IA, 33rd, 1907
Kugan, T.P.	Pvt.	G, 75th Ill. Inf.	23		1928 Feb 28	IA, 55th, 1929
Kuhl, John P.		B, 145th Ill. Inf.	25		1925 May 7	KS, 45th, 1926
Kuhlenbeck, John F.	Pvt.	D, 25th Iowa Inf.	157		1912 Jun 19	IA, 39th, 1913
Kuhn, Albert W.		K, 1st West Va.	18		1910 May 31	KS, 30th, 1911
Kuhn, Conrad		B, 103rd Ill.	97		1919 Dec 31	KS, 39th, 1920
Kuhn, Enos N.		G, 133rd Ind.	12		1930 Apr 9	KS, 50th, 1931
Kuhn, Henry		C, 8th Kans.	1		1900 Jun 11	KS, 20th, 1901
Kuhn, J.B.		G, 128th Ind.	10		1935 Dec 27	NE, 60th, 1936
Kuhn, John	Pvt.	I, 2nd U.S. Cav.	166	48	1884 Dec 14	NE, 9th, 1885
Kuhn, P.		I, 120th Ohio Inf.	40		1899 Jun	KS, 19th, 1900
Kuhn, Peter	Sergt.	K, 40th Iowa Inf.	330	48	1886 Dec 16	IA, 13th, 1887
Kuhn, Samuel		B, 3rd Ind.	87		1909 Nov 18	KS, 29th, 1910
Kuhns, J.A.		A, 20th Penn.	63		1921 May 19	KS, 41st, 1922
Kuhns, J.C.	Pvt.	I, 12th Iowa Inf.	322		1914 Mar 22	IA, 41st, 1915
Kuler, J.F.		I, 2nd Kans.	257		1920 Apr 9	KS, 40th, 1921
Kulms, F.W.		H, 2nd Ind. Cav.	382		1898 Dec 4	KS, 18th, 1899
Kummer, H.C.	Corp.	D, 5th Iowa Cav.	2		1900 Oct 29	IA, 27th, 1901
Kunkel, Ferd		C, 51st Mo.	113		1919 Feb 12	KS, 39th, 1920
Kunkle, Wm.		B, 11th Penn.	25		1926 Mar 26	KS, 46th, 1927
Kunkleman, Adam		E, 135th Penn.	303		1905 Jan 11	KS, 25th, 1906
Kuntz, Adam		D, 4th Ohio Inf.	36		1886	KS, 6th, 1887
Kuntz, C.D.		L, 1st Mo. Cav.	123		1913 Mar 8	NE, 39th, 1915
Kuntz, Henry			55		1924 May 14	IA, 51st, 1925
Kupper, William		F, 2nd U.S. Cav.	22		1885	KS, 5th, 1886
Kurnes, Samuel H.		F, 102nd U.S.C.T.	14		1912 May 17	KS, 32nd, 1913
Kurstered, J.H.		B, 73rd Ind. (died of paralysis)	182	63	1904 Oct 8	NE, 29th, 1905
Kurth, Wm.	Pvt.	K, 47th Wis. Inf.	266	50	1893 Feb 19	IA, 19th, 1893
Kurtz, Christian	1st Lieut.	F, 24th Iowa Inf.	206		1925 Jul 1	IA, 52nd, 1926
Kurtz, D.J.	Corp.	C, 71st Ohio Inf.	324		1930 Feb 2	IA, 57th, 1931
Kurtz, F.	Pvt.	B, 20th N.Y. Inf.	313		1910 Nov 23	IA, 37th, 1911
Kurtz, H.C.	Pvt.	F, 24th Iowa Inf.	140		1920 Oct 1	IA, 47th, 1921
Kurtz, Henry J.		A, 150th Ill. Inf.	35		1941 Jan 28	NE, 66th, 1942
Kurtz, Jacob	Pvt.	K, 2nd Ill. Bat.	305		1919 Dec 27	IA, 46th, 1920
Kusel, Henry, see Kiisel, Henry						
Kuster, Hiram	Pvt.	G, 13th Iowa Inf.	259	76	1894 Jan 17	IA, 21st, 1895
Kutler, Charles	Pvt.	F, 39th Wis. Inf.	78		1916 Mar 5	IA, 43rd, 1917
Kutz, Elon			236		1915	IA, 42nd, 1916
Kyger, N.		A, 147th Inf.	388		1917 May 15	KS, 37th, 1918
Kyle, A.R.		C, 24th Mich.	22		1923 May 30	KS, 43rd, 1924
Kyle, David C.	Pvt.	D, 20th Ohio	108		1926 Mar 8	IA, 53rd, 1927
Kyle, Ira C.		Ill.	34		1916 Aug	KS, 36th, 1917
Kyle, John W.		E, 116th Ill.	51		1916 Nov 26	KS, 36th, 1917
Kyler, S.W.	Pvt.	1st Penn. Art.	1		1916 Mar 21	IA, 43rd, 1917
Kylesberg, Nils		E, 44th Ill. Inf. (died of complication of diseases at Soldiers & Sailors Home, Grand Island; buried in Home Cemetery)	32	77	1905 Dec 30	NE, 30th, 1906
Kyner, James H.		F, 46th Ohio	7		1936 Feb 10	NE, 61st, 1937
Kyte, Francis M.	Lieut.	F, 6th Iowa Inf.	173		1908 Jun 9	IA, 35th, 1909
Kyte, Marshall T.		K, 14th Mich. Inf. (died of paralysis)	204	83	1907 Aug 13	NE, 32nd, 1908
L'mbenhi'm'r, J.	Corp.	I, 5th U.S. Cav. (cause of death: lungs)	69	50	1887 Dec	NE, 12th, 1888
Labar, W.H.		E, 203rd Penn. Inf.	45		1887	KS, 7th, 1888
LaBarre, John	Pvt.	C, 32nd Iowa Inf.	68		1911 Jan 25	IA, 38th, 1912
Labede, Peter			123		1895	KS, 15th, 1896
Labedie, Chas.		F, 14th Kans.	123		1898 Aug 10	KS, 18th, 1899
Labeutt, Daniel		died of dropsy	11		1886	NE, 11th, 1887
Labin, Jas. H.		A, —	32		1906 Jul 12	KS, 26th, 1907
Lablanc, Main J.		U.S. Navy	84		1927 Feb 18	NE, 52nd, 1928
LaBrant, J.B.		G, 58th Ill.	65		1928 Feb 9	KS, 48th, 1929

*See Appendix A, B or C for roster of post names and locations.
†See Introduction for note regarding recording of death date.

Name	Rank	Company, Regiment or Ship	Post*	Age	Death Date†	Journal
LaBrent, L.E.	Pvt.	17th Ill. Cav.	124		1924 Jul 5	IA, 51st, 1925
Lacey, Gates T.		I, 5th Wis.	463		1904 Sep 10	KS, 24th, 1905
Lacey, M.L.		M, 3rd Mich. Cav.	302		1908	KS, 28th, 1909
Lacey, Smith		D, 101st U.S.C.I.	75		1914 Apr 26	KS, 34th, 1915
Lacey, W.F.M.		K, 33rd Ill.	50		1914 Sep 15	KS, 34th, 1915
Lack, J.		144th Ill.	18		1921	IA, 48th, 1922
Lacke, A.G.	Paymaster's Clerk	U.S. Navy	88		1905 Aug 25	IA, 32nd, 1906
Lackey, George	Pvt.	C, 9th Iowa Cav.	84		1928 Apr 19	IA, 55th, 1929
Lackey, Melvin	Pvt.	C, 6th Iowa Cav.	258		1899 May 7	IA, 26th, 1900
Lackey, S.W.		G, 42nd Mass. (former member of Nebraska Dept.; location: Stanton)	190		1937 Nov 6	NE, 62nd, 1938
Lackore, C.H.	Pvt.	C, 2nd Iowa Inf.	151		1902 Nov 11	IA, 29th, 1903
LaCore, G.W.		A, U.S. Reg.	65		1919 Nov 20	KS, 39th, 1920
Lacroix, Eugene		C, 47th Mo.	130		1898 Oct 22	KS, 18th, 1899
Lacy, A.H.	Pvt.	G, 40th Iowa	275		1903-1904	IA, 30th, 1904
Lacy, A.V.		I, 38th Iowa Inf.	150		1st quarter 1885	IA, 11th, 1885
Lacy, J.A.	Pvt.	F, 168th Ohio	7		1907 Jan 18	IA, 34th, 1908
Lacy, John		G, 16th Ind.	12		1915 Mar 19	KS, 35th, 1916
Lacy, John F.	Corp.	H, 3rd Iowa Inf.	40		1913 Sep 29	IA, 40th, 1914
Lacy, P.	Pvt.	K, 26th Ind. Inf.	10		1920 Jul 28	IA, 47th, 1921
Lacy, W.K.		I, 73rd Ill.	180		1914 Nov 11	KS, 34th, 1915
Ladd, A.R.	Pvt.	E, 30th Wis. Inf.	133		1925 Jan 12	IA, 52nd, 1926
Ladd, Andrew		H, 9th Ky.	18		1923 Feb 21	KS, 43rd, 1924
Ladd, Anson	Pvt.	G, 3rd Mo. Cav.	30		1911 Feb 17	IA, 38th, 1912
Ladd, David Asher	Pvt.	F, 1st Iowa Cav.	240		1922 Jan 24	IA, 49th, 1923
Ladd, H.M.			65		1924	KS, 44th, 1925
Ladd, J.A.			125		1915	IA, 42nd, 1916
Ladd, L.O.		D, 110th N.Y.	72		1915 Sep 15	KS, 35th, 1916
LaDee, Henry		A, 200th N.Y. Inf. (died of general debility)	264	54	1895 Dec 3	NE, 20th, 1896
Ladesder, Franz		G, 1st Mo. G, 43rd Ill. Inf. (killed in railroad accident)	380		1891 Sep 28	KS, 11th, 1892
Ladon, Alexander	Sergt.	K, 10th Iowa Inf.	233	89	1899 Aug 13	IA, 26th, 1900
Ladragan, William	Pvt.	G, 26th Iowa Inf.	327		1901 Apr 12	IA, 28th, 1902
Ladwig, Christian	Pvt.	B, 8th Ill. Cav.	90		1918 Jul 21	IA, 45th, 1919
Laevitt, George P.		E, 9th Ind.	117		1911 Mar 18	KS, 31st, 1912
LaFavre, S.	Corp.	H, 33rd Ind.	440		1921 Apr 15	IA, 48th, 1922
LaFayer, Geo.		H, 11th Iowa Inf.	231		1924 Mar 3	IA, 51st, 1925
Lafever, Daniel F.	Pvt.	C, 8th Iowa Cav.	337		1928 Dec 20	IA, 55th, 1929
LaFevre, J.B.		B, 148th N.Y.	209		1919 Jan 19	KS, 39th, 1920
Laffallett, J.W.	Corp.	D, 23rd Iowa	40		1921 Mar 11	IA, 48th, 1922
Laffer, E.	QM	47th Iowa	167		1914 Aug 16	IA, 41st, 1915
Laffer, Phillip	Pvt.	F, 5th Iowa Vol. Inf.	167		1903 Oct 24	IA, 30th, 1904
Lafferty, A.M.	Pvt.	F, 2nd Iowa Cav.	497		1929 Oct 30	IA, 56th, 1930
Lafferty, Geo.	Lieut.	5th Wis. Bat.	329		1919 Apr 11	IA, 46th, 1920
Lafferty, George W.	Pvt.	G, 10th P.R.V.C.[Penn. Res. Vol. Corps?]	40		1912 Dec 24	IA, 39th, 1913
Lafferty, R.W.	Pvt.	B, 50th Ill. Inf.	472		1925 Apr 23	IA, 52nd, 1926
Laffler, Jacob		D, 18th Ohio Inf.	470		1902 Apr 17	KS, 22nd, 1903
Laflin, Lewis H.		I, 1st Neb. (died of diabetes)	169	77	1920 Mar 7	NE, 45th, 1921
Lafmick, William		F, 61st U.S.	9		1923 Jun 8	KS, 43rd, 1924
LaForce, Dan'l A.	Major	Ark.	69		1912 Mar 10	IA, 39th, 1913
Lagel, Benj. E.		12th Ind. Bat.	25		1927 Jul 24	NE, 52nd, 1928
Lagrange, C.M.	Pvt.	I, 50th N.Y. Inf.	88		1917	IA, 44th, 1918
Lagsdon, Geo. W.	Pvt.	G, 13th Iowa	16		1903 Oct 14	IA, 30th, 1904
Lahr, Paul		D, 93rd Ill.	175		1927 Jan 7	KS, 47th, 1928
Lahr, Peter		C, 147th Penn. (died at Alma)	29		1895 Apr	KS, 15th, 1896
Laidlow, W.E.	Pvt.	F, 18th Wis. Inf.	216		1924 Feb 18	IA, 51st, 1925
Lain, Jerome M.		C, 91st Ill.	318		1918 Sep 10	NE, 43rd, 1919
Lain, John M.	Pvt.	A, 3rd Iowa Cav.	100		1926 Feb 24	IA, 53rd, 1927
Laing, Geo. J.	Lieut.	I, 4th Iowa Inf.	192		1930 Oct 20	IA, 57th, 1931
Laing, Robert	Pvt.	I, 4th Iowa Inf.	192		1902 Sep 20	IA, 29th, 1903
Lair, A.S.		I, 152nd Ill. Inf.	153		1899 Aug 19	KS, 19th, 1900

*See Appendix A, B or C for roster of post names and locations.
†See Introduction for note regarding recording of death date.

Name	Rank	Company, Regiment or Ship	Post*	Age	Death Date†	Journal
Laird, A.G.	Pvt.	M, 16th Kans. Cav.	14	57	1887 Aug 23	IA, 14th, 1888
Laird, A.R.		F, 7th Ind.	68		1917 Nov 3	KS, 37th, 1918
Laird, E.E.		A, 63rd Ohio	1		1913 Sep 14	KS, 33rd, 1914
Laird, G.W.	Pvt.	I, 7th Ohio Cav.	20	88	1931 May 6	IA, 58th, 1932
Laird, H.B.	Pvt.	H, 4th Iowa Cav.	132		1925 Dec 24	IA, 52nd, 1926
Laird, H.R.	Corp.	A, 4th Iowa Cav.	263		1918 Jul 14	IA, 45th, 1919
Laird, J.R.			165		1913	IA, 40th, 1914
Laird, James A.	Pvt.	H, 27th Iowa Inf.	16		1910 Jun	IA, 37th, 1911
Laird, Jas. W.		H, 131st Ill.	47		1930	KS, 52nd, 1933
Laird, Jas. W.		H, 131st Ill.	47		1930	KS, 51st, 1932
Laird, John	Pvt.	H, 4th Iowa Cav.	132		1905 May 21	IA, 32nd, 1906
Laird, John M.		H, 13th Ill. Vol. Inf.	1		1909 Apr 12	KS, 29th, 1910
Laird, Levi	Pvt.	G, 4th Iowa Cav.	10	71	1889 Mar 18	IA, 15th, 1889
Laird, M.R.		D, 8th Minn.	265		1891 Mar 7	KS, 11th, 1892
Laird, S.E.	Pvt.	I, 1st Ohio Bat.	16		1915 Jul 2	IA, 42nd, 1916
Lake, Andrew	Pvt.	C, 12th Ill. Cav.	59		1909 Oct 11	IA, 36th, 1910
Lake, Andrew J.	Pvt.	G, 25th Ill. Inf.	59		1909	IA, 36th, 1910
Lake, C.S.	Adjt.	20th Iowa Inf.	206		1917 Jan 18	IA, 44th, 1918
Lake, Delmar	Pvt.	F, 2nd Iowa Cav.	66		1906 Jun 5	IA, 33rd, 1907
Lake, Gibson		West Va.	264		1905 Nov 6	KS, 25th, 1906
Lake, J.D.		D, 48th Ohio Inf.	364		1899 Jan 24	KS, 19th, 1900
Lake, John A.	Pvt.	G, 113th Ohio Inf.	410		1916 Feb 10	IA, 43rd, 1917
Lake, L.H.	Pvt.	I, 16th N.Y. Art.	68		1919 Sep 13	IA, 46th, 1920
Lake, Willis	Pvt.	B, 31st Ohio Inf.	18		1913 Apr 20	IA, 40th, 1914
Lakin, A.G.		K, 4th Ill.	55		1920 Jul 17	KS, 40th, 1921
Lam, L.L.		D, 70th Ind.	142		1904 Aug 8	KS, 24th, 1905
Lam, W.F.		H, 120th Ill.	265		1908 Jun 16	KS, 28th, 1909
Lamadue, J.W.		H, 12th Ill. (died of heart trouble)	27	69	1914 Sep 26	NE, 39th, 1915
Lamar, John		C, 146th Ind.	123		1900 Dec 15	KS, 20th, 1901
Lamaster, Wesley	Pvt.	K, 7th Iowa Inf.	167		1899 Dec 17	IA, 26th, 1900
Lamasters, Geo. L.	Pvt.	E, 78th Ohio Inf.	440, 421	95	1939 Mar 15	IA, 65th, 1939
Lamb, Abel	Corp.	C, 3rd Minn.	1		1916 Sep 10	KS, 36th, 1917
Lamb, B.		B, 71st Ind.	293		1922 Sep 20	KS, 42nd, 1923
Lamb, Basil		B, 72nd Ind.	248		1922 Sep 20	KS, 42nd, 1923
Lamb, C.E.	Pvt.	E, 7th Ill. Cav.	452	86	1931 Feb 19	IA, 58th, 1932
Lamb, Caleb	Capt.	I, 37th Iowa Inf.	16	75	1897 Aug 25	IA, 24th, 1898
Lamb, Curtis A.		A, 16th Ill.	1		1922 Nov 3	KS, 42nd, 1923
Lamb, D.C.	Sergt.	I, 13th Ill. Cav.	181		1912 Dec 2	IA, 39th, 1913
Lamb, D.C.	Sergt.	I, 13th Ill. Cav.	181		1911 Dec 2	IA, 38th, 1912
Lamb, Daniel	Pvt.	F, 8th Iowa Inf.	305		1901 Jul 23	IA, 28th, 1902
Lamb, David	Pvt.	A, 76th Ind. Vols.	347		1904 Apr 27	IA, 31st, 1905
Lamb, David P.		H, 4th Penn. Inf.	1		1899 Apr 19	KS, 19th, 1900
Lamb, Harmon		G, 70th Ill. K, 115th Ind. K, 54th Ill.	55		1919 Aug 1	KS, 39th, 1920
Lamb, J.H.	Pvt.	E, 13th Iowa Inf.	153		1908 Nov 9	IA, 35th, 1909
Lamb, J.M.	Pvt.	H, 36th Iowa Inf.	167	90	1933 May 2	IA, 60th, 1934
Lamb, James		C, 48th Ind.	452		1934	IA, 61st, 1935
Lamb, James B.	Pvt.	H, 39th Iowa Inf.	7		1926 Feb 27	IA, 53rd, 1927
Lamb, Jesse K.	Pvt.	E, 58th Ill. Inf.	16		1913	IA, 40th, 1914
Lamb, Joseph	Corp.	I, 42nd Wis. Inf.	68		1920 Jan 10	IA, 47th, 1921
Lamb, Joseph		A, 33rd Ind.	66		1911 Nov 8	KS, 31st, 1912
Lamb, M.B.	Pvt.	A, 137th Ill. Inf.	5		1913 Feb 21	IA, 40th, 1914
Lamb, Miles		D, Kans. Vol. Cav.	3		1917 Feb 17	KS, 37th, 1918
Lamb, Sylvanus		C, 98th Ohio Inf. (died of old age)	22	85	1916 Jan 23	NE, 41st, 1917
Lamb, Tobias	Pvt.	A, 69th Ill.	321		1899 Oct 29	IA, 26th, 1900
Lamb, Wm.		1st Ind. Cav.	49		1904 Dec 21	KS, 24th, 1905
Lamb, Wm. H.	Pvt.		11		1918 Apr 3	IA, 45th, 1919
Lambdin, Wm. J.		E, 98th Ill. (not a member of the G.A.R.)	18		1912 Nov 10	KS, 32nd, 1913
Lambert, A.J.		151st Ind.	115		1922 Jul 28	KS, 42nd, 1923
Lambert, Elisha		G, 54th Ind.	355		1898 Jan 8	KS, 18th, 1899
Lambert, George	Pvt.	I, 22nd Maine Inf.	3	55	1894 Jun 27	IA, 21st, 1895

*See Appendix A, B or C for roster of post names and locations.
†See Introduction for note regarding recording of death date.
314

Name	Rank	Company, Regiment or Ship	Post*	Age	Death Date†	Journal
Lambert, J.R.		I, 96th Ohio Inf.	66		1917 Sep 6	KS, 37th, 1918
Lambert, Peter	Pvt.	A, 19th Iowa Inf.	12		1910 Oct 13	IA, 37th, 1911
Lambert, R.K.	Pvt.	B, 142nd Ohio Vol. Inf.	16		1918	IA, 45th, 1919
Lambert, Samuel B.		E, 136th Ind. Inf. (died at Osage City)	11		1895 Jul	KS, 15th, 1896
Lambert, Thos. C.		B, Ohio National Guard (died of old age & complication)	77	78	1911 Jul 6	NE, 36th, 1912
Lambert, William		M, 4th Ill. Cav.	340		1921 Oct 19	KS, 41st, 1922
Lambert, Wm. S.	Surg.	6th Iowa Inf.	337	49	1888 Mar 13	IA, 15th, 1889
Lambing, G.W.		B, 133rd Ill.	113		1912 Feb 17	KS, 32nd, 1913
Lambson, J.H.		A, 4th Iowa Inf. (died of cancer)	112	78	1918 Dec 24	NE, 43rd, 1919
Lambson, Jas. F.		A, 4th Iowa (died of cancer)	112	80	1918 Dec 24	NE, 44th, 1920
Lamer, John		E, 81st Ill.	87		1908 Sep 29	KS, 28th, 1909
Lamert, J.G.			384		1899 Sep	KS, 19th, 1900
Lamert, L.G.		15th Batt. Lt. Art. (died of heart trouble)	39		1923 Jul 19	NE, 48th, 1924
Lamken, George	Pvt.	D, 31st Ill. Inf.	155		1929 Dec 21	IA, 56th, 1930
Lamma, C.		I, 152nd Penn. Inf. (died of debility)	112	76	1903 Oct 29	NE, 28th, 1904
Lamme, John W.		E, 153rd Ohio	46		1923 Oct 30	KS, 43rd, 1924
Lammert, L.G., see Lamert, L.G.						
Lammon, John T.	Pvt.	E, 2nd Mich. Inf.	176	45	1887 May 13	IA, 14th, 1888
Lamore, Robert P.		I, 45th Ill. Inf. (died of cancer)	12		1893 Jul 30	NE, 18th, 1894
Lamott, J.P.		I, 66th Ill.	85		1890	KS, 10th, 1891
Lampher, Geo.	Pvt.	D, 10th Ill. Inf.	231		1910 May 9	IA, 37th, 1911
Lamphere, A.D.C.		C, 42nd Ill.	170		1904 Sep 17	KS, 24th, 1905
Lamphere, P.S.		C, 37th Ill. Inf.	259		3rd quarter 1884	IA, 11th, 1885
Lampman, S.		G, 30th Ind.	40		1924 May 5	KS, 44th, 1925
Lampson, W.T.		I, 55th Ohio Inf.	49		1918 Oct 7	KS, 38th, 1919
Lamson, J.H.	Pvt.	G, 9th Iowa Inf.	68		1920 Oct 16	IA, 47th, 1921
Lamson, John			12		1883	KS, 3rd, 1884
Lanage, T.L.	Pvt.	A, 44th Iowa Inf.	329		1907 Jun 13	IA, 34th, 1908
Lanbacher, J.B.	S.M.	11th Iowa Inf.	94		1918 Jun 10	IA, 45th, 1919
Lanbmair, Otto		F, 20th Ill.	164		1909 Aug 8	KS, 29th, 1910
Lancaster, I.J.		Tenn.	266		1912 Mar	KS, 32nd, 1913
Lancaster, Jos.	Pvt.		38		1910 Jun	IA, 37th, 1911
Lancaster, W.H.		D, 130th Ill.	81		1926	NE, 51st, 1927
Lance, C.G.		U.S. Navy	65		1914 Oct 30	KS, 34th, 1915
Lancomber, Geo.		C, 195th Penn. Inf.	265		1927 Apr 2	NE, 51st, 1927
Land, Arthur	Pvt.	12th Chicago Bat.	76		1900 Jun 4	IA, 27th, 1901
Land, Hiram		B, 94th Ill. Inf.	477		1909 Oct 5	KS, 29th, 1910
Land, Jackson		C, 3rd Wis. Inf.	87		1892 Dec 20	NE, 17th, 1893
Landahl, William	Pvt.	B, 24th Iowa Inf.	228	68	1899 Apr 13	IA, 25th, 1899
Landers, F.E.	Pvt.	E, 16th N.Y. Inf.	66		1930 Sep 7	IA, 57th, 1931
Landers, Felix		F, 39th Iowa Inf.	55		1912 Jan 7	IA, 39th, 1913
Landers, Jonas			144		1916 Apr 3	IA, 43rd, 1917
Landin, D.M.	Pvt.	I, 213th Penn. Inf.	1		1908 Dec 26	IA, 35th, 1909
Landin, John		E, 166th Penn.	63		1901 Dec 30	KS, 21st, 1902
Landis, Samuel	Pvt.	I, 208th Penn. Inf.	231		1907 Jan 31	IA, 34th, 1908
Landis, Simon		G, 60th Ill. (died of stomach trouble)	1	74	1920 Jan 7	NE, 45th, 1921
Landon, George W.	Pvt.	I, 23rd N.Y. Inf.	58		1919 Dec 19	IA, 46th, 1920
Landon, Matt	Pvt.	A, 93rd Ill. Inf.	195		1909 Aug	IA, 36th, 1910
Lane, A.		I, 152nd Ill. Inf.	205		1901 Jul 6	KS, 21st, 1902
Lane, A.L.	Pvt.	C, 85th Ill. Inf.	6	42	1887 Apr 2	IA, 14th, 1888
Lane, Chas. E.	Pvt.	C, 21st Iowa	284		1903 Aug 3	IA, 30th, 1904
Lane, E.F.	Pvt.	F, 156th Ill. Inf.	493		1900 Dec 9	IA, 27th, 1901
Lane, Geo. W.	Pvt.	K, 4th Iowa Inf.	211		1909	IA, 36th, 1910
Lane, Henry C.	Corp.	E, 25th Ill. Inf.	72		1903 May 4	IA, 30th, 1904
Lane, I.S.	Pvt.	F, 16th Ill. Inf.	122		1911 Jan 13	IA, 38th, 1912
Lane, J.E.		E, 41st Ohio	170		1921 Feb 18	KS, 41st, 1922
Lane, James		G, 17th Ind. Inf.	113		1899 Jul 14	KS, 19th, 1900
Lane, James F.	Pvt.	I, 164th Ohio	7		1922 Apr 21	IA, 49th, 1923
Lane, John F.		H, 33rd Iowa Inf.	25	81	1920 May 8	NE, 45th, 1921
Lane, Julius	Sergt.	B, 172nd Ohio Inf.	156		1922 Dec 24	IA, 49th, 1923

*See Appendix A, B or C for roster of post names and locations.
†See Introduction for note regarding recording of death date.
315

Name	Rank	Company, Regiment or Ship	Post*	Age	Death Date†	Journal
Lane, Marin		H, 28th N.Y. Inf. (died of rheumatism)	28	77	1921 Aug 22	NE, 46th, 1922
Lane, Martin V.		12th Ill. Cav. (died of Bright's disease)	29		1893 Feb 17	NE, 18th, 1894
Lane, Morgan L.		C, 8th Tenn. Inf.	337		1886	KS, 6th, 1887
Lane, S.S.		16th Ohio	110		1914 Sep 3	KS, 34th, 1915
Lane, T.B.			40		1924	NE, 49th, 1925
Lane, T.J.		U.S. Signal Corps	73	68	1893 Apr 10	IA, 20th, 1894
Lane, W.D.		I, 6th Penn. Cav.	155		1905 Sep 2	KS, 25th, 1906
Lang, A.V.		G, 2nd Ill. Hvy. Art., 16th Corps (born in Erie Co., N.Y., May 14, 1822; died in Albion, Neb.)	42		1883 Nov 21	NE, 8th, 1884
Lang, David H.		D, 2nd Kans.	94		1908 Jun 8	KS, 28th, 1909
Lang, G.S.	Pvt.	K, 4th N.H. Inf.	316		1903 Feb 13	IA, 30th, 1904
Lang, Jacob		H, 192nd Ohio	186		1929 Apr 21	KS, 49th, 1930
Lang, John	Pvt.	I, 9th Iowa Inf.	519		1911 Dec 18	IA, 38th, 1912
Lang, John A.		E, 8th Mo. Inf.	115		1909 May 8	KS, 29th, 1910
Lang, John A.J.		D, 144th Ohio	82		1896 Mar 21	KS, 16th, 1897
Lang, M.			168		1908	IA, 35th, 1909
Lang, William P.		E, 13th Ill.	22		1926 Sep 11	NE, 51st, 1927
Langalier, M.		C, 37th Ill. Inf.	30		1908 May 27	KS, 28th, 1909
Langan, T.M.	Pvt.	E, 166th Ohio	12		1921 Jul 11	IA, 48th, 1922
Langan, W.P.		C, 14th Iowa Inf. (died at National Home)	380		1895 Dec	KS, 15th, 1896
Langdon, Charles E.		C, 7th N.Y. Inf.	1		1912 Jun 4	KS, 32nd, 1913
Langdon, J.H.		G, 2nd Wis.	25		1914 Nov 10	KS, 34th, 1915
Langdon, J.M.		9th Wis.	132		1913 Jan 15	KS, 33rd, 1914
Lange, Adolph	Hosp. Stew.	14th N.Y. Cav.	6		1929 Dec 17	KS, 49th, 1930
Lange, J.H.		I, 32nd Ill.	130		1924 Apr 5	KS, 44th, 1925
Lange, Robert W., see Lauge, Robert W.						
Langenberg, Henry	Pvt.	22nd Iowa Inf.	108		1907 Aug	IA, 34th, 1908
Langford, Melvin		48th Ill.	65		1913 Mar 29	KS, 33rd, 1914
Langford, Tilman	Pvt.	H, 19th Penn. Inf.	122		1912	IA, 39th, 1913
Langh, J.F.	Pvt.	E, 39th Iowa	116		1924 Aug 26	IA, 51st, 1925
Langhein, Z.	Pvt.	K, 4th U.S. Art.	168		1914 Aug 11	IA, 41st, 1915
Langlin, James C.		C, 44th Iowa	441		1908 Oct 1	KS, 28th, 1909
Langsdorf, J.H.		C, 3rd Penn. Hvy. Art.	18		1921 Sep 6	KS, 41st, 1922
Langsha, G.K.		K, 47th Ill.	17		1909 Dec 27	KS, 29th, 1910
Langshaw, Hugh			105		1921	KS, 41st, 1922
Langstaff, J.A.		K, 2nd Neb. Cav.	142		1900 Dec 4	KS, 20th, 1901
Langstaff, L.M.	Pvt.	K, 3rd Iowa Inf.	78		1912 Mar 20	IA, 39th, 1913
Langston, J.C.		G, 110th Ohio	1		1920 Dec 29	KS, 40th, 1921
Langston, W.T.		H, 85th Ill.	63		1918 Nov 25	KS, 38th, 1919
Langton, Michael		D, 13th Ill. Vols.	304		3rd quarter 1884	IA, 11th, 1885
Lanham, Chas.		B, 79th Ind. Inf.	488		1899	KS, 19th, 1900
Lanham, S.M.		D, 8th Kans.	1		1917 Aug 19	KS, 37th, 1918
Laning, Sylvester		48th Ind.	265		1898 Mar 4	KS, 18th, 1899
Lankford, Wm.		G, 79th Ind.	415		1890	KS, 10th, 1891
Lanman, J.		C, 36th Iowa Inf. (cause of death: heart)	193	76	1903 Feb 19	NE, 28th, 1904
Lanning, Nathan	Pvt.	H, 21st & 34th Iowa Inf.	54	92	1937 May 10	IA, 65th, 1939
Lannon, John		A, 4th —	28		1891 May 15	KS, 11th, 1892
Lanphere, C.L.		L, 6th Iowa Cav.	385		1900 Oct 11	KS, 21st, 1902
Lansdown, Harrison		G, 95th Ohio	447		1920 Sep 29	KS, 40th, 1921
Lansing, James W.	Hosp. Stew.	7th Kans. Cav.	293		1886	KS, 6th, 1887
Lansing, Jed		Navy	130		1917 Mar 17	IA, 44th, 1918
Lant, A.R.		C, 91st Ill.	64		1927 Oct 1	KS, 47th, 1928
Lant, Peter Y.	Pvt.	F, 83rd Ill. Inf.	16		1902 Jan 7	IA, 29th, 1903
Lantz, A.J.		C, 162nd Ohio	17		1933 Aug 10	KS, 53rd, 1934
Lantz, F.W.		H, 88th Ohio	1		1925 Sep 1	KS, 45th, 1926
Lantz, Henry		I, 107th Penn. (died of old age)		76	1904 Jun 8	NE, 29th, 1905
Lantz, J.L.		E, 124th Ill.	63		1917 Feb 20	KS, 37th, 1918
Lantz, Jacob	Pvt.	C, 31st Iowa Inf.	68	70	1892 Dec 3	IA, 19th, 1893
Lanwalt, Daniel	Pvt.	E, 145th Ill. Inf.	30		1930 Jul 22	IA, 57th, 1931
Lanwer, James		C, 125th Ohio	36		1914 Jan 17	KS, 34th, 1915

*See Appendix A, B or C for roster of post names and locations.
†See Introduction for note regarding recording of death date.

Name	Rank	Company, Regiment or Ship	Post*	Age	Death Date†	Journal
Lapham, Delos		H, 6th Iowa	303		1905 Feb 17	KS, 25th, 1906
LaPoint, Al		87th —	134		1920 Jan 19	NE, 44th, 1920
Laport, James	Corp.	F, 23rd Ohio Inf.	473		1915 Dec 7	IA, 42nd, 1916
Lapp, Chas. W.		B, 38th Ind.	59		1909 Jun 2	KS, 29th, 1910
Lapsly, William		G, 40th Ohio	16		1902	KS, 22nd, 1903
Laptad, Henry		B, 1st Vt. Hvy. Art.	1		1898 Feb 19	KS, 18th, 1899
Laptad, Peter		L, 14th Vt. Bat., Vt. Art.	12		1927 Sep 5	KS, 47th, 1928
Larabee, J.H.		H, 4th Iowa Cav.	163		1885	KS, 5th, 1886
Larew, John		K, 7th Kans.	92		1889	KS, 9th, 1890
Large, Geo.			292		1918	KS, 38th, 1919
Large, George W.		A, 1st Penn. Res.	167		1914 Sep 21	KS, 34th, 1915
Large, Jos. J.		F, 7th Tenn.	112		1897 Jul 24	KS, 17th, 1898
Largent, D.W.		A, 15th Iowa Inf.	135		1919	IA, 46th, 1920
Largent, Dan	Pvt.	A, 15th Iowa Inf.	135		1920 Mar 13	IA, 47th, 1921
Largent, Gabriel	Recr.	B & C, 57th Ill. Inf.	12		1932 Jul 15	IA, 65th, 1939
Largeny, Gabriel	Pvt.	B, 37th Ind. Inf.	12		1933 Jul 15	IA, 60th, 1934
Larimer, Alex	Pvt.	B, 54th Penn. Inf.	235		1919 Jul 16	IA, 46th, 1920
Larimer, J.M.		C, 20th Ohio Inf.	262		1892 Nov 8	KS, 12th, 1893
Larimer, John A.		C, 33rd Ill. (died of hiccough)	1	81	1920 Mar 22	NE, 45th, 1921
Larimer, John W.		H, 4th Iowa	92		1921 Aug 30	KS, 41st, 1922
Larimer, Thos.		B, 11th Ind.	85		1927 Mar 4	KS, 47th, 1928
Larimore, James F.		K, 9th Iowa Cav.	69	93	1934 May 26	IA, 61st, 1935
Larkin, J.A.		D, 6th Iowa Inf. (died of pneumonia)	32	70	1912 May 3	NE, 37th, 1913
Larkin, James R.		K, 106th Ill. Inf.	43		1902 Jan 29	KS, 22nd, 1903
Larkin, John		B, 40th Iowa (died of paralysis)	13	78	1913 Jul 16	NE, 38th, 1914
Larkin, Rich'd	Pvt.	A, 36th Ill. Inf.	25		1912 Dec 31	IA, 39th, 1913
Larkin, Thomas G.			77		1908 Aug 4	KS, 28th, 1909
Larkin, Thos.	Pvt.	F, 70th N.Y. Inf.	235		1920 Aug 18	IA, 47th, 1921
Larkley, Chas.			29		1905	IA, 32nd, 1906
Larlier, John	Pvt.	H, 11th Iowa Inf.	231		1912 May 5	IA, 39th, 1913
Larne, A.J.		E, 137th Ind.	108		1918 Sep 2	KS, 38th, 1919
Larned, D.W.		B, 27th Mass.	82		1904 Aug 20	KS, 24th, 1905
Laroe, A.		Spencer Co. Legion	12		1912 Apr 2	KS, 32nd, 1913
Larrimore, Hiram		F, 8th Mo. Cav.	32		1921 Oct 29	KS, 41st, 1922
Larrimore, J.R.	Pvt.	A, 35th Iowa	440		1903-1904	IA, 30th, 1904
Larrison, T.J.	Pvt.	B, 24th Iowa Inf.	55		1930 Apr	IA, 57th, 1931
Larrison, Thomas C.		F, 35th Mo.	25		1912 Sep 6	KS, 32nd, 1913
Larry, John	Pvt.	B, 53rd Ill. Inf.	472	59	1895 Oct 31	IA, 22nd, 1896
Larsh, N.B.	Surg.	1st Neb. Cav. (died of congestion of lungs)	24	57	1887 Dec 22	NE, 12th, 1888
Larson, George		E, 91st Ill. Inf.	439		1916 Nov 14	IA, 43rd, 1917
Larson, Hiram	Pvt.	E, 97th Ohio Inf.	414		1913	IA, 40th, 1914
Larson, Johanes	Pvt.	H, 27th Wis.	22		1922 Jan 12	IA, 49th, 1923
Larson, John	Pvt.	F, 8th Iowa Inf.	420		1901 Jul 1	IA, 28th, 1902
Larson, John M.		C, 43rd Ill. (killed by a bull)	111	73	1920 Dec 17	NE, 45th, 1921
Larson, Peter	Pvt.	E, 74th Ill. Inf.	184		1910 Aug 1	IA, 37th, 1911
Larty, Barney		H, 24th N.Y. Cav.	250		4th quarter 1884	IA, 11th, 1885
Larue, Geo. W.		G, 37th Ind.	120		1915 Dec	NE, 40th, 1916
LaRue, T.P.		G, 2nd Iowa Inf.	59		1921 Jan 5	KS, 41st, 1922
Lasalle, J.W.	Pvt.	G, 132nd Ill. Inf.	7		1924 Sep 29	IA, 51st, 1925
Lasell, Edward		C, 2nd Ind.	25		1918 Jul 30	KS, 38th, 1919
LaSelle, H.A.		D, 114th N.Y.	35	84	1922 Mar 3	NE, 47th, 1923
Lash, S.P.		H, 87th Ind. (died of dropsy)	35	80	1918 Sep 2	NE, 43rd, 1919
Lasher, E.A.	Pvt.	H, 193rd N.Y. Inf.	23	84	1932 Dec	IA, 59th, 1933
Lasher, Garrett	Pvt.	D, 28th Wis.	359	56	1899 Jun 29	IA, 26th, 1900
Lasher, Wallace	Pvt.	B, 7th Mo. Cav.	72		1913 Aug 28	IA, 40th, 1914
Lashley, —	Pvt.	F, 25th Ill. Inf.	465		1907 Sep 9	IA, 34th, 1908
Lashly, Geo.	Pvt.	F, 25th Ill. Inf.	440		1919 Mar 19	IA, 46th, 1920
Lashure, James			17		1941 Feb 12	KS, 61st, 1942
Lashure, W.E.			17		1940 Jun 5	KS, 60th, 1941
Lasley, J.H.		C, 53rd Ohio Inf.	28		1912 Jul 15	KS, 32nd, 1913
Lassey, William		A, 4th Mich.	4		1915 Oct 28	KS, 35th, 1916

*See Appendix A, B or C for roster of post names and locations.
†See Introduction for note regarding recording of death date.

Name	Rank	Company, Regiment or Ship	Post*	Age	Death Date†	Journal
Latham, H.E.	Pvt.	G, 147th Ill. Inf.	81		1899 May 19	IA, 26th, 1900
Latham, Henry		G, 116th Ill.	255		1889	KS, 9th, 1890
Lathen, J.E.		G, 16th Kans.	18		1919 Jan 24	KS, 39th, 1920
Lathen, Thos. W.	Pvt.	C, 20th Ky. (died of diabetes)	97	40	1884 Sep 6	NE, 9th, 1885
Lathrop, A.A.		F, 146th Ill.	18		1927 Jan 25	KS, 47th, 1928
Lathrop, Albert M.		E, 18th Conn. Inf. (Hastings; buried in Arlington Cemetery, Washington, D.C.)			1943 May 5	NE, 70th, 1946
Lathrop, Albert M.		E, 18th Conn. Inf.	13		1943 May 5	NE, 67th, 1943
Lathrop, Austin		K, 129th Mass. Inf.	380		1901 Sep 13	KS, 21st, 1902
Lathrop, E.L.	Asst. Surg.	12th Ill. Cav.	69	46	1891 Apr 28	IA, 18th, 1892
Lathrop, G.A.	Pvt.	F, 27th Iowa Inf.	452		1925 May 13	IA, 52nd, 1926
Lathrop, H.T.	Pvt.	A, 9th Ind. Inf.	497		1919 Apr 19	IA, 46th, 1920
Lathrop, J.F.	Pvt.	G, 40th Iowa	40		1921 May 4	IA, 48th, 1922
Lathrop, J.R.	Pvt.	C, 15th Iowa Inf.	335	50	1895 Jul 22	IA, 22nd, 1896
Lathrop, W.D.	Pvt.	A, 32nd Iowa Inf.	25	87	1931 Dec 11	IA, 58th, 1932
Lathrop, W.D.	Pvt.	A, 32nd Iowa Inf.	25		1929	IA, 56th, 1930
Latimer, Augustus		G, 2nd Penn. Cav.	303		1886	KS, 6th, 1887
Latimer, G.H.	Pvt.	at large			1931 Feb 6	IA, 58th, 1932
Latimer, George		I, Mo. State Militia	484		1914 Mar 7	KS, 34th, 1915
Latimer, H.T.	Pvt.	C, 7th Iowa Cav.	101		1924 Nov 8	IA, 51st, 1925
Latimer, John W.	Pvt.	13th Ind. Bat.	140		1917 Oct 24	IA, 44th, 1918
Latimer, R.Z.		C, 12th Iowa Inf. (at large)		89 & 7 mos.	1935 Jun 30	IA, 62nd, 1936
Latimer, Thos. P.	Pvt.	K, 55th Ill. Inf.	56		1911 Nov 10	IA, 38th, 1912
Latimore, W.R.		B, 143rd Penn.	38		1925 Sep 22	KS, 45th, 1926
Latta, J.	Pvt.	A, 22nd Iowa Inf.	110		1917 Dec 21	IA, 44th, 1918
Latta, J.M.	Pvt.	A, 18th Iowa	108		1923 Feb 26	IA, 50th, 1924
Latta, J.R.		D, 116th Ind. Inf. (died at Wellington, Kans.; buried at Prairie Lawn)	57		1894 Jan 10	KS, 14th, 1895
Latta, James	Pvt.	B, 29th Iowa Inf.	38		1920 Feb 4	IA, 47th, 1921
Latta, John	Pvt.	K, 57th Ill. Inf.	267		1915 Jul 3	IA, 42nd, 1916
Latta, R.W.		A, 24th Iowa (died of heart disease)	118	67	1907 Jul 2	NE, 32nd, 1908
Latta, Samuel		H, 2nd Neb.	45		1929	NE, 53rd, 1929
Latta, W.S.		2nd Neb. Cav. (died of old age)	25	76	1891[1901?] Oct	NE, 26th, 1902
Latter, Alexander		F, 125th Ill.	222		1927 Sep 13	KS, 47th, 1928
Lattimer, J.A.	Corp.	I, 83rd Ill. Inf.	56		1917	IA, 44th, 1918
Lattimer, J.M.		112th Ill. Inf. (died of old age)	201	81	1902 Sep	NE, 27th, 1903
Lattimer, John	Pvt.	C, 8th Ill. Cav.	165		1922	IA, 49th, 1923
Latzke, Ferdinand		C, 2nd Kans. Cav.	132		1902 Jun 12	KS, 22nd, 1903
Lau, Henry	Pvt.	E, 2nd Iowa Cav.	1		1931 Feb 13	IA, 57th, 1931
Lau, Henry	Pvt.	E, 2nd Iowa Cav.	1	85	1931 Feb 13	IA, 58th, 1932
Laudreth, Henry		H, 33rd Iowa	253		1910	KS, 30th, 1911
Lauge, Robert W.	Pvt.	K, 17th Mo. Inf.	78		1900 Jun 20	IA, 27th, 1901
Laughery, Francis	Corp.	C, 6th Iowa Inf.	94	51	1887 Apr 23	IA, 14th, 1888
Laughland, Ole C.	Pvt.	A, Ill.	439		1904 Dec 15	IA, 31st, 1905
Laughlin, J.B.		E, 77th Ill.	38		1918 May 20	KS, 38th, 1919
Laughlin, James M.		2nd I.B.[Independent Battery] Kans. Lt. Art.	119		1908 Jul 26	KS, 28th, 1909
Laughlin, John	Pvt.	D, 25th Iowa Inf.	20		1920 Jul 16	IA, 47th, 1921
Laughlin, Wm.			25		1927 May 25	KS, 47th, 1928
Laughton, Alexander		K, 150th Ill.	1		1932 Jun 20	NE, 57th, 1933
Launsbach, Clas	Pvt.	I, 7th Iowa Cav.	22		1917 Oct 22	IA, 44th, 1918
Launtup, James	Pvt.	E, 153rd Ohio	110		1924 Jun 15	IA, 51st, 1925
Launtz, H.A.		A, 7th Kans.	191		1906 Oct 29	KS, 26th, 1907
Launun, Jos.	Pvt.	H, 19th Iowa Inf.	79		1912 Apr	IA, 39th, 1913
Laurence, James B.		U.S. Marine Corps	356		1890	KS, 10th, 1891
Laurma, W.J.			112		1890 Jan 11	NE, 15th, 1891
Lavalle, Michael		E, 12th Ill. Cav.	113		1902 Mar 6	KS, 22nd, 1903
Lavalley, L.	Pvt.	C, 13th Wis.	68		1921 Nov 4	IA, 48th, 1922
Lavelle, Thomas		E, 50th Ill.	12		1897 Jul 19	KS, 17th, 1898
Lavender, —		I, 8th Iowa Inf.			1936 Feb 3	IA, 62nd, 1936
Lavender, R.F.		I, 8th Iowa Inf.	16		1936 Feb 3	IA, 63rd, 1937

*See Appendix A, B or C for roster of post names and locations.
†See Introduction for note regarding recording of death date.

Name	Rank	Company, Regiment or Ship	Post*	Age	Death Date†	Journal
Laverty, J.A.		C, 34th Iowa	23		1889	KS, 9th, 1890
Laverty, Jas. A.			23		1889	KS, 9th, 1890
Lavery, J.L.	Pvt.	L, Penn. Cav.	78		1905 Oct 6	IA, 32nd, 1906
Lavigna, Paul		C, 18th N.Y. Cav.	1		1899 May 23	KS, 19th, 1900
Laville, A.		C, 3rd Kans.	221		1909 Sep 2	KS, 29th, 1910
Lavin, Thos.		F, 2nd R.I.	380		1898 Mar 30	KS, 18th, 1899
Lavo, Frank		E, 12th Kans.	333		1900 Dec 6	KS, 20th, 1901
Lavone, C.	Pvt.	I, 8th Wis. Inf.	222	62	1890 Oct 24	IA, 17th, 1891
Law, Francis	Pvt.	A, 30th Wis.	235		1922 Mar 25	IA, 49th, 1923
Law, Henry	Pvt.	D, 34th Ill. Inf.	18	58	1896 Oct 2	IA, 23rd, 1897
Law, Oscar	Landsman	U.S. Navy	25	79	1919 May 18	NE, 44th, 1920
Law, Sam'l	Pvt.	C, 108th N.Y. Inf.	64		1911 Mar 16	IA, 38th, 1912
Lawhan, James		C, 60th Ind.	3		1906 Sep 8	KS, 26th, 1907
Lawhead, Frank		A, 11th Ind.	14		1922 Nov 23	KS, 42nd, 1923
Lawler, John		D, 25th Ill. Inf. (died of complications)	159	61	1901 Sep	NE, 26th, 1902
Lawler, John		F, 19th U.S. Ind.	1	78	1919 Sep 4	NE, 44th, 1920
Lawler, S.M.		D, 25th Ill. Inf.	293		1918 May 15	KS, 38th, 1919
Lawler, Thos. J.	Sergt.	H, 33rd Iowa Inf.	333		1900 Dec 25	IA, 27th, 1901
Lawn, John		L, 4th U.S. Cav.	147		1914 Mar 4	KS, 34th, 1915
Lawnspack, John	Pvt.	E, 21st Iowa Inf.	78		1928 Feb 16	IA, 55th, 1929
Lawrence, A.K.		D, 91st Ill.	413		1888	KS, 8th, 1889
Lawrence, C.D.	Pvt.	H, 4th Iowa	324		1903 Jul	IA, 30th, 1904
Lawrence, David		A, 33rd N.Y.	293		1919 Dec 31	KS, 39th, 1920
Lawrence, David		A, 3rd N.Y.	293		1919 Dec 31	KS, 40th, 1921
Lawrence, E.C.		A, 22nd Wis. Inf. (died of rheumatism)	214	74	1919 Jun 8	NE, 44th, 1920
Lawrence, Frank P.		A, 22nd Wis. Inf.	4	80	1920 Nov 29	NE, 45th, 1921
Lawrence, G.W.		G, 3rd Mich. Cav.	18		1917 Dec 26	KS, 37th, 1918
Lawrence, George	Pvt.	H, 156th Ill. Inf.	235		1926 Jul 3	IA, 53rd, 1927
Lawrence, H.	Musician	A, 24th Iowa Inf.	57		1912 Jul 25	IA, 39th, 1913
Lawrence, Isaac V.	Sergt.	A, 16th Iowa Inf.	88		1916 Jan 15	IA, 43rd, 1917
Lawrence, J.A.		A, 77th N.Y. Inf. (died of old age)	47		1916 Mar 7	NE, 41st, 1917
Lawrence, J.S.		F, 31st Ohio Inf.	55		1901 Jul 21	KS, 21st, 1902
Lawrence, James		L, 9th Kans. State Militia	12		1916 Nov 13	KS, 36th, 1917
Lawrence, James		B, 11th N.J.	57		1926 Feb 5	KS, 46th, 1927
Lawrence, James B., see Laurence, James B.						
Lawrence, James B.		U.S.M.C. Conn.	356		1889 May 28	KS, 12th, 1893
Lawrence, James B.		Navy	356		1889	KS, 9th, 1890
Lawrence, Jas.	Pvt.	C, 4th Iowa Inf.	12		1916 Sep 4	IA, 43rd, 1917
Lawrence, Jas. B.		C, Con.; U.S. Navy	356		1889 May 28	KS, 11th, 1892
Lawrence, John	Pvt.	I, 9th Iowa	171		1903 Dec 2	IA, 30th, 1904
Lawrence, Joseph W.	Pvt.	H, 4th Iowa Inf.	324	49	1894 Feb 22	IA, 20th, 1894
Lawrence, Phillip		I, 11th Ill. Inf.	250		1915 Sep 12	KS, 36th, 1917
Lawrence, Samuel H.		Batt. C, 2nd Ill. Lt. Art. (former member of department; location: Trenton)	207		1938 Aug 23	NE, 63rd, 1939
Lawrence, Sprague		G, 8th West Va.	129		1908 Aug 24	KS, 28th, 1909
Lawrence, Thomas H.		F, 96th Ill.	465		1912 Nov 1	KS, 32nd, 1913
Lawrence, U.M.		107th Ill. Inf. (died at Wichita; buried at Maple Grove Cemetery)	25		1894 Nov 30	KS, 14th, 1895
Lawrence, W.B.		M, 2nd Colo.	175		1919 Oct	KS, 39th, 1920
Laws, Lewis			294[494?]		1905 Dec 4	KS, 25th, 1906
Lawsha, Jake			3		1928 Dec	NE, 53rd, 1929
Lawson, Andrew		D, 11th R.I. Inf. (born in Providence, R.I.; died in Hebron, Neb.)	17		1883 Apr 9	NE, 8th, 1884
Lawson, Cortland		C, 146th Ohio Vol. Inf.	238		1915 Apr 27	KS, 35th, 1916
Lawson, G.			41		1888	KS, 8th, 1889
Lawson, H.	Pvt.	D, 30th Ind. Inf.	197		1910 Oct 26	IA, 37th, 1911
Lawson, H.	Pvt.	I, 7th Iowa Inf.	40		1920 Mar 24	IA, 47th, 1921
Lawson, J.H.		D, 16th Ill. Inf.	17		1914 Oct 3	KS, 34th, 1915
Lawson, James		Iowa Inf.	197	90	1889	KS, 9th, 1890
Lawson, James Samuel	Pvt.	K, 153rd Ill. Inf. (at large)	130	93	1941 Mar 24	IA, 67th, 1941
Lawson, Jas.	Pvt.	M, 4th Mich. Cav.	12		1900 Apr 18	IA, 27th, 1901

*See Appendix A, B or C for roster of post names and locations.
†See Introduction for note regarding recording of death date.
319

Name	Rank	Company, Regiment or Ship	Post*	Age	Death Date†	Journal
Lawson, Lewis	Pvt.	C & G, 137th Ill. Inf. (at large)	14	93	1940 Apr 1	IA, 66th, 1940
Lawson, Nelson P.		I, 97th Ill.	25		1916 Jun 3	KS, 36th, 1917
Lawson, Richard		C, Ky.	145[147]		1911 May 30	KS, 31st, 1912
Lawson, Robert		B, 47th Ill. (died of heart trouble)	20	74	1908 Jul 3	NE, 33rd, 1909
Lawson, W.J.	Pvt.	H, 8th Ill.	25		1884	KS, 4th, 1885
Lawson, Wm. J.		F, 42nd Mo. (former member of department)			1932 Oct 17	NE, 57th, 1933
Lawton, James		A, 115th Ill.	64		1936 Dec 14	NE, 61st, 1937
Lawton, Russell R.	Corp.	A, 1st Iowa Inf.	452		1926	IA, 53rd, 1927
Laybourn, W.R.				87	1937 Jul 14	IA, 64th, 1938
Laycroft, Frederick		A, 124th Ill. Inf.	191		1912 Nov 15	KS, 32nd, 1913
Layenberger, L.	Pvt.		321		1910 Oct 8	IA, 37th, 1911
Layman, J.P.	1st Lieut.	C, 149th Ind. Vols.	12		1903 Dec 10	IA, 30th, 1904
Layton, Erastus	Pvt.	I, 110th Ohio Inf.	2		1918 May 14	IA, 45th, 1919
Layton, J.R.		G, 86th Ind. Inf.	66		1917 Jan 14	KS, 37th, 1918
Layton, James M.	Corp.	E, 19th Iowa Inf.	251		1901 Sep 4	IA, 28th, 1902
Layton, John F.	Pvt.	D, 34th Iowa	18		1907 Jan	IA, 34th, 1908
Layton, N.J.	Pvt.	I, 21st Iowa Inf.	369		1900 Jul 4	IA, 27th, 1901
Layton, Nathan			141		1886	NE, 11th, 1887
Layton, S.A.		I, 94th Ill. Inf. (died of heart failure)	35	74	1911 Nov 13	NE, 36th, 1912
Lazenby, D.M.	Lieut.	K, 38th Ohio Inf.	79		1926 May 29	IA, 53rd, 1927
Lea, Geo. B.	Corp.	C, 7th Minn. Inf.	88		1915 Jan 29	IA, 42nd, 1916
Lea, J.W.		A, 84th Ill. Inf.	1		1887 Aug 27	KS, 7th, 1888
Leach, F.M.	Corp.	A, 48th Iowa Inf.	26		1901 Aug 29	IA, 28th, 1902
Leach, J.G.	Pvt.	G, 34th Iowa Inf.	137		1919 Aug 25	IA, 46th, 1920
Leach, John Milton	Pvt.	E, 27th Iowa Inf.	184	55	1893 Sep 27	IA, 20th, 1894
Leach, John T.	Pvt.	L, 9th Iowa Cav.	253		1912 Apr 13	IA, 39th, 1913
Leach, L.B.		A, 1st Miss.	38		1927 Jun 5	KS, 47th, 1928
Leach, Marshall		A, 8th Ind.	484		1916 Mar 4	KS, 36th, 1917
Leach, Matthias		L, 7th Ill. Cav.	at large		1931 Dec 14	NE, 56th, 1932
Leach, Melvin G.		H, 18th Mass. Inf. (died of neuralgia of heart)	17	58	1897 Oct 27	NE, 22nd, 1898
Leach, W.S.	Pvt.	E, 95th Ohio	231		1914 Jan 2	IA, 41st, 1915
Leacox, J.M.	Pvt.	B, 19th Ill. Inf.	333	67	1900 Mar 5	IA, 26th, 1900
Leaf, J.H.		I, 44th Ohio Inf. I, 8th Ohio Cav.	250		1915 Oct 1	KS, 36th, 1917
League, J.H.			25		1886	NE, 11th, 1887
League, W. La Fayette		F, 13th Ohio	191		1921 Nov 1	KS, 41st, 1922
Leahey, Jas. C.		D, 123rd Ohio Vol. Inf.	2		1890	KS, 10th, 1891
Leahman, John J.		B, 94th Ohio Inf.	71		1912 Jul 4	KS, 32nd, 1913
Leake, J.W.	Sergt.	6, 1st N.Y. Battery	88		1905 Apr 25	IA, 32nd, 1906
Leallie, J.H.		K, 84th Ill. (died of pneumonia)	217	79	1909 Dec 31	NE, 34th, 1910
Leamer, Geo.	Pvt.	K, 20th Iowa Inf.	1		1921 May 25	IA, 48th, 1922
Leamon, Isaac	Pvt.	F, 133rd Ohio Inf.	236		1910 Dec 10	IA, 37th, 1911
Leamons, H.A.		A, 60th Ohio (died of Bright's disease)	27	76	1914 Aug 12	NE, 39th, 1915
Leanard, A.C.		A, 112th Ill. Inf.	241		1890	KS, 10th, 1891
Leander, Glenn	Pvt.	E, 3rd Ohio Cav.	255		1924 Jun 17	IA, 51st, 1925
Leanord, F.	Pvt.	I, 29th Wis. Inf.	33		1906 Jul	IA, 33rd, 1907
Leapley, W.R.	Pvt.	F, Benton Cadets	74	57	1894 Dec 19	IA, 21st, 1895
Lear, David		died of jaundice	23	69	1913 Aug 6	NE, 38th, 1914
Learnard, O.E.	Lieut. Col.	1st Kans. Inf.	12		1911 Nov 6	KS, 31st, 1912
Leary, J.F., Rev.		I, 15th N.Y. Eng. (see also Appendix D)		60	1906 Feb 21	KS, 25th, 1906
Leary, John O.			383		1922 Jun 16	IA, 49th, 1923
Leary, Peter		F, 83rd U.S.C.T.	365		1914 Aug	KS, 34th, 1915
Leas, W.W.		K, 15th Penn. Inf. (died of old age)	262	56	1896 Feb 8	NE, 21st, 1897
Leasure, John		E, 100th Ill. Inf.	7	53	1896 Jul 14	NE, 21st, 1897
Leatbers, Geo.	Pvt.	D, 18th Penn. Inf.	144		1913	IA, 40th, 1914
Leatherman, John	Pvt.	C, 9th Iowa Inf.	181		1912 Nov 26	IA, 39th, 1913
Leathers, Isaac	Pvt.	D, 37th Iowa Inf.	314	85	1887 Nov 25	IA, 14th, 1888
Leavitt, A.H.		A, 30th Maine Inf.	25		1925 Jan 1	KS, 45th, 1926
Leavitt, George P., see Laevitt, George P.						

*See Appendix A, B or C for roster of post names and locations.
†See Introduction for note regarding recording of death date.

320

Name	Rank	Company, Regiment or Ship	Post*	Age	Death Date†	Journal
Leavitt, Wm. W.	Corp.	K, 152nd Ind. Inf.	168	55	1893 Feb 26	IA, 19th, 1893
Leazer, Robert	Pvt.	B, 3rd Iowa Cav.	192		1923 Nov 1	IA, 50th, 1924
Lebant, Chas.			293		1926	KS, 46th, 1927
Lebey, C.B.		B, 48th Ind.	65		1911 Apr 6	KS, 31st, 1912
Lechey, John	Pvt.	G, 27th Iowa Inf.	134		1924 Sep 9	IA, 51st, 1925
Lechner, M.		B, 13th Kans. Inf.	283		1887 Feb 17	KS, 7th, 1888
Leclare, Oliver	Pvt.	E, 143rd Ohio Inf.	40		1915 Feb 1	IA, 42nd, 1916
Lecompt, F.W.		E, 89th Ind. Inf.	32		1901 Oct 6	KS, 21st, 1902
Ledbeter, S.M.	Pvt.	C, 161st N.Y. Inf.	5	72	1898 Feb 17	IA, 24th, 1898
Ledbetter, John		D, 33rd Ill.	84		1896 Aug 13	KS, 16th, 1897
Ledon, Frank		B, 76th Ill. Inf.	174		1900 Mar 12	KS, 20th, 1901
Ledwick, Robert	Pvt.	A, 2nd N.Y. Inf.	12		1932 Dec 3	IA, 59th, 1933
Ledwick, Thos.	2nd Lieut.	A, 7th N.Y. Cav.	197		3rd quarter 1885	IA, 12th, 1886
Lee, A.G.	Sergt.	H, 53rd Ohio Cav.	433		1910 Jul 27	IA, 37th, 1911
Lee, A.T.		16th Ill.	59		1924 Apr 26	KS, 44th, 1925
Lee, Albert		D, 32nd Iowa	289		1922	KS, 42nd, 1923
Lee, Allen B.			100		1884	KS, 4th, 1885
Lee, C.M.	Pvt.	I, Sioux City Ind. Cav.	154	49	1888 Nov 17	IA, 15th, 1889
Lee, Chas. N.	Capt.	A, 22nd Iowa Inf.	154	48	1885 Sep 11	IA, 12th, 1886
Lee, Chauncey		H, 9th Ill. Inf.	127		1912 Apr 23	KS, 32nd, 1913
Lee, Daniel		A, 4th U.S. Inf.	170		1901 Jun 27	KS, 21st, 1902
Lee, David		C, 3rd Ohio Cav. K, 178th Ohio (died at Marvin)	307		1895 Nov	KS, 15th, 1896
Lee, Don	Pvt.	A, 15th Ill.	66		1921 Oct 7	IA, 48th, 1922
Lee, E.F.	Pvt.	B, 39th Iowa Inf.	26		1920 Nov 13	IA, 47th, 1921
Lee, E.R.		G, 2nd Col.	194		1891 Sep 17	KS, 11th, 1892
Lee, Edward, Rev.	Pvt.	K, 147th N.Y. Inf.	1		1927 Aug 31	IA, 54th, 1928
Lee, Elon Nelson		G, 134th Ill. Inf.	66	98	1938 May 9	IA, 64th, 1938
Lee, Frank M.	Pvt.	13th Ind. Lt. Art.	219		1922 Dec 31	IA, 49th, 1923
Lee, H.			7		1899 Aug 3	KS, 19th, 1900
Lee, H.B.	Pvt.	I, 14th Iowa	12		1921 Feb 2	IA, 48th, 1922
Lee, Henry B.	Pvt.	D, U.S. Sharpshooters	452		1924 May 14	IA, 51st, 1925
Lee, Hiram R.		H, 14th Kans.	1		1905 Feb 7	KS, 25th, 1906
Lee, Israel		D, 9th Iowa Cav.	88		1908 Oct 30	KS, 28th, 1909
Lee, James		1st Mich. Art.	38		1924 Jun 27	KS, 44th, 1925
Lee, James M.	Corp.	F, 39th Iowa Inf.	158		1897 Jan 28	IA, 23rd, 1897
Lee, Jas. W.	Capt.	B, 93rd Ill. Inf.	235		1927 Sep 12	IA, 54th, 1928
Lee, Jasper		F, 9th Iowa	322		1922 Sep 7	KS, 42nd, 1923
Lee, Jesse			142		1883	KS, 3rd, 1884
Lee, Jesse W.		A, Mo. State Militia	98		1897 Nov 1	KS, 17th, 1898
Lee, John		Gunboat	293[493?]		1905	KS, 25th, 1906
Lee, Lafayette		F, 123rd Ohio Inf.	252		1925 Apr 25	KS, 45th, 1926
Lee, Martin R.	Pvt.	G, 27th Wis. Inf.	365	56	1895 Dec 24	IA, 22nd, 1896
Lee, Miles G.		D, 52nd Ind.	257		1917 Oct 11	KS, 37th, 1918
Lee, O.D.		H, 13th Mich.	12		1919 Dec 8	KS, 39th, 1920
Lee, Owen		M, 9th Kans. Inf.	98		1887 Oct 4	KS, 7th, 1888
Lee, R.W.		H, 25th Ill.	51		1926 Oct 19	KS, 46th, 1927
Lee, Samuel		D, 96th Ohio	71		1923 Mar 5	KS, 43rd, 1924
Lee, Silas G.			12		1923 May 1	IA, 50th, 1924
Lee, Spellman		I, 50th Ind.	465		1924 Jun 14	KS, 44th, 1925
Lee, T.J.		K, 143rd Ind.	123		1926 Feb 17	KS, 46th, 1927
Lee, Thomas	Pvt.	K, 25th Iowa Inf.	384		1915	IA, 42nd, 1916
Lee, W.F.		A, 40th Ohio Inf.	100		1935 Jan	KS, 54th, 1935
Lee, W.J.		C, 1st Wis. Art.	118		1885	KS, 5th, 1886
Lee, W.J.		C, 1st Wis. Art.	118		1886	KS, 6th, 1887
Lee, W.S.	Pvt.	A, 4th Minn. Inf.	324		1918 Nov 4	IA, 45th, 1919
Lee, Wm. E.		S, 2nd Neb. Cav.	4	79	1913 Dec 25	NE, 38th, 1914
Lee, Wm. R.		F, 18th Ind.	85		1906 Jan 30	KS, 26th, 1907
Lee, Wm. T.			111		1886	NE, 11th, 1887
Leech, A.H.	Pvt.	H, 94th Ohio Inf.	337		1899 Oct 5	IA, 26th, 1900
Leech, D.J.	Pvt.	F, 124th Ill.	57		1921 Apr 24	IA, 48th, 1922
Leech, F.M.	Pvt.	A, 48th Iowa Inf.	26		1901-1902	IA, 28th, 1902

*See Appendix A, B or C for roster of post names and locations.
†See Introduction for note regarding recording of death date.

Name	Rank	Company, Regiment or Ship	Post*	Age	Death Date†	Journal
Leech, J.C.	Pvt.	D, 3rd Iowa Cav.	100		1920 Aug 12	IA, 47th, 1921
Leech, J.S.		G, 7th Mo.	142		1926 May 30	KS, 46th, 1927
Leech, Louis Josiah, Dr.		B, 2nd Iowa Cav. (at large)	249	91	1937 Sep 23	IA, 64th, 1938
Leech, William J.	Pvt.	E, 149th Ind.	87	53	1900 Feb 16	IA, 26th, 1900
Leedley, Aaron K.		C, Ohio Vol. Inf.	14		1906 Jul 16	KS, 26th, 1907
Leege, H.F.	Pvt.	B, 14th Iowa Inf.	240	59	1898 Jun 30	IA, 25th, 1899
Leek, D.D.	Pvt.	I, 3rd Ohio Cav.	8		1907 Aug 22	IA, 34th, 1908
Leek, Levi		A, 124th Ill.	500		1914 Apr 7	KS, 34th, 1915
Leeke, C.A.		F, 46th Wis. Inf. (died of paralysis)	11	63	1891[1901?] Sep	NE, 26th, 1902
Leeky, Spencer	Pvt.	M, 10th Ohio	88		1926 Mar 22	IA, 53rd, 1927
Leens, Andrew	Pvt.	H, 43rd Ill. Inf.	440	62	1891 Oct 16	IA, 18th, 1892
Leeper, John S.		D, 9th Iowa Inf.	200		1887 Oct 29	KS, 7th, 1888
Leeps, Chas. F.	Corp.	H, 57th Ill. Inf.	198	45	1890 Aug 17	IA, 17th, 1891
Lees, James S.		K, 29th Ind.	145		1917 Nov 3	KS, 37th, 1918
Lees, Samuel		H, 134th Penn. Inf.	14		1909 Jun 20	KS, 29th, 1910
Lees, Wm.		B, 4th Iowa Cav.	59		1918 Jul 23	KS, 38th, 1919
Leet, E.G.	Pvt.	N.Y.C.	108		1919 Aug 13	IA, 46th, 1920
Leffer, Jacob		E, 8th Wis. Inf.	180		1899 Feb 26	KS, 19th, 1900
Leffert, Henry	Pvt.		29		1917 Feb 3	IA, 44th, 1918
Leffler, Marton	Pvt.	A, 17th —	205		1914 Jan 19	IA, 41st, 1915
Lefter, J.H.		A, 14th Iowa Inf. (died of Bright's disease)	32	56	1891[1901?] Mar	NE, 26th, 1902
Leggett, Joseph	Pvt.	A, 1st N.Y. Inf.	130		1927 Feb 4	IA, 54th, 1928
Leggitt, J.H.	Pvt.	16th Iowa Inf.	248		1915	IA, 42nd, 1916
Legitt, G.L.	Sergt.	K, 9th Ill.	116		1905 Jun 1	IA, 32nd, 1906
Leh, Elias		K, 47th Penn. Inf.	66		1900 Sep 8	KS, 20th, 1901
Lehman, John H.		F, 118th Ill. Inf.	95		1941 Sep 15	NE, 66th, 1942
Lehman, John U.		G, 13th Kans.	175		1916 Dec	KS, 36th, 1917
Lehrnickel, Conrad		I, 36th Ill. Inf. (died of pneumonia)	10	60	1900 Jul 12	NE, 25th, 1901
Leib, H.F.		90th Ohio Inf.	198		1912 Nov 5	KS, 32nd, 1913
Leibenhaith, S.	Pvt.	40th N.J. Inf.	515		1908 Jan 16	IA, 35th, 1909
Leichty, Jacob		Ohio (died of apoplexy)	139	63	1905[1904?] Dec 8	NE, 29th, 1905
Leicy, E.W.		H, 7th Penn. Cav.	352		1939 Jun 5	NE, 64th, 1940
Leidig, J.M.		E, 130th Penn.	353		1909 Apr 10	KS, 29th, 1910
Leigh, Samuel	Pvt.		71		1924 Feb 4	IA, 51st, 1925
Leighlon, Byron	Corp.	B, 25th Maine	68		1926 Sep 23	IA, 53rd, 1927
Leighton, C.M.		A, 16th Maine	25		1913 May 16	NE, 38th, 1914
Leighty, D.	Pvt.	G, 9th Iowa	190		1921 Jun 11	IA, 48th, 1922
Leighty, William		C, 85th Penn.	301		1927	KS, 47th, 1928
Leigtner, J.D.		E, 7th Md.	63		1923 Jan 17	KS, 43rd, 1924
Leik, Conrad	Pvt.	D, 198th Penn.	78		1923 Oct 11	IA, 50th, 1924
Leik, Henry	Pvt.	E, 116th Penn. Inf.	70		1910 Dec 21	IA, 37th, 1911
Lein, Thomas A.	Pvt.	K, 33rd Iowa	365		1907 Aug 17	IA, 34th, 1908
Leinbach, T.D.		E, 9th Mich. Cav.	39		1917 Mar 9	KS, 37th, 1918
Leindecker, John	Pvt.	C, 4th Maine Inf.	2		1915 Dec 7	IA, 42nd, 1916
Leindecker, M.	Pvt.	G, 2nd Mo. Res. Corps	2	69	1890 Mar 24	IA, 16th, 1890
Leipert, Jos.	Pvt.	K, 22nd Iowa Inf.	324		1905 Oct	IA, 32nd, 1906
Leiphart, J.P.		B, 18th Penn. Cav. (died of accident)	25		1903 Jan 11	NE, 28th, 1904
Leisering, B.F.		C, 7th Md.	171		1892 Jan 24	KS, 12th, 1893
Leiss, J.B., Rev.		A, 104th Ohio Inf. (died at Kansas City, Mo.)	264		1895 Nov	KS, 15th, 1896
Leisure, Daniel		K, 1st Wis. Cav. (died of cancer)	130	75	1920 Oct 16	NE, 45th, 1921
Leitch, James	Pvt.	I, 18th Wis. Inf.	22	89	1932 Aug 25	IA, 59th, 1933
Leivingston, Heart	Pvt.	H & A, 99th Ind. Inf. (Bright's disease kidneys)	13	45	1885 Dec 1	NE, 10th, 1886
Lekall, Thomas J.		D, 2nd Penn. Cav. (died of old age)	77	80	1925 Aug 3	NE, 50th, 1926
Leland, Cyrus		A, 10th Kans. Vet.	292		1917 Sep	KS, 37th, 1918
Leland, Cyrus, Sr.	QM	15th Kans.	292		1890	KS, 10th, 1891
Lemaster, Eli		E, 11th Ind. Cav.	18		1917 Nov 2	KS, 37th, 1918
LeMaster, Robert		C, 3rd Iowa	117		1920 Feb 9	KS, 43rd, 1924
Lemberger, J.L.	Pvt.	F, 45th Iowa Inf.	69		1932 May 20	IA, 59th, 1933
Lemcke, Chas.		K, 1st Mo.	25		1927 Mar 11	KS, 47th, 1928
Leming, Geo. G.			63		1883	KS, 3rd, 1884

Name	Rank	Company, Regiment or Ship	Post*	Age	Death Date†	Journal
Lemley, Geo.		B, 13th Mo.	132		1900 Mar 24	KS, 20th, 1901
Lemmon, H.W., Dr.			12		1922 Apr 29	KS, 42nd, 1923
Lemning, Fred		born in Germany, 1832; died in Plattsmouth, Neb.	45		1883 Jun 7	NE, 8th, 1884
Lemon, Connie	Capt.	F, 11th Iowa	52		1922 Dec 12	IA, 49th, 1923
Lemon, James		E, 54th Ohio	311		1910 Oct 7	KS, 30th, 1911
Lemon, Stephen E.		I, 24th Iowa	18		1912 Jul 21	KS, 32nd, 1913
Lemont, Thomas			12		1920 Apr 25	KS, 40th, 1921
Lemos, D.A.	Pvt.	G, 174th Penn. Inf.	64		1921 Aug 19	IA, 48th, 1922
Lempke, John	Pvt.	D, 27th Iowa Inf.	184	75	1894 Apr 24	IA, 21st, 1895
Lenahan, Geo. M.	Pvt.	B, 46th Ill. Inf.	117		1911 Jan 30	IA, 38th, 1912
Lendormi, Ernest		17th Ind.	170		1928 Jun 30	IA, 55th, 1929
Lendowski, Michael J.		E, 2nd U.S. Cav. (accidentally killed; died at Soldiers & Sailors Home, Milford)		73	1906 Nov 11	NE, 31st, 1907
Lendzy, Noah H.		K, 25th Ohio	18		1922 Apr 25	KS, 42nd, 1923
Lenger, Henry A.		H, 10th Mo.	77		1931 Apr 8	NE, 56th, 1932
Lengiton, James K.		E, 137th Ill.	122		1922 May 5	IA, 49th, 1923
Lenharr, Sam	Pvt.	M, 17th Penn. Cav.	231		1916 Mar 16	IA, 43rd, 1917
Lenhart, G.C.			25		1886	NE, 11th, 1887
Lenhart, T.M.			497		1906	IA, 34th, 1908
Lennett, J.T.		D, 23rd Maine	296		1892 Nov 5	KS, 12th, 1893
Lennon, J.H.	Cabin Boy	I, *S.S. Hart*	7		1928 Apr 16	NE, 53rd, 1929
Lennon, John		K, 24th Ind.	158		1924 Sep 17	KS, 44th, 1925
Lenon, Geo. W.			14		2nd quarter 1885	IA, 12th, 1886
Lenon, P.H.	Capt.	I, 29th Iowa	52		1923 Apr 27	IA, 50th, 1924
Lenszler, John S.		Sharpshooters, 5th Ohio Inf.	31		1901 Dec 22	KS, 21st, 1902
Lenszler, Peter L.		H, 29th Ohio	31		1921 Jun 17	KS, 41st, 1922
Lent, Ed	Pvt.	92nd Ill. Inf.	113		1913 Sep 17	IA, 40th, 1914
Lent, S.W.	Pvt.	B, 2nd Minn.	22		1921 Feb 13	IA, 48th, 1922
Lentes, J.W.		C, 91st Ohio	71		1923 Jun 2	KS, 43rd, 1924
Lentz, Andrew J.		H, 28th Iowa	17		1916 Dec 15	KS, 36th, 1917
Leo, Andrew	Bugler	C, 1st N.Y. Cav.	8		1922 Jun 5	IA, 49th, 1923
Leonard, A.C., see Leanard, A.C.						
Leonard, Francis, see Leanord, F.						
Leonard, H.B.	Pvt.	C, 75th Ill. Inf.	12	89	1932 Oct 6	IA, 59th, 1933
Leonard, H.H.		A, 112th Ill. Inf. (died at Wichita)	244		1895 Nov	KS, 15th, 1896
Leonard, Hiram	Major	14th Iowa Inf.	157	77	1887 Oct 12	IA, 14th, 1888
Leonard, J.H.	Pvt.	E, 26th Ill. Inf.	94		1911 May 11	IA, 38th, 1912
Leonard, James		died of old age	318		1920	NE, 45th, 1921
Leonard, Jas. M.	Pvt.	E, 21st Ill. Inf.	9		1904 May 15	IA, 31st, 1905
Leonard, John F.		B, 125th Ill.	81		1924 Feb 25	KS, 44th, 1925
Leonard, Joshua	Corp.	M, 2nd Iowa Cav.	247		1901 Dec 9	IA, 28th, 1902
Leonard, M.V.	Pvt.	D, 15th Iowa Inf.	497		1925 Sep 3	IA, 52nd, 1926
Leonard, N.G.		C, 23rd Iowa Inf.	244		1918 May 19	KS, 38th, 1919
Leonard, Orlando		G, 16th Ill. (former member; died at Washington, D.C.)	265		1935 Apr	NE, 60th, 1936
Leonard, S.R.	Pvt.	G, 20th Ohio	55		1926 Feb 8	IA, 53rd, 1927
Leonard, Thomas		C, 112th Penn. Art.	6		1914 Dec 24	KS, 34th, 1915
Leonard, Thomas			99		1916 Jan 21	KS, 36th, 1917
Leonard, W.	Pvt.		24		1914 Jul	IA, 41st, 1915
Leonard, William		G, 38th Ill.	32		1924 May 10	KS, 44th, 1925
Leonard, William		I, 38th Ind. Inf.	25		1925 Sep 27	KS, 45th, 1926
Leonard, Wm. L.	Asst. Surg.	39th Iowa Inf. 7th Ill. Inf.	55	71	1893 Dec 19	IA, 20th, 1894
Leonhardt, Frederick W.		A, 43rd Mo.	25		1934	NE, 59th, 1935
Lepley, R.R.		I, 12th Penn. Cav. (died of paralysis)	95	55	1901 Nov	NE, 26th, 1902
Leppelman, B.F.		F, 169th Ohio	244		1929 Jun 10	KS, 49th, 1930
Leppert, Lawrence		A, 9th West Va. Inf.	294		1901 Apr	KS, 21st, 1902
Leppleman, E.J.		F, 8th Ohio Inf.	105		1902	KS, 22nd, 1903
Leppo, D.W.		E, 2nd Iowa Inf.	19		1921 Sep 8	IA, 48th, 1922
LeQuratte, M.	Pvt.	I, 1st Minn. Inf.	314	77	1897 Jan 9	IA, 24th, 1898

*See Appendix A, B or C for roster of post names and locations.
†See Introduction for note regarding recording of death date.

323

Name	Rank	Company, Regiment or Ship	Post*	Age	Death Date†	Journal
Lerks, J.W.		A, 48th Ohio	3		1916 Mar 14	KS, 36th, 1917
Leroy, L.L.		L, 53rd Ill.	123		1914 Apr 23	KS, 34th, 1915
Leroy, L.L.		B, 53rd Ky.	123		1913 Apr 23	KS, 33rd, 1914
Lescher, Joseph		D, 87th Ill. Inf. (died of old age)	35	73	1907 Feb 21	NE, 32nd, 1908
Lescher, T.H.		A, 3rd Kans.	1		1923 Nov 18	KS, 43rd, 1924
Lesco, Clifford		A, 71st Ill. Inf.	339		1917 Dec 24	KS, 37th, 1918
Lesco, Joseph		A, 21st Ohio	145		1920 May 1	KS, 40th, 1921
Lesieur, Louis		M, 16th Ill. Cav. (died of heart failure)	55	69	1915 May 22	NE, 40th, 1916
Leslee, Thomas		F, 18th Ind. Inf.	123		1891 Oct 6	KS, 11th, 1892
Lesley, F.M.	Pvt.	G, 2nd Iowa Inf.	123		1919 Nov 17	IA, 46th, 1920
Lesley, James		I, 2nd Ill. Inf.	354		1926 Nov 21	NE, 51st, 1927
Lesley, W.S.		I, 2nd Vt.	322		1913 Dec 16	KS, 33rd, 1914
Lesley, Wm. M.	Pvt.	A, 14th Iowa Inf.	123		1919 Sep	IA, 46th, 1920
Leslie, B.F.	Pvt.	B, 32nd Mo. Inf.	53		1899	NE, 24th, 1900
Leslie, Cyrus B.	Pvt.	G, 2nd Iowa Inf.	88		1904-1905	IA, 31st, 1905
Leslie, James		C, 24th Iowa Inf. (former member)	265		1940 Aug 9	NE, 65th, 1941
Leslie, Jas. R.		I, 68th Ill.			1926 Nov 21	NE, 51st, 1927
Leslie, P.	Pvt.	G, 20th Iowa Inf.	123		1919 Nov 17	IA, 47th, 1921
Leson, J.E.			96		1917 Jan 25	IA, 44th, 1918
Lester, Geo. W.		H, 3rd N.J. Cav.	17		1918 Jan 13	KS, 38th, 1919
Lester, John W.	Pvt.	F, —	235		1929 Feb 13	IA, 56th, 1930
Lester, Joseph E.	Pvt.	D, 102nd Ill. Inf.	11	76	1889 Mar 31	IA, 16th, 1890
Lester, Martin	Pvt.		314		1925 Nov 28	IA, 52nd, 1926
Lester, P.J.	Pvt.	H, 9th Ill. Inf.	271		1920 Sep 7	IA, 47th, 1921
Letcher, Henry		C, 56th Mo. Inf.	10		1886	KS, 6th, 1887
Letcher, William E.		A, 29th Ind.	23		1936 Jun 9	NE, 61st, 1937
Lett, John		E, 11th Iowa, Crockers Brigade (see also Appendix D)	32		1937 Jan 12	NE, 62nd, 1938
Letter, William	Pvt.	C, 31st Iowa Inf.	68	55	1900 May 20	IA, 26th, 1900
Letters, William	Pvt.	C, 31st Iowa Inf.	68		1900-1901	IA, 27th, 1901
Letts, J.R.	2nd Lieut.	E, — Ill. Inf.	66		1901 Oct 22	IA, 28th, 1902
LeValley, Stephen E.	Sergt.	F, 102nd Ill. Inf.	375		1915 Mar 7	IA, 42nd, 1916
Levan, John	Pvt. / Pvt.	D, 129th Penn. Inf. / E, 3rd Mo. Lt. Art.	2	73	1896 Mar 31	IA, 22nd, 1896
Levan, Wm. M.		G, 4th Ill.	134		1898 Jan 27	KS, 18th, 1899
Level, James		H, 31st Wis. Inf. (cause of death: heart)	352		1903 Aug 3	NE, 28th, 1904
Leversee, Austin	Pvt.	K, 3rd Iowa Inf.	222		1925 Mar 26	IA, 52nd, 1926
Leviley, E.			108		1909 Dec 4	IA, 36th, 1910
Lewellen, J.M.		G, 7th Iowa	491		1917 Feb 12	KS, 37th, 1918
Lewellyn, Jos.		I, 2nd Kans. Cav. (died of old age)	68	82	1902 Aug	NE, 27th, 1903
Lewis, A.H.		H, 17th Ind. Inf.	51		1925 May 22	KS, 45th, 1926
Lewis, A.H.G.	Pvt.	B, 31st Mass. Inf.	235	51	1893 Oct 6	IA, 20th, 1894
Lewis, A.O.		K, 21st Kans.	40		1914 Apr 29	KS, 34th, 1915
Lewis, Abe		K, 10th Mo.	113		1926 Mar 1	KS, 46th, 1927
Lewis, Alden P.		K, 14th Wis. Inf. (died at Clyde)	159		1895 Dec 2	KS, 15th, 1896
Lewis, Alonzo		K, 9th Mich.	32	81	1916 Feb 28	NE, 41st, 1917
Lewis, Aron	Pvt.		173		1926 Aug 30	IA, 53rd, 1927
Lewis, B.G.		I, 156th Ill.	222		1905 Apr	KS, 25th, 1906
Lewis, B.R.		D, 33rd Ohio Inf.	11		1919 Apr 14	NE, 44th, 1920
Lewis, Barney		I, 10th West Va.	207		1930 Sep 5	NE, 55th, 1931
Lewis, Benj. F.	Pvt.	G, 1st Ill.	497		1923 Jan 4	IA, 50th, 1924
Lewis, C.C.		K, 2nd Mich.	220		3rd quarter 1883	IA, 10th, 1884
Lewis, C.G.	Asst. Surg.	30th Iowa Inf.	69		1900 May 9	IA, 27th, 1901
Lewis, Chas.	Pvt.	H, 27th Iowa Inf.	22		1904 Sep 23	IA, 31st, 1905
Lewis, Chas. H., Dr.		G, 16th Conn.	110		1885	KS, 5th, 1886
Lewis, Chester		E, 89th Ind.	113		1916 Apr 16	KS, 36th, 1917
Lewis, Clark H.	Pvt.	K, 11th Ill. Cav.	56		1925 Mar 3	IA, 52nd, 1926
Lewis, Clinton		H, 53rd Ind. Inf.	25		1911 Nov 22	KS, 31st, 1912
Lewis, D.S.		H, 76th Penn.	171		1919 May 24	KS, 39th, 1920
Lewis, David		G, 11th Kans.	158		1931 May 11	KS, 52nd, 1933
Lewis, David		G, 11th Kans.	158		1931 May 11	KS, 51st, 1932
Lewis, David W.		G, 10th Ill. Cav. (died of lung trouble)	120	67	1918 Jul 28	NE, 43rd, 1919

*See Appendix A, B or C for roster of post names and locations.
†See Introduction for note regarding recording of death date.

324

Name	Rank	Company, Regiment or Ship	Post*	Age	Death Date†	Journal
Lewis, E.	Corp.	H, 8th Iowa Inf.	452		1926 Jan 19	IA, 53rd, 1927
Lewis, E.G.	Pvt.	H, 92nd Inf.	238		1915 Apr 4	IA, 42nd, 1916
Lewis, Ephriam		G, 11th Iowa Inf. (died of hemorrhage of lungs)	77	74	1906 Dec 22	NE, 31st, 1907
Lewis, Ewing B.	Lieut.	I, 11th Iowa	231		1914 Aug 16	IA, 41st, 1915
Lewis, Frederick		E, 6th Tenn.	42		1926 Jun 3	KS, 46th, 1927
Lewis, Geo.		A, 2nd Penn. Bat. A, 206th Penn. Inf. (died of pneumonia)	206	56	1901 Aug	NE, 26th, 1902
Lewis, Geo. H.	Pvt.	C, 15th Ill. Cav.	111		1920 Aug 4	IA, 47th, 1921
Lewis, Geo. H.	Sergt.	F, 14th Conn. Inf.	12		1913 Mar 16	IA, 40th, 1914
Lewis, Geo. W.	Pvt.	E, 14th N.Y. Inf.	8		1904 Mar 11	IA, 31st, 1905
Lewis, Geo. W.		A, 13th Kans.	292		1918	KS, 38th, 1919
Lewis, George		I, 114th Ky.	486		1917 Jan 27	KS, 37th, 1918
Lewis, H.R.		A, 42nd Ill.	38		1914 Mar 28	KS, 34th, 1915
Lewis, Henry		G, 9th Ohio Cav. (died of operation)	231	72	1916 Mar 6	NE, 40th, 1916
Lewis, J.B.	Pvt.	C, 45th Iowa Inf.	186		1921 Jun 26	IA, 48th, 1922
Lewis, J.J.		A, 5th Iowa Cav.	86		3rd quarter 1883	IA, 10th, 1884
Lewis, J.S.	Pvt.	B, 40th Wis. Inf.	78		1910 Sep 14	IA, 37th, 1911
Lewis, Jacob		C, 101st Penn.	241		1897 Nov 27	KS, 17th, 1898
Lewis, James K.		G, 1st Neb. Cav. (former member of department; died at Milford)	77		1939 May	NE, 64th, 1940
Lewis, Jas.	Pvt.	E, 4th Iowa Inf.	7		1920 Jan 15	IA, 47th, 1921
Lewis, John	Pvt.	E, 60th U.S.C. Inf.	11		1897 Mar 22	IA, 24th, 1898
Lewis, John	Pvt.	E, 4th Iowa Inf.	12		1911 Nov 26	IA, 40th, 1914
Lewis, John		K, 111th Ohio	180		1892 Sep 14	KS, 12th, 1893
Lewis, John C.	Pvt.	F, 113th Ill. Inf.	14	55	1896 Sep 2	IA, 23rd, 1897
Lewis, John F.	1st Sergt.	G, 107th Ill.	52		1915 Jan 21	KS, 35th, 1916
Lewis, John W.	Sergt.	Sawyer's Battery	22		1911 Sep 17	IA, 38th, 1912
Lewis, Joseph			59		1919 Mar 31	KS, 39th, 1920
Lewis, L.B.		C, 101st Penn.	112		1902 Jul	KS, 22nd, 1903
Lewis, Llewellyn	Pvt.	C, 16th Wis. Inf. (at large)	101	95	1941 Jan 5	IA, 67th, 1941
Lewis, M.B.	Pvt.	B, 182nd Ohio Inf.	22		1909 Apr 9	IA, 36th, 1910
Lewis, Myron A.		E, 50th N.Y. Hvy. Art.	175		1912 Oct 30	KS, 32nd, 1913
Lewis, Nathan		K, 86th Ohio Inf.	19		1924 Dec 21	KS, 44th, 1925
Lewis, O.B.		D, 38th Ind. Inf. (died of kidney disease)	118	75	1921 Oct 4	NE, 46th, 1922
Lewis, Owen		B, 18th Ind. Inf.	36		1921 Feb 2	KS, 41st, 1922
Lewis, Porter		I, 3rd Ill. Cav.	185		1912 Jul 8	KS, 32nd, 1913
Lewis, R.D.		F, 60th Ohio	418		1922 Jan 17	KS, 42nd, 1923
Lewis, R.D.		E, 60th Ohio	418		1922 Jan 13	KS, 43rd, 1924
Lewis, R.G.	Capt.	B, 98th Ohio Inf.	66		1916 Dec 29	IA, 43rd, 1917
Lewis, R.P.	Lieut.	B, 123rd Ind.	108		1924 Jun 19	IA, 51st, 1925
Lewis, S.D.		C, 50th Ill.	26		1917	KS, 37th, 1918
Lewis, Samuel M.		K, 7th Ill. Inf.	200		1901 Feb 17	KS, 21st, 1902
Lewis, Slater D.		C, 50th Ill.	23		1916 Jul 16	KS, 36th, 1917
Lewis, Stephen	Sergt.	B, 8th Iowa Cav.	279	74	1894 Feb 9	IA, 20th, 1894
Lewis, T.D.		H, 3rd Tenn.	59		1892 Sep 10	KS, 12th, 1893
Lewis, T.J.	Pvt.	D, 1st Iowa Cav.	116		1910 Oct 28	IA, 37th, 1911
Lewis, Theodore	Corp.	G, 50th Penn. Inf.	111		1928 Feb 13	IA, 55th, 1929
Lewis, Thos. J.	Corp.	D, 12th Iowa Inf.	235		1927 Dec 15	IA, 54th, 1928
Lewis, V.C.	Corp.	C, 126th Ohio Inf.	42		1923 Mar 27	IA, 50th, 1924
Lewis, W.A.		C, 86th Ohio Inf.	88		1917 Aug 3	KS, 37th, 1918
Lewis, W.G.		I, 133rd Ohio	63		1919 Feb 27	KS, 39th, 1920
Lewis, W.H.		K, 175th Ohio Vol. Inf.	51		1915 Dec 2	KS, 35th, 1916
Lewis, Wesley		D, 2nd Mo.	271		1916 Apr 17	KS, 36th, 1917
Lewis, William H.		B, 72nd Ill. Inf.	64		1901 Dec 4	KS, 21st, 1902
Lewis, Wm.		D, 2nd Mich. Inf. (died of arteris scleresis)	110	60	1902 Oct	NE, 27th, 1903
Lias, Harvey		M, 2nd Iowa Cav.			1902 Apr 16	IA, 28th, 1902
Lias, John W.	Pvt.	M, 2nd Iowa Cav.	72	75	1892 Jul 30	IA, 19th, 1893
Lias, Thos. W.	Pvt.	M, 2nd Iowa Cav.	461		1907 Mar 26	IA, 34th, 1908
Libbey, Benj.			147		1900 Jul 22	KS, 20th, 1901
Libby, John B.		G, 1st Ill.	81		1927 Jul 2	KS, 47th, 1928
Libby, M.B.			375		1910 Jul 16	IA, 37th, 1911

*See Appendix A, B or C for roster of post names and locations.
†See Introduction for note regarding recording of death date.

325

Name	Rank	Company, Regiment or Ship	Post*	Age	Death Date†	Journal
Lichtberger, J.	Pvt.	G, 24th Iowa Inf.	208		1907 Jun 30	IA, 34th, 1908
Lichteberger, J.	Pvt.	G, 24th Iowa Inf.	208		1911 Apr 27	IA, 38th, 1912
Lichthau, H.		F, 118th Ill.	132		1923 May 11	KS, 43rd, 1924
Lichty, C.W.	Pvt.	D, 30th Iowa Inf.	68		1908 Jul 7	IA, 35th, 1909
Lichty, Cyrus Myers	Pvt.	A, 21st Iowa Inf. (at large)	222	95	1939 Sep 22	IA, 66th, 1940
Lichty, Jacob	Pvt.	D, 107th Ohio Vol. Inf.	12		1924 Oct 30	IA, 51st, 1925
Lichty, Jacob P.		H, 24th Iowa (died of general decline)	245	78	1918 Jan 21	NE, 43rd, 1919
Lichty, Jos. J.		K, 1st —	25	74	1917 Oct 19	NE, 42nd, 1918
Lickliter, J.D.		E, 24th Ohio	25		1926 Jan	KS, 48th, 1929
Liddick, G.W.	Pvt.	C, 77th Penn. Inf.	57		1932 Jan 7	IA, 59th, 1933
Liddle, A.S.	1st Lieut.	12th N.Y. Bat.	30		1924 Apr 26	IA, 51st, 1925
Liebhart, M.		H, 26th Ill. (died of dropsy)	13	79	1921 Jul 3	NE, 46th, 1922
Liebler, Jacob W.	Pvt.	F, 26th Iowa Inf. (at large)		98	1941 Nov 22	IA, 68th, 1942
Liedeman, John	Pvt.	E, 17th Mo. Inf.	1		1905 Jul 31	IA, 32nd, 1906
Lieter, M.L.		G, 178th Ill. Inf.	25		1940 Jan	KS, 60th, 1941
Lievengood, H.H.		F & C, 11th Mo. Cav.	226		1914 Sep 4	KS, 34th, 1915
Liggett, Joseph	Pvt.	C, 73rd Ind. Vol. Inf.	123	54	1900 Jan 13	IA, 26th, 1900
Liggitt, Robert	Sergt.	G, 27th Mo. Inf.	173		1902 Dec 27	IA, 29th, 1903
Light, A.T.	Pvt.	E, 83rd Ind.	156		1922 Jun 8	IA, 49th, 1923
Light, Coleman		L, 6th N.Y.	127		1920 Nov 14	KS, 40th, 1921
Light, I.T.		C, 38th Ind.	129		1918 Feb 7	KS, 38th, 1919
Light, J.H.		A, 49th Ind.	129		1925 Mar 20	KS, 44th, 1925
Light, J.H.		C, 49th Ind. Inf.	129		1925 Mar 20	KS, 45th, 1926
Lightbody, Isaac		C, 12th Ill. Cav.	188	75	1914 May 31	NE, 39th, 1915
Lightfoot, John	Pvt.	H, 12th Iowa Inf.	254		1910 Jul 19	IA, 37th, 1911
Lightfoot, W.L.	Corp.	B, 30th Iowa Inf.	379		1903 Jul 29	IA, 30th, 1904
Lightman, Henry	Pvt.	8th Iowa	30		1903 Nov 6	IA, 30th, 1904
Lightner, John C.		A, 2nd Iowa	25		1929 Feb 17	KS, 49th, 1930
Lihleefer, Henry	Pvt.	C, 4th Iowa Cav.	20		1891 Nov 16	IA, 18th, 1892
Like, D.M.	Drummer	K, 117th Ill. Inf.	12		1913 Jan 10	IA, 40th, 1914
Likens, Samuel		I, 17th Ind. I, 61st Ill.	184		1912 Nov 18	KS, 32nd, 1913
Likes, R.B.	Pvt.	D, 23rd Iowa Inf.	12		1930 May 31	IA, 57th, 1931
Lill, Wm.		dropped dead	318		1923 Dec 1	NE, 48th, 1924
Lillibridge, R.L.	Pvt.	A, 45th Ill. Inf.	42		1917 Dec 2	IA, 44th, 1918
Lillich, George		Navy	28		1925 Dec 27	KS, 45th, 1926
Lillie, George A.	Sergt.	G, 16th Vt. Inf.	206		1901 Sep 16	IA, 28th, 1902
Lillie, R.L.	Pvt.	C, 26th Iowa Inf.	233	59	1891 Dec 18	IA, 18th, 1892
Lilly, B.E.	Pvt.	G, 2nd Iowa Cav.	231		1913 Feb 3	IA, 40th, 1914
Lilly, Chas. E.	Pvt.	H, 22nd Iowa Inf.	235		1911 Nov 27	IA, 38th, 1912
Lilly, W.L.	Pvt.	G, 16th Vt. Inf.	206		1904 Apr	IA, 31st, 1905
Lilly, W.W.	Pvt.	H, 46th Wis. Inf.	5	87	1933 Dec 8	IA, 60th, 1934
Limbacker, Thomas		5th Iowa Cav.	311		1908 Apr 29	KS, 28th, 1909
Limbenhiemer, J., see L'mbenhi'm'r, J.						
Limbocker, L.C.		C, 19th Iowa	232		1918 Sep 20	KS, 38th, 1919
Limbocker, W.A.		K, 11th Kans. Cav.	271		1913 May 31	KS, 33rd, 1914
Limbrey, C.S.		K, 11th Ky. Cav.	1		1921 May	KS, 41st, 1922
Lime, Wm.	Pvt.	F, 102nd Ill. Inf.	22		1904 Apr 17	IA, 31st, 1905
Limes, E.T.		I, 33rd Iowa (died of stomach trouble)	63	68	1915 May 2	NE, 40th, 1916
Limes, J.L.			103		1906 Dec 11	KS, 26th, 1907
Limmons, Richard M.		C, 29th Ind. Inf. (died of dropsy)	112	69	1900 Oct 15	NE, 25th, 1901
Lincoln, Albert	Pvt.	D, 46th Ill. Inf.	68		1917 Jul 31	IA, 44th, 1918
Lincoln, Daniel B.		G, 44th Iowa Inf. (died of paralysis)	22	73	1919 Mar 17	NE, 44th, 1920
Lincoln, Daniel Boone		45th Iowa Inf.	25	76	1919 Mar 17	NE, 44th, 1920
Lincoln, E.		I, 12th Ill. Inf.	127		1908 May 27	KS, 28th, 1909
Lincoln, G.P.		K, 57th Ill. Inf.	83		1925 Nov 8	KS, 45th, 1926
Lincoln, Geo. A.	Pvt.	3rd Wis. Bat.	235		1919 Jul 18	IA, 46th, 1920
Lincoln, Jas.	Pvt.	E, 39th Ill.	440		1903-1904	IA, 30th, 1904
Lincoln, N.N.			87		1884	KS, 4th, 1885
Lindaman, Saml.	Pvt.	A, 11th Ill. Inf.	3	60	1891 Jul 1	IA, 18th, 1892
Lindas, John		A, 29th Wis.	8		1930 Sep 19	KS, 50th, 1931

Name	Rank	Company, Regiment or Ship	Post*	Age	Death Date†	Journal
Lindburg, Andrew	Pvt.	C, 9th Ill. Cav.	59		1917 Oct 15	IA, 44th, 1918
Linder, Fred		B, 186th Ohio Inf. (died of paralysis)	289	75	1904 Dec 5	NE, 29th, 1905
Linder, John		K, 9th Wis. (died of old age)	19		1913 Nov 26	NE, 38th, 1914
Linderman, C.H.		K, 99th Ind. Inf.	103		1900 Feb 9	KS, 20th, 1901
Linderman, Chas.	2nd Lieut.	A, 8th Iowa Cav.	11		1907 Apr	IA, 34th, 1908
Linderman, Christian		A, 133rd Ohio Vol. Inf. (died of infirmities of old age)	115	86	1911 Jul 25	NE, 36th, 1912
Linderman, David		G, 91st Ill.	206		1909 Jul 7	KS, 29th, 1910
Linderman, S.B.			25	46	1887 Jun 26	NE, 12th, 1888
Lindermeyer, Jake		A, 150th Ind. Inf.	262	65	1895 Jul 27	NE, 20th, 1896
Lindermin, John		109th Ill.	147		1923 Jun 23	KS, 43rd, 1924
Lindley, R.J.	Pvt.	A, 37th —	98	74	1886 Aug 6	IA, 13th, 1887
Lindley, W.P.	Pvt.	B, 86th Ill. Inf.	186		1920 Oct 31	IA, 47th, 1921
Lindon, John		B, 2nd Iowa Inf. (died of Bright's disease)	76		1904 Jul	NE, 29th, 1905
Lindsay, A.	Pvt.	D, 6th Vt. Inf.	112	53	1897 Mar 15	IA, 23rd, 1897
Lindsay, Chas.		G, 78th Ohio Inf.	37		1902 Dec 8	KS, 22nd, 1903
Lindsay, Francis M.		G, 72nd Ind.	46		1918 Nov 24	KS, 38th, 1919
Lindsay, G.W.	Pvt.	D, 28th Ind. Col. Inf.	20		1925	IA, 52nd, 1926
Lindsay, H.S.			29		1917	IA, 44th, 1918
Lindsay, John		G, 47th Iowa	233		1934 Oct 20	IA, 61st, 1935
Lindsay, John M.	Pvt.	D, 15th Iowa Inf. (at large)	16, 49	93	1941 Nov 1	IA, 68th, 1942
Lindsay, Nicholas	Pvt.	E, 126th Ill. Inf.	130		1917 Feb	IA, 44th, 1918
Lindsay, R.J.	Pvt.	A, 37th Iowa Inf.	98	61	1886 Aug 16	IA, 17th, 1891
Lindsay, Thos.	Surg.	12th Kans. Inf.	180		1901 Jan 19	KS, 21st, 1902
Lindsey, E.		K, 1st Iowa Cav.	55		1922 Oct 25	KS, 42nd, 1923
Lindsey, J.M.		H, 64th Ill.	115		1933 Jun 8	KS, 53rd, 1934
Lindsey, John D.		H, 64th Ill.	18		1910 Jan 7	KS, 30th, 1911
Lindsey, John H.		E, 3rd Wis. Inf. (died of cancer of stomach)	45	75	1906 Nov 6	NE, 31st, 1907
Lindsey, Samuel C.		A, 50th Ill. Inf.	158		1899 Sep 19	KS, 19th, 1900
Lindsey, Warren		H, 10th Ill. Cav.	203		1921 Apr 30	KS, 41st, 1922
Lindsley, F.D.	Pvt.	A, 140th Ill. Inf.	8		1909 Sep 19	IA, 36th, 1910
Lindsley, Wm. Reinor	Pvt.	H, 29th Wis. Inf. (at large)	236	98	1941 Oct 23	IA, 67th, 1941
Lindt, John	Pvt.	B, Penn. Lt. Art. (see also Appendix D)	29		1912 Aug 30 or Sep 7	IA, 39th, 1913
Line, David		A, 118th Ill.	29		1922 Apr 25	IA, 49th, 1923
Lineaweaver, G.P.	Sergt.	I, 19th Iowa Inf.	516		1905 Nov 9	IA, 32nd, 1906
Lines, W.F.	Pvt.	E, 7th Ill. Cav.	243		1924 Feb 6	IA, 51st, 1925
Linfor, Robert		C, 1st Ill.	25		1933 Nov	KS, 53rd, 1934
Lingar, Robert		C, 1st La.	25		1936	KS, 56th, 1937
Lingenfelter, Chas. H.	Pvt.	D, 23rd Wis. Inf.	346	103, 7 mos. & 6 days	1945 May 11	IA, 71st, 1945
Lingrell, Wm.	Pvt.	A, 12th Mich. Inf.	47	49	1890 Aug 22	IA, 17th, 1891
Lining, C.C.	Sergt.	C, 2nd Iowa Cav.	19		1915 Apr 7	IA, 42nd, 1916
Link, R.C.	Pvt.	I, 29th Wis. Inf.	277	59	1894 Dec 7	IA, 21st, 1895
Linkin, Jacob	Pvt.	K, 26th Penn. Inf.	250		1906 Apr 14	IA, 33rd, 1907
Linley, G.W.		I, 25th Mich.	4		1920 Aug 9	KS, 40th, 1921
Linn, Adam	Pvt.	I, 158th Penn. Inf.	19		1930 Jul	IA, 57th, 1931
Linn, D.D.		B, 6th U.S. Inf. (died of typhoid)	107	59	1895 Dec 3	NE, 20th, 1896
Linn, J.L.		C, 6th Iowa Cav.	66		1892 Sep 2	NE, 17th, 1893
Linn, J.M.		S, 38th Iowa	57		1928 Nov 16	KS, 48th, 1929
Linn, John J.		C, 133rd Penn. Inf.	111		1918 Feb 9	IA, 45th, 1919
Linn, S.B.	Pvt.	A, 9th Penn. Cav.	364		1920 Mar 12	IA, 47th, 1921
Linn, Scott	Pvt.	C, 133rd Penn.	111		1903 Jul 22	IA, 30th, 1904
Linn, Sylvester J.	Pvt.	F, —	103		1923 Sep 16	IA, 50th, 1924
Linnville, Henderson	Sergt.	F, 15th Iowa Inf.	15		1900 Dec 27	IA, 27th, 1901
Linsecum, Geo.		C, 9th Ind. Cav.	84		1927 Jul 10	NE, 52nd, 1928
Linsey, Jas.		26th Iowa	56		1906	KS, 26th, 1907
Linsley, Jacob		H, 47th Iowa	500		1917 Oct 17	KS, 37th, 1918
Lint, Isac		A, 47th Ind.	25		1926 Jan 18	NE, 51st, 1927
Lintacomb, F.		F, 130th Ill.	32		1896 May 20	KS, 16th, 1897
Linthicum, E.P.		G, 11th Wis. Cav.	453		1914 Jun 2	KS, 34th, 1915

*See Appendix A, B or C for roster of post names and locations.
†See Introduction for note regarding recording of death date.
327

Name	Rank	Company, Regiment or Ship	Post*	Age	Death Date†	Journal
Lintleman, R.F.	Sergt.	E, 113th Ill. Inf.	156		1912 Apr 12	IA, 39th, 1913
Linton, C.L.		D, 140th Penn. Inf.	12		1909 Dec 12	KS, 29th, 1910
Linton, Geo.		B, 13th Kans. Inf.	89		1891 Apr 8	KS, 11th, 1892
Linton, Harvey B.		I, 6th Iowa Inf. (former member of department)			1932 Aug 11	NE, 57th, 1933
Linvill, Adam H.		F, 13th Ohio Inf. (died of old age)	47	77	1906 Oct 14	NE, 31st, 1907
Linville, R.		K, 11th Kans.	129		1916 Jul	KS, 36th, 1917
Lip, Andrew J.		G, 9th Ill. Inf.	127		1909 Dec 10	KS, 29th, 1910
Liphold, Gottlieb		D, 2nd Ill. Cav.	241		1917 May 22	KS, 37th, 1918
Lipmann, Chas.			235		1913 Jun 6	IA, 40th, 1914
Lisher, James M.		B, 16th —		94	1938 Feb 19	IA, 64th, 1938
Lisle, Henry	Pvt.	D, 129th Ohio Inf.	26		1927 Feb 12	IA, 54th, 1928
Lisler, Milton		G, 22nd Conn. Cav.	80		1892 Sep 9	NE, 17th, 1893
Lissenbee, H.H.		A, 15th Kans.	463		1909 Jul 25	KS, 29th, 1910
List, G.H.		A, 20th Ill.	49		1920 Jun 8	KS, 40th, 1921
Listen, M.B.		A, 124th Ill.	314		1924 Nov 28	IA, 51st, 1925
Listenwalter, Frank	Pvt.	E, 136th Ohio Inf.	235		1917 Dec 14	IA, 44th, 1918
Lister, J.F.			16		1918	IA, 45th, 1919
Lister, William		I, 41st Ill. Inf.	99		1912 Apr 12	KS, 32nd, 1913
Liston, H.S.	Pvt.	H, 6th West Va. Cav.	395	51	1890 Aug 2	IA, 17th, 1891
Litchfield, Albert H.	Corp.	H, 2nd Ohio Cav.	330		1903 Jan 1	IA, 29th, 1903
Litchfield, Geo.		D, 64th Ill. Inf.	124		1891 Jun	KS, 11th, 1892
Litchfield, James		C, 3rd U.S.C.	17		1927 Dec 26	KS, 47th, 1928
Lithell, W.A.		F, 14th Mo. Cav.	54		1902 Sep 16	KS, 22nd, 1903
Littel, C.A.		D, 11th Ill. Inf.	207		1926 Oct 26	NE, 51st, 1927
Littell, D.W.		C, 7th Kans. State Militia	12		1912 Feb 13	KS, 32nd, 1913
Littell, John	Pvt.	B, 6th Iowa Cav.	452	57	1893 Nov 22	IA, 20th, 1894
Littell, W.H.	Capt.	D, 23rd Iowa Inf.	192		1918 Sep 3	IA, 45th, 1919
Little, Alex	Pvt.	28th Iowa Inf.	314		1925	IA, 52nd, 1926
Little, Alex.	Pvt.	G, 28th Iowa	314		1924 Nov 28	IA, 51st, 1925
Little, C.A.		K, 150th Penn. Inf.	25		1900 Jan 2	KS, 20th, 1901
Little, Charles		D, 4th Iowa	1		1905 Sep 17	KS, 25th, 1906
Little, Geo.	Pvt.	D, 1st Mo. Cav.	452		1925 Apr 19	IA, 52nd, 1926
Little, Geo. H.	Pvt.	I, 1st Minn.	30		1924 Mar 25	IA, 51st, 1925
Little, Geo. M.	Pvt.	F, 47th Iowa Inf.	108	53	1898 Dec 6	IA, 25th, 1899
Little, George W.		G, 7th Iowa Cav.	113		1915 Dec 21	KS, 35th, 1916
Little, H.		Ord. Dept.	132		1924 May 31	KS, 44th, 1925
Little, H.E.		B, 1st Wis. Cav.	75		1902 Nov 26	KS, 22nd, 1903
Little, J.F.	Pvt.	D, 172nd Ohio Inf.	436		1906	IA, 33rd, 1907
Little, John T.		E, 6th Iowa Inf.	313		3rd quarter 1884	IA, 11th, 1885
Little, John T.		E, 134th Ohio	68		1926 Dec 16	KS, 46th, 1927
Little, John W.		K, 106th Ill.	143		1928	NE, 53rd, 1929
Little, Jos.	Pvt.	H, 32nd Mo. Inf.	103	53	1889 Dec 27	IA, 16th, 1890
Little, Robt.		U.S.S. Great Western & Red Rover			1929 Feb 20	NE, 53rd, 1929
Little, Samuel H.		C, 8th Mo. Cav.	25	78	1913 Feb 21	NE, 38th, 1914
Little, W.H.		C, 6th Md. Inf.	205		1899 Dec 14	KS, 19th, 1900
Little, W.R.			88		1884	KS, 4th, 1885
Little, Walter	Pvt.	F, 1st Ill. Art.	88		1918 Nov 27	IA, 46th, 1920
Little, William A.		G, 61st Ohio	134		1913 Oct 22	KS, 33rd, 1914
Littlefield, J.J.	Asst. Surg.	18th Mich.	25		1896 Nov	KS, 16th, 1897
Littler, John E.		E, 94th Ill. Inf.	114		1901 Oct 13	KS, 21st, 1902
Litton, B.C.		C, 155th Ill. Inf.	55		1918 Jan 28	IA, 45th, 1919
Littrell, W.W.		A, 32nd Ill.	17		1911 Jun 25	KS, 31st, 1912
Litts, John G.	Pvt.	C, 27th —	54		1886 May 15	IA, 13th, 1887
Litz, Herman			293[493?]		1905	KS, 25th, 1906
Litzenberg, B.F.	Pvt.	B, 22nd Penn. Cav.	208	52	1894 Jun 14	IA, 21st, 1895
Litzkus, Richard		F, 1st Va. Inf.	66		1916 Aug 17	KS, 36th, 1917
Livengood, Theo. F.		C, —	30		1912 Jul 8	KS, 32nd, 1913
Liveringhouse, Lewis		E, 152nd Ind. (nonmember of department; died at Juniata)			1935 Nov 6	NE, 60th, 1936
Livermore, Albert A.		B, 51st Mass. Inf. (died at Beloit; buried at Edmond Cemetery)	147		1894 Feb 17	KS, 14th, 1895

*See Appendix A, B or C for roster of post names and locations.
†See Introduction for note regarding recording of death date.

Name	Rank	Company, Regiment or Ship	Post*	Age	Death Date†	Journal
Livers, John A.		C, 104th Ill.	78		1922 Dec 6	KS, 42nd, 1923
Livesay, William			54		1920 Oct 22	KS, 40th, 1921
Living, Francis		A, 3rd Ind. Cav.	100		1918 Aug 8	KS, 38th, 1919
Livingood, B.F.		B, 15th Kans. Cav.	30		1916 Aug 1	KS, 36th, 1917
Livingood, H.H., see Lievengood, H.H.						
Livingood, Harlan		F, 11th Mo. Cav.	1		1929 Dec 8	NE, 54th, 1930
Livingston, Alvah H.	Pvt.	19th N.Y. Inf.	59		1923 Mar 6	IA, 50th, 1924
Livingston, Geo. F.		I, 165th Penn. Vol. Inf.	63		1916 Mar 22	KS, 36th, 1917
Livingston, J.A.	Corp.	A, 22nd Iowa	452		1921 Aug 20	IA, 48th, 1922
Livingston, J.T.			25	74	1921 Aug 11	NE, 46th, 1922
Livingston, M.E.	Pvt.	K, 7th Wis. Cav.	3		1922 Nov 26	IA, 49th, 1923
Livingston, Robt. R.	Capt. Brig. Gen.	A, 1st Neb. Inf. 1st Neb. Cav. (died of acute intestinal catarrh)	45	61	1888 Sep 28	NE, 13th, 1889
Livingston, T.M.	Pvt.	E, 86th Ill. Inf.	208	60	1897 Jun 19	IA, 24th, 1898
Livingston, W.A.	Corp.	B, 48th Iowa Vol. Inf.	16		1918	IA, 45th, 1919
Livingston, W.J.		E, 4th Wis. Cav.	25		1926 Jun 28	NE, 51st, 1927
Lizer, A.L.	Pvt.	E, 142nd Ill. Inf.	40		1920 Jan 9	IA, 47th, 1921
Lloyd, John			230		1916 Jul 16	IA, 43rd, 1917
Lloyd, Windsor J.	Pvt.	E, 172nd Penn. Inf.	59		1919 Aug 3	IA, 46th, 1920
Lloyd, Wm. J.		B, 67th Ind.	75		1921 Sep 29	KS, 41st, 1922
Loak, James		K, 1st Colo.	380		1898 May 19	KS, 18th, 1899
Lobaugh, Ben. F.		G, 11th Ill. Cav.	145		1910 Oct 31	KS, 30th, 1911
Lobdell, M.C.	Pvt.		91		1926 Nov 16	IA, 53rd, 1927
Lochart, M.		H, 3rd Ohio Cav.	69		1919 Mar 15	KS, 39th, 1920
Loche, Adolph		12th —	236		1913 Nov 8	IA, 40th, 1914
Lochrie, George	Pvt.	I, 2nd Ill. Cav.	7	91	1932 Feb 13	IA, 59th, 1933
Lock, C.A.	Lieut.	E, 2nd N.H. Inf.	212		1913 Mar 2	IA, 40th, 1914
Lock, Henry		118th Ill. Inf.	110		1908 Sep 14	NE, 33rd, 1909
Lock, Jno.		C, 58th Ill.	158		1911 Apr 1	KS, 31st, 1912
Lock, John, Jr.		H, 14th Kans. State Militia	271		1897 Feb 28	KS, 17th, 1898
Lock, Joshua F.	Pvt.	F, 15th Iowa Inf.	452		1924 Dec 4	IA, 51st, 1925
Lock, P.A.	Pvt.	D, 28th Iowa Inf.	98		1913 May 11	IA, 40th, 1914
Lock, W.H.			193		1908	IA, 35th, 1909
Lockard, Geo. W.	Pvt.	D, 7th Iowa Cav.	192	95	1935 Dec 31	IA, 65th, 1939
Lockart, Robert R.	Corp.	C, 30th Iowa	157		1914 May 26	IA, 41st, 1915
Locke, Chas.	Pvt.	E, 22nd Wis.	142		1903 Dec 6	IA, 30th, 1904
Locke, Jas. B.	Sergt.	C, 47th Iowa Vols.	12		1903 Apr 18	IA, 30th, 1904
Locke, John	Pvt.	I, 24th Iowa Inf.	400		1922 Jan 19	IA, 49th, 1923
Locke, Josiah		H, 11th Maine	26		1926 Apr 24	NE, 51st, 1927
Locke, Wm.		F, 8th Ind. Cav.	36		1908[1909?] Nov 21	KS, 29th, 1910
Locker, J.J.		F, 13th Kans.	93		1888	KS, 8th, 1889
Lockerby, Jason			132		1913 Dec	IA, 40th, 1914
Lockhart, A.		B, 25th Iowa (died of heart trouble)	21	78	1919 Jul 16	NE, 44th, 1920
Lockhart, Alex		F, 45th Ind. (died of general disability)	21	82	1920 Jul 14	NE, 45th, 1921
Lockhart, G.W.		D, 7th Iowa Cav.		95	1936[1935?] Dec 31	IA, 62nd, 1936
Lockie, C.L.	Pvt.		480		1900 Jul 20	IA, 27th, 1901
Locklin, Ralph		H, 1st Vt. Cav.	42		1912 Mar 19	KS, 32nd, 1913
Lockman, J.W.		A, 3rd Iowa	57		1916 Mar 5	KS, 36th, 1917
Lockner, John			10	79	1922 Mar 5	NE, 47th, 1923
Lockridge, John W.		B, 114th Ill. Inf.	88		1908 Apr 25	KS, 28th, 1909
Lockridge, S.B.		B, 16th Iowa Inf.	98		4th quarter 1884	IA, 11th, 1885
Lockridge, S.P.	Pvt.	B, 16th Iowa Inf.	98	51	1884 Oct 12	IA, 17th, 1891
Lockridge, Wm.	Pvt.	B, 10th Iowa Inf.	425	70	1895 Jun 6	IA, 22nd, 1896
Lockwood, A.D.		D, 25th Iowa Inf.	1		1929 Sep 25	KS, 49th, 1930
Lockwood, E.J.	Corp.	G, 11th Iowa Inf.	421	53	1893 Jun 11	IA, 20th, 1894
Lockwood, Ed	Pvt.	D, 77th N.Y. Inf.	200		1915 Oct 7	IA, 42nd, 1916
Lockwood, J.M.			236		1906	IA, 33rd, 1907
Lockwood, James A.		G, 16th Ind.	90		1920 Feb 17	KS, 40th, 1921
Lockwood, John E.		K, 146th Ill. Inf.	32		1899 Dec 29	KS, 19th, 1900
Lockwood, Joseph		F, 6th Ind.	209		1904 Jun 9	KS, 24th, 1905

*See Appendix A, B or C for roster of post names and locations.
†See Introduction for note regarding recording of death date.

Name	Rank	Company, Regiment or Ship	Post*	Age	Death Date†	Journal
Lockwood, O.		C, 6th Conn. (died at National Military Home)	380		1888	KS, 8th, 1889
Lockwood, R.B.	Pvt.	92nd Ill.	72		1914 Dec 25	IA, 41st, 1915
Lockwood, R.B.	Musician	B, 92nd Ill. Inf.	147		1915 Jan 23	IA, 42nd, 1916
Lockwood, W.S.	Pvt.	G, 52nd Ind. Inf.	40		1916 May 31	IA, 43rd, 1917
Lockwood, William E.					1937 Jul 15	IA, 64th, 1938
Lockwood, Wm. Edward	Corp.	K, 29th Wis. Inf.	147	97	1939 Feb 8	IA, 65th, 1939
Loder, John	Pvt.	D, 57th Ohio Inf.	154		1916 Mar 31	IA, 43rd, 1917
Lodge, A.G.	Pvt.	C, 11th Iowa Inf.	223		1905 Jan 22	IA, 32nd, 1906
Lodge, Oscar F.	Pvt.	D, 11th Iowa Inf.	408		1913 Oct 1	IA, 40th, 1914
Loeber, F.C.	Pvt.	K, 112th Ill. Inf.	236	68	1887 Aug 16	IA, 14th, 1888
Loehr, John F.	Pvt.	I, 45th Iowa Inf.	19	80	1931 Apr 14	IA, 58th, 1932
Loffland, Geo.		B, 114th Ohio	265		1898 Nov 27	KS, 18th, 1899
Lofland, John	Capt. Lieut. Col.	D, — 33rd Iowa Inf.	98	62	1892 Sep 27	IA, 19th, 1893
Loften, B.R.	Pvt.	E, 47th Mo. Inf.	2		1908 Feb 12	IA, 35th, 1909
Logan, Chas. W.		H, 27th Iowa Inf.	247		1904 Aug 5	IA, 31st, 1905
Logan, D.E.			25		1919 May 2	NE, 44th, 1920
Logan, D.W.	Pvt.	G, 105th Penn. Inf.	222		1913 Nov 15	IA, 40th, 1914
Logan, David H.		F, 17th Iowa	257		1911 May 26	KS, 31st, 1912
Logan, E.J.	Pvt.	F, 4th Ind. Bat.	86		1924 Feb 7	IA, 51st, 1925
Logan, G.C.	Pvt.	A, 47th Ill.	49		1921 Mar 1	IA, 48th, 1922
Logan, Geo. S.		F, 128th Penn. Inf.	91		1887 Jul 3	KS, 7th, 1888
Logan, Henry		E, 105th Ohio	25	79	1921 Dec 28	NE, 46th, 1922
Logan, Herman N.		D, 34th Ill. Inf.	147		1925 Nov 1	KS, 45th, 1926
Logan, Hugh	Pvt.	E, 37th Iowa Inf.	49		1904 Dec 1	IA, 31st, 1905
Logan, J.D.	Pvt.	G, 145th Penn. Inf.	124		1920 Apr 26	IA, 47th, 1921
Logan, J.E.		H, 118th Ill.	276		1897 Jul 5	KS, 17th, 1898
Logan, Jacob		H, 59th Ind.	66		1913 Dec 9	KS, 33rd, 1914
Logan, James	Pvt.		122		1920	IA, 47th, 1921
Logan, James A.		K, 10th Ind.	259		1923 Dec 27	KS, 43rd, 1924
Logan, John		C, 25th Ill.	203		1916 Dec 27	KS, 36th, 1917
Logan, John B.		E, 135th Ind. Inf.	9		1925 Apr 10	KS, 45th, 1926
Logan, L.M.		L, 43rd Ind.	142		1913 Oct 4	KS, 33rd, 1914
Logan, M.M.	Sergt.	M, 16th Penn. Cav.	57		1918 Dec 27	IA, 45th, 1919
Logan, S.M.	Sergt.	C, 7th Iowa Inf.	108		1918 Jul 26	IA, 45th, 1919
Logan, W.B.		B, 6th Mo.	364		1926	KS, 46th, 1927
Logan, W.C.		B, 8th Iowa	142		1925 Mar 18	KS, 44th, 1925
Logan, W.C.		B, 8th Iowa	142		1925 Mar 18	KS, 45th, 1926
Logan, Wm.		K, 1st Iowa Cav.	293		1913 May 21	KS, 33rd, 1914
Logan, Wm. H.		D, 2nd Ohio Art.	47		1918 Jun 1	KS, 38th, 1919
Loggie, Hans	Pvt.	I, 8th Iowa Inf.	250		1901 Sep 20	IA, 28th, 1902
Loghrey, Joseph B.	Corp.	B, 86th N.Y. Inf. (died of suicide)	96	45	1888 Jan 3	NE, 13th, 1889
Loghry, Alvin		C, 106th Ill. Inf. (died of old age)	22	89	1924 May 16	NE, 49th, 1925
Loghry, Jas. F.		K, 152nd Ind. (died of general debility)	22	77	1906 Sep 10	NE, 31st, 1907
Logie, Chas. J., M.D.		N.Y. Hvy. Art.	130		1889	KS, 9th, 1890
Logston, Joseph		F, 93rd Ill.	47		1911 Jan 10	KS, 31st, 1912
Lohanaten, Andrew		A, 1st Mo. Cav.	64		1923 Dec 24	KS, 43rd, 1924
Loman, Thomas			93		1906	KS, 26th, 1907
Lomax, Perry	Commodore	D, 7th Ill. Cav. (see also Appendix D)	25		1935 Aug 21	NE, 60th, 1936
Lombard, David	Pvt.	K, 27th Iowa Inf.	77	94	1931 Mar 25	IA, 58th, 1932
Lonburger, Geo.		I, 39th Ill.	64		1906 Dec 18	KS, 26th, 1907
London, William	Pvt.	F, Mich. Battery	62		1914 Oct 10	IA, 41st, 1915
Londrey, J.R.		F, 30th Mich.	4		1924 May 21	KS, 44th, 1925
Lone, S.	Pvt.	H, 11th Iowa Inf.	231		1921 Apr 12	IA, 48th, 1922
Lonergan, Jos. M.		K, 12th Tenn.	380		1897 Mar 23	KS, 17th, 1898
Long, A.A.	Pvt.		48		1929 Aug	IA, 56th, 1930
Long, A.D.	Pvt.	F, 29th Iowa Inf.	248		1915	IA, 42nd, 1916
Long, A.R.	Pvt.	H, 8th Iowa Cav.	8		1926 Nov 19	IA, 53rd, 1927
Long, A.S.			1		1893 Aug 9	KS, 13th, 1894
Long, Alonzo		29th Conn. Inf.	110		1908 May 8	NE, 33rd, 1909
Long, D.T.		D, 119th Ill.	50		1914 Sep 4	KS, 34th, 1915

Name	Rank	Company, Regiment or Ship	Post*	Age	Death Date†	Journal
Long, Denis		K, 36th Ill.	129		1922 Oct 16	KS, 42nd, 1923
Long, Geo.	Pvt.	K, 127th —	117	56	1892 Nov 2	IA, 19th, 1893
Long, Geo.		M, 9th Kans. Cav.	277		1899 Nov 1	KS, 19th, 1900
Long, George		I, 30th Penn. Inf.	8		1902 Sep 6	KS, 22nd, 1903
Long, Harden		A, 86th Ill.	25		1889	KS, 9th, 1890
Long, J.	Pvt.	E, 29th Iowa Inf.	263		1921 Sep 12	IA, 48th, 1922
Long, J.A.	Pvt.	B, 26th Ill. Inf.	267	48	1887 Oct 14	IA, 14th, 1888
Long, J.M.	Capt.	C, 53rd Ohio Inf.	123		1917 Apr 25	IA, 44th, 1918
Long, J.W.	Sergt.	C, 33rd Wis. Inf.	42		1926 Nov 10	IA, 53rd, 1927
Long, James		K, 5th Ky. Inf. (died at Atchison, Kans.; buried at Mt. Vernon Cemetery)	93		1894 Aug 30	KS, 14th, 1895
Long, Jeremiah		I, 99th Ind.	252		1915 Dec 1	KS, 35th, 1916
Long, Jesse		H, 11th Kans.	370		1914 Oct 6	KS, 34th, 1915
Long, John	Pvt.	F, 11th Ill. Cav.	440		1919 Jul 19	IA, 46th, 1920
Long, John	Pvt.	A, 35th Iowa Inf.	231		1926 Jan 19	IA, 53rd, 1927
Long, John		I, 30th Ind.	180		1922 Jun 14	KS, 42nd, 1923
Long, John J.	Corp.	H, 164th Ohio	42		1907 May 30	IA, 34th, 1908
Long, John Z.	Pvt.	G, 176th Ohio Inf.	343		1915 Nov 27	IA, 42nd, 1916
Long, Jos. H.		B, 152nd Ill. Inf.	44		1899 Sep 15	KS, 19th, 1900
Long, L.S.		K, 2nd Kans. Cav.	1		1896 Mar 19	KS, 16th, 1897
Long, Levi	Pvt.	C, 33rd Wis. Inf.	42		1921 May 1	IA, 48th, 1922
Long, Marion	Pvt.	B, 50th Ind. Inf.	244		1904 Dec 28	IA, 31st, 1905
Long, Martin		A, 1st Ohio Hvy. Art.	8		1918 Jul 12	KS, 38th, 1919
Long, Michael		A, 47th Ohio	380		1912 Aug 15	KS, 32nd, 1913
Long, N.L.	Pvt.	I, 13th Iowa Inf.	108		1928 Aug 10	IA, 55th, 1929
Long, O.	Pvt.	A, 165th Ohio Inf.	94		1908 Nov 28	IA, 35th, 1909
Long, Peter	Pvt.	G, 147th Ill. Inf.	452		1929 Nov	IA, 56th, 1930
Long, Peter L.	Pvt.	F, 147th Ill. Inf.	452		1930 Jun 5	IA, 57th, 1931
Long, Robert	Pvt.	D, 38th Iowa Inf.	216		1893 Aug 7	IA, 20th, 1894
Long, Samuel		E, 98th N.Y.	25	71	1915 Nov 17	NE, 40th, 1916
Long, Silas		F, 11th Ind.	51		1926 Dec 21	KS, 46th, 1927
Long, Thos. A.	Pvt.	H, 40th Ind. Inf.	197		1926 Oct 2	IA, 53rd, 1927
Long, W.A.			98		1926 May 16	KS, 46th, 1927
Long, W.B.			156		1924 Dec 31	IA, 51st, 1925
Long, W.W.	Pvt.	H, 27th Iowa Inf.	54		1928 Apr 13	IA, 55th, 1929
Long, William		E, 50th Ill.	286		1905	KS, 25th, 1906
Long, William T.		F, 10th Ind. Inf.	90		1925 Feb 18	KS, 45th, 1926
Long, Wm.		G, 45th Ill.	101		1925 May	NE, 51st, 1927
Long, Z.V.			230		1899	NE, 24th, 1900
Longacre, Wm.		Ind.	1		1910 May 4	KS, 30th, 1911
Longbon, David		F, 9th Mich.	260		1898 May 17	KS, 18th, 1899
Longer, P.H.	Pvt.	M, 9th Iowa Cav.	197	83	1897 Aug 25	IA, 24th, 1898
Longerbeam, A.J.	Pvt.	K, 8th Iowa Cav.	228		1916 Aug 14	IA, 43rd, 1917
Longfellow, Chas.		F, 3rd Kans. State Militia	12		1909 Apr 18	KS, 29th, 1910
Longfellow, J.W.		D, 2nd Kans.	256		1922 May 3	KS, 42nd, 1923
Longhery, John	Pvt.	A, 6th U.S. Cav.	92		1903 May 25	IA, 30th, 1904
Longhlin, Thomas	Pvt.	E, 187th Penn. Inf.	14		1905 Dec 20	IA, 32nd, 1906
Longhorn, James	Capt.	I, 19th Ill. Inf.	132		1918 Mar 18	IA, 45th, 1919
Longley, E.K.		H, 16th West Va.	23		1928 May 21	KS, 48th, 1929
Longley, Howard A.	Pvt.	C, 16th Wis. Inf.	5		1901 Jan 15	IA, 27th, 1901
Longmaker, Isaac	Pvt.	A, 39th Iowa	55		1907 Apr 2	IA, 34th, 1908
Longman, Elias		45th Ill.	74		1904 Mar 3	IA, 30th, 1904
Longsdors, A.J.		1st Ind. Bat.	25		1893 Aug 13	KS, 13th, 1894
Longshore, Wm. H.		D, 30th Ohio Inf.	32		1908[1909?] Dec 20	KS, 29th, 1910
Longstreet, T.E.		G, 126th N.Y. Inf.	25	81	1920 Feb 5	NE, 45th, 1921
Longstreth, C.H.		F, 6th Penn. Cav.	364		1921	KS, 41st, 1922
Longwell, J.D.		A, 12th Ohio Cav. (drowned in flood)	165	76	1919 Oct 24	NE, 44th, 1920
Lonie, Edward		H, 2nd Wis.	265		1932 Jan 28	NE, 57th, 1933
Lonker, William		M, 9th Iowa Cav.	174		1919 Sep 2	KS, 39th, 1920
Lonnis, A.B.	Pvt.	G, 87th Ohio Inf.	235		1924 Aug 29	IA, 51st, 1925
Lontner, Jacob	Sergt.	D, 18th Iowa Inf.	424		1902 Dec 15	IA, 29th, 1903
Looby, John H.	Major	62nd U.S.C.T.	12		1909 Dec 23	IA, 36th, 1910

*See Appendix A, B or C for roster of post names and locations.
†See Introduction for note regarding recording of death date.

Name	Rank	Company, Regiment or Ship	Post*	Age	Death Date†	Journal
Loofboro, J.A.	Pvt.	D, 14th Iowa	19		1907 1st term	IA, 34th, 1908
Loofborough, J.A., see Loofboro, J.A.						
Loofborrow, W.P.		20th Ohio	28		1928 Mar 28	KS, 48th, 1929
Looker, Frederic		K, 35th Ind.	383		1906 Nov 3	KS, 26th, 1907
Loomas, A.N.		I, 45th Iowa	89		1926	KS, 46th, 1927
Loomer, Phillip	Pvt.	I, 44th Wis.	220		1914 Jan 3	IA, 41st, 1915
Loomis, A.M.	Capt.	K, 24th Iowa Inf.	130		1909 Dec 5	IA, 36th, 1910
Loomis, E.		F, 2nd Iowa Cav.	113		1926 Mar 2	NE, 51st, 1927
Loomis, Elmer		B, 77th Ohio Vol. Inf.	49		1915 Aug 12	KS, 35th, 1916
Loomis, H.J.	Pvt.	G, 14th Wis. Inf.	46		1913 May 26	IA, 40th, 1914
Loomis, Henry C.	Lieut. Lieut. Col.	C, 64th N.Y. Inf. 154th N.Y. Inf. (see also Appendix D)	85		1905 Oct 14	KS, 25th, 1906
Loomis, Mysiners		I, 102nd Ill. Inf.	25		1917 Sep 17	KS, 37th, 1918
Loomis, S.I.	Sergt.	181st Ohio Inf.	270		1900 Mar 23	IA, 27th, 1901
Loomis, Theron		G, 43rd Wis.	[25?]		1923	NE, 48th, 1924
Loomis, W.B.		E, 24th Iowa Inf. (died of jaundice)	52		1894 Apr 6	NE, 19th, 1895
Loomis, Wm.	Pvt.	4th Iowa Inf.	20		1914	IA, 41st, 1915
Looney, Patrick		A, 8th Kans. Inf. (died at National Military Home; buried at National Military Home Cemetery)	380		1894 Jun 1	KS, 14th, 1895
Loonus, J.R.		H, 134th Ill.	69		1922 Oct 6	KS, 42nd, 1923
Loop, Albert		F, 28th Ohio	147		1918 Jul 20	KS, 38th, 1919
Looper, Thomas			342		1912	KS, 32nd, 1913
Looper, Thomas			342		1915	KS, 35th, 1916
Loos, John	Pvt.	I, 21st Iowa Inf.	369		1900 Jul 14	IA, 27th, 1901
Loose, C.A.		H, 102nd Penn.	89		1893 Nov 4	KS, 13th, 1894
Loose, L.T.		F, 76th Ill.	56		1906 Nov 28	KS, 26th, 1907
Loose, Westley		H, 17th Wis.	51		1924 May 14	KS, 44th, 1925
Lopeman, John J.		H, 16th Kans. Inf.	170		1887 Mar 20	KS, 7th, 1888
Loper, D.D.	Pvt.	G, 34th Iowa Inf.	67		1904 Nov 23	IA, 31st, 1905
Loper, E.		E, 36th Iowa	63		1921 Apr 16	KS, 41st, 1922
Loper, Lewis		F, 11th Ind.	18		1928 Dec 18	KS, 48th, 1929
Loper, Louis (or Lewis) D.	Pvt.	K, 2nd Iowa Cav. C, 30th Iowa Inf.	29	93	1939 Feb 10	IA, 65th, 1939
Loper, Wm.		K, 7th Ill. Inf.	29		1927 Aug 8	IA, 54th, 1928
Loranz, Henry	Pvt.	A, 8th Iowa Cav.	11		1928 Mar	IA, 55th, 1929
Lord, Albert E.		I, 114th N.Y.	87		1898 Nov 2	KS, 18th, 1899
Lord, Elisha N.		C, 17th Penn. Cav.	18		1905 Feb 17	KS, 25th, 1906
Lord, George A.		B, 5th Mich. Cav. (died of rheumatism of heart)	380		1891 Feb 5	KS, 11th, 1892
Lord, J.C.			127		1928 Oct 9	KS, 48th, 1929
Lord, Lucius T.		F, 45th Ill. Inf.	117		1900 Apr 14	KS, 20th, 1901
Lord, Norman H.		D, 33rd Wis.	87		1916 Nov 13	KS, 36th, 1917
Lorence, Frank		D, 44th Iowa Inf. (at large)		91	1936 Feb 18	IA, 63rd, 1937
Lorence, Frank		D, 44th Iowa Inf. (at large)		91	1936 Feb 18	IA, 62nd, 1936
Lorenson, Jens		I, 15th Wis.	87		1906 Jul 22	KS, 26th, 1907
Lorig, Matthias	Pvt.	E, 21st Iowa Inf.	342	58	1888 Feb 21	IA, 15th, 1889
Lorimer, J.C.		I, 84th Ill.	68		1914 Oct 20	KS, 34th, 1915
Lorimer, J.R.		K, 8th Ill. (died of pneumonia)	1	84	1918 Apr 26	NE, 43rd, 1919
Loring, Emory		B, 86th Ohio (died at Soldiers' Home, Leavenworth)	65		1893 Dec	KS, 13th, 1894
Lormier, J.R.	Pvt.	A, 34th Iowa Inf.	440		1906 Nov 1	IA, 33rd, 1907
Lorton, Sam'l	Pvt.	D, 20th Iowa Inf.	1		1923 Dec 6	IA, 50th, 1924
Losch, Andrew		K, 187th Ohio	1		1921 Feb 22	KS, 41st, 1922
Losee, Geo. M.	Pvt.	M, 13th N.Y. Hvy. Art.	156		1927 Dec 25	IA, 54th, 1928
Losey, A.	Corp.	E, 9th Iowa Inf.	306	41	1885 Jul 28	IA, 12th, 1886
Losh, W.H.		E, 137th Penn.	65		1928 Mar 8	KS, 48th, 1929
Lost, Charles		A, 6th Wis.	12		1905 Mar 17	KS, 25th, 1906
Loter, Hiram P.		K, 7th Mo. Cav.	73		1916 May 16	KS, 36th, 1917
Lothrop, Chas. H.	1st Surg.	1st Iowa Cav.	92	59	1890 Feb 6	IA, 16th, 1890
Lothrop, Chas. H.	Surg.	1st Iowa Cav.	92	58	1890 Feb 8	IA, 18th, 1892
Lothrop, J.S.	Capt.	I, 11th Ill. Inf.	22		1913 Jul 1	IA, 40th, 1914

*See Appendix A, B or C for roster of post names and locations.
†See Introduction for note regarding recording of death date.

Name	Rank	Company, Regiment or Ship	Post*	Age	Death Date†	Journal
Lott, C.S.	Pvt.	G, 54th Ill. Inf.	309		1926 Nov 9	IA, 53rd, 1927
Lott, James, see James, Lott						
Lott, Martin	Capt.	I, 16th Iowa Inf.	68		1911 Apr 8	IA, 38th, 1912
Lott, T.J.		B, 21st Penn. Cav.	47		1908 Jul 23	KS, 28th, 1909
Lotz, Jno.	Pvt.	C, Penn. Cav.	22		1925 Jun 24	IA, 52nd, 1926
Loud, R.W.	Lieut.	G, 122nd Ill. Inf.	32		1884	KS, 4th, 1885
Louden, D.S.	Pvt.	I, 49th Penn. Inf.	56	93	1933 Jul 16	IA, 60th, 1934
Louden, Stephen		F, 1st Wis. Art. (cause of death: heart)	140	72	1901 Aug	NE, 26th, 1902
Louder, John		E, 123rd Iowa	88		1931 Jan 16	KS, 52nd, 1933
Louder, John		E, 123rd Iowa	88		1931 Jan 16	KS, 51st, 1932
Louderback, A.		H, 21st Ind.	54		1921 Jul	KS, 41st, 1922
Louderbough, Milton			266		1901 Aug 15	KS, 21st, 1902
Loudon, J.P.		F, 55th Penn. (died of bee sting)	245	72	1918 Mar 16	NE, 43rd, 1919
Loudon, Jos.		F, 58th Ind. Inf. (died of paralysis)	226	72	1902 May	NE, 27th, 1903
Loudon, William		B, 11th Wis.	34		1936 Apr 23	NE, 61st, 1937
Loughary, J.S.		F, 3rd Iowa Cav.	19		1921 Aug 8	IA, 48th, 1922
Loughlin, Thomas, see Longhlin, Thomas						
Loughran, E.	Pvt.	1st Iowa	30		1923 Nov 17	IA, 50th, 1924
Loughridge, J.	Pvt.	K, 33rd Iowa Inf.	40		1910 Aug 4	IA, 37th, 1911
Loughry, A.	Pvt.	G, 135th Penn. Inf.	305		1919 Apr 22	IA, 46th, 1920
Loukd, Chas.			23		1906 Oct 1	IA, 33rd, 1907
Lounsbury, H.W.		E, 33rd Iowa	94		1922 Oct 11	IA, 49th, 1923
Louthan, Henry		K, 120th Ohio	1		1921 Feb 22	KS, 41st, 1922
Loutzenhizer, John		C, 145th Penn. Inf.	147		1925 May 31	KS, 45th, 1926
Loux, Charles L.		C, 99th Ind.	151		1916 Jun 6	KS, 36th, 1917
Love, J.N.		A, 144th N.Y.	130		1904 Mar 3	KS, 24th, 1905
Love, Julian		A, 1st N.Y. Hvy. Art.	32		1925 Apr 13	KS, 45th, 1926
Love, S.D.					1929[1928?] Mar	NE, 53rd, 1929
Love, W.R.	Capt.	L, 7th Mo. Cav.	107	72	1891 Nov 16	IA, 18th, 1892
Love, W.R.		A, 88th Ill.	12		1915 Jan 31	KS, 35th, 1916
Love, William		E, 81st Ind. Inf.	32		1939 Jun 6	NE, 64th, 1940
Love, Wm.		B, 43rd Ohio Inf.	198		1916 Sep 24	KS, 36th, 1917
Lovejoy, A.J.	Sergt.	E, 29th Mich. Inf.	77		1926 Jan 3	IA, 53rd, 1927
Lovejoy, Ami	Pvt.	B, 96th Ill. Inf.	267		1909 Sep 7	IA, 36th, 1910
Lovejoy, Chas. H.		7th Kans.	40		1904 Dec 3	KS, 24th, 1905
Lovejoy, J.A.	Lieut.	186th Ohio Inf.	324		1913 May 9	IA, 40th, 1914
Lovejoy, Miles		D, 6th U.S. Inf.	132		1885	KS, 5th, 1886
Lovejoy, Wm. Emerson		E, 111th N.Y. Inf.	7	93	1938 Jul 28	IA, 64th, 1938
Lovelace, C.F.	QM	22nd Iowa Inf.	8		1909 Jul 19	IA, 36th, 1910
Lovelace, J.R.		F, 9th Ky. Inf.	17		1929 Sep 29	KS, 49th, 1930
Lovelace, Lucius	Pvt.	K, 21st Iowa Inf.	26	88	1933 Sep 7	IA, 60th, 1934
Lovelace, Lucius		K, 21st Iowa	26	88	1934 Sep 7	IA, 61st, 1935
Loveland, P.A.	Pvt.	D, 36th N.J.	69		1923 Sep 7	IA, 50th, 1924
Lovelee, L.S.	Sergt.	M, 14th N.Y. Inf.	74		1916 Jan 3	IA, 43rd, 1917
Lovell, R.M.	Pvt.	G, 20th Penn. Cav.	228		1905 Apr 15	IA, 32nd, 1906
Lovell, Reuben		F, 96th Ohio Inf.	31		1923 Oct 10	NE, 48th, 1924
Lovell, William B.		G, 8th Iowa Cav. (at large)	452	93	1937 Oct 20	IA, 64th, 1938
Loverein, Geo. H.	Pvt.	G, 9th Vt. Inf.	193		1917 Jan 26	IA, 44th, 1918
Loving, F.H.	Corp.	G, 92nd Ohio Inf.	40		1920 May 6	IA, 47th, 1921
Low, Allen		F, 5th Ind.	129		1896 Jul 25	KS, 16th, 1897
Low, Sam	Pvt.	M, Wis. Cav.	67		1916 Oct 7	IA, 43rd, 1917
Low, William H.		A, 20th Maine Inf.	18		1908 Apr 15	KS, 28th, 1909
Lowden, J.W.	Pvt.	H, 6th Iowa	497		1928 Jan 18	IA, 55th, 1929
Lowden, Wm.	Pvt.	F, 40th Iowa Inf.	414		1913	IA, 40th, 1914
Lowder, A.J.		A, 55th Ill.	28		1922 Oct 21	KS, 42nd, 1923
Lowder, James H.		A, 55th Ill. Inf.	28		1912 Jul 10	KS, 32nd, 1913
Lowe, Austin		I, 11th Ill. Cav.	464		1902 Mar 24	KS, 22nd, 1903
Lowe, David	Pvt.	H, 36th Iowa Inf.	497		1928[1927?] Nov 7	IA, 54th, 1928
Lowe, G.N.		D, 36th Ind.	459		1904 Feb 14	KS, 24th, 1905
Lowe, H.G.		B, 126th Ill. Inf. (died of blood poisoning)	59	58	1897 May 28	NE, 22nd, 1898
Lowe, J.H.		G, 132nd Ind.	155		1921 Jun 12	KS, 41st, 1922

*See Appendix A, B or C for roster of post names and locations.
†See Introduction for note regarding recording of death date.

Name	Rank	Company, Regiment or Ship	Post*	Age	Death Date†	Journal
Lowe, Jacob S.		F, 208th Penn.	249		1892 Nov 14	KS, 12th, 1893
Lowe, James		B, 175th Ohio	85		1906 Aug 26	KS, 26th, 1907
Lowe, John W.		I, 7th Kans. Cav.	493		1910 Dec 27	KS, 30th, 1911
Lowe, Phillip	Pvt.	K, 2nd Neb. Cav.	344	65	1899 Jan 15	IA, 25th, 1899
Lowe, Richard		A, 8th Ohio (died of dropsy)	35	70	1912 Nov 7	NE, 37th, 1913
Lowe, Sandy	Col.	23rd Mo. Vols.	74		1902	KS, 22nd, 1903
Lowe, Sandy			40		1902	KS, 22nd, 1903
Lowe, T.J.	1st Lieut.	G, 34th Iowa	426		1901 Nov 7	IA, 28th, 1902
Lowe, W.N.		A, 73rd Ohio	1		1917 Jan 13	KS, 37th, 1918
Lowe, William P.	Pvt.	H, 5th Wis. Inf.	118		1901 Nov 1	IA, 28th, 1902
Lowe, Wm. H.		C, 15th Ill. (died of lung fever)	109	65	1905[1904?] Dec 14	NE, 29th, 1905
Lowell, Freeman A.	Pvt.	K, 28th Ill. Vol. Inf.	375		1903 Sep 27	IA, 30th, 1904
Lowell, J.S.	Pvt.	A, 16th Minn. Inf.	88		1921 Oct 28	IA, 48th, 1922
Lowell, James H.		A, 13th Mass.	46		1925 Feb 19	KS, 45th, 1926
Lowell, R.		D, 47th Iowa Inf. (died of dry gangrene)	70	76	1895 Dec 17	NE, 20th, 1896
Lowenberg, Wm.		H, 36th Iowa Inf.	69		1922 Oct 25	IA, 49th, 1923
Lower, H.S.		B, 125th Penn.	127		1931 Oct 3	KS, 52nd, 1933
Lower, H.S.		B, 125th Penn.	127		1931 Oct 3	KS, 51st, 1932
Lower, Levi			24		1914 Aug	KS, 34th, 1915
Lowerre, Benj. F.	Pvt.	K, 56th N.Y.	124		1926 Mar 5	IA, 53rd, 1927
Lowery, Edward	Corp.	G, 116th Ohio Inf.	79	65	1896 Jun 5	IA, 23rd, 1897
Lowery, James T.		D, 4th Ky.	380		1912 Apr 26	KS, 32nd, 1913
Lowery, Lewis		K, 1st Neb. Inf.	7	66	1906 Apr 27	NE, 31st, 1907
Lowery, O.H.	Pvt.	I, 6th Iowa Inf.	5	47	1887 Feb 18	IA, 13th, 1887
Lowery, O.H.	Sergt.	I, 6th Iowa Inf.	5	47	1887 Feb 8	IA, 14th, 1888
Lowery, Phillip		3rd Mo. Cav.	132		1911 Dec 7	KS, 31st, 1912
Lowery, Thomas	Pvt.	I, 39th Mo. Inf.	254		1923 Sep 23	IA, 50th, 1924
Lowery, W.	Pvt.	M, 4th Iowa Cav.	324		1920 Sep 18	IA, 47th, 1921
Lowery, W.B., see Lowrey, W.B.						
Lowery, William C.		E, 94th Ill.	5		1932 Oct 31	NE, 57th, 1933
Lowman, Geo. W.		B, 11th Penn.	155		1930 Feb 21	KS, 50th, 1931
Lowman, Henry		B, 75th Ill. Inf.	356		1917 Jul 1	KS, 37th, 1918
Lowman, John C.		I, 12th Ind. Cav.	82		1914 Aug 18	KS, 34th, 1915
Lowrey, J.J.	Pvt.	I, 29th Mo. Inf.	254		1920	IA, 47th, 1921
Lowrey, James		G, 36th Iowa	301		1928 Feb 13	KS, 48th, 1929
Lowrey, M.		H, 1st Minn. (died of old age)	231	86	1908 Aug 28	NE, 33rd, 1909
Lowrey, O.W.	Pvt.	I, 6th Iowa Inf.	12	86	1931 Oct 19	IA, 58th, 1932
Lowrey, W.B.		Ohio Lt. Art.	157		1912	NE, 37th, 1913
Lowrey, William	Pvt.	C, 3rd Iowa Cav.	2	63	1894 Apr 4	IA, 20th, 1894
Lowrie, Wm.	Pvt.	A, 2nd Wis. Cav.	22		1922 Sep 27	IA, 49th, 1923
Lowry, J.K.		A, 17th Ohio Inf.	7		1925 Jan 17	NE, 50th, 1926
Lowry, Melvin		I, 2nd Kans. Cav.	160		1911 Oct 13	KS, 31st, 1912
Lowther, A.L.		A, 1st Va. Lt. Art.	89		1917	KS, 37th, 1918
Loy, G.T.	Pvt.	F, 23rd Iowa Inf.	56		1929 Jan	IA, 56th, 1930
Loy, J.	Pvt.	A, 6th Iowa Cav.	235		1919 Jan 9	IA, 46th, 1920
Loy, J.W.		E, 11th Kans.	249		1904 Oct 30	KS, 24th, 1905
Loy, S.W.		E, 11th Kans. Cav.	74		1917 Dec 30	KS, 37th, 1918
Lozier, J.H.	Chaplain	37th Ind.	400		1907 Aug	IA, 34th, 1908
Lozier, Jacob	Pvt.	F, 9th Iowa Cav.	130	85	1931 Aug 4	IA, 58th, 1932
Luas, David		E, 11th Ill. Cav.	66		1911 Nov 18	KS, 31st, 1912
Lubbock, Robt.	Private	G, 35th N.Y. Inf.	235		1916 May 5	IA, 43rd, 1917
Lucas, A.J.		I, 20th Ohio Inf.	117		1891 Oct 24	KS, 11th, 1892
Lucas, Benj. W.	Pvt.	G, 63rd Ind. Vol. Inf.	191	54	1899 Mar 1	IA, 25th, 1899
Lucas, C.A.	Corp.	24th Iowa	8		1907 1st term	IA, 34th, 1908
Lucas, Charles			153		1883	KS, 3rd, 1884
Lucas, Charles S.		I, 8th Penn. (died of cancer)	23	75	1915 Dec 15	NE, 40th, 1916
Lucas, D.W.			167		1927 Dec 24	IA, 55th, 1929
Lucas, F.M.	Pvt.	G, 25th Iowa	246		1924 Jun	IA, 51st, 1925
Lucas, F.M.	Pvt.	G, 25th Iowa Inf.	246		1923 Jun	IA, 50th, 1924
Lucas, Henry S.	Pvt.	G, 40th Ind. Inf.	12		1912 Aug 23	IA, 39th, 1913
Lucas, J.F.	Pvt.	G, 25th Iowa	246		1921 Apr	IA, 48th, 1922

*See Appendix A, B or C for roster of post names and locations.
†See Introduction for note regarding recording of death date.

334

Name	Rank	Company, Regiment or Ship	Post*	Age	Death Date†	Journal
Lucas, John	Pvt.	A, 36th Iowa Inf.	324		1908 May 10	IA, 35th, 1909
Lucas, John		H, 39th Ind.	8		1913 Dec 28	KS, 33rd, 1914
Lucas, John Frederick		6th Div. Eng.		93	1937 Jan 4	IA, 64th, 1938
Lucas, John T.	Pvt.	H, 13th Iowa Inf.	94	83	1932 Aug 16	IA, 59th, 1933
Lucas, Thomas H.		E, 42nd Ill. Inf.	127		1909 Dec 31	KS, 29th, 1910
Lucas, Tipton	Pvt.	A, 93rd Ill.	323		1924 Jun 15	IA, 51st, 1925
Lucas, Wm.		A, 65th Ind.	257		1922 Jun 18	KS, 42nd, 1923
Lucas, Wm. D.	Capt.	F, 5th N.Y. Cav.	12	54	1892 Aug 15	IA, 19th, 1893
Lucas, Wm. M.		A, 2nd Ill. Lt. Art.	253		1893 Oct 6	KS, 13th, 1894
Luce, J.D.		A, 112th Ill.	51		1915 Sep 28	KS, 35th, 1916
Luce, John W.		E, 1st Ohio Art.	122		4th quarter 1883	IA, 10th, 1884
Luce, John W.	Pvt.	E, 1st Ohio Art.	152		1884 Nov 17	IA, 17th, 1891
Luce, Joseph W.		C, 3rd Mich. Cav.	86		1914 Mar 11	KS, 33rd, 1914
Luce, S.	Pvt.	E, 31st Iowa Inf.	46		1921 Jan 3	IA, 48th, 1922
Luce, Sam'l	Pvt.	E, 31st Iowa Inf.	46		1920 Jan 3	IA, 47th, 1921
Luce, W.C.		H, 19th Ill. Inf. (killed by train)	98	89	1920 Nov 15	NE, 45th, 1921
Luce, W.S.			173		1913	IA, 40th, 1914
Luck, Geo. C.	Pvt.	F, 21st Iowa Inf.	75		1903 Sep 24	IA, 30th, 1904
Luckadoo, E.	Pvt.	E, 60th U.S.C.T.	452		1918 Jul 7	IA, 45th, 1919
Luckee, William	Pvt.	A, 1st Neb. Cav. (died of apoplexy)	45	59	1888 Apr 13	NE, 13th, 1889
Luckenbill, Ezra	Pvt.	G, 4th Iowa Cav.	68		1910 Oct 8	IA, 37th, 1911
Luckey, Jeremiah		F, 25th Iowa	59		1913 Apr 23	KS, 33rd, 1914
Lucus, Thos.		F, 1st Penn. Cav.	23		1926	NE, 51st, 1927
Lucy, W.W.		A, 54th Ind.	38		1917 Jan 10	KS, 37th, 1918
Ludden, Enos	Pvt.	G, 27th Iowa Inf.	68		1910 Aug 27	IA, 37th, 1911
Luddington, R.W.		E, 3rd (M) Kans.[Kans. State Militia?]	12		1905 Oct 7	KS, 25th, 1906
Luddington, W.W.	Pvt.	I, 8th Ind. Inf.	7	58	1893 Jan 24	IA, 19th, 1893
Luder, A.J.		B, Iowa Inf.	27		1916 Nov 29	KS, 36th, 1917
Ludington, L.W.		15th Ill. (died of chronic trouble)	147	69	1911 Jan 7	NE, 36th, 1912
Ludlow, J.H.		K, H, B, 63rd Ind. Inf. (member at large)	65		1934 Dec 24	KS, 54th, 1935
Ludlow, J.H.		K, H, B, 63rd Ind.	65		1934 Dec 12	KS, 55th, 1936
Ludlow, James H.		B, 63rd Ind.	65		1911 Mar 17	KS, 31st, 1912
Ludlow, W.O.	Pvt.	D, 1st Iowa Cav.	55		1907 Jun 8	IA, 34th, 1908
Ludwickson, Christianson		H, 5th Minn. Inf.	79		1926 Oct 11	KS, 50th, 1931
Ludwig, Frederick		B, 150th Ill.	252		1920 Apr 20	KS, 40th, 1921
Lueshen, John L.	Sergt.	E, 3rd Wis. Inf.	452		1900-1901	IA, 27th, 1901
Lufkin, James M.		A, 32nd Mass.	26		1892 Oct 22	KS, 12th, 1893
Luke, Elias	Pvt.	C, 3rd Iowa Cav.	79	49	1894 Dec 23	IA, 21st, 1895
Luke, G.		H, 49th Ill.	49		1896 Aug 6	KS, 16th, 1897
Luke, G.W.	Lieut.	K, 96th Ill. Inf.	81		1910 Feb 9	IA, 37th, 1911
Luke, Leopold	Pvt.	K, 3rd Iowa Cav.	49		1922 Jan 15	IA, 49th, 1923
Lukenbill, P.H.		G, 38th Ind.	142		1913 Aug 23	KS, 33rd, 1914
Lull, A.			5		1937	KS, 57th, 1938
Lull, H.M.		C, 1st Neb.	240		1909 Jan 22	KS, 29th, 1910
Lullus, Wm. H.		K, 15th Ind.	49		1889	KS, 9th, 1890
Lumkins, Robert		E, 3rd Mo. Inf.	174		1901 Jan 2	KS, 21st, 1902
Lumm, Cornelius		A, 126th Ohio	81		1918 Jan 14	KS, 38th, 1919
Lund, John		K, 24th Wis. Inf.	8		1887 Oct 5	KS, 7th, 1888
Lund, Stillman G.		C, 91st Ohio Inf.	110	84	1916 Sep 9	NE, 41st, 1917
Lundergran, Victor		U.S. Navy, Sweden (died of heart failure)	110		1918 Apr 21	NE, 43rd, 1919
Lundy, N.J.		E, 26th Ill.	85		1902 Dec 20	KS, 22nd, 1903
Luney, J.L.		I, 1st Ill. Cav.	32	78	1920 May 20	NE, 45th, 1921
Luninghauer, Peter		1st Mo. Art.	133	79	1915 Mar 5	NE, 40th, 1916
Lunn, C.E.		A, 31st Mass.	17		1926 Jan 9	KS, 46th, 1927
Lunt, A.B.		B, 8th Vt.	176		1928 Dec 28	KS, 49th, 1930
Lunt, A.M.		H, 67th Ill. (died of heart trouble)	63		1919 May 22	NE, 44th, 1920
Lupher, A.D.		G, 63rd Penn.	129		1922 May 26	KS, 42nd, 1923
Lurton, Henry A.		K, 45th Iowa	112		1908 Dec 10	NE, 33rd, 1909
Lusader, Isaac	Sergt.	B, 9th Ind. Inf.	116	53	1894 Dec 16	IA, 21st, 1895
Luse, C.I.	Pvt.	B, 2nd Iowa Inf.	255	60	1896 Nov 4	IA, 23rd, 1897
Luse, Marvin R.	1st Lieut.	B, 14th Iowa Inf.	12	60	1892 Jul 7	IA, 19th, 1893
Lushbaugh, Jeromiah		114th Ind. Inf.	68	82	1926 Feb 1	NE, 50th, 1926

*See Appendix A, B or C for roster of post names and locations.
†See Introduction for note regarding recording of death date.

Name	Rank	Company, Regiment or Ship	Post*	Age	Death Date†	Journal
Lusher, H.H.	Sergt.	D, 4th Penn. Cav.	192		1901-1902	IA, 28th, 1902
Lusk, Absalom		K, 124th Ill.	69		1926 Nov 19	NE, 51st, 1927
Lusk, George H.		A, 122nd N.Y.	380		1902 Apr 23	KS, 22nd, 1903
Lusk, John		1st Wis. Hvy. Art.	[18?]		1918 Dec 1	KS, 38th, 1919
Lust, William	Pvt.	H, 17th — Inf.	84	72	1897 May 19	IA, 24th, 1898
Lutgen, Sidney B., Dr.		F, 77th Ohio	104		1927 Feb 14	NE, 52nd, 1928
Lutham, Geo. C.			356		1911	IA, 38th, 1912
Luther, Allen	Pvt.	B, 45th Iowa Inf.	436		1929 Jan 4	IA, 55th, 1929
Luther, Daniel	Pvt.	I, 6th N.Y. Hvy. Art.	173	72	1888[1887?] Apr 29	IA, 14th, 1888
Luther, Frank		E, 50th Ind.	142		1908 Nov	KS, 28th, 1909
Luther, H.G.	Pvt.	C, 23rd Wis. Inf.	3		1915 Apr 16	IA, 42nd, 1916
Lutman, Daniel W.	Corp.	E, 208th —	211		1928 May 9	IA, 55th, 1929
Lutsy, J.C.		C, 54th Penn. Inf. (died of paralysis)	78	74	1918 Mar 27	NE, 43rd, 1919
Lutter, George	Pvt.	F, 4th U.S. Art.	7		1901 Dec 5	IA, 28th, 1902
Luty, C.O.		B, 61st Penn.	87		1923 Feb 25	KS, 43rd, 1924
Lutz, Chas. B.	Pvt.	F, 40th Iowa Inf.	359		1911 Apr 1	IA, 38th, 1912
Lutz, George	Pvt.	E, 2nd Mich. Inf.	26	84	1932 Apr 20	IA, 59th, 1933
Lutz, Jacob	Pvt.	66th Ohio Inf.	12		1913 Feb 15	IA, 40th, 1914
Lutz, W.H.		A, 12th Ill.	20		1922 Mar 2	KS, 42nd, 1923
Lux, J.H.		F, 11th N.Y. Inf.	5		4th quarter 1884	IA, 11th, 1885
Lyas, Olven	Pvt.	G, 35th Iowa Inf.	250	67	1893 Dec 5	IA, 20th, 1894
Lydeck, Dallas		died of fever	118		1886	NE, 11th, 1887
Lydic, J.R.		K, 84th Penn.	1		1914 Oct 6	KS, 34th, 1915
Lydick, T.B.			130		1928 Dec 20	KS, 48th, 1929
Lydig, Wm.		F, 142nd Penn. Inf.	216		1886	KS, 6th, 1887
Lyford, Chas.		E, 16th Mich.	380		1898 Jun 5	KS, 18th, 1899
Lyle, W.M.	Pvt.	I, 46th Iowa	110		1924 Feb 24	IA, 51st, 1925
Lyle, Wm.	Pvt.	B, 93rd N.Y.	22		1911 Dec 28	IA, 38th, 1912
Lyles, J.H.		F, 49th Ill.	64		1919 Jun 5	KS, 39th, 1920
Lyman, A.W.			311		1917 Apr 9	KS, 37th, 1918
Lyman, Alford		F, 25th Ill.	130		1911 Dec 29	KS, 31st, 1912
Lyman, Chas. W.		C, 1st Ohio Art. (died of paralysis)	214	60	1906 Aug 31	NE, 31st, 1907
Lyman, G.W.	Pvt.	I, 105th Ohio Inf.	30		1918 Mar 15	IA, 45th, 1919
Lyman, Geo. Z.	Pvt.	A, 142nd N.Y. Inf.	465		1911 Sep 21	IA, 38th, 1912
Lyman, Homer		D, 10th Vt.	100		1908 Dec 19	KS, 28th, 1909
Lyman, J.M.		3rd U.S.A.[U.S. Art.?]	13	78	1916 Nov 10	NE, 41st, 1917
Lyman, J.P.	Corp.	B, 46th Iowa Inf.	64		1923	IA, 50th, 1924
Lyman, S.B.	Sergt.	A, 65th Ill. Inf.	357	60	1894 May 18	IA, 21st, 1895
Lyman, Sereno	Pvt.	C, 29th Iowa Inf.	358	52	1893 May 27	IA, 20th, 1894
Lyman, T.W.		E, 9th Penn. Cav. (died of abscess of kidneys)	133	67	1911 Jul 3	NE, 37th, 1913
Lymer, R.H.	Pvt.	G, 110th Penn.	11		1905 Jan 12	IA, 32nd, 1906
Lynch, Clark	Pvt.	E, 1st Iowa Cav.	20		1913 Dec 13	IA, 40th, 1914
Lynch, Con		C, 5th Ohio Cav.	89		1929 Sep 15	KS, 49th, 1930
Lynch, George C.		I, 10th Ind. (not a member of the G.A.R.)	129		1913 Feb 28	KS, 32nd, 1913
Lynch, J.	Pvt.	H, 55th Ill. Inf.	12		1924 Apr 17	IA, 51st, 1925
Lynch, Mike	Pvt.	K, 148th Ill. Inf.	452		1922 Aug 23	IA, 49th, 1923
Lynch, P.A.	Pvt.	F, 33rd Iowa Inf.	19		1919 May 4	IA, 46th, 1920
Lynch, Pat	Pvt.	A, 34th Ill. Inf.	24		1910	IA, 37th, 1911
Lynch, Patrick	Pvt.	36th Ill. Inf.	24		1918 Jul 15	IA, 45th, 1919
Lynch, R.B.	Capt.	E & F, 6th & 42nd Ohio Inf.	36		1918 May 22	KS, 38th, 1919
Lynch, T.W.		G, 18th Ohio	35		1898 May 1	KS, 18th, 1899
Lynch, W.J.	Pvt.	C, 13th Ill. Inf.	78		1916 Nov 14	IA, 43rd, 1917
Lynch, Wm.	Pvt.	B, 7th Minn. Inf.	365		1908 Feb 19	IA, 35th, 1909
Lynch, Wm.		Iowa Cav.	434		1922 Apr 27	IA, 49th, 1923
Lynde, Edward	Col.	9th Kans.	117		1897 Mar 27	KS, 17th, 1898
Lynde, Edwin	Pvt.	H, 1st U.S.S.S.N.Y.[1st U.S. Sharpshooters]	418		1903 May 16	IA, 30th, 1904
Lynes, Henry B.		A, 3rd Iowa Cav.	25		1924 Jan 16	KS, 44th, 1925
Lynn, Ebeneezer		E, 19th Iowa	145		1906 Jan 12	KS, 26th, 1907
Lynn, H.C.	Pvt.	I, 1st Iowa Cav.	167		1915 Feb 14	IA, 42nd, 1916
Lynn, H.H.		H, 7th Kans. Cav.	167		1922 Feb 16	KS, 42nd, 1923

Name	Rank	Company, Regiment or Ship	Post*	Age	Death Date†	Journal
Lynn, J.N.		Ind.	125		1913 Mar 17	KS, 33rd, 1914
Lynn, R.B.	Pvt.	D, 11th Iowa Inf.	40		1906	IA, 33rd, 1907
Lyon, A.M.	Pvt.	G, 8th Iowa Inf.	233		1917 Dec 2	IA, 44th, 1918
Lyon, Amos A.			65		1886	NE, 11th, 1887
Lyon, Andrew J.	Capt.		45		1922 May 11	IA, 49th, 1923
Lyon, Augustus E.	Pvt.	E, 37th Iowa Inf.	69	45	1887 Mar 18	IA, 13th, 1887
Lyon, C.H.	Pvt.	A, 1st Iowa Cav.	36		1900 Jun 24	IA, 27th, 1901
Lyon, Chas.		H, 17th Ill. Cav.	3		1929 Jun 16	NE, 54th, 1930
Lyon, Dennis		E, 4th Ind. Cav. (died of abscess)	86	64	1895 Oct 23	NE, 20th, 1896
Lyon, Elishale		D, 23rd Iowa	18		1910 Dec 30	KS, 30th, 1911
Lyon, Francis A.		11th Mo. Inf. 13th Mo. Cav. (was sick less than 24 hours)	32		1910 Dec 16	KS, 30th, 1911
Lyon, George W.	Corp. Pvt.	E, 11th Ill. Cav. A, 11th Ill. Inf.	So. Dak.	100	1940 Feb 2	IA, 66th, 1940
Lyon, H.C.	Pvt.	I, 3rd Ill.	66		1926 Jan 14	IA, 53rd, 1927
Lyon, Isaac B.	Pvt.	G, 11th Mich. Inf.	370	56	1897 Jun 9	IA, 24th, 1898
Lyon, J.B.	Pvt.	B, 9th Iowa Cav.	233	48	1896 Jun 20	IA, 23rd, 1897
Lyon, J.F.		I, 124th Ill. Inf.	36		1900 Feb 12	KS, 21st, 1902
Lyon, J.H.		E, 36th Iowa Inf.	223		1926 Jun 25	NE, 51st, 1927
Lyon, J.W.	Pvt.	F, 152nd Ohio	44		1907 Mar	IA, 34th, 1908
Lyon, James	Pvt.	C, 123rd Ohio Inf.	26		1919 Dec 18	IA, 46th, 1920
Lyon, Justus H.		G, 44th Wis. Inf.	1		1938 Aug 30	NE, 63rd, 1939
Lyon, M.W.	Pvt.	A, 18th U.S. Inf.	403		1911 Jun 28	IA, 38th, 1912
Lyon, O.H.	Capt.	3rd Iowa Battery	377		1904 Jun 18	IA, 31st, 1905
Lyon, S.		E, 45th N.Y.	294		1888	KS, 8th, 1889
Lyon, S.A.	Pvt.	A, 112th N.Y. Inf.	158	43	1890 Oct 23	IA, 17th, 1891
Lyon, T.J.	Corp.	E, 13th Wis. Inf.	150		1916 Jan 26	IA, 43rd, 1917
Lyon, Thomas J.	Corp.	E, 13th Wis. Inf.	150		1915 Jan 26	IA, 42nd, 1916
Lyon, Wm.	Pvt.	M, 4th Penn.	5		1909 May 14	IA, 36th, 1910
Lyons, A.P.	Pvt.	H, 18th Iowa Inf.	452		1927 May 10	IA, 54th, 1928
Lyons, E.P.			431		1913 Aug 13	IA, 40th, 1914
Lyons, Geo.	Pvt.	I, 17th Iowa Inf.	254		1910 Apr 10	IA, 37th, 1911
Lyons, H.H.		E, 33rd Ind. Inf.	32		1917 Nov 26	KS, 37th, 1918
Lyons, I.W.		22nd Ohio Bat.	47		1913 Apr 10	KS, 33rd, 1914
Lyons, J.T.		E, 1st Vt. Cav.	7	81	1925 Dec 20	NE, 50th, 1926
Lyons, James		E, 18th Penn.	147		1928 Apr 20	KS, 48th, 1929
Lyons, Jason		I, 73rd Ill.	13	80	1914 Apr 17	NE, 39th, 1915
Lyons, M.D.			322		1920 Jul 28	KS, 40th, 1921
Lyons, Marion		F, 2nd Kans.	66		1924 Jul 3	KS, 44th, 1925
Lyons, Sanderson	Pvt.	G, 12th Ill. Cav.	114	61	1888 Apr	IA, 15th, 1889
Lyons, Timothy	Pvt.	C, 3rd Tenn. Inf.	231		1916 Jan 25	IA, 43rd, 1917
Lyons, W.D.		D, 8th Ill.	322		1921 May 10	KS, 41st, 1922
Lyons, William	Pvt.	F, 1st Neb. Inf.	57	43	1886 Nov 18	IA, 13th, 1887
Lyons, Wm. T.		A, 18th Wis. (died of heart failure)	110	72	1911 Jun 20	NE, 36th, 1912
Lysander, Asa		Ohio (died of general debility)	151	78	1910 Jul 10	NE, 35th, 1911
Lyster, W.A.		H, 3rd Iowa	[4?]		1920 Jun 13	KS, 40th, 1921
Lytle, Andrew		H, 22nd Wis.	66		1911 Mar 17	KS, 31st, 1912
Lytle, G.W.		E, 11th Mo.	51		1916 Oct 4	KS, 36th, 1917
Lytle, J.M.	Pvt.	C, 19th Iowa Inf.	108		1931 Oct 18	IA, 58th, 1932
Lytle, John G.		D, 150th Ind.	244		1917 May 8	KS, 37th, 1918
Lyttle, Samuel	Sergt.	F, 11th Iowa Inf.	8		1913 Nov 8	IA, 40th, 1914
M'Lin, David		B, 26th Ind.	64		1920 Mar 10	KS, 40th, 1921
Maberry, H.M.			32		1911 Sep 29	KS, 31st, 1912
Maberry, James		M, 1st Mo.	32		1896 May 22	KS, 16th, 1897
Mabon, John P.		A, 33rd Wis. Inf.	136		1923 Oct 9	NE, 48th, 1924
Macauley, Wm.		K, 12th Ill.	22		1919 Nov 18	KS, 39th, 1920
Mace, H.G.		D, 8th Iowa Cav.	75		1908 Jan 31	KS, 28th, 1909
Mace, John			67		1914 Dec 11	IA, 41st, 1915
Mach, J.P.		A, 2nd Ill. Cav.	130		1901 Apr 29	KS, 21st, 1902
Machefky, Fred		A, 2nd Mich. Inf.	6		1921 Nov 7	KS, 41st, 1922

*See Appendix A, B or C for roster of post names and locations.
†See Introduction for note regarding recording of death date.

Name	Rank	Company, Regiment or Ship	Post*	Age	Death Date†	Journal
Macis, John		E, 6th Ohio Cav. (died at National Military Home; buried at National Military Home Cemetery)	380		1894 May 28	KS, 14th, 1895
Mack, Daniel		A, D, 45th Penn. Inf. (died of old age)	182	83	1919 Aug 18	NE, 44th, 1920
Mack, Geo.		C, 140th N.Y. Inf.	432		1891 Jul 21	KS, 11th, 1892
Mack, Green		K, 12th U.S. Col. Inf.	236		1891 Jan 25	KS, 11th, 1892
Mack, H.C.	Pvt.	H, 18th Ill. Inf.	94	89	1931 Jan 6	IA, 58th, 1932
Mack, H.O.	Sergt.	46th Ohio Inf.	133	78	1897 Mar 14	IA, 24th, 1898
Mack, Henry		F, 100th Ind. Inf. (died of consumption)	156	58	1895 Jan 24	NE, 20th, 1896
Mack, Ledyard P.		D, 50th Penn.	82		1890	KS, 10th, 1891
Mack, M.H.	Pvt.	K, 23rd Iowa Inf.	88		1911 Feb 27	IA, 38th, 1912
Mack, R.P.	Corp.	A, 32nd Iowa Inf.	452		1922 Mar 21	IA, 49th, 1923
Mack, W.E.	Pvt.	B, 64th Ohio Inf.	158		1900 Dec 1	IA, 27th, 1901
Mack, Warren		G, 34th N.Y. Inf. H, 152nd N.Y. Inf. (died of old age)	133	79	1901 Dec	NE, 26th, 1902
Mack, William		I, 32nd Ohio Inf.	262		1891 Dec 20	KS, 11th, 1892
Mackay, Thos. J.		F, 42nd Mass. Inf.	110	76	1920 Mar 29	NE, 45th, 1921
Mackenroth, C.J.		C, 50th N.Y.	52		1893 Oct 30	KS, 13th, 1894
Mackenzie, Chas.	Adjt.	9th Iowa Inf.	12		1908 Feb 14	IA, 35th, 1909
MacKenzie, Geo.		D, 16th N.H.	47		1898 Sep 28	KS, 18th, 1899
Mackey, Ezra		F, 122nd Ill. Inf. (died at Belleville; buried at Belleville Cemetery)	44		1894 Aug 11	KS, 14th, 1895
Mackey, H.D.	Pvt.	A, 116th Ill. Inf.	255		1904 Jun 22	IA, 31st, 1905
Mackey, Hiram	Sergt.	54th Ind.	440		1922 Aug 10	IA, 49th, 1923
Mackey, J.G.			32		1883	KS, 3rd, 1884
Mackey, James		died of sickness	190		1920	NE, 45th, 1921
Mackey, Jno. T.	Lieut.	16th U.S. Inf.	2	52	1888 May 25	IA, 15th, 1889
Mackey, Jno. W.		E, 64th Ohio Inf.	85		1934 Mar 23	KS, 54th, 1935
Mackey, John		A, 3rd Cal. Cav. (died at Monticello; buried at Monticello)	318		1894 Sep 15	KS, 14th, 1895
Mackey, M.	Pvt.	H, 155th Ill. Inf.	192		1930 Sep 8	IA, 57th, 1931
Mackey, Patrick		K, 43rd N.Y.	93		1909 Nov 22	KS, 29th, 1910
Mackey, S.E.		C, 6th Ohio	68		1904 Feb 17	KS, 24th, 1905
Mackey, Wm. O.	Pvt.	C, 3rd Iowa Cav.	2	47	1892 Dec 11	IA, 19th, 1893
Macklin, James E.	Brig. Gen.	U.S.A., retired	6		1925 Dec 17	KS, 45th, 1926
Macklin, Wm.	Pvt.	C, 10th Ill. Inf.	254	55	1895 May 26	IA, 22nd, 1896
Mackrill, S.R.	Pvt.	K, 24th Iowa Inf.	130	59	1897 Jan 30	IA, 23rd, 1897
Maclary, C.F.		F, 6th Del.	129		1913 Sep 11	KS, 33rd, 1914
MacMurray, Jonathan		G, 46th Ill. Inf.	354		1914 Sep 12	KS, 34th, 1915
Macomber, A.	Pvt.	I, 4th Iowa Cav.	55		1915 Nov 20	IA, 42nd, 1916
Macomber, H.W.	Sergt.	D, 2nd Maine Inf.	44		1919 Sep	IA, 46th, 1920
Macy, Allen	Pvt.	D, 45th Iowa	12		1922 Mar 6	IA, 49th, 1923
Macy, Edward	Musician	39th Ohio Inf.	200		1886	KS, 6th, 1887
Macy, Jonathan	Pvt.	D, 132nd Ohio Inf.	1		1925 Aug 15	IA, 52nd, 1926
Macy, Joseph D.		I, 15th Ind.	25		1923 Jan 25	KS, 43rd, 1924
Madden, Henry	Pvt.	A, 11th Iowa Inf.	231		1900-1901	IA, 27th, 1901
Madden, Robert		K, —	318	76	1919 Dec 13	NE, 44th, 1920
Madden, Spencer			10		1927 Apr 11	KS, 47th, 1928
Madden, Wm. L.		H, 50th Mo.	354	84	1921 Dec 6	NE, 46th, 1922
Maddock, J.R.		A, 11th Kans. Mil.	55		1918 Feb 26	KS, 38th, 1919
Maddock, Jacob R.		E, 7th Iowa Cav. (died of heart failure)	55	72	1909 Jan 10	NE, 34th, 1910
Maddox, D.E.		H, 70th Ohio	117		1931 Apr 14	KS, 51st, 1932
Maddox, D.E.		H, 70th Ohio	117		1931 Apr 14	KS, 52nd, 1933
Maddox, John Harvey		G, 44th Mo.	57		1930 Jun 1	KS, 50th, 1931
Maddox, Luther		G, 151st Ill.	265		1932 Sep 2	NE, 57th, 1933
Maddox, Richard		A, 19th U.S.C.	18		1921 Aug 10	KS, 41st, 1922
Maddox, Richard P.		B, 44th Mo.	25	73	1916 Dec 3	NE, 41st, 1917
Maddox, W.C.	Pvt.	7th Ill.	1		1915 Oct 28	KS, 35th, 1916
Maddy, John		G, 6th Mo. S.G.	76		1929	KS, 49th, 1930
Madison, Barton W.		E, 20th Iowa	65		1918 Jun 17	KS, 38th, 1919
Madison, Caleb C.		E, 11th Iowa Inf. (died of cancer of stomach)	22	73	1919 Apr 7	NE, 44th, 1920
Madison, Edgar	Pvt.	K, 75th Ill. Inf.	66		1917 Dec 1	IA, 44th, 1918

Name	Rank	Company, Regiment or Ship	Post*	Age	Death Date†	Journal
Madison, Ira		F, 39th Ind.	66		1918 Feb 8	KS, 38th, 1919
Madison, James H.	Pvt.	I, 152nd Wis. Inf.	298		1912 Oct 16	IA, 39th, 1913
Madison, Jno. R.	Capt.	I, 19th Ill. Inf.	190	74	1888 Sep 21	IA, 15th, 1889
Madison, John R.		B, 50th Ky.	1		1927 Feb 18	KS, 47th, 1928
Madison, Luther, see Mattison, Luther						
Mador, James E.		D, 52nd Ky.	81		1915 Mar 31	KS, 35th, 1916
Maffit, A.W.	Pvt.	G, 32nd Iowa Inf.	66		1911 Oct 13	IA, 38th, 1912
Maffitt, Leroy A.	Pvt.	C, 30th Ind. Inf.	12		1912 Oct 25	IA, 39th, 1913
Magar, H.S.			294		1921 Apr 24	KS, 41st, 1922
Magee, A.H.		dropped dead	318		1923 Dec 1	NE, 48th, 1924
Magee, Enock	Pvt.	E, 149th N.Y. Inf.	235		1906	IA, 33rd, 1907
Magee, George	Pvt.	A, 9th N.Y. Cav.	88		1922 Mar 17	IA, 49th, 1923
Magee, Hiram		B, 88th Ohio	25	76	1915 Sep 7	NE, 40th, 1916
Magee, John S.	Pvt.	B, 8th Ill. Inf.	5		1898 Dec 31	IA, 25th, 1899
Magee, Lafayette		D, 147th N.Y.	25		1921 Mar 26	KS, 41st, 1922
Magee, Matthew		E, 46th Ill. Inf.	327		1st quarter 1885	IA, 11th, 1885
Magee, Robt.	Pvt.	H, 6th Iowa Cav.	16		1905 Mar 15	IA, 32nd, 1906
Magher, Mike	Pvt.	B, 4th Ill. Cav.	83		1916 Aug 12	IA, 43rd, 1917
Magill, W.H.		A, 21st N.Y.	171		1931	NE, 56th, 1932
Magmus, Samuel	Pvt.	E, 38th Iowa Inf.	216		1908 Feb 10	IA, 35th, 1909
Magons, Fred.	Pvt.	F, 8th Iowa	167	60	1898 Dec 17	IA, 25th, 1899
Magoon, Chas.	Pvt.	C, 74th Ill. Inf.	42		1920 Jan 1	IA, 47th, 1921
Magruder, Asel D.		E, 18th Ohio	25		1920 Aug 15	KS, 40th, 1921
Magruder, John G.		G, 36th Ohio Inf.	25		1917 Jun 1	KS, 37th, 1918
Maguire, Frank		C, 3rd Mich.	17		1922 May 13	KS, 42nd, 1923
Maguire, L.F.		H, 16th N.Y. Inf. (died of old wound)	262	59	1901 Mar	NE, 26th, 1902
Maguire, Michael		H, 39th N.Y.	380		1912 Mar 24	KS, 32nd, 1913
Mahaffa, John		9th Ind. Legion	147		1916 Oct 19	KS, 36th, 1917
Mahaffey, J.M.		C, 1st Batt. Penn. Lt. Art.	62		1933 Nov 9	NE, 58th, 1934
Mahaffey, J.N.W.		D, 32nd Iowa Inf. (died of stomach trouble)	63	75	1907 Sep 1	NE, 32nd, 1908
Mahaffey, S.		6th Iowa	129		1923 Mar 11	KS, 43rd, 1924
Mahaffy, James	Pvt.	C, 91st Ill. Inf.	57		1909 Sep 28	IA, 36th, 1910
Maham, Daniel P.		I, 9th Mo. State Militia	57		1923 Jul 27	KS, 43rd, 1924
Mahan, —			156		1884	KS, 4th, 1885
Mahan, James Curtis	Corp.	C, 59th Ind. (see also Appendix D)	25	95	1935 May 28	NE, 60th, 1936
Mahan, Michael		C, 113th Ill. (died of kidney trouble)	130	82	1920 Feb 22	NE, 45th, 1921
Mahana, Jas. S.	Sergt.	C, 9th Ohio Cav.	8		1903 Feb 28	IA, 30th, 1904
Mahanna, Thomas		D, 8th N.H. Inf.	1		1899 Oct 8	KS, 19th, 1900
Mahar, C.W.	Pvt.	Quartermaster Dept., Ill. Inf.	236		1923	IA, 50th, 1924
Mahar, Edward		H, 67th Ill.	64		1922 Jul 3	KS, 42nd, 1923
Maher, David	Pvt.	F, 26th Iowa Inf.	92	57	1895 Apr 12	IA, 22nd, 1896
Maher, Patrick		A, 5th Mich. Inf. (died of bowel complaint)	187	78	1902 Oct	NE, 27th, 1903
Mahnke, Fred	Pvt.	G, 32nd Wis.	22		1903 Dec 1	IA, 30th, 1904
Mahoffey, Joseph	Pvt.	I, 50th Ill. Inf.	286		1911	IA, 38th, 1912
Maholm, I.H.		E, 132nd Ind. Inf. (died of old age)	354	89	1925 Aug	NE, 50th, 1926
Mahon, M.			458		1896	KS, 16th, 1897
Mahon, T.G.		A, 66th Ind.	98		1888	KS, 8th, 1889
Mahon, William	Pvt.	F, 13th Ill. Cav.	156		1916 Feb 5	IA, 43rd, 1917
Mahoney, Clement		E, 84th Ind.	14		1920 Oct 5	KS, 40th, 1921
Mahoney, Daniel, see Muhoney, Daniel						
Mahoney, J.W.		3rd Iowa Battery	151		1909 Feb 11	IA, 35th, 1909
Mahoney, Morgan		E, 84th Ind.	500		1917 Sep 10	KS, 37th, 1918
Mahoney, Wm.	Pvt.	G, 99th Penn. Inf.	110		1906 Aug 4	IA, 33rd, 1907
Mahood, J.C.		I, 191st Penn.	59		1919 Jun 30	KS, 39th, 1920
Mahordy, Thomas J.		E, 44th N.Y. Inf. (died of brain disease)	113		1894 Apr 7	NE, 19th, 1895
Mahr, J.M.	Steward	30th Ill.	156		1906 Jun 26	KS, 26th, 1907
Maier, Geo.	Pvt.	C, 19th Iowa Inf.	8	46	1888 Aug 9	IA, 15th, 1889
Mailander, Geo.		G, 58th Ill. Inf.	90	71	1909 Jun 27	NE, 34th, 1910
Main, Joseph	Pvt.	A, 37th Ind. Inf.	96	53	1893 Feb 16	IA, 19th, 1893

Name	Rank	Company, Regiment or Ship	Post*	Age	Death Date†	Journal
Main, L.J.			114		1922	NE, 47th, 1923
Main, Louis A.	Corp.	C, 27th Iowa Inf.	235		1924 Nov 29	IA, 51st, 1925
Maine, Frank W.	Sergt.	C, 12th Iowa Inf.	259		1905 Mar 15	IA, 31st, 1905
Maine, John W.	Pvt.	G, 46th Iowa Inf.	398	73	1894 Sep 30	IA, 21st, 1895
Maine, Jos. U.		G, 13th U.S. Inf.	25		1894 Oct 16	NE, 19th, 1895
Maitland, Thomas F.			85		1920 Nov 25	KS, 40th, 1921
Major, Robt.		F, 5th Ohio Cav.	110	65	1902 Sep	NE, 27th, 1903
Majors, E.W.		C, 1st Iowa Cav.	49		1918 May 10	KS, 38th, 1919
Majors, F.		F, 121st Ohio Inf.	83		1929 May 1	KS, 49th, 1930
Majors, Thomas J.	Col.	1st Neb. Cav. (see also Appendix D)	302		1932 Jul 11 or 12	NE, 57th, 1933
Majors, Wilson E.	Lieut.	C, 1st Neb. Cav. (see also Appendix D)	302		1931 Sep 8	NE, 56th, 1932
Makeany, W.H.		C, 31st Wis.	142		1908 Aug	KS, 28th, 1909
Makemeyer, Henry		H, Ill.	25		1935 Aug 15	KS, 55th, 1936
Makepeace, D.C.	Pvt.	G, 44th Ill. Inf.	3	53	1890 May 7	IA, 17th, 1891
Makepense, E.A.		B, 130th Ind.	244		1923 Nov 23	KS, 43rd, 1924
Makepiece, G.W.			94		1904-1905	IA, 31st, 1905
Maker, Christian		C, 43rd Wis. Inf.	78	90	1936 Apr 22	IA, 63rd, 1937
Maker, Christian		C, 43rd Wis. Inf.	78	90	1936 Apr 22	IA, 63rd, 1937
Maker, Christian		C, 43rd Wis. Inf.	78	90	1936 Apr 22	IA, 62nd, 1936
Makins, Joseph		C, 74th Ill.	39		1911 Nov 6	KS, 31st, 1912
MaKinster, Wm.	Pvt.	A, 15th Iowa	68		1924 Nov 14	IA, 51st, 1925
Malcom, Albertis	Pvt.	D, 112th Ill. Inf.	127		1915 Feb 28	IA, 42nd, 1916
Malenburg, John	Corp.	E, 10th Ill.	57		1924 Feb 28	IA, 51st, 1925
Malia, John O.	Pvt.	E, 28th Iowa Inf.	8		1901 Mar 3	IA, 28th, 1902
Malian, James		I, 7th Kans.	293		1921 Jan 8	KS, 41st, 1922
Malin, W.G.	Sergt.	E, 15th Ohio	24		1922 Apr 25	IA, 49th, 1923
Mall, Joseph		B, 28th Iowa	88		1922 Oct 2	KS, 42nd, 1923
Mall, Sam			88		1929	KS, 49th, 1930
Mallack, A.J.		G, 9th N.Y.	17		1918 Feb 13	KS, 38th, 1919
Mallahan, A.J.			235		1911 Mar 3	IA, 38th, 1912
Mallard, Zacharias		C, 7th Kans. Cav.	332		1911 Aug 3	KS, 31st, 1912
Mallie, Fred			311		1901	NE, 26th, 1902
Mallison, Jos.		E, 105th N.Y.	7		1927 Mar 5	NE, 52nd, 1928
Mallock, P.		K, 8th N.Y. Cav.	271		1909	IA, 36th, 1910
Mallory, D.C.	Pvt.	K, 46th Ill. Inf.	81		1913 Mar 12	IA, 40th, 1914
Mallory, Russell H.		A, 47th & 95th Ill.	25		1921 Feb 4	NE, 46th, 1922
Mallory, Saml. W.	Pvt.	F, 19th Iowa Inf.	153	45	1890 Feb 3	IA, 16th, 1890
Mallory, W.L.	Pvt.	L, 1st Iowa Cav.	389		1910 Sep 29	IA, 37th, 1911
Mallow, J.W.	Pvt.	F, 11th Wis. Inf.	66	53	1895 Mar 20	IA, 22nd, 1896
Mallown, Wm. D.	Hosp. Stew.	I, 1st Iowa Cav.	424	78	1899 Sep 8	IA, 26th, 1900
Malloy, Stephen	Sergt.	C, 9th U.S. Inf. (remained in service till death; died of apoplexy)	2	52	1884 Dec 24	NE, 9th, 1885
Malone, Andrew J.		L, 1st Ohio	25		1916 Nov 7	KS, 36th, 1917
Malone, John		I, 66th Ohio Inf.	40	89	1935 Jun 9	IA, 62nd, 1936
Malone, John R.		D, 1st Ohio Hvy. Art.	101		1902 Dec 5	KS, 22nd, 1903
Malone, John W.		9th Ill. Cav.	17		1908	IA, 35th, 1909
Malone, Joseph H.		D, 20th Ill. Inf. (died of old age)	112	81	1915 Nov 6	NE, 40th, 1916
Malone, K.	Pvt.	G, 4th Iowa Cav.	83		1907 Mar 19	IA, 34th, 1908
Malone, S.S.		K, 10th West Va. Inf. (cause of death: kidney)	52	58	1903 May 14	NE, 28th, 1904
Maloney, J.J.	Artificer	9th Wis. Inf.	155		1910 Apr 13	IA, 37th, 1911
Maloney, John	Pvt.	F, 13th Iowa Inf.	193	60	1891 Feb 14	IA, 17th, 1891
Maloney, Mark B.		Maine	18		1923 Dec 13	KS, 43rd, 1924
Malony, Michael	Pvt.	G, 15th Ill. Inf.	137		1913 Dec 30	IA, 40th, 1914
Malony, Samuel	Pvt.	I, 102nd Ohio Inf.	235		1910 Feb 10	IA, 37th, 1911
Malott, Iradell		L, 9th Ohio Cav. (died of cancer of stomach)	55	59	1907 Jun 29	NE, 32nd, 1908
Maltby, C.A.	Pvt.	G, 105th Ill. Inf.	324		1912 Oct 5	IA, 39th, 1913
Maltby, C.O.	Pvt.	F, 46th N.Y. Inf.	168		1915 Aug 8	IA, 42nd, 1916
Maltby, D.		I, 27th N.Y.	29		1921 Jan 25	IA, 48th, 1922
Maltby, M.H.		D, 121st N.Y. Inf.	411		1899 Dec 22	KS, 19th, 1900
Malvin, John			190		1908 Feb 7	IA, 35th, 1909

See Appendix A, B or C for roster of post names and locations.
†*See Introduction for note regarding recording of death date.*

Name	Rank	Company, Regiment or Ship	Post*	Age	Death Date†	Journal
Manahan, Wm.		K, 148th N.Y.	120		1928 May 6	NE, 53rd, 1929
Manbeck, Elijah	Pvt.	E, 39th Iowa Inf.	7		1926 Feb 26	IA, 53rd, 1927
Manbeck, Henry	Pvt.	B, 39th Iowa Inf.	7		1911 Nov 4	IA, 38th, 1912
Manbeck, Isiah			7		1918 Jul 19	IA, 45th, 1919
Mance, T.J.		F & K, 59th Ohio	53		1912 Dec 27	KS, 32nd, 1913
Manchester, J.C.			69		1903-1904	IA, 30th, 1904
Manchester, John R.		A, 97th N.Y.	7		1931 Jul 8	NE, 56th, 1932
Manchester, W.V.	Pvt.	D, 32nd Iowa Inf.	375		1910 Sep 25	IA, 37th, 1911
Manderson, Charles F.			110		1911	NE, 36th, 1912
Manderson, Chas. F.		19th Ohio (died of heart failure)	110	73	1911 Oct 28	NE, 36th, 1912
Mandeville, B.	Pvt.	A, 16th Wis. Inf.	59		1925 Jun 6	IA, 52nd, 1926
Mandeville, C.R.		G, 153rd Ill.	46		1929 Nov 8	KS, 49th, 1930
Manen, S.P.	Sergt.	A, 42nd Ill. Inf.	211		1897 Jul 29	IA, 24th, 1898
Manerier, Phillip	Pvt.	K, 115th Ill. Inf.	7		1916 Jun 2	IA, 43rd, 1917
Manerty, U.H.		22nd Inf.	68		1887 Sep 29	KS, 7th, 1888
Manger, J.H.	Adjt.	1st H.A.A.V.M.N.Y.	242		1892 Oct 29	KS, 12th, 1893
Mangold, John			8		1916 Jul 8	NE, 41st, 1917
Mangus, D.	Wagoner	I, 22nd Iowa Inf.	321		1913 Jan 5	IA, 40th, 1914
Manker, Lewis		B, 2nd Ind.	1		1911 Feb 14	KS, 31st, 1912
Mankle, Jacob, see Monkel, Jacob						
Manley, B.H.	Pvt.	B, 2nd Tenn. Art.	173		1925 Oct 21	IA, 52nd, 1926
Manley, E.R.		C, 44th Ill. Inf. (died of paralysis)	10	73	1896 Sep 30	NE, 21st, 1897
Manley, R.C.		E, 1st Ohio Inf. (died of paralysis)	25	58	1902 Jun	NE, 27th, 1903
Manlove, C.E.	Pvt.	E, 1st Ill. Art.	1		1917 Nov 25	IA, 44th, 1918
Manly, James			115		1914	IA, 41st, 1915
Manly, W.V.N.		H, 7th Wis. Inf.	175		1916 May 18	KS, 36th, 1917
Mann, A.J.	Pvt.	A, 12th Iowa Inf.	141		1915 Oct 10	IA, 42nd, 1916
Mann, A.L.	1 E. Ens.	*Lexington* (ship)	78		1899 Feb 15	IA, 26th, 1900
Mann, A.W.		C, 29th Ohio Inf.	186		1890 May 8	KS, 11th, 1892
Mann, Alfred		C, 116th Ohio	147		1928 Sep 28	KS, 48th, 1929
Mann, Chapman		H, 34th Ill. Inf.	127		1909 Aug 2	KS, 29th, 1910
Mann, Charles		A, 53rd Ill.	123		1896	KS, 16th, 1897
Mann, G.W.		G, 181st Ohio (died of long sickness)	32	88	1911 Jan 5	NE, 36th, 1912
Mann, H.C.		B, 191st Ohio	289		1924 Jul 17	KS, 44th, 1925
Mann, J.M.	1st Lieut.	63rd U.S.C.	154		1899	NE, 24th, 1900
Mann, James	Pvt.	C, 2nd Iowa Cav.	298		1911 Feb 21	IA, 38th, 1912
Mann, John		G, 12th Kans. Inf.	145		1921 Feb 15	KS, 41st, 1922
Mann, Johnathan B.	Pvt.	C, 14th Wis. Inf.	240		1904 Apr	IA, 31st, 1905
Mann, Josef H.		C, 50th Ohio	1		1917 Mar 21	KS, 37th, 1918
Mann, Marrion		D, 144th Ill.	32		1923 Oct 6	KS, 43rd, 1924
Mann, Samuel B.		died of apoplexy	22	73	1914 May 25	NE, 39th, 1915
Mannahan, D.G.	Corp.	G, 5th Iowa	244		1921 Feb 5	IA, 48th, 1922
Mannder, Samuel H.			5		1909	KS, 29th, 1910
Manners, J.		C, 11th Iowa Inf. (cause of death: bladder)	90	74	1903 Nov 13	NE, 28th, 1904
Manners, James K.		H, 1st West Va. Lt. Art.	18		1912 Dec 4	KS, 32nd, 1913
Manning, Barney		G, 4th Ill. Cav.	65		1899 Jan 6	KS, 19th, 1900
Manning, Edwin C.		H, 17th Kans. Militia	85		1915 Dec 11	KS, 35th, 1916
Manning, James E.	Pvt.	A, 89th N.Y. Inf. (at large)	154, 74	94	1939 Oct 12	IA, 66th, 1940
Manning, Joseph		I, 36th Iowa	9		1923 Feb 24	KS, 43rd, 1924
Manning, L.M.	Lieut.	H, 58th Ill. Inf.	18		1906 Mar 7	IA, 33rd, 1907
Manning, Nathan B.		A, 46th Iowa Inf.	32		1917 Oct 10	KS, 37th, 1918
Manning, Walter			[89?]		1918	KS, 38th, 1919
Manning, William H.	Pvt.	F, 34th Iowa Inf.	235	44	1886 Dec 13	IA, 13th, 1887
Manning, William R.	Lieut.	10th Iowa Inf. (see also Appendix D)	16		1912 Mar 23 or 24	IA, 39th, 1913
Mannington, W.W.		C, 19th Ohio (died of pneumonia)	275	77	1919 Feb 5	NE, 47th, 1923
Mannington, Wallace W.		I, 71st Penn. (died of old age)	275	83	1921 Dec 31	NE, 46th, 1922
Mannis, George B.		E, 40th Ind.	1		1913 Nov 13	KS, 33rd, 1914
Manon, J.G.		G, 128th Ohio Inf.	465		1902 Oct 31	KS, 22nd, 1903
Manor, G.		Iowa Inf.	459		1901 Feb	KS, 21st, 1902
Mansfield, T.B.	Pvt.	E, 52nd Ohio Inf.	284		1910 Feb 11	IA, 37th, 1911
Mansfield, Wm. A.		H, 143rd Ill.	85		1917 Jan 17	KS, 37th, 1918

Name	Rank	Company, Regiment or Ship	Post*	Age	Death Date†	Journal
Manship, Sylvester	Unassigned Pvt. Pvt.	37th Ind. Inf. H, 82nd Ind. Inf. (at large) B, 22nd Ind. Inf.		92	1940 Jun 9	IA, 66th, 1940
Manska, Karl	Pvt.	G, 1st Wis. Inf.	284		1907 Jul 18	IA, 34th, 1908
Mansure, R.F.		I, 10th Kans.	293		1910 Mar	KS, 30th, 1911
Mantor, C.	Pvt.	C, 19th Maine Inf.	165		1928 Jan 11	IA, 55th, 1929
Mantre, D.T.			322		1924	KS, 44th, 1925
Manuel, George W.		C, 11th Ind. H, 55th Mass.	14		1913 Mar 19	KS, 33rd, 1914
Manuel, James		D, 1st N.Y. Cav. (died of pneumonia)	8	72	1913 Dec 5	NE, 38th, 1914
Manuel, Thomas B.	Pvt.	D, 12th U.S. Reg.	5	52	1894 Jun 22	IA, 21st, 1895
Manuring, E.C.		D, 34th Ind. Inf.	36		1887 Oct 13	KS, 7th, 1888
Manville, F.W.		B, 9th Ill. Cav. (died of asthma)	7	70	1903 Dec 10	NE, 28th, 1904
Mapes, Daniel		12th Kans.	260		1904 Feb 5	KS, 24th, 1905
Mapes, Daniel W.	Pvt.	4th Wis. Bat.	348		1900 Mar 14	IA, 27th, 1901
Mapes, E.A.		K, 129th Ill.	123		1919 Mar 18	KS, 39th, 1920
Mapes, William		D, 38th Ohio 14th Ohio	18		1913 Mar 9	KS, 33rd, 1914
Maple, L.F.	Corp.	K, 40th Iowa Inf.	18		1918 Sep 24	IA, 45th, 1919
Maple, Silas		C, 85th Ind.	25		1913 Dec 18	KS, 33rd, 1914
Mappin, Jesse		H, 43rd Mo.	292		1904 Jan 31	KS, 24th, 1905
Marble, Ed. D.	Pvt.	K, 105th Ill. Inf.	68		1925 Jun 5	IA, 52nd, 1926
Marble, Frank B.	Pvt.	K, 40th Wis.	81	53	1898 Dec 3	IA, 25th, 1899
Marcell, Gordon		C, 13th Kans.	191		1923	KS, 43rd, 1924
Marcellus, J.E.		39th Ind.	55		1928 Oct 11	KS, 48th, 1929
Marcellus, Levi		B, 150th Ill. Inf.	117		1884	KS, 4th, 1885
Marcey, E.R.		C, 176th Ohio	55		1937 May 6	KS, 56th, 1937
March, Clement		B, 5th Ill. Cav.	117		1890	KS, 10th, 1891
March, David H.		D, 3rd Iowa Cav.	25	73	1918 Apr 28	NE, 43rd, 1919
March, H.W.		K, 3rd Mich.	85		1923 Aug 23	KS, 43rd, 1924
March, L.M.	Pvt.	C, 186th N.Y. Inf.	3		1913 Jul 24	IA, 40th, 1914
March, Theo. T.		E, Penn. (died of heart failure)	302	70	1904	NE, 29th, 1905
March, W.T.		E, 3rd Iowa Cav.	25		1930 Oct 25	NE, 55th, 1931
March, Wm. T.		A, 123rd Ill.	311		1898 Jul 19	KS, 18th, 1899
Marchant, A.J.	Pvt.	G, 44th Ill. Inf.	377		1910 Jul 20	IA, 37th, 1911
Marcinda, James			1		1926 Sep 22	KS, 46th, 1927
Marcker, S.D.	Corp.	H, 4th N.H. Inf.	26		1902 Aug 6	IA, 29th, 1903
Marcot, Geo.	Pvt.	G, 2nd Kans. Inf.	22		1913 Sep 28	IA, 40th, 1914
Marcum, W.A.		Mo. (died of general decline)	78	91	1917 Oct 12	NE, 43rd, 1919
Marcum, W.A.		G, 5th Mo. Cav.	84		1917 Oct 12	NE, 42nd, 1918
Mardis, Amos		K, 24th Ohio	293		1927	KS, 47th, 1928
Mardis, S.F.	Sergt.	C, 18th Iowa Inf.	55		1908 Apr 7	IA, 35th, 1909
Mardis, W.K.	Pvt.	A, 16th Iowa Inf.	173		1904 Aug 13	IA, 31st, 1905
Mardis, William W.		F, 13th Ky. Inf.	302		1933 Jan 2	NE, 58th, 1934
Margrave, T.E.		H, 20th Ill. (died of bladder trouble)	223	80	1920 Mar 11	NE, 45th, 1921
Marian, Joseph		E, 46th Ill.	13	74	1918 Jun 16	NE, 43rd, 1919
Maris, C.F.			196		1913 Jun 9	IA, 40th, 1914
Marity, J.A.			104		1890	NE, 15th, 1891
Mark, Andrew		K, 1st Iowa Inf. (born in Ohio; died of dropsy at Soldiers & Sailors Home Hospital, Burkett; buried at Home Cemetery)		68	1906 Dec 17	NE, 31st, 1907
Mark, Francis		H, 13th Kans.	380		1911 Jul 6	KS, 31st, 1912
Mark, Gilbert			129		1923 Feb 15	KS, 43rd, 1924
Mark, Henry	Pvt.	C, 35th Iowa Inf.	231		1919 Mar 19	IA, 46th, 1920
Mark, J.M.		I, 50th Ill. Inf.	85		1925 Jul 6	KS, 45th, 1926
Markell, John W.	Sergt.	F, 37th Iowa Inf.	78	75	1891 Feb 26	IA, 18th, 1892
Marker, Dennis		C, 123rd Penn. Inf. (died in railroad accident)	188	61	1901 Mar	NE, 26th, 1902
Marker, Fred		E, 5th Mo. State Militia Cav.	52		1908 Apr 5	KS, 28th, 1909
Marker, W.S.	Pvt.		314		1926	IA, 53rd, 1927
Markey, Thos.	Pvt.	A, 140th N.Y. Inf.	7		1912 Jan 3	IA, 39th, 1913
Markham, Byron		C, 151st Ill.	64		1909 May 8	KS, 29th, 1910

See Appendix A, B or C for roster of post names and locations.
†*See Introduction for note regarding recording of death date.*

Name	Rank	Company, Regiment or Ship	Post*	Age	Death Date†	Journal
Markham, Charles	Pvt.	B, 49th Mass. Inf.	98	58	1899 Dec 17	IA, 26th, 1900
Markham, David	Pvt.	K, 18th Mass. Inf.	98		1927 Dec 30	IA, 54th, 1928
Markham, J.J.		E, 56th Ohio	17		1920 Feb 3	KS, 40th, 1921
Markham, L.H.	Pvt.	G, 49th N.Y. Inf.	7		1910 Nov 19	IA, 37th, 1911
Markham, Wm. H.		I, 12th Iowa	484		1893 Aug 9	KS, 13th, 1894
Markland, R.H.		F, 4th Mo. Cav. (died at Salina)	127		1895 Apr 28	KS, 15th, 1896
Markland, Wm.		died of old age	130	97	1919 Jun 3	NE, 44th, 1920
Markle, Barney	Pvt.	F, 11th Ind. Inf.	167		1926 Mar 10	IA, 53rd, 1927
Markle, S.J.		B, 30th Ohio Inf.	129		1887 Mar 26	KS, 7th, 1888
Markle, Volney A.		I, 21st Ohio (died of paralysis)	30	73	1920 Oct 10	NE, 45th, 1921
Markley, H.H.	Sergt.	2nd Cal. Inf.	222	90	1931 Jun 12	IA, 58th, 1932
Markley, Isreal		Kans. State Militia	47		1909 Feb 12	KS, 29th, 1910
Markley, M.U.		F, 12th Ind.	294		1898 Nov 27	KS, 18th, 1899
Marks, A.L.		13th Ill.	58		1892 Jun 5	KS, 12th, 1893
Marks, B.F.		G, 10th Iowa	20		1915 May 28	KS, 35th, 1916
Marks, C.R.	Pvt.	K, 8th Mass. Inf.	22	91	1932 Dec 19	IA, 59th, 1933
Marks, Ernst	Pvt.	B, 17th Wis. Inf.	102	73	1897 Nov 25	IA, 24th, 1898
Marks, George		H, 7th Mo. Cav.	155		1925 May 4	KS, 45th, 1926
Marks, W.H.		H, 4th Mich.	7		1920 Jan 27	KS, 40th, 1921
Markwell, S.A.	Pvt.	C, 36th Ill. Inf.	163	69	1896 Jan 9	IA, 22nd, 1896
Markwell, S.A.	Pvt.	C, 36th Ill. Inf.	163		1896 Jan 10	IA, 23rd, 1897
Marlay, Joseph K.		60th Ohio Inf. (died of heart failure)	214	73	1897 Apr 15	NE, 22nd, 1898
Marler, Wm. J.	Pvt.	I, 2nd Kans. Inf.	51		1902 Dec 2	IA, 29th, 1903
Marlin, B.T.		A, 78th Penn. Inf. (died at New Cambria)	127		1895 Jul 29	KS, 15th, 1896
Marlow, Albert		C, 1st U.S. Inf.	3		1899 Dec 29	KS, 19th, 1900
Marlow, C.	Pvt.	D, 19th Iowa Inf.	15		1904 Sep 10	IA, 31st, 1905
Marlow, William	Pvt.	A, 36th Ind. Inf.	52		1927 Dec 2	IA, 54th, 1928
Marmon, Frank	Pvt.	B, 35th Iowa Inf.	231		1908 Oct 31	IA, 35th, 1909
Maroney, John		I, 1st U.S. Art., Ireland	354	78	1921 Mar 8	NE, 46th, 1922
Marple, A.A.			439		1911 Jun 23	KS, 31st, 1912
Marquand, H.	Pvt.	Colo. Inf.	259		1916 Jan 22	IA, 43rd, 1917
Marquet, Philip		C, 14th N.Y. Inf. (died of heart failure)	198		1891 Dec 17	KS, 11th, 1892
Marquette, D.		H, 86th Ohio	318	72	1911 Aug 15	NE, 36th, 1912
Marquette, David, Rev.		one of the pioneers of Methodism in Nebraska	[318?]		1911	NE, 36th, 1912
Marquis, C.R.	Pvt.	A, 166th Ohio Inf.	98	58	1896 Jan 23	IA, 23rd, 1897
Marquis, D.R.			36		1930 Apr 5	KS, 50th, 1931
Marr, D.V.		G, 27th Mo. Inf.	63		1909 Feb 4	KS, 29th, 1910
Marr, I.D.	Pvt.	A, 24th Iowa Inf.	163		1902 Nov 30	IA, 29th, 1903
Marrie, Simon T.		M, 12th Ohio Cav.	53		1923 Jan 10	KS, 43rd, 1924
Marringer, N.	Pvt.	G, 16th Iowa	277	65	1890 Sep 9	IA, 17th, 1891
Marriott, David	Pvt.	G, 11th Iowa Inf.	177		1910 Sep 26	IA, 37th, 1911
Marrow, John A.		F, 1st Iowa Cav.	260		1914 Jul 16	KS, 34th, 1915
Marsden, Sam'l	Pvt.	A, 96th Ill. Inf.	163	51	1889 Mar 30	IA, 16th, 1890
Marse, C.R.	Pvt.	I, 1st Iowa	64		1905	IA, 32nd, 1906
Marsell, Joseph	Pvt.	H, 9th Iowa Cav.	248		1923	IA, 50th, 1924
Marsellus, Yan		F, 32nd Ind.	71		1917 Aug 31	KS, 37th, 1918
Marsh, Alonzo	Pvt.	8th Wis. Bat.	124		1922	IA, 49th, 1923
Marsh, Clark		B, 11th Mich.	207		1933 Aug	NE, 58th, 1934
Marsh, Duane	Pvt.	E, 54th N.Y. Inf.	117		1917 Apr 3	IA, 44th, 1918
Marsh, E.A.		E, 95th Ill.	5		1918 Jul 20	KS, 38th, 1919
Marsh, E.L.	Capt.	D, 2nd Iowa Vols.	12		1906 Feb 23	IA, 33rd, 1907
Marsh, Eli		C, 4th Minn. Inf.	88		1916 Sep 9	KS, 36th, 1917
Marsh, F.M.		B, 118th Ohio	25		1914 Jul 1	KS, 34th, 1915
Marsh, F.S.			64		1907 Oct 2	IA, 34th, 1908
Marsh, Frank S.		K, 9th Ill. Cav. (died of old age)	112	77	1915 Apr 20	NE, 40th, 1916
Marsh, I.D.	Capt.	C, 39th Iowa Inf.	45	67	1891 Nov 16	IA, 19th, 1893
Marsh, James E.		E, 148th Ind. Inf.	55		1885	KS, 5th, 1886
Marsh, Jas. B.	Pvt.	B, 11th Iowa Inf.	24		1925	IA, 52nd, 1926
Marsh, Jas. E.		E, 128th Ind. Inf.	55		1886	KS, 6th, 1887
Marsh, Jasper L.	Pvt.	B, Ill. Inf.	127		1929 Jul 21	IA, 56th, 1930
Marsh, Jasper Newton		C, 92nd Ill. Mtd. Inf.	417	95	1938 Jul 30	IA, 64th, 1938

*See Appendix A, B or C for roster of post names and locations.
†See Introduction for note regarding recording of death date.

Name	Rank	Company, Regiment or Ship	Post*	Age	Death Date†	Journal
Marsh, Joel E.	Pvt.	A, 6th Iowa Cav.	101		1926 Mar 13	IA, 53rd, 1927
Marsh, John	Pvt.	D, 157th Ohio Inf.	465		1904 Oct 18	IA, 31st, 1905
Marsh, Joseph		I, 107th Ill.	18		1911 May 16	KS, 31st, 1912
Marsh, Leonard		K, 74th Ill.	250		1922 Aug 1	KS, 42nd, 1923
Marsh, N.B.	Pvt.	E, 67th Ill. Inf.	267		1913 Jun 19	IA, 40th, 1914
Marsh, O.		2nd Ohio	158		1922 Oct 29	KS, 42nd, 1923
Marsh, S.C.		G, 29th Iowa	8		1915 Sep 18	KS, 35th, 1916
Marsh, Thomas	Pvt.	E, 8th Mich.	52		1915 Nov 21	KS, 35th, 1916
Marsh, W.	Pvt.	B, 110th N.Y.	271		1921 Jan 10	IA, 48th, 1922
Marsh, Wesley		M, 9th Iowa Cav.	170		1928 Nov 18	IA, 55th, 1929
Marsh, William		B, 7th Ind.	32		1924 Apr 6	KS, 44th, 1925
Marsh, William T.		E, 134th Ind. Inf.	1		1912 Aug 21	KS, 32nd, 1913
Marsh, Wm. C.	Pvt.	B, 32nd Wis. Inf.	25	98	1939 Jan 12	IA, 65th, 1939
Marsh, Wm. H.	Pvt.	D, 151st Ohio Inf.	466		1912 Jan 4	IA, 38th, 1912
Marsh, Wm. H.	Pvt.	D, 151st Ohio Inf.	466		1912 Jan 4	IA, 39th, 1913
Marshal, John Z.		D, 123rd N.Y. Inf.	25		1911 Feb	NE, 36th, 1912
Marshal, Joseph		C, 153rd Ind.	8		1904 Oct 18	KS, 24th, 1905
Marshal, M.C.		A, 7th Maine Inf.	35		1902 May 19	KS, 22nd, 1903
Marshal, T.R.	Lieut.	121st Ohio Inf.	130		1900 Aug 9	IA, 27th, 1901
Marshal, Warren	Pvt.	A, 18th Iowa Inf.	212		1916 Dec 2	IA, 43rd, 1917
Marshall, A.	Pvt.	G, 8th Iowa Inf.	425		1905 Mar 2	IA, 32nd, 1906
Marshall, A.	Pvt.	C, 67th Ill. Inf.	42		1918 Jun 19	IA, 45th, 1919
Marshall, Andrew			147		1899 Jan 19	KS, 19th, 1900
Marshall, C.W.	Pvt.	D, 13th Iowa Inf.	5		1911 Dec	IA, 38th, 1912
Marshall, D.B.			96		1917 Feb 18	IA, 44th, 1918
Marshall, D.P.		K, 155th Penn. Inf. (died at Arkansas City)	158		1895 Mar 20	KS, 15th, 1896
Marshall, Eli		A, 57th Ind.	186		1925 Mar	KS, 45th, 1926
Marshall, Francis		G, 64th Ill.	104		1927 Apr 24	NE, 52nd, 1928
Marshall, Frank		B, 34th Ill. Inf.	25	72	1917 Jun 22	NE, 42nd, 1918
Marshall, Geo. W.	Pvt.	H, 17th Iowa Inf.	59		1918 Dec 6	IA, 45th, 1919
Marshall, H.H.	Pvt.	B, 140th Ill. Inf.	327		1921 Jun 17	IA, 48th, 1922
Marshall, Isaac	Pvt.	G, 29th Iowa Inf.	51	97	1940 Mar 1	IA, 66th, 1940
Marshall, J.E.	Pvt.	G, 4th Iowa Cav.	254		1923 Nov 26	IA, 50th, 1924
Marshall, J.F.		G, 68th Ill.	28		1913 Mar 30	KS, 33rd, 1914
Marshall, James		F, 134th Penn.	25		1893 Sep 23	KS, 13th, 1894
Marshall, James		K, 55th Ill.	59		1925 Apr 10	KS, 45th, 1926
Marshall, Jeremiah		D, 6th Iowa Cav.	15		3rd quarter 1884	IA, 11th, 1885
Marshall, John C.		I, 112th Ill.	12		1912 May 7	KS, 32nd, 1913
Marshall, Jos. G.		B, 56th Penn.	221		1897 Nov 19	KS, 17th, 1898
Marshall, Joseph L.		A, 6th Kans.	209		1916 Feb 18	KS, 36th, 1917
Marshall, Myron M.	Pvt.	H, 5th R.I. Cav.	327		1911 Nov 21	IA, 38th, 1912
Marshall, N.B.		F, 1st Ohio Hvy. Art.	174		1914 Apr 30	KS, 34th, 1915
Marshall, N.T.	Pvt.	G, 4th Iowa Inf.	286	48	1891 Aug 30	IA, 18th, 1892
Marshall, R.	Pvt.	D, 3rd Ohio Inf.	122	62	1895 Apr 6	IA, 22nd, 1896
Marshall, Robt. A.		C, 5th Ill. Cav.	196		1885	KS, 5th, 1886
Marshall, T.B.		F, 43rd Ohio	293		1913 Mar 3	KS, 33rd, 1914
Marshall, T.C.		I, 5th Kans.	447		1896 Aug 27	KS, 16th, 1897
Marshall, T.H.		B, 1st Kans. Inf.	435		1901 Feb 26	KS, 21st, 1902
Marshall, Thomas		G, 14th Mo.	57		1912 Oct 14	KS, 32nd, 1913
Marshall, Thomas B.		F, 43rd Ohio	52		1913 Mar 4	KS, 33rd, 1914
Marshall, Thomas R.	Pvt.	F, 137th Ill. Inf.	493		1915 Oct 27	IA, 42nd, 1916
Marshall, Thos.		B, 34th Ill.	25		1929 May 18	NE, 54th, 1930
Marshall, W.H.		E, 96th Ohio (died of old age)	1	80	1924 Feb 14	NE, 49th, 1925
Marshall, Wm. A.		G, 78th Penn. Inf.	12		1917 Aug 29	KS, 37th, 1918
Marsland, W.A.		E, 62nd Ill.	85		1902 Jan 30	KS, 22nd, 1903
Marsters, George W.		U.S.N. Massachusetts (on gunboat)	43		1905 Sep 16	KS, 25th, 1906
Marston, J.M.		F, 12th N.H. Inf.	84		1912 Jan 30	KS, 32nd, 1913
Marthar, William		H, 8th Iowa Inf.	357	90	1937 Feb 8	IA, 64th, 1938
Martimus, Smith		A, 9th Minn.	113		1911 Apr 20	KS, 31st, 1912
Martin		died of complications	301	81	1915 Jun 11	NE, 41st, 1917
Martin, A.P.		E, 81st N.Y. Inf. (died of wounds)	25	54	1895 Jul 31	NE, 20th, 1896
Martin, Abram	Pvt.	I, 11th Iowa Inf.	8		1915 Aug 21	IA, 42nd, 1916

*See Appendix A, B or C for roster of post names and locations.
†See Introduction for note regarding recording of death date.

Name	Rank	Company, Regiment or Ship	Post*	Age	Death Date†	Journal
Martin, Alex		G, 51st Ill. Inf. (died of paralysis)	52		1902 Mar	NE, 27th, 1903
Martin, Alfred S.		F, 50th Ill. Inf. (killed in railroad accident)	4		1889	KS, 9th, 1890
Martin, Allen		Navy	267		1899 Feb 18	KS, 19th, 1900
Martin, Andrew W.	Pvt.	K, 84th Ill. Inf.	452		1908 Feb 15	IA, 35th, 1909
Martin, Augustus		F, 1st Penn. Cav. Penn. Lt. Art.	64		1904 May 26	KS, 24th, 1905
Martin, B.F.	Pvt.	B, 20th Iowa Inf.	244		1926 Dec 19	IA, 53rd, 1927
Martin, Bernard		C, 155th N.Y. Vols.	298		1902 Dec 3	KS, 22nd, 1903
Martin, C.A.		3rd Iowa Battery	11		1904 Jul 31	KS, 24th, 1905
Martin, C.E.		11th Ohio Cav. (died at Wichita; buried at Maple Grove Cemetery)	25		1894 Sep 11	KS, 14th, 1895
Martin, C.L.	Pvt.	14th Mass. Battery	370	53	1889 Jun 12	IA, 16th, 1890
Martin, Charles I.	Pvt.	C, 27th Iowa Inf.	240		1917 Nov 14	IA, 44th, 1918
Martin, Charles L.		G, 168th Ohio	284		1917 Jul 2	KS, 37th, 1918
Martin, D.R., Dr.	Surg.	3rd Iowa Inf.	200		1902 Apr 20	KS, 22nd, 1903
Martin, D.S.	Pvt.	B, 194th Ohio Inf.	7		1913 Nov 28	IA, 40th, 1914
Martin, Daniel		C, 18th Mo. (died of old age at Soldiers & Sailors Home, Milford)		77	1906 Sep 26	NE, 31st, 1907
Martin, Daniel S.	Pvt.	D, 194th Ohio Inf.	55		1913 Nov 28	IA, 40th, 1914
Martin, David P.	Pvt.	17th Ill. Cav.	333		1919 Jan 28	IA, 46th, 1920
Martin, David S.		B, 16th Ill. Inf. (died of heart trouble)	22	78	1924 Jun 5	NE, 49th, 1925
Martin, E.H.		C, 7th Kans. Cav.	170		1910 Nov 30	KS, 30th, 1911
Martin, E.L.		D, 2nd Neb. Cav. (died of pneumonia)	2	70	1902 Nov	NE, 27th, 1903
Martin, Edward		A, 77th Ohio	342		1897 Aug 30	KS, 17th, 1898
Martin, F.	Pvt.	B, 17th Wis. Inf.	461		1910 Dec 20	IA, 37th, 1911
Martin, F.H.			377		1913 Aug	KS, 33rd, 1914
Martin, F.M.		A, 104th Ohio	250		1921 Aug 31	KS, 41st, 1922
Martin, Fred		E, 7th Mo. Cav. (died at Baldwin)	231		1895 Oct	KS, 15th, 1896
Martin, Fred		G, 4th Ill. Cav. (died of old age)	299	75	1915 Apr 1	NE, 39th, 1915
Martin, Frederick		E, Mo. Cav. (died at Baldwin)	40		1895 Oct	KS, 15th, 1896
Martin, G.L.	Pvt.		29		1917 Jan 20	IA, 44th, 1918
Martin, G.W.	Pvt.	C, 7th Iowa Inf.	7		1906 Oct 2	IA, 33rd, 1907
Martin, Geo.		C, 78th Ill.	8		1917 Jan 28	KS, 37th, 1918
Martin, George H.		D, 116th Ill.	41		1914 Oct 15	KS, 34th, 1915
Martin, George W.		K, 83rd Ill. Inf.	252		1925 Oct 10	KS, 45th, 1926
Martin, George W.		H, 129th Ill. Inf. (died of complications)	60	82	1910 May 28	NE, 35th, 1911
Martin, Gileo	Pvt.	A, 17th Ind. Inf.	206		1915 Nov 24	IA, 42nd, 1916
Martin, H.F.	Pvt.	C, 172nd Ohio Inf.	127		1919 Nov 25	IA, 46th, 1920
Martin, H.H.	Pvt.	B, 20th Iowa Inf.	244		1926 Jul 19	IA, 53rd, 1927
Martin, Henry		G, 4th Md. Inf.	1		1935 Mar	KS, 54th, 1935
Martin, Henry B.		G, 8th Mo.	246		1892 Mar 7	KS, 12th, 1893
Martin, Henry H.	Pvt.	B, 20th Iowa Inf.	244		1925 Jul 24	IA, 52nd, 1926
Martin, Henry H.		F, 7th Ill. Cav.	22	87	1923 Jul 11	NE, 48th, 1924
Martin, Henry J.		D, 17th Ind. Inf.	57		1886	KS, 6th, 1887
Martin, Ira T.	Pvt.	B, 9th Iowa Cav.	91		1907 Dec 24	IA, 34th, 1908
Martin, Isaac	Pvt.	C, —	244		1906 Mar 24	IA, 33rd, 1907
Martin, Isaac		F, 11th Iowa Inf.	18		1920 Dec 20	KS, 41st, 1922
Martin, J.F.		B, 10th Ind.	18		1933 Mar 18	KS, 53rd, 1934
Martin, J.H.		B, 2nd Ill. Cav.	255		1914 Feb 18	KS, 34th, 1915
Martin, J.J.		C, 129th Ill. Inf.	65		1925 Aug 19	KS, 45th, 1926
Martin, J.R.	Pvt.	I, 120th Ohio	12		1921 Apr 11	IA, 48th, 1922
Martin, J.R.		E, 24th Ill. Inf.	155		1925 Mar 25	KS, 45th, 1926
Martin, J.W.		G, 120th Ind.	380		1896 Mar 8	KS, 16th, 1897
Martin, J.W.		A, 35th Mo.	113		1906 May 16	KS, 26th, 1907
Martin, Jacob	Pvt.	A, Iowa Cav.	231		1909 Oct 5	IA, 36th, 1910
Martin, Jacob		D, 102nd Ohio Vol. Inf.	93		1915 Feb 24	KS, 35th, 1916
Martin, James			74		1910	IA, 37th, 1911
Martin, James		A, 10th Tenn. Cav. (died at Hutchinson)	17		1895 Jul 8	KS, 15th, 1896
Martin, James F.		H, 138th Ohio	85		1900 Jun 30	KS, 20th, 1901
Martin, James M.		D, 2nd Neb. Cav. (died of old age)	55	76	1911 May 5	NE, 36th, 1912
Martin, Jno. N.		B, 33rd Wis. Inf.	38	65	1891[1901?] Nov	NE, 26th, 1902
Martin, Joel T.		A, 86th Ill. Inf.	309		1892 May 7	NE, 17th, 1893

*See Appendix A, B or C for roster of post names and locations.
†See Introduction for note regarding recording of death date.

Name	Rank	Company, Regiment or Ship	Post*	Age	Death Date†	Journal
Martin, John	Pvt.	K, 13th Iowa Inf.	40		1910 Mar 4	IA, 37th, 1911
Martin, John		D, 42nd Ill. Inf.	164		1892 Jan 28	KS, 12th, 1893
Martin, John		H, 51st Ill.	252		1893 Jun 26	KS, 13th, 1894
Martin, John		A, 2nd Kans. Mil.	1		1913 Sep 3	KS, 33rd, 1914
Martin, John		K, 31st Ill.	17		1926 Apr 9	KS, 46th, 1927
Martin, John A.	Col.	8th Kans.	93		1889	KS, 9th, 1890
Martin, John A.	Col.	8th Kans. Inf. (see also Appendix D)	93		1889 Oct 2	KS, 11th, 1892
Martin, John B.		I, 10th Kans. Cav.	90		1924 Jul 24	KS, 44th, 1925
Martin, John K.	Pvt.		150		1924	IA, 51st, 1925
Martin, John L.		I, 1st Iowa Inf.		94	1937 Jan 1	IA, 64th, 1938
Martin, John M.		D, 8th Mass.	25		1914 Oct 13	KS, 34th, 1915
Martin, John S.			296		1922 Sep 15	KS, 42nd, 1923
Martin, John S.		C, 2nd Wis. Cav.	88		1906 Mar 1	KS, 26th, 1907
Martin, Josiah	Pvt.	C, 17th Iowa Inf.	19		1923	IA, 50th, 1924
Martin, L.S.		H, 129th Ill. Inf. (died of heart failure)	60	78	1918 May 4	NE, 43rd, 1919
Martin, Legrand		G, 58th Ind. Inf.	50		1900 Dec 4	KS, 20th, 1901
Martin, Lester B.		C, 6th Wis.	75	68	1904 Aug 29	NE, 29th, 1905
Martin, Levi		B, 5th Iowa Cav.	240		1899 Sep 28	KS, 19th, 1900
Martin, M.M.		E, 14th Kans. Cav.	185		1929 Dec 12	KS, 49th, 1930
Martin, Monroe		F, 132nd Penn. Inf.	324		3rd quarter 1884	IA, 11th, 1885
Martin, Oliver P.	Pvt.		235		1912 Oct 15	IA, 39th, 1913
Martin, Peter	Pvt.	G, 3rd U.S. Art.	251	65	1894 Sep 3	IA, 21st, 1895
Martin, R.B.	Pvt.		66		1920 Aug 1	IA, 47th, 1921
Martin, R.L.		D, 12th Iowa Inf.	180		1899 Jun 11	KS, 19th, 1900
Martin, R.S.	Pvt.	D, 13th Ind. Inf.	167		1926 Nov 1	IA, 53rd, 1927
Martin, R.S.			153		1888	KS, 8th, 1889
Martin, R.S.		D, 12th Iowa	51		1899 Jun 11	KS, 19th, 1900
Martin, Robert		C, 26th N.J.	380		1905 Jan 10	KS, 25th, 1906
Martin, Robt. George	Pvt.	D, 188th Ohio Inf. (at large)	152, 26	95 & 5 days	1944 Aug 30	IA, 70th, 1944
Martin, Rubin		A, 110th Ill.	87		1928 Dec 2	KS, 48th, 1929
Martin, S.D.	Lieut.	D, 8th Ill. Cav.	247		1926 Nov 15	IA, 53rd, 1927
Martin, S.E.		2nd Kans.	1		1910 Dec 7	KS, 30th, 1911
Martin, S.H.			7		1883	KS, 3rd, 1884
Martin, S.M.		B, 13th Ill.	205		1917 Aug 1	KS, 37th, 1918
Martin, Samuel	Pvt.	C, 102nd Ohio Inf.	12		1927 Feb 2	IA, 54th, 1928
Martin, Seth	1st Lieut.	H, 4th Iowa Cav.	277	77	1894 Jan 9	IA, 21st, 1895
Martin, T.B.	Pvt.	C, 39th Ohio Inf.	152		1910 Dec 25	IA, 37th, 1911
Martin, Theodore	Pvt.	B, 5th Iowa Cav.	131	70	1898 Nov 30	IA, 25th, 1899
Martin, Thomas		G, 5th U.S. Cav.	389		1893 Dec 18	KS, 13th, 1894
Martin, Thos. E.			51		1906	KS, 26th, 1907
Martin, V.S.	Pvt.	E, 23rd Iowa Inf.	12		1906 Sep 3	IA, 33rd, 1907
Martin, W.	Pvt.	D, 60th U.S.C. Inf.	18		1913 Dec 1	IA, 40th, 1914
Martin, W.A.		G, 24th Iowa Inf.	7		1927 Jan 5	NE, 52nd, 1928
Martin, W.D.	Pvt.	20th Independent Battery	238		1915 May 23	IA, 42nd, 1916
Martin, W.D.		A, 48th Penn. Inf.	25		1894 Feb 14	NE, 19th, 1895
Martin, W.H.	Musician	F, 142nd Ill. Inf.	497		1912 Jul 5	IA, 39th, 1913
Martin, W.H.H.		117th Ind.	337		1902 Jun 6	KS, 22nd, 1903
Martin, W.J.		H, 173rd Penn.	465		1911 Jan 29	KS, 31st, 1912
Martin, W.M.		C, 131st Ill.	54		1923	KS, 43rd, 1924
Martin, W.W.		B, 154th Ind. Inf. (buried in officers' row at the National Military Home cemetery)			1924 Mar 7	KS, 43rd, 1924
Martin, W.W.		C, B, 55th & 154th Ind.	32		1924 Mar 8	KS, 44th, 1925
Martin, Wesley		C, 2nd N.Y. Hvy. Art.		86	1936 Apr 29	IA, 62nd, 1936
Martin, Wesley		C, 2nd N.Y. Art.	66	86	1935 Apr 29	IA, 62nd, 1936
Martin, Wesley			165		1911	NE, 36th, 1912
Martin, William	Pvt.	D, 7th Iowa Cav.	40		1914 Jun 23	IA, 41st, 1915
Martin, William		C, 11th Iowa	1		1919 Jan 13	KS, 39th, 1920
Martin, Wm.		M, 4th U.S.A.	118		1917 Oct 22	KS, 37th, 1918
Martin, Wm. H.		C, 70th Ind.	12		1902 Jul 17	KS, 22nd, 1903
Martindale, C.D.		C, 1st Ohio Lt. Art.	477		1917 May 11	KS, 37th, 1918
Martindale, Leye		F, 12th Kans.	108		1912 Nov 29	KS, 32nd, 1913

*See Appendix A, B or C for roster of post names and locations.
†See Introduction for note regarding recording of death date.

346

Name	Rank	Company, Regiment or Ship	Post*	Age	Death Date†	Journal
Martindale, Milo		B, 29th Mich. (died of old age)	82	85	1917 Feb 23	NE, 42nd, 1918
Martineau, Wm.			64		1917 Apr 25	IA, 44th, 1918
Marton, Anderson	Pvt.	C, 14th Iowa Inf.	330		1906 Nov 22	IA, 33rd, 1907
Marts, Squire	Pvt.	D, 15th Iowa Inf.	497		1915 Oct 7	IA, 42nd, 1916
Martz, Jacob R.	Pvt.	D, 2nd Md. Inf.	71	89	1933 Mar 1	IA, 60th, 1934
Marvin, David E.	Pvt.	B, 95th Ill. Inf.	284	47	1892 Nov 13	IA, 19th, 1893
Marvin, Richard M.	Sergt.	H, 31st Iowa Inf.	190		1918 Jan 26	IA, 45th, 1919
Masheler, T.K.		C, 140th Ohio	175		1922 Dec 12	KS, 43rd, 1924
Masher, James A.		E, 14th Maine Inf.	44		1929 Oct 20	KS, 49th, 1930
Mason, A.	Sergt.	K, 60th U.S.C.T.	20		1910 Nov 7	IA, 37th, 1911
Mason, A.L.		F, 104th Ill.	240		1895 Apr 3	KS, 16th, 1897
Mason, Abe		D, 48th N.Y.	51		1924 Jan 16	KS, 44th, 1925
Mason, Albert		H, 10th Penn. (died of general breakdown)	32	91	1924 Sep 14	NE, 49th, 1925
Mason, C.B.		A, 13th Ohio	18		1911 Apr 15	KS, 31st, 1912
Mason, Charles W.		3rd Penn. Hvy. Art.		93	1937 Aug 2	IA, 64th, 1938
Mason, E.H.	Pvt.	C, 10th Ill. Inf.	12		1929 Jan 30	IA, 56th, 1930
Mason, E.K.	Pvt.	A, 19th Iowa Inf.	2		1903 Jun 17	IA, 30th, 1904
Mason, E.R.	Pvt.	A, 13th Iowa Inf.	206		1912 Nov 14	IA, 39th, 1913
Mason, Elbert W.		G, 75th Ill. (died of paralysis, heart)	79	75	1917 Dec 20	NE, 42nd, 1918
Mason, Elishua		D, 10th Ind.	64		1893 Nov 15	KS, 13th, 1894
Mason, Isaac		4th Iowa Battery	452	88	1934 Feb 18	IA, 61st, 1935
Mason, J.B.	Hosp. Stew.	3rd Iowa Cav.	12		1920 Jan 11	IA, 47th, 1921
Mason, J.C.	Pvt.	C, 13th Iowa Inf.	271		1914 Apr 2	IA, 41st, 1915
Mason, J.C.	Pvt.	H, 3rd Wis. Inf.	31		1922 Mar 15	IA, 49th, 1923
Mason, James		E, 7th Ill.	18		1906 Sep 10	KS, 26th, 1907
Mason, John		F, 24th Iowa (died of indigestion)	118	66	1897 May 27	NE, 22nd, 1898
Mason, N.	Pvt.	A, 148th Ill. Inf.	39		1900 May 3	IA, 27th, 1901
Mason, N.R.		F, 4th Maine	164		1892 Dec 1	KS, 12th, 1893
Mason, O.S.		E, 129th Ill. Inf. (died of old age)	47	85	1919 May 25	NE, 44th, 1920
Mason, Philip H.	Corp.	F, 28th Iowa Inf.	332		1915 Sep 18	IA, 42nd, 1916
Mason, Pleasant R.		C, 51st Ill. Vol. Inf.	25		1908 May 22	KS, 28th, 1909
Mason, R.B.		H, 123rd Ill.	117		1924 Jul 24	KS, 44th, 1925
Mason, R.P.	Pvt.	C, 15th Iowa Inf.	250		1904 Nov 9	IA, 31st, 1905
Mason, S.M.		C, 105th Ill.	40	75	1916 Mar 28	NE, 41st, 1917
Mason, Thomas	Pvt.	C, 17th Iowa Inf.	40		1919 Oct 27	IA, 46th, 1920
Mason, Thos.		H, 105th Ill. Inf.	1		1899 May 3	KS, 19th, 1900
Mason, Thos. H.		F, 129th Ill. Inf. (died of old age)	188		1923	NE, 48th, 1924
Mason, W.E.		I, 53rd Ill.	293		1911 May 18	KS, 31st, 1912
Mason, W.H.		C, 20th Iowa	43		1910 May 16	KS, 30th, 1911
Mason, Wm.		E, 137th Ill. Inf.	318	63	1910 Aug 25	NE, 35th, 1911
Mason, Wm.		A, 2nd Ill. (died of old age)	29	82	1922 Apr 10	NE, 47th, 1923
Masser, Aug.	Pvt.	D, Penn. Ind. Battery	12		1921 May 31	IA, 48th, 1922
Massey, Fred I.	Pvt.	B, 105th N.Y. Inf.	78		1908 Mar 13	IA, 35th, 1909
Massey, George N.		D, 139th Iowa	53		1919 Sep 8	KS, 39th, 1920
Massey, J.M.		A, 77th Mo.	129		1919 Nov 26	KS, 39th, 1920
Massey, James			24		1890	NE, 15th, 1891
Massey, John		E, 7th Ill.	23		1933 Jan 30	KS, 53rd, 1934
Massey, S.M.			436		1907 Sep 22	IA, 34th, 1908
Masson, Henry		died of old age	197	77	1911 Aug 5	NE, 36th, 1912
Masten, Hiram		F, 150th N.Y.	27	77	1900 Jul 10	NE, 25th, 1901
Master, Jas. G.L.	Corp.	D, 45th Ill. Inf.	130		1925 Jan 12	IA, 52nd, 1926
Masterman, B.F.		E, 5th Ind.	4		1906 Nov 25	KS, 26th, 1907
Masterman, H.		28th Iowa Inf. (died of old age)	25	90	1903 Apr 22	NE, 28th, 1904
Masterman, Henry		died at age 90 years & 20 days	25	90	1903 Apr 23	NE, 27th, 1903
Masters, Irvin		I, 7th Ky. Cav. (died of diabetes)	111	74	1919 Nov 21	NE, 44th, 1920
Masters, J.T.		B, 94th Ill.	36		1919 Dec 30	KS, 39th, 1920
Masters, Jas. L.		L, 6th Ind.	90		1930 Sep 23	KS, 50th, 1931
Masters, W.D.	Pvt.	F, 30th Iowa Inf.	170		1922 Dec 1	IA, 49th, 1923
Mastick, Julius C.		B, 1st Wis. Cav. (died at Soldiers & Sailors Home, Grand Island; buried at Arlington, Neb.)	26	71	1905 Dec 5	NE, 30th, 1906
Mastin, John J.T.		I, 10th Ky. Cav.	274		1901 Oct 22	KS, 21st, 1902

Name	Rank	Company, Regiment or Ship	Post*	Age	Death Date†	Journal
Matchett, Joseph T.		A, 78th Ohio Vol. Inf.	250		1916 Jul 28	KS, 36th, 1917
Mateer, James	Pvt.	C, 40th Iowa Inf.	40	98	1940 Jan 5	IA, 66th, 1940
Materson, James A.		M, 7th Mo.	302		1896 Oct 16	KS, 16th, 1897
Mathena, F.M.		C, 13th Kans.	293		1910 Aug 1	KS, 30th, 1911
Mathency, Jas. M.		C, 22nd Ind. Inf.	1		1885	KS, 5th, 1886
Matheny, A.	Pvt.		51		1917 Jun 25	IA, 44th, 1918
Matheny, A.		F, 31st Iowa Inf.	66		1912 May 17	KS, 32nd, 1913
Mather, Geo. W.		A, 17th Iowa	158		1914 Mar 15	KS, 34th, 1915
Mathers, Francis		I, 7th West Va. Cav.	73		4th quarter 1884	IA, 11th, 1885
Mathers, Henry		H, 1st Ohio Cav.	13		1936	NE, 61st, 1937
Matherson, Francis		C, 126th Ill.	59		1896 Oct 20	KS, 16th, 1897
Matheson, Donald		I, 28th Wis.			1928 Dec 17	NE, 53rd, 1929
Matheus, Mortimer		I, 135th Ohio Inf.	92		1925 Jul 7	KS, 45th, 1926
Mathew, Anthony		K, 51st Ohio (died of old age)	301	76	1915 Dec 15	NE, 41st, 1917
Mathew, Harrison H.		G, 6th Ind. Cav. G, 71st Ind. Inf.	19	93, 6 mos. & 1 day	1937 Jul 10	IA, 64th, 1938
Mathew, John H.	Pvt.	H, 31st Iowa Inf.	54		1922 Dec 18	IA, 49th, 1923
Mathews, C.W.	Pvt.	H, 37th Ohio Cav.	497		1923 Dec 2	IA, 50th, 1924
Mathews, David	Pvt.	C, 13th Iowa Inf.	18	56	1890 Aug 2	IA, 18th, 1892
Mathews, F.M.		A, 9th Kans.	12		1926 May 13	KS, 46th, 1927
Mathews, Fred		H, 96th N.Y.	28		1927 Aug 27	KS, 47th, 1928
Mathews, G.W.		E, 36th Ill.	130		1921 Apr 24	KS, 41st, 1922
Mathews, H.M.	Pvt.	C, 1st Mo.	153		1925 Mar 11	IA, 52nd, 1926
Mathews, Hiram Bennett		G, 99th Ind. Inf. (at large)		91	1938 Apr 15	IA, 64th, 1938
Mathews, Isaac	Pvt.	E, 36th Iowa Inf.	497		1926 Jun 2	IA, 53rd, 1927
Mathews, J.A.		G, 24th Iowa	64		1922 Mar 4	KS, 42nd, 1923
Mathews, J.F.		died of old age	143	81	1915 May	NE, 40th, 1916
Mathews, J.P.		F, 9th N.Y. Cav.	175		1916 Sep 13	KS, 36th, 1917
Mathews, J.W.		I, 10th Ill. Cav.	28		1891 Sep	KS, 11th, 1892
Mathews, J.W.			123		1886	NE, 11th, 1887
Mathews, Jas. C.			35		1897 Sep 4	NE, 22nd, 1898
Mathews, John L.	Lieut.	B, 13th Iowa Inf.	16		1909 Feb 4	IA, 36th, 1910
Mathews, Mark	Sergt.	G, 20th Iowa Inf.	88		1913 Apr 9	IA, 40th, 1914
Mathews, N.A.		B, 134th Ohio	255		1918 Dec 30	KS, 38th, 1919
Mathews, P.H.			98		1927 Oct 16	KS, 47th, 1928
Mathews, Paul	Pvt.	25th N.Y. Battery	12		1927 Jul 22	IA, 54th, 1928
Mathews, Robert		L, 2nd Mo.	17		1927 Jan 8	KS, 47th, 1928
Mathews, T.A.		D, 4th Iowa	258		1892 Jan 28	KS, 12th, 1893
Mathews, W.T.	1st Lieut.	D, 39th Iowa Inf.	173		1900 Jan 2	IA, 27th, 1901
Mathewson, J.B.		B, 101st N.Y. Inf. (died of disease of liver)	10	70	1912 Dec 10	NE, 37th, 1913
Mathias, A.J.			2		1909 Feb 12	IA, 36th, 1910
Mathias, H.M.		H, 53rd Ill.	25		1928 Nov 18	KS, 48th, 1929
Mathias, Joseph		M, 5th Penn. Hvy. Art.	127		1912 Aug 7	KS, 32nd, 1913
Mathias, William R.		K, 15th Iowa	64		1939 Oct 17	KS, 59th, 1940
Mathick, I.A.		15th West Va. Inf. (died of wounds)	155	48	1896 Sep 13	NE, 21st, 1897
Mathies, C.L., see Matthis, C.L.						
Mathis, C.G.			2		1928	IA, 55th, 1929
Mathis, Cal.			231		1929 Jan 19	IA, 55th, 1929
Maths, George	Corp.	E, 82nd Ill. Inf.		96	1939 Nov 9	IA, 66th, 1940
Matlack, J.B.			29		1917	IA, 44th, 1918
Matlick, Jacob G.	Pvt.	B, 2nd West Va. Cav.	12	89	1932 Aug 24	IA, 59th, 1933
Matlock, Joseph B.	Sergt. Major	35th Mo. Inf.	158		1884	KS, 4th, 1885
Matlock, Wm. H.		U.S. Navy	58		1910 Dec 31	IA, 38th, 1912
Matlocks, Wilder M.	Pvt.	H, 38th Iowa Inf.	48		1899 Mar 7	IA, 26th, 1900
Matmaker, John		B, 51st Ohio	256		1920 Jun 12	KS, 40th, 1921
Matrau, Henry C.		G, 6th Wis.	25	72	1917 Jan 5	NE, 42nd, 1918
Matson, Chas. Perry	Pvt.	B, 44th Wis. Inf. (at large)	80	93	1940 Oct 30	IA, 67th, 1941
Matson, W.C.	Pvt.	H & I, 70th & 86th N.Y. Inf.	78		1929 Dec 26	IA, 56th, 1930
Mattack, J.R.		A, 130th Penn.	37		1913 Oct 31	KS, 33rd, 1914
Matteson, D.W.		A, 16th Ill.	5		1913 Nov 12	KS, 33rd, 1914

*See Appendix A, B or C for roster of post names and locations.
†See Introduction for note regarding recording of death date.

Name	Rank	Company, Regiment or Ship	Post*	Age	Death Date†	Journal
Matteson, G.C.		D, 47th Ill.	12	88	1934 Oct 8	IA, 61st, 1935
Matteson, Mark J.		A, 1st Wis. Hvy. Art.	at large		1929	NE, 55th, 1931
Matthews, B.A.	Pvt.	B, 3rd Iowa Inf.	49		1917 May 9	IA, 44th, 1918
Matthews, G.J.		I, 8th Mich. Cav.	356		1916 Sep	KS, 36th, 1917
Matthews, Geo. W.		A, 110th Ill.	100		1911 Nov 28	KS, 31st, 1912
Matthews, Jacob		U.S. Navy	1		1912 Apr 9	KS, 32nd, 1913
Matthews, John		D, 83rd U.S.C.T.	380		1912 Oct 7	KS, 32nd, 1913
Matthews, Lee	Pvt.	E, 42nd Ill. Inf.	452	37	1888 Sep 6	IA, 15th, 1889
Matthews, S.W.		F, 104th Penn.	14		1910 Aug 21	KS, 30th, 1911
Matthews, Samuel S.		I, 127th U.S. Colored Inf.	153		1912 Aug 31	KS, 32nd, 1913
Matthews, T.E.	Pvt.		222		1908 Apr	IA, 35th, 1909
Matthews, Thomas		I, 25th Iowa	257		1915 Jan 5	KS, 35th, 1916
Matthews, W.R.	Pvt.	E, 4th Iowa Cav.	16		1905 Feb 16	IA, 32nd, 1906
Matthews, W.T.	Lieut.	D, 39th Iowa Inf.	173		1899 Jan 2	IA, 26th, 1900
Matthewson, Angel	Capt.	D, 1st N.Y. Lt. Art.	64		1913 Jan 15	KS, 33rd, 1914
Matthewson, Joseph		L, 7th Ill. Cav.	53		1886	KS, 6th, 1887
Matthias, J.J.	Pvt.	E, 3rd Md. Inf.	235	43	1887 Feb 17	IA, 14th, 1888
Matthis, C.L.	Seaman	U.S. gunboat *Benton*	5		1901 May 6	IA, 27th, 1901
Mattingly, G.T.		E, 31st Wis.	1		1928 Jul 7	KS, 48th, 1929
Mattingly, John	Pvt.	E, 11th Ill. Cav.	222		1922 Feb 10	IA, 49th, 1923
Mattison, David		A, 10th Wis.	63		1919 Sep 6	KS, 39th, 1920
Mattison, J.D.		G, 1st N.Y. Art.	77		1925 Jun 28	KS, 45th, 1926
Mattison, James	Pvt.	G, 47th Iowa Inf.	40		1929 Apr 28	IA, 56th, 1930
Mattison, James		H, 16th Wis. (died of old age)	42		1913 Oct 16	NE, 38th, 1914
Mattison, Luther	Pvt.	G, 86th N.Y. (died of cancer)	196	46	1885 Sep 9	NE, 10th, 1886
Mattison, Peter		A, 59th Ill.	7		1930 Feb 20	NE, 55th, 1931
Mattix, Jacob	Pvt.	B, 38th Iowa Inf.	182	53	1892 May 28	IA, 19th, 1893
Matton, David		G, 2nd Neb. (died of dropsy)	66	54	1897 Jun 11	NE, 22nd, 1898
Mattox, C.H.	Pvt.	H, 16th Iowa Inf.	190		1911 Jan 15	IA, 38th, 1912
Mattox, Thos. H.		A, 78th Ill.	156		1906 Aug 21	KS, 26th, 1907
Matz, Marx		B, 16th Iowa (died of paralysis)	4	72	1908 Oct 14	NE, 33rd, 1909
Matz, Simon		B, 2nd Colo. Cav.	2		1908 Feb 6	KS, 28th, 1909
Matzka, Wm.					1929 Jan 3	NE, 53rd, 1929
Maudsley, C.W.	Pvt.	F, 31st Iowa Inf.	4	57	1887 Dec 19	IA, 14th, 1888
Maues, Jacob Eli		L, 5th Ind. Cav.	1		1931 Dec 26	KS, 51st, 1932
Maukley, Michael		D, 107th Ohio Inf.	57		1887 May 6	KS, 7th, 1888
Maul, Ben		K, 57th Ind. Inf.	284		1913 Oct 14	IA, 40th, 1914
Maul, Edward	Pvt.	I, 22nd Iowa Inf.	112		1900 Sep 21	IA, 27th, 1901
Maul, Mathias		U.S. Regulars	25		1905 Jul 14	NE, 30th, 1906
Maul, Matthias		U.S. Regulars	25		1905 Jul 14	NE, 31st, 1907
Maule, C.I.		F, 124th Ohio Inf.	15		1916 Nov 22	KS, 36th, 1917
Maunder, Samuel H., see Mannder, Samuel H.						
Maur, Geo. G.	Lieut.	I, 21st Iowa	78		1907 Feb 19	IA, 34th, 1908
Maur, William	Pvt.	H, 19th U.S. Inf.	452		1911 May	IA, 38th, 1912
Maurer, Abraham		A, 191st Penn.	85		1917 May 13	KS, 37th, 1918
Maurer, Jno. D.		A, 94th Ohio	85		1911 Apr 6	KS, 31st, 1912
Maurice, David		B, 17th Ill.	291		1931	NE, 56th, 1932
Maurice, David		B, 17th Ill.	291		1930 Dec 20	NE, 55th, 1931
Maus, John A.		5th Penn. Res.	85		1913 Sep 18	KS, 33rd, 1914
Maus, John H.		G, 125th Penn.	262		1919 Jan 17	NE, 44th, 1920
Maus, John H.		G, 125th Penn. Inf.	262	74	1919 Jan 17	NE, 43rd, 1919
Mause, J.E.		L, 5th Ind.	1		1931 Dec 28	KS, 52nd, 1933
Maust, Eliza A.		K, 171st Penn. Inf. (died of paralysis)	84	86	1925 Apr 6	NE, 50th, 1926
Maver, John M.G., Rev.		E, 28th Mich.	250		1919 Nov 24	KS, 39th, 1920
Max, Friedly		E, 3rd Mo.			1927 Aug 22	NE, 52nd, 1928
Max, John		C, Battery Ill.	17		prior to 1891	KS, 11th, 1892
Maxen, L.L.		F, 102nd Ill.	463		1909 Aug 15	KS, 29th, 1910
Maxfield, Geo.		F, 112th Ill. (died of heart failure)	18	68	1900 May 1	NE, 25th, 1901
Maxon, —		Neb. (died of old age)	134	82	1916 Oct 25	NE, 41st, 1917
Maxon, C.S.	Pvt.	B, 21st Iowa Inf.	190		1928 Dec 24	IA, 55th, 1929
Maxon, John R.		H, 45th Iowa Inf. (see Appendix D)	91		1924 Dec 23	NE, 49th, 1925

*See Appendix A, B or C for roster of post names and locations.
†See Introduction for note regarding recording of death date.
349

Name	Rank	Company, Regiment or Ship	Post*	Age	Death Date†	Journal
Maxon, Nathan E.	Pvt.	C, 40th Wis. Inf.	150		1904 May 15	IA, 31st, 1905
Maxon, Willard H.	Pvt.	C, 11th Kans. Inf.	249		1927 Dec 6	IA, 54th, 1928
Maxwell, A.F.			55		1919 Sep 21	KS, 39th, 1920
Maxwell, A.J.			64		1884	KS, 4th, 1885
Maxwell, A.W.	Pvt.	F, 25th Wis.	365		1907 Apr 8	IA, 34th, 1908
Maxwell, Andrew J.		D, 3rd Colo.	64		1885	KS, 5th, 1886
Maxwell, Benjamin		E, 174th Ohio Inf.	32		1925 Oct 8	KS, 45th, 1926
Maxwell, C.B.	Landsman	U.S.S. Michigan	1		1898 Oct 14	KS, 18th, 1899
Maxwell, Chas.	Pvt.	F, 15th Ill. Inf.	125		1911 Jul 1	IA, 38th, 1912
Maxwell, Edward L.		15th Ky. Cav.	65		1912 Apr 15	KS, 32nd, 1913
Maxwell, J.H.		A, 17th U.S. Inf.	71		1923 Feb 8	KS, 43rd, 1924
Maxwell, J.N.		A, 32nd Iowa Cav.	66		1919 Aug 19	IA, 46th, 1920
Maxwell, L.B.	Surg.	14th West Va.	256		1906 Jun 19	KS, 26th, 1907
Maxwell, Robt.		I, 2nd Kans. Cav.	119		1895 May 31	KS, 15th, 1896
Maxwell, S.B.		K, 134th Ohio	55		1913 Oct 28	KS, 33rd, 1914
Maxwell, Samuel	Pvt.	E, 125th Ohio Inf.	364		1908 Sep 26	IA, 35th, 1909
Maxwell, T.H.	Capt.	I, 25th Iowa Inf.	108		1899 Jul 27	IA, 26th, 1900
Maxwell, T.J.	Surg.	3rd Iowa Cav.	2		1905 Aug 1	IA, 32nd, 1906
Maxwell, Vincent		I, 25th Iowa	49		1905 Nov 1	KS, 25th, 1906
Maxwell, W.T.	Sergt.	H, 1st Iowa Cav.	440		1919 Aug 24	IA, 46th, 1920
May, Alex.		E, 6th Ohio Inf.	127		1901 Jun 15	KS, 21st, 1902
May, Alexander P.		A, 53rd Iowa	240		1914 Sep 4	KS, 34th, 1915
May, Alonzo M.	Sergt.	B, 40th Wis. Inf.	194		1925 Mar 15	IA, 52nd, 1926
May, Dan		D, 96th Ohio (died of insanity)	151	69	1910 May 28	NE, 35th, 1911
May, David		K, 31st Ind. Inf.	72		1936 Jan 10	KS, 55th, 1936
May, Dexter		A, 7th Kans.	201		1925 Jan 25	KS, 45th, 1926
May, Hollis		6th Vt.	412		1918	KS, 38th, 1919
May, Jacob		K, 88th Penn.	225		1920 Dec 31	KS, 40th, 1921
May, James M.		I, 11th Kans. Cav.	225		1901 Dec 20	KS, 21st, 1902
May, Jerry		52nd U.S. Cav.	132		1911 May 12	KS, 31st, 1912
May, Jesse	Lieut.	B, 7th West Va. Cav.	108		1924 May 16	KS, 44th, 1925
May, John		G, 49th Ohio	1		1910 Jan 18	KS, 30th, 1911
May, N.H.	Pvt.	H, —	22		1923 Feb 5	IA, 50th, 1924
May, Richard	Pvt.	A, 23rd Iowa Inf.	234		1917 Dec 10	IA, 44th, 1918
May, T.P.	Corp.	G, 17th Mich. Inf.	118		1905 May 23	IA, 32nd, 1906
May, Thos. J.		A, 38th N.Y.	46		1922 Aug 30	KS, 42nd, 1923
May, William		not a member of post named, but buried by said post	8		1897	KS, 17th, 1898
May, Wm. J.		I, 11th Kans. Cav.	160		1916 Dec 20	KS, 36th, 1917
Maya, John		6th Mo. Cav. (died of old age)	163	85	1916 Oct 21	NE, 41st, 1917
Mayborn, T.		A, 14th N.Y. (died of cancer)	35	75	1918 Jul 4	NE, 43rd, 1919
Maybury, Alonzo		B, 124th Ohio Inf.	15	87	1935 Oct 10	IA, 62nd, 1936
Mayer, Chas.	Pvt.	F, 1st Iowa Cav.	112		1919 Apr 2	IA, 46th, 1920
Mayer, Geo. W.			515		1912 Dec 30	IA, 40th, 1914
Mayer, Geo. W.			515		1914 Dec 30	IA, 41st, 1915
Mayer, Henry		H, 4th U.S.	36		1914 Oct 17	KS, 34th, 1915
Mayer, J.H.		D, 58th Ohio	378		1926 Oct 21	KS, 46th, 1927
Mayer, W.	Pvt.	H, 23rd Ill. Inf.	452		1924 Sep 12	IA, 51st, 1925
Mayew, W.C.	Pvt.	I, 25th Iowa Inf.	108		1925 Oct 31	IA, 52nd, 1926
Mayfield, Alexander		I, 14th U.S. Cav.	25		1930 Sep 25	KS, 50th, 1931
Mayfield, Alexander			36		1930 Sep 25	KS, 50th, 1931
Mayfield, Isaac		120th Ind. Inf.	210		1900 Dec 25	KS, 20th, 1901
Mayfield, Lee			3		1916 Jun 16	KS, 36th, 1917
Mayhall, G.W.		F, 72nd Ind.	1		1897 Apr 20	KS, 17th, 1898
Mayler, E.			7		1915	KS, 35th, 1916
Maynard, Chas.		D, 37th Penn.	292		1896 Jan 4	KS, 16th, 1897
Maynard, H.H.	Pvt.	H, 145th Penn. Inf.	235		1917 Oct 28	IA, 44th, 1918
Maynard, H.P.		A & E, 86th Ohio A, 189th Ohio	147		1922 Sep	KS, 42nd, 1923
Maynard, L.W.	Pvt.	D, 156th Ill.	22		1926 May 16	IA, 53rd, 1927
Maynard, P.E.	Pvt.	G, 53rd Penn. Inf.	159		1908 Oct 18	IA, 35th, 1909
Maynard, Sam'l M.	Pvt.	9th Vt. Inf.	86		1908 Oct 15	IA, 35th, 1909

*See Appendix A, B or C for roster of post names and locations.
†See Introduction for note regarding recording of death date.

Name	Rank	Company, Regiment or Ship	Post*	Age	Death Date†	Journal
Maynard, W.W.		F, 2nd N.Y.	256		1913 Jun 8	KS, 33rd, 1914
Maynard, Wm.		C, 47th Iowa Inf.	98	91	1935 Sep 21	IA, 62nd, 1936
Mayne, J.B.	Corp.	A, 15th Ill. Inf.	244		1904 Jul 5	IA, 31st, 1905
Mayne, James	Pvt.	A, 3rd Iowa Inf. A, 3rd Iowa Bat.	88	76	1895 May 4	IA, 22nd, 1896
Maynihan, Pat		H, 9th Ill. Inf.	339		1887 Feb 14	KS, 7th, 1888
Maynilken, H.H.	2nd Lieut. Pvt.	G, 8th Res. Corps F, 1st Va. Cav.	2	58	1896 Sep 19	IA, 23rd, 1897
Mayo, Lewis		B, 87th Ill.	6		1911 Jun 28	KS, 31st, 1912
Mayou, Merrill			23		1911 Jun 27	KS, 31st, 1912
Mays, Jas. S.	Pvt.	A, 21st Iowa Inf.	92		1911 Aug 21	IA, 38th, 1912
Mayweatner, Geo.	Pvt.	K, 60th U.S. Colored Inf.	250	54	1899 Jan 9	IA, 25th, 1899
Maze, W.A.		I, 84th Ind. (died of cancer)	1	85	1917 Jul 30	NE, 42nd, 1918
McAdam, John	Pvt.	I, 1st U.S. Cav.	70		1910 Dec 18	IA, 37th, 1911
McAdams, George		G, 74th Ohio	51		1910 May 6	KS, 30th, 1911
McAdams, Henry H.		E, 22nd Ill.	36		1920 Feb 7	KS, 40th, 1921
McAdams, John T.		E, 3rd Ill.	380		1897 Dec 12	KS, 17th, 1898
McAdams, Walter		H, 10th Iowa	65		1910 Sep 21	KS, 30th, 1911
McAfee, Hiram		E, 63rd Ind.	74		1904	KS, 24th, 1905
McAfee, J.A.	Pvt.	D, 4th Ohio Cav.	12	88 & 7 mos.	1932 Jul 4	IA, 59th, 1933
McAfee, J.B.		I, 11th Kans.	1		1908 May 19	KS, 28th, 1909
McAffee, Edwin	Pvt.	C, 67th Ill. Inf.	365		1915 Dec 3	IA, 42nd, 1916
McAlister, J.J.	Sergt.	E, 78th Ohio Inf.	24	48	1894 Jul 15	IA, 21st, 1895
McAlister, John	Sergt.	I, 69th Ohio Inf.	235		1928 Apr 17	IA, 55th, 1929
McAllaster, J.E.		K, 2nd Iowa Cav.	20		1900 Oct 31	KS, 20th, 1901
McAllester, W.A.		B, 2nd Neb. Cav.	9		1923 Jan	NE, 48th, 1924
McAllister, D.J.	Pvt.	K, 14th Wis. Inf.	101	41	1885 May 25	IA, 12th, 1886
McAllister, F.C.	Pvt.	G, 4th Iowa Inf.	322		1900 Aug 24	IA, 27th, 1901
McAllister, F.O.	Pvt.	G, 27th Iowa Inf.	3		1913 Jun 22	IA, 40th, 1914
McAllister, Jas. E.	Pvt.	A, 5th Iowa Inf.	7		1920 Apr 18	IA, 47th, 1921
McAlpin, L.B.	Sergt.	F, 23rd Iowa Inf.	11		1919 Jan 18	IA, 46th, 1920
McAndrew, John	Lieut.	H, 34th Iowa Inf.	55		1914 Nov 25	IA, 41st, 1915
McAndrew, P.D.		K, 9th Ill. Cav.	171		1935 Jul 5	NE, 60th, 1936
McAnnich, Wm.	Pvt.	B, 16th Iowa Inf.	1		1918 May 4	IA, 45th, 1919
McArthur, H.C.		K, 15th Iowa	25		1926 Apr 26	NE, 51st, 1927
McArthur, J.A.	Pvt.	A, 44th Iowa Inf.	78		1911 Jul 28	IA, 38th, 1912
McArthur, W.H.H.		K, 31st Ohio	158		1914 Oct	KS, 34th, 1915
McAtee, Frank M., see Mcater, Frank M.						
McAtee, George		K, 18th Ohio	17		1923 Mar	KS, 43rd, 1924
McAtee, Wm.		E, 19th Ind.	35		1908	NE, 33rd, 1909
Mcater, Frank M.	Pvt.	K, 57th Ohio	212		1907 Dec 15	IA, 34th, 1908
McAuerd, J.F.		B, 117th Ind.	286		1905	KS, 25th, 1906
McAuley, Henry		I, 16th Ill. (killed by cars)	24	73	1910 Oct 20	NE, 35th, 1911
McAuley, John W.		I, 11th Ill. Cav. (cause of death: kicked by horse)	90	67	1913 Sep 23	NE, 38th, 1914
McBeath, Samuel A.		A, 7th Penn. Inf. 17th Penn. Cav.	408		1912 Dec 8	KS, 32nd, 1913
McBetg, Thomas	Pvt.	C, 148th Penn. Inf.	219		1917 Jan	IA, 44th, 1918
McBeth, Wm.			79		1917 May 26	IA, 44th, 1918
McBeth, Wm.		3rd Ohio Bat. Lt. Art. (died of old age)	26	87	1924 Nov 10	NE, 49th, 1925
McBirney, H.G.	Pvt.	E, 11th Iowa Inf.	30		1910 Nov 6	IA, 37th, 1911
McBith, Robt. R.			19		1909 Sep 20	IA, 36th, 1910
McBride, D.A.	Pvt.	1st Reg. State Militia Cav.	235		1915 May 28	IA, 42nd, 1916
McBride, Ezekiel		I, 13th Ohio Vol. Inf.	27		1915 Oct	KS, 35th, 1916
McBride, J.C.		H, 57th Ill. (died of dysentery)	44	83	1920 Sep 24	NE, 45th, 1921
McBride, Jas.		F, 35th Iowa (died of old age)	10	84	1904 Feb 11	NE, 29th, 1905
McBride, L.L.		B, 162nd Ohio	380		1904 Jul 12	KS, 24th, 1905
McBride, Lewis C.		H, 12th Ind. Cav. (see also Appendix D)	25	94	1941 Sep 21	NE, 66th, 1942
McBride, Martin		M, 13th Mo. Cav.	293		1922 Jun 3	KS, 42nd, 1923
McBride, William			18		1926	IA, 53rd, 1927
McBride, William T.		B, 8th Mo. Inf.	6		1901 Jan 28	KS, 21st, 1902

*See Appendix A, B or C for roster of post names and locations.
†See Introduction for note regarding recording of death date.

Name	Rank	Company, Regiment or Ship	Post*	Age	Death Date†	Journal
McBrien, Wm.		I, 15th Mo. Cav.	25		1905 Jun 2	NE, 31st, 1907
McBrien, Wm.		I, 15th Mo. Cav.	25		1905 Jun 2	NE, 30th, 1906
McBrier, J.H.		C, 16th Penn. Cav.	132		1893 Mar 13	KS, 13th, 1894
McBroom, J.D.	Capt.	K, 106th N.Y. Inf.	72		1908 May 11	IA, 35th, 1909
McBroom, John	Sergt.	E, 4th Iowa Cav.	321	49	1886 Dec 9	IA, 13th, 1887
McBurney, J.B.		B, 69th Ohio	265		1918 May 12	KS, 38th, 1919
McBurney, J.H.		K, 13th Ky.	274		1916 Oct 31	KS, 36th, 1917
McBurny, S.	Pvt.	C, 142nd Ill. Inf.	193		1918 Nov 1	IA, 45th, 1919
McCabe, J.B.		H, 1st Wis.	108		1897 Jun 5	KS, 17th, 1898
McCabe, Shepard		C, 86th Ind.	293		1917 Mar 28	KS, 37th, 1918
McCabe, Terry	Pvt.	B, 3rd Wis. Inf.	103		1919 Oct 26	IA, 46th, 1920
McCade, W.A.			22		2nd quarter 1885	IA, 12th, 1886
McCaffery, C.	Pvt.	A, 38th Penn.	2		1921 Dec 22	IA, 48th, 1922
McCaffrey, B.	Pvt.	I, 9th Mich. Inf.	329		1900 Nov 21	IA, 27th, 1901
McCaffrey, Cornelius	Pvt.	C, 43rd Ohio Inf.	40		1915 Dec 9	IA, 42nd, 1916
McCaffrey, John W.		E, 34th Iowa	293		1911 May 29	KS, 31st, 1912
McCahill, Mat.	Pvt.	H, 34th Iowa Inf.	12		1931 Jan 16	IA, 58th, 1932
McCahlend, J.R.		A, 53rd Ill.	18	76	1917 Mar 15	NE, 42nd, 1918
McCain, Geo. D.	Pvt.	F, 47th Iowa Inf.	12		1916 Feb 2	IA, 43rd, 1917
McCain, George	Pvt.	K, 16th Ind. Inf.	26		1930 Jan 25	IA, 57th, 1931
McCain, William	Corp.	F, 2nd Wis. Cav.	466		1901 Mar 4	IA, 27th, 1901
McCall, D.H.		F, 199th Penn. Inf.	147		1899 Jul 22	KS, 19th, 1900
McCall, Daniel E.		C, 12th Iowa	297		1919 Jul 1	KS, 39th, 1920
McCall, Geo. W.	1st Lieut.	H, 6th Iowa Cav.	7	70	1889 Nov 24	IA, 16th, 1890
McCall, George			24		1901 Sep	IA, 28th, 1902
McCall, James		D, 29th Iowa Inf.	23		1918 Jul 31	IA, 45th, 1919
McCall, John	Pvt.	D, 10th Iowa Inf.	67		1902 Mar 6	IA, 29th, 1903
McCall, Samuel		E, 75th Ill. Inf. (died at Columbus; buried at Columbus Cemetery)	59		1894 Aug 15	KS, 14th, 1895
McCall, Solomon			67		1922 Apr 27	IA, 49th, 1923
McCall, Thomas C.	R.Q.M.	M, 32nd Iowa Inf.	31		1892 Aug	IA, 19th, 1893
McCall, Thos.	Pvt.	I, 13th Iowa Inf.	1		1922 Dec 31	IA, 49th, 1923
McCall, W.H.		C, 53rd Penn.	297		1914 Jun 28	KS, 34th, 1915
McCall, W.J.	Pvt.	G, 1st Iowa Cav.	154		1917 Mar 18	IA, 44th, 1918
McCall, W.R.	Pvt.	D, 29th Iowa	22		1923 Mar	IA, 50th, 1924
McCall, W.T.	Pvt.	D, 29th Iowa	22		1926 Sep 20	IA, 53rd, 1927
McCall, William	Pvt.	I, 25th Iowa Inf.	108		1917 Aug 20	IA, 44th, 1918
McCalle, J.B.	Corp.	K, 13th Mo. Inf.	57		1920 Feb 20	IA, 47th, 1921
McCalley, Geo. W.	Pvt.	A, 18th Iowa Inf.	206		1918 Feb 12	IA, 45th, 1919
McCalliff, John	Pvt.	G, 31st Wis. Inf.	81		1910 Aug 22	IA, 37th, 1911
McCalmont, Elisha K.		H, 14th Iowa	265		1930 Jan 20	NE, 55th, 1931
McCammon, George W.		A, 29th Ohio	225		1905 May 15	KS, 25th, 1906
McCampbell, Andrew	Pvt.	19th Iowa Inf.	333		1918 Mar 4	IA, 45th, 1919
McCan, Pat.		Marine Corps	180		1899	KS, 19th, 1900
McCan, W.J.	Pvt.	I, 2nd Iowa Cav.	107		1920 Mar 2	IA, 47th, 1921
McCandles, Milton W.		C, 66th Ind.	98		1932 Dec 6	NE, 57th, 1933
McCandles, Philip S.		E, 18th Ill.	7		1932 Mar 26	NE, 57th, 1933
McCanlon, Miles H.		H, 26th Ind.	81		1915 Sep 22	KS, 35th, 1916
McCann, J.D.		K, 106th Ill. Inf. (died of army disabilities)	84	73	1901 Feb	NE, 26th, 1902
McCann, Mike		B, 4th Minn.	447		1916 Jun 12	KS, 36th, 1917
McCann, Patrick	Pvt.	D, 149th Penn. Inf.	29		1892 Feb 10	IA, 19th, 1893
McCann, Robert H.		G, 11th Wis. (died of old age)	4	78	1924 Oct 10	NE, 49th, 1925
McCann, Robt.		H, 1st N.J.	380		1904 Feb 20	KS, 24th, 1905
McCann, S.S.		C, 3rd Wis.	12		1925 Apr 7	KS, 45th, 1926
McCann, S.S.		C, 3rd Wis. Cav.	12		1925 Apr 7	KS, 44th, 1925
McCann, Thomas	Pvt.	C, 29th Iowa Inf.	52		1914 Nov 9	IA, 41st, 1915
McCans, Jerome		C, 39th Mo. Inf.	265		1928 Feb 23	NE, 52nd, 1928
McCants, Leander	Pvt.	B, 138th Ill. Inf. B, 118th Ill. Inf.	100	93	1938 Dec 18	IA, 65th, 1939
McCardell, C.C.	Pvt.	F, 5th Penn.	68		1922 Apr 6	IA, 49th, 1923
McCarity, Frank		B, 9th Ill.	175		1889	KS, 9th, 1890
McCarky, J.K.	2nd Lieut.	C, 27th Ind. Inf.	97	68	1900 Feb 20	IA, 26th, 1900

*See Appendix A, B or C for roster of post names and locations.
†See Introduction for note regarding recording of death date.

352

Name	Rank	Company, Regiment or Ship	Post*	Age	Death Date†	Journal
McCarmie, Thomas		U.S.N., New York	113		1923	KS, 43rd, 1924
McCart, A.R.	Pvt.	F, 17th Iowa	123		1905 Feb 5	IA, 32nd, 1906
McCarten, J.			112		1923	NE, 48th, 1924
McCarter, C.C.		C, 2nd Ohio	278		1926 Nov 15	KS, 46th, 1927
McCarter, Tyrus		M, 8th Ill. Cav. (died of old age)	180	72	1901 Aug	NE, 26th, 1902
McCartey, A.	Pvt.	C & H, 52nd Ill. Inf. (died of consumption)	44	50	1887 Apr 2	NE, 12th, 1888
McCarthy, D.F.	2nd Lieut.	H, 10th Minn.	12		1899 Jun 19	IA, 26th, 1900
McCarthy, Isaac	Pvt.	E, 7th Ill. Cav.	74	72	1898 Apr 23	IA, 24th, 1898
McCarthy, Timothy		I, 4th Mass. Hvy. Art.	87		1892 Dec 3	KS, 12th, 1893
McCarthy, Timothy		died at his home in Larned (see also Appendix D)			1900 Jun 12	KS, 20th, 1901
McCartney, George		E, 41st Wis. Inf.	231	88	1935 Feb 15	IA, 62nd, 1936
McCartney, J.	Landsman	U.S. gunboat	25		1914 Dec 11	KS, 34th, 1915
McCartney, J.S.		D, 22nd Penn. Cav.	81		1926 Aug	NE, 51st, 1927
McCartney, James	Pvt.	K, 21st Iowa Inf.	332		1927 Jan 28	IA, 54th, 1928
McCartney, James W.		H, 11th Kans.	1		1917 Jul 9	KS, 37th, 1918
McCartney, John A.		D, Ind. Vols.	7		1924[1923?] Feb 12	NE, 48th, 1924
McCartney, M.	Pvt.	B, 13th Iowa	30		1906 Jun 8	IA, 33rd, 1907
McCartney, Theo.	Pvt.	A, 13th Iowa Inf.	66		1901 Aug 10	IA, 28th, 1902
McCartny, John	Pvt.	G, 33rd Mo. Inf.	306		1908 Mar 6	IA, 35th, 1909
McCarty, C.B.		C, 16th Ind.	85		1929 Apr 27	KS, 49th, 1930
McCarty, George W.		H, 15th Ill. Cav. (died at LeRoy, Kans.; buried at LeRoy Cemetery)	190		1894 Jul	KS, 14th, 1895
McCarty, Gilmour		I, 5th Mo. Cav.	25	85	1918 Dec 29	NE, 43rd, 1919
McCarty, H.J.	Pvt.	3rd Ill. Battery	100		1895 May 20	IA, 22nd, 1896
McCarty, John E.		I, 21st Ohio Inf.	42		1921 Jul 18	KS, 41st, 1922
McCarty, Justice		K, 129th Penn.	362		1912 Jan 13	KS, 31st, 1912
McCarty, Levi		B, 62nd Ohio	127		1906 Oct 16	KS, 26th, 1907
McCarty, Thomas		C, 1st La.	380		1897 Apr 19	KS, 17th, 1898
McCarty, Wm.			87		1909 Feb 16	KS, 29th, 1910
McCashland, B.C.		I, 53rd Ill. (died of heart trouble)	22	80	1925 Jul 9	NE, 50th, 1926
McCaslin, Geo.		D, 17th Ind.	1		1926 May 15	KS, 46th, 1927
McCaslin, Harvey		H, 15th Kans.	35		1911 Nov 16	KS, 31st, 1912
McCaslin, J.C.		I, 8th Ind.	129		1908 Apr 14	KS, 28th, 1909
McCauley, C.H.	Pvt.	B, 23rd Iowa Inf.	7		1898 Mar 22	IA, 26th, 1900
McCauley, F.W.		I, 1st Ohio Vol. Inf.	50		1924 Jun 20	KS, 44th, 1925
McCauley, Frank		D, Ill. Inf.	17		1936 May 6	KS, 56th, 1937
McCauley, John		E, 15th Ill.	147		1913 Jun 29	KS, 33rd, 1914
McCaully, Joseph	Sergt.	A, 9th Ill. Cav.	235		1906 Jan 12	IA, 33rd, 1907
McCauly, James		D, 12th Ind.	324	85	1934 Mar 31	IA, 61st, 1935
McCausland, J.A.	Pvt.	I, 20th Ohio Cav.	432		1917 May 1	IA, 44th, 1918
McCausland, W.F.		I, 85th Ill.	90		1927 May 2	KS, 47th, 1928
McCay, John		D, 51st Ohio (died of paralysis)	35	73	1917 May 1	NE, 42nd, 1918
McChafney, Fred		A, 2nd Mich.	6		1922 Nov 2	KS, 42nd, 1923
McCherry, Thomas		B, 115th Ill.	83		1905 Aug 16	KS, 25th, 1906
McChesney, George		A, 34th Iowa	44		1916 Apr 27	KS, 36th, 1917
McChesney, Leander		B, 1st N.J. Art.	88		1909 Nov 15	KS, 29th, 1910
McChesney, R.G.	Sergt.	A, 53rd Ohio Inf.	108		1927 Jan 26	IA, 54th, 1928
McClain, A.H.	Pvt.	F, 123rd Ohio Inf.	363		1904 Jul 8	IA, 31st, 1905
McClain, Arthur		K, 1st Wis. Cav. (died of heart failure)	355		1892 Oct 12	KS, 12th, 1893
McClain, J.					1890	KS, 10th, 1891
McClain, John		H, 40th Ill.	352		1932 Feb 16	NE, 57th, 1933
McClain, Jonathan	Pvt.	F, 40th Iowa Inf.	317	66	1897 May 11	IA, 24th, 1898
McClain, Wm.	Pvt.	H, 13th Iowa Inf.	168		1906 Nov 30	IA, 33rd, 1907
McClain, Wm.	Pvt.	G, 1st Wis. Cav.	77		1906 Feb 3	IA, 32nd, 1906
McClain, Wm., see Mclain, Wm.						
McClanahan, F.M.			96		1908	IA, 35th, 1909
McCland, R.W.		I, 7th Ill.	335		1896 May 4	KS, 16th, 1897
McClaren, Robt.		E, 8th Ohio	382		1896 Mar 20	KS, 16th, 1897
McClaren, W.A.		D, 4th Penn.	36		1917 Dec 22	KS, 37th, 1918
McClaskey, Jno. R.	Sergt.		81		1919 Nov 15	IA, 46th, 1920

*See Appendix A, B or C for roster of post names and locations.
†See Introduction for note regarding recording of death date.
353

Name	Rank	Company, Regiment or Ship	Post*	Age	Death Date†	Journal
McClaskey, John R.	Sergt.	A, 13th Iowa Inf.	343		1919 Jan 24	IA, 46th, 1920
McClean, Alexander	Pvt.	E, 33rd Iowa Inf.	452	91	1935 Oct 5	IA, 65th, 1939
McClearn, R.E.	Pvt.	10th Iowa Inf.	141		1900 Nov	IA, 27th, 1901
McCleary, E.J.		D, 17th Kans.	68		1921 Jan 14	KS, 41st, 1922
McCleary, Geo. W.	Pvt.	C, 46th Iowa Inf.	14		1909 Dec 3	IA, 36th, 1910
McCleary, J.D.	Sergt.		116		1914 Apr 9	IA, 41st, 1915
McCleary, James	Sergt.	H, 55th Ill. Inf.	188		1899	NE, 24th, 1900
McCleary, James A.	Pvt.	21st Ohio Inf.	22		1931 Mar 19	IA, 58th, 1932
McCleary, Mose	Pvt.	F, 8th Kans.	1		1922 Aug 17	IA, 49th, 1923
McClees, J.H.		G, 8th Ind. Cav.	32		1933 Dec 7	NE, 58th, 1934
McClellan, C.B.		K, 22nd Ohio Inf.	18		1899 Feb 24	KS, 19th, 1900
McClellan, F.W.		4th Iowa Bat.	85		1912 May 28	KS, 32nd, 1913
McClellan, J.S.		Ind.	265		1921 Jun 2	KS, 41st, 1922
McClellan, John L.	Pvt.	E, 2nd Penn. Inf.	58		1913 Mar 4	IA, 40th, 1914
McClellan, M.A.		K, 69th N.Y.	244		1922 Mar	KS, 42nd, 1923
McClellan, R.T.		M, 9th Penn. Cav. (died of consumption)	25	68	1902 Aug	NE, 27th, 1903
McClellan, W.L.		H, 27th & 168th Ohio	18		1920 Apr 10	KS, 40th, 1921
McClellan, W.S.	Pvt.	B, 55th Penn. Inf.	11	43	1886 Apr 24	IA, 13th, 1887
McClelland, F.	Asst. Surg.	16th Iowa Inf.	235	66	1896 Feb 13	IA, 22nd, 1896
McClelland, G.P.	Capt.	F, 155th Penn. Inf.	1	55[?]	1898 Dec 27	IA, 25th, 1899
McClelland, J.H.	Pvt.	F, 136th Ohio Inf.	263		1905 Jul 16	IA, 32nd, 1906
McClelland, M.G.	Pvt.	L, 133rd N.Y. Inf.	72	57	1889 Mar 15	IA, 16th, 1890
McClelland, T.L.		C, 114th Ill.	12		1911 Jun 29	KS, 31st, 1912
McClement, Samuel	Pvt.	E, 17th Wis.	101		1901 Jul 7	IA, 28th, 1902
McClenathan, A.	Pvt.	A, 4th Vt.	8		1899	NE, 24th, 1900
McClenehan, Robert		F, 5th Iowa Inf.	167		4th quarter 1883	IA, 10th, 1884
McClenny, W.C.		I, 2nd Kans. Cav.	225		1916 Sep 14	KS, 36th, 1917
McClery, D.D.	Pvt.	H, 162nd Ohio Inf.	255		1909 Jul 15	IA, 36th, 1910
McClester, John		12th Penn.	426		1905 Oct	KS, 25th, 1906
McClintick, Sam W.	Pvt.	K, 98th Ohio Inf.	54		1914 Jul 2	IA, 41st, 1915
McClintick, T.H.		C, 123rd Ohio (died of gastritis)	231	65	1911 Jan 16	NE, 36th, 1912
McClintoc, John			96		1919	NE, 44th, 1920
McClintock, Harvey		K, 134th Ohio	322		1900 Apr 30	KS, 20th, 1901
McClintock, J.R.	Pvt.	H, 12th Ill. Cav.	3		1910 Sep 3	IA, 37th, 1911
McClintock, James P.		K, 171st Penn.	175		1909 Mar 5	KS, 32nd, 1913
McClintock, John		K, 34th Ohio Inf. (died at Moline, Kans.; buried at Moline Cemetery)	110		1894 May 1	KS, 14th, 1895
McClintock, John R.		E, — Ill. (died of liver trouble)	23		1919 Dec 9	NE, 44th, 1920
McClintock, Jos.		H, 76th Ohio	187		1897 Oct 1	KS, 17th, 1898
McClintock, Mathias		K, 212th Penn. Inf.	147		1934 Aug 10	KS, 54th, 1935
McClintock, W.J.		B, 33rd Ill.	447		1926 Dec 2	KS, 46th, 1927
McClintook, John E.	Pvt.	H, 23rd Iowa Inf.	297		1913 Feb 21	IA, 40th, 1914
McClog, Jno.		D, 12th Mich.	85		1904 Sep 26	KS, 24th, 1905
McClosky, —	Corp.	E, 9th Ohio Cav.	158		1925 Nov 5	IA, 52nd, 1926
McClosky, Wm. P.	Corp.	H, 1st Col. Cav.	168		1910 Dec 6	IA, 37th, 1911
McCloud, John		A, 33rd Ind. Inf.	153		1912 Mar 8	KS, 32nd, 1913
McCloud, Williamson		A, 33rd Ind.	153		1905 Aug 15	KS, 25th, 1906
McCluey, Robt.	Pvt.	E, 118th Ill. Inf.	2		1905 Oct 16	IA, 32nd, 1906
McClung, John S.		A, 68th Ill. Inf.	25		1925 Mar 10	KS, 45th, 1926
McClung, Wm.		B, 76th Penn.	100		1926 Feb 15	KS, 46th, 1927
McClung, Zarah		Calif. Vet. Bat.	356		1898 Aug 1	KS, 18th, 1899
McClure, A.W.	Surg.	4th Iowa Cav.	20		1905	IA, 32nd, 1906
McClure, George F.		C, 5th Ill. Cav. (died at Wichita; buried at Maple Grove Cemetery)	25		1894 Jul 13	KS, 14th, 1895
McClure, J.A.		H, 173rd Ohio	380		1913 Apr 6	KS, 33rd, 1914
McClure, J.W.		F, 36th Ill. Inf. (died of old age)	4	79	1922 Dec 14	NE, 47th, 1923
McClure, Jas. F.		B, 123rd Ind.	355		1928 Nov 7	KS, 48th, 1929
McClure, Jno. O.	Sergt.	B, 10th Iowa Cav.	230		1923 Aug 1	IA, 50th, 1924
McClure, Joseph T.		B, 47th Ill.	378		1919 Nov 4	KS, 39th, 1920
McClure, R.B.		G, 159th Ohio	66		1914 Nov 3	KS, 34th, 1915
McClure, R.M.		H, 17th Ind.	33		1927	KS, 47th, 1928
McClure, Reuben		I, 15th Kans.	6		1926 May 18	KS, 46th, 1927

*See Appendix A, B or C for roster of post names and locations.
†See Introduction for note regarding recording of death date.

Name	Rank	Company, Regiment or Ship	Post*	Age	Death Date†	Journal
McClure, Robert		A, 102nd Ohio	43		1900 Nov 27	KS, 20th, 1901
McClure, Robert		B, 1st N.H.	288		1927 Sep	KS, 47th, 1928
McClure, Robert M.		H, 17th Ind.	33		1926 Dec 25	KS, 46th, 1927
McClure, S.A.		A, 48th Iowa	289		1898 May 1	KS, 18th, 1899
McClure, S.H.		C, 54th Ind.	147		1929 Oct 2	NE, 54th, 1930
McClure, Sam'l H.	Pvt.	C, 151st Ohio Inf.	54		1911 Aug 23	IA, 38th, 1912
McClure, T.B.		C, 7th Iowa	85		1929 Jul 11	KS, 49th, 1930
McClure, Thomas		K, B, 60th Ind.	250		1923 May 26	KS, 43rd, 1924
McClure, Thos.	Sergt.	3rd Bat. 18th U.S.	141		1903 Jan 31	IA, 30th, 1904
McClure, Thos.	Pvt.	H, 3rd U.S. Art.	141		1904 Jan 31	IA, 31st, 1905
McClure, W.H.			265		1906 Jul 4	KS, 26th, 1907
McClure, W.H.		H, 71st Ohio	51		1916 Dec 12	KS, 36th, 1917
McClure, Wm.		D, 4th Kans. Cav.	293		1929	KS, 49th, 1930
McClure, Wm.		K, 2nd Mo. Cav.	41		1935 Feb 3	KS, 54th, 1935
McClure, Wm. H.	Lieut.	3rd Iowa Battery	222		1908 Nov 17	IA, 35th, 1909
McClurg, Thomas		D, 102nd Ill. Inf.	115		1886	KS, 6th, 1887
McCollim, A.J.		K, 145th Ohio	85		1912 Aug 12	KS, 32nd, 1913
McCollister, Archibald		D, 5th Kans.	32		1916 Feb 11	KS, 36th, 1917
McCollister, M.M.		K, 94th Ohio	25		1916 Aug 17	KS, 36th, 1917
McCollom, J.N.			122		1913 Mar 39	IA, 40th, 1914
McCollough, J.B.	Pvt.	H, 116th Penn. Inf.	1		1911 Dec 5	IA, 38th, 1912
McCollum, A.		K, 36th Ohio	17		1913 Oct 14	KS, 33rd, 1914
McCollum, Jas.	Surg.	2nd & 25th Wis. Inf.	216	80	1897 Feb 7	IA, 23rd, 1897
McColm, J.L.	Pvt.	A, 30th Ohio Inf.	231		1925 Sep 8	IA, 52nd, 1926
McComant, A.	Pvt.	F, 3rd Wis. Inf.	292		1917 Jan 3	IA, 44th, 1918
McComb, C.I.	Pvt.	C, 206th Penn.	55		1923 Mar 22	IA, 50th, 1924
McComb, Daniel			7		1893 Jan 1	KS, 13th, 1894
McComb, John	Pvt.	G, 16th N.Y. Cav.	48		1919 Sep 25	IA, 46th, 1920
McComb, Samuel		I, 98th Ohio	40		1916 Apr 15	KS, 36th, 1917
McComber, J.A.			25		1936	KS, 56th, 1937
McCombs, John		2nd Iowa Cav.	32		1893 Nov	KS, 13th, 1894
McComel, Theophilus		E, 1st Mich.	55		1910 Jun 28	KS, 30th, 1911
McConahay, John	Pvt.	D, 120th Ohio	22		1907 2nd term	IA, 34th, 1908
McConahughey, A.	Pvt.	D, 40th Ohio Inf.	49		1929 Mar 2	IA, 56th, 1930
McConahy, Frank A.	Pvt.	H, 20th Iowa Inf.	235	56	1899 May 24	IA, 26th, 1900
McConan, W.		K, 4th Iowa	113		1888	KS, 8th, 1889
McConaughy, A.D.		K, 30th Ill. Inf.	93		1890	KS, 10th, 1891
McConihey, E.C.			23		1924 Dec 6	KS, 44th, 1925
McConkey, J.W.	Pvt.	G, 107th Ill. Inf.	392		1911 Dec 3	IA, 38th, 1912
McConnell, A.F.	Sergt.	B, 23rd Wis. Inf.	124		1909 Oct 12	IA, 36th, 1910
McConnell, B.J.		F, 11th Iowa	63		1930 Mar 11	NE, 55th, 1931
McConnell, Cyrus J.		D, 22nd Iowa Inf.	337		1917 Dec 31	IA, 44th, 1918
McConnell, G.B.		A, 93rd Ill. (died of general debility)	43	61	1907 May 24	NE, 32nd, 1908
McConnell, H.K.		B, 71st Ohio	11		1889	KS, 9th, 1890
McConnell, J.A.		E, 155th Penn. Inf.	1		1934 Jun 17	KS, 54th, 1935
McConnell, James	Corp.	G, 47th Ill. Inf.	197	48	1886 Sep 22	IA, 13th, 1887
McConnell, Jos.	Capt.	M, 2nd Iowa Cav.	92		1910 Jan 4	IA, 37th, 1911
McConnell, O.T.		C, 15th Penn. Cav.	13	77	1918 Jun 10	NE, 43rd, 1919
McConnell, Owen		U.S.A.	22		1922 Jun 2	KS, 42nd, 1923
McConnell, W.H.			58		4th quarter 1883	IA, 10th, 1884
McConnell, Wm. K.		K, 3rd Mo. Cav.	134		1889	KS, 9th, 1890
McConoughey, Robert L.		A, 51st Ohio Cav.	25		1920 Jan 6	KS, 40th, 1921
McCool, W.C.		I, 29th Ohio (died of old age)	98	86	1920 Dec 12	NE, 45th, 1921
McCool, W.C.		I, 29th Iowa	48		1926	NE, 51st, 1927
McCord, Blaine M.		G, 14th Penn. Cav. (died of softening of artery)	4	67	1912 Feb 16	NE, 37th, 1913
McCord, J.A.	Sergt.	A, 1st Iowa Cav.	12		1928 Sep 12	IA, 55th, 1929
McCord, James J.	Sergt.	I, 31st Iowa Inf.	269		1897 May 6	IA, 24th, 1898
McCord, M.A.	Pvt.	K, 28th Iowa Inf.	16		1929 Jun 4	IA, 56th, 1930
McCord, R.D.		C, 7th Ill. Cav.	88		1912 Jan 4	KS, 32nd, 1913
McCord, Thos. T.	Pvt.	K, 28th Iowa Inf.	16		1917 Jan 7	IA, 44th, 1918
McCord, W.D.		E, 37th Ill. Inf. (cause of death: heart)	90		1903 Oct	NE, 28th, 1904

*See Appendix A, B or C for roster of post names and locations.
†See Introduction for note regarding recording of death date.

Name	Rank	Company, Regiment or Ship	Post*	Age	Death Date†	Journal
McCorkle, G.W.		K, 7th Lt. Art.	127		1927 May 27	KS, 47th, 1928
McCormack, A.G.		A, 160th Ohio	142		1909 Feb 7	KS, 29th, 1910
McCormack, Doctor		G, 38th Ind.	85		1923 Sep 19	KS, 43rd, 1924
McCormack, J.B.	Pvt.	H, 5th Ind. Inf.	94		1926 Sep 3	IA, 53rd, 1927
McCormack, Jas.		F, 11th Kans.	54		1902 Aug 17	KS, 22nd, 1903
McCormack, William		H, 31st Ill. Cav.	65		1908 Apr 8	KS, 28th, 1909
McCormack, Wm.	Pvt.	H, 45th Ill.	231		1914 Dec 21	IA, 41st, 1915
McCormic, M.		G, 174th Ohio Inf.	83		1925 Jul 7	KS, 45th, 1926
McCormick, Alb't N.	Capt.	H, 1st Iowa Cav.	18	58	1894 Nov 20	IA, 21st, 1895
McCormick, Bernard	Pvt.	C, 32nd Iowa Inf.	68		1909 Aug 21	IA, 36th, 1910
McCormick, J.		D, 3rd Mich.	96		1888	KS, 8th, 1889
McCormick, J.L.	Capt.	E, 8th Iowa Inf.	49		1904 Dec 29	IA, 31st, 1905
McCormick, J.T.	Pvt.	C, 17th Iowa Inf.	313		1910 Jan 22	IA, 37th, 1911
McCormick, J.W.		K, 3rd Ohio	186		1888	KS, 8th, 1889
McCormick, J.W.		K, 3rd Ohio Cav.	186		1886 Nov 23	KS, 11th, 1892
McCormick, James		F, 47th Ill. Inf.	90	72	1910 Aug 3	NE, 35th, 1911
McCormick, James D.		B, 65th U.S. Col.	257		1925 Dec 9	KS, 45th, 1926
McCormick, Jno. W.	Pvt.	E, 6th Ill. Cav.	69	88	1933 Oct 13	IA, 60th, 1934
McCormick, John		E, 1st Iowa Cav.	25		1908 Oct 10	KS, 28th, 1909
McCormick, John W.		B, 151st Ill. (died of cancer of mouth)	21	77	1922 Apr 15	NE, 47th, 1923
McCormick, Joseph		B, 147th Ind. Inf. (died of old age)	84	82	1914 Sep 23	NE, 39th, 1915
McCormick, Owen	Pvt.	F, 5th Mo. Inf.	127	60	1892 Feb 5	IA, 18th, 1892
McCormick, P.H.		D, 3rd Mich. Cav.	96		1887	KS, 7th, 1888
McCormick, Patrick	Pvt.	E, 155th Ill. Inf.	22		1932	IA, 59th, 1933
McCormick, R.	Pvt.	F, 26th Ill. Inf.	26		1912 Jul 24	IA, 39th, 1913
McCormick, R.F.		D, 154th Ill. Inf.	69		1915 Oct 15	IA, 42nd, 1916
McCormick, S.P.	Bugler	A, 4th Iowa Cav.	263		1906 Sep 1	IA, 33rd, 1907
McCormick, T.B.		A, 68th Ill. Inf.	25		1934 Jul	KS, 54th, 1935
McCormick, Thos. J.	Pvt.	G, 151st Ill.	271		1923 Aug 1	IA, 50th, 1924
McCosh, P.	Pvt.		122		1920	IA, 47th, 1921
McCoslin, Frank	Pvt.	I, 40th Wis. Inf.	101		1922 Mar 20	IA, 49th, 1923
McCosna, A.I.		C, 119th Ill.	158		1920 Jul 7	KS, 40th, 1921
McCowan, W.L.	Pvt.	E, 18th Ill. Inf.	124		1930 Mar 22	IA, 57th, 1931
McCowen, A.P.		E, 5th Ohio	25		1927 Aug 20	KS, 47th, 1928
McCoy, A.H.		E, 130th & 202nd Penn.	115		1918 Dec 7	KS, 38th, 1919
McCoy, A.J.	Pvt.	H, 30th Ind. Inf.	122		1919 Feb 9	IA, 46th, 1920
McCoy, Albert R.	Corp.	D, 140th Ill. Inf.	88	50	1896 Sep 30	IA, 23rd, 1897
McCoy, Ben.	Pvt.	H, 47th Iowa Inf.	40		1920 Aug 24	IA, 47th, 1921
McCoy, Benj.	Pvt.	E, 3rd West Va. Inf.	66		1927 Apr 6	IA, 54th, 1928
McCoy, C.M.	Corp.	H, 140th Penn. Inf.	116		1926 Jan 28	IA, 52nd, 1926
McCoy, Charles		E, 7th Iowa Inf. (at large)		89	1935 Sep 20	IA, 62nd, 1936
McCoy, Charles		E, 7th Iowa Inf.	2	89	1935 Sep 20	IA, 62nd, 1936
McCoy, Charles P.		I, 64th Ill.	12		1910 Aug 10	KS, 30th, 1911
McCoy, Chas.	Corp.	E, 2nd U.S. Inf.	515		1912 Jan 13	IA, 38th, 1912
McCoy, Chas.	Pvt.	140th Penn. Inf.	116		1926 Jan 28	IA, 53rd, 1927
McCoy, D.J.	Sergt.	B, 6th Iowa Inf.	208	68	1898 Apr 18	IA, 25th, 1899
McCoy, D.J.	Sergt.	B, 6th Iowa Inf.	208	68	1899 Apr 18	IA, 25th, 1899
McCoy, David J.	Major	6th Iowa Inf.	208	68	1898 Apr 18	IA, 24th, 1898
McCoy, H.C., Dr.	Pvt. & Hosp. Stew. Asst. Surg.	31st Wis. Inf. 3rd Tenn. Cav. (see Appendix D)	165		1901 Mar 10	IA, 27th, 1901
McCoy, H.W.	Capt.	F, 10th Ind. Inf.	49		1927 Sep 22	IA, 54th, 1928
McCoy, Henry	Corp.	K, 6th Iowa Inf.	246		1910 Sep 22	IA, 37th, 1911
McCoy, J.W.	Pvt.	E, 22nd Iowa Vol. Inf.	107		1901 Mar 9	IA, 28th, 1902
McCoy, James B.		A, 87th Ohio	243		1898 Oct 5	KS, 18th, 1899
McCoy, James Gilbert	Corp.	E, 3rd U.S. Inf. (at large)	12	94	1940 Jan 24	IA, 66th, 1940
McCoy, John	Pvt.	G, 23rd Ill. Inf.	311		1916 Aug 4	IA, 43rd, 1917
McCoy, John		F, 1st N.Y. Lt. Art.	101		1914 Jun 27	KS, 34th, 1915
McCoy, John C.		1st Wis. Lt. Art.	124		1928 Dec 19	IA, 55th, 1929
McCoy, Jonas M.		H, 90th Vol. Cav.	51		1914 Dec 30	KS, 34th, 1915
McCoy, Joseph		K, 133rd Ill. Inf.	364		1925 Feb 25	KS, 45th, 1926
McCoy, Joseph T.		C, 11th Iowa	81		1913 Jul 31	KS, 33rd, 1914
McCoy, N.A.	Pvt.	B, 44th Iowa	231		1914 Sep 14	IA, 41st, 1915

*See Appendix A, B or C for roster of post names and locations.
†See Introduction for note regarding recording of death date.
356

Name	Rank	Company, Regiment or Ship	Post*	Age	Death Date†	Journal
McCoy, P.R.		I, 18th Penn. Cav.	318		1913 Jun	NE, 38th, 1914
McCoy, Patrick		H, 14th Wis. Inf. (died of liver enlargement)	86	56	1895 Jan 29	NE, 20th, 1896
McCoy, S.L.		K, 19th Iowa	25		1926 Nov 10	NE, 51st, 1927
McCoy, Sam. Moses			18		1926	IA, 53rd, 1927
McCoy, W.H.	Pvt.	G, 27th Ill. Inf.	231		1915 Jan 8	IA, 42nd, 1916
McCoy, W.H.	Pvt.	H, 17th Ill. Cav.	68		1917 Sep 5	IA, 44th, 1918
McCoy, W.M.	Pvt.	D, 8th Iowa	166		1905 Apr 28	IA, 32nd, 1906
McCoy, W.P.		D, West Va. Lt. Art.	47		1926 Jun	NE, 51st, 1927
McCoy, W.W.		died of old age	92	80	1914 Dec 17	NE, 39th, 1915
McCoy, Wm.		D, 28th Iowa Inf. (died of cancer)	44		1905 Apr	NE, 30th, 1906
McCoy, Wm. A.	Pvt.	H, 5th Kans. Cav.	325	70	1893 Nov 22	IA, 20th, 1894
McCoy, Wm. H.		F, 1st Mo. M. Cav.	18		1916 Nov 28	KS, 36th, 1917
McCoy, Wm. W.	Pvt.	K, 47th Ill. Inf.	321	56	1892 Jun 19	IA, 19th, 1893
McCracken, A.J.		D, 2nd Art. Cav.	164		1909 Aug 14	KS, 29th, 1910
McCracken, Charles T.		K, 12th Conn.	237		1896 Dec 27	KS, 16th, 1897
McCracken, E.W.	Corp.	46th Iowa Inf.	111		1932	IA, 59th, 1933
McCracken, Isaac L.		G, 93rd Ohio Vol. Inf.	14		1908 Aug 26	KS, 28th, 1909
McCracken, J.G.			54		1883	KS, 3rd, 1884
McCracken, J.W.		D, 38th Wis. Inf. (died of paralysis)	81		1894 Feb 11	NE, 19th, 1895
McCracken, Jno. T.		C, 24th Iowa	147		1904 Feb 11	KS, 24th, 1905
McCrady, W.	Pvt.	K, 109th N.Y. Inf.	156		1910 Feb 21	IA, 37th, 1911
McCrady, Wm. A.	Pvt.	C, 5th Iowa Inf.	254	60	1893 Feb 21	IA, 19th, 1893
McCrarey, A.B.			11		1925	IA, 52nd, 1926
McCrary, —			11		1927	IA, 54th, 1928
McCrary, F.M.		29th Ind.	8		1889	KS, 9th, 1890
McCrary, Geo. B.	Corp.	B, 83rd Ill.	156		1922 Aug 19	IA, 49th, 1923
McCrary, J.C.	Major	G, 3rd Iowa Cav.	79	75	1892 Jun 25	IA, 19th, 1893
McCrary, James C.	Pvt.	A, 7th —	177		1907 Dec 19	IA, 34th, 1908
McCrary, Jas. B.		A, 58th Ind. Inf.	85		1886	KS, 6th, 1887
McCrary, Lewis		39th Iowa	311		1921	KS, 41st, 1922
McCrary, M.R.	Pvt.	E, 61st Ill. Inf.	156		1906 Jul 9	IA, 33rd, 1907
McCrary, Miner	Pvt.	G, 3rd Iowa Cav.	254		1923 Sep 17	IA, 50th, 1924
McCray, Addison	Pvt.	8th Iowa Cav.	57		1913 Apr 1	IA, 40th, 1914
McCray, James B.	Lieut.	C, 30th Iowa	157		1914 Mar 17	IA, 41st, 1915
McCray, John		D, 93rd Ohio	244		1919 Aug 18	KS, 39th, 1920
McCray, William	Pvt.	C, 31st Iowa Inf.	68	76	1894 Sep 10	IA, 21st, 1895
McCrea, B.G.		A, 3rd Ind.	180		1911 Jan 11	KS, 31st, 1912
McCready, J.A.		G, 68th Ind.	25		1927 Oct 10	KS, 47th, 1928
McCready, M.P.	Pvt.	K, 17th Iowa Inf.	349	56	1892 Nov 11	IA, 19th, 1893
McCready, Samuel		G, 68th Ind. Inf. (died at Florence; buried at Florence)	202		1894 Dec 1	KS, 14th, 1895
McCreary, J.S.	Pvt.	E, 100th Penn.	156		1905 Mar 24	IA, 32nd, 1906
McCreary, Joseph		K, 184th Ohio	90		1922 Nov 25	KS, 42nd, 1923
McCreath, James		F, 155th Ill. Inf.	12		1909 Aug 22	KS, 29th, 1910
McCree, E.		C, 10th Mo. (died of cancer heart)	35	78	1917 Nov 10	NE, 42nd, 1918
McCrellis, —	Sergt.	A, 25th Wis. Inf.	81		1927 Sep 14	IA, 54th, 1928
McCrew, Mathew S.	Pvt.	K, 184th Ohio Inf.	446		1912 Jan 13	IA, 39th, 1913
McCrew, V.Y.		I, 3rd Ky. Cav.	4		1914 Dec 5	KS, 34th, 1915
McCright, George		C, 177th Ohio (nonmember; died at Fremont)			1936 Dec	NE, 61st, 1937
McCristal, F.B.		E, 3rd Ill. Cav.	22		1906 Sep 30	IA, 33rd, 1907
McCrory, Joseph		H, 80th Ill.	1		1905 Aug 16	KS, 25th, 1906
McCrosky, J.W.		B, 5th Iowa Inf. (died of pneumonia)	45		1894 Aug 12	NE, 19th, 1895
McCubbin, W.H.		44th Mo.	500		1929 Dec 9	KS, 49th, 1930
McCuchon, O.G.			204		1899	IA, 26th, 1900
McCulick, Jonaz		A, 43rd Wis.	127		1918 Apr 2	KS, 38th, 1919
McCulla, Lewis J.	Pvt.	11th Iowa Inf.	219		1926 May	IA, 53rd, 1927
McCulla, Lewis J.	Pvt.	C, Art.	219		1927 Oct	IA, 54th, 1928
McCullaugh, John R.	Pvt.	I, 1st Ind. Bat.	59		1918 May 13	IA, 45th, 1919
McCullock, Jonas		A, 43rd Wis.	127		1918 Jul 18	KS, 38th, 1919
McCullon, Stephen M.	1st Lieut.	B, 64th Ohio	284		1901 Nov 11	IA, 28th, 1902

*See Appendix A, B or C for roster of post names and locations.
†See Introduction for note regarding recording of death date.

357

Name	Rank	Company, Regiment or Ship	Post*	Age	Death Date†	Journal
McCullong, J.A.		K, 14th Iowa	432		1888	KS, 8th, 1889
McCullough, A.R.	Pvt.	D, 20th Iowa Inf.	1		1917 Nov 21	IA, 44th, 1918
McCullough, C.		E, 8th Iowa	25		1914 May 20	KS, 34th, 1915
McCullough, F.M.	Pvt.	B, 126th Ill. Inf.	1		1917 Feb 24	IA, 44th, 1918
McCullough, J.A.		C, 11th Kans. Cav.	196		1902 Apr 30	KS, 22nd, 1903
McCullough, J.C.		E, 2nd Ind. Cav.	59		1929 Oct 12	KS, 50th, 1931
McCullough, John	Pvt.	A, 11th Iowa Inf. (died from explosion of engine)	20	48	1891 Aug 3	NE, 16th, 1892
McCullough, John		B, 3rd Ohio Inf.	68	92	1926 Feb 4	NE, 50th, 1926
McCullough, L.R.			321		1924 Feb 1	IA, 51st, 1925
McCullough, Wm.		K, 32nd Iowa	44		1917 Sep 15	KS, 37th, 1918
McCullow, P.J.	Pvt.	H, 4th Iowa Cav.	216		1910 Nov 10	IA, 37th, 1911
McCullum, Archibal	Pvt.	B, 43rd Wis. Inf.	78		1912 Mar 27	IA, 39th, 1913
McCullum, H.S.		I, 8th Ill. Inf.	324		1917 Feb 28	IA, 44th, 1918
McCully, Jno.		D, 13th Kans.	93		1905 May 3	KS, 25th, 1906
McCully, Lyle		Penn. Cav.	90		1912 Apr 12	KS, 32nd, 1913
McCully, W.A.		65th Ohio (died at Independence)	4		1896 Jan	KS, 15th, 1896
McCumber, C.F.	Pvt.	E, 10th N.Y. Inf.	440		1911 Nov 8	IA, 38th, 1912
McCune, Hugh		C, 65th Ill. Inf. (died of paralysis)	13	82	1920 Sep 1	NE, 45th, 1921
McCune, J.W.		C, 105th Penn.	7		1928 Dec 3	NE, 53rd, 1929
McCune, Jas.	Pvt.	H, 36th Iowa Inf.	385	52	1892 Apr 7	IA, 19th, 1893
McCune, John	Pvt.	D, 78th Ohio Inf.	334		1900 Oct 18	IA, 27th, 1901
McCune, Thomas		died of old age	72	74	1918 Sep	NE, 43rd, 1919
McCune, W.H.	Pvt.	A, 15th Iowa	88		1926 Jun 15	IA, 53rd, 1927
McCune, W.P.		L, 7th Mo.	303		1909 Dec 17	KS, 29th, 1910
McCurdy, J.A.	Pvt.	A, 22nd Wis. Inf.	452		1919 Mar 9	IA, 46th, 1920
McCurdy, J.B.	Corp.	C, 28th Iowa Inf.	40		1926 Oct 6	IA, 53rd, 1927
McCurdy, J.P.		K, 11th Penn.	17		1904 Nov 16	KS, 24th, 1905
McCurdy, Robert		A, 73rd Ill. Inf. (died from rupture of blood vessel in brain)	383		1892 Jul 11	KS, 12th, 1893
McCurdy, T.E.	Pvt.	I, 12th Ill. Inf.	63		1929 Jan 14	IA, 56th, 1930
McCurry, John		A, 3rd Ill. Cav. I, 113th Ill. Inf. B, 120th Ill. Inf.	18		1920 Nov 14	KS, 40th, 1921
McCurry, Joseph F.		I, 1st Tenn.	412		1921 Oct 3	KS, 41st, 1922
McCusker, Patrick	Pvt.	E, 38th Iowa Inf.	168		1902 Oct 2	IA, 29th, 1903
McCutchan, R.P.		A, 42nd Ind. Inf.	11	79	1917 Oct 11	NE, 42nd, 1918
McCutchen, B.F.		F, 8th Penn. Inf.	25		1925 Jun 10	KS, 45th, 1926
McCutchen, M.M.		A, 43rd Ind.	81		1920 Jun 4	KS, 40th, 1921
McCutcheon, W.R.	Pvt.	I, 9th Penn. Inf.	108		1919 Dec 18	IA, 46th, 1920
McDaniel, D.	Pvt.	C, 112th Penn. Inf.	95		1906 May 15	IA, 33rd, 1907
McDaniel, D.M.	Pvt.	C, 4th West Va. Cav.	158	66	1891 Aug 3	IA, 18th, 1892
McDaniel, J.F.	Pvt.		329		1921 Oct 6	IA, 48th, 1922
McDaniel, J.S.	Lieut.	B, 2nd Wis. Cav.	235		1912 Dec 14	IA, 39th, 1913
McDaniel, J.S.			235		1913 Jan 3	IA, 40th, 1914
McDaniel, James		C, 20th Iowa (died of old age)	118	78	1911	NE, 36th, 1912
McDaniel, John W.		E, 5th Ind. Cav.	474		1915 Mar 28	KS, 35th, 1916
McDaniel, Richard		E, 31st Penn.	63		1928 Jul 13	KS, 48th, 1929
McDaniel, Wm.		C, 36th Iowa Inf. (cause of death: kidney)	32	67	1905 Apr 4	NE, 30th, 1906
McDaniel, Wm.		location: Aurora			1927 Dec 31	NE, 52nd, 1928
McDanield, W.H.H.		K, 23rd Ind. Inf.	69		1914 Dec 11	KS, 34th, 1915
McDaniels, E.F.	Sergt.	A, 5th Cal. Cav.	66		1913 Jan 28	IA, 40th, 1914
McDaniels, J.N.		H, 185th N.Y. Inf. (died of consumption)	134	64	1896 Apr 26	NE, 21st, 1897
McDaniels, James	Pvt.	H, 28th Iowa Inf.	321		1892	IA, 19th, 1893
McDaunald, P.H.		33rd Ind.	74		1915 Apr 9	KS, 35th, 1916
McDerby, David		E, Mich. Hvy. Art. (died of Bright's disease)	64		1894 Oct 31	NE, 19th, 1895
McDermott, Jas.	Lieut.	I, 4th Ky. Inf.	85		1918 Apr 26	KS, 38th, 1919
McDermott, Michael	Pvt.	I, 12th Iowa Inf.	78		1919 Feb 18	IA, 46th, 1920
McDevitt, James			144		1913 Feb 11	KS, 33rd, 1914
McDivitt, C.J.		C, 125th Penn. Vol. Inf.	63		1912 Apr 18	KS, 32nd, 1913
McDole, N.C.	Pvt.	34th Iowa Inf.	55	89	1931 Apr 2	IA, 58th, 1932
McDole, Peter	Pvt.	A, 25th Iowa Inf.	108		1921 Sep 21	IA, 48th, 1922

*See Appendix A, B or C for roster of post names and locations.
†See Introduction for note regarding recording of death date.

Name	Rank	Company, Regiment or Ship	Post*	Age	Death Date†	Journal
McDolvell, C.C.			230		1884	KS, 4th, 1885
McDonald, A.	Corp.	D, 32nd Iowa Inf.	451		1907 May	IA, 34th, 1908
McDonald, A.W.	Pvt.	F, 69th Ill. Inf.	123		1911 Nov 11	IA, 38th, 1912
McDonald, A.Y.	Pvt.	I, 21st Iowa Inf.	78	73	1891 Jul 29	IA, 18th, 1892
McDonald, Alex.	Pvt.	H, 23rd Wis. Inf.	212		1929 May 25	IA, 56th, 1930
McDonald, Alexander	Corp.	D, 175th N.Y. Inf.	74	61	1894 Apr 15	IA, 20th, 1894
McDonald, D.	Pvt.	B, 28th Wis. Inf.	22		1920 Feb 10	IA, 47th, 1921
McDonald, Duncan	Lieut. Col.	2nd Wis. Inf.	396	57	1892 Nov 20	IA, 19th, 1893
McDonald, Fred		A, 83rd U.S. A, Kans.	231		1896 Dec 14	KS, 16th, 1897
McDonald, G.D.		F, 166th Ohio	66		1918 Oct 17	KS, 38th, 1919
McDonald, G.W.	Pvt.	H, 13th Wis. Inf.	55		1911 Sep 26	IA, 38th, 1912
McDonald, George		D, — Ky.	25		1916 Jan 19	KS, 36th, 1917
McDonald, H.J.	Lieut. Col.	11th Conn. Inf.	12		1910 Oct 20	IA, 37th, 1911
McDonald, Hugh	Pvt.	I, 2nd Iowa Inf.	29	64	1896 Jun 27	IA, 23rd, 1897
McDonald, J.C., see McDouald, J.C.						
McDonald, J.N.		E, 57th Penn.	35		1904 Jul 1	KS, 24th, 1905
McDonald, J.P.	Pvt.	C, 49th Mass.	327		1907 Oct 7	IA, 34th, 1908
McDonald, James	Pvt.	E, 2nd Iowa Cav.	74		1923 Mar 18	IA, 50th, 1924
McDonald, James		F, 12th Ill. (killed on railroad)	188		1889	KS, 9th, 1890
McDonald, N.B.		H, 24th Ind.	89		1936 Jun 13	KS, 56th, 1937
McDonald, P.		I, 6th Ind.	98		1898 Dec 19	KS, 18th, 1899
McDonald, P.H., see McDaunald, P.H.						
McDonald, Patrick	Pvt.	B, 34th Ill. Inf.	88	51	1887 Mar 13	IA, 13th, 1887
McDonald, R.S.			202		1905	IA, 32nd, 1906
McDonald, Richard H.		M, 2nd Iowa Cav.	36		1914 Nov 5	KS, 34th, 1915
McDonald, Robert S.	Pvt.	H, 8th Iowa Inf.	202		1919 Sep 5	IA, 46th, 1920
McDonald, Robt.			79		1927	IA, 54th, 1928
McDonald, Sylvanus		D, 25th Mich. (died of Bright's disease)	83		1914 Feb 14	NE, 39th, 1915
McDonald, T.E.	Pvt.	I, 47th Iowa Inf.	40		1905 Aug 31	IA, 32nd, 1906
McDonald, W.A.	Corp.	E, 96th —	23		1921 Dec 29	IA, 48th, 1922
McDonald, William B.		E, 13th Ohio	12		1925 Jan 24	KS, 45th, 1926
McDonald, William B.		E, 13th Ohio Inf.	12		1925 Jan 24	KS, 44th, 1925
McDonald, William R.		L, 6th Va. Cav.	85		1915 Jun 17	KS, 35th, 1916
McDonald, Wm. A.		I, 82nd Ohio Inf.	57		1892 Jun 18	KS, 12th, 1893
McDonaly, Fred		A, 83rd —	208		1896	KS, 16th, 1897
McDonough, James P.	Pvt.	C, 7th Iowa Inf. (at large)	5	92	1939 Jul 6	IA, 65th, 1939
McDonough, John	Pvt.	D, 4th Ohio Cav.	452		1918 Sep 23	IA, 45th, 1919
McDonough, P.	Pvt.	B, 8th Iowa Inf.	40		1920 Mar 4	IA, 47th, 1921
McDorwrin, H.C.		A, 16th Mo. Cav.	133		1887 Apr 22	KS, 7th, 1888
McDouald, J.C.	Pvt.	E, 7th Iowa Cav.	5		1920 Jan 31	IA, 47th, 1921
McDougal, Leander		L, 3rd Mich. Cav. (died of rheumatism & pneumonia)	47	78	1912 Dec 13	NE, 37th, 1913
McDougall, Alex	Pvt.	G, 27th Wis.	91		1923 Mar 21	IA, 50th, 1924
McDougall, Jas.	Pvt.	G, 27th Wis. Inf.	91	76	1893 Jul 20	IA, 20th, 1894
McDougall, John		C, 8th Kans.	463		1919 Dec 20	KS, 39th, 1920
McDowall, West	Pvt.	C, 1st Iowa Cav.	135		1918	IA, 45th, 1919
McDowell, Comrade			279		1914	KS, 34th, 1915
McDowell, Geo.	Corp.	H, 25th Wis. Inf.	242		1920 Apr 15	IA, 47th, 1921
McDowell, Isaiah		D, 2nd Colo. Cav.	127		1913 Apr 23	KS, 33rd, 1914
McDowell, J.A.		A, 59th Ill. Inf. (died of old age)	84		1909 Apr 4	NE, 34th, 1910
McDowell, John		H, 1st Iowa	52		1893 Mar 23	KS, 13th, 1894
McDowell, John H.					1937 Aug 6	IA, 64th, 1938
McDowell, M.W.		H, 44th Ind.	250		1906 Aug 1	KS, 26th, 1907
McDowell, Marion		I, 36th Wis. Inf. (died of dropsy)	204	56	1902 May	NE, 27th, 1903
McDowell, O.P.			37		1917	IA, 44th, 1918
McDowell, R.B.		K, 53rd Penn. Battery	107		1892 Mar 3	NE, 17th, 1893
McDowell, Robert		B, 128th Ohio Inf.	1		1891 May 19	KS, 11th, 1892
McDowell, T.C.		B, 32nd Ohio Inf.	180		1929 Dec 22	KS, 49th, 1930
McDowell, W.H., Dr.		H, 31st Ind.	51		1915 Aug 1	KS, 35th, 1916

*See Appendix A, B or C for roster of post names and locations.
†See Introduction for note regarding recording of death date.

359

Name	Rank	Company, Regiment or Ship	Post*	Age	Death Date†	Journal
McDowell, West	Pvt.	C, 1st Iowa Cav.	135		1917 Nov 17	IA, 44th, 1918
McDowell, William		A, 1st Ohio Art.	66		1899 Apr 26	KS, 19th, 1900
McDuff, Wm.	Pvt.	D, 28th Iowa Inf.	235		1908 Nov 10	IA, 35th, 1909
McDuffie, I.J.	Pvt.	F, 33rd N.Y. Inf.	23		1930 Jul	IA, 57th, 1931
McDuffy, David		Mich.	9		1908 Aug	NE, 33rd, 1909
McDuffy, Geo.		B, 14th Wis.	25		1930 Sep 20	KS, 50th, 1931
McDugal, Wm.		M, 2nd Col. Cav.	4		1910 Oct 10	KS, 30th, 1911
McDunn, Ezra	Masters Mate	U.S. Navy	12		1928 Oct 16	IA, 55th, 1929
McDurham, James			[32?]		1896 Feb 15	KS, 16th, 1897
McEarthson, R.C.		M & C, 15th Ill.	18		1930 Nov 8	KS, 50th, 1931
McEleuain, George		G, 131st Ohio	87		1908 Jun 28	KS, 28th, 1909
McElfresh, John		M, 2nd Mo.	355		1921 Sep 11	KS, 41st, 1922
McElheney, John J.		A, 136th N.Y.	258		1921 Jan 6	KS, 41st, 1922
McElheny, P.H.		F, 13th Penn. Cav.	380		1919 Sep	KS, 39th, 1920
McElhose, G.B.	Pvt.	F, 77th Ohio	22		1922 Aug 23	IA, 49th, 1923
McEllroes, Jesse		K & B, 14th Penn. Cav. (died of urenia & gangrene)	143	81	1922 Dec 25	NE, 47th, 1923
McElrath, Robert	Lieut.	K, 19th Mich. Inf.	414		1904 May 23	IA, 31st, 1905
McElray, W.G.	Capt.	I, 5th Iowa Cav.	49		1915 Nov 25	IA, 42nd, 1916
McElroy, Benjamin		H, 17th Ohio	46		1920 Jun 3	KS, 40th, 1921
McElroy, D.W.	Pvt.	A, 78th Penn. Inf.	2		1911 Feb 8	IA, 38th, 1912
McElroy, George			145		1884	KS, 4th, 1885
McElroy, James C.		H, 13th Kans.	1		1908 Jan 31	KS, 28th, 1909
McElroy, John			116		1916	IA, 43rd, 1917
McElroy, M.	Pvt.	K, 40th Iowa	233		1921 Oct 13	IA, 48th, 1922
McElroy, T.D.	Drummer	K, 18th Iowa Inf.	94		1920 Jul 1	IA, 47th, 1921
McElroy, W.B.	Pvt.	D, 4th Penn. Cav.	235	45	1889 Oct 4	IA, 16th, 1890
McElroy, W.T.			72		1911 Nov 15	KS, 31st, 1912
McElvain, D.		G, 35th Mo. Inf.	32		1934 Dec 29	KS, 54th, 1935
McElvain, Daniel		B, 113th Ind.	32		1935 Dec 12	KS, 55th, 1936
McElwain, M.	Sergt. 1st Sergt.	H, 2nd Neb. Cav. B, 1st Neb. (died of paralysis)	45	49	1888 Apr 28	NE, 13th, 1889
McElwain, Thos.		A, 3rd Ill. Cav.	176		1908 Jul 25	KS, 28th, 1909
McElwee, W.W.	Pvt.	D, 194th Penn. Inf.	227	49	1891 Mar 12	IA, 17th, 1891
McElyea, I.B.	2nd Sergt.	I, 89th Ill. Inf.	30	61	1889 Jul 6	IA, 16th, 1890
McEntire, James	Pvt.	E, 30th Ill. Inf.	5		1926 Apr 5	IA, 53rd, 1927
McEvers, C.N.		F, 101st Ill.	49		1916 May 19	KS, 36th, 1917
McEvers, Chester	Pvt.	B, 5th Iowa Cav.	139	53	1892 Dec 11	IA, 19th, 1893
McEvoy, James		D, 2nd Neb. Cav. (died of pneumonia)	55	68	1911 Apr 4	NE, 36th, 1912
McEvoy, Richard		D, 4th Iowa (died at Hartford; buried at Hartford Cemetery)	196		1894 Aug 29	KS, 14th, 1895
McEwen, David			32		1911 May 20	KS, 31st, 1912
McEwen, Jas. C.		C, 5th Ill.	139		1896 Apr 10	KS, 16th, 1897
McFaddan, G.W.	Pvt.	K, 58th Ind.	9		1905 Jun 21	IA, 32nd, 1906
McFadden, Leander W.		G, 31st Iowa (died of old age)	25	70	1916 May 10	NE, 41st, 1917
McFadden, Walter	Musician	A, 29th Iowa Inf.	29		1911 Aug 19	IA, 38th, 1912
McFall, Chas.	Pvt.	H, 8th Iowa	40		1923 Mar 1	IA, 50th, 1924
McFarlan, Thos.	Pvt.	A, 2nd Wis. Inf.	103		1923 Apr 11	IA, 50th, 1924
McFarland, B.W.	Pvt.	A, 32nd Ill. Inf.	309		1904 Sep 16	IA, 31st, 1905
McFarland, Bart		B, 41st Wis. Inf.	131		1931 Feb 13	KS, 51st, 1932
McFarland, Benj.		D, 12th Ohio Inf.	8		1918 Jan 22	KS, 38th, 1919
McFarland, C.W.			426		1907 2nd term	IA, 34th, 1908
McFarland, Cy		A, 117th Ill.	25		1923	NE, 48th, 1924
McFarland, D.T.		F, 6th Iowa	17		1922 Mar 13	KS, 42nd, 1923
McFarland, E.S.		E, 2nd Kans. Cav.	132		1916 Jun 14	KS, 36th, 1917
McFarland, Edward T.		E, 175th Ohio Inf.	493		1912 Nov 15	KS, 32nd, 1913
McFarland, H.C.		9th Kans. Cav.	248		1906 Nov 7	IA, 33rd, 1907
McFarland, J.A.	Pvt.	13th N.Y. Hvy. Art.	89		1904 Aug 14	IA, 31st, 1905
McFarland, J.F.		K, 186th Ohio	225		1913 Aug 6	KS, 33rd, 1914
McFarland, J.H.	Capt.	D, 6th Vt. Cav.	18		1925 Jan 7	IA, 52nd, 1926
McFarland, James		I, 155th Ill. (died of heart disease)	134	78	1922 Apr 7	NE, 47th, 1923
McFarland, Jno.		C, 185th Ind. Inf.	56		1886	KS, 6th, 1887

*See Appendix A, B or C for roster of post names and locations.
†See Introduction for note regarding recording of death date.

Name	Rank	Company, Regiment or Ship	Post*	Age	Death Date†	Journal
McFarland, John	Pvt.	32nd Iowa Inf.	66		1915 May 24	IA, 42nd, 1916
McFarland, Jos.		C, 57th Penn. Inf. (died in railroad accident)	9	69	1891[1901?] Mar	NE, 26th, 1902
McFarland, Michael		C, 10th Ill. Cav.	243		1916 Oct 17	KS, 36th, 1917
McFarland, R.S.		C, 163rd Ohio National Guard	12		1904 Sep 25	KS, 24th, 1905
McFarland, Samuel		D, 39th Iowa Inf.	85		1916 Oct 19	KS, 36th, 1917
McFarland, W.B.		died of bilious fever	36		1904 Oct 28	NE, 29th, 1905
McFarlin, A.D.		F, 53rd Ill.	65		1922 Oct 21	KS, 42nd, 1923
McFarlin, John A.		F, 1st Penn. Art.	302		1908 Oct 21	KS, 28th, 1909
McFarlin, Wm. M.	Pvt.	E, 8th Iowa Inf.	49		1925 Jul 24	IA, 52nd, 1926
McFatridge, J.C.	Pvt.	M, 3rd Iowa Cav.	398		1917 Jun 7	IA, 44th, 1918
McFeren, James		E, 126th Penn.	81		1928	NE, 53rd, 1929
McFerren, Jacob	Pvt.	K, 9th Iowa Inf.	509		1900 Jul 6	IA, 27th, 1901
McFerren, James			13		1928 Aug 21	NE, 53rd, 1929
McFerren, R.B.		A, 7th Ill.	221		1913 May 8	KS, 33rd, 1914
McGaha, Malcomb		E, 2nd Tenn. Battery	61		1929 May 16	KS, 49th, 1930
McGahea, Geo. W.		D, 122nd Ill. Inf.	66		1918 Apr 26	KS, 38th, 1919
McGander, Michael		I, 2nd Colored Miss. Lt. Inf.	57		1909 Sep 15	KS, 29th, 1910
McGarrah, J.D.	Pvt.	E, 14th Iowa Inf.	7		1926 May	IA, 53rd, 1927
McGarvan, S.D.		A, 117th Ohio	47		1927 Apr 30	KS, 47th, 1928
McGaw, H.B.		C, 97th Ohio (died of heart disease)	13	78	1921 Apr 15	NE, 46th, 1922
McGee, David H.		C, 14th Ky.	18		1910 Aug 8	KS, 30th, 1911
McGee, J.H.		M, 2nd Iowa (died of heart trouble)	21	82	1919 Dec 14	NE, 44th, 1920
McGee, J.W.		C, 134th Ill.	49		1931 Mar 3	KS, 52nd, 1933
McGee, J.W.		C, 134th Ill.	49		1931 Mar 3	KS, 51st, 1932
McGee, John		C, 124th Ill.	127		1924 Aug 6	KS, 44th, 1925
McGee, Thos.		E, 146th Ill.	51		1926 Dec 28	KS, 46th, 1927
McGee, William			17		1937 Jan 27	KS, 57th, 1938
McGee, Wm. H.	Pvt.	A, 1st Col. Cav.	78		1908 Dec 31	IA, 35th, 1909
McGeehan, Wm.			6		1913	IA, 40th, 1914
McGeehon, R.S.		H, 124th Penn. Inf.	6	97	1936 Aug 10	IA, 63rd, 1937
McGelason, I.P.		D, 33rd Ill.	42		1909 Aug 16	KS, 29th, 1910
McGeorge, Julius		H, 4th Mich. Inf.	113		1916 Jan 4	KS, 36th, 1917
McGeorge, Julius		H, 4th Mich.	113		1915	KS, 35th, 1916
McGibbons, G.W.	Pvt.	A, 119th Ill.	22		1907 Jan 27	IA, 34th, 1908
McGibbons, G.W.	Pvt.	E, 104th Ill.	22		1907	IA, 34th, 1908
McGill, Henry		F, 4th Wis. Cav.	52		1928 May 11	NE, 53rd, 1929
McGill, James		C, 19th Ill. Inf.	380		1901 Dec 9	KS, 21st, 1902
McGill, M.W.		F, 9th Penn. Inf. (died from effect of wounds)	177		1889	KS, 9th, 1890
McGill, Pat	Pvt.		40		1896 Jan 19	IA, 22nd, 1896
McGill, Tobias		G, 16th Iowa	52		1928 Jul 26	KS, 48th, 1929
McGill, Wm.	Pvt.	E, 7th Iowa Cav.	46		1925 Dec 30	IA, 52nd, 1926
McGill, Wm. H.	Pvt.	H, 45th Iowa Inf.	153		1927 Nov	IA, 54th, 1928
McGillorey, John	Pvt.	F, 105th Ill. Inf.	91	48	1891 Dec 26	IA, 18th, 1892
McGilvrey, Alexander		G, 15th Iowa (died of heart failure)	355		1892 Nov 10	KS, 12th, 1893
McGin, Francis			35		1905	NE, 30th, 1906
McGinness, Joseph		11th Ill. Cav.	311		1921	KS, 41st, 1922
McGinnis, Benj.	Pvt.	A, 29th Iowa Inf.	29		1888 Dec 9	IA, 15th, 1889
McGinnis, Jas.			9		1911	IA, 38th, 1912
McGinnis, Jesse		C, 21st Ill. Inf. (died in Russell County; buried at Russell County Cemetery)	152		1894 Feb 18	KS, 14th, 1895
McGinnis, Lewis A.	Pvt.	A, 61st Ohio Inf.	34	86	1932 May 26	IA, 59th, 1933
McGinnis, M.W.			98		1912	KS, 32nd, 1913
McGinnis, R.W.		F, 20th Ohio Inf. (died of paralysis)	253		1893 Apr 2	NE, 18th, 1894
McGinnis, W.W.	Pvt.		74		1920 Jun 4	IA, 47th, 1921
McGinnis, Wm. H.	Pvt.	D, 37th Penn. Inf.	55		1915 Sep 22	IA, 42nd, 1916
McGinniss, John C.		E, 131st Penn.	64		1890	KS, 10th, 1891
McGinty, James		K, 164th Ohio	81		1931 Apr 12	KS, 51st, 1932
McGinty, James		K, 164th Ohio	81		1931 Apr 12	KS, 52nd, 1933
McGiripey, W.W.	Pvt.	H, 15th Ind.	57		1924 Mar 18	IA, 51st, 1925
McGirr, Frances			35		1912	NE, 37th, 1913

*See Appendix A, B or C for roster of post names and locations.
†See Introduction for note regarding recording of death date.

Name	Rank	Company, Regiment or Ship	Post*	Age	Death Date†	Journal
McGivern, John	Pvt.	F, 15th N.Y. Hvy. Art.	56		1899	NE, 24th, 1900
McGlasson, W.T.		H, 8th Iowa	45		1923	KS, 43rd, 1924
McGlency, James		Iowa	292		1911	KS, 31st, 1912
McGlothlin, H.H.		K, 15th Kans.	3		1926 Jun 4	KS, 46th, 1927
McGlumphry, F.M.	Pvt.	B, 1st Va. Cav.	40		1920 Dec 25	IA, 47th, 1921
McGlynn, Patrick		D, 10th Conn. Inf. (died at National Home)	380		1895 Feb	KS, 15th, 1896
McGonager, J.A.		C, 41st Ohio Inf. (died of consumption)	289		1893 Sep 13	NE, 18th, 1894
McGorrisk, E.J.	Surg.	9th Iowa Inf.	12		1904 Apr 17	IA, 31st, 1905
McGory, D.H.	Pvt.	D, 54th Ind. Inf.	56		1924 Oct 2	IA, 51st, 1925
McGovern, A.B.		D, 96th Ohio	96		1922 Jul 9	KS, 42nd, 1923
McGovney, C.L.		D, 191st Ohio Inf.	90		1930 May 19	KS, 50th, 1931
McGowen, Alex	Pvt.	I, 1st Wis. Cav.	42		1910 Jul 4	IA, 37th, 1911
McGowen, Thomas	Pvt.	F, 12th Iowa	54		1907 Mar 29	IA, 34th, 1908
McGown, Geo.		I, 11th Minn. Inf. (died of consumption)	251		1894 Oct 26	NE, 19th, 1895
McGrall, Thomas		D, 23rd Ill. Inf.	222		1899 Sep 22	KS, 19th, 1900
McGrath, John		B, 48th Ohio Inf.		88	1936 Jan 24	IA, 62nd, 1936
McGrath, John	Pvt.	B, 148th Ohio Inf.	440	88	1935 Jan 24	IA, 65th, 1939
McGrath, W.F.		C, 4th Ill. Cav.	147		1905 Sep 27	KS, 25th, 1906
McGraw, Geo. M.		84th Ind.	120		1927 Jan	NE, 51st, 1927
McGraw, J.W.	Pvt.	F, 40th Wis. Inf.	101		1916 Mar 19	IA, 43rd, 1917
McGray, William		C, 3rd U.S.	171		1911 Apr 3	KS, 31st, 1912
McGrayel, Michael	Capt.	E, 93rd Md. Inf.	152		1885 Jun 28	IA, 12th, 1886
McGreevy, Wm. J.		I, 74th Ohio	52		1914 Mar 21	KS, 34th, 1915
McGregor, Andrew		I, 49th Ill. Inf.	1		1902 Mar 24	KS, 22nd, 1903
McGregor, Geo. S.		K, 1st Md. Potomac Home Bat. (died of general disability)	89	69	1913 Jun 5	NE, 38th, 1914
McGregor, John		D, 19th Ind.	174		1914 Sep 26	KS, 34th, 1915
McGregor, Robert P.		F & B, 30th & 152nd Ind. (see also Appendix D)	123		1897 Aug 22	KS, 17th, 1898
McGrew, B.D.		L, 6th U.S. Cav. (died of general debility)	89	80	1917 Jul 29	NE, 42nd, 1918
McGrew, James		F, 157th Ohio Vol. Inf. (Waco)			1944 Dec 28	NE, 70th, 1946
McGrew, W.A.	Pvt.	A, 96th Ohio Inf.	57		1916 Aug 4	IA, 43rd, 1917
McGrew, Wm. T.	Pvt.	A, 1st Ohio Bat.	235	58	1899 May 1	IA, 25th, 1899
McGriff, Patrick	Pvt.	A, 89th Ind. Inf.	84		1912 Jul 4	IA, 39th, 1913
McGrogan, E.J.	Pvt.	L, 6th N.Y. Cav.	239	65	1897 Aug 26	IA, 24th, 1898
McGuire, A.J.		B, 7th Ill. Cav.	4		1910 Jan 8	KS, 30th, 1911
McGuire, Bernard		D, 144th Ill.	32		1928 May 21	KS, 48th, 1929
McGuire, David W.		I, 8th Ill. Cav.	32		1901 Apr 25	KS, 21st, 1902
McGuire, Elisha		B, 2nd Neb. Cav. (died of general breakdown)	118	87	1920 Mar 27	NE, 45th, 1921
McGuire, Ellis		K, 13th West Va. Inf.	482		1901 Jun 10	KS, 21st, 1902
McGuire, Frank		A, 2nd Mo. Cav.	4		1887 Apr 7	KS, 7th, 1888
McGuire, J.F.		K, 13th Vt. Inf.	49		1925 Mar 26	KS, 45th, 1926
McGuire, S.W.		7th Mo.	23		1914 Sep 20	KS, 34th, 1915
McGumacy, M.		I, 10th Ohio Cav.	328		1911 Oct 21	KS, 31st, 1912
McGurgan, A.C.	Pvt.	B, 2nd Penn. Inf.	440	62	1897 Feb 1	IA, 23rd, 1897
McGuyre, J.A.		H, 10th Ill.	25		1919 Oct 5	KS, 39th, 1920
McHafferty, Samuel		4th Ohio	129		1926 Aug 2	KS, 46th, 1927
McHargue, James M.	Pvt.	E, 1st Ind. Hvy. Art. (at large)		97	1942 Apr 12	IA, 68th, 1942
McHenery, Hiram		B, 65th Ill.	51		1924 Mar 31	KS, 44th, 1925
McHenry, Chambers		B, 8th Iowa	25		1909 Jul 25	KS, 29th, 1910
McHenry, James		D, 1st West Va.	142		1923 Jul 15	KS, 43rd, 1924
McHenry, L.	Pvt.	F, 36th Iowa Inf.	122		1913 Jan 11	IA, 40th, 1914
McHenry, S.V.		D, 35th Wis.	130		1920 Nov 20	KS, 40th, 1921
McHenry, W.A.	Sergt.	L, 8th Ill. Cav.	58		1921 Nov 28	IA, 48th, 1922
McHenry, Wm. H.	Pvt.	B, 38th Iowa Inf.	90	50	1896 Mar 20	IA, 22nd, 1896
McHugh, H.B.			199		1921	KS, 41st, 1922
McHugh, Hugh		I, 88th Ill.	4		1896 Mar 20	KS, 16th, 1897
McIlvain, G.	Pvt.	G, 12th Ill.	452		1921 Sep 2	IA, 48th, 1922
McIney, M.S.		I, 45th Ky. Inf. (died of old age)	77	83	1919 Dec 20	NE, 44th, 1920
McIntire, Andrew J.		I, 5th Ind.	251		1924 Sep 25	KS, 44th, 1925
McIntire, E.M.		G, 35th Ill.	44		1921 Jul 4	KS, 41st, 1922

*See Appendix A, B or C for roster of post names and locations.
†See Introduction for note regarding recording of death date.

362

Name	Rank	Company, Regiment or Ship	Post*	Age	Death Date†	Journal
McIntire, F.C.		G, 16th Kans.	68		1929 Oct 9	KS, 49th, 1930
McIntire, George		11th Kans.	158		1921 Dec 11	KS, 41st, 1922
McIntire, P.		G, 21st Iowa	118		1888	KS, 8th, 1889
McIntire, R.G.	Pvt.	H, 2nd Cal. Cav.	343	61	1892 May 23	IA, 19th, 1893
McIntire, T.A.		K, 18th Mich.	66		1905 Jan 15	KS, 25th, 1906
McIntosh, A.	Pvt.	F, 35th Iowa Inf.	452		1928 Jun 2	IA, 55th, 1929
McIntosh, Alex	Pvt.	A, 18th Iowa Inf.	216		1916 Mar 30	IA, 43rd, 1917
McIntosh, Daniel		C, 55th Ill.	1		1910 May 5	KS, 30th, 1911
McIntosh, E.W.		A, 24th Ill.	7		1927 Jul	NE, 52nd, 1928
McIntosh, J.G.		D, 139th Ind.	274		1913 Nov	KS, 33rd, 1914
McIntosh, John M.		G, 4th Iowa Cav.	2	88	1935 May 9	IA, 62nd, 1936
McIntosh, Jos.		H, 79th Ill. (died of bowel complaint)	192	61	1897 Dec 12	NE, 22nd, 1898
McIntosh, Perry H.	Pvt.	B, 6th Iowa Cav.	190		1913 Sep 28	IA, 40th, 1914
McIntosh, William		I, 5th N.Y.	6		1893 Sep 30	KS, 13th, 1894
McIntosh, Wm.			168		1909 Jul 1	IA, 36th, 1910
McIntyre, B.F.	Sergt.	A, 19th Iowa Inf.	2		1910 Nov 7	IA, 37th, 1911
McIntyre, James		G, 2nd Mich.	63		1891 Oct 28	KS, 12th, 1893
McIntyre, John		E, 8th Mich. Cav.	90		1924 Jun 17	KS, 44th, 1925
McIntyre, W.T.		24th Penn.	25		1905 Dec 13	NE, 31st, 1907
McIntyre, W.T.		24th Penn. Inf.	25		1905 Dec 13	NE, 30th, 1906
McIntyre, William G.		K, 13th Mo. Cav.	58		1924 Nov 6	KS, 44th, 1925
McIntyre, Wm.		K, 75th Ill.	25		1931 Jan 7	NE, 56th, 1932
McIver, Isaac		K, 49th Ill. Inf. (died at Arlington; buried at G.A.R. Cemetery)	242		1894 Nov 10	KS, 14th, 1895
McIvigg, F.D.			96		1923 Mar 27	IA, 50th, 1924
McJillon, John P.		Ind. Bat. 16th Ohio	89		1901 Nov 7	KS, 21st, 1902
McKaig, Jno.		C, 10th Kans.	68		1904 May 7	KS, 24th, 1905
McKain, J.M.	Pvt.	I, 18th Iowa Inf.	19	92	1931 Jun 30	IA, 58th, 1932
McKain, Joseph		B, 123rd Penn.	25		1932 Feb 28	NE, 57th, 1933
McKanna, Amos		A, 5th O.N.G.[Ohio National Guard?]	55		1915 Oct 31	KS, 35th, 1916
McKarg, R.N.	2nd Lieut.	K, 5th Ind. Inf.	22		1925 Aug 18	IA, 52nd, 1926
McKay, A.B.		A, 6th Ill.	23		1928 Jul 19	KS, 48th, 1929
McKay, Allen	Pvt.	G, 83rd Ill. Inf.	235	60	1896 Mar 9	IA, 22nd, 1896
McKay, Cyrus	Sergt.	D, 3rd Iowa Inf.	168	70	1897 Dec 27	IA, 24th, 1898
McKay, D.C.		F, 11th Mo. Cav. (mustered out May 2, Mo. Cav.)	159		1890	KS, 10th, 1891
McKay, Dan	Pvt.	F, 19th Iowa Inf.	153		1930 Feb 20	IA, 57th, 1931
McKay, Edward		K, 15th Mass.	380		1916 Jul 6	KS, 36th, 1917
McKay, G.W.	1st Lieut.	F, 9th Iowa Cav.	194		1902 Nov 19	IA, 29th, 1903
McKay, N.W.	Pvt.	I, 6th Iowa Inf.	153		1917 Apr 15	IA, 44th, 1918
McKay, Wm.	Pvt.		337		1926 Feb 26	IA, 53rd, 1927
McKay, Wm. H.		A, 67th Ill. Inf.	7		1926 Nov 7	NE, 51st, 1927
McKead, C.S.	Pvt.	C, 44th Iowa Inf.	130		1924 Dec 12	IA, 51st, 1925
McKean, Cornelius	Pvt.	E, 4th Iowa Inf.	26		1911 Nov 29	IA, 38th, 1912
McKean, G.W.	Pvt.	C, 46th Iowa Inf.	26		1919 Jun 5	IA, 46th, 1920
McKee, Alexander		I, 101st Penn. Inf.	11		1894 Oct 29	NE, 19th, 1895
McKee, David		E, 1st Ohio	25		1910 Sep 7	KS, 30th, 1911
McKee, Isaac		15th Kans. Bat.	1		1925 Sep 17	KS, 45th, 1926
McKee, J.L.	Lieut.	C, Independent Penn. Art.	5		1903 Jun 30	IA, 30th, 1904
McKee, John		K, 7th Kans.	6		1915 Jun 28	KS, 35th, 1916
McKee, John H.		I, 105th Penn. Inf.	25	87	1919 Jan 29	NE, 44th, 1920
McKee, John S.	Sergt.	K, 9th Iowa Inf.	235		1922 Dec 21	IA, 49th, 1923
McKee, Jonathan	Corp.	M, 14th Ill. Cav.	198	50	1890 May 11	IA, 17th, 1891
McKee, Leonard		E, 151st Ohio	53		1916 Dec 22	KS, 36th, 1917
McKee, Miller	Pvt.	B, 4th Iowa Cav.	308		1910 Jul	IA, 37th, 1911
McKee, Robert A.	Capt. Major	B, 5th Iowa Cav. 5th U.S. Cav.	84	56	1897 Feb 9	IA, 23rd, 1897
McKee, Robert J.	Corp.	B, 70th Ohio Inf.	12		1910 Jul 15	IA, 37th, 1911
McKee, Robert J.		D, 16th Kans. Cav.	25		1920 Mar 4	KS, 40th, 1921
McKee, Samuel	Corp.	A, 25th Iowa Inf.	76		1897 Apr 4	IA, 23rd, 1897
McKee, Samuel	Pvt.	G, 136th Ohio Inf.	84		1908 Apr 15	IA, 35th, 1909
McKee, W.S.		B, 5th Ill.	265		1911 Nov 5	KS, 31st, 1912

*See Appendix A, B or C for roster of post names and locations.
†See Introduction for note regarding recording of death date.

Name	Rank	Company, Regiment or Ship	Post*	Age	Death Date†	Journal
McKee, W.T.	Pvt.	K, 3rd Md. Inf. (at large)			1933 May 5	IA, 60th, 1934
McKee, Wilson			122		1886	NE, 11th, 1887
McKeefy, G.E.		M, 1st Hvy. Art.	80		1906	NE, 31st, 1907
McKeeghan, Wm. A.		B, 11th Ill. Cav. (died of dropsy)	80	50	1895 Dec 15	NE, 20th, 1896
McKeehan, H.C.	Pvt.	I, 3rd Iowa Cav.	122		1917 Mar 17	IA, 44th, 1918
McKeen, J.	Pvt.	C, 7th Ill. Cav.	296		1908 Jan 12	IA, 35th, 1909
McKeen, J.S.		A, 139th Penn. (died of hardening arteries)	1	84	1925 Mar 4	NE, 50th, 1926
McKeeyan, Jas.	Pvt.	F, 21st Iowa Inf.	75		1903 Oct 27	IA, 30th, 1904
McKel, Arthur W.	Pvt.	H, 114th Ill. Inf.	168	63	1894 Nov 11	IA, 21st, 1895
McKelley, C.F.			116		1924 Apr 30	IA, 51st, 1925
McKeloog, Mathew		H, 144th Ohio	260		1924 Nov 10	KS, 44th, 1925
McKelvey, J.C.		1st Ohio	38		1918 Jun 22	KS, 38th, 1919
McKelvey, Mathew		I, 118th N.Y.	1		1923 Mar 24	KS, 43rd, 1924
McKelvie, A.J.		M, 1st Wis. (died of general debility)	140	73	1918 Aug 6	NE, 44th, 1920
McKenna, George		G, 2nd Kans. Inf. (died at Leavenworth; buried at Mt. Calvary Cemetery)	6		1894 Sep 27	KS, 14th, 1895
McKensie, G.W.	Pvt.	B, 8th N.Y.	22		1924 Feb 27	IA, 51st, 1925
McKenzie, B.G.		H, 31st Ind. Art.	7		1926 Sep 28	NE, 51st, 1927
McKenzie, C.N.		E, 19th Iowa Inf.	113		1900 Aug 15	KS, 20th, 1901
McKenzie, C.R.	Pvt.	D, 144th Ohio National Guard	81		1906 Feb 18	IA, 33rd, 1907
McKenzie, J.M.					[1938?]	KS, 58th, 1939
McKenzie, James	Pvt.	F, 30th U.S. Inf.	12		1918 Aug 21	IA, 45th, 1919
McKenzie, N.	Pvt.	A, 2nd Iowa Inf.	2		1920 Jun 3	IA, 47th, 1921
McKenzie, T.C.		Signal Corps, Dept. Tenn.	81		1st quarter 1885	IA, 11th, 1885
McKenzie, Thos. W.		A, 20th Ill.	[51?]		1885	KS, 5th, 1886
McKerrell, Niele			125		1913 Oct 18	IA, 40th, 1914
McKesick, John P.	Pvt.	D, 5th Mo. Cav.	210	43	1892 Dec 15	IA, 19th, 1893
McKey, Geo. W.	Sergt.	H, 1st Iowa	23		1916 Jul 20	KS, 36th, 1917
McKibben, Hugh		C, 164th Penn.	85		1902 Sep 19	KS, 22nd, 1903
McKibben, J.H.	Pvt.	K, 46th Ill. Inf.	57		1912 Apr 7	IA, 39th, 1913
McKibbin, H.H.		B, 25th Ill. Inf.	129		1887 May 1	KS, 7th, 1888
McKibbon, J.T.	Capt.	B, 25th Ill.	4		1916 Dec 15	KS, 36th, 1917
McKim, H.	Pvt.	A, 15th Ohio Inf.	138		1910 Mar 4	IA, 37th, 1911
McKim, John D.	Corp.	D, 7th Iowa Cav.	398		1907 Mar 13	IA, 34th, 1908
McKines, A.B.			29		3rd quarter 1883	IA, 10th, 1884
McKinley, C.C.		K, 58th Ill.	253		1910	KS, 30th, 1911
McKinley, E.M.	Pvt.	K, 31st Iowa Inf.	88		1909 Nov 30	IA, 36th, 1910
McKinley, H.	Pvt.	C, 21st Mo. Inf.	325	70	1896 Apr 26	IA, 23rd, 1897
McKinley, Peter W.		H, 29th Mich.	1		1922 Jan 9	KS, 42nd, 1923
McKinna, H.	Pvt.	D, 40th Iowa Inf.	64		2nd quarter 1889	IA, 16th, 1890
McKinney, —		H, 93rd Ohio (consumptive)	322		1889	KS, 9th, 1890
McKinney, A.			299		1915 Jan 2	NE, 40th, 1916
McKinney, A.W.		31st Ind.	17		1893 Sep 6	KS, 13th, 1894
McKinney, Alfred		D, 86th Ill. Inf. (died of paralysis)	115	73	1905[1904?] Dec 1	NE, 29th, 1905
McKinney, C.C.		8th Mo.	111		1921 Jul 16	KS, 41st, 1922
McKinney, Geo. W.			517		1909 Sep 11	IA, 36th, 1910
McKinney, J.P.	Com. Surg.	27th Iowa	168		1903 Dec 14	IA, 30th, 1904
McKinney, J.W.		E, 125th Ill.	407		1908	KS, 28th, 1909
McKinney, Jas. C.		H, 8th Mo.	263		1893 Dec 29	KS, 13th, 1894
McKinney, Robert	Pvt.	F, 37th Iowa Inf.	447	62	1892 Oct 8	IA, 19th, 1893
McKinney, T.	Capt.	B, 11th Iowa Inf. (at large)			1931 Jun 7	IA, 58th, 1932
McKinney, W.B.	Pvt.	D, 10th Iowa Inf.	16		1905	IA, 32nd, 1906
McKinney, W.B.	Pvt.	D, 10th Iowa Inf.	16		1925 Jul 18	IA, 52nd, 1926
McKinney, Wm.	Pvt.	H, 12th Iowa Inf.	40		1906 Aug 21	IA, 33rd, 1907
McKinnon, Jas. H.		C, 110th Ky. Inf.	25	77	1918 Feb 24	NE, 43rd, 1919
McKinnon, L.	Pvt.	B, 2nd Iowa Cav.	94		1933 Apr 18	IA, 60th, 1934
McKinon, John	Pvt.	D, 14th Ind. Inf.	317	50	1889 Jul 6	IA, 16th, 1890
McKinsbrey, Jas.		C, 135th Ill.	17		1904 Mar	KS, 24th, 1905
McKinzey, Elisha		F, 94th N.Y. Inf. (died of cancer of neck & jaw)	130	72	1907 Dec 25	NE, 33rd, 1909
McKirahan, M.F.		A, 25th Ohio	1		1913 Feb 10	KS, 33rd, 1914
McKirihan, William D.		D, 1st West Va. Cav.	23		1909 Feb 28	KS, 29th, 1910

*See Appendix A, B or C for roster of post names and locations.
†See Introduction for note regarding recording of death date.

Name	Rank	Company, Regiment or Ship	Post*	Age	Death Date†	Journal
McKirtland, R.	Lieut.	2nd Iowa Cav.	22		1917 Oct 7	IA, 44th, 1918
McKish, John	Pvt.	C, 13th Iowa Inf.	168		1913 Oct 10	IA, 40th, 1914
McKisson, I.V.		1st Ill. Lt. Art.	85		1914 Jan 27	KS, 34th, 1915
McKitrick, J.S.		H, 185th Ohio Vol. Inf.	71		1906 Apr 9	KS, 26th, 1907
McKitrick, James		G, 90th Ohio	53		1929 Jan 3	KS, 49th, 1930
McKittrick, J.L.		C, 138th Ohio	115		1896 Apr 6	KS, 16th, 1897
McKittrick, James	Pvt.	C, 16th Iowa Inf.	164		1909 Nov 19	IA, 36th, 1910
McKnight, A.E.		C, 31st Wis. Inf.	25		1905 Dec 22	NE, 30th, 1906
McKnight, A.E.		C, 31st Wis.	25		1905 Dec 22	NE, 31st, 1907
McKnight, G.W.		D, 20th Wis. Inf. (died of heart disease)	10	75	1918 May 31	NE, 43rd, 1919
McKnight, Geo.	Pvt.	D, 11th Ind. Inf.	235		1915 Jun 21	IA, 42nd, 1916
McKnight, Henry		F, 16th Ohio H, 15th M.S.	27		1918 Feb 8	KS, 38th, 1919
McKnight, J.D.		B, 31st Wis.	25		1915 Feb 24	NE, 40th, 1916
McKnight, J.P.		G, 128th Ill. 129th Ind.	130		1917 Sep 8	KS, 37th, 1918
McKnight, Jesse		C, 6th Mo. (died of dyspepsia)	94		1908 Jul 8	NE, 33rd, 1909
McKnight, Josiah		I, 43rd Ohio	36		1923 Feb 19	KS, 43rd, 1924
McKnight, Robert M.		B, 16th Ind. Inf. (at large)	440	92, 9 mos. & 7 days	1937 May 2	IA, 64th, 1938
McKone, John		H, 86th Ill.	12		1921 Mar 10	KS, 41st, 1922
McKrimme, W.W.		L, 11th Ill. Cav.	244		1917 Jul 23	KS, 37th, 1918
McKune, A.B., see McKines, A.B.						
McLain, Albert		D, 19th Kans.	71		1914 Dec 3	KS, 34th, 1915
McLain, Arthur	Pvt.	K, 37th Ind. Inf.	57		1918 Oct	IA, 45th, 1919
McLain, F.E.		26th Ohio Bat.	2		1929 Sep 8	KS, 50th, 1931
McLain, F.T.	Pvt.	G, 14th Iowa Inf.	30		1910 Nov 9	IA, 37th, 1911
McLain, Frank E.		26th Ohio Inf.	2		1929 Sep 8	KS, 49th, 1930
McLain, John	Pvt.	G, 46th Iowa Inf.	231		1926 Jan 12	IA, 53rd, 1927
McLain, Robert	Pvt.	A, 48th Penn. Cav.	77		1929	IA, 56th, 1930
McLain, W.T.	Pvt.	B, 9th Penn. Cav.	5		1920 Oct 27	IA, 47th, 1921
Mclain, Wm.		B, 83rd Ind.	25		1909 Jun 28	KS, 29th, 1910
McLain, Wm. A.		B, 117th Ill. Inf. (died of heart failure)	43		1908 May 19	NE, 33rd, 1909
McLanahan, A.J.		A, 26th Ind. (died of heart disease)	38		1889	KS, 9th, 1890
McLane, James B.	Pvt.	1st Wis. Eng.	49		1913 Jun 18	IA, 40th, 1914
McLarman	Pvt.	C, 5th Iowa Cav.	11		1928 Mar	IA, 55th, 1929
McLaughlin, A.H.		B, 33rd Wis. Inf. (died of abscess)	314		1893 May 9	NE, 18th, 1894
McLaughlin, A.J.	Pvt.	B, 1st Ohio Art.	321		1911 Jan 7	IA, 38th, 1912
McLaughlin, Andrew		I, 13th Kans.	130		1924 Dec 14	KS, 44th, 1925
McLaughlin, Daniel, see McLauglin, Daniel						
McLaughlin, F.J.		E, 47th Iowa Inf.	117		1935 Mar 3	KS, 55th, 1936
McLaughlin, Harrison		D, 73rd Ind. Inf. (died of kidney disease)	47	72	1908 Dec 18	NE, 33rd, 1909
McLaughlin, J.A.		K, 11th Ind. Inf.	1		1890	KS, 10th, 1891
McLaughlin, J.W.	Pvt.	I, 34th Iowa Inf.	410		1908 Mar 28	IA, 35th, 1909
McLaughlin, James	Pvt.	D, 123rd N.Y. Inf.	101		1913 Nov 3	IA, 40th, 1914
McLaughlin, Jas.	Pvt.	G, 142nd Ill. Inf.	63		1924 Apr 19	IA, 51st, 1925
McLaughlin, Jas. R.	Capt.	H, 98th Ohio Inf.	59		1926 Feb 7	IA, 53rd, 1927
McLaughlin, John	Pvt.	C, 11th U.S.	153		1917 Oct 17	IA, 44th, 1918
McLaughlin, M.J.	Pvt.	B, 4th U.S. Cav.	1		1919 Nov 22	IA, 46th, 1920
McLaughlin, Neal, see McLoughlin, Neal						
McLaughlin, O.F.		C, 10th Ind.	117		1920 Feb 17	KS, 43rd, 1924
McLaughlin, Patrick			[28?]		1925 Dec 12	KS, 45th, 1926
McLaughlin, R.	Pvt.	D, 11th Iowa Inf.	163		1911 Dec 19	IA, 38th, 1912
McLaughlin, W.	Pvt.	A, 40th Iowa Inf.	40		1913 May 5	IA, 40th, 1914
McLaughlin, Wesley		F, 74th Penn.	88		1905 Nov 9	KS, 25th, 1906
McLaughlin, Wm. P.		B, 126th Ill. Inf.	266		1899 Jan 3	KS, 19th, 1900
McLauglin, Daniel	Pvt.	C, 17th Wis. Inf.	308	56	1886 Nov 6	IA, 13th, 1887
McLaury, J.N.		E, 109th N.Y. Inf.	66		1911 Jun 24	IA, 38th, 1912
McLean, Neil			9		1911 Dec 10	NE, 36th, 1912

*See Appendix A, B or C for roster of post names and locations.
†See Introduction for note regarding recording of death date.

Name	Rank	Company, Regiment or Ship	Post*	Age	Death Date†	Journal
McLean, T.A.			113		1883	KS, 3rd, 1884
McLean, W.I.	Corp.	D, 13th Iowa Inf.	167		1908 Nov 3	IA, 35th, 1909
McLellan, B.R.	Pvt.	4th Ind. Battery	16		1911 Jul 25	IA, 38th, 1912
McLellan, Melen		H, 11th Tenn. Inf.	464		1901 Nov 8	KS, 21st, 1902
McLellan, T.A.		E, 9th Kans.	51		1916 Aug 29	KS, 36th, 1917
McLelland, Lyman W.		D, 50th Ill. Inf.	87		1899 Apr 6	KS, 19th, 1900
McLennan, F.C.	Pvt.	E, 20th Ill. Inf.	233	53	1892 Dec 11	IA, 19th, 1893
McLeod, Isaac N.		I, 7th Ohio Cav. (died of old age)	47	82	1913 Aug 1	NE, 38th, 1914
McLeroy	Pvt.	D, 1st Wis. Cav.	377		1917 Dec 2	IA, 44th, 1918
McLin, David, see M'Lin, David						
McLin, John H.			23		1913 Apr 14	KS, 33rd, 1914
McLothin, Shad.		F, 45th Ky.	3		1906 Feb 3	KS, 26th, 1907
McLoughlin, Neal	Pvt.	B, 33rd Ohio Inf.	103		1910 Sep 11	IA, 37th, 1911
McMahan, John S.		G, 178th Penn.	384		1913 Apr 19	KS, 32nd, 1913
McMahon, Oliver C.		H, 50th Ind. Inf.	199		1935 Apr 26	KS, 55th, 1936
McMains, J.J.		Ill.	199		1920 Mar 29	KS, 40th, 1921
McMains, Samuel	Pvt.	I, 28th Iowa Inf.	292	83	1887 Jul 4	IA, 14th, 1888
McMaken, C.A.		A, 1st Neb. Art.	493		1910 Jun 12	KS, 30th, 1911
McMall, Charles E.		A, 7th Iowa Inf.	240		1901 Jul 12	KS, 21st, 1902
McMamgal, D.		C, 53rd Ohio (died of old age)	5	83	1925 Nov 29	NE, 50th, 1926
McMamon, John		H, 26th Iowa (died of decline)	1	74	1917 Oct 28	NE, 42nd, 1918
McManamy, John		G, 4th Kans.	91		1893 Dec 3	KS, 13th, 1894
McManis, Charles		G, 118th Ill.	293		1912 Jan 20	KS, 32nd, 1913
McManis, Jno.		D, 24th Ohio (suicide by cutting throat)	182		1889	KS, 9th, 1890
McMannis, Charles		B, 118th Ill.	293		1911 Dec 10	KS, 31st, 1912
McManus, C.H.		E, 5th Ohio Cav.	14		1917 Mar 13	KS, 37th, 1918
McManus, James	Pvt.	K, 1st Ohio Inf.	515		1908 Jan 18	IA, 35th, 1909
McManus, P.W.	1st Lieut.	B, 27th Mass.	1		1922 Nov 28	IA, 49th, 1923
McManus, Thos. P.	Lieut.	I, 105th N.Y. Inf.	68		1909 Jan 20	IA, 36th, 1910
McMartin, D.A.	Pvt.	I, 9th Iowa Inf.	168		1919	IA, 46th, 1920
McMartin, Duncan	Col.	153rd N.Y. Inf.	155	76	1894 Jul 6	IA, 21st, 1895
McMartin, P.	Pvt.	M, 1st Iowa Cav.	168	61	1897 Jan 31	IA, 23rd, 1897
McMasters, C.P.	Pvt.	B, 149th Penn.	192		1899 Oct	IA, 26th, 1900
McMasters, D.B.	Pvt.	I, 1st Mich. Cav.	358		1903 Sep 25	IA, 30th, 1904
McMasters, J.W.C.		D, 23rd Iowa Inf.	176		1916 Feb 4	KS, 36th, 1917
McMasters, Robert B.		G, 73rd Ind.	250		1913 Oct 7	KS, 33rd, 1914
McMath, W.H.		B, 16th Ill.	57		1922 May 22	KS, 42nd, 1923
McMattison, David	Pvt.	K, 44th Wis. Inf.	77		1906 Feb 23	IA, 33rd, 1907
McMeans, J.W.	Lieut.	A, 9th Iowa Inf.	74		1918 Dec 24	IA, 45th, 1919
McMichael, John		F, 83rd Penn. Inf.	1		1912 Dec 10	KS, 32nd, 1913
McMichael, Jos.	Pvt.	C, 23rd Iowa Inf.	21	40	1885 Apr 27	IA, 12th, 1886
McMichael, M.E.	Pvt.	F, 87th Ohio	30		1926 Jan 22	IA, 53rd, 1927
McMichoel, A.M.		G, 155th Ohio Inf. (died of heart trouble)	69	78	1916 Sep 10	NE, 41st, 1917
McMickel, W.H.H.	Pvt.	C, 7th Iowa Cav.	452		1927 Aug 13	IA, 54th, 1928
McMillan, A.C.	Pvt.	C, 3rd Minn. Inf.	216		1907 Nov 15	IA, 34th, 1908
McMillan, David S.	Pvt.	B, 1st Iowa Cav.	12		1913 Jul 21	IA, 40th, 1914
McMillan, E.C.		6th Ind. Cav.	94		1909	IA, 36th, 1910
McMillan, Forgus P.		H, 35th Iowa	19		1909 Jan 10	NE, 34th, 1910
McMillan, J.E.	Pvt.	E, 14th Iowa Inf.	7		1898 Feb 8	IA, 26th, 1900
McMillan, James		G, 5th Ohio	380		1919 Aug	KS, 39th, 1920
McMillan, L.S.	Pvt.	K, 3rd Iowa Cav.	49		1918 Mar 2	IA, 45th, 1919
McMillen, A.P.		A, 156th Ohio	147		1906 Oct 2	KS, 26th, 1907
McMillen, Alex	Pvt.	I, 33rd Iowa Inf.	49		1915 Jan 25	IA, 42nd, 1916
McMillen, D.L.	Sergt.	K, 2nd Wis. Cav.	130		1902 1st term	IA, 28th, 1902
McMillen, J.M.		155th Ind.	158		1921 Aug 19	KS, 41st, 1922
McMiller, Francis	Pvt.	I, 1st Iowa Cav.	389		1917 May 6	IA, 44th, 1918
McMiller, John	Pvt.	A, 32nd Iowa Inf.	4	61	1897 Mar 6	IA, 23rd, 1897
McMillin, Alexander		I, 8th Ill. Cav.	9		1913 May 10	KS, 33rd, 1914
McMillin, Dan		D, 1st Neb.	7		1927 Mar 5	NE, 52nd, 1928
McMillin, G.M.		G, 70th Ind. Inf.	19		1910 Dec 23	KS, 30th, 1911
McMinn, R.W.		B, 126th Ohio Inf. (died of tumor)	112		1893 Dec 14	NE, 18th, 1894

*See Appendix A, B or C for roster of post names and locations.
†See Introduction for note regarding recording of death date.
366

Name	Rank	Company, Regiment or Ship	Post*	Age	Death Date†	Journal
McMoins, Sanford C.	Pvt.	C, 7th Iowa Inf.	40		1919 Jun 12	IA, 46th, 1920
McMullen, George W.		K, 26th Ind.	238		1914 Jul 24	KS, 34th, 1915
McMullen, H.P.			17		1933 Jun 8	KS, 53rd, 1934
McMullen, J.F.		107th Ill.	36		1927 Mar 2	KS, 47th, 1928
McMullen, J.W.	Capt.	C, 7th Iowa Inf.	40		1910 Aug 22	IA, 37th, 1911
McMullen, Jno.	Pvt.	E, 36th Iowa Inf.	497		1925 Dec 6	IA, 52nd, 1926
McMullen, P.	Pvt.	E, 32nd Iowa Inf.	497		1926 Mar 14	IA, 53rd, 1927
McMullin, Calvin	Pvt.	A, 27th Iowa Inf.	82		1911 Jun 26	IA, 38th, 1912
McMuny, C.		C, 46th Ill.	176		1927 May 5	KS, 49th, 1930
McMurray, J.W.			122		1927	IA, 54th, 1928
McMurray, Newton	Pvt.	F, 18th Iowa Inf.	1		1915 May 19	KS, 35th, 1916
McMurray, Wm.			4		1914 Mar 13	IA, 41st, 1915
McMurry, David		U.S. Cav.	269		1905 Nov 3	IA, 32nd, 1906
McMurtrie, P.C.			55		1912 May 7	KS, 32nd, 1913
McNab, A.B.		G, 69th Ill. Inf.	66		1922 Nov 5	IA, 49th, 1923
McNair, James M.	Pvt.	G, 8th Wis. Inf.	168		1913 Jan 25	IA, 40th, 1914
McNall, Alexander B.		E, 15th Penn.	408		1904 Apr	KS, 24th, 1905
McNalley, Alexander	Pvt.	D, 17th Wis. Inf. (at large)		90	1936 Dec 19	IA, 65th, 1939
McNaly, John		D & K, 2nd West Va.	65		1911 Jan 31	KS, 31st, 1912
McNamar, J.V.	Pvt.	A, 46th Ind. Inf.	56		1926 Dec 13	IA, 53rd, 1927
McNamar, Jos. A.	Pvt.	H, 6th West Va. Cav.	437	49	1889 Aug 13	IA, 16th, 1890
McNamar, Wm.		C, 8th Ill. Cav.	94		1928 Jan 4	NE, 52nd, 1928
McNamar, Wm.		E, 8th Ill.	94		1929 May 31	NE, 54th, 1930
McNames, Jere	Pvt.	G, 174th Ill. Inf.	20		1884	KS, 4th, 1885
McNaughton, Wm.	Pvt.	C, 28th Wis. Inf.	3		1913 Jul 4	IA, 40th, 1914
McNaul, James T.	Pvt.	G, 30th Wis. Inf.	46		1917 Feb 6	IA, 44th, 1918
McNawn, John		33rd Ohio (died of paralysis)	302	85	1900 Feb 11	NE, 25th, 1901
McNeal, A.S.	Pvt.	D, 34th Ill. Inf.	329		1904 Jan 16	IA, 31st, 1905
McNeal, Geo. A.		1st Penn. Art.	206		1916 Dec 31	IA, 43rd, 1917
McNeal, James	Pvt.	A, 126th Ohio	98		1919	IA, 46th, 1920
McNeal, W.L.	Corp.	A, 2nd Iowa Cav.	12		1925 May 19	IA, 52nd, 1926
McNealy, G.W.	Pvt.	C, 11th Iowa Inf.	208		1906 Jan 19	IA, 33rd, 1907
McNeeley, Geo.	Sergt.	G, 11th Iowa Inf.	208		1905 Jan 19	IA, 32nd, 1906
McNeeley, Geo.		30th Iowa Inf.	20		1916	IA, 43rd, 1917
McNeely, Francis		F, 10th Kans. (No. Post 42)	87		1905 Sep	KS, 25th, 1906
McNeer, G.H.	Pvt.	E, 2nd Mo.	275		1903-1904	IA, 30th, 1904
McNees, J.A.		F, 13th Kans.	12		1906 Mar 19	KS, 26th, 1907
McNeil, D.H.R.		D, 31st Mo.	32		1922 May 17	KS, 42nd, 1923
McNeil, H.C.	2nd Lieut.	C, 2nd Iowa	22		1924 Mar 25	IA, 51st, 1925
McNeil, J.			1		1887 Aug 17	KS, 7th, 1888
McNeill, J.F.	Sergt. Major	G, 114th Ill. Inf.	40		1930 Dec 21	IA, 57th, 1931
McNelands, Robert J.		D, 140th Penn.	17		1915 Jan 20	KS, 35th, 1916
McNelly, Pennock	Pvt.	I, 175th Penn. Inf.	155		1910 Dec 18	IA, 37th, 1911
McNess, S.			114		1922	NE, 47th, 1923
McNett, Henry		H, 154th Ind.	25		1927 Jun 1	NE, 52nd, 1928
McNett, Nelson	Pvt.	I, 35th N.Y. Inf.	352	84	1891 Jul 14	IA, 18th, 1892
McNew, E.		B, 8th Tenn. Cav.	35		1917 Oct 3	KS, 37th, 1918
McNey, Alfred H.	Pvt.	I, 79th Ohio Inf.	12		1918 May 25	IA, 45th, 1919
McNichols, Patrick	Pvt.	C, 90th Ill. Inf.	31		1912 May	IA, 39th, 1913
McNie, Zeb	Pvt.	D, 34th Iowa Inf.	56		1916 Oct 9	IA, 43rd, 1917
McNight, Thos.		18th Mich. Inf.	473		1913 Nov 3	NE, 38th, 1914
McNinch, Samuel		I, 188th Penn.	63		1928	KS, 48th, 1929
McNulty, Christopher		A, 15th Kans. Inf.	68		1887 May 6	KS, 7th, 1888
McNulty, Robt.	Pvt.	E, 4th Iowa Inf.	7		1907 Aug 8	IA, 34th, 1908
McNulty, Thomas		5th Iowa Cav.	76		1920 Jun 6	KS, 40th, 1921
McNutt, Geo. E.	Pvt.	F, 38th Iowa Inf.	68		1912 Dec 16	IA, 39th, 1913
McNutt, Robert, Dr.	Asst. Surg.	39th Iowa Inf.	7		1893 Dec 9	IA, 20th, 1894
McNutt, Robt. A.	Pvt.	K, 177th Penn. Inf.	247		1911 Feb 28	IA, 38th, 1912
McOmber, S.F.	Pvt.	A, 1st Mich. Cav.	254		1923 Dec 31	IA, 50th, 1924
McOmber, Spencer F.	Pvt.	A, 1st Mich. Cav.	254		1922 Dec 31	IA, 49th, 1923
McPeake, James C.		B, 133rd Ind.	55		1915 Sep 8	KS, 35th, 1916
McPeek, Joseph		K, 92nd Ohio	265		1910 Dec 23	KS, 30th, 1911

See Appendix A, B or C for roster of post names and locations.
†*See Introduction for note regarding recording of death date.*

Name	Rank	Company, Regiment or Ship	Post*	Age	Death Date†	Journal
McPhail, Alex		E, 17th Wis.	28		1913 Mar 6	KS, 33rd, 1914
McPheeters, William		B, 154th Ind.	265		1915 Jun 19	KS, 35th, 1916
McPhelomy, Thos.		E, 2nd Cal. Cav.	493		1922 Feb 24	KS, 42nd, 1923
McPherren, James		E, 61st Ill. (died of paralysis)	22	79	1925 Feb 18	NE, 50th, 1926
McPherrin, J.Q.	Pvt.	G, 145th Penn. Inf.	358		1926 May 27	IA, 53rd, 1927
McPherson, C.E.		C, 1st Neb.	216		1927 May 28	NE, 52nd, 1928
McPherson, Hiram		D, 79th Ohio	418		1926 Apr 2	KS, 46th, 1927
McPherson, J.E.		H, 122nd Ill.	44		1919 Apr 14	KS, 39th, 1920
McPherson, J.W.		D, 23rd Ill.	35		1923	NE, 48th, 1924
McPherson, William		F, 124th Ill. Inf. (died of old age)	105	76	1913 Aug 10	NE, 38th, 1914
McQueen, C.E.		H, 12th Ill. Cav.	50		1911	KS, 31st, 1912
McQueen, Geo.	Pvt.	C, 22nd Iowa Inf.	197		1907 Mar 2	IA, 34th, 1908
McQueen, T.	Pvt.	A, 110th Ill. Inf.	124		1910 Jun 25	IA, 37th, 1911
McQuerry, James		33rd Ky.	466		1918 Jan 14	KS, 38th, 1919
McQuiddy, A.G.			36		1926 Nov 1	KS, 46th, 1927
McQuiddy, H.C.		D, 5th Tenn. Cav.	36		1892 Nov 3	KS, 12th, 1893
McQuigg, Wm.	Asst. Surg.	26th Iowa Inf.	327		1910 Dec 17	IA, 37th, 1911
McQuilkin, Jefferson		C, 143rd Ohio	160		1912 Dec 6	KS, 32nd, 1913
McQuilkin, R.J.	Pvt.		187		1906	IA, 33rd, 1907
McQuillian, T.J.		G, 99th Penn. Inf.	7		1924[1923?] Jun 9	NE, 48th, 1924
McQuirk, E.J.	Pvt.	B, 7th Iowa Cav.	391		1906 Sep 13	IA, 33rd, 1907
McQuiston, D.S.	Pvt.	E, 23rd Iowa Inf.	7		1915 Nov 15	IA, 42nd, 1916
McQuity, Van Buren		I, 10th Iowa Inf. (died of heart failure)	187	77	1906 Jul 25	NE, 31st, 1907
McRacken, J.E.		E, 124th Ind. (former member; died at Blair)	52		1936 Sep 6	NE, 61st, 1937
McRae, Philip	1st Lieut.	L, 8th Ill. Cav. (resident of Blue Rapids, Kans.; a prominent Mason)	328		1906 Mar 14	KS, 25th, 1906
McReynolds, D.	Pvt.	I, 17th Iowa Inf.	84		1906 Dec 3	IA, 33rd, 1907
McReynolds, F.M.	Pvt.	I, 22nd Iowa Inf.	8		1918 Aug 1	IA, 45th, 1919
McReynolds, J.W.	Corp.	C, 20th Wis. (died of dropsy)	31	48	1887 Feb 24	NE, 12th, 1888
McReynolds, L.A.		D, 19th Iowa	1		1924 Dec 10	KS, 44th, 1925
McReynolds, Robert		A, 10th Ill. Cav. (cause of death: lungs & heart)	43	77	1895 Jun 9	NE, 20th, 1896
McReynolds, Thos. P.	Pvt.	A, 4th Iowa Inf.	112		1913 Sep 30	IA, 40th, 1914
McReynolds, W.D.		C, 20th Wis. (died of accident)	31	75	1917 Dec 31	NE, 42nd, 1918
McRoberts, Charles E.		F, C, U.S.V., Ind.	25		1924 Jan 10	KS, 44th, 1925
McRoberts, Wm. H.	Pvt.	7th Iowa Cav.	130		1900 Nov 18	IA, 27th, 1901
McRoe, Philip		L, 8th Ill.	328		1906 Mar 14	KS, 26th, 1907
McRoe, Philip		8th Ill.	328		1906 Mar 14	KS, 25th, 1906
McRoy, Amos	Pvt.	D, 6th Iowa Cav.	168		1905 May 1	IA, 32nd, 1906
McStay, John	Pvt.	K, 15th Iowa Inf.	68		1920 Oct 7	IA, 47th, 1921
McSweeneys, E.W.	Pvt.	F, 8th Iowa Cav.	115	44	1888 Oct 13	IA, 15th, 1889
McVay, Josiah H.	2nd Lieut.	B, 36th Iowa	159		1899 Feb 12	IA, 26th, 1900
McVay, Nathaniel	Pvt.	C, 28th Iowa Inf.	50		1919 Feb 10	IA, 46th, 1920
McVey, A.K.			73		1917	IA, 44th, 1918
McVey, J.D.	Pvt.	B, 36th Iowa Inf.	156		1904 Apr 10	IA, 31st, 1905
McVey, Jno. G.		H, 87th Ohio Vol. Inf.	128		1901 Dec 22	KS, 21st, 1902
McVey, John		B, 5th Mo.	[18?]		1909 Oct 25	KS, 29th, 1910
McVey, W.H.		C, 36th Ohio Inf.	7		1925 Apr 27	NE, 50th, 1926
McVicar, Nathan		A, 25th Iowa	87		1911 Jan 16	KS, 31st, 1912
McVicker, W.H.	Pvt.	D, 32nd Ill. Inf.	465		1913	IA, 40th, 1914
McWharter, R.M.		C, 13th Ky.			[1938?]	KS, 58th, 1939
McWhinney, M.Q.		B, 57th Ind. Inf.	13	72	1918 Jun 3	NE, 43rd, 1919
McWhinney, S.L.		A, 123rd Ill. Inf.	19		1899 Feb 5	KS, 19th, 1900
McWilliams, David			145		1884	KS, 4th, 1885
McWilliams, Issiah	Pvt.	C, 2nd Colo. Cav.	22		1911 May 8	IA, 38th, 1912
McWilliams, J.	Pvt.		64		1921 Apr 3	IA, 48th, 1922
McWilliams, Jno.		A, 2nd Kans.	25	71	1917 Mar 21	NE, 42nd, 1918
McWilliams, L.A.	Pvt.	H, 27th Iowa Inf.	139		1907 Jan 11	IA, 33rd, 1907
McWilliams, L.A.	Pvt.	H, 27th Iowa Inf.	139		1907 Jan 29	IA, 34th, 1908
McWilliams, L.E.	Lieut.	8th Mich.	29		1915 Aug 20	IA, 42nd, 1916
McWilliams, L.H.	Pvt.	C, 29th Iowa Inf.	139		1910 May 6	IA, 37th, 1911

Name	Rank	Company, Regiment or Ship	Post*	Age	Death Date†	Journal
McWilliams, S.		F, 21st Mo.	247		1888	KS, 8th, 1889
McWilliams, T.T.			96		1913 Mar 1	IA, 40th, 1914
McWilliams, Thos. H.		C, 106th Ill. Inf.	117		1930 Aug 20	KS, 50th, 1931
McWilliams, Wm.		E, 12th Ill.	463		1914 Jul 12	KS, 34th, 1915
McWilson, Wm.		A, 2nd Iowa Cav.	59		1899 Oct 16	KS, 19th, 1900
Meacham, C.	Lieut.	H, 100th Ill.	43		1907 Nov	IA, 34th, 1908
Meaclen, J.		K, 21st Mo.	271		1888	KS, 8th, 1889
Mead, A.H.		K, 6th Iowa	58		1914 Oct 5	KS, 34th, 1915
Mead, A.T.		34th Ill. Inf.	305		1913 Sep 23	IA, 40th, 1914
Mead, Daniel	Pvt.	A, 2nd Minn. Inf.	166	68	1897 Jul 28	IA, 24th, 1898
Mead, Giles		B, 2nd Neb. Cav.	52	76	1900 May 9	NE, 25th, 1901
Mead, Giles H.		H, 10th Iowa Inf. (died of paralysis)	188	75	1914 Mar 3	NE, 39th, 1915
Mead, H.H.	Saddler	L, 1st Iowa Cav.	78	59	1898 Jul 8	IA, 25th, 1899
Mead, H.L.		E, 104th Ill. Inf.	7		1926 Jul 21	NE, 51st, 1927
Mead, Jerome B.	Pvt.	H, 12th Wis. Inf.	118	43	1889 May 29	IA, 16th, 1890
Mead, Joseph		C, 9th Ind.	32		1896 Mar 16	KS, 16th, 1897
Mead, Orson			7		1909 May 19	IA, 36th, 1910
Mead, R.W.	Corp.	D, 118th N.Y. Inf.	88		1916 Nov 18	IA, 43rd, 1917
Mead, Simeon P.	Corp.		171		1910 Oct 5	IA, 37th, 1911
Meade, Allen	Sergt.	B, 6th Maine Inf.	154		1903 Dec 3	IA, 30th, 1904
Meade, C.E.	Sergt.	H, 9th Iowa Inf.	168	49	1887 Sep 9	IA, 14th, 1888
Meade, Jos.		C, 16th Mich. Inf.	66		1935 Oct 29	KS, 55th, 1936
Meader, A.	Pvt.	E, 26th Maine Inf.	154		1921 Mar 17	IA, 48th, 1922
Meader, D.G.	Sergt.	B, 6th Maine	154		1905 Aug 13	IA, 32nd, 1906
Meador, Andrew W.		D, 52nd Ky.	81		1914 Oct 24	KS, 34th, 1915
Meador, J.B.		I, 16th Mo.	336		1897 Mar 15	KS, 17th, 1898
Meadows, J.W.		A, 11th Kans.	379		1900 Aug 6	KS, 20th, 1901
Meads, James L.		C, 6th Ind. Cav.	123		1892 Jul 20	KS, 12th, 1893
Meadville, James		C, 208th Penn.	75		1927	NE, 52nd, 1928
Meal, John		G, 117th U.S. (Col.)	171		1911 Jan 17	KS, 31st, 1912
Meal, Marshal		K, 21st Wis. (died at Hartford, Kans.; buried at Hartford Cemetery)	196		1894 Jun 17	KS, 14th, 1895
Mealey, B.F.		B, 54th Penn.	15		1906 Dec 25	KS, 26th, 1907
Mealis, Augustus	Pvt.	F, 142nd Ill. Inf.	[436?]		1915 Mar 20	IA, 42nd, 1916
Meals, William S.		G, 2nd Mo. Cav. (died of dropsy)	39		1893 May 27	NE, 18th, 1894
Meanes, N.F.	Pvt.	K, 2nd Iowa	497		1923 Sep 27	IA, 50th, 1924
Meanor, Elias D.		H, 15th Penn. Cav.	28		1917 Oct 18	KS, 37th, 1918
Means, George H.			52		1914 Jan 5	KS, 34th, 1915
Means, Hugh H.		B, 100th Penn. Inf. (died at Iola, Kans.; buried at Iola Cemetery)	51		1894 Feb 19	KS, 14th, 1895
Means, James Q.		C, 53rd Penn.	2		1905 Jan 5	KS, 25th, 1906
Means, John	Pvt.	I, 32nd Iowa Inf.	193	63	1889 Mar 23	IA, 16th, 1890
Means, L.F.	Corp.	A, 39th Iowa Inf.	440		1926 Aug 19	IA, 53rd, 1927
Means, Otto	Pvt.	A, —	364		1906 Mar 8	IA, 33rd, 1907
Means, Thos. H.		H, 12th West Va.	25		1926 Jun 30	KS, 46th, 1927
Means, W.A.		F, 21st Ill. Inf.	255		1925 Oct 2	KS, 45th, 1926
Means, W.W.	Pvt.	D, 28th Iowa Inf.	98		1889 Sep 2	IA, 16th, 1890
Means, Wm. M.	Pvt.	28th Iowa Inf.	98	57	1889 Sep 2	IA, 17th, 1891
Mears, E.P.		F, 49th Wis.	4		1926 Apr 26	KS, 46th, 1927
Mears, J.W.	Pvt.	E, 35th Iowa Inf.	39		1920	IA, 47th, 1921
Mears, James	Pvt.	F, 75th Ill. Inf.	47		1911 Oct 29	IA, 38th, 1912
Mears, S.H.	Pvt.	K, 66th Ill. Inf.	49		1929 Jan 2	IA, 56th, 1930
Mebler, C.B.		died of cancer	18		1913 Dec 28	NE, 38th, 1914
Mecham, Abner E.		7th Ind. Battery	14		1898 Nov 7	KS, 18th, 1899
Mechion, J.M.		E, 122nd Penn.	18		1923 Aug 25	KS, 43rd, 1924
Medaris, Jno. R.		A, 33rd Ind.	55		1904 Oct 2	KS, 24th, 1905
Medary, T.C.	Pvt.	B, 27th Iowa Inf.	194	53	1893 Jun 21	IA, 20th, 1894
Meddaugh, Joseph	Pvt.	A, 36th Iowa Inf.	31	63	1886 Jan 13	IA, 12th, 1886
Medherst, Wm.		F, 83rd Ill.	293		1913 Jan 25	KS, 33rd, 1914
Medler, John L.		K, 92nd Ill. (died of long sickness)	32	67	1911 May 19	NE, 36th, 1912
Medley, A.D.			76		1919 Jun 8	KS, 39th, 1920
Medley, F.M.		C, 1st Neb. (died of high blood pressure)	302	81	1925 Feb 27	NE, 50th, 1926

*See Appendix A, B or C for roster of post names and locations.
†See Introduction for note regarding recording of death date.

369

Name	Rank	Company, Regiment or Ship	Post*	Age	Death Date†	Journal
Medley, John	Pvt.	K, 5th Mo. Cav.	29	59	1897 Feb 15	IA, 23rd, 1897
Medrow, David			25		1909 Jul 4	KS, 29th, 1910
Mee, Wm. H.	Pvt.	D, 35th Iowa Inf.	231	78	1896 Jul 3	IA, 23rd, 1897
Meean, Michael, see Michael, Meean						
Meed, A.G.		A, 24th Wis. (died of heart failure)	164		1891 Apr 19	KS, 11th, 1892
Meek, Alan S.		I, 99th Ind.	51		1919 Oct 12	KS, 39th, 1920
Meek, Corwin A.		L, 11th Mo. Cav. (died in Wichita, Kans.; buried in Wichita cemetery)	25		1925 Nov 14	KS, 45th, 1926
Meek, M.M.		E, 73rd Ohio Cav.	52		1900 Oct 11	KS, 20th, 1901
Meek, S.S.		B, 10th Ohio	104		1927 May 1	KS, 47th, 1928
Meeker, A.J.		B, 42nd Mo. Inf.	58		1912 Jun 7	KS, 32nd, 1913
Meeker, Geo.		G, 5th Iowa (died of old age)	35	75	1921 Apr 27	NE, 46th, 1922
Meeker, J.W.	Pvt.	A, 11th Iowa Inf.	231		1926 Oct 21	IA, 53rd, 1927
Meeker, Loren S.	Pvt.	D, 10th Minn. Inf.	22		1902 Jul 3	IA, 29th, 1903
Meeker, Thomas	Pvt.	11th Iowa Inf.	115		1918 Jun 27	IA, 45th, 1919
Meeker, Wm. T.	Corp.	D, 36th Iowa Inf.	138		1913 May 8	IA, 40th, 1914
Meerdink, Henry	Pvt.	D, 35th Iowa Inf.	231		1915 Dec 5	IA, 42nd, 1916
Meffert, John L.		B, 172nd Penn.	100		1924 Feb 1	KS, 44th, 1925
Mefford, Eli	Pvt.		235		1912 Mar 24	IA, 39th, 1913
Mefford, James M.		C, 132nd Ohio Vol. Inf. (former member of department; died at Red Cloud)	34		1939 Apr 11	NE, 64th, 1940
Mefford, Sanford		M, Ky. Cav. (died at Baldwin)	40		1895 Jul	KS, 15th, 1896
Meginnis, John		H, 13th Mich.	85		1921 May 18	KS, 41st, 1922
Meglemaie, J.E.		B, 23rd Mo.	25		1922 Apr 17	NE, 47th, 1923
Meglemrie, J.E.		B, 23rd Mo.	25		1922 Apr 17	NE, 47th, 1923
Megrue, Joseph F.		5th Ohio Lt. Art. 146th Ohio Inf. (died of arleria geersin)	60	66	1911 Feb 13	NE, 36th, 1912
Mehan, John	Pvt.	H, 32nd Iowa	81	76	1898 Sep 19	IA, 25th, 1899
Mehan, John	Pvt.	F, 45th Iowa Inf.	384		1906 Dec 19	IA, 33rd, 1907
Mehl, Chas.	Pvt.	G, 16th Iowa Inf.	78		1912 Oct 3	IA, 39th, 1913
Mehlin, A.G.	Pvt.	H, 20th N.Y. Inf.	78	57	1892 Feb 16	IA, 18th, 1892
Mehoom, Robt.		L, 6th West Va. (died of stomach trouble)	63	73	1915 Aug 14	NE, 40th, 1916
Meiers, John, see Meirs, John						
Meinzer, J.W.			2		1909	NE, 34th, 1910
Meir, Joseph		F, 24th Ind.	1		1920 Jun 15	KS, 40th, 1921
Meires, John, see Meirs, John						
Meirs, John	Pvt.	F, 11th N.Y. Inf.	30		1908 Apr 22	IA, 35th, 1909
Meisner, Fred.	Pvt.	E, 9th Iowa Inf.	184	50	1887 Feb 17	IA, 14th, 1888
Mekimson, W.B.	Pvt.	G, 7th Iowa	51		1926 Nov	IA, 53rd, 1927
Melary, Mose	Pvt.	H, 7th Kans.	36		1922	IA, 49th, 1923
Melbourn, Edward		F, 2nd Neb.	50		1909 Dec 8	KS, 29th, 1910
Melcher, Louis	Pvt.	C, 14th Wis.	3		1928	IA, 55th, 1929
Melia, Mike O.	Pvt.	35th Iowa Inf.	231		1916 Jan 18	IA, 43rd, 1917
Melick, Jesse V.	Pvt.	A, 20th Ohio Inf.	493		1909 Jan 19	IA, 36th, 1910
Melick, Stewart P.	Corp.	K, 26th Iowa Inf.	230	53	1897 Jun 18	IA, 24th, 1898
Melins, P.L.			124		1925 Apr 30	IA, 52nd, 1926
Melisen, Chas.		I, 1st Penn. Rifles	11		1892 Dec 22	NE, 17th, 1893
Mellen, Emery		L, 1st Ohio	55		1906 Jan 1	KS, 26th, 1907
Melliman, Jacob		C, 2nd Kans.	79		1891 Dec 21	KS, 11th, 1892
Mellon, M.		M, 9th N.Y. Art.	271		1888	KS, 8th, 1889
Mellott, Peter		G, 7th West Va. Inf. (died at Plainville; buried at Plainville Cemetery)	298		1894 Jun 13	KS, 14th, 1895
Meloy, J.A.		F, 16th Penn. Cav.	65		1898 May 25	KS, 18th, 1899
Melson, H.W.		E, 7th Wis.	267	82	1907 Jul 3	NE, 32nd, 1908
Melson, J.H.		B, 60th Ohio	255		1913 Dec 22	KS, 33rd, 1914
Melter, Daniel	Pvt.	D, 45th Wis. Inf.	25	88	1931 Sep 27	IA, 58th, 1932
Melton, A.		F, 36th Ill.	294		1905 Oct	KS, 25th, 1906
Melton, J.H.		I, 23rd Mo. Inf.	64		1912 Apr 23	KS, 32nd, 1913
Melvgin, A.W.	Pvt.	E, 5th Iowa Cav.	122	85 & 5 mos.	1931 Apr 16	IA, 58th, 1932
Melville, W.H.		C, 4th Mich.	85		1924 Apr 22	KS, 44th, 1925
Melvin, Jos.	Pvt.	E, 2nd Minn. Inf.	344	63	1891 Oct 31	IA, 18th, 1892

*See Appendix A, B or C for roster of post names and locations.
†See Introduction for note regarding recording of death date.

Name	Rank	Company, Regiment or Ship	Post*	Age	Death Date†	Journal
Melzer, H.A.	Pvt.	4th Ind. Battery	192		1923 Sep 10	IA, 50th, 1924
Mencer, Harry	Pvt.	E, 15th Iowa Inf.	337		1927 Jan 2	IA, 54th, 1928
Menchin, Henry	Pvt.	I, 1st Ill. Inf.	332		1915 Jun 6	IA, 42nd, 1916
Mendenhall, B.F.	Pvt.	D, 9th Ind. Inf.	34		1919 Nov 17	IA, 46th, 1920
Mendenhall, Chas. D.		B, 32nd Iowa	222		1926 Oct 7	KS, 46th, 1927
Mendenhall, G.M.	Pvt.	C, 7th Iowa Inf.	452		1905 Apr 25	IA, 32nd, 1906
Mendenhall, H.S.		K, 18th Iowa	25		1918 Dec 4	KS, 38th, 1919
Mendenhall, John A.		E, 75th Ohio Vol. Inf.	85		1915 Feb 22	KS, 35th, 1916
Mendenhall, N.			244		1911 Aug 8	KS, 31st, 1912
Mendenhall, T.P.	Pvt.	C, 154th Ohio	23		1926 Mar 4	IA, 53rd, 1927
Mendenhall, W.B.		E, 156th Ohio	20		1924 Apr 20	KS, 44th, 1925
Mendeth, L.P.			63		1884	KS, 4th, 1885
Mendith, Charles		H, 25th Ky. Mtd. Inf.	90		1915 Aug 3	KS, 35th, 1916
Menelous, Geo.	Corp.	B, 93rd Ill.	7		1905 Sep	IA, 32nd, 1906
Menert, John	Pvt.	D, 23rd Iowa Inf.	466		1914 Nov 5	IA, 41st, 1915
Meng, J.C.		K, 91st Ill.	447		1919 Dec 15	KS, 39th, 1920
Menger, Morits	Bugler	M, 1st Ohio Lt. Art.	117	60	1897 Nov 20	IA, 24th, 1898
Menger, Sam'l			147		1900 Jul 27	KS, 20th, 1901
Menser, Jackson, see Mentzer, Jackson						
Mensing, A.V.		G, 1st Mich. Cav.	40	69	1917 Dec 11	NE, 42nd, 1918
Mentz, Michael	Pvt.	K, 1st Iowa Inf.	235		1900-1901	IA, 27th, 1901
Mentzer, Chas.		D, 50th Penn.	34		1928 Jan 7	NE, 52nd, 1928
Mentzer, Geo. W.	Pvt.	A, 20th Iowa Inf.	235		1916 Nov 18	IA, 43rd, 1917
Mentzer, Jackson		F, 1st Ill. L.I.	80		1903 Aug 12	IA, 30th, 1904
Mentzer, James B.	Pvt.	G, 8th Iowa Inf.	244		1922 Feb 14	IA, 49th, 1923
Mentzer, P.H.	Pvt.	F, 20th Iowa Inf.	56		1921 Oct 21	IA, 48th, 1922
Meossner, C.F.		K, 2nd Minn.	12		1885	KS, 5th, 1886
Mercer, B.C.			170		1926 Mar 29	IA, 53rd, 1927
Mercer, Eli		F, 40th Iowa	12		1912 Jun 26	KS, 32nd, 1913
Mercer, Greenup		A, 19th Ky.	66		1911 Aug 23	KS, 31st, 1912
Mercer, John	Landsman	Navy	1		1926 Apr 5	NE, 51st, 1927
Mercer, Midian		C, 7th West Va.	51		1923 Jan 15	KS, 43rd, 1924
Mercer, P.P.		11th Ill.	289		1922 Jan 6	KS, 42nd, 1923
Mercer, S.F.	Asst. Surg.	49th Ill. Inf.	8		1902 May 17	KS, 22nd, 1903
Mercer, V.T.		F, 174th Ohio Inf.	113		1913 Jan 6	NE, 38th, 1914
Mercer, Wm.		B, 14th West Va. Art.	75		1908 Feb 19	KS, 28th, 1909
Merchant, D.O.			91		1907 1st term	IA, 34th, 1908
Merchant, D.W.	Pvt.	M, 11th Ill. Cav.	67		1909 Dec 3	IA, 36th, 1910
Meredith, David P.	Pvt.	A, 8th Iowa Inf.	92		1908 Jun 2	IA, 35th, 1909
Meredith, F.M.		D, 134th Ind.	75		1905 Mar 3	KS, 25th, 1906
Meredith, J.R.		I, 27th Ky.	1		1917 Oct 7	KS, 37th, 1918
Meredith, W.H.	Pvt.	D, 2nd Neb. Cav.	6		1923	IA, 50th, 1924
Mericas, J.J.			25		1923	NE, 48th, 1924
Mericle, Martin	Corp.	A, 114th Ohio Inf.	343		1914 Sep 28	IA, 41st, 1915
Merida, Wax		A, 8th Ohio Cav.	8		1925 Nov 13	KS, 45th, 1926
Merideth, Jesse	Wagoner	I, 19th Iowa Inf.	516		1916 Feb 5	IA, 43rd, 1917
Merideth, M.	Surg.	68th Ind. Inf.	98		1904 Dec 28	IA, 31st, 1905
Merideth, W.D.		G, 132nd Ind.	71		1920 Nov 18	KS, 40th, 1921
Meridith, George W., see Miridith, Geo. W.						
Meriman, A.G.	Pvt.	F, 1st Iowa Cav.	68		1922 Feb 24	IA, 49th, 1923
Merithew, A.J.		E, 76th Penn. Inf.	36		1899 Nov 10	KS, 21st, 1902
Merithew, H.J.		E, 76th Penn. Inf.	36		1899 Nov 10	KS, 19th, 1900
Merkes, P.B.	Pvt.	E, 12th U.S. Inf.	78		1913 Dec 30	IA, 40th, 1914
Merrell, J.F.		G, 75th N.Y. (died of old age)	13	85	1925 Oct 30	NE, 50th, 1926
Merrell, M.G.		B, 3rd Mo.	23		1928 Dec 15	NE, 53rd, 1929
Merrell, Wm. C.	Pvt.	E, 184th Ohio Inf.	127		1904 Feb 11	IA, 30th, 1904
Merrett, B.L.			487		1910	IA, 37th, 1911
Merriaim, Syrus A.		D, 103rd Ill.	85		1908 Jan 6	KS, 28th, 1909
Merriam, D.J.		37th Ill. Inf.	23		1914	IA, 41st, 1915
Merriam, John Smith	Pvt.	B, 1st Ill. Lt. Art. (at large)	111, 7	96	1941 Aug 21	IA, 67th, 1941

Name	Rank	Company, Regiment or Ship	Post*	Age	Death Date†	Journal
Merrill, G.E.			190		1st quarter 1884	IA, 10th, 1884
Merrill, Geo.	Pvt.	E, 36th Ill. Inf.	66		1912 Jul 23	IA, 39th, 1913
Merrill, Geo. W.	Pvt.	A, 5th Ohio Inf.	52		1919	IA, 46th, 1920
Merrill, Harding I.		B, 47th Ill. Inf.	25		1937 Jun 22	KS, 57th, 1938
Merrill, J.L.		B, 14th Penn. Cav.	130		1901 Feb 14	KS, 21st, 1902
Merrill, J.T.	Pvt.	C, 136th Ind. Inf.	440		1917 Oct 10	IA, 44th, 1918
Merrill, J.W.	Capt. & Major	I, 27th Vol. Inf.	46	73	1899 Jan 26	IA, 25th, 1899
Merrill, Jas. W.	Pvt.	G, 45th Iowa Inf.	157		1908 Oct 16	IA, 35th, 1909
Merrill, John C.		H, 130th Ohio	7		1932 Jan 8	NE, 57th, 1933
Merrill, John H.	Pvt.	G, 15th Iowa Inf.	12		1913 Nov 17	IA, 40th, 1914
Merrill, L.C.		F, 5th Penn.	78		1893 Jun 30	KS, 13th, 1894
Merrill, L.L.	Pvt.		440	53	1889 Jul 25	IA, 16th, 1890
Merrill, Marvin		U.S. Navy	244		1925 Jan 13	KS, 45th, 1926
Merrill, N.A.	Capt.	D, 26th Iowa Inf.	92	70	1896 Dec 31	IA, 24th, 1898
Merrill, R.G.		130th Ohio	25		1905 Aug	NE, 31st, 1907
Merrill, R.G.		130th Ohio Inf.	25		1905 Aug 1	NE, 30th, 1906
Merrill, William	Major & Capt.	D, 144th N.Y.	14		1913 Sep 23	KS, 33rd, 1914
Merrill, Wm.	1st Lieut.	E, 23rd Iowa Inf.	12		1902 Jan 3	IA, 29th, 1903
Merrill, Wm. C.	Pvt.	E, 184th Ohio Inf.	127		1904 Feb 11	IA, 31st, 1905
Merriman, A.G., see Meriman, A.G.						
Merritt, B.		B, 39th Ind. Inf.	4		1934	KS, 54th, 1935
Merritt, I.T.C.	Pvt.	D, 144th Ind. Inf.	306		1906	IA, 33rd, 1907
Merritt, J.M.			233		1927 Jun 16	IA, 54th, 1928
Merritt, John		F, 2nd Iowa	83		1913	KS, 33rd, 1914
Merritt, Robert N.		A, 13th Kans. Inf.	97		1913 Jan 23	KS, 32nd, 1913
Merry, John F.	Lieut.	F, 46th Iowa Inf.	190		1917 Jan 30	IA, 44th, 1918
Merry, N.E.	Sergt.	F, 145th Ohio Inf.	100		1920 Jul 23	IA, 47th, 1921
Merryman, Freeman		C, 102nd Ill.	1		1933 Oct 17	NE, 58th, 1934
Merserve, J.B.		C, 7th Ill. Cav.	25		1913 Dec 26	NE, 38th, 1914
Mershan, James W.	Pvt.	F, 24th Iowa Inf.	12		1927 Feb 7	IA, 54th, 1928
Mersy, T.K.		C, 10th Minn. Inf.	185		1901 Apr 12	KS, 21st, 1902
Mertimore, J.R.		A, 46th Ohio Inf.	75		1899 May 28	KS, 19th, 1900
Mervis, William, see Meves, William						
Merwin, B.W.	Pvt.	9th Iowa Inf.	456		1918 Jul 31	IA, 45th, 1919
Merwin, Francis M.		C, 97th Ohio	127		1914 Jun 26	KS, 34th, 1915
Merwin, W.C.		G, 5th Ohio Cav.	64		1923 May 19	KS, 43rd, 1924
Merz, Edward	Pvt.	1st Iowa Inf.	70		1917 Dec 31	IA, 44th, 1918
Mescher, James	Pvt.	H, 16th Iowa Inf.	110	57	1887 Mar 20	IA, 14th, 1888
Mesendick, Henry		F, 50th Ill.	32		1917 Jan 19	KS, 37th, 1918
Meseraull, I.L.		I, 10th Mich. Inf.	11	63	1908 Feb 5	NE, 33rd, 1909
Meserve, C.E.	1st Lieut.	K, 16th Mass.	190		1901 May 24	IA, 28th, 1902
Mesher, James	Pvt.	H, 16th Iowa Inf.	110	57	1887 Mar 20	IA, 13th, 1887
Mesinger, James		F, 8th Ill.	324		1890	KS, 10th, 1891
Mespley, J.E.		A, 103rd Ill. (died of Bright's disease)	32	75	1920 Aug 7	NE, 45th, 1921
Mesrod, Robert		C, 113th Ill. Inf.	76		1916	NE, 41st, 1917
Messenger, Geo.		F, 19th Kans.	111		1926 Dec 26	KS, 46th, 1927
Messenger, J.W.	Pvt.	19th Ohio Battery	149	68	1891 Dec	IA, 18th, 1892
Messenger, Jasper	Sergt.	I, 117th Ill. Inf.	124		1908 Mar 12	IA, 35th, 1909
Messenger, Philip		B, 22nd N.J. Inf. K, 13th N.J. Inf.	46		1886	KS, 6th, 1887
Messenger, S.C.	Pvt.	B, 18th Iowa Inf.	297		1905 Aug 3	IA, 32nd, 1906
Messer, J.P.	Eng.	*S.S. Colorado*	235		1916 Oct 31	IA, 43rd, 1917
Messer, Jesse	Pvt.	B, Bat. 1 Neb. Cav.	59		1925 Apr 1	IA, 52nd, 1926
Messer, John		E, 126th Ohio	127		1892 Jun 10	KS, 12th, 1893
Messereau, Peter		C, 44th N.Y.	82		1935 May 3	KS, 55th, 1936
Messerschmidt, Ernest		B, 22nd Wis. Inf.	7		1926 Oct 31	NE, 51st, 1927
Messersmith, A.H.		1st Col. Cav.	186		1910 Oct 2	IA, 37th, 1911
Messick, George			340		1890	KS, 10th, 1891
Messick, George		I, 30th Ind.	340		1916 May 7	KS, 36th, 1917
Messick, Henry		A, 57th Ky. Inf.	10		1886	KS, 6th, 1887

*See Appendix A, B or C for roster of post names and locations.
†See Introduction for note regarding recording of death date.

Name	Rank	Company, Regiment or Ship	Post*	Age	Death Date†	Journal
Messinger, J.C.	Pvt.	B, 26th Ill. Inf.	267		1929 Aug 18	IA, 56th, 1930
Messinger, J.F.	Pvt.	B, 14th Iowa Inf.	68		1906 Oct 6	IA, 33rd, 1907
Messinger, James, see Mesinger, James						
Messinger, Theo.	Pvt.	F, 46th Ill. Inf.	63		1901 Aug 2	IA, 28th, 1902
Messler, J.R.		F, 59th Ill. Inf. (died of disability)	84	70	1913 May 14	NE, 38th, 1914
Messler, L.		G, 101st Ind. Inf. (died of paralysis)	84	52	1895 Mar 1	NE, 20th, 1896
Messler, Wm.	Pvt.	G, 2nd Iowa Cav.	452		1917 Aug 11	IA, 45th, 1919
Messner, F.D.	Pvt.	G, 100th Inf.	49	84	1932 Jun 4	IA, 59th, 1933
Metcalf, A.		I, 25th Wis.	211		1888	KS, 8th, 1889
Metcalf, A.C.	Pvt.	I, 33rd Ill. Inf.	244		1926 Nov 17	IA, 53rd, 1927
Metcalf, Christian	Pvt.	B, 21st Ill. Inf.	78		1916 Jan 6	IA, 43rd, 1917
Metcalf, E.W.			209		1905	NE, 30th, 1906
Metcalf, H.T.	Sergt.	D, 1st Iowa Cav.	116		1930 Feb 22	IA, 57th, 1931
Metcalf, Joel		F, 48th Ind. Inf.	64		1901 Dec 1	KS, 21st, 1902
Metcalf, John U.		I, 64th Ill.	7		1934 Dec 20	NE, 59th, 1935
Metcalf, La Fayette		D, 35th Iowa Inf.	32		1892 Apr 20	NE, 17th, 1893
Metcalf, Levi	Corp.	F, 3rd Mich. Vol. Inf.	247		1903 Mar 2	IA, 30th, 1904
Metcalf, O.J.	Pvt.		493		1914 Oct	IA, 41st, 1915
Metcalf, S.H.	Pvt.	E, 46th Iowa Inf.	98		1910	IA, 37th, 1911
Metcalf, W.F.		died at Ottawa	[18?]		1895 Dec	KS, 15th, 1896
Metcalf, W.P.		C, 185th Ohio (died of bronchitis)	188	74	1922	NE, 47th, 1923
Metcalf, Wm.	Pvt.	B, 1st U.S. Cav.	519		1905 May 3	IA, 32nd, 1906
Metler, D.V.	Pvt.	E, 14th Ohio Inf.	222		1903 Jan 26	IA, 29th, 1903
Metler, John T.	Pvt.	B, 2nd Md. Inf.	181		1910 Nov 16	IA, 37th, 1911
Mettlen, John T.		A, 105th Penn.	5	66	1897 Aug 10	NE, 22nd, 1898
Metz, B.C.		Ill.	78	80	1918	NE, 43rd, 1919
Metz, John	Pvt.	G, 33rd Iowa Inf.	49		1918 Aug 4	IA, 45th, 1919
Metzer, Nicholas		I, 9th Wis. (died of old age)	13	80	1917 Dec 30	NE, 42nd, 1918
Metzger, A.E.			71		1914 Nov 25	IA, 41st, 1915
Metzger, D.	Pvt.	E, 26th Iowa Inf.	1		1897 Aug 8	IA, 24th, 1898
Metzger, Eli U.			160		1885	KS, 5th, 1886
Metzger, Geo.	Pvt.	I, 125th N.Y. Inf.	1		1923 Sep 24	IA, 50th, 1924
Metzger, John C.		H, 7th Ill. Cav.	85		1914 Sep 26	KS, 34th, 1915
Meves, William		A, 8th Iowa Inf.	92		1937 May 20	IA, 64th, 1938
Mevis, C.H.	Pvt.	C, Iowa	24		1923 Jan 14	IA, 50th, 1924
Mewis, L.A.		C, 29th Wis.	190		1929	NE, 54th, 1930
Meyer, Alfred		K, 156th Penn. Inf.	63		1925 May 31	KS, 45th, 1926
Meyer, August		H, 16th Ill. Inf.	129		1925 Jan 27	KS, 45th, 1926
Meyer, Fred	Pvt.	I, 9th Wis. Inf.	141	71	1st quarter 1886	IA, 13th, 1887
Meyer, Frederick		B, 1st Ill. Cav. (died of suicide)	95	61	1895 Jun 10	NE, 20th, 1896
Meyer, George	Pvt.	G, 28th Ohio Inf.	2		1912 Dec 30	IA, 39th, 1913
Meyer, Gottlieb		A & F, 2nd U.S.	25	84	1915 Apr 1	NE, 40th, 1916
Meyer, Henry		H, 2nd U.S. Cav.	132		1892 Dec	KS, 12th, 1893
Meyer, Jacob	Pvt.	K, 25th Ind. Inf.	117	50	1887 Apr 30	IA, 14th, 1888
Meyer, Jacob		B, 3rd Iowa Inf. (died of bladder trouble)	90	68	1909 Dec 23	NE, 34th, 1910
Meyer, John	Capt.	K, 28th Iowa Inf.	16		1902 May 13	IA, 29th, 1903
Meyer, John	Pvt.	C, 22nd Iowa Inf.	16		1906 Mar	IA, 33rd, 1907
Meyer, Simon	Pvt.	A, 11th Iowa Inf.	1	86	1931 Jan 16	IA, 58th, 1932
Meyer, Wm.			236		1917 Jan 28	IA, 44th, 1918
Meyerhoff, J.H.	Pvt.	D, 23rd Iowa Inf.	466	50	1890 Feb 6	IA, 17th, 1891
Meyers, A.F.		H, 84th Ill.	83		1926 Aug 17	KS, 46th, 1927
Meyers, August		H, 16th Ill.	129		1925 Jan 27	KS, 44th, 1925
Meyers, Ed. F.		F, 10th Penn. Inf. F, 5th U.S. Cav. (died of paralysis)	69	74	1908 Nov 27	NE, 33rd, 1909
Meyers, Henry		G, 107th Ill.	25		1922 Dec 15	NE, 47th, 1923
Meyers, Isaac B.		H, 2nd Iowa Cav.	8	96	1938 Mar 16	IA, 64th, 1938
Meyers, J.H.		C, 54th Penn. Vols.	429		1908	KS, 28th, 1909
Meyers, M.		D, 115th Ohio Vol. Inf.	1		1908 Jun 6	KS, 28th, 1909
Michael, B.F.		G, 76th Ill.	57		1923 Apr 23	KS, 43rd, 1924
Michael, G.A.		B, 38th Iowa Inf.	68		4th quarter 1883	IA, 10th, 1884
Michael, Henry		C, 105th Penn.	72		1926 Jan 13	KS, 46th, 1927

Name	Rank	Company, Regiment or Ship	Post*	Age	Death Date†	Journal
Michael, Meean			233		1927 Oct 25	IA, 54th, 1928
Michael, William		D, 117th N.Y. Inf.	477		1929 Jun 23	KS, 49th, 1930
Michaels, Samuel		M, Ohio Vol. Cav.	11		1921 Apr 5	KS, 41st, 1922
Michel, F.	Pvt.	A, 3rd Mo. Inf.	254		1903 Sep 13	IA, 30th, 1904
Michel, F.	Pvt.	A, 3rd Mo. Inf.	254		1903 Sep 13	IA, 33rd, 1907
Michner, Wm. H.	Pvt.	B, 122nd Ohio Inf.	249		1929 Dec 25	IA, 56th, 1930
Mick, Isaac A.	Pvt.	G, 34th Ill. Inf.	49		1913 Jun 9	IA, 40th, 1914
Mickel, C.G.		B, 4th Minn.	19		1918 Jul 30	KS, 38th, 1919
Mickel, J.		I, 20th Mich.	25		1922 Oct 4	NE, 47th, 1923
Mickel, J.		I, 20th Mich.	25		1922 Oct 4	NE, 47th, 1923
Mickelborough, R.S.		C, Mo. Cav. & 2 Bat.	18		1922 Nov 16	KS, 42nd, 1923
Mickey, I.	Pvt.	12th Iowa Inf.	194		1912 Jul 31	IA, 39th, 1913
Mickey, John H.		D, 8th Iowa Cav. (died of natural cause)	26	65	1910 Jun 2	NE, 35th, 1911
Mickle, Alexander		E, 145th Ohio (died of heart failure)	274	78	1907 Mar 12	NE, 32nd, 1908
Mickle, Andrew J.		B, 105th Ohio Inf.	25	82	1917 Feb 7	NE, 42nd, 1918
Mickle, Jos.	Corp.	B, 13th Ill. Inf.	57		1910 Jan 28	IA, 37th, 1911
Micklson, Knut	Pvt.	G, 49th Wis. Inf.	465		1917 Apr 1	IA, 44th, 1918
Middaugh, J.	Pvt.	C, 5th Iowa Inf.	167	64	1895 Jan 11	IA, 22nd, 1896
Middlebusher, Wm., see Midlebresher, Wm.						
Middleton, Ashel	Pvt.	F, 65th Ind. Inf.	465	59	1894 Feb 2	IA, 20th, 1894
Middleton, Chas. H.		Penn. Hvy. Art.	516		1918 Mar 7	IA, 45th, 1919
Middleton, John		I, 88th Ind.	39		1915 Oct 3	KS, 35th, 1916
Midlebresher, Wm.		D, 2nd Kans.	314		1920 Jan 29	KS, 40th, 1921
Mielke, Henry	Pvt.	L, 7th Iowa Cav.	22		1904 Feb 2	IA, 31st, 1905
Mierstein, Thos.	Pvt.	H, 45th Ohio Inf.	22		1920 Jul 17	IA, 47th, 1921
Mike, Awalt		E, 320th Iowa Cav.	27		1908 Jun 28	KS, 28th, 1909
Mikesell, Geo.	Pvt.	I, 17th Iowa Inf.	19	82	1892 Apr 15	IA, 18th, 1892
Mikesell, J.R.	Pvt.	F, 3rd Iowa Cav.	19		1918 Dec 7	IA, 45th, 1919
Mikesell, S.P.		Penn.	116	75	1914 Oct 23	NE, 39th, 1915
Milam, J.S.		A, 57th Ind.	17		1909 Jul 28	KS, 29th, 1910
Milby, Edward P.		H, 28th Ill.	303		1913 Oct	KS, 33rd, 1914
Mildebrand, S.M.	Pvt.	H, 33rd Iowa Inf.	358		1913 Nov 18	IA, 40th, 1914
Miler, Charles W.		E, 6th Iowa	1		1924 Mar 25	KS, 44th, 1925
Miles, Archibald		G, 8th Iowa (died of old age)	25	80	1908 Nov 25	NE, 33rd, 1909
Miles, C.C.		A, 124th Ill. (died of old age)	22	84	1917 Dec 27	NE, 42nd, 1918
Miles, E.D.		F, 60th Ohio	25		1892 Nov 19	KS, 12th, 1893
Miles, Edward		K, 1st Wis. Hvy. Art.	4		1902 Jan 22	KS, 22nd, 1903
Miles, Eli			132		1901	KS, 21st, 1902
Miles, F.M.	Pvt.	A, 24th Iowa Inf.	164		1918 Sep 8	IA, 45th, 1919
Miles, Fred G.		H, 57th Ill. Inf.	77		1923 May 15	NE, 48th, 1924
Miles, Henry F.	Sergt. Major	144th N.Y. Inf.	3		1902 Dec 16	IA, 29th, 1903
Miles, I.	Pvt.		55		1910 Apr 1	IA, 37th, 1911
Miles, J.D.		F, 11th Iowa Cav. (died of diabetes)	34		1894 Jul 4	NE, 19th, 1895
Miles, J.J.		C, 6th Ind. Cav.	268		1918 Dec 22	KS, 40th, 1921
Miles, James	Pvt.	D, 105th Ill. Inf.	181		1910 Feb	IA, 37th, 1911
Miles, John	Corp.	B, 33rd Iowa Inf.	167	58	1897 May 24	IA, 24th, 1898
Miles, John		2nd Iowa	59		1896 Apr 1	KS, 16th, 1897
Miles, John			12		1923 Apr 19	KS, 43rd, 1924
Miles, P.M.	Pvt.	E, 7th Iowa Inf.	156		1902 Nov 30	IA, 29th, 1903
Miles, S. July		E, 96th U.S.C. Inf.	7		1941 Jun 12	NE, 66th, 1942
Miles, W.F.			3		1907 Jan	IA, 34th, 1908
Miles, William		A, 9th N.J.	17		1925 Feb 13	KS, 45th, 1926
Miles, Wm.			147		1900 Jul 31	KS, 20th, 1901
Milikan, William		A, 1st Ohio Cav.	252		1924 Feb 24	KS, 43rd, 1924
Millag, Jeremiah	Pvt.	E, 93rd Ill. Inf.	250		1903 Feb 28	IA, 30th, 1904
Millage, Sam'l	Pvt.	C, 50th Ohio Inf.	231		1916 Dec 30	IA, 43rd, 1917
Millar, A.H.	Pvt.	G, 2nd Iowa Cav.	231		1916 Mar 18	IA, 43rd, 1917
Millard, F.O.		F, 8th Minn.	12		1900 Oct 23	KS, 20th, 1901
Millard, Orrin M.		B, 18th Iowa Inf.	45		1885	KS, 5th, 1886
Millard, Q.D.			50		1910 Sep	IA, 37th, 1911
Milledge, M.L.		C, 50th Ill.	293		1911 Nov 30	KS, 31st, 1912

*See Appendix A, B or C for roster of post names and locations.
†See Introduction for note regarding recording of death date.

Name	Rank	Company, Regiment or Ship	Post*	Age	Death Date†	Journal
Millen, H.C.	Pvt.	D, 41st Mo. Inf.	68	59	1887 Dec 29	IA, 15th, 1889
Millen, William R.		I, 22nd Ind.	25		1921 Dec 25	KS, 41st, 1922
Miller, A.	Pvt.		342		1899	IA, 26th, 1900
Miller, A.E.	Pvt.	C, 14th Wis. Inf.	142		1917 Sep 18	IA, 44th, 1918
Miller, A.G.	Pvt.	H, 13th Iowa Inf.	156		1902 Dec 3	IA, 29th, 1903
Miller, A.H.	Pvt.	A, 55th Ohio Inf.	58		1913 Apr 28	IA, 40th, 1914
Miller, A.L.		G, 155th Ohio	36		1914 Jan 23	KS, 34th, 1915
Miller, A.T.		I, 1st West Va. Cav.	94		1st quarter 1885	IA, 11th, 1885
Miller, A.T.		C, 7th Iowa Inf.	231		1924 Feb 11	IA, 51st, 1925
Miller, A.W.		I, 112th N.Y. Inf.	30		1908 Sep 27	KS, 28th, 1909
Miller, Abe	Pvt.	G, 22nd Iowa Inf.	8		1913 Jul 30	IA, 40th, 1914
Miller, Abel		A, 97th Ind.	17		1916 Aug 3	KS, 36th, 1917
Miller, Adam		I, 8th Ind.	464		1896 May 10	KS, 16th, 1897
Miller, Adam B.		A, 134th Penn.	52		1921 Nov 2	KS, 41st, 1922
Miller, Adam B.		A, 8th Mich.	98		1897 Jun 10	KS, 17th, 1898
Miller, Alba	Pvt.	C, 74th Ill. Inf.	42		1920 Jan 14	IA, 47th, 1921
Miller, Albert		B, 67th Tenn. Inf. (at large)	26	95	1938 Nov 17	IA, 64th, 1938
Miller, Alex		5th Ill.	51		1917	KS, 37th, 1918
Miller, Alexander		A, 28th Ill.	17		1920 Sep 2	KS, 40th, 1921
Miller, Alvin M.		F, 76th Ill. (former member; died at Hemingford)	227		1935 Jun 14	NE, 60th, 1936
Miller, Amos		B, 11th Ill. Cav.	10		1930 Apr 22	NE, 55th, 1931
Miller, Arthur O.		B, 12th Ind. Cav.	380		1886	KS, 6th, 1887
Miller, Asa	Pvt.	B, 16th Iowa Inf.	342	67	1899 Jun 26	IA, 26th, 1900
Miller, B.F.	Sergt.	G, 30th Ill. Inf.	34	46	1886 Nov 23	IA, 13th, 1887
Miller, B.F.		B, 9th Mo.	139		1912 Dec 28	KS, 32nd, 1913
Miller, Belfield		E, 94th Ill. Inf.	199		1887 Aug 2	KS, 7th, 1888
Miller, Benj.		G, 6th Kans. Cav.	380		1898 Jul 12	KS, 18th, 1899
Miller, Boreas A.	Musician	H, 14th Ohio Inf.	452		1900-1901	IA, 27th, 1901
Miller, C.E.		G, 12th N.Y. Cav.	464		1888	KS, 8th, 1889
Miller, C.J.		G, 142nd Ind.	25		1914 Jan 9	KS, 34th, 1915
Miller, C.T.	Pvt.	C, 134th Ohio Inf.	2	88	1932 Jun 8	IA, 59th, 1933
Miller, Calvin C.	Pvt.	A, 60th Ohio Inf.	193		1913 Nov 4	IA, 40th, 1914
Miller, Chancey O.	Pvt.	F, 14th Iowa Inf.	516		1901 Nov 6	IA, 28th, 1902
Miller, Charles	Pvt.	B, 25th Mo. Inf.	1		1915 May 25	KS, 35th, 1916
Miller, Chas.		D, 11th Mo. Inf.	14		1909 May 12	KS, 29th, 1910
Miller, Chas. B.	Corp.	C, 4th Wis. Inf.	68		1913	IA, 40th, 1914
Miller, Chas. E.	Pvt.	C, 105th Ohio Inf.	167		1907 Dec 12	IA, 34th, 1908
Miller, Chas. E.		L, 1st Iowa Cav.	191		1904 Oct 17	KS, 24th, 1905
Miller, Christopher		51st Ill. Inf.	91	86	1916 Oct 18	NE, 41st, 1917
Miller, Cyrus H.		K, 51st Wis. Inf. (died of cancer of bowels)	98		1920 Mar 9	NE, 45th, 1921
Miller, D.B.		M, 4th Iowa Cav.	57	95	1935 Nov 27	IA, 62nd, 1936
Miller, D.D.	Corp.	I, 83rd Ill. Inf.	56		1916 Dec 14	IA, 43rd, 1917
Miller, D.S.		M, 4th Mich. Cav. (died of disease)	177		1909 Sep 20	NE, 34th, 1910
Miller, Dan T.		H, 18th Iowa Inf.	354		1926 Dec 18	NE, 51st, 1927
Miller, Daniel		A, 123rd Ill. Inf.	117		1892 Jul 1	KS, 12th, 1893
Miller, Daniel		K, 15th Ohio	18		1906 Feb 11	KS, 26th, 1907
Miller, Daniel		E, 11th Kans. Inf.	18		1929 May 10	KS, 49th, 1930
Miller, David		23rd Ind.	18		1905 Oct 26	KS, 25th, 1906
Miller, David		15th Penn.	56		1906 Aug 30	KS, 26th, 1907
Miller, E.A.		E, 59th Ill.	57		1924 Dec 11	KS, 44th, 1925
Miller, E.B.	Pvt.	K, 130th Penn. Inf.	80		1917 Nov 12	IA, 44th, 1918
Miller, Edward	Fireman	U.S. Navy, N.J.	89		1902 Mar 25	KS, 22nd, 1903
Miller, Edward G.	Capt.	G, 20th Wis. Inf. (see also Appendix D)	68		1906 May 30	IA, 33rd, 1907
Miller, Edward J.	Pvt.	Battery 17th N.Y. Lt. Art. (not a G.A.R. member)		95	1941 Sep 22	IA, 67th, 1941
Miller, Ezra	Pvt.	B, 119th Ill. Inf.	192	87	1932 Dec 26	IA, 59th, 1933
Miller, Ezra W.	Pvt.	B, 23rd	252		1922 Nov 20	IA, 49th, 1923
Miller, F.M.		F, 115th Ind.	12		1913 Oct 27	KS, 33rd, 1914
Miller, F.R.		C, 16th Ill. 3rd Mo.	12		1913 Jul 22	KS, 33rd, 1914
Miller, F.W.		E, 83rd Penn.	158		1922 Jul 16	KS, 42nd, 1923

Name	Rank	Company, Regiment or Ship	Post*	Age	Death Date†	Journal
Miller, Frank		G, 150th Ohio Inf.	262	75	1918 Aug 20	NE, 43rd, 1919
Miller, Frank L.	Pvt.	E, 20th Iowa Inf.	1	89	1931 May 8	IA, 58th, 1932
Miller, Franklin		B, 8th Ind.	123		1914 Feb 26	KS, 34th, 1915
Miller, Franklin		B, 8th Ohio	123		1913 Feb 26	KS, 33rd, 1914
Miller, Franklin		B, 13th U.S. Inf. (died of heart leakage)	107	66	1912 Oct 5	NE, 37th, 1913
Miller, Fred		D, 10th U.S. Inf.	66		1918 Aug 6	KS, 38th, 1919
Miller, Fred		K, 5th Mo. Inf. (died of stomach trouble)	32	56	1900 Jan 10	NE, 25th, 1901
Miller, G.A.	Pvt.	103rd Penn. Inf.	7	89	1931 Jul 20	IA, 58th, 1932
Miller, G.H.		F, 15th West Va. Inf.	202		1891 Nov 23	KS, 11th, 1892
Miller, G.W.	Pvt.	F, 6th Iowa Cav.	194		1913 Nov 3	IA, 40th, 1914
Miller, G.W.		B, 18th Ohio Vol. Inf. (died of chronic intestinal nephritis)	134	72	1914 Jan 12	NE, 39th, 1915
Miller, Geo.	Pvt.	H, 45th Iowa Inf.	170	47	1888 May	IA, 15th, 1889
Miller, Geo.	Pvt.	G, 27th Iowa Inf.	3		1910 Jun 19	IA, 37th, 1911
Miller, Geo.		F, 10th Ill. (died of old age)	2		1915 May 28	NE, 40th, 1916
Miller, Geo. T.	Pvt.	I, 2nd Iowa Inf.	29		1911 Nov 14	IA, 38th, 1912
Miller, Geo. W.	Pvt.	E, 11th Iowa Inf.	110		1913 Dec	IA, 40th, 1914
Miller, Geo. W.		H, 193rd Ohio	244		1926 Sep 2	KS, 46th, 1927
Miller, Geo. W.		H, 68th Ill. (died of kidney trouble)	47	80	1921 Apr 15	NE, 46th, 1922
Miller, George		F, 111th Ohio	3		1929 Sep 8	NE, 54th, 1930
Miller, George A.	Pvt.	B, 73rd Ill. Inf.	56	50	1887 Dec 19	IA, 14th, 1888
Miller, George W.	Corp.	B, 92nd Ill. Inf.	516	51	1896 May 30	IA, 23rd, 1897
Miller, H.A.		F, 102nd Ohio Inf. (died in Anderson County; buried at Oakwood Cemetery)	117		1894 Nov 23	KS, 14th, 1895
Miller, H.B.	Pvt.	D, 13th Ill.	173		1903 Aug 2	IA, 30th, 1904
Miller, H.B.		M, 8th Ohio Cav.	85		1921 Dec 28	KS, 41st, 1922
Miller, H.H.	Artificer	1st Ohio Cav.	12		1929 Apr 15	IA, 56th, 1930
Miller, H.M.		E, 3rd Ohio Cav.	51		1913 Nov 10	KS, 33rd, 1914
Miller, H.P.	Pvt. & Musician	K, 3rd West Va. Inf. (died of dropsy)	52	50	1887 Mar	NE, 12th, 1888
Miller, Harvey	Pvt.	D, 6th Iowa Cav.	365	60	1894 May 26	IA, 20th, 1894
Miller, Henry	1st Lieut.	G, 46th Iowa Inf.	337	61	1890 Mar 19	IA, 16th, 1890
Miller, Henry		F, 4th Ill. Cav.	439		1913 Feb 19	KS, 33rd, 1914
Miller, Henry		M, N.Y. Eng. (died of paralysis)	250	62	1900 Aug 10	NE, 25th, 1901
Miller, Henry		F, 15th Mo. Inf.	90	68	1905	NE, 30th, 1906
Miller, Henry		D, 112th Ill. Inf. (died of cancer)	132	67	1903 Sep 23	NE, 28th, 1904
Miller, Henry		E, 2nd Iowa Cav. (died of cancer)	109	79	1923 Jan 16	NE, 47th, 1923
Miller, Henry J.	Pvt.	H, 156th Ill. Inf.	252, 12	93	1939 Dec 15	IA, 66th, 1940
Miller, Henry S.		E, 117th N.Y.	68		1913 Jan 20	KS, 33rd, 1914
Miller, Henry W.		H, 162nd N.Y. Inf.	77		1925 Nov 26	KS, 45th, 1926
Miller, Henry W.		A, 46th Ill. (former member of Nebraska Dept.; location: Falls City)	84		1937 Jan 4	NE, 62nd, 1938
Miller, Hiram B.		E, 2nd Ohio Cav.	11		1912 Oct	KS, 32nd, 1913
Miller, I.T.		F, 94th Ill. Vols. (died at Tacoma, Wash.)	158		1895 Aug 21	KS, 15th, 1896
Miller, Isaiah		I, 9th Ind.	108		1917 Feb 15	KS, 36th, 1917
Miller, J.	Pvt.		367		1910 Nov	IA, 37th, 1911
Miller, J.	Pvt.	7th Mo. Inf.	231		1926 May 19	IA, 53rd, 1927
Miller, J.A.	Pvt.	D, 187th Ill.	392		1914 Sep 19	IA, 41st, 1915
Miller, J.A.	Pvt.	H, 1st Mich. Cav.	235		1917 Nov 2	IA, 44th, 1918
Miller, J.D.		G, 21st Penn.	258		1927	KS, 47th, 1928
Miller, J.F.	Pvt.	C, 2nd Ohio Inf.	329		1905 Sep 18	IA, 32nd, 1906
Miller, J.F.	Pvt.	C, 2nd Ohio Cav.	67		1905 Sep 18	IA, 32nd, 1906
Miller, J.F.	Pvt.	K, 86th Ill. Inf.	173		1919 Oct 16	IA, 46th, 1920
Miller, J.H.	Corp.	B, 3rd Mich. Cav.	337		1904	IA, 31st, 1905
Miller, J.H.		E, 35th Ohio	59		1918 Mar 26	KS, 38th, 1919
Miller, J.H.		D, 145th Ill.	130	73	1919 May 20	NE, 44th, 1920
Miller, J.J.	Pvt.	B, 14th Iowa Inf.	245	61	1886 Sep 15	IA, 17th, 1891
Miller, J.J.	Pvt.	B, 14th Iowa Inf.	245	60	1886 Sep 15	IA, 13th, 1887
Miller, J.J.			122		1894	NE, 19th, 1895
Miller, J.J.		E, 154th Ind. Inf. (died of typhoid fever)	122	47	1895 Oct 24	NE, 20th, 1896
Miller, J.J.		D, 11th Iowa Inf. (died of gandres)	36	72	1913 Dec	NE, 38th, 1914
Miller, J.K., Rev.		H, 33rd Iowa	71		1920 Jun 18	KS, 40th, 1921
Miller, J.L.	Pvt.	36th Iowa Inf.	69		1911 Feb 8	IA, 38th, 1912

*See Appendix A, B or C for roster of post names and locations.
†See Introduction for note regarding recording of death date.
376

Name	Rank	Company, Regiment or Ship	Post*	Age	Death Date†	Journal
Miller, J.L.	Pvt.	C, 23rd Iowa	7		1922 Jul 11	IA, 49th, 1923
Miller, J.M.		K, 120th Ill.	1		1919 Oct 23	KS, 39th, 1920
Miller, J.M.		A, 12th West Va.	244		1922 May	KS, 42nd, 1923
Miller, J.M.		H, 27th Iowa Inf. (died of heart failure)	70	70	1895 Apr 12	NE, 20th, 1896
Miller, J.M.		M, 1st Ind. Hvy. Art.	13		1926 Jul 15	NE, 51st, 1927
Miller, J.S.		78th Ill. Inf.	20		1916	IA, 43rd, 1917
Miller, J.S.			147		1912 Jun 25	KS, 32nd, 1913
Miller, J.W.	Pvt.	G, 193rd N.Y. Inf.	77	43	1891 Sep 13	IA, 18th, 1892
Miller, J.Y.		E, 47th Ill. Inf. (died of weak heart)	77	79	1921 Oct 21	NE, 46th, 1922
Miller, Jacob	Pvt.	A, 46th Iowa Inf.	70		1910 Sep 28	IA, 37th, 1911
Miller, Jacob	Pvt.	A, 23rd Wis.	81		1922 Oct 25	IA, 49th, 1923
Miller, Jacob		D, 13th Kans.	175		1911 Aug 20	KS, 32nd, 1913
Miller, Jacob		K, 75th Ind. Inf.	4		1914 Mar 28	KS, 34th, 1915
Miller, Jacob		H, 88th Penn.	52		1928 Jul 6	KS, 48th, 1929
Miller, Jacob		B, 1st Neb. Cav.	84		1917 Jan 4	NE, 42nd, 1918
Miller, Jacob P.					1937 Jul 19	IA, 64th, 1938
Miller, James	Asst. Surg.	30th Ind. Inf.	319	66	1886 Feb 2	IA, 12th, 1886
Miller, James	Pvt.	H, 2nd Iowa Inf.	156		1912 May 11	IA, 39th, 1913
Miller, James	Pvt.	D, 2nd Iowa Cav.	26		1920 Apr 7	IA, 47th, 1921
Miller, James	Pvt.	F, 197th Ohio Inf.	74		1925 Aug 18	IA, 52nd, 1926
Miller, James		A, 10th Ill. Inf.	198		1912 Jul 8	KS, 32nd, 1913
Miller, James		K, 174th Ohio	191		1918 Jun 10	KS, 38th, 1919
Miller, James		K, 155th Ohio Inf.	1		1934 Jul 26	KS, 54th, 1935
Miller, James A.	Pvt.	B, 150th Ill. Inf.	292		1912 Oct 6	IA, 39th, 1913
Miller, James A.		B, 87th Ill.	87		1919 Sep 12	KS, 39th, 1920
Miller, James C.		Ill. (died of liver disease)	37	68	1905 Nov 8	NE, 30th, 1906
Miller, James E.			158		1883	KS, 3rd, 1884
Miller, James M.		G, 32nd Iowa (member at large; died at Pawnee City)			1935 Feb 15	NE, 60th, 1936
Miller, James W.		K, 83rd U.S.C.T.	380		1911 Oct 1	KS, 31st, 1912
Miller, James W.		K, 11th Ind.	251		1919 Jun 14	KS, 39th, 1920
Miller, Jas. E.		B, 2nd Iowa	1		1926 Aug 8	NE, 51st, 1927
Miller, Jeremiah H.		L, 7th Iowa Cav.	160		1901 Mar 22	KS, 21st, 1902
Miller, Jesse L.		K, 4th Wis. Inf.	7		1924[1923?] Aug 17	NE, 48th, 1924
Miller, John	Pvt.	E, 93rd Ill. Inf.	250		1911 Nov 19	IA, 38th, 1912
Miller, John	Pvt.	F, 41st Mo. (died of cancer of stomach)	52	42	1884 Feb 28	NE, 9th, 1885
Miller, John		D, 58th Ohio	23		1929	NE, 54th, 1930
Miller, John		D, 140th Ill.	130	80	1925 Aug 13	NE, 50th, 1926
Miller, John F.			20		1904 Jan 23	IA, 30th, 1904
Miller, John F.		F, 209th Penn.	115		1905 Jul 18	KS, 25th, 1906
Miller, John H.		D, 64th Ill. Inf. (died at Pleasanton)	3		1895 Sep	KS, 15th, 1896
Miller, John J.		K & G, 121st Ohio Vol. Inf.	71		1900 Apr 6	KS, 20th, 1901
Miller, John P.			147		1912 Feb 9	KS, 32nd, 1913
Miller, John T.		D, 8th Iowa Inf. (member at large)	127		1934 Mar 15	KS, 54th, 1935
Miller, John T.		D, 8th Iowa	127		1934 Mar 15	KS, 55th, 1936
Miller, John U.	Pvt.	H, 2nd Iowa Cav.	8		1902 Mar 9	IA, 29th, 1903
Miller, John W.		H, 18th Iowa	354	88	1922 Aug 27	NE, 47th, 1923
Miller, Jonathan		E, 93rd Ill. Inf. (died of abscess)	102	68	1901 Jun	NE, 26th, 1902
Miller, Joseph		A, 7th Ohio	53		1914 Mar 6	KS, 34th, 1915
Miller, Joseph			273		1926	KS, 46th, 1927
Miller, Joseph		G, 78th Ohio Inf. (died of tuberculosis of bone)	35	71	1913 Sep 24	NE, 38th, 1914
Miller, Joseph H.	Pvt. Pvt.	I, 46th Iowa Inf. A, 4th Iowa Cav. (at large)	231	93	1941 Mar 1	IA, 67th, 1941
Miller, Joshua	Pvt.	D, 44th Mo.	56		1913 Nov 18	IA, 40th, 1914
Miller, Josiah			235		1912 Feb 3	IA, 39th, 1913
Miller, L.L.	Musician	D, 171st Ohio Inf.	16	78	1898 Nov 6	IA, 25th, 1899
Miller, L.R.		L, 3rd Ohio	294		1924 Apr 4	KS, 44th, 1925
Miller, L.Y.	Pvt.	E, 156th N.Y. Inf.	86		1913 Aug 5	IA, 40th, 1914
Miller, Lake		D, 8th U.S. Inf. (died of pneumonia)	7	53	1895 Dec 9	NE, 20th, 1896
Miller, Larkin	Pvt.	A, 8th Iowa Cav. (at large)	210	94	1940 Oct 18	IA, 67th, 1941
Miller, Levi		died of sickness	190		1920	NE, 45th, 1921

*See Appendix A, B or C for roster of post names and locations.
†See Introduction for note regarding recording of death date.
377

Name	Rank	Company, Regiment or Ship	Post*	Age	Death Date†	Journal
Miller, Luke		B, 32nd Mo.	417		1927 Mar 4	KS, 47th, 1928
Miller, M.M.		F, 1st Mich. Bat.	8		1888	KS, 8th, 1889
Miller, Matt		F, 48th Wis. Inf.	10		1923 Aug 19	NE, 48th, 1924
Miller, Michael		C, 157th N.Y.	171		1898 May 15	KS, 18th, 1899
Miller, Miles M.	Sergt.	C, 30th Iowa Inf.	157		1913 Sep 7	IA, 40th, 1914
Miller, Miner S.			1		1884	KS, 4th, 1885
Miller, N.G.		K, 75th N.Y. Inf.	45		1886	KS, 6th, 1887
Miller, N.H.		G, 29th Ind.	64		1893 Apr 27	KS, 13th, 1894
Miller, Nathan		G, 83rd U.S.C.T.	365		1912 Dec 18	KS, 32nd, 1913
Miller, Nicholas		E, 13th Ill.	10		1920 Aug 9	NE, 45th, 1921
Miller, Nicholaus	Sergt.	K, 102nd N.Y.	1		1916 Aug 15	KS, 36th, 1917
Miller, Obadiah	Pvt.	I, 51st Ind. Inf.	17		1926 Jun 12	IA, 53rd, 1927
Miller, Oscar D.	Pvt.	B, 35th N.Y. Inf.	105	42	1889 Jun 17	IA, 16th, 1890
Miller, Owen B.	Pvt.	H, 19th Iowa Inf.	153	50	1892 Apr 27	IA, 18th, 1892
Miller, P.	Pvt.	E, 45th Inf.	170		1922 Oct 29	IA, 49th, 1923
Miller, P.A.			452		1924	IA, 51st, 1925
Miller, P.G.		Iowa Inf.	459		1901 Aug	KS, 21st, 1902
Miller, P.J.	Pvt.	H, 38th Iowa	147		1903 Dec 28	IA, 30th, 1904
Miller, P.J.		B, 17th West Va. Inf.	127		1921 May 31	KS, 41st, 1922
Miller, Paul	Pvt.	I, 13th Iowa Inf.	10		1915 Apr 7	IA, 42nd, 1916
Miller, Paul	Pvt.	K, 22nd Iowa Inf.	8		1928 May 8	IA, 55th, 1929
Miller, Paul H.		Ram *Avenger*	12		1900 Aug 1	IA, 27th, 1901
Miller, Peter	Pvt.	H, West Va. Inf.	231		1918 May 12	IA, 45th, 1919
Miller, Philip	Pvt.	D, 11th N.Y. Cav.	365	56	1894 Mar 31	IA, 20th, 1894
Miller, Phillip		K, 66th Ind.	131		1904 Dec 2	KS, 24th, 1905
Miller, R.A.	Pvt.		11		1916 Dec 17	IA, 43rd, 1917
Miller, R.C.		C, 81st Ind.	17		1930 Mar 18	KS, 50th, 1931
Miller, R.H.		K, 11th Penn. Inf.	88		1912 Apr 10	KS, 32nd, 1913
Miller, R.K.	Lieut. Col.	14th Iowa Inf.	7	58	1894 Aug 27	IA, 21st, 1895
Miller, Robert S.		H, 5th Penn. Hvy. Art.	85		1913 May 23	KS, 33rd, 1914
Miller, Russell	Pvt.	C, 1st N.Y. Eng.	321		1908 Jul 30	IA, 35th, 1909
Miller, S.F.	Pvt.	13th Kans.	98		1906 Jun 13	IA, 33rd, 1907
Miller, S.F.	Pvt.	C, 9th Iowa Inf.	296		1908 Mar 24	IA, 35th, 1909
Miller, S.S.	Pvt.	H, 38th Ohio	43		1907 Oct	IA, 34th, 1908
Miller, S.S.		A, 92nd N.Y. Inf. (died of congestion of lungs)	112	62	1902 Oct	NE, 27th, 1903
Miller, S.T.		A, 34th Ill.	35	80	1919 Aug 16	NE, 44th, 1920
Miller, Sam		L, 1st Mich. Lt. Art. (died of heart disease)	83		1914 Sep 11	NE, 39th, 1915
Miller, Samuel		F, Penn. Reserve	93		1915 Oct 8	KS, 35th, 1916
Miller, Silas		1st Ill. Lt. Art.	26		1931 Feb 7	NE, 56th, 1932
Miller, Solomon		K, 118th Ind. Inf.	27		1925 Jul 23	KS, 45th, 1926
Miller, Stephen		A, 123rd Ind.	17		1923 Oct 3	KS, 43rd, 1924
Miller, T.B.	Pvt.	16th Ohio	109		1907 Sep 5	IA, 34th, 1908
Miller, T.H.			290		1909 Apr 13	IA, 36th, 1910
Miller, T.J.	Pvt.	A, 23rd Iowa Inf.	30	88	1931 Jun 15	IA, 58th, 1932
Miller, Thompson	Pvt.	F, 69th Ill. Inf.	36		1909	IA, 36th, 1910
Miller, V.G.		46th Ohio	12		1888	KS, 8th, 1889
Miller, W.B.	Pvt. Sergt.	I, 25th Ill. Inf. Signal Corps (died of pneumonia)	46	45	1887 May 18	NE, 12th, 1888
Miller, W.C.		B, 1st Penn.	28		1899 Jul 25	KS, 19th, 1900
Miller, W.F.		A, 129th Ill.	89		1916 Sep 2	KS, 36th, 1917
Miller, W.H.	Pvt.		108		1917 Oct 3	IA, 44th, 1918
Miller, W.J.		G, 100th Penn.	7		1920 Oct 10	KS, 40th, 1921
Miller, W.J.		E, 152nd Ill.	32		1936 Jan 19	KS, 57th, 1938
Miller, W.J.	Pvt.	K, 33rd Iowa Inf. (cause of death: stomach)	52	44	1887 Aug 29	NE, 12th, 1888
Miller, W.T.		F, 147th Ill.	51		1919	KS, 39th, 1920
Miller, W.W.	Pvt.	F, 37th Iowa Inf.	78	85	1893 Jan 15	IA, 19th, 1893
Miller, W.W.			36		1929 Mar 15	KS, 49th, 1930
Miller, William		G, 2nd Iowa	105		1892 Feb	KS, 12th, 1893
Miller, William		C, 79th Del.	129		1913 Sep 4	KS, 33rd, 1914
Miller, William		I, 2nd West Va.	175		1931 Sep 1	KS, 51st, 1932

*See Appendix A, B or C for roster of post names and locations.
†See Introduction for note regarding recording of death date.
378

Name	Rank	Company, Regiment or Ship	Post*	Age	Death Date†	Journal
Miller, William		202nd Penn.	115		1927	KS, 47th, 1928
Miller, William		I, 2nd West Va.	175		1931 Sep 1	KS, 52nd, 1933
Miller, Wm.			77		1899 Jan	IA, 26th, 1900
Miller, Wm.		I, 14th Ohio Inf. (died of La Grippe)	44	71	1895 Dec 23	NE, 20th, 1896
Miller, Wm.	Pvt. Corp.	D, 95th Ill. Inf. D, 47th Ill. Inf. (died of suicide)	52	41	1887 Oct	NE, 12th, 1888
Miller, Wm. F.		C, 105th Ill.	2		1898 Jun 2	KS, 18th, 1899
Miller, Wolf	Pvt.	F, 23rd Iowa	11		1907 Nov	IA, 34th, 1908
Miller, Z.		D, 30th Ind.	51		1916 Oct 22	KS, 36th, 1917
Miller, Z.		K, 25th Penn. Inf. (died of paralysis)	147	51	1896 Dec 3	NE, 21st, 1897
Millett, C.M.		I, 65th N.Y. Inf. (born in New York; died in Hastings, Neb.)	13		1883 Mar 29	NE, 8th, 1884
Millett, William J.		H, 27th Iowa Inf.	190		1919 Apr 13	IA, 46th, 1920
Millgate, Stephen		A, 153rd N.Y. Inf.	11	66	1896 Apr 1	NE, 21st, 1897
Millham, George W.		C, 79th Ohio Vol. Inf.	30		1915 Oct 4	KS, 35th, 1916
Millham, H.		A, 17th Ill.	465		1908 May 27	KS, 28th, 1909
Millham, Wm.		C, 129th Ill. Inf.	131		1900 Oct 18	KS, 20th, 1901
Millhite, E.W.		F, 114th Ill.	244		1928 Mar	KS, 48th, 1929
Millhouse, J.H.		G, 32nd Mo. Inf. (died of old age)	1	93	1924 Jun 2	NE, 49th, 1925
Milligan, Isaac		D, —	17		1918 Jan 15	KS, 38th, 1919
Milligan, Joel B.	Sergt.	D, 168th Penn.	192		1907 Jul 25	IA, 34th, 1908
Milligan, T.W.		G, 72nd Ind.	46		1915 Dec 30	KS, 36th, 1917
Milligan, Thomas	Pvt.	G, 18th Penn. Inf.		94	1939 Jan 25	IA, 65th, 1939
Milligan, William E.		G, 6th Kans. Cav.	339		1916 Sep 13	KS, 36th, 1917
Millikan, M.F.		G, 85th Ohio Inf.	199		1887 Sep	KS, 7th, 1888
Millikan, William, see Milikan, William						
Millikin, F.M.	Corp.	E, 63rd Ind. Inf.	452		1922 Aug 1	IA, 49th, 1923
Milliman, J.C.	Pvt.	E, 46th N.Y. Inf. (at large)		86	1933 Jul 21	IA, 60th, 1934
Milliman, William W.	Corp.	D, 77th N.Y. Inf.	38		1916 Nov 15	IA, 43rd, 1917
Millington, J.G.		I, 11th Ill. Cav.	18		1916 May 14	KS, 36th, 1917
Millirons, John		D, 3rd Mo.	113		1927	KS, 47th, 1928
Millison, E.H.		B, 16th U.S. Inf.	81		1923 Jul 22	KS, 43rd, 1924
Millner, C.W.	Pvt.	I, 17th Iowa Inf.	20		1921 Nov	IA, 48th, 1922
Millner, Wm. G.		E, 175th Ohio	16		1898 Sep 26	KS, 18th, 1899
Mills, A.A.			99		1912 Aug 22	KS, 32nd, 1913
Mills, A.C.	Pvt.	A, 39th Iowa	55		1926 Oct 17	IA, 53rd, 1927
Mills, A.N.		H, 2nd Ill.	142		1933 Mar 12	KS, 53rd, 1934
Mills, A.R.	Capt.	C, 47th U.S. Col.	12		1888	KS, 8th, 1889
Mills, Andrew	Pvt.	C, 6th Iowa Cav.	414	80	1895 Dec 27	IA, 22nd, 1896
Mills, Bannitt	Pvt.	D, 105th Ind. Inf.	6	84 & 6 mos.	1932 Mar 11	IA, 59th, 1933
Mills, Charles W.		I, 98th N.Y. Inf.	77	91	1938 Apr 18	IA, 64th, 1938
Mills, Dan'l A.	Pvt.	2nd Ohio Inf.	222		1911 Aug 14	IA, 38th, 1912
Mills, G.H.			13		1926 Mar 17	NE, 51st, 1927
Mills, G.L.	Pvt.	E, 1st Maine Cav.	163		1910 Apr 14	IA, 37th, 1911
Mills, G.N.		I, 15th N.Y. Eng.	71		1899 Mar 13	KS, 19th, 1900
Mills, Geo. L.	Sergt.	K, 117th N.Y. Inf.	200	47	1889 Dec 4	IA, 16th, 1890
Mills, Isaac A.		C, 118th Ill.	311		1922 Apr 29	KS, 42nd, 1923
Mills, J.B.	Pvt.	F, 93rd Ill. Inf.	26		1899 Apr 12	IA, 26th, 1900
Mills, J.B.		E, 192nd N.Y. Inf.	25		1937 Feb 1	KS, 57th, 1938
Mills, J.H.	Pvt.	C, 7th Iowa Inf.	43		1931 Jan 18	IA, 57th, 1931
Mills, J.H.	Pvt.	H, 39th Iowa Inf.	43	83	1931 Jan 18	IA, 58th, 1932
Mills, J.H.		132nd N.Y. Vols. (died of dropsy)	318		1908 Feb 25	NE, 33rd, 1909
Mills, J.M.		E, 120th Ind.	74		1917 Mar 2	KS, 37th, 1918
Mills, J.P.	Pvt.	E, 43rd Wis. Inf.	124		1927 Apr 29	IA, 54th, 1928
Mills, J.R.		A, 1st Mo. Eng.	493		1922 Mar 2	KS, 42nd, 1923
Mills, J.W.	Pvt.	B, 39th Iowa Inf.	7		1913 Dec 6	IA, 40th, 1914
Mills, James		D, 8th Iowa Inf.	50		1925 Jul 25	KS, 45th, 1926
Mills, James M.		G, 16th Ind. Inf. (died of acute pneumonia)	231		1894 Apr 29	NE, 19th, 1895
Mills, John		D, 87th Ill.	112		1897 Apr 23	KS, 17th, 1898
Mills, John		B, 18th Ohio	259		1902 Mar 31	KS, 22nd, 1903

*See Appendix A, B or C for roster of post names and locations.
†See Introduction for note regarding recording of death date.

379

Name	Rank	Company, Regiment or Ship	Post*	Age	Death Date†	Journal
Mills, Joseph B.	Pvt.	F, 93rd Ill. Inf. D, 4th V.R.C.	26	77	1899 Apr 12	IA, 25th, 1899
Mills, L.C.			96		1918 Sep 7	IA, 45th, 1919
Mills, Levi W.	Pvt.	C, 45th Penn. Inf.	7	52	1894 Jul 3	IA, 21st, 1895
Mills, M.C.	Adjt.		222		1907 2nd term	IA, 34th, 1908
Mills, Mason P.	QM	12th Ill. Cav. (died at Cedar Rapids; buried August 2)	235	53	1896 Jul 31	IA, 23rd, 1897
Mills, Myron H.		K, 84th Ill. Inf.	38	82	1919 May	NE, 44th, 1920
Mills, Richard		I, 17th N.Y.	72		1925 Oct 19	KS, 45th, 1926
Mills, T.K.	Corp.	C, 124th Ill. Inf.	235	51	1893 Aug 29	IA, 20th, 1894
Mills, W.F.			339		1914 Apr 27	IA, 41st, 1915
Mills, W.H.	Pvt.	H, 5th Kans. Cav.	251		1915 Jun 12	IA, 42nd, 1916
Mills, W.H.	Pvt.	C, 12th Wis.	117		1923 May 19	IA, 50th, 1924
Mills, W.M.		B, 48th Iowa Inf. (died of apoplexy)	197	90	1910 Jun 19	NE, 35th, 1911
Millspaugh, Isaac		F, 56th N.Y.	39		1927 May 27	NE, 52nd, 1928
Milner, Geo. S.		I, 73rd Ind.	43		1918 Oct 19	KS, 38th, 1919
Milton, James			95		1890	NE, 15th, 1891
Milton, Robert		K, U.S.C.T.	132		1914 Mar 29	KS, 34th, 1915
Minchen, Wm.		H, 87th Ind. Inf.	153		4th quarter 1883	IA, 10th, 1884
Minehost, F.	Pvt.	I, 65th Ill. Inf.	80		1905 Nov 25	IA, 32nd, 1906
Miner, A.		K, 111th Ill. Inf.	177		1900 Sep 5	KS, 20th, 1901
Miner, Charles J.		K, 36th K, 137th Ill. Inf.	4		1914	KS, 34th, 1915
Miner, Jas. F.	Sergt.	F, Burell's Eng.	78		1902 Aug 25	IA, 29th, 1903
Miner, Joseph	Pvt.	A, 33rd Iowa Inf.	12		1927 May 5	IA, 54th, 1928
Miner, Lyman P.	Corp.	C, 31st Wis. Inf.	3		1917 Sep 19	IA, 44th, 1918
Miner, M.C.		H, 8th Iowa	49		1915 Sep 24	KS, 35th, 1916
Miner, Nelson, see Nelson, Miner						
Miner, W.H.	Corp.	B, 81st N.Y.	127		1916 Aug 1	KS, 36th, 1917
Miner, W.H.		B, 81st N.Y.	51		1916 Aug 11	KS, 36th, 1917
Miner, W.J.	Pvt.	B, 15th Ill. Inf.	472		1916 Jul 26	IA, 43rd, 1917
Miner, Wm.		I, 42nd Ill.	68		1927 Jul 31	NE, 52nd, 1928
Minert, D.M.			55		1919 Aug 13	KS, 39th, 1920
Ming, James		U.S. Navy	17		1914 Aug 23	KS, 34th, 1915
Minger, C.A.		B, 9th Kans. Cav.	12		1910 Feb 24	KS, 30th, 1911
Minger, Reed	Corp.	D, 27th Iowa Inf.	146	56	1897 Sep 3	IA, 24th, 1898
Minhouse, William		C, 9th Kans. Cav.	293		1923 Nov 19	KS, 43rd, 1924
Minick, H.O.	Capt.	A, 49th U.S. Colored Inf. (died of rupture of blood vessel)	53	58	1891 Aug 5	NE, 16th, 1892
Minick, Peter		D, 207th Penn. Inf.	63		1909 Oct 23	KS, 29th, 1910
Minkel, Peter	Pvt.	F, 45th Ohio Inf.	261		1911 Jan 13	IA, 38th, 1912
Minner, L.D., see Minnor, L.D.						
Minnisch, D.R.			116		1920	IA, 47th, 1921
Minnock, John	Pvt.	C, 26th Vt. Inf.	358		1910 Aug 21	IA, 37th, 1911
Minnor, L.D.		B, 8th Mo.	63		1920 Oct 2	KS, 40th, 1921
Minns, Fred		B, 37th Ill.	87		1918 Nov 3	KS, 38th, 1919
Mino, Leonard	Pvt.	H, 97th Ill. Inf.	68		1908 Feb 20	IA, 35th, 1909
Minor, A.C.		G, 13th Ohio	63		1906 Jan 7	KS, 26th, 1907
Minor, Andrew J.		H, 15th Penn. Cav.	25		1911 May 20	NE, 36th, 1912
Minor, Andrew J.			25		1911	NE, 36th, 1912
Minor, E.P.		F, 5th Kans. Cav.	51		1899 Apr 29	KS, 19th, 1900
Minor, J.W.H.		K, 2nd Ohio Inf. (died of consumption)	303		1890	KS, 10th, 1891
Minord, R.J.		B, 22nd Ohio	25		1913 Sep 27	NE, 38th, 1914
Minott, James S.	Pvt.	F, 1st Mich. Sharpshooters	400		1912 Nov 27	IA, 39th, 1913
Minrick, Joshua			7		1899 Aug 10	IA, 26th, 1900
Mint, John C.		A, 32nd Ill.	142		1909 Dec 18	KS, 29th, 1910
Minter, Philip	Pvt.	A, 22nd Wis. Inf.	512		1918 May 18	IA, 45th, 1919
Mintey, Andrew J.	Pvt.	C, 9th Ohio Bat.	216		1903 Jul 31	IA, 30th, 1904
Minton, John H.H.		A, 50th Ill. Inf.	32		1908[1909?] May 23	KS, 29th, 1910
Minton, Timothy			98		1927 May 23	KS, 47th, 1928
Minton, Wm. H.		F, 12th Ky. Inf.	293		1931 Apr 14	KS, 51st, 1932

*See Appendix A, B or C for roster of post names and locations.
†See Introduction for note regarding recording of death date.

Name	Rank	Company, Regiment or Ship	Post*	Age	Death Date†	Journal
Minturn, P.B.			120		1884	KS, 4th, 1885
Minturn, Rufus C.		B, 24th Iowa Inf.	28		1917 Sep 3	KS, 37th, 1918
Minty, Walter J.	Pvt.	F, 34th Iowa Inf.	216		1902 Nov 20	IA, 29th, 1903
Miracle, John L.		F, 36th Ohio	55		1910 May 8	KS, 30th, 1911
Mires, Isaac F.			49		4th quarter 1883	IA, 10th, 1884
Miridith, Geo. W.	Corp.	I, 19th Iowa Inf.	177		1903 Dec 17	IA, 30th, 1904
Miscal, Isaac		B, 5th U.S.	25		1909 Aug 26	KS, 29th, 1910
Misell, Thomas		B, 4th West Va.	113		1904 Jul 23	KS, 24th, 1905
Misenheimer, C.		I, 13th Kans.	130		1916 Aug 1	KS, 36th, 1917
Miser, W.T.		I, 200th Penn.	64		1924 May 2	KS, 44th, 1925
Misner, Jacob		H, 52nd Ill.	175		1910 Feb 12	KS, 32nd, 1913
Misner, Jasper H.		G, 104th Ill.	25		1927 Feb 13	NE, 52nd, 1928
Mitchell, A.J.		K, 22nd Wis.	66		1897 Sep 7	KS, 17th, 1898
Mitchell, A.N.		16th Ohio Bat.	51		1917 Oct	KS, 37th, 1918
Mitchell, Aaron B.		G, 21st Ohio Inf.	25		1913 Jun 6	NE, 38th, 1914
Mitchell, Albert	Pvt.	C, 60th U.S. Colored Inf.	413		1892 Jun 16	IA, 19th, 1893
Mitchell, Alex	Pvt.	Ohio Battery	19		1923	IA, 50th, 1924
Mitchell, Andrew	Capt.	D, 15th Iowa Inf.	420		1902 Jul 17	IA, 29th, 1903
Mitchell, C.A.		K, 151st Ind. Inf.	142		1925 Jul 11	KS, 45th, 1926
Mitchell, C.W.			11		1927	IA, 54th, 1928
Mitchell, C.W.		E, 9th Ky. Cav.	32		1918 Sep 8	KS, 38th, 1919
Mitchell, Casper S.			30		1897 Sep 8	KS, 17th, 1898
Mitchell, Chas. C.	Pvt.	K, 35th Iowa Inf.	181		1912 Sep 23	IA, 39th, 1913
Mitchell, D.B.			45		1919 Aug 11	IA, 46th, 1920
Mitchell, D.E.	Pvt.	A, 133rd Ind. Inf.	39	86	1931 Oct 4	IA, 58th, 1932
Mitchell, D.L.		D, 23rd Ill.	51		1926 Aug 12	KS, 46th, 1927
Mitchell, David		D, 85th Ind.	65		1911 Apr 29	KS, 31st, 1912
Mitchell, Eli		E, 21st Ind.	22		1926 Apr 11	NE, 51st, 1927
Mitchell, F.T.	Pvt.	C, 36th Ill.	7		1903 Feb	IA, 30th, 1904
Mitchell, G.W.	Sergt.	L, 2nd Mo. Art.	46		1899	NE, 24th, 1900
Mitchell, Geo. K.	Pvt.	B, 33rd Iowa Inf.	40	62	1890 Oct	IA, 18th, 1892
Mitchell, Geo. L.		E, 29th Ill. Inf.	50		1930	KS, 50th, 1931
Mitchell, Geo. W.		G, 77th Penn.	52		1921 Jun 17	KS, 41st, 1922
Mitchell, Henry		D, 9th Ky. Inf. (died at Eldorado; buried at Bellvista Cemetery)	66		1894 Mar 5	KS, 14th, 1895
Mitchell, Hugh H.		H, 113th Ohio	209		1909 May 26	KS, 29th, 1910
Mitchell, J.	Pvt.	C, 39th Iowa	203		1921 Oct 15	IA, 48th, 1922
Mitchell, J.C.		H, 10th N.Y.	25		1933 Jan	KS, 53rd, 1934
Mitchell, J.E.	Pvt.	I, 14th Iowa Inf.	2		1930 Jul 7	IA, 57th, 1931
Mitchell, J.M.		B, 66th Ohio	190		1929	NE, 54th, 1930
Mitchell, J.R.		C, 30th Iowa	225		1911 Dec 30	KS, 31st, 1912
Mitchell, J.S.			24		1886	NE, 11th, 1887
Mitchell, J.W.		44th Mo.	51		1917	KS, 37th, 1918
Mitchell, Jacob	Pvt.	C, 39th Iowa Inf.	203		1917 Oct 15	IA, 44th, 1918
Mitchell, James B.		C, 2nd West Va. Cav.	82		1922 Dec 3	KS, 42nd, 1923
Mitchell, James R.	Pvt.	D, 28th Iowa Inf.	98		1916 Apr 6	IA, 43rd, 1917
Mitchell, John	Pvt.	E, 10th Ill. Inf.	57		1933	IA, 60th, 1934
Mitchell, John C.	Lieut.	K, 8th Ill. Cav. (died of wound)	154	53	1861 Apr 10	NE, 13th, 1889
Mitchell, Joshua		D, 8th Kans.	92		1931 Apr 28	KS, 51st, 1932
Mitchell, Joshua		D, 8th Kans.	92		1931 Apr 28	KS, 52nd, 1933
Mitchell, M.R., M.D.	Lieut. Major	B, 88th Ohio 27th U.S.C.T.	250		1928 Dec 27	KS, 48th, 1929
Mitchell, Michael		10th Ohio Bat.	120		1932 Dec 24	NE, 57th, 1933
Mitchell, R.S.		H, 13th Ind. Inf.	11	79	1902 Jun	NE, 27th, 1903
Mitchell, Robt.	Pvt.	H, 21st Mo.	254	47	1891 Sep 17	IA, 18th, 1892
Mitchell, S.D.		C, 7th Kans. Cav.	283		1896 Apr 4	KS, 16th, 1897
Mitchell, S.D.		I, 13th Ill.	25		1919 Sep 29	KS, 39th, 1920
Mitchell, Samuel T.		E, 10th R.I.	355		1929 Jan 12	KS, 51st, 1932
Mitchell, Samuel T.		E, 10th R.I.	355		1929 Jan 12	KS, 52nd, 1933
Mitchell, Samuel T.		K, 10th R.I.	353		1929 Jan 12	KS, 50th, 1931
Mitchell, T.C.			94		1928 Feb 23	IA, 55th, 1929
Mitchell, Thomas		8th Ill.	113		1923	KS, 43rd, 1924

*See Appendix A, B or C for roster of post names and locations.

†See Introduction for note regarding recording of death date.

381

Name	Rank	Company, Regiment or Ship	Post*	Age	Death Date†	Journal
Mitchell, W.B.	Pvt.	F, 47th Iowa Inf.	12		1917 Oct 9	IA, 44th, 1918
Mitchell, W.H.		I, 157th Ohio	249		1904 Apr 6	KS, 24th, 1905
Mitchell, W.H.		K, 38th N.Y. Inf.	147		1914 Aug 1	KS, 34th, 1915
Mitchell, W.J.	Pvt.	G, 83rd Ill. Inf.	12		1928 Feb 14	IA, 55th, 1929
Mitchell, W.W.			63		1884	KS, 4th, 1885
Mitchell, W.W.	Seaman	U.S.S. Oriole	11	77	1923 Jan 27	NE, 48th, 1924
Mitchell, William		C, 34th Ind.	33		1919	KS, 39th, 1920
Mitchell, William H.		A, 24th Ind. Inf. (died in Hutchinson, Kans.; buried in Huntsville cemetery, Reno County)	17		1925 Jun 6	KS, 45th, 1926
Mitchell, Wm.	Pvt.	K, 11th Iowa Inf.	39		1912 Sep 22	IA, 39th, 1913
Mittard, E.J.		A, 197th N.Y.	100		1919 Jan 13	KS, 39th, 1920
Mitten, John H.			36		1926 Feb 5	KS, 46th, 1927
Mitterling, Geo. S.		I, 172nd Penn. (died of old age)	4	84	1924 Aug 13	NE, 49th, 1925
Mittlestadt, Fred	Pvt.	C, 6th Iowa Cav.	48		1899 Feb 24	IA, 26th, 1900
Mitts, J.M.	Pvt.	K, 4th Iowa Cav.	20		1908 Jun	IA, 35th, 1909
Mitzler, George		A, 120th Ohio Inf.	94		1891 Apr 19	KS, 11th, 1892
Mix, H.W.	Pvt.	C, 145th Penn. Inf.	284		1904 Jun 30	IA, 31st, 1905
Mix, Jasper		H, 10th N.Y.	1		1931 Aug 17	KS, 51st, 1932
Mix, S.H.	Pvt.	B, 92nd Ill. Inf.	235		1930 Mar 29	IA, 57th, 1931
Mix, William P.		D, 53rd Ohio	145		1909 Jul 10	KS, 29th, 1910
Mize, James		A, 17th Kans.	256		1936 Jun 12	KS, 56th, 1937
Mize, William H.		D, 14th Ky. Cav.	69		1920 Apr 12	KS, 40th, 1921
Mizner, Henry G.		B, 14th Wis. Inf. (died of heart failure)	60	72	1918 Nov 2	NE, 43rd, 1919
Mizner, Hiram		A, 142nd Ill.	7		1927 Feb 23	NE, 52nd, 1928
Mizner, J.W.		D, 1st Penn. Cav.	63		1923 Apr 3	KS, 43rd, 1924
Moats, Ambrose P.		H, 38th Iowa Inf.	130	91	1937 Feb 3	IA, 64th, 1938
Moats, S.J.	Pvt.	E, 9th Iowa Inf.	29		1920 Feb 8	IA, 47th, 1921
Mobley, Seth		prominent in newspaper circles of the state 20 years ago; died at Manila; mustered out at Grand Island			1911 Jul 11	NE, 36th, 1912
Mobley, Seth P.		B, 7th Iowa Cav.	11	66	1911 Jul 10	NE, 36th, 1912
Mock, Daniel A.		A, 8th Tenn. Inf.	61		1887 May 17	KS, 7th, 1888
Mock, E.K.		G, 112th Ill.	17		1913 Apr 19	KS, 33rd, 1914
Mock, George		I, 62nd Penn. Inf.	82		1914 Mar 4	KS, 34th, 1915
Mock, George		F, 30th Ill.	25		1928 Dec 26	KS, 48th, 1929
Mock, Henry		84th Ind. Inf.	7		1919 Jun 11	IA, 46th, 1920
Mock, L.P.		D, 50th Penn.	82		1890 Jun 22	KS, 16th, 1897
Mock, W.H.		D, 35th Ind.	69		1913 Aug 4	KS, 33rd, 1914
Mockett, John H.		F, 28th Wis.	25		1928 Mar 10	NE, 53rd, 1929
Mockett, Richard		C, 43rd Wis. (nonmember of department; died at Lincoln)			1935 Apr	NE, 60th, 1936
Modlin, Benj.	Pvt.	G, 29th Ind. Inf.	106	63	1896 Jan 12	IA, 23rd, 1897
Modlin, I.N.			186		1899	KS, 19th, 1900
Modlin, W.S.		C, 36th Ind.	129		1916 Mar 22	KS, 36th, 1917
Moehliman, Eury H.		11th Kans.	100		1892 Feb 2	KS, 12th, 1893
Moeller, Herman F.		D, 140th Ill. Inf. (died of heart trouble)	130	68	1908 Jun 3	NE, 33rd, 1909
Moerheke, F.	Pvt.		42		1899 Mar	IA, 26th, 1900
Moessner, C.F., see Meossner, C.F.						
Moestoller, Josiah	Pvt.	D, 10th Maine Inf. (at large)			1931 Feb 7	IA, 58th, 1932
Moffat, John		B, 4th Wis.	52		1919 Dec 12	KS, 39th, 1920
Moffat, Roger		E, 35th Wis.	52		1911 Jul 17	KS, 31st, 1912
Moffat, W.A.		1st Ohio Art.	294		1920 Jan 15	KS, 40th, 1921
Moffatt, S.G.		D, 1st Iowa	270		1919 Jan 31	KS, 39th, 1920
Moffatt, Thomas A.	Pvt.	B, 12th Ill. Inf.	78		1923 Oct 4	IA, 50th, 1924
Moffatt, Thos. H.			110		1890	NE, 15th, 1891
Moffert, Adam		45th Ill. Inf.	147		1901 Dec 22	KS, 21st, 1902
Moffett, Wm. H.		A, 77th Ohio	18		1906 Dec 21	KS, 26th, 1907
Moffit, F.G.	Sergt.	D, 34th Iowa Inf.	12		1921 Aug 1	IA, 48th, 1922
Moffit, William A.		E, 1st Ohio Hvy. Art.	294		1920 Jan 16	KS, 40th, 1921
Moffitt, Henry F.		28th Iowa Inf.	167		1902 Dec 21	IA, 29th, 1903
Moffitt, Robert H.		B, 6th Kans. Cav.	32		1919 Apr 18	KS, 39th, 1920

*See Appendix A, B or C for roster of post names and locations.
†See Introduction for note regarding recording of death date.

Name	Rank	Company, Regiment or Ship	Post*	Age	Death Date†	Journal
Mogg, Conrad		E, 2nd Mo.	75		1889	KS, 9th, 1890
Mogg, John		B, 3rd Del.	22		1922 Dec 25	KS, 42nd, 1923
Mohan, James	Pvt.	B, 6th Iowa Cav.	91		1922 Jul 27	IA, 49th, 1923
Mohler, Harvey		E, 34th Ind.	354	73	1921 Apr 20	NE, 46th, 1922
Mohler, J.L.	Pvt.	I, 50th Ill. Inf.	57		1918 Nov 8	IA, 45th, 1919
Mohler, John		K, 120th Ill. Inf.		91	1936 Apr 22	IA, 62nd, 1936
Mohler, John		K, 120th Ill. Inf.	19	91	1936 Apr 22	IA, 63rd, 1937
Mohler, John H.		B, 6th Mo. Inf.	25		1912 Oct 8	KS, 32nd, 1913
Mohr, Martin			1	43	1885 Apr 18	IA, 12th, 1886
Mohr, Peter		B, 13th Kans.	283		1906 Feb 14	KS, 26th, 1907
Mohrenstecker, G.A.		H, 33rd Mo. Inf. (died of heart failure)	24	66	1895 Apr 1	NE, 20th, 1896
Molamphy, R.B.			91		1911 2nd term	IA, 38th, 1912
Molamphy, R.B.			91		1912	IA, 39th, 1913
Moleneux, N.	Fifer	G, 38th Wis. Inf.	220	56	1896 May 30	IA, 23rd, 1897
Moles, Wilson		H, 1st Ohio Hvy. Art. (died of paralysis)	77	48	1895 Dec 29	NE, 20th, 1896
Molesworth, James		I, 1st Iowa	68		1917 Feb 7	KS, 37th, 1918
Molesworth, John			284		1899	KS, 19th, 1900
Moll, Wm.		I, 12th Kans.	68		1913 Aug 10	KS, 33rd, 1914
Mollenhous, George W.		E, 138th Ind.	118		1923 Sep 20	KS, 43rd, 1924
Moloney, Mike	Pvt.	I, 147th Ill. Inf.	58		1915 Oct 12	IA, 42nd, 1916
Momeyer, Cyrus J.		K, 15th Iowa	52		1919 Jan 8	KS, 39th, 1920
Monahan, John	Pvt.	G, 26th Iowa Inf.	88		1906 Jul 2	IA, 33rd, 1907
Moncrief, T.	Pvt.	F, 146th Ill. Inf.	150	81	1895 Dec 23	IA, 22nd, 1896
Mondt, F.W.	Pvt.	K, 2nd Cal. Cav.	1		1918 Oct 12	IA, 45th, 1919
Mondy, Martin V.		died of stomach disease	153	61	1905 Nov 30	NE, 30th, 1906
Mone, A.A.		N.Y. (died of bronchitis)	27	76	1914 Jun 14	NE, 39th, 1915
Moner, Samuel G.		A, 146th Ill. Inf. (died of disability)	84	70	1913 Dec 15	NE, 38th, 1914
Mong, Wm. H.		E, 150th Ind.	25	75	1921 Sep 1	NE, 46th, 1922
Mongar, I.	Pvt.		173		1921 Jun 28	IA, 48th, 1922
Monk, Ed.		C, 14th Ill.	12		1921 Mar 28	KS, 41st, 1922
Monk, John	Pvt.	H, 168th Ohio	285		1903 Mar 25	IA, 30th, 1904
Monk, William		F, 6th Iowa Cav. (died of old age)	109	80	1922 Feb 2	NE, 47th, 1923
Monkel, Jacob	Pvt.	E, 77th Ill.	248		1923	IA, 50th, 1924
Monlux, Wm.	Sergt.	D, 21st Iowa	184		1903 Aug 21	IA, 30th, 1904
Monohan, Robt.		B, 23rd Wis. Inf.	11	79	1891[1901?] Feb	NE, 26th, 1902
Monroe, A.B.	Pvt.	8th Ind. Battery	156		1927 Nov 24	IA, 54th, 1928
Monroe, A.D.	Corp.	G, 107th Ill. Inf.	316		1901 Dec 4	IA, 28th, 1902
Monroe, Alex A.		F, 23rd Mass.	12		1916 Apr 23	KS, 36th, 1917
Monroe, Hooper		G, 31st & 71st Ill.	25		1926 Jun 7	KS, 46th, 1927
Monroe, J.A.			147		1919 Aug 15	KS, 39th, 1920
Monroe, J.V.	1st Sergt.	C, 7th Iowa Cav.	107		1900 Apr	IA, 27th, 1901
Monroe, Jas. K.		K, 33rd Ill.	244		1927 Apr 26	KS, 47th, 1928
Monroe, John H.	Pvt.	H, 11th Iowa Inf.	231		1908 Nov 19	IA, 35th, 1909
Monroe, John V.	Sergt.	C, 7th Iowa Cav.	107		1899 Nov 20	IA, 26th, 1900
Monroe, John W.		E, 98th Ill.	145		1913 Jan 17	KS, 33rd, 1914
Monroe, L.C.		I, 72nd Ohio	113		1902 Jul 26	KS, 22nd, 1903
Monroe, M.V.		H, 8th Tenn. Cav.	17		1914 Oct 24	KS, 34th, 1915
Monroe, Samuel	Pvt.	D, 2nd Iowa Cav.	12		1928 Apr 20	IA, 55th, 1929
Monroe, W.D.		H, 5th Kans. Cav.	155		1936 Dec 4	KS, 56th, 1937
Monroe, Wm.		A, 13th Wis. Inf. (died of paralysis)	13	54	1895 Jan 7	NE, 20th, 1896
Monroe, Wm. E.		A, 9th Kans. Cav.	12		1889	KS, 9th, 1890
Monroe, Wm. F., see Munroe, Wm. F.						
Monson, Hans	Pvt.	E, 13th Iowa Inf.	194		1930 Feb 4	IA, 57th, 1931
Monson, John		A, 52nd N.Y. Inf.	7		1899 Mar 1	KS, 19th, 1900
Monson, S.S.		B, 155th Ill.	65		1915 May 3	KS, 35th, 1916
Monsure, R.F.		I, 10th Kans. Cav.	293		1909 Mar	KS, 29th, 1910
Montague, C.		H, 22nd Ill.	65		1897 Dec 19	KS, 17th, 1898
Montague, John		1st Colo. Bat.	447		1899 Feb 23	KS, 19th, 1900
Montague, Lyman		A, 126th Ill. Inf.	185		1917 Mar 3	KS, 37th, 1918
Montell, Prosper		U.S. Navy	78		1907 Nov 16	IA, 34th, 1908
Montgomery, A.C.		B, 83rd Penn. Inf. (died of heart trouble)	32	57	1900 Dec 21	NE, 25th, 1901

*See Appendix A, B or C for roster of post names and locations.
†See Introduction for note regarding recording of death date.

Name	Rank	Company, Regiment or Ship	Post*	Age	Death Date†	Journal
Montgomery, Alex.		F, —	94		1891 Aug 20	KS, 11th, 1892
Montgomery, C.A.			126		1883	KS, 3rd, 1884
Montgomery, H.	Pvt.	C, 6th Iowa Inf.	141		1920 Jan 11	IA, 47th, 1921
Montgomery, I.M.		A, 140th Ind.	85		1927 Mar 31	KS, 47th, 1928
Montgomery, J.B.		B, 23rd Wis. Inf.	57		1891 Jan 10	KS, 11th, 1892
Montgomery, J.E.	Corp.	I, 10th Iowa Inf.	84		1924 Jun	IA, 51st, 1925
Montgomery, J.M.	QM	107th Penn.	1		1917 Mar 6	KS, 37th, 1918
Montgomery, Jas. B.	Pvt.	D, 3rd Iowa Cav.	100		1919 Nov 10	IA, 46th, 1920
Montgomery, John			495		1904-1905	IA, 31st, 1905
Montgomery, John	Corp.	B, 28th Iowa Inf.	334		1914 Oct 21	IA, 41st, 1915
Montgomery, L.O.	Pvt.	H, 2nd Iowa Inf.	12		1897 Jan 26	IA, 23rd, 1897
Montgomery, M.W.	Sergt.	G, 4th Ill. Cav.	31		1924 Dec 18	IA, 51st, 1925
Montgomery, Mich'l	Pvt.	G, 2nd Iowa Inf.	181		1916 Apr 4	IA, 43rd, 1917
Montgomery, Moses P.		H, 15th Ill. Inf. (died of heart trouble)	98	76	1910 Jul	NE, 35th, 1911
Montgomery, Nelson C.		H, 117th Ind. Inf. E, 136th Ind. Inf. A, 140th Ind. Inf.	71		1900 Mar 8	KS, 20th, 1901
Montgomery, Patrick		F, 6th Cav.	53		1917 Feb 4	KS, 37th, 1918
Montgomery, R.R.	Pvt.	G, 7th Iowa Inf.	58		1925 Mar 22	IA, 52nd, 1926
Montgomery, W.A.	Pvt.	E, 35th Ind. Inf.	296		1902	IA, 29th, 1903
Montgomery, W.C.		A, 116th Ohio Vol. Inf.	1		1908 Jun 8	KS, 28th, 1909
Montgomery, W.W.		A, 2nd V.R.C. (died at Burlingame)	35		1895 Jan	KS, 15th, 1896
Montgomery, Wesley		A, 1st Neb.	13	70	1909 May 22	NE, 34th, 1910
Montgomery, Wm.	Pvt.	M, 2nd Iowa Cav.	94	69	1897 Mar	IA, 24th, 1898
Moody, Benjamin F.			147		1891 Jul 4	KS, 11th, 1892
Moody, J.J.	Pvt.	B, 14th Iowa Inf.	337		1926	IA, 53rd, 1927
Moody, J.W.	Sergt.	I, 29th Iowa Inf.	52		1910 Oct 19	IA, 37th, 1911
Moody, J.W.	Surg.	182nd Ohio Inf.	260		1914 Dec 18	KS, 34th, 1915
Moody, Jas. A.	Musician	I, 1st Mo. Inf.	56		1924 Oct 10	IA, 51st, 1925
Moody, Jas. T.		C, 5th Ky. Cav. (died of heart failure)	130	75	1910 May 24	NE, 37th, 1913
Moody, Joel		H, 2nd Ind. H.G.[Indian Home Guard?]	1		1914 Feb 18	KS, 34th, 1915
Moody, Levi P.		I, 70th Ind. Inf. (died at Leavenworth; buried at National Military Home Cemetery)	32		1894 May	KS, 14th, 1895
Moody, S.B.		G, 12th Iowa Inf.	177	85	1913 Apr 12	NE, 38th, 1914
Moody, William		H, 144th Ind.	180		1914 Jan 18	KS, 34th, 1915
Moody, William H.		A, 156th Ill. Inf. (born in Illinois; died of urenic poisoning at Soldiers & Sailors Home Hospital, Burkett; buried at Ansley, Neb.)		62	1906 Jul 24	NE, 31st, 1907
Moody, Wm.	Corp.	B, 14th Iowa Inf.	452		1926 Sep 25	IA, 53rd, 1927
Moon, Edwin	Pvt.	I, 115th Ill.	15		1905 Jul 1	IA, 32nd, 1906
Moon, George W.		B, 69th Ohio	72		1925 Dec 1	KS, 45th, 1926
Moon, I.F.		B, 40th Iowa (died of blood pressure)	13	73	1921 Feb 21	NE, 46th, 1922
Moon, I.M.		K, 9th Ill. Cav.	3		1914 Apr 22	KS, 34th, 1915
Moon, J.B.			116		1916 Aug 19	IA, 43rd, 1917
Moon, J.B.			116		1917 Mar 9	IA, 44th, 1918
Moon, J.R.		F, 86th Ill. Inf.	10		1895 Feb 14	NE, 20th, 1896
Moon, Jacob B.		C, 11th Kans. H.G.	55		1916 Oct 16	KS, 36th, 1917
Moon, John E.		D, 14th Ind. Inf.	1		1912 Aug 3	KS, 32nd, 1913
Moon, John M.	Pvt.	K, 104th Penn. Inf.	127		1917 Feb 10	IA, 44th, 1918
Moon, Milo H.		B, 70th Ind.	25		1923 Jun 16	KS, 43rd, 1924
Moon, Richard	Pvt.	C, 24th Iowa Inf.	110		1905 Sep 8	IA, 32nd, 1906
Moon, Simon		B, 4th N.Y. Hvy. Art.	465		1919 Sep 18	KS, 39th, 1920
Moon, W.	Pvt.	G, 11th Wis. Inf.	68		1921 May 13	IA, 48th, 1922
Moon, W.J.	Corp.	D, 34th Iowa Inf.	309		1926 Feb 8	IA, 53rd, 1927
Mooney, F.C.		D, 10th Mo. Inf.	13		1916 May 7	KS, 36th, 1917
Mooney, George Frederick		E, 13th Iowa Inf. (at large)	23, 203 & 264	95	1938 Jul 1	IA, 64th, 1938
Mooney, H.B.		D, 127th Ill.	130		1893 Aug 6	KS, 13th, 1894
Mooney, Hiram		A, 12th N.H. Inf.	350		1886	KS, 6th, 1887
Mooney, James E.		1st Res. Vet. Corps	1		1914 Aug 12	KS, 34th, 1915
Mooney, Richard M.		E, 37th N.Y. Inf. (died at Hutchinson)	17		1895 Jul 13	KS, 15th, 1896

*See Appendix A, B or C for roster of post names and locations.
†See Introduction for note regarding recording of death date.

Name	Rank	Company, Regiment or Ship	Post*	Age	Death Date†	Journal
Mooney, Robt.		G, 8th Ind. Cav.	119		1911 Mar 30	KS, 31st, 1912
Mooney, Thomas		F, 15th Ill. Inf.	1		1912 Dec 27	KS, 32nd, 1913
Mooney, Wm.	Pvt.	D, 5th Iowa Inf.	94		1911	IA, 38th, 1912
Moonnan, E.	Pvt.	H, 9th Cav.	43		1916 Sep 26	IA, 43rd, 1917
Moony, Daniel W.		F, 44th Mo. Inf.	281		1886	KS, 6th, 1887
Moor, John	Pvt.	3rd Wis. Battery	3		1928	IA, 55th, 1929
Moore, A.D.		H, 7th Kans. Cav.	3		1900 Oct 28	KS, 20th, 1901
Moore, A.W.	Pvt.	G, 33rd Iowa Inf.	40		1925 Aug 30	IA, 52nd, 1926
Moore, Aaron		B, 115th Ohio	5		1924 Feb 28	KS, 44th, 1925
Moore, Abraham	Pvt.	K, 9th West Va.	192		1914 Jun 15	IA, 41st, 1915
Moore, Albert C.		A, 5th Iowa Vol. Inf.	25		1908 Jul 8	KS, 28th, 1909
Moore, Alex			371		1904 Sep 11	IA, 31st, 1905
Moore, Alex. S.		B, 3rd Mo. (died at Howard, Kans.; buried at Cresco Cemetery)	23		1894 Oct 16	KS, 14th, 1895
Moore, Alonzo	Pvt.	E, 21st Iowa Inf.	78	48	1888 May 3	IA, 15th, 1889
Moore, Antone		G, 34th Wis. Inf.	324		1917 Mar 13	IA, 44th, 1918
Moore, B.F.		B, 84th Ill.	25		1914 Aug 7	KS, 34th, 1915
Moore, Benj. F.		128th Ind.	176		1914 May 14	KS, 34th, 1915
Moore, Benjamin C.		D, 8th U.S. Colored Hvy. Art.	7		1932 Nov 20	NE, 57th, 1933
Moore, C.E.		K, 202nd Penn.	25		1926 Mar 14	NE, 51st, 1927
Moore, Cornelius L.		D, 136th Ohio Inf.	265		1938 Aug 27	NE, 63rd, 1939
Moore, D.	Pvt.	I, 41st Ohio Inf.	10		1925	IA, 52nd, 1926
Moore, D.C.		16th Ind. Art. 116th Ind.	1		1919 Jun 2	KS, 39th, 1920
Moore, D.J.		H, 100th Ind.	74		1927	KS, 47th, 1928
Moore, D.M.			180		1923 Aug	KS, 43rd, 1924
Moore, Daniel D.	2nd Lieut.	D, 7th Iowa Cav.	167		1904 Nov 25	IA, 31st, 1905
Moore, E.G.	Pvt.	C, 19th Ind. Inf.	10		1918 Sep 2	IA, 45th, 1919
Moore, E.L.		F, 10th Kans. Militia	117		1898 May 29	KS, 18th, 1899
Moore, E.R.		gunboat, Navy	377		1924	IA, 51st, 1925
Moore, E.V.		G, 32nd Iowa	412		1920 Feb	KS, 40th, 1921
Moore, Elias A.	Pvt.	C, 32nd Iowa Inf.	26		1927 Aug 7	IA, 54th, 1928
Moore, Ellis		I, 85th Ill.	74		1909 Jan 8[Mar 7?]	KS, 29th, 1910
Moore, Elmer	Pvt.	F, 31st Iowa Inf.	66	58	1891 Sep 4	IA, 18th, 1892
Moore, Elwood	Pvt.	G, 61st Penn. Inf.	271		1906 Nov 13	IA, 33rd, 1907
Moore, Eph.			55		1924 Jun 10	IA, 51st, 1925
Moore, F.M.		G, 50th Ill. Inf.	293		1914 Mar 11	KS, 34th, 1915
Moore, G. Marion		L, 6th Kans. Cav.	3		1934 May 28	KS, 54th, 1935
Moore, G.W.		C, 96th N.Y. Inf. (cause of death: heart)	132	68	1903 Jan 30	NE, 28th, 1904
Moore, Geo.	Pvt.	H, 4th Vt. Inf.	190		1903 Nov 6	IA, 30th, 1904
Moore, Geo.	Pvt.	D, 22nd Penn. Cav.	8		1919 Jun 23	IA, 46th, 1920
Moore, Geo. P.		G, 8th Iowa Inf.	159		1890	KS, 10th, 1891
Moore, Geo. W.	Pvt.	A, 46th Ill. Inf.	140		1925 Jan 20	IA, 52nd, 1926
Moore, Geo. W.		M, 1st Mich.	52		1926 Oct 30	KS, 46th, 1927
Moore, George		D, 7th Ill.	1		1924 Apr 13	KS, 44th, 1925
Moore, George		D, 104th Ill. Inf. (died of old age)	152	77	1905 Jul	NE, 30th, 1906
Moore, H.G.	Pvt.	K, 8th Iowa Cav.	80		1930 Jul 12	IA, 57th, 1931
Moore, H.L.	Col.	D, 2nd Kans. Inf.	12		1914 May 1	KS, 34th, 1915
Moore, H.R.	Pvt.	B, 19th Iowa Inf.	452		1929 May 11	IA, 56th, 1930
Moore, Harry	Pvt.	B, 13th Ohio Inf.	337		1928 Apr 29	IA, 55th, 1929
Moore, Henry	Pvt.	I, 2nd Iowa	173		1903 Sep 7	IA, 30th, 1904
Moore, I.C.		F, 130th Ind.	113		1928 Jan 23	KS, 48th, 1929
Moore, I.F.		B, 25th Mo.	293		1920 Jun 27	KS, 40th, 1921
Moore, I.Q.		A, 188th Ohio	17		1923 May 22	KS, 43rd, 1924
Moore, I.S.		C, 86th Ind.	441		1912 May 2	KS, 32nd, 1913
Moore, Isaac		H, 80th Ill.	17		1923 Mar 13	KS, 43rd, 1924
Moore, Isaac S.		C, 6th Iowa	77		1893 Dec 26	KS, 13th, 1894
Moore, J.	Pvt.	I, 28th —	233		1921 May 19	IA, 48th, 1922
Moore, J.	Lieut.	N, 6th Vt.	49		1921 Sep 29	IA, 48th, 1922
Moore, J.C.	Corp.	C, 172nd Ohio Inf.	377		1900 Nov	IA, 27th, 1901
Moore, J.D.		E, 107th Ill.	51		1923 Feb 26	KS, 43rd, 1924
Moore, J.F.	Pvt.	G, 19th Ill. Inf.	168	65	1890 Aug 31	IA, 17th, 1891

*See Appendix A, B or C for roster of post names and locations.
†See Introduction for note regarding recording of death date.

Name	Rank	Company, Regiment or Ship	Post*	Age	Death Date†	Journal
Moore, J.H.	Pvt.	A, 2nd Ill. Cav.	452		1919 Oct 19	IA, 46th, 1920
Moore, J.I.	Pvt.	G, 6th Iowa Inf.	123		1917 Feb 25	IA, 44th, 1918
Moore, J.J.		B, 22nd Iowa	352		1929 Jul 18	NE, 54th, 1930
Moore, J.P.		B, 87th Ohio	244		1925 May 20	KS, 45th, 1926
Moore, J.S.	Corp.	F, 3rd Mo. Cav.	26		1910 Sep 27	IA, 37th, 1911
Moore, J. Scott		B, 15th Ohio	293		1921 Jan 30	KS, 41st, 1922
Moore, J.T.			1		1925	NE, 50th, 1926
Moore, J.V.		E, 8th Iowa Cav.	31		1923 Apr 4	NE, 48th, 1924
Moore, J.W.	Pvt.	G, 11th Ill. Inf.	69	84	1933 Mar 12	IA, 60th, 1934
Moore, J.W.			51		1906	KS, 26th, 1907
Moore, J.W.		E, 17th Ind.	465		1924 Nov 11	KS, 44th, 1925
Moore, J.W.		C, 83rd Penn. Inf. (died of heat stroke)	95	73	1913 Aug 14	NE, 38th, 1914
Moore, James	Pvt.	B, 9th Iowa Inf.	347	54	1887 Feb 2	IA, 15th, 1889
Moore, James		121st Ohio Inf.	68		1886	KS, 6th, 1887
Moore, Jas.	Corp.	G, 9th Ill. Cav.	501		1903 Oct 9	IA, 30th, 1904
Moore, John	Pvt.		337		1928 Jun 6	IA, 55th, 1929
Moore, John	Pvt.		67		1926 May 24	IA, 53rd, 1927
Moore, John	Pvt.	C, 45th Penn. Inf.	16		1926 Apr 16	IA, 53rd, 1927
Moore, John		A, 68th Ohio Inf. (died of inflammation of bowels)	122	57	1895 Dec 7	NE, 20th, 1896
Moore, John			122		1894	NE, 19th, 1895
Moore, John C.		D, 8th Kans.	12		1925 Oct 27	KS, 45th, 1926
Moore, John F.		H, 13th Wis.	30		1915 Jan 19	KS, 35th, 1916
Moore, John H.	Pvt.	A, 15th Iowa Inf.	55		1930 Apr	IA, 57th, 1931
Moore, John J.	Pvt.	D, 211th Penn. Inf.	235	72	1897 Jun 19	IA, 24th, 1898
Moore, John J.		K, 166th Ohio (died of kidney trouble)	1	76	1922 Feb 2	NE, 47th, 1923
Moore, John L.	Sergt.	A, 117th Ill. Inf.	40		1914 Nov 13	IA, 41st, 1915
Moore, John Oscar		F, 125th Penn. Inf. (see also Appendix D)	25	92	1936 Dec 11	NE, 61st, 1937
Moore, John W.		D, 142nd Ohio Vol. Inf.	1		1909 Sep 7	KS, 29th, 1910
Moore, John W.		E, 44th Wis.	380		1897 Oct 18	KS, 17th, 1898
Moore, Jos.			170		1899	IA, 26th, 1900
Moore, Jos.	Pvt.	D, 73rd Ind. Inf.	33		1917 Feb 13	IA, 44th, 1918
Moore, Jos. D.	Pvt. & Sergt.	E, 7th Ill. Inf. (died of wounds)	60	50	1887	NE, 12th, 1888
Moore, Josian W.		B, 64th Ill.	265		1893 Aug 21	KS, 13th, 1894
Moore, L.	Corp.	D, 7th Iowa Cav.	7		1914 Dec 22	IA, 41st, 1915
Moore, L.W.		E, 176th N.Y.	71		1906 Sep 8	KS, 26th, 1907
Moore, Mathew			166		1890	NE, 15th, 1891
Moore, McHenry		E, 6th Penn.	[12?]		1936 Mar 9	KS, 56th, 1937
Moore, Oren P.		H, 3rd Iowa Hvy. Art.	81		1892 Jan 17	KS, 12th, 1893
Moore, Orton		H, 45th Ind.	115		1928 Mar 7	KS, 48th, 1929
Moore, P.L.	Gunner	U.S. Gunboat *Chillicothe*	250	68	1887 Dec 29	IA, 14th, 1888
Moore, P.P.		F, 39th Ind. Inf.	92		1900 Feb 7	KS, 20th, 1901
Moore, P.S.		E, 40th Ind.	4		1918 Dec 11	KS, 38th, 1919
Moore, R. Lindsay	Corp.	A, 6th West Va. Inf.	49		1917 Jan 26	IA, 44th, 1918
Moore, R.W.	Corp.	B, 36th Iowa Inf.	40		1930 Apr 28	IA, 57th, 1931
Moore, Reuben F.		Lane's Bat. Colo.	244		1913 May 23	KS, 33rd, 1914
Moore, S.			337		1926 Dec 18	KS, 46th, 1927
Moore, S.A.	Lieut.	G, 2nd Iowa	100		1905 Feb 6	IA, 32nd, 1906
Moore, S.E.		H, 3rd Mo.	57		1916 Mar 3	KS, 36th, 1917
Moore, S.L.	Sergt.		329		1921 May 30	IA, 48th, 1922
Moore, Sample R.		E, 102nd Ill. Inf. (died at Waco, Tex.)	356		1895 Jul	KS, 15th, 1896
Moore, Samuel H.	Pvt.	F, 85th Penn. Inf.	137		1912 Aug 20	IA, 39th, 1913
Moore, Silas		H, 52nd N.Y.	321		1896 Mar 14	KS, 16th, 1897
Moore, Solomon		G, 49th Ind.	270		1898 Feb 20	KS, 18th, 1899
Moore, Sylvester	Pvt.	D, 25th Ohio Inf.	216	53	1886 Sep 2	IA, 13th, 1887
Moore, T.C.		C, 107th Penn. Inf.	1		1918 Jan 7	KS, 38th, 1919
Moore, Thomas	Pvt.	K, 22nd Iowa Inf.	112	52	1886 Feb 27	IA, 12th, 1886
Moore, Thomas	Pvt.	K, 22nd Iowa	112		1886 Feb 27	IA, 17th, 1891
Moore, Thomas	Pvt.	A, 22nd Iowa Inf.	249		1926 Nov 4	IA, 53rd, 1927
Moore, Thomas		K, 154th Ill. Inf. (died of apoplexy)	326		1893 Jun 13	NE, 18th, 1894
Moore, Thomas		K, 96th N.Y.	207		1926 Apr 5	NE, 51st, 1927
Moore, Thomas C.	Pvt.	I, 1st Iowa Cav.	5		1902 Jan 30	IA, 28th, 1902

*See Appendix A, B or C for roster of post names and locations.
†See Introduction for note regarding recording of death date.

Name	Rank	Company, Regiment or Ship	Post*	Age	Death Date†	Journal
Moore, Thomas E.		C, 4th Iowa Cav.	7		1938 Mar 22	NE, 63rd, 1939
Moore, Thos.		A, 114th Ill. Inf.	4		1889	KS, 9th, 1890
Moore, Tilford		D, 6th Mo. State Militia	11		1917 Jun 16	KS, 37th, 1918
Moore, Tomas		K, 16th Ind.	27		1924 Nov 24	KS, 44th, 1925
Moore, W.B.		I, 21st Iowa	18		1927 Jun 21	KS, 47th, 1928
Moore, W.E.		G, 2nd Mo. Cav.	130		1904 Jan 20	KS, 24th, 1905
Moore, W.F.		H, 28th Ill.	378		1922 Aug 27	KS, 42nd, 1923
Moore, W.G.		C, 7th Wis. Vols.	84		2nd quarter 1884	IA, 11th, 1885
Moore, W.H.			7		1900-1901	IA, 27th, 1901
Moore, W.H.	Pvt.	A, 46th Wis. Inf.	220		1913 Feb 11	IA, 40th, 1914
Moore, W.H.		B, 91st Ill.	28		1920 May 12	KS, 40th, 1921
Moore, W.M.		D, 148th Ohio	249		1913 Mar 15	KS, 33rd, 1914
Moore, W.S.	Pvt.	E, 2nd Iowa Inf.	12		1912 Apr 23	IA, 39th, 1913
Moore, W.W.	Sergt.	L, 9th Iowa Cav.	12		1897 Jan 16	IA, 23rd, 1897
Moore, Wallace M.	Corp.	E, 190th Penn. Inf.	400	91 & 9 mos.	1932 Jan 10	IA, 59th, 1933
Moore, William	Pvt.	A, 126th Ohio Inf.	493		1925 Dec 8	IA, 52nd, 1926
Moore, William M.		148th Ohio	249		1913 Mar 15	KS, 32nd, 1913
Moore, William R.		E, 77th Ill.	156		1908 Oct 2	KS, 28th, 1909
Moore, William W.	Pvt.	C, 12th Iowa Inf.	190		1915 Sep 10	IA, 42nd, 1916
Moore, Wm.	Pvt.	A, 48th & G, 4th Iowa Cav.	94	39	1885 Jul 26	IA, 12th, 1886
Moore, Wm.	Corp.	F, 134th Ill. Inf.	29		1925 Oct 10	IA, 52nd, 1926
Moore, Wm.		F, 27th Ill. Inf.	28		1900 Apr 4	KS, 20th, 1901
Moore, Wm. H.		A, 14th Ill. Inf. (died of consumption)	32	70	1912 Dec 13	NE, 37th, 1913
Moore, Wm. J.			226		1901 Nov	KS, 21st, 1902
Moore, Wm. S.	Pvt.	K, 36th Ill. Inf.	156		1910 Dec 4	IA, 37th, 1911
Moorehead, A.J.	Corp.	H, 84th Ill.	97		1907 Mar 30	IA, 34th, 1908
Moorehead, Philip C.		G, 133rd Ohio (former member; died at North Platte)	15		1936 Feb 28	NE, 61st, 1937
Moorehouse, Edward N.		B, 5th Cal. Inf. (died at Topeka, Kans.; buried at Topeka Cemetery)	1		1894 Nov 8	KS, 14th, 1895
Moorhead, E.		E, 11th Kans. Cav.	249		1918 Jun 19	KS, 38th, 1919
Moorhead, Samuel		K, 1st Kans.	53		1919 Nov 8	KS, 39th, 1920
Moorman, W.H.		A, 34th Iowa	83		1916 Dec 17	KS, 36th, 1917
Moose, William	Pvt.	B, 34th Iowa Inf.	49		1919 May 24	IA, 46th, 1920
Mooses, Frank E.		D, 8th Ohio Cav.	7	64	1906 Mar 9	NE, 31st, 1907
Moothart, W.P.			108		1925 Aug 3	IA, 52nd, 1926
Mopman, Jas.		I, 20th Iowa	66		1906 Jan 3	KS, 26th, 1907
Moppin, Albert					1937 Aug 14	IA, 64th, 1938
Moraign, John H.		H, 32nd Ill.	339		1921 Aug 2	KS, 41st, 1922
Moran, J.H.		E, 10th Kans.	269		1891 Jul	KS, 11th, 1892
Moran, James		F, 18th Mo.	325		1906 Sep	KS, 26th, 1907
Moran, James		H, 9th Ky. Cav.	52		1912 Jan 15	KS, 32nd, 1913
Moran, John	Pvt.	91st Ohio Inf.	286		1911	IA, 38th, 1912
Moran, William		A, 60th Ohio Inf. (died at National Military Home; buried at National Military Home Cemetery)	380		1894 Jun 6	KS, 14th, 1895
Moran, William		A, 60th Ohio Inf. (died at National Home)	380		1895	KS, 15th, 1896
Mordica, James		F, 15th Kans. Cav.	211		1889	KS, 9th, 1890
Mordick, T.	Pvt.	A, 48th Iowa Inf.	425		1918	IA, 45th, 1919
More, Jacob M.	Pvt.	A, 11th Penn. Cav.	236		1928 Jan 3	IA, 55th, 1929
More, John W.			380		1925 Mar 19	KS, 45th, 1926
Moredick, David H.		B, 10th Iowa Inf. (died of old age, accident)	77	88	1922 Dec 30	NE, 47th, 1923
Morehead, A.J.	Corp.	H, 84th Ill. Inf.	97		1906 May 30	IA, 33rd, 1907
Morehead, C.L.	Pvt.	I, 20th Iowa Inf.	235		1926 Dec 5	IA, 53rd, 1927
Morehead, Wm.	Saddler	M, 17th Ill. Cav.	300		1911 Apr 27	IA, 38th, 1912
Moreheiser, W.H.	Pvt.	H, 16th Iowa Inf.	78		1926 Jan 20	IA, 53rd, 1927
Morehouse, D.B.	Lieut.	I, 19th Ill. Inf.	1		1913 Jun 11	IA, 40th, 1914
Morehouse, Edward N., see Moorehouse, Edward N.						
Morehouse, J.W.		E, 9th Ind. Inf. (born in Elkhart, Ind.; died in Friend)	130		1883 Nov 9	NE, 8th, 1884

*See Appendix A, B or C for roster of post names and locations.
†See Introduction for note regarding recording of death date.

387

Name	Rank	Company, Regiment or Ship	Post*	Age	Death Date†	Journal
Morehouse, W.E.			479		1905	IA, 32nd, 1906
Moreland, A.L.	Pvt.	E, 28th Iowa Inf.	8		1921 Dec 12	IA, 48th, 1922
Moreland, Daniel		C, 17th Kans.	113		1910 Apr 21	KS, 30th, 1911
Moreland, I.E.	Pvt.	E, 69th Ind. Inf.	7		1913 Nov 4	IA, 40th, 1914
Moreland, John	Pvt.	F, 20th Iowa Inf.	212		1909 Dec 25	IA, 36th, 1910
Moreland, Wm. H.		I, 8th Ill.	55		1896 Aug 29	KS, 16th, 1897
Morey, Charles	Sergt.	A, 25th Wis. Inf.	63		1929 Jul 14	IA, 56th, 1930
Morey, George F.			94		1886 Mar 13	IA, 12th, 1886
Morey, Henry C.	Pvt.	H, 49th Wis. Inf.	118		1918 Oct 27	IA, 45th, 1919
Morey, Ira F.		B, 26th Iowa Inf.	88		1st quarter 1885	IA, 11th, 1885
Morey, J.K.		D, 40th Ill. Inf.	293		1908 Feb 10	KS, 28th, 1909
Morey, Orlando G.	Pvt.	H, 1st Wis. Art.	63		1913 Aug 20	IA, 40th, 1914
Morford, J.M.	Pvt.		96		1920 Feb 13	IA, 47th, 1921
Morford, John		G, 15th Ill.	98		1935 Dec 18	NE, 60th, 1936
Morford, Joseph		G, 2nd Iowa Cav. (died of heart failure)	89	75	1914 Jul 13	NE, 39th, 1915
Morgan, A.	Sergt. Major	37th Ill.	92	51	1892[1891] Aug 31	IA, 18th, 1892
Morgan, B.F.		B, 31st Ind.	49		1931 May 7	KS, 51st, 1932
Morgan, B.F.		B, 31st Ind.	49		1931 May 7	KS, 52nd, 1933
Morgan, Benj. F.			32		1914 Oct 16	KS, 34th, 1915
Morgan, C.P.		G, 9th Ohio Cav.	40		1919 Jan 12	KS, 39th, 1920
Morgan, Chas.		I, 42nd Mo.	45		1931 Aug 8	KS, 52nd, 1933
Morgan, Chas.		I, 42nd Mo.	45		1931 Aug 8	KS, 51st, 1932
Morgan, D.	Pvt.	A, 6th N.Y.	465		1919 May 14	IA, 46th, 1920
Morgan, D.C.		F, 1st Iowa Cav.	49		1904 Dec 11	KS, 24th, 1905
Morgan, D.M.		F, 20th Ind. Inf.	38		1886	KS, 6th, 1887
Morgan, D.T.		K, 12th Kans.	147		1914 Apr 17	KS, 34th, 1915
Morgan, Dan			299		1915 Jun 29	NE, 40th, 1916
Morgan, E.A.		G, 1st Wis. Cav.	25		1894 Mar 4	NE, 19th, 1895
Morgan, E.D.	Musician	20th U.S. Inf.	212	39	1887 May	NE, 12th, 1888
Morgan, E.O.	Pvt.	M, 3rd Ohio Cav.	86		1915 Oct 27	IA, 42nd, 1916
Morgan, Elijah		H, 1st West Va. Inf.	474		1891 May 29	KS, 11th, 1892
Morgan, F.H.	Pvt.	D, 40th Wis. Inf.	58		1927 Oct 3	IA, 54th, 1928
Morgan, Frank P.		F, 47th Iowa Inf.	110	73	1921 Feb 12	NE, 46th, 1922
Morgan, G.F.	Pvt.	H, 46th Ill. Inf.	242		1916 Aug 12	IA, 43rd, 1917
Morgan, G.W.		D, 87th Ohio	17		1913 Mar 30	KS, 33rd, 1914
Morgan, H.A.	Sergt.	H, 2nd Vt. Inf.	94		1902 Dec 11	IA, 29th, 1903
Morgan, H.M.	Pvt.	G, 1st N.Y. Art.	365		1914 Dec 8	IA, 41st, 1915
Morgan, Isaac F.	Pvt.	H, 26th Iowa Inf.	127	68	1898 Oct 22	IA, 25th, 1899
Morgan, Isaac L.		E, 2nd Ill. Cav.	31		1917 Jan	KS, 37th, 1918
Morgan, J.B.	1st Lieut.	K, 12th Iowa	1		1922 May 25	IA, 49th, 1923
Morgan, J.F.		H, 14th Conn.	25		1922 Oct 30	NE, 47th, 1923
Morgan, J.F.		H, 14th Conn. (not a member; buried by Farragut Post)	25		1922 Oct 30	NE, 47th, 1923
Morgan, J.W.	Pvt.	K, 25th Ill. Inf.	156		1921 Feb 14	IA, 48th, 1922
Morgan, James		C, 14th Ill.	49		1914 Jan 4	KS, 34th, 1915
Morgan, James A.		E, 3rd Ohio Inf.	159		1885	KS, 5th, 1886
Morgan, James W.	Pvt.	D, 138th Ill.	244		1922 Aug 10	IA, 49th, 1923
Morgan, Joe			134		1920	NE, 45th, 1921
Morgan, John	Pvt.	H, 1st Penn. Lt. Art.	49	46	1885 Aug 27	IA, 12th, 1886
Morgan, John	Corp.	D, 46th Iowa Inf.	412		1906 Jul 26	IA, 33rd, 1907
Morgan, John Foster	Lieut.	A, 66th Ohio	94		1927 Jan 16	NE, 51st, 1927
Morgan, John R.		Ill.	23		1926 Oct 9	KS, 46th, 1927
Morgan, John R.		C, 62nd Ill.	23		1926 Oct 9	KS, 47th, 1928
Morgan, John S.		H, 14th Ill. Inf. (died of consumption)	318	70	1910 Aug 6	NE, 35th, 1911
Morgan, John W.		M, 2nd Mo. Cav.	49		1900 Jun 25	KS, 20th, 1901
Morgan, John W.		C, 137th Ind.	458		1915	KS, 36th, 1917
Morgan, Joseph S.		F, 14th Ill.	127		1923 Jul 17	KS, 43rd, 1924
Morgan, Josiah		Neb. Indian (died of indigestion)	118		1905 Aug 6	NE, 30th, 1906
Morgan, Marion	Pvt. Pvt. Pvt.	G, 20th Iowa Inf. K, 29th Iowa Inf. I, 44th Iowa Inf.	87	93	1940 Feb 10	IA, 66th, 1940
Morgan, Milo			64		1928	IA, 55th, 1929

*See Appendix A, B or C for roster of post names and locations.
†See Introduction for note regarding recording of death date.
388

Name	Rank	Company, Regiment or Ship	Post*	Age	Death Date†	Journal
Morgan, Milo	Pvt.	C, 28th Iowa Inf.	64		1928	IA, 56th, 1930
Morgan, Rich'd M.	Pvt.	F, 28th Ill. Inf.	395	56	1898 May 25	IA, 25th, 1899
Morgan, Rich'd M.	Pvt.	C, 28th Ill. Inf.	395	57	1898 May 15	IA, 25th, 1899
Morgan, Richard			23		1911 May 1	IA, 38th, 1912
Morgan, Seth H.	Pvt.	C, 13th Iowa Inf.	59		1910 Sep 18	IA, 37th, 1911
Morgan, Stephen	Pvt.	F, 26th Iowa Inf.	92		1913 Jun 6	IA, 40th, 1914
Morgan, T.J.		F, 51st Ind.	112		1914 Jan 14	KS, 33rd, 1914
Morgan, T.W.	Pvt.	A, 21st Iowa Inf.	74		1915 Oct 23	IA, 42nd, 1916
Morgan, W.A.	Pvt.	I, 6th Iowa Cav.	215		1915 Feb 12	IA, 42nd, 1916
Morgan, W.H.		E, 112th Ill.	78		1893 Dec 12	KS, 13th, 1894
Morgan, W.H.		A, 46th Ill.	25		1914 Nov 9	KS, 34th, 1915
Morgan, W.H.		C, 9th Ind.	89		1918	KS, 38th, 1919
Morgan, W.H.		I, 58th Ohio Vol. Inf.	23		1929 Feb 7	KS, 49th, 1930
Morgan, W.W.	Corp.	I, 48th Mo. Inf.	135		1913	IA, 40th, 1914
Morgan, William		H, 27th Iowa	185		1916 Jan 26	KS, 36th, 1917
Morgan, William		A, 13th Ind.	303		1920 Sep 10	KS, 40th, 1921
Morgan, William Albert	Pvt. & 1st Lieut.	D, 23rd Ky. Vol. Inf. (see Appendix D)		76	1917 Mar 24	KS, 36th, 1917
Morgan, William B.		K, 13th Ind. Inf. (died of disability)	84	76	1912 Apr 9	NE, 37th, 1913
Morgan, Wm.		A, 2nd Mo.	85		1916 Jul 23	KS, 36th, 1917
Morgan, Wm. G.		A, 19th Penn. Cav. (died of tuberculosis)	118		1905 May 11	NE, 30th, 1906
Morgan, Wm. H.		C, 51st Mo.	90		1935 Apr 21	KS, 55th, 1936
Morgan, Wm. J.	Pvt.	C, 5th Iowa Cav.	78		1912 Jul 27	IA, 39th, 1913
Morgridge, G.O.	Pvt.	H, 11th Iowa Inf.	231		1909 Feb 11	IA, 36th, 1910
Morgridge, H.S.	Pvt.	C, 1st Iowa Inf.	250	48	1887 Sep 30	IA, 14th, 1888
Moriarty, Bartholomew		C, 17th Kans.	114		1906 Nov 25	KS, 26th, 1907
Moriarty, Michael		H, 15th Kans.	114		1906 Oct 9	KS, 26th, 1907
Morill, C.A.	Pvt.	A, 75th Ill. Inf.	82	50	1895 Apr 1	IA, 22nd, 1896
Morison, J.C.	Pvt.	H, 13th Iowa Inf.	337		1907 Aug 11	IA, 34th, 1908
Morison, Peter	Pvt.	H, 2nd Wis.	506		1899 Dec	IA, 26th, 1900
Morland, James H.		I, 144th Ind.	435		1921 Dec 22	KS, 41st, 1922
Morledge, R.R.		K, 4th Iowa Inf. (died of paralysis)	13	83	1923 Jun 24	NE, 48th, 1924
Morley, Henry		D, 11th Kans. Cav.	28		1914 Nov 3	KS, 34th, 1915
Morley, L.A.	Corp.	G, 2nd Ohio Cav.	97		1913 Feb 20	IA, 40th, 1914
Morley, Marshal		G, 15th Ill. Inf. (died of Bright's disease)	8	64	1902 Oct	NE, 27th, 1903
Morley, W.R.	Pvt.	H, 39th Ill. Inf.	258		1906 Dec 27	IA, 33rd, 1907
Morlin, J.D.	Pvt.	D, 112th Ill. Inf.	11		1915 Sep 10	IA, 42nd, 1916
Morning, F.M.		D, 124th Ill.	426		1897 Feb 17	KS, 17th, 1898
Morning, J.W.	Pvt.	G, 169th Ohio Inf.	245		1899	NE, 24th, 1900
Morony, David David		K, 85th Ohio	119		1917 Mar 5	KS, 37th, 1918
Morrell, A.		I, 32nd Ill.	18		1923 May 7	KS, 43rd, 1924
Morrell, E.		I, 8th Ill. Cav.	385		1900 Sep 5	KS, 21st, 1902
Morrell, Joseph	Pvt.	H, 9th Iowa Cav.	248		1922 Dec 22	IA, 49th, 1923
Morrill, E.N.		C, 7th Kans.	130		1909 Mar 14	KS, 29th, 1910
Morris, A.J.			480	57	1892 Nov 7	IA, 19th, 1893
Morris, Albert		K, 104th Ohio	61		1911	KS, 31st, 1912
Morris, Amos G.		K, 26th Ind.	104		1909 Nov 2	KS, 29th, 1910
Morris, Benjamin			42		1907 Jul 29	NE, 32nd, 1908
Morris, D.			352		1900-1901	IA, 27th, 1901
Morris, D.		H, 57th Ill. Inf.	197	97	1935 Mar 19	IA, 62nd, 1936
Morris, D.W.		H, 126th Ill.	55		1911 Dec 27	KS, 31st, 1912
Morris, Edward T.	Corp.	D, 26th Ill. Inf.	12		1912 Nov 22	IA, 39th, 1913
Morris, Floyd		H, 29th Ohio	36		1922 Dec 5	KS, 42nd, 1923
Morris, Frank		F, 1st Vt.	113		1917 Feb 12	KS, 37th, 1918
Morris, Frank		13th Ill.	129		1929 May 25	KS, 49th, 1930
Morris, Fredrick		A, 59th Ill.	428		1913 Nov 18	KS, 33rd, 1914
Morris, Geo. H.	Sharpshooter	Capt. Jocob Siegle, Ohio	40	79	1908 Dec 30	NE, 33rd, 1909
Morris, Geo. P.	Sergt.	B, 2nd Wis. Cav.	3		1923 Jun 5	IA, 50th, 1924
Morris, H.H.	Corp.	E, 33rd Ill.	64		1923	IA, 50th, 1924
Morris, H.W.		D, 128th N.Y.	500		1931 May 18	KS, 52nd, 1933
Morris, H.W.		D, 128th N.Y.	500		1931 May 18	KS, 51st, 1932
Morris, Isaac		B, 43rd Mo.	469		1924 Sep	KS, 44th, 1925
Morris, Isaac N.		H, 133rd Ill. (died of heart trouble)	91	75	1921 Oct 22	NE, 46th, 1922

*See Appendix A, B or C for roster of post names and locations.
†See Introduction for note regarding recording of death date.

Name	Rank	Company, Regiment or Ship	Post*	Age	Death Date†	Journal
Morris, J.B.		F, 157th Ind.	25		1910 Dec 27	KS, 30th, 1911
Morris, J.G.	Bugler	C, 9th Iowa Cav.	497		1920 Oct 6	IA, 47th, 1921
Morris, J.N.		I, 12th Kans. Inf.	16		1909 Oct 10	KS, 29th, 1910
Morris, J.P.		A, 35th Ind.	42		1913 Apr	NE, 38th, 1914
Morris, J.R.			412		1922	IA, 49th, 1923
Morris, Jas. K.		G, 11th Ohio Inf. (died of acute hepatitis)	110	54	1897 Jul 15	NE, 22nd, 1898
Morris, John		E, 147th Penn. Inf.	49	95	1938 Feb 14	IA, 64th, 1938
Morris, John		H, 5th Ind. Cav.	32		1927	NE, 52nd, 1928
Morris, John D.	Pvt.	I, 148th Ohio Inf.	202	70	1893 Sep 2	IA, 20th, 1894
Morris, John W.		B, 1st Del. Cav.	265		1928 Sep 7	NE, 53rd, 1929
Morris, Joseph	Pvt.	C, 21st Mo.	127		1926 Feb 7	IA, 53rd, 1927
Morris, Nathaniel		1st Ill. Cav.			1890	KS, 10th, 1891
Morris, P.H.	Pvt.	C, 2nd Wis. Cav.	66		1912 Jun 18	IA, 39th, 1913
Morris, Preston		A, 2nd Kans. Cav.	180		1912 Jan 28	KS, 32nd, 1913
Morris, Richard		103rd Ill.	12		1898 Mar 7	KS, 18th, 1899
Morris, T.C.		H, 36th Ohio	81		1927 Dec 29	KS, 47th, 1928
Morris, Thomas			114		1883	KS, 3rd, 1884
Morris, V.R.J.			29		1911 Apr 15	IA, 38th, 1912
Morris, Z.	Pvt.	11th Iowa Inf.	126	69	1895 Oct	IA, 22nd, 1896
Morrison, A.J.		B, 100th Penn.	5		1912 Jun 30	KS, 32nd, 1913
Morrison, Alexander	Pvt.	I, 153rd Ill. Inf.	215		1917 Nov 14	IA, 44th, 1918
Morrison, C.H.		F, 194th Penn.	203		1922 May 24	KS, 42nd, 1923
Morrison, C.M.		C, 2nd Vt.	250		1928 Sep 28	KS, 48th, 1929
Morrison, C.S.		A, 13th Mich.	13	77	1907 Aug 5	NE, 32nd, 1908
Morrison, Fisher	Pvt.	G, 25th Iowa Inf.	19		1903 Sep	IA, 30th, 1904
Morrison, Geo. W.	Pvt.	G, 30th Ill. Vol. Inf.	285	53	1898 Nov 29	IA, 25th, 1899
Morrison, H.H.		G, 15th Kans.	127		1917 Jun 4	KS, 37th, 1918
Morrison, Isaac		K, 85th Penn. Inf.	71	44	1887 Nov 26	IA, 15th, 1889
Morrison, J.A.	Pvt.	K, 53rd Ill. Inf.	322		1917 Jan 4	IA, 44th, 1918
Morrison, J.C., see Morison, J.C.						
Morrison, J.S.		G, Iowa Inf.	71		1915 Dec 24	KS, 36th, 1917
Morrison, J.T.		A, 58th Ohio	184		1910 Jul 3	KS, 30th, 1911
Morrison, James		B, 50th N.Y. Eng. (died of asthma)	90	71	1895 Apr 1	NE, 20th, 1896
Morrison, James N.		B, 31st Wis.	3		1892 May 2	KS, 12th, 1893
Morrison, John	Pvt.	A, 46th Iowa Inf.	70		1910 Aug 21	IA, 37th, 1911
Morrison, John T.	Pvt.	H, 13th Mo.	52		1915 Mar 5	KS, 35th, 1916
Morrison, John T.		H, 13th Mo. Cav.	52		1913 Mar 4	KS, 33rd, 1914
Morrison, N.B.	Pvt.	I, 95th Ill. Inf.	440		1920 Feb 22	IA, 47th, 1921
Morrison, Perry	Pvt.	7th Wis.	452		1919 Jan 21	IA, 46th, 1920
Morrison, Perry		F, 26th Ohio Vol. Inf.	65		1915 May 10	KS, 35th, 1916
Morrison, Peter, see Morison, Peter						
Morrison, R.F.		B, 83rd Ill.	25		1928 Jan 1	KS, 48th, 1929
Morrison, Robert		H, 9th Ill. Inf.	89		1901 May 9	KS, 21st, 1902
Morrison, S.S.		B, 121st Ohio Inf.	66		1918 Jul 9	IA, 45th, 1919
Morrison, Silas A.		K, 86th Ohio	1		1924 Dec 2	KS, 44th, 1925
Morrison, Thomas U.	Pvt.	M, 1st Mo. Cav.	434		1901 May 28	IA, 28th, 1902
Morrison, Thos.	Pvt. 2nd Lieut.	B, 1st Iowa Inf. K, 22nd Iowa Inf.	8	62	1893 Mar 1	IA, 19th, 1893
Morrison, Wm.	Pvt.		52		1921 Dec 4	IA, 48th, 1922
Morrison, Wm. B.	2nd Lieut.	D, 20th Penn. Cav.	88		1889	KS, 9th, 1890
Morrison, Wm. H.		C, 146th Ohio Inf.	2		1900 Aug 24	IA, 27th, 1901
Morrison, Wm. H.			216		1895	NE, 20th, 1896
Morrisy, G.H.	Sergt. Major	16th Iowa Inf.	190		1911 Feb 2	IA, 38th, 1912
Morroll, Richard	Pvt.	A, 44th Iowa Inf.	78		1911 Oct 24	IA, 38th, 1912
Morrow, Ebenezer L.	Pvt.	A, 5th Ind. Cav.	49	40	1888 Aug	IA, 16th, 1890
Morrow, Elias C.		C, 150th Ind.	25		1915 Jun 12	NE, 40th, 1916
Morrow, Henry A.	Col.	24th Mich. Vols. (see Appendix D)		61	1891 Jan 31	NE, 15th, 1891
Morrow, J.K.		E, 88th Ohio	18		1923 Aug 23	KS, 43rd, 1924
Morrow, James		A, 115th Ill.	59		1909 Jan 10	KS, 29th, 1910
Morrow, James		D, 116th Iowa Inf.	155		1930 Jan 10	KS, 50th, 1931

*See Appendix A, B or C for roster of post names and locations.
†See Introduction for note regarding recording of death date.

Name	Rank	Company, Regiment or Ship	Post*	Age	Death Date†	Journal
Morrow, Joseph		H, 63rd Ohio	185		1923 Feb 27	KS, 43rd, 1924
Morrow, Rozzell		I, 15th Iowa	118	70	1917 Nov 7	NE, 42nd, 1918
Morrow, S.E.	Corp.	L, 8th Iowa Cav.	497		1913 Jul 3	IA, 40th, 1914
Morrow, Thos.		B, 29th Iowa Inf.	103		1st quarter 1883	IA, 10th, 1884
Morrow, Thos.	Pvt.	B, 29th Iowa Inf.	103	39	1889 Feb 4	IA, 16th, 1890
Morrow, W.E.			173		1922 Jun 9	IA, 49th, 1923
Morrow, Wm.		F, 15th Iowa Inf. (died of heart failure)		64	1894 Aug	NE, 26th, 1902
Morse, A.			365		1917	KS, 37th, 1918
Morse, A.G.	Pvt.	D, 4th N.Y. Hvy. Art.	178		1917 Mar 13	IA, 44th, 1918
Morse, A.O.	Corp.	I, 37th Ill. Inf.	377	53	1894 Sep 19	IA, 21st, 1895
Morse, Alfred L.		D, 95th Ill. Inf. (died of heart failure)	60	74	1918 Apr 5	NE, 43rd, 1919
Morse, Alpheus A.	Pvt.	F, 27th Iowa Inf.	190		1916 Oct 5	IA, 43rd, 1917
Morse, Alva F.	Pvt.	C, 144th Ill. Inf.	193		1918 Oct 1	IA, 45th, 1919
Morse, Charles		D, 9th Vt.	350		1916 Sep 29	KS, 36th, 1917
Morse, E.S.	Pvt.		96		1927 Jul 27	IA, 54th, 1928
Morse, Edward N.		H, 2nd Ill. Art. (died of old age; see also Appendix D)	4	73	1920 Jun 30	NE, 45th, 1921
Morse, Elisha					1928 Dec 19	NE, 53rd, 1929
Morse, George N.	Corp.	F, 31st Iowa Inf.	302		1918 Sep 27	IA, 45th, 1919
Morse, John		F, 94th N.Y. (died of dropsy)	27	80	1913 Feb 22	NE, 37th, 1913
Morse, John			27		1913 Feb 21	NE, 39th, 1915
Morse, Mark H.	Pvt.	F, 31st Iowa Inf.	130	102, 2 mos. & 7 days	1943 Dec 25	IA, 70th, 1944
Morse, O.E.		D, 5th Kans. Cav.	33		1917 Jul 13	KS, 37th, 1918
Morse, Salem W.	2nd Lieut.	F, 7th Iowa Cav.	184		1903 Nov 19	IA, 30th, 1904
Morse, W.H.	Pvt.	F, 14th N.Y.	181		1905 May 28	IA, 32nd, 1906
Morse, Wm.		National Military Home	6		1936	KS, 55th, 1936
Morsell, M.V.		D, 3rd Wis. Inf.	285		1886	KS, 6th, 1887
Morser, Anderson		I, 79th U.S.	365		1922 Jun 1	KS, 42nd, 1923
Morten, Jesse	Pvt.	H, 27th Iowa Inf.	54		1925 Dec 22	IA, 52nd, 1926
Mortimer, David		A, 6th Mo.	116		1925 Oct 23	KS, 45th, 1926
Mortimore, Daniel T.		L, 9th Iowa Vol. Cav. (died of cancer)	77	71	1911 Nov 6	NE, 36th, 1912
Morton, B.E.		B, 7th Iowa Inf.	77		1890	KS, 10th, 1891
Morton, C.A.			98		1909 Jun 2	KS, 29th, 1910
Morton, Charles A.	Pvt.	3rd Iowa Battery	70	68	1894 Jul 19	IA, 21st, 1895
Morton, Geo. W.	Pvt.	G, 124th Ill. Inf.	56		1925 Feb 25	IA, 52nd, 1926
Morton, George		H, 2nd Kans.	12		1913 Mar 25	KS, 33rd, 1914
Morton, J.E.		A, 3rd Colo.	32		1912 Aug 31	KS, 32nd, 1913
Morton, James	Pvt.	C, 4th N.Y. Hvy. Art.	235	56	1899 Sep 23	IA, 26th, 1900
Morton, Jesse B.		D, 1st Neb. Cav. (died of general decline)	84	80	1921	NE, 46th, 1922
Morton, John T.	Asst. Adjt. Gen.	Gen. Deitzler's staff	1		1901 May 1	KS, 21st, 1902
Morton, John W.	Corp.	C, 19th Iowa Inf.	108		1926 May 26	IA, 53rd, 1927
Morton, Robert		E, 51st Ill. Inf.	112		1900 Nov 29	KS, 20th, 1901
Morton, S.G.		A, 98th Ohio	22		1919 Feb 26	KS, 39th, 1920
Morton, W.C.	Trumpeter	K, 7th Iowa Cav.	132		1905 Oct 14	IA, 32nd, 1906
Moscript, R.O.		I, 137th Penn.	265		1916 Sep 22	KS, 36th, 1917
Moser, C.A.		H, 14th Kans.	81		1927 Oct 27	KS, 47th, 1928
Moser, Philip H.		C, 108th Ind.	71		1919 Jan 1	KS, 39th, 1920
Moses, E.N.		B, 187th Ohio Inf. (died of paralysis)	35		1905 Nov 18	NE, 30th, 1906
Moses, E.N.		B, 187th Ohio (died of paralysis)	35		1905 Nov 18	NE, 37th, 1913
Moses, George N.		I, 15th Ill.	52		1911 Sep 10	KS, 31st, 1912
Moses, Marcus			93		1899 Sep 27	KS, 19th, 1900
Moses, R.H.		I, 1st Ill. Cav. C, 146th Ill.	52		1913 Oct 17	KS, 33rd, 1914
Mosher, A.P.	Pvt.	B, 12th Mich. Cav.	216		1919 Dec 12	IA, 46th, 1920
Mosher, Benjeman		C, 1st Ohio Hvy. Art.	69	89	1922 Nov 29	NE, 47th, 1923
Mosher, C.F.		B, 9th Kans.	40		1915 Jul 31	KS, 35th, 1916
Mosher, Cornelius		B, 34th Ill.	142		1913 Mar 4	KS, 33rd, 1914
Mosher, Cornelius		B, 34th Ill.	142		1913 Mar 4	KS, 32nd, 1913
Mosher, Jeptha		H, 1st N.Y. Marines (died of hardening of arteries)	22	83	1923 Oct 23	NE, 48th, 1924
Mosher, Minor		K, 37th Iowa	25		1897 Sep 28	KS, 17th, 1898

*See Appendix A, B or C for roster of post names and locations.
†See Introduction for note regarding recording of death date.

Name	Rank	Company, Regiment or Ship	Post*	Age	Death Date†	Journal
Mosier, A.N.		C, 15th Iowa Inf. (died of paralysis)	107	62	1902 Jun	NE, 27th, 1903
Mosier, Dan			[153?]		1902	NE, 27th, 1903
Mosier, Joseph		32nd Ind.	14		1902	KS, 22nd, 1903
Mosier, L.J.		G, 1st Minn.	130		1902 Jun 10	KS, 22nd, 1903
Mosler, Edwin	Pvt.	A, 46th Ill. Inf.	68		1919 Sep 13	KS, 39th, 1920
Mosmer, John	Pvt.	A, 4th Ind. Cav.	254		1929 Jul 25	IA, 56th, 1930
Moss, Aaron	Sergt.	A, 21st Iowa Inf.	200		1908 Jul 31	IA, 35th, 1909
Moss, D.M.	Pvt.	I, 23rd Ill. Inf.	111		1919	IA, 46th, 1920
Moss, David W.	Pvt.	D, 149th Penn. Inf.	12	55	1932	IA, 59th, 1933
Moss, George A.		F, 28th Iowa Inf.	147		1896 Apr 17	IA, 22nd, 1896
Moss, James E.	Corp.	E, 36th Ill. Inf.	111		1914 Dec 19	KS, 34th, 1915
Moss, Jorad		F, 8th Cav. (died at Potwin)	377		1932 Nov 18	IA, 59th, 1933
Moss, S.C.	Surg.	78th Ill. Inf.	5	64	1895 Dec	KS, 15th, 1896
Moss, Thos. D.	Pvt.	E, 12th Iowa Inf.	105	55	1892 Sep 7	IA, 19th, 1893
Mossman, B.F.	Pvt.	D, 146th Ill. Inf.	98		1891 Sep 16	IA, 18th, 1892
Mossman, Geo.		G, 27th Iowa	154		1905 Oct 13	IA, 32nd, 1906
Mossman, Wilbur	Pvt.	B, 2nd Iowa Cav.	452		1905 Feb 12	IA, 32nd, 1906
Mosson, Henry C.		B, N.Y. B.S.S.[Berdan Sharpshooters?] (died of dropsy)	39	65	1919 Jul 23	IA, 46th, 1920
					1906 Aug 18	NE, 31st, 1907
Mote, Butler	Pvt.	I, 15th Iowa Inf.	205		1906 May 28	IA, 33rd, 1907
Motes, N.		E, 22nd Iowa	173		1888	KS, 8th, 1889
Motley, Alfonse			252		1937 Mar 23	IA, 64th, 1938
Motram, C.V., Dr.	Surg.	6th Mich.	12		1904 Sep	KS, 24th, 1905
Mott, A.		H, 3rd N.Y. Art.	8		1888	KS, 8th, 1889
Mott, A.P.	Pvt.	E, 135th N.Y. Inf.	68		1908 Nov 11	IA, 35th, 1909
Mott, Alonzo H.	Pvt.	D, 153rd —	220		1919 Dec 20	IA, 46th, 1920
Mott, Fred	Pvt.	K, 115th Ohio Inf.	67		1911 Sep 5	IA, 38th, 1912
Mott, Henry		H, 44th Ill.	155		1923 Feb 16	KS, 43rd, 1924
Mott, John C.		D, 7th Ill. (not a member of the G.A.R.)	18		1912 Dec 30	KS, 32nd, 1913
Mott, John T.		14th N.Y. Lt. Art. (died of Bright's disease)	13	78	1911 Oct 25	NE, 36th, 1912
Mott, Lawrence	Pvt.	E, 13th Iowa	497		1924 May 13	IA, 51st, 1925
Mott, S.E.		F, 150th Ind.	8		1921 Apr 9	KS, 41st, 1922
Moulton, B.		G, 74th Ind.	175		1897 Nov 28	KS, 17th, 1898
Moulton, B.F.	Pvt.	E, 14th N.H. Inf.	216	71	1895 Jul 7	IA, 22nd, 1896
Moulton, E.C.	Pvt.	K, 38th Iowa Inf.	12		1915 Jan 19	IA, 42nd, 1916
Moulton, E.P.		G, 41st Ill. Inf.	145		1899 Feb 14	KS, 19th, 1900
Moulton, Geo.		A, 2nd Kans.	42		1927 Feb 5	KS, 47th, 1928
Moulton, Joseph		H, 11th Kans.	62		1889	KS, 9th, 1890
Moulton, N.H.	Pvt.	F, 3rd Iowa Inf.	47	58	1894 Jul 8	IA, 21st, 1895
Moulton, O.B.			65		1915 Jul 15	KS, 35th, 1916
Moultrof, D.C.		I, 12th Vt. Inf. (died of consumption)	52	61	1903 Jul 31	NE, 28th, 1904
Mount, Cyrus		4th Iowa	435		1908 Oct 2	KS, 28th, 1909
Mount, D.W.		I, 13th Iowa	28		1922 Aug 9	KS, 42nd, 1923
Mountain, J.H.		I, 18th Iowa	142		1904 May 5	KS, 24th, 1905
Mountford, Hugh		H, 132nd Ohio Inf.	96		1929 Dec	KS, 50th, 1931
Mourer, A.D.		H, 2nd Mo. Cav.	71		1904 Feb 18	KS, 24th, 1905
Mourie, J.T.			113		1908 Feb 3	KS, 28th, 1909
Mouroll, Nicholas	Corp.	L, 1st Iowa Cav.	130		1927 Mar 26	IA, 54th, 1928
Mousley, G.E.		7th Kans.	20		1896 Jan 6	KS, 16th, 1897
Mow, Johnathan		21st Ind. Art.	55		1886	KS, 6th, 1887
Mowbray, E.T.		89th Ohio Inf.	25		1911 Sep 26	NE, 36th, 1912
Mowder, Henry		F, 65th Ind. Inf.	151		1901 Mar 5	KS, 21st, 1902
Mowder, James M.	Pvt.	C, 14th Iowa Inf. M, 7th Iowa Cav.	188	52	1894 Aug 18	IA, 21st, 1895
Mowder, Wm. H.	Pvt.	A, 26th Iowa Inf.	188		1915 Jun 23	IA, 42nd, 1916
Mower, George		D, 16th Ohio	104		1927 Feb 16	KS, 47th, 1928
Mower, George R.	Pvt.	H, 1st Neb. Inf.	19		1928 Jan 28	IA, 55th, 1929
Mowery, J.	Pvt.		264[364]		1921	IA, 48th, 1922
Mowery, Joseph		F, 46th Penn. (died of paralysis)	265	65	1910	NE, 35th, 1911
Mowry, T.		Penn. B.T.	172		1912 Oct 7	IA, 39th, 1913
Mowthorp, Wm.	Pvt.	G, 26th Iowa Inf.	118		1906 Feb 5	IA, 33rd, 1907

*See Appendix A, B or C for roster of post names and locations.
†See Introduction for note regarding recording of death date.

392

Name	Rank	Company, Regiment or Ship	Post*	Age	Death Date†	Journal
Moyer, George	Pvt.	A, 105th Ill. Inf.	300		1899 Apr	IA, 26th, 1900
Moyer, Henry	Pvt.	A, 112th Ill. Inf.	349		1902 Sep 21	IA, 29th, 1903
Moyer, Henry		D, 60th Ind.	167		1913 Apr 27	KS, 33rd, 1914
Moyer, J.H.		G, 148th Penn.	130		1909 Jan 15	KS, 29th, 1910
Moyer, J.H.		I, 58th Ohio	378		1927	KS, 47th, 1928
Moyer, John			127		1922 Sep 15	KS, 42nd, 1923
Moyer, John T.	Pvt.	B, 1st Wis. Inf.	68	84	1931 May 8	IA, 58th, 1932
Moyer, Manasseh B.		G, 80th Ill. Inf.	88		1908 Aug 29	KS, 28th, 1909
Moyer, Michael	Pvt.	F, 106th Ind. Inf.	30	46	1887 Jan 25	NE, 12th, 1888
Moyer, Samuel	Pvt.	C, 48th Ind. Inf.	4		1917 Nov 1	IA, 44th, 1918
Moyer, Wm.	Pvt.	H, 5th Iowa Cav.	88	59	1893 Jun 28	IA, 20th, 1894
Moynihan, Pat, see Maynihan, Pat						
Mrisior, N.R.		K, 1st Ind.	294		1906 May 1	KS, 26th, 1907
Mucerhen, Jacob		C, 6th Kans. Inf.	300		1899 Aug	KS, 19th, 1900
Much, Anthony		Mo.	435		1893 Feb	KS, 13th, 1894
Mucheal, Geo.		B, 2nd Iowa Cav.	470		1899 Nov 4	KS, 19th, 1900
Muchmore, Henry	Pvt.	C, 79th Ohio Inf.	497		1911 Dec 13	IA, 38th, 1912
Muchow, Chas.		10th N.Y. Battery	127		1901 Jan 21	KS, 21st, 1902
Muck, A.		I, 44th Mo.	435		1897	KS, 17th, 1898
Mudge, H.P.	Pvt.	K, —	69		1927 Dec 25	IA, 54th, 1928
Mudge, L.C.			5		1925 Oct 14	IA, 52nd, 1926
Mudget, W.	Pvt.	L, 9th Iowa Cav.	16	88	1933 Feb 6	IA, 60th, 1934
Mudgett, C.C.	Major	3rd Iowa Cav.	312	84	1897 Jul 3	IA, 24th, 1898
Mudgett, W.H.	Pvt.	C, 37th Ill. Inf.	179		1901-1902	IA, 28th, 1902
Mueller, Adam H.	Seaman	steamship	8		1902 Jul 2	IA, 29th, 1903
Mueller, Fred		G, 34th Wis. Inf. (died of paralysis)	197	68	1914 Nov 26	NE, 39th, 1915
Mueller, Henry J.		1st Kans. Battery	50		1898 Mar 4	KS, 18th, 1899
Mueller, Paul J.		C, 98th N.Y.	25		1920 Dec 20	KS, 41st, 1922
Muenzemayer, J.J.		I, 1st Kans. Cav.	132		1918	KS, 38th, 1919
Muffly, Jos. W.	1st Lieut.	148th Penn.	12		1908 Dec 31	IA, 36th, 1910
Muhoney, Daniel	Pvt.	D, 33rd Mass.	78		1907 Jun 10	IA, 34th, 1908
Muhrlein, Frank	Sergt.	H, 2nd Iowa Cav.	8	75	1894 Sep	IA, 21st, 1895
Muhs, Peter	Color Bearer	A, 8th Iowa Inf.	88	51	1893 Dec 10	IA, 20th, 1894
Muichen, C.B.	Lieut.	K, 34th Ill. Inf.	48		1913 Jan 5	IA, 39th, 1913
Muier, Thos.		I, 45th Iowa Inf.	412		1906 Nov 5	IA, 33rd, 1907
Muir, Bryce		F, 10th Mo.	127		1928 Mar 21	KS, 48th, 1929
Muir, John		K, 5th Ill. Cav.	127		1929 Nov 26	KS, 49th, 1930
Muir, R.D.		A, 145th Ind.	56	79	1926 Mar 21	NE, 50th, 1926
Muir, W.P.L.	Lieut.	E, 15th Iowa	516		1922 Sep 1	IA, 49th, 1923
Mukes, Philip		A, 116th Ky.	321		1906 Nov 18	KS, 26th, 1907
Mulbry, William	Pvt.	E, 6th Ill. Inf.	150		4th quarter 1885	IA, 12th, 1886
Mulcia, Robert		I, 85th Ill. (died of old age)	38	89	1925 Apr	NE, 50th, 1926
Mulford, M.D.	Pvt.		235		1910 Feb 6	IA, 37th, 1911
Mulford, Sam'l	Corp.	B, 74th Ohio Inf.	34		1923 Oct 1	IA, 50th, 1924
Mulhern, John	Adjt.	29th Ill. Inf.	78		1904-1905	IA, 31st, 1905
Mulholland, Andrew	Pvt.	B, 12th U.S. Inf.	34		1925 Jul	IA, 52nd, 1926
Mulholland, W.	Pvt.	G, 189th Ohio	66		1907 Jul 28	IA, 34th, 1908
Mulick, Jas.	Pvt.		166		1912 Feb 2	IA, 39th, 1913
Mulkey, J.M.			180		1885	KS, 5th, 1886
Mulkins, Jos.	Pvt.	A, 8th Iowa Cav.	11	51	1888 Aug 17	IA, 15th, 1889
Mull, Con. G.		F, 11th Ind.	51		1908 Dec 24	KS, 28th, 1909
Mull, W.H.		K, 79th Penn.	12		1928 Nov 3	KS, 48th, 1929
Mulla, John	Pvt.	31st N.Y. Art.	22		1913 Dec 14	IA, 40th, 1914
Mullan, C.W.	Pvt.	D, 47th Iowa Inf.	68		1919 May 8	IA, 46th, 1920
Mullan, T.A.	Pvt.	I, Ind. Inf.	410		1913 May 27	IA, 40th, 1914
Mullarkey, James		K, 9th U.S. Inf. (born in Ireland; resident of Soldiers & Sailors Home, Burkett; died & buried in Shelton, Neb.)		79	1906 May 2	NE, 31st, 1907
Mullarkey, James		9th U.S. Inf.	354	79	1906 Mar 31	NE, 31st, 1907
Mullary, Chas. L.	Pvt.	F, 14th Vt. Inf.	88		1897 Aug 24	IA, 24th, 1898
Mullen, A.W.	Pvt.	B, 28th Wis. Inf.	42		1887 Apr 20	IA, 14th, 1888

See Appendix A, B or C for roster of post names and locations.
†*See Introduction for note regarding recording of death date.*

Name	Rank	Company, Regiment or Ship	Post*	Age	Death Date†	Journal
Mullen, Daniel	Pvt.	F, 15th Ill. Inf.	75		1899	NE, 24th, 1900
Mullen, E.J.		M, 1st J. Cav.[1st Iowa Cav.] 15th Iowa Cav.	2		1917 Nov 15	KS, 37th, 1918
Mullen, G.M.		D, 153rd Ill.	83		1887 Jul 5	KS, 7th, 1888
Mullen, J.M.	Pvt.	K, 92nd Ill. Inf.	14		1929	IA, 56th, 1930
Mullen, L.D.		L, 3rd Ind. Cav.	123		1914 Apr	NE, 39th, 1915
Mullen, P.		E, 29th Wis.	498		1911 Nov 16	KS, 33rd, 1914
Mullen, T.H.	Pvt.	A, 40th Iowa Inf.	49		1920 Aug 27	IA, 47th, 1921
Mullen, W.C.		L, 14th Ill. Cav.	11		1928	NE, 53rd, 1929
Mullenix, Henry H.		B, 108th Ohio	25		1926 Jun 11	KS, 46th, 1927
Muller, John F.	Pvt.	31st N.Y. Art.	22		1914 Dec 2	IA, 41st, 1915
Mulligan, John	Pvt.	C, 62nd Ill. Inf.	327		1915 Mar 16	IA, 42nd, 1916
Mulligan, Robert	Pvt.	E, 35th Iowa Inf.	2	64	1896 Jul 12	IA, 23rd, 1897
Mullihan, S.		C, 3rd R.I. Art. (died of fever)	32	62	1905 Oct 12	NE, 30th, 1906
Mulliken, Leander		F, 77th N.Y.	59		1912 Oct 31	KS, 32nd, 1913
Mulliken, Leander		F, 77th N.Y.	59		1913 Oct 31	KS, 33rd, 1914
Mullikin, J.W.		K, 18th Ind.	142		1926 Oct 18	KS, 46th, 1927
Mullin, Moses S.		B, 45th Penn.	1		1917 Jan 31	KS, 37th, 1918
Mullin, Peter		E, 25th Wis.	498		1911 Nov 16	KS, 31st, 1912
Mullin, S.C.		E, 107th Penn.	112		1929 Sep 13	NE, 54th, 1930
Mullinex, A.	Pvt.	F, 3rd Iowa Inf.	222		1910	IA, 37th, 1911
Mullis, H.H.	Pvt.	H, 70th Ind. Inf.	359		1906 Jul 2	IA, 33rd, 1907
Mullis, Wm.	Pvt.	B, 17th Ill. Cav.	45		1910	IA, 37th, 1911
Mullock, Peter	Pvt.	N.Y. Cav.	271		1908 Nov	IA, 35th, 1909
Mulvane, Ralph		I, 11th Ind. Cav.	1		1909 Dec 22	KS, 29th, 1910
Mulvaney, Barney		F, 39th Ill.	30		1917 Jul 1	KS, 37th, 1918
Muman, A.R.		F, 11th Kans.	220		1897 May 1	KS, 17th, 1898
Muman, Jonas B.		B, 28th Penn. Inf.	39		1900 Aug 12	KS, 20th, 1901
Muman, T.H.		D, 102nd Penn.	188		1908 Jul 21	NE, 33rd, 1909
Mumford, C.C.		G, 1st Ill. Cav.	25	73	1910 Apr 4	NE, 35th, 1911
Mumm, Peter	Pvt.	E, 2nd Iowa Cav.	403		1902 Jan 26	IA, 29th, 1903
Mummert, Francis		A, 13th Penn. Cav.	98		1928 Sep 11	KS, 48th, 1929
Munch, Henry	Pvt.	E, 9th Wis. Inf.	336	54	1892 Jan	IA, 18th, 1892
Muncy, L.D.		G, 15th Ohio Inf.	1		1889	KS, 9th, 1890
Munday, Chas.		G, 27th Mich.	35		1908 Feb 6	KS, 28th, 1909
Munday, William			35		1893 Jun 20	KS, 13th, 1894
Mundell, James		A, 114th Ohio	129		1916 Oct 20	KS, 36th, 1917
Mundell, Ransom			117		1926 Oct 21	KS, 46th, 1927
Mundhank, H.W.	Pvt.	B, 93rd Ohio Inf.	452		1928 Dec 22	IA, 55th, 1929
Mundhunk, Henry	Pvt.		94		1918 Jun 10	IA, 45th, 1919
Mundt, Peter	Pvt.	M, 2nd Mo. Art.	88		1919 Aug 14	IA, 46th, 1920
Munger, Albert	Pvt.	B, Dubuque Battery	243		1912 Dec	IA, 39th, 1913
Munger, David	Pvt.	20th Ohio Bat.	12		1919 Nov	IA, 46th, 1920
Munger, Frank		C & E, 11th Mo. Cav.	44		1929	KS, 49th, 1930
Munger, Geo.	Pvt.	E, 13th Ill. Inf.	141		1910 Jan 7	IA, 37th, 1911
Munger, Isaac C.	Sergt.	I, 16th Iowa Inf.	68		1912 Nov 22	IA, 39th, 1913
Munger, L.C.		D, 9th Mo. Cav.	51		1908 May 1	KS, 28th, 1909
Munger, N.O.	Pvt.	A, 4th Iowa	68		1926 Jul 3	IA, 53rd, 1927
Munger, S.O.		E, 40th Iowa Inf.	198		1912 Sep 19	KS, 32nd, 1913
Munger, T.C.	Pvt.	C, 17th N.Y. Inf.	235		1912 Mar 19	IA, 39th, 1913
Mungon, Geo. W.		died of old age	209		1905	NE, 30th, 1906
Munhall, C.S.		I, 26th Ill. Inf. (former member of department; location: Kearney)	1		1938 Oct 17	NE, 63rd, 1939
Munk, S.P.		D, 23rd Iowa (died at Barnes; buried at Maplewood Cemetery)	363		1894 Nov 8	KS, 14th, 1895
Munn, H.L.	Pvt.	D, 9th N.Y. Hvy. Art.	30		1920 Sep 2	IA, 47th, 1921
Munn, Silas		B, 24th Iowa Inf.	110	90	1936 Dec 28	IA, 63rd, 1937
Munns, B.P.		G, 7th Mo.	10	80	1920 May 23	NE, 45th, 1921
Munns, W.B.			55		1926 Sep	KS, 46th, 1927
Munns, Wm. B.		G, 152nd Ill.	433		1926 Mar 11	KS, 46th, 1927
Munroe, Wm.		A, 13th Wis. (died of old age)	13	83	1923 May 28	NE, 48th, 1924
Munroe, Wm. F.		G, 151st N.Y.			1928 Dec 21	NE, 53rd, 1929

*See Appendix A, B or C for roster of post names and locations.
†See Introduction for note regarding recording of death date.

Name	Rank	Company, Regiment or Ship	Post*	Age	Death Date†	Journal
Munsell, L.F.		H, 8th Wis. Inf. (died of hemorrhage)	80	71	1895 Mar	NE, 20th, 1896
Munsen, Wm.		B, 14th Vt.	9		1900 Dec 19	KS, 20th, 1901
Munson, A.P.	Lieut.	A, 27th Conn. Inf.	42		1919 Feb 13	IA, 46th, 1920
Munson, Ira C.	Pvt.		91		1908 Mar	IA, 35th, 1909
Munson, J.M.		F, 110th Mich.	265		1919 Jul 14	KS, 39th, 1920
Munson, Zeph		H, 3rd Md. Cav.	35		1928	NE, 53rd, 1929
Munt, John C.		F, 154th Ill. Inf. (cause of death: struck by auto)	2	77	1920 Jun 11	NE, 45th, 1921
Muntz, Henry		E, 134th Penn. Inf.	380		1917 Jun 18	KS, 37th, 1918
Muntz, Josiah P.		G, 24th Iowa Inf.	141		1885	KS, 5th, 1886
Muntz, Peter		A, 13th Iowa Inf. (died of wound received at Atlanta, Georgia)	[187?]	62	1902 Jun	NE, 27th, 1903
Murcer, Francis M.		15th Kans. Cav.	63		1924 Mar 18	KS, 44th, 1925
Murdock, Geo.		I, 93rd Ill.	180		1922 Dec 14	KS, 42nd, 1923
Murdock, Joseph		E, 22nd Ill. Inf. (died of dropsy)	173		1893 Jul 1	NE, 18th, 1894
Murdock, Roland P.		B, — Kans.	25		1906 Oct 17	KS, 26th, 1907
Murdock, T.B.		G & F, 9th Kans. Cav.	66		1909 Nov 4	KS, 29th, 1910
Murdock, W.			168		1908	IA, 35th, 1909
Murnch, Jacob	Pvt.	E, 4th Ill. Cav.	67		1907 Dec 22	IA, 34th, 1908
Murock, S.		I, 47th Ill. Inf.	175		1930 Mar 27	KS, 50th, 1931
Murphey, C.L.		A, 49th Penn. Vol. Inf.	63		1916 Aug 28	KS, 36th, 1917
Murphy, A.D.		B, 16th Iowa Inf. (died of apoplexy)	197	71	1901 Jun	NE, 26th, 1902
Murphy, Alex		D, 16th Ohio Vol. Inf.	144		4th quarter 1884	IA, 11th, 1885
Murphy, Andrew J.		I, 28th U.S. Cav.	100		1925 Feb 3	KS, 44th, 1925
Murphy, Andrew J.		I, 28th U.S. Col.	100		1925 Feb 3	KS, 45th, 1926
Murphy, B.A.		F, 21st Ill.	110		1931 Apr 11	KS, 52nd, 1933
Murphy, B.A.		F, 21st Ill.	110		1931 Apr 11	KS, 51st, 1932
Murphy, B.E.		I, 7th Mo. Cav.	85		1890	KS, 10th, 1891
Murphy, C.L., see Murphey, C.L.						
Murphy, D.W.	Pvt.	24th Ohio Bat.	16		1921 Sep 5	IA, 48th, 1922
Murphy, Daniel		G, 1st Ky. Cav.	356		1892 Jun 15	KS, 12th, 1893
Murphy, E.R.	Seaman	U.S.S. Peoria	92		1919 Oct 4	KS, 39th, 1920
Murphy, Ed	Pvt.		57		1930	IA, 57th, 1931
Murphy, Geo.	Sergt.	G, 8th Wis. Inf.	348		1904 Sep 17	IA, 31st, 1905
Murphy, H.A.			32		1921 Oct 19	NE, 46th, 1922
Murphy, Henry C.	Sergt.	G, 84th Ind. Inf.	12		1917 May 22	IA, 44th, 1918
Murphy, J.C.	Pvt.	H, 13th U.S. Inf.	78		1912 Aug 16	IA, 39th, 1913
Murphy, J.H.		E, 88th Ill. Inf.	134		1892 Nov 9	NE, 17th, 1893
Murphy, J.M.		A, 11th Ky. Cav.	356		1916 Mar	KS, 36th, 1917
Murphy, J.R.	Pvt.	H, 17th Iowa Inf.	22		1931 Nov	IA, 58th, 1932
Murphy, James	Pvt.	C, 1st Iowa Bat.	452		1915	IA, 42nd, 1916
Murphy, Jas. K.	Pvt.	E, 6th Iowa Inf.	49		1911 Jun 6	IA, 38th, 1912
Murphy, John H.		A, 80th Ohio Inf. (died at Cherryvale; buried at Fairview Cemetery)	142		1894 Feb 18	KS, 14th, 1895
Murphy, John J.		C, 68th Penn.	88		1885	KS, 5th, 1886
Murphy, M.		H, 177th Penn. (died of asthma)	267	64	1906 Feb 21	NE, 31st, 1907
Murphy, Michael	Pvt.	F, 16th Iowa Inf.	327		1900 Dec 21	IA, 27th, 1901
Murphy, Michael			44		1892 Feb 23	KS, 12th, 1893
Murphy, Monteville		E, 17th Kans. Inf.	251		1908[1909?] Sep 17	KS, 29th, 1910
Murphy, P.A.	Pvt.	D, 45th N.Y. Inf.	235		1930 Nov 15	IA, 57th, 1931
Murphy, Peter		D, 17th Mich. Inf.	18		1908 Feb 15	KS, 28th, 1909
Murphy, Philip J.			231		1928 Nov 19	IA, 55th, 1929
Murphy, Richard		I, 8th N.Y. Cav.	14		1910 Jan 30	KS, 30th, 1911
Murphy, Roger	Pvt.	B, 146th Ill.	504		1903 Dec 26	IA, 30th, 1904
Murphy, S.J.	Pvt.	D, 37th Iowa Inf.	233	87	1897 Apr 6	IA, 23rd, 1897
Murphy, S.S., Rev.		H, 45th Iowa	40		1916 Nov 8	KS, 36th, 1917
Murphy, W.	Pvt.	H, 33rd Ill.	57		1921 Sep 8	IA, 48th, 1922
Murphy, W.H.	Pvt.	F, 16th Ill.	203		1922 Oct 28	IA, 49th, 1923
Murphy, William		A, 43rd Ind.	144		1896 May 17	KS, 16th, 1897
Murphy, Wm.	Pvt.	H, 5th Iowa Inf.	466	62	1893 Sep 10	IA, 20th, 1894
Murphy, Wm.	Pvt.	F, 157th Ill.	323		1924 Jan 29	IA, 51st, 1925

Name	Rank	Company, Regiment or Ship	Post*	Age	Death Date†	Journal
Murphy, Wm.		H, 34th Ind. Inf.	120	59	1911 Feb 17	NE, 36th, 1912
Murphy, Wm. C.			45		1923 Apr 30	IA, 50th, 1924
Murr, Bartley	Pvt.	E, 13th Iowa Inf.	317		1905 Sep 9	IA, 32nd, 1906
Murray, A.B.		G, 36th Ill.	25		1928 Nov 22	NE, 53rd, 1929
Murray, Alvin R.		A, 181st Ohio	17		1916 Feb 13	KS, 36th, 1917
Murray, Bruce	Pvt.	G, 46th Ohio Inf.	244		1925 Dec 25	IA, 52nd, 1926
Murray, Chas. L.		U.S. Signal Corps	131	44	1887 Oct 23	IA, 14th, 1888
Murray, David S.	Pvt.	I, 17th Iowa Inf.	19		1904 May 4	IA, 31st, 1905
Murray, Edd		E, 84th Ind.	77		1915 Jun 20	KS, 35th, 1916
Murray, Geo. B.		F, 15th Iowa	428		1920 Dec 29	KS, 40th, 1921
Murray, Henry	Pvt.	F, 19th Iowa Inf.	153		1929 Oct 10	IA, 56th, 1930
Murray, J.H.		A, 79th Ohio Inf.	203		1929 Jan 26	KS, 50th, 1931
Murray, J.L.	Pvt.	E, 16th Iowa Inf.	153		1927 Dec	IA, 54th, 1928
Murray, John	Pvt.	D, 7th Wis. Inf.	88		1905 Jan 16	IA, 31st, 1905
Murray, John	Pvt.	G, 50th Ohio Inf.	69		1912 Jan 15	IA, 39th, 1913
Murray, John	Pvt.	B, 34th Ill. Inf. (at large)			1931 Oct 16	IA, 58th, 1932
Murray, Nelson		C, 183rd Ill. Inf.	293		1925 Oct 17	KS, 45th, 1926
Murray, Robert M.		H, 57th Ill. Inf.	234, 347, 6, 52, 302	93	1938 Jul 26	IA, 64th, 1938
Murray, Samuel		I, 93rd Ind.	92		1896 Nov 14	KS, 16th, 1897
Murray, T.			35		1911 Jan 26	NE, 36th, 1912
Murray, T.H.			268		1918 Mar 14	KS, 40th, 1921
Murray, W.B.	Pvt.	M, 4th Iowa Cav.	19		1915 Feb 8	IA, 42nd, 1916
Murray, Wm. A.		A, 4th Iowa Inf.	170	91	1936 Jul 13	IA, 63rd, 1937
Murrell, T.I.		3rd Iowa Bat.	29		1921 Mar 26	IA, 48th, 1922
Murry, A.J.		I, 35th Ind.	92		1893 Jan 7	KS, 13th, 1894
Murry, Andrew		D, 168th Ohio	55		1911 Dec 12	KS, 31st, 1912
Murry, Daniel S.		E, 47th Ill.	68		1890	KS, 10th, 1891
Murry, W.H.H.		A, 30th Ill. Inf.	54		1912 Dec 26	KS, 32nd, 1913
Musgrove, George		M, 3rd Kans.	153		1913 May 1	KS, 33rd, 1914
Musselman, Lewis B.		B, 108th Ill. Inf. (Norfolk)			1946 Oct 12	NE, 73rd, 1949
Musser, Charles O.		A, 29th Iowa Inf.	1		1938 Mar 10	NE, 63rd, 1939
Musser, John S.		Penn. Vols.	297		1902 Mar 19	KS, 22nd, 1903
Musser, William		H, 136th Penn. (died of old age)	354	88	1913 Jul 11	NE, 38th, 1914
Mutchie, Peter		2nd Wis.	112		1913 Jul 17	NE, 38th, 1914
Mutchler, L.H.	Pvt.	H, 5th Ohio Cav.	43		1908 Jan	IA, 35th, 1909
Muzzy, F.J.	Pvt.	D, 1st Ill. Art.	5		1915 Apr 20	IA, 42nd, 1916
Muzzy, H.C.		1st Kans. Bat.	12		1906 Dec 27	KS, 26th, 1907
Muzzy, L.B.	Pvt.	E, 15th Iowa Inf.	2	80	1897 Jan 1	IA, 23rd, 1897
Mychoff, Perry S.	Pvt.	G, 84th Ill. Inf.	122		1917 Mar 20	IA, 44th, 1918
Myer, George H.		I, 12th Tenn. Cav.	7		1938 Feb 27	NE, 63rd, 1939
Myer, John			277		1911 2nd term	IA, 38th, 1912
Myer, John D.	Pvt.	E, 12th Iowa Inf.	243		1919 Oct 3	IA, 46th, 1920
Myer, W.E.	Pvt.	A, 40th Iowa Inf.	49		1920 Dec 25	IA, 47th, 1921
Myer, W.H.	Pvt.	A, 11th Iowa Inf.	1		1920 Dec 25	IA, 47th, 1921
Myer, Z.B.		I, 17th Ind.	85		1919 Jun 6	KS, 39th, 1920
Myers, A.G.		K, 99th Penn.	18		1924 Nov 4	KS, 44th, 1925
Myers, A.L.	Pvt.	A, 27th Ill. Inf.	1		1919 Nov 21	IA, 46th, 1920
Myers, Anthony		C, 7th Kans. Cav.	118		1918 Apr 12	KS, 38th, 1919
Myers, August		B, 25th Mo.	271		1914 Aug 14	KS, 34th, 1915
Myers, B.F.	Pvt.	I, 13th Iowa	122		1905 May 9	IA, 32nd, 1906
Myers, B.F.		A, 9th Ind.	257		1909 Jun 7	KS, 29th, 1910
Myers, C.D.	Pvt.	28th Iowa Inf.	235		1924 Feb 15	IA, 51st, 1925
Myers, C.H.		G, 13th Wis. Inf.	68		1926 Mar 17	NE, 51st, 1927
Myers, C.L.		G, 17th Ill. Inf.	22		1900 Aug 16	KS, 20th, 1901
Myers, Charles	Pvt.	B, 7th Ill. Cav.	222	93	1933 Feb 15	IA, 60th, 1934
Myers, Comrade			279		1914	KS, 34th, 1915
Myers, D.M.		K, 1st Penn.	63		1917 Dec 17	KS, 37th, 1918
Myers, David		F, 74th Penn.	59		1913 Sep 23	KS, 33rd, 1914
Myers, E.H.	Pvt.	B, — Iowa Inf.	206	89	1932 Dec 2	IA, 59th, 1933
Myers, E.W.		E & K, 22nd & 47th Iowa (died of heart trouble)	289	68	1911 Dec 22	NE, 36th, 1912

*See Appendix A, B or C for roster of post names and locations.
†See Introduction for note regarding recording of death date.

Name	Rank	Company, Regiment or Ship	Post*	Age	Death Date†	Journal
Myers, Ed		I, 3rd U.S. Cav.	287		1908	NE, 33rd, 1909
Myers, Edward	Pvt.	K, 15th Ill. Inf.	67		1899 May 20	IA, 26th, 1900
Myers, Eli			73		1917	IA, 44th, 1918
Myers, Elijah			29		1890	NE, 15th, 1891
Myers, F.W.	Pvt.	A, 209th Penn. Inf.	59		1912 Jul 31	IA, 39th, 1913
Myers, Frederick		B, 9th N.Y. Hvy. Art.	25		1936 Feb 8	NE, 61st, 1937
Myers, Geo.	Pvt.	D, 36th Iowa Inf.	323	49	1888 Mar 27	IA, 15th, 1889
Myers, Geo. H.		H, 21st Penn. Cav. (died of general debility)	169	83	1919 Oct 8	NE, 44th, 1920
Myers, H.		I, 94th Ill.	63		1888	KS, 8th, 1889
Myers, H.M.	Pvt.	D, 35th Iowa	255		1922 Mar	IA, 49th, 1923
Myers, Henry		G, 107th Ill.	25		1922 Dec 15	NE, 47th, 1923
Myers, Henry C.		F, 1st Ind. Cav.	54		1922 Feb 26	KS, 42nd, 1923
Myers, Henry P.		36th Penn. (died of Bright's disease)	204	75	1915 Jul 24	NE, 40th, 1916
Myers, I.W.	Pvt.	G, 147th Ill. Inf.	81		1929 Jan 18	IA, 56th, 1930
Myers, J.		A, 17th Ill. Inf. (died of old age)	94	79	1922 Apr 8	NE, 47th, 1923
Myers, J.A.	Pvt.	C, 28th Iowa Inf.	127		1905 Sep 23	IA, 32nd, 1906
Myers, J.A.	Pvt.	G, 151st Ind. Inf.	98		1913 Jun 10	IA, 40th, 1914
Myers, J.A.		G, 51st Ohio	17		1930 Jan 19	KS, 50th, 1931
Myers, J.B.		B, 11th Iowa Inf.	94	89	1935 Mar 20	IA, 62nd, 1936
Myers, J.C.		E, 68th Ind.	52		1920 Jan 12	KS, 40th, 1921
Myers, J.E.	Pvt.	B, 11th Ohio Cav.	323		1924 Aug 29	IA, 51st, 1925
Myers, J.H.	Sergt.	E, 36th Iowa Inf.	497		1914 Dec 3	IA, 41st, 1915
Myers, J.K.	Pvt.	C, 39th Iowa Inf.	26		1930 Nov 15	IA, 57th, 1931
Myers, J.S.	Pvt.	B, 127th Ohio Inf.	127	57	1888 Feb	IA, 18th, 1892
Myers, J.S.		F, 148th Ill.	45		1916 Sep 23	KS, 36th, 1917
Myers, J.V.	Pvt.	D, 44th Iowa Inf.	400	55	1896 Dec 22	IA, 23rd, 1897
Myers, J.V.	Lieut.	H, 37th Iowa Inf.	19	76	1895 Jun 17	IA, 22nd, 1896
Myers, J.W.	Pvt.	E, 140th Ill. Inf.	452		1924 Jul 28	IA, 51st, 1925
Myers, J.W.	Pvt.	I, 10th Iowa Inf.	40	84	1931 Mar 23	IA, 58th, 1932
Myers, J.W.		H, 16th Ind.	28		1925 Mar 6	KS, 45th, 1926
Myers, Jefferson		K, 33rd Iowa Inf.	147		1942 Apr 7	NE, 67th, 1943
Myers, Jno. S.	Pvt.	B, 157th Ohio Inf.	127	57	1888 Feb 18	IA, 15th, 1889
Myers, John	Pvt.	G, 7th Ind. Inf.	384		1910 May 20	IA, 37th, 1911
Myers, John	Pvt.	G, 15th Iowa Inf.	116		1913 Aug 3	IA, 40th, 1914
Myers, John	Pvt.	D, 16th Iowa Art.	297	84	1931 Jun 8	IA, 58th, 1932
Myers, John		B, 54th N.Y.	52		1902 Feb 25	KS, 22nd, 1903
Myers, John C.		I, 161st Ohio	292		1931 May 7	KS, 51st, 1932
Myers, John C.		I, 161st Ohio	292		1931 May 7	KS, 52nd, 1933
Myers, Jos. N.		K, 6th West Va.	20		1890	KS, 10th, 1891
Myers, Joseph	Pvt.	H, 89th Ohio Inf.	111		1928 Dec 22	IA, 55th, 1929
Myers, Joseph		D, 25th Iowa (died at Westmoreland; buried at Westmoreland Cemetery)	151		1894 May 22	KS, 14th, 1895
Myers, Joseph		I, 26th Penn.	13		1926 Jan 15	NE, 51st, 1927
Myers, Joseph		D, 5th Penn. (died of old age)	287	86	1921 Mar 6	NE, 46th, 1922
Myers, Joseph S.		I, 153rd Penn.	39		1913 Sep 16	KS, 33rd, 1914
Myers, Josiah	Pvt.	A, 1st Md. Inf.	235		1918 Jul 20	IA, 45th, 1919
Myers, L.G.	Pvt.	K, 7th Iowa Inf.	108		1928 Sep 16	IA, 55th, 1929
Myers, L.K.		H, 29th Iowa Inf.	57		1890	KS, 10th, 1891
Myers, Levi		E, 74th Ind.	57		1922 Nov 26	KS, 42nd, 1923
Myers, Michael		D, 15th Ohio Inf.	373		1886	KS, 6th, 1887
Myers, Michael		A, 89th Ohio Inf.	196		1891 Mar 10	KS, 11th, 1892
Myers, Murray		E, 44th Ill.	25		1922 Oct 2	KS, 42nd, 1923
Myers, N.M.	Pvt.	B, 12th Mich.	22		1923 Jun	IA, 50th, 1924
Myers, P.H.	Pvt.	I, 92nd Ill. Inf.	185	48	1888 Aug 5	IA, 15th, 1889
Myers, Peter		C, 3rd Mich. Inf. (born in Canada; died in Sparta, Mich.)	70		1883	NE, 8th, 1884
Myers, Phillip		A, 112th Ind.	90		1915 May 25	KS, 35th, 1916
Myers, R.R.	Pvt.	A, 30th Ind. Inf.	7		1912 Jun 1	IA, 39th, 1913
Myers, Reuben	Pvt.	G, 93rd Ill. Inf.	118	57	1889 Mar 8	IA, 15th, 1889
Myers, S.B.	Midshipman	Navy	97		1917 Aug 10	IA, 44th, 1918
Myers, S.H.	Corp.	C, 24th Iowa Cav.	12		1926 Nov 21	IA, 53rd, 1927

Name	Rank	Company, Regiment or Ship	Post*	Age	Death Date†	Journal
Myers, Samuel S.		D, 8th Iowa	151		1897 Jul 4	KS, 17th, 1898
Myers, T.B.		K, 18th Ohio	85		1933 Nov 22	KS, 53rd, 1934
Myers, T.J.			20		1929	IA, 56th, 1930
Myers, T.J.		D, 36th Iowa	155		1922 Dec 27	KS, 43rd, 1924
Myers, T.S.		33rd Iowa	52	76	1913 Mar 1	NE, 38th, 1914
Myers, Thomas W.		C, 31st Ill.	304		1915 Jul 26	KS, 35th, 1916
Myers, Thorton D.	Pvt.	118th Ohio Inf.	12		1915 Aug 14	IA, 42nd, 1916
Myers, W.D.	Pvt.	D, 77th Ill. Inf.	241		1887 Sep 18	IA, 14th, 1888
Myers, W.D.		G, 3rd Colo. (died of heart failure)	22	72	1915 May 9	NE, 40th, 1916
Myers, W.H.H.	Pvt.	H, 38th Iowa	223		1903 Jan 24	IA, 30th, 1904
Myers, W.M.	Sergt.	H, 3rd N.Y. Art.	263		1917 Mar 28	IA, 44th, 1918
Myers, W.M.	Sergt.	H, 5th N.Y. Art.	263		1917 Mar 25	IA, 43rd, 1917
Myers, William H.		G, 34th N.J.	303		1923 Jul 20	KS, 43rd, 1924
Myor, F.M.		H, 4th Penn.	37		1885	KS, 5th, 1886
Myrick, S.B.	Pvt.	G, 25th —	512		1905 Apr 21	IA, 32nd, 1906
Myton, Taylor		H, 125th Penn. Vols.	94		1923 Sep 23	IA, 50th, 1924
Nadelhoffer, Wm.		H, 17th Ill. Cav.	12		1918 Apr 11	KS, 38th, 1919
Naden, J.		E, 91st Ill.	25		1908	NE, 33rd, 1909
Nafus, Dan			64		1930 Dec 8	KS, 50th, 1931
Nafus, J.H.		F, 9th Ind.	311		1913 Aug 31	KS, 33rd, 1914
Nagel, Valentine		A, 1st Mo. Cav.	46		1921 May 27	KS, 41st, 1922
Nagle, Greer		G, 147th Ill.	25		1933 Dec 20	KS, 53rd, 1934
Nagle, J.	Pvt.	C, 92nd Ill. Inf.	163		1910 Sep 4	IA, 37th, 1911
Nagle, M.D.	Pvt.	I, 12th Iowa Inf.	78		1906 Apr 27	IA, 33rd, 1907
Nagle, T.M.	Pvt.	D, 2nd Iowa Inf.	7		1898 Feb 17	IA, 26th, 1900
Nagle, Volney	Pvt.	G, 3rd Iowa Cav.	20		1920 Jul	IA, 47th, 1921
Nagle, Webster	Pvt.	A, 1st Iowa Bat.	7		1917 Sep 22	IA, 44th, 1918
Nair, E.W.		A, 10th Va. Inf.	59		1934 Jul 23	KS, 54th, 1935
Name, John		G, 115th Ill. Inf.	57		1901 Jun 28	KS, 21st, 1902
Names, Dan'l	Pvt.	A, 6th Iowa Cav.	92		1912 May 10	IA, 39th, 1913
Nance, J.M.			118		1884	KS, 4th, 1885
Nance, J.M.			118		1886	KS, 6th, 1887
Nance, J.V.	Corp.	C, 2nd Kans.	97	57	1891 Mar 16	IA, 18th, 1892
Nance, M.V.	Pvt.	B, 18th Iowa Inf.	173		1900	IA, 27th, 1901
Nangle, Edward J.		H, 213th Penn. Inf. (died of Bright's disease)	5	69	1905 Nov 22	NE, 30th, 1906
Nanning, Michael		E, 8th Penn.	380		1904 Jul 23	KS, 24th, 1905
Napier, Isaac		83rd U.S. Inf.	18		1902 Aug 17	KS, 22nd, 1903
Narthey, Herbert	Pvt.	C, 21st Iowa Inf.	68	91	1932 May 31	IA, 59th, 1933
Nash, Aaron		H, 105th Penn. Inf. (died of age & army wound)	13	79	1924 Nov 5	NE, 49th, 1925
Nash, Chester	Pvt.	E, 47th Wis. Inf.	337		1929 Jan 4	IA, 56th, 1930
Nash, D.A.	Pvt.	E, 142nd Ill.	30		1921 Feb 5	IA, 48th, 1922
Nash, David F.		C, 41st Ohio	51		1928 Feb 7	KS, 48th, 1929
Nash, Geo. W.		C, 132nd Ohio	23		1893	KS, 13th, 1894
Nash, J.W.		B, 52nd Ill.	260		1914 Jun 30	KS, 34th, 1915
Nash, John		E, 99th Ill.	364		1913 Mar 23	KS, 33rd, 1914
Nash, Judah		C, 95th Ohio Inf.	123		1886	KS, 6th, 1887
Nash, N.A.		K, 42nd Wis. Inf. (born in New York; died in Hastings)	13		1883 Oct 7	NE, 8th, 1884
Nash, S.S.	Pvt.	E, 75th Ill. Inf.	29		1899 Oct 17	IA, 26th, 1900
Nash, Stephen		K, 42nd Wis. (died of kidney trouble)	13	70	1914 Jul 16	NE, 39th, 1915
Nash, William			168		1884	KS, 4th, 1885
Nash, William S.	Bugler	81st Ohio	92		1914 Nov 14	KS, 34th, 1915
Nasler, H.C.	Pvt.	I, 7th Iowa	69		1923 Oct 10	IA, 50th, 1924
Nason, O.B.		I, 47th Iowa	158		1927 Dec 20	KS, 47th, 1928
Nathany, William		B, 23rd Mo. Inf.	204		2nd quarter 1884	IA, 11th, 1885
Nation, Eligah	Pvt.	G, 58th Ill. Inf.	40		1927 Mar 17	IA, 54th, 1928
Nation, J.C.		K, 89th Ohio Inf. (at large)		90	1936 Nov 10	IA, 63rd, 1937
Nation, Seth		I, 8th Ind. Inf.	311		1918 Jan 17	KS, 38th, 1919
Naueritz, Peter	Pvt.	3rd Wis. Cav.	171		1908 Apr 21	IA, 35th, 1909
Nauerth, Jacob		G, 14th Iowa	244		1925 Aug 16	KS, 45th, 1926

*See Appendix A, B or C for roster of post names and locations.
†See Introduction for note regarding recording of death date.
398

Name	Rank	Company, Regiment or Ship	Post*	Age	Death Date†	Journal
Nauke, Frederick	Pvt.	C, 19th Wis. Inf.	238	75	1897 Apr 28	IA, 24th, 1898
Nauslar, J.W.		I, 125th Ill. Inf.	84		1917 Apr 21	NE, 42nd, 1918
Naylon, Michael	Pvt.	C, 45th Ill.	297		1907 Oct 28	IA, 34th, 1908
Naylor, James		B, 1st Mo. Eng.	1		1931 Oct 20	KS, 51st, 1932
Naylor, James F.		I, 62nd Ohio	46		1920 Aug 31	KS, 40th, 1921
Naylor, James M.		I, 81st Ohio	25		1913 Aug 23	KS, 33rd, 1914
Neal, A.E.		I, 50th Ill.	9		1936 Mar	KS, 55th, 1936
Neal, A.H.		I, 50th Ill.	9		1936 Mar	KS, 56th, 1937
Neal, Barnett		15th Ill. Inf. (died of complications, old age)	188	85	1919 Aug 26	NE, 44th, 1920
Neal, C.W.	Sergt.	K, 31st Maine Inf.	1		1914	IA, 42nd, 1916
Neal, C.W.		D, 39th Iowa Inf.	173		1923 Sep 19	IA, 50th, 1924
Neal, C.W.		H, 46th Iowa Inf.	173		1924 Apr 18	IA, 51st, 1925
Neal, Daniel		G, 8th Ill.	8		1889	KS, 9th, 1890
Neal, J.Q.			84		1884	KS, 4th, 1885
Neal, John	Pvt.	A, 9th Ind. Cav.	36	65	1898 Nov 28	IA, 25th, 1899
Neal, John	Pvt.	A, 9th Ind. Cav.	36		1899 Nov 28	IA, 26th, 1900
Neal, John	Pvt.	K, 13th Iowa Inf.	103		1913 Aug 31	IA, 40th, 1914
Neal, John W.		C, 84th Ill.	238		1926 Jun 12	KS, 46th, 1927
Neal, Mithias T.		A, 7th Kans. Cav.	84		1904 Feb 29	KS, 24th, 1905
Neal, P.T.		A, 48th Mo.	209		1926 Feb 15	KS, 46th, 1927
Neal, Pridnus		D, 60th Ill. (U.S.C.T.)	486		1905 Dec 21	KS, 25th, 1906
Neal, Samuel M.		C, 11th Mo. Inf.	311		1886	KS, 6th, 1887
Neal, Thos. J.		D, 98th Ill.	17		1926 Apr 27	KS, 46th, 1927
Neal, W.A.	Pvt.	F, 82nd Ohio Inf.	461		1929 Mar 27	IA, 56th, 1930
Neal, Wm. M.		H, 143rd Ill.	7		1930 Mar 2	NE, 55th, 1931
Neal, Wm. P.	Drummer	I, 25th Iowa Inf.	40		1913 Oct 19	IA, 40th, 1914
Neale, A.H.		I, 50th Ill.	9		1936 Mar 8	KS, 57th, 1938
Neally, William	Corp.	F, 2nd Colo. Cav.	516		1901 Aug 7	IA, 28th, 1902
Nealy, George F.		B, Mo. Rifle Bat.	500		1916	KS, 36th, 1917
Near, John		B, 20th Ill.	145		1918 Apr 11	KS, 38th, 1919
Neas, Levi M.			167		1912 Dec	IA, 39th, 1913
Nebb, Geo. W.		F, 201st Penn.	52		1918 May 30	KS, 38th, 1919
Nebergall, Andrew C.S.		B, 16th Ill.	36		1924 Oct 19	KS, 44th, 1925
Neckleton, Geo.	Musician	G, 72nd Ill. Inf.	512		1912	IA, 39th, 1913
Neddo, John	Pvt.	E, 48th Ind.	1		1906 Nov 1	KS, 26th, 1907
Needham, D.L.	Pvt.		167		1927 Apr 9	IA, 54th, 1928
Needham, Frank	Pvt.	C, 5th Iowa Cav.	16		1905 Mar 16	IA, 32nd, 1906
Needham, H.V.	Pvt.	G, 134th Ill. Inf.	66	90	1933 Jul 19	IA, 60th, 1934
Needham, W.H.	Lieut.	22nd Iowa	167		1924 Oct 15	IA, 51st, 1925
Needles, A.H.	Pvt.	I, 4th Iowa Cav.	34		1910 Sep 5	IA, 37th, 1911
Needs, Walter		C, 8th Ohio	81		1928 Apr 18	KS, 48th, 1929
Neel, Jonathan		K, 68th Penn.	422		1905 Aug 12	KS, 25th, 1906
Neeland, John		B, 13th Kans.	26		1918 Jan 28	KS, 38th, 1919
Neeley, A.F.		I, 2nd Kans. Militia	81		1920 May 3	KS, 40th, 1921
Neeley, D.J.	Pvt.	A, 59th Ill. Inf.	271		1906 Mar 1	IA, 33rd, 1907
Neeley, Robert	Corp.	C, 24th Iowa	110		1922 Oct 25	IA, 49th, 1923
Neely, A.D.		Navy (died at Blue Ridge)	328		1895 Dec	KS, 15th, 1896
Neely, Bert N.		E, 57th Ind. Inf. (died at Hartford, Tex.)	205		1895 Aug	KS, 15th, 1896
Neely, Charles H.	Pvt.	E, 66th Ill.	66		1926 Feb 21	IA, 53rd, 1927
Neely, Henry	Fifer	E, 8th Iowa	49		1923 Mar 2	IA, 50th, 1924
Neely, Joseph	Pvt.	E, 8th Iowa	49		1926 Sep 4	IA, 53rd, 1927
Neferson, A.A.	Pvt.	E, 91st Ill.	234		1922 Jan 7	IA, 49th, 1923
Neff, Henry C.		G, 1st Ohio Inf.	130		1935 May 24	KS, 55th, 1936
Neff, J.J.	Pvt.	H, 32nd Iowa Vol. Inf.	84	57	1899 Mar 18	IA, 25th, 1899
Neff, J.M.	Pvt.	G, 23rd Ohio Inf.	283		1926 Mar 16	IA, 53rd, 1927
Neff, J.W.	Pvt.	21st Mo. Inf.	122		1919 May 2	IA, 46th, 1920
Neff, John H.	Pvt.	F, 94th Ill. Inf.	408		1909 Jun 4	IA, 36th, 1910
Neff, Robert		A, 133rd Ind. Inf.	12		1925 Jul 9	KS, 45th, 1926
Negle, Henry	Pvt.	K, 82nd Penn. Inf.	147		1922	IA, 49th, 1923
Negley, D.F.	Pvt.	E, 76th Penn. Inf.	410		1917 Mar 22	IA, 44th, 1918
Negley, John	Pvt.	B, 208th Penn. Cav.	410		1910 Jun 10	IA, 37th, 1911

*See Appendix A, B or C for roster of post names and locations.
†See Introduction for note regarding recording of death date.

Name	Rank	Company, Regiment or Ship	Post*	Age	Death Date†	Journal
Negley, John F.		I, 77th Ill.	301		1925 Apr 3	KS, 45th, 1926
Negly, J.W.	Sergt.	B, 157th Ill.	95		1901 Apr 6	IA, 28th, 1902
Negus, David	Corp.	C, 143rd Ohio	249		1907 May 14	IA, 34th, 1908
Nehrbass, C.			161		1899 Dec 2	KS, 19th, 1900
Nehrhood, E.F.		B, 5th Minn.	68		1922 Mar 29	KS, 42nd, 1923
Neiderwieser, J.	Corp.	B, Mo. Art.	7	49	1885 May 13	NE, 10th, 1886
Neidig, Samuel		I, 24th Iowa	7	91	1934 Jun 8	IA, 61st, 1935
Neidigh, Wm. H.	Sergt.	E, 3rd Iowa Cav.	473		1910 Nov 11	IA, 37th, 1911
Neighbor, George W.		D, 55th Ohio	30		1923 Sep 13	KS, 43rd, 1924
Neil, C.	Pvt.	C, 60th N.Y.	292		1903 Nov 17	IA, 30th, 1904
Neil, Geo.	Pvt.	D, 15th Penn. Cav.	94		1914 Jan 24	IA, 40th, 1914
Neil, George		I, 2nd Kans. Cav.	1		1931 Nov 20	KS, 51st, 1932
Neil, George S.	Pvt.	A, 70th Ohio Inf.	66	89	1931 Jul 1	IA, 58th, 1932
Neil, John A.		I, 10th Ind. Cav.	95	87	1920	NE, 45th, 1921
Neil, Thomas		A, 12th Ill. Cav.	158		1906 Apr 3	KS, 26th, 1907
Neill, John		Ill.	88		1924 Jul 26	KS, 44th, 1925
Neirmeyer, Simon	Pvt.	I, 15th Iowa Inf.	400		1899 Sep	IA, 26th, 1900
Neling, W.H.	Sergt.	E, 27th Iowa Inf.	222		1920 Feb 22	IA, 47th, 1921
Nellis, A.	Pvt.	A, 127th Ill. Inf.	329		1897 Jan 25	IA, 23rd, 1897
Nelsom, J.	Pvt.	E, 36th Iowa Inf.	40		1920 Feb 16	IA, 47th, 1921
Nelson, Adam	Pvt.	G, 198th Ohio Inf.	116	84	1933 Jan 24	IA, 60th, 1934
Nelson, Andrew		E, 91st Ill. Inf. (at large)			1935 Nov 29	IA, 62nd, 1936
Nelson, B.F.		D, 16th Ky. Inf.	63		1916 Nov 9	KS, 36th, 1917
Nelson, Briley		A, 14th Ill. Cav.	25		1920 Dec 24	KS, 40th, 1921
Nelson, C.C.	Pvt.	C, 18th Ohio Inf.	337		1900 Feb 19	IA, 27th, 1901
Nelson, C.C.		G, 104th Ill.	66		1922 Jan 9	IA, 49th, 1923
Nelson, C.G.	Pvt.	I, 4th Iowa Inf.	192	57	1895 Nov 6	IA, 22nd, 1896
Nelson, Eldrige		E, 22nd Vol. Reserve	99		1890	KS, 10th, 1891
Nelson, Eli	Pvt.	D, 5th Iowa Cav.	74		1923 Sep 14	IA, 50th, 1924
Nelson, G.M.		H, 168th Ill.	51		1917	KS, 37th, 1918
Nelson, Geo. W.		G, 18th Ill.	84		1909 Nov 19	KS, 29th, 1910
Nelson, Henry	Pvt.	K, 11th Ill. Inf.	271		1927 May 13	IA, 54th, 1928
Nelson, Henry		H, 4th Wis. Cav. (died of old age)	201	74	1910 Feb 8	NE, 35th, 1911
Nelson, J.D.	Pvt.	G, 15th Ill. Inf.	12		1931 May 21	IA, 58th, 1932
Nelson, J.E.		A, 53rd Ill. Inf. (died at Waco; buried at Waco Cemetery)	262		1894 Sep 24	KS, 14th, 1895
Nelson, J.I.		C, 148th Iowa Inf. K, 44th Iowa Inf.	10		1894 Mar 2	NE, 19th, 1895
Nelson, J.K.		E, 12th Ill. Inf.	66		1917 Apr 21	KS, 37th, 1918
Nelson, J.V.	Pvt.	I, 70th Ohio Inf.	55		1897 Aug 24	IA, 24th, 1898
Nelson, James	Pvt.	E, 35th Mo. Inf.	2	50	1896 Mar 20	IA, 22nd, 1896
Nelson, James R.		C, 1st Mo.	150		1896 Jan 30	KS, 16th, 1897
Nelson, Jerry			142		1925 Aug 14	KS, 45th, 1926
Nelson, John	Pvt.	B, 32nd Iowa	101		1901 Nov 21	IA, 28th, 1902
Nelson, John		B, 1st Md. Cav. (died at Soldiers Home, Leavenworth)	210		1893 Jun 5	KS, 13th, 1894
Nelson, John M.		G, 30th Iowa (former member; died at Axtell)	342		1936	NE, 61st, 1937
Nelson, John R.		H, 12th Ill.	158		1895 Jan 6	KS, 16th, 1897
Nelson, Julius	Sergt.	B, 27th Iowa Inf.	344	68	1897 Jan 30	IA, 24th, 1898
Nelson, L.F.		H, 13th U.S. Inf.	168		1899 May 3	IA, 26th, 1900
Nelson, Miner	Corp.	C, 15th West Va. Inf.	250		1907 Sep 16	IA, 34th, 1908
Nelson, Oley		D, 40th Wis. Inf.	30	93	1938 Apr 15	IA, 64th, 1938
Nelson, Paul H.		F, 29th Iowa	193	76	1904 May	NE, 29th, 1905
Nelson, Peter	Pvt.	H, 2nd Minn. Inf.	151	64	1898 Jan 30	IA, 24th, 1898
Nelson, R.O.		C, 57th Ill.	89		1917	KS, 37th, 1918
Nelson, S.A.		I, 4th Ky. Inf.	13	70	1916 Dec 27	NE, 41st, 1917
Nelson, S.G.	Pvt.	A, 12th Ill. Cav.	42		1920 Jul 16	IA, 47th, 1921
Nelson, Samuel			64		1st quarter 1885	IA, 11th, 1885
Nelson, Thomas		K, 13th Mo.	50		1919 Jan 1	KS, 39th, 1920
Nelson, W.A.	Corp.	F, 12th Iowa Inf.	63		1920 May 18	IA, 47th, 1921
Nelson, W.T.			110		1913	IA, 40th, 1914

*See Appendix A, B or C for roster of post names and locations.
†See Introduction for note regarding recording of death date.

400

Name	Rank	Company, Regiment or Ship	Post*	Age	Death Date†	Journal
Nelson, William D.	Pvt.	A, 36th Iowa Inf.	286	49	1894 Dec 22	IA, 21st, 1895
Nelson, Wm.	Pvt.	1st Colo. Cav.	313	48	1889 Jun 24	IA, 16th, 1890
Neptune, Eli		G, 186th Ohio	47		1928 Sep 4	KS, 48th, 1929
Neptune, Sam'l	Pvt.	122nd Ohio Inf.	18		1930 Aug 1	IA, 57th, 1931
Neptune, W.H.		D, 27th Ohio	25		1925 Jan 13	KS, 45th, 1926
Nerb, John	Pvt.	C, 16th U.S. Inf.	78		1908 Nov 2	IA, 35th, 1909
Nerbert, Jacob	Pvt.	C, 35th Iowa Inf.	231	54	1896 Jun 13	IA, 23rd, 1897
Nesbit, James		12th Ohio Battery	93		1912 Nov 12	KS, 32nd, 1913
Nesbit, James		Penn. (died of cancer of stomach)	217	65	1910 Jan 31	NE, 34th, 1910
Nesbit, Nathaniel		G, 111th Penn.	12		1896 Sep 17	KS, 16th, 1897
Nesbit, Robert M.		L, 7th Ohio Cav.	179		1912 May 18	KS, 32nd, 1913
Nesbitt, Wm. B.	Pvt.	G, 38th Ind. Inf.	321		1908 Jul 25	IA, 35th, 1909
Nesling, D.A.	Pvt.	E, 27th Iowa Inf.	496	64	1895 Oct 19	IA, 22nd, 1896
Nesmith, Jas.	Pvt.	F, 14th Penn. Cav.	8		1925 Feb 27	IA, 52nd, 1926
Nesselroad, C.C.	Pvt.	C, 29th Iowa Inf.	52		1915 Aug 25	IA, 42nd, 1916
Nester, Joshua		H, 20th Ill. Inf.	158		1929 Jun 12	KS, 49th, 1930
Neth, Jacob			92		1913	IA, 40th, 1914
Neth, Joab		L, 12th Mo. Cav.	32		1935	KS, 55th, 1936
Neth, John J.	Pvt.	I, 3rd Iowa Cav.	452		1911 Mar 27	IA, 38th, 1912
Nethercutt, John			190		1899	IA, 26th, 1900
Netteekiend, N.			141		1894	NE, 19th, 1895
Nettler, W.H.	Pvt.	A, 7th Mo. Cav.	231		1914 Mar 9	IA, 41st, 1915
Nettles, Andy		E, 49th U.S.C.T.	25		1923	NE, 48th, 1924
Nettleton, Chas.	Pvt.	H, 3rd Wis. Cav.	12		1918 Nov 28	IA, 45th, 1919
Nettleton, D.M.		I, 4th Ill. (died of old age)	13	81	1922 Mar 24	NE, 47th, 1923
Nettleton, J.A.		I, 37th Ill. Inf. (died at Burlingame; buried at Burlingame Cemetery)	35		1894 Jun 26	KS, 14th, 1895
Nettleton, Wm.	Sergt.	K, 75th Ill. Inf.	42		1916 May 10	IA, 43rd, 1917
Neuby, Jeremiah		K, 10th Ill.	203		1926 Aug 11	KS, 46th, 1927
Neudeck, Ed	Pvt.	2nd Wis. Bat.	57		1913 Jul 17	IA, 40th, 1914
Neufind, Wm. R.	Pvt.	K, 32nd Ill. Inf.	59		1910 Jan 14	IA, 37th, 1911
Neufren, Julius N.		D, 2nd Iowa (died of stomach trouble)	12	68	1904 Oct 3	NE, 29th, 1905
Neullough, D.P.		3rd Ohio Inf.	68		1926 Feb 4	NE, 51st, 1927
Neuman, Frederick		B, 42nd Ill. (former member of Nebraska Dept.; location: Exeter)	76		1937 May 7	NE, 62nd, 1938
Neuman, Jacob J.	Musician	I, 148th Ill. Inf. (at large)	154, 12	97, 3 mos. & 17 days	1943 Nov 21	IA, 70th, 1944
Nevarre, D.D.		B, 7th Mich.	142		1921 Aug 28	KS, 41st, 1922
Nevil, William		H, 59th Ill.	25		1914 Mar 21	KS, 34th, 1915
Neville, Blanchard		F, 33rd Wis. Inf. (at large)		91	1936 Jun 4	IA, 63rd, 1937
Neville, Hiram	Pvt.	C, 13th West Va. Inf.	235		1918 Sep 30	IA, 45th, 1919
Nevins, S.		C, 133rd Ill. (died of kidney trouble)	100	71	1905 Jan 1	NE, 29th, 1905
Nevus, Geo.	Pvt.	K, 43rd Ind.	40		1923 Jul 26	IA, 50th, 1924
New, John		H, 8th Ill. Cav.	159		1899 Dec 22	KS, 19th, 1900
New, N.W.		C, 44th Ill.	87		1920 Dec 20	KS, 40th, 1921
Newall, C.		E, 5th U.S. Cav.	132		1888	KS, 8th, 1889
Newall, S.A.		D, 9th Ill.	36		1902 Jan 4	KS, 22nd, 1903
Newberry, Ed		F, 37th Ind.	59		1896 May 12	KS, 16th, 1897
Newberry, J.S.	Sergt.	D, 8th Wis. Inf.	77		1925 Jun	IA, 52nd, 1926
Newbold, Jacob C.		C, 25th Iowa	25		1916 Feb 3	KS, 36th, 1917
Newbold, Samuel		A, 8th Ind.	32		1923 Nov 22	KS, 43rd, 1924
Newburn, Noah			200		1st quarter 1886	IA, 12th, 1886
Newby, James T.	Pvt.	G, 18th Ind. Inf.	359	54	1896 Mar 3	IA, 22nd, 1896
Newby, Jeremiah, see Neuby, Jeremiah						
Newby, John		A, 33rd Ind.	445		1916 Jul 29	KS, 36th, 1917
Newby, R.G.		Ind.	423		1908 Dec 13	KS, 28th, 1909
Newcomb, C.D.	Sergt.	I, 62nd Ohio Inf.	440		1912 Jan 17	IA, 39th, 1913
Newcomb, D.C.			495		1911 May 6	IA, 38th, 1912
Newcomb, Edwin M.	Capt.	H, 16th Iowa Inf.	78		1918 Apr 14	IA, 45th, 1919
Newcomb, Samuel B.	Pvt.	B, 166th Ohio Inf.	147	59	1894 Jul 26	IA, 21st, 1895

*See Appendix A, B or C for roster of post names and locations.
†See Introduction for note regarding recording of death date.

Name	Rank	Company, Regiment or Ship	Post*	Age	Death Date†	Journal
Newcombe, Calvin B.		C, 50th N.Y.	52		1913 Apr 11	KS, 33rd, 1914
Newcome, James		E, 11th Iowa	127		1905 Aug 7	KS, 25th, 1906
Newcome, Joseph		died of heart trouble	44	58	1900 Jun	NE, 25th, 1901
Newel, Marien	Pvt.	B, 38th Iowa Inf.	267		1915 Apr 10	IA, 42nd, 1916
Newell, A.		A, 1st Wis. Cav.	239		1912 Jun 15	KS, 32nd, 1913
Newell, C.C.		Ill.	271		1909	IA, 36th, 1910
Newell, C.P.		B, 44th Iowa	355		1898 Dec 25	KS, 18th, 1899
Newell, I.D.		F, 7th Ill.	13	77	1914 Oct 24	NE, 39th, 1915
Newell, Isaac		C, 11th Kans.	55		1921 Mar 11	KS, 41st, 1922
Newell, J.A.		A, 11th Mo. Inf. C, 136th Ill.	209		1888	KS, 8th, 1889
Newell, J.H.		E, 152nd Ind.	311		1917 Dec 18	KS, 37th, 1918
Newell, John	Corp.	K, 19th Wis. Inf.	81		1914 Jun 24	IA, 41st, 1915
Newell, Oren		D, 60th Ohio	240		1904 Apr 10	KS, 24th, 1905
Newell, Richard			25		1938 Jan 9	KS, 59th, 1940
Newell, Rufus H.	Pvt.	F, 33rd N.Y. Inf.	298		1911 Mar 18	IA, 38th, 1912
Newell, S.H.		A, 1st Iowa Cav.	46		1920 Jul 6	KS, 40th, 1921
Newell, W.H.		F, 91st Ill.	45	84	1925	NE, 50th, 1926
Newell, Wm.		H, 3rd Iowa Cav.	25	80	1918 May 6	NE, 43rd, 1919
Newhall, M.H.		A, 12th Vt.	303		1909 Mar 6	KS, 29th, 1910
Newhoff, Wm.	Pvt.	I, 5th Mich. Cav.	22		1930	IA, 57th, 1931
Newhoff, Wm.	Pvt.	I, 5th Mich.	22	94	1933 Dec 10	IA, 60th, 1934
Newhouse, Henry Andrew	Pvt.	D, 22nd Conn. Inf. (at large)	18	94	1940 Jul 25	IA, 66th, 1940
Newhouse, J.R.	Pvt.	E, 11th Iowa Inf.	75		1914 Sep 19	IA, 41st, 1915
Newhouse, James V.	Sergt.	C, 10th Ind.	1		1916 Dec 22	KS, 36th, 1917
Newhunter, A.B.	Pvt.	G, 19th Iowa Inf.	153		1904-1905	IA, 31st, 1905
Newkirk, W.C.		G, 50th Ind. Inf.	128		1900 Apr 9	KS, 21st, 1902
Newland, Hamilton D.	Sergt.	F, 23rd Ohio	244		1922 Nov 20	IA, 49th, 1923
Newland, Isaac		D, 18th Ill.	25		1923 Feb 18	KS, 43rd, 1924
Newland, Joseph T.	Pvt.	H, 44th Iowa Inf.	26	47	1894 Feb 9	IA, 20th, 1894
Newland, W.R.	Pvt.	1st Ohio Bat.	20		1910 Sep 8	IA, 37th, 1911
Newlin, Henry		D, 12th Ill. Inf.	39		1902 Feb 27	KS, 22nd, 1903
Newlin, James		C, 11th Kans. Cav.	464		1917 Feb	KS, 37th, 1918
Newlin, W.H.		D, 12th Ill. Inf.	39		1901 Feb 27	KS, 21st, 1902
Newman, A.A.		K, 10th Maine	158		1922 Jul 31	KS, 42nd, 1923
Newman, Adam		C, 43rd Ill.	158		1896 Nov 12	KS, 16th, 1897
Newman, Albert	Surg.	3rd Kans.	12		1905 Apr 28	KS, 25th, 1906
Newman, Albert N.	Pvt.	F, 23rd Iowa Inf.	57	56	1892 Sep 21	IA, 19th, 1893
Newman, C.	Pvt.	H, Art.	457		1905 Feb	IA, 32nd, 1906
Newman, David A.	Pvt.	I, 20th Iowa	244		1914 Feb 5	IA, 41st, 1915
Newman, Geo. A.	Pvt.	G, 6th N.Y. Cav.	222		1920 Jun 15	IA, 47th, 1921
Newman, Geo. S.		R, 38th Ind. Inf.	32	70	1909 Nov 7	NE, 34th, 1910
Newman, George		G, 59th Ind.	83		1910 Dec 27	KS, 30th, 1911
Newman, George W.	Pvt.	D, 97th Ohio Inf.	364	52	1892 Aug 10	IA, 19th, 1893
Newman, Isaac		H, 6th Ohio	293		1921 May 11	KS, 41st, 1922
Newman, J.B.			173		1927 Sep 9	IA, 54th, 1928
Newman, M.		F, 21st Ill. Inf.	63		1925 Dec 12	KS, 45th, 1926
Newman, Thomas	Pvt.	A, 31st Iowa Inf.	206		1915 Oct 7	IA, 42nd, 1916
Newman, Wesley		E, 61st Ill. Inf.	32		1899 Jul 13	KS, 19th, 1900
Newman, William		G, 208th Penn.	127		1923 Nov 4	KS, 43rd, 1924
Newman, Wm. E.	Pvt.	B, 7th Iowa Inf.	132		1902 Dec 6	IA, 29th, 1903
Newmarks, G.W.		K, 47th Iowa	52		1905 Feb 4	KS, 25th, 1906
Newnham, Howard		C, 57th Ill. (died of pneumonia)	19	78	1918 Jun 22	NE, 43rd, 1919
Newport, Ephriam		H, 82nd Ind.	55		1928 Sep 5	KS, 48th, 1929
Newport, J.B.		H, 73rd Ill. Inf.	49		1894	KS, 14th, 1895
Newsome, John, see Nowsome, John						
Newson, H.H.			54		1905 Mar 29	KS, 25th, 1906
Newton, C.W.		E, 105th Ill.	236	90	1934 Jul	IA, 61st, 1935
Newton, E.B.		H, 156th Ill.	118		1931	KS, 51st, 1932
Newton, E.B.		H, 156th Ill.	118		1932	KS, 52nd, 1933
Newton, Edward		E, 11th Wis. (died of cancer of stomach)	116	79	1910 Dec 28	NE, 35th, 1911

Name	Rank	Company, Regiment or Ship	Post*	Age	Death Date†	Journal
Newton, Elisha	Pvt.	G, 25th Ind. Inf.	337	62	1893 Apr 9	IA, 20th, 1894
Newton, F.E.	Capt.	29th U.S.C.T. Inf.	25	65	1903 Jul 1	NE, 28th, 1904
Newton, Goodman		C, 53rd Ill. Inf.	35		1917 Jan 30	KS, 37th, 1918
Newton, H.B.			104		1912 Sep 20	KS, 32nd, 1913
Newton, H.P.		location: Madrid			1927 May 8	NE, 52nd, 1928
Newton, Henry	Pvt.	E, 33rd Iowa Inf.	40		1913 Sep 10	IA, 40th, 1914
Newton, Hiram		D, 112th Ill.	4		1923 Mar 9	KS, 43rd, 1924
Newton, Ira C.	Pvt.	147th Ill. Inf.	519		1925 Jul 1	IA, 52nd, 1926
Newton, Kenneth		K, 38th Ill.	251		1917 Jul 24	KS, 37th, 1918
Newton, M.C.		H, 9th N.Y.	1		1920 Jul 12	KS, 40th, 1921
Newton, N.M.		C, 139th Ill. Inf. (died of apoplexy)	134		1894 May 24	NE, 19th, 1895
Newton, Revilo		A, 88th Ill.	142		1921 Mar 19	KS, 41st, 1922
Newton, S.B.		K, 18th Ohio	64		1916 Aug 22	KS, 36th, 1917
Newton, T.U.		H, 161st Ohio 4th Mo. (died at Spring Hill)	104		1895 Dec 6	KS, 15th, 1896
Newton, W.O.	Pvt.	B, 13th Ill. Inf.	59		1910 Feb 10	IA, 37th, 1911
Neyens, H.K.	Pvt.	I, 42nd Wis. Inf.	118		1905 Jul 23	IA, 32nd, 1906
Niblack, N.A.	Pvt.	C, 2nd Mo. State Militia	434	51	1888 Jun 15	IA, 15th, 1889
Nicedemus, Jos.	Pvt.	I, 149th Penn. Inf.	206		1925 Apr 29	IA, 52nd, 1926
Nicely, A.	Corp.	I, 63rd Ind.	86		1921 Nov 22	IA, 48th, 1922
Nicely, Anthony		C, Ind. Penn. Lt. Art.	1		1917 Mar 11	KS, 37th, 1918
Nicely, C.S.		D, 7th Penn.	1		1926 Jan 27	KS, 46th, 1927
Nicely, W.R.		C, 63rd Ind.	6		1913 May 1	KS, 33rd, 1914
Nichles, Henry		D, 130th Penn.	395		1909 Oct 8	KS, 29th, 1910
Nichol, Newton W.	Pvt.	B, 3rd Iowa Inf.	49		1919 Oct 15	IA, 46th, 1920
Nicholas, H.R.		B, 2nd Ill. Art.	74		1921 Mar 27	KS, 41st, 1922
Nicholas, S.T.			47		1904	KS, 24th, 1905
Nicholas, Thomas			20		1925	KS, 45th, 1926
Nicholay, M.		G, 20th Ill.	63		1921 Feb 19	KS, 41st, 1922
Nicholos, Ganet		C, 15th Mo. Cav.	123		1930 Apr 28	KS, 50th, 1931
Nichols, A.	Corp.	B, 37th Iowa Inf.	455	74	1891 Jan 4	IA, 17th, 1891
Nichols, Albert O.	Pvt.	C, 15th N.J. Inf.	29		1913 Aug 28	IA, 40th, 1914
Nichols, Alden S.		F, 47th Mass. Inf. (died of heart failure)	44	71	1915 Dec 8	NE, 40th, 1916
Nichols, Alex	Pvt.	A, 38th Iowa Inf.	78		1909 Jul 15	IA, 36th, 1910
Nichols, B.F.		H, 128th Ind.	25		1928 May 10	KS, 48th, 1929
Nichols, C.H.		E, 50th Wis.	42		1926 Apr 20	NE, 51st, 1927
Nichols, Cornelius		H, 1st Ill. Lt. Art.	7		1931 Apr 12	NE, 56th, 1932
Nichols, Elias L.	Pvt.	B, 3rd Iowa Inf.	49		1917 Jan 29	IA, 44th, 1918
Nichols, F.D.		D, 5th U.S. Art.	8		1941 Apr 14	KS, 61st, 1942
Nichols, G.M.	Pvt.	D, 20th Iowa Inf.	1		1921 Oct 2	IA, 48th, 1922
Nichols, Garret		C, 15th Mo. Cav.	123		1929 Apr 28	KS, 49th, 1930
Nichols, Geo. C.	Pvt.	C, 22nd Iowa Inf.	7		1911 Sep 14	IA, 38th, 1912
Nichols, George	Pvt.	C, 46th Iowa Inf.	7	90	1932 Feb 4	IA, 59th, 1933
Nichols, George A.		F, 12th U.S. Inf.	12		1911 Oct 20	KS, 31st, 1912
Nichols, H.B.		B, 39th Iowa	71		1905 Sep 6	KS, 25th, 1906
Nichols, H.J.			58		2nd quarter 1885	IA, 12th, 1886
Nichols, H.L.			23		1926 Apr 10	KS, 46th, 1927
Nichols, Harrison		H, 11th Kans.	1		1892 Feb 17	KS, 12th, 1893
Nichols, Henry	Pvt.	I, 13th Iowa Inf.	108	51	1892 Nov 10	IA, 19th, 1893
Nichols, Henry B.		K, 100th Ohio	92		1909 Jan	KS, 29th, 1910
Nichols, Hiram		G, 51st Ill.	344		1927 Apr 16	KS, 47th, 1928
Nichols, I.S.	Pvt.	B, 5th Iowa Cav.	40		1926 Jan 3	IA, 53rd, 1927
Nichols, J.	Pvt.		167		1921 Nov 26	IA, 48th, 1922
Nichols, J.T.		G, 170th Ohio	68		1916 Feb 16	KS, 36th, 1917
Nichols, James J.		C, 123rd Ind.	119		1898 Nov 3	KS, 18th, 1899
Nichols, John	Pvt.	K, 6th Ind.	285		1903 May 21	IA, 30th, 1904
Nichols, John	Pvt.	E, 25th Wis. Inf.	236	88	1931 Jan 4	IA, 58th, 1932
Nichols, John L.		B, 2nd Ill. Cav.	260		1902 Feb 10	KS, 22nd, 1903
Nichols, John P.	Pvt.	I, 4th Conn. Inf.	461	69	1894 Nov 15	IA, 21st, 1895
Nichols, Joseph N.			85		1920 Aug 17	KS, 40th, 1921
Nichols, Nelson		B, 168th Penn.	96		1913 Jun 15	KS, 33rd, 1914
Nichols, Nicholas	Pvt.	C, 92nd Ill. Inf.	71	55	1893 Jan 5	IA, 19th, 1893

*See Appendix A, B or C for roster of post names and locations.
†See Introduction for note regarding recording of death date.

Name	Rank	Company, Regiment or Ship	Post*	Age	Death Date†	Journal
Nichols, O.P.		D, 9th Iowa Cav.	290		1913 Nov 2	IA, 40th, 1914
Nichols, O.P.		A, 4th Wis.	59		1920 Jun 9	KS, 40th, 1921
Nichols, Robert		D, 9th Mich.	13	84	1925 Oct 24	NE, 50th, 1926
Nichols, Samuel	Pvt.	I, 38th Penn. Inf.	216		1918 Nov 20	IA, 45th, 1919
Nichols, Slocum	Pvt.	D, 6th Iowa Cav.	22		1907 May 1	IA, 34th, 1908
Nichols, W.A.	Corp.	B, 2nd Iowa Inf.	255		1907 Oct 13	IA, 34th, 1908
Nichols, W.H.		E, 132nd Ohio (died of asthma at Soldiers & Sailors Home, Milford)		72	1906 Dec 28	NE, 31st, 1907
Nichols, William		B, 6th Kans.	64		1936 Aug 15	KS, 56th, 1937
Nichols, William R., see Nicols, William R.						
Nicholson, H.H.		B, 49th Wis. Inf. (former member)	25		1940 Aug 17	NE, 65th, 1941
Nicholson, J.F.		H, 25th Mo. Inf. (died of kidney & heart disease)	204	86	1908 Sep 1	NE, 33rd, 1909
Nicholson, J.T.	Pvt.	K, 31st Iowa Inf.	74		1924 Oct 11	IA, 51st, 1925
Nicholson, John A.		I, 3rd Iowa Cav.	7	91	1937 Sep 30	IA, 64th, 1938
Nicholson, Smith		C, 50th Ill.	118		1917 Jun 17	KS, 37th, 1918
Nicholson, Thos.		B, 25th Iowa Inf.	100		1918 May 3	KS, 38th, 1919
Nicholson, Wm.		A, 27th N.Y. Inf. (died at National Home)	380		1895 Jul	KS, 15th, 1896
Nickel, Thomas		A, 36th Iowa	448		1925 May	KS, 45th, 1926
Nickell, J.H.		A, 8th Mo. Cav.	25		1928 Feb 2	KS, 48th, 1929
Nicker, J.N.	Pvt.	B, 86th Ill. Inf.	465		1904 Nov 8	IA, 31st, 1905
Nickerson, Alexander		I, 73rd Ind. Inf.	176		1916 Aug 2	KS, 36th, 1917
Nickerson, J.B.		K, 7th Wis. Inf.	378		1888	KS, 8th, 1889
Nickerson, Nelson		I, 1st Wis. Cav.	52		1912 Mar 12	KS, 32nd, 1913
Nickle, W.F.		H, 25th Iowa Inf. Penn.	89	78	1919 Sep 12	NE, 44th, 1920
Nickle, William		D, 11th Ind. Cav. (died of uraemic poisoning)	10	70	1915 Apr 14	NE, 40th, 1916
Nickles, John		D, 21st Penn.	2		1909 May 3	KS, 29th, 1910
Nickodemus, W.H.	Pvt.	L, 11th Iowa Inf.	122		1919	IA, 46th, 1920
Nickols, H.		E, 28th Iowa Inf.	25		1886	KS, 6th, 1887
Nicodemus, John		F, 57th Ind.	36		1916 Jun 24	KS, 36th, 1917
Nicodemus, Jos., see Nicedemus, Jos.						
Nicodemus, P.H.	Pvt.	H, 13th Iowa Inf.	94	53	1887 Dec 2	IA, 14th, 1888
Nicodemus, Theodore		I, 106th Ill. Inf.	18		1908 Sep 18	KS, 28th, 1909
Nicol, Alexander F.	Sergt.	B, 14th Iowa Inf.	240		1922 Dec 6	IA, 49th, 1923
Nicola, John			231		1928 Aug 11	IA, 55th, 1929
Nicolia, Henry	Pvt.	I, 179th Penn. Vol. Inf.	270		1901 Dec 28	IA, 28th, 1902
Nicoll, David	Pvt.	G, 137th Ill. Inf.	57		1929	IA, 56th, 1930
Nicols, William R.		I, 8th Iowa Cav. (died of heart failure)	1	67	1910	NE, 35th, 1911
Niday, James L.	Pvt.	E, 34th Iowa Inf.	137		1919 Dec 19	IA, 46th, 1920
Niehaus, Jules W.		B, 40th Mo. Inf.	6		1914 Apr 17	KS, 34th, 1915
Niehl, H.			118		1915 Jun	IA, 42nd, 1916
Nield, Wm. C.	Corp.	E, 144th N.Y. Inf.	300		1910 Sep 7	IA, 37th, 1911
Nietter, Thomas	Pvt.	E, 8th Iowa Inf.	49		1919 Jan 20	IA, 46th, 1920
Nieumuister, Gotlieb		B, 14th Mo. Inf. (died of disability)	61		1908 Jan 12	NE, 33rd, 1909
Nifful, P.		A, 6th Wis.	147		1906 Aug 19	KS, 26th, 1907
Nigh, Isaac		G, 115th Ill.	72		1916 Oct 17	KS, 36th, 1917
Nigh, J.C.		A, 49th Ohio	49		1924 Jul 2	KS, 44th, 1925
Nihart, George		G, 203rd Penn.	38		1898 Aug 3	KS, 18th, 1899
Nikerk, S.H.		H, 65th Ill.	132		1923 Jun 23	KS, 43rd, 1924
Niles, Albert G.		C, 55th Ohio	85		1917 Apr 25	KS, 37th, 1918
Niles, Elbert S.		I, 47th Penn.	35		1896 Nov 29	KS, 16th, 1897
Niles, Geo. A.		D, 75th N.Y. Inf.	63		1899 Apr 9	KS, 19th, 1900
Niles, J.Y.	1st Lieut.	A, 110th N.Y. 78th U.S.C.T.	1		1916 Feb 2?	KS, 36th, 1917
Niles, L.P.			102		1883	KS, 3rd, 1884
Niles, Peter H.		H, 23rd Mass.	71		1898 Aug 20	KS, 18th, 1899
Niles, R.S.	Pvt.	G, 38th Iowa Inf.	48		1915 Dec 4	IA, 42nd, 1916
Nill, John M.	Pvt.	C, 5th Ohio Inf.	231		1915 May 14	IA, 42nd, 1916
Nilson, David	Seaman	U.S. Navy	42		1923 Oct 8	IA, 50th, 1924
Nims, T.O.		B, 56th Ill.	25		1908	NE, 33rd, 1909

*See Appendix A, B or C for roster of post names and locations.
†See Introduction for note regarding recording of death date.

Name	Rank	Company, Regiment or Ship	Post*	Age	Death Date†	Journal
Nims, W.E.		K, 63rd Penn.	5		1918 Aug 9	KS, 38th, 1919
Ninemier, J.J.	Pvt.	K, 26th Ill. Inf.	497		1914 Nov 18	IA, 41st, 1915
Nininger, A.J.		C, 6th Cal. Inf.	71		1899 May 30	KS, 19th, 1900
Ninus, David A.		C, 14th Ky. Inf.	257		1901 Aug 29	KS, 21st, 1902
Nipps, Jacobs			[77?]		1904 Sep 9	KS, 24th, 1905
Nirk, John	Pvt.	A, 117th Ill.	72	56	1890 Oct 20	IA, 17th, 1891
Nisenger, Ayers		A, 121st Ohio Inf. (died of heart trouble)	182	65	1906	NE, 31st, 1907
Nisle, Geo.		54th Ohio Inf.	108		1908 Apr 10	IA, 35th, 1909
Nisley, Fred	Pvt.	F, 13th Iowa Inf.	140		1913 Nov 1	IA, 40th, 1914
Nisson, Christian		B, 15th Wis. Inf.	13		1928 Feb 28	NE, 53rd, 1929
Niterauer, D.D.	Pvt.	E, 21st Iowa	78		1923 Nov 29	IA, 50th, 1924
Nixon, A.J.		D, 143rd Ill.	50		1906 May 3	KS, 26th, 1907
Nixon, A.W.		I, 35th Ill.	434		1889	KS, 9th, 1890
Nixon, C.		B, 40th Ill.	100		1933 May 12	KS, 53rd, 1934
Nixon, G.T.A.			69		1886	NE, 11th, 1887
Nixon, Isaac	Pvt.	D, 18th Iowa Inf.	158		1920 Mar 28	IA, 47th, 1921
Nixon, J.	Pvt.	H, 19th Iowa Inf.	79	74	1888 Oct 25	IA, 15th, 1889
Nixon, J.P.	1st Lieut.	E, 70th Ohio Inf.	43		1899	NE, 24th, 1900
Nixon, Jacob	Sergt.	I, 19th Iowa Inf.	516		1918 Sep 28	IA, 45th, 1919
Nixon, James	Pvt.	I, 47th Ill. Inf.	284		1892 Jun 26	IA, 19th, 1893
Nixon, John	Pvt.	H, 19th Iowa Inf.	79	62	1888 Oct 25	IA, 16th, 1890
Nixon, M.			29		4th quarter 1883	IA, 10th, 1884
Nixon, Perry		C, 10th Ill.	142		1917 Oct 4	KS, 37th, 1918
Nixon, W.F.	Pvt.	C, 26th Iowa Inf.	88		1925 Jul 25	IA, 52nd, 1926
Nixon, W.W.	Lieut.	K, 33rd Ohio Inf.	329	68	1893 May 21	IA, 20th, 1894
Nixson, Geo. W.	Pvt.	H, 153rd Ill. Inf.	2		1919 Sep 29	IA, 46th, 1920
Nixton, S.M.		H, 159th Ind.	445		1924 May 4	IA, 51st, 1925
Noah, Hanks		H, 20th Ohio	20		1905 Jan 23	KS, 25th, 1906
Noah, M.M.		A, 4th Iowa	25		1926 Aug 13	NE, 51st, 1927
Noble, C.H.		I, 2nd Ill. Lt. Art.	1		1889	KS, 9th, 1890
Noble, Cherrick J.		I, 6th Penn. Res. Vol. Corps (died of paralysis at Soldiers & Sailors Home, Grand Island; buried in Home Cemetery)	17	61	1905 Aug 7	NE, 30th, 1906
Noble, Cyrus W.		C, 91st Ill.	46		1910 Nov 18	KS, 30th, 1911
Noble, George W.	Capt.	C, 31st Ind.	1		1915 Oct 1	KS, 35th, 1916
Noble, Norman J.	Pvt.	E, 20th Iowa Inf.	64		1912 Sep 30	IA, 39th, 1913
Noble, Oscar H.	Corp.	E, 140th Ill. Inf.	440		1902 Jun 18	IA, 29th, 1903
Noble, Scott O.		U.S. Navy, Ill.	123		1931 Feb 2	KS, 51st, 1932
Noble, Scott O.		U.S. Navy, Ill.	123		1931 Feb 2	KS, 52nd, 1933
Noble, W.	Pvt.	C, 6th Iowa Cav.	132		1921 Jan 27	IA, 48th, 1922
Noble, Wm.			255		1895 Jul 5	NE, 20th, 1896
Noblett, T.W.		F, 24th Ind.	153		1897 Mar	KS, 17th, 1898
Noddings, William		C, 44th Ind.	10		1929 Feb 21	NE, 54th, 1930
Nodurft, William		K, 33rd Ind.	20		1924 Oct 19	KS, 44th, 1925
Noe, Albert		C, 15th Ohio	7		1923 Jan	NE, 48th, 1924
Noe, Geo. F.	Pvt.	E, 4th Ill. Cav.	325	55	1891 Apr 29	IA, 18th, 1892
Noe, Lafayette		H, 8th Kans.	282		1905 Dec 21	KS, 25th, 1906
Noetticap, J.R.		C, 20th N.Y.	28		1891 Jun 21	KS, 16th, 1897
Noggle, I.P.	Pvt.	E, 96th Ill. Inf.	105	53	1889 Oct 17	IA, 16th, 1890
Nolan, A.A.		F, 4th Iowa	69		1898 Dec 30	KS, 18th, 1899
Nolan, C.A.	Pvt.	I, 36th Ohio Inf.	30		1911 Apr 16	IA, 38th, 1912
Nolan, Geo.		C, 69th N.Y.	8		1918 Apr 7	KS, 38th, 1919
Nolan, John		G, 50th Ill. Inf.	440		1915 Dec 10	IA, 42nd, 1916
Nolan, John		K, 26th Ohio	142		1923 Mar 4	KS, 43rd, 1924
Nolan, Patrick	Pvt.	K, 38th Iowa Inf.	168	67	1887 Feb 6	IA, 15th, 1889
Nolan, Patrick	Pvt.	K, 38th Iowa Inf.	168	67	1887 Feb 7	IA, 14th, 1888
Nolan, Peter	Pvt.	M, Iowa Cav.	497		1927 Sep	IA, 54th, 1928
Nolan, W.C.		1st Kans. Battery	12		1893 Feb 5	KS, 13th, 1894
Nolan, W.J.	Pvt.	M, 13th Ill. Cav.	349		1904 Mar 15	IA, 31st, 1905
Noland, Abraham		G, 7th Mo.	304		1900 Nov 12	KS, 20th, 1901
Noland, Silas	Pvt.	H, 25th Ohio Inf.	186		1913 Nov 29	IA, 40th, 1914
Nolder, Amos B.		B, 34th Ind. Inf.	432		1899 May 14	KS, 19th, 1900

*See Appendix A, B or C for roster of post names and locations.
†See Introduction for note regarding recording of death date.

405

Name	Rank	Company, Regiment or Ship	Post*	Age	Death Date†	Journal
Noler, Moses		B, 10th Ind.	1		1930	KS, 50th, 1931
Nolin, E.B.		I, 2nd Ill. Cav.	264	60	1896 Jul 29	NE, 21st, 1897
Noling, W.H.	Pvt.	C, 78th Ind. Inf.	12		1916 Dec 11	IA, 43rd, 1917
Noll, Thomas Jefferson	Pvt.	C, 146th Ill. Inf. (at large)	71, 64	98, 8 mos. & 19 days	1943 Aug 31	IA, 70th, 1944
Nolte, Chas.	Pvt.	F, 98th Ill. Inf.	247		1919 Mar 5	IA, 46th, 1920
Nolte, Chas. F.	Pvt.	F, 98th N.Y. Inf.	247		1919 Mar 5	IA, 46th, 1920
Nonemaker, Wilson		B, 113th Penn.	100		1930 Nov 25	KS, 50th, 1931
Nonis, T.J.		G, 3rd Iowa	68		1898 Jan 20	KS, 18th, 1899
Nookes, J.L.		A, 27th Mo.	112		1911 Jan 3	KS, 31st, 1912
Noonan, Thomas		A, 15th Ill.	98		1937 Jul 23	NE, 62nd, 1938
Nord, J.M.		D, 57th Ill.	30		1926 Oct 7	NE, 51st, 1927
Nordhaus, F.H.			109		1904-1905	IA, 31st, 1905
Nordike, S.B.	Pvt.	F, 88th Ohio	271		1921 Oct 7	IA, 48th, 1922
Nordike, Wm. W.		K, 1st Mo. Cav.	81		1916 Jan 31	KS, 36th, 1917
Nordyke, S.A.		A, 110th Ind.	28		1915 Mar 19	KS, 35th, 1916
Norelius, A.	Pvt.	D, 3rd Minn. Inf.	58		1927 Apr 10	IA, 54th, 1928
Norhous, H.F.	Corp.	D, 5th N.Y.	109		1903 Dec 17	IA, 30th, 1904
Norman, H.W.	Pvt.	H, 13th Iowa Inf.	337	57	1897 Dec 3	IA, 24th, 1898
Norman, James		A, 17th Iowa Inf.	29		1919 Jun 21	IA, 46th, 1920
Norman, Lewis		F, 6th Ind. Cav.	55		1918 Apr 17	KS, 38th, 1919
Norman, T.J.		F, 10th Ind.	145		1898 Aug 17	KS, 18th, 1899
Norman, William		C, 6th Mo.	123		1910 Sep 2	KS, 30th, 1911
Norris, Albert L.		G, 1st Ohio Lt. Art. (died of dropsy)	105	68	1913 Sep 22	NE, 38th, 1914
Norris, C.H.		G, 2nd Neb. (died of stricture of throat)	165	75	1911 May 28	NE, 36th, 1912
Norris, Chas. B.		E, 19th Maine Inf.	11	77	1917 Jul 25	NE, 42nd, 1918
Norris, Geo. R.	Pvt.	A, 2nd N.Y. Cav.	68		1918 Apr 11	IA, 45th, 1919
Norris, I.N.		F, 26th Ind.	221		1922 Oct 22	KS, 42nd, 1923
Norris, Israel P.		E, 7th Ill.	47-297		1919 Oct 4	KS, 39th, 1920
Norris, Israel P.		E, 7th Ill.	297		1919 Oct 4	KS, 39th, 1920
Norris, J.H.		D, 86th Ill. Inf.	8		1902 Sep 4	KS, 22nd, 1903
Norris, James			123		1895	KS, 15th, 1896
Norris, Joseph		F, 3rd Mo. Cav.	25		1925 Jan 14	KS, 45th, 1926
Norris, Lee	Pvt.	D, 69th Ill. Inf.	73[75?]		1899	NE, 24th, 1900
Norris, T.J.	Corp.	I, 2nd Iowa Cav.	59		1904 Oct 13	IA, 31st, 1905
Norris, W.W.			147		1904	IA, 31st, 1905
North, Charles			75		1884	KS, 4th, 1885
North, J.A.	Lieut.	F, 31st Ohio Inf.	244		1918 Aug 2	IA, 45th, 1919
North, Jacob		B, 35th Wis.	15		1914 Nov 21	KS, 34th, 1915
North, John W.		E, 1st Wis.	280[380?]		1911 Feb 3	KS, 31st, 1912
North, Luther H.		K, 2nd Neb. Cav.	9		1935 Apr 18	NE, 60th, 1936
Northcut, John		20th Kans.	[35?]		1914	KS, 34th, 1915
Northorp, Thomas	Pvt.	K, 35th Iowa Inf.	93		1917 Aug 1	IA, 44th, 1918
Northrop, John P.		B, 2nd N.Y.	28		1891 Jun 26	KS, 11th, 1892
Northrop, S.	Pvt.	I, 136th Penn. Inf.	465		1905 Apr 1	IA, 32nd, 1906
Northrup, Rollin		G, 19th Conn. Inf.	150		1886	KS, 6th, 1887
Northrup, T.G.	Pvt.		52		1906	IA, 33rd, 1907
Northstein, Noah			127		1922 Mar 20	KS, 42nd, 1923
Northup, C.P.	Eng.	B, 4th Iowa Inf.	7		1917 Feb 22	IA, 44th, 1918
Northup, Ira J.		C, 2nd U.S. Sharpshooters	122		1885	KS, 5th, 1886
Northup, Wilton	Pvt.	H, 8th Ohio Vols.	12		1926 Apr 6	IA, 53rd, 1927
Northway, D.C.	Corp.	B, 16th U.S.A.	73		1899	NE, 24th, 1900
Norton, A.A.			87[187?]		1887 Oct 3	KS, 7th, 1888
Norton, A.H.		I, 4th Ill. Cav.	43		1914 Apr 7	KS, 34th, 1915
Norton, Andy			385		1914 Apr 19	KS, 33rd, 1914
Norton, C.M.	Pvt.	M, 1st Mich. Cav.	94		1907 2nd term	IA, 34th, 1908
Norton, Charles		13th Iowa Inf.	314		1916	IA, 43rd, 1917
Norton, Chas. A.	Pvt.	K, 49th Mass. Inf.	267		1903 Jun	IA, 30th, 1904
Norton, D.D.			173		1910	IA, 37th, 1911
Norton, D.W.		C, 24th Iowa	43		1918	KS, 38th, 1919

*See Appendix A, B or C for roster of post names and locations.
†See Introduction for note regarding recording of death date.

Name	Rank	Company, Regiment or Ship	Post*	Age	Death Date†	Journal
Norton, E.A.	Pvt.	E, 43rd Wis. Inf.	81		1918 Oct 1	IA, 45th, 1919
Norton, E.H.	Pvt.	2nd Iowa Bat.	123		1917 Mar 15	IA, 44th, 1918
Norton, H.	Pvt.	D, 30th Maine Inf.	22		1920 Aug 30	IA, 47th, 1921
Norton, J.W.	Pvt.	F, 104th Ohio Inf.	497		1917 Jan 3	IA, 44th, 1918
Norton, John Q.A.		E, 7th Ohio Cav.	12		1929 Nov 26	KS, 49th, 1930
Norton, L.M.		E, 5th Iowa Cav.	82	69	1915 Jan 4	NE, 40th, 1916
Norton, Luther M.		E, 45th Ohio	71		1889	KS, 9th, 1890
Norton, R.D.		H, 107th Ill. Inf. (cause of death: kidney)	32		1905 Sep 11	NE, 30th, 1906
Norton, Tracy	Pvt.	C, 17th Kans.	49		1906 Apr 6	IA, 33rd, 1907
Norton, W.H.		K, 89th Ill. (died of old age)	104	83	1921 May 30	NE, 46th, 1922
Norton, Washington	Pvt.	K, 23rd Ill. Inf.	114		1899	NE, 24th, 1900
Norton, Wm.		C, 17th Kans. Inf.	15		1908 Jun 12	KS, 28th, 1909
Norvell, Thomas V.		I, 2nd Ind.	7		1931 Jul 29	NE, 56th, 1932
Norwood, Job		K, 76th N.Y. (died of cerebral hemorrhage)	287	72	1912 Dec 25	NE, 37th, 1913
Norwood, W.W.		T, 6th Kans. Cav. (died from fall from tree)	15	63	1904	NE, 29th, 1905
Notestine, J.A.	Pvt.	C, 57th Ill.	275		1924 Mar 28	IA, 51st, 1925
Notestine, T.H.		A, 30th Ind.	85		1921 Apr 28	KS, 41st, 1922
Nott, Julius H.	Sergt.	A, 6th Iowa Inf.	206		1915 Oct 11	IA, 42nd, 1916
Nott, Perrin R.	Pvt.	K, 89th Ill. Inf.	115		1923 Dec 10	IA, 50th, 1924
Nott, Thos. P.	Corp.	H, 5th Wis. Inf.	219		1910 Mar	IA, 37th, 1911
Notting, Frederick		H, 99th Ill.	244		1904 Nov 2	KS, 24th, 1905
Nottingham, A.R.		E, 1st Ore. Cav.	12		1917 Jun 8	KS, 37th, 1918
Nourse, Horace D.	Pvt.	L, 12th Penn. Cav.	87	50	1897 Oct 28	IA, 24th, 1898
Novell, Wm.		H, 10th N.Y. Hvy. Art.	9	63	1906 Aug 1	NE, 31st, 1907
Novenger, Isaac	Capt.	B, 30th Iowa Inf.	7		1905 Mar	IA, 32nd, 1906
Novinger, A.J.	Capt.	K, 46th Penn. Inf.	173		1918	IA, 45th, 1919
Novinger, John	Pvt.	F, 1st Iowa Cav.	45		1902 Dec 20	IA, 29th, 1903
Novotny, Frank		G, 5th Mich. Vol. Inf.	140		1908 Oct 14	NE, 33rd, 1909
Nowells, James T.	Pvt.	A, 8th Iowa Inf. (at large)	452	93	1940 Jan 4	IA, 67th, 1941
Nowels, Stephen			239		1917	KS, 37th, 1918
Nowlin, James F.		L, 1st Iowa Cav.	78		1st quarter 1883	IA, 10th, 1884
Nownes, Charles		1st Vt. Cav. (died of operation for nose)	55	67	1910 Jul 12	NE, 35th, 1911
Nowsome, John	Sergt.	B, 25th Penn. Inf.	18		1905 Jul 15	IA, 32nd, 1906
Noyes, Charles J.		A, 11th Maine	17		1910 Jan 29	KS, 30th, 1911
Noyes, David F.		L, 2nd N.Y. Cav. (former member of department; location: Falls City)			1933 Oct 2	NE, 58th, 1934
Noyes, H.		I, 11th Mo. Cav.	130		1922 Nov 30	KS, 42nd, 1923
Noyes, James F.		K, 30th Wis.	167		1914 May 15	KS, 34th, 1915
Noyes, James H.	Surg.	6th N.H. Inf.	300		1918 Jan 31	IA, 45th, 1919
Noyes, John H.	Pvt.	C, 29th Iowa Inf.	103		1915 Jun 13	IA, 42nd, 1916
Noyes, N., see Eoyes, N.						
Noyes, N.B.	Pvt.	F, 29th Ohio Inf.	130		1915 Nov 5	IA, 42nd, 1916
Noyes, Wm.	Pvt.	C, 97th Ohio Inf.	103		1911 May 9	IA, 38th, 1912
Nuckolls, Ezra	2nd Lieut.	9th Iowa Inf.	154		1925 Apr 1	IA, 52nd, 1926
Nuesser, John	Pvt.	I, 22nd Iowa Inf.	8		4th quarter 1885	IA, 12th, 1886
Nuff, Maurier		A, 6th Kans. Cav.	2		1931 Jan 11	KS, 52nd, 1933
Nugent, Wm.	Pvt.	H, 13th N.Y. Inf.	12		1908 Oct 13	IA, 35th, 1909
Nulick, Thos.	Pvt.	B, 4th Iowa Inf.	166		1911 Dec 16	IA, 38th, 1912
Null, W.F.		G, 134th & 147th Ind.	4		1928 Apr 15	KS, 48th, 1929
Nults, J.F.		14th Ill.	4		1924 Jan 26	KS, 44th, 1925
Nungesser, Horace		K, 47th Iowa Inf.	316		1925	KS, 45th, 1926
Nunn, George R.	Capt.	H, 6th Iowa Inf.	2		1901 Oct 29	IA, 28th, 1902
Nunn, Robert	Pvt.	D, 46th Ill. Inf.	327		1917 Jul 15	IA, 44th, 1918
Nunnick, Anthony J.		I, 11th Kans. Cav.	28		1912 Dec	KS, 32nd, 1913
Nuss, S.E.		D, 10th Ind. Inf.	206		1887 Dec 10	KS, 7th, 1888
Nute, Edward	Pvt.	A, 36th Ill. Inf.	82		1910 Nov 26	IA, 37th, 1911
Nutt, Thomas	Pvt.	Penn. Ringold Cav.	116		1905 Oct 18	IA, 32nd, 1906
Nutt, Wm. M.		F, 88th Ind.	207		1933 Jul	NE, 58th, 1934
Nutter, F.M.	Pvt.	B, 3rd Iowa Cav.	6		1926 Mar 11	IA, 53rd, 1927
Nutting, A.J.	Pvt.	H, 11th Wis. Inf.	154		1908 Jan 23	IA, 35th, 1909
Nutting, S.M.	Corp.	G, 6th Iowa Cav.	342	70	1898 Sep 22	IA, 25th, 1899
Nyce, John F.		A, 44th Ind.	13		1935 Feb 8	NE, 60th, 1936

Name	Rank	Company, Regiment or Ship	Post*	Age	Death Date†	Journal
Nye, B.F.		I, 14th Ill.	129		1917 Apr 19	KS, 37th, 1918
Nye, Daniel	Pvt.	F, 4th N.Y. Art.	122		1905 Nov 3	IA, 32nd, 1906
Nye, Geo. L.	QM Sergt.	B, 7th Iowa	117		1922 Nov 15	IA, 49th, 1923
Nye, Henry		D, 33rd Ohio	127		1928 May	KS, 48th, 1929
Nye, J.W.	Pvt.	F, 7th Iowa Cav.	337		1908 Dec 26	IA, 35th, 1909
Nye, James		C, 60th Ohio	66		1911 May 8	KS, 31st, 1912
Nye, Nelson B.		K, 9th Mich.	6		1915 Jul 23	KS, 35th, 1916
Nye, O.J.	Pvt.	B, 2nd West Va. Cav.	235	87	1931 May 9	IA, 58th, 1932
Nye, Oliver H.	Pvt.	G, 21st Mo. Inf.	268		1905 Feb 9	IA, 31st, 1905
Nye, W.W.					[1938?]	KS, 58th, 1939
Nypher, David		L, 1st N.Y. Cav.	1		1921 Feb 21	KS, 41st, 1922
O'Beermis, L.	Pvt.	A, 1st Iowa Cav.	2		1905 Jul 4	IA, 32nd, 1906
O'Brian, Alfred		A, 2nd West Va. Inf.	96		1912 Oct 14	KS, 32nd, 1913
O'Briand, Edw.	Pvt.	D, 112th Ill. Inf.	231		1925 Oct 11	IA, 52nd, 1926
O'Brien, F.H.		F, 16th Iowa	127		1917 Sep 22	KS, 37th, 1918
O'Brien, Geo. M.		died at his home in Omaha			1887 Jan 8	NE, 10th, 1886
O'Brien, Geo. M., see Obrien, Geo. M.						
O'Brien, J., see Brien, J.O.						
O'Brien, John J.	Pvt.	D, 7th Cal. Inf.	22		1914 Dec 23	IA, 41st, 1915
O'Brien, Joseph	Pvt.	K, 187th Penn. Inf.	124		1922 Apr 2	IA, 49th, 1923
O'Brien, M., see Obrien, M.						
O'Brien, Patrick	Pvt.	F, 52nd Ill. Inf.	452		1925 Jul 4	IA, 52nd, 1926
O'Brien, Patrick		K, 148th Ill. Inf. (died of cancer)	127	63	1895 Sep 6	NE, 20th, 1896
O'Brien, S.P.	Lieut.	A, 23rd Iowa Inf.	30		1912 Mar 17	IA, 39th, 1913
O'Brien, Thos.		B, 68th Inf.	7		1924[1923?] Dec 7	NE, 48th, 1924
O'Bryan, Geo.		G, 5th Iowa Inf.	250		1930 Apr 9	KS, 50th, 1931
O'Bryen, George		E, 76th Ill. Inf.	250		1930[1929?] Apr 9	KS, 49th, 1930
O'Conley, Henry	Pvt.	K, 8th Iowa Cav.	343	54	1898 Nov 22	IA, 25th, 1899
O'Connell, J.G.		I, 69th Ill. Inf. (died of hardening of arteries)	47	77	1919 Jul 27	NE, 44th, 1920
O'Connell, James		B, 92nd N.Y.	123		1898 Oct 3	KS, 18th, 1899
O'Conner, R.			92		1900 Mar 27	IA, 27th, 1901
O'Conner, Thos.		A, 143rd N.Y.	77		1898 Sep 19	KS, 18th, 1899
O'Connor, Patrick		E, 24th Penn. Inf. (died at Kansas City, Mo.; buried at Eudora Cemetery)	333		1894 Oct 1	KS, 14th, 1895
O'Dell, L.R.	Pvt.	C, 65th Ill.	68		1905 Feb 18	IA, 32nd, 1906
O'Donnell, F.O.	Pvt.	F, 23rd Ill. Inf.	78		1925 Sep 9	IA, 52nd, 1926
O'Halloran, Daniel	Pvt.	C, 13th Iowa Inf.	150		1901 Feb 10	IA, 27th, 1901
O'Hana, Dan'l J.		F, 3rd Wis. Cav.	7		1926 Oct 13	NE, 51st, 1927
O'Hanlon, James		H, 17th Ohio	25		1916 Feb 11	KS, 36th, 1917
O'Hare, Barney	Pvt.	B, 93rd Ill. Inf.	18		1904 Nov 22	IA, 31st, 1905
O'Harra, H.C.		E, 7th Wis. Inf.	17		1929 May 7	KS, 49th, 1930
O'Kane, John W.		E, 92nd Ill. Inf. (died of consumption)	90	68	1909 Aug 31	NE, 34th, 1910
O'Kell, Ralph R.	Pvt.	L, 4th Iowa Cav.	201		1913 Nov 16	IA, 40th, 1914
O'Laughlin, D.M.	Corp.	K, 13th Iowa Inf.	108		1931 Feb 26	IA, 58th, 1932
O'Leary, Daniel		A, 5th Ohio Inf.	98		1914 Jun 6	KS, 34th, 1915
O'Leary, Michael	Pvt.	A, 53rd Ill. Inf.	22		1910 Oct 9	IA, 37th, 1911
O'Mara, John			165		1883	KS, 3rd, 1884
O'Neal, Lemuel			203		1923	IA, 50th, 1924
O'Neal, P.J., see Oneal, P.J.						
O'Neil, Jasper		B, 3rd Iowa Cav.	14		1892 Feb 22	KS, 12th, 1893
O'Neil, John	Pvt.	I, 8th Iowa Cav.	31		1917 Nov 12	IA, 44th, 1918
O'Neil, Michael		Navy	32		1889	KS, 9th, 1890
O'Neil, Wm.	Pvt.	L, 1st Wis. Hvy. Art.	269		1907 Oct 11	IA, 34th, 1908
O'Neil, Wm.	Pvt.	6th Mo.	1		1906 Jul 29	KS, 26th, 1907
O'Neill, Augustus	Corp.	A, 43rd Minn. Inf.	101	95	1939 Jun 8	IA, 65th, 1939
O'Neill, J.W.		3rd U.S.A. Hvy. Art.	244		1928 Mar	KS, 48th, 1929
O'Toole, Terry	Pvt.	C, 1st Minn. Art.	78		1925 Jul 22	IA, 52nd, 1926
Oakford, William M.		53rd Ill.	98		1910 Dec 15	KS, 30th, 1911
Oakley, J.J.		H, 6th Kans.	293		1920 Mar 2	KS, 40th, 1921
Oakly, F.M.		I, 24th Ky.	18		1924 Aug 24	KS, 44th, 1925

*See Appendix A, B or C for roster of post names and locations.
†See Introduction for note regarding recording of death date.

Name	Rank	Company, Regiment or Ship	Post*	Age	Death Date†	Journal
Oaks, Abraham		G, 40th Iowa	18		1912 Jun 27	KS, 32nd, 1913
Oaks, Geo.		F, 34th Iowa Inf.	18		1900 Jan 3	KS, 20th, 1901
Oaks, J.S.		B, 55th Ohio Inf.	4		1887 Mar 12	KS, 7th, 1888
Oaks, Jessie	Pvt.	A, 11th Iowa Inf.	231		1927 Jan 22	IA, 54th, 1928
Oaks, Levi			173		1912	IA, 39th, 1913
Oaldes, Warren	Pvt.	H, 26th Iowa Inf.	111		1911 Jul 1	IA, 38th, 1912
Oard, Geo. W.		F, 83rd Ind.	19		1893 Feb 28	KS, 13th, 1894
Oath, Andrew	Pvt.	G, 15th Mo. Inf.	78		1910 Nov 2	IA, 37th, 1911
Oathweigh, Henry	Corp.	B, 5th Wis. Inf.	452		1926 Sep 9	IA, 53rd, 1927
Oatman, A.G.		E, 108th Ill.	12		1911 Jan 4	KS, 31st, 1912
Oatman, John H.		F, 110th N.Y.	13	75	1912 May 15	NE, 37th, 1913
Obenchain, J.W.	Pvt.	K, 48th Ind. Inf.	22		1920 Mar 25	IA, 47th, 1921
Obenchain, W.L.		H, 144th Ohio	38		1918 Aug 2	KS, 38th, 1919
Oberlies, John		55th Ill. (died of old age)	318	88	1919	NE, 44th, 1920
Oberlies, John		E, 40th Iowa Inf. (nonmember)	25	74	1913 May 11	NE, 38th, 1914
Oberly, Cavier	Pvt.	E, 1st Minn.	222		1923 Feb 13	IA, 50th, 1924
Oberman, Wm.		K, 100th Ill. Inf.	56		1889	KS, 9th, 1890
Obley, Christian		I, 96th Ill. Inf.	464		1902 Sep 23	KS, 22nd, 1903
Obricht, Jacob	Pvt.	K, 12th Ill. Inf.	247		1905 Feb 11	IA, 32nd, 1906
Obrien, Geo. M.	Major & Bvt. Brig. Gen.	7th Iowa Cav. (died of pneumonia)	7	57	1887 Jan 9	NE, 12th, 1888
Obrien, M.		H, 23rd Ohio Reg. (died of dropsy)	354	72	1912 Jul 5	NE, 37th, 1913
Ochel, Dan'l		D, 178th N.Y. Inf.	380		1899 May 27	KS, 19th, 1900
Ochel, T.W.		176th Ohio	68		1929 Nov 8	KS, 49th, 1930
Ochiltree, T.J.	Sergt.	M, 8th Iowa Cav.	153	90	1932 Jan 1	IA, 59th, 1933
Ocker, Henry G.		A, 151st Ind. Inf.	25	73	1918 Dec 11	NE, 43rd, 1919
Ockerson, D.J.	Pvt.	K, 1st Calif.	57		1903-1904	IA, 30th, 1904
Oddy, William		1st Colo. Battery	66		1892 Jul 9	KS, 12th, 1893
Odell, H.C.	Pvt.	D, 1st Mich. Inf.	88		1924 Nov 16	IA, 51st, 1925
Odell, H.C.		B, 7th Ind.	28		1905 Sep 9	KS, 25th, 1906
Odell, John L.		A, 49th Ind.	64		1890	KS, 10th, 1891
Odell, W.H.		I, 118th Ill.	52		1892 Jul 30	KS, 12th, 1893
Odell, W.H.		B, 118th Ill.	52		1896 Jul 30	KS, 16th, 1897
Odell, W.H.		B, 118th Ill.	52		1898 May 4	KS, 18th, 1899
Oden, Chas. W.	Lieut.	C, 29th Iowa Inf.	139		1913 Feb 13	IA, 40th, 1914
Oden, L.		U.S.C.T.	321		1897	KS, 17th, 1898
Oder, Wm. S.	Pvt.	E, 145th Ill. Inf.	66		1928 Apr 23	IA, 55th, 1929
Oderfield, Henry		E, 58th Ohio	6		1897 Feb 3	KS, 17th, 1898
Oesharn, Calab		E, 13th Kans.	53		1924 Feb 22	KS, 44th, 1925
Offen, Benjamin		G, 153rd N.Y. Inf. (died of bladder disease)	52	79	1925 Jan 23	NE, 50th, 1926
Offensberger, W.H.	Pvt.	E, 9th Iowa Cav.	12		1927 Sep 14	IA, 54th, 1928
Offer, Sebastian		D, 24th Ill.	88		1893 Jun 10	KS, 13th, 1894
Officer, J.W.		A, 51st Ohio Inf.	49		1890	KS, 10th, 1891
Offie, J.F.	Pvt.	I, 3rd Iowa Cav.	7		1924 Jan 9	IA, 51st, 1925
Offut, W.L.		B, 4th Mo.	130		1906 Sep 15	KS, 26th, 1907
Ogborn, John E.		G, 1st Ill. Art. (died of consumption)	35		1911 Jul 16	NE, 36th, 1912
Ogden, Andrew		C, 5th Mo. Cav.	48		1925	NE, 50th, 1926
Ogden, J.D.		B, 5th Mo.	51		1916 Nov 10	KS, 36th, 1917
Ogden, James	Sergt.	H, 37th Ky. Inf.	300		1906 May 31	IA, 33rd, 1907
Ogden, James M.	Musician	E, 33rd Iowa Inf.	40	56	1894 Jun 12	IA, 21st, 1895
Ogden, W.G.		K, 101st Penn.	5		1919 Sep 2	KS, 39th, 1920
Ogden, William A.	Capt.	enlisted August 1, 1862, in Co. I, 15th N.J., & later in Co. B, 39th N.J., & served until close of war (born in Odgensburg, N.J., Oct. 9, 1843; died in Jamesburg, N.J.)	30	71	1914 Oct 31	KS, 33rd, 1914
Ogen, John	Corp.	C, 24th Iowa Inf.	452		1926 Mar 31	IA, 53rd, 1927
Ogg, George E.		B, 11th Ill. Inf.	339		1917 Mar 19	KS, 37th, 1918
Ogg, George W.		G, 3rd Ill. Cav.	22		1931 Aug 27	NE, 56th, 1932
Ogg, Jeff		D, 15th Iowa Inf.	25		1902	NE, 27th, 1903
Ogg, Wm. A.		G, 31st Iowa (died of cancer)	6	66	1908 Jul	NE, 33rd, 1909
Ogle, A.B.		D, 43rd Mo.	209		1926 Feb 19	KS, 46th, 1927

*See Appendix A, B or C for roster of post names and locations.
†See Introduction for note regarding recording of death date.

Name	Rank	Company, Regiment or Ship	Post*	Age	Death Date†	Journal
Ogle, Elija M.		K, 68th Ohio (died of the result of a wound)	39	71	1911 Sep 2	NE, 36th, 1912
Ogle, Louis A.		B, 156th Ind.	221		1905 Apr 12	KS, 25th, 1906
Ogle, W.T.	Pvt.	I, 10th Mo. Inf.	496	63	1898 Oct 9	IA, 25th, 1899
Oglesbee, W.H.	Pvt.	I, 3rd Mo. Inf.	184		1911 Mar 8	IA, 38th, 1912
Oglesby, Joe		F, 65th Ill.	137		1st quarter 1884	IA, 10th, 1884
Oglesby, Wm. T.		H, 119th Ill. Inf.	2		1913 Nov 30	IA, 40th, 1914
Ohlemyer, Henry		F, 150th Ill.	115		1898 Aug 14	KS, 18th, 1899
Ohlweiler, John			3		1910	NE, 35th, 1911
Ohmert, J.E.	Pvt.	I, 3rd Ill. Cav.	78		1916 Nov 13	IA, 43rd, 1917
Ojers, R.H.		H, 46th Ill. Inf.	89		1928 Sep 9	NE, 53rd, 1929
Okee, Joseph L.		G, 23rd Iowa	68		1931 Aug 1	NE, 56th, 1932
Okey, W.S.	Pvt.	E, 1st Wis. Hvy. Art.	76		1901 Jan 14	IA, 27th, 1901
Olcott, Geo.	Pvt.	11th Penn. Cav.	480		1917 Mar 12	IA, 44th, 1918
Olden, E.L.		K, 1st Minn.	493		1926 Nov 18	KS, 46th, 1927
Oldes, E.		C, 38th Wis. Inf.	79		1886	KS, 6th, 1887
Oldfield, David		D, 8th Kans.	84		1900 Dec 27	KS, 20th, 1901
Oldfield, Geo.			233		1924	IA, 51st, 1925
Oldfield, L.H.		B, 64th Ohio	25		1921 Jul 19	KS, 41st, 1922
Oldfield, Silas P.	Pvt.	E, 102nd Ohio Inf.	17		1917 Sep 19	IA, 44th, 1918
Oldham, J.S.		A, 13th Iowa	66		1913 Jul 13	KS, 33rd, 1914
Oldham, Jesse	Pvt.	H, 23rd Iowa	55		1901 Dec 7	IA, 28th, 1902
Oldham, S.H.		G, 37th Ind.	25		1929 Sep 9	NE, 54th, 1930
Oldham, Thos. R.		D, 110th U.S. Colored	36		1919 Aug 17	KS, 39th, 1920
Oldridge, Francis		H, 2nd Ky. Cav.	130		1915 Dec 21	KS, 35th, 1916
Oldroyd, Charles W.		C, 16th Ohio	18		1912 Mar 3	KS, 32nd, 1913
Olds, H.D.	Sergt.	H, 3rd Vt. Inf.	235	68	1899 May 2	IA, 25th, 1899
Olds, Jonathan		B, 57th Ill. (cause of death: railroad)	354	68	1908 Jul 24	NE, 33rd, 1909
Olds, Lester		D, 121st Ohio	81		1923 Jul 10	KS, 43rd, 1924
Oldson, James R.		E, 1st Ohio Hvy. Art.	232		1897 Sep 25	KS, 17th, 1898
Oler, W.H.		A, 44th Wis.	267		1908	NE, 33rd, 1909
Oleson, Thomas	Pvt.	G, 20th Wis. Inf.	488	65	1897 Dec	IA, 24th, 1898
Olin, J.L.	Pvt.	A, 1st Ohio Inf.	290	42	1887 Jun 13	IA, 14th, 1888
Olin, Martin S.		G, 117th N.Y.	171		1933 May 1	NE, 58th, 1934
Olin, Sidney S.	Pvt.	I, 11th N.Y. Cav.	88		1916 Jan 4	IA, 43rd, 1917
Olin, Thomas		F, 8th Wis. (died of old age)	182	87	1920 Feb 18	NE, 45th, 1921
Olinger, A.W.		B, 45th Ky. (died of cancer)	299	72	1915 Oct 17	NE, 40th, 1916
Olinger, John		E, 153rd Ill.	316		1916 Aug 1	KS, 36th, 1917
Olinger, T.H.	Pvt.		20		1916	IA, 43rd, 1917
Oliphant, A.R.		K, 154th Ohio Inf. (died of lung fever)	13	71	1906 Mar 19	NE, 31st, 1907
Oliphant, Joel	Pvt.	B, 98th Penn. Inf.	12		1914 Dec 28	IA, 41st, 1915
Oliphant, R.A.			6		1910 Sep 27	IA, 37th, 1911
Oliphant, S.D.		A, 7th Mo.	142		1921 Aug 12	KS, 41st, 1922
Oliver, C.N.		F, 14th Ill.	25		1919 Nov 9	KS, 39th, 1920
Oliver, F.N.	Pvt.	I, 84th Ill.	51		1926 Apr	IA, 53rd, 1927
Oliver, Henry		F, 29th Ind.	322		1921 May 1	KS, 41st, 1922
Oliver, Joseph W.		B, 11th Ill. Cav.	244		1914 Jan	KS, 34th, 1915
Oliver, L.	Pvt.		37		1906	IA, 33rd, 1907
Oliver, Lanty		F, 124th Ill. Inf.	159		1892 Jan 19	KS, 12th, 1893
Oliver, M. Joseph	Pvt.	A, 3rd Iowa Cav.	69		1926	IA, 53rd, 1927
Oliver, R.W.	Chaplain	Washington Vols.	1		1899	NE, 24th, 1900
Oliver, Stephen H.		B, 79th Ohio	25		1913 Nov 9	KS, 33rd, 1914
Oliver, Thomas		F, 77th Ohio	464		1914 Nov 16	KS, 34th, 1915
Oliver, W.J.		I, 84th Penn. Inf. (died of consumption)	204	61	1902 Feb	NE, 27th, 1903
Oliver, W.P.			311		1917 Mar 20	KS, 37th, 1918
Oliverson, T.R.		B, 57th Ill.	85		1917 Dec 26	KS, 37th, 1918
Oliverson, W.B.	Pvt.	B, 57th Ill.	40		1905 Feb 20	IA, 32nd, 1906
Ollinger, Samuel H.		A, 5th Iowa Inf.	200		1901 Oct 23	KS, 21st, 1902
Olliver, E.W.		C, 33rd Ind. Inf. (died of paralysis)	354	78	1913 Sep 17	NE, 38th, 1914
Ollthoff, A.		C, 46th Ill. Inf. (died of paralysis)	65	59	1895 Feb 14	NE, 20th, 1896
Olmstead, F.	Lieut. Col.	59th Ohio Inf.	12	68	1898 Apr 16	IA, 24th, 1898
Olmstead, H.			288		1897 Jun 9	IA, 24th, 1898

Name	Rank	Company, Regiment or Ship	Post*	Age	Death Date†	Journal
Olmstead, Henry		5th Ohio Inf. (died of old age)	111	77	1924 Jun 11	NE, 49th, 1925
Olmstead, N.G.		A, 32nd Iowa Inf.	66		1919 Sep 25	IA, 46th, 1920
Olmstead, O.K.		L, 4th N.Y.	3		1926 Dec 5	NE, 51st, 1927
Olmstead, O.P., see Omstead, O.P.						
Olmstead, Theodore	Pvt.	E, 32nd Iowa Inf.	243		1919 Apr 17	IA, 46th, 1920
Olmstead, Wm. P.		K, 13th Vt.	61		1918 May 27	KS, 38th, 1919
Olmsted, Phillip		M, 1st Col. Cav.	12		1909 Feb 2	KS, 29th, 1910
Olney, Levi	Pvt.	C, 4th Ohio Inf.	117		1925 Feb 18	IA, 52nd, 1926
Olney, S.W.	Capt.	B, 8th Iowa Cav.	497		1925 Apr 19	IA, 52nd, 1926
Olsen, Emeric	Pvt.	E, 9th Iowa Cav.	48		1900 Aug 4	IA, 27th, 1901
Olson, Abraham	Pvt.	H, 1st Ill. Lt. Art.	375	52	1894 Feb 3	IA, 21st, 1895
Olson, Abraham	Pvt.	H, 1st Ill. Lt. Art.	375	50	1894 Feb 1	IA, 20th, 1894
Olson, H.L.			142		1904-1905	IA, 31st, 1905
Olson, H.L.	Pvt.	B, Iowa Inf.	142		1926 Dec 30	IA, 53rd, 1927
Olson, Iver A.		A, 88th Ill. (died of old age)	35	78	1918 May 14	NE, 43rd, 1919
Olson, L.	Pvt.	E, 88th Penn. Inf.	123	50	1885 Sep 26	IA, 14th, 1888
Olson, Peter		H, 1st Ill. Lt. Art.	271		1916 Jan 1	KS, 36th, 1917
Olson, Wm.		C, 30th Iowa (died of heart disease)	86		1889	KS, 9th, 1890
Olswald, A.		D, 138th Penn.	185		1922 Nov 24	KS, 44th, 1925
Oman, Levi		E, 43rd R.I. O.V.I.[43rd Ohio Vol. Inf.]	180		1909 Mar 6	KS, 29th, 1910
Omer, John M.	Pvt.	K, 25th Mo. Cav.	263		1923 Sep 12	IA, 50th, 1924
Omstead, O.P.	Pvt.	E, 32nd Iowa Inf.	81		1926 Jun 13	IA, 53rd, 1927
Omyher, S.	Corp.	G, 15th Wis. Inf.	365		1905 May 14	IA, 32nd, 1906
Oneal, P.J.	Pvt.	E, 46th Ill. Inf.	141		1917 Feb 28	IA, 44th, 1918
Oneal, P.J.		E, 100th Ohio	6		1923 Apr 20	KS, 43rd, 1924
Oney, Marion	Pvt.	G, 3rd Mo. Cav.	251		1894 Apr	IA, 21st, 1895
Oppelt, S.C.	Pvt.	D, 28th Iowa Inf.	98		1918 Aug 1	IA, 45th, 1919
Opperman, Chris.	Pvt.	A, 25th Wis. Inf.	259	61	1887 Dec 25	IA, 14th, 1888
Opperman, J.B.		17th Ohio Bat.	123		1924 Oct 15	KS, 44th, 1925
Oppie, John		1st Neb.	24		1915	NE, 40th, 1916
Orange, W.H.	Pvt.	F, 11th Ind. Inf.	436	51	1892 Jan 17	IA, 18th, 1892
Orchard, Elihn	Pvt.	A, 34th Iowa Inf.	77		1914 Sep 30	IA, 41st, 1915
Orchard, George	Pvt.	K, 31st Iowa Inf.	132		1917 Feb 8	IA, 44th, 1918
Orenn, Thomas		D, U.S. Art., N.Y.	41	78	1921 Jul 15	NE, 46th, 1922
Orgt, B.C.		E, 135th Ind.	265		1917 Feb 18	KS, 37th, 1918
Orin, Byron		A, 33rd Ohio	177		1887 Aug	KS, 7th, 1888
Orin, C.F.			99		1919 Jun 21	KS, 39th, 1920
Orin, J.T.	Pvt.	E, 24th Iowa Inf.	145	70	1893 Nov 29	IA, 20th, 1894
Orland, Eddy	Major	G, 5th Minn.	30		1905 Aug 20	IA, 32nd, 1906
Orme, Geo. V.		H, 124th Ill.			1928 Jul 31	NE, 53rd, 1929
Ormes, Thos.		G, 55th Ky.	333		1898 Sep 1	KS, 18th, 1899
Ormiston, A.		F, 63rd Ohio Inf.	4		1902 Mar 10	KS, 22nd, 1903
Ormond, Samuel	Pvt.	E, 15th Iowa Inf.	79		1916	IA, 43rd, 1917
Ormsbee, C.W.		H, 6th Vt. Inf.	7		1925 Apr 17	NE, 50th, 1926
Ormsbee, Mansel A.	Pvt. Pvt.	G, 2nd Vt. Inf. A, 5th Vt. Inf.	22		1912 Nov 1	IA, 39th, 1913
Ormsby, O.W.	Pvt.	28th N.Y. Ind. Bat.	10		1916 Oct 1	IA, 43rd, 1917
Ormsley, A.L.	Pvt.	L, 1st Mich. E.N.M.	150		1900 May 18	IA, 27th, 1901
Orndorff, Benjamin		G, 6th West Va. Inf. (born in Virginia; died of heart failure at Home Cottage; buried at Petersburg, Neb.)		70	1907 Feb 20	NE, 31st, 1907
Orner, Theo. F.		K, 7th Ind.	1		1904 Oct 21	KS, 24th, 1905
Ornes, Joseph		G, 5th Tenn. Cav.	333		1899 Apr	KS, 19th, 1900
Orons, L.A.	Corp.	25th Ind. Inf.	55		1921 Mar 24	IA, 48th, 1922
Orr, David		F, 35th Ill. Inf.	32		1918 Sep 23	KS, 38th, 1919
Orr, E.J.	Pvt.	6th Wis. Art.	271		1930 Sep 8	IA, 57th, 1931
Orr, J.B.	Pvt.	K, 12th Iowa Inf.	465		1912 Oct 13	IA, 39th, 1913
Orr, J.G.	Musician	H, 126th Ill. Inf.	39		1897 Jun 10	IA, 24th, 1898
Orr, James	Pvt.		69		1932 Mar	IA, 59th, 1933
Orr, James C.		I, 53rd Ill. Inf.	6		1925 Feb 5	KS, 45th, 1926
Orr, James E.	Pvt.	C, 21st Penn. Cav.	69		1931 Nov 31	IA, 58th, 1932

Name	Rank	Company, Regiment or Ship	Post*	Age	Death Date†	Journal
Orr, Joseph		A, 102nd Ohio	18		1910 Jan 30	KS, 30th, 1911
Orr, Mayburg		G, 4th Mo.	56		1906 Dec 27	KS, 26th, 1907
Orr, S.C.		C, 169th Ohio	100		1920 Dec 11	KS, 40th, 1921
Orr, Stephen S.		C, 9th Mo. Inf. (died of heart trouble)	84	84	1925 Sep 3	NE, 50th, 1926
Orr, T.J.		D, 2nd Ohio	270		1913 Mar 5	KS, 32nd, 1913
Orr, William		G, 144th Ill. Inf.	36		1914 Aug 15	KS, 34th, 1915
Orr, William		H, 120th Ohio	25		1928 May 25	NE, 53rd, 1929
Orr, Wm. F.	Pvt.	C, 11th Iowa	115		1907 Mar 2	IA, 34th, 1908
Orr, Wm. H.		I, 7th Mo. Cav. (died of Bright's disease)	26	76	1917 Aug 31	NE, 42nd, 1918
Orr, Wm. L.	Surg.	21st Iowa Inf.	69		1908 Apr 1	IA, 35th, 1909
Orr, Wm. T.	Pvt.	C, 5th Iowa Inf.	55		1912 Oct 3	IA, 39th, 1913
Orrick, C.W.		Troop 5 Kans.	12		1926 Nov 18	KS, 46th, 1927
Orris, M.L.			108		1911 Apr 14	IA, 38th, 1912
Orris, Reuben S.	Sergt.	C, 8th Iowa Inf.	55		1916 Sep 5	IA, 43rd, 1917
Orsman, John H.	Pvt.	F, 1st Penn. Rifles F, 190th Penn. Inf.	250	50	1893 Mar 13	IA, 20th, 1894
Ort, Jacob		E, 1st Ill. Art.	25		1935 Jul 31	NE, 60th, 1936
Orton, Edward		A, 7th Ill. (died of paralysis)	13	81	1923 Mar 2	NE, 48th, 1924
Orton, John W.	Pvt.	D, 67th Penn.	22		1903 Mar 7	IA, 30th, 1904
Orton, W.H.		B, 13th Iowa	147		1928 Dec 10	NE, 54th, 1930
Orvis, Henry C.		D, 17th Ill. (died of complications)	354	74	1920 Oct 3	NE, 45th, 1921
Orvis, Theo. W.	Pvt.		26		1900 Feb 11	IA, 27th, 1901
Orvis, Theodore W.	Capt.	I, 2nd Iowa Cav.	26	52	1900 Feb 11	IA, 26th, 1900
Orwig, Thos. G.	Pvt.	D, 5th Penn. Inf.	12		1911 Jun 26	IA, 38th, 1912
Osa, L.		D, 3rd — (died of old age)	104	75	1910	NE, 35th, 1911
Osbor, Wm. H.		C, 20th Ohio	98	75	1920 Dec 20	NE, 45th, 1921
Osborn, A.	Pvt.	E, 43rd Mo. Inf.	96		1929 Oct 4	IA, 56th, 1930
Osborn, Alfred	Pvt.	F, 17th Iowa Inf.	467	54	1891 Feb 16	IA, 17th, 1891
Osborn, Andrew	Pvt.	E, 3rd Mo. Cav.	306		1901 Aug 12	IA, 28th, 1902
Osborn, Felix		H, 33rd Ohio	58		1916 Nov 18	KS, 36th, 1917
Osborn, Geo.		B, 2nd Neb. Cav.	118	74	1908 Apr	NE, 33rd, 1909
Osborn, Hiram	Bugler	G, 2nd Mo. Inf.	325		1911 Apr 25	IA, 38th, 1912
Osborn, J.B.		K, 121st Ohio	311		1926 May 4	KS, 46th, 1927
Osborn, J.H.		M, 7th & 17th Ky. 9th & 65th Ohio	293		1924 Feb 4	KS, 44th, 1925
Osborn, J.O.		H, 11th Ind.	180		1909 Jul 18	KS, 29th, 1910
Osborn, J.P.	Pvt.	H, 147th Ind. Inf.	330	41	1888 Mar 30	IA, 15th, 1889
Osborn, John M.		I, 97th Ind.	95	76	1920	NE, 45th, 1921
Osborn, John R.		K, 39th Iowa Inf. (died of locomotor ataxia)	110		1893 Feb 5	NE, 18th, 1894
Osborn, L.W.		E, 142nd N.Y. Inf. (cause of death: heart)	52	59	1891[1901?] Oct	NE, 26th, 1902
Osborn, Lou		F, 149th Ill.	51		1927	KS, 47th, 1928
Osborn, Lyman	Pvt.	I, 47th Wis.	130		1907 2nd term	IA, 34th, 1908
Osborn, Lyman			130		1908	IA, 35th, 1909
Osborn, R.F.	1st Lieut.	H, 137th N.Y. Inf.	383		4th quarter 1885	IA, 12th, 1886
Osborn, T.W.	Pvt.	B, 62nd Ohio Inf.	466		1914 Aug 12	IA, 41st, 1915
Osborn, W.F.		11th & 13th Penn.	40		1914 Jan 27	KS, 34th, 1915
Osborne, A.P.		D, 35th Ill.	158		1927 Feb 15	KS, 47th, 1928
Osborne, C.B.	Pvt.	D, 134th Ill. Inf.	6		1929 Oct 9	IA, 56th, 1930
Osborne, H.D.	Pvt.	E, 18th Mich. Inf.	22		1917 May 7	IA, 44th, 1918
Osborne, J.A.		L, 16th N.Y. Inf. (died of paralysis)	32		1891[1901?] Feb	NE, 26th, 1902
Osborne, J.K.		E, 21st Ky.	127		1895 Oct 5	KS, 16th, 1897
Osborne, J.W.			11		1927	IA, 54th, 1928
Osborne, John		K, 39th Ohio	85		1923 Apr 27	KS, 43rd, 1924
Osborne, Robt.		I, 6th Kans.	32		1935	KS, 55th, 1936
Osgood, Chas. L.	Pvt.	B, 18th Iowa Inf.	297		1919 Jul 13	IA, 46th, 1920
Osgood, Edward N.		B, 1st Cal. Cav.	6		1925 May 2	KS, 45th, 1926
Osgood, J.S.		E, 6th Ohio Cav.	47		1907 Feb 11	IA, 34th, 1908
Osgood, O.S.	Pvt.	C, 15th Mass. Inf.	20	51	1890 Mar 6	IA, 16th, 1890
Osgood, W.C.		E, 40th Ohio Inf.	388		1912 Oct 12	KS, 32nd, 1913
Osier, Cyrus M.		D, 68th Ohio (died of stomach complications)	10	70	1915 Mar 18	NE, 40th, 1916

*See Appendix A, B or C for roster of post names and locations.
†See Introduction for note regarding recording of death date.

Name	Rank	Company, Regiment or Ship	Post*	Age	Death Date†	Journal
Osler, J.K.	Pvt.	F, 106th Ill. Inf.	414		1915 Nov 1	IA, 42nd, 1916
Osler, J.W.	Pvt.	H, 38th Ill. Inf.	161	44	1887 Oct 8	IA, 14th, 1888
Osmer, E.B.	Pvt.	E, 37th Ill. Inf.	63		1911 May 11	IA, 38th, 1912
Ostenberg, Otto		A, 11th Wis. Inf. (former member)	90		1940 Oct 22	NE, 65th, 1941
Osterlo, John		A, 2nd Neb. Cav. (died of old age)	133	80	1915 Jun 2	NE, 40th, 1916
Ostrander, Cornelius E.		F, 52nd Ill. Inf.	380		1917 Apr 18	KS, 37th, 1918
Ostrander, Jacob	Pvt.	E, 105th Ill. Inf.	66		1916 Dec 30	IA, 43rd, 1917
Ostrum, J.B.		E, 147th N.Y. (died of old age)	120	77	1921 Oct 2	NE, 46th, 1922
Osure, E.B.	Pvt.	E, 37th Ill. Inf.	63		1911 May 5	IA, 41st, 1915
Oswald, A., see Olswald, A.						
Oswald, William		H, 44th Ohio	84		1933 Jul 19	NE, 58th, 1934
Oswalt, Geo. W.	Pvt.	H, 2nd Ind. Cav. (died of consumption; dis. caused by fall from horse in service)	45	43	1884 Mar 15	NE, 9th, 1885
Othmer, August	Pvt.	C, 35th Iowa Inf.	231		1911 Jan 10	IA, 38th, 1912
Otis, Anson M.		D, 16th Wis. Inf.			1929 Jan 19	NE, 53rd, 1929
Otis, George W.		H, 17th Mich.	269		1905 Mar 23	KS, 25th, 1906
Otis, J.F.	Pvt.	I, 38th Wis. Inf.	329		1931 Jan 20	IA, 58th, 1932
Otis, J.F.	Pvt.	I, 38th Wis. Inf.	329		1930 Jan 20	IA, 57th, 1931
Otis, John	Corp.	F, 12th Iowa Inf.	190		1st quarter 1886	IA, 12th, 1886
Ott, George	Pvt.	G, 48th Ind. Inf.	11	67	1894 Nov 13	IA, 21st, 1895
Ott, John		K, 136th Ind.	5		1925 Dec 31	NE, 51st, 1927
Ott, M.C.	Pvt.	I, 24th N.Y. Inf.	250		1907 Apr 12	IA, 34th, 1908
Ott, Wm.		1st Neb.	24		1911	NE, 36th, 1912
Ottemiller, Frederick		K, 166th Penn. Inf.	354	80	1915 May 30	NE, 40th, 1916
Otterman, C.		C, 5th U.S. Cav. (cause of death: heart)	12	65	1891[1901?] Aug	NE, 26th, 1902
Ottman, Henry		F, 6th Kans. Cav.	127		1912 Feb 24	KS, 32nd, 1913
Otto, E.W.		21st Mo. Inf.	311		1908 Feb 29	KS, 28th, 1909
Otwell, C.W., Dr.		G, 40th Ohio	4		1914 Jan 10	KS, 34th, 1915
Ours, J.H.			440		1911 Jan 14	IA, 38th, 1912
Ouston, W.H.		C, 4th Ohio	83		1925 Jan 6	KS, 45th, 1926
Ovenstake, Peter		A, 60th Ohio	187		1927 Apr 17	NE, 51st, 1927
Overfilt, C.A.	Corp.	G, 6th Iowa Inf.	108		1928 Nov 18	IA, 55th, 1929
Overhocker, C.N.	Corp.	A, 10th N.Y. Art.	147		1904	IA, 31st, 1905
Overholser, Wm.	Pvt.	B, 72nd Ill. Inf.	22		1927 Mar 20	IA, 54th, 1928
Overman, John Q.			35		1911 Nov 29	NE, 36th, 1912
Overman, Joseph R.		D, 11th Ind. Inf.	14		1899 Mar 24	KS, 19th, 1900
Overman, O.F.		B, 103rd Ill.	238		1908 Jan 3	KS, 28th, 1909
Overman, T.W.	Pvt.	C, 29th Iowa Inf.	26		1909 Jan 18	IA, 36th, 1910
Overmire, S.B.	Pvt.	F, 28th Iowa Inf.	316		1931 May 15	IA, 58th, 1932
Overmire, S.B.	Pvt.	F, 28th Iowa Inf. (at large)			1931 May 15	IA, 58th, 1932
Overmyer, David		not a member of the G.A.R.; died suddenly at his home in Topeka; lawyer, statesman & patriot			1907 Jan 9	KS, 26th, 1907
Overoaker, Simeon	Pvt.	A, 32nd Iowa Inf.	133	68	1886 Dec 30	IA, 13th, 1887
Overshelp, Phillp	Pvt.	H, 4th Mo. Cav.	5	57	1898 Sep 11	IA, 25th, 1899
Overstreet, Jas.		I, 13th Ky.	25		1933 Apr	KS, 53rd, 1934
Overtiuf, C.S.	Pvt.	F, 19th Penn. Cav.	364		1912 May 10	IA, 39th, 1913
Overton, Allen S.		B, 3rd Iowa	1		1923 Jun 26	KS, 43rd, 1924
Overton, C.F.	Corp.	C, 15th Iowa Inf.	2		1933	IA, 60th, 1934
Overton, Charles G.		F, 44th N.Y.	71		1905 Jan 1	KS, 25th, 1906
Overton, F.	Pvt.	A, 58th Ill. Inf.	150		1910 Feb 20	IA, 37th, 1911
Overton, F.C.	Pvt.		2		1932	IA, 59th, 1933
Overton, S.C.		H & G, 2nd Penn. Hvy. Art.	302		1929 Dec	NE, 54th, 1930
Overton, S.C.		H & G, 2nd Penn. Hvy. Art.	302		1930 Jan 20	NE, 55th, 1931
Overturf, S.N.		G, 4th Wis. Cav.	113		1914 Sep 5	NE, 39th, 1915
Oviatt, E.L.	Sergt.	D, 5th Iowa Inf.	93		1907 Sep 15	IA, 34th, 1908
Ovington, Chas.	Pvt.	A, 6th Iowa Inf.	88		1907 Feb 25	IA, 34th, 1908
Owen, Alex W.	Pvt.	G, 156th Ill. Inf.	343		1926 Nov 29	IA, 53rd, 1927
Owen, E.E.	Pvt.	B, 7th Iowa Inf.	8		1915 Feb 14	IA, 42nd, 1916
Owen, E.M.	Pvt.	E, 10th Minn. Inf.	48	79	1897 Aug 30	IA, 24th, 1898
Owen, F.N.		F, 3rd Wis. Cav.	7		1928 Apr 16	NE, 53rd, 1929
Owen, Geo.	Pvt.	G, 75th Ind. Inf.	11		1906 Mar	IA, 33rd, 1907

*See Appendix A, B or C for roster of post names and locations.
†See Introduction for note regarding recording of death date.
413

Name	Rank	Company, Regiment or Ship	Post*	Age	Death Date†	Journal
Owen, Henry W.	Pvt.	F, 30th Ill. Inf.	400		1904 Jun 28	IA, 31st, 1905
Owen, J.J.		I, 37th Ind.	25		1922 Jan 7	NE, 47th, 1923
Owen, J.J.		I, 37th Ind.	25		1922 Jan 7	NE, 47th, 1923
Owen, Maroni			4		1904 Jul 9	NE, 29th, 1905
Owen, O.E.		I, 19th Kans.	12		1926 Mar 16	KS, 46th, 1927
Owen, T.J.		H, 9th Iowa Cav.	8		1888	KS, 8th, 1889
Owene, Robert	Pvt.	C, 105th Penn. Inf.	62		1923 Jul 4	IA, 50th, 1924
Owens, A.B.		K, 16th Ohio	459		1892 Aug 19	KS, 12th, 1893
Owens, D.B.		F, 16th Ill.	71		1927 Feb 26	KS, 47th, 1928
Owens, David C.		H, 6th Ind. Cav. (died at Neodesha; buried at Varner Cemetery)	145		1894 Jul 19	KS, 14th, 1895
Owens, E.		D, 125th Ind.	25		1926 Feb 27	NE, 51st, 1927
Owens, Elias	Corp.	A, 29th Iowa Inf.	38		1928 Dec 16	IA, 55th, 1929
Owens, Eric		U.S. Sharpshooters	12		1915 Jan 6	KS, 35th, 1916
Owens, Frederick	Pvt.	F, 45th Ill. Inf.	1		1919 Sep 6	IA, 46th, 1920
Owens, G.T.		119th Ill.	4		1924 Sep 15	KS, 44th, 1925
Owens, Geo. W.		C, 174th Ohio	118		1908 Nov 19	KS, 28th, 1909
Owens, Henry		C, 23rd Iowa	25		1897 Nov 25	KS, 17th, 1898
Owens, Henry D.	Pvt.	G, 15th Iowa Inf.	49		1917 Jan 22	IA, 44th, 1918
Owens, Isaac T.		E, 1st Kans. Inf. (died of cancer)	11	72	1911 May 5	NE, 36th, 1912
Owens, Isaac T.		G, 1st Mo. Inf.	354	73	1911 May 5	NE, 36th, 1912
Owens, J.B.			82		1883	KS, 3rd, 1884
Owens, J.H.		I, 7th Mo.	174		1923 Dec 13	KS, 43rd, 1924
Owens, J.L.	Pvt.	E, 107th Penn. Inf.	321		1905 Apr 8	IA, 32nd, 1906
Owens, James			3		1928	IA, 55th, 1929
Owens, John	Pvt.	G, 27th Ky. Inf.	56		1927 May 22	IA, 54th, 1928
Owens, John		B, 152nd Ind.	153		1906 Apr 25	KS, 26th, 1907
Owens, Joseph	Pvt.	A, 11th Penn. Inf.	62		1900 Oct 8	IA, 27th, 1901
Owens, L.H.			69		1925	IA, 52nd, 1926
Owens, Londorn	Pvt.	F, 45th Iowa Inf.	5		1915 May 21	IA, 42nd, 1916
Owens, P.		I, 53rd Mass. (died at National Military Home)	380		1888	KS, 8th, 1889
Owens, R.P.		B, 40th Ind. Inf.	243		1891 Apr 16	KS, 11th, 1892
Owens, Robert	Pvt.	I, 2nd Iowa Cav.	153		1929 Oct 3	IA, 56th, 1930
Owens, Robert		15th Kans. Inf.	225		1912 Dec 1	KS, 32nd, 1913
Owens, S.		C, 48th Ind.	64		1888	KS, 8th, 1889
Owens, Thomas W.	Pvt.	G, 8th Iowa Inf.	233		1915 Aug 28	IA, 42nd, 1916
Owens, Thos.	Pvt. Pvt.	A, 1st Neb. Inf. A, 1st Neb. Cav. (died of general debility)	45	56	1888 Dec 29	NE, 13th, 1889
Owens, W.P.		B, 2nd Mo. Cav.	7		1892 Jan 1	KS, 12th, 1893
Owens, W.W.	Pvt.	B, Ind.	107		1918	IA, 45th, 1919
Owens, Wm. P.			122		1925 May 28	IA, 52nd, 1926
Owings, Ephraim		A, 86th Ind.	32		1898 Mar 25	KS, 18th, 1899
Oxberger, Irwin	Pvt.	B, 112th Ill. Inf.	7		1905 Dec	IA, 32nd, 1906
Oxenrider, S.	Pvt.	G, 10th Iowa Inf.	309		1929 Mar	IA, 56th, 1930
Oxley, James	Sergt.	H, 24th Iowa Inf.	206	93	1932 Jan 19	IA, 59th, 1933
Oxley, Stewart	Pvt.	I, 51st Ohio Inf.	168		1915 Aug 4	IA, 42nd, 1916
Oxley, Thos.	Pvt.	G, 7th Mo. Cav.	305		1910 Oct 23	IA, 37th, 1911
Oxley, W.H.	Pvt.	C, 9th Iowa Inf.	168	60	1897 Jan 27	IA, 23rd, 1897
Oyle, B.F.		A, 8th Ohio	52		1906 Jan 3	KS, 26th, 1907
Oyler, Thomas		A, 3rd Mo. Cav.	25		1921 Dec 23	NE, 46th, 1922
Pace, Cad C.		H, 21st Mo. Inf. (died of dropsy)	214	62	1906 Mar 18	NE, 31st, 1907
Pace, J.W.	Pvt.	G, 3rd Cav.	49		1924 Jan 6	IA, 51st, 1925
Pace, James		C, 23rd Wis. Inf.	203		4th quarter 1883	IA, 10th, 1884
Pace, James		C, 23rd Wis. Inf.	203		2nd quarter 1884	IA, 11th, 1885
Pace, Robt.	Pvt.	E, 55th Penn. Inf.	49		1918 Jan 1	IA, 45th, 1919
Pace, W.H.	Pvt.	14th Iowa Inf.	110		1900-1901	IA, 27th, 1901
Pace, Wm.	Pvt.	L, 3rd Iowa Cav.	251		1916 Apr 20	IA, 43rd, 1917
Packard, A.C.		E, 2nd U.S. Sharpshooters	117		1902 Dec 6	KS, 22nd, 1903
Packard, Charles	Corp.	A, 32nd Iowa	307		1901 Sep 18	IA, 28th, 1902
Packard, George W.		A, 9th Kans.	1		1912 Oct 26	KS, 32nd, 1913
Paddock, A.E.	Pvt.	F, 20th Ill. Inf.	71		1910 Feb 19	IA, 37th, 1911

*See Appendix A, B or C for roster of post names and locations.
†See Introduction for note regarding recording of death date.

Name	Rank	Company, Regiment or Ship	Post*	Age	Death Date†	Journal
Paddock, A.J.	Pvt.	D, 96th —	124		1919 Jan 2	IA, 46th, 1920
Paddock, Charles		I, 95th Ill. Inf. K, 47th Ill. Inf.	198		1916 Oct 9	KS, 36th, 1917
Paddock, H.C.	Sergt.	C, 25th Ill. Inf. I, 76th Ill. Inf.	192		1926 Aug 13	IA, 53rd, 1927
Paddock, Joseph W.		K, 1st Neb. Inf. (died of pneumonia)	110	69	1895 Jan 20	NE, 20th, 1896
Paden, J.L.		I, 12th Ill. Inf. (died of pneumonia)	34		1903	NE, 28th, 1904
Padget, William H.		A, 3rd Ind. Cav.	88	95	1937 Jul 3	IA, 64th, 1938
Padgett, G.W.	Pvt.	B, 15th Ill. Vol. Inf. Cav. (died of rheumatism)	24	51	1891 Mar 14	NE, 16th, 1892
Padgett, L.D.		D, 45th Iowa	147		1925 Jan 12	KS, 45th, 1926
Padgett, W.H.		H, 8th Iowa	43		1918 Dec	KS, 39th, 1920
Padgett, Wm.		H, 8th Iowa	43		1918	KS, 38th, 1919
Pagan, J.	Pvt.	G, 2nd Iowa Inf.	100		1921 Jan 6	IA, 48th, 1922
Page, Alva	Pvt.	C, 32nd Iowa Inf.	68		1927 Jun 25	IA, 54th, 1928
Page, David D.		E, 6th N.H.	52		1919 Nov 30	KS, 39th, 1920
Page, Geo. W.		F, 8th Ill. Cav.	37		1920 Jan 9	KS, 40th, 1921
Page, H.R.	Pvt.	B, 46th Iowa Inf.	7	49	1891 Oct 30	IA, 18th, 1892
Page, I.E.		F, 44th Ohio Inf.	176		1916 Jun 1	KS, 36th, 1917
Page, John		H, 11th Ill. Inf.	49		3rd quarter 1884	IA, 11th, 1885
Page, Jos.	Pvt.	F, 101st Ill. Inf.	9		1911	IA, 38th, 1912
Page, L.K.	Pvt.	F, 16th Iowa Inf.	93		1910 Jan 6	IA, 36th, 1910
Page, W.P.		A, 4th Ohio (died at Netawaka)	135		1895 Mar 3	KS, 15th, 1896
Page, William			122		1925	IA, 52nd, 1926
Paige, G.W.	Sergt.	E, 29th Iowa Inf.	209		1913 Apr 30	IA, 40th, 1914
Paige, H.B.	Pvt.	K, 7th Cal. Inf.	124		1910 Jan 12	IA, 37th, 1911
Pain, Jordan	Pvt.		79		1899	IA, 26th, 1900
Paine, H.O.			171		1908 Jun	NE, 33rd, 1909
Paine, J.O.		G, 36th Iowa	32	82	1920 Jan 1	NE, 44th, 1920
Paine, Phelps		E, 9th Ill. Inf. (died at Omaha; buried in Wyuka Cemetery in Lincoln)	25	75	1919 May 3 or 4	NE, 44th, 1920
Painter, D.F.			177		1923	KS, 43rd, 1924
Painter, Daniel		E, 12th Ohio Inf.	4		1925 Sep 22	KS, 45th, 1926
Painter, Geo.		A, 11th Ind.	49		1896 Aug 10	KS, 16th, 1897
Painter, Geo. B.	Pvt.	C, 4th U.S. Cav.	168		1917 Aug 13	IA, 44th, 1918
Painter, Henry H.		I, 72nd Ill.	225		1913 Dec 24	KS, 33rd, 1914
Painter, J.		B, 1st Mich. Eng. (died of blood poison)	354	76	1904 Mar 28	NE, 29th, 1905
Painter, J.C.	Pvt.	D, 2nd Iowa Inf.	7		1917 Mar 7	IA, 44th, 1918
Painter, J.W.		D, 137th Ill.	1		1917 May 7	KS, 37th, 1918
Painter, John	Pvt.	E, 50th Penn. Mil. Inf.	7		1917 Jun 24	IA, 44th, 1918
Painter, Louis	Capt.		418		1900 Aug 11	IA, 27th, 1901
Painter, Robt. M.		K, 9th Iowa Inf. (of Meade)	388		1925 Mar 31	KS, 45th, 1926
Painter, W.B.		I, 8th Ind. B, 85th Ind.	12		1927 Jul 8	KS, 47th, 1928
Painton, Thomas		G, 39th Iowa Inf.	49		1890	KS, 10th, 1891
Painton, Thomas			49		1884	KS, 4th, 1885
Painton, Thomas		G, 39th Iowa Inf.	49		1884 Mar 2	KS, 12th, 1893
Paintor, Geo. B.		C, 4th U.S. Cav.	168		1918	IA, 45th, 1919
Paisley, Isaiah		C, 16th Iowa Inf. (died of dropsy)	102	65	1909 Mar 7	NE, 34th, 1910
Palen, J.E.			96		1916 Jun 14	IA, 43rd, 1917
Palen, Sidney	Pvt.	A, 12th N.Y. Cav.	94	89	1933 Oct 25	IA, 60th, 1934
Palm, A.		C, 3rd Kans. State Militia	12		1906 Nov 5	KS, 26th, 1907
Palmatier, Anson J.	Pvt.	B, 77th N.Y. Inf.	303		1899	NE, 24th, 1900
Palmer, A.R.		B, 86th Ohio Inf.	15		1891 Oct 12	KS, 11th, 1892
Palmer, A.S.		G, 86th Ohio	1		1922 Jan 23	KS, 42nd, 1923
Palmer, A.S.		U.S. Navy	284	87	1917 Aug 26	NE, 42nd, 1918
Palmer, Albert		3rd Iowa Bat. Art. (died of heart trouble)	130	62	1908 Nov 6	NE, 33rd, 1909
Palmer, Alfred H.		H, 146th N.Y. Inf.	110		1908 Feb 13	NE, 33rd, 1909
Palmer, Alpheus	Capt.	C, 16th Iowa Inf.	78	69	1893 Dec 26	IA, 20th, 1894
Palmer, Chris	Pvt.	K, 7th Iowa Cav.	101		1920 Nov 20	IA, 47th, 1921
Palmer, Clarkson	Pvt.	G, 42nd Wis.	101		1907 Feb 5	IA, 34th, 1908
Palmer, D.C.	Pvt.	D, 35th Wis. Inf.	124		1920 Sep	IA, 47th, 1921
Palmer, D.J.	Col.	25th Iowa Inf.	108		1928 Nov 19	IA, 55th, 1929

*See Appendix A, B or C for roster of post names and locations.
†See Introduction for note regarding recording of death date.

Name	Rank	Company, Regiment or Ship	Post*	Age	Death Date†	Journal
Palmer, David			47		1913 Jun 15	IA, 40th, 1914
Palmer, David L.		A, 6th Iowa Inf.	58		1925 Apr 17	KS, 45th, 1926
Palmer, E.D.		E, 2nd Mich. Cav.	35		1919 Jan 24	KS, 39th, 1920
Palmer, Geo.		E, 9th Penn. Cav.	171		1917	KS, 37th, 1918
Palmer, Geo. E.	Pvt.	A, 16th Ill. Inf.	42	47	1890 Mar 23	IA, 16th, 1890
Palmer, George			386		1912 Feb 12	KS, 32nd, 1913
Palmer, H.		D, 38th Iowa Inf. (died of old age)	80	76	1895 Apr 6	NE, 20th, 1896
Palmer, H.H.	Corp.	B, 2nd Ohio Vol. Cav.	57		1912 Jan 6	IA, 39th, 1913
Palmer, Henry E.		1st Kans. Battery (died of heart failure; see also Appendix D)	110	70	1911 Apr 2	NE, 36th, 1912
Palmer, J.B.			32		1911 Oct 1	KS, 31st, 1912
Palmer, J.C.		H, 9th Mo.	8		1935 Feb	KS, 56th, 1937
Palmer, J.C.		H, 9th Mo.	8		1937 Feb	KS, 57th, 1938
Palmer, J.C.		H, 9th Mo. Cav.	8		1935 Feb	KS, 55th, 1936
Palmer, J.D.	Pvt.	D, 50th N.Y.	49		1907 Apr 29	IA, 34th, 1908
Palmer, James F.	Pvt.	C, 14th Ohio Inf.	57		1913 Aug 13	IA, 40th, 1914
Palmer, John H.	Capt.	A, 156th N.Y. Inf.	11		1902	IA, 29th, 1903
Palmer, Jos. W.		E, 21st Ind. & 1st Hvy. Art.	250		1922 Dec 2	KS, 42nd, 1923
Palmer, R.S.	Pvt.	E, 12th Ill. Cav.	10		1920 Jul 14	IA, 47th, 1921
Palmer, Robert		I, 91st Ohio Inf.	356		1918 Feb 20	KS, 38th, 1919
Palmer, Samuel		14th Ill.	174		1893 Dec 18	KS, 13th, 1894
Palmer, Samuel		K, 126th Penn.	12		1921 Jul 30	KS, 41st, 1922
Palmer, Thomas		G, 34th Ill.	123		1896 Nov 23	KS, 16th, 1897
Palmer, W.A.		G, 33rd Ohio	158		1920 Apr 22	KS, 40th, 1921
Palmer, W.H.		F, 9th Ind. Inf. (died of disease of head)	94	71	1911 May 14	NE, 36th, 1912
Palmer, W.H.		E, 53rd Ill.	52	82	1922 May 31	NE, 47th, 1923
Palmer, Wm.	Pvt.	G, 2nd Iowa Cav.	329		1922 Oct 19	IA, 49th, 1923
Palmeter, John		E, 4th Mich.	12		1915 Jun 17	KS, 35th, 1916
Palsgrove, Andrew J.	Pvt.	A, 146th Ill. Inf.	88		1917	IA, 44th, 1918
Palsgrove, David L.	Corp.	D, 126th Penn. Inf.	88		1917 Jan 22	IA, 44th, 1918
Pamell, D.B.		C, 16th Wis.	42		1923 Jan 5	KS, 43rd, 1924
Pancoast, W.M.		E, 31st Ohio Inf.	176		1902 Dec 3	KS, 22nd, 1903
Pangburn, F.	Pvt.	L, 2nd Mo. Cav.	452		1925 May	IA, 52nd, 1926
Panley, Jacob	Pvt.	H, 8th Iowa Cav.	210	73	1888 Mar 30	IA, 15th, 1889
Panley, Jeremiah	Pvt.	I, 40th Iowa Inf.	40	67	1894 Jun 25	IA, 21st, 1895
Pannell, Wm.	Pvt.	F, 31st Wis. Inf.	365		1915 Apr 8	IA, 42nd, 1916
Pape, William		F, 94th Ill.	32		1927	KS, 47th, 1928
Parady, Alson		C, 2nd Wis.	129	77	1912 Mar 10	NE, 37th, 1913
Parady, Joseph	Pvt.	K, 16th N.Y. Cav.	29		1897 Feb 19	IA, 24th, 1898
Parcells, B.C.		A, 102nd Ind.	364		1888	KS, 8th, 1889
Parcells, John W.		B, 116th Ind. Inf.	12		1900 Aug 9	KS, 20th, 1901
Parcels, James		K, 155th Penn.	92		1917 Aug 16	KS, 37th, 1918
Parch, Geo. S.			111		1886	NE, 11th, 1887
Parcher, D.M.	Pvt.	D, 29th Iowa Inf.	466	59	1892 Nov 16	IA, 19th, 1893
Pardee, A.	Pvt.	D, 8th Ill. Cav.	42		1905 Jun 6	IA, 32nd, 1906
Pardee, E.L.	Pvt.	G, 22nd Iowa Inf.	197		1911 Apr 10	IA, 38th, 1912
Pardoe, Geo. W.	Pvt.	C, 12th Penn.	22		1915 Jan 14	IA, 42nd, 1916
Pardun, John J.		C, 17th Ill.	206		1889	KS, 9th, 1890
Pardy, Henry M., see Bardy, Henry M.						
Parell, Joseph		C, 27th Iowa	175		1922 Mar 18	KS, 42nd, 1923
Parent, Thomas H.		K, 31st Ind. Inf.	90		1912 Oct 3	KS, 32nd, 1913
Paris, John M.		I, 16th Ind. Inf.	294		1901 Mar	KS, 21st, 1902
Paris, W.L.		H, 79th Ohio Inf.	18		1899 Apr 11	KS, 19th, 1900
Parish, Ambros H.			52		1923 Mar 10	NE, 48th, 1924
Parish, Eber	Pvt.	H, 102nd Ill.	49		1905 Jul 24	IA, 32nd, 1906
Parish, G.R.		died of dropsy	94	68	1903 May 3	NE, 28th, 1904
Parish, I.F.		G, 17th Iowa	18		1927 Dec 31	KS, 47th, 1928
Parish, L.L.		E, 74th Ill. (died of decline)	1	83	1920 Mar 11	NE, 45th, 1921
Parish, N.	Pvt.	G, 24th N.Y. Inf.	284		1911 Oct 6	IA, 38th, 1912
Park, Ben S.	Pvt.	F, 16th Mich. Inf.	88		1910 Apr 16	IA, 37th, 1911
Park, Edward		14th Mo.	20		1922 Jul 20	KS, 42nd, 1923

*See Appendix A, B or C for roster of post names and locations.

†See Introduction for note regarding recording of death date.

Name	Rank	Company, Regiment or Ship	Post*	Age	Death Date†	Journal
Park, J.C.	Pvt.	B, 2nd Iowa Inf.	255		1921 May 6	IA, 48th, 1922
Park, James M.		H, 93rd Ill. Inf.	185		1912 Aug 18	KS, 32nd, 1913
Park, John W.		D, 13th Mo.	12		1900 Aug 19	KS, 20th, 1901
Park, Ruban	Seaman	U.S. Navy (died of inf. stomach)	51	63	1887 Oct 23	NE, 12th, 1888
Park, William A.	Pvt.	D, 17th West Va. Inf.	186		1915 Dec 8	IA, 42nd, 1916
Park, Wm.	Pvt.		235		1912 Oct 1	IA, 39th, 1913
Park, Wm.		H, 12th Ill. Cav. (died of old age)	140	83	1925 Jan 6	NE, 49th, 1925
Park, Wm. P.	Pvt.	D, 30th Iowa Inf.	192		1930 May 22	IA, 57th, 1931
Parke, John H.		A, 85th Penn. Inf. (died of heart failure)	55	74	1909 Mar 29	NE, 34th, 1910
Parke, Norman	Pvt.	D, 3rd Col. Inf.	132		1923 Nov 25	IA, 50th, 1924
Parker, A.			277		1911 2nd term	IA, 38th, 1912
Parker, A.J.	Pvt.	186th Penn. Inf.	324		1918 Aug 17	IA, 45th, 1919
Parker, Albert G.		A, 13th Ind. (died of old age)	44[24?]	82	1907 Jan 14	NE, 34th, 1910
Parker, B.	Pvt.	G, 27th Iowa Inf.	132		1911 Nov 30	IA, 38th, 1912
Parker, C.C.			261		1890	NE, 15th, 1891
Parker, C.G.		C, 86th Ill. Inf. (died of apoplexy)		65	1903 Dec 23	NE, 28th, 1904
Parker, C.M.		A, 46th Ind. Inf.	25	78	1919 Mar 10	NE, 44th, 1920
Parker, Charles	Pvt.	M, 5th N.Y. Hvy. Art.	97	53	1898 May 24	IA, 25th, 1899
Parker, Charrey		G, 61st N.Y.	59		1885	KS, 5th, 1886
Parker, D.H.	Pvt.	L, 9th Iowa Cav.	116		1926 Jul 8	IA, 53rd, 1927
Parker, David G.		A, 25th Ohio	129		1921 Jul 26	KS, 41st, 1922
Parker, Edward W., Dr.				93	1937 Dec 26	IA, 64th, 1938
Parker, Edwin E.	Pvt.	B, 21st Iowa Inf.	22		1899 Jul 18	IA, 26th, 1900
Parker, Francis M.		C, 11th Kans.	55		1923 Aug 14	KS, 43rd, 1924
Parker, Geo.		G, 45th Ill. Inf.	29		1921 Jul 26	IA, 48th, 1922
Parker, George			160		1884	KS, 4th, 1885
Parker, Gordon W.		F, 10th N.Y. Art.	176		1909 Apr 26	KS, 29th, 1910
Parker, H.B.	Capt.	A, 39th Ill. Inf.	97		1913 Jan 15	IA, 40th, 1914
Parker, H.S.	Pvt.	I, 142nd Ind. Inf.	456		1926 Jun	IA, 53rd, 1927
Parker, H.S.	Pvt.	I, 42nd Ind. Inf.	456		1927	IA, 54th, 1928
Parker, Hanes	Pvt.	D, 8th Iowa Inf.	44		1917 Mar	IA, 44th, 1918
Parker, Hobson	Pvt.	D, 40th Iowa Inf.	127	77	1887 Aug 3	IA, 14th, 1888
Parker, Hobson	Pvt.	B, 40th Iowa Inf.	127	73	1877 Aug 3	IA, 18th, 1892
Parker, J.H.		K, 44th N.Y. (not a member; buried by Farragut Post)	25		1922 Sep 19	NE, 47th, 1923
Parker, J.H.		K, 44th N.Y.	25		1922 Sep 19	NE, 47th, 1923
Parker, J.M.	Pvt.	B, 15th Iowa Inf.	12		1919 Oct 18	IA, 46th, 1920
Parker, J.M.			94		1919 Jun 5	IA, 46th, 1920
Parker, J.M.		C, 47th Kans. Inf. (died at Arkansas City)	49		1895 Dec	KS, 15th, 1896
Parker, J.W.		E, 118th Ill.	180		1912 Sep 25	KS, 32nd, 1913
Parker, James		F, 7th Ind. Cav.	37		1923 Jan 14	KS, 43rd, 1924
Parker, James G.	Pvt.	5th Ind. Cav.	349	60	1895 Dec 26	IA, 22nd, 1896
Parker, Joel	Pvt.	C, 15th Mo. Militia	271	64	1887 Jul 22	IA, 14th, 1888
Parker, John		13th Kans.	332		1902 Sep 19	KS, 22nd, 1903
Parker, John M.		G, 151st Ill.	185		1911 May 24	KS, 31st, 1912
Parker, L.F.	Lieut.	B, 46th Iowa Inf.	64		1911 Dec 11	IA, 38th, 1912
Parker, L.G.		A, 2nd Ill. Lt. Art.	198		1916 Jan 6	KS, 36th, 1917
Parker, L.S.	Pvt.	C, 26th Mass. Inf.	7		1929 Mar 2	IA, 56th, 1930
Parker, M.F.		1st Iowa Battery	464		1902 Oct 26	KS, 22nd, 1903
Parker, M.V.		E, 35th Mo.	117		1924 Jul 18	KS, 44th, 1925
Parker, Marion	Pvt.	E, 4th Mo. State Militia	10		1922 Dec 7	IA, 49th, 1923
Parker, N.C.		C, 3rd Minn.	252		1926 Apr 15	KS, 46th, 1927
Parker, P.	Corp.	H, 39th Iowa Inf.	43		1908 Feb 4	IA, 35th, 1909
Parker, Robt. S.		K, 20th Kans.	18		1930 May 17	KS, 50th, 1931
Parker, S.G.	Capt.	B, 5th Kans. Cav.	122		1905 Mar 23	IA, 31st, 1905
Parker, S.W.	Corp.	C, 52nd Ohio Inf.	297		1913 Mar 23	IA, 40th, 1914
Parker, Sam'l B.		G, 29th Mo. (died of kidney trouble)	47	69	1911 Aug 30	NE, 36th, 1912
Parker, Samuel		F, 13th U.S.C.T.	25		1923	NE, 48th, 1924
Parker, Silas	Pvt.	H, 5th Mo. Cav.	122		1923 Aug	IA, 50th, 1924
Parker, Silas	Pvt.	D, 6th Iowa Inf. (at large)	122	100	1940 Dec 31	IA, 67th, 1941
Parker, Stephen		I, 12th U.S. Col.	321		1925 Sep 14	KS, 45th, 1926
Parker, W.E.	Pvt.	H, 128th Ohio Inf.	236	95	1931 Mar 15	IA, 58th, 1932

*See Appendix A, B or C for roster of post names and locations.
†See Introduction for note regarding recording of death date.

Name	Rank	Company, Regiment or Ship	Post*	Age	Death Date†	Journal
Parker, W.E.			54		1931	IA, 58th, 1932
Parker, W.G.		K, 10th Iowa Inf.	108		1913	IA, 40th, 1914
Parker, W.H.	Pvt.	K, 1st Vt. Cav.	12	47	1888 Jul 1	IA, 15th, 1889
Parker, W.H.	Lieut.	B, 36th Wis. Inf.	277		1912	IA, 39th, 1913
Parker, W.M.	Pvt.	M, 16th Penn. Cav.	343	57	1897 Feb 26	IA, 24th, 1898
Parker, Wyman		H, 5th Iowa Cav.	100		1886	KS, 6th, 1887
Parkes, A.P.		F, 157th N.Y.	36		1906 Oct	KS, 26th, 1907
Parkhill, Sml.	Corp.	K, 100th Ind. Inf.	167		1927 Oct 17	IA, 54th, 1928
Parkhurst, B.F.		H, 37th Ill. (died of dropsy)	220	57	1897 Jun 6	NE, 22nd, 1898
Parkhurst, E.J.		B, 42nd Iowa	32		1931 May 17	KS, 52nd, 1933
Parkhurst, E.J.		B, 42nd Iowa	32		1931 May 17	KS, 51st, 1932
Parkhurst, F.H.		D, 40th Wis.	1		1927 Nov 3	KS, 47th, 1928
Parkhurst, Joel		D, 91st Ill. Inf.	354	79	1906 Jan 24	NE, 31st, 1907
Parkin, J.	Pvt.	C, 29th Penn. Inf.	491		1908 Nov 2	IA, 35th, 1909
Parkins, Stephen		K, 19th Iowa Inf.	19	88	1935 Oct 27	IA, 62nd, 1936
Parkins, Wm.	Pvt.	C, 1st Iowa Inf.	231	72	1893 Nov 18	IA, 20th, 1894
Parkinson, Henry	Lieut.	C, 17th West Va. Inf.	108		1926	IA, 53rd, 1927
Parkinson, Joseph		I, 103rd Ill. Inf.	25	76	1911 Apr 29	NE, 36th, 1912
Parks, A.			363		1903-1904	IA, 30th, 1904
Parks, Austin	Pvt.	E, 17th Iowa Inf.	452		1915 Dec 18	IA, 42nd, 1916
Parks, B.T.		G, 147th Penn. Inf.	25	74	1919 Dec 21	NE, 44th, 1920
Parks, Chas.	Pvt.	C, 38th Iowa Inf.	132		1908 Jun 11	IA, 35th, 1909
Parks, D.H.	Pvt.	C, 11th Penn. Inf.	222		1920 Jun 11	IA, 47th, 1921
Parks, D.M.			67		1922 Apr 26	IA, 49th, 1923
Parks, E.P.		B, 42nd Mass.	129		1914 Aug 24	KS, 34th, 1915
Parks, E.R.		E, 7th Wis. Inf.	10		1920 May 16	NE, 45th, 1921
Parks, E.W.		I, 2nd N.J.	129		1933 Nov 26	KS, 53rd, 1934
Parks, Elias	Sergt.	E, 36th Iowa Inf.	1		1911 1st term	IA, 38th, 1912
Parks, Geo. W.	Pvt.	D, 10th Mo. Inf.	325		1902 Mar 26	IA, 29th, 1903
Parks, George		E, 3rd Wis.	47		1910 Dec 15	KS, 30th, 1911
Parks, George S.		D, 26th Ill.	13		1935 May 26	NE, 60th, 1936
Parks, H.H.	Pvt.	C, 13th Wis. Inf.	104		1921 Dec 11	IA, 48th, 1922
Parks, J.G.			5		1896	KS, 16th, 1897
Parks, Jas. R.	Pvt.	5th Wis. Inf.	219		1925 Mar 7	IA, 52nd, 1926
Parks, John		C, 2nd Iowa Inf. (died of cancer)	52		1902 Sep	NE, 27th, 1903
Parks, R.N.		K, 8th Ky.	407		1908	KS, 28th, 1909
Parks, Robt. B.		140th Ill.	130		1928	NE, 52nd, 1928
Parks, S.A.		H, 163rd N.Y. Inf. (died of pneumonia)	40		1893 Apr 7	NE, 18th, 1894
Parks, Silas		G, 21st N.Y. Cav.	87		1934 Oct 9	KS, 55th, 1936
Parks, T.	Pvt.	K, 13th Mich. Inf.	201	72	1895 Jan 1	IA, 21st, 1895
Parks, Tim	Pvt.	K, 13th Mich. Inf.	201	75	1895 Jan 1	IA, 22nd, 1896
Parks, W.R.	Pvt.	D, 19th Wis.	101		1901 Sep 25	IA, 28th, 1902
Parks, William	Pvt.	A, 46th Wis. Inf.	81		1925 Aug 27	IA, 52nd, 1926
Parll, Charles		C, 3rd Iowa Cav.	12	88	1935 Oct 12	IA, 62nd, 1936
Parmenter, K.K.	Pvt.	G, 140th Ill.	10		1907 Nov 25	IA, 34th, 1908
Parmenter, Potter	Pvt.	H, 26th Iowa Inf.	136	69	1892 Jan 31	IA, 18th, 1892
Parmenter, Walter		B, 11th Kans.	46		1917 Sep 16	KS, 37th, 1918
Parmer, Clark		A, 105th Ill. Inf.	75	74	1891[1901?] Jul	NE, 26th, 1902
Parmeter, W.L.	Pvt.	A, 28th Iowa Inf.	98		1913 Jun 6	IA, 40th, 1914
Parmlee, E.A.		A, 23rd Ohio Inf.	7		1925 Jan 13	NE, 50th, 1926
Parmler, Geo.		E, 7th Conn.	232		1896 Nov 12	KS, 16th, 1897
Parmley, Silas	Pvt.	K, 46th Iowa Inf.	204		1911	IA, 38th, 1912
Parnell, E.		A, 7th Iowa Vol. Cav.	418		1921 Jul 20	KS, 41st, 1922
Parnell, Edward		A, 7th Iowa	35		1928 Dec 1	KS, 48th, 1929
Parnell, N.W.			14		1913	KS, 33rd, 1914
Parnell, W.G.		F, 6th West Va.	128		1900 Jan 6	KS, 19th, 1900
Parnila, J.B.	Pvt.	H, 51st Wis. Inf.	141		1926 Jun 20	IA, 53rd, 1927
Parr, E.T.		D, 17th Ind. Inf.	1		1900 Jul 16	KS, 20th, 1901
Parr, J.P.		K, 7th Ind. Cav.	59		1935 Mar 17	KS, 55th, 1936
Parr, James		H, 47th Ill. Inf.	116		1st quarter 1885	IA, 11th, 1885
Parr, Robert C.	Pvt.	K, 74th Ohio Inf.	116		1926 Mar 11	IA, 53rd, 1927
Parr, Wm.	Sergt.	F, 3rd Iowa Cav.	5	68	1892 Mar 25	IA, 19th, 1893

*See Appendix A, B or C for roster of post names and locations.
†See Introduction for note regarding recording of death date.

Name	Rank	Company, Regiment or Ship	Post*	Age	Death Date†	Journal
Parrett, Robt. T.	Pvt.	K, 43rd Mo. Inf.	68	86	1933 Aug 20	IA, 60th, 1934
Parriott, Marion	Pvt.	B, 71st Ill.	365		1907 Aug 8	IA, 34th, 1908
Parris, C.W.		I, 3rd Iowa Cav.	85		1886	KS, 6th, 1887
Parris, F.J.		G, 14th Vt. Inf.	32	61	1905 May 30	NE, 30th, 1906
Parrish, E.		B, 8th Wis. Inf.	29		1919 Sep 13	IA, 46th, 1920
Parrish, F.W.		6th Wis. Battery	11		1905 Feb 3	IA, 31st, 1905
Parrish, Isaac		A, 97th Ill. Inf.	47		1894 Oct 1	NE, 19th, 1895
Parrish, J.C.	Pvt.	D, 36th Iowa	12	60	1890 Sep 25	IA, 17th, 1891
Parrot, F.I.	Pvt.	H, 2nd Iowa Cav.	8		1905 Sep 22	IA, 32nd, 1906
Parrott, Fred		T, 153rd Ind. Inf.	203		1929 May 20	KS, 50th, 1931
Parrott, James C.	Capt.	E, 7th Iowa Inf. (see also Appendix D)	2	87	1898 Oct 17	IA, 25th, 1899
Parrott, Matthew		A, 42nd Ind.	25		1897 Feb 20	KS, 17th, 1898
Parrott, Thomas M.		C, 49th Iowa Inf.		92	1936 Feb 23	IA, 62nd, 1936
Parrott, Thos. M.	Pvt.	C, 44th Iowa Inf.	452	91	1935 Feb 22	IA, 65th, 1939
Parry, D.D.		F, 3rd Ohio Inf. (died at Arkansas City)	158		1895 Jan 4	KS, 15th, 1896
Parselo, Charles	Pvt.	H, 22nd Iowa Inf.	98	65	1899 Aug 31	IA, 26th, 1900
Parshel, J.K.		K, —	290		1918 Jan 21	IA, 45th, 1919
Parsons, A.W.	Corp.	A, 3rd Ill. Cav.	215		1901 Sep 2	IA, 28th, 1902
Parsons, Byron C.	Pvt.	F, 29th Wis. Inf.	193		1915 Sep 17	IA, 42nd, 1916
Parsons, Charles		E, 31st Iowa	244		1911 Dec 26	KS, 31st, 1912
Parsons, D.M.	Pvt.	A, 13th Iowa Inf.	11		1918 Jun 2	IA, 45th, 1919
Parsons, Daniel	Pvt.	H, 44th Ill. Inf.	68	61	1894 Jan 3	IA, 20th, 1894
Parsons, E.J.		C, 29th Wis.	76		1930	NE, 55th, 1931
Parsons, Geo. B.	Capt.	B, 4th Penn. Cav.	133		1899	NE, 24th, 1900
Parsons, George E.		D, 13th Kans. (died of heart disease)	339		1891 Oct 24	KS, 11th, 1892
Parsons, H.H.			96		1917 Mar 23	IA, 44th, 1918
Parsons, Henry H.		B, 118th Ill. (died of paralysis)	13	81	1921 Nov 22	NE, 46th, 1922
Parsons, Horace C.	Pvt.	C, 6th Mich. Inf.	165		1922	IA, 49th, 1923
Parsons, J.L.		K, 7th Ky.	85		1926 Jul 25	KS, 46th, 1927
Parsons, James D.		B, 78th Ill. Inf.	50		1900 Mar 15	KS, 20th, 1901
Parsons, John W.	Pvt.	B, 3rd Iowa Cav.	301	45	1893 Dec 14	IA, 20th, 1894
Parsons, Josiah	Pvt.	C, 14th Iowa Inf.	68		1904 Dec 29	IA, 31st, 1905
Parsons, Luke F.	Lieut.	F, 6th Kans. Cav. (of Salina; was the last Kansan associated with the noted John Brown; buried in Salina cemetery)		92	1926 Apr 23	KS, 45th, 1926
Parsons, M.	Pvt.		516		1918 Oct 14	IA, 45th, 1919
Parsons, M.	Pvt.	A, 5th Iowa	110		1924 Apr 16	IA, 51st, 1925
Parsons, Rufus D.	Pvt.	D, 44th Iowa Inf.	400	93 & 6 mos.	1932 May 24	IA, 59th, 1933
Parsons, S.		K, 36th Ill. Inf.	74	52	1895 Nov 7	NE, 20th, 1896
Parsons, S.F.		F, 6th Kans.	127		1926 Apr 23	KS, 46th, 1927
Parsons, Samuel	Pvt.	B, 3rd Iowa Cav.	268		1916 Jul 19	IA, 43rd, 1917
Parsons, Thomas T.	Pvt.	D, 1st Kans. Inf.	4	57	1893 Feb 5	IA, 19th, 1893
Parsons, W.H.	Pvt.	E, 10th Mich. Inf.	29		1904	IA, 31st, 1905
Parsons, Z.J.		G, 2nd Neb. Cav. (died of stomach trouble)	166		1893 Jul 21	NE, 18th, 1894
Partch, W.W.	Pvt.	A, 47th Ind. Inf.	452		1927 Aug 1	IA, 54th, 1928
Partridge, E.R.		E, 3rd Wis.	1		1919 Nov 8	KS, 39th, 1920
Partridge, James		D, 130th Ohio	175		1911 Jan 11	KS, 32nd, 1913
Partridge, W.E.	Pvt.	F, 36th Ill. Inf.	82		1910 Mar 16	IA, 37th, 1911
Partridge, Z.B.		F, 13th Ill. Inf.	11	72	1917 Nov 12	NE, 42nd, 1918
Paschke, Julius	Pvt.	A, 49th Wis. Inf.	132		1912 Aug 8	IA, 39th, 1913
Pasko, E.K.		B, 32nd Wis.	5		1923 Mar 8	KS, 43rd, 1924
Pasley, Albert			477		1923	KS, 43rd, 1924
Pasley, William		B, 21st Ill.	1		1924 May 8	KS, 44th, 1925
Passel, Daniel		H, 20th Penn.	71		1931 Dec 5	KS, 51st, 1932
Passel, Daniel		H, 20th Penn.	71		1931 Dec 5	KS, 52nd, 1933
Pastlow, N.H.		F, 182nd Ohio (died of stroke)	13	81	1924 Oct 25	NE, 49th, 1925
Pastus, Thomas		died of Bright's disease	47		1921 Oct 31	NE, 46th, 1922
Patch, Nelson		K, 4th Iowa Inf. (died at Palco, Kans.; buried at Palco Cemetery)	469		1894 Jun 16	KS, 14th, 1895
Pate, John W.		H, 2nd Ky. Inf.	244		1930 Jan 23	KS, 50th, 1931
Paterson, Jos. B.		H, 126th Ohio	153		1906 Sep 1	KS, 26th, 1907

*See Appendix A, B or C for roster of post names and locations.
†See Introduction for note regarding recording of death date.
419

Name	Rank	Company, Regiment or Ship	Post*	Age	Death Date†	Journal
Paterson, L.F.		L, 6th Kans.	3		1918 Nov 7	KS, 38th, 1919
Paterson, S.S.	Pvt.	F, 12th Ohio Inf.	16	63	1899 Feb 25	IA, 25th, 1899
Patnode, Israel		E, 53rd Ill. Inf.	38		1908 Nov 12	KS, 28th, 1909
Patrick, A.J.			58		1916 Sep 9	IA, 44th, 1918
Patrick, Albert H.		F, 29th Iowa Inf.	64		1925	KS, 45th, 1926
Patrick, H.	Pvt.	H, 87th Ohio Inf.	252		1897 Jan 24	IA, 23rd, 1897
Patrick, J.C.	Pvt.	K, 35th N.Y. Inf.	231	58	1893 Jul 2	IA, 20th, 1894
Patrick, J.M.	Pvt.	3rd Iowa	10		1921 Dec	IA, 48th, 1922
Patrick, James	Pvt.	H, 37th Ind. Inf.	67		1918 May 28	IA, 45th, 1919
Patrick, John	Pvt.	H, 121st Ohio Vol. Inf.	7		1901 Sep 15	IA, 28th, 1902
Patrick, P.F.	Pvt.	I, 22nd Wis. (died of dysentery)	66	38	1884 Oct 6	NE, 9th, 1885
Patrick, R.B.		D, 17th Ind.	28		1920 May 28	KS, 40th, 1921
Patrick, Robt. E.		E, 97th Ill. Inf.	110		1908 Dec 30	NE, 33rd, 1909
Patrick, S.L.		E, 34th Ill.	18		1923 Sep 20	KS, 43rd, 1924
Patrick, Sam			54		1917 Jun	KS, 37th, 1918
Patrick, Warren	Pvt.	H, 37th Iowa Inf.	67		1911 Aug 21	IA, 38th, 1912
Patrick, William			226		1923	KS, 43rd, 1924
Pattee, D.J.	Capt.	F, 47th Iowa Inf.	26		1912 Jul 19	IA, 39th, 1913
Pattee, J.F.	Corp.	F, 86th Ill. Inf.	357		1889 Aug 24	IA, 16th, 1890
Patten, John M.	Pvt.	F, 60th Ohio	271		1914 Nov 7	IA, 41st, 1915
Patten, L.J.		E, 136th Ill.	36		1913 Dec 25	KS, 33rd, 1914
Patten, L.K.		1st Maine Art.	417		1904 Sep 8	KS, 24th, 1905
Patten, Rubert		G, 35th Iowa	231		1924 Oct 6	IA, 51st, 1925
Patten, Samuel		A, 12th Ill. Cav. (died of old age)	50	70	1918 Apr 26	NE, 43rd, 1919
Patter, Geo. N.	Pvt.	G, 27th Iowa Inf.	132		1914 Feb 14	IA, 41st, 1915
Patterson, A.A.	Pvt.	F, 141st Ohio Inf.	306		1905 Dec 2	IA, 32nd, 1906
Patterson, A.H.	Pvt.	H, 20th Iowa Inf.	244		1929	IA, 56th, 1930
Patterson, Alma	Pvt.	B, 5th Iowa Cav.	202		1919 Dec 30	IA, 46th, 1920
Patterson, Andrew	Pvt.	A, 2nd Iowa Cav.	170		1905 Dec 26	IA, 32nd, 1906
Patterson, C.A.	Pvt.	M, 11th N.Y. Cav.	365		1907 May 16	IA, 34th, 1908
Patterson, Dan.		A, 184th Ill.	64		1928	KS, 48th, 1929
Patterson, David	Pvt.	G, 9th Iowa Cav.	2		1906 Jan 29	IA, 33rd, 1907
Patterson, Edwin	Pvt.	C, 52nd Ohio Inf.	206		1917 Apr 6	IA, 44th, 1918
Patterson, Enoch	Pvt.	I, 107th Ill.	68		1924 Apr 2	IA, 51st, 1925
Patterson, F.J.	Pvt.	F, 21st Iowa Inf.	7		1927 Feb 15	IA, 54th, 1928
Patterson, Frank	Pvt.	A, 105th Ill. Inf.	220		1906 Sep	IA, 33rd, 1907
Patterson, Franklin		D, 3rd Ohio Cav.	52		1924 Apr 19	KS, 44th, 1925
Patterson, G.D.		F, 54th Penn. Inf.	1		1916 Apr 29	KS, 36th, 1917
Patterson, G.W.	Pvt.	D, 60th N.Y. Col. Inf.	8		1924 Jun 20	IA, 51st, 1925
Patterson, G.W.		I, 3rd West Va. Inf.	4		1915 Jul 22	KS, 35th, 1916
Patterson, Geo. W.	Corp.	G, 2nd Iowa Cav.	56	53	1889 Oct 18	IA, 16th, 1890
Patterson, H.C.			12		1922 Mar 6	KS, 42nd, 1923
Patterson, H.E.	Pvt.	B, 28th Iowa Inf.	233		1909 Feb 24	IA, 36th, 1910
Patterson, Henry G.		F, 86th Ohio E, 182nd Ohio	484		1913 Nov 29	KS, 33rd, 1914
Patterson, Ira D.	Pvt.	K, 2nd Iowa Cav.	157		1907 Feb 25	IA, 34th, 1908
Patterson, J.A.		M, 4th Ill. Cav.	39		1918 Sep 17	IA, 45th, 1919
Patterson, J.B.	Pvt.	D, 32nd Iowa Inf.	67		1923 Oct 20	IA, 50th, 1924
Patterson, J.H.		H, 7th Ill. Inf.	158		1929 Aug 4	KS, 49th, 1930
Patterson, J.N.		41st Wis. Inf.	55		1911 Dec 16	IA, 38th, 1912
Patterson, J.S.	Pvt.	C, 132nd Ohio Inf.	118		1906 Dec 3	IA, 33rd, 1907
Patterson, J.W.	Pvt.	F, 176th Ohio Inf.	78		1913 Apr 30	IA, 40th, 1914
Patterson, Jas.			233		1924	IA, 51st, 1925
Patterson, John	Pvt.	I, 28th Iowa Inf.	450	70	1894 May 16	IA, 21st, 1895
Patterson, John	Pvt.	E, 92nd Ill. Inf.	386		1900 Sep 18	IA, 27th, 1901
Patterson, John		G, 12th Ill.	55		1896 Nov 3	KS, 16th, 1897
Patterson, John			123		1895	KS, 15th, 1896
Patterson, John		F, Ill. U.S. Eng. (died of old age)	169	87	1914 Apr	NE, 39th, 1915
Patterson, John		F, 31st Wis. (died of old age)	23	81	1925 Oct 6	NE, 50th, 1926
Patterson, Joseph B., see Paterson, Jos. B.						

*See Appendix A, B or C for roster of post names and locations.
†See Introduction for note regarding recording of death date.

Name	Rank	Company, Regiment or Ship	Post*	Age	Death Date†	Journal
Patterson, L.F., see Patterson, L.F.						
Patterson, L.H.		F, 6th Kans. Cav.	100		1918 Feb 3	KS, 38th, 1919
Patterson, Lewis	Pvt.	E, 86th Ind. Inf.	56		1906 Sep 10	IA, 33rd, 1907
Patterson, M.		E, 19th U.S.C.T.	378		1912 Mar 22	KS, 32nd, 1913
Patterson, M.F.	Pvt.	B, 67th Ill. Inf.	107		1930 Aug 3	IA, 57th, 1931
Patterson, Martin A.		F, 1st Col. Cav. (killed on S.F.R.R.)	64		1892 Jan 8[?]	KS, 12th, 1893
Patterson, Milton	Pvt.	F, 23rd Iowa Inf.	271		1926 Jan 8	IA, 53rd, 1927
Patterson, R.E.		F, 57th Ill.	55		1928 Feb 9	KS, 48th, 1929
Patterson, S.S.	Capt.	staff officer	16		1899 Feb 4	IA, 26th, 1900
Patterson, S.S., see Patterson, S.S.						
Patterson, Samuel		B, 10th Ind. Inf.	35		1918 Jul 23	KS, 38th, 1919
Patterson, Stephen		A, 49th U.S.C.	321		1927	KS, 47th, 1928
Patterson, T.C.		E, 19th Ill.	69		1929 Nov 21	NE, 54th, 1930
Patterson, W.E.	Pvt.	E, 3rd Iowa Cav.	107	53	1897 Jan 31	IA, 24th, 1898
Patterson, W.H.		C, 7th Ind. Cav.	1		1922 Mar 5	KS, 42nd, 1923
Patterson, W.I.		130th Ind.	1		1911 Aug 13	KS, 31st, 1912
Patterson, W.M.		F, 12th N.Y. Inf.	1		1893 Jun	NE, 18th, 1894
Patterson, Wm.	Pvt.	I, 68th Ohio Inf.	175	53	1888 Nov 26	IA, 15th, 1889
Patterson, Wm.	Pvt.	B, 39th Iowa Inf.	26		1922 Sep 29	IA, 49th, 1923
Patterson, Wm.		K, 138th Ill.	71		1928 Oct 3	KS, 48th, 1929
Patterson, Wm.		K, 32nd N.Y. Inf. (died of jaundice)	68	71	1905 Nov 10	NE, 30th, 1906
Patteson, J.W.	Corp.	G, 20th Iowa Inf.	423		1896 Nov 7	IA, 24th, 1898
Pattison, F.L.		B, 117th Ind.	68		1911 May 30	KS, 31st, 1912
Pattison, J.D.		D, 206th Penn. Inf.	250		1912 Jul 1	KS, 32nd, 1913
Patton, A.J.		G, 6th M.S. Cav.	100		1913 Nov 18	KS, 33rd, 1914
Patton, George		I, 86th Ind.	1		1919 Apr 13	KS, 39th, 1920
Patton, J.D.		F, 116th Ill.	65		1910 Oct 18	KS, 30th, 1911
Patton, J.S.		2nd Iowa Inf. (died of old age)	25	77	1903 Mar 30	NE, 28th, 1904
Patton, James R.		I, 9th Ill. Cav.	500		1913 Oct 13	IA, 40th, 1914
Patton, John	Pvt.	M, 6th N.Y. Hvy. Art.	124		1909 Sep 5	IA, 36th, 1910
Patton, John S.		6th West Va.	17		1919 Dec 29	KS, 39th, 1920
Patton, R.D.	Pvt.	F, 26th N.Y. Inf.	42		1915 May 27	IA, 42nd, 1916
Patton, Richard L.		F, 60th Ohio	12		1930 Jun 14	KS, 50th, 1931
Patton, Robert M.		F, 139th Ill.	130		1912 Dec 20	KS, 32nd, 1913
Patton, T.B.		A, 88th Ohio H, 174th Ohio	1		1919 Aug 19	KS, 39th, 1920
Patton, W.H.	Sergt.	C, 33rd Iowa Inf.	40		1925 Jun 15	IA, 52nd, 1926
Patton, W.H.		H, 4th Ohio	322		1921 Nov 10	KS, 41st, 1922
Patton, Wm. G.		C, 1st Mo. Inf.	464		1899 Jan 15	KS, 19th, 1900
Patty, Amos D.		I, —	262		1919 Nov 25	NE, 44th, 1920
Paugborn, Chas.	Pvt.	M, 4th Iowa Cav.	20		1922 Oct 7	IA, 49th, 1923
Paul, C.A.		M, 3rd Ill. Cav.	20		1911 Aug 7	KS, 31st, 1912
Paul, C.H.		A, 7th N.H.	13		1930 Feb 1	NE, 55th, 1931
Paul, Edward	Pvt.	E, 39th Ill. Inf.	512		1919 Dec 29	IA, 46th, 1920
Paul, F.	Pvt.	E, 20th Wis. Inf.	132	61	1896 Jan 23	IA, 22nd, 1896
Paul, G.N.			173		1915	IA, 42nd, 1916
Paul, H.F.	Pvt.	K, 24th Iowa Inf.	130	90	1932 Aug 10	IA, 59th, 1933
Paul, Henry	Pvt.	K, 21st Iowa Inf. (died of heart disease)	42	58	1887 Feb 24	NE, 12th, 1888
Paul, J.W.	Pvt.	B, 91st Ill. Inf.	10		1918 Jan 8	IA, 45th, 1919
Paul, J.W.		I & B, 14th Kans. State Militia	271		1914 Mar 9	KS, 34th, 1915
Paul, Jacob	Pvt.	K, 7th Iowa Inf.	324		1920 Mar 30	IA, 47th, 1921
Paul, John Fred		B, 13th Kans. (killed by cars)	283		1891 Dec 2	KS, 11th, 1892
Paul, John K.		B, 58th Mass.	303		1902 Mar 29	KS, 22nd, 1903
Paul, L.J.	Pvt.	I, 30th Wis.	38		1906 Apr 5	IA, 33rd, 1907
Paul, Lewis	Pvt.	C, 12th Wis.	223		1922 Sep 11	IA, 49th, 1923
Paul, Sylvester		K, 49th Wis. Inf.	18		1908 Apr 3	KS, 28th, 1909
Paul, W.		F, 11th Kans.	180		1916 Oct 14	KS, 36th, 1917
Paul, West	Pvt.	H, 11th Kans. Cav.	7	84	1931 Apr 1	IA, 58th, 1932
Paul, Wm.		13th Kans. Inf.	328		1889	KS, 9th, 1890
Pauline, Enos T.	Pvt.	F, 38th Ill. Inf.	337		1902 Oct 30	IA, 29th, 1903

*See Appendix A, B or C for roster of post names and locations.
†See Introduction for note regarding recording of death date.

421

Name	Rank	Company, Regiment or Ship	Post*	Age	Death Date†	Journal
Paulis, John		B, 22nd Iowa Inf.	8		2nd quarter 1884	IA, 11th, 1885
Paull, Robert		F, 88th Ill.	4		1930 May 11	KS, 50th, 1931
Paulson, C.F.	Adjt.		321		1918 Aug 2	IA, 45th, 1919
Paulson, John	Chaplain	8th Kans.	32		1893 Jun	KS, 13th, 1894
Paulus, Valentine		C, 34th Wis. E, 45th Wis. (died of old age)	60	82	1915 Apr 30	NE, 39th, 1915
Paulus, Valentine		C, 34th Wis. Inf. E, 45th Wis. Inf. (died of heart failure due to age)	60	82	1915 Apr 30	NE, 40th, 1916
Paup, D.A.		I, 12th Iowa Inf.	284		1918 Jan 25	IA, 45th, 1919
Pawalka, Jos.	Pvt.	I, 26th Iowa Inf.	130		1919 Aug 6	IA, 46th, 1920
Paxson, W.F.	Pvt.	B, 29th Ind. Inf.	188		1916 Apr 22	IA, 43rd, 1917
Paxton, J.N.	Pvt.	F, 10th Iowa Inf.	67		1921 Sep 5	IA, 48th, 1922
Paxton, James		Indiana Battery	105		1898 Aug	KS, 18th, 1899
Payden, D.W.	Pvt.	139th Ill. Inf.	440		1919 Apr 18	IA, 46th, 1920
Paye, S.A.	Pvt.	G, 10th Vt. Inf.	187		1910 Nov 24	IA, 37th, 1911
Paymal, Isdore P.	Pvt.	L, 11th Ill. Cav.	283		1915 Apr 28	IA, 42nd, 1916
Payn, Thomas	Pvt.	D, 32nd Iowa Inf.	329		1905 Sep 17	IA, 32nd, 1906
Payne, A.C.			170		1927 Jun 2	IA, 54th, 1928
Payne, Alexander		B, 4th U.S.C.I.	321		1930 Apr 3	KS, 50th, 1931
Payne, Colson	Pvt.	H, 118th Ill. Inf.	275	64	1889 Oct 23	IA, 16th, 1890
Payne, D.L.			25		1884	KS, 4th, 1885
Payne, David	Pvt.	G, 125th U.S. Colored	1	6?	1898 Nov 26	IA, 25th, 1899
Payne, Ferguson		H, 87th Ind.	265		1910 Nov 8	KS, 30th, 1911
Payne, G.W.		K, 153rd Ill.	116		1921 Mar 6	KS, 41st, 1922
Payne, Henry J.		C, 139th Ill.	209		1904 Aug 3	KS, 24th, 1905
Payne, J.H.			7		1900-1901	IA, 27th, 1901
Payne, J.S.	Pvt.	K, 87th —	290		1924 Apr 17	IA, 51st, 1925
Payne, James M.		G, 2nd & 6th Ill. Cav.	32		1923 Jul 19	KS, 43rd, 1924
Payne, John E.		21st Ill.	339		1911 May 21	KS, 31st, 1912
Payne, P.J.	Surg.	10th Mo. Inf.	2		1905 Aug 24	IA, 32nd, 1906
Payne, R.A.	Capt.	Penn. Cav.	404		1922 May 31	IA, 49th, 1923
Payne, Thomas	Pvt.	D, 32nd Iowa	67		1905 Sep 17	IA, 32nd, 1906
Payne, Thomas		A, 12th Kans.	463		1914 Oct 10	KS, 34th, 1915
Payne, Wm.	Pvt.	E, 5th Iowa Inf.	493		1926 Aug 25	IA, 53rd, 1927
Payne, Wm. T.			176		3rd quarter 1883	IA, 10th, 1884
Payton, J.L.	Pvt.	K, 7th Ill. Cav.	10		1927	IA, 54th, 1928
Payton, J.W.	Pvt.	D, 112th Ill. Inf.	11		1911 Mar 5	IA, 38th, 1912
Payton, Jno. M.	Pvt.	K, 6th Iowa Inf.	181		1927 Oct 8	IA, 54th, 1928
Payton, John	Pvt.	K, 7th Ill. Cav.	10		1926 Jun 3	IA, 53rd, 1927
Payton, W.F.	Sergt.	G, 140th Ill. Inf.	10		1927 Sep	IA, 54th, 1928
Pazon, D.C.			10		1922 Sep 9	KS, 42nd, 1923
Peabody, J.H.	Asst. Surg.		7	72	1906 Sep 9	NE, 31st, 1907
Peabody, T., see Peobody, T.						
Peach, I.L.		V, 138th Ill.	106		1892 Dec 22	KS, 12th, 1893
Peach, M.W.			55		1920	IA, 47th, 1921
Peachin, Adolpheus		G, 38th Ohio	64		1885	KS, 5th, 1886
Peacock, Gordon		133rd Ill.	122		1922 Sep	IA, 49th, 1923
Peacock, H.L.	Lieut.	G, 9th Iowa Inf.	1		1921 Dec	IA, 48th, 1922
Peacock, Samuel D.		C, 18th Iowa	258		1922	KS, 43rd, 1924
Peacock, T.		I, 77th N.Y. Inf.	229		1892 Oct 18	NE, 17th, 1893
Peak, J.W.		D, 65th Ohio	81		1919 Feb 24	KS, 39th, 1920
Peake, George W.		K, 132nd Ill. Inf. (not a member but living in Nebraska; location: Blair)			1938 Jul 13	NE, 63rd, 1939
Peaker, Charles	Pvt.	G, 63rd Ohio	219		1901 Oct 1	IA, 28th, 1902
Pealer, B.F.			127		1922 Jul 24	KS, 42nd, 1923
Peaper, Charles		U.S. Navy	6		1897 Oct 11	KS, 17th, 1898
Pearce, Azel		M, 1st Neb.	37		1927 Dec 29	KS, 47th, 1928
Pearce, Daniel		E, 29th Ill. Inf. (died at Girard)	49		1895 Oct	KS, 15th, 1896
Pearce, J.T.	Lieut.	B, 23rd Mo. State Militia	257		1915 Jul 15	KS, 35th, 1916
Pearce, J.W.	Lieut.	D, 21st Ill. Inf.	66		1914 Sep 29	IA, 41st, 1915
Pearce, Joseph M.		H, 6th Ind. Inf.	339		1916 Sep 17	KS, 36th, 1917

*See Appendix A, B or C for roster of post names and locations.
†See Introduction for note regarding recording of death date.
422

Name	Rank	Company, Regiment or Ship	Post*	Age	Death Date†	Journal
Pearce, Joshua C.	Corp.	H, 9th Iowa Cav.	440	98	1845[?] Aug 25	IA, 70th, 1944
Pearce, Leonard S.		B, 12th Kans.	12		1930 Jun 8	KS, 50th, 1931
Pearman, Nathan		B, 1st Mo.	283		1885	KS, 5th, 1886
Pears, Daniel		E, 101st Penn.	71		1889	KS, 9th, 1890
Pears, Jno. S.		A, 20th Ohio	336		1904 Nov 27	KS, 24th, 1905
Pearse, H.N.			66		1884	KS, 4th, 1885
Pearson, Albert		K, 1st Ark. Cav. (died of pneumonia)	95	73	1908 Dec 31	NE, 33rd, 1909
Pearson, B.F.			79		4th quarter 1883	IA, 10th, 1884
Pearson, Ira A.		I, 33rd Iowa Inf. (died of paralysis)	77	57	1901 Nov	NE, 26th, 1902
Pearson, J.R.		H, 2nd Kans. Cav.	293		1922 Jan 22	KS, 42nd, 1923
Pearson, James		E, 8th N.Y. Art. (died of general disability)	116		1894 May 16	NE, 19th, 1895
Pearson, Jas. B.	Pvt.	F, 4th Iowa Cav.	40		1916 May 12	IA, 43rd, 1917
Pearson, Leonard		G, 132nd Ill.	72		1926 Dec 28	KS, 46th, 1927
Pearson, Phinneas A.	Pvt.	G, 36th Iowa Inf.	79	55	1894 May	IA, 21st, 1895
Pearson, R.N.		F, 1st Kans.	96		1893 Feb 9	KS, 13th, 1894
Pearson, Silas	Pvt.	F, 3rd Iowa Cav.	19		1926 Mar 19	IA, 53rd, 1927
Pearson, T.J.		H, 19th Iowa Inf.	5		1929 Feb 10	KS, 49th, 1930
Pearson, William		F, 70th N.Y.	17		1915 Sep 12	KS, 35th, 1916
Pease, A.T.		G, 61st Ill. Inf. (died of stomach disease)	[153?]	71	1902 Sep	NE, 27th, 1903
Pease, E.N.	Pvt.	E, 29th Iowa Inf.	56	69	1898 Mar 7	IA, 24th, 1898
Pease, Edward		A, 124th Ill.	12		1898 Jul 26	KS, 18th, 1899
Pease, G.A.	Pvt.	K, 83rd Ill. Inf.	7		1919 Oct 28	IA, 46th, 1920
Pease, G.L.		F, 28th Conn.	35	79	1923 Feb 22	NE, 48th, 1924
Pease, Geo. W.	Pvt.	I, 16th Wis.	81		1926 Jul 19	IA, 53rd, 1927
Pease, Hugh A.		D, 40th Iowa Inf.	253	96	1938 Sep 16	IA, 64th, 1938
Pease, J.W.			209		1st quarter 1885	IA, 11th, 1885
Pease, Martin		F, 1st Mich. Cav.	395		1916 May 2	KS, 36th, 1917
Pease, Reuben			69		1892	NE, 17th, 1893
Pease, Sherman	Pvt.	E, 105th Ohio Inf.	231		1913 Sep 14	IA, 40th, 1914
Peaslee, J.J.		F, 8th Ill. Cav. N.Y.	4		1896 May 12	KS, 16th, 1897
Peasley, John J.		C, 7th Ohio Vol. Inf.	32		1915 Jul 30	KS, 35th, 1916
Peasley, R.L.	Fifer	I, 23rd Iowa	139		1904 Mar 12	IA, 30th, 1904
Peavey, Benj. S.		K, 5th Wis. Bat.	145		1913 Dec 12	KS, 33rd, 1914
Peck, Allen	Pvt.	A, 178th Ohio	211		1915 Jan 10	IA, 41st, 1915
Peck, Amos		H, 2nd Kans. Cav. (died of pneumonia)	38	73	1909 Feb	NE, 34th, 1910
Peck, Charles			72		1884	KS, 4th, 1885
Peck, Charles F.	Pvt.	B, 128th Ohio Vol. Inf.	1		1915 Mar 24	KS, 35th, 1916
Peck, Clark	Pvt.	C, 49th Wis. Inf.	165		1927 Dec 13	IA, 54th, 1928
Peck, Duane		E, 186th N.Y.	259		1913 Jul 17	KS, 33rd, 1914
Peck, E.J.		H, 4th Wis.	32		1898 Feb 25	KS, 18th, 1899
Peck, G.C.		G, 1st Ohio Lt. Art.	214		1898 Jun 4	KS, 18th, 1899
Peck, George R.		K, 31st Wis. Inf.	1		1931 Nov 13	KS, 51st, 1932
Peck, Henry W.	Col.	2nd Wis. Inf.	410	64	1895 Jun 6	IA, 22nd, 1896
Peck, Ira O.		E, 55th & 166th Ohio	32		1921 Apr 16	KS, 41st, 1922
Peck, John	Pvt.	B, 34th Iowa Inf.	302		1909 Apr 3	IA, 36th, 1910
Peck, N.C.	Pvt.	D, 4th N.Y. Inf.	63		1912 Nov 18	IA, 39th, 1913
Peck, N.C.	Pvt.	D, 4th N.Y. Inf.	63		1913 Nov 18	IA, 41st, 1915
Peck, Richard		B, 146th Ill.	336		1906 Jul 5	KS, 26th, 1907
Peck, S.E.	Pvt.	C, 14th Iowa	117		1923 Jun 11	IA, 50th, 1924
Peck, Sam'l E.	Pvt.	G, 4th Iowa Cav.	236		1911 Jun 13	IA, 38th, 1912
Peck, Sheldon		I, 6th Iowa Cav.	52		1932 Feb 23	NE, 57th, 1933
Peck, W.G.			1		1st quarter 1884	IA, 10th, 1884
Peck, Wm.	Capt.	H, 10th N.Y. Cav.	199		1885	KS, 5th, 1886
Peck, Wm. H.	Sergt.	F, 31st Iowa Cav.	130	68	1896 Mar 28	IA, 22nd, 1896
Peck, Wm. S.	Sergt.	E, 5th Iowa Inf.	231		1909 May 11	IA, 36th, 1910
Peckham, W.R.	Pvt.	A, 166th Ohio Inf.	286	52	1884 May 16	IA, 15th, 1889
Peckham, Wm. R.		A, 166th Ohio Inf.	286		2nd quarter 1884	IA, 11th, 1885
Peckover, A.B.		F, 10th Iowa	25		1928 Dec 11	KS, 48th, 1929
Peden, J.H.		F, 21st Ky. Inf.	147		1914 Oct 17	KS, 34th, 1915
Peden, Jas.			72		1912 Jul 10	IA, 39th, 1913
Peder, Christon		F, 18th Iowa	51		1923 Feb 12	KS, 43rd, 1924
Peebles, J.M.	Pvt.	I, 46th Wis. Inf.	101	56	1893 Oct 24	IA, 20th, 1894

*See Appendix A, B or C for roster of post names and locations.
†See Introduction for note regarding recording of death date.

Name	Rank	Company, Regiment or Ship	Post*	Age	Death Date†	Journal
Peek, F.M.		B, 63rd Ind. Inf.	158		1912 Aug 16	KS, 32nd, 1913
Peek, S.E.	2nd Lieut.	1st Mo.	24		1905	IA, 32nd, 1906
Peek, S.E.	Pvt.	L, 1st Iowa Cav.	94	89	1931 Jun 29	IA, 58th, 1932
Peel, H.		I, 7th Ill.	111		1922	KS, 42nd, 1923
Peer, Henry C.	Pvt.	I, 10th Iowa Inf.	36		1909	IA, 36th, 1910
Peery, James		H, 38th Ill.	72		1919 May 26	KS, 39th, 1920
Peffer, Jacob J.		E, 111th Penn. Inf.	32		1917 Jan 14	KS, 37th, 1918
Peffer, William A.		83rd Ill. Inf.	1		1912 Oct 7	KS, 32nd, 1913
Pegg, G.D.		I, 8th Iowa Cav.	94		1921 May 18	IA, 48th, 1922
Pegs, J.S.		I, 104th Ohio Inf.	184		1901 Nov 13	KS, 21st, 1902
Peick, Adolph	Corp.	G, 16th Iowa Inf.	120	66	1893 Apr 8	IA, 20th, 1894
Peiper, Jonathan		I, 9th Penn. Cav.	244		1916 Jul 13	KS, 36th, 1917
Peirce, H.E.	Pvt.	B, 141st Penn. Vols.	242		1903 Aug 21	IA, 30th, 1904
Peison, B.	Pvt.	D, 26th Wis. Inf.	154		1915 Feb 2	IA, 42nd, 1916
Pelen, Chas.		H, 13th Ill. Inf. (died of apoplexy)	81	69	1896 Sep 1	NE, 21st, 1897
Pelet, James L.		B, 3rd Iowa Inf. (died of apoplexy)	274	73	1913 May 11	NE, 37th, 1913
Pelham, A.	Pvt.	F, 4th Iowa Cav.	452		1920 Oct 24	IA, 47th, 1921
Pelham, L.G.		D, 11th Ind.	158		1927 May 16	KS, 47th, 1928
Pellitt, Wm.		H, 12th Kans.	68		1922 Dec 3	KS, 42nd, 1923
Pelson, Isaiah	Sergt.	H, 10th Ill. Cav.	52		1918 Jan 1	KS, 38th, 1919
Pelsue, J.W.		F, 9th Mo. Cav.	231		1890	KS, 10th, 1891
Peltier, Louis E.		G, 45th Mo. Inf.	78	91	1936 Nov 7	IA, 63rd, 1937
Pelton, A.J.	Pvt.	B, 155th Ind. Inf.	88		1920 Jun 23	IA, 47th, 1921
Pelton, D.R., Dr.		K, 27th Iowa Inf.	1		1896 Nov 4	KS, 16th, 1897
Pelton, Oshea	Pvt.	K, 40th Iowa Inf.	267	69	1899 Feb 7	IA, 25th, 1899
Pelton, Watson		D, 105th Ohio Inf.	25		1912	IA, 39th, 1913
Pember, D.E.		K, 64th N.Y. Inf.	85		1912 Dec 28	KS, 32nd, 1913
Pemberton, Moses		A, 173rd Ohio Vol. Inf.	8		1908 Jun 17	KS, 28th, 1909
Pembleton, M.L.		A, 104th Penn. (died of rupture)	32	69	1915 May 20	NE, 40th, 1916
Pembrook, Charles		E, 104th Ill.	60		1930 Aug 11	NE, 55th, 1931
Pence, D.N.		D, 62nd Ill. Inf.	123		1891 Dec 31	KS, 11th, 1892
Pence, John	Pvt.	B, 3rd Ill. Cav.	115		1909 Jan 2	IA, 35th, 1909
Pence, O.P.	Pvt.	C, 11th Ind. Inf.	12		1897 Jan 27	IA, 23rd, 1897
Pence, Peter			221		1909 Feb 3	KS, 29th, 1910
Pendarvis, Geo. F.		D, 138th Ill.	81		1920 Apr 10	KS, 40th, 1921
Pendarvis, Jas. C.		B, 91st Ill.	147		1930 Jan 29	NE, 55th, 1931
Pendel, G.M.	Pvt.	D, 75th N.Y. Inf.	22		1927 Apr 15	IA, 54th, 1928
Pendergast, James		GBN[gunboat, Navy?]	193	67	1904 Jan 22	NE, 29th, 1905
Pendergast, John	Pvt.	B, 6th Kans. Cav.	186	65	1899 Mar 15	IA, 25th, 1899
Pendergrast, C.P.		C, 16th Ind. Inf.	63		1912 Oct 7	KS, 32nd, 1913
Penderson, Wm.			482		1898 Nov 2	KS, 18th, 1899
Pendigras, James	Pvt.	C, 50th N.Y. Inf.	123	65	1893 Nov 7	IA, 20th, 1894
Pendlebury, Isaac		C, 2nd Conn. Inf.	383		1886	KS, 6th, 1887
Pendleton, John	Pvt.	G, 3rd Wis. Cav.	461		1920 Dec 27	IA, 47th, 1921
Pendleton, S.E., Rev.		E, 7th Ill.	40		1904 Jul 12	KS, 24th, 1905
Pendray, John	Pvt.	G, 14th Iowa	123		1905 Jun 30	IA, 32nd, 1906
Pendry, R.T.	Pvt.	B, 34th Iowa Inf.	169	50	1899 Dec 7	IA, 26th, 1900
Penfield, C.G.	Pvt.	E, 4th Iowa Cav.	64		1921 May 7	IA, 48th, 1922
Penhollow, Henry	Pvt.	H, Penn. Bucktail Rifles	46	59	1899 Oct 21	IA, 26th, 1900
Penn, J.B.	Pvt.	H, 45th Ill. Inf.	95		1901 Jun 27	IA, 28th, 1902
Penn, Stacy		E, 9th Kans. Cav. (died at Neodesha; buried at Shelly Cemetery)	145		1894 Mar 5	KS, 14th, 1895
Penn, W.H.	1st Lieut.	E, 13th Iowa Vols.	12		1906 Jan 12	IA, 33rd, 1907
Penn, W.R.			116		1909	KS, 29th, 1910
Pennell, J.S.		E, 1st West Va.	167		1934 Jan 11	IA, 61st, 1935
Penney, E.W.	Lieut. Col.	D, 6th Ind. 130th Ind.	1		1919 Oct 23	KS, 39th, 1920
Penney, S.		D, 66th Ohio	26		1888	KS, 8th, 1889
Pennfield, J.H.	Pvt.	15th Ill. Inf.	133		1927 Jun 4	IA, 54th, 1928
Pennington, J.L.	Pvt.	K, 42nd Penn. Inf.	59	86	1931 Aug 6	IA, 58th, 1932
Pennington, Josiah	Pvt. Landsman	I, 36th Ind. Inf. U.S. Navy Prince, Mass.	2		1903 Dec 23	IA, 30th, 1904

*See Appendix A, B or C for roster of post names and locations.
†See Introduction for note regarding recording of death date.
424

Name	Rank	Company, Regiment or Ship	Post*	Age	Death Date†	Journal
Pennington, Sam'l W.		A, 18th Mo.	85		1890	KS, 10th, 1891
Pennington, Thomas	Pvt.	E, 61st Ohio Vols.	12		1905 Jun 3	IA, 32nd, 1906
Pennington, Wm. R.		G, 156th Ill.	17		1926 Apr 3	KS, 46th, 1927
Pennington, Wm. T.			11		1913	IA, 40th, 1914
Penny, J.L.		C, 111th Ohio	1		1916 May 10	KS, 36th, 1917
Penny, Louis C.	Pvt.	H, 21st Iowa Inf.	88		1919 Feb 11	IA, 46th, 1920
Penny, Newton	Pvt.	H, 32nd Iowa Inf.	311		1904 Sep 24	IA, 31st, 1905
Penny, Noah R.			23		1900 Nov 8	KS, 20th, 1901
Penny, Thomas R.		D, 68th Ill.	7		1935 Sep 3	NE, 60th, 1936
Penny, Thos. R.		D, 68th Ill.	7		1929 Mar 23	NE, 54th, 1930
Penrod, Frank		A, 54th Penn.	176		1913 May 30	KS, 33rd, 1914
Penrose, Jno. R.	Pvt.	E, 24th Wis. Inf.	220	46	1890 Feb 8	IA, 16th, 1890
Pense, J.C.	Pvt.	E, 172nd Ohio Inf.	440		1918 Sep 26	IA, 45th, 1919
Penson, Robert		F, 103rd Ohio	113		1907 Oct 17	NE, 32nd, 1908
Pentz, C.	Pvt.	G, 126th Penn.	235		1921 Dec 26	IA, 48th, 1922
Pentz, William J.	Pvt.	K, 107th Penn. Inf. (at large)	305, 235	94	1939 Sep 20	IA, 66th, 1940
Penwell, G.C.		K, 9th Kans. Cav.	31		1901 May 30	KS, 21st, 1902
Penyard, A.A.		D, 65th Ohio	17		1928 Jan 8	KS, 48th, 1929
Peobody, T.	Pvt.	B, 23rd Ohio Inf.	97		1916 Apr 20	IA, 43rd, 1917
Pepin, C.M.	Pvt.	I, 38th Iowa Inf.	216		1913 Nov 11	IA, 40th, 1914
Pepin, F.J.	Pvt.	I, 9th Iowa Inf.	130		1929 Feb 5	IA, 56th, 1930
Pepoon, J.B.		A, 1st Ore. (died of old age)	214	83	1921 Aug 25	NE, 46th, 1922
Pepper, Clark		E, 3rd Wis. Inf. (died of consumption)	31		1893 Jun 5	NE, 18th, 1894
Pepper, Ezra		E, 5th Wis. (died of heart disease)	354	80	1918 Jul 25	NE, 43rd, 1919
Pepper, Hubbell		F, 38th Iowa Inf. (died of heart disease)	10	71	1913 Mar 13	NE, 38th, 1914
Pepper, J.S.		86th Ill.	4		1916 Mar 20	KS, 36th, 1917
Peppmeyer, J.H.		E, 8th Kans.	1		1914 Jun 28	KS, 34th, 1915
Percey, John H.		F, 2nd Mo. Eng.	13		1908 Jul 5	KS, 28th, 1909
Percival, C.S.	Chaplain	12th N.Y. Inf.	68	70	1892-1893	IA, 19th, 1893
Percival, Henry	Lieut.	C, 7th N.Y. Inf.	190		1912 Oct 7	IA, 39th, 1913
Perego, Jos.			235		1911 Feb 28	IA, 38th, 1912
Peret, Victor N.		I, 124th Ind. Inf.	92		1921 Oct 6	KS, 41st, 1922
Perine, Henry	Pvt.	F, 3rd Wis. Inf.	29		1929 Jan 17	IA, 56th, 1930
Perine, Jacob	Pvt.	H, 25th Iowa Inf.	20	67	1897-1898	IA, 24th, 1898
Perkins, A.G.	Capt.	Mississippi Squadron	179		1885	KS, 5th, 1886
Perkins, A.W.	Pvt.	H, 27th Iowa Inf.	493		1920 Jul	IA, 47th, 1921
Perkins, Albert Aylette	2nd Lieut., Capt. & Major	25th Iowa Inf. (born Jan. 22, 1839, in Rushville, Illinois; died at his home in Los Angeles, California; see Appendix D)	5	77	1916 May 20	IA, 42nd, 1916
Perkins, Andrew		K, 24th Ind.	25		1935 Aug 16	KS, 55th, 1936
Perkins, Bishop W.		D, 83rd Ill. 16th U.S. Colored (died at Washington, D.C.; buried at Washington, Rock Creek Cemetery)	64		1894 Jun 21	KS, 14th, 1895
Perkins, D.E.	Pvt.	H, 11th Ill. Cav.	7		1912 Apr 11	IA, 39th, 1913
Perkins, Elisha		E, 27th Ind. Inf.	59		1899 Dec 19	KS, 19th, 1900
Perkins, Geo. W.		I, 2nd Col.	238		1906 Mar 27	KS, 26th, 1907
Perkins, George		I, 177th Ohio Inf.	6		1935	KS, 54th, 1935
Perkins, George D.	Pvt.	B, 31st Iowa Inf.	22		1914 Feb 2	IA, 41st, 1915
Perkins, H.C.		A, 53rd Ind. Inf.	6		1918 Mar 16	KS, 38th, 1919
Perkins, Isaac		D, 15th Kans.	238		1890	KS, 10th, 1891
Perkins, J.D.	Pvt.		277		1925 Mar 17	IA, 52nd, 1926
Perkins, Jennings			64		1914 Nov 27	KS, 34th, 1915
Perkins, Joshua		E, 53rd Ky. (died of cancer of stomach)	96	76	1920 Mar 3	NE, 45th, 1921
Perkins, Levi	Pvt.	F, 65th U.S. Col. Inf.	254		1925 Dec 22	IA, 52nd, 1926
Perkins, Levi F.		D, 44th Mo.	7		1932 Oct 30	NE, 57th, 1933
Perkins, Louis		H, 10th N.J.	150		1915 Nov 29	KS, 35th, 1916
Perkins, O.F.	Corp.	F, 4th Minn.	142		1922 Oct 27	IA, 49th, 1923
Perkins, R.C.		Ky. (died of old age)	318		1921 May 26	NE, 46th, 1922
Perkins, Stephen	Pvt.	K, 19th Iowa Inf.	19	88	1935 Oct 25	IA, 65th, 1939
Perkins, Stephen, see Parkins, Stephen						
Perkins, T.H.		H, 78th Ill.	100		1926 Oct 28	KS, 46th, 1927

See Appendix A, B or C for roster of post names and locations.
†See Introduction for note regarding recording of death date.*

Name	Rank	Company, Regiment or Ship	Post*	Age	Death Date†	Journal
Perkins, W.J.		M, 1st N.H. Cav. (died of paralytic stroke)	1	75	1918 Jul 22	NE, 43rd, 1919
Perkins, Willard, see Perknis, Willard						
Perkins, Wm. W.	Pvt.	A, 38th Ohio Inf.	59		1919 Feb 28	IA, 46th, 1920
Perknis, Willard	Pvt.	G, 154th N.Y. Inf.	66		1903 Oct 7	IA, 30th, 1904
Perley, George R.		M, 2nd Minn. Cav.	28		1912 Oct 16	KS, 32nd, 1913
Perrigo, George		Vt.	125		1886	KS, 6th, 1887
Perrigo, W.P.		B, 51st Ind.	73		1913 Feb 1	KS, 32nd, 1913
Perrill, N.A.		18th Ohio Bat.	35		1917 Oct 13	KS, 37th, 1918
Perrin, E.H.	Pvt.	C, 18th Iowa Inf.	84		1917 May 8	IA, 44th, 1918
Perrin, Frank	Pvt.	A, 5th Iowa Cav.	313		1903 Sep 11	IA, 30th, 1904
Perrin, Jacob		C, 8th N.J.	57		1926 May 4	KS, 46th, 1927
Perrin, O.D.		D, 5th Kans.	3		1919 Feb 27	KS, 40th, 1921
Perrin, T.R.	Pvt.	H, 20th Iowa Inf.	112		1912 Mar 9	IA, 39th, 1913
Perrin, T.R.	Pvt.	H, 20th Iowa Inf.	112		1912 Mar 9	IA, 38th, 1912
Perrin, W.B.	Lieut.	3rd Vt. Bat. Lt. Art.	132		1907	IA, 34th, 1908
Perrin, W.B.	Pvt.	B, 1st R.I. Cav.	132		1907 2nd term	IA, 34th, 1908
Perrin, William	Corp.	K, 6th R.M.H.A.	102		1901 Feb 11	IA, 28th, 1902
Perrine, T.J.		I, 14th Ill.	158		1923	KS, 43rd, 1924
Perry, A.		Marine Corps	37		1885	KS, 5th, 1886
Perry, A.M.	Pvt.	A, 9th Iowa Inf.	168		1916 Sep	IA, 43rd, 1917
Perry, A.S.	Pvt.	K, 30th Iowa Inf.	20		1897-1898	IA, 24th, 1898
Perry, Aaron	Sergt.	C, 15th Ill.	59		1905 Mar 29	IA, 32nd, 1906
Perry, B.F.	Pvt.	B, 35th Iowa Inf.	231		1912 Nov 29	IA, 39th, 1913
Perry, B.F.W.		I, 9th Kans.	196		1909 Dec 16	KS, 29th, 1910
Perry, C.M.		A, 10th Wis. Inf.	251		1912 Dec 22	KS, 32nd, 1913
Perry, Chauncey		E, 3rd Mich. Cav. (died at Wray, Colo.; buried at Belleville Cemetery)	44		1894 Aug 17	KS, 14th, 1895
Perry, D.E.	Sergt.	C, 4th Iowa Cav.	20	66	1889 May 17	IA, 16th, 1890
Perry, D.W.C.		A, 60th N.Y.	81		1914 Jul 25	KS, 34th, 1915
Perry, Daniel	Pvt.	E, 29th Regiment	209		1899 Jan 6	IA, 26th, 1900
Perry, Edward	Pvt.	C, 2nd Iowa Cav.	382		1897 Nov 14	IA, 24th, 1898
Perry, Edwin	Pvt.	L, 2nd Iowa Cav. (not a G.A.R. member)		93	1941 Jan 20	IA, 67th, 1941
Perry, F.H., see Pirry, F.H.						
Perry, G.	Pvt.	F, 20th Iowa	212		1921	IA, 48th, 1922
Perry, Geo. E.	Pvt.	B, 41st Wis. Inf.	118		1907 Sep 4	IA, 34th, 1908
Perry, George		H, 12th Ky. Art.	82		1905 Oct 13	KS, 25th, 1906
Perry, George W.		A, 12th Ill.	465		1897 Aug 26	KS, 17th, 1898
Perry, Henry		G, 161st Ohio	457		1905	KS, 25th, 1906
Perry, Henry		C, 31st Wis. (died of heart failure)	231	70	1915 Mar 5	NE, 40th, 1916
Perry, Homer		died of old age	318		1924 Aug 27	NE, 49th, 1925
Perry, J.B.		K, 105th Ill.	1		1917 Jun 12	KS, 37th, 1918
Perry, J.B.		I, 1st Mo.	61		1923 Sep 27	KS, 43rd, 1924
Perry, J.E.	Pvt.	27th Mass. Inf.	499		1913 Apr 4	IA, 40th, 1914
Perry, J.S.		K, 43rd Mass. E, 58th Mass.	12		1921 Apr 12	KS, 41st, 1922
Perry, J.W.		D, 8th Wis.	113		1888	KS, 8th, 1889
Perry, John		L, 12th Mo. Cav.	58		1923 Dec 18	KS, 43rd, 1924
Perry, John E.	Pvt.	E, 16th Ill.	18		1924 Mar 19	IA, 51st, 1925
Perry, John I.	Pvt.	D, 1st Wis. Hvy. Art.	339		1901 Aug 14	IA, 28th, 1902
Perry, Marion		F, 11th Mich. Inf.	66		1934	KS, 54th, 1935
Perry, Marion		F, 11th Mich.	66		1935 Apr 20	KS, 57th, 1938
Perry, Oliver H.	Sergt.	I, 36th Iowa Inf.	325		1907 Feb 28	IA, 34th, 1908
Perry, Philip		M, 2nd N.Y. Mtd. Rifles (died of consumption)	25	70	1902 Nov	NE, 27th, 1903
Perry, Washington		11th U.S., Ark.	365		1919 Dec	KS, 40th, 1921
Perry, Wm. H.	Pvt.	H, 44th Iowa Inf.	91		1912 Jul 18	IA, 39th, 1913
Pershall, C.W.		A, 9th Kans.	12		1888	KS, 8th, 1889
Persing, Riley		F, 12th Penn.	225		1930 Dec 13	KS, 50th, 1931
Persing, Riley		A, 12th Penn.	225		1929 Dec 18	KS, 49th, 1930
Personett, Geo. W.		E, 114th & 58th Ill.	44		1914 Mar 4	KS, 34th, 1915
Persons, Fred		G, 6th Vt.	23		1926	NE, 51st, 1927

*See Appendix A, B or C for roster of post names and locations.
†See Introduction for note regarding recording of death date.

Name	Rank	Company, Regiment or Ship	Post*	Age	Death Date†	Journal
Persons, H.W.		G, 6th Vt. Inf. (died of paralysis)	23	75	1896 Mar 17	NE, 21st, 1897
Pervines, F.M.			23		1920 Dec 11	KS, 40th, 1921
Peshak, Francis	Pvt.	K, 1st Wis. Cav.	479	54	1893 Dec 17	IA, 20th, 1894
Pestana, H.L.		H, 2nd Penn. Hvy. Art.	2		1925 Mar 14	KS, 45th, 1926
Peter, Post		I, 5th Iowa Inf.	77		1900 Oct 12	KS, 20th, 1901
Peterman, James			25		1905 Jun	NE, 30th, 1906
Peterman, W.P.	Sergt.	F, 23rd Iowa Inf.	10		1920 Aug 7	IA, 47th, 1921
Peters, A.R.		G, 91st Penn. Inf.	50		1909 Dec 30	KS, 29th, 1910
Peters, Claus	Pvt.	E, 43rd Ill. Inf.	67		1910 Dec 6	IA, 37th, 1911
Peters, G.W.		B, 11th Iowa	7	89	1934 Feb 17	IA, 61st, 1935
Peters, Henry			185		1896 Sep 6	KS, 16th, 1897
Peters, Henry		H, 153rd Ohio Vol. Inf.	8		1914 Jan 22	KS, 34th, 1915
Peters, Henry		C, 28th N.Y. (died of pneumonia)	206	74	1917 Nov 6	NE, 42nd, 1918
Peters, James K.	Pvt.	F, 21st Iowa	369		1923 Mar 1	IA, 50th, 1924
Peters, John	Pvt.	H, 10th Iowa Inf.	67		1897 Nov 29	IA, 24th, 1898
Peters, John	Pvt.	I, 2nd Ill. Art.	116	76	1899 Jan 15	IA, 25th, 1899
Peters, John		I, 68th N.Y. Inf. (died of general debility)	147	62	1895 Jan 3	NE, 20th, 1896
Peters, L.		A, 40th Ind.	385		1913 Dec 4	KS, 33rd, 1914
Peters, Oliver E.		B, 133rd Ohio Vol. Inf.	64		1901 Dec 5	KS, 21st, 1902
Peters, S.R.		E, 73rd Ohio	36		1910 Apr 23	KS, 30th, 1911
Peters, S.S.		B, 2nd Ohio	110	64	1910	NE, 35th, 1911
Peters, Samuel	Pvt.	A, 1st Neb. Cav.	173	84	1894 Jan 11	IA, 20th, 1894
Peters, T.H.	Capt.	B, 4th Iowa Cav.	190		1921 Jul 19	IA, 48th, 1922
Peters, W.H.			64		1928	IA, 55th, 1929
Peters, Y.R.		Marines, Ohio	129		1887 Jan 12	KS, 7th, 1888
Petersen, Andrew M.		C, 17th Ill. Cav. (died of old age)	197	80	1914 Sep 26	NE, 39th, 1915
Peterson, A.F.		D, 110th Ohio	90		1916 Jul 11	KS, 36th, 1917
Peterson, August		K, 139th Ill. Inf.	271	89	1938 Aug 19	IA, 64th, 1938
Peterson, George W., see Petterson, George W.						
Peterson, Gus		B, 104th Ill.	433		1929 Sep 15	KS, 49th, 1930
Peterson, Holden	Pvt.	K, 27th Iowa Inf.	479		1904 Dec 1	IA, 31st, 1905
Peterson, J.S.			371		1904 Nov	IA, 31st, 1905
Peterson, John	Pvt.	A, 112th Ill. Inf.	152		1908	IA, 35th, 1909
Peterson, John		M, 2nd Ill. Art.	308		1902 Jun 22	KS, 22nd, 1903
Peterson, John		E, 47th Penn.	13	73	1918 Dec 13	NE, 43rd, 1919
Peterson, Lewis		B, 2nd Neb. Cav. California	118	75	1908 Sep 2	NE, 33rd, 1909
Peterson, M.C.	Pvt.	G, 55th Ill. Inf.	440		1920 Feb 7	IA, 47th, 1921
Peterson, M.P.		I, 8th Ill.	145		1906 Apr	KS, 26th, 1907
Peterson, M.S.		H, 4th Kans. Inf.	493		1908 Jan 20	KS, 28th, 1909
Peterson, Myron J.		E, 75th Ill. Inf.	44		1926	NE, 51st, 1927
Peterson, Nels		B, 4th Wis.	164		1896 Jun 7	KS, 16th, 1897
Peterson, Oley		K, 7th Iowa Cav.	67	95	1936 Dec 19	IA, 63rd, 1937
Peterson, Peter		B, 18th Mo.	244		1911 Jan 27	KS, 31st, 1912
Peterson, Peter A.		H, 27th Wis. Inf.	190		1919 Sep 22	IA, 46th, 1920
Peterson, S.A.		I, 4th Ill. Inf.	132	89	1935 Apr 7	IA, 62nd, 1936
Peterson, S.S.		A, 10th Ill. (died at Barteville, I.T.)	28		1895 Nov 27	KS, 15th, 1896
Peterson, Sven		K, 105th Ill. Inf.	127		1899 Sep 29	KS, 19th, 1900
Peterson, T.S.		130th Ill.	28		1895 Mar 27	KS, 16th, 1897
Peterson, Thomas		A, 2nd Neb. Cav. (died of old age)	354	88	1913 Aug 27	NE, 38th, 1914
Peterson, William		E, 15th Iowa	1		1925 Nov 21	KS, 45th, 1926
Pethic, T.M.		A, 42nd Ill. (died of Bright's disease)	29	67	1908 Nov 22	NE, 33rd, 1909
Petit, Daniel		I, 1st Ill. Art.	175		1900 Apr 8	KS, 20th, 1901
Petitt, Frank R.		K, 15th Ill. Inf.	77		1923 Sep 3	NE, 48th, 1924
Petitt, Samuel		A, 1st West Va. Inf. (died of accident)	138	51	1895 Nov 4	NE, 20th, 1896
Petre, W.G.	Pvt.	F, 130th N.Y.	206		1922 Dec 8	IA, 49th, 1923
Petrie, F.	Pvt.	F, 15th Ill. Inf.	88		1921 Jan 11	IA, 48th, 1922
Petrie, Myron			436		1907 Jan 20	IA, 34th, 1908
Petro, George M.		E, 151st Ind. Inf.	354	75	1918 Feb 3	NE, 43rd, 1919
Pettebone, E.D.		B, 74th Ill. Inf.	4		1893 May 7	NE, 18th, 1894
Petterson, George W.		F, 51st Ill.	288		1926 Apr 28	NE, 51st, 1927
Pettet, G.W.		E, 26th Ind.	4		1924 Jun 23	KS, 44th, 1925

Name	Rank	Company, Regiment or Ship	Post*	Age	Death Date†	Journal
Pettibone, Sanford		D, 33rd Ill.	65		1913 Nov 2	KS, 33rd, 1914
Pettingell, C.H.		E, 7th Wis. Inf.	12		1917 Feb 22	KS, 37th, 1918
Pettinger, Nic.			431		1906 Oct 24	IA, 33rd, 1907
Pettis, Morris E.	Pvt.	D, 9th Ind. Inf.	56		1913 Oct	IA, 40th, 1914
Pettit, C.	Corp.	D, 9th Ohio Cav.	14		1914 Mar 7	IA, 41st, 1915
Pettit, D.D.	Pvt.	K, 61st Ohio Inf.	39		1928 Oct 30	IA, 55th, 1929
Petty, A.H.	Pvt.	D, 20th Mich. Inf.	22		1917 Jan 13	IA, 44th, 1918
Petty, Joshua		C, Ind. V.R.C. (died of dropsy)	37		1900	NE, 25th, 1901
Petty, Josiah	Pvt.	G, 2nd Iowa Cav.	26		1926 Jun 25	IA, 53rd, 1927
Petty, R.J.		E, 6th Kans. Cav.	12		1900 Jan 25	KS, 20th, 1901
Petty, W.H.H.	Sergt.	B, 11th West Va. Inf.	458	54	1896 Mar 8	IA, 22nd, 1896
Pettychord, W.H.H.	Pvt.	K, 33rd Iowa Inf.	40	89	1933 Mar 1	IA, 60th, 1934
Pettygrove, Frederick		C, 2nd Wis. Inf.	124	97	1938 Feb 9	IA, 64th, 1938
Pettygrove, N.P.		H, 97th Penn. (died of heart trouble)	111	78	1924 Apr 1	NE, 49th, 1925
Pew, J.B.		I, 57th Penn.	17		1933 Nov 12	KS, 53rd, 1934
Peyton, Chas. L.	Pvt.	I, 18th Ohio Inf.	139		1909 Jun 11	IA, 36th, 1910
Peyton, John Q.A.		D, 78th Ohio Inf.	250		1917 Jul 6	KS, 37th, 1918
Peyton, M.			154		1904-1905	IA, 31st, 1905
Peyton, R.L.		D, 25th Ky. (murdered in Oklahoma)	98		1892 Sep 25	KS, 12th, 1893
Pezton, J.D.		C, 53rd U.S. Inf. (cause of death: kidney & heart)	2	63	1909 Oct 27	NE, 34th, 1910
Pfaff, George		B, 88th Ind.	81		1919 Jun 9	KS, 39th, 1920
Pfannebecker, Henry	Pvt.	9th Iowa Cav.	167		1905 Dec 28	IA, 32nd, 1906
Pfeaster, J.		D, 60th Ohio Inf.	36		1899 Jan 31	KS, 19th, 1900
Pfefferkom, Urban		1st Kans. Inf.	6		1908 Nov 17	KS, 28th, 1909
Pfefferman, S.		B, 129th Ill. (died of old age)	35	85	1920 Feb 24	NE, 45th, 1921
Pfeiffer, E.W.	Pvt.	B, 39th Ohio Inf.	74		1916 Nov 13	IA, 43rd, 1917
Pfester, Daniel		D, 28th Ohio	52		1897 Sep 11	KS, 17th, 1898
Pflough, Henry	Pvt.	A, 6th Iowa Cav.	58		1914 Feb 23	IA, 41st, 1915
Pflug, Jacob			76		1923 May 21	NE, 48th, 1924
Pfotzer, Ed	Pvt.	B, 13th M. Inf.	78		1911 Apr 9	IA, 38th, 1912
Pfouty, Jacob		I, 1st Iowa Cav.	19		1907 Jan 7	IA, 34th, 1908
Pfremer, Michael	Corp.	B, 5th Minn. Inf.	67		1897 Jul 13	IA, 24th, 1898
Pfrimer, G.W.	Pvt.	C, 66th Ind. Inf.	40		1926 Jan 23	IA, 53rd, 1927
Pfrinner, G.W., see Pfrimer, G.W.						
Phebus, Joseph			32		1921	NE, 46th, 1922
Pheister, Jacob		D, 60th Ohio Inf. (died at Newton)	36		1895 Feb	KS, 15th, 1896
Phel, A.D.	Pvt.	A, 47th Iowa Inf.	49		1919 Nov 16	IA, 46th, 1920
Phelan, J.A.		G, 71st Ill.	25		1930 Feb 14	NE, 55th, 1931
Phelps, Benjamin		F, 129th Ohio	7		1932 Oct 30	NE, 57th, 1933
Phelps, Cicero		D, 11th Ill. Cav.	68		1924 Nov 6	KS, 44th, 1925
Phelps, Geo.	Q.M.S.	36th Mass. Inf.	29		1919 Sep	IA, 46th, 1920
Phelps, Geo. D.		H, 17th Penn. Cav. (died of general disability)	187	69	1902 Aug	NE, 27th, 1903
Phelps, Homer H.	Pvt.	D, 8th Iowa Inf.	235		1918 Sep 27	IA, 45th, 1919
Phelps, J.W.	Pvt.	I, 20th Iowa Inf.	124		1910 May 4	IA, 37th, 1911
Phelps, L.S.		I, 62nd Penn. Inf.	156		1886	KS, 6th, 1887
Phelps, Marcus E.		G, 8th Iowa	140		1925 Dec 25	NE, 51st, 1927
Phelps, Uriah		G, 22nd Ill.	50		1898 Jul 9	KS, 18th, 1899
Phelps, W.H.	Sergt.	A, 36th Iowa	49		1907 Oct 16	IA, 34th, 1908
Phenicie, Geo. W.		E, 152nd Ind.	12		1927 Feb 4	KS, 47th, 1928
Phenix, J.		Penn.	464		1917 Apr	KS, 37th, 1918
Phennig, Michael		A, 13th Kans.	292		1900 Jul 9	KS, 20th, 1901
Pherrin, Wm. H.	Pvt.	H, 24th Iowa Inf.	270		1924 Sep 26	IA, 51st, 1925
Philbrick, Charles		H, 2nd Minn.	148		1905 Jun 14	KS, 25th, 1906
Philippi, Chas.		B, 40th Iowa Inf.	127		1912 Oct 2	IA, 39th, 1913
Philips, Benjamin		E, 104th Ill. Inf. (died of wound in face)	119		1894 May 4	NE, 19th, 1895
Philips, Ed	Pvt.	E, 38th Wis. Inf.	77		1933 Jan 12	IA, 60th, 1934
Philips, S.R.			3		1910	NE, 35th, 1911
Philips, Stephen			3		1910	NE, 35th, 1911
Philips, W.M.L.	Pvt.	L, 6th Iowa Cav.	452		1927 Oct 30	IA, 54th, 1928

*See Appendix A, B or C for roster of post names and locations.
†See Introduction for note regarding recording of death date.

Name	Rank	Company, Regiment or Ship	Post*	Age	Death Date†	Journal
Philleo, W.W.		D, 43rd Ill. 12th Ill. (died of dropsy)	152	74	1914 Sep 17	NE, 39th, 1915
Phillipie, Jacob		I, 135th Ohio Inf.	28		1901 Mar 20	KS, 21st, 1902
Phillipps, Martin R.		I, 135th Penn.	1		1911 Feb 24	KS, 31st, 1912
Phillips, A.	Pvt.	C, 7th Iowa Inf.	40		1910 Oct 26	IA, 37th, 1911
Phillips, A.J.		A, 8th Kans.	12		1928 May 23	KS, 48th, 1929
Phillips, A.M.	Capt.	I, 31st Iowa Inf.	74		1918 Jan 21	IA, 45th, 1919
Phillips, Albert, see Philps, Albert						
Phillips, Albert J.	Pvt.	B, 18th Iowa	12		1922 Mar 5	IA, 49th, 1923
Phillips, B.		U.S.C.T.	321		1897	KS, 17th, 1898
Phillips, B.F.		M, 1st Maine Cav.	55		1915 Mar 29	KS, 35th, 1916
Phillips, C.W.		L, 6th Mich.	17		1918 May 31	KS, 38th, 1919
Phillips, Charles	Pvt.	C, 17th Iowa Inf.	376	66	1893 Nov 14	IA, 20th, 1894
Phillips, Charles M.		K, 149th Penn.	76		1932 Jun	NE, 57th, 1933
Phillips, Chas. E.			52		1890 Feb 4	NE, 15th, 1891
Phillips, Chas. W.		L, 8th Ind.	12		1927 May 8	KS, 47th, 1928
Phillips, D.C.		H, 20th U.S. Eng. (died of apoplexy at Soldiers & Sailors Home, Milford)		49	1907 Jan 2	NE, 31st, 1907
Phillips, Daniel H.	Pvt.	G, 28th Iowa Inf.	403		1913 Feb 10	IA, 40th, 1914
Phillips, E.	Pvt.	C, 181st Ohio	271		1914 Sep 13	IA, 41st, 1915
Phillips, E.		B, 28th Iowa	186		1898 Dec 24	KS, 18th, 1899
Phillips, E.D.F., Dr.			12		1922 Dec 24	KS, 42nd, 1923
Phillips, E.W.		B, 11th Ill. Cav.	25		1941 Mar 20	KS, 61st, 1942
Phillips, F.S.		G, 30th N.J. Inf.	203		1899 Jul 9	KS, 19th, 1900
Phillips, G.K.		A, 171st Ohio	96		1920 Dec 22	KS, 40th, 1921
Phillips, G.W.	Pvt.	L, 9th Ohio Cav.	2		1922 Nov 9	IA, 49th, 1923
Phillips, George		G, 26th Ind.	25		1924 Apr 8	KS, 44th, 1925
Phillips, H.H.		I, 10th Iowa Inf.	16		1918 Apr 12	IA, 45th, 1919
Phillips, I.H.	Pvt.	B, 142nd Ohio Inf.	176	48	1888 Apr 13	IA, 15th, 1889
Phillips, I.S.	Musician	C, 34th Iowa Inf.	383		1905 Nov 2	IA, 32nd, 1906
Phillips, J.H.		C, 86th Ohio	68		1929 Apr 29	KS, 49th, 1930
Phillips, J.M.		I, 179th Ohio	42		1912 Jul 21	KS, 32nd, 1913
Phillips, J.V.	Sergt.	B, 44th Ind. Inf.	322		1917 Sep 30	IA, 44th, 1918
Phillips, J.W.	Capt.	H, 9th Iowa (murdered)	179	56	1884 Nov 7	NE, 9th, 1885
Phillips, James		79th U.S., Mo.	365		1919 Jul	KS, 40th, 1921
Phillips, James H.	Pvt.	I, 4th Iowa Cav.	49		1913 May	IA, 40th, 1914
Phillips, Jesse S.		C, 13th Tenn.	129		1931 May 31	KS, 51st, 1932
Phillips, Jesse S.		C, 13th Tenn.	129		1931 May 31	KS, 52nd, 1933
Phillips, Jno.		H, 35th Ill.	451		1904 Oct 31	KS, 24th, 1905
Phillips, John	Pvt.	C, 5th Iowa Cav.	88		1913 Sep 4	IA, 40th, 1914
Phillips, John W.	Sergt.	E, 29th Wis. Inf.	101		1914 Oct 27	IA, 41st, 1915
Phillips, John W.		5th Mo. Battery	145		1936 Jul 23	KS, 56th, 1937
Phillips, L.C.	Pvt.	18th Iowa	48		1926 May 26	IA, 53rd, 1927
Phillips, L.M.	Sergt.	B, 121st Ohio	192		1907 Jun 5	IA, 34th, 1908
Phillips, Luke	Pvt.	I, 1st Mich. Battery	154		1914 Dec 12	IA, 41st, 1915
Phillips, Marvin	Pvt.	F, 10th N.Y. Hvy. Art.	23		1908 May 27	IA, 35th, 1909
Phillips, Mordecai		A, 40th Ind. Inf.	477		1916 Feb 29	KS, 36th, 1917
Phillips, Nelson		A, 16th Iowa	17		1910 Jul	KS, 30th, 1911
Phillips, Orvill	Pvt. & Sergt.	B, 18th Penn. (died of heart disease)	35	44	1884 Mar 5	NE, 9th, 1885
Phillips, P.M.	Lieut.	A, 10th Kans. Inf.	28		1912 Mar 5	IA, 39th, 1913
Phillips, P.W.		7th Ind. Cav.	176		1928 Aug 20	KS, 49th, 1930
Phillips, Peter	Corp.	L, 62nd Penn. Inf.	67	77	1896 Nov 3	IA, 23rd, 1897
Phillips, Philip	Sergt.	16th & 66th Ohio	9		1927 Nov 20	KS, 47th, 1928
Phillips, Robt.		D, 65th Ind.	65		1918 Jan 15	KS, 38th, 1919
Phillips, S.B.	Pvt.	B, 14th Iowa Inf.	222		1917 Jan 15	IA, 44th, 1918
Phillips, Thomas			452		1916 Mar 12	IA, 43rd, 1917
Phillips, U.S.		B, 3rd Kans. Cav.	150		1905 Dec	KS, 25th, 1906
Phillips, W.A.		3rd Kans.	127		1893 Nov 30	KS, 13th, 1894
Phillips, W.F.		D, 145th Ill.	51		1904 Oct 15	KS, 24th, 1905
Phillips, W.H.		F, 57th Ill.	50		1928	KS, 48th, 1929
Phillips, W.W.	Pvt.	D, 99th Ohio Cav.	7		1898 Jun 11	IA, 26th, 1900

*See Appendix A, B or C for roster of post names and locations.
†See Introduction for note regarding recording of death date.

Name	Rank	Company, Regiment or Ship	Post*	Age	Death Date†	Journal
Phillips, W.W.		I, 50th Ohio	202		1911 Jul 25	KS, 32nd, 1913
Phillips, Wm.		H, 7th Iowa Inf. (died of stomach trouble)	63	67	1907 Sep 20	NE, 32nd, 1908
Phillips, Wm. A.		A, 51st Ind.	1		1914 Feb 8	KS, 34th, 1915
Phills, Luther	Pvt.	L, 7th Iowa Cav.	25		1924 Jul	IA, 51st, 1925
Philme, M.H.		H, 20th Ark.	25		1914 Nov 3	KS, 34th, 1915
Philo, F.B.		G, 12th Mich.	4		1899 May 9	KS, 19th, 1900
Philpot, Geo.	Pvt.	K, 3rd Iowa Inf.	222		1926 Apr 1	IA, 53rd, 1927
Philpot, John	Pvt.	K, 3rd Iowa Inf.	222		1907 2nd term	IA, 34th, 1908
Philpot, Robt.		D, 176th Ohio (died of dropsy)	66	75	1897 Feb 28	NE, 22nd, 1898
Philpott, Jas. E.	Major	80th Ohio	25		1927 Sep 5	NE, 52nd, 1928
Philpott, Jas. M.	Pvt.	K, 25th Iowa Inf.	440		1925 Nov 27	IA, 52nd, 1926
Philps, Albert		15th Iowa Inf.	25		1901-1902	IA, 28th, 1902
Philson, J.W.		H, 104th Ill. (died of dropsy)	273		1912 Feb 19	NE, 37th, 1913
Phinecy, Wm. C.		H, 15th Ind.	12		1920 Sep 11	KS, 40th, 1921
Phinney, C.E.		15th Iowa Inf. (died of paralysis)	139	75	1903 Mar 2	NE, 28th, 1904
Phinney, John N.		M, 4th Mich.	36		1904 Feb 2	KS, 24th, 1905
Phinney, L.D.		G, 46th Iowa	25		1908	NE, 33rd, 1909
Phinney, Wm.	Lieut.	D, 22nd Iowa Inf.	337	50	1888 Mar 10	IA, 15th, 1889
Phipps, E.	Pvt.	F, 107th Ill. Inf.	309	77	1892 Aug 6	IA, 19th, 1893
Phipps, James	Pvt.	A, 9th Iowa Inf.	518		1899 Aug	IA, 26th, 1900
Phoenix, J.R.	Pvt.	2nd —	124		1929 May 22	IA, 56th, 1930
Piatt, Amos		D, 1st Col. Cav.	53		1912 Aug 12	KS, 32nd, 1913
Piatt, J.I.		A, 151st Ill.	81		1927 Mar 31	KS, 47th, 1928
Pickard, Elmer		G, 12th Mich. Inf.	29		1919 Jul 22	IA, 46th, 1920
Pickard, H.J.	Pvt.	D, 7th Iowa Inf.	245		1900 May 5	IA, 27th, 1901
Pickard, J.	Pvt.	H, 1st Mich. Eng.	29	78	1897 Feb 6	IA, 23rd, 1897
Pickard, John E.		F, 8th Kans.	85		1936 Apr 7	KS, 56th, 1937
Pickard, T.E.	Pvt.	E, 1st Iowa Cav.	20		1930	IA, 57th, 1931
Pickell, H.M.	Lieut.	D, 4th Iowa Cav.	12		1921 Mar 17	IA, 48th, 1922
Picken, Alphues	Pvt.	F, 4th Iowa Cav.	68		1909 Apr 6	IA, 36th, 1910
Pickens, Chas.	Musician	B, 40th Iowa Inf.	253		2nd quarter 1885	IA, 12th, 1886
Pickens, H.M.		D, 6th N.Y. Cav.	98		1927 Jan 3	NE, 52nd, 1928
Pickerel, David		B, 116th Ind.	1		1931	NE, 56th, 1932
Pickerel, N.C.	Pvt.	8th Iowa Cav.	19		1923 Jan 8	IA, 50th, 1924
Pickerell, G.N.	Pvt.	A, 7th Ohio Inf.	7		1920 Apr 15	IA, 47th, 1921
Pickerell, Thomas H.		F, 15th Kans. Cav.	30		1920 May 7	KS, 40th, 1921
Pickering, Eli	Pvt.	B, 2nd Mo. Inf.	325		1918 May 28	IA, 45th, 1919
Pickering, J.B.		G, 98th Ohio (died of general disability)	198	66	1904 Jun 25	NE, 29th, 1905
Pickering, J.O.		H, 19th Kans.	68		1923 May 6	KS, 43rd, 1924
Pickering, Jos.		I, 18th Penn. Cav.	77		1918	NE, 43rd, 1919
Pickett, A.	Pvt.	F, 2nd Iowa Inf.	79		1902 Sep 4	IA, 29th, 1903
Pickett, Jacob	Pvt.	D, 1st Iowa Cav.	452		1920 Feb 16	IA, 47th, 1921
Pickett, James M.		K, 2nd & 3rd Iowa Inf. (consolidated)			1937 Sep 7	IA, 64th, 1938
Pickett, Jerry	Pvt.	M, 8th Ill. Cav.	24		1910 Nov 25	IA, 37th, 1911
Pickett, W.T.	Pvt.	D, 32nd Ill. Inf.	7		1915 Feb 3	IA, 42nd, 1916
Pickham, M.L.	Corp.	B, 2nd Minn. Inf.	193		1913 Apr 4	IA, 40th, 1914
Pickle, L.F.			181		1897 Dec 24	KS, 17th, 1898
Pickrell, William T.		C, 11th Mo. Inf.	18		1908 Nov 23	KS, 28th, 1909
Pickvel, Bengt F.		E, 22nd Ind.	68		1925 Mar 20	KS, 45th, 1926
Picter, John	Pvt.	B, 46th Ill. Inf.	154		1913 Feb 1	IA, 40th, 1914
Pidco, H.M.		F, 1st Penn.	53		1897 Aug 8	KS, 17th, 1898
Piele, Herman		K, 28th Ind. Cav.	244		1921 Dec	KS, 41st, 1922
Pierce, A.C.	Capt.	G, 11th Kans. Cav. (see also Appendix D)	132		1926 Oct 28	KS, 46th, 1927
Pierce, A.D.		I, 11th Wis. Inf. (died of softening of brain)	204	66	1908 Nov 11	NE, 33rd, 1909
Pierce, Ames		C, 138th Ill.	44		1913 Mar 8	KS, 33rd, 1914
Pierce, Amos		E, 138th Ill.	44		1914 Mar 8	KS, 34th, 1915
Pierce, Brinkley	Pvt.	H, 92nd Ill. Inf.	222		1928 Apr 5	IA, 55th, 1929
Pierce, C.C.		E, 100th Ind. Inf. (died of paralysis)	11	71	1891[1901?] Oct	NE, 26th, 1902
Pierce, C.W.		C, 95th Ill. (died of pneumonia)	38	83	1907 Feb	NE, 34th, 1910
Pierce, Charles Wilson	1st Lieut. & Major	V.R.C. (died at Federal Point, Florida; see Appendix D)	38		1907 Feb 24	NE, 31st, 1907
Pierce, D.			40		1906 Jan 22	NE, 31st, 1907

*See Appendix A, B or C for roster of post names and locations.
†See Introduction for note regarding recording of death date.

430

Name	Rank	Company, Regiment or Ship	Post*	Age	Death Date†	Journal
Pierce, F.M.		G, 13th Ill.	293		1925 Dec 15	KS, 45th, 1926
Pierce, G.R.	Pvt.	Vt.	20		1915 Dec	IA, 42nd, 1916
Pierce, Geo. W.	Pvt.	F, 51st Mo.	57		1924 Jan 12	IA, 51st, 1925
Pierce, George	Corp.	C, 13th Wis. Inf.	371	36	1886 Jul 17	IA, 13th, 1887
Pierce, George		I, 2nd N.Y. Cav.	1		1931 Oct 9	KS, 51st, 1932
Pierce, H.E., see Peirce, H.E.						
Pierce, Isaac	Pvt.	B & H, 17th Ohio Vol. Inf.	98	84	1899 Aug 11	IA, 26th, 1900
Pierce, J.B.		E, 15th Mich. Inf.	50		1899 May 2	KS, 19th, 1900
Pierce, J.P.			299		1915 Mar 15	NE, 40th, 1916
Pierce, J.V.		C, 147th N.Y.	114		1904 Dec 15	KS, 24th, 1905
Pierce, Jas. M.	Pvt.	C, 7th Ill. Cav.	247		1900 Sep 18	IA, 27th, 1901
Pierce, John			38		1915 Feb 15	IA, 42nd, 1916
Pierce, John		F, 1st West Va. Inf.	25	75	1895 Jul 21	NE, 20th, 1896
Pierce, L.G.	Capt.	7th Ill. Cav.	37		1905	IA, 32nd, 1906
Pierce, Laban	Pvt.	B, 4th Iowa Cav.	342		1913[1912?] Dec 22	IA, 39th, 1913
Pierce, Norman O.		I, 14th Mich. Inf.	303		1901 Jan 8	KS, 21st, 1902
Pierce, S.N.	Surg.	14th Iowa Inf.	222		1900 Sep 23	IA, 27th, 1901
Pierce, S.N.		G, 106th Ill. Inf.	42		1925 Aug 24	KS, 45th, 1926
Pierce, Samuel S.	1st Lieut.	A, 33rd Iowa Inf.	49		1904 Aug 8	IA, 31st, 1905
Pierce, W.H.		F, 2nd Ohio Hvy. Art.	113		1916 May 1	KS, 36th, 1917
Pierce, William		K, 19th Wis.	30		1910 Jun 23	KS, 30th, 1911
Pierce, William		H, 2nd N.Y. Cav.	7		1936 Nov 26	NE, 61st, 1937
Pierce, Wm. B.	Pvt.	C, 8th Iowa Inf.	141		1918 Oct 9	IA, 45th, 1919
Pierce, Wm. L.	Pvt.	D, 24th Iowa Inf.	110	63	1895 Oct 30	IA, 22nd, 1896
Piercy, J.T.			45		1919 May 30	IA, 46th, 1920
Piersol, John B.	Pvt.	A, 45th Ill. Inf.	126		1904 Sep 29	IA, 31st, 1905
Piersol, Silas		D, 101st Ind. Inf.	18		1914 Dec 16	KS, 34th, 1915
Pierson, Geo. W.		H, 22nd Iowa Cav.	20		1892 Sep 30	NE, 17th, 1893
Pierson, Geo. W.		A, 7th Iowa Inf. (died of Bright's disease)	54	54	1897 Oct 24	NE, 22nd, 1898
Pierson, George W.		E, 14th Kans. Cav. (died at Pittsburg, Kans.)	65		1894 Mar 9	KS, 14th, 1895
Pierson, J.W.		F, 40th Ind. Inf.	293		1899 Aug 20	KS, 19th, 1900
Pierson, Orson		B, 2nd N.Y. Cav.	2	80	1923 Jan 2	NE, 48th, 1924
Pierson, R.H.			40		1906	KS, 26th, 1907
Pierson, Robert B.	Pvt.	12th Mass. Bat.	516		1913 Jul 30	IA, 40th, 1914
Pierson, W.P.		C, 22nd Ind.	43		1906 Oct 22	KS, 26th, 1907
Pietzuch, Joseph		I, 32nd Ind. Inf.	380		1900 Jun 1	KS, 20th, 1901
Pigg, C.C.		H, 1st Mo. State Militia	71		1929	KS, 49th, 1930
Pigg, John M.	Pvt.	C, 118th Ill. Inf.	2		1915 Feb 13	IA, 42nd, 1916
Pigman, J.H.	Pvt.		115		1921 Jun 10	IA, 48th, 1922
Pigott, Edward		C, 3rd U.S. Cav.	12		1911 Feb 9	KS, 31st, 1912
Pigott, George		C, 3rd U.S. Cav.	12		1910 Mar	KS, 30th, 1911
Pike, Delos		I, 11th Minn.	151		1902 Feb 11	KS, 22nd, 1903
Pike, E.J.	Adjt.	18th Iowa Inf.	403		1904 Nov 3	IA, 31st, 1905
Pike, Geo. W.			85		1920 Jun 20	KS, 40th, 1921
Pike, Gilman L.		D, 39th Iowa (died of hardening of the arteries)	60	70	1911 Jan 12	NE, 36th, 1912
Pike, H.C.	Pvt.	F, 19th Iowa Inf.	153		1929 Feb 14	IA, 56th, 1930
Pike, James L.	Pvt.	K, 17th Iowa Inf.	191		1910 Jun 5	IA, 37th, 1911
Pike, William	Pvt.	E, 25th Iowa Inf.	299		1899	NE, 24th, 1900
Pikes, Perley		D, 1st Colo. Cav.	28		1898 May 3	KS, 18th, 1899
Pilgrim, J.R.	Pvt.	C, 33rd Iowa Inf.	40		1906	IA, 33rd, 1907
Pilgrim, William		I, 2nd Neb. Cav.	22		1928 Dec	IA, 55th, 1929
Pilkington, J.	Pvt.	K, 155th Ill. Inf.	120	72	1897 Jan 9	IA, 23rd, 1897
Pilliar, Edward D.			25		1913 Mar 27	KS, 33rd, 1914
Pilling, Isaiah	Pvt.	K, 2nd Iowa Cav.	452	57	1889 Jan 5	IA, 16th, 1890
Pillond, Frank	Sergt.	E, 2nd Iowa Cav.	284	53	1888 Jul 25	IA, 15th, 1889
Pillsbury, M.G.		D, 2nd U.S. Cav.	55		1925 Sep 26	KS, 45th, 1926
Pillsbury, W.H.H.		I, 17th Maine Inf. (died of blood poison; see also Appendix D)	147	55	1895 Dec 28	NE, 20th, 1896
Pilzer, Benjamin F.		A, 6th West Va.	37		1925 Feb 17	KS, 45th, 1926
Pimby, Robert		F, 96th Ill. Inf.	281		3rd quarter 1884	IA, 11th, 1885

Name	Rank	Company, Regiment or Ship	Post*	Age	Death Date†	Journal
Pinckney, John B.	Pvt.	E, Border Brigade	22		1914 Feb 1	IA, 41st, 1915
Pindell, J.T.	Medical Cadet		96		1911 May 22	KS, 31st, 1912
Pine, George W.		K, 99th Ill.	32		1934 Feb 23	NE, 59th, 1935
Pine, R.D.		D, 23rd Ill. B, 53rd Ill.	25		1916 Aug 10	NE, 41st, 1917
Pinegar, P.J.	Pvt.		173		1921 Aug 2	IA, 48th, 1922
Piner, R.M.	Pvt.		290		1906	IA, 33rd, 1907
Ping, Mathias	Pvt.	G, 39th Iowa Inf.	157	70	1892 Dec 31	IA, 19th, 1893
Ping, P.I.B.		I, 1st Iowa Cav.	49		1890 Aug 22	KS, 12th, 1893
Ping, P.J.B.		I, 1st Iowa Cav.	49		1890	KS, 10th, 1891
Ping, Thomas		17th Iowa	49		1885	KS, 5th, 1886
Pingaman, W.H.	Pvt.	G, 3rd Iowa Cav.	79	59	1889 May 3	IA, 16th, 1890
Pingel, John D.		K, 15th Ill. Cav.	255		1917 Sep 26	KS, 37th, 1918
Pingree, Jno. T.G.	Pvt.	A, 65th Ill. Inf.	211	56	1898 Nov 7	IA, 25th, 1899
Pingree, Thomas, Rev.		B, 11th Ind.	[40?]		1916 Aug 4	KS, 36th, 1917
Pingrey, Darious	Pvt.	C, 2nd Iowa Inf.	255		1908 Jul 17	IA, 35th, 1909
Pink, Stanton			10		1922 Sep 7	KS, 42nd, 1923
Pinkerton, Isaac H.		K, 11th Kans. Inf.	88		1909 Mar 28	KS, 29th, 1910
Pinkerton, Merwin	Pvt.	A, 7th Iowa Cav.	263	68	1897 Dec 20	IA, 24th, 1898
Pinney, Geo. B.	Pvt.	D, 22nd Conn. Inf.	283		1911 Nov 20	IA, 38th, 1912
Pinney, J.A.		F, 22nd Iowa	115		1925 Nov 3	KS, 45th, 1926
Pinney, J.C.		B, 9th Kans. Cav. (died at Longton)	91		1895 Apr 8	KS, 15th, 1896
Pinney, W.T.		120th Ill. Inf.	25		1905 Oct 3	NE, 30th, 1906
Pinney, W.T.		129th Ill.	25		1905 Oct 3	NE, 31st, 1907
Pinnock, W.D.		I, 38th Ind.	123		1925 Dec 18	KS, 45th, 1926
Pinvey, F.H.	Pvt.	B, 1st M.S.S.	78		1907 Jun 20	IA, 34th, 1908
Piper, E.T.		E, 34th Ill. Inf. (died of old age)	62	86	1903 May 23	NE, 28th, 1904
Piper, G.W.		G, 7th Mich.	47		1928 Dec 23	KS, 48th, 1929
Piper, H.J.		83rd Ill. Inf.			1929 Jan 10	NE, 53rd, 1929
Piper, J.W.		D, 147th Ind.	293		1924	KS, 44th, 1925
Piper, R.H.		D, 7th Ind.	4		1915 May 6	KS, 35th, 1916
Piper, Ralph R.		D, 177th Ohio Inf.	354	75	1915 Jul 3	NE, 40th, 1916
Piper, W.B.		D, 32nd Ill.	380		1912 Sep 4	KS, 32nd, 1913
Pirry, F.H.		I, 40th Ill. (buried in post grounds)	127		1888	KS, 8th, 1889
Pitcher, Luther S.	Pvt.	14th Iowa Inf.	267		1925 Oct 14	IA, 52nd, 1926
Pitcher, Wm.			35		1905	NE, 30th, 1906
Pitcher, Wm.			35		1912	NE, 37th, 1913
Pitcker, A.J.			32		1911 Jan 22	KS, 31st, 1912
Pithan, Henry	Pvt.	E, 26th Iowa	44		1905 Aug 12	IA, 32nd, 1906
Pitman, Jas. Henry	Pvt.	K, 7th Mo. Cav. (at large)	251	96	1940 Sep 25	IA, 67th, 1941
Pitman, W.G.		4th Iowa (died of heart failure)	318		1904	NE, 29th, 1905
Pitman, Wm.		G, U.S. Vols.	328		1906	KS, 26th, 1907
Pitser, G.M.	Musician	I, 17th Wis. Inf.	30		1908 Jul 25	IA, 35th, 1909
Pitsor, C.W.	Capt.	I, 17th Wis. Inf.	284		1900 Feb 6	IA, 27th, 1901
Pitt, John F.	Pvt.	F, 6th Iowa Cav.	194		1919 May 25	IA, 46th, 1920
Pittenger, R.S.		B, 8th Ill. Cav. (died of Bright's disease)	169	73	1915 Jan 17	NE, 39th, 1915
Pittman, Harry	Bugler	A, 7th Mo. Cav.	100		1919 Jun 23	IA, 46th, 1920
Pittman, J.F.		F, 55th Penn. Inf.	18		1917 Sep 10	KS, 37th, 1918
Pittman, Thomas		B, 85th Ind.	32		1905 Nov 29	KS, 25th, 1906
Pitts, Fountain			236		1921 Jul 16	KS, 41st, 1922
Pitts, John		B, 134th Ohio	68		1893 Aug 20	KS, 13th, 1894
Pitts, John R.	Pvt. & Corp.	C, 12th Wis. Vol. Inf.	91		1924 Jul 16[?]	IA, 51st, 1925
Pitts, L.M.		K, 16th Ky. Inf.	118		1917 Aug 30	KS, 37th, 1918
Pitts, W.H.	Pvt.	H, 7th Iowa Inf.	98		1931 Mar 5	IA, 58th, 1932
Pitts, William			69	88	1925 Dec 11	NE, 50th, 1926
Pitts, Z.		E, 142nd Ill.	24		1897 Jul 25	KS, 17th, 1898
Pitzer, Joseph H.		H, 1st Md. Inf.	79		1886	KS, 6th, 1887
Pitzer, Thomas B.		A, 11th Kans. Cav.	250		1917 Apr 4	KS, 37th, 1918
Pixley, A.F.	Pvt.	F, 11th Md. Inf.	122		1913 May 28	IA, 40th, 1914
Pixley, L.E.		I, 66th Ill.	55		1905 Jan 31	KS, 25th, 1906
Pixley, Luther		H, 74th Ind. Inf. (died of accidental injury)	110		1921 Mar 17	NE, 46th, 1922
Pixley, Moses A.		G, 13th Mich.	8		1897 Sep 24	KS, 17th, 1898

*See Appendix A, B or C for roster of post names and locations.
†See Introduction for note regarding recording of death date.

Name	Rank	Company, Regiment or Ship	Post*	Age	Death Date†	Journal
Pixley, T.S.		E, 10th Ill. Inf.	85		1914 Aug 14	KS, 34th, 1915
Pixley, W.M.		17th Iowa Inf.	20		1916	IA, 43rd, 1917
Place, E.B.		F, 11th Conn.	289		1920 Feb 20	KS, 40th, 1921
Place, J.W.		D, 13th N.H. Inf. (died of heart failure)	11	77	1922 Sep 27	NE, 47th, 1923
Place, James D.	Pvt.	F, 75th Ill. Inf.	68		1909 Apr 6	IA, 36th, 1910
Placik, F.A.		47th Iowa	94		1921 May 7	IA, 48th, 1922
Plaffley, John		G, 7th Kans.	283		1892 Feb 19	KS, 12th, 1893
Plank, George H.			295[495?]		1905 Jan 4	KS, 25th, 1906
Plank, Jacob		E, 132nd Ohio Inf. (died of cancer)	30	63	1896 Nov 19	NE, 21st, 1897
Plank, John		H, 18th Mich. Inf.	13		1893 Jun 6	NE, 18th, 1894
Plank, W.W.	Pvt.	C, 8th Iowa Inf.	236		1928 Apr 2	IA, 55th, 1929
Plant, Daniel A.		B, 39th Ohio Inf.	1		1901 Jan 5	KS, 21st, 1902
Plant, Jacob		E, 32nd Ohio Inf. (died of general debility)	25	63	1896 Nov 19	NE, 21st, 1897
Plantz, V.A.	Pvt.	E, 46th Ill. Inf.	12		1919 Dec 9	IA, 46th, 1920
Platt, George W.	1st Lieut.	F, 122nd N.Y.	1		1916 Aug 25	KS, 36th, 1917
Platt, Jas. A.	Pvt.	G, 193rd Penn.	88		1924 Sep 6	IA, 51st, 1925
Platt, Joseph N.	Corp.	I, 9th Ohio Cav. (at large)	231	94	1940 Feb 14	IA, 66th, 1940
Platt, Nathan		I, 9th Mich. Inf. (died of consumption)	11	54	1895 Aug 1	NE, 20th, 1896
Platt, Nicholas		G, 9th Kans. Cav.	72		1892 Dec 29	KS, 12th, 1893
Platt, S.D.	Pvt.	K, 9th Iowa Inf.	165		1906 Sep 2	IA, 33rd, 1907
Platter, C.C.	Capt.	D, 81st Ohio Inf.	57		1909 Dec 30	IA, 36th, 1910
Platter, George Wm.	Pvt.	A, 17th Iowa Inf.	84		1916 Sep 13	IA, 43rd, 1917
Platti, Purdy		I, 16th Ind. (died of old age)	47	78	1921 Dec 29	NE, 46th, 1922
Platts, Wesley E.		F, 156th Ill.	12		1915 Jul 19	KS, 35th, 1916
Plein, John M.	Pvt.	D, 1st Iowa Cav.	70		1911 Jun 11	IA, 38th, 1912
Pletcher, Daniel	Pvt.	D, 72nd Ind. Inf.	149		1914 Aug 25	IA, 41st, 1915
Pletcher, J.B.		C, 69th Penn. Inf.	190		1886	KS, 6th, 1887
Pletcher, John C.			89		1919 Oct 29	NE, 44th, 1920
Plondaux, C.H.	Pvt.	D, 48th —	168		1916 Jan 5	IA, 42nd, 1916
Plotts, M.L.		H, 119th Ill. Inf.	7		1928 Jul 6	NE, 53rd, 1929
Plowman, Charles E.		A, 46th Ill.	58		1910 Dec 12	KS, 30th, 1911
Plowman, Oliver		F, 12th Penn. Cav.	142		1923 Jun 4	KS, 43rd, 1924
Plucknett, Jas.		F, 2nd Iowa Cav. (died of old age)	89		1923 Aug 6	NE, 48th, 1924
Plum, George		H, 15th Ind.	12		1915 Sep 25	KS, 35th, 1916
Plumb, Geo.		B, 9th Kans.	55		1933 Oct 12	KS, 53rd, 1934
Plumb, Geo. M.		40th Wis. Inf.	25	73	1919 Mar 7	NE, 44th, 1920
Plumb, Henry	Lieut.	C, 109th N.Y. Inf.	12		1917 Mar 2	IA, 44th, 1918
Plumb, Henry	Surg.	19th Conn. Inf.	3		1929 Jan 4	KS, 49th, 1930
Plumb, Preston B.	Col.	11th Kans. Inf. (died in Washington, D.C.; U.S. senator; see also Appendix D)	55		1891 Dec 20	KS, 11th, 1892
Plumb, S.H.	Pvt.	G, 17th Iowa Inf.	1	60	1887 Jan 7	IA, 14th, 1888
Plumb, T.F.		died of consumption	84		1910 Nov 13	NE, 35th, 1911
Plumb, Z.	Pvt.	F, 26th Iowa Inf.	14	62	1887 Jun 8	IA, 14th, 1888
Plumer, A.		F, 107th Ill. Inf. (died of heart failure)	134	76	1896 Oct 1	NE, 21st, 1897
Plumer, Wm.		81st N.Y.	262		1908	NE, 33rd, 1909
Plumley, S.I.	Pvt.	E, 1st Ind. Hvy. Art.	165	50	1893 Aug 6	IA, 20th, 1894
Plumly, J.S.	Sergt.	E, 33rd Iowa Vols.	12		1905 Oct 8	IA, 32nd, 1906
Plummer, A.L.	Pvt.	E, 4th Iowa Inf.	7		1920 Dec 20	IA, 47th, 1921
Plummer, Benj. Franklin		A, 17th Kans. Inf.	7	92, 3 mos. & 12 days	1937 Dec 26	IA, 64th, 1938
Plummer, C.	Pvt.	C, 137th Ind. Inf.	104		1927 Jan 8	IA, 54th, 1928
Plummer, D.	Capt.	A, 22nd Mich. Inf.	222		1910	IA, 37th, 1911
Plummer, E.E.		G, 12th Kans.	180		1922 Jan 31	KS, 42nd, 1923
Plummer, H.		H, 30th Ind. Inf.	7		1899 Feb 4	KS, 19th, 1900
Plummer, Hiram	Pvt.	A, 112th Ill. Vol. Inf.	7		1901 Aug 2	IA, 28th, 1902
Plummer, I.J.	Sergt.	K, 8th Iowa Inf.	330	54	1886 Dec 6	IA, 13th, 1887
Plummer, J.E.		E, 17th Ind.	129		1916 Dec 14	KS, 36th, 1917
Plummer, J.W.		H, 3rd Ind.	71		1918 Mar 18	KS, 38th, 1919
Plummer, John W.	Pvt.	E, 32nd Iowa Inf.	243		1908 Mar 14	IA, 35th, 1909
Plummer, R.L.	Pvt.	H, 7th Md. Inf.	452		1903 Sep 22	IA, 30th, 1904

Name	Rank	Company, Regiment or Ship	Post*	Age	Death Date†	Journal
Plummer, T.J.		A, 2nd Mo. Inf.	7	85	1925 Nov 3	NE, 50th, 1926
Plummer, Wm.		5th Inf. Bat. (nearly 85 years old)	129		1889	KS, 9th, 1890
Plunkett, John N.		F, 114th Ill. Inf.	142		1900 Jan 1	KS, 20th, 1901
Pluskey, William		C, 1st Ind. Art.	209		1910 Dec 26	KS, 30th, 1911
Plybon, John		G, 11th Penn. Inf. (died of consumption)	84	80	1909 Aug 17	NE, 34th, 1910
Plymefser, Samuel J.		G, 6th Iowa Inf. (died of old age)	193	87	1916 Jun 11	NE, 41st, 1917
Plympton, C.H.	Pvt.	K, 97th Ohio Inf.	452		1925 Sep 23	IA, 52nd, 1926
Pocock, J.W.		H, 2nd Neb. Cav.	40	82	1920 Dec 19	NE, 45th, 1921
Poe, Amos		F, 39th Mo.	244		1917 Aug 11	KS, 37th, 1918
Poe, Daniel W.		I, 111th Ohio Inf. (died of chronic diarrhea contracted in army)	125		1891 Sep 28	KS, 11th, 1892
Poe, Isaac S.		E, 12th Ind.	209		1909 Nov 20	KS, 29th, 1910
Poeverlien, Geo.		D, 10th Kans.	379		1898 Dec 6	KS, 18th, 1899
Poff, Henry W.		I, 39th Ill. Inf. (died at Clinton)	450		1895 Dec	KS, 15th, 1896
Poff, J.A.		E, 17th Ind.	12		1908 Apr 3	KS, 28th, 1909
Poffinbarger, J.H.		D, 23rd Mo.	377		1917 Oct 21	KS, 37th, 1918
Pogue, John W.	Pvt.	E, 10th Ill. Inf.	57		1917 Feb 16	IA, 44th, 1918
Pogue, Milton B.		C, 4th Ill.	209		1926 Jun 3	KS, 46th, 1927
Pohlman, Wm.		C, 3rd Ind. Cav.	10		1926 Apr 2	NE, 51st, 1927
Poinsett, W.B.		A, 15th Ind.	28		1900 Jun 5	KS, 20th, 1901
Point, Stephen	Pvt.	F, 25th Ohio	88		1926 Sep 7	IA, 53rd, 1927
Pointer, J.F.		E, 7th Mo. Cav. (died of dropsy)	289	71	1903 May 6	NE, 28th, 1904
Pointer, Robt.	Pvt.	D, 2nd Colo. Cav.	96	56	1891 Sep 17	IA, 18th, 1892
Pointer, W.L.			7		1928 Mar	IA, 55th, 1929
Poisal, George C.	Pvt.	G, 32nd Iowa	42	60	1899 Jul 18	IA, 26th, 1900
Pokett, Sylvester	Pvt.	C, 1st Neb. Cav. (at large)	83, 136, 304	95, 1 mo. & 23 days	1943 Dec 7	IA, 70th, 1944
Polaga, John H.	Pvt.	F, 77th Penn. Inf.	93		1918 Feb 7	IA, 45th, 1919
Poland, George		C, 67th Penn.	175		1916 Aug 13	KS, 36th, 1917
Poland, James H.	Pvt.	L, 7th Iowa Cav.	8		1912 May 26	IA, 39th, 1913
Poland, Silas	Pvt.	I, 22nd Iowa Inf.	125		1906 May 22	IA, 33rd, 1907
Polen, Samuel		107th Ohio	421		1901-1902	IA, 28th, 1902
Polin, Henry		E, 1st Neb. Cav.	88		1886	KS, 6th, 1887
Polin, N.		K, 11th West Va.	77		1922 Jul 20	KS, 42nd, 1923
Poling, Silas	Pvt.	B, 13th Iowa Inf.	253		1917 Aug 3	IA, 44th, 1918
Polk, A.D.		A, 1st Penn. Cav.	85		1912 Jun 10	KS, 32nd, 1913
Polk, Charles H.		D, 138th Ill. Inf.	209	88	1937 Jan 28	IA, 64th, 1938
Polk, Chas.	Lieut.	21st Ind. Hvy. Art.	55		1918 Jun 9	IA, 45th, 1919
Polla, S.H.		A, 4th Ky.	322		1922 Mar 24	KS, 42nd, 1923
Pollard, Dudley H.		B, 8th Iowa Cav.	31	74	1918 Oct 4	NE, 43rd, 1919
Pollard, J.A.			2		1928	IA, 55th, 1929
Pollars, E.E.		E, 4th Ill.	36		1930 Mar 5	KS, 50th, 1931
Pollett, Daniel		F, 3rd Ohio Inf.	90		1929 Mar 17	KS, 49th, 1930
Pollett, Henry		A, 135th Ind.	90		1921 Nov 24	KS, 41st, 1922
Pollinberger, W.C.			45		1919 Jul 15	IA, 46th, 1920
Polling, Matin	Pvt.	B, 13th Iowa Inf.	197		1907 Jan 12	IA, 34th, 1908
Pollock, A.	Pvt.	C, 36th Ill. Inf.	286		1911	IA, 38th, 1912
Pollock, Addison	Pvt.	C, 36th Ill. Inf.	286		1906 May	IA, 33rd, 1907
Pollock, J.T.		A, 174th Ind.	25		1931 Oct 2	NE, 56th, 1932
Pollock, John S.		F, 21st Ill. Inf. (died at Winfield; buried at New Salem, Kans.)	85		1894 Dec 8	KS, 14th, 1895
Pollock, Joseph	Pvt.	F, 1st Col. Cav.	46		1899	NE, 24th, 1900
Polsgrove, A.			32		1883	KS, 3rd, 1884
Polston, A.	Pvt.	G, 40th Iowa	169	45	1886 Feb 1	IA, 17th, 1891
Polton, Edward	Pvt.	G, 45th Ohio Inf.	112	50	1894 Feb 5	IA, 20th, 1894
Pomeroy, Daniel	Farrier	M, 8th Mich. Cav.	230		1903 Jan 30	IA, 29th, 1903
Pomeroy, E.D.		B, 148th Ill.	33		1927	KS, 47th, 1928
Pomeroy, P.L.		E, 68th Ohio	142		1913 Mar 2	KS, 33rd, 1914
Pomeroy, Peter		K, 83rd Ill.	203		1916 Sep 26	KS, 36th, 1917
Pomeroy, Timothy		E, 68th Ohio	142		1913 Mar 2	KS, 32nd, 1913
Pomery, Joseph		G, 43rd Ill. Inf.		91	1936 Jan 14	IA, 62nd, 1936

*See Appendix A, B or C for roster of post names and locations.
†See Introduction for note regarding recording of death date.

Name	Rank	Company, Regiment or Ship	Post*	Age	Death Date†	Journal
Pomery, Joseph		G, 43rd Ill. Inf.	231	91	1936 Jan 14	IA, 63rd, 1937
Pond, D.B.	Pvt.	A, 2nd Ill. Cav.	111		1905 May 15	IA, 32nd, 1906
Pond, Geo. F.		3rd Mich.	32		1911 Jun 21	KS, 31st, 1912
Pond, Homer W.		C, 3rd Wis. Cav. (see also Appendix D)	32		1909 Jan 14	KS, 28th, 1909
Pond, Hugh	Sergt.	I, 212th Ill.	111		1905 May 17	IA, 32nd, 1906
Pond, John O.		B, 150th Ind.	64		1920 Nov 4	KS, 40th, 1921
Pontzius, James	Pvt.	G, 19th Iowa Inf.	153	89	1933 Dec 29	IA, 60th, 1934
Pool, August	Pvt.	F, 11th Wis. (died of blood poison)	13	42	1885 May 11	NE, 10th, 1886
Pool, F.M.		O, 7th Colo. Inf.	113		1913 Aug 5	KS, 33rd, 1914
Pool, Horace	Lieut.	I, 1st Iowa Inf.	78		1916 Feb 16	IA, 43rd, 1917
Pool, S.G.	Pvt.	F, 11th Iowa Inf.	197		1914 Sep 24	IA, 41st, 1915
Pool, Savage	Pvt.	E, 13th Iowa	263	50	1891 May 9	IA, 18th, 1892
Poole, J.M.	Pvt.	G, 29th Iowa Inf.	96		1908 May 29	IA, 35th, 1909
Pooler, A.M.		F, 6th Kans.	1		1908 Nov 25	KS, 28th, 1909
Poor, Bailey E., see Porr, Baley E.						
Poor, Elijah	Pvt.	H, 29th Ind. Inf.	84		1899	NE, 24th, 1900
Poor, James A.	1st Lieut.	C, 27th Iowa Inf.	54		1901 Jan 6	IA, 28th, 1902
Poor, John S.		K, 50th Mass.	at large		1929 Dec 28	NE, 55th, 1931
Poor, M.	Pvt.	G, 47th Iowa Inf.	8		1921 Mar 29	IA, 48th, 1922
Poor, William		E, 26th Ind.	170		1919 Jan 21	KS, 39th, 1920
Poor, Wm.		E, 26th Ind.	170		1918 Jan 13	KS, 38th, 1919
Poore, Thomas J.		B, 5th Iowa Inf.	91	77	1916 Oct 19	NE, 41st, 1917
Pope, A.J.	Major	13th Iowa Inf.	167		4th quarter 1883	IA, 10th, 1884
Pope, Abran		F, 92nd Ill. (died of old age)	35	83	1925 Feb 6	NE, 50th, 1926
Pope, August		K, 11th Kans. Cav.	35		1913 Dec 28	KS, 33rd, 1914
Pope, Benj. F.		B, 22nd Wis.	47		1930 Sep 20	NE, 55th, 1931
Pope, C.	Pvt.	E, 14th Iowa (died of accident)	164	41	1884 Feb 1	NE, 9th, 1885
Pope, J.A.		I, 3rd Kans.	43		1888	KS, 8th, 1889
Pope, John			4		1904 Aug 31	NE, 29th, 1905
Pope, L.E.		D, 2nd Iowa	25		1926 Nov 17	NE, 51st, 1927
Pope, S.A.	Pvt.	D, 20th Iowa Inf.	4		1905	IA, 32nd, 1906
Popejoy, T.J.	Pvt.	B, 40th Iowa Inf.	103		1917 Jan 11	IA, 44th, 1918
Popenoe, P.D.		B, 60th Bat.	12		1920 May 22	KS, 40th, 1921
Popham, Elias		A, 74th Ind.	47		1918 Jan 7	KS, 38th, 1919
Popino, S.C.			129		1923 May 5	KS, 43rd, 1924
Porr, Baley E.		H, 1st N.Y. Lt. Art.	354	85	1913[1912?] Dec 27	NE, 37th, 1913
Porr, Charles		G, 13th Kans.	175		1916 Dec	KS, 36th, 1917
Port, H.H.	Pvt.	B, 2nd Iowa Inf.	461		1917 Nov 10	IA, 44th, 1918
Port, I.		F, 169th Penn.	51		1902 Sep 12	KS, 22nd, 1903
Porter, A.G.		A, 8th Conn. Inf.	25		1893 Nov 23	NE, 18th, 1894
Porter, Abraham		D, 9th Mich. Cav.	47		1921 Jun 13	KS, 41st, 1922
Porter, Albert		A, 14th U.S.C.T.	1		1916 Jun 26	KS, 36th, 1917
Porter, E.J.		D, 28th Penn.	12		1921 Apr 28	KS, 41st, 1922
Porter, Elias L.		H, 100th Ind. Inf.	89		1901 Mar 21	KS, 21st, 1902
Porter, F.	Musician	15th Army Corps	12		1920 Oct 30	IA, 47th, 1921
Porter, F.J.	Pvt.	L, 9th Iowa Cav.	86		1924 Feb 22	IA, 51st, 1925
Porter, H.G.	Pvt.	K, 21st Iowa Inf.	190	87	1931 Mar 21	IA, 58th, 1932
Porter, Harvey T.		C, 150th Penn. Inf.	35		1900 Aug 26	KS, 20th, 1901
Porter, J.B.		H, 65th Ohio Inf. H, 67th Ohio Inf.	136		1920	NE, 45th, 1921
Porter, J.C.		K, 45th Penn.	63		1920 Apr 27	KS, 40th, 1921
Porter, J.H.	Pvt.	C, 28th Iowa	127		1921 Jan 6	IA, 48th, 1922
Porter, J.N.	Pvt.	C, 129th Ohio Inf.	302		1905 Dec 1	IA, 32nd, 1906
Porter, J.R.	Pvt.	B, 10th Iowa Inf.	296		2nd quarter 1885	IA, 12th, 1886
Porter, J.S.		D, 15th Iowa Inf. (cause of death: heart)	192	75	1901 Dec	NE, 26th, 1902
Porter, J.W.		D, 205th Penn.	25		1919 Jul 24	KS, 39th, 1920
Porter, James		F, 24th Iowa	43		1905 Jun 29	KS, 25th, 1906
Porter, John		E, 9th Kans. Inf.	16		1901 Nov 17	KS, 21st, 1902
Porter, John E.		K, 33rd Iowa	258		1913 Mar 26	KS, 33rd, 1914
Porter, John G.	Pvt.	H, 34th N.Y. Inf.	212		1907 Nov 22	IA, 34th, 1908
Porter, John M.	Capt.	A, 36th Iowa Inf.	337		1908 Dec 31	IA, 35th, 1909

*See Appendix A, B or C for roster of post names and locations.
†See Introduction for note regarding recording of death date.

Name	Rank	Company, Regiment or Ship	Post*	Age	Death Date†	Journal
Porter, John S.		K, 30th Mich.	207	82	1913 Nov 19	NE, 38th, 1914
Porter, Joll J.		G, 7th Ind.	50		1924	KS, 44th, 1925
Porter, Josiah		B, 2nd Col. Cav.	36		1890	KS, 10th, 1891
Porter, Julius P.		G, 61st Ill. Inf.	44		1890	KS, 10th, 1891
Porter, Nelson G.	Corp.	K, 34th Ill. Inf.	1		1922 Apr 22	IA, 49th, 1923
Porter, Robt. B.		I, 132nd Ohio	8		1893 Jul 25	KS, 13th, 1894
Porter, S.	Corp.	80th Ohio Inf.	309		1919 Jun	IA, 46th, 1920
Porter, S.D.		H, 2nd Iowa Cav. (died of paralysis)	47		1896 May 7	NE, 21st, 1897
Porter, S.M.		I, 27th Ill. Inf.	66		1919 Mar 6	IA, 46th, 1920
Porter, Seth		G, 6th Vt.	339		1918 Apr 23	KS, 38th, 1919
Porter, Silas		G, 21st N.Y. Cav. (member at large)	87		1934 Oct 9	KS, 54th, 1935
Porter, T.	Pvt.	B, 24th Iowa Inf.	254	53	1895 Apr 18	IA, 22nd, 1896
Porter, Thomas		F, 44th Ill. Inf.	32	74	1909 Jun 1	NE, 34th, 1910
Porter, W.A.	Pvt.	B, 64th N.Y. Inf.	452		1929 Jan 23	IA, 56th, 1930
Porter, W.A.		B, 53rd Ohio	4		1921 May 22	KS, 41st, 1922
Porter, W.C.			32		1911 Mar 21	KS, 31st, 1912
Porter, W.W.	Pvt.	78th Ohio Inf.	55		1925 Nov 9	IA, 52nd, 1926
Porter, W.Y.	Pvt.	B, 10th Ind. Inf.	290	50	1891 Aug 11	IA, 18th, 1892
Porter, Wm.	Pvt.	F, 70th Ind. Inf.	302		1902 Nov 20	IA, 29th, 1903
Porter, Wm.		F, 105th Ill. Inf.	147		1909 Oct 15	KS, 29th, 1910
Porter, Wm.			193		1886	NE, 11th, 1887
Porterfield, J.C.		B, 11th Kans. Cav.	46		1920 Sep 17	KS, 40th, 1921
Posey, Dudley		A, 92nd Ohio	8		1921 Jul 25	KS, 41st, 1922
Posson, A.Z.		F, 13th Wis. (died of heart trouble)	18	80	1922 Feb 5	NE, 47th, 1923
Posson, Charles W.		I, 44th Wis.	209		1913 Feb 15	KS, 33rd, 1914
Post, C.W.	Pvt.	H, 24th Iowa Inf.	270		1912	IA, 39th, 1913
Post, J.M.		A, 87th Ind.	25		1920	KS, 40th, 1921
Post, Joseph		F, 16th Ill. Cav.	158		1886	KS, 6th, 1887
Post, McPherson			44		1913	NE, 38th, 1914
Post, Parley	Pvt.	I, 6th U.S. Cav.	7		1922 Feb 9	IA, 49th, 1923
Post, Peter, see Peter, Post						
Post, T.J.		B, 160th Ohio Inf.	45		1886	KS, 6th, 1887
Poster, James		E, 17th Kans.	16		1904 Nov 16	KS, 24th, 1905
Postlethwait, Wm.		D, 28th Iowa	47		1911 Jan 30	KS, 31st, 1912
Potter, A.G.		A, 10th Kans.	68		1892 Aug 2	KS, 12th, 1893
Potter, A.P.		I, 84th Ind.	142		1908 Dec 15	KS, 28th, 1909
Potter, Adin H.		D, 6th N.Y. Inf. (died of heart disease)	231	61	1905 Jun 13	NE, 30th, 1906
Potter, B.F.		G, 12th Kans.	129		1917 Feb 21	KS, 37th, 1918
Potter, C.W.		G, 56th Ill. Inf. (died of hernia)	171	83	1924 Oct 10	NE, 50th, 1926
Potter, Charles R.		F, 19th Iowa	94		1931 Jul	NE, 56th, 1932
Potter, Dennis G.		F, 23rd Ohio Inf.	269		1900 Sep 13	KS, 20th, 1901
Potter, E.			170		1915	IA, 42nd, 1916
Potter, Geo. O.	Pvt.	K, 29th Iowa Inf.	194	63	1891 Mar 17	IA, 18th, 1892
Potter, Henry W.	Sergt.	G, 96th N.Y. Inf.	88		1909 Dec 2	IA, 36th, 1910
Potter, Horace		42nd Ohio	263		1906 Nov 14	KS, 26th, 1907
Potter, Ira M.		M, 5th U.S. Cav. (died of apoplexy)	112		1916 May 12	NE, 41st, 1917
Potter, Isaac	Pvt.	A, 1st Maine Inf.	452		1918 Jul 18	IA, 45th, 1919
Potter, J.	Corp.	A, 25th Mich. Inf.	452		1926 Feb 19	IA, 53rd, 1927
Potter, J.M.		E, 81st Ohio	47		1927 May 30	KS, 47th, 1928
Potter, James G.	Sergt.	I, 24th Iowa Inf.	492		1918 May 25	IA, 45th, 1919
Potter, James W.	Pvt.	F, 12th Iowa Inf.	104	92	1932 Jul 19	IA, 59th, 1933
Potter, John	Pvt.	I, 101st Ill. Inf.	16		1912 May 20	IA, 39th, 1913
Potter, John		D, 8th Mo. Inf. (member at large)			1934 May 12	KS, 54th, 1935
Potter, John F.	Pvt.	9th Wis. Bat.	67		1917 Apr 13	IA, 44th, 1918
Potter, John J.		D, 8th Mo. Inf. (at large)			1934 May 12	KS, 55th, 1936
Potter, Lester	Pvt.	F, 142nd N.Y. Inf.	132		1919 Mar 15	IA, 46th, 1920
Potter, Lewis S.	Pvt.	G, 8th Mo. Inf.	34		1903 Mar 21	IA, 30th, 1904
Potter, Marvin	Capt.	F, 142nd N.Y. Inf.	132		1916	IA, 43rd, 1917
Potter, Matt. R.	Landsman	Vessel, Mo.	12		1909 Mar 27	KS, 29th, 1910
Potter, O.O.	Lieut. Col., AQM, 5 years	B, 31st N.Y.	57		1892 May 8	KS, 12th, 1893
Potter, Richard		F, 10th Ill.	142		1898 Jul 19	KS, 18th, 1899

Name	Rank	Company, Regiment or Ship	Post*	Age	Death Date†	Journal
Potter, Sam'l	Pvt.	I, 1st Wis. Inf.	493		1920 Oct	IA, 47th, 1921
Potter, Simeon V.	Sergt.	K, 21st Wis. Inf.	168		1910 Apr 15	IA, 37th, 1911
Potter, W.H.					1909 Aug 13	KS, 29th, 1910
Potter, Warren	Sergt.	K, 142nd N.Y. Inf.	182	55	1891 Mar 8	IA, 18th, 1892
Potter, Wm.		K, 51st Ohio Inf.	17		1914 Dec 21	KS, 34th, 1915
Potter, Wm. M.M.		A, 68th Ind.	203		1919 Mar 29	KS, 39th, 1920
Potthoff, Henry	Pvt.	C, 41st Mo. Inf.	5		1911 Dec 8	IA, 38th, 1912
Pottle, W.H.		C, 8th Maine Inf.	158		1899 Nov 7	KS, 19th, 1900
Potts, Chas.	Pvt.	H, 28th Ill. Inf.	7		1910 Nov 19	IA, 37th, 1911
Potts, J.B.	Pvt.	E, 1st Penn. Reserves	22	54	1897 Dec 10	IA, 24th, 1898
Potts, Jas. F.	Pvt.	H, 28th Ill. Inf.	279		3rd quarter 1885	IA, 12th, 1886
Potts, John W.		G, 7th Mo. Cav.	32		1937 Sep 16	KS, 56th, 1937
Potts, Jonathan J.		H, 1st Neb. (died of apoplexy)	201	84	1915 Oct 17	NE, 40th, 1916
Potts, Lewis F.		C, 119th Ill. Inf.	110	59	1905 Jan 24	NE, 30th, 1906
Potts, Nelson	Pvt.	H, 28th Ill. Inf.	279	59	1897 Feb 19	IA, 23rd, 1897
Potts, W.T.		E, 10th Kans.	32		1928 Feb 24	KS, 48th, 1929
Potts, W.W.	Pvt.	Art.	251		1912 Sep 9	IA, 39th, 1913
Potts, William		H, 28th Ill. Vols.	153		1909 Dec 7	KS, 29th, 1910
Poucher, Hiram	Pvt.	B, 25th Iowa	18		1924 Mar 12	IA, 51st, 1925
Poulson, John W.		A, 18th U.S. Inf.	27		1914 Sep 2	KS, 34th, 1915
Poulton, Wm.		K, 1st U.S. Art.	17		1910 May 28	KS, 30th, 1911
Pound, Louis C.		B, 49th Ind.	17		1915 Feb 2	KS, 35th, 1916
Powal, Leander	Pvt.	14th Iowa Inf.	251		1907 Nov 15	IA, 34th, 1908
Powel, T.P.	Pvt.	K, 50th Wis. Inf.	124		1916	IA, 43rd, 1917
Powel, W.H.	Pvt.	D, 7th Iowa Inf.	122		1919 Jul 2	IA, 46th, 1920
Powell, A.W.		L, 15th N.Y. Inf. (died of accident)	155		1897 Jun 27	NE, 22nd, 1898
Powell, Alex B.	Major	19th Ill. Inf.	90		1925 Jan 15	KS, 45th, 1926
Powell, Alfred		G, 10th Ind.	65		1928 Feb 19	KS, 48th, 1929
Powell, Allen		B, 83rd U.S. Col. Inf.	236		1891 Jan 14	KS, 11th, 1892
Powell, E.L.	Pvt.	C, 140th Penn. Inf.	515		1915 Jul 8	IA, 42nd, 1916
Powell, E.O.		C, 23rd Iowa	328		1892 Jul 15	KS, 12th, 1893
Powell, F.			245		1890	NE, 15th, 1891
Powell, Gideon		G, 6th Ind. Inf. (died of heart disease)	129	80	1906 Dec 31	NE, 31st, 1907
Powell, Isaac		H, 36th Iowa	468		1893 Dec 16	KS, 13th, 1894
Powell, J.B.		E, 62nd Ohio Inf. (died at Lawrence)	12		1895 Aug	KS, 15th, 1896
Powell, J.C.	Pvt.	B, 26th Ill. Inf.	159	73	1893 Nov 7	IA, 20th, 1894
Powell, J.J.			235		1908 Jan 6	IA, 35th, 1909
Powell, Jas. M.	Pvt.	B, 40th Iowa Inf.	40		1916 Dec 24	IA, 43rd, 1917
Powell, John	Pvt.	1st Minn. Bat.	110		1900 Oct	IA, 27th, 1901
Powell, John		D, 2nd Ohio	85		1905 May 21	KS, 25th, 1906
Powell, John		K, 12th Kans.	32		1915 Dec 26	KS, 35th, 1916
Powell, John		D, 49th Wis. Inf. (died of Bright's disease)	42	70	1895 Sep 19	NE, 20th, 1896
Powell, L.B., Dr.		G, 126th Ill.	12		1913 Feb 6	KS, 33rd, 1914
Powell, N.		14th Kans.	365		1917	KS, 37th, 1918
Powell, R.M.			125		1911	IA, 38th, 1912
Powell, Robt.	Pvt.	C, 29th Wis. Inf.	125		1926 Mar 6	IA, 53rd, 1927
Powell, Thos.	Corp.	I, 145th Ind. Inf.	452		1926 Jun 2	IA, 53rd, 1927
Powell, W.G.S.		F, 6th West Va. Inf.	128		1900 Jan 6	KS, 21st, 1902
Powell, W.J.	Pvt.	H, 36th Iowa Inf.	497		1918	IA, 45th, 1919
Powell, W.W.		C, 6th Ohio	17		1893 Jan 28	KS, 13th, 1894
Powell, William		A, 1st Neb. (died of dropsy)	21	75	1919 Jan 28	NE, 43rd, 1919
Powell, Wm.		A, 1st Neb. (died of dropsy)	21	76	1919 Jan 8	NE, 44th, 1920
Powell, Wm.		C, 1st Neb. (died of general disability)	21	76	1919 Jan 28	NE, 45th, 1921
Power, John C.	Capt.	8th Iowa Cav.	5		1927	IA, 54th, 1928
Power, L.B.	Surg.		157		1894 Jul	IA, 21st, 1895
Power, W.G.	Pvt.	G, 39th Iowa Inf.	400		1928 Oct 31	IA, 55th, 1929
Power, W.W.	Pvt.	D, 45th Iowa Inf.	100		1920 Jun 15	IA, 47th, 1921
Powers, Albert	Pvt.	A, 3rd Iowa Cav.	100		1923 Apr 26	IA, 50th, 1924
Powers, Chester B.		M, 1st Ill. Battery (died of old age)	155	82	1909 May 19	NE, 33rd, 1909
Powers, Dan		H, 4th Penn.	286		1905	KS, 25th, 1906
Powers, E.B.	Corp.	I, 4th Ill. Cav.	111		1917 Apr 10	IA, 44th, 1918
Powers, F.G.		D, 112th N.Y.	85		1911 Oct 7	KS, 31st, 1912

*See Appendix A, B or C for roster of post names and locations.
†See Introduction for note regarding recording of death date.

Name	Rank	Company, Regiment or Ship	Post*	Age	Death Date†	Journal
Powers, George H.			84		1907 Apr 5	KS, 26th, 1907
Powers, H.C.	Pvt.	G, 6th Wis. Inf.	22		1911 Sep 9	IA, 38th, 1912
Powers, H.H.		C, 21st Ohio Inf.	69		1887 May 2	KS, 7th, 1888
Powers, Henry C.		E, 89th Ind. Inf.	4		1887 May 11	KS, 7th, 1888
Powers, Isaiah		B, 126th Ill. Inf. (died of blood poison)	287		1894 Jun 3	NE, 19th, 1895
Powers, J.K.			29		1915	IA, 42nd, 1916
Powers, Joseph		K, 2nd Mo.	463		1910 Oct 5	KS, 30th, 1911
Powers, Julius H.	Capt.	I, 9th Iowa Inf.	277		1907 May 21	IA, 34th, 1908
Powers, M.		Kans. State Militia	271		1910 Jun 6	KS, 30th, 1911
Powers, M.S.		K, 24th Iowa Inf.	250		1927 Jun 11	KS, 47th, 1928
Powers, Michael		H, 39th Wis. Inf.	117		1916 Dec 12	KS, 36th, 1917
Powers, O.C.	Pvt.		190		1929 Oct 20	IA, 56th, 1930
Powers, William H.		I, 192nd N.Y. Inf.	452	92, 4 mos. & 19 days	1938 Sep 22	IA, 64th, 1938
Pragger, C.B.	Pvt.	F, 44th Iowa Inf.	492		1906 Jul 2	IA, 33rd, 1907
Prall, C.C.		C, 3rd Iowa Cav.		88	1936[1935?] Oct 12	IA, 62nd, 1936
Pramer, Walter	Pvt.	K, 2nd Wis. Cav.	101		1917 Sep 30	IA, 44th, 1918
Pranty, A.		G, 27th Ill.	36		1906 Jan	KS, 26th, 1907
Prater, J.S.		B, 180th Ohio	85		1922 Jun 21	KS, 42nd, 1923
Prater, James F.	Pvt.	L, 9th Mich. Cav.	86		1919 Jun 11	IA, 46th, 1920
Prather, B.G.		G, 24th Ind.	238		1906 Jul 2	KS, 26th, 1907
Prather, F.A.		G, 16th Kans. Cav.	96		1912 Sep 21	KS, 32nd, 1913
Pratt, A.J.	Pvt.	D, 42nd Iowa Inf.	122		1920	IA, 47th, 1921
Pratt, A.R.	Pvt.	B, 7th Ill. Cav.	57		1923 Oct 6	IA, 50th, 1924
Pratt, Abraham		I, 86th Ill. (died of old age)	133	83	1914 Jun 27	NE, 39th, 1915
Pratt, Adelbert		G, 15th Minn.	35	78	1923 Dec 8	NE, 48th, 1924
Pratt, B.R.		B, 7th N.H.	27		1928 Feb 5	KS, 48th, 1929
Pratt, Benton	Pvt.		108		1899 Jul	IA, 26th, 1900
Pratt, Chas. H.		I, 3rd Wis.	256		1931 Mar 15	KS, 51st, 1932
Pratt, Chas. H.		I, 3rd Wis.	256		1931 Mar 15	KS, 52nd, 1933
Pratt, D.W.	Pvt.	5th Wis. Art.	219		1904 Dec 6	IA, 31st, 1905
Pratt, E.F.	Pvt.	C, 101st N.Y. Inf.	235	53	1892 Feb 19	IA, 18th, 1892
Pratt, E.W.	Pvt.	K, 36th Ill. Inf.	194		1916	IA, 43rd, 1917
Pratt, Edward T.		I, 66th Ill.	11	75	1915 Jul 15	NE, 40th, 1916
Pratt, G.W.		E, 9th Ind.	84		1888	KS, 8th, 1889
Pratt, Geo.		B, 10th Mo. Inf. (died of Bright's disease)	10	72	1913 Apr 12	NE, 38th, 1914
Pratt, H.L.	Pvt.	A, 88th Ohio Inf.	236		1930 Feb 4	IA, 57th, 1931
Pratt, I.V.		18th Mo.	2		1893 May	KS, 13th, 1894
Pratt, J.R.		E, 13th Iowa	58		1923 Oct 21	KS, 43rd, 1924
Pratt, Joseph	Pvt.	H, 151st Ill. Inf.	236		1930 Oct 11	IA, 57th, 1931
Pratt, L.M.		E, 33rd Ill. Inf. (died of heart failure)	26	85	1925 Sep 30	NE, 50th, 1926
Pratt, Lewelyn F.		C, 2nd Maine Cav.	380		1917 Sep 1	KS, 37th, 1918
Pratt, Lorenzo	Pvt.	B, 105th Ill. Inf.	247		1908 Jul 5	IA, 35th, 1909
Pratt, Lyman	Corp.	C, 8th Ill. Cav.	38		1925 Mar 29	IA, 52nd, 1926
Pratt, M.A.		K, 3rd Ill. Cav.	244		1921 Dec	KS, 41st, 1922
Pratt, M.S.	Pvt.	H, 3rd N.Y. Lt. Art.	260	55	1892 Oct 8	IA, 19th, 1893
Pratt, M.S.	Sergt.	C, 5th Iowa Inf.	235		1917 Dec 5	IA, 44th, 1918
Pratt, Myron		E, 126th Ill. Inf.	25		1892	NE, 17th, 1893
Pratt, N.H.	Lieut.	I, 95th Ill.	194		1918	IA, 45th, 1919
Pratt, O.A.		H, 3rd Iowa Cav.	85		1919 Feb 18	KS, 39th, 1920
Pratt, O.P.	Pvt.	5th Wis. Inf.	110	92	1933 May 1	IA, 60th, 1934
Pratt, R.G.	Pvt.	A, 12th Iowa Inf.	339		1900 Oct 10	IA, 27th, 1901
Pratt, S.	Pvt.	K, 6th U.S. Cav.	10		1908 Jan	IA, 35th, 1909
Pratt, W.S.		G, 139th Ill.	354		1926 Jun 10	KS, 46th, 1927
Pratt, William H.		E, 4th Penn. Cav. (born in New Jersey; died of paralysis at Soldiers & Sailors Home Hospital, Burkett; buried at Home Cemetery)		72	1907 Feb 3	NE, 31st, 1907
Pratt, Wm. A.		C, 48th Ohio	68		1916 Sep 30	KS, 36th, 1917
Pratz, Stephen B.		K, 47th Ill. Inf.	87[187?]		1887 Oct 29	KS, 7th, 1888
Pray, Eli		D, 70th Ind.	28		1927 Sep 6	KS, 47th, 1928

*See Appendix A, B or C for roster of post names and locations.
†See Introduction for note regarding recording of death date.

Name	Rank	Company, Regiment or Ship	Post*	Age	Death Date†	Journal
Pray, John		L, 2nd Wis. Inf.	7		1926 Jul 25	NE, 51st, 1927
Pray, Robert		E, 23rd Ind. Inf.	192	92	1936 Jun 8	IA, 63rd, 1937
Preble, Henry J.	Q.M.S.	3rd Iowa Bat.	193		1915 May 17	IA, 42nd, 1916
Predden, F.L.		C, 7th Mo. Cav.	54		1922 Mar 4	KS, 42nd, 1923
Predmore, Clark		G, 8th Ind.	75		1905 Aug 19	KS, 25th, 1906
Pregler, John	Corp.	E, 5th Iowa Cav.	70	49	1892 Aug 17	IA, 19th, 1893
Prentice, C.T.K.		E, 17th Kans.	12		1915 Jan 17	KS, 35th, 1916
Prentice, Charles	Pvt.	E, 48th Wis. Inf.	391		1926 Jun 29	IA, 53rd, 1927
Prentice, Franklin	Pvt.	M, 9th Iowa Cav.	67		1923 Jun 27	IA, 50th, 1924
Prentice, Geo. R.		117th Ill. Inf.	25		1935 May 14	KS, 55th, 1936
Prentice, Jos. R.		C, 19th U.S. Inf.	17		1908 Aug 7	NE, 33rd, 1909
Prentice, T.J.	Pvt.	I, 14th Iowa Inf.	330		1897 Mar 24	IA, 24th, 1898
Prentiss, S.B., Dr.	Surg.	U.S. Vols.	12		1892 Oct 9	KS, 12th, 1893
Prescott, Alfonso		A, 104th Ill.	66		1910 Aug 31	KS, 30th, 1911
Prescott, Chas. T.	Pvt.	K, 1st Iowa Cav.	485		1902 Aug 28	IA, 29th, 1903
Prescott, Ivry	1st Lieut.	148th Ind.	139		1929 May 12	KS, 49th, 1930
Prescott, Ivy		E, 26th & 148th Ind. Inf.	139		1930 May 12	KS, 50th, 1931
Prescott, John H.		F, 12th N.H. Inf.	127		1891 Jul 14	KS, 11th, 1892
Presler, Laomin M.		1st Mo. Lt. Art.	131		1911 Jun 25	KS, 31st, 1912
Pressler, Martin	Pvt.	A, 50th Penn. Inf.	64		1908 Mar 12	IA, 35th, 1909
Pressley, Jacob F.		I, 58th Ill.	5		1910 Sep 30	KS, 30th, 1911
Pressnal, J.S.	1st Lieut.	F, 63rd Ind. Inf.	6	92	1932 Feb 4	IA, 59th, 1933
Presson, Charles A.		E, 3rd Iowa Cav.	65		1930 Oct 4	KS, 50th, 1931
Presson, Chas.		E, 3rd Iowa	65		1931 Oct 4	KS, 51st, 1932
Presson, Chas.		E, 3rd Iowa	65		1931 Oct 4	KS, 52nd, 1933
Presson, H.		F, 55th Ill. (not a member of Farragut Post)	25	96	1913 May 1	NE, 38th, 1914
Presson, Joseph H.		A, 55th Ill. Inf. (see Appendix D)	7	84	1924 Jun 11	NE, 49th, 1925
Pressy, E.M.		B, 9th Mich.	118		1922 Dec 20	KS, 42nd, 1923
Prestine, F.L.	Pvt.	C, 46th Ill.	62		1906 Dec 1	IA, 33rd, 1907
Preston, —			380		1923	KS, 43rd, 1924
Preston, A.G.	Pvt.	B, 3rd N.Y. Cav.	488	55	1894 Mar 10	IA, 21st, 1895
Preston, A.G.	Pvt.	B, 3rd N.Y. Cav.	488	55	1894 Mar 9	IA, 20th, 1894
Preston, C.N.	Pvt.	G, 35th Iowa Inf.	271		1908 Oct	IA, 35th, 1909
Preston, Chandler	Pvt.	A, 36th Ill. Inf.	7	83	1898 Dec 20	IA, 25th, 1899
Preston, Charles	Pvt.	A, 6th Iowa Cav.	492		1900 May 16	IA, 27th, 1901
Preston, David	Pvt.	B, 86th Ill. Inf.	55		1930 May	IA, 57th, 1931
Preston, F.M.		I, 57th Ohio	123		1936 May 20	KS, 57th, 1938
Preston, F.M.		I, — Ohio	123		1936 May 20	KS, 56th, 1937
Preston, Henry M.	Corp.	F, 12th Iowa Inf.	236		1912 Nov 12	IA, 39th, 1913
Preston, J.D.			10		1927	IA, 54th, 1928
Preston, J.W.			180		1894	NE, 19th, 1895
Preston, Jacob	Sergt.	G, 89th Ill. Inf.	18		1905 Jul 27	IA, 32nd, 1906
Preston, Jerry C.		F, 2nd Minn. (died from cancer and wound received in battle)	164		1890	KS, 10th, 1891
Preston, John B.	Pvt.	B, 1st Wis. Cav.	26	58	1899 Jul 9	IA, 26th, 1900
Preston, W.F.	Pvt.	K, 21st Iowa Inf.	492		1893 Feb 18	IA, 20th, 1894
Preston, W.H.		C, 20th Iowa	294		1918 Apr 23	KS, 38th, 1919
Preston, W.M.		A, 1st Minn.	235		1906 Nov 4	IA, 33rd, 1907
Preston, Wm. E.		H, 25th Ill. Inf.	11	83	1925 Dec 9	NE, 50th, 1926
Pret, Jas. W.		19th Ind. Bat.	167		1906 Sep 9	KS, 26th, 1907
Preterbaugh, S.G.		B, 3rd Ill.	17		1918 Oct 29	KS, 38th, 1919
Pretz, W.H.		B, 57th Ill.	29		1922 Mar 20	IA, 49th, 1923
Prewitt, William, see Pruitt, William						
Price, C.C.	Pvt.	G, 42nd Ind.	190		1924 Jul 27	IA, 51st, 1925
Price, C.H.	Corp.	A, 4th Wis. Cav.	332		1930 Jan 14	IA, 57th, 1931
Price, C.P.		D, 6th Kans.	123		1891 Mar 8	KS, 11th, 1892
Price, Charles		I, 46th Ohio	47		1926 Jul 7	KS, 46th, 1927
Price, D.A.		F, 13th Ill.	123		1927 Apr 27	KS, 47th, 1928
Price, Euclid		H, 81st Ill.	113		1917 Jul 27	KS, 37th, 1918
Price, F.J.	Sergt.	E, 4th Iowa	425		1922 Dec 18	IA, 49th, 1923
Price, F.M.		B, 12th Kans.	40		1913 Aug 22	KS, 33rd, 1914

*See Appendix A, B or C for roster of post names and locations.
†See Introduction for note regarding recording of death date.

439

Name	Rank	Company, Regiment or Ship	Post*	Age	Death Date†	Journal
Price, Furman		A, 3rd Ill.	25		1885	KS, 5th, 1886
Price, G.V.D.		D, 12th Iowa	28		1920 Nov 22	KS, 40th, 1921
Price, George		E, 3rd U.S.	380		1897 Dec 11	KS, 17th, 1898
Price, Gilbert S.		B, 2nd Neb. Cav.	7		1924[1923?] Mar 8	NE, 48th, 1924
Price, H.	Pvt.	B, 2nd Iowa Cav.	94		1920 Apr 24	IA, 47th, 1921
Price, Herbert T.	Pvt.	I, 4th Wis. Cav.	332		1927 Jun 9	IA, 54th, 1928
Price, Ira A.	Pvt.	C, 3rd Mich. Inf.	22		1916 Jan 18	IA, 43rd, 1917
Price, Israel		D, 10th Iowa	40		1913 Feb 18	KS, 33rd, 1914
Price, J.C.	Pvt.	C, 5th Iowa	153		1926 Jul 14	IA, 53rd, 1927
Price, J.F.	Pvt.	F, 56th Penn. Vol. Inf.	8		1924 Jan 20	IA, 51st, 1925
Price, J.R.		A, 2nd Penn.	119		1923 Jun 24	KS, 43rd, 1924
Price, J.W.		D, 2nd Ky. Inf.	5		1906 Feb 8	IA, 33rd, 1907
Price, James	Pvt.	A, 2nd Penn. Reserves	452		1907 Nov 14	IA, 34th, 1908
Price, John		G & D, 2nd Ind. Cav.	28		1916 Jan 2	KS, 36th, 1917
Price, John		G, 1st Neb. Vet. Vols.	118		1939 Nov 17	NE, 64th, 1940
Price, John D.	Pvt.	D, 1st Mo.	54	54	1892 Jun 25	IA, 19th, 1893
Price, John H.		C, 5th Iowa Cav.	40		1917 Jan 4	KS, 37th, 1918
Price, John S.		B, 37th Ind. Inf. (died of general disability)	77	76	1916 Mar 14	NE, 41st, 1917
Price, M.S.		F, 34th Ill.	127		1913 Dec 30	KS, 33rd, 1914
Price, Robt.			287		1925	NE, 50th, 1926
Price, S.A.		M, 102nd Penn.	1		1908 Apr 10	KS, 28th, 1909
Price, Sam	Pvt.	D, 9th Iowa Inf.	502		1900 Apr 14	IA, 27th, 1901
Price, Thompson	Corp.	G, 82nd Ohio Inf.	205	58	1899 Jul 4	IA, 26th, 1900
Price, Thos.	Pvt.	G, 27th Iowa Inf.	132	51	1888 Feb 1	IA, 15th, 1889
Price, Thos. E.		B, 2nd Neb. Inf.	7		1926 Dec 28	NE, 51st, 1927
Price, W.G.		D, 12th Iowa Inf.	58		1928 Mar 1	KS, 49th, 1930
Price, W.J.			214		1922	NE, 47th, 1923
Price, W.M.		L, 14th Kans. Cav.	66		1911 Oct 1	KS, 31st, 1912
Price, W.P.	Pvt.	J, 11th Wis. Inf.	357		1905 May 23	IA, 32nd, 1906
Price, Wm. H.	Pvt.	E, 4th Iowa Cav.	321		1900 Feb 17	IA, 27th, 1901
Prichett, Robert C.		A, 8th Tenn.	153		1910 Aug 23	KS, 30th, 1911
Prickett, Aaron A.			203		1900 Apr 3	KS, 20th, 1901
Priddy, D.M.	Pvt.	D, 9th Iowa Cav.	39		1909 Aug 15	IA, 36th, 1910
Priddy, J.T.		C, 10th Kans.	293		1912 Aug 24	KS, 32nd, 1913
Priddy, James W.		A, 13th Ind. Cav. (see Appendix D)	250		1934 May 17 or 18	KS, 54th, 1935
Priddy, W.H.		H, 15th Ohio	265		1918 Dec 28	KS, 38th, 1919
Prideaux, Thomas	Pvt.	A, 33rd Wis. Inf.	258		1916 Aug 29	IA, 43rd, 1917
Pridemore, Jeremiah		B, 48th Ill. Inf. (died of old age)	36	79	1913 Feb	NE, 38th, 1914
Pridemore, Jeremiah		B, 48th Ind. Vol. Inf. (died of pneumonia)	36	83	1913 Apr 27	NE, 37th, 1913
Pridle, J.W.	Pvt.	G, 2nd Iowa	100		1905 May 7	IA, 32nd, 1906
Priest, George		I, 1st Iowa Cav.	73		2nd quarter 1884	IA, 11th, 1885
Priest, George		F, 140th Ind. Inf.	[18?]		1901 Nov 22	KS, 21st, 1902
Priest, J.D.	Pvt.	D, 2nd Iowa Inf.	4		1897-1898	IA, 24th, 1898
Priestly, William		Wis.	28		1905 May 6	KS, 25th, 1906
Prime, John R.			12		1923 May 24	IA, 50th, 1924
Primmer, Abram		H, 33rd Ohio	19		1897 Feb 28	KS, 17th, 1898
Primmer, Abram		I, 151st Ohio	19		1897 Feb 28	KS, 16th, 1897
Primrose, Alex.		F, 39th N.Y. Inf.	380		1899 Mar 18	KS, 19th, 1900
Prince, H.R.		A, 41st Ohio Cav. (died of consumption)	289		1893 Sep 24	NE, 18th, 1894
Prince, W.E.		I, 23rd Mo.	263		1904 Aug 15	KS, 24th, 1905
Princehouse, W.H.		K, 20th Ohio	57		1927 May 12	KS, 47th, 1928
Princi, Andrew		C, 23rd Mo.	294		1896 Mar 5	KS, 16th, 1897
Prindle, E.R.			63		1928 Dec 28	IA, 56th, 1930
Prindle, Owen I.		E, 6th Iowa Inf.	1		1932 Jul 30	NE, 57th, 1933
Prine, M.M.	Corp.	4th Iowa Bat.	40		1920 Mar 10	IA, 47th, 1921
Prine, Wm.		E & A, 47th & 50th Mo.	500		1913 Feb 13	KS, 33rd, 1914
Pring, W.H.	Pvt.	H, 8th Iowa Inf.	40		1908 Oct 17	IA, 35th, 1909
Pritchard, J.O.			42		1909 Aug	IA, 36th, 1910
Pritchard, P.W.	Pvt.	I, 7th Iowa Cav.	22		1897 Jun 27	IA, 24th, 1898
Pritchett, George E.		E, 126th N.Y. Inf.	110	70	1912 Mar 12	NE, 37th, 1913
Prnyn, James W.		F, 23rd Iowa (died of heart trouble)	90	71	1912 Sep 12	NE, 37th, 1913
Pro, George			265		1913 Jun 16	KS, 33rd, 1914

*See Appendix A, B or C for roster of post names and locations.
†See Introduction for note regarding recording of death date.

Name	Rank	Company, Regiment or Ship	Post*	Age	Death Date†	Journal
Probasco, Geo.		I, 76th Ill.	63		1921 Dec 27	KS, 41st, 1922
Probst, Daniel			127		1919 Mar 2	KS, 39th, 1920
Probst, O.M.	Pvt.	E, 129th Ohio Inf.	23		1912 Mar 29	IA, 39th, 1913
Procter, Jas. M.		D, 16th Ill.	81		1898 Oct 22	KS, 18th, 1899
Proctor, A.E.	Sergt.	K, 74th Ohio Inf.	9		1917 Oct 20	IA, 44th, 1918
Proctor, A.H.		K, 28th Mich.	356		1890	KS, 10th, 1891
Proctor, A.H.		K, 28th Mich. Inf.	356		1888 Mar 25	KS, 11th, 1892
Proctor, A.H.		K, 28th Mich.	356		1888	KS, 8th, 1889
Proctor, A.H.		K, 28th Mich. Inf.	356		1888 Mar 25	KS, 12th, 1893
Proctor, Geo. N.	Pvt.	B, 34th Iowa Inf.	173		1897 Nov 13	IA, 24th, 1898
Proctor, J.G.			222		1916	IA, 43rd, 1917
Proctor, James M.		D, 16th Ill.	114		1898 Oct 22	KS, 18th, 1899
Proctor, John		C, 52nd Ind.	83		1923 Oct 4	KS, 43rd, 1924
Proctor, John C.		H, 13th Kans.	1		1923 Nov 6	KS, 43rd, 1924
Proctor, Wallace	Pvt.	A, 92nd N.Y. Inf.	452		1914 Dec 28	IA, 41st, 1915
Proeger, George H.		C, 11th Kans. Cav.	55		1917 Apr 10	KS, 37th, 1918
Prose, Henry B.		H, 25th Ill. Inf.	20		1921 Sep 11	KS, 41st, 1922
Prose, L.B.	Pvt.		86	58	1893 Jun 20	IA, 20th, 1894
Prose, W.L.		H, 25th Ill.	244		1924 Nov 28	KS, 44th, 1925
Prosper, Claud	Pvt.	F, 53rd Ill. Inf.	66		1908 Aug 18	IA, 35th, 1909
Prosser, C.H.	Pvt.	H, 36th Iowa	497		1921 Dec 14	IA, 48th, 1922
Protexter, Geo.	Pvt.	D, 12th Ill.	147		1922	IA, 49th, 1923
Proudfit, W.H.		G, 36th Ill.	25		1928 Jul 18	NE, 53rd, 1929
Prouty, A.S.	Sergt.	H, 38th Wis. Inf.	263		1897 Jul 10	IA, 24th, 1898
Prouty, C.C.	Capt.	E, 33rd Iowa Inf.	12		1909 Dec 28	IA, 36th, 1910
Prouty, D.A.		D, 18th Mo.	38		1922 Feb 14	KS, 42nd, 1923
Prouty, James N.	Sergt.	A, 92nd Ill. Inf.	193		1915 Dec 28	IA, 42nd, 1916
Prouty, John M.		G, 27th Ill. 9th Ill. Inf.	36		1921 Dec 30	KS, 41st, 1922
Prouty, Levi O.			452		1932	IA, 59th, 1933
Provine, John S.		C, 84th Ill.	7		1889	KS, 9th, 1890
Provinsky, D.	Pvt.	K, 4th Ill. Cav.	22		1927 Apr 12	IA, 54th, 1928
Pruden, L.		C, 33rd Ind. Inf.	294		1916 May	KS, 36th, 1917
Prudham, Chas.		E, 44th N.Y.	8		1909 Aug 15	KS, 29th, 1910
Prueatt, B.L.		I, 145th Penn.	477		1910 May 25	KS, 30th, 1911
Pruess, E.F.A.	Pvt.	E, 2nd Iowa Cav.	236		1921 Dec	IA, 48th, 1922
Pruess, E.F.A.			236		1922	IA, 49th, 1923
Pruett, John		I, 21st Mo.	147		1893 Oct 2	KS, 13th, 1894
Pruett, W.H.		G, 20th Ind. Inf.	7		1926 Nov 9	NE, 51st, 1927
Pruitt, John R.			36		1926 Oct 16	KS, 46th, 1927
Pruitt, William		H, 50th Ind. Inf.		95	1937 Jun 22	IA, 64th, 1938
Prunty, —			12		1923 Mar 12	IA, 50th, 1924
Prunty, David		E, 15th Mo. Cav.	38		1904 Sep 23	KS, 24th, 1905
Prunty, David		G, 28th Kans.	38		1921 Sep 10	KS, 41st, 1922
Prusell, Martin	Pvt.	C, 14th Iowa Inf.	4	64	1892 May 4	IA, 19th, 1893
Prutsman, Christian M.		I, 7th Wis. Inf. (died of dropsy)	112	81	1915 Sep 30	NE, 40th, 1916
Pryce, Sam D.	Capt.	A, 22nd Iowa Inf.	8		1923 Dec 20	IA, 50th, 1924
Pryor, Charles		H, 148th Ill.	170		1921 Feb 15	KS, 41st, 1922
Pryor, Hiram		E, 7th Ind. Inf.	4		1925 Aug 8	KS, 45th, 1926
Pryor, J.H.	Pvt.	I, 35th Ill. Inf.	31		1926 Jan 20	IA, 53rd, 1927
Pryor, R.T.		M, 5th Iowa Cav. (died at Fredonia)	98		1895 Jul 24	KS, 15th, 1896
Psett, S.G.			72		1924 Jan 1	KS, 44th, 1925
Pucher, James P.		died of dropsy	1	75	1905 Dec 20	NE, 30th, 1906
Pucket, James A.	Pvt.	B, 13th Ohio Inf.	384	52	1893 May 14	IA, 20th, 1894
Puckett, —			98		1926 May	KS, 46th, 1927
Puffer, A.E.		*U.S.S. Undilla*	12		1918 Jan 23	IA, 45th, 1919
Puffer, Wm.		7th Ill.	464		1904 Nov 4	KS, 24th, 1905
Pugh, Booz Franklin		K, 5th Penn. Hvy. Art. (see also Appendix D)	18	75	1923 Mar 9	KS, 43rd, 1924
Pugh, E.D.		K, 36th Iowa	12		1904 May 29	KS, 24th, 1905
Pugh, E.M.		died of heart failure	73	64	1904 Dec	NE, 29th, 1905
Pugh, F.H.		M, 9th Ohio Cav.	7		1924[1923?] Jun 20	NE, 48th, 1924

Name	Rank	Company, Regiment or Ship	Post*	Age	Death Date†	Journal
Pugh, J.W.	Pvt.	F, 23rd Ohio Inf.	235		1915 Jun 7	IA, 42nd, 1916
Pugh, James		K, 43rd Mo.	88		1928 Sep 19	KS, 48th, 1929
Pugh, William	Pvt.	G, 19th Iowa Inf.	56		1922 Oct 12	IA, 49th, 1923
Pugh, Wm. H.	Pvt.	F, 4th Iowa Cav.	40		1927 Jan 21	IA, 54th, 1928
Pugsley, John L.		134th Ohio Inf.	343		1912 Jan 1	IA, 38th, 1912
Pulk, Wm.		2nd Minn. Bat.	462		1889	KS, 9th, 1890
Pullen, Archy		C, 60th U.S. Colored Inf.	25		1937 Dec 3	NE, 62nd, 1938
Pulver, B.F.	Pvt.	D, 93rd Ill. Inf.	94		1917 Jul 23	IA, 44th, 1918
Pulver, Cassius M.		D, 8th Calif.	7		1931 Oct 1	NE, 56th, 1932
Pulver, G.	Sergt.	K, 3rd Iowa Inf.	271		1914 Nov 28	IA, 41st, 1915
Pulver, Isaac L.			333		1928 Jun 14	IA, 55th, 1929
Pulver, Myron	Pvt.	H, 75th Ill. Inf.	188		1913 Oct 23	IA, 40th, 1914
Pump, Frederick		B, 37th Ohio (died of old age)	62	83	1917 May 4	NE, 42nd, 1918
Pumpelly, B.A.		I, 10th Kans. Cav.	74		1918 Jun 3	KS, 38th, 1919
Pumroy, D.C.	Pvt.	D, 29th Iowa Inf.	334		1897 Mar 21	IA, 24th, 1898
Puntenney, Parker S.	Pvt.	C, 4th Iowa Cav.	454		1906 May 21	IA, 33rd, 1907
Purcell, Geo. W.	Pvt.	H, 45th Ohio Inf.	10		1919 Jan 12	IA, 46th, 1920
Purcell, W.D., see Pursell, W.D.						
Purcell, W.W.		E, 10th Iowa Inf. (died of wounds)	25	65	1895 Mar 26	NE, 20th, 1896
Purdey, D.S.	Pvt.	B, 10th N.Y. Hvy. Art.	111		1904 Jul 10	IA, 31st, 1905
Purdum, William T.		E, 3rd Enrolled Mo. Militia	250		1924 Nov 8	KS, 44th, 1925
Purdy, Clark		E, 12th Ohio (died of diabetes)	27	69	1912 Oct 24	NE, 39th, 1915
Purdy, James		A, 7th Kans. Cav.	63		1919 Jun 28	KS, 39th, 1920
Purdy, S.C.		E, 12th & 22nd Ohio (died of diabetes)	27	68	1912 Oct 24	NE, 37th, 1913
Purdy, S.K.		C, 4th N.Y. Hvy. Art.	124		3rd quarter 1884	IA, 11th, 1885
Purington, L.A.		I, 2nd Iowa Cav.	67		1912 Dec 26	IA, 39th, 1913
Purkhiser, M.	Pvt.	B, 66th Ind. Inf.	31		1908 Aug	IA, 35th, 1909
Pursell, I.N.	Pvt.	B, 35th Iowa Inf.	231		1906 Dec 7	IA, 33rd, 1907
Pursell, W.D.		E, 10th Ill. (died of army trouble)	32	74	1915 Feb 16	NE, 40th, 1916
Pursell, William		D, 4th Iowa Cav.	47		1909 Jan 17	KS, 29th, 1910
Pursing, Jacob	Pvt.	B, 16th Iowa Inf.	163	56	1893 Apr 21	IA, 20th, 1894
Purvis, Elijah	Sergt.	B, 2nd Iowa Cav.	30		1912 Sep 23	IA, 39th, 1913
Purvis, Frank		C, 26th Ind. Inf.	252		1901 Feb 1	KS, 21st, 1902
Purvis, J.C.		F, 11th Iowa	108	87	1934 May 15	IA, 61st, 1935
Pusel, Jacob		E, 10th Ill. Inf. (died of dropsy)	23	65	1896 Feb 6	NE, 21st, 1897
Putman, H.	Pvt.	F, 103rd Ill. Inf.	235	65	1891 Feb 27	IA, 17th, 1891
Putman, H., see Puttman, H.						
Putman, L.	Pvt.	E, 1st Ill. Art.	88		1907 Sep 15	IA, 34th, 1908
Putman, S.C.	Pvt.	H, 8th Vt. Inf.	10		1920 Dec 17	IA, 47th, 1921
Putman, W.S.	Pvt.	D, 3rd Iowa Cav.	235		1921 Feb 9	IA, 48th, 1922
Putman, William		F, 21st Iowa	49	87	1934 Jul 15	IA, 61st, 1935
Putnam, A.D.	Lieut.	H, 3rd Mo. Cav.	414		1904 Jan 30	IA, 31st, 1905
Putnam, C.F.			1		1893 Oct 21	KS, 13th, 1894
Putnam, Chas. E.			235		1913 May	IA, 40th, 1914
Putnam, Gilbert		D, 28th Mich.	318	90	1917 Oct 12	NE, 42nd, 1918
Putnam, Jacob E.		A, 13th Md.	8		1885	KS, 5th, 1886
Putnam, P.S.		47th Ind. Inf. (died of old age)	25	80	1903 Mar 29	NE, 28th, 1904
Putnam, Peter	Pvt.	E, 5th Iowa Inf.	63		1923 Dec 14	IA, 50th, 1924
Putnam, S.C., see Putman, S.C.						
Putnam, W.H.		D, 127th Ill.	100		1913 Dec 8	KS, 33rd, 1914
Putnam, W.S., see Putman, W.S.						
Putnam, William, see Putman, William						
Putney, W.A.			18		1886	NE, 11th, 1887
Putney, W.G.		I, 2nd Ill. Art. (died of paralysis)	214	76	1919 Oct 27	NE, 44th, 1920
Putney, Wm.			168		1909 Oct 7	IA, 36th, 1910
Putt, Geo. W.		G, 122nd Ohio (died of old age)	35	73	1910 Dec 15	NE, 35th, 1911
Puttman, H.		died of brain fever	59		1895 Apr 24	NE, 20th, 1896
Pyer, W.M.	Pvt.	F, 15th Vt. Inf.	172		1905 Jun 24	IA, 32nd, 1906
Pygal, John		32nd Wis. (died of old age)	38	87	1925 Dec	NE, 50th, 1926

*See Appendix A, B or C for roster of post names and locations.
†See Introduction for note regarding recording of death date.

Name	Rank	Company, Regiment or Ship	Post*	Age	Death Date†	Journal
Pygall, John O., see Pzzal, John O.						
Pyle, A.L.		A, 3rd Ill. Inf. A, 7th Ill. Cav.	52		1916 Sep 20	KS, 36th, 1917
Pyle, G.W.			7		1919	IA, 46th, 1920
Pyle, J.B.		L, 14th Kans. Cav.	91		1891 Dec 19	KS, 11th, 1892
Pyle, J.S.	Capt.	H, 100th Penn. Inf.	208	56	1897 Aug 12	IA, 24th, 1898
Pyle, Samuel W.		B, 15th Kans.	32		1919 Jun 5	KS, 39th, 1920
Pyle, T.J.		E, 2nd Mo.	18		1933 Oct 17	KS, 53rd, 1934
Pyle, Wm.		M, 5th Kans. Cav. B, 15th Kans. Cav.	23		1922 Jun 16	KS, 42nd, 1923
Pyles, Jacob B.		4th West Va.	247		1916 Apr 28	KS, 36th, 1917
Pyser, Alfred		G, 2nd Colo. Cav. (died of typhoid fever)	123	58	1895 Nov 1	NE, 20th, 1896
Pzzal, John O.		A, 32nd Wis. (died of sleeping sickness)	38	86	1924 May	NE, 49th, 1925
Quackenbush, A.		K, 15th Kans. Cav.	1		1922 Jul 13	KS, 42nd, 1923
Quade, Frank L.	Pvt.	G, 8th Iowa Cav.	78	98, 4 mos. & 16 days	1945 May 9	IA, 71st, 1945
Quaifft, A.E.	Capt.	H, 28th Iowa Inf.	132		1906 Jun 15	IA, 33rd, 1907
Quarterman, W.H.		B, 7th Iowa	17		1918 Feb 12	KS, 38th, 1919
Queen, Wesley		F, 2nd Neb. (died of old age)	25	79	1915 Dec 12	NE, 40th, 1916
Quest, Charles		E, 25th Ill. Inf.	74		1912 Dec 7	KS, 32nd, 1913
Quick, A.W.			123		1914 Dec 27	KS, 34th, 1915
Quick, Charles	Sergt.	K, 3rd Iowa Cav.	49	72	1893 Sep 22	IA, 20th, 1894
Quick, Eli J.	Pvt.	I, Tyler Rangers	29	86 & 6 mos.	1932 Jan 7	IA, 59th, 1933
Quick, J.M.	Pvt.	D, 3rd Ohio Inf.	9		1911	IA, 38th, 1912
Quick, James	Pvt.	K, 7th Kans. Cav.	101	76	1895 Jun 2	IA, 22nd, 1896
Quick, Lorenzo		D, 138th Ill.	25		1915 Sep 4	NE, 40th, 1916
Quick, P.V.	Pvt.	L, 7th Ill. Cav.	1	90	1931 Mar 17	IA, 58th, 1932
Quick, T.M.		L, 2nd Mo. (died of senility)	354	79	1904 Mar 6	NE, 29th, 1905
Quicksell, Jas. W.	Pvt.	A, 2nd Iowa Inf. C, 3rd Iowa Cav.	515	57	1898 Aug 16	IA, 25th, 1899
Quier, Levi		H, 58th Ill. Inf.	172		1929 Sep 3	KS, 49th, 1930
Quiett, John L.		F, 13th Kans. Inf.	493		1902 Dec 27	KS, 22nd, 1903
Quigley, John S.	Pvt.	A, 32nd Iowa Inf.	141		1913 Oct 16	IA, 40th, 1914
Quigley, W.A.		C, 67th Ind.	4		1920 Apr 13	KS, 40th, 1921
Quigley, Wm. L.		D, 86th N.Y. Inf. (born in New York; resident of Soldiers & Sailors Home, Burkett; died & buried in Wolbach, Neb.)		73	1906 May 25	NE, 31st, 1907
Quigly, Geo. W.		F, 13th Ohio Inf. (died of heart disease)	44	61	1897 Feb 20	NE, 22nd, 1898
Quim, John		F, 110th Ohio Inf.	15		1887 Feb 4	KS, 7th, 1888
Quimby, D.C.		F, 37th Iowa (died of old age)	11	91	1904 Jun 28	NE, 29th, 1905
Quimby, Freeman B.		C, 7th Wis.			1928 Dec 21	NE, 53rd, 1929
Quimby, S.J.		61st U.S.C.T. (died of old age)	110	79	1912 Sep 8	NE, 37th, 1913
Quinlick, Martin		H, 9th Mo. Cav.	280		1892 Nov 29	KS, 12th, 1893
Quinn, J.D.		C, 85th N.Y.	63		1921 Mar 19	KS, 41st, 1922
Quinn, John	Pvt.	B, 75th Ill. Inf.	136		3rd quarter 1885	IA, 12th, 1886
Quinn, L.		I, 1st Neb. Inf.	240		1916 Jan 4	KS, 36th, 1917
Quinn, Leonidas		I, 1st Neb.	240		1915 Jan 4	KS, 35th, 1916
Quinn, R.M.	Sergt.	G, 1st Kans. Inf.	39		1928 Dec 20	IA, 55th, 1929
Quinn, Richard H.	Pvt.	A, 3rd Col. Inf.	98		1902 Jul 30	IA, 29th, 1903
Quinn, T.A.		F, 1st Wis. Hvy. Art.	86		1919 Dec 28	KS, 39th, 1920
Quinn, Thomas	Pvt.	B, 52nd Ill. Inf.	349	52	1898 Jul 20	IA, 25th, 1899
Quint, S.C.	Pvt.	K, 12th Mich. Inf.	44		1925 Apr 14	IA, 52nd, 1926
Quishenberry, Thos.		C, 14th Kans.	161		1898 Nov 23	KS, 18th, 1899
Quisling, Einar		G, 14th Wis. Inf.	190		1918 Jun 21	KS, 38th, 1919
Quixby, B.W.		L, 1st Ohio	57		1933 Mar 29	KS, 53rd, 1934
Quontz, August		M, 1st Ind. (sudden death)	104	75	1920 Apr 22	NE, 45th, 1921
Raaliff, W.H.		77th Ind. Inf.	14		1899 Jan 19	KS, 19th, 1900
Raber, Lewis		D, 194th Penn.	7		1933 Sep 7	NE, 58th, 1934
Raber, P.H.	Pvt.	F, 12th Ky. Cav.	452		1915	IA, 42nd, 1916

*See Appendix A, B or C for roster of post names and locations.
†See Introduction for note regarding recording of death date.

Name	Rank	Company, Regiment or Ship	Post*	Age	Death Date†	Journal
Race, G.W.		F, 130th N.J.	106		1892 Dec 27	KS, 12th, 1893
Racey, Samuel	Pvt.	K, 30th Ohio Inf.	69		1928 May 19	IA, 55th, 1929
Rachford, J.M.	Pvt.	4th Ohio Cav.	434	58	1891 May 15	IA, 18th, 1892
Rachford, N.D.	Pvt.	A, 2nd Mo. Cav.	40		1924 Jul 1	IA, 51st, 1925
Radcliff, B.T.		E, 22nd Iowa Inf. (died at Overbrook; buried at Overbrook Cemetery)	237		1894 Apr 25	KS, 14th, 1895
Radcliff, J.C.		G, 13th Kans. Vols.	355		1902 Apr 27	KS, 22nd, 1903
Radcliff, Samuel		G, Ohio Hvy. Art.	119		1922 — 7	KS, 42nd, 1923
Radefer, Silas		F, 50th Ohio	68		1933 Aug 17	NE, 58th, 1934
Rader, Abraham		D, 79th Ill.	262		1897 Sep 2	KS, 17th, 1898
Rader, S.J.	Pvt.	B, 36th Iowa Inf.	69		1912 Sep 4	IA, 39th, 1913
Rader, W.A.		K, 14th Kans.	130		1931 Apr 11	KS, 51st, 1932
Rader, W.A.		K, 14th Kans.	130		1931 Apr 11	KS, 52nd, 1933
Rader, W.H.H.		G, 46th Ind. Inf. (died of alcoholism)	25	63	1891[1901?] Jun	NE, 26th, 1902
Radford, Jos.	Pvt.	C, 21st Iowa Inf.	78		1915 Nov 17	IA, 42nd, 1916
Radford, W.T., see Rauford, W.T.						
Radford, William T.		U.S. Navy, *Ozark* (died at Oklahoma City, Oklahoma Terr.)	2		1894 Jan 25	KS, 14th, 1895
Radford, Wm.		E, 3rd Iowa Battery	130		1889	KS, 9th, 1890
Radges, Samuel		H, 74th Ohio	1		1921 Jan 5	KS, 41st, 1922
Radnich, Stephen	Pvt.		251		1912 Sep 13	IA, 39th, 1913
Radtke, Wm.	Pvt.	H, 4th Vt. Inf.	202		1903 Nov 4	IA, 30th, 1904
Raff, A.K.	Corp.	I, 19th Ohio	231		1903 Oct 30	IA, 30th, 1904
Raff, E.J.	Pvt.	A, 20th Ohio Inf.	1		1927 Dec 20	IA, 54th, 1928
Raff, George		2nd Iowa	193		1913 Feb 18	KS, 32nd, 1913
Raff, William		I, 16th Iowa	250		1928 Nov 10	KS, 48th, 1929
Raffensperger, J.J.	Pvt.	C, 24th Iowa Inf.	135		1917 Jan 28	IA, 44th, 1918
Raffensperger, Joe	Pvt.	C, 24th Iowa Inf.	135		1918 Jan 28	IA, 45th, 1919
Raffsenperger, J.		C, 9th Penn.	87		1930 Apr 23	KS, 50th, 1931
Ragan, Cal.			167		1928 Feb 7	IA, 55th, 1929
Ragan, Geo.		G, 145th Ill.	32		1926 Mar 15	NE, 51st, 1927
Ragan, Jas. W.		C, 15th Kans.	243		1896 Aug 9	KS, 16th, 1897
Ragan, Josiah		I, 18th Ill. Inf.	397	96	1937 Feb 17	IA, 64th, 1938
Ragsdale, G.H., see Hagsdale, G.H.						
Ragsdale, Jas. M.			36		1930 Mar 12	KS, 50th, 1931
Ragsdale, W.H.		C, 13th Iowa	68		1929 Dec 16	KS, 49th, 1930
Raikes, John H.	Pvt.	H, 115th Ind. Inf.	192		1917 Jan 10	IA, 44th, 1918
Raines, H.F.		H, 49th Ky.	59		1918 Sep 15	KS, 38th, 1919
Raines, Hiram		D, 49th Ky.	59		1919 Sep 5	KS, 39th, 1920
Raines, Isaac C.	Pvt.	C, 75th Ind. Inf.	40		1912 Nov 8	IA, 39th, 1913
Raines, Peter R.		D, 7th Ill. Cav.	243		1908 Jun 25	KS, 28th, 1909
Rainey, D.B.		78th Ohio Inf. (died at Dodge City, Kans.; buried at Dodge City G.A.R. Cemetery)	294		1894 Mar 7	KS, 14th, 1895
Rains, Allen M.	Pvt.	D, 4th Penn. Inf.	252		1901 May 15	IA, 27th, 1901
Rains, George W.		C, 29th Ind.	90		1923 Dec 9	KS, 43rd, 1924
Rains, R.F.	Pvt.	G, 32nd Iowa Inf.	220		1904 Sep 30	IA, 31st, 1905
Rains, Zebadee	Pvt.	B, 25th Iowa Inf.	384		1911 Nov 15	IA, 38th, 1912
Rake, Asher W.		B, 1st Ill. Bat. (died of dropsy of heart)	70		1893 Oct 25	NE, 18th, 1894
Rake, George W.		M, 5th Kans. Cav.	71		1924 Feb 2	KS, 44th, 1925
Rake, John	Pvt.	A, 116th Ohio Inf.	23		1918 Jan 25	IA, 45th, 1919
Ralf, Marion	Pvt.	I, 12th Iowa Inf.	74		1904 Mar 7	IA, 30th, 1904
Rall, E.B.		A, 84th Ill.	244		1929 Oct 27	KS, 49th, 1930
Ralph, G.W.		D, 9th N.Y.	113		1914 Jan 23	KS, 34th, 1915
Ralph, H.C.		D, 9th N.Y. Cav.	116		1898 Jun 14	KS, 18th, 1899
Ralph, J.B.		C, 104th Ill.	7		1929 Mar 29	NE, 54th, 1930
Ralston, E.D.		F, 21st Penn. Cav.	34		1928 Apr 26	NE, 53rd, 1929
Ralston, J.N.	Pvt.	I, 102nd Ill. Inf.	94		1931 Jul 17	IA, 58th, 1932
Ralston, John	Pvt.	E, 30th Iowa Inf.	333		1916	IA, 43rd, 1917
Ralston, John			461		1917	IA, 44th, 1918
Ralston, John			333		1917	IA, 44th, 1918

*See Appendix A, B or C for roster of post names and locations.
†See Introduction for note regarding recording of death date.

Name	Rank	Company, Regiment or Ship	Post*	Age	Death Date†	Journal
Ralston, S.F.		K, 1st Penn.	68		1917 Jan 12	KS, 37th, 1918
Ralston, W.		D, 12th Ill.	129		1916 Jul 19	KS, 36th, 1917
Rama, I.W.	Pvt.	D, 8th[?] Wis. Inf.	452	51	1897 Jan 7	IA, 23rd, 1897
Ramay, Wm. R.		25th Iowa	116		1924 Sep 1	IA, 51st, 1925
Rambach, M.	Pvt.	K, 3rd Iowa Inf.	11		1910 Jun	IA, 37th, 1911
Ramey, Wm.	Pvt.	K, 18th Iowa Inf.	12		1929 Mar 24	IA, 56th, 1930
Ramfle, Michael	Pvt.	A, 31st Iowa Inf.	233		1910 Mar 24	IA, 37th, 1911
Ramier, Wm.	Pvt.	C, 26th Iowa	38		1905 May	IA, 32nd, 1906
Ramillian, N.		K, 76th Ill. Inf.	331		1900 Aug 5	KS, 20th, 1901
Ramsay, J.F.	Sergt.	I, 149th Penn. Inf.	8		1930 Sep 11	IA, 57th, 1931
Ramsay, J.M.		A, 46th Penn. Inf.	35		1894	NE, 19th, 1895
Ramsdell, William		L, 6th Mich. (former member; died at Exeter)	76		1936 Nov 2	NE, 61st, 1937
Ramsey, A.C.		C, 132nd Ohio	66		1920 May 23	KS, 40th, 1921
Ramsey, A.O.		F, 7th Mo. Cav.	1		1920 Feb 20	KS, 40th, 1921
Ramsey, A.T.		D, 7th Mo. Cav.	244		1901 Nov 3	KS, 21st, 1902
Ramsey, D.	Pvt.	I, 6th Iowa Inf.	5		1920 Apr 21	IA, 47th, 1921
Ramsey, E.B.	Pvt.	13th Penn. Inf.	16		1916	IA, 43rd, 1917
Ramsey, Edward I.		B, 43rd Ind. Inf.			1937 (1936?) Jun 29	IA, 64th, 1938
Ramsey, F.M.		K, 79th Ind.	32		1923 Aug 9	KS, 43rd, 1924
Ramsey, J.H.		I, 3rd Iowa (died of cancer)	35	78	1921 Mar 15	NE, 46th, 1922
Ramsey, James	Sergt.	K, 31st Iowa Inf.	88		1930 Feb 14	IA, 57th, 1931
Ramsey, James	Pvt.	I, 2nd Penn. Sharpshooters	1		1915 Apr 21	KS, 35th, 1916
Ramsey, James M.			35		1897 Dec 14	NE, 22nd, 1898
Ramsey, M.K.	Pvt.	E, 3rd Iowa Inf.	329		1904 Apr 26	IA, 31st, 1905
Ramsey, R.P.	Pvt.	K, 45th Iowa Inf.	79		1926 Jul 23	IA, 53rd, 1927
Ramsey, Robert		B, 3rd N.Y. Cav.	91	59	1893 Jun 7	IA, 20th, 1894
Ramsey, T.B.		D, 4th Iowa Cav.	407		1908	KS, 28th, 1909
Ramsey, W.H.H.		A, 5th N.Y.	40		1919 Apr 28	NE, 44th, 1920
Ramsey, W.T.		E, 10th Kans.	12		1910 Nov 4	KS, 30th, 1911
Ramsey, Wm. F.		I, 2nd Iowa Cav.	25		1940 Jan 24	NE, 65th, 1941
Ran, Jacob		M, 1st West Va.	435		1906 Sep 10	KS, 26th, 1907
Rand, Geo. D.	Paymaster	U.S. Navy	2		1903 Nov 12	IA, 30th, 1904
Rand, W.V.		B, 126th Ill.	24		1898 Dec 22	KS, 18th, 1899
Randal, A.K.	Sergt.	G, 1st Wis. Cav.	400		1911 Jul 22	IA, 38th, 1912
Randall, Alonzo		E, 1st Mich. Art.	354	77	1906 Mar 28	NE, 31st, 1907
Randall, C.M.		17th N.Y. Inf.	1		1890	KS, 10th, 1891
Randall, C.M.		17th N.Y. Bat.	1		1918 May 28	KS, 38th, 1919
Randall, C.W.		B, 13th N.H.	35		1926 Apr 10	NE, 51st, 1927
Randall, David H.		D, 21st Ohio	25		1912 Jul 8	KS, 32nd, 1913
Randall, E.F.		3rd Mich.	76		1926 Aug 23	KS, 46th, 1927
Randall, George		G, 90th N.Y. Inf.	88		1914 Jan 1	KS, 34th, 1915
Randall, H.E.	Pvt.	K, 3rd Iowa Cav.	49		1918 Sep 28	IA, 45th, 1919
Randall, H.T.		K, 33rd Ill.	176		1913 Feb 19	KS, 33rd, 1914
Randall, I.W.		K, 3rd Iowa Inf.	259		1925 Jun 28	KS, 45th, 1926
Randall, J.M.			311		1917 Mar 17	KS, 37th, 1918
Randall, J.M.	Capt.	G, 21st Ohio K, 65th Ohio	66		1921 Jul 19	KS, 41st, 1922
Randall, J.W.		F, 6th Mo.	68		1919	KS, 39th, 1920
Randall, L.M.		B, 25th Iowa Inf.	7		1921	IA, 48th, 1922
Randall, M.M.		I, 32nd Wis.	65		1898 Nov 16	KS, 18th, 1899
Randall, Murray N.		I, 32nd Wis. Inf.	65		1899	KS, 19th, 1900
Randall, P.E.	Pvt.	I, 27th Wis.	124		1905 Dec	IA, 32nd, 1906
Randall, R.R.			25	82	1910 Feb 3	NE, 35th, 1911
Randall, Steve	Pvt.	F, 50th Ill. Inf.	208		1915 Aug 21	IA, 42nd, 1916
Randall, T.R.		E, 10th Mo.	147		1927 Nov 17	KS, 47th, 1928
Randall, W.H.		C, 8th Iowa Inf. (died of lung fever)	43	50	1896 Jan 6	NE, 21st, 1897
Randall, W.S.		C, 8th Iowa Inf. (died of diabetes)	43		1893 Apr 22	NE, 18th, 1894
Randall, W.W.	Pvt.	D, 30th Wis. Inf.	48		1917 Mar 2	IA, 44th, 1918
Randall, William	Pvt.	C, 102nd Penn. Inf.	40		1915 Jul 23	IA, 42nd, 1916
Randle, Abraham		B, 114th Ohio Inf.	88		1909 Dec 26	KS, 29th, 1910
Randolph, A.G.		G, 22nd Penn. Cav.	55		1924 May 27	KS, 44th, 1925

*See Appendix A, B or C for roster of post names and locations.
†See Introduction for note regarding recording of death date.

Name	Rank	Company, Regiment or Ship	Post*	Age	Death Date†	Journal
Randolph, Wm. H.	Pvt.	G, 3rd Iowa Inf.	116	52	1893 May 24	IA, 20th, 1894
Rands, J.G.	Sergt.	C, 27th Minn. Inf.	12		1927 Oct 17	IA, 54th, 1928
Raney, Geo. C.		A, 17th Ohio	55		1896 Nov 5	KS, 16th, 1897
Rank, A.C.	Pvt.	K, 196th Penn. Inf.	29		1923 Nov 23	IA, 50th, 1924
Rankard, Michael		C, 160th N.Y.	184		1902 Aug 7	KS, 22nd, 1903
Rankin, Allison		F, 18th Ill.	74		1932 May 10	NE, 57th, 1933
Rankin, C.H.		C, 1st Iowa	174		1919 May 15	KS, 39th, 1920
Rankin, David K.		A, 78th Penn. Inf.	88		1916 Mar 6	KS, 36th, 1917
Rankin, E.	Pvt.		86		1916 Feb 14	IA, 43rd, 1917
Rankin, Ezra	Corp.	H, 7th Va. Inf.	100		1918	IA, 45th, 1919
Rankin, J.C.		E, 7th Ohio	221		1916 Jun 16	KS, 36th, 1917
Rankin, J.M.	Pvt.	F, 143rd Ill. Inf.	42		1913 Jun 31	IA, 40th, 1914
Rankin, Jesse					1937 Aug 16	IA, 64th, 1938
Rankin, John	Pvt.	I, 2nd Iowa Cav.	78		1905 Nov 5	IA, 32nd, 1906
Rankin, John K.	Col.	D, C, & H, 2nd Kans.	12		1913 Oct 29	KS, 33rd, 1914
Rankin, Silas P.		E, 138th Ill. Inf. (at large)			1932 Jan 16	IA, 59th, 1933
Rankin, Wm.		G, 21st Iowa Inf.	20		1931	KS, 51st, 1932
Ranney, A.B.		F, 19th Mich.	158		1904 Dec 15	KS, 24th, 1905
Ranney, A.O.		B, 22nd Wis.	322		1912 Mar 12	KS, 32nd, 1913
Ransdell, Wm. F.		C, 156th Ind.	284		1936 Feb 19	NE, 61st, 1937
Ransom, Amos		G, 2nd Ill. Inf.	447		1899 Apr 26	KS, 19th, 1900
Ransom, C.S.	Pvt.	I, 34th Ill. Inf. / G, 142nd Ill. Inf.	132		1929 Nov 8	IA, 56th, 1930
Ransom, Chas. H.		C, 186th N.Y.			1921 Apr 22	KS, 41st, 1922
Ransom, Isaac		C, 49th Ind.	244		1897 Aug 4	KS, 17th, 1898
Ransom, John	Pvt.		3		1917 Mar 3	IA, 44th, 1918
Ransom, John			29		1883	KS, 3rd, 1884
Ransom, W.H.		27th Ill.	26		1926 Mar 27	KS, 46th, 1927
Ransom, William H.		F, 125th Ohio Inf.	244		1925 Dec 7	KS, 45th, 1926
Rany, A.J.			6		1890	NE, 15th, 1891
Rapeen, H.G.	Pvt.	A, 14th Iowa Inf.	149		1924 Oct 24	IA, 51st, 1925
Raper, F.A.		K, 84th Ill. Inf. (died of La Grippe)	24	78	1891[1901?] Feb	NE, 26th, 1902
Raper, R.	Pvt.	82nd Ill.	32		1921 May 24	IA, 48th, 1922
Raper, T.J.			11		1917	IA, 44th, 1918
Raper, W.B.		C, 2nd Neb. Cav.	5		1914 Dec 29	NE, 39th, 1915
Rapp, Frederick	Pvt.	G, 10th N.J. Inf.	95		1908 Dec 18	IA, 35th, 1909
Rapp, John			77		1922 May 22	KS, 42nd, 1923
Rapp, Paul	Pvt.	I, 6th N.Y. Hvy. Art.	294		1925 Oct 3	IA, 52nd, 1926
Rarick, J.J., see Rarrick, J.J.			231			
Rarick, Nathan B.		F, 39th Ill. Inf.	78		1902 Jul 2	KS, 22nd, 1903
Rarick, O.S.		B, 6th Iowa Inf.	158		1912 May 10	KS, 32nd, 1913
Rariden, M.D.		D, 59th Ind. Vol. Inf.	87		1890	KS, 10th, 1891
Rarrick, J.J.		K, 11th Ohio / E, 69th Ohio	12		1904 Dec 3	KS, 24th, 1905
Raser, Adam H.		K, 112th Ill.	82		1923 Mar 1	KS, 43rd, 1924
Rash, John C.		F, Home Guards, Mo.	127		1892 Aug	KS, 12th, 1893
Rash, Larson		died at Ottawa	[18?]		1895 Dec	KS, 15th, 1896
Rashaw, Orin C.		K, 1st Wis. Art. (former member of department; died at Grand Island)	354		1939 Apr 18	NE, 64th, 1940
Rasher, Frank	Pvt.		1		1924 Apr 17	IA, 51st, 1925
Rasler, John	Corp.	C, 100th Ind. Inf.	12		1900-1901	IA, 27th, 1901
Rasler, John	Corp.	C, 100th Ind. Inf.	17		1901-1902	IA, 28th, 1902
Rasp, Jacob		C, 10th Tenn. (died of heart trouble)	68	78	1921 Nov 20	NE, 46th, 1922
Rasph, Daniel		C, 147th Ind. Inf.	36		1900 Feb 19	KS, 21st, 1902
Rassing, T.A.	Capt.	E, 15th Wis. Inf.	193		1913 Nov 1	IA, 40th, 1914
Ratcliff, Jas. R.		B, 43rd Ind. Inf. (died of heart trouble)	23		1923 May 17	NE, 48th, 1924
Ratekin, J.R.	Pvt.	I, 11th Iowa Inf.	56		1928	IA, 55th, 1929
Rath, John	Pvt.	B, 31st Iowa	311		1914 Jun 20	IA, 41st, 1915
Rath, William	Pvt.	F, 5th Iowa Cav.	78		1918 Mar 21	IA, 45th, 1919
Rathborne, H.L.		M, 2nd Neb. Cav.	100		1930 Apr 15	KS, 50th, 1931
Rathbun, J.O.C.		K, 2nd Mo. Cav.	52		1913 Dec 17	KS, 33rd, 1914
Rathbun, Robert S.	Pvt.	B, 24th Iowa	88		1923 Feb 18	IA, 50th, 1924

*See Appendix A, B or C for roster of post names and locations.
†See Introduction for note regarding recording of death date.

Name	Rank	Company, Regiment or Ship	Post*	Age	Death Date†	Journal
Rathbun, S.D.	Com. Sergt.	C, 4th Wis. Cav.	247		1901 Feb 14	IA, 28th, 1902
Rathbun, S.W.	Capt.	B, 24th Iowa	206		1921 Jul 11	IA, 48th, 1922
Rathburn, A.H.		C, 50th N.Y. Inf.	262	71	1914 May 18	NE, 39th, 1915
Rathburn, E.C.	Pvt.	E, 9th N.Y. Cav.	222		1900 Dec 7	IA, 27th, 1901
Rathburn, Geo. R.		I, 24th Iowa	7		1927 Jan 6	NE, 52nd, 1928
Rathburn, Wm.	Corp.	M, 12th Ind. Cav.	298		1899 Oct 14	IA, 26th, 1900
Raub, A.A.		H, 1st Penn.	1		1926 Oct 3	KS, 46th, 1927
Rauford, W.T.		E, 6th Mo. Cav.	303		1904 Nov 22	KS, 24th, 1905
Raum, Jerry	Pvt.	K, 15th Iowa Inf.	164		1916 Apr	IA, 43rd, 1917
Rausser, Joshua		G, 112th Ill.	89		1910 Aug 16	KS, 30th, 1911
Ravenscraft, A.R.	Capt.	I, 22nd Ind. Inf.	170		1896 Nov 13	IA, 23rd, 1897
Rawitzer, Wm.		A, 41st Wis. Inf. (died of pneumonia)	7	71	1902 Nov	NE, 27th, 1903
Rawley, J.B.			68		1890	KS, 10th, 1891
Rawlings, J.L.		H, 23rd Iowa	455		1896 Feb 10	KS, 16th, 1897
Rawlings, Nichlos V.		E, 111th Ill.	32		1924 May 12	KS, 44th, 1925
Rawlings, Wm. J.		G, 70th Ind.	322		1902 Dec 17	KS, 22nd, 1903
Rawlins, A.		1st Ohio	130		1920 Nov 1	KS, 40th, 1921
Rawlins, J.M.			17		1911 Sep 27	KS, 31st, 1912
Raworth, George		J, 64th Ill. (died of old age)	2	89	1918 Jun 17	NE, 43rd, 1919
Rawson, C.H.			12		2nd quarter 1884	IA, 11th, 1885
Rawson, John G.	Pvt.	G, 11th Wis. Inf.	165		1928 Feb 18	IA, 55th, 1929
Ray, Allen	Sergt.	G, 46th Wis. Inf.	408	58	1896 Jan 9	IA, 22nd, 1896
Ray, Allen C.	Sergt.	G, 46th Wis. Inf.	408	58	1896 Jan 9	IA, 23rd, 1897
Ray, Alphonso		F, 2nd N.Y. Cav.	85		1912 Dec 18	KS, 32nd, 1913
Ray, Amos		H, 87th Ill.	158		1920 Dec 23	KS, 40th, 1921
Ray, Charles D.		B, 12th Ill. Inf. (born in Rhode Island; died at Soldiers & Sailors Home Hospital, Burkett; buried at Home Cemetery)		65	1906 Nov 26	NE, 31st, 1907
Ray, Charles D.		I, 55th Ill. Inf.	354	64	1906 Nov 26	NE, 31st, 1907
Ray, Chas. E.	Pvt.	M, 17th Ill. Cav.	403	46	1892 Jan 23	IA, 18th, 1892
Ray, Geo.	Pvt.	C, 6th Mo.	22		1921 Feb 8	IA, 48th, 1922
Ray, Hugh		D, 52nd Ind. Inf. (died of cancer of stomach)	10	61	1905 May 28	NE, 30th, 1906
Ray, J.H.		D, 52nd Ohio	55		1933 Feb 18	KS, 53rd, 1934
Ray, J.M.		F, 76th Penn.	25		1933 Oct 28	NE, 58th, 1934
Ray, James A.		B, 30th Mo. Inf.	17		1914 Apr 18	KS, 34th, 1915
Ray, James M.	Sergt.	B, 34th Iowa Inf.	169	68	1897 Sep 4	IA, 24th, 1898
Ray, James M.	Sergt.	B, 34th Iowa Inf.	169	67	1896 Sep 4	IA, 23rd, 1897
Ray, John		G, 1st Mich. Lt. Art. (died of heart disease)	34		1893 Nov 7	NE, 18th, 1894
Ray, John F.	Pvt.	H, 8th Wis. Inf.	235		1910 Apr	IA, 37th, 1911
Ray, John I.		H, 30th Ill.	25		1922 Jun 3	KS, 42nd, 1923
Ray, Samuel D.		A, 42nd Ohio	17		1918 Oct 10	KS, 38th, 1919
Ray, Thos.	Pvt.	F, 39th Iowa	55		1905 Mar 8	IA, 32nd, 1906
Ray, W.L.			122		1898 Aug	KS, 18th, 1899
Ray, Wm.		F, 49th Wis. Inf. (died of complications)	262	81	1920 Nov 30	NE, 45th, 1921
Rayan, David	Pvt.	E, 81st Iowa	12		1905 Jun 19	IA, 32nd, 1906
Rayburn, A.F.		B, 40th Iowa Inf.	127		1912 Jun 28	IA, 39th, 1913
Rayburn, Joseph N.	Pvt.	F, 3rd Iowa Inf.	16		1912 Feb 14	IA, 39th, 1913
Rayburn, T.D.	Sergt.	F, 10th Iowa Inf.	452		1906 Jan 3	IA, 33rd, 1907
Rayfield, Chas.		B, 7th Ohio Cav.	453		1922 Sep 18	KS, 42nd, 1923
Rayle, James E.		D, 58th Ind. Inf.	196		1899 Oct 12	KS, 19th, 1900
Rayles, Jacob		F, 11th Ill. Cav. (died of old age)	149	84	1916 Nov 12	NE, 41st, 1917
Raymond, E.	Pvt.	H, 4th Iowa Cav. (died of exhausted vitality)	17	46	1884 Jan 1	NE, 9th, 1885
Raymond, H.C.	Capt.	C, 32nd Iowa Inf.	3		1908 Apr 18	IA, 35th, 1909
Raymond, H.L.	Pvt.	B, 40th Wis. Inf.	22		1918 Aug 6	IA, 45th, 1919
Raymond, Horace H.	Pvt.	B, 16th N.Y. Inf.	88		1913 Dec 4	IA, 40th, 1914
Raymond, John N.	Farrier	I, 2nd Wis. Cav.	98	62	1894 Sep 15	IA, 21st, 1895
Raymond, Joseph	Pvt.	L, 2nd Iowa Cav.	74		1901 Dec 5	IA, 28th, 1902
Raymond, L.B.	Sergt.	G, 6th Wis. Inf. (see also Appendix D)	81		1911 Apr 18	IA, 38th, 1912
Raymond, Ransom		A, 8th Mo. Cav.	17		1912 Oct 21	KS, 32nd, 1913
Raymond, Seth		C, 3rd Wis. (died of paralysis)	265	74	1910	NE, 35th, 1911

Name	Rank	Company, Regiment or Ship	Post*	Age	Death Date†	Journal
Raymond, T.W.	Pvt.	A, 36th Ill.	22		1924 May 6	IA, 51st, 1925
Raymor, J.W.		Navy	132		1930 Mar 26	KS, 50th, 1931
Rayney, E.R.	Eng.	U.S. Navy	4		1906	KS, 26th, 1907
Rayston, A.M.		C, 3rd Ohio Inf.	36		1899 Sep 9	KS, 21st, 1902
Razor, W.W.		G, 24th Ky.	42		1917 Apr 28	KS, 37th, 1918
Rea, John W.		A, 106th Penn.	17		1920 Dec 28	KS, 40th, 1921
Rea, R.I.		H, 13th Kans.	130		1920 Jun 20	KS, 40th, 1921
Reach, Chas.			260		1899	NE, 24th, 1900
Read, Chas. P.	Pvt.	M, 2nd Iowa Cav.	235	49	1891 Jan 25	IA, 17th, 1891
Read, Elijah T.		H, 26th Ind.	150		1916 Feb 20	KS, 36th, 1917
Read, Geo. M.	Pvt.	H, 42nd Ohio Inf.	12		1908 Jul 5	IA, 35th, 1909
Read, H.A.		G, 19th Ill. Inf.	270		3rd quarter 1884	IA, 11th, 1885
Read, I.H.		I, 177th Penn. Inf. (died of Bright's disease)	140	56	1895 May 18	NE, 20th, 1896
Read, J.P.	Pvt.	I, 84th Penn. Inf.	452		1919 May 8	IA, 46th, 1920
Read, W.L.	Pvt.	B, 110th Ohio Inf.	94		1900-1901	IA, 27th, 1901
Read, Z.S.		1st Iowa Cav.	55		1911 Nov 7	IA, 38th, 1912
Reader, Samuel J.	1st Lieut. & QM	2nd Kans. M.	250		1914 Sep 15	KS, 34th, 1915
Reading, August	Drum Major	D, 20th Iowa Inf.	1	91	1932 Jun 15	IA, 59th, 1933
Reading, James E.		E, 5th & G, 13th Mo. Cav. (died at Lawrence)	12		1895 Oct	KS, 15th, 1896
Ready, J.W.		G, 41st —	71		1917 Mar 18	KS, 37th, 1918
Ready, Joseph C.	Pvt.	A, 12th Ill. Cav.	42		1932 Jan 8	IA, 59th, 1933
Reagan, J.W.		C, 73rd Ill. (died of heart disease & dropsy)	265		1890	KS, 10th, 1891
Reager, John			2	71	1916 Sep 4	NE, 41st, 1917
Real, George		B, 154th N.Y.	301		1913 Apr	KS, 32nd, 1913
Ream, David		B, 2nd Ill. Cav.	113		1902 Jul 6	KS, 22nd, 1903
Ream, F.S.			80		1918	IA, 45th, 1919
Ream, J.C.	Pvt.	86th Penn. Inf.	24		1918 Apr 18	IA, 45th, 1919
Ream, Leroy R.		G, 69th Ind. Inf. (died at Osage City; buried at Swedish Cemetery)	11		1894 Sep 15	KS, 14th, 1895
Ream, Phillip H.	Pvt.	B, 2nd Iowa Cav.	234		1900 Nov 5	IA, 27th, 1901
Ream, Samuel E.		C, Penn & Ind. Bat.	46		1923 Sep 4	KS, 43rd, 1924
Reamer, W.R.		1st Ohio Inf.	108		1908 Jun 27	IA, 35th, 1909
Reames, Jeremiah		L, 5th Mo.	332		1897 Aug 3	KS, 17th, 1898
Reamy, Cyrus		D, 17th Kans. Inf.	250		1914 Dec 25	KS, 34th, 1915
Rean, J.T.	Pvt.	C, 33rd Iowa Inf.	40		1916 Jan 6	IA, 43rd, 1917
Reardon, Albert P.		L, 123rd Ohio	279		1918 Nov 24	KS, 38th, 1919
Reardon, Charles	Pvt.	B, 2nd Wis. Inf.	141		1892 Sep 4	IA, 19th, 1893
Rearick, John M.		G, 98th N.Y.	52		1919 Nov 3	KS, 39th, 1920
Reaser, Cornelius		K, 75th Ind.	206		1931 Jan 6	NE, 56th, 1932
Reason, T.	Pvt.	B, 40th Ohio Inf.	222		1924 Nov 3	IA, 51st, 1925
Reaves, E.A.	Corp.	A, 4th Iowa Cav.	209		1909 Nov 13	IA, 36th, 1910
Reaves, F.M.		M, 15th N.Y. Eng.	68		1930 Aug 29	KS, 50th, 1931
Reavis, James Washington					1937 Mar 6	IA, 64th, 1938
Rebman, W.H.	Pvt.	E, 5th Iowa Cav.	70		1910 Jul	IA, 37th, 1911
Rebstock, C.		F, 11th Kans. Cav.	180		1899 Apr 10	KS, 19th, 1900
Reckard, Barrett		E, 44th Ind.	190		1933 Feb 9	NE, 58th, 1934
Reckler, Fred A.	Pvt.	C, 2nd Wis. Inf.	16		1916	IA, 43rd, 1917
Rector, J.N.	Pvt.	B, 30th Iowa Inf.	100		1929 Aug 14	IA, 56th, 1930
Rector, Levi C.		D, 8th Ill. Inf. (died of paralysis)	62	72	1916 Sep 14	NE, 41st, 1917
Rector, Sam'l		B, 2nd Neb. Cav. (died of paralysis)	61	80	1902 Dec	NE, 27th, 1903
Red, John			12		1923 Jan 8	KS, 43rd, 1924
Redd, George W.		D, 140th Penn.	17		1915 Jul 23	KS, 35th, 1916
Redden, Isaac	Pvt.	D, 15th Iowa Inf.	29	46	1893 Jan 21	IA, 19th, 1893
Reddick, John		C, 1st Va.	17		1897 Feb 20	KS, 17th, 1898
Reddick, W.H.	Lieut.	B, 33rd Ohio	153		1903 Nov 9	IA, 30th, 1904
Redding, C.C.	Pvt.	B, 19th Wis.	22		1923 Feb 13	IA, 50th, 1924
Reddington, John W.		A, 57th Ind. Inf.	117		1912 Mar 31	KS, 32nd, 1913
Redeman, Philip	Pvt.	E, 9th Wis. Inf.	240	61	1893 Jul 6	IA, 20th, 1894
Redenbaugh, Jno.	Corp.	K, 58th Ill. Inf.	38		1925 Apr 17	IA, 52nd, 1926

*See Appendix A, B or C for roster of post names and locations.
†See Introduction for note regarding recording of death date.

Name	Rank	Company, Regiment or Ship	Post*	Age	Death Date†	Journal
Reder, Anton	Corp.	A, 169th N.Y. Inf.	147		1916 May 26	IA, 43rd, 1917
Redfield, Franklin A.		I, 77th Ill. (died of rheumatism)	169	69	1905[1904?] Aug 26	NE, 29th, 1905
Redfield, J.W.	2nd Lieut.	I, 39th Iowa Inf.	43	57	1896 May 28	IA, 23rd, 1897
Redfield, L.E.	Pvt.	F & M, 7th N.Y. Art.	64		1907 May 18	IA, 34th, 1908
Redfield, Nathan		F, 2nd Neb. Cav. (died of old age)	24	79	1900 Aug 18	NE, 25th, 1901
Redfield, Stephen D.	2nd Lieut.	A, 37th Iowa Inf.	98	85	1893 Apr 20	IA, 20th, 1894
Redford, F.W.		F, 40th Wis. Inf.	214	70	1915 Dec 15	NE, 40th, 1916
Redford, Wm.		I, Wis. (died of stomach trouble)	3	63	1904	NE, 29th, 1905
Redford, Wm.		A, 4th Wis. Inf. (died of fever)	3	63	1905 Jan	NE, 30th, 1906
Redgate, Thos. J.		Navy	17		1922 Jul 8	KS, 42nd, 1923
Rediger, Jacob		F, 77th Ill.	52		1922 Apr 16	KS, 42nd, 1923
Redington, Henry	Pvt.	H, 1st Bat. U.S. Inf.	267	44	1889 May 13	IA, 16th, 1890
Redman, W.B.		K, 25th Ind.	140		1928	NE, 53rd, 1929
Redman, W.H.	Pvt.	C, 12th Ill. Cav.	7		1901-1902	IA, 28th, 1902
Redman, W.H.	Pvt.	C, 5th Iowa Cav.	78		1910 Aug 2	IA, 37th, 1911
Redman, William		H, 126th Ill.	115		1928 Feb 28	KS, 48th, 1929
Redmon, H.W.	Pvt.	E, 38th Wis. Inf.	25		1933	IA, 60th, 1934
Redmon, Wm.	Pvt.	D, 15th Iowa Inf.	57		1916 May 13	IA, 43rd, 1917
Redpath, J.T.	Sergt.	E, 33rd Iowa Inf.	126		1904 Oct 22	IA, 31st, 1905
Redpears, Herman E.		B, 9th Ohio	190		1896 Aug 14	KS, 16th, 1897
Reece, E.B.		F, Kans. State Militia	3		1916 May 26	KS, 36th, 1917
Reece, Herbert		F, 1st Wis.	500		1920	KS, 40th, 1921
Reece, L.C.		Navy	50		1917 Mar 9	KS, 37th, 1918
Reece, Lowell		B, 25th Ohio Inf. H, 82nd Ohio	18		1917 Apr 13	KS, 37th, 1918
Reed, A.B.	Pvt.	14th Ohio Inf.	235	52	1892 Mar 23	IA, 18th, 1892
Reed, Alfred A.		D, 64th Ohio	18		1902 May 12	KS, 22nd, 1903
Reed, Alpheus N.		H, 14th N.Y. Hvy. Art.	25		1935 Aug 24	NE, 60th, 1936
Reed, Byron H.		D, 12th Kans. Inf.	18		1908 Apr 15	KS, 28th, 1909
Reed, C.	Corp.	D, 15th Ohio Inf.	52		1924 Jun 9	IA, 51st, 1925
Reed, C.L.		A, 126th N.Y.	342		1905	KS, 25th, 1906
Reed, Chas. F.			17		1933 Jun 8	KS, 53rd, 1934
Reed, D.R.		C, 57th N.Y.	98		1896 Apr 20	KS, 16th, 1897
Reed, D.S.		A, 86th Ohio (died of old age)	21	80	1919 Dec 11	NE, 44th, 1920
Reed, D.V.		K, 34th Iowa	81		1928 Jan 29	KS, 48th, 1929
Reed, David			500		1910	IA, 37th, 1911
Reed, David		F, 30th Ind. Inf.	65		1899 Jan 13	KS, 19th, 1900
Reed, E.F.			246		1904 Mar 14	IA, 31st, 1905
Reed, E.S.	Sergt.	H, 74th Ill. Inf.	377		1900 Feb	IA, 27th, 1901
Reed, Elmer	Pvt.	A, 1st Iowa Cav.	75		1914 Oct 15	IA, 41st, 1915
Reed, Enis H.		A, 93rd Ill. (cause of death: kidney)	35	76	1915 Apr 14	NE, 40th, 1916
Reed, Enos		K, 34th Iowa	12		1925	KS, 45th, 1926
Reed, Ephriam		G, 152nd Ohio Inf. (died at his home in Auburn, Kans.)	1		1934 Jun 5	KS, 54th, 1935
Reed, F.B.		I, 1st Neb. (died of heart failure)	302	74	1904	NE, 29th, 1905
Reed, Fred W.		E, 3rd Kans. State Militia Inf.	12		1901 Jun 8	KS, 21st, 1902
Reed, Geo.			24		1912 Jul 8	IA, 39th, 1913
Reed, George		A, 26th U.S. Inf.	117		1899 Dec 10	KS, 19th, 1900
Reed, George W.		K, 10th Ohio Cav.	82		1924 Apr 14	KS, 44th, 1925
Reed, George W.		H, 14th Maine	71		1914 Nov 11	KS, 34th, 1915
Reed, H.G.		I, 78th Ill.	71		1928 Feb 7	KS, 48th, 1929
Reed, H.L.		B, 9th Kans.	252		1914 Jul 11	KS, 34th, 1915
Reed, H.M.			275		1919 Aug 19	IA, 46th, 1920
Reed, H.P.		D, 92nd Ill. Inf.	25		1899 Sep 8	KS, 19th, 1900
Reed, Harvey			316		1919	IA, 46th, 1920
Reed, Henry M.		K, 4th Ky.	380		1912 Dec 13	KS, 32nd, 1913
Reed, Hiram H.		G, 122nd N.Y. Inf. (died of consumption)	110		1894 Aug 22	NE, 19th, 1895
Reed, J.A.		F, 151st Ill.	25		1927 Mar 12	KS, 47th, 1928
Reed, J.G.		E, 2nd Ohio Cav.	47		1922 May 26	KS, 42nd, 1923
Reed, J.J.			429		1911	KS, 31st, 1912
Reed, J.R.	Capt.	2nd Iowa Battery	29		1925 Apr 2	IA, 52nd, 1926
Reed, Jacob H.			25		1919 Jan 10	KS, 39th, 1920

*See Appendix A, B or C for roster of post names and locations.
†See Introduction for note regarding recording of death date.
449

Name	Rank	Company, Regiment or Ship	Post*	Age	Death Date†	Journal
Reed, James		E, 3rd Colo. Cav.	429		1908	KS, 28th, 1909
Reed, James S.	Pvt.	B, 34th Iowa Inf.	252	60	1893 Dec 26	IA, 20th, 1894
Reed, James W.		G, 110th Penn. Inf.	20		1891 Oct 6	KS, 11th, 1892
Reed, Jas.	Pvt.	F, 32nd Iowa Inf.	338		1900 May 13	IA, 27th, 1901
Reed, John	Pvt.	E, 1st Iowa Cav.	270		1905 Feb 26	IA, 32nd, 1906
Reed, John A.		E, 11th U.S. Inf. (died of paralysis)	80		1906 Sep 3	NE, 31st, 1907
Reed, John A.		E, 1st Iowa (died of paralysis at Soldiers & Sailors Home, Milford)		75	1906 Sep 3	NE, 31st, 1907
Reed, John P.	Pvt.	G, 8th Iowa Cav.	231		1904 Apr 8	IA, 31st, 1905
Reed, John W.		3rd Wis. Cav.	12		1914 Nov 16	KS, 34th, 1915
Reed, John W.		H, 29th Mich.	31		1917 May	KS, 37th, 1918
Reed, John W.		B, 70th Ohio	20		1926 Nov 1	KS, 46th, 1927
Reed, John W.		I, 1st Ohio Hvy. Art.	53		1919 Nov 21	KS, 39th, 1920
Reed, Joseph O.		G, 154th Ill. Inf.	172		1900 Jul 31	KS, 20th, 1901
Reed, Julius		4th Mo. Inf. (died of congestion of lungs)	21	77	1919 Jan 8	NE, 44th, 1920
Reed, M.D.			29		1907 Oct 1	IA, 34th, 1908
Reed, Madison		H, 133rd Ill.	293		1913 Aug 12	KS, 33rd, 1914
Reed, Miles		A, 3rd Mich.	100		1912 Dec 13	KS, 32nd, 1913
Reed, N.C.		G, 122nd Ohio	63		1921 Aug 21	KS, 41st, 1922
Reed, Oliver Curry (Col.)		E, 60th U.S. Col. Inf. (at large)		92	1938 Jun 18	IA, 64th, 1938
Reed, Philander	Pvt.	D, 75th N.Y.	7		1904 Mar 9	IA, 31st, 1905
Reed, R.W.		E, 16th Ind. Inf.	63		1886	KS, 6th, 1887
Reed, S.W.	Pvt.	M, 31st Iowa Inf.	191		1904 Feb 12	IA, 31st, 1905
Reed, Samuel		K, 42nd Penn.	474		1915 Jan 18	KS, 35th, 1916
Reed, Samuel P.	Pvt.	A, 15th Iowa Inf.	88		1917 Sep 20	IA, 44th, 1918
Reed, Samuel R.		L, 21st Minn. Cav.	105		1918	KS, 38th, 1919
Reed, T.R.		G, 47th Ill.	1		1917 May 12	KS, 37th, 1918
Reed, T.V.		C & B, 34th Iowa	25		1922 Dec 13	KS, 42nd, 1923
Reed, Thomas	Pvt.	I, 4th Iowa Cav.	55		1913 Apr 2	IA, 40th, 1914
Reed, Thomas		D, 2nd N.Y. Hvy. Art.	4		1935 Jan 28	NE, 60th, 1936
Reed, W.		E, 115th Ill.	38		1926 Sep	NE, 51st, 1927
Reed, W.B.			239		1917	KS, 37th, 1918
Reed, W.D.	Pvt.	B, 46th Ill.	68		1923 Jul 3	IA, 50th, 1924
Reed, W.R.		I, 78th Ill.	1		1925 Nov 21	KS, 45th, 1926
Reed, W.T.		E, 105th Penn. Inf.		94	1936[1935?] Jun 10	IA, 62nd, 1936
Reed, W.T.		G, 81st Ind. (killed by accident)	328		1888	KS, 8th, 1889
Reed, Wm.			5		1909	KS, 29th, 1910
Reed, Wm. B.	Pvt.	A, 21st Iowa Inf.	90	51	1896 Feb 29	IA, 22nd, 1896
Reed, Wm. T.		E, 106th Penn. Inf.	29	94	1935 Jun 10	IA, 62nd, 1936
Reede, Joel		K, 33rd Ind.	4		1923 Mar 14	KS, 43rd, 1924
Reeder, A.C.	Pvt.	C, 24th Iowa Inf.	110		1917 Jun 15	IA, 44th, 1918
Reeder, Isom S.		G, 13th Ill. Cav.	32		1918 Nov 15	KS, 38th, 1919
Reeder, T.D.	Pvt.	C, 6th Iowa Cav.	48		1928 Oct 29	IA, 55th, 1929
Reeder, T.D.	Pvt.	C, 4th Iowa Cav.	48		1929	IA, 56th, 1930
Reeder, Wm.		D, 85th Ind.	292		1904 Jun 19	KS, 24th, 1905
Reeder, Zachariah		F, 99th Ill.	71		1913 Apr 18	KS, 33rd, 1914
Reeds, John A.		H, 12th Kans. Vol. Inf.	32		1908 Mar 29	KS, 28th, 1909
Reedy, Thomas J.		A, 1st Md. Regt. (died of Bright's disease)	173	73	1912 Apr 24	NE, 37th, 1913
Reel, John		E, 104th Ohio	63		1923 Nov 1	KS, 43rd, 1924
Reel, Peter	Pvt.	D, 16th U.S. Inf.	26		1921 Jan 15	IA, 48th, 1922
Reel, Wm.	Pvt.	I, 24th Iowa Inf.	74		1918 Sep 25	IA, 45th, 1919
Rees, D.C.		Kans. State Militia	47		1911 Mar 19	KS, 31st, 1912
Rees, David	Pvt.	B, 10th Iowa Inf.	425		1918	IA, 45th, 1919
Rees, E.M.	Pvt.	G, 15th Iowa Inf.	26		1920 Jun 26	IA, 47th, 1921
Rees, Geo. O.		H, 12th Kans.	447		1923 Dec 24	KS, 43rd, 1924
Rees, O.G.		F, 92nd Ill.	175		1926 May 12	KS, 46th, 1927
Rees, Spencer	Pvt.	B, 48th Iowa Inf.	16		1920 Aug 4	IA, 47th, 1921
Reese, Alanson		H, 30th Ill.	131		1925 Nov 2	KS, 45th, 1926
Reese, Isaac W.		E, 30th Ky.	7		1920 Aug 21	KS, 40th, 1921
Reese, J.G.		F, 11th Kans.	180		1912 Jan 9	KS, 32nd, 1913
Reese, J.W.	Pvt.	K, 35th Iowa Inf.	329		1911 Jun 18	IA, 38th, 1912
Reese, John	Pvt.	I, Iowa Inf.	18		1930 Aug 12	IA, 57th, 1931

*See Appendix A, B or C for roster of post names and locations.
†See Introduction for note regarding recording of death date.

Name	Rank	Company, Regiment or Ship	Post*	Age	Death Date†	Journal
Reese, John		A, 113th Ohio (see also Appendix D)	98		1935 Jul 5	NE, 60th, 1936
Reese, Joseph	Pvt.	D, 5th Ohio Cav.	88		1925 Oct 23	IA, 52nd, 1926
Reese, Thos.		C, 8th Kans.	336		1904 Jul 5	KS, 24th, 1905
Reese, W.H.		B, 102nd Ill.	3		1928 Dec 17	KS, 48th, 1929
Reesman, J.T.	Pvt.	155th Ohio National Guard	254		1906	IA, 33rd, 1907
Reesman, S.H.		H, 155th Ohio	318	66	1910 Sep 16	NE, 35th, 1911
Reeve, Arthur T.	Pvt.	K, 7th Kans. Cav.	81	54	1889 Oct 25	IA, 16th, 1890
Reeve, E.D.	Pvt.	E, 11th Iowa	110		1903 Nov 6	IA, 30th, 1904
Reeve, George C.	Pvt.	F, 1st Wis. Hvy. Art.	512		1899 Oct 5	IA, 26th, 1900
Reeve, O.G.	Pvt.	G, 8th Iowa Cav.	81	86	1932 May 5	IA, 59th, 1933
Reeve, W.T.	Musician	D, 193rd N.Y.	22		1926 Jun 1	IA, 53rd, 1927
Reeve, Wm.	Pvt.	E, 22nd Iowa Inf.	107		1917	IA, 44th, 1918
Reeves, C.C.		D, 104th Ohio	28		1919 Dec 4	KS, 39th, 1920
Reeves, C.L.		F, 123rd Ind. Inf.	136		1899 Feb 9	KS, 19th, 1900
Reeves, F.M.		M, 15th N.Y.	69		1930 Aug 29	KS, 51st, 1932
Reeves, F.M.		M, 15th N.Y.	69		1930 Aug 29	KS, 52nd, 1933
Reeves, F.M., see Reaves, F.M.						
Reeves, J.N.	Pvt.	I, 92nd Ohio Inf.	7		1920 Apr 20	IA, 47th, 1921
Reeves, J.N.		C, 8th N.Y. Cav.	257		1898 Dec 27	KS, 18th, 1899
Reeves, James R.		K, 117th Ill.	465		1906 Feb 28	KS, 26th, 1907
Reeves, Jno. H.	Pvt.	D, 4th Ohio Inf.	1		1925 Feb 17	IA, 52nd, 1926
Reeves, John		B, 8th Ill. Cav.	25		1935 Aug 2	KS, 55th, 1936
Reeves, Jos. N.		G, 39th Ill.	112		1927 Dec 7	NE, 52nd, 1928
Reeves, L.	Pvt.	H, 148th Ohio	253		1921 May	IA, 48th, 1922
Reeves, Marcus D.		A, 107th Ill.	117		1923 Jan 23	KS, 43rd, 1924
Reeves, S.M.		D, 1st Mo.	81		1904 Dec 22	KS, 24th, 1905
Reeves, W.	Pvt.	B, 33rd Ind. Inf.	10		1917 Jan 27	IA, 44th, 1918
Reeves, W.A.	Pvt.	A, 9th Iowa Cav.	68		1926 May 19	IA, 53rd, 1927
Reeves, Wm. L.	Pvt.	G, 7th Ill. Cav.	139		1904 Jul 6	IA, 31st, 1905
Reffell, W.G.	Pvt.	G, 13th West Va. Inf.	107		1906 Jul 20	IA, 33rd, 1907
Refimeter, Wm.	Pvt.	G, 27th Iowa	68		1924 Mar 9	IA, 51st, 1925
Regan, A.W.	Pvt.	G, 11th Kans.	137		1923 Aug 12	IA, 50th, 1924
Regennitter, De.	Pvt.	F, 44th Iowa Inf.	1		1917 May 7	IA, 44th, 1918
Regester, Robert			182		1902	KS, 22nd, 1903
Regna, James			32		1911 Oct 14	KS, 31st, 1912
Regnier, Charles F.	Pvt.	H, 1st Ohio Lt. Art. (at large)	255	96	1942 Jan 22	IA, 68th, 1942
Regur, L.G.	Capt.	N.J.	79		1915	IA, 42nd, 1916
Rehmel, A.B.	Pvt.	I, 30th Ohio Inf.	231		1908 Feb 8	IA, 35th, 1909
Rehse, Heinrich		G, 47th N.Y.	24	75	1912 Dec 4	NE, 37th, 1913
Rei, Phillip		A, 9th Ohio Cav.	32		1922 Aug 31	KS, 42nd, 1923
Reichart, Arnold		U.S. Navy	380		1900 May 25	KS, 20th, 1901
Reichart, Emanuel	Sergt.	C, 143rd Penn. Inf. (not a member in Iowa at time of death)	29, 225	95	1940 Oct 3	IA, 67th, 1941
Reichely, George S.		C, 35th Iowa Inf.	153		1918 Nov	IA, 45th, 1919
Reichenbach, F.	Corp.	C, 107th Ohio Inf.	67		1925 Dec 15	IA, 52nd, 1926
Reichneker, George B.		G, 10th Kans.	3		1885	KS, 5th, 1886
Reick, Matthew		Ordnance Dept.	6		1891 Apr 12	KS, 11th, 1892
Reid, Geo.	Pvt.	D, 125th Ohio Inf.	10		1925 Jan 30	IA, 52nd, 1926
Reid, Harvey			74		1910	IA, 37th, 1911
Reid, Hugh		D, 211th Penn.	3		1928 Jan 9	KS, 48th, 1929
Reid, J.R.		D, 152nd Penn. Inf.	25		1929 May 19	KS, 49th, 1930
Reid, Jas. M.	Capt.	A, 2nd Iowa Inf.	2	66	1892 Apr 22	IA, 18th, 1892
Reid, John R.		D, 152nd Ill.	407		1908	KS, 28th, 1909
Reid, Julius		C, 96th Ill. Inf. (died of pneumonia)	21	76	1919 Jan 28	NE, 43rd, 1919
Reid, Julius		C, — Ohio Inf. (died of heart trouble)	21	78	1920 Jan 28	NE, 45th, 1921
Reid, Robert			104		1923 May 3	KS, 43rd, 1924
Reid, William W.		C, 16th Ohio Inf.	250		1912 Jan 7	KS, 32nd, 1913
Reid, Wm.		E, 6th Iowa Cav.	263		2nd quarter 1884	IA, 11th, 1885
Reiderman, Henry	Pvt.	Navy gunboat *Tyler*	97		1915 Nov 25	IA, 42nd, 1916
Reiff, John	Pvt.	26th Iowa Inf.	391		1913 May 26	IA, 40th, 1914
Reiga, Rudolph		F, 3rd Mass. Cav.	6		1910 Jun 13	KS, 30th, 1911
Reigand, Geo.			294		1937 May 1	KS, 57th, 1938

*See Appendix A, B or C for roster of post names and locations.
†See Introduction for note regarding recording of death date.

451

Name	Rank	Company, Regiment or Ship	Post*	Age	Death Date†	Journal
Reigert, E.H.	Surg.	35th Iowa	7		1899 Mar 11	IA, 26th, 1900
Reighard, George			294		1936 Aug 23	KS, 56th, 1937
Reigle, David	Pvt.	B, 28th Iowa	324		1903-1904	IA, 30th, 1904
Reiley, R.	Corp.	A, 31st Iowa	206		1921 Sep 14	IA, 48th, 1922
Reiley, W.H.	Pvt.	I, 1st Iowa Cav.	40		1908 Jul 15	IA, 35th, 1909
Reiley, W.H.			118		1883	KS, 3rd, 1884
Reily, Peter	Pvt.	L, 2nd Iowa Cav.	97		1915 Oct 10	IA, 42nd, 1916
Reiman, Aug.		K, 6th West Va. Inf.	124		1909 Jan 4	NE, 33rd, 1909
Reiman, F.	Pvt.	B, 13th Iowa	62		1921 Dec 9	IA, 48th, 1922
Reiman, F.	Pvt.	B, —	62		1923 Dec 9	IA, 50th, 1924
Reiman, H.C.		B, 13th Iowa	33		1923	KS, 43rd, 1924
Reimers, August	Lieut.	E, 15th Mo. Inf.	1		1908 Dec 25	IA, 35th, 1909
Reimers, Fred		G, 103rd N.Y.	25		1910 Jul 25	NE, 35th, 1911
Reimers, Rimer	Pvt.	I, 1st Mo. Battery	154	64	1888 May 20	IA, 15th, 1889
Reimert, H.		D, 168th Penn.	51		1920 Oct 15	KS, 40th, 1921
Reimert, John		D, 12th Penn.	51		1898 Sep 14	KS, 18th, 1899
Reineke, Wm. A.	Pvt.	D, 13th Iowa Inf.	44		1903 Jun 21	IA, 30th, 1904
Reiner, Joseph	Pvt.	K, 30th Iowa Inf.	108		1929 Apr 25	IA, 56th, 1930
Reinert, Michael	Pvt.	B, 2nd Iowa	167		1927 Nov 18	IA, 54th, 1928
Reinhardt, John	Pvt.	F, 4th Iowa Inf.	184		1903 Nov 30	IA, 30th, 1904
Reinhart, Christopher	Pvt.	A, 34th Ill. Inf.	327		1901 Sep 19	IA, 28th, 1902
Reinhart, Fred	Pvt.	C, 92nd Ill.	68		1924 Apr 7	IA, 51st, 1925
Reinig, Jacob	Pvt.	C, 10th Iowa Inf.	343		1909 Dec 15	IA, 36th, 1910
Reiniger, R.G.	Capt.	B, 7th Iowa Inf.	3		1910 Oct 15	IA, 37th, 1911
Reinke, Charles W.	Pvt.	B, 12th Ill. Cav.	311		1918 Oct 16	IA, 45th, 1919
Reinkey, Fred	Pvt.	12th Wis. Bat.	81		1923 Aug 18	IA, 50th, 1924
Reis, C.W.	Corp.	H, 2nd Col. Cav.	297		1926 Jun 18	IA, 53rd, 1927
Reisinger, A.R.		D, 42nd Ill. F, 15th Ill.	94		1922 Jan 13	IA, 49th, 1923
Reisinger, E.			32		1921 Oct 29	NE, 46th, 1922
Reisinger, Peter	Pvt.	H, 34th Ill. Inf.	88		1917	IA, 44th, 1918
Reisner, Chas. J.	Pvt.	B, 3rd Iowa Cav.	122		1912 Nov 28	IA, 39th, 1913
Reitenour, Elias		E, 8th Mo.	132		1889	KS, 9th, 1890
Reiter, Adolph		B, 7th U.S.	380		1897 Mar 9	KS, 17th, 1898
Reiter, Henry	Pvt.	A, 19th Iowa Inf.	2		1922 Dec 17	IA, 49th, 1923
Reitz, Jacob M.		F, 11th West Va.	337		1908 Oct 7	KS, 28th, 1909
Reitz, Nicholas, see Rietz, Nicholas						
Reitzel, M.L.		E, 21st Ind.	260		1914 Dec 6	KS, 34th, 1915
Reitzell, Blair	Sergt.	H, 1st Iowa Cav.	12		1926 Feb 5	IA, 53rd, 1927
Reller, Henry C.		B, 56th Ohio Inf.	25		1899	NE, 24th, 1900
Remaley, Edw.		H, 15th Ohio	25		1929 Apr 26	NE, 54th, 1930
Remele, E.		E, 18th Mich.	112		1929 Mar 5	NE, 53rd, 1929
Remey, Thomas S.	Pvt.	I, 20th Wis. Inf.	337		1928 Dec 29	IA, 55th, 1929
Remick, Levi		I, 15th Mass.	51		1904 Aug 1	KS, 24th, 1905
Remick, M.F.		H, 150th Ind.	142		1908 Oct	KS, 28th, 1909
Remin, P.B.	Pvt.	D, 20th Iowa	1		1907 Nov 14	IA, 34th, 1908
Remington, G.L.		C, 21st N.Y. (died at Independence)	4		1895	KS, 15th, 1896
Remington, J.B.		D, 89th N.Y. (died in St. Luke's Hospital, Kansas City; remains were taken to his home in Osawatomie)	322		1912 May 12	KS, 32nd, 1913
Remington, S.W.	Pvt.	I, 112th Ill. Inf.	222		1926 Oct 24	IA, 53rd, 1927
Remmer, Nick		C, Kans. Militia	72		1914 Jul 22	KS, 34th, 1915
Remnio, Jas. A.	Pvt.	D, 35th Ind. Inf.	56		1924 Nov 18	IA, 51st, 1925
Rempe, Jacob	Pvt.	A, 30th Iowa Inf.	2		1911 Jul 5	IA, 38th, 1912
Remskar, Jacob		K, 37th Ind.	66		1920 Dec 1	KS, 40th, 1921
Remy, Thomas	Pvt.		337		1929 Jan 10	IA, 56th, 1930
Renberger, Pleasant			74		1883	KS, 3rd, 1884
Renceler, Joe E.		D, 5th Ind. Cav.	18		1914 Sep 12	KS, 34th, 1915
Rendel, John	Pvt.	B, 32nd Iowa Inf.	142		1917 Sep 15	IA, 44th, 1918
Renner, J.W.		K, 14th Va.	83		1924 Jun 25	KS, 44th, 1925
Renner, Jalentine		A, 6th Kans.	318		1892 Oct 12	KS, 12th, 1893

*See Appendix A, B or C for roster of post names and locations.
†See Introduction for note regarding recording of death date.

452

Name	Rank	Company, Regiment or Ship	Post*	Age	Death Date†	Journal
Renner, W.A.		C, 4th Tenn. Inf.	4		1914 Apr 7	KS, 34th, 1915
Renney, Wm.		D, 13th Kans. Inf. (died at Effingham)	276		1895 Aug	KS, 15th, 1896
Rennie, James	Pvt.	A, 553rd Ill. Inf.	465		1905 Dec 21	IA, 32nd, 1906
Rennison, J.C.	Capt.	I, 15th N.Y. Cav.	22		1906 Feb 24	IA, 33rd, 1907
Reno, B.F.	Lieut.	H, 2nd Iowa Cav.	233		1908 Aug 24	IA, 35th, 1909
Reno, J.T.		A, 84th Ill.	51		1916 Aug 27	KS, 36th, 1917
Reno, Wm. B.		B, 76th Penn.	32		1901 Dec 19	KS, 22nd, 1903
Reno, Wm. G.		D, 9th Kans.	111		1931 Mar 10	KS, 51st, 1932
Reno, Wm. G.		D, 9th Kans.	111		1931 Mar 10	KS, 52nd, 1933
Renolds, D.C.	Pvt.	E, 11th Mich. Inf.	29	92	1933 Mar	IA, 60th, 1934
Renting, Nicholas		I, 7th Wis. Cav.	11	69	1896 Mar 20	NE, 21st, 1897
Renville, Knapp	Pvt.	K, 76th Ill. Inf.	219	48	1892 Feb 13	IA, 18th, 1892
Repp, A.X.	Pvt.	K, 36th Iowa Inf.	337		1926 Jan 12	IA, 53rd, 1927
Repstock, William			180		1923 Mar	KS, 43rd, 1924
Requa, George H.		2nd Kans. Battery	32		1915 Dec 25	KS, 35th, 1916
Reschke, F.W.		E, 36th Iowa Inf.	25		1934 Mar	KS, 54th, 1935
Resenoun, James			231		1928 Dec 2	IA, 55th, 1929
Reser, James A.		G, 4th Tenn.	127		1911 Aug 14	KS, 31st, 1912
Resley, M.G.	Pvt.	I, 11th Iowa Inf.	231		1905 May 15	IA, 32nd, 1906
Rester, Al H.	Pvt.	I, 45th Iowa Inf.	5		1915 Dec 2	IA, 42nd, 1916
Rettig, Louis		G, 3rd Ill. Cav. (died of stomach trouble)	111	78	1911 Mar 8	NE, 36th, 1912
Reuhlin, J.C.		K, 136th Ohio	130		1922 Jun 6	KS, 42nd, 1923
Reuires, Bendix	Pvt.	A, 19th Iowa Inf.	2		1905 Apr 27	IA, 32nd, 1906
Reum, Fred	Pvt.	H, 10th Ohio Inf.	168	59	1897 Apr 6	IA, 23rd, 1897
Reusrier, Chas.	Corp.	I, 72nd Ill. Inf.	266	58	1892 Jan 11	IA, 18th, 1892
Reust, Abraham		E, 129th Ind.	1		1914 Jan 3	KS, 34th, 1915
Reute, T.W.	Hosp. Stew.	103rd N.Y. Inf.	78		1913 Oct 1	IA, 40th, 1914
Reveal, Michael M.		A, 101st Ind. Eng.	7		1913 Aug 6	KS, 33rd, 1914
Revert, B.F.		M, 112th Penn.	199		1896 Mar 20	KS, 16th, 1897
Reves, Daniel			7		1918 Nov 15	IA, 45th, 1919
Rew, M.D.	Corp.	E, 5th N.Y. Cav.	192		1913 Mar 9	IA, 40th, 1914
Rews, C.H.		B, 155th Ind.	419		1888	KS, 8th, 1889
Rex, J.L.	Capt.	B, 149th Penn. Inf.	156		1905 Aug 4	IA, 32nd, 1906
Rexroad, Adam F.		A, 34th Ill. Inf. (see also Appendix D)	7		1942 Nov 13	NE, 67th, 1943
Reyburn, —	Col.		241		1908[1909?] Feb 10	KS, 29th, 1910
Reyburn, John C.	Pvt.	F, 33rd Iowa Inf.	414		1908 Aug 4	IA, 35th, 1909
Reyburn, John G.		C, 28th Iowa Inf.	127		1913 Sep 30	IA, 40th, 1914
Reyman, Jacob	Pvt.	E, 49th Wis. Inf.	503		1911 Aug 17	IA, 38th, 1912
Reynard, Peter		D, 1st Ore.	75		1885	KS, 5th, 1886
Reyner, Franklin	Physician	9th Iowa Inf.	78		1927 Sep 2	IA, 54th, 1928
Reyner, Henry C. (or G)		A, 9th Iowa Inf.		92 & 15 days	1937 Feb 4	IA, 64th, 1938
Reynolds, A.R.	Pvt.	G, 6th Iowa Cav.	236		1929 Jan 17	IA, 56th, 1930
Reynolds, Albert	Pvt. & Hosp. Stew.	D, 92nd N.Y. Inf.	88	61	1899 Feb 23	IA, 25th, 1899
Reynolds, Aleck	Pvt.	B, 45th Ill. Inf.	512		1919 May 30	IA, 46th, 1920
Reynolds, Amos	Pvt.	D, 8th Iowa Inf.	400		1912 Sep 22	IA, 39th, 1913
Reynolds, B.H.	Pvt.	G, 28th Iowa Inf.	8		1925 Jul 31	IA, 52nd, 1926
Reynolds, B.J.			156		1924 May 23	IA, 51st, 1925
Reynolds, C.P.	Pvt.	G, 83rd Penn. Inf.	118	89	1931 Apr 2	IA, 58th, 1932
Reynolds, C.S.	Pvt.	K, 8th Ill. Inf.	153		1917 Feb 8	IA, 44th, 1918
Reynolds, Charles, D.D.	Chaplain	2nd Kans.	132		1885	KS, 5th, 1886
Reynolds, Clark		16th Kans.	40		1911 Mar 30	KS, 31st, 1912
Reynolds, D.D.			235		1908	IA, 35th, 1909
Reynolds, D.D.	Pvt.	A, 34th Iowa Inf.	166		1916 Jun	IA, 43rd, 1917
Reynolds, D.M.			38		1910 Apr 12	KS, 30th, 1911
Reynolds, David		F, 9th Kans.	185		1893 Aug 25	KS, 13th, 1894
Reynolds, E.M.		6th Wis. Lt. Art.	85		1902 Feb 4	KS, 22nd, 1903
Reynolds, Ed			147		1912 Sep 3	KS, 32nd, 1913
Reynolds, Ed		K, 1st Iowa Cav. (died of surgical operation)	147	69	1909 Nov 11	NE, 34th, 1910
Reynolds, Edward		B, 1st Mo. Inf.	84		1911 Dec 26	KS, 31st, 1912

*See Appendix A, B or C for roster of post names and locations.
†See Introduction for note regarding recording of death date.

453

Name	Rank	Company, Regiment or Ship	Post*	Age	Death Date†	Journal
Reynolds, Eli		A, 7th Iowa Inf.	231		1924 Jan 30	IA, 51st, 1925
Reynolds, Fred		U.S. Navy	110	72	1905 May 25	NE, 30th, 1906
Reynolds, H.H.	Pvt.	K, 12th Wis. Inf.	81		1914 Sep 19	IA, 41st, 1915
Reynolds, Harly	Pvt.	G, 147th Ill. Inf.	298		1917 Feb 20	IA, 44th, 1918
Reynolds, I.B.	Pvt.	I, 12th Ill. (died of apoplexy)	43	47	1884 Mar 3	NE, 9th, 1885
Reynolds, J.H.	Pvt.	F, 42nd Ind. Inf.	197		1927 Apr 7	IA, 54th, 1928
Reynolds, J.L.	2nd Lieut.	F, 4th Iowa Cav.	107	58	1898 Jul 9	IA, 25th, 1899
Reynolds, J.M.		H, 2nd West Va.	18		1898 Jul 2	KS, 18th, 1899
Reynolds, J.N.		K, 9th Iowa Cav.	3		1926 Apr 3	KS, 46th, 1927
Reynolds, J.P.		G, 7th Ohio Cav.	63		1916 Nov 6	KS, 36th, 1917
Reynolds, J.R.	Pvt.	A, 40th Iowa Inf.	49		1920 Feb 7	IA, 47th, 1921
Reynolds, J.S.	Pvt.	G, 83rd Penn. Inf.	118		1905 Oct 21	IA, 32nd, 1906
Reynolds, James	Pvt.	D, 5th Iowa Inf.	322		1908 Feb	IA, 35th, 1909
Reynolds, James	Corp.	D, 5th Iowa Inf.	156		1911 Mar 22	IA, 38th, 1912
Reynolds, John	Pvt.	E, 92nd Ill.	238		1903 Jan 16	IA, 30th, 1904
Reynolds, John	Pvt.	E, 92nd Ill. Inf.	238		1903 Jan 16	IA, 29th, 1903
Reynolds, John		D, 9th N.Y. Inf.	25		1899 Nov 28	KS, 19th, 1900
Reynolds, John P.	Pvt.	B, 96th Ohio Inf.	343		1911 Dec 30	IA, 38th, 1912
Reynolds, L.A.		F, 11th Mich.	19		1896 Jun 26	KS, 16th, 1897
Reynolds, P.B.		K, 34th Ill. Inf. (died of old age)	112	80	1901 Aug	NE, 26th, 1902
Reynolds, R.		K, 14th Ind.	117		1888	KS, 8th, 1889
Reynolds, R.M.	Sergt.	50th N.Y.	465		1911 Apr 25	KS, 31st, 1912
Reynolds, R.W.	Sergt.	C, 166th Ohio	22		1906 Jul 24	IA, 33rd, 1907
Reynolds, Robt.		C, 1st Ind. (died of lack of blood)	1	76	1918 May 22	NE, 43rd, 1919
Reynolds, S.A.	Sergt.	F, 20th Ohio Inf.	2		1920 Mar 26	IA, 47th, 1921
Reynolds, S.H.	Sergt.	H, 73rd Ind. Inf.	28		1909	IA, 36th, 1910
Reynolds, S.M.		L, 3rd Kans.	12		1927 Mar 9	KS, 47th, 1928
Reynolds, S.W.	Pvt.	F, 8th Iowa Inf.	167		1898 Jul 8	IA, 25th, 1899
Reynolds, T.W.			3		1921 Apr 4	IA, 48th, 1922
Reynolds, T.W.		F, 3rd Ohio	311		1927	KS, 47th, 1928
Reynolds, Thos. M.	Pvt.	I, 3rd Iowa Cav. (died of melanosis & chr. peritonitis)	70	48	1889 Mar 25	NE, 13th, 1889
Reynolds, W.E.	Sergt.	C, 66th Ohio Inf.	22		1927 Jan 31	IA, 54th, 1928
Reynolds, W.R.	Pvt.	L, 9th Iowa Cav.	211		1903 Oct 17	IA, 30th, 1904
Reynolds, Wm.			89		1918 Jan 4	IA, 45th, 1919
Reynolds, Wm.		A, 8th N.Y. Hvy. Art. (died of paralysis)	354	75	1912 Oct 6	NE, 37th, 1913
Reynolds, Wm. H.	Sergt.	K, 56th Penn.	271		1914 Oct 30	IA, 41st, 1915
Reynolds, Wm. R.			[40?]		1904 Sep 26	KS, 24th, 1905
Rhea, David			74		1914 Sep 28	IA, 41st, 1915
Rhea, W.M.		H, 133rd Tenn. Inf.	8		1899 Apr 3	KS, 19th, 1900
Rhenstrong, Peter	Sergt.	D, 1st Ill. Cav.	271	71	1891 Sep 7	IA, 18th, 1892
Rhine, Jas. W.		I, 34th Ind.	75		1910 Apr 14	NE, 35th, 1911
Rhine, Robt. H.	Corp.	I, 34th Ind. Inf.	40	93	1935 Aug 13	IA, 65th, 1939
Rhinehart, G.L.			230		1916 Jun 5	IA, 43rd, 1917
Rhinehart, J.A.	Pvt.	H, 75th Ind. Inf.	40		1916 May 30	IA, 43rd, 1917
Rhinehart, John		D, 2nd Neb. Cav. (died of old age & army service)	47	74	1904 Mar 29	NE, 29th, 1905
Rhinhart, Iret		E, 78th Ohio	104		1906 Dec 9	KS, 26th, 1907
Rhoades, F.N.	Sergt.	F, 2nd Iowa	74		1905	IA, 32nd, 1906
Rhoades, F.N.	Sergt.	L, 2nd Iowa Cav.	74		1911 Jul 11	IA, 38th, 1912
Rhoades, Henry		E, 44th Ind.	447		1911 Jun 16	KS, 31st, 1912
Rhoades, Hiram	Pvt.	D, 10th Iowa Inf.	252	51	1892 Dec 9	IA, 19th, 1893
Rhoades, Oliver D.		E, 2nd Ill. Cav. (died of old age at Soldiers & Sailors Home, Grand Island; buried in Home Cemetery)	13	83	1905 Jun 25	NE, 30th, 1906
Rhoads, Cicero		A, 7th Iowa Cav.	98		1909 Mar 10	KS, 29th, 1910
Rhoads, G.S.		C, 72nd Ill. Inf.	329		1919 Apr 10	IA, 46th, 1920
Rhoads, J.L.		I, 1st Neb.	177		1887 Nov 17	KS, 7th, 1888
Rhoads, John J.	Pvt.	A, 7th Mo. Cav.	433		1919 Jun	IA, 46th, 1920
Rhoady, William D.		F, 14th Ill.	11		1917 Jan 25	KS, 37th, 1918
Rhode, Henry	Sergt.	E, 19th —	138		1915 Nov 28	IA, 42nd, 1916
Rhodenbach, W.		S, 27th Ill. Inf.	251		1886	KS, 6th, 1887

*See Appendix A, B or C for roster of post names and locations.
†See Introduction for note regarding recording of death date.

Name	Rank	Company, Regiment or Ship	Post*	Age	Death Date†	Journal
Rhodes, A.J.	Pvt.	B, 1st Wis. Bat.	7		1918 Mar 1	IA, 45th, 1919
Rhodes, Andrew J.		E, 4th Ky.	1		1905 Apr 7	KS, 25th, 1906
Rhodes, C.C.		A, 94th Ohio	55		1904 Oct 30	KS, 24th, 1905
Rhodes, David		H, 25th Mo.	136		1899 Jul 4	KS, 19th, 1900
Rhodes, Elijah		G, 94th Ill. Inf.	1		1896 Mar 28	KS, 16th, 1897
Rhodes, George H.		G, 13th U.S. Inf. (died of heart failure)	354	66	1913 Nov 23	NE, 38th, 1914
Rhodes, H.	Pvt.	I, 88th Ind. Inf.	12		1920 May 21	IA, 47th, 1921
Rhodes, Henry		B, 81st Ind.	54		1916 Nov 29	KS, 36th, 1917
Rhodes, J.N.		E, 27th Mich.	57		1936 Jan	KS, 55th, 1936
Rhodes, Jacob	Pvt.	K, 102nd Penn. Inf.	68		1912 Sep 9	IA, 39th, 1913
Rhodes, Jacob		K, 27th Mich.	25		1919 Jan 19	KS, 39th, 1920
Rhodes, Jeremiah		F, 6th Iowa Inf.	45		1885	KS, 5th, 1886
Rhodes, John W.	Pvt.	C, 42nd Mo.	11		1914 Oct 10	IA, 41st, 1915
Rhodes, John W.		E, 193rd Penn. Inf. (died at Elk City)	128		1895 Feb 15	KS, 15th, 1896
Rhodes, Milton	Sergt.	I, 14th Iowa Inf.	20		1922 Jun 18	IA, 49th, 1923
Rhodes, Milton B.		E, 18th U.S. Inf.	85		1901 Mar 16	KS, 21st, 1902
Rhodes, N.J.		I, 24th Inf.	388		1917 Apr 11	KS, 37th, 1918
Rhodes, P.M.		A, 39th Iowa Inf.	185		1917 Oct 25	KS, 37th, 1918
Rhodes, P.O.		I, 60th Ohio	23		1930 Aug 11	KS, 50th, 1931
Rhodes, Samuel		C, 1st Ore. Cav.	289		1898 Sep 15	KS, 18th, 1899
Rhodes, Samuel		B, 8th Ky.	209		1910 Apr 10	KS, 30th, 1911
Rhodes, W.B.		F, 15th Ill. Inf. (died at the Veterans' Hospital in Wichita)	25	95	1941 Feb 10 or 21	KS, 61st, 1942
Rhodes, Wm.	Pvt.	B, 32nd Iowa Inf.	42		1918 Dec 17	IA, 45th, 1919
Rhoren, Henry			3		1908	NE, 33rd, 1909
Rhue, Geo.	Pvt.	12th Ohio Batt.	472		1925 Sep 10	IA, 52nd, 1926
Rhue, William		A, — Ohio	52		1905 Apr 19	KS, 25th, 1906
Rhyman, F.F.			272		1908	NE, 33rd, 1909
Rhymn, Francis		C, 85th Penn.	272	78	1907	NE, 32nd, 1908
Riblet, Thomas C.		U.S. Navy	88		1905 Oct 11	KS, 25th, 1906
Rice, A.D.		I, 1st Mich.	1		1929 Jun 16	NE, 54th, 1930
Rice, Abijah		E, 11th Ind. Cav.	384		1914 Apr 27	KS, 33rd, 1914
Rice, Calvin		D, 99th Ill. Inf.	128		1901 Sep 20	KS, 21st, 1902
Rice, E.L.	Pvt.	F, 10th Iowa Inf.	7		1905 Mar	IA, 32nd, 1906
Rice, E.S.	Pvt.	H, 88th Ill. Inf.	30		1916 Apr 22	IA, 43rd, 1917
Rice, E.W.	Brig. Gen.	C, 7th Iowa Inf.	396	51	1887 Jun 21	IA, 17th, 1891
Rice, E.W.	Br. M. Gen.	C, 7th Iowa Inf.	396	52	1887 Jun 21	IA, 14th, 1888
Rice, E.W.	Sergt.	C, 7th Iowa Inf.	22		1927 Feb 23	IA, 54th, 1928
Rice, Geo. D.		M, 9th Kans. Cav.	72		1899 Jul 22	KS, 19th, 1900
Rice, H.H.	1st Lieut.	K, 9th Vt.	22		1924 Nov 6	IA, 51st, 1925
Rice, H.W.	Capt.	K, 61st U.S.C.	22		1915 Jul 2	IA, 42nd, 1916
Rice, Henry	Pvt.	E, 97th Ohio Inf.	156		1922 Mar 18	IA, 49th, 1923
Rice, Henry	Pvt.	A, 151st Ill. Inf.	137		1926 May 9	IA, 53rd, 1927
Rice, J.H.		K, 106th Ill. (died of general debility)	115	69	1909 Oct	NE, 34th, 1910
Rice, J.J.			25		1910 Jan 18	NE, 35th, 1911
Rice, J.S.	Lieut.	K, 13th Iowa Inf.	1		1916 Sep 18	IA, 43rd, 1917
Rice, James	Pvt.	E, 3rd Iowa Cav.	63		1894 Nov 10	IA, 21st, 1895
Rice, Joe (colored)	Pvt.		343		1926 Dec 28	IA, 53rd, 1927
Rice, John		A, 39th Iowa	3		1892 Jun 11	KS, 12th, 1893
Rice, Lane		D, 104th Mich. Inf. (died of dropsy)	112	81	1916 Jul 12	NE, 41st, 1917
Rice, Martin	Pvt.	A, 140th Ill. Inf.	97	64	1899 May 23	IA, 26th, 1900
Rice, N.H.	Pvt.	G, 11th Iowa Inf.	231		1917 Oct 10	IA, 44th, 1918
Rice, Nathaniel N.		G, 77th N.Y. Inf.	334[354?]	75	1906 Feb 10	NE, 31st, 1907
Rice, P.W.		A, 4th Vt.	116		1925 Mar 17	KS, 45th, 1926
Rice, Ravilla	Sergt.	B, 128th Ohio Inf.	210		1905 Mar 16	IA, 32nd, 1906
Rice, Robt.	Pvt.		167		1920 May 23	IA, 47th, 1921
Rice, S.B.	Pvt.	B, 76th Penn. Inf.	78		1910 Jul 11	IA, 37th, 1911
Rice, S.S.	Pvt.	B, 24th Ill. Inf.	58		1925 Oct 6	IA, 52nd, 1926
Rice, Samuel H.		H, 7th Penn. Cav.	56	81	1915 Oct 30	NE, 40th, 1916
Rice, T.	Pvt.	L, 24th Penn. Inf.	284		1918 Sep 26	IA, 45th, 1919
Rice, Truman			105		1922 May	KS, 42nd, 1923
Rice, W.H.		L, 8th Ill. Cav.	383		1899 Jun 26	KS, 19th, 1900

*See Appendix A, B or C for roster of post names and locations.
†See Introduction for note regarding recording of death date.
455

Name	Rank	Company, Regiment or Ship	Post*	Age	Death Date†	Journal
Rice, W.H.		G, 12th Mass.	52		1923 Apr 17	KS, 43rd, 1924
Rice, W.J.		L, 8th Iowa Cav.	98		1930 Nov 25	NE, 55th, 1931
Rice, W.W.		B, 10th Mass. Inf.	9		1902	NE, 27th, 1903
Rice, William	Pvt.	C, 34th Ill. Inf.	126		1905 Nov 6	IA, 33rd, 1907
Rice, William L.		C, 142nd Ill.	1		1924 Mar 4	KS, 44th, 1925
Rice, Wm. M.	Pvt.	I, 31st Iowa Inf.	74		1915 Jul 28	IA, 42nd, 1916
Ricedorff, Ezra	Pvt.	H, 47th Iowa	211	43	1890 Oct 7	IA, 17th, 1891
Rich, A.H.		B, 3rd Penn. Cav.	375		1899 Jul 12	KS, 19th, 1900
Rich, Chas.			57		1917	NE, 42nd, 1918
Rich, Chas.		G, 14th Vt.	32		1927	NE, 52nd, 1928
Rich, Francis M.		K, 120th Ill. Inf.	354	66	1906 Mar 13	NE, 31st, 1907
Rich, Nelson A.	Corp.	G, 5th Vt. Inf.	236	42	1886 Jun 3	IA, 13th, 1887
Richard, Eli	Pvt.	A, 43rd Wis. Inf.	2		1911 Feb 21	IA, 38th, 1912
Richard, Josiah	Sergt.	G, 173rd Penn. Inf.	140		1901 Feb 18	IA, 28th, 1902
Richards, A.B.	Pvt.	H, 7th Wis.	78	53	1891 May 10	IA, 18th, 1892
Richards, A.L.		148th Ohio Inf.	286		1911	IA, 38th, 1912
Richards, Aaron	Seaman	U.S. Ships	266		1905 Nov 5	IA, 32nd, 1906
Richards, Andrew		F, 8th Kans. Inf.	127		1916 Jul 6	KS, 36th, 1917
Richards, Barney		B, 12th Ohio	87		1909 Feb 12	KS, 29th, 1910
Richards, C.H.		H, 42nd Ind. Inf.	163	62	1896 Oct 9	NE, 21st, 1897
Richards, C.R.	Corp.	B, 75th Ill. Inf.	266		1904 Dec 29	IA, 31st, 1905
Richards, Charles		C, 4th N.Y. Lt. Art.	113		1902 May 27	KS, 22nd, 1903
Richards, D.	Pvt.	D, 11th Iowa	255		1922 Apr	IA, 49th, 1923
Richards, E.	Pvt.	F, 6th Iowa Cav.	440		1908 Jul 14	IA, 35th, 1909
Richards, E.A.	Pvt.	A, 6th Maine	332		1906 Jan 24	IA, 33rd, 1907
Richards, Elwood A.		A, 130th Ind.	20		1929 Jun 5	KS, 49th, 1930
Richards, Franklin	Pvt.	E, 13th U.S. Inf.	216		1905 Jun 27	IA, 32nd, 1906
Richards, G.R.		F, 7th Ohio Art.	383		1929 Nov	KS, 49th, 1930
Richards, H.C.		E, 15th N.H. (not a member of Farragut Post)	25		1913 Nov 18	NE, 38th, 1914
Richards, H.V.	Pvt.	K, 14th Penn. Cav. (died of old age)	4	71	1891 May 28	NE, 16th, 1892
Richards, J.H.		D, 124th Ill.	32		1918 Apr 17	KS, 38th, 1919
Richards, J.H.	Pvt.	K, 82nd Ind. (died of disability)	210	58	1887 Feb	NE, 12th, 1888
Richards, J.L.	Lieut.	G, 11th Ohio Inf.	170		1910 Jan 31	IA, 37th, 1911
Richards, J.L.			130		1911 Jan 15	IA, 38th, 1912
Richards, J.M.		C, 13th U.S. Inf.	110		1906 Apr 3	NE, 31st, 1907
Richards, J.P.		E, 8th Kans.	35		1908 May 15	KS, 28th, 1909
Richards, John	Pvt.		115		1917 Oct 28	IA, 44th, 1918
Richards, John J.		D, 15th Ill. Cav.	64		1912 Oct 17	KS, 32nd, 1913
Richards, Jos.	Pvt.	F, 7th Iowa Cav.	216	72	1891 Jan 6	IA, 17th, 1891
Richards, Lewis		E, 8th Iowa Cav.	1		1887 May 14	KS, 7th, 1888
Richards, Lucius D.		I, 15th Vt. K, 17th Vt. (see also Appendix D)	4		1931 Aug 19	NE, 56th, 1932
Richards, Myron		1st Ohio Ill.	25		1913 Jun 14	NE, 38th, 1914
Richards, N.	Sergt.	D, 38th Iowa Inf.	464	59	1896 Feb 7	IA, 23rd, 1897
Richards, N.	Pvt.	I, 16th Wis. Inf.	3	92	1933 Aug 8	IA, 60th, 1934
Richards, Nathan		H, 40th Iowa	17		1915 Jan 20	KS, 35th, 1916
Richards, Noble	Pvt.	D, 21st Iowa Inf.	57		1909 Aug 29	IA, 36th, 1910
Richards, R.A.	Pvt.	C, 192nd N.Y. Inf.	235		1912 Oct 24	IA, 39th, 1913
Richards, Samuel		died of Bright's disease	89		1908	NE, 33rd, 1909
Richards, W.C.	Pvt.	H, 11th Iowa Inf.	231		1911 Mar 16	IA, 38th, 1912
Richards, W.S.	Pvt.	E, 3rd Conn. Inf.	315		1899	NE, 24th, 1900
Richards, Wm. H.	Corp.	A, 96th Ill. Inf.	81		1918 Jul 31	IA, 45th, 1919
Richardson, A.		K, 22nd Iowa	144		1917 Nov 6	KS, 37th, 1918
Richardson, Aden	Pvt.	A, 24th Iowa	164		1901 Jul 5	IA, 28th, 1902
Richardson, Alfred	Pvt.	D, 12th Ohio Vol. Inf.	267	60	1899 Feb 1	IA, 25th, 1899
Richardson, Benjamin F.		F, 8th Iowa Inf.		98	1938 Mar 23	IA, 64th, 1938
Richardson, C.	Pvt.	A, 6th Iowa Cav.	375		1910 Aug 9	IA, 37th, 1911
Richardson, C.H.	Chaplain	92-8 N.Y.	22		1903 May 11	IA, 30th, 1904
Richardson, D.B.		I, 112th Iowa Inf.			1928 Apr 5	NE, 53rd, 1929
Richardson, Dick		G, 16th Kans. Cav.	25		1908 Feb 25	NE, 33rd, 1909
Richardson, F.C.		B, 7th Minn. Inf.	293		1909 May 15	KS, 29th, 1910

*See Appendix A, B or C for roster of post names and locations.
†See Introduction for note regarding recording of death date.
456

Name	Rank	Company, Regiment or Ship	Post*	Age	Death Date†	Journal
Richardson, Fredrick		G, 21st Iowa	143		1928 Dec 21	NE, 53rd, 1929
Richardson, G.C.	Pvt.	G, 33rd Iowa Inf.	432		1916 Feb 7	IA, 43rd, 1917
Richardson, Geo. S.		G, 6th Iowa	59		1897 Sep 2	KS, 17th, 1898
Richardson, H.	Pvt.	E, 103rd Ill. Inf.	40		1908 Aug 31	IA, 35th, 1909
Richardson, Ira F.	Corp.	A, 16th U.S. Inf.	348	48	1886 Jun 1	IA, 13th, 1887
Richardson, J.		H, 9th Kans. Cav.	210		1893 Aug 7	KS, 13th, 1894
Richardson, J.H.		C, 122nd Ind. or Ill. Inf.	25		1938 Jan	KS, 57th, 1938
Richardson, J.W.	Musician	8th Wis. Inf. K, 23rd Wis. Inf.	1		1886	KS, 6th, 1887
Richardson, James H.		C, 10th Iowa Inf.	87		1916 Jul 24	KS, 36th, 1917
Richardson, Jas. A.		F, 104th N.Y. Inf.	11		1919 Dec 17	NE, 44th, 1920
Richardson, John L.	Corp.	A, 20th Iowa Inf.	58		1917 Sep 20	IA, 45th, 1919
Richardson, Joseph		A, 1st Ark.	63		1905 Oct 26	KS, 25th, 1906
Richardson, L.G.	Pvt.	D, 1st Minn. Inf.	298		1907 Apr 3	IA, 34th, 1908
Richardson, M.		D, 9th N.Y.	293		1906 Nov 7	KS, 26th, 1907
Richardson, M.A.		H, 83rd Ind.	129		1908 Aug 3	KS, 28th, 1909
Richardson, M.H.		K, 142nd N.Y.	23		1914	IA, 41st, 1915
Richardson, Milford		D, 9th Minn.	25		1906 Oct 21	KS, 26th, 1907
Richardson, Ole		died of heart failure	18		1913 Dec 28	NE, 38th, 1914
Richardson, Ozear		H, 6th Va. Inf.	388		1917 Apr 15	KS, 37th, 1918
Richardson, Robert N.		H, 14th West Va. Inf.	243		1914 Aug 2	KS, 34th, 1915
Richardson, S.H.		C, 7th Ill. Cav.	60		1927 Nov 17	NE, 52nd, 1928
Richardson, T.F.		A, 79th Ind.	51		1928 Feb 21	KS, 48th, 1929
Richardson, T.S.		F, 2nd Ky. Cav.	57		1910 Jul 9	KS, 30th, 1911
Richardson, Thos.		Grampus, Ohio (died of cancer)	262	57	1900 Feb 3	NE, 25th, 1901
Richardson, Thos. D.		A, 45th Mo.	61		1909	KS, 29th, 1910
Richardson, W.H.		C, 52nd Ind. (died of old age)	169	83	1915 Oct 21	NE, 40th, 1916
Richardson, W.T.		A, 2nd Conn. Art.	10	46	1895 Mar 31	NE, 20th, 1896
Richardson, Wm.	Corp.	H, 18th U.S. Colored Inf.	88		1916 Sep 18	IA, 43rd, 1917
Richardson, Wm.		8th Kans.	35		1900 Jan 27	KS, 20th, 1901
Richardson, Wm. B.	Pvt.	13th Iowa Inf.	245		1899 Mar	IA, 26th, 1900
Richart, Cyrus		H, 78th Ill. Inf. (died at Oswego, Kans.; buried at Mt. Moriah Cemetery)	150		1894 Nov 1	KS, 14th, 1895
Riche, Frank	Pvt.	K, 6th Iowa Cav.	346		1928 Nov 28	IA, 56th, 1930
Richenbach, W.F.C.	Asst. Eng.	U.S. Navy	1		1920 Mar 26	KS, 40th, 1921
Richer, John	Pvt.	G, 65th Ill. Inf.	42		1911 May 8	IA, 38th, 1912
Richeson, James		K, 4th Iowa Cav.	13	80	1918 Feb 10	NE, 43rd, 1919
Richey, John		H, 208th Penn.	293		1920 Feb 22	KS, 40th, 1921
Richey, S.P.			25		1890	NE, 15th, 1891
Richey, Samuel		A, M.M. Brigade[Mississippi Marine Brigade]	25		1892 Nov 11	KS, 12th, 1893
Richey, Wm. A.		K, 78th Penn. Inf.	25		1890 Sep 6	KS, 11th, 1892
Richie, Anthony	Pvt.	Ill. Regiment	116		1922 Apr 28	IA, 49th, 1923
Richie, John		A, 5th Kans. Cav.	1		1887 Aug 31	KS, 7th, 1888
Richie, W.S.	Pvt.	A, 1st Iowa Inf.	231		1899 Nov 14	IA, 26th, 1900
Richley, Philip	Pvt.	G, 19th Iowa Inf.	153		1927 Feb	IA, 54th, 1928
Richman, Jos. H.		A, 29th U.S.C. Inf.	14		1901 Dec 14	KS, 21st, 1902
Richmond			17		1902 May 29	KS, 22nd, 1903
Richmond, Frank		B, 44th Iowa	231	88	1934 Feb 7	IA, 61st, 1935
Richmond, Frank		G, 44th Iowa Inf.	231	88	1935 Feb 7	IA, 62nd, 1936
Richmond, H.J.		A, 112th Inf. (at large)			1932 Jan 10	IA, 59th, 1933
Richmond, J.D.			342		1915	KS, 35th, 1916
Richmond, J.F.	Pvt.	K, 16th Wis. Inf.	71		1910 Nov 12	IA, 37th, 1911
Richmond, J.M.		E, 15th Iowa	256		1928 Jun 23	KS, 48th, 1929
Richmond, Jas. T.	Pvt.	B, 11th Mo. Cav.	122		1930	IA, 57th, 1931
Richmond, John	Pvt.	A, 112th Ill. Inf.	113	76	1892 Nov 27	IA, 19th, 1893
Richmond, Norris C.	Pvt.	D, 126th Ill.	235		1922 Jul 12	IA, 49th, 1923
Richmond, Royal		K, 9th Iowa	257		1892 Jun 15	KS, 12th, 1893
Richmond, S.S.		G, 105th Ohio	27		1921 Feb 28	KS, 41st, 1922
Richmond, T.V.		D, 41st Ohio	199		1923 Oct 2	KS, 46th, 1927
Richmond, Wm. S.	Pvt.	H, 23rd Iowa	55	57	1891 Mar 7	IA, 17th, 1891
Richston, Jacob	Pvt.	B, 72nd Ind. Inf.	68		1928 Jan 10	IA, 55th, 1929

Name	Rank	Company, Regiment or Ship	Post*	Age	Death Date†	Journal
Richter, A.		G, 24th Ill. Inf. (died of paralysis)	65	57	1895 Nov 24	NE, 20th, 1896
Richter, E.		I, 5th Ohio Cav.	55		1893 Sep 2	KS, 13th, 1894
Richter, Harry E.		I, 123rd Ind.	7		1911 Dec 15	KS, 31st, 1912
Rick, John	Sergt.	A, 2nd Penn. Art.	431		1911 Apr 2	IA, 38th, 1912
Rick, John		Kans.	241		1908[1909?] Oct 15	KS, 29th, 1910
Rickabaugh, J.G.	Pvt.	I, 18th Iowa Inf.	235	58	1898 Mar 2	IA, 24th, 1898
Rickabaugh, Joe		H, 2nd Kans.	55		1904 Jul 26	KS, 24th, 1905
Rickal, Joel H.		H, 24th Ohio	129		1924 Jun 29	KS, 44th, 1925
Rickard, P.G.		K, 39th Wis.	335		1926 Feb 4	KS, 46th, 1927
Rickards, Charles H.		F, 7th Ohio Cav. (died of dropsy)	84	79	1925 Mar 3	NE, 50th, 1926
Rickehaupt, Phillip		C, 8th Ill. Cav.	250		1908 Apr 6	KS, 28th, 1909
Rickel, Henry	Lieut.	C, 6th Iowa Cav.	235		1925 Jun 18	IA, 52nd, 1926
Rickel, J.H.		G, 24th Ohio Inf.	129		1925 Jun 19	KS, 45th, 1926
Rickel, Joel H.		G, 24th Ohio Infantry (of Chanute)			1924 Jun 29	KS, 44th, 1925
Rickell, F.W.		I, 112th Ill.	7		1927 Mar 25	NE, 53rd, 1929
Ricker, A.		cause of death: heart	25		1903 Jun 4	NE, 28th, 1904
Ricker, A.		N.Y. (died of paralysis)	43		1903	NE, 28th, 1904
Ricker, H.B.	Pvt.	G, 17th Mass.	156		1903 Nov 8	IA, 30th, 1904
Ricker, J.N.		H, 48th Ind. Inf. (died of heart failure)	84	68	1896 Nov 22	NE, 21st, 1897
Ricker, S.F.		B, 1st Maine	55		1897 Aug 20	KS, 17th, 1898
Ricker, William		K, 45th Ill. Inf.	25		1893 Oct 16	NE, 18th, 1894
Rickerson, C.D.G.	Pvt.	39th Iowa Inf.	45		1912	IA, 39th, 1913
Rickerson, Gardner		M, 5th N.Y. Art.	13	81	1918 May 29	NE, 43rd, 1919
Rickets, A.C.	Pvt.	H, 80th Ohio	19		1907 1st term	IA, 34th, 1908
Rickett, C.	Pvt.	B, 22nd Iowa Inf.	27		1908	IA, 35th, 1909
Rickett, Harry		I, 78th Ill. Inf. (born in Warren County, Ill.; died in Sidney, Neb.)	12		1883 Jul 26	NE, 8th, 1884
Rickett, W.H.		C, 12th Kans.	51		1921 Jun 27	KS, 41st, 1922
Ricketts, A.C.		E, 135th Ohio	25		1932 Jun 18	NE, 57th, 1933
Ricketts, Alex		K, 107th Ill.	117		1885	KS, 5th, 1886
Rickey, J.M.		F, 53rd Ohio Inf.	77		1916 Mar 13	KS, 36th, 1917
Rickey, Wm.	Pvt.	I, 18th Iowa Inf.	112	47	1884 Mar 14	IA, 17th, 1891
Rickey, Wm.		I, 18th Iowa Inf.	112		2nd quarter 1884	IA, 11th, 1885
Rickman, J.		I, 14th U.S.C.T. Inf.	36		1911 Aug 13	KS, 31st, 1912
Rickman, Jno. W.		L, 4th Iowa Cav.	58		1927 Jan 17	IA, 54th, 1928
Rickman, W.H.	Pvt.	4th Iowa	29		1928 Jun 26	IA, 55th, 1929
Rickoff, Henry S.	Pvt.	I, 78th N.Y. Inf.	88		1915 Dec 28	IA, 42nd, 1916
Rickords, T.F.	Corp.	G, 27th N.J. Inf.	2		1909 Oct 10	IA, 36th, 1910
Rickring, Jess		died at asylum	81		1914	NE, 39th, 1915
Ricks, J.A.	Pvt.	F, 21st Ill.	22		1924 May 21	IA, 51st, 1925
Ricleard, James		H, 8th N.Y. Inf. (cause of death: heart)	262	64	1901 May	NE, 26th, 1902
Riddell, Joseph H.		I, 33rd Iowa (died of paralysis)	9	82	1924 Dec 16	NE, 49th, 1925
Riddell, S.T.	Pvt.	A, 8th N.Y. Cav.	34		1899	NE, 24th, 1900
Riddings, Henry	Pvt.	D, 1st Kans. Inf.	22		1911 Jan 5	IA, 38th, 1912
Riddle, F.M.		H, 8th Iowa	1		1913 May 10	KS, 33rd, 1914
Riddle, Frank M.		3rd Ind. Battery (died at Phoenix, Arizona, where he was temporarily residing; buried in Blue Rapids cemetery)	1		1913 May 10	KS, 33rd, 1914
Riddle, James L.		A, 30th Ill. Inf. (died of paralysis)	10	57	1902 Feb	NE, 27th, 1903
Riddle, John T.	Pvt.	A, 36th Iowa Inf.	313		1912 Apr 29	IA, 39th, 1913
Riddle, O.S.			305		1903-1904	IA, 30th, 1904
Riddle, P.G.			36		1924 Sep 24	KS, 46th, 1927
Riddle, Wm.	Pvt.	D, 2nd Iowa Inf.	7		1916 Nov 6	IA, 43rd, 1917
Ridell, J.		B, 18th U.S. Ohio (died of dyspepsia)	147	64	1905[1904?] Jan 15	NE, 29th, 1905
Ridemong, Walter			190		1899	IA, 26th, 1900
Rideneour, Joseph	Pvt.	I, 13th Iowa Inf.	48	65	1893 Apr 23	IA, 20th, 1894
Ridenhour, Frank		A, 187th Ohio	293		1914 Apr 10	KS, 34th, 1915
Ridenour, D.W.		E, 22nd Ohio Inf.	66		1902 Jan	KS, 22nd, 1903
Ridenour, James		H, 95th Ohio	158		1893 Oct 2	KS, 13th, 1894
Ridenour, John L.			297		1922 Sep 17	KS, 42nd, 1923
Ridenour, Martin		K, 11th West Va.	32		1898 Dec 21	KS, 18th, 1899
Rider, Charles J.	Capt.	H, 106th N.Y. Inf.	176	89	1898 Mar 22	IA, 24th, 1898

*See Appendix A, B or C for roster of post names and locations.
†See Introduction for note regarding recording of death date.

458

Name	Rank	Company, Regiment or Ship	Post*	Age	Death Date†	Journal
Rider, D.		E, 33rd Ill. Inf. (died of general debility)	25	58	1896 Jul 24	NE, 21st, 1897
Rider, E.P.		G, 9th Iowa Cav. (died of heart failure)	43		1908 Jun 9	NE, 33rd, 1909
Rider, J.Q.A.	Lieut.	E, 91st Ill.	68		1907 May 15	IA, 34th, 1908
Ridgely, Eli		C, 11th Mo. Cav. (former member; died at Grand Island)	69		1936 May 18	NE, 61st, 1937
Ridgeway, James			2		1929 Feb 9	IA, 56th, 1930
Ridgley, Richard			192		1890	NE, 15th, 1891
Ridinger, D.		A, 93rd Ind. Inf.	36		1911 Jan 15	KS, 31st, 1912
Ridings, C.C.		B, 60th Ohio	2[27?]		1918 Mar 4	KS, 38th, 1919
Ridler, C.C.	Pvt.	K, 16th Ind. Inf.	49	52	1890 Mar 14	IA, 17th, 1891
Ridler, Calvin C.	Pvt.	K, 16th Ind. Inf.	49	50	1890 Mar 15	IA, 16th, 1890
Ridler, J.W.	Pvt.	H, 21st Iowa Inf.	391		1915 Dec 8	IA, 42nd, 1916
Ridley, Reson		K, 116th Ohio Inf.	12		1908 Jan 2	KS, 28th, 1909
Ridley, Robert	Com. Sergt.	K, 14th R.I. Hvy. Art.	413	58	1887 Mar 18	IA, 15th, 1889
Ridlon, J.F.		I, 35th Ill.	447		1916	KS, 36th, 1917
Ridpath, Jos.	Pvt.	E, 33rd Iowa Inf.	34		1911 Aug 27	IA, 38th, 1912
Rieley, L.A.	Pvt.	45th Iowa Inf.	153		1914 Dec 26	IA, 41st, 1915
Rielke, P.A.	Pvt.	K, 169th Ohio Inf.	50		1918 Apr 1	IA, 45th, 1919
Rietz, Nicholas		H, 117th Ill.	68		1922 Nov 21	KS, 42nd, 1923
Riffe, Jno. F.		A, 42nd Penn.	[25?]		1923	NE, 48th, 1924
Riffer, Henry		D, 119th Ill. Inf.	175		1929 Jan 12	KS, 49th, 1930
Riffle, C.C.	Pvt.	C, 139th Penn. Inf.	12		1920 Jan 27	IA, 47th, 1921
Riffley, C.F.	Pvt.	A, 30th Iowa Inf.	2	54	1891 Aug 23	IA, 18th, 1892
Rigby, A.L.	Pvt.	K, 1st Iowa Inf.	25		1929 May 9	IA, 56th, 1930
Rigby, Henry	Chaplain	20th Ohio Inf.	30	71	1894 Jun 10	IA, 21st, 1895
Rigby, M.F.		B, 24th Iowa Inf.	400		1918	IA, 45th, 1919
Rigby, Simon		A, 2nd Md. Inf. (died of old age & disability)	180	79	1911 Mar 22	NE, 36th, 1912
Rigby, Washington H.	Pvt.	M, 1st Iowa Cav.	109	52	1893 Apr	IA, 20th, 1894
Rigdon, Robert W.		A, 8th Ind.	250		1924 May 1	KS, 44th, 1925
Rigg, Jas. C.		I, 5th Ill. Cav. (leave a needy family)	125		1889	KS, 9th, 1890
Riggan, M.M.		E, 65th Ind. Inf.	147		1934 Feb 9	KS, 54th, 1935
Riggs, Andrew		E, 3rd Wis.	31	61	1904 Jan 27	NE, 29th, 1905
Riggs, Daniel C.		C, 17th Kans.	380		1905 Dec 30	KS, 25th, 1906
Riggs, F.M.	Pvt.	24th Ind. Lt. Art.	235		1920 Aug 6	IA, 47th, 1921
Riggs, G.W.	Pvt.	B, 20th Conn. Inf.	452		1922 Feb 15	IA, 49th, 1923
Riggs, J.T.		F, 2nd Minn. Inf. (died of old age)	24	77	1902 Jul	NE, 27th, 1903
Riggs, James W.	Sergt.	K, 25th Iowa Inf.	263		1911 Dec 26	IA, 39th, 1913
Riggs, James W.	Sergt.	K, 25th Ind. Inf.	263		1911 Dec 26	IA, 38th, 1912
Riggs, Jeremiah		Va. Cav.	40		1915 Feb 2	IA, 42nd, 1916
Riggs, Nathan		E, 12th Kans. Inf.	414		1891 Jan 8	KS, 11th, 1892
Riggs, S.F.		B, 9th Kans.	1		1911 Feb 3	KS, 31st, 1912
Right, E.W.		B, 154th Ill. Inf.	68		1926 Dec 14	NE, 51st, 1927
Rigney, Patrick		A, 36th Ill. Inf. (died at Ellsworth)	22		1895 Aug	KS, 15th, 1896
Rike, J.L.		B, 44th Ohio	158		1924 Nov 26	KS, 44th, 1925
Rila, T.F.		E, 25th Ill. Inf.	173		1924 Feb 6	IA, 51st, 1925
Rilea, T.J.	Pvt.	D, 175th Ohio Inf.	173		1925 Feb 6	IA, 52nd, 1926
Riley, Alex		10th Kans.	195		1892 May	KS, 12th, 1893
Riley, Anderson		E, U.S.C. In. Chero	46		1904 Aug 11	KS, 24th, 1905
Riley, Bernard	Pvt.	1st Iowa Cav.	434		1909 Mar	IA, 36th, 1910
Riley, D.F.		A, 46th Wis.	64		1926 Sep	NE, 51st, 1927
Riley, E.L.		H, 7th Wis. Inf. (died of paralysis)	77	77	1920 Nov 4	NE, 45th, 1921
Riley, Geo. W.		D, 119th Ill.	25		1910 Sep 7	KS, 30th, 1911
Riley, I.L.		D, 72nd Ind.	270		1913 May 6	KS, 32nd, 1913
Riley, J.B.		D, 30th Ohio	469		1915 Dec 15	KS, 36th, 1917
Riley, J.H.		F, 3rd Iowa Cav.	63		1921 Nov 12	KS, 42nd, 1923
Riley, J.H.		D, 16th Mo.	293		1927	KS, 47th, 1928
Riley, J.O.		E, 28th Iowa	13		1930 Sep 9	NE, 55th, 1931
Riley, J.W.	Pvt.	E, 6th Iowa Cav.	139	65	1893 Jul 17	IA, 20th, 1894
Riley, James A.		K, 9th Iowa Inf.	71		1901 Aug 21	KS, 21st, 1902
Riley, James B.		G, 16th Ohio Vol. Inf.	469		1915 Dec 15	KS, 35th, 1916
Riley, John	Pvt.	G, 15th Iowa Inf.	497	48	1894 Nov 22	IA, 21st, 1895

*See Appendix A, B or C for roster of post names and locations.
†See Introduction for note regarding recording of death date.
459

Name	Rank	Company, Regiment or Ship	Post*	Age	Death Date†	Journal
Riley, John	Pvt.	C, 12th Ill. Cav.	124		1911 Aug 15	IA, 38th, 1912
Riley, L.S.		D, 195th Ohio Inf.	164		1899 Jul 2	KS, 19th, 1900
Riley, M.V.			2		1909 Feb 27	IA, 36th, 1910
Riley, Madison		E, 134th Ind. Inf. (died of old age)	318		1922 Apr 25	NE, 47th, 1923
Riley, Peter		H, 6th Kans. Cav.	32		1908 Mar 23	KS, 28th, 1909
Riley, R.F.	Pvt.	K, 13th Iowa Inf.	108	66	1898 Dec 3	IA, 25th, 1899
Riley, Roswell J.		C, 55th Ill. Inf.	71		1900 Dec 4	KS, 20th, 1901
Riley, S.S.		C, 23rd Ind.	65		1927 Oct 25	KS, 47th, 1928
Riley, Samuel		C, 15th Mo. Inf.	244		1921 Jun	KS, 41st, 1922
Riley, T.J.		B, 10th Ill. Cav.	17		1916 Aug 3	KS, 36th, 1917
Riley, Thomas N.		A, 5th Ohio	100		1931 Sep 24	KS, 52nd, 1933
Riley, Thomas N.		A, 5th Ohio	100		1931 Sep 24	KS, 51st, 1932
Riley, W.H.		E, 50th Ill. Inf.	118		1886	KS, 6th, 1887
Riley, W.H.		E, 3rd West Va. Cav.	270		1899 Mar 16	KS, 19th, 1900
Riley, W.L.		G, 21st N.Y. Cav.	66		1922 May 2	KS, 42nd, 1923
Riley, Wm.		A, 95th Ill. (died of diabetes)	130	86	1912 Dec 22	NE, 37th, 1913
Riley, Z.F.		H, 175th Ohio	1		1896 Dec 6	KS, 16th, 1897
Rime, Wirter		K, 14th Ill. Cav.	286		1893 Jan 10	KS, 12th, 1893
Rimochl, Henry	Pvt.	E, 55th Ill.	68		1907 Jul 24	IA, 34th, 1908
Rincher, William		K, 56th U.S.C.T.	25		1920 Oct 20	KS, 40th, 1921
Rinck, E.N.			36		1926 Mar 16	KS, 46th, 1927
Rine, Michael P.		L, 7th Ill.	57		1930 Apr 30	KS, 50th, 1931
Rineborger, T.M.	Pvt.	55th Ohio	88		1923 Feb 24	IA, 50th, 1924
Rinehart, Alexander		G, 17th Iowa Vols.	381		1902 Apr 22	KS, 22nd, 1903
Rinehart, John	Pvt.	B, 5th Iowa Inf.	84		1905 Mar 31	IA, 31st, 1905
Rinehart, John T.		K, 5th Iowa Inf. & 9th Iowa Cav. (died of pneumonia)	284	58	1904 Nov 4	NE, 29th, 1905
Rinehart, S.	Pvt.	K, 47th Ill. Inf.	440		1921 Feb 26	IA, 48th, 1922
Rinehart, Samuel		E, 14th Ill. Inf.	17		1914 Jan 9	KS, 34th, 1915
Rinerd, I.W.	Pvt.	B, 4th Iowa Cav.	55		1913 Jan 18	IA, 40th, 1914
Ring, G.W.		G, 25th Wis.	209		1911 Apr	KS, 31st, 1912
Ring, Henry		K, 7th N.Y.	235		1914 Nov 14	IA, 41st, 1915
Ring, Lawrence		U.S. Navy	380		1911 Dec 26	KS, 32nd, 1913
Ring, R.C.	Pvt.	B, —	244		1906 May 2	IA, 33rd, 1907
Ring, T.R.	Pvt.	D, 83rd Penn. Inf.	7		1921	IA, 48th, 1922
Ringer, Brad		C, 2nd Ohio	25		1908 Apr 5	NE, 33rd, 1909
Ringer, Frank E.		I, 48th Penn.	250		1905 Dec 24	KS, 25th, 1906
Ringer, Wm. G.		C, 84th Ill.	117		1913 Jan 27	KS, 33rd, 1914
Ringston, S.			54		1921	KS, 41st, 1922
Rinnal, Jacob		H, 192nd Ohio	117		1924 Oct 1	KS, 44th, 1925
Rinner, Peter	Sergt.	K, 2nd Dragoons	297		1912 Mar 10	IA, 39th, 1913
Rinsworth, O.	Pvt.	A, 32nd Wis. Inf.	58		1908 Dec 7	IA, 35th, 1909
Ripley, David			231		1929 Jan 14	IA, 55th, 1929
Ripley, E.W.	Pvt.	F, 34th N.Y. Inf.	147		1920 Aug 28	IA, 47th, 1921
Ripley, Edward		G, 155th Ohio	68		1924 Apr 27	KS, 44th, 1925
Ripley, Geo. W.			4		1883	KS, 3rd, 1884
Ripley, Herman		A, 76th N.Y.	40		1919 Jun 13	KS, 39th, 1920
Ripley, J.H.	Pvt.	C, 2nd Iowa Inf.	110		1923 Aug 12	IA, 50th, 1924
Ripley, Robert J.	Pvt.	E, 29th Iowa Inf.	56		1914 Sep 9	IA, 41st, 1915
Rippeleaw, J.E.		18th Ind. Batt.	13		1928 Jan 8	NE, 53rd, 1929
Risden, M.R.		G, 115th Ohio (died of Bright's disease)	110	75	1917 Feb 15	NE, 42nd, 1918
Risden, Watson	Pvt.	H, 128th Ind. Inf.	235	89	1932 Jun 30	IA, 59th, 1933
Risenger, Joe		C, 124th Ind.	98		1926 Jun	KS, 46th, 1927
Rishel, Jacob	Pvt.	B, 9th Iowa Cav.	26		1926 Nov 29	IA, 53rd, 1927
Rising, J.R.		I, 60th N.Y. Inf. (died of cancer of bowels)	354		1891 Apr 22	KS, 11th, 1892
Risler, Nathaniel		F, 62nd Ohio Inf.	98		1914 Apr 1	KS, 34th, 1915
Risley, John Parker		D, 20th Iowa Inf. E, 29th Iowa Inf.	1	91	1938 Mar 27	IA, 64th, 1938
Risley, Samuel M.		E & L, 140th & 7th Ill. Cav. (died of rheumatism)	60	66	1909 Oct 10	NE, 34th, 1910
Riss, C.M.		B, 11th Mo.	174		1917 Nov 3	KS, 37th, 1918
Ristine, H.G.			236		1917 Jan 30	IA, 44th, 1918

See Appendix A, B or C for roster of post names and locations.
†*See Introduction for note regarding recording of death date.*

Name	Rank	Company, Regiment or Ship	Post*	Age	Death Date†	Journal
Ristine, Henry	Surg.	20th Iowa Inf.	235	74	1893 Apr 28	IA, 20th, 1894
Riswick, John	Pvt.	C, —	49		1923 Jan 14	IA, 50th, 1924
Ritchey, F.G.		F, 138th Penn.	98		1919 Nov 21	KS, 39th, 1920
Ritchey, J.C.	Pvt.	C, 1st Iowa Cav.	12		1930 Oct 22	IA, 57th, 1931
Ritchey, Jonathan		G, 13th Iowa	34		1919 Sep 27	KS, 39th, 1920
Ritchey, Lafe		I, 61st Ill.	25		1923	NE, 48th, 1924
Ritchie, Clement		K, 15th Penn. Inf.	32		1908[1909?] Nov 30	KS, 29th, 1910
Ritchie, David		G, 102nd Ill.	14		1902 Dec 1	KS, 22nd, 1903
Ritchie, Geo. W.		National Military Home			1936 Apr 5	KS, 55th, 1936
Ritchie, James T.		A, 137th Ohio Inf.	100		1914 Jul 20	KS, 34th, 1915
Ritchie, Thomas W.		A, 5th Iowa Cav. (died of cancer)	55	67	1909 Mar 8	NE, 34th, 1910
Ritchie, W.H.		B, 155th Ind.	83		1933 Jan 10	KS, 53rd, 1934
Ritchie, Wm.	Pvt.	C, 47th Ill. Inf.	235		1908 Dec 18	IA, 35th, 1909
Ritchison, Walter	Pvt.	C, 29th Iowa Vol. Inf.	103		1901 Dec 21	IA, 28th, 1902
Ritmour, Geo. W.	Pvt.	B, 168th Penn. Inf.	466		1924 Apr	IA, 51st, 1925
Ritner, B.D.	Pvt.	E, 16th Penn. Inf.	88		1907 Oct 8	IA, 34th, 1908
Ritter, Benj. F.		D, 30th Ind.	90		1915 Feb 23	KS, 35th, 1916
Ritter, Francis	Pvt.	K, 9th Iowa Inf. (at large)	67	98, 2 mos. & 23 days	1944 Jun 21	IA, 70th, 1944
Ritter, Henry		G, 49th Penn.	12		1914 Mar 20	KS, 34th, 1915
Ritter, I.L.		H, 67th Penn. Inf. (killed at Chapman)	105	70	1913 Apr 4	NE, 38th, 1914
Ritter, Jacob			261		1890	NE, 15th, 1891
Ritter, Jonas		F, 25th Iowa	83		1916 Mar 17	KS, 36th, 1917
Ritzman, John B.	Corp.	E, 5th Iowa Cav.	5		1918 Jan 11	IA, 45th, 1919
Rivers, Harry, see Cooper, Edwin R.						
Rix, John	Pvt.	A, 4th Mich. Cav.	170	54	1893 Dec 15	IA, 20th, 1894
Roach, C.A.		E, 129th Ohio Inf. (died at White Water)	375		1895 Oct	KS, 15th, 1896
Roach, David		I, 18th Iowa Inf.	31		1899 Jul 23	KS, 19th, 1900
Roach, J.A.	Pvt.	C, 85th Ohio	324		1907 Sep 28	IA, 34th, 1908
Roach, J.A.		F, 151st Ill.	25		1927 May 20	KS, 47th, 1928
Roach, J.B.	Pvt.	C, 28th Iowa Inf.	127		1917 Jan 14	IA, 44th, 1918
Roach, J.P.	Capt.	G, 23rd Iowa Inf.	7	71	1893 Jul 20	IA, 20th, 1894
Roach, Robert		E, 10th Wis.	180		1892 Apr 20	KS, 12th, 1893
Roach, S.C.		H, 138th Ind.	25		1930 Dec 7	KS, 50th, 1931
Roach, S.T.		43rd Ind. Inf.	180		1886	KS, 6th, 1887
Roach, T.C.		H, 185th Ohio	453		1913 Dec 22	KS, 33rd, 1914
Roach, Thomas		A, N.Y. Art.	293		1910 Apr	KS, 30th, 1911
Roache, Michael		I, 5th U.S.A.	6		1891 Jan 10	KS, 11th, 1892
Roades, John R.	Pvt.	A, 13th Iowa Inf.	74		1915 Apr 23	IA, 42nd, 1916
Roads, David		K, 8th Ill. Inf. (died of heart disease)	24	65	1902 May	NE, 27th, 1903
Roakey, Lewis F.		D, 1st Penn. Cav.	58		1912 Jul 25	KS, 32nd, 1913
Roan, J.M.	Pvt.	A, 33rd Iowa Inf.	452		1918 Sep 18	IA, 45th, 1919
Roat, Chas. A.		L, 2nd Colo. Cav.	12		1908 Jul 1	KS, 28th, 1909
Robb, Alexander G.	Sergt.	H, 5th Wis. Inf.	250		1918 Sep 8	KS, 38th, 1919
Robb, Andrew		I, 8th Iowa	14		1892 Dec 29	KS, 12th, 1893
Robb, Geo. L.	Pvt.	E, 33rd Iowa Inf.	337		1926 May 6	IA, 53rd, 1927
Robb, George H.		C, 8th Kans. Inf.	191		1912 Mar 1	KS, 32nd, 1913
Robb, H.M.		D, 83rd Ill.	30	70	1888	KS, 8th, 1889
Robb, James		I, 15th Penn.	18		1898 Mar 3	KS, 18th, 1899
Robb, James Edgar	Pvt.	C, 14th Iowa Inf.	16		1901 Oct 27	IA, 28th, 1902
Robb, S.W.		M, 10th Mo. Cav.	153		1912 Jan 15	KS, 32nd, 1913
Robb, Sam'l H.		K, 1st Ky.	113		1908 Feb 12	NE, 33rd, 1909
Robb, Wallace N.		C, 76th Ill. Inf.	262	70	1915 May 12	NE, 39th, 1915
Robb, Wilson	Chaplain	18th Iowa Inf.	173		1916	IA, 43rd, 1917
Robbins, A.	Pvt.	C, 2nd Mo. State Militia	467	46	1890 Apr 3	IA, 17th, 1891
Robbins, Charles C.	Pvt.	A, 118th Ill. Inf.	2		1902 Nov 12	IA, 29th, 1903
Robbins, E.H.	Lieut.	I, 27th Iowa Inf.	194		1908 Dec 7	IA, 35th, 1909
Robbins, Enoch		A, 5th Ind. Cav. (died of heart trouble)	201	70	1908 Nov 26	NE, 33rd, 1909
Robbins, Ephraim	Pvt.	H, 14th Ill. Inf.	66		1930 Dec 27	IA, 57th, 1931

Name	Rank	Company, Regiment or Ship	Post*	Age	Death Date†	Journal
Robbins, Evans	Pvt.	I, 16th Ill. Inf.	97	57	1895 May 23	IA, 22nd, 1896
Robbins, Frank		K, 6th U.S. Cav.	131		1910 May 28	KS, 30th, 1911
Robbins, Geo. W.	Pvt.	B, 64th Ill. Inf.	5		1903 Feb 25	IA, 29th, 1903
Robbins, H.	Pvt.	I, 32nd Ohio Inf.	238		1910 Sep 12	IA, 37th, 1911
Robbins, Henry		A, 24th Iowa	164[165?]		1st quarter 1884	IA, 10th, 1884
Robbins, J.B.	Pvt.		5		1930 Jun 28	IA, 57th, 1931
Robbins, J.E.		E, 4th Vt.	66		1905 Feb 28	KS, 25th, 1906
Robbins, J.L.		120th Ind. Inf.	55	91	1935 Sep 19	IA, 62nd, 1936
Robbins, J.M.		120th Ind. Inf.		91 & 9 mos.	1936[1935?] Sep 19	IA, 62nd, 1936
Robbins, Jacob B.		K, 78th Ill.	249		1897 Jul 21	KS, 17th, 1898
Robbins, James M.		1st Battery Kans. Lt. Art.	18		1913 Jan 22	KS, 33rd, 1914
Robbins, Jasper	Pvt.	F, 8th Iowa Cav.	66		1928 Oct 28	IA, 57th, 1931
Robbins, John B.	Sergt.	H, 13th U.S. Inf.	247		1913 Jun 18	IA, 40th, 1914
Robbins, John Y.		A, 44th Ind.	129		1905 Jan 7	KS, 25th, 1906
Robbins, L.B.		B, 8th Mich. Cav., 23rd Corps (died in Bellwood)	83		1883 May	NE, 8th, 1884
Robbins, M.F.C.	Pvt.	K, 38th Iowa Inf.	258	51	1886 Dec 25	IA, 13th, 1887
Robbins, Mont, see Robins, Mont						
Robbins, R.B.	Pvt.	G, 123rd Ill. Inf.	156		1917 Feb 4	IA, 44th, 1918
Robbins, Thomas, see Robins, Thomas						
Robbins, Thornton		B, 24th Ohio Inf.	500		1916 Feb 14	KS, 36th, 1917
Robbins, W.M.		E, 17th Mich. (died of heart failure)	164		1891 Sep 30	KS, 11th, 1892
Robe, J.E.		K, 34th Iowa	52		1905 Apr 26	KS, 25th, 1906
Robens, John P.		E, 176th N.Y.	32		1905 Jul 21	KS, 25th, 1906
Roberson, T.B.		138th Ill.	104		1924 Sep 27	KS, 44th, 1925
Robert A.	Sergt.	C, 25th —	2		1921 Aug 6	IA, 48th, 1922
Robert, Paul T.		G, 14th Wis.	336		1898 Jul 7	KS, 18th, 1899
Roberts, A.	Sergt.	D, 36th Iowa Inf.	73		1910 Nov	IA, 37th, 1911
Roberts, A.	Col.	C, 1st Iowa Inf. 11th U.S. Inf. A, 30th Iowa Inf.	20	70	1907 Jun 5	NE, 32nd, 1908
Roberts, A.A.	Pvt.	K, 8th Ind. Inf.	52		1897 Feb 16	IA, 24th, 1898
Roberts, A.C.	Pvt.	K, 8th Vt. Inf.	300	55	1896 Jan 30	IA, 23rd, 1897
Roberts, A.E.		I, 1st Tenn. Cav.	311		1918 Mar 17	KS, 38th, 1919
Roberts, Abel C.	Surg.	21st Mo. Vet. Vol. Inf.	170		1901 Jul 27	IA, 28th, 1902
Roberts, Abel W.	Pvt.	2nd Iowa Lt. Art. (at large)		90	1935 Apr 1	IA, 65th, 1939
Roberts, B.F.	Sergt.	C, 29th Iowa	83		1922	IA, 49th, 1923
Roberts, B.F.		12th Kans. Inf.	173		1913	NE, 38th, 1914
Roberts, C.G.	Sergt.	L, 2nd Ill. Art.	88	58	1892 May 4	IA, 19th, 1893
Roberts, C.H.		C, 40th Iowa	85		1930 Jan 29	KS, 50th, 1931
Roberts, Chas.		M, 5th Ill. Cav.	11	80	1919 Dec 11	NE, 44th, 1920
Roberts, Cyrus	Pvt.	C, 12th Wis.	81		1922 Aug 16	IA, 49th, 1923
Roberts, D.B.		I, 23rd Ky. Inf.	118		1918 May 23	KS, 38th, 1919
Roberts, D.H.	Pvt.	I, 32nd Iowa Inf.	118		1903 Aug 17	IA, 31st, 1905
Roberts, D.H.		K, 184th Ohio	356		1931 Oct 26	KS, 52nd, 1933
Roberts, D.H.		K, 184th Ohio	356		1931 Oct 26	KS, 51st, 1932
Roberts, E.R.	Pvt.	B, 21st Iowa Inf.	42		1921 Sep	IA, 48th, 1922
Roberts, Edward	Pvt.	G, 28th Iowa Inf.	403		1900 Apr 26	IA, 27th, 1901
Roberts, Edward		G, 18th Mo.	147		1904 Dec 1	KS, 24th, 1905
Roberts, G.B.		E, 106th Ill.	17		1917 Nov 21	KS, 37th, 1918
Roberts, Geo.	Pvt.	G, 112th Ill. Inf.	321		1920 Apr 2	IA, 47th, 1921
Roberts, Geo. F.	Pvt.	E, 37th Mass. Inf.	223		1909 Nov 4	IA, 36th, 1910
Roberts, Geo. H.	Pvt.	H, 6th Iowa Inf.	440		1925 Nov 20	IA, 52nd, 1926
Roberts, Geo. W.		A, 40th Ohio	191		1923	KS, 43rd, 1924
Roberts, H.C.		C, 24th Ind. Inf. (killed by accident)	476		1891 Oct 10	KS, 11th, 1892
Roberts, J.E.	Pvt.	I, 42nd Iowa	118		1903 Aug 2	IA, 30th, 1904
Roberts, J.J.	Pvt.	D, 36th Iowa Inf.	138		1916 Mar 17	IA, 43rd, 1917
Roberts, J.L.		A, 117th Ind.	13		1896 Feb 3	KS, 16th, 1897
Roberts, J.M.M.	Corp.	K, 12th West Va. Inf.	313		1908 Oct 26	IA, 35th, 1909
Roberts, J.W.			26		1917	KS, 37th, 1918

*See Appendix A, B or C for roster of post names and locations.
†See Introduction for note regarding recording of death date.

Name	Rank	Company, Regiment or Ship	Post*	Age	Death Date†	Journal
Roberts, Jacob		K, 25th Ill.	250		1912 Nov 25	KS, 33rd, 1914
Roberts, James H.		M, 4th Kans. State Militia	12		1910 Aug 10	KS, 30th, 1911
Roberts, James T.		E, 9th Iowa Cav. (died of paralysis)	112		1911 Jul 1	NE, 36th, 1912
Roberts, Jas.	Pvt.	C, 84th Ohio Inf.	72		1918 Jun 9	IA, 45th, 1919
Roberts, Jas.	Pvt.	B, 23rd Wis. Inf.	472		1920 Feb 14	IA, 47th, 1921
Roberts, Jas. D.		K, 8th Ind. Inf.	51		1891 Nov 9	KS, 11th, 1892
Roberts, John M.	Pvt.	B, 6th Iowa Inf.	26	58	1892 Apr 18	IA, 18th, 1892
Roberts, John N.		C, 19th Ohio O, 6th Ohio	12		1927 Nov 21	KS, 47th, 1928
Roberts, Johnson F.		11th Ill. Inf. (died of physical breakdown)	47	84	1919 Jun 9	NE, 44th, 1920
Roberts, Meredith		D, 62nd U.S.C.I.	405		1913 Mar 9	KS, 33rd, 1914
Roberts, Moses		K, 1st Ohio Cav.	47		1937 Apr 9	NE, 62nd, 1938
Roberts, O.W.		E, 116th Ill. (died of general decline)	169		1916 Dec 18	NE, 41st, 1917
Roberts, R.M.	Pvt.	B, 2nd Iowa Inf.	57		1920 Dec 23	IA, 47th, 1921
Roberts, R.R.		I, 73rd Ill. Inf.	26		1902 Oct 17	KS, 22nd, 1903
Roberts, Richards		G, 3rd Kans.	6		1904	KS, 24th, 1905
Roberts, Robert	Pvt.	A, 52nd Wis. Inf.	124	59	1886 Jun 4	IA, 13th, 1887
Roberts, S.D.		C, 75th Ill. Inf.	25		1893 Aug 21	NE, 18th, 1894
Roberts, S.S.		G, 155th Ill. Inf. (cause of death: heart)	107	68	1903 Jun 5	NE, 28th, 1904
Roberts, Samuel		H, 152nd Ohio	5		1921 Jul 12	KS, 41st, 1922
Roberts, Samuel L.		G, 15th Iowa (died of heart trouble)	94	69	1916 Jul 23	NE, 41st, 1917
Roberts, Stewert	Pvt.	H, 161st Ohio Inf.	81		1913 Mar 13	IA, 40th, 1914
Roberts, T.	Pvt.	6th Mass. Vols.	12		1926 Jun 26	IA, 53rd, 1927
Roberts, T.F.		D, 10th Kans.	117		1923 May 23	KS, 43rd, 1924
Roberts, Thomas	Pvt.	C, 12th Wis. Inf.	124		1912 Aug 17	IA, 39th, 1913
Roberts, Thomas	Pvt.	C, 120th N.Y. Inf.	503		1922 May 27	IA, 49th, 1923
Roberts, Thos.	Pvt.	B, 30th Iowa Inf.	158		1924 Feb 26	IA, 51st, 1925
Roberts, Thos. M.		A, 26th Mo.	118	74	1917 Oct	NE, 42nd, 1918
Roberts, W.S.		B, 32nd Ohio Inf. (died of heart disease)	118	74	1921 Sep 10	NE, 46th, 1922
Roberts, Wallace		E, 6th Iowa	238		1916 Nov 5	KS, 36th, 1917
Roberts, William	Pvt.	D, 140th Ind. Inf.	45		1928 Feb 21	IA, 55th, 1929
Roberts, William R.		I, 47th Iowa Inf. (died of old age)	110	89	1921 Aug 17	NE, 46th, 1922
Roberts, Wm.	Pvt.	I, 141st Ill. Inf.	222		1909 Oct 26	IA, 36th, 1910
Roberts, Wm. A.	Pvt.	B, 8th Iowa Cav.	138		1912 Nov 2	IA, 40th, 1914
Roberts, Wm. E.	Corp.	G, 1st Wis. Inf.	97		1909 Sep 19	IA, 36th, 1910
Roberts, Wm. M.			25	83	1910 May 13	NE, 35th, 1911
Roberts, Zeph		F, 14th Ill.	257		1925 Jun 20	KS, 45th, 1926
Robertson, Alex.	Pvt.	G, 43rd Ohio Inf.	452		1912 Oct 25	IA, 39th, 1913
Robertson, Anthony		A, 79th Ill.	108		1892 Dec 27	KS, 12th, 1893
Robertson, C.H.		K, 17th Ill. Cav.	7		1925 Mar 5	NE, 50th, 1926
Robertson, D.A.	Pvt.	A, 19th Iowa Inf.	5		1909 May 23	IA, 36th, 1910
Robertson, D.A.	Lieut.	K, 13th Iowa Cav.	431		1910 Sep 29	IA, 37th, 1911
Robertson, F.M.		A & D, 11th Md.	248		1926 Jan 4	KS, 46th, 1927
Robertson, Henry C.		G, 2nd Neb. Cav.	66		1929	NE, 54th, 1930
Robertson, Horace	Pvt.	F, 10th Iowa Inf.	249		1923 Apr 7	IA, 49th, 1923
Robertson, J.A.		B, 45th Iowa Inf.	108		1916 Jan 18	IA, 43rd, 1917
Robertson, J.A.		A, 74th N.Y.	100		1927 Sep 21	KS, 47th, 1928
Robertson, J.L.	Pvt.	F, 1st Maine Art.	118		1905 Nov 4	IA, 32nd, 1906
Robertson, J.T.		C, 19th Iowa Inf.	7		1926 Mar 1	NE, 51st, 1927
Robertson, Jno.	Pvt.	C, 35th N.Y. Inf.	231	41	1884 Jan	IA, 14th, 1888
Robertson, John		C, 35th N.Y. Inf.	231		2nd quarter 1884	IA, 11th, 1885
Robertson, John H.		I, 35th Wis. (died of pneumonia)	60		1923 Jan 1	NE, 48th, 1924
Robertson, Joseph F.		A, 3rd Iowa Cav.	23		1909 Mar 22	KS, 29th, 1910
Robertson, Julius		D, 7th Ky.	4		1917 Dec 8	KS, 37th, 1918
Robertson, N.		E, 11th La.	25		1913 Aug 14	NE, 38th, 1914
Robertson, Robt.	Pvt.	D, 10th Iowa Inf.	347	64	1887 Feb 8	IA, 15th, 1889
Robertson, S.S.			55		1911 Jun 8	IA, 38th, 1912
Robertson, Samuel		H, 79th Ill.	112		1904 Apr 15	KS, 24th, 1905
Robertson, T.S.		2nd Mo. Cav.	515		1919 Oct 12	IA, 46th, 1920
Robertson, W.M.	Pvt.	G, 116th Ind. Inf.	153		1930 Jan 28	IA, 57th, 1931
Robertson, W.S.	Major	5th Iowa Inf.	231	52	1887 Jan 28	IA, 14th, 1888
Robertson, W.S.	Major	died at his home in Muscatine, Iowa	231		1886 Jan 20	IA, 13th, 1887

Name	Rank	Company, Regiment or Ship	Post*	Age	Death Date†	Journal
Robeson, Wm.	Pvt.	1st Iowa Battery	68		1911 Oct 26	IA, 38th, 1912
Robey, C.A.	Pvt.	E, 1st Iowa Cav.	194		1924	IA, 51st, 1925
Robey, Truman A.		C, 90th Ill.	25		1915 Mar 12	NE, 40th, 1916
Robinett, A.G.		C, 21st Ohio	1		1910 Feb 25	KS, 30th, 1911
Robinett, J.W.		C, 36th Ohio	64		1927 Aug 28	KS, 47th, 1928
Robins, D.C.		I, 104th Ill. Inf.	13		1893 Aug 24	NE, 18th, 1894
Robins, Henry	Pvt.	A, 24th Iowa Inf.	164	36	1st quarter 1887	IA, 13th, 1887
Robins, Mont		K, 68th Ind. Inf.	32	76	1916 Jan 19	NE, 41st, 1917
Robins, Thomas		8th Mo.	264		1906 Nov 26	KS, 26th, 1907
Robinson, A.		E, 21st Wis. Inf. (died of abscess of liver)	119		1893 Jul 26	NE, 18th, 1894
Robinson, A.W.		G, 4th Ill. Inf.	28		1921	KS, 41st, 1922
Robinson, Alonzo		K, 12th Iowa Inf.	25		1919 Nov 16	NE, 44th, 1920
Robinson, Amos H.		C, 3rd Vt.	17		1898 Oct 11	KS, 18th, 1899
Robinson, Calvin F.		B, 32nd Ohio	18		1926 Oct 23	KS, 46th, 1927
Robinson, Charles		E, 3rd Kans. State Militia (died in Grant Township; buried at Oak Hill Cemetery)	12		1894 Aug 17	KS, 14th, 1895
Robinson, Charles E.			130		1914 Jul 15	KS, 34th, 1915
Robinson, D.		B, 21st Kans.	370		1902 Apr 29	KS, 22nd, 1903
Robinson, D.C.	Pvt.	F, 26th Ind. Inf.	66		1916 Apr 3	IA, 43rd, 1917
Robinson, D.L.		New York	54		1886 Jun 5	IA, 13th, 1887
Robinson, D.W.		14th Kans. Cav.	92		1898 Aug 15	KS, 18th, 1899
Robinson, David		G, 33rd Mo.	18		1922 Jan 4	KS, 42nd, 1923
Robinson, David		G, 33rd Mo. Inf.	18		1920 Dec 20	KS, 41st, 1922
Robinson, E.		E, 7th Ill.	482		1920 Feb 8	KS, 40th, 1921
Robinson, E.B.		B, 1st Minn.	19		1898 Oct 30	KS, 18th, 1899
Robinson, Earl		A, 10th Ill. Inf.	395		1934	KS, 55th, 1936
Robinson, Edmond J.		Virginia, U.S.N.	481		1914 Feb 8	KS, 34th, 1915
Robinson, Elisha D.		F, 147th Ill. Inf.	144		1891 Apr 16	KS, 11th, 1892
Robinson, F.	Pvt.	K, 7th Iowa Cav.	170	64	1888 Feb 21	IA, 15th, 1889
Robinson, G.A.		I, 4th Iowa	87		1930 Jan 24	KS, 50th, 1931
Robinson, G.D.		K, 54th Ill.	193		1929 Oct 26	NE, 54th, 1930
Robinson, G.S.		H, 115th Ill. Inf. (at large)		93	1936 May 28	IA, 63rd, 1937
Robinson, G.W.	Pvt.	F, Eng. of West	400	55	1889 Jun 8	IA, 16th, 1890
Robinson, G.W.		19th Iowa	173		1907 Nov 3	IA, 34th, 1908
Robinson, G.W.	Pvt.	G, 52nd Ill. Inf.	485		1911 Jun 28	IA, 38th, 1912
Robinson, G.W.		B, 101st Ill.	301		1934	KS, 55th, 1936
Robinson, Gabriel		31st & 67th Ind.	85		1904 Jun 10	KS, 24th, 1905
Robinson, George		2nd & 7th N.Y. Hvy. Art.	25		1911 Nov 17	NE, 36th, 1912
Robinson, H.			168		1908	IA, 35th, 1909
Robinson, Harvey		K, 112th Ill.	32		1934 Apr	NE, 59th, 1935
Robinson, Henry C.		164th Ohio	61		1909 Dec 4	KS, 29th, 1910
Robinson, I.J.	Pvt.	4th Iowa Ind. Battery	210		1904 Jun 19	IA, 31st, 1905
Robinson, Isaac		E, 103rd Ill.	58		1926 Aug	NE, 52nd, 1928
Robinson, J.B.		B, 34th Iowa	10	80	1920 Mar 19	NE, 45th, 1921
Robinson, J.G.			222		1916	IA, 43rd, 1917
Robinson, J.W.	Pvt.	H, 1st N.H. Inf.	222		1915	IA, 42nd, 1916
Robinson, J.Y.			221		1923	KS, 43rd, 1924
Robinson, Jack		A, 89th U.S.C.T.	380		1909 Mar 17	KS, 29th, 1910
Robinson, Jacob W.		F, 9th Ky. Inf.	250		1921 Apr 19	KS, 41st, 1922
Robinson, James		1st Cal. Cav.	20		1919 Oct	IA, 46th, 1920
Robinson, James	Pvt.	C, 17th Mass. Inf.	11		1899	NE, 24th, 1900
Robinson, James K.		D, 132nd Ill. Inf.	25		1911 Feb 24	NE, 36th, 1912
Robinson, Jasper		M, 1st Col. Cav.	1		1916 Apr 9	KS, 36th, 1917
Robinson, Jay		E, 24th N.Y. Inf. (died of old age)	264	78	1921 Jan 25	NE, 46th, 1922
Robinson, Job, see Robison, Job						
Robinson, John	Corp.	K, 7th Ohio Cav.	286		1903 Nov 21	IA, 31st, 1905
Robinson, John	Lieut.	I, 2nd Mich. Cav.	66		1917 Oct 29	IA, 44th, 1918
Robinson, John		B, 1st Wis.	49		1899 Jan 8	KS, 19th, 1900
Robinson, John D.		E, 135th Ind. Inf.	25		1911 May 21	NE, 36th, 1912
Robinson, John F.		E, 10th Ill.	1		1916 Dec 26	KS, 36th, 1917
Robinson, John S.	Pvt.	A, 23rd Ind. Bat.	283		1915 Apr 8	IA, 42nd, 1916

Name	Rank	Company, Regiment or Ship	Post*	Age	Death Date†	Journal
Robinson, Johnson			20		1904 Feb 19	IA, 30th, 1904
Robinson, Joseph		A, 6th Ky. Inf.	244		1899 Apr 29	KS, 19th, 1900
Robinson, Joseph		B, 134th Penn.	185		1912 Mar 7	KS, 32nd, 1913
Robinson, Lander		E, 6th Kans.	12		1910 Dec 12	KS, 30th, 1911
Robinson, Levi S.	Pvt.	I, 8th Ohio Inf.	452		1907 Apr 15	IA, 34th, 1908
Robinson, Mike		A, 75th Ind.	7		1927	NE, 52nd, 1928
Robinson, Moses H.	Corp.	E, 5th Iowa Inf.	267		1919 Dec 2	IA, 46th, 1920
Robinson, Parsons	Pvt.	K, 83rd Ill.	306		1907 Apr 13	IA, 34th, 1908
Robinson, R.F.		C, 42nd Ill.	28		1928 Feb	KS, 48th, 1929
Robinson, Robert	Pvt.	I, 4th Iowa Inf.	457	65	1896 Nov 1	IA, 23rd, 1897
Robinson, S.N.		F, 8th Kans.	51		1920 Feb 7	KS, 40th, 1921
Robinson, S.S.	Pvt.	I, 27th Iowa Inf.	349		1906 Jul 3	IA, 33rd, 1907
Robinson, Samuel		K, 161st Ohio	69		1911 Jun 25	KS, 31st, 1912
Robinson, T.B.	Pvt.	A, 36th Ill.	12		1922 Sep 26	IA, 49th, 1923
Robinson, W.D.		A, 9th Iowa Inf. (cause of death: heart)	228	62	1901 Dec	NE, 26th, 1902
Robinson, W.H.	Pvt.	E, 39th Iowa	253		1924 Dec 14	IA, 51st, 1925
Robinson, Walter	Pvt.	D, 10th N.Y. Inf.	314		1910 May 21	IA, 37th, 1911
Robinson, Wm.	1st Lieut.	H, 9th Kans.	102		1899	KS, 19th, 1900
Robinson, Wm.		60th Ill. Rifles	297		1904 Jul 21	KS, 24th, 1905
Robinson, Wm. H.	Pvt.	184th N.Y. Inf.	416		1916 Jun 5	IA, 43rd, 1917
Robinson, Wm. R.	Pvt.	H, 35th Iowa Inf.	228		1912 Aug 11	IA, 39th, 1913
Robinston, William	Pvt.	A, 11th Iowa Inf.	153		1919 Oct 21	IA, 46th, 1920
Robison, D.R.	Pvt.	E, 60th U.S. Colored	107	62	1892 Mar 12	IA, 18th, 1892
Robison, J.S.	Pvt.	Iowa Inf.	167		1913 May 19	IA, 40th, 1914
Robison, Jasper C.	Pvt.	F, 8th Iowa Cav.	66		1928 Oct 28	IA, 55th, 1929
Robison, Job		9th Kans.	40		1911 Mar 30	KS, 31st, 1912
Robison, Lem		I, 141st Penn. Inf. (died of kidney trouble)	136	74	1912 Apr 6	NE, 37th, 1913
Robison, Robert D.		B, 25th Wis.	110	69	1910 Jun 8	NE, 35th, 1911
Robmetle, J.			15		1888	KS, 8th, 1889
Robock, W.H.	Pvt.	E, 8th Iowa Inf.	49		1924 Jul 9	IA, 51st, 1925
Robson, Norton		G, 60th —	10		1909 Nov 4	KS, 29th, 1910
Roby, Barton		I, 151st Ohio	46		1912 Apr 7	KS, 32nd, 1913
Roby, Isaac	Pvt.	H, 8th Iowa Cav.	497		1930 Aug 22	IA, 57th, 1931
Roby, James		M, 8th Ill. Cav. (died of dropsy at Soldiers & Sailors Home, Grand Island; buried in Home Cemetery)	22	61	1905 Sep 16	NE, 30th, 1906
Rochelle, M.S.		C, 46th Ohio Vol. Inf.	25		1908 Jun 21	KS, 28th, 1909
Rock, Geo. M.	Pvt.	E, 45th Ill. Inf.	139		1913 Jan 7	IA, 40th, 1914
Rockefeller, C.L.	Pvt.	I, 20th Wis. Cav.	337		1929 Apr 10	IA, 56th, 1930
Rockefellow, F.M.		K, 56th Ill. Inf.	139		1930	KS, 50th, 1931
Rockenfield, John	Pvt.	28th Iowa Inf.	24		1912 Jan 30	IA, 39th, 1913
Rockerfeller, F.M.		K, 65th Ill.	139		1927 Dec 8	KS, 47th, 1928
Rockerhill, J.W.		34th Ohio Vol. Inf.	33		1884	KS, 4th, 1885
Rockey, Jacob	Pvt.	C, 25th Iowa Inf.	246		1902 Oct 13	IA, 29th, 1903
Rockford, M.		A, 23rd Mich. Inf. (died at Sedgwick; buried at Hillside Cemetery)	255		1894 Jan	KS, 14th, 1895
Rockhill, J.W.			33		1884	KS, 4th, 1885
Rockhill, Jonathan		B, 149th Ohio Inf. (died of diabetes)	345	55	1901 May	NE, 26th, 1902
Rockrow, Andrew	Pvt.	E, 4th N.Y. Art.	452		1907 Mar 31	IA, 34th, 1908
Rockwell, B.		C, 34th Iowa	132		1930 Apr 15	KS, 50th, 1931
Rockwell, Geo.		E, 7th Mo. Cav. (died at Junction City)	132		1896 Jan 14	KS, 15th, 1896
Rockwell, H.			440		1911 Apr 1	IA, 38th, 1912
Rockwell, T.L.		B, 7th Ohio	199		1926 Jul 10	KS, 46th, 1927
Rockwell, W.H.		I, 83rd Ill.	85		1927 Apr 27	KS, 47th, 1928
Rockwood, John N., see Kockwood, John N.						
Rodabeck, J.C.	Capt.	15th Ill. Inf.	29		1905 Aug 5	IA, 32nd, 1906
Roddewig, Fritz	Pvt.	G, 20th Iowa Inf.	1		1917 Dec 30	IA, 45th, 1919
Roddy, D.R.P.		I, 149th Penn.	8		1929 Dec 12	KS, 50th, 1931
Roddy, Martin		D, 1st Wis. (died of pneumonia)	24	74	1915 Nov 12	NE, 40th, 1916
Rodenbaugh, H.J.	Pvt.	D, 29th Ohio	12		1921 May 24	IA, 48th, 1922
Rodenburg, John H.		F, 5th Mo.	65		1928 May 10	KS, 48th, 1929

Name	Rank	Company, Regiment or Ship	Post*	Age	Death Date†	Journal
Roderick, D.C.		E, 10th Mass.	50		1924 Aug 28	NE, 49th, 1925
Roderick, J.S.		K, 61st Ill. Inf.	39		1925	KS, 45th, 1926
Roderick, Thomas	Sergt.	F, 24th Iowa Inf.	454	67	1895 Feb 23	IA, 21st, 1895
Rodermel, Robert J.		K, 92nd Ill. Mtd. Inf.	94 & 452	96 & 5 mos.	1937 May 17	IA, 64th, 1938
Rodgers, A.H.	Pvt.	I, 47th Iowa Inf.	40	85	1931 Feb 25	IA, 58th, 1932
Rodgers, Alpheus H.		B, 146th Ind.	1		1916 Mar 10	KS, 36th, 1917
Rodgers, E.J.		B, 1st N.Y. (died of weakness)	157	63	1905[1904?] Nov 14	NE, 29th, 1905
Rodgers, George D.	Pvt.	H, 16th Iowa	157		1914 Jan 15	IA, 41st, 1915
Rodgers, H.B.		D, 50th Penn.	12		1896 Jul 1	KS, 16th, 1897
Rodgers, J.A.		H, 8th Kans.	410		1897 Jul 17	KS, 17th, 1898
Rodgers, J.R.	Capt.	B, 5th & 48th Iowa Inf.	16		1930 Dec 5	IA, 57th, 1931
Rodgers, James		D, 2nd Iowa	130		1896 Feb 19	KS, 16th, 1897
Rodgers, James L.		E, 52nd Ohio Inf.	127	91	1935 Dec 2	IA, 62nd, 1936
Rodgers, Joel A.	Pvt.	B, 147th Ill. Inf.	22		1915 Aug 7	IA, 42nd, 1916
Rodgers, S.H.	Capt.	K, 102nd Ill.	381		1912 Sep 14	KS, 32nd, 1913
Rodgers, Sam'l	Pvt.	A, 12th Ill. Cav.	394		1909 Apr 2	IA, 36th, 1910
Rodgers, W.M.		G, 23rd Ill. Inf.	117		1887	KS, 7th, 1888
Rodman, A.A.	2nd Lieut.	C, 8th Iowa	108		1905	IA, 32nd, 1906
Roe, Adam	Pvt.	F, 35th Iowa	333		1923 Feb 8	IA, 50th, 1924
Roe, Chas. E.	Pvt.	B, 12th Iowa	68		1907 Nov 2	IA, 34th, 1908
Roe, Geo.		A, 9th Kans.	12		1927 Jul 8	KS, 47th, 1928
Roe, James	Pvt.	D, 23rd Iowa Inf.	186		1913 May	IA, 40th, 1914
Roe, John			209		[1903-1904?] Mar 4	IA, 30th, 1904
Roe, W.E.		I, 5th Mo. Cav.	123		1893 Aug 1	KS, 13th, 1894
Roeder, S.A.	Pvt.	I, 11th Ill. Inf.	22		1913 Oct 9	IA, 40th, 1914
Roemer, Fred		A, 11th Wis.	129		1913 Aug 27	KS, 33rd, 1914
Roeske, Chas.		13th Wis.	193	66	1904 Jan 7	NE, 29th, 1905
Roessler, P.H.			1		1884	KS, 4th, 1885
Roff, J.W.		E, 97th Ohio	265		1909 Apr 1	KS, 29th, 1910
Roff, Martin	Pvt.	C, 2nd Ky. Inf.	74	69	1894 Nov 4	IA, 21st, 1895
Roff, Peter		D, 27th Ky. Inf.	36		1936 Feb 12	KS, 55th, 1936
Roger, B.T.	Pvt.	3rd Iowa Inf.	68		1906 Oct 2	IA, 33rd, 1907
Roger, J.H.	Pvt.	I, 44th Iowa Inf.	86		1905 Aug 21	IA, 32nd, 1906
Roger, J.W.	Sergt.	B, 8th Mich. Cav.	233		1899	NE, 24th, 1900
Rogers, A.		C, 1st Ill. Cav.	299	71	1911 Dec 6	NE, 36th, 1912
Rogers, A.J.	Pvt.	A, 34th Iowa Inf. 47th Iowa Inf.	116		1912 Apr 21	IA, 39th, 1913
Rogers, A.J.			116		1916 Jul 27	IA, 43rd, 1917
Rogers, A.N.			37		1923	IA, 50th, 1924
Rogers, A.T.		B, 142nd Ind.	1		1889	KS, 9th, 1890
Rogers, Adrian		K, 129th Ind.	179		1919 Aug 6	KS, 39th, 1920
Rogers, C.E.	Pvt.	G, 31st Iowa Inf.	67		1923 Jan 18	IA, 50th, 1924
Rogers, Charles	Pvt.	D, 13th U.S. Inf. (at large)		86	1933 Jun 4	IA, 60th, 1934
Rogers, Charles			37		1884	KS, 4th, 1885
Rogers, Eli	Pvt.	E, 10th Ill. Inf.	134		1906 Apr 26	IA, 33rd, 1907
Rogers, F.E.		I, 21st Iowa (died of heart failure)	226	70	1909 Feb 17	NE, 34th, 1910
Rogers, Fred J.		M, 2nd N.Y. Cav.	25		1928 Oct 7	NE, 53rd, 1929
Rogers, Geo.			236		1914 Nov 7	IA, 41st, 1915
Rogers, H.S.	Sergt.	D, 19th Iowa	57		1926 Jan	IA, 53rd, 1927
Rogers, Horace P.		K, 161st N.Y. Inf. (died of pleuro pneumonia)	113		1894 Jan 25	NE, 19th, 1895
Rogers, I.N.		D, 156th Ohio Inf. (died of disease)	265		1893 Nov 20	NE, 18th, 1894
Rogers, J.C.	Pvt.	B, 147th Ill. Inf.	209		1901 Nov 18	IA, 28th, 1902
Rogers, J.M.		D, 163rd Ohio	19		1916	KS, 36th, 1917
Rogers, J.W.		F, 133rd Ill.	17		1920 Nov 21	KS, 40th, 1921
Rogers, J.W.		C, 7th Ill. Cav. (died of heart failure)	76		1893 Aug 3	NE, 18th, 1894
Rogers, James		E, 10th Iowa Inf.		99	1936 May 11	IA, 62nd, 1936
Rogers, James	Pvt.	E, 10th Iowa Inf.	231	99	1935 May 11	IA, 65th, 1939
Rogers, James		I, 15th West Va.	19		1930 Dec 18	KS, 50th, 1931
Rogers, Jas.		C, 105th Ohio Inf.	354		1926 Feb 28	NE, 51st, 1927

*See Appendix A, B or C for roster of post names and locations.
†See Introduction for note regarding recording of death date.
466

Name	Rank	Company, Regiment or Ship	Post*	Age	Death Date†	Journal
Rogers, Jason		H, 2nd Iowa Inf. (died of rheumatism of heart)	31	52	1895 Aug 15	NE, 20th, 1896
Rogers, Jesse C.		C, 5th Ill. H, 12th Ill. Cav. (died at Fort Scott)	32		1895 Jul	KS, 15th, 1896
Rogers, John	Pvt.	H, 29th Wis. Inf. (died of old age)	20	77	1891 Dec 26	NE, 16th, 1892
Rogers, John C.	Pvt.	B, 8th Iowa Inf.	57		1911 Jul 24	IA, 38th, 1912
Rogers, Jonathan		B, 43rd Ohio	64		1897 Dec 17	KS, 17th, 1898
Rogers, Jonathan		E, 145th Ind. Inf.	85		1933 Dec 23	KS, 54th, 1935
Rogers, Joseph	Pvt.	I, 21st Iowa Inf.	78		1917 Jul 16	IA, 44th, 1918
Rogers, Joshua	Pvt.	H, 12th Mich. Inf.	33	62	1897 Jun 22	IA, 24th, 1898
Rogers, Lewis		B, 33rd Ill. Inf.	23		1913 Sep 12	IA, 40th, 1914
Rogers, N.E.	Pvt.	F, 15th Ill. Inf.	242		1904 Sep 3	IA, 31st, 1905
Rogers, Nelson	Pvt.	14th Iowa Inf.	186	75	1896 Mar 10	IA, 22nd, 1896
Rogers, O.C.		95th Ill. (died of pneumonia)	318		1921 Mar 19	NE, 46th, 1922
Rogers, Oscar		I, 124th Ind.	185		1908	KS, 28th, 1909
Rogers, Pat		D, 95th Ohio	453		1917 Sep 17	KS, 37th, 1918
Rogers, R.S.			310		1894	NE, 19th, 1895
Rogers, Reuben S.		B, 116th Ill.	72		1916 Nov 16	KS, 36th, 1917
Rogers, Solon		A, 46th Ind.	68		1923 Aug 29	KS, 43rd, 1924
Rogers, T.M.	Pvt.	C, 22nd Iowa	16		1921 Sep 24	IA, 48th, 1922
Rogers, Thomas		D, 105th Ill.	158		1906 Jan 6	KS, 26th, 1907
Rogers, Thomas C.	Pvt.	E, 21st Wis. Inf.	78		1918 Sep 20	IA, 45th, 1919
Rogers, Thos.	Pvt.	L, 7th Iowa Cav.	50		1918	IA, 45th, 1919
Rogers, W.B.		F, 1? Ohio	25		1919 Nov 9	KS, 39th, 1920
Rogers, W.K.		H, 8th Ill.	185		1920 Dec 10	KS, 40th, 1921
Rogers, W.T.		L, 2nd Ohio	380		1922 Jun 20	KS, 42nd, 1923
Rogers, Warren		B, 64th Ill.	51		1916 May 6	KS, 36th, 1917
Rogers, Webber L.		K, 13th Iowa	240		1913 Mar 6	KS, 33rd, 1914
Rogers, Wilbur L.		K, 13th Iowa Inf.	240		1913 Mar 6	KS, 32nd, 1913
Rogers, Wm.	Pvt.	I, 35th Wis.	284		1914 Oct 5	IA, 41st, 1915
Rogers, Wm.		F, 74th Ill. Inf.	25	76	1919 Feb 14	NE, 44th, 1920
Rogers, Wm. N.		D, 35th Ohio	36		1904 Feb 15	KS, 24th, 1905
Rogler, C.W.			15		1888	KS, 8th, 1889
Rohe, Adam			12		1923 Mar 24	KS, 43rd, 1924
Rohestrow, Cornelius		I, 142nd Ind. Inf.	14		1901 May 23	KS, 21st, 1902
Rohr, John		A, 123rd Ill.	89		1922 Nov	KS, 42nd, 1923
Rohr, John			[89]		1923	KS, 43rd, 1924
Rohr, Silas		A, 10th Iowa (died of cancer)	39		1920 Dec 26	NE, 45th, 1921
Rohrbaugh, S.B.	Col.		18		1906	KS, 26th, 1907
Rohrer, Daniel	Pvt.	A, 22nd Penn.	22		1922 Apr 4	IA, 49th, 1923
Roine, Sam		A, 47th Ill.	63		1917 Oct 29	KS, 37th, 1918
Rokes, Jas.	Pvt.	E, 24th Iowa Inf.	418	60	1888 Mar 24	IA, 15th, 1889
Rokes, Phillip	Pvt.	E, 24th Iowa Inf.	418		1888 Sep 19	IA, 15th, 1889
Roland, John			207	84	1913 Nov 27	NE, 38th, 1914
Roland, Marshall, see Rolland, Marshall						
Roland, R.H.		F, 92nd Ohio	17		1923 Jun 16	KS, 43rd, 1924
Role, R.H.			120		1910	NE, 35th, 1911
Roleson, J.C.	Pvt.	K, 14th Iowa Inf.	337		1906 Jul 16	IA, 33rd, 1907
Rolfe, Thomas E.		F, 46th Ill. Inf.	167		1912 Jan 5	KS, 32nd, 1913
Rolker, Henry W.			515		1919 Oct 10	IA, 46th, 1920
Roll, Richard E.		K, 83rd Ind.	244		1920 Jul 30	KS, 40th, 1921
Rolland, Marshall	Pvt. Pvt.	A, 45th Ill. Inf. B, 7th Ill. Cav.	235	73	1898 Dec 20	IA, 25th, 1899
Roller, E.	Pvt.	K, 195th Ohio Inf.	137		1912 May 19	IA, 39th, 1913
Roller, Joseph		D, 6th U.S. (died of paralysis)	35	73	1917 May 18	NE, 42nd, 1918
Rollett, Geo.	Sergt.	D, 7th Iowa Inf.	170		1919 May 19	IA, 46th, 1920
Rollette, E.C.	Corp.	C, 6th N.Y. Hvy. Art.	46		1920 Dec 31	IA, 47th, 1921
Rollins, J.S.	Pvt.	B, 24th Iowa Inf.	64		1928	IA, 56th, 1930
Rollins, Jas.	Pvt.	M, 1st Art.	58		1925 Apr 3	IA, 52nd, 1926
Rollins, N.A.	Pvt.	D, 40th Iowa Inf.	16		1910 Apr 12	IA, 37th, 1911
Rolstin, Porter	Pvt.	A, 39th Iowa Inf.	55		1913 Dec 20	IA, 40th, 1914

Name	Rank	Company, Regiment or Ship	Post*	Age	Death Date†	Journal
Rolston, Hugh	Pvt.	H, 21st Ohio Inf.	466	49	1890 Dec 17	IA, 17th, 1891
Roman, I.C.		G, 63rd Ohio Inf. (died of old age)	77	66	1906 Jan 30	NE, 31st, 1907
Rome, H.B.	Pvt.	I, 9th Iowa Inf.	452		1921 Jun 11	IA, 48th, 1922
Romey, A.	Pvt.	3rd Iowa Inf.	118		1915 Feb	IA, 42nd, 1916
Romig, Owen T.		F, 161st Ohio Inf.	90		1935 Mar 8	KS, 55th, 1936
Romine, David C.		F, 72nd Ind.	1		1924 Dec 10	KS, 44th, 1925
Rommel, D.G.	Pvt.		26		1930 Jun 29	IA, 57th, 1931
Rommel, H.A.	Pvt.	C, 10th Iowa	12		1890 Apr	IA, 17th, 1891
Rommel, Wm.		D, 3rd Ill. Cav.	118		1913 Jul 10	KS, 33rd, 1914
Rone, Lewis		G, 3rd Ill. Cav.	32		1898 Oct 25	KS, 18th, 1899
Rood, Anson	2nd Lieut.	38th Wis. Inf.	374	74	1898 Jan 12	IA, 24th, 1898
Rood, H.H.	Lieut.	A, 13th Iowa Inf.	400		1915	IA, 42nd, 1916
Rood, H.M.		F, 74th Ill. (died of pneumonia)	147	72	1905[1904?] Apr 20	NE, 29th, 1905
Rood, W.H.		37th Wis. (died of cancer)	57	68	1917 Oct 20	NE, 42nd, 1918
Roodhouse, J.D.		G, 91st Ill.	32		1904 Jul 30	KS, 24th, 1905
Roof, J.M.		G, 87th Ind. Inf.	250		1908[1909?] Aug 3	KS, 29th, 1910
Rooker, W.D.	Pvt.	D, 2nd Iowa Cav.	17		1921 Jun 6	IA, 48th, 1922
Rooney, Thomas		A, 8th Kans. Inf.	380		1887 Sep 25	KS, 7th, 1888
Roop, August	Pvt.	A, 44th Iowa Inf.	78		1924 Nov 27	IA, 51st, 1925
Roops, David	Pvt.	I, 82nd Penn. Inf.	93		1915 Apr	IA, 42nd, 1916
Roose, Chas. S.	Pvt.	A, 144th Ohio	298		1907 Jan 24	IA, 34th, 1908
Root, A.D.		B, 1st Iowa Cav.	3		1893 Nov 9	KS, 13th, 1894
Root, A.P.	Pvt.	I, 5th U.S.M.[Mo. State Militia?]	297		1917 Mar 19	IA, 44th, 1918
Root, A.P.		L, 111th Cal.	42		1925 Jul 19	NE, 51st, 1927
Root, Albert	Pvt.	B, 6th Kans. Cav.	11		1915 Nov	IA, 42nd, 1916
Root, E.E.	Capt.	B, 33rd N.Y. Inf.	98		1916 Feb 25	KS, 36th, 1917
Root, Harry C.		A, 187th Penn.	1		1932 Mar 15	KS, 52nd, 1933
Root, J.P., Dr.	Surg.	7th Kans. P.L.	55		1885	KS, 5th, 1886
Root, Joseph		8th Ind.	26		1921 Jun 22	KS, 41st, 1922
Root, Levings W.		I & B, 37th & 2nd N.Y. Inf. (cause of death: liver)	193	64	1906 Sep 2	NE, 31st, 1907
Root, Lewis			32		1913 Jul 27	KS, 33rd, 1914
Root, Marvin			5		1890 Jan 10	NE, 15th, 1891
Root, R.H.	Pvt.	C, 88th Ohio Inf.	142		1917 Jul 15	IA, 44th, 1918
Root, Richard	Major Lieut.	8th Iowa Cav. K, 19th Iowa Inf.	2		1903 Jul 28	IA, 30th, 1904
Root, Ruben L.		H, 96th Ill.	176		1915	KS, 35th, 1916
Root, Samuel P.		B, 17th Ill. Cav.	176		1905 Oct 21	KS, 25th, 1906
Root, W.G.		L, 2nd Col. Cav.	196		1909 Aug 16	KS, 29th, 1910
Roots, Geo. F.		F, 36th Ill.	92		1927 Dec 13	KS, 47th, 1928
Roper, John M.		M, 2nd Penn. Hvy. Art. (died of cancer of stomach)	214	71	1912 Feb 8	NE, 37th, 1913
Roper, W.H.		not a member of Farragut Post	25		1913	NE, 38th, 1914
Rorabaugh, D.	Pvt.	C, 20th Iowa Inf.	16		1910 Sep 29	IA, 37th, 1911
Rordan, T.W.	Pvt.	C, 39th Wis.	22		1923 Feb 19	IA, 50th, 1924
Rork, Curtis		K, 79th Ill.	4		1926 Apr 3	KS, 46th, 1927
Rorsehach, Emile		A, 72nd Ohio	64		1926 Oct 19	KS, 46th, 1927
Rosa, Francis	Pvt.	G, 24th Iowa Inf.	111		1903 May 25	IA, 30th, 1904
Rosa, Isaac	Pvt.	G, 89th Ill. Inf.	45		1911 Sep 26	IA, 38th, 1912
Rose, A.N.	Pvt.	H, 89th Ill. Inf.	139	64	1893 Mar 18	IA, 20th, 1894
Rose, Albert W.	Pvt.	H, 82nd Ohio Inf.	235		1925 Apr 17	IA, 52nd, 1926
Rose, Alex		M, 11th Kans. Cav.	12		1914 Dec 7	KS, 34th, 1915
Rose, Amos		E, 53rd Ill. Inf.	14		1914 Nov 13	KS, 34th, 1915
Rose, Arch	Pvt.	D, 28th Iowa Inf.	296		1905 Jun	IA, 32nd, 1906
Rose, B.F.			113		1908 Nov 1	KS, 28th, 1909
Rose, C.A.	Pvt.	I, 25th Wis. Inf.	57		1920 Jul 21	IA, 47th, 1921
Rose, C.J.	Pvt.	E, 10th Iowa Inf.	67	89	1932 Oct 21	IA, 59th, 1933
Rose, D.N.		B, 64th Ill.	259		1921 May 21	KS, 41st, 1922
Rose, Edward W.		B, 15th N.Y.	25	91	1934 May 13	IA, 61st, 1935
Rose, Geo. D.	Pvt.	K, 14th Iowa Inf.	7		1913 Dec 16	IA, 40th, 1914
Rose, Geo. S.		H, 55th Ill. Inf.	127		1900 Mar 27	KS, 20th, 1901
Rose, H.N.		I, 3rd Ohio	81		1906 Nov 21	KS, 26th, 1907

Name	Rank	Company, Regiment or Ship	Post*	Age	Death Date†	Journal
Rose, Hiram		H, 8th N.C.	120	82	1924 Sep 27	NE, 49th, 1925
Rose, Joseph		E, 7th N.Y.	400		1918	KS, 38th, 1919
Rose, Joseph T.		B, 1st Maine Cav. (died of old age, heart trouble)	83	78	1923 Mar 11	NE, 47th, 1923
Rose, Lemuel		K, 1st Ark. (died at Turon)	403		1895 Jul	KS, 15th, 1896
Rose, Millard	Pvt.	F, 22nd N.Y. Cav.	88		1929 Nov 9	IA, 56th, 1930
Rose, Mose	Pvt.	B, 6th Wis. Art.	68		1925 Jan 17	IA, 52nd, 1926
Rose, Perry	Pvt.	K, 28th Iowa Inf.	271		1920 Aug 21	IA, 47th, 1921
Rose, Peter		A, 5th Iowa	152		1908 Jul 3	NE, 33rd, 1909
Rose, R.R.	Pvt.	E, 54th Ohio Inf.	216	88	1931 Nov 16	IA, 58th, 1932
Rose, T.E.		I, 32nd Ohio	38		1914 Mar 27	KS, 34th, 1915
Rose, Thomas	Pvt.	I, 20th Iowa Inf.	270	60	1887 Oct 28	IA, 14th, 1888
Rose, Thomas	Pvt.		314		1915	IA, 42nd, 1916
Rose, W.C.		D, 113th Ohio	225		1896 Apr 18	KS, 16th, 1897
Rose, W.L.		16th Ill.	244		1911 May 28	KS, 31st, 1912
Rose, William		B, 38th Iowa Inf.	124		1928 Jun 21	IA, 55th, 1929
Roseberg, Jas. M.	Musician	G, 21st Mo. Inf.	268		1902 Feb 14	IA, 29th, 1903
Roseberry, C.W.		C, 82nd Ind.	142		1909 Sep	KS, 29th, 1910
Roseberry, Jasper		F, 25th Ind.	81		1930 May 27	KS, 50th, 1931
Roseberry, John		D, 2nd Mo. Cav.	244		1913	KS, 33rd, 1914
Roseberry, Loren T.		G, 148th Ill.	9		1916 Jun 2	KS, 36th, 1917
Rosebush, Oliver		U.S. Navy	311		1912 Mar 15	KS, 32nd, 1913
Rosecrans, Wm. H.		G, 81st Ind. Inf.	244		1916 Sep 18	KS, 36th, 1917
Rosellins, A.C.		B, 4th U.S. Cav. (died of heart failure)	24	58	1896 Sep 21	NE, 21st, 1897
Rosemire, Richard		G, 8th Iowa Cav.	78	91	1935 May	IA, 63rd, 1937
Rosenbarger, William			51		1896	KS, 16th, 1897
Rosenberg, D.			24		1913 Apr 25	IA, 40th, 1914
Rosenberg, Robert A.		I, 23rd Ohio Inf. (died at Meade, Kans.; buried at Graceland Cemetery)	388		1894 Mar 30	KS, 14th, 1895
Rosenberger, D.	Pvt.	F, 6th Iowa Cav.	24		1919 Dec 2	IA, 46th, 1920
Rosenburg, A.B.	Pvt.	E, 4th Minn. (died of blood poison)	36	40	1884 Aug 13	NE, 9th, 1885
Rosencrantz, I.P.	Pvt.	K, 81st Ind.	472		1901 Feb 5	IA, 28th, 1902
Rosenger, A.F.	Pvt.		142		1920 May	IA, 47th, 1921
Rosengrants, H.H.		D, 33rd Ill. Inf.	292		1892 May 3	NE, 17th, 1893
Rosh, N.R.	Pvt.	97th Ohio Inf.	108		1923 Jan 21	IA, 50th, 1924
Ross, A.C.	Pvt.	E, 3rd Iowa Inf.	300		1920 Mar 1	IA, 47th, 1921
Ross, A.J.	Pvt.	K, West Va. Inf.	122		1911 Jan 29	IA, 38th, 1912
Ross, A.S.	Pvt.	G, 1st Minn. Cav.	3		3rd quarter 1885	IA, 12th, 1886
Ross, C.B.	Pvt.	H, 112th N.Y. Inf.	159		1909 Oct 25	IA, 37th, 1911
Ross, D.		G, 188th Ohio	4		1912 Dec 19	KS, 32nd, 1913
Ross, Daniel	Pvt.	I, 22nd Iowa Inf.	8	58	1889 Nov 1	IA, 16th, 1890
Ross, Diego C.	1st Lieut.	B, 47th Ill. Inf.	312	59	1889 Mar 18	IA, 16th, 1890
Ross, Edwin R.		C, 83rd Ohio	25		1893 Sep 12	KS, 13th, 1894
Ross, F.M.	Pvt.	B, 42nd Ind. Inf.	75		1915 Jul 3	IA, 42nd, 1916
Ross, Felix W.	Pvt.	D, 137th Ill. Inf.	56		1924 Nov 20	IA, 51st, 1925
Ross, Frank		Iowa Cav.	108		1913	IA, 40th, 1914
Ross, Geo. D.	Sergt.	G, 21st Wis. Inf.	197		1925 Mar 24	IA, 52nd, 1926
Ross, Geo. H.	Pvt.	G, 49th Wis. Inf.	141		1927 Aug 4	IA, 54th, 1928
Ross, Geo. H.		G, 101st Ill.	25		1923	NE, 48th, 1924
Ross, Grant L.	Sergt.	K, 34th Ill. Inf.	22		1929 Apr 18	IA, 56th, 1930
Ross, Henry H.	Pvt.	M, 3rd Iowa Cav.	96		1917 Sep 2	IA, 44th, 1918
Ross, J.	Pvt.		251		1921 Dec 8	IA, 48th, 1922
Ross, J.N.C.		C, 8th Mo.	17		1921 Apr 22	KS, 41st, 1922
Ross, J.P.		I, 12th Ill.	55		1920 Oct 8	KS, 40th, 1921
Ross, James	Pvt.	H, 29th Wis. Inf.	97		1901 May 3	IA, 27th, 1901
Ross, Jesse D.		C, 13th Mo. Cav.	500		1916 Dec 22	KS, 36th, 1917
Ross, Jno. B.		F, 13th Kans.	40		1904 Dec 1	KS, 24th, 1905
Ross, John			380		1923	KS, 43rd, 1924
Ross, John J.		H, 134th Penn.	185		1912 Aug 28	KS, 32nd, 1913
Ross, John P.		H, 1st Iowa Cav.	30		1914 Oct 20	KS, 34th, 1915
Ross, John W.	Pvt.	F, 149th Ill.	1		1915 Apr 20	KS, 35th, 1916
Ross, Jos.	Pvt.	D, 150th Ind.	115	60	1890 Aug 11	IA, 17th, 1891

*See Appendix A, B or C for roster of post names and locations.
†See Introduction for note regarding recording of death date.
469

Name	Rank	Company, Regiment or Ship	Post*	Age	Death Date†	Journal
Ross, Joseph T.		K, 46th Ind. (died of stroke)	134	82	1925 Sep 14	NE, 50th, 1926
Ross, M.H.	Pvt.	C, 6th Iowa Inf.	81		1915 Apr 23	IA, 42nd, 1916
Ross, Mason		D, 187th Ohio	38		1892 Oct 22	KS, 12th, 1893
Ross, O.A.		I, 27th Iowa	17		1918 Jun 9	KS, 38th, 1919
Ross, P.B.		D, 21st Wis.	1		1919 Aug 20	KS, 39th, 1920
Ross, R.W.		L, 11th Ind.	25		1916 Sep 3	KS, 36th, 1917
Ross, Robt. M.		E, 102nd Ill.	156		1906 Mar 12	KS, 26th, 1907
Ross, Sterling A.		F, 25th Wis.	380		1912 Mar 9	KS, 32nd, 1913
Ross, T.F.		14th Kans.	163		1888	KS, 8th, 1889
Ross, T.H.B.		K, 89th Ill.	27		1885	KS, 5th, 1886
Ross, T.S.	Pvt.	B, 25th Iowa Inf.	67		1910 Jun 28	IA, 37th, 1911
Ross, Thomas		E, 79th U.S. Col.	153		1910 Jul 4	KS, 30th, 1911
Ross, Thomas		E, 79th Okla. U.S. Inf.	153		1909 Jul 4	KS, 29th, 1910
Ross, Thomas F.		D, 14th Kans. Cav. (died of consumption)	24	59	1904 Apr 18	NE, 29th, 1905
Ross, W.A.		A, 15th Iowa	452		1934	IA, 61st, 1935
Ross, W.D.		D, 98th Penn. Inf.	242		1899 Dec 28	KS, 19th, 1900
Ross, W.D.		D, 148th Penn.	28		1918 Jul	KS, 38th, 1919
Ross, W.H.		K, Penn. Hvy. Art.	440		1923 Jan 23	IA, 50th, 1924
Ross, W.L.		B, 13th Mo. Cav.	54		1914 Aug 11	KS, 34th, 1915
Ross, Whitfield		F, 9th Kans.	68		1926 Mar 11	KS, 46th, 1927
Rossel, J.E.		H, 41st Ill.	50		1919 Oct 30	KS, 39th, 1920
Rosser, Edwin A.		I, 2nd West Va.	90		1922 Jan 25	KS, 42nd, 1923
Rosser, W.H.	Surg.	46th Iowa Inf.	100		1915 Aug 12	IA, 42nd, 1916
Rossiter, Floyd	Pvt.	12th Ohio Battery	7	56	1891 Nov 23	IA, 18th, 1892
Rossiter, Geo. W.		C, 106th Ill. Inf.	32	66	1909 Mar 7	NE, 34th, 1910
Rosswick, Henry		K, 5th N.J.	11	79	1916 May 19	NE, 41st, 1917
Roth, Anthony		K, 3rd Mo. Cav.	250		1922 Feb 3	KS, 42nd, 1923
Roth, Henry A.	Pvt.	C, 19th Wis. Inf.	42	66	1889 Nov 24	IA, 16th, 1890
Roth, J.M.		E, 16th Kans. Cav.	55		1929 May 24	KS, 49th, 1930
Roth, Joel W.		E, 176th Penn. Inf.	93		1912 Jan 20	KS, 32nd, 1913
Roth, John	Pvt.	25th Iowa Inf.	5		1927	IA, 54th, 1928
Roth, John		I, 4th Ind.	72		1930 Jan 20	KS, 50th, 1931
Roth, Joseph A.	Pvt.	D, 96th Ill. Inf.	72	61	1893 Mar 29	IA, 19th, 1893
Roth, W.T.		H, 26th Iowa	293		1923 Apr 23	KS, 43rd, 1924
Rothemeyer, W.C.		C, 4th Mo.	17		1909 Jun 20	KS, 29th, 1910
Rother, F.M.	Pvt.	L, 4th Iowa Cav.	284	63	1891 Dec 31	IA, 18th, 1892
Rothimil, George	Pvt.	A, 2nd Iowa Vols.	222		1899 Apr 10	IA, 25th, 1899
Rothrock, Jas. H.	Lieut. Col.	35th Iowa Inf.	23	70	1899 Jan 14	IA, 25th, 1899
Rothrock, John W.	Pvt.	E, 7th Penn. Cav.	16		1912 Jun 23	IA, 39th, 1913
Rothschild, Lee		G, *U.S. Romeo*, U.S. Navy	110	74	1914 Aug 21	NE, 39th, 1915
Rothwell, William		D, 117th Ill.	158		1914 Nov	KS, 34th, 1915
Rotzell, John C.		D, 2nd Del. Inf.	380		1901 Feb 24	KS, 21st, 1902
Rouen, J.D.	Pvt.		122		1910 Jan 25	IA, 37th, 1911
Rough, Daliel		D, 147th Penn.	2		1917 May 17	KS, 37th, 1918
Roun, Pat H.		C, 7th Ill.	49		1919 Jan 15	KS, 39th, 1920
Roundy, P.W.	Lieut.	K, 2nd Wis. Cav.	1		1921 Feb 3	IA, 48th, 1922
Rourke, P.J.D.	1st Lieut. Lieut. Col.	E, 1st Penn. Res. 1st Penn. Res. (died of pneumonia)	69	70	1885 Jan 20	NE, 10th, 1886
Rouse, Chas. G.		B, 33rd Wis. Inf. (died of kidney trouble)	89	85	1921 Apr 26	NE, 46th, 1922
Rouse, Henry, see Rrouse, Henry						
Rouse, R.E.		34th Ill. Inf.	68		1925 Nov	NE, 51st, 1927
Rouse, R.E.		C, 34th Ill. Inf.	68		1926 Nov 29	NE, 50th, 1926
Roush, James G.		E, 10th Kans. Inf.	51		1914 Sep 29	KS, 34th, 1915
Roush, John		193rd Ohio	378		1912 Jul 12	KS, 32nd, 1913
Roush, John M.		D, 74th Ill.	65		1928 Mar 12	KS, 48th, 1929
Roush, William	Pvt.	L, 2nd Ohio Cav.	84		1923 Feb 13	IA, 50th, 1924
Roush, Wm.			80		1899 Jun	KS, 19th, 1900
Roushton, J.		A, 117th Ind. (died of paralysis)	35	76	1921 May 23	NE, 46th, 1922
Rousseau, Wm.	Pvt.	E, 42nd Mo. Inf.	192		1929 Sep 1	IA, 56th, 1930
Roustin, A.J.			7		1928 Jan 1	IA, 55th, 1929
Routh, James P.		3rd Mo.	340		1931	KS, 51st, 1932

*See Appendix A, B or C for roster of post names and locations.
†See Introduction for note regarding recording of death date.

470

Name	Rank	Company, Regiment or Ship	Post*	Age	Death Date†	Journal
Routh, James P.		3rd Mo.	340		1931	KS, 52nd, 1933
Row, R.L.		K, 114th Ohio	180		1920 Mar 20	KS, 40th, 1921
Rowan, J.A.	Pvt.	A, 8th Iowa Inf.	231		1919 Aug 25	IA, 46th, 1920
Rowand, John H.		B, 31st Iowa	232		1912 Dec 31	KS, 32nd, 1913
Rowdon, David C.		E, 84th Ind.	[25?]		1923	NE, 48th, 1924
Rowe, A.M.	Pvt.	F, 2nd N.Y. Cav.	98		1917 Feb 10	IA, 44th, 1918
Rowe, Chas.		G, 89th Ill. Inf.	423	53	1889 May 23	IA, 16th, 1890
Rowe, Davia B.		H, 8th N.H.	262	75	1900 Jan 27	NE, 25th, 1901
Rowe, David P.		G, 144th Ill. Inf.	17		1912 Jun 9	KS, 32nd, 1913
Rowe, Henry	Pvt.	F, 7th Ill. Cav.	181		1924 Oct 31	IA, 51st, 1925
Rowe, J.F.	Pvt.	G, 93rd N.Y. Inf.	150		1905 Dec 20	IA, 32nd, 1906
Rowe, Jacob	Pvt.	C, 28th Iowa	100		1924 Dec	IA, 51st, 1925
Rowe, Myron E.		D, 1st Mich. Art.		90, 4 mos. & 4 days	1937 May 10	IA, 64th, 1938
Rowe, Simeon W.		H, 5th Minn.	134		1904 Sep 25	KS, 24th, 1905
Rowe, W.J.		E, 11th Kans.	248		1926 Nov 5	KS, 46th, 1927
Rowe, Wm. H.	Pvt.	7th Iowa Cav.	248		1922 Mar 1	IA, 49th, 1923
Rowell, C.S.	Pvt.	C, 11th Vt. Inf.	193		1912 Mar 16	IA, 39th, 1913
Rowell, W.R.		E, 18th Mo.	61		1923 May 4	KS, 43rd, 1924
Rowen, Jasper		B, 11th Iowa	94	89	1934 Oct 25	IA, 61st, 1935
Rowland, D.H.		D, 65th Inf.	71		1917 Feb 4	KS, 37th, 1918
Rowland, David W.			25		1911 Mar 26	NE, 36th, 1912
Rowland, H.W.	Pvt.	A, 21st Iowa Inf.	479		1899 Mar 7	IA, 26th, 1900
Rowland, J.		K, 94th Ohio	83		1917 Nov 28	KS, 37th, 1918
Rowland, J.B.		F, 14th Kans.	491		1919 May 3	KS, 39th, 1920
Rowland, J.H.		I, 149th Ohio Inf. 168th Ohio	18		1917 Dec 27	KS, 37th, 1918
Rowland, Marshall, see Rolland, Marshall						
Rowland, P.H.	Pvt.	I, 2nd Wis. Inf.	78		1913 Mar 8	IA, 40th, 1914
Rowland, Perry		B, 9th Ohio	17		1916 Nov 25	KS, 36th, 1917
Rowland, Wm. C.		H, 116th Ohio	60		1916 Aug 1	KS, 36th, 1917
Rowley, A.J.	Pvt.	D, 15th Iowa Inf.	332		1908 Mar	IA, 35th, 1909
Rowley, C.M.	Pvt.	D, 13th Wis. Inf.	88	41	1886 Oct 7	IA, 13th, 1887
Rowley, D.L.		E, 44th N.Y.	78		1888	KS, 8th, 1889
Rowley, Henry K.		B, 50th N.Y.	90		1926 Oct 16	KS, 46th, 1927
Rowley, John M.		F, 98th Ohio (died of long sickness)	32		1911 Apr 25	NE, 36th, 1912
Rowley, L.H.	Pvt.	B, 85th N.Y. Inf.	173		1920 Nov 1	IA, 47th, 1921
Rowley, M.E.		I, 74th Ill.	54		1888	KS, 8th, 1889
Rowley, W.R.	Pvt.	K, 12th N.Y.	231		1921 Aug 23	IA, 48th, 1922
Rowlinson, J.D.		A, 82nd Ind.	290		1890	KS, 10th, 1891
Rown, John	Pvt.	I, 25th Iowa Inf.	108		1906	IA, 33rd, 1907
Rownd, S.H.	Pvt.	B, 31st Iowa Inf.	222		1917 Mar 3	IA, 44th, 1918
Rowray, J.W.			235		1911 Apr	IA, 38th, 1912
Rowsey, Lafayette		C, 8th Ill.	25		1912 Dec 23	KS, 32nd, 1913
Roy, G.D.		I, 2nd Ind.	3		1930 Sep 14	KS, 50th, 1931
Roy, J.O.		I, 56th Inf.	22		1887	KS, 7th, 1888
Roy, L.D.	Pvt.	H, 8th Wis. Inf.	348	45	1893 Dec 26	IA, 20th, 1894
Royce, B.R.		C, 54th Ill. Inf.	43	58	1891[1901?] Jul	NE, 26th, 1902
Royce, E.Y.	Pvt.	8th Wis. Battery	72		1907 Jan 15	IA, 34th, 1908
Royce, P.B.		F, B, 61st N.Y. (died of pneumonia)	10		1919 Dec 12	NE, 44th, 1920
Royell, J.B.		28th Ill.	98		1924 Dec 18	IA, 51st, 1925
Royer, Daniel		G, 148th Penn.	225		1923 Apr 30	KS, 43rd, 1924
Royer, I.A.		I, 65th Ill.	25		1931 Jul 10	NE, 56th, 1932
Royer, J.H.	Pvt.	I, 44th Iowa Inf.	86		1906	IA, 33rd, 1907
Royer, John F.	Pvt.	A, 25th Iowa Inf.	112	50	1895 Dec 29	IA, 22nd, 1896
Royke, Chas.		D, 40th West Va. Mt. Inf.	66		1899 Mar 31	KS, 19th, 1900
Royster, R.D.	Pvt.	K, 18th Iowa	329		1924 Jul 19	IA, 51st, 1925
Royston, A.C.		C, 23rd Mo. Inf.	36		1899 Sep 14	KS, 19th, 1900
Rozelle, N.W.			7		1900-1901	IA, 27th, 1901
Rrouse, Henry		E, 3rd Wis. Inf. (died of pneumonia)	151	60	1900 Apr 1	NE, 25th, 1901

Name	Rank	Company, Regiment or Ship	Post*	Age	Death Date†	Journal
Rubey, Kinzer		Ill. Cav.	423		1908 Nov 23	KS, 28th, 1909
Ruble, Henry		D, 6th Reg. Cav.	116		1924 Oct 28	IA, 51st, 1925
Ruble, S.B.		D, 11th Kans.	128		1897 Jul 29	KS, 17th, 1898
Ruble, W.S.		C, 10th Kans.	4		1917 Jul 8	KS, 37th, 1918
Ruby, A.S.		D, 8th Iowa Cav.	116	95	1936 Mar 5	IA, 63rd, 1937
Ruby, B.R.F.	Pvt.	D, 8th Iowa Cav.	285	76	1898 Apr 13	IA, 24th, 1898
Ruby, J.W.		I, 4th Iowa Cav.	158		1913 Jul 26	KS, 33rd, 1914
Ruby, J.W.		D, 42nd Ohio Inf. (died of wounds)	298	55	1895 Nov 13	NE, 20th, 1896
Ruby, Mathew		I, 7th Ill.	8		1890	KS, 10th, 1891
Ruby, W.S.	Pvt.	H, 8th Iowa Cav.	56	57	1898 Dec 25	IA, 25th, 1899
Ruch, Phillip			32		1922 Nov 7	NE, 47th, 1923
Rucker, A.L.	Pvt.	A, 20th Iowa Inf.	124		1916	IA, 43rd, 1917
Rucker, Henry			105		1899 Jan 8	KS, 19th, 1900
Rucker, James	Pvt.	G, 28th Iowa Inf.	314		1908 Feb 4	IA, 34th, 1908
Rucker, Jas.	Pvt.	G, 28th Iowa Inf.	314		1908 Feb 4	IA, 35th, 1909
Rucker, T.H.	Pvt.	A, 12th Minn. Inf.	216		1910 Nov 8	IA, 37th, 1911
Ruckle, W.H.		D, 16th Ohio Inf.	66		1916 Mar 1	KS, 36th, 1917
Ruckman, Thomas	Pvt.	E, 100th Ill. Inf.	365		1915 Jun 24	IA, 42nd, 1916
Ruckman, Wm.	Pvt.	D, 32nd Ohio Inf.	211		1908 Apr 8	IA, 35th, 1909
Rudd, Alonzo E.			25		1913 Jun 2	KS, 33rd, 1914
Rudd, Anderson		B, 6th Mo. Inf.	79		1886	KS, 6th, 1887
Rudd, James A.	Pvt.	I, 13th Iowa	75		1907 May 15	IA, 34th, 1908
Ruder, E.W.	Pvt.	F, 29th Iowa Inf.	55		1919 Nov 7	IA, 46th, 1920
Rudolf, John		H, 44th Mo. Inf.	52		1912 Aug 8	KS, 32nd, 1913
Rudolph, Herman		C, 30th Ind. Inf.	92		1900 Jun 28	KS, 20th, 1901
Rudrow, Ezra V.			45		1926 Aug 5	IA, 53rd, 1927
Rudy, Aaron		G, 181st Ohio Inf.	105		1902	KS, 22nd, 1903
Rudy, Samuel		D, 159th Ohio	166		1905 Apr 6	KS, 25th, 1906
Ruedy, Louis	Pvt.	B, 15th N.Y. Hvy. Art.	1		1914 Oct 2	IA, 41st, 1915
Ruff, B.V.	Corp.	A, 148th Ill. Inf.	64		1921 Nov 16	IA, 48th, 1922
Ruff, Chas.		C, 56th Penn.	82		1927 Sep 8	KS, 47th, 1928
Ruffcorn, P.H.	Pvt.	B, 85th Penn. Inf.	197		1932	IA, 59th, 1933
Ruffeorn, Lewis	Pvt.	C, 18th Ohio Inf.	103		1911 Jan 28	IA, 38th, 1912
Rugan, E.A.	Pvt.	H, 149th Ind. Inf.	1		1930 Mar 22	IA, 57th, 1931
Ruggles, H.G.		H, 105th Ohio	25		1913 Oct 31	KS, 33rd, 1914
Ruggles, J.W.	Pvt.	C, 34th Iowa	50		1921 May 2	IA, 48th, 1922
Ruggles, M.E.		H, 22nd Mich.	289		1898 Jan 28	KS, 18th, 1899
Ruggles, O.M.	Pvt.	A, 16th Wis.	377		1907 Jan 17	IA, 34th, 1908
Ruhl, D.C.		C, 6th Ohio Cav.	40	82	1920 Apr 26	NE, 45th, 1921
Ruhland, Ben		12th Wis.	91		1922 Mar 25	IA, 49th, 1923
Ruks, J.O.	Pvt.	I, 55th U.S.C.	141		1915 Apr 28	IA, 42nd, 1916
Rulison, Wm. A.		I, 3rd Mich.	314		1892	KS, 12th, 1893
Rull, Adam		K, 69th Ind. Inf.	127		1901 Jul 5	KS, 21st, 1902
Rulledge, W.J.		M, 8th Ill. Cav.	17		1925 Dec 17	KS, 45th, 1926
Rumbaugh, Jesse B.	Pvt.	G, 23rd Iowa Inf.	40		1919 Dec 12	IA, 46th, 1920
Rumbaugh, W.H., see Rumbo, W.H.						
Rumble, Fred	Pvt.	A, 58th Ill.	88		1914 Oct 26	IA, 41st, 1915
Rumble, H.J.			400		1918	IA, 45th, 1919
Rumble, James P.	Pvt.	D, 4th Iowa Cav.	12		1915 Nov 20	IA, 42nd, 1916
Rumbo, W.H.	Pvt.	G, 1st Iowa Cav.	154		1912 Jun 5	IA, 39th, 1913
Rumbolz, Wm. R.		F, 7th Ill. Inf. B, 1st Mo. Cav. F, 7th Vols.	25	80	1920 Jul 16	NE, 45th, 1921
Rumelhart, George		L, 8th Ill. Cav. (former member)	42		1941 Jul 25	NE, 66th, 1942
Rumley, T.J.		D, 9th Kans. Cav.	18		1915 Mar 6	KS, 35th, 1916
Rummel, D.E.	Corp.	B, 9th Iowa Inf.	191		1910 Jan 20	IA, 37th, 1911
Rummer, P.	Pvt.	F, 92nd Ohio Inf.	143	42	1887 Feb 18	IA, 14th, 1888
Rummery, Jas.	Pvt.	F, 35th Iowa Inf.	447	71	1891 Apr 4	IA, 18th, 1892
Rumple, J.N.W.	Pvt.	H, 2nd Iowa Cav.	233		1903 Jan 31	IA, 29th, 1903
Rumple, John W.	Pvt.	B, 55th Ohio Inf.	17		1910 Dec 24	IA, 38th, 1912
Runckle, J.M.	Pvt.	F, 4th Iowa Inf.	12		1924 Feb 24	IA, 51st, 1925

*See Appendix A, B or C for roster of post names and locations.
†See Introduction for note regarding recording of death date.
472

Name	Rank	Company, Regiment or Ship	Post*	Age	Death Date†	Journal
Rundle, P.H.		F, 106th Ill.	115		1922 May 3	KS, 42nd, 1923
Rundorff, Emil			4		1914 Dec 28	IA, 41st, 1915
Runkin, J.W.		I, — Iowa	185		1908	KS, 28th, 1909
Runkle, A.J.	Pvt.	F, 24th Iowa Inf.	235		1926 Feb 14	IA, 53rd, 1927
Runkle, C.M.	Lieut.	A, 12th Iowa Inf.	154		1912 Feb 1	IA, 39th, 1913
Runkle, James		B, 46th Ill. Inf.	124	96	1935 Jun 5	IA, 62nd, 1936
Runyan, Geo. W.	Pvt.	3rd Ind. Battery Iowa	67		1901 Jun 9	IA, 28th, 1902
Runyan, Levi	Sergt.	A, 15th N.J. Inf.	88		1915 Mar 12	IA, 42nd, 1916
Runyan, S.T.	Pvt.	K, 42nd Ohio	275		1924 Jul 28	IA, 51st, 1925
Runyand, Joseph			236		1912 Sep 28	IA, 39th, 1913
Runyon, John H.		F, 68th Ill. Inf.	13	86	1920 Jun 29	NE, 45th, 1921
Runyon, O.N.		5th Ohio Bat.	47		1910 Mar 9	KS, 30th, 1911
Rupard, B.F.		I, 16th Mo. Cav.	142		1918 Jan 15	KS, 38th, 1919
Rupe, John M.	Pvt.	E, 3rd Iowa Inf.	69		1926	IA, 53rd, 1927
Rupert, Jno. C.		C, 139th Penn. (cause of death: liver & kidney)	291	78	1925 Feb 21	NE, 50th, 1926
Rupert, John		F, 41st Ill.	52		1921	KS, 41st, 1922
Rupert, John N.			25		1910 Jul 30	NE, 35th, 1911
Rupert, Wm. H.	Lieut.	C, 148th Ill. Inf.	200		1915 Dec 20	IA, 42nd, 1916
Rupiper, J.A.		F, 39th Wis. Inf. (died of tuberculor laryngeitis)	345	63	1902 Dec	NE, 27th, 1903
Rupp, Jno. A.	Pvt.	H, 114th N.Y. Inf.	371	66	1892 May 11	IA, 19th, 1893
Ruppel, Lewis F.		I, 47th Iowa (died at his farm home in Loup County, Neb.; see also Appendix D)	at large	84	1931 Oct 6	NE, 56th, 1932
Rusch, Eli		H, 214th Penn. Inf.	63		1900 Sep 8	KS, 20th, 1901
Rush, F.L.	Pvt.		96		1909 Jun 22	IA, 36th, 1910
Rush, J.	Pvt.	D, 46th Ill. Inf.	141		1921 May 3	IA, 48th, 1922
Rush, J.J.	Pvt.	G, 184th Ohio Inf.	236		1903 Jul 26	IA, 30th, 1904
Rush, J.W.		L, 3rd Ohio Inf.	8		1902 Jan 31	KS, 22nd, 1903
Rush, Jacob		D, 8th Ill. Vols.	12		1906 Sep 9	KS, 26th, 1907
Rush, James H.		F, 4th West Va. D, 5th U.S.	129		1921 Nov 1	KS, 41st, 1922
Rush, John	Pvt.	A, 171st Ohio	68		1903 Nov 3	IA, 30th, 1904
Rusher, James H.		I, 23rd Ind. (died of pneumonia)	77	69	1913 May 15	NE, 38th, 1914
Rushmore, J.B.		D, 207th Penn. Inf.	31		1925 May 17	IA, 52nd, 1926
Rushon, James		I, 20th Ind. Inf. (died of bullet)	274		1893 Mar 31	NE, 18th, 1894
Rusk, James K.		K, 44th Mo.	87		1919 Jun 25	KS, 39th, 1920
Russ, John N.	Pvt.	D, 44th Ill. Inf.	25		1901 Jan 27	IA, 28th, 1902
Russel, Sam			74		1905	IA, 32nd, 1906
Russell, A.			235		1909 Aug	IA, 36th, 1910
Russell, A.D.		K, 128th Ohio Inf.	203		1929 Feb 27	KS, 50th, 1931
Russell, A.M.		I, 35th Iowa	1		1920 Feb 4	KS, 40th, 1921
Russell, Andrew J.	Pvt.	C, 8th Minn. Inf.	74		1908 Jun 2	IA, 35th, 1909
Russell, B.H.	Capt.	G, 16th Ill. Inf.	111		1893 Aug 7	IA, 20th, 1894
Russell, C.P.		D, 14th Ohio Inf. (died of suicide)	180		1902	NE, 27th, 1903
Russell, Charles F.		M, 3rd Ill. Cav.	156		1902 Oct 13	KS, 22nd, 1903
Russell, Chas.	Pvt.	D, 134th Ohio Inf.	49		1916 Sep 4	IA, 43rd, 1917
Russell, David C.	Pvt.	H, 132nd Ind. Inf.	17		1913	IA, 40th, 1914
Russell, E.E.		B, 102nd Ill.	51		1916 May 1	KS, 36th, 1917
Russell, E.R.		I, 83rd Ill.	72		1928 Jan 3	KS, 48th, 1929
Russell, Enoch		I, 11th Kans.	35		1896 Nov 19	KS, 16th, 1897
Russell, F.M.		H, 27th Ohio	98		1910 Apr 21	KS, 30th, 1911
Russell, G.W.		C, 11th Ill. Cav.	69		1922 Mar 14	IA, 49th, 1923
Russell, Geo. W.	Pvt.	C, 55th Ill. Inf.	200		1917 Aug 2	IA, 44th, 1918
Russell, Henry C.		K, 2nd Iowa Inf. (died of Bright's disease)	34	58	1902 Jul 3	NE, 27th, 1903
Russell, Henry C.			34		1902 Jul 3	NE, 27th, 1903
Russell, J.B.		F, 72nd Ohio	25		1932	NE, 58th, 1934
Russell, J.F.		H, 3rd Wis. Inf. (died of cancer of liver)	10	72	1912 Jan 14	NE, 37th, 1913
Russell, J.H.	Pvt.	E, 47th Iowa Inf.	156		1915 Nov 8	IA, 42nd, 1916
Russell, J.J.	1st Lieut.	Ill.	23		1901-1902	IA, 28th, 1902
Russell, J.J.	Pvt.	C, 14th Iowa Inf.	42		1911 Oct 3	IA, 38th, 1912
Russell, J.W.		H, 4th Ill. Cav.	8		1915 Sep 19	KS, 35th, 1916

Name	Rank	Company, Regiment or Ship	Post*	Age	Death Date†	Journal
Russell, James M.		B, 5th Kans. Cav.	348		1901 Jul 9	KS, 21st, 1902
Russell, John		C, 44th Ill. Inf.	112		1900 Aug 7	KS, 20th, 1901
Russell, Jonathan		M, 11th Kans. Cav.	12		1911 Oct 10	KS, 31st, 1912
Russell, L.	Pvt.		52		1921 Oct 21	IA, 48th, 1922
Russell, L.G.	Pvt.	A, 77th Ill. Inf.	195		1904 Jul 16	IA, 31st, 1905
Russell, M.	Pvt.	I, 2nd Iowa Inf.	164		1920 Apr 8	IA, 47th, 1921
Russell, M.P.		B, 59th Inf.	143		1894 Sep 14	NE, 19th, 1895
Russell, M.T.	Capt.	A, 51st Ind. Inf.	12		1908 Jul 2	IA, 35th, 1909
Russell, O.J.		H, 33rd Ind.	55		1908 Nov 20	KS, 28th, 1909
Russell, R.S.		E, 25th Ohio Inf.	362		1895 May	KS, 15th, 1896
Russell, S.	Corp.	D, 58th Reg.	74		1921 Nov 9	IA, 48th, 1922
Russell, S.A.	Capt.	I, 25th Iowa Inf.	108	77	1893 Sep 28	IA, 20th, 1894
Russell, S.C.	Adjt.	8th Kans.	12		1904 Jan 18	KS, 24th, 1905
Russell, S.M.		C, 29th Penn. Inf. (died of insanity)	25		1903	NE, 28th, 1904
Russell, Thos.		10th Ill. Inf. (died at Gardner, Kans.; buried at Olathe)	447		1894	KS, 14th, 1895
Russell, Vinton		Ohio	133		1902 Nov 12	KS, 22nd, 1903
Russell, W.D.	Pvt.	K, 15th Iowa Cav.	433		1910 Jul 17	IA, 37th, 1911
Russell, W.F.	Pvt.	L, 9th Iowa Cav.	52		1930 Jan 15	IA, 57th, 1931
Russell, W.H.		I, 11th Ind.	97		1905 Jun 28	KS, 25th, 1906
Russell, W.H.		A, 17th Mich.	7		1936 Feb 14	NE, 61st, 1937
Russell, W.O.	Pvt.	C, 1st Mass. Cav.	181		1908 Oct 14	IA, 35th, 1909
Russell, W.S.	Pvt.	K, 2nd Iowa Cav.	157		1910 Dec 21	IA, 38th, 1912
Russell, W.S.	Corp.	F, 11th Iowa Inf.	235		1924 Feb 14	IA, 51st, 1925
Russell, William	Pvt.	A, 13th Wis. Inf.	168	75	1897 Aug 1	IA, 24th, 1898
Russell, Wm.	Pvt.	B, 38th Wis. Inf.	216		1930 Apr 28	IA, 57th, 1931
Russell, Wm.		D, 179th Ohio	169		1909 Jun 25	KS, 29th, 1910
Russum, B.D.		I, 11th Kans.	1		1904 Apr 2	KS, 24th, 1905
Rust, H.P.	Pvt.	E, 147th Ill. Inf.	333	48	1892 Jan 30	IA, 18th, 1892
Rust, John S.		D, 2nd Kans. (died of disease contracted in army)	275		1891 Dec 22	KS, 11th, 1892
Rust, S.C.		K, 63rd Penn. Inf.	5		1916 Jun 30	KS, 36th, 1917
Rust, W.E.	Musician	B, 8th Iowa Inf.	1	66	1890 Jul 29	IA, 17th, 1891
Ruth, Alex			55		1911 Jan 28	IA, 38th, 1912
Ruth, John B.		A, 13th Penn. Inf. (died of softening of brain)	110	76	1913 Dec 31	NE, 38th, 1914
Rutherford, A.E.		I, 115th Ill.	256		1920 Jul 13	KS, 40th, 1921
Rutherford, C.P.		E, 174th Ohio	6		1923 Apr 23	KS, 43rd, 1924
Rutherford, John	Pvt.	A, 10th Iowa Inf.	503		1914 Feb 14	IA, 41st, 1915
Ruthroff, J.C.		L, 4th Iowa Cav.	22	89	1935 Nov 13	IA, 62nd, 1936
Rutledge, Geo. W.		K, 145th Ill.	51		1921 Sep 17	KS, 41st, 1922
Rutledge, John		G, 45th Iowa	18		1928 Apr 14	KS, 48th, 1929
Rutledge, Thos.		F, 8th Kans.	51		1926 Nov 12	KS, 46th, 1927
Rutledge, W.	Pvt.	H, 160th Ohio Inf.	283		1920 Dec 2	IA, 47th, 1921
Rutledge, W.B.		C, 8th Iowa Cav.	239		1917	KS, 37th, 1918
Rutledge, W.B.		C, 10th Iowa Cav.	239		1918 Jul	KS, 38th, 1919
Rutlidge, Joseph		A, 3rd Ohio	244		1926	KS, 46th, 1927
Rutt, Joseph W.	Capt.	H, 179th Penn. Vols.	359		1902 Apr 22	IA, 28th, 1902
Rutter, John H.		A, 53rd Penn. G, 145th Penn.	25		1913 Jul 14	KS, 33rd, 1914
Ruttinger, Frank		G, 67th Penn.	68		1921 Jun 20	KS, 41st, 1922
Ruwe, August		A, 27th Ill. Inf. (died of old age)	4	84	1920 Nov 5	NE, 45th, 1921
Ruzor, W.W.		A, 28th Iowa (died of heart disease)	23	79	1915 Oct 5	NE, 40th, 1916
Ryan, A.W.		M, 18th N.Y. Cav.	11		1928	NE, 53rd, 1929
Ryan, Edward	Sergt.	9th Iowa Inf. 9th Iowa Cav.	194	61	1892 Nov 27	IA, 19th, 1893
Ryan, Edward	Pvt.	D, 35th Wis. Inf.	193		1913 Oct 23	IA, 40th, 1914
Ryan, Geo. F.		C, 60th N.W.[N.Y.?]	11		1928	NE, 53rd, 1929
Ryan, Ira L.		H, 122nd Ill. (died of general breakdown)	35	74	1915 Apr 12	NE, 40th, 1916
Ryan, J.M.	Pvt.	4th Iowa Cav.	138		1916 Dec 28	IA, 43rd, 1917
Ryan, J.P.	Capt.	F, 14th Wis. Inf.	22		1916 Mar 3	IA, 43rd, 1917
Ryan, James	Pvt.	E, 10th Wis. Inf.	14		1906 Mar 10	IA, 33rd, 1907
Ryan, Jos. F.	Pvt.	A, 7th Mo. Inf.	78		1900 Mar 20	IA, 27th, 1901

*See Appendix A, B or C for roster of post names and locations.
†See Introduction for note regarding recording of death date.

Name	Rank	Company, Regiment or Ship	Post*	Age	Death Date†	Journal
Ryan, Michael	Corp.	K, 8th Iowa Inf.	153		1910 Oct 28	IA, 37th, 1911
Ryan, R.H.			24		1927	IA, 54th, 1928
Ryan, Thomas		D, 141st Penn.	1		1914 Apr 5	KS, 34th, 1915
Ryan, W.H.		C, 8th Ill. Inf.	12		4th quarter 1884	IA, 11th, 1885
Ryan, Wm. S.			35		1897 Sep 28	NE, 22nd, 1898
Ryden, Charles A.	Pvt.	I, 12th Ill. Vol. Inf.	7		1901 Jul 10	IA, 28th, 1902
Ryder, G.H.	Pvt.	H, 26th Iowa Inf.	92		1911 May 26	IA, 38th, 1912
Ryder, S.P.	Pvt.	A, 44th Iowa Inf.	78		1916 Mar 2	IA, 43rd, 1917
Rye, John		B, 2nd U.S. Mil. (died at Topeka)	71		1895 Apr 17	KS, 15th, 1896
Ryerson, William	Pvt.	F, 15th Iowa Inf.	233		1902 Mar 14	IA, 28th, 1902
Ryker, William R.		A, 6th Ind. (former member; died at Guide Rock)	138		1935 Feb	NE, 60th, 1936
Rymer, B.F.		L, 7th Ind. Cav. (died of old age)	25	72	1903 Mar	NE, 28th, 1904
Rymon, L.D.	Sergt.	G, 27th Iowa Inf.	3		1925 Oct 9	IA, 52nd, 1926
Rympson, Hugh	Pvt.	17th Iowa Inf.	472		1911 Apr	IA, 38th, 1912
Rynder, John B.	Pvt.	K, 27th Iowa Inf.	77		1916 Nov 15	IA, 43rd, 1917
Ryno, N.		C, 11th Kans.	464		1897 May 24	KS, 17th, 1898
Saal, Boja		F, 2nd Mo. Inf. (cause of death: heart)	166	64	1901 Oct	NE, 26th, 1902
Saar, Henry		E, 19th Iowa	129		1921 Apr 3	KS, 41st, 1922
Sabine, Andrew	Surg.	26th Ohio Vol. Inf.	257		1915 Feb 13	KS, 35th, 1916
Sacket, E.	Pvt.	114th Ill. Inf.	29		1928 May 24	IA, 55th, 1929
Sackett, Charles	Lieut.	I, 3rd Ill. Cav.	39		1927 Nov 15	IA, 54th, 1928
Sackett, Chas.			29		1912 Oct 5	IA, 39th, 1913
Sackett, E.P.	Corp.	3rd U.S. Art.	1		1905 Jan 8	IA, 32nd, 1906
Sackett, Geo. C.	Pvt.	C, 1st Cav.	55		1922 Apr 16	IA, 49th, 1923
Sackett, S.L.		H, 38th N.Y. Inf.	292		1892 Dec 20	NE, 17th, 1893
Sackman, Rufus C.		C, 13th Mo.	500		1917 Oct 28	KS, 37th, 1918
Sackrider, D.	Pvt.	K, 121st Iowa Inf.	74		1910 Oct 2	IA, 37th, 1911
Sackrison, Jones Peter		B, 9th Ill. Inf. (died of blood poison at Soldiers & Sailors Home, Grand Island; buried at Edgar, Neb.)	23	71	1905 Sep 27	NE, 30th, 1906
Sacks, Benj. F.	Pvt.	A, 179th Penn. Inf. F, 15th Ill. Inf.	300		1927 Mar 17	IA, 54th, 1928
Sacora, Joseph	Pvt.	C, 15th Iowa Inf.	130	86	1932 Sep 15	IA, 59th, 1933
Sacrider, J.H., see Saouder, J.H.						
Sadler, E.R.		G, 1st Ky. Cav.	356		1891 Mar 14	KS, 11th, 1892
Sadler, E.R.		G, 1st Ky. Cav.	356		1891 Mar 14	KS, 12th, 1893
Sadler, Harry		F, 4th Iowa Cav.	59		1921 May 12	KS, 41st, 1922
Sadler, J.M.	Corp.	B, 20th Iowa Inf.	472		1910 Nov 24	IA, 37th, 1911
Sadler, W.G.		D, 13th Ky. Cav.	13		1932 Feb 5	NE, 57th, 1933
Saenger, Fritz	Pvt.	B, 16th Iowa Inf.	327	58	1887 Apr 26	IA, 14th, 1888
Safely, John	Sergt.	K, 11th Iowa Inf.	400	46	1889 Apr 19	IA, 16th, 1890
Safford, R.W.	Pvt.	G, 5th Iowa Cav.	54		1907 Mar 11	IA, 34th, 1908
Safton, W.M.	Pvt.	K, 32nd Iowa Inf.	154		1922 Mar 28	IA, 49th, 1923
Sage, E.H.		died of cancer of stomach	308		1913 Dec 1	NE, 38th, 1914
Sage, H.D.	Capt.	C, 26th Iowa Inf.	80		1914 Jan 10	IA, 40th, 1914
Sage, Henry		D, 122nd N.Y.	1		1892 Jan 24	KS, 12th, 1893
Sage, John		A, 37th Ind.	5		1919 Jan 27	KS, 39th, 1920
Sage, John R.	Pvt.	A, 121st N.Y. Inf.	12		1919 May 28	IA, 46th, 1920
Sage, L.B.		E, 3rd Wis. (died of cancer)	76	70	1909 Jul 26	NE, 34th, 1910
Sagertz, G.B.		Navy, Ohio	113		1918 Mar 30	KS, 38th, 1919
Sagor, M.A.		D, 29th Iowa	202		1896 Nov 24	KS, 16th, 1897
Said, Jefferson	Pvt.	F, 31st Iowa Inf.	298	53	1893 Aug 19	IA, 20th, 1894
Sailor, H.	Lieut.	D, Penn. Bat.	140		1921 Nov 27	IA, 48th, 1922
Sailor, Robert		D, 38th Ind. Inf.	179		1918 Mar 9	KS, 38th, 1919
Saint, H.	Pvt.	I, 14th Iowa Inf.	20		1915 Oct	IA, 42nd, 1916
Saint, James	Sergt.	E, 23rd Penn. Inf.	9		1906 Dec	IA, 33rd, 1907
Sala, Edward		H, 42nd Wis. (died of heart trouble)	5	80	1924 Dec 11	NE, 49th, 1925
Salem, R.J.	Pvt.	F, 29th Iowa	10		1907 Sep 19	IA, 34th, 1908
Salisbury, —	Pvt.	E, 5th Iowa Cav.	216		1922 Apr 21	IA, 49th, 1923
Salisbury, John	Drum Major	A, 46th Iowa Inf.	216	72	1889 Feb 15	IA, 15th, 1889
Salisbury, L.H.	Pvt.	E, 39th Iowa Inf.	452		1919 Feb 8	IA, 46th, 1920

*See Appendix A, B or C for roster of post names and locations.
†See Introduction for note regarding recording of death date.
475

Name	Rank	Company, Regiment or Ship	Post*	Age	Death Date†	Journal
Salisbury, O.A.	Pvt.	K, 95th Ill. Inf.	365	62	1898 Jul 7	IA, 25th, 1899
Salisbury, Sam'l L.		E, 139th Penn.	25		1908	NE, 33rd, 1909
Salkeld, A.		F, 77th Ohio	271		1913 Jul 17	KS, 33rd, 1914
Salkeld, James		2nd Kans. Battery	264		1898 Sep	KS, 18th, 1899
Salkon, Herman	Pvt.	G, 92nd Ill. Inf.	469		1908 Aug 27	IA, 35th, 1909
Sallady, Milton	Pvt.	A, 25th Iowa	170		1905	IA, 32nd, 1906
Sallard, A.B., Dr.		D, 40th Ky.	12		1913 Apr 20	KS, 33rd, 1914
Sallee, Benj. F.		E, 17th Ill.	3		1923 Mar 25	KS, 43rd, 1924
Sallee, N.V.		C, 9th M.S.M.	14		1902 Sep 15	KS, 22nd, 1903
Sallee, W.A.			66		1883	KS, 3rd, 1884
Sallee, W.A.	Sergt.	C, 3rd Ky. Cav.	66		1884	KS, 4th, 1885
Salmon, G.W.	Pvt.	I, 128th Ohio	511		1921 Jun 14	IA, 48th, 1922
Salmon, Isaiah			17		1917 Jan 30	KS, 37th, 1918
Salmon, J.D.		E, 3rd Ky.	85		1906 Jul 11	KS, 26th, 1907
Salmons, L.C.		A, 123rd Ill. Inf.	25		1935 Mar 30	KS, 55th, 1936
Salsgiun, Henry	Pvt.	2nd Penn. Bat.	11		1911 Jan	IA, 38th, 1912
Salt, Thos.	Pvt.	A, 12th R.I. Inf.	386		1904 Sep 30	IA, 31st, 1905
Salter, James H.		G, 13th Mich. Inf. (died of heart failure)	28	76	1921 May 2	NE, 46th, 1922
Salter, John	Pvt.	H, 86th Ill. Inf.	38		1920 Dec 9	IA, 47th, 1921
Salters, John W.		D, 116th Ill.	405		1914 Mar 7	KS, 33rd, 1914
Salters, John W.		D, 116th Ill. Inf.	405		1914 Mar 7	KS, 34th, 1915
Salts, Peter		G, 76th Ohio	35	80	1923 Apr 25	NE, 48th, 1924
Saltz, A.J.	Pvt.	22nd Ind.	324		1903 Nov	IA, 30th, 1904
Sammers, Thomas		G, 5th Kans.	40		1914 Mar 5	KS, 34th, 1915
Sample, A.E.		A, 30th Ill.	20		1927 Jul 17	KS, 47th, 1928
Sample, Alex		C, 8th Iowa (died of heart failure)	35	81	1922 Nov 5	NE, 47th, 1923
Sample, Jas. F.		C, 60th Ohio Inf. (died of lung trouble)	13	76	1913 Mar 10	NE, 38th, 1914
Sample, John		K, 66th Ind. (accidentally killed)	199		1889	KS, 9th, 1890
Sample, John		C, 50th Ohio	51		1920 Dec 18	KS, 40th, 1921
Sample, Josiah		A, 2nd Kans. Cav.	50		1917 Jun 14	KS, 37th, 1918
Sample, Mathew I.	Pvt.	A, 32nd Iowa Inf.	193		1916 Jan 5	IA, 43rd, 1917
Sample, Richard		F, 48th U.S.C.T.	100		1912 Jun 7	KS, 32nd, 1913
Samples, J.		L, 1st Mo. Cav.	65		1916 Apr 15	KS, 36th, 1917
Samples, Wm. T.		K, 1st Wis. Cav.	47		1912 Nov 4	KS, 32nd, 1913
Sampson, Charles	Pvt.	B, 156th Ill. Inf.	69		1899	NE, 24th, 1900
Sampson, E.	Pvt.	I, 45th Iowa Inf.	227	58	1896 Feb 8	IA, 22nd, 1896
Sampson, S.V.	Pvt.	H, 3rd Iowa Inf.	107		1911 Sep 8	IA, 38th, 1912
Sampson, Seth		F, — Iowa	40		1918 Nov 24	KS, 38th, 1919
Sampson, W.B.		C, 47th Ill. Inf.	3		1889	KS, 9th, 1890
Sams, Samuel	Pvt.	H, 7th Ind. Cav.	163	48	1893 Jul 20	IA, 20th, 1894
Samson, C.E.	Pvt.	B, 1st Iowa Cav.	39	48	1891 Apr 10	IA, 18th, 1892
Samuels, Edmund	Pvt.	I, 71st N.Y. Inf.	13	54	1892 Jun 15	IA, 19th, 1893
Samuels, Joseph A.	Bugler	C, 3rd Iowa Cav.	2		1917 Nov 21	IA, 44th, 1918
Samuels, Lewis			6		1916 Jul 15	KS, 36th, 1917
Sanborn, A.H.		G, 79th Ill.	49		1931 Oct 19	KS, 51st, 1932
Sanborn, A.H.		G, 79th Ill.	49		1931 Oct 19	KS, 52nd, 1933
Sanborn, Chas. S.		G, 11th N.H. (died of diabetes)	13	73	1917 Dec 11	NE, 42nd, 1918
Sanborn, E.M.	Pvt.	B, 41st Ohio Inf.	48		1910 Dec 22	IA, 37th, 1911
Sanborn, F.B.			24		1927	IA, 54th, 1928
Sanborn, George	Corp.	E, 4th Wis. Inf.	383		1926 Jun 13	IA, 53rd, 1927
Sanborn, J.	Pvt.	I, 4th Ill. Inf.	18		1919 Nov 1	IA, 46th, 1920
Sanborn, Jas. D.			24		1915 Feb 6	IA, 41st, 1915
Sandage, Abraham		A, 26th Ind. Inf. (died of paralysis)	22	72	1912 Sep 4	NE, 37th, 1913
Sanderlin, Isaac S.		I, 100th Ohio	244		1917 May 8	KS, 37th, 1918
Sanders, Anderson		B, 3rd Hvy. Art.	71		1919 Mar 3	KS, 39th, 1920
Sanders, D.M.		F, 17th Ill. Cav.	76		1912	KS, 32nd, 1913
Sanders, Daniel		C, 12th Mich. Vols.	266		1902 Oct 19	KS, 22nd, 1903
Sanders, Daniel		B, 11th Ind. Cav.	344		1934 Dec 25	KS, 54th, 1935
Sanders, Elza	Pvt.	K, 13th Iowa Inf.		94	1939 Oct 3	IA, 66th, 1940
Sanders, Franklin		F, 10th Iowa	343		1890	KS, 10th, 1891
Sanders, Geo. L.		E, 73rd Ind.	46		1918 Mar 7	KS, 38th, 1919
Sanders, George		A, 1st U.S. Col. Art.	17		1925 Nov 27	KS, 45th, 1926

*See Appendix A, B or C for roster of post names and locations.
†See Introduction for note regarding recording of death date.

Name	Rank	Company, Regiment or Ship	Post*	Age	Death Date†	Journal
Sanders, H.H.		E, 5th Ill. Cav. (died of consumption)	3	63	1905 Feb	NE, 30th, 1906
Sanders, Henry		B, 7th Mo. Cav. (died at Ottawa)	18		1895 Aug	KS, 15th, 1896
Sanders, Henry		E, 53rd Ill. (member at large)			1936 Nov 24	NE, 61st, 1937
Sanders, James M.		32nd Ill. Inf. (died of old age)	35	73	1907 May 4	NE, 32nd, 1908
Sanders, Jamuel	Pvt.	H, 12th Kans. Inf.	127		1902 Oct 3	IA, 29th, 1903
Sanders, John F.	Pvt.	C, 28th Iowa	127		1923 Feb 6	IA, 50th, 1924
Sanders, Morgan	Pvt.	A, 11th Iowa Inf.	256	63	1892 Jan 13	IA, 18th, 1892
Sanders, R.W.		C, 54th Ky.	252		1897 Apr 30	KS, 17th, 1898
Sanders, S.C.	Pvt.	C, 13th Wis. Inf.	63		1906 May 6	IA, 33rd, 1907
Sanders, S.F., Dr.		I, 137th Ill. Inf. (died at his home in Holdrege, Neb., see Appendix D)			1926 Sep 9	NE, 51st, 1927
Sanders, Thos.		L, 11th Kans. Cav.	88		1922 May 4	KS, 42nd, 1923
Sanders, Thos. S.		G, 97th N.Y. Inf. (born in England; died of heart failure at Grand Island; buried at Soldiers & Sailors Home Cemetery, Burkett)		66	1906 Oct 12	NE, 31st, 1907
Sanders, U.B.		176th Penn. Inf.	235		1909 Aug	IA, 36th, 1910
Sanders, Wm.	Pvt.	E, 15th Iowa Inf.	20		1902 Apr	IA, 29th, 1903
Sanderson, A.W.	Pvt.	K, 34th Iowa Inf.	400	91	1933 May 7	IA, 60th, 1934
Sanderson, John		K, 58th Ohio	1		1914 Dec 13	KS, 34th, 1915
Sanderson, Oliver		C, 11th Mo.	459		1908 Oct 21	KS, 28th, 1909
Sanderson, Sam		D, 149th Ind. Inf.	500		1934 Oct 8	KS, 54th, 1935
Sanderson, Samuel W.		C, 3rd Ohio Inf.	12		1901 Jul 10	KS, 21st, 1902
Sanderson, W.A.		K, 34th Iowa Inf. (cause of death: kidneys)	32		1893 Dec	NE, 18th, 1894
Sandford, Noble		B, 45th Ill.	1		1926 May 8	NE, 51st, 1927
Sandford, W.H.	Pvt.	H, 49th N.Y. Inf.	337		1925 Mar 24	IA, 52nd, 1926
Sands, C.H.	Corp.	E, 50th Wis.	357	58	1890 Nov	IA, 17th, 1891
Sands, Israel		A, 108th Ill.	85		1911 Jul 3	KS, 31st, 1912
Sands, J.D.	Chaplain	19th Iowa Inf.	247		1909 Mar 9	IA, 36th, 1910
Sands, Jacob		A, 123rd Ind.	127		1931	KS, 51st, 1932
Sands, Jacob		A, 123rd Ind.	127		1932	KS, 52nd, 1933
Sands, Jno. W.	Pvt.	A, 14th Iowa Vol. Inf.	108		1924 Feb 10	IA, 51st, 1925
Sandusky, George W.		H, 1st Ky.	475		1892 Aug 18	KS, 12th, 1893
Sandy, J.A.		H, 3rd Wis. (died of paralysis)	120	73	1913 Sep	NE, 38th, 1914
Sandy, John		G, 43rd Mo.	292		1916 Jul 7	KS, 36th, 1917
Sanford, A.	Pvt.		316		1915	IA, 42nd, 1916
Sanford, Don H.	Corp.	F, 6th Mich. Inf.	81		1919 Jun 24	IA, 46th, 1920
Sanford, G.W.		G, 18th U.S. Inf. G, 17th Ill. Cav.	18		1924 Oct 3	KS, 44th, 1925
Sanford, O.E.		C, 10th Wis.	16		1928 Jan 1	KS, 48th, 1929
Sanford, Owen C.		G, 152nd Ill. Inf.	301		1929 Jan 4	KS, 49th, 1930
Sanford, W.C.		Eng. M. Squ. New York	176		1908 Sep 5	KS, 28th, 1909
Sanger, A.T.		C, 86th Ill.	113		1915 Oct 4	KS, 35th, 1916
Sanger, John C.	Pvt.	C, 136th N.Y.	18		1924 May 1	IA, 51st, 1925
Sanger, M.E.		K, 86th Ill.	256		1912 Feb 4	KS, 32nd, 1913
Sankey, Ezekiel J.	Pvt.	L, 3rd Iowa Cav. (at large)	251	92	1935 Sep 29	IA, 65th, 1939
Santee, E.M.	Pvt.	G, 1st Ill. Lt. Art.	94		1915 Oct 2	IA, 42nd, 1916
Santo, August	Musician	6th Iowa Inf.	2		1922 Mar 22	IA, 49th, 1923
Saouder, J.H.		D, 65th Ill.	10		1926 Sep 1	NE, 51st, 1927
Sapp, Daniel		K, 5th Mo. (died of heart trouble)	283		1893 Dec 10	KS, 13th, 1894
Sapp, W.F., Sr.	Lieut. Col.	2nd Neb. Cav.	29	66	1890 Nov 20	IA, 17th, 1891
Sappenfald, Robt.		F, 17th Kans. Inf.	57		1929 Feb 22	KS, 49th, 1930
Sarber, R.B.		F, 6th Kans. Inf.	271		1899 Mar 17	KS, 19th, 1900
Sarbook, Arnold	Pvt.	A, 36th Ill. Inf.	170	79	1896 Jan 13	IA, 22nd, 1896
Sarchett, Chas.	Pvt.	C, 9th Iowa Inf.	165		1918	IA, 45th, 1919
Sarchett, Thomas			165		1918	IA, 45th, 1919
Sargeant, L.S.		A, 17th Kans.	55		1908 Jan 8	KS, 28th, 1909
Sargent, A.C.		L, 50th N.Y. Eng.	46		1916 Jun 10	KS, 36th, 1917
Sargent, Chas. H.		E, 8th Mass.	25		1913 Nov 9	NE, 38th, 1914
Sargent, D.D.			288		1922	KS, 42nd, 1923
Sargent, D.D.		C, 9th Minn.	288		1921 Sep 27	KS, 41st, 1922
Sargent, Daniel B.		M, S.S. Kearsarge	110	82	1921 Apr 17	NE, 46th, 1922

*See Appendix A, B or C for roster of post names and locations.
†See Introduction for note regarding recording of death date.

477

Name	Rank	Company, Regiment or Ship	Post*	Age	Death Date†	Journal
Sargent, E.A.	Pvt.	D, 1st Bat. Mass. Hvy. Art.	377		1901 Jul 1	IA, 28th, 1902
Sargent, E.M.	Capt.	K, 59th Iowa Inf.	71		1904 Jan 7	IA, 31st, 1905
Sargent, Geo. H.	Wagoner	23rd Reserve C.[Corps]	231		1917	IA, 44th, 1918
Sargent, Ira		D, 4th Iowa Inf.		90	1936[1935?] Dec 6	IA, 62nd, 1936
Sargent, Ira H., see Sergant, Ira H.						
Sargent, J.M.	Pvt.		235		1912 May 23	IA, 39th, 1913
Sargent, J.S.	Q.M.S.	G, Mo. Cav.	364		1922 Jul 8	IA, 49th, 1923
Sargent, W.G.	Major	63rd U.S.C.T.	175		1899 Jan 28	KS, 19th, 1900
Sargent, W.S.	Pvt.	1st Minn. Bat.	67		1921 Mar 9	IA, 48th, 1922
Sargent, W.W.	Pvt.	H, 8th Iowa Inf.	64		1908 Jan 6	IA, 35th, 1909
Sarger, John			249		4th quarter 1885	IA, 12th, 1886
Saronson, John			299		1915 Feb 2	NE, 40th, 1916
Sarper, J.		K, 9th Kans.	271		1916 Nov	KS, 36th, 1917
Sarver, Samuel C.		B, 134th Ohio	250		1931 Jan 13	KS, 52nd, 1933
Sarver, Samuel C.		B, 134th Ohio	250		1931 Jan 13	KS, 51st, 1932
Sassey, A.			114		1922	NE, 47th, 1923
Satchell, J.W.	Pvt.	I, 13th Iowa Inf.	64		1899	IA, 26th, 1900
Satchell, N.M.	Sergt.	F, 10th Iowa Inf.	40		1912 Jul 13	IA, 39th, 1913
Sater, A.H.	Sergt.	K, 86th Ind. Inf.	20		1915 Oct	IA, 42nd, 1916
Satterhwait, Wm.	Pvt.	A, 35th Iowa Inf.	231		1915 Oct 22	IA, 42nd, 1916
Satterlee, F.E.		I, 46th Wis.	147		1928 Jul 21	NE, 54th, 1930
Satterly, I.J.	Corp.	M, 4th Wis. Cav.	67		1910 Feb 5	IA, 37th, 1911
Sattes, Emil R.G.		D, 1st U.S. Cav.	7		1893 Feb 14	NE, 18th, 1894
Sauer, Peter	Pvt.	H, 15th Mo. Inf.	2	61	1894 Jul 16	IA, 21st, 1895
Saulsbury, B.L.	Pvt.	B, 34th Iowa Inf.	10	50	1887 Jul 23	IA, 14th, 1888
Saulter, Martin		H, 128th Ind. Inf. (died of heart failure)	36		1893 Jul 5	NE, 18th, 1894
Saunders, Billy		Ky.	51		1931 Jun 2	KS, 52nd, 1933
Saunders, Billy		Ky.	51		1931 Jun 2	KS, 51st, 1932
Saunders, Charles		M, 2nd U.S. Art.	25		1915 Aug 19	NE, 40th, 1916
Saunders, Charles W.		C, 17th Kans. Inf.	85		1901 Mar 6	KS, 21st, 1902
Saunders, Frank	Pvt.	F, 10th Iowa Inf.	127	46	1890 Nov 4	IA, 18th, 1892
Saunders, H.H.	Pvt.	E, — Cal. Cav.	68	57	1893 Apr 17	IA, 20th, 1894
Saunders, Isaac	Corp.	B, 4th Iowa Cav.	342		1907 Apr 26	IA, 34th, 1908
Saunders, J.H.	Pvt.	H, 18th Iowa Inf.	7		1918 Apr 3	IA, 45th, 1919
Saunders, J.W.		A, 57th Mass. Inf.	253		1st quarter 1884	IA, 10th, 1884
Saunders, John		C, 1st Kans.	6		1927 May 27	KS, 47th, 1928
Saunders, L.W.		H, 8th Ill. Cav.	77		1928 Mar 6	NE, 53rd, 1929
Saunders, M.V.	Pvt.	K, 28th Iowa Reg.	16		1923 Mar 24	IA, 50th, 1924
Saunders, S.F.		I, 137th Ill.	111		1926 Sep 9	NE, 51st, 1927
Saunders, S.H.		D, 14th Ill. Inf.	98		1916 Jun 6	KS, 36th, 1917
Saunders, S.L.	Pvt.	I, 55th Ohio Inf.	8		1911 May 30	IA, 38th, 1912
Saunders, S.S.			100		1890 Nov	NE, 15th, 1891
Saunders, Stephen		E, 32nd Wis. Inf.	477		1899 Dec 17	KS, 19th, 1900
Saunders, T.J.	Paymaster	U.S.A.	1		1897 Oct 19	IA, 24th, 1898
Saunders, W.C.	Pvt.	M, 8th Iowa Cav.	153		1927 May 28	IA, 54th, 1928
Saunderson, Henry	Capt.	E, 6th Iowa Inf.	337	71	1894 Jul 16	IA, 21st, 1895
Saur, Fred	Landsman		12		1909 Apr 16	KS, 29th, 1910
Savage, Abel	Pvt.	K, 34th Iowa Inf.	18		1900 Nov 20	IA, 27th, 1901
Savage, James E.		K, 8th U.S. Inf.	52		1912	KS, 32nd, 1913
Savage, James S.		D, 54th Ill. Inf.	85		1918 Nov 19	KS, 38th, 1919
Savage, James W.	Col.	died at Omaha			1890 Nov 22	NE, 15th, 1891
Savage, Samuel	Pvt.	B, 29th Iowa Inf.	263		1916 Apr 29	IA, 43rd, 1917
Savidge, Wm.		G, 45th Ohio Inf.	81	88	1935 Mar 11	IA, 62nd, 1936
Sawger, J.A.	Pvt.	B, 65th Ill. Inf.	284		1920 Oct 9	IA, 47th, 1921
Sawin, G.T.	Pvt.	D, 151st Ill. Inf.	452		1929 Apr 5	IA, 56th, 1930
Sawtell, Zephaniah		E, 23rd Md.	81		1928 Sep 18	KS, 48th, 1929
Sawter, Oswald		G, 37th Ind.	64		1921 Oct 16	KS, 41st, 1922
Sawvel, A.	Pvt.	C, 27th Iowa Inf.	165	57	1893 Aug 4	IA, 20th, 1894
Sawyer, A.D.		I, 56th Penn.	28		1922 Sep 2	KS, 42nd, 1923
Sawyer, C.H.	Pvt.	H, 20th Iowa Inf.	212		1906 Jan 18	IA, 33rd, 1907
Sawyer, Charles W.	Sergt.	I, 38th Iowa Inf.	216		1902 Dec 14	IA, 29th, 1903

*See Appendix A, B or C for roster of post names and locations.
†See Introduction for note regarding recording of death date.

Name	Rank	Company, Regiment or Ship	Post*	Age	Death Date†	Journal
Sawyer, David H.		B, 141st Ill. Inf. (died of old age)	291	77	1917 Jun 3	NE, 42nd, 1918
Sawyer, F.A.	Pvt.	G, 1st Wis. Cav.	10		1915 Jul 28	IA, 42nd, 1916
Sawyer, Geo.	Pvt.	E, 5th Mass. Inf.	212		1907 Nov 16	IA, 34th, 1908
Sawyer, I.A.			2		1909 May 12	IA, 36th, 1910
Sawyer, James	Pvt.	F, 22nd Wis.	98		1914 Oct 30	IA, 41st, 1915
Sawyer, L.L.	Sergt.	D, 100th Ind. Inf.	300		1913 May 2	IA, 40th, 1914
Sawyer, P.L.	Pvt.	D, 28th Maine Inf.	97	53	1899 Aug 11	IA, 26th, 1900
Sawyer, S.N.		Mo.	437		1917 Mar 15	KS, 37th, 1918
Sawyer, Spencer A.	Sergt.	D, 41st Ohio Inf.	500		1918 Oct 20	IA, 45th, 1919
Sawyer, Thos. A.		died of kidney disease	209		1905	NE, 30th, 1906
Sawyer, W.J.	Sergt.	F, 16th Iowa Inf.	466		1907 Sep 14	IA, 34th, 1908
Sawyers, Sylvester H.	Capt.	C, 36th Iowa Inf.	328	60	1892 Feb 5	IA, 19th, 1893
Sax, A.C.	Pvt.	K, 111th Ill.	100		1924 Apr 2	IA, 51st, 1925
Saxer, P.J.		D, 14th Wis. (died of apoplexy)	13	80	1922 Sep 12	NE, 47th, 1923
Saxton, George W.	Pvt.	M, 7th Iowa Cav.	88	84	1931 Jan 10	IA, 58th, 1932
Saxton, James P.	Pvt.	M, 7th Iowa Cav.	92		1897 Dec 25	IA, 24th, 1898
Saxton, John H.	Pvt.	A, 18th Iowa Inf.	92	50	1895 Apr 7	IA, 22nd, 1896
Sayer, S.B.	Sergt.	E, 18th Ill. Inf.	71		1914 Dec 29	IA, 41st, 1915
Sayers, D.N.		F, 30th Ill.	27		1911 Aug 9	KS, 31st, 1912
Sayles, Adam	Pvt.	C, 55th U.S.C.T.	88		1901 Dec 8	IA, 28th, 1902
Saylor, Samuel		K, 1st Ohio Art.	36		1890	KS, 10th, 1891
Saylor, Thos. J.	Pvt.	E, 23rd Iowa Inf.	7		1912 Oct 5	IA, 39th, 1913
Sayre, J.P.		B, 21st Ill.	202		1896 May 7	KS, 16th, 1897
Sayre, Peter W.	Corp.	C, 27th Ohio	1		1916 Feb 27	KS, 36th, 1917
Sayres, John D.	Corp.	H, 8th Iowa Cav.	325	52	1895 Sep 24	IA, 22nd, 1896
Scafferd, Robt.		G, 20th Ill.	191		1893 Aug 25	KS, 13th, 1894
Scaggs, W.H.	Pvt.	G, 3rd Col. Cav.	58		1907 May 30	IA, 35th, 1909
Scaggs, Wm.	Pvt.	G, 3rd Col.	58		1907 May 30	IA, 34th, 1908
Scales, W.H.	Pvt.	G, 5th Mich. Cav.	192		1926 Nov 13	IA, 53rd, 1927
Scalley, Patrick		G, 12th Iowa	19		1907	IA, 34th, 1908
Scally, Patrick	Sergt.	K, 22nd Ill. Inf.	236		1897 Apr	IA, 24th, 1898
Scandland, C.W.	Pvt.	C, 34th Iowa Inf.	116		1910 Jun 11	IA, 37th, 1911
Scanlan, M.T.	Pvt.	B, 12th U.S. Inf.	12	87	1933 Jan 25	IA, 60th, 1934
Scannel, Columbus		B, 5th Cal.	23		1911 Aug 23	KS, 31st, 1912
Scarborough, D.L.	Pvt.	G, 2nd Iowa Inf.	152		1920 Jul 11	IA, 47th, 1921
Scarbrough, Cooper	Pvt.	H, 5th Maine Inf.	68		1919 Dec 29	IA, 46th, 1920
Scarth, F.O.	2nd Lieut.	B, 113th Ohio Vol. Inf.	16	50	1886 Feb 28	IA, 12th, 1886
Schaaff, Chas. A.		B, 46th U.S. Colored Inf.	380		1899 May 18	KS, 19th, 1900
Schaap, William	Sergt. Major	18th Mo.	93		1918 Jan 2	KS, 38th, 1919
Schack, Johnson	Pvt.	G, 22nd Ohio	497		1924 Apr 14	IA, 51st, 1925
Schad, Henry		E, 1st N.Y.	25		1927 Apr 20	KS, 47th, 1928
Schadt, William	Pvt.	E, 9th Ill. Inf.	124	88	1932 Jan 26	IA, 59th, 1933
Schaefer, Michael		1st Neb. (cause of death: paralyzed)	118		1907 Sep	NE, 32nd, 1908
Schaeffer, Chas. A.	Pvt.	1st Penn. Battery Lt. Art.	8	54	1898 Sep 23	IA, 25th, 1899
Schaeffer, J.A.		6th Ohio Vol. Cav.	36		1908 Jul 17	KS, 28th, 1909
Schafer, Aaron	Pvt.	H, 3rd Iowa Inf.	40	59	1892 Apr 3	IA, 18th, 1892
Schafer, Conrade	Pvt.	A, 19th Iowa Inf.	2		1914 Nov 21	IA, 41st, 1915
Schafer, John	Pvt.	E, 25th Iowa Inf.	19		1924 Apr 5	IA, 51st, 1925
Schaffer, A.T.			80		1912	IA, 39th, 1913
Schaffer, Henry		H, 43rd Ill.	52		1928 Jan 31	KS, 48th, 1929
Schaffer, Herman	Pvt.	F, 16th Iowa Inf.	174	47	1891 Sep 23	IA, 18th, 1892
Schaffer, William C.		C, 7th Ill.	381		1909 Jul 9	KS, 29th, 1910
Schafnet, Jacob		D, 13th Ill. Inf.	231		1924 Jan 31	IA, 51st, 1925
Schall, A.		K, 11th Penn. Inf.	12		1899 Nov 19	KS, 19th, 1900
Schall, Wm. B.		B, 11th Ill.	17		1926 Jan 21	KS, 46th, 1927
Schaller, Nicolas	Pvt.	K, 1st U.S.V.V.	359		1908 Jul 26	IA, 35th, 1909
Schaller, Phil	Sergt.	E, 27th Iowa Inf. (see also Appendix D)	284		1911 Jul 21 or 1912 Jun 21	IA, 38th, 1912
Schallerf, Wm.	Pvt.	C, 20th Iowa Inf.	256	52	1886 Nov 2	IA, 17th, 1891
Schallert, William	Pvt.	C, 20th Iowa Inf.	256	52	1886 Nov 2	IA, 13th, 1887
Schallion, Zeo	Pvt.	F, 21st Iowa Inf.	81		1912 Oct 18	IA, 39th, 1913
Schamp, Robert C.	Pvt.	F, 44th Ind.	17		1910 Feb 23	KS, 30th, 1911

*See Appendix A, B or C for roster of post names and locations.
†See Introduction for note regarding recording of death date.

Name	Rank	Company, Regiment or Ship	Post*	Age	Death Date†	Journal
Schanerberg, Fred			4		1914 Mar 30	IA, 41st, 1915
Schank, Edward M.	Pvt.	F, 12th Ill. Inf.	132		1902 Oct 22	IA, 29th, 1903
Schanten, Geo. P.		K, 151st N.Y.	255		1921 Jun 27	KS, 41st, 1922
Schardine, John		C, 11th Ind.	83		1916 Mar 31	KS, 36th, 1917
Schardt, G.		D, 17th Mo. Inf. (died of cancer)	120		1893 Sep 9	NE, 18th, 1894
Schastine, Henry		F, 44th Ill.	33		1896 Dec	KS, 16th, 1897
Schatti, Werner		C, 26th Mo.	380		1913 Dec 29	KS, 33rd, 1914
Schaub, Frederick	Bugler	6th Iowa Cav.	64		1921 Nov 29	KS, 41st, 1922
Schechter, Henry		I, 89th Ill. Inf.	2		1908 Nov 27	KS, 28th, 1909
Schecker, Chas.	Sergt.	D, 27th Iowa Inf.	184		1907 Oct 13	IA, 33rd, 1907
Scheckle, John		A, 46th Ill.	5		1922 Jun 10	KS, 42nd, 1923
Scheel, Wm.		F, 64th Ill. Inf.	55		1917 Aug 3	KS, 37th, 1918
Scheiner, Elias		G, 34th Wis.	53		1917 Feb 22	KS, 37th, 1918
Scheinkoenig, Frank		I, 4th N.Y. Hvy. Art.	88		1914 Dec 8	KS, 34th, 1915
Schelds, J.H.C.	Pvt.	H, 18th Iowa Inf.	297		1912 Sep 29	IA, 39th, 1913
Schell, J.F.		F, 2nd Penn.	13	70	1916 Apr 15	NE, 41st, 1917
Schell, W.A.		L, 133rd Ill.	25		1931 Jul 7	NE, 56th, 1932
Schemmorhorn, B.			493		1904 Mar	IA, 31st, 1905
Schenck, D.M.	Sergt.	G, 3rd Ill. Inf.	135		1905	IA, 32nd, 1906
Schenck, Fred		G, 48th Ind. Inf.	33		1900 Nov 24	KS, 20th, 1901
Schenck, Obediah		1st Iowa Lt. Art.	142		1914 Nov 3	KS, 34th, 1915
Schenck, Paul		H, 2nd Ill. Art.	52		1911 Feb 22	KS, 31st, 1912
Schenck, W.L.			1		1910 Jan 4	KS, 30th, 1911
Schenert, Fred		B, 4th Mo.	18		1905 Sep 30	KS, 25th, 1906
Schenk, Cyreniss		D, 3rd Iowa Cav.	293		1909 Jun	KS, 29th, 1910
Schenk, E.T.	Lieut. Col.		255		1910 Oct 26	IA, 37th, 1911
Scheonaman, W.D.	Pvt.	F, 49th Wis. Inf.	408	65	1897 Jan 12	IA, 23rd, 1897
Scherf, Edward		3rd Wis. Cav.		90	1938 Jun 8	IA, 64th, 1938
Scherfe, A.			170		1915	IA, 42nd, 1916
Schibler, G.A.		215th Ill.	47		1918 Jul 31	KS, 38th, 1919
Schick, John			4		1914 Feb 27	IA, 41st, 1915
Schickler, Charles					1901 Feb 17	IA, 27th, 1901
Schierer, John	Pvt.	G, 16th Iowa Inf.	1		1916 Oct 10	IA, 43rd, 1917
Schilling, Edward		G, 32nd Ind.	453		1926 May 7	KS, 46th, 1927
Schilling, Joseph	Band	44th Ill. Vol. Inf.	266		1901 May 25	IA, 27th, 1901
Schima, Joseph	Pvt.	B, 2nd Mo. Inf. A, 2nd U.S. Inf.	2	82	1897 Feb 8	IA, 23rd, 1897
Schimelfenig, J.	Pvt.	C, 38th N.Y. Inf.	116		1910 Jul 20	IA, 37th, 1911
Schimmelpfennig, F.J.		D, 105th Ill. Inf. (died of accident)	240		1893 Apr 21	NE, 18th, 1894
Schimner, C.J.	Pvt.	G, 11th Iowa	20		1907 Mar 24	IA, 34th, 1908
Schindler, Jacob	Pvt.	I, 37th Wis. Inf.	22		1925 Jan 2	IA, 52nd, 1926
Schindler, Jacob			34		1890	NE, 15th, 1891
Schira, Frederick		C, 2nd U.S. Art.	120		1899 Nov 21	KS, 19th, 1900
Schirringer, Gabriel	Pvt.	D, 20th Iowa Inf.	349	53	1891 Dec 21	IA, 18th, 1892
Schlapp, Henry	Pvt.	F, 5th Iowa Cav.	170	53	1893 Jun 4	IA, 20th, 1894
Schley, Jacob	Pvt.	F, 1st Penn. Mtd.	235		1918 May	IA, 45th, 1919
Schlosser, Frank			84		1927 Nov 27	NE, 52nd, 1928
Schlupp, Jacob		31st Iowa	175		1921 Nov 29	KS, 41st, 1922
Schmalzried, John Frederick		16th Ind. Lt. Art. (former member; died at North Platte)	69		1936 Sep 23	NE, 61st, 1937
Schmetzer, E.		A & E, 75th Ohio	64		1917	KS, 37th, 1918
Schmid, Adam		Wis.	9		1922 Jan 6	NE, 46th, 1922
Schmid, Geo.		D, 10th — (died of old age)	287	89	1909 Jul 28	NE, 34th, 1910
Schmid, Jacob		A, 60th Ind. Vols.	9		1926 Mar 10	NE, 51st, 1927
Schmid, Joseph	Pvt.	E, 21st Iowa Inf.	78		1919 Aug 27	IA, 46th, 1920
Schmidt, C.C.	Pvt.	H, 32nd Iowa Inf.	81	56	1896 Mar 26	IA, 23rd, 1897
Schmidt, George		K, 3rd Mo. Cav. (died of old age)	55	67	1911 Oct 25	NE, 36th, 1912
Schmidt, Gustave	Pvt.	G, Benton Hussars	231		1910 Mar 16	IA, 37th, 1911
Schmidt, Herman		C, 35th Iowa	231		1923 Sep 14	IA, 50th, 1924
Schmidt, John		A, 57th Ill. Inf.		93	1936 Mar 9	IA, 62nd, 1936
Schmidt, John		A, 57th Ill. Inf.	68	93	1935 Mar 9	IA, 62nd, 1936
Schmidt, John D.	Musician	3rd Colo.	44		1900 Jun 18	IA, 27th, 1901

Name	Rank	Company, Regiment or Ship	Post*	Age	Death Date†	Journal
Schmidt, John D.		K, 150th Ind.	185		1921 Sep 1	KS, 41st, 1922
Schmidt, R.	Band	B, 7th Iowa Inf.	231		1920 Mar 9	IA, 47th, 1921
Schmidt, Wm. H.	Pvt.	H, 38th Iowa Inf.	495		1916 Dec	IA, 43rd, 1917
Schminkey, Samuel		B, 9th Iowa Cav.	235		4th quarter 1884	IA, 11th, 1885
Schmitt, Wm.		I, 13th Kans. Inf. (died of Bright's disease)	48		1894 Sep 5	NE, 19th, 1895
Schmitten, Fritz	Capt.	M, 2nd Mo. Art.	163		1911 Dec 26	IA, 39th, 1913
Schnack, John		B, 79th Ill.	8		1915 Jul 9	KS, 35th, 1916
Schnack, Peter		B, 79th Ill.	8		1917 Jan 16	KS, 37th, 1918
Schnatterly, H.L.		H, 46th Ind.	241		1908[1909?] Feb 5	KS, 29th, 1910
Schneider, Adam	Pvt.	B, 22nd Iowa Vol. Inf.	8		1924 Mar 23	IA, 51st, 1925
Schneider, John		H, 20th Ky. (died at Lawrence)	12		1895 Sep	KS, 15th, 1896
Schneider, Mike	Pvt.	1st Wis. Hvy. Art.	3		1930 Dec 10	IA, 57th, 1931
Schneidewind, Otto		G, 16th Mich. Inf. (died of apoplexy)	7	65	1903 Jul 9	NE, 28th, 1904
Schnell, J.F.		M, 1st Penn.	32		1927	KS, 47th, 1928
Schneph, F.	Pvt.	I, 27th Wis. Inf.	152		1912 May 10	IA, 39th, 1913
Schnepp, Isaac, see Scnepp, Isaac						
Schnier, F.W.		D, 35th Iowa	231		1923 Jul 3	IA, 50th, 1924
Schnoering, John	Pvt.	E, 5th Iowa Cav.	70		1919 Jul	IA, 46th, 1920
Schober, P.F.	Sergt.	G, 15th N.Y. Art.	7	55	1890 Mar 28	IA, 17th, 1891
Schoeb, Wm.		D, 1st Neb. Cav.	105		1921	KS, 41st, 1922
Schoeck, Jacob G.		E, 11th Ind.	55		1915 Oct 28	KS, 35th, 1916
Schoeming, Henry	Pvt.	K, 10th Iowa Inf.	1	59	1893 Aug 12	IA, 20th, 1894
Schoen, John		L, 3rd Ill. Cav.	43		1919 May 6	KS, 39th, 1920
Schoen, W.	Pvt.	I, 16th Iowa Inf.	55		1910 May 6	IA, 37th, 1911
Schoenaman, W.D., see Scheonaman, W.D.						
Schoffler, Sol H.		L, 6th U.S. Cav.	25		1917 Nov 12	KS, 37th, 1918
Schofield, Darius	Asst. Surg.	47th U.S.C.T.	108	59	1893 Apr 15	IA, 20th, 1894
Schofield, G.W.	Pvt.	K, 4th Iowa Cav.	153		1913 Nov 13	IA, 40th, 1914
Scholes, A.J.			7		1900-1901	IA, 27th, 1901
Scholl, J.L.	Pvt.	L, 7th Ill. Cav.	56		1912 Jan 7	IA, 39th, 1913
Scholler, John			7		1886	NE, 11th, 1887
Scholtz, Robert			170		1899	IA, 26th, 1900
Schomberg, Jacob	Pvt.	C, 35th Iowa Inf.	231		1918 Dec 26	IA, 45th, 1919
Schoning, John	Pvt.	M, 2nd Mo. Lt. Art.	88		1912 May 23	IA, 39th, 1913
Schonwrtz, Geo.		D, 166th Penn.	87		1922 Feb 11	KS, 42nd, 1923
Schooler, Lewis, Dr.	Corp.	A, 145th Ind. Inf.	12		1928 Oct 10	IA, 55th, 1929
Schooley, I.N.	Pvt.	K, 8th Iowa Cav.	403		1911 Sep 14	IA, 38th, 1912
Schooltree, John	Pvt.	E, 28th Iowa Inf.	183	62	1889 Sep 7	IA, 16th, 1890
Schoon, W.H.		F, 72nd Ind. Inf.	20		1901 Mar 16	KS, 21st, 1902
Schoononn, G.A.	Pvt.	A, 28th Iowa	98		1924 Oct 19	IA, 51st, 1925
Schoonover, N.B.	Pvt.	G, 132nd Penn. Inf.	111		1906 Aug 9	IA, 33rd, 1907
Schoonover, Oscar A.	Pvt.	50th N.Y. Eng.	465		1928 Nov 1	IA, 55th, 1929
Schoothal, Henry	Pvt.	M, 6th Iowa Cav.	78		1923 Feb 24	IA, 50th, 1924
Schott, George	Pvt.	K, 192nd Ohio Inf.	231	86	1935 Feb 7	IA, 65th, 1939
Schott, Joseph	Pvt.	H, 26th Iowa Inf.	92		1909 Dec 30	IA, 36th, 1910
Schotte, Chas.		B, 66th Ill.	25		1922 Mar 18	NE, 47th, 1923
Schotte, Chas.		B, 66th Ill.	25		1922 Mar 18	NE, 47th, 1923
Schrader, Chris. D.		F, 10th N.Y.	301		1897 Jul 1	KS, 17th, 1898
Schrader, John J., see Shrader, John J.						
Schrawger, A.F.		C, 185th & 154th Ohio (died of apoplexy)	27	84	1922 Dec 22	NE, 47th, 1923
Schreckengast, Samuel, see Shreckengast, Samuel						
Schreener, Gustave	Pvt.	D, 15th N.Y. Art.	88		1915 Jan 29	IA, 42nd, 1916
Schreiner, E.L.	Pvt.	F, 1st Iowa Inf.	337		1911 May 8	IA, 38th, 1912
Schreiner, J.A.	Pvt.	45th Iowa Inf.	20		1916 Sep	IA, 43rd, 1917
Schrend, J.W.		H, 9th Ohio Cav.	7		1925 Aug	NE, 50th, 1926
Schreurs, Garrett	Pvt.	A, 7th Iowa Inf.	231		1915 Sep 7	IA, 42nd, 1916
Schreve, T.J.	Lieut.	E, 83rd Ind.	81		1923 Jun 11	IA, 50th, 1924
Schriber, Henry	Pvt.	M, 4th Cal.	19		1924 Mar 3	IA, 51st, 1925

Name	Rank	Company, Regiment or Ship	Post*	Age	Death Date†	Journal
Schriddie, Henry		H, 43rd Ill.	52		1916 Sep 28	KS, 36th, 1917
Schrimper, Wm.	Pvt.	F, 20th Iowa Inf.	206		1913 Jan 30	IA, 40th, 1914
Schriver, Nicholas	Pvt.	M, 2nd Mo. Lt. Art.	327		1923 Jan 7	IA, 50th, 1924
Schrode, C.	Pvt.	E, 42nd Ill. Inf.	512		1913 Jul 10	IA, 40th, 1914
Schroder, A.W.	Pvt.	C, 26th Iowa	92		1921 Apr 27	IA, 48th, 1922
Schroder, Aug.		10th Wis. Inf.	311		1901	NE, 26th, 1902
Schroder, Chas.	Pvt.	C, 46th Ill. Inf.	3		1913 Oct 27	IA, 40th, 1914
Schroder, Jacob	Pvt.	C, 10th Ill. Inf.	440		1917 Sep 16	IA, 44th, 1918
Schrody, Wm.	Pvt.	A, 27th Iowa Inf.	194		1913 Dec 2	IA, 40th, 1914
Schroeder, Carl		Wis.	311	65	1907 Dec 29	NE, 32nd, 1908
Schroeder, J.H.	Pvt.	H, 10th Iowa Inf.	24		1909 Sep 15	IA, 36th, 1910
Schroger, William		B, 165th Penn.	71		1905 Oct 10	KS, 25th, 1906
Schrorder, August	Pvt.	E, 2nd Iowa Cav.	261		1916 Dec 30	IA, 43rd, 1917
Schroyer, Samuel		I, 15th Ind. Cav.	9		1911 Oct 5	KS, 31st, 1912
Schroyer, William		E, 13th Kans. Inf.	9		1911 Sep 25	KS, 31st, 1912
Schuele, Adolph	2nd Lieut.	C, 13th Ill. Cav.	1		1888	KS, 8th, 1889
Schuelte, Conrad		C, 21st Iowa	69		1911 Jun 11	KS, 31st, 1912
Schuittger, Frederick	Pvt.	A, 57th Ill. Vol. Inf.	5		1901 Jul 16	IA, 28th, 1902
Schuler, John		2nd Neb.	84	67	1901 Mar	NE, 26th, 1902
Schuler, Joseph		A, 4th Iowa Cav.		89	1936 Feb 17	IA, 62nd, 1936
Schuler, Joseph		A, 4th Iowa Cav.	68	89	1935 Feb 17	IA, 62nd, 1936
Schuler, Joseph A.		Penn. Cav. 42nd Ind.	14		1896 Jul 6	KS, 16th, 1897
Schull, John	1st Lieut.	A, 2nd Kans. Inf.	257	75	1891 Dec 3	IA, 18th, 1892
Schultz, August		C, 32nd Ind. Inf. (died at Canton)	84		1895 Jan 28	KS, 15th, 1896
Schultz, August F.		D, 1st Iowa Inf.	127		1902 Apr 8	KS, 22nd, 1903
Schultz, C.		I, 2nd Iowa Cav.	134		1925	NE, 50th, 1926
Schultz, George C.	Capt.	171st Penn. Inf.	389	64	1885 Nov 23	IA, 12th, 1886
Schultz, Philip	Pvt.	I, 89th Ill. Inf.	200		1927 Nov 8	IA, 54th, 1928
Schultz, R.	Pvt.	C, 36th Iowa Inf.	434		1929 Sep 15	IA, 56th, 1930
Schumacher, Leo	Capt.	A, 16th Iowa Inf.	1		1912 Dec 16	IA, 39th, 1913
Schundemier, Jacob			38		1911 1st term	IA, 38th, 1912
Schurdevin, Germain	Pvt.	C, 152nd Ind. Inf.	97		1912 Oct 14	IA, 39th, 1913
Schurr, Godfrey		K, 178th Ohio	47		1914 Mar 20	KS, 34th, 1915
Schute, Richard		A, 42nd Ohio	52		1908 Jun 24	KS, 28th, 1909
Schuyler, H.P.	Pvt.	I, 95th Ill.	235		1923 Feb 24	IA, 50th, 1924
Schuyter, H.P.	Pvt.	A, 95th Ill. Inf.	231		1923 Feb 22	IA, 50th, 1924
Schwalbagh, Joseph		A, 9th Ill. (died of old age at Soldiers & Sailors Home, Milford)		76	1907 Jan 11	NE, 31st, 1907
Schwanp, Joseph		A, 153rd Penn.	69		1923 Aug 23	KS, 44th, 1925
Schwartes, Carl W.		K, 53rd Ill. Inf. A, 6th West Va.	16		1889	KS, 9th, 1890
Schwartz, Chas.		gunboat & Ohio Inf.	499		1913 Jun 22	IA, 40th, 1914
Schwartz, J.C.			185		1883	KS, 3rd, 1884
Schwartz, John F.		D, 12th Kans.	40		1908 Feb 14	KS, 28th, 1909
Schwartz, John N.		Kans. Militia	196		1910 Oct 6	KS, 30th, 1911
Schwartz, William		H, 1st Ohio Cav.	190		1928 Jun 18	KS, 48th, 1929
Schwarz, Chas.		Dept. of Ordnance (died of old age)	89	83	1922 May 12	NE, 47th, 1923
Schwarzott, John		6th Mo. Inf.	380		1901 Jul 2	KS, 21st, 1902
Schwaup, Joseph		A, 153rd Penn.	69		1923 Aug 25	KS, 46th, 1927
Schweager, Wm.	Pvt.	E, 21st Iowa	70		1907 Nov 27	IA, 34th, 1908
Schwesinger, Erhard C.		*S.S. Lexington*		96	1938 Mar 4	IA, 64th, 1938
Schwickler, John	Pvt.	A, 46th Iowa Inf.	452		1924 Mar 16	IA, 51st, 1925
Scllan, W.R.		F, 9th Mich. Inf.	5		1906 May 16	IA, 33rd, 1907
Scnepp, Isaac	Pvt.	D, 154th Ind. Inf.	130		1928 Jan 6	IA, 55th, 1929
Scofield, G.D.	Pvt.	H, 1st Iowa Lt. Art.	500		1920 Dec 30	IA, 47th, 1921
Scofield, Jos. P.	Pvt.	K, 13th Wis. Inf.	142		1918	IA, 45th, 1919
Scofield, P.D.	Sergt.	E, 27th Wis.	12		1926 May 11	IA, 53rd, 1927
Scofield, R.L.		B, 52nd N.Y.	113		1914 Jan 10	KS, 34th, 1915
Scoles, C.W.	Corp.	G, 18th Iowa Inf.	49		1899 Dec 31	IA, 26th, 1900
Scoles, H.J.	Asst. Surg.	40th Iowa Inf.	49	72	1897 Jan 25	IA, 23rd, 1897
Scollard, Patrick		I, 2nd Neb. Cav. (died of apoplexy)	116	50	1895 May 1	NE, 20th, 1896

*See Appendix A, B or C for roster of post names and locations.
†See Introduction for note regarding recording of death date.

Name	Rank	Company, Regiment or Ship	Post*	Age	Death Date†	Journal
Scothorn, L.M.		B, 21st Ohio Inf.	25	76	1919 Mar 12	NE, 44th, 1920
Scott, A.J.	Pvt.	A, 11th Ill. Inf.	316		1897-1898	IA, 24th, 1898
Scott, A.J.	Lieut.	C, 24th Iowa Inf.	322		1916 Oct 16	IA, 43rd, 1917
Scott, A.L.		B, 4th Ohio	4		1920 Sep 17	KS, 40th, 1921
Scott, A.P.		E, 23rd N.Y.	35		1913 Jan 7	KS, 33rd, 1914
Scott, A.R.		C, 54th Penn. Inf.	84		1917 Apr 28	NE, 42nd, 1918
Scott, A.W.	Major	42nd U.S.	488		1899 Mar 18	KS, 19th, 1900
Scott, Albert		A, 105th Ill. Inf. (died of heart failure)	107	62	1906 Sep 11	NE, 31st, 1907
Scott, Albert Winfield		A, 46th Wis. Inf.	7	88	1937 Jun 22	IA, 64th, 1938
Scott, Alex O.	Sergt.	E, 157th Ohio Inf.	158		1904 Sep 18	IA, 31st, 1905
Scott, B.F.	Pvt.	C, 141st Ohio	275		1924 Jul 12	IA, 51st, 1925
Scott, B.F.		F, 113th Ill. Inf.	16		1925 Jun 20	KS, 45th, 1926
Scott, B.R.		B, 77th Ohio Inf.	7		1922 Nov 10	KS, 45th, 1926
Scott, C.C.	Corp.	G, 46th Iowa Inf.	297		1921 Jan 10	IA, 48th, 1922
Scott, Charles A.		H, 80th Ohio	134		1919 Nov 16	KS, 39th, 1920
Scott, D.O.	Pvt.	B, 19th Wis. Inf.	469		1910 Jun 1	IA, 37th, 1911
Scott, Daniel B.	Pvt.	I, 46th Iowa	111		1926 May 6	IA, 53rd, 1927
Scott, Edward B.		K, 6th U.S. Inf.	9		1921 Sep 9	KS, 41st, 1922
Scott, F.A.	Pvt.	H, 62nd Mo. Inf.	71	53	1896 May 11	IA, 23rd, 1897
Scott, G.W.	Pvt.	D, 9th Iowa Inf.	502		1906 Jan 24	IA, 33rd, 1907
Scott, G.W.		B, 80th Ohio	325		1906 Aug 25	KS, 26th, 1907
Scott, G.W.		E, 4th Mo.	130		1926 Nov 17	KS, 46th, 1927
Scott, Gary T.		A, 9th Conn.	17		1912 Jan 7	KS, 32nd, 1913
Scott, Geo. G.	Pvt.	A, 44th Iowa	78		1923 Jan 6	IA, 50th, 1924
Scott, Geo. H.	Pvt.	K, 105th Ill. Inf.	156		1927	IA, 54th, 1928
Scott, Geo. M.	Pvt.	C, 96th Ohio Inf.	497		1908 Jul 25	IA, 35th, 1909
Scott, Geo. W.	Corp.	H, 6th Mo. Inf.	11		1910 Dec 2	IA, 37th, 1911
Scott, George	Pvt.	I, 24th Iowa Inf.	255		1925	IA, 52nd, 1926
Scott, Grant		B, 1st Conn.	3		1893 Feb 15	KS, 13th, 1894
Scott, H.		D, 14th Iowa	180		1915 Dec 6	KS, 35th, 1916
Scott, H.C.		E, 23rd N.Y.	35		1908 Nov 18	KS, 28th, 1909
Scott, H.W.		H, 105th Iowa	38		1926 Aug	NE, 51st, 1927
Scott, Harmon		H, 3rd Ind. H.G.[Indian Home Guard?]	51		1891 Aug 14	KS, 11th, 1892
Scott, Harper	Pvt.	A, 93rd Ill. Inf.	98		1904 Dec 4	IA, 31st, 1905
Scott, Hiram		B, 45th Iowa (died of old age)	38	82	1925 Feb	NE, 50th, 1926
Scott, Hugh		D, 14th Iowa	180		1916 Jan 11	KS, 36th, 1917
Scott, Hugh P.	Pvt.	Ind. Battery	1		1920 Jul 22	IA, 47th, 1921
Scott, Ira		L, 2nd Ohio Cav.	55		1914 Feb 15	KS, 34th, 1915
Scott, J.		D, 122nd U.S. Cav.	36		1906 Sep	KS, 26th, 1907
Scott, J.A.	Pvt.	A, 60th N.J. Inf.	96		1930 Jul 6	IA, 57th, 1931
Scott, J.A.		C, 129th Ill. Inf.	17		1914 Mar 17	KS, 34th, 1915
Scott, J.A.		1st Va. Inf. (died of dropsy & old age)	9		1894 Sep	NE, 19th, 1895
Scott, J.C.		126th N.Y.	132		1917 Oct 2	KS, 37th, 1918
Scott, J.H.		K, 29th Ill.	4		1919 Jan 14	KS, 39th, 1920
Scott, J.M.	Pvt.	C, 39th Iowa Inf.	54		1929 Jun 10	IA, 56th, 1930
Scott, J.M.		14th Ohio Battery (died of heart failure)	152	61	1905[1904?] Dec 4	NE, 29th, 1905
Scott, J.W.		H, 5th Kans. Cav.	4		1916 Jul 16	KS, 36th, 1917
Scott, Jacob	Pvt.	G, 12th Wis.	150		1923 Feb 10	IA, 50th, 1924
Scott, James	Corp.	F, 15th Iowa Inf.	15	46	1887 Apr 2	IA, 14th, 1888
Scott, James	Pvt.	K, 77th Ohio Inf.	472		1916 May 10	IA, 43rd, 1917
Scott, James		K, 15th Kans. Cav. (died at Gardner)	447		1895 Feb	KS, 15th, 1896
Scott, James F.		H, 160th Ohio	260		1917 Aug 22	KS, 37th, 1918
Scott, Jason	Pvt.	H, 38th Ohio Inf.	91		1928 Apr 25	IA, 55th, 1929
Scott, Job		B, 91st Ohio Inf. (died of heart failure)	134	50	1896 Feb 4	NE, 21st, 1897
Scott, John	Capt.	H, 50th Ind.	17		1893 Feb 26	KS, 13th, 1894
Scott, John		L, 9th Penn. Cav.	158		1918 Jan 10	KS, 38th, 1919
Scott, John		123rd Ill.	59		1928 Mar 15	KS, 48th, 1929
Scott, John H.		A, 13th Kans.	493		1922 Jan 30	KS, 42nd, 1923
Scott, John H.	Pvt.	M, 1st Hvy. Art. (died of pneumonia)	13	45	1884 Nov	NE, 9th, 1885
Scott, John J.		D, 13th Kans.	93		1902 Jun 16	KS, 22nd, 1903
Scott, John W.		10th Kans.	51		1899 Jan 19	KS, 19th, 1900
Scott, John W.		F, 54th Ind. Inf.	25	81	1918 Oct 28	NE, 43rd, 1919

*See Appendix A, B or C for roster of post names and locations.
†See Introduction for note regarding recording of death date.

Name	Rank	Company, Regiment or Ship	Post*	Age	Death Date†	Journal
Scott, Jos. W.	Pvt.	A, 7th Mo. Cav.	177		1911 May 26	IA, 38th, 1912
Scott, Joseph		F, 122nd U.S.C.T.	321		1909 Dec 3	KS, 29th, 1910
Scott, Joseph A.		18th Ind. Bat.	46		1924 Jun 7	KS, 44th, 1925
Scott, M.		I, 59th Ohio Inf.	173		1913 Oct 8	NE, 38th, 1914
Scott, M.M.			1		1927 May 26	KS, 47th, 1928
Scott, M.M.		I, 68th Ohio Inf.	27		1892 Sep 20	NE, 17th, 1893
Scott, M.P.		24th Iowa (died of old age)	13	82	1923 Feb 16	NE, 48th, 1924
Scott, Matthew H.		L, 1st Iowa (died of old age)	22	81	1921 Dec 20	NE, 46th, 1922
Scott, N.M.	Pvt.	H, 6th Kans. Cav.	122		1910 Jan 4	IA, 37th, 1911
Scott, N.S.		112th N.Y. Inf.	25		1892	NE, 17th, 1893
Scott, Newton	Pvt.	A, 36th Iowa Inf.	173		1925 Mar 2	IA, 52nd, 1926
Scott, O.M.	Pvt.	F, 13th N.Y.	105		1899	NE, 24th, 1900
Scott, R.A.		C, 9th Ill. Cav.	1		1900 Sep 22	KS, 20th, 1901
Scott, R.M., Rev.		E, 132nd Ill. Inf.	65		1925 Oct 29	KS, 45th, 1926
Scott, Robert		B, 19th Ill. (died of cancer of stomach)	95		1914 Nov 20	NE, 39th, 1915
Scott, Robert J.		F, 12th Mo. Cav. (former member; died at Beaver City)	163		1936 Nov 29	NE, 61st, 1937
Scott, S.G.	Musician	33rd Ill. Inf.	87	80	1892 Mar 18	IA, 18th, 1892
Scott, S.H.		18th Ind. Bat.	46		1927 Aug 20	KS, 47th, 1928
Scott, S.S.		L, 16th Kans. Cav.	96		1925 Mar 10	KS, 45th, 1926
Scott, Sam			25	76	1910 Dec 10	NE, 35th, 1911
Scott, Sam'l	Pvt.	F, 34th Iowa Inf.	192		1903 Nov 20	IA, 30th, 1904
Scott, Samuel	Pvt.	B, 8th Iowa Cav.	19		1916 Jun 21	IA, 43rd, 1917
Scott, T.H.	Pvt.	A, 30th Wis. Inf.	2	59	1888 May 26	IA, 15th, 1889
Scott, T.J.	Pvt.	D, 4th Iowa Inf.	259		1905 May 30	IA, 32nd, 1906
Scott, T.J.	Pvt.	B, 3rd Iowa Inf.	398		1913 Feb 1	IA, 40th, 1914
Scott, Thomas		B, 51st Ind.	25		1911 Feb 3	KS, 31st, 1912
Scott, Thomas H.		G, Penn. Bat.	253		1910	KS, 30th, 1911
Scott, Thomas W.	Pvt.	A, 15th Iowa Inf.	206		1918 Aug 25	IA, 45th, 1919
Scott, Thos. J.	Pvt.	L, 6th Iowa Cav.	269		1905 Feb 5	IA, 31st, 1905
Scott, W.H.			77		1898 Jan 29	KS, 18th, 1899
Scott, W.H.		I, 8th Ind.	244		1931 Aug 24	KS, 52nd, 1933
Scott, W.H.		I, 8th Ind.	244		1931 Aug 24	KS, 51st, 1932
Scott, W.S.	Pvt.	L, 8th Iowa Cav.	337		1925 May 12	IA, 52nd, 1926
Scott, W.W.	Pvt.	D, 8th Iowa Cav.	108		1923 Mar 6	IA, 50th, 1924
Scott, W.W.			51		1896	KS, 16th, 1897
Scott, W.W.		E, 5th Kans.	16		1912 Jan 21	KS, 32nd, 1913
Scott, Waldon		F, 7th Mo.	32		1905 Sep 9	KS, 25th, 1906
Scott, William		D, 18th Ohio	7		1913 Jul 14	KS, 33rd, 1914
Scott, William		E, 155th Ohio Vol. Inf.	8		1915 Mar 26	KS, 35th, 1916
Scott, William		C, 111th Ohio Inf.	64		1925	KS, 45th, 1926
Scott, William A.		E, 15th Iowa Inf.	22		1913 Jan 11	KS, 32nd, 1913
Scott, Winfield		D, 75th Ind. 3rd Iowa Cav.	113		1917 Jan 27	KS, 37th, 1918
Scott, Wm. A.	Pvt.	I, 180th Ohio Inf.	358		1927 Jun 30	IA, 54th, 1928
Scott, Wm. A.		E, 15th Iowa	68		1913 Jan 12	KS, 33rd, 1914
Scouten, Daniel G.		C, 8th Ill.	380		1913 Aug 23	KS, 33rd, 1914
Scovel, H.J.	Pvt.	D, 4th Iowa Inf.	416	92	1931 Nov 23	IA, 58th, 1932
Scovel, Palmer F.	1st Lieut.	C, 1st Ill. Lt. Art.	18		1899 Nov 20	IA, 26th, 1900
Scovelle, F.E.	Pvt.	K, 8th Ill. Cav.	425		1905 Dec 19	IA, 32nd, 1906
Scovil, C.W.	Corp.	C, 22nd Wis. Inf.	493		1912 Jul	IA, 39th, 1913
Scovill, Frederick		I, 8th N.Y.	32		1905 Jul 5	KS, 25th, 1906
Scoville, D.A.		A, 46th Ill. Inf. (died of pneumonia)	44	61	1903 Apr	NE, 28th, 1904
Scoville, E.W.	Pvt.	A, 2nd U.S. Sharpshooters 1st Minn.	90	53	1887 Jun 15	IA, 14th, 1888
Scoville, E.W.	Pvt.	A, 2nd U.S. Sharpshooters	90	52	1887 Jun 15	IA, 17th, 1891
Scoville, G.W.	Sergt.	G, 103rd Ill. Inf.	395	61	1897 Mar 21	IA, 24th, 1898
Scranton, Albert		I, 135th Ohio	381		1906	KS, 26th, 1907
Scranton, Charles		B, 1st Mich. Cav.	185		1923 Mar 19	KS, 43rd, 1924
Scranton, George T.		H, 119th Ill. Inf.	4		1914	KS, 34th, 1915
Scranton, R.E.		K, 2nd Ohio (died of asthma, pneumonia)	228	59	1904 Mar 21	NE, 29th, 1905
Scriber, B.	Pvt.	4th Ohio Cav.	20		1905	IA, 32nd, 1906

*See Appendix A, B or C for roster of post names and locations.
†See Introduction for note regarding recording of death date.

Name	Rank	Company, Regiment or Ship	Post*	Age	Death Date†	Journal
Scribner, C.L.		H, 1st Maine Cav.	10		1927 Aug 7	NE, 52nd, 1928
Scribner, H.W.		C, 13th Vt.	46		1933	KS, 53rd, 1934
Scribner, H.W.		C, 13th Vt. Inf.	46		1934 Oct 4	KS, 54th, 1935
Scritchfield, Wm.	Pvt.	I, 4th Iowa Inf.	325		1912 Sep 19	IA, 39th, 1913
Scritsmeier, R.P.		C, 1st Wis. Hvy. Art.	98		1933	NE, 58th, 1934
Scroggins, Y.A.		B, 50th Ill.	147		1922 Jun	KS, 42nd, 1923
Scroggs, W.H.	Lieut. Col.	C, 81st Ohio Inf.	116		1921 Jul 13	IA, 48th, 1922
Scudder, Joseph S.		K, 1st U.S. Chas.	145		1916 Nov 26	KS, 36th, 1917
Scull, James M.		H, 45th Iowa Inf.	135	91	1937 Feb 19	IA, 64th, 1938
Scullen, Wm. H.	Pvt.	1st Ill. Art.	88		1923 Dec 10	IA, 50th, 1924
Seabury, Jerome			338		1909 Jun 17	IA, 36th, 1910
Seachrist, John W.		K, 154th Penn.	500		1916 Apr 10	KS, 36th, 1917
Seacord, James C.	Pvt.	E, 151st Ill. Inf.	23	74	1894 Dec 17	IA, 21st, 1895
Seafers, Isaac		B, 118th Ill. Inf.	18		1940 Aug 20	KS, 60th, 1941
Seagrane, W.A.		A, 9th Ohio (died of pontinesus)	32		1890	KS, 10th, 1891
Seagraves, W.L.		G, 57th Ind. Inf. D, 6th Ind. Inf.	17		1912 Oct 18	KS, 32nd, 1913
Seales, J.N.	Pvt.	A, 9th No. Va.	242		1924 Feb 4	IA, 51st, 1925
Seals, J.M.	Pvt.	A, 9th West Va. Inf.	242		1925 Feb 4	IA, 52nd, 1926
Seaman, August			6		1908	IA, 35th, 1909
Seaman, C.O.	Pvt.	A, 4th Minn. Cav.	12	83	1931 Nov 25	IA, 58th, 1932
Seaman, Geo.		G, 2nd Neb. Cav.	130		1918 Nov 8	KS, 38th, 1919
Seaman, Horace	Pvt.	E, 118th N.Y. Inf.	64	59	1887 Oct 16	IA, 14th, 1888
Seaman, J.J.	Capt.	C, 40th Ind. Inf.	186		1921 May 30	IA, 48th, 1922
Seaman, John		D, 3rd Ohio Cav.	1		1913 Sep 25	KS, 33rd, 1914
Seaman, John H.		B, 88th Ohio Inf. (died at Girard, Kans.; buried at Girard Cemetery)	49		1894 Apr 2	KS, 14th, 1895
Seaman, R.G.	Pvt.	F, 88th Ohio Inf.	23	87	1931 Dec 16	IA, 58th, 1932
Seaman, W.P.		C, 111th Mo. Inf.	23		1908 Oct 21	IA, 35th, 1909
Seaman, William E.		F, 89th Ill.	85		1915 Mar 18	KS, 35th, 1916
Seamands, M.V.	Pvt.	M, 2nd Iowa Cav.	461		1916 Jun 15	IA, 43rd, 1917
Seamond, S.	Pvt.	M, 2nd Iowa Cav.	93		1921 May 30	IA, 48th, 1922
Seapy, James		A, 105th Ill. Inf.	151		1900 Mar 12	KS, 20th, 1901
Search, James W.		F, 3rd Ill. Cav. (born in Pennsylvania; died of paralysis at Soldiers & Sailors Home Hospital, Burkett; buried at Home Cemetery)		70	1907 Jan 31	NE, 31st, 1907
Search, W.R.	Pvt.	F, 50th Ill.	22		1924 Dec 27	IA, 51st, 1925
Searcy, Edward C.		L, 59th Ill.	142		1913 Mar 31	KS, 32nd, 1913
Searcy, Edward C.		L, 59th Ill.	142		1913 Mar 31	KS, 33rd, 1914
Searing, J.W.	Pvt.	I, 29th N.J. Inf.	22		1917 Jan 12	IA, 44th, 1918
Searle, A.P.			392		1907 1st term	IA, 34th, 1908
Searle, B.W.	Pvt.	I, 1st Iowa Cav.	69		1911 Feb 16	IA, 38th, 1912
Searles, B.	Pvt.		264		1912	IA, 39th, 1913
Searles, B.	Pvt.	B, 5th N.Y. Art.	264		1913	IA, 40th, 1914
Searles, G.W.		C, 21st Mich. Inf.	93		1912 Jul 28	KS, 32nd, 1913
Searles, Jacob	Pvt.	H, 3rd Ohio Cav.	235		1918 Jan 8	IA, 45th, 1919
Searles, James M.	Pvt.	C, 21st Wis. Inf.	235		1913 Aug 1	IA, 40th, 1914
Sears, Francis A.		A, 67th Ind. Inf.	65		1886	KS, 6th, 1887
Sears, Geo.	Pvt.	H, 2nd Iowa Cav.	130		1919 May 13	IA, 46th, 1920
Sears, J.M.	Pvt.	F, 15th Ill. Inf.	392		1900 Sep 11	IA, 27th, 1901
Sears, J.R.	Pvt.	F, 25th Ill. Inf.	497		1930 May 7	IA, 57th, 1931
Sears, John W.		C, 1st Ky. Cav.	81		1913 Sep 1	KS, 33rd, 1914
Sears, Sackett			6		1899 Mar	IA, 26th, 1900
Sears, Thomas B.	Sailor		12		1925 Dec 9	KS, 45th, 1926
Searson, Edwin		B, 148th Penn. Inf.	11	65	1910 Jan 22	NE, 35th, 1911
Seatin, Sam'l		G, 3rd Kans. Inf.	12		1899 Dec 18	KS, 19th, 1900
Seaton, J.C.		G, 9th Penn. Res. Corps	63		1919 May 22	KS, 39th, 1920
Seaton, John		B, 22nd Ill. Inf.	93		1912 Jan 12	KS, 32nd, 1913
Seaton, Lambertson M.		H, 103rd Penn.	1		1928 Jan 2	KS, 48th, 1929
Seaton, Lee R.		C, 2nd Iowa Cav.	2		4th quarter 1883	IA, 10th, 1884
Seaton, W.W.	Pvt.	D, 74th Ill. Inf.	59		1905 Feb 15	IA, 32nd, 1906
Seatts, E.R.	Pvt.	H, 35th Iowa	191		1907 Jul 12	IA, 34th, 1908

*See Appendix A, B or C for roster of post names and locations.
†See Introduction for note regarding recording of death date.
485

Name	Rank	Company, Regiment or Ship	Post*	Age	Death Date†	Journal
Seaver, B.R.		K, 2nd U.S. Cav.	292		1892 Sep 9	NE, 17th, 1893
Seaver, Leonard	Pvt.	E, 58th N.Y. Inf.	74		1917 Sep 19	IA, 44th, 1918
Seavey, W.H.	Pvt.	1st Co. Andrews Sharpshooters	35	52	1894 Mar 27	IA, 21st, 1895
Seaward, J.C.		E, 13th Ind.	14		1915 Nov 24	KS, 35th, 1916
Seber, Jacoq	Pvt.	A, 152nd N.Y. Inf.	101	49	1889 Feb 14	IA, 15th, 1889
Seberg, John		H, 28th Ill. Inf. (member at large)			1941 Aug[Apr?] 25	NE, 66th, 1942
Sebern, J.J.	Pvt.	G, 132nd Ind. Inf.	113		1917 Nov 20	IA, 44th, 1918
Secor, Abram	Corp.	F, 1st N.Y. Eng.	222	49	1890 Dec 18	IA, 17th, 1891
Secord, Robert A.		G, 126th Ill. (died of old age)	44[24?]	83	1909 Jul 5	NE, 34th, 1910
Sedam, Abram	Pvt.	H, 45th Ill. Inf.	22		1916 Feb 26	IA, 43rd, 1917
Sedam, Thomas R.		B, 126th Ill. Inf. (died of old age)	28	86	1912 Jul	NE, 37th, 1913
Sedan, Frank		B, 76th Ill. Inf.	174		1899 Mar 12	KS, 19th, 1900
Sedgwick, E.W.		A, 61st Mass. Inf.	190		1918 Jan 25	IA, 45th, 1919
Sedgwick, T.H.	Pvt.	D, 95th Ill. Inf.	88		1901 Apr 18	IA, 27th, 1901
Sedgwick, Thomas N.		B, 36th Ill. Inf.	190	97	1938 Jun 29	IA, 64th, 1938
Sedore, James		7th Ohio Lt. Bat.	2		1893	NE, 18th, 1894
Sedoris, A.I.		C, 2nd Neb. (died of dropsy)	63	88	1917 Aug 29	NE, 42nd, 1918
See, A.N.		I, 136th Penn.	127		1924 Dec 17	KS, 44th, 1925
See, Silas N.	Pvt.	K, 32nd Iowa Inf.	31		1912 Jan	IA, 39th, 1913
Seeber, F.C.		C, 10th Ill. Inf.	52		1908 Nov 15	KS, 28th, 1909
Seeber, Gideon L.	Pvt.	E, 12th Iowa Inf.	176	53	1894 Feb 22	IA, 20th, 1894
Seebers, Henry	Pvt.	11th Md. Inf.	68	86	1932 May 28	IA, 59th, 1933
Seeds, Jesse		I, 43rd Ind.	257		1908 Apr 28	KS, 28th, 1909
Seefridge, John T.		C, 91st Ill.	14		1913 Jun 11	KS, 33rd, 1914
Seegriff, M.R.	Pvt.	G, 89th Ill. Inf.	466		1921 Jul 8	IA, 48th, 1922
Seeley, B.L.		M, 10th N.Y. Hvy. Art.	71		1921 Dec 3	KS, 41st, 1922
Seeley, Enoch S.	Pvt.	I, 17th Ill. Inf.	440	56	1891 Oct 21	IA, 18th, 1892
Seeley, F.M.		K, 1st Wis.	69		1922 Mar 28	KS, 42nd, 1923
Seeley, Fredrick O.		2nd Conn. Lt. B.	65		1908 Jul 23	KS, 28th, 1909
Seeley, John		H, 1st Mich.	147		1914 Dec 16	KS, 34th, 1915
Seeley, R.P.	Col.	G, 45th Ill. Inf.	29	52	1888 Mar 13	IA, 15th, 1889
Seeley, W.H.	Pvt.	I, 78th N.Y. Inf.	327		1921 Dec 10	IA, 48th, 1922
Seely, Levi		B, 104th Ohio	274		1916 Sep 27	KS, 36th, 1917
Seelye, William H.		H, 62nd Ill.	1		1937 Jan 26	NE, 62nd, 1938
Seems, T.	Pvt.	B, 5th Penn. Inf.	17		1904 Aug 11	IA, 31st, 1905
Seeright, D.J.	Lieut.		79		1918 Dec 3	IA, 45th, 1919
Sees, John		H, 21st Iowa	59		1924 Jul 9	KS, 44th, 1925
Sees, Wm. E.		K, 206th Penn.	131		1904 Apr 25	KS, 24th, 1905
Sefort, John	Pvt.	F, 194th N.Y. Inf.	216	76	1899 Mar 22	IA, 25th, 1899
Seggerman, John		K, 108th Ill. Vol. Inf. (died of paralysis)	77	72	1910 Aug 7	NE, 35th, 1911
Sego, J.M.	Pvt.	C, 7th Iowa Cav.	7		1929 Aug 7	IA, 56th, 1930
Segrin, John	Pvt.	D, 32nd Ill. Inf.	347		1905 May 30	IA, 32nd, 1906
Segrist, Samuel		A, 28th Iowa	46		1928 Feb 5	KS, 48th, 1929
Segster, Joshua		G, 74th Ill. Inf.	113		1909 May 17	KS, 29th, 1910
Seibel, A.	Corp.	F, 8th Iowa Inf.	124		1923 Feb 3	IA, 50th, 1924
Seibert, John C.	Pvt.	C, 31st Iowa Inf.	12		1910 Jul 11	IA, 37th, 1911
Seibert, William K.		E, 10th Wis.	1		1890	KS, 10th, 1891
Seidle, J.M.		C, 8th Col.	50		1909 Feb	KS, 29th, 1910
Seidler, Ferdinand	Pvt.	F, 14th U.S. Inf.	322		1917 Sep 20	IA, 44th, 1918
Seifken, Hero S.		G, 10th Ill.	60		1933 Dec 2	NE, 58th, 1934
Seigle, George F.		27th N.Y. Bat.	100		1912 May 26	KS, 32nd, 1913
Seigler, A.E.		2nd Mo. State Militia	25		1919 Oct 9	KS, 39th, 1920
Seiler, John	Pvt.	B, 35th Iowa Inf.	231		1905 Dec 12	IA, 32nd, 1906
Seitz, Frederick	Pvt.	D, 20th Iowa Inf.	284	69	1894 Jan 28	IA, 20th, 1894
Seitz, J.L.		K, 52nd Ill.	87		1928 Sep 30	KS, 48th, 1929
Seitz, Oscar		Mo. Battery	127		1906 Jul 8	KS, 26th, 1907
Selby, J.W.		H, 186th Ohio	271		1916 Sep 15	KS, 36th, 1917
Sellars, I.N.		15th Iowa	43		1923 May 29	IA, 50th, 1924
Selleck, Albert			464		1892 Jan 20	KS, 12th, 1893
Sellens, Thomas		C, 7th Ind. Inf.	152		1901 Oct 14	KS, 21st, 1902
Sellers, Andrew J.		I, 30th Iowa	1		1930	KS, 50th, 1931
Sellers, Edward P.	1st Sergt.	I, 93rd Ill. Inf.	283		1901 Dec 1	IA, 28th, 1902

See Appendix A, B or C for roster of post names and locations.
†*See Introduction for note regarding recording of death date.*

Name	Rank	Company, Regiment or Ship	Post*	Age	Death Date†	Journal
Sellers, John		H, 21st Penn. Cav.	475		1893 Aug 13	KS, 13th, 1894
Sellers, S.F.		H, 48th Ill.	50		1902 Jul 15	KS, 22nd, 1903
Sellman, C.O.	Pvt.	E, 40th Iowa Inf.	16	43	1886 Jun 13	IA, 13th, 1887
Sellon, W.R., see Scllan, W.R.						
Sells, David		I, 7th Cal. Inf.	380		1901 Feb 6	KS, 21st, 1902
Sells, Emanuel	Pvt.	K, 43rd Ohio Inf.	243	64	1887 Apr 10	IA, 14th, 1888
Sells, George A.		G, 13th Iowa	8		1896 Mar 30	KS, 16th, 1897
Sells, Lewis R.		L, 11th Mo. Cav. (died at Douglass, Kans.; buried at R.C. Township Cemetery)	97		1894 Oct 4	KS, 14th, 1895
Selly, Tallmon	Pvt.	C, 13th Ill. Inf.	391		1927 Oct 26	IA, 54th, 1928
Semmell, William		K, 13th Iowa Inf.	7		1909 Jan 30	KS, 29th, 1910
Semple, A.E.		of Lyons, Kans.; was one of Sherman's fifers & a member of the Wichita Drum Corps			1927 Apr 20	KS, 46th, 1927
Semple, Frank H.	Pvt.	E, 19th Iowa Inf.	2	48	1889 Dec 3	IA, 16th, 1890
Semple, H.E.	Pvt.	H, 12th Penn. Inf.	515		1900 Sep 20	IA, 27th, 1901
Semple, R.H.		B, 155th Penn.	1		1926 Feb 9	KS, 46th, 1927
Semple, Smith		H, 100th Penn.	222		1892 Dec 26	KS, 12th, 1893
Senburn, W.H.		B, 1st Ill. Hvy. Art.	38		1916 Dec 21	KS, 36th, 1917
Seneff, Albert		L, 57th Penn.	69		1929 May 1	NE, 54th, 1930
Senior, M.D.L.		F, 25th Mo.	292		1890	KS, 10th, 1891
Sennott, M.M.		E, 21st Mo.	158		1925 Jan 8	KS, 45th, 1926
Senter, W.J.		K, 1st Mich.	147		1926 Jun 11	KS, 46th, 1927
Sephens, S.S.		F, 12th West Va.	240		1904 Jan 21	KS, 24th, 1905
Septer, Samuel		I, 43rd Ohio	69		1893 Aug 20	KS, 13th, 1894
Serena, George		F, 135th Penn.	45		1916 Feb 15	KS, 36th, 1917
Sergant, Ira H.		D, 4th Iowa Inf.		90	1935 Dec 5	IA, 62nd, 1936
Sergeant, Geo. H., see Sargent, Geo. H.						
Servia, A.J.	Capt.	I, 4th Penn.	51		1916 Sep 25	KS, 36th, 1917
Servis, A.E.	Saddler	I, 5th Ind. Cav.	66	56	1892 Dec 11	IA, 19th, 1893
Servis, John	Pvt.	A, 54th Ohio Inf.	83		1912 Jan 27	IA, 39th, 1913
Sessler, Martin J.M.		B, 32nd Ill.	52		1913 Apr 10	KS, 33rd, 1914
Setter, Martin		G, 7th Kans. Cav.	180		1905 Nov 10	KS, 25th, 1906
Settle, Nelson		K, 60th Ind.	42		1931	KS, 52nd, 1933
Settle, Nelson		K, 60th Ind.	42		1931	KS, 51st, 1932
Sever, H.K.	Pvt.	G, 1st Iowa Inf.	8		1905 Sep 12	IA, 32nd, 1906
Severence, G.W.		G, 3rd Ky.	71		1898 Aug 8	KS, 18th, 1899
Severide, John O.	Pvt.	E, 91st Ill. Inf.	234		1915 Dec 2	IA, 42nd, 1916
Severin, L.H.	Pvt.	A, 36th Ill. Inf.	222		1918 Dec	IA, 45th, 1919
Severson, Barnard	Pvt.	F, 38th Iowa	211		1915 Jan 13	IA, 41st, 1915
Sevrens, W.S.	Pvt.	B, 88th Ohio Inf.	252		1897 Apr 16	IA, 23rd, 1897
Seward, Atwell C.		C, 3rd Col. Cav.	28		1911 May 24	KS, 31st, 1912
Seward, George W.		K, 32nd Ohio Inf.	85		1914 Jun 29	KS, 34th, 1915
Seward, Horatio L.		L, 2nd Calif. Cav.	2		1892 May 3	NE, 17th, 1893
Seward, Thos. R.	Pvt.	I, 38th Iowa	31		1901 Aug	IA, 28th, 1902
Sewell, Francis		I, 79th U.S.C. (died at Bethel)	10		1895 May	KS, 15th, 1896
Sewell, L.A.	Pvt.	F, 1st Art.	58		1905 Mar 4	IA, 32nd, 1906
Sewell, Lawrence		D, 137th Ind.	88		1918 Jul 26	KS, 38th, 1919
Sewell, Samuel	Pvt.	B, 38th Iowa Inf.	267		1917 Jan 16	IA, 44th, 1918
Sexsmith, Joseph D.		I, 144th N.Y.	113		1920 Dec 7	KS, 40th, 1921
Sexton, Isiac		I, 23rd Ohio R. Vet.	250	68	1900 Mar 28	NE, 25th, 1901
Sexton, Wiley		B, 116th Ill.	486		1917 Nov 9	KS, 37th, 1918
Seydel, J.M.	Pvt.	G, 47th Iowa Inf.	8		1911 May 18	IA, 38th, 1912
Seydel, Wm.	Pvt.	C, 17th Wis. Inf.	333		1902 Sep 10	IA, 29th, 1903
Seymore, —		Ohio (died at Latham)	340		1895	KS, 15th, 1896
Seymour, John S.		B, 38th Wis. Inf.	235	88	1935 May 17	IA, 62nd, 1936
Seymour, Silas A.		F, 189th N.Y.	35		1930	NE, 55th, 1931
Shackelford, J.M.		F, 8th Ky.	244		1898 May 28	KS, 18th, 1899
Shackleford, J.B.	Pvt.	K, 7th Ill. Cav.	63		1928 Jun 27	IA, 55th, 1929
Shackleford, W.M.		B, 35th Mo. Inf. (died at Courtland, Kans.; buried at Courtland Cemetery)	344		1894 Dec 13	KS, 14th, 1895
Shackleton, Robt.	Pvt.	D, 187th N.Y. Inf.	30		1905 Oct 27	IA, 32nd, 1906

*See Appendix A, B or C for roster of post names and locations.
†See Introduction for note regarding recording of death date.
487

Name	Rank	Company, Regiment or Ship	Post*	Age	Death Date†	Journal
Shadbolt, Jerome	Pvt.	15th Iowa Inf.	220		1906 Oct	IA, 33rd, 1907
Shadduck, Wm.		I, 9th N.Y. Inf.	17		1929 Mar 24	KS, 49th, 1930
Shaddy, Frank		C, 3rd Ind. Cav.	4		1921 Feb 16	KS, 41st, 1922
Shade, Jacob	Pvt.	K, 68th Ohio Inf.	12	87	1931 Apr 7	IA, 58th, 1932
Shadeewily, F.W.		K, 7th Ill.	28		1896 Apr 11	KS, 16th, 1897
Shader, Arthur L.		A, 52nd Wis.	25		1934 Feb 25	NE, 59th, 1935
Shadford, Wm.	1st Sergt.	H, 37th Iowa Inf.	107	84	1893 Dec 13	IA, 20th, 1894
Shadle, R.E.		E, 42nd Ind.	88		1926	KS, 46th, 1927
Shadley, Frank		G, 99th Ind. Inf.	32		1934 Aug 7	KS, 54th, 1935
Shadley, Jno.	Pvt.	A, 104th Ohio Inf.	7		1925 May 3	IA, 52nd, 1926
Shaeffer, A.F.			166		1894	NE, 19th, 1895
Shaeffer, A.M.		K, 16th Iowa Inf.	329	92	1935 Nov 25	IA, 62nd, 1936
Shaeffer, Geo. H.		L, 6th Ohio Cav.	25	77	1918 Jan 30	NE, 43rd, 1919
Shaeffer, Jacob			233		1922 Mar 27	IA, 49th, 1923
Shaeffer, Sam G.		I, 127th Penn.	30		1916 May 31	KS, 36th, 1917
Shafe, John		K, 14th Iowa	15		1893 Jul 27	KS, 13th, 1894
Shafer, A.B.	Musician	B, 3d Md. Inf.	485		1902 Jun 26	IA, 29th, 1903
Shafer, Albert C.		A, 11th Mich. Inf.	246		1899 Dec 18	KS, 19th, 1900
Shafer, Erastus		B, 2nd Neb. Cav.	19		1907 Apr 9	IA, 34th, 1908
Shafer, Fred	Pvt.	F, 28th Iowa Inf.	343		1911 Oct 11	IA, 38th, 1912
Shafer, Geo.	Pvt.	C, 51st Ohio Inf.	66		1925 May 12	IA, 52nd, 1926
Shafer, H.D.		E, 119th Ill. Inf.	240		1914 Dec 10	KS, 34th, 1915
Shafer, H.P.		D, 145th Ohio D, 1st Ohio Cav.	130		1933 Dec 10	KS, 53rd, 1934
Shafer, Joseph	Pvt.	A, 133rd Ill. Inf.	231		1914 Apr 10	IA, 41st, 1915
Shafer, Samuel		K, 11th Iowa Inf.	235	98	1937 Dec 13	IA, 64th, 1938
Shafer, Samuel			340		1890	KS, 10th, 1891
Shafer, Tobias	Pvt.	F, 138th Penn. Inf.	16		1902 Feb 25	IA, 29th, 1903
Shaffer, A.J.		D, 8th Ill.	1		1918 Jan 18	KS, 38th, 1919
Shaffer, Alexander	Sergt.	G, 13th Wis. Inf.	68		1897 Feb 22	IA, 24th, 1898
Shaffer, Allen		E, 32nd Ohio Inf.	17		1912 Mar 16	KS, 32nd, 1913
Shaffer, E.F.			135		1908	IA, 35th, 1909
Shaffer, Geo. C.	QM Sergt.	M, 4th Wis. Cav.	267		1904 Apr 27	IA, 31st, 1905
Shaffer, George H.		L, 6th Ohio Cav. (died of Bright's disease)	89	78	1918 Jan 29	NE, 43rd, 1919
Shaffer, J.A.	Pvt.	C, 13th Wis. Inf.	68		1911 Feb 15	IA, 38th, 1912
Shaffer, J.H.			7		1909 Sep 24	IA, 36th, 1910
Shaffer, J.M.			2		1913 Mar 25	IA, 40th, 1914
Shaffer, J.W.		D, 142nd Ohio	25		1921 Jul 21	KS, 41st, 1922
Shaffer, John	Pvt.	D, 35th Iowa Inf.	153		1919 May 30	IA, 46th, 1920
Shaffer, John		B, E, 13th Mo. State Militia	58		1923 Jun 29	KS, 43rd, 1924
Shaffer, John W.		Penn. Inf.	284		1901 Nov 13	KS, 21st, 1902
Shaffer, L.H.	Pvt.	H, 2nd Ohio Cav.	98	59	1898 Dec 9	IA, 25th, 1899
Shaffer, N.D.		C, 54th Penn.	2		1931 Nov 8	KS, 51st, 1932
Shaffer, N.D.		C, 54th Penn.	2		1931 Nov 8	KS, 52nd, 1933
Shaffer, S.W.	Pvt.	K, 2nd Penn. Inf.	212		1918 Jan 12	IA, 45th, 1919
Shaffer, Samuel B.		B, 125th Penn.	64		1930[1939?] Apr 29	KS, 59th, 1940
Shaffer, Thomas		A, 98th Ill.	293		1912 Oct 10	KS, 32nd, 1913
Shaffer, Valentine		A, 197th Ohio	92		1924 Nov 16	KS, 44th, 1925
Shaffer, W.A.			108	90	1936 Nov 21	IA, 63rd, 1937
Shaffer, W.B., Dr.		108th Ohio	108		1892 Feb 29	KS, 12th, 1893
Shaffer, W.H.	Saddler	K, 8th Iowa Cav.	339		1901-1902	IA, 28th, 1902
Shaffer, W.H.		E, 8th N.Y. Cav.	65		1921 Feb 8	KS, 41st, 1922
Shaffer, Washington		G, 110th Penn.	17		1916 Dec 12	KS, 36th, 1917
Shaffer, Wesley	Pvt.	I, 109th N.Y. Inf.	67		1928 Jul 17	IA, 55th, 1929
Shaffer, William		H, 9th Penn.	61		1933 Mar 13	KS, 53rd, 1934
Shaffer, Wm.	Pvt.	D, 99th Ind. Inf.	81		1911 Mar 17	IA, 38th, 1912
Shaffler, Robert		124th Ill. (died of tuberculosis)	60	76	1907 Nov 22	NE, 32nd, 1908
Shafley, A.H.		B, 17th Ill. Cav.	177		1892 Apr 15	KS, 12th, 1893
Shafmer, J.F.		B, 2nd Minn.	35	79	1923 Oct 5	NE, 48th, 1924
Shafroth, Fred	Pvt.	E, 116th Ohio Inf.	324		1913 Jan 15	IA, 40th, 1914
Shaftsberry, John		E, 58th N.Y.	26		1905 Sep 14	KS, 25th, 1906
Shakespeare, A.B.	Pvt.	F, 20th Iowa	212		1924 Jan 30	IA, 51st, 1925

*See Appendix A, B or C for roster of post names and locations.
†See Introduction for note regarding recording of death date.

Name	Rank	Company, Regiment or Ship	Post*	Age	Death Date†	Journal
Shaler, Elon S.		I, 142nd Ohio	1		1926 Dec 14	KS, 46th, 1927
Shall, Simon		G, 63rd Penn.	118		1918 Oct 17	KS, 38th, 1919
Shaller, Joseph	Pvt.	F, 6th Iowa Cav.	24		1911 Jul	IA, 38th, 1912
Shalty, Henry F.		C, 45th Ohio Vols.	2		1885	KS, 5th, 1886
Shamberger, Phil H.	Pvt.	A, 7th Penn. Cav.	77		1899	NE, 24th, 1900
Shammo, T.H.		E, 9th Penn. Cav.	31		1925 Feb 14	IA, 52nd, 1926
Shamp, W.A.		H, 30th —	25		1927 Aug 17	NE, 52nd, 1928
Shan, Alex.		C, 3rd Kans. State Militia	12		1904 Jun 27	KS, 24th, 1905
Shandlemeier, J.	Pvt.	F, 3rd Penn. Inf.	329	58	1896 Jun 15	IA, 23rd, 1897
Shane, Isaac W.		E, 149th Ind.	85		1933 Jul 24	KS, 53rd, 1934
Shane, J.T.	Pvt.	C, 4th Iowa Cav.	20		1906	IA, 33rd, 1907
Shane, Wm. E.		E, 46th Ill. (died of gastritis & irr. stomach)	308	61	1908 Feb 16	NE, 33rd, 1909
Shaner, A.J.		31st Ohio			1913 May 24	KS, 33rd, 1914
Shaner, Ellis		D, 7th Penn.	25		1937 Nov 11	KS, 57th, 1938
Shangrah, Paul		D, 14th Wis.	263		1904 Jul 8	KS, 24th, 1905
Shank, H.W.	Pvt.	B, 1st Md. Cav.	235		1929 Jan 25	IA, 56th, 1930
Shank, Jacob			49		1884	KS, 4th, 1885
Shank, Philip		I, 176th Ohio Inf.	97		1891 Oct 20	KS, 11th, 1892
Shank, Wm.			103		1906 Sep 8	KS, 26th, 1907
Shankland, J.M.	Sergt.	C, 161st Ohio Inf.	12		1912 May 10	IA, 39th, 1913
Shankland, R.B.	Pvt.	I, 36th Ill. Inf.	84		1912 Apr 26	IA, 39th, 1913
Shanklin, A.T.	Sergt.	H, 6th Iowa Cav.	270		1924 Feb 21	IA, 51st, 1925
Shanklin, F.C.		I, 91st Ill.	18		1926 Feb 5	KS, 46th, 1927
Shanklin, John		C, 11th Kans.	42		1927 Aug 25	KS, 47th, 1928
Shanks, B.F.		D, 7th Marine (died of consumption)	274	64	1907 Jul 23	NE, 32nd, 1908
Shanks, Christ. C.	Pvt.	D, 11th Ill. Inf.	77		1904 Dec 15	IA, 31st, 1905
Shanks, J.		D, 190th Penn.	89		1888	KS, 8th, 1889
Shanley, John	Pvt.	I, 39th Iowa Inf.	7		1916 Apr 13	IA, 43rd, 1917
Shanlis, E.M.			13	66	1909 Sep 19	NE, 34th, 1910
Shannon, A.J.		12th Kans.	117		1898 Jul 21	KS, 18th, 1899
Shannon, Aaron		A, 16th Ill.	13	76	1917 Nov 15	NE, 42nd, 1918
Shannon, Absalom	Pvt.	E, 30th Wis. Inf.	90		1900 Dec 20	IA, 27th, 1901
Shannon, Daniel	Pvt.		316		1924 Jul 13	IA, 51st, 1925
Shannon, George		F, 16th Kans.	256		1911 Dec 16	KS, 31st, 1912
Shannon, I.H.		B, 11th Ind.	49		1913 Dec 29	KS, 33rd, 1914
Shannon, J.	Pvt.	F, 45th Ill. Inf.	68		1920 Dec 10	IA, 47th, 1921
Shannon, J.B.P.	Pvt.	A, 45th Ill. Inf.	23		1912 Jun 10	IA, 39th, 1913
Shannon, J.P.		C, 73rd Ill. Inf.	81		1900 Nov 23	KS, 20th, 1901
Shannon, J.P.		K, 78th Ill.	241		1905 Nov 30	KS, 25th, 1906
Shannon, John A.	Pvt.	D, 33rd Iowa	40		1923 Jan 7	IA, 50th, 1924
Shannon, John D.	1st Lieut.	C, 15th Iowa Inf.	12		1902 Jul 7	IA, 29th, 1903
Shannon, John T.		L, 1st Ind. Art. (Cav.)	174		1905 Feb 6	KS, 25th, 1906
Shannon, Joseph	Pvt.	I, 83rd Ohio Inf.	55		1912 Jul 13	IA, 39th, 1913
Shannon, Patrick		A, 88th N.Y.	293		1921 Sep 2	KS, 41st, 1922
Shannon, Robt. J.	Lieut.	D, 32nd Iowa	329	71	1898 Nov 8	IA, 25th, 1899
Shannon, T.F.	Pvt.	E, 9th Iowa Cav.	68		1928 Nov 11	IA, 55th, 1929
Shannon, T.R.			340		1890	KS, 10th, 1891
Shannon, W.A.	Pvt.	A, 25th Iowa Inf.	108		1919 Nov 10	IA, 46th, 1920
Shannon, W.W.			241		1902 Feb 10	KS, 22nd, 1903
Shannon, Walter		D, 124th Ill.	85		1931 Sep 25	KS, 52nd, 1933
Shannon, Walter		D, 124th Ill.	85		1931 Sep 25	KS, 51st, 1932
Shannon, William		F, 18th Ill. Inf. (died at Topeka, Kans.; buried at Topeka Cemetery)	71		1894 Feb 26	KS, 14th, 1895
Shannon, Wm.			105		1898 Dec 26	KS, 18th, 1899
Shapstall, Solomon	Pvt.	A, 12th Ohio Cav.	297		1925 Mar 17	IA, 52nd, 1926
Sharer, Joseph		H, 159th Ill.	237		1898 Nov 5	KS, 18th, 1899
Sharmon, Wm. H.		A, 52nd N.Y.	69	76	1922 Aug 24	NE, 47th, 1923
Sharon, C.C.	Pvt.	D, 36th Iowa Inf.	49		1927 Sep 7	IA, 54th, 1928
Sharp, Alonzo	Pvt.	I, 12th Ill.	68		1924 Jun 21	IA, 51st, 1925
Sharp, B.F.		F, 150th Ill. Inf. (Merna)			1944 Jan	NE, 70th, 1946
Sharp, David	Pvt.	I, 18th Inf.	7		1927 Aug 12	IA, 54th, 1928

*See Appendix A, B or C for roster of post names and locations.
†See Introduction for note regarding recording of death date.

Name	Rank	Company, Regiment or Ship	Post*	Age	Death Date†	Journal
Sharp, Davis	Pvt.	K, 19th Iowa Inf.	170	87	1932 Oct 19	IA, 59th, 1933
Sharp, E.E.		D, 6th Ind.	465		1907 Dec 18	KS, 28th, 1909
Sharp, Geo.	Pvt.	C, 33rd Iowa Inf.	40		1915 Jan 23	IA, 42nd, 1916
Sharp, Geo. E.	Pvt.	A, 34th Iowa Inf.	309		1904 Apr 1	IA, 31st, 1905
Sharp, George		F, 4th Ind.	123		1896 Nov 24	KS, 16th, 1897
Sharp, James	Pvt.	L, 1st Mo. Cav.	84		1907 Apr 21	IA, 34th, 1908
Sharp, James R.		L, 3rd N.Y. Cav.	69	83	1922 Nov 29	NE, 47th, 1923
Sharp, Jno. N.		I, 116th Ind. Inf.	25	84	1918 Apr 27	NE, 43rd, 1919
Sharp, John		M, 1st Col.	253		1910	KS, 30th, 1911
Sharp, Nimrod		B, 122nd Ill. Inf.	32		1908 Jul 20	KS, 28th, 1909
Sharp, Peter		H, 121st N.J.	65		1926 Dec 3	KS, 46th, 1927
Sharp, Robert		C, 2nd Mich. (died of rheu. & heart failure)	36	65	1907 Dec 25	NE, 32nd, 1908
Sharp, Samuel F.		F, 155th Ill.	339		1927 Aug 19	KS, 48th, 1929
Sharp, Wm.	Pvt.	A, 5th Ohio Batt.	12		1929 Jul 13	IA, 56th, 1930
Sharpe, M.B.		K, 15th Ind.	129	67	1912 Oct 18	NE, 37th, 1913
Sharpe, Stephen			463		1921 May 24	KS, 41st, 1922
Sharpless, J.F.		E, 15th N.Y. Inf.	180		1908	NE, 33rd, 1909
Sharrock, J.B.		I, 77th Ohio	1		1928 Sep 17	KS, 48th, 1929
Shatto, Ralph	Sergt.	C, 19th Iowa Vol. Inf.	343		1899 Aug 21	IA, 26th, 1900
Shattuck, J.V.		C, 161st N.Y. (nonmember; died at Central City)			1936 Apr 23	NE, 61st, 1937
Shaughnessy, M.		A, 7th Ill. Cav. (died of cancer)	47	64	1904 Jan 7	NE, 29th, 1905
Shaull, David Milton		C, 20th Ohio Inf.		91	1937 Jan 13	IA, 64th, 1938
Shaull, M.S.	Musician	E, 24th Iowa Inf.	145		1917 Jul 2	IA, 44th, 1918
Shaull, S.R.	Pvt.	H, 65th N.Y. Inf.	145		1913 Jun 7	IA, 40th, 1914
Shaver, Jacob	Pvt.	A, 13th Iowa Inf.	235		1924 Jan 31	IA, 51st, 1925
Shaver, Peter			167		1924 Apr 9	IA, 51st, 1925
Shaw, A.	Sergt.	G, 136th Ohio Inf.	334	63	1894 Oct 24	IA, 22nd, 1896
Shaw, A.D.	Pvt.	A, 85th Penn. Inf.	472		1920 Jul 8	IA, 47th, 1921
Shaw, A.R.			108		1915	IA, 42nd, 1916
Shaw, Bartlet		H, 1st Mass.	379		1896 Feb 15	KS, 16th, 1897
Shaw, Charles G.	Sergt.	E, 83rd Ill. Inf.	116	62	1898 Jan 3	IA, 24th, 1898
Shaw, Daniel D.	Pvt.	A, 2nd Ill. Cav.	239	56	1893 Dec 2	IA, 20th, 1894
Shaw, Daniel R.	Pvt.	G, 3rd Iowa Cav.	51	61	1898 Mar 31	IA, 24th, 1898
Shaw, David		H, 2nd Ohio Hvy. Art.	17		1919 Jul 20	KS, 39th, 1920
Shaw, E.B.	Pvt.	G, 21st Ohio Inf.	48		1908 Nov 12	IA, 35th, 1909
Shaw, Edward A.		114th U.S. (killed in tornado)	110	68	1913 Mar 23	NE, 38th, 1914
Shaw, Egbert		H, 1st Neb. Cav. (died of spinal disease)	100	70	1895 Oct 7	NE, 20th, 1896
Shaw, F.	Corp.	F, 4th Minn.	142		1923 Nov 25	IA, 50th, 1924
Shaw, F.Y.	Pvt.	A, 30th Ind. Inf.	220	51	1895 Jan 10	IA, 21st, 1895
Shaw, Frank G.		B, 34th Ohio Inf.	50		1900 Oct 27	KS, 20th, 1901
Shaw, Frank V.	Capt.	A, 57th Penn.	9		1921 Mar 8	KS, 41st, 1922
Shaw, George E.		D, 11th N.Y. Cav.	198		1912 Sep 1	KS, 32nd, 1913
Shaw, Harley		F, 3rd N.Y.	35		1926 Mar 28	NE, 51st, 1927
Shaw, J.H.	Pvt.	B, 101st Iowa Inf.	24		1905 Jul 26	IA, 32nd, 1906
Shaw, J.H.		G, 36th Iowa Inf.	49		1912 Feb 23	KS, 32nd, 1913
Shaw, James N.		E, 17th Iowa	493		1900 Feb 5	KS, 20th, 1901
Shaw, Jerry		E, 4th Ind.	1		1927 May 18	KS, 47th, 1928
Shaw, Joel	Pvt.	H, 75th Ill. Inf.	23		1930 Apr	IA, 57th, 1931
Shaw, John		K, 99th Ind.	35	86	1923 Sep 16	NE, 48th, 1924
Shaw, John C.	Pvt.	H, 13th Ohio Inf.	265	58	1893 Nov 22	IA, 20th, 1894
Shaw, John Wesley		E, 15th Ill. Inf. (died of wounds)	165	82	1920 Oct 9	NE, 45th, 1921
Shaw, Joseph		L, 39th Ohio Inf.	256		1934 Mar 15	KS, 54th, 1935
Shaw, L.W.	Pvt.	E, 17th Iowa Inf.	107		1920 Mar 6	IA, 47th, 1921
Shaw, Levi	Pvt.	E, 33rd Iowa Inf.	40		1920 Feb 9	IA, 47th, 1921
Shaw, Levi		D, 13th Iowa	78		1906 Aug 13	KS, 26th, 1907
Shaw, Nelson		I, 89th Ohio	25		1922 Jan 12	KS, 42nd, 1923
Shaw, Nelson M.	Pvt.	C, 143rd Ohio Inf.	84	50	1893 Sep 18	IA, 20th, 1894
Shaw, Rufus F.			39		3rd quarter 1883	IA, 10th, 1884
Shaw, Samuel	Pvt.	I, 132nd Ohio	275		1924 Mar 17	IA, 51st, 1925
Shaw, Smith		F, 1st Ohio Lt. Art. (died at Bonner Springs; buried at Elm Grove Cemetery)	256		1894 Sep 3	KS, 14th, 1895

*See Appendix A, B or C for roster of post names and locations.
†See Introduction for note regarding recording of death date.

Name	Rank	Company, Regiment or Ship	Post*	Age	Death Date†	Journal
Shaw, Volney		H, 49th Iowa	132	88	1934 May 11	IA, 61st, 1935
Shaw, W.H.	Sergt.	K, 33rd Iowa Inf.	40		1926 Jun 23	IA, 53rd, 1927
Shaw, Warren		F, 111th Ohio	4		1921 Aug 16	KS, 41st, 1922
Shaw, William		G, 11th Iowa	84		1910 Jun 27	KS, 30th, 1911
Shaw, William		C, 5th Ky. Inf.	127		1914 Jun 29	KS, 34th, 1915
Shaw, Willis O.	Pvt.	A, 142nd Ohio Inf.	100		1918 Sep 25	IA, 45th, 1919
Shaw, Wilson		B, 68th Ind. Inf.	85		1908 Mar 21	KS, 28th, 1909
Shawger, Stephen W.			65		1916 Jan 17	KS, 36th, 1917
Shawver, Samuel		B, 11th Mo. Inf.	18		1929 Mar 28	KS, 49th, 1930
Shay, James	Pvt.	H, 29th Ind. Inf.	57		1927 Jul 5	IA, 54th, 1928
Shay, James	Pvt.	H, 29th Ind. Inf.	57		1928 Jul 5	IA, 55th, 1929
Shay, Joshua		K, 4th Iowa Inf.	177		1899 Jun 26	KS, 19th, 1900
Shea, Andrew J.		D, 4th Iowa Inf.	142		1886	KS, 6th, 1887
Shea, John R.		E, 35th Iowa	7		1922 Oct 14	IA, 49th, 1923
Sheafer, W.U.	Pvt.	D, 10th Mo. Inf.	153		1906 Nov 30	IA, 33rd, 1907
Sheaffer, Chas. H.		C, 9th Penn. Cav.	265		1929 Jan 31	NE, 53rd, 1929
Sheafor, M.V.B.		M, 4th Iowa Cav.	113		1909 Jan 15	KS, 29th, 1910
Sheafor, P.M.		L, 8th Iowa Cav.	1		1916 Jan 7	KS, 36th, 1917
Sheahaw, Edward		F, 37th Ind.	353		1918 Dec 18	KS, 38th, 1919
Shealey, Tobias	Pvt.	A, 145th N.Y. Inf.	493		1900-1901	IA, 27th, 1901
Shearer, J.H.	Pvt.	B, 25th Wis.	156		1903 Sep 30	IA, 30th, 1904
Shearer, J.L.		H, 36th Iowa	94		1923 Jun 4	IA, 50th, 1924
Shearer, J.R.			347		1911 2nd term	IA, 38th, 1912
Shearer, J.S.		B, 50th Ohio	113		1889	KS, 9th, 1890
Shearer, James		C, 3rd Tenn. Cav.	322		1934 Apr 17	KS, 54th, 1935
Shearer, John	Pvt.	12th Battery, Wis. Lt. Art. (was Dept. Commander of Texas at time of death)	30, 89	94	1941 Oct 9	IA, 67th, 1941
Shearer, N.F.		A, 95th Ill.	50		1904 Nov 29	KS, 24th, 1905
Shearer, Robert H.		I, 16th Kans. Cav.	117		1914 Aug 31	KS, 34th, 1915
Sheaver, L.V.	Pvt.	K, 52nd Ind. Inf.	107		1906 Jul 19	IA, 33rd, 1907
Shedd, C.E.	Pvt.	K, 8th Iowa Cav.	31	50	1896 Jul 23	IA, 23rd, 1897
Shedd, C.F.		E, 48th N.Y.	25		1922 Feb 21	NE, 47th, 1923
Shedd, C.F.		E, 48th N.Y.	25		1922 Feb 21	NE, 47th, 1923
Shedd, H.P.	Pvt.	F, 51st Mass. Inf.	222		1917 Apr 17	IA, 44th, 1918
Sheddinger, Lewis	Pvt.	103rd Penn. Inf.	80		1913 Oct 30	IA, 40th, 1914
Shedeck, Joseph	Pvt.	F, 44th Iowa Inf.	130		1927 Mar 4	IA, 54th, 1928
Sheehan, M.M., see Shehan, M.M.						
Sheehey, Roger	Pvt.	I, 46th Ill. Inf.	30		1918 May 13	IA, 45th, 1919
Sheeks, E.H.		Minn. Battery	17		1935 Dec 30	KS, 56th, 1937
Sheeks, Isaac			32		1911 Feb 8	NE, 36th, 1912
Sheeler, I.	Pvt.	A, 40th Iowa Inf.	84	62	1896 Jun 2	IA, 23rd, 1897
Sheeley, Granville		F, 10th Iowa	209		1916 Mar 17	KS, 36th, 1917
Sheeley, Tobias	Pvt.	H, 145th N.Y. Inf.	493		1900 Jun 14	IA, 27th, 1901
Sheener, A.J.		C, 6th Kans. Cav.	14		1917 Nov 7	KS, 37th, 1918
Sheets, Benj.	Pvt.	G, 62nd Ohio Inf.	400		1926 Oct 25	IA, 53rd, 1927
Sheets, D.C.			64		1917	KS, 37th, 1918
Sheets, E.E.		I, 35th Iowa	5		1885	KS, 5th, 1886
Sheets, Geo. F.			45		1926 Mar 21	IA, 53rd, 1927
Sheets, Jesse		F, 151st Ohio	42		1916 Feb 5	KS, 36th, 1917
Sheets, Jocob		A, 40th Ind.	272	64	1907	NE, 32nd, 1908
Sheets, John		H, 104th Penn.	250		1920 May 24	KS, 40th, 1921
Sheets, Levi	Pvt.	I, 4th Ind. Cav.	200		1908 May 8	IA, 35th, 1909
Sheets, Peyton		E, 133rd Ill. Inf. (died of dropsy at Soldiers & Sailors Home, Grand Island; buried in Home Cemetery)	19	55	1905 Aug 23	NE, 30th, 1906
Sheets, Solomon		A, 12th Ill. Cav. (died of general debility)	118	67	1907 Mar 9	NE, 32nd, 1908
Sheets, T.		D, 26th Ill. Inf.	111		1917 Oct 19	KS, 37th, 1918
Sheetz, Aaron		I, 188th Penn. Inf.	250		1918 Feb 15	KS, 38th, 1919
Sheetz, Leander	Adjt.	8th Ill.	165	54	1898 Jul 18	IA, 25th, 1899
Sheffer, Robert	Pvt.	I, 61st Ill. Inf.	364		1908 Dec 14	IA, 35th, 1909
Sheffer, T.J.	Pvt.	E, 20th Penn. Inf.	312		1910 May 6	IA, 37th, 1911

Name	Rank	Company, Regiment or Ship	Post*	Age	Death Date†	Journal
Sheffield, Charles H.		I, 35th Ind. Inf.	71		1901 Mar 30	KS, 21st, 1902
Sheffield, D.A.			346		1910	IA, 37th, 1911
Sheffield, Frank			94		1919 Jan	IA, 46th, 1920
Sheffield, R.P.		H, 8th Iowa Cav. (at large)			1932 Mar 3	IA, 59th, 1933
Shefler, F.J.	Pvt.	C, 14th Iowa Inf.	235		1918 Dec 13	IA, 46th, 1920
Shehan, M.M.	Pvt.	B, 20th Ind. Inf.	267	53	1888 Nov 29	IA, 15th, 1889
Shehi, Harrison		E, 13th Ill. Cav.	53		1930 Sep 22	KS, 50th, 1931
Sheibly, G.W.	Sergt.	B, 13th Penn. Res.	22		1924 Jan 3	IA, 51st, 1925
Sheitz, M.A.	Pvt.	H, 8th Ill. Inf.	403		1904 Aug 21	IA, 31st, 1905
Shelby, Nelson	Pvt.	A, 60th U.S. Inf.	19	56	1897 Jan 9	IA, 23rd, 1897
Shelden, J.W.	Pvt.	E, 4th Ind. Cav. (died of cancer)	67	54	1884 Dec 2	NE, 9th, 1885
Sheldon, B.O.	Pvt.	A, 4th Iowa Inf.	263		1920 Dec 15	IA, 47th, 1921
Sheldon, C.D.	Pvt.	D, 153rd Ill. Inf.	141		1915 Feb 8	IA, 42nd, 1916
Sheldon, E.O.	Sergt.	A, 4th Iowa Inf.	263		1921 Dec 15	IA, 48th, 1922
Sheldon, F.L.	Pvt.	C, 24th Iowa Inf.	110		1925 Nov 26	IA, 52nd, 1926
Sheldon, Geo. R.		H, 143rd Penn.	1		1910 Jun 8	KS, 30th, 1911
Sheldon, Geo. W.	1st Lieut.	E, 68th Ind.	12		1922 Jan 1	IA, 49th, 1923
Sheldon, Henry		L, 8th Ill. Cav. (see also Appendix D)	22		1937 Jan 23	NE, 62nd, 1938
Sheldon, Horace J.	Pvt.	K, 15th Iowa Inf.	193		1912 Mar 22	IA, 39th, 1913
Sheldon, J.J.	Surg.	35th Ohio Vol. Inf.	101		1884	KS, 4th, 1885
Sheldon, M.R.	Pvt.	2nd Ill. Cav.	55		1910 Aug 15	IA, 37th, 1911
Sheldon, O.H.		H, 20th Wis. Inf.	52	73	1903 Mar 20	NE, 28th, 1904
Sheldon, S.E.	Asst. Surg.	32nd Ohio Inf.	1		1900 Apr 10	KS, 20th, 1901
Sheldon, W.A.	Corp.	H, 8th Ill. Cav.	155		1907 Sep 8	IA, 34th, 1908
Sheley, Martin	Pvt.	C, 28th Iowa Inf.	392		1918 Aug 22	IA, 45th, 1919
Sheley, Samuel		E, 14th Kans. Cav.	92		1918 Jan 5	KS, 38th, 1919
Shelhart, Valentine		died of pneumonia	262		1900 Jan 13	NE, 25th, 1901
Shell, Charley		H, 31st Ind. (died of old age)	55	82	1920	NE, 45th, 1921
Shell, H.C.	Wagon Master	175th Ohio Inf.	127		1920 Nov 16	IA, 47th, 1921
Shell, William		I, 48th Mo.	50		1937 Nov 21	KS, 56th, 1937
Shellabarger, Joseph		A, 116th Ill.	1		1905 Sep 22	KS, 25th, 1906
Shellebarger, Abram		K, 85th Ill.	45		1935 Jul 8	NE, 60th, 1936
Shelley, L.P.		A, 15th Ill.	265		1908 Jun 29	KS, 28th, 1909
Shellhorn, A.		I, 8th N.Y.	12		1921 Sep 20	KS, 41st, 1922
Shellhorn, E.J.			25	73	1910 Apr 7	NE, 35th, 1911
Shellor, Wm.					1929 Jan 22	NE, 53rd, 1929
Shelly, Geo. C.			165		1926	IA, 53rd, 1927
Shelmadine, J.W.	Pvt.	A, 26th Iowa Inf.	284		1915 May 24	IA, 42nd, 1916
Shelstead, John		B, 15th Wis.	4		1915 Jan 2	KS, 35th, 1916
Shelton, Caleb	Pvt.	F, 145th Ind.	18		1924 Aug 15	IA, 51st, 1925
Shelton, Dirk	Pvt.	A, 7th Iowa Inf.	231		1904 Sep 6	IA, 31st, 1905
Shelton, Jesse V.		D, 123rd Ill.	465		1924 Apr 29	KS, 44th, 1925
Shelton, P.	Pvt.	F, 195th Ind. Inf.	18		1920	IA, 47th, 1921
Shenk, John		G, 100th Ill.	185		1918 May 19	KS, 38th, 1919
Shepard, Alonzo	Pvt.	G, 25th Iowa Inf.	231	53	1897 Nov 28	IA, 24th, 1898
Shepard, Joel L.		B, 83rd Ind. Inf. (died in Reno County)	17		1895 Dec 14	KS, 15th, 1896
Shepard, L.D.	Pvt.	F, 9th N.J. Inf.	2		1930 Jun 9	IA, 57th, 1931
Shepard, Peter A.		B, 11th Kans. Cav.	259		1904 Mar 14	KS, 24th, 1905
Shepardson, H.A.		F, 18th Mich. Inf. (died of old age)	318		1923 May 14	NE, 48th, 1924
Sheperson, N.B.	Pvt.	F, 14th Iowa Inf.	145		1911 Feb 1	IA, 38th, 1912
Shephard, A.P.		106th Ill. Vol. Inf.	4		1926 Nov 15	NE, 51st, 1927
Shepherd, Alfred		A, 77th Penn.	25		1913 Jul 26	KS, 33rd, 1914
Shepherd, B.F.		H, 46th Iowa	127		1924 Oct 3	KS, 44th, 1925
Shepherd, C.		H, 14th Ill. Inf. (died of accident)	199	60	1901 Nov	NE, 26th, 1902
Shepherd, Emory O.		A, 20th N.Y. Cav.	25		1910 Jul 21	NE, 35th, 1911
Shepherd, H.M.		I, 50th Ill.	100		1917 Nov 24	KS, 37th, 1918
Shepherd, I.N.		F, 23rd Iowa Inf. (died of old age)	207		1925 Jun	NE, 50th, 1926
Shepherd, John H.		F, 26th Ill.	18		1910 Jun 11	KS, 30th, 1911
Shepherd, S.D.			120		1886	NE, 11th, 1887
Shepherd, Samuel	Pvt.	F, 33rd Iowa Inf.	167	56	1889 Jan 27	IA, 16th, 1890
Shepherd, T.A.	S.M.	M, 125th Penn. Cav.	22		1920 Jun 6	IA, 47th, 1921
Sheppard, J.C.	Pvt.	K, 113th Ohio Inf.	56	66	1887 Jul 23	IA, 14th, 1888

*See Appendix A, B or C for roster of post names and locations.
†See Introduction for note regarding recording of death date.
492

Name	Rank	Company, Regiment or Ship	Post*	Age	Death Date†	Journal
Sheppard, J.H.		C, 16th Ind. Vol. Inf.	25		1908 Sep 10	KS, 28th, 1909
Sheppard, James	Pvt.	F, 2nd Iowa Inf.	69		1917 Feb 8	IA, 44th, 1918
Sheppard, Jeremiah			271		1913 Mar 24	IA, 40th, 1914
Sheppard, Jos.			96		1913 Jan 23	IA, 40th, 1914
Sheppard, S.P.H.	Pvt.	A, 48th Iowa Inf.	12		1917 Nov 3	IA, 44th, 1918
Sheppardson, M.J.	Sergt.	F, 15th Iowa Inf.	263		1904 Aug 10	IA, 31st, 1905
Sheppardson, W.H.	Musician	F, 15th Iowa Inf.	15		1904 Mar 10	IA, 31st, 1905
Shepperd, Elias		C, 15th Kans.	102		1906 Apr 3	KS, 26th, 1907
Sheppherd, C.A.		E, 12th Penn. Cav. (died of dropsy)	151	68	1910 Jun 25	NE, 35th, 1911
Sherarer, A.		17th Iowa	77		1928 Apr 25	KS, 48th, 1929
Sherburne, L.U.		E, 14th Maine (died of arterio sclerosis)	204	87	1912 Jul 24	NE, 37th, 1913
Shere, Thomas A.	Pvt.	B, 12th Ill. Inf.	193		1915 Dec 20	IA, 42nd, 1916
Sherer, C.G.		C, 7th N.H. Vols.	71		1912 Dec 14	KS, 32nd, 1913
Sherer, H.F.	Pvt.	G, 13th Ind. Inf.	440		1903 Jul	IA, 30th, 1904
Sherfey, N.A.	Pvt.	I, 1st Minn. Inf.	231		1913 Feb 1	IA, 40th, 1914
Sheridan, Andrew J.		E, 124th Ill.	28		1914 Mar 25	KS, 34th, 1915
Sheriff, Edward, see Scherf, Edward						
Sherland, R.C.		C, 6th Wis.	209		1919	KS, 39th, 1920
Sherman, A.	Pvt.	2nd Wis. Cav.	215		1914 Dec 16	IA, 41st, 1915
Sherman, A.S.		E, 3rd Mich.	35		1926 Jul 3	NE, 51st, 1927
Sherman, Adrain C.	Pvt.	E, 18th Ind.	1		1906 Jul 8	KS, 26th, 1907
Sherman, Alexander	Pvt.	H, 4th Iowa Cav.	68		1919 Oct 15	IA, 46th, 1920
Sherman, Asher D.			127		1920 Mar 25	KS, 40th, 1921
Sherman, Buren R.	Sergt.	G, 13th Iowa Inf.	68		1904 Nov 11	IA, 31st, 1905
Sherman, C.A.	QM	11th Penn. Cav.	67		1908 Dec 20	IA, 35th, 1909
Sherman, G.C.			77		1910 Jun 8	IA, 37th, 1911
Sherman, George		K, 127th Ill.	127		1905 Nov 18	KS, 25th, 1906
Sherman, Hoyt	Major	Gen. Staff	12		1904 Jan 26	IA, 31st, 1905
Sherman, Joseph	Pvt.	C, 83rd Ill. Inf.	27		1917 Feb 4	IA, 44th, 1918
Sherman, Milo			104		1916	IA, 43rd, 1917
Sherman, O.H.		F, 28th Mich.	17		1923 Jun 24	KS, 43rd, 1924
Sherman, P.W.			236		1906 Apr 1	IA, 33rd, 1907
Sherman, S.M.		I, 16th Wis.	25		1904 Feb 8	NE, 29th, 1905
Sherman, W.B.	Pvt.	F, 4th Ill. Cav.	67	85	1931 Dec 17	IA, 58th, 1932
Sherman, W.D.	Pvt.	C, 19th Iowa Inf.	419	57	1897 May 4	IA, 23rd, 1897
Shermerhorn, A.C.			17		1902 Oct 30	KS, 22nd, 1903
Sherod, M.C.	Pvt.	F, 2nd Iowa Inf.	79	77	1896 May 18	IA, 23rd, 1897
Sherrard, D.S.		B, 14th Penn.	85		1933 Apr 5	KS, 53rd, 1934
Sherrill, John		U.S. Gunboat *Star*	75	68	1901 Oct	NE, 26th, 1902
Sherwin, I.F.		152nd Ind.	110		1911 Aug 10	KS, 31st, 1912
Sherwin, N.W.	1st Lieut.	E, 129th Ind.	408		1903 Jul 30	IA, 30th, 1904
Sherwin, S.L.C.		E, 7th Iowa Cav.	147		1935 Mar 1	KS, 55th, 1936
Sherwood, Benj.	Pvt.	E, 8th Iowa Inf.	317	41	2nd quarter 1885	IA, 12th, 1886
Sherwood, Frank		E, 19th Iowa Inf. (died of heart trouble)	35		1913 Apr 20	NE, 38th, 1914
Sherwood, J.D.		G, 4th Penn. Cav. E, 138th Ind. Inf. (died of cancer)	7	48	1895 Aug	NE, 20th, 1896
Sherwood, J.M.		B, 66th Ind.	142		1922 Aug 20	KS, 42nd, 1923
Sherwood, James		E, 9th Ind.	113		1918 Aug 31	KS, 38th, 1919
Sherwood, Sidney	Pvt.	E, 10th Iowa Inf.	505	68	1895 Oct 28	IA, 22nd, 1896
Sherwood, Wm. H.	Corp.	A, 8th N.Y. Hvy. Art.	140		1924 Dec 25	IA, 51st, 1925
Shetler, Jerrymiah		H, 115th Ill. (died of old age)	124	84	1918	NE, 43rd, 1919
Shetterby, W.S.		C, 34th Iowa	113		1892 Sep	KS, 12th, 1893
Shew, A.L.		H, 1st N.Y. Vet. Cav.	325		1919 Sep 27	KS, 39th, 1920
Shick, Henry		D, 177th Penn.	81		1927	NE, 52nd, 1928
Shick, Henry		B, 172nd Penn.	81		1928 Aug 5	NE, 53rd, 1929
Shickley, J.B.		A, 74th Ohio Inf. (died of paralysis)	22	72	1909 Jul 8	NE, 34th, 1910
Shide, Wimer		50th Mo.	81		1928 Feb 4	KS, 48th, 1929
Shideler, Isaac		H, 116th Ind.	20		1898 Oct 1	KS, 18th, 1899
Shields, C.B.		F, 4th Ohio	225		1913 Nov 18	KS, 33rd, 1914
Shields, C.R.	Pvt.	D, 151st Ill. Inf.	57		1913 Dec 18	IA, 40th, 1914
Shields, David		G, 143rd Ohio	158		1930 Jun 6	KS, 50th, 1931

Name	Rank	Company, Regiment or Ship	Post*	Age	Death Date†	Journal
Shields, G.T.		F, 10th Iowa Inf.	17		1886	KS, 6th, 1887
Shields, J.B.	Pvt.	H, 85th Ill. Inf.	302		1905 Jul 30	IA, 32nd, 1906
Shields, J.C.	Pvt.	G, 13th Iowa Inf.	235		1924 Dec 14	IA, 51st, 1925
Shields, J.T.		B, 46th Ind.	72		1916 Jul 13	KS, 36th, 1917
Shields, J.W.		K, 49th Penn.	293		1922 Feb 26	KS, 42nd, 1923
Shields, Jas. A.		H, 49th Penn. Vol. Inf.	25		1908 Oct 14	KS, 28th, 1909
Shields, John	Pvt.		132		1915	IA, 42nd, 1916
Shields, John		G, 100th Penn. Inf.	108	90	1936 May 22	IA, 63rd, 1937
Shields, Lewis William		H, 120th Ind. Inf.	235	89	1937 Mar 26	IA, 64th, 1938
Shields, Robert P.		K, 155th Penn. Inf.	61		1901	KS, 21st, 1902
Shields, W.H.		F, 206th Ill. (died of apoplexy)	110		1916 May 2	NE, 41st, 1917
Shields, Wm.	Sergt.	G, 40th Iowa Inf.	49		1918 Mar 10	IA, 45th, 1919
Shields, Wm. H.	Pvt.	C, 7th Iowa Cav.	497	90	1936 May 3	IA, 65th, 1939
Shiffer, Elias	Pvt.		126		1899	IA, 26th, 1900
Shiffer, R.W.	Pvt.	I, 46th Ill. Inf.	7		1919 Mar 13	IA, 46th, 1920
Shiffer, Solomon		3rd Penn. Art.	130		1917 Jun 22	KS, 37th, 1918
Shiffert, S.H.		L, 1st Penn. Cav.	127		1902 Nov 26	KS, 22nd, 1903
Shiley, G.P.	Pvt.	L, 16th N.Y. Hvy. Art.	59		1928 May 11	IA, 55th, 1929
Shilling, John	Pvt.	A, 33rd Iowa	49		1921 Nov 25	IA, 48th, 1922
Shilling, John		C, 13th Kans.	130		1911 Dec 2	KS, 31st, 1912
Shimeall, C.F.		F, 13th Wis.	1		1918 May 18	KS, 38th, 1919
Shimer, Jesse		G, 8th Ind. Inf.	451		1916	KS, 36th, 1917
Shimer, Moses		A, 4th Colo.	345		1898 Dec 16	KS, 18th, 1899
Shinault, Jacob		H, 91st Ill. (died of stomach trouble)	63	77	1922 Feb 1	NE, 47th, 1923
Shindall, Augustus		I, 31st Wis.	43		1904 Feb 3	KS, 24th, 1905
Shiney, L.		32nd Wis. Inf.	22		1892 Jul 28	IA, 19th, 1893
Shink, John		F, 75th Ind. Inf.	182		1901 Nov 15	KS, 21st, 1902
Shinkle, E.R.	Corp.	G, 15th Ill. Inf.	66		1915 Oct 31	IA, 42nd, 1916
Shinkle, William		F, 1st Ill. Cav.	4		1902 Sep 11	KS, 22nd, 1903
Shinn, A.C.		G, 12th Ill. Cav.	18		1924 Sep 3	KS, 44th, 1925
Shinn, Josiah		B, 3rd Va. Inf. 6th West Va. Cav.	127		1909 Sep 7	KS, 29th, 1910
Shipe, Jonas		Penn.	127		1911 Apr 16	KS, 31st, 1912
Shiplett, J.H.	Pvt.	D, 11th Iowa Inf.	250		1906 Feb 11	IA, 33rd, 1907
Shipley, B.R.		D, 36th Iowa Inf.		96	1936 Jan 15	IA, 62nd, 1936
Shipley, B.R.		D, 36th Iowa Inf.	116	96	1936 Jan 15	IA, 63rd, 1937
Shipley, John H., see Shpiley, John H.						
Shipley, L.D.		53rd Ind.	51		1906 Jan 24	KS, 26th, 1907
Shipley, Robert		B, 122nd Ill. Inf.	354	74	1911 Dec 16	NE, 36th, 1912
Shipley, W.H.		Trade Battery	7		1922 Apr 27	IA, 49th, 1923
Shipley, William	Pvt.	B, 7th Ill. Inf.	40	67	1894 Jun 22	IA, 21st, 1895
Shipley, Wm.	Pvt.	K, 47th Wis.	67		1903 Dec 19	IA, 30th, 1904
Shipman, A.B.			23		1906 Jul 27	IA, 33rd, 1907
Shipman, G.A.	Pvt.	H, 13th N.Y. Hvy. Art.	147		1926 May 19	IA, 53rd, 1927
Shipman, Henry		C, 154th Ind.	49		1914 Feb 2	KS, 34th, 1915
Shipman, J.O.			230		1899	NE, 24th, 1900
Shipman, J.R.	Pvt.	H, 19th Iowa Inf.	153		1913 Nov 6	IA, 40th, 1914
Shipman, John W.	Sergt.	E, 2nd Ill. (not member of the post, but buried by it)	[64?]		1885	KS, 5th, 1886
Shipman, R.C.		K, 6th Iowa (died of heart trouble)	32	75	1915 Aug 12	NE, 40th, 1916
Shipman, T.B.	Corp.	K, 9th Iowa Cav.	272	39	1885 Sep 30	IA, 12th, 1886
Shipman, W.O.		E, 4th Ill. Cav. (died of old age)	94	80	1922 Mar 2	NE, 47th, 1923
Shipman, Wm.	Pvt.	D, 153rd Ill.	512	62	1898 Sep 2	IA, 25th, 1899
Shippu, Geo. W.		G, 29th Ind. (died of age, flu)	182	87	1925 Jun 19	NE, 50th, 1926
Shipton, P.M.	Sergt.	C, 2nd Ark. Cav.	68		1911 Nov 23	IA, 38th, 1912
Shipton, Robt. H.	Sergt.	A, 18th Ohio Inf.	191		1900 Aug 20	IA, 27th, 1901
Shipton, Wallace	Pvt.	E, 2nd Minn. Inf.	26		1930 May 25	IA, 57th, 1931
Shiras, O.P.		General Heren's staff	78		1916 Jan 7	IA, 43rd, 1917
Shiras, Peter		G, 4th Ohio Cav.	18		1918 Nov 5	KS, 38th, 1919
Shire, Samuel		I, 54th Ill.	25		1927 Mar 6	KS, 47th, 1928
Shireman, Henry B.	Pvt.	B, 45th Penn. Inf.	206		1916 Feb 2	IA, 43rd, 1917

*See Appendix A, B or C for roster of post names and locations.
†See Introduction for note regarding recording of death date.

494

Name	Rank	Company, Regiment or Ship	Post*	Age	Death Date†	Journal
Shires, Thomas J.		A, 93rd Ill. (died of paralysis)	22	71	1915 Jan 14	NE, 40th, 1916
Shirk, David		B, 107th Penn.	63		1914 Jun 28	KS, 34th, 1915
Shirk, J.S.		B, 32nd Ohio	65		1919	KS, 39th, 1920
Shirk, M.H.	Pvt.	K, 15th Penn. Cav.	19		1926 Mar 5	IA, 53rd, 1927
Shirk, Martin B.		E, 13th Penn.	25		1930 Sep 25	KS, 50th, 1931
Shirk, N.B.			140		1926 Jan 17	IA, 53rd, 1927
Shirk, S.G.		I, 25th Ohio	74		1920 Nov 11	KS, 40th, 1921
Shirk, W.A.		E, 15th Iowa	1	94	1934 Mar 1	IA, 61st, 1935
Shirkey, Harvey		C, Mo. Cav.	7		1922 Dec 25	IA, 49th, 1923
Shirky, O.	Pvt.	A, 6th Ill.	231		1921 Apr 13	IA, 48th, 1922
Shirley, George		1st Col. Cal. 2nd Penn.	126		1896 Dec 21	KS, 16th, 1897
Shirley, Ira		A, 5th Ind.	17		1928 May 31	KS, 48th, 1929
Shirley, T.H., see Shurley, T.H.						
Shive, John W.		K, 9th Ky.	37		1919 Aug 22	KS, 39th, 1920
Shiveley, Geo.		C, 21st Mo.	22		1926	KS, 46th, 1927
Shivers, David		A, 5th Ohio Inf. (died at Clay Center)	88		1895 Jul 28	KS, 15th, 1896
Shivers, Wm.		F, 57th Ohio	429		1908	KS, 28th, 1909
Shives, John A.		I, 7th Iowa	176		1915 Aug 19	KS, 35th, 1916
Shoafstall, J.	Pvt.	M, 9th Iowa Cav.	440		1917 Jun 6	IA, 44th, 1918
Shobe, E.		F, 20th Ohio Inf.	16		1929 Jun 6	KS, 49th, 1930
Shock, George W.		B, 169th Ohio	84		1935 May 2	NE, 60th, 1936
Shockey, Mid		F, 4th Ill. Cav.	51		1923 Sep 23	KS, 43rd, 1924
Shockey, Thomas P.		K, 7th Ky. Cav.	90		1917 Sep	KS, 37th, 1918
Shockley, John		G, 83rd Ill.	45		1914	KS, 34th, 1915
Shockley, Thos. H.	Corp.	K, 79th Ohio Inf.	40		1927 Sep 3	IA, 54th, 1928
Shocknect, Joe	Pvt.	I, 52nd Ill. Inf.	267	45	1892 Nov 29	IA, 19th, 1893
Shoely, Geo.		C, 21st Mo.	22		1923 Jul 10	KS, 43rd, 1924
Shoemaker, Burton H.		B, 132nd Penn.	25		1915 May 15	NE, 40th, 1916
Shoemaker, F.M.	Capt.	I, 14th Ohio	68		1906 May 3	IA, 33rd, 1907
Shoemaker, G.			197		1921 Oct 15	IA, 48th, 1922
Shoemaker, Geo.		F, 21st Ohio	145		1920 Feb 20	KS, 40th, 1921
Shoemaker, Henry	Pvt.	F, 45th Ill. Inf.	156		1905 Sep 30	IA, 32nd, 1906
Shoemaker, Henry	Corp.	F, 116th N.Y. Inf.	78		1915 Aug 12	IA, 42nd, 1916
Shoemaker, J.L.		K, 4th Iowa Inf. (died of apoplexy)	204	77	1912 Sep 24	NE, 37th, 1913
Shoemaker, O.		27th Ill.	500		1923	KS, 43rd, 1924
Shoemaker, S.			63		1925 May	KS, 45th, 1926
Shoemaker, W.S.		O, 1st Colo. Inf. (died of chronic dis.)	204	25	1902 May	NE, 27th, 1903
Shoemaker, Wilson S.		D, 1st Neb. Ind. (died of pneumonia)	110	69	1913 Aug 27	NE, 38th, 1914
Shoemaker, Wm. R.	Pvt.	B, 92nd Ill.	247		1899 Dec 9	IA, 26th, 1900
Shoesmith, James	Pvt.		52		1920 Sep	IA, 47th, 1921
Shoesmith, Thomas		Phila. Eng. (died of old age)	69	83	1908 Feb 1	NE, 33rd, 1909
Shoffner, S.		H, 2nd Iowa	50		1924 Sep 27	KS, 44th, 1925
Shomber, Chas.		C, 6th Penn.	18		1927 Dec 30	KS, 47th, 1928
Shomber, Daniel		A, —	443		1910 Jun 21	KS, 30th, 1911
Shomhill, A.W.	Pvt.	H, 36th Wis. Inf.	68	87	1932 Jul 8	IA, 59th, 1933
Shook, Andrew		I, 63rd Ill. Inf.	82		1914 Jul	KS, 34th, 1915
Shook, George W.		A, 2nd Penn. Cav.	77		1937 Jun 5	NE, 62nd, 1938
Shook, Isase		A, 116th U.S.	236		1924 Feb 2	KS, 44th, 1925
Shook, John	Pvt.	K, 18th Iowa Inf.	127		1911 Feb 15	IA, 38th, 1912
Shook, L.W.		F, 93rd Ohio	4		1910 Jul 13	KS, 30th, 1911
Shoop, W.H.	Pvt.	B, 2nd Ohio Inf.	425		1915 Mar 6	IA, 42nd, 1916
Shope, Comrade			265		1913 Jun 20	KS, 33rd, 1914
Shope, T.R.	Lieut.	D, 45th Penn. Inf.	132		1920 Apr 16	IA, 47th, 1921
Shopley, A.	Pvt.	H, 16th Iowa Cav.	118		1901 Oct	IA, 28th, 1902
Shore, H.P.		K, 2nd Iowa Inf. (died of old age)	26	87	1921 May 12	NE, 46th, 1922
Shore, Jno. D.	Pvt.	E, 4th Wis. Cav.	423	48	1889 Dec 16	IA, 16th, 1890
Shore, O.M.		D, 87th Ind.	318	66	1911 Apr 4	NE, 36th, 1912
Shores, Josiah	Corp.	B, 32nd Ill. Inf.	77		1920 Jul 29	IA, 47th, 1921
Shores, T.B.		K, 11th Kans. Cav.	40		1908[1909?] Sep 28	KS, 29th, 1910
Shorey, J.V.	Pvt.	97th N.Y. Inf.	37		1919 Apr 26	IA, 46th, 1920
Short, C.M.	Pvt.	C, 50th Wis. Inf.	219		1907 Jul	IA, 34th, 1908

*See Appendix A, B or C for roster of post names and locations.
†See Introduction for note regarding recording of death date.

Name	Rank	Company, Regiment or Ship	Post*	Age	Death Date†	Journal
Short, Chas. A.		B, 2nd Mass. Cav.	25	79	1918 Dec 27	NE, 43rd, 1919
Short, David T.		E, 7th Mo. Cav.	40		1892 Dec 4	KS, 12th, 1893
Short, Ed		F, 87th Ind.	24		1892 Jan 30	KS, 12th, 1893
Short, Henry		C, 18th Wis.	286		1905	KS, 25th, 1906
Short, J.L.		G, 7th Ill. Inf.	63		1914 Oct 6	KS, 34th, 1915
Short, J.P.		M, 8th N.Y.	85		1926 Aug 11	KS, 46th, 1927
Short, J.S.		I, 63rd Ill.	150		1896 Jan 2	KS, 16th, 1897
Short, Luther	Pvt.	E, 39th —	291		1924 Apr 30	IA, 51st, 1925
Short, N.M.		G, 149th Ind.	132		1888	KS, 8th, 1889
Short, W.A.			1		1884	KS, 4th, 1885
Short, W.J.			380		1924 Dec 17	KS, 44th, 1925
Short, Wm.		H, 19th Ind.	98		1898 Aug 9	KS, 18th, 1899
Short, Y.W.	Musician	C, 70th Ind. Inf.	192		1915 Jan 29	IA, 42nd, 1916
Shorten, Richard		K, 12th Kans.	32		1926 Jun 10	KS, 46th, 1927
Shorts, Edward		E, 30th Ill.	46		1928 Sep 5	KS, 48th, 1929
Shottle, Emil	Pvt.		140		1910	IA, 37th, 1911
Shotts, D.T.		A, 18th Ohio	185		1928 Mar 2	KS, 49th, 1930
Shoup, C.F.		E, 1st Vt. Eng.	64		1918 Aug 23	KS, 38th, 1919
Shoup, George		H, 9th Ind. (former member; died at Hubbell)	50		1936	NE, 61st, 1937
Shoup, Leslie J.F.			54		1900 May 12	KS, 20th, 1901
Shoup, S.	Pvt.	D, 106th Ill. Inf.	34		1920 Jul 15	IA, 47th, 1921
Shoup, Solomon O.		5th Ind. Art.	145		1886	KS, 6th, 1887
Shoup, Wm. J.	Pvt.	H, 48th Ill. Inf.	78	47	1893 Nov 11	IA, 20th, 1894
Shouts, John	Pvt.	H, 52nd Ill. Inf.	234		1905 Nov 13	IA, 32nd, 1906
Shove, Thomas B.		K, 11th Kans.	18		1909 Sep 29	KS, 29th, 1910
Show, T.R.	Pvt.	K, 62nd Ohio Inf.	11		1915 Jun 23	IA, 42nd, 1916
Showalter, B.F.		A, 25th Iowa (former member; died at Lincoln)	38		1935 Jun 8	NE, 60th, 1936
Showalter, D.H.	Pvt.	B, 21st Penn. Cav.	11		1905 Nov 22	IA, 32nd, 1906
Showalter, J.H.		6th Va.	4	83	1914 May 21	NE, 39th, 1915
Showater, John T.		B, 9th Ill.	57		1922 Jul 14	KS, 42nd, 1923
Showe, J.I.		K, 37th Iowa Inf. (died of bladder disease)	98	70	1895 Mar 25	NE, 20th, 1896
Shown, Peter		E, 12th Ky. Inf.	289		1900 Mar 3	KS, 20th, 1901
Shpiley, John H.	Pvt.		324		1922 Apr 6	IA, 49th, 1923
Shrader, J.A.	Pvt.	G, 63rd Ohio Inf.	84		1930 May 23	IA, 57th, 1931
Shrader, J.C.	Capt.	H, 22nd Iowa Inf.	8		1906 Oct 29	IA, 33rd, 1907
Shrader, J.W.		11th Kans. Cav.	155		1929 Dec 23	KS, 49th, 1930
Shrader, John J.		F, 9th Ill. Cav. (former member of department)			1932 Dec 1	NE, 57th, 1933
Shrader, Samuel	Pvt.	C, 2nd Ky. Cav.	22		1933 Apr 9	IA, 60th, 1934
Shreckengast, Samuel		K, 12th Penn. Inf. (died of heart failure)	19	80	1911 Feb 9	NE, 36th, 1912
Shreeve, John S.			69		1900 Sep	IA, 27th, 1901
Shreeve, Walter		D, 2nd U.S. Art. (former member of Nebraska Dept.; location: Elm Creek)	178		1937 Jan 24	NE, 62nd, 1938
Shreeves, U.S.		C, 6th West Va. Art.	132		1914 Mar 5	KS, 34th, 1915
Shreffler, Edmund		B, 7th Ill. Inf. (died of old age)	22	85	1909 Jun 19	NE, 34th, 1910
Shreve, A.P.	Major & Paymaster	B, 6th Ohio Vol. Inf. U.S. Vols.	71		1902 Jun 27	KS, 22nd, 1903
Shreve, Jonathan	Pvt.	B, 29th Iowa Inf.	363		1902 Feb 12	IA, 29th, 1903
Shreves, B.F.	Pvt.	B, 79th Ill. Inf.	100		1921 Dec 19	IA, 48th, 1922
Shreves, M.	Pvt.		52		1916 Jun 16	IA, 43rd, 1917
Shriner, Alfred		G, 1st Md. Inf.	258		1887 Mar 15	KS, 7th, 1888
Shriver, Adam		I, 1st Penn.	19		1931 Jan 25	KS, 51st, 1932
Shriver, Adam		I, 1st Penn.	19		1932 Jan 25	KS, 52nd, 1933
Shriver, Chas.	Pvt.	E, 13th Iowa Inf.	122		1910 Mar 21	IA, 37th, 1911
Shriver, Henry		B, 106th Wis.	127		1924 Mar 17	KS, 44th, 1925
Shriver, Isaak		F, 165th Penn. Inf. (died of old age)	105	80	1913 Mar 16	NE, 38th, 1914
Shriver, J.		E, 74th Ind. Inf.	66		1916 Sep 15	KS, 36th, 1917
Shriver, W.R.	Lieut.	D, 1st Iowa Cav.	55		1915 Dec 20	IA, 42nd, 1916
Shrockmorton, John	Sergt.	E, 34th Iowa Inf.	491		1907 1st term	IA, 34th, 1908
Shrontz, J.F.		D, 18th Penn. Cav.	46		1916 Nov 13	KS, 36th, 1917
Shropshire, Thomas		3rd Colo. Cav.	58	87	1935 Nov 12	IA, 62nd, 1936

*See Appendix A, B or C for roster of post names and locations.
†See Introduction for note regarding recording of death date.

Name	Rank	Company, Regiment or Ship	Post*	Age	Death Date†	Journal
Shrout, H.E.		C, 50th Mo.	177		1887 Oct 9	KS, 7th, 1888
Shroyer, James		K, 91st Ind.	9		1923 Jul 20	KS, 43rd, 1924
Shroyer, Jas. M.	Pvt.	3rd Iowa Bat.	40		1918 Nov 28	IA, 45th, 1919
Shuch, W.	Pvt.	F, 75th Ohio Inf.	5	52	1897 Feb 13	IA, 24th, 1898
Shuck, G.C.		B, 31st Ohio	25		1930 Jul	NE, 55th, 1931
Shuck, J.S.		E, 7th Ind.	46		1898 May 15	KS, 18th, 1899
Shuck, Wm. Jasper	Corp.	B, 30th Iowa Inf. (at large)	328	99	1941 Mar 23	IA, 67th, 1941
Shuey, J.	Pvt.	I, 44th Iowa Inf.	456		1899 Jan	IA, 26th, 1900
Shuey, R.G.	Pvt.	H, 22nd Iowa Cav.	235		1919 Apr 25	IA, 46th, 1920
Shufeldt, Hiram W.		B, 17th Ill. Cav. (former member of department; location: Friend)	130		1938 Aug	NE, 63rd, 1939
Shugart, J.H.		H & A, 15th & 69th Iowa	110		1916 Mar 22	NE, 41st, 1917
Shuggard, Thos. B.	Pvt.	K, 2nd Iowa Cav.	5		1904 Oct 7	IA, 31st, 1905
Shukers, J.A.		B, 1st Ohio Lt. Art.	74		1922 May 15	KS, 42nd, 1923
Shuler, George	Pvt.	C, 31st Iowa Inf.	81		1933	IA, 60th, 1934
Shuler, John A.	Pvt.	B, 1st Ind. Hvy. Art.	116		1930 Jun 21	IA, 57th, 1931
Shull, Alonzo		F, 22nd Ind.	203		1918 Aug 20	KS, 38th, 1919
Shull, Chas. M.			7		1927	IA, 54th, 1928
Shull, D.A.		D, 72nd Ind.	21	75	1909 Jun 29	NE, 34th, 1910
Shull, Elias		B, 86th Ohio	1		1914 Nov 2	KS, 34th, 1915
Shull, Solomon		E, 132nd Ohio Cav.	293		1924	KS, 44th, 1925
Shultes, Adrian	Pvt.	C, 5th Wis. Inf.	157		1911 Oct 30	IA, 38th, 1912
Shultice, C.H.		H, 39th Ohio	127		1926 Aug 16	KS, 46th, 1927
Shultz, Calvin D.		H, S.S. (died of pneumonia)	110	72	1913 Feb 22	NE, 38th, 1914
Shultz, Eli		I, 39th Ill.	25		1927 Feb 21	NE, 52nd, 1928
Shultz, G.		E, 27th Ill.	380		1916 Jul 9	KS, 36th, 1917
Shultz, Henry A.	Sergt.	K, 34th Wis. Inf.	436		1911 Sep 29	IA, 38th, 1912
Shultz, J.N.		F, 11th Kans.	4		1926 Sep 23	KS, 46th, 1927
Shultz, John W.		Ill. (died of accident)	34	74	1921 Nov 2	NE, 46th, 1922
Shultz, Joseph	Pvt.	F, 76th Penn.	416		1923 Oct 25	IA, 50th, 1924
Shultz, Luis	Pvt.	B, 2nd Mo. Inf. D, U.S.R.C.	267	59	1898 Sep 3	IA, 25th, 1899
Shultz, Thomas		C, 18th U.S.	131		1906 Sep 20	KS, 26th, 1907
Shumaker, J.W.	Pvt.	E, 12th Iowa Inf.	68		1928 Jan 6	IA, 55th, 1929
Shumaker, M.H.	Pvt.	B, 25th Iowa Inf.	20		1922 Aug 15	IA, 49th, 1923
Shuman, H.C.		D, 63rd Ohio Inf.	17		1914 Mar 4	KS, 34th, 1915
Shumard, W.T.		A, 70th Ohio	49		1927	KS, 47th, 1928
Shumart, A.N.		G, 48th Ohio Inf. (died of old age)	284		1923 Oct 8	NE, 48th, 1924
Shumate, J.B.		K, 45th Ill.	144		1928	KS, 48th, 1929
Shumate, J.M.		B, 30th Ill.	53		1913 Mar 13	KS, 32nd, 1913
Shumate, John W.		H, 9th West Va.	1		1925	KS, 45th, 1926
Shumway, Henry L.		B, 2nd Mo.	1		1909 Feb 9	KS, 29th, 1910
Shumway, Lewelyn		D, 40th Ohio	71		1905 Sep 11	KS, 25th, 1906
Shumway, R.B.		F, 140th Ohio Inf.	20		1914 Jun 2	KS, 34th, 1915
Shunk, Allen		B, 133rd Penn.	42		1893 Feb 25	KS, 13th, 1894
Shupe, Daniel		E, 123rd Ill.	31	73	1918 Nov 2	NE, 43rd, 1919
Shupe, J.M.			309		1922	IA, 49th, 1923
Shupp, M.O.		I, 44th Ohio	110		1911 Nov 30	KS, 31st, 1912
Shurley, T.H.		E, 39th Ind.	286		1905	KS, 25th, 1906
Shurtleff, J.V.G.		K, 1st Maine Cav.	25	50	1895 May 19	NE, 20th, 1896
Shurtleff, Norman		H, 3rd Wis. Cav.	85		1925 Jul 6	KS, 45th, 1926
Shurtliff, C.	Pvt.	D, 4th Iowa Inf.	263		1905 Jun 1	IA, 32nd, 1906
Shurtz, H.H.		A, 2nd Car.	1		1917 Feb 19	KS, 37th, 1918
Shuster, William S.		H, 9th Kans. Cav. (died of old age)	22	84	1924 Sep 21	NE, 49th, 1925
Shute, Wm. R.		D, Penn. Berdan's Sharpshooters	11	55	1897 May 22	NE, 22nd, 1898
Shutterley, W.H.	Corp.	F, 36th Iowa Inf.	398		1909 Sep 16	IA, 36th, 1910
Shutterly, S.R.	Pvt.	E, 29th Iowa Inf.	56		1908 Mar 31	IA, 35th, 1909
Shutts, H.M.	Pvt.	E, 1st N.Y. Eng.	98		1902 Nov 13	IA, 29th, 1903
Shutts, L.E.	Pvt.	G, 13th Iowa Inf.	98		1929 Oct 15	IA, 56th, 1930
Shwal, Jacob		A, 2nd Ohio Cav. (died of cancer)	133	75	1916 Aug 29	NE, 41st, 1917
Sibbett, David		F, 2nd Kans.	3		1902 Nov 6	KS, 22nd, 1903
Sibert, J.G., M.D.	Hosp. Stew.	E, 56th Iowa Inf.	386	54	1897 Sep 25	IA, 24th, 1898

*See Appendix A, B or C for roster of post names and locations.
†See Introduction for note regarding recording of death date.
497

Name	Rank	Company, Regiment or Ship	Post*	Age	Death Date†	Journal
Siberts, Cyrus	Pvt. Corp.	G, 4th Iowa Inf. H, 45th Iowa Inf.	20		1903 Jul 11	IA, 30th, 1904
Sibil, John	Musician	37th Iowa Inf.	246		1904 Jan 6	IA, 31st, 1905
Sibrey, I.M.		K, 16th Ind. Inf.	216		1892 Mar	KS, 12th, 1893
Sickels, Daniel E.	Pvt.	G, 16th Penn. Cav.	190		1917 Nov 20	IA, 44th, 1918
Sickendick, George		H, 44th Ill.	17		1898 Jun 1	KS, 18th, 1899
Sickman, Daniel		96th Ohio	17		1909 Apr 15	KS, 29th, 1910
Sickofooce, M.		E, 44th Ind.	318	75	1917 Feb 1	NE, 42nd, 1918
Siddens, Jas. H.		C, 98th Ill. (died of old age)	25	78	1916 Apr 19	NE, 41st, 1917
Siddens, T.B.			25	65	1910 Jan 12	NE, 35th, 1911
Siddons, W.H.		C, 14th Ill.	57		1921 May 25	KS, 41st, 1922
Sidener, Jos. E.	Pvt.	A, 113th Ohio Inf.	7		1917 Mar 16	IA, 44th, 1918
Sider, H.A.	Pvt.	153rd Ind. Inf.	7		1927 Mar 25	IA, 54th, 1928
Sides, Alexander		I, 126th Ill. (died of paralysis)	13	74	1917 Nov 25	NE, 42nd, 1918
Sides, Jacob A.			170		1890	NE, 15th, 1891
Sides, John B.		G, 122nd Penn.	25	78	1910 Oct 16	NE, 35th, 1911
Sides, Sam'l	Pvt.	D, 4th Penn. Cav.	77		1905 Oct 25	IA, 32nd, 1906
Sidewell, Wm.	Pvt.	F, 17th Iowa Inf.	434		1904 Aug 28	IA, 31st, 1905
Sidle, D.M.		F, 134th Ohio	85		1929 Jul 5	KS, 49th, 1930
Sidler, Teater	Pvt.	B, 6th Kans. Inf.	122		1905 Dec 1	IA, 32nd, 1906
Sidles, James Z.		E, 46th Ill.	25		1927 Sep 6	NE, 52nd, 1928
Sidlinger, S.H.		E, 14th Ohio	17		1935 Dec 28	KS, 56th, 1937
Sidlow, J.W.		K, 8th Ill. Cav.	294		1931 Jul 1	KS, 52nd, 1933
Sidlow, J.W.		K, 8th Kans. Cav.	294		1931 Jul 1	KS, 51st, 1932
Sidner, W.M.		C, 140th Ill.	262	72	1904 Oct 25	NE, 29th, 1905
Sidney, E.		C, 8th Ill. Cav.	118		3rd quarter 1884	IA, 11th, 1885
Sidney, Edward	Pvt.	H, 49th U.S. Colored	256	43	1885	IA, 17th, 1891
Sidney, Edward	Pvt.	H, 49th U.S. Colored Inf.	256	43	1886 Feb	IA, 13th, 1887
Sidney, Woodridge		K, 13th Kans. Cav.	142		1923 Sep 2	KS, 43rd, 1924
Sidwell, J.W.		40th U.S. Cav.	1		1918 Sep 13	KS, 38th, 1919
Sidwell, Thos. R.	Pvt.	188th Penn. Inf.	343		1919 Nov 14	IA, 46th, 1920
Sieck, Henry	Corp.	B, 56th Ohio Inf.	75	56	1891 Jul 12	NE, 16th, 1892
Sieck, John J.D.		B, 32nd Ill.	284		1935 Mar 13	NE, 60th, 1936
Siever, George		F, 120th —	380		1914 May 14	KS, 34th, 1915
Siffler, G.L.		40th Iowa	448		1911 Dec 11	KS, 31st, 1912
Sigafoose, Lewis F.	Pvt.	K, 22nd Iowa Inf. (at large)	108	99, 8 mos. & 18 days	1943 Sep 25	IA, 70th, 1944
Sigerson, Wm.		E, 1st Ark. Inf.	25		1902 Jan 1	KS, 22nd, 1903
Sigler, Martin V.B.			291		1919	IA, 46th, 1920
Sigler, William H.		F, 12th V.R.C.	85		1915 Sep 23	KS, 35th, 1916
Signor, S.A.		C, 104th Ill. (died of heart trouble)	63	83	1917 Nov 1	NE, 42nd, 1918
Silas, Washington			236		1928 Jan 28	KS, 49th, 1930
Silcott, James A.	Pvt.	C, 34th Iowa	116		1905 Apr 17	IA, 32nd, 1906
Silcott, John			116		1917 Jan 15	IA, 44th, 1918
Siler, A.C.		I, 65th Ohio	12		1920 Feb 9	KS, 40th, 1921
Silick, Asher	Pvt.	I, 1st Mo. Inf.	153		1920 Mar 8	IA, 47th, 1921
Sill, H.F.	Capt.	C, 27th Iowa Inf.	54		1925 Feb 24	IA, 52nd, 1926
Sillett, Henry		E, 16th Ind.	1		1922 Feb 25	KS, 42nd, 1923
Sills, Burne			236		1927 Jul 4	KS, 47th, 1928
Sills, Edwin		A, 46th Ill.	1		1923 Apr 14	KS, 43rd, 1924
Sills, James B.		B, 1st Ohio Vol. Inf.	265		1915 Mar 29	KS, 35th, 1916
Sills, John		I, 11th Kans. Cav.	225		1911 Sep 21	KS, 31st, 1912
Silsby, L.S.G.	Pvt.	F, 138th Ohio Inf.	139	68	1894 Sep 7	IA, 21st, 1895
Silvernail, Geo. H.		K, 5th Wis. Inf.	113		1911 Jan 23	NE, 36th, 1912
Silvers, John	Pvt.	G, Ind. Inf.	186		1909 Oct 17	IA, 36th, 1910
Silverthorn, R.G.	Pvt.	B, 22nd Iowa Inf.	440		1904 Nov 28	IA, 31st, 1905
Silverthorn, Wm.	Pvt.	C, 7th Iowa Inf.	40		1906	IA, 33rd, 1907
Silvey, W.T.		G, 84th Ind. Inf.	57		1912 Sep 4	KS, 32nd, 1913
Simcox, Jacob		C, 55th Ill. Inf. (died at Neal)	269		1895 Apr	KS, 15th, 1896
Simeral, Jas. M.		L, 1st Iowa Cav. (died of exhaustion)	110	79	1902 Oct	NE, 27th, 1903

*See Appendix A, B or C for roster of post names and locations.
†See Introduction for note regarding recording of death date.
498

Name	Rank	Company, Regiment or Ship	Post*	Age	Death Date†	Journal
Simerson, Jos.	Pvt.	M, 2nd Wis. Cav.	216		1917 Aug 8	IA, 44th, 1918
Simmers, W.H.	Pvt.	H, 16th Iowa Inf.	235		1919 Oct 23	IA, 46th, 1920
Simmonds, E.L.		A, 80th Ill. Inf.	55		1937 May 17	KS, 56th, 1937
Simmonds, G.D.		I, 8th Ohio H, 41st Ohio	184		1911 Nov 6	KS, 31st, 1912
Simmonds, W.H.		E, 129th Ohio Vols.	184		1902 Apr 11	KS, 22nd, 1903
Simmons, B.R.		2nd Iowa Bat. (died of uremic trouble)	32	74	1913 Feb 5	NE, 38th, 1914
Simmons, Benj.	Pvt.	F, 3rd Iowa City	192		1911 Nov 16	IA, 38th, 1912
Simmons, C.R.		A, 13th Iowa	32		1900 Dec 6	KS, 20th, 1901
Simmons, C.S.	Pvt.	E, 14th N.Y. Inf.	222		1928 Jan 23	IA, 55th, 1929
Simmons, D.M.			116		1920	IA, 47th, 1921
Simmons, G.H.	Corp.	A, 1st Mich. Cav.	67		1924 Jun 26	IA, 51st, 1925
Simmons, J.W.	Pvt.	I, 44th Mo. Inf.	56		1920 Dec 4	IA, 47th, 1921
Simmons, James L.		H, 133rd Ill.	364		1911 Apr 25	KS, 31st, 1912
Simmons, L.A.		A, 84th Ill.	57		1888	KS, 8th, 1889
Simmons, Samuel W.	Pvt.	C, 24th Iowa Inf.	110	67	1892 Nov 7	IA, 19th, 1893
Simmons, W.B.		F, 40th Ohio	379		1888	KS, 8th, 1889
Simmons, W.H.	Pvt.	C, 2nd Iowa Cav.	452		1914 Aug	IA, 41st, 1915
Simmons, Wm.		K, 6th Mo. Cav.	12		1906 Dec 24	KS, 26th, 1907
Simms, George	Pvt.	F, 4th Iowa Inf.	7		1929 Mar 8	IA, 56th, 1930
Simms, James		K, 107th Ill.	18		1912 Mar 2	KS, 32nd, 1913
Simon, D.C.	Saddler	G, 2nd Ill. Cav.	235	53	1899 Mar 23	IA, 25th, 1899
Simon, Fred	Musician	D, 1st Md.	235		1922 May 23	IA, 49th, 1923
Simon, Henry		B, 41st N.Y.	414		1902 Aug 20	KS, 22nd, 1903
Simon, Wilhelm	Pvt.	H, 11th Iowa Inf.	231		1930 Sep 21	IA, 57th, 1931
Simonds, George		6th Mich. Cav.	93		1902 Jun 9	KS, 22nd, 1903
Simons, A.		L, 16th Ohio	180		1911 Jul 20	KS, 31st, 1912
Simons, D.E.	Pvt.	C, 35th N.Y. Inf.	23		1930 Feb 1	IA, 57th, 1931
Simons, Daniel	Pvt.	A, 25th Iowa Vol. Inf.	108		1924 Jan 8	IA, 51st, 1925
Simons, E.I.			8		1883	KS, 3rd, 1884
Simons, G.W.		F, 11th Kans. Inf.	180		1886	KS, 6th, 1887
Simons, J.M.	Pvt.	E, 36th Iowa Inf.	5		1905 Jan	IA, 32nd, 1906
Simons, L.		Kans.	282		1912 Aug	KS, 32nd, 1913
Simons, M.L.	Pvt.	C, 2nd Iowa Cav.	109		1907 Sep 1	IA, 34th, 1908
Simons, W.H.		A, 77th Ohio	12		1897 Jun 26	KS, 17th, 1898
Simonson, H.	Pvt.	H, 9th Iowa Inf.	194		1908	IA, 35th, 1909
Simonton, C.A.		G, 7th Ind.	1		1897 Jun 18	KS, 17th, 1898
Simonton, S.S.		D, 7th Iowa Inf. (died in Oklahoma Territory)	1		1895 Jul	KS, 15th, 1896
Simpkins, A.W.		D, 2nd Neb. Cav. (died of pneumonia)	36	74	1916 Dec 21	NE, 41st, 1917
Simpkins, Alpheus W.	Pvt.	D, 2nd Neb. Cav.		92	1936 May 24	IA, 65th, 1939
Simpkins, Alpheus W.		D, 2nd Neb. Cav.	10		1936 May 24	NE, 61st, 1937
Simpkins, G.W.		G, 83rd Ill. Inf.	68		1929 Jan 8	NE, 53rd, 1929
Simplot, Chas.	Com. Sergt.	46th Iowa Inf.	78		1900 Dec 2	IA, 27th, 1901
Simpson, A.H.		I, 28th Iowa (died at Kansas City)	28		1895 Mar 16	KS, 15th, 1896
Simpson, A.M.		C, 9th Ind. (died of paralysis)	111	83	1924 Mar 18	NE, 49th, 1925
Simpson, A.P.	Pvt.	E, 22nd N.Y.	74		1907 Dec 5	IA, 34th, 1908
Simpson, B.D.		E, 78th Ill. Inf.	174		1900 Sep 28	KS, 20th, 1901
Simpson, Basil M.	Sergt.	D, 43rd Ohio Inf.	58		1915 Aug 15	IA, 42nd, 1916
Simpson, Daniel		F, 38th Iowa	431		1898 Nov 22	KS, 18th, 1899
Simpson, Edward	Pvt.	A, 96th Ill. Inf.	267	57	1893 Feb 18	IA, 20th, 1894
Simpson, F.L.		D, 39th Ohio	129		1923 Jul 11	KS, 43rd, 1924
Simpson, George		B, 2nd Colo.	38		1914 Oct 6	KS, 34th, 1915
Simpson, Gilead	Pvt.	C, 6th Mo. Cav.	379		1902 Dec 2	IA, 29th, 1903
Simpson, H.E.		A, 154th Ill. Inf.	198		1916 Nov 13	KS, 36th, 1917
Simpson, Horace	Pvt.	H, 26th Iowa	117	52	1891 Feb 27	IA, 17th, 1891
Simpson, J.E.	2nd Lieut.	G, 12th Iowa Inf.	168		1904 Sep 22	IA, 31st, 1905
Simpson, J.E.			29		1911 Feb 6	IA, 38th, 1912
Simpson, J.P.					[1938?]	KS, 58th, 1939
Simpson, James H.		L, 11th Kans. Cav.	88		1908 Nov 19	KS, 28th, 1909
Simpson, John F.		E, Ill.	63		1939 May 1	KS, 59th, 1940
Simpson, Jos.		E, 13th Ill.	104		1931 May 15	KS, 51st, 1932

*See Appendix A, B or C for roster of post names and locations.
†See Introduction for note regarding recording of death date.

Name	Rank	Company, Regiment or Ship	Post*	Age	Death Date†	Journal
Simpson, Jos.		E, 13th Ill.	104		1931 May 15	KS, 52nd, 1933
Simpson, Nathan	Pvt.	C, 21st Iowa	78		1907 Apr 28	IA, 34th, 1908
Simpson, R.S.		G, 41st Ill.	87		1926 Jan 2	KS, 46th, 1927
Simpson, Robert		K, 9th Kans.	38		1930 Oct 7	KS, 50th, 1931
Simpson, Walter A.			67		1900 Jan 12	IA, 27th, 1901
Simpson, Wm.	Pvt.	G, 142nd Ill. Inf.	163		1909 Apr 5	IA, 36th, 1910
Sims, David	Corp.	I, 142nd Ohio Inf.	55		1915 Aug 3	IA, 42nd, 1916
Sims, F.W.	Pvt.	I, 92nd Ill. Inf.	7		1929 Dec 15	IA, 56th, 1930
Sims, George	Pvt.	D, 40th Iowa Inf.	252	67	1894 Jun 17	IA, 21st, 1895
Sims, George D.		D, 38th Iowa Inf.	36		1900 May 12	KS, 21st, 1902
Sims, John	Pvt.	1st Minn. Inf.	216		1924 Mar 26	IA, 51st, 1925
Sims, M.		G, 79th —	365		1917	KS, 37th, 1918
Sims, Milton		G, 79th U.S.C.	365		1928	KS, 48th, 1929
Sims, W.A.		I, 2nd Mo. Cav.	47		1913 Jan 24	KS, 33rd, 1914
Sims, Wm.		G, 8th Mo. Inf. (died of stomach trouble)	22	67	1909 Jan or Jun 5	NE, 34th, 1910
Sinclair, Archie	Pvt.	H, 1st Iowa Cav.	337		1916 Apr 26	IA, 43rd, 1917
Sinclair, C.C.		B, 132nd Penn.	1		1935	KS, 55th, 1936
Sinclair, Frank	Pvt.	G, 136th N.Y. Inf.	5		1913 Aug 18	IA, 40th, 1914
Sinclair, John		A, 13th Ind. Cav.	345		1892 Apr 19	KS, 12th, 1893
Sinclair, Sam	Pvt.	Washington Cav.	40	71	1890 Jul 22	IA, 18th, 1892
Sinclair, W.T.		A, 165th N.Y.	12		1914 May 1	KS, 34th, 1915
Sinclair, William		H, 130th Ind.	293		1914 Sep 22	KS, 34th, 1915
Sinclair, Wm.		E, 121st Penn.	72		1933 Oct 4	KS, 53rd, 1934
Sindlinger, Wm.	Pvt.	G, 46th Ill. Inf.	68		1909 May 1	IA, 36th, 1910
Sine, John	Pvt.	F, 31st Wis. Inf.	68		1911 Oct 2	IA, 38th, 1912
Singer, A.	Pvt.	6th Iowa Inf.	20		1914	IA, 41st, 1915
Singer, David		C, 38th Ohio	26		1921 Nov 21	KS, 41st, 1922
Singer, F.A.	Pvt.	A, 46th Iowa Inf.	22		1930	IA, 57th, 1931
Singleton, Adolph		H, 21st Mo.	185		1926 Dec 28	KS, 46th, 1927
Singleton, John	Pvt.	E, 20th Ind. Inf.	98	53	1892 Nov 21	IA, 19th, 1893
Singleton, John W.		I, 25th Mo.	81		1924 Jan 28	KS, 44th, 1925
Singleton, William			106		1884	KS, 4th, 1885
Singley, William		K, 194th Penn.	17		1920 Aug 20	KS, 40th, 1921
Sinix, Chas.			[89]		1923	KS, 43rd, 1924
Sinkhorn, W.F.		A, 4th Ky.	125		1912 May 20	KS, 32nd, 1913
Sinn, John		A, 195th Penn.	17		1924 Jun 30	KS, 44th, 1925
Sipes, Ed		D, 13th Kans.	1		1921 Feb 22	KS, 41st, 1922
Sipes, Geo. W.	Lieut.	C, 9th Penn. Cav.	44		1912 Jul 18	IA, 39th, 1913
Sipes, John		D, 13th Kans.	1		1927 Jun 26	KS, 47th, 1928
Sipes, Samuel	Pvt.		52		1931 Jan	IA, 58th, 1932
Sipes, Samuel	Pvt.		52		1931 Jan	IA, 57th, 1931
Siphers, John M.		E, 83rd Ill. Inf. (died of Bright's disease)	55	66	1906 Apr 1	NE, 31st, 1907
Sipna, S.R.	Pvt.	G, 33rd Iowa Inf.	22		1932 Oct 30	IA, 59th, 1933
Sipp, W.J.		E, 88th Ill.	113		1928 Jan 15	KS, 48th, 1929
Sisley, A.S.	Pvt.	C, 142nd Ind.	2		1921 Oct 23	IA, 48th, 1922
Sisson, Francis L.		5th Wis. Battery	140		1923 Feb 27	NE, 49th, 1925
Sisson, J.J.		B, 13th Iowa	418		1931	KS, 51st, 1932
Sisson, J.J.		B, 13th Iowa	418		1931	KS, 52nd, 1933
Sisson, Joseph F.	Pvt.	K, 27th Wis. Inf.	339		1900 Aug 9	IA, 27th, 1901
Sisson, W.C.		D, 13th Iowa	40		1922 Aug 12	KS, 42nd, 1923
Sitler, H.L.		I, 2nd Penn. Cav.	294		1917 Oct 30	KS, 37th, 1918
Sitler, J.R.	1st Lieut.	L, 9th Penn. Cav.	16		1914 Dec 27	IA, 41st, 1915
Sitler, L.C.	Pvt.	A, 25th Iowa Inf.	108		1912	IA, 39th, 1913
Sitley, Joseph B.		G, 65th N.Y.	380		1897 Dec 18	KS, 17th, 1898
Siton, William	Sergt.	E, 12th N.Y.	15		1901 May 25	IA, 28th, 1902
Sitterly, Abram		K, 91st N.Y.	100		1930 Mar 5	KS, 50th, 1931
Sitts, J.W.		G, 8th Ill.	87		1926 Mar 28	KS, 46th, 1927
Siuniford, Oscar	Sergt.	B, 102nd Ohio (not member of the post, but buried by it)	[64?]		1885	KS, 5th, 1886
Sivard, H.H.			85		1893 Oct 25	KS, 13th, 1894
Sivearenger, Geo.	Pvt.	F, 84th Ill. Inf.	16		1909 Feb 21	IA, 36th, 1910
Siverly, George		H, 45th Iowa Inf.	8	93	1937 Dec 28	IA, 64th, 1938

*See Appendix A, B or C for roster of post names and locations.
†See Introduction for note regarding recording of death date.

Name	Rank	Company, Regiment or Ship	Post*	Age	Death Date†	Journal
Sivers, Wm. E.			294		1923 Dec 8	KS, 43rd, 1924
Six, Lewis	Corp.		18		1920 Mar	IA, 47th, 1921
Sixberry, Chas. H.		A, 15th Mich. Inf. (died of heart failure)	229	58	1895 May 11	NE, 20th, 1896
Sixbury, C.E.	Sergt.	A, 105th Ill. Inf.	252		1917 Sep 4	IA, 44th, 1918
Sizer, Geo.	Pvt.	A, 24th Iowa Inf.	164		1906 Apr 13	IA, 33rd, 1907
Sizer, Geo.	Pvt.	A, 24th Iowa Inf.	164		1906 Apr 13	IA, 32nd, 1906
Skea, J.P.	Musician	D, 8th Iowa Inf.	235		1921 Jul 26	IA, 48th, 1922
Skeers, Charles			33		1923	KS, 43rd, 1924
Skeers, Charles		M, 4th Iowa Cav.	34		1922 Oct 31	KS, 42nd, 1923
Skibauske, L.		F, 1st N.J. Cav. (died of paralysis)	197		1894 Jun 17	NE, 19th, 1895
Skidmore, James		G, 7th Mo. Cav.	25		[1939?]	KS, 59th, 1940
Skiff, H.S.	Pvt.	B, 13th Iowa Inf.	16		1904 Nov 12	IA, 32nd, 1906
Skiles, James M.		C, 3rd Mo. Cav. (died of general debility)	111	78	1919 May 6	NE, 44th, 1920
Skiles, Robert		Iowa, in Navy (died of natural causes)	5	80	1922 Sep 15	NE, 47th, 1923
Skiles, William		G, 5th Ill. Cav.	89		1916 Jul 29	KS, 36th, 1917
Skinner, Alfred J.	Pvt.	I, 22nd Mich. Inf.	366		1918 Mar 7	IA, 45th, 1919
Skinner, Benj. F.	Pvt.	G, 1st Iowa Cav.	190	49	1892 May 3	IA, 19th, 1893
Skinner, C.R.	Pvt.	D, 92nd Ill. Inf.	235		1920 Mar 9	IA, 47th, 1921
Skinner, Charles			22		1925 Sep 28	KS, 45th, 1926
Skinner, Cooper	Pvt.	G, 45th Ohio Inf.	57		1919 Dec 11	IA, 46th, 1920
Skinner, Elias	Chaplain	24th Iowa Inf.	68		1912 May 1	IA, 39th, 1913
Skinner, F.S.		I, 1st Md. Cav.	46		1913 Nov 14	KS, 33rd, 1914
Skinner, G.W.		I, 97th N.Y.	96		1886 Aug 26	KS, 12th, 1893
Skinner, I.H.		A, 20th Ind.	28		1919 May 18	KS, 39th, 1920
Skinner, J.O.			7		1909 Jan 15	IA, 36th, 1910
Skinner, James M.		F, 44th Iowa	25		1915 Oct 3	NE, 40th, 1916
Skinner, James T.			226		1901 Sep	KS, 21st, 1902
Skinner, Jas. L.		E, 2nd Neb.	90		1933 Mar 17	KS, 53rd, 1934
Skinner, John	Pvt.	A, 1st Iowa Cav.	12	92	1935 Mar 14	IA, 65th, 1939
Skinner, Joseph B.		F, 1st Vt. Art.	250		1917 Mar 11	KS, 37th, 1918
Skinner, S.S.		E, 8th N.Y. Hvy. Art. Neb. (died of neuralgia of heart)	118	61	1908 Oct 4	NE, 33rd, 1909
Skinner, T.E.		G, 1st Colo. Cav. (died at Beverly)	422		1895 Oct	KS, 15th, 1896
Skinner, W.H.	Pvt.	I, 147th Ill. Inf.	371	62	1888 Apr 23	IA, 15th, 1889
Skinner, W.H.		E, 112th N.Y.	43		1917 Dec 22	KS, 37th, 1918
Skinner, Wm. T.		E, 3rd Iowa Cav.	12		1920 Oct 29	KS, 40th, 1921
Skipton, Wm.		92nd Ohio Inf.	108		1913	IA, 40th, 1914
Skuls, H. Clay	Pvt.	A, 146th Ill. Inf.	242		1918 Feb 20	IA, 45th, 1919
Slaae, George E.		E, 113th Ill. Inf. (died of pneumonia)	54		1893 Nov 20	NE, 18th, 1894
Slack, J.R.		K, 22nd Penn. Cav. (died of tumor)	156		1893 Nov 13	NE, 18th, 1894
Slack, Samuel			17		1909 May 28	KS, 29th, 1910
Slad, Franklin	Pvt.	E, 31st Iowa Inf.	70		1919	IA, 46th, 1920
Slade, Clark M.	Pvt.	L, 1st Iowa Cav.	452	85	1931 Apr 19	IA, 58th, 1932
Slade, Edward		I, 81st Ohio Inf.	301		1929 Apr 10	KS, 49th, 1930
Slade, George E., see Slaae, George E.						
Slagle, Henry			497		1907 Mar 3	IA, 34th, 1908
Slaight, Chas. P.	Pvt.	A, 7th Iowa Cav.	8	55	1890 Mar 7	IA, 16th, 1890
Slain, John		N, 8th Ill.	294		1909 Sep	KS, 29th, 1910
Slama, Joseph	Pvt.	D, 22nd Wis. Inf.	236	49	1895 Jan 15	IA, 21st, 1895
Slancell, Wm. L.		D, 1st Ark.	92		1922 Apr 22	KS, 42nd, 1923
Slaneost, Joel		D, 191st Ohio Inf.	18		1901 Feb 27	KS, 21st, 1902
Slapman, Elias		H, 8th U.S. Inf.	252		1922 Aug 31	KS, 42nd, 1923
Slater, Thomas	Pvt.	K, 12th Wis. Inf.	150		1916 Jan 17	IA, 42nd, 1916
Slater, Wilson		K, 182nd Ohio Inf. (died of rheumatism of heart)	282		1893 Oct 29	NE, 18th, 1894
Slater, Wm.			45		1908 Dec 16	NE, 33rd, 1909
Slattery, James		I, 55th Ill.	58		1917 Dec 24	KS, 37th, 1918
Slatton, James		C, 31st Ill. Cav.	54		1913 Aug 26	KS, 33rd, 1914
Slaughter, Frank		A, 3rd Ohio	171		1928 Feb 26	KS, 48th, 1929
Slaughter, J.M.		F, 1st West Va.	265		1892 Nov 28	KS, 12th, 1893
Slaughter, John	Pvt.	17th Ind.	69		1924 Mar 19	IA, 51st, 1925

*See Appendix A, B or C for roster of post names and locations.
†See Introduction for note regarding recording of death date.
501

Name	Rank	Company, Regiment or Ship	Post*	Age	Death Date†	Journal
Slaughter, Taylor		A, 25th U.S.C.T.	52		1922 Apr 22	KS, 42nd, 1923
Slaughter, W.H.	Pvt.	K, 20th Iowa Inf.	1		1917 Feb 15	IA, 44th, 1918
Slauson, James	Pvt.	K, 21st Iowa Inf.	206		1918 Mar 8	IA, 45th, 1919
Slauter, Geo.		K, 8th Iowa Cav.	110		1917 Feb 7	IA, 44th, 1918
Slavins, Jos.	Pvt.	L, 1st Ohio Lt. Art.	186	45	1888 Mar	IA, 15th, 1889
Slavon, James (alias McKinney, Barney)		B, 40th N.Y. Inf. (died of paralysis at Soldiers & Sailors Home, Grand Island; buried in Home Cemetery)	1	67	1905 Jan 5	NE, 30th, 1906
Slawson, A.C.	Pvt.	5th Wis. Battery	25		1927 Oct	IA, 54th, 1928
Slawson, Chas. H.		I, 8th Kans.	49		1899 Jan 31	KS, 19th, 1900
Slawson, Earl B.		B, 34th Wis.	25		1913 Aug 4	NE, 38th, 1914
Slawson, John		E, 81st Ill.	322		1922 Feb 12	KS, 42nd, 1923
Slaymaker, Henry, see Sleymaker, Henry						
Sleanmon, F.		G, 178th Penn.	294		1906 Apr 5	KS, 26th, 1907
Sleath, Amos		D, 123rd Ill.	444		1893 Aug 14	KS, 13th, 1894
Sleath, Wm. M.		A, 78th Ohio	158		1906 Sep 26	KS, 26th, 1907
Sleeper, E.N.	Pvt.	I, 34th Iowa Inf.	42		1913 May 25	IA, 40th, 1914
Sleeper, S.A.	Pvt.	K, 4th Maine Inf.	408	46	1887 May 16	IA, 14th, 1888
Sleeth, Addison		G, 52nd Ind.	72		1912 Sep 18	KS, 32nd, 1913
Sleggel, D.C.	Pvt.	M, 9th Ohio Cav.	321		1920 May 30	IA, 47th, 1921
Sleigal, D.C.			321		1919 May 30	IA, 46th, 1920
Sleiumety, John		E, 57th Ohio	28		1908[1909?] Dec 3	KS, 29th, 1910
Slemniety, Jacob		B, 186th Ohio Inf.	207		1912 Oct 3	NE, 37th, 1913
Sleymaker, Henry		C, Wis. Brackets B.	39	71	1906 Nov 4	NE, 31st, 1907
Slider, Jacob		K, 200th Penn.	25	86	1919 Jul 12	NE, 44th, 1920
Slife, James	Pvt.	G, 24th Iowa Inf.	212		1917 May 10	IA, 44th, 1918
Sloan, Henry	Pvt.	E, 150th N.Y. Inf.	327	74	1894 Jun 20	IA, 21st, 1895
Sloan, J.G.		D, 47th Ohio Inf. (died of consumption)	95	65	1903 Oct 9	NE, 28th, 1904
Sloan, J.M.	Pvt.	B, 1st Ohio Art.	49		1917 Apr 7	IA, 44th, 1918
Sloan, James			150		1884	KS, 4th, 1885
Sloan, S.B.			190		1929 Oct 10	IA, 56th, 1930
Sloan, Wm.		170th Ohio Inf.	29		1927 Jan 2	IA, 54th, 1928
Sloane, Thos. O.	Corp.	K, 137th Ohio Inf.	22		1929 Dec 17	IA, 56th, 1930
Sloat, Burget R.		B, 2nd Calif.	60		1926 May 16	NE, 51st, 1927
Slocum, A.J.		F, 160th N.Y. (died of heart trouble)	182	76	1922 Nov 30	NE, 47th, 1923
Slocum, C.A.	Capt.	G, 27th Iowa Inf.	3		1912 Apr 30	IA, 39th, 1913
Slocum, C.B.		C, 136th Ill. Inf. (born in White County, Ill.; died in Lincoln, Neb.)	77		1883 Feb 7	NE, 8th, 1884
Slocum, Ed. R.	Pvt.	A, 124th Ill. Inf.	116	49	1895 Nov 20	IA, 22nd, 1896
Slocum, J.W.	Pvt.	D, 17th Penn. Cav.	141	74[?]	1899 Jan 4	IA, 25th, 1899
Slocum, John		M, 1st Mo.	46		1928 Feb 5	KS, 48th, 1929
Slocum, John R.	Pvt.	K, 22nd Wis. Inf.	68		1900-1901	IA, 27th, 1901
Slocum, John R.	Pvt.	D, 22nd Wis. Inf.	68	53	1900 Apr 9	IA, 26th, 1900
Slocum, Jonah		U.S. Navy	1		1891 Apr 10	KS, 11th, 1892
Slocum, W.T.	Pvt.	H, 83rd Ill. Inf.	235		1926 Nov 28	IA, 53rd, 1927
Slocum, Willis		1st N.Y. Bat.	259		1912 Jun 10	KS, 32nd, 1913
Sloniger, J.K.P.		G, 27th Mo.	52		1914 Mar 6	KS, 34th, 1915
Sloop, B.		B, 2nd Mo.	25		1927 Apr 16	KS, 47th, 1928
Sloop, Jacob		1st Ill. Lt. Art.	84		1913 Sep 17	KS, 33rd, 1914
Slosson, Nathaniel		G, 13th Kans. Inf.	175		1886	KS, 6th, 1887
Slote, James		11th Mich. Inf. (died of pneumonia)	231	59	1902 Jan	NE, 27th, 1903
Slothower, J.B.		H, 87th Penn. Inf. (died of cancer)	55	67	1902 Apr	NE, 27th, 1903
Slunner, Thomas W.		C, 2nd Wis.	185		1915 Jan 23	KS, 35th, 1916
Slup, William		B, 47th Ill.	209		1908 May 3	KS, 28th, 1909
Sluss, Henry C.		E, 12th Ill.	25		1926 Aug 7	KS, 46th, 1927
Slusser, Obadiah B.		E, 48th Ind.	225		1919 Nov 28	KS, 39th, 1920
Smail, Geo. W.		B, 140th Penn.	239		1921 Oct 23	KS, 41st, 1922
Small, F.M.			[65?]		1898 Apr 9	KS, 18th, 1899
Small, H.L.		C, 6th Vt. Inf. (died of general debility)	9		1902 Jan	NE, 27th, 1903
Small, J.W.		G, 2nd Ill. Lt. Art. (died of pneumonia)	32		1893 Mar	NE, 18th, 1894
Small, James	Pvt.	I, 22nd Iowa Inf.	37		1922 Oct 27	IA, 49th, 1923

*See Appendix A, B or C for roster of post names and locations.
†See Introduction for note regarding recording of death date.

Name	Rank	Company, Regiment or Ship	Post*	Age	Death Date†	Journal
Small, Jno. A.	Pvt.	A, 194th Penn.	40		1923 Dec 26	IA, 50th, 1924
Small, John		B, 67th Ohio Vol. Inf.	159		1899 Nov 28	KS, 19th, 1900
Small, John W.	Sergt.	E, 147th Ill. Inf.	132		1885 Oct 14	IA, 12th, 1886
Small, Robert	Pvt.	F, 191st Ohio Inf.	168	66	1894 Mar 10	IA, 20th, 1894
Small, S.F.	Pvt.	K, 7th Ill.	153		1924	IA, 51st, 1925
Smalldon, John		K, 26th Ill. (died of paralysis, age)	79	76	1917 Jun 7	NE, 42nd, 1918
Smalley, H.D.		H, 162nd Ohio	132		1910 Jun 31	KS, 30th, 1911
Smalley, J.H.		G, 8th Ind.	28		1922 Sep 28	KS, 42nd, 1923
Smalley, John W.		C, 70th Ohio	428		1914 Jul 2	KS, 34th, 1915
Smally, E.	Pvt.	C, 1st Ill. Art.	118	44	1889 Dec 11	IA, 16th, 1890
Smarngin, E.E.	Capt.	F, 17th Iowa	113		1890	KS, 10th, 1891
Smart, F.C.		A, 145th Penn.	301		1923 Apr 6	KS, 43rd, 1924
Smart, M.J.		G, 11th Wis. Inf.	51		1925 Dec 14	KS, 45th, 1926
Smart, W.		H, 22nd Iowa Inf.	75	72	1905 Jul 25	NE, 30th, 1906
Smedley, Edwin	Pvt.	E, 4th Ohio Inf.	78		1908 Sep 7	IA, 35th, 1909
Smedley, Jacob		D, 10th Ill. Inf.	339		1930 Jun 7	KS, 50th, 1931
Smeed, E.O.			299		1915 Apr 10	NE, 40th, 1916
Smeltzer, D.B.		D, 11th Ill.	[51?]		1937 Jul 19	KS, 56th, 1937
Smidt, H.D.	Pvt.	E, 16th Ill. Cav.	40		1925 Apr 17	IA, 52nd, 1926
Smiley, J.F.	Pvt.	E, 139th Ill.	9		1898 Dec 26	IA, 25th, 1899
Smiley, John	Pvt.	G, —	8		1908	IA, 35th, 1909
Smiley, John	Lieut.	G, 22nd Iowa Inf.	8		1908 Apr 24	IA, 35th, 1909
Smiley, John A.		F, 20th Ind.	23		1916 Jun 27	KS, 36th, 1917
Smiley, R.M.		A, 23rd Mo. Inf.	63		1914 Mar 10	KS, 34th, 1915
Smiley, Thomas	Pvt.	K, 36th Iowa Inf.	337		1901 Apr 15	IA, 28th, 1902
Smirce, Wm. L.		D, 12th Kans.	18		1906 Jun 26	KS, 26th, 1907
Smith, A.A.	Pvt.	1st Wis. Inf.	132	52	1897 Mar 14	IA, 24th, 1898
Smith, A.D.	Pvt.	F, 31st Wis. Inf.	452		1910 Aug	IA, 37th, 1911
Smith, A.H.	Pvt.	G, 24th Iowa Inf.	235		1905 Dec 15	IA, 32nd, 1906
Smith, A.H.		H, 12th Kans.	8		1904 Apr 5	KS, 24th, 1905
Smith, A.J.	Pvt.	19th Iowa Inf.	384		1897 Sep 3	IA, 24th, 1898
Smith, A.L.	Pvt.	C, 123rd Ohio	12		1922 Oct 31	IA, 49th, 1923
Smith, A.M.	Pvt.	F, 16th Ill. Inf.	8		1927 Mar 3	IA, 54th, 1928
Smith, A. Starr	Pvt.	B, 13th U.S. Inf.	235		1916 Apr 20	IA, 43rd, 1917
Smith, A.T.	Pvt.	G, 40th Ohio Inf.	59		1921 Jul 2	IA, 48th, 1922
Smith, A.W.			24		1906 May	KS, 25th, 1906
Smith, A.W.		49th Ohio	43		1906 May 8	KS, 26th, 1907
Smith, A.W.	Sergt.	B, 1st Battalion, 19th U.S. Inf. (see also Appendix D)	87		1919 Jan 2	KS, 39th, 1920
Smith, A.W.		E, 10th —	4		1923 Oct 13	KS, 43rd, 1924
Smith, Aaron	Pvt.	B, 133rd Ohio Vol. Inf.	30	68	1885 Jul 23	IA, 12th, 1886
Smith, Ab. C.	Corp.	F, 9th Iowa	48		1891 May 18	IA, 18th, 1892
Smith, Abraham W.	Sergt.	B, 1st Battalion, 19th U.S. Inf. (see Appendix D)		76	1919 Jan 2	KS, 38th, 1919
Smith, Adam	Pvt.	L, 21st Penn. Cav.	333		1926 May 3	IA, 53rd, 1927
Smith, Adam		K, 12th Kans.	3		1898 Sep 5	KS, 18th, 1899
Smith, Adam		B, 153rd Penn.	69		1921 Feb 22	KS, 41st, 1922
Smith, Adam		B, 26th Ind. Inf. (died of comp[lication] of diseases)	40	82	1918 Apr 29	NE, 43rd, 1919
Smith, Adam N.	Pvt.	F, 31st Iowa Inf.	207	50	1886 Jul 23	IA, 13th, 1887
Smith, Albert	Pvt.	F, 46th Iowa Inf.	78	45	1887 Jun 23	IA, 14th, 1888
Smith, Albert		B, 102nd Ill.	46		1931 Jan 18	KS, 52nd, 1933
Smith, Albert		B, 102nd Ill.	46		1931 Jan 18	KS, 51st, 1932
Smith, Alvin H.		73rd Ind.	63		1924 Aug 8	KS, 44th, 1925
Smith, Anderson		C, 128th Ind. Inf. (died of old age)	4	80	1920 Sep 20	NE, 45th, 1921
Smith, Anson			38		1919	IA, 46th, 1920
Smith, Anson		H, 75th Ill.	18		1909 Aug 23	KS, 29th, 1910
Smith, Aron	Pvt.	B, 3rd Iowa Inf.	16	92	1932 Jun 28	IA, 59th, 1933
Smith, Asa		C, 148th Ind. Inf. (died at Girard, Kans.; buried at Girard Cemetery)	49		1894 Dec 3	KS, 14th, 1895
Smith, Asa B.	Corp.	C, 97th Ohio Inf.	400		1930 Jul 25	IA, 57th, 1931
Smith, Asa W.		E, 50th Ohio	222		1912 Nov 30	KS, 32nd, 1913

Name	Rank	Company, Regiment or Ship	Post*	Age	Death Date†	Journal
Smith, Ashley	Sergt.	E, 38th Wis. Inf.	124		1902	IA, 29th, 1903
Smith, B.A.	Pvt.	G, 31st Iowa Inf.	130	60	1889 Apr 18	IA, 16th, 1890
Smith, B. Carl		H, 47th Ind. Inf. (died at Sedgwick; buried at Pleasant Valley Cemetery)	255		1894 Feb 3	KS, 14th, 1895
Smith, B.F.		D, 73rd Ind. Cav.	25		1938 Jul 6	KS, 59th, 1940
Smith, B.P.		G, 80th Penn. Inf.	17		1912	KS, 32nd, 1913
Smith, Barney	Corp.	E, 92nd Ill. Inf.	222		1917 Oct	IA, 44th, 1918
Smith, Barney		E, 10th Tenn.	103		1900 Feb 25	KS, 20th, 1901
Smith, Benj.	Pvt.	C, 76th Ill. Inf.	165		1892 Feb 17	IA, 18th, 1892
Smith, Benj.		G, 149th Ohio Inf.	50		1900 Jun 12	KS, 20th, 1901
Smith, Benjamin	Pvt.	C, 76th Ill. Inf.	165		1892 Feb 17	IA, 19th, 1893
Smith, Bond		I, 12th U.S. Hvy. Art.	321		1909 Sep 27	KS, 29th, 1910
Smith, Buntin	Capt.	A, 2nd Kans. State Militia	322		1905 Jul 22	KS, 25th, 1906
Smith, C.		A, 116th —	18		1921	IA, 48th, 1922
Smith, C.A.			69		1913 Oct	IA, 40th, 1914
Smith, C.A.		C, 4th Mich. Cav.	28	72	1906 Mar 19	NE, 31st, 1907
Smith, C.C.		K, 21st Wis. Inf. (died at Alton, Kans.; buried at Ashbrook Cemetery)	106		1894 Jun 16	KS, 14th, 1895
Smith, C.C.		Md.			1902 Nov	KS, 22nd, 1903
Smith, C.M.		97th Ill. Inf.	51		1899 Feb 8	KS, 19th, 1900
Smith, C.N.	Pvt.	A, 4th Iowa Cav.	56		1928 Dec 27	IA, 55th, 1929
Smith, C.O.	Col.	B, 15th Ky.	17		1938 Feb 26	KS, 57th, 1938
Smith, C.S.			25		1900 Jan 14	KS, 20th, 1901
Smith, C.T.		F, 27th Mass. Inf.	7		1928 Feb 27	NE, 53rd, 1929
Smith, Charles		C, 61st Mass.	5		1924 Mar 23	KS, 44th, 1925
Smith, Charles A.		13th Ill. Cav.	52		1917 Apr 13	KS, 37th, 1918
Smith, Charles A.		C, 17th Mich.	35		1932 Aug	NE, 57th, 1933
Smith, Charles H.	Lieut.	C, 4th Iowa Cav. (see also Appendix D)	20		1910 Sep 25	IA, 37th, 1911
Smith, Chas.	Pvt.	D, 57th Ohio	166		1907 Mar 3	IA, 34th, 1908
Smith, Chas.		K, 96th Ill. Inf. (died of blood poison)	48		1894 Apr 14	NE, 19th, 1895
Smith, Chas. M.			45		1924 Jun 14	IA, 51st, 1925
Smith, Chas. M.		A, 11th Mass.	72		1930 Jun 25	KS, 50th, 1931
Smith, Chas. R.		M, 2nd Penn. Art. (died of apoplexy)	318		1923 May 10	NE, 48th, 1924
Smith, Chas. W.J.			424		1902 Jul 18	KS, 22nd, 1903
Smith, Comdr.			10		1922 Nov 17	KS, 42nd, 1923
Smith, D.C.		B, 5th West Va. Inf. (died of accident)	7	53	1895 Feb 14	NE, 20th, 1896
Smith, D.J.		C, 6th Ill.	262		1919 May 13	NE, 44th, 1920
Smith, D.O.	Pvt.	G, 34th Iowa Inf.	48		1925 Nov 15	IA, 52nd, 1926
Smith, D.O.	Pvt.	G, 34th Iowa	48		1926 Nov	IA, 53rd, 1927
Smith, D.R.	Pvt.	C, 9th Ind. Inf.	110		1924 Jul 25	IA, 51st, 1925
Smith, D.W.		M, 13th Mo.	142		1927 Oct 22	KS, 47th, 1928
Smith, D.W.		H, 145th Ind. Inf.	25		1919 Dec 14	NE, 44th, 1920
Smith, D.W.		A, 166th Ohio	7		1927 Nov 26	NE, 52nd, 1928
Smith, D.W.C.		G, Wis. U.S. Colored Inf.	96	67	1904 Jan 21	NE, 29th, 1905
Smith, Dana R.		K, 12th Kans.	8		1925 May 30	KS, 45th, 1926
Smith, Daniel	Pvt.	G, 31st Iowa Inf.	67		1901 Mar 13	IA, 28th, 1902
Smith, Daniel		L, 12th N.Y. Cav. (died at Bronson)	482		1895 Apr	KS, 15th, 1896
Smith, Daniel L.		B, 5th Mich. Inf. (died at Grand Township; buried at Long Island Cemetery)	181		1894 Dec 2	KS, 14th, 1895
Smith, Daniel M.		B, 86th Ill. Inf. (died of old age)	22	73	1924 Aug 18	NE, 49th, 1925
Smith, Daniel T.		A, 21st Ind.	395		1917 Sep 18	KS, 37th, 1918
Smith, David			173		1922 May 21	IA, 49th, 1923
Smith, David		K, 10th Mo. Inf. (died at Latham)	340		1895 Dec	KS, 15th, 1896
Smith, David		D, 6th Penn.	53		1913 Oct 8	KS, 33rd, 1914
Smith, David		G, 21st Mich.	64		1916 Oct 14	KS, 36th, 1917
Smith, David		L, 3rd Ohio Cav.	84	61	1901 Nov	NE, 26th, 1902
Smith, David C.		H, 30th Mo.	82		1917 Oct 21	KS, 37th, 1918
Smith, David M.		C, 2nd Ohio	41		1917 Jul 17	KS, 37th, 1918
Smith, E.	Pvt.	C, 72nd Ohio Inf.	123		1915 Mar	IA, 42nd, 1916
Smith, E.F.		I, 81st Ind.	257		1928	KS, 48th, 1929
Smith, E.H.	Pvt.	H, 26th Iowa Inf.	58		1911 May 9	IA, 38th, 1912
Smith, E.H.	Major	13th U.S. Art.	70		1916	IA, 43rd, 1917

*See Appendix A, B or C for roster of post names and locations.
†See Introduction for note regarding recording of death date.
504

Name	Rank	Company, Regiment or Ship	Post*	Age	Death Date†	Journal
Smith, E.J.		K, 2nd Tenn.	47		1917 Aug 19	KS, 37th, 1918
Smith, E.L.		163rd Ill. Inf.	28	67	1912 Feb 28	NE, 37th, 1913
Smith, E.M.		F, 12th Ind.	117		1890	KS, 10th, 1891
Smith, E.N.		C, 92nd Ohio	66		1911 Aug 6	KS, 31st, 1912
Smith, E.P.	Pvt.	B, 2nd Iowa Cav.	118	65	1893 Jan 7	IA, 20th, 1894
Smith, E.R.		D, 44th Iowa	59		1885	KS, 5th, 1886
Smith, E.W.		K, 12th Wis. Inf. (died of cancer)	38	68	1895 May 22	NE, 20th, 1896
Smith, Ed. C.	Sergt.	G, 68th Ind. Inf.	12	50	1897 Dec 18	IA, 24th, 1898
Smith, Ed S.		G, 2nd Iowa	150		1918	KS, 38th, 1919
Smith, Edward	Pvt.	D, 21st Iowa	81		1922 Mar 21	IA, 49th, 1923
Smith, Edward		20th Ill. (died of old age)	35	84	1921 Jan 11	NE, 46th, 1922
Smith, Edwin		G, 139th Ill. (died of cancer)	13	79	1922 Jan 9	NE, 47th, 1923
Smith, Edwin T.		K, 3rd Mich. Cav.	4		1892 Nov 5	NE, 17th, 1893
Smith, Eli	Pvt.	I, 39th Iowa	12	54	1891 Feb 7	IA, 17th, 1891
Smith, Eli	Pvt.	G, 11th Iowa Inf.	192	93	1939 Dec 6	IA, 66th, 1940
Smith, Elias	Corp.	H, 55th Ohio Inf.	432		1890 Jan	IA, 17th, 1891
Smith, Elijah			[153?]		1902	NE, 27th, 1903
Smith, Emory P.	Pvt.	G, 52nd Ohio Inf. (at large)	195	100	1939 Oct 8	IA, 66th, 1940
Smith, Erastus		K, 21st Iowa Inf.	235	95	1937 Aug 4	IA, 64th, 1938
Smith, Erastus		D, 7th Kans. Cav. (died of paralytic stroke)	1	77	1918 Oct 11	NE, 43rd, 1919
Smith, F.A.		C, 54th Penn. Inf.	63		1925 Nov 29	KS, 45th, 1926
Smith, F.C.			99		1917 Feb 18	KS, 37th, 1918
Smith, F.M.	Pvt.	9th Iowa Cav.	251		1912 Dec 8	IA, 39th, 1913
Smith, Findley	Pvt.	H, 96th Ill.	364		1899 Oct 4	IA, 26th, 1900
Smith, Fitch		D, 104th Ill.	29		1922 Aug 10	IA, 49th, 1923
Smith, Francis G.		B, 18th Wis. Inf. (died of Bright's disease)	44	73	1915 Nov 12	NE, 40th, 1916
Smith, Francis M.		D, 4th Iowa Inf.	20		1931	KS, 51st, 1932
Smith, Frank B.		I, 14th Wis.	474		1919 Mar 26	KS, 39th, 1920
Smith, Frank W.	Capt.	A, 5th Maine Inf.	1		1919 Jun 6	IA, 46th, 1920
Smith, Fred	Pvt.	F, 21st U.S. Art.	54		1929 Aug 29	IA, 56th, 1930
Smith, Fred		E, 152nd Ohio	458		1897 Feb 10	KS, 16th, 1897
Smith, Fred. A.			180		1929	KS, 49th, 1930
Smith, Frederick		D, 45th Penn. Inf. (died of general debility)	39	72	1895 Oct 8	NE, 20th, 1896
Smith, G.A.		C, 18th Ind.	108		1887 Oct 14	KS, 7th, 1888
Smith, G.B.		F, 4th Ind.	4		1928 May 5	KS, 48th, 1929
Smith, G.K.	Pvt.	A, 141st Ill. Inf.	132		1916	IA, 43rd, 1917
Smith, G.O.		F, 92nd N.Y.	36		1913 Mar 1	KS, 33rd, 1914
Smith, G.P.	Col.	129th Ill.	72		1889	KS, 9th, 1890
Smith, G.W.		G, 2nd Tenn.	47		1918 Dec 6	KS, 38th, 1919
Smith, Geo.			243		1922 Apr 13	KS, 42nd, 1923
Smith, Geo. B.		F, 38th Ill. Inf. (died of pneumonia)	154		1922 Jul 6	NE, 47th, 1923
Smith, Geo. F.		B, 143rd Ind.	158		1898 Jan	KS, 18th, 1899
Smith, Geo. H.		H, 73rd Ind.	25		1921 Nov 21	KS, 41st, 1922
Smith, Geo. M.	Pvt.	H, 8th Kans. Inf.	147		1911 Nov 26	IA, 38th, 1912
Smith, Geo. O.		F, 17th Ill.	243		1920	KS, 40th, 1921
Smith, Geo. P.	1st Lieut.	G, 27th Iowa Inf.	5		1900 Sep 5	IA, 27th, 1901
Smith, Geo. Pratt		A, 36th Ohio	104		1920 May 17	KS, 40th, 1921
Smith, Geo. W.	Pvt.	A, 33rd Iowa Inf.	49		1900 Sep 20	IA, 27th, 1901
Smith, Geo. W.	Pvt.	F, 4th Iowa Inf.	158		1907 May 3	IA, 34th, 1908
Smith, Geo. W.		U.S. Marines	78		1924 Nov 12	IA, 51st, 1925
Smith, Geo. W.		A, 123rd Ohio	292		1927 May	KS, 47th, 1928
Smith, Geo. Y.		F, 129th Ind.	180		1919 Feb 18	KS, 39th, 1920
Smith, George	Pvt.	B, 60th Ohio Inf.	28	54	1894 Jul 31	IA, 21st, 1895
Smith, George	Pvt.	G, 2nd N.Y. Mtd. Inf.	236		1929 Jan 8	IA, 56th, 1930
Smith, George			32		1914 May 7	KS, 34th, 1915
Smith, George		F, 5th Wis. Inf. (died of paralysis)	171	83	1924 May 10	NE, 50th, 1926
Smith, George A.		E, 86th Ill.	179		1919 Apr 25	KS, 39th, 1920
Smith, George F.		A, 11th Penn. Cav.	93		1912 May 8	KS, 32nd, 1913
Smith, George H.		C, 134th Penn.	65		1915 Feb 27	KS, 35th, 1916
Smith, George L.		F, 27th Iowa Inf. (member at large; location: Ulysses)			1938 Mar 17	NE, 63rd, 1939
Smith, George W.	Pvt.	I, 3rd Ind. Cav.	206		1897 May 20	IA, 24th, 1898

*See Appendix A, B or C for roster of post names and locations.
†See Introduction for note regarding recording of death date.

Name	Rank	Company, Regiment or Ship	Post*	Age	Death Date†	Journal
Smith, George W.		B, 1st Nev. Cav. (died of pneumonia at Soldiers & Sailors Home, Grand Island; buried in Home Cemetery)	29	69	1905 Dec 4	NE, 30th, 1906
Smith, Guy		K, 2nd Ill.	28		1897 Oct 21	KS, 17th, 1898
Smith, H.	Pvt.	I, 47th Ill. Inf.	14		1928 Dec 13	IA, 55th, 1929
Smith, H.B.	Pvt.	G, 60th —	117		1914 Feb 1	IA, 41st, 1915
Smith, H.C.	Pvt.	F, 59th Ohio Inf.	88	51	1889 Jul 26	IA, 16th, 1890
Smith, H.C.			486		1900-1901	IA, 27th, 1901
Smith, H.C.	Pvt.	G, 30th Iowa Inf.	19		1920	IA, 47th, 1921
Smith, H.C.			64		1928	IA, 55th, 1929
Smith, H.C.		F, 20th Mich.	36		1927 Apr 13	KS, 47th, 1928
Smith, H.D.		C, 48th Wis. Inf. (died of paralysis)	32		1905 Dec 23	NE, 30th, 1906
Smith, H.D.		F, 13th Kans.	72		1913 May 10	KS, 33rd, 1914
Smith, H.H.		F, 89th N.Y.	1		1914 Jul 12	KS, 34th, 1915
Smith, H.I.	Capt.	H, 3rd Mo.	25		1909 Sep 30	KS, 29th, 1910
Smith, H.M.		B, 7th Iowa Inf.	42		1910 Nov 12	IA, 37th, 1911
Smith, H.N.		E, 10th Mo. Cav.	225		1916 Jan 11	KS, 36th, 1917
Smith, H.W.		14th Wis.	8		1916	NE, 41st, 1917
Smith, H.W.	Pvt.	F, 1st Neb. Cav.	97	39	1888 Sep 17	IA, 15th, 1889
Smith, Hamilton	Pvt.	H, 23rd Ill.	452		1907 Jul 14	IA, 34th, 1908
Smith, Harrison		K, 2nd Ohio Inf.	19		1907 Aug 3	IA, 34th, 1908
Smith, Harrison H.		H, 2nd Ind. Cav.	241		1920 Sep 12	KS, 40th, 1921
Smith, Harry C.	Pvt.	D, 13th Ind. Cav.	259		1904 Oct 23	IA, 31st, 1905
Smith, Harry F.	Pvt.	K, 10th Kans. Inf.	8		1922 Dec 19	IA, 49th, 1923
Smith, Harvey		H, 134th Ohio	4		1917 May 29	KS, 37th, 1918
Smith, Harvey	Pvt.	E, 12th Iowa Inf.	68	88	1931 Jul 16	IA, 58th, 1932
Smith, Henry		B, 44th Ind.	85		1924 Nov 11	KS, 44th, 1925
Smith, Henry	Musician	K, 11th Iowa Inf.	235	65	1897-1898	IA, 24th, 1898
Smith, Henry	Pvt.	I, 14th Ill.	68		1924 Jan 29	IA, 51st, 1925
Smith, Henry		G, 35th Iowa Vols.	357		1902 Apr 12	KS, 22nd, 1903
Smith, Henry		I, 57th Ill.	311		1916 Nov 10	KS, 36th, 1917
Smith, Henry B.		K, 5th Kans. State Militia	322		1909 Aug 18	KS, 29th, 1910
Smith, Henry C.	Pvt.	D, 2nd Iowa Cav.	37		1924 Mar 18	IA, 51st, 1925
Smith, Henry C.		M, 9th Con. Inf.	52		1930 Mar 1	KS, 50th, 1931
Smith, Henry D.	Pvt.	E, 11th Ill. Inf.	193		1917 Jan 22	IA, 44th, 1918
Smith, Henry L.	Pvt.	A, 1st Ore. Vol. Inf.	153	62	1898 Aug 27	IA, 25th, 1899
Smith, Henry T.		A, 76th Ohio	47		1913 Nov 25	KS, 33rd, 1914
Smith, Hiram J.			424		1921	KS, 41st, 1922
Smith, Hiram J.			424		1920	KS, 40th, 1921
Smith, Hiram M.		D, 130th Ill.	264		1904 Dec 16	KS, 24th, 1905
Smith, Hollis A.		E, 100th Ill. Inf.	8		1887 Sep	KS, 7th, 1888
Smith, Horace J.	Lieut.	K, 92nd Ill.	18		1906 Dec 2	KS, 26th, 1907
Smith, Hubbard C.		3rd Maine	101		1902 Oct 14	KS, 22nd, 1903
Smith, I.K.		B, 88th Ill.	451		1893 Jun 9	KS, 13th, 1894
Smith, I.L.	Capt.	C, 54th Penn. Inf.	31		1908 Oct	IA, 35th, 1909
Smith, I.N.		K, 57th Ohio	130		1908 Nov 14	KS, 28th, 1909
Smith, I.S.	Pvt.	H, 33rd Ill. Inf.	149	56	1887 Mar 2	IA, 13th, 1887
Smith, I.W.		A, 37th Ohio	318		1917 Oct 11	NE, 42nd, 1918
Smith, Ichabod		89th Ind.	435		1917 Aug 14	KS, 37th, 1918
Smith, Ira	Pvt.	H, 43rd Ohio Inf.	258		1915 Jan 21	IA, 42nd, 1916
Smith, Ira	Corp.	A, 2nd Iowa Cav.	67		1920 Sep 15	IA, 47th, 1921
Smith, Ira H.	Pvt.	A, 2nd Wis. Cav.	76	52	1887 Aug 31	IA, 14th, 1888
Smith, Isaac		I, 13th Kans. Inf. (died of heart disease)	48	53	1897 Mar 11	NE, 22nd, 1898
Smith, Isaac		A, 25th Wis. Inf. (died of typhoid fever)	333	70	1895 Sep 2	NE, 20th, 1896
Smith, Isaac, see Smyth, Isaac						
Smith, Isaac C.		C, 36th Iowa	380		1897 Aug 29	KS, 17th, 1898
Smith, Isaac S.		G, 1st Penn. Lt. Art.	100		1929 Oct 6	KS, 49th, 1930
Smith, Iva	Pvt.	H, 43rd Ohio Inf.	258		1915 Jan 21	IA, 41st, 1915
Smith, J.	Pvt.	H, 39th Iowa Inf.	6	55	1894 Jul 22	IA, 21st, 1895
Smith, J.		G, 151st Ill. Inf. (died of dropsy)	338	61	1896 Feb 15	NE, 21st, 1897
Smith, J.A.	Pvt.	K, 48th Ill. Inf.	7	40	1891 Nov 8	IA, 18th, 1892
Smith, J.A.	Pvt.	E, 74th Ill. Inf.	503		1915 Nov 3	IA, 42nd, 1916

*See Appendix A, B or C for roster of post names and locations.
†See Introduction for note regarding recording of death date.

Name	Rank	Company, Regiment or Ship	Post*	Age	Death Date†	Journal
Smith, J.A.	Pvt.	I, 78th Ill. Inf.	153		1914 Sep 27	IA, 41st, 1915
Smith, J.A.	Pvt.	B, 2nd Bat. U.S. Art.	101		1916 Apr 1	IA, 43rd, 1917
Smith, J.C.	Lieut.	I, 2nd Iowa Cav.	108	64	1894 Oct 4	IA, 21st, 1895
Smith, J.C.	Pvt.	B, 176th Ohio	398		1914 Dec 11	IA, 41st, 1915
Smith, J.C.		M, 5th Ill.	293		1906 Nov 20	KS, 26th, 1907
Smith, J.C.		26th Ill.	65		1913 Oct	KS, 33rd, 1914
Smith, J.C.G.		D, 46th Ind. Inf.	98		1914 Feb 14	KS, 34th, 1915
Smith, J.D.			133		1922	IA, 49th, 1923
Smith, J.D.	Capt.	E, 176th N.Y.	1		1906 Apr 21	KS, 26th, 1907
Smith, J.D.		H, 12th Ohio Cav. (died of old age)	13	90	1923 Sep 9	NE, 48th, 1924
Smith, J.E.	Pvt.	F, 35th N.Y. Inf.	88		1921 Feb 21	IA, 48th, 1922
Smith, J.H.	Sergt.	K, 28th Iowa Inf.	511		1915 Jan 9	IA, 42nd, 1916
Smith, J.H.			167		1917	IA, 44th, 1918
Smith, J.H.		G, 7th Iowa	127		1888	KS, 8th, 1889
Smith, J.H.		E, 28th Ill.	364		1926	KS, 46th, 1927
Smith, J.J.		C, 79th Ohio	433		1922 Mar 13	KS, 42nd, 1923
Smith, J.K.	Pvt.	G, 6th Iowa Inf.	6		1908	IA, 35th, 1909
Smith, J.L.	Pvt.	C, 36th Iowa Inf.	398		1908 May 28	IA, 35th, 1909
Smith, J.L.		12th Kans. Hvy. Art.	170		1908 Dec	KS, 28th, 1909
Smith, J.N.		K, 16th Ill.	76		1912	KS, 32nd, 1913
Smith, J.N.		G, 105th Ill. 11th U.S. Col.	127		1917 Nov 23	KS, 37th, 1918
Smith, J.O.		H, 8th Minn. Inf.	39		1892 Feb 16	NE, 17th, 1893
Smith, J.P.	Pvt.	B, Penn. Militia	26		1910 Mar 20	IA, 37th, 1911
Smith, J.P.		F, 100th Penn. Inf.	28	72	1906 May 16	NE, 31st, 1907
Smith, J.P.		I, 17th Penn. Cav. (died of old age)	32	80	1912 Jan 26	NE, 37th, 1913
Smith, J.Q.		E, 7th Ohio Cav.	65		1917 Apr 1	KS, 37th, 1918
Smith, J.R.	Pvt.	C, 5th Inf.	115		1921 Mar 30	IA, 48th, 1922
Smith, J.S.			55		1921 Jul 25	IA, 48th, 1922
Smith, J.T.		L, 2nd Minn. Cav.	5	89	1935 Nov 16	IA, 62nd, 1936
Smith, J.T.		L, 16th Ohio Cav.	180		1911 Jun 5	KS, 31st, 1912
Smith, J.T., Rev.		G, 16th Ill.	24	69	1912 Feb 7	NE, 37th, 1913
Smith, J.W.	Pvt.	E, 39th Iowa Inf.	23		1916 Nov 6	IA, 43rd, 1917
Smith, J.W.		C, 151st N.Y. Inf.	20	92	1935 Oct 27	IA, 62nd, 1936
Smith, J.W.		C, 151st Inf.		92	1936[1935?] Oct 27	IA, 62nd, 1936
Smith, J.W.		H, 30th Iowa Inf.	17		1912 Apr 21	KS, 32nd, 1913
Smith, J.W.		I, 130th Ind. Inf.	25		1893 Jun	NE, 18th, 1894
Smith, J. Wesley		C, 71st N.Y. Mil.	18		1936 Mar 17	KS, 56th, 1937
Smith, Jackson F.	Pvt.	E, 52nd Wis. Inf.	37	59	1894 Sep 12	IA, 21st, 1895
Smith, Jacob		G, 54th Ill. Inf. (died at Goffs, Kans.; buried at Goffs Cemetery)	411		1894 Dec 20	KS, 14th, 1895
Smith, Jacob		E, 2nd Kans. State Militia	1		1908 Nov 30	KS, 28th, 1909
Smith, Jacob		G, 8th Iowa Cav.	127		1911 Feb 8	KS, 31st, 1912
Smith, Jacob		H, 30th Ind. Inf. (died of heart failure)	13	72	1913 Dec 3	NE, 38th, 1914
Smith, Jacob		E, 24th Iowa	32	76	1924 Feb 21	NE, 49th, 1925
Smith, Jacob W.	Pvt.	B, 2nd Neb. Cav.	59		1916 Oct 31	IA, 43rd, 1917
Smith, James	Pvt.	K, 124th Ind. Inf.	172	57	1886 Jun 21	IA, 13th, 1887
Smith, James		3rd Iowa Cav.	100		1918	IA, 45th, 1919
Smith, James		E, 2nd U.S. Inf.	380		1900 Feb 16	KS, 20th, 1901
Smith, James		C, 17th Mass. Inf.	88		1912 Dec 3	KS, 32nd, 1913
Smith, James		A, 7th Kans.	71		1914 May 25	KS, 34th, 1915
Smith, James		H, 94th Ill. Inf. (died of kidney trouble)	130	70	1913 Oct 17	NE, 38th, 1914
Smith, James A.	Pvt.	I, 10th Iowa Vol. Inf.	92		1901 Jul 16	IA, 28th, 1902
Smith, James A.	Pvt.	A, 74th Ohio Inf.	233	53	1898 Jan 24	IA, 24th, 1898
Smith, James A.		F, 17th Ill.	49		1921 Nov 23	KS, 41st, 1922
Smith, James A.		A, 22nd Iowa	216		1935 Jun 30	NE, 60th, 1936
Smith, James E.	Pvt.	F, 35th N.Y. Inf.	88		1917	IA, 44th, 1918
Smith, James E.	Pvt.	A, 64th Ill. Cav.	141		1931 Aug 20	IA, 58th, 1932
Smith, James H.	Pvt.	C, 24th Iowa Inf.	236		1928 Apr 12	IA, 55th, 1929
Smith, James H.		C, 117th & 140th Ind.	14		1915 Apr 20	KS, 35th, 1916
Smith, James H.		68th Ky.	500		1923	KS, 43rd, 1924
Smith, James M.	Pvt.	C, 21st Iowa Inf.	42		1901 Oct 20	IA, 28th, 1902

*See Appendix A, B or C for roster of post names and locations.
†See Introduction for note regarding recording of death date.
507

Name	Rank	Company, Regiment or Ship	Post*	Age	Death Date†	Journal
Smith, Jas. A.	Pvt.	F, 124th Ill. Inf.	235		1916 Dec 3	IA, 43rd, 1917
Smith, Jas. S.		A, Mich.	51		1917	KS, 37th, 1918
Smith, Jas. T.		G, 145th Ind.	17		1911 Feb 12	KS, 31st, 1912
Smith, Jas. Thos.	Pvt.	L, 2nd Minn. Cav.	5	89	1935 Nov 16	IA, 65th, 1939
Smith, Jeremiah	Pvt.	F, 92nd Ohio Inf.	122	63	1893 Sep 1	IA, 20th, 1894
Smith, Jerry L.		96th Ill.	385		1889	KS, 9th, 1890
Smith, Jno.	Pvt.	G, 55th Ill. Inf.	47	49	1883 Apr 27	IA, 14th, 1888
Smith, Jno. H.	Pvt.	H, 9th Ind. Inf.	7	50	1888 Nov 17	IA, 15th, 1889
Smith, Job		E, 43rd Ind. Inf.	18		1899 Jan 26	KS, 19th, 1900
Smith, John	Pvt.	I, 15th Ill. Inf.	231	61	1898 Feb 6	IA, 24th, 1898
Smith, John		G, 2nd N.Y. Hvy. Art.	72		1892 Feb 23	KS, 12th, 1893
Smith, John		I, 20th Ind. Inf. (died at Cleveland)	265		1895 Nov	KS, 15th, 1896
Smith, John		13th Penn. Regulars	199		1899 Oct 11	KS, 19th, 1900
Smith, John		16th Ind. Lt. Art.	64		1901 Sep	KS, 21st, 1902
Smith, John		I, 49th Ky. Inf.	147		1908 Mar 4	KS, 28th, 1909
Smith, John		E, 92nd Ill.	303		1902 Nov 11	KS, 22nd, 1903
Smith, John			14		1913	KS, 33rd, 1914
Smith, John		A, 7th N.Y.	1		1913 Jul 27	KS, 33rd, 1914
Smith, John		G, 88th Ohio	25		1923 Nov 13	KS, 43rd, 1924
Smith, John		L, 8th Mich.	5		1927 Apr 4	KS, 47th, 1928
Smith, John		B, 145th Ohio (died of hardening of arteries)	223	76	1922 Jan 4	NE, 47th, 1923
Smith, John A.		B, 51st Mo. Inf. (died at Marysville; buried at Savannah, Mo.)	9		1894 Jan 10	KS, 14th, 1895
Smith, John C.		H, 8th Ill. (died of heart trouble)	15	77	1916 Oct 10	NE, 41st, 1917
Smith, John D.			233		1924	IA, 51st, 1925
Smith, John D.	Pvt.	B, 147th Ill. Inf.	88		1912 Aug 6	IA, 39th, 1913
Smith, John E.	Pvt.	G, 3rd Iowa Cav.	408		1897 Jun 8	IA, 24th, 1898
Smith, John F.		F, 4th Iowa	40		1914 Nov 22	KS, 34th, 1915
Smith, John H.	Sergt.	K, 28th Iowa Inf.	511		1915[1914?] Dec 9	IA, 41st, 1915
Smith, John H.		G, 7th Iowa Cav. (died at Salina)	127		1895 Apr 14	KS, 15th, 1896
Smith, John M.W.		F, 86th Ill. (died of heart disease)	44	73	1918 Feb 12	NE, 43rd, 1919
Smith, John N.			233		1924	IA, 51st, 1925
Smith, John N.		E, 11th Kans. Inf.	271		1899 Aug 14	KS, 19th, 1900
Smith, John R.		E, 111th Ill. Inf.	85		1925 Mar 8	KS, 45th, 1926
Smith, John R.		F, 37th Iowa Inf. (died at Osborne, Kans.; buried at Osborne Cemetery)	69		1894 Oct 13	KS, 14th, 1895
Smith, John S.	Pvt.	G, 10th Iowa Inf.	12		1915 Apr 26	IA, 42nd, 1916
Smith, John W.		A, 79th Ill. Inf.	250		1908 Nov 8	KS, 28th, 1909
Smith, Jonathan		C, Ill.	47		2nd quarter 1883	IA, 10th, 1884
Smith, Jos.	Corp.	F, 102nd Ill. Inf.	491	58	1892 Jan 10	IA, 18th, 1892
Smith, Jos.		I, 145th Ind.	158		1906 Jan 1	KS, 26th, 1907
Smith, Jos.		D, 14th N.Y. Inf. (died of brain disease)	112	68	1902 Dec	NE, 27th, 1903
Smith, Jos. M.	Sergt.	F, 6th Iowa Cav.	59		1910 Apr 29	IA, 37th, 1911
Smith, Jos. W.		I, 130th Ind.	25		1928 Dec 22	NE, 53rd, 1929
Smith, Joseph L.		E, 67th Ind. Inf. N, 24th Ind. Inf. (died of paralysis)	44	72	1914 Oct 4	NE, 39th, 1915
Smith, Joseph W.	Pvt.	I, 8th Penn. Inf.	235	55	1894 Feb 26	IA, 20th, 1894
Smith, Josiah			253		1890	NE, 15th, 1891
Smith, Justin M.		L, 5th Ill. Cav.	32		1920 Feb 24	KS, 40th, 1921
Smith, L.B.	Pvt. & Sergt.	G, 1st Wis. Art. (died of dyspepsia)	58	50	1887 Oct 19	NE, 12th, 1888
Smith, L.D.	Pvt.	C, 34th Iowa Inf.	309		1906 May 1	IA, 33rd, 1907
Smith, L.G.		B, 4th West Va.	27		1936 Jul 28	KS, 55th, 1936
Smith, L.L.	Pvt.	E, 44th Iowa Inf.	243		1919 Oct 18	IA, 46th, 1920
Smith, L.W.	Pvt.	A, 112th Ill. Inf.	175		4th quarter 1885	IA, 12th, 1886
Smith, L.W.		K, 8th Ind.	71		1926 Oct 26	KS, 46th, 1927
Smith, Levi	Pvt.	D, 112th Ill. Inf.	56		1926 Mar 1	IA, 53rd, 1927
Smith, Lewis		D, 13th Mo. S.M.	388		1925	KS, 45th, 1926
Smith, Lewis G.		K, 146th Ill. Inf.	64		1899 Jan 5	KS, 19th, 1900
Smith, Lorenzo		E, 121st N.Y.	1		1927 Apr 11	NE, 52nd, 1928
Smith, Louis A.		A, 14th Ill. Cav.	209		1910 Apr 23	KS, 30th, 1911
Smith, Lucien		33rd Ill. Inf.	54		1912 Dec 26	KS, 32nd, 1913

*See Appendix A, B or C for roster of post names and locations.
†See Introduction for note regarding recording of death date.

Name	Rank	Company, Regiment or Ship	Post*	Age	Death Date†	Journal
Smith, Luke A.	Pvt.	E, 7th Iowa Cav.	55	91	1936 Dec 9	IA, 65th, 1939
Smith, Lurentz	Pvt.	I, 11th Penn. Cav.	259		1908 Jul 21	IA, 35th, 1909
Smith, Luther H.		A, 127th Ill.	25		1922 Nov 21	KS, 42nd, 1923
Smith, M.	Pvt.	K, 3rd N.Y. Inf.	34		1921 Jun 30	IA, 48th, 1922
Smith, M.		H, 120th Ohio	257		1919 Feb 7	KS, 39th, 1920
Smith, M.		F, 40th Iowa Inf. (died of heart failure)	74	68	1896 May 11	NE, 21st, 1897
Smith, M.C.	Pvt.	I, 103rd Penn. Inf.	22		1920 Feb 7	IA, 47th, 1921
Smith, M.D.		A, 1st N.Y.	198		1897 Jun 17	KS, 17th, 1898
Smith, M.F.		113th Ill.	18		1896 Feb 19	KS, 16th, 1897
Smith, M.H.	Pvt.	F, 60th U.S.	1		1928 Oct 19	IA, 55th, 1929
Smith, M.J.	Q.M.S.	I, 7th Iowa Cav.	223		1914 Nov 26	IA, 41st, 1915
Smith, M.L.		9th Kans.	54		1926	KS, 46th, 1927
Smith, M.M.	Pvt.	E, 3rd Wis. Vet. Inf.	124		1901 Feb 23	IA, 27th, 1901
Smith, M.V.		G, 7th Kans.	4		1912 Dec 11	KS, 32nd, 1913
Smith, Marion A.		A, 3rd Mich. Cav.	25		1923 Nov 14	KS, 43rd, 1924
Smith, Marshel B.		L, 10th Ill. Cav.	49		1887 Nov 36	KS, 7th, 1888
Smith, Martin V.	Corp.	I, 5th Iowa Inf.	130		1925 Mar 29	IA, 52nd, 1926
Smith, Milo P.	Capt.	C, 31st Iowa Inf.	235		1926 Apr 28	IA, 53rd, 1927
Smith, Milone	1st Lieut.	F, 105th Ill.	22		1905 Sep 14	IA, 32nd, 1906
Smith, Morgan J.	Pvt.	I, 16th Wis. Inf.	78		1908 Jan 8	IA, 35th, 1909
Smith, Moses	Pvt.	F, 8th Kans. Inf.	59		1915 Jan 5	IA, 42nd, 1916
Smith, Myron C.		I, 77th Ill. (died of arterio sclerosis)	318	82	1924 Sep 4	NE, 49th, 1925
Smith, N.			133		1921 Mar	IA, 48th, 1922
Smith, N.		B, 17th Ohio	49		1887 Sep 34	KS, 7th, 1888
Smith, N.B.		K, 77th Ohio	378		1916	KS, 36th, 1917
Smith, N.P.F.		D, 22nd Iowa	25		1920 Aug 4	NE, 51st, 1927
Smith, N.S.		K, 112th Ill.	175		1926 Apr 29	KS, 46th, 1927
Smith, N.T.	Pvt.	G, 129th Ohio	52		1926 Sep 9	IA, 53rd, 1927
Smith, N.W.		C, 100th Ill. Inf.	88		1912 Mar 23	KS, 32nd, 1913
Smith, Nathan	Pvt.	M, 2nd Iowa Cav.	176	64	1899 May 30	IA, 26th, 1900
Smith, Nathan		B, 118th N.Y. Inf.	293		1901 Aug 6	KS, 21st, 1902
Smith, Nathan		C, 34th Iowa	240		1911 Mar 22	KS, 31st, 1912
Smith, Nathan			276		1890 Jan 6	NE, 15th, 1891
Smith, Neri		H, 43rd Ohio	32		1926 Nov 28	NE, 51st, 1927
Smith, Newton H.	Pvt.	G, 4th Iowa Inf.	516		1906 Jul 3	IA, 33rd, 1907
Smith, O.B.		E, 77th Ill. (died of general breakdown)	1	76	1918 Mar 29	NE, 43rd, 1919
Smith, O.F.		F, 4th Iowa	20		1928 Nov 29	KS, 48th, 1929
Smith, O.H.		C, 95th Ill. (served 3 years as cap)	3		1892 Jun 13	KS, 12th, 1893
Smith, O.J.		H, 4th Mich.	34		1928 Jun 16	NE, 53rd, 1929
Smith, O.W.		F, 13th Kans.	4		1924 Dec 13	KS, 44th, 1925
Smith, Oliver	Pvt.	F, 6th Mich. Inf.	327		1913 Jun 10	IA, 40th, 1914
Smith, Ordel		G, 10th Kans.	142		1923 Oct 19	KS, 43rd, 1924
Smith, Orin		F, 2nd Ohio Cav.	25		1923 Mar 26	KS, 43rd, 1924
Smith, Oscar F.			132		1923 Aug 27	IA, 50th, 1924
Smith, Owen	Pvt.	B, 44th Iowa Inf.	231		1916 Apr 20	IA, 43rd, 1917
Smith, P.A.	Pvt.	A, 8th Iowa Inf.	111		1910 Dec 25	IA, 37th, 1911
Smith, P.H.		I, 1st Kans. Inf.	6		1906 Jan 17	KS, 26th, 1907
Smith, Pat		M, U.S. F, 3rd Penn. Hvy. Art.	50		1903 Oct 9	IA, 30th, 1904
Smith, Patrick	Pvt.	G, 102nd Ill.	57		1905 Apr 6	IA, 32nd, 1906
Smith, Philander	Pvt.	D, 2nd Iowa Inf.	12		1917 Jun 15	IA, 44th, 1918
Smith, Philip			314		1906 Sep 23	IA, 33rd, 1907
Smith, Philip		B, 78th Penn.	377		1917 Mar 19	KS, 37th, 1918
Smith, Philip		D, 45th Wis. Inf. (died of heart disease)	10	68	1913 Jan 9	NE, 38th, 1914
Smith, Phinneas	Pvt.	B, 27th Iowa Inf.	235		1912 May 17	IA, 39th, 1913
Smith, Pleasent		K, 6th Ky. Cav.	65		1893 Jun 3	KS, 13th, 1894
Smith, Pressly		B, 6th Mo. Cav.	47		1921 Jul 27	KS, 41st, 1922
Smith, Preston T.		F, 9th Mo. Inf.	25		1911 Nov 21	KS, 31st, 1912
Smith, R.A.	Capt.	F, 13th Ill. Inf.	156		1919 Feb 24	IA, 46th, 1920
Smith, R.B.	Pvt.	G, 2nd Iowa Cav.	127		1919 Nov 6	IA, 46th, 1920
Smith, R.H.	Pvt.	F, 46th Iowa Inf.	416	84	1931 Mar 25	IA, 58th, 1932
Smith, R.J.		A, 70th Ohio Inf.	57		1918 Jul 30	KS, 38th, 1919

*See Appendix A, B or C for roster of post names and locations.
†See Introduction for note regarding recording of death date.
509

Name	Rank	Company, Regiment or Ship	Post*	Age	Death Date†	Journal
Smith, R.M.		H, 89th Ill. Inf. G, 9th Ill.	18		1917 Nov 16	KS, 37th, 1918
Smith, R.P.	Pvt.	A, 3rd West Va. Cav.	10		1901 Apr 1	IA, 28th, 1902
Smith, Ralph	Pvt.	L, 13th N.Y. Hvy. Art.	22		1899 Aug 4	IA, 26th, 1900
Smith, Richard H.		B, 113th Ill.	259		1896 Jun 29	KS, 16th, 1897
Smith, Robert			1		3rd quarter 1883	IA, 10th, 1884
Smith, Robert		I, 76th —	40	75	1904 Aug	NE, 29th, 1905
Smith, Robert C.	Corp.	I, 50th Ill.	374		1903 Nov	IA, 30th, 1904
Smith, Robt. S.		G, 5th Ill.	18		1906 Nov 23	KS, 26th, 1907
Smith, Rudolph		A, 24th Iowa	260		1916 Nov 17	KS, 36th, 1917
Smith, S.A.		D, 12th Ohio Cav.	32	71	1916 May 30	NE, 41st, 1917
Smith, S.B.	Sergt.	F, 209th Penn. Inf.	117		1911 May 24	IA, 38th, 1912
Smith, S.B.	Pvt.	B, 65th Ill. Inf.	88		1925 May 3	IA, 52nd, 1926
Smith, S.G.	Major	40th Iowa Inf.	16	59	1890 Nov 7	IA, 17th, 1891
Smith, S.G.		A, 13th Iowa Inf.	440		1915 Jan 7	IA, 42nd, 1916
Smith, S.M.	Sergt.	H, 112th Ill. Inf.	39		1921 Sep	IA, 48th, 1922
Smith, S.M.		G, 57th & 152nd Ill.	99		1897 Apr	KS, 17th, 1898
Smith, S.M.		G, 3rd Tenn. Inf.	98		1934	KS, 54th, 1935
Smith, S.S.	Pvt.	F, 17th Ill. Inf.	92		1914 Dec 12	IA, 41st, 1915
Smith, S.T.		E, 2nd West Va.	12		1933 Dec 25	KS, 53rd, 1934
Smith, S.W.	Pvt.	B, 47th Wis. Inf.	42		1917 Mar 7	IA, 44th, 1918
Smith, Samuel	Pvt.	B, 2nd Iowa Cav.	86		1901 Aug 9	IA, 28th, 1902
Smith, Samuel	Pvt.	F, 21st Iowa Inf.	78		1908 Mar 31	IA, 35th, 1909
Smith, Samuel	Pvt.	A, 89th Ill. Inf.	40	93	1931 Sep 5	IA, 58th, 1932
Smith, Sidney	Pvt.	B, 29th Wis. Inf.	77		1912 Dec 8	IA, 39th, 1913
Smith, Silas			[55?]		1926 Oct 6	KS, 46th, 1927
Smith, Simeon			386		1904 May 6	IA, 31st, 1905
Smith, Simeon		E, 124th N.Y. (died of apoplexy)	284	77	1908 Nov 20	NE, 33rd, 1909
Smith, Sumner	Pvt.	K, 8th Iowa Inf.	337		1913 Jun 13	IA, 40th, 1914
Smith, Swift B.	Pvt.	G, 2nd Conn. Art.	222		1899	NE, 24th, 1900
Smith, T.J.		27th Iowa Inf.	62		1923 Feb 16	NE, 48th, 1924
Smith, Thomas	Pvt.	I, 14th Ill. Inf.	321		1915 Nov 29	IA, 42nd, 1916
Smith, Thomas	Pvt.	G, 13th Kans. Cav.	252		1914 Dec 25	IA, 41st, 1915
Smith, Thomas		A, 18th U.S.C.T.	10		1925	KS, 45th, 1926
Smith, Thomas		C, 38th Ohio (died of heart failure)	19	66	1900 Sep 9	NE, 25th, 1901
Smith, Thomas J.		E, 6th Iowa Vol. Inf.	337		3rd quarter 1884	IA, 11th, 1885
Smith, Thomas J.		F, 13th U.S. Inf. 1st Batt. (see also Appendix D)	207		1933 Apr 23	NE, 58th, 1934
Smith, Thomas S.	Sergt.	C, 30th Iowa Inf.	374		1901 Sep 8	IA, 28th, 1902
Smith, Thomas W.		I, 103rd Ohio	123		1912 Nov 10	KS, 32nd, 1913
Smith, Thomas W.		I, 183rd Ohio	123		1912 Nov 3	KS, 33rd, 1914
Smith, Thos.		A, 69th Ill. Inf. (died of old age)	44	70	1896 May 18	NE, 21st, 1897
Smith, Thos. D.	Pvt.	I, 7th Ohio Cav.	29		1920 Apr 21	IA, 47th, 1921
Smith, U.B.			69		1926	IA, 53rd, 1927
Smith, W.A.		19th Iowa Inf.	20		1917 Mar	IA, 44th, 1918
Smith, W.A.		H, 42nd Ohio	46		1909 Dec 15	KS, 29th, 1910
Smith, W.D.	Pvt.	G, 4th Iowa Inf.	473		1906	IA, 33rd, 1907
Smith, W.D.	Pvt.	13th Ohio Battery	377		1910 Nov 10	IA, 37th, 1911
Smith, W.D.			463		1921 Jun 3	KS, 41st, 1922
Smith, W.E.	Pvt.	C, 10th Iowa Inf.	88		1910 Mar 13	IA, 37th, 1911
Smith, W.G.			96		1916 Jul 15	IA, 43rd, 1917
Smith, W.H.	Pvt.	B, 61st Penn. Inf.	8	70	1892 Nov 8	IA, 19th, 1893
Smith, W.H.	Pvt.	I, 23rd Penn. Inf.	9		1911	IA, 38th, 1912
Smith, W.H.	Pvt.	G, 97th N.Y. Inf.	12		1916 Dec 9	IA, 43rd, 1917
Smith, W.H.		M, 7th Iowa	130	93	1934 Sep 29	IA, 61st, 1935
Smith, W.H.		I, 11th Kans.	11		1889	KS, 9th, 1890
Smith, W.H.		D, 62nd Penn.	9		1924 Jun 17	KS, 44th, 1925
Smith, W.H.H.			50		1920 Aug	KS, 40th, 1921
Smith, W.H.H.		U.S.C.T.	22		1921 May 14	KS, 41st, 1922
Smith, W.H.M.	Pvt.	F, 47th Iowa	12		1922 May 1	IA, 49th, 1923
Smith, W.J.C.			204		1899	IA, 26th, 1900
Smith, W.K.	Pvt.	E, 6th Iowa Inf.	79		1912 Oct 23	IA, 39th, 1913

*See Appendix A, B or C for roster of post names and locations.
†See Introduction for note regarding recording of death date.

Name	Rank	Company, Regiment or Ship	Post*	Age	Death Date†	Journal
Smith, W.L.		K, 21st Penn. Cav.	115		1925 Apr 6	KS, 45th, 1926
Smith, W.M.	Pvt.	E, 74th Ohio	400		1899 Aug	IA, 26th, 1900
Smith, W.P.		A, 17th Ill. Cav.	80		1906 Jun 27	NE, 31st, 1907
Smith, W.R.		F, 12th Kans.	12		1910 Apr 10	KS, 30th, 1911
Smith, W.S.	Pvt.	E, 35th Mo. Inf.	497		1911 Jul 20	IA, 38th, 1912
Smith, W.S.		A, 36th Ill. Inf.	15		1890 Jan 28	KS, 12th, 1893
Smith, W.T.	Pvt.	D, 33rd Iowa Inf.	40		1905 Dec 4	IA, 32nd, 1906
Smith, W.V.		D, 96th Ill. Inf.	25	89	1920 Dec 29	NE, 45th, 1921
Smith, W.W.		C, 1st Mich. Inf.	207		1912 Sep 28	NE, 37th, 1913
Smith, Wallace	Sergt.	B, 3rd Wis. Inf.	223		1912 Nov 21	IA, 39th, 1913
Smith, Wallace E.	Pvt.	K, 45th Iowa Inf.	516		1910 Nov 15	IA, 37th, 1911
Smith, Walter A.	Pvt.	B, 2nd Neb. Cav.	59		1923 Feb 1	IA, 50th, 1924
Smith, Willard R.		L, 33rd Penn.	25		1915 Apr 24	NE, 40th, 1916
Smith, William	Pvt.	F, 22nd Iowa Inf.	83		1916 Feb 22	IA, 43rd, 1917
Smith, William		K, 21st Penn.	115		1925 Apr 6	KS, 44th, 1925
Smith, William F.		K, 89th Ohio	17		1923 Jun 2	KS, 43rd, 1924
Smith, William H.		E, 118th Ind. Inf. (died at Osage Mission; buried at Bond Cemetery)	114		1894 Apr 10	KS, 14th, 1895
Smith, William H.		A, 79th U.S.C.T.	321		1916 Oct 19	KS, 36th, 1917
Smith, William P.		A, 17th Ill. Cav. (died of dropsy & paralysis at Soldiers & Sailors Home, Milford)		66	1906 Jun 27	NE, 31st, 1907
Smith, William W.	Lieut. Col.	17th Mass. (see also Appendix D)	1		1919 Dec 22	KS, 39th, 1920
Smith, Wm.	Pvt.		22		1905 Jan 23	IA, 32nd, 1906
Smith, Wm.	Pvt.	C, 146th Ill. Inf.	298		1905	IA, 32nd, 1906
Smith, Wm.	Pvt.	E, 1st U.S. Eng.	57		1916 Jul 3	IA, 43rd, 1917
Smith, Wm.	Sergt.	D, 31st Iowa	68		1923 Jul 1	IA, 50th, 1924
Smith, Wm.	Pvt.	M, 8th Ill. Cav.	436		1929 Dec 18	IA, 56th, 1930
Smith, Wm.		M, 4th Ind. Cav.	456		1889	KS, 9th, 1890
Smith, Wm.		F, 15th Iowa	20		1904	KS, 24th, 1905
Smith, Wm.			35		1911 Jun 24	NE, 36th, 1912
Smith, Wm. A.	Pvt.	gunboat *Lexington*	94		1916 Nov	IA, 43rd, 1917
Smith, Wm. B.	Pvt.	G, 126th Ill. Inf.	184	82	1893 Nov 13	IA, 20th, 1894
Smith, Wm. H.	Pvt.	C, 15th Ill. Inf.	91		1908 Jul 17	IA, 35th, 1909
Smith, Wm. H.	Sergt.	H, 9th Iowa Cav.	155		1913 Nov 7	IA, 40th, 1914
Smith, Wm. H.	Corp.	I, 5th Iowa Inf.	269		1908 Mar 10	IA, 35th, 1909
Smith, Wm. H.		K, 118th Ind.	55		1920 Jun 15	KS, 40th, 1921
Smithburg, G.A.	Pvt.	M, 4th Iowa Cav.	19		1930 Aug	IA, 57th, 1931
Smithers, Wm.		D, 9th Kans.	50		1917 Feb 6	KS, 37th, 1918
Smithline, John Adams	Pvt. Pvt.	G, 36th Ill. Inf. F, 4th Veteran Reserve	5, 19	93	1940 Jul 3	IA, 66th, 1940
Smithson, Geo. W.			96		1918 Sep 6	IA, 45th, 1919
Smithwick, John			134		1890	NE, 15th, 1891
Smock, C.G.		C, 3rd Ky. Cav.	12		1914 Oct 3	KS, 34th, 1915
Smock, Chas.	1st Lieut.	D, 15th Iowa Inf.	279	45	1889 May 15	IA, 16th, 1890
Smock, S.J.		G, 70th Ind.	12		1914 Dec 2	KS, 34th, 1915
Smock, T.	Pvt.	I, 95th Ill.	124		1905 Dec	IA, 32nd, 1906
Smock, T.C.	Pvt.	G, 13th Iowa Inf.	7		1925 Mar 10	IA, 52nd, 1926
Smoke, W.H.		not a member of post named, but buried by said post	63		1897	KS, 17th, 1898
Smothers, Geo.		G, 55th Mass.	158		1911 Feb 16	KS, 31st, 1912
Smouse, W.H.	Lieut.	24th Iowa Inf.	235		1911 Dec 15	IA, 38th, 1912
Smoyer, Samuel	Pvt.	E, 2nd Mo. Cav.	22		1923 May	IA, 50th, 1924
Smuck, J.B.	Pvt.		141		1900 Jun	IA, 27th, 1901
Smurr, John	Pvt.	A, 5th Iowa Inf.	23		1918 Jan 27	IA, 45th, 1919
Smyser, P.C.	Pvt.	H, 27th Iowa Inf.	54		1911 Feb 19	IA, 38th, 1912
Smyth, Isaac		C, 128th Penn. (died of old age)	81	85	1922 Mar 18	NE, 47th, 1923
Smyth, Patrick		B, 9th Bat.	39		1908 Aug 6	NE, 33rd, 1909
Smythe, B.B.		A, 1st U.S. Dragoons	1		1913 Aug 12	KS, 33rd, 1914
Smythe, J.H.		E, 49th Penn.	50		1917 May 23	KS, 37th, 1918
Snakenburg, Wm.	Pvt.	E, 13th Ind. Inf.	167		1926 Nov 6	IA, 53rd, 1927
Snarly, David			113		1883	KS, 3rd, 1884

*See Appendix A, B or C for roster of post names and locations.
†See Introduction for note regarding recording of death date.

Name	Rank	Company, Regiment or Ship	Post*	Age	Death Date†	Journal
Snavely, Michael F.	Pvt.	E, 28th Iowa Inf.	8		1902 Oct 19	IA, 29th, 1903
Snead, Zachariah W.	Pvt.	H, 8th Iowa Cav.	56	46	1894 Oct 19	IA, 21st, 1895
Snee, H.R.		E, 39th Ill. (location: Hayes Center)			1927 Oct 24	NE, 52nd, 1928
Snell, George		D, 3rd Wis.	113		1913 Feb 17	KS, 33rd, 1914
Snelling, Elliott R.		H, 17th Ind. Inf. (died at Soldiers & Sailors Home, Grand Island; buried in New Harmony, Ind.)	9	78	1905 May 1	NE, 30th, 1906
Snelling, Geo. T.		I, 10th Ill. Hvy. Art. (died of consumption)	69		1894 Jun 29	NE, 19th, 1895
Snelling, William H.		I, 10th Ill. Cav.	25		1893 May 20	NE, 18th, 1894
Snetterly, Abraham		B, 34th Iowa	176		1926 Aug 29	KS, 46th, 1927
Sneyden, Geo.		B, 44th U.S.C.T.	380		1904 Nov 6	KS, 24th, 1905
Snider, C.H.		I, 20th Wis. Inf.	68		1926 Mar 10	NE, 51st, 1927
Snider, Carlisle		L, 120th Ind. (former member; died at Maywood)	303		1936 Mar 22	NE, 61st, 1937
Snider, David D.		G, 43rd Wis. Inf.	44	80	1915 Dec 11	NE, 40th, 1916
Snider, Ferdinand		K, 208th Penn.	6		1906	KS, 26th, 1907
Snider, Frank R.	Pvt.		5		1927	IA, 54th, 1928
Snider, Henry E.	Pvt.	A, 129th Ill. Inf.	40		1915 Jan 17	IA, 42nd, 1916
Snider, Jacob		C, 3rd Tenn.	196		1906 Oct 14	KS, 26th, 1907
Snider, John	Pvt.	A, 33rd Iowa Inf.	49		1918 Apr 1	IA, 45th, 1919
Snider, Lemuel N.		E, 2nd Mo.	40		1908 Aug 27	KS, 28th, 1909
Snider, S.	Pvt.	D, 53rd Penn. Inf. (died of inf. kidneys)	141	59	1885 Sep 16	NE, 10th, 1886
Sniff, Amos		F, 16th Iowa Inf. (died of heart disease)	123	59	1895 May 1	NE, 20th, 1896
Snively, Silas	Pvt.	I, 152nd Ind. Inf.	231		1902 Nov 11	IA, 29th, 1903
Snoddy, Jas. D.		G, 7th Kans. Vol. Cav. Ill. Cav.	3		1917 Oct 28	KS, 37th, 1918
Snoddy, L.O.	Capt.	I, 18th Col. Inf.	35		1918 Jun 19	KS, 38th, 1919
Snode, J.W.		E, 62nd Ohio	17		1926 Apr 1	KS, 46th, 1927
Snodgrass, A.		E, 86th Ohio	448		1908 Mar 1	KS, 28th, 1909
Snodgrass, Geo. T.		Iowa (died of fever)	22	60	1908 Apr 7	NE, 33rd, 1909
Snodgrass, Geo. W.		D, 15th Ind.	193		1911 Aug 15	KS, 31st, 1912
Snodgrass, Hugh	Pvt.	B, 26th Iowa Inf.	418	63	1895 Dec 9	IA, 22nd, 1896
Snodgrass, J.C.	Pvt.	I, 17th Iowa Vol. Inf.	55		1906 Feb 9	IA, 33rd, 1907
Snodgrass, J.M.		E, 12th Ind. Cav.	328		1918 Nov	KS, 38th, 1919
Snodgrass, James R.	Pvt.	I, 39th Iowa Inf.	313		1904 Mar 14	IA, 31st, 1905
Snodgrass, Jas.		F, 11th Ind. Inf. (died of general disability)	79	73	1902 Jun	NE, 27th, 1903
Snodgrass, John T.		K, 134th Ohio	144		1917 Feb 10	KS, 37th, 1918
Snodgrass, T.J.		D, 118th Ohio	53		1916 Aug 19	KS, 36th, 1917
Snodgrass, W.U.		H, 21st Ind.	53		1924 Oct 18	KS, 44th, 1925
Snodgrass, Wm.	Pvt.	F, 31st Iowa Inf.	68		1926 Sep 26	IA, 53rd, 1927
Snodgrass, Wm.			17		1935 Jun 26	KS, 55th, 1936
Snoffer, Joshua	Sergt.	3rd U.S. Dragoons	235		1906 May 5	IA, 33rd, 1907
Snoffer, S.R.		B, 46th Ohio	117		1896 Nov 17	KS, 16th, 1897
Snook, C.P.	Pvt.	4th Ill. Cav.	236	99	1933 Jul 14	IA, 60th, 1934
Snook, Isaac	Pvt.	C, 17th Iowa Inf.	38		1920 Jul 5	IA, 47th, 1921
Snook, J.H.	Pvt.	C, 157th Ill. Inf.	56		1913 Nov 19	IA, 40th, 1914
Snook, Thos. B.	Pvt.	D, 34th Iowa Inf.	235		1912 Nov 22	IA, 39th, 1913
Snook, W.W.		H, 1st Iowa Cav.	130		1908 Aug 14	KS, 28th, 1909
Snook, Wm.	Pvt.	K, 11th Mich. Inf.	16		1917 Jan 20	IA, 44th, 1918
Snooks, M.J.		H, 37th Ind. Inf.	116		1886	KS, 6th, 1887
Snouffer, F.J.			6		1925	IA, 52nd, 1926
Snouffer, Joshua, see Snoffer, Joshua						
Snover, Frank	Sergt.	K, 1st Wis. Cav.	163		1912 Dec 18	IA, 39th, 1913
Snow, E.S.		C, 60th Ohio	364		1926	KS, 46th, 1927
Snow, F.M.		F, 19th Mich. Inf. D, 17th U.S.	209		1912 Nov 16	KS, 32nd, 1913
Snow, Jno. M.		E, 24th Iowa Inf. (died of cancer)	79		1894 Sep 28	NE, 19th, 1895
Snow, Nathan	Pvt.		210		1901 Sep 16	IA, 28th, 1902
Snow, Nathan S.		F, 5th Mo. State Militia	210		1901 Mar 13	IA, 27th, 1901
Snow, W.A.		C, 2nd Mass. Hvy. Art.	241		1909 Nov 10	KS, 29th, 1910
Snowden, Geo. O.	Pvt.	D, 39th Ill. Inf.	68		1914 Apr	IA, 41st, 1915
Snowden, J.W.		11th Ill. Cav. (died of paralysis)	25	65	1903 Feb 28	NE, 28th, 1904

*See Appendix A, B or C for roster of post names and locations.
†See Introduction for note regarding recording of death date.

Name	Rank	Company, Regiment or Ship	Post*	Age	Death Date†	Journal
Snowdon, A.J.		B, 15th Va. (died of debility)	1	72	1918 Sep 29	NE, 43rd, 1919
Snyder, A.	Pvt.	A, 31st Iowa	244		1901 May 29	IA, 28th, 1902
Snyder, A.C.		G, 3rd Wis. Cav. (died of Bright's disease)	8	73	1913 Sep 22	NE, 38th, 1914
Snyder, A.J.	Pvt.	H, 34th Iowa Inf.	55		1916 Dec 22	IA, 43rd, 1917
Snyder, A.L.	Pvt.	G, 12th Wis. Inf.	12		1908 Sep 8	IA, 35th, 1909
Snyder, Alvin			92		1914 Aug 12	KS, 34th, 1915
Snyder, Anthony	Pvt.	B, 35th Ind. Inf. (at large)		94	1941 Aug 20	IA, 67th, 1941
Snyder, B.P.	Musician	Gen. Harrison's Brigade Band	441	45	1889 Aug 31	IA, 16th, 1890
Snyder, C.L.	Pvt.	C, 20th Iowa Inf.	1		1910 Oct 17	IA, 37th, 1911
Snyder, C.M.	Musician	E, 1st Iowa Cav.	20		1911 Feb	IA, 38th, 1912
Snyder, C.W.			74		1914 Sep 23	IA, 41st, 1915
Snyder, Carlton	Pvt.	B, 34th Iowa Inf.	473		1915 Jun 15	IA, 42nd, 1916
Snyder, Christian		D, 82nd Penn.	117		1913 Jul 11	KS, 33rd, 1914
Snyder, D.A.			25		1909 Jun 19	KS, 29th, 1910
Snyder, Daniel	Pvt.	C, 2nd Iowa Cav.	92		1923 Jan 8	IA, 50th, 1924
Snyder, Daniel W.	Corp.	D, 19th Ill. Inf.	68		1910 Jan 10	IA, 37th, 1911
Snyder, David		G, 35th Ill.	3		1927 Aug 21	KS, 47th, 1928
Snyder, Davis		K, 150th Ill.	65		1919 Jan 21	KS, 39th, 1920
Snyder, E.A.	Lieut.	H, 46th Ill. Inf.	222		1916	IA, 43rd, 1917
Snyder, Ed L.		B, 34th Iowa Inf.	16		1918 Mar 12	IA, 45th, 1919
Snyder, Edwin		E, 123rd Ohio Vol. Inf.	1		1915 Dec 24	KS, 35th, 1916
Snyder, Gotlieb	Pvt.	E, 178th Ohio Inf.	236		1925 May 28	IA, 52nd, 1926
Snyder, H.W.		E, 5th Iowa Inf.	17		1911 May 26	KS, 31st, 1912
Snyder, Henry	Pvt.	G, 9th Iowa Cav.	52		1926 Apr 10	IA, 53rd, 1927
Snyder, Henry H.		H, 74th Ind.	129		1909 Feb 10	KS, 29th, 1910
Snyder, J.C.	Pvt.	F, 93rd Ill. Inf.	1		1930 Sep 12	IA, 57th, 1931
Snyder, J.E.	Sergt.	2nd Iowa Bat.	26		1918 Apr 6	IA, 45th, 1919
Snyder, J.H.		I, 77th Ill.	1		1928 Feb 24	KS, 48th, 1929
Snyder, J.H.		H, 38th Wis.	25		1936	KS, 56th, 1937
Snyder, J.H.		A, 18th Ohio Inf. (died of old age)	1	84	1919 Aug 10	NE, 44th, 1920
Snyder, J.K.		E, 51st Penn. Inf.	4		1925 Oct 24	KS, 45th, 1926
Snyder, J.M.	Corp.	D, 92nd Ill.	365		1914 Jul 5	IA, 41st, 1915
Snyder, J.P.		B, 7th Cal. Inf.	465		1899 Mar 11	KS, 19th, 1900
Snyder, J.T.	Pvt.	G, 3rd Iowa Cav.	433		1910 Dec 10	IA, 37th, 1911
Snyder, J.W.	Col.	9th N.Y. Hvy. Art.	25		1914 Oct 27	KS, 34th, 1915
Snyder, James		C, 129th Ohio	69	76	1922 Nov 3	NE, 47th, 1923
Snyder, James A.		11th Ind. Battery	96		1902 Mar 12	KS, 22nd, 1903
Snyder, John	Sergt.	L, 2nd Iowa Cav.	163	58	1892 Oct 1	IA, 19th, 1893
Snyder, John	Pvt.	F, 32nd Iowa Vol. Inf.	149	72	1899	IA, 26th, 1900
Snyder, John	Pvt.	G, 36th Ind. Inf.	219		1913 Nov 29	IA, 40th, 1914
Snyder, John		E, 118th Ill. (died of kidney trouble)	21	67	1907 Jul 22	NE, 32nd, 1908
Snyder, John, see Synder, John						
Snyder, John C.		F, 95th N.Y.	167		1910 May 30	KS, 30th, 1911
Snyder, John G.	Pvt.	G, 8th Iowa Cav.	22		1917 Mar 4	IA, 44th, 1918
Snyder, John W.		K, 35th Iowa	85		1900 Jul 22	KS, 20th, 1901
Snyder, John W.		G, 123rd Ill.	68		1930 Sep 27	KS, 50th, 1931
Snyder, John W.		F, 123rd Ill.	68		1930 Sep 27	KS, 52nd, 1933
Snyder, John W.		G, 56th Ind. Inf.	25		1917 Sep 6	KS, 37th, 1918
Snyder, John W.		F, 123rd Ill.	68		1930 Sep 27	KS, 51st, 1932
Snyder, Joseph		E, 9th Wis.	4		1936 Jul 27	NE, 61st, 1937
Snyder, Lawrance D.		M, N.Y. Lt. Art.	165	76	1920 Jul 28	NE, 45th, 1921
Snyder, M.W.		H, 198th Ohio Inf.	311		1918 Jun 14	KS, 38th, 1919
Snyder, Sam'l B.	Pvt.	F, 35th Iowa Inf.	231		1912 Nov 18	IA, 39th, 1913
Snyder, T.H.		H, 39th Mo.	25		1933 May	KS, 53rd, 1934
Snyder, Wm. C.		G, 18th Mo.	303		1900 Sep 18	KS, 20th, 1901
Soden, W.R.	Pvt.	L, 15th N.Y. Inf.	296		1905 Jun 30	IA, 32nd, 1906
Soedt, Henry	Lieut.	A, 6th Iowa Cav.	403		1910 Sep 13	IA, 37th, 1911
Sohl, Ludwig	Pvt.	E, 5th Iowa Cav.	78		1906 Sep 29	IA, 33rd, 1907
Sohner, Casper	Pvt.	I, 31st Mass. Inf.	68		1905 Feb 23	IA, 32nd, 1906
Solace, C.L.			269		1899	NE, 24th, 1900
Soldier, Peter	Pvt.	11th Neb.	24		1907 Mar 16	IA, 33rd, 1907
Soles, A.L.	Pvt.	B, 1st Cal. Cav.	10		1920 Feb 1	IA, 47th, 1921

*See Appendix A, B or C for roster of post names and locations.
†See Introduction for note regarding recording of death date.

Name	Rank	Company, Regiment or Ship	Post*	Age	Death Date†	Journal
Soles, Geo.	Corp.	B, 70th Ohio Inf.	49		1905 Aug 18	IA, 32nd, 1906
Soliday, S.D.	Corp.	D, 90th Ohio	57		1924 Jul 8	IA, 51st, 1925
Solifelt, George		E, 20th Penn. Cav.	51		1936 Feb 3	KS, 55th, 1936
Sollars, Peter		I, 131st Ohio Inf. (died at Cedarvale; buried at Cedarvale Cemetery)	99		1894 Sep 25	KS, 14th, 1895
Soloman, Wm.	Pvt.	F, 3rd U.S. Cav.	12		1907	IA, 34th, 1908
Soloman, Wm.	Pvt.	D, 186th Ohio	12		1907 Mar 9	IA, 34th, 1908
Somer, Geo. W.		B, 44th Penn. Inf. (died of Bright's disease)	110	69	1913 Sep 1	NE, 38th, 1914
Somerhalter, Bernard	Pvt.	F, 43rd Ill. Inf.	2		1910 Aug 17	IA, 37th, 1911
Somers, David		C, 61st R.I.	256		1919 Feb 19	KS, 39th, 1920
Somers, E.C.	Pvt.	F, 106th Ill.	19		1903 Feb 7	IA, 30th, 1904
Somers, Edwin R.	Pvt. Pvt.	K, 77th Ill. Inf. C, 130th Ill. Inf.	236	99, 4 mos. & 9 days	1944 Jul 3	IA, 70th, 1944
Somers, J.W.	1st Lieut. & QM	76th Ill.	93		1919 Aug 2	IA, 46th, 1920
Somers, S.W.		D, 39th Ind.	55		1925 Aug 24	KS, 45th, 1926
Somerville, W.S.	Pvt.	K, 17th Iowa Inf.	79		1912 Oct 23	IA, 39th, 1913
Somes, Conrad	Pvt.	G, 11th Iowa Inf.	20	52	1892 Mar 23	IA, 18th, 1892
Sommer, Andy		died of paralysis	256	75	1920 Jan 30	NE, 45th, 1921
Sommer, Fred.		H, 29th Iowa (not reported before)	25		1889	KS, 9th, 1890
Sommerfield, John		G, 56th U.S.C.T.	25		1926 Oct 23	NE, 51st, 1927
Sommers, A.P.	Pvt.	I, 12th Wis. Inf.	132		1930 Oct 7	IA, 57th, 1931
Sommerville, John		H, 1st Wis. Cav. (died of old age)	1		1894 Jan 17	NE, 19th, 1895
Somors, J.W.		H, 12th Wis.	293		1924	KS, 44th, 1925
Soper, E.B.	Capt.	D, 12th Iowa Inf.	150		1917	IA, 44th, 1918
Soper, Eben	Pvt.	B, 18th Wis.	81		1922 Dec 19	IA, 49th, 1923
Soper, George W.	Pvt.	K, 35th Iowa Vol. Inf.	181		1901 Dec 16	IA, 28th, 1902
Soper, J.F.		A, 31st Ill. Inf.	147		1908 Dec 23	KS, 28th, 1909
Soper, Lyman		K, 10th Wis. Inf. (died of general disability)	89	71	1913 Jun 12	NE, 38th, 1914
Soper, M.H.		5th Cav. 37th Ind.	453		1914 Apr 17	KS, 34th, 1915
Sopher, Abijah T.	Corp.	G, 79th Ind. Inf.	40		1912 May 3	IA, 39th, 1913
Sopher, Walter F.		E, 87th Ind.	145		1918 Sep 25	KS, 38th, 1919
Sorrell, Nelson	Pvt.	A, 5th Penn. Cav.	7	64	1892 Jul 6	IA, 19th, 1893
Soth, W.P.	Corp.	C, 146th Ohio Inf.	343		1900 Sep 28	IA, 27th, 1901
Souder, George B.		H, 3rd Md. Cav. (died at Leavenworth; buried at National Military Home Cemetery)	415		1894 Apr 26	KS, 14th, 1895
Souders, J.A.		E, 78th Ohio	25		1921 Jan 7	KS, 41st, 1922
Souders, James		F, 2nd Mo. State Militia	35		1914 Jan 15	KS, 34th, 1915
Souders, James B.	Pvt.	10th Iowa Inf.	98		1900 Jun 13	IA, 27th, 1901
Souders, John P.		E, 151st Ill.	47		1934 Oct	NE, 59th, 1935
Souders, W.P.		E, 77th Ill.	47		1931 Aug 24	NE, 56th, 1932
Sough, F.M.	Pvt.	D, 9th Iowa	190		1921 Oct 14	IA, 48th, 1922
Sough, J.F.			116		1923 Oct 28	IA, 50th, 1924
Soule, Edwin		C, 7th Mo. Cav. (died of apoplexy)	35	68	1911 Aug 23	NE, 36th, 1912
Soule, M.B.		E, 16th Ind.	4		1927 Jun 10	KS, 47th, 1928
Sourbeer, Frank		H, 50th Penn.	388		1921 Apr 7	KS, 41st, 1922
Souter, James	Pvt.	F, 20th Ohio Inf.	399		1900 Oct 18	IA, 27th, 1901
South, James		L, 16th Kans. Cav.	220		1892 Mar 2	KS, 12th, 1893
Southard, N.C.	Pvt.	C, 19th Iowa	28		1907 Oct 4	IA, 34th, 1908
Southard, Wm. R.		A, 32nd Iowa (died of heart disease)	8	58	1900 Nov 17	NE, 25th, 1901
Souther, Wm.	Pvt.	A, 6th Iowa Inf.	44		1906 Nov 13	IA, 33rd, 1907
Southerland, A.M.		A, 59th N.Y. (died of typhoid fever)	94		1890	KS, 10th, 1891
Southern, Daniel					1890	KS, 10th, 1891
Southern, Wm.	Pvt.	I, 22nd Ind. Inf.	434		1900 Sep	IA, 27th, 1901
Southwick, A.B.		D, 2nd Colo. Inf. (died of consumption)	261		1894 May 26	NE, 19th, 1895
Southwick, Albert		C, 10th Kans. Inf.	127		1891 Jan 18	KS, 11th, 1892
Southwick, H.R.	Pvt.	I, 3rd Wis. Inf.	254	47	1886 Jul 7	IA, 13th, 1887
Southwick, H.R.	Pvt.	I, 3rd Wis. Inf.	254	47	1886 Jul 7	IA, 17th, 1891
Southwick, John H.	Pvt.	D, 7th Ill. Inf.	359		1912 Jun 24	IA, 39th, 1913
Southy, I.T.		D, 1st Ind.	8		1928 Dec 17	KS, 48th, 1929

*See Appendix A, B or C for roster of post names and locations.
†See Introduction for note regarding recording of death date.

Name	Rank	Company, Regiment or Ship	Post*	Age	Death Date†	Journal
Sovereign, Lewis		F, 83rd Ill.	25		1922 Oct 8	KS, 42nd, 1923
Sovereign, Milton		A, 39th Ill.	32		1933 Jan 2	NE, 58th, 1934
Soward, H.J.		C, 21st Ind.	271		1913 May 5	KS, 33rd, 1914
Soward, John L.		F, 151st Ind.	28		1916 Jun 29	KS, 36th, 1917
Soward, Thomas Howard	2nd Lieut. 1st Lieut.	L, 2nd Ky. Vol. Cav. B, 2nd Ky. Vol. Cav. (died at Guthrie, Okla.; see Appendix D)		78	1918 Aug 31	KS, 38th, 1919
Sowards, John		E, 33rd Ohio	36		1919 Mar 15	KS, 39th, 1920
Sowash, J.B.	Pvt.	A, 2nd Iowa Cav.	440	57	1899 Mar 30	IA, 25th, 1899
Sowash, Wm. M.	Pvt.	7th Iowa Inf.	108		1929 May 7	IA, 56th, 1930
Sowber, Jas. C.	Pvt.	K, 34th Iowa Inf.	208		1911 Oct 21	IA, 38th, 1912
Sowder, H.N.		H, 82nd Ind.	269		1897 Dec 9	KS, 17th, 1898
Sowell, Ira W.		K, 4th Iowa Cav.	43		1912 Apr 1	KS, 32nd, 1913
Sowerine, George		G, 2nd Calif. Cav.	265		1931 Aug 21	NE, 56th, 1932
Sowers, A.J.	Pvt.	K, 136th Ohio Inf.	10		1919 Oct 4	IA, 46th, 1920
Sowers, Alfred B.		34th Ohio Inf.	40		1917 May 15	KS, 37th, 1918
Sowers, John		B, 166th Ohio Inf.	293		1925 Dec 1	KS, 45th, 1926
Sowles, Velie	Pvt.	F, 2nd Ill. Lt. Art.	26	86	1933 Nov 5	IA, 60th, 1934
Spader, Geo.	Pvt.	C, 28th Penn. Inf.	12		1915 Nov 16	IA, 42nd, 1916
Spaht, Z.		H, 35th Ill.	36		1906 Feb	KS, 26th, 1907
Spain, J.H.	Pvt.	C, 33rd —	126		1904 Jul 30	IA, 31st, 1905
Spain, John J.		A, 30th Iowa Inf.	25		1911 Oct 2	KS, 31st, 1912
Spalding, Henry C.		F, 167th Ohio	433		1912 Nov 12	KS, 32nd, 1913
Spalding, Jas. T.		G, 83rd Ill. Inf. (died of bronchitis)	47	69	1908 Dec 25	NE, 33rd, 1909
Spalding, S.K., Dr.		K, 2nd Iowa Cav. (see Appendix D)			1915 Sep 29	NE, 40th, 1916
Spangler, F.G.			4		1922 Nov	KS, 42nd, 1923
Spangler, Francis M.		H, 107th Ill. Inf.	14		1912 Dec 27	KS, 32nd, 1913
Spangler, Harrison	Pvt.	A, 38th Ohio Inf.	50		1911 2nd term	IA, 38th, 1912
Spangler, Simon M.		A, 148th Penn.	36		1922 Oct 17	KS, 42nd, 1923
Spangler, T.P.	Pvt.	C, 149th Penn. Inf.	408		1911 Sep 24	IA, 38th, 1912
Spangler, W.A.	Pvt.	K, 1st Wis. Cav.	66		1917 Nov 26	IA, 44th, 1918
Spanpaltz, Chas.	Pvt.	K, 10th Penn. Inf.	5		1908	IA, 35th, 1909
Spanton, John		K, 9th Iowa Inf.	25	76	1911 Nov 23	NE, 36th, 1912
Spar, L.		F, 11th Kans. Cav.	142		1889	KS, 9th, 1890
Sparacy, Jas.			51		1906	KS, 26th, 1907
Sparer, John R.	Pvt.	D, 16th Iowa Inf.	347		1912	IA, 39th, 1913
Sparks, Benjamin			18		1926	IA, 53rd, 1927
Sparks, Edwin C.		D, 152nd Ill.	18		1911 May 9	KS, 31st, 1912
Sparks, G.M.	Pvt.	C, 10th Iowa Inf.	94	87	1931 Jul 17	IA, 58th, 1932
Sparks, H.M.	Pvt.	F, 4th Iowa Cav.	138		1906 Apr 3	IA, 33rd, 1907
Sparks, J.T.		H, 58th Ind. Inf.	200		1886	KS, 6th, 1887
Sparks, Jeremiah J.	Pvt.	E, 4th Iowa Cav.	199		1917 Jul 3	IA, 44th, 1918
Sparks, M.E.		C, 30th Mo.	142		1917 Dec 4	KS, 37th, 1918
Sparks, R.H.		124th Ind. Inf.	18		1917 Jan 23	KS, 37th, 1918
Sparks, W.A.	Pvt.	I, 145th Ill.	323		1924 Mar 10	IA, 51st, 1925
Sparling, Almon		B, 20th Wis.	209		1909 Sep 2	KS, 29th, 1910
Sparling, Isaac W.		H, 63rd Ill. (died of old age)	94	76	1916 Nov	NE, 41st, 1917
Sparr, John R.		H, 3rd Ky. Cav.	12		1917 Aug 6	KS, 37th, 1918
Sparr, W.R.		A, 3rd Kans. State Militia	12		1902 Aug 25	KS, 22nd, 1903
Sparrow, Harry		I, 12th Ind.	81		1921 Jul 8	KS, 41st, 1922
Sparrowgrove, James	Pvt.	B, 78th Ohio Inf.	233		1931 Apr	IA, 58th, 1932
Spates, Jacob R.	Pvt.	D, 9th Iowa Inf.	40		1924 Feb 7	IA, 51st, 1925
Spaulding, Dudley	Pvt.	G, 140th Ind. Inf.	56		1919 Jul 19	IA, 46th, 1920
Spaulding, E.B.	Lieut.	51st Ill. Inf.	22		1920 Mar 4	IA, 47th, 1921
Spaulding, James	Pvt.	F, 38th Iowa Inf.	235		1917 Jan 4	IA, 44th, 1918
Spaulding, O.A.		I, 34th Ind. Inf. (died at Harper, Kans.; buried at Harper Cemetery)	251		1894 Apr 22	KS, 14th, 1895
Spaulding, S.W.		G, 142nd Ill. Inf.	13		1925 May 27	IA, 52nd, 1926
Spaulis, Simon	Pvt.	C, 142nd Penn. Inf.	68	87	1931 Dec 26	IA, 58th, 1932
Speadling, A.H.	Pvt.	D, 45th Wis. Inf.	142		1924 Aug 24	IA, 51st, 1925
Speaker, Henry		D, 10th Kans.	380		1921 Oct 17	KS, 41st, 1922
Speaker, W.P.	Pvt.	G, 17th Ill. Inf.	392		1905	IA, 32nd, 1906

*See Appendix A, B or C for roster of post names and locations.
†See Introduction for note regarding recording of death date.

515

Name	Rank	Company, Regiment or Ship	Post*	Age	Death Date†	Journal
Speakman, James	Pvt.	H, 124th Penn. Inf.	519		1905 Sep 15	IA, 32nd, 1906
Spear, B.F.		I, 27th Mo.	116	89	1934 Dec 12	IA, 61st, 1935
Spear, J.A.	Pvt.	G, 11th Iowa Inf.	222	98	1932 Apr 4	IA, 59th, 1933
Spear, Johnson	Pvt.	B, 24th Iowa Inf.	110		1928 Mar 24	IA, 55th, 1929
Spear, Robt.		H, 103rd Penn. Inf.	420		1899 May 6	KS, 19th, 1900
Spear, S.C.	Pvt.	C, 42nd Mass. Inf.	165		1927 Dec 7	IA, 54th, 1928
Spear, T.J.		H, 116th Ohio	198		1923 Aug 12	KS, 43rd, 1924
Spear, W.H.	Pvt.	H, 92nd Ill. Inf.	440		1917 Dec 4	IA, 44th, 1918
Spear, William		7th Wis. Bat. (died of broken hip)	84	77	1920 Dec 30	NE, 45th, 1921
Spearman, C.T.	Major	4th Iowa Cav.	20		1922 Feb 28	IA, 49th, 1923
Spearman, J.D.			106		1890 Jan 11	NE, 15th, 1891
Spears, Charles G.	Pvt.	F, 38th Iowa Inf.	68		1910 Dec 5	IA, 37th, 1911
Spears, Chas.		B, 151st Ind. Inf.	38		1899 Nov 25	KS, 19th, 1900
Spears, Daniel		C, 6th Kans. Cav.	33		1900 Aug 13	KS, 20th, 1901
Spears, Irvin			186		1910 Aug 8	IA, 37th, 1911
Spears, Joseph		C, 119th Ind.	28		1896 Jun 11	KS, 16th, 1897
Spears, N.H.	Pvt.	C, 12th Iowa Inf.	47		1912 May 10	IA, 39th, 1913
Spears, Stephen J.		A, 8th Kans.	35		1916 Oct 30	KS, 36th, 1917
Spears, T.M.	Pvt.	H, 54th Ill. Inf.	42		1919 Jun 26	IA, 46th, 1920
Spease, G.S.	Pvt.	C, 7th Ohio Inf.	519		1905 Oct 10	IA, 32nd, 1906
Speece, Thomas B.		C, 106th Ill.	87		1923 Nov 21	KS, 43rd, 1924
Speed, R.		D, 1st Kans.	74		1913 Oct 20	KS, 33rd, 1914
Speekman, James			22		1905	IA, 32nd, 1906
Speer, A.G.		A, 7th Kans. Cav.	130		1911 Oct 13	KS, 31st, 1912
Speer, Austin G.		G, 50th Ind. Inf.	185		1885	KS, 5th, 1886
Speer, James H.		Signal Corps	63		1913 Feb 7	KS, 33rd, 1914
Speer, Joseph	Pvt.	G, 20th Iowa Inf.	68		1904 May	IA, 31st, 1905
Speer, Robert	Surg.	G, 20th Iowa Inf.	125		1913 Jun 15	IA, 40th, 1914
Speer, William S.		C, 48th Ohio Inf.	68		1925 Jul 27	KS, 45th, 1926
Speer, Wm.		G, 5th Ky.	407		1908	KS, 28th, 1909
Speers, H.V.	Sergt.	G, Penn. Hvy. Art.	94		1912 Nov 14	IA, 39th, 1913
Spekn, H.S.					1909 Sep 25	KS, 29th, 1910
Spellman, Chas. E.		F, 19th Ind.	32	91	1924 Dec 22	NE, 49th, 1925
Spelts, Louis		K, 26th Ill. Inf. (died of paralysis)	10	61	1905 Dec 17	NE, 30th, 1906
Spence, E.F.			35		1911 Jan 28	NE, 36th, 1912
Spence, John		11th Ohio	130		1914 Dec 2	KS, 34th, 1915
Spencer, D.J.			211		1918	IA, 45th, 1919
Spencer, David	Pvt.	36th Ill. Inf.	42		1922 Feb 3	IA, 49th, 1923
Spencer, David C.	Major	33rd Mo. Inf.	354	65	1905 Jul 14	NE, 30th, 1906
Spencer, David C.	Sergt. Major	33rd Mass. Inf. (died of paralysis at Soldiers & Sailors Home, Grand Island; buried in Home Cemetery)	14	65	1905 Jul 14	NE, 30th, 1906
Spencer, E.	Pvt.	G, 10th Iowa Inf.	425		1911 Sep 25	IA, 38th, 1912
Spencer, E.G.		15th Iowa Inf.	19		1921 Jan 14	IA, 48th, 1922
Spencer, Elihu D.			425		1917	IA, 44th, 1918
Spencer, Geo. J.		E, 137th N.Y. Inf. (died of general debility)	11	76	1903 Dec 24	NE, 28th, 1904
Spencer, Geo. S.	Pvt.	H, 10th Mich. Cav.	452		1907 Sep 8	IA, 34th, 1908
Spencer, Geo. W.		K, 117th Ill. Inf.	51		1891 Dec 19	KS, 11th, 1892
Spencer, George K.		B, 35th Iowa	6		1925	KS, 45th, 1926
Spencer, H.L.	Pvt.	B, 9th Ohio Cav.	40		1919 Jun 13	IA, 46th, 1920
Spencer, I.N.			205		1911	KS, 31st, 1912
Spencer, J.M.	Pvt.	K, 33rd Ill. Inf.	192		1919 Nov 23	IA, 46th, 1920
Spencer, J.M.	QMS	Wis. Cav.	12		1916 May 13	KS, 36th, 1917
Spencer, James	Pvt.	K, 24th Iowa Inf.	130	94	1939 Mar 29	IA, 65th, 1939
Spencer, James		H & E, 120th Ohio	129		1904 Mar 23	KS, 24th, 1905
Spencer, James R.	Pvt.	F, 2nd Col. Inf.	49	70	1894 Dec 31	IA, 21st, 1895
Spencer, Jesse			104		1923 Jan 3	KS, 43rd, 1924
Spencer, John		E, 156th N.Y.	71		1925 May 4	KS, 45th, 1926
Spencer, John A.	Pvt.	Mo.	12		1911 Aug 30	IA, 38th, 1912
Spencer, John F.		H, 146th Ill.	25		1928 Dec 20	NE, 53rd, 1929

*See Appendix A, B or C for roster of post names and locations.
†See Introduction for note regarding recording of death date.

Name	Rank	Company, Regiment or Ship	Post*	Age	Death Date†	Journal
Spencer, L.D.		A, 6th Ill. Cav. (died in Wallace County, Kans.; buried at Sharon Township Cemetery)	473		1894 Sep 26	KS, 14th, 1895
Spencer, L.H.		H, 15th Conn. Inf.	51		1892 Jul 3	NE, 17th, 1893
Spencer, M.J.		E, 100th Penn.	337		1928	KS, 48th, 1929
Spencer, M.V.	Corp.	G, 65th Ill. Inf.	324		1916 Mar 24	IA, 43rd, 1917
Spencer, Mark H.	Pvt.	L, 3rd Mich. Cav.	1		1923 Oct 3	IA, 50th, 1924
Spencer, Milton		L, 6th Iowa Cav.	113		1916 Mar 4	KS, 36th, 1917
Spencer, N.C.	Pvt.	F, 81st N.Y. Inf.	205		1902 May 23	IA, 29th, 1903
Spencer, R.K.	Pvt.	D, 88th Ohio Inf.	12		1900 Aug 4	IA, 27th, 1901
Spencer, Richard	Pvt.	A, 34th Ill. Inf.	56		1915 Dec 15	IA, 42nd, 1916
Spencer, Romanzo D.	Pvt.	H, 4th Iowa Cav.	132	44	1890 Feb 6	IA, 16th, 1890
Spencer, S.M.		K, 52nd Ind.	339		1928	KS, 48th, 1929
Spencer, T.B.		D, 14th Iowa	25		1928 Dec 10	KS, 48th, 1929
Spencer, W.	Pvt.	D, 10th Conn. Cav.	12		1928 May 26	IA, 55th, 1929
Spencer, W.A.	Pvt.	A, 16th Wis. Inf.	22		1909 Jan 29	IA, 36th, 1910
Spencer, William	Pvt.	C, 13th Iowa Inf.	138		1894 Nov 14	IA, 21st, 1895
Spencer, William		D, 5th N.J.	60		1928 Oct 26	NE, 53rd, 1929
Spencer, Wm.		2nd Col. Cav.	294		1909 Nov 7	KS, 29th, 1910
Spencer, Wm.	Lieut.	F, 21st Ky. Inf.	98		1916 Dec 16	KS, 36th, 1917
Spencer, Wm. T.		H, 45th Ohio (died of old age)	77	85	1925 Jan 25	NE, 50th, 1926
Speort, William E.		F, 114th Ill. Inf.	18		1908 Jun 3	KS, 28th, 1909
Sperlock, Milton		I, 7th Iowa	155		1910 Apr	KS, 30th, 1911
Sperner, Jacob	Pvt.	B, 2nd Mo. Art.	369		1911 Apr 5	IA, 38th, 1912
Spero, Wm. S.	Pvt.	K, 92nd Ill. Inf.	302		1915 Sep 20	IA, 42nd, 1916
Sperry, E.F.	Pvt.	B, 3rd Iowa Inf.	12		1910 Jan 16	IA, 37th, 1911
Sperry, L.E.	Pvt.	G, 1st Wis. Hvy. Art.	71		1914 Apr 9	IA, 41st, 1915
Sperry, L.J.		M, 11th Kans. Cav.	12		1900 Dec 25	KS, 20th, 1901
Sperry, Luther		A, 7th Kans. Cav.	71		1918	KS, 38th, 1919
Sperry, N.F.		K, 2nd Wis. Inf. (died of cancer)	9		1902 Jan	NE, 27th, 1903
Sperry, W.H.		K, 7th Iowa Inf.	7		1915 Mar 1	IA, 42nd, 1916
Spicer, J.A.	Pvt.	A, 17th Wis.	57		1926 Oct	IA, 53rd, 1927
Spicer, J.W.	Pvt.	C, 27th Wis. Inf.	57		1920 May 22	IA, 47th, 1921
Spicer, John W.	Pvt.	G, Wis. Inf.	57		1917 Oct 26	IA, 44th, 1918
Spidel, Albert		F, 57th Ill. (died of paralysis)	54	76	1924 May 31	NE, 49th, 1925
Spidol, David		C, 5th Ind.	46		1926 Nov 15	KS, 46th, 1927
Spiegelmire, J.H.		H, 104th Ohio	265		1910 Nov 8	KS, 30th, 1911
Spielman, John A.	2nd Lieut.	K, 17th Iowa Inf.	19		1914 Dec 27	IA, 41st, 1915
Spiers, Alexander		A, 1st N.Y. Eng.	1		1916 Apr 25	KS, 36th, 1917
Spiker, J.F.	Pvt.	C, 19th Ill. Inf.	18		1915 Aug 15	IA, 42nd, 1916
Spiker, S.R.		G, 10th Ill. Inf.	52	56	1900 Jun 9	NE, 25th, 1901
Spiker, T.L.		G, 118th Ill. (died of old age)	35	81	1920 Mar 3	NE, 45th, 1921
Spiller, Wm.		C, 76th Ill.	46		1920 Nov 28	KS, 40th, 1921
Spilman, P.P.	Capt.	B, 146th Ind. 52nd Ind.	69		1922 Jul 16	IA, 49th, 1923
Spilman, R.B.		K, 86th Ind.	100		1898 Oct 10	KS, 18th, 1899
Sping, David		H, 73rd Ohio	83		1919 Feb 19	KS, 39th, 1920
Spitler, Rufus B.		K, 13th Ohio	93		1909 Jul 8	KS, 29th, 1910
Spittle, Emanuel	Pvt.	3rd Mich. Cav.	461		1926 Mar 20	IA, 53rd, 1927
Spivey, N.		K, 58th Ill. Inf. (died of cancer)	22	73	1920 Sep 27	NE, 45th, 1921
Spondale, J.W.		B, 8th Ohio	142		1937 Nov 30	KS, 57th, 1938
Sponer, J.W.	Pvt.	I, 4th Vt.	231		1923 Mar 13	IA, 50th, 1924
Spong, David, see Sping, David						
Spooner, B.F.		F, 10th N.J.	18		1924 Sep 3	KS, 44th, 1925
Spoor, Isaac		G, 15th Iowa	68	88	1934 May 14	IA, 61st, 1935
Spoor, Joseph	Pvt.	G, 26th N.Y. Inf.	12		1917 Oct 30	IA, 44th, 1918
Spore, D.W.	Pvt.	K, 96th Ill. Inf.	7		1926 Mar	IA, 53rd, 1927
Spore, R.S.		died at his home in Sedgwick, Kans.	255 or 225		1906 Feb 2	KS, 25th, 1906
Sporks, George		D, 12th Colo. Lt. Art.	18		1908 Jan 27	KS, 28th, 1909
Sporleader, A.J.		G, 124th Ill.	147		1905 Aug 31	KS, 25th, 1906
Spradling, J.O.		G, 9th Ind.	311		1927	KS, 47th, 1928
Spradling, Jacob		G, 9th Ind.	311		1926 Nov 28	KS, 46th, 1927

*See Appendix A, B or C for roster of post names and locations.
†See Introduction for note regarding recording of death date.

517

Name	Rank	Company, Regiment or Ship	Post*	Age	Death Date†	Journal
Spragg, D.S.	Corp.	C, 27th Iowa Inf.	80		1923 Oct 15	IA, 50th, 1924
Sprague, Abel A.		9th Iowa Cav.	25		1927 Dec 9	NE, 52nd, 1928
Sprague, C.G.		I, 7th N.Y. State M.	110	66	1905 Jan 19	NE, 30th, 1906
Sprague, D.L.	Pvt.	E, 22nd Wis. Inf.	101		1926 Dec 16	IA, 53rd, 1927
Sprague, Edward F.		I, 56th Ill. F, 13th Ill.	55		1914 Dec 11	KS, 34th, 1915
Sprague, Herman T.		E, 5th Iowa Inf.	258		1890	KS, 10th, 1891
Sprague, Lawrence, see Lawrence, Sprague						
Sprague, Oscar	Pvt.	G, 1st Wis.	77		1928 Nov	IA, 55th, 1929
Sprague, Philip		K, 18th Ill.	1		1905 Jan 17	KS, 25th, 1906
Sprague, Silas		A, 46th Ohio (died of kidney disease)	25	65	1900 Jul 18	NE, 25th, 1901
Sprague, W.H.	Pvt.	99th N.Y. Inf.	329		1918 Sep 26	IA, 45th, 1919
Sprague, Wales O.		A, 7th Ill. Cav.	356	71	1915 Feb 20	NE, 40th, 1916
Spraguins, J.D.		E, 45th Ill. Inf.	84		1926 Mar 31	NE, 51st, 1927
Sprangle, A.L.		8th Ind.	4		1926 Jan 2	KS, 46th, 1927
Spreecher, Geo.		K, 34th Ohio Inf. (died of old age)	34	93	1891[1901?] Nov	NE, 26th, 1902
Sprelman, D.H.		I, 43rd Ohio Inf.	93		1891 Jun 3	KS, 11th, 1892
Spreng, Phillip J.	Lieut.	H, 26th Ill.	1		1916 Apr 10	KS, 36th, 1917
Spriggins, Emanuel		C, 6th Cav.	25	77	1918 Apr 15	NE, 43rd, 1919
Spring, Ezra T.		D, 191st Ohio Inf.	52		1930 Jul 25	KS, 50th, 1931
Spring, James Adam		K, 129th Ohio Inf.	45	92 & 6 mos.	1937 Nov 5	IA, 64th, 1938
Spring, Martin	Pvt.	H, 15th Mo. Inf.	75	61	1897 Oct 31	IA, 24th, 1898
Springer, Alfred	Pvt.	H, 4th Minn.	57		1899	NE, 24th, 1900
Springer, E.B.		B, 12th Mo.	8		1898 Apr 9	KS, 18th, 1899
Springer, Francis		A, 3rd N.J.	4		1921 Mar 12	KS, 41st, 1922
Springer, G.W.	Pvt.	F, 10th Iowa Inf.	7		1915 Nov 27	IA, 42nd, 1916
Springer, O.H.P.	Pvt.	L, 9th Iowa Cav.	7		1925 Sep 28	IA, 52nd, 1926
Springer, Oliver	Sergt.	L, 34th Iowa Inf.	116		1905 Feb 24	IA, 31st, 1905
Springer, S.A.	Pvt.	F, 39th Ill. Inf.	290	45	1887 Nov 14	IA, 14th, 1888
Springer, Wm. B.		G, 7th Kans.	174		1912 Mar 23	KS, 32nd, 1913
Springoton, S.A.		B, 18th Iowa	180		1911 May 27	KS, 31st, 1912
Springsteen, David	Pvt.	F, 19th Iowa Inf.	410		1913 Sep 13	IA, 40th, 1914
Springsteen, John	Pvt.	E, 12th Mich. Inf.	40		1910 Aug 15	IA, 37th, 1911
Springton, S.A., see Springoton, S.A.						
Sprinkle, Calvin		K, 9th Penn.	380		1902 Jun 27	KS, 22nd, 1903
Spronkle, Peter		G, 105th Penn.	199		1923 Dec 6	KS, 46th, 1927
Sproul, John S.	Pvt.	C, 7th Iowa Inf.	59		1912 Feb 20	IA, 39th, 1913
Sproul, W.H.	Pvt.	D, 191st Ohio	440		1923 Dec 30	IA, 50th, 1924
Sproule, Ceo.	Pvt.	G, 94th Ill. Inf.	210		1905 Apr 28	IA, 32nd, 1906
Sprouse, Samuel C.		A, 97th Ill.	118		1918 Dec 31	KS, 38th, 1919
Sprout, William		H, 141st Ill. (not a member of the department but living in Nebraska; location: Franklin)			1937 Sep 23	NE, 62nd, 1938
Spry, Geo. W.	Sergt.	B, 34th Iowa Inf.	7		1887 Apr 6	IA, 14th, 1888
Spry, George W.	Sergt.	B, 34th Iowa Inf.	7		1887 Apr 6	IA, 13th, 1887
Spry, John	Pvt.	F, 103rd Ohio	363		1907 2nd term	IA, 34th, 1908
Spunangle, W.J.	Artificer	C, 1st Mo. Eng.	11		1909 Oct	IA, 36th, 1910
Spurbeck, Andrew		D, 47th Ill.	10	76	1920 Aug 18	NE, 45th, 1921
Spurgeon, Stanford		D, 9th Kans.	81		1923 Jan 9	KS, 43rd, 1924
Spurling, John D.		I, 59th U.S. C.F.[U.S.C.T.?]	132		1899 Jun	KS, 19th, 1900
Spurlock, L.B.		C, 130th Mo. A, 7th Iowa Cav.	113		1921 Apr 26	KS, 41st, 1922
Spurlock, W.B.		L, 5th Kans. Cav.	132		1929 Jan	KS, 51st, 1932
Spurlock, W.B.		I, 5th Kans. Cav.	132		1929 Jan 19	KS, 49th, 1930
Spurrier, Francis M.	Sergt.	D, 32nd Iowa Inf.	300		1912 Nov 17	IA, 39th, 1913
Spurrier, Thos. B.		D, 14th Iowa Vol. Inf.	25		1908 Aug 14	KS, 28th, 1909
Squire, G.B.	Pvt.	B, 3rd Ohio Cav.	383		1903 Jul 25	IA, 30th, 1904
Squires, Albian C.		A, 16th Ill. G, 22nd Wis.	250		1924 Jun 27	KS, 44th, 1925
Squires, E.V.		D, 48th Ind.	32		1902 Mar 15	KS, 22nd, 1903

*See Appendix A, B or C for roster of post names and locations.
†See Introduction for note regarding recording of death date.

Name	Rank	Company, Regiment or Ship	Post*	Age	Death Date†	Journal
Squires, G.E.		I, 44th Iowa Inf. (died of apoplexy)	110	74	1918 Feb 18	NE, 43rd, 1919
Squires, H.D.	Pvt.	A, 14th Iowa	30		1921 Apr	IA, 48th, 1922
Squires, Henry		A, 27th Ind.	344		1920 May 9	KS, 40th, 1921
Squires, J.		H, 1st Neb. (died of general debility)	42		1894 Aug 3	NE, 19th, 1895
Squires, J.W.	Pvt.	K, 67th Ill. Inf.	29		1918 Aug 18	IA, 45th, 1919
Squires, S.L.	Pvt.	K, 44th Ind.	16		1921 Jul 7	IA, 48th, 1922
Squires, Thos.	Pvt.	B, 6th Conn. Inf.	7		1904 Apr 26	IA, 31st, 1905
Squirs, Grison		G, 125th Penn. Inf. (died of old age)	1	80	1924 May 26	NE, 49th, 1925
Squiver, E.W.	Pvt.	F, 1st Neb. Inf.	11		1912	IA, 39th, 1913
Sreeisor, Jacob H.		I, 68th Ind.	14		1889	KS, 9th, 1890
Srevers, Hans	Pvt.	A, 14th Iowa Inf.	44	57	1896 May 8	IA, 23rd, 1897
Sroufe, Geo. W.		H, 112th Ill. Inf.	8		1886	KS, 6th, 1887
St. Clair, A.J.		B, 81st Ind.	87		1922 Mar 4	KS, 42nd, 1923
St. Clair, Alexander	2nd Lieut.	I, 43rd U.S.C. Inf.	12		1900 Sep 25	IA, 27th, 1901
St. Clair, Enoch		C, 15th West Va. Inf.	500		1916 Mar 26	KS, 36th, 1917
St. Clair, Wm.	Pvt.	D, 28th Iowa Inf.	166		1915 Feb	IA, 42nd, 1916
St. Criss, see Criss, St.						
St. Dennis, G.			25		1900 Mar	KS, 20th, 1901
St. John	Pvt.	D, 32nd Penn.	154		1926 Jun 28	IA, 53rd, 1927
St. John, D.J.			172		1913	IA, 40th, 1914
St. John, H.D.	Pvt.	G, 2nd Iowa Inf.	235		1907 Jun 26	IA, 34th, 1908
St. John, Henry		A, 7th Mo.	25		1916 Jan 19	KS, 36th, 1917
St. John, L.G.	Pvt.	I, 11th Minn. Inf.	216		1904 Feb 6	IA, 30th, 1904
St. John, L.G.	Pvt.	I, 11th Minn. Inf.	216		1904 Feb 6	IA, 31st, 1905
St. John, L.S.	Pvt.	H, 1st Minn. Inf.	216		1913 Jun 26	IA, 40th, 1914
St. John, Marcena		E, 11th Kans. Cav.	18		1917 Jul 5	KS, 37th, 1918
St. John, Mark B.		D, 32nd Wis.	28		1921	KS, 41st, 1922
St. John, Milton		L, 13th Ohio Cav.	35		1919 Jan 27	KS, 39th, 1920
St. John, Robert Thomas		A, 7th Ill. Cav.	512	91	1937 Apr 28	IA, 64th, 1938
St. John, T.R.	Pvt.	B, 185th Ill. Inf.	12		1928 Mar 8	IA, 55th, 1929
St. John, Y.E.		K, 14th Wis. Cav.	4		1887 Apr 30	KS, 7th, 1888
St. Ledger, John	Sergt.	C, 59th Ill. Inf.	231		1908 Oct 20	IA, 35th, 1909
St. Ledger, John		H, 87th Ind. Inf.	25		1917 Jan 1	KS, 37th, 1918
St. Louis, John F.		H, 17th Mo.	35		1896 Dec 23	KS, 16th, 1897
St. Perrie, Houre		D, 76th Ill.	71		1904 Apr 23	KS, 24th, 1905
St. Perrie, Jas.	Pvt.	K, 147th Ill.	23		1926 Jan	IA, 53rd, 1927
St. Peter, Theo.		A, 35th Iowa	63		1919 Jul 16	KS, 39th, 1920
Staab, Geo.	Pvt.	H, 4th Wis. Inf.	140	72	1891 Sep	IA, 18th, 1892
Staats, Abram		F, 74th Ill.	258		1931 Apr	KS, 52nd, 1933
Staats, Abram		F, 74th Ill.	258		1931 Apr	KS, 51st, 1932
Stabler, George W.		C, 2nd Kans. Cav.	93		1911 May 12	KS, 31st, 1912
Stacey, Clinton		D, 51st Mo.	359		1897 Aug	KS, 17th, 1898
Stack, John		H, 15th N.Y. Hvy. Art. (died of consumption)	25	62	1900 May 24	NE, 25th, 1901
Stack, Thos. W.		U.S. Navy	25		1905 Jul 20	NE, 30th, 1906
Stack, Thos. W.		U.S. Navy	25		1905 Jul 24	NE, 31st, 1907
Stackhouse, Allen	Pvt.	D, 112th Ill. Inf.	127	55	1894 Jun 15	IA, 21st, 1895
Stacy, F.M.	Pvt.	G, 151st Ohio Inf.	173		1920 Aug 24	IA, 47th, 1921
Stacy, Judson C.	Pvt.	K, 20th Iowa Inf.	382		1900 Sep	IA, 27th, 1901
Stadden, I.		6th Kans.	32		1888	KS, 8th, 1889
Stader, Chas. E.	Pvt.	F, 1st La. Inf.	7		1916 Nov 17	IA, 43rd, 1917
Staens, James F.		C, 7th Kans.	175		1924 May 23	KS, 44th, 1925
Stafford, Alfred		A, 85th Ind.	1		1924 Mar 29	KS, 44th, 1925
Stafford, E.J.	Corp.	A, 2nd Iowa Cav.	231		1920 Aug 6	IA, 47th, 1921
Stafford, Frank		B, 16th Ohio Cav.	69		1919 Mar 15	KS, 39th, 1920
Stafford, Jas. M.		H, 72nd Ind. Inf.	25		1891 Sep 22	KS, 11th, 1892
Stafford, Thomas		K, 50th N.Y. Inf.	64		1893 May 3	IA, 20th, 1894
Stafford, W.C.	Pvt.	E, 50th Mass.	123		1905 Apr 21	IA, 32nd, 1906
Stagg, W.J.		D, 132nd Ind.	1		1932 Dec 26	KS, 52nd, 1933
Staggers, A.		C, 17th West Va.	85		1929 Jun 11	KS, 49th, 1930
Stahl, Daniel			140		1926 Jan 16	IA, 53rd, 1927
Stahl, Daniel W.	Pvt.	D, 78th Ohio Inf.	316, 335	93	1939 Oct 11	IA, 66th, 1940

*See Appendix A, B or C for roster of post names and locations.
†See Introduction for note regarding recording of death date.

Name	Rank	Company, Regiment or Ship	Post*	Age	Death Date†	Journal
Stahl, H.	Pvt.		94		1921 Mar 8	IA, 48th, 1922
Stahl, Henry	Pvt.	B, 13th Iowa Inf.	285	73	1897 Feb 15	IA, 24th, 1898
Stahl, J.W.	Pvt.	D, 21st Iowa Inf.	235		1907 Apr 4	IA, 34th, 1908
Stahl, Jerome	Pvt.	2nd Kans. Mil.	1		1915 Apr 22	KS, 35th, 1916
Stakebrake, I.L.		F, 156th Ohio	132		1924 Feb 3	KS, 44th, 1925
Stakes, G.H.	Pvt.	B, 34th Ill. Inf.	122		1917 Jan 8	IA, 44th, 1918
Stakes, Joseph			35		1905	NE, 30th, 1906
Staley, Charles H.		A, 51st Mo. Inf.	93		1914 Aug 22	KS, 34th, 1915
Staley, F.M.		E, 132nd Penn.	32		1926 Apr 27	NE, 51st, 1927
Staley, George		L, 12th Ind.	77		1928 Nov 7	NE, 53rd, 1929
Staley, James	Pvt.	L, 4th Iowa Cav.	81		1908 Dec 23	IA, 35th, 1909
Staley, John A.		E, 10th West Va. Inf.	17		1915 Sep 29	KS, 35th, 1916
Staley, Paren		E, 7th Md.	25		1915 May 5	NE, 40th, 1916
Staley, Wm.	Pvt.	D, 153rd Ill. Inf.	440		1919 Nov 3	IA, 46th, 1920
Stalker, J.A.	Pvt.	I, 6th Wis. Inf.	36	74	1897 May 17	IA, 24th, 1898
Stalker, John		G, 71st Ind. Vols.	71		1909 Aug 1	KS, 29th, 1910
Stall, A.	Pvt.	G, 43rd Iowa Inf.	48		1916 Jul 6	IA, 43rd, 1917
Stall, Arthur	Pvt.	C, 1st Neb. Cav.	38	63	1892 Dec 14	IA, 19th, 1893
Stall, Edward K.	Pvt.	H, 94th Ill. Inf.	20		1932	IA, 59th, 1933
Stall, Johnathan		G, 178th Ohio	111		1921 Aug 12	KS, 41st, 1922
Stall, Robt.		died of heart trouble	62	63	1908 Apr 18	NE, 33rd, 1909
Stall, Sigman		B, 148th N.Y.	318	73	1912	NE, 37th, 1913
Stallard, W.D.		I, 1st Neb.	74		1898	KS, 18th, 1899
Stallcop, Benjamin K.		G, 18th Iowa Inf.	85		1901 Jul 21	KS, 21st, 1902
Stalter, C.W.	Corp.	H, 122nd Ohio Inf.	293		1929	KS, 49th, 1930
Stalter, David		F, 123rd Ohio	85		1906 Feb 4	KS, 26th, 1907
Stambo, Joshua	Pvt.	C, 48th Ohio Inf.	67	97	1933 Sep 29	IA, 60th, 1934
Stamm, Christian		G, 20th Ill. Inf.	82	94	1938 Mar 14	IA, 64th, 1938
Stamm, J.F.	Pvt.	E, 2nd Iowa Inf.	118		1909 Apr 7	IA, 36th, 1910
Stamm, R.	Sergt.	E, 2nd Iowa Inf.	118	57	1897 Jan 30	IA, 23rd, 1897
Stanchfield, C.A.			5		1911 1st term	IA, 38th, 1912
Standidge, Thomas		K, 141st Ill. Inf. (former member)	254		1942 Mar 15	NE, 67th, 1943
Standish, George	Pvt.	C, 2nd Iowa Art.	11		1928	IA, 55th, 1929
Standish, R.M.		died of cancer	36		1904 Sep	NE, 29th, 1905
Standish, W.J.		9th N.Y. Cav.	68		1902 Aug 12	IA, 29th, 1903
Standley, Wm. M.		K, 5th Mo. Inf. (died of heart failure)	288		1895 Oct 15	NE, 20th, 1896
Stanfield, Ferdinan		D, 106th Ohio	7		1897 Jul 1	NE, 22nd, 1898
Stanfield, George	Pvt.	2nd Iowa Bat.	55		1915 Apr 11	IA, 42nd, 1916
Stanfield, I.J.		A, 23rd Iowa	34		1927 Dec 20	KS, 47th, 1928
Stanfield, P.H.	Pvt.	C, 22nd Iowa Inf.	440		1917 May 6	IA, 44th, 1918
Stanfield, R.T.		K, 120th Ind.	44		1916 May 15	KS, 36th, 1917
Stanfield, S.N.	Pvt.	H, 24th Iowa Inf.	101	77	1897 Jan 13	IA, 23rd, 1897
Stanfield, Samuel		G, 154th Ohio	129		1908 May 16	KS, 28th, 1909
Stanford, A.K.	Pvt.	H, 27th Iowa Inf.	166		1909 Nov 7	IA, 36th, 1910
Stanford, J.W.		D, 51st Ohio	158		1914 Mar 20	KS, 34th, 1915
Stanger, Albert Moore	Pvt.	B, 22nd Penn. Cav.	98	94	1939 May 14	IA, 65th, 1939
Stanley, A.J.			25		1909 Aug 16	KS, 29th, 1910
Stanley, Chas.	1st Sergt.	K, 18th Iowa Inf.	40		1904 Jun 7	IA, 31st, 1905
Stanley, D.W.		D, 29th Wis.	46		1928 Feb 5	KS, 48th, 1929
Stanley, J.H.		F, 35th Wis.	355		1913 Aug 29	KS, 33rd, 1914
Stanley, John	Pvt.	C, 5th Kans. Cav.	251		1899	IA, 26th, 1900
Stanley, R.C.		D, 73rd Ind. Inf.	47		1899 Jul 20	KS, 19th, 1900
Stanley, Samuel R.			14		1923 May 25	IA, 50th, 1924
Stanley, W.E.		Mass. Hvy. Art.	54		1926 Dec 16	IA, 53rd, 1927
Stanley, W.E.	PDChap.		154		1927	IA, 54th, 1928
Stanly, I.M.		K, 9th Ill. Cav.	32		1925 Nov 27	KS, 45th, 1926
Stanly, Thomas		B, 95th Penn. Inf.	132		1925 Apr 11	KS, 45th, 1926
Stansberry, George			130		1914 Nov 25	KS, 34th, 1915
Stansbury, Geo. A.		L, 7th Ill.	130		1913 Nov 24	KS, 33rd, 1914
Stanter, Louis		B, 154th Ill. Inf. (died of paralysis at Soldiers & Sailors Home, Grand Island; buried in Home Cemetery)	15	76	1905 Jul 16	NE, 30th, 1906

*See Appendix A, B or C for roster of post names and locations.
†See Introduction for note regarding recording of death date.

Name	Rank	Company, Regiment or Ship	Post*	Age	Death Date†	Journal
Stanton, Amon	Pvt.	A, 14th Ill. Cav.	192		1923 Jun 19	IA, 50th, 1924
Stanton, C.A.	Major	3rd Iowa Cav.	122		1913 Jun	IA, 40th, 1914
Stanton, Edwin W.		Unc., 3rd Wis. Bat.	184	90	1938 Mar 31	IA, 64th, 1938
Stanton, Green	Pvt.	C, 82nd Ohio Inf.	251		1916 Mar 17	IA, 43rd, 1917
Stanton, Sandford A.		F, 17th Iowa	32		1924 Dec 2	KS, 44th, 1925
Stanwood, M.O.	Pvt.	B, 3rd Iowa Inf.	231		1908 Feb 11	IA, 35th, 1909
Stapleford, Dan'l	Pvt.	C, 30th Iowa	275		1903-1904	IA, 30th, 1904
Staples, A.	Pvt.	G, 4th Maine	324		1921 Jan 29	IA, 48th, 1922
Staples, D.K.		died of paralysis	68		1913	NE, 38th, 1914
Staples, George M.	Surg.	14th Iowa Inf.	78	68	1895 Sep 7	IA, 22nd, 1896
Staples, Jotham S.		D, 28th Maine	22	85	1908 Sep 8	NE, 33rd, 1909
Staples, M.M.			44		1922 Jun 5	KS, 42nd, 1923
Stapleton, James		H, 1st Neb. Cav. (location: Blair)			1927 Aug 5	NE, 52nd, 1928
Staplin, Geo.		C, 15th Ill. Inf.	171		1917	KS, 37th, 1918
Starbuck, Elisha		K, 39th Iowa Inf.	15	98	1937 Oct 28	IA, 64th, 1938
Starbuck, J.		10th Ind. Inf.	28	62	1902 Oct	NE, 27th, 1903
Staring, Chas. M.	Musician	G, 1st Wis. Art.	23		1922 Feb 10	IA, 49th, 1923
Stark, B.G.		E, 37th Ind. Inf.	193		1908 Oct 10	IA, 35th, 1909
Stark, L.B.	Wagoner	143rd Penn.	212		1903-1904	IA, 30th, 1904
Stark, Martin	Pvt.	B, 33rd Ill. Inf.	68		1918 Apr 10	IA, 45th, 1919
Stark, R.C.		H, 116th Penn. Inf.	118		1912 Jan 6	KS, 32nd, 1913
Stark, S.B.		D, 2nd Iowa	63		1920 Nov 10	KS, 40th, 1921
Starke, John	Pvt.	B, 1st Neb. Cav.	231		1917	IA, 44th, 1918
Starkey, John		E, 191st Ohio	19		1914 Mar 7	KS, 34th, 1915
Starks, L.H.	Pvt.	G, 5th Iowa Inf. I, 5th Iowa Cav.	98	61	1900 Jan 2	IA, 26th, 1900
Starns, Levi		B, 86th Ind.	293		1923 Dec 19	KS, 43rd, 1924
Starr, A.D.	Pvt.	H, 4th Iowa Inf.	466		1918 Sep 7	IA, 45th, 1919
Starr, Barnard		A, 38th Iowa Inf.	46		2nd quarter 1884	IA, 11th, 1885
Starr, J.B.		E, 87th Ind.	110	65	1910 Jan 9	NE, 35th, 1911
Starr, James T.	Pvt.	C, 42nd Ill. Inf.	255		1922 Sep	IA, 49th, 1923
Starr, Loring	Pvt.	F, 21st Mo. Inf.	254		1923 Apr 8	IA, 50th, 1924
Starr, Nathan A.		C, 21st Conn.	88		1904 Jul 13	KS, 24th, 1905
Starr, W.H.		D, 8th Ill.	265		1918 Nov 16	KS, 38th, 1919
Starr, William		B, 13th Ill.	25		1897 Jan 21	KS, 17th, 1898
Starr, Wm.	Pvt.	F, 7th Iowa Cav.	68		1915 Sep 19	IA, 42nd, 1916
Starrett, H.M.	Corp.	H, 7th Iowa Inf.	263		1903 Aug 27	IA, 30th, 1904
Starritt, W.H.		F, 59th Iowa	59		1924 Dec 21	KS, 45th, 1926
Starrs, M.C.	Pvt.	K, 4th Iowa Inf.	55		1903 Feb 23	IA, 30th, 1904
Start, James		E, 2nd N.Y. Hvy. Art.	448		1919 Oct 2	KS, 39th, 1920
Starter, —		H, 12th Iowa	293		1924	KS, 44th, 1925
Statcup, Usher J.		E, 32nd Iowa			1908	KS, 28th, 1909
State, Adam	Pvt.	I, 34th Ky. Inf.	231		1907 Feb 24	IA, 34th, 1908
Staten, Jack			243		1920	KS, 40th, 1921
Statler, Charles S.		E, 36th Iowa	2		1919 Sep 2	KS, 39th, 1920
Staton, Robert		C, 10th Mo. Inf. (died of gunshot wound, head)	1		1894 Feb 28	NE, 19th, 1895
Staton, Thos.		E, 76th Ill. Inf.	3		1918 Dec 11	KS, 38th, 1919
Stattlemeyer, D.T.			290		1915 Jul 18	IA, 42nd, 1916
Stattman, F.H.		C, 77th Penn.	17		1922 Jul 29	KS, 42nd, 1923
Statton, Curtis H.		G, 63rd Ind. Inf.	68		1939 Apr	NE, 64th, 1940
Statton, Joseph S.	Pvt.	C, 38th Iowa Inf.	277		1903 Sep 16	IA, 30th, 1904
Statts, E.P.	Corp.	H, 89th N.Y. Inf.	77		1910 Dec 14	IA, 37th, 1911
Staub, Libnius		C, 45th Wis. Inf. (died of old age)	273	72	1901 Aug	NE, 26th, 1902
Stauffer, Henry		B, 7th Ill. Inf. (died of chronic bronchitis)	95	68	1906 Sep 14	NE, 31st, 1907
Stauffer, Isaac	Pvt.	B, 28th Penn. Inf.	483		1902 May 10	IA, 29th, 1903
Stauffer, J.W.	Pvt.	D, 88th Ill. Inf.	26		1930 Oct 17	IA, 57th, 1931
Stautz, F.M.	Pvt.	A, 18th Iowa Inf.	235	49	1891 Dec 15	IA, 18th, 1892
Staver, H.Q.		A, 11th Ill. Inf. (died of heart disease)	48	60	1897 Sep 7	NE, 22nd, 1898
Staves, M.C.	Pvt.	K, 11th Iowa Inf.	7		1910 Mar 25	IA, 37th, 1911
Stavlus, Lewis		A, 52nd Wis.	57		1913 May 3	KS, 33rd, 1914
Steadman, Dow		B, 18th Penn.	13	79	1916 Aug 31	NE, 41st, 1917

*See Appendix A, B or C for roster of post names and locations.
†See Introduction for note regarding recording of death date.

Name	Rank	Company, Regiment or Ship	Post*	Age	Death Date†	Journal
Steadman, E.A.			487		1910	IA, 37th, 1911
Steadman, E.D.	Pvt.	D, 12th Iowa Inf.	98	53	1891[?]	IA, 22nd, 1896
Steadman, Geo. O.	Pvt.	A, 31st Iowa Inf.	12		1914 Sep 15	IA, 41st, 1915
Steadman, James S.		B, 18th Wis.	71		1914 Jan 26	KS, 34th, 1915
Steadman, John J.	Drummer	H, 171st Ohio Inf. (not a member in Iowa at time of death)	61, 29	92	1941 Apr 19	IA, 67th, 1941
Steadman, L.		G, 1st Colo.	114		1892 Sep 5	KS, 12th, 1893
Stearinan, Marion		A, 76th Ill.	14		1908 Mar 7	KS, 28th, 1909
Stearn, W.W.		K, 2nd West Va. (died of broken hip)	35	80	1922 Apr 3	NE, 47th, 1923
Stearns, Bradshaw	Sergt.	H, 11th Wis. Inf.	97	63	1898 Apr 20	IA, 24th, 1898
Stearns, Chas. S.	Pvt.	F, 15th Iowa Inf.	54		1911 Sep 26	IA, 38th, 1912
Stearns, E.	Pvt.		122		1911 Mar 18	IA, 38th, 1912
Stearns, G.A.	Pvt.	I, 7th Ill. Cav.	42		1922 Mar 22	IA, 49th, 1923
Stearns, G.L.	Corp.	B, 31st Iowa Inf.	206		1906 Oct 24	IA, 33rd, 1907
Stearns, Henry H.	Pvt.	K, 58th Ind. Inf.	12		1918 Mar 11	IA, 45th, 1919
Stearns, John	Pvt.	D, 9th Iowa Inf.	18		1929 Apr 19	IA, 56th, 1930
Stearns, John O.		B, 37th Ill. Inf. (died of heart failure)	55	70	1909 Aug 11	NE, 34th, 1910
Stearns, John S., Rev.		B, 43rd Ill. Inf. (died from injuries)	1		1925 Nov 19 or 20	KS, 45th, 1926
Stearns, Thos. J.		I, 60th N.Y. 17th Wis. (died of paralysis)	27	76	1914 Jan 3	NE, 39th, 1915
Stearns, W.T.	Sergt.	A, 3rd Mo. Cav.	208		1911 Feb 7	IA, 38th, 1912
Stears, Samuel			321		1923	KS, 43rd, 1924
Stebbins, A.H.	Pvt.		487		1920	IA, 47th, 1921
Stebbins, Gardiner B.		I, 7th Ohio Cav.	7		1913 May 15	KS, 33rd, 1914
Stebbins, H.D.		D, 18th Ohio Inf. (died at Denver, Colo.)	22		1889	KS, 9th, 1890
Stebbins, Martin V.		F, 1st Iowa Cav.	267	92	1938 Feb 27	IA, 64th, 1938
Stebens, E.J.	Pvt.	F, 39th Ill. Inf.	26		1906 Mar 25	IA, 33rd, 1907
Stech, Philip L.	Pvt.	F, 34th Iowa Inf.	288	62	1893 Dec 5	IA, 20th, 1894
Stedman, E.H.	Lieut.	A, 37th Iowa Inf.	98	73	1887 Oct 10	IA, 14th, 1888
Stedman, E.H.	Pvt.	A, 37th Iowa Inf.	98	73	1887 Oct 10	IA, 17th, 1891
Steece, James	Pvt.	G, 4th Ohio Cav.	451	70	1898 Jan 3	IA, 24th, 1898
Steel, James A.		Ill.	175		1914 Jan	KS, 33rd, 1914
Steel, Jatsen		F, 6th West Va.	18		1923 Feb 16	KS, 43rd, 1924
Steel, Leonard J.		B, 10th Kans. Inf.	64		1901 Sep	KS, 21st, 1902
Steel, R.H.		E, 1st Penn. Vol. Rifles	66		1885	KS, 5th, 1886
Steel, W.H.	Pvt.	A, 8th Ohio Inf.	206		1921 Jan 29	IA, 48th, 1922
Steel, W.M.	Pvt.	A, 144th Ill. Inf.	150	68	1896 Mar 19	IA, 23rd, 1897
Steel, Wm.	Pvt.	A, 1st Wis. Cav.	124		1909 Feb 21	IA, 36th, 1910
Steel, Wm.		G, 16th Ill.	85		1921 Feb 1	KS, 41st, 1922
Steele, A.C.	Sergt.	D, 74th Ill. Inf.	188		1915 May 29	IA, 42nd, 1916
Steele, Calvin F.		A, 2nd Ill. Cav. (see also Appendix D)	77		1910 Mar 5	NE, 35th, 1911
Steele, H.S.		1st U.S. Lt. Art.	1		1918 Jul 14	KS, 38th, 1919
Steele, H.S.		A, 54th Ohio (died of blood poison)	1	77	1918 Nov 12	NE, 43rd, 1919
Steele, J.M., Col.	Lieut. Col.	11th Kans. Cav.	55		1916 Jan 27	KS, 36th, 1917
Steele, John T.		A, 28th Ill.	100		1923 Sep 18	KS, 43rd, 1924
Steele, Joseph	Pvt.	I, 137th Ill. Inf. D, 151st Ill. Inf. (at large)	452	96	1942 Nov 2	IA, 69th, 1943
Steele, L.S.		K, 2nd Colo. Cav.	12		1916 Jun 14	KS, 36th, 1917
Steele, Miner	Pvt.	E, 31st Wis. Inf.	519		1914 May 2	IA, 41st, 1915
Steele, S.L.	Lieut.	B, 25th Iowa Inf.	20		1897-1898	IA, 24th, 1898
Steele, William H.		K, 191st Penn.	1		1892 Aug 28	KS, 12th, 1893
Steelman, Thos. B.		B, 130th Ill. Inf.	18		1901 Dec 12	KS, 21st, 1902
Steen, F.	Pvt.	F, 12th Iowa Inf.	184		1912 Jan 18	IA, 39th, 1913
Steen, James		H, 9th Kans. Cav.	68		1913 Sep 28	KS, 33rd, 1914
Steen, Robert P.		B, 1st Penn. Battery	91		1892 Mar 21	NE, 17th, 1893
Steene, James C.		H, 1st Iowa Vol. Inf.	44		1892 Mar 2	KS, 12th, 1893
Steenrod, Geo. W.		C, 85th N.Y.	25		1920 Sep 10	KS, 40th, 1921
Steere, R.A.	Pvt.	A, 2nd Minn. Inf.	34	67	1890 Sep 3	IA, 17th, 1891
Steere, Solan		A, 67th Ill.	144		1929 Dec 27	KS, 49th, 1930
Steere, Thomas		I, 18th Conn.	147		1896 May 4	KS, 16th, 1897
Steers, David S.	Pvt.	E, 160th Ohio Inf.	440		1914 Dec 31	IA, 41st, 1915
Steers, Solon		A, 57th Ind.	147		1928 Dec 28	KS, 48th, 1929

*See Appendix A, B or C for roster of post names and locations.
†See Introduction for note regarding recording of death date.

Name	Rank	Company, Regiment or Ship	Post*	Age	Death Date†	Journal
Steffey, Henry		D, 86th Ind.	23	69	1907 Jul 26	NE, 32nd, 1908
Steffin, Charles		G, 5th Kans.	185		1910 Sep	KS, 30th, 1911
Steffins, James	Pvt. Sergt.	K, 15th Ill. G, 15th Ill. (died of heart disease)	13	45	1885 Nov 11	NE, 10th, 1886
Steffins, W.E.	Seaman	U.S. Frigate *Constitution*	225		1914 Jun 24	KS, 34th, 1915
Steffy, George		E & K, 10th Iowa Inf. & 35th Iowa Inf.	67		2nd quarter 1884	IA, 11th, 1885
Stegenga, Durk		J, 25th Mich.	354	76	1921 Apr 13	NE, 46th, 1922
Steigerwalt, Frank	Pvt.	D, 194th Penn. Inf.	111	49	1893 Dec 20	IA, 20th, 1894
Steinberg, Henry		C, 148th Ill.	127		1934 Feb 25	KS, 55th, 1936
Steinblock, D.H.	Pvt.	A, 32nd Iowa Inf.	154		1916 Dec 8	IA, 43rd, 1917
Steiner, David	Pvt.	F, 31st Wis. Inf.	383		1905 Feb 26	IA, 32nd, 1906
Steingraeber, W.G.	Pvt.	E, 25th Iowa Inf.	5		1915 Jul 20	IA, 42nd, 1916
Steinhauer, C.W.		I, — N.Y.	17		1910 May 30	KS, 30th, 1911
Steinman, Peter	Pvt.	G, 19th Iowa Inf.	231		1926 Apr 20	IA, 53rd, 1927
Stella, J.M.	Sergt.	H, 56th N.Y.	133		1914 Jul 16	IA, 41st, 1915
Stellrecht, Henry	Pvt.	G, 9th N.Y. Inf.	231		1926 May 26	IA, 53rd, 1927
Stennett, Chas.	Pvt.	B, 13th Regulars	57		1920 Sep 19	IA, 47th, 1921
Stenzel, William		F, 5th Wis.	201		1914 May 1	KS, 34th, 1915
Stepens, William		M, 2nd Ill. Cav.	153		1910 May 12	KS, 30th, 1911
Stephens, A.C.	Pvt.	H, 10th Iowa Inf.	231		1917 Dec 15	IA, 44th, 1918
Stephens, Alexander W.		E, 1st Ill.	89		1910 Dec 17	KS, 30th, 1911
Stephens, E.G.	Pvt.	I, 13th Iowa Vol. Inf.	5	68	1899 Sep 10	IA, 26th, 1900
Stephens, E.W.		89th Ill.	89		1911 Sep 12	KS, 31st, 1912
Stephens, George		I, 79th N.Y. Inf.	132		1899 Aug	KS, 19th, 1900
Stephens, Handy	Pvt.	H, 93rd Ill. Inf.	12		1918 Dec	IA, 45th, 1919
Stephens, John		D, 10th N.Y.	269		1906 Nov 28	KS, 26th, 1907
Stephens, Marcey	Pvt.	A, Ensign[Engineers?] of West Mo. Inf.	110		1899	NE, 24th, 1900
Stephens, S.S., see Sephens, S.S.						
Stephens, T.W.		K, 20th Ind.	250		1922 Oct 28	KS, 42nd, 1923
Stephens, Thos. L.	2nd Lieut.	D, 44th Iowa Inf.	15		1925 Jun 29	IA, 52nd, 1926
Stephens, W.N.		A, 17th Iowa	51		1915 Apr 19	KS, 35th, 1916
Stephens, W.N.		A, 17th Iowa	51		1916 Apr 19	KS, 36th, 1917
Stephens, William, see Stepens, William						
Stephenson, Albert		B, 36th Iowa	369		1896 Oct 14	KS, 16th, 1897
Stephenson, C.W.	Pvt.	H, 152nd N.Y. Inf.	22		1913 Mar 20	IA, 40th, 1914
Stephenson, J.E.	Pvt.	G, 20th Iowa Inf.	231		1910 Oct 14	IA, 37th, 1911
Stephenson, J.H.		K, 43rd Mo.	177		1887 Aug	KS, 7th, 1888
Stephenson, John P.		I, 17th Iowa Inf.	2	91	1937 Jun 11	IA, 64th, 1938
Stephenson, Louis	Pvt.	I, 17th Iowa Inf.	515		1916 Apr 13	IA, 43rd, 1917
Stephenson, Robert	Sergt.	D, 47th Iowa Inf.	112	51	1892 May 22	IA, 19th, 1893
Stephenson, Thos.			7		1909 Nov	IA, 36th, 1910
Stephenson, Thos.		B, 13th Iowa Inf. (cause of death: brain)	115	67	1895 Feb 16	NE, 20th, 1896
Stephenson, W.H.		A, 19th U.S. Inf.	179		1929 Sep	NE, 54th, 1930
Stephenson, W.S.		H, 4th Ind. Cav.	17		1925 May 2	KS, 45th, 1926
Stepleton, Jessie L.		A, 3rd Ind.	25		1936 Nov	KS, 56th, 1937
Stepleton, Wesley			36		1930 Aug 11	KS, 50th, 1931
Sterling, J.W.	1st Lieut.	M, 22nd Iowa Inf.	8		1905 Jul 18	IA, 32nd, 1906
Sterling, Martin V.	Pvt.	E, 4th Iowa Cav.	321	61	1899 Feb 1	IA, 25th, 1899
Sterling, Robt.	Pvt.	F, 142nd Ill. Inf.	242	61	1898 Jul 1	IA, 25th, 1899
Stern, Frank		I, 88th Penn. (nonmember; died at Pleasant Dale)			1936 Jan 5	NE, 61st, 1937
Stern, John		B, 28th Penn. Inf.	110	75	1920 May 19	NE, 45th, 1921
Stern, John		B, 28th Penn.	113		1920 May 17	NE, 45th, 1921
Sternberg, Theo.			[22]		1929	KS, 49th, 1930
Sternberg, Thomas		121st N.Y.	22		1926	KS, 46th, 1927
Sternbergh, T.J.		D, 2nd Kans. Inf.	12		1912 Dec 12	KS, 32nd, 1913
Sterneman, C.H.			231		1911 Jul 24	IA, 38th, 1912
Sterner, William D.		A, 130th Penn. Inf. (died of cancer of bladder)	143	85	1921 Sep 27	NE, 47th, 1923
Sterns, Smith	Pvt.	H, 4th Iowa Cav.	132		1925 Dec 16	IA, 52nd, 1926

*See Appendix A, B or C for roster of post names and locations.
†See Introduction for note regarding recording of death date.

Name	Rank	Company, Regiment or Ship	Post*	Age	Death Date†	Journal
Sterrett, Geo. T.	Pvt.	G, 35th Iowa Inf.	250		1911 Aug 20	IA, 38th, 1912
Sterrett, Howard					1937 Jul 10	IA, 64th, 1938
Sterrett, J.A.		B, 75th Ohio	271		1913 Aug 7	KS, 33rd, 1914
Sterrett, Perry	Pvt.	D, 11th Iowa Inf.	12	95	1939 Jan 5	IA, 65th, 1939
Sterrett, Robert		K, 3rd Iowa Cav.	26		1894 Nov 16	NE, 19th, 1895
Stetler, John		6th U.S. Cav.	57		1902 Feb 1	KS, 22nd, 1903
Stetson, F.P.			113		1908 Nov 3	KS, 28th, 1909
Steuben, A.M., see Stueben, A.M.						
Steuben, F.W.	Pvt.	E, 92nd Ill. Inf.	377		1924 Dec 21	IA, 51st, 1925
Steven, Archibald		I, 153rd Ill.	22		1934 Jan 19	NE, 59th, 1935
Stevens, A.F.	Pvt.		71		1924 Apr 19	IA, 51st, 1925
Stevens, A.F.		25th Wis.	80		1924 Apr 19	IA, 51st, 1925
Stevens, A.J.		A, 21st Ill.	17		1927 May 21	KS, 47th, 1928
Stevens, Albert	Pvt.	M, 2nd Iowa Cav.	391	52	1888 Mar 16	IA, 15th, 1889
Stevens, B.W.	Pvt.	K, 2nd Mass. Art.	3		1901-1902	IA, 28th, 1902
Stevens, Ben	Pvt.	G, 148th Ill. Inf.	284		1916 Aug 12	IA, 43rd, 1917
Stevens, C.H.		G, 28th Mich. Inf. (died of dropsy)	111	69	1918 Dec 3	NE, 43rd, 1919
Stevens, C.J.	Pvt.	H, 2nd Mich. Cav.	42		1917 Feb 26	IA, 44th, 1918
Stevens, C.L.	Pvt.	I, 44th Wis. Inf.	222		1924 Mar 8	IA, 51st, 1925
Stevens, Colver		I, 20th Maine	117		1898 Jan 12	KS, 18th, 1899
Stevens, Daniel	Pvt.	B, 30th Wis. Inf.	194		1912 Mar 8	IA, 39th, 1913
Stevens, David		I, 33rd Iowa	25		1923	NE, 48th, 1924
Stevens, David E.		B, 13th Wis.	209		1913 May 12	KS, 33rd, 1914
Stevens, E.F.	Pvt.	A, 1st Maine Cav.	200		1909 Nov 25	IA, 36th, 1910
Stevens, E.J.M.	Pvt.	B, 14th Iowa	12		1922 Dec 30	IA, 49th, 1923
Stevens, E.R.		122nd N.Y.	50		1920 Oct	KS, 40th, 1921
Stevens, Erial	Pvt.	C, 31st Ohio	57		1922 Dec 18	IA, 49th, 1923
Stevens, Ezra	Pvt.	B, 7th Iowa	497		1922 Dec 17	IA, 49th, 1923
Stevens, F.C.	Pvt.	C, 7th Ill. Cav.	141		1930 Jul 13	IA, 57th, 1931
Stevens, F.I.	Pvt.	F, 57th Ill. Inf.	132		1911	IA, 38th, 1912
Stevens, Frank P.		F, 11th N.H. Inf. (died of lung disease)	321	51	1895 Mar 4	NE, 20th, 1896
Stevens, George P.		I, 19th Iowa Inf. (murdered)	244		1893 May 20	NE, 18th, 1894
Stevens, Henry	Pvt.	B, 31st Iowa Inf.	68		1908 Feb 21	IA, 35th, 1909
Stevens, Henry		A, 99th Ill.	1		1930 May 20	NE, 55th, 1931
Stevens, Henry R.		60th Ohio Vol. Inf.	64		1912 Mar 31	KS, 32nd, 1913
Stevens, Hiram		C, 1st Wis. Cav.	28		1899 Nov 20	KS, 19th, 1900
Stevens, J.A.			12		1923 Aug 15	IA, 50th, 1924
Stevens, J.B.		E, 138th Penn. Inf.	209		1929	KS, 49th, 1930
Stevens, J.B.		E, 138th Penn.	209		1928 Dec 9	KS, 48th, 1929
Stevens, J.H.	Pvt.	G, 2nd Iowa Inf.	100		1915 Oct 24	IA, 42nd, 1916
Stevens, J.M.		55th Ohio Vol. Inf. (died at Garnett)	180		1895 Aug 25	KS, 15th, 1896
Stevens, Jas. T.		A, 69th Ill.	12		1889	KS, 9th, 1890
Stevens, John H.	Pvt.	I, Ill. Marines	42		1927 Apr 11	IA, 54th, 1928
Stevens, Jos. W.	Sergt.	I, 7th Iowa Cav.	22		1910 May 15	IA, 37th, 1911
Stevens, Joseph		K, 149th Ind.	87		1911 Jun 12	KS, 31st, 1912
Stevens, Lyman G.	Pvt.	B, 1st Minn.	42		1926 Feb 26	IA, 53rd, 1927
Stevens, Mahlon		G, 6th Kans. Cav.	30		1920 Jul 20	KS, 40th, 1921
Stevens, Peter		G, 2nd Neb. Cav.	165		1927 Apr 3	NE, 52nd, 1928
Stevens, Seth B.	Pvt.	C, 14th Iowa Inf.	42		1904 Oct 6	IA, 31st, 1905
Stevens, W.F.		B, 29th Ohio Inf. (died at Tacoma, Ore.; buried at Tacoma Cemetery)	14		1894 May 12	KS, 14th, 1895
Stevens, W.F.		B, 65th Ind.	25		1914 May 19	KS, 34th, 1915
Stevens, W.M.			34		1885	KS, 5th, 1886
Stevens, William H.	Chaplain	148th Penn. Vol. Inf.	364		1901 Jun 10	IA, 28th, 1902
Stevens, Wm. H.	Pvt.	1st Wis. Hvy. Art.	68		1927 Nov 5	IA, 54th, 1928
Stevenson, A.	Pvt.	A, 88th Ohio Inf.	286	56	1896 Nov 23	IA, 23rd, 1897
Stevenson, B.F.		F, 85th Ohio Inf.	23		1915 Sep 14	IA, 42nd, 1916
Stevenson, C.F.		H, 18th U.S.	201	94	1938 May 9	IA, 64th, 1938
Stevenson, Chas.	Pvt.	13th Ohio Inf.	434		1925 May 15	IA, 52nd, 1926
Stevenson, E.J.	Pvt.	K, 7th Ill. Cav.	39		1910 Jan 10	IA, 36th, 1910
Stevenson, Geo.			68		1899 Mar 24	KS, 19th, 1900

Name	Rank	Company, Regiment or Ship	Post*	Age	Death Date†	Journal
Stevenson, J.A.		K, 11th Ind.	17		1923 Jan 27	KS, 43rd, 1924
Stevenson, Jas.		C, 119th Ill. Inf.	25	77	1918 Apr 12	NE, 43rd, 1919
Stevenson, Jno. P.	Pvt.	A, 19th Iowa Inf.	7		1918 Jan 1	IA, 45th, 1919
Stevenson, John		F, 10th Mo. Inf.	127		1908 Sep 14	KS, 28th, 1909
Stevenson, N.P.			94		1928 Jun 14	IA, 55th, 1929
Stevenson, Peter C.	Corp.	H, 16th Wis. (died of wounds)	65	58	1884 Nov 4	NE, 9th, 1885
Stevenson, R.E., Dr.		B, 10th Ill.	68		1919 Apr 15	KS, 39th, 1920
Stevenson, R.S.	1st Lieut.	A, 14th Ill. Cav.	236	76	1894 Mar 17	IA, 21st, 1895
Stevenson, S.E.		B, 26th Ind.	64		1927 Dec 14	KS, 47th, 1928
Stevenson, S.L.	Pvt.	B, 85th Ill. Inf.	193		1912 Jun 26	IA, 39th, 1913
Stevenson, Silas	Pvt.	B, 9th Ind. Inf.	24		1931 Apr	IA, 58th, 1932
Stevenson, W.		K, 18th Wis. Inf.	116	84	1903 Jan	NE, 28th, 1904
Stevenson, W.N.	Pvt.	B, 57th Ill. Inf.	67		1930 Jun	IA, 57th, 1931
Stever, Franklin		M, 16th Mo. Cav.	170		1916 Apr 13	KS, 36th, 1917
Steward, A.			94		1919	IA, 46th, 1920
Steward, David		G, 76th Ohio	416		1896 Nov 11	KS, 16th, 1897
Steward, Geo.	Corp.	K, 148th Ohio	40		1907 Nov 18	IA, 34th, 1908
Steward, Geo. W.		K, 1st Wis. Cav.	140		1929 May 4	NE, 53rd, 1929
Steward, Wm.		I, 1st U.S. Sharpshooters	104	59	1895 Jun 12	NE, 20th, 1896
Stewart, A.		L, 49th Ill.	117		1916 Oct 7	KS, 36th, 1917
Stewart, A.C.	Lieut.	H, 30th Mo.	64		1889	KS, 9th, 1890
Stewart, A.J.		E, 22nd Iowa	25		1921 Nov 21	NE, 46th, 1922
Stewart, Albert C.		H, 9th U.S. Cav.	88		1919 Feb 15	KS, 39th, 1920
Stewart, Alex.	Pvt.	H, 28th Wis. Inf.	333	60	1894 Mar 10	IA, 20th, 1894
Stewart, Alga M.		D, 96th Ill. Inf.	11	77	1920 Dec 26	NE, 45th, 1921
Stewart, Alva T.	Pvt.	D, 34th Iowa Inf.	94		1911 Jul 6	IA, 38th, 1912
Stewart, Amos		B, 6th Kans.	97		1923 Jul 1	KS, 43rd, 1924
Stewart, C.		A, 53rd Ohio (died of stomach trouble)	10		1904 Mar 10	NE, 29th, 1905
Stewart, C.A.		E, 20th Ill. Inf.	12		1908 Sep 11	KS, 28th, 1909
Stewart, C.N.	Pvt.	H, 2nd Iowa Inf.	108		1904 Dec 11	IA, 31st, 1905
Stewart, Charles S.	Pvt.	13th Iowa	127		1923 Apr 6	IA, 50th, 1924
Stewart, Charles W.			39		1924 Nov 12	KS, 44th, 1925
Stewart, Chas. H.		B, 1st N.Y. Lt. Art.	66		1904 Aug 19	KS, 24th, 1905
Stewart, Cyrus G.		G, — N.Y. (died of chronic disease)	356	70	1910 Jan 16	NE, 35th, 1911
Stewart, D.F.		I, 133rd Penn.	65		1909 Jul 30	KS, 29th, 1910
Stewart, David	Surg.	28th Iowa Inf.	8		1910 Jun 10	IA, 37th, 1911
Stewart, David A.	Pvt.	F, 36th Iowa Inf.	306	65	1898 Dec 14	IA, 25th, 1899
Stewart, David H.		D, 1st Kans.	6		1918 May 20	KS, 38th, 1919
Stewart, David S.		A, 76th Ill.	130		1909 Jul 10	KS, 29th, 1910
Stewart, E.R.		C, 140th Ohio	54		1917 Jul 6	KS, 37th, 1918
Stewart, Edwin		K, 1st Wis. Cav. (died of complication of diseases)	57	74	1915 Nov 2	NE, 40th, 1916
Stewart, F.E.	Pvt.	F, 13th Wis. Inf.	101		1926 Jul 29	IA, 53rd, 1927
Stewart, Flavius A.			117		1925 Feb 14	KS, 45th, 1926
Stewart, Geo. J.			5		1908	IA, 35th, 1909
Stewart, George A.		H, 2nd West Va. Cav.	76		1925 Oct 14	KS, 45th, 1926
Stewart, Henry	Pvt.	I, 19th Inf.	19		1916 Apr 30	IA, 43rd, 1917
Stewart, J.F.	Pvt.	K, 45th Iowa Inf.	12		1927 Dec 19	IA, 54th, 1928
Stewart, J.H.	Lieut.	H, 2nd Iowa Inf.	108		1917 Oct 17	IA, 44th, 1918
Stewart, J.M.	Pvt.	H, 22nd Iowa Inf.	156		1914 Nov 12	IA, 41st, 1915
Stewart, J.O.	Capt.	B, 20th Iowa Inf.	235	95	1932 Sep 11	IA, 59th, 1933
Stewart, J.S.		H, 145th Ind.	142		1924 Aug 8	KS, 44th, 1925
Stewart, J.W.		D & Q, 139th Ill. Inf. (died of diabetes)	34	51	1902 Apr	NE, 27th, 1903
Stewart, J.W.		E, 86th Ill. Inf. (died of heart disease)	228	58	1902 Nov	NE, 27th, 1903
Stewart, James		F, 3rd Iowa Inf. (died at Topeka)	1		1895 Apr 3	KS, 15th, 1896
Stewart, James	Col.		23		1898 Sep 3	KS, 18th, 1899
Stewart, James		C, 65th Ill.	132		1923 Mar 22	KS, 43rd, 1924
Stewart, James			63		1925 Feb 3	KS, 45th, 1926
Stewart, James, see Stewert, James						
Stewart, Jas.	Pvt.	G, 13th U.S. Inf.	1		1913 Aug 23	IA, 40th, 1914
Stewart, John	Corp.	K, 60th N.Y. Inf.	308	54	1892 Apr 26	IA, 19th, 1893

Name	Rank	Company, Regiment or Ship	Post*	Age	Death Date†	Journal
Stewart, John					1901 Jan 27	IA, 27th, 1901
Stewart, John Gregg		D, 4th Iowa Cav.	271	91	1938 Feb 19	IA, 64th, 1938
Stewart, John H.			64		1899	NE, 24th, 1900
Stewart, John J.		A, 6th Kans. Cav.	32		1908[1909?] Jul 26	KS, 29th, 1910
Stewart, John W.		9th Kans. (died of old age)	311		1892 Sep 12	KS, 12th, 1893
Stewart, Jos. W.		C, 30th Iowa	252		1893 Aug 9	KS, 13th, 1894
Stewart, Joseph		B, 1st Kans. Inf.	32		1921 May 8	KS, 41st, 1922
Stewart, Joseph E.		E, 15th Ohio	1		1916 Sep 10	KS, 36th, 1917
Stewart, R.	Pvt.	C, 44th Ind. Inf.	141		1920 May 19	IA, 47th, 1921
Stewart, R.M.		B, 43rd Mo.	130		1916 Nov 6	KS, 36th, 1917
Stewart, Ray H.		H, 6th Iowa Hvy. Art. (died of cancer of stomach)	69		1894 Sep 5	NE, 19th, 1895
Stewart, S.G., Dr.		D, 74th Ohio	1		1919 Feb 6	KS, 39th, 1920
Stewart, S.J.	Capt.	H, 10th Kans.	72		1918 Apr 19	KS, 38th, 1919
Stewart, S.S.		G, 4th N.J.	100		1920 May 20	KS, 40th, 1921
Stewart, Sanford			122		1925 Sep 11	IA, 52nd, 1926
Stewart, T.C.	Yeoman	Gunboat *Pittsburg*	156	51	1888 Mar 29	IA, 15th, 1889
Stewart, Thos. B.		Dept. of Monongahela, Penn.	353		1900 Mar 2	KS, 20th, 1901
Stewart, W.C.			68		1906 Apr 18	IA, 33rd, 1907
Stewart, W.H.		A, 21st Ill.	461		1912 Aug 2	KS, 32nd, 1913
Stewart, W.M.		C, 35th Ind.	257		1923 Feb 17	KS, 43rd, 1924
Stewart, W.M.		E, 45th Ohio (died of old age)	13	82	1923 Nov 7	NE, 48th, 1924
Stewart, W.S.		D, 172nd Ohio	127		1931 Oct 21	KS, 52nd, 1933
Stewart, W.S.		D, 172nd Ohio	127		1931 Oct 21	KS, 51st, 1932
Stewart, Watson		3rd Ohio Bat.	72		1910 Aug 3	KS, 30th, 1911
Stewart, William H.		B, 134th Ind.	22		1926 Dec 25	NE, 51st, 1927
Stewart, Wm.		155th Ohio	113		1921 Aug 20	KS, 41st, 1922
Stewart, Wm. B.	Pvt.	C, 57th Ill. Vol. Inf.	343		1901 Oct 24	IA, 28th, 1902
Stewart, Wm. E.	Corp. & Sergt.	G, 92nd Ill. (died of gravel)	130	57	1884 Aug 11	NE, 9th, 1885
Stewart, Wm. H.		H, 4th Mo. Cav.	92		1918 Feb 9	KS, 38th, 1919
Stewart, Wm. H.	Pvt.	B, 134th Ind. (see Appendix D)	22		1926 Dec 25	NE, 51st, 1927
Stewart, Z.J.	Pvt.	F, 134th Penn. Inf.	7		1911 Jan 17	IA, 38th, 1912
Stewert, J.H.	Pvt.	E, 4th Iowa Cav.	64		1908 Feb 16	IA, 35th, 1909
Stewert, James	Pvt.	C, 8th Iowa Inf.	337		1907 Jan 9	IA, 34th, 1908
Stichter, Henry	Pvt.	E, 48th Ohio Inf.	108		1915 Dec 30	IA, 42nd, 1916
Stick, C.	Pvt.	K, 3rd Iowa Inf.	48		1924 Dec 30	IA, 51st, 1925
Stick, C.	Pvt.	F, 3rd Iowa	48		1923 Dec 30	IA, 50th, 1924
Stickel, Isaiah		A, 2nd Ill.	40		1911 Nov 20	KS, 31st, 1912
Stickel, Joseph H.	1st Lieut.	F, 33rd Wis. Inf.	17		1899	NE, 24th, 1900
Stickleman, Henry	Pvt.	K, 40th Ohio	10		1922	IA, 49th, 1923
Stickler, G.M.			56		1918	IA, 45th, 1919
Stickley, D.T.		K, 4th West Va.	17		1930 Jun 3	KS, 50th, 1931
Stickley, Robt.	Pvt.	C, 31st Iowa Inf.	235		1916 Jun 27	IA, 43rd, 1917
Stickney, —			14		1928	IA, 55th, 1929
Stickney, George	Sergt.	B, 146th Ill. Inf.	102	59	1896 May 21	IA, 23rd, 1897
Stickney, J.H.		E, 169th N.Y. Vol. Inf.	25		1908 May 26	KS, 28th, 1909
Stickney, John M.	Pvt.	I, 2nd Ill. Cav.	76		1904 Dec 31	IA, 31st, 1905
Stickney, Judson		D, 8th Kans.	52		1918 Oct 4	KS, 38th, 1919
Stickney, W.N.	Pvt.	C, 2nd N.Y. Cav.	98		1915 Jun 7	IA, 42nd, 1916
Stier, W.S.	Pvt.	47th Iowa Inf.	122		1913 Aug 13	IA, 40th, 1914
Stiers, Joseph		C, 9th Ohio	259		1927 May 14	KS, 47th, 1928
Stiff, W.W.		H, 60th Ill. Inf.	85		1925 Dec 22	KS, 45th, 1926
Stiffler, G.B.		F, 101st Ind. Inf.	182		1902	KS, 22nd, 1903
Stigenwalt, J.M.		2nd Kans. Lt. Art.	142		1892 Aug 18	KS, 12th, 1893
Stiles, Asa D.	Pvt.	F, 22nd Iowa Inf.	8		1915 Oct 5	IA, 42nd, 1916
Stiles, B.F.	Capt.	A, 2nd Iowa Cav.	222		1915	IA, 42nd, 1916
Stiles, David		G, 3rd Iowa (died of paralysis)	60	70	1914 Feb 19	NE, 39th, 1915
Stiles, Henry	Pvt.	A, 2nd Vt. Inf.	222		1924 Jun 20	IA, 51st, 1925
Stiles, J.E.	Pvt.	C, 46th Iowa Inf.	43		1924 Dec 9	IA, 51st, 1925
Stiles, J.E.	Pvt.	C, 46th Iowa	43		1923 Dec 9	IA, 50th, 1924
Stiles, J.E.	Pvt.	C, 46th Iowa Inf.	43		1925 Dec 9	IA, 52nd, 1926
Stiles, John R.	Pvt.	D, 7th Ill. Cav.	196		1909 Sep 14	IA, 36th, 1910

*See Appendix A, B or C for roster of post names and locations.
†See Introduction for note regarding recording of death date.

Name	Rank	Company, Regiment or Ship	Post*	Age	Death Date†	Journal
Stiles, Mortimer		B, 13th Ind. Inf.	14		1912 Jan 24	KS, 32nd, 1913
Stiles, T.W.	Capt.	F, 39th Iowa Inf.	55		1905 Dec 10	IA, 32nd, 1906
Stiles, W.A.	Sergt.	A, 2nd Iowa Inf.	108		1902 Dec 30	IA, 29th, 1903
Stiles, W.H.	Pvt.	B, 22nd Iowa Inf.	12	90	1933 Feb 14	IA, 60th, 1934
Stiles, Wm.		C, 8th Kans.	195		1885	KS, 5th, 1886
Still, C.C.	Pvt.	H, 5th Kans. Cav.	7		1916 Feb 7	IA, 43rd, 1917
Stilley, W.F.		C, 9th Ill. Inf.	147		1934 Apr 28	KS, 54th, 1935
Stilley, William W.		G, 111th Ill. Vol. Inf.	131		1885	KS, 5th, 1886
Stillman, A.P.		C, 86th Ill.	278		1920 Jan 25	KS, 40th, 1921
Stillman, L.P.	Pvt.	F, 6th Iowa Cav.	150	43	1887 Apr 11	IA, 14th, 1888
Stillman, T.J.	Pvt.	A, 11th Mich. Cav.	94		1930 Dec 11	IA, 57th, 1931
Stillwater, Jacob R.		I, 9th Kans. Cav.	257		1920 Jan 4	KS, 40th, 1921
Stillwell, A.	Pvt.	A, 2nd Wis. Inf.	44		1912 Jan 14	IA, 39th, 1913
Stillwell, A.W.		B, 5th Wis.	25		1928 Mar 4	KS, 48th, 1929
Stillwell, Geo. W., see Stillwell, Geo. W.						
Stillwell, J.R., Rev.	Capt.	C, 79th Ohio Inf.	12	54	1887 Sep 8	IA, 15th, 1889
Stillwell, John	Pvt.	G, 17th Iowa Inf.	49		1898 Sep 5	IA, 25th, 1899
Stillwell, Lem	Pvt.	B, 98th Ohio Inf.	197	90	1933 Jul 15	IA, 60th, 1934
Stillwell, Thos.			305		1903-1904	IA, 30th, 1904
Stilson, A.R.		B, 19th Ohio Inf.	18		1914 Feb 10	KS, 34th, 1915
Stilson, Chester B.	Pvt.	A, 14th Iowa Inf.	68		1911 Aug 13	IA, 38th, 1912
Stilson, L.D.		D, 49th N.Y. Inf. (died of exposure)	32	70	1912 May 9	NE, 37th, 1913
Stilson, Samuel		D, 4th Ill. Cav.	4		1931 Mar 7	NE, 56th, 1932
Stilwell, Geo. W.		E, 34th —	106		1891 Sep 5	KS, 11th, 1892
Stimmel, B.B.		H, 201st Penn. Inf.	127		1908 Sep 27	KS, 28th, 1909
Stimmel, D.W.		77th Ill.	17		1909 Dec 2	KS, 29th, 1910
Stimmell, M.D.		I, 86th Ohio Vol. Inf.	36		1908[1909?] Dec 23	KS, 29th, 1910
Stimpson, K.E.		G, 1st Mich.	159		1908 Dec 26	KS, 28th, 1909
Stine, Albert L.	Pvt.	D, 44th Iowa Inf.	236	85	1931 May 22	IA, 58th, 1932
Stine, F.		E, 93rd Ohio Inf.	220	52	1896 Jan 14	NE, 21st, 1897
Stine, J.D.		I, 154th Ohio Inf.	63	68	1903 Jan	NE, 28th, 1904
Stine, Jno. B.	Pvt.	K, 11th Iowa Inf.	235		1918 Apr 20	IA, 45th, 1919
Stine, John L.		B, Ind. Art., Penn.	46		1929 Sep 20	KS, 49th, 1930
Stine, W.H.		A, 34th Ind.	4		1923 Feb 10	KS, 43rd, 1924
Stinebaugh, George D.		E, 14th Ohio	18		1912 Apr 19	KS, 32nd, 1913
Stinebaugh, J.B.		H, 38th Ohio H, 8th H.V.C.	18		1916 Jun 14	KS, 36th, 1917
Stiner, Abe		H, 7th U.S.	25		1934	IA, 61st, 1935
Stinger, Jacob		3rd U.S. Art.	7		1885	KS, 5th, 1886
Stinger, John R.		A, 2nd D.C. Inf.	11	68	1900 Nov 16	NE, 25th, 1901
Stingle, John			153		1925 Aug 12	IA, 52nd, 1926
Stingley, Absalom L.		H, 13th Mo.	18		1910 Dec 14	KS, 30th, 1911
Stinson, A.D.	Capt.	I, 30th Ind. Inf.	57		1912 Apr 8	IA, 39th, 1913
Stinson, Andrew		D, 23rd Mo.	55		1914 Feb 21	KS, 34th, 1915
Stinson, C.M.	Pvt.	Ohio	108		1920 Jul 20	IA, 47th, 1921
Stinson, E.H.	Pvt.	I, 74th Ill.	81		1922 May 19	IA, 49th, 1923
Stinson, J.W.		D, 72nd Ind.	51		1920 Nov 15	KS, 40th, 1921
Stinson, John			55		1929 Jan 5	IA, 56th, 1930
Stinson, Stephen			11		1925	IA, 52nd, 1926
Stinson, Stephen			11		1927	IA, 54th, 1928
Stipe, David J.		B, 74th Ohio Inf.	176		1916 Mar 24	KS, 36th, 1917
Stipp, J.W.		E, 136th Ind., 5 K, 148th Ind.	339		1918 Feb 3	KS, 38th, 1919
Stire, P.C.			116		1928 Jul 14	IA, 55th, 1929
Stires, P.J.		K, 155th Ill.	65		1929 Mar 29	KS, 49th, 1930
Stirk, Jos. W.		H, 34th Iowa	272	60	1907	NE, 32nd, 1908
Stirts, J.M.		I, 20th Ohio	158		1927 Aug 31	KS, 47th, 1928
Stiteler, David			49		1884	KS, 4th, 1885
Stitger, D.H.		H, 48th Penn.	448		1911 Sep 13	KS, 31st, 1912
Stith, Henry T.	2nd Lieut.	D, 16th Kans. Inf.	18		1916 Feb 24	KS, 36th, 1917
Stitler, William		A, 77th Ill.	32		1905 Nov 23	KS, 25th, 1906
Stitson, F.A.		D, 111th Penn. Inf.	113		1925 Mar 11	KS, 45th, 1926

Name	Rank	Company, Regiment or Ship	Post*	Age	Death Date†	Journal
Stitt, W.K.		H, 8th Ind.	322		1906 Feb 5	KS, 26th, 1907
Stitzell, George		56th Penn. Inf. (died at Wichita; buried at Maple Grove Cemetery)	25		1894 Dec 2	KS, 14th, 1895
Stiver, Barnard		D, 12th Ill. Inf.	66		1916 Jul 23	KS, 36th, 1917
Stivers, Jeremiah		A, 1st Wis. Hvy. Art. (died at Atchison)	336		1895 May	KS, 15th, 1896
Stock, Theodore F.		E, 142nd Ill.	13		1934 Feb 1	NE, 59th, 1935
Stock, William		K, 10th Tenn. Inf.	380		1909 Aug 6	KS, 29th, 1910
Stockard, W.R.		G, 96th Ohio	147		1926 Nov 13	KS, 46th, 1927
Stockdale, J.S.	Musician	G, 25th Ind. Inf.	512		1912	IA, 39th, 1913
Stockebrand, Wm.		H, 9th Kans.	185		1921 Jan 6	KS, 41st, 1922
Stocker, J.C.		C, 189th Ohio Inf.	185		1917 Aug 6	KS, 37th, 1918
Stocker, John W.	Lieut.	C, 29th Iowa Inf.	38	58	1893 Sep 7	IA, 20th, 1894
Stocking, Henry		G, 107th N.Y. Inf.	17		1899 Jul 30	KS, 19th, 1900
Stockman, Isaac	Pvt.	F, 22nd Ind.	108		1926 Apr 14	IA, 53rd, 1927
Stocks, G.W.	Pvt.	I, 3rd Iowa Inf.	132		1906	IA, 33rd, 1907
Stockton, A.J.		13th Ky. Cav.	115		1922 Jun 19	KS, 42nd, 1923
Stockton, R.L.		E, 106th Ill. Inf. (died of suicide)	41		1923 Jun 28	NE, 48th, 1924
Stockton, S.J.	Pvt.	D, 138th Ill. Inf.	154		1899	NE, 24th, 1900
Stockwell, G.W.		K, 95th Ill.	152		1893 Nov 10	KS, 13th, 1894
Stockwell, H.O.		C, 3rd Vt.	263		1890	KS, 10th, 1891
Stockwell, William			117		1923	KS, 43rd, 1924
Stockwell, Wm. A.	Pvt.	F, 31st Mass. Inf.	147		1904	IA, 31st, 1905
Stodard, C.N.	Pvt.	D, 25th Iowa Inf.	271		1923 Apr 14	IA, 50th, 1924
Stoddard, E.		F, 27th Mass.	7		1929 Jan 28	NE, 54th, 1930
Stoddard, Frank		K, 144th N.Y.	209		1905 Sep 4	KS, 25th, 1906
Stoddard, J.C.	Pvt.	D, 8th Iowa Inf.	235	89	1931 Mar 29	IA, 58th, 1932
Stoddard, L.F.	Lieut.	B, 2nd Iowa Cav.	452		1917 Jul 21	IA, 45th, 1919
Stoddard, W.H.	Capt.	C, 10th Iowa Inf.	24		1924 Nov 19	IA, 51st, 1925
Stoeffler, Louis	Pvt.	D, 27th Iowa Inf.	146	52	1896 Nov 19	IA, 23rd, 1897
Stoel, O.A.	Pvt.	H, 12th Ill. Cav.	461		1923 Apr 6	IA, 50th, 1924
Stoffer, John		A, 64th Ohio	63		1923 Jan 6	KS, 43rd, 1924
Stoffer, S.		E, 112th Ill.	294		1905 Sep 10	KS, 25th, 1906
Stogsdell, James			201		1918 Jan 18	KS, 38th, 1919
Stoker, George W.	Pvt.	H, 35th Ind. Inf.	231		1919 Aug 8	IA, 46th, 1920
Stokes, C.	Pvt.	H, 47th Wis.	68		1921 Apr 12	IA, 48th, 1922
Stokes, Conrad	Pvt.	E, 35th Iowa Inf.	231		1912 Aug 18	IA, 39th, 1913
Stokes, E.E.	Pvt.	G, 14th Iowa Inf.	125		1911 Dec 3	IA, 38th, 1912
Stokes, George	Pvt.		44		1929 May 24	IA, 56th, 1930
Stokes, John	Sergt.	E, 82nd Ind. Inf.	255		1906 Oct 24	IA, 33rd, 1907
Stokes, John W.		F, 134th Ohio	25		1923 Feb 20	KS, 43rd, 1924
Stokes, Joseph			35		1912	NE, 37th, 1913
Stokes, Thos. B.	Act. Ensign	U.S. Navy	352	52	1887 Oct 15	IA, 14th, 1888
Stokes, W.S.	Sergt.	I, 124th Ill. Inf.	68		1905 Nov 9	IA, 32nd, 1906
Stolts, James P.		F, 5th Ill. Cav.	25		1920 Nov 3	KS, 40th, 1921
Stoltzman, C.		I, 8th Ill. Inf. (cause of death: heart)	197	64	1901 Oct	NE, 26th, 1902
Stombaugh, Jacob		F, 46th Wis. Cav.	17		1912 Feb 21	KS, 32nd, 1913
Stompkins, J.S.		B, 177th Ohio (died of heart failure)	116	74	1897 Nov 12	NE, 22nd, 1898
Stone, A.C.	Pvt.	I, 36th Iowa Inf.	497		1929 Nov 27	IA, 56th, 1930
Stone, A.L.		F, 4th Ind.	71		1914 Aug 4	KS, 34th, 1915
Stone, Adison		I, 154th N.Y. (died of asthma)	23	62	1904 Jul	NE, 29th, 1905
Stone, Bradford		D, 16th N.Y. (died of heart disease)	60	75	1907 Mar 8	NE, 32nd, 1908
Stone, Charles L.		G, 33rd Mo.	1		1914 Nov 25	KS, 34th, 1915
Stone, Chas. L.		B, Ill. M. Bat. (died of heart failure)	13	77	1919 Nov 26	NE, 44th, 1920
Stone, Chas. T.	Pvt.	M, 1st Minn. Hvy. Art.	36		1913 Sep 20	IA, 40th, 1914
Stone, Cyrus B.		B, 168th Ohio Inf.	55		1911 May 12	KS, 31st, 1912
Stone, Ezekial		1st N.Y. Art. (died of paralysis)	60	71	1911 Nov 1	NE, 36th, 1912
Stone, Ezekial J.		H, 1st N.Y. Lt. Art. (died of heart failure)	60	71	1910 Nov 1	NE, 35th, 1911
Stone, F.C.	Pvt.	B, 5th Mass. Inf.	40		1929 May 25	IA, 56th, 1930
Stone, F.M.	Pvt.	K, 15th Iowa Inf.	49		1919 May 25	IA, 46th, 1920
Stone, Fred P.		F, — Iowa (died of paralysis)		70	1910 Nov 12	NE, 35th, 1911
Stone, Geo. H.	Pvt.	K, 8th Iowa	206		1903 Feb 19	IA, 30th, 1904
Stone, Geo. W.		E, 3rd Mich. Cav.	25		1923	NE, 48th, 1924

*See Appendix A, B or C for roster of post names and locations.
†See Introduction for note regarding recording of death date.
528

Name	Rank	Company, Regiment or Ship	Post*	Age	Death Date†	Journal
Stone, H.D.	lt. Seaman		125		1926 Oct 14	IA, 53rd, 1927
Stone, H.S.		F, 112th Ill.	13	72	1909 Sep 11	NE, 34th, 1910
Stone, J.D.	Pvt.	K, 6th Iowa Cav.	270		1907 Feb 14	IA, 34th, 1908
Stone, J.D.			7		1926 Sep	IA, 53rd, 1927
Stone, J.S.		I, 40th Iowa	37		1927 Jan 26	KS, 47th, 1928
Stone, Jacob		E, 65th U.S. Colored Inf.	127		1900 Apr 15	KS, 20th, 1901
Stone, John E.		I, 13th Ind.	293		1911 Jul 15	KS, 31st, 1912
Stone, Jos. C.	Capt.	1st Iowa Cav.	5		1902 Dec 3	IA, 29th, 1903
Stone, L.S.	Wagoner	K, 21st Iowa Inf.	342		1903 Sep 2	IA, 30th, 1904
Stone, Phillip S.	Pvt.	D, 22nd Iowa Inf.	170		1902 Dec 29	IA, 29th, 1903
Stone, R.M.		U.S. Navy	110	58	1905 Aug 14	NE, 30th, 1906
Stone, W.G.		C, 1st Iowa Inf. (died of heart failure)	169	57	1896 Jan 24	NE, 21st, 1897
Stone, W.H.		C, 14th Kans. (died of pneumonia)	283		1892 Jan 9	KS, 12th, 1893
Stone, W.H.H.		E, 79th Ohio	96		1913 Nov 10	KS, 33rd, 1914
Stone, W.M.		C, 17th Kans.	148		1905 Oct 22	KS, 25th, 1906
Stone, Walter B.			171		1910 Jun 10	IA, 37th, 1911
Stone, William		H, 18th Ill. V.R.C. (died of paralysis)	73	62	1900 Feb 25	NE, 25th, 1901
Stone, William		A, 27th Wis. Inf. (died of stone in bladder)	34		1900 Apr 15	NE, 25th, 1901
Stone, Wm. T.		E, 68th Ind.	55		1928 Feb 7	KS, 48th, 1929
Stonebarger, Daniel		I, 63rd Ill. (died of paralysis)	28	75	1920 May 16	NE, 45th, 1921
Stonebraker, A.R.		K, 19th Ind. Inf.	127		1908 Mar 1	KS, 28th, 1909
Stonebraker, E.J.		E, 46th Ill. Inf.	81	87	1935 Jul 15	IA, 62nd, 1936
Stonebraker, Wm.		K, 1st Ind.	127		1917 Feb 19	KS, 37th, 1918
Stoneking, David W.		K, 14th West Va.	90		1921 Jan 19	KS, 41st, 1922
Stoneking, Edward		E, 2nd Va.	1		1930	KS, 50th, 1931
Stoneking, Geo.	Pvt.	I, 20th Iowa Inf.	235		1928 Oct 31	IA, 55th, 1929
Stoneman, L.	Pvt.	H, 27th Iowa Inf.	493		1906 Oct 5	IA, 33rd, 1907
Stoneman, M.S.	Pvt.	H, 27th —	493		1906 Oct	IA, 34th, 1908
Stoneman, R.R.	Pvt.	9th Iowa Inf.	493		1916 Mar	IA, 43rd, 1917
Stoner, D.F.		D, 77th Penn. Inf.	25		1911 Jul	NE, 36th, 1912
Stoner, George W.	Pvt.	G, 9th Iowa Cav.	90	61	1896 Jan 23	IA, 22nd, 1896
Stoner, Henry F.		E, 10th Mo.	87		1911 Jun 28	KS, 31st, 1912
Stoner, Jacob		H, 57th Penn.	2		1898 Nov 27	KS, 18th, 1899
Stoner, Wm.	Pvt.		68		1917	IA, 44th, 1918
Stonerook, S.B.	Sergt.	C, 110th Penn. Inf.	110		1917 May 10	IA, 44th, 1918
Stoors, Geo. W.		A, 1st N.Y. Eng.	35		1926 Jul	KS, 46th, 1927
Stoors, T.H.	Pvt.	C, 33rd Ill. Inf.	118		1907 Sep 7	IA, 34th, 1908
Storey, I.K.	Pvt.	8th Iowa Inf.	116		1927 May 10	IA, 54th, 1928
Storey, J.D.		F, 14th Ind. (died of paralysis)	40	87	1922 Aug 7	NE, 47th, 1923
Storey, Joseph		F, 19th Iowa	64		1897 Nov 25	KS, 17th, 1898
Stork, John H.		A, 2nd Neb. (died of indigestion)	118	69	1905[1904?] Oct 6	NE, 29th, 1905
Storm, John	Pvt.	A, 24th Iowa	164		1914 Jul 18	IA, 41st, 1915
Stormont, S.B.		D, 173rd Ohio	415		1897 Sep 7	KS, 17th, 1898
Storr, John O.		A, 20th Iowa	14		1915 Mar 6	KS, 35th, 1916
Storrs, Jno. L.	Pvt.	D, 9th Mich. Inf.	94		1927 Aug 14	IA, 54th, 1928
Story, D.M.		G, 33rd Iowa	59		1919 Jan 7	KS, 39th, 1920
Story, N.H.		E, 86th Ill. Inf.	252		1914 Apr 19	KS, 34th, 1915
Story, Thomas A.		H, 26th Ind.	85		1890	KS, 10th, 1891
Stote, John M.		H, 62nd Penn.	1		1909 Jan 13	KS, 29th, 1910
Stotle, Lewis	Pvt.	E, 210th Penn. Inf.	16		1915 Feb 25	IA, 42nd, 1916
Stotsberry, John S.	Pvt.	E, 19th Ohio Cav.	79		1918 Oct 7	IA, 45th, 1919
Stott, W.G.	Pvt.	I, 39th N.Y. Inf.	142	39	1887 May 15	IA, 15th, 1889
Stott, W.H.	Pvt.	K, 110th Penn. Inf.	42		1918 Dec 11	IA, 45th, 1919
Stottle, Joseph	Pvt.	K, 17th Mo. Inf.	78		1905 Dec 22	IA, 32nd, 1906
Stough, Daniel		E, 126th Ill.	74		1915 Jul 28	KS, 35th, 1916
Stoughton, Aaron		G, 41st Penn. Inf. (died of paralysis)	311		1901 Feb	NE, 26th, 1902
Stoughton, C.A.	Pvt.	B, 52nd Ill. Inf.	26		1922 Jun 3	IA, 49th, 1923
Stoughton, M.		8th Vt. V.R.C.	25	60	1903 Oct	NE, 28th, 1904
Stoughton, S.B.		H, 93rd Ill.	59		1918 Apr 20	KS, 38th, 1919
Stoury, T.L.		B, 6th Ind. Cav.	25		1914 May 20	KS, 34th, 1915
Stout, Abner		12th Ohio Bat. (died of paralysis)	97	78	1902 Nov	NE, 27th, 1903
Stout, Amos		B, 12th Mich.	51		1915 Jan 6	KS, 35th, 1916

*See Appendix A, B or C for roster of post names and locations.
†See Introduction for note regarding recording of death date.
529

Name	Rank	Company, Regiment or Ship	Post*	Age	Death Date†	Journal
Stout, Amos		B, 12th Mich.	51		1916	KS, 36th, 1917
Stout, D.B.		G, 126th Ill. Inf.	263		1902 Aug 14	KS, 22nd, 1903
Stout, Dow	Pvt.	H, 39th Iowa Inf.	43		1919 Jun 23	IA, 46th, 1920
Stout, F.E.	Corp.	D, 33rd Iowa Inf.	40	65	1895 Jan 17	IA, 21st, 1895
Stout, Geo. W.	Pvt.	A, 28th Iowa Inf.	98		1903 Aug 10	IA, 30th, 1904
Stout, Jackson		C, 28th Ill.	25		1914 Feb 12	KS, 34th, 1915
Stout, N.		B, 9th Minn. Inf.	464		1899 Jun 26	KS, 19th, 1900
Stout, P.B.		Mass.	117		1918 Oct 16	KS, 38th, 1919
Stout, Septimas		A, 101st Penn.	85		1924 Oct 14	KS, 44th, 1925
Stout, Thomas		G, 147th Ind. Inf.	26		1911 Oct 12	KS, 31st, 1912
Stout, Thos. J.		M, 7th Ill.	256		1911 Dec 6	KS, 31st, 1912
Stout, W.J.	Pvt.	C, 188th Ohio Inf.	15		1928 Jun 13	IA, 55th, 1929
Stout, W.M.		I, 140th Ill.	85		1928 Jan 11	KS, 48th, 1929
Stout, Wm.		B, 69th Ohio	63		1918 Apr 18	KS, 38th, 1919
Stout, Wm. G.		D, 78th Ill.	185		1926 May 23	KS, 46th, 1927
Stouter, Jacob	Pvt.	H, 11th Penn. Inf. (died of fever)	147	56	1888 Oct 15	NE, 13th, 1889
Stouter, John		F, 203rd Penn. Inf. (died of leakage heart)	289	82	1920 Aug 5	NE, 45th, 1921
Stovall, Geo. W.		B, 79th Ill. Inf.	1		1899 Apr 21	KS, 19th, 1900
Stover, —			7		1928 Feb 15	IA, 55th, 1929
Stover, B.B.			262		1919 May 16	NE, 44th, 1920
Stover, Ben T.		A, 1st Ohio	117		1906 Feb 7	KS, 26th, 1907
Stover, David	Pvt.	B, 13th Iowa Inf.	16		1909 Sep 24	IA, 36th, 1910
Stover, G.W.		died of Bright's disease	44		1903 Sep 10	NE, 28th, 1904
Stover, H.F.		C, 3rd Penn.	1		1923 Dec 8	KS, 43rd, 1924
Stover, J.W.		D, 7th Ind. Inf.	98		1930 Mar 3	KS, 50th, 1931
Stover, Joseph		U.S. Navy Ship *Benton*	81		1906 Apr 18	KS, 26th, 1907
Stover, M.W.	Sergt.	K, 22nd Iowa Inf.	233		1902 Oct 16	IA, 29th, 1903
Stover, T.S.		D, 31st Maine	51		1922 Oct 6	KS, 42nd, 1923
Stow, Benj. F.		H, 45th Iowa Inf.	7	88	1936 Jul 23	IA, 63rd, 1937
Stow, J.S.	Pvt.	A, 11th Ill. Inf.	130		1921 Mar 6	IA, 48th, 1922
Stowe, Burdette Allen		C, 28th Iowa Inf.	64	94	1938 Aug 28	IA, 64th, 1938
Stowe, John W.		G, 7th Mo. Cav.	23		1911 Feb 22	KS, 31st, 1912
Stowell, —	Pvt.	B, 6th N.Y. Hvy. Art.	22		1929 Feb 5	IA, 56th, 1930
Stowell, E.G.	Lieut.		52		1917 Apr	IA, 44th, 1918
Stowell, J.G.		D, 9th Iowa	22		1922 Feb 16	KS, 42nd, 1923
Stowell, J.G.		H, 9th Iowa	22		1921	KS, 41st, 1922
Stowell, Luther E.		A, 86th Ill. Inf. (died of heart failure)	22	73	1913 Dec 20	NE, 38th, 1914
Stowell, M.T.		D, 1st Wis. Hvy. Art.	14		1932	NE, 57th, 1933
Stowell, R.W.		K, 113th Ill. Inf. (Ohiowa)			1944 Jan 13	NE, 70th, 1946
Stowelt, Lafe		A, 42nd Ill.	14		1893 Jul 26	KS, 13th, 1894
Stowers, D.J.		B, 2nd Kans.	65		1921 Jul 26	KS, 41st, 1922
Stowis, C.E.	Pvt.	39th Iowa Inf.	55		1908 Oct 8	IA, 35th, 1909
Stoyell, A.		L, 9th N.Y.	293		1914 May 16	KS, 34th, 1915
Strachan, Louis		E, 72nd Ill.	23		1927 Oct 25	KS, 47th, 1928
Strachan, W.L.		E, 72nd Ill.	23		1919 Jan 18	KS, 39th, 1920
Straight, Francis M.		E, 20th Mo. Inf.		93	1938 Sep 5	IA, 64th, 1938
Straight, J.S.	Pvt.	I, 8th Iowa Cav.	42		1906 Dec 29	IA, 33rd, 1907
Straight, M.A.		F, 34th N.Y.	117		1893 Jul 3	KS, 13th, 1894
Strain, A.L.	Pvt.	A, 46th Ind. Inf.	190		1926 Apr 17	IA, 53rd, 1927
Strain, Chas. T.		B, 137th Ind.	174		1908 Jul 23	KS, 28th, 1909
Strain, David M.		B, 11th Iowa	354		1927 Nov	NE, 52nd, 1928
Strain, Frank		G, 18th Ind.	77		1924 Sep 16	KS, 44th, 1925
Strait, Oscar		E, 41st Ill. Inf. (died at Ft. Scott, Kans.)	32		1894 Nov	KS, 14th, 1895
Strait, W.B.		A, 34th Iowa	123		1896 Nov 24	KS, 16th, 1897
Straley, Amos		I, 26th Ind.	89		1916 Dec 19	KS, 36th, 1917
Stran, J.W.	Pvt.		29		1916 Feb 5	IA, 43rd, 1917
Stranahan, John	Pvt.	4th Iowa Battery	204		1891 Jul 6	IA, 18th, 1892
Stranathan, Sam'l		B, 29th Iowa	355		1897 Aug 9	KS, 17th, 1898
Stranathan, W.B.		B, 29th Iowa Vol. Inf.	355		1916 Apr 6	KS, 36th, 1917
Strandhan, P.			167		1924 Apr 26	IA, 51st, 1925
Strane, Robert E.	Pvt.	F, 21st Iowa Inf.	78		1912 Jun 18	IA, 39th, 1913
Strange, A.A.		D, 56th Ill.	407		1898 Nov 14	KS, 18th, 1899

*See Appendix A, B or C for roster of post names and locations.
†See Introduction for note regarding recording of death date.

Name	Rank	Company, Regiment or Ship	Post*	Age	Death Date†	Journal
Strange, James A.			127		1922 Jul 26	KS, 42nd, 1923
Strasser, J.		44th Ill. Inf.	1		1912 Mar 14	IA, 39th, 1913
Straton, G.M.		C, 6th Wis.	88		1924 Jul 12	KS, 44th, 1925
Straton, Geo.		H, 3rd N.Y.	13	62	1907 Apr 22	NE, 32nd, 1908
Straton, Joel		C, 53rd Mass.	28		1923 Jan 19	KS, 43rd, 1924
Stratten, Zaccheus		D, 176th Ohio Inf.	25		1893 May 6	NE, 18th, 1894
Stratton, A.L.		C, 2nd Wis.	88		1897 Mar 27	KS, 17th, 1898
Stratton, Charles	Pvt.	E, 27th Iowa Inf.	495		1908 Jun 20	IA, 35th, 1909
Stratton, E.T.	Sergt.	D, 6th Iowa Inf.	122	51	1890 Sep 30	IA, 17th, 1891
Stratton, G.W.	Pvt.	B, 104th Ohio Inf.	497		1916 Apr 25	IA, 43rd, 1917
Stratton, Gilmore		H, 1st Ohio	1		1898 Jul 12	KS, 18th, 1899
Stratton, J.C.		G, 15th Mo. Cav.	17		1910 Aug 25	KS, 30th, 1911
Stratton, J.L.		G, 10th Ohio Cav.	5		1922 Jan 17	KS, 41st, 1922
Stratton, J.L.		G, 10th Ohio Cav.	5		1922 Jan 17	KS, 42nd, 1923
Stratton, John W.	Capt.	D, 143rd Ohio Inf.	440		1930 Dec 5	IA, 57th, 1931
Straub, F.J.		D, 12th Mo.	142		1937 May 1	KS, 57th, 1938
Straus, H.	Pvt.	H, 3rd Colo.	5		1904 Jan 25	IA, 31st, 1905
Strauss, Charles E.		C, 184th Ohio	1		1914 Mar 11	KS, 34th, 1915
Straw, H.B.	Pvt.	I, 29th Iowa Inf.	29		1912 Jan 4	IA, 39th, 1913
Strawn, Miles		B, 9th Iowa Cav.	296		1937 May 3	IA, 64th, 1938
Strawn, W.H.	Drummer	A, 45th Iowa Inf.	20		1911 Oct	IA, 38th, 1912
Strayer, Samuel		A, 148th Penn.	151		1933 Mar 18	NE, 58th, 1934
Stream, F.S.	Pvt.	B, 9th Iowa Cav.	23		1911 Jun 2	IA, 38th, 1912
Stream, S.A.	Pvt.	E, 16th Iowa Inf.	440		1919 Mar 25	IA, 46th, 1920
Strean, J.G.		A, 76th Ill. Inf. (died at Paola, Kans.; buried at Oakwood Cemetery)	117		1894 Jul 19	KS, 14th, 1895
Streator, H.C.		G, 129th Ill. Inf. (died of apoplexy)	92	69	1902 Mar	NE, 27th, 1903
Streckbine, Louis	Pvt.	M, 7th Ill. Cav.	92		1919 Oct 14	IA, 46th, 1920
Streepey, Geo.	Pvt.	I, 36th Iowa Inf.	325		1916	IA, 43rd, 1917
Streepy, Edward, Jr.	Pvt.	I, 36th Iowa Inf. (at large)	328	98	1942 Dec 13	IA, 69th, 1943
Street, James S.		I, 1st Iowa Cav.	28		1912 Nov 30	KS, 32nd, 1913
Streeter, E.R.	Pvt.	D, 10th N.Y. Cav.	94		1926 Jul 20	IA, 53rd, 1927
Streeter, Edwin M.	Pvt.	E, 40th Iowa Inf.	511		1910 Jun 8	IA, 37th, 1911
Streeter, F.M.					1911 Feb 4	KS, 31st, 1912
Streeter, G.D.		B, 31st Iowa Inf. (died of apoplexy)	75	70	1903 Sep 13	NE, 28th, 1904
Streeter, H.P.		H, 11th Kans. Cav.	1		1885	KS, 5th, 1886
Streeter, Silas	Pvt.	H, 7th Wis. Inf.	58		1920 Apr 16	IA, 47th, 1921
Streets, Aaron		E, 31st Iowa Inf.	25	78	1920 Nov 1	NE, 45th, 1921
Streight, F.M.		A, 5th Ohio Cav.	13	68	1907 Aug 14	NE, 32nd, 1908
Stretch, A.	Pvt.	F, 35th Iowa Inf.	10		1905 Jul 25	IA, 32nd, 1906
Stretch, M.B.	Pvt.	A, 11th Ind. Inf.	10		1903 Apr 19	IA, 30th, 1904
Stribling, George		D, 3rd Ind. Cav.	84		1902 Feb 2	KS, 22nd, 1903
Stricker, J.C.		D, U.S. Cav.	293		1910 Jun 29	KS, 30th, 1911
Strickler, E.L.	Musician		91		1928 Apr 28	IA, 55th, 1929
Strickler, R.P.		B, 16th Ill.	12		1894[1893?] Aug 9	KS, 13th, 1894
Strickler, W.B.		I, 126th Ohio	142		1926 Feb 16	KS, 46th, 1927
Stricklerm, F.	Pvt.	A, 146th Ill. Inf.	200		1925 Mar 8	IA, 52nd, 1926
Strickley, John W.	Pvt.	4th West Va. Inf.	108		1928 Apr 26	IA, 55th, 1929
Strider, Thos.		A & F, 7th Ill. Cav.	18		1937 Apr 16	KS, 56th, 1937
Striffler, Martin	Pvt.	K, 151st Ind. Inf.	377	73	1897 Mar 24	IA, 24th, 1898
Striker, John	Pvt.	F, 2nd Iowa Cav.	465		1917 Jun 16	IA, 44th, 1918
Strine, M.A.		C, 41st Ohio	4		1926 Aug 12	KS, 46th, 1927
Strine, W.T.		A, 20th Penn. Cav.	395		1923 Aug 6	KS, 43rd, 1924
Stringer, Eli		D, 3rd Iowa Cav.	270		1908 Apr 26	KS, 28th, 1909
Stringer, Justice J.	Pvt.	B, 3rd Ill. Cav.	259		1909 Mar 3	IA, 36th, 1910
Stringer, Mark		died of cancer	5	69	1910	NE, 35th, 1911
Stringham, Irving A.	Sergt.	K, 23rd Ohio Vols.	190		1901 Jul 7	IA, 28th, 1902
Strite, Levi E.			400		1935 Dec 29	IA, 62nd, 1936
Stroble, J.J.		H, 188th Ohio Inf.	24		1892 Oct 26	NE, 17th, 1893
Stroble, Louis		D, 15th U.S. Inf. (died of lagrippe)	24	59	1897 Dec 5	NE, 22nd, 1898
Strode, Jesse B.	Sergt. & 2nd Lieut.	G, 50th Ill. Inf. (see Appendix D)	25	79	1924 Nov 10	NE, 49th, 1925
Strode, Newton		B, 15th Iowa (died of paralysis)	354	76	1920 Oct 2	NE, 45th, 1921

Name	Rank	Company, Regiment or Ship	Post*	Age	Death Date†	Journal
Stroebele, Wunibald	Pvt.	3rd Iowa Bat.	358		1919 Oct 31	IA, 46th, 1920
Strofflett, G.W.	Corp.	A, 5th Cal. Inf.	235		1910 Apr 10	IA, 37th, 1911
Strohm, Isaac	Pvt.	F, 31st Iowa	88		1926 Aug 30	IA, 53rd, 1927
Strohm, R.H.			519		1916	IA, 43rd, 1917
Strohm, Solomon		C, 158th Penn. Inf.	63		1914 Oct 28	KS, 34th, 1915
Strohn, I.N.		C, 113th Ohio	1		1917 May 28	KS, 37th, 1918
Strom, J.H.		F, 3rd Penn.	238		1892 Mar 26	KS, 12th, 1893
Stroman, Samuel		D, 44th Ind. Inf. A, 21st Ind. Hvy. Art.	10		1921 Feb 12	NE, 46th, 1922
Strong, A.W.		H, 114th N.Y. Inf.	48		1899	KS, 19th, 1900
Strong, Abram C.		I, 38th N.Y. (died of heart failure)	342	70	1911 Nov 2	NE, 36th, 1912
Strong, Alvah		F, 2nd Neb. Inf.	100		1887 May 19	KS, 7th, 1888
Strong, Amanzie	Lieut.	G, 27th Wis. Inf.	156		1915 Sep 6	IA, 42nd, 1916
Strong, C.B.		H, 12th Mich. Inf.	12		1934 Jan 7	KS, 54th, 1935
Strong, H.A.		K, 12th Kans.	33		1927 Nov 29	KS, 47th, 1928
Strong, Haydn		A & F, 94th N.Y. Inf. (died of paralysis)	57	77	1915 May 30	NE, 40th, 1916
Strong, Henry F.	Pvt.	12th Wis. Inf.	431	58	1896 Sep 20	IA, 23rd, 1897
Strong, Henry V.	Pvt.	G, 5th Wis. Inf.	365	57	1893 Dec 25	IA, 20th, 1894
Strong, James	Pvt.	B, 128th N.Y. Inf.	76	45	1885 Sep 3	IA, 12th, 1886
Strong, Reuben		B, 1st N.Y. Cav.	353		1912 Jun 1	KS, 32nd, 1913
Strong, T.L.	Pvt.	K, 34th Iowa	208	69	1890 Sep 1	IA, 17th, 1891
Strong, W.N.		14th Ohio Battery	72		1910 Jul 27	IA, 37th, 1911
Strongh, John		I, 59th Ohio	244		1924 Jun 4	KS, 44th, 1925
Strongham, J.S.		D, 154th Ill.	50		1927	KS, 47th, 1928
Strope, J.R.	Pvt.	K, 33rd Ill. Inf.	254		1916 Dec 7	IA, 43rd, 1917
Strother, A.H.	Pvt.	B, 88th Ohio Inf.	270		1926 Nov 19	IA, 53rd, 1927
Strother, Robert S.		H, 22nd Ky. Inf.	85		1918 Dec 21	KS, 38th, 1919
Strotsteffen, John		C, 1st Mo. Eng.	25		1915 May 30	NE, 40th, 1916
Stroud, James	Pvt.	E, 34th Mo. Inf.	18		1919 Jul 4	IA, 46th, 1920
Stroup, J.L.		D, 8th Kans.	106		1914 Sep 16	KS, 34th, 1915
Stroup, Michael	Pvt.	G, 4th Ohio Cav.	84		1927 Oct 18	IA, 54th, 1928
Strovermer, Isaac	Pvt.		167		1916 Dec	IA, 43rd, 1917
Strow, W.P.		D, 9th Iowa Cav.	17		1926	NE, 51st, 1927
Strubble, Asa	Pvt.	E, 2nd Iowa Cav.	74		1918 May 20	IA, 45th, 1919
Struble, Alpheus		D, 15th N.J.	2		1892 Nov 13	KS, 12th, 1893
Struble, C.	Pvt.	C, 76th Ill. Inf.	97		1917 Aug 13	IA, 44th, 1918
Struble, I.S.			91		1913 Feb 17	IA, 40th, 1914
Struble, Riley	Pvt.	B, 6th Iowa Inf.	74		1911 Jan 1	IA, 38th, 1912
Struck, A.T.	Pvt.	5th Ill. Cav.	220		1927 Sep 4	IA, 54th, 1928
Strunk, A.D.		E, 9th Iowa	95		1914 Oct 14	NE, 39th, 1915
Strunk, Geo.			[35?]		1926	KS, 46th, 1927
Strunk, H.C.		A, 8th Penn. Cav.	11	74	1891[1901?] Jan	NE, 26th, 1902
Strunk, Levi		B, 15th Ill.	61		1916 May 6	KS, 36th, 1917
Stryker, C.W.		D, 144th Ind. Inf.	139		1899 Feb 18	KS, 19th, 1900
Stuart, A.H.	Sergt.	G, 21st Iowa Inf.	78	54	1890 Aug 1	IA, 17th, 1891
Stuart, Alman		I, 9th Ind. (died of cancer)	91	87	1909 Aug 19	NE, 34th, 1910
Stuart, Basil		C, 23rd Iowa	7	90	1934 Aug 19	IA, 61st, 1935
Stuart, C.F.	Corp.	B, 9th Iowa	30		1923 Feb 26	IA, 50th, 1924
Stuart, George W.		D, 2nd Iowa Cav.	40		1912 Feb 28	KS, 32nd, 1913
Stuart, J.W.		died of accident	220		1887	NE, 12th, 1888
Stuart, John W.	Corp.	C, 23rd Iowa Inf.	7		1931 Jan 16	IA, 57th, 1931
Stuart, John W.	Corp.	C, 23rd Iowa Inf.	7	89	1931 Jan 16	IA, 58th, 1932
Stuart, Richard	Pvt.	H, 26th N.Y. Inf.	12		1900 Oct 23	IA, 27th, 1901
Stuart, V.A.		D, 129th Ill. (died of Bright's disease)	18	62	1908 Nov 25	NE, 33rd, 1909
Stuart, William		F, 1st Kans.	271		1911 Apr 28	KS, 31st, 1912
Stubbs, Oscar		dropped dead	354		1925	NE, 50th, 1926
Stubbs, Sylvames T.		I, 11th Ohio	14		1904 Jul 16	KS, 24th, 1905
Stuck, John	Pvt.	E, 26th Iowa Inf.	223		1904 Mar 16	IA, 31st, 1905
Stuckel, R.K.		I, 46th Penn.	251		1918 Jul 15	KS, 38th, 1919
Stucker, J.K.		19th Ohio Battery (died of cancer)	61	65	1902 Jul	NE, 27th, 1903
Stucker, Joseph		I, 65th Ind. Inf.	6		1901 Dec 17	KS, 21st, 1902
Stucker, W.H.	Pvt.	L, 2nd Penn. Hvy. Art.	1		1923 May 6	IA, 50th, 1924

Name	Rank	Company, Regiment or Ship	Post*	Age	Death Date†	Journal
Stuckey, Fred		H, 51st Ind.	55		1905 Nov 20	KS, 25th, 1906
Stuckey, J.J.	Corp.	14th Ill. Inf.	12		1908 Apr 6	IA, 35th, 1909
Stuckey, John S.		D, 138th Penn. (died of dropsy)	112	63	1897 Feb 23	NE, 22nd, 1898
Stuckey, M.M.		D, 47th Ill.	25		1912 Dec 30	KS, 32nd, 1913
Studd, J.W.		H, 49th Ill. Inf.	239		1892 Jan 26	KS, 12th, 1893
Studebaker, Jno. R.		A, 112th Ohio	18		1897 Jun 10	KS, 17th, 1898
Studley, H.O.		M, 5th Mich. Cav.	9		1928 Nov 12	NE, 53rd, 1929
Stueben, A.M.	Corp.	B, 122nd N.Y. Inf.	377	48	1886 Nov 30	IA, 13th, 1887
Stuelke, Friedrich	Pvt.	F, 33rd Wis. Inf.	132	94	1939 Jan	IA, 65th, 1939
Stuffel, M.	Pvt.	E, 26th Iowa Inf.	123		1915 Mar	IA, 42nd, 1916
Stukey, John F.		H, 15th Ohio	398		1889	KS, 9th, 1890
Stukey, John T.		H, 15th Ohio Inf.	3		1889	KS, 9th, 1890
Stull, Frank	Pvt.	G, 3rd Iowa Cav.	79	50	1892 Nov 18	IA, 19th, 1893
Stull, Jacob	2nd Corp.	K, 22nd Wis. Inf.	155		1925 Jul 23	IA, 52nd, 1926
Stull, James		B, 15th Ill. Cav.	106		1890	KS, 10th, 1891
Stull, James F.		F, 53rd Ky. Mt. Inf.	469		1928 Aug 19	KS, 48th, 1929
Stull, James H.	Pvt.	E, 19th Wis. Inf.	68		1912 Apr 19	IA, 39th, 1913
Stullken, Gerhardt		9th Wis. Cav.	222		1916 Mar 17	KS, 36th, 1917
Stultz, Adam		I, 5th Ill.	57		1916 Oct 4	KS, 36th, 1917
Stultz, George L.	Pvt.	D, 5th Wis. Inf.	22	52	1892 Oct 5	IA, 19th, 1893
Stumbaugh, F.S.	Col.	2nd & 77th Penn.	1		1897 Feb 25	KS, 17th, 1898
Stump, J.B.		Miss. Squadron, Navy	40		1916 Aug 16	KS, 36th, 1917
Stumph, Oliver P.			295		1922 Jul 4	KS, 42nd, 1923
Sturdevant, D.G.		F, 52nd Penn. Inf.	113		1911 Jul 27	NE, 36th, 1912
Sturdevant, J.L.	Corp.	E, 44th Iowa Inf.	267		1911 Jan 21	IA, 38th, 1912
Sturdvant, W.M.			109		1904-1905	IA, 31st, 1905
Sturgeon, J.L.		A, 18th Wis. Inf. (died of general debility)	9		1902 Oct	NE, 27th, 1903
Sturgeon, J.M.	Lieut.	D, 12th N.Y. Cav.	466		1916 Apr 28	IA, 43rd, 1917
Sturgeon, Wm. C.	Pvt.	A, 77th Ill. Inf.	35		1914 Apr 14	IA, 41st, 1915
Sturges, E.F.		H, 14th Kans.	130		1926 Feb 15	KS, 46th, 1927
Sturges, Henry A.		C, 133rd Ill.	1		1911 May 27	KS, 31st, 1912
Sturgess, Henry B.	Capt.	U.S. Inf.	12		1911 Jan 23	IA, 38th, 1912
Sturgie, R.L.		F, 135th Ind.	4		1930 Dec 5	KS, 50th, 1931
Sturgis, Wm.	Pvt.	A, 4th Iowa Inf.	209		1905 Feb	IA, 32nd, 1906
Sturk, John	Pvt.	I, 12th Mo. Inf.	364		1915 Aug 19	IA, 42nd, 1916
Sturm, J.T.		H, 14th West Va.	27		1920 Jul 25	KS, 40th, 1921
Sturman, W.H.		H, 9th Mo. Cav.	25		1925 Feb 24	KS, 45th, 1926
Sturtevant, S.L.		C, 142nd N.Y. Inf.	147	71	1911 Dec 11	NE, 36th, 1912
Sturtevent, O.L.		F, 92nd Ill. Inf. (died of consumption)	32		1902 Aug	NE, 27th, 1903
Sturtz, Wm.	Bugler	D, 9th Iowa Cav.	19		1929 Nov 21	IA, 56th, 1930
Stutsman, D.C.	Pvt.	F, 13th Iowa	5	80	1891 Feb 2	IA, 17th, 1891
Stutsman, Sol	Pvt.	C, 1st Iowa Bat.	7		1915 Dec 20	IA, 42nd, 1916
Stutson, Howard F.	Pvt.	H, 27th Iowa Inf.	493	91	1935 Oct 10	IA, 65th, 1939
Suberkrup, Henry		69th Wis. Inf. F, 2nd Mo. Lt. Art.	6		1917 Sep 7	KS, 37th, 1918
Suberkrup, Henry		E, 2nd Mo. L.H.[Lt. Art.]	6		1918	KS, 38th, 1919
Such, George		H, 112th Ill. Inf. (died at Fredonia; buried at Fredonia)	98		1894 Jan 2	KS, 14th, 1895
Suenin, August		E, 9th Ill. (died of old age)	218	90	1925 Jan 18	NE, 49th, 1925
Suer, Bernard		C, 1st Wis. Cav.	236	89	1935 Aug 10	IA, 62nd, 1936
Sughone, P.S.		G, 95th Ill.	293		1906 May 2	KS, 26th, 1907
Sughrue, P.			293		1906 May 9	KS, 25th, 1906
Suits, W.B.	Pvt.	D, 15th Iowa Inf.	173	61	1898 Oct 23	IA, 25th, 1899
Sulivan, D.		B, 55th Ill. Inf. (died of consumption)	267	65	1900 Jun 27	NE, 25th, 1901
Sulivan, M.E.		B, 32nd Ohio (died of heart trouble)	187	73	1917 Jul 21	NE, 42nd, 1918
Sullivan, A.L.		B, 134th Ohio	318	71	1911 Jul 9	NE, 36th, 1912
Sullivan, Chas. E.		L, 2nd Colo. Cav.	25		1886	KS, 6th, 1887
Sullivan, Cornelius	Corp.	H, 56th Mass. Inf.	11		1900 Oct 11	IA, 27th, 1901
Sullivan, Daniel		K, 1st Wis.	6		1897 Dec 25	KS, 17th, 1898
Sullivan, E.P.			38		1888	KS, 8th, 1889
Sullivan, J.B.	Pvt.	K, Iowa Inf.	153		1905 Dec 25	IA, 32nd, 1906
Sullivan, J.B.		B, 104th Ill.	88	87	1934 Feb 28	IA, 61st, 1935

Name	Rank	Company, Regiment or Ship	Post*	Age	Death Date†	Journal
Sullivan, J.E.		B, 43rd Ohio	180		1913 Jul 15	KS, 33rd, 1914
Sullivan, J.F.		K, 113th Ohio	203		1927 Sep 1	KS, 47th, 1928
Sullivan, J.G.		3rd Kans. State Militia	12		1916 Jul 19	KS, 36th, 1917
Sullivan, J.M.		70th Ohio Inf.	40		1900 Jul 14	KS, 20th, 1901
Sullivan, J.W.		D, 136th Ill.	51		1927	KS, 47th, 1928
Sullivan, Jas. S.		E, 60th Ill.	303		1896 May 9	KS, 16th, 1897
Sullivan, Jere	Pvt.	G, 36th N.Y. Inf.	27	66	1891 Mar 29	IA, 18th, 1892
Sullivan, Jno. D.	Pvt.	C, 2nd Iowa Inf.	369		1925 Mar 17	IA, 52nd, 1926
Sullivan, John J.	Bugler	6th U.S. Cav.	59		1926 Sep 27	IA, 53rd, 1927
Sullivan, Joseph F.		G, 17th Ill. Cav.	117		1892 Mar 10	KS, 12th, 1893
Sullivan, Josiah		I, 146th Ind. (former member; died at McCook)	250		1935 May 19	NE, 60th, 1936
Sullivan, Michael	Pvt.	K, 25th Iowa Inf.	312	62	1892 Oct 27	IA, 19th, 1893
Sullivan, Mike		C, 100th Ill.	130		1927	NE, 52nd, 1928
Sullivan, W.H.	Pvt.	B, 3rd Iowa Cav.	19		1919 Aug 4	IA, 46th, 1920
Sultzer, W.B.		Sailor on Man-of-War	448		1925 Aug 1	KS, 45th, 1926
Sumerson, J.R.	Pvt.	8th Mo. Inf.	26		1923 Jan 5	IA, 50th, 1924
Summerfield, Elias		E, 24th Ill.	12		1924 Oct 31	KS, 44th, 1925
Summerhaks, Wm.	Pvt.	D, 7th Iowa Cav.	8		1927 Oct 3	IA, 54th, 1928
Summers, E.J.		D, 4th Ind. Cav.	32		1933	NE, 58th, 1934
Summers, J.H.		C, 5th Kans. Cav.	147		1902 Jan 12	KS, 22nd, 1903
Summers, Jonathan	Pvt.	I, 6th Minn. Inf.	236		1930 Jan 4	IA, 57th, 1931
Summers, Joseph		H, 30th Iowa	19	85	1934 Jul	IA, 61st, 1935
Summers, N.P.			45		1921 Feb 5	IA, 48th, 1922
Summers, Nineveh		F, 2nd Mo. Cav.	112		1892 Aug 20	NE, 17th, 1893
Summers, O.P.		H, 20th Penn.	433		1926 May 4	KS, 46th, 1927
Summers, Thos. H.		E, 9th Tenn. Inf.	32		1918 Mar 6	KS, 38th, 1919
Sumner, A.A.	Pvt.	B, 50th Wis. Inf.	2		1900 Sep 18	IA, 27th, 1901
Sumner, Henry	Pvt.	B, 22nd Iowa Inf.	452		1924 Mar 25	IA, 51st, 1925
Sumpter, S.C.		11th Mo.	388		1911 Jul	KS, 31st, 1912
Sunderland, J.		I, 100th Ohio	265		1917 Jun 8	KS, 37th, 1918
Sunt, W.H.	Pvt.	4th West Va.	497		1923 Aug 14	IA, 50th, 1924
Supplee, Jonathan	Pvt.	F, 25th Iowa Inf.	44	51	1893 Sep	IA, 20th, 1894
Surber, Eratus		I, 18th Iowa	142		1933 Jul 2	KS, 53rd, 1934
Sussong, H.W.		D, 32nd Iowa Cav.	32		1924 Feb 24	KS, 44th, 1925
Suter, Jacob		A, 44th Ill.	65		1898 Jul 20	KS, 18th, 1899
Suter, Martin	Capt.	G, 4th Md. Inf.	215		1917 Jan 11	IA, 44th, 1918
Sutherin, John		G, 2nd West Va.	1		1930 Aug 4	KS, 50th, 1931
Sutherland, Abram		E, 22nd Ind.	52		1931 Jul 23	NE, 56th, 1932
Sutherland, Albert		A, 59th N.Y. Inf.	94		1890 Nov 21	KS, 11th, 1892
Sutherland, Andrew	Major	D, 31st Iowa	68		1922 Jul 14	IA, 49th, 1923
Sutherland, D.E.	Pvt.	K, 16th Wis. Inf.	31		1918 Jan 19	IA, 45th, 1919
Sutherland, D.W.	Pvt.	C, 44th Iowa	33		1926 Mar 25	IA, 53rd, 1927
Sutherland, E.H.		E, 113th Ill. Inf.	407		1917 Oct 15	KS, 37th, 1918
Sutter, F.M.		B, 2nd Iowa (not a member of Farragut Post)	25		1913 Oct 25	NE, 38th, 1914
Sutters, Ab A.	Pvt.	M, 7th Iowa Cav.	74		1918 Nov 7	IA, 45th, 1919
Sutton, E.L.		146th Ill.	113		1923	KS, 43rd, 1924
Sutton, Ed	Steward	U.S.S. Lackawanna	22		1907 2nd term	IA, 34th, 1908
Sutton, Ezra		39th Iowa Inf.	177		1899 Jul 26	KS, 19th, 1900
Sutton, Geo.	Pvt.	E, 160th Ohio Inf.	491		1908 Nov 2	IA, 35th, 1909
Sutton, George			340		1890	KS, 10th, 1891
Sutton, George		I, 36th Iowa Inf.	340		1895 Dec	KS, 15th, 1896
Sutton, Guier		G, 82nd Ohio Inf.	301		1929 Feb 19	KS, 49th, 1930
Sutton, J.B.			180		1884	KS, 4th, 1885
Sutton, J.R.			69		1905 Sep 8	IA, 32nd, 1906
Sutton, Jerry L.	Pvt.	H, 3rd Iowa Cav.	19		1917 May 15	IA, 44th, 1918
Sutton, Louis	Corp.	G, 46th Ind. (died of dysentery)	192	53	1887 Mar 20	NE, 12th, 1888
Sutton, Michael W.		B, 6th N.Y. Hvy. Art. (see also Appendix D)	294		1918 Jun 12	KS, 38th, 1919
Sutton, Milton		Ohio	144		1923	KS, 43rd, 1924
Sutton, O.B.	Pvt.	I, 141st Ohio Inf.	192		1917 Mar 18	IA, 44th, 1918

*See Appendix A, B or C for roster of post names and locations.
†See Introduction for note regarding recording of death date.

Name	Rank	Company, Regiment or Ship	Post*	Age	Death Date†	Journal
Sutton, P.M.	Pvt.	A, 6th Iowa Cav.	94		1901-1902	IA, 28th, 1902
Sutton, R.B.		B, 126th N.Y. Inf. (died of paralysis)	275	72	1910 Jan 15	NE, 35th, 1911
Sutton, Reuben		I, 55th Ohio Inf.	64		1899 Dec	KS, 19th, 1900
Sutton, T.W.			88		1886	NE, 11th, 1887
Sutton, Wm.		I, 3rd Mo. Cav.	165		1930 Jun 5	NE, 55th, 1931
Svensden, Edward, see Sveusden, Edward						
Sveusden, Edward	Capt.	E, 26th Iowa Inf.	88		1910 Jan 1	IA, 37th, 1911
Swain, Byron		D, 11th Ill. Cav.	12		1924 Apr 8	KS, 44th, 1925
Swain, James W.	Corp.	D, 40th Wis.	300		1922 Apr 13	IA, 49th, 1923
Swald, A.E.		D, 138th Penn.	185		1922 Nov 24	KS, 42nd, 1923
Swalley, Abe		8th Ohio	123		1935 Apr 30	KS, 55th, 1936
Swallow, Alexander		I, 12th Mass. (died of neuralgia of the heart)	60	69	1911 Jun 12	NE, 36th, 1912
Swallow, Andrew		3rd Vt. Battery	160		1901 Oct 23	KS, 21st, 1902
Swalm, Alb. W.	Pvt.	D, 33rd Inf.	40		1922 Aug 23	IA, 49th, 1923
Swan, A.H.		Kans.	344		1930 Oct 31	KS, 50th, 1931
Swan, A.W.		A, 52nd Ill.	8		1917 Nov 28	KS, 37th, 1918
Swan, Alex		E, 2nd Ohio Lt. Art. (died at Marion; buried at Marion Cemetery)	202		1894 Aug 1	KS, 14th, 1895
Swan, Charles		C, 4th Iowa Cav. (died of paralysis of brain)	342	55	1897 Feb 19	NE, 22nd, 1898
Swan, Clark	Pvt.	F, 20th N.Y. Cav.	59		1906 Jun 3	IA, 33rd, 1907
Swan, D.I.		H, 101st Ind.	129		1926 Jul 8	KS, 46th, 1927
Swan, Daniel		F, 85th Penn.	65		1912 Dec 12	KS, 32nd, 1913
Swan, James		F, 6th Kans.	1		1912 Dec 11	KS, 32nd, 1913
Swan, John P.	Pvt.	K, 9th Iowa Inf.	206		1930 May 25	IA, 57th, 1931
Swan, Milo		K, 6th Kans. Cav.	32		1904 Sep 12	KS, 24th, 1905
Swan, Robert G.	Pvt.	H, 3rd Ohio Inf.	12	50	1894 Jun 2	IA, 21st, 1895
Swan, W.G.		2nd Neb. Vols. (died of heart trouble)	318		1908 Sep 10	NE, 33rd, 1909
Swan, W.L.			5		1929 Jul 6	IA, 56th, 1930
Swan, William G.	Sergt.	C, 2nd Neb. Cav. (died of heart trouble)	47	72	1908 Sep 13	NE, 33rd, 1909
Swan, Wm. H.	Pvt.	G, 3rd Iowa Inf.	6		1917 Nov 21	IA, 44th, 1918
Swan, Wm. H.	Pvt.	C, 15th Ill. Inf.	36		1899	NE, 24th, 1900
Swanbeck, F.H.		B, 9th Wis.	107		1918	KS, 38th, 1919
Swander, W.J.		K, 20th Ohio Inf.	87		1887 Sep 13	KS, 7th, 1888
Swane, J.A.	Pvt.	M, 8th Cav.	114		1899 Jul 6	IA, 26th, 1900
Swanger, E.	Pvt.	I, 50th Wis. Inf.	104		1925 May 2	IA, 52nd, 1926
Swank, E.	Pvt.	E, 133rd Penn. Inf.	68		1927 May 11	IA, 54th, 1928
Swank, Frank		Calif.	374		1893	KS, 13th, 1894
Swank, Samuel	Pvt.	H, 8th Kans. Inf.	54		1899	NE, 24th, 1900
Swank, W.H.H.			96		1915 Mar 4	IA, 42nd, 1916
Swanser, John	Pvt.	F, 102nd Ill. Inf.	155		1907 Dec 2	IA, 34th, 1908
Swanson, G.W.		C, 3rd Ill. Cav.	207		1912 Sep 30	NE, 37th, 1913
Swanson, Swan		Mo. Eng.	32	78	1909 Apr 6	NE, 34th, 1910
Swanton, Joseph		C, 11th Ill.	429		1896 Jul 6	KS, 16th, 1897
Swarm, Henry		C, 1st Penn. Cav.	167		1918 Sep 30	KS, 38th, 1919
Swart, B.C.		K, 41st Ill.	158		1905 Sep	KS, 25th, 1906
Swart, I.T.		A, 10th Kans.	457		1905	KS, 25th, 1906
Swart, Jno.	Pvt.	D, 140th Penn. Inf.	34	70	1890 Mar 18	IA, 16th, 1890
Swart, John	Pvt.	D, 104th Penn. Inf.	34	77	1890 Jan 18	IA, 17th, 1891
Swarthout, Henry		A, 85th N.Y.	17		1919 Jun 17	KS, 39th, 1920
Swarts, J.A.	Pvt.	A, 15th Penn. Inf.	14		1929	IA, 56th, 1930
Swarts, Robert	Pvt.	B, 2nd Wis. Inf.	63		1916 Jan 10	IA, 42nd, 1916
Swartwood, Charles		H, 17th Ill. Inf.	214		1917 Mar	KS, 37th, 1918
Swartz, C.F.	Pvt.	K, 7th Ohio Inf.	168	62	1892 Jan 13	IA, 18th, 1892
Swartz, D.W.	Pvt.	C, 7th Mo. Cav.	2		1905 May 21	IA, 32nd, 1906
Swartz, David		F, 46th Ohio	175		1923 Jan 29	KS, 43rd, 1924
Swartz, Francis		D, 55th Penn. 1st U.S. Art.	207		1928 May 21	NE, 53rd, 1929
Swartz, Henry C.		F, 46th Ohio	44		1913 Oct 21	KS, 33rd, 1914
Swartz, J.B.		48th Ind.	142		1889	KS, 9th, 1890
Swartz, J.L.	Pvt.	A, 46th Ill. Inf.	141	88	1932 Mar 26	IA, 59th, 1933

*See Appendix A, B or C for roster of post names and locations.
†See Introduction for note regarding recording of death date.

Name	Rank	Company, Regiment or Ship	Post*	Age	Death Date†	Journal
Swartz, J.W.		R, 6th West Va.	104		1927 May 21	KS, 47th, 1928
Swartz, Jacob		L, 10th Ill. Cav.	85		1908 Jan 2	KS, 28th, 1909
Swartz, Michael		58th Ill.	113		1914 Feb 16	KS, 34th, 1915
Swartz, Samuel W.	Pvt.	B, 71st Ill. Inf.	197		1902 Nov 20	IA, 29th, 1903
Swartz, W.E.	Sergt.	D, 16th Ohio	22		1907 2nd term	IA, 34th, 1908
Swartz, Wm. M.		F, 46th Ohio Inf.	1		1925 Jul 5	KS, 45th, 1926
Swartzlander, Fred		B, 2nd Penn. Cav.	110	72	1920 Feb 22	NE, 45th, 1921
Swarz, Oswald		A, 13th Ill.	380		1898 Apr 29	KS, 18th, 1899
Swatzell, Jeremiah P.		I, 17th Ky. Inf.	128		1901 Oct 15	KS, 21st, 1902
Swayne, Oscar	Pvt.	B, 10th Iowa Inf.	7		1917 Feb 16	IA, 44th, 1918
Swayze, D.C.		H, 13th Kans.	40		1906 Feb 15	KS, 26th, 1907
Swayze, D.W.			28		1890 Apr 13	NE, 15th, 1891
Swayze, W.H.		11th Ind.	437		1919 Jan 29	KS, 39th, 1920
Swayze, W.H.		11th Ohio Lt. Art.	437		1919 Jan 29	KS, 41st, 1922
Sweany, Y.B.		K, 4th Ohio Inf.	129		1887 Jan 6	KS, 7th, 1888
Swearengen, Jas.		H, 140th Penn.	25		1922 Aug 20	NE, 47th, 1923
Swearengen, Jos. P.		9th Battery Ind. Lt. Art.	51		1891 May 29	KS, 11th, 1892
Swearengin, A.K.	Pvt.	B, 25th Iowa Inf.	497		1928 Feb 26	IA, 55th, 1929
Swearingen, A.T.	Pvt.	D, 9th Minn. Inf.	26		1915 Feb 18	IA, 42nd, 1916
Swearinger, Jas.		H, 140th Penn.	25		1922 Aug 20	NE, 47th, 1923
Swearington, R.O.		B, 24th Iowa	77		1922 Jul 6	KS, 42nd, 1923
Sweasey, W.M.	Pvt.	B, 65th Ind. Inf. (died of lung trouble)	76	44	1888 Dec 15	NE, 13th, 1889
Sweatt, T.J.	Pvt.	E, —	343		1913 May 15	IA, 40th, 1914
Sweazey, Byron O.		I, 38th N.Y. Inf. F, 8th N.Y. Mtd. Inf.	110	81	1921 Jul 25	NE, 46th, 1922
Sweeley, L.Z.		K, 54th Ill. (died of catarrh trouble)	231	63	1908 Nov 6	NE, 33rd, 1909
Sweeney, Charles	Pvt.	K, 27th Iowa Inf.	77		1917 Apr 7	IA, 44th, 1918
Sweeney, D.L.	QM	H, 14th N.Y. Inf.	25		1934 Jul	KS, 54th, 1935
Sweeney, D.L.	QM	H, 14th N.Y.	25		1936	KS, 56th, 1937
Sweeney, David		K, 59th Ind. Inf.	206		1891 Dec 8	KS, 11th, 1892
Sweeney, H.L.		B, 10th Mo. (died of accident)	301	78	1915 May 12	NE, 41st, 1917
Sweeney, H.L.		B, 10th Mo. (died of accident)	301	78	1915 Jun 25	NE, 40th, 1916
Sweeney, Ira		4th Tenn.	129		1906 Mar 23	KS, 26th, 1907
Sweeney, J.H.	Pvt.	K, 27th Iowa Inf.	77		1918 Nov 11	IA, 45th, 1919
Sweeney, Moses T.	Pvt.	C, 26th Iowa Inf.	88	63	1886 Apr 3	IA, 13th, 1887
Sweenie, James H.	Pvt.	B, 30th Iowa Inf.	100		1917 Sep 12	IA, 44th, 1918
Sweeny, G.W.	Lieut.	H, 11th Iowa Inf.	173		1920 Jul 26	IA, 47th, 1921
Sweet, Alva A.	Pvt.	K, 8th Iowa Cav.	235	86	1931 Feb 4	IA, 58th, 1932
Sweet, Amos		K, 1st Wis. Hvy. Art.	159		1891 Dec 15	KS, 11th, 1892
Sweet, Andrew		K, 160th Ohio	100		1922 May 4	KS, 42nd, 1923
Sweet, C.J.	Pvt.	G, 2nd Iowa Inf.	8		1915 Apr 25	IA, 42nd, 1916
Sweet, E.L.	Pvt.	A, 1st Iowa Cav. (at large)		88	1933 Dec 29	IA, 60th, 1934
Sweet, Eli	Pvt.	G, 7th Iowa Inf.	292		1926 Nov 25	IA, 53rd, 1927
Sweet, George		B, 4th Mo.	18		1902 May 27	KS, 22nd, 1903
Sweet, J.B.	Pvt.	K, 32nd Iowa Vol. Inf.	476	76	1898 Jun 14	IA, 25th, 1899
Sweet, James	Pvt.	G, 19th Wis. Inf.	452		1925 May 30	IA, 52nd, 1926
Sweet, M.H.	Pvt.	E, 2nd Iowa Cav.	108		1917 Feb 6	IA, 44th, 1918
Sweet, M.W.	Pvt.	F, 13th Iowa Inf.	235		1916 May 10	IA, 43rd, 1917
Sweet, Noah	Pvt.	F, 12th Ill. Inf.	3	84	1932 Oct 3	IA, 59th, 1933
Sweet, W.W.		E, 28th Conn.	25		1896 May 7	KS, 16th, 1897
Sweet, William		I, 3rd & 5th Mich.	325		1893 Apr 20	KS, 13th, 1894
Sweet, Wm.		F, 55th Ohio	41		1906 Oct	KS, 26th, 1907
Sweeting, Olin	Pvt.	G, 26th Iowa Inf.	235		1923 May 2	IA, 50th, 1924
Sweetland, B.F.			[175?]		1929 Feb 23	KS, 49th, 1930
Sweetland, Isaac		D, 8th Kans. Inf.	175		1902 Dec 2	KS, 22nd, 1903
Sweetland, John M.		H, 4th Ohio Cav. (died of heart failure)	448		1893 May 19	KS, 13th, 1894
Sweetman, John W.	Pvt.	A, 29th Mo. Inf.	210		1902 Jan 12	IA, 28th, 1902
Sweeton, Wiley		B, 23rd Mo. Inf.	7		1925 Jan 27	NE, 50th, 1926
Sweezey, W.H.		E, 17th Mich.	1		1917 Mar 14	KS, 37th, 1918
Sweezy, George		G, 22nd N.Y. Inf.	233	94	1935 Dec 7	IA, 62nd, 1936
Sweezy, George		G, 22nd N.Y. Inf. (at large)		94	1935 Dec 7	IA, 62nd, 1936
Sweezy, W.		C, 17th Iowa	325		1888	KS, 8th, 1889

*See Appendix A, B or C for roster of post names and locations.
†See Introduction for note regarding recording of death date.

536

Name	Rank	Company, Regiment or Ship	Post*	Age	Death Date†	Journal
Sweger, Henry	Pvt.	I, 208th Penn. Inf.	57		1933	IA, 60th, 1934
Swegle, R.Z.		K, 11th Ill. Cav.	50		1924 Nov 5	KS, 44th, 1925
Swehla, F.J.		D, 6th Iowa Cav.	115		1921	KS, 41st, 1922
Swelm, Thos. C.	Pvt.	B, 3rd Iowa Inf.	40		1916 Jan 14	IA, 43rd, 1917
Swem, E.L.	Corp. Lieut.	C, 1st Iowa Inf. G, 59th U.S. Colored	235		1918 May 4	IA, 45th, 1919
Swenney, William		G, 25th Ind.	50		1924 Nov 25	KS, 44th, 1925
Swenson, O.	Pvt.	C, 15th Wis. Inf.	216		1906 Jun 27	IA, 33rd, 1907
Swerringer, D.K.			1		1893 Jun 5	KS, 13th, 1894
Swett, J.H.		F, 15th Ill.	294		1906 May 1	KS, 26th, 1907
Swift, A.	Pvt.	B, 6th Iowa Inf.	434		1920 Jun 6	IA, 47th, 1921
Swift, Charles Henry		D, 4th Iowa Cav.		86, 11 mos. & 27 days	1937 Aug 30	IA, 64th, 1938
Swift, F.B.	Capt.	D, 1st Kans.	49		1916 Mar 7	KS, 36th, 1917
Swift, O.B.	Pvt.	A, 31st Wis. Inf.	42		1922 Aug 28	IA, 49th, 1923
Swigart, H.M.			13	67	1913 Aug 5	NE, 38th, 1914
Swiggit, John		I, 7th Kans.	292		1896 Jan 9	KS, 16th, 1897
Swiggitt, T.C.		A, 8th Ind.	107		1906 Apr 24	KS, 26th, 1907
Swihart, Wm. E.		C, 1st Neb. Cav.	52	75	1922 Nov 13	NE, 47th, 1923
Swinger, Truman		K, 7th Vt. (died of heart disease)	1	82	1922 Dec 11	NE, 47th, 1923
Swingle, John F.		A, 137th Penn.	100		1930 Mar 4	KS, 50th, 1931
Swingle, S.M.	Pvt.	E, 1st Mo. Cav.	1		1920 Aug 17	IA, 47th, 1921
Swink, John		I, 137th Ill.	340		1916 Feb 11	KS, 36th, 1917
Swinson, John		C, 17th Kans. Inf. (died at Concordia)	113		1895 Jun 20	KS, 15th, 1896
Swinson, Swin		E, 83rd Ill. Inf. (died of heart trouble & dropsy)	147	69	1911 Dec 15	NE, 36th, 1912
Swisher, J.G.		E, 31st Ind.	83		1927 Feb 11	KS, 47th, 1928
Swisher, Jacob H.			25		1906	KS, 26th, 1907
Swisher, James		E, 70th Ill.	90		1928 Jun 16	KS, 48th, 1929
Swisher, Jerome		K, 17th West Va.	465		1925	KS, 45th, 1926
Swisher, John		Ohio	90		1916 Oct 28	KS, 36th, 1917
Swisher, Peter		K, 22nd Penn. Cav.	271		1919 Dec 7	IA, 46th, 1920
Swisher, W.H.	Pvt.	K, 82nd Ohio Inf.	231		1908 Jun 26	IA, 35th, 1909
Switzer, A.M.		A, 185th Ohio	17		1919 Mar 19	KS, 39th, 1920
Switzer, Alpheus	Pvt.	K, 35th Iowa Inf.	473		1906	IA, 33rd, 1907
Switzer, J.C.		U.S. Navy	8		1887 Mar 3	KS, 7th, 1888
Switzer, W.L.		F, 57th Ohio	87		1916 Jan 16	KS, 36th, 1917
Switzer, W.P.		35th Ill.	105		1922 Mar	KS, 42nd, 1923
Swope, B.A.	Pvt.	G, 8th Iowa Inf.	292		1926 Mar 27	IA, 53rd, 1927
Swope, H.H.	Pvt.	B, 23rd Iowa Inf.	7		1906 Apr 4	IA, 33rd, 1907
Swope, Thomas		H, 59th Ohio	142		1925 Apr 11	KS, 44th, 1925
Swope, Thomas		H, 59th Ohio Inf.	142		1925 Apr 10	KS, 45th, 1926
Swords, D.		D, 6th[?] Wis. Inf. (died of lung)	140	63	1901 Feb	NE, 26th, 1902
Swygard, F.W.	Sergt.	C, 30th Iowa Inf.	157		1912 Jul 21	IA, 39th, 1913
Swygart, A.N.		F, 15th Ind.	51		1928 Sep 26	KS, 48th, 1929
Sydenstricker, C.A.S.	Pvt.	G, 36th Ohio Inf.	91		1902 Sep 18	IA, 29th, 1903
Sydow, Chas.	2nd Lieut.	D, 27th Iowa Inf.	168		1902 Dec 19	IA, 29th, 1903
Syees, William	Pvt.	A, 14th Iowa Inf.	244		1918 Feb 21	IA, 45th, 1919
Syferd, Phillip W.	Pvt.	F, 34th Iowa Inf.	28		1903 Dec 14	IA, 30th, 1904
Sykes, Geo.	Pvt.	I, 26th Iowa Inf.	365		1908	IA, 35th, 1909
Sykes, James H.		E, 12th Tenn. Cav.	74	95	1938 Oct 6	IA, 64th, 1938
Sykes, R.F.	Pvt.	E, 96th Ohio Vol. Inf.	130		1901 Jul 2	IA, 28th, 1902
Sykes, T.P.			13		1905	NE, 30th, 1906
Sylvester, Chas.			45		1926 Jun 21	IA, 53rd, 1927
Sylvester, J.W.	Pvt.	M, 4th Penn. Cav.	235		1913 Jun 28	IA, 40th, 1914
Sylvester, John	Pvt.	G, 4th Iowa Cav.	306		1906	IA, 33rd, 1907
Sylvester, L.S.	Pvt.	F, 8th Iowa Cav.	337	64	1896 Apr 1	IA, 22nd, 1896
Sylvia, Thomas		I, 51st Ill. Inf. (died at Pittsburg)	65		1894 Feb 17	KS, 14th, 1895
Symes, E.		K, 36th Ill.	418		1923 Jan 3	KS, 43rd, 1924
Symes, Edwin		K, 76th Ill.	418		1923 Jan 3	KS, 42nd, 1923
Symmes, G.D.		D, 38th Iowa	36		1900 Jul 29	KS, 20th, 1901

*See Appendix A, B or C for roster of post names and locations.
†See Introduction for note regarding recording of death date.

537

Name	Rank	Company, Regiment or Ship	Post*	Age	Death Date†	Journal
Symons, O.E.	Pvt.	H, 9th Iowa Inf.	66		1912 Nov 17	IA, 39th, 1913
Synder, John	Pvt.	F, 32nd Iowa	149		1899 Jul	IA, 26th, 1900
Sypher, Samuel		I, 140th Ill. Inf. (died of lightning)	59	49	1895 Aug 22	NE, 20th, 1896
Syphers, A.L.	Pvt.	A, 7th Maine Inf.	111	52	1893 Nov 20	IA, 20th, 1894
Taber, F.H.		A, 3rd Wis. Cav. (died of dropsy)	23	67	1891[1901?] Mar	NE, 26th, 1902
Taber, Ira J.	Adjt.	11th Kans. Cav.	46		1890	KS, 10th, 1891
Tabor, Freeman H.		H, 3rd Wis. Cav.	23		1900 Mar 28	NE, 25th, 1901
Tabor, Jabez B.		B, 25th Ill.	29		1898 May 19	KS, 18th, 1899
Tabor, O.F.		B, Iowa	8		1892 Jun 15	KS, 12th, 1893
Taffe, John W.		I, 2nd Cal. Cav. (died at Kansas City, Mo.; buried at Oak Grove Cemetery)	28		1894 Jul 20	KS, 14th, 1895
Taffee, J.W.		I, 2nd Col.	28		1894 Jan 10	KS, 16th, 1897
Taft, Daniel E.	Pvt.	K, 2nd Ill. Art.	88		1912 Jun 25	IA, 39th, 1913
Taft, Joel	Pvt.	C, 23rd Iowa	7		1922 Jan 7	IA, 49th, 1923
Taft, Loel		C, 23rd Iowa	7		1921	IA, 48th, 1922
Taft, M.A.	Sergt.	F, 34th Iowa Inf.	216		1908	IA, 35th, 1909
Taft, R.M.	Pvt.	C, 1st Ill. Lt. Art.	12		1916 May 17	IA, 43rd, 1917
Taggart, Albert		D, 4th Ind. Cav.	25		1913 Sep 26	KS, 33rd, 1914
Taggart, S.L.	Lieut. Col.	3rd Iowa Inf.	78		1907 Feb 4	IA, 34th, 1908
Tague, David	Pvt.	H, 5th Ind. Inf.	98		1927 Feb 18	IA, 54th, 1928
Talbitzer, C.W.		E, 19th Ohio (died of influenza)	275	78	1919 Feb 5	NE, 44th, 1920
Talbot, B.M.			321		1928 Oct	IA, 55th, 1929
Talbot, B.M.	Pvt.		321		1927 Oct	IA, 54th, 1928
Talbot, E.J.	Pvt.	E, 40th Iowa Inf.	16		1910 Aug 30	IA, 37th, 1911
Talbot, Edward	Pvt.	G, 39th Iowa Inf.	20		1922 Dec 19	IA, 49th, 1923
Talbot, John		E, 12th Ohio	96		1936	KS, 55th, 1936
Talbot, R.C.		H, 132nd Ind.	98		1934	NE, 59th, 1935
Talbot, Robert D.		C, 75th Ill.	64		1921 Jun 12	KS, 41st, 1922
Talbot, William		H, 13th U.S. Inf. 1st Batt.	113		1933 Apr 12	NE, 58th, 1934
Talbott, Geo. W.	Pvt.	G, 28th Iowa Vol. Inf.	233	65	1899 Feb 19	IA, 25th, 1899
Talbott, J.P.	Sergt.	B, 3rd Iowa Cav.	254		1916 Aug 4	IA, 43rd, 1917
Talbott, K.T.	Pvt.	B, 3rd Iowa Cav.	2		1911 Dec 26	IA, 38th, 1912
Talbott, L.W.		B, 1st Iowa Inf.	8		4th quarter 1884	IA, 11th, 1885
Talbott, Seth		I, 22nd Iowa	18		1930 Apr 8	KS, 50th, 1931
Talbott, Wm. H.	Pvt.	D, 33rd Iowa Inf.	275		1907 Dec 5	IA, 34th, 1908
Talcott, L.C.		F, 27th Iowa	116		1927 Aug 17	KS, 47th, 1928
Talcott, L.D.			47		1916 Mar 20	IA, 43rd, 1917
Talcott, R.W.		C, 3rd U.S. Cav.	25		1923	NE, 48th, 1924
Talcutt, Horace T.	Pvt.	B, 21st Iowa Inf.	259		1910 Jun 22	IA, 37th, 1911
Talefero, W.H.	Pvt.	D, 33rd Ind.	22		1905 Sep 14	IA, 32nd, 1906
Tales, R.W.		A, 31st Mass.	294		1905 Jan	KS, 25th, 1906
Talkington, L.B.		I, 14th Ill. Inf.	22	83	1923 Nov 19	NE, 48th, 1924
Tallman, Albert	Pvt.	A, 1st N.Y. Dragoons	77		1903 Dec 26	IA, 30th, 1904
Tallman, J.H.	Pvt.	E, 31st Iowa Inf.	197		1905 Feb 16	IA, 32nd, 1906
Tallman, Joseph B.		B, 50th Wis. (died of pleura pneumonia)	274	64	1910 Jan 3	NE, 34th, 1910
Tallman, M.	Pvt.	K, 11th Iowa Inf.	452		1921 Apr 8	IA, 48th, 1922
Talmage, C.H.		I, 3rd Iowa Inf.	48		1907 May 2	IA, 34th, 1908
Talmage, J.W.		21st Ind. (died of heart trouble)	18	71	1910 Mar 10	NE, 35th, 1911
Talmage, John	Pvt.	A, 6th Iowa Inf.	259		1906 Sep 19	IA, 33rd, 1907
Talman, M.		K, 11th Iowa Inf.	452		1922 Apr 10	IA, 49th, 1923
Tamer, B.L.	Pvt.	A, 5th Iowa Inf.	80		1902 Sep 25	IA, 29th, 1903
Tamlinson, T.T.	Pvt.	K, 12th Iowa Inf.	171		1905 Aug 19	IA, 32nd, 1906
Tandy, Jackson P.			92		1914	KS, 34th, 1915
Tanenson, Byron		B, 6th N.Y. Hvy. Art. (died of cancer)	352	75	1922 Jan 8	NE, 47th, 1923
Tankersly, A.J.		A, 78th Ill.	113		1911 Aug 16	KS, 31st, 1912
Tannehill, Jas.		B, 137th Ill.	142		1933	KS, 53rd, 1934
Tanner, D.A.	Lieut.	C, 40th Iowa Inf.	399	61	1888 Feb 22	IA, 15th, 1889
Tanner, J.W.		F, 198th Ill.	38		1930	KS, 50th, 1931
Tanner, Oscar		E, 3rd Ohio	36		1922 Aug 27	KS, 42nd, 1923
Tansey, Daniel			426		1908	IA, 35th, 1909
Tapping, Moses	Pvt.	A, 9th Mo. Cav.	452		1928 Jan 15	IA, 55th, 1929
Tarabee, William		H, 13th Ill.	409		1893 Aug 21	KS, 13th, 1894

*See Appendix A, B or C for roster of post names and locations.
†See Introduction for note regarding recording of death date.

538

Name	Rank	Company, Regiment or Ship	Post*	Age	Death Date†	Journal
Tarbel, John A.		G, 112th Ill. Inf. (died of Bright's disease)	102	80	1910 Sep 14	NE, 35th, 1911
Tarbell, James M.		E, 2nd Vt.	147		1917 Feb 1	KS, 37th, 1918
Tarbin, E.B.		C, 53rd Ky.	9		1933 Mar 16	KS, 53rd, 1934
Tarbox, A.P.		F, 28th Maine	25		1926 May 27	NE, 51st, 1927
Tarpey, Thomas		B, 151st N.Y. Inf.	171		1899 Apr 30	KS, 19th, 1900
Tarren, G.W.		F, 15th Ill. Inf.	18		1901 May 5	KS, 21st, 1902
Tart, H.P.			55		1920	IA, 47th, 1921
Tascha, Garrett		G, 15th Ill. Cav.	72		1918 Jun 15	KS, 38th, 1919
Tasker, George W.	Pvt.	A, 47th Iowa Inf.	216	79	1893 Dec 22	IA, 20th, 1894
Tasters, Herman		E, 6th Ohio Inf.	14		1899 Apr 11	KS, 19th, 1900
Tate, Daniel	Pvt.	K, 60th U.S. Inf.	413	46	1892 May 3	IA, 19th, 1893
Tate, Geo. W.		L, 8th Penn. Inf.	293		1899 Aug 8	KS, 19th, 1900
Tate, George H.		I, 1st Ill. Cav.	364		1917 Jan 29	KS, 36th, 1917
Tate, M.V.	Pvt.	H, 33rd Iowa Inf.	33		1924 Jun 1	IA, 51st, 1925
Tate, S.T.		D, 141st Penn.	118		1911 Mar 5	KS, 31st, 1912
Tate, Thomas B.	Pvt.	D, 22nd Iowa Inf.	337		1912 Jun 30	IA, 39th, 1913
Tatman, Brazillian		G, 91st Ill.	147		1929 Feb 22	KS, 49th, 1930
Taton, Augustus F.		G, 81st Ind.	85		1917 Apr 21	KS, 37th, 1918
Tatro, C.		C, 12th Iowa Inf.	68	93	1935 Jul 27	IA, 62nd, 1936
Tatroe, D.B.S.		G, 42nd N.Y.	13	89	1918 Feb 16	NE, 43rd, 1919
Tauber, George			68		1913 May 15	KS, 33rd, 1914
Tault, H.T.			54		1923	KS, 43rd, 1924
Taut, Benjamin		H, 79th Ind. Inf.	[18?]		1901 Apr 12	KS, 21st, 1902
Taviner, Nimrod		A, 124th Ohio	129		1931 Jul 14	KS, 52nd, 1933
Tawney, Horacio		C, 100th Ohio	111		1928 Sep 17	KS, 48th, 1929
Taxton, J.T.	Pvt.	H, 26th Iowa Inf.	10		1911 Nov 5	IA, 38th, 1912
Tayer, W.H.		K, 38th Ohio	25		1914 May 5	KS, 34th, 1915
Taylor, A.E.		7th Mo.	17		1904 Jul 19	KS, 24th, 1905
Taylor, A.M.		A, 19th Iowa Inf. (at large) (dropped [dead] because of insanity)			1932	IA, 59th, 1933
Taylor, A.R.	Pvt.	A, 8th Mo. Inf.	267		1912 Nov 10	IA, 39th, 1913
Taylor, A.S.	Pvt.	G, 24th Iowa Inf.	67		1918 Jun 4	IA, 45th, 1919
Taylor, Alfred		D, 40th Ind. Inf. (died of kidney disease)	118	75	1917 Nov 5	NE, 42nd, 1918
Taylor, Andrew W.		I, 1st Vt.	11	76	1920 Aug 29	NE, 45th, 1921
Taylor, Arnold B.		B, 17th Kans.	40		1914 Aug 30	KS, 34th, 1915
Taylor, C.G.	Pvt.	D, 16th Mich. Inf.	116		1913 Oct 30	IA, 40th, 1914
Taylor, Charles		C, 8th U.S. Col.	6		1928 Nov	KS, 48th, 1929
Taylor, Charles H.		F, 15th Conn.	35		1897 Sep 8	KS, 17th, 1898
Taylor, Chas. W.	Sergt.	C, 3rd Iowa Cav.	2		1913 Jul 24	IA, 40th, 1914
Taylor, David		B, 113th Ohio 116th Ohio	464		1919 Oct	KS, 39th, 1920
Taylor, David		8th U.S. Inf.	17		1922 Sep 27	KS, 42nd, 1923
Taylor, Dorsey	Pvt.	F, 10th Iowa Inf.	22		1918 Jun 7	IA, 45th, 1919
Taylor, Edward D.		B, 31st N.J.	241		1911 Dec 15	KS, 31st, 1912
Taylor, Elliott Paddock	Pvt.	M, 4th Iowa Cav.	227, 19	98, 5 mos. & 13 days	1944 Jun 5	IA, 70th, 1944
Taylor, F.E.		A, 21st Ind. Hvy. Art.	4		1917 Mar 1	KS, 37th, 1918
Taylor, Francis M.		C, 10th Ind. (died of fever)	1	82	1920 Sep 1	NE, 45th, 1921
Taylor, Frank	Pvt.	A, 29th Wis. Inf.	101		1900 Apr 5	IA, 27th, 1901
Taylor, Fred. N.	Pvt.	B, 147th Ill.	66		1926 Aug 4	IA, 53rd, 1927
Taylor, G.W.	Pvt.	E, 77th Ill. Inf.	194		1915	IA, 42nd, 1916
Taylor, G.W.		A, 23rd Iowa	185		1919 May 12	KS, 39th, 1920
Taylor, G.W.		B, 34th Iowa	69		1926 Mar 26	KS, 46th, 1927
Taylor, Galveston		F, 148th Ill.	127		1933 May 30	KS, 53rd, 1934
Taylor, Geo.		H, 2nd Ill. Art.	182		1898 Oct 7	KS, 18th, 1899
Taylor, Geo.		A, 25th Conn.	130	75	1918 Oct 5	NE, 43rd, 1919
Taylor, Geo. R.	Pvt.	E, 65th Ind. Inf.	56		1908 Jan 9	IA, 35th, 1909
Taylor, Geo. W.	Pvt.	G, 200th Penn. Inf.	116		1930 Aug 10	IA, 57th, 1931
Taylor, Geo. W.		B, 66th Ind.	85		1922 Aug 15	KS, 42nd, 1923
Taylor, George		H, 42nd Ohio	160		1897 Jul 30	KS, 17th, 1898

*See Appendix A, B or C for roster of post names and locations.
†See Introduction for note regarding recording of death date.
539

Name	Rank	Company, Regiment or Ship	Post*	Age	Death Date†	Journal
Taylor, George		M, 9th Kans. Cav. (died at Hallowell; buried at McKee Cemetery)	200		1894 Jan 29	KS, 14th, 1895
Taylor, George P.		A, 1st Penn. Res.	171		1919 May 31	KS, 39th, 1920
Taylor, George W.		B, 36th Iowa	69		1925 Mar 26	KS, 44th, 1925
Taylor, George W.		C, 25th Iowa Inf. Illinois (died of old age)	354	80	1919 Apr 15	NE, 44th, 1920
Taylor, H.A.		C, 2nd Kans.	68		1904 Sep 21	KS, 24th, 1905
Taylor, Henry		K, 5th U.S. Art.	1		1888	KS, 8th, 1889
Taylor, Henry H.		C, 45th Ill. Inf.	88		1909 May 3	KS, 29th, 1910
Taylor, Huston L.	Col.	H, 59th Ill.	25		1906 Jul 2	KS, 26th, 1907
Taylor, Isaac A.		H, 122nd Ill. Vol. Cav.	196		1892 Nov 24	KS, 12th, 1893
Taylor, Isiah			108		1913	IA, 40th, 1914
Taylor, J.C.	Pvt.	B, 10th Iowa Vols.	12		1906 May 21	IA, 33rd, 1907
Taylor, J.G.	Pvt.	C, 9th Penn.	22		1922 Nov 23	IA, 49th, 1923
Taylor, J.H.	Pvt.	M, 4th Iowa Cav.	57		1920 Sep 4	IA, 47th, 1921
Taylor, J.H.		D, 32nd Ill. Inf. (died at Weaver, Kans.; buried at Weaver Cemetery)	131		1894 Apr 8	KS, 14th, 1895
Taylor, J.H.		G, 135th Penn.	63		1917 Feb 17	KS, 37th, 1918
Taylor, J.H.		B, 55th Ind.	57		1926 Feb 11	KS, 46th, 1927
Taylor, J.I.		A, 59th Ind. Inf.	91		1896 Mar 24	NE, 21st, 1897
Taylor, J.L.	Pvt.	E, 146th Ill.	311		1901 Apr 15	IA, 28th, 1902
Taylor, J.M.	Pvt.	H, 2nd Iowa Cav.	337		1908 May 21	IA, 35th, 1909
Taylor, J.M.		I, 11th Ill. Cav.	12		1886	KS, 6th, 1887
Taylor, J.S.	Sergt.	C, 20th Ind. Inf.	235		1928 Mar 3	IA, 55th, 1929
Taylor, Jacob		H, 53rd Ind.	185		1913 Dec 7	KS, 33rd, 1914
Taylor, James C.		B, 43rd Wis.			1929 Jan 21	NE, 53rd, 1929
Taylor, James P.	Pvt.	9th Bat. Wis. Lt. Art.	132		1902 Feb 15	IA, 28th, 1902
Taylor, Jasper		E, 18th Wis.	127		1923 Apr 16	KS, 43rd, 1924
Taylor, Jerry	Pvt.	A, 121st Ohio Vol. Inf.	466		1924 Jan 6	IA, 51st, 1925
Taylor, Jno. W.	Pvt.	L, 8th Iowa Cav.	497		1925 Aug 6	IA, 52nd, 1926
Taylor, John		F, 11th Kans.	477		1893 Feb 21	KS, 13th, 1894
Taylor, John		B, 139th Ohio Inf.	63		1900 Feb 16	KS, 20th, 1901
Taylor, John J.	Pvt.	G, 124th N.Y. Inf.	215	75	1899 Oct 8	IA, 26th, 1900
Taylor, John L.			493		1917 Oct 25	IA, 44th, 1918
Taylor, John R.		H, 33rd Ind.	1		1923 Feb 16	KS, 43rd, 1924
Taylor, John T.		G, 5th Ohio	6		1926 Dec 5	KS, 46th, 1927
Taylor, John W.	Pvt.	B, 7th Mo. Cav.	2	66	1896 Nov 21	IA, 23rd, 1897
Taylor, Jonathan		C, 150th Penn.	301		1893 Jan	KS, 13th, 1894
Taylor, Joshua		H, 11th Wis.	1		1927 Jul 3	KS, 47th, 1928
Taylor, L.D.		G, 5th Iowa Cav. (died of pneumonia)	50	69	1895 Dec 24	NE, 20th, 1896
Taylor, L.P.		34th Ill. Inf.	335		1886	KS, 6th, 1887
Taylor, L.S.	Pvt.	H, 15th Iowa Inf.	2		1914 Oct 13	IA, 41st, 1915
Taylor, Leander W.		C, 90th Ohio Inf. (nonmember)			1941 Nov 25	NE, 66th, 1942
Taylor, Levi	Pvt.	F, 85th Penn.	173		1905 Jan 17	IA, 32nd, 1906
Taylor, M.	Pvt.	C, 28th Iowa Inf.	127	66	1894 Jun 8	IA, 21st, 1895
Taylor, M.V.	Sergt.	A, 13th Iowa	206		1924 Nov 18	IA, 51st, 1925
Taylor, Matthew		F, 155th Ill. Inf.	302	90	1937 Jan 2	IA, 64th, 1938
Taylor, Moses		died of heart failure	22	78	1916 Dec 19	NE, 41st, 1917
Taylor, N.C.	Pvt.	C, 142nd Ill. Inf.	165		1911 Oct	IA, 38th, 1912
Taylor, Nelson		K, 102nd Ill.	318	68	1912	NE, 37th, 1913
Taylor, Nicholas		C, 5th Mo. Cav.	28		1922 Mar 12	KS, 42nd, 1923
Taylor, Noble		118th Ill. (died of dropsy)	288	74	1920 Jun 5	NE, 45th, 1921
Taylor, Noble D.			54		1920	NE, 45th, 1921
Taylor, O.H.		C, 2nd Neb. Cav.	11	65	1902 Apr	NE, 27th, 1903
Taylor, Orville J.	Pvt.	B, 42nd Wis. Inf. (former member)	22		1941 Nov	IA, 68th, 1942
Taylor, Ozro C.	Pvt.	L, 1st N.Y. Art.	48	42	1890 Dec 8	IA, 17th, 1891
Taylor, R.E.	Pvt.	G, 30th Iowa Inf.	440		1912 Dec 1	IA, 39th, 1913
Taylor, Robert		C, 11th Ky.	85		1906 Jan 9	KS, 26th, 1907
Taylor, Robert		178th Ohio Inf. (died of infirmities)	124		1893 Apr 2	NE, 18th, 1894
Taylor, S.		C, 27th Iowa	5		1926 Mar 11	NE, 51st, 1927
Taylor, Samuel		K, 91st Ill. Inf.	127		1900 May 5	KS, 20th, 1901
Taylor, Silas		K, 5th Ohio	85		1890	KS, 10th, 1891
Taylor, Simon			112		1906	IA, 33rd, 1907

*See Appendix A, B or C for roster of post names and locations.
†See Introduction for note regarding recording of death date.

Name	Rank	Company, Regiment or Ship	Post*	Age	Death Date†	Journal
Taylor, Stephen			80		1884	KS, 4th, 1885
Taylor, T.		G, 61st Ill. Inf.	54		1912 Feb 1	KS, 32nd, 1913
Taylor, T.A.		F, 8th Penn. Res.	11	80	1921 Oct 11	NE, 46th, 1922
Taylor, W.E.	Pvt.	M, 4th Iowa Cav.	20		1920 Jul	IA, 47th, 1921
Taylor, W.H.C.		L, 1st Tenn. Cav. (died at Gaylord, Kans.; buried at Gaylord Cemetery)	184		1894 Feb 27	KS, 14th, 1895
Taylor, William	Pvt.	D, 111th Penn. Inf.	258		1901 Feb 15	IA, 27th, 1901
Taylor, William P.		24th Ind. Bat.	185		1914 Jun 25	KS, 34th, 1915
Taylor, Wm.	Pvt.	2nd Ind. Bat.	88		1913 Jun 12	IA, 40th, 1914
Taylor, Wm.	Pvt.	10th Wis. Inf.	497		1915 Jun 24	IA, 42nd, 1916
Taylor, Wm.	Pvt.	A, 93rd Ill. Inf.	231		1914 May 8	IA, 41st, 1915
Taylor, Wm. E.		A, 11th Iowa	52		1926 Feb 1	NE, 51st, 1927
Tea, George W.		I, 19th Ohio Inf. (died at Kiowa, Kans.; buried at Riverview Cemetery)	384		1894 Sep 13	KS, 14th, 1895
Teachman, Joseph		H, 15th N.Y. (died of consumption)	90	38	1884 Mar 21	NE, 9th, 1885
Teal, Geo.	Pvt.		352		1900 Jan 9	IA, 27th, 1901
Teal, Thos.	Sergt.	T, Ill.	251		1924 Mar 6	IA, 51st, 1925
Teale, Geo. H.	Pvt.		96		1927 Nov 20	IA, 54th, 1928
Teale, Jas. E.	Pvt.	B, 12th Ill. Inf.	306		1900 Jul	IA, 27th, 1901
Teale, Thomas	Sergt.	F, 4th Ill.	251		1923 Mar 6	IA, 50th, 1924
Teas, Geo. W.	Pvt.	C, 1st Cal. Inf.	40	65	1895 Dec 25	IA, 22nd, 1896
Teas, J.B.	Pvt.	H, 1st Iowa Cav.	18		1919 Feb 6	IA, 46th, 1920
Teas, W.C.		D, 2nd Col. Cav.	68		1912 Jun 16	KS, 32nd, 1913
Teator, L.M.		B, 6th Kans. Cav.	30		1916 Feb 28	KS, 36th, 1917
Tebay, J.A.	Pvt.	C, 7th Ill. Cav.	81		1921 Aug 19	IA, 48th, 1922
Tebbe, Wm.		F, 6th Mo. Inf.	368		1887 Dec 8	KS, 7th, 1888
Tebbins, John H.		D, 1st Mo. Inf.	7		1926 Dec 12	NE, 51st, 1927
Tebo, D.G.	Pvt.	K, 24th Iowa	130		1926 Jul 10	IA, 53rd, 1927
Tebus, William	Pvt.	B, 15th Iowa Inf.	347	67	1897 Sep 20	IA, 24th, 1898
Tedford, W.H.	Corp.	F, 11th Iowa Inf.	192		1917 Jul 25	IA, 44th, 1918
Tedro, J.D.		L, 1st Iowa Cav.	40	69	1915 Oct 31	NE, 40th, 1916
Tedrone, M.K.		36th Iowa Inf.	192		1905 Jan 13	IA, 32nd, 1906
Tedrow, C.W.		A, 5th Ohio	55		1921 Apr 24	KS, 41st, 1922
Tedrow, Jacob		H, 62nd Ill.	93		1909 Mar 28	KS, 29th, 1910
Tee, R.V.		A, 56th Penn. Inf. (died of consumption)	327		1894 Dec 12	NE, 19th, 1895
Teeman, C.	Pvt.	4th Iowa Art.	271		1931 Nov 7	IA, 58th, 1932
Teemans, Fred	Pvt.	K, 4th Iowa Cav.	20		1907 Apr 7	IA, 34th, 1908
Teeple, George			16		1912 Oct 15	KS, 32nd, 1913
Teer, William		H, 98th Ohio	46		1893 Feb 27	KS, 13th, 1894
Teeter, D.	Pvt.	I, 2nd Neb. Cav.	233		1921 Dec 15	IA, 48th, 1922
Teeter, J.R.	Pvt.	M, 4th Iowa Cav.	19		1916 Feb 16	IA, 43rd, 1917
Teeter, Joseph	Corp., 2nd Lieut. & Capt.	I, 34th Ill. Inf. (see also Appendix D)	25	74	1921 Feb 28 or Mar 2	NE, 46th, 1922
Teeter, Moses J.	Pvt.	K, 1st Minn. Inf.	206		1917 Jan 12	IA, 44th, 1918
Teeter, S.P.		K, 26th Ill. Inf.	17		1929 Jan 3	KS, 49th, 1930
Teeters, Louis		A, 129th Ind.	63		1922 May 2	KS, 42nd, 1923
Teffer, J.J.			4		1893 Dec	KS, 13th, 1894
Tegtmeyer, Henry		K, 119th N.Y. Inf.	11	70	1911 Nov 8	NE, 36th, 1912
Teidt, John	Pvt.	K, 1st Ill. Art.	267	54	1893 Mar 30	IA, 20th, 1894
Telcamp, William		O, 94th Ill.	38		1927 Dec 29	KS, 47th, 1928
Teller, Ralph R.	Pvt. Lieut. Col.	A, 2nd Iowa Inf. 60th U.S.C.T.	2	64	1893 Feb	IA, 21st, 1895
Tellus, H.B.		F, 43rd Ill.	293		1906 Oct 27	KS, 26th, 1907
Telyea, Peter		H, 19th Wis. Inf.	66	87	1891 Dec 29	KS, 11th, 1892
Temple, W.B.	Pvt.	M, 9th Iowa Cav.	6		1923	IA, 50th, 1924
Temple, William H.	Pvt.	B, 52nd Mass. Inf.	267		1919 Nov 14	IA, 46th, 1920
Templeman, E.W.	Pvt.	23rd Wis. Inf.	55		1910 Oct 24	IA, 37th, 1911
Templeman, J.N.	Pvt.	G, 32nd Iowa Inf.	8	42	1890 Mar? 22	IA, 17th, 1891
Templeton, J.H.	Pvt.	E, 10th Penn. Inf.	40		1929 Mar 11	IA, 56th, 1930
Templeton, J.S.		H, 6th Vt.	25		1936 Oct 19	NE, 61st, 1937
Templeton, Thomas H.		D, 11th Minn.	125		1885	KS, 5th, 1886
Templeton, W.G.		D, 8th Iowa Cav.	7		1921 Feb 6	NE, 48th, 1924

*See Appendix A, B or C for roster of post names and locations.
†See Introduction for note regarding recording of death date.

Name	Rank	Company, Regiment or Ship	Post*	Age	Death Date†	Journal
Templin, W.D.	Lieut.	D, 32nd Iowa Inf.	67		1920 Feb 13	IA, 47th, 1921
Tenis, Annica		H, 135th Ohio Inf.	375		1901 Jul 16	KS, 21st, 1902
Tennant, A.E.	Pvt.	C, 7th Ill. Cav.	236		1926 Nov 19	IA, 53rd, 1927
Tennant, David L.		K, 14th Iowa	25		1913 Oct 15	KS, 33rd, 1914
Tennant, John		F, 6th Kans. Cav.	271		1918 Oct 5	KS, 38th, 1919
Tennant, W.S.	Pvt.	K, 14th Iowa Inf.	96		1913 Dec 23	IA, 40th, 1914
Terhufen, Henry	Pvt.	C, 9th Kans. Cav.	485		1903 Dec 23	IA, 30th, 1904
Termaine, Henry J.		4th Lt. Art. Bat. Iowa	257		1915 Sep 27	KS, 35th, 1916
Ternes, Mathias		K, 44th Ill. Inf.	142		1899 Feb 15	KS, 19th, 1900
Terrell, Chas. A.		E, 85th Ind.	64		1897 Nov 23	KS, 17th, 1898
Terrell, Mathew		E, 134th Ohio Inf.	127		1901 Jun 4	KS, 21st, 1902
Terrill, Aaron B.	Pvt.	I, 4th Mich. Cav.	190		1915 Jul 13	IA, 42nd, 1916
Terrill, Edmond		G, 3rd Ill. Cav. (died at Hutchinson)	17		1895 Jul 17	KS, 15th, 1896
Terrill, R.W.	Sergt.	F, 12th Iowa Inf.	190		1926 Oct 2	IA, 53rd, 1927
Terry, Chas. M.		K, 4th N.Y.	7		1904 Sep 18	KS, 24th, 1905
Terry, Chas. W.	Pvt.	I, 12th Ill. Cav.	96		1917 Aug 23	IA, 44th, 1918
Terry, Dennis Stevens		I, 33rd Iowa Inf.	49	90	1938 Aug 27	IA, 64th, 1938
Terry, F.M.		B, 3rd Iowa Cav.	378		1912 Jul 5	KS, 32nd, 1913
Terry, G.F.		K, 13th Ind. Cav.	435		1912 Jun 3	KS, 32nd, 1913
Terry, Jefferson		C, 83rd Ohio	36		1913 Mar 30	KS, 33rd, 1914
Terry, John M.	Lieut.	C, 166th Ohio Inf.	235		1916 Dec 24	IA, 43rd, 1917
Terry, John M.		B, 103rd Ill.	127		1927 May 14	KS, 47th, 1928
Terry, Wm. L.		C, 144th Ind. Inf.	35		1908 Jan 29	NE, 33rd, 1909
Tersey, G.W.	Pvt.	1st Wis. Hvy. Art.	124		1925 Oct 30	IA, 52nd, 1926
Terwilleger, A.B.		E, 14th Mich. Inf.	88		1921 Apr 6	KS, 41st, 1922
Terwilliger, Chas. F.		A, 1st H.E.S.C.	354	77	1914 Mar 29	NE, 40th, 1916
Tesson, Joe	Pvt.	7th Iowa Inf.	24		1921 Feb	IA, 48th, 1922
Teter, J.P.	Chaplain	F, 94th Ill. Inf.	69		1900 Feb	IA, 27th, 1901
Teter, Jonathan		G, 77th Ill. Inf. (died of consumption)	17		1899 Aug 8	KS, 19th, 1900
Teter, Wm.	Corp.	G, 7th Iowa Inf.	88	39	1885 Mar 30	NE, 10th, 1886
Tetwiler, Henry	Pvt.	B, 108th Ill. Inf.	31		1924 Dec 20	IA, 51st, 1925
Tew, V.	Pvt.	A, 73rd Ill. Inf. (died of heart failure)	23		1931 Dec 1	IA, 58th, 1932
Thaler, W.M.		B, 47th Ill.	54		1894 Jun 28	NE, 19th, 1895
Thamer, Henry		25th N.Y. Battery	154		1922 Jun 4	IA, 49th, 1923
Tharnish, Peter	Pvt.	I, 34th Iowa	35		1912 Jan 1	IA, 39th, 1913
Tharp, Albert		I, 20th Iowa Inf.	11		1930 Jun 20	NE, 55th, 1931
Tharp, James	Pvt.	I, 72nd Ill. (died of pneumonia, liver com.)	98		1903 Dec 27	IA, 30th, 1904
Tharp, L.R.		G, 20th Iowa Inf. (former member of department; location: Wahoo)	5	68	1910 May 11	NE, 35th, 1911
Tharp, Nathan D.		K, 45th Ill.	90		1938 Aug 26	NE, 63rd, 1939
Tharp, Orville R.		M, 78th Ind. Inf.	25		1911 Mar 18	KS, 31st, 1912
Tharp, Robert	Pvt.	C, 124th Ill.	359		1916 Jan 28	IA, 43rd, 1917
Thatcher, C.B.		D, 7th Iowa Cav.	[25?]		1918 Jul 18	KS, 38th, 1919
Thatcher, C.N.		G or D, 52nd Ill. Inf. (of Great Bend)	31		1925 Feb 19	IA, 52nd, 1926
Thatcher, George W.		F, 16th Kans.	52		1924 Dec 24	KS, 44th, 1925
Thatcher, I.		I, 29th Ohio Inf.	283		1910 Dec 15	KS, 30th, 1911
Thatcher, John T.	Pvt.	C, 3rd Kans. State Militia (died at Lawrence)	519		1908 Aug 6	IA, 35th, 1909
Thatcher, S.O.		I, 24th Iowa Inf.	12		1895 Aug	KS, 15th, 1896
Thayer, A.H.	Pvt.	K, 11th Mich. Inf.	30		1919 Oct 8	IA, 46th, 1920
Thayer, A.J.	Pvt.	D, 39th Ill. Inf. (died at Medicine Lodge)	247		1908 Jan 25	IA, 35th, 1909
Thayer, E.J.		K, 5th Mich.	51		1895 Jul	KS, 15th, 1896
Thayer, Election		E, 19th Ind. Inf.	81		1904 Jun 6	KS, 24th, 1905
Thayer, Enos	Pvt.	buried in Wyuka Cemetery at Lincoln (see Appendix D)	80		1910	IA, 37th, 1911
Thayer, John M.	Gen.	A, 146th N.Y. Inf.	25		1906 Mar 19	NE, 30th, 1906
Thayer, L.F.	Pvt.	B, 12th Iowa Inf.	141		1921 Dec 24	IA, 48th, 1922
Thebodo, Stephen	Pvt.	E, 8th Kans.	495		1902 Jun 16	IA, 29th, 1903
Theibaut, C.T.		D, 27th Iowa Inf.	25		1926 Mar 11	NE, 51st, 1927
Thein, Peter	Pvt.	A, 48th Ohio	44		1901 Nov 20	IA, 28th, 1902
Theis, C.P.		G, 83rd Penn.	55		1928 May 11	KS, 48th, 1929
Thenburg, Adam			182	78	1916 Mar 28	NE, 41st, 1917

*See Appendix A, B or C for roster of post names and locations.
†See Introduction for note regarding recording of death date.
542

Name	Rank	Company, Regiment or Ship	Post*	Age	Death Date†	Journal
Thewles, Wm.		A, 39th Ill. Inf.	14		1886	KS, 6th, 1887
Thoburn, T.C.		58th Ohio	89		1911 Sep 19	KS, 31st, 1912
Thom, Nathan		H, 93rd Ill. Inf.	45		1927 Apr 1	IA, 54th, 1928
Thomas, A.	Pvt.	8th Ind. Lt. Art.	197		1908 Aug 16	IA, 35th, 1909
Thomas, A.D.	Pvt.	88th Ohio Inf.	2		1922 May 30	IA, 49th, 1923
Thomas, A.N.		C, 73rd Ind. (died of pneumonia)	44	64	1904 Mar 26	NE, 29th, 1905
Thomas, A.S.		G, 49th Ohio	25		1937 Jan 2	KS, 57th, 1938
Thomas, Albert		D, 8th Iowa Inf.	89	74	1918 Jan 21	NE, 43rd, 1919
Thomas, Amos	Pvt.	K, 11th Minn. Inf.	101		1913 Apr 28	IA, 40th, 1914
Thomas, B.F.	Sergt.	G, 14th Iowa Inf.	125		1912 Jun 16	IA, 39th, 1913
Thomas, B.F.			125		1915	IA, 42nd, 1916
Thomas, B.F.		L, 12th Ind. Cav.	176		1916 Jan 5	KS, 36th, 1917
Thomas, C.	Sergt.	G, 98th Ohio Inf.	12		1909 Jun 15	IA, 36th, 1910
Thomas, Creighton		G, 113th Ohio	65		1893 Jun 1	KS, 13th, 1894
Thomas, D.F.	Corp.	B, 150th Ill. Inf.	192		1913 Aug 23	IA, 40th, 1914
Thomas, D.L.	Pvt.	H, 129th Ohio Inf.	34		1929 May 21	IA, 56th, 1930
Thomas, David	Pvt.	133rd Penn. Inf.	190		1930 Apr 16	IA, 57th, 1931
Thomas, David F.	Pvt.	B, 150th Ill. Inf.	235		1927 Sep 15	IA, 54th, 1928
Thomas, E.	Pvt.	G, 28th Wis. Inf.	216		1918 Oct 20	IA, 45th, 1919
Thomas, E.D.		D, 10th Ill. Inf.	179		1912 Mar 10	KS, 32nd, 1913
Thomas, E.W.			328		1892 Feb 3	KS, 12th, 1893
Thomas, F.M.		D, 3rd Penn.	100		1927 Dec 7	KS, 47th, 1928
Thomas, F.S., Dr.	Pvt.	A, 137th Ill. Inf.	29		1899 Aug 14	IA, 26th, 1900
Thomas, Frank		D, 7th Wis. Inf. (died of dropsy)	59		1893 Aug 5	NE, 18th, 1894
Thomas, G.K.		B, 44th Ind.	182		1891 Jun 1	KS, 11th, 1892
Thomas, G.S.		K, 99th Ind.	22		1929	NE, 55th, 1931
Thomas, Geo. D.	Pvt.	G, 4th West Va. Cav.	12		1918 Dec 20	IA, 45th, 1919
Thomas, Geo. N.		G, 10th Iowa	147		1926 Jan	KS, 46th, 1927
Thomas, George A.		I, 29th Wis.	6		1924 Jun 23	KS, 44th, 1925
Thomas, Griffith J.		C, 32nd Wis. Inf. B, 1st Wis. Art. (see also Appendix D)	60		1926 Feb 28	NE, 51st, 1927
Thomas, H.	Pvt.	I, 53rd Ill. Inf.	452	86	1933 Oct 18	IA, 60th, 1934
Thomas, H.		D, 4th Ill.	35	76	1922 Mar 23	NE, 47th, 1923
Thomas, H.W.	Pvt.	D, 3rd Colo. Inf.	12	92	1933 Jul 21	IA, 60th, 1934
Thomas, Henry Burt		E, 83rd Penn. Inf.		99	1937 Jul 18	IA, 64th, 1938
Thomas, Hugh			55		1920 Apr 1	KS, 40th, 1921
Thomas, J.	Pvt.	C, 31st Mass.	68		1921 Dec 12	IA, 48th, 1922
Thomas, J.B.		K, 25th Mo. Inf.	91		1887 Feb 2	KS, 7th, 1888
Thomas, J.C.		G, 1st Ohio Art. B, 21st Ohio Inf. (died at Ponca, O.T.)	158		1895 Dec 6	KS, 15th, 1896
Thomas, J.C.			3		1928 May 29	NE, 53rd, 1929
Thomas, J.D.		K, 25th Ohio Inf.	282		1892 Jan 3	NE, 17th, 1893
Thomas, J.F.		B, 54th Ohio	85		1933 Sep 15	KS, 53rd, 1934
Thomas, J.S.		G, 50th Ind.	257		1919 Jan 18	KS, 39th, 1920
Thomas, Jacob		I, 76th Ill.	63		1922 Dec 31	KS, 42nd, 1923
Thomas, James	Pvt.	H, 50th Wis. Inf.	215	63	1894 Oct 30	IA, 21st, 1895
Thomas, James	Pvt.	F, 6th Iowa Inf. (at large)			1933 Nov 16	IA, 60th, 1934
Thomas, James		E, 65th Ill.	118		1926 Aug 25	NE, 51st, 1927
Thomas, James H.	Pvt.	I, 32nd Iowa Inf.	236	65	1887 Nov 26	IA, 14th, 1888
Thomas, Jas. R.		G, 27th Ohio Inf. (died at Halstead; buried at Halstead Cemetery)	199		1894 Jan 27	KS, 14th, 1895
Thomas, John	Pvt.	E, 37th Wis. Inf.	324	57	1896 Jun 4	IA, 23rd, 1897
Thomas, John	Pvt.	K, 36th Iowa Inf.	40		1930 Nov 22	IA, 57th, 1931
Thomas, John		A, 86th U.S. Colored (died at Ft. Scott; buried at Ft. Scott National Cemetery)	486		1894 Jun 12	KS, 14th, 1895
Thomas, John		B, 40th Mo.	428		1910 Jun 21	KS, 30th, 1911
Thomas, John W.		A, 28th M.S. Inf. Col.[U.S. Colored Inf.]	17		1929 Jan 28	KS, 49th, 1930
Thomas, Jos.	Pvt.	B, 7th Wis. Inf.	519		1906 Jun	IA, 33rd, 1907
Thomas, Julius O.			18		1884	KS, 4th, 1885
Thomas, L.J.		L, 2nd Neb.	371		1889	KS, 9th, 1890
Thomas, Levi	Pvt.	D, 6th Iowa Inf.	122		1917 Jan 22	IA, 44th, 1918
Thomas, Lyman		E, 34th Ind. Inf.	108		1934	KS, 54th, 1935

Name	Rank	Company, Regiment or Ship	Post*	Age	Death Date†	Journal
Thomas, M.B.	Pvt.	E, 78th Mo. Inf.	292		1911 Feb 26	IA, 38th, 1912
Thomas, M.K.		K, 17th Ill. Cav.	53		1921 Apr 16	KS, 41st, 1922
Thomas, M.W.	Surg.	13th Iowa Inf.	12		1887 Oct 17	IA, 15th, 1889
Thomas, Malin		D, 26th —	98		1904 Nov 9	KS, 24th, 1905
Thomas, Martin		G, 57th Ind.	17		1893 Mar 25	KS, 13th, 1894
Thomas, O.J.	Pvt.	H, 45th Penn.	436		1914 Jun 23	IA, 41st, 1915
Thomas, Pleasant W.	Pvt.	D, 6th Cav.	122		1923 Aug 25	IA, 50th, 1924
Thomas, Richard		Mo.	10		1909 Aug 26	KS, 29th, 1910
Thomas, Robert S.		F, 40th Iowa Inf. (died in Trego County, Kans.; buried at WaKeeney Cemetery)	157		1894 Jun 8	KS, 14th, 1895
Thomas, S.C.		I, 15th Iowa (died of heart disease)	18	74	1920 Apr 1	NE, 45th, 1921
Thomas, S.E.		F, 77th Inf. (died of paralysis)	115		1910 Sep 20	NE, 35th, 1911
Thomas, S.H.			180		1923 Aug 18	KS, 43rd, 1924
Thomas, S.O.	Pvt.	D, 85th Penn. Inf.	5		1911 Feb 10	IA, 38th, 1912
Thomas, S.S.	Pvt.	F, 29th Iowa Inf.	248	66	1892 May 28	IA, 19th, 1893
Thomas, Samuel		K, 9th Ind.	126		1896 Sep 5	KS, 16th, 1897
Thomas, Samuel		2nd Wis. Inf.	[18?]		1918 Jan	KS, 38th, 1919
Thomas, Scott		B, 169th Ohio Inf.	191		1917 Apr 21	KS, 37th, 1918
Thomas, Simon A.	Pvt.	B, 86th Ohio Vol. Inf.	56		1922 Jun 22	IA, 49th, 1923
Thomas, Stephen		K, 6th Mich. (died of nervous prostration)	2	76	1897 Jan 12	NE, 22nd, 1898
Thomas, T.F.		U.S. Cav.	25		1919 Apr 2	KS, 39th, 1920
Thomas, Theo.		B, 92nd Ill. Inf.	81	91	1935 Apr 22	IA, 62nd, 1936
Thomas, Thompson	Sergt.	A, 123rd Ohio Inf.	147		1913 May 12	IA, 40th, 1914
Thomas, Timothy		E, 8th U.S. Cav. Inf. (died of insanity)	24	58	1905 Jan 22	NE, 30th, 1906
Thomas, W.H.	Pvt.	B, —	472		1919 Nov 16	IA, 46th, 1920
Thomas, W.H.		G, 14th N.Y. Art.	147		1919 Mar 31	IA, 46th, 1920
Thomas, W.S.	Pvt.	A, 16th Ill. Inf.	78		1911 May 30	IA, 38th, 1912
Thomas, W.W.	Capt.	H, 46th Iowa Inf.	192	85	1899 Feb 19	IA, 26th, 1900
Thomas, William P.		D, 10th Kans. (former member of Nebraska Dept.; location: Adams)	100		1937 Feb	NE, 62nd, 1938
Thomas, Wm.		K, 46th Ill.	44		1931 Oct	NE, 56th, 1932
Thomas, Wm. H.		A, 153rd Ohio Inf.	187	70	1895 Jan 16	NE, 20th, 1896
Thomas, Wm. M.		F, 16th Ind. Inf.	25	77	1919 Oct 20	NE, 44th, 1920
Thomas, Wm. R.	Pvt.	E, 50th Wis. Inf.	101		1925 Mar 1	IA, 52nd, 1926
Thomas, Zachariah		C, 25th Wis.	238		1913 Jan 8	KS, 33rd, 1914
Thomason, Janes		F, 4th Tenn.	311		1927	KS, 47th, 1928
Thompkins, E.C.	Pvt.	D, 5th N.Y.	22		1926 Aug 3	IA, 53rd, 1927
Thompson, A.J.	Pvt.	A, 78th Ohio Inf.	10		1927 Feb	IA, 54th, 1928
Thompson, A.J.	Pvt.	A, 78th Ohio Inf.	10		1926 Dec 20	IA, 53rd, 1927
Thompson, A.S.		E, 10th Ill.	25		1937 Nov	KS, 56th, 1937
Thompson, Abram		G, 187th N.Y.	25	89	1917 May 17	NE, 42nd, 1918
Thompson, Agustus S.		B, 112th Ill.	142		1906 Jul 1	KS, 26th, 1907
Thompson, Allen W.	Pvt.	H, 76th N.Y. Inf.	277		1910 May	IA, 37th, 1911
Thompson, Alonzo F.		A, 142nd Ill.	176		1919 Apr 18	KS, 39th, 1920
Thompson, Andrew B.		A, 102nd Ill.	142		1913 Nov 4	KS, 33rd, 1914
Thompson, Arad	Pvt.	K, 20th Maine Inf.	98		1916 Jul 22	IA, 43rd, 1917
Thompson, B.F.	Pvt.	A, 103rd Ohio Inf.	458	46	1889 Dec 27	IA, 16th, 1890
Thompson, B.F.		K, 43rd Mo. Inf.	78		1908 Nov 27	KS, 28th, 1909
Thompson, Benj. F.	Pvt.	K, 2nd Ill. Cav.	283		1901 Jul 28	IA, 28th, 1902
Thompson, Byron J.		D, 20th Wis.	240		1890	KS, 10th, 1891
Thompson, C.B.		A, 142nd Penn. Inf. (died of apoplexy)	18	68	1906 Feb 19	NE, 31st, 1907
Thompson, C.E.	Pvt.	B, 1st Iowa Inf.	233	62	1898 Mar 21	IA, 24th, 1898
Thompson, C.N.		I, 148th Ill.	42		1923 Dec 10	KS, 43rd, 1924
Thompson, C.O., see Tompson C.O.						
Thompson, C.W.		K, 8th Ill. Cav.	250		1901 Jun 23	KS, 21st, 1902
Thompson, Charles	Pvt.	D, 1st Mo. Cav.	1		1918 Jan 21	IA, 45th, 1919
Thompson, Chas. B.	Pvt.	E, 8th Iowa Inf.	49		1889 May 14	IA, 16th, 1890
Thompson, Chas. E.		A, 148th Ill.	25		1927 Feb 13	NE, 52nd, 1928
Thompson, Chas. G.		G, 11th Kans.	158		1906 Apr 28	KS, 26th, 1907
Thompson, D.B.		I, 1st Ohio Vol. Art.	4		1915 Mar 11	KS, 35th, 1916
Thompson, D.L.		E, 4th Mo. Cav. (died of pneumonia)	84	61	1895 Nov 9	NE, 20th, 1896

*See Appendix A, B or C for roster of post names and locations.
†See Introduction for note regarding recording of death date.
544

Name	Rank	Company, Regiment or Ship	Post*	Age	Death Date†	Journal
Thompson, D.M.		C, 2nd Mo.	55		1904 Jun 3	KS, 24th, 1905
Thompson, D.M.		11th Kans.	166		1906 Mar 24	KS, 26th, 1907
Thompson, D.R.	Pvt.	D, 33rd Iowa Inf.	210	67	1895 Jun 9	IA, 22nd, 1896
Thompson, D.T.		G, 75th Ind.	[51?]		1885	KS, 5th, 1886
Thompson, Daniel L.		B, 128th Ind.	46		1923 Jan 3	KS, 43rd, 1924
Thompson, David		F, 172nd Ohio	75		1911 Aug 30	KS, 31st, 1912
Thompson, David		M, 4th Iowa Cav. (died of bloody flux)	88	77	1895 Aug 12	NE, 20th, 1896
Thompson, E.A.		E, 10th Ky. Inf.	17		1914 Apr 18	KS, 34th, 1915
Thompson, E.C.	Pvt.	I, 1st Iowa Cav.	107		1909 Nov	IA, 36th, 1910
Thompson, E.O.	Pvt.	C, 47th Iowa	497		1923 Mar 16	IA, 50th, 1924
Thompson, E.T.		C, 191st Ohio	199		1923 Nov 23	KS, 46th, 1927
Thompson, Ed D.	Adjt.	2nd Kans.	12		1906 Jun 22	KS, 26th, 1907
Thompson, Edwin	Pvt.	K, 1st Wis. Hvy. Art.	47	49	1893 Oct	IA, 20th, 1894
Thompson, Enoch	Pvt.	A, 115th Ohio Inf.	497		1929 Jan 6	IA, 56th, 1930
Thompson, Eugene	Pvt.	C, 1st Wis. Cav.	154		1923 Oct 9	IA, 50th, 1924
Thompson, Ezra	Corp.	F, 170th Ohio Inf.	8		1925 Sep 4	IA, 52nd, 1926
Thompson, F.E.		E, 91st Ill. Inf.	260		1901 May 1	KS, 21st, 1902
Thompson, F.J.		H, 39th Wis.	25		1924 Jan 24	KS, 44th, 1925
Thompson, F.M.	Pvt.	L, 3rd Iowa Cav.	205	58	1889 Apr 19	IA, 16th, 1890
Thompson, F.M.		I, 6th Penn. Res. Corps	81		1933 Aug 13	NE, 58th, 1934
Thompson, G.C.		H, 1st Cav.	337		1905	IA, 32nd, 1906
Thompson, G.L.			221		1888	KS, 8th, 1889
Thompson, G.S.	Pvt.	B, 3rd Vt. Inf.	42		1928 Feb 16	IA, 55th, 1929
Thompson, G.W.	Sergt.	K, 26th Ind. Inf.	122		1910 Mar 20	IA, 37th, 1911
Thompson, Geo.	Pvt.	M, 1st Iowa Cav.	400		1924 Apr 25	IA, 51st, 1925
Thompson, Geo. W.	Sergt.	L, 4th Iowa Cav.	40	60	1895 Mar 1	IA, 21st, 1895
Thompson, Geo. W.	Corp.	E, 5th Iowa Cav.	78		1922 Sep 5	IA, 49th, 1923
Thompson, Geo. W.		C, 12th Ill.	72		1904 Oct 22	KS, 24th, 1905
Thompson, H.			7		1918 Sep 2	IA, 45th, 1919
Thompson, H.		E, 44th N.Y.	113		1907 Dec 9	NE, 32nd, 1908
Thompson, H.C.	Pvt.	K, 9th Iowa Cav.	270		1930	IA, 57th, 1931
Thompson, Harvey	Pvt.	C, 8th Iowa Cav.	19		1914 Feb 14	IA, 41st, 1915
Thompson, I.I.	Pvt.	E, 19th Mich. Inf.	101		1913 Aug 28	IA, 40th, 1914
Thompson, I.N.		A, 79th Ill. (former member of department)			1932 Jun 5	NE, 57th, 1933
Thompson, Isaac	Pvt.	102nd Ill.	57		1923 Aug 24	IA, 50th, 1924
Thompson, Isaac M.		F, 97th Ohio (died of pneumonia)	2	82	1923 May 23	NE, 48th, 1924
Thompson, J.		H, 13th Kans.	292		1895 Mar	KS, 15th, 1896
Thompson, J.B.	Pvt.	I, 2nd Iowa Cav.	342		1913 Feb 22	IA, 40th, 1914
Thompson, J.B.	Band	6th Iowa Inf.	173		1916	IA, 43rd, 1917
Thompson, J.C.	Sergt.	D, 15th Ill. Inf.	98		1906 Feb 15	IA, 33rd, 1907
Thompson, J.C.	Pvt.	5th Wis. Inf.	152		1915 Nov 11	IA, 42nd, 1916
Thompson, J.C.	Pvt.	22nd Penn.	39		1922 Dec 6	IA, 49th, 1923
Thompson, J.C.		D, 36th Ill.	239		1897 Feb 24	KS, 17th, 1898
Thompson, J.F.		F, 34th Ind.	51		1904 Oct 13	KS, 24th, 1905
Thompson, J.G.		H, 75th Ind.	203		1921 Sep 24	KS, 41st, 1922
Thompson, J.H.			299		1915 Apr 2	NE, 40th, 1916
Thompson, J.J.	Pvt.	A, 41st Penn. (died of pneumonia)	46	60	1884 Mar 16	NE, 9th, 1885
Thompson, J.J.		A, 149th Penn. (died of cancer of stomach)	84	53	1897 May 10	NE, 22nd, 1898
Thompson, J.M.	1st Lieut.	H, 36th Iowa Inf.	10		1906 Mar	IA, 33rd, 1907
Thompson, J.M.		F, 11th Ohio	108	88	1934 Jun 13	IA, 61st, 1935
Thompson, J.M.		7th Ind.	4		1923 Oct 10	KS, 43rd, 1924
Thompson, J.R.		A, 169th Penn.	85		1921 Feb 1	KS, 41st, 1922
Thompson, J.R.		C, 40th Ind.	209		1923 Apr 14	KS, 43rd, 1924
Thompson, J.S.		H, 111th Ill.	132		1911 Dec 12	KS, 31st, 1912
Thompson, J.S.		F, 55th P.T. (died of age)	18	72	1919 Apr 7	NE, 44th, 1920
Thompson, J.W.		G, 24th Ind.	27		1925 Jan 21	KS, 45th, 1926
Thompson, James			14		1905 Dec 4	KS, 25th, 1906
Thompson, James D.		C, 38th Mo. Vols.	1		1909 Dec 19	KS, 29th, 1910
Thompson, James K.P.	Musician	D, 21st Iowa (see also Appendix D)	147		1903 Jan 15	IA, 30th, 1904
Thompson, James M.		A, 28th Ill.	125		1912 Oct 8	KS, 32nd, 1913
Thompson, James R.	Lieut.	H, 111th Ohio	90		1899	NE, 24th, 1900
Thompson, James W.		G, 50th Ill.	127		1924 Jul 14	KS, 44th, 1925

*See Appendix A, B or C for roster of post names and locations.
†See Introduction for note regarding recording of death date.

Name	Rank	Company, Regiment or Ship	Post*	Age	Death Date†	Journal
Thompson, Jas. L.		I, 12th Iowa Inf.	25	72	1918 Jan 17	NE, 43rd, 1919
Thompson, Jno. B.	Pvt.	G, 12th Iowa Inf.	168	54	1893 Feb 18	IA, 19th, 1893
Thompson, Jno. B.	Pvt.	F, 9th Iowa Inf.	48	69	1898 Jul 8	IA, 25th, 1899
Thompson, Jo.	Pvt.	K, 40th Ind. Inf.	98		1910	IA, 37th, 1911
Thompson, John	Sergt.	F, 151st Ind. Inf.	68		1900 Dec 31	IA, 27th, 1901
Thompson, John	Pvt.	6, 29th Iowa Inf.	59		1905 Apr 1	IA, 32nd, 1906
Thompson, John G.		2nd Col. Cav.	318		1917 Feb 10	KS, 36th, 1917
Thompson, Jos. A.	Pvt.	F, 23rd Iowa Inf.	16		1909 Nov 20	IA, 36th, 1910
Thompson, Jos. B.	Pvt.	I, 2nd Iowa Cav.	190		1913 Feb 22	IA, 40th, 1914
Thompson, Joseph		I, 21st Ill.	158		1896 Feb 4	KS, 16th, 1897
Thompson, Joseph		H, 5th U.S. Col. Inf.	321		1915 May 5	KS, 35th, 1916
Thompson, Joseph G.	Pvt.	G, 3rd Iowa Cav.	497		1922 Sep 23	IA, 49th, 1923
Thompson, L.F.		B, 87th Ind. Inf.	52		1912 Jan 22	KS, 32nd, 1913
Thompson, L.R.	Pvt.	C, 36th Iowa Inf.	122		1919 Sep 2	IA, 46th, 1920
Thompson, Lewis		B, 17th Ill. Cav.	481		1917 May 11	KS, 37th, 1918
Thompson, Lorin		B, 26th Ill.	143		1927 Mar 8	NE, 51st, 1927
Thompson, M.V.	Pvt.	I, 146th Ill. Inf.	436		1911 Mar 12	IA, 38th, 1912
Thompson, Martin B.		D, 72nd Ind. Inf. (died at Girard; buried at Girard Cemetery)	49		1894 Apr 27	KS, 14th, 1895
Thompson, Mathew H.		D, 38th Ind.	78		1918 Jan 4	KS, 38th, 1919
Thompson, Matthew		D, 38th Ind. Inf.	78		1918 Jan 4	KS, 38th, 1919
Thompson, Michael	Pvt.	I, 15th Wis. Inf.	479		1917 Nov 27	IA, 44th, 1918
Thompson, P.	Pvt.	K, 102nd Ill.	400		1921 Jun 10	IA, 48th, 1922
Thompson, Perry		G, 12th U.S. Col.	321		1925 Oct 17	KS, 45th, 1926
Thompson, R.E.	Pvt.	I, 2nd Iowa Inf.	98		1901 Dec 3	IA, 28th, 1902
Thompson, R.L.			55		1926 Mar 27	IA, 53rd, 1927
Thompson, R.W.	Pvt.	B, 4th Ind. Cav.	98		1907 Nov 10	IA, 34th, 1908
Thompson, Robt.		C, U.S. Inf.	18		1930 Sep 29	KS, 50th, 1931
Thompson, Robt. M.	Pvt.	C, 42nd Ohio	12		1907 Jul 18	IA, 34th, 1908
Thompson, S.D.		3rd Iowa Battery	206		1911 Apr 7	IA, 38th, 1912
Thompson, S.F.		D & C, 83rd Ill.	274		1916 Dec 13	KS, 36th, 1917
Thompson, S.M.	Pvt.	D, 35th Iowa Inf.	231	68	1891 Jul 22	IA, 18th, 1892
Thompson, Sam'l	Pvt.	E, 7th Mo. Cav.	100		1911 Jun 24	IA, 38th, 1912
Thompson, Samuel	Pvt.	I, 25th Iowa Inf.	108		1917	IA, 44th, 1918
Thompson, Senaca	Pvt.	K, 8th Ill. Cav.	71		1913 Feb 25	IA, 40th, 1914
Thompson, Smith		H, 91st Ohio	244		1926 Mar 28	KS, 46th, 1927
Thompson, T.J.		H, 33rd Ind.	451		1913 Nov 6	KS, 33rd, 1914
Thompson, Thos. J.	Musician	I, 19th Ill. Inf.	67		1900 Aug 19	IA, 27th, 1901
Thompson, W.G.	Major	20th Iowa Inf.	206		1911 Apr 2	IA, 38th, 1912
Thompson, W.H.		D, 114th Ill.	183		1892	KS, 12th, 1893
Thompson, W.H.		U.S. Navy (died at National Military Home; buried at National Military Home Cemetery)	380		1894 Apr 4	KS, 14th, 1895
Thompson, W.H.		K, 25th Mo.	45		1916 Jul 15	KS, 36th, 1917
Thompson, W.L.	Sergt.	B, 1st Vols.	113		1905	IA, 32nd, 1906
Thompson, W.M.		D, 114th Ill. Inf.	183		1891 Sep 2	KS, 11th, 1892
Thompson, W.S.	Pvt.	C, 11th U.S. Inf.	153		1920 Jul 8	IA, 47th, 1921
Thompson, William	Pvt.	B, 86th U.S. Inf.	497		1928 Apr 26	IA, 55th, 1929
Thompson, William		F, 85th Ind.	259		1930 Oct 30	KS, 50th, 1931
Thompson, Wm.	Pvt.	52nd Ill. Inf.	13		1918 Jan 18	IA, 45th, 1919
Thompson, Wm.	Pvt.	E, 45th Inf.	153		1923 Mar 12	IA, 50th, 1924
Thompson, Wm.		A, 28th Iowa	99		1897 Aug 27	KS, 17th, 1898
Thompson, Wm.		K, 5th West Va.	4		1921 Feb 26	KS, 41st, 1922
Thompson, Wm. A.	Pvt.	D, 8th Iowa Inf.		87	1936 Mar 23	IA, 65th, 1939
Thompson, Wm. H.	Pvt.	I, 85th N.Y. Inf.	88		1909 Apr 15	IA, 36th, 1910
Thompson, Wm. H.		I, 83rd Ill.	19	66	1907 May 12	NE, 32nd, 1908
Thompson, Wm. H.		I, 83rd Ill.	174		1913 Mar 10	KS, 33rd, 1914
Thompson, Wm. L.	Pvt.	G, 3rd Iowa Cav.	2		1904 Jun 28	IA, 31st, 1905
Thomson, John	Pvt.	L, 7th Ill. Cav.	147		1925 Mar	IA, 52nd, 1926
Thoran, Christian	Pvt.	H, 12th Iowa Inf.	267		1904 Oct 28	IA, 31st, 1905
Thoren, Henry	Pvt.	B, 26th Ill. Inf.	311		1915 Oct 26	IA, 42nd, 1916
Thorla, Silas		22nd Ohio Lt. Art.	85		1925 Jul 27	KS, 45th, 1926

*See Appendix A, B or C for roster of post names and locations.
†See Introduction for note regarding recording of death date.

Name	Rank	Company, Regiment or Ship	Post*	Age	Death Date†	Journal
Thorn, John	Pvt.	A, 17th Penn. Cav.	348		1909 Dec	IA, 36th, 1910
Thorn, L.H.	Pvt.	D, 63rd Ohio	92		1921 Aug 10	IA, 48th, 1922
Thorn, Nathaniel G.	Pvt.	A, 49th Wis. Inf.	42	91	1940 Oct 16	IA, 67th, 1941
Thornberry, W.H.		A, 8th Kans. Cav.	92		1929 May 15	KS, 49th, 1930
Thornborg, J.T.		B, 47th Iowa Inf.	1		1908 Sep 7	KS, 28th, 1909
Thornbrue, A.		G, 9th Iowa Inf.	7		1921	IA, 48th, 1922
Thornburg, J.T.		147th Ind. Inf.	35	70	1910 Dec 13	NE, 35th, 1911
Thornburg, Marion F.		G, 11th Ohio Cav.	84		1936 Mar 31	NE, 61st, 1937
Thornburg, William	Pvt.	F, 39th Iowa Inf.	55		1914 Jun 10	IA, 41st, 1915
Thorne, B.F.		E, 30th Iowa Inf. (died of heart disease)	11	64	1906 Jun 3	NE, 31st, 1907
Thorne, Edgar	Pvt.	C, 9th West Va. Cav.	497	92	1933 Apr 14	IA, 60th, 1934
Thorne, G.A.		I, 12th Kans.	447		1912 Sep 30	KS, 32nd, 1913
Thorne, J.		D, 2nd Ill.	104		1888	KS, 8th, 1889
Thorne, J.E.	Corp.	9th N.Y. Hvy. Art.	322	56	1896 Dec 11	IA, 23rd, 1897
Thornell, L.M.		C, 40th Ind.	49		1914 Feb 7	KS, 34th, 1915
Thornhill, Asbury		D, 2nd Kans. Cav.	145		1885	KS, 5th, 1886
Thornley, Edward		C, 15th Iowa Inf. (died of old age)	303	80	1901 Oct	NE, 26th, 1902
Thornley, Hiram	Sergt.	E, 31st Iowa	519		1907 Apr 8	IA, 34th, 1908
Thornson, Ed	Pvt.	I, 15th Wis. Inf.	168		1913 Apr 5	IA, 40th, 1914
Thornton, Alex W.	Pvt.	C, 9th Tenn. Cav.	246		1912 May 16	IA, 39th, 1913
Thornton, E.F.		G, 45th Iowa	12		1924 Dec 15	KS, 44th, 1925
Thornton, E.V., see Thorton, E.V.						
Thornton, F.M.	Pvt.	F, 7th Iowa Cav.	231		1920 Aug 8	IA, 47th, 1921
Thornton, J.T.	Pvt.	B, 19th Ill. Inf.	379		1906 May 22	IA, 33rd, 1907
Thornton, J.W.		I, 15th Ohio Inf.	380		1900 Jan 22	KS, 20th, 1901
Thornton, James		G, 11th Mo. Cav.	90		1929 Sep 8	KS, 49th, 1930
Thornton, James M.		D, 7th Mo.	500		1917 Nov 19	KS, 37th, 1918
Thornton, Lyman F.		F, 17th Wis. Inf. (died of rupture)	114		1894 Dec 6	NE, 19th, 1895
Thornton, O.E.		C, 30th Iowa (died at Lawrence)	12		1895 May	KS, 15th, 1896
Thornton, Sam			235		1900-1901	IA, 27th, 1901
Thornton, Serrill	Pvt.	E, 118th N.Y. Inf.	159	87	1894 Jan 23	IA, 20th, 1894
Thornton, Stephen		B, 62nd Mo.	7		1933 Jul 22	NE, 58th, 1934
Thornton, Wm. A.	Pvt.	G, 46th Ohio Inf.	261		1899	NE, 24th, 1900
Thornton, Wm. E.		I, 24th Mich.	85		1897 Jul 3	KS, 17th, 1898
Thorp, A.A.		K, 45th Ill.	8		1912 Mar 26	KS, 32nd, 1913
Thorp, C.F.	Pvt.		159		1899	NE, 24th, 1900
Thorp, C.O.		H, 45th Ill.	25		1921 Nov 28	KS, 41st, 1922
Thorp, H.M.		G, 117th Ill.	42		1927 Jul 28	KS, 47th, 1928
Thorp, Jefferson		F, 8th Kans.	64		1927 Feb 14	KS, 47th, 1928
Thorp, R.J.		B, 123rd Ind. Inf.	85		1914 Mar 12	KS, 34th, 1915
Thorp, Robt.	Pvt.	E, 26th Ind. Inf.	359		1917 Jan 28	IA, 44th, 1918
Thorp, T.F.	Corp.	E, 116th Ind. Inf.	452		1922 Jan 17	IA, 49th, 1923
Thorp, Thomas	Pvt.	D, 23rd Iowa Inf.	192		1928 Mar 31	IA, 55th, 1929
Thorp, Thos.	Pvt.	I, 11th Iowa Inf.	231		1916	IA, 43rd, 1917
Thorp, Zeno		A, 34th Iowa	17		1909 Oct 16	KS, 29th, 1910
Thorpe, Franklin		B, 115th Ill. Inf.	362		1917 Dec 1	KS, 37th, 1918
Thorpe, Lee	Pvt.	K, 8th Iowa Inf.	255		1899	IA, 26th, 1900
Thorpe, Levi	Pvt.	A, 92nd Ill. Inf.	141		1916 Nov 18	IA, 43rd, 1917
Thorpe, Moses E.		E, 34th Iowa Inf.	500		1914 Aug 9	KS, 34th, 1915
Thorton, E.V.		C, 6th Wis.	261		1893 Aug 13	KS, 13th, 1894
Thrall, Daniel G.		C, 27th Ohio Inf.	380		1902 Jul 3	KS, 22nd, 1903
Thrasher, J.T.	Pvt.	G, 40th Iowa Inf.	7		1929 Jan 10	IA, 56th, 1930
Thrasher, Oscar B.		A, 44th Ind.	81		1913 Jun 5	KS, 33rd, 1914
Thrasher, W.C.		F, 9th Kans.	51		1917 Apr 18	KS, 37th, 1918
Threewit, W.R.		A, 1st Kans. Inf. (died of disease of lungs)	200		1890	KS, 10th, 1891
Thriefty, Frederick	Lieut.	F, 154th Ill. Inf.	56		1926 Dec 15	IA, 53rd, 1927
Thrift, D.V.	Pvt.	E, 82nd Ohio	31		1921	IA, 48th, 1922
Thrift, S.J.		I, 9th Ind. Cav.	118		1922 Mar 17	KS, 42nd, 1923
Throckmorton, A.W.		A, 1st Neb. Cav. (died of blood poison)	40	73	1918 Jul 22	NE, 43rd, 1919
Throckmorton, D.J.	Corp.	A, 115th Ill. Inf.	20		1909 Aug	IA, 36th, 1910
Throckmorton, Jno.	Sergt.	E, 34th Iowa Inf.	491		1906 Aug 7	IA, 33rd, 1907

*See Appendix A, B or C for roster of post names and locations.
†See Introduction for note regarding recording of death date.
547

Name	Rank	Company, Regiment or Ship	Post*	Age	Death Date†	Journal
Throdsnorton, Job	Capt.	F, 15th Iowa Inf.	209		1905 Feb	IA, 32nd, 1906
Throop, J.A.		C, 8th Ill. Cav.	5		1921 Sep 16	KS, 41st, 1922
Thuerer, Hen	Pvt.	I, 8th Ill. Cav.	124		1908 Sep 23	IA, 35th, 1909
Thumm, John Michael	Pvt. Pvt.	K, 73rd Ohio Inf. K, 12th Ohio Lt. Art. (at large)		94	1940 May 6	IA, 66th, 1940
Thurben, F.R.	Capt.	B, 39th Iowa Inf.	7		1924 Nov 29	IA, 51st, 1925
Thurber, Justin W.	Pvt.	D, 12th Iowa Inf.	259		1908 Dec 6	IA, 35th, 1909
Thurber, N.H.	Pvt.	B, 15th Ohio Inf.	78		1911 Feb 13	IA, 38th, 1912
Thurbey, Edward	Corp.	M, 2nd Penn. Hvy. Art.	7	48	1895 Dec 7	IA, 22nd, 1896
Thurman, Andrew		F, 15th Kans. Cav.	87		1924 Nov 30	KS, 44th, 1925
Thurman, Richard S.		E, 14th Kans. Cav.	90		1934 Jan 12	KS, 54th, 1935
Thurston, C.T.		B, 64th N.Y. Inf.	158		1912 Jul	KS, 32nd, 1913
Thurston, D.C.		C, 15th Ohio	81		1931 Apr 11	KS, 52nd, 1933
Thurston, D.C.		C, 15th Ohio	81		1931 Apr 11	KS, 51st, 1932
Thurston, L.S.	Pvt.	K, 40th Iowa Inf.	74		1924 May 28	IA, 51st, 1925
Thutcher, A.H.	Musician	G, 31st Wis.	48		1901 Apr 12	IA, 28th, 1902
Tibbetts, Chas. E.		Conn.	328		1889	KS, 9th, 1890
Tibbetts, John B.		G, 9th Kans. Cav.	72		1892 Jun 20	KS, 12th, 1893
Tibbetts, O.T., see Tibetts, O.T.						
Tibbits, Horace			43		1886	NE, 11th, 1887
Tibbitts, J.J.	Pvt.	E, 5th Kans. Cav.	122		1913 Jan 21	IA, 40th, 1914
Tibeighen, James	Pvt.	H, 10th Iowa Inf.	284		1915 Jan 4	IA, 42nd, 1916
Tibetts, O.T.		E, 16th Ind.	68		1896 Jul 17	KS, 16th, 1897
Tice, D.M.	Pvt.	C, 147th Ill. Inf.	101		1913 Feb 6	IA, 40th, 1914
Tice, John		E, 31st Iowa Inf.	17		1912 Mar	KS, 32nd, 1913
Tichenor, Joahn D.		B, 8th Iowa Inf.	1		1912 Feb 2	IA, 39th, 1913
Tichnor, Elias W.		K, 27th Ill. Inf.	110		1906 Aug 5	NE, 31st, 1907
Tidball, D.A.		H, 3rd Iowa Cav.	11	69	1907 Feb 16	NE, 32nd, 1908
Tidball, Hugh		B, G, 16th Ohio	107		1924 Sep 9	KS, 44th, 1925
Tidrick, Miller R.	Lieut.	G, 3rd Iowa Inf.	55		1914 Nov 13	IA, 41st, 1915
Tiernan, Thomas, see Turnan, Thomas						
Tiernan, Thos.	Pvt.	D, 21st Ill. Inf.	113		1919 May 6	IA, 46th, 1920
Tiernaw, James L.	Pvt.	G, 26th Iowa Inf.	58	58	1894 Nov 15	IA, 21st, 1895
Tierney, Daniel	Pvt.	B, 146th Ill.	125		1926 Nov 25	IA, 53rd, 1927
Tierney, Michael	Pvt.	E, 10th Iowa	88		1922 Feb 16	IA, 49th, 1923
Tierney, Patrick	Pvt.	B, 15th Iowa Vol. Inf.	83		1901 Jul 24	IA, 28th, 1902
Tietsort, J.W.	Pvt.	N, 10th Iowa	111		1903 Aug 25	IA, 30th, 1904
Tiffany, Cyrus A.		E, 188th Penn. Inf. (died of old age)	354	79	1919 Jun 4	NE, 44th, 1920
Tiffany, Herman		K, 14th Wis.	121		1890	KS, 10th, 1891
Tiffany, J.W.		F, 27th Mich.	130		1904 Aug 26	KS, 24th, 1905
Tiffany, N.B.		B, 138th Ill.	62		1928 Sep 30	NE, 53rd, 1929
Tiffany, Peter		B, 138th Ill.	32		1921 Apr 11	KS, 41st, 1922
Tiffeny, Cyrus		E, 188th Penn.	354		1918 Dec 10	NE, 43rd, 1919
Tiffin, J.H.		H, 133rd Ind.	293		1911 Aug 31	KS, 31st, 1912
Tigard, Simon		D, 10th West Va. (died of Bright's disease)	107	65	1909 Feb 28	NE, 33rd, 1909
Tilberry, W.M.		F, 17th Ohio	17		1926 Jun 4	KS, 46th, 1927
Tilden, Frederick Carl	Corp.	M, 11th Vt. Inf. (at large)	30	92	1939 Oct 10	IA, 66th, 1940
Tilden, George G.	C. & B.M.	H, 1st Vt. Hvy. Art.	30	50	1892 Jul 31	IA, 19th, 1893
Tilden, Josiah		B, 139th Ill.	25		1928 Aug 10	NE, 53rd, 1929
Tilgman, C.M.	Pvt.	B, 94th Ill. Inf.	431		1916 Feb 24	IA, 43rd, 1917
Tilgner, Fred		C, 24th Wis.	127		1896 Apr 28	KS, 16th, 1897
Tillatson, Francis		A, 99th Ind.	110		1896 Dec 14	KS, 16th, 1897
Tillinzhorst, C.E.		F, 7th R.I.	1		1908 Jun 5	KS, 28th, 1909
Tillman, G.W.		110th Ill.	25		1926 Jan 7	KS, 46th, 1927
Tillotson, Chas. S.	Pvt.	F, 1st Wis. Hvy. Art.	168		1902 Sep 17	IA, 29th, 1903
Tillotson, Elijah	Pvt.	18th Iowa Inf.	173		1918 May 18	IA, 45th, 1919
Tillotson, F.M.	Sergt.	E, 12th Iowa Inf.	1		1908 Mar 14	IA, 35th, 1909
Tillotson, Francis, see Tillatson, Francis						
Tilton, A.F.	Pvt.	H, 92nd Ill. Inf.	71		1922 Dec 25	IA, 49th, 1923

*See Appendix A, B or C for roster of post names and locations.
†See Introduction for note regarding recording of death date.
548

Name	Rank	Company, Regiment or Ship	Post*	Age	Death Date†	Journal
Tilton, J.H.		C, 4th Iowa	1		1904 Feb 6	KS, 24th, 1905
Tilton, John F.		G, 10th Iowa	52		1927 Oct	KS, 48th, 1929
Tilton, R.S.		F, 4th Iowa	147		1900 Jan	KS, 20th, 1901
Tilton, Samuel		B, 128th Ind. (died of kidney & liver)	62	72	1915 May 16	NE, 40th, 1916
Tilton, T.V.	Pvt.	G, 45th Iowa Inf.	40		1929 Jul 20	IA, 56th, 1930
Timans, George		D, 185th Ohio	68		1923 Dec 10	KS, 43rd, 1924
Timberlake, W.H.	Lieut.	C, 8th Maine Inf.	59		1899 Oct 2	KS, 19th, 1900
Timbers, Geo.		H, 15th Ohio	147		1921 Dec 15	KS, 41st, 1922
Timbrel, Lot	Pvt.	C, 33rd Iowa	23		1922 Dec 11	IA, 49th, 1923
Timm, Christopher		K, 39th Ill. Inf.	26		1926 Feb 26	NE, 51st, 1927
Timm, Fredrick		A, 11th Mich. Inf.	26		1926 Mar 26	NE, 51st, 1927
Timmel, F.P.		I, 1st West Va. (died of paralysis)	209	79	1922 Apr 27	NE, 47th, 1923
Timmons, Jas. F.	Pvt.	A, 27th Ohio Inf.	12		1912 Jan 8	IA, 39th, 1913
Timmons, S.F.		F, 11th Ohio	89		1931 Oct 18	KS, 51st, 1932
Timmons, S.F.		F, 11th Ohio	89		1931 Oct 18	KS, 52nd, 1933
Timson, A.A.	Wagoner	C, 44th Iowa Inf.	263		1910 Mar 21	IA, 37th, 1911
Tincher, G.M.		A, 27th Ind.	250		1920 Jun 14	KS, 40th, 1921
Tincher, James H.		E, 10th Ill. Cav.	1		1912 Apr 3	KS, 32nd, 1913
Tindall, J.	Pvt.	E, 58th Ill. Inf.	124		1925 May 10	IA, 52nd, 1926
Tindell, Geo. E.		D, 17th Ill. Cav. (died of bladder trouble)	56	71	1916 Sep 26	NE, 41st, 1917
Tingley, G.W.		A, 128th Ind. (died of general debility)	43	62	1907 Sep 13	NE, 32nd, 1908
Tinker, E.J.			92		1899 Jul 5	IA, 26th, 1900
Tinkham, C.G.	Pvt.	H, 1st Vol. Art.	124		1906 Feb 1	IA, 33rd, 1907
Tinkham, J.L.	Lieut.	D, 8th Iowa Inf.	98		1919	IA, 46th, 1920
Tinkler, David	Pvt.	F, 10th Iowa Inf.	292	71	1894 Jan 1	IA, 21st, 1895
Tinshall, E.O.		G, 2nd Neb.	84	78	1901 Mar	NE, 26th, 1902
Tinsley, T.A.	Lieut.	D, 102nd N.Y.	12		1905 Feb 11	IA, 32nd, 1906
Tinsley, T.B.		G, 32nd Ill.	158		1911 Mar 20	KS, 31st, 1912
Tipple, Jonathan		H, 25th Iowa Vol. Inf. (died of infirmities of old age)	115		1911 Aug 4	NE, 36th, 1912
Tipton, B.F.	Pvt.	A, 25th Iowa Inf.	112		1917 Sep 11	IA, 44th, 1918
Tipton, Joe		G, 59th Ind.	87		1922 Jun 10	KS, 42nd, 1923
Tipton, John E.		A, 60th Ohio Inf.	1		1900 Apr 6	KS, 20th, 1901
Tipton, R.A.		I, 133rd Ind.	180		1919 Dec 11	KS, 39th, 1920
Tipton, Winfield S.	Pvt.	F, 11th Ohio Cav.	94		1904[1903] Dec 31	IA, 30th, 1904
Titcomb, George H.		K, 9th Kans.	260		1910 Sep 8	KS, 30th, 1911
Tittsworth, H.		B, 13th N.J.	278		1920 Aug 24	KS, 40th, 1921
Titus, Chas. E.		F, 63rd Ohio	1		1920 Apr 15	KS, 40th, 1921
Titus, Elisha B.		E, 129th Ill.	257		1898 Mar 8	KS, 18th, 1899
Titus, J.M.		G, 27th Mo.	293		1910 Sep 20	KS, 30th, 1911
Titus, Joseph		A, 3rd N.T.[N.J.] Cav.	301		1901 Mar 13	KS, 21st, 1902
Titus, L.J.		I, 62nd N.Y. (died of paralysis)	111	70	1913 Dec 24	NE, 38th, 1914
Titus, Morgan	Pvt.	I, 3rd Iowa Inf.	77		1928 May	IA, 55th, 1929
Titus, W.D.	Pvt.	G, 2nd Mo. Cav.	40		1926 May 29	IA, 53rd, 1927
Tobey, E.P.	Pvt.	C, 44th Iowa Inf.	7		1927	IA, 54th, 1928
Tobey, Henry			73		1890	NE, 15th, 1891
Tobey, Samuel W.	Pvt.	B, 72nd Inf.	297		1922 Jul 4	IA, 49th, 1923
Tobias, Joseph W.		H, 27th Ind.	1		1915 Dec 18	KS, 35th, 1916
Tobias, Mailon		G, 48th Ind. Inf.	127		1916 Aug 19	KS, 36th, 1917
Tobias, Norwood		K, 12th Ind.	100		1912 Jul 7	KS, 32nd, 1913
Tobin, G.		U.S.C.T.	130		1919 Apr 23	KS, 39th, 1920
Toburen, Herman		E, 13th Kans.	100		1927 Oct 29	KS, 47th, 1928
Todd, A.G.		I, 11th Kans. Cav.	127		1901 Sep 5	KS, 21st, 1902
Todd, Benj. A.		G, 21st Ohio	293		1913 Aug 20	KS, 33rd, 1914
Todd, C.D.	Pvt.	32nd Iowa Inf.	436		1920 Nov 20	IA, 47th, 1921
Todd, Christopher	Pvt.	D, 38th Iowa Inf.	216	61	1893 Aug 13	IA, 20th, 1894
Todd, Daniel		I, 64th Ohio Vol. Inf.	32		1917 Dec 24	KS, 37th, 1918
Todd, E.C.		K, 91st N.Y.	145		1888	KS, 8th, 1889
Todd, E.C.		K, 91st N.Y. Inf.	145		1886	KS, 6th, 1887
Todd, E.C.		K, 91st N.Y.	145		1885	KS, 5th, 1886
Todd, E.C.		I, 91st N.Y.	145		1889	KS, 9th, 1890
Todd, Enoch		T, 116th Ill. Inf.	498		1930	KS, 50th, 1931

*See Appendix A, B or C for roster of post names and locations.
†See Introduction for note regarding recording of death date.

Name	Rank	Company, Regiment or Ship	Post*	Age	Death Date†	Journal
Todd, F.M.		F, 116th Ill. Inf.	74		1918 Jun 21	KS, 38th, 1919
Todd, F.P.		E, 96th Ill.	4		1915 Mar 21	KS, 35th, 1916
Todd, George		D, 140th U.S.C.T.	17		1914 Feb 12	KS, 34th, 1915
Todd, Henry W.	Pvt.	F, 2nd Iowa Cav.	452		1912 Oct 22	IA, 39th, 1913
Todd, J.E.			12		1922 Oct 29	KS, 42nd, 1923
Todd, J.W.			404		1919 Mar 7	IA, 45th, 1919
Todd, John			477		1919 Oct	KS, 39th, 1920
Todd, John D.		D, 11th Kans.	47		1922 Jan 26	KS, 42nd, 1923
Todd, John S.		H, 14th Penn. Cav.	1		1921 May 16	KS, 41st, 1922
Todd, Joseph		K, 76th Ill.	74		1910 Sep 2	KS, 30th, 1911
Todd, Luke	Pvt.	B, 42nd Wis. Inf.	168		1890 Jan	IA, 16th, 1890
Todd, Sam'l	Pvt.	D, 21st Ohio Inf.	44		1917 Jan	IA, 44th, 1918
Todd, T.S.	Pvt.	A, 185th N.Y.	88	48	1890 Jun 20	IA, 17th, 1891
Todd, Wm.	Pvt.	D, 10th Iowa	203		1924 Feb 3	IA, 51st, 1925
Toft, John	Pvt.	E, 12th Iowa Inf.	56		1928 Oct 2	IA, 55th, 1929
Tofte, George		D, 13th Kans.	93		1902 Jan	KS, 22nd, 1903
Toiland, E.		K, 59th Ill.	50		1924 Feb 25	KS, 44th, 1925
Toland, D.C.		D, 124th Ohio	129		1928 Sep 28	KS, 48th, 1929
Toland, D.C.		D, 124th Ohio	129		1928 Sep 27	KS, 50th, 1931
Toland, James			271		1912 Dec 28	IA, 40th, 1914
Toliver, G.S.	Pvt.	K, 10th Iowa Inf.	23	93	1933 Oct 24	IA, 60th, 1934
Toll, P.R.	Sergt.	I, 93rd Ill. Inf.	365		1915 Sep 3	IA, 42nd, 1916
Tolle, John		D, 84th Ill. Inf.	413		1900 Feb 4	KS, 20th, 1901
Tolles, Henry L.		C, 66th Ill.	88		1913 Feb 9	KS, 33rd, 1914
Tolliffe, G.W.		C, 14th West Va. (died at Burlingame)	35		1895 Apr	KS, 15th, 1896
Tolliver, Henry	Pvt.	U.S.C.T.	7		1926 Nov 28	IA, 53rd, 1927
Tolman, Anson	Sergt.	D, 21st Wis. Inf.	147		1918 Jun 23	IA, 45th, 1919
Tolman, Nathaniel H.		G, 2nd Ill.	92		1917 Apr 13	KS, 37th, 1918
Tomelson, E.G.		123rd Ill.	50		1920 Nov	KS, 40th, 1921
Tomkins, Wm. M.	Pvt.	F, 46th Iowa Inf.	190		1917 Oct 23	IA, 44th, 1918
Tomle, P.S.	Act. Asst. Paymaster	U.S. Navy	88	62	1898 Jul 18	IA, 25th, 1899
Tomlin, George	Pvt.	B, 22nd Iowa Inf.	8		1899 Jul 16	IA, 26th, 1900
Tomlin, Henry		D, 151st N.Y.	120	75	1910 Jul 11	NE, 35th, 1911
Tomlinson, C.C.		M, 7th Iowa	1		1923 Mar 9	KS, 43rd, 1924
Tomlinson, D.E.			55		1906 Feb 23	IA, 33rd, 1907
Tomlinson, E.C.	Pvt.	C, 52nd Ohio Inf.	249		1913	IA, 40th, 1914
Tomlinson, H. Sylvester		F, 123rd Ill. Inf.	452	90	1937 Jan 27	IA, 64th, 1938
Tomlinson, John O.		F, 8th Ind. Cav.	85		1915 Apr 7	KS, 35th, 1916
Tomlinson, R.W.	Pvt.	E, 111th N.J. Inf.	247		1917 Jan 14	IA, 44th, 1918
Tomlinson, Vincent	Lieut.	K, 32nd Iowa Inf.	329	65	1892 Feb 18	IA, 18th, 1892
Tompkins, E.	Pvt.	L, 6th Iowa Cav.	259	54	1888 Nov 29	IA, 15th, 1889
Tompkins, E.C., see Thompkins, E.C.						
Tompkins, J.S., see Stompkins, J.S.						
Tompkins, Milton			99		1883	KS, 3rd, 1884
Tompkins, Monroe		D, 68th Ky.	155		1922 Jan 15	KS, 42nd, 1923
Tompkins, W.C.	Pvt.	C, 12th Wis. Inf.	101		1921 Jun 25	IA, 48th, 1922
Tompson, C.O.		27th Iowa	155		1888	KS, 8th, 1889
Toms, A.R.		H, 4th Iowa Cav.	132		1919 Oct 17	KS, 39th, 1920
Toms, Hiram	Pvt.	G, 22nd Iowa Inf.	8		1916 Feb 25	IA, 43rd, 1917
Toms, William H.		I, 3rd West Va. Cav.	31	92	1938 Aug 21	IA, 64th, 1938
Tomson, H.B.		2nd Ohio Lt. Art. (died of paralysis)	25		1903 Sep	NE, 28th, 1904
Toner, Thomas		G, 4th Ind. Cav.	308		1900 Jul 26	KS, 20th, 1901
Tonkinson, John		A, 7th Penn. Cav. (died of paralysis)	38	65	1911 Mar 10	NE, 36th, 1912
Tonkinson, Joseph T.		I, 101st Penn. Inf.	4		1887 Feb 24	KS, 7th, 1888
Tonnehill, Wm.		E, 93rd Ind.	57		1928 Nov 19	KS, 48th, 1929
Tonont, John		G, 16th Kans.	18		1906 Apr 22	KS, 26th, 1907
Toof, Henry A.		C, 14th Ill. (died of cancer)	44	72	1915 Aug 4	NE, 40th, 1916
Toogood, T.			75		1886	NE, 11th, 1887
Tooker, —		died of old age	354		1919 Apr 19	NE, 44th, 1920
Tooker, Albert		G, 1st Wis. (died of accident)	19	60	1900 Aug 22	NE, 25th, 1901

*See Appendix A, B or C for roster of post names and locations.
†See Introduction for note regarding recording of death date.

Name	Rank	Company, Regiment or Ship	Post*	Age	Death Date†	Journal
Tooker, R.B.	Pvt.	D, 136th Penn.	31		1926 Oct 26	IA, 53rd, 1927
Toole, N.B.	Pvt.	M, Ind. Cav.	284		1918 Nov 14	IA, 45th, 1919
Tooley, H.B.	Pvt.	C, 1st Ill. Art.	414		1911 1st term	IA, 38th, 1912
Toomb, J.W.	Pvt.	E, 3rd Cav.	100		1905 Apr 20	IA, 32nd, 1906
Toombs, A.C.		H, 13th U.S. Inf.	85		1913 Oct 2	KS, 33rd, 1914
Toombs, J.P.	Pvt.	D, 45th Iowa Inf.	100		1923 Jul 10	IA, 50th, 1924
Toops, Nathan	Pvt.	G, 2nd Mo. Inf.	452		1915	IA, 42nd, 1916
Toops, W.R.		C, 7th Mo. Cav.	198		1923 Dec 7	KS, 43rd, 1924
Toot, M.		I, 98th Ill. Inf. (died of old age)	289	91	1912 Nov 19	NE, 37th, 1913
Topfer, Hermance	Pvt.	C, 37th Ill. Inf.	329		1918 Nov 15	IA, 45th, 1919
Topham, David B.		B, 5th Iowa Cav. (died of heart failure)	91	83	1917 Jul 5	NE, 42nd, 1918
Toplef, J.C.		Navy paymaster	158		1922 Nov 23	KS, 42nd, 1923
Topper, Conrad	Pvt.		329		1922 Sep 6	IA, 49th, 1923
Topping, Albert	Pvt.	H, 115th Ill. Inf.	38		1899 Nov 28	IA, 26th, 1900
Topping, E.N.	Col.	D, 110th Ill. Inf.	252		1887 Jan 13	KS, 7th, 1888
Torbitt, T.B.		F, 113th Ill. Inf. (died at Green Valley)	3		1895 Mar	KS, 15th, 1896
Torble, Fred		E, 157th N.Y. (died of rupture)	350	80	1914 Apr 24	NE, 39th, 1915
Torillott, E.T.		E, 76th Ill.	2		1923 Aug 5	KS, 43rd, 1924
Tornoff, George		I, 7th Ill. Cav. (died of bronchitis)	77		1893 Aug 23	NE, 18th, 1894
Torrance, Robert		A, 30th Mo.	7		1913 Nov 24	KS, 33rd, 1914
Torrence, Chas.	Pvt.	A, 133rd Ill. Inf.	40		1914 Jul 22	IA, 41st, 1915
Torrey, William H.		E, 22nd Wis. (died of kidney trouble)	195	76	1916 Apr 7	NE, 41st, 1917
Torrington, J.E.		C, 1st Ind. Cav.	1		1925 Dec 19	KS, 45th, 1926
Torry, C.O.	Corp.	F, 27th Iowa	190		1921 Mar 5	IA, 48th, 1922
Torry, Wm.		I, 1st Ohio Inf.	52		1918 Mar 15	KS, 38th, 1919
Torvine, Edward	Pvt.	D, 16th U.S. Inf.	68		1919 Mar 22	IA, 46th, 1920
Totten, Johnson		C, 15th Iowa Inf.	11	68	1907 Dec 31	NE, 33rd, 1909
Totten, T.B.		F, 44th Ind. Inf.	14		1914 Feb 11	KS, 34th, 1915
Totten, T.B.		F, 44th Ind. Inf.	17		1914 Feb 10	KS, 34th, 1915
Toubert, John	Pvt.	I, 28th Iowa Inf.	292		1926 Mar 30	IA, 53rd, 1927
Toulouse, J.	Pvt.	H, 25th Wis. Inf.	12		1920 Nov 9	IA, 47th, 1921
Toulouse, John	Corp.	H, 25th Wis. Inf.	101		1917 Aug	IA, 44th, 1918
Tout, J.M.		D, 8th Ind. Inf. (died of Bright's disease)	115	63	1903 Oct 20	NE, 28th, 1904
Tout, James		I, 6th Ohio Inf.	11	78	1910 Jan 8	NE, 35th, 1911
Tovera, John	Pvt.	G, 15th Iowa Inf.	40		1914 Jun 10	IA, 41st, 1915
Tower, D.A.	Pvt.	K, 23rd Iowa Inf.	154	58	1895 Oct 12	IA, 23rd, 1897
Tower, D.W.		F, 2nd Iowa Inf.	69		1st quarter 1885	IA, 11th, 1885
Tower, H.	Corp.	E, 46th Wis. Inf.	168		1900 Jan 29	IA, 27th, 1901
Tower, Silas		H, 146th Ill. Inf. (died at National Military Home; buried at Leavenworth)	19		1894 Mar 10	KS, 14th, 1895
Towers, C.J.	Drummer	H, 17th Ill.	231		1922 Aug 13	IA, 49th, 1923
Towers, Z.T.		H, 144th Ind.	461		1897 Dec 5	KS, 17th, 1898
Towle, A.S.		died of heart trouble	125		1910 Jul 8	NE, 35th, 1911
Towle, Abner C.		H, 1st Wis. Hvy. Art.	256		1936 Aug 7	NE, 62nd, 1938
Towle, E.A.	Pvt.	H, 63rd Ohio Inf.	88		1928	IA, 55th, 1929
Town, Geo. S.		E, 111th N.Y. Inf. (died of la grippe)	42		1891 Dec 25	KS, 11th, 1892
Town, Marion	Pvt.	39th —	43		1910 Oct 16	IA, 37th, 1911
Town, S.D.	Pvt.	D, 38th Iowa Inf.	216		1916 Jul 12	IA, 43rd, 1917
Towne, David		C, 46th Wis.	63		1921 May 12	KS, 41st, 1922
Towne, L.S.	Corp.	B, 1st Vt. Inf.	441		1905 Jul 25	IA, 32nd, 1906
Towner, H.F.			22		1922 Jan 22	KS, 42nd, 1923
Towner, M.D.		H, 2nd Neb. Cav.	318		1913 Apr	NE, 38th, 1914
Towner, O.W.	Pvt.	23rd N.Y. Battery	456		1914 Oct 1	IA, 41st, 1915
Towner, W.E.		G, 11th Kans. (died at Kansas City)	71		1894 Nov 27	KS, 14th, 1895
Townsend, Albert H.		A, 11th Penn. (died of paralysis)	265		1925 Oct 27	NE, 50th, 1926
Townsend, B.	Pvt.	C, 3rd Iowa Cav.	2		1912 Oct 10	IA, 39th, 1913
Townsend, C.H.	Sergt.	A, 9th Iowa Inf.	374	77	1897 Mar 25	IA, 24th, 1898
Townsend, D.B.		F, 148th Ill.	69		1922 Mar 1	KS, 42nd, 1923
Townsend, E.	Lieut.	B, 31st Iowa Inf.	222		1900-1901	IA, 27th, 1901
Townsend, F.S.			64		1907 Aug 25	IA, 34th, 1908
Townsend, George W.		D, 97th, 156th Ind.	271		1914 Aug 4	KS, 34th, 1915
Townsend, H.N.			7		1918 Aug 12	IA, 45th, 1919

Name	Rank	Company, Regiment or Ship	Post*	Age	Death Date†	Journal
Townsend, Harrison	Sergt.	E, 78th Ohio Inf.	84		1913 Nov 20	IA, 40th, 1914
Townsend, J.J.		G, 4th Kans.	1		1896 Apr 22	KS, 16th, 1897
Townsend, J.N.		K, 3rd Mich.	47		1910 Jan 17	KS, 30th, 1911
Townsend, Nat.	Pvt.	C, 22nd Iowa Cav.	16		1905 Jul 14	IA, 32nd, 1906
Townsend, P.G.		E, 9th Ill.	68		1925 Oct 6	IA, 52nd, 1926
Townsend, Sol.			3		1884	KS, 4th, 1885
Townsend, W.H.H.	Lieut.	I, 16th Wis. Inf.	94		1920 Apr 28	IA, 47th, 1921
Townsend, W.S.		F, 6th Mo. Cav.	85		1930 Feb 19	KS, 50th, 1931
Townsend, Wm. B.		F, 8th Mich. Inf. (died of consumption, exp. in service)	131			KS, 10th, 1891
Townsley, Thomas		Knapp's Independent Batt. E, Penn.	25		1933 May 16	NE, 58th, 1934
Townsley, W.A.	Pvt.	9th Ill. Cav.	68		1931 Apr 4	IA, 58th, 1932
Townsley, Wm.		A, 101st Penn. Inf. (died of tuberculosis of hip)	60	78	1920 Sep 19	NE, 45th, 1921
Toy, S.P.	Pvt.	B, 24th Iowa Inf.	110		1917 Dec 15	IA, 44th, 1918
Toy, T.D.		I, 47th Ill.	142		1926 Jun 4	KS, 46th, 1927
Toyne, George	Pvt.	E, 13th Iowa Inf.	291		1911 Jun 25	IA, 38th, 1912
Toyne, Wilson	Pvt.	D, 28th Ill. Inf.	231		1918 Jun 7	IA, 45th, 1919
Tozier, Wilbur S.	Pvt.	K, 24th Iowa Inf.	22		1916 Mar 13	IA, 43rd, 1917
Trace, James		D, 160th Ohio	105		1897	KS, 17th, 1898
Tracey, Dennis		D, 26th Ind. Inf.	74		1923 Nov 2	NE, 48th, 1924
Tracht, R.	Pvt.		110		1921 Aug 8	IA, 48th, 1922
Tracy, Adison		K, 12th Wis. (died of old age)	1	83	1924 Oct 10	NE, 49th, 1925
Tracy, Alex F.		A, 21st Mo. Inf.	40		2nd quarter 1884	IA, 11th, 1885
Tracy, David			[22]		1929	KS, 49th, 1930
Tracy, Edward		C, 5th U.S. Vols.	125		1885	KS, 5th, 1886
Tracy, G.H.		A, 14th Ill. (died of chronic diarrhea)	42	77	1919 Jul 7	NE, 44th, 1920
Tracy, G.T.		B, 10th Kans.	170		1918 Oct 19	KS, 38th, 1919
Tracy, G.W.	Pvt.	D, 1st Lt. Art.	132		1912 Sep	IA, 39th, 1913
Tracy, Geo.	Pvt.	G, 13th Wis. Inf.	16		1902 Feb 8	IA, 29th, 1903
Tracy, Ira A.	Pvt. & Sergt.	F, 3rd N.Y. Inf. (died of pneumonia)	69	41	1887 Mar	NE, 12th, 1888
Tracy, Jonathan	Pvt.	H, 81st Ohio Inf.	262		1899	NE, 24th, 1900
Tracy, T.H.		A, 8th Ill. Cav. (cause of death: heart)	109	66	1902 Jan	NE, 27th, 1903
Tracy, W.H.		H, 7th Ohio Inf.	11	73	1918 Nov 4	NE, 43rd, 1919
Trahn, John J.	Pvt.	D, 33rd Wis. Inf.	25		1912	IA, 39th, 1913
Trainer, Henry	Pvt.	C, 16th Ill. Inf.	311		1905 Dec 16	IA, 32nd, 1906
Trainer, James			38		1916	KS, 36th, 1917
Tramel, Jas. J.	Musician	D, 40th Iowa Inf.	511		1912 Jan 7	IA, 39th, 1913
Trant, Geo.		A, 9th Iowa	38		1911 Aug 7	KS, 31st, 1912
Trant, J.M.		B, 8th U.S.C.T.	292		1901 Feb 4	KS, 22nd, 1903
Trapp, Elias		F, 100th Ohio	152		1897 Jul 18	KS, 17th, 1898
Trask, Theo. P.		G, 8th Iowa (died of hemorrhage)	82	72	1917 Dec 14	NE, 42nd, 1918
Trask, Z.A.	Pvt.	F, 71st Ill. Inf.	200		1917 Jul 24	IA, 44th, 1918
Trauernicht, Peter T.					1929 Jan 10	NE, 53rd, 1929
Traul, Levi		C, 23rd Ohio Inf.	69	96	1935 Nov 6	IA, 62nd, 1936
Trautman, Geo.	Corp.	D, 28th Wis. Inf.	94		1912 Feb 8	IA, 39th, 1913
Travelpiece, James		F, 178th Penn. Inf.	1		1940 Jun 5	NE, 65th, 1941
Travelute, Andrew J.		A, 67th Ill.	9		1917 Jun 12	KS, 37th, 1918
Traver, J.A.	Pvt.	M, 9th Iowa Cav.	452		1918 Oct 16	IA, 45th, 1919
Travers, F.H.		A, 128th N.Y.	71		1914 Nov 14	KS, 34th, 1915
Travers, J.P.		Wis.	116	70	1914 Mar 11	NE, 39th, 1915
Traverse	Pvt.	F, 30th Iowa Inf.	100		1909 Sep 24	IA, 36th, 1910
Traviner, Nimrod		A, 124th Ohio	129		1931 Jul 14	KS, 51st, 1932
Travis		L, 5th Ky. Cav.	301	78	1915 Mar 5	NE, 40th, 1916
Travis, Edmond R.	Capt.	B, 48th N.Y. Inf.	267	60	1896 Feb 4	IA, 22nd, 1896
Travis, F.G.W.		M, 16th Kans. Cav.	1		1922 Mar 11	KS, 42nd, 1923
Travis, G.W.		H, 144th Ill.	81		1927 Apr 27	KS, 47th, 1928
Travis, H.M.	Capt.	I, 124th N.Y.	51		1915 Dec 4	KS, 35th, 1916
Travis, James F.		8th Iowa Cav.	235		1906 Jul 1	IA, 33rd, 1907
Travis, John H.		I, 10th Wis. Inf. (died of paralysis)	38	78	1919 Sep	NE, 44th, 1920
Travis, Vincent	Pvt.	H, 112th Penn. Inf.	452		1908 May 9	IA, 35th, 1909
Travise, Hiram		K, 80th N.Y.	47		1926 Apr 27	KS, 46th, 1927

*See Appendix A, B or C for roster of post names and locations.
†See Introduction for note regarding recording of death date.

Name	Rank	Company, Regiment or Ship	Post*	Age	Death Date†	Journal
Traylor, Geo. M.		K, 8th Ill. Cav.	28		1921	KS, 41st, 1922
Traynor, Andrew		D, 1st Mich. Cav. (see also Appendix D)	110	78	1920 Jul 6	NE, 45th, 1921
Treadway, F.B.		F, 155th Ill.	311		1912 Feb 28	KS, 32nd, 1913
Treadwell, Chas.		Ill. (died of runaway accident)	35	61	1907 June 5	NE, 32nd, 1908
Treadwell, T.P.	Pvt.	C, 74th Ill. Cav.	22		1911 Sep 10	IA, 38th, 1912
Treat, John		A, 16th Mo. Cav.	54		1913 Jun 4	KS, 33rd, 1914
Treavitt, C.S.	1st Lieut.	D, 37th N.Y. Inf. (died of miasmatic)	214	79	1903 Jan	NE, 28th, 1904
Treble, Wilhelm	Pvt.	B, 46th Ill. Inf.	24		1917 May 22	IA, 44th, 1918
Treeburg, N.	Pvt.	G, 2nd N.Y. Inf.	3		1920 Mar 23	IA, 47th, 1921
Treffer, G.E.		Wis.	58		1902 Oct 5	KS, 22nd, 1903
Trefren, G.F.		B, 186th Ohio	40	68	1915 Nov 20	NE, 40th, 1916
Tregloon, G.W.	Pvt.	I, 1st Mo. Cav.	44		1925 Aug 14	IA, 52nd, 1926
Trego, A.J.	Pvt.	I, 7th Iowa Cav.	452		1918 Nov 1	IA, 45th, 1919
Trego, Jesse		K, 17th Ind.	1		1920 Dec 16	KS, 40th, 1921
Treibble, Frank		F, 7th Ill. Cav.	1		1894 Jun 11	KS, 15th, 1896
Trenany, James		B, 53rd Ill.	123		1917 Jun 27	KS, 37th, 1918
Trent, A.I.		C, 23rd Iowa	412		1912 Mar	KS, 33rd, 1914
Trent, E.M.	Pvt.	I, 9th Iowa Inf.	7		1930 Aug 31	IA, 57th, 1931
Trent, J.M.	Pvt.	42nd Mo. Inf.	325		1917 Sep 1	IA, 44th, 1918
Trent, James R.		B, 59th Ind. Inf.	428		1912 Dec 18	KS, 32nd, 1913
Trent, T.A.	Pvt.		173		1926 Apr 16	IA, 53rd, 1927
Tressler, J.E.		H, 133rd Penn.	89		1931 Jul 14	KS, 52nd, 1933
Tressler, J.E.		H, 133rd Penn.	89		1931 Jul 14	KS, 51st, 1932
Trester, M.L.		C, 134th Ind. Inf. (cause of death: heart)	25	62	1903 Nov 16	NE, 28th, 1904
Trewin, Richard	Pvt.	2nd Penn. Battery	74		1907 Nov 9	IA, 34th, 1908
Trezise, John		F, 21st Penn. Cav.	71		1913 Jan 6	KS, 32nd, 1913
Trezise, John		F, 21st Penn. Cav.	71		1913 Jan 16	KS, 33rd, 1914
Trible, E.J.		F, 123rd Ill.	4		1930 Jun 16	KS, 50th, 1931
Trice, John S.		Ohio	1		1908 Jan 3	KS, 28th, 1909
Trickey, George M.		E, 76th Ill.	198		1914 Mar 7	KS, 34th, 1915
Triem, Peter		K, 8th Ill. Cav.	25	86	1921 Sep 6	NE, 46th, 1922
Trigg, J.S.	Pvt.	E, 10th Minn. Vols.	12		1906 Jun 6	IA, 33rd, 1907
Trimble, Albert M.		K, 93rd Ill. Inf. (see also Appendix D)	25	81	1921 Mar 11	NE, 46th, 1922
Trimble, Jasper	Pvt.	A, 19th Iowa Inf.	516		1926 Apr 4	IA, 53rd, 1927
Trimble, Jasper	Pvt.	A, 19th Iowa Inf.	516		1925 Apr 4	IA, 52nd, 1926
Trinetts, P.	Pvt.	K, 173rd Penn. Inf.	329	57	1896 Nov 8	IA, 23rd, 1897
Triplett, Eli		D, 7th Kans. Cav.	118		1929 Jul 26	NE, 54th, 1930
Triplett, T.M.		B, 39th Ill.	25		1931 Sep 30	NE, 56th, 1932
Triplett, Wm. H.		G, 86th Ill.	201		1921 Apr 10	KS, 41st, 1922
Tripp, Jonathan R.		K, 114th Ohio			1913 Sep 24	KS, 33rd, 1914
Tripp, R.O.	Pvt.	H, 15th Ill. Inf.	476		1899 Mar 22	IA, 26th, 1900
Tripp, Ralph E.	Pvt.	A, 31st Iowa Inf.	206		1925 May 31	IA, 52nd, 1926
Tripp, Stephen		K, 11th Penn.	18		1926 Jan	KS, 46th, 1927
Tritt, John B.		Penn.	57		1925 Dec 2	KS, 45th, 1926
Trivilpiece, Wm.		B, 2nd Penn. Hvy. Art.	113		1913 Jan 27	NE, 38th, 1914
Trobert, George	Pvt.	E, 2nd Iowa Cav.	1		1915 Aug 16	KS, 35th, 1916
Trobridge, L.	Pvt.	13th Wis. Art.	12		1921 Jun 16	IA, 48th, 1922
Trodner, Geo.		D, 2nd Ohio	71		1923 Jun 6	KS, 43rd, 1924
Trogdon, Solomon Clinton		H, 8th Iowa Cav.	192	94	1937 Jan 29	IA, 64th, 1938
Trollope, Wesley		H, 117th Ill. Inf. (died of old age)	41	79	1908 Jul 10	NE, 33rd, 1909
Tromblie, Julius		G, 8th Wis. (died of cancer of liver)	35	72	1915 Nov 30	NE, 40th, 1916
Trombly, Jos.			371		1904 Dec	IA, 31st, 1905
Troop, Robt.		E, 20th Iowa	45		1930 Dec 14	NE, 55th, 1931
Trostle, Isaac B.		A, 20th Penn. Cav. G, 133rd Penn. Inf. E, 7th Penn. Bat.	250		1925 Apr 11	KS, 45th, 1926
Trot, James	Pvt.	K, 24th Ohio (died of typhoid fever)	58	50	1884 Mar	NE, 9th, 1885
Trotel, John F.	Pvt.	G, 3rd Md. Inf. (died of disease of stomach)	96	40	1888 Sep	NE, 13th, 1889
Trotler, H.B.	Capt.	F, 11th Iowa Inf.	66		1917	IA, 44th, 1918
Trott, C.H.	A.A.G.	7th Iowa	132		1916 Mar 2	KS, 36th, 1917
Trott, Geo. F.		44th Mass.	132		1921 Jun 17	KS, 41st, 1922

Name	Rank	Company, Regiment or Ship	Post*	Age	Death Date†	Journal
Trotter, B.N.		C, 116th Ind.	190		1927 Jul 11	KS, 47th, 1928
Trotter, John		91st Ohio (location: Nebraska City)			1927 Jun 25	NE, 52nd, 1928
Trotter, Jonas B.		L, 13th Ind. Art.	59		1923 Jul 9	KS, 43rd, 1924
Trotter, M.L.		B, 2nd Ind. Cav.	81		1918 Apr 13	KS, 38th, 1919
Trotter, Robert		D, 10th N.Y. Cav.	241		1916 Sep 7	KS, 36th, 1917
Trout, A.W.	Pvt.	H, 70th Ill. Inf.	26		1925 Jan 8	IA, 52nd, 1926
Trout, Abraham		E, 90th Ohio Inf.	11	74	1914 Apr 27	NE, 39th, 1915
Trout, E.A.	Pvt.	A, 76th Penn. Inf.	170	85	1933 Apr 26	IA, 60th, 1934
Trout, H.C.	Sergt.	G, 11th Penn. Inf.	7		1918 Mar 1	IA, 45th, 1919
Trout, John W.		D, 7th Iowa Cav.	49		1915 Nov 24	KS, 35th, 1916
Trout, W.M.	Pvt.	A, 9th Iowa Inf.	74		1906 Sep 8	IA, 33rd, 1907
Troutner, J.F.	Pvt.	K, 3rd Iowa Inf.	132		1929 Jun 27	IA, 56th, 1930
Trow, William S.		A, 2nd Colo. Cav. (died of old age)	206		1917 Sep 26	NE, 42nd, 1918
Trowbridge, J.D.	Corp.	K, 19th Iowa Inf.	20		1908	IA, 35th, 1909
Trowbridge, J.F.		M, 1st Ill. Lt. Art.	463		1922	KS, 42nd, 1923
Trowbridge, James F.		M, 1st Ill.	463		1916 May 30	KS, 36th, 1917
Trowbridge, L., see Trobridge, L.						
Trowbridge, Leander M.		F, 6th West Va. Inf.	88		1909 Apr 18	KS, 29th, 1910
Trowbridge, W.H.	Pvt.	D, 12th Iowa Inf.	7		1929 Apr 5	IA, 56th, 1930
Trowbridge, Wm.	Pvt.	C, 32nd Iowa Inf.	44		1919 Oct 25	IA, 46th, 1920
Troxel, M.E.		H, 153rd Penn.	23	90	1934 Jun 27	IA, 61st, 1935
Troxell, W.D.	Pvt.	H, 36th Iowa Inf.	497		1916 Dec 29	IA, 44th, 1918
Troy, S.S.	Capt.	H, 4th Iowa Cav.	68		1908 Nov 11	IA, 35th, 1909
Troyer, W.	Pvt.	A, 112th Ill. Inf.	107		1899	NE, 24th, 1900
Tru eib, Henry		H, 4th Mo. Cav.	93		1893 Jul 28	KS, 13th, 1894
Truair, H.A.		L, 16th Ill. Cav.	68		1915 May 3	IA, 42nd, 1916
Truax, F.M.		E, 14th Mo.	17		1918 Jul 13	KS, 38th, 1919
Truax, John		D, 25th Mo. Inf. (cause of death: heart)	25	60	1891[1901?] Oct	NE, 26th, 1902
Truax, John H.	Sergt.	F, 1st Wis. Cav.	297		1928 Jan	IA, 55th, 1929
Truax, Louis	Pvt.	E, —	79		1912 Oct 23	IA, 39th, 1913
Truby, Wm.	Pvt.	D, 86th Ill. Inf.	124		1916	IA, 43rd, 1917
Trude, Geo. W.	Pvt.	I, 8th Wis. Inf.	12		1915 May 29	IA, 42nd, 1916
True, L.C.	Col.	E, 62nd Ill.	28		1918 Feb 8	KS, 38th, 1919
True, R.S.		B, 44th Wis.	132		1926 Mar 26	KS, 46th, 1927
Trueblood, A.L.		G, 13th Ind.	93		1904 Apr 19	KS, 24th, 1905
Trueblood, H.S.		K, 14th Ind.	185		1927 Jul 9	KS, 47th, 1928
Truell, Ferd A.		F, 12th Wis.	25		1928 May 25	NE, 53rd, 1929
Truesdale, C.M., see Trusdale, C.M.						
Truesdale, James		1st Line Cav.	144		1st quarter 1885	IA, 11th, 1885
Truesdel, John	Sailor	U.S. Navy	11		1928	IA, 55th, 1929
Truesdell, Andrew J.		K, 14th Minn.	172		1913 Feb 3	KS, 32nd, 1913
Truesdell, James P.	Pvt.	B, 47th Wis. Inf.	170		1901 Apr 9	IA, 28th, 1902
Truesdell, M.V.B.	Pvt.	H, 95th Ill. Inf.	452		1920 May 23	IA, 47th, 1921
Truesdell, Richard R., see Tuesdell, Richard R.						
Truitt, Jesse	Sergt.	H, 23rd Iowa	55		1903 Dec 9	IA, 30th, 1904
Truman, A.B.		C, 15th Ill. Inf.	63		1914 Jul 6	KS, 34th, 1915
Trumble, Abner W.		D, 2nd Neb. Cav. (died of heart failure)	55	82	1912 Sep 4	NE, 37th, 1913
Trumble, John E.		K, 114th Ill.	459		1913 Nov 9	KS, 33rd, 1914
Trumble, Wm.	Sergt.	C, 29th Wis. Inf.	38		1899	NE, 24th, 1900
Trumbull, A.S.			45		1883	KS, 3rd, 1884
Trump, D.W.	Pvt.	A, 15th Iowa Inf.	74	48	1892 Mar 15	IA, 18th, 1892
Trundy, J.H.	Pvt.	E, 6th Maine Inf.	8	47	1888 Aug 27	IA, 15th, 1889
Trunmell, J.J.		A, 71st Ill.	119		1906 Dec 25	KS, 26th, 1907
Trunnell, Thomas D.	Pvt.	B, 18th Mo. Inf.	186		1919 Apr 28	IA, 46th, 1920
Trusdale, C.M.		B, 117th Penn.	35		1908[1909?] Mar 3	KS, 29th, 1910
Trusdell, J.P.	Pvt.	H, 15th Iowa Inf.	163		1901 Mar 23	IA, 27th, 1901
Trusley, Chas.		C, 61st Ill. Inf. (died of Bright's disease)	13	68	1913 Jan 17	NE, 38th, 1914
Trussler, Edward J.	Pvt. & Capt.	6th N.Y. Ind. Bat.	254		1901 Sep 11	IA, 28th, 1902
Trusty, J.S.M.	Pvt.	I, 32nd Iowa Inf.	236		1900 Jul	IA, 27th, 1901

*See Appendix A, B or C for roster of post names and locations.
†See Introduction for note regarding recording of death date.

Name	Rank	Company, Regiment or Ship	Post*	Age	Death Date†	Journal
Tryon, G.H.	Pvt.	I, 47th Iowa Inf.	23	46	1894 Nov 17	IA, 21st, 1895
Tschudy, J.B., see Tscudy, J.B.						
Tscudy, J.B.		G, 2nd Minn. Inf. (died of cancer in throat)	9		1894 Dec 4	NE, 19th, 1895
Tubbs, Freeland G.		A, 5th Iowa Inf.	74		1904 Feb 19	IA, 30th, 1904
Tubbs, S.P.		C, 23rd Mich.	50		1896 Dec 5	KS, 16th, 1897
Tucker, Andrew			464		1899	KS, 19th, 1900
Tucker, Charles H.		I, 24th Iowa	65		1910 Dec 1	KS, 30th, 1911
Tucker, D.		D, 85th & 33rd Ind.	4		1918 Apr 13	KS, 38th, 1919
Tucker, David		D, 7th Ill. (died of dropsy)	180	72	1911 May	NE, 36th, 1912
Tucker, Eli		D, 44th Mass.	75		1920 Jun 7	KS, 40th, 1921
Tucker, George B.		A, 33rd Mass. Inf. I, 44th Mass. Inf.	242		1891 Jun 13	KS, 11th, 1892
Tucker, George E.		E, 1st Ind. Cav.	14		1910 Jan 16	KS, 30th, 1911
Tucker, Henry C.		A, 161st Ohio	262		1897 May 27	KS, 17th, 1898
Tucker, Isaac		died of consumption	79		1891 May 9	NE, 16th, 1892
Tucker, J.H.		C, 1st Neb. Inf. (died of pneumonia)	1	75	1919 Aug 9	NE, 44th, 1920
Tucker, J.S.		C, 9th Maine Inf.	255		1925 Nov 9	KS, 45th, 1926
Tucker, J.W.	Lieut. Col.	80th Ind. Inf. (died of general debility)	208	69	1901 Sep	NE, 26th, 1902
Tucker, James P.		E, 39th Iowa Inf. (died at Soldiers & Sailors Home, Grand Island; buried at Kearney, Neb.)	30	74	1905 Dec 28	NE, 30th, 1906
Tucker, James W.		C, 134th Ind.	1		1911 Mar 28	KS, 31st, 1912
Tucker, Jas.	Pvt.	B, 31st Wis. Cav.	168		1889 Dec 4	IA, 16th, 1890
Tucker, John	Pvt.	F, 1st Neb.	22		1926 Oct 26	IA, 53rd, 1927
Tucker, Leander O.		K, 33rd Iowa	295		1915 Jul 16	KS, 35th, 1916
Tucker, Nathaniel		B, 126th Ill.	114		1898 Dec 18	KS, 18th, 1899
Tucker, Pearley		I, 15th Vt. Inf. (died at Omaha, Neb.)	71		1895 Mar 29	KS, 15th, 1896
Tucker, Preston	Pvt.	K, 4th Ohio Cav.	461		1900 Oct 17	IA, 27th, 1901
Tucker, R.		F, 16th Mo. Cav. (died of old age)	35	75	1920 Jan 23	NE, 45th, 1921
Tucker, R.E.	Sergt.	G, 76th N.Y. Inf.	34	48	1890 Jun 3	IA, 17th, 1891
Tucker, R.H.		H, 26th Ill.	17		1918 Sep 15	KS, 38th, 1919
Tucker, Richard		2nd Ohio Bat.	293		1921 Nov 17	KS, 41st, 1922
Tucker, Samuel	Asst. Surg.	2nd Wis. Inf.	372	75	1887 Mar 10	IA, 14th, 1888
Tucker, W.E.	Pvt.	I, 2nd Iowa Cav.	42		1906 Sep 19	IA, 33rd, 1907
Tucker, William		E, 10th —	443		1897 Mar 17	KS, 17th, 1898
Tucker, Wm.		E, 10th Ill.	443		1889	KS, 9th, 1890
Tueling, William	Pvt.	E, 5th Iowa Cav.	70		1897-1898	IA, 24th, 1898
Tuesdell, Richard R.		H, 3rd N.Y. Art.	14		1909 Feb 7	KS, 29th, 1910
Tufrie, Francis	Pvt.	H, 13th Iowa Inf.	94	91	1931 May	IA, 58th, 1932
Tufts, Winfield		I, 27th N.Y.	113		1917 Mar 4	KS, 37th, 1918
Tuggle, A.P.		A, 20th Mo. State Militia	85		1925 Apr 20	KS, 45th, 1926
Tuley, L.W.	Lieut. Col.	44th Ohio Inf.	29		1928 Mar 9	IA, 55th, 1929
Tull, Alonzo	Pvt.	B, 19th Ill. Inf.	297		1905 Mar 3	IA, 32nd, 1906
Tull, M.L.		B, 99th Ill.	87		1918 Jan 18	KS, 38th, 1919
Tulley, Thomas		K, 20th Ohio	44		1913 May 23	KS, 33rd, 1914
Tullis, Henry C.		A, 132nd Ill.	25		1927 Dec 30	NE, 52nd, 1928
Tullis, J.S.	Pvt.	A, 39th Iowa Inf.	14	59	1887 Dec 8	IA, 14th, 1888
Tullis, J.W.	Pvt.	G, 34th Iowa Inf.	18		1918 Nov 24	IA, 45th, 1919
Tullis, John H.		A, 12th Kans. Inf.	160		1916 Sep 13	KS, 36th, 1917
Tullis, R.D.M.		D, 174th Ohio	23		1897 Jan 26	KS, 17th, 1898
Tullis, Thos. S.	Pvt.	C, 5th Kans. Cav.	410		1912 Oct 20	IA, 39th, 1913
Tullis, Wm.			91		1911 1st term	IA, 38th, 1912
Tullis, Wm.			91		1911 2nd term	IA, 38th, 1912
Tullis, Wm.			91		1912	IA, 39th, 1913
Tuman, David M.		F, 29th Wis.	311		1924 Oct 16	KS, 44th, 1925
Tumbleson, J.K.	Pvt.	A, 92nd Ill. Inf.	252		1897 Feb 12	IA, 23rd, 1897
Tumbulson, F.M.		H, 75th Ind.	252		1900 Oct 13	KS, 20th, 1901
Tumey, Patrick		formerly member of Ransom Post 198, Oberlin	198		1892 Aug	KS, 12th, 1893
Tunison, B.		H, 1st Neb. Inf. (died of paralysis)	55	59	1903 Nov 15	NE, 28th, 1904
Tunks, Alfred		G, 147th Ill.	23		1928 May 1	NE, 53rd, 1929
Tunnell, I.B.		F, 122nd Ill.	87		1926 Dec 10	KS, 46th, 1927

*See Appendix A, B or C for roster of post names and locations.
†See Introduction for note regarding recording of death date.

Name	Rank	Company, Regiment or Ship	Post*	Age	Death Date†	Journal
Tupper, Thos. J.	Pvt.	K, 1st Iowa Cav.	147		1913 Apr 24	IA, 40th, 1914
Tupper, W.H.	Pvt.	K, 17th Wis. Inf.	132	53	1895 Oct 16	IA, 22nd, 1896
Turbett, T.B.	Pvt.	E, 142nd Ill.	142		1922 Oct 8	IA, 49th, 1923
Turbush, Charles		F, 126th N.Y.	265		1915 May 12	KS, 35th, 1916
Turbush, Geo.		K, 8th Vt.	83		1918	KS, 38th, 1919
Turbut, Geo. A.	Pvt.	H, 64th Ohio Inf.	7		1910 May 2	IA, 37th, 1911
Turgon, John	Pvt.	D, 8th Iowa Cav.	153		1911 Oct 19	IA, 38th, 1912
Turk, Andes	Pvt.	E, 4th Iowa Cav.	16		1907 Nov 29	IA, 34th, 1908
Turk, Jason		H, 15th O.B. Ohio	92		1909 Dec 24	KS, 29th, 1910
Turk, Lewis H.			29		1894	NE, 19th, 1895
Turnan, Thomas	Pvt.	D, 21st Ill. Inf.	113		1919 May 22	IA, 46th, 1920
Turnbull, T.	Pvt.	E, 74th Ill. Inf.	42		1910 Mar 16	IA, 37th, 1911
Turner, A.		3rd Iowa Battery	175		1897 Aug 19	KS, 17th, 1898
Turner, A.P.	Pvt.	A, 12th Ill. Inf.	1		1929 Apr 23	IA, 56th, 1930
Turner, Allen M.		B, 187th Ohio	18		1909 Sep 18	KS, 29th, 1910
Turner, Andrew		I, 133rd Ill.	49		1923 Jun 2	KS, 43rd, 1924
Turner, Asa		H, 8th Iowa Inf.	305		1923 Sep 2	IA, 50th, 1924
Turner, Asa		8th Iowa Inf.	305		1922 Sep	IA, 49th, 1923
Turner, B.F.		C, 133rd Ill. Inf. (died of hardening of arteries)	11		1919 Jun 1	NE, 44th, 1920
Turner, B.H.	Pvt.	B, 6th Mich. Cav. (died of neuralgia of bowels)	18	46	1884 Apr 13	NE, 9th, 1885
Turner, Burton		F, 146th Ind. Inf.	290		1900 Dec 1	KS, 20th, 1901
Turner, C.H.	Pvt.	I, 16th Iowa Inf.	165		1923 Oct 6	IA, 50th, 1924
Turner, Chris		96th Ill. Inf. (died of fever)	3	73	1905 Dec	NE, 30th, 1906
Turner, David		E, 118th Ill.	52		1914 Jan 28	KS, 34th, 1915
Turner, Dennis		H, 133rd Ind.	83		1917 Apr 25	KS, 37th, 1918
Turner, E.B.		A, 119th Ill. Inf.	59		1887 Nov 10	KS, 7th, 1888
Turner, E.F.	Pvt.	K, 139th Ill. Inf.	456		1915 Jan 27	IA, 42nd, 1916
Turner, E.J.		D, 118th Ohio	255		1914 Jun 9	KS, 34th, 1915
Turner, E.M.		F, 66th Ohio	493		1924 Nov 1	KS, 44th, 1925
Turner, E.R.		14th Ohio	265		1898 Apr 3	KS, 18th, 1899
Turner, F.W.		I, 21st Wis.	76		1925 Apr 20	KS, 45th, 1926
Turner, Free			15		1907 2nd term	IA, 34th, 1908
Turner, G.C.	Pvt.	I, 16th Iowa	165		1921 Dec 20	IA, 48th, 1922
Turner, G.W.	Corp.	61st Penn. Vol. Inf.	108		1924 Jul 14	IA, 51st, 1925
Turner, Geo. A.	Lieut.	51st Ill.	94		1921 Apr 27	IA, 48th, 1922
Turner, Geo. F.	Pvt.	23rd Independent Bat. N.Y. Lt. Art.		91	1935 Oct 28	IA, 65th, 1939
Turner, Henry H.		H, 27th Iowa	60		1934 Aug 14	NE, 59th, 1935
Turner, Hercules	Pvt.	G, 3rd Iowa	57		1923 Jan 10	IA, 50th, 1924
Turner, J.B.		D, 27th Ohio	71		1931 Apr 17	KS, 52nd, 1933
Turner, J.B.		D, 27th Ohio	71		1931 Apr 17	KS, 51st, 1932
Turner, J.D.	Pvt.		96		1927 Jul 11	IA, 54th, 1928
Turner, J.J.		K, 116th Ind. (died of consumption)	24	54	1897 Dec 5	NE, 22nd, 1898
Turner, J.M.		K, 22nd Ohio Inf.	12		1916 Apr 4	KS, 36th, 1917
Turner, J.P.	Sergt.	C, 15th Penn. Cav.	27		1916 Jun 15	IA, 43rd, 1917
Turner, J.R.		G, 125th Ill. Inf. (died at Wichita; buried at Maple Grove Cemetery)	25		1894 May 15	KS, 14th, 1895
Turner, J.S.		A, 211th Penn. (died of blood poison)	169	77	1922 Oct 7	NE, 47th, 1923
Turner, J.W.		G, 1st Ky. Cav.	185		1892 Sep 17	KS, 12th, 1893
Turner, James	Pvt.	E, 13th Iowa Inf.	6		1901 Sep 7	IA, 28th, 1902
Turner, James C.	Pvt.	A, 22nd Ohio Inf.	12		1913 Jan 12	IA, 40th, 1914
Turner, James R.		F, 17th Ill. Inf.	142		1891 Nov 18	KS, 11th, 1892
Turner, Jas.		H, 37th Ill. Inf.	1		1885	KS, 5th, 1886
Turner, Jno. A.		B, 145th Ind.	464		1904 May 21	KS, 24th, 1905
Turner, John	Pvt.	G, 11th Ill. Cav.	35		1913 Sep 18	IA, 40th, 1914
Turner, John	Pvt.	N.Y. Eng.	495		1915	IA, 42nd, 1916
Turner, John	Pvt.	B, 151st Ill. Inf.	186		1930	IA, 57th, 1931
Turner, John H.	Pvt.	G, 148th Ill. Inf.	324		1925 Oct 9	IA, 52nd, 1926
Turner, Lafayette	Pvt.	4th V.R.C.	165		2nd quarter 1885	IA, 12th, 1886
Turner, Lyman	Pvt.	K, Penn.	133		1905 Dec 17	IA, 32nd, 1906

*See Appendix A, B or C for roster of post names and locations.
†See Introduction for note regarding recording of death date.

556

Name	Rank	Company, Regiment or Ship	Post*	Age	Death Date†	Journal
Turner, M.K.		K, 170th Ohio National Guard (died of heart failure)	9		1902 May	NE, 27th, 1903
Turner, Martin		E, 5th Tenn.	4		1911 Jul 21	KS, 31st, 1912
Turner, Michael	Corp.	H, 7th Iowa Cav.	68		1910 Jun 2	IA, 37th, 1911
Turner, Moses	Pvt.	G, 17th Wis. Inf.	329	74	1897 Mar 10	IA, 24th, 1898
Turner, Robert	Pvt.	F, 42nd Wis. Inf.	358		1915 Apr 20	IA, 42nd, 1916
Turner, Robt. L.	Pvt. & Sergt.	H, 8th Iowa Inf.	40		1912 Feb 26	IA, 39th, 1913
Turner, S.			50		1927	IA, 54th, 1928
Turner, S.B.	Farrier	M, 4th Iowa Cav.	19	91	1932 Jan 25	IA, 59th, 1933
Turner, S.R.		64th Wis. Inf.	37	69	1905 Oct 8	NE, 30th, 1906
Turner, Thomas	Pvt.	C, 4th Iowa Inf.	37	67	1898 Nov 22	IA, 25th, 1899
Turner, Thomas E.		E, 34th Ill. Inf. (died of heart disease)	60	80	1922 Jul 8	NE, 47th, 1923
Turner, W.H.	Major	2nd Wis. Inf.	2		1900 Nov 25	IA, 27th, 1901
Turner, W.H.	Pvt.	U.S. Navy	193		1910 Oct 3	IA, 37th, 1911
Turner, W.H.		E, 1st Kans.	1		1928 Feb 14	KS, 47th, 1928
Turner, W.J.	Pvt.	B, 7th Ind. Inf.	10		1911 Apr 11	IA, 38th, 1912
Turner, Waren B.	Pvt.	E, 92nd N.Y. Inf.	88		1927 Mar 23	IA, 54th, 1928
Turner, William H.		C, 7th Cal.	380		1912 Jul 11	KS, 32nd, 1913
Turner, Wm. H.		A, 2nd Neb. Cav. (died of old age)	4	80	1920 Feb 23	NE, 45th, 1921
Turney, Alex	Pvt.	D, 7th Ohio Inf.	297	67	1887 May 5	IA, 15th, 1889
Turney, D.M.		H, 41st Ill.	50		1905 Dec 8	KS, 25th, 1906
Turney, Isaac		D, 7th Iowa	251		1906 Jul 20	KS, 26th, 1907
Turney, Thomas		H, 69th N.Y. Inf. (died at National Military Home; buried at National Military Home Cemetery)	380		1894 May 27	KS, 14th, 1895
Turpin, David	Pvt.	G, 94th Ill. Inf.	66		1929 Nov 2	IA, 56th, 1930
Turpin, J.H.		H, 6th Ohio B. Res. Corps	250	67	1902 Jan	NE, 27th, 1903
Turrell, H.A.	Corp.	G, 211th Penn. Inf.	23	53	1891 Nov 19	IA, 18th, 1892
Turton, E.J.	Pvt.	E, 8th Iowa Cav.	254		1924 Aug 13	IA, 51st, 1925
Turvey, David	Pvt.	I, 89th Ill. Vol. Inf.	484		1901 Mar 31	IA, 28th, 1902
Tusant, J.H.	Pvt.	M, 10th N.Y. Hvy. Art.	12		1920 Oct 30	IA, 47th, 1921
Tusner, Wm.	Pvt.	G, 13th Iowa Inf.	98		1907 Apr 21	IA, 34th, 1908
Tuten, Robert P.		E, 26th N.Y. Cav. (died of paralysis of brain)	110	74	1918 Dec 24	NE, 43rd, 1919
Tuthill, Geo.	Pvt.	K, 3rd Iowa Inf.	222		1917 May 6	IA, 44th, 1918
Tuthill, W.C.		K, 5th Ill.	127		1931 Jun 12	KS, 52nd, 1933
Tuthill, W.C.		K, 5th Ill.	127		1931 Jun 12	KS, 51st, 1932
Tuttle, Arby		E, 3rd Wis.	58		1916 Mar 12	KS, 36th, 1917
Tuttle, C.		D, 10th Kans.	36		1908 Oct 31	KS, 28th, 1909
Tuttle, F.M.		E, 42nd Ohio	129		1918 Sep 23	KS, 38th, 1919
Tuttle, I.C.	Pvt.		96		1920 Feb 21	IA, 47th, 1921
Tuttle, J.C.			17		1911 Aug 24	KS, 31st, 1912
Tuttle, J.M.		H, 8th Ill. Cav.	15		1901 Apr 6	KS, 21st, 1902
Tuttle, Jas. M.	Col. Brig. Gen.	2nd Iowa Inf. (died at Casa Grande, Arizona)	12	66	1892 Oct 24	IA, 19th, 1893
Tuttle, John W.		C, 140th Ind.	89		1910 Nov 10	KS, 30th, 1911
Tuttle, L.M.		B, 2nd Ohio Cav.	127		1899 Sep 11	KS, 19th, 1900
Tuttle, Nathaniel P.		F, 11th Ind.	337		1908	KS, 28th, 1909
Tuttle, Percy C.	Pvt.	E, 11th Kans. Cav.	440	54	1899 Apr 25	IA, 25th, 1899
Tutwiler, Jacob	Pvt.	I, 21st Mo. Inf.	497		1915 Oct 18	IA, 42nd, 1916
Tuxham, John		K, 2nd Kans. Cav.	173		1913 Oct 31	NE, 38th, 1914
Twidale, Wm.		F, 9th Mich.	13	75	1914 Jul 8	NE, 39th, 1915
Twiggs, Alonzo	Pvt.	F, 60th U.S. Inf.	1		1910 Jul 14	IA, 37th, 1911
Twin, Dick	Pvt.	I, 80th Ohio Inf.	122		1905 Nov 7	IA, 32nd, 1906
Twiss, Loren		B, 123rd Ohio	142		1918 May 3	KS, 38th, 1919
Twogood, A.J.	Com. Sergt.	31st Iowa Inf.	206	74	1887 Oct 31	IA, 15th, 1889
Twogood, Albert	Pvt.	C, 74th Ill. Inf.	519		1913 Jun 10	IA, 40th, 1914
Twogood, O.J.		A, 67th Ill.	6		1919 Jun 29	KS, 39th, 1920
Twogood, Wm. E.			71		1916 Feb 26	IA, 43rd, 1917
Twombly, V.P.	Capt.	K, 2nd Iowa Inf.	7		1918 Feb 24	IA, 45th, 1919
Twyning, H.H.		I, 11st Wis.	18		1925 Jul	KS, 45th, 1926
Tye, Matt		D, 9th Kans.	129		1916 May 25	KS, 36th, 1917
Tyler (or Fry), Bartlett		K, 22nd Ky. Inf.	281		1887 Dec 9	KS, 7th, 1888

*See Appendix A, B or C for roster of post names and locations.
†See Introduction for note regarding recording of death date.
557

Name	Rank	Company, Regiment or Ship	Post*	Age	Death Date†	Journal
Tyler, A.G.	Pvt.	A, 11th Iowa Inf.	231		1921 Mar 14	IA, 48th, 1922
Tyler, A.H.	Pvt.	E, 27th Iowa Inf.	371	52	1892 Nov 24	IA, 19th, 1893
Tyler, Chas. E.		B, 32nd Ohio	53		1890	KS, 10th, 1891
Tyler, Edwin		C, 50th Ill.	52		1923 Jul 3	KS, 43rd, 1924
Tyler, Geo. B.		B, 6th Iowa Cav. (died of arthritis)	13	72	1920 Dec 15	NE, 45th, 1921
Tyler, Geo. C.		BB, 1st Iowa Cav.	92		1909 Oct 23	IA, 36th, 1910
Tyler, Geo. W.		G, 106th Ill. Inf.	318	76	1917 Feb 22	NE, 42nd, 1918
Tyler, George	Pvt.	I, 3rd Mo. Inf.	42		1928 Jun 3	IA, 55th, 1929
Tyler, Henry		H, 12th Maine Inf.	120		1940 Oct 10	NE, 65th, 1941
Tyler, Isham		G, 15th Kans. Cav.	12		1904 Mar 3	KS, 24th, 1905
Tyler, J.N.		I, 26th Mich.	98		1926 Nov 15	KS, 46th, 1927
Tyler, James M.		G, 111th Penn.	433		1912 Oct 24	KS, 32nd, 1913
Tyler, Jas. D.		106th Penn. Inf.	29		1927 Apr 18	IA, 54th, 1928
Tyler, Milton		A, 7th Ill. Cav.	25		1921 Dec 20	KS, 41st, 1922
Tyler, Roswell P.	Pvt.	C, 8th Mo. Inf.	168		1899 Feb 20	IA, 26th, 1900
Tyler, Seneca		D, 20th Iowa	7		1918	KS, 38th, 1919
Tyler, Wm. C.		E, 27th Iowa (died of congestive chill)	65	83	1897 Nov 13	NE, 22nd, 1898
Tylor, H.V.	Sergt.		264		1912	IA, 39th, 1913
Tynan, J.M.		I, 53rd Ill.	51		1922 Nov 26	KS, 42nd, 1923
Tynell, W.S., M.D.	Surg.	Co. Portsm'th, Ohio	301		1885	KS, 5th, 1886
Tyner, Wm.		I, Ill.	256		1929 Sep 21	KS, 49th, 1930
Typer, John		A, 118th Ill.	52		1904 Jan 12	KS, 24th, 1905
Tyrrell, Isaac M.	Pvt.	I, 2nd Kans. Cav.	313		1908 Jan 14	IA, 35th, 1909
Tyrrell, S.G.	Pvt.	E, 7th Ill. Cav.	512		1915 Oct 1	IA, 42nd, 1916
Tyson, C.S.			23		1914	IA, 41st, 1915
Tyson, Enos	Pvt.	F, 146th Ill. Inf.	440		1913 Mar 7	IA, 40th, 1914
Tyson, Jared		I, 15th Kans. Cav.	12		1925 Mar 16	KS, 44th, 1925
Tyson, Jared		I, 15th Kans.	12		1925 Mar 16	KS, 45th, 1926
Tysor, Andrew	Pvt.	K, 1st Mo. Eng.	333	69	1896 Nov 18	IA, 23rd, 1897
Ubanks, A.J.	Sergt.	I, 47th Iowa Inf.	40		1922 Feb 24	IA, 49th, 1923
Udall, Frank O.	Pvt.	B, 6th Iowa Cav.	78		1906 Apr 2	IA, 33rd, 1907
Udish, Chas.	Pvt.	I, 11th Iowa Inf.	231		1918 Jun 25	IA, 45th, 1919
Uebel, Ferdinand	Pvt.	A, 20th Iowa Inf.	235		1911 Dec 28	IA, 38th, 1912
Uebel, Geo. W.		G, 108th Ill.	25		1929 Nov 27	NE, 54th, 1930
Ufford, A.H.	Corp.	C, 110th N.Y.	222		1921 Nov 3	IA, 48th, 1922
Uglow, J.W.		H, 49th Wis.	113		1917 Mar 30	KS, 37th, 1918
Uglow, Samuel		B, 2nd Penn. Inf.	25	51	1895 Mar 11	NE, 20th, 1896
Uhl, Albert	Pvt.	166th Ohio Inf.	493		1914 Jan 2	IA, 40th, 1914
Uhler, Carroll	Pvt.	I, 16th Ill. Inf.	521		1904-1905	IA, 31st, 1905
Uhler, F.M.		H, 78th Ill.	25		1923	NE, 48th, 1924
Uhrig, Simon		K, 39th N.Y. Inf. (died of heart trouble)	118		1906 Nov 24	NE, 31st, 1907
Uidkiff, Preston	Pvt.	K, 21st Iowa Inf.	342		1905 Jul 10	IA, 32nd, 1906
Ukele, Fred		I, 146th Ill.	175		1923 Mar 3	KS, 43rd, 1924
Ulch, Joseph		G, 147th Penn.	164		1913 Dec 9	KS, 33rd, 1914
Ulery, John		D, 14th Ky.	23		1928 Nov 12	KS, 48th, 1929
Ulrey, S.C.		H, 118th Ill. (died of complications)	182	74	1922 Mar 7	NE, 47th, 1923
Ulrich, Aug. G.	Pvt.	F, 5th Iowa Cav.	2		1920 May 8	IA, 47th, 1921
Ulrich, Fred	Pvt.	I, 7th Iowa Cav.	231		1914 May 8	IA, 41st, 1915
Ulum, J.C.	Pvt.	H, 22nd Iowa Inf.	31		1916 Jan 30	IA, 43rd, 1917
Ulum, Luther	Pvt.	H, 22nd Iowa Inf.	235		1928 Jul 7	IA, 55th, 1929
Umbarger, Rudolph		I, 146th Ill. Inf.	206		1900 Jul 6	KS, 20th, 1901
Umbaugh, E.	Pvt.	G, 89th Ill. Inf.	111		1921 Aug 5	IA, 48th, 1922
Umberhour, Frank		E, 133rd Ill. (died of pneumonia)	1	82	1925 Feb 19	NE, 50th, 1926
Umphrey, John H.		D, 5th Kans.	3		1899 Oct 2	KS, 19th, 1900
Umpleby, S.C.	Pvt.	I, 167th N.Y. Inf.	12	85	1933 Aug 4	IA, 60th, 1934
Unangst, Franklin	Corp.	D, 93rd Ill. Inf.	57		1914 Oct 16	IA, 41st, 1915
Unangst, J.S.		H, 8th N.J. Inf.	25		1903 Dec	NE, 28th, 1904
Underhill, G.			125		1915	IA, 42nd, 1916
Underhill, J.B.		E, 42nd Ohio	4		1921 Apr 14	KS, 41st, 1922
Underhill, John W.		died of cancer of stomach	207	82	1922 Mar 18	NE, 47th, 1923
Underhill, N.P.		114th —	262		1919 Nov 7	NE, 44th, 1920
Underventer, H.	Pvt.	I, 1st Iowa	500		1924	IA, 51st, 1925

*See Appendix A, B or C for roster of post names and locations.
†See Introduction for note regarding recording of death date.

Name	Rank	Company, Regiment or Ship	Post*	Age	Death Date†	Journal
Underwood, A.J.		B, 8th Inf.	124		1893 Aug 25	KS, 13th, 1894
Underwood, A.T.	Sergt. Major	89th Ill. Inf.	127	56	1895 Apr 23	IA, 22nd, 1896
Underwood, C.W.		K, 36th Ill. Inf. (died at Blue Rapids; buried at Prospect Hill Cemetery)	328		1894 Oct	KS, 14th, 1895
Underwood, Colloway H.		H, 8th Mo. Cav.	265		1929 Jan 10	NE, 53rd, 1929
Underwood, E.B.		I, 83rd Ill.	66		1897 Dec 24	KS, 17th, 1898
Underwood, Ed.	Pvt.	A, 96th Ill. Inf.	81		1927 Dec 30	IA, 54th, 1928
Underwood, Geo.	Pvt.	E, 1st Wis. Cav.	277		1905 Nov 19	IA, 32nd, 1906
Underwood, Hiram		D, 36th Iowa	155		1915 Sep 14	KS, 35th, 1916
Underwood, James	Pvt.	F, 32nd Iowa Inf.	152		1901 Nov 12	IA, 28th, 1902
Underwood, L.	Pvt.	F, 29th Iowa Inf.	10		1896 Jun 6	IA, 23rd, 1897
Underwood, R.J.	Pvt.	D, 15th Ill. Inf.	283		1905 Jul 31	IA, 32nd, 1906
Underwood, Thomas	Pvt.	I, 5th Wis. Inf.	63		1923 Mar 30	IA, 50th, 1924
Underwood, Thomas	Pvt.	I, 5th Wis. Inf	63		1922 Mar 30	IA, 49th, 1923
Underwood, W.R.		F, 75th Ind.	17		1911 Dec 16	KS, 31st, 1912
Underwood, Wm. H.		D, 15th Ill.	88		1911 Sep 27	KS, 31st, 1912
Unebleby, John		F, 7th Penn. Cav.	71		1893 Mar 18	KS, 13th, 1894
Unger, John W.		K, 75th Ill. (died of old age)	13	81	1919 Dec 17	NE, 44th, 1920
Ungles, Robert B.		I, 17th Ill. Inf.	14		1909 May 7	KS, 29th, 1910
Unkofer, S.M.		A, 2nd Ill. Inf.	130		1912 Jun 21	KS, 32nd, 1913
Unsel, Henry B.		B, 3rd Ky.	311		1897 Dec 19	KS, 17th, 1898
Unthark, W. Collins		B, 137th Ill. Inf.	29		1925 Feb 27	IA, 52nd, 1926
Updegraph, Jacob	Pvt.	M, 4th Iowa Cav.	49		1913 Mar 31	IA, 40th, 1914
Updike, Edward		G, 14th N.Y.	7		1931 Jul 29	NE, 56th, 1932
Upham, Jas.		I, 17th Ill.	49		1905 Feb	KS, 25th, 1906
Upton, David		B, 40th Iowa (died of old age)	188	82	1914 Dec 30	NE, 39th, 1915
Upton, Mark A.	Pvt.	A, 3rd Colo. Cav.	110		1899	NE, 24th, 1900
Urfer, Sam'l	Pvt.		321		1910 Oct 15	IA, 37th, 1911
Urie, J.		A, 11th Kans. Cav.	68		1919 Dec 9	KS, 39th, 1920
Urmy, S.S.		F, 3rd Ind. Cav.	250		1916 Aug 12	KS, 36th, 1917
Urquhart, A.D.		B, 173rd Ohio Inf. (died at Lenora)	290		1895 Aug	KS, 15th, 1896
Urquhart, M.H.	Pvt.	E, 86th Ohio Inf.	22		1917 Jun 17	IA, 44th, 1918
Usher, Dyer	Sergt.	A, 31st Iowa Inf.	235	80	1894 Dec 11	IA, 21st, 1895
Usher, H.H.	Pvt.	I, 20th Iowa Inf.	235		1918 Jan 19	IA, 45th, 1919
Utich, H.W.	Pvt.	H, 22nd Ill. Inf.	141		1920 Jul 9	IA, 47th, 1921
Utley, Chas. L.	Corp.	F, 27th Iowa Inf.	190		1917 Mar 20	IA, 44th, 1918
Utley, M.S., see Uttley, M.S.						
Utter, W.H.		B, 11th Wis. (died of old age)	143	80	1911 Dec 28	NE, 36th, 1912
Utterbach, J.T.		G, 46th Ill. (died of cancer)	190		1920 May 30	NE, 45th, 1921
Utterbark, Jefferm	Pvt.	B, 33rd Iowa Inf.	167	59	1897 Mar 18	IA, 24th, 1898
Uttley, M.S.	Pvt.	G, 13th Iowa Inf.	98		1912 Jan 14	IA, 39th, 1913
Utz, Josephus		F, 154th Ind.	255		1904 Jul 20	KS, 24th, 1905
Uzzell, W.F.		C, 26th Ill. (died of Bright's disease)	88	68	1912	NE, 37th, 1913
Vabeld, John	Sergt.		154		1899	NE, 24th, 1900
Vadee, H.S.		D, 7th Mo.	93		1904 Oct 14	KS, 24th, 1905
Vader, Jacob		B, 12th Mich.	34		1920 Jan	KS, 40th, 1921
Vail, Hubbard F.		E, 129th Ill. Inf. (died of heart failure)	25	71	1913 Jan 21	NE, 38th, 1914
Vail, Isaac		H, 33rd Ill.	18		1909 Aug 23	KS, 29th, 1910
Vail, James W.		M, 1st Wis. Art. (died of heart failure)	95		1894 May 25	NE, 19th, 1895
Vail, Thos. C.		H, 6th Ind. Inf.	1		1900 Dec 14	KS, 20th, 1901
Vale, Eli		H, 67th —	63		1926 Jul 10	NE, 51st, 1927
Vale, O.T.		D, 7th Iowa	8		1912 Apr 21	KS, 32nd, 1913
Valentine, D.S.		F, 32nd Iowa Inf.	338		1918	IA, 45th, 1919
Valentine, H.C.			15		1905	IA, 32nd, 1906
Valentine, I.B.	Pvt.	K, 146th Ill. Inf.	297		1904 Feb 2	IA, 31st, 1905
Valentine, J.H.		F, 32nd Iowa (died of diabetes)	25		1916 Jul 6	NE, 41st, 1917
Valentine, L.	Pvt.	G, 21st N.Y. Inf.	34		1921 Aug 8	IA, 48th, 1922
Van, W.H.	Pvt.	K, 24th Iowa Inf.	9		1916 May 6	IA, 43rd, 1917
VanAkin, A.O.	Pvt.	C, 135th Ill. Inf.	170	85	1931 Dec 2	IA, 58th, 1932
Vanander, J.W.	Pvt.	I, 83rd Ill. Inf.	167	57	1890 Jan 27	IA, 16th, 1890
Vanardale, P.V.		D, 113th Ill.	18		1921	IA, 48th, 1922
Vanardman, C.P.		G, 7th Ill.	129		1906 Dec 30	KS, 26th, 1907

Name	Rank	Company, Regiment or Ship	Post*	Age	Death Date†	Journal
VanArsdale, Adnah E.		E, 1st N.Y. Cav.	293		1931	KS, 51st, 1932
Vanarsdale, W.W.	Pvt.	H, 40th Iowa Inf.	322		1910 Apr 22	IA, 37th, 1911
VanArsdall, John		cause of death: paralytic	105	79	1914	NE, 39th, 1915
Vanasdall, Samuel A.		F, 15th Iowa	23		1911 Jan 15	KS, 31st, 1912
Vanaster, David		I, 1st Ohio Art.	257		1921 Aug 15	KS, 41st, 1922
VanAuken, J.B.	Pvt.	D, 28th Iowa Inf.	261	59	1886 Dec 25	IA, 13th, 1887
VanAusdale, Amos		F, 136th Ohio Vol. Inf.	115		1915 Dec 28	KS, 35th, 1916
VanAusdale, Isaac *		H, 167th Ohio	25		1936 Dec 2	KS, 56th, 1937
VanBarcum, D.			17		1933 Nov 12	KS, 53rd, 1934
Vanbeck, Geo.	1st Lieut.	C, 1st Iowa Cav.	20		1906	IA, 33rd, 1907
Vanbeck, Geo. D.	Corp.	B, 2nd U.S. Art.	306		1904 Mar 21	IA, 31st, 1905
VanBenthusen, W.	Capt.	A, 3rd Iowa Cav.	100		1905 Dec 27	IA, 32nd, 1906
VanBlaricom, Sidney		B, 142nd Ill.	24		1919 May 19	KS, 39th, 1920
VanBogart, Frank	Pvt.	K, 153rd Ill. Inf.	48		1918 Oct 8	IA, 45th, 1919
VanBremer, William		H, 4th Ohio	380		1905 Sep 10	KS, 25th, 1906
Vanburen, Chas. H.		C, 13th Wis. Inf.	98		1914 Apr 14	KS, 34th, 1915
VanBuren, Evert	Surg.	147th Ill. Inf. (died of apoplexy)	354	66	1905 Oct 26	NE, 30th, 1906
VanBuren, Evert		E, 132nd Ill. Inf. (died of apoplexy at Soldiers & Sailors Home, Grand Island; buried at Hooper, Neb.)	25	66	1905 Oct 26	NE, 30th, 1906
VanBuren, H.F.		H, 44th Ind.	92		1928 Mar 17	KS, 48th, 1929
VanBuren, J.E.	Seaman	Gunboat Atlantic Squadron	12		1890	KS, 10th, 1891
Vanburen, Wm. H.	Pvt.	F, 8th Ill. Inf.	22		1910 Nov 8	IA, 37th, 1911
VanBuskink, D.F.		K, — Ind.	33		1922 Dec 29	KS, 42nd, 1923
Vanbuskirk, M.			81		1886 Oct 17	NE, 11th, 1887
VanCamp, H.C.	Pvt.	F, 21st Mo. Inf.	515		1905	IA, 32nd, 1906
Vancampen, D.D.	Pvt.	I, 89th Ill. Inf.	329		1897 Aug 10	IA, 24th, 1898
Vance, A.M.		H, 17th Iowa Inf.	7		1928 Nov 22	IA, 55th, 1929
Vance, Adam	Pvt.	I, 9th Iowa Inf.	168		1919	IA, 46th, 1920
Vance, Amos		C, 54th Ind.	144		1918 Aug 9	KS, 38th, 1919
Vance, Andrew J.	Pvt.	M, 1st Mo. Eng.		91	1936 Oct 7	IA, 65th, 1939
Vance, Ezra F.		E, 17th Iowa Inf.	25	81	1919 Feb 21	NE, 44th, 1920
Vance, George C.		C, 2nd Maine QM Corps (died of old age)	77	94	1908 Mar 31	NE, 33rd, 1909
Vance, H.W.		C, 12th Ill.	114		1898	KS, 18th, 1899
Vance, J.C.		E, 13th Kans.	4		1928 Jan 11	KS, 48th, 1929
Vance, J.R.		I, 39th Ohio	13		1927 Nov 6	NE, 52nd, 1928
Vance, O.H.		E, 7th Iowa Cav.	40		1927 Jun 4	IA, 54th, 1928
Vance, Zachery T.	Pvt.	9th Iowa Cav.	254		1922 Sep 4	IA, 49th, 1923
Vanchorck, Ed.	Pvt.	D, 31st Iowa	68		1924 Oct 27	IA, 51st, 1925
Vancicle, F.W.		K, 54th Ill. Inf.	55		1936 Feb 15	KS, 55th, 1936
VanCleave, B.F.		B, 10th Ind. K, 22nd Iowa	1		1925 Apr 10	KS, 45th, 1926
VanCleve, B.M.		B, 10th Ind.	1		1928 Nov 21	KS, 48th, 1929
VanCorder, C.	Capt.	B, 39th Iowa Inf.	34		1924 May 28	IA, 51st, 1925
Vancouver, John			482		1917 Aug 20	KS, 37th, 1918
VanCuren, Edward	Pvt.	C, 145th Penn. Inf.	284		1892 Oct 11	IA, 19th, 1893
VanDeBogart, L.	Pvt.	D, 21st Wis. Inf.	3		1901 Dec 6	IA, 28th, 1902
VanDeMark, D.		A, 1st N.Y.	17		1923 Apr 6	KS, 43rd, 1924
Vanderberg, John W.	Pvt.	H, 9th N.Y. Inf.	12		1919 May 29	IA, 46th, 1920
Vanderberg, W.H.	Pvt.	G, 6th Iowa Cav.	22		1915 Dec 9	IA, 42nd, 1916
Vanderbilt, P.D.		C, 9th Iowa	113		1905 Mar 25	KS, 25th, 1906
Vanderbilt, W.H.		C, 27th Iowa (died of old age)	352	86	1922 Sep 20	NE, 47th, 1923
Vanderburg, P.D.	Pvt.	K, 149th Ohio Inf.	436		1903 Nov 26	IA, 30th, 1904
Vandergriff, E.B.		D, 11th Kans. (died of Bright's disease)	289	64	1908 Jan 23	NE, 33rd, 1909
Vanderhoof, H.		F, 12th Mich.	3		1929 Oct 28	NE, 54th, 1930
Vanderhoof, Herman		7th Mich.	262		1919 Nov 23	NE, 44th, 1920
Vanderhoof, Nathan		I, 155th Ind. (former member; died at St. Edward)	140		1936 Sep 11	NE, 61st, 1937
Vanderlip, H.	Pvt.	B, 25th Ill. Inf.	339		1913 Sep 23	IA, 40th, 1914
Vanderlip, Wm.		I, 2nd Kans.	94		1905 Sep 19	KS, 25th, 1906
Vanderly, John	Pvt.	8th Iowa Inf.	137		1919 Jul 31	IA, 46th, 1920
Vanderman, C.P.		G, 7th Ill.	129		1905 May 31	KS, 25th, 1906

*See Appendix A, B or C for roster of post names and locations.
†See Introduction for note regarding recording of death date.
560

Name	Rank	Company, Regiment or Ship	Post*	Age	Death Date†	Journal
Vanderment, O.D.		G, 8th Ill. Inf.	54		1899 Jan 19	KS, 19th, 1900
Vanderpool, Elisha	Capt.	C, 35th Mo. Inf.	210		1897 Aug 23	IA, 24th, 1898
Vanderveer, Uriah	Pvt.	E, 5th Ohio Cav.	64		1914 Nov 5	IA, 41st, 1915
Vanderver, A.B.		E, 146th Ohio	104		1906	KS, 26th, 1907
VanDervoont, Paul		M, 16th Ill. Cav. (died of heart failure)	2	60	1902 Jul	NE, 27th, 1903
VanDervoort, Paul		died at Puetre Principe, Cuba	2		1902 Jul 29	NE, 27th, 1903
Vanderwalker, George		C, 1st Wis. Art.	267	91	1938 Feb 21	IA, 64th, 1938
Vanderwege, Martin		F, 47th Wis.	101		1926	NE, 51st, 1927
Vanderwert, Theodore		A, 3rd Iowa Cav.	22	91	1937 Dec 15	IA, 64th, 1938
Vandeventer, C.C.		K, 46th Ill. Inf.	1		1934 Nov	KS, 54th, 1935
Vandeventer, John		B, 15th Ill.	380		1920 Feb 22	KS, 40th, 1921
VanDeventer, John M.		B, 15th Ill.	380		1921 Feb 22	KS, 41st, 1922
Vandever, M.			145		1883	KS, 3rd, 1884
Vandewater, J.		J, 5th Ohio	85		1928 Jun 29	KS, 48th, 1929
Vandine, Walter			32		1911 Jan 13	KS, 31st, 1912
Vandiver, J.S.		G, 132nd Ind.	25		1920 Apr 27	KS, 40th, 1921
Vandiver, Marion		C, 11th Mo. Cav.	209		1919 Dec 24	KS, 39th, 1920
Vandivert, F.A.	Pvt.	K, 8th Iowa Inf.	153		1899 Dec 12	IA, 26th, 1900
Vandling, A.		B, 22nd N.J.	8		1915 Apr 16	KS, 35th, 1916
VanDoran, J.F.	Pvt.	F, 3rd Penn. Inf.	74		1921 Jun 3	IA, 48th, 1922
VanDoren, Charles	Pvt.	B, 155th Ill. Inf. (at large)	64	95	1940 Sep 29	IA, 67th, 1941
VanDusen, G.S.		U.S. Navy, N.J. (died of heart failure)	52	81	1924 Mar 3	NE, 49th, 1925
VanDusen, Nelson	Pvt.	K, 1st Wis. Cav.	22		1915 May 8	IA, 42nd, 1916
VanDuser, James M.	Pvt.	A, 14th Iowa Inf.	382		1901 Dec 2	IA, 28th, 1902
VanDuyn, J.N.		I, 14th Iowa	35	65	1910 Dec 15	NE, 35th, 1911
VanDuzee, A.J.	Lieut.	44th Iowa Inf.	78		1912 Nov 15	IA, 39th, 1913
VanDyke, H.H.	Pvt.		167		1911 Jan	IA, 38th, 1912
VanDyke, W.		G, 3rd Iowa Cav.	25		1914 May 20	KS, 34th, 1915
VanDyne, Martin		B, 4th Mich. Inf. (died in Oklahoma)	167		1895	KS, 15th, 1896
Vaneman, Nicolas D.	Pvt.	C, 27th Iowa Inf.	63		1913 Jan 13	IA, 41st, 1915
VanEpps, C.E.	Pvt.	Mississippi Marine Brigade	72		1918 Jan 6	IA, 45th, 1919
VanEpps, C.E.	Pvt.	Miss. Marine	72		1917 Jun	IA, 44th, 1918
Vanepps, Chas. H.	Pvt.	C, 26th Iowa Inf.	88		1911 Sep 19	IA, 38th, 1912
VanEpps, Wm. W.H.		D, 20th Iowa	171		1932 Nov 13	NE, 57th, 1933
VanFlete, G.B.		C, 136th Ohio	258		1923	KS, 43rd, 1924
VanFossen, John		B, 1st Kans.	6		1930 Jan 4	KS, 51st, 1932
VanFossen, John		B, 1st Kans.	6		1930 Jan 4	KS, 52nd, 1933
VanFossen, John		I, 1st Kans. Cav.	6		1930 Jan 15	KS, 50th, 1931
VanFossin, L.C.		Mulhouse Ill. Bat.	123		1892 Dec 7	KS, 12th, 1893
VanGieson, Henry H.	Asst. Surg.	Navy	110	65	1905 Mar 7	NE, 30th, 1906
VanGrundy, David		I, 2nd Kans. Cav. (died at Neosho Rapids)	233		1895 Sep	KS, 15th, 1896
VanGundy, Elmer		K, 46th Ohio	25		1921 Jul 15	KS, 41st, 1922
VanHageman, see Hageman, Van						
VanHoesen, I.N.		G, 10th Mo.	12		1897 Jan 6	KS, 17th, 1898
Vanhon, T.J.		H, 155th Ill. Inf.	20		1913	IA, 40th, 1914
Vanhoosen, L.J.		D, 7th Iowa (died of apoplexy)	26		1908 Nov 25	NE, 33rd, 1909
VanHorn, A.I.	Corp.	F, 26th Iowa Inf.	92	65	1889 Jul 9	IA, 18th, 1892
VanHorn, Ambrose	Pvt.	B, 57th Ill.	292		1907 Mar 1	IA, 34th, 1908
VanHorn, Arthur		G, 5th Iowa Inf. (died of complication)	57	77	1917 Oct 13	NE, 42nd, 1918
Vanhorn, B.F.		I, 1st Kans. (Col.)	47		1911 Sep 28	KS, 31st, 1912
VanHorn, B.F.		B, 12th Kans. Inf.	18		1917 Jan 13	KS, 37th, 1918
VanHorn, D.M.		C, 22nd Iowa	130		1921 Jan 26	KS, 41st, 1922
Vanhorn, D.P.	Pvt.	K, 85th Ill. Inf.	115		1912 Oct 24	IA, 39th, 1913
VanHorn, David		G, 39th Ohio	83		1928 Jun 27	KS, 48th, 1929
VanHorn, J.D.	Pvt.	D, 26th Iowa	418		1909 Sep 23	IA, 36th, 1910
VanHorn, James H.		B, 48th Wis. (former member; died at Norfolk)	109		1936 Nov 1	NE, 61st, 1937
VanHorn, John E.		I, 10th Iowa	131		1920 Jan 13	KS, 40th, 1921
VanHorn, Rich'd	Pvt.	I, Cav.	219		1927 Jul	IA, 54th, 1928
VanHorn, S.		V.R.C., Ohio	18		1897 Jul 15	KS, 17th, 1898
VanHusen, N.K.		B, 100th N.Y. Inf.	110	80	1920 Dec 21	NE, 45th, 1921

Name	Rank	Company, Regiment or Ship	Post*	Age	Death Date†	Journal
Vanlandingham, L.J.			36		1893 Dec 18	KS, 13th, 1894
Vanlaudingham, —			40		1902 Mar 1	KS, 22nd, 1903
VanLawrence, J.B.		F, 83rd Ill. Inf.	163	63	1896 Oct 2	NE, 21st, 1897
Vanleas, N.		G, 15th West Va. Inf. (died of inflammation of bladder)	[153?]	60	1902 Sep	NE, 27th, 1903
Vanleer, J.W.		B, 63rd Ind.	147		1931 Apr 18	NE, 56th, 1932
VanLeuven, Geo. M., Sr.	Pvt.	B, 7th Iowa Inf.	217	81	1893 Jun 15	IA, 20th, 1894
VanLew, James		C, 177th Penn.	253		1910	KS, 30th, 1911
Vanlone, F.	Pvt.	A, 1st N.H. Art.	42		1915 Mar 26	IA, 42nd, 1916
VanLuman, Cornelius		A, 1st Kans. (killed on S.F.R.R.)	278		1892 Jan 22	KS, 12th, 1893
VanLuven, Geo. M.	Pvt.	D, 3rd Iowa Inf.	77		1915 Feb 24	IA, 42nd, 1916
VanMeter, A.P.		K, 4th West Va.	96		1928 Dec 2	KS, 48th, 1929
VanMeter, Jacob H.		E, 156th Ill.	131		1898 Sep	KS, 18th, 1899
VanMetre, F.M.		location: Grand Island			1927 May 27	NE, 52nd, 1928
Vann, Jessie	Pvt.	I, N.Y. Art.	78		1924 Sep 20	IA, 51st, 1925
Vanname, Frank	Pvt.		29		1916 Feb 5	IA, 43rd, 1917
VanNardstran, Ira		H, 37th Ill.	87		1885	KS, 5th, 1886
VanNess, B.	Pvt.	K, 49th Ohio Inf.	275		1920 Jan 24	IA, 48th, 1922
VanNess, Ralph G.		U, Red Rover (died of old age)	110	93	1913 Sep 10	NE, 38th, 1914
VanNorden, J.J.	Pvt.	B, 3rd Iowa Inf.	222		1909 Dec 20	IA, 36th, 1910
VanNordshand, J.M.		D, 30th Iowa	87		1920 Feb 27	KS, 40th, 1921
Vannosdoll, Wm.	Pvt.	B, 52nd Penn. Inf.	236	69	1898 Feb 10	IA, 24th, 1898
VanNote, V.	Pvt.	F, 127th Ill. Inf.	42		1921 Jan 27	IA, 48th, 1922
Vannuys, John H.		F, 7th Ind.	51		1924 Dec 1	KS, 44th, 1925
VanOrman, C.		B, 35th Ill. Inf.	238		1887 Dec 7	KS, 7th, 1888
VanOrman, H.		E, 83rd Ill.	129		1904 Jun 18	KS, 24th, 1905
VanOrman, J.G.	Lieut.	A, 71st N.Y. Inf.	94		1906	IA, 33rd, 1907
VanOrsdal, F.M.		I, 4th Iowa	71		1928 Aug 17	KS, 48th, 1929
Vanorsdale, Amos		F, 136th Ohio	115		1914 Oct 27	KS, 34th, 1915
VanOrsdall, C.		B, 58th Ill.	265		1920 Dec 12	KS, 40th, 1921
VanOrsdel, D.	Pvt.	K, 3rd Ill. Cav.	22		1918 Jan 28	IA, 45th, 1919
Vanorsdol, G.W.		E, 1st Iowa Cav.	250		1919 Aug 24	KS, 39th, 1920
Vanosdel, R.H.		I, 47th Ill. Inf.	18		1917 Jun 5	KS, 37th, 1918
Vanover, S.M.		D, 80th Ind.	130		1926 Aug 10	KS, 46th, 1927
Vanoy, F.G.		G, 9th Kans. Cav.	54		1904 Mar 7	KS, 24th, 1905
VanPatten, M., Dr.		I, — N.Y.	14		1932	KS, 52nd, 1933
VanPatten, M., Dr.		I, — N.Y.	14		1931	KS, 51st, 1932
VanPelt, H.V.	Pvt.	A, 38th N.Y. Inf.	324	89	1931 Jan 19	IA, 58th, 1932
VanPelt, Hiram		M, 3rd Iowa Cav.	147		1922 Nov 13	KS, 42nd, 1923
VanRiper, J.		F, 48th Ind.	81	89	1934 Aug 31	IA, 61st, 1935
VanRoyne, Peter		F, 4th Iowa	23		1893	KS, 13th, 1894
VanSaul, W.H.	Pvt.	E, 7th Iowa Inf.	2	49	1892 Feb 10	IA, 18th, 1892
VanSchneider, Frederick	Pvt. Corp.	M, 4th Ill. Cav. I, 12th Ill. Cav.	98	59	1892 Sep 22	IA, 19th, 1893
Vanscoy, John		I, 1st Ohio Art.	40	81	1918 Apr 18	NE, 44th, 1920
Vanscoyk, A.J.	Pvt.	E, 4th Iowa	425		1914 Apr 3	IA, 41st, 1915
Vanscoyoc, James		B, 3rd Iowa Cav.	251		1914 Mar 1	KS, 34th, 1915
Vanscoyoc, O.K.		D, 14th Iowa Inf., 17th Corps (born in Ohio, Oct. 23, 1831; died in Louisville, Neb.)	175		1883 Dec 18	NE, 8th, 1884
Vanscoys, O.K.	Pvt.	D, 14th Iowa (died of typhoid pneumonia)	175	52	1884 Dec	NE, 9th, 1885
VanSickle, A.J.		8th Ind. Bat.	301		1921	KS, 41st, 1922
VanSickle, Selah	Pvt.	M, 3rd Ohio Cav.	159		1913 Oct 23	IA, 40th, 1914
VanSkike, J.N.	Capt.	L, 4th Ind. Cav.	166	64	1885 Nov 23	IA, 12th, 1886
VanSlancomb, W.M.		B, 106th Ill.	87		1920 Dec 8	KS, 40th, 1921
Vanslyke, J.P.		I, 6th Mich. Inf. (died of consumption)	18		1894 Jul 9	NE, 19th, 1895
VanSlyke, Jay	Pvt.	C, 15th N.Y. Inf.	216		1905 May 6	IA, 32nd, 1906
VanSlyke, W.H.	Sergt.	F, 116th —	83		1923 Feb 23	IA, 50th, 1924
Vansteenberg, Robert		W, 2nd Wis. Cav. (died of paralysis)	136	73	1913 Nov 2	NE, 38th, 1914
VanSteenwyk, Wm.	Pvt.	H, 17th Iowa Inf.	2		1912 Mar 22	IA, 39th, 1913
VanTilburg, —	Pvt.	G, 93rd Ill. Inf.	222		1926 Aug 21	IA, 53rd, 1927
Vantine, Chas.	Lieut.	F, 128th N.Y.	47		1918 Mar 23	KS, 38th, 1919

Name	Rank	Company, Regiment or Ship	Post*	Age	Death Date†	Journal
VanTreese, Thos.		D, 68th Ind.	86		1922 Aug 27	KS, 42nd, 1923
Vantrump, I.C.		G, 45th Iowa Inf. (died of inflammation of bowels)	74		1893 Aug 8	NE, 18th, 1894
VanValkinburg, R.V.			452		1900-1901	IA, 27th, 1901
VanVleck, Andrew	Pvt.	G, Hvy. Art.	235		1922 Oct 1	IA, 49th, 1923
VanVlete, John		K, 52nd Ill.	284		1934 Aug	IA, 61st, 1935
VanVolkenberg, Wm.		B, 1st N.Y.	25		1928 Jul 27	KS, 48th, 1929
VanVoorhis, A.T.		B, 22nd Penn. Cav. (died at St. Joe, Mo.)	122		1895 Dec	KS, 15th, 1896
VanVoorhis, K.S.	Lieut. Col.	137th N.Y.	8		1888	KS, 8th, 1889
VanWalkenb'rg, R.B.	Pvt.	H, 14th Iowa Inf.	452		1900 Jun 19	IA, 27th, 1901
VanWert, C.C.	Corp.	C, 16th Ill. Cav.	134		1924 Jun 15	IA, 51st, 1925
VanWert, R.	Pvt.	N.Y. Battery	271		1908 Nov	IA, 35th, 1909
VanWest, Geo. T.	Musician	F, 93rd Ill.	81		1907 Sep 12	IA, 34th, 1908
Vanwie, J.H.	Pvt.	E, 19th Wis. Inf.	42		1916 Nov 27	IA, 43rd, 1917
VanWie, J.J.	Pvt.	A, 44th Iowa Inf.	78		1897 Aug	IA, 24th, 1898
VanWie, Nelson			42		1909 Dec 1	IA, 36th, 1910
Vanwinkle, Henry	Pvt.	K, 25th Iowa Inf.	96	85	1931 Jun 1	IA, 58th, 1932
VanWinkle, Isaiah	Pvt.	K, 25th Iowa Inf.	290		1915 Sep 10	IA, 42nd, 1916
VanWinkle, Perry	Pvt.	F, 11th Penn. Inf.	108		1918 May 27	IA, 45th, 1919
VanWyck, Charles H.	Col.	56th N.Y. Inf. (died of paralysis)	24	70	1895 Oct 23	NE, 20th, 1896
VanZandt, Cornelius		E, 18th Iowa Inf.	250		1909 Dec 26	IA, 36th, 1910
VanZant, J.R.		D, 6th Kans. Cav.	17		1914 Jan 31	KS, 34th, 1915
Vanzant, William		A, 38th Ind.	64		1885	KS, 5th, 1886
VanZant, William			64		1884	KS, 4th, 1885
Varble, J.B.	Pvt.	B, 86th Ill. Inf.	195		1909 Sep	IA, 36th, 1910
Vargason, John	Pvt.	C, 9th Iowa Cav.	63		1924	IA, 51st, 1925
Varner, Harvey	Pvt.	G, 2nd Iowa Cav.	231		1902 Aug 20	IA, 29th, 1903
Varney, H.L.		H, 8th Ohio	186		1904 Aug 22	KS, 24th, 1905
Varney, S.A.		D, 12th Wis.	5		1920 Jan 17	KS, 40th, 1921
Varney, W.E.	Corp.	H, 2nd Iowa Inf.	235	94	1932 Feb 20	IA, 59th, 1933
Varnum, T.B.		B, 9th Kans.	12		1919 Feb 5	KS, 39th, 1920
Vassar, John G.	Corp.	I, 23rd Ill. Inf.	58		1916 Mar 24	IA, 43rd, 1917
Vaughn, Baily	Pvt.	A, 9th Iowa Inf.	88		1917	IA, 44th, 1918
Vaughn, E.G.	Pvt.	K, 2nd Iowa Inf.	2		1904 Nov 14	IA, 31st, 1905
Vaughn, Elsa		H, 8th Iowa Cav. (location: Alliance)			1927 Jul 18	NE, 52nd, 1928
Vaughn, Geo. B.		D, 38th Wis.	25		1908 Apr 10	NE, 33rd, 1909
Vaughn, Job		D, 55th Ill.	59		1889	KS, 9th, 1890
Vaughn, John E.		13th Ind.	168		1897 Dec 28	KS, 17th, 1898
Vaughn, S.H.		25th Ill. Inf.	25		1905 May 14	NE, 30th, 1906
Vaughn, S.H.		25th Ill.	25		1905 May 14	NE, 31st, 1907
Vaughn, Thos.		5th Iowa	85		1927 May 17	KS, 47th, 1928
Vaughn, William		Iowa	129		1923 Jan 29	KS, 43rd, 1924
Vaughn, Wm. J.		B, 52nd Penn. Inf.	35		1914 Jul 20	KS, 34th, 1915
Vaught, Wm.			51		1908 Nov 14	KS, 28th, 1909
Vawter, J.B.	Sergt.	C, 4th Ky. Mtd. Inf.	17		1897-1898	IA, 24th, 1898
Vawters, A.F.		H, 73rd Ohio	255		1905 Jan 18	KS, 25th, 1906
Veale, Geo. W.	Lieut. Col.	E, 4th Kans. Cav. 6th Kans. Cav.	71		1916 Nov 28	KS, 36th, 1917
Veasie, J.H.		E, 33rd Iowa Inf. (died of old age)	11		1893 Apr 7	NE, 18th, 1894
Veatch, Simeon		L, 3rd Mo. Cav.	192		2nd quarter 1884	IA, 11th, 1885
Veatch, Simeon		L, 3rd Iowa Cav.	192		1st quarter 1884	IA, 10th, 1884
Veazie, Chas. B.		G, 2nd Maine	4		1930 Apr 13	NE, 55th, 1931
Veberg, August		I, 2nd Iowa	18		1926 Feb 11	KS, 46th, 1927
Veits, John		H, 34th Mich.	12		1910 May 10	KS, 30th, 1911
Velie, Jas. M.	Pvt.	M, 16th N.Y. Cav.	56		1927 Feb 24	IA, 54th, 1928
Vencel, Tichenor		E, 78th Ill.	52		1902 Aug 9	KS, 22nd, 1903
Veneman, W.J.			305		1916	IA, 43rd, 1917
Venner, William		E, 134th Ind.	45		1933 Apr 24	NE, 58th, 1934
Vennum, A.R.		F, — Ill. (died of consumption)	76		1913	NE, 38th, 1914
Ventle, R.		H, 123rd Ind. Cav.	59		1934 Aug 17	KS, 54th, 1935
Venus, Joseph A.		A, 17th Va.	164		1909 Apr 7	KS, 29th, 1910
Verhi, Jacob	Pvt.	C, 3rd Iowa Inf.	371	62	1890 Jul 29	IA, 17th, 1891

*See Appendix A, B or C for roster of post names and locations.
†See Introduction for note regarding recording of death date.

Name	Rank	Company, Regiment or Ship	Post*	Age	Death Date†	Journal
Verley, Frank M.		B, 31st Wis. Inf. (died of pneumonia)	121		1893 Nov 23	NE, 18th, 1894
VerMenlen, John	Pvt.	E, 36th Iowa Inf.	12		1924 Apr 30	IA, 51st, 1925
Vermillion, W.H.			55		1913 Oct 2	KS, 33rd, 1914
Vermillon, W.H.		I, 37th Ill.	314		1892	KS, 12th, 1893
Verney, Jas. B.		D, N.Y. Hvy. Art. (died of pneumonia)	32	60	1908 Jan 10	NE, 33rd, 1909
Vernon, E.S.		F, 78th Ohio	259		1926 Dec 10	KS, 46th, 1927
Vernon, James H.	Pvt.	G, 39th N.J. Inf.	29	86	1931 Apr 1	IA, 58th, 1932
Vernon, William E.	Pvt. Pvt.	A, 33rd Iowa Inf. A, 34th/38th Consolidated Iowa	49	100	1939 Oct 11	IA, 66th, 1940
Versaw, Levi	Corp.	C, 22nd Iowa	62		1907 Dec 7	IA, 34th, 1908
Vertrees, J.W.	Pvt.	C, 15th Ill. Inf.	83		1920 Dec 10	IA, 47th, 1921
Vertrus, Sam'l D.		F, 129th Ill. (died of pneumonia)	35		1910	NE, 35th, 1911
Vesper, George	Pvt.		122		1928	IA, 55th, 1929
Vest, Henry		C, 9th Mo.	167		1905 Jul 14	KS, 25th, 1906
Vestal, H.C.		A, 23rd Iowa	331		1900 Oct 28	KS, 20th, 1901
Vester, Conrad		N.Y.	94		1902 Jul 26	KS, 22nd, 1903
Vetter, Albert		G, 72nd Ohio	112		1932 Aug 17	NE, 57th, 1933
Vetter, J.J.		K, 12th Mich.	47		1931 Mar 10	NE, 56th, 1932
Vial, E.			45		1925 Sep 25	IA, 52nd, 1926
Vibbard, W.	Pvt.	K, 116th N.Y. Inf.	24		1915 Jun 21	IA, 42nd, 1916
Vick, Henry		D, 104th Ohio Inf. (died at Junction City)	132		1895	KS, 15th, 1896
Vickers, Andrew J.	Lieut.	17th West Va. Inf.	65		1915 Sep 7	KS, 35th, 1916
Vickers, James X.		D, 142nd Ind.	14		1893 Jul 21	KS, 13th, 1894
Vickers, N.C.	Lieut.	D, 143rd Ohio Inf.	440		1919 May 20	IA, 46th, 1920
Victor, Andrew	Pvt.	B, 12th & 27th Iowa	344	52	1898 Jan 8	IA, 24th, 1898
Victor, Lycurgus	Pvt.	F, 70th Ind. Inf.	309	57	1898 Jan 7	IA, 24th, 1898
Victor, M.A.	Pvt.	B, 40th Iowa Inf.	127	55	1894 Mar 10	IA, 21st, 1895
Videll, J.L.			96		1906	IA, 33rd, 1907
Vie, Wm.	Pvt.	C, 40th Iowa	144		1922	IA, 49th, 1923
Viele, Sydney B.		H, 95th N.Y. (died of old age)	47	74	1897 Oct 13	NE, 22nd, 1898
Vierling, B.S.	Pvt.		55		1905 May 31	IA, 32nd, 1906
Viers, Thomas H.B.	Pvt.	B, 70th Ohio Inf.	5	58	1899 Jun 14	IA, 26th, 1900
Viertman, A.W.	Pvt.	G, 153rd Ill. Inf.	30		1920 Jul	IA, 47th, 1921
Vieth, Fred A.		E, 49th Mo. (died of paralysis and cancer)	79		1917 Oct 26	NE, 42nd, 1918
Viets, John		D, 13th Mo. Cav.	49		1918 Dec 4	KS, 38th, 1919
Villemont, F.G.		C, 31st Wis.	35		1927	KS, 47th, 1928
Villian, Paul	Pvt.	E, 20th Iowa Inf.	1		1897 Feb 24	IA, 24th, 1898
Villiers, Francis	Pvt.	H, 19th Iowa Inf.	55		1914 Sep 27	IA, 41st, 1915
Vilmer, Joseph		B, 62nd Ill.	47		1926 Mar 26	KS, 46th, 1927
Vilzes, V.		2nd Kans. Inf.	12		1891 Oct 8	KS, 11th, 1892
Vinall, H.G.	Pvt.	C, 20th Iowa Inf.	222		1926 Jan 31	IA, 53rd, 1927
Vince, R.E.		F, 9th Kans.	293		1922 Apr 11	KS, 42nd, 1923
Vincen, Daniel C.		H, 53rd Ill.	354	79	1921 Apr 28	NE, 46th, 1922
Vincent, A.E.			26		1888 Jan 2	NE, 12th, 1888
Vincent, B.	Pvt.	C, 32nd Iowa Inf.	236		1930 Dec 24	IA, 57th, 1931
Vincent, Beth		C, 32nd Iowa	236		1934 Apr 20	IA, 61st, 1935
Vincent, Chas. S.	Sergt.	A, 92nd Ill. Inf.	101		1909 Oct 15	IA, 36th, 1910
Vincent, Geo. W.	Pvt.	H, 14th Ill. Inf.	297		1916 Jun 11	IA, 43rd, 1917
Vincent, John	Pvt.	A, 96th Ill. Inf.	81		1927 Feb 5	IA, 54th, 1928
Vincent, R.		E, 157th Ind.	5		1912 Apr 17	KS, 32nd, 1913
Vincent, Thatcher		H, 43rd Ohio Inf.	68		1912 Nov 17	KS, 32nd, 1913
Vincent, Thos.	Pvt.	A, 46th Ill. Inf.	49		1924 Aug 8	IA, 51st, 1925
Vincent, W.H.		H, 25th Penn.	320		1893 Oct 29	KS, 13th, 1894
Vincent, Wm.	Pvt.	B, 45th Iowa Inf.	333		1913	IA, 40th, 1914
Vincent, Wm. Alonzo	Corp.	A, 152nd N.Y. Inf. (at large)	314	96	1943 Apr 20	IA, 69th, 1943
Vinegar, W.H.	Pvt.	A, 31st Ill. Inf.	74		1920 Feb 15	IA, 47th, 1921
Vinsil, J.K.	Pvt.	E, 143rd Ohio Inf.	208	65	1897 Jan 4	IA, 23rd, 1897
Vinton, S.J.			12		1899	NE, 24th, 1900
Virchone, Wm.			479		1905	IA, 32nd, 1906
Virgil, William	Pvt.	17th Ill. Cav.	219		1910 Nov	IA, 37th, 1911
Virmilyea, G.E.	Pvt.	I, 3rd Wis. Inf.	71	38	1888 Jan 18	IA, 15th, 1889
Visnow, Sam'l	Pvt.	G, 5th Wis. Inf.	461		1916 May 25	IA, 43rd, 1917

Name	Rank	Company, Regiment or Ship	Post*	Age	Death Date†	Journal
Viso, Wm.		F, 11th Kans. Cav.	180		1909 Jul 16	KS, 29th, 1910
Vliet, David	Pvt.	C, 84th Ill. Inf.	11		1899 Apr 15	IA, 26th, 1900
Voelker, Jo.	Pvt.	I, 43rd Ill. Inf.	5		1920 Nov 3	IA, 47th, 1921
Vogal, Frederick		A, 3rd Kans.	380		1911 Aug 3	KS, 31st, 1912
Vogan, Joseph R.		D, 23rd Mo.	428		1914 Aug 13	KS, 34th, 1915
Vogel, A.J.	Pvt.	F, 8th Iowa Inf.	167		1915 Feb 27	IA, 42nd, 1916
Vogel, Gotlieb		K, 25th Ind. Inf.	25		1905 Nov 28	NE, 30th, 1906
Vogel, Gottlole		K, 25th Ind.	25		1905 Nov 28	NE, 31st, 1907
Vogel, John T.	Sergt.	2nd Kans.	20		1897 Feb 11	KS, 17th, 1898
Vogel, Lewis		2nd Ill. Cav. (died at Topeka, Kans.; buried at Topeka Cemetery)	71		1894 May 20	KS, 14th, 1895
Vogel, Simon	Pvt.	G, 45th Iowa Inf.	2		1906 Dec 7	IA, 33rd, 1907
Vogelsong, Geo. D.		D, 187th Penn.	6		1927 Jun 18	KS, 47th, 1928
Voght, Samuel			170		1899	IA, 26th, 1900
Vogl, Frederick		D, U.S. Surgeon	132		1899 Dec 4	KS, 19th, 1900
Vogus, Francis	Pvt.	C, 9th Ill. Cav.	230		1912 Oct 26	IA, 39th, 1913
Voight, H.		D, 33rd Wis. Inf. (died at Topeka)	71		1895 Jun 4	KS, 15th, 1896
Voigtlander, Theo.		D, 45th Wis. (died of paralysis)	22	69	1917 Jan 30	NE, 42nd, 1918
Voigtlander, Theodore		D, 45th Wis. (died of paralysis)	22	69	1917 Jan 30	NE, 41st, 1917
Volbehr, F.	Pvt.	D, 10th Iowa Inf.	163		1909 Mar 27	IA, 36th, 1910
Volburg, Jas. H.		H, 49th Ohio Inf. (died at Longton)	91		1895 Aug 5	KS, 15th, 1896
Voliket, Chas.	Pvt.	K, 46th Wis. Inf.	84		1920 Sep 29	IA, 47th, 1921
Volk, John C.		H, 110th Ohio	64		1920 Apr 7	KS, 40th, 1921
Vollmer, F., see Vollnur, F.						
Vollmer, Morritz	Pvt.	G, 16th Iowa Vols.	70		1899 Oct 5	IA, 26th, 1900
Vollnur, F.		A, 1st Colo. Cav.	52		1908 May 5	KS, 28th, 1909
Volz, Daniel		H, 94th Ohio	295		1906 Jun 29	KS, 26th, 1907
VonSchentz, Oscar		B, 107th Penn. (died of paresis)	21		1909 Sep 17	NE, 34th, 1910
Voorhees, Isaac	Pvt.	K, 2nd Wis. Cav.	68		1910 Jun 21	IA, 37th, 1911
Voorhies, Lemuel E., see Vorhes, Lemuel E.						
Voorhis, A.L.		B, 46th Ind.	164		1913 Aug 19	KS, 33rd, 1914
Vorce, Wm.	Pvt.	C, 100th Ill. Inf.	68		1925 Jun 15	IA, 52nd, 1926
Vore, I.D.	Capt.	B, 11th Ill.	231		1899 Oct 26	IA, 26th, 1900
Vore, Mahlon	Corp.	E, 26th Ind. Inf.	7	60	1895 Nov 4	IA, 22nd, 1896
Vore, Malon		E, 26th Ind. Inf.	44	59	1895 Nov 1	NE, 20th, 1896
Vorees, Isaac			24		1926	IA, 53rd, 1927
Vorheas, James	Pvt.	K, 14th Iowa Inf.	18		1918 Mar 16	IA, 45th, 1919
Vorhees, Daniel		D, 10th Ind.	369		1892 Feb 6	KS, 12th, 1893
Vorhes, Lemuel E.		I, 14th Iowa	52		1926 Jul 9	NE, 51st, 1927
Voris, Miles		C, 42nd Ill.	64		1906 Nov	KS, 26th, 1907
Vorney, Edgar		D, 14th N.Y. Hvy. Art.	180		1908 Oct 23	NE, 33rd, 1909
Vosburg, Wm.	Capt.	F, 31st Iowa Inf.	88	75	1891 Aug 8	IA, 18th, 1892
Voshall, W.P.	Pvt.	B, 28th Ohio Inf.	233		1904 Nov 1	IA, 31st, 1905
Voss, Hans	Pvt.	I, 1st Iowa Inf.	17		1908 Aug 2	IA, 35th, 1909
Vought, Geo. W.	Pvt.	D, 39th Iowa	426		1903 Nov	IA, 30th, 1904
Vought, Lewis	Pvt.	L, 4th Iowa Cav.	370	68	1896 Jul 25	IA, 23rd, 1897
Vreeland, M.V.	Sergt.	H, 11th Ill. Cav.	40	87	1931 Oct 24	IA, 58th, 1932
Vroom, J.H.	Sergt.	F, 17th Ill. Cav.	68	56	1897 Apr	IA, 24th, 1898
Vrooman, D.K.	Pvt.	E, 49th Wis. Inf.	72	67	1896 Mar 10	IA, 23rd, 1897
Vrooman, W.L.		G, 31st Iowa	191		1899	IA, 26th, 1900
Waatherbee, S.S.		B, 133rd Ohio	12		1924 Jul 22	KS, 44th, 1925
Wachtell, U.R.		G, 5th Mo. Cav.	318	74	1917	NE, 42nd, 1918
Wadda, Simon B.	Pvt.	H, 80th Ohio Vol. Inf.	1		1915 Jul 2	KS, 35th, 1916
Waddel, Josiah		H, 79th U.S.C. Inf.	7		1939 Jan 14	NE, 64th, 1940
Waddell, Charles			96		1918	IA, 45th, 1919
Waddell, John		H, 23rd Eng.	185		1918 Mar 21	KS, 38th, 1919
Waddle, Charles F.			150		1884	KS, 4th, 1885
Waddle, S.H.		G, 45th Iowa	131		1929 Oct 4	KS, 49th, 1930
Wade, A.F.			85		1893 Jul	KS, 13th, 1894
Wade, B.		F, 63rd Ind.	112		1918 Aug 12	KS, 38th, 1919
Wade, Benj. F.		Ind. Scouts	95		1926	NE, 51st, 1927

Name	Rank	Company, Regiment or Ship	Post*	Age	Death Date†	Journal
Wade, George		H, 9th N.Y. Cav. (died of hardening of nerves)	107	66	1908 Aug 23	NE, 33rd, 1909
Wade, George G.		H, 47th Ind.	222		1919 Sep 10	KS, 39th, 1920
Wade, Ira		C, 23rd Ill. (died of blood poison)	89	75	1915 Jul 11	NE, 40th, 1916
Wade, J.H.	Pvt.	H, 9th Iowa Vol. Cav.	173		1918	IA, 45th, 1919
Wade, John	Pvt.	C, 2nd Iowa Cav.	400		1923 Dec 15	IA, 50th, 1924
Wade, John		K, 111th Penn.	151		1909 Sep 15	KS, 29th, 1910
Wade, John			98		1927 Nov	KS, 47th, 1928
Wade, John H.	Pvt.	F, 168th Penn. Inf.	343	58	1886 Mar 16	IA, 12th, 1886
Wade, John W.	Pvt.	96th Ill. Inf.	271		1908 Apr	IA, 35th, 1909
Wade, Louis A.		K, 11th Mo.	32		1919 Jun 26	KS, 39th, 1920
Wade, S.B.	Lieut.	A, 5th Kans. Cav.	1		1915 Apr 17	KS, 35th, 1916
Wade, Spencer		E, 11th Kans.	1		1908 Feb 24	KS, 28th, 1909
Wade, T.I.	Pvt.	K, 25th Mich.	81		1926 Aug 2	IA, 53rd, 1927
Wade, W.S.	Sergt.	H, 5th Ill. Cav.	97		1902 Jan 22	IA, 28th, 1902
Wadell, W.R.		C, 15th Iowa	22	89	1934 Aug 15	IA, 61st, 1935
Wadkins, A.		H, 7th Ill.	255		1905 Aug 2	KS, 25th, 1906
Wadkins, Dorchester		2nd Kans.	464		1904 Dec 21	KS, 24th, 1905
Wadle, John			74		1910	IA, 37th, 1911
Wadleigh, Jonathan			63		1890	NE, 15th, 1891
Wadsack, Fred		G, 27th Ill. Inf.	150		1885	KS, 5th, 1886
Wadsworth, James Henry		B, 92nd Ill. Inf.		87	1937 Sep 27	IA, 64th, 1938
Wadsworth, O.F.	Pvt.	K, 89th Ill. Inf.	44		1905 Feb 7	IA, 32nd, 1906
Wadsworth, Samuel W., see Wadworth, Sam'l W.						
Wadsworth, W.F.		A, 169th N.Y.	25		1932 Jun 12	NE, 57th, 1933
Wadworth, Sam'l W.		I, 13th Ill.	463		1896 Feb	KS, 16th, 1897
Waens, J.G.		I, 20th Ohio Inf.	12		1925 Aug 15	IA, 52nd, 1926
Waers, W.H.	Pvt.	H, 195th Ohio	12		1922 Oct 21	IA, 49th, 1923
Wager, Charles	Sergt.	A, 24th Iowa Inf.	164		1922 Jul 16	IA, 49th, 1923
Wager, J.A.	Sergt.	F, 20th Iowa Inf.	212		1904 May 21	IA, 31st, 1905
Wagg, C.	Pvt.	E, 25th Iowa Inf.	5		1912 Dec 8	IA, 39th, 1913
Waggoner, Alfred		C, 158th Penn. (died of heart disease)	245	62	1904 Jul 11	NE, 29th, 1905
Waggoner, H.M.	Pvt.	F, 208th Penn. Inf.	117	60	1895 Feb 24	IA, 22nd, 1896
Waggoner, Isacher R.		H, 25th Mo. Inf.	250		1914 Feb 2	KS, 34th, 1915
Waggoner, S.		A, 104th Ill.	59		1888	KS, 8th, 1889
Wagner, Ammi H.	Pvt.	F, 3rd Penn. Hvy. Art.	503		1902	IA, 29th, 1903
Wagner, B.	Sergt.	A, Cav.	50		1923 Jun 29	IA, 50th, 1924
Wagner, C.		G, 12th Ill. Inf.	342		1900 Aug 17	KS, 20th, 1901
Wagner, C.F.	Pvt.	E, 25th Iowa Inf.	1		1911 1st term	IA, 38th, 1912
Wagner, Calvin			132		1920 Nov 14	KS, 40th, 1921
Wagner, Christian		F, 8th Kans.	256		1921 May 11	KS, 41st, 1922
Wagner, Gideon	Pvt.	A, 34th Iowa Inf.	7		1913 Dec 22	IA, 40th, 1914
Wagner, H.D.			7		1909 Feb 5	IA, 36th, 1910
Wagner, Henry	Pvt.	D, 142nd Ill. Inf.	436		1927 Oct 26	IA, 54th, 1928
Wagner, Henry		A, 75th Ind. (died of old age)	206	85	1922 Jul	NE, 47th, 1923
Wagner, Isaac L.			1		1904 Feb 13	KS, 24th, 1905
Wagner, Isiah	Pvt.	H, 34th Ill.	311		1914 Jun 29	IA, 41st, 1915
Wagner, Jacob J.		G, 88th Penn. Inf.	1		1899 Mar 3	KS, 19th, 1900
Wagner, James H.		O, 24th Iowa Inf.	147		4th quarter 1884	IA, 11th, 1885
Wagner, John	Pvt.	D, 32nd Ill.	95		1905 Aug 26	IA, 32nd, 1906
Wagner, John J.		K, 47th Wis. Inf.	120		1926 Nov 22	NE, 51st, 1927
Wagner, Lawrence	Pvt.	I, 12th Ill. Cav.	55	56	1896 Mar 29	IA, 22nd, 1896
Wagner, M.V.	Pvt.	D, 51st Ohio	233		1907 2nd term	IA, 34th, 1908
Wagner, Michael	Pvt.	H, 1st Iowa Inf.	70	63	1892 Jan 12	IA, 18th, 1892
Wagner, W.H.		K, 85th Ill.	68		1914 Oct 22	KS, 34th, 1915
Wagner, Wm. M.	Pvt.	K, 46th Ill. Inf.	452		1929	IA, 56th, 1930
Wagoner, J.L.		I, 157th Ohio	12		1920 Jun 10	KS, 40th, 1921
Wagoner, James		F, 20th Wis. Cav.	115		1922 Oct 22	KS, 42nd, 1923
Wagoner, Joseph		H, 10th Ill. (died at Olpe)	369		1895 Aug	KS, 15th, 1896
Wagoner, S.C.		G, 13th Wis. Inf.	63		1914 Aug 14	KS, 34th, 1915
Wagstaff, D.R.		A, 2nd Colo.	127		1919 Feb 5	KS, 39th, 1920

*See Appendix A, B or C for roster of post names and locations.
†See Introduction for note regarding recording of death date.

Name	Rank	Company, Regiment or Ship	Post*	Age	Death Date†	Journal
Wagstaff, Richard		A, 83rd Ill. Inf.	12		1901 Sep 19	KS, 21st, 1902
Wahaven, M.	Pvt.	G, 33rd Iowa	40		1921 Feb 14	IA, 48th, 1922
Wahl, Joseph		B, 68th Ohio	25		1929 Jun 20	NE, 54th, 1930
Waid, A.O.	Pvt.	K, 150th Penn. Inf.	149		1909 Mar 29	IA, 36th, 1910
Waid, G.A.		I, 55th Ind.	142		1917 Feb 11	KS, 37th, 1918
Waid, William H.		D, 29th Ind. Inf. (died at National Military Home; buried at Leavenworth, Kans.)	42		1894 May 26	KS, 14th, 1895
Waide, J.B.	Pvt.	M, 17th Ill. Cav.	197		1914 Dec 26	IA, 41st, 1915
Wailes, G.W.	Pvt.	6th Iowa Inf.	122		1915 Jan 25	IA, 42nd, 1916
Wails, G.W.	Pvt.	6th Iowa Inf.	122		1916 Aug 20	IA, 43rd, 1917
Wait, H.B.		H, 13th Mich.	25		1892 Nov 8	KS, 12th, 1893
Wait, John	Corp.	F, 31st N.Y. Inf.	235	58	1891 Oct 20	NE, 16th, 1892
Wait, John D.		E, 91st Ill.	300		1889	KS, 9th, 1890
Wait, Lee		135th Ill.	23		1911 Aug 31	KS, 31st, 1912
Wait, W.R.	Pvt.	A, 9th Iowa Inf.	492		1916 Jun 23	IA, 43rd, 1917
Wait, Warren	Corp.	G, 12th Iowa Inf.	132		1902 Nov 6	IA, 29th, 1903
Waite, A.C.			127		1922 Jul 22	KS, 42nd, 1923
Waite, Edgar		F, 15th Iowa	55		1921 Jul 30	KS, 41st, 1922
Waite, G.L.		H, 16th Kans.	243		1888	KS, 8th, 1889
Waite, G.W.	Pvt.	B, 12th Penn. Inf.	259		1905 May 20	IA, 32nd, 1906
Waite, John W.	Pvt.	G, 6th Iowa Inf.	112		1907 Jan 17	IA, 34th, 1908
Waite, W.E.			86		1907 2nd term	IA, 34th, 1908
Waite, W.F.		M, 16th Kans.	28		1910 Nov 11	KS, 30th, 1911
Waite, Wm. H.	Sergt.	K, 56th Ohio	8		1904 Oct 27	IA, 31st, 1905
Waitt, H., Rev.		F, B, 6th Mass.	25		1923 Mar 3	KS, 43rd, 1924
Wake, Alphazo		B, 9th Iowa Cal.[Cav.] (murdered)	166	54	1900 Nov 3	NE, 25th, 1901
Wakefield, A.W.	Col.	49th Penn. (six months prisoner of war)	47		1891 Dec 17	KS, 11th, 1892
Wakefield, C.A.		C, 143rd Ill.	50		1896 Oct 12	KS, 16th, 1897
Wakefield, G.W.	Pvt.	F, 41st Ill.	22		1905 Mar 27	IA, 32nd, 1906
Wakefield, H.T.	Pvt.	M, 1st Wis. Cav.	39		1928 Feb	IA, 55th, 1929
Wakefield, J.C.		K, 177th Penn.	127		1933 Mar 9	KS, 53rd, 1934
Wakefield, Jacob	Pvt.	C, 6th Iowa Cav.	46	64	1885 Jul 2	IA, 12th, 1886
Wakefield, Joseph		F, 125th U.S.C.T.	18		1910 Feb 16	KS, 30th, 1911
Wakefield, Orson		F, 18th Ind. Inf.	25	82	1917 May 28	NE, 42nd, 1918
Wakefield, Schuyler	Pvt.	K, 95th Ill. Inf. (died of LaGrippe)	7	50	1891 Apr 8	NE, 16th, 1892
Wakefield, Wm.		G, 35th N.Y.	42		1908 Mar 28	KS, 28th, 1909
Wakeland, P.D.		H, 70th Ind. Inf. (died of kidney complaint)	56	68	1896 Jun 7	NE, 21st, 1897
Wakelee, Chas. L.	Pvt.	B, 14th Iowa Inf.	112		1916 Jan 16	IA, 43rd, 1917
Wakely, Henry		I, 37th Iowa Inf.	94		3rd quarter 1884	IA, 11th, 1885
Wakeman, F.M.		B, 72nd Ind.	394		1898 Oct 16	KS, 18th, 1899
Wakeman, R.S.	Pvt.	C, 3rd Mo. Cav.	31		1912 Oct	IA, 39th, 1913
Walace, David		E, 7th Iowa	470		1896 Jul 1	KS, 16th, 1897
Walace, J.M.		G, 62nd Ohio	314		1888	KS, 8th, 1889
Walbridge, J.		G, 6th Kans.	427		1898 Mar 17	KS, 18th, 1899
Walcott, Albert G.			28		1883	KS, 3rd, 1884
Walcott, E.S.	Pvt.	12th N.Y. Cav.	1		1924 Sep 22	IA, 51st, 1925
Walcott, N.M.	Corp.	E, 47th Iowa Inf.	247		1925 May 6	IA, 52nd, 1926
Walde, Anton	Pvt.	K, 146th Ill. Inf.	88		1919 Sep 20	IA, 46th, 1920
Walden, Calvin		F, 7th Iowa	28		1911 Nov 30	KS, 31st, 1912
Walden, G.W.		G, 47th Ill. Inf.	11	79	1908 Feb 4	NE, 33rd, 1909
Walden, Joseph	Pvt.	B, 30th Iowa	337		1907 Jul 1	IA, 34th, 1908
Walden, M.M.	Capt.	D, 6th Iowa Inf.	122	54	1891 Jul 24	IA, 18th, 1892
Waldman, Mark		G, 1st Cal.	1		1917 Mar 1	KS, 37th, 1918
Waldo, Jno.	Pvt.	C, 3rd Wis. Inf.	7		1925 Jul 3	IA, 52nd, 1926
Waldock, John	Sergt.	B, 15th Ill. Inf.	176		1899 Aug 10	KS, 19th, 1900
Waldon, Simeon		D, 28th U.S. Colored Inf.	17		1918 Sep 4	KS, 38th, 1919
Waldron, Arnold		G, 94th Ill.	117		1926 Jan 14	KS, 46th, 1927
Waldron, I.H.		C, 105th Ill. Inf.	11	78	1916 Mar 5	NE, 41st, 1917
Waldron, Jasper		B, 1st Mo. Eng. (died of pneumonia)	32	74	1912 Oct 1	NE, 37th, 1913
Waldron, Philip		A, 53rd Ohio	145		1885	KS, 5th, 1886
Waldron, Sam'l J.	Pvt.	B, 14th Iowa Inf.	57		1911 Aug 15	IA, 38th, 1912
Waldron, W.O.	Com. Sergt.	L, 7th Iowa Inf.	7		1907 Apr 17	IA, 34th, 1908

Name	Rank	Company, Regiment or Ship	Post*	Age	Death Date†	Journal
Wales, Alanson			[42?]		1909 Apr 17	KS, 29th, 1910
Wales, Thos. H.	Sergt.	K, 1st Colo. Cav. (died of Bright's disease; also had rheumatism contracted in service)	45	42	1884 Oct 6	NE, 9th, 1885
Walford, James	Pvt.	H, 64th N.Y.	33		1907 Mar 24	IA, 34th, 1908
Walgemuth, Jno.	Pvt.	D, 7th Iowa Inf.	170		1904 Jan	IA, 30th, 1904
Walgren, August	Pvt.	M, 4th Iowa Cav.	19		1914 Mar 17	IA, 41st, 1915
Walizer, E.R.	Pvt.	G, 54th Penn. Inf.	7		1906 Apr 4	IA, 33rd, 1907
Walizer, Jonathan		D, 1st Penn. Res.	493		1916 Dec 28	KS, 36th, 1917
Walke, Constastine		H, 36th Iowa Inf.	380		1901 Feb 22	KS, 21st, 1902
Walkenshaw, J.C.		I, 9th R.R.C.V.[Penn. Res. Vol. Corps]	6		1909 Dec 16	KS, 29th, 1910
Walker, A.	Pvt.	A, 35th Iowa	231		1921 Aug 15	IA, 48th, 1922
Walker, A.		I, 103rd Penn.	5		1926 Nov 9	KS, 46th, 1927
Walker, A.B.	Pvt.	I, 154th Ohio Inf.	29		1924 May 13	IA, 51st, 1925
Walker, A.C.	Pvt.	B, 23rd N.Y. Inf.	452		1915 Aug 26	IA, 42nd, 1916
Walker, A.D.	Pvt.	B, 23rd Iowa Inf.	7		1898 Nov 2	IA, 25th, 1899
Walker, A.F.		K, 10th Ill. Inf.	59		1916 Oct 15	KS, 36th, 1917
Walker, A.J.		F, 23rd Iowa Inf.	30		1900 May 30	KS, 20th, 1901
Walker, A.N.		H, 47th Ill. Inf. (died at Ottawa)	18		1895 Dec	KS, 15th, 1896
Walker, Albert		B, 32nd Ky.	236		1925 Jul	KS, 45th, 1926
Walker, Alex.		I, 52nd Penn. Inf.	347		1900 May	KS, 20th, 1901
Walker, Alexander		C, 13th Ill. Cav.	448		1910 Dec 13	KS, 30th, 1911
Walker, Alfred	Pvt.	C, 1st Iowa Cav.	208		1912 Oct 1	IA, 39th, 1913
Walker, Alonza		H, 142nd N.Y.	17		1918 Mar 14	KS, 38th, 1919
Walker, Ancil	Pvt.	D, 2nd Mich. Inf.	222	88	1932 Nov 18	IA, 59th, 1933
Walker, Andrew		K, 3rd Tenn. (13)	185		1918 Mar 1	KS, 38th, 1919
Walker, Charles N.		F, 98th Ohio	448?		1912 Sep 13	KS, 32nd, 1913
Walker, Chas.		M, 21st Penn. Cav. (died of heart failure, other com[plications?])	148	62	1911 Jun 25	NE, 36th, 1912
Walker, D.B.		G, 13th Kans.	53		1927 Oct 12	KS, 47th, 1928
Walker, D.R.	Pvt.	A, 27th Iowa Inf.	194	92	1931 Jun 22	IA, 58th, 1932
Walker, Daniel		I, 1st U.S. Colored Art.	321		1914 Sep 16	KS, 34th, 1915
Walker, E.D.		C, 25th Wis.	226		1924 Jul 12	KS, 44th, 1925
Walker, F.E.	Pvt.	F, 29th Iowa Inf.	10		1926 Oct	IA, 53rd, 1927
Walker, F.G.		D, 32nd Wis. Inf.	36		1918 Jul 28	KS, 38th, 1919
Walker, F.M.	Pvt.		251		1914 Oct 17	IA, 41st, 1915
Walker, G.A.	Pvt.	I, 103rd Penn.	108		1923 Feb 6	IA, 50th, 1924
Walker, G.A.		B, 149th Ind.	28		1927 Jul 14	KS, 47th, 1928
Walker, G.M.		C, 11th Kans. Cav.	127		1918 Dec 12	KS, 38th, 1919
Walker, G.W.	Eng.	Navy	24		1916	IA, 43rd, 1917
Walker, Geo. R.		I, 2nd Conn. Hvy. Art.	34		1922 Apr 10	KS, 42nd, 1923
Walker, Henry J.		A, 12th Wis. Inf. (died in Florida)	190		1891 Jan 22	KS, 11th, 1892
Walker, Hiram	Corp.	G, 2nd Iowa Cav.	446?		1900 Apr 14	IA, 27th, 1901
Walker, Isaac	Pvt.	G, 14th Iowa Inf.	31		1893 Oct	IA, 20th, 1894
Walker, J.	Pvt.	D, 17th Iowa Inf.	231		1921 Mar 28	IA, 48th, 1922
Walker, J.A.	Pvt.	B, 4th Iowa Cav.	12		1908 Dec 16	IA, 35th, 1909
Walker, J.D.	Pvt.	D, 17th Iowa	7		1921	IA, 48th, 1922
Walker, J.G.	Pvt.	E, 1st U.S. Inf.	109		1925 Oct 1	IA, 52nd, 1926
Walker, J.I.		22nd Ohio Battery	23		1908 Apr 6	NE, 33rd, 1909
Walker, J.M.	Pvt.	F, 36th Iowa Inf.	122		1928 Dec	IA, 55th, 1929
Walker, J.M.		G, 172nd Ohio Vol. Inf. (died of paralysis)	22	78	1925 Feb 18	NE, 50th, 1926
Walker, J.N.	Pvt.	G, 17th Iowa Inf.	7		1920 Aug 11	IA, 47th, 1921
Walker, James	Pvt.	C, 9th Penn. Inf. H, 32nd Iowa Inf.	22		1930 Mar 27	IA, 57th, 1931
Walker, James V.		A, 39th Iowa Inf.	55		1912 May 22	IA, 39th, 1913
Walker, John			175		1925 May	KS, 45th, 1926
Walker, John (Col.)		C, 1st Kans. Col. Inf.	7	97	1937 Jul 25	IA, 64th, 1938
Walker, John R.			25		1913 Jan 9	KS, 33rd, 1914
Walker, John R.		H, 32nd Ky. Inf.	130		1925 Feb 4	KS, 45th, 1926
Walker, Joseph			29		1884	KS, 4th, 1885
Walker, Joseph	Pvt.	G, 74th Ohio Inf.	100		1899	NE, 24th, 1900
Walker, K.	Pvt.	H, 15th Vt. Inf.	358		1912 Sep 15	IA, 39th, 1913
Walker, Landy A.		H, 15th Ind.	111		1937 Jan 12	NE, 62nd, 1938

Name	Rank	Company, Regiment or Ship	Post*	Age	Death Date†	Journal
Walker, Leicester		K, 2nd U.S. Cav. (died of kidney trouble; see also Appendix D)	69	80	1916 Apr 9 or 10	NE, 41st, 1917
Walker, Lige		C, 9th Kans.	38		1918 Feb 16	KS, 38th, 1919
Walker, Martin	Pvt.	M, 6th Iowa Cav.	12		1899 Oct 17	IA, 26th, 1900
Walker, Nathan		B, 122nd Ill. Inf.	87		1914 Dec 11	KS, 34th, 1915
Walker, Peter H.		E, 14th Wis. Inf. (died of rheumatism)	38	67	1909 Jan 29	NE, 34th, 1910
Walker, R.A.		C, 99th Ill. Inf.	171		1914 Nov 6	KS, 34th, 1915
Walker, R.C.		I, 19th Ill. Inf. (final discharge Company C, 149th Ill. Vol. Inf.)	55		1890	KS, 10th, 1891
Walker, Ransom		E, 1st Iowa Cav.	25	70	1913 Oct 10	NE, 38th, 1914
Walker, Robert			74		1916 Feb 9	IA, 43rd, 1917
Walker, Robt. F.	Sergt.	C, 98th Ohio Inf.	358		1926 Apr 10	IA, 53rd, 1927
Walker, Ross			284		1908	NE, 33rd, 1909
Walker, Sam'l T.			113		1908 Feb 29	NE, 33rd, 1909
Walker, Samuel	Lieut. Col.	16th Kans. Cav.	12		1893 Feb 26	KS, 13th, 1894
Walker, Samuel		D, 14th Ill.	4		1931 Jan 19	KS, 52nd, 1933
Walker, Samuel		D, 14th Ill.	4		1931 Jan 19	KS, 51st, 1932
Walker, Thomas A.	Pvt.	G, 15th Iowa Inf.	116		1922 Aug	IA, 49th, 1923
Walker, W.		47th Ill.	54		1904 Dec 17	KS, 24th, 1905
Walker, W.A.		B, 16th Mich. Sharpshooters	88		1st quarter 1885	IA, 11th, 1885
Walker, W.B.	Pvt.	C, 71st N.Y. Inf.	16		1901 Aug 29	IA, 28th, 1902
Walker, W.D.		M, 12th Ohio	56		1914 Feb 11	KS, 33rd, 1914
Walker, W.F.		B, 139th Ind.	[25?]		1918 Aug 7	KS, 38th, 1919
Walker, W.H.	Pvt.	C, 36th Ohio	17		1921 May 20	IA, 48th, 1922
Walker, W.H.		A, 43rd Ind.	59		1920 Apr 18	KS, 40th, 1921
Walker, W.H.		E, 93rd Ill. (died of paralysis)	35	91	1919 Jun 20	NE, 44th, 1920
Walker, W.H.		C, 36th Ohio Vol. Inf. (died of heart trouble)	22	82	1925 Dec 4	NE, 50th, 1926
Walker, W.H.		A, 70th Ohio Vols.	22		1925 Dec 4	NE, 51st, 1927
Walker, W.J.		E, 104th Penn.	64		1919 Nov 13	KS, 39th, 1920
Walker, W.J.		13th Ill.	129		1929 Nov 8	KS, 49th, 1930
Walker, W.P.		5th Wis.	34		1927 Nov	KS, 47th, 1928
Walker, Walter		I, 1st Neb. Cav.	7	53	1895 Jun 24	NE, 20th, 1896
Walker, William			122		1922 Sep	IA, 49th, 1923
Walker, William	Pvt.	F, 19th Iowa Inf.	153		1929 Nov 5	IA, 56th, 1930
Walker, William		A, 79th U.S.C. (died at Argentine)	10		1895 Apr	KS, 15th, 1896
Walker, William	Pvt. & Corp.	G, 45th Mass. Inf. (died of heart disease)	34	44	1888 Feb 7	NE, 13th, 1889
Walker, Wm.	Pvt.	I, 3rd Iowa Inf.	122		1909	IA, 36th, 1910
Walker, Wm.	Corp.	B, 2nd Iowa Cav.	133		1926 Mar 2	IA, 53rd, 1927
Walker, Wm. A.	Pvt.	F, 142nd Ind. Inf.	262		1899	NE, 24th, 1900
Walker, Wm. L.		C, 66th Ill.	209		1904 Mar 19	KS, 24th, 1905
Walkins, Edward		C, 92nd Ohio	25		1922 Mar 28	KS, 42nd, 1923
Walkinshaw, J.C., see Walkenshaw, J.C.						
Walkinshaw, Joseph Cowan	2nd Lieut. & 1st Lieut.	I, 9th Penn. Res. (see Appendix D)		78	1909 Dec 16	KS, 29th, 1910
Walkup, A.		H, 4th Iowa (died of gallstones)	40	70	1912 Jul 18	NE, 37th, 1913
Walkup, John		D, 19th Iowa	7		1933 Oct 6	NE, 58th, 1934
Wall, A.F.	Pvt.	E, 1st Iowa Inf.	5		1915 Apr 5	IA, 42nd, 1916
Wall, A.T.	Pvt.	3rd Ind. Battery	22		1906 Sep 11	IA, 33rd, 1907
Wall, J.J.	Seaman	U.S. Navy	1		1919 Aug 21	KS, 39th, 1920
Wall, John	Pvt. Pvt.	D, 1st Neb. A, 1st Neb. (died of accident)	34		1884 Jul	NE, 9th, 1885
Wall, Lewis		I, 1st Kans.	6		1904 Nov 7	KS, 24th, 1905
Wallace, A.		A, 9th Ill.	293		1923 Jun 23	KS, 43rd, 1924
Wallace, Alex.	Pvt.	B, U.S. Eng.	6		1926 Jun 20	IA, 53rd, 1927
Wallace, D.W.		2nd Mo. Scouts (died of cancer of throat)	255		1893 Jun 20	NE, 18th, 1894
Wallace, David, see Walace, David						
Wallace, F.S.		M, 2nd Mich. Cav.	113		1920 May 13	KS, 40th, 1921
Wallace, G.S.		A, 1st Ind. Cav.	76		1928 Sep 30	NE, 53rd, 1929
Wallace, Geo. A.		K, 119th N.Y.	380		1904 Dec 6	KS, 24th, 1905
Wallace, Geo. W.	Pvt.	B, 7th Ill. Cav.	369		1919 Mar 19	IA, 46th, 1920

*See Appendix A, B or C for roster of post names and locations.
†See Introduction for note regarding recording of death date.

Name	Rank	Company, Regiment or Ship	Post*	Age	Death Date†	Journal
Wallace, Geo. W.		K, 121st N.Y.	88		1931 Jan 16	KS, 52nd, 1933
Wallace, Geo. W.		K, 121st N.Y.	88		1931 Jan 16	KS, 51st, 1932
Wallace, George		D, 4th West Va. Inf.	68	90	1936 Jun 1	IA, 62nd, 1936
Wallace, George	Pvt.	D, 4th West Va. Inf.	68	90	1935 May 25	IA, 65th, 1939
Wallace, J.G.	Pvt.	B, 6th Penn. Art.	158		1900 Dec 19	IA, 27th, 1901
Wallace, J.M., see Walace, J.M.						
Wallace, J.O.		F, 100th Penn.	68		1922 Mar 22	KS, 42nd, 1923
Wallace, J.W.			426		1907 2nd term	IA, 34th, 1908
Wallace, James	Pvt.	44th Wis. Inf.	215	64	1893 Jun 1	IA, 20th, 1894
Wallace, John R.	Corp.	G, 115th Ill. Inf.	300		1910 Dec 16	IA, 37th, 1911
Wallace, Joseph		D, 18th Ohio	54		1917 Jan 1	KS, 36th, 1917
Wallace, Joseph			54		1917 Jun 1	KS, 37th, 1918
Wallace, L.H.	Pvt.		108		1933	IA, 60th, 1934
Wallace, R.A.		D, 168th Ohio	1		1911 May 8	KS, 31st, 1912
Wallace, R.B.	Sergt.	K, 1st Colo. Cav.	94	90	1931 Jun 30	IA, 58th, 1932
Wallace, R.B.		I, 73rd Ohio	1		1921 Jun	KS, 41st, 1922
Wallace, Robert S.		D, 104th Ill. Inf. (born in Illinois; died of paralysis at Soldiers & Sailors Home Hospital, Burkett; buried at Paxton, Neb.)		73	1906 Sep 8	NE, 31st, 1907
Wallace, Thomas	Pvt.	G, 46th Wis. Inf.	133		1923 Jul 3	IA, 50th, 1924
Wallace, W.B.	Pvt.	B, 80th Ohio Inf.	94		1929 Aug 18	IA, 56th, 1930
Wallace, W.H.			5		1925 Oct 21	IA, 52nd, 1926
Wallace, W.M.		H, 1st Mich. Art.	88		1911 Oct 21	KS, 31st, 1912
Wallace, W.R.	Pvt.	E, 70th Ohio Inf.	199		1912 Mar 19	IA, 39th, 1913
Wallace, W.S.		C, 106th Ill. Inf.	337		1935 Feb 25	KS, 55th, 1936
Wallace, William	Pvt.	B, 4th Iowa Cav.	54	85	1933 Nov 29	IA, 60th, 1934
Wallace, William	Pvt.	D, 8th Ohio Cav.	98	65	1899 Mar 23	IA, 25th, 1899
Wallace, William		I, 35th Iowa Inf. (died of old age)	77	82	1924 Nov 3	NE, 49th, 1925
Wallace, Wm.	Pvt.	B, 2nd Iowa Cav.	94		1908 Oct 8	IA, 35th, 1909
Wallack, B.F.		D, 17th Kans.	276		1897 May 11	KS, 17th, 1898
Wallar, John R.	Pvt.	A, 44th Iowa Inf.	78	51	1891 Aug 20	IA, 18th, 1892
Wallen, M.	Pvt.	G, 44th Iowa	465		1921 Dec 20	IA, 48th, 1922
Wallen, M.	Pvt.	G, 44th —	495		1921 Dec 20	IA, 48th, 1922
Wallenford, N.N.		G, 10th Ky.	437		1922 Jan 15	KS, 42nd, 1923
Waller, Geo. L.	Corp.	8th Penn. Cav.	197		1902 Mar 5	IA, 28th, 1902
Waller, H.M.		D, 12th Wis.	209		1913 Aug 13	KS, 33rd, 1914
Waller, Wm. H.	Pvt.	C, 52nd Ill. Inf. (at large)			1933 Aug	IA, 60th, 1934
Walles, Henry		H, 1st Ohio	64		1923 Feb 21	KS, 43rd, 1924
Walley, John J.		H, 152nd N.Y.	16		1932 Aug 31	NE, 57th, 1933
Walley, T.B.	Pvt.	I, 13th Iowa Inf.	98		1913 Mar 6	IA, 40th, 1914
Wallice, J.C.			317		1893 Mar	KS, 13th, 1894
Wallick, D.H.		G, 102nd Ohio	68		1909 Dec 1	KS, 29th, 1910
Walling, A.M.		A, 8th Iowa Inf.	10		1927 Dec 17	NE, 52nd, 1928
Walling, Hermann	Pvt.	D, 15th Iowa Inf.	458	49	1891 Jul 29	IA, 18th, 1892
Walling, J.H.		B, 144th N.Y. Inf.	12		1925 Jun 17	IA, 52nd, 1926
Walling, James		F, 149th N.Y. (died of paralysis)	13	71	1914 Apr 8	NE, 39th, 1915
Wallingford, C.M.		H, 10th Ky. Cav.	139		1912 Nov 9	KS, 32nd, 1913
Wallis, B.L.		C, 46th Ind. Inf.	51		1918 Sep 20	KS, 38th, 1919
Wallis, N.W.		H, 80th Ill.	139		1916 Sep 25	KS, 36th, 1917
Wallis, S.W.	Pvt.	F, 15th Ill. Inf.	101		1916 Jan 22	IA, 43rd, 1917
Walliser, Henry	Pvt.	H, 27th Iowa Inf.	132		1913 Feb	IA, 40th, 1914
Walls, C.	Pvt.	C, 26th Iowa Inf.	88		1921 Dec 11	IA, 48th, 1922
Walls, Daniel		F, 53rd Ohio	12		1911 May 1	KS, 31st, 1912
Walls, Joseph G.		H, 13th Ohio Inf. (died of consumption)	303		1890	KS, 10th, 1891
Walls, S.		D, 31st Ind.	223	74	1920 Dec 30	NE, 45th, 1921
Walls, Thomas A.		F, 34th Iowa	258		1902 May 30	KS, 22nd, 1903
Wallweber, C.W.	Pvt.	A, 44th Iowa Inf.	78		1916 Dec 8	IA, 43rd, 1917
Walm, S.J.		A, 27th Ind.	1		1927 Feb 17	KS, 47th, 1928
Walmer, Daniel	Pvt.	E, 2nd Iowa Inf.	19		1918 Jul 31	IA, 45th, 1919
Walmoth, Joseph	Pvt.	D, 10th Iowa Inf.	212	47	1885 Jul 8	IA, 16th, 1890
Walmsley, J.W.		B, 14th Ky. Cav.	111		1932 Sep 12	NE, 57th, 1933

*See Appendix A, B or C for roster of post names and locations.
†See Introduction for note regarding recording of death date.

570

Name	Rank	Company, Regiment or Ship	Post*	Age	Death Date†	Journal
Walrad, Horace		B, 55th Ill.	23		1914	IA, 41st, 1915
Walrath, G.A.		G, 14th Iowa Inf.	66		1922 Jul 16	IA, 49th, 1923
Walrath, O.G.	Pvt.	D, 39th N.Y. Inf.	25		1933 Jan	IA, 60th, 1934
Walrod, T.E.	Pvt.	F, 26th Iowa Inf.	236		1929 Oct 7	IA, 56th, 1930
Walsh, E.	Pvt.	A, 19th Penn. Cav.	235		1921 Nov 26	IA, 48th, 1922
Walsh, J.B.	Pvt.	E, 35th Iowa Inf.	231		1910 Sep 13	IA, 37th, 1911
Walsh, Jas.	Pvt.	H, 1st Mich. Sharpshooters	132	52	1889 Aug 15	IA, 16th, 1890
Walsh, John		U.S. Marine Corps	380		1898 Jul 5	KS, 18th, 1899
Walsh, John		R, 64th Ill. Inf.	32	64	1909 Jun 31	NE, 34th, 1910
Walsh, John K.	Surgeon	Navy (died at Soldiers Home, Leavenworth)	50		1889	KS, 9th, 1890
Walsh, Patrick		U.S. Marines	1		1924 Apr 13	KS, 44th, 1925
Walsh, Robert		G, 25th Ill.			1929 Jan 1	NE, 53rd, 1929
Walsh, Thomas	Corp.	I, 43rd Wis. Inf.	216		1928 Apr 18	IA, 55th, 1929
Walsh, Thomas		A, 13th N.J. Inf.	380		1900 Apr 17	KS, 20th, 1901
Walsh, William L.		H, 19th Ill. Inf. (died of paralysis)	4	63	1897 Jul 26	NE, 22nd, 1898
Walston, H.W.	Pvt.	I, 91st N.Y.	165		1905	IA, 32nd, 1906
Walten, Vincent		M, 9th Iowa	119		1912 May 31	KS, 32nd, 1913
Waltenbaugh, Jacob	Pvt.	F, 139th Penn. Inf.	281	49	1887 Sep 20	IA, 14th, 1888
Walter, A.H.		20th Wis. Inf.	5		1887 Sep 3	KS, 7th, 1888
Walter, B.S.		F, 86th Ill.	10	88	1919 Apr 29	NE, 44th, 1920
Walter, Corwin S.		8th & 9th Kans. Cav.	25		1925 May 9	KS, 45th, 1926
Walter, Elias		D, 63rd Ill.	441		1896 Feb 14	KS, 16th, 1897
Walter, John F.		48th Ind.	132		1911 Mar 5	KS, 31st, 1912
Walter, John L.		A, 28th Penn.	25		1928 Jan 6	NE, 53rd, 1929
Walter, Joseph		D, 59th Ill. Inf.	117		1899 Oct 7	KS, 19th, 1900
Walter, Joseph A.		C or G, 74th Penn. (of Great Bend)	52		1924 Oct 24	KS, 44th, 1925
Walter, R.C.		F, 86th Ill.	10	82	1919 Aug 1	NE, 44th, 1920
Walter, Scott	Pvt.	C, 9th Penn. Cav.	68		1924 Feb 24	IA, 51st, 1925
Walters, Daniel	Pvt.	I, 4th Iowa Cav.	67		1915 Nov 30	IA, 42nd, 1916
Walters, Floyd	Pvt.	77th Ohio Inf.	52		1912 Jan 28	IA, 39th, 1913
Walters, G.W.		G, 28th Iowa Inf.	301	50	1896 Jun 6	NE, 21st, 1897
Walters, H.B.	Sergt.	G, 2nd Iowa Cav.	255		1920 Jun 8	IA, 47th, 1921
Walters, Harry	Pvt.	H, 4th Iowa Cav.	118		1901 Aug	IA, 28th, 1902
Walters, J.B.	Pvt.	M, 4th Iowa Cav.	124		1915	IA, 42nd, 1916
Walters, James	Saddler	G, 2nd Iowa Cav.	17		1929 Feb 18	IA, 56th, 1930
Walters, John	Pvt.	B, 90th Ohio Inf.	7	61	1897 Nov 19	IA, 24th, 1898
Walters, John		F, 39th Iowa	48		1889	KS, 9th, 1890
Walters, John		B, 11th Mo.	253		1910	KS, 30th, 1911
Walters, John		C, 102nd Ohio	132		1914 Aug 7	KS, 34th, 1915
Walters, John H.		E, 9th Kans. Cav.	51		1924 Feb 2	KS, 44th, 1925
Walters, Jos.		F, 61st Ill.	25		1908 Jun 26	NE, 33rd, 1909
Walters, L.	Pvt.	F, 2nd Iowa Cav.	452		1925 Mar 14	IA, 52nd, 1926
Walters, Moses		C, 64th Ohio Vol. Inf.	130		1915 Dec 4	KS, 35th, 1916
Walters, Noah			80		1899 May 8	KS, 19th, 1900
Walters, Samuel		B, 114th Ohio	179		1902 Nov 5	KS, 22nd, 1903
Walters, Simon		C, 152nd Ind.	24		1924	KS, 44th, 1925
Walters, W.W.	Pvt.	H, 92nd Ill. Mtd. Inf.	322	55	1895 Aug 24	IA, 22nd, 1896
Walters, William		C, 64th Ohio	130		1905 Apr 12	KS, 25th, 1906
Waltham, R.		G, 8th Iowa	100		1908 Jun 13	KS, 28th, 1909
Walther, Chas. F.		provost marshal under Sidney Clark at Leavenworth, Kansas (died of blood poison)	84	53	1888 Sep 1	NE, 13th, 1889
Walther, Chas. W.		E, 77th Wis.	25		1929 Jul 19	NE, 54th, 1930
Waltman, J.A.	Pvt.	H, 7th Ill. Inf.	440		1918 Feb 6	IA, 45th, 1919
Walton, A.C.		I, 2nd Kans. Cav.	418		1923 Jan 14	KS, 43rd, 1924
Walton, Abraham		Ind. (nonmember; died at Milford)			1936 Aug	NE, 61st, 1937
Walton, Amos	Pvt.	B, 7th Ind. Inf.	175	44	1887 Jan 21	IA, 13th, 1887
Walton, Amos		G, 8th Kans.	158		1898 Sep	KS, 18th, 1899
Walton, Andrew D.		H, 67th Ill. Inf. (died of paralysis at Soldiers & Sailors Home, Grand Island; buried in Home Cemetery)	5	66	1905 Feb 23	NE, 30th, 1906
Walton, B.F.	Sergt.	B, 4th Iowa Inf.	139		1905 Apr 11	IA, 31st, 1905

*See Appendix A, B or C for roster of post names and locations.
†See Introduction for note regarding recording of death date.

Name	Rank	Company, Regiment or Ship	Post*	Age	Death Date†	Journal
Walton, Cary		I, 2nd Kans. Cav.	418		1923 Jan 14	KS, 42nd, 1923
Walton, Charles		Wis.	436		1914 May 8	IA, 41st, 1915
Walton, Eli		1st Kans. Bat.	418		1916 Jan 9	KS, 36th, 1917
Walton, Geo. D.	Pvt.	28th Iowa Inf.	314		1915	IA, 42nd, 1916
Walton, Geo. W.	Pvt.	G, 1st Iowa Cav.	93		1917 Oct 30	IA, 44th, 1918
Walton, Henry		F, 16th Ill. Eng. (died at Weir City, Kans.; buried at Weir Cross Road Cemetery)	200		1894 Aug 17	KS, 14th, 1895
Walton, Henry W.		I, 15th Iowa	142		1897 Mar 24	KS, 17th, 1898
Walton, J.C.		5th Ind. Bat.	12		1914 Aug 27	KS, 34th, 1915
Walton, James		G, 28th Wis.	203		1925 Mar 19	KS, 45th, 1926
Walton, James		G, 28th Wis.	203		1924 Mar 19	KS, 44th, 1925
Walton, James		D, 122nd Ill. Inf.	52		1928 May 8	NE, 53rd, 1929
Walton, John		B, 9th Kans.	12		1928 May 4	KS, 48th, 1929
Walton, N.			204		1894	NE, 19th, 1895
Walton, Ralph R.		I, 17th Ill. Cav.	90		1915 Jun 2	KS, 35th, 1916
Walton, Thomas	Pvt.	H, 77th Penn. Inf.	3		1919 Apr 22	IA, 46th, 1920
Walton, W.H.	Pvt.	E, 11th Iowa Inf.	121	51	1892 May 1	IA, 19th, 1893
Walts, John	Pvt.	I, 40th Iowa Inf.	127	60	1887 Jul 15	IA, 14th, 1888
Waltz, Henry	Pvt.	F, 1st Wis. Cav.	7		1922 Jul 21	IA, 49th, 1923
Waltz, Jacob M.	Pvt.	F, 2nd Iowa Cav.	247		1914 Dec 22	IA, 41st, 1915
Waltz, Philip	Pvt.	I, 25th Wis. Inf.	78		1929 Feb 1	IA, 56th, 1930
Waluto, A.G.			28		1884	KS, 4th, 1885
Walworth, Jos.	Pvt.	D, 10th Iowa Inf.	212		2nd quarter 1885	IA, 12th, 1886
Walz, George		E, 17th Ill. Cav.	85		1912 Sep 7	KS, 32nd, 1913
Walz, Gottfried	Corp.	I, 8th Kans. Inf.	26		1911 Nov 17	IA, 38th, 1912
Wambold, Wm. W.	Pvt.	I, 75th Ill. Inf.	465		1915 Jan 3	IA, 42nd, 1916
Wampler, William A.		C, 68th Ill. Inf. G, 115th Ind. Inf. K, 17th Ind. Inf. (died at Topeka, Kans.; buried at Topeka Cemetery)	1		1894 Nov 13	KS, 14th, 1895
Wamsley, J.	Pvt.	B, 10th Wis. Inf.	124		1911 Aug 1	IA, 38th, 1912
Wamsley, Wm.		D, 21st Ill.	185		1885	KS, 5th, 1886
Wanamaker, B.F.		20th Ohio (died of pneumonia)	301	73	1916 Jan 20	NE, 40th, 1916
Wanamaker, B.F.		Ohio (died of pneumonia)	301	72	1916 Jan 20	NE, 41st, 1917
Wandall, John M.		H, 11th Ill. Cav.	179		1916 Oct 16	KS, 36th, 1917
Wandler, J.M.		F, 6th Kans. Cav. (died at Lyons, Kans.; buried at Morris Cemetery)	132		1894 Dec 28	KS, 14th, 1895
Wandling, J.H.			167		1924 Oct 25	IA, 51st, 1925
Wandling, Jacob		N, 33rd Iowa Inf. (died of old age)	112	87	1910 Dec 17	NE, 35th, 1911
Wands, L.		A, 95th Ill.	122		1890	KS, 10th, 1891
Wanser, Wm.		D, 47th Ill. Inf.	193		1908 Nov 5	NE, 33rd, 1909
Want, Joshua F.		D, 5th Kans. Vol. Cav.	32		1908 Apr 16	KS, 28th, 1909
Wanty, J.J.		B, 47th Ind.	185		1893 Nov 30	KS, 13th, 1894
Wanzer, S.A.		K, 36th Ill.	65		1921 Oct 22	KS, 41st, 1922
Wapels, John		C, 44th Ill. Inf. (died of old age)	77	76	1906 Jan 22	NE, 31st, 1907
Wapler, Otto		A, 87th Ind.	147		1919	KS, 39th, 1920
Warbasse, J.	Pvt.	K, 4th N.J. Cav.	212		1915 Dec 29	IA, 42nd, 1916
Warburton, G.L.		B, 36th Wis.	159		1897 Mar 28	KS, 17th, 1898
Warbutton, J.W.		G, 11th Ind.	180		1922 Dec 12	KS, 42nd, 1923
Ward, A.		A, 48th Iowa	40	96	1916 Jan 14	NE, 41st, 1917
Ward, Allen H.		C, 20th Penn.	47		1896 Sep 20	KS, 16th, 1897
Ward, Byron C.	Pvt.	G, 2nd Vt.	12		1922 Jan 18	IA, 49th, 1923
Ward, C.C.		G, 12th Vt.	257		1908 Jun	KS, 28th, 1909
Ward, Cornelius			194		1915 May 12	IA, 42nd, 1916
Ward, David		F, 23rd N.Y. Vol. Inf.	69		1908 Aug 15	KS, 28th, 1909
Ward, E.	Pvt.	G, 25th Iowa	440		1901 Dec 29	IA, 28th, 1902
Ward, E.A.	Pvt.	G, 24th Iowa Inf.	72		1913 Apr 7	IA, 40th, 1914
Ward, E.C.F.		K, 55th Ind.	49		1923 Jan 24	KS, 43rd, 1924
Ward, E.E.		K, 7th Kans.	129		1908 Oct 7	KS, 28th, 1909
Ward, E.H.	Pvt.	A, 3rd Iowa Inf.	206		1919 Apr 14	IA, 46th, 1920
Ward, E.R.	Sergt.	G, 2nd Vt. Vols.	12		1906 May 8	IA, 33rd, 1907
Ward, G.H.	Pvt.	G, 141st Ohio Inf.	255		1905 Jun 4	IA, 32nd, 1906
Ward, Geo. R.	Pvt.	B, 29th Iowa Inf.	124		1917 Apr 25	IA, 44th, 1918

*See Appendix A, B or C for roster of post names and locations.
†See Introduction for note regarding recording of death date.
572

Name	Rank	Company, Regiment or Ship	Post*	Age	Death Date†	Journal
Ward, Geo. S.	2nd Lieut.	C, 12th Ill. Inf.	68	73	1890 Jun 5	IA, 17th, 1891
Ward, George W.		A, 81st Ill. Inf.	6		1908 Aug 22	KS, 28th, 1909
Ward, George W.R.		I, 38th Ind. Inf.	250		1912 Aug 18	KS, 32nd, 1913
Ward, Hiram		C, Kans. Reserve (died at Harveyville)	418		1895 Nov	KS, 15th, 1896
Ward, Isaac			4		1914 Feb 21	IA, 41st, 1915
Ward, J.B.		E, —	447		1916 Feb 23	KS, 36th, 1917
Ward, J.D.		I, 9th Kans.	491		1917 Nov 14	KS, 37th, 1918
Ward, J.E.		K, 3rd Mich. Inf.	379		1908 Oct 17	IA, 35th, 1909
Ward, J.H.			29		1915 Dec 14	IA, 42nd, 1916
Ward, J.R.		K, 55th Ky. Inf.	57		1886	KS, 6th, 1887
Ward, J.T.		G, 139th Ill.	71		1906 Dec 31	KS, 26th, 1907
Ward, J.W.	Corp.	H, 12th Iowa Inf.	5		1926 Apr 27	IA, 53rd, 1927
Ward, J.W.		F, 6th Ind.	158		1927 Apr 8	KS, 47th, 1928
Ward, James	Corp.	C, 24th Iowa Inf.	452		1926 Mar 31	IA, 53rd, 1927
Ward, John			38		1894	NE, 19th, 1895
Ward, John	Pvt.	C, 14th U.S. Inf. (cause of death: heart)	185	40	1887 Apr	NE, 12th, 1888
Ward, John		C, 55th Ind. Inf. (died of heart disease)	95	60	1905 Jul 28	NE, 30th, 1906
Ward, John A.	Pvt.	B, 28th Iowa Inf.	233		1919 Mar 24	IA, 46th, 1920
Ward, Jos.			307		1891 Apr 1	IA, 18th, 1892
Ward, M.L.	Pvt.	A, 20th Ill. Inf.	104		1906 May	IA, 33rd, 1907
Ward, O.S.		F, 1st Ohio Inf.	25	78	1919 Mar 26	NE, 44th, 1920
Ward, Peter		16th Kans. Cav.	380		1905 Mar 16	KS, 25th, 1906
Ward, R.		C, 6th Iowa Cav. (died of Bright's disease)	182	69	1903 Dec 23	NE, 28th, 1904
Ward, S.B.		K, Ind. Art.	268		1888	KS, 8th, 1889
Ward, S.L.	Lieut.	K, 3rd Iowa Cav.	45		1910	IA, 37th, 1911
Ward, Stephen		D, 2nd Iowa Cav. (died of amputation of foot)	52	77	1923 Jul 2	NE, 48th, 1924
Ward, Thomas	Capt.	I, 34th Iowa Inf.	410		1906 Mar 9	IA, 33rd, 1907
Ward, Thomas		A, 6th Kans.	32		1905 Oct 1	KS, 25th, 1906
Ward, W.G.		89th Ill. Inf.	434		1919 Apr 13	IA, 46th, 1920
Ward, W.H.		E, 6th Kans. Cav.	3		1929 Jul 7	KS, 49th, 1930
Ward, W.H.		B, 47th Ohio	28		1927 Nov 17	KS, 47th, 1928
Ward, W.R.	Lieut.	F, 26th Iowa Inf.	92		1912 Jan 4	IA, 39th, 1913
Ward, Wm. A.		F, 113th Ill. Inf.	174		1901 Aug 15	KS, 21st, 1902
Wardell, Henry W.		A, 100th Ill.	17		1936 Mar 16	KS, 56th, 1937
Wardell, W.W.		A, 100th Ill. Inf.			1937 Mar 16	KS, 57th, 1938
Warden, Elijah H.		D, 6th Kans. Cav.	82		1920 Feb 18	KS, 40th, 1921
Warden, Geo.			347		1900 Sep 28	IA, 27th, 1901
Warden, Geo. W.	Pvt.	B, 23rd Iowa Inf.	347		1900 Sep 25	IA, 27th, 1901
Warden, J.B.			75		1913	IA, 40th, 1914
Warden, John H.	Pvt.	G, 24th Iowa Inf.	235		1924 Jan 24	IA, 51st, 1925
Warden, R.	Corp.	H, 52nd Ill. Inf.	88		1905 May 16	IA, 31st, 1905
Warden, Wm.		H, 30th Ky.	428		1906 Oct 21	KS, 26th, 1907
Warder, Clark		A, 45th Ky. Inf.	293		1929	KS, 49th, 1930
Wardrum, P.		H, 39th Ill.	235		1893 Apr 1	KS, 13th, 1894
Ware, C.M.	Sergt.	B, 3rd Iowa Cav.	40		1924 Mar 14	IA, 51st, 1925
Ware, Elias M.	Pvt.	F & K, 2nd Iowa Inf.	177	56	1895 May 13	IA, 22nd, 1896
Ware, Eugene F.			32		1911 Jul 2	KS, 31st, 1912
Ware, Reuben		E, 3rd Iowa Cav.	69	92	1936 Apr 4	IA, 63rd, 1937
Ware, Ruben		E, 3rd Iowa Cav.			1936 Apr 4	IA, 62nd, 1936
Ware, V.I.	Pvt.	D, 6th Iowa Inf.	122	58	1893 Dec 22	IA, 20th, 1894
Ware, W.F.		D, 21st Kans. Inf. (died of paralysis)	77	79	1921 Jan 19	NE, 46th, 1922
Wareham, R.A.	Capt.	C, 49th Wis. Inf.	42	48	1890 Jan 13	IA, 16th, 1890
Warehan, James K.		E, 1st Penn. Bat. (died of flu)	206	78	1923 Mar 23	NE, 48th, 1924
Waren, William H.		128th Ohio	63		1924 Feb 12	KS, 44th, 1925
Warener, J.G.	Pvt.	G, 8th Iowa Inf.	500		1919 Feb 10	IA, 46th, 1920
Warfield, J.B.		K, 15th N.Y. Eng.	63		1912 Feb 15	KS, 32nd, 1913
Warhurst, Wm.	Pvt.	D, 11th Ill. Cav.	424	52	1890 Feb 23	IA, 17th, 1891
Warick, John H.		5th Battery Wis. Lt. Art.	134		1911 Jan 25	KS, 31st, 1912
Warick, Samuel R.		5th Wis. Battery	58		1925 Sep 10	KS, 45th, 1926
Waring, Charles		G, 11th Kans.	100		1913 Jan 4	KS, 33rd, 1914
Wark, Aaron		F, 71st Ind.	46		1917 May 14	KS, 37th, 1918

Name	Rank	Company, Regiment or Ship	Post*	Age	Death Date†	Journal
Wark, Emanuel M.		F, 6th Ind. Cav.	4		1915 Jun 24	KS, 35th, 1916
Wark, S.H.	Pvt.	E, 18th Ill. Inf.	135		1920 Nov 3	IA, 47th, 1921
Warlmut, Joseph		H, 9th Ill.	36		1920 Oct 23	KS, 40th, 1921
Warn, Edward W.	Pvt.	G, 21st Iowa Inf.	371	57	1894 Aug 21	IA, 21st, 1895
Warn, Sylvester	Pvt.	E, 38th Iowa Inf.	168		1916 May 5	IA, 43rd, 1917
Warner, B.F.		C, 115th Ill. Inf.	256		1909 Dec 16	KS, 29th, 1910
Warner, C.A.		F, 34th Ill. (died of appendicitis)	22	62	1907 Nov 20	NE, 32nd, 1908
Warner, C.W.		D, 8th N.Y. Art.	35		1904 May 19	KS, 24th, 1905
Warner, D.C.		A, 108th Ill.	238		1930 Apr 28	KS, 50th, 1931
Warner, David		B, 42nd Ill. (died of paralysis)	22	80	1908 Mar 2	NE, 33rd, 1909
Warner, E.A.	Capt.	H, 14th Iowa	212		1903-1904	IA, 30th, 1904
Warner, E.A.		I, 5th Mich. Cav. (cause of death: kidneys)	32	73	1915 Jul 18	NE, 40th, 1916
Warner, E.W.		74th Ill.	122		1920 Feb 8	KS, 40th, 1921
Warner, Elven K.	Pvt.	I, 35th Wis. Inf.	16		1908 Nov 3	IA, 35th, 1909
Warner, Ephraim D.		H, 10th N.Y. Cav.	68		1920 Nov 19	KS, 40th, 1921
Warner, G.L.		144th Ohio Inf.	28	82	1902 Aug	NE, 27th, 1903
Warner, Geo.		G, 11th Kans.	100		1928 Oct 15	KS, 48th, 1929
Warner, Geo. W.		H, 15th Kans.	18		1892 Jan 2	KS, 12th, 1893
Warner, Grove A.	Pvt.	C, 29th Mich. Inf.	519		1910 Jul 11	IA, 37th, 1911
Warner, Henry		A, 108th Ill. (died of paralysis)	109	70	1912 Oct	NE, 37th, 1913
Warner, J.	Pvt.	H, 71st Ill. Inf.	156		1910 Jan 17	IA, 37th, 1911
Warner, John		G, 11th Kans.	100		1921 Jan 3	KS, 41st, 1922
Warner, John H.	Pvt.	E, 103rd Penn. Inf.	496		1901 Feb 19	IA, 27th, 1901
Warner, Joseph		H, 86th Ohio Inf.		89	1936 Mar 6	IA, 62nd, 1936
Warner, Joseph		B, 182nd Ohio Inf.		89	1936 Mar 6	IA, 62nd, 1936
Warner, Joseph		H, 86th Ohio Inf.	96	89	1936 Mar 6	IA, 63rd, 1937
Warner, Joseph		B, 2nd Mo.	100		1920 Feb 12	KS, 40th, 1921
Warner, L.F.		A, 16th Kans.	238		1905 Apr 10	KS, 25th, 1906
Warner, Richard		A, 3rd Ky.	46		1930 Oct 23	KS, 52nd, 1933
Warner, Richard		A, 3rd Ky.	48		1930 Oct 29	KS, 50th, 1931
Warner, S.B.	Capt.	I, 23rd Ohio	55		1893 May 30	KS, 13th, 1894
Warner, Thomas E.		A, 125th Ill. (died of apoplexy)	112	78	1918 Dec 6	NE, 44th, 1920
Warner, W.B.	Pvt.	C, 12th Iowa Inf.	48		1899 Oct 27	IA, 26th, 1900
Warner, W.C.		B, 9th Ind.	57		1933 May 18	KS, 53rd, 1934
Warner, W.H.	Pvt.	C, 75th Ill. Inf.	34		1906 Jan 13	IA, 33rd, 1907
Warner, W.N.		D, 46th Ill.	[417]		1932	KS, 52nd, 1933
Warner, W.N.		D, 46th Ill.	[417]		1931	KS, 51st, 1932
Warner, William C.		A, 27th Wis.	43		1905 May 5	KS, 25th, 1906
Warner, Wm.	Pvt.	F, 7th Iowa Cav.	452		1908 May 1	IA, 35th, 1909
Warner, Wm. N.	Surg.	3rd Wis.	49		1897 Jul 10	KS, 17th, 1898
Warnick, Austin W.	Sergt.	C, 23rd Iowa Inf.	425		1925 Apr 21	IA, 52nd, 1926
Warnick, John	Pvt.	Ohio	108		1918 Sep 15	IA, 45th, 1919
Warnock, J.G.	Pvt.	E, 4th Mo. Militia	252		1917 Sep 14	IA, 44th, 1918
Warns, Jonathan		H, 54th Ind.	175		1922 May 2	KS, 42nd, 1923
Warren, C.H.	Pvt.	C, 50th Mass. Inf.	29		1929 Mar 8	IA, 56th, 1930
Warren, C.Y.		14th Ill. Cav. (died of heart failure)	306	70	1905 Apr 24	NE, 29th, 1905
Warren, Christy			79		1917	IA, 44th, 1918
Warren, Dan		F, 128th N.Y.	71		1919 May 2	KS, 39th, 1920
Warren, Frank L.		A, 4th Minn.	26	88	1934 Feb 17	IA, 61st, 1935
Warren, G.K.			114		1896	KS, 16th, 1897
Warren, G.N.	Pvt.	H, 30th Wis. Vols.	54	57	1890 Jul 24	IA, 17th, 1891
Warren, Geo.	Pvt.	F, 16th Mich. Inf.	250		1904 Jul 26	IA, 31st, 1905
Warren, Geo. F.		A, 4th Ill. Cav. (died of paralysis)	60	86	1916 Jul 24	NE, 41st, 1917
Warren, George	Pvt.	E, 38th Iowa Inf.	168	52	1893 Feb 10	IA, 19th, 1893
Warren, George W.		B, 20th Ind. Inf.	17		1914 Mar 15	KS, 34th, 1915
Warren, H.H.		D, 12th Wis. Inf.	15		1893 Sep 20	NE, 18th, 1894
Warren, Henry		Kans.	241		1909 Mar 16	KS, 29th, 1910
Warren, I.H.		H, 8th Kans. (died of heart trouble)	63	77	1917	NE, 42nd, 1918
Warren, J.C.	Pvt.	F, 44th Iowa Inf.	22		1932 Feb 6	IA, 59th, 1933
Warren, Jack		D, 39th U.S. Inf.	25		1934 May	KS, 54th, 1935
Warren, Jack		D, 59th U.S.C.	25		1937 Dec	KS, 56th, 1937
Warren, Joseph	Pvt.	B, 86th Ill. Inf.	17		1927 Jun 23	IA, 54th, 1928

*See Appendix A, B or C for roster of post names and locations.
†See Introduction for note regarding recording of death date.

Name	Rank	Company, Regiment or Ship	Post*	Age	Death Date†	Journal
Warren, Louis		K, 47th Mass. Inf. (died of epilepsy at Soldiers & Sailors Home, Grand Island; buried in Home Cemetery)	8	78	1905 Apr 24	NE, 30th, 1906
Warren, Lucian	Pvt.	B, 104th Ill. Inf.	52		1927 Apr 4	IA, 54th, 1928
Warren, Miles	Capt.	B, 8th Mich. Cav. (died of heart trouble)	83		1891 Jun 14[11?]	NE, 16th, 1892
Warren, Park S.		Maine	25		1925 Apr 27	KS, 45th, 1926
Warren, S.I.		H, 48th Ind. (died of stomach trouble)	1	80	1918 Jul 6	NE, 43rd, 1919
Warren, Solomon S.		K, 182nd Ohio Vol. Inf. (see also Appendix D)	25		1939 Jan 26	NE, 64th, 1940
Warren, T.J.		A, 62nd Ill.	18		1919 Sep 7	KS, 39th, 1920
Warren, Thomas E.		A, 135th Ill. (died of apoplexy)	112	78	1918 Dec	NE, 43rd, 1919
Warren, W.A.	Capt. & QM	Army of the Cumberland	131		1st quarter 1884	IA, 10th, 1884
Warren, W.B.		H, 1st U.S. Lancers	1		1914 Mar 24	KS, 34th, 1915
Warren, W.C.		G, 22nd Iowa Inf.	64		4th quarter 1884	IA, 11th, 1885
Warren, W.R.			69		1906	IA, 33rd, 1907
Warren, Wm.	Pvt.	4th Wis. Battery	456		1926 Apr	IA, 53rd, 1927
Warren, Wm.	Pvt.		200		1925	IA, 52nd, 1926
Warrick, Jno. G.		I, 205th Penn. Inf.	52	70	1903 Jan 23	NE, 28th, 1904
Warriner, C.E.			25		1883	KS, 3rd, 1884
Warriner, Chester	Pvt.		222		1901 Mar 20	IA, 27th, 1901
Warriner, S.C.		B, 4th Wis. Cav. (died of paralysis)	214	75	1920 Oct 17	NE, 45th, 1921
Warrington, Jas. C.		F, 13th Iowa	259		1906 May 26	KS, 26th, 1907
Warritt, Mahlon S.		A, 64th Ill. (died of cancer)	94	71	1916 Jul 18	NE, 41st, 1917
Warson, W.O.V.			128		1st quarter 1883	IA, 10th, 1884
Warthen, Wm. F.	1st Lieut.	E, 15th West Va.	116	48	1890 Dec 26	IA, 17th, 1891
Wartick, Joseph		A, 6th Mo.	125		1910 May 23	KS, 30th, 1911
Wartman, Paul	Pvt.	I, 18th Wis.	222		1899 May 30	IA, 26th, 1900
Warwick, Noble	Pvt.	B, 13th U.S. Inf.	2		1911 Dec 10	IA, 38th, 1912
Wash, G.W.	Pvt.	72nd Ohio Inf.	56		1917	IA, 44th, 1918
Wash, P.		5th U.S. Inf.	28	73	1902 Nov	NE, 27th, 1903
Washaliska, W.H.		F, 79th Penn.	448		1926 Mar 5	KS, 46th, 1927
Washbarn, George P.		H, 21st Mo. (died at his home in Ottawa)	18		1922 May 16	KS, 42nd, 1923
Washburn, D.		not a member of the G.A.R.	76		1912	KS, 32nd, 1913
Washburn, David	Pvt.	B, 37th Iowa	231		1903-1904	IA, 30th, 1904
Washburn, E.G.		G, 184th N.Y.	447		1918	KS, 38th, 1919
Washburn, George	Pvt.		231	89	1932 Dec 23	IA, 59th, 1933
Washburn, L.J.	Sergt.	A, 2nd Iowa Cav.	363		1908 May 1	IA, 35th, 1909
Washburn, Thos. H.		I, 12th Iowa Inf.	284		1891 Feb 1	KS, 11th, 1892
Washington, Geo.	Pvt.	F, 116th U.S.C. Inf.	44	63	1898 Mar 11	IA, 24th, 1898
Washington, Geo.		I, 83rd Kans.	365		1931 Dec 26	KS, 51st, 1932
Washington, Geo.		I, 83rd Kans.	365		1931 Dec 26	KS, 52nd, 1933
Washington, George		C, 63rd N.S. Inf.	60		1893 May 28	KS, 13th, 1894
Washington, George		L, 79th —	365		1917	KS, 37th, 1918
Washington, P.	Pvt.	G, 15th Iowa Inf.	4	49	1894 Mar 12	IA, 21st, 1895
Wasserfall, Jacob		E, 11th Mo. Cav.	85		1925 Jul 3	KS, 45th, 1926
Wasson, G.M.		G, 12th Wis.	25		1928 Feb 10	NE, 53rd, 1929
Wasson, J.P.		I, 129th Ohio	96		1898 Jan 17	KS, 18th, 1899
Wasson, James R.			12		1923 May 5	IA, 50th, 1924
Wasson, Jesse	Surg.	9th Iowa Cav.	187	67	1889 May 15	IA, 17th, 1891
Wasson, Jesse	Surg.	9th Iowa Cav.	187	67	1889 May 15	IA, 16th, 1890
Wasson, John A.			37		1923	IA, 50th, 1924
Wasson, William		B, Penn. Lt. Art.	209		1909 Nov 12	KS, 29th, 1910
Waste, Thos. L.	Pvt.	A, 3rd Wis. Inf.	46		1924 Aug 2	IA, 51st, 1925
Watenpaugh, M.F.	Pvt.	K, 15th Ill. Cav.	240		1915 Jun 10	IA, 42nd, 1916
Waterberry, E.S.		A, 11th & 69th Ill.	55		1924 Jan	KS, 44th, 1925
Waterbery, Henry	Pvt.	H, 17th Conn. Inf.	461		1900 Dec 23	IA, 27th, 1901
Waterbury, Daniel	Pvt.	M, 9th Iowa Cav.	123		1905 Nov 5	IA, 32nd, 1906
Waterbury, Geo.	Pvt.	H, 17th Conn. Inf.	461		1916 Aug 10	IA, 43rd, 1917
Waterbury, O.P.	Hosp. Stew.	A, 65th Ill. Inf.	42		1927 Aug 24	IA, 54th, 1928
Waterhouse, E.A.		I, —	380		1920 Oct 18	KS, 40th, 1921
Waterman, A.J.	Pvt.	G, 6th Iowa Cav.	240		1908 Nov 18	IA, 35th, 1909
Waterman, H.L.	Lieut.	C, 1st N.Y. Eng.	69		1918 May 20	IA, 45th, 1919

*See Appendix A, B or C for roster of post names and locations.
†See Introduction for note regarding recording of death date.
575

Name	Rank	Company, Regiment or Ship	Post*	Age	Death Date†	Journal
Waterman, Henry	Pvt.	B, Q.M. Ohio Cav.	153		1922 Feb 28	IA, 49th, 1923
Waterman, Henry		H, 125th Ind.	25		1930 Jun 8	KS, 50th, 1931
Waterman, Moses	Pvt.	I, 11th Ind. Inf.	94		1903 Apr 21	IA, 30th, 1904
Watermon, Ford	Pvt.	B, 15th Iowa Inf.	252		1906 Jul	IA, 33rd, 1907
Waters, D.O.	Pvt.	L, 4th Iowa Cav.	102		1910 Dec 9	IA, 37th, 1911
Waters, Ed		K, 93rd N.Y.	294		1896 Jan 26	KS, 16th, 1897
Waters, G.A.	Pvt.	H, 171st Ohio Inf.	127		1910 Apr 3	IA, 37th, 1911
Waters, Geo. R.		U.S. Navy	321		1918	KS, 38th, 1919
Waters, H.M.		H, 2nd Ohio Vol. Cav.	4		1915 Feb 20	KS, 35th, 1916
Waters, I.N.		A, 13th Ill.	81		1906 Jul 24	KS, 26th, 1907
Waters, J.	Pvt.	3rd Iowa Bat.	222		1915	IA, 42nd, 1916
Waters, J.T.			92		1913	IA, 40th, 1914
Waters, James		G, 30th Ill.	25		1926 Feb 8	KS, 46th, 1927
Waters, Jos. G.		A, 84th Iowa	1		1926 May 16	KS, 46th, 1927
Waters, L.C.		B, 41st Ohio	1		1922 Jan 9	KS, 42nd, 1923
Waters, M.D.			100		1884	KS, 4th, 1885
Waters, Samuel		C, 40th Ind. Inf. (died of diarrhea)	260	64	1895 Nov 11	NE, 20th, 1896
Waters, T.S.	Pvt.	B, 19th & 45th Iowa Inf.	19		1929 Nov 13	IA, 56th, 1930
Waters, Thos.		B, 91st Ill.	179		1918 Jun 24	KS, 38th, 1919
Waters, W.B.	Surg.	32nd Iowa Inf.	452		1892 Oct 20	IA, 19th, 1893
Waters, W.H.	Pvt.	D, 26th Iowa Inf.	74		1924 Dec 2	IA, 51st, 1925
Wathan, George		B, 8th Iowa (died of old age)	104	80	1922 Jan 14	NE, 47th, 1923
Watkins, A., see Wadkins, A.						
Watkins, C.		Kans.	365		1913 Jul 14	KS, 33rd, 1914
Watkins, C.M.		C, 12th Kans.	96		1927 Mar 22	KS, 47th, 1928
Watkins, D.	Pvt.	A, 92nd Ohio Inf.	364		1920 Jan 20	IA, 47th, 1921
Watkins, Daniel K.		K, 11th Ind.	18		1912 Apr 22	KS, 32nd, 1913
Watkins, Dorchester, Wadkins, Dorchester						
Watkins, Edward		H, 17th Penn. Cav. (died of blood poison)	187	78	1922 Aug 4	NE, 47th, 1923
Watkins, Edward, see Walkins, Edward						
Watkins, F.		C, 92nd Ohio	265		1936 Jan 8	KS, 57th, 1938
Watkins, I.		A, 145th Ohio	96		1919 Jan 6	KS, 39th, 1920
Watkins, S.L.	Pvt.	C, 28th Iowa Inf.	127		1925 Jul	IA, 52nd, 1926
Watkins, W.A.		K, 76th Ill.	17		1916 Jan 15	KS, 36th, 1917
Watkins, W.W.		I, 8th Ind. Cav.	4		1905 Aug 20	KS, 25th, 1906
Watkins, Wm.		G, 202nd Penn. Inf.	328		1901 Nov 12	KS, 21st, 1902
Watkinson, Thomas		H, 79th Ohio Inf. (died of paralysis)	112		1911 Jul 3	NE, 36th, 1912
Watland, Jacob	Pvt.	C, 53rd Ill. Inf. (at large)	199	97	1941 Feb 28	IA, 67th, 1941
Watron, Samuel		G, 13th Ky. Inf.	142		1912 Nov 12	KS, 32nd, 1913
Watrous, Chas. L.	Capt.	D, 76th N.Y. Inf.	12		1916 Feb 9	IA, 43rd, 1917
Watrous, Geo.	Pvt.	A, 13th Iowa Inf.	222		1919 May	IA, 46th, 1920
Watrous, James H.		L, 5th Kans. Cav.	16		1902 May 30	KS, 22nd, 1903
Watson, A.B.		B, 9th Kans. Cav.	15		1909 Feb 4	KS, 28th, 1909
Watson, A.M.		52nd Ill.	65		1912 Dec 19	KS, 32nd, 1913
Watson, Andrew	Pvt.	B, 27th Mich.	1		1906 May 19	KS, 26th, 1907
Watson, C.W.		D, 14th Ill.	12		1910 Aug 14	KS, 30th, 1911
Watson, Charles		6th Kans. Cav.	65		1916 Apr 21	KS, 36th, 1917
Watson, Charles		F, 13th Ind.	63		1936 Jul 28	NE, 61st, 1937
Watson, Cornelius			227		1921 Aug 10	NE, 47th, 1923
Watson, D.		F, 101st Penn.	498		1912 Apr 18	KS, 33rd, 1914
Watson, D.U.		C, 143rd Ill.	118		1932	KS, 52nd, 1933
Watson, D.U.		C, 143rd Ill.	118		1931	KS, 51st, 1932
Watson, Dan'l	Pvt.	E, 1st Iowa Inf.	157		1920 May 8	IA, 47th, 1921
Watson, David		F, 101st Penn.	498		1912 Apr 18	KS, 32nd, 1913
Watson, Geo.	Pvt.	E, Penn.	58		1913 Jun 28	IA, 40th, 1914
Watson, Geo. R.		6th Iowa	258		1923	KS, 43rd, 1924
Watson, George W.		K, 33rd Ind.	241		1912 Jan 6	KS, 32nd, 1913
Watson, J.C., Capt.	2nd Lieut. 1st Lieut.	F, 17th Ohio Vol. Inf. 12th Ohio Vol. Inf.	55		1914 Feb 14	KS, 34th, 1915
Watson, J.H.			98		1911 May 25	KS, 31st, 1912

*See Appendix A, B or C for roster of post names and locations.
†See Introduction for note regarding recording of death date.
576

Name	Rank	Company, Regiment or Ship	Post*	Age	Death Date†	Journal
Watson, J.M.		D, 67th & 62nd Penn.	53		1937 Aug 2	KS, 56th, 1937
Watson, J.W.		B, 150th Ill. Inf.	64		1937 Dec 29	KS, 56th, 1937
Watson, J.W.		B, 150th Ill.	64		1935 Dec 29	KS, 55th, 1936
Watson, John		D, 33rd Ky. Inf.	128		1900 Feb 28	KS, 21st, 1902
Watson, John		D, 33rd Ky. Inf.	128		1900 Feb 2	KS, 19th, 1900
Watson, John		C, 7th Kans.	6		1915 Mar 11	KS, 35th, 1916
Watson, John B.	Pvt.	M, 9th Iowa Inf.	364		1915 Jun 16	IA, 42nd, 1916
Watson, John H.	Pvt.	C, 2nd Iowa Inf.	167		1899 Sep 15	IA, 26th, 1900
Watson, John M.	Pvt.	C, 27th Iowa	298		1903 Oct 16	IA, 30th, 1904
Watson, M.D.	Pvt.	1st R.I. Lt. Art.	74		1912 Sep 8	IA, 39th, 1913
Watson, Marion		F, 7th Ill.	25		1933 May	KS, 53rd, 1934
Watson, N.	Pvt.	K, 2nd Wis. Cav.	154		1900 Jun 21	IA, 27th, 1901
Watson, N.	Pvt.	D, 4th U.S. Inf.	122		1920	IA, 47th, 1921
Watson, Nathan	Pvt.	I, 29th Ind. Inf.	97	62	1896 Feb 29	IA, 23rd, 1897
Watson, R.H.		H, 1st Iowa Cav.	147		1901 Jan 1	KS, 21st, 1902
Watson, S.W.		E, 23rd Mo.	286		1905	KS, 25th, 1906
Watson, Samuel		I, 17th Ill.	113		1933 Aug 3	NE, 58th, 1934
Watson, W.M.C.		30th Iowa Inf.	173		1901 Apr 7	IA, 28th, 1902
Watson, W.Z.		C, 16th N.Y. Inf. (died of brain disease)	247	57	1895 Mar 29	NE, 20th, 1896
Watt, Charles R.		A, 119th Ill. Inf. (murdered)	311		1891 Jul 6	KS, 11th, 1892
Watt, Frank		E, 156th Ind. Inf.	255		1931 Jan 4	KS, 51st, 1932
Watt, I.K.	Pvt. & Sergt.	A, 4th Iowa Inf. (died of heart disease)	33	54	1884 Mar 10	NE, 9th, 1885
Watt, Jno. R.	Pvt.	H, 115th N.Y. Inf.	235		1919 Jan 16	IA, 46th, 1920
Watters, Isaac	Pvt.	D, 16th Penn. Cav.	38		1899 Dec 23	IA, 26th, 1900
Watters, L.K.	Pvt.	B, 35th Iowa Inf.	64		1930	IA, 57th, 1931
Watters, Steve	Corp.	K, 120th N.Y. Inf.	22		1929 Jul	IA, 56th, 1930
Watters, W.W.		F, 36th Ill. Inf. (died of cancer)	11	62	1906 Jan 13	NE, 31st, 1907
Watts, C.A.			380		1918	KS, 38th, 1919
Watts, David	Pvt.	H, 21st Iowa Inf.	54	58	1896 May 29	IA, 23rd, 1897
Watts, J.C.		A, 3rd Kans. State Militia	12		1904 Sep 2	KS, 24th, 1905
Watts, J.M.	Pvt.	A, 2nd Ohio Inf.	100		1920 May 10	IA, 47th, 1921
Watts, J.R.	Pvt.	H, 39th Iowa Inf.	43	59	1896 Mar 18	IA, 23rd, 1897
Watts, J.S.		F, 116th Ill. Inf.	11	62	1903 Feb 19	NE, 28th, 1904
Watts, John	Pvt.	I, 40th Iowa Inf.	127	48	1877 Jul 15	IA, 18th, 1892
Watts, John		H, 21st Iowa	124		1926 Feb 6	IA, 53rd, 1927
Watts, Jonathan J.	Pvt.	A, 201st Penn. Inf.	36	61	1893 Jan 27	IA, 19th, 1893
Watts, Joseph B.		I, 52nd Ill. Inf.	132	91	1937 Dec 1	IA, 64th, 1938
Watts, St. Claire		B, 13th Mo.	293		1927	KS, 47th, 1928
Watts, Thomas		C, 7th N.H. Inf. (died at Arkansas City, Kans.; buried at Riverside Cemetery)	158		1894 Jul 28	KS, 14th, 1895
Watts, Tiffin		F, 5th Ill. Cav.	185		1904 Dec	KS, 24th, 1905
Waudby, Thomas P.		D, 46th Iowa Inf.		88	1936 Apr 20	IA, 62nd, 1936
Waudly, Thomas P.		D, 6th Iowa Inf. (at large)		88	1936 Apr 20	IA, 63rd, 1937
Waudly, Thos.		D, 6th Iowa Inf. (at large)		88	1936 Apr 20	IA, 62nd, 1936
Waugh, John		H, 8th Kans. (died of heart failure)	34		1893 Dec 31	KS, 13th, 1894
Waughop, W.H.	Pvt.	G, 86th Ill. Inf.	100		1906 Oct 28	IA, 33rd, 1907
Waukenhauser, J.	Pvt.	D, 152nd Penn. Inf.	329		1900 Sep 14	IA, 27th, 1901
Wauker, Ignacious		B, 18th Iowa Inf. (died of heart failure)	171	79	1924 Apr 30	NE, 50th, 1926
Waupler, R.	Pvt.	B, 17th Inf.	194		1923	IA, 50th, 1924
Wax, Sidney I.		G, 5th Conn. Inf.	380		1917 Mar 28	KS, 37th, 1918
Wax, W.W.H.		E, 29th Iowa Inf.	56	91	1935 Jun 16	IA, 62nd, 1936
Waxham, James		E, 18th Penn.	35	75	1915 May 18	NE, 40th, 1916
Waxler, A.J.		C, 182nd Ohio	53		1923 Feb 6	KS, 43rd, 1924
Way, A.J.		F, 86th Ill. Inf.	46		1934 Feb	KS, 54th, 1935
Way, H.H.		F, 57th Ohio	33		1914 Nov 29	KS, 34th, 1915
Way, J.S.		C, 69th Ind.	4		1917 Dec 14	KS, 37th, 1918
Way, Jacob		D, 7th Ill. Cav.			1928 Oct	NE, 53rd, 1929
Way, Philo P.		E, 89th Ind.	113		1920 Mar 28	KS, 40th, 1921
Way, Thomas P.		F, 7th Iowa	18		1911 Aug 29	KS, 31st, 1912
Way, W.A.		K, 156th Ohio	113		1909 Jan 14	KS, 29th, 1910
Waychoff, J.D.	Pvt.	H, 15th Penn. Inf.	454		1910 Jun 5	IA, 37th, 1911
Wayman, T.C.	Corp.	A, 38th Iowa Inf.	48		1915 May 28	IA, 42nd, 1916

*See Appendix A, B or C for roster of post names and locations.
†See Introduction for note regarding recording of death date.

Name	Rank	Company, Regiment or Ship	Post*	Age	Death Date†	Journal
Waymire, A.W.		B, 40th Ind. (died of heart failure)	201	70	1912 Dec 26	NE, 37th, 1913
Waymire, Jacob		G, 12th Kans. Inf.	33		1917 Dec 5	KS, 37th, 1918
Waymire, Nathaniel		K, 48th Ind. (died of effects of gun wound)	200		1892 Feb 16	KS, 12th, 1893
Waymore, Hiram		H, 135th Ind.	185		1908	KS, 28th, 1909
Wayne, H.N.	Pvt.	A, 15th Ill. Inf.	244		1915 Jan 15	IA, 42nd, 1916
Waynner, H.	Pvt.	H, 12th Ind. Cav.	209		1899	NE, 24th, 1900
Weaber, E.		A, 42nd Ill.	164		1888	KS, 8th, 1889
Weaber, J.P.		K, 153rd Ind. Inf. (died of heart failure)	171	88	1925 May 5	NE, 50th, 1926
Wead, J.C.F.	Pvt.	F, 154th Ohio Inf.	108		1928 Jan	IA, 55th, 1929
Weakley, W.C.		149th Penn.	25		1926 May 21	NE, 51st, 1927
Wean, S.	Pvt.	B, 4th Mich. Inf.	98		1918 Oct 11	IA, 45th, 1919
Weaner, Adam		F, 13th Ohio	18		1923 Jul 13	KS, 43rd, 1924
Wear, Richard		D, 9th Wis. Cav.	293		1920 Jul 27	KS, 40th, 1921
Weatherby, S.S., see Waatherbee, S.S.						
Weatherholt, C.S.		L, 3rd Ky. Cav. (died at Arkansas City)	158		1895 Sep 17	KS, 15th, 1896
Weatherly, C.L.		D, Michigan City, Mich.	150		1885	KS, 5th, 1886
Weatherly, J.G.			94		1919 Oct	IA, 46th, 1920
Weatherly, Wm. H.	Lieut.	B, 11th Iowa Inf.	94	74	1897 Apr 2	IA, 24th, 1898
Weatherman, T.A.		H, 9th Kans. Cav.	51		1922 Sep 7	KS, 42nd, 1923
Weathers, John L.		D, 16th Iowa (died of old age at Soldiers & Sailors Home, Milford)		81	1906 Nov 16	NE, 31st, 1907
Weatherwax, A.T.	Pvt.	K, 8th Iowa Cav.	3	87	1932 Jul 8	IA, 59th, 1933
Weave, W.B.	Pvt.	F, 125th Ill.	329		1903 Oct 12	IA, 30th, 1904
Weaver, A.J.		A, 3rd Penn.	244		1923 Nov 4	KS, 43rd, 1924
Weaver, Alfred		H, 11th Kans. Cav.	12		1917 Apr 4	KS, 37th, 1918
Weaver, B.F.		F, 4th Mo. Cav. (died at Doniphan County; buried at Fanning Cemetery)	292		1894 Aug 15	KS, 14th, 1895
Weaver, C.B.		117th Ind.	429		1908	KS, 28th, 1909
Weaver, C.B.			429		1911	KS, 31st, 1912
Weaver, Daniel R.	Pvt.	B, 105th Ill. Inf.	68		1912 Sep 7	IA, 39th, 1913
Weaver, David	Pvt.	C, 1st Mo. Cav.	1		1922 Mar 28	IA, 49th, 1923
Weaver, Edward F.		B, 76th Ohio	25		1912 Nov 5	KS, 32nd, 1913
Weaver, Frank		C, 46th Penn. Inf.	69		1917 Nov 7	KS, 37th, 1918
Weaver, Geo. T.			113		1908 Jan 5	KS, 28th, 1909
Weaver, George	Pvt.	G, 141st Penn. Inf.	469	56	1896 Feb 9	IA, 22nd, 1896
Weaver, Harry C.		H, 16th Ind. Inf.	85		1901 Feb 6	KS, 21st, 1902
Weaver, Henry		F, 65th Penn. Inf.	15		1909 Nov 7	KS, 29th, 1910
Weaver, J.H.	Pvt.	B, 6th Iowa Inf.	5		1911 Jan 31	IA, 38th, 1912
Weaver, J.J.		I, 4th West Va.	51		1921 Apr 13	KS, 41st, 1922
Weaver, J.S.		N, 11th Penn. Vol. Inf.	32		1918 Oct 31	KS, 38th, 1919
Weaver, Jacob	Corp.	C, 135th Penn.	332		1899 Jul 29	IA, 26th, 1900
Weaver, Jacob	Corp.	C, 135th Penn. Inf.	332	60	1899 Aug 4	IA, 26th, 1900
Weaver, James B.		G, 19th Ill. Inf.	270		1889	KS, 9th, 1890
Weaver, James D.	Gen.	2nd Iowa Inf.	12		1912 Feb 6	IA, 39th, 1913
Weaver, Jas. B.		G, 19th Ill. (sudden death)	270		1890	KS, 10th, 1891
Weaver, Joe M.		G, 134th Ohio	17		1925 Jul 9	KS, 45th, 1926
Weaver, John	Pvt.	G, 38th Iowa Inf.	48		1915 Mar 22	IA, 42nd, 1916
Weaver, John		H, 3rd N.Y.	2		1890	KS, 10th, 1891
Weaver, John W.		C, 83rd Ill. Inf.	92		1900 Jun 22	KS, 20th, 1901
Weaver, Jonathan		E, 69th Ind.	64		1910 Jul 1	KS, 30th, 1911
Weaver, Moses	Corp.	E, 153rd Ill. Inf.	204		1909 May 28	IA, 36th, 1910
Weaver, R.B.	Pvt.	A, 9th Iowa Cav.	7		1912 Feb 4	IA, 39th, 1913
Weaver, S.		4th Iowa	43		1923 Jun 29	IA, 50th, 1924
Weaver, Sanford		H, 45th Ind.	130		1912 Jan 13	KS, 32nd, 1913
Weaver, Thos. C.		A, 53rd Ill. Inf.	123		1934 May 19	KS, 54th, 1935
Weaver, W.M.	Pvt.	K, 5th Ohio Inf.	22		1927 Feb 8	IA, 54th, 1928
Weaver, Wm.		B, 150th Ill.	84		1912 Jun 30	KS, 32nd, 1913
Weaver, Wm.		I, 94th N.Y. Hvy. Art.	13	78	1920 Aug 21	NE, 45th, 1921
Webb, A.G.			96		1906	IA, 33rd, 1907
Webb, D.W.		A, 95th Ill. Inf.	235		1906 May 23	IA, 33rd, 1907
Webb, Delorma		I, 73rd Ind.	14		1913 May 24	KS, 33rd, 1914

*See Appendix A, B or C for roster of post names and locations.
†See Introduction for note regarding recording of death date.

Name	Rank	Company, Regiment or Ship	Post*	Age	Death Date†	Journal
Webb, Edgar C.		A, 98th N.Y.	1		1915 Dec 13	KS, 35th, 1916
Webb, F.W.	Pvt.	K, 3rd Iowa Inf.	25		1933 Dec	IA, 60th, 1934
Webb, Geo. M.	Capt.	E, 14th Iowa Inf.	452		1916 Nov 19	IA, 43rd, 1917
Webb, George	Pvt.	A, 26th Iowa Inf.	164	57	1893 Jul 3	IA, 20th, 1894
Webb, Henry			497		1911 Aug 29	IA, 38th, 1912
Webb, J.B.		E, 18th Iowa Inf. (born in Penn.; died in Lincoln)	25		1883	NE, 8th, 1884
Webb, J.C.		G, 5th Iowa	158		1925 Jan 10	KS, 45th, 1926
Webb, J.F.		A, 5th Iowa Inf. (died of old age)	89	80	1922 Oct 14	NE, 47th, 1923
Webb, J.P.		C, 5th Ind. Cav.	422		1912 Jun 19	KS, 32nd, 1913
Webb, James	Pvt.	I, 4th Iowa Cav.	26		1906 Aug 26	IA, 33rd, 1907
Webb, Jas. M.	Pvt.	K, 5th Iowa Inf.	400	49	1891 Jul 3	IA, 18th, 1892
Webb, John		not a member of post named, but buried by said post	117		1897	KS, 17th, 1898
Webb, John		I, 118th Ill. (died of broken hip)	35	82	1920 Nov 29	NE, 45th, 1921
Webb, John H.		H, 75th Ohio Inf.	278		1899 Jun 12	KS, 19th, 1900
Webb, Leland J.		died at Topeka	1		1893 Feb 21	KS, 13th, 1894
Webb, Madison			235		1930 Feb 6	IA, 57th, 1931
Webb, Soloman D.B.		E, 2nd Iowa Inf.	113		1915 Sep 3	KS, 35th, 1916
Webb, T.F.		H, 154th Ind. Inf.	422		1912 Jul 16	KS, 32nd, 1913
Webb, W.C.	Col.	37th Wis.	1		1898 Apr 20	KS, 18th, 1899
Webb, W.D.	Pvt.	39th Mo.	52		1923 Oct	IA, 50th, 1924
Webb, W.H.		28th Ill.	26		1917 Jan 29	KS, 36th, 1917
Webb, W.S.	Capt.	H, 130th Ohio Inf.	8		1901 Nov 28	KS, 21st, 1902
Webb, William		D, 3rd U.S. Cav.	36		1923 Jun 3	KS, 43rd, 1924
Webber, John L.		H, 9th Kans. Cav.	12		1890	KS, 10th, 1891
Webber, Samuel		F, 5th Mo. Cav. (died of disease contracted in army)	412		1891 Jun 26	KS, 11th, 1892
Webber, Samuel F.		C, 33rd Ind.	23		1916 Jan 13	KS, 36th, 1917
Webbert, David		G, 131st Ohio Inf.	1		1893 Aug	NE, 18th, 1894
Weber, Geo.		G, 37th Ohio Inf.	25		1904 Jun 17	NE, 29th, 1905
Weber, George		D, 11th Penn.	19		1917 May 15	KS, 37th, 1918
Weber, Jacob		K, 7th Ind. (shot by bandit)	95	77	1921 Nov 22	NE, 46th, 1922
Weber, John		E, 4th Ill. Inf.	151		1899 Jan 19	KS, 19th, 1900
Weber, L.C.		H, 65th Ind. Inf. (died of Bright's disease)	46	67	1909 Sep	NE, 34th, 1910
Webster, A.B.			3		1921 Aug 28	IA, 48th, 1922
Webster, B.F.			87		1893 Mar	KS, 13th, 1894
Webster, Byron		D, 92nd Ill.	142		1931 Jul 27	KS, 51st, 1932
Webster, Byron		D, 92nd Ill.	142		1931 Jul 27	KS, 52nd, 1933
Webster, C.J.	Pvt.	A, 17th —	102		1920 Mar 25	IA, 47th, 1921
Webster, Dan.		A, 3rd Kans. Inf.	208		1899 Feb 13	KS, 19th, 1900
Webster, F.D.		I, 11th Ill.	87		1893 Mar 9	KS, 16th, 1897
Webster, F.F.		H, 10th N.Y. Art.	117		1st quarter 1885	IA, 11th, 1885
Webster, Frank N.	Pvt.	K, 50th N.Y. Eng.	270	46	1894 Nov 30	IA, 21st, 1895
Webster, G.A.		I, 1st N.H. Cav.	201		1921 Jun	IA, 48th, 1922
Webster, I.N.			12		1923 May 26	IA, 50th, 1924
Webster, J. Lee		B, 170th Ohio	7		1929 Sep 1	NE, 54th, 1930
Webster, J.R.		G, 11th Ind.	25		1917 Jan 9	NE, 42nd, 1918
Webster, John E.	Sergt.	D, 43rd Mass. Inf.	165	59	1889 May 3	IA, 16th, 1890
Webster, N.L.	Corp.	H, 7th Ill. Cav.	168		1900 May 4	IA, 27th, 1901
Webster, O.W.			25	77	1921 Jun 20	NE, 46th, 1922
Webster, Samuel C.		5th Wis. Bat. (died at Delphos)	116		1895 Jan 16	KS, 15th, 1896
Webster, W.H.	Sergt.	C, 3rd Penn. Cav.	312		1918 Mar 31	IA, 45th, 1919
Webster, William I.		I, 15th Iowa (nonmember; died at Beatrice)			1936 Apr 4	NE, 61st, 1937
Wedding, James W.	Pvt.	I, 12th Ill. Inf.	66		1927 Aug 17	IA, 54th, 1928
Weddle, D.C.			87		1884	KS, 4th, 1885
Wedgewood, Geo. F.		I & C, 3rd & 7th Maine Inf.	214	62	1905	NE, 30th, 1906
Weeber, Jno. C.		53rd Ill. Inf. (cause of death: heart)	195	65	1901 Dec	NE, 26th, 1902
Weed, A.G.		A, 24th Wis.	164		1891 Apr 19	KS, 12th, 1893
Weed, A.G.		A, 24th Wis.	164		1891 Apr 19	KS, 16th, 1897
Weed, A.G.		A, 24th Wis.	164		1897 Apr 19	KS, 17th, 1898
Weed, B.M.		G, 1st Ohio Bat., N.Y.	354	66	1911 Jan 3	NE, 36th, 1912

*See Appendix A, B or C for roster of post names and locations.
†See Introduction for note regarding recording of death date.

579

Name	Rank	Company, Regiment or Ship	Post*	Age	Death Date†	Journal
Weed, Charles		C, 2nd Mo. Cav., Va. (drowned in bath tub)	52	81	1924 Jun 24	NE, 49th, 1925
Weed, F.F.	Pvt.	G, 44th Ill. Inf.	338	42	[1889?]	IA, 17th, 1891
Weed, Geo. W.		B, 10th Kans. D, 7th N.Y. Hvy. Art.	1		1917 Dec 10	KS, 37th, 1918
Weed, James		K, 8th Wis.	140		1926 Nov 17	NE, 51st, 1927
Weed, U.R.			65		1924	KS, 44th, 1925
Weeden, William		K, 55th Ill. Inf.	67	94	1937 Jun 9	IA, 64th, 1938
Weekerly, Hiram J.		3rd Ohio Bat.	47		1900 Aug 17	KS, 20th, 1901
Weekly, Artemus		C, 7th Iowa	209		1920 Nov 23	KS, 40th, 1921
Weeks, A.J.	Pvt.	H, 2nd Mo. Cav.	22		1925 Apr 26	IA, 52nd, 1926
Weeks, C.E.		B, 7th Wis.	25		1925 Nov 18	NE, 53rd, 1929
Weeks, C.H.		H, 46th Ind. Inf.	147		1926 Dec 24	NE, 51st, 1927
Weeks, Chas.		K, 14th Wis. Inf. (died of hardening arteries)	262	77	1920 Jan 18	NE, 45th, 1921
Weeks, Cyrus		A, 9th Ill. Cav.	293		1921 Oct 22	KS, 41st, 1922
Weeks, J.H.	Pvt.	I, 32nd Ohio Inf.	197	57	1895 Dec 29	IA, 22nd, 1896
Weeks, James		A, Miss. (1st Bat. Bri.)	156		1905 Aug 18	KS, 25th, 1906
Weeks, Joseph		K, 188th Ohio Inf. (died of old age)	354	85	1925 Apr 23	NE, 50th, 1926
Weeks, Lucas A.		D, 15th Iowa	69		1897 Jul 14	KS, 17th, 1898
Weeks, P.	Pvt.		277		1925	IA, 52nd, 1926
Weeks, Peter H.		I, 5th Mo.	12		1928 Oct 3	KS, 48th, 1929
Weeks, W.W.	Pvt.	E, 91st —	234		1920 Feb 21	IA, 47th, 1921
Weeks, Weir W.	Pvt.	E, 91st Ill.	234		1922 Feb 21	IA, 49th, 1923
Weenes, Geo. W.			45		1918 Oct 5	IA, 45th, 1919
Weetks, J.W.S.		H, 7th Kans. Cav.	6		1906	KS, 26th, 1907
Weever, T.L.	Surgeon	7th Kans. Cav.	6		1905 Sep 11	KS, 25th, 1906
Wehn, Lewis		G, 192nd Penn.	35		1908 Apr 11	NE, 33rd, 1909
Wehrheim, John	Pvt.	C, 13th U.S. Inf.	66		1913 Aug 7	IA, 40th, 1914
Wehrman, H.C.		M, 10th Ohio Cav.	13	72	1914 Nov 24	NE, 39th, 1915
Wehrman, H.J.		D, H, 6th Wis.	47		1926 Feb 14	KS, 46th, 1927
Weichbradt, A.		F, 45th Ill. Inf. (died at National Military Home; buried at National Military Home Cemetery)	380		1894 Oct 24	KS, 14th, 1895
Weichman, John			10		1902	NE, 27th, 1903
Weide, August		K, 9th Wis.	301		1922 Jul 24	KS, 42nd, 1923
Weidner, David		47th Ind. Inf.	60		1899 Oct 19	KS, 19th, 1900
Weidner, Ernest	Pvt.	H, 1st Iowa Inf.	78	84	1933 Oct 4	IA, 60th, 1934
Weidner, J.H.	Pvt.	K, 19th Ind. Inf.	11		1911 Jun	IA, 38th, 1912
Weigant, Henry		K, 10th Kans. Inf.	283		1925 Oct 22	KS, 45th, 1926
Weigle, Jacob		I, 132nd Ill.	14		1926 Mar 13	KS, 46th, 1927
Weigle, Louis		C, 15th Penn. Cav.	83		1925 Jul 1	KS, 45th, 1926
Weigle, William		H, 47th Wis. Inf.		94	1936 Feb 16	IA, 62nd, 1936
Weigle, Wm.		H, 47th Wis. Inf.	235	94	1936 Feb 16	IA, 63rd, 1937
Weiler, James		H, 152nd Ind.	265		1889	KS, 9th, 1890
Weimer, Edward		I & H, 34th Ill.	60		1923 Oct 31	NE, 48th, 1924
Weingard, Abram		D, 39th N.Y. Art. (died of accident)	262	71	1905 Apr 1	NE, 30th, 1906
Weingard, Abram		D, 39th N.Y. (died of accident)	262	71	1911 Apr 1	NE, 36th, 1912
Weinheimer, J.A.		E, 37th Ill. Inf.	251		1912 Mar 30	KS, 32nd, 1913
Weinheimer, V.		A, 2nd Kans. Cav.	18		1900 Jan 7	KS, 20th, 1901
Weinrich, Phillip		C, 48th Mo. Inf.	85		1941 Jul 15	KS, 61st, 1942
Weinshenk, Antone	Corp.	I, 5th Iowa Inf.	131	50	1893 May 31	IA, 20th, 1894
Weir, John S.		A, 96th Ind.	1		1917 Jan 27	KS, 37th, 1918
Weise, August		F, 19th Iowa Inf.	1		1912 Nov 26	IA, 39th, 1913
Weiser, E.J.	Capt.	D, 3rd Iowa Inf.	168		1902 Oct 28	IA, 29th, 1903
Weiser, Martin		I, 99th Ohio Inf.	71		1914 Feb 19	KS, 34th, 1915
Weisman, C.A.		G, 22nd Ill.	12		1885	KS, 5th, 1886
Weisner, J.W.	Pvt.	Wis. Inf.	29		1920 Dec 19	IA, 47th, 1921
Weiss, Fred	Pvt.	I, 25th Iowa Inf.	5		1900-1901	IA, 27th, 1901
Weiss, Frederick	Pvt.	E, 25th Iowa Inf.	5	58	1900 Feb 21	IA, 26th, 1900
Weitnaur, A.B.	Musician	F, Penn. Lt. Art.	68		1904 Dec 3	IA, 31st, 1905
Weitz, A.		K, 21st N.Y.	28		1888	KS, 8th, 1889
Welch, B.T.		K, 13th Iowa	1		1920 Sep 6	KS, 40th, 1921

*See Appendix A, B or C for roster of post names and locations.
†See Introduction for note regarding recording of death date.

Name	Rank	Company, Regiment or Ship	Post*	Age	Death Date†	Journal
Welch, C.M.	Pvt.	E, 11th Ind. Inf.	1		1896 Mar 2	KS, 16th, 1897
Welch, Charles A.		A, 19th Ill. Inf.	8		1914 May 22	KS, 34th, 1915
Welch, Darius		92nd Ohio	265		1897 Apr 20	KS, 17th, 1898
Welch, E.H.	Pvt.	E, 14th Ill. Inf.	56	51	1886 Oct 20	IA, 13th, 1887
Welch, Eben Smith		G, 12th N.H.	45		1914 Nov 9	KS, 34th, 1915
Welch, Fred			92		1914	NE, 39th, 1915
Welch, Isaac			51		1896	KS, 16th, 1897
Welch, J.	Pvt.		115		1921 Oct 11	IA, 48th, 1922
Welch, J.			159		1925	IA, 52nd, 1926
Welch, J.	Pvt.		159		1926 Nov	IA, 53rd, 1927
Welch, J.A.		G, 15th Iowa	17		1921 Jul 22	KS, 41st, 1922
Welch, Jacob		H, 12th Ohio	241		1917 Sep 2	KS, 37th, 1918
Welch, Jas. H.	Pvt.	G, 165th Penn. Inf.	55		1913 Jun 21	IA, 40th, 1914
Welch, John S.	Pvt.	C, 40th Ind. Inf.	23		1910 Dec 27	IA, 37th, 1911
Welch, Jos.	Pvt.	B, 48th Ohio Inf.	69		1908 Jul	IA, 35th, 1909
Welch, L.W.		F, 52nd Penn.	81		1916 Jul	KS, 36th, 1917
Welch, Martin	Pvt.	I, 118th N.Y.	383	63	1890 Mar 10	IA, 16th, 1890
Welch, Mitchel	Pvt.	E, 35th Iowa Inf.	250		1913 Nov 16	IA, 40th, 1914
Welch, P.C.			12		1906	KS, 26th, 1907
Welch, Robt.	Pvt.	H, 147th Ill. Inf.	231		1920 Jun 21	IA, 47th, 1921
Welch, Robt.		F, 136th N.Y.	311		1917 Jun 24	KS, 37th, 1918
Welch, Ross L.		H, 38th Ill.	339		1931 Mar 12	KS, 51st, 1932
Welch, Ross L.		H, 38th Ill.	339		1931 Mar 12	KS, 52nd, 1933
Welch, S.S.		I, 18th Iowa	5		1912 Jun	KS, 32nd, 1913
Welch, Stephen		I, 116th U.S.C.T.	241		1909 Jun 6	KS, 29th, 1910
Welch, W.H.		G, 154th Ill.	156		1917 Dec 12	KS, 37th, 1918
Welch, Wm.	Pvt.	H, 83rd Penn. Inf.	231		1913 Jan 4	IA, 40th, 1914
Welch, Wm. A.	Pvt.	A, 9th N.Y. Hvy. Art.	22		1908 Aug 2	IA, 35th, 1909
Welcher, B.S.	Pvt.	E, 1st Ohio Lt. Art.	49		1915 Nov 2	IA, 42nd, 1916
Welcome, Wm. M.		16th Wis. Inf.	1		1914 Sep 7	KS, 34th, 1915
Weld, Lewy T.	Corp.	B, 9th Mich. St. Art.	235		1923 Oct 14	IA, 50th, 1924
Welden, Clark		I, 75th Ill.	240		1904 Mar 1	KS, 24th, 1905
Welden, Thos.	Pvt.	3rd Bat.	168		1920 Jul 12	IA, 47th, 1921
Weldin, Samuel		K, 78th Ill.	147		1919 Jan 24	KS, 39th, 1920
Weldin, Z.A.		I, 86th Ohio (died of blood poison)	1	77	1918 Jan 27	NE, 43rd, 1919
Weldon, E.D., see Welldon, E.D.						
Weldon, John J.C.	Pvt.	E, 4th West Va.	103		1922 Dec 21	IA, 49th, 1923
Weldon, L.A.	Pvt.	A, 92nd Ill. Inf.	497		1926 Jan 26	IA, 53rd, 1927
Weldon, L.W.		G, 16th Ohio (died of old age)	131	84	1917 Sep 29	NE, 42nd, 1918
Welein, John	Pvt.	E, 128th Ill. Inf.	68		1920 Feb 10	IA, 47th, 1921
Weliver, Samuel		G, 18th Ohio	17		1904 Mar	KS, 24th, 1905
Welker, Fred	Major	G, 1st Mo. Art.	231		1914 Jul 14	IA, 41st, 1915
Welker, Joshua	Pvt.	B, 7th Wis. Inf.	132		1902 Sep 14	IA, 29th, 1903
Welker, W.S.	Pvt.	D, 115th Ill. Inf.	29		1928 Sep 10	IA, 55th, 1929
Welldon, E.D.	Pvt.	I, 75th Ill. Inf.	168		1910 Jan 23	IA, 37th, 1911
Weller, F.M.			342		1912	KS, 32nd, 1913
Weller, F.M.			342		1915	KS, 35th, 1916
Weller, Phillip	Pvt.	E, 16th Ind. (died of consumption)	107	43	1884 Jan 6	NE, 9th, 1885
Weller, William H.		I, 11th Mich. Inf.	10	83	1913 Mar 15	NE, 38th, 1914
Weller, Wm.	Teamster	H, — Mich.	318		1913	NE, 38th, 1914
Welles, C.			112		1923	NE, 48th, 1924
Welles, James		K, 9th Kans.	126		1908 Oct 27	KS, 28th, 1909
Wellhouse, Fredrick		I, 19th Kans.	1		1911 Jan 10	KS, 31st, 1912
Wellhouse, Peter		I, 41st Ill.	1		1890	KS, 10th, 1891
Wellhouse, Walter		A, 11th Kans. Cav.	1		1914 May 2	KS, 34th, 1915
Wellier, Jacob		A, 18th U.S.	1		1923 Jan 20	KS, 43rd, 1924
Wellis, Geo. S.	Pvt.	G, 19th Iowa Inf.	153		1907 Apr	IA, 34th, 1908
Welliver, M.	Pvt.	I, 16th Ill. Inf.	25		1912	IA, 39th, 1913
Wellman, A.J.		C, 10th Vt.	255		1918 Jan 10	KS, 38th, 1919
Wellman, John F.		B, 154th N.Y.	12		1911 Oct 12	KS, 31st, 1912
Wellman, Wm.	Pvt.	N.Y. Inf.	495		1915 Feb	IA, 42nd, 1916

*See Appendix A, B or C for roster of post names and locations.
†See Introduction for note regarding recording of death date.

Name	Rank	Company, Regiment or Ship	Post*	Age	Death Date†	Journal
Wells, A.		B, 14th Kans. State Militia	271		1898 Nov 17	KS, 18th, 1899
Wells, A.C.	Pvt.	C, 2nd Iowa Cav.	23		1930 Apr	IA, 57th, 1931
Wells, A.E.		C, 1st Wis. (died of general breakdown)	118	75	1919 Jun 24	NE, 44th, 1920
Wells, A.W.		E, 9th Ind.	1		1910 May 19	KS, 30th, 1911
Wells, Absolam	Lieut.		434		1916 Jul 26	IA, 43rd, 1917
Wells, Albert		63rd Ohio Inf. (died at Ellsworth)	22		1895 Oct	KS, 15th, 1896
Wells, Alfred			190		1925 Apr	IA, 52nd, 1926
Wells, Benjamin F.			244		1925 Jan 17	KS, 45th, 1926
Wells, C.E.		B, 74th Ill. Inf. (died of heart failure)	18	64	1909 Mar 20	NE, 34th, 1910
Wells, C.F.	Pvt.	B, 29th Iowa Inf.	263		1918 Mar 22	IA, 45th, 1919
Wells, C.S.	Capt.	H, 8th Iowa Inf.	49		1915 Jan 9	IA, 42nd, 1916
Wells, Damon E.	Pvt.	I, 157th N.Y. Inf.	88		1924 May 5	IA, 51st, 1925
Wells, Daniel W.		C, 6th Mo. Cav. (died at Elk Falls; buried at Elk Falls Cemetery)	289		1894 Dec 20	KS, 14th, 1895
Wells, Edmond S.	Saddler	B, 2nd Minn. Cav.	365		1900 Sep 26	IA, 27th, 1901
Wells, Ephriam		E, 44th Mass. Inf.	16		1900 Apr 28	NE, 25th, 1901
Wells, Fred T.	Sergt.	I, 44th Iowa Inf.	94		1926 Dec 16	IA, 53rd, 1927
Wells, G.M.		K, 11th Mich. Cav.	52		1898 Dec 2	KS, 18th, 1899
Wells, G.S.			152		1883	KS, 3rd, 1884
Wells, Geo. T.		D, 14th Ill. Inf.	25		1921 Mar 10	KS, 41st, 1922
Wells, Geo. W.		F, 51st Ill.	388		1921 Feb 25	KS, 41st, 1922
Wells, H.C.		H, 81st N.Y. (died of old age)	289	84	1920 Sep 23	NE, 45th, 1921
Wells, H.H.			17		1911	KS, 31st, 1912
Wells, H.M.		C, 36th Wis.	75		1910	NE, 35th, 1911
Wells, Henry Clay		B, 10th Kans.	102		1905 May 13	KS, 25th, 1906
Wells, Henry R.		K, 102nd Ill.	252		1922 Nov 13	KS, 42nd, 1923
Wells, Henry S.	Pvt.	F, 166th Ohio Inf.	193		1912 May 1	IA, 39th, 1913
Wells, J.B.	Pvt.	C, 33rd Iowa Inf.	173		1919 Jan 27	IA, 46th, 1920
Wells, J.C.	Pvt.	K, 197th Penn. Inf.	122		1917 Jan 10	IA, 44th, 1918
Wells, J.C.		H, 91st Ill.	311		1926 Jul 12	KS, 46th, 1927
Wells, J.D.		A, 34th Ohio	304		1922 Nov 2	KS, 43rd, 1924
Wells, J.L.	Pvt.	H, 32nd Ohio Inf.	440		1918 Nov 5	IA, 45th, 1919
Wells, J.T.			98		1913	KS, 33rd, 1914
Wells, James		E, 1st Ohio Cav.	117		1884	KS, 4th, 1885
Wells, James	Sergt.	33rd N.Y. Inf.	32		1904 Apr 16	KS, 24th, 1905
Wells, John		A, 102nd Ill.	380		1898 Dec 8	KS, 18th, 1899
Wells, John B.		H, 41st Ill.	66		1893 Aug 20	KS, 13th, 1894
Wells, John F.		C, 152nd Ind. Inf. (died at Belleville; buried at Belleville Cemetery)	44		1894 Oct 4	KS, 14th, 1895
Wells, John F.		15th Iowa	143		1928 Dec 14	NE, 53rd, 1929
Wells, John M.		D, 39th Iowa Inf.	336		1902 Mar 10	KS, 22nd, 1903
Wells, John S.		82nd Ind.	251		1930 Feb 28	KS, 50th, 1931
Wells, John S.		K, 82nd Ind. Inf.	251		1930 Feb 28	KS, 49th, 1930
Wells, Leander		H, 23rd Wis. Inf. (died of old age)	50	70	1918 Apr 14	NE, 43rd, 1919
Wells, M.		F, 3rd Mich.	28		1902 Apr 7	KS, 22nd, 1903
Wells, M.E.		G, 101st Ohio	45		1916 Dec 28	KS, 36th, 1917
Wells, Nicholas T.	Corp.	K, 40th Wis. Inf. (at large)	25	97	1943 Apr 14	IA, 69th, 1943
Wells, O.F.		I, 28th Ill. Inf.	7	56	1896 Jul 14	NE, 21st, 1897
Wells, Oliver C.		H, 46th Ill. Inf. (died of paralysis)	22		1912 Sep 26	NE, 37th, 1913
Wells, P.	Lieut.	D, 106th N.Y. Inf.	329		1906 Apr 13	IA, 33rd, 1907
Wells, R.A.	Capt.	K, 6th Iowa Inf.	204		1914 Nov	IA, 41st, 1915
Wells, Sidney	Pvt.	H, 1st Iowa Cav.	208		1901 Nov 18	IA, 28th, 1902
Wells, Simon	Pvt.	C, 34th Iowa Inf.	215		1900 May 29	IA, 27th, 1901
Wells, T.J.		5th Wis. Battery	275		1913 Aug 3	IA, 40th, 1914
Wells, T.J.		A, 55th Mass.	198		1916 Nov 5	KS, 36th, 1917
Wells, Troy		A, 62nd Ohio Inf. (died of heart failure)	256	62	1902 May	NE, 27th, 1903
Wells, W.B.	Pvt.	B, 140th Ohio	206		1899 May 23	IA, 26th, 1900
Wells, W.H.		B, 11th Kans.	23		1897 Jun 14	KS, 17th, 1898
Wells, W.W.		A, 70th Ill.	44		1905 Jan 10	KS, 25th, 1906
Wells, William F.		E, 4th West Va.	52		1923 May 31	KS, 43rd, 1924
Welsh, E.		H, 52nd Ind.	117		1916 Sep 12	KS, 36th, 1917
Welsh, Geo.	Pvt.	B, 32nd Iowa Inf.	67		1911 Sep 11	IA, 38th, 1912

*See Appendix A, B or C for roster of post names and locations.
†See Introduction for note regarding recording of death date.

Name	Rank	Company, Regiment or Ship	Post*	Age	Death Date†	Journal
Welsh, James		H, 95th Ill. Inf. (died of tuberculosis)	38	64	1910 Jan 16	NE, 35th, 1911
Welsh, John B.		D, 25th Ohio (died of old age)	77	83	1925 Aug 29	NE, 50th, 1926
Welsh, W.G.		9th Ohio Bat.	36		1899 Dec 4	KS, 19th, 1900
Welsh, W.H.		F, 31st Ind.	50		1926 Aug 22	KS, 46th, 1927
Welso, C.			18		1921	IA, 48th, 1922
Welstead, James		I, 136th N.Y. Inf.	4		1940 Feb 7	NE, 65th, 1941
Welt, J.K.	Pvt.	E, 52nd Ohio Inf.	337		1916	IA, 43rd, 1917
Welter, M.	Pvt.	3rd Iowa Bat.	78		1920 Dec 18	IA, 47th, 1921
Welton, B.		A, 1st Minn. Lt. Art. (died of heart failure)	86		1894 Feb 27	NE, 19th, 1895
Welton, James A.		B, 17th Ill. Cav.	4		1926 Jul 4	NE, 51st, 1927
Welton, M.		K, 51st Ill. Inf. (died of heart disease)	149		1893 Jun 3	NE, 18th, 1894
Welton, N.L.	Pvt.	H, 93rd Ill. Inf.	57		1916 Mar 2	IA, 43rd, 1917
Welton, O.	Pvt.	B, 20th Wis. Inf.	11		1912 Aug 31	IA, 39th, 1913
Welts, W.H.		died suddenly	284	71	1910	NE, 35th, 1911
Welty, Aaron		H, 34th Ind.	12		1919 Oct 30	KS, 39th, 1920
Welty, Adam			98		1911 Sep 14	KS, 31st, 1912
Welty, Francis J.		C, 2nd Ky. Cav.	41		1911 Jun 21	KS, 31st, 1912
Welty, H.		F, 68th Ohio	26		1917	KS, 37th, 1918
Welty, Sam'l H.	Pvt.	D, 92nd Ill.	408		1907 Aug 13	IA, 34th, 1908
Welty, W.H.	Pvt.	E, 5th Wis. Bat.	81		1916	IA, 43rd, 1917
Welver, Zenas		A, 8th N.Y. Cav.	12		1925 Nov 19	IA, 52nd, 1926
Weman, F.E.		E, 11th Ill.	32		1933 Mar 13	KS, 53rd, 1934
Wemple, E.A.		I, 26th Iowa Inf.	262	79	1919 Mar 4	NE, 43rd, 1919
Wemple, Mindret	Capt. & Major	H, 41st Ill. Vol. Cav.	312	69	1900 Feb 6	IA, 26th, 1900
Wemple, P.		K, 7th Iowa Cav.	242		1906 Nov 15	IA, 33rd, 1907
Wendel, C.		Kans.	199		1920 Aug 17	KS, 40th, 1921
Wendell, Anthony		B, 53rd Ind.	57		1915 Dec 27	KS, 35th, 1916
Wendell, John		C, 19th Mich.	42		1893 Sep 28	KS, 13th, 1894
Wendeln, Mathias		A, 97th Ill. Inf. (died of dropsy)	21	67	1905 Nov 2	NE, 30th, 1906
Wendt, August		M, 6th Kans. Cav.	68		1913 Sep 15	KS, 33rd, 1914
Wendt, F.	Pvt.	C, 20th Iowa Inf.	1		1926 Feb 5	IA, 53rd, 1927
Wendt, Fred		I, 139th Ill. Inf.	354	62	1906 Mar 29	NE, 31st, 1907
Wenke, Herman		F, 7th Penn. (died of old age)	112		1916 Jan 13	NE, 41st, 1917
Wensel, Pete		H, 105th Penn.	113		1926 Jun 2	NE, 51st, 1927
Wentrode, Jeheil T.		B, 76th —	1		1911 Jan 23	KS, 31st, 1912
Wentsel, S.J.	Pvt.	H, 208th Penn. Inf.	290		1919 Dec 19	IA, 46th, 1920
Wentworth, C.A.	Pvt.	M, 1st Maine Cav.	30		1929 Jan 25	IA, 56th, 1930
Wentworth, G.T.			122		4th quarter 1883	IA, 10th, 1884
Wentworth, H.E.		D, 14th N.Y.	1		1927 Nov 21	KS, 47th, 1928
Wentworth, H.P., see Wintworth, H.P.						
Wentworth, Hiram E.		G, 11th Ill. Cav.	251		1914 Aug 17	KS, 34th, 1915
Wentz, Charles		F, 1st Dragoons	2		1890	KS, 10th, 1891
Wentz, Geo. H.	Capt.	G, 51st Ill. Inf.	418	80	1894 Mar 28	IA, 20th, 1894
Wentz, H.		F, 112th N.Y. Inf.	159		1892 Jul 15	KS, 12th, 1893
Wentz, J.G.		H, 88th Ill.	7		1920 Nov 2	KS, 40th, 1921
Wentz, Wm.		F, 196th Ohio (died in Oklahoma City)	343		1890	KS, 10th, 1891
Wentzel, John	Pvt.	F, 5th Penn. Hvy. Art.	28		1911 Jul 4	IA, 38th, 1912
Werdner, Wm. H.		O, 2nd Kans.	174		1908 Jan 2	KS, 28th, 1909
Were, Newton S.		C, 54th Ind.	19		1913 Feb 2	KS, 33rd, 1914
Werneke, Herman		E, 49th Mo.	27		1933 Jan 4	KS, 53rd, 1934
Werner, Benj. F.		E, 130th Ind.	265		1927 Nov 18	NE, 52nd, 1928
Werner, F.J.		B, 104th Ohio	16		1929 Jan 14	NE, 53rd, 1929
Werner, Joseph		A, 89th Ind. Inf.	117		1886	KS, 6th, 1887
Werner, Richard		A, 3rd Ky.	46		1930 Oct 23	KS, 51st, 1932
Wernner, Samuel		D, 9th Ohio Inf.	477		1928 Jan 28	KS, 48th, 1929
Wert, D.M.	Pvt.	D, 9th Iowa Cav.	16		1911 Jun 11	IA, 38th, 1912
Wert, E.N.		D, 120th Ind.	72		1919 Sep 24	KS, 39th, 1920
Wert, Jno. J.	Pvt.	A, 196th Ohio Inf.	130	42	1888 Oct 19	IA, 15th, 1889
Werth, Fritz		M, 3rd Mo. (died of old age)	7		1904 Mar 6	NE, 29th, 1905
Werts, James		I, 3rd Ohio Inf.	71		1912 Jan 21	KS, 32nd, 1913
Werts, Soloman		D, 122nd Ohio	12		1928 Oct 24	KS, 48th, 1929

Name	Rank	Company, Regiment or Ship	Post*	Age	Death Date†	Journal
Wertz, Elias	Corp.	C, 9th Ind. Inf.	12		1925 May 11	IA, 52nd, 1926
Wertz, J.C.		B, 10th Penn.	129		1904 Jul 25	KS, 24th, 1905
Wertz, John		D, 26th Iowa	407		1908	KS, 28th, 1909
Wertz, John		D, 26th Iowa	407		1915 Oct 18	KS, 35th, 1916
Wertz, John S.	Pvt.	K, 14th Iowa Vol. Inf.	5		1901 Jun 7	IA, 28th, 1902
Wescoat, C.R.	Pvt.	H, 9th Iowa Cav.	466	60	1893 Feb 2	IA, 19th, 1893
Wescott, A.R.	1st Lieut.	B, 31st Maine Inf.	235	51	1891 Jul 1	IA, 18th, 1892
Wescott, Erskine	Pvt.		583		1900-1901	IA, 27th, 1901
Wescott, G.C.	Pvt.	I, 2nd Wis. Cav.	343		1911 Oct 9	IA, 38th, 1912
Wescott, H.H.		F, 27th Wis. Inf.	16		1918	IA, 45th, 1919
Wescott, J.	Pvt.	E, 11th Mich.	68		1921 Oct 30	IA, 48th, 1922
Weskimen, Allen		H, 40th Ohio	39		1913 Apr 17	KS, 33rd, 1914
Wesley, John	Pvt.	C, 15th Ill. Inf.	45		1906 Jun 6	IA, 33rd, 1907
Wesson, Daniel P.		F, 35th Ill.	4	81	1914 May 2	NE, 39th, 1915
Wesson, E.W.	Pvt.	C, 185th Ohio Inf.	235		1908 Jul 30	IA, 35th, 1909
West, A.J.		E, 25th Ill.	173		1923 Feb 6	IA, 50th, 1924
West, A.J.		D, 39th Iowa Inf.	173		1924 Sep 19	IA, 51st, 1925
West, Adelbert	Pvt.	K, 31st Wis. Inf.	12		1927 Apr 27	IA, 54th, 1928
West, Albert		B, 175th Ohio Inf. (died at Emporia)	464		1895 Sep	KS, 15th, 1896
West, Alexander		B, 10th U.S.	127		1912 Apr 6	KS, 32nd, 1913
West, Alexander		B, 10th U.S. Colored Inf. (not a member of Farragut Post)	25		1913 Apr 6	NE, 38th, 1914
West, B.S.	Pvt.	E, 8th Ind.	266		1901 Sep 21	IA, 28th, 1902
West, C.H.		F, 93rd Ill. Inf.	25		1902 Dec 2	KS, 22nd, 1903
West, Charles		B, 14th Ill. Cav.	55[25?]		1892	NE, 17th, 1893
West, Chas. S.		D, 17th Conn.	25	78	1917 Apr 19	NE, 42nd, 1918
West, David A.	Pvt.	G, 43rd Wis. Inf.	329	49	1889 Apr 23	IA, 16th, 1890
West, E.R.	Pvt.	E, 4th Iowa Inf.	7		1919 Dec 18	IA, 46th, 1920
West, Frank K.		C, 50th Ill. (died of erysipelas)	354	68	1904 Aug 18	NE, 29th, 1905
West, Geo.	Pvt.	F, 6th N.Y. Hvy. Art.	365		1909 Dec 13	IA, 36th, 1910
West, Geo. R.	Lieut. Col.	37th Iowa Inf.	78	83	1892 Mar 20	IA, 18th, 1892
West, George W.		E, 115th Ind.	79		1892 Oct 20	KS, 12th, 1893
West, Henry			380		1918	KS, 38th, 1919
West, Humphrey	Pvt.	L, 7th Ill. Cav.	192		1927 Apr 26	IA, 54th, 1928
West, I.G.		L, 9th Iowa Cav. (dropped dead)	10		1924 Jan 1	NE, 48th, 1924
West, I.J.		L, 9th Iowa Cav. (David City)			1944 Mar	NE, 70th, 1946
West, J.B.		I, 66th Ill. Inf. (died at Ottawa)	18		1885[1895?] Nov	KS, 15th, 1896
West, J.B.		I, 54th Ill.	64		1919 Mar 29	KS, 39th, 1920
West, J.M.	Pvt.	E, 40th Iowa Inf.	7		1912 Dec 25	IA, 39th, 1913
West, J.V.	Pvt.	C, 23rd Iowa Inf.	7		1913 May 10	IA, 40th, 1914
West, James O.		F, 20th Ind. Inf. (died of fever)	11	55	1900 Jan 9	NE, 25th, 1901
West, James P.			179		1899	NE, 24th, 1900
West, Jas.	Pvt.	C, 39th Iowa Inf.	67		1916 Jan 20	IA, 43rd, 1917
West, John	Pvt.	B, 32nd Iowa Inf.	42		1901 Sep 29	IA, 28th, 1902
West, John		E, 3rd Iowa	25	67	1915 Jan 10	NE, 40th, 1916
West, John P.			32		1913 Mar 11	KS, 33rd, 1914
West, Joseph A.		E, 12th Kans.	12		1925 Jul 10	KS, 45th, 1926
West, L.C.		B, 148th Ohio National Guards	104		1922 Nov 5	KS, 42nd, 1923
West, Lewis	Pvt.	D, 13th Mich. Inf.	3		1915 Aug 2	IA, 42nd, 1916
West, P.B.		B, 65th Ill. Inf. C, 137th Ill. Inf. (died of old age)	171		1923 Jan 27	NE, 48th, 1924
West, P.B.		K, 153rd Ind. Inf. (died of heart failure)	171	80	1923 Jan 27	NE, 50th, 1926
West, P.B.		died of old age	171		1923 Jan 28	NE, 47th, 1923
West, R.P.		D, 21st Ill.	113		1902 Dec 11	KS, 22nd, 1903
West, Randle C.	Corp.	B, 11th Mich. Inf.	139		1911 Apr 3	IA, 37th, 1911
West, Robt. L.		K, 3rd Iowa	464		1904 Mar 5	KS, 24th, 1905
West, S.M.	Pvt.	M, 7th Iowa Cav.	136	59	1891 Nov 5	IA, 18th, 1892
West, Sam		G, 12th Iowa Inf.	80		1906 Jan 27	NE, 31st, 1907
West, Simon Pope	Pvt.	G, 3rd Army Corps (not a G.A.R. member)		93	1940 Sep 29	IA, 67th, 1941
West, Thomas O.	Pvt.	K, 27th Ohio Inf.	11	79	1886 Jul 6	IA, 13th, 1887
West, William	Pvt.	B, 3rd Iowa Cav.	2	67	1899 May 11	IA, 26th, 1900
West, William	Pvt.	F, 129th Ohio Inf.	34		1899	NE, 24th, 1900

*See Appendix A, B or C for roster of post names and locations.
†See Introduction for note regarding recording of death date.

Name	Rank	Company, Regiment or Ship	Post*	Age	Death Date†	Journal
West, Wm.		B, 161st Ohio	35	72	1919 Apr 5	NE, 44th, 1920
West, Zachariah	Sergt.	G, 8th Mo. Inf.	59	93	1933 Jul 19	IA, 60th, 1934
Westbrook, Milton H.	Pvt.	E, 134th Ill. Inf.	327		1902 Sep 28	IA, 29th, 1903
Westburg, Louis	Pvt.	I, 8th Iowa	94		1924 Dec 5	IA, 51st, 1925
Westburger, J.W.		A, 13th Ohio Inf. (at large)			1932 Jan 28	IA, 59th, 1933
Westcott, Emory	Sergt.	F, 22nd Iowa Inf.	8		1923 Feb 14	IA, 50th, 1924
Westerman, H.	Pvt.	H, 95th Ill. Inf.	30		1920 Jan 9	IA, 47th, 1921
Westervelt, P.N.		H, 146th Ill. Inf. (died of old age)	32	79	1902 Oct	NE, 27th, 1903
Westfall, J.	Pvt.	H, 100th La. Inf.	93		1921 Dec 11	IA, 48th, 1922
Westfall, Marion		E, 134th Ohio	354	74	1922 Nov 29	NE, 47th, 1923
Westgate, S.S.	Pvt.	F, 2nd Iowa Cav.	141		1921 Dec 22	IA, 48th, 1922
Westheffer, Edwin		H, 87th Ind.	12		1926 Jun 23	KS, 46th, 1927
Westhoff, C.	Pvt.	H, 148th N.Y. Inf.	132		1911	IA, 38th, 1912
Westlake, M.M.	Pvt.	G, 16th Ill. Inf.	208		1911 Nov 2	IA, 38th, 1912
Westman, Norman			85		1920 Sep 25	KS, 40th, 1921
Weston, A.C.	Pvt.	A, 36th Wis. Inf.	7		1920 Jan 17	IA, 47th, 1921
Weston, C.B.	Sergt.	B, 73rd Ind.	200		1924 Oct 24	IA, 51st, 1925
Weston, C.F.	1st Lieut.	E, 21st Wis.	66		1906 Mar 12	IA, 33rd, 1907
Weston, J.A.	Pvt.	B, 1st Penn. Bat.	472		1916 Feb 17	IA, 43rd, 1917
Weston, John	Pvt.	A, 1st Wis. Hvy. Art.	163		1911 Oct 25	IA, 38th, 1912
Weston, Joseph B.		K, 25th Ill. Inf. (died at Wellsville)	96		1894 Apr 9	KS, 14th, 1895
Weston, Martin S.			500		1919	KS, 39th, 1920
Weston, Martin S.		L, 12th Mo. Cav.	500		1920	KS, 40th, 1921
Weston, Perry E.		G, 39th Ill.	62		1929 Aug 27	NE, 54th, 1930
Weston, Solon H.		C, 16th Wis.	293		1902 Dec 24	KS, 22nd, 1903
Weston, W.J.			50		1927	IA, 54th, 1928
Westover, L.H.		I, 127th Ill.	18		1913 Jan 10	KS, 33rd, 1914
Westrup, J.F.		E, 35th Ind.	63		1926 Mar 3	KS, 46th, 1927
Wetherbee, E.			124		1913	IA, 40th, 1914
Wetherbee, M.E.			29		1915 Jun 30	IA, 42nd, 1916
Wetherbee, W.C.		D, 140th Ill. Inf.	94		1923 Mar 13	IA, 50th, 1924
Wetherell, Henry	Sergt.	1st Ohio Lt. Art.	40		1917 Aug 28	IA, 44th, 1918
Wetherell, John, see Witherell, John						
Wetzel, C.F.	Pvt.	D, 15th N.Y.	125		1930	IA, 57th, 1931
Weuve, Ulyses	Pvt.	A, 104th Ill. Inf.	266		1904 Apr 15	IA, 31st, 1905
Wexberg, Francis	Pvt.	C, 15th N.Y. Hvy. Art.	497		1908 Mar 2	IA, 35th, 1909
Weyer, George		E, 13th Kans.	246		1912 Aug 3	KS, 32nd, 1913
Weywaud, Christian	Pvt.	F, 45th Wis. Inf.	231		1904 Feb 4	IA, 31st, 1905
Whaley, A.M.	Capt.	K, 17th N.Y. Inf.	242		1911 Oct 29	IA, 38th, 1912
Whaley, S.O.		I, 28th Ohio (died of cancer)	26	79[?]	1920 Mar 1	NE, 45th, 1921
Whaley, Warren		G, 15th Iowa	52		1917 Dec 14	KS, 37th, 1918
Whalley, B.R.	Pvt.	42nd Ohio	501		1907 Apr 18	IA, 34th, 1908
Whan, John	Pvt.	E, 174th Ohio	271		1914 Mar 20	IA, 41st, 1915
Wharrum, Thomas	Pvt.	A, 128th Ohio Inf.	63		1910 Nov 8	IA, 37th, 1911
Whealer, James H.		37th Ind.	104		1924 Aug 23	KS, 44th, 1925
Wheat, A.H.	Pvt.	F, 15th Ill. Inf.	68		1928 Dec 3	IA, 55th, 1929
Wheat, Jefferson			55		1928 Sep 6	IA, 55th, 1929
Wheaton, J.S.	Pvt.	B, 39th Iowa Inf.	7	72	1893 Aug	IA, 20th, 1894
Wheeland, C.D.	Pvt.	E, 209th Penn. Inf.	312		1916 Dec 24	IA, 43rd, 1917
Wheeler, A.C.		A, 110th Ill.	209		1919 Oct 16	KS, 39th, 1920
Wheeler, A.C.		K, 67th Ind. Inf. (died of fever)	81	75	1906 Aug 1	NE, 31st, 1907
Wheeler, A.C.		A, 55th Ill.	77		1934 Mar 9	NE, 59th, 1935
Wheeler, Alfred F.	Pvt.	A, 32nd Wis. Inf.	149		1909 Mar 11	IA, 36th, 1910
Wheeler, Allen W.	Pvt.	E, 38th Iowa Inf.	277		1901-1902	IA, 28th, 1902
Wheeler, Alonzo	Pvt.	I, 3rd Penn. Hvy. Art.	108		1933 Sep 8	IA, 60th, 1934
Wheeler, Bass		C, 15th U.S. Colored	321		1886	KS, 6th, 1887
Wheeler, Chas. G.		G, 17th Vt.	78		1927	KS, 48th, 1929
Wheeler, Curtis	Pvt.	K, 45th Iowa Inf.	347	56	1892 Apr 15	IA, 19th, 1893
Wheeler, Dan			75		1920	NE, 45th, 1921
Wheeler, E.A.		I, 64th Ill. Inf.	127		1912 Jan 28	IA, 39th, 1913
Wheeler, G.L.	Pvt.	F, 44th Iowa Inf.	92		1919 Mar 23	IA, 46th, 1920

*See Appendix A, B or C for roster of post names and locations.
†See Introduction for note regarding recording of death date.
585

Name	Rank	Company, Regiment or Ship	Post*	Age	Death Date†	Journal
Wheeler, Geo. B.		E, 1st Mo. Inf.	138		1901 Jul 1	KS, 21st, 1902
Wheeler, Geo. O.	Pvt.	A, 5th Iowa Inf.	7		1922 Mar 28	IA, 49th, 1923
Wheeler, H.H.		9th N.Y. Hvy. Art.	25		1928 Feb 11	NE, 53rd, 1929
Wheeler, H.N.		E, 135th Ohio (died of old age)	118	85	1919 Nov 5	NE, 44th, 1920
Wheeler, H.O.	Pvt.	C, 27th N.Y. Inf.	235		1919 Oct 26	IA, 46th, 1920
Wheeler, Hiram	Pvt.	I, 47th Wis.	168		1905 Jan 9	IA, 32nd, 1906
Wheeler, Holland		A, 3rd Kans.	12		1920 Apr 14	KS, 40th, 1921
Wheeler, Hubbard		G, 169th Penn. Inf.	11		1919 Dec 16	NE, 44th, 1920
Wheeler, Ira Calvin		G, 47th Wis. Inf.	216	87, 8 mos. & 11 days	1937 Jan 19	IA, 64th, 1938
Wheeler, J.B.		I, 34th N.Y.	155		1923 May 13	KS, 43rd, 1924
Wheeler, J.E.		L, 12th Ill. Cav.	60		1928 Nov	NE, 53rd, 1929
Wheeler, J.K.		E, 10th Kans. Inf.	118		1918 Dec 18	KS, 38th, 1919
Wheeler, J.M.	Pvt.	H, 14th Ill. Inf.	88		1925 Apr 26	IA, 52nd, 1926
Wheeler, J.O.		I, 98th Ill.	83		1919 Mar 6	KS, 39th, 1920
Wheeler, J.W.		F, 105th Ill. Inf.	83		1925 Oct 3	KS, 45th, 1926
Wheeler, James H., see Whealer, James H.						
Wheeler, John	Pvt.	E, 40th Iowa Inf.	16		1906 Mar 15	IA, 33rd, 1907
Wheeler, John H.	Pvt.	A, 22nd Iowa	52		1922 Oct	IA, 49th, 1923
Wheeler, Jos. K.		E, 3rd Penn. Bat. Art.	206		1923 Mar 23	NE, 48th, 1924
Wheeler, Louis		I, 14th N.Y.	18		1923 Apr 9	KS, 43rd, 1924
Wheeler, Myron		A, 55th Ill. Inf.	77		1927 Dec 9	NE, 52nd, 1928
Wheeler, Nehemiah	Sergt.	141st Ill. Inf.	436		1915 Dec 19	IA, 42nd, 1916
Wheeler, P.A.	Pvt.	F, 8th Ill.	12		1922 Oct 28	IA, 49th, 1923
Wheeler, P.A.	Sergt.	H, 8th Iowa Inf.	12		1927 Oct 20	IA, 54th, 1928
Wheeler, Seth		B, 3rd N.Y. Art.	260		1922 May 30	KS, 42nd, 1923
Wheeler, T.H.	Pvt.	E, 14th Ohio Inf.	211		1909	IA, 36th, 1910
Wheeler, T.W.	Pvt.	A, 21st Iowa Inf.	88		1925 Dec 29	IA, 52nd, 1926
Wheeler, Theodore		D, 2nd Iowa Inf.	244		1930 Jul 21	KS, 50th, 1931
Wheeler, Thomas	Pvt.	A, 10th Iowa Inf.	252		1912 Jun 7	IA, 39th, 1913
Wheeler, Thomas H.	Pvt.	K, 7th Iowa Inf.	136	47	1895 Mar 3	IA, 21st, 1895
Wheeler, W.C.	Steward		251		1905	IA, 32nd, 1906
Wheeler, W.W.		Mich. (died of old age)	97	82	1917 Dec 30	NE, 43rd, 1919
Wheeler, Wm.		A, 16th N.Y. Cav., Sheridan's Corps (born in Canada; died in Jewell Co., Kans.)	63		1883 Dec 5	NE, 8th, 1884
Wheeling, John		C, 141st Ill.	182	83	1920 Oct 8	NE, 45th, 1921
Wheelock, A.E.	Pvt.	E, 3rd Wis. Inf.	165	49	1889 Aug 8	IA, 16th, 1890
Wheelock, Chas.	Sergt.	B, 5th Iowa	202		1907 Nov 30	IA, 34th, 1908
Wheelock, W.H.		K, 116th N.Y.	42		1908 Jun 3	KS, 28th, 1909
Whelan, T.R.		A, 7th Ill.	142		1909 Jan 16	KS, 29th, 1910
Whelchel, Benjamin		D, 6th Kans. Cav. (died at Arkansas Springs; buried at Arkansas Springs)	4		1894 Jun	KS, 14th, 1895
Whelock, David			338		1918	IA, 45th, 1919
Wherett, I.N.		K, 101st Ind.	311		1910 Oct 2	KS, 30th, 1911
Wherfel, J.B.		I, 16th Ohio	1		1913 Oct 10	KS, 33rd, 1914
Whetsel, James		F, 35th Ohio Vols.	200		1902 Aug 19	KS, 22nd, 1903
Whetstine, R.S.	Pvt.	I, 18th Iowa Inf.	112		1917 Apr 2	IA, 44th, 1918
Whetstone, Mathias		I, 13th Iowa (died at Linn)	31		1895 Aug	KS, 15th, 1896
Whiffen, T.U.		A, 124th Ill.	89		1934 Apr 22	NE, 59th, 1935
Whilker, W.A.		E, 47th Ohio (died of paralysis)	84	77	1921 Apr 2	NE, 46th, 1922
Whims, Jasper		H, 140th Penn. Inf.	55		1899 Jan 18	KS, 19th, 1900
Whims, Jasper		H, 140th Penn. Inf.	464		1899 Jan 18	KS, 19th, 1900
Whiner, David		B, 12th Ohio	243		1920	KS, 40th, 1921
Whinery, C.	Pvt.	E, 16th Ohio Inf.	7	55	1895 Oct 9	IA, 22nd, 1896
Whinery, David			243		1922 May 5	KS, 42nd, 1923
Whinery, Isaiah		G, 17th Ohio	3		1919 Nov 11	KS, 39th, 1920
Whinnery, Arthur	Seaman	Gunboat Silver Lake	93		1909 Nov 14	IA, 36th, 1910
Whinnery, J.S.	Pvt.	G, 104th Ohio Inf.	94		1901 Jan 6	IA, 27th, 1901
Whipp, Henry		D, 83rd Ill.	113		1896 Sep 1	KS, 16th, 1897
Whipple, E.J.		A, 1st Vt.	31		1926	NE, 51st, 1927

*See Appendix A, B or C for roster of post names and locations.
†See Introduction for note regarding recording of death date.

Name	Rank	Company, Regiment or Ship	Post*	Age	Death Date†	Journal
Whipple, Orlo		E, 19th Ill.	12		1912 Oct 19	KS, 32nd, 1913
Whipple, Rockwell	Pvt.	E, 4th Wis. Cav.	42	101	1941 Apr 14	IA, 67th, 1941
Whipple, William, see Wipple, William						
Whips, F.N.		I, 24th Ind.	at large		1932 Apr 3	NE, 57th, 1933
Whisler, C.	Pvt.	F, 15th Iowa Inf.	231		1913 Jan 2	IA, 40th, 1914
Whismand, W.S.		D, 34th Iowa	18		1896 Jun 23	KS, 16th, 1897
Whismore, E.		G, 102nd Ohio	433		1924 Feb 9	KS, 44th, 1925
Whisner, Sam		H, 9th Kans. Inf.	170		1901 Jul 26	KS, 21st, 1902
Whissett, J.W.			311		1917 Jan 21	KS, 37th, 1918
Whistler, John H.			98		1910 Nov 4	KS, 30th, 1911
Whistler, W.C.		D, 47th Wis. Inf. (died at Harrisville)	144		1894 Jan 16	KS, 15th, 1896
Whitaker, A.J.		C, 54th Mich. Inf. (died of chronic diarrhea)	9		1893 Sep 18	NE, 18th, 1894
Whitaker, Alven		H, 39th Ill.	18		1930 Mar 28	KS, 50th, 1931
Whitaker, Charles	Pvt., Capt., & Lieut. Col.	28th Wis. Inf.	30	69	1892 Dec 11	IA, 19th, 1893
Whitaker, D.J.	Pvt.	G, 2nd Iowa Bat.	7		1914 Nov 25	IA, 41st, 1915
Whitaker, E.C.		I, 29th Ohio	79		1898 Apr 4	KS, 18th, 1899
Whitaker, Francis M., see Whiteker, Francis M.						
Whitaker, John C.		D, 19th Mich. (died of old age)	95	78	1913[1912] Nov 1	NE, 37th, 1913
Whitaker, John P.		D, 12th Kans.	18		1906 Jul 24	KS, 26th, 1907
Whitaker, T.C.		I, 13th Ohio	185		1910 Oct	KS, 30th, 1911
Whitamore, Thomas		B, 85th Ind.	150		1915 Nov 4	KS, 35th, 1916
Whitbeck, G.R.			67		1916	IA, 43rd, 1917
Whitcomb, A.H.		E, 2nd Md.	12		1910 Feb 26	KS, 30th, 1911
Whitcomb, C.S.	Pvt.	113th Ill.	104		1923 May 24	IA, 50th, 1924
Whitcomb, Chas. P.	Pvt.	C, 5th Iowa Cav.	12		1916 Mar 6	IA, 43rd, 1917
Whitcomb, E.		A, 34th Ill.	130	81	1925 Jun 6	NE, 50th, 1926
Whitcomb, W.A.		I, 15th Ill.	130		1928	NE, 52nd, 1928
Whitcraft, J.L.		I, 151st Ohio	46		1913 Nov 5	KS, 33rd, 1914
Whitcraft, John A.		K, 145th Ohio National Guard	55		1898 Jan 16	KS, 18th, 1899
Whitcraft, L.V.		B, 31st Ohio	46		1908 Dec 10	KS, 28th, 1909
White, A.B.	1st Lieut.	K, 2nd Minn.	22		1903 May 12	IA, 30th, 1904
White, A.D.	Pvt.	F, 174th Ohio Inf.	247		1925 Jun 5	IA, 52nd, 1926
White, Abner C.		K, 18th Iowa (died of chronic intestinal nephritis)	134	69	1914 Oct 6	NE, 39th, 1915
White, Albert P.	Pvt.	G, 38th Iowa Inf.	48	60	1891 Sep 11	IA, 18th, 1892
White, Albin J.		J, 12th Wis. (died in Idaho)	149	71	1924 Sep 14	NE, 49th, 1925
White, Andrew J.	Pvt.	K, 39th Mo. Inf.	297		1927 Nov 19	IA, 54th, 1928
White, Armitstead		F, 15th U.S.C.T.	462		1897 Feb 20	KS, 17th, 1898
White, B.F.	Pvt.	E, 30th Iowa Inf.	363	44	1889 May 27	IA, 16th, 1890
White, Benjamin		G, 116th Ill.	244		1931 Oct 19	KS, 51st, 1932
White, Benjamin		G, 116th Ill.	244		1931 Oct 19	KS, 52nd, 1933
White, Charles		2nd M.O. Cav.	306		1891 Aug 22	KS, 11th, 1892
White, Charles C.		I, 1st Wis. Inf.	104		4th quarter 1884	IA, 11th, 1885
White, Chas. I.	Lieut.	A, 22nd Wis. Inf.	216		1909 Sep 30	IA, 36th, 1910
White, Chas. R.		C, 7th Ill.	3		1920 Feb 11	KS, 40th, 1921
White, David	Chaplain	107th Ill. Inf.	12		1901 Oct 24	KS, 21st, 1902
White, David A.		B, 119th U.S.	150		1896 Nov 4	KS, 16th, 1897
White, E.			277		1917	IA, 44th, 1918
White, Eli J.		4th Wis. Bat.	175		1914 Apr 23	KS, 33rd, 1914
White, Erastus			191		1883	KS, 3rd, 1884
White, Frank		H, 7th Ill. Cav.	32		1902 Feb 8	KS, 22nd, 1903
White, Frank		D, 14th Kans.	293		1923 Feb 11	KS, 43rd, 1924
White, Fred W.	Pvt.	D, 47th Iowa Inf.	68		1912 Oct 16	IA, 39th, 1913
White, Frederick			28		1912	KS, 32nd, 1913
White, G.L.	Pvt.	I, 38th Wis. Inf.	3		1899	IA, 26th, 1900
White, G.W.	Pvt.	H, 73rd Iowa Cav.	259		1905 Feb 24	IA, 32nd, 1906
White, Geo. E.	Pvt.	I, 140th Ohio Inf.	1	50	1892 Nov 4	IA, 19th, 1893
White, Geo. J.		G, 21st Iowa Inf. (died of apoplexy)	228	61	1901 May	NE, 26th, 1902
White, George		E, 5th Mich. Inf.	354		1923 Jan 2	NE, 47th, 1923

*See Appendix A, B or C for roster of post names and locations.
†See Introduction for note regarding recording of death date.

Name	Rank	Company, Regiment or Ship	Post*	Age	Death Date†	Journal
White, George		F, 148th Ill.	22		1933 Nov 10	NE, 58th, 1934
White, H.G.		A, 94th N.Y. Inf.	255		1900 Apr 3	KS, 19th, 1900
White, Henry		A, 123rd Ill. Inf.	94		1923 Mar 8	IA, 50th, 1924
White, Henry	Pvt.	I, 20th Iowa (died of broken back)	35	38	1885 Jun 16	NE, 10th, 1886
White, Henry A.	Pvt.	H, 184th N.Y. Inf.	40	100, 6 mos. & 8 days	1945 Feb 20	IA, 71st, 1945
White, Henry G.	Fife Major	B, 15th Ill. Inf.	389		1925 Nov 13	IA, 52nd, 1926
White, Henry S.		C, 57th Ind.	147		1928 Sep 22	KS, 48th, 1929
White, Henry Thos.	Pvt.	A, 168th Penn. Inf. (at large)	40	98	1943 Mar 5	IA, 69th, 1943
White, Horatio G.	Pvt.	H, 193rd Ohio	1		1906 Jan 3	KS, 26th, 1907
White, Isaac	Pvt.	H, —	236		1908 Feb	IA, 35th, 1909
White, Isaac O.	Pvt.	A, 15th Ohio Inf.	321		1900 Oct 20	IA, 27th, 1901
White, J.B.		K, 178th Ohio	265		1911 May 5	KS, 31st, 1912
White, J.C.	Pvt.	C, 9th Mo. Cav.	79		1921 Dec 20	IA, 48th, 1922
White, J.C.		I, 15th Ill. Cav. (died of Bright's disease)	350	76	1903 Oct 1	NE, 28th, 1904
White, J.C.		H, 172nd Ohio Inf. (cause of death: heart)	25	58	1903 Aug 8	NE, 28th, 1904
White, J.H.	Pvt.	D, 152nd Ohio Inf.	40		1910 Feb 28	IA, 37th, 1911
White, J.M., Rev.		I, 10th Tenn.			1937 Feb 7	KS, 57th, 1938
White, J.O.	Corp.	G, 13th Penn.	156		1907 Jul 17	IA, 34th, 1908
White, J.R.	Pvt.	K, 39th Ill.	66		1926 Apr 30	IA, 53rd, 1927
White, J.T.		Ohio	266		1913 May 5	KS, 32nd, 1913
White, J.W.	Pvt.	C, 2nd Wis. Cav.	452		1929 Jul 20	IA, 56th, 1930
White, J.W.		I, 26th Ind.	54		1920 May 8	KS, 40th, 1921
White, Jacob		Ohio (died of dropsy)	311	70	1907 Apr 13	NE, 32nd, 1908
White, James		K, 11th Penn. Inf.	12		1899 Apr 20	KS, 19th, 1900
White, James		B, 117th Ill. Inf.	354	75	1906 Mar 30	NE, 31st, 1907
White, James A.		A, 31st Iowa	58		1920 Jul 22	KS, 40th, 1921
White, James S.		H, 28th Ill.	25		1935 Apr 29	NE, 60th, 1936
White, Jesse		G, 11th Kans.	100		1926 Aug 20	KS, 46th, 1927
White, John	Pvt.	B, Ohio National Guard	10		1913 Jul 8	IA, 40th, 1914
White, John	Lieut.	E, 11th Iowa Inf.	130	92	1932 Feb 24	IA, 59th, 1933
White, John		A, 99th Ill. Inf.	251		1912 Nov 11	KS, 32nd, 1913
White, John		177th Ohio	25		1905 Aug 20	NE, 31st, 1907
White, John		177th Ohio Inf.	25		1905 Aug 20	NE, 30th, 1906
White, John		20th Ill. (died of pneumonia)	114	72	1916 May	NE, 41st, 1917
White, John		7th Kans. (died of stomach trouble)	63	73	1919 Nov 17	NE, 44th, 1920
White, John, Rev.		I, 10th Tenn.			1937 Feb 7	KS, 56th, 1937
White, John Andrew		F, 10th Ill. Cav.	14		1918 Jan 13	KS, 38th, 1919
White, John H.	Pvt.	B, 159th Ohio Inf.	10		1913 Jul	IA, 40th, 1914
White, John W.		H, 143rd Penn. Inf.	31		1st quarter 1885	IA, 11th, 1885
White, John W.		G, 187th Penn. Inf. (died of general debility)	129	78	1907 Nov 18	NE, 32nd, 1908
White, Jos. B.		I, 3rd Iowa Inf. C, 31st Iowa Inf. (died of heart disease)	23	82	1921 May 7	NE, 46th, 1922
White, Joseph	Pvt.	K, 29th Ohio Inf.	131	53	1898 Apr 17	IA, 24th, 1898
White, L.C.			24		1908 Jan 9	IA, 35th, 1909
White, L.J.		D, 7th Iowa	25		1897 Mar 3	KS, 17th, 1898
White, L.M.	Pvt.	M, 4th Iowa Cav.	19		1929 Feb 18	IA, 56th, 1930
White, L.U.		K, 26th Iowa Inf. (died of general breakdown)	118	85	1920 Nov 12	NE, 45th, 1921
White, L.U.		K, 26th Iowa Inf. (died of old age)	118	86	1920 Nov 12	NE, 46th, 1922
White, Lilborn		D, 12th U.S.	18		1909 Jun 6	KS, 29th, 1910
White, Obediah H.		B, 5th U.S.C.T.	14		1912 Apr 25	KS, 32nd, 1913
White, Peter	Pvt.	I, 45th Ill. Inf.	436	62	1892 Jul 21	IA, 19th, 1893
White, Reuben		A, 46th Ind.	156		1908 Nov 2	KS, 28th, 1909
White, Richard H.		3rd Wis. Cav.	127		1887 Jul 3	KS, 7th, 1888
White, S.A.			108		1915	IA, 42nd, 1916
White, S.L.	Pvt.	B, 1st Lt. Art.	358		1907 Aug 28	IA, 34th, 1908
White, S.W.	Pvt.	A, 9th Iowa Inf.	57		1929	IA, 56th, 1930
White, T.M.		4th Pro. Regulars	279		1911 Dec 25	KS, 32nd, 1913
White, T.W.	Pvt.		96		1927 May 16	IA, 54th, 1928

*See Appendix A, B or C for roster of post names and locations.
†See Introduction for note regarding recording of death date.

Name	Rank	Company, Regiment or Ship	Post*	Age	Death Date†	Journal
White, Thomas		C, 77th Ill. 1st Minn.	158		1896 Apr 7	KS, 16th, 1897
White, Thomas		D, 1st Mo. Eng.	380		1900 Dec 20	KS, 20th, 1901
White, Thos. J.		I, 37th Ind. Inf.	128		1901 Nov 22	KS, 21st, 1902
White, W.	Pvt.	I, 3rd Md.	22		1921 Aug 25	IA, 48th, 1922
White, W.E.	Pvt.	K, 74th Penn. Inf.	271	60	1891 Jun 17	IA, 18th, 1892
White, W.H.		2nd Mass.	132		1917 Sep 18	KS, 37th, 1918
White, W.L.	Pvt.	D, 33rd Iowa Vols.	12		1926 Mar 20	IA, 53rd, 1927
White, Warren	Pvt.	C, 29th Iowa Inf.	38	59	1888 Jun 18	IA, 15th, 1889
White, William	Pvt.	E, 18th N.Y. Cav.	8	45	1892 Sep 14	IA, 19th, 1893
White, William	Pvt.	I, 170th Ohio Inf.	64		1930 Jan 23	IA, 57th, 1931
White, William		29th Ohio	110		1931 Sep 13	KS, 52nd, 1933
White, William		29th Ohio	110		1931 Sep 13	KS, 51st, 1932
White, William F.	Pvt.	F, 63rd Md.	1		1915 Jan 7	KS, 35th, 1916
White, Wm.			67		1913 May 21	IA, 40th, 1914
White, Wm.			28		1921	KS, 41st, 1922
Whitead, Isaac		D, 2nd Iowa Cav.	25		1905 Mar 4	NE, 30th, 1906
Whitebread, Mark		E, 95th Penn.	18		1925 Dec 21	KS, 45th, 1926
Whitecotten, A.		K, 8th Ind.	293		1923 Oct 4	KS, 43rd, 1924
Whited, Isaac		D, 2nd Iowa Cav.	25		1905 Mar 4	NE, 29th, 1905
Whited, John		I, 15th Mo. Inf.	22		1939 Nov 3	NE, 64th, 1940
Whitehair, John		K, 13th Kans.	278		1925 Feb 8	KS, 45th, 1926
Whitehead, Frederick	Pvt.	I, 10th Iowa Inf.	84		1917 Mar 17	IA, 44th, 1918
Whitehead, James		D, 19th Wis. 55th U.S. Cav.	55		1920 Nov 20	KS, 40th, 1921
Whitehead, John M.		15th Ind.	1		1909 Mar 8	KS, 29th, 1910
Whitehead, Samuel		H, 2nd Tenn. Cav.	325		1917 Sep 27	KS, 37th, 1918
Whitehorn, Lorenzo		I, 2nd Neb. Cav.	110	78	1921 Jul 20	NE, 46th, 1922
Whiteker, Francis M.		C, 4th Ill. Cav. (died of paralysis)	22	75	1916 May 1	NE, 41st, 1917
Whiteley, Geo. W.	Pvt.	C, 6th Iowa Cav.	46		1902 Apr 12	IA, 29th, 1903
Whitell, Isaac		D, 2nd Iowa Cav.	25		1905 Mar 4	NE, 31st, 1907
Whiteman, John C.	Pvt.	C, 3rd Mo. Cav.	471	55	1895 Dec 27	IA, 22nd, 1896
Whitemore, S.P.	Pvt.	J, 55th Ill.	1		1906 Feb 22	KS, 26th, 1907
Whitenach, Robt. H.	Capt.		94		1899	IA, 26th, 1900
Whitenack, Peter	Pvt.	I, 20th Iowa Inf.	206	75	1892 Nov	IA, 19th, 1893
Whiteneck, Wm.	Pvt.	D, 12th Iowa Inf.	452		1927 Aug 2	IA, 54th, 1928
Whiteneck, Wm. W.	Pvt.	D, 12th Iowa Inf.	68		1927 Aug 2	IA, 54th, 1928
Whitenhal, C.T.		U.S.C.T.	175		1911 Sep 6	KS, 32nd, 1913
Whitesell, John	Pvt.	G, 8th Iowa Inf.	8	56	1898 Jan 26	IA, 24th, 1898
Whitesell, John M.		B, 206th Penn. Inf.	356		1899 Feb 18	KS, 19th, 1900
Whiteside, Benjamin	Sergt.	I, 6th U.S. Cav.	7		1899	NE, 24th, 1900
Whiteside, J.E.			145		1936 Feb 20	KS, 55th, 1936
Whitesides, Garrett C.		H, 17th Mich. Inf.	32		1908[1909?] Aug 22	KS, 29th, 1910
Whitford, Geo.	Pvt.	C, 85th N.Y. Inf.	98		1912 Jul 2	IA, 39th, 1913
Whitford, J.H.		36th Ohio Inf.	180		1886	KS, 6th, 1887
Whitford, L.		F, 1st Minn. Inf.	209		1908 Nov 5	KS, 28th, 1909
Whitford, W.D.	Pvt.	B, 5th Mich. Inf.	1		1902 Jul 12	IA, 29th, 1903
Whiticar, T.M.		162nd Ohio Inf.	40	63	1890 Sep	IA, 18th, 1892
Whiting, A.V.		G, 43rd Mass. Vol. Mil. Inf.	77		1926 Dec 27	NE, 51st, 1927
Whiting, Charles		F, 2nd N.Y. Cav.	11		1893 Mar 19	NE, 18th, 1894
Whiting, F.S.	Capt.	M, 4th Iowa Cav.	12		1912 Nov 16	IA, 39th, 1913
Whiting, John A.	Pvt.	H, 20th Ill. Inf.	247	53	1895 Jan 14	IA, 23rd, 1897
Whiting, L.H.		F, 50th N.Y.	42	84	1920 Nov 19	NE, 45th, 1921
Whiting, Luther		A, 12th Ill.	53		1921 Nov 25	KS, 41st, 1922
Whitlatch, Adam	Pvt.	A, 13th Iowa Inf.	400		1915	IA, 42nd, 1916
Whitley, H.C.		7th La.	55		1919 Oct 16	KS, 39th, 1920
Whitley, Robert		D, 17th Kans.	116		1921 Jul 6	KS, 41st, 1922
Whitlock, J.G.		A, 1st Neb. (died of heart failure)	31	70	1904 May 9	NE, 29th, 1905
Whitlock, T.J.	Pvt.	C, 11th Tenn. Cav.	108		1927	IA, 54th, 1928
Whitman, James E.		H, 37th Iowa Inf. (died at Pleasanton)	3		1895 Dec	KS, 15th, 1896
Whitman, Mark	Pvt.	G, 7th Iowa Cav.	357		1901 Jan 24	IA, 27th, 1901
Whitman, Robert W.		E, 7th Iowa Cav.	176		1913 Apr 3	KS, 33rd, 1914

See Appendix A, B or C for roster of post names and locations.
†*See Introduction for note regarding recording of death date.*

Name	Rank	Company, Regiment or Ship	Post*	Age	Death Date†	Journal
Whitmore, H.		A, 2nd Ill. Lt. Art. (died of heart failure)	136	70	1912 Apr 7	NE, 37th, 1913
Whitmore, Horace			147		1908 Apr 22	KS, 28th, 1909
Whitmore, Roscoe			29		1907 Sep 10	IA, 34th, 1908
Whitmore, W.S.	Pvt.	E, 6th Iowa Inf.	398		1897 Feb 6	IA, 24th, 1898
Whitney, A.	Pvt.	H, 12th Ind. Cav.	45		1909 Jul 15	IA, 36th, 1910
Whitney, Brayton	Pvt.	B, 29th Wis. Inf.	168	64	1892 Aug 5	IA, 19th, 1893
Whitney, Chas.	Pvt.	B, 2nd Minn. Cav.	383		1909 Jun 3	IA, 36th, 1910
Whitney, David	Pvt.	G, 15th Vt. Inf.	118		1927 Sep 16	IA, 54th, 1928
Whitney, E.E.	Pvt.	K, 7th Wis. Inf.	147		1904 Dec 8	IA, 31st, 1905
Whitney, F.B.	Pvt.	H, 12th Ill. Inf.	81		1929 Jan 28	IA, 56th, 1930
Whitney, Geo. A.	Pvt.	K, 2nd N.Y. Inf.	497		1925 Dec 18	IA, 52nd, 1926
Whitney, George		I, 16th Kans. Cav. (died at Emporia)	464		1895 Mar	KS, 15th, 1896
Whitney, H.	Musician	K, 76th N.Y. Inf. (cause of death: kidneys)	11	43	1887 Mar 18	NE, 12th, 1888
Whitney, J.R.	Pvt.	D, 12th N.Y. Cav.	231		1916 Jan 19	IA, 43rd, 1917
Whitney, Leroy	Sergt.	C, 146th Iowa Inf.	124		1931 Dec	IA, 58th, 1932
Whitney, M.M.R.		F, 1st Ill. Cav.	58		1934 Sep 15	KS, 54th, 1935
Whitney, Mark	Pvt.	K, 13th Wis. Inf.	79		1925 Aug 2	IA, 52nd, 1926
Whitney, R.B.		I, H, 1st Mich.	1		1914 Jan 8	KS, 34th, 1915
Whitney, W.E.		I, 120th N.Y.	44		1919 Dec 9	KS, 39th, 1920
Whitney, W.M.		D, 1st Ill. Cav.	58		1934 Sep 11	KS, 54th, 1935
Whitney, William Clifford	Gen.	see Appendix D			1907 Jun 16	KS, 27th, 1908
Whitright, Joseph		G, 101st & 58th Ind. Cav. (member at large)	87		1934 May 28	KS, 54th, 1935
Whitright, Joseph		G, 101st & 58th Ind.	87		1934 May 8	KS, 55th, 1936
Whitsel, Chas. J.	Pvt.	I, 9th Iowa Cav.	40		1916 Oct 25	IA, 43rd, 1917
Whitsell, John		F, 73rd Ind.	145		1936 Mar 6	KS, 56th, 1937
Whitsit, Henry C.		F, 145th Ind.	23		1916 Apr 26	KS, 36th, 1917
Whitsitt, John	Pvt.	F, 36th Iowa Inf.	358		1912 Jul 9	IA, 39th, 1913
Whitson, Aaron		Ohio	257		1908	KS, 28th, 1909
Whitson, C.C.	QM	5th Ohio	15		1897 Apr 14	KS, 17th, 1898
Whitt, James		H, 13th Mo. Cav.	at large		1930	NE, 55th, 1931
Whittaker, E.S.		D, 9th Ohio (died of paralysis)	21	66	1907 Nov 10	NE, 32nd, 1908
Whittaker, H.B.		B, 72nd Ohio	49		1920 Feb 25	KS, 40th, 1921
Whittaker, John C., see Whitaker, John C.						
Whittaker, Newton		B, 128th Ind. Inf.	447		1901 Jul 4	KS, 21st, 1902
Whitted, J.A.		K, 51st Ind.	64		1933 Jan 10	KS, 53rd, 1934
Whitted, J.M.		D, 2nd Neb. Cav. (died of old age)	55	92	1918 Apr 30	NE, 43rd, 1919
Whittel, H.B.			29		1916 Nov 18	IA, 43rd, 1917
Whittemore, A.B.		E, 31st Iowa (died of suicide)	23		1919 May 14	NE, 44th, 1920
Whitten, D.T.		H, 120th Ind.	4		1928 Jan 27	KS, 48th, 1929
Whitten, John	Pvt.	H, 5th Iowa Inf.	254		1902 Sep 7	IA, 29th, 1903
Whittenbrg, Benj. F.		D, 10th Mo. Cav.	90		1920 Aug 16	KS, 40th, 1921
Whittikind, W.J.		H, 20th Ill.	71		1914 Aug 1	KS, 34th, 1915
Whittington, A.B.K.		I, 60th Ill. Inf.	61		1886	KS, 6th, 1887
Whittlery, C.H.		E, 23rd N.Y.	147		1925 Mar 27	KS, 45th, 1926
Whittlesey, Rollins		C, 151st Ill.	440	91	1934 May 24	IA, 61st, 1935
Whittmore, Geo. L.	Pvt.	H, 16th Iowa Inf.	78		1902 Jul 16	IA, 29th, 1903
Whittum, Geo. D.	Pvt.	K, 10th Maine Inf.	14		1921 Sep 16	IA, 48th, 1922
Whitworth, Herbert			294		1913 Jun	KS, 33rd, 1914
Whitworth, Wm.			55		1929 Dec 12	IA, 56th, 1930
Whitzel, Peter D.		H, 64th Ill. Inf.	12		1901 Sep 3	KS, 21st, 1902
Whitzell, John		F, 73rd Ind.	145		1936 Feb 20	KS, 55th, 1936
Wholstenholm, John	Pvt.	K, 77th Ill. Inf.	306		1899	NE, 24th, 1900
Wiall, S.E.		C, 3rd Penn.	7		1927 Aug 10	NE, 52nd, 1928
Wiant, George W.			25		1936	KS, 56th, 1937
Wible, I.W.		D, 21st Penn.	18		1923 Feb 21	KS, 43rd, 1924
Wiboat, John	Pvt.	K, 9th Ill. Cav.	26		1919 Sep 15	IA, 46th, 1920
Wicher, Wiley			231		1928 Oct 8	IA, 55th, 1929
Wick, Henry	Pvt.	C, 29th Iowa Inf.	211		1900 May 9	IA, 27th, 1901
Wick, John	Pvt.	L, 1st Mo. Lt. Art.	5		1913 Dec 12	IA, 40th, 1914
Wickam, Azel J.	Pvt.	A, 12th Iowa Inf.	247		1897 May 19	IA, 24th, 1898

*See Appendix A, B or C for roster of post names and locations.
†See Introduction for note regarding recording of death date.

Name	Rank	Company, Regiment or Ship	Post*	Age	Death Date†	Journal
Wickam, O.			86		1883	KS, 3rd, 1884
Wicker, Fred	Pvt.	F, 44th Iowa Vol. Inf.	505	51	1899 Mar 31	IA, 25th, 1899
Wicker, H.A.		D, 12th Kans.	187		1892 Jan 18	KS, 12th, 1893
Wicker, W.G.	Pvt.	F, 38th Ill.	497		1923 Sep 27	IA, 50th, 1924
Wickersham, Bayard			3		1928 Sep	NE, 53rd, 1929
Wickersham, C.H.	Pvt.	B, 12th Ohio Cav.	12		1926 Dec 10	IA, 53rd, 1927
Wickersham, Israel M.		F, 2nd Ohio Art.	271		1937 Nov 11	IA, 64th, 1938
Wickersham, J.O.	Corp.	A, 122nd Ill. Inf.	197		1916 Jan 1	IA, 43rd, 1917
Wickersham, W.G.		G, 12th Kans.	112		1904 Dec 17	KS, 24th, 1905
Wickham, B.	Pvt.	A, 13th Iowa Inf.	141		1916 Nov 28	IA, 43rd, 1917
Wickham, B.P.	Corp.	H, 20th Iowa Inf.	206	67	1893 Oct 11	IA, 20th, 1894
Wickham, C.H.	Pvt.	F, 3rd Mich. Vols.	57		1906 Oct 12	IA, 33rd, 1907
Wickham, J.M.		H, 29th Iowa Inf.	84		1912 Sep 3	KS, 32nd, 1913
Wickham, James W.		D, 3rd Ohio Cav.	33		1920 Sep 3	KS, 40th, 1921
Wickham, John		F, 9th Penn. (died of old age)	1	80	1918 Sep 28	NE, 43rd, 1919
Wickham, T.			235		1911 Mar 2	IA, 38th, 1912
Wickins, David D.		G, 20th Ill.	175		1917 Dec 26	KS, 37th, 1918
Wickman, Angus	Pvt.	E, 48th Wis. Inf.	277		1912 Aug 2	IA, 39th, 1913
Wickman, John D.	Pvt.	H, 28th Iowa Inf.	321		1917 May 28	IA, 44th, 1918
Wicks, A.A.	Pvt.	H, 29th Wis. Inf.	66		1916 Aug 9	IA, 43rd, 1917
Wicks, C.S.		K, 51st Ill.	98		1910 Oct 13	KS, 30th, 1911
Wicks, G.W.	Pvt.	E, 29th Wis. Inf.	66		1906 Nov 4	IA, 33rd, 1907
Wicks, Jas.	Pvt.	60th Col. Inf.	20		1914	IA, 41st, 1915
Wicks, M.		F, 32nd Ind. Inf. (died at Topeka Reunion)	380		1888	KS, 8th, 1889
Wickwire, Frank E.		B, 21st Wis.	4		1934 Mar 18	NE, 59th, 1935
Wickwire, Myron R.		B, Penn. Mil.	4	74	1913 Mar 1	NE, 38th, 1914
Widdows, M.		H, 185th Ohio Inf.	293		1929	KS, 49th, 1930
Wideburg, E.		1st Mo. Inf. (died of general debility)	25	66	1896 Mar 17	NE, 21st, 1897
Widener, John		F, 37th Ill. Inf.			1890	KS, 10th, 1891
Widick, Andrew		B, 9th Iowa Cav.			1929 Jan 27	NE, 53rd, 1929
Widner, Gustave	Pvt.	H, 1st Iowa Inf.	78		1915 Sep 22	IA, 42nd, 1916
Widner, Jas.		H, 4th Iowa Inf.	324		1906 Jan 25	IA, 33rd, 1907
Widney, O.A.		K, 11th Kans. Cav.	127		1929 Oct 3	KS, 49th, 1930
Widoes, David A.		176th Ohio	25		1927 Jun 8	KS, 47th, 1928
Widup, C.S.		I, 152nd Ind.	81		1919 May 5	KS, 39th, 1920
Wiebrock, Fridric		A, 27th Ill.	72		1889	KS, 9th, 1890
Wiemer, Joe			233		1924	IA, 51st, 1925
Wier, J.A.		D, 21st Ind. (died of hardening of arteries)	223	86	1921 Mar 20	NE, 46th, 1922
Wier, John		K, 24th Ohio	24	70	1912 Nov 4	NE, 37th, 1913
Wier, Thos. M.		I, 25th Ind. Inf.	7		1909 Oct 14	KS, 29th, 1910
Wierman, J.H.		A, 69th Ind.	38		1898 Apr 8	KS, 18th, 1899
Wieser, Gideon	Pvt.	I, 47th Penn. Inf.	10		1913 Sep 7	IA, 40th, 1914
Wiesner, Sam'l	Pvt.	G, 8th N.Y. Inf.	154		1906 Nov 25	IA, 33rd, 1907
Wiggins, A.J.	Pvt.	E, 10th Iowa Inf.	27		1916 Apr	IA, 43rd, 1917
Wiggins, C.D.	Pvt.	C, 83rd Ill.	27		1907 Nov 13	IA, 34th, 1908
Wiggins, Jas. W.	Pvt.	A, 135th Penn. Inf.	65		1886 May 5	IA, 14th, 1888
Wiggins, John		H, 80th Ohio	20		1926 Dec 11	KS, 46th, 1927
Wiggins, S.W.	Pvt.	K, 16th Wis. Inf.	23		1924 Jul 1	IA, 51st, 1925
Wiggins, Walter W.		C, 11th Ind. Inf. (died at Grinnell; buried at Grinnell Cemetery)	127		1894 Jan 30	KS, 14th, 1895
Wight, A.G.	Pvt.	A, 141st Ill. Inf.	97		1917 May 3	IA, 44th, 1918
Wight, Geo. W.		G, 48th Ind.	35		1921 Aug 4	KS, 41st, 1922
Wight, W.H., Dr.		H, 2nd Ill.	52		1913 May 16	KS, 33rd, 1914
Wight, William		C, 5th N.Y. Hvy. Art.	329		1901 Apr 14	IA, 27th, 1901
Wight, Wm.	Pvt.	C, 5th N.Y. Hvy. Art.	329		1901 Apr 14	IA, 28th, 1902
Wighton, Chas. C.	Pvt.	C, 58th Ill. Inf.	284	65	1892 Nov 26	IA, 19th, 1893
Wigren, S.P.	Sergt.	D, 57th Ill. Inf.	18		1905 Dec 10	IA, 32nd, 1906
Wigton, A.L.		G, 88th Ohio Inf. (died of pneumonia)	110	74	1914 Dec 20	NE, 39th, 1915
Wilber, A.A.		23rd Ind. Battery	198		1897 Sep 8	KS, 17th, 1898
Wilber, C.H.	Pvt.	H, 15th Iowa	46		1906 Mar 23	IA, 33rd, 1907
Wilber, Chas.	Pvt.	A, 3rd Iowa Inf.	452		1925 May 10	IA, 52nd, 1926
Wilbern, T.O.		C, 155th Ill. Inf. (at large)			1936 Jun 30	IA, 63rd, 1937

Name	Rank	Company, Regiment or Ship	Post*	Age	Death Date†	Journal
Wilbur, E.L.		G, 2nd C. Mich.[2nd Mich. Cav.]	25		1930 Jul 26	KS, 50th, 1931
Wilbur, Wm.		D, 33rd Ind.	25		1922 May 26	KS, 42nd, 1923
Wilburn, Geo. W.		2nd Neb. Cav.	273	58	1901 Aug	NE, 26th, 1902
Wilch, Jacob			41		1919	NE, 44th, 1920
Wilcox, A.A.	Landsman	U.S. Navy	365		1911 Jun 3	IA, 38th, 1912
Wilcox, Abner		H, 4th Mich. Cav.	32		1928	NE, 53rd, 1929
Wilcox, Baley	Pvt.	B, 45th Ohio Inf.	211		1912	IA, 39th, 1913
Wilcox, C.C.	Major	G, 13th Tenn. Cav.	55		1893 Mar 23	KS, 13th, 1894
Wilcox, Clark		H, 2nd Neb. (died of paralysis at Soldiers & Sailors Home, Milford)		72	1906 Apr 24	NE, 31st, 1907
Wilcox, Eli J.		E, 1st Colo. Cav. (died of heart failure)	344	64	1897 Mar 14	NE, 22nd, 1898
Wilcox, H.W.	Pvt.	F, 105th Ill. Inf.	91		1902 Aug 19	IA, 29th, 1903
Wilcox, H.W.	Pvt.	B, 91st Ill. Inf.	67		1899 Jan	IA, 26th, 1900
Wilcox, Henry			45		1925 Jan 31	IA, 52nd, 1926
Wilcox, J.A.		128th N.Y. Inf. (died of paralysis)	207	83	1925 Oct 16	NE, 50th, 1926
Wilcox, J.B.	Pvt.	F, 106th Ill. Inf.	26		1926 Oct 16	IA, 53rd, 1927
Wilcox, J.W.	Pvt.	B, 91st Ill. Inf.	300	50	1888 Oct 9	IA, 15th, 1889
Wilcox, Jeremiah		G, 95th Ill.	443		1892 Sep 22	KS, 12th, 1893
Wilcox, Jeremiah		G, 95th Ill.	443		1892 Sep 21	KS, 17th, 1898
Wilcox, Jesse B.			267		1925 Sep 5	IA, 52nd, 1926
Wilcox, John	Pvt.	L, 1st Iowa Cav.	132		1906 Jan 13	IA, 32nd, 1906
Wilcox, John	Pvt.	D, 7th Iowa Inf.	80		1911 Feb 26	IA, 38th, 1912
Wilcox, John			25		1915	NE, 40th, 1916
Wilcox, John F.	Pvt.	D, 44th Iowa Inf.	164	48	1893 Nov 10	IA, 20th, 1894
Wilcox, Joseph M.		I, 3rd Ohio	1		1914 Jul 12	KS, 34th, 1915
Wilcox, Josiah		D, 8th N.Y.	1		1911 May 2	KS, 31st, 1912
Wilcox, L.T.	Pvt.	F, 106th Ill. Inf.	26		1920 Apr 7	IA, 47th, 1921
Wilcox, R.R.	Pvt.	C, 55th Ill. Inf.	339		1908 May 31	IA, 35th, 1909
Wilcox, Robert S.		E, 1st N.Y. Lt. Art. C, 179th N.Y. Inf. (see also Appendix D)	7		1933 Apr 11	NE, 58th, 1934
Wilcox, S.		C, 142nd Ill.	40	78	1916 Aug 25	NE, 41st, 1917
Wilcox, S.C.	Corp.	L, 1st Mich. Cav.	12		1925 Feb 20	IA, 52nd, 1926
Wilcox, U.T.	Pvt.	D, 102nd N.Y. Inf.	124		1924	IA, 51st, 1925
Wilcox, W.T.		D, 4th Kans. Inf.	25		1905 Mar 15	NE, 30th, 1906
Wilcox, W.T.		D, 4th Kans.	25		1907 Mar 15	NE, 31st, 1907
Wilcox, W.V.	Bugler	H, 8th Iowa Cav.	12		1925 Oct 12	IA, 52nd, 1926
Wilcox, Wm. T.		B, 11th Kans. Cav.	46		1920 Aug 17	KS, 40th, 1921
Wilcox, Z.T.		H, 10th N.Y. Inf.	4		1894	NE, 19th, 1895
Wilcox, Zadok	Pvt.	D, 10th Mich. Cav.	153		1908 Dec 26	IA, 35th, 1909
Wilcoxen, Thos. M.	Sergt.	E, 22nd Iowa Inf.	107		1904 Jun 14	IA, 31st, 1905
Wilcoxon, J.	Capt.	A, 27th Ind.	293		1888	KS, 8th, 1889
Wilcoxon, M.		A, 62nd U.S.C.T.	464		1902 Sep 19	KS, 22nd, 1903
Wilcoxson, Caleb		12th Ind.	206		3rd quarter 1883	IA, 10th, 1884
Wild, David	Pvt.	I, 2nd U.S. Inf.	270		1920 Sep 1	IA, 47th, 1921
Wild, John	Pvt.	I, 1st Ohio Lt. Art.	343		1907 Oct 2	IA, 34th, 1908
Wildasin, George	Pvt.	G, 35th Iowa Inf.	250	51	1893 Jun 9	IA, 20th, 1894
Wilde, M.M.		E, 31st Iowa Inf.	227		1892 Jan 10	NE, 17th, 1893
Wilde, W.T., Sr.		29th Iowa Inf. (killed by cars at Logan, Iowa)	422		1891 Nov 12	KS, 11th, 1892
Wilder, Dempsey		63rd U.S.C. (died in Colorado)	100		1892 Dec 14	KS, 12th, 1893
Wilder, J.J.	Pvt.	G, 23rd Wis. Inf.	298		1911 Dec 21	IA, 38th, 1912
Wilder, M.S.	Pvt.	F, 24th Iowa Inf.	200	44	1890 Dec 27	IA, 17th, 1891
Wilder, S.W.		G, 6th Vt.	1		1904 Sep 11	KS, 24th, 1905
Wilderman, R.B.		K, 1st Art. (died of infirmities)	262	79	1920 May 27	NE, 45th, 1921
Wildes, B.B.	Pvt. Pvt.	G, 3rd Maine Inf. C, 146th Ill.	68		1912 Nov 12	IA, 39th, 1913
Wildman, J.E.			94		1916 May 13	IA, 43rd, 1917
Wildre, C.L.	Pvt.	I, 9th Iowa Inf.	329		1930 Jun 18	IA, 57th, 1931
Wildy, Joseph		K, 85th Ohio	1		1909 Feb 17	KS, 29th, 1910
Wiles, A.B.		I, 11th Iowa	56		1889	KS, 9th, 1890
Wiles, A.B.	Capt.	11th Iowa	56		1893 Mar 27	KS, 13th, 1894
Wiles, Geo. H.	Pvt.	A, 35th Iowa Inf.	231		1918 Feb 28	IA, 45th, 1919

*See Appendix A, B or C for roster of post names and locations.
†See Introduction for note regarding recording of death date.
592

Name	Rank	Company, Regiment or Ship	Post*	Age	Death Date†	Journal
Wiles, Thos.		B, 29th Iowa	45		1928 Jun 16	NE, 53rd, 1929
Wiley, A.D.		F, 88th Ohio	155	94	1934 Nov 6	IA, 61st, 1935
Wiley, D.W.			54		1884	KS, 4th, 1885
Wiley, F.P.	Pvt.		329		1924 Mar 15	IA, 51st, 1925
Wiley, Fred W.		I, 3rd Wis. Inf.	15		1891 Dec 19	KS, 11th, 1892
Wiley, Geo. W.		G, 11th Iowa	92		1909 Dec 23	KS, 29th, 1910
Wiley, H.G.	Pvt.	I, 25th Wis. Inf.	452		1915	IA, 42nd, 1916
Wiley, Henry B.		H, 4th Mo. Cav.	50		1918 Jan 22	KS, 38th, 1919
Wiley, Jno. M.	Pvt.	B, 8th Iowa Cav.	377	50	1888 Feb 25	IA, 15th, 1889
Wiley, Joe		D, 100th Ohio	174		1918	KS, 38th, 1919
Wiley, John H.		F, 45th Ill.	112		1933 Jan 1	NE, 58th, 1934
Wiley, Joseph S.		K, 8th Ill. Inf.	1		1940 Sep 29	NE, 65th, 1941
Wiley, Robert		G, 33rd Ind.	32		1924 Jul 17	KS, 44th, 1925
Wiley, Solon L.		A, 52nd Ill. Inf.	7		1926 Jul 5	NE, 51st, 1927
Wiley, W.T.		B, 75th Ind.	1		1932 Feb 11	KS, 52nd, 1933
Wiley, Wm.		K, 11th Kans. Cav.	153		1900 Jun 7	KS, 20th, 1901
Wiley, Wm. B.		I, 14th Kans.	251		1921 Jun 21	KS, 41st, 1922
Wilfong, David	Pvt.	8th Iowa Cav.	17		1923 May 28	IA, 50th, 1924
Wilheit, J.R.		E, 14th Ill.	84		1932 Feb 26	NE, 57th, 1933
Wilhelm, Jeremiah		A, 3rd Md. Inf.	25		1942 Jun 11	NE, 67th, 1943
Wilhelm, Jos. B.	Pvt.	H, 11th Iowa Inf.	231		1907 Apr 5	IA, 34th, 1908
Wilhelm, S.S.			54		1890	NE, 15th, 1891
Wilhelm, S.S.			54		1894	NE, 19th, 1895
Wilhite, E.M., see Wilkite, E.M.						
Wilhite, J.H.		B, 9th Ill.	55		1904 Dec 16	KS, 24th, 1905
Wilhite, J.R., see Wilheit, J.R.						
Wilhour, Wm. H.		I, 102nd Ohio	30		1919 Aug 8	KS, 39th, 1920
Wilkelm, Samuel	Pvt.	B, 37th Iowa Inf.	250	84	1894 Nov 9	IA, 21st, 1895
Wilkenson, Jno. W.		C, 28th N.Y. Inf.	366		1886	KS, 6th, 1887
Wilkers, D.G.		Navy	293		1918 May 10	KS, 38th, 1919
Wilkerson, Frank		4th U.S. Art.	465		1913 Apr 22	KS, 33rd, 1914
Wilkerson, Gerry N.		K, 32nd Ill.	12		1914 Oct 25	KS, 34th, 1915
Wilkerson, J.M.		G, 15th Kans.	1		1913 Jul 14	KS, 33rd, 1914
Wilkerson, J.W.	Pvt.	G, 79th Ohio Inf.	96		1932 Jan 14	IA, 59th, 1933
Wilkerson, John		F, 25th Iowa	19		1907 Dec 14	IA, 34th, 1908
Wilkerson, S.E.			73		1917	IA, 44th, 1918
Wilkerson, W.J.	Pvt.	K, 1st Va. Cav.	7	89	1932 Oct 10	IA, 59th, 1933
Wilkey, H.M.		H, 21st Ind.	4		1926 Nov 22	KS, 46th, 1927
Wilkie, Robert		H, 9th Ill.	271		1922 Jan 20	IA, 49th, 1923
Wilkie, W.F.	Pvt.	D, 23rd Iowa Inf.	192		1919 Nov	IA, 46th, 1920
Wilkin, E.E.		C, 8th Iowa	246		1923 Feb 8	KS, 43rd, 1924
Wilkin, George		A, 19th Penn.	69		1909 Dec 3	KS, 29th, 1910
Wilkin, Neal			5		1926 Jun 27	IA, 53rd, 1927
Wilkin, T.M.	Pvt.	C, 19th Iowa	108		1923 Jan 23	IA, 50th, 1924
Wilkins, A.R.			71		1888	KS, 8th, 1889
Wilkins, Ben		C, 11th Ohio Inf. (died of hardening of arteries)	21	83	1919 Mar 15	NE, 44th, 1920
Wilkins, Ben		C, 11th Ill. (died of general disability)	21	78	1920 Mar 15	NE, 45th, 1921
Wilkins, Charles	Pvt.	11th Mich. Cav.	20		1918 Dec	IA, 45th, 1919
Wilkins, Chas.	Pvt.	E, 27th Iowa Inf.	165	57	1889 Mar 5	IA, 16th, 1890
Wilkins, D.A.		17th Iowa Inf.	515		1916 Apr 5	IA, 43rd, 1917
Wilkins, Geo. W.	Sergt.	B, 8th Iowa Cav.	297		1908 Jun 30	IA, 35th, 1909
Wilkins, George		H, 6th Mass. Inf. (died of sunstroke)	197	66	1895 Aug 15	NE, 20th, 1896
Wilkins, Isaac		B, 12th Kans.	40		1920 May 12	KS, 40th, 1921
Wilkins, J.E.	Pvt.	G, 112th Ill. Inf.	7		1901 Jun 9	IA, 28th, 1902
Wilkins, J.M.	Pvt.	C, 23rd Ohio Inf.	69		1932 May	IA, 59th, 1933
Wilkins, James E.		K, 15th West Va.	17		1893 Oct 8	KS, 13th, 1894
Wilkins, Jesse		A, 9th Kans. Cav.	221		1889	KS, 9th, 1890
Wilkins, Nelson		G, 3rd Ohio Cav.	35		1917 Jun 7	KS, 37th, 1918
Wilkins, W.	Drum Major	29th Iowa Inf.	10		1928	IA, 55th, 1929
Wilkins, W.L.	Pvt.	G, 5th Vt. Inf.	22		1918 Feb 14	IA, 45th, 1919

*See Appendix A, B or C for roster of post names and locations.
†See Introduction for note regarding recording of death date.

Name	Rank	Company, Regiment or Ship	Post*	Age	Death Date†	Journal
Wilkinson, A.C.		B, 145th Ill.	147		1924 Feb 13	KS, 44th, 1925
Wilkinson, E.M.		H, 28th Ind.	17		1913 Aug 23	KS, 33rd, 1914
Wilkinson, Ed C.	Pvt.	H, 8th Iowa	30		1926 Dec 21	IA, 53rd, 1927
Wilkinson, Geo. C.		F, 93rd Ill. (died of old age)	35	87	1910 Dec 37	NE, 35th, 1911
Wilkinson, J.	Pvt.	M, 6th Iowa Cav.	82		1914 Nov 25	IA, 41st, 1915
Wilkinson, J.E.			73		1916	IA, 43rd, 1917
Wilkinson, J.M.			1		1883	KS, 3rd, 1884
Wilkinson, J.O.		C, 2nd U.S.	25		1918 Sep 30	KS, 38th, 1919
Wilkinson, J.S.		H, 15th West Va. Cav.	7		1928 Dec 15	IA, 55th, 1929
Wilkinson, James		D, 18th U.S.C.T.	294		1916	KS, 36th, 1917
Wilkinson, Jno.	Pvt.	H, 1st Wis. Art.	223	50	1887 Feb 12	IA, 14th, 1888
Wilkinson, John	Pvt.	K, 2nd Iowa Inf.	23		1911 Feb 18	IA, 38th, 1912
Wilkinson, Samuel			130		1918 Feb 13	KS, 38th, 1919
Wilkinson, W.		A, 14th Kans.	31		1888	KS, 8th, 1889
Wilkinson, W.		H, 29th Ind. (died of cancer)	180	81	1922 Sep	NE, 48th, 1924
Wilkinson, W.S.	Pvt.	F, 39th Iowa Inf.	55		1914 Jun 4	IA, 41st, 1915
Wilkite, E.M.	Pvt.	E, 8th Iowa Inf.	44		1919 Jan 3	IA, 46th, 1920
Wilks, Thomas	Pvt.	K, 45th Ill. Vol. Inf.	84		1922 Jan 18	IA, 49th, 1923
Will, Henry	Pvt.	I, Denver Guards	231		1910 Mar 31	IA, 37th, 1911
Will, John	Farrier	F, 25th Iowa Inf.	129	51	1891 Apr 22	IA, 18th, 1892
Will, Jurgen		M, 1st Iowa Cav. (died of catarrh of bowels)	344	63	1897 Feb 5	NE, 22nd, 1898
Willantt, John			173		1922 Dec 7	IA, 49th, 1923
Willard, A.		6th Kans.	123		1910 Feb 19	KS, 30th, 1911
Willard, D.B.		C, 15th Wis.	5		1917 Mar 25	KS, 37th, 1918
Willard, Dennis		F, 8th Ill. Inf.	66		1916 Sep 9	KS, 36th, 1917
Willard, J.S.		G, 20th Ind.	17		1926 Jun 11	KS, 46th, 1927
Willard, Sam'l	Pvt.	G, 136th N.Y. Inf.	270		1915 Oct 10	IA, 42nd, 1916
Willard, Whitcomb		Kans.	282		1913 Jan 23	KS, 32nd, 1913
Willett, Geo. A.	Pvt.	D, 1st Iowa Inf.	5		1912 Apr 17	IA, 39th, 1913
Willett, Geo. R.	Capt.	D, 3rd Iowa Vol. Inf.	168	73	1898 Dec 12	IA, 25th, 1899
Willett, James William	Boatswain's Mate	Gunboat *Springfield*, U.S. Navy	24	94	1940 May 13	IA, 66th, 1940
Willett, L.D.	Pvt.	A, 3rd Vt. Inf.	86		1930 Jan 9	IA, 57th, 1931
Willett, Thos.	Pvt.	G, 30th Ill. Inf.	22		1929 Mar 26	IA, 56th, 1930
Willey, A.L.		L, 7th Ohio Cav.	179		1913 Sep 28	KS, 33rd, 1914
Willey, F.W.		I, 3rd Wis.	15		1891 Dec 19	KS, 12th, 1893
Willey, Henry		D, 17th U.S. (died of pneumonia)	28	72	1914 May 16	NE, 39th, 1915
Willey, John W.		D, 2nd Kans.	12		1915 Aug 7	KS, 35th, 1916
Willey, William W.		K, 136th Ind.	88		1911 Aug 21	KS, 31st, 1912
Willfly, Fenton		C, 48th U.S.C.T.	174		1912 Jun 22	KS, 32nd, 1913
Willfony, Eli		G, 26th Mich. Inf.	415		1887 Feb 27	KS, 7th, 1888
Willford, Cyrus		H, 120th Ohio	496		1912 Mar 4	KS, 32nd, 1913
Willharm, C.	Sergt.	K, 100th Ill. Inf.	240	52	1896 Apr 1	IA, 22nd, 1896
Willhite, Jos. H.		D, 7th Kans. Inf.	18		1899 Apr 21	KS, 19th, 1900
William, D.	Pvt.	F, 20th Ill. Inf.	155		1921 Jan 14	IA, 48th, 1922
William, John F.		E, 4th Iowa (died of pleurisy)	267	70	1910 Apr 2	NE, 35th, 1911
Williams, A.		C, 145th Ill.	8		1885	KS, 5th, 1886
Williams, A.H.		B, 11th Kans.	46		1912 Mar 26	KS, 32nd, 1913
Williams, A.J.		A, 41st Ill. Inf.	32		1918 Oct 29	KS, 38th, 1919
Williams, A.P.		A, 6th Mass. Inf.	12		1908 Apr 10	KS, 28th, 1909
Williams, A.W.	Pvt.	G, 13th Iowa Inf.	497		1928 May 22	IA, 55th, 1929
Williams, Alexander		A, 99th Ind. Inf.	142		1925 Mar 20	KS, 45th, 1926
Williams, Alexander		A, 99th Ind.	142		1925 Mar 25	KS, 44th, 1925
Williams, Alexander		Ill.	337		1923 Feb	KS, 43rd, 1924
Williams, Amos		B, 14th Ill.	49		1916 Feb 14	KS, 36th, 1917
Williams, Ashley R.		E, 50th Ohio Inf.	92		1925 Jan 18	KS, 45th, 1926
Williams, B.F.		C, 15th Iowa	406		1910	KS, 30th, 1911
Williams, Ben		E, 32nd Mo.	27		1904 Oct 24	KS, 24th, 1905
Williams, C.E.		B, 204th Penn.	20		1896 Mar 21	KS, 16th, 1897
Williams, C.E.			[87?]		1919 Aug 25	KS, 39th, 1920
Williams, C.R.		C, 15th Mich. Inf. (at large)		92 & 5 mos.	1935 Oct 3	IA, 62nd, 1936

*See Appendix A, B or C for roster of post names and locations.
†See Introduction for note regarding recording of death date.
594

Name	Rank	Company, Regiment or Ship	Post*	Age	Death Date†	Journal
Williams, C.T.	Pvt.	A, 8th Iowa Inf.	503		1907 Sep 14	IA, 34th, 1908
Williams, Charles		E, 111th Ohio Inf. (died at Valley Falls; buried at Rose Hill Cemetery)	225		1894 Nov 16	KS, 14th, 1895
Williams, Charles W.		I, 1st Ill.	18		1911 Dec 11	KS, 31st, 1912
Williams, Chas. H.		B, 15th Ohio	46		1917 May 13	KS, 37th, 1918
Williams, Chas. O.	Pvt.	H, 1st Conn. Hvy. Art.	452		1917 Jan 13	IA, 45th, 1919
Williams, D.		A, 118th N.Y.	100		1904	KS, 24th, 1905
Williams, D.B.			32		1913 Feb 25	KS, 33rd, 1914
Williams, D.W.	Pvt.	B, 36th Iowa Inf.	497		1926 May 26	IA, 53rd, 1927
Williams, David			1		1910 Jul 11	KS, 30th, 1911
Williams, David A.	Lieut. Col.	136th Ohio Vol. Inf.	1		1915 Oct 6	KS, 35th, 1916
Williams, E.		G, 14th K.C.	129		1924 Jan 13	KS, 44th, 1925
Williams, E.B.	Sergt.	C, 32nd Iowa Inf.	259		1897 May 20	IA, 24th, 1898
Williams, E.P.		H, 8th Iowa Inf.	94		4th quarter 1884	IA, 11th, 1885
Williams, Ed H.		H, 107th Ill.	174		1918 Apr 27	KS, 38th, 1919
Williams, Ed. H.	Pvt.	A, 11th Wis.	23		1926 Mar 11	IA, 53rd, 1927
Williams, Edmond		E, 10th Ky. Cav.	38		1892 Nov 15	KS, 12th, 1893
Williams, Edward O.	Pvt.	C, 4th Ill. Cav.		91	1938 Feb 1	IA, 65th, 1939
Williams, Elijah		A, 54th Ohio Vols.	142		1902 Aug 4	KS, 22nd, 1903
Williams, F.D.	Pvt.	B, 15th Vt. Inf.	307	46	1885 Aug 6	IA, 12th, 1886
Williams, Francis E.		E, 146th Ill. Inf.	250		1925 Mar 11	KS, 45th, 1926
Williams, G.W.	Pvt.	K, 3rd Iowa Cav.	322		1914 Nov 6	IA, 41st, 1915
Williams, Geo.	Pvt.	2nd N.Y. Inf.	144		1913	IA, 40th, 1914
Williams, Geo.		D, 6th Iowa Cav. (died of heart failure)	180	75	1922 Sep 14	NE, 47th, 1923
Williams, Geo. D.		F, 57th Penn. Inf.	28	65	1910 Dec 30	NE, 35th, 1911
Williams, Geo. P.			45		1926 Jan 27	IA, 53rd, 1927
Williams, George		D, 6th Iowa (died of heart trouble)	180	79	1922 Sep	NE, 48th, 1924
Williams, George D.		G, 6th Mo. Cav. (died of heart trouble)	218	76	1915 Dec 24	NE, 40th, 1916
Williams, George H.		B, 2nd Colo. Cav.	27		1914 Jul 23	KS, 34th, 1915
Williams, George P.		E, 51st Wis.	151		1st quarter 1884	IA, 10th, 1884
Williams, George P.	Sergt.	25th Lt. Art.	16		1901 Oct 30	IA, 28th, 1902
Williams, George W.			25		1884	KS, 4th, 1885
Williams, H.D.	Capt.	I, 16th Iowa Inf.	68		1914	IA, 41st, 1915
Williams, H.E.	Capt.	B, 31st Iowa Inf.	222		1902 Jun 7	IA, 29th, 1903
Williams, H.K.	Capt.	D, 4th Ohio Cav.	20		1927 Jan 30	IA, 54th, 1928
Williams, H.W.		H, 123rd Ill. Inf.	51		1901 Jun 27	KS, 21st, 1902
Williams, Hill		H, 76th Wis. Cav.	71		1917 Feb 2	KS, 37th, 1918
Williams, Hiram		A, 34th Iowa Inf.	77		1918 Feb 1	NE, 43rd, 1919
Williams, Hobart		D, 151st N.Y. Inf.	7	86	1925 Nov 18	NE, 50th, 1926
Williams, I.H.		D, 9th Ind. Inf. (died of pneumonia)	147	61	1895 Jan 14	NE, 20th, 1896
Williams, Isaac	Pvt.	H, 20th Iowa Inf.	7		1918 Apr 23	IA, 45th, 1919
Williams, Isaac			80		1927 Jan 18	IA, 54th, 1928
Williams, Isaiah		I, 6th Wis.	259		1928 Dec 7	KS, 50th, 1931
Williams, Isaiah		I, 6th Wis.	259		1928 Dec 7	KS, 48th, 1929
Williams, J.A.		A, 27th Iowa	315		1897 Aug 15	KS, 17th, 1898
Williams, J.B.		I, 68th U.S. Col.	63		1922 May 21	KS, 42nd, 1923
Williams, J.C.	Pvt.	C, 40th Iowa Inf.	144		1918 Jul 1	IA, 45th, 1919
Williams, J.D.	Capt.	K, 24th Iowa Inf.	81		1900 Sep 24	IA, 27th, 1901
Williams, J.G.	Pvt.	B, 148th Ind. Inf.	59		1906 Feb 8	IA, 33rd, 1907
Williams, J.H.		D, 59th Ill. Inf. (died at St. Louis, Mo.; buried at Hillsdale Cemetery)	117		1894 Sep 15	KS, 14th, 1895
Williams, J.K.		B, 14th Ind. Inf.	202		1917 Nov 28	KS, 37th, 1918
Williams, J.M.	Pvt.	H, 26th Iowa	57		1901 Sep 23	IA, 28th, 1902
Williams, J.W.			127		1927 Mar 15	KS, 47th, 1928
Williams, Jacob		B, 43rd Wis.	110	63	1910 Aug 14	NE, 35th, 1911
Williams, James	Pvt.	K, 139th Ind. Inf. (at large)	84, 167	97	1942 Sep 18	IA, 69th, 1943
Williams, James		A, 13th Kans. (died at Bigelow, Kans.; buried at Antioch Cemetery)	330		1894 Oct 31	KS, 14th, 1895
Williams, James C.	Pvt.	L, 3rd Iowa Cav.	195	57	1886 Jun 6	IA, 13th, 1887
Williams, James E.		D, 46th Ill.	288		1928	NE, 53rd, 1929
Williams, Jas. P.		C, 35th Ill. Inf.	380		1900 Aug 27	KS, 20th, 1901
Williams, Jeremiah		K, 47th Tenn.	321		1911 Mar 14	KS, 31st, 1912

*See Appendix A, B or C for roster of post names and locations.
†See Introduction for note regarding recording of death date.

Name	Rank	Company, Regiment or Ship	Post*	Age	Death Date†	Journal
Williams, Jno. C.		D, 18th Wis. Inf.	214	62	1906	NE, 31st, 1907
Williams, Jno. G.	Pvt.	D, 1st Iowa Cav.	235		1924 Jul 27	IA, 51st, 1925
Williams, Jno. Henry	Pvt.	F, 32nd Iowa Inf.	154		1904 Dec 17	IA, 31st, 1905
Williams, Jno. S.		A, 2nd Iowa	292		1904 Mar 6	KS, 24th, 1905
Williams, Jno. W.		E, 36th Ohio Inf.	22	77	1923 Jan 6	NE, 48th, 1924
Williams, John	Pvt.	I, 34th Iowa Inf.	410		1908 Mar 29	IA, 35th, 1909
Williams, John		U.S. Navy	22		1918 Dec 2	IA, 45th, 1919
Williams, John		C, 14th Kans.	129		1921 Mar 25	KS, 41st, 1922
Williams, John		E, 126th Ill. (died of old age)	87	73	1904 Sep 9	NE, 29th, 1905
Williams, John L.		B, 7th Mo. State Militia	27		1929 Mar 9	KS, 49th, 1930
Williams, John M.		E, 53rd Ill. Inf.	29	90	1938 Mar 24	IA, 64th, 1938
Williams, John R.	Pvt.	B, 142nd Ill. Inf.	42	94	1940 Aug 11	IA, 66th, 1940
Williams, John R.		B, 8th Ba. I.	380		1896 Jun 14	KS, 16th, 1897
Williams, John S.		B, 13th Kans. Inf.	191		1890	KS, 10th, 1891
Williams, Joseph		A, 122nd Ill.	142		1917 Apr 14	KS, 37th, 1918
Williams, Joseph S.		M, 8th Ill. Cav. (died of old age)	354	83	1919 Apr 6	NE, 44th, 1920
Williams, L.S.	Capt.	I, 6th Vt. Inf.	365		1905 Jul 25	IA, 32nd, 1906
Williams, L.V.	Pvt.	8th Ill. Cav.	29		1906 Feb 16	IA, 33rd, 1907
Williams, Lane		M, 11th Mo.	59		1917 Jul 24	KS, 37th, 1918
Williams, Lewis	Corp.	B, 7th Kans. Cav.	12		1917 Feb 14	IA, 44th, 1918
Williams, Lloyd James		member at large			1940 Jan 8	KS, 60th, 1941
Williams, Lorena	Pvt.	G, 20th Wis. Inf.	222		1913 Jan 14	IA, 40th, 1914
Williams, Monroe		F, 79th Kans.	321		1909 Nov 20	KS, 29th, 1910
Williams, N.H.	Pvt.	K, 34th Iowa Inf.	168	75	1896 Mar 1	IA, 23rd, 1897
Williams, N.L.	Pvt.	E, 74th Ill. Inf.	46		1926 Aug 9	IA, 53rd, 1927
Williams, Nathan		K, 139th Ill. Inf. A, 65th Ill. K, 112th Ill.	7	93	1938 Mar 3	IA, 64th, 1938
Williams, Nathan		I, 7th Kans.	321		1910 Nov 2	KS, 30th, 1911
Williams, Newton	Pvt.	E, 30th Iowa Inf.	19		1915 Dec 8	IA, 42nd, 1916
Williams, Newton H.		A, 1st Mo. Cav.	46		1912 Oct 27	KS, 32nd, 1913
Williams, O.C.		U.S. Navy, Ill. (died of heart trouble)	63		1916 Nov 26	NE, 41st, 1917
Williams, O.L.	Sergt.	C, 45th Ill. Inf.	24		1909 Nov 13	IA, 36th, 1910
Williams, Owen	Pvt.	I, 2nd Ohio Hvy. Art.	235	74	1891 Apr 29	IA, 18th, 1892
Williams, P.			493		1906 Apr 24	IA, 33rd, 1907
Williams, P.M.		B, 3rd Colo. Cav.	47		1917 Nov 17	KS, 37th, 1918
Williams, Park	Pvt.	D, 3rd Iowa Cav.	18		1912 Jun 19	IA, 39th, 1913
Williams, Perry		K, 5th Ill.	273		1926	KS, 46th, 1927
Williams, Pomeroy	Corp.	12th Ind. Cav.	358		1916 Jan 17	KS, 36th, 1917
Williams, Porter S.		H, 17th Ohio	115		1906 Sep 30	KS, 26th, 1907
Williams, R.A.		F, 14th Kans. Cav.	129		1925 Jul 13	KS, 45th, 1926
Williams, R.G.		K, 124th Ill. (died of general debility)	18	81	1908 Jun 6	NE, 33rd, 1909
Williams, R.M.	Pvt.	F, 34th Ill. Inf.	10		1912 Jun 17	IA, 39th, 1913
Williams, R.P.			55		1883	KS, 3rd, 1884
Williams, R.S.	Lieut.		130		1900	IA, 27th, 1901
Williams, Richard		L, 2nd Mich. Cav.	140		1926 Apr 1	NE, 51st, 1927
Williams, Robert P.		A, 7th Iowa Cav.	5		1937 Aug 1	NE, 62nd, 1938
Williams, Robert W.		E, 29th Wis.	453		1921 Oct 18	KS, 41st, 1922
Williams, Robt.			72		1929 Dec 5	KS, 49th, 1930
Williams, S.F.	Pvt.	M, 6th Iowa Cav.	78		1911 Aug 7	IA, 38th, 1912
Williams, S.H.		B, 84th Ind.	25		1927 Aug 18	NE, 52nd, 1928
Williams, S.T.		I, 12th Ill.	335		1904 Sep 22	KS, 24th, 1905
Williams, Sampson		B, 84th Ind. (location: Franklin)			1927	NE, 52nd, 1928
Williams, Samuel	Corp.	I, 35th Iowa Inf.	88		1916 Jan 8	IA, 43rd, 1917
Williams, Sherman A.	Capt.	A, 26th Iowa Inf.	88		1900 May 6	IA, 27th, 1901
Williams, Solomon H.		E, 86th Ill.	127		1885	KS, 5th, 1886
Williams, Steve	Pvt.	D, 15th Iowa Inf.	497		1926 Apr 25	IA, 53rd, 1927
Williams, T.			277		1917	IA, 44th, 1918
Williams, T.B.	Pvt.	I, 32nd Iowa Inf.	236		1903 Aug 26	IA, 30th, 1904
Williams, T.J.	Pvt.		31		1920 Mar	IA, 47th, 1921
Williams, T.M.		I, 2nd Kans. Cav.	334		1892 Apr	KS, 12th, 1893
Williams, T.W.		C, 6th Penn. (died of old age)	96		1915 Aug 26	NE, 40th, 1916

*See Appendix A, B or C for roster of post names and locations.
†See Introduction for note regarding recording of death date.

Name	Rank	Company, Regiment or Ship	Post*	Age	Death Date†	Journal
Williams, Thomas		G, 39th Ohio	19		1914 Dec 16	KS, 34th, 1915
Williams, Thomas J.		D, 120th Ind.	265		1935 Jun 13	KS, 55th, 1936
Williams, Thomas M.		B, 4th Iowa Inf.	225		1914 Jul 13	KS, 34th, 1915
Williams, W.B.			3		1926 Sep 7	IA, 53rd, 1927
Williams, W.B.	Farrier	E, 9th Iowa Cav.	94	87	1933 Dec 14	IA, 60th, 1934
Williams, W.C.			64		1928	IA, 55th, 1929
Williams, W.F.		G, 89th Ohio	25		1922 Jan 25	KS, 42nd, 1923
Williams, W.L.		1st Mich. Inf.	282		1892 Feb 19	NE, 17th, 1893
Williams, W.M.	Pvt.	H, 1st Battalion 13th U.S. Inf.	54	49	1888 May 1	IA, 15th, 1889
Williams, W.M.	1st Sergt.	F, 27th Iowa Inf.	166		1900 Dec 18	IA, 27th, 1901
Williams, W.W.			158		1919 Jun 5	IA, 46th, 1920
Williams, W.W.	Pvt.	K, 4th Iowa Cav.	153	85	1932 Jul 6	IA, 59th, 1933
Williams, William		B, 64th Ill. Inf. (died of old age)	50	76	1911 Oct 24	NE, 36th, 1912
Williams, William X.		F, 88th Penn.	113		1905 Oct 22	KS, 25th, 1906
Williams, Wm.	Pvt.	B, 29th Mass. Inf.	190		1902 Aug 9	IA, 29th, 1903
Williams, Wm. C.		I, 16th Wis.	88		1919 Oct 1	KS, 39th, 1920
Williams, Zudoc	Pvt.	G, 11th Ill. Cav.	67		1901 Jan 22	IA, 28th, 1902
Williamson, B.P.		H, 3rd Ind. Inf.	41		1902	KS, 22nd, 1903
Williamson, Ebenezer		C, 51st Ohio Inf.	73	96	1937 Sep 9	IA, 64th, 1938
Williamson, Elija	Pvt.	A, Iowa Lt. Art.	452	87	1931 Dec 10	IA, 58th, 1932
Williamson, Elijah	Pvt.	Iowa Lt. Art.	452		1930 Dec 10	IA, 57th, 1931
Williamson, Frank		G, 14th Ill. (died of old age)	24	74	1915 Dec 27	NE, 40th, 1916
Williamson, Fred	Pvt.	12th Reserve Corps	112		1900 Jun 1	IA, 27th, 1901
Williamson, Fuel		A, 15th U.S. Colored Inf.	321		1902 Apr 26	KS, 22nd, 1903
Williamson, G.F.		2nd Reserve Corps & V.R.C.	112		1900 Jun 1	IA, 27th, 1901
Williamson, Geo.	Pvt.	H, 169th Ohio Inf.	327		1920 Mar	IA, 47th, 1921
Williamson, H.F.		C, 112th Ill. Inf. (died of heart disease)	23	87	1921 Oct 6	NE, 46th, 1922
Williamson, J.I.		C, 128th Ohio	270		1908 Sep 26	KS, 28th, 1909
Williamson, James H.		G, 12th Penn. Cav.	340		1924 Apr 17	KS, 44th, 1925
Williamson, L.J.			211		1917	IA, 44th, 1918
Williamson, R.C.		C, 10th Kans.	27		1924 Nov 21	KS, 44th, 1925
Williamson, S.F.		B, 13th Ind. Cav. (died of accident)	24	66	1908 Jan 17	NE, 33rd, 1909
Williamson, T.	Pvt.	A, 108th Ill. Inf.	34		1920 Nov 23	IA, 47th, 1921
Williamson, T.M.		F, 1st Ohio Lt. Art.	271		1909	IA, 36th, 1910
Williamson, Theo.		G, 106th Ind.	267		1914 Sep 5	KS, 34th, 1915
Williamson, W.	Pvt.		43		1920 Jul 19	IA, 47th, 1921
Williamson, W.I.	Lieut.	F, 11th Iowa Inf.	49		1917 Nov 10	IA, 44th, 1918
Williamson, Wm.		B, 14th Inf.	9		1920 Aug 10	NE, 45th, 1921
Willie, Clement	Pvt.	I, 2nd Wis. Cav.	452		1929 Jan 28	IA, 56th, 1930
Willie, James A.		H, 2nd Kans. Cav.	12		1911 Mar 15	KS, 31st, 1912
Williford, W.A.			54		1904 Dec 19	KS, 24th, 1905
Williman, Thomas M.		A, 192nd Ohio Vol. Inf.	23		1939 Nov 12	NE, 64th, 1940
Willin, A.J.		B, 20th Wis. Inf. (died of apoplexy)	272	65	1896 Oct 2	NE, 21st, 1897
Willing, James T.	Pvt.	F, 4th Ill. Inf.	452		1912 Jan 21	IA, 39th, 1913
Willis, A.G.	Pvt.	M, 2nd Iowa Cav.	80		1899	NE, 24th, 1900
Willis, E.D.		G, 17th Iowa Inf.	293		1931 Jan 15	KS, 51st, 1932
Willis, E.L.	Pvt.	C, 56th Ill. Inf.	440	83	1932 Feb 5	IA, 59th, 1933
Willis, Harvey D.	Hosp. Stew.	122nd U.S.C.T.	12		1919	IA, 46th, 1920
Willis, Irvin	Pvt.	G, 18th Iowa Vols.	306		1903 Mar 23	IA, 30th, 1904
Willis, J.D.		A, 15th West Va. Cav.	170		1928 Mar 23	IA, 55th, 1929
Willis, J.H.	Pvt.	E, 41st Ill.	40		1907 Dec 17	IA, 34th, 1908
Willis, Jno. G.		K, 17th Ill. Cav.	7		1925 Mar 25	NE, 50th, 1926
Willis, John K.		G, 11th Ind. Cav.	181		1893 Feb 15	KS, 13th, 1894
Willis, R.A.		D, 8th Minn. Inf. (died of pneumonia)	262	78	1920 Apr 22	NE, 45th, 1921
Willis, S.		E, 31st Ind.	130		1933 Jul 29	KS, 53rd, 1934
Willis, W.A.	Pvt.	K, 74th Ill. Inf.	8		1915 Oct 22	IA, 42nd, 1916
Willis, W.A.	Pvt.	10th Iowa Inf.	309		1918 Jul 2	IA, 45th, 1919
Willis, W.A.		K, Ohio National Guard	55		1926 Apr 9	KS, 46th, 1927
Willis, Willet A.	Corp.	E, 24th Iowa Inf.	77		1912 Dec 12	IA, 39th, 1913
Willison, Peter	Pvt.	E, 6th Kans. Cav.	153		1916 May 19	IA, 43rd, 1917
Willit, Edward A.		30th Ill.	51		1912 Jul 10	KS, 32nd, 1913
Willits, H.		G, 27th Ill.	27		1928	NE, 53rd, 1929

Name	Rank	Company, Regiment or Ship	Post*	Age	Death Date†	Journal
Willits, L.P.			316		1927 Jun 30	IA, 54th, 1928
Willkin, W.J.		U.S. Navy	40		1922 Feb 14	KS, 42nd, 1923
Willmer, E.P.	Pvt.	B, 131st Ohio Inf.	57		1933	IA, 60th, 1934
Willoon, Samuel	Lieut.	F, 81st N.Y. Inf.	68		1917 Feb 18	IA, 44th, 1918
Willoughby, L.B.		C, 31st Ind. Inf. (died of dropsy)	23	64	1900 Dec	NE, 26th, 1902
Willoughby, Levi P.		C, 31st Ind. Inf. (died of asthma)	23	63	1900 Dec 25	NE, 25th, 1901
Willoughby, Theo.		G, 2nd West Va. Cav.	40	87	1934 Dec 14	IA, 61st, 1935
Willoughby, Wm.		U.S. Navy	25		1905 Jul 19	NE, 30th, 1906
Willoughby, Wm.		U.S. Navy	25		1905 Jul	NE, 31st, 1907
Willowby, B.	Pvt.	I, 61st Penn. Inf.	18		1919 Aug 6	IA, 46th, 1920
Wills, A.H.		A, 148th Ohio	380		1898 May 21	KS, 18th, 1899
Wills, Peter			25		1934 May	KS, 54th, 1935
Wills, Robt. S.	Pvt.	C, 130th Ind. Inf.	452		1924 Mar 20	IA, 51st, 1925
Wills, Wm. F.	Pvt.	6, 15th Iowa	59		1905 Jun 3	IA, 32nd, 1906
Willson, Amos			12		1923 Dec 21	KS, 43rd, 1924
Willson, Henry	Pvt.	E, 9th Iowa Cav.	452		1914 Oct	IA, 41st, 1915
Willson, J.D.	Pvt.	M, 7th Mo. Cav.	379		1906 Jul 15	IA, 33rd, 1907
Willson, John, Dr.		F, 106th Ill. Inf.	72		1929 Apr 29	KS, 49th, 1930
Willson, Wm.	Pvt.	F, 13th Iowa Inf.	329		1919 Dec 2	IA, 46th, 1920
Willson, Wm. S.	Pvt.	F, 9th Ill. Cav.	88		1909 Nov 20	IA, 36th, 1910
Willy, Wm.	Pvt.	D, 44th Iowa Inf.	26		1916 Mar 21	IA, 43rd, 1917
Wilmarth, George O.		A, 2nd Kans. M.[Kans. State Militia?]	1		1914 Feb 12	KS, 34th, 1915
Wilmer, A.			429		1911	KS, 31st, 1912
Wilmer, Rudolph		K, 24th Ill. Inf.	429		1908	KS, 28th, 1909
Wilmot, C.A.		E, 151st Ill.	44		1904 Nov 14	KS, 24th, 1905
Wilmot, J.W.		H, 50th Ill.	176		1913 Mar 6	KS, 33rd, 1914
Wilmoth, J.W.	Pvt.	F, 18th Ill. Inf.	497		1920 Feb 27	IA, 47th, 1921
Wilshire, John	Pvt.	F, 47th Iowa Inf.	362	46	1889 Jun 12	IA, 16th, 1890
Wilsin, Geo. N.	Pvt.	E, 5th Mich. Cav.	503		1916 Sep 5	IA, 43rd, 1917
Wilson, A.L.		G, 34th N.Y.	66		1911 Feb 7	KS, 31st, 1912
Wilson, A.P.		F, 36th Ohio	147		1905 Sep 8	KS, 25th, 1906
Wilson, A.P.		B, 18th Ky. Inf. (died of apoplexy)	22	75	1914 Dec 24	NE, 39th, 1915
Wilson, A.R.		H, 9th Iowa Cav.	25		1930 Mar 11	NE, 55th, 1931
Wilson, Amos		G, 71st Ill.	255		1912 Sep 29	KS, 32nd, 1913
Wilson, Amos			81		1886 Dec 9	NE, 11th, 1887
Wilson, Andrew		B, 59th Ind. Inf. (in Mexican War)	388	73	1891 Jun 24	KS, 11th, 1892
Wilson, Arthur D.		B, 141st Ill.	171		1933 Dec 5	NE, 58th, 1934
Wilson, B.F.	Pvt.	K, 1st Mo. Inf.	7		1920 Jan 30	IA, 47th, 1921
Wilson, B.G.		K, 84th Ind. Inf.	19		1910 Mar 22	KS, 30th, 1911
Wilson, B.L.		I, 186th Ohio	127		1917 Jan 22	KS, 37th, 1918
Wilson, B.W.	Lieut. Col.	28th Iowa Inf.	24		1907 Mar 4	IA, 33rd, 1907
Wilson, B.W.	Col.		24		1907 Mar 1	IA, 34th, 1908
Wilson, C.	Pvt.	I, 7th Cal.	253		1921 Apr	IA, 48th, 1922
Wilson, C.A.	Pvt.	K, 15th Ill. Inf.	95		1910 Oct 1	IA, 37th, 1911
Wilson, C.C.	Pvt.	I, 118th Ohio	238		1903 Jul 27	IA, 30th, 1904
Wilson, C.C.	Pvt.	F, 40th N.Y. Inf.	10		1918 Jan 24	IA, 45th, 1919
Wilson, C.C.		C, 65th Ind.	1		1913 Nov 24	KS, 33rd, 1914
Wilson, C.C.		A, 83rd Ill. E, 61st Ill.	301		1922 Feb 13	KS, 42nd, 1923
Wilson, C.L.		G, 25th Iowa	153	90	1934 Jul 6	IA, 61st, 1935
Wilson, C.L.		L, 11th Kans.	1		1900 Apr 28	KS, 20th, 1901
Wilson, C.S.	Pvt.	D, 1st Iowa Cav.	12		1915 Aug 18	IA, 42nd, 1916
Wilson, C.W.			18		1922	IA, 49th, 1923
Wilson, C.W.		E, 104th Ill. Inf.	156		1899 Nov 19	KS, 19th, 1900
Wilson, C.W.		A, 8th Iowa	13	78	1918 Oct 3	NE, 43rd, 1919
Wilson, Carson		B, 18th Iowa	3		1904 Oct 16	KS, 24th, 1905
Wilson, Charles A.	Pvt.	K, 15th Ill. Inf.	343		1910 Oct 9	IA, 37th, 1911
Wilson, Charles B.		A, 34th Ill. (not a member of the department but living in Nebraska; location: Lincoln)			1937 Jun 19	NE, 62nd, 1938
Wilson, Charles C.	Pvt.	K, 4th N.Y. Inf.	283		1915 Jun 9	IA, 42nd, 1916
Wilson, Charles E.		I, 25th Ill.	85		1911 Mar 31	KS, 31st, 1912

*See Appendix A, B or C for roster of post names and locations.
†See Introduction for note regarding recording of death date.

Name	Rank	Company, Regiment or Ship	Post*	Age	Death Date†	Journal
Wilson, Chas.		F, 26th Ill. (died of dropsy)	35	77	1917 Jul 8	NE, 42nd, 1918
Wilson, Chas. H.			24		1890	NE, 15th, 1891
Wilson, Clark	Pvt.	C, 33rd Iowa Inf.	34	88	1932 Jun 21	IA, 59th, 1933
Wilson, D.K.		B, 58th Ill. Inf.	156		1885	KS, 5th, 1886
Wilson, David			28		1915 Sep 24	KS, 35th, 1916
Wilson, David G.		B, 93rd Ill.	493		1921 Dec 24	KS, 41st, 1922
Wilson, E.D.	Corp.	A, 18th Iowa Inf.	181	55	1893 Mar 4	IA, 20th, 1894
Wilson, E.E.		C, 2nd West Va. Cav. (died at Independence; buried at Mt. Hope Cemetery)	4		1894 Aug 28	KS, 14th, 1895
Wilson, E.M.		A, 10th Mo. Inf.	293		1914 Nov 3	KS, 34th, 1915
Wilson, E.M., Dr.		died of heart disease	84		1886 Nov 6	NE, 11th, 1887
Wilson, E.W.		A, 119th Ill.	35		1911 Jun 6	KS, 31st, 1912
Wilson, Eldridge		K, 15th Iowa Inf. (at large)	222	98	1938 Apr 26	IA, 64th, 1938
Wilson, Eli C.		F, 64th Ohio	25		1922 Apr 26	KS, 42nd, 1923
Wilson, Erastus		B, 7th Iowa Cav. Indiana (died of paralysis)	89	71	1919 Aug 4	NE, 44th, 1920
Wilson, Evan		66th Ill. Inf.	7		1923 Sep	NE, 48th, 1924
Wilson, F.	Pvt.	C, 38th Iowa Inf.	281	45	1887 Jul 4	IA, 14th, 1888
Wilson, Francis M.		H, 8th Ky.	190		1897 Aug 27	KS, 17th, 1898
Wilson, Frank		K, 86th Ind. Inf.	69		1887 Feb 17	KS, 7th, 1888
Wilson, Garison		A, 2nd Iowa	435		1913 Nov 17	KS, 33rd, 1914
Wilson, Geo. B.		K, 2nd Ill.	142		1917 Aug 1	KS, 37th, 1918
Wilson, Geo. N., see Wilsin, Geo. N.						
Wilson, George		M, 1st Wis. Cav.	25		1913 Oct 30	NE, 38th, 1914
Wilson, H.C.	Lieut.	K, 23rd Iowa Inf.	94		1907 Feb 4	IA, 34th, 1908
Wilson, H.W.	Pvt.	F, 145th Ohio Inf.	34		1920 Jan 15	IA, 47th, 1921
Wilson, H.W.		D, 124th Ind.	12		1928 May 19	KS, 48th, 1929
Wilson, Henry	Corp.	H, 1st Mass. Inf.	30		1915 Jun 18	IA, 42nd, 1916
Wilson, Henry	Pvt.	G, 13th Iowa Inf.	164		1915 Oct 15	IA, 42nd, 1916
Wilson, Henry, see Willson, Henry						
Wilson, Henry M.	Capt.	D, 28th Iowa Inf.	98		1912 Mar 2	IA, 39th, 1913
Wilson, Henry W.		E, 86th Ill. Inf.	64		1902 May 15	KS, 22nd, 1903
Wilson, Herman	Pvt.	42nd Wis. Inf.	258		1909 Dec 10	IA, 36th, 1910
Wilson, Hiram		K, 116th Ind. Inf. (died of Brights disease)	289		1891 Mar 21	KS, 11th, 1892
Wilson, Hosea	Pvt.	E, 7th Cal. Inf.	253		1920 Aug 9	IA, 47th, 1921
Wilson, I.G.		D, 104th Ohio	42		1911 Jul 5	KS, 31st, 1912
Wilson, J.		F, 1st Iowa Cav.	84		1917 Nov 14	NE, 42nd, 1918
Wilson, J.A.	Pvt.	F, 32nd Iowa Inf.	154	51	1888 Mar 20	IA, 15th, 1889
Wilson, J.A.	Pvt.	K, 25th Iowa Inf.	122		1910 Mar 12	IA, 37th, 1911
Wilson, J.C.			13		1926 Feb 23	NE, 51st, 1927
Wilson, J.H.		F, 15th West Va.	51		1916 Feb 16	KS, 36th, 1917
Wilson, J.M.	Pvt.	C, 81st Ohio	500		1903 Dec 13	IA, 30th, 1904
Wilson, J.O.		B, 115th Ohio	139		1928 Jan 22	KS, 48th, 1929
Wilson, J.P.	Pvt.	A, 45th Iowa Inf.	440		1920 Mar 18	IA, 47th, 1921
Wilson, J.P.		E, 29th Ind.	147		1898 Dec 14	KS, 18th, 1899
Wilson, J.W.	1st Lieut.	K, 28th Iowa Inf.	16	51	1887 May 6	IA, 14th, 1888
Wilson, J.W.	Sergt.	C, 28th Iowa Inf.	127		1920 Jan 21	IA, 47th, 1921
Wilson, Jacob B.	Pvt.	11th Iowa Inf.	109		1923 Dec 20	IA, 50th, 1924
Wilson, James		D, 25th Ill.	72		1928 Dec 28	KS, 48th, 1929
Wilson, James		F, 13th Ky.	25		1913 Feb 14	NE, 38th, 1914
Wilson, James		B, 11th Mo.	1		1927 Mar 28	NE, 52nd, 1928
Wilson, James A.	Pvt.	G, 3rd Iowa Cav.	403		1901 Apr 25	IA, 28th, 1902
Wilson, James K.P.		H, 11th Ill. Cav.	250		1920 Jun 3	KS, 40th, 1921
Wilson, James P.		F, 138th Ill.	247		1910 Apr 28	KS, 30th, 1911
Wilson, James R.		F, 23rd Iowa Inf.	248		1st quarter 1885	IA, 11th, 1885
Wilson, Jas. A.	Pvt.	H, 24th Ind. Inf.	12		1911 Jun 8	IA, 38th, 1912
Wilson, Jas. S.	Corp.	B, 22nd Iowa Inf.	8		1903 Dec 25	IA, 30th, 1904
Wilson, Jas. T.	Pvt.	C, 4th Ill. Cav.	71		1916 Feb 21	IA, 43rd, 1917
Wilson, Jeremiah P.	Pvt.	A, 103rd Penn. Inf.	190		1918 Jul 16	IA, 45th, 1919
Wilson, Jerry			[4?]		1918 Apr 12	KS, 38th, 1919

*See Appendix A, B or C for roster of post names and locations.
†See Introduction for note regarding recording of death date.

Name	Rank	Company, Regiment or Ship	Post*	Age	Death Date†	Journal
Wilson, Jesse		F, 88th Ind.	4		1930 Jun 24	KS, 50th, 1931
Wilson, John	Pvt.	H, 15th Iowa	150		1903 Dec 25	IA, 30th, 1904
Wilson, John		G, 2nd Mo.	380		1896 Sep 3	KS, 16th, 1897
Wilson, John		B, 7th Kans. Cav.	39		1921 May 20	KS, 41st, 1922
Wilson, John		D, U.S.C.T.	52		1926 Nov 19	KS, 46th, 1927
Wilson, John		F, 12th Ill. Inf. (died of old age)	47	80	1905 Feb 26	NE, 30th, 1906
Wilson, John			32		1921	NE, 46th, 1922
Wilson, John B.	Pvt.	I, 52nd Ohio Inf.	125	72	1897 Nov 5	IA, 24th, 1898
Wilson, John C.	Corp.	K, 28th Iowa	16		1901 Aug 20	IA, 28th, 1902
Wilson, John H.	Pvt.	B, 43rd Ind. Inf.	12		1915 Jan 3	IA, 42nd, 1916
Wilson, John L.		G, 114th Ill. Inf.	32	80	1909 Nov 8	NE, 34th, 1910
Wilson, John M.	Corp.	D, 4th Iowa Inf.	20		1912 Sep 19	IA, 39th, 1913
Wilson, John W.	Sergt.	H, 2nd Iowa Inf.	250		1915 Mar 4	IA, 42nd, 1916
Wilson, John W.		G, 19th Iowa Inf.	14		1912 Dec 18	KS, 32nd, 1913
Wilson, John W.		B, 49th Ind. (not a member of the G.A.R.)	18		1912 Oct 9	KS, 32nd, 1913
Wilson, John W.		G, U.S. Regulars (died at Scammon, Kans.; buried at Scammon Cemetery)	59		1894 Dec 1	KS, 14th, 1895
Wilson, John W.		26th Ohio Bat.	110		1918 Oct 10	KS, 38th, 1919
Wilson, Jonathan	Pvt.	H, 25th Iowa Inf.	20		1904 Jun 21	IA, 31st, 1905
Wilson, Jos.	Pvt.	I, 7th Mo. Cav.	454		1890 Jun 13	IA, 17th, 1891
Wilson, Jos. D.		H, 7th Penn. Cav. (died of dropsy)	188	77	1920 Mar 24	NE, 45th, 1921
Wilson, Jos. L.	Pvt.	D, 34th Iowa Inf.	275	49	1891 Dec 14	IA, 18th, 1892
Wilson, Joseph		K, 194th Ohio	14		1922 Apr 19	KS, 42nd, 1923
Wilson, Joseph M.		A, 4th Iowa Cav.	209		1916 Sep 27	IA, 43rd, 1917
Wilson, Josiah		Iowa (died of old age)	78	82	1917 Nov 15	NE, 43rd, 1919
Wilson, L.A.	Paymaster Clerk	U.S.S. San Jacinto	323		1924 Jul 2	IA, 51st, 1925
Wilson, L.I.	Pvt.	L, 3rd Iowa Cav.	173		1920 Jul 3	IA, 47th, 1921
Wilson, L.L.	Pvt.	A, 20th Iowa Inf.	244		1916 May 12	IA, 43rd, 1917
Wilson, L.N.		U.S. Navy	30		1924 Jul 1	KS, 44th, 1925
Wilson, Lemuel		C, 91st Ind.	85		1925 Mar 26	KS, 45th, 1926
Wilson, Levi	Pvt.	G, 159th Ohio	17		1921 Oct 17	IA, 48th, 1922
Wilson, Luther A.		D, 10th Ill.	25		1906 Dec 17	KS, 26th, 1907
Wilson, M.S.	Pvt.	I, 1st Ill. Lt. Art.	3		1903 Jun 6	IA, 30th, 1904
Wilson, M.W.		G, 2nd Ind.	25		1916 Mar 2	KS, 36th, 1917
Wilson, Matt	Pvt.	D, 35th Iowa Cav.	255		1924 Sep 3	IA, 51st, 1925
Wilson, O.W.	Pvt.	B, 106th N.Y. Inf.	31		1912 May	IA, 39th, 1913
Wilson, Oliver P.		K, 113th Ill.	25	70	1915 Jan 10	NE, 40th, 1916
Wilson, Peter	Corp.	G, 14th Iowa Inf.	125	50	1887 Apr 23	IA, 14th, 1888
Wilson, R.B.		B, 15th Ill.	334		1913 Jun 19	KS, 33rd, 1914
Wilson, R.C.			63		1883	KS, 3rd, 1884
Wilson, R.J.		E, 46th Iowa	235	89	1934 Oct 26	IA, 61st, 1935
Wilson, R.P.	Pvt.	A, 46th Ill. Inf.	141		1929 Mar 29	IA, 56th, 1930
Wilson, R.S.		F, 95th Ohio Inf. (died at Winfield)	85		1895 Jun 20	KS, 15th, 1896
Wilson, Robert	Sergt.	I, 8th Ill. Inf.	516		1901 Aug 13	IA, 28th, 1902
Wilson, Robert J.		D, 26th Ill.	60		1925 Jun 20	NE, 51st, 1927
Wilson, Roger		D, 19th Wis. Inf. (died of pneumonia)	124	58	1895 Dec 19	NE, 20th, 1896
Wilson, Royal	Pvt.	G, 30th Wis. Inf.	377		1917 Feb 21	IA, 44th, 1918
Wilson, S.H.F.	Pvt.	C, 1st Iowa Cav.	157		1911 Dec 16	IA, 39th, 1913
Wilson, S.S.	Sergt.	D, 16th Ill.	2		1923 Jun 6	IA, 50th, 1924
Wilson, Scott W.	Pvt.	F, 49th Mass. Inf.	235	87	1932 Feb 7	IA, 59th, 1933
Wilson, Smith		G, 11th Penn.	17		1893 Oct 9	KS, 13th, 1894
Wilson, Solomon			292		1913	KS, 33rd, 1914
Wilson, T.J.	Pvt.	I, 12th Iowa Inf.	74		1910 Nov 10	IA, 37th, 1911
Wilson, T.K.			440		1911 Jan 26	IA, 38th, 1912
Wilson, T.M.		C, 102nd Ill. Inf. (died of cancer)	9	74	1891[1901?] May	NE, 26th, 1902
Wilson, Tarleton	Bugler	G, 6th Kans. Cav.	153	86	1932 Jun 20	IA, 59th, 1933
Wilson, Thomas	Pvt.	H, 104th Ill. Inf.	324		1910 Feb 25	IA, 37th, 1911
Wilson, Thomas	Sergt.	F, 40th Iowa Inf.	49		1916 May 27	IA, 43rd, 1917
Wilson, Thomas B.	Pvt.	L, 2nd U.S. Cav.	305		1901 Jul 1	IA, 28th, 1902
Wilson, Thomas G.	Pvt.	I, 50th Ill. Inf.	5	47	1893 May 28	IA, 20th, 1894
Wilson, Thomas H.		D, 160th Neb. (died of heart failure)	342	75	1922 Feb 24	NE, 46th, 1922
Wilson, Thomas J.	Pvt.	D, 12th Iowa Inf.	317	63	1894 Feb 28	IA, 20th, 1894

*See Appendix A, B or C for roster of post names and locations.
†See Introduction for note regarding recording of death date.

Name	Rank	Company, Regiment or Ship	Post*	Age	Death Date†	Journal
Wilson, Thomas J.		M, 2nd Iowa	59		1913 Jan 26	KS, 33rd, 1914
Wilson, Thomas R.	Pvt.	B, 1st Cav.	59		1922 Jun 16	IA, 49th, 1923
Wilson, W.C.	Pvt.		2		1932	IA, 59th, 1933
Wilson, W.F.	Pvt.	A, 11th Ind. Inf.	235		1920 Mar 9	IA, 47th, 1921
Wilson, W.H.	Pvt.	D, 29th Iowa Inf.	271		1923 Aug	IA, 50th, 1924
Wilson, W.H.		E, 7th Iowa Cav.	69	87	1936 Apr 2	IA, 63rd, 1937
Wilson, W.H.		C, 1st Ohio Cav.	166		1887 Apr 7	KS, 7th, 1888
Wilson, W.H.		C, 134th N.Y. Inf.	1		1925 Dec 9	KS, 45th, 1926
Wilson, W.J.	Pvt.	H, 4th U.S.	22		1899 Oct 9	IA, 26th, 1900
Wilson, W.J.		D, 95th Ohio 48th Ky.	293		1918 Mar 12	KS, 38th, 1919
Wilson, W.L.		F, 118th Ind.	129		1921 Jun 1	KS, 41st, 1922
Wilson, W.L.		H, 142nd Penn.	24	70	1912 Oct 18	NE, 37th, 1913
Wilson, W.P.	Pvt.	E, 28th Iowa Inf.	8		1929 Jul 3	IA, 56th, 1930
Wilson, W.R.	Pvt.	A, 9th Iowa Cav.	440		1916 Dec 3	IA, 43rd, 1917
Wilson, W.W.		H, 3rd Ohio	179		1892 Jan 11	KS, 12th, 1893
Wilson, Walker	Pvt.	A, 1st Iowa Cav.	75		1906 Aug 5	IA, 33rd, 1907
Wilson, William	Pvt.	128th Ohio Inf.	52		1927 Apr 1	IA, 54th, 1928
Wilson, William		D, 13th Mo. Inf. C, 1st Mo. Inf.	405		1899 Aug 30	KS, 19th, 1900
Wilson, William		D, 7th Ohio Cav.	19		1908 May 10	KS, 28th, 1909
Wilson, William		H, 99th Ohio	1		1922 Dec 28	KS, 43rd, 1924
Wilson, William		B, 1st Mich. Cav.	185		1925 Mar 19	KS, 44th, 1925
Wilson, William		E, 99th Ind. Inf. (died of acute rheumatism)	57		1893 Apr 16	NE, 18th, 1894
Wilson, William		F, 36th Penn. Inf. (died of pneumonia)	4	50	1896 Feb 11	NE, 21st, 1897
Wilson, William H.		E, 44th Iowa Inf. & 7th Cav.		87	1936 Apr 2	IA, 62nd, 1936
Wilson, William H.		F, 10th Ind. Inf.	12		1924 May 4	KS, 44th, 1925
Wilson, Willis			85		1920 May 6	KS, 40th, 1921
Wilson, Wm.		D, 143rd Ill.	52		1930 Mar 11	NE, 55th, 1931
Wilson, Wm. C.		B, 83rd Ill. Inf.	25	72	1917 Jul 17	NE, 42nd, 1918
Wilson, Wm. H.			45		1918 Nov 6	IA, 45th, 1919
Wilson, Wm. S.		G, 136th N.Y. Inf.	25		1901 Nov 23	KS, 21st, 1902
Wilt, Andrew		I, 9th Penn. Cav.	25		1914 Apr 13	KS, 34th, 1915
Wilt, J.A.		G, 87th Penn.	1		1931	NE, 56th, 1932
Wilt, Levi		Unassigned, 140th Penn.	14		1915 Jun 8	KS, 35th, 1916
Wilton, Wm.		F, 83rd Ill. Inf.	163		1892 Nov 29	NE, 17th, 1893
Wiltse, Albert		F, 112th N.Y.	182		1930 Apr 3	NE, 55th, 1931
Wiltse, Geo. W.	Pvt.	D, 21st Iowa Inf.	127	85	1931 Jul 13	IA, 58th, 1932
Wiltse, George W.	Pvt.	D, 21st Iowa Inf.	127		1930 Jul 13	IA, 57th, 1931
Wiltse, Jerome		K, 48th Mo. Inf. (died of paralytic stroke)	84	90	1925 Dec 1	NE, 50th, 1926
Wiltse, N.P.	Pvt.	3rd Battery	3		1906 Aug	IA, 33rd, 1907
Wiltse, Robert		U.S. Navy N.Y.	40		1926 Mar 14	KS, 46th, 1927
Wiltse, W.C.	Pvt.		3		1927	IA, 54th, 1928
Wiltsie, J.J.	Corp.	A, 23rd Iowa Inf.	7		1915 Aug 9	IA, 42nd, 1916
Wiltsie, J.P.	Pvt.	A, 112th N.Y. Inf.	258		1912 Jun 24	IA, 39th, 1913
Wiltz, C.		A, 44th Iowa Inf. (died of heart disease)	147		1894 Dec 2	NE, 19th, 1895
Wimberley, F.M.		H, 1st Iowa Cav. (died of cancer of bladder)	73	64	1897 Mar 31	NE, 22nd, 1898
Wimple, E.A.		I, 26th Iowa Inf.	262		1919 Mar 2	NE, 44th, 1920
Winagar, M.	Pvt.	E, 6th Iowa Cav.	97		1916	IA, 43rd, 1917
Winans, Geo. S.			294		1923 Dec 12	KS, 43rd, 1924
Winans, H.K.			180		1899 Sep 30	KS, 19th, 1900
Winans, H.W.	Pvt.	H, 24th Iowa	270		1914	IA, 41st, 1915
Winans, Ira W.J.		B, 31st Ind.	36		1902 Apr 4	KS, 22nd, 1903
Wince, Phillip W.	Pvt.	A, 129th Ill. Inf.	57		1914 Nov 5	IA, 41st, 1915
Winch, Frederick		D, 27th Iowa Inf.	25	76	1917 Jun 4	NE, 42nd, 1918
Winch, Wm.			91		1923 Oct 29	IA, 50th, 1924
Winchel, John	Pvt.		231		1929 Oct 8	IA, 56th, 1930
Winchel, John K.		B, 132nd Ill.	52		1928 Nov 3	NE, 53rd, 1929
Winchell, Abner			56		1913	KS, 33rd, 1914
Winchell, D.A.			267		1926 Jan 26	IA, 53rd, 1927

Name	Rank	Company, Regiment or Ship	Post*	Age	Death Date†	Journal
Winchell, E.S.		F, 12th Iowa	342		1885	KS, 5th, 1886
Winchester, A.		14th U.S. Colored Inf.	241		1900 Jun 3	KS, 20th, 1901
Winchester, Alexander		G, 12th U.S. Colo. Inf.	321		1918	KS, 38th, 1919
Winchester, Isaac A.		B, 85th Ill.	127		1921 Jul 25	KS, 41st, 1922
Winck, Jacob	Pvt.	A, 5th Iowa Inf.	110		1902 Jul 27	IA, 29th, 1903
Windbigler, J.L.		B, 142nd Ind. Inf.	81		1925 Nov 27	KS, 45th, 1926
Windecker, John	Pvt.	A, 46th Ill. Inf.	141		1922 Feb 15	IA, 49th, 1923
Windell, Wm.		D, 46th Ill. Inf.	84	58	1901 Mar	NE, 26th, 1902
Winder, J.E.	Pvt.	D, 17th Iowa Inf.	10		1919 May 20	IA, 46th, 1920
Winders, Henry C.	2nd Lieut.	H, 2nd Colored Kans.	1		1906 Nov 17	KS, 26th, 1907
Windham, Robert Baxter		K, 46th Iowa (died of general breakdown; see Appendix D)	45	78	1925	NE, 50th, 1926
Windhorst, John		K, 9th Ind.	5		1912 Mar 4	KS, 32nd, 1913
Windmiller, Chard	Pvt.	H, 49th Mo. Inf.	98		1912 Jun 8	IA, 39th, 1913
Windnes, J.	Pvt.	G, 16th Iowa Inf.	78		1910 Dec 31	IA, 37th, 1911
Windsor, David		B, 91st N.Y.	293		1920 Apr 24	KS, 40th, 1921
Windsor, Henry C.			12		1923 Jul 19	IA, 50th, 1924
Windsor, Zacharias		E, 8th Ind.	63		1913 Sep 21	KS, 33rd, 1914
Wineband, John		F, 25th Iowa	69		1925	KS, 45th, 1926
Winegar, G.W.	Pvt.	K, 15th Wis. Inf.	452		1930 Dec 15	IA, 57th, 1931
Wineke, H.J.	Pvt.	B, 14th Iowa	8		1923 Feb 19	IA, 50th, 1924
Winekroop, Geo.		F, 62nd Ill.	8		1928 Apr 8	KS, 48th, 1929
Wineland, John		F, 23rd Iowa	69		1926 Mar 2	KS, 46th, 1927
Winfield, S.		F, 138th Ind.	129		1904 Jun 8	KS, 24th, 1905
Wing, A.E.			463		1923	KS, 43rd, 1924
Wing, D.E.	Pvt.	G, 74th Ill. Inf.	215		1901 Apr 6	IA, 27th, 1901
Wing, Guy		G, 100th N.Y.	2		1922 Nov 20	KS, 43rd, 1924
Wing, Harrison		A, 95th Ill. Inf. (died of heart failure)	60	81	1921 Jun 17	NE, 46th, 1922
Wing, Hiram		8th Ohio	294		1909 Dec 18	KS, 29th, 1910
Wing, J.H.			129		1929 Jun 20	KS, 49th, 1930
Wing, Jesse P.	Pvt.	D, 112th Ill. Inf.	16	42	1888 Apr 29	IA, 15th, 1889
Wing, John P.	Pvt.	H, 140th N.Y. Inf.	497		1915 May 5	IA, 42nd, 1916
Wing, Seneca		I, 35th Wis. (died of diabetes)	60	76	1912 Aug 1	NE, 37th, 1913
Winger, J.W.		2nd Penn. Art.	25		1905 Apr 29	NE, 31st, 1907
Winger, J.W.	Capt.	2nd Penn. Art.	25		1905 Apr 29	NE, 30th, 1906
Wingert, Henry		E, 178th Ohio	89		1896 May 23	KS, 16th, 1897
Wingett, T.A.		K, 16th Penn.	57		1919 Aug 26	KS, 39th, 1920
Wingfield, Cicero	Pvt.	D, 28th Iowa Inf.	40		1928 Jan 29	IA, 55th, 1929
Wingfield, James	Pvt.	B, 91st Ill. Inf.	67	87	1931 Nov 13	IA, 58th, 1932
Wingrove, Wm.	Pvt.	F, 15th Iowa Inf.	464	67	1891 Jul 12	IA, 18th, 1892
Winkels, Ben		C, 7th Kans. Cav.	130		1904 Mar 4	KS, 24th, 1905
Winkle, Fred	Pvt.	E, 9th Wis.	284		1928	IA, 55th, 1929
Winklepleck, Sam'l		E, 2nd Kans. Battery & Cav.	32		1905 Sep 19	KS, 25th, 1906
Winkler, Geo. J.		I, 101st Penn.	9		1931 Oct 17	KS, 51st, 1932
Winkler, Geo. J.		I, 101st Penn.	9		1931 Oct 17	KS, 52nd, 1933
Winkler, Henry		I, 27th Wis. Inf. (died of pneumonia)	81		1893 Oct 9	NE, 18th, 1894
Winkler, J.W.	Pvt.	E, 20th Ill. Inf. E, 66th Ill. Inf.	252	50	1895 Mar 31	IA, 22nd, 1896
Winkler, Sidney	Pvt.	G, 27th Iowa Inf.	200	62	1887 Jul 10	IA, 15th, 1889
Winkley, Wm.	Pvt.	H, 27th Iowa Inf.	290		1911 Oct 11	IA, 38th, 1912
Winn, A.G.		I, 143rd Ill. Inf. (died of cancer)	68	64	1906 Dec 4	NE, 31st, 1907
Winn, Frank	Pvt.	E, 3rd Iowa Cav.	279		1914 Oct 26	IA, 41st, 1915
Winn, J.M.			69		1926	IA, 53rd, 1927
Winn, James		K, 46th Ky. Inf.	10		1886	KS, 6th, 1887
Winn, Peter	Pvt.	E, 50th Ill. Inf.	69	48	1891 Jan 20	IA, 18th, 1892
Winne, F.		G, 11th Kans.	36		1927 Jul 20	KS, 47th, 1928
Winner, J.C.		K, 37th Ind. Inf.	440		1913 Sep 15	IA, 40th, 1914
Winner, W.H.			98		1913 Sep 26	KS, 33rd, 1914
Winnett, Gilbert M.	Pvt.	C, 9th Ohio Cav.	454		1910 Feb 10	IA, 37th, 1911
Winnett, Gilbert M.	Pvt.	C, 9th Ohio Cav.	454		1910 Feb 10	IA, 36th, 1910
Winnie, J.G.		L, 16th N.Y. Hvy. Art.	25		1909 Oct 10	KS, 29th, 1910
Winnie, W.W.	Pvt.	D, 177th Ohio Inf.	101		1920 Jun 10	IA, 47th, 1921

*See Appendix A, B or C for roster of post names and locations.
†See Introduction for note regarding recording of death date.

Name	Rank	Company, Regiment or Ship	Post*	Age	Death Date†	Journal
Winrott, James	Pvt.	G, —	241		1902 Feb 7	IA, 29th, 1903
Winsel, David	Pvt.	E, 18th Iowa	301		1907 Sep 12	IA, 34th, 1908
Winsker, Wm.	Pvt.	C, 106th Ill. Inf.	234	56	1892 Feb 8	IA, 18th, 1892
Winslow, Edward		F, 3rd Kans. State Militia (died at Lawrence)	12		1895 Jan	KS, 15th, 1896
Winslow, I.N.	Pvt.	H, 39th Iowa Inf.	67		1917 Nov 3	IA, 44th, 1918
Winslow, J.		E, 43rd Ind.	1		1926 Apr 20	NE, 51st, 1927
Winslow, Jabez	Pvt.	H, 7th Iowa Inf.	37		1899 Aug 12	IA, 26th, 1900
Winslow, Jesse		G, 24th Ind.	210		1893	KS, 13th, 1894
Winslow, W.G.		15th Wis. Lt. Art. (died of paralysis)	130	75	1909 Mar 21	NE, 37th, 1913
Winsor, H.L.	Pvt.	E, 1st Wis. Inf.	267	59	1892 Jan 1	IA, 18th, 1892
Winsor, Henry		I, 148th Ohio	32		1933 May 29	NE, 58th, 1934
Winsor, James H.	Pvt.	C, 39th Wis.	88		1926 Mar 6	IA, 53rd, 1927
Winston, Thomas		149th Ill.	12		1928 May 14	KS, 48th, 1929
Winter, D.R.	Pvt.		29		1926	IA, 53rd, 1927
Winter, F.J.	Pvt.	P, 10th Iowa Inf.	23		1924 Sep 14	IA, 51st, 1925
Winter, Wm. P.	Pvt.	B, 12th Iowa Inf.	165		1910 May 13	IA, 37th, 1911
Winterbum, J.J.	Pvt.	K, 13th Vt. Inf.	200		1906 May 20	IA, 33rd, 1907
Wintermute, R.K.	Pvt.	H, 11th Iowa Inf.	231		1907 Apr 7	IA, 34th, 1908
Winters, Abraham		H, 26th Ill.	156		1906 Jul 3	KS, 26th, 1907
Winters, Cornelius		F, 39th Mo.	156		1906 Feb 5	KS, 26th, 1907
Winters, Geo.		65th Ill. Inf.	99	57	1896	NE, 21st, 1897
Winters, Henry		D, 7th Va. Vols.	2		1897	KS, 17th, 1898
Winters, Isaac		D, 39th Iowa Inf.	7		1937 Jan 1	IA, 64th, 1938
Winters, J.R.		B, 46th Ind.	27		1918 Sep 4	KS, 38th, 1919
Winters, Jas.			68		1926 May 12	KS, 46th, 1927
Winters, Solomon		J, 56th Mass.	123		1931 Jan 14	KS, 52nd, 1933
Winters, Solomon		J, 56th Mass.	123		1931 Jan 14	KS, 51st, 1932
Winters, Wm.		A, 59th Ind.	239		1921 Apr 21	KS, 41st, 1922
Winters, Wm. S.	1st Sergt.	C, 15th Iowa Inf.	12		1891 Jan 4	IA, 18th, 1892
Winterstein, Wm.	Pvt.	K, 23rd Iowa Inf.	9		1917 Feb 10	IA, 43rd, 1917
Wintworth, H.P.		B, 15th Iowa Inf. (died of disability)	84	58	1903 Nov 28	NE, 28th, 1904
Winz, Jackson		C, 2nd Mo. Cav. (died of hemorrhage)	120	74	1917 Sep 28	NE, 42nd, 1918
Wipple, William	Pvt.	Wis. Inf.	488	77	1897 Sep	IA, 24th, 1898
Wirick, Hiram A.	Pvt.	K, 139th Ind. Inf. (at large)	173	94	1941 Mar 20	IA, 67th, 1941
Wirt, A.W.		B, 18th U.S. Inf.	32	77	1916	NE, 41st, 1917
Wiscarer, Geo. A.		I, 7th Iowa (died of stomach trouble)	63		1915	NE, 40th, 1916
Wisconsin, John		K, 1st Minn. Inf.	328		1909 Oct 21	KS, 29th, 1910
Wisdom, T.G.		A, 84th Ill. Inf. (died at Elk City)	128		1895 Mar 3	KS, 15th, 1896
Wise, A.H.		I, 65th Ind. Inf.	1		1887 Sep 28	KS, 7th, 1888
Wise, Christian		E, 11th Kans. Inf.	464		1899 Nov 30	KS, 19th, 1900
Wise, E.F.		I, 5th West Va. Cav.	68	93	1935 Apr 7	IA, 62nd, 1936
Wise, Elijah	Pvt.	C, 13th Iowa Inf.	234		1907 Jun 18	IA, 34th, 1908
Wise, Fred.		M, 11th Penn.	20		1897 Oct 2	KS, 17th, 1898
Wise, Fredericks C.		E, 186th Ohio	84		1910 Jan 23	KS, 30th, 1911
Wise, George W.		K, 34th Iowa	85		1913 May 14	KS, 33rd, 1914
Wise, J.D.			6		1908	IA, 35th, 1909
Wise, J.W.		F, 94th Ill.	71		1919 Mar 17	KS, 39th, 1920
Wise, John		D, 146th Ohio	255		1904 Apr 24	KS, 24th, 1905
Wise, Jonathan	Pvt.	D, 27th Ohio Inf	271		1925 Mar 25	IA, 52nd, 1926
Wise, Lafayette		H, 107th Ill.	85		1885	KS, 5th, 1886
Wise, Martin	Pvt.	G, 27th Iowa	42		1926 Nov 10	IA, 53rd, 1927
Wise, S.B.		G, 35th Iowa Inf.	231		1924 Feb 10	IA, 51st, 1925
Wise, Samuel	Corp.	B, Ill. Inf.	23		1913 Dec 30	IA, 40th, 1914
Wisecarver, Jacob		E, 13th Iowa	64	90	1934 Jun 10	IA, 61st, 1935
Wiseman, John		H, 10th Ill. (died at Ingleside)	1	76	1918 May 15	NE, 43rd, 1919
Wiseman, John F.			25		1910 May 31	NE, 35th, 1911
Wiseman, Wm.		K, 7th Wis.	25		1931 Jan 18	NE, 56th, 1932
Wiser, C.F.		K, 97th Ill. Inf. (died of old age)	120	89	1918 Oct 9	NE, 43rd, 1919
Wiser, T.F.		N.Y.	12	59	1904 Jul 10	NE, 29th, 1905
Wisner, F.O.		D, 8th Wis. Inf. (died of operation for gallstones)	350	69	1906 Mar 18	NE, 31st, 1907

Name	Rank	Company, Regiment or Ship	Post*	Age	Death Date†	Journal
Wisner, G.J.		G, 14th Kans.	51		1902 Nov 7	KS, 22nd, 1903
Wisner, J.R.		I, 15th N.Y.	13	92	1918 Feb 8	NE, 43rd, 1919
Witcher, Jackson	Pvt.	L, 7th Iowa Cav.	38		1900 Feb 10	IA, 27th, 1901
Witcher, T.K.		B, 11th Mo.	68		1911 Jan 15	KS, 31st, 1912
Witham, Amos		F, 13th Kans. Inf. (died at Vermillion)	246		1895 Jul	KS, 15th, 1896
Witham, J.C.		C, 12th Ind.	142		1927 Nov 2	KS, 47th, 1928
Witham, Otis		Navy	357		1898 Sep 19	KS, 18th, 1899
Witherell, John	Hosp. Stew.	H, 35th Iowa Inf.	140		1902 Aug 25	IA, 29th, 1903
Withers, A.J.		I, 14th Ill. Cav.	218		1928 Aug	NE, 53rd, 1929
Withers, A.J.		I, 14th Ill. Cav.	218		1927 Jul 28	NE, 52nd, 1928
Witherspoon, Thomas	Musician	58th Ind. Inf.	25		1899	NE, 24th, 1900
Withrow, M.			118		1884	KS, 4th, 1885
Withrow, M.		A, 73rd Ind. Inf.	118		1886	KS, 6th, 1887
Witmar, Samuel J.		G, 162nd Ohio Vols.	153		1885	KS, 5th, 1886
Witmer, F.R.	Pvt.	B, 214th Penn. Inf.	16		1928 May 31	IA, 55th, 1929
Witmer, J.W.	Pvt.	H, 133rd Penn. Inf.	12		1913 Jun 14	IA, 40th, 1914
Witmer, Jacob R.	Lieut.	B, 214th Penn. Inf.	511		1911 Apr 8	IA, 38th, 1912
Witt, F.L.	Pvt.	K, 12th Ill. Inf.	12	93	1932 Sep 8	IA, 59th, 1933
Witt, Henry		A, 65th Ohio	145		1913 Mar 12	KS, 33rd, 1914
Witte, Geo.			235		1915 Sep 18	IA, 42nd, 1916
Witter, Benj. O.	Pvt.	B, 7th Ill. Inf.	26		1933 Oct 19	IA, 60th, 1934
Witter, D.F.	Pvt.	G, 4th Iowa Cav.	12		1922 Oct 29	IA, 49th, 1923
Witter, George E.		E, 55th Ill.	25		1927 Aug 17	NE, 52nd, 1928
Witter, W.L.	Pvt.	G, 4th Iowa Cav.	7	87	1931 Nov 11	IA, 58th, 1932
Witters, Geo. W.		H, 208th Penn. (died of cancer of stomach)	91	74	1919 Oct 24	NE, 44th, 1920
Wittig, Chas. M.	Pvt.	C, 1st Mo. Cav.	1		1918 Jan 30	IA, 45th, 1919
Wittkop, Frederick	Pvt.	H, 4th Mo. Cav.	240		1914 Nov 6	IA, 41st, 1915
Wittman, John	Pvt.	H, 156th Ill. Inf.	193		1917 Feb 6	IA, 44th, 1918
Witts, John		1st Kans. Bat.	38		1924 Jun 12	KS, 44th, 1925
Wittstruck, Chas. M.		M, 11th Ill. Cav. (died of paralysis)	25	71	1916 Feb 23	NE, 41st, 1917
Witworth, Wm.	Pvt.		55		1929 Dec	IA, 57th, 1931
Wochlk, Amos	Pvt.	C, 14th Iowa Inf.	386	73	1898 Jan 27	IA, 24th, 1898
Wocka, Henry	Pvt.	B, 107th Ohio Inf.	86		1925 Jan 20	IA, 52nd, 1926
Woelflinger, Geo.		E, 1st Wis. Hvy. Art. (died of pneumonia)	60	65	1908 Jan 4	NE, 33rd, 1909
Woelflinger, George		E, 1st Wis. Hvy. Art. (died of Bright's disease)	60	72	1907 Jan 4	NE, 32nd, 1908
Woffard, G.W.		G, 178th Ind.	293		1924	KS, 44th, 1925
Woffender, Wm. H.		M, 5th Mo. Cav.	255		1917 May 5	KS, 37th, 1918
Woherer, Wm.	Corp.	127th Ill. Inf.	395	64	1899 Mar	IA, 26th, 1900
Wohlford, Cyrus	Pvt.	C, 13th Iowa Inf.	168	45	1891 Jan 10	IA, 17th, 1891
Wohlgamuth, J.J.		died of old age	32	81	1910 May 18	NE, 35th, 1911
Wohrer, Geo. H.		I, 26th Iowa Inf.	23		1918 Dec 1	IA, 45th, 1919
Wolcott, Alfred W.		B, — Iowa	88		1919 Apr 10	KS, 39th, 1920
Wolcott, George W.		A, 2nd Neb. Cav. (died of accident)	133	72	1907 Apr 18	NE, 32nd, 1908
Wolcott, H.P.	Paymaster	C, —	71		1906 Mar 1	KS, 26th, 1907
Wolf, A.M.		I, 53rd Ind.	25		1923 Dec 10	KS, 43rd, 1924
Wolf, Casper	Pvt.	I, 23rd Wis. Inf.	81		1914 Oct 16	IA, 41st, 1915
Wolf, Daniel	Pvt.	E, 21st Iowa	78		1907 Jun 3	IA, 34th, 1908
Wolf, Franklin		E, 149th Penn.	5		1913 May 10	KS, 33rd, 1914
Wolf, G.R.		A, 175th Ohio	13		1926 Jun 8	NE, 51st, 1927
Wolf, Geo. W.		D & I, 130th & 191st Penn. Inf.	115		1934 Jun 7	KS, 54th, 1935
Wolf, George	Pvt.	F, 5th Mo. Cav.	241		1901 Apr 21	IA, 28th, 1902
Wolf, George	Pvt.	E, 5th Iowa Cav.	184		1904 Dec 5	IA, 31st, 1905
Wolf, George W.		A, 8th Iowa Inf. (died of dementia at Soldiers & Sailors Home, Grand Island; buried in Home Cemetery)	31	58	1905 Dec 27	NE, 30th, 1906
Wolf, Gottlick	Pvt.	B, 15th Iowa Inf.	146		1905 Feb 14	IA, 32nd, 1906
Wolf, Henry		C, 47th Penn. (not a member of the department but living in Nebraska; location: Stella)			1937 Mar 19	NE, 62nd, 1938
Wolf, Henry A.		F, 10th Ohio Vol. Inf.	250		1916 Oct 30	KS, 36th, 1917
Wolf, Horace G.		B, 31st Wis. Inf.	158		1899 Aug 12	KS, 19th, 1900
Wolf, J.H.		F, 8th Mich.	57		1924 Sep 15	KS, 44th, 1925

Name	Rank	Company, Regiment or Ship	Post*	Age	Death Date†	Journal
Wolf, J.W.		D, 23rd Iowa	87		1927 Jun 4	KS, 47th, 1928
Wolf, Jerry	Pvt.	A, 151st Ill. Inf.	300		1915 May 21	IA, 42nd, 1916
Wolf, John	Pvt.	D, 71st Ill. Inf.	359		1910 Jun 30	IA, 37th, 1911
Wolf, John	Pvt.	L, 2nd Ill. Lt. Art.	283		1918 Oct 18	IA, 45th, 1919
Wolf, Lambert B.	Capt.	E, 142nd Ohio Inf.	30		1918 Aug 29	KS, 38th, 1919
Wolf, Peter		I, 35th Ill.	18		1909 Oct 8	KS, 29th, 1910
Wolf, W.			6		1921	IA, 48th, 1922
Wolf, W.A.		I, 159th O.N.G.[Ohio National Guard?]	18		1915 Nov 23	KS, 35th, 1916
Wolf, Wm.	Pvt.	G, 1st Wis.	81		1927 Nov 3	IA, 54th, 1928
Wolf, Wm. P.	Capt.	I, 46th Iowa Inf.	110	50	1896 Sep 19	IA, 23rd, 1897
Wolfe, H.C.		K, 79th Ill.	80		1933	NE, 58th, 1934
Wolfe, J.A.		D, 1st Md. Eng.	105	65	1903 Dec 22	NE, 28th, 1904
Wolfe, J.R.	Pvt.	D, 6th Iowa Cav.	179		1908 Jul 11	IA, 35th, 1909
Wolfe, Jacob	Pvt.	D, 153rd Ill. Inf.	57		1933 Jan 8	IA, 60th, 1934
Wolfe, James	Drummer	D, 15th Iowa Inf.	49	89	1931 Oct 6	IA, 58th, 1932
Wolfe, James H.	Musician	17th Ohio Inf.	26		1914 Dec 15	IA, 41st, 1915
Wolfe, John		C, 51st Ohio Inf. (died of cancer)	115		1910 Oct 26	NE, 35th, 1911
Wolfe, John L.	Pvt.	H, 1st Art.	222		1923 May 16	IA, 50th, 1924
Wolfe, L.A.		K, 3rd Va.	289		1924 Jul 4	KS, 44th, 1925
Wolfersberg, Isaac			17		1902 Jul 12	KS, 22nd, 1903
Wolff, Julius		K, Ill.	127		1911 Nov 8	KS, 31st, 1912
Wolfinger, James	Pvt.	B, 6th Kans. Inf.	325		1915 Oct 30	IA, 42nd, 1916
Wolfley, Louis		A, 145th Ohio	68		1916 Jan 6	KS, 36th, 1917
Wolford, L.E.		F, 8th Iowa Cav.	32		1927	NE, 52nd, 1928
Wolford, S.C.	Pvt.	H, 97th Ohio Inf.	8		1919 Jul 3	IA, 46th, 1920
Woll, Gilbert W.		K, 122nd —	236		1926 Apr 24	KS, 46th, 1927
Woltmire, James		H, 16th Penn.	380		1920 Jan 14	KS, 40th, 1921
Wolven, George		H, 99th Ind.	119		1919 Oct 16	KS, 39th, 1920
Wolverton, Perry	Pvt.	A, 34th Iowa Inf.	137		1919 Nov 23	IA, 46th, 1920
Womacks, L.T.			45		1919 Nov 8	IA, 46th, 1920
Wommon, F.J.		2nd Iowa Cav.	314		1916	IA, 43rd, 1917
Wompon, Robert			365		1900 Sep 3	KS, 20th, 1901
Wonsetler, Josiah		A, 6th Kans. 2nd Mo. Cav.	8		1918 Sep 19	KS, 38th, 1919
Wood, A.H.		D, 24th Wis.	1		1926 Aug 26	KS, 46th, 1927
Wood, A.S.		G, 147th Ill. Inf.	12		1906 Aug 12	KS, 26th, 1907
Wood, Abram		E, 78th Ohio Inf.	91	79	1919 Jul 4	NE, 44th, 1920
Wood, Alfred F.		K, 96th Ill. Inf. (died of paralysis)	48	84	1916 Oct 10	NE, 41st, 1917
Wood, B.F.		K, 3rd Wis. (at large)			1925 Apr 30	KS, 45th, 1926
Wood, Benj. F.		E, 3rd Wis. (at large)	164		1925 Apr 30	KS, 46th, 1927
Wood, Bingham	Pvt.	G, 22nd Iowa Inf.	455	49	1893 Oct 17	IA, 20th, 1894
Wood, C.E.		C, 171st Penn.	35		1904 Oct 6	KS, 24th, 1905
Wood, C.M.		C, 96th Ohio	85		1890	KS, 10th, 1891
Wood, C.W.	Pvt.	G, 27th Iowa Inf.	267	51	1887 Mar 8	IA, 14th, 1888
Wood, C.W.		D, 22nd Ill. U.S. Cav.	25		1921 Jan 20	KS, 41st, 1922
Wood, Calvin		F, 50th Ind.	3		1919 Jun 8	KS, 39th, 1920
Wood, Charles W.	Pvt.	K, 35th Mass. Inf.	267		1929 Jan 13	IA, 56th, 1930
Wood, Chas. J.		A, 6th Kans.	75		1907 Aug 14	NE, 32nd, 1908
Wood, Chauncey	Pvt.	A, 37th Iowa Inf.	235	80	1890 Jan 28	IA, 16th, 1890
Wood, Dewitt C.	Pvt.	B, 21st Wis.	68		1903 Dec 17	IA, 30th, 1904
Wood, E.A.	Pvt.	F, 103rd Ohio Inf.	123		1917 Mar 8	IA, 44th, 1918
Wood, E.R.	1st Lieut.	A, 53rd Wis. Inf.	339		1906 Nov 25	IA, 33rd, 1907
Wood, E.R.			337		1911 Mar 24	KS, 31st, 1912
Wood, E.W.		E, 3rd Kans. State Militia	12		1902 Oct 31	KS, 22nd, 1903
Wood, Edgar		H, 16th Wis.	165		1928 Feb 9	NE, 52nd, 1928
Wood, Edgar		H, 16th Wis.	165		1928 Feb 9	NE, 53rd, 1929
Wood, F.P.	Sergt.	H, 8th Ky. Inf.	462		1903 Nov 27	IA, 30th, 1904
Wood, F.W.	Pvt.	L, 6th Iowa Cav.	7		1912 Jun 29	IA, 39th, 1913
Wood, G.J.		D, 1st Kans. Art.	50		1898 Feb 27	KS, 18th, 1899
Wood, Henry		E, 21st N.Y.	89		1905 Dec 3	KS, 25th, 1906
Wood, I.L.		G, 179th Ohio Vol. Inf. (Tekamah)			1944 Sep 6	NE, 70th, 1946

*See Appendix A, B or C for roster of post names and locations.
†See Introduction for note regarding recording of death date.
605

Name	Rank	Company, Regiment or Ship	Post*	Age	Death Date†	Journal
Wood, Ira B.		L, 9th Ill. (died of heart disease)	245	69	1904	NE, 29th, 1905
Wood, J.	Pvt.	D, 168th Penn. Inf.	398		1911 Mar 2	IA, 38th, 1912
Wood, J.			45		1923	NE, 48th, 1924
Wood, J.E.		D, 6th Ohio	113		1926 Mar 11	KS, 46th, 1927
Wood, J.G.		Squirrel Hunters, Ohio	1		1928 Sep 12	KS, 48th, 1929
Wood, J.M.	Corp.	M, 17th Ill. Cav.	31		1919 Aug 22	IA, 46th, 1920
Wood, James		B, 2nd Colo. Cav.	132		1886	KS, 6th, 1887
Wood, James		H, 58th Ind. Inf.	1		1901 Jan 8	KS, 21st, 1902
Wood, James		E, 50th Penn. Inf.	88		1916 Jan 17	KS, 36th, 1917
Wood, Jesse		H, 2nd Ill. Art.	284		1890	NE, 15th, 1891
Wood, Jno. H.	Sergt.	I, 11th Ind. Inf.	252		1886	KS, 6th, 1887
Wood, Joel			337	47	1888 Aug 20	IA, 15th, 1889
Wood, John	Pvt.	F, 10th Iowa Inf.	39		1923	IA, 50th, 1924
Wood, John G.	Sergt.	A, 53rd Ill. Inf.	127		1908 Oct 16	IA, 35th, 1909
Wood, John H.	Pvt.	K, 119th Ill. Inf.	83	62	1894 Mar 31	IA, 21st, 1895
Wood, John N.		F, 19th Iowa Inf. (died of general debility)	321		1906 Dec 30	IA, 33rd, 1907
Wood, John S.	Major	7th Iowa Cav.	169	83	1919 Apr 28	NE, 44th, 1920
Wood, John W.		I, 43rd Iowa Inf.	69		1912 Jul 5	IA, 39th, 1913
Wood, Jos.	Pvt.		42		1908 Sep 23	IA, 35th, 1909
Wood, Joseph		A, 15th Ohio Vol. Inf.	316		1910 Nov	IA, 37th, 1911
Wood, K.O.		H, 15th Ill. Cav. (died of heart failure)	253		1885	KS, 5th, 1886
Wood, L.M.			125	75	1912 Dec 14	NE, 37th, 1913
Wood, Leman A.	Sergt.	E, 10th Ohio Cav.	6		1908	IA, 35th, 1909
Wood, Lyman		F, 146th Iowa	501		1911 Sep 10	IA, 38th, 1912
Wood, M.R.		79th Ind.	65		1908 May 21	KS, 28th, 1909
Wood, M.T.	Corp.	D, 11th N.Y. Cav.	118		1911 Mar 5	KS, 31st, 1912
Wood, Martin		K, 122nd Ill.	156		1918 Mar 8	IA, 45th, 1919
Wood, N.N.		I, 1st N.Y.	339		1896 Jul 6	KS, 16th, 1897
Wood, N.R.	Sergt.	E, 3rd Iowa Inf.	265		1917 Jun 25	KS, 37th, 1918
Wood, Nelson S.		A, 28th Iowa	305		1905 Mar 6	IA, 32nd, 1906
Wood, Norman F.	Pvt.	G, 102nd Ill.	7		1893 Sep 21	KS, 13th, 1894
Wood, P.H.		M, 10th Ohio	108		1922 Aug 9	IA, 49th, 1923
Wood, P.R.	Sergt.	C, 12th Iowa Inf.	1		1927 Jan 8	KS, 47th, 1928
Wood, Parker J.	Pvt.	B, 76th Ohio Inf.	24		1919 Dec 30	IA, 46th, 1920
Wood, R.A.		A, 84th Ill. Inf.	100		1927 May 15	IA, 54th, 1928
Wood, R.R.	Capt.	C, 2nd Wis. Cav.	252		1887 Jul 18	KS, 7th, 1888
Wood, R.R.	Capt.	C, 2nd Wis. Cav.	101		1906 Jan 7	IA, 33rd, 1907
Wood, Robt.	Pvt.	M, 2nd Iowa Cav.	101		1905 Jan 17	IA, 32nd, 1906
Wood, S.W.		I, 153rd Ill. Inf.	74		1923 May 3	IA, 50th, 1924
Wood, Samuel	Pvt.	G, 184th N.Y. Inf.	477		1909 Mar 24	KS, 29th, 1910
Wood, Samuel D.		L, 7th Ohio	223		1913 Aug 21	IA, 40th, 1914
Wood, Samuel M.		I, 10th Ill.	68		1920 Oct 16	KS, 40th, 1921
Wood, Samuel S.	Pvt.	A, 7th Iowa Inf.	1		1923 Sep 10	KS, 43rd, 1924
Wood, Solomon		K, 80th Ill. Inf.	231		1915 Feb 6	IA, 42nd, 1916
Wood, W.		F, 2nd Mo. Cav.	63		1901 Apr 27	KS, 21st, 1902
Wood, W.C.			426		1888	KS, 8th, 1889
Wood, W.J.	Pvt.	I, 1st Neb. Inf.	156		1908 Jul 20	IA, 35th, 1909
Wood, W.J.		I, 134th Penn.	10	48	1885 Jul 21	IA, 12th, 1886
Wood, W.J.		I, 134th Penn. Inf.	51		1917 Aug 25	KS, 37th, 1918
Wood, Warren		A, 1st Ore.	51		1918 Aug 20	KS, 38th, 1919
Wood, William C.		K, 25th Mass.	85		1923 Aug 5	KS, 43rd, 1924
Wood, William W.		A, 11th Mich. Inf.	500		1920	KS, 40th, 1921
Wood, Wm.				94	1937 Feb 27	IA, 64th, 1938
Wood, Wm. C.	Pvt.	1st Mo. Eng.	32		1906	KS, 26th, 1907
Wood, Wm. H.		F, 59th Ill. Inf.	324		1915 Feb 21	IA, 41st, 1915
Woodall, T.N.			91		1886	KS, 6th, 1887
Woodard, Asa C.		4th Iowa Cav. (died of general disability)	36		1929 Apr 17	KS, 49th, 1930
Woodard, C.E.		B, 1st N.Y. Art.	36		1893 Jun 4	NE, 18th, 1894
Woodard, H.D.		F, 141st Ill. Inf. (Malcolm)	19		1919 Jul 29	KS, 39th, 1920
Woodard, Hibbard D.		F, 141st Ill. Inf. (member at large)			1943 May 29	NE, 70th, 1946
Woodard, J.J.	Pvt.	18th Iowa	203		1943 May 29	NE, 67th, 1943
					1921 Jul 31	IA, 48th, 1922

See Appendix A, B or C for roster of post names and locations.
†See Introduction for note regarding recording of death date.

Name	Rank	Company, Regiment or Ship	Post*	Age	Death Date†	Journal
Woodard, Sidney D.		14th Wis.	500		1929 Nov 28	KS, 49th, 1930
Woodard, W.R.	Pvt.	A, 2nd Neb.	156		1899	NE, 24th, 1900
Woodburn, D.M.		F, 58th Ohio	52		1917 May 16	KS, 37th, 1918
Woodburn, W.L.	Sergt.	E, 10th Iowa Inf.	325	61	1897 Mar 6	IA, 23rd, 1897
Woodbury, Nathan		H, 84th Ind.	5		1913 Jul 26	KS, 33rd, 1914
Woodcock, A.C.	Pvt.	D, 1st West Va. Cav.	22		1918 Jul 1	IA, 45th, 1919
Woodcock, Abner C.		A, B, 10th Kans.	22		1924 Oct 4	KS, 44th, 1925
Woodcock, Jacob		B, 21st Mo. (killed by lightning)	433		1890	KS, 10th, 1891
Wooden, Alfred			371		1906	IA, 33rd, 1907
Woodford, E.B.		M, 7th Iowa Cav.	22	90	1936 Jun 1	IA, 63rd, 1937
Woodford, Henry	Pvt.	D, 20th Iowa Inf.	1		1908 Dec 14	IA, 35th, 1909
Woodford, Samuel D.	Pvt.	I, 154th N.Y. Inf.	215		1913 Feb 27	IA, 40th, 1914
Woodin, Amos	Pvt.	B, 49th Wis. Inf.	465	92	1897 Jun 30	IA, 24th, 1898
Woodin, C.S.	Pvt.	K, 15th Ill. Inf.	57		1912 Aug 21	IA, 39th, 1913
Woodin, D.W.	Pvt.	M, 3rd Mich. Cav.	12		1912 Jun 16	IA, 39th, 1913
Woodin, James L.		B, 11th Ill. Cav. (died at Iola, Kans.; buried at Iola Cemetery)	51		1894 May 27	KS, 14th, 1895
Woodland, G.W.		C, 114th Ohio	50		1914 Jan 25	KS, 34th, 1915
Woodland, Joseph	Pvt.	20th Wis. Inf.	209		1916 Nov 27	IA, 43rd, 1917
Woodland, R.	Pvt.	E, 6th Wis. Inf.	172		1899	NE, 24th, 1900
Woodlief, Wm. H.		G, 1st Ohio	18		1912 Sep 24	KS, 32nd, 1913
Woodring, Henry	Pvt.	C, 55th Ill. Inf.	267		1914 Nov 3	IA, 41st, 1915
Woodring, J.F.	Pvt.	M, 74th Ill. Cav.	267		1925 Jun 1	IA, 52nd, 1926
Woodring, Peter	Pvt.	H, 37th Ill. Inf. (at large)	68	94	1939 Jan 8	IA, 65th, 1939
Woodring, W.F.	Pvt.	D, 13th Ill. Inf.	88		1925 Jan	IA, 52nd, 1926
Woodrow, H.H.	Sergt.	K, 29th Iowa Inf.	204		1917 Sep 29	IA, 44th, 1918
Woodrow, Henry C.		F, 18th Mich.	356		1922 Nov 20	KS, 42nd, 1923
Woodruff, C.L.		D, 15th Ill.	192		1889	KS, 9th, 1890
Woodruff, Calvin	Lieut.	A, 62nd Ohio Inf.	40		1916 Jan 11	IA, 43rd, 1917
Woodruff, E.K.	2nd Lieut.	A, 33rd Iowa Inf.	49	73	1897 Feb 9	IA, 23rd, 1897
Woodruff, Elias B.	Lieut.	F, 4th Iowa Cav.	49		1907 Jul 18	IA, 34th, 1908
Woodruff, Henry	Pvt.	B, 85th Ohio Inf.	168		1904 Aug 6	IA, 31st, 1905
Woodruff, J.H.	Pvt.	E, 4th Iowa	58		1905 Dec 16	IA, 32nd, 1906
Woodruff, Jesse		I, 33rd Ohio Inf.	67		1912 Sep 30	IA, 39th, 1913
Woodruff, O.D.		F, 74th Ill.	85		1921 Oct 20	KS, 41st, 1922
Woodrum, Nathan		A, 15th Va.	252		1926 Mar 10	KS, 46th, 1927
Woods, A.	Pvt.	16th Wis. Inf.	76		1900 May 7	IA, 27th, 1901
Woods, A.R.	Pvt.	A, 2nd Ind. Cav.	488	57	1895 Feb 2	IA, 22nd, 1896
Woods, Aaron		1st Art.	119		1912 Dec 18	KS, 32nd, 1913
Woods, B.F.		B, 9th Iowa	334		1900 Oct 14	KS, 20th, 1901
Woods, D.H.		F, 36th Iowa	172		1924 Jul 16	KS, 44th, 1925
Woods, F.M.		5th Ill. Lt. Art.	25		1928 Jul 31	NE, 53rd, 1929
Woods, George		D, 2nd N.Y. Cav. (cause of death: heart)	308	82	1914 Oct	NE, 39th, 1915
Woods, George H.		A, 140th Ill. (former member; died at Lincoln)	61		1935 Sep 2	NE, 60th, 1936
Woods, Gideon M.		K, 138th Ill. Vol. Inf.	25		1908 Dec 11	KS, 28th, 1909
Woods, H.D.		F, 36th Iowa Inf.	172		1925	KS, 45th, 1926
Woods, Harry H.		H, 115th Ohio	34		1926 Dec 1	NE, 51st, 1927
Woods, Henry			44	83	1924 Apr	NE, 49th, 1925
Woods, J.A.		C, 1st Mo. Eng.	12		1924 Oct 29	KS, 44th, 1925
Woods, J.F.	Pvt. Pvt. Pvt. & Sergt.	K, 85th Ohio Vol. Inf. K, 87th Ohio Vol. Inf. L, 2nd Ohio Hvy. Art.	34	44	1888 Jan 18	NE, 13th, 1889
Woods, J.G.		A, 5th Mo. Cav.	57		1912 Jun 9	KS, 32nd, 1913
Woods, J.N.		F, 141st Ill.	18		1926 Apr 4	KS, 46th, 1927
Woods, James		2nd Ohio Art. (died of heart trouble)	34	75	1919 Mar	NE, 44th, 1920
Woods, James M.	Pvt.	E, 35th Iowa Inf.	403		1909 Dec 7	IA, 36th, 1910
Woods, Jerry D.		D, 132nd Ill.	25		1928 Dec 15	NE, 53rd, 1929
Woods, John		G, 7th Ohio Cav.	3		1930 Mar 7	NE, 55th, 1931
Woods, John H.		B, 18th Iowa Inf.		91	1937 Nov 26	IA, 64th, 1938
Woods, John T.		F, 42nd Ill.	36		1924 Mar 2	KS, 44th, 1925
Woods, Jonathan		C, 74th Ohio	443		1910 Mar 12	KS, 30th, 1911

*See Appendix A, B or C for roster of post names and locations.
†See Introduction for note regarding recording of death date.

607

Name	Rank	Company, Regiment or Ship	Post*	Age	Death Date†	Journal
Woods, Joshua G.	Pvt.	H, 115th Ohio Vol. Inf.	34	45	1888 Feb	NE, 13th, 1889
Woods, L.B.		K, 148th Penn.	10		1932 Aug 24	NE, 57th, 1933
Woods, L.M.	Pvt.	A, 60th N.Y. Inf.	231		1908 Jul 27	IA, 35th, 1909
Woods, Lewis	Pvt.	F, 13th Iowa Inf.	140		1920 Jan 15	IA, 46th, 1920
Woods, Mitchell		B, 40th U.S. Colored	321		1910 Apr 25	KS, 30th, 1911
Woods, N.B.		A, 133rd Ohio	34		1935 May 14	NE, 60th, 1936
Woods, Neri	Pvt.	A, 38th Iowa Inf.	63		1908 Apr 4	IA, 35th, 1909
Woods, O.W.		G, 33rd Ill. (dropped dead)	1		1925	NE, 50th, 1926
Woods, Silas S.			380		1918	KS, 38th, 1919
Woods, Thomas		Kans.	292		1924 Mar	KS, 44th, 1925
Woods, Timothy		K, 10th Minn.	380		1890	KS, 10th, 1891
Woods, W.H.		B, 10th Mo. Inf. (location: Blair)			1927 Feb 8	NE, 52nd, 1928
Woods, W.S.		G, U.S. Vol. Ohio	196		1906 Jan 6	KS, 26th, 1907
Woods, Wm.	Lieut.	H, 18th Iowa Inf.	98		1917 Jan 26	IA, 44th, 1918
Woods, Wm.			32		1911 Nov 13	KS, 31st, 1912
Woods, Z.T.		gunboat Indiana (found dead in bed)	63	82	1925 Nov 20	NE, 50th, 1926
Woodseem, Jno L.	Landsman	U.S. Navy	18		1909 Feb 9	KS, 29th, 1910
Woodside, W.J.	Pvt.	M, 19th Ill. Cav.	71		1911 Jan 26	IA, 38th, 1912
Woodward, B.F.	Pvt.	Marine Corps	44		1919 Dec 4	IA, 46th, 1920
Woodward, B.W.		E, 3rd Kans. State Militia	12		1900 Oct 19	KS, 20th, 1901
Woodward, Benj., Dr.		15th Ill. Inf.	68		1887 Jun 29	KS, 7th, 1888
Woodward, Charles	Pvt.	C, 10th Iowa Inf.	231		1926 Apr 13	IA, 53rd, 1927
Woodward, E.M.	Pvt.	C, 142nd Ill. Inf.	344	49	1898 Jan 2	IA, 24th, 1898
Woodward, Frank B.		C, 7th Kans. Inf. (died at Manhattan; buried at Manhattan Cemetery)	100		1893 Mar 15	KS, 14th, 1895
Woodward, J.J.	Pvt.	18th La. Inf.	203		1920 Jul 31	IA, 47th, 1921
Woodward, J.W.	Pvt.	C, 13th U.S. Inf.	495	60	1896 Feb 1	IA, 23rd, 1897
Woodward, Jno. M.		K, 34th Ind. Inf.	46		1934 Sep 8	KS, 54th, 1935
Woodward, Joel		D, 99th Ill.	36		1904 Jul 2	KS, 24th, 1905
Woodward, John	Pvt.	I, 9th Ill. Cav.	200		1918 Apr 2	IA, 45th, 1919
Woodward, John			463		1924 Mar 10	KS, 44th, 1925
Woodward, L.H.	Pvt.	K, 102nd Ill. Inf.	88		1911 Apr 20	IA, 38th, 1912
Woodward, Seth		B, 128th Ohio Inf.	66		1900 Feb 10	KS, 20th, 1901
Woodward, Thomas		G, 31st Iowa Inf. (died of heart trouble)	118	82	1925 May 30	NE, 50th, 1926
Woodward, Wm. H.	Pvt.	E, 23rd Iowa Inf.	7		1927 Sep 22	IA, 54th, 1928
Woodworth, C.D.		E, 53rd N.Y. Inf. (died of apoplexy)	110	70	1916 Sep 18	NE, 41st, 1917
Woodworth, Edwin		E, 123rd Ill.	68		1920 Apr 18	KS, 40th, 1921
Woodworth, Geo. E.	Pvt.	L, 21st N.Y. Cav.	236		1917	IA, 44th, 1918
Woodworth, Homer S.		B, 100th Ind. Inf. (see also Appendix D)	7	98	1941 May 19	NE, 66th, 1942
Woodworth, James		F, 81st Ohio	265		1912 Jul 6	KS, 32nd, 1913
Woodworth, Matthew		H, 154th N.Y.	46		1914 Dec 21	KS, 34th, 1915
Woodworth, O.H.		died of heart trouble	284	65	1910	NE, 35th, 1911
Woody, A.C.		K, 29th Iowa	25		1925 Dec 14	NE, 51st, 1927
Woody, C.M.		A, 69th Ind.	1		1928 Aug 29	KS, 48th, 1929
Woody, W.D.		A, 4th Ohio Hos. (died of general breakdown)	1	72	1919 Jan 23	NE, 44th, 1920
Woolard, Chester		K, 89th Ohio Inf.	113		1916 May 8	KS, 36th, 1917
Woolard, I.L.		C, 15th Kans.	68		1916 Jul 30	KS, 36th, 1917
Wooldrige, J.A.	Pvt.	B, 39th Iowa	49		1921 Nov 18	IA, 48th, 1922
Wooley, David	Pvt.	G, 11th Iowa Inf.	440		1899 Oct 29	IA, 26th, 1900
Wooley, J.L.		C, 78th Ill.	226		1929 Sep	KS, 49th, 1930
Wooley, John	Pvt.	5th Penn. Inf.	150		1906 Oct 12	IA, 33rd, 1907
Wooley, Sam'l S.	Pvt.	C, 34th Ill. Inf.	329		1913 Apr 17	IA, 40th, 1914
Woolf, Aaron		I, 79th Penn.	5		1897 May 14	KS, 17th, 1898
Woolhiser, W.A.	Pvt.	F, 25th Wis. Inf.	22	57	1887 Apr 21	IA, 14th, 1888
Woolley, Wm. V.			10	84	1921 Nov 23	NE, 46th, 1922
Woolm, J.H.			143		1900 Feb 6	IA, 27th, 1901
Woolsey, H.C.		E, 37th Ill.	6	90	1934 Jul 8	IA, 61st, 1935
Woolsey, J.L.			6		1921	IA, 48th, 1922
Woolworth, J.H.	Pvt.	A, 11th Wis. Inf.	22		1915 Jul 12	IA, 42nd, 1916
Woomer, M.V.		D, 11th Ind.	240		1923 Dec 27	KS, 43rd, 1924

*See Appendix A, B or C for roster of post names and locations.
†See Introduction for note regarding recording of death date.

Name	Rank	Company, Regiment or Ship	Post*	Age	Death Date†	Journal
Woore, Henry		F, 39th Ill. Inf.	68	96, 1 mo. & 14 days	1938 Oct 14	IA, 64th, 1938
Wooster, Charles		G, 2nd Mich. (died of heart failure)	29	79	1922 Dec 30	NE, 47th, 1923
Wooster, Jacob		A, 36th Ohio	13	76	1918 May 6	NE, 43rd, 1919
Wooten, Geo.		B, 4th Mo. Cav.	98		1921	KS, 41st, 1922
Wooten, S.		B, 2nd Penn.	51		1920	KS, 40th, 1921
Worcester, A.	Pvt.	B, 31st Iowa Inf.	222		1905 Mar	IA, 32nd, 1906
Worcester, H.A.		3rd Ill. Battery	93		4th quarter 1883	IA, 10th, 1884
Worden, Amariah			63		1926	NE, 51st, 1927
Worden, Charles B.		F, 8th West Va. G, 7th West Va. Cav.	52		1919 Mar 14	KS, 39th, 1920
Worden, G.W.		I, 66th Ill.	257		1908	KS, 28th, 1909
Worden, W.C.	Pvt.	I, 5th Iowa Inf.	74		1921 Aug 24	IA, 48th, 1922
Worick, Samuel R., see Warick, Samuel R.						
Work, A.B.		D, 31st Ill. Inf.	451		1901 Sep	KS, 21st, 1902
Work, A.D.	Corp.	F, 74th Ill. Inf.	190		1913 Feb 19	IA, 40th, 1914
Work, D.C.		K, 28th Iowa	25		1933 Jul 6	NE, 58th, 1934
Work, Fleming	Pvt.	A, 8th Iowa Cav.	210		1897 Sep 14	IA, 24th, 1898
Work, George F.		B, 5th Iowa Inf.	13		1937 Dec 4	NE, 62nd, 1938
Work, J.H.	Pvt.	B, Iowa Vol. Inf.	8		1924 Mar 19	IA, 51st, 1925
Work, W.A.		U.S. Navy Sp. *Louisiana*	69		1919 May 19	IA, 46th, 1920
Workessien, G.	Pvt.	E, 17th Ill. Cav.	123		1901 Oct 21	IA, 28th, 1902
Working, D.W.		A, 4th Minn. Inf.	63		1908 Mar 24	KS, 28th, 1909
Working, Samuel K.		C, 49th Penn. Inf. (died at Abilene; buried at Abilene Cemetery)	63		1894 Aug 13	KS, 14th, 1895
Workman, W.S.	Pvt.	G, 10th Ill. Cav.	81		1899	NE, 24th, 1900
Works, A.B.		D, 31st Ill.	451		1902	KS, 22nd, 1903
Worley, Andrew		D, 9th Kans.	46		1926 May 22	KS, 46th, 1927
Worley, E.J.			292		1911	KS, 31st, 1912
Worley, George W.		K, 5th Mo. (died of old age)	123	85	1921 Jan 7	NE, 46th, 1922
Worley, J.	Asst. Surg.	26th Ohio Inf.	314		1912 May 12	IA, 39th, 1913
Worley, James	Pvt.	C, 14th Mo. Cav.	122		1920	IA, 47th, 1921
Worley, John		H, 6th Mo.	42		1889	KS, 9th, 1890
Worley, L.J.		E, 101st Penn.	63		1920 Dec 6	KS, 40th, 1921
Worley, O.H.		A, 7th Ind.	23		1928 Jun 25	KS, 48th, 1929
Worley, Robt.	Pvt.	F, 25th Iowa Inf.	115		1908 Sep 6	IA, 35th, 1909
Worley, Wesley		died at Soldiers Home	18		1896	KS, 16th, 1897
Worley, William	Pvt.	C, 78th Ill. Inf.	6		1930 Apr 3	IA, 57th, 1931
Worline, Wm.		A, 94th Ill. (died of heart failure)	13	74	1908 Dec 19	NE, 33rd, 1909
Worloy, S.T.	Capt.	A, 119th Ill. Inf.	2		1915 Dec 5	IA, 42nd, 1916
Worman, Chas. L.		A, 131st Penn.	52		1917 Apr 17	KS, 37th, 1918
Worman, Thomas	Pvt.	H, 1st Col. Cav.	63		1915 Dec 9	IA, 42nd, 1916
Wormser, M.		Mo.	266		1911 May 30	KS, 32nd, 1913
Wornom, C.T.	Pvt.	I, 17th Ill. Inf.	6		1907 2nd term	IA, 34th, 1908
Worrall, James P.		E, 79th Ill. Inf.	7		1909 May 24	KS, 29th, 1910
Worrell, A.A.	Pvt.	A, 34th Ill. Inf.	26		1929 Aug 25	IA, 56th, 1930
Worrell, E.A.	Pvt.	C, 8th Ill. Cav.	88		1921 Mar 13	IA, 48th, 1922
Worrell, James R.	Pvt.	A, 13th Ind. Cav.	16		1899	NE, 24th, 1900
Worsley, Henry		A, 132nd Ill.	88		1928 Aug 27	KS, 48th, 1929
Worst, Jacob	Musician	7th Iowa Inf.	231		1909 Oct 16	IA, 36th, 1910
Worster, Jefferson Hugh		C, 2nd Iowa Inf.		95, 9 mos. & 9 days	1937 Aug 25	IA, 64th, 1938
Worth, Fred	Pvt.	E, 5th N.Y. Art.	1	87	1933 May 21	IA, 60th, 1934
Worth, Geo. W.	Pvt.	A, 144th Ohio Inf.	26		1926 Jul 31	IA, 53rd, 1927
Worth, Mathias	Pvt.	E, 16th Ill. Inf.	8	67	1889 Apr 17	IA, 16th, 1890
Worth, W.J.	Pvt.	H, 14th Iowa Inf.	202		1912 Dec 1	IA, 39th, 1913
Worthingham, Elias		G, 155th Ill.	17		1930 Apr 18	KS, 50th, 1931
Worthington, C.F.		C, 1st Mich.	117		1918 Mar 11	KS, 38th, 1919
Worthington, C.F.		C, 1st Mich.	117		1917	KS, 37th, 1918

*See Appendix A, B or C for roster of post names and locations.

†See Introduction for note regarding recording of death date.

Name	Rank	Company, Regiment or Ship	Post*	Age	Death Date†	Journal
Worthington, Edward		A, 61st Ill. Inf.	87		1885	KS, 5th, 1886
Worthington, Elias		G, 155th Ill.	17		1918 Sep 4	KS, 38th, 1919
Worthington, J.E.	Pvt.	A, 172nd Ohio Inf.	55		1933 Oct 15	IA, 60th, 1934
Worthington, L.M.			129		1929 Apr 26	KS, 49th, 1930
Wortman, J.G.		E, 96th Ohio Vol. Inf.	128		1900 Oct 10	KS, 21st, 1902
Wortman, J.H.		D, 1st Ind. Hvy. Art.	65		1918 Aug 8	KS, 38th, 1919
Wortz, John M.	Pvt. & Corp.	B & H, 12th Penn. Vol. Inf. & 20th Cav.	88	72	1900 Jan 24	IA, 26th, 1900
Woster, J.T.F.			50		1903-1904	IA, 30th, 1904
Woy, J.L.	Pvt.	K, 5th Penn. Hvy. Art.	452		1920 Jun 7	IA, 47th, 1921
Wray, Emereth		K, 25th Mich. Inf.	209		1929	KS, 49th, 1930
Wray, Hiram			294		1922 May 2	KS, 42nd, 1923
Wreath, W.		G, 126th Ill.	271		1920 Jun 22	KS, 40th, 1921
Wrede, Chas.		F, 2nd U.S. Inf.			1928 Dec	NE, 53rd, 1929
Wren, F.P.		B, 20th Ohio	117		1921 Apr 28	KS, 43rd, 1924
Wren, Lewis		C, 45th Ohio	251		1923 Sep 8	KS, 43rd, 1924
Wren, M.N.		C, 66th Ill.	85		1921 Apr 24	KS, 41st, 1922
Wrench, John		E, 155th Ohio	147		1925 Nov 29	KS, 45th, 1926
Wrenn, R.			112		1923	NE, 48th, 1924
Wrenn, Thos. J.	Pvt.	C, 40th — Vols.	78	45	1889 Apr 11	IA, 16th, 1890
Wright, A.M.			83		1914 Mar 3	KS, 34th, 1915
Wright, Albert D.		D, 23rd Mich. (cause of death: heart)	35	72	1915 Apr 30	NE, 40th, 1916
Wright, Albert G.	Pvt.	B, 30th Iowa Inf.	100		1914 Nov 5	IA, 41st, 1915
Wright, Albert S.		E, 24th Ill. Inf.	33		1902 Feb 17	KS, 22nd, 1903
Wright, Alford		H, 71st Ill.	32		1905 Mar 2	KS, 25th, 1906
Wright, Alpha	Chaplain Capt.	25th Mo. Inf. U.S.A. (died of Bright's disease)	45	75	1888 Nov 30	NE, 13th, 1889
Wright, Andrew J.		A, 2nd Iowa	25		1924 Apr 5	KS, 44th, 1925
Wright, B.F.	2nd Lieut.	G, 19th Iowa Inf.	153	67	1896 Apr 9	IA, 23rd, 1897
Wright, C.M.	Pvt.	E, 16th Mich. Inf.	78	48	1887 Dec 12	IA, 14th, 1888
Wright, Carl C.		B, 47th Ill.	18		1913 Aug 9	KS, 33rd, 1914
Wright, Chas. A.	Pvt.	A, 19th Iowa Inf.	2		1919 Nov 22	IA, 46th, 1920
Wright, Chas. H.	Pvt.	C, 27th Iowa Inf.	134		1925 Jul 12	IA, 52nd, 1926
Wright, Chas. H.	Pvt.	C, 27th Iowa Inf.	134		1927 Jul 12	IA, 54th, 1928
Wright, D.M.		C, 115th Ill.	17		1898 May 3	KS, 18th, 1899
Wright, Dan	Pvt.	A, 93rd Ill. Inf.	67		1918 Mar	IA, 45th, 1919
Wright, David	Pvt.	C, 11th Ind. Inf.	65		1887 Jan 15	IA, 14th, 1888
Wright, E.A.		E, 44th Iowa Inf. (at large)			1935 Sep 27	IA, 62nd, 1936
Wright, E.A.		E, 44th Iowa Inf.		88	1936[1935?] Sep 27	IA, 62nd, 1936
Wright, E.L.	Pvt.	D, 26th Iowa Inf.	5		1929 May 23	IA, 56th, 1930
Wright, E.W., see Right, E.W.						
Wright, Ed	Lieut. Col.	24th Iowa Inf.	7	68	1895 Dec 7	IA, 22nd, 1896
Wright, Edgar		F, 15th Iowa	55		1917 Feb 14	KS, 37th, 1918
Wright, Edward R.	Pvt.	D, 35th Iowa Inf.	7	57	1888 Feb 27	NE, 13th, 1889
Wright, Enos	Pvt.	D, 28th Iowa Inf.	40		1905 Apr 30	IA, 32nd, 1906
Wright, Eugene A.	Pvt.	E, 44th Iowa Inf.	222	88	1935 Dec 26	IA, 65th, 1939
Wright, F.F.	Pvt.	F, 147th Ill. Inf.	124		1927 Oct 4	IA, 54th, 1928
Wright, F.W.		K, 17th Mich.	395		1935	KS, 55th, 1936
Wright, Geo.			124		1913	IA, 40th, 1914
Wright, George J.		D, 74th Ind.	69		1920 Jan 26	KS, 40th, 1921
Wright, Gilmore J.		B, 128th Ohio (died of old age)	318	79	1925 Feb 15	NE, 49th, 1925
Wright, H.B.	Pvt.	E, 2nd Ill. Cav.	23		1925 Feb 20	IA, 52nd, 1926
Wright, H.H., see Write, H.H.						
Wright, H.J.		A, 134th Ill. Inf.	7		1925 Oct 30	KS, 45th, 1926
Wright, Henry		G, 5th Mo. Colored Inf.	332		1897 Sep 16	KS, 17th, 1898
Wright, Isaac	Pvt.	D, 12th Ill. Inf.	68		1927 Apr 28	IA, 54th, 1928
Wright, Isaac N.		H, 36th Iowa Inf.	380		1901 Mar 8	KS, 21st, 1902
Wright, J.D.	Sergt.	47th Iowa Inf.	18		1905 Dec 26	IA, 32nd, 1906
Wright, J.D.H.	Pvt.	I, 1st Dragoons	124		1912 Aug 20	IA, 39th, 1913
Wright, J.F.		A, 12th Ind.	71		1916 Jun 3	KS, 36th, 1917
Wright, J.H.		H, 80th Ohio	17		1913 Apr 30	KS, 33rd, 1914
Wright, J.H.		G, 69th Ill. (died of pneumonia)	13	89	1906 Nov 26	NE, 31st, 1907
Wright, J.R.		G, 34th Ohio	87		1926 Mar 19	KS, 46th, 1927

*See Appendix A, B or C for roster of post names and locations.
†See Introduction for note regarding recording of death date.

No Joshua Wright

Name	Rank	Company, Regiment or Ship	Post*	Age	Death Date†	Journal
Wright, J.R.		8th Ohio	13		1927 Aug 1	NE, 52nd, 1928
Wright, J.S.	Pvt.	B, 30th Iowa Inf.	271	47	1887 Oct 29	IA, 14th, 1888
Wright, J.W.		G, 6th Iowa Cav.	255		1st quarter 1884	IA, 10th, 1884
Wright, Jacob	Pvt.	C, 4th Iowa Cav.	20		1906	IA, 33rd, 1907
Wright, James	Sergt.	D, 1st Iowa Inf.	56	90	1932	IA, 58th, 1932
Wright, James		H, 5th Kans.	125		1910 Dec 1	KS, 30th, 1911
Wright, James			[180?]		1932	KS, 52nd, 1933
Wright, Jno. J.	Pvt.	D, 10th Ohio Inf.	440	43	1889 Oct 1	IA, 16th, 1890
Wright, John			515		1919 Sep	IA, 46th, 1920
Wright, John		B, 86th Ill.	57		1893 Nov 18	KS, 13th, 1894
Wright, John B.		I, 28th Iowa	25		1927 Mar 22	NE, 52nd, 1928
Wright, John C.		C, 57th Ind.	255		1916 Mar 7	KS, 36th, 1917
Wright, John G.		C, 38th Iowa Inf.	132	98	1936 Jul 9	IA, 63rd, 1937
Wright, John P.	Pvt.	F, 29th Iowa Inf.	10		1913 Jul 31	IA, 40th, 1914
Wright, John W.		B, 10th Iowa	18		1919 Apr 29	KS, 39th, 1920
Wright, Jos. C.	Pvt.	B, 31st Iowa Inf.	298		1911 May 7	IA, 38th, 1912
Wright, K.D.	Pvt.	F, 13th Iowa	497		1922 Jun 22	IA, 49th, 1923
Wright, Lyman	Pvt.	D, 35th Iowa Inf.	304	46	1887 Oct 4	IA, 14th, 1888
Wright, M.D.	Corp.	C, 1st N.Y. Lt. Art.	58		1909 Jul 21	IA, 36th, 1910
Wright, M.K.		D, 168th Ohio	57		1916 Jan 17	KS, 36th, 1917
Wright, Mark W.	Pvt.	C, 44th Iowa Inf.	78		1913 Sep 21	IA, 40th, 1914
Wright, O.H.		B, 12th Mich. Inf. (died of general breakdown)	155	86	1920 Sep 27	NE, 45th, 1921
Wright, O.P.	Pvt.	A, 47th Iowa Inf.	49		1927 Feb 17	IA, 54th, 1928
Wright, Oscar		I, 48th Ill. (died of old age)	36	77	1913 Jul	NE, 38th, 1914
Wright, Owen T.		D, 14th Ind.	293		1910 Dec 20	KS, 30th, 1911
Wright, P.S.	Pvt.	C, 27th Ind. Cav.	440		1908 Mar 1	IA, 35th, 1909
Wright, Rich	Pvt.	M, 5th Iowa Cav.	452		1922 Mar 27	IA, 49th, 1923
Wright, Richard N.		L, 9th Iowa Cav.	25		1940 Jul 14	NE, 65th, 1941
Wright, Robert W., Dr.		C, 9th Iowa (see also Appendix D)	150		1906 Mar 24	KS, 25th, 1906
Wright, Samuel		I, 5th Md. Inf. (died of heart failure)	81	59	1895 Oct 21	NE, 20th, 1896
Wright, Samuel L.		B, 7th Minn. Inf. (died at Independence; buried at Mt. Hope Cemetery)	4		1894 Jun 18	KS, 14th, 1895
Wright, T.A.	Pvt.	A, 37th Ind.	29		1923 Dec 11	IA, 50th, 1924
Wright, T.J.		F, 38th Ill. Inf.	338	52	1896 May 7	NE, 21st, 1897
Wright, Thomas			218		1883	KS, 3rd, 1884
Wright, V.H.	Pvt.	K, 8th Iowa Cav.	63		1921 Jul 26	IA, 48th, 1922
Wright, W.C.	Pvt.	4th Iowa Cav.	10		1926	IA, 53rd, 1927
Wright, W.G.		E, 34th Penn.	14		1898 Jun 23	KS, 18th, 1899
Wright, W.J.			68		1899 Apr 24	KS, 19th, 1900
Wright, W.K.		H, 112th Ill. Inf.	113		1903 Dec 12	NE, 28th, 1904
Wright, W.T.	Pvt.	E, 70th Ohio Inf.	66		1916 Jul 6	IA, 43rd, 1917
Wright, W.W.	Pvt.	H, 9th Iowa Cav.	7		1924 Feb 22	IA, 51st, 1925
Wright, William E.	Sergt.	B, 3rd Iowa Inf.	49		1901 Jun 19	IA, 28th, 1902
Wright, Wm.	Pvt.	C, 12th Ill. Cav.	171	80	1887 Oct 5	IA, 14th, 1888
Write, H.H.	Lieut.	D, 6th Iowa	122		1905 Apr 28	IA, 32nd, 1906
Wulfekuhler, Fred		A, 3rd Mo.	6		1927 May 12	KS, 47th, 1928
Wunderlich, J.C.		C, 35th Iowa (died of blood poisoning)	10	72	1913 Sep 30	NE, 38th, 1914
Wundoff, Geo.	Pvt.	C, 24th Iowa Inf.	222		1912 Nov 20	IA, 39th, 1913
Wuthring, J.W.		C, 57th Ill.	47		1918 Aug 20	KS, 38th, 1919
Wutner, John	Pvt.	B, 54th Ill. Inf.	139	58	1897 Feb 12	IA, 23rd, 1897
Wyant, H.S.	Pvt.	B, 64th Ill. Inf.	145		1906 Dec 11	IA, 33rd, 1907
Wyant, M.B.		G, 52nd Ohio	50		1927	KS, 47th, 1928
Wyant, Samuel	Pvt.	K, 107th Penn. Inf.	31		1913 May	IA, 40th, 1914
Wyant, W.W.		D, 11th Mich.	293		1912 Aug 15	KS, 32nd, 1913
Wyatt, Daniel Franklin	Pvt.	B, 36th Ohio Inf. (see also Appendix D)	1	67	1906 Jan 10	KS, 26th, 1907
Wyatt, Davis		G, 42nd Ill.	76		1916 Jul 1	KS, 36th, 1917
Wyatt, Frank			64		1906 Mar 6	IA, 33rd, 1907
Wyatt, John		146th Ind. Inf.	4		1899 Dec 11	KS, 19th, 1900
Wyckofef, Wm.		B, 2nd U.S.	240		1904 Apr 4	KS, 24th, 1905
Wyckoff, Edward		F, 16th Ill. Inf. (died of cancer)	298		1893 Jul 5	NE, 18th, 1894
Wyckoff, Simon Dennis		K, 2nd Iowa Inf. (at large)	302	90	1937 Feb 16	IA, 64th, 1938

Name	Rank	Company, Regiment or Ship	Post*	Age	Death Date†	Journal
Wyckoff, Thos. R.	Pvt.	G, 129th Ill. Inf.	60		1899	NE, 24th, 1900
Wyckoff, W.H.		A, 78th Ill.	85		1922 Sep 20	KS, 42nd, 1923
Wycoff, Henry	Pvt.	B, 30th Ill. Inf.	49		1917 Sep 19	IA, 44th, 1918
Wycoff, W.		H, 3rd Iowa Cav.	378		1927	KS, 47th, 1928
Wycoff, William		I, 47th Iowa	180		1914 Mar 26	KS, 34th, 1915
Wycoff, Wm.		K, 3rd Iowa	378		1928	KS, 48th, 1929
Wykoff, John N.	Sergt.	C, 22nd Iowa	12		1907 Apr 6	IA, 34th, 1908
Wykoff, Wm. R.			29		1914 Jul 18	IA, 41st, 1915
Wylie, James E.		G, 106th Ill. Inf. (died of Bright's disease)	91	82	1917 Oct 30	NE, 42nd, 1918
Wyman, C.L.		A, 12th Ill. Cav.	142		1900 Nov 2	KS, 20th, 1901
Wyman, Henry C.		E, 8th Iowa	112		1926 Dec	NE, 51st, 1927
Wyman, Horance		6, 11th Kans.	66		1904 Jun 29	KS, 24th, 1905
Wymark, Wm.	Pvt.	F, 14th Iowa Inf.	246	64	1897 Oct 14	IA, 24th, 1898
Wymore, C.S.		2nd Kans.	170		1908 Mar	KS, 28th, 1909
Wymore, John W.	Pvt.	C, 40th Iowa Inf.	59		1929 Jun 10	IA, 56th, 1930
Wymore, S.N.	Pvt.	K, 33rd & 34th Iowa Inf.	399		1927	IA, 54th, 1928
Wynkoop, John	Pvt.	K, 11th Ind.	440		1901 Aug 7	IA, 28th, 1902
Wynn, Henry		F, 45th Ill. Inf.	66		1912 Sep 30	KS, 32nd, 1913
Yager, H.C.		E, 7th Penn. (died at Kansas City)	28		1895 Feb 16	KS, 15th, 1896
Yale, Francis B.		G, 8th Iowa Inf.	25		1908 Mar 30	NE, 33rd, 1909
Yale, Frank B.		E, 8th Iowa Inf. (died of heart failure)	41	64	1908 Apr 10	NE, 33rd, 1909
Yancey, John		K, 45th Ill. Inf.	354	64	1906 Mar 18	NE, 31st, 1907
Yancey, John		K, 45th Inf.	7		1906 Mar 8	NE, 31st, 1907
Yarger, Israel	1st Sergt.	F, 40th Iowa Vol. Inf.	56	65	1898 Dec 18	IA, 25th, 1899
Yargus, Wm.	Pvt.	F, 3rd Ill. Inf.	246		1911 Oct 23	IA, 38th, 1912
Yarham, William		E, 133rd Ill.	111		1914 Jul 9	KS, 34th, 1915
Yarnell, David	Sergt.	F, 44th Ind. Inf.	133	53	1899 Feb 16	IA, 25th, 1899
Yarner, W.H.	Pvt.	11th Ohio Inf.	108		1921 Sep 11	IA, 48th, 1922
Yarno, Ezra		F, 156th Ill. Inf. (died of cancer of stomach)	23	61	1909 Aug 12	NE, 34th, 1910
Yarrow, Carl	Pvt.	G, 35th Mass. Inf.	1		1925 Nov 9	IA, 52nd, 1926
Yarrow, F.	Pvt.	G, 35th Mass. Inf.	1		1926 Jan	IA, 53rd, 1927
Yates, Andrew E.	Pvt.	A, 3rd Iowa Cav.	400	93	1936 Jan 3	IA, 65th, 1939
Yates, Elias	Pvt.	A, 100th Ill. Inf.	40	63	1893 Jun 30	IA, 20th, 1894
Yates, John		G, 16th Ky. Inf. (died of pneumonia)	84	56	1895 Jan 1	NE, 20th, 1896
Yates, John W.		I, 137th Md. (died of paralysis)	22	77	1921 Dec 9	NE, 46th, 1922
Yates, Joshua O.	Pvt.	A, 90th Ohio Inf.	113	64	1892 May 14	IA, 19th, 1893
Yates, LeRoy	Lieut.	6th Ky.	130		1897 Feb 21	KS, 17th, 1898
Yates, W.J.		G, 137th Ind.	57		1926 Feb 20	KS, 46th, 1927
Yates, W.W.		A, 2nd Ill. Lt. Art. (died of paralysis)	50		1894 Jun 30	NE, 19th, 1895
Yates, William J.		G, 137th Ind.	22		1926 Feb 20	NE, 51st, 1927
Yates, Wm. H.	Pvt.	I, 40th Wis.	124		1926 Jul 9	IA, 53rd, 1927
Yatmas, A.H.	Pvt.	K, 1st N.Y. Cav.	440		1920 Feb 8	IA, 47th, 1921
Yauger, Jacob A.		B, 141st N.Y.	448		1919 Jun 4	KS, 39th, 1920
Yaw, John L.		E, 17th Mich.	130		1911 Jan 13	KS, 31st, 1912
Yeager, A.B.		D, 11th Ind.	4		1909 Sep	KS, 29th, 1910
Yeager, B.	Pvt.	H, 1st Iowa Inf.	54	61	1897 May 6	IA, 24th, 1898
Yeager, Cornelius		B, 15th Iowa	94		1922 Oct 22	IA, 49th, 1923
Yeager, Geo. M.		H, 1st Ohio Hvy. Art.	386		1892 Apr 6	KS, 13th, 1894
Yeager, John		D, 12th Ill. Inf. (died of heart failure)	13	79	1920 Oct 10	NE, 45th, 1921
Yeager, Joseph	Pvt.	G, 11th Iowa Inf.	440	57	1895 May 26	IA, 22nd, 1896
Yeakle, S.K.	Pvt.	H, 3rd Penn. Res.	156		1911 Dec 21	IA, 38th, 1912
Yearick, John	Pvt.	E, 28th Iowa Inf.	8		1926 Jan 3	IA, 53rd, 1927
Yearin, Frederick		M, 2nd Iowa Cav.	344		1892 Sep 26	KS, 12th, 1893
Yeatman, G.			13		1886	NE, 11th, 1887
Yeauger, W.B.	Pvt.	G, 116th Ohio Inf.	122	85	1931 Apr 24	IA, 58th, 1932
Yegge, Joseph	Pvt.	H, 26th Iowa Inf.	44	58	1893 Feb 19	IA, 19th, 1893
Yehner, Conrad		D, 16th Kans.	29		1893 Oct 28	KS, 13th, 1894
Yeho, S.S.		C, 6th Mo. Inf.	235	95	1935 Jan 18	IA, 62nd, 1936
Yeley, Geo.	Pvt.	I, 12th Iowa Inf.	1		1921 Feb 4	IA, 48th, 1922
Yelland, Albert	Pvt.	H, 2nd Ill. Hvy. Art.	42		1925 Nov 21	IA, 52nd, 1926
Yenler, Martin	Pvt.	M, 2nd Iowa Cav.	311	40	1887 Mar 5	IA, 14th, 1888

*See Appendix A, B or C for roster of post names and locations.
†See Introduction for note regarding recording of death date.

Name	Rank	Company, Regiment or Ship	Post*	Age	Death Date†	Journal
Yenter, Martin	Pvt.	M, 2nd Iowa Cav.	311	40	1887 Mar 5	IA, 17th, 1891
Yeoman, F.F.		136th Ind. Inf. (died of consumption)	132	64	1903 Apr	NE, 28th, 1904
Yeoman, I.		H, 11th Wis.	17		1911 Nov 23	KS, 31st, 1912
Yeoman, J.A.O.	Capt.	A, 1st Ohio Cav.	236		1900 Nov 17	IA, 27th, 1901
Yeomans, Charles		H, 51st Ohio Inf.	36		1914 Aug 26	KS, 34th, 1915
Yeomans, S.P.	Sergt.	7th Iowa Cav.	3		1903 Sep 8	IA, 30th, 1904
Yeryan, John H.		G, 69th Ind.	25		1926 Feb 22	KS, 46th, 1927
Yetley, C.J.			94		1928 Mar 6	IA, 55th, 1929
Yetts, Theodore F.	Pvt. Pvt.	K, 116th Ind. Inf. K, 129th Ind. Inf. (at large)	323	94	1941 Jun 23	IA, 67th, 1941
Yieth, Wm.	Pvt.	Wis. Lt. Art.	379	53	1895 Dec 24	IA, 22nd, 1896
Yochum, Nicholas	Pvt.	C, 2nd Batt., 16th U.S. Inf.	139, 29	95	1939 Sep 23	IA, 66th, 1940
Yockey, John	Pvt.	G, 22nd Iowa Inf.	322	90	1933 Mar 28	IA, 60th, 1934
Yocum, Frederick		G, 14th Ind. (died of cancer of stomach)	96	83	1922 Dec 31	NE, 47th, 1923
Yocum, I.		E, 75th Ill. Inf.	133		1920 May	IA, 48th, 1922
Yocum, Joseph		E, 62nd Ohio	13		1926 Apr 30	NE, 51st, 1927
Yoder, A.J.			54		1918 Dec 7	KS, 38th, 1919
Yoder, James		D, 85th Penn. Art.	262	76	1914 Aug 21	NE, 39th, 1915
Yoder, Josiah		F, 129th Ill.	113		1911 Sep 10	KS, 31st, 1912
Yoder, S.C.	Pvt.	I, 101st Penn.	12		1921 Mar 10	IA, 48th, 1922
Yoders, W.N.	Sergt.	A, 18th Penn. Cav.	116	89	1932 Dec 11	IA, 59th, 1933
Yoe, W.T.		K, 137th Ill.	4		1923 Apr 29	KS, 43rd, 1924
Yohng, B.C.		C, 87th Ind. Inf.	231		1924 Feb 10	IA, 51st, 1925
Yonley, Jesse		G, 51st Ohio Inf.	63		1887 Dec 27	KS, 7th, 1888
Yontz, Edwin A.		92nd Ill. Inf.	77		1918 Jan	NE, 43rd, 1919
York, A.	Pvt.	H, 2nd Mo. Inf.	100		1920 Dec 29	IA, 47th, 1921
York, Andrew J.	Pvt.	B, 86th Ind. Inf.	74		1923 Feb 18	IA, 50th, 1924
York, Eli		C, 40th Ill. Inf.	274		1899 Aug 20	KS, 19th, 1900
York, Geo. E.	Pvt.	A, 3rd Iowa Cav.	100		1917 Mar 10	IA, 44th, 1918
York, Matthew D.		I, 94th Ill. Inf.	244		1930 Aug 3	KS, 50th, 1931
York, N.	Pvt.		321		1910 Dec 10	IA, 37th, 1911
York, W.A.	Pvt.	I, 40th Iowa Inf.	452		1928 Apr 25	IA, 55th, 1929
Yost, L.M.			36		1929 Jun 23	KS, 49th, 1930
Young, A.F.	Corp.	A, 14th Ill. Cav.	189	47	1893 Mar 18	IA, 19th, 1893
Young, A.F.	Corp.	A, 14th Ill. Cav.	189	48	1893 Mar 18	IA, 21st, 1895
Young, A.F.	Pvt.	H, 42nd Wis. Inf.	111		1917 May 2	IA, 44th, 1918
Young, A.G.		B, 1st Wis. Hvy. Art.	231		1913 Apr 20	IA, 40th, 1914
Young, A.H.			108		1909	IA, 36th, 1910
Young, A.S.	Pvt.	G, 12th Iowa Inf.	132		1911	IA, 38th, 1912
Young, A. William		G, 31st Ind.	71		1924 Jul 22	KS, 44th, 1925
Young, Aaron		C, 105th Penn. Inf. (cause of death: heart)	25	60	1891[1901?] Oct	NE, 26th, 1902
Young, Alex	Pvt.	A, 1st Ky. Inf.	7		1910 Nov 19	IA, 37th, 1911
Young, Alex.		C, 122nd Ohio	1		1927 Feb 11	NE, 52nd, 1928
Young, Alexander			188		1907 2nd term	IA, 34th, 1908
Young, America	Pvt.	H, 17th Wis. Inf.	18		1904 Oct 16	IA, 31st, 1905
Young, B.C., see Yohng, B.C.						
Young, C.C.		H, 186th Ohio	[40?]		1914 Nov 23	KS, 34th, 1915
Young, Charles			32	74	1910 Apr	NE, 35th, 1911
Young, Chas.		E, 100th Ill.	175		1906 Oct 15	KS, 26th, 1907
Young, Chas. C.	Pvt.	A, 9th Iowa Inf.	74		1924 Apr 15	IA, 51st, 1925
Young, Cyras		E, 92nd U.S.C.T.	88		1904 Jan 24	KS, 24th, 1905
Young, D.M.	Pvt.	B, 21st Penn. Cav.	329		1904 Mar 20	IA, 31st, 1905
Young, Daniel		D, 4th Iowa Inf.	330		1886	KS, 6th, 1887
Young, David	Pvt.	D, 2nd Iowa Cav.	173		1899 Oct	IA, 26th, 1900
Young, E.O.	Pvt.	E, 1st Ill. Art.	42		1904 Nov 16	IA, 31st, 1905
Young, Emanuel	Corp.	B, 23rd Iowa Inf.	7		1917 Oct 27	IA, 44th, 1918
Young, Francis M.		G, 22nd Ind. (died of heart trouble)	83	76	1918 Apr 21	NE, 43rd, 1919
Young, G.A.	Pvt.	A, 7th Ind. Cav.	349		1902 Nov 13	IA, 29th, 1903
Young, G.W.	Pvt.	D, 44th Iowa Inf.	400		1929 Jul 12	IA, 56th, 1930
Young, G.W.			25		1940 Feb 20	KS, 60th, 1941
Young, Geo. B.		I, 4th Penn. Cav.	71		1930 Jan 25	KS, 50th, 1931
Young, Geo. L.	Corp.	B, 5th Iowa Cav.	78		1922 Dec 14	IA, 49th, 1923

*See Appendix A, B or C for roster of post names and locations.
†See Introduction for note regarding recording of death date.
613

Name	Rank	Company, Regiment or Ship	Post*	Age	Death Date†	Journal
Young, H.H.	Corp.	I, 34th Iowa Inf.	376		1890 Sep	IA, 17th, 1891
Young, Hezekiah	Pvt.	F, 37th Iowa Inf.	78	75	1891 Jul 14	IA, 18th, 1892
Young, Hiram L.		B, 2nd Colo. Cav.	91		1911 Jul 23	KS, 31st, 1912
Young, Israel W.		B, 13th Wis. Inf. (died of paralysis)	11	70	1911 Jul 4	NE, 36th, 1912
Young, J.B.	Pvt.	A, 48th Iowa Inf.	7		1927 May 8	IA, 54th, 1928
Young, J.L.	Lieut.	Iowa Inf.	251		1912	IA, 39th, 1913
Young, J.L.		I, 3rd Mo.	47		1929 Mar 25	NE, 54th, 1930
Young, J.T.	Sergt.	K, 36th Iowa	337		1907 Nov 11	IA, 34th, 1908
Young, J.U.	Pvt.	B, 24th Iowa Inf.	39		1912 Jul 9	IA, 39th, 1913
Young, J.W.		B, 40th Ind.	265		1911 Apr 21	KS, 31st, 1912
Young, Jacob	Pvt.	E, 2nd Iowa Inf.	69		1911 Jun 16	IA, 38th, 1912
Young, James	Pvt.	F, 39th Iowa Inf.	158		1900-1901	IA, 27th, 1901
Young, James	Pvt.	F, 39th Iowa Inf.	158		1900 Jun 4	IA, 27th, 1901
Young, James	Pvt.	1st Iowa Bat.	384		1917	IA, 44th, 1918
Young, James Cull		I, 31st Ind.	1		1911 Sep 16	KS, 31st, 1912
Young, Jas. A.		H, 1st Neb.	25	74	1917 Mar 24	NE, 42nd, 1918
Young, John	Pvt.	A, 44th Iowa Inf.	116		1905 Jan 22	IA, 31st, 1905
Young, John	Pvt.	K, 19th Iowa Inf.	18		1910 Oct 25	IA, 37th, 1911
Young, John	Corp.	G, 6th U.S. Cav.	452		1926 Oct 26	IA, 53rd, 1927
Young, John		F, 143rd Ill.	25		1929 Jun 10	NE, 54th, 1930
Young, John M.	Pvt.	G, 1st Iowa Cav.	40		1919 Jul 19	IA, 46th, 1920
Young, John W.	Pvt.	C, 19th Iowa Inf.	49		1924 Dec 26	IA, 51st, 1925
Young, Joseph		C, 76th Ill. Inf.	25		1892	NE, 17th, 1893
Young, L.D.	Pvt.	K, 8th Iowa Cav.	343	49	1892 Aug	IA, 19th, 1893
Young, Lewis	Pvt.	A, 14th Iowa Inf.	329		1913 Apr 18	IA, 40th, 1914
Young, M.	Pvt.	A, 128th Ind. Inf.	40		1920 May 10	IA, 47th, 1921
Young, M.M.		E, 46th Ind.	15		1892 Oct 2	KS, 12th, 1893
Young, M.R.			158		1919 Jan 4	IA, 46th, 1920
Young, Marion		K, 168th Ohio Inf.	39		1918 Mar 21	IA, 45th, 1919
Young, Mathew		G, 89th Ind.	318	70	1911 Oct 22	NE, 36th, 1912
Young, Moses	Pvt.	L, 5th Kans. Cav.	205	63	1888 Mar 30	IA, 15th, 1889
Young, N.A.J.			20		1913 Aug	IA, 40th, 1914
Young, N.E.		17th Kans.	221		1909	KS, 29th, 1910
Young, P.W.	Pvt.	K, 208th Penn. Inf.	44		1925 Aug 24	IA, 52nd, 1926
Young, Peter		I, 64th Ohio	74		1910 Jul 24	KS, 30th, 1911
Young, Robert	Pvt.	G, 6th Iowa Cav.	116		1917 Sep 21	IA, 44th, 1918
Young, Robert	Pvt.	E, 5th Ohio Inf.	12		1927 Jul 22	IA, 54th, 1928
Young, Robert		H, 143rd N.Y.	14		1887 Dec 25	KS, 7th, 1888
Young, Robert C.	Pvt.	G, 46th Ill.	88		1926 Jan 17	IA, 53rd, 1927
Young, S.M.		E, 144th N.Y.	127		1926 May 18	KS, 46th, 1927
Young, Samuel		G, 111th Penn.	131		1914 Mar 12	KS, 34th, 1915
Young, Samuel A.	2nd Lieut. Corp.	K, 1st Penn. Reserves G, 101st Reserve Corps	37		1901 Jan 8	IA, 27th, 1901
Young, Simon		D, 95th Ill. Inf.	25	78	1920 Nov 28	NE, 45th, 1921
Young, Squire S.		G, 21st Ind. Inf.	1		1899 Jun 6	KS, 19th, 1900
Young, T.J.	Pvt.	E, 16th Iowa Inf.	512		1914 Dec 7	IA, 41st, 1915
Young, Temple E.	Pvt.	G, 27th Iowa Inf.	440		1914 Jul 11	IA, 41st, 1915
Young, Thomas L.	Pvt.	I, 5th Iowa Inf.	176	58	1894 Jun 7	IA, 21st, 1895
Young, W.J.	Pvt.	A, 14th Ill. Cav.	50		1893 Jan 19	IA, 20th, 1894
Young, W.P.	Pvt.	K, 4th Iowa Cav.	20		1923 Mar 22	IA, 50th, 1924
Young, W.S.		M, 17th Penn.	113		1911 Nov 28	KS, 31st, 1912
Young, W.T.		I, 115th Ill.	32		1922 Sep 4	KS, 42nd, 1923
Young, W.W.	Pvt.	B, 4th Iowa Cav.	190	40	1888 May 23	IA, 15th, 1889
Young, William		H, 19th U.S. Inf. D, 10th Ind. Cav.	18		1915 Dec 4	KS, 35th, 1916
Young, Wm. A.		B, 11th Kans. Cav.	259		1919	KS, 39th, 1920
Young, Wm. H.	Corp.	D, 13th Iowa Inf.	167	96	1939 Mar 30	IA, 65th, 1939
Younglon, E.J.			95		1911 Apr 7	IA, 38th, 1912
Youngman, James T.		G, 98th Ill.	151		1914 May 24	KS, 34th, 1915
Youngman, John W.		A, 38th Ill.	25		1928 Apr 29	KS, 48th, 1929
Younker, Chas. E.	Pvt.	4th Wis. Bat.	66		1925 Jan 14	IA, 52nd, 1926
Younker, James		F, 35th Ind.	75		1893 Sep 17	KS, 13th, 1894

*See Appendix A, B or C for roster of post names and locations.
†See Introduction for note regarding recording of death date.

Name	Rank	Company, Regiment or Ship	Post*	Age	Death Date†	Journal
Younkin, Aaron S.		C, 5th Iowa Cav.	25		1941 Feb 14	NE, 66th, 1942
Younkin, John Franklin		D, 24th Iowa Inf.		94	1937 Aug 14	IA, 64th, 1938
Yount, A.H.	Pvt.	G, 147th Inf.	86		1917 Nov 9	IA, 44th, 1918
Yount, D.	Pvt.	D, 8th Iowa Inf.	206		1915 Dec 30	IA, 48th, 1922
Yount, Daniel	Pvt.	F, 8th Iowa Inf.	206		1915 Nov 30	IA, 42nd, 1916
Yount, Daniel		G, 46th Penn. (died of paralysis of heart)	265	67	1910	NE, 35th, 1911
Yovorsky, H.F.	Pvt.	A, 13th U.S. Art.	8		1924 Dec 21	IA, 51st, 1925
Yule, Erastus D.	Asst. Surg.	2nd Iowa Cav.	94	77	1891 Dec 13	IA, 18th, 1892
Yule, Thos.			35		1905	NE, 30th, 1906
Yule, Thos.			35		1905 May 30	NE, 37th, 1913
Yutzy, J.H.	Sergt.	K, 5th Penn. Hvy. Art.	22		1915 Oct 26	IA, 42nd, 1916
Zable, John		K, 11th Kans. Cav.	39		1902 May 26	KS, 22nd, 1903
Zabriskie, A.C.	Pvt.	K, 32nd Iowa Inf.	63		1915 Aug 6	IA, 42nd, 1916
Zach, John	Pvt.	H, 16th Iowa Vet. Inf.	222	55	1890 Apr 5	IA, 17th, 1891
Zane, W.L.			437		1923 Mar 10	KS, 43rd, 1924
Zane, William		F, 19th Ill. Inf.	71		1899 Apr 12	KS, 19th, 1900
Zappe, F.			472		1903-1904	IA, 30th, 1904
Zarger, John B.			100		1909 Dec 8	KS, 29th, 1910
Zediker, John R.	Pvt.	H, 11th Iowa Inf.	231	54	1895 Apr 8	IA, 22nd, 1896
Zeigenbine, Christopher		B, 83rd Ind.	1		1924 May 4	KS, 44th, 1925
Zeigler, A.M.	Pvt.	46th Ill. Vols.	371		1899 Apr 7	IA, 26th, 1900
Zeigler, Gottleib		M, 1st Ohio Lt. Art.	127		1911 Nov 20	KS, 31st, 1912
Zeigler, Jacob		B, 90th Ohio Inf. (died at Ottumwa, Kans.; buried at Hickory Creek Cemetery)	108		1894 Apr 15	KS, 14th, 1895
Zeigler, Philip		F, 208th Penn.	81		1933 Oct 14	NE, 58th, 1934
Zeilinger, John, Sr.		I, 180th Ohio (died of old age)	10	90	1919 Nov 17	NE, 44th, 1920
Zeim, William	Pvt.	I, 39th Wis. Inf.	476		1900 Nov 28	IA, 27th, 1901
Zeitler, H.	Pvt.	A, 5th Iowa	23		1914	IA, 41st, 1915
Zelle, Godfrey	Pvt.	D, 2nd Iowa	12		1909 Oct 26	IA, 36th, 1910
Zeller, E.R.		K, 167th Ohio Inf.	55	90	1935 Jul 22	IA, 62nd, 1936
Zeller, E.R.		K, 157th Ohio Inf.		90	1936[1935?] Jul 22	IA, 62nd, 1936
Zeller, F.J.R.		E, 132nd Penn. Inf. (died at Cheney)	325		1895 Jan	KS, 15th, 1896
Zellers, Jas. T.			233		1924	IA, 51st, 1925
Zentz, Levi H.		F, 36th Iowa Inf.		93	1937 Apr 11	IA, 64th, 1938
Zerbel, Fred	Pvt.	E, 26th Wis. Inf.	42		1917 Mar 14	IA, 44th, 1918
Ziders, Geo. W.		A, 1st Ill. Cav.	274		1898 Jul 29	KS, 18th, 1899
Ziegenfus, L.J.C.	Pvt.	K, 1st Iowa Inf.	88		1921 Mar 27	IA, 48th, 1922
Ziegler, A.M., see Zeigler, A.M.						
Ziegler, J.B.		A, 101st Penn.	4		1908 Dec 6	KS, 28th, 1909
Ziegler, John		C, 2nd Minn.	94		1928 Dec 22	NE, 53rd, 1929
Zike, G.W.		I, 16th Kans. Cav.	51		1904 Oct 17	KS, 24th, 1905
Zimerman, —		died of paralysis	78		1918	NE, 43rd, 1919
Zimmer, Jacob		F, 29th Ind.	90		1915 Feb 3	KS, 35th, 1916
Zimmer, Jacob		I, 122nd Ohio	52		1928 Feb 21	KS, 48th, 1929
Zimmer, N.			13		1886	NE, 11th, 1887
Zimmerer, Ferdinand		H, 53rd Ill. Inf. (died of heart failure)	112	83	1924 Nov 11	NE, 49th, 1925
Zimmerman, A.J.		Q, 36th Ill. Inf.	84		1917 Aug 16	NE, 42nd, 1918
Zimmerman, Geo.		M, 2nd Col. Cav. (born in Prussia; died in Sidney, Neb.)	12		1883 Jul 19	NE, 8th, 1884
Zimmerman, H.			172		1900-1901	IA, 27th, 1901
Zimmerman, Henry		F, 13th Iowa Inf.	235	95	1938 Mar 28	IA, 64th, 1938
Zimmerman, Henry		1st N.Y. Art.	132		1911 Apr 7	KS, 31st, 1912
Zimmerman, Henry O.			6		1910 Nov 2	KS, 30th, 1911
Zimmerman, J.J.	Corp.	E, 8th Iowa Cav.	452		1920 Jul 23	IA, 47th, 1921
Zimmerman, J.W.		H, 72nd Ind. Inf.	61		4th quarter 1883	IA, 10th, 1884
Zimmerman, John	Pvt.	11th N.Y. Battery	236	53	1894 Aug 3	IA, 21st, 1895
Zimmerman, Joseph		H, 3rd Iowa Inf.	192	91	1935 Feb 19	IA, 62nd, 1936
Zimmerman, P.J.		H, 26th Wis.	35		1929	NE, 54th, 1930
Zimmerman, S.B.			17		1887 May 30	KS, 7th, 1888
Zimmerman, Wm.		F, 81st Ind.	68		1922 Jan 7	KS, 42nd, 1923
Zink, H.C.		H, 6th Iowa	87		1916 Jun 6	KS, 36th, 1917

Name	Rank	Company, Regiment or Ship	Post*	Age	Death Date†	Journal
Zinn, Wm.		F, 7th Calif. Inf. (died of old age)	22	84	1919 Dec 11	NE, 44th, 1920
Zins, German		D, 10th Kans.	23		1917 Jun 13	KS, 37th, 1918
Zollars, Morgan W.	Capt.	B, 85th Penn. Inf.	195	74	1894 Jul 6	IA, 21st, 1895
Zoller, Michael		E, 4th Penn.	259		1920 Jun 4	KS, 40th, 1921
Zollner, John H.	Corp.	H, 11th Iowa Inf.	231		1912 Aug 9	IA, 39th, 1913
Zook, I.J.	Pvt.	H, 16th Iowa Inf.	51		1919 Jan 26	IA, 46th, 1920
Zook, Joseph	Pvt.	G, 209th Penn. Inf.	312	43	1890 Jun 26	IA, 17th, 1891
Zook, W.R.		M, 29th Neb.	113		1925 Jul 8	KS, 45th, 1926
Zorger, Emanuel	Musician	11th Ind. Inf.	1		1886	KS, 6th, 1887
Zornes, Jas. N.	Pvt.	I, 7th Iowa Inf.	452		1924 Feb 24	IA, 51st, 1925
Zoung, D.C.		D, 348th Ill.	18		1896 Mar 2	KS, 16th, 1897
Zuborg, Henry H.	Pvt.	K, 3rd Wis. Cav.	12		1916 Jun 5	IA, 43rd, 1917
Zuebler, John	Pvt.	E, 211th —	291		1924 Feb 17	IA, 51st, 1925
Zueck, James M.	Pvt.	E, 47th Wis. Inf.	409		1897 Jan 14	IA, 24th, 1898
Zumbroegel, Clem.	Pvt.	A, 1st Md. Inf.	170		1926 Nov 22	IA, 53rd, 1927
Zumbrunn, B.C.	Pvt.	F, 6th Mo. Cav. (died of general debility)	84	65	1884 Mar 15	NE, 9th, 1885
Zurcher, D.A.		G, 4th Mo.	39		1919 Nov 15	KS, 39th, 1920
Zutavern, William H.	Pvt.	C, 184th Ohio Vol. Inf.	52		1915 Apr 26	KS, 35th, 1916
Zuver, B.P.		D, 12th Iowa Inf. (died of disease of lungs & brain)	100		1893 Mar 21	NE, 18th, 1894
Zwanziger, Wm.	Pvt.	I, 25th Wis. Inf.	132		1909 Oct 12	IA, 36th, 1910
Zweig, W.		E, 1st Wis. Cav.	32		1926 Dec 20	NE, 51st, 1927
Zylewicz, Edward		A, 14th N.Y.	380		1897 Dec 19	KS, 17th, 1898

*See Appendix A, B or C for roster of post names and locations.
†See Introduction for note regarding recording of death date.
616

APPENDIX A

Roster of Department of Iowa post names and locations

This roster was compiled from several volumes of the *Journal of the Annual Encampment, Department of Iowa, Grand Army of the Republic* (title varies slightly). In cases in which the name and/or location of a post changed over the years, these changes are noted in the far right column. Please note that the roster of post names and locations was not consulted in every volume of the *Journal of the Annual Encampment*, thus this roster may not reflect all the changes in post names and locations that occurred over the years.

No.	Name	Location
1	August Wentz Post	Davenport
2	Torrence Post	Keokuk
3	Charles City Post	Charles City
4	Fred Steele Post	Anamosa
5	C.L. Matthies Post	Burlington
6	Sam Rice Post	Atlantic
7	Kinsman Post	Des Moines
8	Iowa City (or Kirkwood) Post	Iowa City
9	W.H. Worthington Post	Griswold
10	Sedgwick Post	Bedford
11	Warren Post	Clarinda
12	Crocker Post	Des Moines
13	William Hoyman Post	Clarence
14	Maxwell Post	Stuart
15	A. Ke(a)rney Post	Glenwood
16	Garrett Post	Newton
17	War(r) Post	Mitchellville
18	Iseminger (or Issinger) Post	Chariton
19	George H. Strong Post	Fairfield
20	McFarland Post	Mt. Pleasant
21	Joe Hooker Post	Des Moines
22	B.F. Smith (or Gen. Hancock) Post	Sioux City
23	Geo. H. Thomas Post	Jefferson
24	T.F. Bradford Post	Tama
25	Custer Post	Cherokee
26	Redfield Post	Perry
27	McCray Post	Prairie City
28	David Harding Post	Allerton
29	Abe Lincoln Post	Council Bluffs
30	Ellsworth Post	Ames
31	J.D. (or J.G.) Ferguson Post	Nevada
32	Clemens Post	Marysville
33	McPherson Post	Manning
34	Allison Post	Audubon
35	O.P. Morton Post	Exira
36	Wadsworth Post	Dexter
37	Charles Baker Post	Panora
38	Fuller Post	Logan
39	Myers Post	Greenfield
40	Phil Kearney Post	Oskaloosa
41	A.C. Hopson Post	Greeley
42	C.H. Huntley Post	Mason City

43	Marshall Post	Redfield	
44	Jeff C. Davis Post	Carroll	
45	Col. Mills Post	Adel	
46	W.W. Warner Post	Fayette	
47	Reynolds Post	Maynard	
48	Abernathy (or Abernethy) Post	West Union	
49	J.C. Ferguson Post	Knoxville	
50	Meade Post	Anita	
51	Thomas Houston (or Huston) Post	Redding	
52	Tracy Post	Guthrie Center	
53	J.A. Davis Post	Jesup	
54	E.C. Little Post	Independence	
55	Pitzer Post	Winterset	
56	Burnside Post	Shenandoah	
57	Garfield Post	Red Oak	
58	John A. Logan Post	Denison	
59	Beldon (or Belden) Post	Missouri Valley	
60	Jewett Post	Nevinville	
61	J.A. Rawlins Post	Creston	
62	Dorr Post	Altoona	
63	G.W. Nelson Post	Hazleton	
64	Gordon Granger Post	Grinnell	
65	Page Post	Coin	
66	Winfield Scott Post	Webster City	
67	J.G. Miller Post	Boonesboro	
68	Robert Anderson Post	Waterloo	
69	Cloutman Post	Ottumwa	
70	Lookout Post	Dubuque	
71	Wilson (or Wilston, Wilton, Milton) Post	Grundy Center	
72	McKinzie (or McKenzie) Post	Sheldon	
73	Voorhees (or Vorhies) Post	Eldon	
74	A.W. Drips Post	Maquoketa	
75	Tip Best Post	Montrose	
76	Cotrell (or Cottrell) Post	Pattersonville	1882
	Cotrell (or Cottrell) Post	Hull	1888 and after
77	F.A. Brush Post	Osage	
78	Hyde Clark Post	Dubuque	
79	W.C. Harper Post	Keosauqua	
80	E.D. Baker Post	Storm Lake	
81	J.W. McKinzie (or McKenzie) Post	Hampton	
82	S.A. Hurlbut Post	Alta	
83	Shields Post	Dunlap	
84	Shelladay (or Shelledy) Post	Monroe	
85	Canby Post	Portlandville	
86	Eaton Post	Woodbine	
87	Hoskins Post	Mapleton	
88	N.B. Baker Post	Clinton	
89	F. Bentl(e)y Post	Gilbert Station	
90	George H. Gardner (or Gardiner) Post	Nora Springs	
91	Mower Post	Le Mars	
92	N.B. Howard Post	DeWitt	
93	Matthew Gray Post	Ida Grove	
94	Frank M. Thomas Post	Marshalltown	
95	Farragut Post	Gilman	
96	E.C. (or E.G.) Miller Post	Mt. Ayr	

97	Hanscom (or Hanscomb) Post	Onawa
98	P.M. Coder Post	Vinton
99	James Cantwell Post	Wiota	1882
	John Lewis Post	Harvard	1889 and after
100	Elisha B. Townsend Post	Bloomfield
101	Tom Howard Post	Clear Lake
102	Mulligan Post	Sheffield
103	Barnes Post	Mondamin
104	S.V. (or J.V.) Carpenter Post	Fredericksburg
105	Surfus Post	Bristow
106	Alloway Post	Lynnville
107	E.F. Winslow Post	Agency
108	I.G. (or J.G.) White Post	Washington
109	J.Q. Wilds (or Wild, Wilde) Post	Stanwood
110	William Beaver Post	Tipton
111	N.H. Powers Post	Scranton
112	Ed. Hamlin Post	Wellman
113	Allee Post	Manson
114	Blake Post	Morning Sun
115	Todd Post	Columbus Junction
116	J.T. Randolph Post	Indianola
117	Col. Goodrich Post	Odebolt
118	L.C. Ireland Post	Sibley
119	Vandover (or Vandever) Post	Ute
120	A.J. Smith Post	Elkport
121	Lentz Post	Fontanelle
122	J.L. Bashore Post	Centerville
123	U.S. Grant Post	Avoca
124	Annett(e) Post	Spencer
125	J.G. Safely Post	Traer
126	Shiloh Post	Peoria
127	Wisner Post	Montezuma
128	J.M. Rentz Post	Charleston
129	Joe Neal Post	Columbus City
130	Ben Paul Post	Wyoming
131	Iuka Post	Bellevue
132	George W.S. Dodge Post	Nashua
133	Gen. Lyon Post	Clarion
134	Griffith Post	Oelwein
135	Washington Post	Adair
136	J.R. Slack Post	Irwin
137	Wayne (or Wagner) Post	Humeston
138	John (or Joe) Wilcox Post	Eddyville
139	Neitzsch Post	Little Sioux
140	John A. Buck Post	Lisbon
141	Charles Payne Post	Iowa Falls
142	Rendall (or Rendell) Post	Northwood
143	Charlton (or Chariton) Post	Richland
144	Humes (or Hurnes) Post	What Cheer
145	Bricker Post	Ladora
146	Hassendeufel Post	Guttenberg
147	Dunlap Post	Rock Rapids
148	Compton Post	Churdan
149	Hartman Post	Goldfield
150	Henry Dillon Post	Emmetsburg

151	Hayden Post	Forest City	
152	H.O. Johnson Post	Grand Junction	
153	A.M. Taylor Post	Wapello	
154	E.C. Buckner Post	Eldora	
155	Andersonville Post	Beaman	
156	Lander(s) Post	Lake City	
157	Shep(p)ard Post	Mediapolis	
158	John Miller Post	St. Charles	
159	General Reynolds (or Mansfield) Post	Calliope	1883-1897
	Mansfield Post	Hawarden	1898 and after
160	Washburn Post	Winthrop	
161	W.W. Updegraph (or Updegraff) Post	Macedonia	
162	Wilsey Post	Bussey	1883-1890
	Wilsey Post	Hamilton	1892 and after
163	C. Lawrence Post	Sabula	
164	Alf. Schofield Post	Miles	
165	J.C. Taylor Post	Algona	
166	L.S. Schuiler (or Shuiler, Shuler, Shuller) Post	Brandon	
167	R.F. Lowe Post	Sigourney	
168	Col. Hughes Post	Decorah	
169	O.P. Lewin Post	Hartford	
170	James B. Sample Post	Fort Madison	
171	Sutherland Post	Waucoma	
172	Janesville Post	Janesville	
173	Osceola Post	Osceola	
174	Virtue Post	Polk City	
175	Whin(n)ery Post	DeSoto	
176	J.O. Duer Post	Monticello	
177	Shriver Post	Vernon	
178	Sisco Post	Elma	
179	Howe Post	Britt	
180	Sully Post	Lake Mills	
181	C.G. (or C.C.) Francis Post	Walker	
182	Capt. Folks Post	Plainfield	
183	George A. Remley Post	Oxford	
184	Elisha Boardman Post	Elkader	
185	Rippey Post	Rippey	
186	William Kellogg Post	Seymour	
187	F.M. Thompson Post	La Porte	
188	Perry Wright Post	Coon Rapids	
189	Knox Center Post	La Celle	
190	W.A. Morse Post	Manchester	
191	Don A. Carpenter Post	Olin	
192	Robt. Jackson Post	Corydon	
193	A. Rowley Post	Humboldt	
194	John J. Stillman Post	Waukon	
195	J.A. (or J.J.) Adams Post	Cromwell	
196	R. Henderson Post	Bayard	
197	Harlan Post	Harlan	
198	J.D. Craven Post	Macksburg	
199	H.C. (or W.C.) Leighton Post	New Sharon	
200	Greene Post	Greene	
201	C.A. Abbott Post	Lewis	
202	Bedsaul Post	Magnolia	
203	R.L. Clingan Post	Minburn	

204	M. Summers Post	Malvern	
205	Van Wert Post	Van Wert	
206	R. Mitchell Post	Marion	
207	Bud Hazen Post	Lucky Valley	
208	Frank Nolan Post	Russell	
209	Joe Ross Post	Sidney	
210	M.S. Holtzinger Post	Hamburg	
211	Henry Keating Post	Afton	
212	Marvin Mills Post	Central City (or Waubeck)	
213	N.L. McKinnie Post	Crawfordsville	
214	H. Robinson Post	Oxford Junction	
215	Launtz Post	Ireton	
216	Memorial Post	Cresco	
217	Lauman Post	Lime Springs	
218	McCullough Post	Henderson	
219	E.O.C. Ord Post	Sutherland	
220	James Butler Post	Clarksville	
221	Lee Post	Smithland	
222	James Brownell Post	Cedar Falls	
223	Hallar (or Wallar, Waller) Post	Milford	
224	Emerson Post	Emerson	
225	J.I. Gilbert Post	Neola	
226	Winget (or Wingate) Post	Spirit Lake	
227	A.R. Pierce (or Price) Post	Glasgow	
228	G.S. (or G.J.) Comstock Post	Mechanicsville	
229	R. Crawford Post	Oakland	
230	Richmond Post	Dallas (or Dallas Center)	
231	Shelby Norman Post	Muscatine	
232	P.A. Newell Post	Birmingham	
233	John Dillon Post	Marengo	
234	Ersland Post	Cambridge	
235	T.Z. Cook Post	Cedar Rapids	
236	Ft. Donelson Post	Ft. Dodge	
237	Rogers Post	Lineville	
238	J.B. Steadman Post	Colo	
239	J.A. Patton Post	Zearing	
240	O'Brien Post	Tripoli	
241	Gettysburg Post	Northboro	
242	John Braden (or Brayden) Post	Parkersburg	
243	Robert Olmstead Post	New Hartford	
244	Denison Post	Center Point	
245	A. Kimple Post	Salem	
246	J.L. Jordon (or Jordan) Post	Hillsboro	
247	Whited Post	Belmond	
248	Upton Post	New Market	
249	Noel Morrison Post	West Branch	
250	H. Seibert (or Siebert) Post	Wilton Junction	
251	Leon Post	Leon	
252	J.H. (or J.W.) Guthrie Post	Woodward	
253	E.D. Duncan Post	Colfax	
254	Miles King Post	Farmington	
255	S. (or J., J.J., Silas) Jackson Post	West Liberty	
256	Maj. Lightfoot Post	Buffalo	
257	James P. Milligan (or Milliken) Post	Drakesville	
258	Brush Creek Post	Brush Creek	up through 1893
	Brush Creek Post	Arlington	1899 and after

259	Henry Howard Post	Strawberry Point	
260	Burke Post	Frederika	
261	H.M. Miller Post	Dysart	
262	Shell Rock Post	Shell Rock	
263	John Allen Post	Tabor	
264	Mays Post	Bagley	
265	Van Meter Post	Van Horne	
266	O.G. Hunt Post	State Center	
267	Robbins Post	Waverly	
268	G.H. Emerson Post	Vincennes	up through 1893
	G.H. Emerson Post	Belfast	1897 and after
269	R.M. Smith Post	Andrew	
270	William Carbee (or Oarbee, Crabtree) Post	Springville	
271	William Lundy (or Villisca) Post	Villisca	
272	E.S. Collins Post	South English	
273	Trego Post	Laurens	
274	Marne Post	Marne	
275	Milo Post	Milo	
276	Center Post	Randalia	
277	O.P. (or A.P.) Morton Post	New Hampton	
278	Bent Post	Sumner	1884
	J.P. Jones Post	Earlham	1889-1890
279	D.G. (or L.G.) Balding Post	Libertyville	
280	M. Hobart Post	Winfield	
281	Bevins Post	Volga	
282	C. Washburn Post	Grant City	
283	Rice Post	Conway	
284	Sac (or Gen. Wm. T. Sherman) Post	Sac City	
285	J. Conley (or Conway) Post	Goshen	up through 1889
	J. Conley (or Conway) Post	Diagonal	1890 and after
286	B. Talbot(t) Post	Tingley	
287	Campbell Post	Quincy	
288	Messenger Post	New York	
289	Hawkeye Post	Hawkeye	
290	Ed. Otis Post	Clearfield	
291	Newport Perry Wright Post	Glidden	
292	James Cross Post	Millersburg	
293	Thomas Henderson Post	Postville	
294	John C. Channer Post	Bassett	
295	John Knight Post	Castalia	1884
	Summers Post	Shellsburg	1889
296	J.C. Summers Post	Shellsburg	
297	William Dufar Post	Murray	
298	William Baker Post	Correctionville	
299	Hiram Steele Post	Edgewood	
300	Buford Post	Ogden	
301	T.J. Nutt Post	Douds	
302	C.D. Murray Post	Massena	
303	Thornton Post	Waukee	
304	Defiance Post	Defiance	
305	J.H. Ewing Post	Maxwell	
306	Davis City Post	Davis City	
307	C.H. Packard Post	Renwick	
308	Marble Rock Post	Marble Rock	
309	Lacona Post	Lacona	

310	Shenkle Post	Collins
311	E.H. Mix Post	Ackley
312	Henry Walton Post	Garden Grove
313	J.R. Castle Post	Avery
314	John B. Hancock (or Hancox) Post	Belle Plaine
315	Randolph Post	Burt
316	Lenox Post	Lenox
317	Geo. R. Taylor Post	Columbia
318	E. Harlin Post	Runnells
319	Clough Post	Sioux Rapids
320	G. Foster Post	Lucas
321	J.T. Drake Post	Brooklyn
322	Op(e)dyke Post	Rockwell City
323	Wilson Post	Hopeville
324	Llewellyn Post	Corning
325	Henry Jaquiss Post	Cincinnati
326	Thos. Canada Post	Swan
327	Albert Winchell Post	Lyons
328	Allen W. Miller Post	Unionville
329	W.C. Crooks Post	Boone
330	R. Ruckman (or Buckman) Post	Pleasantville
331	C.H. Wheeler Post	Malcom
332	Gen. Bell Post	Kingsley
333	Ed. Carris Post	Keota
334	William Prather Post	Mt. Etna
335	J.H. Wagner Post	Prescott
336	H. Ellsworth Post	West Bend
337	Orman Post	Albia
338	Ben. Kersey (or John Lockard) Post	Union
339	Kenyon Post	Sanborn
340	J. Talbot Post	Elliott
341	Jacob Nauman Post	Blairstown
342	J.M. Holbrook Post	Delhi
343	S.S. Dil(l)man Post	Toledo
344	Hemenway Post	Lansing
345	C.H. Abbott Post	West Point
346	O.R. Whitman (or O.S. Fowler) Post	Lamont
347	J. Fil(l)mer (or Fillmore or R.L. Clingan) Post	Madrid
348	Floyd Post	Floyd
349	Howland (or Lohr) Post	Lohrville
350	V. Van Pelt Post	Rhodes
351	Job Stout Post	Radcliff
352	Buckner Post	Ruthven
353	Webb Post	Persia
354	Leslie Post	Pilot Grove
355	Jas. Bell Post	Norwalk
356	Lieut. Braden Post	Allison
357	Andrew Mills Post	Rolfe
358	W. Layton Post	Oakland
359	Stanfield Post	Casey
360	S. Caldwell Post	Letts
361	Jas. Buttercase Post	Riverton
362	Chas. Mich(e)ner Post	Atalissa
363	Geo. Lyon (or Logan) Post	Brighton
364	Dick Yates Post	Shelby

365	I. Mattson (or M.A. Vanderberg) Post	Estherville	
366	Geary Post	Peterson	
367	Fairbank Post	Fairbank	
368	Clayton Post	Van Meter	
369	Cascade Post	Cascade	
370	Maj. Hutchinson Post	Livermore	
371	Harvey Dix (or James Miller) Post	McGregor	
372	Dan Hill Post	Stratford	
373	Kit Carson Post	Ashton	
374	C.R. Weaver (S.S. Perry) Post	Randolph	
375	Dayton (Capt. A. Doud) Post	Dayton	
376	Andrews Post	Westerville	up through 1890
	Andrews Post	Grand River	1892 and after
377	Charles J. Pixley Post	Rockford	
378	F.M. Paul Post	Plum Hollow	
379	Ransom Post	Farragut	
380	Hagler Post	Cantrill	
381	A. Waldron Post	Quasqueton	
382	I.R. Buckman Post	Leclaire	
383	Fonda Post	Fonda	
384	W. Hardin Post	New London	
385	Davenport Post	Woodburn	
386	Thompson Post	Reinbeck	
387	Rock Valley (or Jerry Rusk or Jones) Post	Rock Valley	
388	Lehigh Post	Lehigh	
389	Atlanta Post	Rockwell	
390	Wm. Lock(e) Post	Mt. Sterling	
391	Gen. McDowell Post	Early	
392	Wm. D. Price Post	Schaller	
393	Col. W.S. Brooks Post	Batavia	
394	I.M. Huston Post	Victor	
395	John C. (or Jesse) Brown Post	Cumberland	
396	Gen. Hancock Post	Sioux City	
397	Boyd Post	Modale	
398	Samuel Sumner (or Summer) Post	Moravia	
399	Tom Connor (or Conner) Post	Rose Hill	
400	Wilbur C. Dimmitt Post	Mt. Vernon	
401	William Cady Post	Camanche	
402	Geo. Lickey Post	Martinsburg	
403	Reese Lloyd Post	Williamsburg	
404	Albert Hobbs Post	Pella	
405	J.W. May Post	Confidence	
406	Hamilton Scott Post	Fremont	
407	Henry Osborn(e) Post	Council Bluffs	
408	John A. Dix Post	Walnut	
409	W.A. Roberts Post	Hopkinton	
410	Decatur Post	Decatur	
411	Bayer (or Boyer) Post	Sloan	
412	A. Bevar (or Bevan) Post	Deep River	
413	Pratt Post	Keokuk	
414	Robt. Provard Post	Carson	
415	Kilpatrick Post	West Side	
416	Newell Post	Newell	
417	S.F. Jordan Post	Primghar	
418	A.J. Filloon (or Folloon) Post	Garwin	

419	Houston Post	Gilmore City (or Gilmore)	
420	Eugene Springer Post	Norway	
421	J.P. Shively Post	Kent	
422	Jackson Elrod Post	Floris	
423	Gen. Geddes Post	Holstein	
424	J.M. Hedrick Post	Hedrick	
425	J.B. Sexton Post	Carlisle	
426	Weldon Post	Weldon	
427	Simmons Post	Gowrie	
428	Foster Post	Harveyville	up through 1891
	Foster Post	Tracy	1892 and after
429	Silver City Post	Silver City	
430	McMillen (or McMillan) Post	Menlo	
431	Cassius Fairchild Post	Williams	
432	Kellogg (or Gen. Wilson) Post	Kellogg	
433	Charles W. Fisher Post	Milton	
434	W.A. Clark Post	Moulton	
435	Wm. McDonald Post	Kellerton	
436	W. Fairbanks Post	Alden	
437	Abe Flick Post	Blockton	
438	A.T. Phelps Post	Manilla	
439	Erick L. Sheldahl Post	Story City	
440	T.J. Potter (or Trotter) Post	Creston	
441	Union Post	Creston	
442	Watt Truman Post	Abingdon	
443	Russell Barnes Post	Hastings	
444	Samuel Ervin (or Irvin) Post	New Virginia	
445	James Welch Post	Orient	
446	Isaiah Dodder Post	Grandview	
447	William Vail Post	Fruitland	
448	James Cantrill (or Joseph Cantwell) Post	Gravity	
449	Jonathan Roby Post	Truro	
450	B.F. Kirby Post	North English	1889
	B.F. Kirby Post	Kirby	1892
	B.F. Kirby Post	North English	1896
451	Hartley Post	Hartley	
452	Gen. Sheridan Post	Marshalltown	
453	E.N. Kirk Post	Imogene	
454	W.S. Wynett (or Winnett) Post	Dedham	
455	Robert Allen Post	Riverside	
456	Van Davis Post	Peterson	
457	John Kyle Post	Coggon	
458	Sidney Fuller Post	Oto	
459	J.B. Bonney Post	Denmark	
460	Pleasanton Post	Pleasanton	
461	Jas. Biddlecome Post	Akron	
462	Charles Schubert Post	Earlville	
463	McMillan (or McMillin) Post	Baxter	
464	Bud Smith Post	Dow City	
465	Wm. B. Griffith Post	Eagle Grove	
466	M(e)yerhoff Post	Nodaway	
467	John F. Walden Post	Mystic	
468	Jas. B. McCullock Post	Lorimore (or Laramore)	
469	Emery (or Emory) Post	Larrabee	
470	Samuel Neal Post	Booneville	

471	Bradford Post	Quick
472	Dick Rout (or Rowett) Post	Grant
473	Henry Damon Post	Shannon City
474	Gen. Geo. Crook Post	Laurens
475	Panama Post	Panama
476	W.H. M(e)yers Post	Liscomb
477	John C. Fremont Post	Brayton
478	Dorrance Post	Bridgewater
479	Vanderpoel (or Vanderpool) Post	West Mitchell
480	Pomeroy Post	Pomeroy
481	L.B. Sutton Post	Emeline
482	J.W. McLean Post	Paton
483	E.R.S. Canby Post	Gladbrook
484	Jacob Miller Post	Briscoe
485	P.S. Dow(e) Post	Garner
486	John Rutan (or Ben Kersey) Post	New Providence
487	John R. Andrews Post	Lamoni
488	A.B. Wallace Post	Dows
489	Bent Post	Sumner
490	Denbow Post	Albion
491	McKnight Post	Derby
492	A.P. Hovey Post	Monmouth
493	Winthrop Post	Winthrop
494	G.W. Roberts Post	Portsmouth
495	Monona Post	Monona
496	Bancroft Post	Bancroft
497	Lyon (or J.M. Tuttle) Post	South Ottumwa
498	F.M. Paul Post	Thurman
499	Col. Connell Post	Marengo
500	Lockridge Post	Urbana
501	J.W. Johns(t)on Post	Thornburg
502	Major Lyman Post	Crescent
503	James Miller Post	Marathon
504	Tom Clark Post	Thornton
505	H.J. Simpson (or Wall Lake) Post	Wall Lake
506	Battle Creek Post	Battle Creek
507	Jamaica Post	Jamaica
508	Jerry Rusk Post	Superior
509	Arwine Post	Troy Mills
510	Capt. Bryant Post	Castana
511	E.H. Keyes Post	Mingo
512	G.W. Young Post	Riceville
513	Armstrong Post	Princeton
514	Will Ellis Post	Delta
515	Belknap Post	Keokuk
516	Elias M. Ware Post	Bonaparte
517	S.G. Knee (or S.C./S.G. Keene) Post	Colesburg
519	Peter Van Norman Post	Moville

APPENDIX B

Roster of Department of Kansas post names and locations

This roster was compiled from several volumes of the *Journal of the Annual Encampment of the Department of Kansas, Grand Army of the Republic* (title varies slightly) and a publication titled *Roster of the Members and the Posts, Grand Army of the Republic, Department of Kansas* (1894). In cases in which the name and/or location of a post changed over the years, these changes are noted in the far right column. Please note that the *Journal of the Annual Encampment* did not always include a roster of post names and locations, thus the roster below may not reflect all the changes in post names and locations that occurred over the years.

No.	Name	Location	
1	Lincoln Post	Topeka, Shawnee County	
2	D.M. Vance Post	Hays (or Hays City), Ellis County	
3	Jewell Post	Pleasanton, Linn County	
4	McPherson Post	Independence, Montgomery County	
5	Kearney Post	Washington, Washington County	
6	Custer Post	Leavenworth, Leavenworth County	
7	Wadsworth Post	Council Grove, Morris County	
8	B.F. Larned Post	Larned, Pawnee County	
9	Lyon Post	Marysville, Marshall County	
10	Charles Sumner Post	Wyandotte	up through 1884
	Charles Sumner Post	Kansas City, Wyandotte County	1895 and after
11	Canby Post	Osage City, Osage County	
12	Washington Post	Lawrence, Douglas County	
13	Austerhaus Post	Prescott, Linn County	up through 1889
	Elsmore Post	Elsmore, Allen County	1890-1910
	Elsmore Post	Savonburg	1913 and after
14	Meade Post	Sterling, Rice County	
15	John W. Geary Post	Cottonwood Falls, Chase County	
16	Allison Post	Burlington, Coffey County	
17	Joe Hooker Post	Hutchinson, Reno County	
18	George H. Thomas Post	Ottawa, Franklin County	
19	Lyndon Post	Lyndon, Osage County	
20	Kit Carson Post	Lyons, Rice County	
21	Johnson Post	Hanover	up through 1886
	Mound Post	Gridley, Coffey County	1888-1895
	Ft. Donelson Post	St. Mary's	1902 and after
22	E.E. Ellsworth Post	Ellsworth, Ellsworth County	
23	E.M. Stanton Post	Howard, Elk County	
24	Sedgwick Post	Clifton, Washington County	
25	Garfield Post	Wichita, Sedgwick County	
26	Rawlins Post	Elk Falls, Elk County	
27	Upton (or G.D. Bayard) Post	Caldwell, Sumner County	
28	Burnside Post	Wyandotte	up through 1884
	Burnside Post	Kansas City, Wyandotte County	1895 and after
29	Ed. Lines Post	Alma, Waubaunsee County	
30	Sherman Post	Ness City, Ness County	
31	J.G. Blunt Post	Linn, Washington County	
32	Wm. H. Lytle Post	Fort Scott, Bourbon County	
33	Montgomery Post	Mound City, Linn County	
34	Jim Lane Post	Mankato, Jewell County	
35	E.P. Sheldon Post	Burlingame, Osage County	

36	Judson Kilpatrick Post	Newton, Harvey County	
37	Farragut Post	Burrton	
38	O.P. Morton Post	Wamego, Pottawatomie County	
39	Custard Post	Onaga, Pottawatomie County	
40	E.D. Baker Post	Baldwin (or Baldwin City), Douglas County	
41	Winfield Scott Post	Millbrook	up through 1884
	Hill City Post	Hill City, Graham County	1900 and after
42	Pollock Post	Marion, Marion County	
43	Reynolds Post	Cawker City, Mitchell County	
44	John Brown Post	Belleville, Republic County	
45	Robert Anderson Post	Smith Center, Smith County	
46	Will Wendell Post	Holton, Jackson County	
47	Kennesaw Post	Minneapolis	
48	S.A. Hurlbut Post	Ellinwood, Barton County	
49	Gen. Bailey Post	Girard, Crawford County	
50	Dick Yates Post	Eureka, Greenwood County	
51	McCook Post	Iola, Allen County	
52	Pap Thomas Post	Great Bend, Barton County	
53	Henderson Post	Frankfort, Marshall County	
54	Frank P. Blair Post	Galena, Cherokee County	
55	P.B. Plumb Post	Emporia, Lyon County	
56	Shiloh Post	Cherokee, Crawford County	
57	James Shields Post	Wellington, Sumner County	
58	Deach Post	Jewell (or Jewell City), Jewell County	
59	John A. Dix Post	Columbus, Cherokee County	
60	Dahlgren Post	Walnut City	up through 1884
	Alta Vista Post	Alta Vista, Waubaunsee County	1888-1904
	Kirkpatrick Post	La Harpe	1917
61	Benton (or W.H. Anthony) Post	Anthony, Harper County	
62	Jesse Nelson Post	Tecumseh, Shawnee County	
63	Abilene Post	Abilene, Dickinson County	
64	Antietam Post	Parsons, Labette County	
65	Gen. Russell Post	Pittsburg, Crawford County	
66	W.H.L. Wallace Post	El Dorado, Butler County	
67	Chickamauga Post	Scranton, Osage County	
68	Franklin Post	Olathe, Jewell County	
69	O.M. Mitchell Post	Osborne, Osborne County	
70	Gettysburg Post	Hollenberg, Washington County	up through 1903
		Labette	1908
71	Topeka (or Gen. Rice) Post	Topeka, Shawnee County	
72	Vicksburg Post	Humboldt, Allen County	
73	B.F. Goss (or Neosho Falls) Post	Neosho Falls, Woodson County	
74	Stone River Post	Sedan, Chautauqua County	
75	W.H. Earl(e) (or Eskridge) Post	Eskridge, Waubaunsee County	
76	Stockton Post	Stockton, Rooks County	
77	Phillipsburg Post	Phillipsburg, Phillips County	
78	Ionia Post	Ionia, Jewell County	
79	Brownlow Post	Gould	1883
	Brownlow Post	Severy, Greenwood County	1884 and after
80	Resaca (or Williamsburg) Post	Williamsburg, Franklin County	
81	Kirby Smith Post	Haddam	1883-1884
	Ness Post	Bazine, Ness County	1888-1895
	Parsons Post	Parsons	1898 and after
82	Gen. Strong Post	Jetmore, Hodgeman County	
83	Reno Post	Nickerson, Reno County	

84	Silas Miller Post	Canton, McPherson County	
85	Siverd (or Winfield) Post	Winfield, Cowley County	
86	Pomona Post	Pomona	1883-1884
	L.P. Wilkes Post	Dwight, Morris County	1888 and after
87	James B. McPherson Post	McPherson, McPherson County	
88	Phil Sheridan (or Clay Center) Post	Clay Center, Clay County	
89	Peabody Post	Peabody, Marion County	
90	John Goldy (or Milan) Post	Milan, Sumner County	up through 1907
	Sheridan Post	Coffeyville	1909 and after
91	Mulligan Post	Longton, Elk County	
92	George Graham (or Seneca) Post	Seneca, Nemaha County	
93	John A. Martin (or Atchison) Post	Atchison, Atchison County	
94	Col. J. Hays Post	Carbondale, Osage County	
95	Gere Post	Gere	1883
	Gen. Mower Post	Galatia, Barton County	1884 and after
96	Lookout Post	Wellsville, Franklin County	
97	Douglass Post	Douglass, Butler County	
98	Phil Harvey (or Fredonia) Post	Fredonia, Wilson County	
99	Cedar Vale Post	Cedar Vale, Chautauqua County	
100	Lew Gove (or Manhattan) Post	Manhattan, Riley County	
101	Chase Post	Beattie, Marshall County	
102	A.J. Smith (or Fontana) Post	Fontana, Miami County	
103	C.F. Smith (or DeLong) Post	St. John, Stafford County	
104	Gen. Curtis (or Spring Hill) Post	Spring Hill, Jewell County	
105	L.E. (or R.L.) King Post	Augusta, Butler County	
106	Gen. Bull (or H.C. Buell) Post	Bull City	up through 1884
	Gen. Bull (or H.C. Buell) Post	Alton, Osborne County	1894 and after
107	Collyer Post	Collyer, Trego County	
108	Knowlton Post	Ottumwa, Coffey County	up through 1907
		Hall's Summit	1908
	Knowlton Post	Ottumwa, Coffey County	1909-1917
	Knowlton Post	Ottawa	1919
	Knowlton Post	Burlington	1922 and after
109	J.R. (or J.B.) Richardson Post	Miltonvale, Cloud County	1883-1895
	Wabaunsee Post	Wabaunsee	1898
	Richardson Post	Miltonvale, Cloud County	1900 and after
110	Solomon City Post	Solomon City	1883
	E.O.C. Ord Post	Moline, Elk County	1884 and after
111	Princeton Post	Princeton, Franklin County	up through 1926
		Richmond	1927 and after
112	Fall River Post	Fall River, Greenwood County	
113	W.T. Sherman (or Concordia) Post	Concordia, Cloud County	
114	G.K. Warren Post	Osage Mission, Neosho County	up through 1895
		St. Paul	1900
	G.K. Warren Post	Osage Mission, Neosho County	1901
	G.K. Warren Post	St. Paul	1902 and after
115	Wilson Post	Wilson, Ellsworth County	
116	Wilderness (or Delphos) Post	Delphos, Ottawa County	
117	McCaslin (or Paola) Post	Paola, Miami County	
118	Pea Ridge Post	Chetopa, Labette County	
119	New Albany Post	New Albany, Wilson County	
120	Leavenworth Post	Leavenworth, Leavenworth County	up through 1895
	Newton Post	Newton	1898 and after
121	Cumberland Post	Salem	up through 1895
	G.W. Harrison Post	Andover, Butler County	1900 and after
122	Kirwin Post	Kirwin, Phillips County	

123	Baxter Springs Post	Baxter Springs, Cherokee County	
124	Prairie Grove Post	Kansas Center	up through 1884
	Prairie Grove Post	Frederick, Rice County	1894 and after
125	Leon Post	Leon, Butler County	
126	Sackett Post	Irving, Marshall County	
127	John A. Logan (or Salina) Post	Salina, Saline County	
128	Elk City Post	Elk City, Montgomery County	
129	Neosho (or Chanute) Post	Chanute, Neosho County	
130	Hiawatha Post	Hiawatha, Brown County	
131	Bridge Post	Bridge	1883
	Bridge Post	Pliny	1884
	Bridge Post	Chico, Saline County	1895-1903
	Bridge Post	Gypsum	1904 and after
132	Junction City Post	Junction City, Geary County	
133	H.C. McDorman (or Dexter) Post	Dexter, Cowley County	up through 1898
	Wabaunsee Post	Wabaunsee	1900 and after
134	Greenleaf Post	Greenleaf, Washington County	
135	O.R. Powers Post	Netawaka, Jackson County	
136	Buffalo Post	Buffalo	1883
	Medicine Post	Raceburg	1884
	Ad Astra Post	Chanute, Neosho County	1895 and after
137	Scandia (or Wallace) Post	Scandia	up through 1884
	Sandy Valley Post	Middleton, Woodson County	1898 and after
138	N.B. Page Post	Whiting, Jackson County	
139	Mound Valley Post	Mound Valley, Labette County	
140	Jayhawker Post	Air	1883
	Jayhawker Post	Waushara	1884
	Jayhawker Post	Admire, Lyon County	1894 and after
141	Cora (or Pawnee) Post	Cora	up through 1884
	Galesburg Post	Galesburg, Neosho County	1894 and after
142	Hackleman (or Henkleman) Post	Cherryvale, Montgomery County	
143	Hepler Post	Hepler, Crawford County	up through 1889
	W.D. Conn Post	Alanthus, Gove County	1890
	Natoma Post	Natoma, Osborne County	1894 and after
144	Havensville Post	Havensville, Pottawatomie County	
145	Humphrey (or Neodesha) Post	Neodosha, Wilson County	
146	Circleville Post	Circleville, Jackson County	
147	Beloit Post	Beloit, Mitchell County	
148	9th Cavalry (or G.W. Smith) Post	Ft. Riley	up through 1884
	C.C. Myers Post	Toledo, Chase County	1887 and after
149	Tonganoxie Post	Tonganoxie	up through 1884
	S.S. Perry Post	Wallace, Wallace County	1894 and after
150	Oswego Post	Oswego, Labette County	
151	Westmoreland Post	Westmoreland, Pottawatomie County	
152	Bunker Hill Post	Bunker Hill, Russell County	
153	Coffeyville Post	Coffeyville, Montgomery County	
154	Jas. Montgomery (or Uniontown) Post	Uniontown, Bourbon County	
155	Jules Williams (or Oskaloosa) Post	Oskaloosa, Jefferson County	
156	Osage (or McCune) Post	McCune, Crawford County	
157	Corinth Post	Monmouth	1883
	John Anderson Post	Wilder, Jewell County	1884 and after
158	Arkansas City Post	Arkansas City, Cowley County	
159	Cornforth Post	Clyde, Cloud County	
160	Meriden Post	Meriden, Jefferson County	
161	Winchester Post	Custer	1884
	Slocum (or Tonganoxie) Post	Tonganoxie	1900 and after

162	Gaylord Post	Crystal Plains	1884
	James Fear Post	Brownell, Ness County	1890 and after
163	Oneida Post	Oneida, Nemaha County	
164	Larrabee Post	Russell, Russell County	
165	H.Z. Curtis Post	Keelville	1884
	H.Z. Curtis Post	Melrose, Cherokee County	1894 and after
166	James B. Kyle (or Soldier) Post	Soldier, Jackson County	
167	John L. Graham Post	Wetmore, Nemaha County	
168	Sumter Post	Winchester, Jefferson County	
169	Dunlap Post	Dunlap	
170	Robert B. Mitchell Post	La Cygne, Linn County	
171	George Ellis Post	Ellis, Ellis County	
172	Burden Post	Burden, Cowley County	
173	Scottsville Post	Scottsville, Mitchell County	
174	Eldred Post	Medicine Lodge, Barber County	
175	Sabetha Post	Sabetha, Nemaha County	
176	Cloud Post	Central City	1884
	R.B. Hayes Post	Pratt, Pratt County	1894 and after
177	Logan Post	Logan, Phillips County	
178	Ohio Grove Post	Minneapolis, Ottawa County	1884-1889
	Steadman Hatch Post	Partridge, Reno County	1890-1895
		Sylvan Grove	1902
179	Meacham Post	Colony, Anderson County	up through 1907
		Holliday	1908
		Colony, Anderson County	1909 and after
180	Rufus Gilpatrick Post	Garnett, Anderson County	
181	Long Island Post	Long Island, Phillips County	
182	J.B. (or J.P.) Milroy Post	Star	1884
	J.B. (or J.P.) Milroy Post	Lenora, Norton County	1894 and after
183	Mulberry Post	Mulberry (or Mulberry Grove), Crawford County	
184	Charley Aldrich Post	Cedarville, Smith County	up through 1903
	Charley Aldrich Post	Cedar	1914 and after
185	Woodson Post	Yates Center, Woodson County	
186	H.H. Free Post	Burr Oak, Jewell County	
187	Madison Post	Madison, Greenwood County	
188	Centralia Post	Centralia, Nemaha County	
189	Buford Post	Halstead, Harvey County	
190	Orloff Norton Post	Leroy, Coffey County	
191	Severance Post	Severance, Doniphan County	
192	Rosseau Post	Shady Bend	1884
	Bies Post	Brewster, Thomas County	1890 and after
193	Sargent Post	Little River	1884
	Russell Springs Post	Russell Springs, Logan County	1890-1895
	Little River Post	Little River	1900 and after
194	R. Mercer Post	Leonard	1884
	Richardson Post	Admire	1902 and after
195	Wier (or Weir) Post	Pardee, Atchison County	
196	I.A. Taylor (or Hartford) Post	Hartford, Lyon County	
197	Capt. Trego Post	Wakeeney, Trego County	
198	T.E.G. Ransom Post	Oberlin, Decatur County	
199	Toronto Post	Toronto, Woodson County	
200	Col. Givens Post	Hallowell, Cherokee County	
201	Everest Post	Everest	1884
	U.S. Grant Post	Elmdale, Chase County	1886 and after
202	Gen. Francis Marion Post	Florence, Marion County	
203	Mulvane Post	Mulvane, Sumner County	

204	Col. H.T. Johnson Post	Urbana	1884
	Ulysses Post	Ulysses, Grant County	1887 and after
205	Westphalia Post	Westphalia	1884
	Liberal Post	Liberal, Seward County	1890 and after
206	Armourdale Post	Armourdale	1884
	Earlton Post	Earlton, Neosho County	1887 and after
207	Silver Lake Post	Silver Lake, Shawnee County	
208	Gen. R.G. Shaw Post	Leavenworth, Leavenworth County	
209	Capt. Jarvis Post	Norton, Norton County	
210	Sergeant McCoy Post	Garrison	1884
	Sergeant McCoy Post	Randolph, Riley County	1894 and after
211	White Rock Valley Post	White Rock	1884
	Capt. H.M. Dobyns Post	Opolis, Crawford County	1886 and after
212	Harbine Post	Harbine	1884
	Harbine Post	Byron, Republic County	1895
213	Knoxville Post	Kingston	1884
	Floral Post	Floral, Cowley County	1895 and after
214	Atwood Post	Atwood, Rawlins County	
215	Bennington Post	Bennington, Ottawa County	
216	McElvane Post	Lura	1884
	J.Y. Smith Post	Brainard, Butler County	1890
	Winfield Scott Post	Scott City, Saline County	1895 and after
217	Roanoke Post	Oak Valley, Elk County	
218	Chautauqua (or Chautauqua Springs) Post	Chautauqua (or Chautauqua Springs)	
219	Col. Shane Post	Hollyrood	1884
	Banner City Post	Banner City, Dickinson County	1888 and after
220	T.R. Stanley Post	Weir	1884
	Greeley Post	Greeley, Anderson County	1894-1898
221	Quenemo Post	Quenemo, Osage County	
222	La Crosse Post	La Crosse, Rush County	
223	Elmwood Post	Shiboleth	1884
	Elmwood Post	Dresden, Decatur County	1894 and after
224	Eagle Post	Chase, Rice County	
225	Capt. Lewis Stafford Post	Valley Falls, Jefferson County	
226	Omio Post	Onion	1884
	Col. J.J. Jones Post	Formosa, Jewell County	1894 and after
227	Rough and Ready Post	Star Valley	1884
	Tim McCarthy Post	Burdette, Pawnee County	1888 and after
228	Delaware Post	Ozawkie, Jefferson County	
229	Bridgeport Post	Bridgeport, Saline County	
230	Belmont Post	Crestline, Cherokee County	1884-1890
	J.W. Mackey Post	Pomona, Franklin County	1894 and after
231	Walnut Post	Walnut, Crawford County	
232	Capt. Ben Greenman Post	Downs, Osborne County	
233	A.W. Farr Post	Empire City	1884
		Simpson, Mitchell County	1889
	McConnell Post	Blakeman, Rawlins County	1890
		Neosho Rapids	1898 and after
234	Ed. Kitchen Post	Montana	1884
	W.S. Harney Post	Coolidge, Hamilton County	1890 and after
235	Brookville Post	Brookville, Saline County	
236	W.H. Grimes Post	Atchison, Atchison County	
237	F.H. Warner Post	Netherland	1884
	Conrad Baker Post	Voltaire, Sherman County	1888
	Overbrook Post	Overbrook, Osage County	1890 and after

238	Melvern Post	Melvern, Osage County	
239	Glasco Post	Glasco, Cloud County	
240	Lebanon Post	Lebanon, Smith County	
241	T.O. Howe Post	Kinsley, Edwards County	
242	Perryville Post	Arlington, Reno County	
243	Altoona Post	Altoona, Wilson County	
244	Wm. Creighton Post	Covert	1884
	Ingalls Post	Ingalls, Gray County	1890
	Eggleston Post	Wichita, Sedgwick County	1894 and after
245	Equity Post	Rich	1884
	Equity Post	Lone Elm, Anderson County	1895 and after
246	Thompson (or Mason) Post	Vermillion, Marshall County	
247	Waverly Post	Waverly, Coffey County	
248	Volunteer Post	Coyville, Wilson County	
249	Americus Post	Americus, Lyon County	
250	Blue Post	North Topeka, Shawnee County	
251	Harper Post	Harper, Harper County	
252	Louisburg Post	Louisburg, Miami County	
253	Axtell Post	Axtell, Marshall County	
254	Sanders Post	Morantown, Allen County	
255	Stephenson Post	Sedgwick, Harvey County	
256	Ft. Donelson Post	St. Mary's	1884
	McDaniel(s) Post	Bonner Springs, Wyandotte County	1890 and after
257	James R. Fulton (or Garden City) Post	Garden City, Finney County	
258	Gen. Hazen (or Hackelman) Post	Lincoln, Lincoln County	
259	Corning Post	Corning	
260	Waterville Post	Waterville, Marshall County	
261	Galesburg Post	Galesburg	1884
	Glen Elder Post	Glen Elder, Mitchell County	1894 and after
262	Dover Post	Dover	1884
	John Morgan Post	Rago, Kingman County	1888
	Centropolis Post	Centropolis, Franklin County	1890
	Baldwin Post	Derby	1895 and after
263	Portis Post	Portis, Osborne County	
264	R.B. Burleigh (or Burley) Post	Blue Mound, Linn County	
265	Kingman Post	Kingman, Kingman County	
266	Griffin Post	Ada, Ottawa County	
267	Copeland-Goodwin Post	Iuka	1884
	J.H. Howe Post	Kanorado	1895
		Lamborn	1898 and after
268	Col. Topping Post	Altamont, Labette County	
269	W.H. Washburn Post	Twin Falls	1884
	W.H. Washburn Post	Neal, Greenwood County	1894 and after
270	Atlanta Post	Burgeville	1884
	Atlanta Post	Vilas, Wilson County	1895-1901
		Rest	1902 and after
271	Gen. Lander Post	Lane	1884-1895
	Manhattan Post	Manhattan, Riley County	1895 and after
272	Cato Post	Cato, Crawford County	
273	Grub(b) Post	Jamestown, Cloud County	
274	Bronson Post	Bronson	1884
	Barnhill Post	Lost Springs, Marion County	1895 and after
275	Jack Judy Post	Lancaster, Atchison County	
276	Effingham (or Agniel) Post	Effingham, Atchison County	
277		South Cedar	1884
	Chapin Post	Virgil	1901 and after

278	Monitor Post	Nortonville, Jefferson County	
279	McLouth Post	McLouth, Jefferson County	
280	Fisher Post	White City	
281	McFarland Post	Muscotah, Atchison County	
282	Huron Post	Huron	1884
	Grinter Post	Edwardsville	1898 and after
283	Nathan Price Post	Wathena, Doniphan County	
284	Bristow Post	Bristow	1884
	Sylvester Griffin Post	Milford, Geary County	1890-1903
		Perry	1910
	Griffin Post	Milford	1917
285	Virgil Post	Virgil	1884
	Achilles Post	Achilles	1900 and after
286	Cedron Post	Cedron, Lincoln County	1884-1901
	Cedron Post	Blue Hill	1902
	Cedron Post	Cedron	1903
		Blue Hill	1907
287	Center Ridge Post	Center Ridge	1884
	Buffalo Post	Buffalo, Wilson County	1895 and after
288	Corinth Post	Perry, Jefferson County	
289	Appomattox Post	Grenola, Elk County	
290	Drywood Post	Memphis	1884
	McDowell Post	Hoxie, Sheridan County	1894 and after
291	Chattanooga Post	Peoria, Franklin County	
292	Kennedy Post	Troy, Doniphan County	
293	Grant Post	Lancing, Leavenworth County	1886
	Victor Post	Ft. Dodge	1898 and after
294	Lewis Post	Dodge City	
295	Goodspeed (or W.S. Rosecrans) Post	Reading, Lyon County	
296	James A. Garfield Post	Garfield	
297	Bald Hill Post	Windsor	1884
	Richard Rowett Post	Culver, Ottawa County	1894 and after
298	Plainville Post	Plainville, Rooks County	
299	Miles Keogh Post	Kinsley	1884
	Rosedale Post	Rosedale, Wyandotte County	1886
	Englewood Post	Englewood, Clark County	1888 and after
300	Sylvan Grove Post	Sylvan Grove	1884
	James M. Arthur Post	Goodrich, Linn County	1890 and after
301	Henry Hopkins Post	Stafford, Stafford County	
302	Steadman Post	Terra Cotta	1884
	Chas. O. Rovohl Post	Colby, Thomas County	1887 and after
303	Haskell Post	Arcadia, Crawford County	1884-1886
	George I. Ransom Post	Armourdale, Wyandotte County	1887-1902
	George I. Ransom Post	Kansas City	1903 and after
304	Iuka Post	Melville, Ottawa County	1885
	Iuka Post	Oak Hill, Clay County	1894 and after
305	Private Samuel Pike Post	Towanda, Butler County	
306	Fulton Post	Fulton, Bourbon County	1885
	Gen. Rawlings Post	Bushton, Rice County	1888
307	Judson Post	Xenia, Bourbon County	1885
	Marvin Post	Marvin, Phillips County	1890 and after
308	Marquette Post	Marquette, McPherson County	
309	Marcus Amsden Post	Palmer, Washington County	1885
	Claflin Post	Claflin, Barton County	1888 and after
310	Billy Hugh(e)s Post	Republic City, Republic County	

311	Erie Post	Erie, Neosho County	
312	Edmond Post	Edmond, Norton County	
313	Pine Bluff Post	Edgerton, Jewell County	
314	Thomas Doan(e) Post	Lebo, Coffey County	
315	J.M. Frank Post	Greely, Anderson County	1885
	H.D. Washburn Post	Alden, Rice County	1888
		Bigelow	1898
316	Joe Butterfield Post	Greensburg, Kiowa County	
317	M.M. Crocker Post	Galva, McPherson County	
318	Capt. Ames Post	Shawnee, Jewell County	
319	Raymond Post	Raymond, Rice County	
320	Dick Root Post	Delhi, Osborne County	1885
	Crook Post	Weir (or Weir City), Cherokee County	1894 and after
321	Fort Pillow Post	Topeka, Shawnee County	
322	Fletcher Webster Post	Roxbury, McPherson County	1885
	Ossawatomie Post	Ossawatomie, Miami County	1890 and after
323	New Salem Post	New Salem, Cowley County	
324	Grand Center Post	Baltimore, Cowley County	1885
	Cowley Post	Atlanta, Cowley County	1894 and after
325	W.H. Rankin Post	Cheney, Sedgwick County	
326	Gregory Post	Pawnee Rock, Barton County	1885
	Uric Dahlgren Post	Fort Gibson, Indian Territory	1890
	Gordon Granger Post	Aurora, Cloud County	1895 and after
327	Col. Fulton Post	Rossville, Shawnee County	
328	Robert Hale (or Hall) Post	Blue Rapids, Marshall County	
329	Gen. Merrill Post	Torrance, Cowley County	1885
	Morton Post	Wilsey, Morris County	1895 and after
330	Veteran Post	Blaine, Marshall County	1885
	Veteran Post	Barrett, Marshall County	1894 and after
331	Liberty Post	Liberty, Montgomery County	1885
	Harker Post	Luray, Russell County	1890
	Wadleigh Post	Webber	1898 and after
332	White Cloud Post	White Cloud, Doniphan County	
333	Eudora Post	Eudora, Douglas County	
334	Caney Post	Caney, Montgomery County	1885
	Miles Hart (or Maple City) Post	Maple City, Cowley County	1890 and after
335	C.E. Warriner Post	Valley Center, Sedgwick County	
336	Private E.C. Johnson Post	Atchison, Atchison County	
337	Belle Plaine (or Gen. Geo. Crook) Post	Belle Plaine, Sumner County	
338	General Carlin Post	Stuart, Smith County	1885-1886
		Springfield, Clay County	1887
	Dick Kendall Post	Broughton, Clay County	1898 and after
339	Thayer Post	Thayer, Neosho County	
340	Latham Post	Latham, Butler County	
341	J.N. Parsons Post	Ogden, Riley County	
342	Argonia Post	Argonia, Sumner County	
343	Gardner Post	Udall, Cowley County	
344	Courtland Post	Courtland, Republic County	
345	Chas. Culver Post	Cloverdale, Chautauqua County	
346	F.G. Rockwell Post	Oklahoma City, Indian Territory	1890
	George A. Noker Post	Cuba, Republic County	1895 and after
347	S.J. Willis Post	Skiddy, Morris County	
348	Chalk Mound Post	Chalk Mound, Waubaunsee County	
350	Columbia Post	Lamar, Ottawa County	
351	Albert F. Peck Post	Hazelton, Barber County	

352	Tucker (or Tincher) Post	Garden Plain, Sedgwick County	
353	Frontier Post	Spearville, Ford County	
354	S.A. Gilbert Post	Mount Hope, Sedgwick County	
355	Glenwood Post	Crow, Phillips County	1886
	Gaylord Post	Gaylord, Smith County	1895 and after
356	McGooney (or McGovney) Post	Clearwater, Sedgwick County	
357	Bavaria Post	Bavaria, Saline County	1886
	Agra Post	Agra, Phillips County	1890
358	M.D. (or W.D.) Updegraff Post	Iuka, Pratt County	
359	Parson Brownlow Post	Wayne, Republic County	
360	Charles G. Harker Post	Attica, Harper County	
361	Glen Elder Post	Glen Elder, Mitchell County	1886
	Th. W. Sweeny Post	Pawnee Rock, Barton County	1890 and after
362	Chapman Post	Chapman, Dickinson County	
363	Barnes Post	Barnes, Washington County	
364	Lakin Post	Lakin, Kearney County	
365	Sam Walker (or Lawrence) Post	Lawrence, Douglas County	
366	Capt. Hudson Post	Cimarron, Gray County	
367	Buffalo Park Post	Buffalo Park, Gove County	
368	George B. McClellan Post	Morgansville, Clay County	
369	Thomas James Post	Bittertown, Lyon County	1885
	Thomas James Post	Olpe, Lyon County	1894 and after
370	Richland Post	Richland, Shawnee County	
371	Mission Ridge Post	De Soto, Jewell County	
372	Sun City Post	Sun City, Barber County	1885
	T.C. Cory Post	Dennis, Labette County	1894 and after
373	Corp. Hagar Post	Protection, Comanche County	1886
	John M. Corse Post	La Fontaine, Wilson County	1894 and after
374	Solomon Post	Solomon City, Dickinson County	
375	Dan McCook Post	Annelly, Harvey County	1886
	W.C. Ward Post	Whitewater, Butler County	1890
376	Linwood Post	Linwood	
377	Potwin Post	Potwin, Butler County	
378	John D. Wilson Post	Concordia, Cloud County	1886
	C.P. Taylor Post	Conway Springs, Sumner County	1894 and after
379	North Lawrence Post	North Lawrence, Douglas County	1886
	Capt. G.D. Wallace Post	Sarcoxie, Jefferson County	1894 and after
380	Thomas Brennan Post	National Military Home, Leavenworth County	
381		Syracuse	1886
382	Hancock Post	Colwich, Sedgwick County	
383		Vine Creek, Ottawa County	1886-1898
		Manchester, Dickinson County	1900
	Reed Post	Vine Creek, Ottawa County	1901-1902
	Reed Post	Manchester, Dickinson County	1903 and after
384	Barricklow Post	Kiowa (or New Kiowa), Barber County	
385		Germantown, Smith County	1887
	Kensington Post	Kensington, Smith County	1894 and after
386		Conway Springs, Sumner County	1887
	Sylvia Post	Sylvia, Reno County	1888 and after
387		Kendall, Hamilton County	
388	Meade Post	Meade (or Meade Center), Meade County	
389	Webster Post	Webster, Rooks County	
390		Cambridge, Cowley County	
391		Windom, McPherson County	1887
	J.J. Baldwin Post	Cairo, Pratt County	1888 and after

No.	Post	Location	Year
392		Crisfield, Harper County	1887
	Major Collins Post	Stark, Neosho County	1895
393		Norwich, Kingman County	1887
	John Fremont Post	Nonchalanta, Ness County	1894 and after
394	Old Flag Post	Fowler City, Meade County	
395	Hope Post	Hope, Dickinson County	
396		Fargo Springs, Seward County	1887
	Enterprise Post	Enterprise, Dickinson County	1894 and after
397	O.P. Morton Post	Beaumont, Butler County	
398	Scott Post	Coldwater, Comanche County	
399	John F. Miller Post	Leoti, Wichita County	
400	Almena Post	Almena, Norton County	
401		Neosho Rapids, Lyon County	1887
	John A. Savage Post	Lewis, Edwards County	1890 and after
402		Ravanna, Hodgeman County	1887
	Mart. E. Bacon Post	Fact, Clay County	1895-1901
	Mart. E. Bacon Post	Green	1902
403	Fremont Post	Turon, Reno County	
404	Richfield Post	Richfield, Morton County	
405	Oakley Post	Oakley, Logan County	
406	Woodston Post	Woodston, Rooks County	
407	South Haven Post	South Haven, Sumner County	
408	Perth Post	Perth, Sumner County	
409	H.W. Beck Post	Benton, Butler County	
410		Scott, Scott County	1887
	Seth Kelley Post	Vinland, Douglas County	1890 and after
411	Chester A. Arthur Post	Goffs, Nemaha County	
412		Wano, Cheyenne County	1887
	Sam Webber Post	St. Francis, Cheyenne County	1894 and after
413	Norcatur Post	Norcatur, Decatur County	
414		Eunice City, Logan County	1887
	Inman Post	Inman, McPherson County	1894 and after
415	Dighton Post	Dighton, Lane County	
416	Dick Curry Post	Oronoque, Norton County	
417	Violenta Post	Violenta, Sheridan County	1887
	Selden Post	Selden, Sheridan County	1894 and after
418	Harveyville Post	Harveyville, Waubaunsee County	
419	Col. Putnam Post	Haddam, Washington County	
420		Hartland, Hamilton County	1887
	John A. Anderson Post	Louisville, Pottawatomie County	1894 and after
421	S.S. Perry Post	Wallace, Wallace County	1888
	Savonburg Post	Savonburg	1894 and after
422	Lewis Christie Post	Beverly, Lincoln County	
423	Santa Fe Post	Santa Fe, Haskell County	
424	Herington Post	Herington, Dickinson County	
425	T.J. Harrison Post	Belmont, Kingman County	
426	Corbin Post	Corbin, Sumner County	1888
	J.M. Gaston Post	Kimball, Neosho County	1894 and after
427	J.H. McWilliams Post	Nescatunga, Comanche County	1888
	J.D. Austin Post	Riley, Riley County	1894 and after
428	W.S. Robertson Post	Eustis, Sherman County	1888
	W.S. Robertson Post	Goodland, Sherman County	1894 and after
429	Geo. J. Stannard Post	Wakefield, Clay County	
430	Cullison Post	Cullison	
431	Beacher Post	Jennings, Decatur County	

432	B.H. Porter Post	Macksville, Stafford County	
433	Charles A. Nichols Post	Gove City, Gove County	
434	Bear Valley Post	Shockey, Grant County	
435	Haven Post	Haven, Reno County	
436		Grainfield, Gove County	1889
	Cap. W. Catcher Post	Tahlequah, Indian Territory	1890
	J.D. Bain Post	Hoisington, Barton County	1894 and after
437	Major Elliott Post	Ashland, Clark County	
438	R.Q. Thompson Post	Tribune, Greeley County	
439	Major Rankin Post	Kincaid, Anderson County	
440	Industry Post	Industry, Clay County	
441	Kalvesta Post	Kalvesta, Garfield County	1889
	Liberty Post	Liberty, Montgomery County	1894 and after
442	Hugo Post	Hugoton, Stevens County	
443	Walton Post	Walton, Harvey County	
444	Gen. A.H. Terry Post	Riverside, Hodgeman County	
445	Havana Post	Havana	
446	Bird City Post	Bird City, Cheyenne County	
447	Kingfisher Post	Kingfisher, Indian Territory	1890
	O.B. (or O.P.) Gardner Post	Gardner, Jewell County	1894 and after
448	Rush Post	McCracken, Rush County	
449	Woodsdale Post	Woodsdale, Stevens County	
450	Gen. Lane Post	Clinton, Douglas County	
451	Bacon (or Beacon) Post	Bluff City, Harper County	
453	Black Eagle Post	Horton, Brown County	
454	McNeal Post	Homewood, Franklin County	
455	A. McDonald Post	Strong City, Chase County	
456	Henry Fuller Post	Narka, Republic County	
457	Hartranft Post	Guthrie, Indian Territory	1890
	W.R. Anderson Post	Tescott, Ottawa County	1894 and after
458	Knoxville Post	Edna, Labette County	
459	Blackburn Post	Randall, Jewell County	
461	W.H. Gibson Post	Leeds, Chautauqua County	
462	Lucas Post	Lucas, Russell County	
463	Capt. Kingscott Post	Argentine, Wyandotte County	
464	W.S. Hancock Post	Emporia, Lyon County	
465	J.B. Ste(a)dman Post	Gypsum (or Gypsum City), Saline County	
466	Bucklin Post	Bucklin, Ford County	
467	John P. Bugh Post	Nashville, Kingman County	
468	Robinson Post	Robinson, Brown County	
469	Farmer City Post	Farmer City, Wichita County	1889
	Palco Post	Palco, Rooks County	1893
470	Geneseo Post	Geneseo, Rice County	1888
	Esbon Post	Esbon, Jewell County	1893 and after
471	Hill City Post	Hill City, Graham County	1889
	J.W. Vance Post	Wellsford, Kiowa County	1894 and after
472	Arcadia Post	Arcadia, Crawford County	
473	B.F. Butler Post	Sharon Springs, Wallace County	
474	George D. Wagner Post	Armourdale, Wyandotte County	1888
	Dahlgren Post	Rush Center, Rush County	1894 and after
475	Arney Post	Colocan, Greeley County	1888
	Arney Post	Astor, Greeley County	1894 and after
476	Geuda Springs Post	Geuda Springs, Sumner County	
477	Oketo Post	Oketo, Marshall County	1888
	Buney (or Birney) Post	Caney, Montgomery County	1893 and after

478	Motor Post	Motor, Rooks County	1889
	Motor Post	Codell, Rooks County	1894 and after
479	Banner (or Sidney A. Bean) Post	Banner, Trego County	
480	Houston (or Robt. Huston) Post	Morehead, Neosho County	
481	Oklahoma Post	Beaver, Indian Territory	1889
	Lecompton Post	Lecompton, Douglas County	1893 and after
482	Bronson Post	Bronson, Bourbon County	
483	Edward Vass Post	McAlester, Indian Territory	1890
	Clem Chivington Post	Goddard, Sedgwick County	1893 and after
484	E.E. Kimball Post	Rexford, Thomas County	
485	Osterhaus Post	Prescott, Linn County	
486	Albert Carter Post	Norman, Indian Territory	1890
	Norwich Post	Norwich, Kingman County	1893-1895
	Richard Steel(e) Post	Fort Scott, Bourbon County	1898 and after
487	Tom May Post	Mapleton, Bourbon County	
488	Hamilton Post	Hamilton, Greenwood County	
489	General Slocum Post	Tonganoxie	1895
	Tyler Post	Shaw	1898
490		White City	1898
	Buell Post	Cedarvale	1900 and after
491	Haughey Post	Hillsdale	
492	Hiattsville Post	Hiattsville	
493	A.S. Everest Post	Atchison	
494	Coats Post	Coats	
495		Topeka	
496	Pomona Post	Pomona	
497	Fulton Post	Fulton	
498	Peru Post	Peru	
500	Gen. U.B. Pearsall Post	National Military Home	

APPENDIX C

Roster of Department of Nebraska post names and locations

This roster was compiled from several volumes of the *Journal of the Annual Encampment, Department of Nebraska, Grand Army of the Republic* (title varies slightly), and then compared to Dave Wells' "History of the Nebraska G.A.R. Posts" (http://www.civil-warmuseumnc.org/; accessed October 26, 2006). In cases in which the name and/or location of a post changed over the years, these changes are noted in the far right column. Please note that the roster of post names and locations was not consulted in every volume of the *Journal of the Annual Encampment*, thus this roster may not reflect all the changes in post names and locations that occurred over the years.

No.	Name	Location	
1	Sedgwick Post	Kearney	
2	Phil Kearney Post	Ft. Omaha	up through 1896
	Phil Kearney Post	South Omaha	1896 and after
3	Seward Post	Seward	
4	McPherson Post	Fremont	
5	Casey Post	Wayne	
6	Union Post	Stella	up through 1892
	Union Post	Shubert	1893 and after
7	George A. Custer Post	Omaha	
8	Canby Post	St. Paul	
9	Baker Post	Columbus	
10	Abraham Lincoln Post	David City	
11	Lyon Post	Grand Island	
12	E.V. Sumner Post	Sidney	
13	Silas A. Strickland Post	Hastings	
14	E.A. Rice Post	Steele City	
15	George A. Thomas Post	Nelson	
16	Edgar Post	Edgar	
17	Morton Post	Hebron	
18	W.A. Webb Post	Fairmont	
19	George G. Meade Post	Sutton	
20	E.M. Stanton Post	Rising City	
21	Wadsworth Post	Syracuse	
22	Wilson Post	Geneva	
23	Buford Post	Central City	
24	William Baumer Post	Nebraska City	
25	Farragut Post	Lincoln	
26	J.F. Reynolds Post	Osceola	
27	Thornburg Post	Clarks	
28	Joe Hooker Post	Shelton	
29	E.E. Ellsworth Post	Silver Creek	
30	Col. Kane Post	Raymond	
31	Bob McCook Post	Ashland	
32	Robert Anderson Post	York	
33	James Shields Post	Grafton	
34	Phil Sheridan Post	Schuyler	
35	Rawlins Post	Beatrice	
36	T.E.G. Ransom Post	Scotia	
37	Gen. Scott Post	Blue Springs	

38	Mitchell Post	Waverly	
39	Edward Lennox Post	Atkinson	
40	Commodore Foote Post	Ord	
41	Dick Yates Post	Waco	
42	Kit Carson Post	Albion	
43	George C. Oliver Post	Fairfield	
44	Chandler Post	Aurora	
45	John McConihie Post	Plattsmouth	
46	Carrigan Post	Arlington	
47	Heckathorn Post	Tecumseh	
48	Commodore Porter Post	Salem	
49	Wright Woolsey Post	Elk Creek	
50	Lew Wallace Post	Hubbell	
51	Harker Post	Wilber	
52	John A. Dix Post	Blair	
53	Boston Corbett Post	Nemaha City	
54	Mansfield Post	Palmyra	
55	Dahlgren Post	Papillion	
56	Winslow Post	Milford	
57	Lombard Post	North Loup	
58	A.L. Gates Post	Lyons	
59	J.A. Mower Post	Stromsburg	
60	Richardson Post	Harvard	
61	LaFayette Post	Weeping Water	
62	Elizabeth Upright Post	Bennett	
63	Old Abe Post	Superior	
64	Sherman Post	Valparaiso	
65	A.J. Smith Post	Doniphan	
66	William Mix Post	Humboldt	
67	Capt. James P. Mead Post	Long Pine	
68	Fremont Post	Neligh	
69	Stephen A. Douglas Post	North Platte	
70	Col. Schrontz Post	Creighton	
71	Star Post	Lerton	up through 1884
	Star Post	Seaton	1885-1887
	Star Post	Bromfield	1888 and after
72	Dick Beadle Post	Hardy	
73	Farnsworth Post	Ulysses	
74	Caddell Post	Cedar Rapids	
75	Holland Post	Crete	
76	John Brown Post	Exeter	
77	Russell Post	Fairbury	
78	Norton Post	Western	
79	Ambrose E. Burnside Post	Wells	up through 1888
	Ambrose E. Burnside Post	Bladen	1889 and after
80	James A. Garfield Post	Red Cloud	
81	Geary Post	Juniata	
82	Kilpatrick Post	Oakdale	
83	Charles Russell Lowell Post	Bellwood	
84	Veteran Post	Falls City	
85	Sergt. Key Post	Eight-Mile Grove	
86	Gen. John O'Neill Post	O'Neill	
87	Griffin Post	Stockham	
88	Elliott Post	Davenport	
89	S.R. Curtis Post	DeWitt	

90	John A. Andrew Post	Wahoo	
91	Strong Post	Minden	
92	Simon Cameron Post	Cameron	up through 1890
	Simon Cameron Post	Cairo	1891 and after
93	Stephen A. Hurlbut Post	Hampton	
94	Van Meter Post	Alma	
95	John Ingham Post	Pawnee City	
96	Tucker Post	Kent	up through 1887
	Tucker Post	Taylor	1888 and after
97	Noble Graves Post	Bradshaw	
98	C.C. Washburn Post	Broken Bow	
99	Gen. Sill Post	Sterling	
100	Sergt. Cox Post	Adams	
101	Wyman Post	Firth	
102	R.O.D. Cummings Post	Shelby	
103	Pollock Post	Brownville	
104	Gen. Roberts Post	Brock	up through 1885
	Gen. Roberts Post	Talmage	1886 and after
105	Sully Post	North Bend	
106	Kirkwood Post	Springfield	
107	Coates Post	Dorchester	
108	Crocker Post	Oxford	
109	Mathewson Post	Norfolk	
110	Omaha Post	Omaha	
111	Sergeant Glover Post	Holdrege	
112	Reno Post	Plum Creek or Lexington	
113	G.K. Warren Post	Gibbon	
114	Whitehead Post	Orleans	
115	Coleman Post	Wymore	
116	Gen. Stoneman Post	Ponca	
117	Collins Post	Glenville	
118	Boomer Post	Tekamah	
119	Gordon Granger Post	Decatur	
120	Garrett Post	Arapahoe	
121	Col. Cruft Post	Brainard	
122	Hunter Post	Ohiowa	
123	Kenesaw Post	Elmwood	
124	Shiloh Post	Loup City	
125	Lander Post	Niobrara	
126	Buckingham Post	Bazile Mills	
127	Lookout Mountain Post	Saxon	up through 1890
	Lookout Mountain Post	Friend	1891 and after
128	Gen. Mulligan Post	Sacramento	
129	Finnicum Post	Wisner	
130	W.F. Stacy (or William T. Sherman) Post	Friend	
131	Antietam Post	Bloomington	
132	B.F. Stephenson Post	Wayland	up through 1889
	B.F. Stephenson Post	Gresham	1890 and after
133	Upton Post	Hooper	
134	Bradley Post	Wood River	
135	Logan Post	Blue Hill	
136	Benjamin Franklin Post	Franklin	
137	Major Keenan Post	Beaver Crossing	
138	Timothy O. Howe Post	Guide Rock	
139	Winchester Post	Utica	

140	Kinsman Post	St. Edward	
141	C.H. Slocum Post	Endicott	
142	Putnam Post	Marquette	
143	Salmon P. Chase Post	Madison	
144	Parson Brownlow Post	Chester	
145	Bob Mercer Post	South Bend	
146	John E. Kleven Post	Culbertson	
147	Live Eagle Post	Fullerton	
148	Reserve Post	Odell	
149	Mission Ridge Post	Greenwood	
150	Frank P. Blair Post	Riverton	
151	Memorial Post	Momence	up through 1888
	Memorial Post	Shickley	1889 and after
152	Herron Post	Ayr	
153	Corinth Post	Genoa	
154	Indianola Post	Indianola	
155	Mathias Post	Kenesaw	
156	Valley Post	Lowell	up through 1887
	Valley Post	Minden	1888-1893
	Valley Post	Hartwell	1902 and after
157	Potter Post	Reynolds	
158	Clark Elder Post	Chapman	
159	William F. Barry Post	Liberty	
160	Hansen Post	Hansen	
161	Rocky Face Post	Morseville	
162	Thayer Post	Alexandria	
163	Capt. J.H. Freas Post	Beaver City	
164	Volunteer Post	Dawson	
165	John N. Gere Post	Table Rock	
166	Trego Post	Rulo	
167	Baldwin Post	St. Joe	
168	E.O.C. Ord Post	Carleton	
169	A.L. Mason Post	Crab Orchard	
170	Crittenden Post	Dakota City	
171	Ainsworth Post	Ainsworth	
172	William Butler Post	Burchard	
173	Auburn Post	Auburn	
174	Atlanta Post	Waterloo	up through 1894
	Atlanta Post	Elk City	1895-1904
	Atlanta Post	Valley	1905 and after
175	A.B. Fox Post	Louisville	
176	Belmont Post	Wakefield	
177	Col. Stewart Post	Stuart	
178	Hutton Post	Elm Creek	
179	Ossawattomie Post	Hartington	
180	Steedman Post	Westerville	up through 1888
	Steedman Post	Ansley	1889 and after
181	Gratehouse Post	Humphrey	
182	Gov. Harvey Post	Burnett	up through 1888
	Gov. Harvey Post	Tilden	1891 and after
183	William Inman Post	Inman	
184	Monitor Post	Cortland	
185	C.R. Wever Post	Emerson	
186	J.L. Wright Post	Grand Rapids	
187	Cambridge Post	Cambridge	
188	Jesse B. Morehouse Post	Tobias	

189	Amzi Garrison Post	Fletcher	
190	Kendall Post	Stanton	
191	Pierce Post	Pierce	
192	Gen. Augur Post	Ewing	
193	J.G. Lauman Post	Plainview	
194	Chickamauga Post	Unadilla	
195	Sweet Post	West Union	up through 1888
	Sweet Post	Sargent	1889 and after
196	Excelsior Post	Arnold	
197	D.S. Crawford Post	West Point	
198	Stout Post	Homerville	up through 1890
	Elwood Post	Elwood	1892 and after
199	Sanford Staley Post	Swanton	
200	U.S. Grant Post	Naponee	
201	Strain Post	Plymouth	
202	Williams Post	Axtell	
203	Geo. Vandeventor Post	Verdon	
204	A.A. Plumb Post	Wilsonville	
205	Lindsay Post	Cozad	
206	Thomas Martin Post	Gothenburg	
207	J.K. Barnes Post	McCook	
208	Col. Wood Post	Valentine	
209	Mulligan Post	Western	
210	Garland Post	Garwood Hall	up through 1888
	Garland Post	Doty	1889 and after
211	H.S. Kaley Post	Cowles	
212	Springview Post	Springview	
213	Geo. B. McClellan Post	Bertrand	
214	Appomattox Post	Lincoln	
215	J.M. Thayer Post	Ogallala	
216	Gould Post	Republican City	
217	Gen. Edwards Post	Benkelman	
218	Crocker Post	Chappell	
219	Corinth Post	Stratton	
220	Cedar Mountain Post	Ravenna	
221	Picket Post	Kimball	
222	Clearwater Post	Clearwater	
223	Hay Springs Post	Hay Springs	up through 1906
	Sheridan County Post	Rushville	1910-1911
	Sheridan County Post	Gordon	1911 and after
224	Wm. Whitaker Post	Apple Creek	up through 1888
	Wm. Whitaker Post	Dorsey	1889 and after
225	Col. J.R. Scott Post	Ono	
226	A. Doan Post	Gandy	
227	Lennington Post	Chadron	
228	R. Jewett Post	Armada	up through 1893
	R. Jewett Post	Miller	1902 and after
229	Newport Post	Newport	
230	P.A. Porter Post	Blyville	up through 1888
	P.A. Porter Post	Peoria	1889-1891
	P.A. Porter Post	Bloomfield	1892 and after
231	Perryville Post	Litchfield	
232	Chickamauga Post	Lodgepole	
233	Gettysburg Post	Trenton	
234	Hancock Post	Willow Springs	

235	T.T. Dow Post	Arcadia	
236	Hackleman Post	Cairo	
237	Stone River Post	Mason City	
238	Wauhatchie Post	Howells	
239	John A. Jordan Post	Clay Center	
240	Gen. Hazen Post	Bartlett	
241	O'Brien Post	Turner	
242	C.A. Arthur Post	Lawrence	up through 1896
	C.A. Arthur Post	Negunda	1897 and after
243	Campbell Post	Campbell	
244	J.W. McLane Post	Farnam	
245	Nickajack Post	Diller	
246	Emerich Post	Emerich	
247	Mark Goodham Post	Chambers	
248	A.C. Harding Post	Wilcox	
249	Col. Gillespie Post	Norden	
250	Heintzelman Post	Stockville	
251	Gen. Colburn Post	Leonie	
252	Vicksburg Post	Strang	
253	Ricketts Post	Arborville	
254	Carleton Post	Imperial	
255	Putnam Post	Grant	
256	Samuel Rice Post	Merna	
257	R.B. Marcy Post	Brewster	
258	Wm. F. Cody Post	Wallace	
259	E.D. Fancher Post	Johnstown	
260	Iuka Post	Carrico	up through 1894
	Iuka Post	Hayes Center	1895 and after
261	Robinson Post	Ft. Robinson	up through 1889
	Robinson Post	Crawford	1890 and after
262	George Crook Post	Omaha	
263	Myrtle Post	Lee Park	up through 1892
	Myrtle Post	Kingston	1893 and after
264	Wm. Hayes Post	Callaway	
265	Gering Post	Gering	
266	Norton Post	Daykin	
267	T.F. Meagher Post	Greeley	
268	Non Pariel Post	Non Pariel	
269	H.B. Hull Post	Palisade	
270	Little Phil. Post	Tecumseh	
271	A.W. Howard Post	Alexandria	
272	John W. Vance Post	Battle Creek	
273	Boston Corbett Post	Leigh	
274	Crittenden Post	Wescott	up through 1899
	Crittenden Post	Comstock	1900 and after
275	Atlanta Post	Platte Center	up through 1895
	Atlanta Post	Monroe	1896 and after
276	Meredith Post	Petersburg	
277	W.H.L. Wallace Post	Filley	
278	Drury Post	Pender	
279	Col. Jewell Post	Barada	
280	Hurlbut Post	Madrid	
281	Hemingford Post	Hemingford	
282	Robert Livingston Post	South Omaha	
283	Harrison Post	Trumbull	

284	Dick Oglesby Post	Huntley	
285	Sackett Post	Haigler	
286	Prosser Post	Prosser	
287	Corp. Tanner Post	Curtis	
288	Eagle Post	Eagle	
289	Gen. Willich Post	Palmer	
290	Oak Post	Oak	
291	J.A. Stafford Post	Bassett	
292	Joshua B. Davis Post	Craig	
293	Gretna Post	Gretna	
294	Beemer Post	Beemer	
295	Cheney Post	Cheney	
296	James Laird Post	Bartley	
297	Capt. Keyes Post	Lebanon	
298	F.M. Graham Post	Danbury	
299	Smith Gavitt Post	Kearney	
300	James Isom Post	Florence	
301	Champion Post	Champion	up through 1901
	Champion Post	Imperial	1902 and after
302	Martin Stowell Post	Peru	
303	Sibley Post	Maywood	
304	Edward Hatch Post	Whitney	
305	George Weeks Post	Harrisburg	
306	C.W. Hayes Post	Lushton	
307	Berwyn Post	Berwyn	
308	Banner Post	South Sioux City	
309	Ben Thompson Post	Brownville	
310	Rushville Post	Rushville	
311	D.A. Woodbury Post	Scribner	
312	Jerry Sullivan Post	Hickman	
313	Emerick Post	Newman Grove	
314	John Bryner Post	Sumner	
315	Gossard Post	Herman	
316	A.H. Terry Post	Neligh	
317	Orchard Post	Orchard	
318	Belknap Post	University Place	
319	Gen. Morrow Post	Overton	
320	Stinehope Post	Catherine	
321	Gen. Dayton Post	Alliance	
322	Resaca Post	Creston	
323	S.V. Brewer Post	Gordon	
324	A.N. Snyder Post	Powell	
325	Ch. Davenport Post	Dubois	
326	John H. Allen Post	Dodge	
327	Rutherford B. Hayes Post	Elgin	
328	Wm. Burgess Post	Spencer	
329	Detwiller Post	Upland	
330	66 Post	Hull	
331	Dr. C.H. Wilson Post	Nebraska City	
332	Purdam Post	Moorefield	
333	John Lamason Post	Page	
334	Harvey Pratt Post	Loomis	up through 1896
	Harvey Pratt Post	Atlanta	1897 and after
335	George Washington Post	Dorsey	
336	Gov. Curtin Post	Douglas	

337	Samuel Dennis Post	South Omaha
338	Wm. S. Hooten Post	Butte
339	Stone River Post	Mason City
340	Lester Baker Post	Waunetta
341	E.W. Ellis Post	Venango
342	Capt. Cooper Post	Axtell
343	Curtis Post	Curtis
344	Jerry Rusk Post	Harrison
345	Fairchild Post	Harvard
346	Nathan Bailey Post	Edison
347	Holbrook Post	Holbrook
348	Arapahoe Post	Arapahoe
349	M.L. Hayward Post	Carroll
350	Robinson Post	Bayard
351	McKinley Post	Stella
352	Randolph Post	Randolph
353	John A. Logan Post	Gross
354	A.W. Whipple Post	Soldiers and Sailors Home, Burkett
355	W.R. Akers Post	Mitchell
356	Jack Horton Post	Lynch

APPENDIX D

References to Grand Army of the Republic members with obituaries

In some cases the *Journal of the Annual Encampment* contains obituaries of G.A.R. members. The list below contains references to these obituaries. The following libraries contain extensive holdings of the *Journal of the Annual Encampment* of the G.A.R. Departments of Iowa, Kansas and Nebraska: Library of Congress, University of Illinois Library, State Historical Society of Iowa Library, Kansas State Historical Society Library, Nebraska State Historical Society Library, and Wisconsin Historical Society Library.

Adams, Clarendon E. — See *48th Journal of the Annual Encampment, Department of Nebraska* (1924), pages 74-75.

Alexander, Silas J. — See *35th Journal of the Annual Encampment, Department of Nebraska* (1911), page 100.

Anderson, Thomas P. — See *34th Journal of the Annual Encampment, Department of Kansas* (1915), page 99.

Aulabaugh, Josiah A. — See *60th Journal of the Annual Encampment, Department of Nebraska* (1936), page 38.

Bedell, Gilbert — See *26th Journal of the Annual Encampment, Department of Kansas* (1907), pages 37a, 212.

Bell, Ortha C. — See *56th Journal of the Annual Encampment, Department of Nebraska* (1932), page 53; *57th Journal of the Annual Encampment, Department of Nebraska* (1933), page 42.

Blackmar, Wilmon W. — See *25th Journal of the Annual Encampment, Department of Kansas* (1906), pages 142-144.

Blue, Richard Whiting — See *26th Journal of the Annual Encampment, Department of Kansas* (1907), pages 212-214.

Blystone, W.J. — See *48th Journal of the Annual Encampment, Department of Nebraska* (1924), pages 76-77.

Booth, Henry — See *17th Journal of the Annual Encampment, Department of Kansas* (1898), pages 138-139.

Botkin, Theodosius — See *38th Journal of the Annual Encampment, Department of Kansas* (1919), pages 18, 40.

Bowman, Elias Wesley — See *48th Journal of the Annual Encampment, Department of Kansas* (1929), page 19.

Brockman, John M. — See *31st Journal of the Annual Encampment, Department of Nebraska* (1907), pages 95-96.

Bross, Harmon — See *52nd Journal of the Annual Encampment, Department of Nebraska* (1928), pages 47-49.

Brown, Edwin F. — See *67th Journal of the Annual Encampment, Department of Nebraska* (1943), page 28.

Bryson, David — See *63rd Journal of the Annual Encampment, Department of Nebraska* (1939), pages 36-37.

Buckner, Allen — See *20th Journal of the Annual Encampment, Department of Kansas* (1901), pages 43, 94.

Burke, James H. — See *26th Journal of the Annual Encampment, Department of Kansas* (1907), pages 185-186.

Campbell, Robert A. — See *42nd Journal of the Annual Encampment, Department of Kansas* (1923), pages 19-20, 117.

Carmichael, M.A. — See *22nd Journal of the Annual Encampment, Department of Kansas* (1903), pages 14 and unnumbered page.

Church, Alonzo H. — See *19th Journal of the Annual Encampment, Department of Nebraska* (1895), page 155.

Clark, Charles Armory — See *40th Journal of the Annual Encampment, Department of Iowa* (1914), pages 56-58.

Clark, John R. — See *15th Journal of the Annual Encampment, Department of Nebraska* (1891), page 70.

Clarkson, Thaddeus S. — See *39th Journal of the Annual Encampment, Department of Nebraska* (1915), page 102.

Collins, C.C. — See *46th Journal of the Annual Encampment, Department of Kansas* (1927), page 54.

Conrad, William F. — See *28th Journal of the Annual Encampment, Department of Iowa* (1902), pages 22, 75-76.

Consigny, Eugene A. — See *27th Journal of the Annual Encampment, Department of Iowa* (1901), pages 62-66.

Cook, Bradford Pierce — See *36th Journal of the Annual Encampment, Department of Nebraska* (1912), pages 80-81, 96.

Cook, John B. — See *19th Journal of the Annual Encampment, Department of Iowa* (1893), page 97.

Crapo, Philip M. — See *30th Journal of the Annual Encampment, Department of Iowa* (1904), pages 52-55.

Creigh, Thomas A. — See *34th Journal of the Annual Encampment, Department of Nebraska* (1910), page 101.

Culver, Jacob H. — See *46th Journal of the Annual Encampment, Department of Nebraska* (1922), pages 57-58.

Damewood, Francis A. — See *56th Journal of the Annual Encampment, Department of Nebraska* (1932), pages 41-42.

Davis, Joshua B. — See *14th Journal of the Annual Encampment, Department of Nebraska* (1890), unnumbered page.

Davis, Madison Bartlett — See *41st Journal of the Annual Encampment, Department of Iowa* (1915), pages 32-33.

Davis, Samuel D. — See *31st Journal of the Annual Encampment, Department of Nebraska* (1907), pages 93-94.

Davisson, John S. — See *66th Journal of the Annual Encampment, Department of Nebraska* (1942), pages 35-36.

Dempster, John A. — See *39th Journal of the Annual Encampment, Department of Nebraska* (1915), pages 101-103, 133-134.

Diener, John F. — See *42nd Journal of the Annual Encampment, Department of Nebraska* (1918), page 80.

Durand, O.H. — See *41st Journal of the Annual Encampment, Department of Nebraska* (1917), page 114.

Dyer, Henry A. — See *39th Journal of the Annual Encampment, Department of Iowa* (1913), page 55.

Eastman, D.W. — See *32nd Journal of the Annual Encampment, Department of Kansas* (1913), pages 82-83.

Eberly, John — See *38th Journal of the Annual Encampment, Department of Nebraska* (1914), page 80.

Ehrhardt, John A. — See *50th Journal of the Annual Encampment, Department of Nebraska* (1926), page 37.

Elliott, David Stewart — See *18th Journal of the Annual Encampment, Department of Kansas* (1899), pages 226-227.

Estelle, Lee S. — See *45th Journal of the Annual Encampment, Department of Nebraska* (1921), page 81.

Fancher, Elias B. — See *50th Journal of the Annual Encampment, Department of Nebraska* (1926), page 38.

Feighan, John W. — See *18th Journal of the Annual Encampment, Department of Kansas* (1899), pages 224-225.

Fisher, Hugh D., Rev. — See *25th Journal of the Annual Encampment, Department of Kansas* (1906), page 166.

Gage, James D. — See *48th Journal of the Annual Encampment, Department of Nebraska* (1924), page 75.

Geddes, James Loraine — See *13th Journal of the Annual Encampment, Department of Iowa* (1887), pages 14, 148-155.

Given, Josiah — See *34th Journal of the Annual Encampment, Department of Iowa* (1908), pages 26-27.

Green, Albert R. — See *38th Journal of the Annual Encampment, Department of Kansas* (1919), pages 17-18, 40.

Griswold, Hurlbut Edward — See *35th Journal of the Annual Encampment, Department of Iowa* (1909), pages 34-35, 124-125.

Guthrie, John — See *26th Journal of the Annual Encampment, Department of Kansas* (1907), pages 125-126.

Hanback, Lewis — See *17th Journal of the Annual Encampment, Department of Kansas* (1898), pages 130-133.

Harper, Samuel Houston — See *38th Journal of the Annual Encampment, Department of Iowa* (1912), pages 32, 113-114.

Harris, Charles — See *39th Journal of the Annual Encampment, Department of Kansas* (1920), pages 104-105.

Harris, John P. — See *36th Journal of the Annual Encampment, Department of Kansas* (1917), page 81.

Hemry, Charles W., Rev. — See *49th Journal of the Annual Encampment, Department of Nebraska* (1925), page 30.

Hibbert, T.E. — See *29th Journal of the Annual Encampment, Department of Nebraska* (1905), pages 74-75.

Hoagland, Henry V. — See *54th Journal of the Annual Encampment, Department of Nebraska* (1930), page 41.

Hoagland, Joseph S. — See *45th Journal of the Annual Encampment, Department of Nebraska* (1921), page 70.

Hobble, P.R. — See *38th Journal of the Annual Encampment, Department of Kansas* (1919), pages 41-42.

Hogin, George B. — See *21st Journal of the Annual Encampment, Department of Iowa* (1895), page 100.

Holman, Harrison West — See *31st Journal of the Annual Encampment, Department of Iowa* (1905), pages 40-48.

Horton, Laurens Jackson — See *31st Journal of the Annual Encampment, Department of Nebraska* (1907), pages 94-95.

Howe, P.D.C. Church — See *40th Journal of the Annual Encampment, Department of Nebraska* (1916), pages 103-104, 120-121.

Hudson, Joseph Kennedy — See *26th Journal of the Annual Encampment, Department of Kansas* (1907), pages 85-86, 105-107; *27th Journal of the Annual Encampment, Department of Kansas* (1908), pages 94-95.

Jackson, Thomas Jefferson — See *25th Journal of the Annual Encampment, Department of Kansas* (1906), pages 167-168.

Johnson, George — See *60th Journal of the Annual Encampment, Department of Nebraska* (1936), pages 34-35.

Kelly, Bernard — See *45th Journal of the Annual Encampment, Department of Kansas* (1926), page 25.

King, Martin V. — See *43rd Journal of the Annual Encampment, Department of Nebraska* (1919), pages 39, 74.

Kinney, Charles H. — See *63rd Journal of the Annual Encampment, Department of Nebraska* (1939), page 36.

Leary, J.F., Rev. — See *25th Journal of the Annual Encampment, Department of Kansas* (1906), pages 20, 90-91, 174-175.

Lett, John — See *61st Journal of the Annual Encampment, Department of Nebraska* (1937), pages 42-43.

Lindt, John — See *39th Journal of the Annual Encampment, Department of Iowa* (1913), pages 57, 107-108.

Lomax, Perry — See *60th Journal of the Annual Encampment, Department of Nebraska* (1936), pages 37-38.

Loomis, Henry C. — See *25th Journal of the Annual Encampment, Department of Kansas* (1906), pages 165-166.

Mahan, James Curtis — See *60th Journal of the Annual Encampment, Department of Nebraska* (1936), pages 34-35.

Majors, Thomas J. — See *57th Journal of the Annual Encampment, Department of Nebraska* (1933), pages 44-45.

Majors, Wilson E. — See *56th Journal of the Annual Encampment, Department of Nebraska* (1932), pages 43-44.

Manning, William R. — See *38th Journal of the Annual Encampment, Department of Iowa* (1912), pages 33-36, 113-114.

Martin, John A. — See *9th Journal of the Annual Encampment, Department of Kansas* (1890), pages 76-77.

Maxon, John R. — See *49th Journal of the Annual Encampment, Department of Nebraska* (1925), pages 34-35.

McBride, Lewis C. — See *66th Journal of the Annual Encampment, Department of Nebraska* (1942), pages 36-37.

McCarthy, Timothy — See *20th Journal of the Annual Encampment, Department of Kansas* (1901), pages 42-43, 94.

McCoy, H.C., Dr. — See *27th Journal of the Annual Encampment, Department of Iowa* (1901), pages 56-57.

McGregor, Robert P. — See *17th Journal of the Annual Encampment, Department of Kansas* (1898), pages 131-133.

Miller, Edward G. — See *32nd Journal of the Annual Encampment, Department of Iowa* (1906), pages 32-37.

Moore, John Oscar — See *61st Journal of the Annual Encampment, Department of Nebraska* (1937), page 42.

Morgan, William Albert — See *36th Journal of the Annual Encampment, Department of Kansas* (1917), page 81.

Morrow, Henry A. — See *15th Journal of the Annual Encampment, Department of Nebraska* (1891), pages 65-67.

Morse, Edward N. — See *45th Journal of the Annual Encampment, Department of Nebraska* (1921), pages 68-69.

Palmer, Henry E. — See *35th Journal of the Annual Encampment, Department of Nebraska* (1911), page 99.

Parrott, James C. — See *25th Journal of the Annual Encampment, Department of Iowa* (1899), pages 96-98, 178.

Perkins, Albert Aylette — See *42nd Journal of the Annual Encampment, Department of Iowa* (1916), pages 44-46.

Pierce, A.C. — See *45th Journal of the Annual Encampment, Department of Kansas* (1926), page 25; *46th Journal of the Annual Encampment, Department of Kansas* (1927), page 52.

Pierce, Charles Wilson — See *31st Journal of the Annual Encampment, Department of Nebraska* (1907), page 96.

Pillsbury, W.H.H. — See *20th Journal of the Annual Encampment, Department of Nebraska* (1896), page 101.

Plumb, Preston B. — See *11th Journal of the Annual Encampment, Department of Kansas* (1892), pages 80-81, 102.

Pond, Homer W. — See *28th Journal of the Annual Encampment, Department of Kansas* (1909), pages 27, 111-112.

Presson, Joseph H. — See *49th Journal of the Annual Encampment, Department of Nebraska* (1925), pages 28-30.

Priddy, James W. — See *54th Journal of the Annual Encampment, Department of Kansas* (1935), page 4; *55th Journal of the Annual Encampment, Department of Kansas* (1936), pages 39-40.

Pugh, Booz Franklin — See *42nd Journal of the Annual Encampment, Department of Kansas* (1923), pages 20-21, 117.

Raymond, L.B. — See *37th Journal of the Annual Encampment, Department of Iowa* (1911), pages 42-43.

Reese, John — See *60th Journal of the Annual Encampment, Department of Nebraska* (1936), pages 36-37.

Remington, J.B. — See *31st Journal of the Annual Encampment, Department of Kansas* (1912), pages 27-28.

Rexroad, Adam F. — See *66th Journal of the Annual Encampment, Department of Nebraska* (1942), page 28.

Richards, Lucius D. — See *56th Journal of the Annual Encampment, Department of Nebraska* (1932), page 41.

Ruppel, Lewis F. — See *56th Journal of the Annual Encampment, Department of Nebraska* (1932), page 46.

Sanders, S.F., Dr. — See *51st Journal of the Annual Encampment, Department of Nebraska* (1927), pages 41-42.

Schaller, Phil — See *38th Journal of the Annual Encampment, Department of Iowa* (1912), pages 30-31, 34-36.

Sheldon, Henry — See *61st Journal of the Annual Encampment, Department of Nebraska* (1937), page 43.

Smith, Abraham W. — See *38th Journal of the Annual Encampment, Department of Kansas* (1919), pages 17, 40.

Smith, Charles H. — See *37th Journal of the Annual Encampment, Department of Iowa* (1911), pages 40-41.

Smith, Thomas J. — See *57th Journal of the Annual Encampment, Department of Nebraska* (1933), page 52.

Smith, William W. — See *39th Journal of the Annual Encampment, Department of Kansas* (1920), page 105.

Soward, Thomas Howard — See *38th Journal of the Annual Encampment, Department of Kansas* (1919), page 41.

Spalding, S.K., Dr. — See *40th Journal of the Annual Encampment, Department of Nebraska* (1916), pages 102-103, 122.

Steele, Calvin F. — See *34th Journal of the Annual Encampment, Department of Nebraska* (1910), pages 69, 103.

Stewart, Wm. H. — See *51st Journal of the Annual Encampment, Department of Nebraska* (1927), pages 42-43.

Strode, Jesse B. — See *49th Journal of the Annual Encampment, Department of Nebraska* (1925), pages 33-34.

Sutton, Michael W. — See *38th Journal of the Annual Encampment, Department of Kansas* (1919), pages 39-40.

Teeter, Joseph — See *45th Journal of the Annual Encampment, Department of Nebraska* (1921), page 77.

Thayer, John M. — See *30th Journal of the Annual Encampment, Department of Nebraska* (1906), pages 97-98.

Thomas, Griffith J. — See *50th Journal of the Annual Encampment, Department of Nebraska* (1926), page 39.

Thompson, James K.P. — See *29th Journal of the Annual Encampment, Department of Iowa* (1903), pages 78-80.

Traynor, Andrew — See *45th Journal of the Annual Encampment, Department of Nebraska* (1921), page 69.

Trimble, Albert M. — See *45th Journal of the Annual Encampment, Department of Nebraska* (1921), pages 51-52, 78.

Walker, Leicester — See *40th Journal of the Annual Encampment, Department of Nebraska* (1916), pages 104-105.

Walkinshaw, Joseph Cowan — See *29th Journal of the Annual Encampment, Department of Kansas* (1910), pages 143-144.

Warren, Solomon S. — See *63rd Journal of the Annual Encampment, Department of Nebraska* (1939), page 37.

Whitney, William Clifford — See *27th Journal of the Annual Encampment, Department of Kansas* (1908), pages 96-97.

Wilcox, Robert S. — See *57th Journal of the Annual Encampment, Department of Nebraska* (1933), pages 51-52.

Windham, Robert Baxter — See *49th Journal of the Annual Encampment, Department of Nebraska* (1925), pages 35-36.

Woodworth, Homer S. — See *66th Journal of the Annual Encampment, Department of Nebraska* (1942), pages 34-35.

Wright, Robert W., Dr. — See *25th Journal of the Annual Encampment, Department of Kansas* (1906), pages 179-180.

Wyatt, Daniel Franklin — See *25th Journal of the Annual Encampment, Department of Kansas* (1906), pages 172-174.

APPENDIX E

Statistical summary of states and territories from which comrades in this book served

Arizona Territory	1	Nebraska Territory	225
Arkansas	27	Nevada	3
California	66	New Hampshire	68
Colorado Territory	83	New Jersey	100
Connecticut	89	New Mexico Territory	2
Dakota Territory	6	New York	1,585
Delaware	17	North Carolina	3
District of Columbia	4	Ohio	3,591
Illinois	6,354	Oregon	9
Indiana	2,892	Pennsylvania	1,639
Iowa	8,064	Rhode Island	28
Kansas	1,523	Tennessee	95
Kentucky	342	Vermont	182
Louisiana	10	Virginia	40
Maine	128	West Virginia	242
Maryland	75	Wisconsin	1,860
Massachusetts	227		
Michigan	596	U.S. Army	468
Minnesota	217	U.S.C.T. (U.S. Colored Troops)	248
Mississippi	7	U.S. Navy	187
Missouri	1,257	Veteran Reserve Corps	28

APPENDIX F

Annotated bibliography of Grand Army of the Republic department-level rosters and indexes

Colorado
"Colorado Civil War Grand Army of the Republic Members," Denver Public Library website, http://denverlibrary.org/research/genealogy/gar.html, accessed October 26, 2006.
Online membership roster compiled from rosters of the Department of Colorado published in 1895, 1910, and 1931; entries include member's name, rank, company, regiment or ship, and post number; also includes roster of posts showing name, number, and location of post.

Illinois
Grand Army of the Republic, Department of Illinois. *Roster of the Department of Illinois, Grand Army of the Republic.* Kansas City, Mo.: Western Veteran, 1896.
Arranged by post (neither numerically nor by location); entries include member's name, company, and regiment or ship.

Northcott, Dennis, and Thomas Brooks. *Grand Army of the Republic, Department of Illinois: Transcription of the Death Rolls, 1879–1947.* St. Louis, Mo.: Dennis Northcott, 2003.
Arranged alphabetically by member's name; entries include member's name, rank, company, regiment or ship, death date, and name, number, and location of post; some entries include age or place of burial.

Shaw, William C. *Illustrated Roster of the Department of Illinois, Grand Army of the Republic.* 1914.
Arranged numerically by post number; entries include member's name, rank, and regiment or ship.

Indiana
Northcott, Dennis. *Indiana Civil War Veterans: Transcription of the Death Rolls of the Department of Indiana, Grand Army of the Republic, 1882-1948.* St. Louis, Mo.: Dennis Northcott, 2005.
Arranged alphabetically by member's name; entries include member's name, rank, company, regiment or ship, age, death date, and name, number, and location of post.

Kansas
"Necrology of the Grand Army of the Republic," Kansas State Historical Society website, http://www.kshs.org/genealogists/military/gar/garnecrologies.htm, accessed October 26, 2006.
Searchable index to death notices published in the encampment proceedings of the Department of Kansas; entries include member's name and number and page of the encampment proceedings that includes the death notice.

Roster of the Members and the Posts, Grand Army of the Republic, Department of Kansas. Topeka, Department of Kansas, 1894.
Arranged alphabetically by county then by post; entries include member's name, rank, and regiment or ship.

Massachusetts
Sargent, A. Dean. *Grand Army of the Republic: Civil War Veterans, Department of Massachusetts, 1866 to 1947.* Bowie, Md.: Heritage Books, 2002.
Arranged numerically by post number; entries include member's name, rank, company, regiment or ship, name and location of post, birth date or death date, and place of residence or birth.

Sargent, A. Dean. *Grand Army of the Republic: Civil War Veterans, Department of Massachusetts, 1866 to 1947.* CD-ROM. Bowie, Md.: Heritage Books, 2002.

Minnesota
Richardson, Antona Hawkins. *Roll of the Dead, 1886–1906: Department of Minnesota, Grand Army of the Republic.* St. Paul, Minn.: Paduan Press, 2000.
Arranged alphabetically by member's name; entries include member's name, rank, company, regiment or ship, death date, and name, number, and location of post; some entries include age, cause of death, and place of burial.

Missouri

Concannon, Marie, and Josiah Parkinson. *Grand Army of the Republic—Missouri Division—Index to Death Rolls, 1882–1940*. Columbia, Mo.: State Historical Society of Missouri, 1995. Accessible on the Virtually Missouri website, http://www.virtuallymissouri.org/, accessed October 26, 2006.
Arranged alphabetically by member's name; entries include member's name, number and location of post, age, and year and page number of report from which extracted.

Grand Army of the Republic, Department of Missouri. *Roster of the Department of Missouri, Grand Army of the Republic, and Its Auxiliaries*. Kansas City, Mo.: Western Veteran, 1895.
Arranged by post—St. Louis posts are listed numerically, followed by other posts listed alphabetically by county; entries include member's name, company, and regiment or ship.

Roster of the Department of Missouri, Grand Army of the Republic, 1895. Edited and indexed by members of Phelps Camp #66, Sons of Union Veterans of the Civil War, Springfield, Missouri. Springfield, Mo.: The Camp, ca. 1999.
Arranged alphabetically by member's name; entries include member's name, company, regiment or ship, and name and location of post; some officers' ranks included.

Nebraska

"Nebraska Civil War Veterans," Denver Public Library website, http://denverlibrary.org/research/genealogy/gar.html, accessed October 26, 2006.
Online membership roster compiled from a roster of the Department of Nebraska published in 1911; entries include member's name, regiment or ship, and post number; also includes roster of posts showing name, number, and location of post.

Oregon

Myers, Jane. *Honor Roll of Oregon Grand Army of the Republic, 1881–1935: Deaths Reported in Oregon of Members of the GAR, Extracted from Proceedings of the Annual Encampments of the Department of Oregon, Grand Army of the Republic*. Cottage Grove, Ore.: Cottage Grove Genealogical Society, ca. 1980.
Arranged alphabetically by member's name; entries include member's name, company, regiment or ship, death date, age, and post number; also includes roster of posts showing name, number, and location of post.

ORDER FORM

Founded in 1866, the Grand Army of the Republic became the largest association of Union Civil War veterans. The following three books contain death records of more than 90,000 G.A.R. members.

Use this order form to order additional copies, or share it with a friend, your local library, genealogical/historical society, or Civil War interest group.

Name:_____

Address:_____

City:_____ State:_____ Zip:_____

Phone:_____ E-mail Address:_____

PLEASE SEND ME

Grand Army of the Republic, Department of Illinois:
Transcription of the Death Rolls, 1879–1947.._____copy/copies

Indiana Civil War Veterans: Transcription of the Death Rolls
of the Department of Indiana, Grand Army of the Republic, 1882–1948 ...._____copy/copies

Iowa, Kansas and Nebraska Civil War Veterans: Compilation
of the Death Rolls of the Departments of Iowa, Kansas and
Nebraska, Grand Army of the Republic, 1883-1948 ...._____copy/copies

TOTAL COST

Total Number of Books _____ χ $30.00 *(per book)* = _____

Shipping Cost *(Add $4 shipping for one book, and $1 for each additional book.)* = _____

Missouri residents add 7.616% sales tax. = _____

Total Amount Enclosed = _____

Make check payable to Dennis Northcott and send to:
Dennis Northcott
P.O. Box 11801
St. Louis, MO 63105

Library purchase orders are welcome.

COMING NEXT
COMPILATION OF THE DEATH ROLLS OF THE DEPARTMENT OF PENNSYLVANIA, GRAND ARMY OF THE REPUBLIC

For more information, visit *www.ngpublications.com*